D MAP PAGES

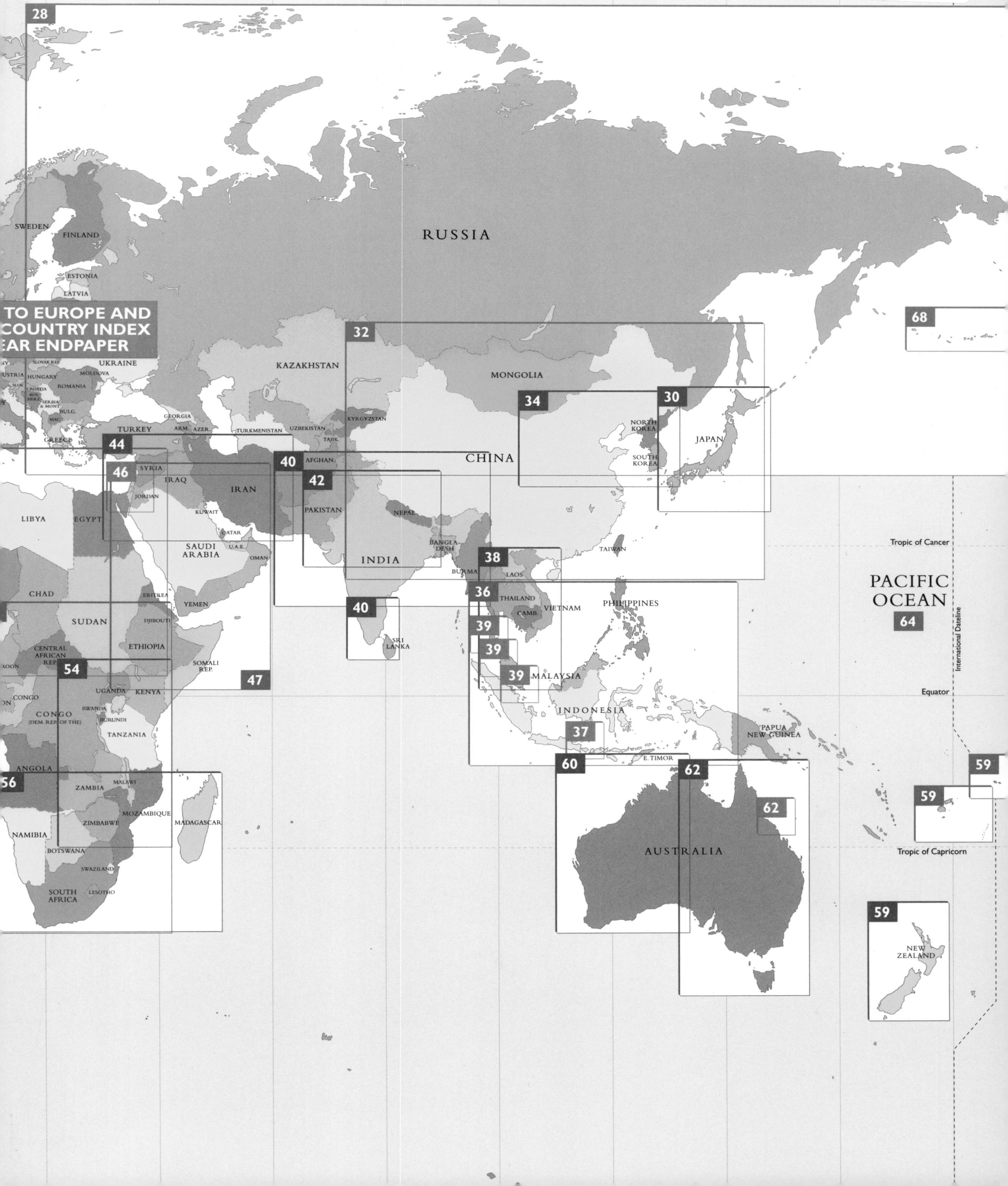

28

SWEDEN
FINLAND

ESTONIA
LATVIA

RUSSIA

**TO EUROPE AND
COUNTRY INDEX
EAR ENDPAPER**

68

UKRAINE
SLOVAK REP.
USTRIA HUNGARY
CROATIA
Y ROMANIA
SON. SERBIA
HERZ. & MONT. BULG.
MAC.
GREECE

KAZAKHSTAN

MONGOLIA

32

34

30

GEORGIA
ARM. AZER.
TURKMENISTAN UZBEKISTAN
TAJIK.

KYRGYZSTAN

NORTH
KOREA

JAPAN

TURKEY

44

46 SYRIA
IRAQ
JORDAN

40 AFGHAN.

42

CHINA

SOUTH
KOREA

IRAN

LIBYA EGYPT

KUWAIT

QATAR
U.A.E.

SAUDI
ARABIA

OMAN

PAKISTAN

NEPAL

INDIA

BANGLA-
DESH

BURMA

38

TAIWAN

Tropic of Cancer

CHAD

ERITREA

YEMEN

SUDAN

DJIBOUTI

40

SRI
LANKA

36 THAILAND
CAMB.

LAOS

VIETNAM

PHILIPPINES

PACIFIC
OCEAN

64

CENTRAL
AFRICAN
REP.

ETHIOPIA

SOMALI
REP.

54

UGANDA KENYA

47

39

39

39 MALAYSIA

CON
CONGO
(DEM. REP. OF THE)

RWANDA
BURUNDI

TANZANIA

INDONESIA

37

PAPUA
NEW GUINEA

Equator

ON

ANGOLA

56

ZAMBIA

MALAWI

MOZAMBIQUE

MADAGASCAR

60

E. TIMOR

62

62

59

59

NAMIBIA

ZIMBABWE

BOTSWANA

AUSTRALIA

Tropic of Capricorn

SWAZILAND

SOUTH
AFRICA

LESOTHO

59

NEW
ZEALAND

International Dateline

PHILIP'S

WORLD ATLAS

CONSULTANTS

Philip's are grateful to the following people for acting as specialist geography consultants on '*The World in Focus*' front section:

Professor D. Brunsden, Kings College, University of London, UK
Dr C. Clarke, Oxford University, UK
Dr I. S. Evans, Durham University, UK
Professor P. Haggett, University of Bristol, UK
Professor K. McLachlan, University of London, UK
Professor M. Monmonier, Syracuse University, New York, USA
Professor M-L. Hsu, University of Minnesota, Minnesota, USA
Professor M. J. Tooley, University of St Andrews, UK
Dr T. Unwin, Royal Holloway, University of London, UK

THE WORLD IN FOCUS
Cartography by Philip's

Picture Acknowledgements
NASA/GSFC page 14

Illustrations: Stefan Chabluk

WORLD CITIES
Cartography by Philip's

Page 11, Dublin: The town plan of Dublin is based on Ordnance Survey Ireland by permission of the Government Permit Number 7617. © Ordnance Survey Ireland and Government of Ireland.

Page 11, Edinburgh, and page 15, London:
This product includes mapping data licensed from Ordnance Survey® with the permission of the Controller of Her Majesty's Stationery Office. © Crown copyright 2003. All rights reserved. Licence number 100011710.

Vector data: Courtesy of Gräfe and Unser Verlag GmbH, München, Germany
(city centre maps of Bangkok, Beijing, Cape Town, Jerusalem, Mexico City, Moscow, Singapore, Sydney, Tokyo and Washington D.C.)

All satellite images in this section courtesy of NPA Group Limited, Edenbridge, Kent (www.satmaps.com)

Published in Great Britain in 2003
by Philip's,
a division of Octopus Publishing Group Limited,
2–4 Heron Quays, London E14 4JP

Copyright © 2003 Philip's

Cartography by Philip's

ISBN 0–540–08408–5

A CIP catalogue record for this book is available from the British Library.

Printed in Hong Kong

Details of other Philip's titles and services can be found on our website at: www.philips-maps.co.uk

Philip's World Atlases are published in association with The Royal Geographical Society (with The Institute of British Geographers).

The Society was founded in 1830 and given a Royal Charter in 1859 for 'the advancement of geographical science'. It holds historical collections of national and international importance, many of which relate to the Society's association with and support for scientific exploration and research from the 19th century onwards. It was pivotal in establishing geography as a teaching and research discipline in British universities close to the turn of the century, and has played a key role in geographical and environmental education ever since.

Today the Society is a leading world centre for geographical learning – supporting education, teaching, research and expeditions, and promoting public understanding of the subject.

The Society welcomes those interested in geography as members. For further information, please visit the website at: www.rgs.org

PHILIP'S

WORLD ATLAS

IN ASSOCIATION WITH
THE ROYAL GEOGRAPHICAL SOCIETY
WITH THE INSTITUTE OF BRITISH GEOGRAPHERS

Contents

World Statistics

Countries	vi
Physical Dimensions	vii
Philip's World Maps	viii

The World in Focus

Planet Earth	2–3
Restless Earth	4–5
Landforms	6–7
Oceans	8–9
Climate	10–11
Water and Vegetation	12–13
Environment	14–15
Population	16–17
The Human Family	18–19
Wealth	20–21
Quality of Life	22–23
Energy	24–25
Production	26–27
Trade	28–29
Travel and Tourism	30–31
Index	32

World Cities

Amsterdam	2
Athens	2
Atlanta	3
Baghdad	3
Bangkok	3
Barcelona	4
Beijing	4
Berlin	5
Boston	6
Brussels	6
Budapest	7
Buenos Aires	7
Cairo	7
Calcutta (Kolkata)	8
Canton (Guangzhou)	8
Cape Town	8
Chicago	9
Copenhagen	10
Delhi	10
Dublin	11
Edinburgh	11
Helsinki	12
Hong Kong	12
Istanbul	12
Jakarta	13
Jerusalem	13
Johannesburg	13
Karachi	14
Lagos	14
Lisbon	14
London	15
Lima	16
Los Angeles	16
Madrid	17
Manila	17
Melbourne	17
Mexico City	18
Miami	18
Milan	18
Montréal	19
Moscow	19
Mumbai (Bombay)	20
Munich	20
New York	21
Osaka	22
Oslo	22
Paris	23
Prague	24
Rio de Janeiro	24
Rome	25
San Francisco	25
St Petersburg	26
Santiago	26
São Paulo	26
Seoul	26
Shanghai	27
Singapore	27
Stockholm	28
Sydney	28
Tokyo	29
Tehran	30
Tianjin	30
Toronto	30
Vienna	31
Warsaw	31
Washington	32
Wellington	32
Index to City Maps	33–39
World Cities Satellite Images	40–48

World Maps

Map Symbols	1
The World: Political 1:95 000 000	2–3
Arctic Ocean 1:35 000 000	4
Antarctica 1:35 000 000	5

Europe

Europe: Physical 1:20 000 000	6
Europe: Political 1:20 000 000	7

Scandinavia 1:5 000 000
Iceland 1:5 000 000

8–9

Ireland 1:2 000 000

10

Scotland 1:2 000 000

11

England and Wales 1:2 000 000

12–13

British Isles 1:5 000 000

14

Netherlands, Belgium and Luxembourg 1:2 500 000

15

Central Europe 1:5 000 000

16–17

Eastern Europe and Turkey 1:10 000 000

18–19

France 1:5 000 000

20

Spain and Portugal 1:5 000 000

21

Italy and the Balkan States 1:5 000 000

22–23

Balearics, Canaries and Madeira 1:1 000 000 / 1:2 000 000

24

Malta, Crete, Corfu, Rhodes and Cyprus 1:1 000 000 / 1:1 300 000

25

Asia

Asia: Physical 1:50 000 000	26
Asia: Political 1:50 000 000	27

Russia and Central Asia 1:20 000 000

28–29

Japan 1:5 000 000

30–31

China and the Far East 1:15 000 000
Hong Kong and Macau 1:1 000 000
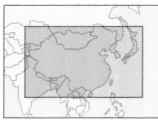
32–33

Northern China and Korea 1:6 000 000

34–35

Indonesia and the Philippines 1:12 500 000

36–37

Mainland South-east Asia 1:6 000 000
Ko Phuket 1:1 000 000
Ko Samui 1:1 000 000
Pinang 1:1 000 000
Singapore 1:1 000 000

38–39

South Asia 1:10 000 000

40–41

Northern India and Nepal
1:6 000 000
Jammu and Kashmir   1:6 000 000

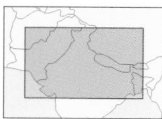

42–43

The Middle East
1:7 000 000

44–45

The Near East   1:2 500 000

46

**Arabia and the Horn
of Africa**   1:15 000 000

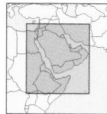

47

Africa

Africa: Physical
1:42 000 000   48

Africa: Political
1:42 000 000   49

Northern Africa
1:15 000 000

50–51

Central and Southern Africa
1:15 000 000

52–53

East Africa   1:8 000 000

54–55

Southern Africa
1:8 000 000
Madagascar 1:8 000 000

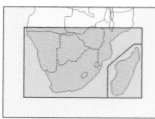

56–57

Australia and Oceania

**Australia and Oceania:
Physical and Political**
1:50 000 000   58

New Zealand   1:6 000 000
Samoan Islands 1:12 000 000
Fiji and Tonga 1:12 000 000

59

Western Australia
1:8 000 000

60–61

Eastern Australia
1:8 000 000
Whitsunday Islands 1:2 500 000

62–63

Pacific Ocean
1:54 000 000   64–65

North America

North America: Physical
1:35 000 000   66

North America: Political
1:35 000 000   67

Canada   1:15 000 000
Alaska   1:30 000 000

68–69

Western Canada   1:7 000 000

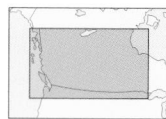

70–71

Eastern Canada   1:7 000 000

72–73

United States   1:12 000 000
Hawaii 1:10 000 000

74–75

Western United States
1:6 000 000

76–77

**Central and Southern
California and Washington**
1:2 500 000

78–79

Middle United States
1:6 000 000

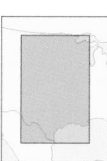

80–81

Eastern United States
1:6 000 000

82–83

North-eastern United States
1:2 500 000

84–85

Mexico   1:8 000 000

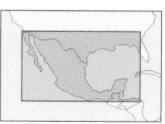

86–87

**Central America and the
West Indies**   1:8 000 000
Jamaica 1:3 000 000
Guadeloupe 1:2 000 000
Martinique 1:2 000 000
Puerto Rico 1:3 000 000
Virgin Islands 1:2 000 000
St Lucia 1:2 000 000
Barbados 1:2 000 000

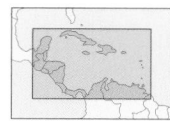

88–89

South America

South America: Physical
1:35 000 000   90

South America: Political
1:35 000 000   91

South America – North
1:16 000 000
Trinidad and Tobago 1:2 500 000

92–93

Central South America
1:8 000 000

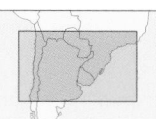

94–95

South America – South
1:16 000 000

96

Index to World Maps
97–176

World: Regions in the News   177

World Statistics: Countries

This alphabetical list includes all the countries and territories of the world. If a territory is not completely independent, the country it is associated with is named. The area figures give the total area of land, inland water and ice. The population figures are 2002 estimates. The annual income is the Gross Domestic Product per capita† in US dollars. The figures are the latest available, usually 2001 estimates.

Country/Territory	Area km^2 Thousands	Area $miles^2$ Thousands	Population Thousands	Capital	Annual Income US $
Afghanistan	652	252	27,756	Kabul	800
Albania	28.8	11.1	3,545	Tirana	3,800
Algeria	2,382	920	32,278	Algiers	5,600
American Samoa (US)	0.2	0.08	69	Pago Pago	8,000
Andorra	0.45	0.17	68	Andorra La Vella	19,000
Angola	1,247	481	10,593	Luanda	1,330
Anguilla (UK)	0.1	0.04	12	The Valley	8,600
Antigua & Barbuda	0.44	0.17	67	St John's	10,000
Argentina	2,767	1,068	37,813	Buenos Aires	12,000
Armenia	29.8	11.5	3,330	Yerevan	3,350
Aruba (Netherlands)	0.19	0.07	70	Oranjestad	28,000
Australia	7,687	2,968	19,547	Canberra	24,000
Austria	83.9	32.4	8,170	Vienna	27,000
Azerbaijan	86.6	33.4	7,798	Baku	3,100
Azores (Portugal)	2.2	0.87	234	Ponta Delgada	12,600
Bahamas	13.9	5.4	301	Nassau	16,800
Bahrain	0.68	0.26	656	Manama	13,000
Bangladesh	144	56	133,377	Dhaka	1,750
Barbados	0.43	0.17	277	Bridgetown	14,500
Belarus	207.6	80.1	10,335	Minsk	8,200
Belgium	30.5	11.8	10,275	Brussels	26,100
Belize	23	8.9	263	Belmopan	3,250
Benin	113	43	6,788	Porto-Novo	1,040
Bermuda (UK)	0.05	0.02	64	Hamilton	34,800
Bhutan	47	18.1	2,094	Thimphu	1,200
Bolivia	1,099	424	8,445	La Paz/Sucre	2,600
Bosnia-Herzegovina	51	20	3,964	Sarajevo	1,800
Botswana	582	225	1,591	Gaborone	7,800
Brazil	8,512	3,286	176,030	Brasília	7,400
Brunei	5.8	2.2	351	Bandar Seri Begawan	18,000
Bulgaria	111	43	7,621	Sofia	6,200
Burkina Faso	274	106	12,603	Ouagadougou	1,040
Burma (= Myanmar)	677	261	42,238	Rangoon	1,500
Burundi	27.8	10.7	6,373	Bujumbura	600
Cambodia	181	70	12,775	Phnom Penh	1,500
Cameroon	475	184	16,185	Yaoundé	1,700
Canada	9,976	3,852	31,902	Ottawa	27,700
Canary Is. (Spain)	7.3	2.8	1,694	Las Palmas/Santa Cruz	18,200
Cape Verde Is.	4	1.6	409	Praia	1,500
Cayman Is. (UK)	0.26	0.1	36	George Town	30,000
Central African Republic	623	241	3,643	Bangui	1,300
Chad	1,284	496	8,997	Ndjaména	1,030
Chile	757	292	15,499	Santiago	10,000
China	9,597	3,705	1,284,304	Beijing	4,300
Colombia	1,139	440	41,008	Bogotá	6,300
Comoros	2.2	0.86	614	Moroni	710
Congo	342	132	2,958	Brazzaville	900
Congo (Dem. Rep. of the)	2,345	905	55,225	Kinshasa	590
Cook Is. (NZ)	0.24	0.09	21	Avarua	5,000
Costa Rica	51.1	19.7	3,835	San José	8,500
Croatia	56.5	21.8	4,391	Zagreb	8,300
Cuba	111	43	11,224	Havana	2,300
Cyprus	9.3	3.6	767	Nicosia	11,500
Czech Republic	78.9	30.4	10,257	Prague	14,400
Denmark	43.1	16.6	5,369	Copenhagen	28,000
Djibouti	23.2	9	473	Djibouti	1,400
Dominica	0.75	0.29	70	Roseau	3,700
Dominican Republic	48.7	18.8	8,722	Santo Domingo	5,800
East Timor	14.9	5.7	953	Dili	500
Ecuador	284	109	13,447	Quito	3,000
Egypt	1,001	387	70,712	Cairo	3,700
El Salvador	21	8.1	6,354	San Salvador	4,600
Equatorial Guinea	28.1	10.8	498	Malabo	2,100
Eritrea	94	36	4,466	Asmara	740
Estonia	44.7	17.3	1,416	Tallinn	10,000
Ethiopia	1,128	436	67,673	Addis Ababa	700
Faroe Is. (Denmark)	1.4	0.54	46	Tórshavn	20,000
Fiji	18.3	7.1	856	Suva	5,200
Finland	338	131	5,184	Helsinki	25,800
France	552	213	59,766	Paris	25,400
French Guiana (France)	90	34.7	182	Cayenne	6,000
French Polynesia (France)	4	1.5	258	Papeete	5,000
Gabon	268	103	1,233	Libreville	5,500
Gambia, The	11.3	4.4	1,456	Banjul	1,770
Gaza Strip (OPT)*	0.36	0.14	1,226	–	630
Georgia	69.7	26.9	4,961	Tbilisi	3,100
Germany	357	138	83,252	Berlin	26,200
Ghana	239	92	20,244	Accra	1,980
Gibraltar (UK)	0.007	0.003	28	Gibraltar Town	17,500
Greece	132	51	10,645	Athens	17,900
Greenland (Denmark)	2,176	840	56	Nuuk (Godthåb)	20,000
Grenada	0.34	0.13	89	St George's	4,750
Guadeloupe (France)	1.7	0.66	436	Basse-Terre	9,000
Guam (US)	0.55	0.21	161	Agana	21,000
Guatemala	109	42	13,314	Guatemala City	3,700
Guinea	246	95	7,775	Conakry	1,970
Guinea-Bissau	36.1	13.9	1,345	Bissau	900
Guyana	215	83	698	Georgetown	3,600
Haiti	27.8	10.7	7,064	Port-au-Prince	1,700
Honduras	112	43	6,561	Tegucigalpa	2,600
Hong Kong (China)	1.1	0.4	7,303	–	25,000
Hungary	93	35.9	10,075	Budapest	12,000
Iceland	103	40	279	Reykjavik	24,800
India	3,288	1,269	1,045,845	New Delhi	2,500
Indonesia	1,890	730	231,328	Jakarta	3,000
Iran	1,648	636	66,623	Tehran	6,400
Iraq	438	169	24,002	Baghdad	2,500
Ireland	70.3	27.1	3,883	Dublin	27,300
Israel	20.6	7.96	6,030	Jerusalem	20,000
Italy	301	116	57,716	Rome	24,300
Ivory Coast (= Côte d'Ivoire)	322	125	16,805	Yamoussoukro	1,550
Jamaica	11	4.2	2,680	Kingston	3,700
Japan	378	146	126,975	Tokyo	27,200
Jordan	89.2	34.4	5,307	Amman	4,200
Kazakhstan	2,717	1,049	16,742	Astana	5,900
Kenya	580	224	31,139	Nairobi	1,000
Kiribati	0.72	0.28	96	Tarawa	840
Korea, North	121	47	22,224	Pyŏngyang	1,000
Korea, South	99	38.2	48,324	Seoul	18,000
Kuwait	17.8	6.9	2,112	Kuwait City	15,100
Kyrgyzstan	198.5	76.6	4,822	Bishkek	2,800
Laos	237	91	5,777	Vientiane	1,630
Latvia	65	25	2,367	Riga	7,800
Lebanon	10.4	4	3,678	Beirut	5,200
Lesotho	30.4	11.7	2,208	Maseru	2,450
Liberia	111	43	3,288	Monrovia	1,100
Libya	1,760	679	5,369	Tripoli	7,600
Liechtenstein	0.16	0.06	33	Vaduz	23,000
Lithuania	65.2	25.2	3,601	Vilnius	7,600
Luxembourg	2.6	1	449	Luxembourg	43,400
Macau (China)	0.02	0.006	462	–	17,600
Macedonia (FYROM)	25.7	9.9	2,055	Skopje	4,400
Madagascar	587	227	16,473	Antananarivo	870
Madeira (Portugal)	0.81	0.31	241	Funchal	16,800
Malawi	118	46	10,702	Lilongwe	660
Malaysia	330	127	22,662	Kuala Lumpur/Putrajaya	9,000
Maldives	0.3	0.12	320	Malé	3,870
Mali	1,240	479	11,340	Bamako	840
Malta	0.32	0.12	397	Valletta	15,000
Marshall Is.	0.18	0.07	74	Dalap-Uliga-Darrit	1,600
Martinique (France)	1.1	0.42	422	Fort-de-France	11,000
Mauritania	1,030	398	2,829	Nouakchott	1,800
Mauritius	2	0.72	1,200	Port Louis	10,800
Mayotte (France)	0.37	0.14	171	Mamoundzou	600
Mexico	1,958	756	103,400	Mexico City	9,000
Micronesia, Fed. States of	0.7	0.27	136	Palikir	2,000
Moldova	33.7	13	4,435	Chişinău	2,550
Monaco	0.002	0.001	32	Monaco	27,000
Mongolia	1,567	605	2,694	Ulan Bator	1,770
Montserrat (UK)	0.1	0.04	8	Plymouth	2,400
Morocco	447	172	31,168	Rabat	3,700
Mozambique	802	309	19,608	Maputo	900
Namibia	825	318	1,821	Windhoek	4,500
Nauru	0.02	0.008	12	Yaren District	5,000
Nepal	141	54	25,874	Katmandu	1,400
Netherlands	41.5	16	16,068	Amsterdam/The Hague	25,800
Netherlands Antilles (Neths)	0.99	0.38	214	Willemstad	11,400
New Caledonia (France)	18.6	7.2	208	Nouméa	15,000
New Zealand	269	104	3,908	Wellington	19,500
Nicaragua	130	50	5,024	Managua	2,500
Niger	1,267	489	10,640	Niamey	820
Nigeria	924	357	129,935	Abuja	840
Northern Mariana Is. (US)	0.48	0.18	77	Saipan	12,500
Norway	324	125	4,525	Oslo	30,800
Oman	212	82	2,713	Muscat	8,200
Pakistan	796	307	147,663	Islamabad	2,100
Palau	0.46	0.18	19	Koror	9,000
Panama	77.1	29.8	2,882	Panamá	5,900
Papua New Guinea	463	179	5,172	Port Moresby	2,400
Paraguay	407	157	5,884	Asunción	4,600
Peru	1,285	496	27,950	Lima	4,800
Philippines	300	116	84,526	Manila	4,000
Poland	313	121	38,625	Warsaw	8,800
Portugal	92.4	35.7	9,609	Lisbon	17,300
Puerto Rico (US)	9	3.5	3,958	San Juan	11,200
Qatar	11	4.2	793	Doha	21,200
Réunion (France)	2.5	0.97	744	St-Denis	4,800
Romania	238	92	22,318	Bucharest	6,800
Russia	17,075	6,592	144,979	Moscow	8,300
Rwanda	26.3	10.2	7,398	Kigali	1,000
St Kitts & Nevis	0.36	0.14	39	Basseterre	8,700
St Lucia	0.62	0.24	160	Castries	4,400
St Vincent & Grenadines	0.39	0.15	116	Kingstown	2,900
Samoa	2.8	1.1	179	Apia	3,500
San Marino	0.06	0.02	28	San Marino	34,600
São Tomé & Príncipe	0.96	0.37	170	São Tomé	1,200
Saudi Arabia	2,150	830	23,513	Riyadh	10,600
Senegal	197	76	10,590	Dakar	1,580
Serbia & Montenegro	102.3	39.5	10,657	Belgrade	2,250
Seychelles	0.46	0.18	80	Victoria	7,600
Sierra Leone	71.7	27.7	5,615	Freetown	500
Singapore	0.62	0.24	4,453	Singapore	24,700
Slovak Republic	49	18.9	5,422	Bratislava	11,500
Slovenia	20.3	7.8	1,933	Ljubljana	16,000
Solomon Is.	28.9	11.2	495	Honiara	1,700
Somalia	638	246	7,753	Mogadishu	550
South Africa	1,220	471	43,648	C. Town/Pretoria/Bloem.	9,400
Spain	505	195	38,383	Madrid	18,900
Sri Lanka	65.6	25.3	19,577	Colombo	3,250
Sudan	2,506	967	37,090	Khartoum	1,360
Suriname	163	63	436	Paramaribo	3,500
Swaziland	17.4	6.7	1,124	Mbabane	4,200
Sweden	450	174	8,877	Stockholm	24,700
Switzerland	41.3	15.9	7,302	Bern	31,100
Syria	185	71	17,156	Damascus	3,200
Taiwan	36	13.9	22,548	Taipei	17,200
Tajikistan	143.1	55.2	6,720	Dushanbe	1,140
Tanzania	945	365	37,188	Dodoma	610
Thailand	513	198	62,354	Bangkok	6,600
Togo	56.8	21.9	5,286	Lomé	1,500
Tonga	0.75	0.29	106	Nuku'alofa	2,200
Trinidad & Tobago	5.1	2	1,164	Port of Spain	9,000
Tunisia	164	63	9,816	Tunis	6,600
Turkey	779	301	67,309	Ankara	6,700
Turkmenistan	488.1	188.5	4,689	Ashkhabad	4,700
Turks & Caicos Is. (UK)	0.43	0.17	19	Cockburn Town	7,300
Tuvalu	0.03	0.01	11	Fongafale	1,100
Uganda	236	91	24,699	Kampala	1,200
Ukraine	603.7	233.1	48,396	Kiev	4,200
United Arab Emirates	83.6	32.3	2,446	Abu Dhabi	21,100
United Kingdom	243.3	94	59,778	London	24,700
United States of America	9,373	3,619	280,562	Washington, DC	36,300
Uruguay	177	68	3,387	Montevideo	9,200
Uzbekistan	447.4	172.7	25,563	Tashkent	2,500
Vanuatu	12.2	4.7	196	Port-Vila	1,300
Vatican City	0.0004	0.0002	1	Vatican City	N/A
Venezuela	912	352	24,288	Caracas	6,100
Vietnam	332	127	81,098	Hanoi	2,100
Virgin Is. (UK)	0.15	0.06	21	Road Town	16,000
Virgin Is. (US)	0.34	0.13	123	Charlotte Amalie	15,000
Wallis & Futuna Is. (France)	0.2	0.08	16	Mata-Utu	2,000
West Bank (OPT)*	5.86	2.26	2,164	–	1,000
Western Sahara	266	103	256	El Aaiún	N/A
Yemen	528	204	18,701	Sana	820
Zambia	753	291	9,959	Lusaka	870
Zimbabwe	391	151	11,377	Harare	2,450

*OPT = Occupied Palestinian Territory   N/A = Not Available

† Gross Domestic Product per capita has been measured using the purchasing power parity method. This enables comparisons to be made between countries through their purchasing power (in US dollars), showing real price levels of goods and services.

World Statistics: Physical Dimensions

Each topic list is divided into continents and within a continent the items are listed in order of size. The bottom part of many of the lists is selective in order to give examples from as many different countries as possible. The order of the continents is the same as in the atlas, beginning with Europe and ending with South America. The figures are rounded as appropriate.

World, Continents, Oceans

	km²	miles²	%
The World	509,450,000	196,672,000	–
Land	149,450,000	57,688,000	29.3
Water	360,000,000	138,984,000	70.7
Asia	44,500,000	17,177,000	29.8
Africa	30,302,000	11,697,000	20.3
North America	24,241,000	9,357,000	16.2
South America	17,793,000	6,868,000	11.9
Antarctica	14,100,000	5,443,000	9.4
Europe	9,957,000	3,843,000	6.7
Australia & Oceania	8,557,000	3,303,000	5.7
Pacific Ocean	179,679,000	69,356,000	49.9
Atlantic Ocean	92,373,000	35,657,000	25.7
Indian Ocean	73,917,000	28,532,000	20.5
Arctic Ocean	14,090,000	5,439,000	3.9

Ocean Depths

Atlantic Ocean		m	ft
Puerto Rico (Milwaukee) Deep		9,220	30,249
Cayman Trench		7,680	25,197
Gulf of Mexico		5,203	17,070
Mediterranean Sea		5,121	16,801
Black Sea		2,211	7,254
North Sea		660	2,165
Indian Ocean		**m**	**ft**
Java Trench		7,450	24,442
Red Sea		2,635	8,454
Pacific Ocean		**m**	**ft**
Mariana Trench		11,022	36,161
Tonga Trench		10,882	35,702
Japan Trench		10,554	34,626
Kuril Trench		10,542	34,587
Arctic Ocean		**m**	**ft**
Molloy Deep		5,608	18,399

Mountains

Europe		m	ft
Elbrus	Russia	5,642	18,510
Mont Blanc	France/Italy	4,807	15,771
Monte Rosa	Italy/Switzerland	4,634	15,203
Dom	Switzerland	4,545	14,911
Liskamm	Switzerland	4,527	14,852
Weisshorn	Switzerland	4,505	14,780
Taschorn	Switzerland	4,490	14,730
Matterhorn/Cervino	Italy/Switzerland	4,478	14,691
Mont Maudit	France/Italy	4,465	14,649
Dent Blanche	Switzerland	4,356	14,291
Nadelhorn	Switzerland	4,327	14,196
Grandes Jorasses	France/Italy	4,208	13,806
Jungfrau	Switzerland	4,158	13,642
Grossglockner	Austria	3,797	12,457
Mulhacén	Spain	3,478	11,411
Zugspitze	Germany	2,962	9,718
Olympus	Greece	2,917	9,570
Triglav	Slovenia	2,863	9,393
Gerlachovka	Slovak Republic	2,655	8,711
Galdhöpiggen	Norway	2,468	8,100
Kebnekaise	Sweden	2,117	6,946
Ben Nevis	UK	1,343	4,406
Asia		**m**	**ft**
Everest	China/Nepal	8,850	29,035
K2 (Godwin Austen)	China/Kashmir	8,611	28,251
Kanchenjunga	India/Nepal	8,598	28,208
Lhotse	China/Nepal	8,516	27,939
Makalu	China/Nepal	8,481	27,824
Cho Oyu	China/Nepal	8,201	26,906
Dhaulagiri	Nepal	8,172	26,811
Manaslu	Nepal	8,156	26,758
Nanga Parbat	Kashmir	8,126	26,660
Annapurna	Nepal	8,078	26,502
Gasherbrum	China/Kashmir	8,068	26,469
Broad Peak	China/Kashmir	8,051	26,414
Xixabangma	China	8,012	26,286
Kangbachen	India/Nepal	7,902	25,925
Trivor	Pakistan	7,720	25,328
Pik Kommunizma	Tajikistan	7,495	24,590
Demavend	Iran	5,604	18,386
Ararat	Turkey	5,165	16,945
Gunong Kinabalu	Malaysia (Borneo)	4,101	13,455
Fuji-San	Japan	3,776	12,388
Africa		**m**	**ft**
Kilimanjaro	Tanzania	5,895	19,340
Mt Kenya	Kenya	5,199	17,057
Ruwenzori (Margherita)	Ug./Congo (D.R.)	5,109	16,762
Ras Dashan	Ethiopia	4,620	15,157
Meru	Tanzania	4,565	14,977
Karisimbi	Rwanda/Congo (D.R.)	4,507	14,787
Mt Elgon	Kenya/Uganda	4,321	14,176
Batu	Ethiopia	4,307	14,130
Toubkal	Morocco	4,165	13,665
Mt Cameroon	Cameroon	4,070	13,353
Oceania		**m**	**ft**
Puncak Jaya	Indonesia	5,030	16,503
Puncak Trikora	Indonesia	4,750	15,584

		m	ft
Puncak Mandala	Indonesia	4,702	15,427
Mt Wilhelm	Papua New Guinea	4,508	14,790
Mauna Kea	USA (Hawaii)	4,205	13,796
Mauna Loa	USA (Hawaii)	4,169	13,681
Mt Cook (Aoraki)	New Zealand	3,753	12,313
Mt Kosciuszko	Australia	2,237	7,339
North America		**m**	**ft**
Mt McKinley (Denali)	USA (Alaska)	6,194	20,321
Mt Logan	Canada	5,959	19,551
Pico de Orizaba	Mexico	5,610	18,405
Mt St Elias	USA/Canada	5,489	18,008
Popocatepetl	Mexico	5,452	17,887
Mt Foraker	USA (Alaska)	5,304	17,401
Ixtaccihuatl	Mexico	5,286	17,342
Lucania	Canada	5,227	17,149
Mt Steele	Canada	5,073	16,644
Mt Bona	USA (Alaska)	5,005	16,420
Mt Whitney	USA	4,418	14,495
Tajumulco	Guatemala	4,220	13,845
Chirripó Grande	Costa Rica	3,837	12,589
Pico Duarte	Dominican Rep.	3,175	10,417
South America		**m**	**ft**
Aconcagua	Argentina	6,962	22,841
Bonete	Argentina	6,872	22,546
Ojos del Salado	Argentina/Chile	6,863	22,516
Pissis	Argentina	6,779	22,241
Mercedario	Argentina/Chile	6,770	22,211
Huascaran	Peru	6,768	22,204
Llullaillaco	Argentina/Chile	6,723	22,057
Nudo de Cachi	Argentina	6,720	22,047
Yerupaja	Peru	6,632	21,758
Sajama	Bolivia	6,542	21,463
Chimborazo	Ecuador	6,267	20,561
Pico Colon	Colombia	5,800	19,029
Pico Bolivar	Venezuela	5,007	16,427
Antarctica		**m**	**ft**
Vinson Massif		4,897	16,066
Mt Kirkpatrick		4,528	14,855

Rivers

Europe		km	miles
Volga	Caspian Sea	3,700	2,300
Danube	Black Sea	2,850	1,770
Ural	Caspian Sea	2,535	1,575
Dnepr (Dnipro)	Black Sea	2,285	1,420
Kama	Volga	2,030	1,260
Don	Black Sea	1,990	1,240
Petchora	Arctic Ocean	1,790	1,110
Oka	Volga	1,480	920
Dnister (Dniester)	Black Sea	1,400	870
Vyatka	Kama	1,370	850
Rhine	North Sea	1,320	820
N. Dvina	Arctic Ocean	1,290	800
Elbe	North Sea	1,145	710
Asia		**km**	**miles**
Yangtze	Pacific Ocean	6,380	3,960
Yenisey–Angara	Arctic Ocean	5,550	3,445
Huang He	Pacific Ocean	5,464	3,395
Ob–Irtysh	Arctic Ocean	5,410	3,360
Mekong	Pacific Ocean	4,500	2,795
Amur	Pacific Ocean	4,400	2,730
Lena	Arctic Ocean	4,400	2,730
Irtysh	Ob	4,250	2,640
Yenisey	Arctic Ocean	4,090	2,540
Ob	Arctic Ocean	3,680	2,285
Indus	Indian Ocean	3,100	1,925
Brahmaputra	Indian Ocean	2,900	1,800
Syrdarya	Aral Sea	2,860	1,775
Salween	Indian Ocean	2,800	1,740
Euphrates	Indian Ocean	2,700	1,675
Amudarya	Aral Sea	2,540	1,575
Africa		**km**	**miles**
Nile	Mediterranean	6,670	4,140
Congo	Atlantic Ocean	4,670	2,900
Niger	Atlantic Ocean	4,180	2,595
Zambezi	Indian Ocean	3,540	2,200
Oubangi/Uele	Congo (D.R.)	2,250	1,400
Kasai	Congo (D.R.)	1,950	1,210
Shaballe	Indian Ocean	1,930	1,200
Orange	Atlantic Ocean	1,860	1,155
Cubango	Okavango Delta	1,800	1,120
Limpopo	Indian Ocean	1,600	995
Senegal	Atlantic Ocean	1,600	995
Australia		**km**	**miles**
Murray–Darling	Indian Ocean	3,750	2,330
Darling	Murray	3,070	1,905
Murray	Indian Ocean	2,575	1,600
Murrumbidgee	Murray	1,690	1,050
North America		**km**	**miles**
Mississippi–Missouri	Gulf of Mexico	6,020	3,740
Mackenzie	Arctic Ocean	4,240	2,630
Mississippi	Gulf of Mexico	3,780	2,350
Missouri	Mississippi	3,780	2,350
Yukon	Pacific Ocean	3,185	1,980
Rio Grande	Gulf of Mexico	3,030	1,880
Arkansas	Mississippi	2,340	1,450
Colorado	Pacific Ocean	2,330	1,445

		m	ft
Red	Mississippi	2,040	1,270
Columbia	Pacific Ocean	1,950	1,210
Saskatchewan	Lake Winnipeg	1,940	1,205

South America		km	miles
Amazon	Atlantic Ocean	6,450	4,010
Paraná–Plate	Atlantic Ocean	4,500	2,800
Purus	Amazon	3,350	2,080
Madeira	Amazon	3,200	1,990
São Francisco	Atlantic Ocean	2,900	1,800
Paraná	Plate	2,800	1,740
Tocantins	Atlantic Ocean	2,750	1,710
Paraguay	Paraná	2,550	1,580
Orinoco	Atlantic Ocean	2,500	1,550
Pilcomayo	Paraná	2,500	1,550
Araguaia	Tocantins	2,250	1,400

Lakes

Europe		km²	miles²
Lake Ladoga	Russia	17,700	6,800
Lake Onega	Russia	9,700	3,700
Saimaa system	Finland	8,000	3,100
Vänern	Sweden	5,500	2,100
Asia		**km²**	**miles²**
Caspian Sea	Asia	371,800	143,550
Lake Baykal	Russia	30,500	11,780
Aral Sea	Kazakhstan/Uzbekistan	28,687	11,086
Tonlé Sap	Cambodia	20,000	7,700
Lake Balqash	Kazakhstan	18,500	7,100
Africa		**km²**	**miles²**
Lake Victoria	East Africa	68,000	26,000
Lake Tanganyika	Central Africa	33,000	13,000
Lake Malawi/Nyasa	East Africa	29,600	11,430
Lake Chad	Central Africa	25,000	9,700
Lake Turkana	Ethiopia/Kenya	8,500	3,300
Lake Volta	Ghana	8,500	3,300
Australia		**km²**	**miles²**
Lake Eyre	Australia	8,900	3,400
Lake Torrens	Australia	5,800	2,200
Lake Gairdner	Australia	4,800	1,900
North America		**km²**	**miles²**
Lake Superior	Canada/USA	82,350	31,800
Lake Huron	Canada/USA	59,600	23,010
Lake Michigan	USA	58,000	22,400
Great Bear Lake	Canada	31,800	12,280
Great Slave Lake	Canada	28,500	11,000
Lake Erie	Canada/USA	25,700	9,900
Lake Winnipeg	Canada	24,400	9,400
Lake Ontario	Canada/USA	19,500	7,500
Lake Nicaragua	Nicaragua	8,200	3,200
South America		**km²**	**miles²**
Lake Titicaca	Bolivia/Peru	8,300	3,200
Lake Poopo	Bolivia	2,800	1,100

Islands

Europe		km²	miles²
Great Britain	UK	229,880	88,700
Iceland	Atlantic Ocean	103,000	39,800
Ireland	Ireland/UK	84,400	32,600
Novaya Zemlya (N.)	Russia	48,200	18,600
Sicily	Italy	25,500	9,800
Corsica	France	8,700	3,400
Asia		**km²**	**miles²**
Borneo	South-east Asia	744,360	287,400
Sumatra	Indonesia	473,600	182,860
Honshu	Japan	230,500	88,980
Sulawesi (Celebes)	Indonesia	189,000	73,000
Java	Indonesia	126,700	48,900
Luzon	Philippines	104,700	40,400
Hokkaido	Japan	78,400	30,300
Africa		**km²**	**miles²**
Madagascar	Indian Ocean	587,040	226,660
Socotra	Indian Ocean	3,600	1,400
Réunion	Indian Ocean	2,500	965
Oceania		**km²**	**miles²**
New Guinea	Indonesia/Papua NG	821,030	317,000
New Zealand (S.)	Pacific Ocean	150,500	58,100
New Zealand (N.)	Pacific Ocean	114,700	44,300
Tasmania	Australia	67,800	26,200
Hawaii	Pacific Ocean	10,450	4,000
North America		**km²**	**miles²**
Greenland	Atlantic Ocean	2,175,600	839,800
Baffin Is.	Canada	508,000	196,100
Victoria Is.	Canada	212,200	81,900
Ellesmere Is.	Canada	212,000	81,800
Cuba	Caribbean Sea	110,860	42,800
Hispaniola	Dominican Rep./Haiti	76,200	29,400
Jamaica	Caribbean Sea	11,400	4,400
Puerto Rico	Atlantic Ocean	8,900	3,400
South America		**km²**	**miles²**
Tierra del Fuego	Argentina/Chile	47,000	18,100
Falkland Is. (E.)	Atlantic Ocean	6,800	2,600

Philip's World Maps

The reference maps which form the main body of this atlas have been prepared in accordance with the highest standards of international cartography to provide an accurate and detailed representation of the Earth. The scales and projections used have been carefully chosen to give balanced coverage of the world, while emphasizing the most densely populated and economically significant regions. A hallmark of Philip's mapping is the use of hill shading and relief colouring to create a graphic impression of landforms: this makes the maps exceptionally easy to read. However, knowledge of the key features employed in the construction and presentation of the maps will enable the reader to derive the fullest benefit from the atlas.

Map sequence

The atlas covers the Earth continent by continent: first Europe; then its land neighbour Asia (mapped north before south, in a clockwise sequence), then Africa, Australia and Oceania, North America and South America. This is the classic arrangement adopted by most cartographers since the 16th century. For each continent, there are maps at a variety of scales. First, physical relief and political maps of the whole continent; then a series of larger-scale maps of the regions within the continent, each followed, where required, by still larger-scale maps of the most important or densely populated areas. The governing principle is that by turning the pages of the atlas, the reader moves steadily from north to south through each continent, with each map overlapping its neighbours.

Map presentation

With very few exceptions (e.g. for the Arctic and Antarctica), the maps are drawn with north at the top, regardless of whether they are presented upright or sideways on the page. In the borders will be found the map title; a locator diagram showing the area covered; continuation arrows showing the page numbers for maps of adjacent areas; the scale; the projection used; the degrees of latitude and longitude; and the letters and figures used in the index for locating place names and geographical features. Physical relief maps also have a height reference panel identifying the colours used for each layer of contouring.

Map symbols

Each map contains a vast amount of detail which can only be conveyed clearly and accurately by the use of symbols. Points and circles of varying sizes locate and identify the relative importance of towns and cities; different styles of type are employed for administrative, geographical and regional place names. A variety of pictorial symbols denote features such as glaciers and marshes, as well as man-made structures including roads, railways, airports and canals.

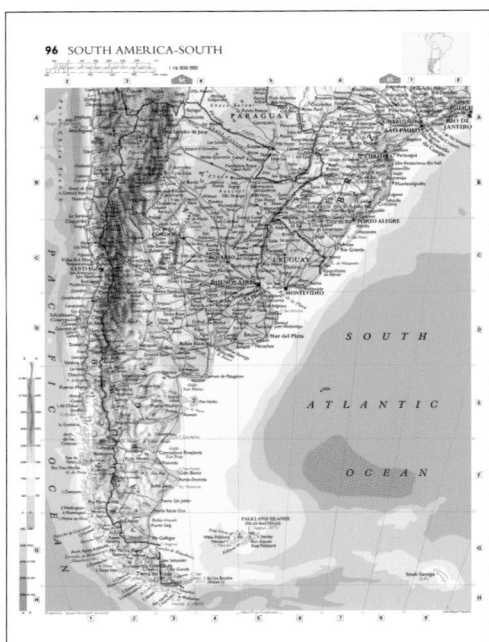

International borders are shown by red lines. Where neighbouring countries are in dispute, for example in the Middle East, the maps show the *de facto* boundary between nations, regardless of the legal or historical situation. The symbols are explained on the first page of the World Maps section of the atlas.

Map scales

The scale of each map is given in the numerical form known as the 'representative fraction'. The first figure is always one, signifying one unit of distance on the map; the second figure, usually in millions, is the number by which the map unit must be multiplied to give the equivalent distance on the Earth's surface. Calculations can easily be made in centimetres and kilometres, by dividing the Earth units figure by 100 000 (i.e. deleting the last five 0s). Thus 1:1 000 000 means 1 cm = 10 km. The calculation for inches and miles is more laborious, but 1 000 000 divided by 63 360 (the number of inches in a mile) shows that the ratio 1:1 000 000 means approximately 1 inch = 16 miles. The table below provides distance equivalents for scales down to 1:50 000 000.

LARGE SCALE		
1:1 000 000	1 cm = 10 km	1 inch = 16 miles
1:2 500 000	1 cm = 25 km	1 inch = 39.5 miles
1:5 000 000	1 cm = 50 km	1 inch = 79 miles
1:6 000 000	1 cm = 60 km	1 inch = 95 miles
1:8 000 000	1 cm = 80 km	1 inch = 126 miles
1:10 000 000	1 cm = 100 km	1 inch = 158 miles
1:15 000 000	1 cm = 150 km	1 inch = 237 miles
1:20 000 000	1 cm = 200 km	1 inch = 316 miles
1:50 000 000	1 cm = 500 km	1 inch = 790 miles
SMALL SCALE		

Measuring distances

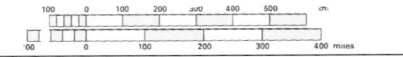

Although each map is accompanied by a scale bar, distances cannot always be measured with confidence because of the distortions involved in portraying the curved surface of the Earth on a flat page. As a general rule, the larger the map scale (i.e. the lower the number of Earth units in the representative fraction), the more accurate and reliable will be the distance measured. On small-scale maps such as those of the world and of entire continents, measurement may only be accurate along the 'standard parallels', or central axes, and should not be attempted without considering the map projection.

Latitude and longitude

Accurate positioning of individual points on the Earth's surface is made possible by reference to the geometrical system of latitude and longitude. Latitude *parallels* are drawn west–east around the Earth and numbered by degrees north and south of the Equator, which is designated 0° of latitude. Longitude *meridians* are drawn north–south and numbered by degrees east and west of the *prime meridian*, 0° of longitude, which passes through Greenwich in England. By referring to these co-ordinates and their subdivisions of minutes (¹⁄₆₀th of a degree) and seconds (¹⁄₆₀th of a minute), any place on Earth can be located to within a few hundred metres. Latitude and longitude are indicated by blue lines on the maps; they are straight or curved according to the projection employed. Reference to these lines is the easiest way of determining the relative positions of places on different maps, and for plotting compass directions.

Name forms

For ease of reference, both English and local name forms appear in the atlas. Oceans, seas and countries are shown in English throughout the atlas; country names may be abbreviated to their commonly accepted form (e.g. Germany, not The Federal Republic of Germany). Conventional English forms are also used for place names on the smaller-scale maps of the continents. However, local name forms are used on all large-scale and regional maps, with the English form given in brackets only for important cities – the large-scale map of Russia and Central Asia thus shows Moskva (Moscow). For countries which do not use a Roman script, place names have been transcribed according to the systems adopted by the British and US Geographic Names Authorities. For China, the Pin Yin system has been used, with some more widely known forms appearing in brackets, as with Beijing (Peking). Both English and local names appear in the index, the English form being cross-referenced to the local form.

THE
WORLD
IN FOCUS

PLANET EARTH	2	WATER & VEGETATION	12	QUALITY OF LIFE	22
RESTLESS EARTH	4	ENVIRONMENT	14	ENERGY	24
LANDFORMS	6	POPULATION	16	PRODUCTION	26
OCEANS	8	THE HUMAN FAMILY	18	TRADE	28
CLIMATE	10	WEALTH	20	TRAVEL & TOURISM	30

Planet Earth

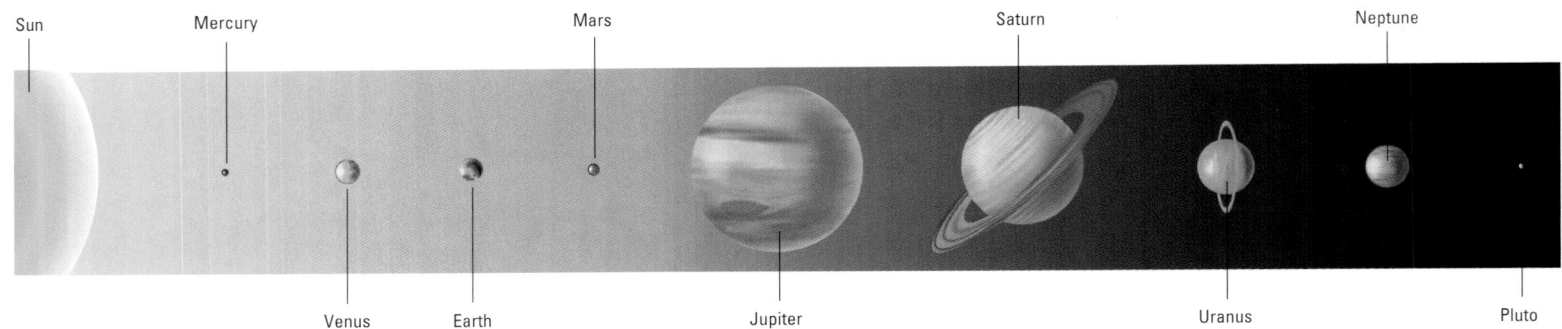

Sun Mercury Mars Saturn Neptune
Venus Earth Jupiter Uranus Pluto

The Solar System

A minute part of one of the billions of galaxies (collections of stars) that comprises the Universe, the Solar System lies some 27,000 light-years from the centre of our own galaxy, the 'Milky Way'. Thought to be about 4,600 million years old, it consists of a central sun with nine planets and their moons revolving around it, attracted by its gravitational pull. The planets orbit the Sun in the same direction – anti-clockwise when viewed from the Northern Heavens – and almost in the same plane. Their orbital paths, however, vary enormously.

The Sun's diameter is 109 times that of Earth, and the temperature at its core – caused by continuous thermonuclear fusions of hydrogen into helium – is estimated to be 15 million degrees Celsius. It is the Solar System's only source of light and heat.

Profile of the Planets

	Mean distance from Sun (million km)	Mass (Earth = 1)	Period of orbit (Earth days/years)	Period of rotation (Earth days)	Equatorial diameter (km)	Number of known satellites
Mercury	57.9	0.055	87.97 days	58.67	4,878	0
Venus	108.2	0.815	224.7 days	243.00	12,104	0
Earth	149.6	1.0	365.3 days	1.00	12,756	1
Mars	227.9	0.11	687.0 days	1.028	6,794	2
Jupiter	778	317.9	11.86 years	0.411	143,884	60
Saturn	1,427	95.2	29.46 years	0.427	120,536	31
Uranus	2,870	14.6	84.01 years	0.748	51,118	21
Neptune	4,497	17.2	164.8 years	0.710	50,538	11
Pluto	5,900	0.002	247.7 years	6.39	2,324	1

All planetary orbits are elliptical in form, but only Pluto and Mercury follow paths that deviate noticeably from a circular one. Near perihelion – its closest approach to the Sun – Pluto actually passes inside the orbit of Neptune, an event that last occurred in 1983. Pluto did not regain its station as outermost planet until February 1999.

The Seasons

Seasons occur because the Earth's axis is tilted at an angle of approximately 23½°. When the northern hemisphere is tilted to a maximum extent towards the Sun, on 21 June, the Sun is overhead at the Tropic of Cancer (latitude 23½° North). This is midsummer, or the summer solstice, in the northern hemisphere.

On 22 or 23 September, the Sun is overhead at the Equator, and day and night are of equal length throughout the world. This is the autumn equinox in the northern hemisphere. On 21 or 22 December, the Sun is overhead at the Tropic of Capricorn (23½° South), the winter solstice in the northern hemisphere. The overhead Sun then tracks north until, on 21 March, it is overhead at the Equator. This is the spring (vernal) equinox in the northern hemisphere.

In the southern hemisphere, the seasons are the reverse of those in the north.

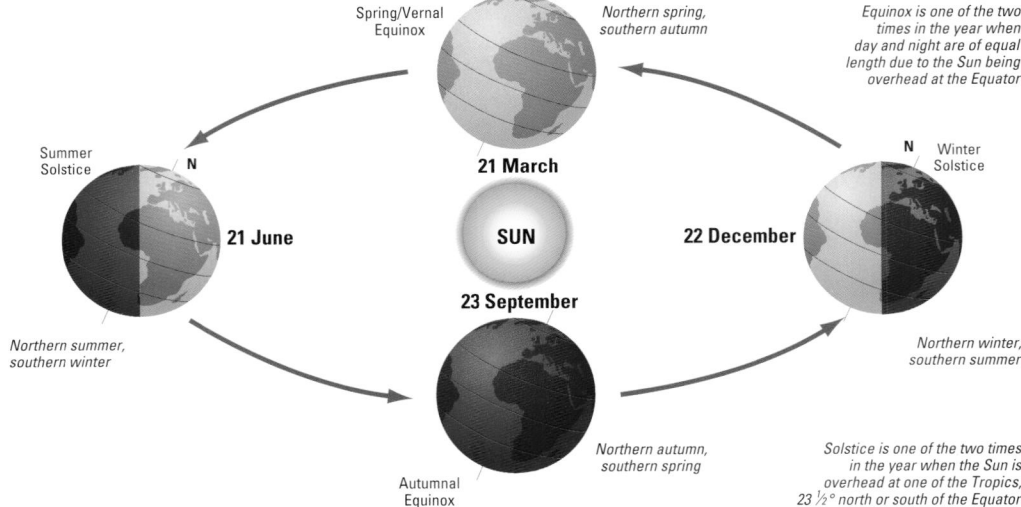

Spring/Vernal Equinox — Northern spring, southern autumn

Equinox is one of the two times in the year when day and night are of equal length due to the Sun being overhead at the Equator

Summer Solstice — 21 June

21 March

SUN

22 December — Winter Solstice

23 September

Northern summer, southern winter

Autumnal Equinox — Northern autumn, southern spring

Northern winter, southern summer

Solstice is one of the two times in the year when the Sun is overhead at one of the Tropics, 23 ½° north or south of the Equator

Day and Night

The Sun appears to rise in the east, reach its highest point at noon, and then set in the west, to be followed by night. In reality, it is not the Sun that is moving but the Earth rotating from west to east. The moment when the Sun's upper limb first appears above the horizon is termed sunrise; the moment when the Sun's upper limb disappears below the horizon is sunset.

At the summer solstice in the northern hemisphere (21 June), the Arctic has total daylight and the Antarctic total darkness. The opposite occurs at the winter solstice (21 or 22 December). At the Equator, the length of day and night are almost equal all year.

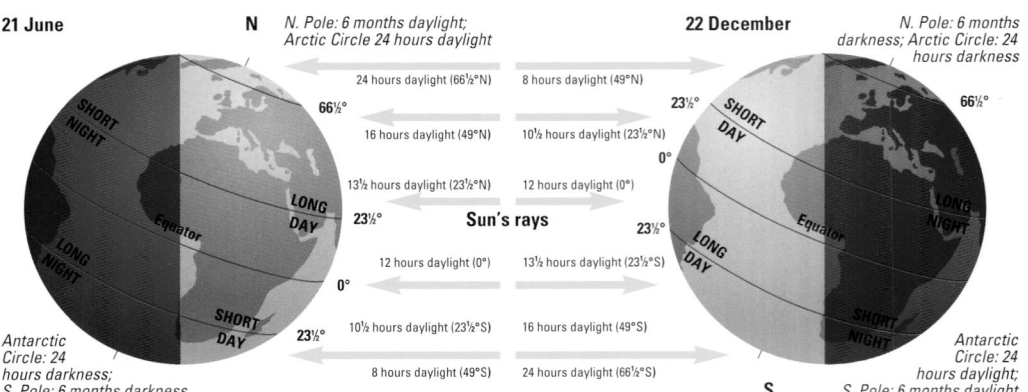

21 June — N. Pole: 6 months daylight; Arctic Circle 24 hours daylight

24 hours daylight (66½°N) 8 hours daylight (49°N)
16 hours daylight (49°N) 10½ hours daylight (23½°N)
13½ hours daylight (23½°N) 12 hours daylight (0°)
Sun's rays
12 hours daylight (0°) 13½ hours daylight (23½°S)
10½ hours daylight (23½°S) 16 hours daylight (49°S)
8 hours daylight (49°S) 24 hours daylight (66½°S)

SHORT NIGHT LONG DAY LONG NIGHT SHORT DAY
Equator

Antarctic Circle: 24 hours darkness; S. Pole: 6 months darkness

22 December — N. Pole: 6 months darkness; Arctic Circle: 24 hours darkness

SHORT DAY LONG NIGHT LONG DAY SHORT NIGHT
Equator

Antarctic Circle: 24 hours daylight; S. Pole: 6 months daylight

Time

Year: The time taken by the Earth to revolve around the Sun, or 365.24 days.

Leap Year: A calendar year of 366 days, 29 February being the additional day. It offsets the difference between the calendar and the solar year.

Month: The approximate time taken by the Moon to revolve around the Earth. The 12 months of the year in fact vary from 28 (29 in a Leap Year) to 31 days.

Week: An artificial period of 7 days, not based on astronomical time.

Day: The time taken by the Earth to complete one rotation on its axis.

Hour: 24 hours make one day. Usually the day is divided into hours AM (ante meridiem or before noon) and PM (post meridiem or after noon), although most timetables now use the 24-hour system, from midnight to midnight.

Sunrise

Sunset

The Moon

The Moon rotates more slowly than the Earth, making one complete turn on its axis in just over 27 days. Since this corresponds to its period of revolution around the Earth, the Moon always presents the same

Phases of the Moon

Distance from Earth: 356,410 km – 406,685 km; Mean diameter: 3,475.1 km; Mass: approx. 1/81 that of Earth; Surface gravity: one-sixth of Earth's; Daily range of temperature at lunar equator: 200°C; Average orbital speed: 3,683 km/h

New Moon — Crescent — First quarter — Gibbous — Full Moon — Gibbous — Last quarter — Crescent — New Moon

hemisphere or face to us, and we never see 'the dark side'. The interval between one full Moon and the next (and between new Moons) is about 29½ days – a lunar month. The apparent changes in the

shape of the Moon are caused by its changing position in relation to the Earth; like the planets, it produces no light of its own and shines only by reflecting the rays of the Sun.

Eclipses

When the Moon passes between the Sun and the Earth it causes a partial eclipse of the Sun (1) if the Earth passes through the Moon's outer shadow (P), or a total eclipse (2) if the inner cone shadow crosses the Earth's surface. In a lunar eclipse, the Earth's shadow crosses the Moon and, again, provides either a partial or total eclipse.

Eclipses of the Sun and the Moon do not occur every month because of the 5° difference between the plane of the Moon's orbit and the plane in which the Earth moves. In the 1990s only 14 lunar eclipses were possible, for example, seven partial and seven total; each was visible only from certain, and variable, parts of the world. The same period witnessed 13 solar eclipses – six partial (or annular) and seven total.

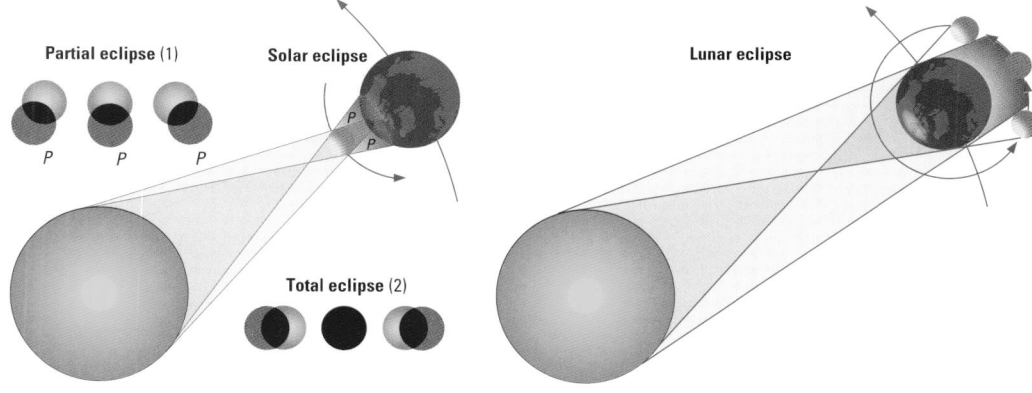

Tides

The daily rise and fall of the ocean's tides are the result of the gravitational pull of the Moon and that of the Sun, though the effect of the latter is only 46.6% as strong as that of the Moon. This effect is greatest on the hemisphere facing the Moon and causes a tidal 'bulge'. When the Sun, Earth and Moon are in line, tide-raising forces are at a maximum and Spring tides occur: high tide reaches the highest values, and low tide falls to low levels. When lunar and solar forces are least coincidental with the Sun and Moon at an angle (near the Moon's first and third quarters), Neap tides occur, which have a small tidal range.

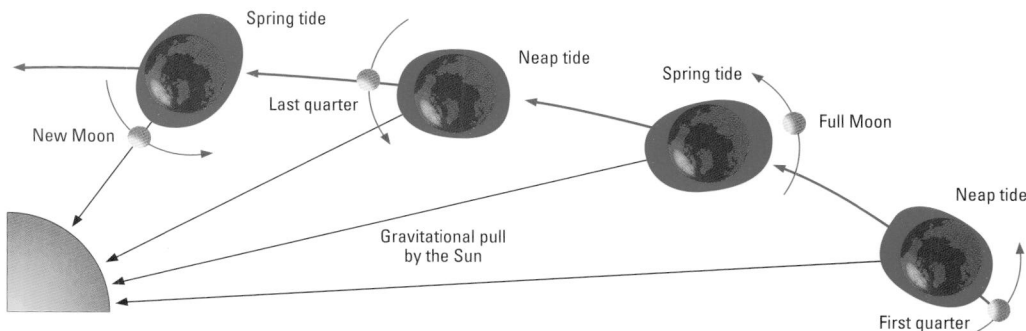

Restless Earth

The Earth's Structure

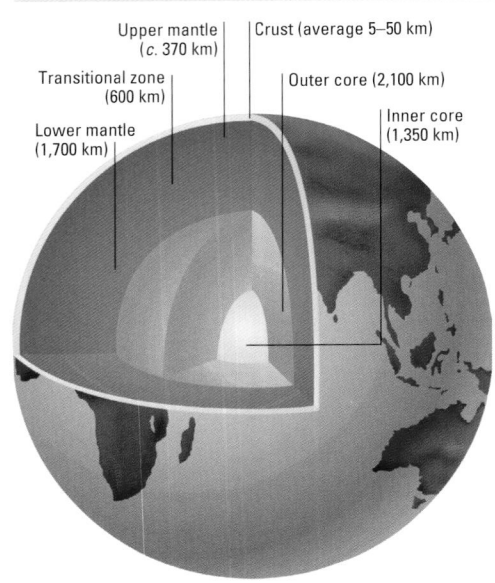

- Upper mantle (c. 370 km)
- Crust (average 5–50 km)
- Transitional zone (600 km)
- Outer core (2,100 km)
- Lower mantle (1,700 km)
- Inner core (1,350 km)

Continental Drift

About 200 million years ago the original Pangaea landmass began to split into two continental groups, which further separated over time to produce the present-day configuration.

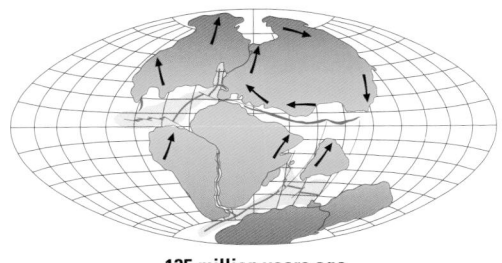

135 million years ago

Trench
Rift
New ocean floor
Zones of slippage

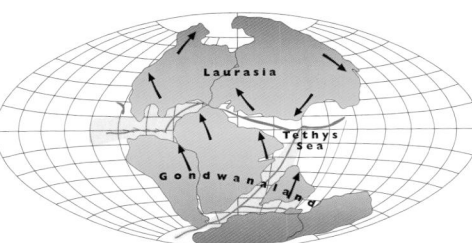

180 million years ago

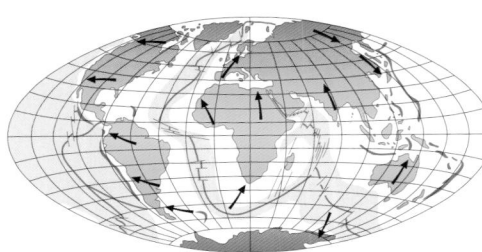

Present day

Notable Earthquakes Since 1900

Year	Location	Richter Scale	Deaths
1906	San Francisco, USA	8.3	503
1906	Valparaiso, Chile	8.6	22,000
1906	San Francisco, USA	7.7	3,000
1906	Valparaiso, Chile	8.6	22,000
1908	Messina, Italy	7.5	83,000
1915	Avezzano, Italy	7.5	30,000
1920	Gansu (Kansu), China	8.6	180,000
1923	Yokohama, Japan	8.3	143,000
1927	Nan Shan, China	8.3	200,000
1932	Gansu (Kansu), China	7.6	70,000
1933	Sanriku, Japan	8.9	2,990
1934	Bihar, India/Nepal	8.4	10,700
1935	Quetta, India (now Pakistan)	7.5	60,000
1939	Chillan, Chile	8.3	28,000
1939	Erzincan, Turkey	7.9	30,000
1960	S. W. Chile	9.5	2,200
1960	Agadir, Morocco	5.8	12,000
1962	Khorasan, Iran	7.1	12,230
1964	Anchorage, USA	9.2	125
1968	N. E. Iran	7.4	12,000
1970	N. Peru	7.7	66,794
1972	Managua, Nicaragua	6.2	5,000
1974	N. Pakistan	6.3	5,200
1976	Guatemala	7.5	22,778
1976	Tangshan, China	8.2	255,000
1978	Tabas, Iran	7.7	25,000
1980	El Asnam, Algeria	7.3	20,000
1980	S. Italy	7.2	4,800
1985	Mexico City, Mexico	8.1	4,200
1988	N.W. Armenia	6.8	55,000
1990	N. Iran	7.7	36,000
1992	Flores, Indonesia	6.8	1,895
1993	Maharashtra, India	6.4	30,000
1994	Los Angeles, USA	6.6	51
1995	Kobe, Japan	7.2	5,000
1995	Sakhalin Is., Russia	7.5	2,000
1996	Yunnan, China	7.0	240
1997	N. E. Iran	7.1	2,400
1998	Takhar, Afghanistan	6.1	4,200
1998	Rostaq, Afghanistan	7.0	5,000
1999	Izmit, Turkey	7.4	15,000
1999	Taipei, Taiwan	7.6	1,700
2001	Gujarat, India	7.7	14,000
2002	Afyon, Turkey	6.5	44
2002	Baghlan, Afghanistan	6.1	1,000
2003	Boumerdes, Algeria	6.8	2,200

Earthquakes

Earthquake magnitude is usually rated according to either the Richter or the Modified Mercalli scale, both devised by seismologists in the 1930s. The Richter scale measures absolute earthquake power with mathematical precision: each step upwards represents a tenfold increase in shockwave amplitude. Theoretically, there is no upper limit, but the largest earthquakes measured have been rated at between 8.8 and 8.9. The 12–point Mercalli scale, based on observed effects, is often more meaningful, ranging from I (earthquakes noticed only by seismographs) to XII (total destruction); intermediate points include V (people awakened at night; unstable objects overturned), VII (collapse of ordinary buildings; chimneys and monuments fall) and IX (conspicuous cracks in ground; serious damage to reservoirs).

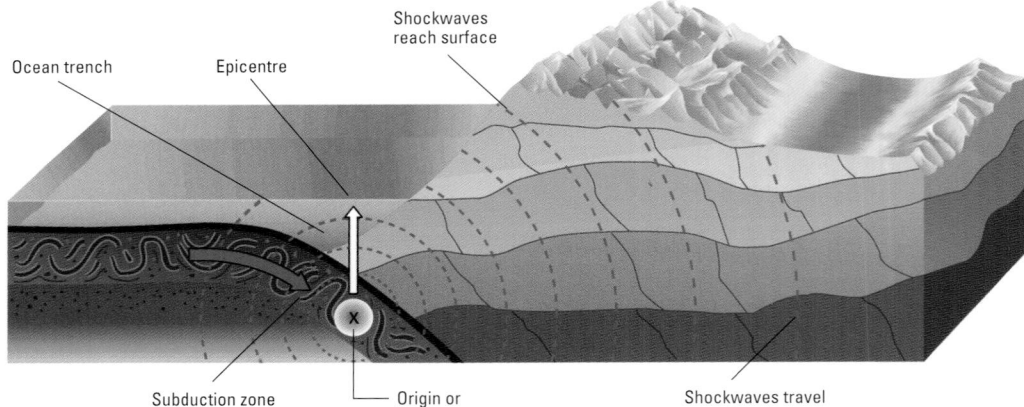

- Shockwaves reach surface
- Ocean trench
- Epicentre
- Subduction zone
- Origin or focus
- Shockwaves travel away from focus

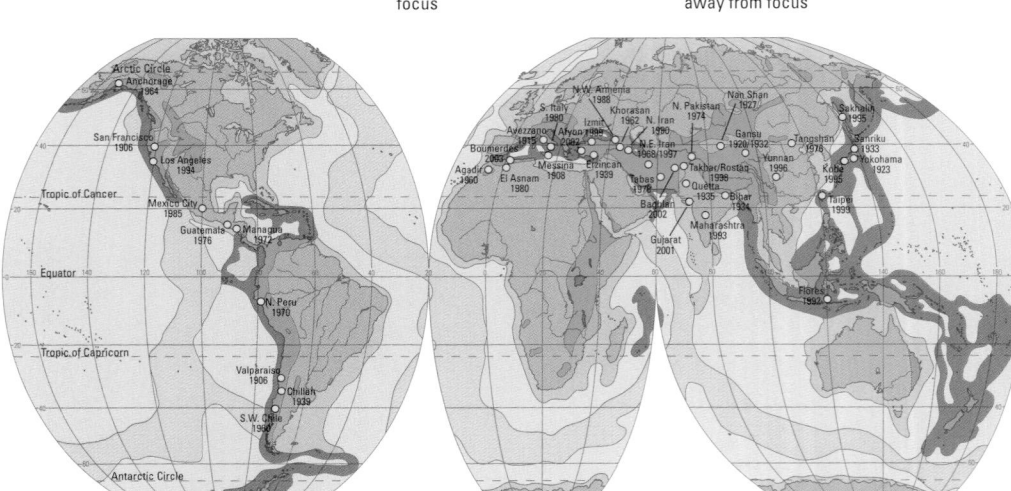

Projection: Interrupted Mollweide

Structure and Earthquakes

- Mobile land areas
- Submarine zones of mobile land areas
- Stable land platforms
- Submarine extensions of stable land platforms
- Mid-oceanic volcanic ridges
- Oceanic platforms

1976○ Principal earthquakes and dates (since 1900)

Earthquakes are a series of rapid vibrations originating from the slipping or faulting of parts of the Earth's crust when stresses within build up to breaking point. They usually happen at depths varying from 8 km to 30 km. Severe earthquakes cause extensive damage when they take place in populated areas, destroying structures and severing communications. Most initial loss of life occurs due to secondary causes such as falling masonry, fires and flooding.

Plate Tectonics

Plate boundaries — PACIFIC Major plates

→ Direction of plate movements and rate of movement (cm/year)

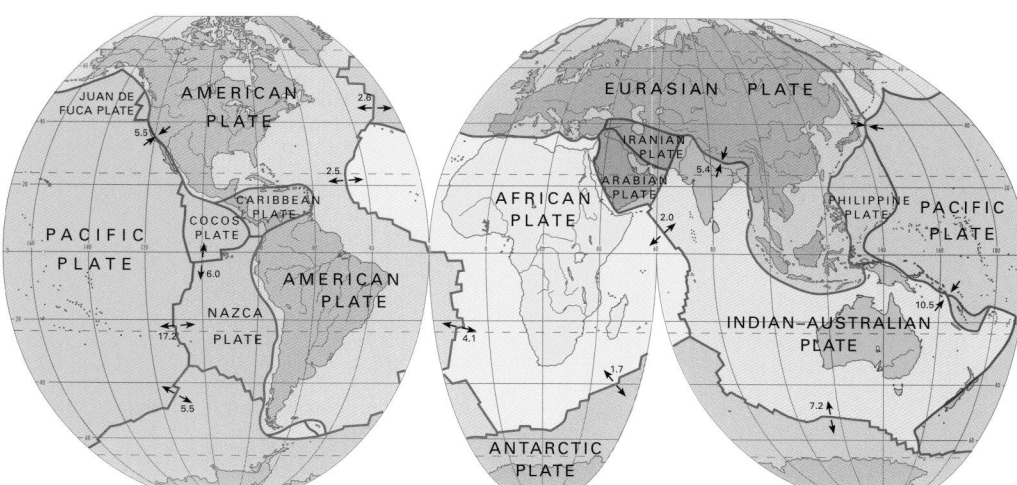

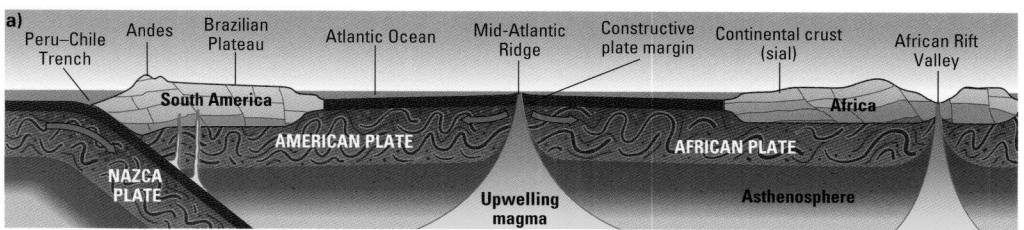

a) Peru–Chile Trench | Andes | Brazilian Plateau | Atlantic Ocean | Mid-Atlantic Ridge | Constructive plate margin | Continental crust (sial) | African Rift Valley — South America — AMERICAN PLATE — Africa — NAZCA PLATE — AFRICAN PLATE — Upwelling magma — Asthenosphere

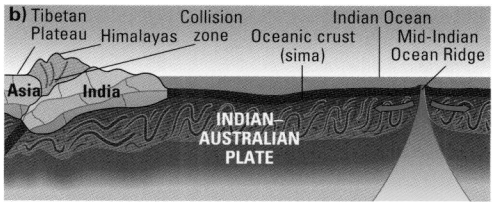

b) Tibetan Plateau | Collision zone | Indian Ocean | Himalayas | Oceanic crust (sima) | Mid-Indian Ocean Ridge — Asia | India — INDIAN–AUSTRALIAN PLATE

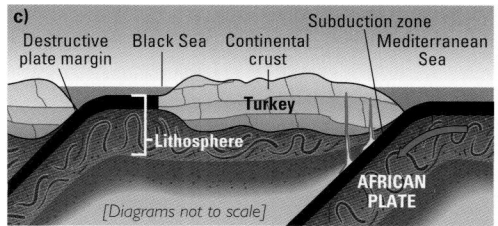

c) Destructive plate margin | Black Sea | Continental crust | Subduction zone | Mediterranean Sea — Turkey — Lithosphere — AFRICAN PLATE — [Diagrams not to scale]

The drifting of the continents is a feature that is unique to Planet Earth. The complementary, almost jigsaw-puzzle fit of the coastlines on each side of the Atlantic Ocean inspired Alfred Wegener's theory of continental drift in 1915. The theory suggested that the ancient super-continent, which Wegener named Pangaea, incorporated all of the Earth's landmasses and gradually split up to form today's continents.

The original debate about continental drift was a prelude to a more radical idea: plate tectonics. The basic theory is that the Earth's crust is made up of a series of rigid plates which float on a soft layer of the mantle and are moved about by continental convection currents within the Earth's interior. These plates diverge and converge along margins marked by seismic activity. Plates diverge from mid-ocean ridges where molten lava pushes upwards and forces the plates apart at rates of up to 40 mm [1.6 in] a year.

The three diagrams, left, give some examples of plate boundaries from around the world. Diagram (a) shows sea-floor spreading at the Mid-Atlantic Ridge as the American and African plates slowly diverge. The same thing is happening in (b) where sea-floor spreading at the Mid-Indian Ocean Ridge is forcing the Indian–Australian plate to collide into the Eurasian plate. In (c) oceanic crust (sima) is being subducted beneath lighter continental crust (sial).

Volcanoes

Volcanoes occur when hot liquefied rock beneath the Earth's crust is pushed up by pressure to the surface as molten lava. Some volcanoes erupt in an explosive way, throwing out rocks and ash, whilst others are effusive and lava flows out of the vent. There are volcanoes which are both, such as Mount Fuji. An accumulation of lava and cinders creates cones of variable size and shape. As a result of many eruptions over centuries, Mount Etna in Sicily has a circumference of more than 120 km [75 miles].

Climatologists believe that volcanic ash, if ejected high into the atmosphere, can influence temperature and weather for several years afterwards. The 1991 eruption of Mount Pinatubo in the Philippines ejected more than 20 million tonnes of dust and ash 32 km [20 miles] into the atmosphere and is believed to have accelerated ozone depletion over a large part of the globe.

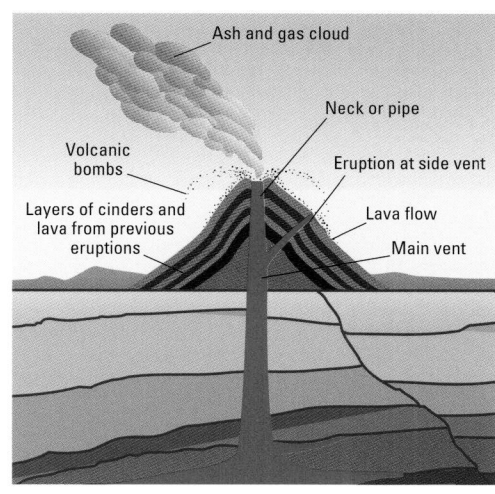

Ash and gas cloud | Neck or pipe | Volcanic bombs | Eruption at side vent | Layers of cinders and lava from previous eruptions | Lava flow | Main vent

Distribution of Volcanoes

Volcanoes today may be the subject of considerable scientific study but they remain both dramatic and unpredictable: in 1991 Mount Pinatubo, 100 km [62 miles] north of the Philippines capital Manila, suddenly burst into life after lying dormant for more than six centuries. Most of the world's active volcanoes occur in a belt around the Pacific Ocean, on the edge of the Pacific plate, called the 'ring of fire'. Indonesia has the greatest concentration with 90 volcanoes, 12 of which are active. The most famous, Krakatoa, erupted in 1883 with such force that the resulting tidal wave killed 36,000 people and tremors were felt as far away as Australia.

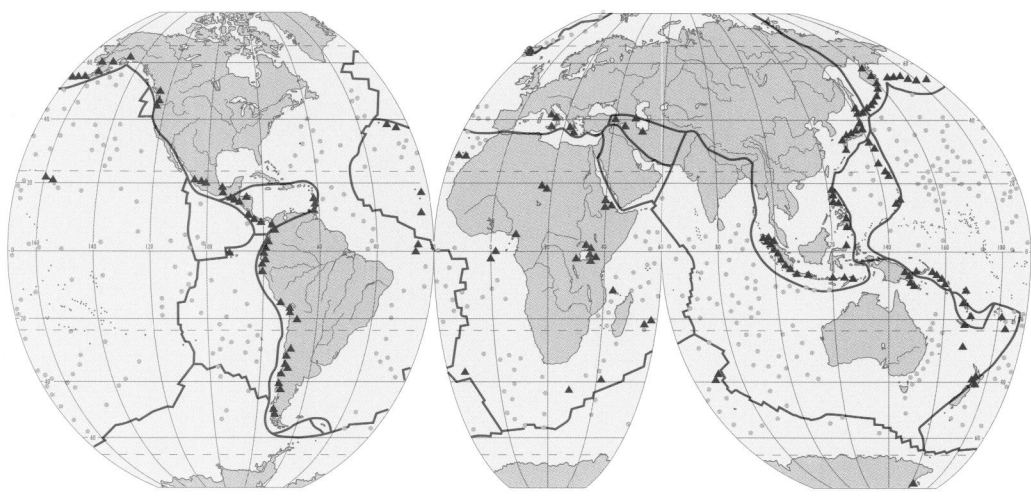

○ Submarine volcanoes

▲ Land volcanoes active since 1700

— Boundaries of tectonic plates

Landforms

The Rock Cycle

James Hutton first proposed the rock cycle in the late 1700s after he observed the slow but steady effects of erosion.

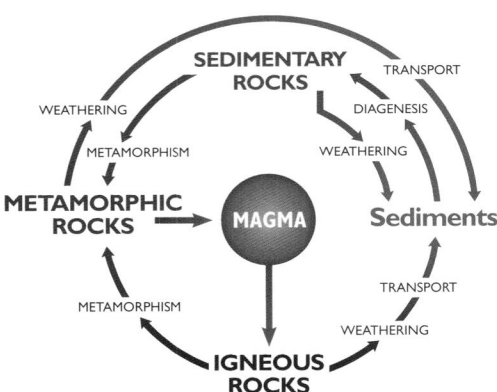

Above and below the surface of the oceans, the features of the Earth's surface are constantly changing. The phenomenal forces generated by convection currents in the molten core of our planet carry the vast segments or 'plates' of the crust across the globe in an endless cycle of creation and destruction. A continent may travel little more than 25 mm [1 in] per year, yet in the vast span of geological time this process throws up giant mountain ranges and creates new land.

Destruction of the landscape, however, begins as soon as it is formed. Wind, water, ice and sea, the main agents of erosion, mount a constant assault that even the most resistant rocks cannot withstand. Mountain peaks may dwindle by as little as a few millimetres each year, but if they are not uplifted by further movements of the crust they will eventually be reduced to rubble and transported away.

Water is the most powerful agent of erosion – it has been estimated that 100 billion tonnes of sediment are washed into the oceans every year. Three Asian rivers account for 20% of this total, the Huang He, in China, and the Brahmaputra and Ganges in Bangladesh.

Rivers and glaciers, like the sea itself, generate much of their effect through abrasion – pounding the land with the debris they carry with them. But as well as destroying they also create new landforms, many of them spectacular: vast deltas like those of the Mississippi and the Nile, or the deep fjords cut by glaciers in British Columbia, Norway and New Zealand.

Geologists once considered that landscapes evolved from 'young', newly uplifted mountainous areas, through a 'mature' hilly stage, to an 'old age' stage when the land was reduced to an almost flat plain, or peneplain. This theory, called the 'cycle of erosion', fell into disuse when it became evident that so many factors, including the effects of plate tectonics and climatic change, constantly interrupt the cycle, which takes no account of the highly complex interactions that shape the surface of our planet.

Mountain Building

Mountains are formed when pressures on the Earth's crust caused by continental drift become so intense that the surface buckles or cracks. This happens where oceanic crust is subducted by continental crust or, more dramatically, where two tectonic plates collide: the Rockies, Andes, Alps, Urals and Himalayas resulted from such impacts. These are all known as fold mountains because they were formed by the compression of the rocks, forcing the surface to bend and fold like a crumpled rug. The Himalayas are formed from the folded former sediments of the Tethys Sea which was trapped in the collision zone between the Indian and Eurasian plates.

The other main mountain-building process occurs when the crust fractures to create faults, allowing rock to be forced upwards in large blocks; or when the pressure of magma within the crust forces the surface to bulge into a dome, or erupts to form a volcano. Large mountain ranges may reveal a combination of those features; the Alps, for example, have been compressed so violently that the folds are fragmented by numerous faults and intrusions of molten igneous rock.

Over millions of years, even the greatest mountain ranges can be reduced by the agents of erosion (most notably rivers) to a low rugged landscape known as a peneplain.

Types of faults: Faults occur where the crust is being stretched or compressed so violently that the rock strata break in a horizontal or vertical movement. They are classified by the direction in which the blocks of rock have moved. A normal fault results when a vertical movement causes the surface to break apart; compression causes a reverse fault. Horizontal movement causes shearing, known as a strike-slip fault. When the rock breaks in two places, the central block may be pushed up in a horst fault, or sink (creating a rift valley) in a graben fault.

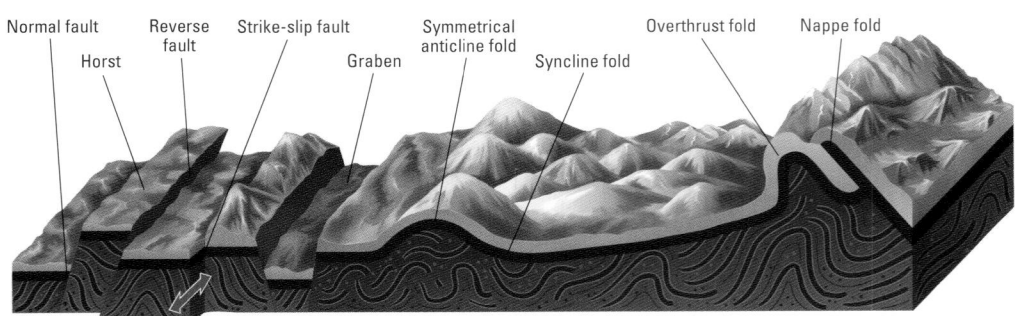

Types of fold: Folds occur when rock strata are squeezed and compressed. They are common therefore at destructive plate margins and where plates have collided, forcing the rocks to buckle into mountain ranges. Geographers give different names to the degrees of fold that result from continuing pressure on the rock. A simple fold may be symmetric, with even slopes on either side, but as the pressure builds up, one slope becomes steeper and the fold becomes asymmetric. Later, the ridge or 'anticline' at the top of the fold may slide over the lower ground or 'syncline' to form a recumbent fold. Eventually, the rock strata may break under the pressure to form an overthrust and finally a nappe fold.

Continental Glaciation

Ice sheets were at their greatest extent about 200,000 years ago. The maximum advance of the last Ice Age was about 18,000 years ago, when ice covered virtually all of Canada and reached as far south as the Bristol Channel in Britain.

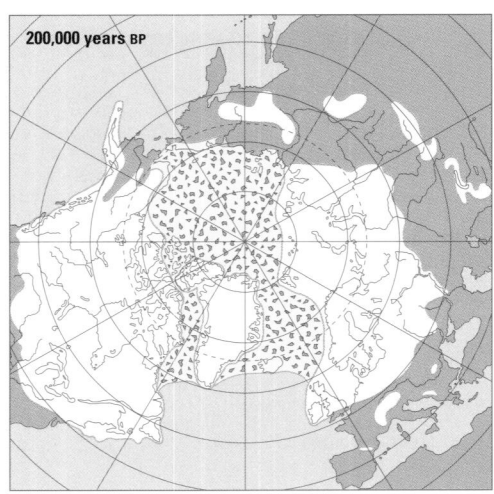

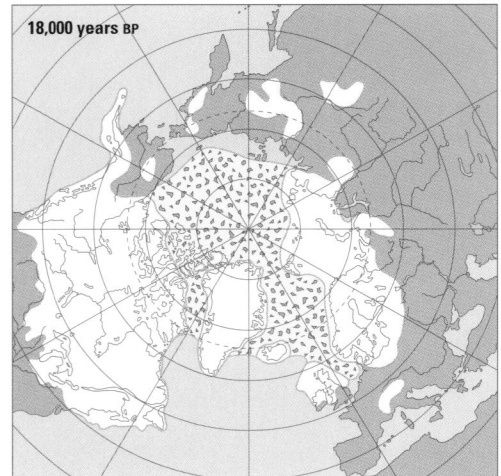

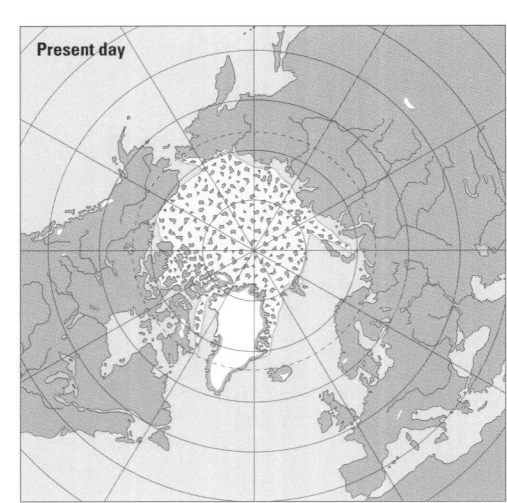

A stylized diagram to show a selection of landforms found in the mid-latitudes.

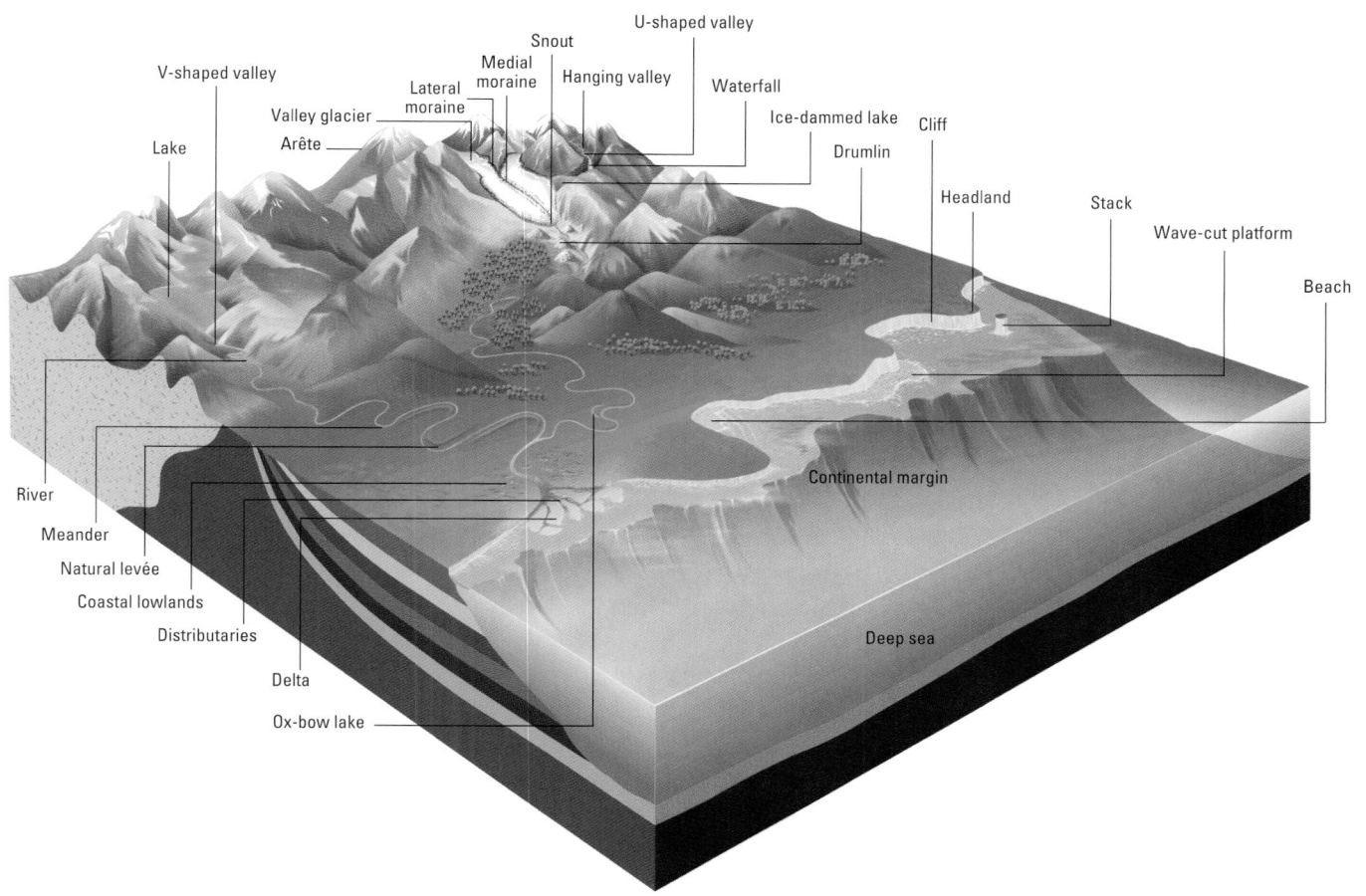

V-shaped valley

Valley glacier

Arête

Lateral moraine

Medial moraine

Snout

Hanging valley

U-shaped valley

Waterfall

Ice-dammed lake

Cliff

Drumlin

Headland

Stack

Wave-cut platform

Beach

Lake

River

Meander

Natural levée

Coastal lowlands

Distributaries

Delta

Ox-bow lake

Continental margin

Deep sea

Desert Landscapes

The popular image that deserts are all huge expanses of sand is wrong. Despite harsh conditions, deserts contain some of the most varied and interesting landscapes in the world. They are also one of the most extensive environments – the hot and cold deserts together cover almost 40% of the Earth's surface.

The three types of hot desert are known by their Arabic names: sand desert, called *erg*, covers only about one-fifth of the world's desert; the rest is divided between *hammada* (areas of bare rock) and *reg* (broad plains covered by loose gravel or pebbles).

In areas of *erg*, such as the Namib Desert, the shape of the dunes reflects the character of local winds. Where winds are constant in direction, crescent-shaped *barchan* dunes form. In areas of bare rock, wind-blown sand is a major agent of erosion. The erosion is mainly confined to within 2 m [6.5 ft] of the surface, producing characteristic, mushroom-shaped rocks.

Erg

Hammada

Reg

Surface Processes

Catastrophic changes to natural landforms are periodically caused by such phenomena as avalanches, landslides and volcanic eruptions, but most of the processes that shape the Earth's surface operate extremely slowly in human terms. One estimate, based on a study in the United States, suggested that 1 m [3 ft] of land was removed from the entire surface of the country, on average, every 29,500 years. However, the time-scale varies from 1,300 years to 154,200 years depending on the terrain and climate.

In hot, dry climates, mechanical weathering, a result of rapid temperature changes, causes the outer layers of rock to peel away, while in cold mountainous regions, boulders are prised apart when water freezes in cracks in rocks. Chemical weathering, at its greatest in warm, humid regions, is responsible for hollowing out limestone caves and decomposing granites.

The erosion of soil and rock is greatest on sloping land and the steeper the slope, the greater the tendency for mass wasting – the movement of soil and rock downhill under the influence of gravity. The mechanisms of mass wasting (ranging from very slow to very rapid) vary with the type of material, but the presence of water as a lubricant is usually an important factor.

Running water is the world's leading agent of erosion and transportation. The energy of a river depends on several factors, including its velocity and volume, and its erosive power is at its peak when it is in full flood. Sea waves also exert tremendous erosive power during storms when they hurl pebbles against the shore, undercutting cliffs and hollowing out caves.

Glacier ice forms in mountain hollows and spills out to form valley glaciers, which transport rocks shattered by frost action. As glaciers move, rocks embedded into the ice erode steep-sided, U-shaped valleys. Evidence of glaciation in mountain regions includes cirques, knife-edged ridges, or arêtes, and pyramidal peaks.

Oceans

Relative sizes of the world's oceans

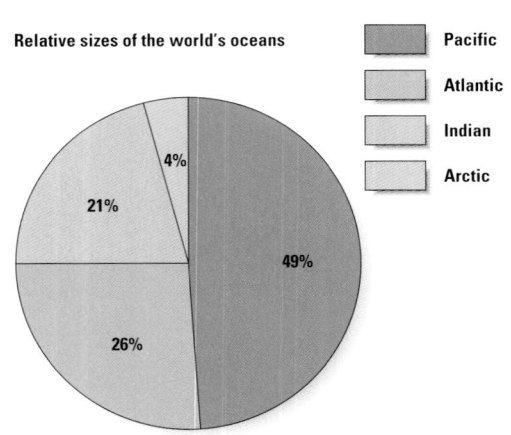

■	Pacific
■	Atlantic
■	Indian
■	Arctic

4%
21%
49%
26%

In a strict geographical sense there are only four true oceans – the Atlantic, Indian, Pacific and Arctic. The International Hydrographic Bureau does not recognize the Antarctic Ocean (even less the 'Southern Ocean') as a separate entity. From ancient times to about the 15th century, the legendary 'Seven Seas' comprised the Red Sea, Mediterranean Sea, Persian Gulf, Black Sea, Adriatic Sea, Caspian Sea and Indian Sea.

The Earth is a watery planet: more than 70% of its surface – over 360,000,000 sq km [140,000,000 sq miles] – is covered by the oceans and seas. The mighty Pacific alone accounts for nearly 36% of the total, and 49% of the sea area. Gravity holds in around 1,400 million cu. km [320 million cu. miles] of water, of which over 97% is saline.

The vast underwater world starts in the shallows of the seaside and plunges to depths of more than 11,000 m [36,000 ft]. The continental shelf, part of the landmass, drops gently to around 200 m [650 ft]; here the seabed falls away suddenly at an angle of 3° to 6° – the continental slope. The third stage, called the continental rise, is more gradual with gradients varying from 1 in 100 to 1 in 700. At an average depth of 5,000 m [16,500 ft] there begins the aptly-named abyssal plain – massive submarine depths where sunlight fails to penetrate and few creatures can survive.

From these plains rise volcanoes which, taken from base to top, rival and even surpass the tallest continental mountains in height. Mauna Kea, on Hawaii, reaches a total of 10,203 m [33,400 ft], some 1,355 m [4,500 ft] more than Mount Everest, though scarcely 40% is visible above sea level.

In addition, there are underwater mountain chains up to 1,000 km [600 miles] across, whose peaks sometimes appear above sea level as islands such as Iceland and Tristan da Cunha.

The Ocean Depths

Average and maximum depths of the world's great oceans, in metres

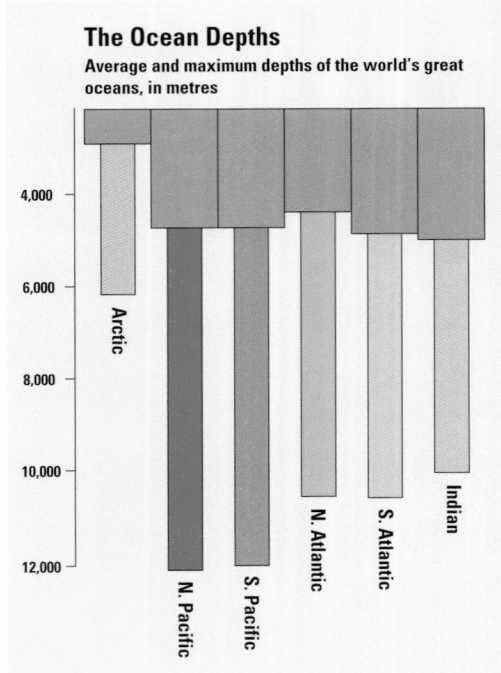

January ocean currents

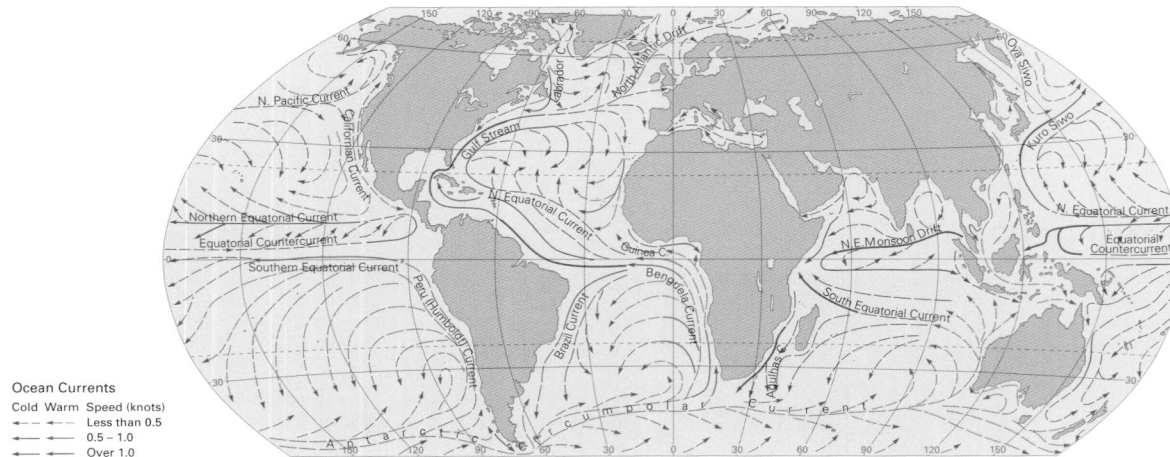

Ocean Currents
Cold Warm Speed (knots)
Less than 0.5
0.5 – 1.0
Over 1.0

July ocean currents

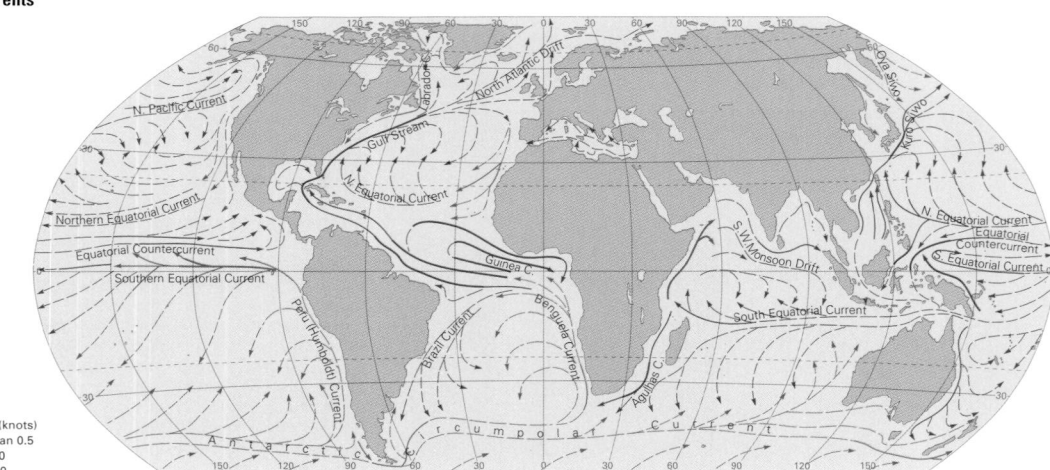

Ocean Currents
Cold Warm Speed (knots)
Less than 0.5
0.5 – 1.0
Over 1.0

Moving immense quantities of energy as well as billions of tonnes of water every hour, the ocean currents are a vital part of the great heat engine that drives the Earth's climate. They themselves are produced by a twofold mechanism. At the surface, winds push huge masses of water before them; in the deep ocean, below an abrupt temperature gradient that separates the churning surface waters from the still depths, density variations cause slow vertical movements.

The pattern of circulation of the great surface currents is determined by the displacement known as the Coriolis effect. As the Earth turns beneath a moving object – whether it is a tennis ball or a vast mass of water – it appears to be deflected to one side. The deflection is most obvious near the Equator, where the Earth's surface is spinning eastwards at 1,700 km/h [1,050 mph]; currents moving polewards are curved clockwise in the northern hemisphere and anti-clockwise in the southern.

The result is a system of spinning circles known as gyres. The Coriolis effect piles up water on the left of each gyre, creating a narrow, fast-moving stream that is matched by a slower, broader returning current on the right. North and south of the Equator, the fastest currents are located in the west and in the east respectively. In each case, warm water moves from the Equator and cold water returns to it. Cold currents often bring an upwelling of nutrients with them, supporting the world's most economically important fisheries.

Depending on the prevailing winds, some currents on or near the Equator may reverse their direction in the course of the year – a seasonal variation on which Asian monsoon rains depend, and whose occasional failure can bring disaster to millions.

World Fishing Areas

Main commercial fishing areas (numbered FAO regions)

Catch by top marine fishing areas, thousand tonnes (2000)

1.	Pacific, NW	[61]	23,141	24.4%
2.	Pacific, SE	[87]	15,822	16.7%
3.	Atlantic, NE	[27]	10,920	11.5%
4.	Pacific, WC	[71]	9,899	10.4%
5.	Indian, E	[57]	4,708	5.0%
6.	Indian, W	[51]	3,902	4.1%
7.	Atlantic, EC	[34]	3,523	3.7%
8.	Pacific, NE	[67]	2,518	2.7%
9.	Atlantic, NW	[21]	2,063	2.2%
10.	Atlantic, WC	[31]	1,831	1.9%

Principal fishing areas

Leading fishing nations

China 17.9% Peru 11.2% Japan 5.3% USA 5.0% Chile 4.5% Indonesia 4.4% Russia 4.2%

World total (2000): 94,849,000 tonnes
(Marine catch 90.7% Inland catch 9.3%)

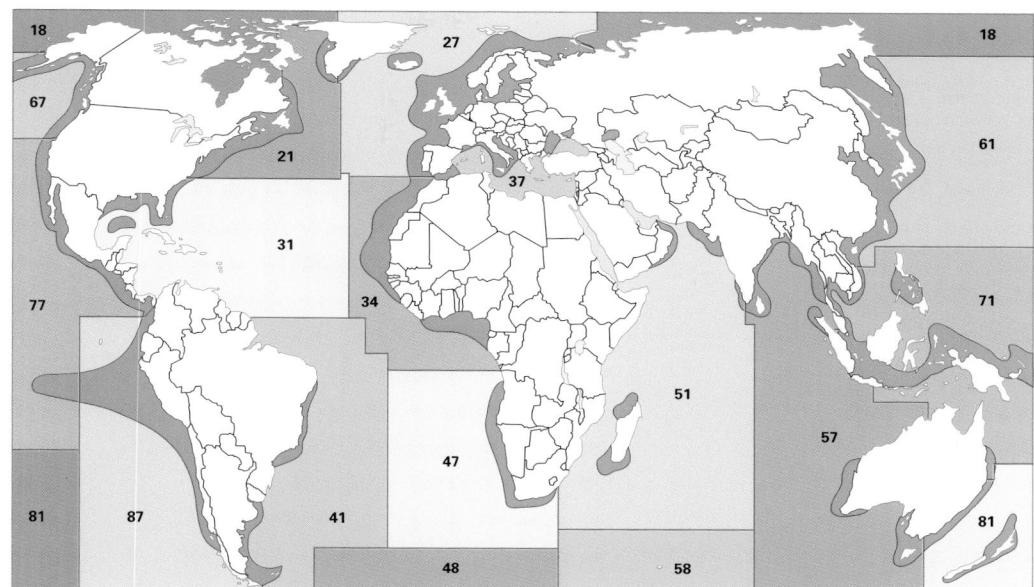

Marine Pollution

Sources of marine oil pollution (latest available year)

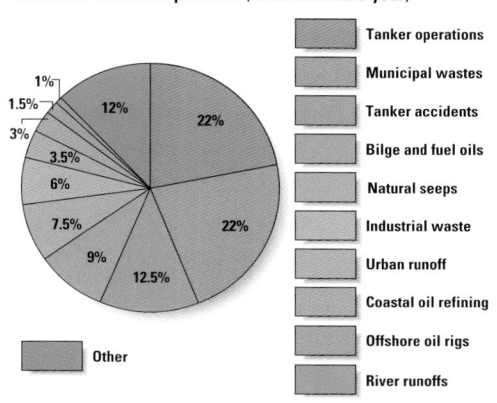

- Tanker operations
- Municipal wastes
- Tanker accidents
- Bilge and fuel oils
- Natural seeps
- Industrial waste
- Urban runoff
- Coastal oil refining
- Offshore oil rigs
- River runoffs
- Other

Oil Spills

Major oil spills from tankers and combined carriers

Year	Vessel	Location	Spill (barrels)**	Cause
1979	Atlantic Empress	West Indies	1,890,000	collision
1983	Castillo De Bellver	South Africa	1,760,000	fire
1978	Amoco Cadiz	France	1,628,000	grounding
1991	Haven	Italy	1,029,000	explosion
1988	Odyssey	Canada	1,000,000	fire
1967	Torrey Canyon	UK	909,000	grounding
1972	Sea Star	Gulf of Oman	902,250	collision
1977	Hawaiian Patriot	Hawaiian Is.	742,500	fire
1979	Independenta	Turkey	696,350	collision
1993	Braer	UK	625,000	grounding
1996	Sea Empress	UK	515,000	grounding

Other sources of major oil spills

1983	Nowruz oilfield	The Gulf	4,250,000[†]	war
1979	Ixtoc 1 oilwell	Gulf of Mexico	4,200,000	blow-out
1991	Kuwait	The Gulf	2,500,000[†]	war

** 1 barrel = 0.136 tonnes/159 lit./35 Imperial gal./42 US gal.   [†] estimated

River Pollution

Sources of river pollution, USA (latest available year)

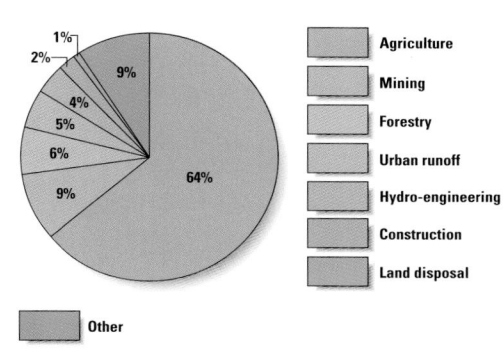

- Agriculture
- Mining
- Forestry
- Urban runoff
- Hydro-engineering
- Construction
- Land disposal
- Other

Water Pollution

- Severely polluted sea areas and lakes
- Polluted sea areas and lakes
- Areas of frequent oil pollution by shipping

- ◣ Major oil tanker spills
- ▲ Major oil rig blow-outs
- ▼ Offshore dumpsites for industrial and municipal waste
- — Severely polluted rivers and estuaries

The most notorious tanker spillage of the 1980s occurred when the *Exxon Valdez* ran aground in Prince William Sound, Alaska, in 1989, spilling 267,000 barrels of crude oil close to shore in a sensitive ecological area. This rates as the world's 28th worst spill in terms of volume.

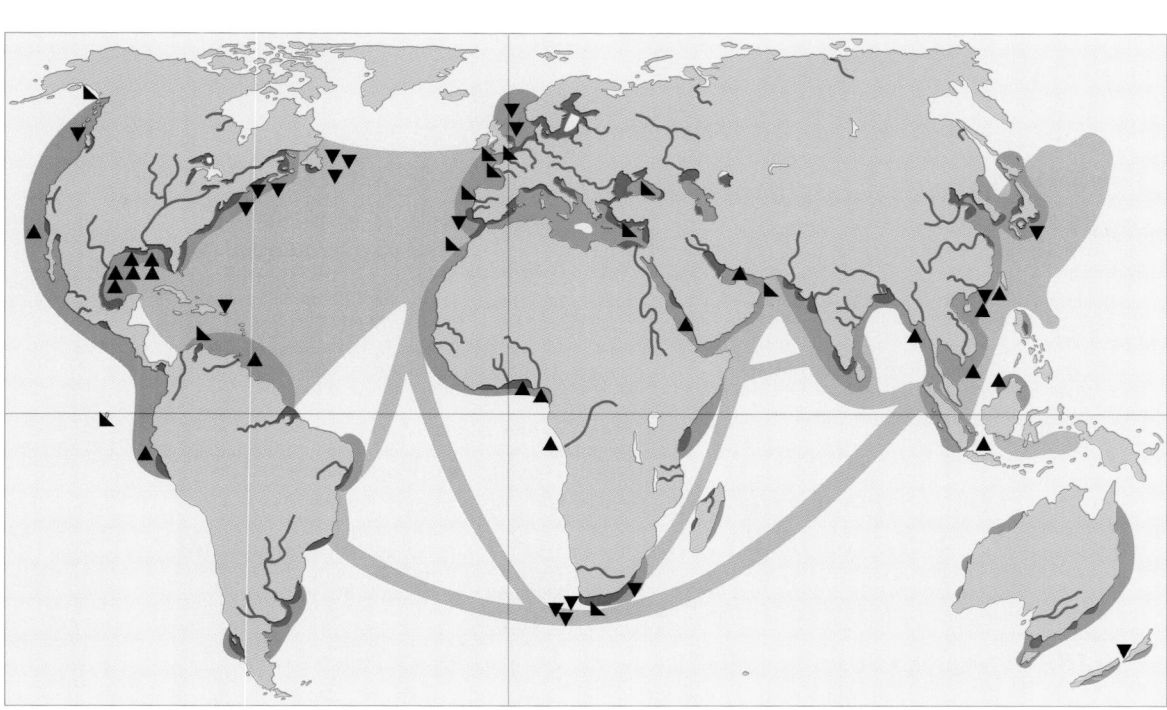

Climate

Climatic Regions

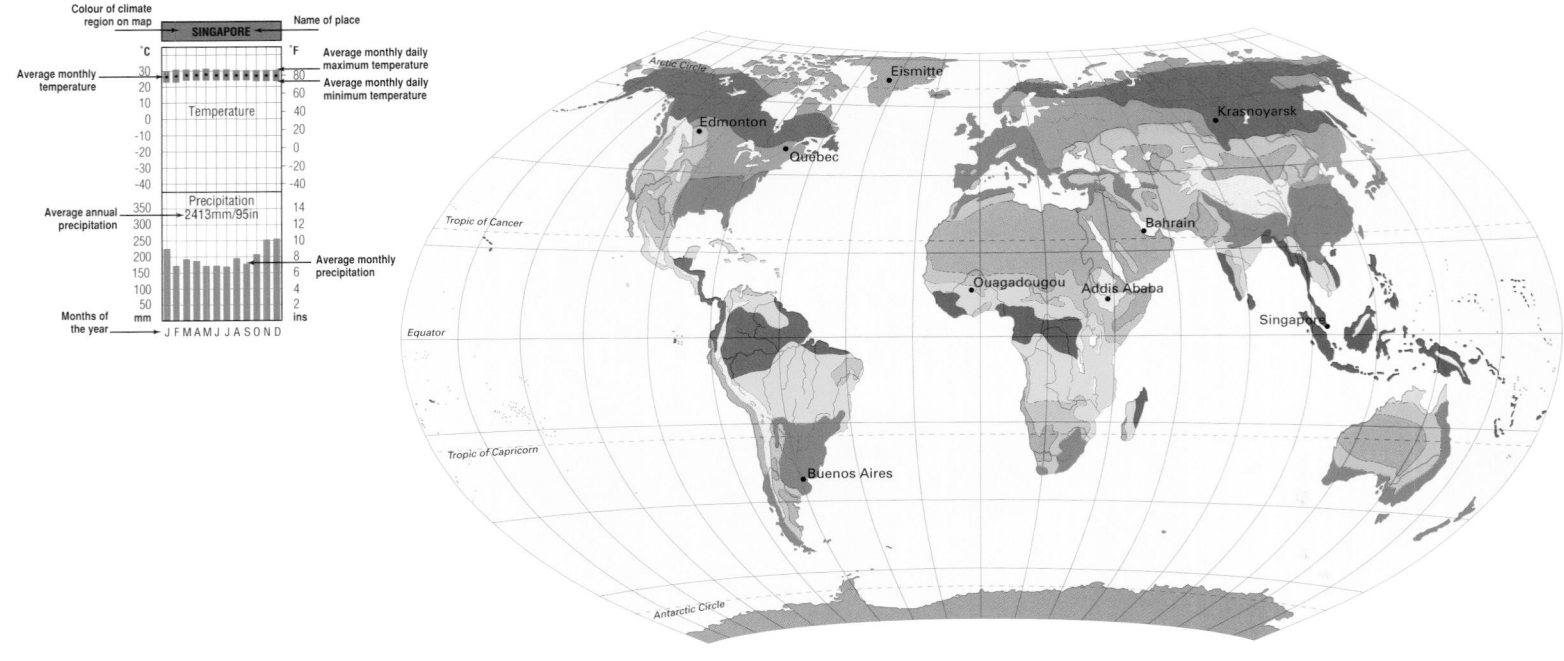

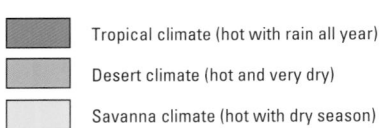 Tropical climate (hot with rain all year)

Desert climate (hot and very dry)

Savanna climate (hot with dry season)

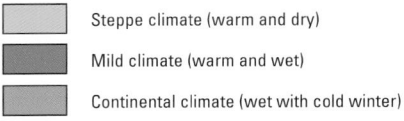 Steppe climate (warm and dry)

Mild climate (warm and wet)

Continental climate (wet with cold winter)

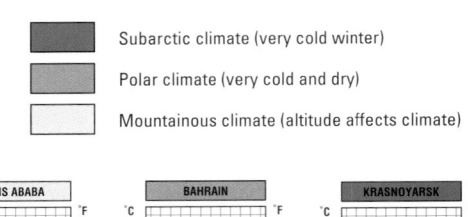 Subarctic climate (very cold winter)

Polar climate (very cold and dry)

Mountainous climate (altitude affects climate)

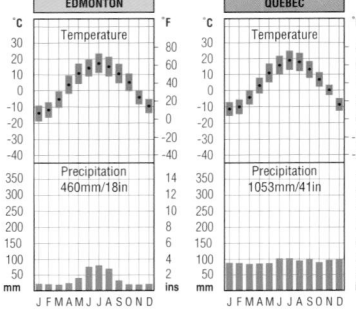

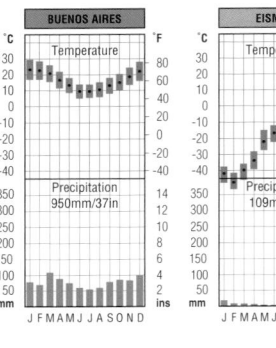

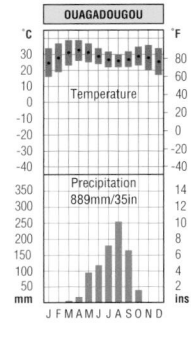

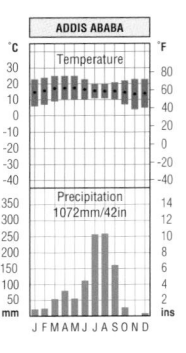

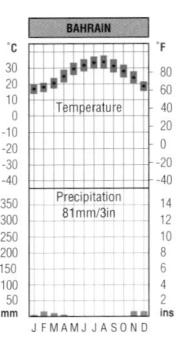

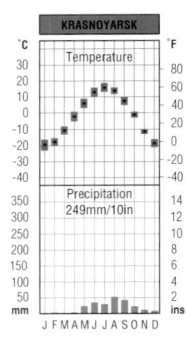

Climate Records

Temperature

Highest recorded shade temperature: Al Aziziyah, Libya, 58°C [136.4°F], 13 September 1922.

Highest mean annual temperature: Dallol, Ethiopia, 34.4°C [94°F], 1960–66.

Longest heatwave: Marble Bar, W. Australia, 162 days over 38°C [100°F], 23 October 1923 to 7 April 1924.

Lowest recorded temperature (outside poles): Verkhoyansk, Siberia, –68°C [–90°F], 6 February 1933.

Lowest mean annual temperature: Plateau Station, Antarctica, –56.6°C [–72.0°F].

Precipitation

Longest drought: Calama, N. Chile, no recorded rainfall in 400 years to 1971.

Wettest place (12 months): Cherrapunji, Meghalaya, N. E. India, 26,470 mm [1,040 in], August 1860 to August 1861. Cherrapunji also holds the record for the most rainfall in one month: 2,930 mm [115 in], July 1861.

Wettest place (average): Mawsynram, India, mean annual rainfall 11,873 mm [467.4 in].

Wettest place (24 hours): Cilaos, Réunion, Indian Ocean, 1,870 mm [73.6 in], 15–16 March 1952.

Heaviest hailstones: Gopalganj, Bangladesh, up to 1.02 kg [2.25 lb], 14 April 1986 (killed 92 people).

Heaviest snowfall (continuous): Bessans, Savoie, France, 1,730 mm [68 in] in 19 hours, 5–6 April 1969.

Heaviest snowfall (season/year): Paradise Ranger Station, Mt Rainier, Washington, USA, 31,102 mm [1,224.5 in], 19 February 1971 to 18 February 1972.

Pressure and winds

Highest barometric pressure: Agata, Siberia (at 262 m [862 ft] altitude), 1,083.8 mb, 31 December 1968.

Lowest barometric pressure: Typhoon Tip, Guam, Pacific Ocean, 870 mb, 12 October 1979.

Highest recorded wind speed: Mt Washington, New Hampshire, USA, 371 km/h [231 mph], 12 April 1934. This is three times as strong as hurricane force on the Beaufort Scale.

Windiest place: Commonwealth Bay, Antarctica, where gales frequently reach over 320 km/h [200 mph].

Climate

Climate is weather in the long term: the seasonal pattern of hot and cold, wet and dry, averaged over time (usually 30 years). At the simplest level, it is caused by the uneven heating of the Earth. Surplus heat at the Equator passes towards the poles, levelling out the energy differential. Its passage is marked by a ceaseless churning of the atmosphere and the oceans, further agitated by the Earth's diurnal spin and the motion it imparts to moving air and water. The heat's means of transport – by winds and ocean currents, by the continual evaporation and recondensation of water molecules – is the weather itself. There are four basic types of climate, each of which can be further subdivided: tropical, desert (dry), temperate and polar.

Composition of Dry Air

Nitrogen	78.09%	Sulphur dioxide	trace
Oxygen	20.95%	Nitrogen oxide	trace
Argon	0.93%	Methane	trace
Water vapour	0.2–4.0%	Dust	trace
Carbon dioxide	0.03%	Helium	trace
Ozone	0.00006%	Neon	trace

El Niño

In a normal year, south-easterly trade winds drive surface waters westwards off the coast of South America, drawing cold, nutrient-rich water up from below. In an El Niño year (which occurs every 2–7 years), warm water from the west Pacific suppresses up-welling in the east, depriving the region of nutrients. The water is warmed by as much as 7°C [12°F], disturbing the tropical atmospheric circulation. During an intense El Niño, the south-east trade winds change direction and become equatorial westerlies, resulting in climatic extremes in many regions of the world, such as drought in parts of Australia and India, and heavy rainfall in south-eastern USA. An intense El Niño occurred in 1997–8, with resultant freak weather conditions across the entire Pacific region.

Normal year

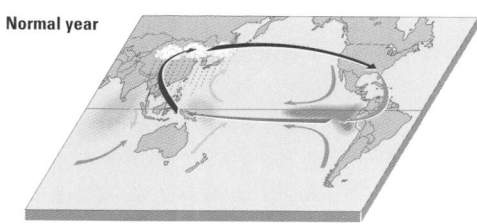

El Niño event

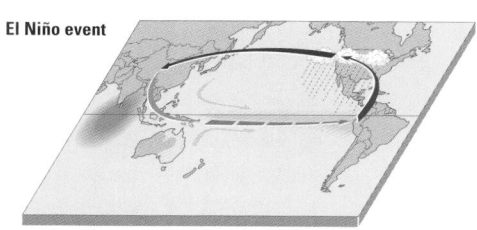

Beaufort Wind Scale

Named after the 19th-century British naval officer who devised it, the Beaufort Scale assesses wind speed according to its effects. It was originally designed as an aid for sailors, but has since been adapted for use on the land.

Scale	Wind speed km/h	mph	Effect
0	0–1	0–1	**Calm** Smoke rises vertically
1	1–5	1–3	**Light air** Wind direction shown only by smoke drift
2	6–11	4–7	**Light breeze** Wind felt on face; leaves rustle; vanes moved by wind
3	12–19	8–12	**Gentle breeze** Leaves and small twigs in constant motion; wind extends small flag
4	20–28	13–18	**Moderate** Raises dust and loose paper; small branches move
5	29–38	19–24	**Fresh** Small trees in leaf sway; wavelets on inland waters
6	39–49	25–31	**Strong** Large branches move; difficult to use umbrellas
7	50–61	32–38	**Near gale** Whole trees in motion; difficult to walk against wind
8	62–74	39–46	**Gale** Twigs break from trees; walking very difficult
9	75–88	47–54	**Strong gale** Slight structural damage
10	89–102	55–63	**Storm** Trees uprooted; serious structural damage
11	103–117	64–72	**Violent storm** Widespread damage
12	118+	73+	**Hurricane**

Conversions
°C = (°F − 32) × 5/9; °F = (°C × 9/5) + 32; 0°C = 32°F
1 in = 25.4 mm; 1 mm = 0.0394 in; 100 mm = 3.94 in

Temperature

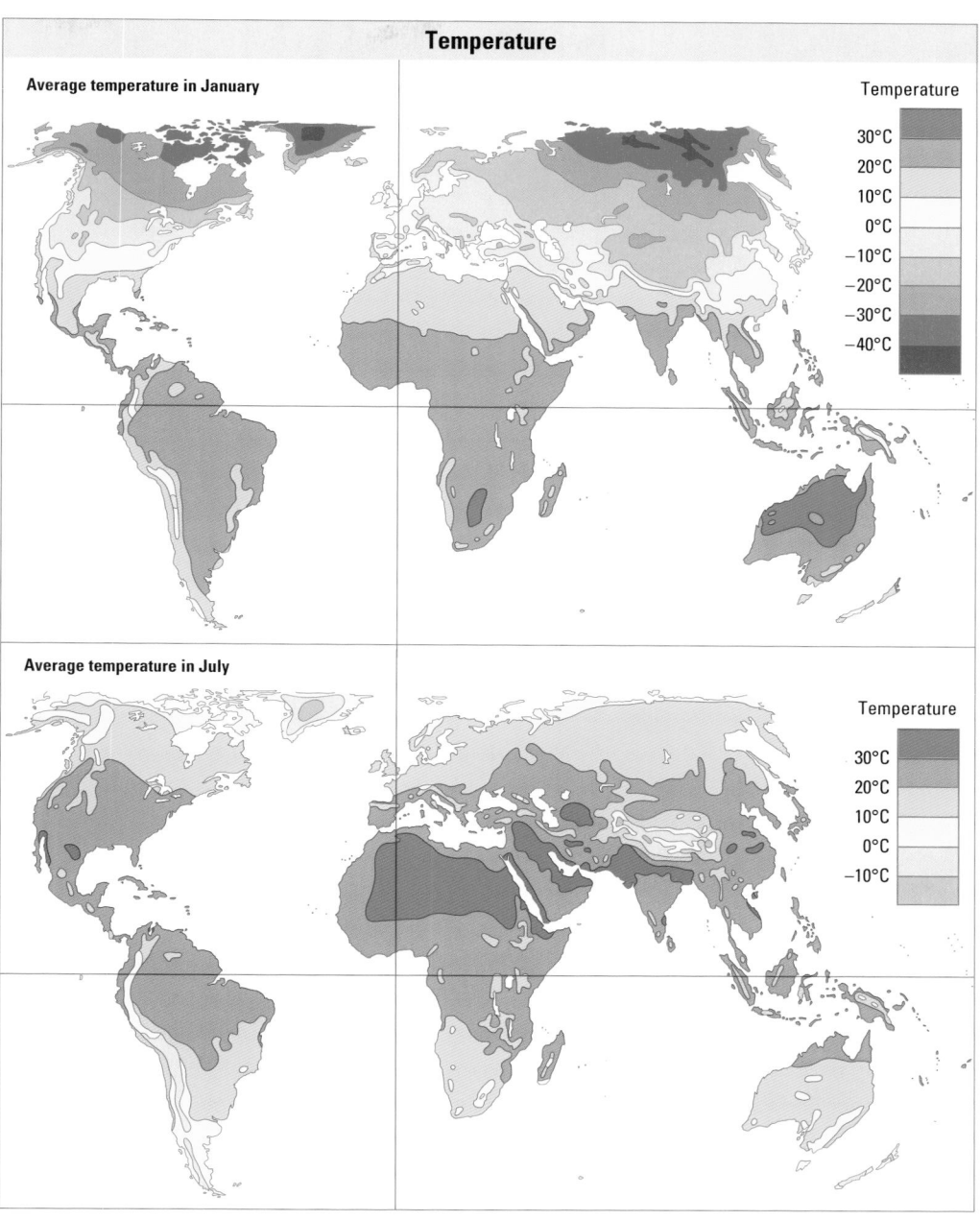

Average temperature in January

Temperature
30°C
20°C
10°C
0°C
−10°C
−20°C
−30°C
−40°C

Average temperature in July

Temperature
30°C
20°C
10°C
0°C
−10°C

Precipitation

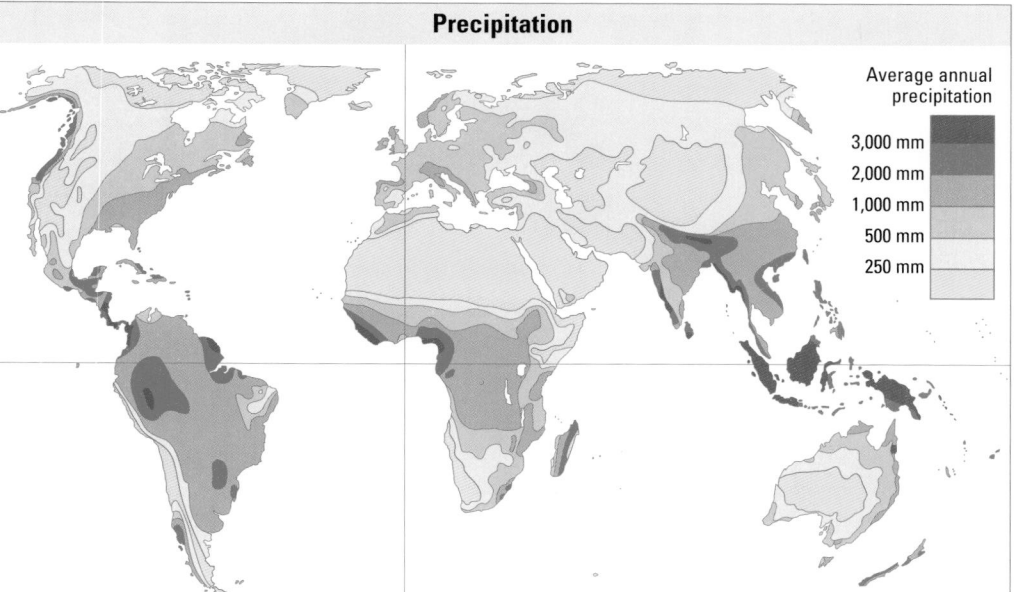

Average annual precipitation
3,000 mm
2,000 mm
1,000 mm
500 mm
250 mm

Water and Vegetation

The Hydrological Cycle

The world's water balance is regulated by the constant recycling of water between the oceans, atmosphere and land. The movement of water between these three reservoirs is known as the hydrological cycle. The oceans play a vital role in the hydrological cycle: 74% of the total precipitation falls over the oceans and 84% of the total evaporation comes from the oceans.

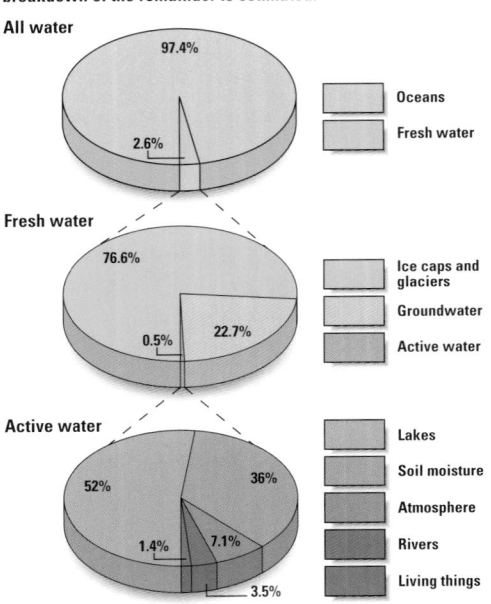

Water Distribution

The distribution of planetary water, by percentage. Oceans and ice caps together account for more than 99% of the total; the breakdown of the remainder is estimated.

All water
- 97.4% Oceans
- 2.6% Fresh water

Fresh water
- 76.6% Ice caps and glaciers
- 22.7% Groundwater
- 0.5% Active water

Active water
- 52% Lakes
- 36% Soil moisture
- 7.1% Atmosphere
- 3.5% Rivers
- 1.4% Living things

Water Utilization

Domestic | Industrial | Agriculture

The percentage breakdown of water usage by sector, selected countries (latest available year)

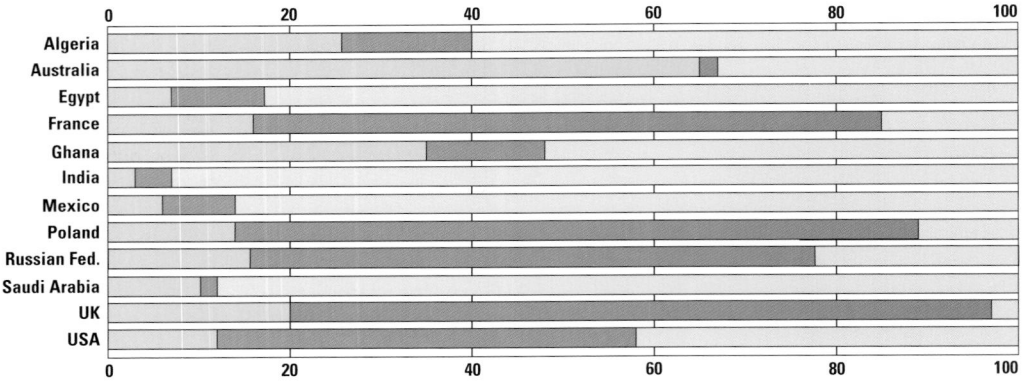

Algeria, Australia, Egypt, France, Ghana, India, Mexico, Poland, Russian Fed., Saudi Arabia, UK, USA

Water Usage

Almost all the world's water is 3,000 million years old, and all of it cycles endlessly through the hydrosphere, though at different rates. Water vapour circulates over days, even hours, deep ocean water circulates over millennia, and ice-cap water remains solid for millions of years.

Fresh water is essential to all terrestrial life. Humans cannot survive more than a few days without it, and even the hardiest desert plants and animals could not exist without some water. Agriculture requires huge quantities of fresh water: without large-scale irrigation most of the world's people would starve. In the USA, agriculture uses 42% and industry 45% of all water withdrawals.

The United States is one of the heaviest users of water in the world. According to the latest figures the average American uses 380 litres a day and the average household uses 415,000 litres a year. This is two to four times more than in Western Europe.

Water Supply

Percentage of total population with access to safe drinking water (2000)

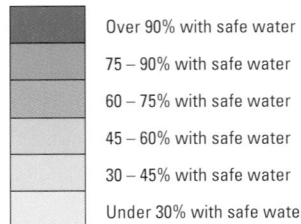

- Over 90% with safe water
- 75 – 90% with safe water
- 60 – 75% with safe water
- 45 – 60% with safe water
- 30 – 45% with safe water
- Under 30% with safe water

△ Under 80 litres per person per day domestic water consumption

▲ Over 320 litres per person per day domestic water consumption

NB: 80 litres of water a day is considered necessary for a reasonable quality of life.

Least well-provided countries

Afghanistan	13%	Sierra Leone	28%
Ethiopia	24%	Cambodia	30%
Chad	27%	Mauritania	37%

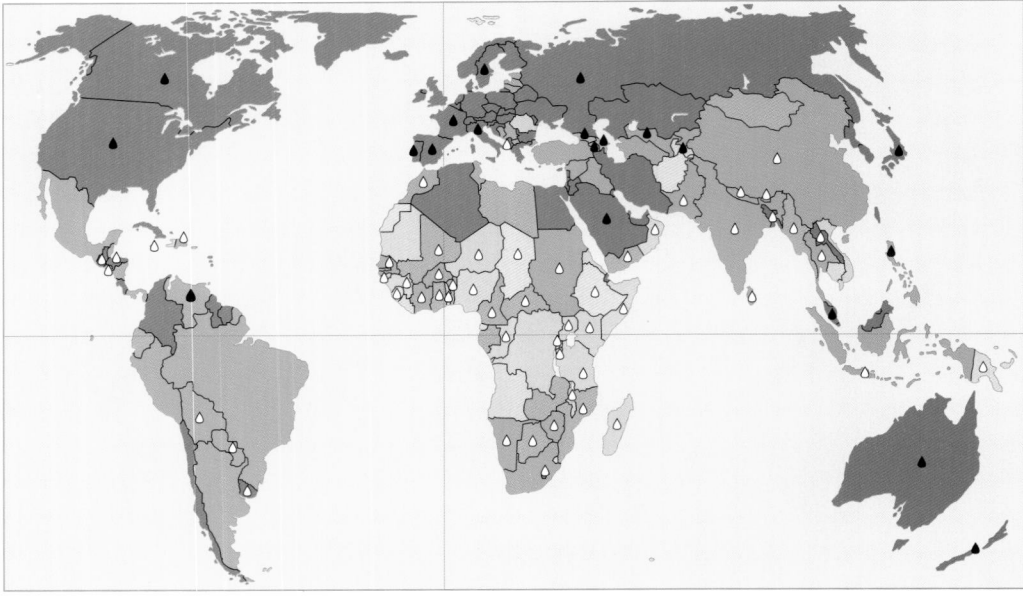

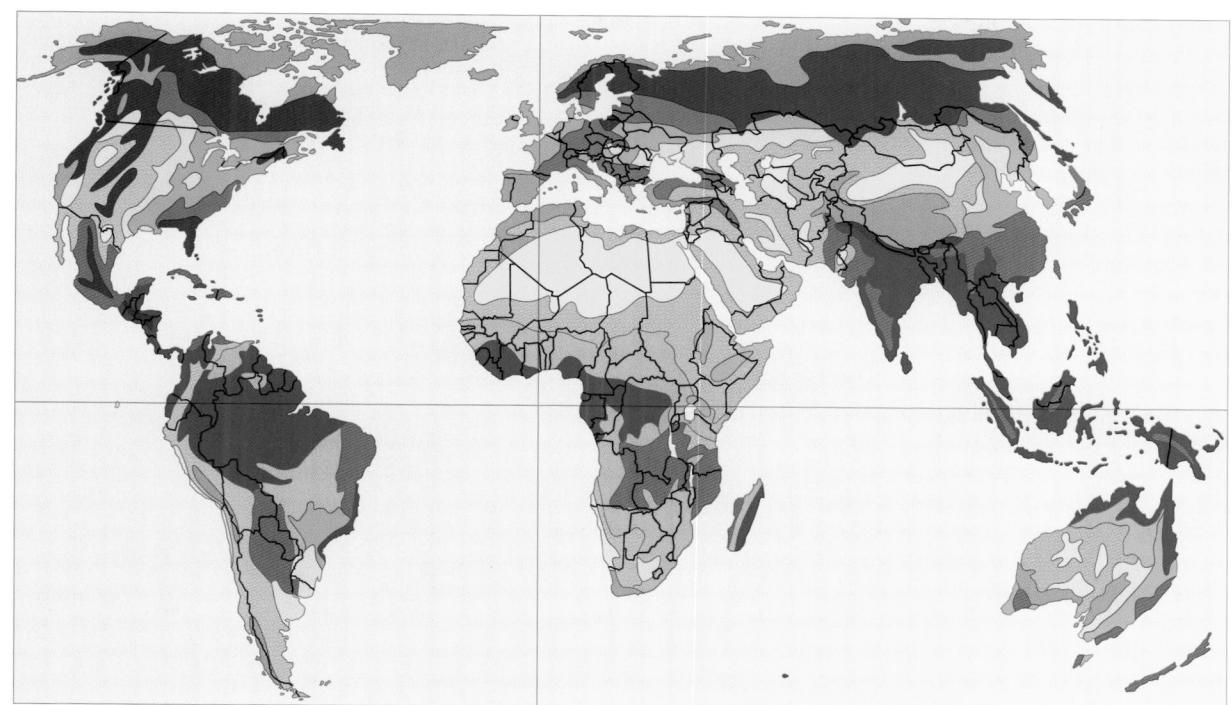

Natural Vegetation

Regional variation in vegetation

	Tundra and mountain vegetation
	Needleleaf evergreen forest
	Mixed needleleaf evergreen & broadleaf deciduous trees
	Broadleaf deciduous woodland
	Mid-latitude grassland
	Evergreen broadleaf and deciduous trees & shrubs
	Semi-desert scrub
	Desert
	Tropical grassland (savanna)
	Tropical broadleaf rainforest and monsoon forest
	Subtropical broadleaf and needleleaf forest

The map shows the natural 'climax vegetation' of regions, as dictated by climate and topography. In most cases, however, agricultural activity has drastically altered the vegetation pattern. Western Europe, for example, lost most of its broadleaf forest many centuries ago, while irrigation has turned some natural semi-desert into productive land.

Land Use by Continent

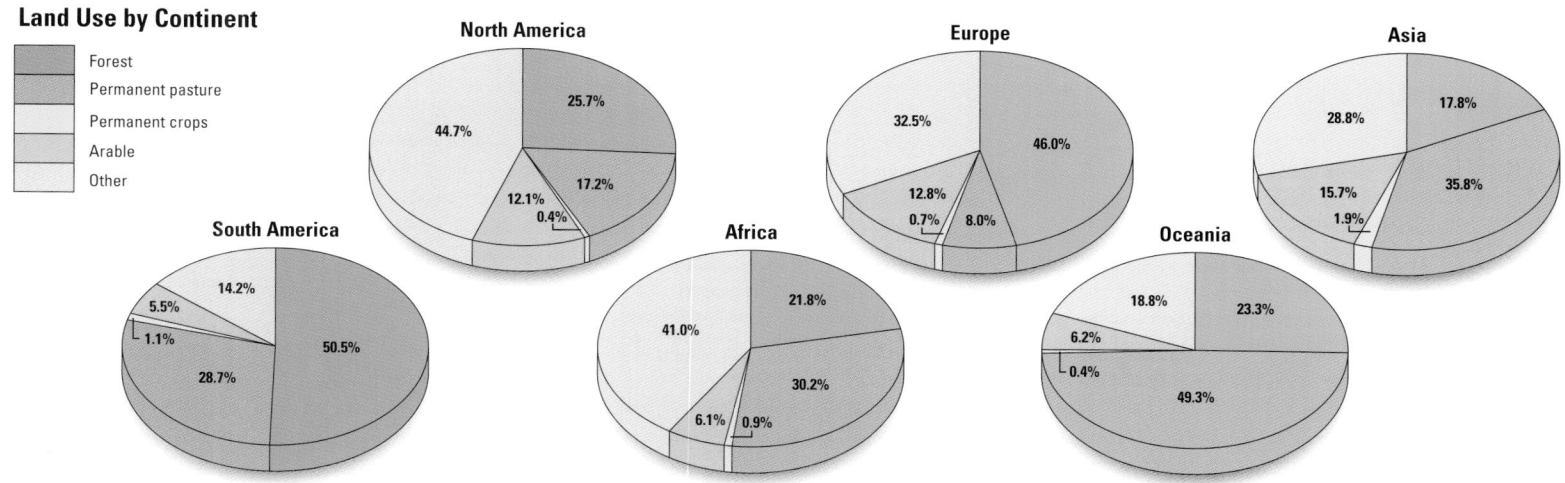

	Forest
	Permanent pasture
	Permanent crops
	Arable
	Other

North America: 25.7%, 17.2%, 0.4%, 12.1%, 44.7%

Europe: 46.0%, 8.0%, 0.7%, 12.8%, 32.5%

Asia: 17.8%, 35.8%, 1.9%, 15.7%, 28.8%

South America: 50.5%, 28.7%, 1.1%, 5.5%, 14.2%

Africa: 21.8%, 30.2%, 0.9%, 6.1%, 41.0%

Oceania: 23.3%, 49.3%, 0.4%, 6.2%, 18.8%

Forestry: Production

	Forest and woodland (million hectares)	Annual production (2001, million cubic metres)	
		Fuelwood	Industrial roundwood*
World	*3,869.5*	*1,784.3*	*1,543.3*
Europe	1,039.3	98.1	462.5
S. America	885.6	189.2	151.1
Africa	649.9	534.5	68.1
N. & C. America	549.3	154.5	596.6
Asia	547.8	795.5	216.0
Oceania	197.6	12.6	48.9

Paper and Board

Top producers (2001)**		Top exporters (2001)**	
USA	81,529	Canada	14,540
China	35,529	Finland	10,875
Japan	31,794	Germany	8,830
Canada	19,865	Sweden	8,733
Germany	17,879	USA	8,355

* roundwood is timber as it is felled
** in thousand tonnes

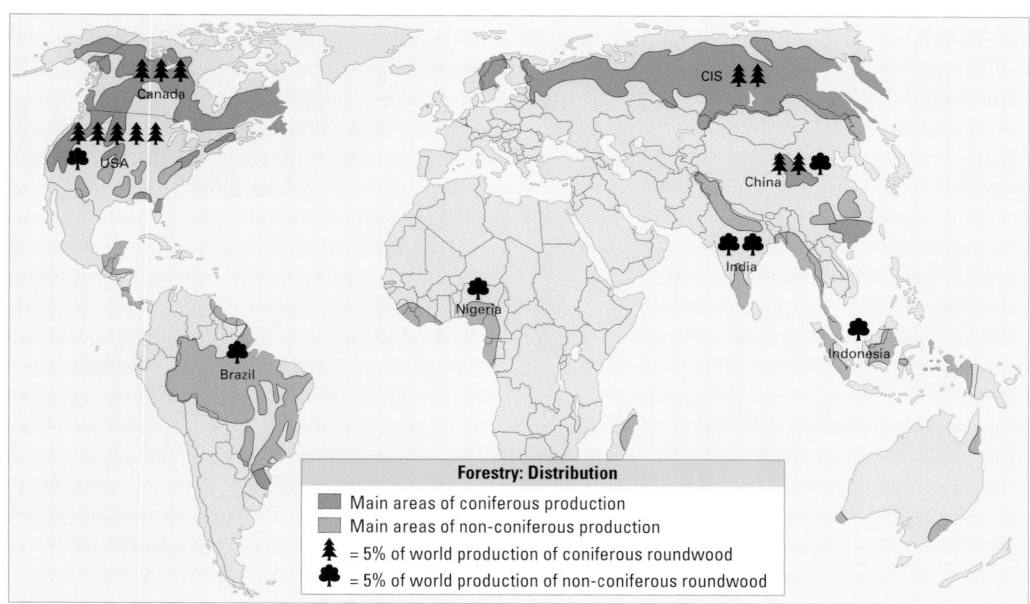

Forestry: Distribution

	Main areas of coniferous production
	Main areas of non-coniferous production
♣	= 5% of world production of coniferous roundwood
♣	= 5% of world production of non-coniferous roundwood

Environment

Humans have always had a dramatic effect on their environment, at least since the development of agriculture almost 10,000 years ago. Generally, the Earth has accepted human interference without obvious ill effects: the complex systems that regulate the global environment have been able to absorb substantial damage while maintaining a stable and comfortable home for the planet's trillions of lifeforms. But advancing human technology and the rapidly-expanding populations it supports are now threatening to overwhelm the Earth's ability to compensate.

Industrial wastes, acid rainfall, desertification and large-scale deforestation all combine to create environmental change at a rate far faster than the great slow cycles of planetary evolution can accommodate. As a result of overcultivation, overgrazing and overcutting of groundcover for firewood, desertification is affecting as much as 60% of the world's croplands. In addition, with fire and chain-saws, humans are destroying more forest in a day than their ancestors could have done in a century, upsetting the balance between plant and animal, carbon dioxide and oxygen, on which all life ultimately depends.

The fossil fuels that power industrial civilization have pumped enough carbon dioxide and other so-called greenhouse gases into the atmosphere to make climatic change a near-certainty. As a result of the combination of these factors, the Earth's average temperature has risen by approximately 0.5°C [1°F] since the beginning of the 20th century, and it is still rising.

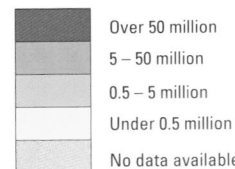

Global Warming

Carbon dioxide emissions in tonnes (1998)

- Over 50 million
- 5 – 50 million
- 0.5 – 5 million
- Under 0.5 million
- No data available

High atmospheric concentrations of heat-absorbing gases appear to be causing a rise in average temperatures worldwide – up to 1.5°C [3°F] by the year 2020, according to some estimates. Global warming is likely to bring about a rise in sea levels that may flood some of the world's densely populated coastal areas.

Greenhouse Power

Relative contributions to the Greenhouse Effect by the major heat-absorbing gases in the atmosphere.

The chart combines greenhouse potency and volume. Carbon dioxide has a greenhouse potential of only 1, but its concentration of 350 parts per million makes it predominate. CFC 12, with 25,000 times the absorption capacity of CO_2, is present only as 0.00044 ppm.

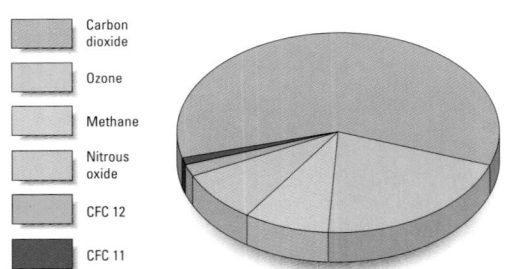

- Carbon dioxide
- Ozone
- Methane
- Nitrous oxide
- CFC 12
- CFC 11

Ozone Layer

The ozone 'hole' over the northern hemisphere in March 2000.

The colours represent Dobson Units (DU). The ozone 'hole' is seen as the dark blue and purple patch in the centre, where ozone values are around 120 DU or lower. Normal levels are around 280 DU. The ozone 'hole' over Antarctica is much larger.

Carbon Dioxide

Estimated percentage share of total world CO_2 emissions (2000)

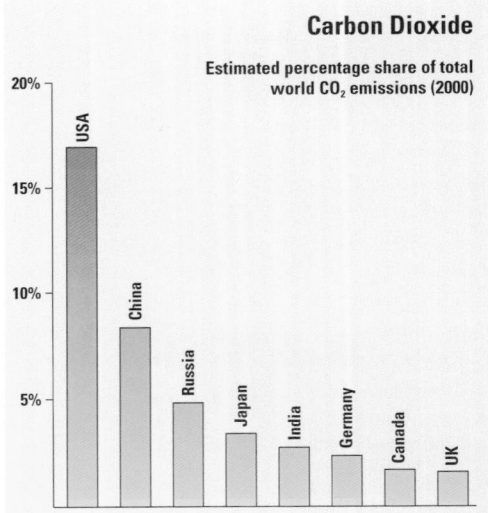

The Greenhouse Effect

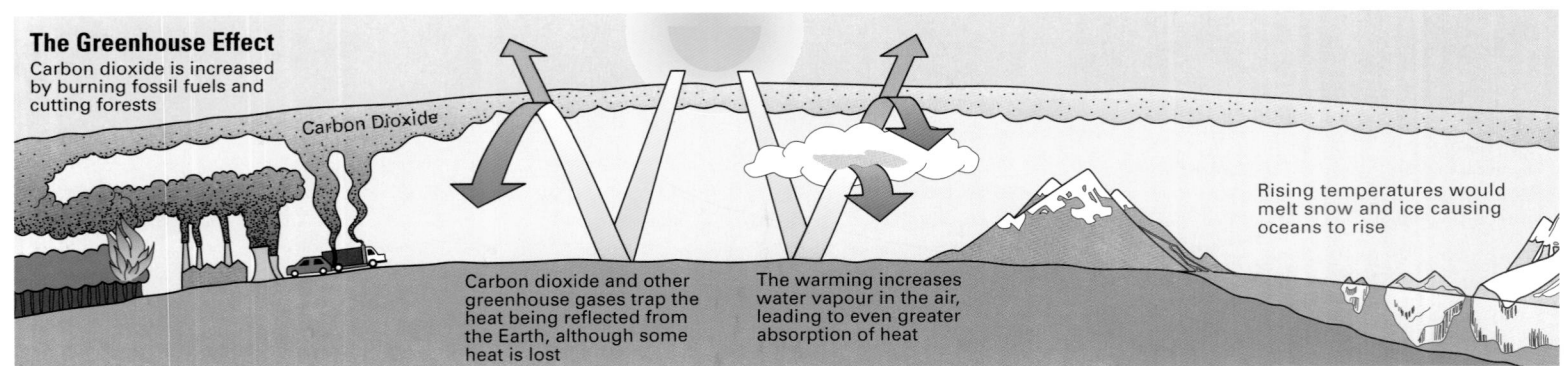

Carbon dioxide is increased by burning fossil fuels and cutting forests

Carbon Dioxide

Carbon dioxide and other greenhouse gases trap the heat being reflected from the Earth, although some heat is lost

The warming increases water vapour in the air, leading to even greater absorption of heat

Rising temperatures would melt snow and ice causing oceans to rise

Desertification

- Existing deserts
- Areas with a high risk of desertification
- Areas with a moderate risk of desertification
- Former areas of rainforest
- Existing rainforest

Forest Clearance

Thousands of hectares of forest cleared annually, tropical countries surveyed 1981–85, 1987–90 and 1990–5. Loss as a percentage of remaining stocks is shown in figures on each column.

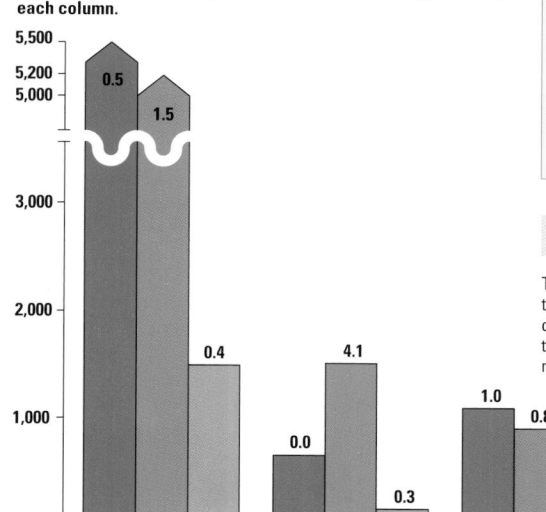

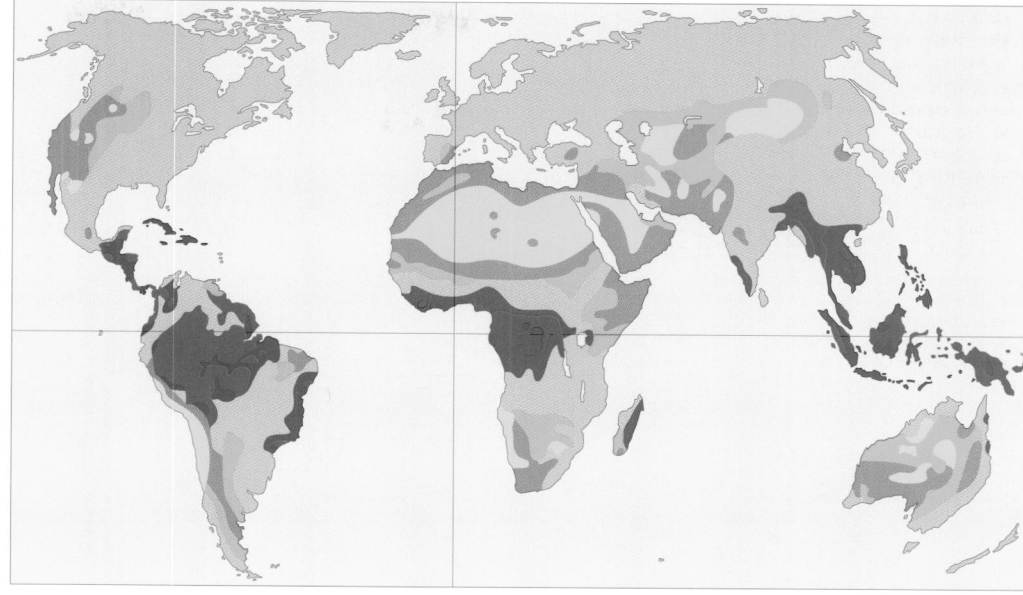

Deforestation

The Earth's remaining forests are under attack from three directions: expanding agriculture, logging, and growing consumption of fuelwood, often in combination. Sometimes deforestation is the direct result of government policy, as in the efforts made to resettle the urban poor in some parts of Brazil; just as often, it comes about despite state attempts at conservation. Loggers, licensed or unlicensed, blaze a trail into virgin forest, often destroying twice as many trees as they harvest. Landless farmers follow, burning away most of what remains to plant their crops, completing the destruction.

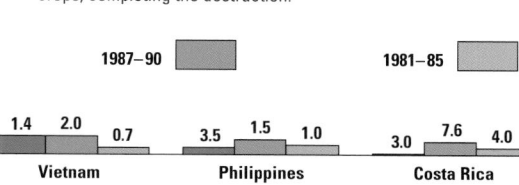

Bar chart legend: 1990–95, 1987–90, 1981–85

Brazil: 0.5, 1.5, 0.4
India: 0.0, 4.1, 0.3
Indonesia: 1.0, 0.8, 0.5
Burma: 1.4, 2.1, 0.3
Thailand: 2.6, 2.5, 2.4
Vietnam: 1.4, 2.0, 0.7
Philippines: 3.5, 1.5, 1.0
Costa Rica: 3.0, 7.6, 4.0

Ozone Depletion

The ozone layer, 25–30 km [15–18 miles] above sea level, acts as a barrier to most of the Sun's harmful ultra-violet radiation, protecting us from the ionizing radiation that can cause skin cancer and cataracts. In recent years, however, two holes in the ozone layer have been observed during winter: one over the Arctic and the other, the size of the USA, over Antarctica. By 1996, ozone had been reduced to around a half of its 1970 amount. The ozone (O_3) is broken down by chlorine released into the atmosphere as CFCs (chlorofluorocarbons) – chemicals used in refrigerators, packaging and aerosols.

Air Pollution

Sulphur dioxide is the main pollutant associated with industrial cities. According to the World Health Organization, at least 600 million people live in urban areas where sulphur dioxide concentrations regularly reach damaging levels. One of the world's most dangerously polluted urban areas is Mexico City, due to a combination of its enclosed valley location, 3 million cars and 60,000 factories. In May 1998, this lethal cocktail was added to by nearby forest fires and the resultant air pollution led to over 20% of the population (3 million people) complaining of respiratory problems.

Acid Rain

Killing trees, poisoning lakes and rivers and eating away buildings, acid rain is mostly produced by sulphur dioxide emissions from industry and volcanic eruptions. By the mid 1990s, acid rain had sterilized 4,000 or more of Sweden's lakes and left 45% of Switzerland's alpine conifers dead or dying, while the monuments of Greece were dissolving in Athens' smog. Prevailing wind patterns mean that the acids often fall many hundred kilometres from where the original pollutants were discharged. In parts of Europe acid deposition has slightly decreased, following reductions in emissions, but not by enough.

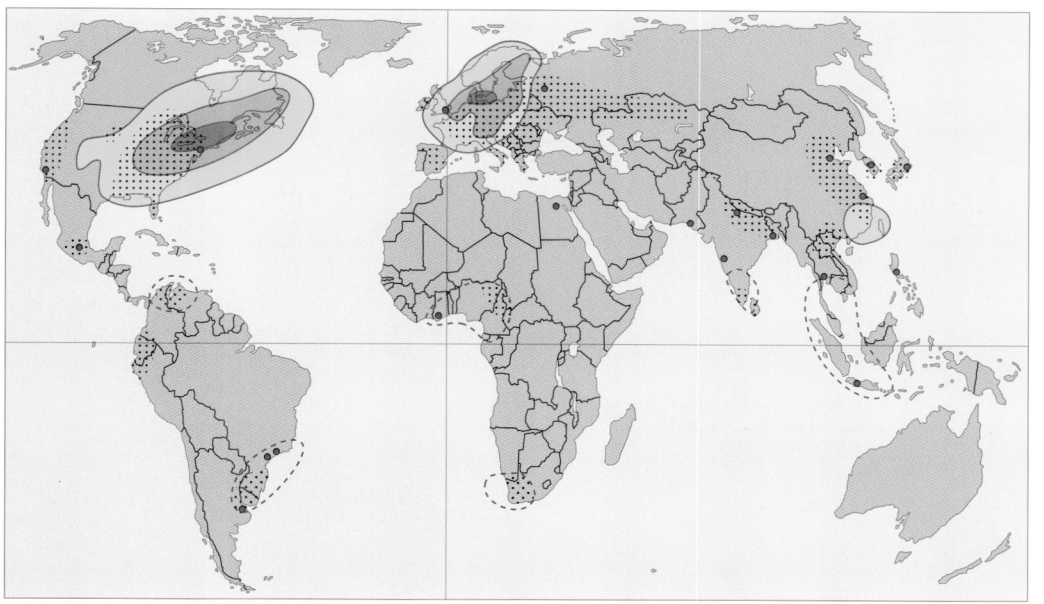

World Pollution

Acid rain and sources of acidic emissions (latest available year)

Acid rain is caused by high levels of sulphur and nitrogen in the atmosphere. They combine with water vapour and oxygen to form acids (H_2SO_4 and HNO_3) which fall as precipitation.

- Regions where sulphur and nitrogen oxides are released in high concentrations, mainly from fossil fuel combustion
- Major cities with high levels of air pollution (including nitrogen and sulphur emissions)

Areas of heavy acid deposition

pH numbers indicate acidity, decreasing from a neutral 7. Normal rain, slightly acid from dissolved carbon dioxide, never exceeds a pH of 5.6.

- pH less than 4.0 (most acidic)
- pH 4.0 to 4.5
- pH 4.5 to 5.0
- Areas where acid rain is a potential problem

Population

Demographic Profiles

Developed nations such as the UK have populations evenly spread across the age groups and, usually, a growing proportion of elderly people. The great majority of the people in developing nations, however, are in the younger age groups, about to enter their most fertile years. In time, these population profiles should resemble the world profile (even Nigeria has made recent progress with reducing its birth rate), but the transition will come about only after a few more generations of rapid population growth.

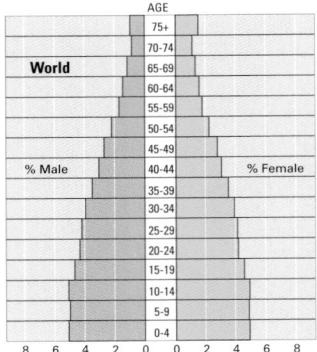

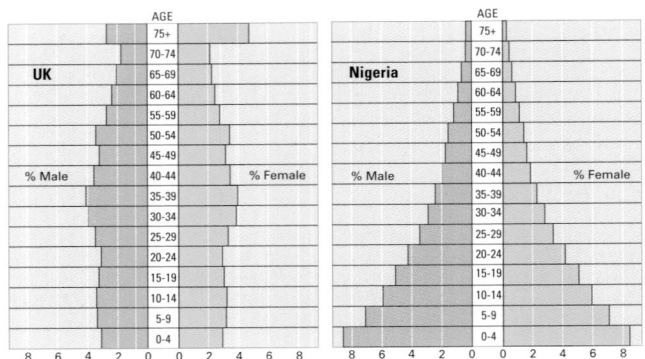

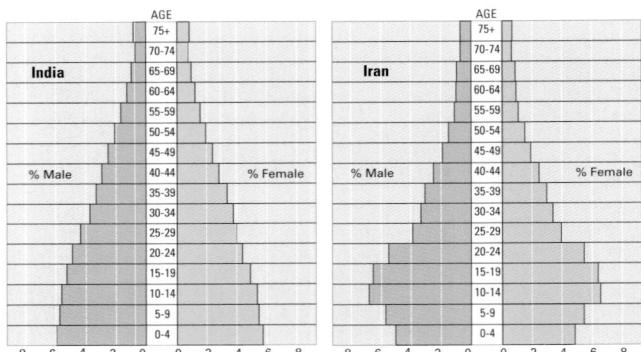

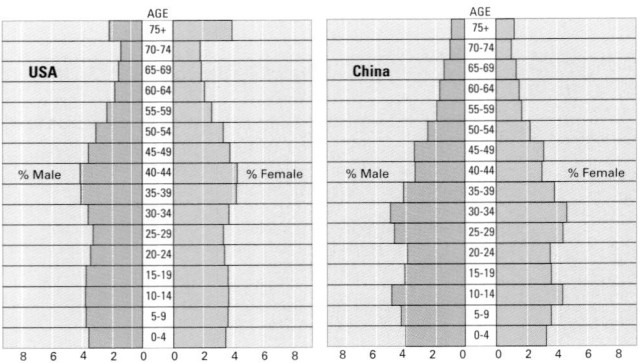

Most Populous Nations [in millions (2002 estimates)]

1.	China	1,284	9. Nigeria	130	17. Turkey	67
2.	India	1,046	10. Japan	127	18. Iran	67
3.	USA	281	11. Mexico	103	19. Thailand	62
4.	Indonesia	231	12. Philippines	85	20. UK	60
5.	Brazil	176	13. Germany	83	21. France	60
6.	Pakistan	148	14. Vietnam	81	22. Italy	58
7.	Russia	145	15. Egypt	71	23. Congo (Dem. Rep.)	55
8.	Bangladesh	133	16. Ethiopia	68	24. Ukraine	48

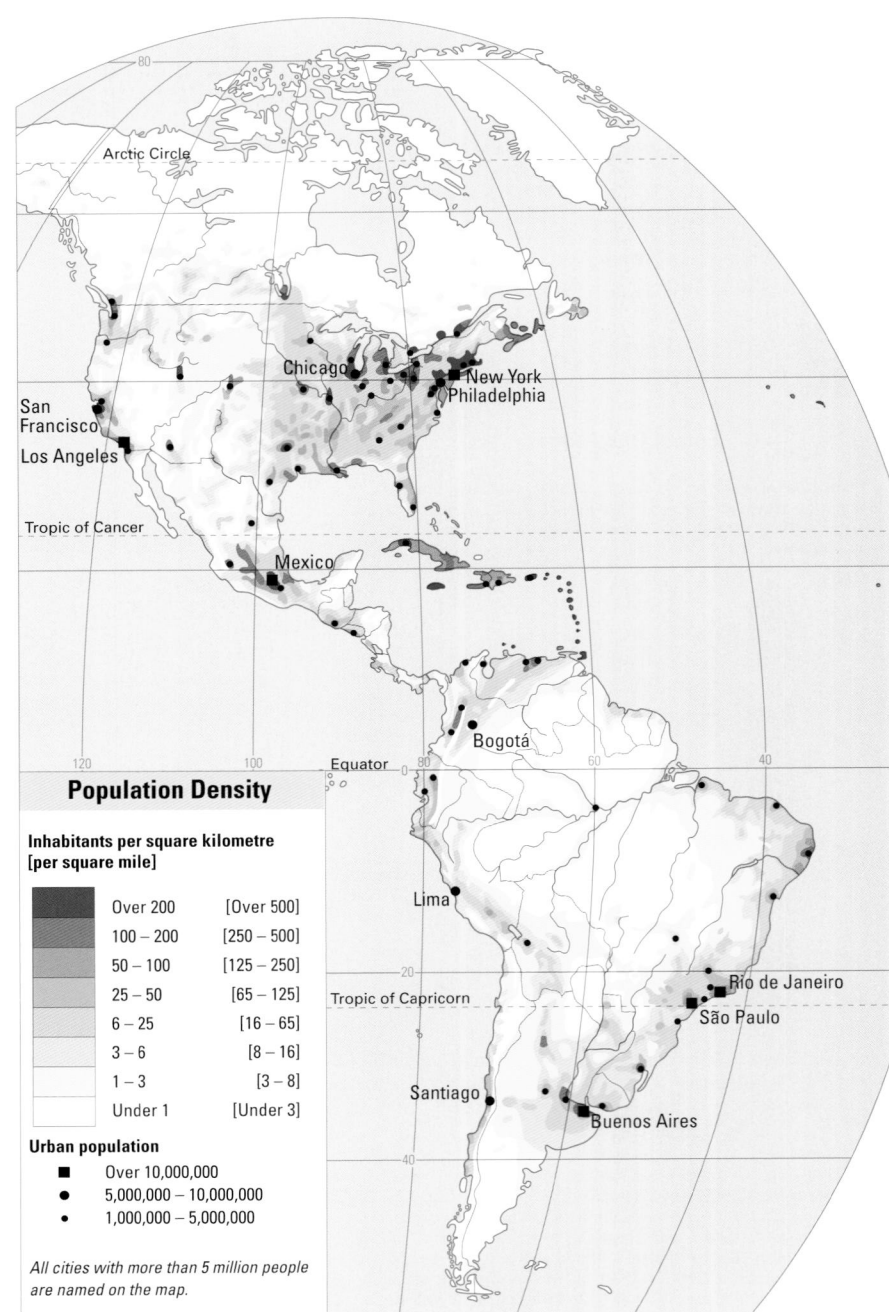

Population Density

Inhabitants per square kilometre [per square mile]

Over 200	[Over 500]
100 – 200	[250 – 500]
50 – 100	[125 – 250]
25 – 50	[65 – 125]
6 – 25	[16 – 65]
3 – 6	[8 – 16]
1 – 3	[3 – 8]
Under 1	[Under 3]

Urban population

■ Over 10,000,000

● 5,000,000 – 10,000,000

• 1,000,000 – 5,000,000

All cities with more than 5 million people are named on the map.

Continental Comparisons

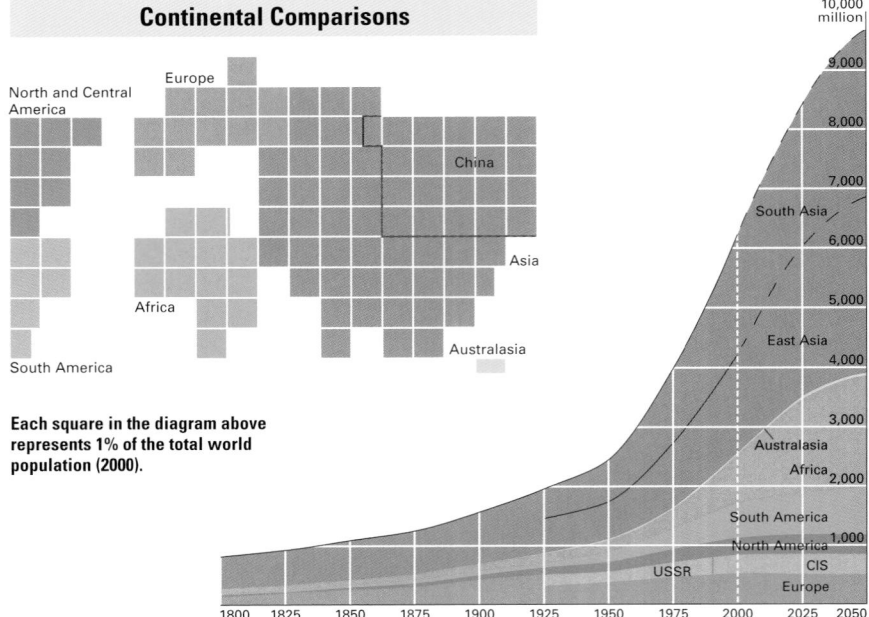

Each square in the diagram above represents 1% of the total world population (2000).

16

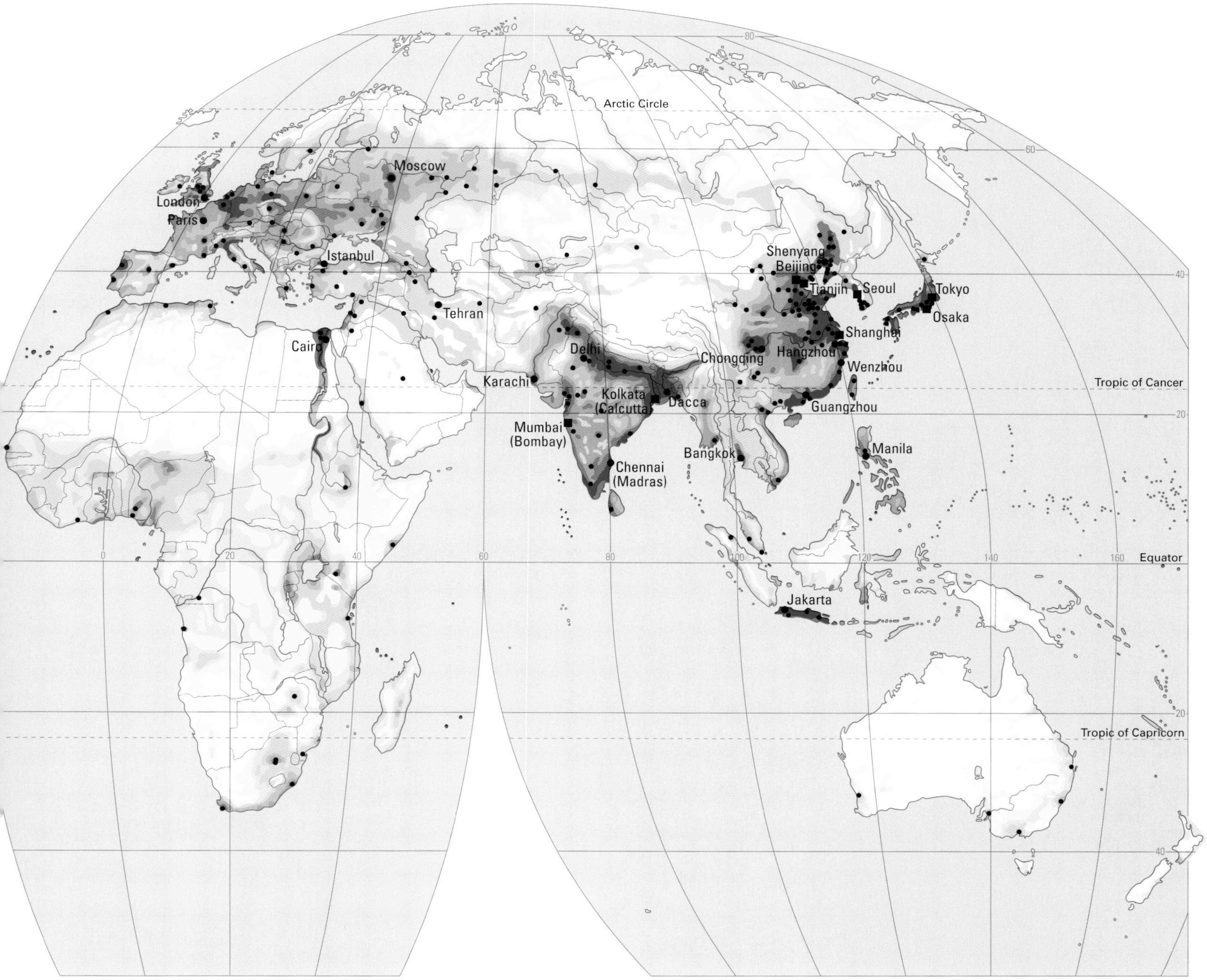

Arctic Circle

London
Paris
Moscow
Istanbul
Tehran
Cairo
Karachi
Delhi
Kolkata
(Calcutta)
Mumbai
(Bombay)
Dacca
Chennai
(Madras)
Bangkok
Shenyang
Beijing
Tianjin
Chongqing
Hangzhou
Shanghai
Wenzhou
Guangzhou
Seoul
Tokyo
Osaka
Manila
Jakarta

Tropic of Cancer

Equator

Tropic of Capricorn

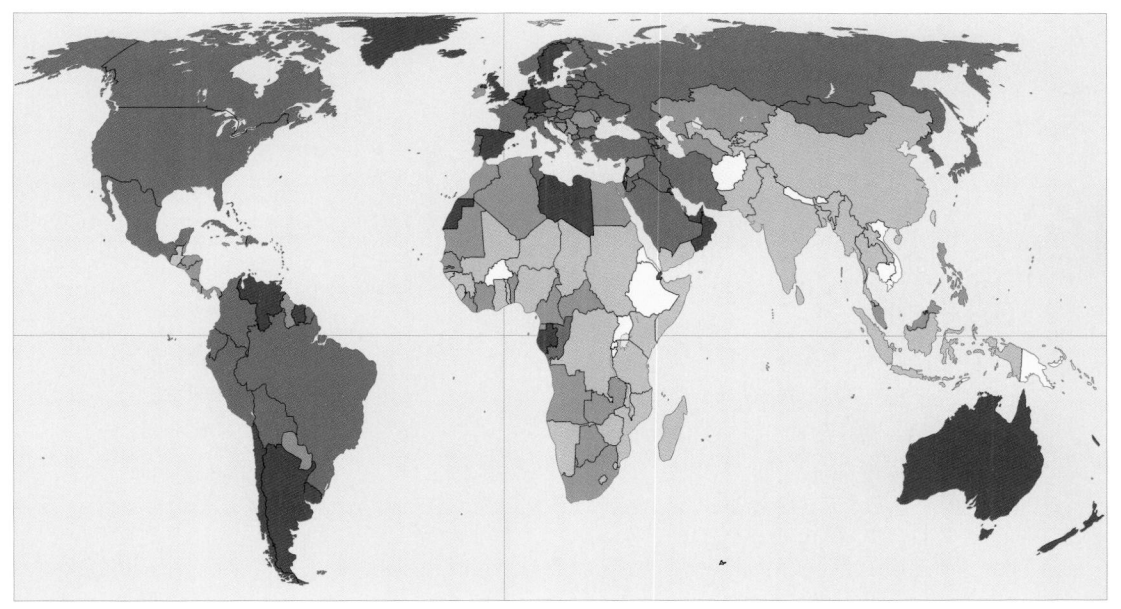

Urban Population

Percentage of total population living in towns and cities (2000)

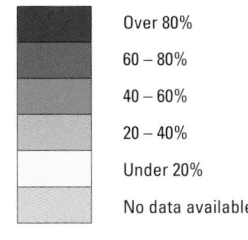

	Over 80%
	60 – 80%
	40 – 60%
	20 – 40%
	Under 20%
	No data available

Most urbanized

Singapore 100%
Nauru 100%
Monaco 100%
Vatican City 100%
Belgium 97.3%

Least urbanized

Rwanda 6.4%
Bhutan 7.3%
East Timor 7.4%
Burundi 9.2%
Nepal 10.8%

The Human Family

Predominant Languages

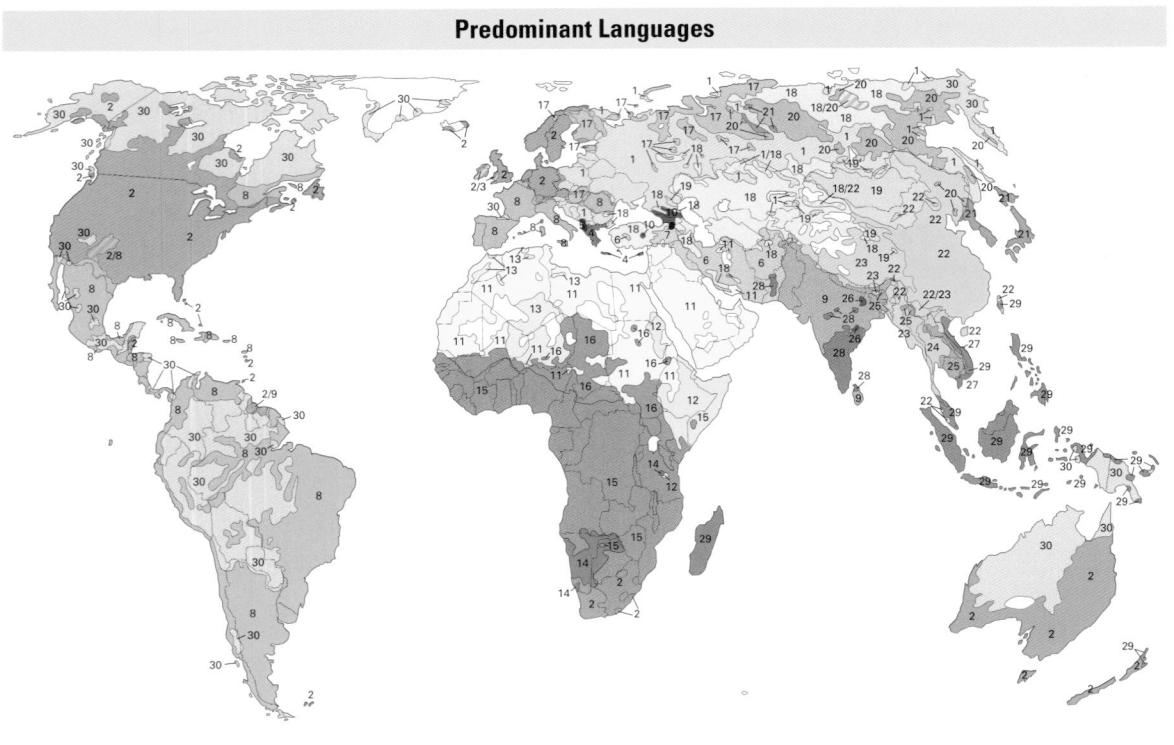

INDO-EUROPEAN FAMILY

1	Balto-Slavic group (incl. Russian, Ukrainian)
2	Germanic group (incl. English, German)
3	Celtic group
4	Greek
5	Albanian
6	Iranian group
7	Armenian
8	Romance group (incl. Spanish, Portuguese, French, Italian)
9	Indo-Aryan group (incl. Hindi, Bengali, Urdu, Punjabi, Marathi)
10	CAUCASIAN FAMILY

AFRO-ASIATIC FAMILY

11	Semitic group (incl. Arabic)
12	Kushitic group
13	Berber group

14	KHOISAN FAMILY
15	NIGER-CONGO FAMILY
16	NILO-SAHARAN FAMILY
17	URALIC FAMILY

ALTAIC FAMILY

18	Turkic group (incl. Turkish)
19	Mongolian group
20	Tungus-Manchu group
21	Japanese and Korean

SINO-TIBETAN FAMILY

| 22 | Sinitic (Chinese) languages (incl. Mandarin, Wu, Yue) |
| 23 | Tibetic-Burmic languages |

| 24 | TAI FAMILY |

AUSTRO-ASIATIC FAMILY

25	Mon-Khmer group
26	Munda group
27	Vietnamese

28	DRAVIDIAN FAMILY (incl. Telugu, Tamil)
29	AUSTRONESIAN FAMILY (incl. Malay-Indonesian, Javanese)
30	OTHER LANGUAGES

Languages of the World

Language can be classified by ancestry and structure. For example, the Romance and Germanic groups are both derived from an Indo-European language believed to have been spoken 5,000 years ago.

First-language speakers, 1999 (in millions)
Mandarin Chinese 885, Spanish 332, English 322, Bengali 189, Hindi 182, Portuguese 170, Russian 170, Japanese 125, German 98, Wu Chinese 77, Javanese 76, Korean 75, French 72, Vietnamese 68, Yue Chinese 66, Marathi 65, Tamil 63, Turkish 59, Urdu 58.

Official languages (% of total population)
English 27%, Chinese 19%, Hindi 13.5%, Spanish 5.4%, Russian 5.2%, French 4.2%, Arabic 3.3%, Portuguese 3%, Malay 3%, Bengali 2.9%, Japanese 2.3%.

Predominant Religions

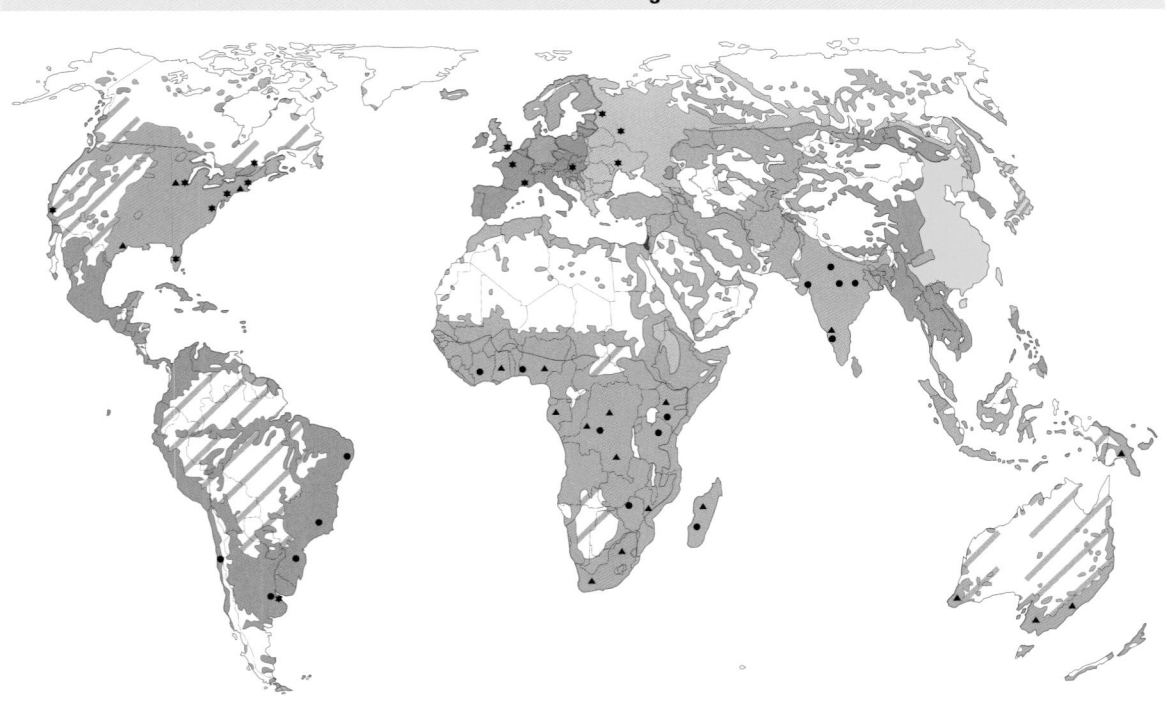

Religious Adherents

Religious adherents in millions (2001)

Christianity	2 019	Hindu	820
Roman Catholic	*1 067*	Chinese folk	387
Protestant	*346*	Buddhism	362
Orthodox	*216*	Ethnic religions	242
Anglican	*80*	New religions	103
Independent	*392*	Sikhism	24
Others	*139*	Judaism	14
Islam	1 207	Spiritism	12
Sunni	*1 002*	Baha'i	7
Shiite	*193*	Confucianism	6
Others	*12*	Jainism	4
Non-religious/		Shintoism	3
Agnostic/Atheist	921		

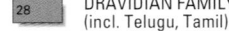

- ▲ Roman Catholicism
- Orthodox and other Eastern Churches
- • Protestantism
- Sunni Islam
- Shiite Islam
- Buddhism
- Hinduism
- Confucianism
- ● Judaism
- Shintoism
- Tribal Religions

United Nations

Created in 1945 to promote peace and co-operation and based in New York, the United Nations is the world's largest international organization, with 191 members and an annual budget of US $1.3 billion (2002). Each member of the General Assembly has one vote, while the five permanent members of the 15-nation Security Council – China, France, Russia, UK and USA – hold a veto. The Secretariat is the UN's principal administrative arm. The 54 members of the Economic and Social Council are responsible for economic, social, cultural, educational, health and related matters. The UN has 16 specialized agencies – based in Canada, France, Switzerland and Italy, as well as the USA – which help members in fields such as education (UNESCO), agriculture (FAO), medicine (WHO) and finance (IFC). By the end of 1994, all the original 11 trust territories of the Trusteeship Council had become independent.

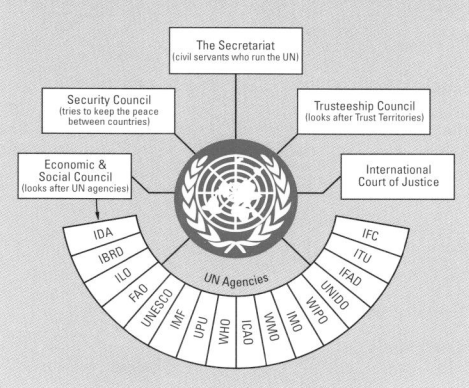

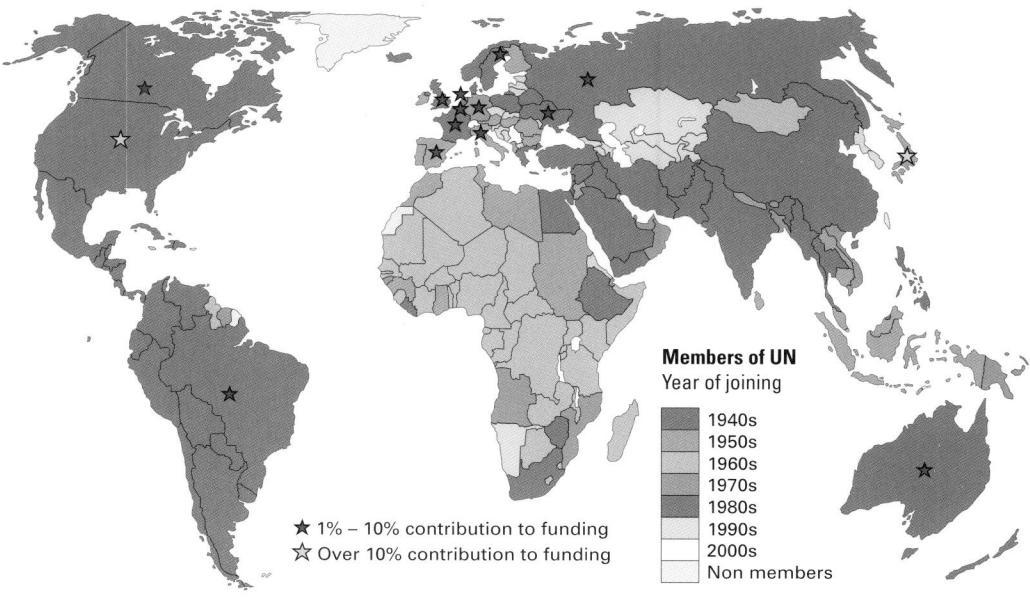

Members of UN
Year of joining

- 1940s
- 1950s
- 1960s
- 1970s
- 1980s
- 1990s
- 2000s
- Non members

★ 1% – 10% contribution to funding
☆ Over 10% contribution to funding

MEMBERSHIP OF THE UN In 1945 there were 51 members; by the end of 2002 membership had increased to 191 following the admission of East Timor and Switzerland. There are 2 independent states which are not members of the UN – Taiwan and the Vatican City. All the successor states of the former USSR had joined by the end of 1992. The official languages of the UN are Chinese, English, French, Russian, Spanish and Arabic.

FUNDING The UN regular budget for 2002 was US $1.3 billion. Contributions are assessed by the members' ability to pay, with the maximum 22% of the total (USA's share), the minimum 0.01%. The 15-country European Union pays over 37% of the budget.

PEACEKEEPING The UN has been involved in 54 peacekeeping operations worldwide since 1948.

International Organizations

ACP African-Caribbean-Pacific (formed in 1963). Members have economic ties with the EU.
ARAB LEAGUE (formed in 1945). The League's aim is to promote economic, social, political and military co-operation. There are 21 member nations.
ASEAN Association of South-east Asian Nations (formed in 1967). Cambodia joined in 1999.
AU The African Union replaced the Organization of African Unity (formed in 1963) in 2002. Its 53 members represent over 94% of Africa's population. Arabic, French, Portuguese and English are recognized as working languages.
CIS The Commonwealth of Independent States (formed in 1991) comprises the countries of the former Soviet Union except for Estonia, Latvia and Lithuania.
COLOMBO PLAN (formed in 1951). Its 25 members aim to promote economic and social development in Asia and the Pacific.
COMMONWEALTH The Commonwealth of Nations evolved from the British Empire; it comprises 16 Queen's realms, 32 republics and 5 indigenous monarchies, giving a total of 53. Nigeria was suspended in 1995, but reinstated in 1999.
EFTA European Free Trade Association (formed in 1960). Portugal left the original 'Seven' in 1989 to join what was then the EC, followed by Austria, Finland and Sweden in 1995. Only 4 members remain: Norway, Iceland, Switzerland and Liechtenstein.
EU European Union (evolved from the European Community in 1993). The 15 members – Austria, Belgium, Denmark, Finland, France, Germany, Greece, Ireland, Italy, Luxembourg, Netherlands, Portugal, Spain, Sweden and the UK – aim to integrate economies, co-ordinate social developments and bring about political union. These members, of what is now the world's biggest market, share agricultural and industrial policies and tariffs on trade. The original body, the European Coal and Steel Community (ECSC), was created in 1951 following the signing of the Treaty of Paris.
LAIA Latin American Integration Association (1980). Its aim is to promote freer regional trade.
NATO North Atlantic Treaty Organization (formed in 1949). It continues after 1991 despite the winding up of the Warsaw Pact. The Czech Republic, Hungary and Poland were the latest members to join in 1999.
OAS Organization of American States (formed in 1948). It aims to promote social and economic co-operation between developed countries of North America and developing nations of Latin America.

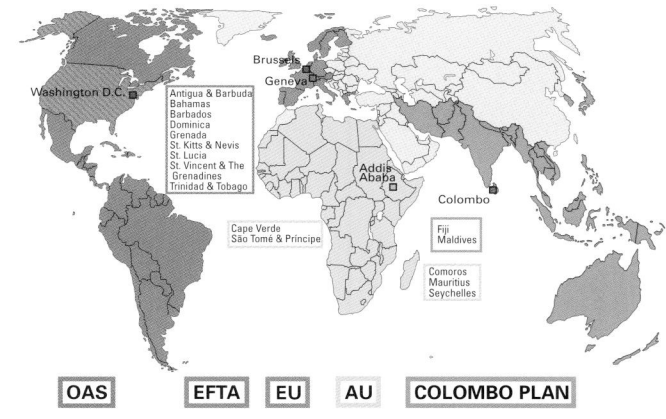

OAS | EFTA | EU | AU | COLOMBO PLAN

OECD Organization for Economic Co-operation and Development (formed in 1961). It comprises 30 major free-market economies. Poland, Hungary and South Korea joined in 1996. 'G8' is its 'inner group' of leading industrial nations, comprising Canada, France, Germany, Italy, Japan, Russia, UK and USA.
OPEC Organization of Petroleum Exporting Countries (formed in 1960). It controls about three-quarters of the world's oil supply. Gabon left the organization in 1996.

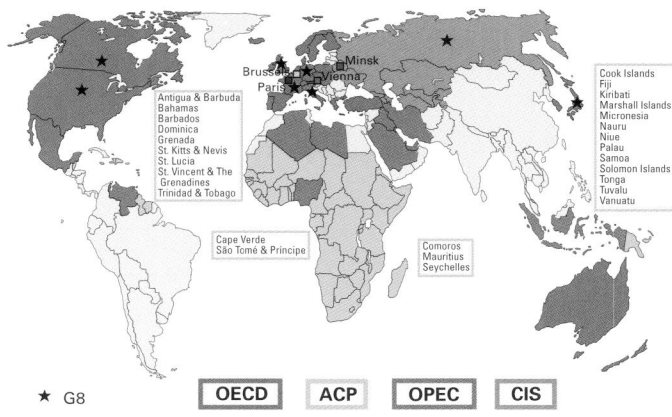

★ G8 | OECD | ACP | OPEC | CIS

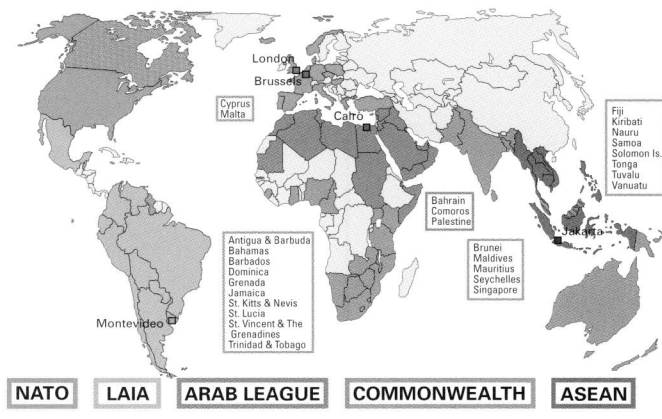

NATO | LAIA | ARAB LEAGUE | COMMONWEALTH | ASEAN

Wealth

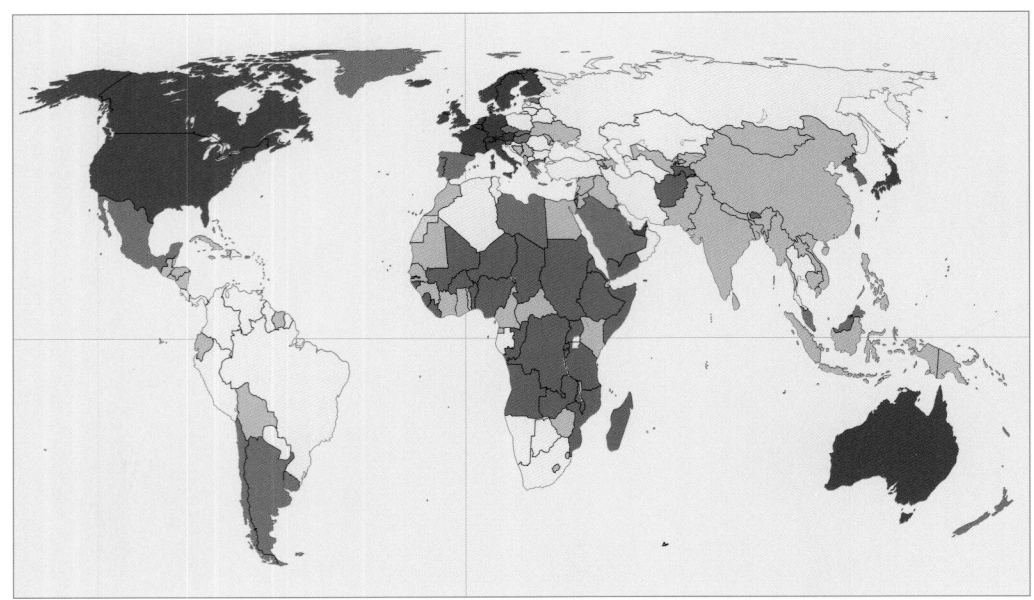

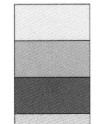

Wealth Creation

The Gross Domestic Product (GDP) of the world's largest economies, US $ million (2001)

1.	USA	10,082,000	23.	Taiwan		386,000
2.	China	5,560,000	24.	Poland		340,000
3.	Japan	3,450,000	25.	Philippines		335,000
4.	India	2,500,000	26.	Pakistan		299,000
5.	Germany	2,174,000	27.	Belgium		268,000
6.	France	1,510,000	28.	Egypt		258,000
7.	UK	1,470,000	29.	Colombia		255,000
8.	Italy	1,402,000	30.	Saudi Arabia		241,000
9.	Brazil	1,340,000	31.	Bangladesh		230,000
10.	Russia	1,200,000	32.	Switzerland		226,000
11.	Mexico	920,000	33.	Austria		220,000
12.	Canada	875,000	34.	Sweden		219,000
13.	South Korea	865,000	35.	Ukraine		205,000
14.	Spain	757,000	36.	Malaysia		200,000
15.	Indonesia	687,000	37.	Greece		190,000
16.	Australia	466,000	38.	Hong Kong		180,000
17.	Argentina	453,000	39.	Algeria		177,000
18.	Turkey	443,000	40.	Portugal		174,000
19.	Iran	426,000	41.	Vietnam		168,000
20.	Netherlands	413,000	42.	Chile		153,000
21.	South Africa	412,000	43.	Romania		153,000
22.	Thailand	410,000	44.	Denmark		150,000

The Wealth Gap

The world's richest and poorest countries, by Gross Domestic Product per capita in US $ (2001)

1.	Luxembourg	43,400	1.	Sierra Leone	500
2.	USA	36,300	2.	East Timor	500
3.	San Marino	34,600	3.	Somalia	550
4.	Norway	31,800	4.	Congo (D. Rep.)	590
5.	Switzerland	31,100	5.	Burundi	600
6.	Denmark	29,000	6.	Tanzania	610
7.	Canada	27,700	7.	Malawi	660
8.	Ireland	27,300	8.	Ethiopia	700
9.	Japan	27,200	9.	Comoros	710
10.	Austria	27,000	10.	Eritrea	740
11.	Monaco	27,000	11.	Afghanistan	800
12.	Finland	26,200	12.	Yemen	820
13.	Germany	26,200	13.	Niger	820
14.	Belgium	26,100	14.	Nigeria	840
15.	Netherlands	25,800	15.	Mali	840
16.	France	25,700	16.	Kiribati	840
17.	Sweden	25,400	17.	Zambia	870
18.	Hong Kong (China)	25,000	18.	Madagascar	870
19.	Iceland	24,800	19.	Mozambique	900
20.	Singapore	24,700	20.	Guinea-Bissau	900

GDP per capita is calculated by dividing a country's Gross Domestic Product by its total population.

Continental Shares

Shares of population and of wealth (GNP) by continent

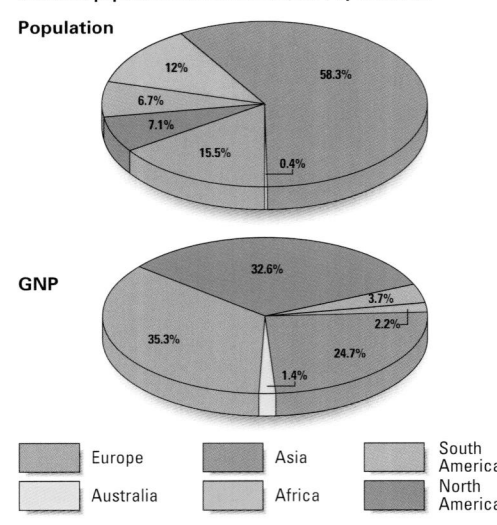

Population

GNP

- Europe
- Australia
- Asia
- Africa
- South America
- North America

Inflation

Average annual rate of inflation (2002)

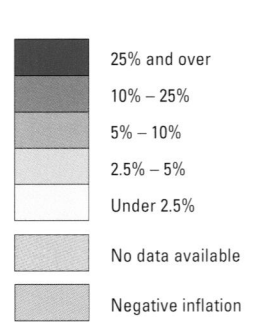

- 25% and over
- 10% – 25%
- 5% – 10%
- 2.5% – 5%
- Under 2.5%
- No data available
- Negative inflation

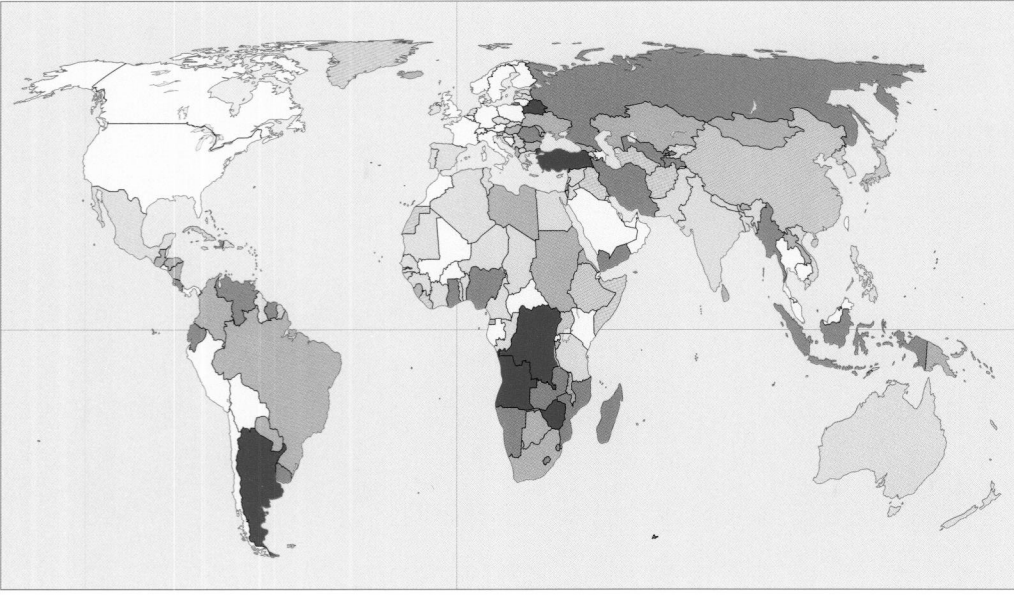

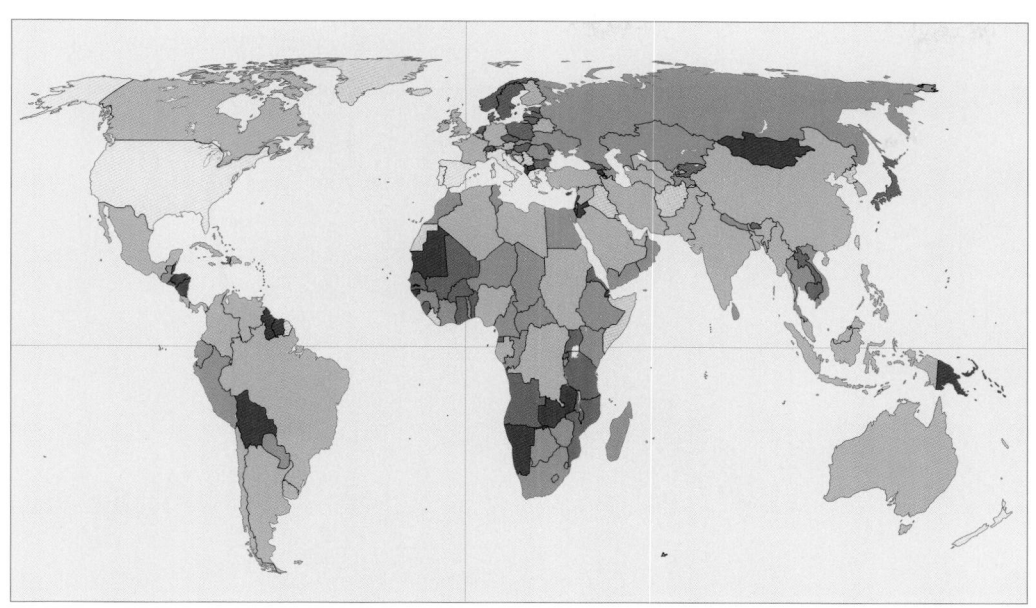

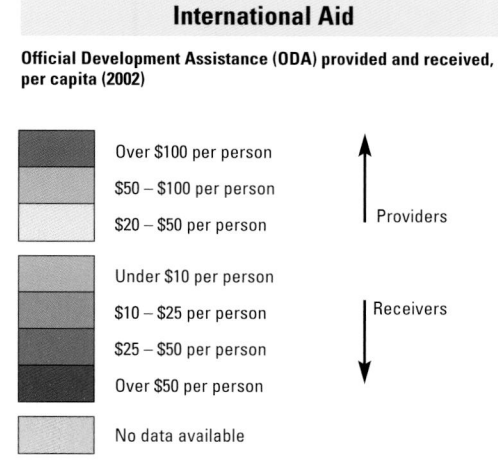

Official Development Assistance (ODA) provided and received, per capita (2002)

Over $100 per person
$50 – $100 per person
$20 – $50 per person
} Providers

Under $10 per person
$10 – $25 per person
$25 – $50 per person
Over $50 per person
} Receivers

No data available

Debt and Aid

International debtors and the aid they receive

Although aid grants make a vital contribution to many of the world's poorer countries, they are usually dwarfed by the burden of debt that the developing economies are expected to repay. It is estimated that the total debt burden of developing countries is US $410 billion, while the cost of servicing that debt amounts to US $25 billion a year.

Debt, US $ per capita (2000)

Aid, US $ per capita (2000)

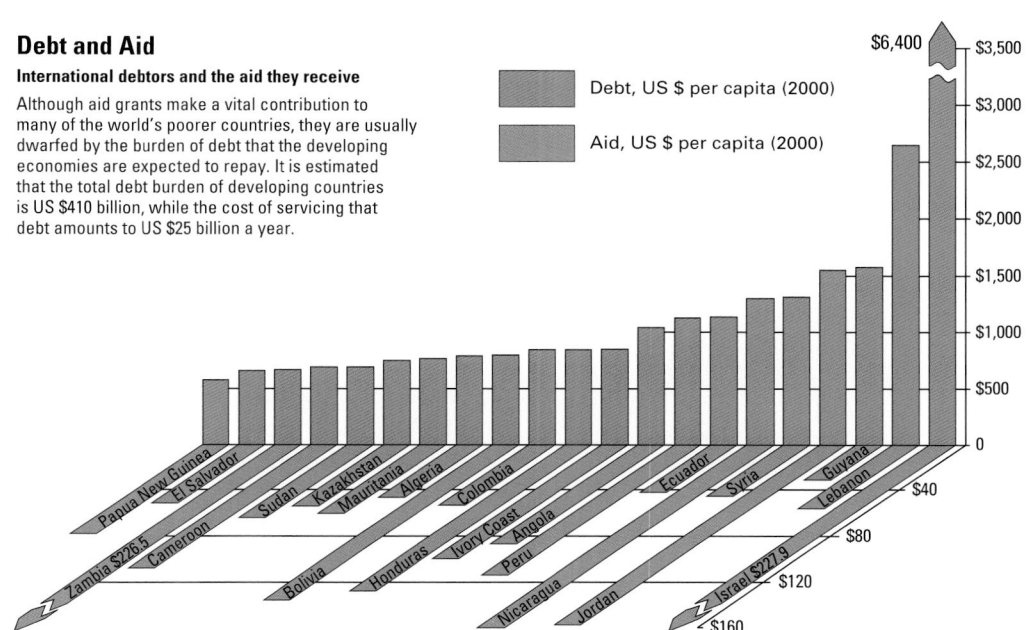

Distribution of Spending

Percentage share of household spending, selected countries

Food
Medicine & Education
Clothing
Transport
Energy & Housing
Other

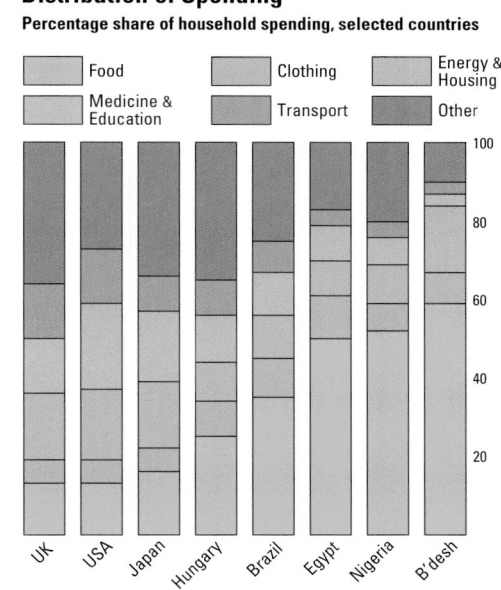

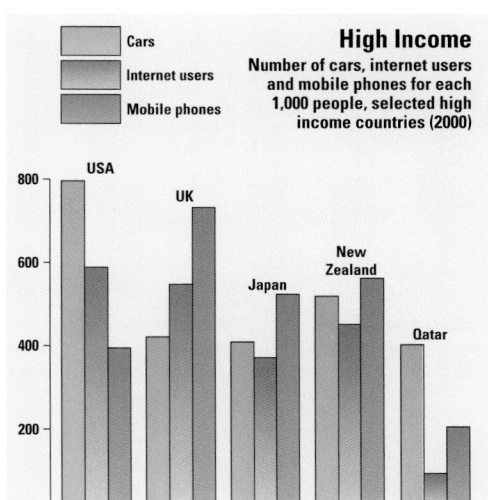

High Income

Cars
Internet users
Mobile phones

Number of cars, internet users and mobile phones for each 1,000 people, selected high income countries (2000)

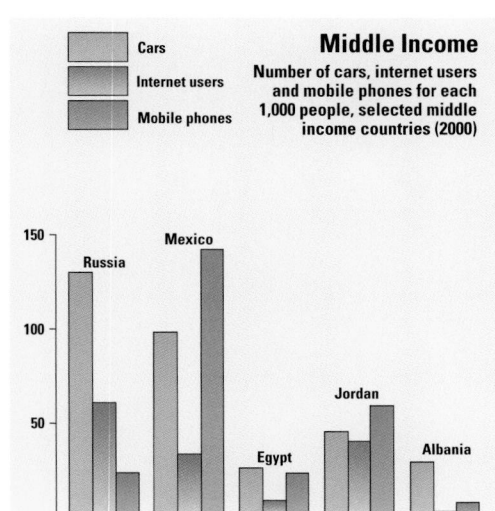

Middle Income

Cars
Internet users
Mobile phones

Number of cars, internet users and mobile phones for each 1,000 people, selected middle income countries (2000)

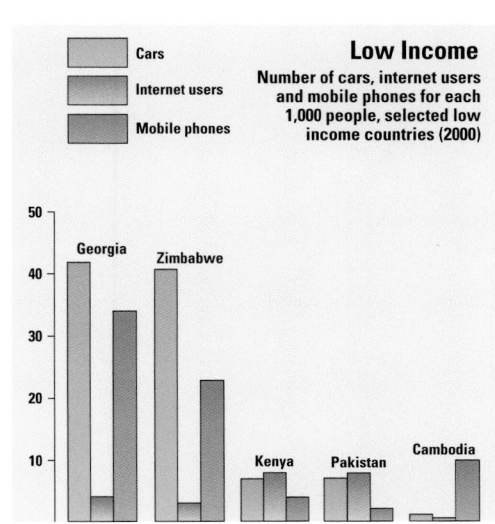

Low Income

Cars
Internet users
Mobile phones

Number of cars, internet users and mobile phones for each 1,000 people, selected low income countries (2000)

Quality of Life

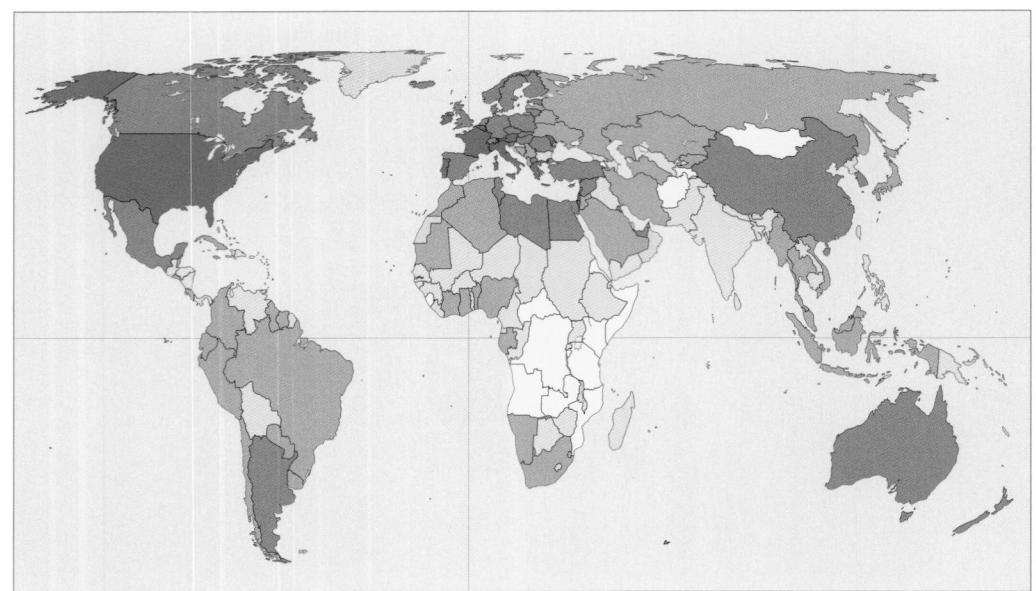

Daily Food Consumption

Average daily food intake in calories per person (2000)

Over 3,500 calories per person

3,000 – 3,500 calories per person

2,500 – 3,000 calories per person

2,000 – 2,500 calories per person

Under 2,000 calories per person

No data available

Hospital Capacity

Hospital beds available for each 1,000 people (latest available year)

Highest capacity		Lowest capacity	
Switzerland	20.8	Benin	0.2
Japan	16.2	Nepal	0.2
Tajikistan	16.0	Afghanistan	0.3
Norway	13.5	Bangladesh	0.3
Belarus	12.4	Ethiopia	0.3
Kazakhstan	12.2	Mali	0.4
Moldova	12.2	Burkina Faso	0.5
Ukraine	12.2	Niger	0.5
Latvia	11.9	Guinea	0.6
Russia	11.8	India	0.6

[UK 4.9] [USA 4.2]

Although the ratio of people to hospital beds gives a good approximation of a country's health provision, it is not an absolute indicator. Raw numbers may mask inefficiency and other weaknesses: the high availability of beds in Kazakhstan, for example, has not prevented infant mortality rates over three times as high as in the United Kingdom and the United States.

Life Expectancy

Years of life expectancy at birth, selected countries (2001)

The chart shows combined data for both sexes. On average, women live longer than men worldwide, even in developing countries with high maternal mortality rates. Overall, life expectancy is steadily rising, though the difference between rich and poor nations remains dramatic.

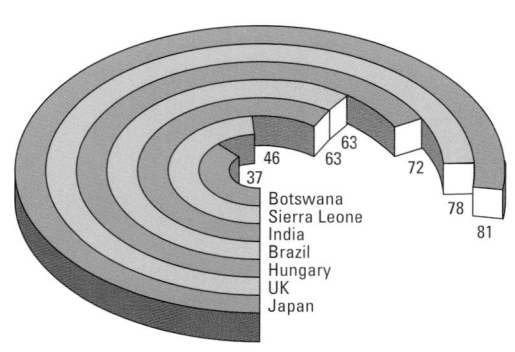

37 46 63 63 72 78 81

Botswana
Sierra Leone
India
Brazil
Hungary
UK
Japan

Causes of Death

Causes of death for selected countries by percentage

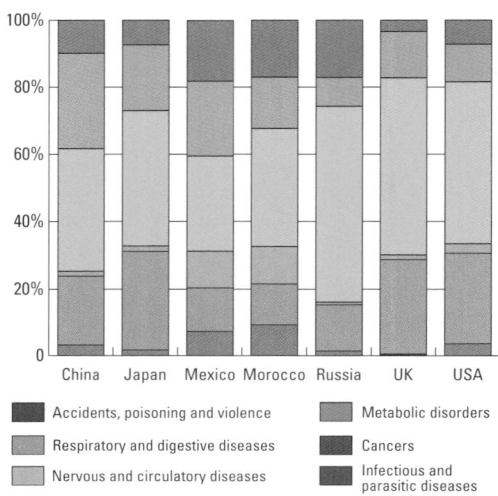

China Japan Mexico Morocco Russia UK USA

Accidents, poisoning and violence

Respiratory and digestive diseases

Nervous and circulatory diseases

Metabolic disorders

Cancers

Infectious and parasitic diseases

Infant Mortality

Number of babies who died under the age of one, per 1,000 live births (2001)

100 deaths and over per 1,000 births

50 – 100 deaths per 1,000 births

25 – 50 deaths per 1,000 births

10 – 25 deaths per 1,000 births

Under 10 deaths per 1,000 births

No data available

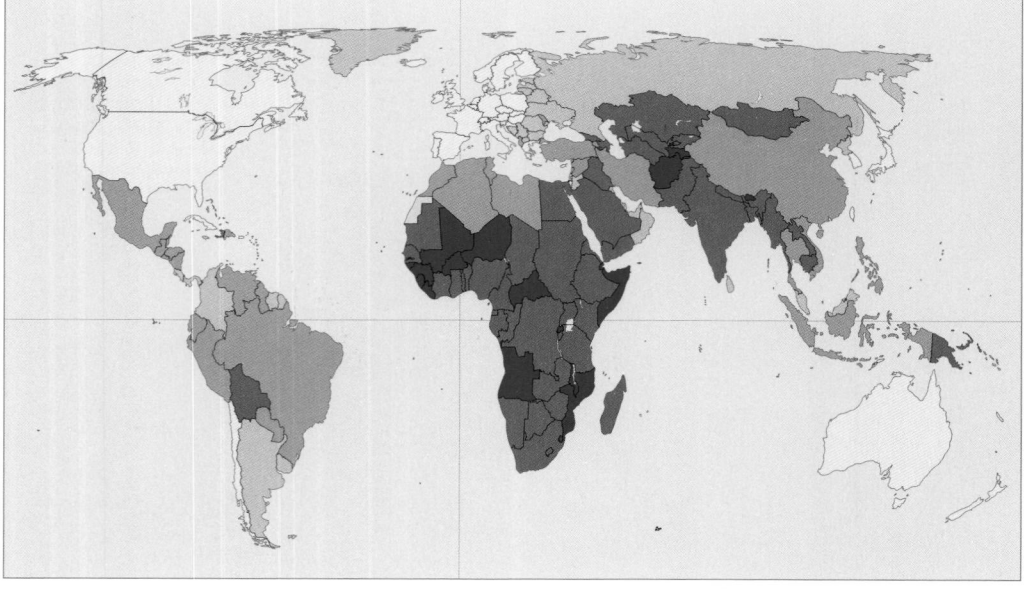

Highest infant mortality		Lowest infant mortality	
Angola	194 deaths	Sweden	3 deaths
Afghanistan	147 deaths	Iceland	4 deaths
Sierra Leone	147 deaths	Singapore	4 deaths
Mozambique	139 deaths	Finland	4 deaths
Liberia	132 deaths	Japan	4 deaths

[UK 6 deaths]

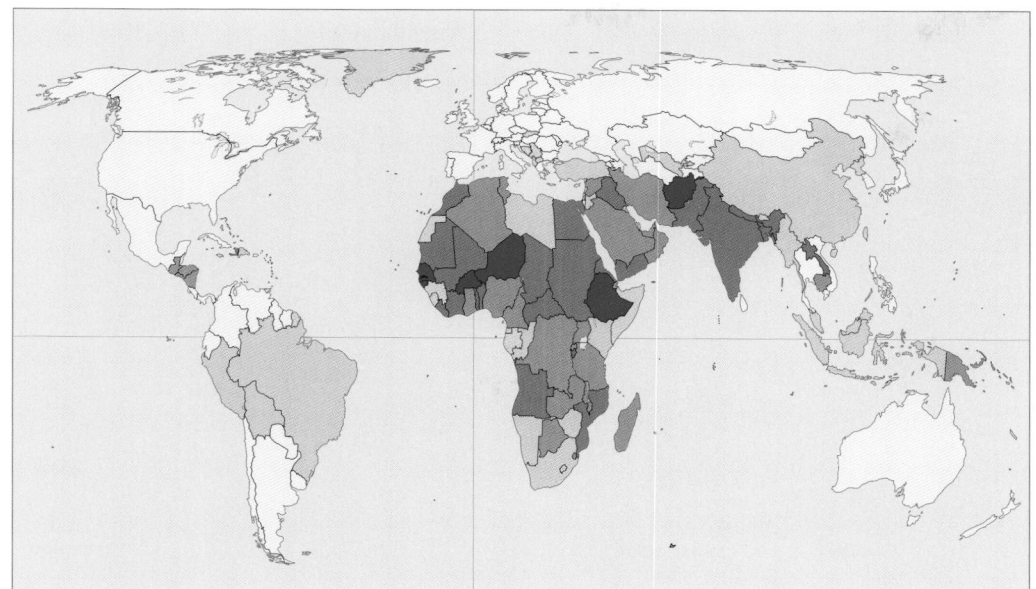

Illiteracy

Percentage of the total adult population unable to read or write (2000)

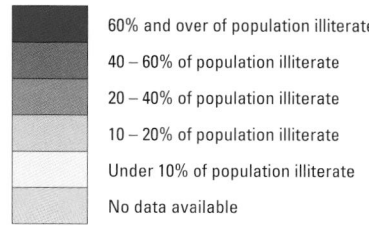

- 60% and over of population illiterate
- 40 – 60% of population illiterate
- 20 – 40% of population illiterate
- 10 – 20% of population illiterate
- Under 10% of population illiterate
- No data available

Countries with the highest and lowest illiteracy rates

Highest		Lowest	
Niger	84	Australia	0
Burkina Faso	76	Denmark	0
Gambia	63	Estonia	0
Afghanistan	63	Finland	0
Senegal	63	Luxembourg	0

[UK 1%]

Fertility and Education

Fertility rates compared with female education, selected countries (1995–2000)

Percentage of females aged 12–17 in secondary education

Fertility rate: average number of children borne per woman

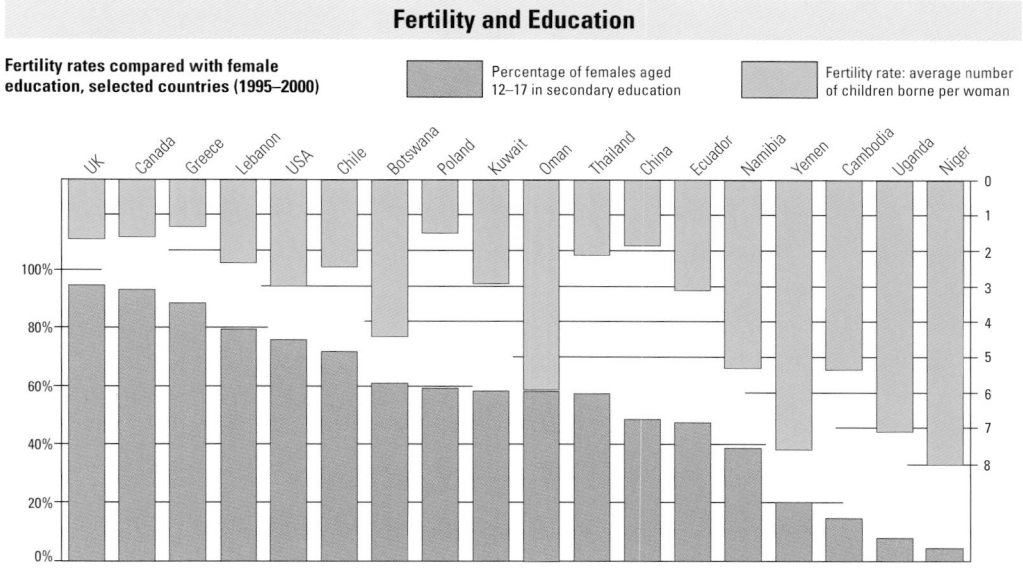

Living Standards

At first sight, most international contrasts in living standards are swamped by differences in wealth. The rich not only have more money, they have more of everything, including years of life. Those with only a little money are obliged to spend most of it on food and clothing, the basic maintenance costs of their existence; air travel and tourism are unlikely to feature on their expenditure lists. However, poverty and wealth are both relative: slum dwellers living on social security payments in an affluent industrial country have far more resources at their disposal than an average African peasant, but feel their own poverty nonetheless. A middle-class Indian lawyer cannot command a fraction of the earnings of a counterpart living in New York, London or Rome; nevertheless, he rightly sees himself as prosperous.

The rich not only live longer, on average, than the poor, they also die from different causes. Infectious and parasitic diseases, all but eliminated in the developed world, remain a scourge in the developing nations. On the other hand, more than two-thirds of the populations of OECD nations eventually succumb to cancer or circulatory disease.

Human Development Index

The Human Development Index (HDI), calculated by the UN Development Programme, gives a value to countries using indicators of life expectancy, education and standards of living in 2000. Higher values show more developed countries.

- 0.9 and over
- 0.8 – 0.9
- 0.7 – 0.8
- 0.4 – 0.7
- Under 0.4
- No data available

Highest values		Lowest values	
Norway	0.942	Sierra Leone	0.275
Sweden	0.941	Niger	0.277
Canada	0.940	Burundi	0.313
USA	0.939	Mozambique	0.322
Belgium	0.939	Burkina Faso	0.325

[UK 0.928]

Energy

Production

Each square represents 1% of world energy production (2000)

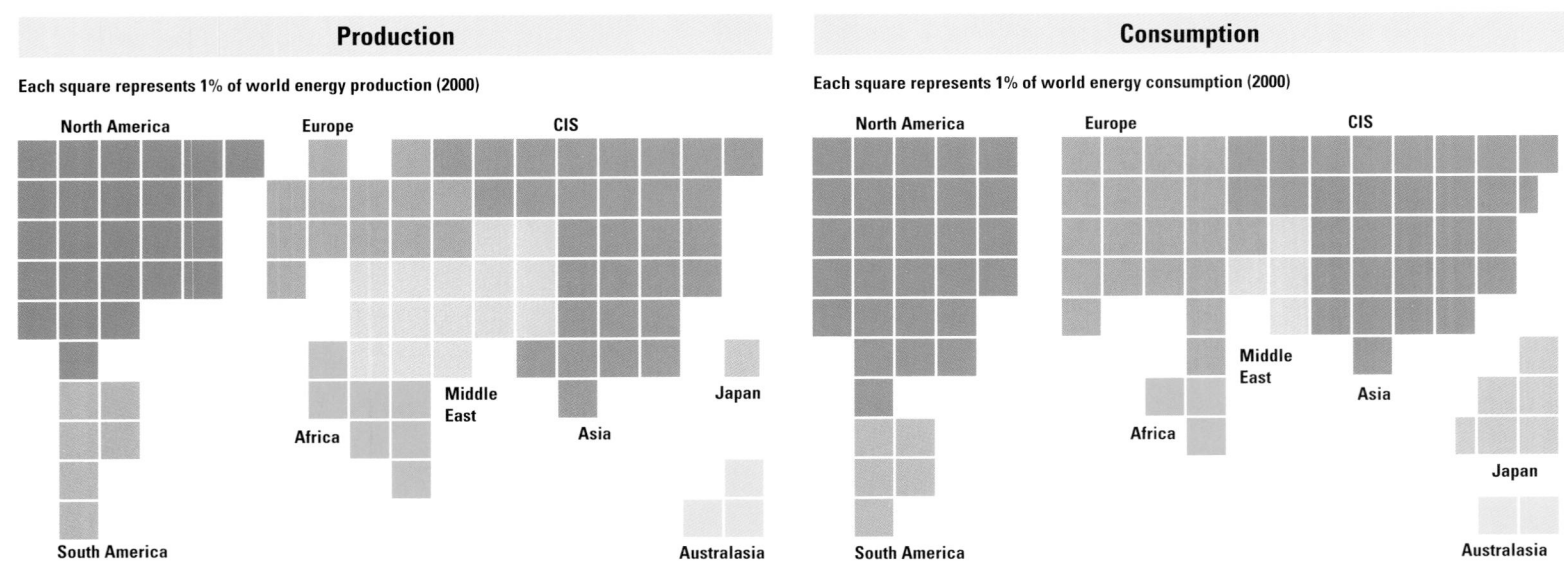

North America · Europe · CIS · Middle East · Africa · Asia · Japan · South America · Australasia

Consumption

Each square represents 1% of world energy consumption (2000)

North America · Europe · CIS · Middle East · Africa · Asia · Japan · South America · Australasia

Energy Balance

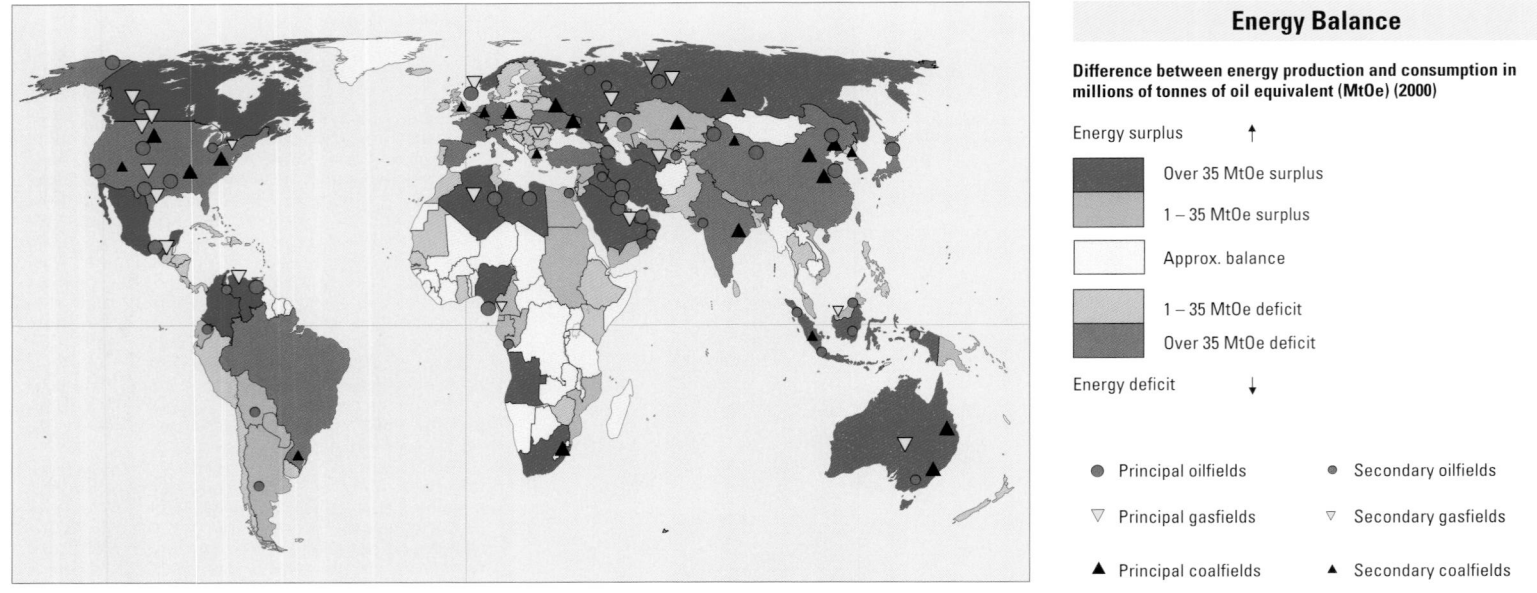

Difference between energy production and consumption in millions of tonnes of oil equivalent (MtOe) (2000)

Energy surplus ↑

- Over 35 MtOe surplus
- 1 – 35 MtOe surplus
- Approx. balance
- 1 – 35 MtOe deficit
- Over 35 MtOe deficit

Energy deficit ↓

- ● Principal oilfields
- ● Secondary oilfields
- ▽ Principal gasfields
- ▽ Secondary gasfields
- ▲ Principal coalfields
- ▲ Secondary coalfields

World Energy Consumption

Energy consumed by world regions, measured in million tonnes of oil equivalent in 2001. Total world consumption was 9,125 MtOe. Only energy from oil, gas, coal, nuclear and hydroelectric sources are included. Excluded are fuels such as wood, peat, animal waste, wind, solar and geothermal which, though important in some countries, are unreliably documented in terms of consumption statistics.

Oil · Gas · Coal · Nuclear · Hydro

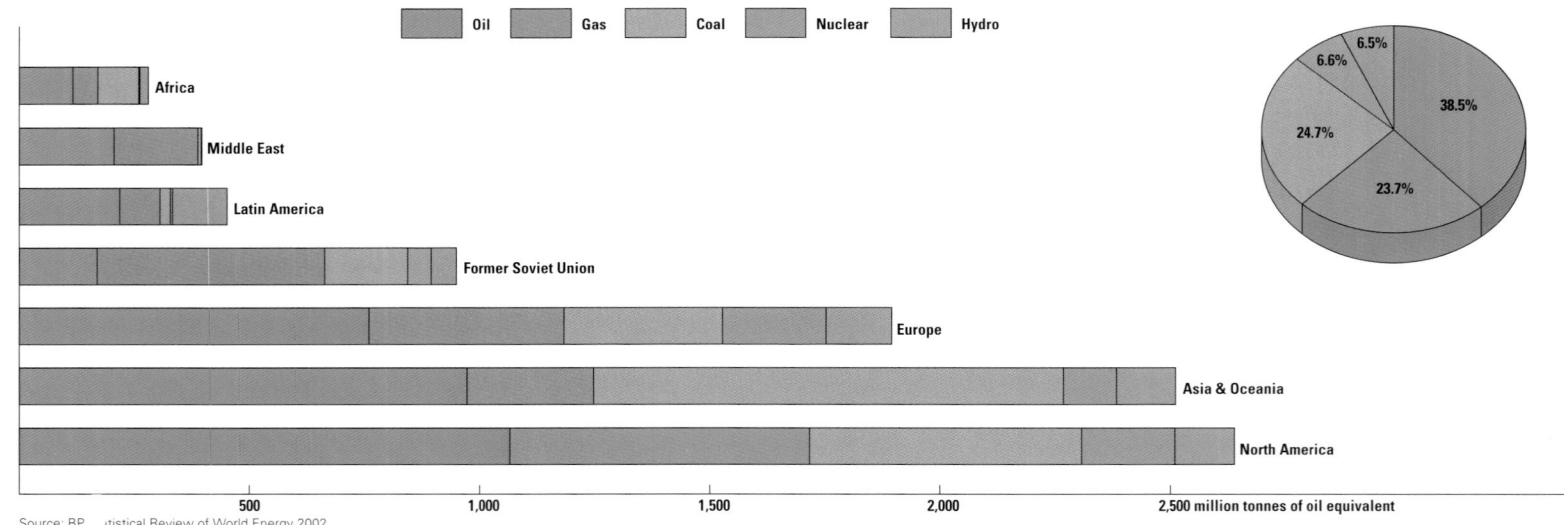

Africa · Middle East · Latin America · Former Soviet Union · Europe · Asia & Oceania · North America

500 · 1,000 · 1,500 · 2,000 · 2,500 million tonnes of oil equivalent

6.5% · 6.6% · 38.5% · 24.7% · 23.7%

Source: BP ıtistical Review of World Energy 2002

Energy

Energy is used to keep us warm or cool, fuel our industries and our transport systems, and even feed us; high-intensity agriculture, with its use of fertilizers, pesticides and machinery, is heavily energy-dependent. Although we live in a high-energy society, there are vast discrepancies between rich and poor; for example, a North American consumes 13 times as much energy as a Chinese person. But even developing nations have more power at their disposal than was imaginable a century ago.

The distribution of energy supplies, most importantly fossil fuels (coal, oil and natural gas), is very uneven. In addition, the diagrams and map opposite show that the largest producers of energy are not necessarily the largest consumers. The movement of energy supplies around the world is therefore an important component of international trade. In 1999, total world movements in oil amounted to 2,025 million tonnes.

As the finite reserves of fossil fuels are depleted, renewable energy sources, such as solar, hydro-thermal, wind, tidal and biomass, will become increasingly important around the world.

Nuclear Power

Major producers by percentage of world total (2000) and by percentage of domestic electricity generation (1999)

Country	% of world total production	Country	% of nuclear as proportion of domestic electricity
1. USA	30.5%	1. Lithuania	76.1%
2. France	15.7%	2. France	75.1%
3. Japan	12.6%	3. Belgium	58.2%
4. Germany	6.7%	4. Slovak Rep.	47.5%
5. Russia	4.6%	5. Sweden	44.2%
6. South Korea	4.1%	6. Ukraine	41.6%
7. UK	3.8%	7. Bulgaria	41.4%
8. Canada	2.9%	8. South Korea	39.1%
9. Ukraine	2.8%	9. Hungary	38.1%
= Sweden	2.8%	10. Slovenia	35.9%

Although the 1980s were a bad time for the nuclear power industry (major projects ran over budget and fears of long-term environmental damage were heavily reinforced by the 1986 disaster at Chernobyl), the industry picked up in the early 1990s. Whilst the number of reactors is still increasing, however, orders for new plants have shrunk. In 1997, the Swedish government began to decommission the country's 12 nuclear power plants.

Hydroelectricity

Major producers by percentage of world total (2000) and by percentage of domestic electricity generation (1999)

Country	% of world total production	Country	% of hydroelectric as proportion of domestic electricity
1. Canada	13.1%	1. Bhutan	99.9%
2. USA	12.0%	2. Paraguay	99.8%
3. Brazil	11.1%	= Zambia	99.8%
4. China	8.5%	4. Norway	99.1%
5. Russia	6.1%	5. Ethiopia	98.1%
6. Norway	4.6%	6. Congo (Rep. Dem.)	97.9%
7. Japan	3.3%	7. Tajikistan	97.8%
8. India	3.1%	8. Cameroon	97.8%
9. France	2.8%	9. Albania	97.2%
10. Sweden	2.7%	= Laos	97.2%

Countries heavily reliant on hydroelectricity are usually small and non-industrial: a high proportion of hydroelectric power more often reflects a modest energy budget than vast hydroelectric resources. The USA, for instance, produces only 8.5% of its power requirements from hydroelectricity; yet that 8.5% amounts to more than three times the hydropower generated by most of Africa.

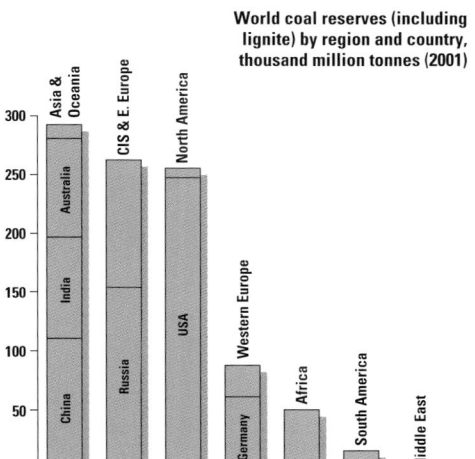

Fuel Exports

Fuels as a percentage of total value of exports (1999)

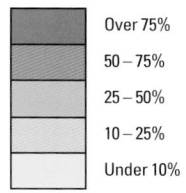

- Over 75%
- 50 – 75%
- 25 – 50%
- 10 – 25%
- Under 10%

In the 1970s, oil exports became a political issue when OPEC sought to increase the influence of developing countries in world affairs by raising oil prices and restricting production. But its power was short-lived, following a fall in demand for oil in the 1980s, due to an increase in energy efficiency and development of alternative resources.

Conversion Rates

1 barrel = 0.136 tonnes or 159 litres or 35 Imperial gallons or 42 US gallons

1 tonne = 7.33 barrels or 1,185 litres or 256 Imperial gallons or 261 US gallons

1 tonne oil = 1.5 tonnes hard coal or 3.0 tonnes lignite or 12,000 kWh

1 Imperial gallon = 1.201 US gallons or 4.546 litres or 277.4 cubic inches

Measurements
For historical reasons, oil is traded in 'barrels'. The weight and volume equivalents (shown right) are all based on average-density 'Arabian light' crude oil.

The energy equivalents given for a tonne of oil are also somewhat imprecise: oil and coal of different qualities will have varying energy contents, a fact usually reflected in their price on world markets.

World Coal Reserves

World coal reserves (including lignite) by region and country, thousand million tonnes (2001)

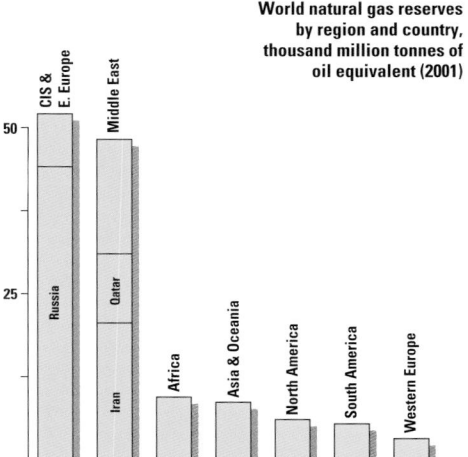

World Gas Reserves

World natural gas reserves by region and country, thousand million tonnes of oil equivalent (2001)

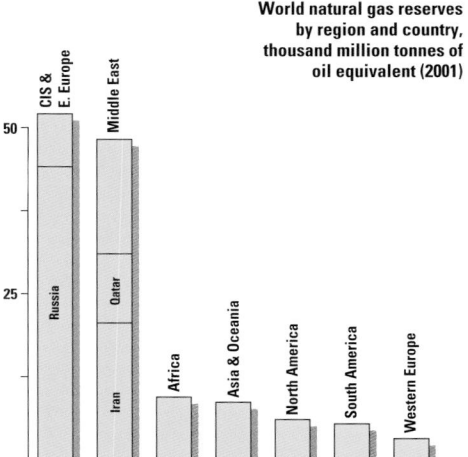

World Oil Reserves

World oil reserves by region and country, thousand million tonnes (2001)

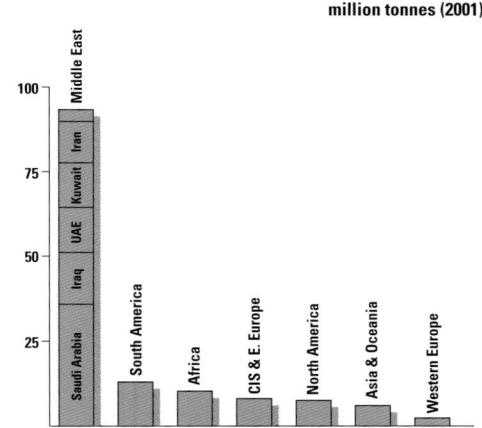

Production

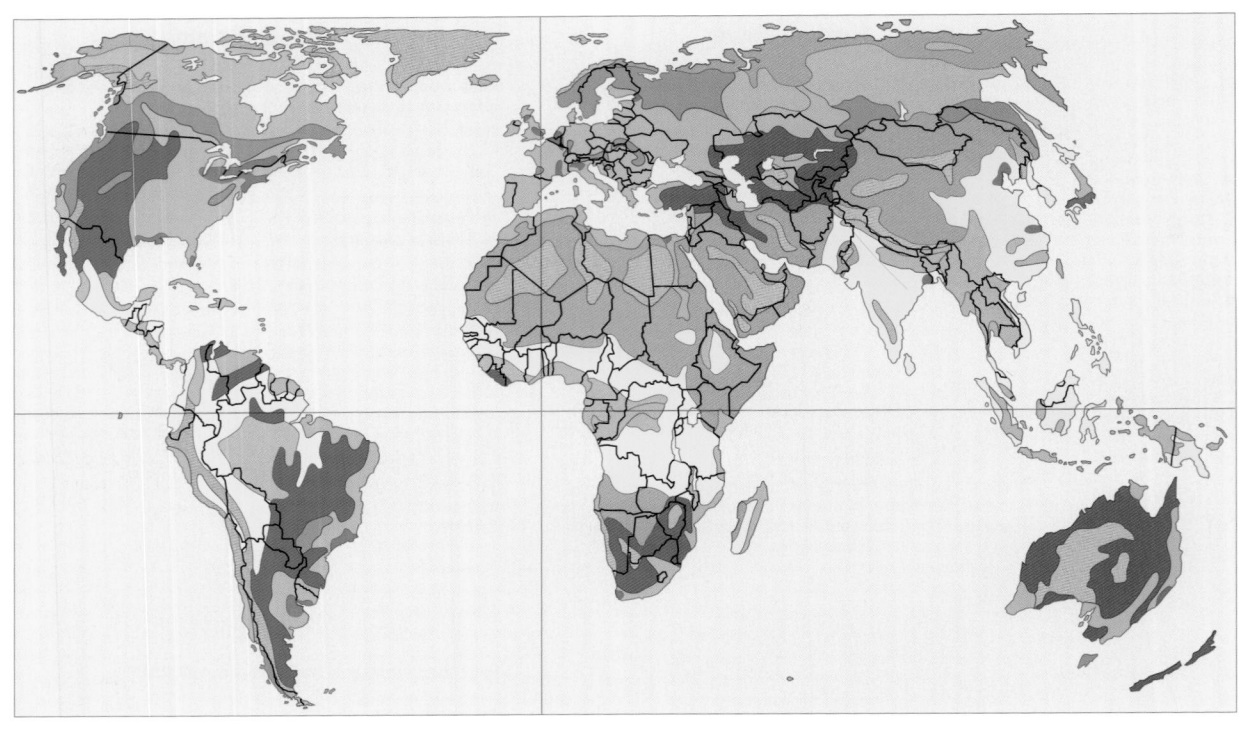

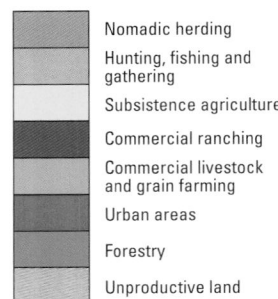
The development of agriculture has transformed human existence more than any other. The whole business of farming is constantly developing: due mainly to the new varieties of rice and wheat, world grain production has increased by over 70% since 1965. New machinery and modern agricultural techniques enable relatively few farmers to produce enough food for the world's 6 billion or so people.

Staple Crops

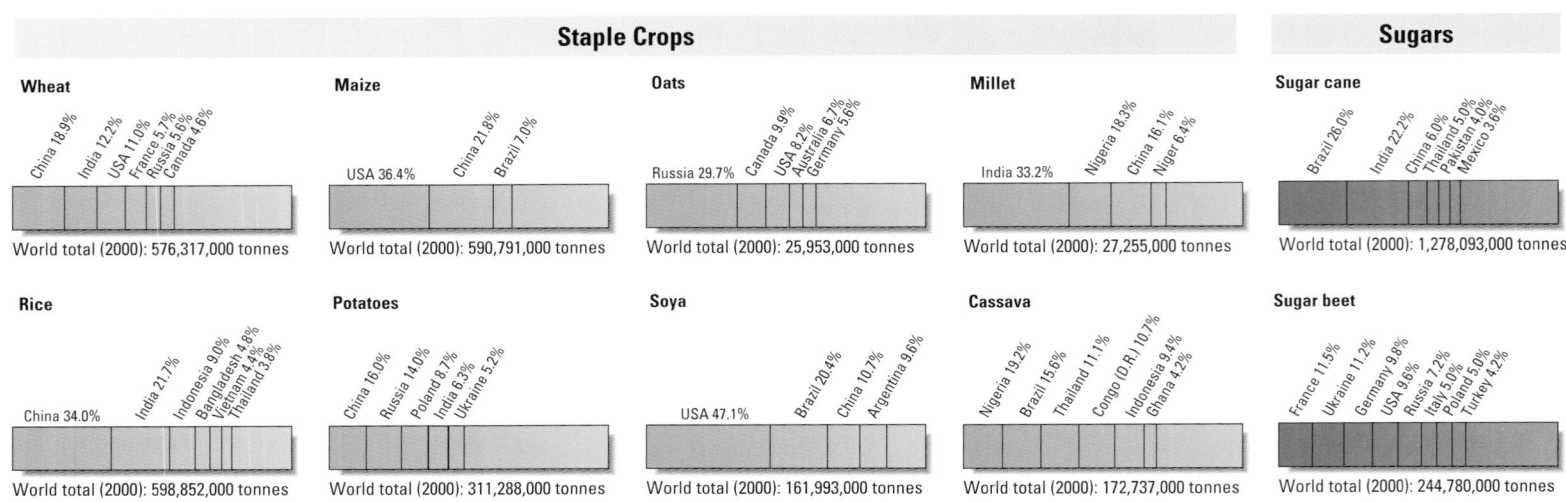

Wheat

China 18.9% | India 12.2% | USA 11.0% | France 5.7% | Russia 5.6% | Canada 4.6%

World total (2000): 576,317,000 tonnes

Maize

USA 36.4% | China 21.8% | Brazil 7.0%

World total (2000): 590,791,000 tonnes

Oats

Russia 29.7% | Canada 9.9% | USA 8.2% | Australia 6.7% | Germany 5.6%

World total (2000): 25,953,000 tonnes

Millet

India 33.2% | Nigeria 18.3% | China 16.1% | Niger 6.4%

World total (2000): 27,255,000 tonnes

Rice

China 34.0% | India 21.7% | Indonesia 9.0% | Bangladesh 4.8% | Vietnam 4.4% | Thailand 3.8%

World total (2000): 598,852,000 tonnes

Potatoes

China 16.0% | Russia 14.0% | Poland 8.7% | India 6.3% | Ukraine 5.2%

World total (2000): 311,288,000 tonnes

Soya

USA 47.1% | Brazil 20.4% | China 10.7% | Argentina 9.6%

World total (2000): 161,993,000 tonnes

Cassava

Nigeria 19.2% | Brazil 15.6% | Thailand 11.1% | Congo (D.R.) 10.7% | Indonesia 9.4% | Ghana 4.2%

World total (2000): 172,737,000 tonnes

Sugars

Sugar cane

Brazil 26.0% | India 22.2% | China 6.0% | Thailand 5.0% | Pakistan 4.0% | Mexico 3.6%

World total (2000): 1,278,093,000 tonnes

Sugar beet

France 11.5% | Ukraine 11.2% | Germany 9.8% | USA 9.6% | Russia 7.2% | Italy 5.0% | Poland 5.0% | Turkey 4.2%

World total (2000): 244,780,000 tonnes

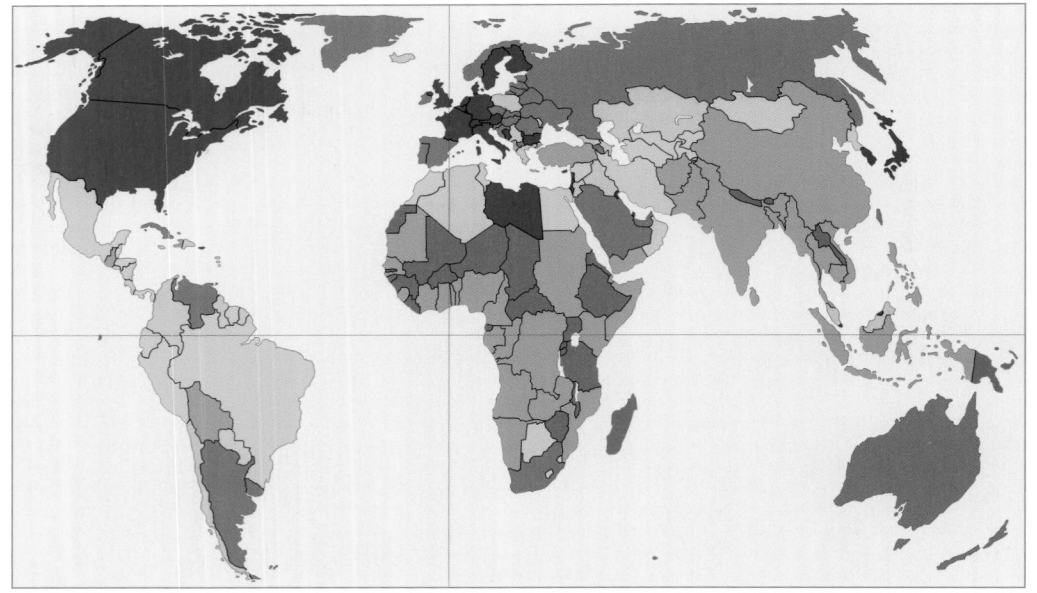

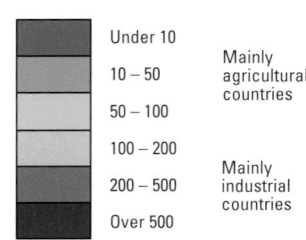
Selected countries (latest available year)

Singapore 8,860	Germany 800
Hong Kong 3,532	Kuwait 767
UK 1,270	Bahrain 660
Belgium 820	USA 657
Former Yugoslavia 809	Israel 633

Mineral Production

*Figures for aluminium are for refined metal; all other figures refer to ore production.

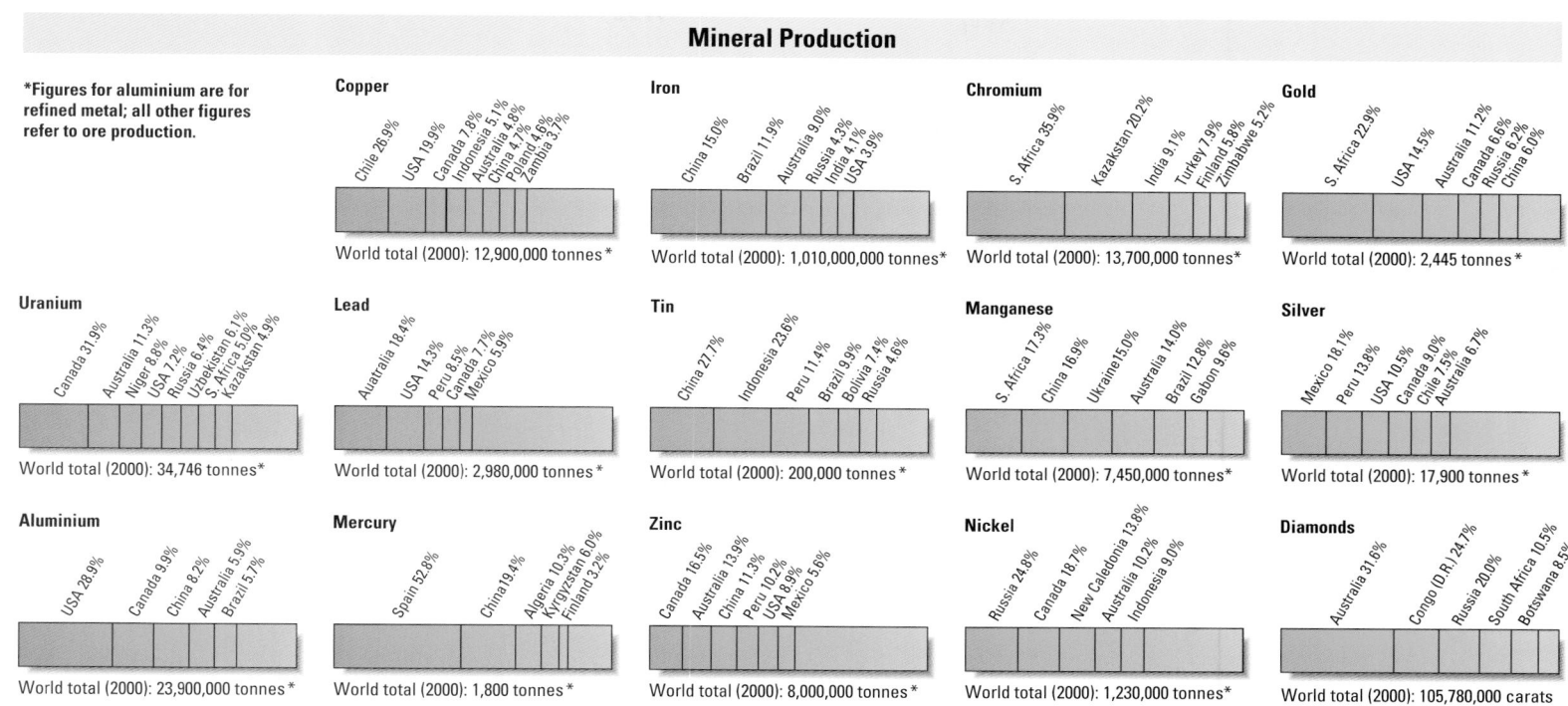

Copper
Chile 26.9% | USA 19.9% | Canada 7.8% | Indonesia 5.1% | Australia 4.8% | China 4.7% | Poland 4.6% | Zambia 3.7%
World total (2000): 12,900,000 tonnes*

Iron
China 15.0% | Brazil 11.9% | Australia 9.0% | Russia 4.3% | India 4.1% | USA 3.9%
World total (2000): 1,010,000,000 tonnes*

Chromium
S. Africa 35.9% | Kazakstan 20.2% | India 9.1% | Turkey 7.9% | Finland 5.8% | Zimbabwe 5.2%
World total (2000): 13,700,000 tonnes*

Gold
S. Africa 22.9% | USA 14.5% | Australia 11.2% | Canada 6.6% | Russia 6.2% | China 6.0%
World total (2000): 2,445 tonnes*

Uranium
Canada 31.9% | Australia 11.3% | Niger 8.8% | USA 7.2% | Russia 6.4% | Uzbekistan 6.1% | S. Africa 5.0% | Kazakstan 4.9%
World total (2000): 34,746 tonnes*

Lead
Australia 18.4% | USA 14.3% | Peru 8.5% | China 7.7% | Canada 5.9% | Mexico 5.9%
World total (2000): 2,980,000 tonnes*

Tin
China 27.7% | Indonesia 23.6% | Peru 11.4% | Brazil 9.9% | Bolivia 7.4% | Russia 4.6%
World total (2000): 200,000 tonnes*

Manganese
S. Africa 17.3% | China 16.9% | Ukraine 15.0% | Australia 14.0% | Brazil 12.8% | Gabon 9.6%
World total (2000): 7,450,000 tonnes*

Silver
Mexico 18.1% | Peru 13.8% | USA 10.5% | Canada 9.0% | Chile 7.5% | Australia 6.7%
World total (2000): 17,900 tonnes*

Aluminium
USA 28.9% | Canada 9.9% | China 8.2% | Australia 5.9% | Brazil 5.7%
World total (2000): 23,900,000 tonnes*

Mercury
Spain 52.8% | China 19.4% | Algeria 10.3% | Kyrgyzstan 6.0% | Finland 3.2%
World total (2000): 1,800 tonnes*

Zinc
Canada 16.5% | Australia 13.9% | China 11.3% | Peru 10.2% | USA 8.9% | Mexico 5.6%
World total (2000): 8,000,000 tonnes*

Nickel
Russia 24.8% | Canada 18.7% | New Caledonia 13.8% | Australia 10.2% | Indonesia 9.0%
World total (2000): 1,230,000 tonnes*

Diamonds
Australia 31.6% | Congo (D.R.) 24.7% | Russia 20.0% | South Africa 10.5% | Botswana 8.5%
World total (2000): 105,780,000 carats

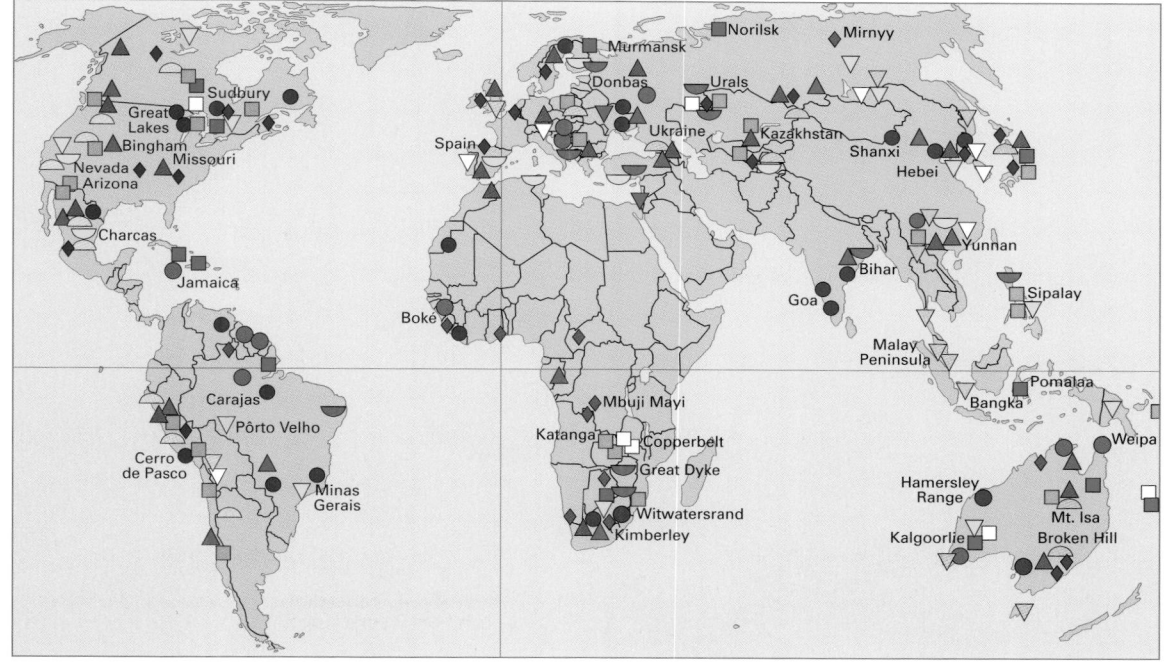

Mineral Distribution

The map shows the richest sources of the most important minerals. Major mineral locations are named.

▽ Gold
◗ Silver
◆ Diamonds
▽ Tungsten
● Iron Ore
■ Nickel
◗ Chrome
▲ Manganese
☐ Cobalt
▲ Molybdenum
▤ Copper
▲ Lead
● Bauxite
▽ Tin
◆ Zinc
◗ Mercury

The map does not show undersea deposits, most of which are considered inaccessible.

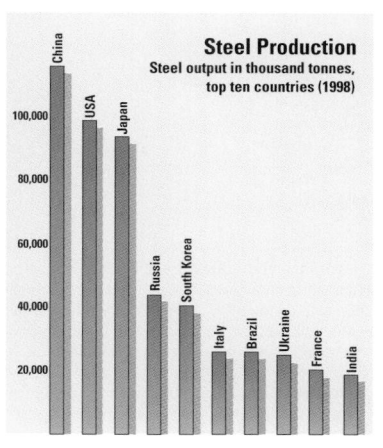

Steel Production
Steel output in thousand tonnes, top ten countries (1998)

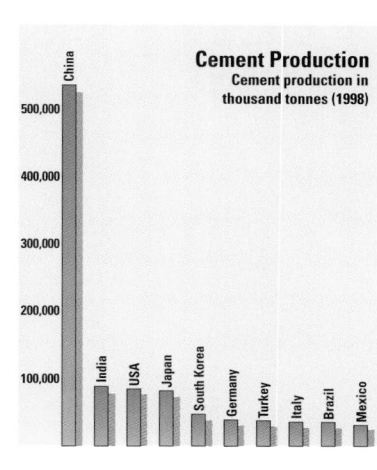

Cement Production
Cement production in thousand tonnes (1998)

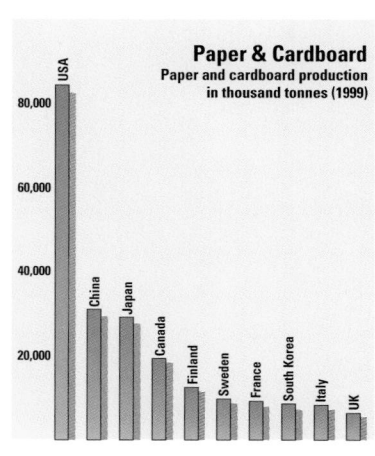

Paper & Cardboard
Paper and cardboard production in thousand tonnes (1999)

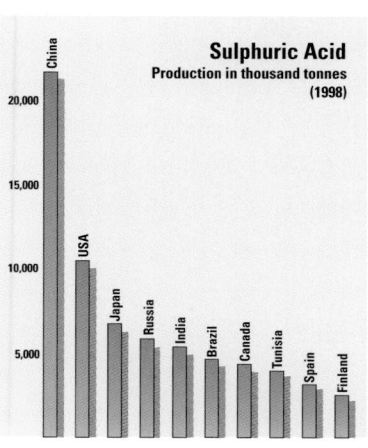

Sulphuric Acid
Production in thousand tonnes (1998)

Trade

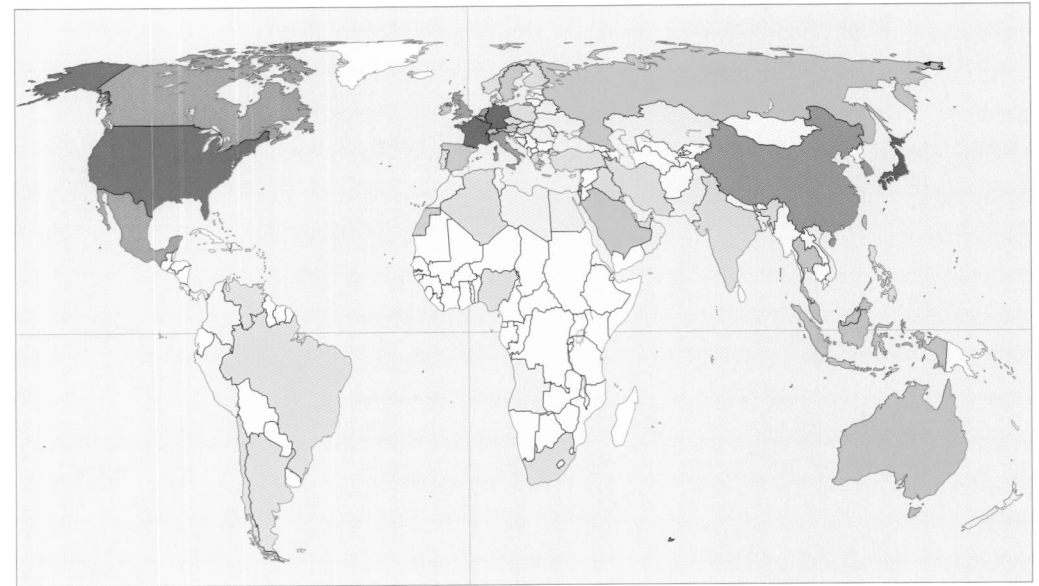

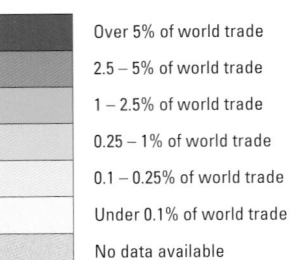
International trade is dominated by a handful of powerful maritime nations. The members of 'G8', the inner circle of OECD (see page 19), and the top seven countries listed in the diagram below, account for more than half the total. The majority of nations – including all but four in Africa – contribute less than one quarter of 1% to the worldwide total of exports; the EU countries account for 35%, the Pacific Rim nations over 50%.

The Main Trading Nations

The imports and exports of the top ten trading nations as a percentage of world trade (2001). Each country's trade in manufactured goods is shown in dark blue.

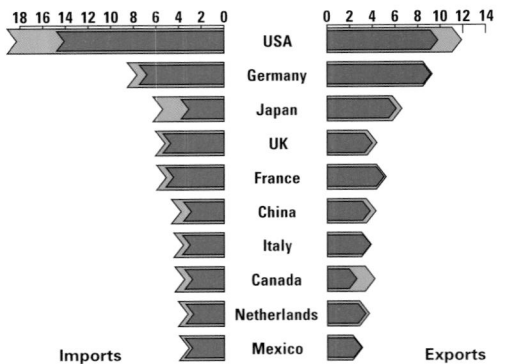

18 16 14 12 10 8 6 4 2 0   0 2 4 6 8 10 12 14

USA
Germany
Japan
UK
France
China
Italy
Canada
Netherlands
Mexico

Imports   Exports

Major exports

Leading manufactured items and their exporters (2000)

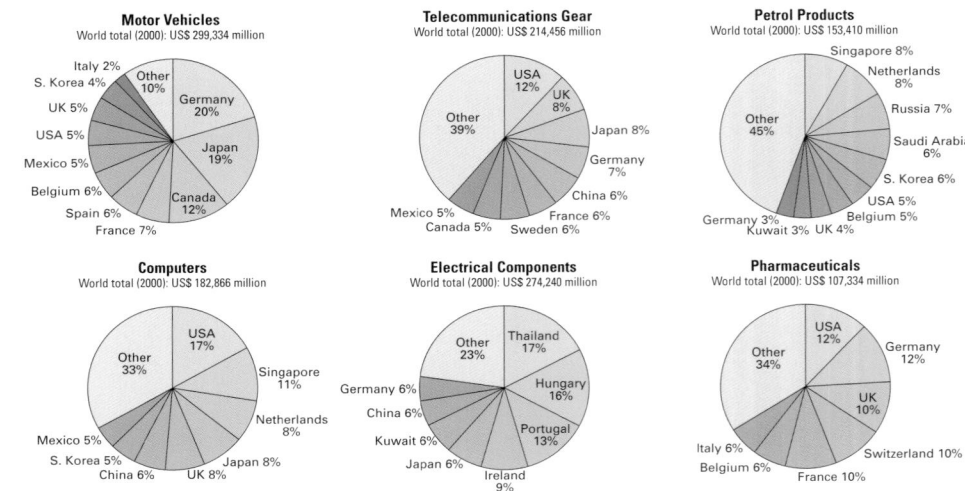

Motor Vehicles
World total (2000): US$ 299,334 million
Italy 2%, S. Korea 4%, Other 10%, Germany 20%, UK 5%, USA 5%, Japan 19%, Mexico 5%, Belgium 6%, Canada 12%, Spain 6%, France 7%

Telecommunications Gear
World total (2000): US$ 214,456 million
USA 12%, UK 8%, Other 39%, Japan 8%, Germany 7%, China 6%, Mexico 5%, France 6%, Canada 5%, Sweden 6%

Petrol Products
World total (2000): US$ 153,410 million
Singapore 8%, Netherlands 8%, Russia 7%, Other 45%, Saudi Arabia 6%, S. Korea 6%, USA 5%, Germany 3%, Belgium 5%, Kuwait 3%, UK 4%

Computers
World total (2000): US$ 182,866 million
USA 17%, Other 33%, Singapore 11%, Netherlands 8%, Mexico 5%, S. Korea 5%, China 6%, Japan 8%, UK 8%

Electrical Components
World total (2000): US$ 274,240 million
Other 23%, Thailand 17%, Germany 6%, Hungary 16%, China 6%, Portugal 13%, Kuwait 6%, Japan 6%, Ireland 9%

Pharmaceuticals
World total (2000): US$ 107,334 million
USA 12%, Germany 12%, Other 34%, UK 10%, Italy 6%, Switzerland 10%, Belgium 6%, France 10%

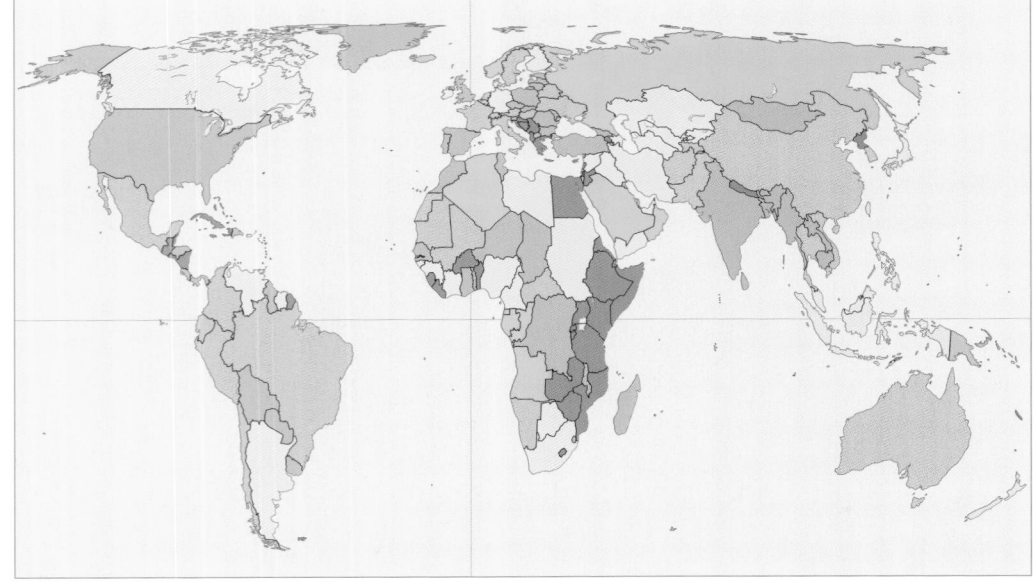

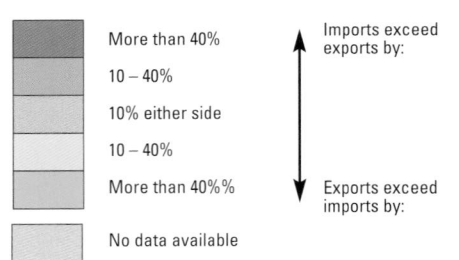
The total world trade balance should amount to zero, since exports must equal imports on a global scale. In practice, at least $100 billion in exports go unrecorded, leaving the world with an apparent deficit and many countries in a better position than public accounting reveals. However, a favourable trade balance is not necessarily a sign of prosperity: many poorer countries must maintain a high surplus in order to service debts, and do so by restricting imports below the levels needed to sustain successful economies.

CARTOGRAPHY BY PHILIP'S. COPYRIGHT PHILIP'S

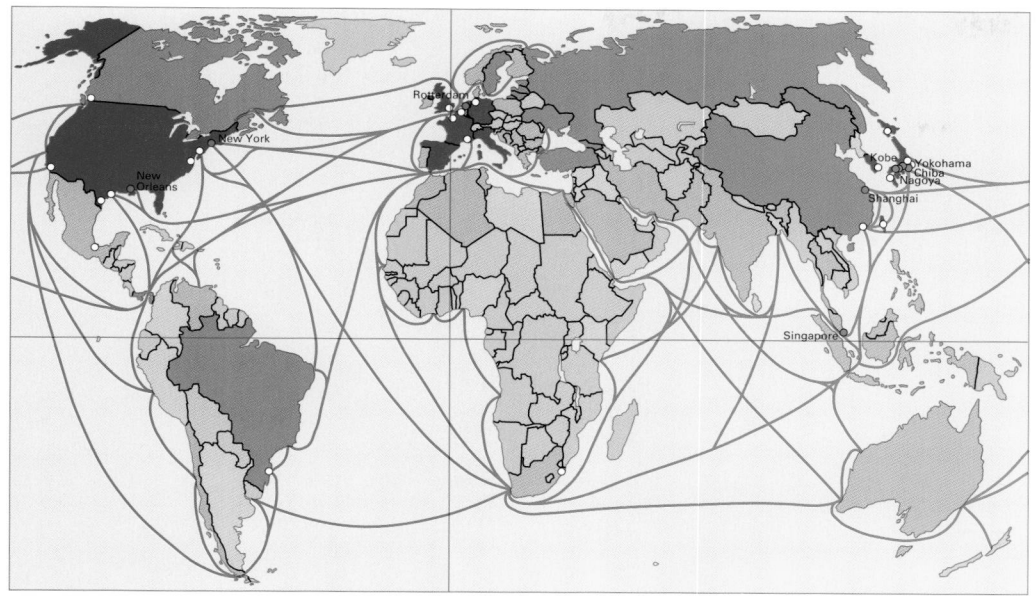

Seaborne Freight

Freight unloaded in millions of tonnes (latest available year)

- Over 100
- 50 – 100
- 10 – 50
- 5 – 10
- Under 5
- Landlocked countries

Major seaports

- ● Over 100 million tonnes per year
- ○ 50–100 million tonnes per year
- — Major shipping routes

Cargoes

Type of seaborne freight

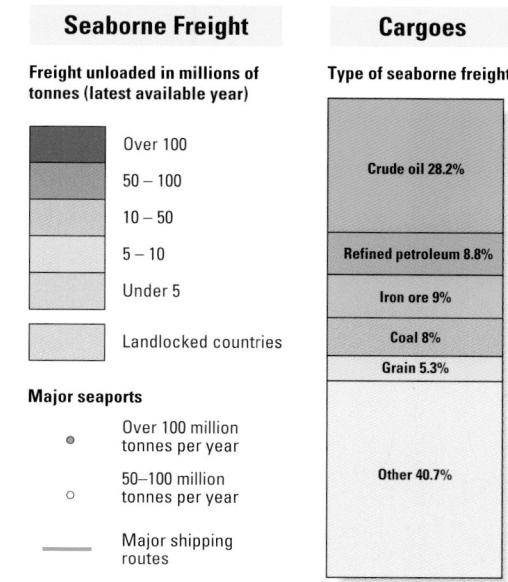

- Crude oil 28.2%
- Refined petroleum 8.8%
- Iron ore 9%
- Coal 8%
- Grain 5.3%
- Other 40.7%

Merchant Fleets

Merchant fleets in thousand gross registered tonnage (2000). Although a large number of vessels are registered in Liberia and Panama, they are not part of the national fleet.

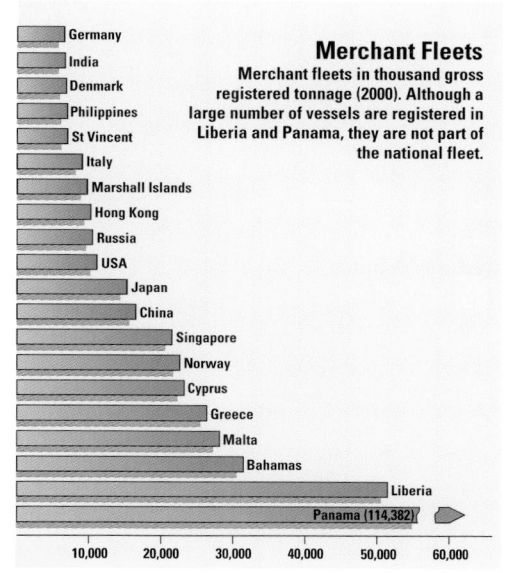

Germany, India, Denmark, Philippines, St Vincent, Italy, Marshall Islands, Hong Kong, Russia, USA, Japan, China, Singapore, Norway, Cyprus, Greece, Malta, Bahamas, Liberia, Panama (114,382)

10,000 20,000 30,000 40,000 50,000 60,000

The Great Ports

Total cargo traffic, in million tonnes (latest available year)

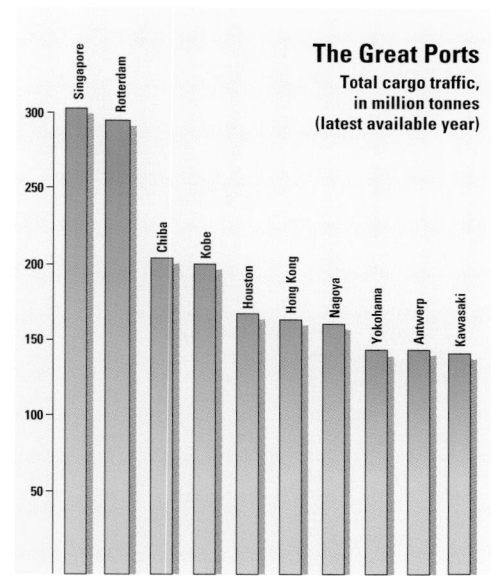

Singapore, Rotterdam, Chiba, Kobe, Houston, Hong Kong, Nagoya, Yokohama, Antwerp, Kawasaki

World Shipping

World merchant fleet by type of vessel and deadweight tonnage (2000)

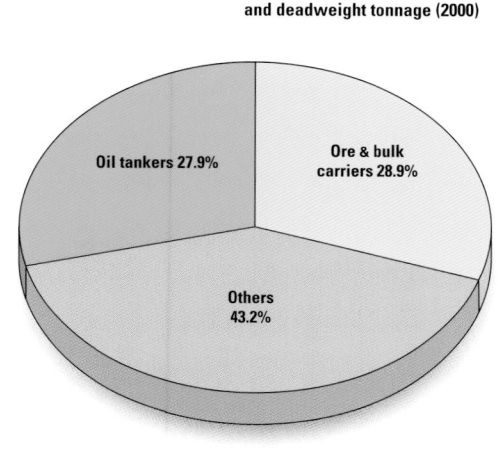

- Oil tankers 27.9%
- Ore & bulk carriers 28.9%
- Others 43.2%

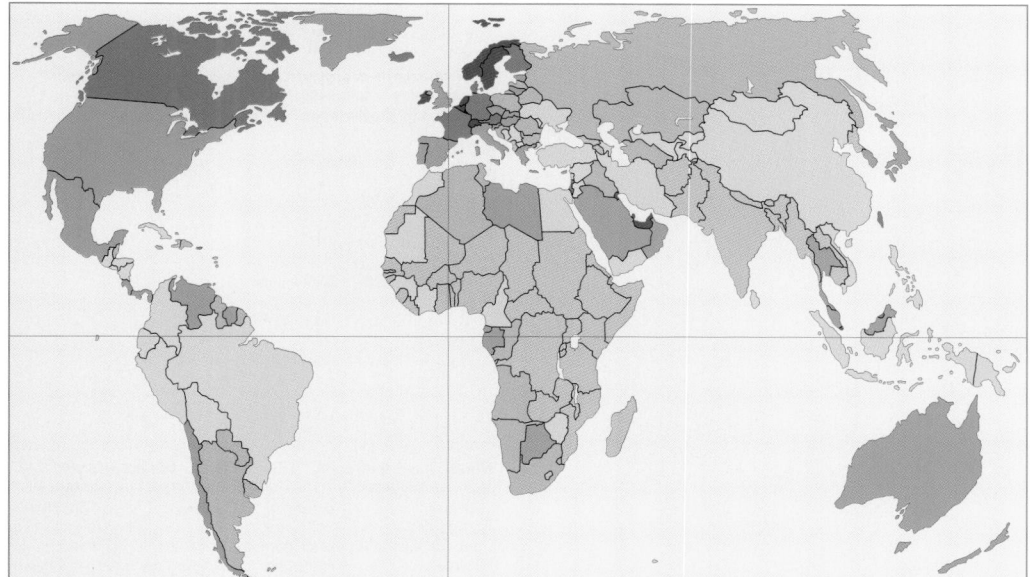

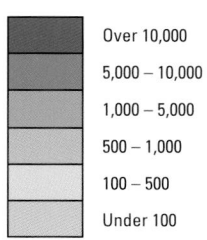

Exports Per Capita

Value of exports in US $, divided by total population (2000)

- Over 10,000
- 5,000 – 10,000
- 1,000 – 5,000
- 500 – 1,000
- 100 – 500
- Under 100

[UK 4,728] [USA 2,791]

Highest per capita

Kuwait	113,614
Liechtenstein	78,848
Singapore	31,860
Aruba (Neths)	31,429
Hong Kong (China)	28,290
Ireland	19,136

Travel and Tourism

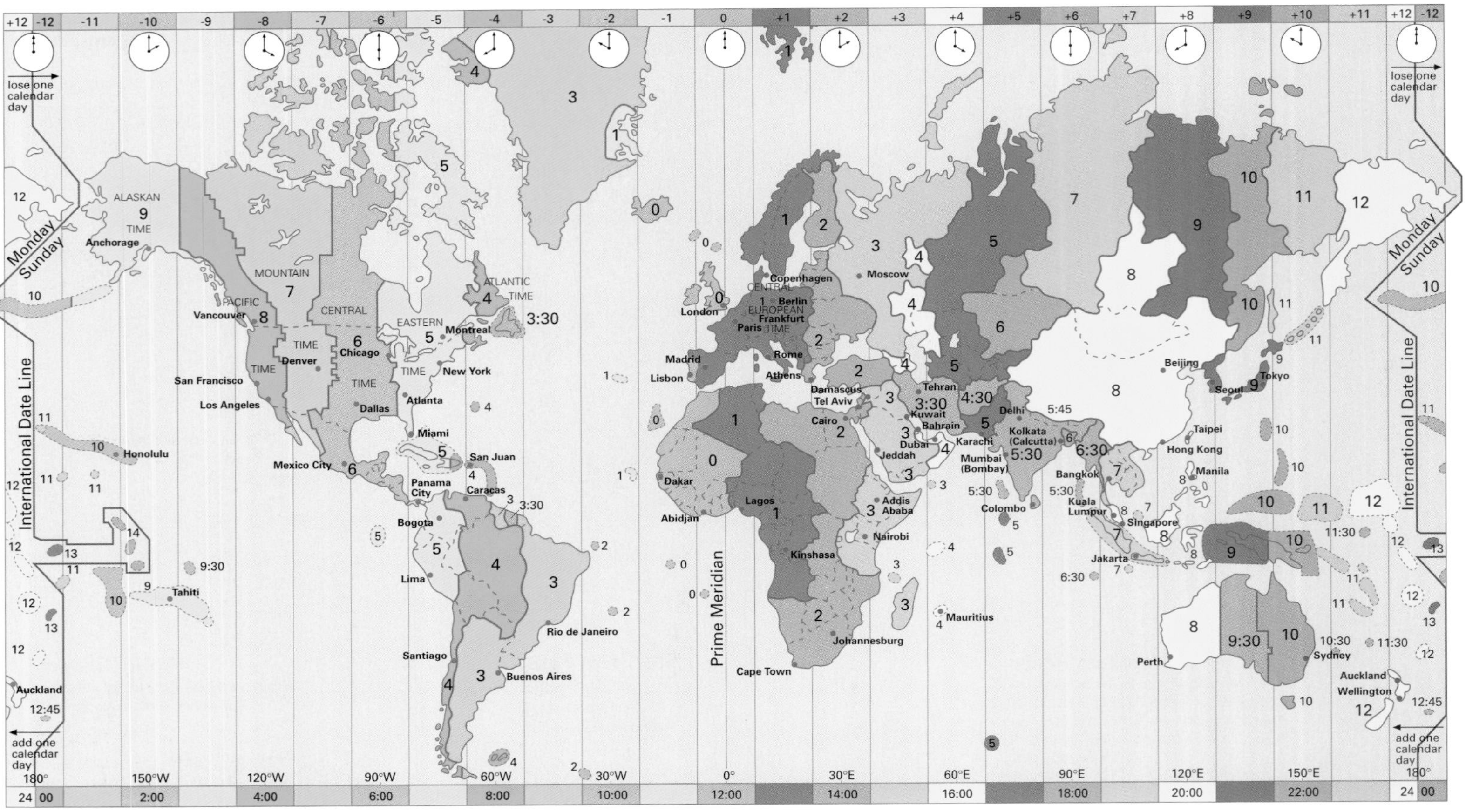

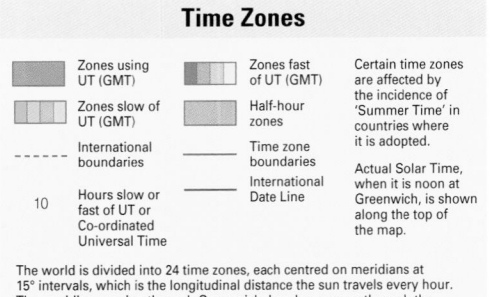

Projection: Mercator

Time Zones

Zones using UT (GMT)	Zones fast of UT (GMT)	Certain time zones are affected by the incidence of 'Summer Time' in countries where it is adopted.
Zones slow of UT (GMT)	Half-hour zones	
International boundaries	Time zone boundaries	Actual Solar Time, when it is noon at Greenwich, is shown along the top of the map.
10 Hours slow or fast of UT or Co-ordinated Universal Time	International Date Line	

The world is divided into 24 time zones, each centred on meridians at 15° intervals, which is the longitudinal distance the sun travels every hour. The meridian running through Greenwich, London, passes through the middle of the first zone.

Rail and Road: The Leading Nations

Total rail network ('000 km)		Passenger km per head per year		Total road network ('000 km)		Vehicle km per head per year		Number of vehicles per km of roads	
1. USA	235.7	Japan	2,017	USA	6,277.9	USA	12,505	Hong Kong	284
2. Russia	87.4	Belarus	1,880	India	2,962.5	Luxembourg	7,989	Taiwan	211
3. India	62.7	Russia	1,826	Brazil	1,824.4	Kuwait	7,251	Singapore	152
4. China	54.6	Switzerland	1,769	Japan	1,130.9	France	7,142	Kuwait	140
5. Germany	41.7	Ukraine	1,456	China	1,041.1	Sweden	6,991	Brunei	96
6. Australia	35.8	Austria	1,168	Russia	884.0	Germany	6,806	Italy	91
7. France	31.9	Argentina	1,011	Canada	849.4	Denmark	6,764	Israel	87
8. France	31.9	Netherlands	994	France	811.6	Austria	6,518	Thailand	73
9. Mexico	26.5	Latvia	918	Australia	810.3	Netherlands	5,984	Ukraine	73
10. South Africa	26.3	Denmark	884	Germany	636.3	UK	5,738	UK	67
11. Poland	24.9	Slovak Rep.	862	Romania	461.9	Canada	5,493	Netherlands	66
12. Ukraine	22.6	Romania	851	Turkey	388.1	Italy	4,852	Germany	62

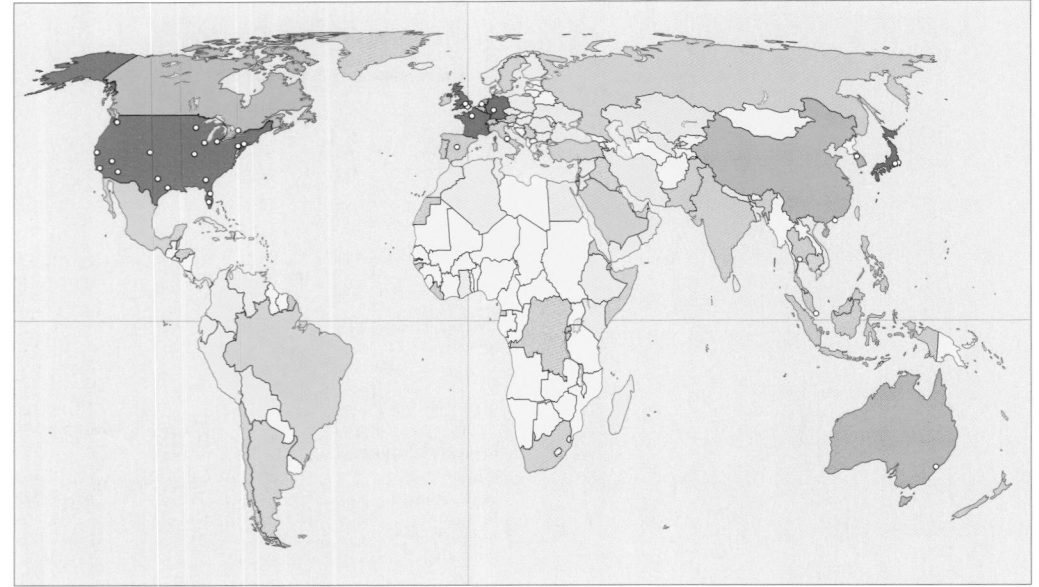

Air Travel

Passenger kilometres flown on scheduled flights (the number of passengers in thousands – international and domestic – multiplied by the distance flown from the airport of origin) (1999)

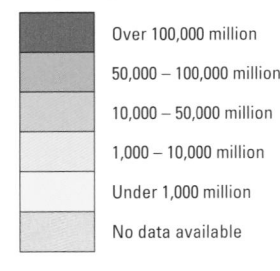

	Over 100,000 million
	50,000 – 100,000 million
	10,000 – 50,000 million
	1,000 – 10,000 million
	Under 1,000 million
	No data available

○ Major airports (handling over 25 million passengers in 2001)

World's busiest airports (total passengers)
1. Atlanta (Hartsfield)
2. Chicago (O'Hare)
3. Los Angeles (International)
4. London (Heathrow)
5. Tokyo (Haneda)

World's busiest airports (international passengers)
1. London (Heathrow)
2. Paris (Charles de Gaulle)
3. Frankfurt (International)
4. Amsterdam (Schipol)
5. Hong Kong (International)

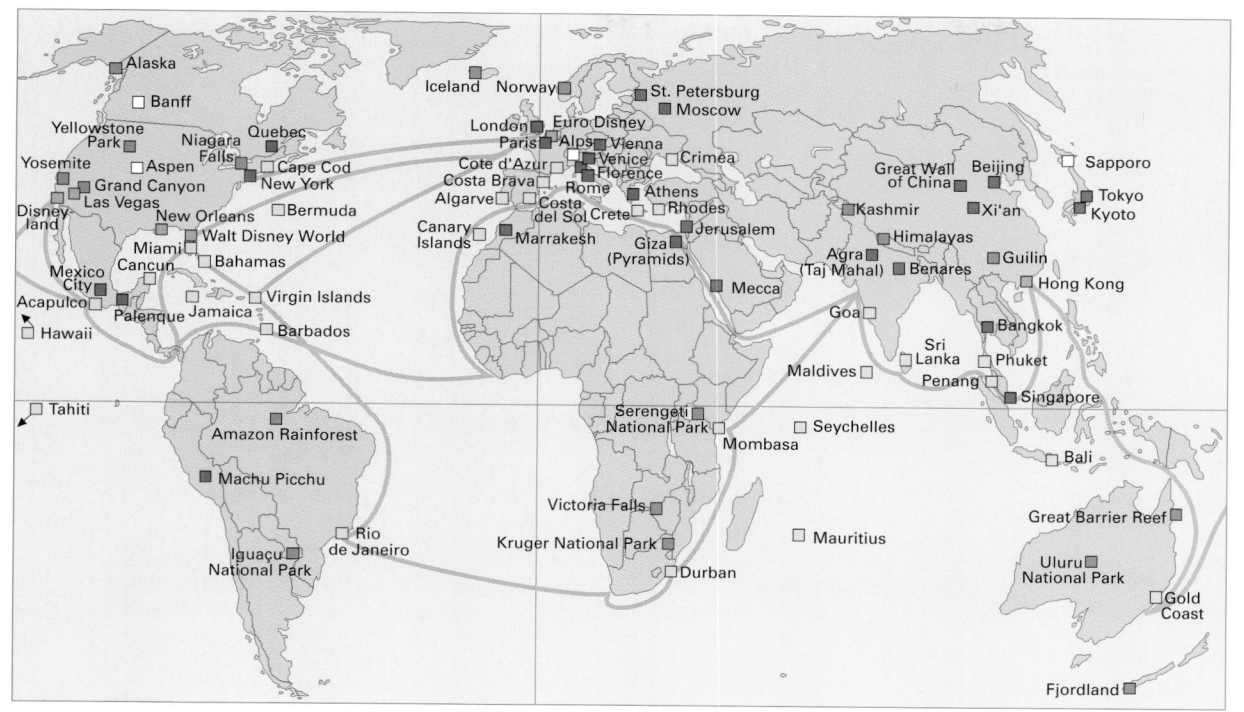

Destinations

- ■ Cultural and historical centres
- □ Coastal resorts
- □ Ski resorts
- ■ Centres of entertainment
- ■ Places of pilgrimage
- ■ Places of great natural beauty
- — Popular holiday cruise routes

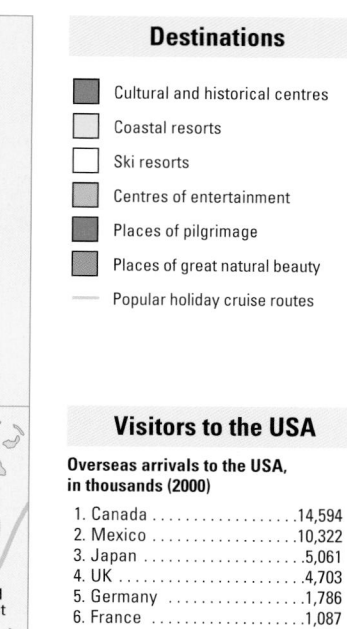

Visitors to the USA

Overseas arrivals to the USA, in thousands (2000)

1. Canada		14,594
2. Mexico		10,322
3. Japan		5,061
4. UK		4,703
5. Germany		1,786
6. France		1,087
7. Brazil		737
8. South Korea		662
9. Venezuela		577
10. Australia		540

Tourist Spending

Countries spending the most on overseas tourism, US$ million (2000)

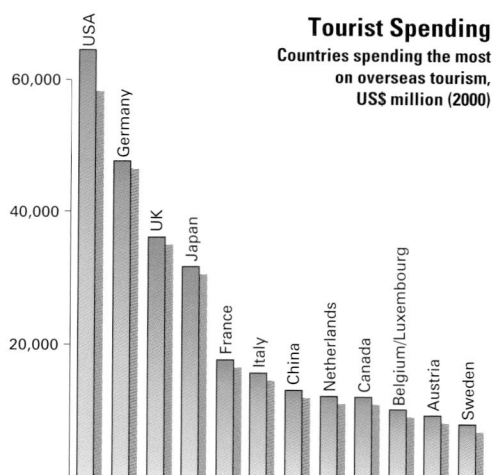

Importance of Tourism

		Arrivals from abroad (2001)	% of world total (2001)
1.	France	76,500,000	11.0%
2.	Spain	49,500,000	7.1%
3.	USA	45,500,000	6.6%
4.	Italy	39,000,000	5.6%
5.	China	33,200,000	4.8%
6.	UK	23,400,000	3.4%
7.	Russia	21,200,000	3.0%
8.	Mexico	19,800,000	2.9%
9.	Canada	19,700,000	2.8%
10.	Austria	18,200,000	2.6%
11.	Germany	17,900,000	2.6%
12.	Hungary	15,300,000	2.2%

In 2001, there was a 0.6% drop in the number of tourist arrivals compared to the previous year, to 693 million. This was partly due to the impact of the terrorist attacks in New York City on 11 September 2001, but was also a result of the weakening economies of tourism-generating markets worldwide.

Tourist Earnings

Countries receiving the most from overseas tourism, US$ million (2000)

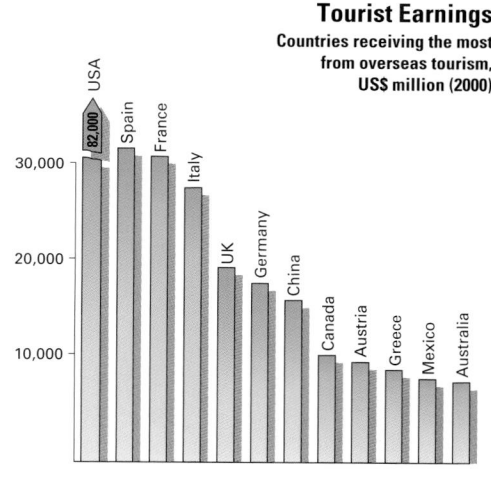

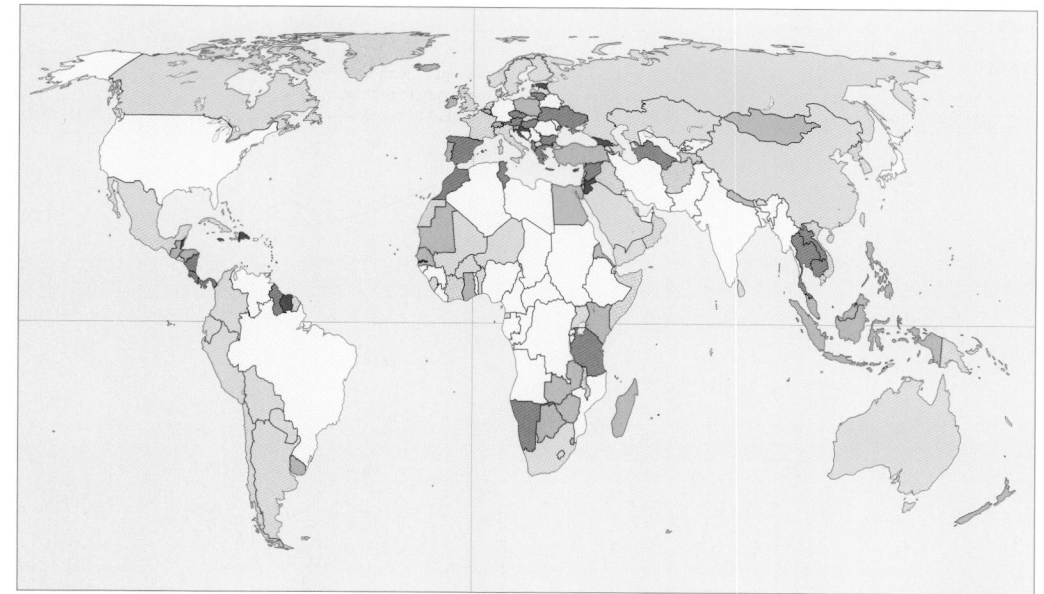

Tourism

Tourism receipts as a percentage of Gross National Income (1999)

- ■ 10% and over
- ■ 5 – 10%
- ■ 2.5 – 5%
- ■ 1 – 2.5%
- □ Under 1%
- □ No data available

Percentage change in tourist arrivals from 2000 to 2001 (top six countries in total number of arrivals)

China	+6.2%
Spain	+3.4%
France	+1.2%
Italy	–5.3%
UK	–7.4%
USA	–10.6%

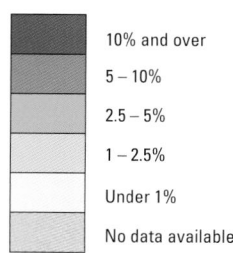

(increase)

(decrease)

The World In Focus: Index

A
Acid rain 15
Agriculture 26
Aid 21
Airports 30
Air travel 30

B
Beaufort Wind Scale 11

C
Carbon dioxide 10, 14
Cement production 27
Climate regions 10
Coal 25
Continental drift 4
Crops 26
Crust 4–5
Currents 8

D
Day and night 2
Debt 21
Deforestation 15
Desertification 15

E
Earth's structure 4
Earthquakes 4
Eclipses 3
Education 23
El Niño 11
Employment 26
Energy balance 24
Epicentre 4
Equinox 2–3

Erosion 7
European Union 19
Exports 28

F
Faults 6
Female employment 23
Fertility 23
Fishing 9
Folds 6
Food consumption 22
Forestry 13
Fuel exports 25

G
Geothermal energy 25
Glaciers 7
Global warming 14
Greenhouse effect 14
Gross Domestic Product 29
Gross National Product 20

H
Holiday destinations 31
Hospital beds 22
Household spending 21
Human Development Index 23
Hydroelectricity 25
Hydrological cycle 12

I
Illiteracy 23
Imports 28
Infant mortality 22
Infectious diseases 22
Inflation 20

International organizations 19

L
Land use 13
Language 18
Life expectancy 22

M
Mantle 4–5
Mercalli Scale 4
Merchant fleets 29
Metals 27
Mid-ocean ridge 5
Minerals 27
Moon 3
Mountain building 6

N
Nuclear power 25

O
OECD 19, 28
Oil 24–25
Ozone 14–15

P
Paper and cardboard 27
Planets 2
Plate tectonics 5
Pollution 9
Population density 16–17
Ports 29
Precipitation 10–12

R
Railways 30

Rainforest 13, 15
Richter Scale 4
Religions 18
Rivers 7
Roads 30

S
Sea-floor spreading 5
Seasons 2
Shipping 29
Solar System 2
Subduction zone 6
Sulphuric acid 27

T
Telecommunications gear 28
Temperature 11
Tides 3
Time zones 30
Tourism 31
Trading nations 28
Transport networks 30

U
United Nations 19
Urban population 17

V
Vegetation 13
Vehicles 28, 30
Volcanoes 5

W
Water 12
Wealth gap 20
Wind power 25

WORLD CITIES

AMSTERDAM	2	EDINBURGH	11	MOSCOW	19	TEHRAN	30
ATHENS	2	HELSINKI	12	MUMBAI	20	TIANJIN	30
ATLANTA	3	HONG KONG	12	MUNICH	20	TORONTO	30
BAGHDAD	3	ISTANBUL	12	NEW YORK	21	VIENNA	31
BANGKOK	3	JAKARTA	13	OSAKA	22	WARSAW	31
BARCELONA	4	JERUSALEM	13	OSLO	22	WASHINGTON	32
BEIJING	4	JOHANNESBURG	13	PARIS	23	WELLINGTON	32
BERLIN	5	KARACHI	14	PRAGUE	24	INDEX	33–39
BOSTON	6	LAGOS	14	RIO DE JANEIRO	24		
BRUSSELS	6	LISBON	14	ROME	25	WORLD CITIES	
BUDAPEST	7	LONDON	15	SAN FRANCISCO	25	SATELLITE IMAGES	
BUENOS AIRES	7	LOS ANGELES	16	ST PETERSBURG	26	CAPE TOWN	40
CAIRO	7	LIMA	16	SANTIAGO	26	CHICAGO	41
CALCUTTA	8	MADRID	17	SÃO PAULO	26	KARACHI	42
CANTON	8	MANILA	17	SEOUL	26	LONDON	43
CAPE TOWN	8	MELBOURNE	17	SHANGHAI	27	NEW YORK	44
CHICAGO	9	MEXICO CITY	18	SINGAPORE	27	SAN FRANCISCO	45
COPENHAGEN	10	MIAMI	18	STOCKHOLM	28	SANTIAGO	46
DELHI	10	MILAN	18	SYDNEY	28	SYDNEY	47
DUBLIN	11	MONTREAL	19	TOKYO	29	TOKYO	48

CITY MAPS

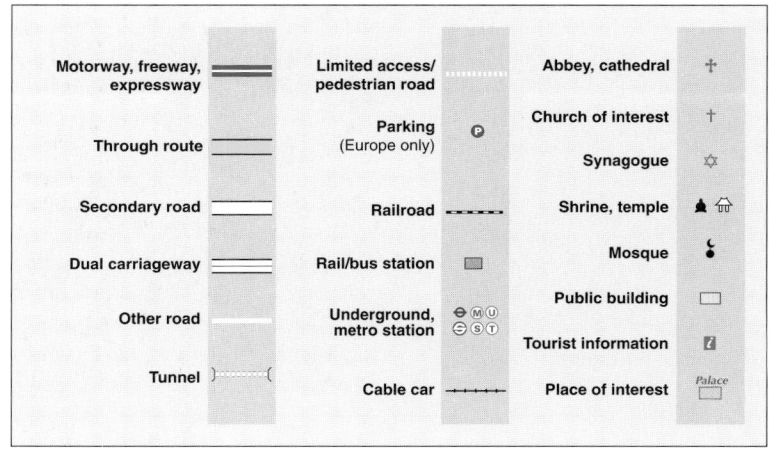

Motorway, freeway, expressway with toll – with road number	A10	
Motorway, freeway, expressway – with European road number	E51	
Road junction	○	
Under construction	= = =	
Tunnel	)======(	
Primary road – with road number dual carriageway single carriageway	14 / 14	
Secondary road – with road number dual carriageway single carriageway	96 / 96	
Other road		
Ferry		
Railroad		
Principal station	Estacion del Norte	
Height above sea level (m)	705 ▲	
Airport	✈	
Airfield	⊕	
Central area coverage		
Urban area		
Woodlands and parks		

CENTRAL AREA MAPS

Motorway, freeway, expressway		
Through route		
Secondary road		
Dual carriageway		
Other road		
Tunnel	)·····(	
Limited access/ pedestrian road		
Parking (Europe only)	P	
Railroad		
Rail/bus station	▢	
Underground, metro station	⊖ M U ⊖ S T	
Cable car	+····+	
Abbey, cathedral	✝	
Church of interest	†	
Synagogue	✡	
Shrine, temple	♨ 卍	
Mosque	☪	
Public building	▢	
Tourist information	i	
Place of interest	Palace ▢	

AMSTERDAM

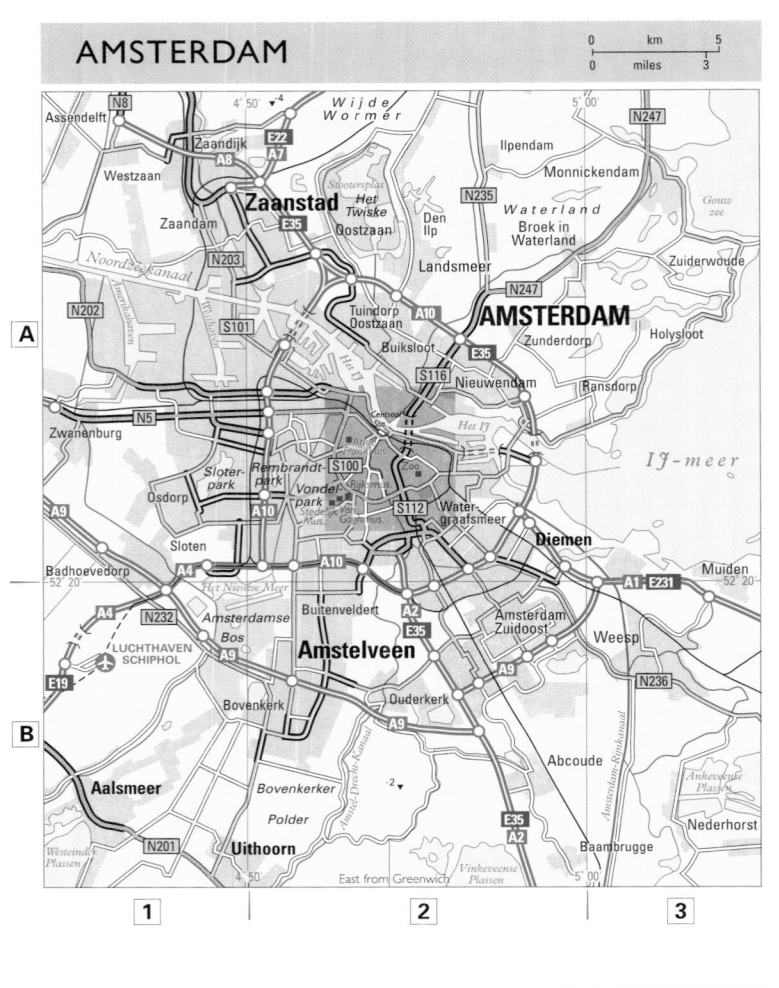

CENTRAL AMSTERDAM

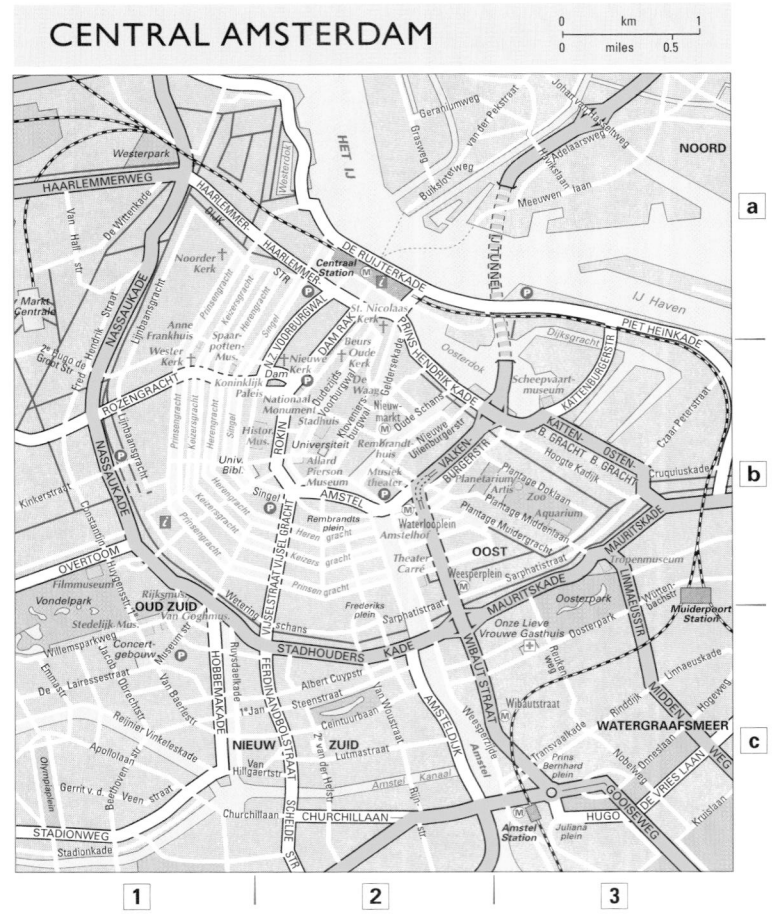

ATHENS

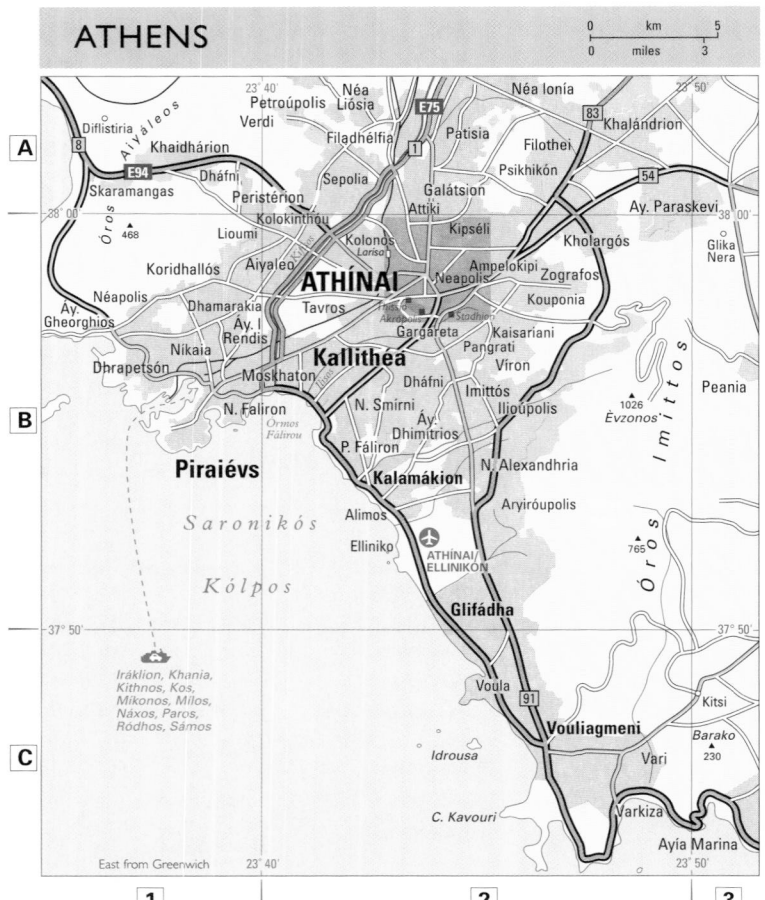

CENTRAL ATHENS

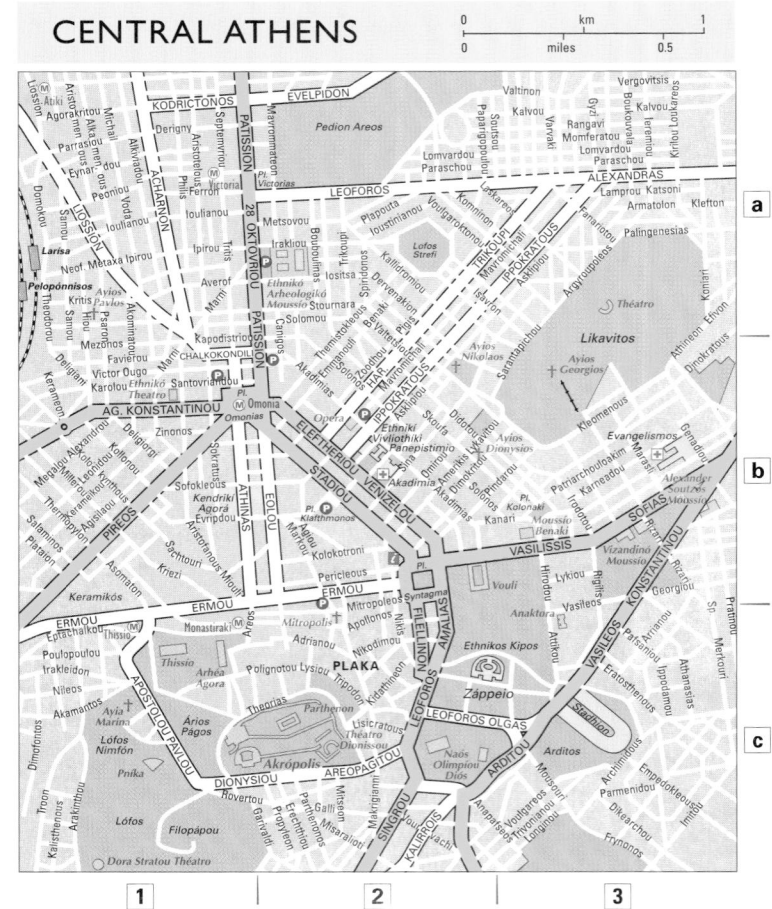

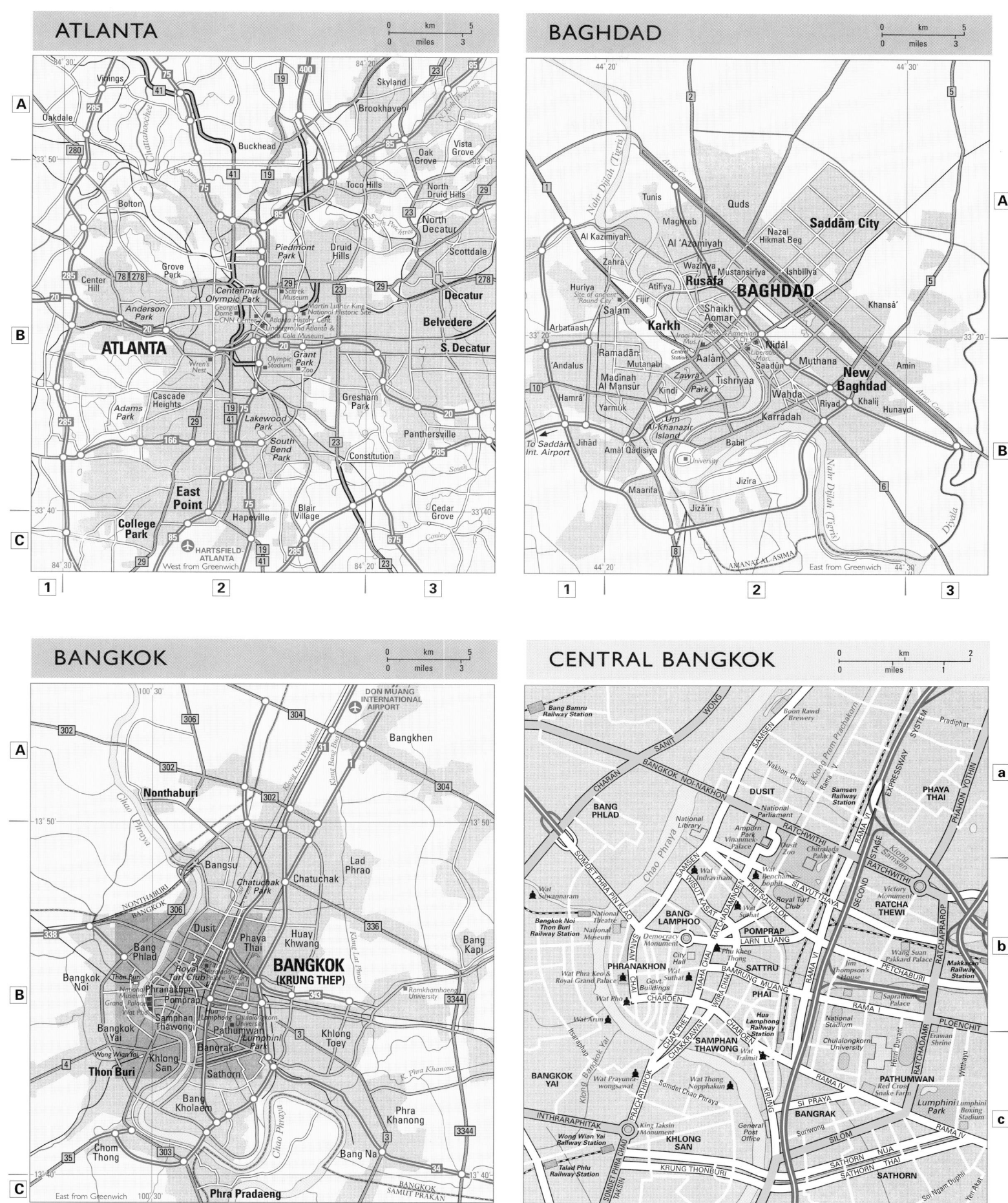

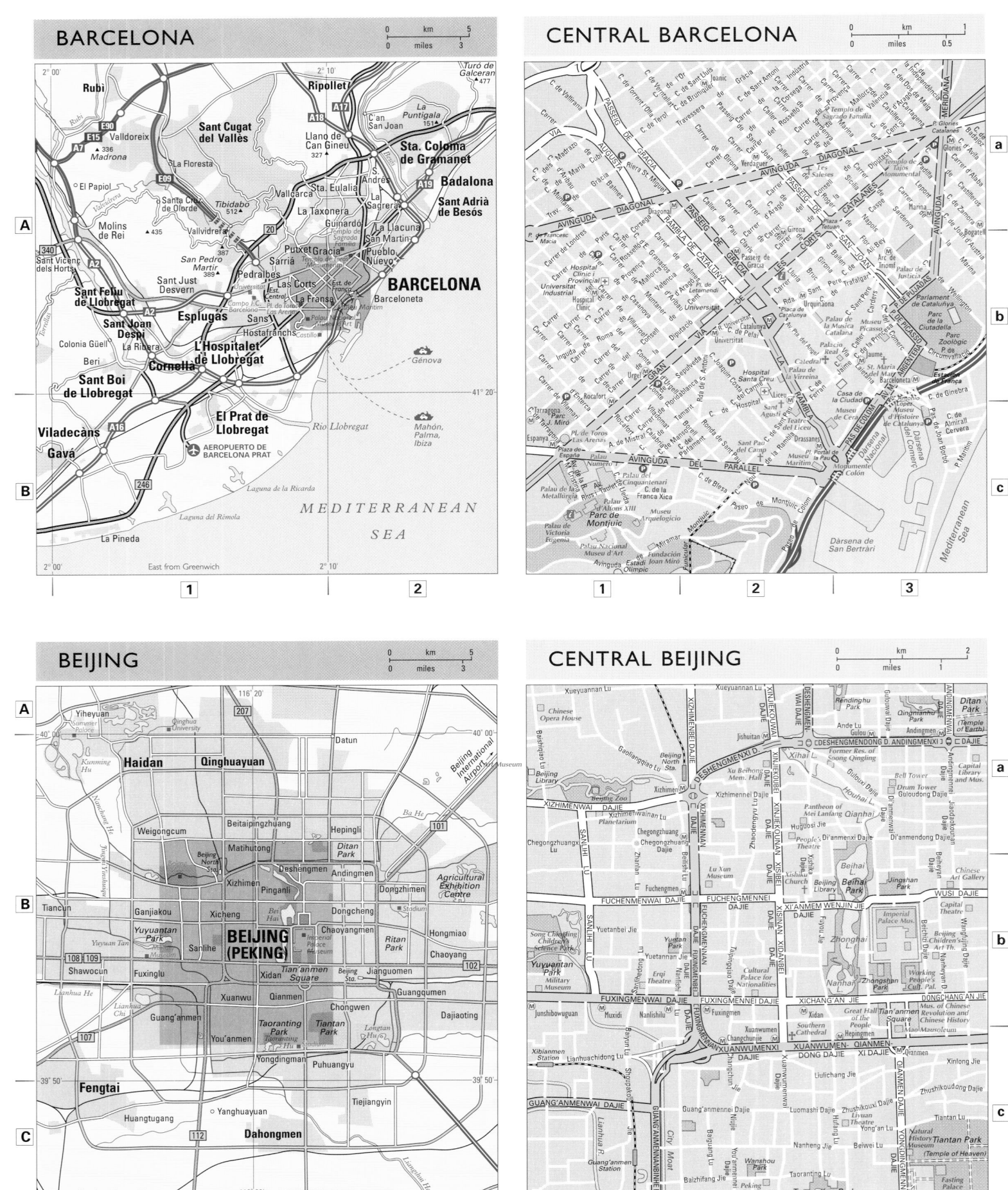

BERLIN

km
0 _____ 5
miles
0 _____ 3

Wansdorf Hennigsdorf E26 Hermsdorf Schulzendorf Lübars Blankenfelde Bucholz Schwanebeck A10 E55 Neu Buch E28 Birkholz Birkholzaue 89 Löhme Werneuchen Rudolfshöhe

Alter Finkenkrug Nieder Neuendorf Heiligensee 111 Waidmannslust 96a Karow Neu Lindenberg A114 Lindenberg Blumberg Krummensee 158 Seefeld

Waldheim **Falkensee** Siedlung Schönwalde Johannesstift Tegelort Tegel Wittenau 96 Niederschönhausen Blankenburg Melchow Wartenberg Ahrensfelde Mehrow Trappenfelde Altlandsberg Nord

A Finkenkrug Falkenhagen Tegeler See Scharfenberg A111 **Reinickendorf** 109 **Weissensee** Hohenschönhausen Falkenburg Heinersdorf Eiche 67 Eiche Süd Hönow A10 Seeberg Friedrichslust **A**

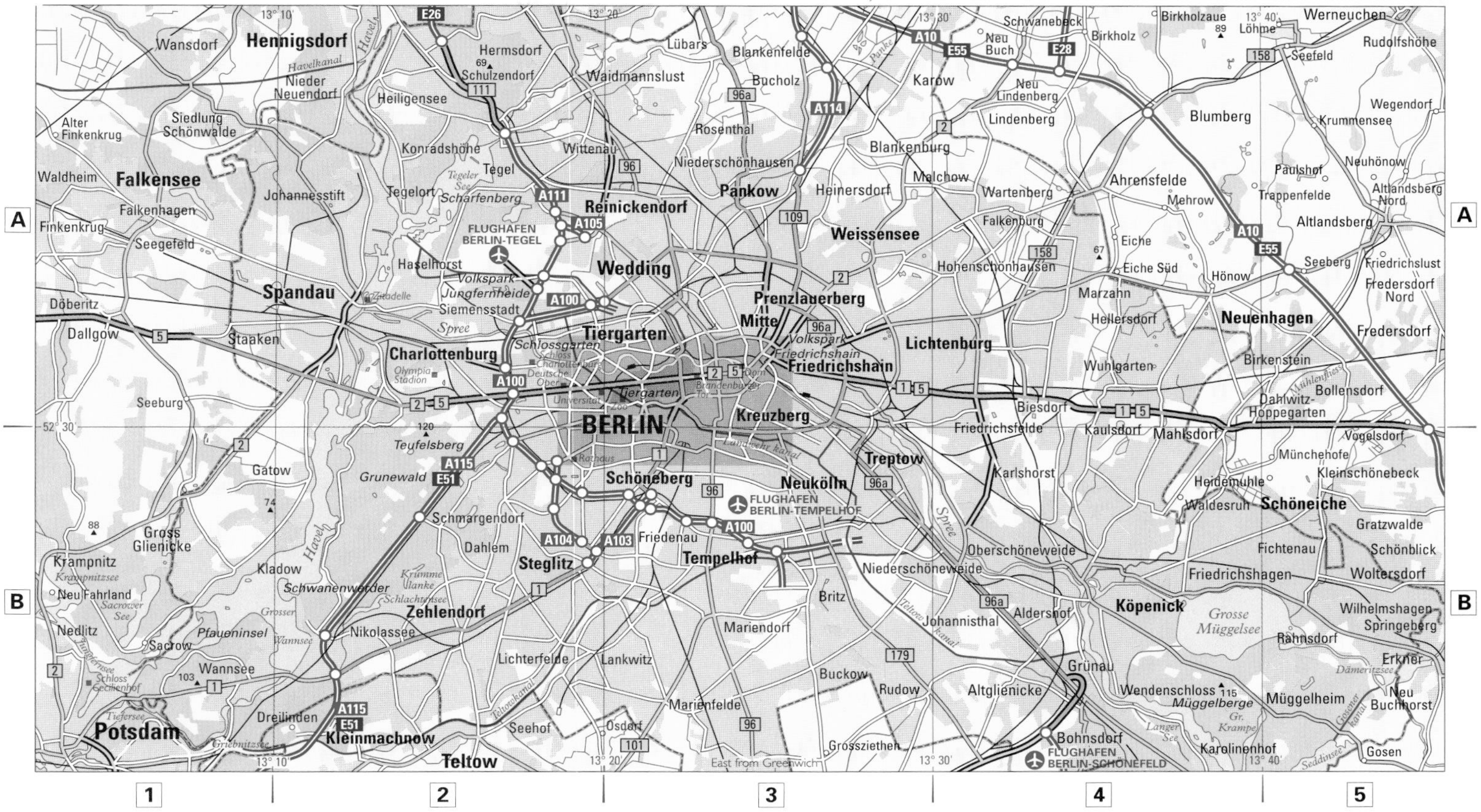

Seegefeld FLUGHAFEN BERLIN-TEGEL A105 **Wedding** Marzahn Heilersdorf E55 Frederdsorf Nord

Spandau Haselhorst Volkspark Jungfernheide Siemensstadt A100 **Prenzlauerberg** **Mitte** 96a Volkspark Friedrichshain **Neuenhagen**

Döberitz Staaken Spree Schlossgarten Deutsche Oper **Tiergarten** **Lichtenburg** Wuhlgarten Birkenstein Fredersdorf

Dallgow 5 **Charlottenburg** Olympia Stadion A100 5 Tiergarten Brandenburger **Friedrichshain** 1 5 Biesdorf Kaulsdorf Mahlsdorf Dahlwitz-Hoppegarten Vogelsdorf

52 30 **BERLIN** 1 **Kreuzberg** Friedrichsfelde Münchehofe

Teufelsberg **Schöneberg** 96 **Treptow** Karlshorst Heidemühle Kleinschönebeck

Gatow 74 Grunewald A115 E51 Neukölln FLUGHAFEN BERLIN-TEMPELHOF Waldesruh **Schöneiche** Fichtenau Schönblick

88 Schmargendorf Dahlem A104 A103 Friedenau A100 Oberschöneweide Gratzwalde Woltersdorf

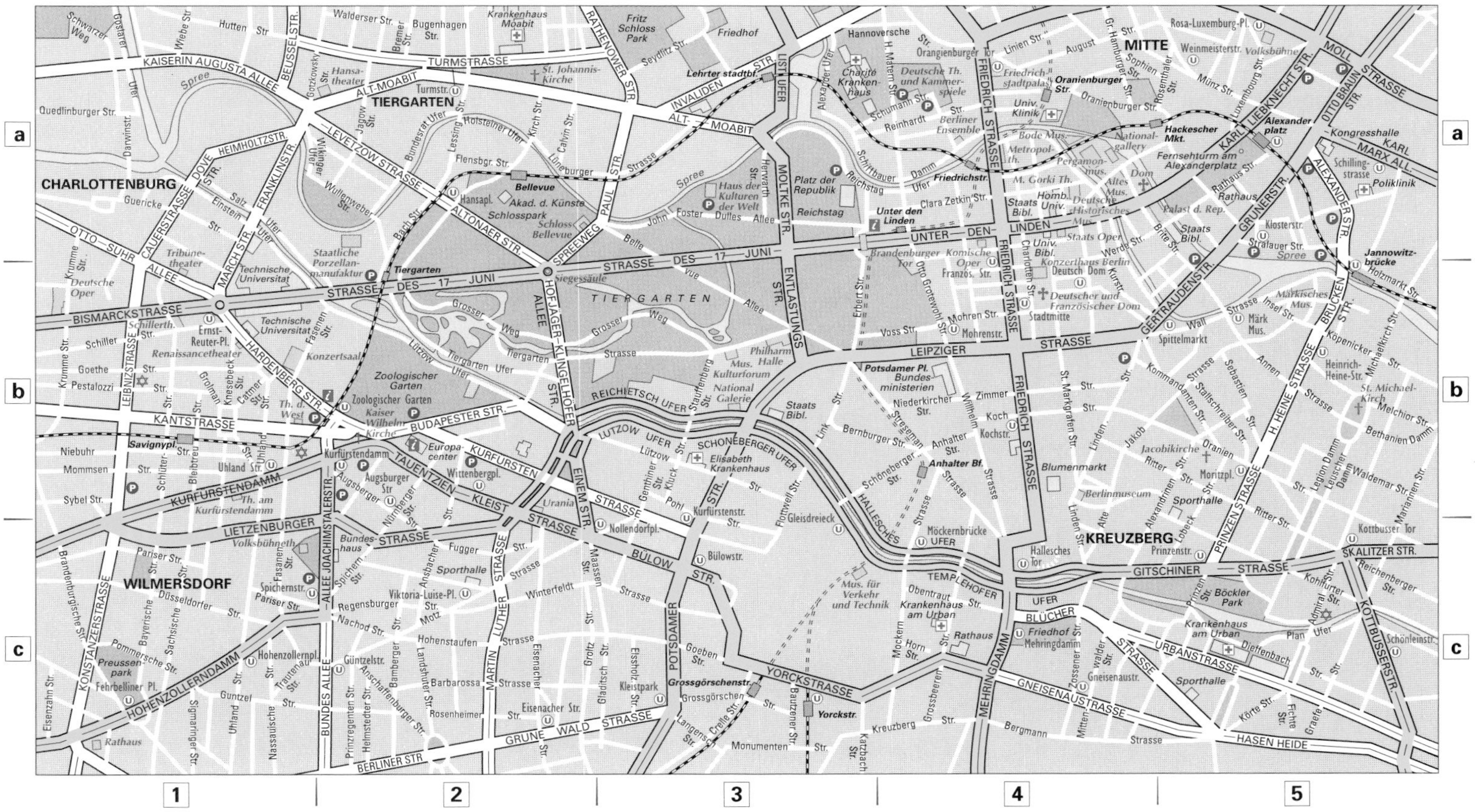

B Gross Glienicke Krampnitz Kladow Krumme Lanke **Steglitz** 1 **Tempelhof** Niederschöneweide **Köpenick** Grosse Müggelsee **B**

Neu Fahrland Sacrow Schwanenwerder Schlachtensee **Zehlendorf** Lichterfelde Lankwitz Britz Johannisthal Adlershof **Wilhelmshagen** Springberg Rahnsdorf Erkner

Nedlitz Pfaueninsel Wannsee **Nikolassee** Mariendorf Buckow 179 Grünau Wendenschloss Müggelberge Müggelheim Neu Buchhorst

2 Sacrow 103 Wannsee Lichtenrade Marienfelde Rudow Altglienicke Bohnsdorf Karolinenhof Gosen

Potsdam Dreilinden A115 E51 **Kleinmachnow** **Teltow** Seehof Osdorf 96 101 Grossziethen FLUGHAFEN BERLIN-SCHÖNEFELD

13 10 13 20 East from Greenwich 13 30 13 40

1 **2** **3** **4** **5**

CENTRAL BERLIN

km
0 _____ 1
miles
0 _____ 0.5

a **CHARLOTTENBURG** **TIERGARTEN** **MITTE** Hackescher Mkt. Alexanderplatz **a**

b Zoologischer Garten **TIERGARTEN** Potsdamer Pl. Jannowitzbrücke **b**

c **WILMERSDORF** Anhalter Bf. **KREUZBERG** **c**

1 **2** **3** **4** **5**

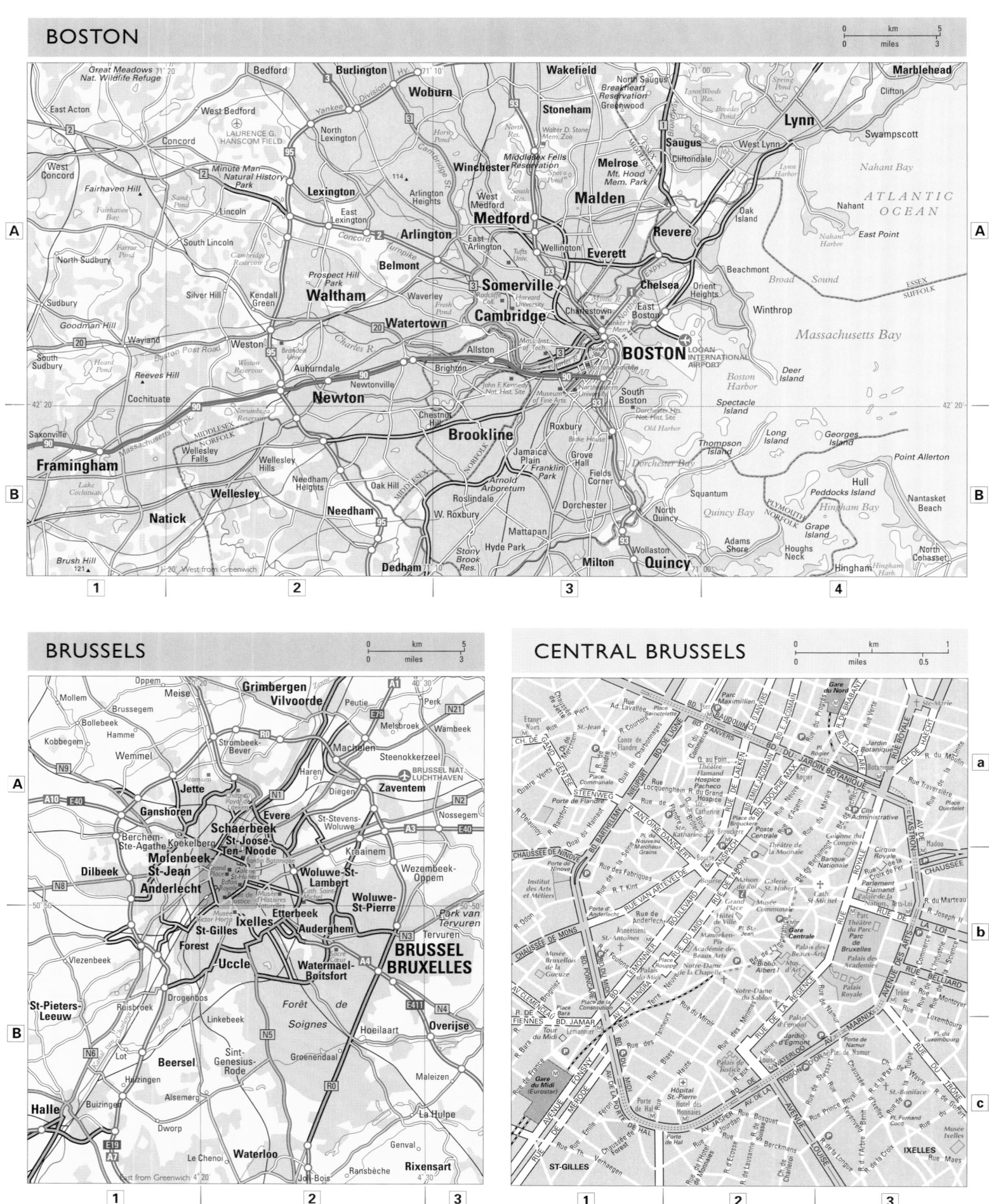

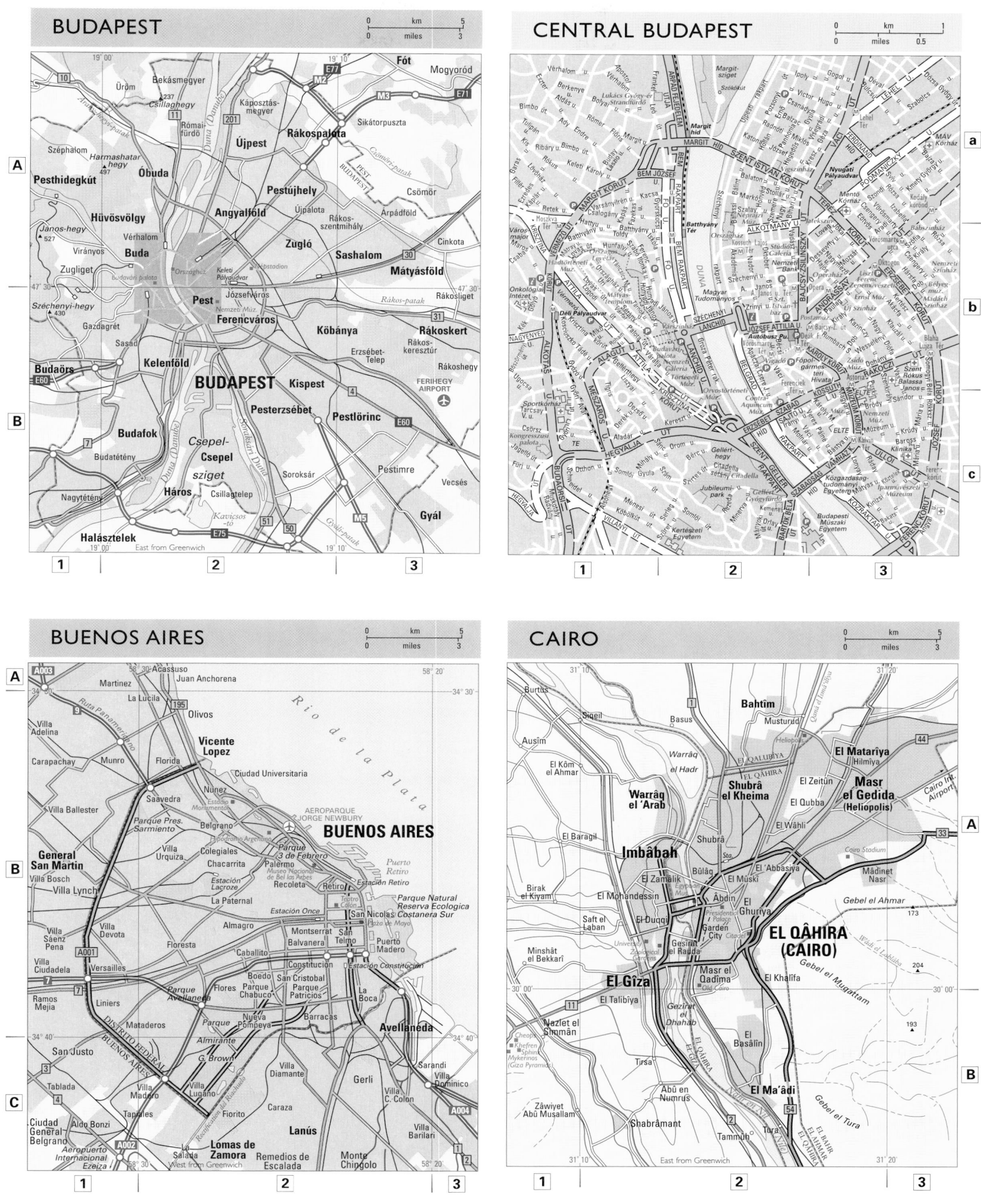

CALCUTTA

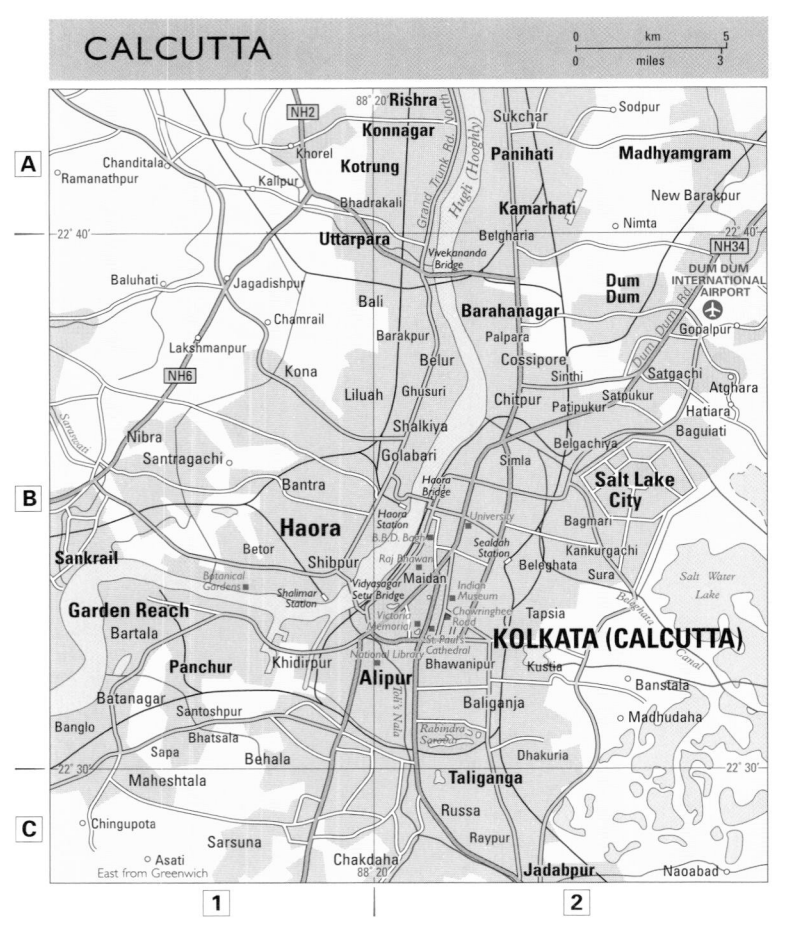

CANTON

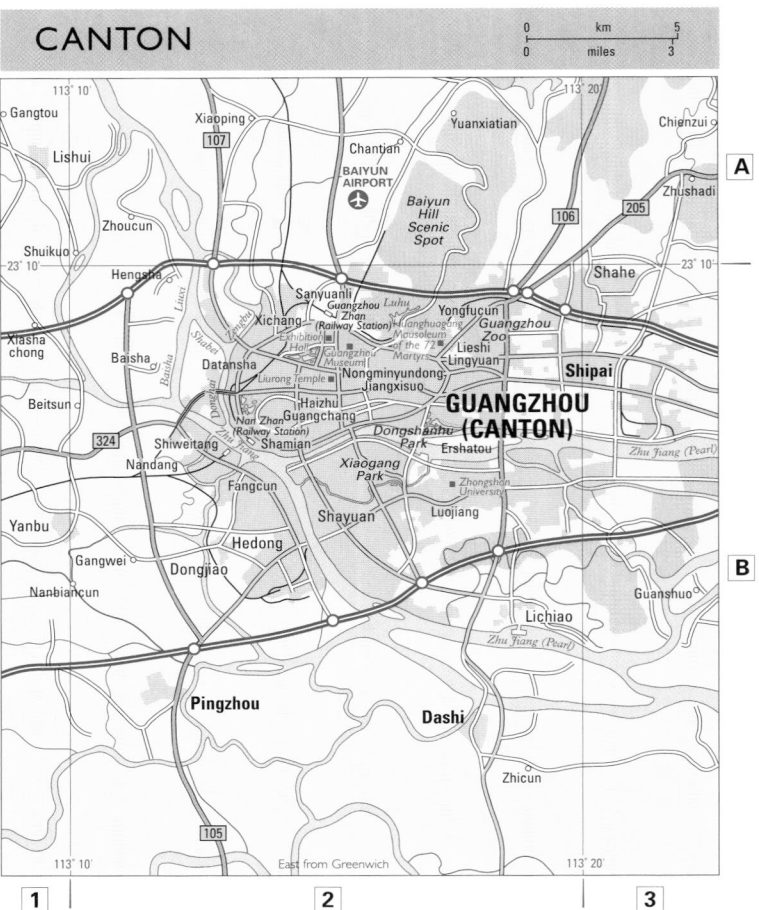

CAPE TOWN

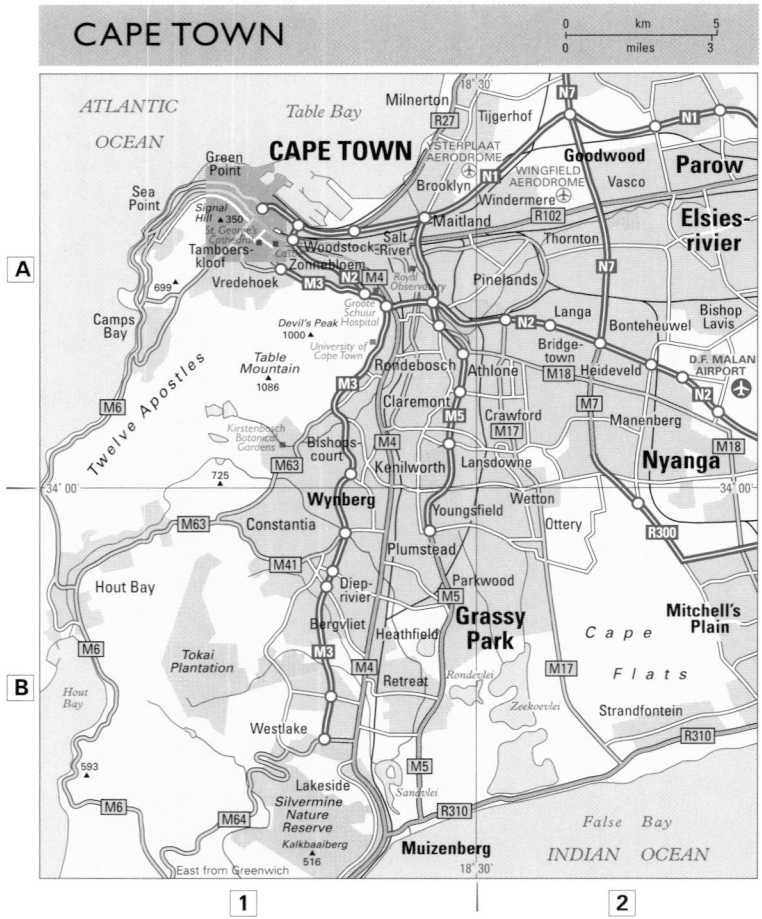

CENTRAL CAPE TOWN

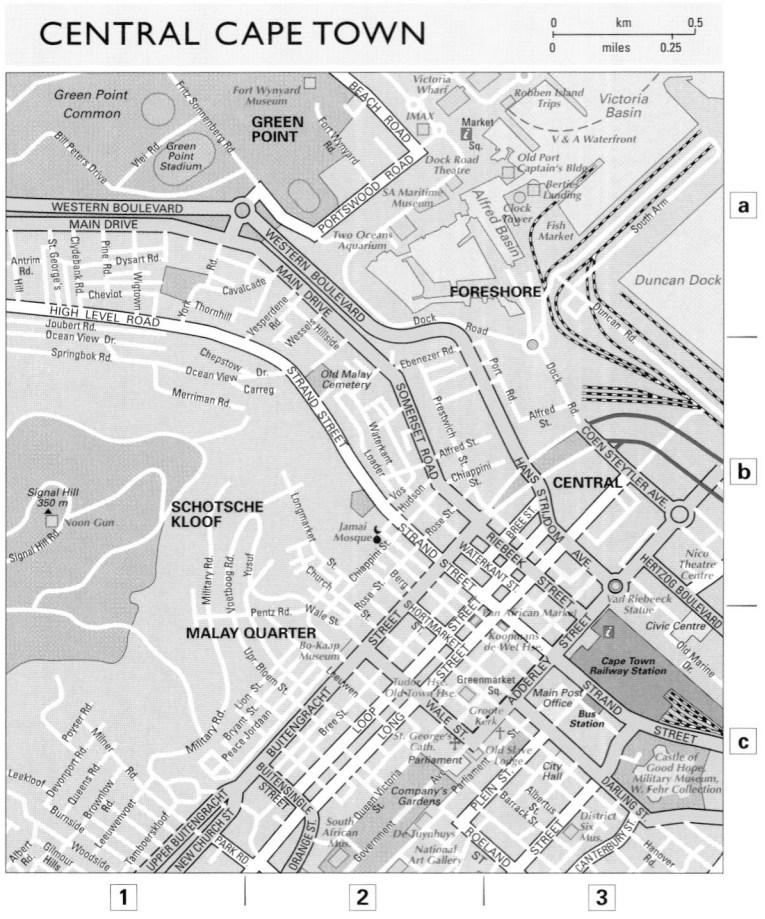

CHICAGO

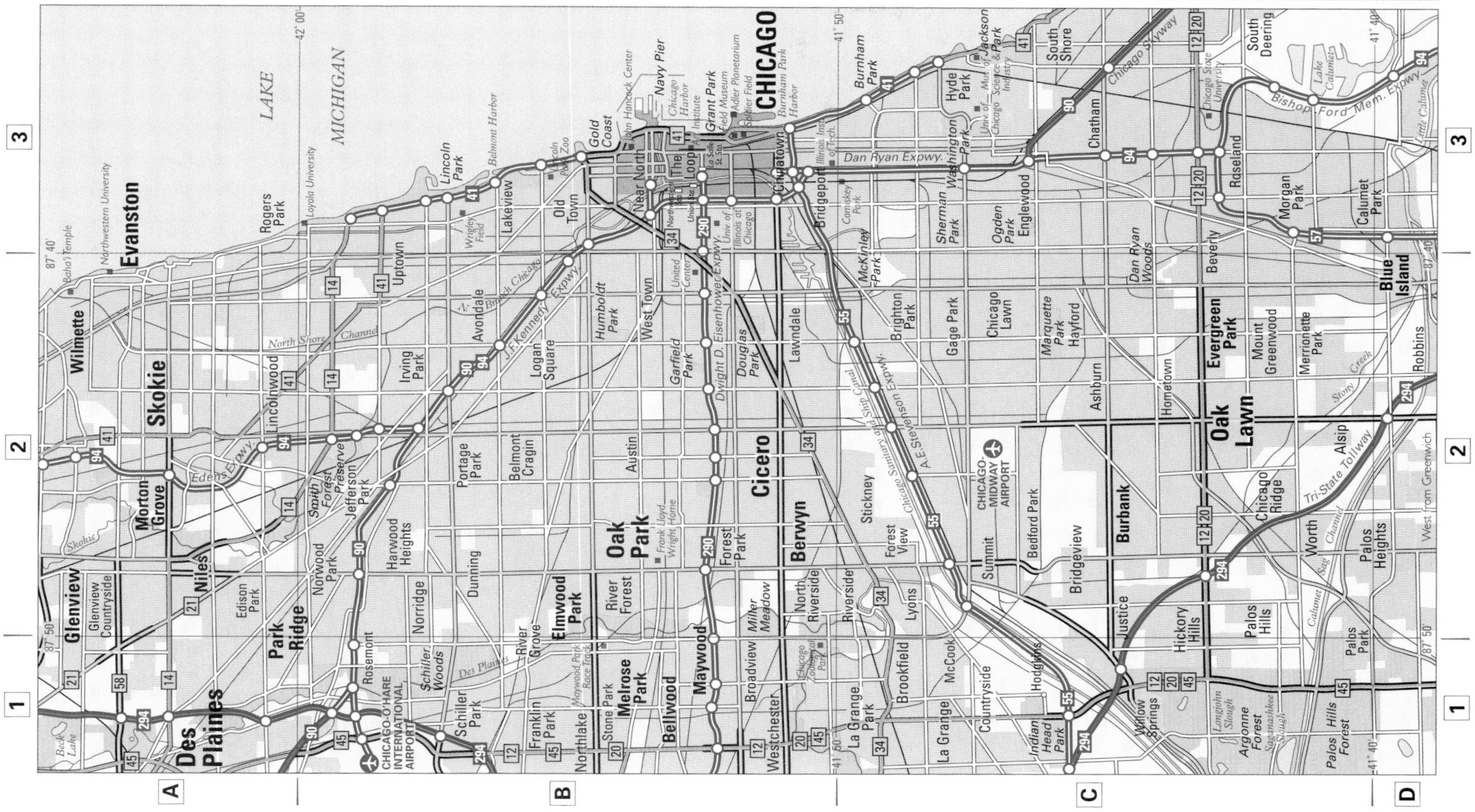
0 km 5
0 miles 3
LAKE MICHIGAN
CHICAGO
Evanston
Wilmette
Skokie
Morton Grove
Glenview
Niles
Park Ridge
Des Plaines
Rosemont
CHICAGO-O'HARE INTERNATIONAL AIRPORT
Oak Park
Cicero
Berwyn
Maywood
Melrose Park
Elmwood Park
Bellwood
Westchester
La Grange
Burbank
Oak Lawn
Evergreen Park
Blue Island
CHICAGO MIDWAY AIRPORT
Dan Ryan Expwy.
Chicago Skyway
Bishop Ford Mem. Expwy.
Tri-State Tollway
A B C D
1 2 3

CENTRAL CHICAGO

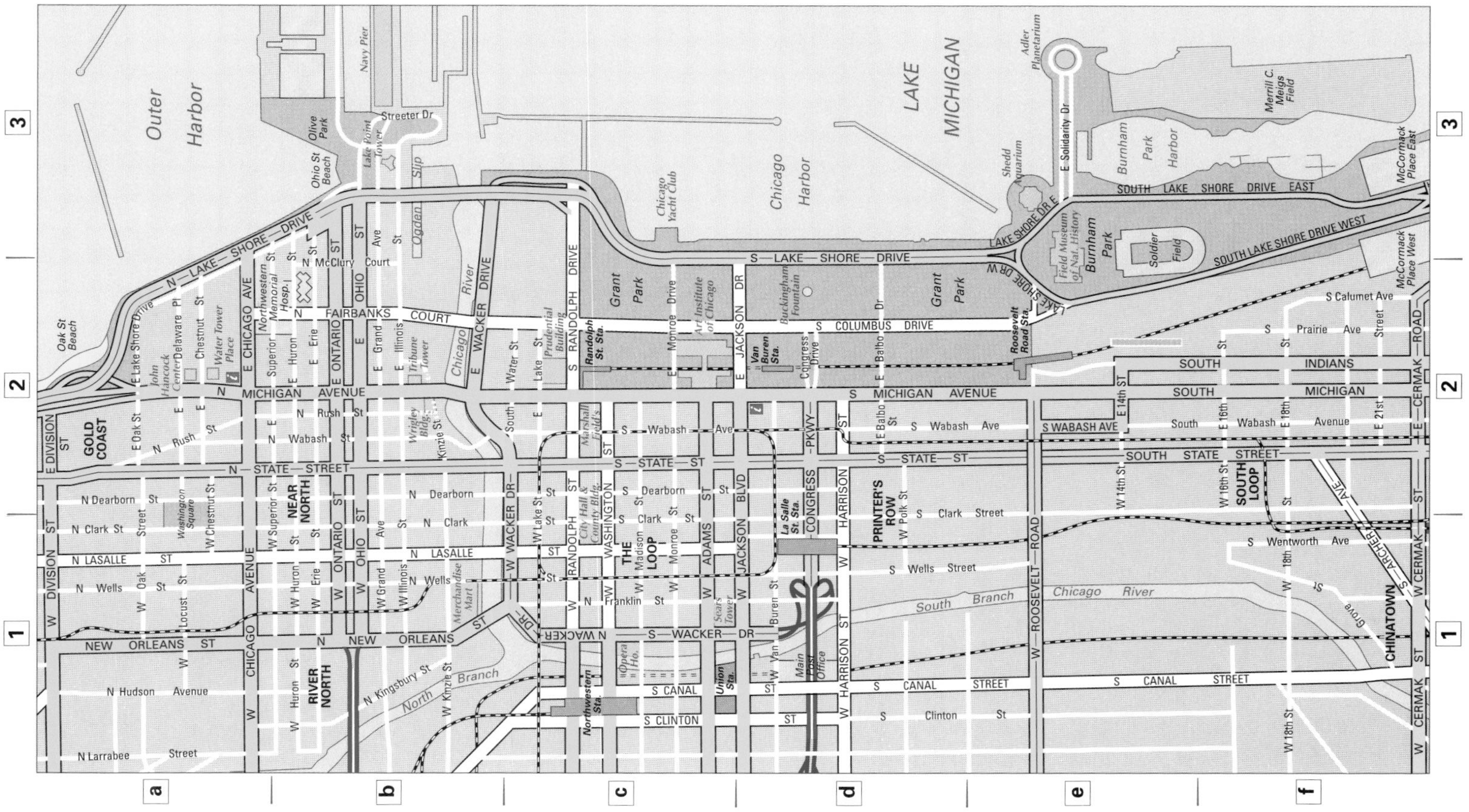
0 km 1
0 miles 0.5
LAKE MICHIGAN
Outer Harbor
Chicago Harbor
Navy Pier
Grant Park
Burnham Park
Soldier Field
Adler Planetarium
Shedd Aquarium
GOLD COAST
NEAR NORTH
RIVER NORTH
THE LOOP
PRINTER'S ROW
SOUTH LOOP
CHINATOWN
MICHIGAN AVENUE
STATE STREET
LAKE SHORE DRIVE
ROOSEVELT ROAD
a b c d e f
1 2 3

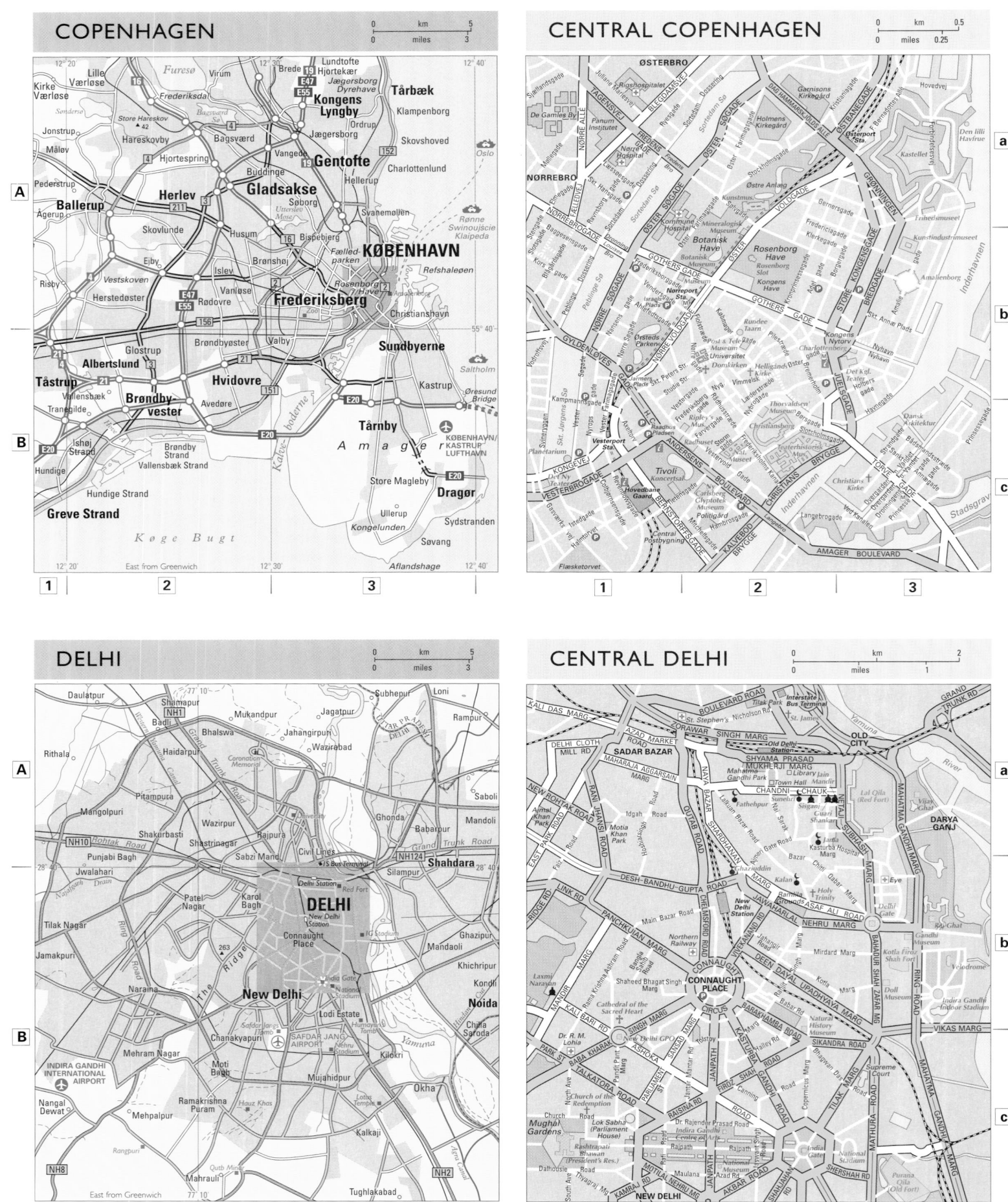

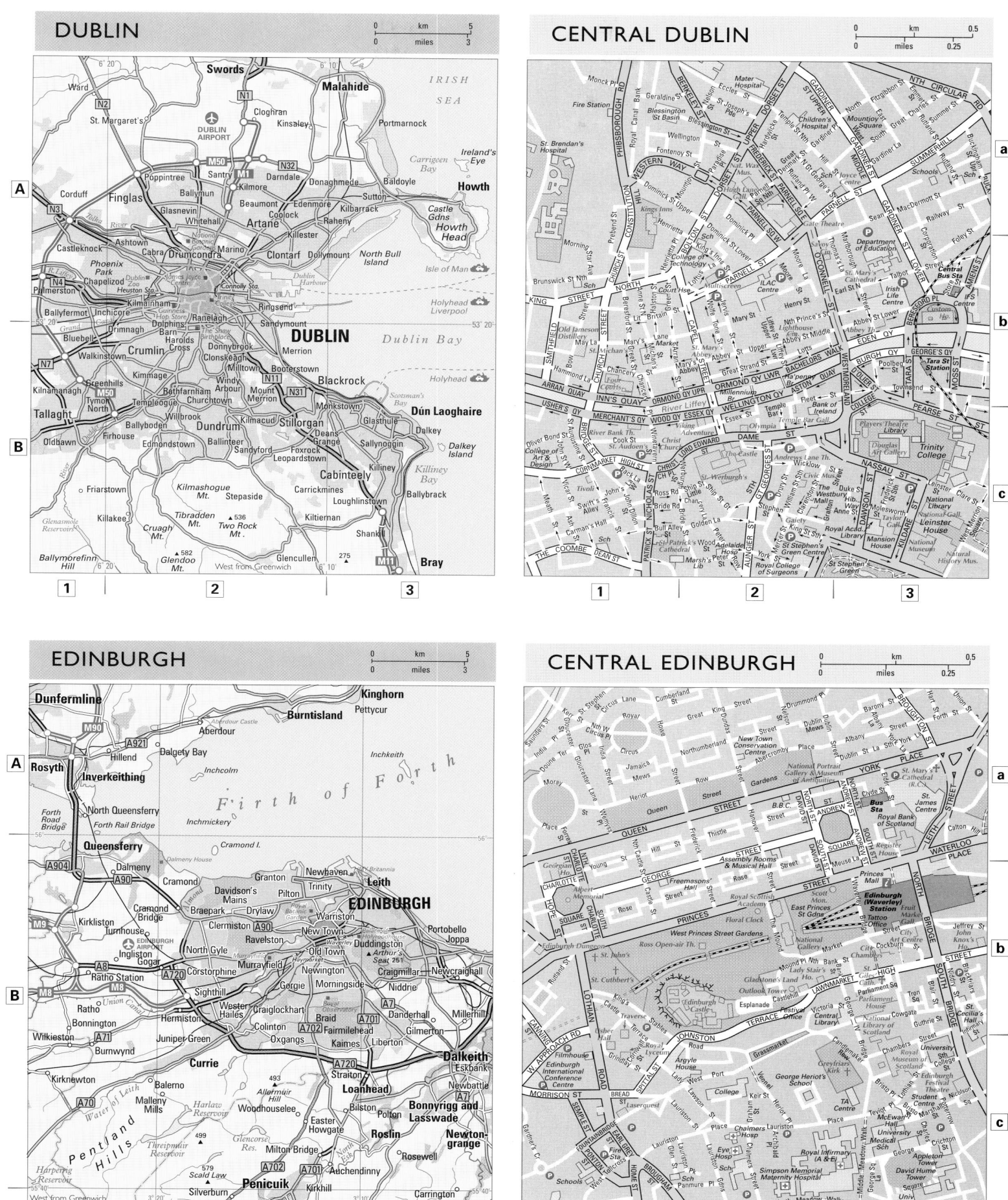

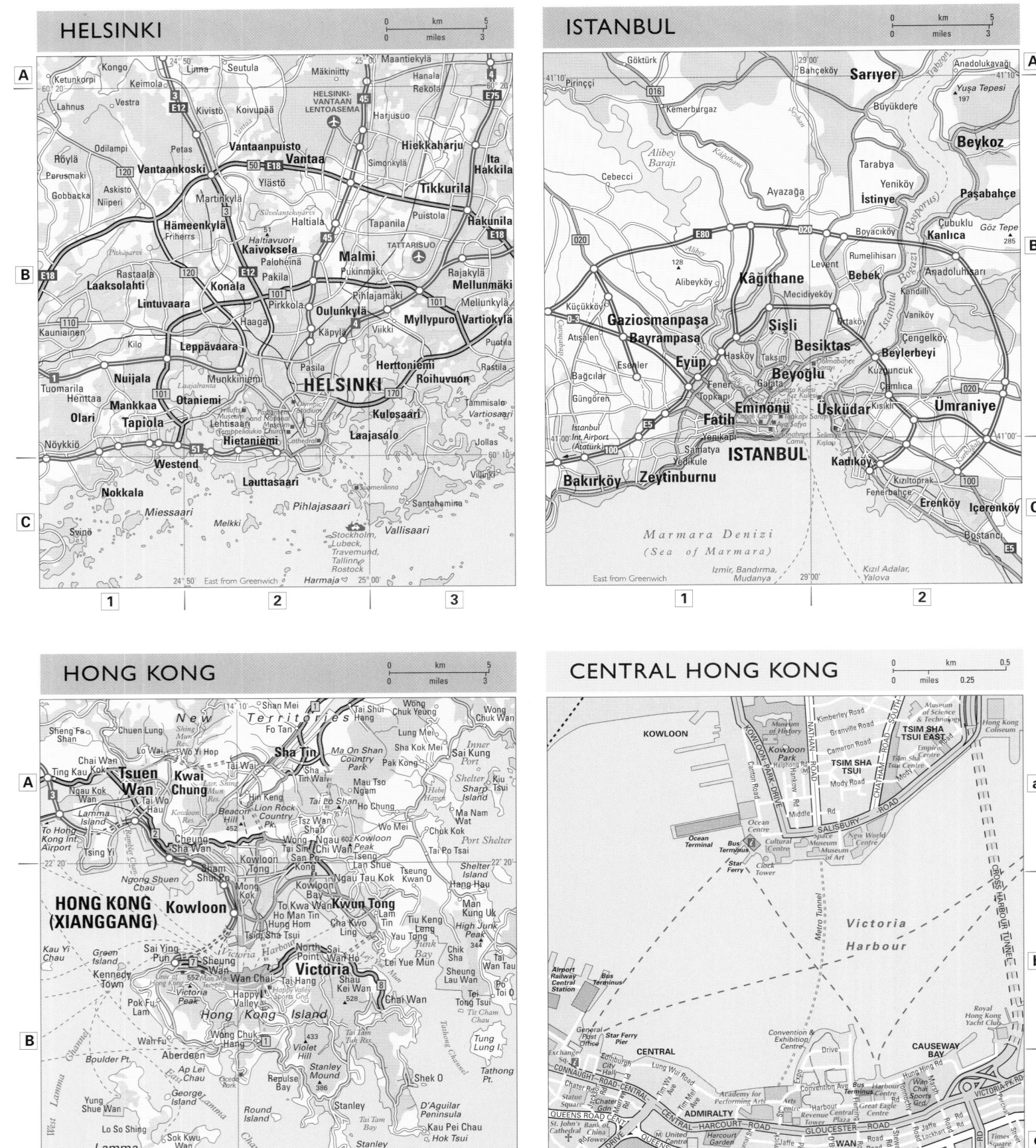

HELSINKI

ISTANBUL

HONG KONG

CENTRAL HONG KONG

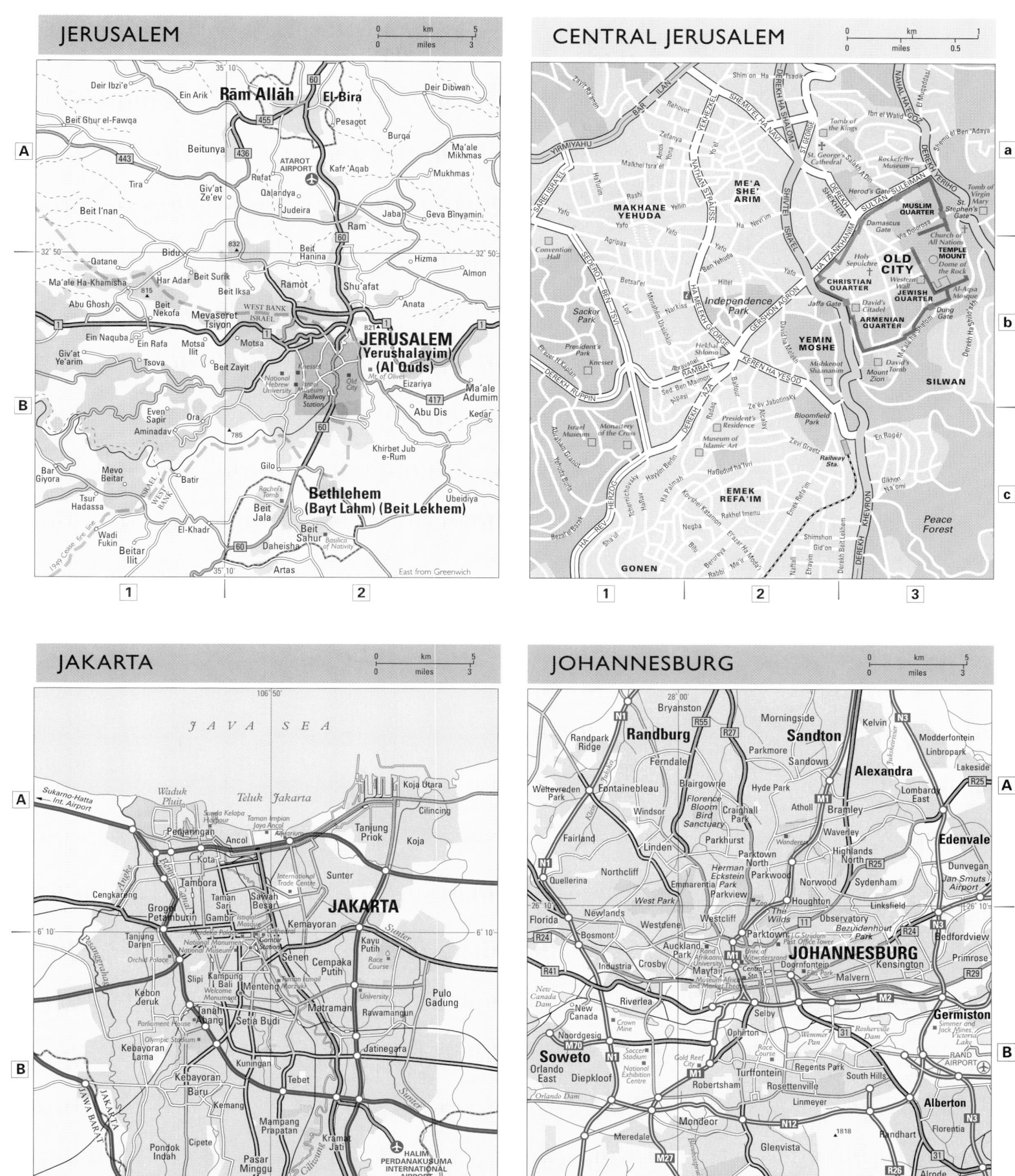

JERUSALEM

km 0 — 5
miles 0 — 3

35° 10'

Deir Ibzi'e · Ein Arik · **Rām Allāh** · **El-Bira** · Deir Dibwan
Beit Ghur el-Fawqa · 455 · Pesagot · Burqa
A · Beitunya · 436 · Rafat · Ma'ale Mikhmas
443 · Giv'at Ze'ev · Kafr 'Aqab · Mukhmas
Tira · Qalandya · Jaba · Geva Binyamin
Beit I'nan · ATAROT AIRPORT · Judeira · Ram
32° 50' · 832 · Beit Hanina · 32° 50' · Hizma · Almon
Qatane · Bidu · 60 · Shu'afat · Anata
Ma'ale Ha-Khamisha · Beit Surik · Ramòt
Har Adar · Beit Iksa · WEST BANK ISRAEL
Abu Ghosh · 815 · Beit Nekofa · Mevaseret Tsiyon · JERUSALEM · 1
B · 1 · Ein Naquba · Motsa Ilit · **(Yerushalayim) (Al Quds)** · 417
Giv'at Ye'arim · Ein Rafa · Motsa · Knesset · Eizariya
Tsova · Beit Zayit · National Hebrew University · Mt. of Olives · Ma'ale Adumim
Even Sapir · Israel Museum Railway Station · Old City · 60 · Abu Dis · Kedar
Ora · Aminadav · 785
Bar Giyora · Mevo Beitar · Khirbet Jub e-Rum
Tsur Hadassa · Batir · Gilo · **Bethlehem**
Wadi Fukin · **(Bayt Lahm) (Beit Lekhem)** · Ubeidiya
Beitar Ilit · El-Khadr · Beit Jala · Rachel's Tomb
Daheisha · Beit Sahur · Basilica of Nativity · 60
East from Greenwich · Artas

1 | **2**

CENTRAL JERUSALEM

km 0 — 1
miles 0 — 0.5

Shim on Ha · Tsadik
Zayit Ha · Tomb of the Kings · Ibn el Walid
BAR ILAN · Rehovot · YEHEZKEL · St. George's Cathedral · Rockefeller Museum · Siyemi el Ben 'Adaya
YIRMIYAHU · Zefaniya · SHEMU'EL HA NAVI · DEREKH YERIHO · **a**
Malkhei Isra él · Amos Yona · Herod's Gate · SULEIMAN · Tomb of Virgin Mary
HaTurim · Yo él · NATHAN STRAUSS · SULTAN · St. Stephen's Gate
MAKHANE YEHUDA · Rashi · Yellin · **ME'A SHE'ARIM** · Ha Nevi'im · Damascus Gate · **MUSLIM QUARTER** · Via Dolorosa · Church of All Nations
Yafo · Agripas · Yafo · **TEMPLE MOUNT**
Convention Hall · Betsal'el · Yafo · Ben Yehuda · Holy Sepulchre · **OLD CITY** · Dome of the Rock
SHIVTEI ISRAEL · Hillél · **CHRISTIAN QUARTER** · Western · Al-Aqsa Mosque
Sacker Park · Narkiss · Independence Park · Jaffa Gate · David's Citadel · **JEWISH QUARTER** · **b**
President's Park · Knesset · Hekhal Shlomo · **ARMENIAN QUARTER** · Dung Gate
Israel Museum · Abravanel · RAMBAN · **YEMIN MOSHE** · David's Tomb
Monastery of the Cross · Sed. Ben Maimon · KEREN HA YESOD · Mishkenot Shaananim · Mount Zion · **SILWAN**
Alkalai Granot · Museum of Islamic Art · President's · Ze'ev Jabotinsky · Bloomfield Park
c · HERZOG · DEREKH RUPPIN · HaGedud ha 'Ivri · Railway Sta. · En Rogé' · Peace Forest
EMEK REFA'IM · Gikhon Na omi
GONEN · Derekh Beit Lehem · DEREKH KHEVRON

1 | **2** | **3**

JAKARTA

km 0 — 5
miles 0 — 3

106° 50'

J A V A   S E A
Koja Utara
Waduk Pluit · *Teluk Jakarta* · Cilincing
A · Sukarno-Hatta Int. Airport · Sunda Kelapa Harbour · Taman Impian Jaya Ancol · Tanjung Priok · Koja
Penjaringan · Ancol · Oceanarium
Cengkareng · Kota · Sunter
Grogol Petamburin · Tambora · Taman Sari · Sawah Besar · **JAKARTA**
Tanjung Duren · Gambir · Kemayoran · Kayu Putih · Sunter
6° 10' · Istiqlal Mosque · Gambir Station · 6° 10'
National Monument National Museum · Senen · Cempaka Putih · Pulo Gadung
Orchid Palace · Merdeka Palace · Kampung Ismail Marzuki · University · Rawamangun
Slipi · Kampung I Bali Welcome Monument · Menteng · Matraman
Kebon Jeruk · **Tanah Abang** · Setia Budi · Jatinegara
Parliament House · Olympic Stadium
B · Kebayoran Lama · Kuningan · Tebet
Kebayoran Baru · Kemang · Mampang Prapatan · Kramat Jati
Pondok Indah · Cipete · Pasar Minggu · **HALIM PERDANAKUSUMA INTERNATIONAL AIRPORT**
East from Greenwich · Cilandak · 106° 50'

1 | **2**

JOHANNESBURG

km 0 — 5
miles 0 — 3

28° 00'
Bryanston · Morningside · Kelvin · N3
Randpark Ridge · R55 · R27 · Parkmore · **Sandton** · Modderfontein · Linbropark
Randburg · Ferndale · Sandown · Lakeside
Weltevreden Park · Fontainebleau · Blairgowrie · Hyde Park · M1 · **Alexandra** · Lombardy East · R25 · **A**
Florence Bloom Bird Sanctuary · Craighall Park · Atholl · Bramley
Fairland · Windsor · Parkhurst · Waverley · **Edenvale**
N1 · Linden · Parktown North · Wanderers · Highlands North · R25 · Dunvegan · Jan Smuts Airport
Quellerina · Northcliff · Herman Eckstein Park · Parkwood · Norwood · Sydenham · Linksfield
West Park · Zoo · Houghton
Florida · 26° 10' · Newlands · Westdene · Westcliff · The Wilds · Observatory · Bezuidenhout Park · 26° 10' · N3
R24 · Bosmont · Parktown · J.G. Strijdom Post Office Tower · R24 · Bedfordview
Auckland Park · Univ. of Witwatersrand · M1 · **JOHANNESBURG** · Kensington · Primrose
New Canada Dam · Industria · Crosby · Mayfair · Museum Africa and Market Theatre · Central Sta. · Doornfontein · Ellis Park · Malvern · R29
New Canada · Riverlea · Selby · M2
Noordgesig · Crown Mine · Ophirton · Wemmer Pan · Rosherville Dam · **Germiston** · Sumner and Jack Mines, Victoria Lake
Soweto · M70 · Soccer Stadium · Race Course · RAND AIRPORT
Orlando East · National Exhibition Centre · Gold Reef City · Turffontein · Regents Park · South Hills
Diepkloof · M1 · Robertsham · Rosettenville · Linmeyer · **Alberton** · N3
Orlando Dam · Mondeor · Meredale · Linmeyer · 1818 · Randhart · Florentia
N12 · Glenvista · R31
M27 · Klipriviersberg Nature Reserve · R26 · Mulbarton · Meyersdal · Alrode
East from Greenwich · Kibler Park · 28° 00'

1 | **2**

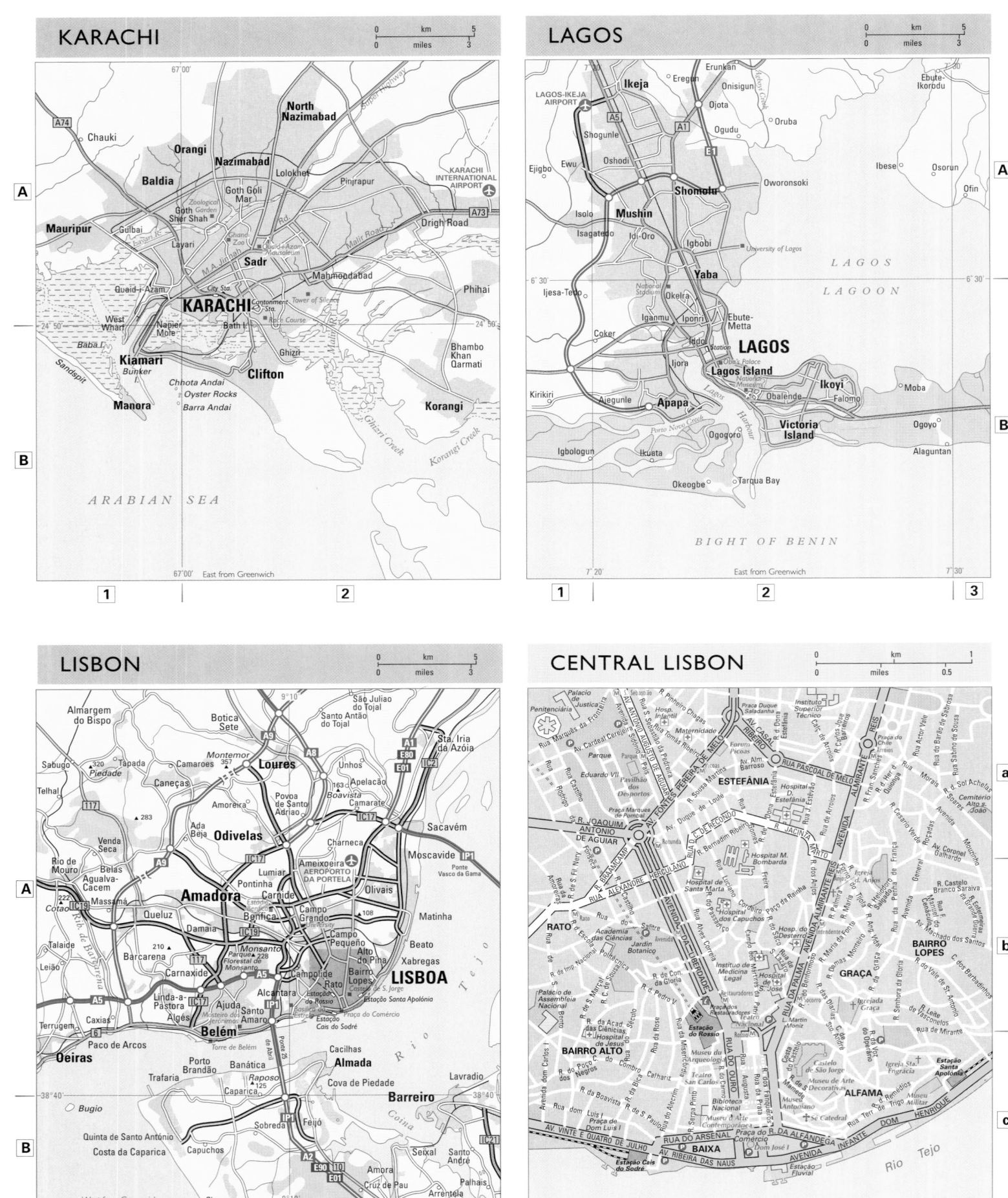

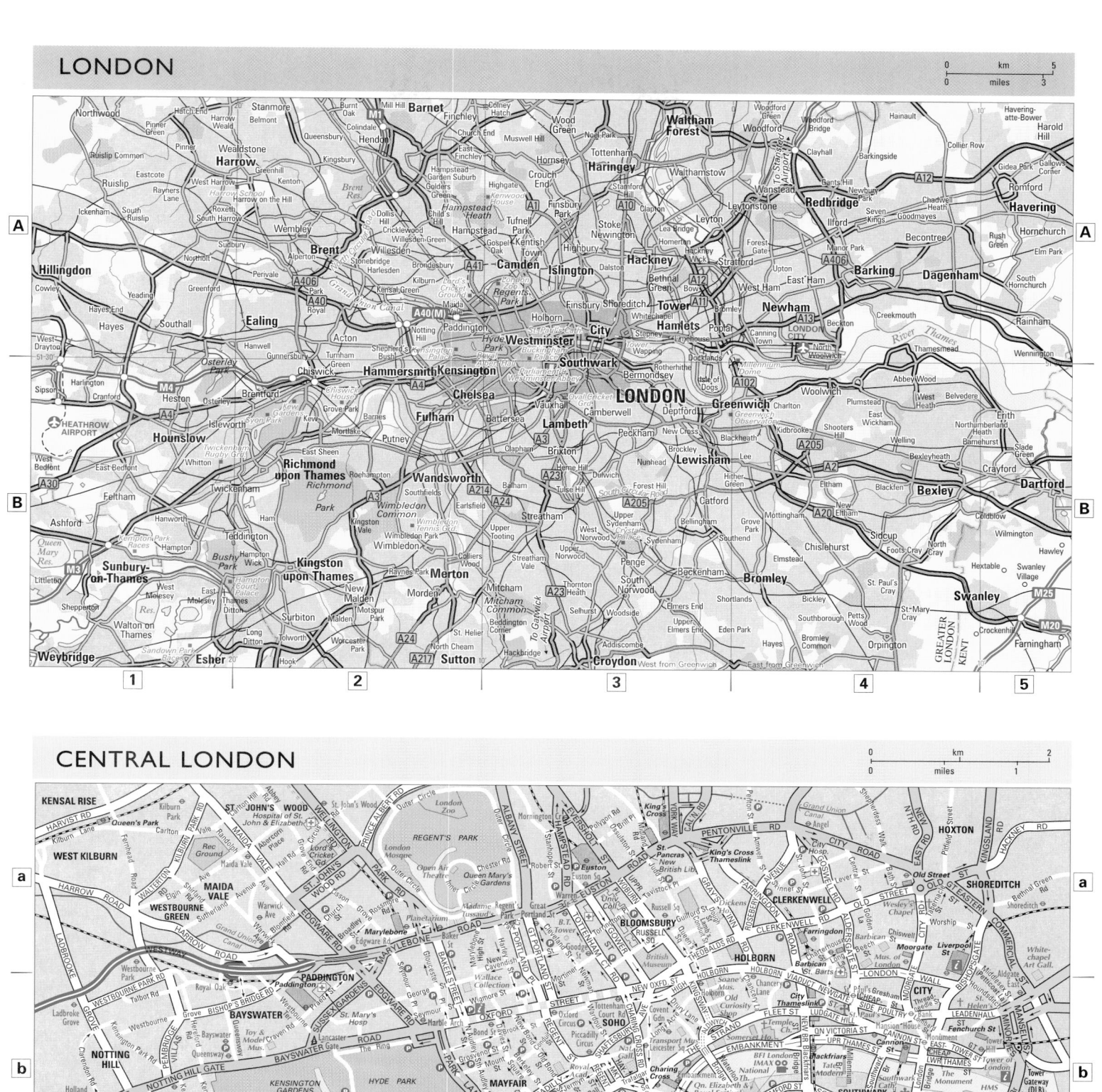

LONDON

CENTRAL LONDON

LOS ANGELES

km 0 — 5
miles 0 — 3

Tarzana, 101, Van Nuys, 170, Burbank, Verdugo Mts., Altadena, San Gabriel Mts., A

Sepulveda Flood Control Basin, San Fernando Valley, Flint Peak 575, Rose Bowl, 210, Pasadena, Sierra Madre, Colorado Fwy.

Encino, 101, North Hollywood, Disney Studios, 134, Glendale, 134, 210, Monrovia

216, Sherman Oaks, 405, Studio City, C.B.S. Studios, Warner Bros. Studios, Universal Studios, Cahuenga Peak 555, Glendale Galleria, Eagle Rock, California Inst. of Tech., Arcadia

Encino Reservoir, Stone Canyon Reservoir, Mts., Hollywood Bowl, Hollywood Lake, Griffith Park, Zoo, Golden State Fwy., Highland Park, Garvanza, South Pasadena, San Marino, 19, Temple City

Santa Monica, 459, 405, Beverly Glen, Hollywood, Mann's Chinese Theatre, Sunset Blvd., Santa Monica Blvd., Silver Lake Reservoir, El Sereno, Southwest Museum, Pasadena Fwy., San Gabriel

Bel Air, Franklin Reservoir, Beverly Hills, West Hollywood, Paramount Studios, Santa Monica Blvd., Hollywood Fwy., 2, Dodger Stadium, Lincoln Heights, California State Univ., Alhambra, Rosemead, 10, El Monte, B

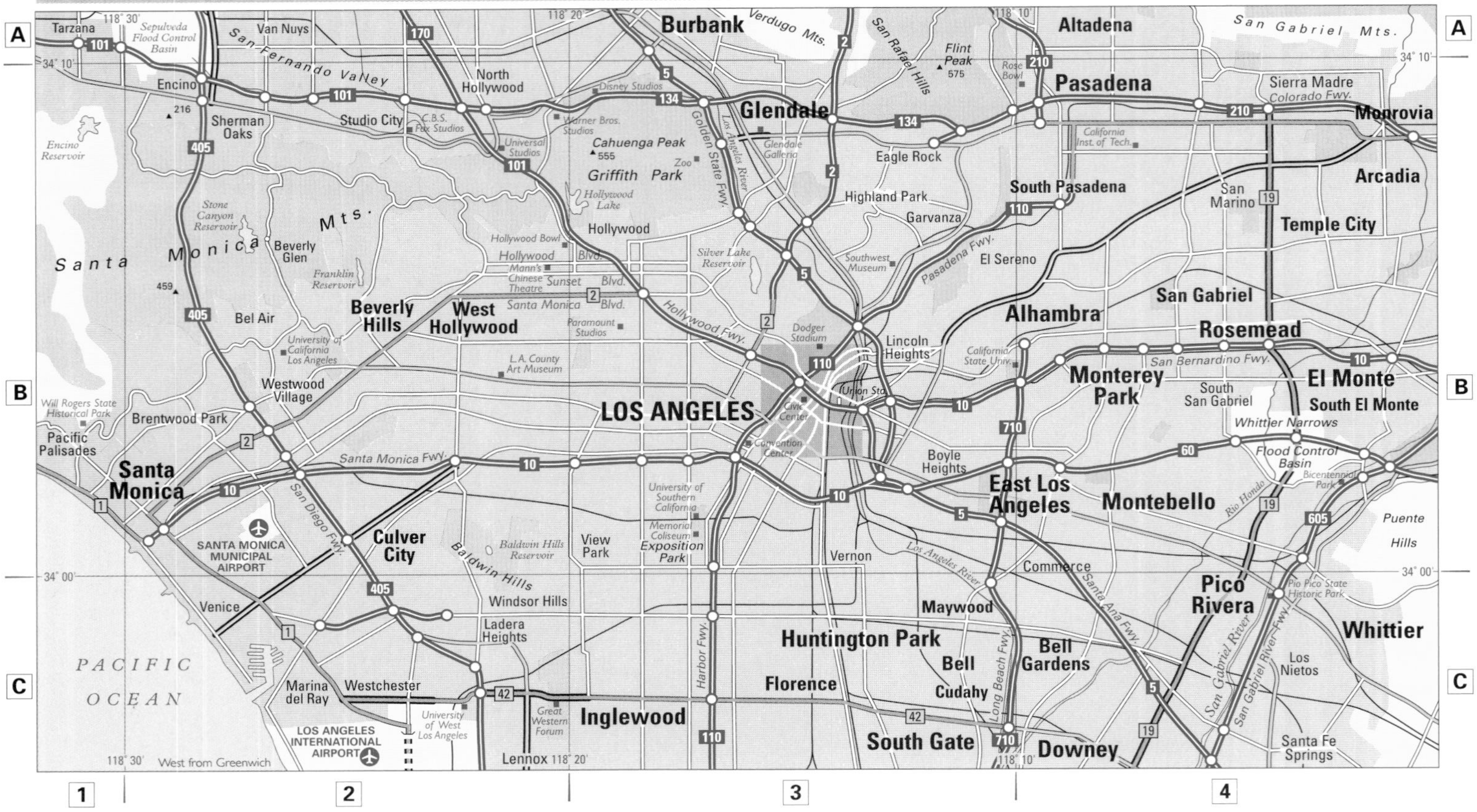

Will Rogers State Historical Park, Westwood Village, University of California Los Angeles, L.A. County Art Museum, 110, Union Sta., San Bernardino Fwy., Monterey Park, South San Gabriel, South El Monte

Brentwood Park, 2, Santa Monica Fwy., 10, LOS ANGELES, Civic Center, Convention Center, Boyle Heights, 710, 60, Flood Control Basin, Bicentennial Park, Whittier Narrows

Pacific Palisades, Santa Monica, 10, San Diego Fwy., University of Southern California, Memorial Coliseum, Exposition Park, 10, 5, East Los Angeles, Montebello, Rio Hondo, 19, 605, Puente Hills

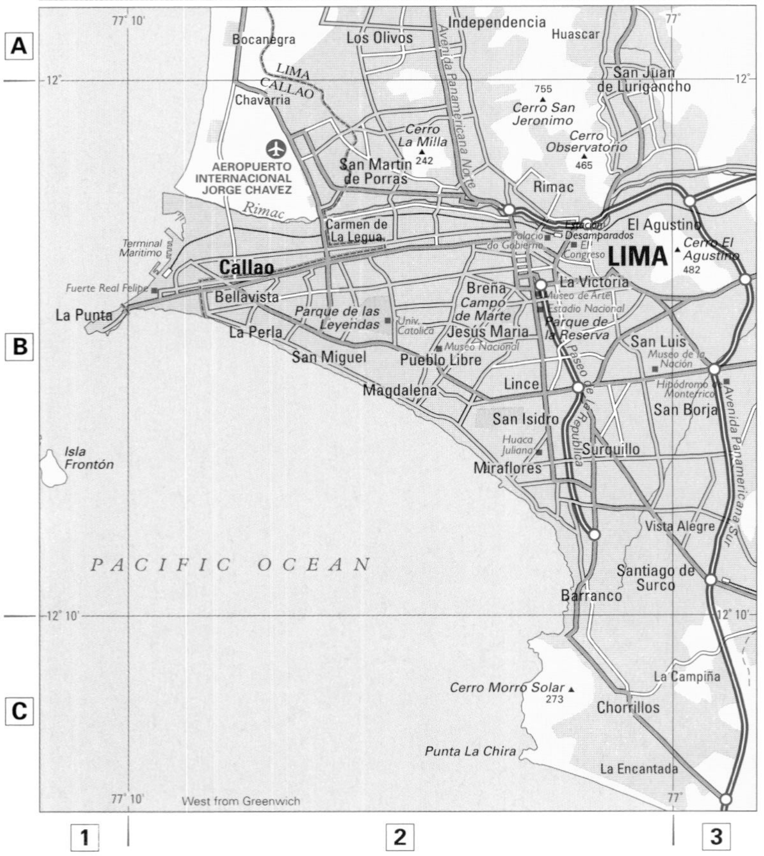

Santa Monica Municipal Airport, Culver City, Baldwin Hills, Baldwin Hills Reservoir, View Park, Vernon, Commerce, Santa Ana Fwy., Pico Rivera, Pio Pico State Historic Park, 34° 00'

Venice, 405, Windsor Hills, Harbor Fwy., Maywood, Bell Gardens, Long Beach Fwy., San Gabriel River, San Gabriel River Fwy., Whittier

Marina del Ray, Westchester, 1, Ladera Heights, 42, Huntington Park, Bell, Cudahy, Florence, 5, Los Nietos, C

Pacific Ocean, Great Western Forum, Inglewood, 110, South Gate, 42, 710, Downey, 19, Santa Fe Springs

Los Angeles International Airport, University of West Los Angeles, Lennox, 118° 20', 118° 10'

West from Greenwich

1 2 3 4

LIMA

km 0 — 5
miles 0 — 3

Bocanegra, Los Olivos, Independencia, Huascar, A

77° 10', 77°, LIMA CALLAO, Chavarria, Cerro San Jeronimo 755, San Juan de Lurigancho, 12°

Cerro La Milla, Cerro Observatorio 465, Cerro San Jeronimo

Aeropuerto Internacional Jorge Chavez, San Martin de Porras 242, Rimac

Terminal Maritimo, Rimac, Carmen de La Legua, Palacio de Gobierno, Desamparados, El Agustino, Cerro El Agustino 482

Callao, Breña, La Victoria, LIMA, Museo de Arte, B

Fuerte Real Felipe, Bellavista, Parque de las Leyendas, Campo de Marte, Estadio Nacional, Parque de la Reserva, San Luis, Museo Nacional

La Punta, La Perla, R. Univ. Catolica, Jesús Maria, Museo de la Nación, La Victoria

San Miguel, Pueblo Libre, Lince, Hipódromo Monterrico, San Borja

Magdalena, San Isidro, Avenida Panamericana Sur

Huaca Juliana, Surquillo

Isla Frontón, Miraflores

Pacific Ocean, Vista Alegre

12° 10', Santiago de Surco, Barranco

Cerro Morro Solar 273, La Campiña, Chorrillos, C

Punta La Chira, La Encantada

77° 10', 77°

West from Greenwich

1 2 3

CENTRAL LOS ANGELES

km 0 — 1
miles 0 — 0.5

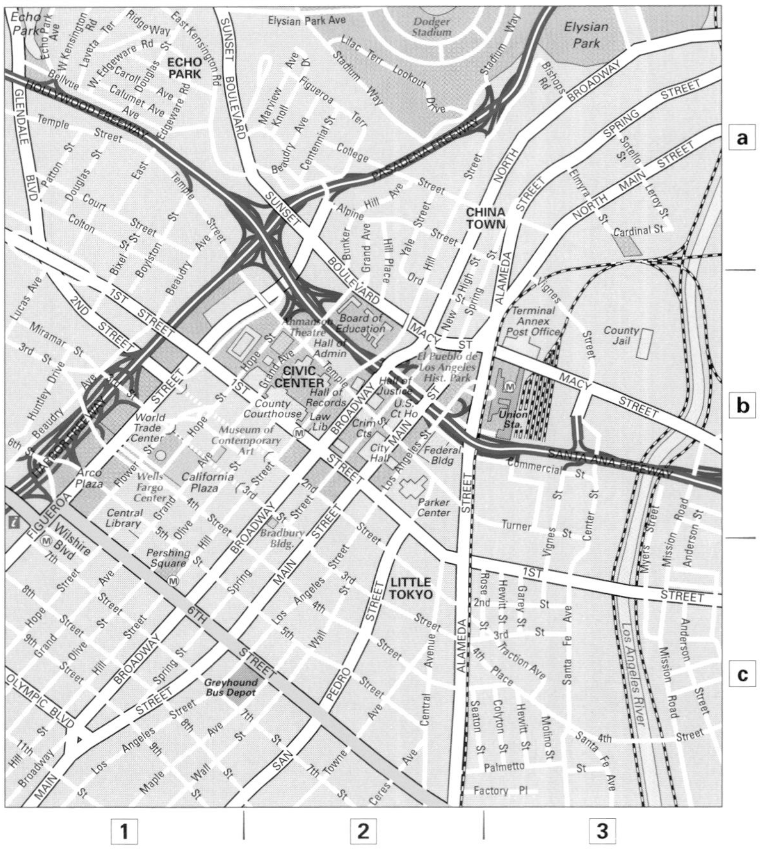

Echo Park, Elysian Park Ave, Dodger Stadium, Elysian Park, a

Echo Park, Sunset Boulevard, Broadway, Spring Street, North Main Street

Glendale Blvd, China Town, Cardinal St, Alameda, Terminal Annex Post Office

Civic Center, World Trade Center, Board of Education, County Jail, Macy Street, b

Arco Plaza, Wells Fargo Center, California Plaza, Museum of Contemporary Art, Parker Center, Union Sta., Commercial St

Central Library, Pershing Square, Bradbury Bldg., Little Tokyo, c

Olympic Blvd, Wilshire Blvd, Broadway, Main Street, San Pedro, Greyhound Bus Depot, Alameda, Santa Fe Ave, Los Angeles River

1 2 3

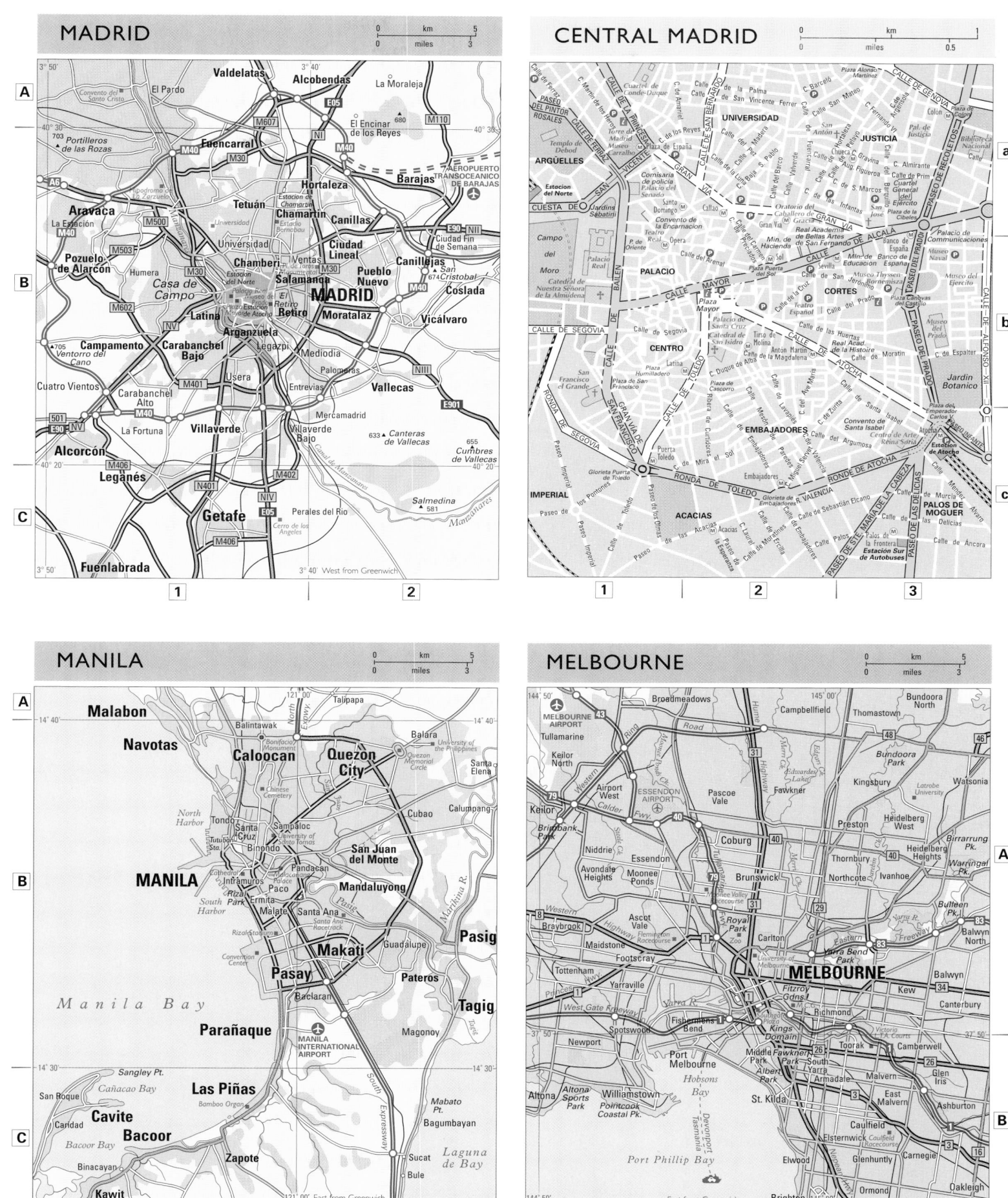

MEXICO CITY

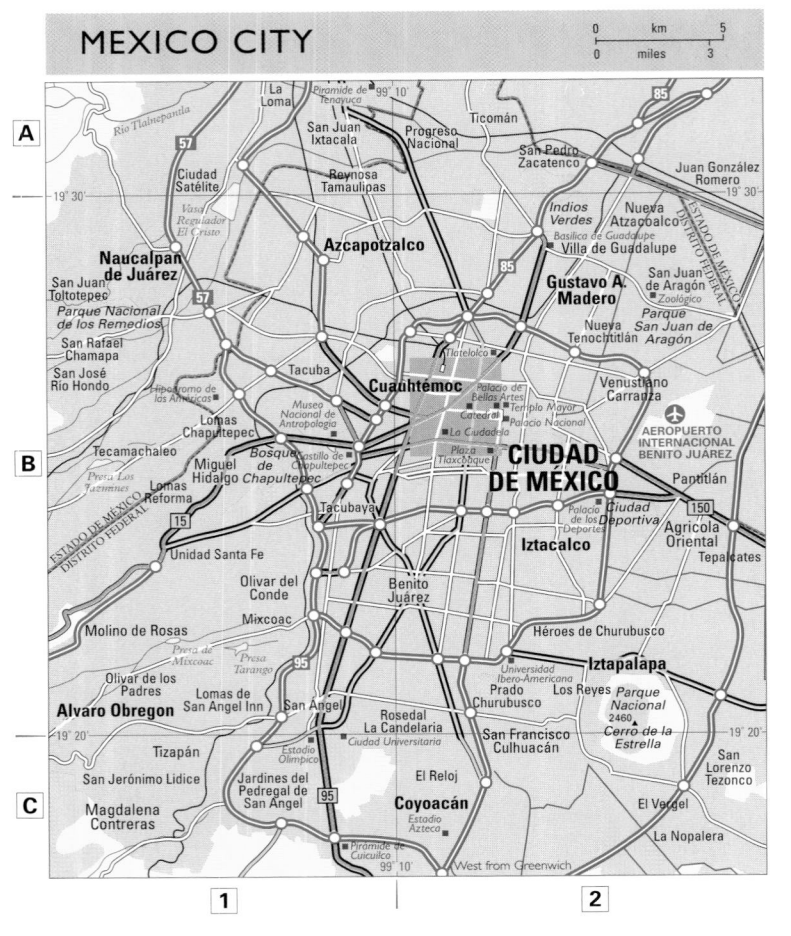

CENTRAL MEXICO CITY

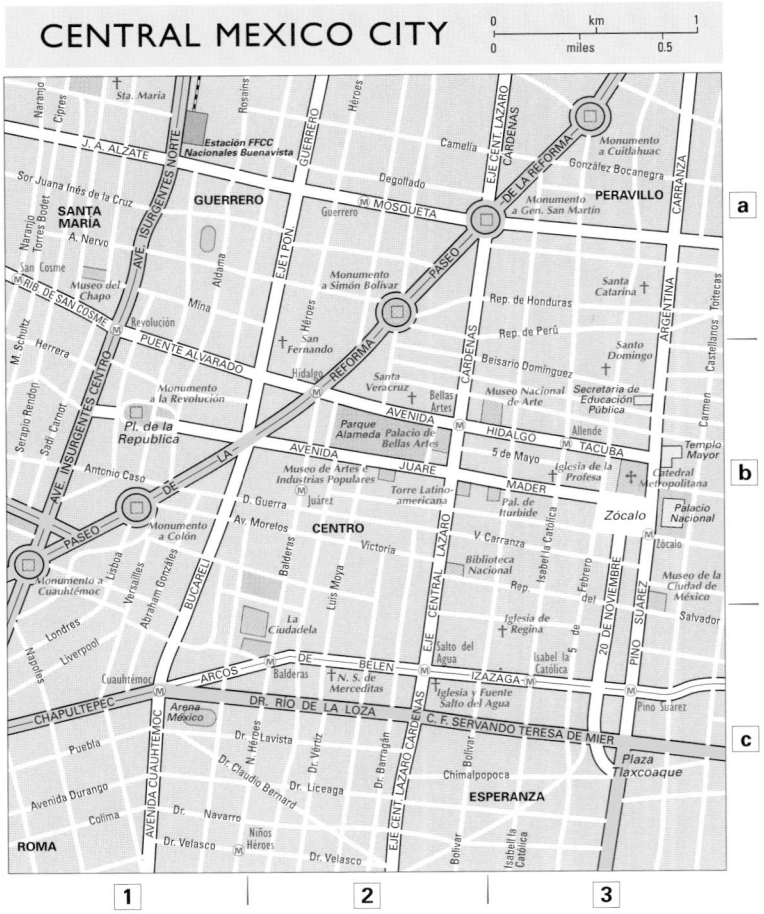

MIAMI

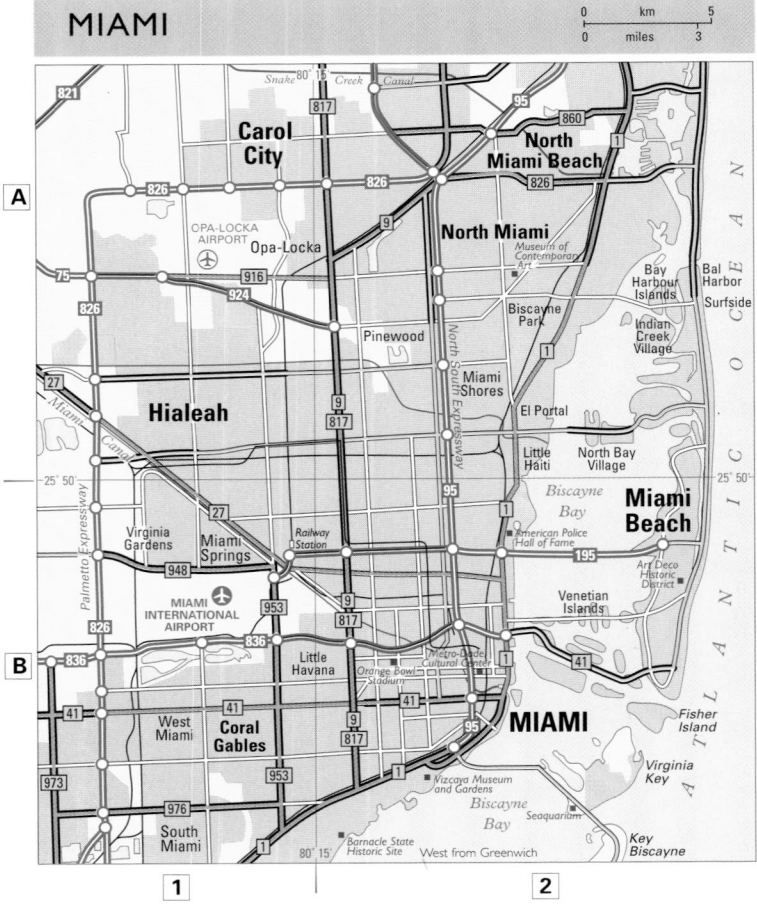

MILAN

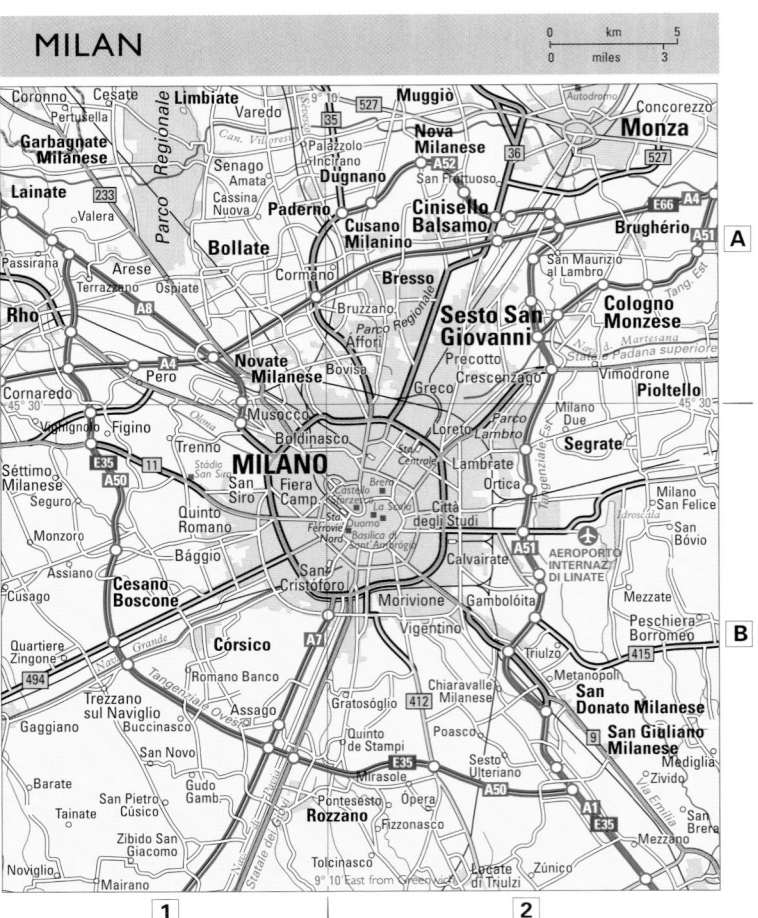

MOSCOW

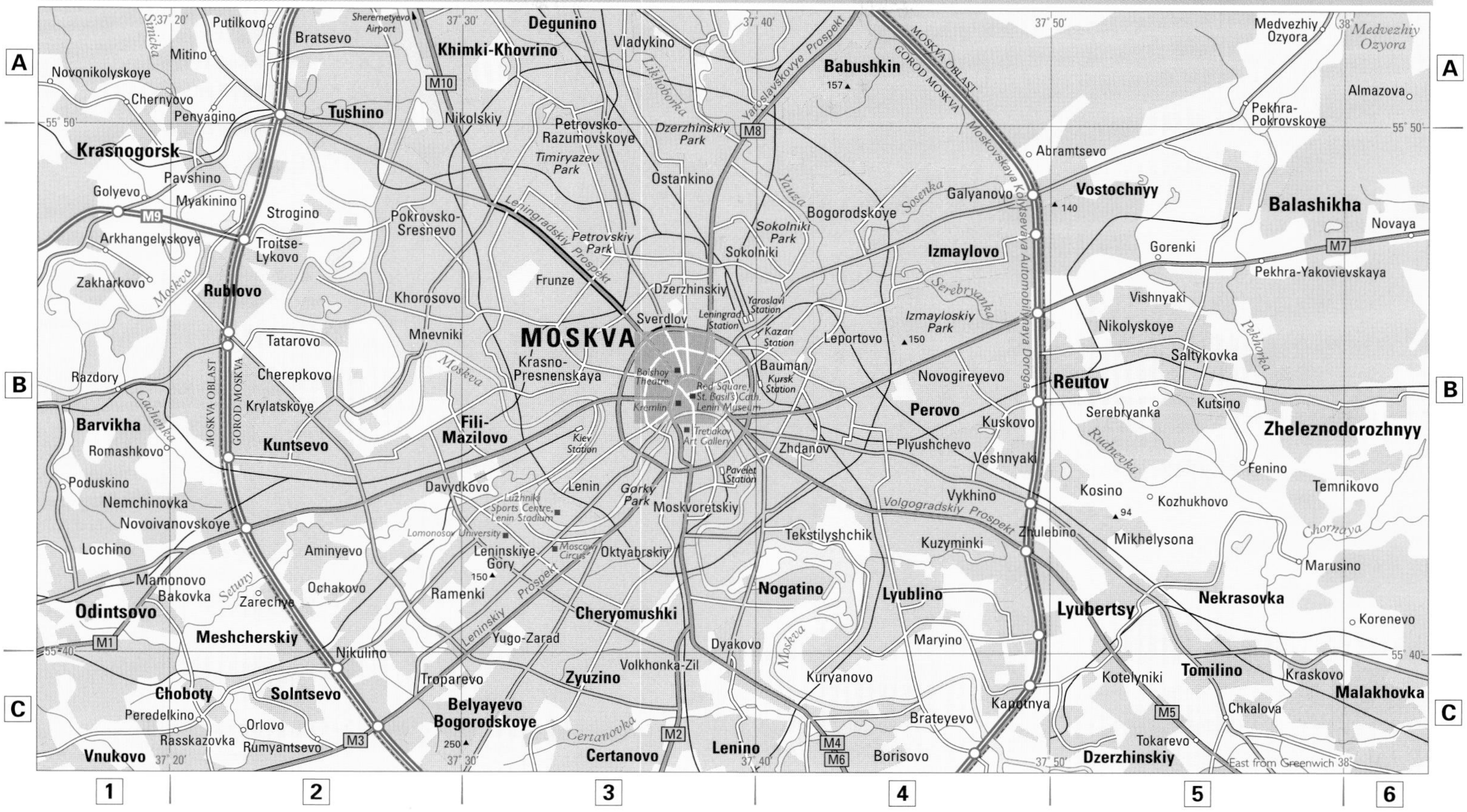

km 0 5
miles 0 3

Novonikolyskoye · Putilkovo · Mitino · Bratsevo · Degunino · Vladykino · Khimki-Khovrino · Sheremetyevo Airport · Medvezhiy Ozyora · Medvezhiy Ozyora

A · Chernovo · Penyagino · Nikolskiy · Petrovsko-Razumovskoye · Dzerzhinskiy Park · Babushkin · 157 · Abramtsevo · Almazova · Pekhra-Pokrovskoye **A**

Tushino · Timiryazev Park · M10 · M8 · Ostankino · Vostochnyy · 140 · **Balashikha** · Novaya

Krasnogorsk · Pavshino · Golyevo · Myakinino · Strogino · Pokrovsko-Sresnevo · Petrovskiy Park · Frunze · Sokolniki Park · Sokolniki · Galyanovo · **Izmaylovo** · Gorenki · M7 · Pekhra-Yakovievskaya

Arkhangelyskoye · Troitse-Lykovo · Khorosovo · Dzerzhinskiy · Leningrad Station · Yaroslavl Station · Izmaylskiy Park · 150 · Vishnyaki · Nikolyskoye · Saltykovka

Zakharkovo · **Rublovo** · Tatarovo · Cherepkovo · Krylatskoye · Mnevniki · **Krasno-Presnenskaya** · Bolshoy Theatre · Kazan Station · Kursk Station · Bauman · Novogireyevo · **Reutov** · Serebryanka · Kutsino

B · **Barvikha** · **MOSKVA** · Red Square St Basil's Cath · Lenin Museum · **Perovo** · Kuskovo · Veshnyaki · **Zheleznodorozhnyy** **B**

Romashkovo · **Kuntsevo** · **Fili-Mazilovo** · Kiev Station · Kremlin · Tretiakov Art Gallery · Zhdanov · Plyushchevo · Fenino

Poduskino · Nemchinovka · Davdkovo · Lenin · Gorky Park · Moskvoretskiy · Vykhino · Kosino · Kozhukhovo · Temnikovo

Novoivanovskoye · Luzhniki Sports Centre Lenin Stadium · Leninskiye Gory · Oktyabrskiy · Moscow Circus · Tekstilyshchik · Kuzminki · 94 · Mikhelysona · Marusino

Lochino · Lomonosov University · Aminyevo · Ochakovo · Ramenki · 150 · **Cheryomushki** · **Nogatino** · **Lyublino** · **Lyubertsy** · **Nekrasovka** · Korenevo

Mamonovo · Bakovka · Zarechye · Yugo-Zarad · Dyakovo · **Tomilino** · Kraskovo

Odintsovo · **Meshcherskiy** · Nikulino · Troparevo · Maryino · Kuryanovo · Kotelniki · **Malakhovka**

C · **Choboty** · **Solntsevo** · **Zyuzino** · Volkhonka-Zil · M5 · Chkalova **C**

Peredelkino · Orlovo · **Belyayevo Bogorodskoye** · Kapotnya · Brateyevo

Rasskazovka · Rumyantsevo · M3 · 250 · **Lenino** · M2 · M4 M6 · Borisovo · Tokarevo · **Dzerzhinskiy**

Vnukovo · **Certanovo** · East from Greenwich 38°

1 **2** **3** **4** **5** **6**

MONTRÉAL

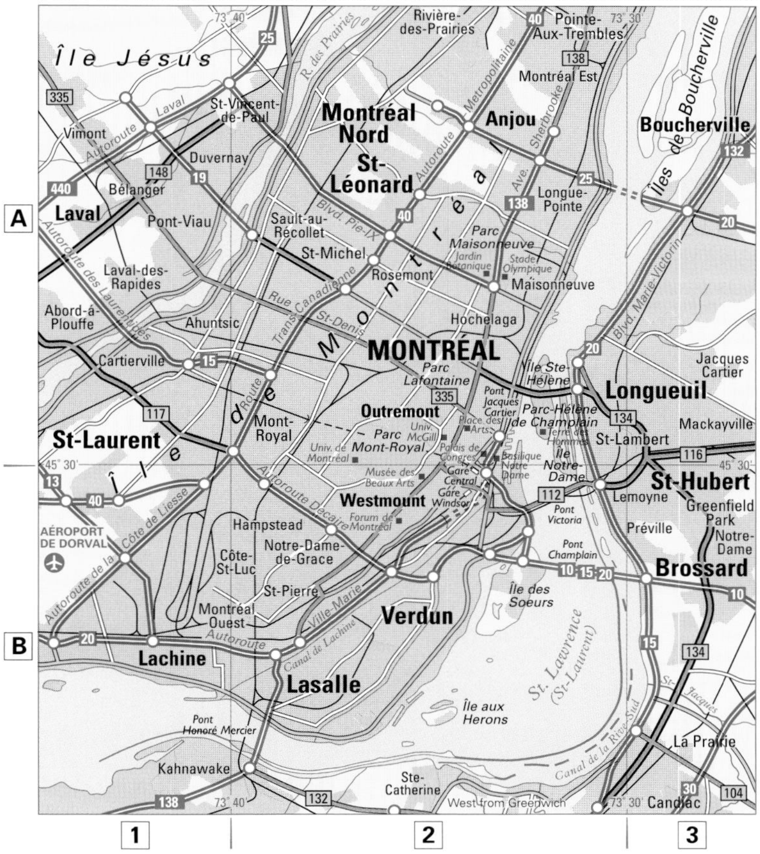

km 0 5
miles 0 3

Île Jésus · Rivière-des-Prairies · Pointe-Aux-Trembles · Boucherville · Montréal Est

Vimont · Laval · St-Vincent-de-Paul · **Montréal Nord** · **Anjou** · **Boucherville**

440 · 148 · Duvernay · **St-Léonard** · Longue-Pointe · Îles de Boucherville · 132

A · **Laval** · Pont-Viau · Sault-au-Récollet · Parc Maisonneuve · Jardin Botanique · Stade Olympique · **A**

Laval-des-Rapides · St-Michel · Rosemont · Maisonneuve

Abord-à-Plouffe · Ahuntsic · Hochelaga · Jacques Cartier

Cartierville · **MONTRÉAL** · Île Ste Hélène · **Longueuil**

Parc Lafontaine · Pont Jacques Cartier · Parc Hélène Champlain · Mackayville · St-Lambert

St-Laurent · Mont-Royal · **Outremont** · Univ. de Montréal · 134 · 116

Parc Mont-Royal · Musée des Beaux Arts · Basilique Notre-Dame · St-Hubert · Lemoyne

Westmount · Gare Windsor · Pont Victoria · Greenfield Park · Notre-Dame · Préville

AÉROPORT DE DORVAL · Hampstead · Forum de Montréal · **Brossard**

Notre-Dame-de-Grace · Côte-St-Luc · St-Pierre · Île des Soeurs

Montréal Ouest · **Verdun** · Île aux Herons · La Prairie

Lachine · Pont Honoré Mercier · **Lasalle** · Kahnawake · Ste-Catherine · West from Greenwich · Candiac · 104

1 **2** **3**

CENTRAL MOSCOW

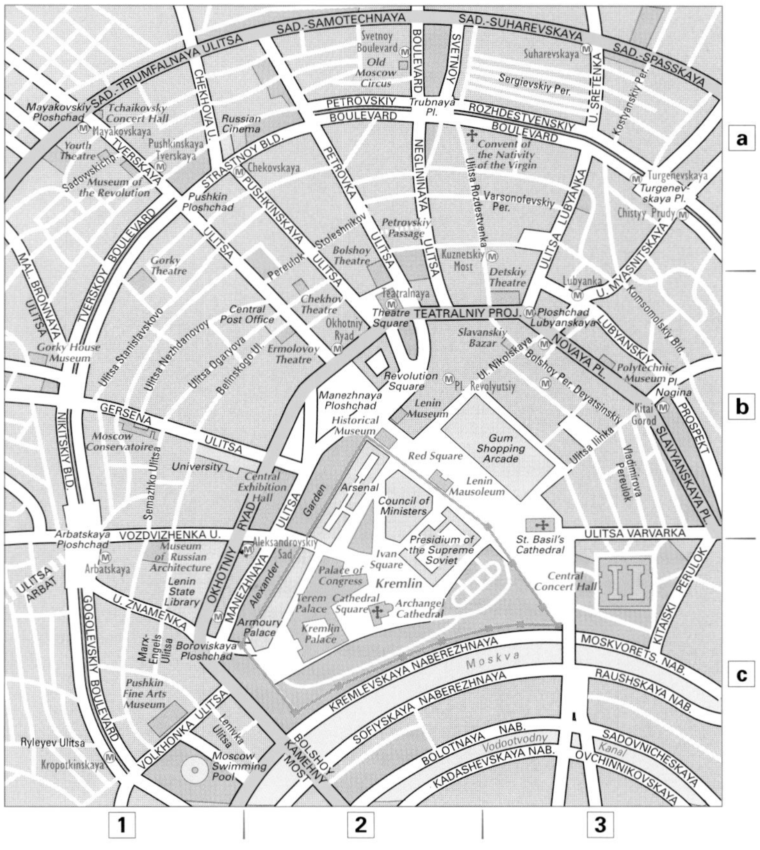

km 0 1
miles 0 0.5

SAD.-SAMOTECHNAYA · SAD.-SUHAREVSKAYA · SAD.-SPASSKAYA · Svetnoy Boulevard · Old Moscow Circus · Suharevskaya · Sergievskiy Per.

Mayakovskiy Ploshchad · Tchaikovsky Concert Hall · Russian Cinema · PETROVSKIY BOULEVARD · ROZHDESTVENSKIY BOULEVARD · Trubnaya Pl. · Convent of the Nativity of the Virgin · Turgenevskaya Turgenevskaya Pl. · Chistry Prudy

a · Youth Theatre · Pushkinskaya · Chekovskaya · Petrovskaya Passage · Kuznetskaya · Varsonofevskiy Per. · Lubyanka

Museum of the Revolution · Pushkinskaya Ploshchad · Stoleshnikov Per. · Bolsho Theatre · Kuznetskiy Most · Detskiy Theatre · Polyclinic · Museum

Gorky Theatre · Perelova · Chekhov Theatre · Teatralnaya · TEATRALNIY PROJ. · Ploshchad Lubyanskiy · Kitai-Gorod

Gorky House Museum · Central Post Office · Okhotny Ryad · Slavanskiy Bazar · Nogina

b · Moscow Conservatoire · Revolution Square · Manezhnaya Ploshchad · Lenin Museum · Gum Shopping Arcade · Vladimirskiy Peredulok **b**

University · Central Exhibition Hall · Historical Museum · Red Square · Lenin Mausoleum

Arbatskaya Ploshchad · VOZDVIZHENKA U. · Museum of Russian Architecture · Alexandrovskiy Sad · Arsenal · Council of Ministers · St Basil's Cathedral · ULITSA VARVARKA · Central Concert Hall

ULITSA ARBAT · Museum · Ivan Square · Presidium of the Supreme Soviet

Lenin State Library · Palace of Congress · Kremlin · Terem Cathedral Square · Archangel Cathedral

c · Borovitskaya Ploshchad · Marx-Engels Ulitsa · Armoury Palace · Borovitskaya · Kremlin Palace · MOSKVORETS. NAB. · RAUSHSKAYA NAB. **c**

Pushkin Fine Arts Museum · KREMLEVSKAYA NABEREZHNAYA · Moskva

Ryleyev Ulitsa · Kropotkinskaya · Moscow Swimming Pool · SOFIYSKAYA NABEREZHNAYA · Vodootvodny Kanal · OVCHINNIKOVSKAYA · SADOVNICHESKAYA · BOLOTNAYA NAB. · KADASHEVSKAYA NAB.

1 **2** **3**

MUMBAI

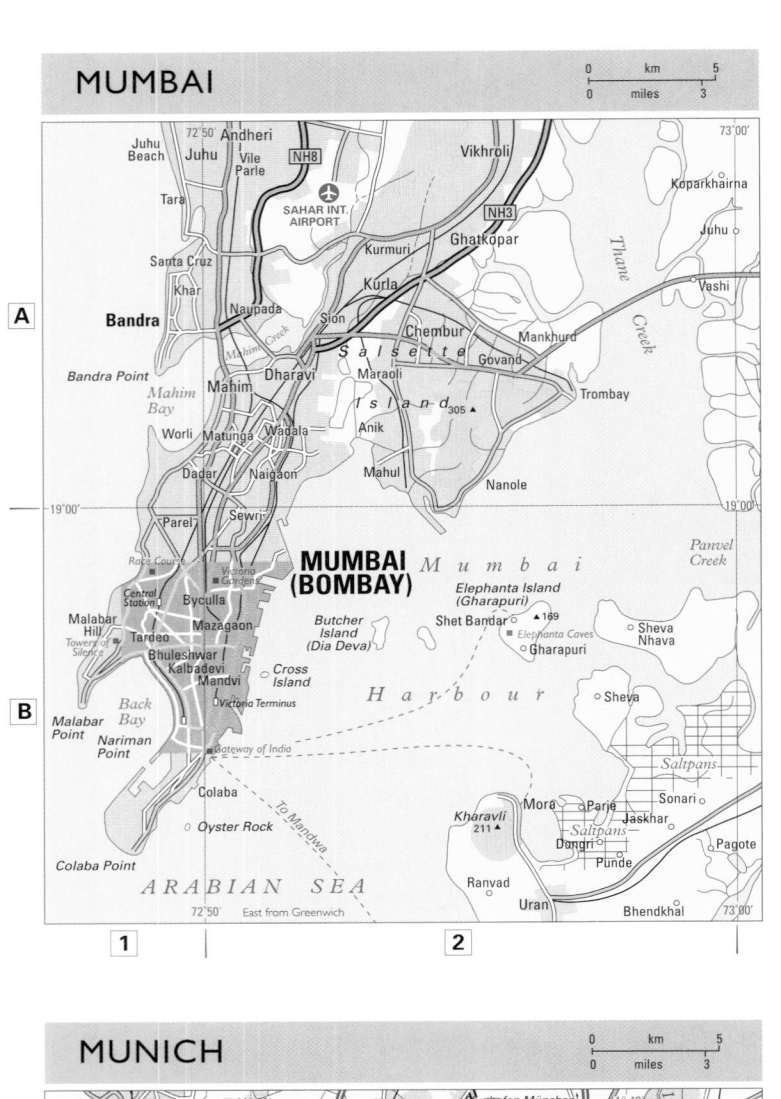

CENTRAL MUMBAI

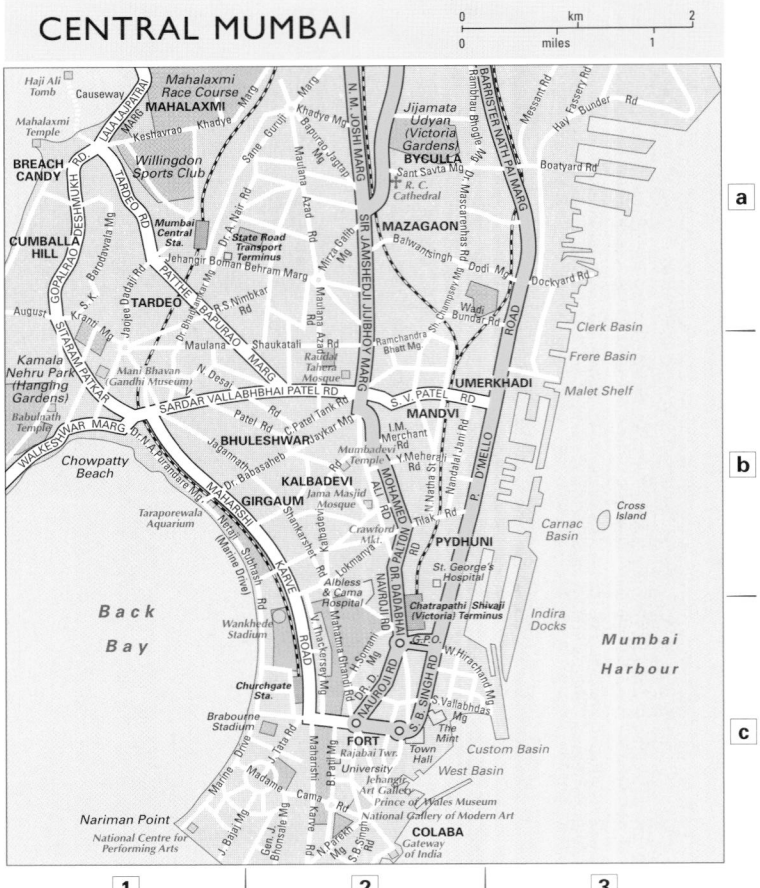

MUNICH

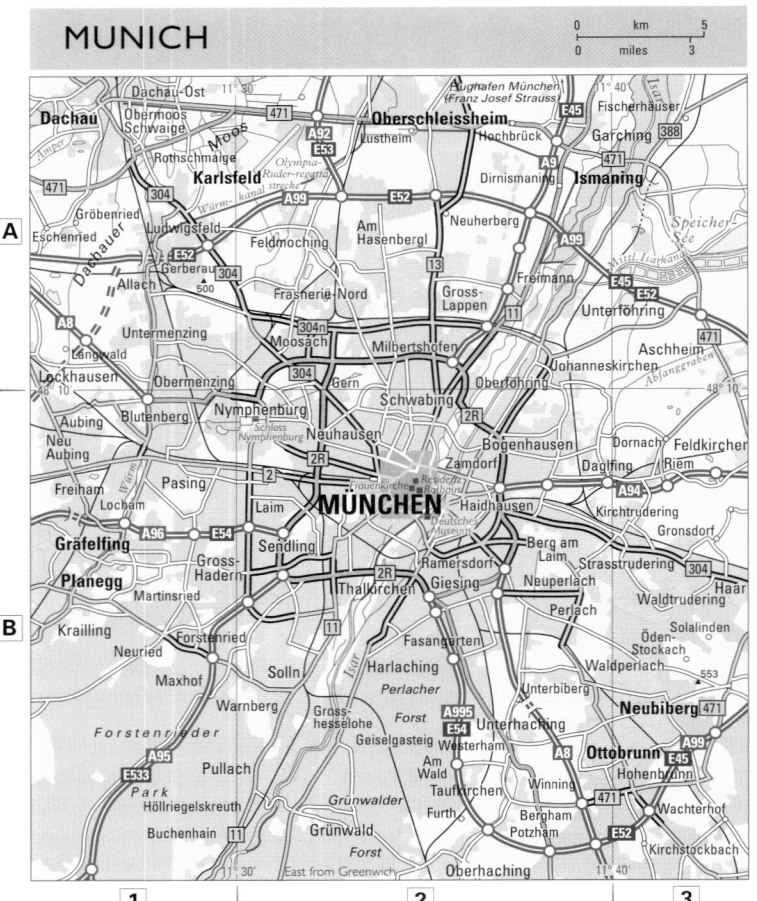

CENTRAL MUNICH

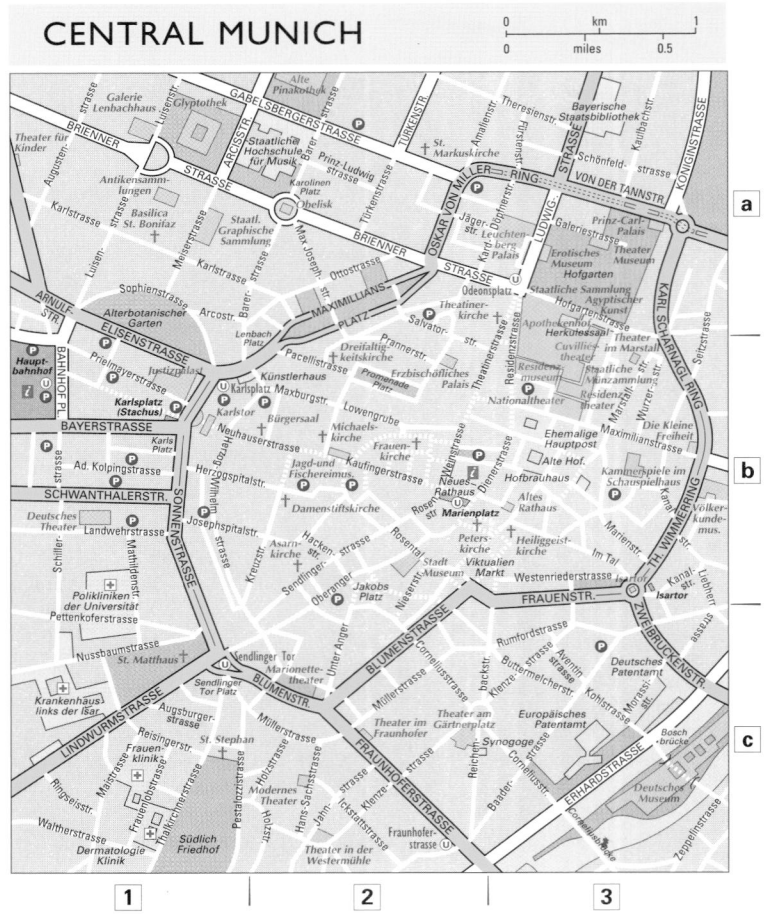

NEW YORK

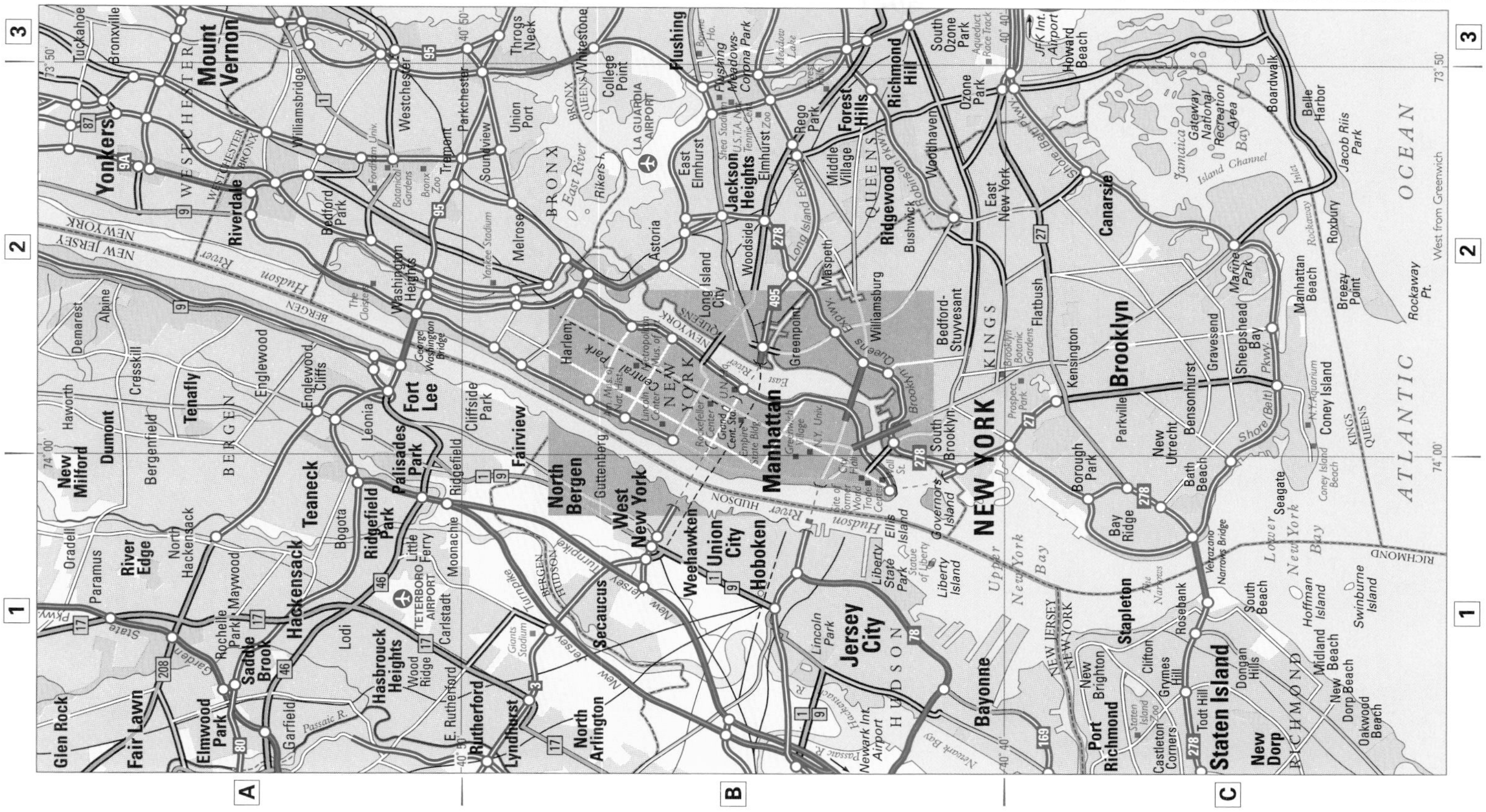

km 0 — 5
miles 0 — 3

3 | 2 | 1 (grid rows)

A | B | C (grid columns)

Tuckahoe • Bronxville • Mount Vernon • Yonkers • Riverdale • WESTCHESTER • Williamsbridge • Westchester • Parkchester • Throgs Neck • Whitestone • Flushing • College Point • Bronx • Rikers I. • La Guardia Airport • Astoria • Jackson Heights • Elmhurst • Rego Park • Forest Hills • Richmond Hill • Ozone Park • South Ozone Park • JFK Int. Airport • Howard Beach • Boardwalk • Belle Harbor • OCEAN

New Milford • Dumont • Tenafly • Englewood • Englewood Cliffs • Fort Lee • George Washington Bridge • Washington Heights • Harlem • Central Park • NEW YORK • Long Island City • Woodside • Maspeth • Middle Village • Ridgewood • Bushwick • East New York • Canarsie • Worthaven

BERGEN • Teaneck • Bogota • Ridgefield Park • Palisades Park • Ridgefield • Cliffside Park • Fairview • North Bergen • West New York • Weehawken • Union City • Hoboken • Guttenberg • MANHATTAN • East River • Hudson • Brooklyn • KINGS • Bedford-Stuyvesant • Flatbush • Kensington • Borough Park • New Utrecht • Bensonhurst • Bath Beach • Gravesend • Sheepshead Bay • Marine Park • Flatlands • Manhattan Beach • Breezy Point • Rockaway Pt. • ATLANTIC

Glen Rock • Fair Lawn • Elmwood Park • Saddle Brook • Hackensack • Hasbrouck Heights • Wood Ridge • Carlstadt • E. Rutherford • Rutherford • Lyndhurst • North Arlington • Secaucus • TETERBORO AIRPORT • Moonachie • Little Ferry • Lincoln Tunnel • Jersey City • Bayonne • NEW JERSEY • NEW YORK • Upper New York Bay • Staten Island • Port Richmond • New Brighton • Clifton • Grymes Hill • Todt Hill • Stapleton • RICHMOND • New Dorp • Dongan Hills • Oakwood Beach • Verrazano Narrows Bridge • Coney Island • Bay Ridge

CENTRAL NEW YORK

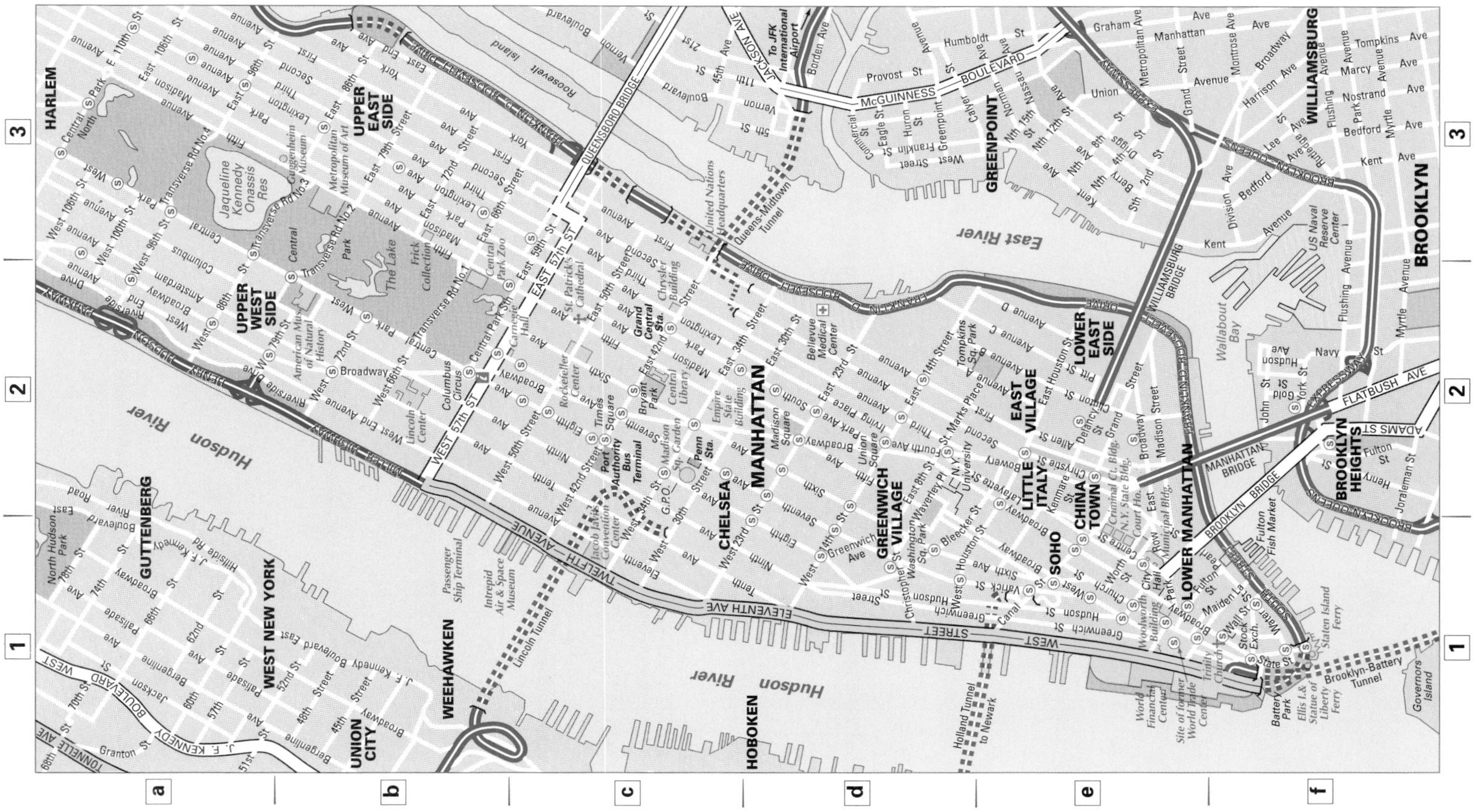

km 0 — 2
miles 0 — 1

3 | 2 | 1 (grid rows)

a | b | c | d | e | f (grid columns)

HARLEM • UPPER WEST SIDE • UPPER EAST SIDE • Central Park • Jacqueline Kennedy Onassis Res. • The Lake • Metropolitan Museum of Art • Frick Collection • Guggenheim Museum • American Museum of Natural History • Lincoln Center • Columbus Circle • Hudson River • East River • Roosevelt Island • Queensboro Bridge • United Nations Headquarters • WILLIAMSBURG • GREENPOINT • QUEENS • Queens–Midtown Tunnel • Grand Central Sta. • Chrysler Building • St. Patrick's Cathedral • Rockefeller Center • Times Square • Port Authority Bus Terminal • G.P.O. • Madison Sq. Garden • Penn Sta. • Empire State Building • N.Y. Public Library • Bryant Park • MANHATTAN • CHELSEA • GREENWICH VILLAGE • EAST VILLAGE • LOWER EAST SIDE • Washington Sq. • N.Y. Univ. • LITTLE ITALY • SOHO • CHINA TOWN • BROOKLYN • Williamsburg Bridge • Manhattan Bridge • Brooklyn Bridge • BROOKLYN HEIGHTS • US Naval Reserve Center • FLATBUSH AVE • ADAMS ST • LOWER MANHATTAN • World Financial Center • World Trade Center Site • Battery Park • Ellis Island • Statue of Liberty Ferry • Governors Island • Staten Island Ferry • Brooklyn–Battery Tunnel • Fulton Fish Market • Holland Tunnel • GUTTENBERG • WEST NEW YORK • WEEHAWKEN • UNION CITY • HOBOKEN • Hudson River • Intrepid Air & Space Museum • Passenger Ship Terminal • Jacob K. Javits Convention Center

TWELFTH AVENUE • ELEVENTH AVE • WEST STREET

OSAKA

0 km 5
0 miles 3

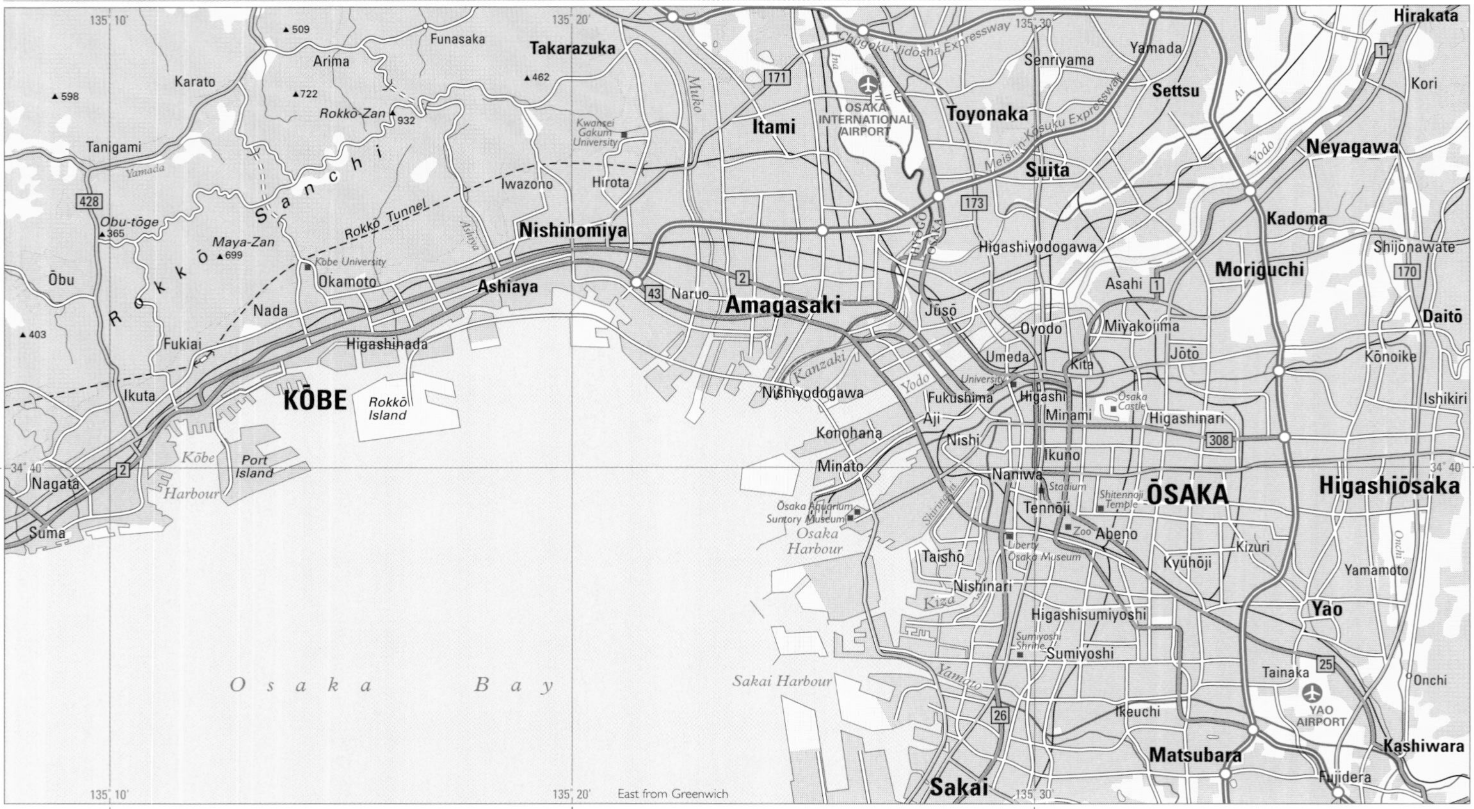

135° 10' 135° 20' 135° 30'

Funasaka
▲509
Takarazuka
Arima
Karato
▲722
Rokkō-Zan ▲932
▲598
Tanigami
▲462
171
Yamada
Senriyama
Hirakata
11
Kori
Itami
OSAKA INTERNATIONAL AIRPORT
Toyonaka
Settsu
Yamada
Kwansei Gakuin University
Iwazono
Rokkō Tunnel
Suita
173
Neyagawa
Obu-tōge
365
Maya-Zan ▲699
Kōbe University
Okamoto
Nishinomiya
Higashiyodogawa
Asahi
Kadoma
Moriguchi
Shijonawate
▲428
Nada
Ashiaya
Naruo
43
Amagasaki
Jūsō
Asahi
1
170
Daitō
Ôbu
▲403
Fukiai
Higashinada
2
Naruo
Umeda
Oyodo
Miyakojima
Jōtō
Kōnoike
Ikuta
Rokkō Island
Nishiyodogawa
Fukushima
Kita
Osaka Castle
Higashinari
308
Ishikiri
Nagata
2
Kōbe Harbour
Port Island
Aji
Higashi
Minami
Nishi
Ikuno
Higashiōsaka
Suma
Konohana
Minato
Naniwa
Stadium
Tennōji
Zoo
Abeno
Kizuri
Yamamoto
Osaka Aquarium Suntory Museum
Osaka Harbour
Taishō
Liberty Osaka Museum
Kyūhōji
Yao
Nishinari
Higashisumiyoshi
Sakai Harbour
Sumiyoshi Shrine
Sumiyoshi
Tainaka
25
Onchi
O s a k a   B a y
26
Ikeuchi
YAO AIRPORT
Matsubara
Kashiwara
Sakai
Fujidera

East from Greenwich

34° 40'

OSLO

0 km 5
0 miles 3

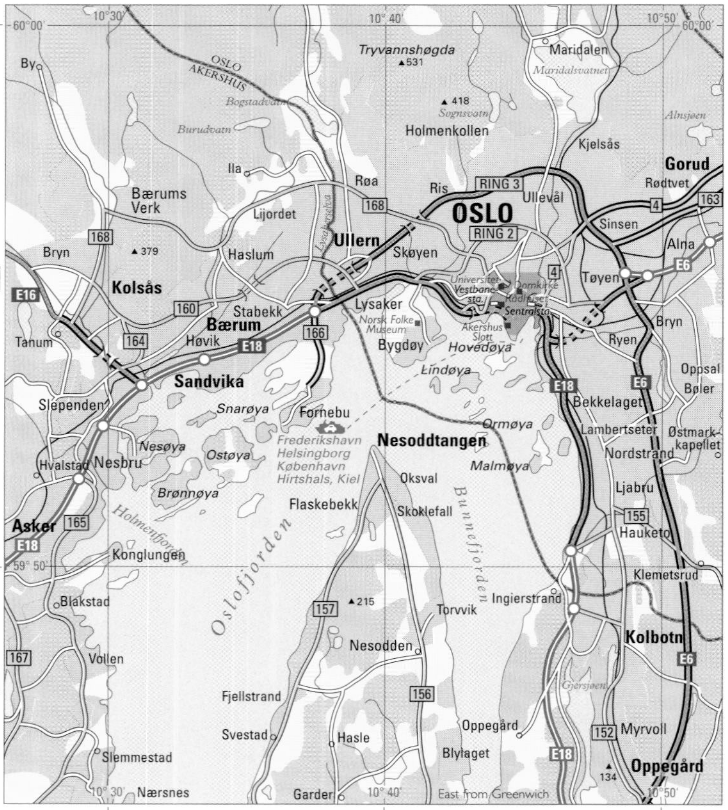

60°00' 10°30' 10°40' 10°50' 60°00'

By
OSLO AKERSHUS
Tryvannshøgda ▲531
Maridalen
Maridalsvatnet
Bogstadvatn
Burudvatn
Sognsvatn
▲418
Albujen
Holmenkollen
Kjelsås
Bærums Verk
Ila
Røa
Ris
RING 3
Ulleval
Gorud
Rødtvet
168
168
▲379
Lijordet
Haslum
Ullern
OSLO RING 2
Skøyen
Sinsen
4
163
Alna
E6
Kolsås
160
Stabekk
Lysaker
Universitet Vestbane
Tøyen
Bryn
Bærum
166
Norsk Folke-museum
Akershus Slott
4
Ryen
164
Høvik
E18
Bygdøy
Hovedøya
Oppsal
Bøler
Tanum
Sandvika
Snarøya
Fornebu
Bekkelaget
E18
E6
Slependen
Nesøya
Lindøya
Ormøya
Lambertseter
Østmark-kapellet
Hvalstad
Nesbru
Brønnøya
Frederikshavn Helsingborg København Hirtshals, Kiel
Nesoddtangen
Malmøya
Nordstrand
Asker
165
Holmefjord
Østøya
Oksval
Flaskebekk
Skoklefall
Ljabru
E18
Konglungen
155
Hauketo
Blåstad
167
Vollen
Bunnefjorden
Nesodden
Klemetsrud
Kolbotn
E6
Svestad
Fjellstrand
157
▲215
Ingierstrand
Torvik
Slemmestad
Hasle
Oppegård
156
Nærsnes
Garder
Svartad
Blylaget
E18
152
Myrvoll
134
Oppegård

East from Greenwich

59° 50'

CENTRAL OSLO

0 km 0.5
0 miles 0.25

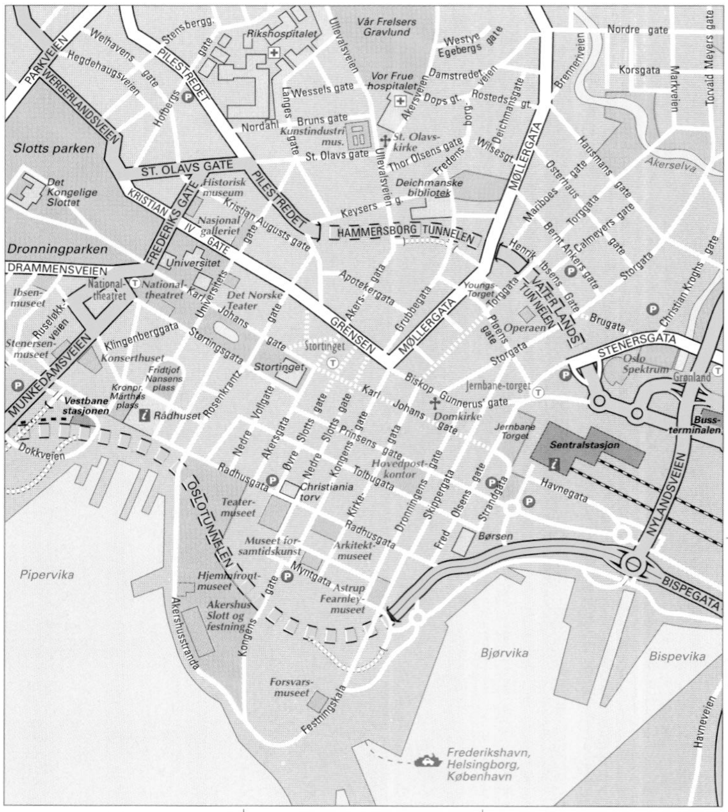

Rikshospitalet
Vår Frelsers Gravlund
Westye Egebergs gate
Nordre gate
Stensberg.
Universitetet
Korsgata
PARKVEIEN
VERGELANDSVEIEN
Weltovens gate
PILESTREDET
Hegdehaugsveien
Wessels gate
Vor Frue hospitalet
Damstreder
Bremnesveien
Markveien
Akerselva
Slotts parken
ST. OLAVS GATE
St. Olavs gate
HAMMERSBORG TUNNELEN
MØLLERGATA
a
Det Kongelige Slottet
KRISTIAN IV GATE
Historisk museum
Deichmanske bibliotek
DRAMMENSVEIEN
Dronningparken
Universitet
Nasjonal galleriet
GRENSEN
Operaen
Ibsen-museet
National-theatret Tårn
Det Norske Teater
Oslo Spektrum
b
Stenersen-museet
MUNKEDAMSVEIEN
Vestbane stasjonen
Rådhuset
Stortinget
Karl Johans gate
STENERSGATA
Sentralstasjon
Buss-terminalen
Christiania torv
OSLO TUNNELEN
Rådhusgata
Hovedpost kontor
NYLANDSVEIEN
Pipervika
Museet for samtidskunst
Arkitekt museet
Børsen
BISPEGATA
Hjemmefront-museet
Myntgata
Astrup Fearnley-museet
Havnegata
Akershus Slott og festning
Bjørvika
Bispevika
Forsvars-museet
Frederikshavn, Helsingborg, København
Havneveien

PARIS

0 — km — 5
0 — miles — 3

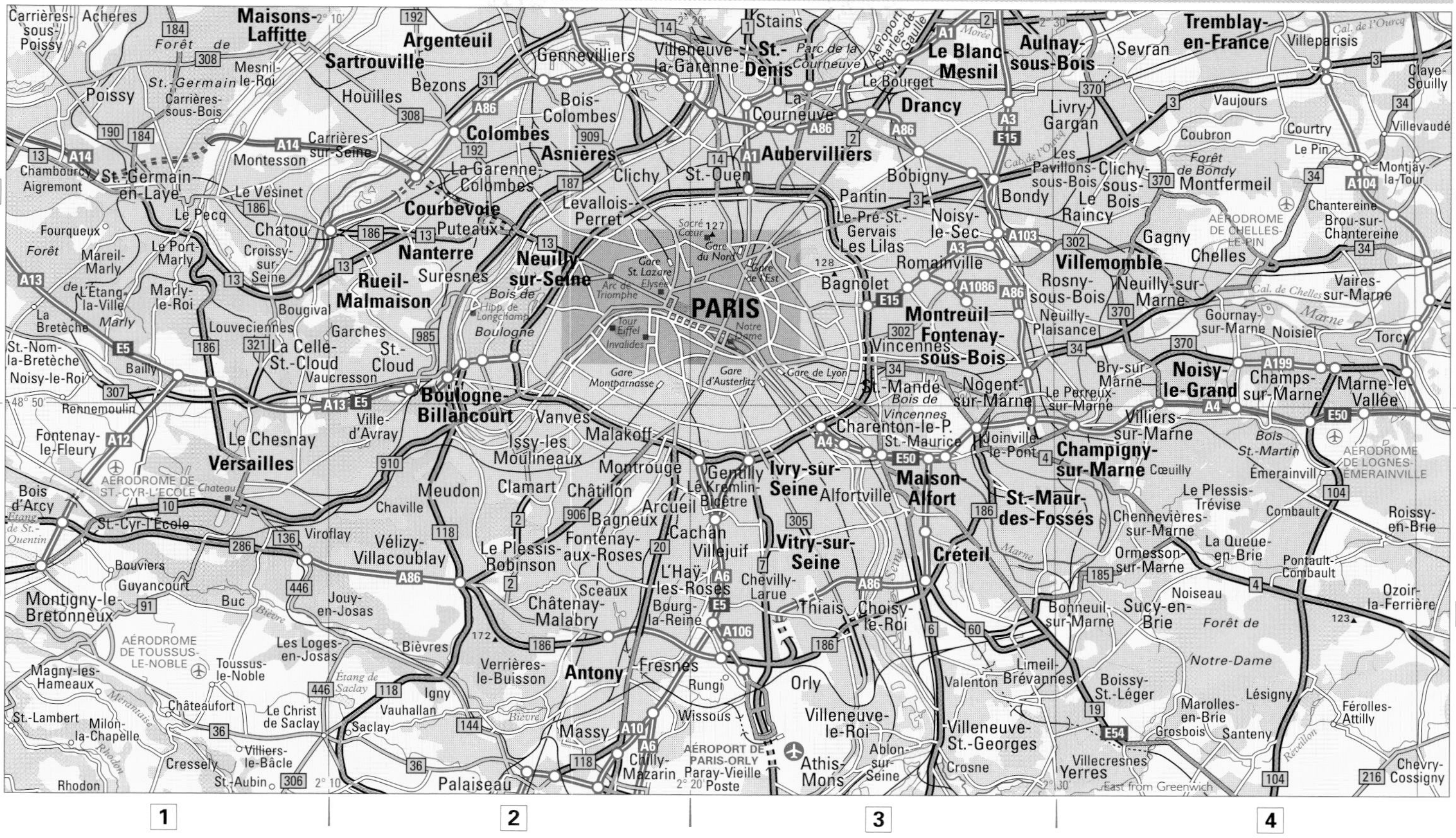

Carrières-sous-Poissy · Achères · Poissy · Maisons-Laffitte · Argenteuil · Sartrouville · Gennevilliers · Villeneuve-la-Garenne · St.-Denis · Stains · Parc de la Courneuve · Le Bourget · Le Blanc Mesnil · Aulnay-sous-Bois · Sevran · Tremblay-en-France · Villeparisis · Claye-Souilly · Villevaudé

Houilles · Bezons · Bois-Colombes · Colombes · Asnières · La Courneuve · Drancy · Livry-Gargan · Les Pavillons-sous-Bois · Clichy-sous-Bois · Montfermeil · Coubron · Le Pin · Courtry

Carrières-sous-Bois · Montesson · La Garenne-Colombes · Clichy · St.-Ouen · Aubervilliers · Pantin · Bobigny · Bondy · Le Raincy · Gagny · Chelles · Vaires-sur-Marne

St.-Germain-en-Laye · Le Pecq · Le Vésinet · Courbevoie · Puteaux · Levallois-Perret · Noisy-le-Sec · Romainville · Villemomble · Chanteloup · Brou-sur-Chantereine

Fourqueux · Le Port-Marly · Chatou · Croissy-sur-Seine · Nanterre · Neuilly-sur-Seine · Gare St.-Lazare · Gare du Nord · Gare de l'Est · Le Pré-St.-Gervais · Les Lilas · Bagnolet · Rosny-sous-Bois · Neuilly-sur-Marne · Gournay-sur-Marne · Noisiel · Torcy

Mareil-Marly · Rueil-Malmaison · Suresnes · Bois de Boulogne · Arc de Triomphe · **PARIS** · Notre Dame · Montreuil · Vincennes · Fontenay-sous-Bois · Bry-sur-Marne · Noisy-le-Grand · Champs-sur-Marne · Marne-la-Vallée

Louveciennes · Garches · St.-Cloud · Vaucresson · Boulogne-Billancourt · Tour Eiffel · Invalides · Gare Montparnasse · Gare d'Austerlitz · Gare de Lyon · St.-Mandé · Nogent-sur-Marne · Le Perreux-sur-Marne · Villiers-sur-Marne

Bailly · Marly-le-Roi · La Celle-St.-Cloud · Ville-d'Avray · Vanves · Malakoff · Charenton-le-P. · St.-Maurice · Joinville-le-Pont · Champigny-sur-Marne · Émerainville

Rennemoulin · Le Chesnay · Issy-les-Moulineaux · Montrouge · Gentilly · Le Kremlin-Bicêtre · Ivry-sur-Seine · Alfortville · Maison-Alfort · St.-Maur-des-Fossés · Chennevières-sur-Marne · Le Plessis-Trévise · Combault · Roissy-en-Brie

Fontenay-le-Fleury · Versailles · Meudon · Clamart · Châtillon · Arcueil · Cachan · Vitry-sur-Seine · Créteil · Ormesson-sur-Marne · Sucy-en-Brie

Bois d'Arcy · St.-Cyr-l'École · Vélizy-Villacoublay · Viroflay · Chaville · Bagneux · Fontenay-aux-Roses · Villejuif · Bonneuil-sur-Marne · Noiseau · Ozoir-la-Ferrière

Montigny-le-Bretonneux · Guyancourt · Buc · Le Plessis-Robinson · Sceaux · L'Haÿ-les-Roses · Chevilly-Larue · Thiais · Choisy-le-Roi · Boissy-St.-Léger · Forêt de Notre-Dame · Lésigny

Jouy-en-Josas · Bièvres · Châtenay-Malabry · Bourg-la-Reine · Villeneuve-le-Roi · Valenton · Brévannes · Marolles-en-Brie · Santeny · Férolles-Attilly

Magny-les-Hameaux · Toussus-le-Noble · Les Loges-en-Josas · Verrières-le-Buisson · Antony · Fresnes · Rungis · Orly · Ablon-sur-Seine · Crosne · Villecresnes · Yerres · Chevry-Cossigny

St.-Lambert · Milon-la-Chapelle · Châteaufort · Igny · Vauhallan · Saclay · Massy · Wissous · Villeneuve-St.-Georges

Cressely · St.-Aubin · Rhodon · Palaiseau · Chilly-Mazarin · AÉROPORT DE PARIS-ORLY Paray-Vieille-Poste · Athis-Mons

1 · 2 · 3 · 4

CENTRAL PARIS

0 — km — 1
0 — miles — 0.5

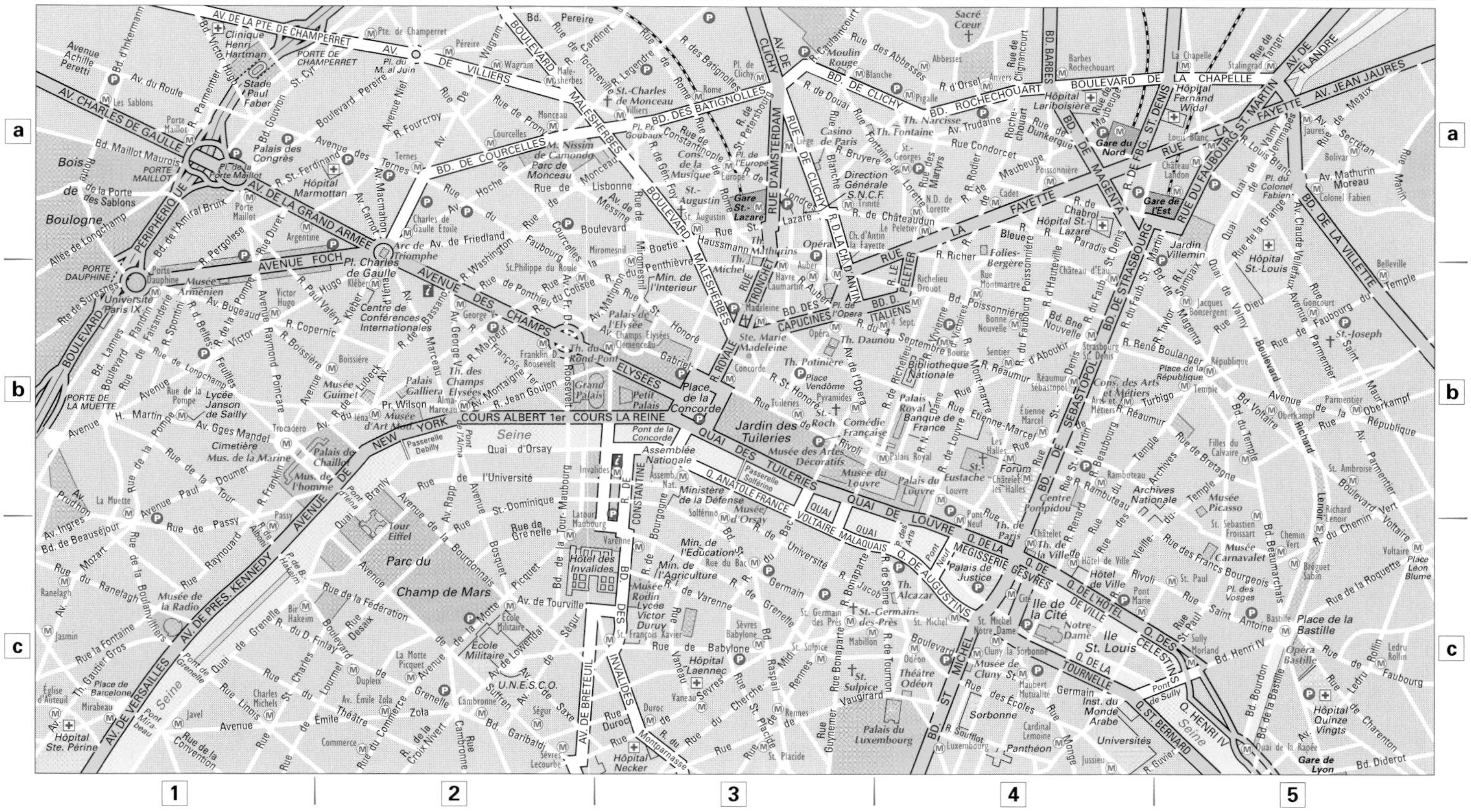

a · b · c

1 · 2 · 3 · 4 · 5

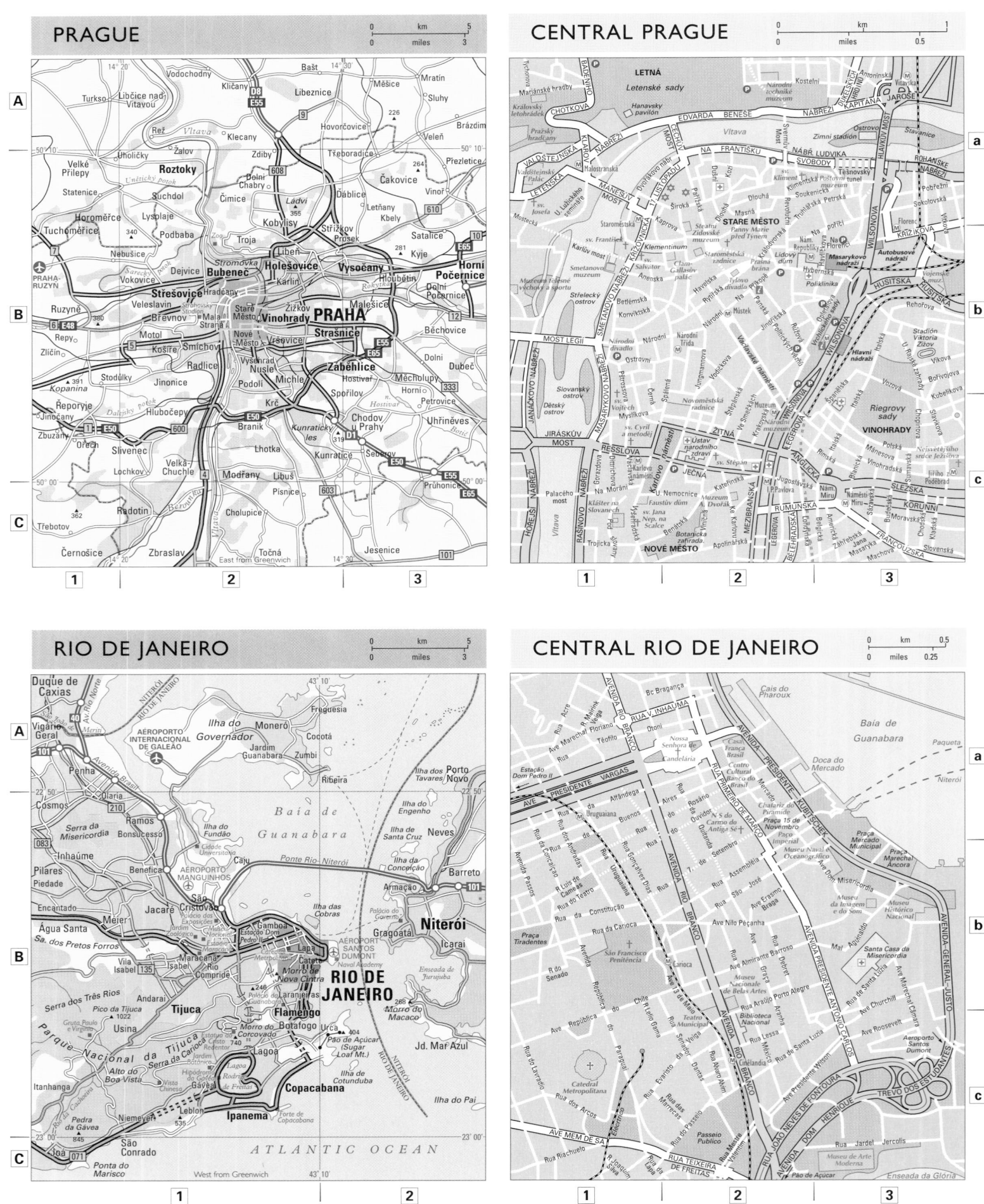

ROME

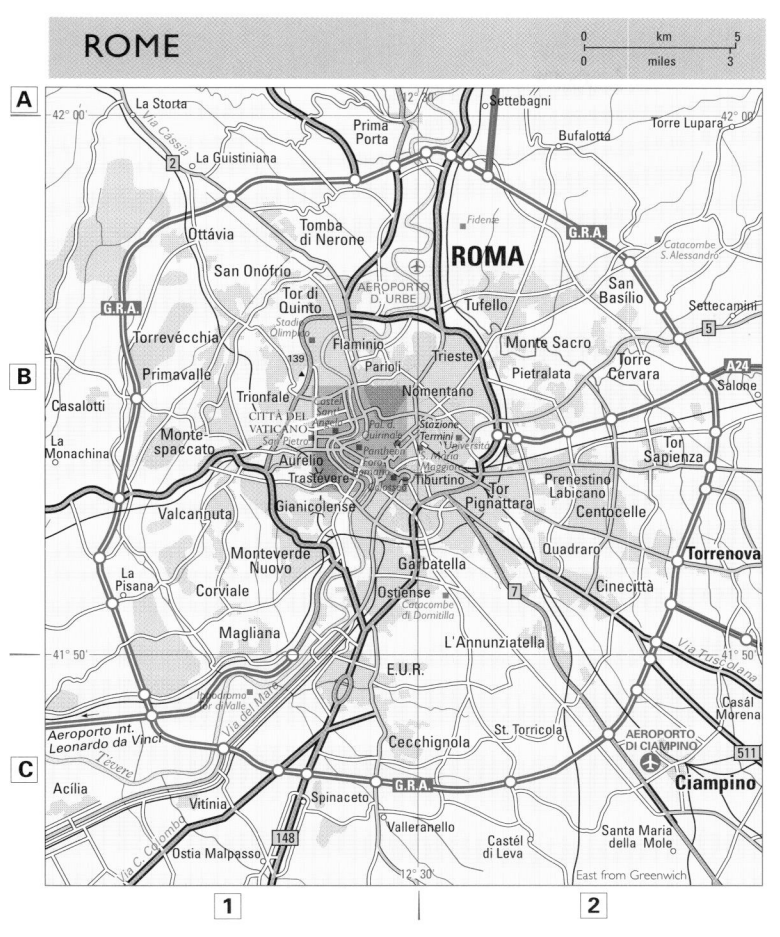

CENTRAL ROME

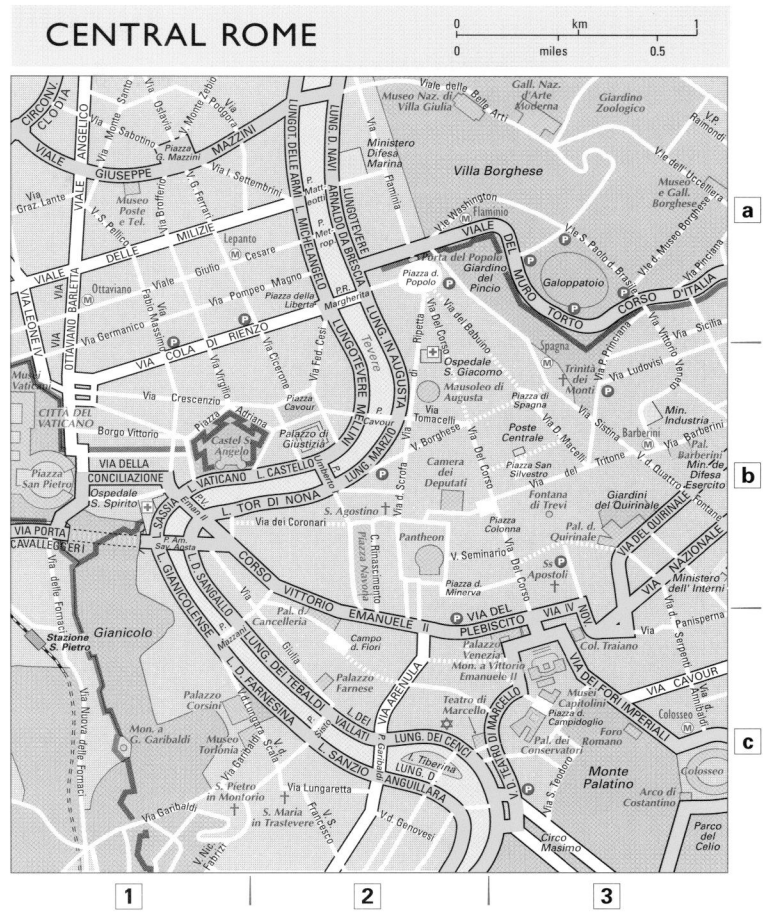

SAN FRANCISCO

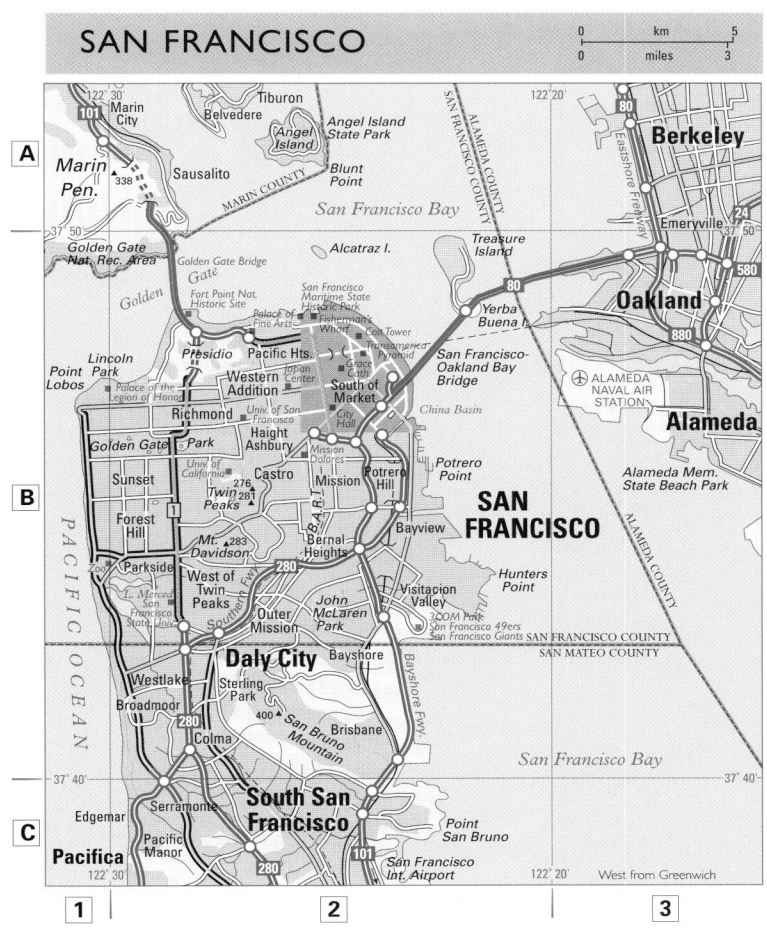

CENTRAL SAN FRANCISCO

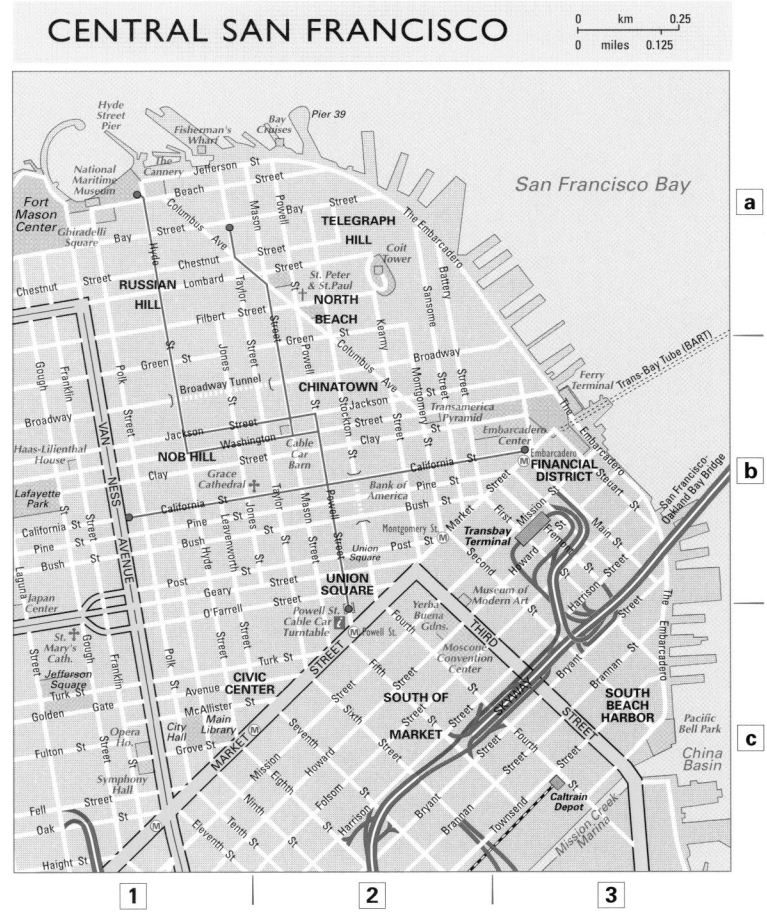

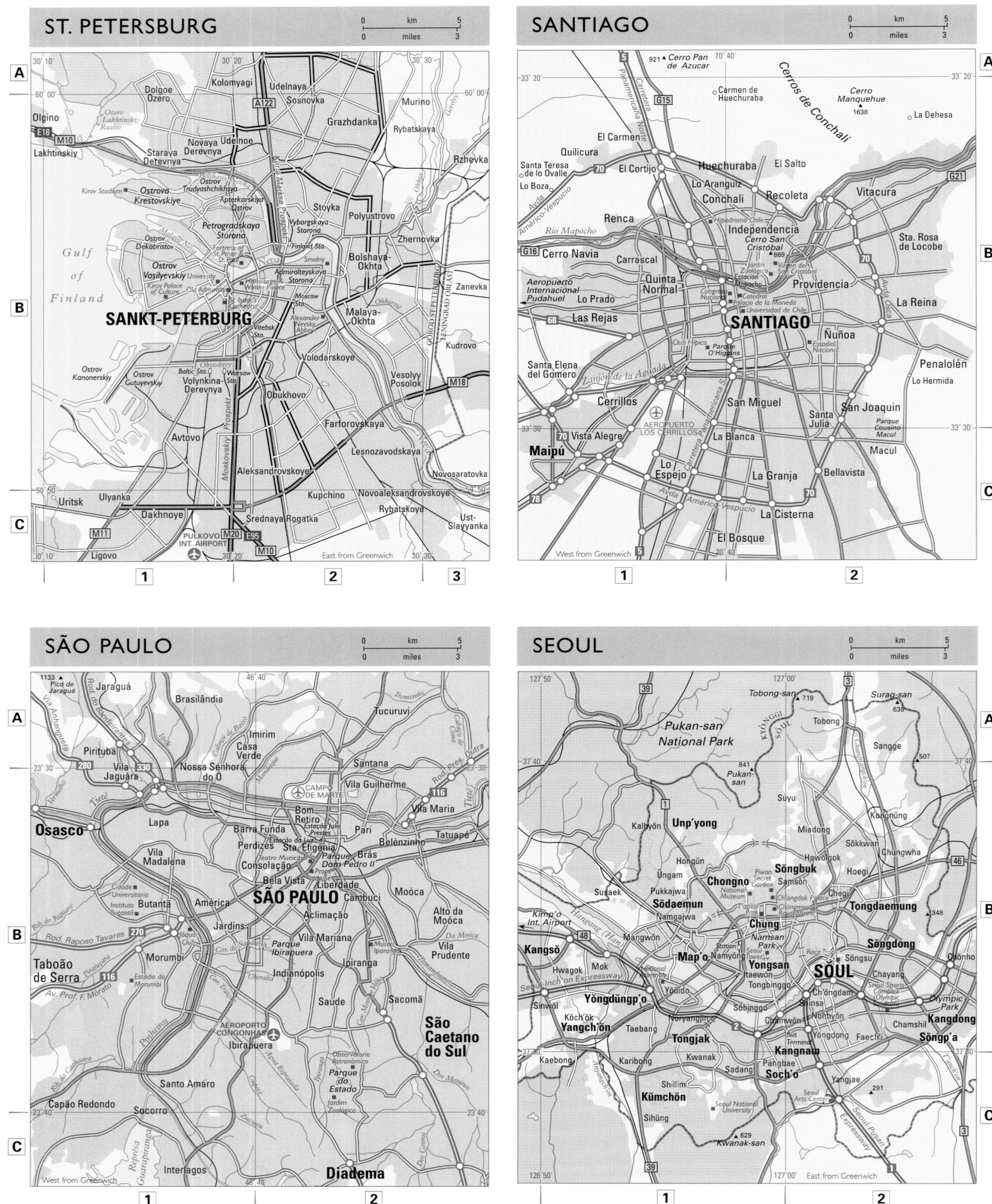

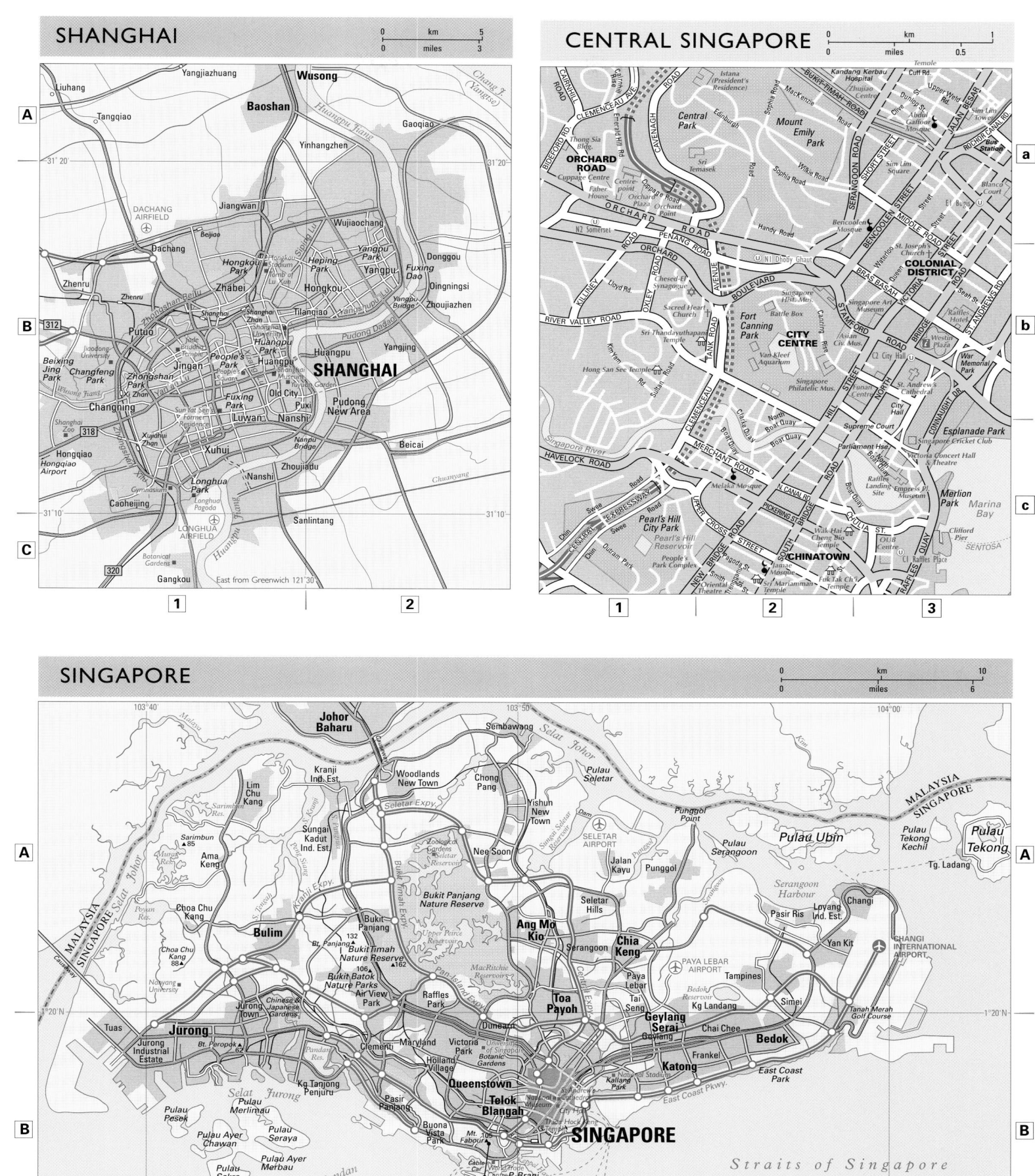

SHANGHAI

km 5 / miles 3

A
Liuhang
Yangjiazhuang
Wusong
Tangqiao
Baoshan
Gaoqiao
31°20'
Yinhangzhen
Huangpu Jiang
Chang J. (Yangtse)
DACHANG AIRFIELD
Jiangwan
Dachang
Wujiaochang
Donggou
Beijiao
Fuxing Dao
Qingningsi
Zhenru
Heping Park
Yangpu Park
Yangpu
Zhenru Beilu
Hongkou Park
Zhabei
Hongkou
Yangpu Bridge
Zhoujiazhen
312
Putuo
Huangpu Park
Shanghai
Tilanqiao
Yangjing
Beixing Jing Park
Changfeng Park
Jingan
People's Park
Huangpu
Zhongshan Park
Xi Zhan
Yuyuan Garden
Old City
Pudong New Area
Changning
Fuxing Park
Puxi
Luwan
Nanshi
Hongqiao
Hongqiao Airport
Former Residence
Xuhui
Nanpu Bridge
Beicai
318
Longhua Park
Nanshi
Zhoujiadu
Chuanyang
31°10'
Caoheijing
Longhua Pagoda
Sanlintang
LONGHUA AIRFIELD
C
Botanical Gardens
320
Gangkou
Huangpu Jiang
East from Greenwich 121°30'

1   2

CENTRAL SINGAPORE

km 1 / miles 0.5

Temple
CAIRNHILL ROAD
CLEMENCEAU AVE.
Istana (President's Residence)
Kandang Kerbau Hospital
Cuff Rd.
Upper Weld Rd.
BUKIT TIMAH ROAD
ALJAN BESAR
a
BIDEFORD RD
Central Park
Edinburgh
Sophia Road
MacKenzie
SERANGOON ROAD
SHORTT STREET
MIDDLE ROAD
ROCHOR CANAL RD
Bus Station
ORCHARD ROAD
Sri Temasek
Mount Emily Park
Wilkie Road
Sim Lim Square
Abdul Gaffoor Mosque
Cuppage Centre
Faber House
Orchard Point
Handy Road
Bencoolen Mosque
St. Joseph's Church
COLONIAL DISTRICT
ORCHARD ROAD
PENANG ROAD
Dhoby Ghaut
Waterloo St
BRAS BASAH
VICTORIA
Raffles Hotel
ST ANDREW'S RD
b
KILLINEY
Chesed-El Synagogue
Somerset
BOULEVARD
Singapore Hist. Mus.
Battle Box
ROAD
RIVER VALLEY ROAD
OXLEY
Sacred Heart Church
Fort Canning Park
Van Kleef Aquarium
CLEMENCEAU
TANK ROAD
Sri Thandayuthapani Temple
HILL STREET
STAMFORD
City Hall
St. Andrew's Cathedral
War Memorial Park
Hong San See Temple
Singapore Philatelic Mus.
NORTH
Clarke Quay
Supreme Court
Esplanade Park
Singapore Cricket Club
c
Singapore River
HAVELOCK ROAD
MERCHANT ROAD
Boat Quay
Parliament Hse.
CONNAUGHT DR
Victoria Concert Hall & Theatre
UPPER CROSS STREET
Melaka Mosque
PICKERING ST
SOUTH CANAL RD
Empress Pl. Museum
Merlion Park
Marina Bay
CENTRAL EXPRESSWAY
Pearl's Hill City Park
Pearl's Hill Reservoir
NEW BRIDGE
CHULIA
RAFFLES QUAY
Clifford Pier
SENTOSA
People's Park Complex
Jamae Mosque
CHINATOWN
Sri Mariamman Temple
Fuk Tak Ch'i Temple

1   2   3

SINGAPORE

km 10 / miles 6

103°40'
Johor Baharu
Sembawang
Selat Johor
103°50'
104°00'
MALAYSIA SINGAPORE
A
Kranji Ind. Est.
Woodlands New Town
Chong Pang
Pulau Seletar
Punggol Point
Pulau Ubin
Pulau Tekong Kechil
Pulau Tekong
Lim Chu Kang
Sarimbun Res.
Yishun New Town
SELETAR AIRPORT
Pulau Serangoon
Tg. Ladang
MALAYSIA SINGAPORE
Sarimbun 85
Sungei Kadut Ind. Est.
Zoological Gardens
Nee Soon
Jalan Kayu
Punggol
Serangoon Harbour
Changi
Ama Keng
Choa Chu Kang
Bukit Panjang Nature Reserve
Seletar Hills
Pasir Ris
Loyang Ind. Est.
CHANGI INTERNATIONAL AIRPORT
Bukit Panjang
132 Bt. Panjang
Upper Peirce Reservoir
Ang Mo Kio
Serangoon
Chia Keng
Yan Kit
1°20'N
Bulim
Bukit Timah Nature Reserve 162
106 Bukit Batok Nature Parks
MacRitchie Reservoir
PAYA LEBAR AIRPORT
Tampines
Choa Chu Kang 88
Air View Park
Raffles Park
Paya Lebar
Bedok Reservoir
Kg Landang
Simei
Tanah Merah Golf Course
Nanyang University
Chinese & Japanese Gardens
Jurong Town
Toa Payoh
Tai Seng
1°20'N
Jurong
Dunearn
Geylang Serai
Chai Chee
Jurong Industrial Estate
Bt. Peropok 62
Clementi
Maryland
Victoria Park
Geylang
Bedok
Tuas
Pandan Res.
Holland Village
Botanic Gardens
Katong
Frankel
East Coast Park
Pulau Pesek
Pasir Panjang
Queenstown
Kallang Park
East Coast Pkwy.
B
Pulau Merlimau
Telok Blangah
National Stadium
Pulau Ayer Chawan
Buona Vista Park
Mt. Faber 105
SINGAPORE
Straits of Singapore
Pulau Seraya
Selat Jurong
Kg Tanjong Penjuru
Cable Car
World Trade Centre
P. Brani
Pulau Ayer Merbau
Pulau Sakra
Selat Pandan
Selat Sinki
Sentosa
Pulau Bukum
East from Greenwich
103°40'   103°50'   104°00'

1   2   3   4

STOCKHOLM

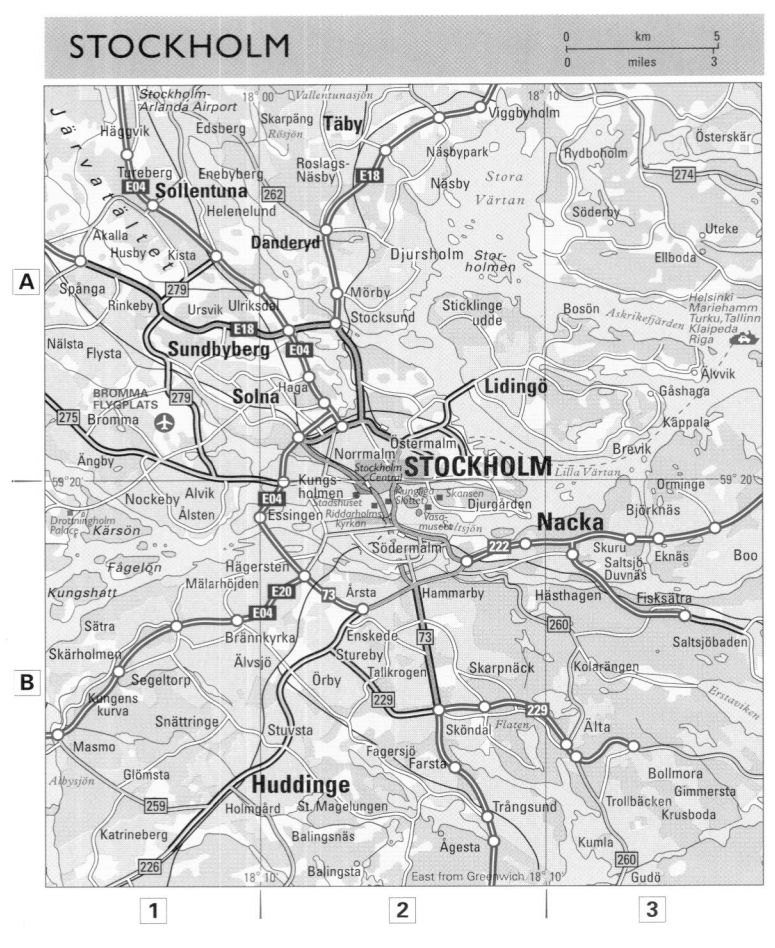

CENTRAL STOCKHOLM

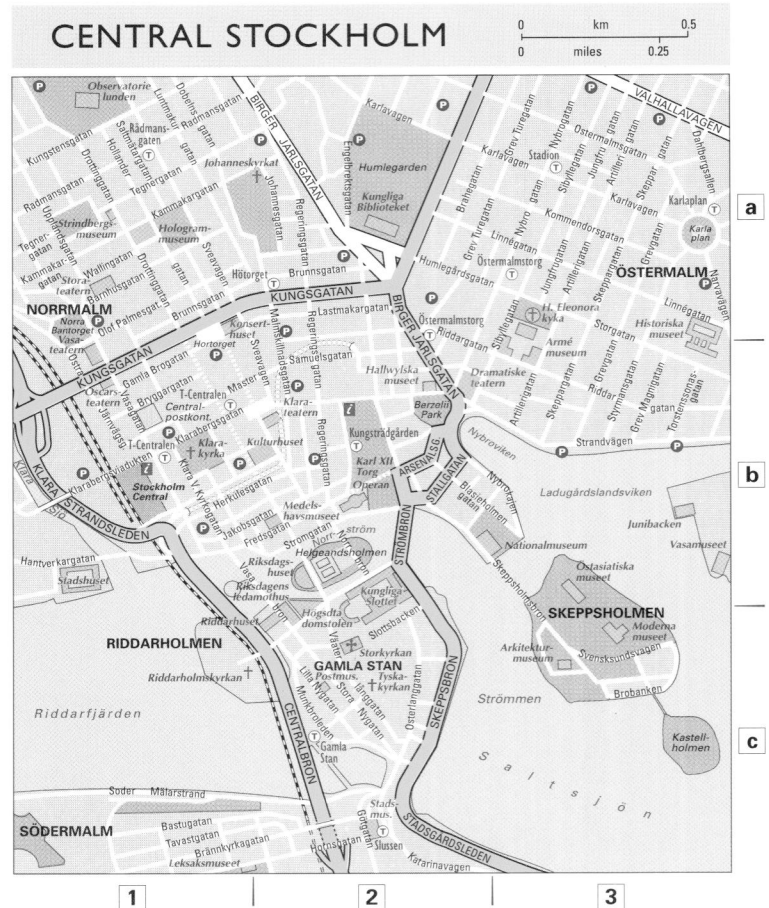

SYDNEY

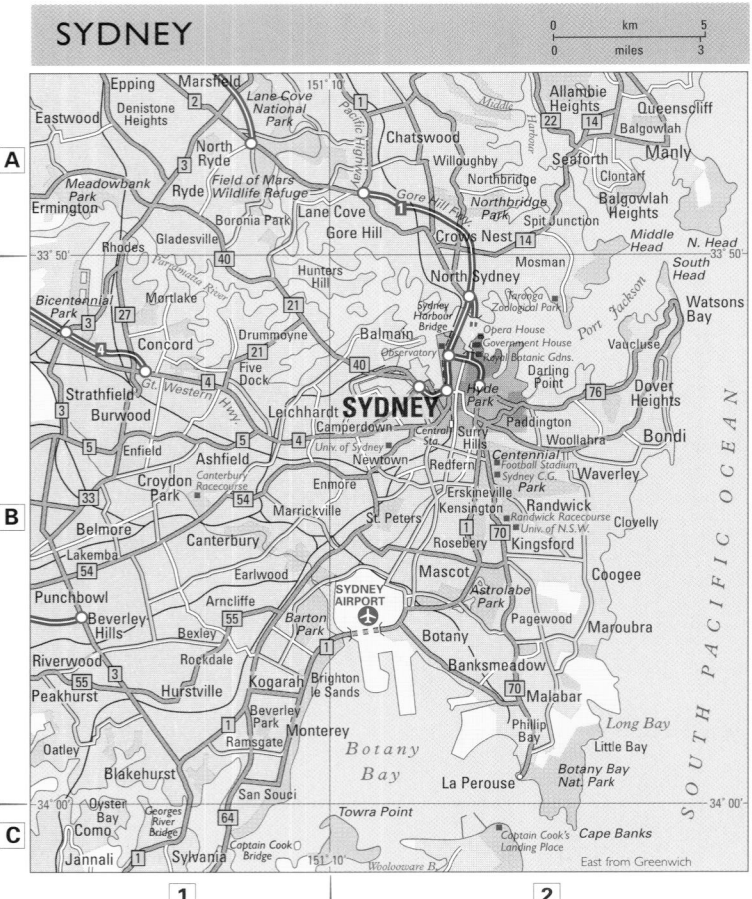

CENTRAL SYDNEY

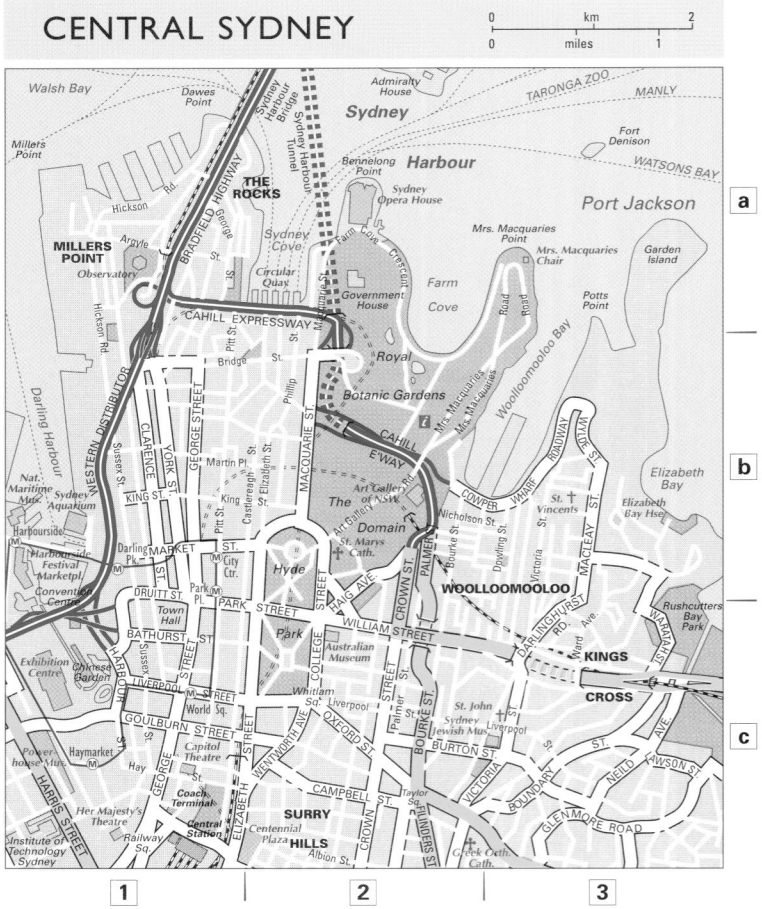

TOKYO

km 5
miles 3

A
B

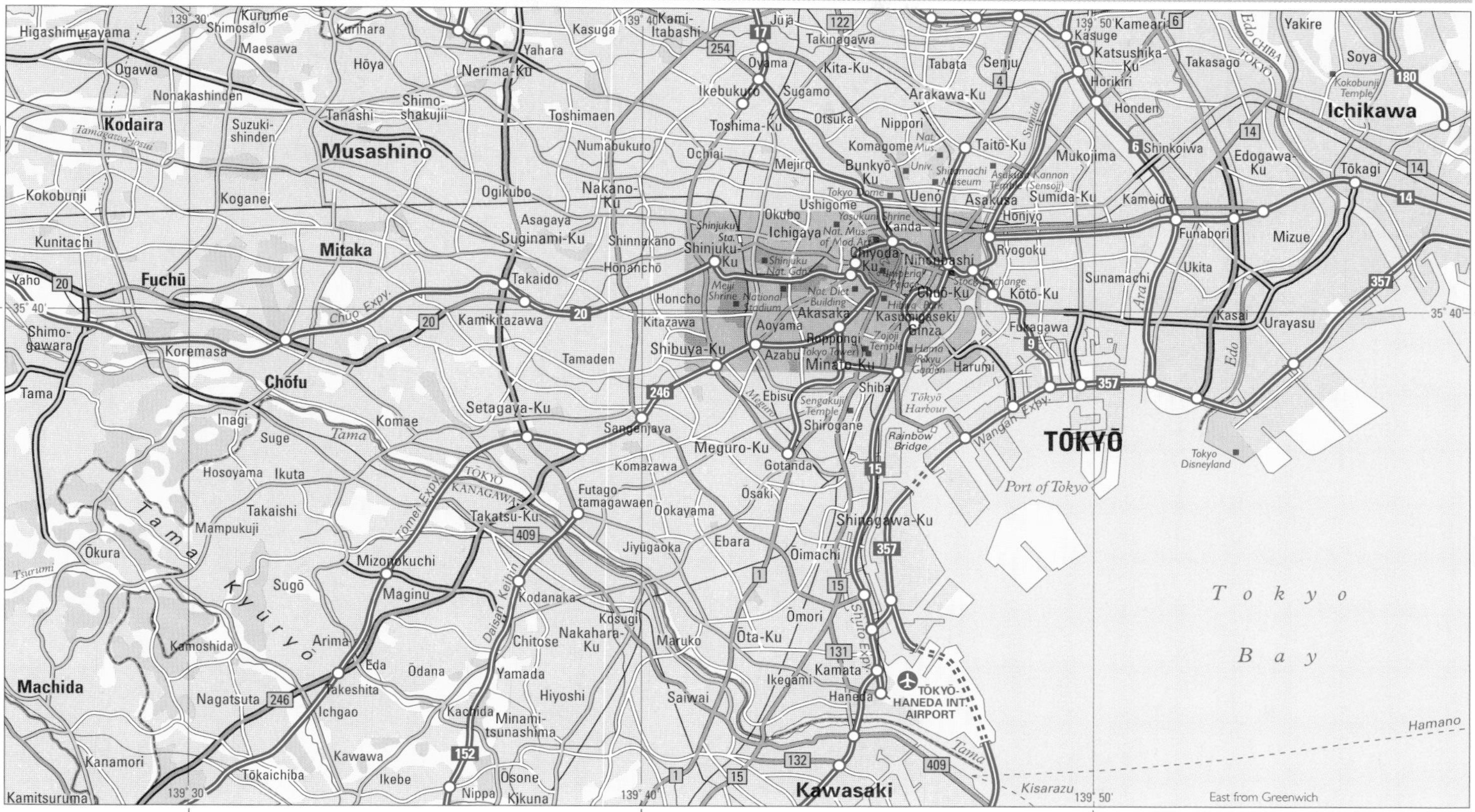

Higashimurayama Kurume Kamigome Kami-Itabashi Takinogawa Kameari Soya
Shimosalo Kunihara Kasuga Kita-Ku Tabata Senju Kasuge Takasago Yakire
Ogawa Nonakashinden Yahara Oyama Ikebukuro Sugamo Arakawa-Ku Horikiri Honden Kokobunji Temple
Hōya Toshimaen Toshima-Ku Otsuka Nippori Shinkoiwa Funabori
Kodaira Suzuki-shinden Tanashi Shimo-shakujii Numabukuro Ochiai Mejiro Komagome Mus. Taitō-Ku Mukōjima Edogawa-Ku Tōkagi
Musashino Nakano-Ku Bunkyō-Ku Ueno Asakusa Honjo Sumida-Ku
Kokunji Koganei Ogikubo Asagaya Shinnakano Shinjuku Okubo Ushigome Kanda Nihonbashi Ryogoku Mizue
Kunitachi Mitaka Suginami-Ku Honanchō Akasaka Chūō-Ku Kōtō-Ku Ukita 357
Yaho Fuchū Takaido Honcho Kamikitazawa Aoyama Roppongi Ginza Fukagawa Kasai Urayasu
Shimo-gawara Koremasa Kitazawa Shibuya-Ku Azabu Minato-Ku Harumi
Chōfu Tamaden Ebisu Shiba Tōkyō Harbour TŌKYŌ Tokyo Disneyland
Tama Inagi Suge Setagaya-Ku Sangenjaya Sengakuji Temple Shirogane Rainbow Bridge Port of Tokyo
Komae Meguro-Ku Gotanda
Hosoyama Ikuta Futago-tamagawaen Komazawa Shinagawa-Ku
Takaishi Takatsu-Ku Ookayama Ebara Ōimachi
Mampukuji Mizonokuchi Jiyūgaoka Ōmori
Ōkura Sugō Maginu Kodanaka Ōta-Ku
Kamoshida Arima Chitose Nakahara-Ku Maruko Kamata
Machida Eda Ōdana Yamada Hiyoshi Ikegami Haneda TŌKYŌ-HANEDA INT. AIRPORT
Nagatsuta Takeshita Kachida Ichigao Minami-tsunashima Saiwai
Kanamori Kawana Ikebe Ōsone Kawasaki Kisarazu Hamano
Kamitsuruma Tōkaichiba Nippa Kikuna

Kodaira Kanagawa Kyūryō Tama East from Greenwich

1 2 3 4

CENTRAL TOKYO

km 1
miles 0.5

a
b
c

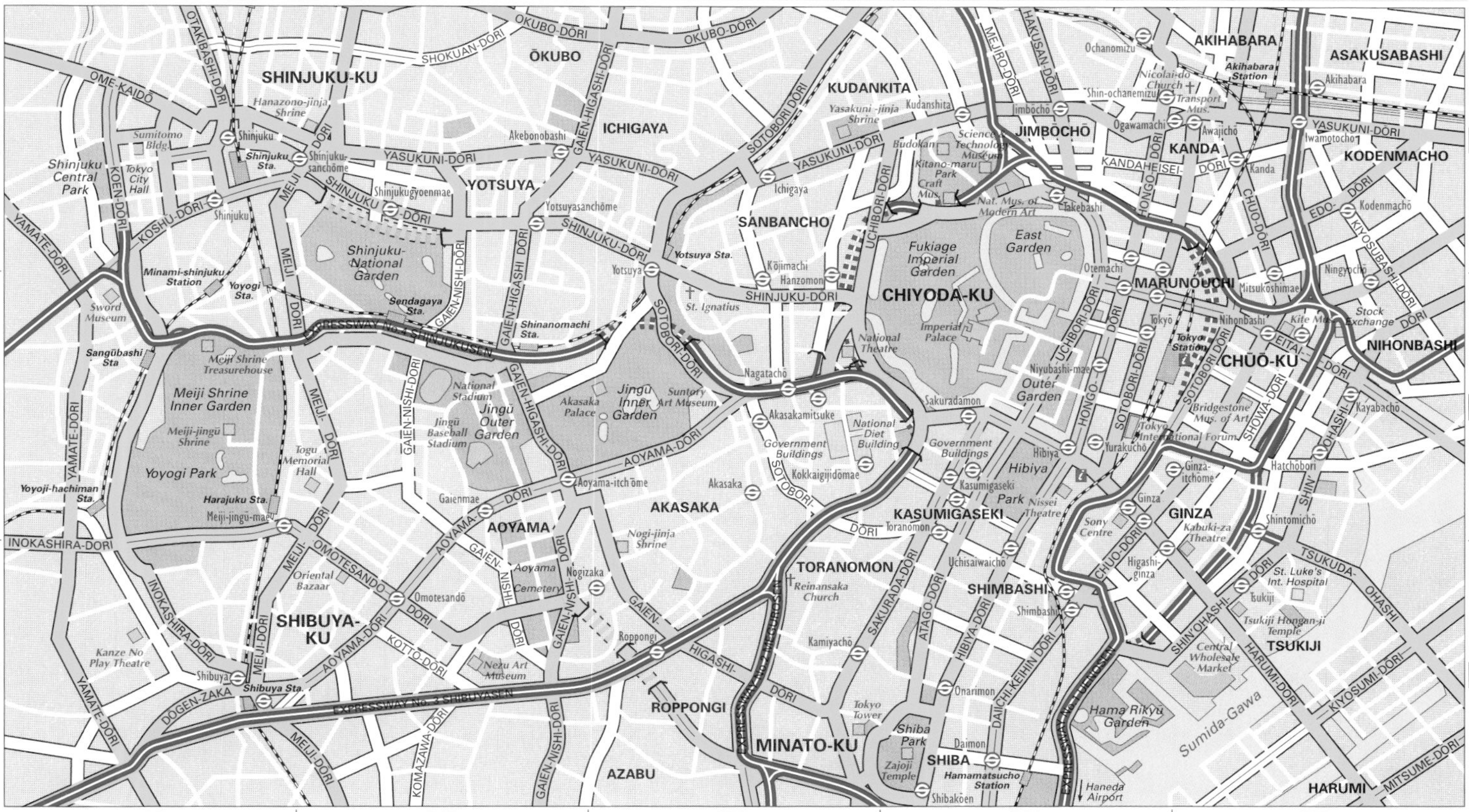

ŌKUBO AKIHABARA ASAKUSABASHI
SHINJUKU-KU KUDANKITA Ochanomizu Akihabara Station
ICHIGAYA Yasukuni-jinja Shrine Kudanshita Nicolai-do Church KANDA KODENMACHO
Hanazono-jinja Shrine Akebonobashi JIMBOCHO Iwatocho
Sumitomo Bldg. Shinjuku YASUKUNI-DORI Budokan Science Museum
Shinjuku Central Park Tokyo City Hall Shinjuku Sta. Shinjuku-sanchōme Ichigaya KANDAHEISEI KODENMACHO
YOTSUYA SANBANCHO Nat. Mus. of Modern Art Takebashi MARUNOUCHI Stock Exchange
Shinjuku-gyoenmae Yotsuya-sanchōme Fukiage Imperial Garden East Garden NIHONBASHI
Minami-shinjuku Station Shinjuku-National Garden Yotsuya Sta. Kōjimachi Hanzōmon CHIYODA-KU Ōtemachi Nihonbashi
Sword Museum Yoyogi Sta. Sendagaya Sta. Shinanomachi Sta. Nagatachō Imperial Palace Tokyo Station CHŪO-KU
Sangūbashi Sta. Meiji Shrine Treasurehouse National Stadium National Theatre Niyubashi-mae Outer Garden Kayabacho
Meiji Shrine Inner Garden Jingū Baseball Stadium Jingū Inner Garden Suntory Art Museum National Diet Building Hibiya Tokyo International Forum Hatchobori
Jingū Outer Garden Akasaka Palace Government Buildings Government Buildings Sakuradamon Yurakucho Bridgestone Mus. of Art
Meiji-jingū Shrine Akasakamitsuke Hibiya Park Ginza-itchome Takaracho
Togu Memorial Hall Gaienmae Aoyama-itchōme Kasumigaseki Nissei Theatre GINZA TSUKUDA
Yoyogi Park Harajuku Sta.   AKASAKA Kokkaigijidomae KASUMIGASEKI Sony Centre Kabuki-za Theatre
Meiji-jingū-mae Aoyama AOYAMA Kokkai Higashi-Ginza St. Luke's Int. Hospital TSUKIJI
Oriental Bazaar Omotesandō Nogi-jinja Shrine TORANOMON Toranomon Shintomicho
Kanze No Play Theatre Omotesando SHIBUYA-KU Aoyama Cemetery Nogizaka Reinanzaka Church SHIMBASHI Central Wholesale Market
Shibuya Sta. Netu Art Museum Roppongi Kamiyachō Shimbashi Tsukiji Hongan-ji Temple
Shibuya ROPPONGI Tokyo Tower Onarimon Hama Rikyū Garden HARUMI
AZABU MINATO-KU Shiba Park Daimon
Zōjoji Temple SHIBA Hamamatsucho Station Haneda Airport
Shibakōen

COPYRIGHT GEORGE PHILIP LTD

1 2 3 4 5

TEHRAN

0 km 5
0 miles 3

Reshteh-ye Kūhhā-ye Alborz
(Elburz Mts.)

Towchāl Cable Car
Darakeh
Darband
Evin
Niāvarān
Sowhānak
Tajrish
Darus
Lavīzān
Sa'ādatābād
Pārk-e Mellat
International Trade Fair
Qolhak
Hesārak
Shahrak-e Qods (Gharb)
Pūnak
Vanak
Dāvūdīyeh
Qāsemābād
Tehrān Pārs
Bāgh-e Feyż
Yūsofābād
Hasanābād
Amīrābād
Nārmak
Karaj Expwy
Jamshīdīyeh
University
Farahābād
Tehran West Bus Terminal
Freedom Tower
Jey
TEHRĀN
Carpet Mus.
MEHRĀBĀD AIRPORT
National Mus. of Iran
Golestan Palace
Ethnographical Mus.
Akbarābād
Shah Mosque
Bāzār
Dūlāb
Qasr-e Fīrūzeh
Tehran Station
Javādīyeh
Qal'eh Morghī
Tehran South Bus Terminal
Afsarīyeh
Vasfenārd
Yaftābād
N'ematābād
Dowlatābād
Shahrak-e Golshahr
Azādegān Expwy
Dom Expwy
Shahr-e Rey (Rey)
Mesgarābād
East from Greenwich

TIANJIN

0 km 5
0 miles 3

Xiaodian
Da Yunhe
Beicang
Dabizhuang
Yixingbu
Xinkai He
Hanjiashu
Zhangguizhuang
Dingzigu
Xigu Park
Ziya He
Tianjin Xi Zhan (Railway Station)
Xigu
Hebei
Nandian
104
Hongqiao
The Sparks
Dabei (Grand Mercy) Temple
Old Chinese District
Ximenwai
Dongmenwai
Tianjin Zhan (Railway Station)
Dongjuzi
Zhangguizhuang
Da Yunhe (Grand Canal)
Nanmenwai
Hedong
TIANJIN (TIENTSIN)
Heping
Antiques Market
Dazhigu
Tianjin University
Nankai University
Nankai
Tiaoyuan Pavilion
Balitai
Xinanlou
Shuishang Park
Natural History Museum
Jianshan Park
Aquatic Park
Renmin Park
Hexi
Hai He
Liqizhuang
Huidui
105
205
East from Greenwich 117°10'

TORONTO

0 km 5
0 miles 3

Fairport
Metro Toronto Zoo
Markham
Thornhill
407
Brown
West Rouge
Rouge Hill
Concord
Newtonbrook
Agincourt
Malvern
Highland Creek
Port Union
Pine Grove
27
Edgeley
404
YORK TORONTO
Woodbridge
Fisherville
Willowdale
11
Northmount
48
York University
North York
Lansing
401
York Mills
Woburn
West Hill
Humber Summit
Black Creek Pioneer Village
Wexford
Bendale
Beaumonte Heights
Armour Heights
Don Mills
Scarborough
Highland Creek
Thistletown
400
DOWNSVIEW AIRPORT
Cliffside
Kipling Heights
Downsview
Lawrence Heights
Wilket Creek Park
Ontario Science Centre
427
Rexdale
Humberlea
401
Danforth
Malton
Woodbine Race Track
Weston
11
Leaside
Thorncliffe
2
409
Forest Hill
Dentonia Park
Birch Cliff
401
Humber Valley Village
York
Casa Loma
East York
5
TORONTO INTERNATIONAL AIRPORT (LESTER B. PEARSON)
Mount Dennis
Kew Gardens
Hanlon
Lambton Mills
Swansea
University of Toronto
Parliament Buildings
City Hall
Riverdale Park
Etobicoke
Islington
Kingsway
High Park
CN Tower & SkyDome
Old Fort York
TORONTO
427
Markland Wood
Humber Bay
Parkdale
Exhibition Place
TORONTO CITY CENTRE AIRPORT
Union Sta.
Gardiner Expwy
Burnhamthorpe
YORK
Summerville
Ontario Place
Toronto Harbour
LAKE ONTARIO
Mimico
Way
Elizabeth
Toronto Islands
Island Park
New Toronto
Gibraltar Point
2
Cooksville
Mississauga
Long Branch
West from Greenwich

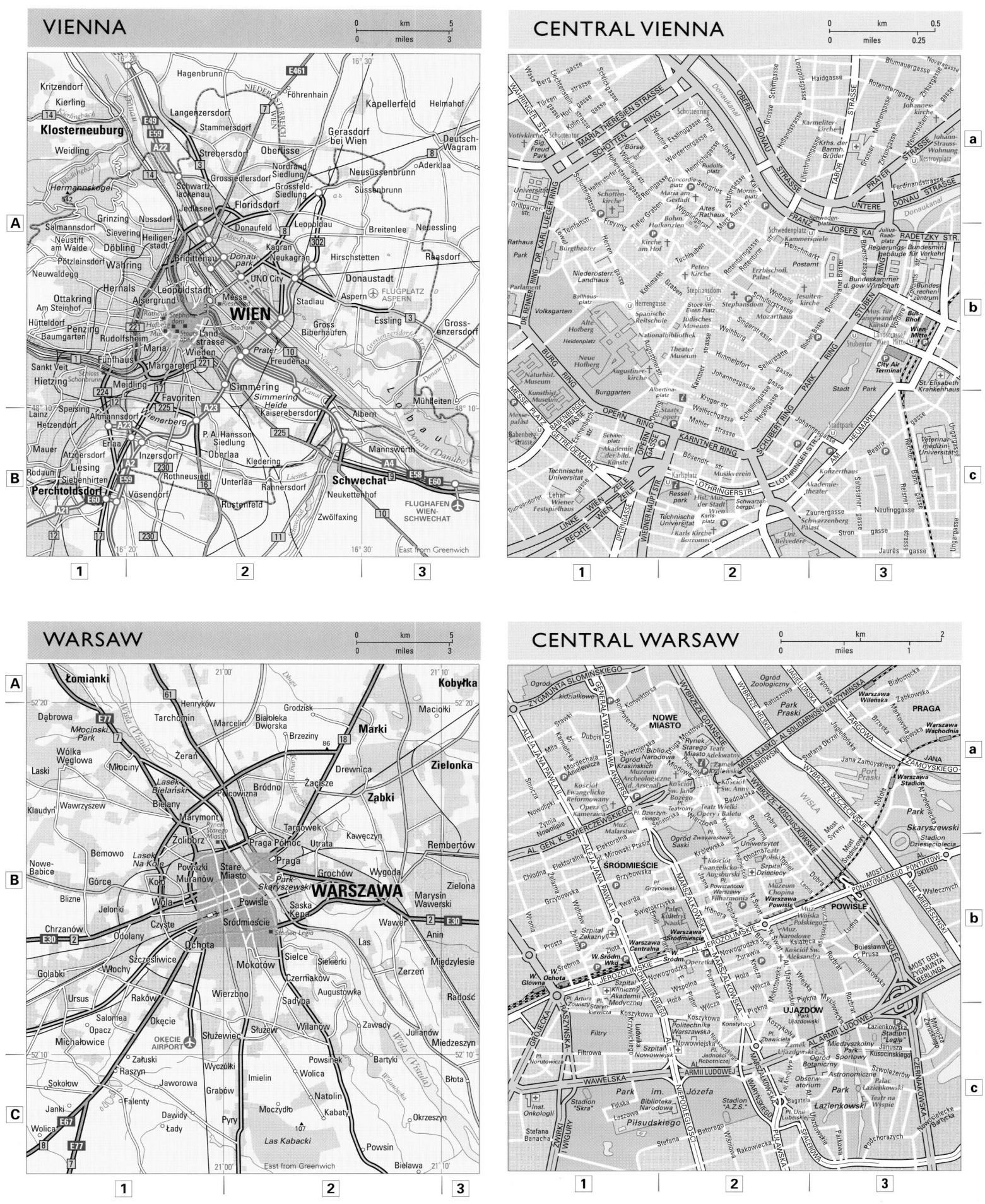

WASHINGTON

0 km 5
0 miles 3

CENTRAL WASHINGTON

0 km 1
0 miles 0.5

WELLINGTON

0 km 5
0 miles 3

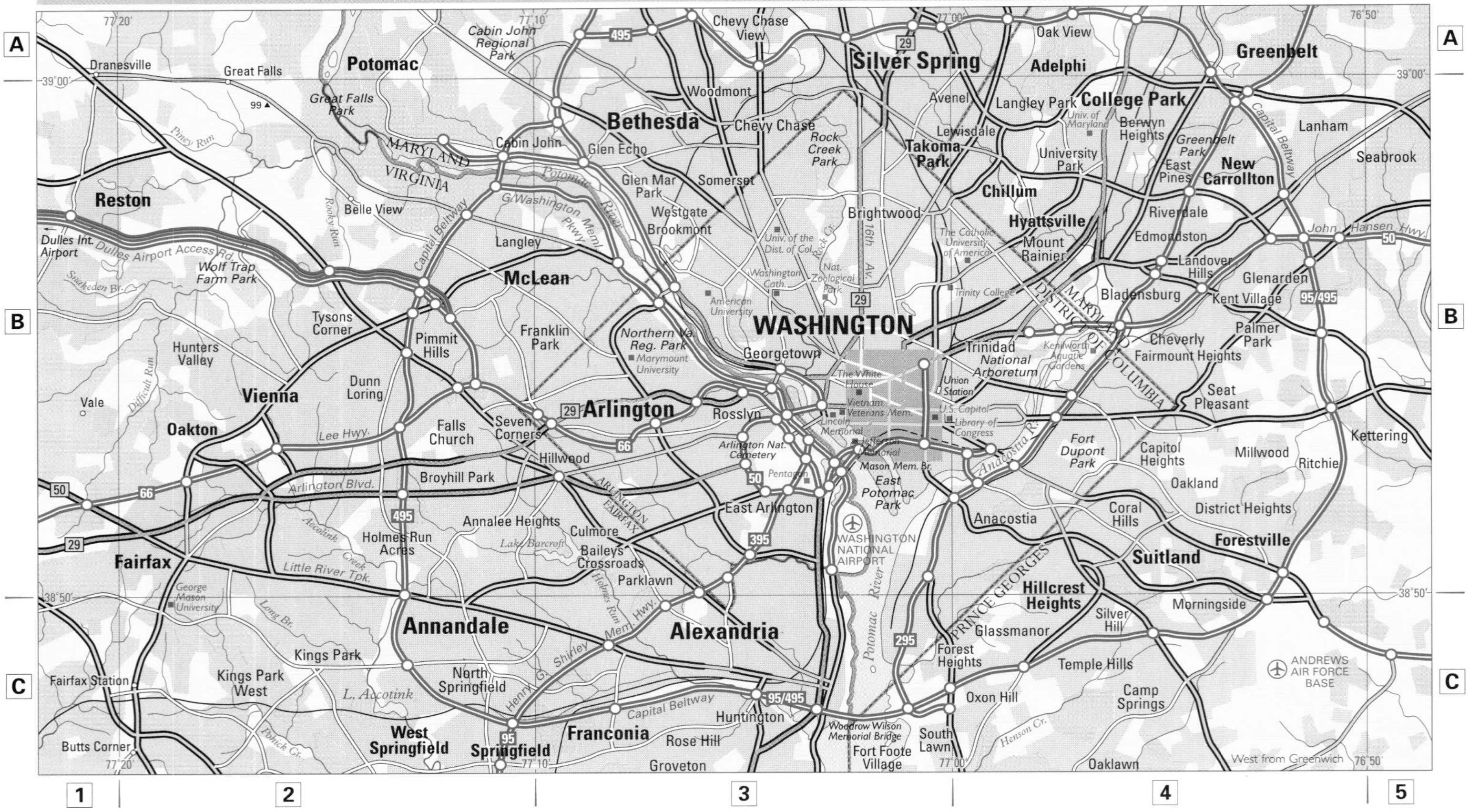

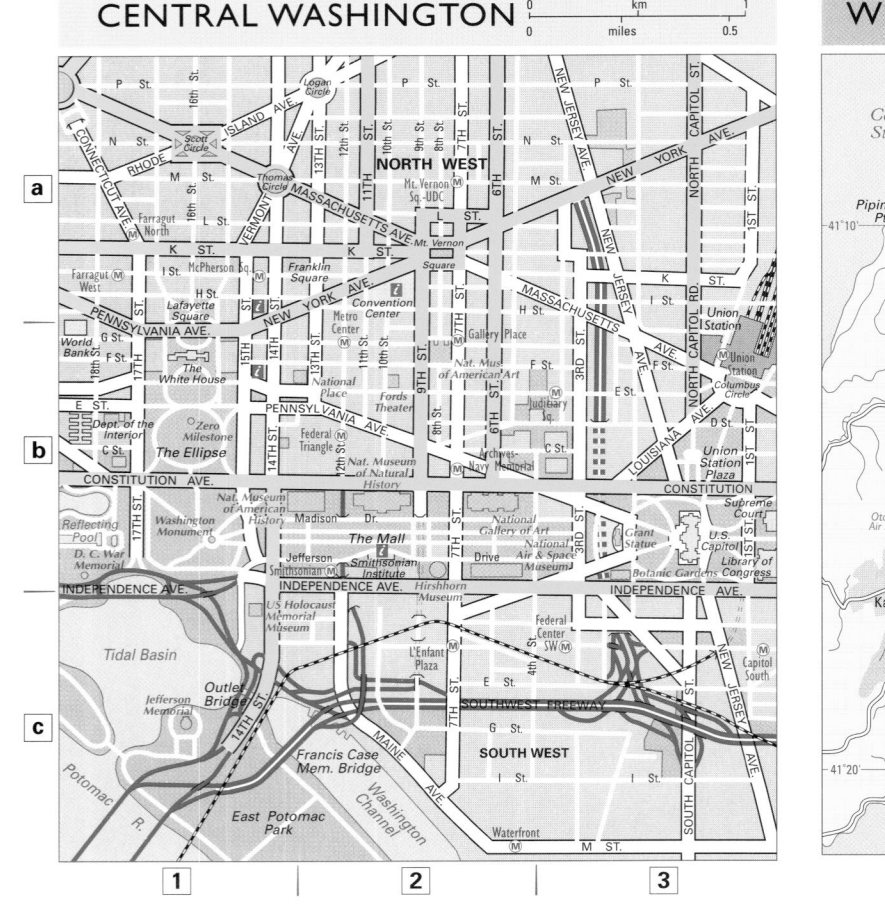

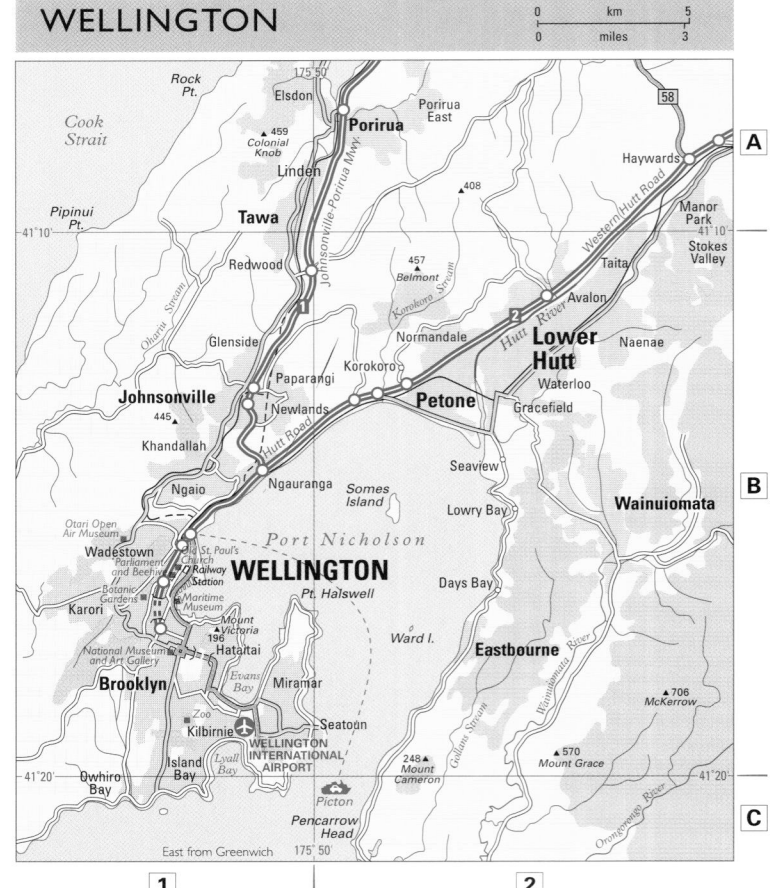

INDEX TO CITY MAPS

The index contains the names of all the principal places and features shown on the City Maps. Each name is followed by an additional entry in italics giving the name of the City Map within which it is located.

The number in bold type which follows each name refers to the number of the City Map page where that feature or place will be found.

The letter and figure which are immediately after the page number give the grid square on the map within which the feature or place is situated. The letter represents the latitude and the figure the longitude. Upper case letters refer to the City Maps, lower case letters to the Central Area Maps. The full geographic reference is provided in the border of the City Maps.

The location given is the centre of the city, suburb or feature and is not necessarily the name. Rivers, canals and roads are indexed to their name. Rivers carry the symbol → after their name.

An explanation of the alphabetical order rules and a list of the abbreviations used are to be found at the beginning of the World Map Index.

A

Aalām, *Baghdad* **3** B2
Aalsmeer, *Amsterdam* **2** B1
Abbey Wood, *London* **15** B4
Abcoude, *Amsterdam* **2** B2
Âbdin, *Cairo* **7** A2
Abeno, *Osaka* **22** B4
Aberdeen, *Hong Kong* **12** B2
Aberdour, *Edinburgh* **11** A2
Aberdour Castle, *Edinburgh* **11** A2
Abfanggraben →, *Munich* **20** A3
Ablon-sur-Seine, *Paris* **23** B3
Abord-à-Plouffe, *Montreal* **19** A1
Abramtsevo, *Moscow* **19** B4
Abu Dis, *Jerusalem* **13** B2
Abû en Numrus, *Cairo* **7** B2
Abu Ghosh, *Jerusalem* **13** B1
Acacias, *Madrid* **17** c2
Acassuso, *Buenos Aires* **7** A1
Accotink Cr. →, *Washington* **32** B2
Acheres, *Paris* **23** A1
Acília, *Rome* **25** C1
Aclimação, *São Paulo* **26** B2
Acton, *London* **15** A2
Açúcar, Pão de, *Rio de Janeiro* **24** B2
Ada Beja, *Lisbon* **14** A1
Adams Park, *Atlanta* **3** B2
Adams Shore, *Boston* **6** B4
Addiscombe, *London* **15** B3
Adelphi, *Washington* **32** A4
Aderklaa, *Vienna* **31** A3
Admiralteyskaya Storona, *St. Petersburg* **26** B2
Áffori, *Milan* **18** A2
Aflandshage, *Copenhagen* **10** B3
Afsarīyeh, *Tehran* **30** B2
Agboyi Cr. →, *Lagos* **14** A2
Ågerup, *Copenhagen* **10** A1
Ågesta, *Stockholm* **28** B2
Agincourt, *Toronto* **30** A3
Agora, Arhéa, *Athens* **2** c1
Agra Canal, *Delhi* **10** B2
Agricola Oriental, *Mexico City* **18** B2
Agua Espraiada →, *São Paulo* **26** B2
Agualva-Cacem, *Lisbon* **14** A1
Agustino, Cerro El, *Lima* **16** B2
Ahrensfelde, *Berlin* **5** A4
Ahuntsic, *Montreal* **19** A1
Ai →, *Osaka* **22** A4
Aigremont, *Paris* **23** A1
Air View Park, *Singapore* **27** A2
Airport West, *Melbourne* **17** A1
Aiyaleo, *Athens* **2** B2
Aiyáleos, Óros, *Athens* **2** B1
Ajegunle, *Lagos* **14** B2
Aji, *Osaka* **22** A3
Ajuda, *Lisbon* **14** A1
Akalla, *Stockholm* **28** A1
Akasaka, *Tokyo* **29** b3
Akbarābād, *Tehran* **30** A2
Akershus Slott, *Oslo* **22** A3
Akihabara, *Tokyo* **29** a5
Akrópolis, *Athens* **2** c2
Al 'Azamiyah, *Baghdad* **3** A2
Al Quds = Jerusalem, *Jerusalem* **13** B2
Alaguntan, *Lagos* **14** B2
Alameda, *San Francisco* **25** B3
Alameda, Parque, *Mexico City* **18** b2
Alameda Memorial State Beach Park, *San Francisco* **25** B3
Albern, *Vienna* **31** B2
Albert Park, *Melbourne* **17** B1
Alberton, *Johannesburg* **13** B2
Albertslund, *Copenhagen* **10** B2
Albysjön, *Stockholm* **28** B1
Alcantara, *Lisbon* **14** A1
Alcatraz I., *San Francisco* **25** B2
Alcobendas, *Madrid* **17** A2
Alcorcón, *Madrid* **17** B1
Aldershof, *Berlin* **5** B4
Aldo Bonzi, *Buenos Aires* **7** C1
Aleksandrovskoye, *St. Petersburg* **26** B2
Alexander Nevsky Abbey, *St. Petersburg* **26** B2
Alexander Soutzos Moussío, *Athens* **2** b3
Alexandra, *Johannesburg* **13** A2
Alexandra, *Singapore* **27** B2
Alexandria, *Washington* **32** C3
Alfama, *Lisbon* **14** c3
Alfortville, *Paris* **23** B3
Algés, *Lisbon* **14** A1
Alhambra, *Los Angeles* **16** B4
Alibey →, *Istanbul* **12** B1
Alibey Barajı, *Istanbul* **12** B1
Alibeyköy, *Istanbul* **12** B1
Alimos, *Athens* **2** B2
Alipur, *Calcutta* **8** B1
Allach, *Munich* **20** A1
Allambie Heights, *Sydney* **28** A2
Allard Pierson Museum, *Amsterdam* **2** b2
Allermuir Hill, *Edinburgh* **11** B2
Allerton, Pt., *Boston* **6** B4
Allston, *Boston* **6** A3
Almada, *Lisbon* **14** A2
Almagro, *Buenos Aires* **7** B2
Almargem do Bispo, *Lisbon* **14** A1
Almazovo, *Moscow* **19** A6
Almirante G. Brown, Parque, *Buenos Aires* **7** C2
Almon, *Jerusalem* **13** B2
Almond →, *Edinburgh* **11** B2
Alnabru, *Oslo* **22** A4
Alnsjøen, *Oslo* **22** A4
Alperton, *London* **15** A2
Alpine, *New York* **21** A2
Alrode, *Johannesburg* **13** B2
Alsemerg, *Brussels* **6** B1
Alsergrund, *Vienna* **31** A2
Alsip, *Chicago* **9** C2
Ålsten, *Stockholm* **28** B1
Älta, *Stockholm* **28** B3
Altadena, *Los Angeles* **16** A4
Alte-Donau →, *Vienna* **31** A2
Alte Hofburg, *Vienna* **31** b1
Alter Finkenkrug, *Berlin* **5** A1
Altes Rathaus, *Munich* **20** b3
Altglienicke, *Berlin* **5** B4
Altlandsberg, *Berlin* **5** A5
Altlandsberg Nord, *Berlin* **5** A5
Altmannsdorf, *Vienna* **31** B1
Alto da Moóca, *São Paulo* **26** B2
Alto do Pina, *Lisbon* **14** A2
Altona, *Melbourne* **17** B1
Alvaro Obregon, *Mexico City* **18** B1
Alvik, *Stockholm* **28** B1
Älvsjo, *Stockholm* **28** B2
Älvvik, *Stockholm* **28** A3
Am Hasenbergl, *Munich* **20** A2
Am Steinhof, *Vienna* **31** A1
Am Wald, *Munich* **20** B2
Ama Keng, *Singapore* **27** A2
Amadora, *Lisbon* **14** A1
Amagasaki, *Osaka* **22** A3
Amager, *Copenhagen* **10** B3
Amāl Qādisiya, *Baghdad* **3** B2
Amalienborg, *Copenhagen* **10** b3
Amata, *Milan* **18** A1
Ameixoeira, *Lisbon* **14** A2
América, *São Paulo* **26** B1
Amin, *Baghdad* **3** B2
Aminadov, *Jerusalem* **13** B1
Aminyevo, *Moscow* **19** B2
Amīrābād, *Tehran* **30** A2
Amora, *Lisbon* **14** B2
Amoreira, *Lisbon* **14** A1
Ampelokipi, *Athens* **2** B2
Amper →, *Munich* **20** A1
Amstel, *Amsterdam* **2** b2
Amstel →, *Amsterdam* **2** c2
Amstel-Drecht-Kanaal, *Amsterdam* **2** B2
Amstel Station, *Amsterdam* **2** c3
Amstelhof, *Amsterdam* **2** b2
Amstelveen, *Amsterdam* **2** B2
Amsterdam, *Amsterdam* **2** A2
Amsterdam-Rijnkanaal, *Amsterdam* **2** B3
Amsterdam Zoo, *Amsterdam* **2** b3
Amsterdam Zuidoost, *Amsterdam* **2** B2
Amsterdamse Bos, *Amsterdam* **2** B1
Anacostia, *Washington* **32** B4
Anadoluhisarı, *Istanbul* **12** B2
Anadolukavağı, *Istanbul* **12** A2
Anata, *Jerusalem* **13** B2
Ancol, *Jakarta* **13** A1
'Andalus, *Baghdad* **3** B1
Andarai, *Rio de Janeiro* **24** B1
Anderlecht, *Brussels* **6** A1
Anderson Park, *Atlanta* **3** B2
Andingmen, *Beijing* **4** B2
Andrews Air Force Base, *Washington* **32** C4
Ang Mo Kio, *Singapore* **27** A3
Ängby, *Stockholm* **28** A1
Angel I., *San Francisco* **25** A2
Angel Island State Park, *San Francisco* **25** A2
Angke, Kali →, *Jakarta* **13** A1
Angyalföld, *Budapest* **7** A2
Anik, *Mumbai* **20** A2
Anin, *Warsaw* **31** B2
Anjou, *Montreal* **19** A2
Annalee Heights, *Washington* **32** B2
Annandale, *Washington* **32** C2
Anne Frankhuis, *Amsterdam* **2** a1
Antony, *Paris* **23** B2
Anyangch'on, *Seoul* **26** C1
Aoyama, *Tokyo* **29** b2
Ap Lei Chau, *Hong Kong* **12** B1
Apapa, *Lagos* **14** B2
Apelacão, *Lisbon* **14** A2
Apterkarskiy Ostrov, *St. Petersburg* **26** B2
Ar Kazimiyah, *Baghdad* **3** B1
Ara →, *Tokyo* **29** A4
Arakawa-Ku, *Tokyo* **29** A3
Arany-hegyi-patak →, *Budapest* **7** A2
Aravaca, *Madrid* **17** B1
Arbataash, *Baghdad* **3** A1
Arc de Triomphe, *Paris* **23** a2
Arcadia, *Los Angeles* **16** B4
Arceuil, *Paris* **23** B2
Arco Plaza, *Los Angeles* **16** b1
Arese, *Milan* **18** A1
Arganzuela, *Madrid* **17** B1
Argenteuil, *Paris* **23** A2
Argonne Forest, *Chicago* **9** C1
Argüelles, *Madrid* **17** a1
Arima, *Osaka* **22** A2
Arima, *Tokyo* **29** B2
Ários Págos, *Athens* **2** c1
Arkhangelyskoye, *Moscow* **19** B1
Arlington, *Boston* **6** A2
Arlington, *Washington* **32** B3
Arlington Heights, *Boston* **6** A2
Arlington Nat. Cemetery, *Washington* **32** B3
Armação, *Rio de Janeiro* **24** B2
Armadale, *Melbourne* **17** B2
Armenian Quarter, *Jerusalem* **13** b3
Armour Heights, *Toronto* **30** A2
Arncliffe, *Sydney* **28** B1
Arnold Arboretum, *Boston* **6** B3
Árpádföld, *Budapest* **7** A3
Arrentela, *Lisbon* **14** B2
Årsta, *Stockholm* **28** B2
Art Institute, *Chicago* **9** c2
Artane, *Dublin* **11** A2
Artas, *Jerusalem* **13** B2
Arthur's Seat, *Edinburgh* **11** B3
Aryiróupolis, *Athens* **2** B2
Asagaya, *Tokyo* **29** A2
Asahi, *Osaka* **22** A4
Asakusa, *Tokyo* **29** A3
Asakusabashi, *Tokyo* **29** a5
Asati, *Calcutta* **8** C1
Aschheim, *Munich* **20** A3
Ascot Vale, *Melbourne* **17** A1
Ashburn, *Chicago* **9** C2
Ashburton, *Melbourne* **17** B2
Ashfield, *Sydney* **28** B1
Ashford, *London* **15** B1
Ashiya, *Osaka* **22** A2
Ashiya →, *Osaka* **22** A2
Ashtown, *Dublin* **11** A2
Askisto, *Helsinki* **12** B1
Askrikefjärden, *Stockholm* **28** A3
Asnières, *Paris* **23** A2
Aspern, *Vienna* **31** A2
Aspern, Flugplatz, *Vienna* **31** A3
Assago, *Milan* **18** B1
Assemblée Nationale, *Paris* **23** b3
Assendelft, *Amsterdam* **2** A1
Assiano, *Milan* **18** B1
Astoria, *New York* **21** B2
Astrolabe Park, *Sydney* **28** B2
Atarot Airport, *Jerusalem* **13** A2
Atghara, *Calcutta* **8** B2
Athens = Athínai, *Athens* **2** B2
Athínai, *Athens* **2** B2
Athinai-Ellinikón Airport, *Athens* **2** B2
Athis-Mons, *Paris* **23** B3
Athlone, *Cape Town* **8** A2
Atholl, *Johannesburg* **13** A2
Atīfīya, *Baghdad* **3** A2
Atişalen, *Istanbul* **12** B1
Atlanta, *Atlanta* **3** B2
Atlanta History Center, *Atlanta* **3** B2
Atomium, *Brussels* **6** A2
Attiki, *Athens* **2** A2
Atzgersdorf, *Vienna* **31** B1
Aubervilliers, *Paris* **23** A3
Aubing, *Munich* **20** B1
Auburndale, *Boston* **6** A2
Aucherdinny, *Edinburgh* **11** B2
Auckland Park, *Johannesburg* **13** B2
Auderghem, *Brussels* **6** B2
Augusta, Mausoleo di, *Rome* **25** b2
Augustówka, *Warsaw* **31** B2
Aulnay-sous-Bois, *Paris* **23** A3
Aurelio, *Rome* **25** B1
Ausîm, *Cairo* **7** A1
Austerlitz, Gare d', *Paris* **23** A3
Austin, *Chicago* **9** B2
Avalon, *Wellington* **32** B2
Avedøre, *Copenhagen* **10** B2
Avellaneda, *Buenos Aires* **7** C2
Avenel, *Washington* **32** B4
Avondale, *Chicago* **9** B2
Avondale Heights, *Melbourne* **17** A1
Avtovo, *St. Petersburg* **26** B1
Ayazağa, *Istanbul* **12** B1
Ayer Chawan, P., *Singapore* **27** B2
Ayer Merbau, P., *Singapore* **27** B2
Ayía Marina, *Athens* **2** C3
Ayía Paraskevi, *Athens* **2** A2
Áyios Dhimitrios, *Athens* **2** B2
Áyios Ioánnis Rendis, *Athens* **2** B1
Azabu, *Tokyo* **29** c3
Azcapotzalco, *Mexico City* **18** B1
Azteca, Estadia, *Mexico City* **18** C2
Azucar, Cerro Pan de, *Santiago* **26** A1

B

Baambrugge, *Amsterdam* **2** B2
Baba I., *Karachi* **14** B1
Babarpur, *Delhi* **10** A2
Babushkin, *Moscow* **19** A4
Back B., *Mumbai* **20** B1
Baclaran, *Manila* **17** B2
Bacoor, *Manila* **17** C1
Bacoor B., *Manila* **17** C1
Badalona, *Barcelona* **4** A2
Badhoevedorp, *Amsterdam* **2** A1
Badli, *Delhi* **10** A1
Bærum, *Oslo* **22** A2
Bağcılar, *Istanbul* **12** B1
Bággio, *Milan* **18** B1
Bāgh-e-Feyz, *Tehran* **30** A1
Baghdād, *Baghdad* **3** A2
Bagmari, *Calcutta* **8** B2
Bagneux, *Paris* **23** B2
Bagnolet, *Paris* **23** A3
Bagsværd, *Copenhagen* **10** A2
Bagsværd Sø, *Copenhagen* **10** A2
Baguiati, *Calcutta* **8** B2
Bagumbayan, *Manila* **17** C2
Bahçeköy, *Istanbul* **12** A1
Bahtîm, *Cairo* **7** A2
Baileys Crossroads, *Washington* **32** B3
Bailly, *Paris* **23** A1
Bairro Alto, *Lisbon* **14** c1
Bairro Lopes, *Lisbon* **14** b3
Baisha, *Canton* **8** B2
Baisha →, *Canton* **8** B2
Baixa, *Lisbon* **14** c2
Baiyun Airport, *Canton* **8** A2
Baiyun Hill Scenic Spot, *Canton* **8** B2
Bakırköy, *Istanbul* **12** C1
Bakovka, *Moscow* **19** B2
Bal Harbor, *Miami* **18** A2
Balara, *Manila* **17** B2
Balashikha, *Moscow* **19** B5
Baldia, *Karachi* **14** A1
Baldoyle, *Dublin* **11** A3
Baldwin Hills, *Los Angeles* **16** B2
Baldwin Hills Res., *Los Angeles* **16** B2
Balgowlah, *Sydney* **28** A2
Balgowlah Heights, *Sydney* **28** A2
Balham, *London* **15** B3
Bali, *Calcutta* **8** B1
Baliganja, *Calcutta* **8** B2
Balingsnäs, *Stockholm* **28** B2
Balingsta, *Stockholm* **28** B2
Balintawak, *Manila* **17** B1
Balitai, *Tianjin* **30** B2
Ballerup, *Copenhagen* **10** A2
Ballinteer, *Dublin* **11** B2
Ballyboden, *Dublin* **11** B2
Ballybrack, *Dublin* **11** B3
Ballyfermot, *Dublin* **11** A1
Ballymorefinn Hill, *Dublin* **11** B1
Ballymun, *Dublin* **11** A2
Balmain, *Sydney* **28** B2
Baluhati, *Calcutta* **8** B1
Balvanera, *Buenos Aires* **7** B2
Balwyn, *Melbourne* **17** A2
Balwyn North, *Melbourne* **17** A2
Banática, *Lisbon* **14** A1
Banco do Brasil, Centro Cultural, *Rio de Janeiro* **24** a2
Bandra, *Mumbai* **20** A1
Bandra Pt., *Mumbai* **20** A1
Bang Kapi, *Bangkok* **3** B2
Bang Kholaem, *Bangkok* **3** A2
Bang Na, *Bangkok* **3** B2
Bang Phlad, *Bangkok* **3** a1
Bangkhen, *Bangkok* **3** A2
Bangkok = Krung Thep, *Bangkok* **3** B2
Bangkok Noi, *Bangkok* **3** B1
Bangkok Yai, *Bangkok* **3** B1
Banglamphoo, *Bangkok* **3** b2
Banglo, *Calcutta* **8** B1
Bangrak, *Bangkok* **3** B2
Bangsu, *Bangkok* **3** B2
Bank, *London* **15** b5
Bank of America, *San Francisco* **25** b2
Bank of China Tower, *Hong Kong* **12** c1
Banks, C., *Sydney* **28** C2
Banksmeadow, *Sydney* **28** B2
Banstala, *Calcutta* **8** B2
Bantra, *Calcutta* **8** B1
Baoshan, *Shanghai* **27** A1
Bar Giyora, *Jerusalem* **13** B1
Barahanagar, *Calcutta* **8** B2
Barajas, *Madrid* **17** B2
Barajas, Aeropuerto Transoceanico de, *Madrid* **17** B2
Barakpur, *Calcutta* **8** A2
Barberini, Palazzo, *Rome* **25** b3
Barbican, *London* **15** a4
Barcarena, *Lisbon* **14** A1
Barcarena, Rib. de →, *Lisbon* **14** A1
Barcelona, *Barcelona* **4** A2
Barcelona-Prat, Aeropuerta de, *Barcelona* **4** B1
Barceloneta, *Barcelona* **4** A2
Barking, *London* **15** A4
Barkingside, *London* **15** A4
Barnes, *London* **15** B2
Barnet, *London* **15** A2
Barra Andai, *Karachi* **14** B2
Barra Funda, *São Paulo* **26** B2
Barracas, *Buenos Aires* **7** B2
Barranco, *Lima* **16** B2
Barreiro, *Lisbon* **14** B2
Barreto, *Rio de Janeiro* **24** B2
Bartala, *Calcutta* **8** B1
Barton Park, *Sydney* **28** B1
Bartyki, *Warsaw* **31** C2
Barvikha, *Moscow* **19** B1
Bastille, Place de la, *Paris* **23** c5
Basus, *Cairo* **7** A2
Batanagar, *Calcutta* **8** B1
Bath Beach, *New York* **21** C1
Bath I., *Karachi* **14** B2
Batir, *Jerusalem* **13** B1
Batok, Bukit, *Singapore* **27** A2
Battersea, *London* **15** B3
Battery Park, *New York* **21** f1
Bauman, *Moscow* **19** B4
Baumgarten, *Vienna* **31** A1
Bay Harbour Islands, *Miami* **18** A2
Bay Ridge, *New York* **21** C1
Bayonne, *New York* **21** B1
Bayshore, *San Francisco* **25** B3
Bayswater, *London* **15** b2
Bayt Lahm = Bethlehem, *Jerusalem* **13** B2
Bayview, *San Francisco* **25** B2
Bāzār, *Tehran* **30** A2
Beachmont, *Boston* **6** A4
Beacon Hill, *Hong Kong* **12** A2
Beato, *Lisbon* **14** A2
Beaumont, *Dublin* **11** A2
Beaumonte Heights, *Toronto* **30** A1
Bebek, *Istanbul* **12** B2
Běchovice, *Prague* **24** B3
Beck L., *Chicago* **9** A1
Beckenham, *London* **15** B3
Beckton, *London* **15** A4
Becontree, *London* **15** A4
Beddington Corner, *London* **15** B3
Bedford, *Boston* **6** A2
Bedford Park, *Chicago* **9** C2
Bedford Park, *New York* **21** A2
Bedford Stuyvesant, *New York* **21** B2
Bedford View, *Johannesburg* **13** B2
Bedok, *Singapore* **27** B3
Bedok, Res., *Singapore* **27** A3
Beersel, *Brussels* **6** B1
Behala, *Calcutta* **8** B1
Bei Hai, *Beijing* **4** B2
Beicai, *Shanghai* **27** B2
Beicang, *Tianjin* **30** A1
Beihai Park, *Beijing* **4** b2
Beijing, *Beijing* **4** B1
Beit Ghur el-Fawqa, *Jerusalem* **13** A1
Beit Hanina, *Jerusalem* **13** B2
Beit Iksa, *Jerusalem* **13** B2
Beit I'nan, *Jerusalem* **13** A1
Beit Jala, *Jerusalem* **13** B2
Beit Lekhem = Bethlehem, *Jerusalem* **13** B2
Beit Nekofa, *Jerusalem* **13** B1
Beit Sahur, *Jerusalem* **13** B2
Beit Surik, *Jerusalem* **13** B1
Beit Zayit, *Jerusalem* **13** B1
Beitaipingzhuan, *Beijing* **4** B1
Beitar Ilit, *Jerusalem* **13** B1
Beitsun, *Canton* **8** B2
Beitunya, *Jerusalem* **13** A2
Beixing Jing Park, *Shanghai* **27** B1
Békásmegyer, *Budapest* **7** A2
Bekkelaget, *Oslo* **22** A3
Bel Air, *Los Angeles* **16** B2
Bela Vista, *São Paulo* **26** B2
Bélanger, *Montreal* **19** A1
Belas, *Lisbon* **14** A1
Belas Artes, Museu Nacionale de, *Rio de Janeiro* **24** b2
Beleghata, *Calcutta* **8** B2
Belém, *Lisbon* **14** A1
Belém, Torre de, *Lisbon* **14** A1
Belènzinho, *São Paulo* **26** B2
Belgachiya, *Calcutta* **8** B2
Belgharia, *Calcutta* **8** B2
Belgrano, *Buenos Aires* **7** B2
Belgravia, *London* **15** c3
Bell, *Los Angeles* **16** C3
Bell Gardens, *Los Angeles* **16** C4
Bell Tower, *Beijing* **4** a2
Bellavista, *Lima* **16** B2
Bellavista, *Santiago* **26** C2
Belle Harbor, *New York* **21** C2
Belle View, *Washington* **32** B2
Bellevue, Schloss, *Berlin* **5** a2
Bellingham, *London* **15** B3
Bellwood, *Chicago* **9** B1
Belmont, *Boston* **6** A2
Belmont, *London* **15** A2
Belmont, *Wellington* **32** B2
Belmont Harbor, *Chicago* **9** B3
Belmore, *Sydney* **28** B1
Belur, *Calcutta* **8** B2
Belvedere, *Atlanta* **3** B3
Belvedere, *London* **15** B4
Belvedere, *San Francisco* **25** A2
Belyayevo Bogorodskoye, *Moscow* **19** C3
Bemowo, *Warsaw* **31** B1
Benaki, Moussío, *Athens* **2** b3
Bendale, *Toronto* **30** A3
Bendkhal, *Mumbai* **20** B2
Benefica, *Rio de Janeiro* **24** B1
Benfica, *Lisbon* **14** A1
Benito Juárez, *Mexico City* **18** B2
Benito Juárez, Aeropuerto Int., *Mexico City* **18** B2
Bensonhurst, *New York* **21** C2
Berchem-Sainte-Agathe, *Brussels* **6** A1
Berg am Laim, *Munich* **20** B2
Bergenfield, *New York* **21** A2
Bergham, *Munich* **20** B2
Bergvliet, *Cape Town* **8** B1
Beri, *Barcelona* **4** A1
Berkeley, *San Francisco* **25** A3
Berlin, *Berlin* **5** A3
Bermondsey, *London* **15** B3
Bernabeu, Estadio, *Madrid* **17** B1
Bernal Heights, *San Francisco* **25** B2
Berwyn, *Chicago* **9** B2
Berwyn Heights, *Washington* **32** B4
Besiktas, *Istanbul* **12** B2
Besós →, *Barcelona* **4** A2
Bethesda, *Washington* **32** B3
Bethlehem, *Jerusalem* **13** B2
Bethnal Green, *London* **15** A3
Betor, *Calcutta* **8** B1
Beurs, *Amsterdam* **2** b2
Beverley Hills, *Sydney* **28** B1
Beverley Park, *Sydney* **28** B1
Beverly, *Chicago* **9** C3
Beverly Glen, *Los Angeles* **16** B2
Beverly Hills, *Los Angeles* **16** B2
Bexley, *London* **15** B4
Bexley, *Sydney* **28** B1
Bexleyheath, *London* **15** B4
Beykoz, *Istanbul* **12** B2
Beylerbeyi, *Istanbul* **12** B2
Beyoğlu, *Istanbul* **12** B1
Bezons, *Paris* **23** A2
Bezuidenhout Park, *Johannesburg* **13** B2
Bhadrakali, *Calcutta* **8** A2
Bhalswa, *Delhi* **10** A2
Bhambo Khan Qarmati, *Karachi* **14** B2
Bhatsala, *Calcutta* **8** B1
Bhawanipur, *Calcutta* **8** B2
Bhuleshwar, *Mumbai* **20** b2
Białołeka Dworska, *Warsaw* **31** B2
Biblioteca Nacional, *Rio de Janeiro* **24** c2
Bicentennial Park, *Sydney* **28** B1
Bickley, *London* **15** B4
Bidu, *Jerusalem* **13** B1
Bielany, *Warsaw* **31** B1
Bielawa, *Warsaw* **31** C2
Biesdorf, *Berlin* **5** A4
Bièvre →, *Paris* **23** B1
Bièvres, *Paris* **23** B2
Bilston, *Edinburgh* **11** B2
Binacayan, *Manila* **17** C1
Binondo, *Manila* **17** B1
Birak el Kiyam, *Cairo* **7** A1
Birch Cliff, *Toronto* **30** A3
Birkenstein, *Berlin* **5** A5
Birkholz, *Berlin* **5** A4
Birkholzaue, *Berlin* **5** A4
Birrarrung Park, *Melbourne* **17** A2
Biscayne Bay, *Miami* **18** B2
Biscayne Park, *Miami* **18** A2
Bishop Lavis, *Cape Town* **8** A2
Bishopscourt, *Cape Town* **8** A1
Bispebjerg, *Copenhagen* **10** A3
Biwon Secret Garden, *Seoul* **26** B1
Björknas, *Stockholm* **28** B3
Black Cr. →, *Toronto* **30** A2
Blackfen, *London* **15** B4
Blackheath, *London* **15** B4
Blackrock, *Dublin* **11** B2
Bladensburg, *Washington* **32** B4
Blair Village, *Atlanta* **3** C2
Blairgowrie, *Johannesburg* **13** A2
Blakehurst, *Sydney* **28** B1
Blakstad, *Oslo* **22** B1
Blankenburg, *Berlin* **5** A3
Blankenfelde, *Berlin* **5** A3
Blizne, *Warsaw* **31** B1
Bloomsbury, *London* **15** a3
Błota, *Warsaw* **31** C3
Blue Island, *Chicago* **9** C2
Bluebell, *Dublin* **11** B1
Bluff Hd., *Hong Kong* **12** B2
Blumberg, *Berlin* **5** A4
Blunt Pt., *San Francisco* **25** A2
Blutenberg, *Munich* **20** B1
Blylaget, *Oslo* **22** B3
Bo-Kaap Museum, *Cape Town* **8** c2
Boa Vista, Alto do, *Rio de Janeiro* **24** B1
Boardwalk, *New York* **21** C3
Boavista, *Lisbon* **14** A2
Bobigny, *Paris* **23** A3
Bocanegra, *Lima* **16** A2
Boedo, *Buenos Aires* **7** B2
Bogenhausen, *Munich* **20** B2
Bogorodskoye, *Moscow* **19** B4
Bogota, *New York* **21** A1
Bogstadvatnet, *Oslo* **22** A2
Bohnsdorf, *Berlin* **5** B4
Bois-Colombes, *Paris* **23** A2
Bois-d'Arcy, *Paris* **23** B1
Boissy-St.-Léger, *Paris* **23** B4
Boldinasco, *Milan* **18** B1
Bøler, *Oslo* **22** A4
Bollate, *Milan* **18** A1
Bollebeek, *Brussels* **6** A1
Bollensdorf, *Berlin* **5** A5
Bollmora, *Stockholm* **28** B3
Bolshaya-Okhta, *St. Petersburg* **26** B2
Bolton, *Atlanta* **3** B2
Bom Retiro, *São Paulo* **26** B2
Bombay = Mumbai, *Mumbai* **20** B2
Bondi, *Sydney* **28** B2
Bondy, *Paris* **23** A3
Bondy, Forêt de, *Paris* **23** A4
Bonifacio Monument, *Manila* **17** B1
Bonneuil-sur-Marne, *Paris* **23** B4
Bonnington, *Edinburgh* **11** B1
Bonnyrig and Lasswade, *Edinburgh* **11** B3
Bonsucesso, *Rio de Janeiro* **24** B1
Bonteheuwel, *Cape Town* **8** A2
Boo, *Stockholm* **28** A3
Booterstown, *Dublin* **11** B2
Borisovo, *Moscow* **19** C4
Borle, *Mumbai* **20** A2
Boronia Park, *Sydney* **28** A1
Borough Park, *New York* **21** C2
Bosmont, *Johannesburg* **13** B1
Bosön, *Stockholm* **28** A3
Bosporus = Istanbul Boğazi, *Istanbul* **12** B2
Bostancı, *Istanbul* **12** C2
Boston Harbor, *Boston* **6** A4
Botafogo, *Rio de Janeiro* **24** B1
Botanisk Have, *Copenhagen* **10** b2
Botany, *Sydney* **28** B2
Botany B., *Sydney* **28** B2
Botany Bay Nat. Park, *Sydney* **28** B2
Botič →, *Prague* **24** B3
Botica Sete, *Lisbon* **14** A1
Boucherville, *Montreal* **19** A3
Boucherville, Îs. de, *Montreal* **19** A3
Bougival, *Paris* **23** A1
Boulder Pt., *Hong Kong* **12** B1
Boulogne, Bois de, *Paris* **23** A2
Boulogne-Billancourt, *Paris* **23** A2
Bourg-la-Reine, *Paris* **23** B2
Bouviers, *Paris* **23** B1
Bovenkerk, *Amsterdam* **2** B2
Bovenkerker Polder, *Amsterdam* **2** B2
Bovisa, *Milan* **18** A2
Bow, *London* **15** A3
Bowery, *New York* **21** e2
Boyacıköy, *Istanbul* **12** B2
Boyle Heights, *Los Angeles* **16** B3
Bradbury Building, *Los Angeles* **16** b2
Braepark, *Edinburgh* **11** B2
Braid, *Edinburgh* **11** B2
Bramley, *Johannesburg* **13** A2
Brandenburger Tor, *Berlin* **5** A3
Brani, P., *Singapore* **27** B3
Branik, *Prague* **24** B2
Brännkyrka, *Stockholm* **28** B2
Brás, *São Paulo* **26** B2
Brasilândia, *São Paulo* **26** A1
Brateyevo, *Moscow* **19** C4
Bratsevo, *Moscow* **19** A2
Bray, *Dublin* **11** B3
Braybrook, *Melbourne* **17** A1
Brázdim, *Prague* **24** A3
Breach Candy, *Mumbai* **20** a1
Breakheart Reservation, *Boston* **6** A3
Brede, *Copenhagen* **10** A3
Breeds Pond, *Boston* **6** A4
Breezy Point, *New York* **21** C2
Breitenlee, *Vienna* **31** A3
Breña, *Lima* **16** B2
Brent, *London* **15** A2
Brent Res., *London* **15** A2
Brentford, *London* **15** B2
Brentwood Park, *Los Angeles* **16** B2
Brera, *Milan* **18** B2
Bresso, *Milan* **18** A2
Brevik, *Stockholm* **28** A3
Břevnov, *Prague* **24** B2
Bridgeport, *Chicago* **9** B3
Bridgetown, *Cape Town* **8** A2
Bridgeview, *Chicago* **9** C2
Brighton, *Boston* **6** A3
Brighton, *Melbourne* **17** B1
Brighton le Sands, *Sydney* **28** B1
Brighton Park, *Chicago* **9** C2
Brightwood, *Washington* **32** B3
Brigittenau, *Vienna* **31** A2
Brimbank Park, *Melbourne* **17** A1
Brisbane, *San Francisco* **25** B2
British Museum, *London* **15** a3
Britz, *Berlin* **5** B3
Brixton, *London* **15** B3
Broad Sd., *Boston* **6** A4
Broadmeadows, *Melbourne* **17** A1
Broadmoor, *San Francisco* **25** B2
Broadview, *Chicago* **9** B1
Broadway, *New York* **21** e1
Brockley, *London* **15** B3
Bródno, *Warsaw* **31** B2
Bródnowski, Kanal, *Warsaw* **31** B2
Broek in Waterland, *Amsterdam* **2** A2
Bromley, *London* **15** B4
Bromley Common, *London* **15** B4
Bromma, *Stockholm* **28** A1
Bromma flygplats, *Stockholm* **28** A1
Brompton, *London* **15** c2
Brøndby Strand, *Copenhagen* **10** B2
Brøndbyøster, *Copenhagen* **10** B2
Brøndbyvester, *Copenhagen* **10** B2
Brondesbury, *London* **15** A2
Brønnøya, *Oslo* **22** A2
Brønshøj, *Copenhagen* **10** A2

Bronxville, *New York* **21 A3**
Brookfield, *Chicago* **9 C1**
Brookhaven, *Atlanta* **3 A2**
Brookline, *Boston* **6 B3**
Brooklyn, *Cape Town* **8 A1**
Brooklyn, *New York* **21 C2**
Brooklyn, *Wellington* **32 B3**
Brooklyn Bridge, *New York* **21 f2**
Brookmont, *Washington* **32 B3**
Brossard, *Montreal* **19 B3**
Brou-sur-Chantereine, *Paris* **23 A4**
Brown, *Toronto* **30 A3**
Broyhill Park, *Washington* **32 B2**
Brughério, *Milan* **18 A2**
Brunswick, *Melbourne* **17 A1**
Brush Hill, *Boston* **6 B1**
Brussegem, *Brussels* **6 A1**
Brussel Nat. Luchthaven, *Brussels* **6 A2**
Brussels = Bruxelles, *Brussels* **6 A2**
Bruxelles, *Brussels* **6 A2**
Bruzzano, *Milan* **18 A2**
Bry-sur-Marne, *Paris* **23 A4**
Bryanston, *Johannesburg* **13 A1**
Bryn, *Oslo* **22 A3**
Brzeziny, *Warsaw* **31 B2**
Bubeneč, *Prague* **24 B2**
Buc, *Paris* **23 B1**
Buchenhain, *Munich* **20 B1**
Buchholz, *Berlin* **5 A3**
Buckhead, *Atlanta* **3 B2**
Buckingham Palace, *London* **15 b3**
Buckow, *Berlin* **5 B3**
Buda, *Budapest* **7 A2**
Budafok, *Budapest* **7 B2**
Budaörs, *Budapest* **7 B1**
Budapest, *Budapest* **7 B2**
Budatétény, *Budapest* **7 B2**
Budavaripalota, *Budapest* **7 b2**
Buddinge, *Copenhagen* **10 A3**
Budokan, *Tokyo* **29 a4**
Buena Vista, *San Francisco* **25 B2**
Buenos Aires, *Buenos Aires* **7 B2**
Bufalotta, *Rome* **25 B2**
Bugio, *Lisbon* **14 A3**
Buiksloot, *Amsterdam* **2 A2**
Buitenveldert, *Amsterdam* **2 A2**
Buizingen, *Brussels* **6 B1**
Bukit Panjang Nature Reserve, *Singapore* **27 A2**
Bukit Timah Nature Reserve, *Singapore* **27 A2**
Bukum, P., *Singapore* **27 B2**
Bûlâq, *Cairo* **7 A2**
Bule, *Manila* **17 C2**
Bulim, *Singapore* **27 A2**
Bullen Park, *Melbourne* **17 A2**
Bundoora North, *Melbourne* **17 A2**
Bundoora Park, *Melbourne* **17 A2**
Bunker I., *Karachi* **14 B1**
Bunkyo-Ku, *Tokyo* **29 A3**
Bunnefjorden, *Oslo* **22 A3**
Buona Vista Park, *Singapore* **27 B2**
Burbank, *Chicago* **9 C2**
Burbank, *Los Angeles* **16 A3**
Burlington, *Boston* **6 A2**
Burnham Park, *Chicago* **9 c2**
Burnham Park Harbor, *Chicago* **9 B3**
Burnhamthorpe, *Toronto* **30 B1**
Burnt Oak, *London* **15 A2**
Burntisland, *Edinburgh* **11 A1**
Burnwynd, *Edinburgh* **11 B1**
Burqa, *Jerusalem* **13 A2**
Burtus, *Cairo* **7 A1**
Burudvatn, *Oslo* **22 A2**
Burwood, *Sydney* **28 B1**
Bushwick, *New York* **21 B2**
Bushy Park, *London* **15 B1**
Butantã, *São Paulo* **26 B1**
Butcher I., *Mumbai* **20 B2**
Butts Corner, *Washington* **32 C2**
Büyükdere, *Istanbul* **12 B1**
Bycolla, *Mumbai* **20 B2**
Bygdøy, *Oslo* **22 A3**

C

C.N. Tower, *Toronto* **30 B2**
Cabaçu de Cima →, *São Paulo* **26 A2**
Caballito, *Buenos Aires* **7 B2**
Cabin John, *Washington* **32 B2**
Cabin John Regional Park, *Washington* **32 A2**
Cabinteely, *Dublin* **11 B3**
Cabra, *Dublin* **11 A2**
Cabuçu de Baixo →, *São Paulo* **26 A1**
Cachan, *Paris* **23 B2**
Cachenka →, *Moscow* **19 B1**
Cachoeira, Rib. da →, *São Paulo* **26 B1**
Cacilhas, *Lisbon* **14 A2**
Cahuenga Pk., *Los Angeles* **16 B3**
Cairo = El Qâhira, *Cairo* **7 A2**
Caju, *Rio de Janeiro* **24 B1**
Čakovice, *Prague* **24 B3**
Calcutta = Kolkata, *Calcutta* **8 B2**
California Inst. of Tech., *Los Angeles* **16 B4**
California Plaza, *Los Angeles* **16 b1**
California State Univ., *Los Angeles* **16 B3**
Callao, *Lima* **16 B2**
Caloocan, *Manila* **17 B1**
Calumet Park, *Chicago* **9 C3**
Calumet Sag Channel →, *Chicago* **9 C2**
Calumpang, *Manila* **17 B2**
Calvairate, *Milan* **18 B2**
Camarate, *Lisbon* **14 A2**
Camaroes, *Lisbon* **14 A1**
Camberwell, *London* **15 B3**
Camberwell, *Melbourne* **17 B2**
Cambridge, *Boston* **6 A3**
Cambridge Res., *Boston* **6 A2**
Cambuci, *São Paulo* **26 B2**
Camden, *London* **15 A3**
Cameron, Mt., *Wellington* **32 B2**
Çamlıca, *Istanbul* **12 C2**
Camp Springs, *Washington* **32 C4**
Campamento, *Madrid* **17 B1**
Campbellfield, *Melbourne* **17 A1**
Camperdown, *Sydney* **28 B2**
Campidoglio, *Rome* **25 c3**
Campo, Casa de, *Madrid* **17 B1**
Campo F.C. Barcelona, *Barcelona* **4 A1**
Campo Grando, *Lisbon* **14 A2**
Campo Pequeño, *Lisbon* **14 A2**
Campolide, *Lisbon* **14 A2**
Camps Bay, *Cape Town* **8 A1**
C'an San Joan, *Barcelona* **4 A1**
Cañacao B., *Manila* **17 C1**

Canarsie, *New York* **21 C2**
Cancelleria, Palazzo dei, *Rome* **25 c2**
Candiac, *Montreal* **19 B3**
Caneças, *Lisbon* **14 A1**
Canillas, *Madrid* **17 B2**
Canillejas, *Madrid* **17 B2**
Canning Town, *London* **15 A4**
Canterbury, *Melbourne* **17 A2**
Canterbury, *Sydney* **28 B1**
Canton = Guangzhou, *Canton* **27 B1**
Caohejing, *Shanghai* **27 B1**
Capão Redondo, *São Paulo* **26 B1**
Caparica, *Lisbon* **14 A2**
Caparica, Costa da, *Lisbon* **14 A2**
Cape Flats, *Cape Town* **8 B2**
Cape Town, *Cape Town* **8 A1**
Capitol Heights, *Washington* **32 B4**
Capitol Hill, *Washington* **32 B4**
Capitolini, Musei, *Rome* **25 c3**
Captain Cook Bridge, *Sydney* **28 C1**
Captain Cook Landing Place Park, *Sydney* **28 C2**
Capuchos, *Lisbon* **14 B1**
Carabanchel Alto, *Madrid* **17 B1**
Carabanchel Bajo, *Madrid* **17 B1**
Carapachay, *Buenos Aires* **7 B1**
Caraza, *Buenos Aires* **7 C2**
Caridad, *Manila* **17 C1**
Carioca, Sa. da, *Rio de Janeiro* **24 B1**
Carlstadt, *New York* **21 A1**
Carlton, *Melbourne* **17 A1**
Carmen de Huechuraba, *Santiago* **26 B1**
Carmen de la Legua, *Lima* **16 B2**
Carnaxide, *Lisbon* **14 A1**
Carnegie, *Melbourne* **17 B2**
Carnegie Hall, *New York* **21 c2**
Carnide, *Lisbon* **14 A1**
Carol City, *Miami* **18 A1**
Carrascal, *Santiago* **26 B1**
Carrickmines, *Dublin* **11 B3**
Carrières-sous-Bois, *Paris* **23 A1**
Carrières-sous-Poissy, *Paris* **23 A1**
Carrières-sur-Seine, *Paris* **23 A2**
Carrigeen Bay, *Dublin* **11 A3**
Cartierville, *Montreal* **19 A1**
Casa Verde, *São Paulo* **26 A1**
Casál Morena, *Rome* **25 C2**
Casaloti, *Rome* **25 B1**
Cascade Heights, *Atlanta* **3 B2**
Castél di Leva, *Rome* **25 C2**
Castel Sant'Angelo, *Rome* **25 B1**
Castle, *Dublin* **11 c2**
Castle, *Edinburgh* **11 b2**
Castle of Good Hope, *Cape Town* **8 c3**
Castleknock, *Dublin* **11 A1**
Castleton Corners, *New York* **21 C1**
Catedral Metropolitana, *Mexico City* **18 b3**
Catedral Metropolitana, *Rio de Janeiro* **24 c1**
Catete, *Rio de Janeiro* **24 B1**
Catford, *London* **15 B3**
Caulfield, *Melbourne* **17 B2**
Causeway Bay, *Hong Kong* **12 c3**
Cavite, *Manila* **17 C1**
Caxias, *Lisbon* **14 A1**
Cebecci, *Istanbul* **12 B1**
Cecchignola, *Rome* **25 C2**
Cecilienhof, Schloss, *Berlin* **5 B1**
Cedar Grove, *Atlanta* **3 C3**
Cempaka Putih, *Jakarta* **13 B2**
Çengelköy, *Istanbul* **12 C2**
Cengkareng, *Jakarta* **13 A1**
Centennial Park, *Sydney* **28 B2**
Center Hill, *Atlanta* **3 B2**
Centocelle, *Rome* **25 B2**
Centraal Station, *Amsterdam* **2 a2**
Central Park, *New York* **21 B2**
Cerillos, *Santiago* **26 B1**
Cerro de la Estrella, *Mexico City* **18 B2**
Cerro de los Angeles, *Madrid* **17 C1**
Cerro Navia, *Santiago* **26 B1**
Certanovka →, *Moscow* **19 C3**
Certanovo, *Moscow* **19 C3**
Cesano Boscone, *Milan* **18 B1**
Cesate, *Milan* **18 A1**
Cha Kwo Ling, *Hong Kong* **12 B2**
Chacarrita, *Buenos Aires* **7 B2**
Chadwell Heath, *London* **15 A4**
Chai Chee, *Singapore* **27 B3**
Chai Wan, *Hong Kong* **12 B2**
Chai Wan Kok, *Hong Kong* **12 A1**
Chaillot, Palais de, *Paris* **23 A2**
Chakdaha, *Calcutta* **8 C1**
Chamartin, *Madrid* **17 B1**
Chamberi, *Madrid* **17 B1**
Chambourcy, *Paris* **23 A1**
Champ de Mars, Parc du, *Paris* **23 c2**
Champigny-sur-Marne, *Paris* **23 B4**
Champlain, Pont, *Montreal* **19 B2**
Champs Elysées, Avenue des, *Paris* **23 b2**
Champs-sur-Marne, *Paris* **23 A4**
Chamrail, *Calcutta* **8 B1**
Chamshil, *Seoul* **26 B2**
Chamwŏn, *Seoul* **26 B2**
Chanakyapuri, *Delhi* **10 B2**
Chanditala, *Calcutta* **8 A1**
Changfeng Park, *Shanghai* **27 B1**
Changi, *Singapore* **27 A3**
Changi Int. Airport, *Singapore* **27 A3**
Changning, *Shanghai* **27 B1**
Chantereine, *Paris* **23 A4**
Chantian, *Canton* **27 B2**
Chao Phraya →, *Bangkok* **3 B2**
Chaoyang, *Beijing* **4 B2**
Chaoyangmen, *Beijing* **4 B2**
Chapelizod, *Dublin* **11 A1**
Chapultepec, Bosque de, *Mexico City* **18 B1**
Chapultepec, Castillo de, *Mexico City* **18 B1**
Charenton-le-Pont, *Paris* **23 B3**
Charing Cross, *London* **15 b4**
Charleroi, Kanal de →, *Brussels* **6 B1**
Charles Bridge, *Prague* **24 b1**
Charles Square, *Prague* **24 b2**
Charlestown, *Boston* **6 A3**
Charlottenburg, *Berlin* **5 A2**
Charlottenburg, Schloss, *Berlin* **5 A2**
Charlottenlund, *Copenhagen* **10 A3**
Charlton, *London* **15 A4**
Charneca, *Lisbon* **14 A2**
Charneca, *Lisbon* **14 A2**
Châteaufort, *Paris* **23 B1**
Chatham, *Chicago* **9 C3**
Châtillon, *Paris* **23 B2**
Chatou, *Paris* **23 A1**

Chatpur, *Calcutta* **8 B2**
Chatswood, *Sydney* **28 A2**
Chatuchak, *Bangkok* **3 B2**
Chatuchak Park, *Bangkok* **3 B2**
Chauki, *Karachi* **14 A1**
Chavarria, *Lima* **16 B2**
Chaville, *Paris* **23 B2**
Chayang, *Seoul* **26 B2**
Chegi, *Seoul* **26 B2**
Chells, *Paris* **23 A4**
Chelles, Canal de, *Paris* **23 A4**
Chells-le-Pin, Aérodrome, *Paris* **23 A4**
Chelsea, *Boston* **6 A3**
Chelsea, *London* **15 B2**
Chelsea, *New York* **21 c1**
Chembur, *Mumbai* **20 A2**
Chennevières-sur-Marne, *Paris* **23 B4**
Cheops, *Cairo* **7 B1**
Cherepkovo, *Moscow* **19 B2**
Chernyovo, *Moscow* **19 A1**
Cheryomuski, *Moscow* **19 B3**
Chestnut Hill, *Boston* **6 B2**
Cheung Sha Wan, *Hong Kong* **12 A1**
Cheverly, *Washington* **32 B4**
Chevilly-Larue, *Paris* **23 B3**
Chevry-Cossigny, *Paris* **23 B4**
Chevy Chase, *Washington* **32 B3**
Chevy Chase View, *Washington* **32 A3**
Chia Keng, *Singapore* **27 A3**
Chiaravalle Milanese, *Milan* **18 B2**
Chicago, *Chicago* **9 B3**
Chicago Harbor, *Chicago* **9 B3**
Chicago Lawn, *Chicago* **9 C2**
Chicago-Midway Airport, *Chicago* **9 C2**
Chicago-O'Hare Int. Airport, *Chicago* **9 B1**
Chicago Ridge, *Chicago* **9 C2**
Chicago Sanitary and Ship Canal →, *Chicago* **9 A3**
Chienzui, *Canton* **8 A3**
Chik Sha, *Hong Kong* **12 B2**
Child's Hill, *London* **15 A2**
Chilla Saroda, *Delhi* **10 B2**
Chillum, *Washington* **32 B4**
Chilly-Mazarin, *Paris* **23 B3**
Chinatown, *Los Angeles* **16 a3**
Chinatown, *New York* **21 e2**
Chinatown, *San Francisco* **25 b2**
Chinatown, *Singapore* **27 c2**
Chingupota, *Calcutta* **8 C1**
Chislehurst, *London* **15 B4**
Chitose, *Tokyo* **29 B2**
Chitralada Palace, *Bangkok* **3 B2**
Chiyoda-Ku, *Tokyo* **29 b4**
Chkalova, *Moscow* **19 C5**
Choa Chu Kang, *Singapore* **27 A2**
Choboty, *Moscow* **19 C2**
Chodov u Prahy, *Prague* **24 B3**
Chôfu, *Tokyo* **29 B2**
Choisy-le-Roi, *Paris* **23 B3**
Cholupice, *Prague* **24 C2**
Chom Thong, *Bangkok* **3 B1**
Chong Pang, *Singapore* **27 A2**
Ch'ŏngdam, *Seoul* **26 B2**
Chongmyo Royal Shrine, *Seoul* **26 B1**
Chongno, *Seoul* **26 B1**
Chongwen, *Beijing* **4 B2**
Chônho, *Seoul* **26 B2**
Chopin, Muzeum, *Warsaw* **31 b2**
Chornaya →, *Moscow* **19 B6**
Chorrillos, *Lima* **16 C2**
Chowpatty Beach, *Mumbai* **20 b1**
Christian Quarter, *Jerusalem* **13 b3**
Christiansborg, *Copenhagen* **10 A3**
Christianshavn, *Copenhagen* **10 A3**
Chrysler Building, *New York* **21 c2**
Chrzanów, *Warsaw* **31 B1**
Chuen Lung, *Hong Kong* **12 A1**
Chuk Kok, *Hong Kong* **12 A2**
Chulalongkom Univ., *Bangkok* **3 B2**
Chung, *Seoul* **26 B1**
Chunghwa, *Seoul* **26 B2**
Chungnangch'on →, *Seoul* **26 B1**
Chūō-Ku, *Tokyo* **29 b5**
Church End, *London* **15 A2**
Churchtown, *Dublin* **11 B2**
Ciampino, *Rome* **25 C2**
Ciampino, Aeroporto di, *Rome* **25 C2**
Cicero, *Chicago* **9 B2**
Cilandak, *Jakarta* **13 B1**
Cilincing, *Jakarta* **13 B2**
Ciliwung →, *Jakarta* **13 B2**
Cimice, *Prague* **24 B2**
Cinecittà, *Rome* **25 C2**
Cinisello Bálsamo, *Milan* **18 A2**
Cinkota, *Budapest* **7 A3**
Cipete, *Jakarta* **13 B1**
Citadella, *Budapest* **7 c2**
Citta degli Studi, *Milan* **18 B2**
Città del Vaticano, *Rome* **25 B1**
City, *London* **15 A3**
City Hall, *New York* **21 e1**
Ciudad Deportiva, *Mexico City* **18 B2**
Ciudad Fin de Semana, *Madrid* **17 B2**
Ciudad General Belgrano, *Buenos Aires* **7 C1**
Ciudad Lineal, *Madrid* **17 B1**
Ciudad Satélite, *Mexico City* **18 A1**
Ciudad Universitaria, *Buenos Aires* **7 B2**
Ciudad Universitaria, *Mexico City* **18 B1**
Ciutadella, Parc de la, *Barcelona* **4 b3**
Civic Center, *Los Angeles* **16 b2**
Clamart, *Paris* **23 B2**
Clapham, *London* **15 B3**
Clapton, *London* **15 A3**
Clayhall, *London* **15 A4**
Clerkenwell, *London* **15 a4**
Clermiston, *Edinburgh* **11 B2**
Clichy, *Paris* **23 A2**
Clichy-sous-Bois, *Paris* **23 A4**
Cliffside, *Toronto* **30 B2**
Cliffside Park, *New York* **21 B2**
Clifton, *Boston* **6 A4**
Clifton, *Karachi* **14 B2**
Clifton, *New York* **21 C1**
Cliftondale, *Boston* **6 A3**
Cloghran, *Dublin* **11 A2**
Clonskeagh, *Dublin* **11 B2**
Clontarf, *Dublin* **11 A2**
Clovelly, *Sydney* **28 B2**
Cobras, I. das, *Rio de Janeiro* **24 B1**
Coburg, *Melbourne* **17 A1**

Cochituate, *Boston* **6 A1**
Cochituate, L., *Boston* **6 B1**
Cocotá, *Rio de Janeiro* **24 A1**
Cœuilly, *Paris* **23 B4**
Coina, *Lisbon* **14 B2**
Coit Tower, *San Francisco* **25 a2**
Coker, *Lagos* **14 B2**
Colaba, *Mumbai* **20 B1**
Colaba Pt., *Mumbai* **20 B1**
Colegiales, *Buenos Aires* **7 B2**
Colindale, *London* **15 A2**
Colinton, *Edinburgh* **11 B2**
College Park, *Atlanta* **3 C2**
College Park, *Washington* **32 B4**
College Point, *New York* **21 B2**
Collégien, *Paris* **23 A4**
Collier Row, *London* **15 A4**
Colliers Wood, *London* **15 B2**
Colma, *San Francisco* **25 B2**
Colney Hatch, *London* **15 A3**
Cologno Monzese, *Milan* **18 A2**
Colombes, *Paris* **23 A2**
Colón, Monumente, *Barcelona* **4 c3**
Colon, Plaza de, *Madrid* **17 a3**
Colonia Güell, *Barcelona* **4 A1**
Colonial Knob, *Wellington* **32 A1**
Colosseo, *Rome* **25 c3**
Columbus Circus, *New York* **21 b2**
Combault, *Paris* **23 B4**
Comércio, Praça do, *Lisbon* **14 A2**
Commerce, *Los Angeles* **16 B4**
Como, *Sydney* **28 C1**
Company's Gardens, *Cape Town* **8 c2**
Conceição, I. da, *Rio de Janeiro* **24 B2**
Concertgebouw, *Amsterdam* **2 c1**
Conchali, *Santiago* **26 B2**
Concord, *Boston* **6 A1**
Concord, *Sydney* **28 B1**
Concord, *Toronto* **30 A1**
Concorde, Place de la, *Paris* **23 b3**
Concorezzo, *Milan* **18 A2**
Coney Island, *New York* **21 C2**
Congonhas, Aéroporto, *São Paulo* **26 B2**
Connaught Place, *Delhi* **10 B2**
Conservatori, Palazzo dei, *Rome* **25 c3**
Consolação, *São Paulo* **26 B2**
Constantia, *Cape Town* **8 B1**
Constitution, *Buenos Aires* **7 B2**
Constitution, *Atlanta* **3 B2**
Convention and Exhibition Centre, *Hong Kong* **12 b3**
Coogee, *Sydney* **28 B2**
Cook Str., *Wellington* **32 A1**
Cooksville, *Toronto* **30 B1**
Coolock, *Dublin* **11 A2**
Copacabana, *Rio de Janeiro* **24 B1**
Copenhagen = København, *Copenhagen* **10 A2**
Coral Gables, *Miami* **18 B2**
Coral Hills, *Washington* **32 B4**
Corcovado, Morro do, *Rio de Janeiro* **24 B1**
Corduff, *Dublin* **11 A1**
Cormano, *Milan* **18 A2**
Cornaredo, *Milan* **18 A1**
Córsico, *Milan* **18 B1**
Corsini, Palazzo, *Rome* **25 B1**
Corviale, *Rome* **25 B1**
Coslada, *Madrid* **17 B2**
Cossigny, *Paris* **23 B4**
Cossipore, *Calcutta* **8 B2**
Costantino, Arco di, *Rome* **25 c3**
Costorphine, *Edinburgh* **11 B2**
Cotao, *Lisbon* **14 A1**
Côte St.-Luc, *Montreal* **19 B2**
Cotundubu, I. de, *Rio de Janeiro* **24 B2**
Coubron, *Paris* **23 A4**
Countryside, *Chicago* **9 C1**
Courbevoie, *Paris* **23 A2**
Courtry, *Paris* **23 A4**
Covent Garden, *London* **15 b4**
Cowgate, *Edinburgh* **11 b3**
Cowley, *London* **15 A1**
Coyoacán, *Mexico City* **18 B2**
Cragin, *Chicago* **9 B2**
Craighall Park, *Johannesburg* **13 A2**
Craiglockhart, *Edinburgh* **11 B2**
Craigmillar, *Edinburgh* **11 B3**
Cramond, *Edinburgh* **11 B2**
Cramond Bridge, *Edinburgh* **11 B1**
Cramond I., *Edinburgh* **11 B2**
Cranford, *London* **15 B1**
Crawford, *Cape Town* **8 A2**
Crayford, *London* **15 B5**
Creekmouth, *London* **15 A4**
Crescenzago, *Milan* **18 A2**
District Heights, *Washington* **32 B4**
Cressely, *Paris* **23 B1**
Cresskill, *New York* **21 A2**
Creteil, *Paris* **23 B3**
Cricklewood, *London* **15 A2**
Cristo Redentor, Estatua do, *Rio de Janeiro* **24 B1**
Crockenhill, *London* **15 B4**
Croissy-Beaubourg, *Paris* **23 B4**
Croissy-sur-Seine, *Paris* **23 A1**
Crosby, *Johannesburg* **13 B1**
Crosne, *Paris* **23 B3**
Cross I., *Mumbai* **20 B2**
Crouch End, *London* **15 A3**
Crown Mine, *Johannesburg* **13 B1**
Crows Nest, *Sydney* **28 A2**
Croydon, *London* **15 B3**
Croydon Park, *Sydney* **28 B1**
Cruagh Mt., *Dublin* **11 B2**
Crumlin, *Dublin* **11 B2**
Cruz de Pau, *Lisbon* **14 B2**
Crystal Palace, *London* **15 B3**
Csepel, *Budapest* **7 B2**
Csepelsziget, *Budapest* **7 B2**
Csillaghegy, *Budapest* **7 A2**
Csillagtelep, *Budapest* **7 B2**
Csömör, *Budapest* **7 A3**
Csömöri-patak →, *Budapest* **7 A3**
Cuatro Vientos, *Madrid* **17 B1**
Cuauhtémoc, *Mexico City* **18 B2**
Cubao, *Manila* **17 B2**
Çubuklu, *Istanbul* **12 B2**
Cudahy, *Los Angeles* **16 C3**
Cuicuilco, Pirámido de, *Mexico City* **18 C2**
Culver City, *Los Angeles* **16 B2**
Cumballa Hill, *Mumbai* **20 a1**
Cumbres de Vallecas, *Madrid* **17 B2**
Cupecé, *São Paulo* **26 B1**
Currie, *Edinburgh* **11 B2**
Cusago, *Milan* **18 B1**
Cusano Milanino, *Milan* **18 A2**
Cusset, *São Paulo* **26 B1**
Custom House, *Dublin* **11 b3**
Çuvuşabaşı →, *Istanbul* **12 B1**
Czernieków, *Warsaw* **31 B2**
Czyste, *Warsaw* **31 B1**

D

D.F. Malan Airport, *Cape Town* **8 A2**
Da Mooca →, *São Paulo* **26 B2**
Da Yunhe →, *Tianjin* **30 A1**
Dabizhuang, *Tianjin* **30 A2**
Dablice, *Prague* **24 B2**
Dąbrowa, *Warsaw* **31 B1**
Dachang, *Shanghai* **27 B1**
Dachang Airfield, *Shanghai* **27 B1**
Dachau-Ost, *Munich* **20 A1**
Dachauer Moos, *Munich* **20 A1**
Dadar, *Mumbai* **20 A1**
Dagenham, *London* **15 A4**
Daglfing, *Munich* **20 B2**
Dahcisha, *Jerusalem* **13 B2**
Dahlem, *Berlin* **5 B2**
Dahlwitz-Hoppegarten, *Berlin* **5 A5**
Dahongmen, *Beijing* **4 C2**
Daitō, *Osaka* **22 A4**
Dajiaoting, *Beijing* **4 B2**
Dakhnoye, *St. Petersburg* **26 C1**
Dalejsky potok →, *Prague* **24 B2**
Dalgety Bay, *Edinburgh* **11 A1**
Dalkeith, *Edinburgh* **11 B3**
Dalkey, *Dublin* **11 B3**
Dalkey Island, *Dublin* **11 B3**
Dallgow, *Berlin* **5 A1**
Dalmeny, *Edinburgh* **11 B1**
Dalston, *London* **15 A3**
Daly City, *San Francisco* **25 B2**
Dam, *Amsterdam* **2 b2**
Dam Rak, *Amsterdam* **2 a2**
Damaia, *Lisbon* **14 A1**
Dämeritzsee, *Berlin* **5 B5**
Dan Ryan Woods, *Chicago* **9 C2**
Danderhall, *Edinburgh* **11 B3**
Danderyd, *Stockholm* **28 A2**
Danforth, *Toronto* **30 A3**
Darakeh, *Tehran* **30 A2**
Darband, *Tehran* **30 A2**
Darling Harbour, *Sydney* **28 b1**
Darling Point, *Sydney* **28 B2**
Darndale, *Dublin* **11 A2**
Darrûs, *Tehran* **30 A2**
Dartford, *London* **15 B5**
Darya Ganj, *Delhi* **1 a3**
Dashi, *Canton* **8 B2**
Datansha, *Canton* **8 B2**
Datun, *Beijing* **4 B2**
Daulatpur, *Delhi* **10 A1**
David's Citadel, *Jerusalem* **13 b3**
David's Tomb, *Jerusalem* **13 b3**
Davidson, Mt., *San Francisco* **25 B2**
Davidson's Mains, *Edinburgh* **11 B2**
Dāvūdiyeh, *Tehran* **30 A2**
Davydkovo, *Moscow* **19 B2**
Dawidy, *Warsaw* **31 C1**
Days Bay, *Wellington* **32 B2**
Dazhigu, *Tianjin* **30 B2**
De Waag, *Amsterdam* **2 b2**
Decatur, *Atlanta* **3 B3**
Dedham, *Boston* **6 B2**
Deguinmo, *Moscow* **19 A3**
Deir Dibwan, *Jerusalem* **13 A2**
Deir Ibzi'e, *Jerusalem* **13 A1**
Dejvice, *Prague* **24 B2**
Dekabristov, Ostrov, *St. Petersburg* **26 B1**
Delhi, *Delhi* **10 B2**
Delhi Gate, *Delhi* **1 b3**
Demarest, *New York* **21 A2**
Den Ilp, *Amsterdam* **2 A2**
Denistone Heights, *Sydney* **28 A1**
Dentonia Park, *Toronto* **30 A3**
Deptford, *London* **15 B3**
Deputati, Camera dei, *Rome* **25 b2**
Des Plaines, *Chicago* **9 A1**
Des Plaines →, *Chicago* **9 B2**
Deshengmen, *Beijing* **4 B2**
Deutsch-Wagram, *Vienna* **31 A3**
Deutsche Oper, *Berlin* **5 A2**
Deutscher Museum, *Munich* **20 b3**
Devil's Peak, *Cape Town* **8 A1**
Dhāfni, *Athens* **2 B2**
Dhakuria, *Calcutta* **8 B2**
Dhamarakia, *Athens* **2 A2**
Dharavi, *Mumbai* **20 A2**
Dhrapersón, *Athens* **2 B1**
Diadema, *São Paulo* **26 C2**
Diegem, *Brussels* **6 A2**
Diemen, *Amsterdam* **2 A2**
Diepkloof, *Johannesburg* **13 B1**
Dieprivier, *Cape Town* **8 B1**
Difficult Run →, *Washington* **32 B1**
Dilbeek, *Brussels* **6 A1**
Dinzigu, *Tianjin* **30 A1**
Dirnismaning, *Munich* **20 A2**
Ditan Park, *Beijing* **4 a2**
Diyála →, *Baghdad* **3 B2**
Djursholm, *Stockholm* **28 A2**
Döbertiz, *Berlin* **5 A1**
Döbling, *Vienna* **31 A2**
Docklands, *London* **15 A3**
Dodder, R. →, *Dublin* **11 B2**
Dodger Stadium, *Los Angeles* **16 B3**
Dolgoe Ozero, *St. Petersburg* **26 A1**
Doll Museum, *Delhi* **1 b3**
Dollis Hill, *London* **15 A2**
Dollymount, *Dublin* **11 A2**
Dolni Chabry, *Prague* **24 B2**
Dolni Počernice, *Prague* **24 B3**
Dolphins Barn, *Dublin* **11 B2**
Dom Pedro II, Parque, *São Paulo* **26 B2**
Domain, The, *Sydney* **28 b2**
Dome of the Rock, *Jerusalem* **13 b3**
Don Mills, *Toronto* **30 A2**
Don Muang Int. Airport, *Bangkok* **3 A2**
Donaghmede, *Dublin* **11 A3**
Donau-Oder Kanal, *Vienna* **31 A3**
Donaufeld, *Vienna* **31 A2**
Donaustadt, *Vienna* **31 A2**
Dongan Hills, *New York* **21 C1**
Dongcheng, *Beijing* **4 B2**
Dongjiao, *Canton* **8 B2**
Dongjuan, *Tianjin* **30 B2**
Dongmenwai, *Tianjin* **30 B2**
Dongri, *Mumbai* **20 b2**
Dongshanhu Park, *Canton* **8 B2**
Dongzhimen, *Beijing* **4 B2**
Doornfontein, *Johannesburg* **13 B2**
Dorchester, *Boston* **6 B3**
Dorchester B., *Boston* **6 B3**
Dornach, *Munich* **20 B3**
Dorval, Aéroport de, *Montreal* **19 B1**
Dos Couros →, *São Paulo* **26 C2**

Dos Moninos →, *São Paulo* **26 C2**
Douglas Park, *Chicago* **9 B2**
Dover Heights, *Sydney* **28 B2**
Dowlatābād, *Tehran* **30 B2**
Downey, *Los Angeles* **16 C4**
Downsview, *Toronto* **30 A1**
Dragor, *Copenhagen* **10 B3**
Drancy, *Paris* **23 A3**
Dranesville, *Washington* **32 A1**
Dreilinden, *Berlin* **5 B2**
Drewnica, *Warsaw* **31 B2**
Drigh Road, *Karachi* **14 A2**
Drimnagh, *Dublin* **11 B2**
Drogenbos, *Brussels* **6 B1**
Druid Hills, *Atlanta* **3 B2**
Drum Towwer, *Beijing* **4 a2**
Drumcondra, *Dublin* **11 A2**
Drummoyne, *Sydney* **28 B1**
Drylaw, *Edinburgh* **11 B2**
Dubeč, *Prague* **24 B3**
Dublin, *Dublin* **11 B2**
Dublin Airport, *Dublin* **11 A2**
Dublin Bay, *Dublin* **11 B3**
Dublin Harbour, *Dublin* **11 B3**
Duddingston, *Edinburgh* **11 B3**
Dugnano, *Milan* **18 A2**
Dūlāb, *Tehran* **30 B2**
Dulwich, *London* **15 B3**
Dum Dum, *Calcutta* **8 B2**
Dum Dum Int. Airport, *Calcutta* **8 B2**
Dumont, *New York* **21 A2**
Dùn Laoghaire, *Dublin* **11 B3**
Dundrum, *Dublin* **11 B2**
Dunearn, *Singapore* **27 B2**
Dunfermline, *Edinburgh* **11 A1**
Dunn Loring, *Washington* **32 B2**
Dunning, *Chicago* **9 B2**
Dunvegan, *Johannesburg* **13 A2**
Duque de Caxias, *Rio de Janeiro* **24 A1**
Dusit, *Bangkok* **3 B2**
Dusit Zoo, *Bangkok* **3 a2**
Duvernay, *Montreal* **19 A1**
Dworp, *Brussels* **6 B1**
Dyakovo, *Moscow* **19 C3**
Dzerzhinskiy, *Moscow* **19 C5**
Dzerzhinskiy, *Moscow* **19 B3**
Dzerzhinskiy Park, *Moscow* **19 B3**

E

Eagle Rock, *Los Angeles* **16 B3**
Ealing, *London* **15 A1**
Earl's Court, *London* **15 c1**
Earlsfield, *London* **15 B2**
Earlwood, *Sydney* **28 B1**
East Acton, *London* **15 A2**
East Arlington, *Boston* **6 A3**
East Arlington, *Washington* **32 B3**
East Bedfont, *London* **15 B1**
East Boston, *Boston* **6 A3**
East Don →, *Toronto* **30 A2**
East Elmhurst, *New York* **21 B2**
East Finchley, *London* **15 A2**
East Ham, *London* **15 A4**
East Humber →, *Toronto* **30 A1**
East Lamma Channel, *Hong Kong* **12 B1**
East Lexington, *Boston* **6 A2**
East Los Angeles, *Los Angeles* **16 B3**
East Molesey, *London* **15 B1**
East New York, *New York* **21 B2**
East Pines, *Washington* **32 B4**
East Point, *Atlanta* **3 C2**
East Potomac Park, *Washington* **32 B3**
East Pt., *Boston* **6 A4**
East River →, *New York* **21 B2**
East Rutherford, *New York* **21 A1**
East Sheen, *London* **15 B2**
East Village, *New York* **21 e2**
East Wickham, *London* **15 A4**
East York, *Toronto* **30 A2**
Eastbourne, *Wellington* **32 B2**
Eastcote, *London* **15 A1**
Easter Howgate, *Edinburgh* **11 B2**
Eastwood, *Sydney* **28 A1**
Ebara, *Tokyo* **29 B3**
Ebisu, *Tokyo* **29 B3**
Ebute-Ikorodu, *Lagos* **14 A2**
Ebute-Metta, *Lagos* **14 B2**
Echo Park, *Los Angeles* **16 a1**
Eda, *Tokyo* **29 B2**
Edendale, *Johannesburg* **13 A2**
Edenmore, *Dublin* **11 A2**
Edgars Cr. →, *Melbourne* **17 A1**
Edgeley, *Toronto* **30 A1**
Edgemar, *San Francisco* **25 C2**
Edinburgh, *Edinburgh* **11 B2**
Edison Park, *Chicago* **9 A2**
Edmondson, *Washington* **32 B4**
Edmondstown, *Dublin* **11 B2**
Edo →, *Tokyo* **29 A4**
Edogawa-Ku, *Tokyo* **29 A4**
Edsberg, *Stockholm* **28 A1**
Edwards L., *Melbourne* **17 A1**
Eiche, *Berlin* **5 A4**
Eiche Sud, *Berlin* **5 A4**
Eiffel, Tour, *Paris* **23 c2**
Ein Arik, *Jerusalem* **13 A1**
Ein Naquba, *Jerusalem* **13 B1**
Ein Rafa, *Jerusalem* **13 B1**
Eizariya, *Jerusalem* **13 B2**
Ejby, *Copenhagen* **10 A2**
Ejigbo, *Lagos* **14 A1**
Ekeberg, *Oslo* **22 A3**
Eknäs, *Stockholm* **28 B3**
El 'Abbasiya, *Cairo* **7 A2**
El Agostino, *Lima* **16 B2**
El Baragil, *Cairo* **7 A1**
El Basâlîn, *Cairo* **7 A2**
El-Bira, *Jerusalem* **13 A2**
El Bosque, *Santiago* **26 B2**
El Carmen, *Santiago* **26 B1**
El Cortijo, *Santiago* **26 B1**
El Duqqi, *Cairo* **7 A2**
El Encinar de los Reyes, *Madrid* **17 A2**
El Ghurlya, *Cairo* **7 A2**
El Gîza, *Cairo* **7 A2**
El-Khadr, *Jerusalem* **13 B1**
El Kôm el Ahmar, *Cairo* **7 A2**
El Ma'âdi, *Cairo* **7 B2**
El Matarîya, *Cairo* **7 A2**
El Mohandessin, *Cairo* **7 A2**
El Muski, *Cairo* **7 A2**
El Pardo, *Madrid* **17 A1**

El Portal, *Miami* **18 A2**
El Prat de Llobregat, *Barcelona* **4 B1**
El Pueblo de L.A. Historic Park, *Los Angeles* **16 b2**
El Qâhira, *Cairo* **7 A2**
El Qubba, *Cairo* **7 A2**
El Reloj, *Mexico City* **18 C2**
El Retiro, *Madrid* **17 B1**
El Salto, *Santiago* **26 B2**
El Sereno, *Los Angeles* **16 B3**
El Talbîya, *Cairo* **7 A2**
El Vergel, *Mexico City* **18 C2**
El Wâhli, *Cairo* **7 A2**
El Zamâlik, *Cairo* **7 A2**
El Zeitûn, *Cairo* **7 A2**
Elephanta Caves, *Mumbai* **20 B2**
Elephanta I., *Mumbai* **20 B2**
Ellboda, *Stockholm* **28 A3**
Ellinikón, *Athens* **2 B2**
Ellis I., *New York* **21 B1**
Elm Park, *London* **15 A5**
Elmers End, *London* **15 B3**
Elmhurst, *New York* **21 B2**
Elmstead, *London* **15 B4**
Elmwood Park, *Chicago* **9 B2**
Elmwood Park, *New York* **21 A1**
Elsdon, *Wellington* **32 A1**
Elsiesrivier, *Cape Town* **8 A2**
Elsternwick, *Melbourne* **17 B2**
Eltham, *London* **15 B4**
Elwood, *Melbourne* **17 B1**
Elysée, *Paris* **23 b2**
Elysian Park, *Los Angeles* **16 a3**
Embajadores, *Madrid* **17 c2**
Embarcadero Center, *San Francisco* **25 b3**
Emek Refa'im, *Jerusalem* **13 c2**
Émerainville, *Paris* **23 B4**
Emeryville, *San Francisco* **25 A3**
Eminönü, *Istanbul* **12 B1**
Emmarentia, *Johannesburg* **13 A2**
Empire State Building, *New York* **21 c2**
Encantado, *Rio de Janeiro* **24 B1**
Encino, *Los Angeles* **16 B2**
Encino Res., *Los Angeles* **16 B2**
Enebyberg, *Stockholm* **28 A1**
Enfield, *Sydney* **28 B1**
Engenho, I. do, *Rio de Janeiro* **24 B2**
Englewood, *Chicago* **9 C3**
Englewood, *New York* **21 A2**
Englewood Cliffs, *New York* **21 A2**
Enmore, *Sydney* **28 B2**
Enskede, *Stockholm* **28 B2**
Entrevias, *Madrid* **17 B1**
Epping, *Sydney* **28 A1**
Erawan Shrine, *Bangkok* **3 c3**
Eregun, *Lagos* **14 A2**
Erenköy, *Istanbul* **12 C2**
Erith, *London* **15 B5**
Erlaa, *Vienna* **31 B1**
Ermington, *Sydney* **28 A1**
Ermita, *Manila* **17 B1**
Ershatou, *Canton* **8 B2**
Erskineville, *Sydney* **28 B2**
Érsekujvár, *Budapest* **7 B3**
Erzsébet-Telep, *Budapest* **7 B3**
Eschenried, *Munich* **20 A1**
Esenler, *Istanbul* **12 B1**
Esher, *London* **15 B1**
Eskbank, *Edinburgh* **11 B3**
Esperanza, *Mexico City* **18 c3**
Esplanade Park, *Singapore* **27 c3**
Esplugas, *Barcelona* **4 A1**
Esposizione Univ. di Roma (E.U.R.), *Rome* **25 C1**
Essendon, *Melbourne* **17 A1**
Essendon Airport, *Melbourne* **17 A1**
Essingen, *Stockholm* **28 B1**
Essling, *Vienna* **31 A3**
Est, Gare de l', *Paris* **23 a5**
Estádio Maracanã, *Rio de Janeiro* **24 B1**
Estado, Parque do, *São Paulo* **26 B2**
Estefânia, *Lisbon* **14 A2**
Esthnikó, Basílica da, *Lisbon* **14 A2**
Ethnikó Arheologiko Moussío, *Athens* **2 a2**
Etobicoke, *Toronto* **30 B1**
Etobicoke Cr. →, *Toronto* **30 B1**
Etterbeek, *Brussels* **6 B2**
Euston, *London* **15 a3**
Evanston, *Chicago* **9 A2**
Even Sapir, *Jerusalem* **13 B1**
Evere, *Brussels* **6 A2**
Everett, *Boston* **6 A3**
Evergreen Park, *Chicago* **9 C2**
Evin, *Tehran* **30 A2**
Evjona, *Athens* **2 B2**
Ewu, *Lagos* **14 A1**
Exchange Square, *Hong Kong* **12 c1**
Exposições, Palácio das, *Rio de Janeiro* **24 B1**
Eyüp, *Istanbul* **12 B1**

F

Fabour, Mt., *Singapore* **27 B2**
Facchi, *Seoul* **26 B2**
Fælledparken, *Copenhagen* **10 A3**
Fagersjö, *Stockholm* **28 B1**
Fagersö, *Stockholm* **28 B3**
Fair Lawn, *New York* **21 A1**
Fairfax, *Washington* **32 B1**
Fairfax Station, *Washington* **32 C2**
Fairhaven Bay, *Boston* **6 A1**
Fairhaven Hill, *Boston* **6 A1**
Fairland, *Johannesburg* **13 A1**
Fairmilehead, *Edinburgh* **11 B2**
Fairmount Heights, *Washington* **32 B4**
Fairport, *Toronto* **30 A4**
Fairview, *New York* **21 A1**
Falenty, *Warsaw* **31 C1**
Fâlirou, Órmos, *Athens* **2 B2**
Falkenberg, *Berlin* **5 A4**
Falkenhagen, *Berlin* **5 A1**
Falls Church, *Washington* **32 B2**
Falomo, *Lagos* **14 B2**
False Bay, *Cape Town* **8 B2**
Fangcun, *Canton* **8 B2**
Farforovskaya, *St. Petersburg* **26 B2**
Farningham, *London* **15 B5**
Farrar Pond, *Boston* **6 A1**
Farsta, *Stockholm* **28 B2**
Fasangarten, *Munich* **20 B2**
Fasanerie-Nord, *Munich* **20 A2**
Fasting Palace, *Beijing* **4 c2**
Fatih, *Istanbul* **12 B1**
Favoriten, *Vienna* **31 B2**
Fawkner, *Melbourne* **17 A1**

Fawkner Park, *Melbourne* .. **17 B1**
Feijó, *Lisbon* **14 B2**
Feldkirchen, *Munich* **20 B3**
Feltham, *London* **15 B1**
Fener, *Istanbul* **12 B1**
Fenerbahçe, *Istanbul* ... **12 C2**
Fengtai, *Beijing* **4 C1**
Fenino, *Moscow* **19 B5**
Ferencváros, *Budapest* .. **7 B2**
Ferihegyi Airport, *Budapest* . **7 B3**
Ferndale, *Johannesburg* . **13 B2**
Férolles-Attilly, *Paris* . **23 B4**
Fichtenau, *Berlin* **5 B5**
Fields Corner, *Boston* .. **6 B3**
Fiera Camp, *Milan* **18 B1**
Fifth Avenue, *New York* . **21 b3**
Figino, *Milan* **18 B1**
Fijir, *Baghdad* **3 A2**
Filadhélfia, *Athens* **2 A2**
Fili-Mazilovo, *Moscow* .. **19 B2**
Filothei, *Athens* **2 A2**
Finchley, *London* **15 A3**
Finglas, *Dublin* **11 A2**
Finsbury, *London* **15 A3**
Finsbury Park, *London* .. **15 A3**
Fiorito, *Buenos Aires* .. **7 C2**
Firhouse, *Dublin* **11 B2**
Fischerhäuser, *Munich* .. **20 A3**
Fisher Island, *Miami* ... **18 B2**
Fisherman Bend, *Melbourne* . **17 A1**
Fisherman's Wharf,
  San Francisco **25 a1**
Fisherville, *Toronto* ... **30 A2**
Fisksätra, *Stockholm* ... **28 B3**
Fitzroy Gardens, *Melbourne* . **17 A1**
Five Dock, *Sydney* **28 B1**
Fjellstrand, *Oslo* **22 A2**
Flamengo, *Rio de Janeiro* . **24 B1**
Flaminio, *Rome* **25 B1**
Flaskebekk, *Oslo* **22 A2**
Flatbush, *New York* **21 C2**
Flaten, *Stockholm* **28 B2**
Flemington Racecourse,
  Melbourne **17 A1**
Flint Pk., *Los Angeles* . **16 B3**
Florence, *Los Angeles* .. **16 C3**
Florence Bloom Bird
  Sanctuary, *Johannesburg* . **13 A2**
Florentia, *Johannesburg* . **13 B2**
Flores, *Buenos Aires* ... **7 B2**
Floresta, *Buenos Aires* . **7 B2**
Florida, *Buenos Aires* .. **7 B2**
Florida, *Johannesburg* .. **13 B1**
Floridsdorf, *Vienna* **31 A2**
Flushing, *New York* **21 B3**
Flushing Meadows Corona
  Park, *New York* **21 B2**
Flysta, *Stockholm* **28 A1**
Fo Tan, *Hong Kong* **12 A2**
Fontaine, *Vienna* **31 A2**
Fontainebleau, *Johannesburg* . **13 A1**
Fontenay-aux-Roses, *Paris* . **23 B2**
Fontenay-le-Fleury, *Paris* . **23 B1**
Fontenay-sous-Bois, *Paris* . **23 B2**
Foots Cray, *London* **15 B4**
Footscray, *Melbourne* ... **17 A1**
Foreshore, *Cape Town* ... **8 a3**
Forest, *Brussels* **6 B1**
Forest Gate, *London* **15 A4**
Forest Heights, *Washington* . **32 C3**
Forest Hill, *London* **15 B3**
Forest Hill, *Toronto* ... **30 A2**
Forest Hills, *New York* . **21 B2**
Forest Park, *Chicago* ... **9 B2**
Forest View, *Chicago* ... **9 C2**
Forestville, *Washington* . **32 B4**
Fornebu, *Oslo* **22 A2**
Fornebu Airport, *Oslo* .. **25 c3**
Foro Romano, *Rome* **25 c3**
Forstenried, *Munich* **20 B1**
Forstenrieder Park, *Munich* . **20 B1**
Fort, *Mumbai* **20 a2**
Fort Canning Park, *Singapore* **27 b2**
Fort Dupont Park,
  Washington **32 B4**
Fort Foote Village,
  Washington **32 C3**
Fort Lee, *New York* **21 A2**
Fort Mason Center,
  San Francisco **25 a1**
Forth, Firth of, *Edinburgh* . **11 A2**
Forth Rail Bridge, *Edinburgh* **11 A1**
Forth Road Bridge,
  Edinburgh **11 A1**
Fót, *Budapest* **7 A3**
Fourqueux, *Paris* **23 A1**
Foxrock, *Dublin* **11 B2**
Framingham, *Boston* **6 B1**
Franconia, *Washington* .. **32 C3**
Frankel, *Singapore* **27 B3**
Franklin Park, *Boston* .. **6 B3**
Franklin Park, *Chicago* . **9 B1**
Franklin Park, *Washington* . **32 B3**
Franklin Res., *Los Angeles* . **16 B2**
Frauenkirche, *Munich* ... **20 b2**
Frederiksberg, *Copenhagen* . **10 A3**
Frederiksdal, *Copenhagen* . **10 A2**
Fredersdorf, *Berlin* **5 A5**
Freguesia, *Rio de Janeiro* . **24 A1**
Freidrichshain, Volkspark,
  Berlin **5 A3**
Freiham, *Munich* **20 B1**
Freimann, *Munich* **20 A2**
Fresh Pond, *Boston* **6 A3**
Fresnes, *Paris* **23 B2**
Freudenau, *Vienna* **31 A2**
Friarstown, *Dublin* **11 B1**
Frick Collection, *New York* . **21 b3**
Friedenau, *Berlin* **5 B3**
Friedrichsfelde, *Berlin* . **5 B4**
Friedrichshagen, *Berlin* . **5 B4**
Friedrichshain, *Berlin* . **5 A3**
Friedrichslust, *Berlin* . **5 A5**
Friherrs, *Helsinki* **12 B1**
Frontón, I., *Lima* **16 B1**
Frunze, *Moscow* **19 B3**
Fuchū, *Tokyo* **29 A1**
Fuencarral, *Madrid* **17 B1**
Fuenlabrada, *Madrid* **17 C1**
Fujidera, *Osaka* **22 B4**
Fukagawa, *Tokyo* **29 B3**
Fukiage Imperial Garden,
  Tokyo **29 a4**
Fukiai, *Osaka* **22 A2**
Fukushima, *Osaka* **22 A3**
Fulham, *London* **15 B2**
Funabori, *Tokyo* **29 A4**
Funasaka, *Osaka* **22 A2**
Fundão, I. do, *Rio de Janeiro* . **24 B1**
Fünfhaus, *Vienna* **31 A2**
Furesø, *Copenhagen* **10 A2**
Furth, *Munich* **20 B3**
Futago-tamagawen, *Tokyo* . **29 B2**
Fuxing Dao, *Shanghai* ... **27 B2**
Fuxing Park, *Shanghai* .. **27 B1**
Fuxinglu, *Beijing* **4 B1**

G

Gage Park, *Chicago* **9 C2**
Gagny, *Paris* **23 A4**
Galata, *Istanbul* **12 B1**
Galátsion, *Athens* **2 A1**
Galeão, Aéroporto Int. de,
  Rio de Janeiro **24 A1**
Galvanovo, *Moscow* **19 B4**
Gambir, *Jakarta* **13 A1**
Gamboa, *Rio de Janeiro* . **24 B1**
Gambolóita, *Milan* **18 B2**
Gamla Stan , *Stockholm* . **28 c2**
Gamlebyen, *Oslo* **22 A3**
Gangwci, *Canton* **8 A1**
Gangwci, *Canton* **8 A2**
Ganjiaxue, *Beijing* **4 B1**
Gaoqiao, *Shanghai* **27 A2**
Garbagnate Milanese, *Milan* . **18 A1**
Garbatella, *Rome* **25 B2**
Garches, *Paris* **23 A2**
Garching, *Munich* **20 A3**
Garden City, *London* **7 A2**
Garden Reach, *Calcutta* . **8 B1**
Garder, *Oslo* **22 B2**
Garfield, *New York* **21 A1**
Garfield Park, *Chicago* . **9 B2**
Gargareta, *Athens* **2 B2**
Garvanza, *Los Angeles* .. **16 B3**
Gåshaga, *Stockholm* **28 A3**
Gateway National Recreation
  Area, *New York* **21 C2**
Gateway of India, *Mumbai* . **20 b2**
Gatow, *Berlin* **5 B1**
Gávea, *Rio de Janeiro* .. **24 B1**
Gávea, Pedra da,
  Rio de Janeiro **24 B1**
Gazdagrét, *Budapest* **7 B1**
Gebel el Ahmar, *Cairo* .. **7 A2**
Gebel el Muqattam, *Cairo* . **7 A2**
Gebel el Tura, *Cairo* ... **7 B2**
Geiselgasteig, *Munich* .. **20 B2**
General San Martin,
  Buenos Aires **7 B1**
Gennevilliers, *Paris* ... **23 A2**
Gentilly, *Paris* **23 B3**
Gentofte, *Copenhagen* ... **10 A3**
Genval, *Brussels* **6 B2**
George I., *Hong Kong* ... **12 B1**
Georges I., *Boston* **6 B4**
Georges River Bridge, *Sydney* **28 C1**
Georgetown, *Washington* . **32 B3**
Georgia Dome, *Atlanta* .. **3 B2**
Gerasdorf bei Wien, *Vienna* . **31 A2**
Gerberau, *Munich* **20 A1**
Gerli, *Buenos Aires* **7 C2**
Germiston, *Johannesburg* . **13 B2**
Gern, *Munich* **20 B2**
Gesìrat el Rauda, *Cairo* . **7 A2**
Getafe, *Madrid* **17 C1**
Geva Binyamin, *Jerusalem* . **11 A2**
Geylang Serai, *Singapore* . **27 B3**
Gezìrat el Dhahab, *Cairo* . **7 B2**
Gharapuri, *Mumbai* **20 B2**
Ghatkopar, *Mumbai* **20 A2**
Ghazipur, *Delhi* **10 B2**
Ghizri, *Karachi* **14 B2**
Ghizri Cr. →, *Karachi* .. **14 B2**
Ghonda, *Delhi* **10 A2**
Ghusuri, *Calcutta* **8 B1**
Gianicolense, *Rome* **25 B1**
Gianicolo, *Rome* **25 c1**
Gibraltar Pt., *Toronto* . **30 B2**
Gidea Park, *London* **15 A5**
Giesing, *Munich* **20 B2**
Gilmerton, *Edinburgh* ... **11 B3**
Gilo, *Jerusalem* **13 B2**
Gimmersta, *Stockholm* ... **28 B3**
Ginza, *Tokyo* **29 b5**
Girgaum, *Mumbai* **20 b2**
Giv'at Ye'arim, *Jerusalem* . **13 B1**
Giv'at Ze'ev, *Jerusalem* . **13 A2**
Giza Pyramids = Pyramids,
  Cairo **7 B1**
Gjersjøen, *Oslo* **22 B3**
Gladesville, *Sydney* **28 B1**
Gladsakse, *Copenhagen* .. **10 A2**
Glasnevin, *Dublin* **11 A2**
Glassmanor, *Washington* . **32 C3**
Glasthule, *Dublin* **11 B2**
Glen Iris, *Melbourne* ... **17 B2**
Glen Mar Park, *Washington* . **32 B3**
Glen Rock, *New York* **21 A1**
Glenardin, *Washington* .. **32 B4**
Glenasmole Reservoirs,
  Dublin **11 B1**
Glencorse Res., *Edinburgh* . **11 B2**
Glencullen, *Dublin* **11 B2**
Glendale, *Los Angeles* .. **16 B3**
Glendoo Mt., *Dublin* **11 B2**
Glenhuntly, *Melbourne* .. **17 B2**
Glenside, *Wellington* ... **32 B1**
Glenview, *Chicago* **9 A2**
Glenview Countryside,
  Chicago **9 A2**
Glenvista, *Johannesburg* . **13 B2**
Glifádha, *Athens* **2 B2**
Glömsta, *Stockholm* **28 B1**
Glostrup, *Copenhagen* ... **10 B2**
Gogar, *Edinburgh* **11 B2**
Göktürk, *Istanbul* **12 A1**
Golabari, *Calcutta* **8 B2**
Golabki, *Warsaw* **31 B1**
Gold Coast, *Chicago* **9 a2**
Golden Gate, *San Francisco* . **25 B2**
Golden Gate Bridge,
  San Francisco **25 B1**
Golden Gate Park,
  San Francisco **25 B2**
Golden Horn, *Istanbul* .. **12 B1**
Golders Green, *London* .. **15 A2**
Gollans Stream →,
  Wellington **32 B2**
Golyevo, *Moscow* **19 B1**
Goodman Hill, *Boston* ... **6 A1**
Goodmayes, *London* **15 A4**
Goodwood, *Cape Town* **8 A2**
Gopalpur, *Calcutta* **8 B2**
Górce, *Warsaw* **31 B1**
Gore Hill, *Sydney* **28 A1**
Gorelyy →, *St. Petersburg* . **26 B2**
Gorenki, *Moscow* **19 B5**
Gorgie, *Edinburgh* **11 B2**
Gorky Park, *Moscow* **19 B3**
Gosen, *Berlin* **5 B5**
Gosener kanal, *Berlin* .. **5 B5**
Gospel Oak, *London* **15 A3**
Gotanda, *Tokyo* **29 B3**
Goth Goli Mar, *Karachi* . **14 A2**
Goth Sher Shah, *Karachi* . **14 A1**
Gournay-sur-Marne, *Paris* . **23 A4**
Governador, I. do,
  Rio de Janeiro **24 A1**
Governor's L., *New York* . **21 B1**

Graben, *Vienna* **31 b2**
Grabów, *Warsaw* **31 C1**
Graça, *Lisbon* **14 b3**
Grace, Mt., *Wellington* . **32 B2**
Grace Cathedral,
  San Francisco **25 b1**
Gracefield, *Wellington* . **32 B2**
Gracia, *Barcelona* **4 A2**
Gräfelfing, *Munich* **20 B1**
Gragoatá, *Rio de Janeiro* . **24 B2**
Grand Central Station,
  New York **21 c2**
Grand Union Canal, *London* . **15 A2**
Grande Place, *Brussels* . **6 b2**
Grant Park, *Atlanta* **3 B2**
Grant Park, *Chicago* **9 c2**
Granton, *Edinburgh* **11 B2**
Grape I., *Boston* **6 B4**
Grassy Park, *Cape Town* . **8 B2**
Gratosóglio, *Milan* **18 B2**
Gratzwalde, *Berlin* **5 B5**
Gravesend, *New York* **21 C2**
Grazhdanka, *St. Petersburg* . **26 B2**
Great Falls, *Washington* . **32 B2**
Great Falls Park, *Washington* . **32 B2**
Great Hall of the People,
  Beijing **4 b2**
Great Meadows National
  Wildlife Refuge, *Boston* . **6 A1**
Greco, *Milan* **18 A2**
Green I., *Hong Kong* **12 B1**
Green Point, *Cape Town* . **8 A1**
Greenbelt, *Washington* .. **32 A4**
Greenbelt Park, *Washington* . **32 A4**
Greenfield Park, *Montreal* . **19 B3**
Greenford, *London* **15 A1**
Greenhill, *London* **15 A2**
Greenhills, *Dublin* **11 B1**
Greenmarket Square,
  Cape Town **8 c2**
Greenpoint, *New York* ... **21 B2**
Greenwich, *London* **15 B3**
Greenwich Observatory,
  London **15 B3**
Greenwich Village, *New York* . **21 b2**
Greenwood, *Boston* **6 A3**
Grefsen, *Oslo* **22 A3**
Gresham Park, *Atlanta* .. **3 B2**
Greve Strand, *Copenhagen* . **10 B1**
Greyfriars Kirk, *Edinburgh* . **11 c2**
Griebnitzsee, *Berlin* ... **5 B1**
Griffen Park, *Los Angeles* . **16 B3**
Grimbergen, *Brussels* ... **6 A2**
Grinzing, *Vienna* **31 A2**
Gröbenried, *Munich* **20 A1**
Grochów, *Warsaw* **31 B2**
Grodzisk, *Warsaw* **31 B2**
Groenendaal, *Brussels* .. **6 B2**
Grogol Petamburan, *Jakarta* . **13 A1**
Gronsdorf, *Munich* **20 B3**
Grorud, *Oslo* **22 A4**
Gross Glienicke, *Berlin* . **5 B1**
Gross-Hadern, *Munich* ... **20 B1**
Gross-Lappen, *Munich* ... **20 A2**
Grosse Krampe, *Berlin* .. **5 B5**
Grosse Müggelsee, *Berlin* . **5 B4**
Grossenzersdorf, *Vienna* . **31 A3**
Grossenzersdorfer Arm →,
  Vienna **31 A3**
Grosser Biberhaufen, *Vienna* . **31 A2**
Grosser Wannsee, *Berlin* . **5 B2**
Grossfeld-Siedlung, *Vienna* . **31 A2**
Grosshesselohe, *Munich* . **20 B2**
Grossjedlersdorf, *Vienna* . **31 A2**
Grosszeithen, *Berlin* ... **5 B3**
Grove Hall, *Boston* **6 B3**
Grove Park, *Atlanta* **3 B2**
Grove Park, *London* **15 B4**
Grove Park, *London* **15 B2**
Groveton, *Washington* ... **32 C3**
Grünau, *Berlin* **5 B4**
Grunewald, *Berlin* **5 B2**
Grünwald, *Munich* **20 B2**
Grünwalder Forst, *Munich* . **20 B2**
Grymes Hill, *New York* .. **21 C1**
Guadalupe, *Manila* **17 B2**
Guadalupe, Basílica de,
  Mexico City **18 B2**
Guanabara, B. de,
  Rio de Janeiro **24 B2**
Guanabara, Jardim,
  Rio de Janeiro **24 A1**
Guanabara, Palácio da,
  Rio de Janeiro **24 B1**
Guang'anmen, *Beijing* ... **4 B1**
Guanggumen, *Beijing* **4 B2**
Guangzhou, *Canton* **8 B2**
Guanshuo, *Canton* **8 B3**
Gudö, *Stockholm* **28 B3**
Güell, Parque de, *Barcelona* . **4 A2**
Guerrero, *Mexico City* .. **18 a1**
Guggenheim Museum,
  New York **21 b3**
Guinardó, *Barcelona* **4 A2**
Gulbai, *Karachi* **14 A1**
Güngören, *Istanbul* **12 C1**
Gunnersbury, *London* **15 B2**
Gustavo A. Madero,
  Mexico City **18 B2**
Guttenberg, *New York* ... **21 B1**
Gutuyevskiy, Ostrov,
  St. Petersburg **26 B1**
Guyancourt, *Paris* **23 B1**
Gyál, *Budapest* **7 B3**
Gyáli-patak →, *Budapest* . **7 B2**

H

Haaga, *Helsinki* **12 B2**
Haar, *Munich* **20 B3**
Hackbridge, *London* **15 B3**
Hackensack, *New York* ... **21 A1**
Hackensack →, *New York* . **21 B1**
Hackney, *London* **15 A3**
Hackney Wick, *London* ... **15 A3**
Haga, *Stockholm* **28 A2**
Hagenbrunn, *Vienna* **31 A2**
Hägersten, *Stockholm* ... **28 B1**
Haggvik, *Stockholm* **28 A1**
Hai He →, *Tianjin* **30 B2**
Haidan, *Beijing* **4 B1**
Haidarpur, *Delhi* **10 A1**
Haidhausen, *Munich* **20 B2**
Haight-Ashbury,
  San Francisco **25 b1**
Hainault, *London* **15 A4**
Haizhu Guangchang, *Canton* . **8 B2**
Hakunila, *Helsinki* **12 B3**
Halásztelek, *Budapest* .. **7 B1**
Haliç = Golden Horn,
  Istanbul **12 B1**
Halim Perdanakusuma
  International Airport,
  Jakarta **13 B2**

Halle, *Brussels* **6 B1**
Haltiala, *Helsinki* **12 B2**
Haltiavuori, *Helsinki* .. **12 B2**
Ham, *London* **15 B2**
Hämeenkylä, *Helsinki* ... **12 B1**
Hammarby, *Stockholm* **28 B2**
Hamme, *Brussels* **6 A1**
Hammersmith, *London* **15 B2**
Hampstead, *London* **15 A2**
Hampstead, *Montreal* **19 B2**
Hampstead Garden Suburb,
  London **15 A2**
Hampstead Heath, *London* . **15 A2**
Hampton, *London* **15 B1**
Hampton Court Palace,
  London **15 B1**
Hampton Wick, *London* ... **15 B1**
Hamra', *Baghdad* **3 B1**
Hanala, *Helsinki* **12 B3**
Haneda, *Tokyo* **29 B3**
Hang Hau, *Hong Kong* **12 B2**
Hanging Gardens, *Mumbai* . **20 b1**
Hanjiashu, *Tianjin* **30 A1**
Hanlon, *Toronto* **30 B1**
Hanwell, *London* **15 A1**
Hanworth, *London* **15 B1**
Haora, *Calcutta* **8 B1**
Hapeville, *Atlanta* **3 C2**
Happy Valley, *Hong Kong* . **12 B2**
Har Adar, *Jerusalem* **13 B1**
Haren, *Brussels* **6 A2**
Hareskovby, *Copenhagen* . **10 A2**
Haringey, *London* **15 A3**
Harjusuo, *Helsinki* **12 B3**
Harlaching, *Munich* **20 B2**
Harlaw Res., *Edinburgh* . **11 B2**
Harlem, *New York* **21 B2**
Harlesden, *London* **15 A2**
Harlington, *London* **15 B1**
Harmaja, *Helsinki* **12 C2**
Harmashatar hegy, *Budapest* . **7 A2**
Harolds Cross, *Dublin* .. **11 B2**
Háros, *Budapest* **7 B2**
Harperrig Reservoir,
  Edinburgh **11 B1**
Harrow, *London* **15 A1**
Harrow on the Hill, *London* . **15 A1**
Harrow School, *London* .. **15 A1**
Harrow Weald, *London* ... **15 A1**
Hartsfield-Atlanta
  International Airport,
  Atlanta **3 C2**
Harumi, *Tokyo* **29 c5**
Harvard Univ., *Boston* .. **6 A3**
Harwood Heights, *Chicago* . **9 B2**
Hasanäbäd, *Tehran* **30 A1**
Hasbrouck Heights,
  New York **21 A1**
Haselhorst, *Berlin* **5 A2**
Hasköy, *Istanbul* **12 B1**
Hasle, *Oslo* **22 A3**
Haslum, *Oslo* **22 A2**
Hästhagen, *Stockholm* ... **28 B3**
Hataitai, *Wellington* ... **32 B1**
Hatch End, *London* **15 A1**
Hatiara, *Calcutta* **8 B2**
Hauketo, *Oslo* **22 A3**
Havel →, *Berlin* **5 A2**
Havelkanal, *Berlin* **5 A2**
Havering, *London* **15 A5**
Havering-atte-Bower,
  London **15 A5**
Hawölgok, *Seoul* **26 B2**
Haworth, *New York* **21 A1**
Hayes, *London* **15 B4**
Hayes, *London* **15 A1**
Hayes End, *London* **15 A1**
Hayford, *Chicago* **9 C2**
Haywards, *Wellington* ... **32 A2**
Heard Pond, *Boston* **6 A1**
Heathfield, *Cape Town* .. **8 B2**
Heathrow Airport, *London* . **15 B1**
Hebe Haven, *Hong Kong* .. **12 A2**
Hebei, *Tianjin* **30 B2**
Hedong, *Canton* **8 B2**
Hedong, *Tianjin* **30 B2**
Heidelberg Heights,
  Melbourne **17 A2**
Heidelberg West, *Melbourne* . **17 A2**
Heidemühle, *Berlin* **5 B5**
Heideveld, *Cape Town* ... **8 A2**
Heiligensee, *Berlin* **5 A2**
Heiligenstadt, *Vienna* .. **31 A2**
Heinersdorf, *Berlin* **5 A3**
Heldenplatz, *Vienna* **31 b1**
Hélène Champlain, Parc,
  Montreal **19 A2**
Helenelund, *Stockholm* .. **28 A2**
Heliopolis = Masr el Gedida,
  Cairo **7 A2**
Hellersdorf, *Berlin* **5 A4**
Hellerup, *Copenhagen* ... **10 A3**
Hevik, *Oslo* **22 A3**
Hovorčovice, *Prague* **24 A3**
Howard Beach, *New York* . **21 C2**
Howth, *Dublin* **11 A3**
Howth Head, *Dublin* **11 A3**
Hoxton, *London* **15 a5**
Höya, *Tokyo* **29 A2**
Hradčany, *Prague* **24 B2**
Huanghuagang Mausoleum of
  the 72 Martyrs, *Canton* . **8 B2**
Huangpu, *Shanghai* **27 B2**
Huangpu Jiang →, *Shanghai* . **27 B1**
Huangpu Park, *Shanghai* . **27 B1**
Huangtugang, *Beijing* ... **4 C1**
Huascar, *Lima* **16 A2**
Huay Khwang, *Bangkok* ... **3 B2**
Huddinge, *Stockholm* **28 B2**
Hudson →, *New York* **21 A2**
Huechuraba, *Santiago* ... **26 B1**
Hueserde san Beltran,
  Barcelona **4 A1**
Hugli, *Calcutta* **8 B2**
Hugli = Hugli →, *Calcutta* . **8 B2**
Hŏnor, *Berlin* **5 A4**
Höngg, *Vienna* **31 A2**

Higashiyodogawa, *Osaka* . **22 A3**
High Park, *Toronto* **30 B2**
Highbury, *London* **15 A3**
Highgate, *London* **15 A3**
Highland Cr. →, *Toronto* . **30 A3**
Highland Creek, *Toronto* . **30 A3**
Highland Park, *Los Angeles* . **16 B3**
Highlands North,
  Johannesburg **13 A2**
Hillcrest Heights, *Washington* . **32 C4**
Hillend, *Edinburgh* **11 A1**
Hillingdon, *London* **15 A1**
Hillwood, *Washington* ... **32 B3**
Hilmīya, *Cairo* **7 A2**
Hin Keng, *Hong Kong* **12 A2**
Hingham, *Boston* **6 B4**
Hingham B., *Boston* **6 B4**
Hingham Harbor, *Boston* . **6 B4**
Hirakata, *Osaka* **22 A4**
Hirota, *Osaka* **22 A3**
Hirschstetten, *Vienna* .. **31 A2**
Histórico Nacional, Museu,
  Rio de Janeiro **24 b3**
Hither Green, *London* ... **15 B3**
Hiyoshi, *Tokyo* **29 B2**
Hizma, *Jerusalem* **13 B2**
Hjortekær, *Copenhagen* .. **10 A3**
Hjortespring, *Copenhagen* . **10 A2**
Hlubočeoy, *Prague* **24 B2**
Ho Chung, *Hong Kong* **12 A2**
Ho Man Tin, *Hong Kong* .. **12 B2**
Hoboken, *New York* **21 B1**
Hobsons B., *Melbourne* .. **17 B1**
Hochbrück, *Munich* **20 A2**
Hochelaga, *Montreal* **19 A2**
Hodgkins, *Chicago* **9 C1**
Hoegi, *Seoul* **26 B2**
Hoeilaart, *Brussels* **6 B2**
Hofberg, *Vienna* **31 A2**
Hoffman I., *New York* ... **21 C1**
Hofgarten, *Munich* **20 a3**
Högsdadomstolen,
  Stockholm **28 c2**
Hohenbrunn, *Munich* **20 B3**
Hohenschönhausen, *Berlin* . **5 A4**
Holborn, *London* **15 b4**
Hollešovice, *Prague* **24 B2**
Holland Village, *Singapore* . **27 B2**
Höllriegelskreuth, *Munich* . **20 B1**
Hollywood, *Los Angeles* . **16 B3**
Holmenkollen, *Oslo* **22 A3**
Holmes Run Acres,
  Washington **32 B2**
Holmgård, *Stockholm* **28 B1**
Holysloot, *Amsterdam* ... **2 A3**
Homerton, *London* **15 A3**
Hometown, *Chicago* **9 C2**
Hōnanchō, *Tokyo* **29 B2**
Honcho, *Tokyo* **29 A3**
Honden, *Tokyo* **29 A4**
Hondo, Rio →, *Los Angeles* . **16 B4**
Hong Kong, *Hong Kong* ... **12 B1**
Hong I., *Hong Kong* **12 B2**
Hong Kong Park, *Hong Kong* . **12 a2**
Hongkou, *Shanghai* **27 B1**
Hongkou Park, *Shanghai* . **27 B1**
Hongmiao, *Beijing* **4 B2**
Hongqiao, *Shanghai* **27 B1**
Hongqiao, *Tianjin* **30 B1**
Hongqiao Airport, *Shanghai* . **27 B1**
Hongün, *Seoul* **26 B1**
Honjyo, *Tokyo* **29 A3**
Honoré Mercier, Pont,
  Montreal **19 B1**
Hooghly = Hugli →, *Calcutta* . **8 B2**
Hook, *London* **15 B2**
Horikiri, *Tokyo* **29 A4**
Horn Pond, *Boston* **6 A3**
Hornchurch, *London* **15 A5**
Horni, *Prague* **24 B3**
Horni Počernice, *Prague* . **24 A3**
Hornsey, *London* **15 A3**
Hortaleza, *Madrid* **17 B2**
Hosoyama, *Tokyo* **29 B2**
Hostafranchs, *Barcelona* . **4 A1**
Hôtel des Invalides, *Paris* . **23 B2**
Houbětín, *Prague* **24 B3**
Houghs Neck, *Boston* **6 B4**
Houghton, *Johannesburg* . **13 B2**
Houilles, *Paris* **23 A2**
Hounslow, *London* **15 B1**
Houses of Parliament,
  London **15 c3**
Hout Bay, *Cape Town* **8 B1**
Hove A →, *Copenhagen* ... **10 A1**
Hovedøya, *Oslo* **22 A3**

Hutt R. →, *Wellington* .. **32 B2**
Hütteldorf, *Vienna* **31 A1**
Hüvösvölgy, *Budapest* ... **7 A2**
Hvalstad, *Oslo* **22 A1**
Hvalstrand, *Oslo* **22 A2**
Hvidovre, *Copenhagen* ... **10 B2**
Hwagok, *Seoul* **26 B1**
Hyattsville, *Washington* . **32 B4**
Hyde Park, *Boston* **6 B3**
Hyde Park, *Chicago* **9 C3**
Hyde Park, *Johannesburg* . **13 A2**
Hyde Park, *London* **15 A3**
Hyde Park, *Sydney* **28 B2**

I

Ibese, *Lagos* **14 A2**
Ibirapuera, *São Paulo* .. **26 B1**
Ibirapuera, Parque, *São Paulo* . **26 B2**
Icarai, *Rio de Janeiro* . **24 B2**
Içerenköy, *Istanbul* **12 C2**
Ichgao, *Tokyo* **29 B2**
Ichigaya, *Tokyo* **29 a3**
Ichikawa, *Tokyo* **29 A4**
Ickenham, *London* **15 A1**
Iddo, *Lagos* **14 B2**
Idi-Oro, *Lagos* **14 A2**
Iganmu, *Lagos* **14 B2**
Igbobi, *Lagos* **14 A2**
Igbologun, *Lagos* **14 B1**
Igny, *Paris* **23 B2**
Iju, Het →, *Amsterdam* .. **2 A2**
IJ-meer, *Amsterdam* **2 A3**
IJtunnel, *Amsterdam* **2 c3**
Ikebe, *Tokyo* **29 B2**
Ikebukuro, *Tokyo* **29 A3**
Ikegami, *Tokyo* **29 B3**
Ikeja, *Lagos* **14 A2**
Ikeuchi, *Osaka* **22 B4**
Ikoyi, *Lagos* **14 B2**
Ikuata, *Lagos* **14 B2**
Ikuno, *Osaka* **22 A4**
Ikuta, *Osaka* **22 A2**
Ikuta, *Tokyo* **29 B2**
Ila, *Oslo* **22 A3**
Ilford, *London* **15 A4**
Ilioúpolis, *Athens* **2 B2**
Ilpendam, *Amsterdam* **2 A2**
Ilsós →, *Athens* **2 B2**
Imagem e do Som, Museu da,
  Rio de Janeiro **24 b3**
Imbábah, *Cairo* **7 A2**
Imielin, *Warsaw* **31 C2**
Imirim, *São Paulo* **26 A2**
Imittós, *Athens* **2 B2**
Imittós, Óros, *Athens* .. **2 B2**
Imperial Palace Museum,
  Beijing **4 b2**
Inagi, *Tokyo* **29 B2**
Inchcolm, *Edinburgh* **11 A2**
Inchicore, *Dublin* **11 B2**
Inchkeith, *Edinburgh* ... **11 A3**
Inchmickery, *Edinburgh* . **11 A2**
Incirano, *Milan* **18 A1**
Independencia, *Lima* **16 A2**
Independencia, *Santiago* . **26 B2**
India Gate, *Delhi* **1 c2**
Indian Creek Village, *Miami* . **18 A2**
Indian Head Park, *Chicago* . **9 C1**
Indianópolis, *São Paulo* . **26 B2**
Indios Verdes, *Mexico City* . **18 B2**
Indira Ghandi International
  Airport, *Delhi* **10 B1**
Industria, *Johannesburg* . **13 B2**
Ingierstrand, *Oslo* **22 B3**
Inglewood, *Los Angeles* . **16 C3**
Ingliston, *Edinburgh* ... **11 B1**
Inhaüme, *Rio de Janeiro* . **24 B1**
Inner Port Shelter,
  Hong Kong **12 A2**
Interlagos, *São Paulo* .. **26 C1**
Intramuros, *Manila* **17 B1**
Invalides, *Paris* **23 A2**
Inverkeithing, *Edinburgh* . **11 A1**
Inzersdorf, *Vienna* **31 B2**
Ipanema, *Rio de Janeiro* . **24 B1**
Ipiranga →, *São Paulo* .. **26 B2**
Iponri, *Lagos* **14 B2**
Ireland's Eye, *Dublin* .. **11 A3**
Irving Park, *Chicago* ... **9 B2**
Isabel, *Rio de Janeiro* . **24 A1**
Isagatedo, *Lagos* **14 A1**
Isar →, *Munich* **20 A3**
Ishbìliya, *Baghdad* **3 A1**
Ishikiri, *Osaka* **22 A4**
Island Bay, *Wellington* . **32 B1**
Island Park, *Toronto* ... **30 B2**
Isle of Dogs, *London* ... **15 B3**
Isleworth, *London* **15 B2**
Islington, *London* **15 A3**
Islington, *Toronto* **30 B1**
Ismaning, *Munich* **20 A3**
Ismayloskiy Park, *Moscow* . **14 A1**
Isolo, *Lagos* **14 A2**
Issy-les-Moulineaux, *Paris* . **23 B2**
Istanbul, *Istanbul* **12 C1**
Istanbul Boğazi, *Istanbul* . **12 B2**
Istinye, *Istanbul* **12 B2**
Itä Hakkila, *Helsinki* .. **12 B3**
Itaewon, *Seoul* **26 B1**
Itahanga, *Rio de Janeiro* . **24 B1**
Itami, *Osaka* **22 A3**
Ivanhoe, *Melbourne* **17 A2**
Ivry-sur-Seine, *Paris* .. **23 B3**
Iwazono, *Osaka* **22 A3**
Ixelles, *Brussels* **6 B2**
Izmaylovo, *Moscow* **19 B4**
Iztacalco, *Mexico City* . **18 B2**
Iztapalapa, *Mexico City* . **18 B2**

J

Jaba, *Jerusalem* **13 A2**
Jababpur, *Calcutta* **8 B2**
Jacaré, *Rio de Janeiro* . **24 B1**
Jackson Heights, *New York* . **21 B2**
Jackson Park, *Chicago* .. **9 C3**
Jacques Cartier, *Montreal* . **19 A3**
Jacques Cartier, Pont,
  Montreal **19 A2**
Jade Buddha Temple,
  Shanghai **27 B1**
Jægersborg, *Copenhagen* . **10 A3**
Jægersborg Dyrehave,
  Copenhagen **10 A3**
Jagadishpur, *Calcutta* .. **8 B1**
Jagatpur, *Delhi* **10 A2**

Jaguaré, Rib. do →,
  São Paulo **26 B1**
Jahangirpur, *Delhi* **10 A2**
Jakarta, *Jakarta* **13 A2**
Jakarta, Teluk, *Jakarta* . **13 A1**
Jalan Kayu, *Singapore* .. **27 A3**
Jamaica Plain, *Boston* .. **6 B3**
Jamakpuri, *Delhi* **10 B1**
Jamshidieh, *Tehran* **30 A2**
Janki, *Warsaw* **31 C1**
Jannali, *Sydney* **28 C1**
Japan Center, *San Francisco* . **25 c1**
Jaraguá, *São Paulo* **26 A1**
Jaraguá, Pico de, *São Paulo* . **26 A1**
Jardim Botânico, *Brussels* . **6 a3**
Järvatälet, *Stockholm* .. **28 A1**
Jaskhar, *Mumbai* **20 B2**
Jatinegara, *Jakarta* **13 B2**
Javádiyeh, *Tehran* **30 B2**
Jaworowa, *Warsaw* **31 C1**
Jedlesee, *Vienna* **31 A2**
Jefferson Memorial,
  Washington **32 c1**
Jefferson Park, *Chicago* . **9 B2**
Jelonki, *Warsaw* **31 B1**
Jerónimos, Mosteiro dos,
  Lisbon **14 A1**
Jersey City, *New York* .. **21 B1**
Jerusalem, *Jerusalem* ... **13 B2**
Jésus, I., *Montreal* **19 A1**
Jesús Maria, *Lima* **16 B2**
Jette, *Brussels* **6 A1**
Jewish Quarter, *Jerusalem* . **13 b3**
Jey, *Tehran* **30 B2**
Jianguomen, *Beijing* **4 B2**
Jiangwan, *Shanghai* **27 B1**
Jianshan Park, *Tianjin* . **30 B1**
Jihād, *Baghdad* **3 B1**
Jim Thompson's House,
  Bangkok **3 b2**
Jimbōchō, *Tokyo* **29 a4**
Jingan, *Shanghai* **27 B1**
Jingu Outer Garden, *Tokyo* . **29 b2**
Jinočany, *Prague* **24 B1**
Jinonice, *Prague* **24 B2**
Jiyūgaoka, *Tokyo* **29 B3**
Jizā'ir, *Baghdad* **3 B2**
Jizira, *Baghdad* **3 A2**
Johannesburg, *Johannesburg* . **13 B2**
Johanneskirchen, *Munich* . **20 A2**
Johannesstift, *Berlin* .. **5 A2**
Johannisthal, *Berlin* ... **5 B4**
John Hancock Center,
  Chicago **9 a2**
John McLaren Park,
  San Francisco **25 B2**
Johnsonville, *Wellington* . **32 B1**
Joinville-le-Pont, *Paris* . **23 B3**
Joli-Bois, *Brussels* **6 B2**
Jollas, *Helsinki* **12 B3**
Jonstrup, *Copenhagen* ... **10 A2**
Joppa, *Edinburgh* **11 B3**
Jorge Chavez, Aeropuerto
  Int., *Lima* **16 B2**
Jorge Newbury, Aeroparque,
  Buenos Aires **7 B2**
Jósefa Piłsudskiego Park,
  Warsaw **31 B1**
Jōtō, *Osaka* **22 A4**
Jouy-en-Josas, *Paris* ... **23 B2**
Juan Anchorena,
  Buenos Aires **7 A2**
Juan González Romero,
  Mexico City **18 A2**
Judeira, *Jerusalem* **13 A2**
Juhu, *Mumbai* **20 A2**
Jūjā, *Tokyo* **29 A3**
Jukskeirivier →,
  Johannesburg **13 A1**
Julianów, *Warsaw* **31 B2**
Jugfernheide, Volkspark,
  Berlin **5 A2**
Jungfernsee, *Berlin* **5 B1**
Juniper Green, *Edinburgh* . **11 B2**
Junk B., *Hong Kong* **12 B2**
Jurong, *Singapore* **27 B2**
Jurong, Selat, *Singapore* . **27 B2**
Jurong Industrial Estate,
  Singapore **27 B2**
Jurujuba, Enseada de,
  Rio de Janeiro **24 B2**
Jūsō, *Osaka* **22 A3**
Justice, *Chicago* **9 C2**
Justicia, *Madrid* **17 a3**
Jwalahari, *Delhi* **10 B1**

K

Kabaty, *Warsaw* **31 C2**
Kadıköy, *Istanbul* **12 C2**
Kadoma, *Osaka* **22 A4**
Kaebong, *Seoul* **26 C1**
Kâğıthane, *Istanbul* **12 B1**
Kâğıthane →, *Istanbul* .. **12 B1**
Kagran, *Vienna* **31 A2**
Kahnawake, *Montreal* **19 B1**
Kaimes, *Edinburgh* **11 B3**
Kaisariani, *Athens* **2 B2**
Kaiser Wilhelm Kirche, *Berlin* . **5 b2**
Kaiserebersdorf, *Vienna* . **31 B2**
Kaivoksela, *Helsinki* ... **12 B2**
Kalamákion, *Athens* **2 B2**
Kalbadevi, *Mumbai* **20 b2**
Kalipur, *Calcutta* **8 B1**
Kalkaji, *Delhi* **10 B2**
Kalkatha, *Athens* **2 B2**
Kalveboderne, *Copenhagen* . **10 B3**
Kamarhati, *Calcutta* **8 B2**
Kamata, *Tokyo* **29 B3**
Kameari, *Tokyo* **29 A4**
Kameido, *Tokyo* **29 A4**
Kami-Itabashi, *Tokyo* ... **29 A3**
Kamikitazawa, *Tokyo* **29 B2**
Kamisuruma, *Tokyo* **29 B2**
Kampong Landang, *Singapore* . **27 A3**
Kampong Tanjong Penjuru,
  Singapore **27 B2**
Kampung Bali, *Jakarta* .. **13 B2**
Kanamori, *Tokyo* **29 B1**
Kanda, *Tokyo* **29 a5**
Kandilli, *Istanbul* **12 B2**
Kangdong, *Seoul* **26 B2**
Kangnam, *Seoul* **26 B1**
Kangsŏ, *Seoul* **26 B1**
Kankurgachi, *Calcutta* .. **8 B2**
Kanlıca, *Istanbul* **12 B2**
Kanonerskiy, Ostrov,
  St. Petersburg **26 B1**
Kanzaki →, *Osaka* **22 A3**
Kapellerfeld, *Vienna* ... **31 A2**

KÁPOSZTÁSMEGYER

Káposztásmegyer, *Budapest* 7 A2
Kapotnya, *Moscow* 19 C4
Käppala, *Stockholm* 28 A3
Käpylä, *Helsinki* 12 B2
Karachi, *Karachi* 14 A2
Karachi Int. Airport, *Karachi* 14 A2
Karato, *Osaka* 22 A2
Karibong, *Seoul* 26 C1
Karkh, *Baghdad* 3 A2
Karlin, *Prague* 24 B2
Karlsfeld, *Munich* 20 A1
Karlshorst, *Berlin* 5 B4
Karlsplatz, *Munich* 20 b1
Karntner Strasse, *Vienna* 31 b2
Karol Bagh, *Delhi* 10 B2
Karolinenhof, *Berlin* 5 B4
Karori, *Wellington* 32 B1
Karow, *Berlin* 5 A3
Karrādah, *Baghdad* 3 B2
Kärsön, *Stockholm* 28 B1
Kasai, *Tokyo* 29 B4
Kashiwara, *Osaka* 22 B4
Kastellet, *Copenhagen* 10 a3
Kastrup, *Copenhagen* 10 B3
Kastrup Lufthavn, *Copenhagen* 10 B3
Kasuga, *Tokyo* 29 A2
Kasuge, *Tokyo* 29 A3
Kasumigaseki, *Tokyo* 29 b4
Katong, *Singapore* 27 B3
Katrineberg, *Stockholm* 28 B1
Katsushika-Ku, *Tokyo* 29 A4
Kau Pei Chau, *Hong Kong* 12 B2
Kau Yi Chau, *Hong Kong* 12 B1
Kaulsdorf, *Berlin* 5 B4
Kauniainen, *Helsinki* 12 B1
Kawasaki, *Tokyo* 29 B3
Kawawa, *Tokyo* 29 B2
Kawęczyn, *Warsaw* 31 B2
Kayu Putih, *Jakarta* 13 B2
Kbely, *Prague* 24 B3
Kebayoran Baru, *Jakarta* 13 B1
Kebayoran Lama, *Jakarta* 13 B1
Kebon Jeruk, *Jakarta* 13 B1
Kedar, *Jerusalem* 13 B2
Keilor, *Melbourne* 17 A1
Keilor North, *Melbourne* 17 A1
Keimola, *Helsinki* 12 A1
Kelenföld, *Budapest* 7 B2
Kelvin, *Johannesburg* 13 A2
Kemang, *Jakarta* 13 B1
Kemayoran, *Jakarta* 13 B2
Kemerburgaz, *Istanbul* 12 B1
Kempton Park Races, *London* 15 B1
Kendall Green, *Boston* 6 A2
Kenilworth, *Cape Town* 8 A1
Kennedy Town, *Hong Kong* 12 B1
Kennington, *London* 15 c4
Kensal Green, *London* 15 A2
Kensal Rise, *London* 15 a1
Kensington, *Johannesburg* 13 B2
Kensington, *London* 15 B2
Kensington, *New York* 21 C2
Kensington, *Sydney* 28 B2
Kensington Palace, *London* 15 A2
Kent Village, *Washington* 32 B4
Kentish Town, *London* 15 A3
Kenton, *London* 15 A2
Kenwood House, *London* 15 A3
Kepa, *Warsaw* 31 B2
Keppel Harbour, *Singapore* 27 B2
Keramíkos, *Athens* 2 b1
Kettering, *Washington* 32 B5
Kew, *London* 15 B2
Kew, *Melbourne* 17 A2
Kew Gardens, *London* 15 B2
Kew Gardens, *Toronto* 30 B3
Key Biscayne, *Miami* 18 B2
Khaidhárion, *Athens* 2 A1
Khalándrion, *Athens* 2 A2
Khalīj, *Baghdad* 3 B2
Khandallah, *Wellington* 32 B1
Khansā', *Baghdad* 3 A2
Kharavli, *Mumbai* 20 B2
Khefren, *Cairo* 7 B1
Khichripur, *Delhi* 10 B2
Khidirpur, *Calcutta* 8 B1
Khimki-Khovrino, *Moscow* 19 A3
Khirbet Jub e-Rum, *Jerusalem* 13 B2
Khlong San, *Bangkok* 3 B2
Khlong Toey, *Bangkok* 3 B2
Kholargós, *Athens* 2 B2
Khorel, *Calcutta* 8 A1
Khorosovo, *Moscow* 19 B2
Kiamari, *Karachi* 14 B1
Kierling, *Vienna* 31 A1
Kierlingbach →, *Vienna* 31 A1
Kifisós →, *Athens* 2 B2
Kikuna, *Tokyo* 29 B2
Kilbarrack, *Dublin* 11 A3
Kilbirnie, *Wellington* 32 B1
Kilburn, *London* 15 A2
Killakee, *Dublin* 11 B2
Killester, *Dublin* 11 A2
Killiney, *Dublin* 11 B3
Killiney Bay, *Dublin* 11 B3
Kilmacud, *Dublin* 11 B2
Kilmainham, *Dublin* 11 A2
Kilmashogue Mt., *Dublin* 11 B2
Kilmore, *Dublin* 11 A2
Kilnamanagh, *Dublin* 11 B1
Kilo, *Helsinki* 12 B1
Kilokri, *Delhi* 10 B2
Kiltiernan, *Dublin* 11 B2
Kimmage, *Dublin* 11 B2
Kindi, *Baghdad* 3 B2
Kinghorn, *Edinburgh* 11 A2
King's Cross, *London* 15 a4
Kings Cross, *Sydney* 28 c3
Kings Domain, *Melbourne* 17 A1
Kings Park, *Washington* 32 C2
Kings Park West, *Washington* 32 C2
Kingsbury, *London* 15 A2
Kingsbury, *Melbourne* 17 A2
Kingsford, *Sydney* 28 B2
Kingston upon Thames, *London* 15 B2
Kingston Vale, *London* 15 B2
Kingsway, *Toronto* 30 B1
Kinsaley, *Dublin* 11 A2
Kipling Heights, *Toronto* 30 A1
Kipséli, *Athens* 2 B2
Kirchstockbach, *Munich* 20 B3
Kirchtrudering, *Munich* 20 B3
Kirikiri, *Lagos* 14 B1
Kirke Værløse, *Copenhagen* 10 A1
Kirkhill, *Edinburgh* 11 B2
Kirkliston, *Edinburgh* 11 B1
Kirknewton, *Edinburgh* 11 B1
Kirov Palace of Culture, *St. Petersburg* 26 B1
Kısıklı, *Istanbul* 12 B2
Kispest, *Budapest* 7 B2
Kista, *Stockholm* 28 A1
Kita, *Osaka* 22 A4
Kita-Ku, *Tokyo* 29 A3
Kitazawa, *Tokyo* 29 B3
Kiu Tsiu, *Hong Kong* 12 A2
Kivistö, *Helsinki* 12 B2
Kızıltoprak, *Istanbul* 12 C2
Kizu →, *Osaka* 22 B3
Kizuri, *Osaka* 22 B4
Kjelsås, *Oslo* 22 A3
Kladow, *Berlin* 5 B1
Klampenborg, *Copenhagen* 10 A3
Klaudyń, *Warsaw* 31 B1
Klecany, *Prague* 24 A2
Kledering, *Vienna* 31 B2
Klein Jukskei →, *Johannesburg* 13 A1
Kleinmachnow, *Berlin* 5 B2
Kleinschönebeck, *Berlin* 5 B5
Klemetsrud, *Oslo* 22 A4
Kličany, *Prague* 24 A2
Klipriviersberg Nature Reserve, *Johannesburg* 13 B2
Klosterneuburg, *Vienna* 31 A1
Knesset, *Jerusalem* 13 b1
Knightsbridge, *London* 15 c2
Kőbánya, *Budapest* 7 B2
Kobbegem, *Brussels* 6 A1
Kōbe, *Osaka* 22 A2
Kōbe Harbour, *Osaka* 22 B2
København, *Copenhagen* 10 A2
Kobylisy, *Prague* 24 B2
Kobyłka, *Warsaw* 31 A3
Kŏch'ŏk, *Seoul* 26 B1
Kodaira, *Tokyo* 29 A1
Kodanaka, *Tokyo* 29 B2
Kodenmacho, *Tokyo* 29 a5
Koekelberg, *Brussels* 6 A1
Koganei, *Tokyo* 29 A2
Kogarah, *Sydney* 28 B1
Køge Bugt, *Copenhagen* 10 B2
Koivupää, *Helsinki* 12 B2
Koja, *Jakarta* 13 A2
Koja Utara, *Jakarta* 13 A2
Kokobunji, *Tokyo* 29 A1
Kokobunji-Temple, *Tokyo* 29 A4
Kolarängen, *Stockholm* 28 B3
Kolbotn, *Oslo* 22 B3
Kolkata, *Calcutta* 8 B2
Koło, *Warsaw* 31 B1
Kolokinthóu, *Athens* 2 B2
Kolomyagi, *St. Petersburg* 26 A1
Kolónos, *Athens* 2 B2
Kolsås, *Oslo* 22 A2
Komae, *Tokyo* 29 B2
Komagome, *Tokyo* 29 A3
Komazawa, *Tokyo* 29 B3
Kona, *Calcutta* 8 B1
Konala, *Helsinki* 12 B2
Kondli, *Delhi* 10 B2
Kongelige Slottet, *Oslo* 22 a1
Kongelunden, *Copenhagen* 10 B3
Kongens Lyngby, *Copenhagen* 10 A3
Kongnŭng, *Seoul* 26 B2
Kongo, *Helsinki* 12 A1
Koninklijk Paleis, *Amsterdam* 2 b2
Konnagar, *Calcutta* 8 A2
Konohana, *Osaka* 22 A3
Kōnoike, *Osaka* 22 A4
Konradshöhe, *Berlin* 5 A2
Kopanina, *Prague* 24 B1
Koparkhairna, *Mumbai* 20 A2
Köpenick, *Berlin* 5 B4
Korangi, *Karachi* 14 B2
Koremasa, *Tokyo* 29 B1
Korenevo, *Moscow* 19 B6
Kori, *Osaka* 22 A4
Koridhallós, *Athens* 2 B1
Korokoro, *Wellington* 32 B2
Korokoro Stream →, *Wellington* 32 B2
Kosino, *Moscow* 19 B5
Kosugi, *Tokyo* 29 B2
Kota, *Jakarta* 13 A1
Kotelyniki, *Moscow* 19 C5
Kōtō-Ku, *Tokyo* 29 A3
Kotrung, *Calcutta* 8 A2
Kouponia, *Athens* 2 B2
Kowloon, *Hong Kong* 12 B1
Kowloon Park, *Hong Kong* 12 a2
Kowloon Peak, *Hong Kong* 12 A2
Kowloon Res., *Hong Kong* 12 A1
Kowloon Tong, *Hong Kong* 12 A2
Kozhukhovo, *Moscow* 19 B5
Kraainem, *Brussels* 6 A2
Krailling, *Munich* 20 B1
Krampnitz, *Berlin* 5 B1
Krampnitzsee, *Berlin* 5 B1
Kranji, Sungei →, *Singapore* 27 A2
Kranji Industrial Estate, *Singapore* 27 A2
Kraskovo, *Moscow* 19 C5
Krasno-Presnenskaya, *Moscow* 19 B3
Krasnogorsk, *Moscow* 19 B1
Krč, *Prague* 24 B2
Krestovskiye, Ostrov, *St. Petersburg* 26 B1
Kreuzberg, *Berlin* 5 A3
Kritzendorf, *Vienna* 31 A1
Krumme Lanke, *Berlin* 5 B2
Krummensee, *Berlin* 5 A5
Krung Thep, *Bangkok* 3 B2
Krusboda, *Stockholm* 28 B3
Krylatskoye, *Moscow* 19 B2
Küçükköy, *Istanbul* 12 B1
Kudankita, *Tokyo* 29 a3
Kudrovo, *St. Petersburg* 26 B3
Kulosaari, *Helsinki* 12 B3
Kulturforum, *Berlin* 5 b3
Kultury i Nauki, Palac, *Warsaw* 31 b2
Kŭmch'ŏn, *Seoul* 26 C1
Kumla, *Stockholm* 28 B3
Kungens kurva, *Stockholm* 28 B1
Kungliga Slottet, *Stockholm* 28 b2
Kungshatt, *Stockholm* 28 B1
Kungsholmen, *Stockholm* 28 A2
Kuningan, *Jakarta* 13 B1
Kunitachi, *Tokyo* 29 A1
Kunming Hu, *Beijing* 4 B1
Kunratice, *Prague* 24 B2
Kunsthistorischesmuseum, *Vienna* 31 b1
Kuntsevo, *Moscow* 19 B2
Kupchino, *St. Petersburg* 26 B2
Kurbağalı →, *Istanbul* 12 C2
Kurihara, *Tokyo* 29 A2
Kurla, *Mumbai* 20 A2
Kurmuri, *Mumbai* 20 A2
Kurume, *Tokyo* 29 A2
Kuryanovo, *Moscow* 19 C4
Kuskovo, *Moscow* 19 B4
Kustia, *Calcutta* 8 B2
Kutsino, *Moscow* 19 B5
Kuzguncuk, *Istanbul* 12 B2
Kuzyminki, *Moscow* 19 B4
Kwai Chung, *Hong Kong* 12 A1
Kwanak, *Seoul* 26 C1
Kwanak-san, *Seoul* 26 C1
Kyje, *Prague* 24 B3
Kyūhōji, *Osaka* 22 B4

L

La Blanca, *Santiago* 26 C2
La Boca, *Buenos Aires* 7 B2
La Bretèche, *Paris* 23 A1
La Campiña, *Lima* 16 C2
La Celle-St.-Cloud, *Paris* 23 A1
La Ciudadela, *Mexico City* 18 c2
La Courneuve, *Paris* 23 A3
La Dehesa, *Santiago* 26 B2
La Encantada, *Lima* 16 C2
La Estación, *Madrid* 17 B1
La Floresta, *Barcelona* 4 A1
La Fortuna, *Madrid* 17 B1
La Fransa, *Barcelona* 4 A1
La Garenne-Colombes, *Paris* 23 A2
La Giustiniana, *Rome* 25 B1
La Grange, *Chicago* 9 C1
La Grange Park, *Chicago* 9 C1
La Granja, *Santiago* 26 C2
La Guardia Airport, *New York* 21 B2
La Hulpe, *Brussels* 6 B2
La Llacuna, *Barcelona* 4 A2
La Loma, *Mexico City* 18 A1
La Lucila, *Buenos Aires* 7 B2
La Maladrerie, *Paris* 23 A1
La Milla, Cerro, *Lima* 16 B2
La Monachina, *Rome* 25 B1
La Moraleja, *Madrid* 17 A2
La Nopalera, *Mexico City* 18 C2
La Paternal, *Buenos Aires* 7 B2
La Perla, *Lima* 16 B2
La Perouse, *Sydney* 28 B2
La Pineda, *Barcelona* 4 B1
La Pisana, *Rome* 25 B1
La Prairie, *Montreal* 19 B3
La Punta, *Lima* 16 B1
La Puntigala, *Barcelona* 4 A2
La Queue-en-Brie, *Paris* 23 B4
La Reina, *Santiago* 26 B2
La Ribera, *Barcelona* 4 A1
La Sagrera, *Barcelona* 4 A2
La Salada, *Buenos Aires* 7 C2
La Scala, *Milan* 18 B2
La Storta, *Rome* 25 A1
La Taxonera, *Barcelona* 4 A2
La Victoria, *Lima* 16 B2
Laajalahti, *Helsinki* 12 B1
Laajasalo, *Helsinki* 12 B3
Laaksolahti, *Helsinki* 12 B1
Lablâba, W. el →, *Cairo* 7 A2
Lac Cisterna, *Santiago* 26 C2
Lachine, *Montreal* 19 B1
Lad Phrao, *Bangkok* 3 B2
Ladera Heights, *Los Angeles* 16 C2
Ládví, *Prague* 24 B2
Łady, *Warsaw* 31 C1
Lafontaine, Parc, *Montreal* 19 A2
Lagoa, *Rio de Janeiro* 24 B1
Lagos, *Lagos* 14 B2
Lagos Harbour, *Lagos* 14 B2
Lagos-Ikeja Airport, *Lagos* 14 A1
Lagos Island, *Lagos* 14 B2
Lagos Lagoon, *Lagos* 14 B2
Laguna de B., *Manila* 17 C2
Laim, *Munich* 20 B2
Lainate, *Milan* 18 A1
Lainz, *Vienna* 31 B1
Lakemba, *Sydney* 28 B1
Lakeside, *Cape Town* 8 B1
Lakeside, *Johannesburg* 13 A2
Lakeview, *Chicago* 9 B3
Lakewood Park, *Atlanta* 3 B2
Lakhtinskiy, *St. Petersburg* 26 B1
Lakhtinskiy Razliv, Oz., *St. Petersburg* 26 B1
Lakshmanpur, *Calcutta* 8 B1
Lal Qila, *Delhi* 1 a3
Lam Tin, *Hong Kong* 12 B2
Lambert, *Oslo* 22 A3
Lambeth, *London* 15 B3
Lambrate, *Milan* 18 B2
Lambro, Parco, *Milan* 18 B2
Lambton Mills, *Toronto* 30 B1
Lamma I., *Hong Kong* 12 B1
Landover Hills, *Washington* 32 B4
Landsmeer, *Amsterdam* 2 A2
Landstrasse, *Vienna* 31 A2
Landwehr kanal, *Berlin* 5 B3
Lane Cove, *Sydney* 28 A1
Lane Cove National Park, *Sydney* 28 A1
Langa, *Cape Town* 8 A2
Langenzersdorf, *Vienna* 31 A2
Langer See, *Berlin* 5 B4
Langley, *Washington* 32 B2
Langley Park, *Washington* 32 B4
Langwald, *Munich* 20 A1
Lanham, *Washington* 32 B4
Lankwitz, *Berlin* 5 B3
L'Annunziatella, *Rome* 25 C2
Lansdowne, *Cape Town* 8 A2
Lansing, *Toronto* 30 A2
Lanús, *Buenos Aires* 7 C2
Lapa, *Rio de Janeiro* 24 B1
Laranjeiras, *Rio de Janeiro* 24 B1
Larísa Sta., *Athens* 2 a1
Las, *Warsaw* 31 B2
Las Corts, *Barcelona* 4 A1
Las Kabacki, *Warsaw* 31 C2
Las Pinas, *Manila* 17 C1
Las Rejas, *Santiago* 26 B1
Lasalle, *Montreal* 19 B2
Lasek Bielański, *Warsaw* 31 B1
Lasek Na Kole, *Warsaw* 31 B1
Laski, *Warsaw* 31 B1
Latina, *Madrid* 17 B1
Laurence G. Hanscom Field, *Boston* 6 A2
Lauttasaari, *Helsinki* 12 C2
Laval, *Montreal* 19 A1
Laval-des-Rapides, *Montreal* 19 A1
Lavīzān, *Tehran* 30 A2
Lavradio, *Lisbon* 14 A2
Lawndale, *Chicago* 9 B2
Lawrence Heights, *Toronto* 30 A2
Layari, *Karachi* 14 A2
Layari →, *Karachi* 14 A1
Lazare, Gare St., *Paris* 23 a3
Łazienkowski, Palac, *Warsaw* 31 c3
Łazienkowski Park, *Warsaw* 31 B2
Le Blanc-Mesnil, *Paris* 23 A3
Le Bourget, *Paris* 23 A3
Le Chenoi, *Brussels* 6 B2
Le Chesnay, *Paris* 23 B1
Le Christ de Saclay, *Paris* 23 B2
Le Kremlin-Bicêtre, *Paris* 23 B3
Le Mesnil-le-Roi, *Paris* 23 A1
Le Pecq, *Paris* 23 A1
Le Perreux, *Paris* 23 A3
Le Pin, *Paris* 23 A4
Le Plessis-Robinson, *Paris* 23 B2
Le Plessis-Trévise, *Paris* 23 B4
Le Port-Marly, *Paris* 23 A1
Le Pré-St.-Gervais, *Paris* 23 A3
Le Raincy, *Paris* 23 A4
Le Vésinet, *Paris* 23 A1
Lea Bridge, *London* 15 A3
Leaside, *Toronto* 30 A2
Leblon, *Rio de Janeiro* 24 B1
Lee, *London* 15 B4
Leganés, *Madrid* 17 C1
Legazpi, *Madrid* 17 B1
Lehtisaari, *Helsinki* 12 B2
Lei Yue Mun, *Hong Kong* 12 B2
Leião, *Lisbon* 14 A1
Leicester Square, *London* 15 b3
Leichhardt, *Sydney* 28 B1
Leith, *Edinburgh* 11 B3
Lemoyne, *Montreal* 19 B3
Lenin, *Moscow* 19 B3
Lenino, *Moscow* 19 C3
Leninskiye Gory, *Moscow* 19 B3
Lennox, *Los Angeles* 16 C2
Leonia, *New York* 21 A2
Leopardstown, *Dublin* 11 B2
Leopoldau, *Vienna* 31 A2
Leopoldstadt, *Vienna* 31 A2
Leportovo, *Moscow* 19 B4
Leppävaara, *Helsinki* 12 B1
Les Lilas, *Paris* 23 A3
Les Loges-en-Josas, *Paris* 23 B1
Les Pavillons-sous-Bois, *Paris* 23 A4
Lésigny, *Paris* 23 B4
Lesnozavodskaya, *St. Petersburg* 26 B2
L'Étang-la-Ville, *Paris* 23 A1
Letná, *Prague* 24 a1
Letňany, *Prague* 24 B3
Levallois-Perret, *Paris* 23 A2
Levent, *Istanbul* 12 B2
Lewisdale, *Washington* 32 B4
Lewisham, *London* 15 B3
Lexington, *Boston* 6 A2
Leyton, *London* 15 A3
Leytonstone, *London* 15 A4
L'Hay-les-Roses, *Paris* 23 B3
L'Hospitalet de Llobregat, *Barcelona* 4 A1
Lhotka, *Prague* 24 B2
Liangshui He →, *Beijing* 4 C2
Lianhua Chi, *Beijing* 4 B1
Lianhua He →, *Beijing* 4 B1
Libčice nad Vitavou, *Prague* 24 A2
Libeň, *Prague* 24 B2
Liberdade, *São Paulo* 26 B2
Liberdade, Ave da, *Lisbon* 14 b1
Liberton, *Edinburgh* 11 B3
Liberty I., *New York* 21 B1
Liberty State Park, *New York* 21 B1
Libeznice, *Prague* 24 A2
Library of Congress, *Washington* 32 c3
Libuš, *Prague* 24 B2
Lichiao, *Canton* 8 B2
Lichtenburg, *Berlin* 5 A4
Lichterfelde, *Berlin* 5 B2
Lidingö, *Stockholm* 28 A2
Lieshi Lingyuan, *Canton* 8 B2
Liesing, *Vienna* 31 B1
Liesing →, *Vienna* 31 B2
Liffey, R. →, *Dublin* 11 A1
Ligovo, *St. Petersburg* 26 C1
Lijordet, *Oslo* 22 A2
Likavitos, *Athens* 2 b3
Likhoborka →, *Moscow* 19 A3
Lilla Värtan, *Stockholm* 28 A3
Lille Værløse, *Copenhagen* 10 A2
Liluah, *Calcutta* 8 B1
Lim Chu Kang, *Singapore* 27 A2
Lima, *Lima* 16 B2
Limbiate, *Milan* 18 A1
Limehouse, *London* 15 A3
Limeil-Brévannes, *Paris* 23 B3
Linate, Aeroporto Internazionale di, *Milan* 18 B2
Linbropark, *Johannesburg* 13 A2
Lincoln, *Boston* 6 A2
Lincoln Center, *New York* 21 b2
Lincoln Heights, *Los Angeles* 16 B3
Lincoln Park, *Chicago* 9 B3
Lincoln Park, *New York* 21 B1
Lincoln Park, *San Francisco* 25 B1
Lincolnwood, *Chicago* 9 A2
Linda-a-Pastora, *Lisbon* 14 A1
Linden, *Johannesburg* 13 A2
Linden, *Wellington* 32 A1
Lindenberg, *Berlin* 5 A4
Lindøya, *Oslo* 22 A3
Liniers, *Buenos Aires* 7 B1
Linkebeek, *Brussels* 6 B2
Linksfield, *Johannesburg* 13 A2
Linmeyer, *Johannesburg* 13 B2
Linna, *Helsinki* 12 A2
Lintuvaara, *Helsinki* 12 B1
Lion Rock Country Park, *Hong Kong* 12 A2
Lioúmi, *Athens* 2 B2
Liqizhuang, *Tianjin* 30 B2
Lisboa, *Lisbon* 14 A2
Lisbon = Lisboa, *Lisbon* 14 A2
Lishui, *Canton* 8 A1
Little B., *Sydney* 28 B2
Little Calumet →, *Chicago* 9 D3
Little Ferry, *New York* 21 A1
Little Italy, *New York* 21 e2
Little Mermaid, *Copenhagen* 10 a3
Little Rouge →, *Toronto* 30 A4
Little Tokyo, *Los Angeles* 16 c2
Liuhang, *Shanghai* 27 A1
Liurong Temple, *Canton* 8 B2
Liuxi →, *Canton* 8 B2
Liverpool Street, *London* 15 a5
Livry-Gargan, *Paris* 23 A4
Ljan, *Oslo* 22 A3
Llano de Can Gineu, *Barcelona* 4 A2
Llobregat →, *Barcelona* 4 A1
Lo Aranguiz, *Santiago* 26 B2
Lo Boza, *Santiago* 26 B1
Lo Chau, *Hong Kong* 12 B2
Lo Espejo, *Santiago* 26 C1
Lo Hermida, *Santiago* 26 B2
Lo Prado, *Santiago* 26 B1
Lo So Shing, *Hong Kong* 12 B1
Lo Wai, *Hong Kong* 12 A1
Loanhead, *Edinburgh* 11 B3
Lobau, *Vienna* 31 A3
Lobos, Pt., *San Francisco* 25 B1
Locham, *Munich* 20 B1
Lochino, *Moscow* 19 B1
Lochkov, *Prague* 24 B2
Lockhausen, *Munich* 20 A1
Lodi, *New York* 21 A1
Lodi Estate, *Delhi* 10 B2
Logan Int. Airport, *Boston* 6 A4
Logan Square, *Chicago* 9 B2
Lognes-Émerainville, Aérodrome de, *Paris* 23 B4
Löhme, *Berlin* 5 A5
Lolokhet, *Karachi* 14 A2
Lomas Chapultepec, *Mexico City* 18 B1
Lomas de San Angel Inn, *Mexico City* 18 B1
Lomas de Zamora, *Buenos Aires* 7 C2
Lombardy East, *Johannesburg* 13 A2
Łomianki, *Warsaw* 31 A1
Lomus Reforma, *Mexico City* 18 B1
London, *London* 15 A3
London Bridge, *London* 15 b5
London City Airport, *London* 15 A4
London Zoo, *London* 15 A3
Long B., *Sydney* 28 B2
Long Branch, *Toronto* 30 B1
Long Brook →, *Washington* 32 C2
Long Ditton, *London* 15 B2
Long I., *Boston* 6 B4
Long Island City, *New York* 21 B2
Long Street, *Cape Town* 8 c2
Longchamp, Hippodrôme de, *Paris* 23 A2
Longhua Pagoda, *Shanghai* 27 B1
Longhua Park, *Shanghai* 27 B1
Longjohn Slough, *Chicago* 9 C1
Longtan Hu →, *Beijing* 4 B2
Longue-Pointe, *Montreal* 19 A2
Longueuil, *Montreal* 19 A3
Loni, *Delhi* 10 A2
Loop, The, *Chicago* 9 c1
Lord's Cricket Ground, *London* 15 A2
Loreto, *Milan* 18 B2
Los Angeles Int. Airport, *Los Angeles* 16 C2
Los Cerrillos, Aeropuerto, *Santiago* 26 B1
Los Nietos, *Los Angeles* 16 C4
Los Olivos, *Lima* 16 A2
Los Reyes, *Mexico City* 18 B2
Lot, *Brussels* 6 B1
Loughlinstown, *Dublin* 11 B3
Loures, *Lisbon* 14 A1
Louveciennes, *Paris* 23 A1
Louvre, Musée du, *Paris* 23 b4
Louvre, Palais du, *Paris* 23 b4
Lower East Side, *New York* 21 e2
Lower Hutt, *Wellington* 32 B2
Lower Manhattan, *New York* 21 e1
Lower New York B., *New York* 21 C1
Lower Shing Mun Res., *Hong Kong* 12 A1
Lowry Bay, *Wellington* 32 B2
Lu Xun Museum, *Beijing* 4 b1
Lübars, *Berlin* 5 A3
Ludwigsfeld, *Munich* 20 A1
Luhu, *Canton* 8 B2
Lumiar, *Lisbon* 14 A2
Lumphini Park, *Bangkok* 3 B2
Lundtofte, *Copenhagen* 10 A3
Lung Mei, *Hong Kong* 12 A2
Luojiang, *Canton* 8 B2
Lustheim, *Munich* 20 A2
Luwan, *Shanghai* 27 B1
Luxembourg, Palais du, *Paris* 23 c4
Luzhniki Sports Centre, *Moscow* 19 B3
Lyndhurst, *New York* 21 B1
Lynn, *Boston* 6 A4
Lynn Harbor, *Boston* 6 A4
Lynn Woods Res., *Boston* 6 A3
Lyon, Gare de, *Paris* 23 c5
Lyons, *Chicago* 9 C2
Lysaker, *Oslo* 22 A2
Lysakerselva →, *Oslo* 22 A2
Lysolaje, *Prague* 24 B2
Lyubertsy, *Moscow* 19 B5
Lyublino, *Moscow* 19 B4

M

Ma Nam Wat, *Hong Kong* 12 A2
Ma On Shan Country Park, *Hong Kong* 12 A2
Ma'ale Adumim, *Jerusalem* 13 B2
Ma'ale Ha Khamisha, *Jerusalem* 13 B1
Ma'ale Mikhmas, *Jerusalem* 13 A2
Maantiekylä, *Helsinki* 12 A3
Maarifa, *Baghdad* 3 B2
Mabato Pt., *Manila* 17 C2
Macaco, Morro do, *Rio de Janeiro* 24 B2
McCook, *Chicago* 9 C2
Machelen, *Brussels* 6 A2
Machida, *Tokyo* 29 B1
Maciołki, *Warsaw* 31 B2
Mackayville, *Montreal* 19 A3
McKerrow, *Wellington* 32 B2
McKinley Park, *Chicago* 9 C2
Mclean, *Washington* 32 B2
Macopocho, R. →, *Santiago* 26 B1
MacRitchie Res., *Singapore* 27 A2
Macul, *Santiago* 26 C2
Madame Tussaud's, *London* 15 a3
Madhudaha, *Calcutta* 8 B2
Madhyamgram, *Calcutta* 8 A2
Madīnah Al Mansūr, *Baghdad* 3 B2
Mâdinet Nasr, *Cairo* 7 A2
Madison Avenue, *New York* 21 c2
Madison Square, *New York* 21 d2
Madrid, *Madrid* 17 B1
Madrona, *Barcelona* 4 A1
Maesawa, *Tokyo* 29 A2
Magdalena, *Lima* 16 B2
Magdalena Contreras, *Mexico City* 18 C1
Maghreb, *Baghdad* 3 A2
Maginu, *Tokyo* 29 B2
Magliana, *Rome* 25 B1
Magny-les-Hameaux, *Paris* 23 B1
Magonoy, *Manila* 17 B2
Mahalaxmi, *Mumbai* 20 a1
Maheshtala, *Calcutta* 8 C1
Mahim, *Mumbai* 20 A2
Mahim B., *Mumbai* 20 A1
Mahlsdorf, *Berlin* 5 A4
Mahmoodabad, *Karachi* 14 A2
Mahrauli, *Delhi* 10 B1
Mahul, *Mumbai* 20 A2
Maida Vale, *London* 15 a1
Maidstone, *Melbourne* 17 A1
Maipú, *Santiago* 26 C1
Maisonneuve, Parc, *Montreal* 19 A2
Maisons-Alfort, *Paris* 23 B3
Maisons-Laffitte, *Paris* 23 A1
Maissoneuve, *Montreal* 19 A2
Maitland, *Cape Town* 8 A1
Makati, *Manila* 17 B2
Mäkiniitty, *Helsinki* 12 A2
Mala Straná, *Prague* 24 B2
Malabar, *Mumbai* 20 B1
Malabar, *Sydney* 28 B2
Malabar Hill, *Mumbai* 20 B1
Malabar Pt., *Mumbai* 20 B1
Malabon, *Manila* 17 B1
Malacañang Palace, *Manila* 17 B1
Malahide, *Dublin* 11 A3
Malakhovka, *Moscow* 19 C6
Malakoff, *Paris* 23 B2
Mälarhöjaen, *Stockholm* 28 B1
Malate, *Manila* 17 B1
Malay Quarter, *Cape Town* 8 c2
Malaya Neva, *St. Petersburg* 26 B1
Malaya-Okhta, *St. Petersburg* 26 B2
Malchow, *Berlin* 5 A3
Malden, *Boston* 6 A3
Malden, *London* 15 B2
Maleizen, *Brussels* 6 B3
Malešice, *Prague* 24 B3
Malir →, *Karachi* 14 B2
Mall, The, *Washington* 32 b2
Malleny Mills, *Edinburgh* 11 B2
Malmi, *Helsinki* 12 B2
Malmøya, *Oslo* 22 A3
Måløv, *Copenhagen* 10 A2
Malpasso, Ost., *Rome* 25 C1
Malton, *Toronto* 30 A1
Malvern, *Johannesburg* 13 B2
Malvern, *Melbourne* 17 B2
Malvern, *Toronto* 30 A3
Mamonovo, *Moscow* 19 B2
Mampang Prapatan, *Jakarta* 13 B1
Mampukuji, *Tokyo* 29 B2
Man Budrukh, *Mumbai* 20 A2
Man Khurd, *Mumbai* 20 A2
Mandaluyong, *Manila* 17 B2
Mandaoli, *Delhi* 10 B2
Mandaqui →, *São Paulo* 26 A2
Mandoli, *Delhi* 10 A2
Mandvi, *Mumbai* 20 B2
Manenberg, *Cape Town* 8 A2
Mang Kung Uk, *Hong Kong* 12 B2
Mangolpuri, *Delhi* 10 A1
Manguinhos, Aéroporto, *Rio de Janeiro* 24 B1
Mangwŏn, *Seoul* 26 B1
Manhattan, *New York* 21 B2
Manhattan Beach, *New York* 21 C2
Manila, *Manila* 17 B1
Manila B., *Manila* 17 B1
Manila Int. Airport, *Manila* 17 B2
Mankkaa, *Helsinki* 12 B1
Manly, *Sydney* 28 A2
Mannswörth, *Vienna* 31 B3
Manor Park, *London* 15 A4
Manor Park, *Wellington* 32 A2
Manora, *Karachi* 14 B1
Manquehue, Cerro, *Santiago* 26 B2
Manzanares, Canal de, *Madrid* 17 C2
Mao Mausoleum, *Beijing* 4 c2
Map'o, *Seoul* 26 B1
Maracanã, *Rio de Janeiro* 24 B1
Maraoli, *Mumbai* 20 A2
Marblehead, *Boston* 6 A4
Marcelin, *Warsaw* 31 B1
Mareil-Marly, *Paris* 23 A1
Margareten, *Vienna* 31 A2
Maria, *Vienna* 31 A2
Maridalen, *Oslo* 22 A3
Maridalsvatnet, *Oslo* 22 A3
Mariendorf, *Berlin* 5 B3
Marienfelde, *Berlin* 5 B3
Marienplatz, *Munich* 20 b2
Marikina →, *Manila* 17 B2
Marin City, *San Francisco* 25 A1
Marin Headlands State Park, *San Francisco* 25 A2
Marin Pen., *San Francisco* 25 A1
Marina del Rey, *Los Angeles* 16 C2
Marine Drive, *Mumbai* 20 b1
Marino, *Dublin* 11 A2
Maritim, Museu, *Barcelona* 4 c2
Markham, *Toronto* 30 A2
Marki, *Warsaw* 31 B2
Markland Wood, *Toronto* 30 B1
Marly, Forêt de, *Paris* 23 A1
Marly-le-Roi, *Paris* 23 A1
Marne →, *Paris* 23 B3
Marne-la-Vallée, *Paris* 23 A4
Marolles-en-Brie, *Paris* 23 B4
Maroubra, *Sydney* 28 B2
Marquette Park, *Chicago* 9 C2
Marrickville, *Sydney* 28 B1
Marsfield, *Sydney* 28 A1
Marshall Field's, *Chicago* 9 c2
Marte, Campo de, *São Paulo* 26 B2
Martesana, Navíglio della, *Milan* 18 A2
Martin Luther King National Historic Site, *Atlanta* 3 B2
Martinez, *Buenos Aires* 7 A1
Martinkylä, *Helsinki* 12 B2
Martinsried, *Munich* 20 B1
Maruko, *Tokyo* 29 B3
Marunouchi, *Tokyo* 29 b4
Marusino, *Moscow* 19 B5
Maryino, *Moscow* 19 B4
Maryland, *Singapore* 27 B2
Marylebone, *London* 15 A2
Marymont, *Warsaw* 31 B1
Marysin Wawerski, *Warsaw* 31 B2
Marzahn, *Berlin* 5 A4
Mascot, *Sydney* 28 B2
Masmo, *Stockholm* 28 B1
Maspeth, *New York* 21 B2
Masr el Gedida, *Cairo* 7 A2
Masr el Qadîma, *Cairo* 7 A2
Massachusetts B., *Boston* 6 A4
Massachusett's Inst. of Tech., *Boston* 6 A3
Massamá, *Lisbon* 14 A1
Massey →, *Toronto* 30 A3
Massy, *Paris* 23 B2
Matihutong, *Beijing* 4 B1
Matinha, *Lisbon* 14 A2
Matramam, *Jakarta* 13 B2
Matsubara, *Osaka* 22 B4
Mattapan, *Boston* 6 B3
Mátyásföld, *Budapest* 7 A3
Mátyástemplom, *Budapest* 7 b1
Mau Tso Ngam, *Hong Kong* 12 A2
Mauer, *Vienna* 31 B1
Mauripur, *Karachi* 14 A1
Maxhof, *Munich* 20 B1
Maya-Zan, *Osaka* 22 A2
Mayfair, *Johannesburg* 13 B2
Mayfair, *London* 15 b3
Mayor, Plaza, *Madrid* 17 b2
Maywood, *Chicago* 9 B1
Maywood, *Los Angeles* 16 C3
Maywood, *New York* 21 A1
Mazagaon, *Mumbai* 20 a2
Me'a She' Arim, *Jerusalem* 13 a2
Meadowbank Park, *Sydney* 28 A1
Měcholupy, *Prague* 24 B3
Měčice, *Prague* 24 A3
Mecidiyeköy, *Istanbul* 12 B2
Medford, *Boston* 6 A3
Mediodia, *Madrid* 17 B2
Medvezhiy Ozyora, *Moscow* 19 A5
Meguro →, *Tokyo* 29 B3
Meguro-Ku, *Tokyo* 29 B3
Mehpalpur, *Delhi* 10 B1
Mehrābād Airport, *Tehran* 30 A1
Mehram Nagar, *Delhi* 10 B1
Mehrow, *Berlin* 5 A4
Mei Lanfang, *Beijing* 4 a2
Meidling, *Vienna* 31 A2
Méier, *Rio de Janeiro* 24 B1
Meiji Shrine, *Tokyo* 29 b1
Meise, *Brussels* 6 A1
Mejiro, *Tokyo* 29 A3
Melbourne, *Melbourne* 17 A1
Melbourne Airport, *Melbourne* 17 A1
Melkki, *Helsinki* 12 C2
Mellunkylä, *Helsinki* 12 B3
Mellunmäki, *Helsinki* 12 B3
Melrose, *Boston* 6 A3
Melrose, *New York* 21 B2
Melrose Park, *Chicago* 9 B1
Melsbroek, *Brussels* 6 A2
Menteng, *Jakarta* 13 B1
Mérantaise →, *Paris* 23 B1
Mercamadrid, *Madrid* 17 B2
Merced, L., *San Francisco* 25 B2
Meredale, *Johannesburg* 13 B1
Merlimau, P., *Singapore* 27 B2
Merri Cr. →, *Melbourne* 17 A1
Merrion, *Dublin* 11 B2
Merrionette Park, *Chicago* 9 C2
Merton, *London* 15 B2
Mesgarābād, *Tehran* 30 B3
Meshcherskiy, *Moscow* 19 B2
Messe, *Vienna* 31 A2
Messe-palast, *Vienna* 31 c1
Metanópoli, *Milan* 18 B2
Metropolitan Museum of Art, *New York* 21 b3
Meudon, *Paris* 23 B2
Mevaseret Tsiyon, *Jerusalem* 13 B1
Mevo Beitar, *Jerusalem* 13 B1
México, Ciudad de, *Mexico City* 18 B1
Meyersdal, *Johannesburg* 13 B2
Mezzano, *Milan* 18 B2
Mezzate, *Milan* 18 B2
Miadong, *Seoul* 26 B2
Miami, *Miami* 18 B2
Miami Beach, *Miami* 18 B2
Miami Canal →, *Miami* 18 A1
Miami Int. Airport, *Miami* 18 B1
Miami Shores, *Miami* 18 A2
Miami Springs, *Miami* 18 B1
Miasto, *Warsaw* 31 B2
Michałowice, *Warsaw* 31 B1
Michigan Avenue, *Chicago* 9 b2
Michle, *Prague* 24 B2
Middle Harbour, *Sydney* 28 A2
Middle Hd., *Sydney* 28 A2
Middle Park, *Melbourne* 17 B1
Middle Village, *New York* 21 B2
Middlesex Fells Reservation, *Boston* 6 A3
Midi, Gare du, *Brussels* 6 c1
Midland Beach, *New York* 21 C1
Miedzeszyn, *Warsaw* 31 B3
Międzylesie, *Warsaw* 31 B3
Miessaari, *Helsinki* 12 C1
Miguel Hidalgo, *Mexico City* 18 B1
Mikhelysona, *Moscow* 19 B5
Milano, *Milan* 18 B1
Milano Due, *Milan* 18 B2
Milano San Felice, *Milan* 18 B2
Milbertshofen, *Munich* 20 A2
Mill Hill, *London* 15 A2
Millennium Dome, *London* 15 A4
Miller Meadow, *Chicago* 9 B2
Millerhill, *Edinburgh* 11 B3
Millers Point, *Sydney* 28 a1
Milltown, *Dublin* 11 B2
Millwood, *Washington* 32 B4
Milnerton, *Cape Town* 8 A1
Milon-la-Chapelle, *Paris* 23 B1
Milton, *Boston* 6 B3
Milton Bridge, *Edinburgh* 11 B2
Mimico, *Toronto* 30 B2
Minami, *Osaka* 22 A4
Minamitsunashima, *Tokyo* 29 B2
Minato, *Osaka* 22 B3
Minato-Ku, *Tokyo* 29 c3
Minshât el Bekkarî, *Cairo* 7 A1
Minute Man Nat. Hist. Park, *Boston* 6 A2
Miraflores, *Lima* 16 B2
Miramar, *Wellington* 32 B1
Misericordia, Sa. da, *Rio de Janeiro* 24 B1
Mission, *San Francisco* 25 B2
Mississauga, *Toronto* 30 B1
Mitaka, *Tokyo* 29 A2
Mitcham, *London* 15 B2
Mitcham Common, *London* 15 B3
Mitchell's Plain, *Cape Town* 8 B2
Mitino, *Moscow* 19 A2
Mitte, *Berlin* 5 A3
Mittel Isarkanal →, *Munich* 20 A3
Mixcoac, *Mexico City* 18 B1
Mixcoac, Presa de, *Mexico City* 18 B1
Miyakojima, *Osaka* 22 A4
Mizonokuchi, *Tokyo* 29 B2
Mizue, *Tokyo* 29 A4
Młocinski Park, *Warsaw* 31 B1
Młociny, *Warsaw* 31 B1
Mnevniki, *Moscow* 19 B2
Moba, *Lagos* 14 B2
Moczydło, *Warsaw* 31 C2
Modderfontein, *Johannesburg* 13 A2
Modřany, *Prague* 24 B2
Mogyoród, *Budapest* 7 A3
Moinho Velho, Cor. →, *São Paulo* 26 B2
Mok, *Seoul* 26 B1
Mokotów, *Warsaw* 31 B2
Molenbeek-Saint-Jean, *Brussels* 6 A1
Molino de Rosas, *Mexico City* 18 B1
Mollem, *Brussels* 6 A1
Mollins de Rey, *Barcelona* 4 A1
Mondeor, *Johannesburg* 13 B2
Moneda, Palacio de la, *Santiago* 26 B2
Moneró, *Rio de Janeiro* 24 A1
Mong Kok, *Hong Kong* 12 B2
Monkstown, *Dublin* 11 B3
Monnickendam, *Amsterdam* 2 A3
Monrovia, *Los Angeles* 16 B4
Monsanto, *Lisbon* 14 A1
Monsanto, Parque Florestal de, *Lisbon* 14 A1
Mont Royal, *Montreal* 19 A2
Mont-Royal, Parc, *Montreal* 19 A2
Montana de Montjuich, *Barcelona* 4 A1
Monte Chingolo, *Buenos Aires* 7 C2

Monte Palatino, *Rome* ... **25** c3
Montebello, *Los Angeles* ... **16** B4
Montemor, *Lisbon* ... **14** A1
Monterey Park, *Los Angeles* ... **16** B4
Montespaccato, *Rome* ... **25** B1
Montessori, *Paris* ... **23** A1
Monteverde Nuovo, *Rome* ... **25** B1
Montfermeil, *Paris* ... **23** A4
Montigny-le-Bretonneux,
  Paris ... **23** B1
Montjay-la-Tour, *Paris* ... **23** A4
Montjuic, Parc de, *Barcelona* ... **4** c1
Montparnasse, Gare, *Paris* ... **23** A2
Montréal, *Montreal* ... **19** A2
Montréal, I. de, *Montreal* ... **19** A2
Montréal, Univ. de, *Montreal* ... **19** B2
Montréal Est, *Montreal* ... **19** A2
Montréal Nord, *Montreal* ... **19** A2
Montréal Ouest, *Montreal* ... **19** B1
Montreuil, *Paris* ... **23** A3
Montrouge, *Paris* ... **23** B2
Montserrat, *Buenos Aires* ... **7** B2
Monza, *Milan* ... **18** B1
Monoro, *Milan* ... **18** B1
Mooca, *São Paulo* ... **26** B2
Moonachie, *New York* ... **21** B1
Moonee Ponds, *Melbourne* ... **17** A1
Moonee Valley Racecourse,
  Melbourne ... **17** A1
Moosach, *Munich* ... **20** A2
Mora, *Mumbai* ... **20** B2
Moratalaz, *Madrid* ... **17** B2
Mörby, *Stockholm* ... **28** A2
Morden, *London* ... **15** B2
Morée →, *Paris* ... **23** A3
Morgan Park, *Chicago* ... **9** C3
Moriguchi, *Osaka* ... **22** A4
Morivione, *Milan* ... **18** B2
Morningside, *Edinburgh* ... **11** B2
Morningside, *Johannesburg* ... **13** A2
Morningside, *Washington* ... **32** C4
Morro Solar, Cerro, *Lima* ... **16** C2
Mortlake, *London* ... **15** B2
Mortlake, *Sydney* ... **28** B1
Morton Grove, *Chicago* ... **9** A2
Morumbi, *São Paulo* ... **26** B1
Moscavide, *Lisbon* ... **14** A2
Moscow = Moskva, *Moscow* ... **19** B3
Moskhaton, *Athens* ... **2** B2
Moskva →, *Moscow* ... **19** B3
Moskvoretskiy, *Moscow* ... **19** B3
Mosman, *Sydney* ... **28** B2
Móstoles, *Madrid* ... **17** C1
Moti Bagh, *Delhi* ... **10** B2
Motol, *Prague* ... **24** B1
Motsa, *Jerusalem* ... **13** B2
Motsa Ilit, *Jerusalem* ... **13** B2
Motspur Park, *London* ... **15** B2
Mottingham, *London* ... **15** B4
Moulin Rouge, *Paris* ... **23** a3
Mount Dennis, *Toronto* ... **30** A2
Mount Greenwood, *Chicago* ... **9** C2
Mount Hood Memorial Park,
  Boston ... **6** A3
Mount Merrion, *Dublin* ... **11** B2
Mount Rainier, *Washington* ... **32** B4
Mount Vernon, *New York* ... **21** A3
Mount Vernon Square,
  Washington ... **32** a2
Mount Zion, *Jerusalem* ... **13** B2
Mustamäki, *Vienna* ... **31** b2
Müggelberge, *Berlin* ... **5** B4
Müggelheim, *Berlin* ... **5** B5
Muggió, *Milan* ... **18** A2
Mughal Gardens, *Delhi* ... **1** c1
Mühleiten, *Vienna* ... **31** A3
Mühlenfliess →, *Berlin* ... **5** A5
Muiden, *Amsterdam* ... **2** A3
Muiderpoort Station,
  Amsterdam ... **2** b3
Muizenberg, *Cape Town* ... **8** B2
Mujahidipur, *Delhi* ... **10** A2
Mukandpur, *Delhi* ... **10** A2
Mukhmas, *Jerusalem* ... **13** A2
Muko →, *Osaka* ... **22** A3
Mukojima, *Tokyo* ... **29** A3
Mulbarton, *Johannesburg* ... **13** B2
Mumbai, *Mumbai* ... **20** B2
Mumbai Harbour, *Mumbai* ... **20** B2
Mumbedobe, *Berlin* ... **5** B5
München, *Munich* ... **20** B2
Munich = München, *Munich* ... **20** B2
Munkkiniemi, *Helsinki* ... **12** B2
Munro, *Buenos Aires* ... **7** B1
Murai Res., *Singapore* ... **27** A2
Muranów, *Warsaw* ... **31** B1
Murino, *St. Petersburg* ... **26** B2
Murrayfield, *Edinburgh* ... **11** B2
Musashino, *Tokyo* ... **29** A2
Museu Nacional,
  Rio de Janeiro ... **24** B1
Mushin, *Lagos* ... **14** A2
Musiektheater, *Amsterdam* ... **2** b2
Muslim Quarter, *Jerusalem* ... **13** a3
Musocco, *Milan* ... **18** B1
Mustansiriya, *Baghdad* ... **3** A2
Musturud, *Cairo* ... **7** A2
Muswell Hill, *London* ... **15** A3
Mutanabi, *Baghdad* ... **3** B2
Muthana, *Baghdad* ... **3** B2
Myakinino, *Moscow* ... **19** B2
Mykerinos, *Cairo* ... **7** B1
Myllypuro, *Helsinki* ... **12** B3

N

Nacka, *Stockholm* ... **28** B3
Nada, *Osaka* ... **22** A2
Naenae, *Wellington* ... **32** B2
Nærsnes, *Oslo* ... **22** A2
Nagata, *Osaka* ... **22** B1
Nagatsuta, *Tokyo* ... **29** B2
Nagytétény, *Budapest* ... **7** B1
Nahant, *Boston* ... **6** A4
Nahant B., *Boston* ... **6** A4
Nahant Harbor, *Boston* ... **6** A4
Nahr Dijlah →, *Baghdad* ... **3** A2
Najafgarh Drain →, *Delhi* ... **10** B1
Nakahara-Ku, *Tokyo* ... **29** B3
Nakano-Ku, *Tokyo* ... **29** A2
Namgajwa, *Seoul* ... **26** B1
Namsan Park, *Seoul* ... **26** B1
Namyŏng, *Seoul* ... **26** B1
Nanbiancun, *Canton* ... **8** B1
Nanchang He →, *Beijing* ... **4** B1
Nandang, *Canton* ... **8** B2
Nandian, *Tianjin* ... **30** A2
Nangal Dewat, *Delhi* ... **10** B1
Naniwa, *Osaka* ... **22** B3
Nankai, *Tianjin* ... **30** B2
Nanmenwai, *Tianjin* ... **30** B2
Nanole, *Mumbai* ... **20** A2
Nanpu Bridge, *Shanghai* ... **27** B1

Nanshi, *Shanghai* ... **27** B1
Nantasket Beach, *Boston* ... **6** B4
Nanterre, *Paris* ... **23** A2
Naoabad, *Calcutta* ... **8** C2
Napier Mole, *Karachi* ... **14** B1
Naraina, *Delhi* ... **10** B1
Nariman Point, *Mumbai* ... **20** c1
Nariman Pt., *Mumbai* ... **20** c1
Närmak, *Tehran* ... **30** A2
Naruo, *Osaka* ... **22** A3
Näsby, *Stockholm* ... **28** A2
Näsbypark, *Stockholm* ... **28** A2
Nathan Road, *Hong Kong* ... **12** a2
Natick, *Boston* ... **6** B2
National Maritime Museum,
  San Francisco ... **25** a1
National Museum, *Bangkok* ... **3** b1
Nationalmuseum, *Stockholm* ... **28** b2
Natolin, *Warsaw* ... **31** C2
Naturhistorischesmuseum,
  Vienna ... **31** b1
Naucalpan de Juárez,
  Mexico City ... **18** B1
Naupada, *Mumbai* ... **20** A2
Navíglio di Pavia, *Milan* ... **18** B1
Navíglio Grande, *Milan* ... **18** B1
Navona, Piazza, *Rome* ... **25** b2
Navotas, *Manila* ... **17** B1
Navy Pier, *Chicago* ... **9** b3
Nazal Hikmat Beg, *Baghdad* ... **3** A2
Nazimabad, *Karachi* ... **14** A2
Nazlet el Simmân, *Cairo* ... **7** B1
Néa Alexandria, *Athens* ... **2** B2
Néa Faliron, *Athens* ... **2** B1
Néa Ionía, *Athens* ... **2** A2
Néa Liósia, *Athens* ... **2** A1
Néa Smírni, *Athens* ... **2** B2
Neapolis, *Athens* ... **2** B2
Near North, *Chicago* ... **9** b2
Nebušice, *Prague* ... **24** B1
Nederhorst, *Amsterdam* ... **2** B3
Nedlitz, *Berlin* ... **5** B1
Nee Soon, *Singapore* ... **27** A2
Needham Heights, *Boston* ... **6** B2
Nekrasovka, *Moscow* ... **19** B4
N'ematábád, *Tehran* ... **30** B2
Nemchinovka, *Moscow* ... **19** B1
Nemzeti Muz, *Budapest* ... **7** c3
Neponsit, *New York* ... **21** C2
Nesodden, *Oslo* ... **22** B3
Nesoddtangen, *Oslo* ... **22** B3
Nesøya, *Oslo* ... **22** A2
Neu Aubing, *Munich* ... **20** B1
Neu Buch, *Berlin* ... **5** A4
Neu Buchhorst, *Berlin* ... **5** B5
Neu Fahrland, *Berlin* ... **5** A1
Neu Lindenberg, *Berlin* ... **5** A4
Neubiberg, *Munich* ... **20** B3
Neue Hofburg, *Vienna* ... **31** b1
Neuenhagen, *Berlin* ... **5** A5
Neuessling, *Vienna* ... **31** A3
Neuhausen, *Munich* ... **20** B2
Neuherberg, *Munich* ... **20** A2
Neuhönow, *Berlin* ... **5** A5
Neuilly-Plaisance, *Paris* ... **23** A4
Neuilly-sur-Marne, *Paris* ... **23** A4
Neuilly-sur-Seine, *Paris* ... **23** A2
Neukagran, *Vienna* ... **31** A2
Neukettenhof, *Vienna* ... **31** B2
Neukölln, *Berlin* ... **5** B3
Neuperlach, *Munich* ... **20** B2
Neuried, *Munich* ... **20** B1
Neustift am Walde, *Vienna* ... **31** A1
Neusüssenbrunn, *Vienna* ... **31** A2
Neuwaldegg, *Vienna* ... **31** A1
Neva →, *St. Petersburg* ... **26** B2
Neves, *Rio de Janeiro* ... **24** B2
New Baghdad, *Baghdad* ... **3** B2
New Barakpur, *Calcutta* ... **8** A2
New Brighton, *New York* ... **21** C1
New Canada, *Johannesburg* ... **13** B1
New Canada Dam,
  Johannesburg ... **13** B1
New Carrollton, *Washington* ... **32** B4
New Cross, *London* ... **15** B3
New Delhi, *Delhi* ... **10** B2
New Dorp, *New York* ... **21** C1
New Dorp Beach, *New York* ... **21** C1
New Malden, *London* ... **15** B2
New Milford, *New York* ... **21** A1
New Territories, *Hong Kong* ... **12** A1
New Toronto, *Toronto* ... **30** B1
New Town, *Edinburgh* ... **11** B2
New Utrecht, *New York* ... **21** C2
Newark B., *New York* ... **21** B1
Newbattle, *Edinburgh* ... **11** B3
Newbury Park, *London* ... **15** A4
Newcraighall, *Edinburgh* ... **11** B3
Newham, *London* ... **15** A4
Newhaven, *Edinburgh* ... **11** B2
Newington, *Edinburgh* ... **11** B2
Newington, *London* ... **15** c5
Newlands, *Johannesburg* ... **13** B2
Newlands, *Wellington* ... **32** B2
Newport, *Melbourne* ... **17** B1
Newton, *Boston* ... **6** A2
Newtonbrook, *Toronto* ... **30** A2
Newtongrange, *Edinburgh* ... **11** B3
Newtonville, *Boston* ... **6** A2
Newtown, *Sydney* ... **28** B2
Neyagawa, *Osaka* ... **22** A4
Ngaio, *Wellington* ... **32** B1
Ngau Chi Wan, *Hong Kong* ... **12** A2
Ngau Tau Kok, *Hong Kong* ... **12** A2
Ngauranga, *Wellington* ... **32** B1
Ngong Shuen Chau,
  Hong Kong ... **12** B1
Ngua Kok Wan, *Hong Kong* ... **12** A1
Nhå Bè, *Ho Chi Minh City* ... ...
Nibra, *Calcutta* ... **8** B1
Nidāl, *Baghdad* ... **3** B2
Niddrie, *Edinburgh* ... **11** B3
Niddrie, *Melbourne* ... **17** A1
Nieder Neuendorf, *Berlin* ... **5** A2
Niederschönewiede, *Berlin* ... **5** B3
Niederschönhausen, *Berlin* ... **5** A3
Niemeyer, *Rio de Janeiro* ... **24** B1
Nieuw Zuid, *Amsterdam* ... **2** c2
Nieuwe Kerk, *Amsterdam* ... **2** a2
Nieuwendam, *Amsterdam* ... **2** A2
Nihonbashi, *Tokyo* ... **29** b5
Niikaia, *Athens* ... **2** B1
Nijkaia, *Athens* ... **2** B1
Nikolassee, *Berlin* ... **5** B2
Nikolskiy, *Moscow* ... **19** B5
Nikulino, *Moscow* ... **19** B2
Nil, *Nahr en* →, *Cairo* ... **7** B2
Nile = Nil, Nahr en →, *Cairo* ... **7** B2
Niles, *Chicago* ... **9** A2
Nimta, *Calcutta* ... **8** A2
Ninguyan, *Tianjin* ... **30** B2
Nippa, *Tokyo* ... **29** B3
Nippori, *Tokyo* ... **29** A3
Nishi, *Osaka* ... **22** A3
Nishinari, *Osaka* ... **22** B3

Nishiyodogawa, *Osaka* ... **22** A3
Niterói, *Rio de Janeiro* ... **24** B2
Nob Hill, *San Francisco* ... **25** b1
Nockeby, *Stockholm* ... **28** B1
Noel Park, *London* ... **15** A3
Nogatino, *Moscow* ... **19** B4
Nogent-sur-Marne, *Paris* ... **23** A3
Noida, *Delhi* ... **10** B2
Noiseau, *Paris* ... **23** B4
Noisiel, *Paris* ... **23** A4
Noisy-le-Grand, *Paris* ... **23** A4
Noisy-le-Roi, *Paris* ... **23** A1
Noisy-le-Sec, *Paris* ... **23** A3
Nokkala, *Helsinki* ... **12** C1
Nomentano, *Rome* ... **25** B2
Nonakashinden, *Tokyo* ... **29** A2
Nongminyundong Jiangxisuo,
  Canton ... **8** B2
Nonhyŏn, *Seoul* ... **26** B2
Nonthaburi, *Bangkok* ... **3** b1
Noon Gun, *Cape Town* ... **8** b1
Noorder Kerk, *Amsterdam* ... **2** a1
Noordgesig, *Johannesburg* ... **13** B2
Noordzeekanaal, *Amsterdam* ... **2** A1
Nord, Gare du, *Paris* ... **23** a4
Nordrand-Siedlung, *Vienna* ... **31** A2
Nordstrand, *Oslo* ... **22** A3
Normandale, *Wellington* ... **32** B2
Nørrebro, *Copenhagen* ... **10** a1
Norridge, *Chicago* ... **9** b3
Norrmalm, *Stockholm* ... **28** a1
North Arlington, *New York* ... **21** B1
North Bay Village, *Miami* ... **18** A2
North Bergen, *New York* ... **21** B1
North Branch Chicago
  River →, *Chicago* ... **9** B2
North Bull Island, *Dublin* ... **11** A3
North Cambridge, *Boston* ... **6** A3
North Cheam, *London* ... **15** B2
North Cohasset, *Boston* ... **6** B4
North Cray, *London* ... **15** B4
North Decatur, *Atlanta* ... **3** B3
North Druid Hills, *Atlanta* ... **3** B3
North Esk →, *Edinburgh* ... **11** B3
North Gyle, *Edinburgh* ... **11** B2
North Hackensack, *New York* ... **21** A1
North Harbor, *Manila* ... **17** B1
North Hd., *Sydney* ... **28** A2
North Hollywood,
  Los Angeles ... **16** B2
North Lexington, *Boston* ... **6** A2
North Miami, *Miami* ... **18** A2
North Miami Beach, *Miami* ... **18** A2
North Nazimabad, *Karachi* ... **14** A2
North Pt., *Hong Kong* ... **12** B2
North Queensferry,
  Edinburgh ... **11** A1
North Quincy, *Boston* ... **6** B3
North Res., *Boston* ... **6** A3
North Riverside, *Chicago* ... **9** B2
North Saugus, *Boston* ... **6** A3
North Shore Channel →,
  Chicago ... **9** B2
North Springfield, *Washington* ... **32** C2
North Sudbury, *Boston* ... **6** A1
North Sydney, *Sydney* ... **28** B2
North Woolwich, *London* ... **15** A4
North York, *Toronto* ... **30** A2
Northbridge, *Sydney* ... **28** A2
Northbridge Park, *Sydney* ... **28** A2
Northcliff, *Johannesburg* ... **13** A1
Northcote, *Melbourne* ... **17** A2
Northlake, *Chicago* ... **9** B1
Northmount, *Toronto* ... **30** A2
Northolt, *London* ... **15** A1
Northumberland Heath,
  London ... **15** B5
Northwood, *London* ... **15** A1
Norumbega Res., *Boston* ... **6** A2
Norwood, *Johannesburg* ... **13** A2
Norwood Park, *Chicago* ... **9** B2
Norwegian, *Seoul* ... **26** B1
Nossa Senhora de Candelária,
  Rio de Janeiro ... **24** a2
Nossa Senhora da Ó,
  São Paulo ... **26** B1
Nossegem, *Brussels* ... **6** A3
Notre-Dame, *Montreal* ... **19** B3
Notre-Dame, *Paris* ... **23** c4
Notre-Dame, Bois, *Paris* ... **23** B4
Notre-Dame-de-Grace,
  Montreal ... **19** B2
Notting Hill, *London* ... **15** b1
Nova Milanese, *Milan* ... **18** A1
Novate Milanese, *Milan* ... **18** A1
Novaya Derevnya,
  St. Petersburg ... **26** A1
Nové Město, *Prague* ... **24** B2
Novoaleksandrovskoye,
  Moscow ... **26** B2
Novogireyevo, *Moscow* ... **19** B4
Novonavanovskoye, *Moscow* ... **19** B4
Novonikolyskoye, *Moscow* ... **19** A1
Novosaratovka, *St. Petersburg* ... **26** B3
Nowe-Babice, *Warsaw* ... **31** B1
Nöykkiö, *Helsinki* ... **12** B1
Nueva Atzacoalco,
  Mexico City ... **18** B2
Nueva Pompeya,
  Buenos Aires ... **7** C2
Nueva Tenochtitlán,
  Mexico City ... **18** B2
Nuijala, *Helsinki* ... **12** B1
Numabukuro, *Tokyo* ... **29** A2
Nunez, *Buenos Aires* ... **7** B2
Nunhead, *London* ... **15** B3
Nuñoa, *Santiago* ... **26** B2
Nusle, *Prague* ... **24** B2
Nussdorf, *Vienna* ... **31** A2
Nyanga, *Cape Town* ... **8** B2
Nymphenburg, *Munich* ... **20** B2
Nymphenburg, Schloss,
  Munich ... **20** B2

O

Oak Grove, *Atlanta* ... **3** A3
Oak Island, *Boston* ... **6** A4
Oak Lawn, *Chicago* ... **9** C2
Oak Park, *Chicago* ... **9** B2
Oak View, *Washington* ... **32** A4
Oakdale, *Atlanta* ... **3** B2
Oakland, *San Francisco* ... **25** B3
Oakland, *Washington* ... **32** B4
Oakland, *Washington* ... **32** C4
Oakleigh, *Melbourne* ... **17** B2
Oakton, *Washington* ... **32** B2
Oakwood Beach, *New York* ... **21** C1
Oatley, *Sydney* ... **28** B1
Obalende, *Lagos* ... **14** B2
Oba's Palace, *Lagos* ... **14** B2
Oberföhring, *Munich* ... **20** B2
Oberhaching, *Munich* ... **20** B2
Oberlaa, *Vienna* ... **31** B2

Oberlisse, *Vienna* ... **31** A2
Obermenzing, *Munich* ... **20** A1
Obermozings Schwaige, *Munich* ... **20** A1
Oberschleissheim, *Munich* ... **20** A2
Oberschöneweide, *Berlin* ... **5** B4
Observatory, *Johannesburg* ... **13** B2
Observatory, *Sydney* ... **28** a1
Obu, *Osaka* ... **22** A1
Obu-Osaka, *Osaka* ... **22** A1
Óbuda, *Budapest* ... **7** A2
Obukhovo, *St. Petersburg* ... **26** B2
Obvodnyy Kanal,
  St. Petersburg ... **26** B2
Ocean Park, *Hong Kong* ... **12** B2
Ochakovo, *Moscow* ... **19** B2
Ochota, *Warsaw* ... **31** B1
O'Connell Street, *Dublin* ... **11** b2
Ödana, *Tokyo* ... **29** B2
Öden-Stockach, *Munich* ... **20** B3
Odilampi, *Helsinki* ... **12** B2
Odintsovo, *Moscow* ... **19** B1
Odivelas, *Lisbon* ... **14** A1
Oeiras, *Lisbon* ... **14** A1
Ofín, *Lagos* ... **14** A1
Ogawa, *Tokyo* ... **29** A1
Ogden Park, *Chicago* ... **9** C2
Ogikubo, *Tokyo* ... **29** A2
Ogogoro, *Lagos* ... **14** B2
Ogoyo, *Lagos* ... **14** B2
Ogudu, *Lagos* ... **14** A2
Ohariu Stream →, *Wellington* ... **32** B1
O'Higgins, Parque, *Santiago* ... **26** B2
Ōimachi, *Tokyo* ... **29** B3
Ojota, *Lagos* ... **14** A2
Okamoto, *Osaka* ... **22** A2
Okęcie, *Warsaw* ... **31** B1
Okęcie Airport, *Warsaw* ... **31** B1
Okelra, *Lagos* ... **14** B2
Okeogbe, *Lagos* ... **14** B2
Okha, *Delhi* ... **10** B2
Okhta, →, *St. Petersburg* ... **26** B2
Okkervil →, *St. Petersburg* ... **26** B2
Oksvall, *Oslo* ... **22** A1
Oktyabrskiy, *Moscow* ... **19** B3
Okubo, *Tokyo* ... **29** a2
Okura, *Tokyo* ... **29** B3
Olari, *Helsinki* ... **12** B1
Olaria, *Rio de Janeiro* ... **24** B1
Old Admiralty, *St. Petersburg* ... **26** b2
Old City, *Delhi* ... **1** A2
Old City, *Jerusalem* ... **13** B2
Old City, *Shanghai* ... **27** B1
Old Fort = Purana Qila, *Delhi* ... **1** b3
Old Harbor, *Boston* ... **6** B3
Old Town, *Chicago* ... **9** B3
Old Town, *Edinburgh* ... **11** B2
Oldbawn, *Dublin* ... **11** B1
Olgino, *St. Petersburg* ... **26** A1
Olímpico, Estadio,
  Mexico City ... **18** C1
Olivais, *Lisbon* ... **14** A2
Olivar de los Padres,
  Mexico City ... **18** C1
Olivar del Conde, *Mexico City* ... **18** B1
Olivos, *Buenos Aires* ... **7** B2
Olona →, *Milan* ... **18** B1
Olympia, *London* ... **15** c2
Olympic Stadium, *Helsinki* ... **12** B2
Olympique, Stade, *Montreal* ... **19** A2
Omonias, Pl., *Athens* ... **2** b1
Ōmori, *Tokyo* ... **29** B3
Onchi, *Osaka* ... **22** B4
Onchi-Osaka, *Osaka* ... **22** B4
Onisigun, *Lagos* ... **14** A2
Ookayama, *Tokyo* ... **29** B3
Oosterpark, *Amsterdam* ... **2** b3
Oostzaan, *Amsterdam* ... **2** A2
Opa-Locka, *Miami* ... **18** A1
Opa-Locka Airport, *Miami* ... **18** A1
Opacz, *Warsaw* ... **31** B1
Opera House, *Sydney* ... **28** a2
Ophirton, *Johannesburg* ... **13** B2
Opgegård, *Oslo* ... **22** B3
Oppem, *Brussels* ... **6** A1
Oppsal, *Oslo* ... **22** A4
Ora, *Jerusalem* ... **13** B1
Oradell, *New York* ... **21** A1
Orange Bowl Stadium, *Miami* ... **18** B2
Orangi, *Karachi* ... **14** A1
Orchard Road, *Singapore* ... **27** a1
Orech, *Prague* ... **24** B1
Ørestad, *Copenhagen* ... **10** B3
Orient Heights, *Boston* ... **6** A4
Orlando Dam, *Johannesburg* ... **13** B1
Orlando East, *Johannesburg* ... **13** B2
Orlovo, *Moscow* ... **19** C2
Orly, *Paris* ... **23** B3
Ormesson-sur-Marne, *Paris* ... **23** B4
Ormond, *Melbourne* ... **17** B2
Orméya, *Oslo* ... **22** A2
Orpington, *London* ... **15** B4
Orsay, Musée d', *Paris* ... **23** b3
Országház, *Budapest* ... **7** b2
Országos Levétár, *Budapest* ... **7** b1
Ortaköy, *Istanbul* ... ...
Ortica, *Milan* ... **18** B2
Oruba, *Lagos* ... **14** A2
Orvostörteneti Múz.,
  Budapest ... **7** c2
Ōsaka, *Osaka* ... **22** B4
Ōsaka B., *Osaka* ... **22** A3
Osdorf, *Berlin* ... **5** B3
Osdorp, *Amsterdam* ... **2** A1
Oshodi, *Lagos* ... **14** A2
Oslo, *Oslo* ... **22** A3
Oslofjorden, *Oslo* ... **22** B2
Osøyro, *Oslo* ... **22** B3
Osorun, *Lagos* ... **14** A2
Ospiate, *Milan* ... **18** A1
Ostankino, *Moscow* ... **19** B3
Östasiatiskamuséet,
  Stockholm ... **28** a3
Österåm, *Stockholm* ... **28** a3
Østerbro, *Copenhagen* ... **10** a2
Osterley, *London* ... **15** B1
Osterley Park, *London* ... **15** B1
Östermalm, *Stockholm* ... **28** a3
Österskär, *Stockholm* ... **28** A3
Ostiense, *Rome* ... **25** B1
Ostmarkkapellet, *Oslo* ... **22** A3
Ostøya, *Oslo* ... **22** A2
Østre Aker, *Oslo* ... **22** A3
Ōta-Ku, *Tokyo* ... **29** B3
Otaniemi, *Helsinki* ... **12** B1
Otari Open Air Museum,
  Wellington ... **32** B1
Ōtsuka, *Tokyo* ... **29** A3
Ottakring, *Vienna* ... **31** A1

Ottávia, *Rome* ... **25** B1
Ottery, *Cape Town* ... **8** B2
Ottobrunn, *Munich* ... **20** B3
Oud Zuid, *Amsterdam* ... **2** b1
Oude Kerk, *Amsterdam* ... **2** a2
Ouderkerk, *Amsterdam* ... **2** B2
Oulunkylä, *Helsinki* ... **12** B2
Ourcq, Canal de l', *Paris* ... **23** A3
Outer Mission, *San Francisco* ... **25** B2
Outremont, *Montreal* ... **19** A2
Overijse, *Brussels* ... **6** B3
Owhiro Bay, *Wellington* ... **32** C1
Oworonsoki, *Lagos* ... **14** A2
Oxford Street, *London* ... **15** b3
Oxon Hill, *Washington* ... **32** C4
Oyodo, *Osaka* ... **22** A3
Oyster B., *Sydney* ... **28** C1
Oyster Rock, *Mumbai* ... **20** B1
Oyster Rocks, *Karachi* ... **14** B2
Ozoir-la-Ferrière, *Paris* ... **23** B4
Ozone Park, *New York* ... **21** B2

P

Pacific Heights, *San Francisco* ... **25** B2
Pacific Manor, *San Francisco* ... **25** C2
Pacific Palisades, *Los Angeles* ... **16** B1
Pacifica, *San Francisco* ... **25** C2
Paco, *Manila* ... **17** B2
Paco de Arcos, *Lisbon* ... **14** A1
Paco Imperial, *Rio de Janeiro* ... **24** a2
Paddington, *London* ... **15** b2
Paddington, *Sydney* ... **28** B2
Paderno, *Milan* ... **18** A1
Pagewood, *Sydney* ... **28** B2
Pagote, *Mumbai* ... **20** B2
Pai, I. do, *Rio de Janeiro* ... **24** B2
Pak Kong, *Hong Kong* ... **12** A2
Pakila, *Helsinki* ... **12** B2
Palacio de Bellas Artes,
  Mexico City ... **18** b2
Palacio Nacional, *Mexico City* ... **18** b3
Palacio Real, *Barcelona* ... **4** b3
Palacio Real, *Madrid* ... **17** b1
Palaión Fáliron, *Athens* ... **2** B2
Palais de Justice, *Brussels* ... **6** c2
Palais Royal, *Paris* ... **23** b4
Palais Royale, *Brussels* ... **6** b3
Palaiseau, *Paris* ... **23** B2
Palau Nacional Museu d'Art,
  Barcelona ... **4** c1
Palazzolo, *Milan* ... **18** A1
Palermo, *Buenos Aires* ... **7** B2
Palhais, *Lisbon* ... **14** B2
Palisades Park, *New York* ... **21** A1
Palmer Park, *Washington* ... **32** B4
Palmerston, *Dublin* ... **11** A1
Paloheinä, *Helsinki* ... **12** B2
Palomeras, *Madrid* ... **17** B2
Palos Heights, *Chicago* ... **9** D2
Palos Hills, *Chicago* ... **9** C2
Palos Hills Forest, *Chicago* ... **9** C1
Palos Park, *Chicago* ... **9** C1
Palpara, *Calcutta* ... **8** B2
Panchur, *Calcutta* ... **8** B1
Pandacan, *Manila* ... **17** B2
Pandan, Selat, *Singapore* ... **27** B2
Pandan Res., *Singapore* ... **27** B2
Panepistimio, *Athens* ... **2** b2
Pangati, *Athens* ... **26** C1
Pangati, *Athens* ... **2** b2
Pangrati, *Athens* ... **2** b3
Pangsua, Sungei →,
  Singapore ... **27** A2
Panihati, *Calcutta* ... **8** A2
Panjang, Bukit, *Singapore* ... **27** A2
Panje, *Mumbai* ... **20** B2
Panke →, *Berlin* ... **5** A3
Pankow, *Berlin* ... **5** A3
Panthéon, *Paris* ... **23** c4
Pantheon, *Rome* ... **25** b2
Pantin, *Paris* ... **23** A3
Pantitlán, *Mexico City* ... **18** B2
Panvel Cr. →, *Mumbai* ... **20** B2
Paparangi, *Wellington* ... **32** B1
Papiol, *Barcelona* ... **4** A1
Paramus, *New York* ... **21** A1
Paranaque, *Manila* ... **17** B1
Paray-Vieille-Poste, *Paris* ... **23** B3
Parco Regionale, *Milan* ... **18** A2
Parel, *Mumbai* ... **20** B1
Pari, *São Paulo* ... **26** B2
Parioli, *Rome* ... **25** B1
Paris, *Paris* ... **23** A3
Paris-Orly, Aéroport de, *Paris* ... **23** B3
Párk-e Mellat, *Tehran* ... **30** A2
Park Ridge, *Chicago* ... **9** A1
Park Royal, *London* ... **15** A2
Parkchester, *New York* ... **21** B2
Parkdale, *Toronto* ... **30** B2
Parkhurst, *Johannesburg* ... **13** A2
Parklawn, *Washington* ... **32** B3
Parklawn, *Johannesburg* ... **13** B2
Parkside, *San Francisco* ... **25** B2
Parktown, *Johannesburg* ... **13** B2
Parktown North,
  Johannesburg ... **13** A2
Parkview, *Johannesburg* ... **13** A2
Parkville, *New York* ... **21** C2
Parkwood, *Johannesburg* ... **13** A2
Parnell, *Cape Town* ... **8** A2
Parow, *Cape Town* ... **8** A1
Parque Chabuco,
  Buenos Aires ... **7** B2
Parque Patricios,
  Buenos Aires ... **7** B2
Parramatta →, *Sydney* ... **28** A1
Pasadena, *Los Angeles* ... **16** B4
Pasar Ris, *Singapore* ... **27** A3
Pasay, *Manila* ... **17** B1
Pasco Vale, *Melbourne* ... **17** A1
Paseo de la Reforma,
  Mexico City ... **18** b2
Pasig, *Manila* ... **17** B2
Pasig →, *Manila* ... **17** B2
Pasila, *Helsinki* ... **12** B2
Pasing, *Munich* ... **20** B1
Pasir Panjang, *Singapore* ... **27** B2
Passaic →, *New York* ... **21** A1
Passirana, *Milan* ... **18** A1
Patel Nagar, *Delhi* ... **10** B1
Pateros, *Manila* ... **17** B2
Pathersville, *Atlanta* ... **3** B3
Pathumwan, *Bangkok* ... **3** B2
Patipukur, *Calcutta* ... **8** B2
Patisia, *Athens* ... **2** A2
Paulo E. Virginia, Gruta,
  Rio de Janeiro ... **24** B1
Paulshof, *Berlin* ... **5** A5

Pavshino, *Moscow* ... **19** B1
Paya Lebar, *Singapore* ... **27** A3
Peachtree →, *Atlanta* ... **3** B2
Peakhurst, *Sydney* ... **28** B1
Peania, *Athens* ... **2** B2
Peckham, *London* ... **15** B3
Peddocks I., *Boston* ... **6** B4
Pederstrup, *Copenhagen* ... **10** A2
Pedregal de San Angel,
  Jardines del, *Mexico City* ... **18** C1
Pekhorka →, *Moscow* ... **19** C6
Pekhra-Pokrovskoye, *Moscow* ... **19** A5
Pekhra-Yakovievskaya,
  Moscow ... **19** B5
Peking = Beijing, *Beijing* ... **4** B2
Pelcowizna, *Warsaw* ... **31** B2
Pelopónnisos Sta., *Athens* ... **2** a1
Penalolén, *Santiago* ... **26** B2
Pencarrow Hd., *Wellington* ... **32** C2
Peng Siang →, *Singapore* ... **27** A2
Penge, *London* ... **15** B3
Penha, *Rio de Janeiro* ... **24** A1
Penicuik, *Edinburgh* ... **11** B2
Penjaringan, *Jakarta* ... **13** A1
Penn Station, *New York* ... **21** a2
Pennsylvania Avenue,
  Washington ... **32** b1
Penyagino, *Moscow* ... **19** A2
Penzing, *Vienna* ... **31** A1
People's Park, *Shanghai* ... **27** B1
People's Square, *Shanghai* ... **27** B1
Perales del Rio, *Madrid* ... **17** C2
Peravillo, *Mexico City* ... **18** a3
Perchtoldsdorf, *Vienna* ... **31** B1
Perdizes, *São Paulo* ... **26** B2
Peredelkino, *Moscow* ... **19** C2
Pergamon Museum, *Berlin* ... **5** a4
Peristérion, *Athens* ... **2** A1
Perivale, *London* ... **15** A2
Perk, *Brussels* ... **6** A2
Perlach, *Munich* ... **20** B2
Perlacher Forst, *Munich* ... **20** B2
Pero, *Milan* ... **18** B1
Péronville, *Montreal* ... **19** B3
Přezletice, *Prague* ... **24** B3
Prima Porta, *Rome* ... **25** B1
Primavalle, *Rome* ... **25** B1
Primrose, *Johannesburg* ... **13** B2
Princes Street, *Edinburgh* ... **11** b2
Printer's Row, *Chicago* ... **9** d2
Progreso Nacional,
  Mexico City ... **18** A2
Prosek, *Prague* ... **24** B3
Prospect Hill Park, *Boston* ... **6** A2
Providencia, *Santiago* ... **26** B2
Prudential Building, *Chicago* ... **9** c2
Průhonice, *Prague* ... **24** C3
Psikhikón, *Athens* ... **2** A2
Pudong New Area, *Shanghai* ... **27** B2
Pueblo Libre, *Lima* ... **16** B2
Pueblo Nuevo, *Barcelona* ... **4** A2
Pueblo Nuevo, *Madrid* ... **17** B2
Puerta del Sol, Plaza, *Madrid* ... **17** b2
Puerto Madero, *Buenos Aires* ... **7** B2
Puerto Retiro, *Buenos Aires* ... **7** B2
Puhuangyu, *Beijing* ... **4** B2
Puistola, *Helsinki* ... **12** B3
Pukan-san, *Seoul* ... **26** B1
Pukinmäki, *Helsinki* ... **12** B2
Pukkajwa, *Seoul* ... **26** B1
Pulkovo Int. Airport,
  St. Petersburg ... **26** C1
Pullach, *Munich* ... **20** B1
Pulo Gadung, *Jakarta* ... **13** B2
Pünak, *Tehran* ... **30** A2
Punchbowl, *Sydney* ... **28** B1
Punde, *Mumbai* ... **20** B2
Punggol, *Singapore* ... **27** A3
Punggol, Sungei →,
  Singapore ... **27** A3
Punggol Pt., *Singapore* ... **27** A3
Punjabi Bagh, *Delhi* ... **10** A1
Puotila, *Helsinki* ... **12** B3
Purana Qila, *Delhi* ... **1** c3
Puteaux, *Paris* ... **23** A2
Putilkovo, *Moscow* ... **19** A2
Putney, *London* ... **15** B2
Putuo, *Shanghai* ... **27** B1
Putxet, *Barcelona* ... **4** A1
Puxi, *Shanghai* ... **27** B1
Pydhuni, *Mumbai* ... **20** c2
Pyramids, *Cairo* ... **7** B1
Pyry, *Warsaw* ... **31** C1

Q

Qalandya, *Jerusalem* ... **13** A2
Qal'eh Morghi, *Tehran* ... **30** B2
Qamā el Ismā'ilīya, *Cairo* ... **7** A2
Qásembábá, *Tehran* ... **30** A3
Qasr-e Firozeh, *Tehran* ... **30** B3
Qatane, *Jerusalem* ... **13** B1
Qianmen, *Beijing* ... **4** B2
Qinghuayuan, *Beijing* ... **4** B1
Qingningxi, *Shanghai* ... **27** B2
Qolhak, *Tehran* ... **30** A2
Quadraro, *Rome* ... **25** B2
Quaid-i-Azam, *Karachi* ... **14** A1
Quartiere Zingone, *Milan* ... **18** B1
Quds, *Baghdad* ... **3** A2
Queen Mary Res., *London* ... **15** B1
Queen Street, *Edinburgh* ... **11** a1
Queensbury, *London* ... **15** A2
Queenscliffe, *Sydney* ... **28** A2
Queensferry, *Edinburgh* ... **11** B1
Queenstown, *Singapore* ... **27** B2
Quellerina, *Johannesburg* ... **13** A1
Queluz, *Lisbon* ... **14** A1
Quezon City, *Manila* ... **17** B2
Quezon Memorial Circle,
  Manila ... **17** B2
Quilicura, *Santiago* ... **26** B1
Quincy, *Boston* ... **6** B3
Quincy B., *Boston* ... **6** B4
Quinta Normal, *Santiago* ... **26** B1
Quinto de Stampi, *Milan* ... **18** B2
Quinto Romano, *Milan* ... **18** B1
Quirinale, *Rome* ... **25** B1
Quirinale, Palazzo dei, *Rome* ... **25** b3

R

Raasdorf, *Vienna* ... **31** A3
Rådhuset, *Oslo* ... **22** A3
Radlice, *Prague* ... **24** B2
Radość, *Warsaw* ... **31** B2
Radotin, *Prague* ... **24** C2
Rafat, *Jerusalem* ... **13** A2
Raffles Hotel, *Singapore* ... **27** B3
Raffles Park, *Singapore* ... **27** B2

Raheny, Dublin — 11 A3
Rahnsdorf, Berlin — 5 B5
Rainham, London — 15 A5
Raj Ghat, Delhi — 1 b3
Rajakylä, Helsinki — 12 B3
Rajpath, Delhi — 1 c2
Rajpura, Delhi — 10 A2
Rákos-patak →, Budapest — 7 B3
Rákoshegy, Budapest — 7 B3
Rákoskeresztúr, Budapest — 7 B3
Rákoskert, Budapest — 7 B3
Rákosliget, Budapest — 7 B3
Rákospalota, Budapest — 7 A2
Rákosszentmihály, Budapest — 7 A2
Rákow, Warsaw — 31 B1
Ram, Jerusalem — 13 A2
Rām Allāh, Jerusalem — 13 A2
Ramādān, Baghdad — 3 B2
Ramakrishna Puram, Delhi — 10 B1
Ramanathpur, Calcutta — 8 A1
Rambla, La, Barcelona — 4 b2
Rambler Channel, Hong Kong — 12 A1
Ramenki, Moscow — 19 B2
Ramersdorf, Munich — 20 B2
Ramos, Rio de Janeiro — 24 B1
Ramos Mejia, Buenos Aires — 7 B1
Ramot, Jerusalem — 13 B2
Rampur, Delhi — 10 A2
Ramsgate, Sydney — 28 B1
Rand Afrikaans Univ., Johannesburg — 13 B2
Rand Airport, Johannesburg — 13 A2
Randburg, Johannesburg — 13 A1
Randhart, Johannesburg — 13 B2
Randpark Ridge, Johannesburg — 13 A1
Randwick, Sydney — 28 B2
Ranelagh, Dublin — 11 A2
Rannersdorf, Vienna — 31 B2
Ransbèche, Brussels — 6 B2
Ransdorp, Amsterdam — 2 A2
Ranvad, Mumbai — 20 B2
Raposo, Lisbon — 14 A1
Rashtrapati Bhawan, Delhi — 1 c1
Rasskazovka, Moscow — 19 C2
Rastaala, Helsinki — 12 B1
Rastila, Helsinki — 12 B3
Raszyn, Warsaw — 31 C1
Ratcha Thewi, Bangkok — 3 b3
Rathfarnham, Dublin — 11 B1
Ratho, Edinburgh — 11 B1
Ratho Station, Edinburgh — 11 B1
Rato, Lisbon — 14 A2
Raveston, Edinburgh — 11 B2
Rawamangun, Jakarta — 13 B2
Rayners Lane, London — 15 A1
Raynes Park, London — 15 B2
Raypur, Calcutta — 8 C2
Razdory, Moscow — 19 B1
Real Felipe, Fuerte, Lima — 16 B2
Recoleta, Buenos Aires — 7 B2
Recoleta, Santiago — 26 B2
Red Fort = Lal Qila, Delhi — 1 a3
Redbridge, London — 15 A4
Redfern, Sydney — 28 B2
Redwood, Wellington — 32 B1
Reeves Hill, Boston — 6 A1
Refshaløen, Copenhagen — 10 A3
Regents Park, Johannesburg — 13 B2
Regent's Park, London — 15 a2
Rego Park, New York — 21 B2
Reina Sofia, Centro de Arte, Madrid — 17 c3
Reinickendorf, Berlin — 5 A3
Rekola, Helsinki — 12 B3
Rembertów, Warsaw — 31 B2
Rembrandthuis, Amsterdam — 2 b2
Rembrandtpark, Amsterdam — 2 A1
Rembrandtplein, Amsterdam — 2 b2
Remedios, Parque Nacional de los, Mexico City — 18 B1
Remedios de Escalada, Buenos Aires — 7 C2
Rémola, Laguna del, Barcelona — 4 B1
Renca, Santiago — 26 B1
Renmin Park, Tianjin — 30 B2
Rennemoulin, Paris — 23 A1
Reporyje, Prague — 24 B1
Republica, Plaza de la, Mexico City — 18 b1
République, Place de la, Paris — 23 b5
Repulse Bay, Hong Kong — 12 B2
Repy, Prague — 24 B1
Residenz, Munich — 20 B2
Residenzmuseum, Munich — 20 b3
Reston, Washington — 32 B2
Retiro, Buenos Aires — 7 B2
Retiro, Madrid — 17 B1
Retreat, Cape Town — 8 B1
Reutov, Moscow — 19 B5
Réveillon →, Paris — 23 B4
Revere, Boston — 6 A3
Rexdale, Toronto — 30 A1
Reynosa Tamaulipas, Mexico City — 18 A1
Rho, Milan — 18 A1
Rhodes, Sydney — 28 A1
Rhodon, Paris — 23 B1
Rhodon →, Paris — 23 B1
Ribeira, Rio de Janeiro — 24 A1
Ricarda, Laguna de la, Barcelona — 4 B1
Richmond, Melbourne — 17 A2
Richmond, San Francisco — 25 B2
Richmond Hill, New York — 21 B2
Richmond Park, London — 15 B2
Richmond upon Thames, London — 15 B2
Riddarholmen, Stockholm — 28 c1
Riddarhuset, Stockholm — 28 c1
Ridgefield, New York — 21 B1
Ridgefield Park, New York — 21 A1
Ridgewood, New York — 21 B2
Riem, Munich — 20 B3
Rijksmuseum, Amsterdam — 2 b1
Rikers I., New York — 21 B2
Riksdagensledamothus, Stockholm — 28 b2
Riksdagshuset, Stockholm — 28 b2
Rimac, Lima — 16 B2
Ringsend, Dublin — 11 A2
Rinkeby, Stockholm — 28 A1
Rio Compride, Rio de Janeiro — 24 B1
Rio de Janeiro, Rio de Janeiro — 24 B1
Rio de la Plata, Buenos Aires — 7 B2
Rio de Mouro, Lisbon — 14 A1
Ripollet, Barcelona — 4 A1
Ris, Oslo — 22 A3
Risby, Copenhagen — 10 A1
Rishra, Calcutta — 8 A2
Ritchie, Washington — 32 B4
Rithala, Delhi — 10 A1
Rive Sud, Canal de la, Montreal — 19 B2

River Edge, New York — 21 A1
River Forest, Chicago — 9 B2
River Grove, Chicago — 9 B1
Riverdale, New York — 21 A2
Riverdale, Washington — 32 B4
Riverdale Park, Toronto — 30 A2
Riverlea, Johannesburg — 13 B1
Riverside, Chicago — 9 C2
Riverwood, Sydney — 28 B1
Rivière-des-Prairies, Montreal — 19 A2
Rixensart, Brussels — 6 B3
Riyad, Baghdad — 3 B2
Rizal Park, Manila — 17 B1
Rizal Stadium, Manila — 17 B1
Røa, Oslo — 22 A2
Robbins, Chicago — 9 D2
Robertsham, Johannesburg — 13 B2
Rochelle Park, New York — 21 A1
Rock Cr. →, Washington — 32 B3
Rock Creek Park, Washington — 32 B3
Rock Pt., Wellington — 32 A1
Rockaway Pt., New York — 21 C2
Rockdale, Sydney — 28 B1
Rockefeller Center, New York — 21 c2
Rodaon, Vienna — 31 B1
Rødovre, Copenhagen — 10 A2
Rodrigo de Freitas, L., Rio de Janeiro — 24 B1
Roehampton, London — 15 B2
Rogers Park, Chicago — 9 A2
Roihuvuori, Helsinki — 12 B3
Roissy-en-Brie, Paris — 23 B4
Rokin, Amsterdam — 2 b2
Rokkō I., Osaka — 22 A2
Rokkō Sanchi, Osaka — 22 A2
Rokkō-Zan, Osaka — 22 A2
Rokytka →, Prague — 24 B3
Roma, Rome — 25 B1
Római-Fürdö, Budapest — 7 A2
Romainville, Paris — 23 A3
Romano Banco, Milan — 18 B1
Rome = Roma, Rome — 25 B1
Romford, London — 15 A5
Rondebosch, Cape Town — 8 A1
Roppongi, Tokyo — 29 c3
Rose Hill, Washington — 32 C3
Rosebank, New York — 21 C1
Rosebery, Sydney — 28 B2
Rosedal La Candelaria, Mexico City — 18 B2
Roseland, Chicago — 9 C3
Rosemead, Los Angeles — 16 B4
Rosemont, Montreal — 19 A2
Rosenborg Have, Copenhagen — 10 a2
Rosenthal, Berlin — 5 A3
Rosettenville, Johannesburg — 13 B2
Rosewell, Edinburgh — 11 B3
Rosherville Dam, Johannesburg — 13 B2
Rösjön, Stockholm — 28 A2
Roslags-Näsby, Stockholm — 28 A2
Roslin, Edinburgh — 11 B3
Roslindale, Boston — 6 B3
Rosny-sous-Bois, Paris — 23 A4
Rosslyn, Washington — 32 B3
Rosyth, Edinburgh — 11 A1
Rotherhithe, London — 15 B3
Rothneusiedl, Vienna — 31 B2
Rothschmaige, Munich — 20 A1
Rouge Hill, Toronto — 30 A4
Round I., Hong Kong — 12 B2
Roxbury, Boston — 6 A3
Roxeth, London — 15 A1
Royal Botanic Garden, Edinburgh — 11 B2
Royal Botanic Gardens, Sydney — 28 b2
Royal Grand Palace, Bangkok — 3 b1
Royal Observatory, Edinburgh — 11 B2
Royal Park, Melbourne — 17 A1
Royal Turf Club, Bangkok — 3 b2
Röyla, Helsinki — 12 B1
Rozas, Portilleros de las, Madrid — 17 B1
Roztoky, Prague — 24 B2
Rozzano, Milan — 18 B1
Rubí →, Barcelona — 4 A1
Rublovo, Moscow — 19 B2
Rudnevka →, Moscow — 19 B5
Rudolfsheim, Vienna — 31 A2
Rudolfshöhe, Berlin — 5 A5
Rudow, Berlin — 5 B3
Rueil-Malmaison, Paris — 23 A2
Ruisbroek, Brussels — 6 B1
Ruislip, London — 15 A1
Rumelihisar, Istanbul — 12 B2
Rumyantsevo, Moscow — 19 C2
Rungis, Paris — 23 B3
Rusafa, Baghdad — 3 A2
Rush Green, London — 15 A5
Russa, Calcutta — 8 C2
Russian Hill, San Francisco — 25 a1
Rustenfeld, Vienna — 31 B2
Rutherford, New York — 21 B1
Ruzyně, Prague — 24 B1
Rybatskaya, St. Petersburg — 26 B3
Rydboholm, Stockholm — 28 A3
Ryde, Sydney — 28 A1
Rynek, Warsaw — 31 b1
Ryogoku, Tokyo — 29 A3
Rzhevka, St. Petersburg — 26 B3

S

Sa'ādatābād, Tehran — 30 A2
Saadún, Baghdad — 3 B2
Saavedra, Buenos Aires — 7 B2
Saboli, Delhi — 10 A2
Sabugo, Lisbon — 14 A1
Sabzi Mand, Delhi — 10 A2
Sacavém, Lisbon — 14 A2
Saclay, Paris — 23 B2
Saclay, Étang de, Paris — 23 B2
Sacomã, São Paulo — 26 B2
Sacré Cœur, Paris — 23 a4
Sacrow, Berlin — 5 B1
Sacrower See, Berlin — 5 B1
Sadang, Seoul — 26 C1
Sadar Bazar, Delhi — 1 a1
Saddām City, Baghdad — 3 A2
Saddle Brook, New York — 21 A1
Sadr, Karachi — 14 A2
Sadyba, Warsaw — 31 B2
Saft el Laban, Cairo — 7 A1
Saganoshakee Slough, Chicago — 9 C1
Sagene, Oslo — 22 A3
Sagrada Família, Templo de, Barcelona — 4 A2
Sagrada Família, Templo de la, Barcelona — 4 b2
Sahar Int. Airport, Mumbai — 20 A2

Sai Kung, Hong Kong — 12 A2
Sai Wan Ho, Hong Kong — 12 B2
Sai Ying Pun, Hong Kong — 12 B1
St.-Aubin, Paris — 23 B2
St.-Cloud, Paris — 23 A2
St.-Cyr-l'École, Aérodrome de, Paris — 23 B1
St.-Denis, Paris — 23 A3
St.-Germain, Forêt de, Paris — 23 A1
St.-Germain-en-Laye, Paris — 23 A1
St. Giles Cathedral, Edinburgh — 11 b2
St. Helier, London — 15 B2
St.-Hubert, Montreal — 19 B3
St. Hubert, Galerie, Brussels — 6 b2
St. Isaac's Cathedral, St. Petersburg — 26 B1
St. Jacques →, Montreal — 19 B3
St. James's, London — 15 b3
St. John's Cathedral, Hong Kong — 12 c1
St. Kilda, Melbourne — 17 B1
St. Lambert, Montreal — 19 B3
St.-Lambert, Paris — 23 B1
St.-Laurent, Montreal — 19 A1
St. Lawrence →, Montreal — 19 B2
St.-Lazare, Gare, Paris — 23 A2
St.-Léonard, Montreal — 19 A2
St. Magelungen, Stockholm — 28 B2
St.-Mandé, Paris — 23 A3
St. Margaret's, Dublin — 11 A2
St.-Martin, Bois, Paris — 23 B4
St. Mary Cray, London — 15 B4
St.-Maur-des-Fossés, Paris — 23 B3
St.-Maurice, Paris — 23 B3
St.-Michel, Montreal — 19 A2
St. Nikolaus-Kirken, Prague — 24 B2
St.-Ouen, Paris — 23 A3
St. Patrick's Cathedral, Dublin — 11 c1
St. Patrick's Cathedral, New York — 21 c2
St. Paul's Cathedral, London — 15 b4
St. Paul's Cray, London — 15 B4
St. Peter's, London — 15 A3
St. Peters, Sydney — 28 B2
St. Petersburg = Sankt Peterburg, St. Petersburg — 26 B1
St.-Pierre, Montreal — 19 B2
St.-Quentin, Étang de, Paris — 23 B1
St. Stephen's Green, Dublin — 11 c3
St.-Vincent-de-Paul, Montreal — 19 A2
Ste.-Catherine, Montreal — 19 A2
Ste.-Hélène, Î., Montreal — 19 A2
Saiwai, Tokyo — 29 B3
Sakai, Osaka — 22 B3
Sakra →, Singapore — 27 B2
Salam, Baghdad — 3 A2
Salamanca, Madrid — 17 B1
Sállynoggin, Dublin — 11 B3
Salmannsdorf, Vienna — 31 A1
Salmedina, Madrid — 17 C2
Salomea, Warsaw — 31 B1
Salsette I., Mumbai — 20 A2
Salt Lake City, Calcutta — 8 B2
Salt River, Cape Town — 8 A1
Salt Water L., Calcutta — 8 B2
Saltsjö-Duvnäs, Stockholm — 28 B3
Saltykovka, Moscow — 19 B5
Samatya, Istanbul — 12 C1
Sampaloc, Manila — 17 B1
Samphan Thawong, Bangkok — 3 B2
Samsón, Seoul — 26 B2
San Andrés, Barcelona — 4 A1
San Angel, Mexico City — 18 B1
San Angelo, Castel, Rome — 25 b1
San Basilio, Rome — 25 B2
San Borja, Lima — 16 B3
San Bóvio, Milan — 18 B2
San Bruno, Pt., San Francisco — 25 C2
San Bruno Mt., San Francisco — 25 B2
San Cristobal, Buenos Aires — 7 B2
San Cristóbal, Madrid — 17 B2
San Cristóbal, Cerro, Santiago — 26 B2
San Cristoforo, Milan — 18 B1
San Donato Milanese, Milan — 18 B2
San Francisco, San Francisco — 25 B2
San Francisco B., San Francisco — 25 B3
San Francisco Culhuacán, Mexico City — 18 C2
San Fruttuoso, Milan — 18 A2
San Gabriel, Los Angeles — 16 B4
San Giuliano Milanese, Milan — 18 B2
San Isidro, Lima — 16 B2
San Jerónimo Lídice, Mexico City — 18 C1
San Joaquín, Santiago — 26 B2
San José Río Hondo, Mexico City — 18 B1
San Juan →, Manila — 17 B2
San Juan de Aragón, Mexico City — 18 B2
San Juan de Aragón, Parque, Mexico City — 18 B2
San Juan de Lurigancho, Lima — 16 A2
San Juan del Monte, Manila — 17 B2
San Juan Ixtacala, Mexico City — 18 B1
San Juan Toltotepec, Mexico City — 18 B1
San Just Desvern, Barcelona — 4 A1
San Justo, Buenos Aires — 7 C1
San Lorenzo Tezonco, Mexico City — 18 C2
San Luis, Lima — 16 B2
San Marino, Los Angeles — 16 B4
San Martín, Buenos Aires — 7 B1
San Martín de Porras, Lima — 16 A2
San Miguel, Lima — 16 B2
San Miguel, Santiago — 26 B2
San Nicolas, Buenos Aires — 7 B2
San Onófrio, Rome — 25 B1
San Pedro Martir, Barcelona — 4 A1
San Pedro Zacatenco, Mexico City — 18 A2
San Pietro, Piazza, Rome — 25 b1
San Po Kong, Hong Kong — 12 A2
San Rafael Chamapa, Mexico City — 18 B1
San Rafael Hills, Los Angeles — 16 A3
San Roque, Manila — 17 C2
San Siro, Milan — 18 B1
San Souci, Sydney — 28 B1
San Telmo, Buenos Aires — 7 B2
San Vicenc dels Horts, Barcelona — 4 A1
Sanbancho, Tokyo — 29 a3
Sandown, Johannesburg — 13 A2
Sandown Park Races, London — 15 B1
Sandton, Johannesburg — 13 A2
Sandvika, Oslo — 22 A2
Sandy Pond, Boston — 6 A2
Sandyford, Dublin — 11 B2
Sandymount, Dublin — 11 B2

Sangenjaya, Tokyo — 29 B2
Sangge, Seoul — 26 B2
Sangley Pt., Manila — 17 C1
Sankrail, Calcutta — 8 B1
Sankt Peterburg, St. Petersburg — 26 B1
Sankt Veit, Vienna — 31 A1
Sanlihe, Beijing — 14 B2
Sanlintang, Shanghai — 27 C1
Sans, Barcelona — 4 A1
Sant Agusti, Barcelona — 4 c2
Sant Ambrogio, Basilica di, Milan — 18 B1
Sant Boi de Llobregat, Barcelona — 4 A1
Sant Cugat, Barcelona — 4 A1
Sant Feliu de Llobregat, Barcelona — 4 A1
Sant Joan Despi, Barcelona — 4 A1
Sant Maria del Mar, Barcelona — 4 b3
Sant Pau del Camp, Barcelona — 4 c2
Santa Ana, Manila — 17 B2
Santa Coloma de Gramenet, Barcelona — 4 A2
Santa Cruz, Manila — 17 B1
Santa Cruz, Mumbai — 20 A1
Santa Cruz, I. de, Rio de Janeiro — 24 B2
Santa Cruz de Olorde, Barcelona — 4 A1
Santa Efigénia, São Paulo — 26 B2
Santa Elena, Manila — 17 B2
Santa Elena del Gomero, Santiago — 26 B1
Santa Eulalia, Barcelona — 4 A2
Santa Iria da Azóia, Lisbon — 14 A2
Santa Julia, Santiago — 26 C2
Santa Maria, Mexico City — 18 B1
Santa Monica, Los Angeles — 16 B2
Santa Monica Mts., Los Angeles — 16 B2
Santa Rosa De Locobe, Santiago — 26 B2
Santa Teresa de la Ovalle, Santiago — 26 B1
Santahamina, Helsinki — 12 C3
Santana, São Paulo — 26 B2
Santeny, Paris — 23 B4
Santiago, Santiago — 26 B2
Santiago de Surco, Lima — 16 B2
Santo Amaro, Lisbon — 14 A2
Santo Amaro, São Paulo — 26 B2
Santo Andre, Lisbon — 14 A2
Santo Antão do Tojal, Lisbon — 14 A2
Santo Tomas, Univ. of, Manila — 17 B1
Santos Dumont, Aéroport, Rio de Janeiro — 24 B2
Santoshpur, Calcutta — 8 B1
Santragachi, Calcutta — 8 B1
Santry, Dublin — 11 A2
Sanyuanli, Canton — 8 B2
São Caetano do Sul, São Paulo — 26 B2
São Conrado, Rio de Janeiro — 24 C1
São Cristovão, Rio de Janeiro — 24 B1
São Francisco Penitência, Rio de Janeiro — 24 b1
São Jorge, Castelo de, Lisbon — 14 A2
São Juliao do Tojal, Lisbon — 14 A2
São Paulo, São Paulo — 26 B2
Sapa, Calcutta — 8 B1
Sapateiro, Cor. do →, São Paulo — 26 B2
Sarandi, Buenos Aires — 7 C2
Saraswati →, Calcutta — 8 A1
Sarecky potok →, Prague — 24 B2
Sarimbun, Singapore — 27 A2
Sarimbun Res., Singapore — 27 A2
Sariyer, Istanbul — 12 B2
Saronikós Kólpos, Athens — 2 B1
Sarriá, Barcelona — 4 A1
Sarsuna, Calcutta — 8 C1
Sarrouville, Paris — 23 A2
Sasad, Budapest — 7 B2
Sashalom, Budapest — 7 A3
Saska, Warsaw — 31 B2
Satalice, Prague — 24 B3
Satgachi, Calcutta — 8 B2
Sathorn, Bangkok — 3 B2
Satpukur, Calcutta — 8 B2
Satte, Stockholm — 28 B1
Sattra Tha, Bangkok — 3 b2
Saúde, São Paulo — 26 B2
Saugus, Boston — 6 A3
Saugus →, Boston — 6 A3
Sault-au-Récollet, Montreal — 19 A2
Sausalito, San Francisco — 25 A2
Sawah Besar, Jakarta — 13 A1
Saxonville, Boston — 6 B1
Scald Law, Edinburgh — 11 B2
Scarborough, Toronto — 30 A3
Sceaux, Paris — 23 B2
Schaerbeek, Brussels — 6 A2
Scharfenberg, Berlin — 5 A2
Scheepvaartmuseum, Amsterdam — 2 b3
Schiller Park, Chicago — 9 B1
Schiller Woods, Chicago — 9 B1
Schiphol, Luchthaven, Amsterdam — 2 B1
Schlachtensee, Berlin — 5 B2
Schlossgarten, Berlin — 5 B2
Schmargendorf, Berlin — 5 B2
Schönblick, Berlin — 5 B5
Schönbrunn, Schloss, Vienna — 31 A1
Schöneberg, Berlin — 5 B3
Schöneiche, Berlin — 5 B5
Schönwalde, Berlin — 5 A1
Schotschekloof, Cape Town — 8 b1
Schulzendorf, Berlin — 5 A4
Schwabing, Munich — 20 B2
Schwanebeck, Berlin — 5 A4
Schwarzackenau, Vienna — 31 A2
Schwechat, Vienna — 31 A2
Scitrek Museum, Atlanta — 3 B2
Scott Monument, Edinburgh — 11 b2
Scottdale, Atlanta — 3 A3
Sea Point, Cape Town — 8 A1
Seabrook, Washington — 32 B5
Seacliff, San Francisco — 25 A2
Seaforth, Sydney — 28 A2
Seagate, New York — 21 C1
Seat Pleasant, Washington — 32 B4
Seaview, Wellington — 32 B2
Seberov, Prague — 24 B3
Secaucus, New York — 21 B1
Seddinsee, Berlin — 5 B5
Seeberg, Berlin — 5 A5
Seeburg, Berlin — 5 A1
Seefeld, Berlin — 5 A5

Seegefeld, Berlin — 5 A1
Seehof, Berlin — 5 B2
Segeltorp, Stockholm — 28 B1
Segrate, Milan — 18 B2
Seguro, Milan — 18 B1
Seine →, Paris — 23 B3
Seixal, Lisbon — 14 B2
Selby, Johannesburg — 13 B2
Seletar, Singapore — 27 A3
Seletar Hills, Singapore — 27 A3
Seletar Res., Singapore — 27 A3
Selhurst, London — 15 B3
Selsdon, London — 15 B3
Senago, Milan — 18 A1
Sendinger Tor Platz, Munich — 20 c1
Sendling, Munich — 20 B2
Senju, Tokyo — 29 A3
Senriyama, Osaka — 22 A4
Sentosa, P., Singapore — 27 B2
Sepolia, Athens — 2 A2
Seoul National Univ., Seoul — 26 C1
Seoul Tower, Seoul — 26 B1
Sepulveda Flood Control Basin, Los Angeles — 16 A2
Serangoon, Singapore — 27 A3
Serangoon, P., Singapore — 27 A3
Serangoon, Sungei →, Singapore — 27 A3
Serangoon Harbour, Singapore — 27 A3
Seraya, P., Singapore — 27 B2
Serebryanka, Moscow — 19 B5
Serebryanka →, Moscow — 19 B4
Serramonte, San Francisco — 25 C2
Sesto San Giovanni, Milan — 18 A2
Sesto Ulteriano, Milan — 18 B2
Setagaya-Ku, Tokyo — 29 B2
Seter, Oslo — 22 A3
Setia Budi, Jakarta — 13 B1
Settebagni, Rome — 25 A2
Settecamini, Rome — 25 B2
Séttimo Milanese, Milan — 18 B1
Settsu, Osaka — 22 A4
Setuny →, Moscow — 19 B2
Scutula, Helsinki — 12 A2
Seven Corners, Washington — 32 B3
Seven Kings, London — 15 A4
Sevran, Paris — 23 A4
Sèvres, Paris — 23 A2
Sewri, Mumbai — 20 B2
Sforzesso, Castello, Milan — 18 B2
Sha Kok Mei, Hong Kong — 12 A2
Sha Tin, Hong Kong — 12 A2
Sha Tin Wai, Hong Kong — 12 A2
Shabrámant, Cairo — 7 B2
Shahdara, Delhi — 10 A2
Shahe, Canton — 8 B2
Shahr-e Rey, Tehran — 30 B2
Shahrak-e Golshahr, Tehran — 30 B1
Shahrak-e Qods, Tehran — 30 A2
Shaikh Aomar, Baghdad — 3 A2
Shakurbasti, Delhi — 10 A1
Shalkiya, Calcutta — 8 B1
Sham Shui Po, Hong Kong — 12 B1
Shamapur, Delhi — 10 A1
Shamian, Canton — 8 B2
Shan Mei, Hong Kong — 12 A2
Shanghai, Shanghai — 27 B2
Shankill, Dublin — 11 B3
Sharp I., Hong Kong — 12 A2
Shastrinagar, Delhi — 10 A2
Shau Kei Wan, Hong Kong — 12 B2
Shawocun, Beijing — 14 B1
Shayuan, Canton — 8 B2
Sheepshead Bay, New York — 21 C2
Shek O, Hong Kong — 12 B2
Shelter I., Hong Kong — 12 B2
Sheng Fa Shan, Hong Kong — 12 A1
Shepherds Bush, London — 15 A2
Shepperton, London — 15 B1
Sherman Oaks, Los Angeles — 16 B2
Sherman Park, Chicago — 9 C2
Shet Bandar, Mumbai — 20 B2
Sheung Lau Wan, Hong Kong — 12 B2
Sheung Wan, Hong Kong — 12 B1
Sheva, Mumbai — 20 B2
Shewa Nhava, Mumbai — 20 B2
Shiba, Tokyo — 29 c4
Shibpur, Calcutta — 8 B1
Shibuya-Ku, Tokyo — 29 B2
Shijōnawate, Osaka — 22 A4
Shillim, Seoul — 26 C1
Shimogawara, Tokyo — 29 B1
Shimosalo, Tokyo — 29 A2
Shimoshakujii, Tokyo — 29 A2
Shinagawa-Ku, Tokyo — 29 B3
Shin Mun Res., Hong Kong — 12 A1
Shinjuku-Ku, Tokyo — 29 B2
Shinjuku National Garden, Tokyo — 29 a2
Shinkoiwa, Tokyo — 29 A4
Shinnakano, Tokyo — 29 A2
Shinsa, Seoul — 26 B2
Shipai, Canton — 8 B3
Shirinashi →, Osaka — 22 B3
Shirogane, Tokyo — 29 B3
Shiweitang, Canton — 8 B2
Shogunle, Lagos — 14 A2
Shomolu, Lagos — 14 A2
Shooters Hill, London — 15 B4
Shoreditch, London — 15 a5
Shortlands, London — 15 B4
Shu' afat, Jerusalem — 13 B2
Shubrã, Cairo — 7 A2
Shubrã el Kheima, Cairo — 7 A2
Shuikou, Canton — 8 B1
Shuishang Park, Tianjin — 30 B1
Sidcup, London — 15 B4
Siebenhirten, Vienna — 31 B1
Siedlung, Berlin — 5 A5
Siekierki, Warsaw — 31 B2
Sielce, Warsaw — 31 B2
Siemensstadt, Berlin — 5 A2
Sierra Madre, Los Angeles — 16 B4
Sievering, Vienna — 31 A1
Sighthill, Edinburgh — 11 B2
Signal Hill, Cape Town — 8 A1
Sihüng, Seoul — 26 C1
Sikátorpuszta, Budapest — 7 A3
Silampur, Delhi — 10 B2
Silver Hill, Boston — 6 A3
Silver Hill, Washington — 32 C4
Silver Spring, Washington — 32 A3
Silvermine Nature Reserve, Cape Town — 8 B1
Silvolanträjet, Helsinki — 12 A2
Simei, Singapore — 27 A3
Simla, Calcutta — 8 B2
Simmering, Vienna — 31 A2
Simmering Heide, Vienna — 31 A2
Simonkylä, Helsinki — 12 B3
Singapore, Singapore — 27 B3
Singapore, Univ. of, Singapore — 27 B2
Sinicka →, Moscow — 19 A1
Sinki, Selat, Singapore — 27 B2

Sint-Genesius-Rode, Brussels — 6 B2
Sinwól, Seoul — 26 B1
Sion, Mumbai — 20 A2
Sipson, London — 15 B1
Siqeil, Cairo — 7 A1
Şişli, Istanbul — 12 B1
Skansen, Stockholm — 28 B2
Skärholmen, Stockholm — 28 B1
Skarpa, Stockholm — 28 B2
Skarpnäck, Stockholm — 28 B2
Skaryszewski Park, Warsaw — 31 B2
Skeppsholmen, Stockholm — 28 c3
Skokie, Chicago — 9 A2
Skokie →, Chicago — 9 A2
Sköndal, Stockholm — 28 B2
Skovlunde, Copenhagen — 10 A2
Skovshoved, Copenhagen — 10 A3
Skuru, Stockholm — 28 B3
Skyland, Atlanta — 3 A3
Slade Green, London — 15 B5
Slemmestad, Oslo — 22 B1
Slependen, Oslo — 22 A2
Slipi, Jakarta — 13 B1
Slivenec, Prague — 24 B2
Sloten, Amsterdam — 2 A1
Sloterpark, Amsterdam — 2 A1
Sluhy, Prague — 24 A3
Służew, Warsaw — 31 B2
Służewiec, Warsaw — 31 B2
Smíchov, Prague — 24 B2
Smith Forest Preserve, Chicago — 9 B2
Smithsonian Institute, Washington — 32 b2
Smolny, St. Petersburg — 26 B2
Snake Creek Canal →, Miami — 18 A2
Snarøya, Oslo — 22 A2
Snättringe, Stockholm — 28 B1
Sóbinggo, Seoul — 26 B1
Sobreda, Lisbon — 14 B1
Soch'o, Seoul — 26 C1
Södacmun, Seoul — 26 B1
Söderby, Stockholm — 28 A3
Söder, Stockholm — 28 A3
Södermalm, Stockholm — 28 B2
Sodpur, Calcutta — 8 A2
Soeurs, I. des, Montreal — 19 B2
Sognsvatn, Oslo — 22 A3
Soho, London — 15 b3
Soho, New York — 21 e1
Soignes, Forêt de, Brussels — 6 B2
Sok Kwu Wan, Hong Kong — 12 B1
Sökkwan, Seoul — 26 B2
Sokolniki, Moscow — 19 B3
Sokolniki Park, Moscow — 19 B4
Sokolów, Warsaw — 31 B1
Solalinden, Munich — 20 B3
Soldier Field, Chicago — 9 e3
Sollentuna, Stockholm — 28 A1
Solln, Munich — 20 B2
Solna, Stockholm — 28 A2
Solntsevo, Moscow — 19 C2
Somerset, Washington — 32 B3
Somerville, Boston — 6 A3
Somes Is., Wellington — 32 B2
Sonari, Mumbai — 20 B2
Sønderso, Copenhagen — 10 A2
Söngbuk, Seoul — 26 B2
Söngdong, Seoul — 26 B2
Söngp'a, Seoul — 26 B2
Sóngsu, Seoul — 26 B2
Soong Qingling, Former Res. of, Beijing — 14 a2
Soroksár, Budapest — 7 B2
Soroksári Duna →, Budapest — 7 B2
Sosenka →, Moscow — 19 B4
Sosnovka, St. Petersburg — 26 B2
Sóul, Seoul — 26 B2
Soundview, New York — 21 B2
South Beach, New York — 21 C1
South Beach Harbor, San Francisco — 25 c3
South Bend Park, Atlanta — 3 B2
South Boston, Boston — 6 A3
South Brooklyn, New York — 21 B2
South Decatur, Atlanta — 3 B3
South Deering, Chicago — 9 C3
South El Monte, Los Angeles — 16 B4
South Gate, Los Angeles — 16 B3
South Harbor, Manila — 17 B1
South Harrow, London — 15 A1
South Hd., Johannesburg — 13 B2
South Hills, Johannesburg — 13 B2
South Hornchurch, London — 15 A5
South Kensington, London — 15 c2
South Lawn, Washington — 32 C3
South Lincoln, Boston — 6 A2
South Miami, Miami — 18 B1
South Norwood, London — 15 B3
South of Market, San Francisco — 25 c3
South Ozone Park, New York — 21 B3
South Pasadena, Los Angeles — 16 B3
South Res., Boston — 6 A3
South Ruislip, London — 15 A1
South San Francisco, San Francisco — 25 C2
South San Gabriel, Los Angeles — 16 B4
South Shore, Chicago — 9 C3
South Sudbury, Boston — 6 A1
Southall, London — 15 A1
Southborough, London — 15 B4
Southend, London — 15 B4
Southfields, London — 15 B2
Southwark, London — 15 b4
Søvang, Copenhagen — 10 B3
Soweto, Johannesburg — 13 B1
Sowhänak, Tehran — 30 A3
Soya, Tokyo — 29 A4
Spandau, Berlin — 5 A2
Spånga, Stockholm — 28 A1
Spanische Reitschule, Vienna — 31 b1
Spectacle I., Boston — 6 A3
Speicher-See, Munich — 20 A3
Speising, Vienna — 31 A1
Sphinx, Cairo — 7 B1
Spinaceto, Rome — 25 C1
Spit Junction, Sydney — 28 A2
Spořilov, Prague — 24 B3
Spot Pond, Boston — 6 A3
Spreewood, Melbourne — 17 B1
Spree →, Berlin — 5 A2
Springberg, Berlin — 5 A5
Springfield, Washington — 32 C2
Squantum, Boston — 6 B3
Srednaya Rogatka, St. Petersburg — 26 C2
Śródmieście, Warsaw — 31 B2
Staaken, Berlin — 5 A1

Stabekk, Oslo — 22 A2
Stadhion, Athens — 2 c3
Stadhuis, Amsterdam — 2 b2
Stadlau, Vienna — 31 A2
Stadshuset, Stockholm — 28 b1
Stains, Paris — 23 A3
Stamford Hill, London — 15 A3
Stammersdorf, Vienna — 31 A2
Stanley, Hong Kong — 12 B2
Stanley Mound, Hong Kong — 12 B2
Stanley Pen., Hong Kong — 12 B2
Stanmore, London — 15 A2
Stapleton, New York — 21 C1
Star Ferry, Hong Kong — 12 a2
Staraya Derevnya, St. Petersburg — 26 B1
Stare, Warsaw — 31 B2
Staré Mesto, Prague — 24 B2
Starego Miasto, Warsaw — 31 a2
Staten Island Zoo, New York — 21 C1
Statenice, Prague — 24 B1
Statue Square, Hong Kong — 12 c1
Stedelijk Museum, Amsterdam — 2 c1
Steele Creek, Melbourne — 17 A1
Steenokkerzeel, Brussels — 6 A2
Steglitz, Berlin — 5 B2
Stepaside, Dublin — 11 B2
Stephansdom, Vienna — 31 b2
Stepney, London — 15 A3
Sterling Park, San Francisco — 25 a2
Stickling udde, Stockholm — 28 A2
Stickney, Chicago — 9 B2
Stillorgan, Dublin — 11 B2
Stockholm, Stockholm — 28 B2
Stocksund, Stockholm — 28 A2
Stodůlky, Prague — 24 B1
Stoke Newington, London — 15 A3
Stokes Valley, Wellington — 32 B2
Stone Canyon Res., Los Angeles — 16 B2
Stone Park, Chicago — 9 B1
Stonebridge, London — 15 A2
Stoneham, Boston — 6 A3
Stony Brook Res., Boston — 6 B3
Stora Värtan, Stockholm — 28 A2
Store Hareskov, Copenhagen — 10 A2
Store Magleby, Copenhagen — 10 B3
Storholmen, Stockholm — 28 A2
Stoyka, St. Petersburg — 26 B2
Straiton, Edinburgh — 11 B2
Strand, London — 15 b4
Strandfontein, Cape Town — 8 B2
Strašnice, Prague — 24 B2
Strasstrudering, Munich — 20 B3
Stratford, London — 15 A4
Strathfield, Sydney — 28 B1
Streatham, London — 15 B3
Streatham Vale, London — 15 B3
Strebersdorf, Vienna — 31 A2
Strogino, Moscow — 19 B2
Strombeek-Bever, Brussels — 6 A2
Stromovka, Prague — 24 B2
Studio City, Los Angeles — 16 B2
Stureby, Stockholm — 28 B2
Stuvsta, Stockholm — 28 B2
Subhepur, Delhi — 10 A2
Sucat, Manila — 17 C2
Suchdol, Prague — 24 B2
Sucy-en-Brie, Paris — 23 B4
Sudbury, Boston — 6 A1
Sugamo, Tokyo — 29 A3
Sugar Loaf Mt. = Açúcar, Pão de, Rio de Janeiro — 24 B2
Suginami-Ku, Tokyo — 29 B2
Sugō, Tokyo — 29 B2
Suitland, Washington — 32 B4
Sukchar, Calcutta — 8 A2
Suma, Osaka — 22 B1
Sumida →, Tokyo — 29 B3
Sumida-Ku, Tokyo — 29 A3
Sumiyoshi, Osaka — 22 B4
Summerville, Toronto — 30 B1
Summit, Chicago — 9 C2
Sunamachi, Tokyo — 29 A3
Sunbury-on-Thames, London — 15 B1
Sundbyberg, Stockholm — 28 A1
Sundbyerne, Copenhagen — 10 B3
Sungei Kadut Industrial Estate, Singapore — 27 A2
Sungei Selatar Res., Singapore — 27 A3
Sunter, Jakarta — 13 A2
Sunter, Kali →, Jakarta — 13 B2
Suomenlinna, Helsinki — 12 C2
Supreme Court, Washington — 32 b3
Sura, Calcutta — 8 B1
Surag-san, Seoul — 26 A2
Surbiton, London — 15 B2
Suresnes, Paris — 23 A2
Surfside, Miami — 18 A2
Surquillo, Lima — 16 B2
Surrey Hills, Sydney — 28 b2
Susack, Seoul — 26 B1
Süssenbrunn, Vienna — 31 A2
Sutton, Dublin — 11 A3
Sutton, London — 15 B2
Suyu, Seoul — 26 B2
Suzukishinden, Tokyo — 29 A2
Svanemøllen, Copenhagen — 10 A3
Svestad, Oslo — 22 B2
Svinö, Helsinki — 12 C2
Swampscott, Boston — 6 A4
Swanley, London — 15 B4
Swanley Village, London — 15 B5
Swansea, Toronto — 30 B2
Swinburne, I., New York — 21 C1
Swords, Dublin — 11 A2
Sydenham, Johannesburg — 13 A2
Sydney, Sydney — 28 B2
Sydney Airport, Sydney — 28 B2
Sydney Harbour Bridge, Sydney — 28 B2
Sydstranden, Copenhagen — 10 B3
Sylvania, Sydney — 28 C1
Syntagma, Pl., Athens — 2 b3
Syon Park, London — 15 B2
Szczęśliwice, Warsaw — 31 B1
Széchenyi-hegy, Budapest — 7 B1
Szent Istvánbáz, Budapest — 7 a2
Széphalom, Budapest — 7 A1

T

Tabata, Tokyo — 29 A3
Tablada, Buenos Aires — 7 C1
Table Bay, Cape Town — 8 A1
Table Mountain, Cape Town — 8 A1
Taboão da Serra, São Paulo — 26 B1
Taby, Stockholm — 28 A2

Tacuba, *Mexico City* **18** B1
Tacubaya, *Mexico City* **18** B1
Taebang, *Seoul* **26** B1
Tagig, *Manila* **17** B2
Tagig ↦, *Manila* **17** B2
Tai Hang, *Hong Kong* **12** A2
Tai Lo Shan, *Hong Kong* **12** A2
Tai Po Tsai, *Hong Kong* **12** A2
Tai Seng, *Singapore* **27** A3
Tai Shui Hang, *Hong Kong* .. **12** A2
Tai Tam B., *Hong Kong* **12** B2
Tai Tam Tuk Res.,
  Hong Kong **12** B2
Tai Wai, *Hong Kong* **12** A1
Tai Wan Tau, *Hong Kong* **12** A2
Tai Wo Hau, *Hong Kong* **12** B2
Tainaka, *Osaka* **22** B4
Taishō, *Osaka* **22** A2
Taita, *Wellington* **32** B2
Tajrīsh, *Tehran* **30** A2
Takaido, *Tokyo* **29** A1
Takaishi, *Tokyo* **29** B1
Takarazuka, *Osaka* **22** A2
Takasago, *Tokyo* **29** A4
Takatsu-Ku, *Tokyo* **29** A2
Takeshita, *Tokyo* **29** B2
Takimegawa, *Tokyo* **29** A2
Takoma Park, *Washington* ... **32** B3
Taksim, *Istanbul* **12** B1
Talaide, *Lisbon* **14** A1
Taliganga, *Calcutta* **8** B2
Talipapa, *Manila* **17** A2
Tallaght, *Dublin* **11** B1
Tallkrogen, *Stockholm* **28** B1
Tama, *Tokyo* **29** B2
Tama ↦, *Tokyo* **29** B2
Tama Kyūryō, *Tokyo* **29** B1
Tamaden, *Tokyo* **29** A2
Tamagawa-josui ↦, *Tokyo* ... **29** A1
Taman Sari, *Jakarta* **13** A1
Tamanduateí ↦, *São Paulo* .. **26** B2
Tamboerskloof, *Cape Town* .. **8** A1
Tambora, *Jakarta* **13** A1
Tammisalo, *Helsinki* **12** B3
Tammūn, *Cairo* **7** B2
Tampines, *Singapore* **27** A3
Tanah Abang, *Jakarta* **13** B1
Tanigami, *Osaka* **22** A2
Tanjung Duren, *Jakarta* **13** B1
Tanjung Priok, *Jakarta* **13** B1
Tanum, *Oslo* **28** A1
Taoranting Park, *Beijing* .. **4** c2
Tapada, *Lisbon* **14** A1
Tapanila, *Helsinki* **12** B3
Tapiales, *Buenos Aires* **7** C1
Tapiola, *Helsinki* **12** B1
Tapsia, *Calcutta* **8** B2
Tara, *Mumbai* **20** A1
Tarabya, *Istanbul* **12** B2
Tarango, *Mexico City* **18** A2
Târbæk, *Copenhagen* **10** A3
Tarchomin, *Warsaw* **31** B1
Tardeo, *Mumbai* **20** B1
Targówek, *Warsaw* **31** B2
Tårnby, *Copenhagen* **10** B3
Tarqua Bay, *Lagos* **14** B2
Tåstrup, *Copenhagen* **10** B1
Tatarovo, *Moscow* **19** B2
Tathong Channel, *Hong Kong* **12** B2
Tathong Pt., *Hong Kong* **12** B2
Tatuapé, *São Paulo* **26** B2
Taufkirchen, *Munich* **20** B2
Tavares, I. dos, *Rio de Janeiro* **24** B2
Távros, *Athens* **2** B2
Tawa, *Wellington* **32** A1
Teaneck, *New York* **21** A1
Teatro Municipal,
  Rio de Janeiro **24** c2
Tebet, *Jakarta* **13** B2
Tecamachaleo, *Mexico City* . **18** B1
Teddington, *London* **15** B1
Tegel, *Berlin* **5** A2
Tegel, Flughafen, *Berlin* .. **5** A2
Tegeler See, *Berlin* **5** A2
Tegelort, *Berlin* **5** A2
Tehrān, *Tehran* **30** A2
Tehrān Pārs, *Tehran* **30** A3
Tei Tong Tsui, *Hong Kong* .. **12** B2
Tejo, Rio ↦, *Lisbon* **14** A1
Tekstilyshchik, *Moscow* **19** B4
Telegraph Hill, *San Francisco* **25** a2
Telhal, *Lisbon* **14** A1
Telok Blangah, *Singapore* .. **27** B2
Teltow, *Berlin* **5** B3
Teltow kanal, *Berlin* **5** B3
Temnikovo, *Moscow* **19** B6
Tempelhof, *Berlin* **5** B3
Tempelhof, Flughafen, *Berlin* **5** B3
Temple City, *Los Angeles* .. **16** B4
Temple Hills Park,
  Washington **32** C4
Temple Mount, *Jerusalem* ... **13** B2
Templeogue, *Dublin* **11** B2
Templo Mayor, *Mexico City* . **18** b3
Tenafly, *New York* **21** A2
Tenayuca, Piramide de,
  Mexico City **18** A1
Tengah ↦, *Singapore* **27** A2
Tennoji, *Osaka* **22** B4
Tepalcates, *Mexico City* ... **18** B2
Terrazzano, *Milan* **18** A1
Terrugem, *Lisbon* **14** A1
Tervuren, *Brussels* **6** B3
Tervuren, Park van, *Brussels* **6** B3
Tetuán, *Madrid* **17** B1
Tévere ↦, *Rome* **25** B3
Thalkirchen, *Munich* **20** B2
Thames ↦, *London* **15** A4
Thames Ditton, *London* **15** B1
Thamesmead, *London* **15** A4
Thana Cr. ↦, *Mumbai* **20** A2
The Loop, *Chicago* **9** B3
The Ridge, *Delhi* **10** B2
The Wilds, *Johannesburg* ... **13** B2
Theater Carré, *Amsterdam* .. **2** b2
Théatro Dionissou, *Athens* . **2** c2
Thiais, *Paris* **23** B3
Thissío, *Athens* **2** b1
Thistletown, *Toronto* **30** A1
Thomastown, *Melbourne* **17** A2
Thompson I., *Boston* **6** B4
Thon Buri, *Bangkok* **3** B1
Thornbury, *Melbourne* **17** A2
Thorncliffe, *Toronto* **30** A2
Thornhill, *Toronto* **30** A2
Thornton, *Cape Town* **8** A2
Thornton Heath, *London* **15** B3
Threipmuir Res., *Edinburgh* **11** B2
Throgs Neck, *New York* **21** B3
Thyssen Bornemisza, Museo,
  Madrid **17** b3
Tian'anmen Square, *Beijing* **4** B2
Tiancun, *Beijing* **4** B1
Tianjin, *Tianjin* **30** B1
Tiantan Park, *Beijing* **4** c2
Tibidabo, *Barcelona* **4** A1

Tibradden Mt., *Dublin* **11** B2
Tiburon, *San Francisco* **25** A2
Tiburtino, *Rome* **25** B2
Ticomán, *Mexico City* **18** A2
Tiefersee, *Berlin* **5** B1
Tiejiangyin, *Beijing* **4** C2
Tientsin = Tianjin, *Tianjin* **30** B1
Tiergarten, *Berlin* **5** A3
Tietê ↦, *São Paulo* **26** B2
Tigerhof, *Cape Town* **8** A2
Tigris = Nahr Dijlah ↦,
  Baghdad **3** B2
Tijuca, *Rio de Janeiro* **24** B1
Tijuca, Parque Nacional da,
  Rio de Janeiro **24** B1
Tijuca, Pico da, *Rio de Janeiro* **24** B1
Tikkurila, *Helsinki* **12** B3
Tilak Nagar, *Delhi* **10** B1
Tilanqiao, *Shanghai* **27** B1
Timah, Bukit, *Singapore* ... **27** A2
Times Square, *New York* **21** c2
Timiryazev Park, *Moscow* ... **19** B3
Ting Kau, *Hong Kong* **12** A1
Tira, *Jerusalem* **13** A1
Tirsa, *Cairo* **7** B2
Tishrīyaa, *Baghdad* **3** B2
Tiu Keng Leng, *Hong Kong* .. **12** B2
Tivoli, *Copenhagen* **10** a3
Tizapán, *Mexico City* **18** C1
Tlalnepantla ↦, *Mexico City* **18** A1
To Kwai Wan, *Hong Kong* **12** B2
Toa Payoh, *Singapore* **27** A3
Tobong, *Seoul* **26** B2
Tobong-san, *Seoul* **26** A2
Točná, *Prague* **24** C2
Toco Hills, *Atlanta* **3** B2
Todt Hill, *New York* **21** C1
Tōkagi, *Tokyo* **29** B2
Tokai Plantation, *Cape Town* **8** B1
Tōkaichiba, *Tokyo* **29** B2
Tokarevo, *Moscow* **19** C5
Tōkyō, *Tokyo* **29** B3
Tokyo B., *Tokyo* **29** B4
Tokyo-Haneda Int. Airport,
  Tokyo **29** A3
Tokyo Harbour, *Tokyo* **29** B3
Tolka R. ↦, *Dublin* **11** A2
Tolworth, *London* **15** B2
Tomb of Lu Xun, *Shanghai* .. **27** B1
Tomb of the Kings, *Jerusalem* **13** a2
Tomba di Nerone, *Rome* **25** A1
Tomilino, *Moscow* **19** C5
Tondo, *Manila* **17** B1
Tongbang, *Seoul* **26** B1
Tongbang-san, *Seoul* **26** A2
Tongjameong, *Seoul* **26** B1
Tongqiao, *Shanghai* **27** A1
Toorak, *Melbourne* **17** A1
Topkapı, *Istanbul* **12** B1
Tor di Quinto, *Rome* **25** A2
Tor Pignattara, *Rome* **25** B2
Tor Sapienza, *Rome* **25** B2
Toranomon, *Tokyo* **29** c3
Torcy, *Paris* **23** A4
Toronto, *Toronto* **30** A3
Toronto, Univ. of, *Toronto* **30** B2
Toronto Harbour, *Toronto* .. **30** B2
Toronto I., *Toronto* **30** B2
Toronto Int. Airport, *Toronto* **30** A1
Toros Las Arenas, Pl. de,
  Barcelona **4** c1
Toros Monumental, Templo
  de, *Barcelona* **4** a3
Torre Latino-americana,
  Mexico City **18** b2
Torre Lupara, *Rome* **25** B2
Torre Nova, *Rome* **25** B2
Torrellas ↦, *Barcelona* **4** A1
Torrevécchia, *Rome* **25** A1
Toshima-Ku, *Tokyo* **29** A2
Toshimaen, *Tokyo* **29** A2
Tottenham, *London* **15** A3
Tottenham, *Melbourne* **17** A1
Tour Eiffel, *Paris* **23** b1
Toussus-le-Noble, *Paris* ... **23** B1
Toussus-le-Noble, Aérodrome
  de, *Paris* **23** B1
Tower Bridge, *London* **15** b5
Tower Hamlets, *London* **15** A3
Tower of London, *London* ... **15** A3
Towra Pt., *Sydney* **28** B2
Tøyen, *Oslo* **22** A3
Toyonaka, *Osaka* **22** A2
Trafalgar Square, *London* .. **15** b3
Trafaria, *Lisbon* **14** A1
Traição, Cor. ↦, *São Paulo* **26** B2
Traneglide, *Copenhagen* **10** B2
Trångsund, *Stockholm* **28** B2
Transamerica Pyramid,
  San Francisco **25** a2
Transbay Terminal,
  San Francisco **25** b3
Trappenfelde, *Berlin* **5** A4
Trastévere, *Rome* **25** c2
Treasure I., *San Francisco* **25** A2
Tréboradice, *Prague* **24** B3
Trebotov, *Prague* **24** C1
Tremblay-en-France, *Paris* . **23** A4
Tremembe ↦, *São Paulo* **26** A2
Tremont, *New York* **21** A2
Trenno, *Milan* **18** A1
Trenton, *Milan* **18** B1
Treptow, *Berlin* **5** B3
Trés Rios, Sa. dos,
  Rio de Janeiro **24** B1
Trevi, Fontana di, *Rome* ... **25** b2
Trezzano sul Navíglio, *Milan* **18** B1
Tríglime Tower, *Chicago* ... **9** B2
Trieste, *Rome* **25** B2
Trinidad, *Washington* **32** B4
Trinity, *Edinburgh* **11** A2
Trinity College, *Dublin* ... **11** c3
Trionfale, *Rome* **25** B2
Triulzo, *Milan* **18** B2
Trocadero, *Paris* **23** b1
Troitse-Lykovo, *Moscow* **19** B2
Troja, *Prague* **24** B2
Trollbäcken, *Stockholm* **20** A2
Trombay, *Mumbai* **20** A2
Troparevo, *Moscow* **19** C2
Tropenmuseum, *Amsterdam* ... **2** b3
Trudyashchikhsya, Ostrov,
  St. Petersburg **26** B1
Tryvasshøgda, *Oslo* **22** A3
Tseng Lan Shue, *Hong Kong* . **12** A2
Tsim Sha Tsui, *Hong Kong* .. **12** A2
Tsing Yi, *Hong Kong* **12** A1
Tsova, *Jerusalem* **13** B1
Tsuen Wan, *Hong Kong* **12** A1
Tsukiji, *Tokyo* **29** c5
Tsur Hadassa, *Jerusalem* ... **13** B1
Tsurumi ↦, *Tokyo* **29** B3
Tsz Wan Shan, *Hong Kong* ... **12** B2
Tuas, *Singapore* **27** B1
Tuchoměřice, *Prague* **24** B1
Tuckahoe, *New York* **21** A3
Tucuruvi, *São Paulo* **26** A2
Tufello, *Rome* **25** B2

Tufnell Park, *London* **15** A3
Tughlakabad, *Delhi* **10** B2
Tuileries, Jardin des, *Paris* **23** b3
Tuindorp Oostzaan,
  Amsterdam **2** A2
Tullamarine, *Melbourne* **17** A1
Tulse Hill, *London* **15** B3
Tung Lung I., *Hong Kong* ... **12** B2
Tung O, *Hong Kong* **12** B1
Tunis, *Baghdad* **3** A2
Tuomaria, *Helsinki* **12** B1
Tureberg, *Stockholm* **28** A1
Turffontein, *Johannesburg* . **13** B2
Turkso, *Prague* **24** A1
Turnham Green, *London* **15** B2
Turnhouse, *Edinburgh* **11** B1
Tuscolana, Via, *Rome* **25** B2
Tushino, *Moscow* **19** A2
Twelve Apostles, *Cape Town* **8** A1
Twickenham, *London* **15** B1
Twickenham Rugby Ground,
  London **15** B1
Twin Peaks, *San Francisco* . **25** B2
Two Rock Mt., *Dublin* **11** B2
Tymon North, *Dublin* **11** B1
Tysons Corner, *Washington* . **32** B2

U

U.S. Capitol, *Washington* .. **32** b3
Ubeidiya, *Jerusalem* **13** B2
Uberaba ↦, *São Paulo* **26** B2
Ubin, P., *Singapore* **27** A3
Uccle, *Brussels* **6** B2
Udelnaya, St. *Petersburg* .. **26** A2
Udelnoe, St. *Petersburg* ... **26** B1
Udding, *Munich* **20** A1
Ueno, *Tokyo* **29** A3
Úholičky, *Prague* **24** B1
Uhřínèves, *Prague* **24** B3
Uithoorn, *Amsterdam* **2** B1
Újpalota, *Budapest* **7** A2
Újpest, *Budapest* **7** A2
Ukita, *Tokyo* **29** A4
Ullerup, *Copenhagen* **10** B3
Ulleval, *Oslo* **22** A3
Ulriksdal, *Stockholm* **28** A1
Ulyanka, St. *Petersburg* ... **26** B1
Um Al-Khanazir Island,
  Baghdad **3** B2
Umeda, *Osaka* **22** A3
Umerkhadi, *Mumbai* **20** A1
Umm el-Fahm, *Jerusalem* **13** A2
Underground Atlanta, *Atlanta* **3** B2
Unětický potok ↦, *Prague* .. **24** B1
Úngam, *Seoul* **26** B1
Unhos, *Lisbon* **14** A2
Unidad Santa Fe, *Mexico City* **18** B1
Union City, *New York* **21** B1
Union Port, *New York* **21** B2
Union Square, *New York* **21** d2
Union San Francisco, *San Francisco* **25** b2
Union Station, *Washington* . **32** b3
United Nations H.Q.,
  New York **21** c3
Universidad, *Madrid* **17** B1
Universidad de Chile,
  Santiago **32** B2
University Park, *Washington* **32** B4
Unp'yong, *Seoul* **26** B1
Unter den Linden, *Berlin* .. **5** a4
Unterföhring, *Munich* **20** A2
Unterföhring, *Munich* **20** A3
Unterhaching, *Munich* **20** B2
Unterlaa, *Vienna* **31** B2
Untermenzing, *Munich* **20** A1
Upper East Side, *New York* . **21** b3
Upper Elmers End, *London* .. **15** B3
Upper New York B.,
  New York **21** C1
Upper Norwood, *London* **15** B3
Upper Peirce Res., *Singapore* **27** A2
Upper Sydenham, *London* **15** B3
Upper Tooting, *London* **15** B3
Upper West Side, *New York* . **21** a2
Upton, *London* **15** A4
Uptown, *Chicago* **9** B2
Uran, *Mumbai* **20** B2
Urayasu, *Tokyo* **29** B4
Urca, *Rio de Janeiro* **24** B2
Uritsk, St. *Petersburg* **26** C1
Úröm, *Budapest* **7** A2
Ursus, *Warsaw* **31** B1
Ursvik, *Stockholm* **28** A1
Usera, *Madrid* **17** B1
Ushigome, *Tokyo* **29** A3
Usina, *Rio de Janeiro* **24** B1
Üsküdar, *Istanbul* **12** B2
Ust-Slavyanka, St. *Petersburg* **26** B2
Uteke, *Stockholm* **28** A3
Utrata, *Warsaw* **31** B2
Uttarpara, *Calcutta* **8** B1
Utterslev Mose, *Copenhagen* **10** A2

V

Vadaul, *Mumbai* **20** A2
Vaires-sur-Marne, *Paris* ... **23** A4
Valby, *Copenhagen* **10** B2
Valcamuta, *Rome* **25** A2
Valdelatas, *Madrid* **17** A1
Valenton, *Paris* **23** B3
Valera, *Milan* **18** A1
Vallcarca, *Barcelona* **4** A1
Valldoreix, *Barcelona* **4** A1
Vallecas, *Madrid* **17** B2
Vallensbæk, *Copenhagen* **10** B2
Vallensbæk Strand,
  Copenhagen **10** B2
Vallentunasjön, *Stockholm* . **28** A2
Valleranello, *Rome* **25** C1
Vallisaari, *Helsinki* **12** C3
Valvidrera, *Barcelona* **4** A1
Valvidrera ↦, *Barcelona* ... **4** A1
Van Goghmuseum,
  Amsterdam **2** c1
Vanak, *Tehran* **30** A2
Vangede, *Copenhagen* **10** A3
Vaniköy, *Istanbul* **12** B2
Vanløse, *Copenhagen* **10** A2
Vantaa, *Helsinki* **12** B2
Vantaa ↦, *Helsinki* **12** B2
Vantaankoski, *Helsinki* **12** B2
Vantaanpuisto, *Helsinki* ... **12** B2
Vanves, *Paris* **23** B2
Varkiza, *Athens* **2** C2
Varsánliget, *Budapest* **7** b2
Vartiokylä, *Helsinki* **12** B3

Vartiosaari, *Helsinki* **12** B3
Vasamuseet, *Stockholm* **28** A2
Vasco, *Cape Town* **8** A2
Vasfanärd, *Tehran* **30** B2
Vashi, *Mumbai* **20** A2
Vasilyevsky, Ostrov,
  St. *Petersburg* **26** B1
Vaso Regulador El Cristo,
  Mexico City **18** B1
Vaucluse, *Sydney* **28** B2
Vaucresson, *Paris* **23** A1
Vauhallan, *Paris* **23** B2
Vaujours, *Paris* **23** A4
Vauxhall, *London* **15** c4
Vecsés, *Budapest* **7** B3
Veleň, *Prague* **24** A2
Veleslavin, *Prague* **24** B2
Vélizy-Villacoublay, *Paris* **23** B2
Velka-Chuchle, *Prague* **24** B2
Velké Přílepy, *Prague* **24** B1
Venda Seca, *Lisbon* **14** A1
Venetian Islands, *Miami* ... **16** B2
Venezia, Palazzo, *Rome* **25** c2
Venice, *Los Angeles* **16** C2
Venice, Madrid **17** B1
Ventorro del Cano, *Madrid* . **17** B1
Venustiano Carranza,
  Mexico City **18** B2
Verde ↦, *São Paulo* **26** A1
Verdi, *Athens* **2** A2
Verdun, *Montreal* **19** B2
Vérhalom, *Budapest* **7** A2
Vermelho ↦, *São Paulo* **26** B2
Vernon, *Los Angeles* **16** C3
Verrières-le-Buisson, *Paris* **23** B2
Versailles, *Buenos Aires* .. **7** B1
Versailles, *Paris* **23** B1
Veshnyaki, *Moscow* **19** B4
Vesolyy Posolok,
  St. *Petersburg* **26** B2
Vestra, *Helsinki* **12** B1
Vestskoven, *Copenhagen* **10** A2
Vicálvaro, *Madrid* **17** B2
Vicente Lopez, *Buenos Aires* **7** B2
Victoria, *Hong Kong* **12** B1
Victoria, *London* **15** c3
Victoria, Mt., *Wellington* . **32** B1
Victoria, Pont, *Montreal* .. **19** B2
Victoria and Albert
  Waterfront, *Cape Town* .. **8** a1
Victoria Gardens, *Mumbai* .. **20** A2
Victoria Harbour, *Hong Kong* **12** B1
Victoria Island, *Lagos* **14** B2
Victoria L., *Johannesburg* . **13** B2
Victoria Lawn Tennis Courts,
  Melbourne **17** B2
Victoria Park, *Singapore* .. **27** B2
Victoria Peak, *Hong Kong* .. **12** B1
Victoria Wharf, *Cape Town* . **8** a2
Vienna = Wien, *Vienna* **31** A2
Vienna, *Washington* **32** B3
View Park, *Los Angeles* **16** B3
Vigário Geral, *Rio de Janeiro* **24** A1
Vigentino, *Milan* **18** B2
Vighignolo, *Milan* **18** B1
Vlikki, *Helsinki* **12** B3
Vikhroli, *Mumbai* **20** A2
Vila Guilherme, *São Paulo* . **26** B2
Vila Isabel, *Rio de Janeiro* **24** B1
Vila Jaguará, *São Paulo* ... **26** B1
Vila Madalena, *São Paulo* .. **26** B1
Vila Maria, *São Paulo* **26** B2
Vila Mariana, *São Paulo* ... **26** B2
Vila Prudente, *São Paulo* .. **26** B2
Viladecans, *Barcelona* **4** B1
Vile Parle, *Mumbai* **20** A2
Villa Adelina, *Buenos Aires* **7** B1
Villa Ballester, *Buenos Aires* **7** B1
Villa Barilari, *Buenos Aires* **7** C2
Villa Borghese, *Rome* **25** a3
Villa Bosch, *Buenos Aires* . **7** B1
Villa C. Colon, *Buenos Aires* **7** C2
Villa de Guadalupe,
  Mexico City **18** B2
Villa Devoto, *Buenos Aires* **7** B1
Villa Diamante, *Buenos Aires* **7** C2
Villa Dominico, *Buenos Aires* **7** C3
Villa Lugano, *Buenos Aires* **7** C2
Villa Lynch, *Buenos Aires* . **7** B1
Villa Madero, *Buenos Aires* **7** C1
Villa Sáenz Pena,
  Buenos Aires **7** B1
Villa Urquiza, *Buenos Aires* **7** B2
Villaverde, *Madrid* **17** B1
Villaverde Bajo, *Madrid* ... **17** B1
Ville-d'Avray, *Paris* **23** B2
Villecresnes, *Paris* **23** B4
Villejuif, *Paris* **23** B3
Villemomble, *Paris* **23** A4
Villeneuve-la-Garenne, *Paris* **23** A2
Villeneuve-le-Roi, *Paris* .. **23** B3
Villeneuve-St.-Georges, *Paris* **23** B3
Villeparisis, *Paris* **23** A4
Villevaudé, *Paris* **23** A4
Villiers-le-Bâcle, *Paris* .. **23** B1
Villiers-sur-Marne, *Paris* . **23** B4
Villinki, *Helsinki* **12** C3
Villoresi, Canale, *Milan* .. **18** A1
Vilvoorde, *Brussels* **6** A2
Vimodrone, *Milan* **18** A2
Vimont, *Montreal* **19** A1
Vinanmek Palace, *Bangkok* .. **3** a2
Vincennes, *Paris* **23** B3
Vincennes, Bois de, *Paris* . **23** B3
Vinings, *Atlanta* **3** A2
Vinohrady, *Prague* **24** B2
Vinof, *Prague* **24** C3
Violet Hill, *Hong Kong* **12** B2
Virányos, *Budapest* **7** A1
Virgen del San Cristóbal,
  Santiago **26** B2
Virginia Gardens, *Miami* ... **18** B1
Virginia Key, *Miami* **16** B2
Viroflay, *Paris* **23** B2
Virum, *Copenhagen* **10** A2
Vishnyaki, *Moscow* **19** B5
Visitacion Valley,
  San Francisco **25** B2
Vista Alegre, *Lima* **16** B3
Vista Alegre, *Santiago* **26** B2
Vitacura, *Santiago* **26** B2
Vitinia, *Rome* **25** C1
Vitry-sur-Seine, *Paris* **23** B3
Vizandinó, Moussío, *Athens* **2** c2
Vladykino, *Moscow* **19** A3
Vlezenbeek, *Brussels* **6** B1
Vltava ↦, *Prague* **24** A2
Vnukovo, *Moscow* **19** C2
Vokovice, *Prague* **24** B1
Voldarskoye, St. *Petersburg* **26** B2
Volhonka-Zil, *Moscow* **19** C3
Vollen, *Oslo* **22** B1
Volodarskoye, St. *Petersburg* **26** B2

Volynkina-Derevnya,
  St. *Petersburg* **26** B1
Vondelpark, *Amsterdam* **2** A2
Vösendorf, *Vienna* **31** B2
Vostochnyy, *Moscow* **19** B4
Vostochnyy, *Moscow* **19** B5
Voula, *Athens* **2** C2
Vouliagmeni, *Athens* **2** C2
Vredehoek, *Cape Town* **8** A1
Vršovice, *Prague* **24** B2
Vyborgskaya Storona,
  St. *Petersburg* **26** B1
Vykhino, *Moscow* **19** B4
Vyšehrad, *Prague* **24** B2

W

Wachterhof, *Munich* **20** B3
Wadala, *Mumbai* **20** A2
Wadestown, *Wellington* **32** B1
Wadi Fukin, *Jerusalem* **13** B1
Wah Fu, *Hong Kong* **12** B1
Wahda, *Baghdad* **3** B2
Währing, *Vienna* **31** A2
Waidmannslust, *Berlin* **5** A3
Wainuiomata, *Wellington* ... **32** B2
Wainuiomata R. ↦,
  Wellington **32** B2
Wakefield, *Boston* **6** A3
Waldesruh, *Berlin* **5** B4
Waldperlach, *Munich* **20** B3
Waldtrudering, *Munich* **20** B3
Walkinstown, *Dublin* **11** B1
Wall Street, *New York* **21** f1
Waltham, *Boston* **6** A2
Waltham Forest, *London* **15** A3
Walthamstow, *London* **15** A3
Walton on Thames, *London* .. **15** B1
Wambeek, *Brussels* **6** B1
Wan Chai, *Hong Kong* **12** B2
Wan Chai Lanes, *Hong Kong* . **12** c2
Wandsworth, *London* **15** B2
Wankhede Stadium, *Mumbai* .. **20** c2
Wannsee, *Berlin* **5** B1
Wansdorf, *Berlin* **5** A4
Wapping, *London* **15** A3
Ward, *Dublin* **11** A1
Ward I., *Wellington* **32** B2
Warnberg, *Munich* **20** B2
Warráq el 'Arab, *Cairo* **7** A2
Warráq el Hadr, *Cairo* **7** A2
Warringen Park, *Melbourne* . **17** A2
Warriston, *Edinburgh* **11** B2
Warsaw = Warszawa, *Warsaw* . **31** B2
Warszawa, *Warsaw* **31** B2
Wartenberg, *Berlin* **5** A4
Washington, *Washington* **32** B3
Washington Heights,
  New York **21** A2
Washington Monument,
  Washington **32** b1
Washington Nat. Airport,
  Washington **32** B3
Washington Park, *Chicago* .. **9** C3
Wat Arun, *Bangkok* **3** b1
Wat Pho, *Bangkok* **3** b1
Wat Phra Keo, *Bangkok* **3** b1
Wat Traimit, *Bangkok* **3** c2
Water of Leith, *Edinburgh* . **11** B1
Water Tower Place, *Chicago* **9** a2
Watergraafsmeer, *Amsterdam* **2** B2
Waterland, *Amsterdam* **2** A2
Waterloo, *Brussels* **6** B2
Waterloo, *London* **15** B2
Waterloo International,
  London **15** b4
Watermael-Boitsfort, *Brussels* **6** B2
Watertown, *Boston* **6** A2
Watsonia, *Melbourne* **17** A2
Waverley, *Boston* **6** A2
Waverley, *Johannesburg* **13** B2
Waverley, *Sydney* **28** B2
Waverley Station, *Edinburgh* **11** b3
Wawer, *Warsaw* **31** B2
Wawrzyszew, *Warsaw* **31** B1
Wayland, *Boston* **6** A1
Wazirabad, *Delhi* **10** A2
Wazīrīya, *Baghdad* **3** A2
Wazirpur, *Delhi* **10** A2
Wealdstone, *London* **15** A2
Wedding, *Berlin* **5** A3
Weehawken, *New York* **21** B1
Weesp, *Amsterdam* **2** B2
Weidling, *Vienna* **31** A1
Weidlingbach, *Vienna* **31** A1
Weigongcun, *Beijing* **4** B1
Weijin He ↦, *Tianjin* **30** B2
Weissensee, *Berlin* **5** A3
Welborn, *Boston* **6** B2
Wellesley, *Boston* **6** B1
Wellesley Falls, *Boston* ... **6** B2
Wellesley Hills, *Boston* ... **6** B2
Welling, *London* **15** B4
Wellington, *Boston* **6** A3
Wellington, *Wellington* **32** B1
Wells Fargo Cenier,
  Los Angeles **16** b1
Weltevreden Park,
  Johannesburg **13** A1
Wembley, *London* **15** A2
Wemmel, *Brussels* **6** A1
Wemmer Pan, *Johannesburg* .. **13** B2
Wenceslas Square, *Prague* .. **24** b2
Wendenschloss, *Berlin* **5** B4
Wengern, *London* **15** A5
Wennington, *London* **15** A5
Werneuchen, *Berlin* **5** A5
West Bedford, *Boston* **6** A1
West Concord, *Boston* **6** A1
West Don ↦, *Toronto* **30** A2
West Drayton, *London* **15** A1
West Ham, *London* **15** A4
West Harrow, *London* **15** A2
West Heath, *London* **15** B4
West Hill, *Toronto* **30** A3
West Hollywood, *Los Angeles* **16** B2
West Kensington, *London* ... **15** c1
West Kilburn, *London* **15** a1
West Lamma Channel,
  Hong Kong **12** B1
West Lynn, *Boston* **6** A3
West Medford, *Boston* **6** A3
West Miami, *Miami* **16** B1
West Molesey, *London* **15** B1
West New York, *New York* ... **21** B1
West Park, *Johannesburg* ... **13** B1
West Rouge, *Toronto* **30** A4
West Roxbury, *Boston* **6** B3
West Springfield, *Washington* **32** C2
West Town, *Chicago* **9** B2
West Wharf, *Karachi* **14** B1
Westbourne Green, *London* .. **15** a1
Westchester, *Chicago* **9** B1

Westchester, *Los Angeles* .. **16** C2
Westchester, *New York* **21** A2
Westcliff, *Johannesburg* ... **13** B2
Westdene, *Johannesburg* **13** B1
Westend, *Helsinki* **12** C1
Wester Hailes, *Edinburgh* .. **11** B2
Westerham, *Munich* **20** B2
Western Addition,
  San Francisco **25** B2
Western Wall, *Jerusalem* ... **13** b3
Westlake, *Cape Town* **8** B1
Westlake, *San Francisco* ... **25** B2
Westminster, *London* **15** A3
Westmount, *Montreal* **19** B2
Weston, *Boston* **6** A2
Weston, *Toronto* **30** A1
Weston Pts., *Boston* **6** A2
Westwood Village,
  Los Angeles **16** B2
Westzaan, *Amsterdam* **2** A1
Wetton, *Cape Town* **8** A2
Wexford, *Toronto* **30** A3
Weybridge, *London* **15** B1
Wezembeek-Oppem, *Brussels* . **6** A2
White House, The,
  Washington **32** b1
Whitechapel, *London* **15** A3
Whitehall, *Dublin* **11** A2
Whitehall, *London* **15** b3
Whittier, *Los Angeles* **16** C4
Whitton, *London* **15** B2
Wieden, *Vienna* **31** A2
Wien, *Vienna* **31** A2
Wien-Schwechat, Flughafen,
  Vienna **31** B3
Wienerberg, *Vienna* **31** B2
Wierzbno, *Warsaw* **31** B2
Wijde Wormer, *Amsterdam* ... **2** A2
Wilanów, *Warsaw* **31** B2
Wilanówka ↦, *Warsaw* **31** C2
Wilhelmshagen, *Berlin* **5** B5
Wilket Creek Park, *Toronto* **30** A2
Wilkieston, *Edinburgh* **11** B1
Willbrook, *Dublin* **11** B2
Willesden, *London* **15** A2
Willesden Green, *London* ... **15** A2
Williamsbridge, *New York* .. **21** A2
Williamstown, *Melbourne* ... **17** B1
Willoughby, *Sydney* **28** A2
Willow Springs, *Chicago* ... **9** C1
Wilmersdorf, *Berlin* **5** c1
Wilmette, *Chicago* **9** A2
Wilmington, *London* **15** B5
Wilshire Boulevard,
  Los Angeles **16** c1
Wimbledon, *London* **15** B2
Wimbledon Common,
  London **15** B2
Wimbledon Tennis Ground,
  London **15** B2
Winchester, *Boston* **6** A3
Windermere, *Cape Town* **8** A2
Windhoek, *Johannesburg* **13** B1
Windsor Hills, *Los Angeles* **16** C2
Windy Arbour, *Dublin* **11** B2
Winning, *Munich* **20** B2
Winthrop, *Boston* **6** A4
Wissous, *Paris* **23** B2
Wittenau, *Berlin* **5** A2
Witwatersrand, Univ. of,
  Johannesburg **13** B2
Włochy, *Warsaw* **31** B1
Wo Mei, *Hong Kong* **12** A2
Wo Yi Hop, *Hong Kong* **12** A1
Woburn, *Boston* **6** A3
Woburn, *Toronto* **30** A3
Woduk Pluit, *Jakarta* **13** A1
Wola, *Warsaw* **31** B1
Wolf Trap Farm Park,
  Washington **32** B2
Wolica, *Warsaw* **31** C1
Wolica, *Warsaw* **31** C1
Wólka Węglowa, *Warsaw* **31** B1
Wollaston, *Boston* **6** B3
Woltersdorf, *Berlin* **5** B5
Woluwe-Saint-Lambert,
  Brussels **6** A2
Woluwe-Saint-Pierre, *Brussels* **6** A2
Wong Chuk Hang,
  Hong Kong **12** B2
Wong Chuk Wan, *Hong Kong* .. **12** A2
Wong Chuk Yeung,
  Hong Kong **12** A2
Wong Tai Sin, *Hong Kong* ... **15** A3
Wood Green, *London* **15** A3
Wood Ridge, *New York* **21** A1
Woodbridge, *Toronto* **30** A1
Woodford, *London* **15** A4
Woodford Bridge, *London* ... **15** A4
Woodford Green, *London* **15** A4
Woodhaven, *New York* **21** B2
Woodhouselee, *Edinburgh* ... **11** B2
Woodlands New Town,
  Singapore **27** A2
Woodmont, *Washington* **32** B3
Woodside, *New York* **21** B2
Woodside, *Cape Town* **8** A1
Woodstock, *Cape Town* **8** A1
Woollahra, *Sydney* **28** B2
Woolloomooloo, *Sydney* **28** b2
Woolooware B., *Sydney* **28** C1
Woolwich, *London* **15** B4
Woolworth Building,
  New York **21** e1
Worli, *Mumbai* **20** A1
Worth, *Chicago* **9** C2
Wren's Nest, *Atlanta* **3** B2
Wrigley Building, *Chicago* . **9** a3
Wuhlgarten, *Berlin* **5** A4
Wujiaochang, *Shanghai* **27** B2
Würm ↦, *Munich* **20** A1
Würm-kanal, *Munich* **20** A1
Wusong, *Shanghai* **27** A2
Wyczółki, *Warsaw* **31** C1
Wynberg, *Cape Town* **8** B1

X

Xabregas, *Lisbon* **14** A2
Xianggang = Hong Kong,
  Hong Kong **12** B1
Xiaodian, *Tianjin* **30** A2
Xiaogang Park, *Canton* **8** B2
Xiasha chong, *Canton* **8** B1
Xicheng, *Beijing* **4** B1

Xidan, *Beijing* **4** B2
Xigu Park, *Tianjin* **30** A2
Xigucun, *Tianjin* **30** A1
Ximenwai, *Tianjin* **30** B1
Xinanlou, *Tianjin* **30** B1
Xinkai He ↦, *Tianjin* **30** B2
Xizhimen, *Beijing* **4** B1
Xu Beihong Mem. Hall,
  Beijing **4** a1
Xuanwu, *Beijing* **4** B1
Xuhui, *Shanghai* **27** B1

Y

Yaba, *Lagos* **14** A2
Yaftābād, *Tehran* **30** B1
Yahara, *Tokyo* **29** A1
Yaho, *Tokyo* **29** A1
Yakire, *Tokyo* **29** B2
Yamada, *Osaka* **22** A4
Yamada, *Tokyo* **29** B2
Yamamoto, *Osaka* **22** B4
Yamato ↦, *Osaka* **22** B3
Yamuna ↦, *Delhi* **10** B2
Yan Kit, *Singapore* **27** B2
Yanbu, *Canton* **8** B1
Yangch'ŏn, *Seoul* **26** B1
Yanghuayuan, *Beijing* **4** C1
Yangjae, *Seoul* **26** C2
Yangjiazhuang, *Shanghai* ... **27** A1
Yangpu, *Shanghai* **27** B2
Yangpu Park, *Shanghai* **27** B2
Yao, *Osaka* **22** B4
Yao Airport, *Osaka* **22** B4
Yarmūk, *Baghdad* **3** B1
Yarra ↦, *Melbourne* **17** A1
Yarra Bend Park, *Melbourne* **17** A1
Yarraville, *Melbourne* **17** A1
Yau Tong, *Hong Kong* **12** B2
Yauza ↦, *Moscow* **19** B3
Yeading, *London* **15** A1
Yedikule, *Istanbul* **12** C1
Yemin Moshe, *Jerusalem* **13** b3
Yenikapı, *Istanbul* **12** B1
Yeniköy, *Istanbul* **12** B2
Yerba Buena Gardens,
  San Francisco **25** c2
Yerba Buena I., *San Francisco* **25** B2
Yerres, *Paris* **23** B4
Yerushalayim = Jerusalem,
  Jerusalem **13** B2
Yiheyuan, *Beijing* **4** B1
Yinhangzhen, *Shanghai* **27** A2
Yishun New Town, *Singapore* **27** A3
Yixingbu, *Tianjin* **30** A2
Ylästö, *Helsinki* **12** B2
Yodo ↦, *Osaka* **22** A3
Yongdingman, *Beijing* **4** B2
Yŏngdong, *Seoul* **26** C2
Yŏngdûngp'o, *Seoul* **26** B1
Yongfucun, *Canton* **8** B2
Yongjing, *Shanghai* **27** B2
Yongsan, *Seoul* **26** B1
Yonkers, *New York* **21** A2
York, *Toronto* **30** A2
York Mills, *Toronto* **30** A2
Yotsuya, *Tokyo* **29** a2
You'anmen, *Beijing* **4** B2
Yōdido, *Seoul* **26** B1
Youndsfield, *Cape Town* **8** B1
Yuanxiatian, *Canton* **8** B1
Yugo-Zarad, *Moscow* **19** B3
Yung Shue Wan, *Hong Kong* .. **12** B1
Yūsofābād, *Tehran* **30** A2
Yuyuantan Park, *Beijing* ... **4** b2

Z

Zaandam, *Amsterdam* **2** A1
Zaandijk, *Amsterdam* **2** A1
Zaanstad, *Amsterdam* **2** A1
Zábehlice, *Prague* **24** B2
Zabki, *Warsaw* **31** B2
Zacisze, *Warsaw* **31** B2
Zahrā, *Baghdad* **3** A1
Zakharkovo, *Moscow* **19** A2
Zalov, *Prague* **24** A2
Załuski, *Warsaw* **31** C1
Zamdorf, *Munich* **20** B2
Zamek Królewski, *Warsaw* ... **31** c3
Zamek Ujazdowski, *Warsaw* .. **31** B3
Zapote, *Manila* **17** C1
Záppeio, *Athens* **2** c2
Zarechye, *Moscow* **19** B2
Zaventem, *Brussels* **6** A2
Zawady, *Warsaw* **31** B2
Zâwiyet Abû Musallam, *Cairo* **7** B1
Zawrâ' Park, *Baghdad* **3** B2
Zbraslav, *Prague* **24** C2
Zbuzany, *Prague* **24** B1
Zdiby, *Prague* **24** B2
Zeekorsici, *Cape Town* **8** B2
Zehlendorf, *Berlin* **5** B2
Zenne ↦, *Brussels* **6** A2
Zerañ, *Warsaw* **31** B2
Zerzeñ, *Warsaw* **31** B2
Zeytinburnu, *Istanbul* **12** C1
Zhabei, *Shanghai* **27** B1
Zhangguizhuang, *Tianjin* ... **30** B2
Zhdanov, *Moscow* **19** B4
Zheleznodorozhnyy, *Moscow* . **19** B6
Zhenru, *Shanghai* **27** B1
Zhernovka, St. *Petersburg* . **26** B2
Zhicun, *Canton* **8** B2
Zhongshan Park, *Beijing* ... **4** b2
Zhongshan Park, *Shanghai* . **27** B1
Zhoucun, *Canton* **8** B2
Zhoujiadu, *Shanghai* **27** B2
Zhoujiazhen, *Shanghai* **27** A2
Zhu Jiang ↦, *Canton* **8** B2
Zhubrino, *Moscow* **19** B5
Zhushadi, *Canton* **8** B2
Zielona, *Warsaw* **31** B2
Zielonka, *Warsaw* **31** B2
Ziya He ↦, *Tianjin* **30** A1
Žižkov, *Prague* **24** B2
Zličin, *Prague* **24** B1
Zócalo, *Mexico City* **18** b3
Zografos, *Athens* **2** B2
Zoliborz, *Warsaw* **31** B1
Zonnenbloem, *Cape Town* **8** A1
Zoo, *Beijing* .... **4** al
Zugliget, *Budapest* **7** B1
Zugló, *Budapest* **7** A2
Zuiderwoude, *Amsterdam* **2** A3
Zumbi, *Rio de Janeiro* **24** B2
Zunderdorp, *Amsterdam* **2** A2
Zuuvuu ↦, *São Paulo* **26** C1
Zwanenburg, *Amsterdam* **2** A2
Zwölfaxing, *Vienna* **31** B2
Zyuzino, *Moscow* **19** C3

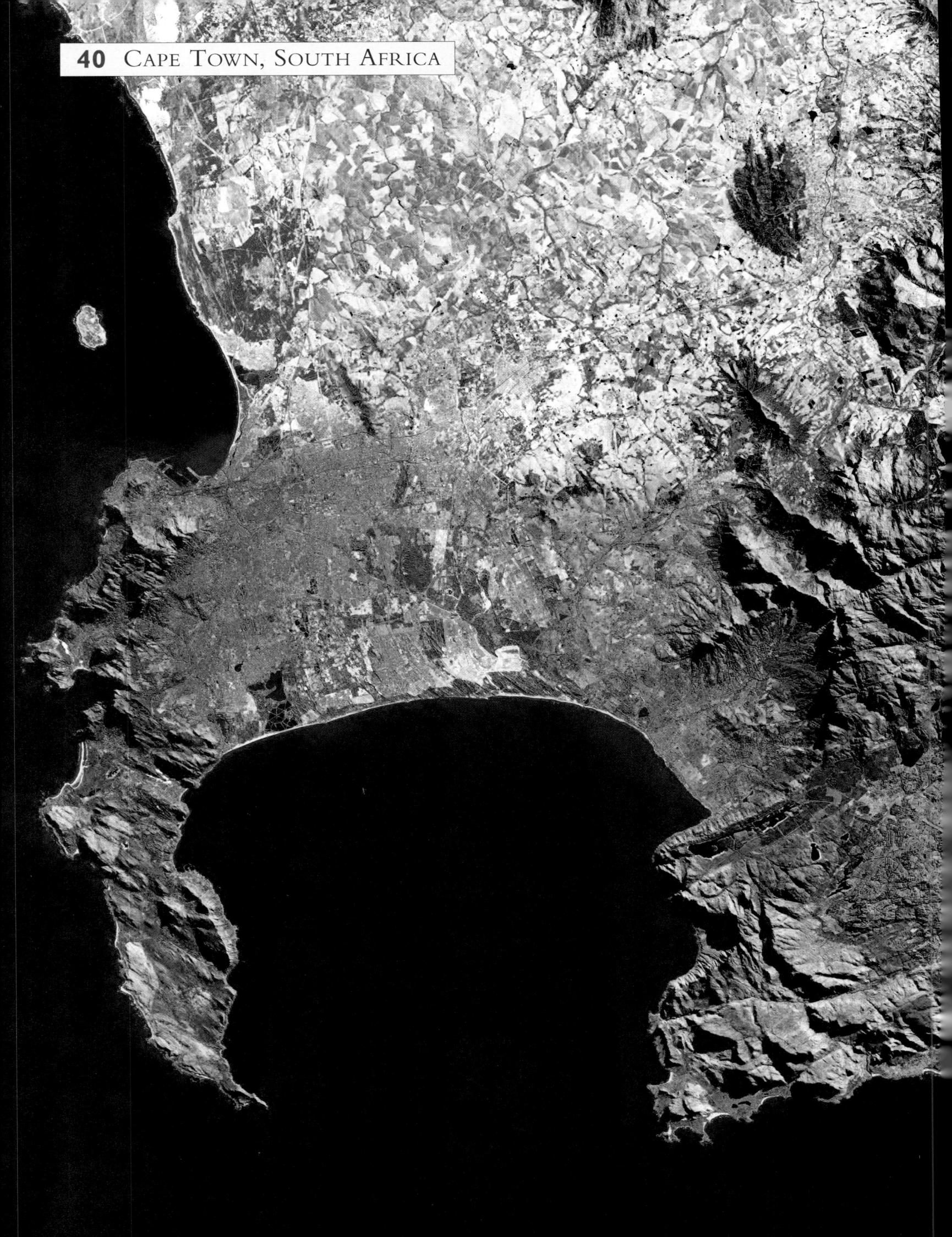

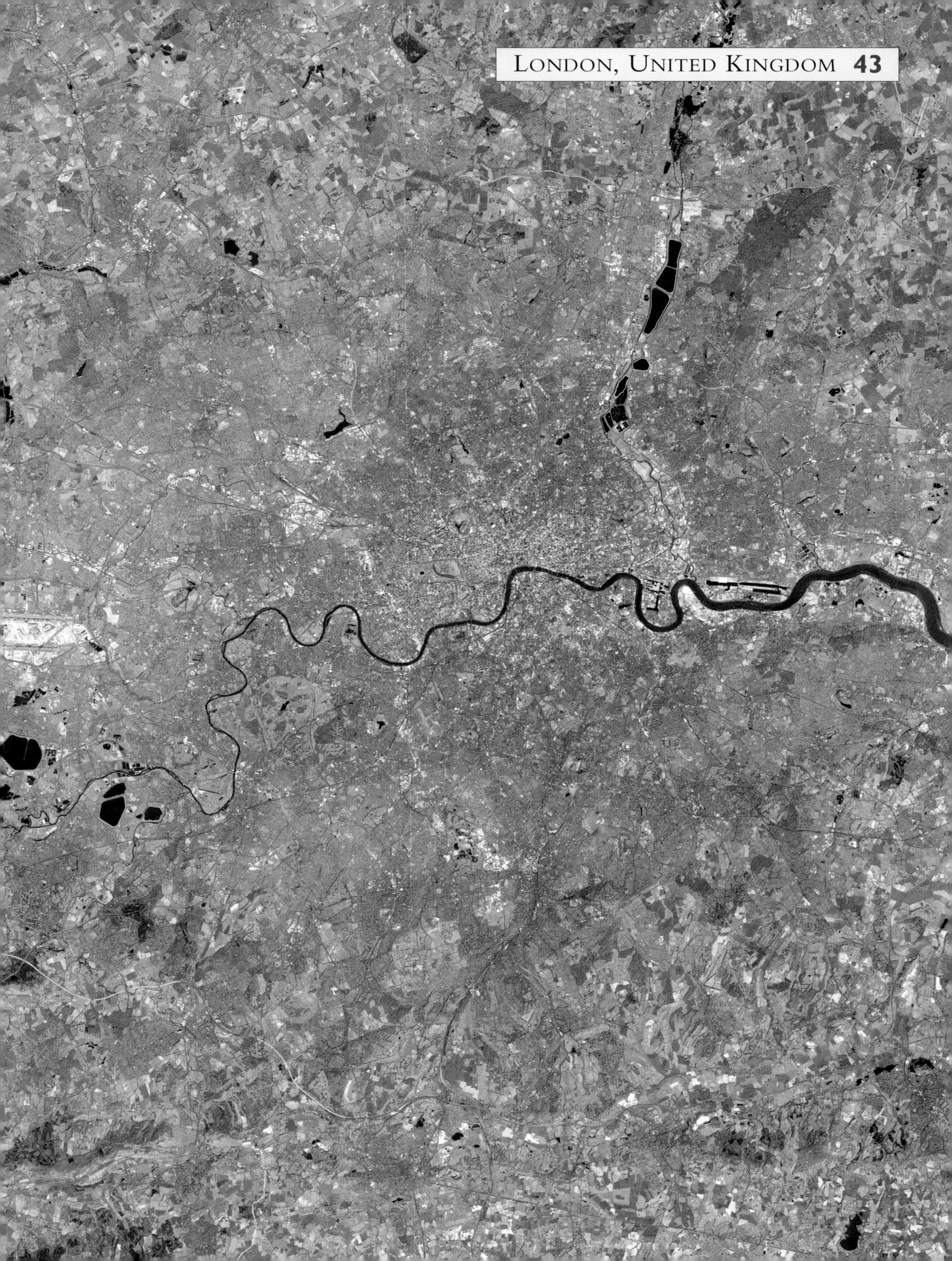

WORLD
MAPS

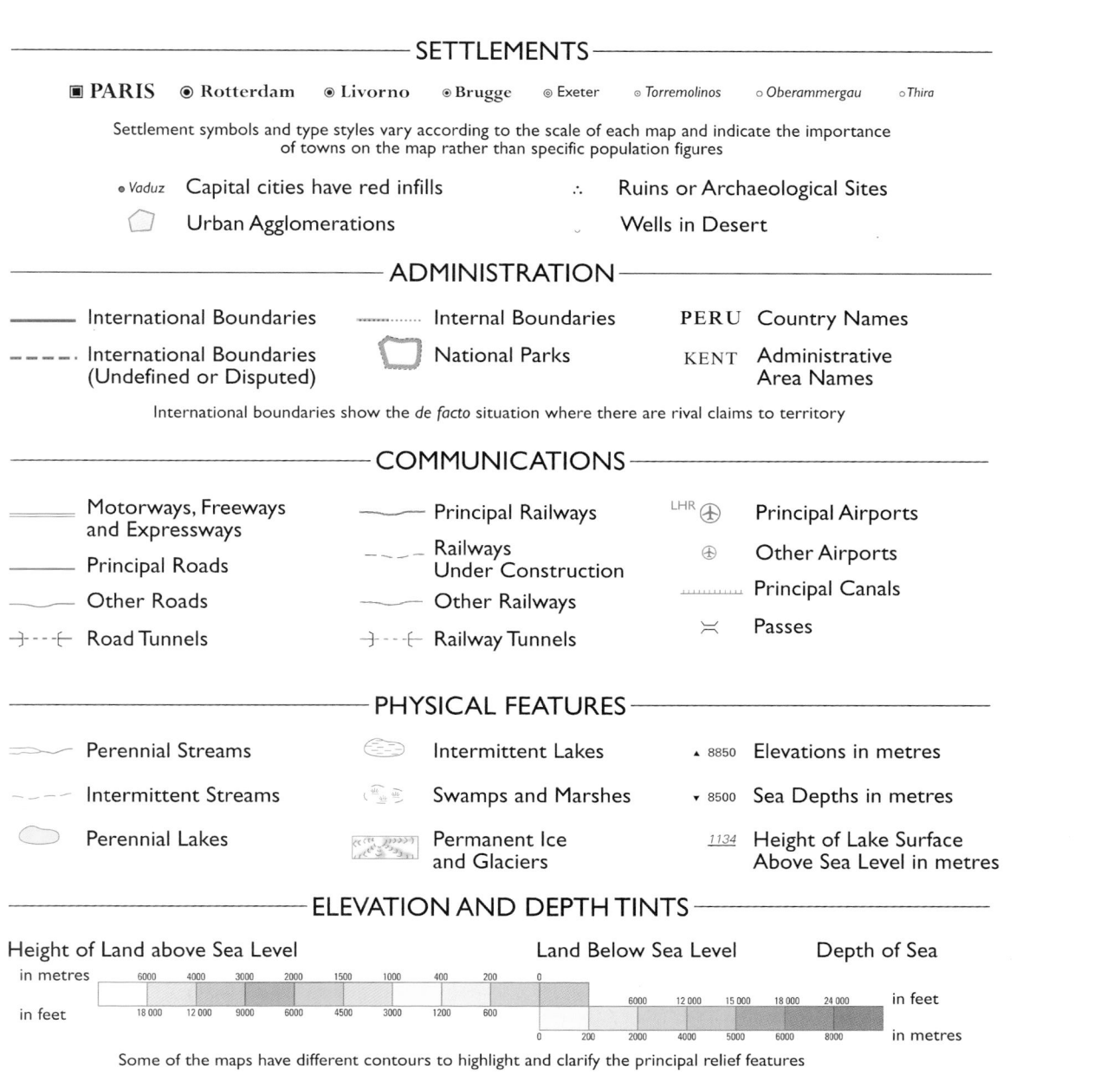

SETTLEMENTS

■ **PARIS**   ◉ **Rotterdam**   ◉ **Livorno**   ◉ Brugge   ◉ Exeter   ◌ *Torremolinos*   ○ *Oberammergau*   ○ *Thira*

Settlement symbols and type styles vary according to the scale of each map and indicate the importance
of towns on the map rather than specific population figures

● *Vaduz*   Capital cities have red infills   ∴   Ruins or Archaeological Sites

⬠   Urban Agglomerations   ˳   Wells in Desert

ADMINISTRATION

───── International Boundaries   ┄┄┄┄ Internal Boundaries   **PERU**   Country Names

─ ─ ─ ∙ International Boundaries   ⬡ National Parks   KENT   Administrative
(Undefined or Disputed)   Area Names

International boundaries show the *de facto* situation where there are rival claims to territory

COMMUNICATIONS

═════ Motorways, Freeways   ───── Principal Railways   LHR ✈ Principal Airports
and Expressways
                                   ─ ─ ─ Railways   ⊕ Other Airports
───── Principal Roads   Under Construction
                                   ───── Other Railways   ┄┄┄┄ Principal Canals
───── Other Roads
                                                            ⤫ Passes
╾┄┄╼ Road Tunnels   ╾┄┄╼ Railway Tunnels

PHYSICAL FEATURES

╌╌╌ Perennial Streams   ⬭ Intermittent Lakes   ▲ 8850 Elevations in metres

─ ─ ─ Intermittent Streams   ⬭ Swamps and Marshes   ▾ 8500 Sea Depths in metres

⬭ Perennial Lakes   ▨ Permanent Ice   *1134* Height of Lake Surface
and Glaciers   Above Sea Level in metres

ELEVATION AND DEPTH TINTS

Height of Land above Sea Level   Land Below Sea Level   Depth of Sea

in metres	6000	4000	3000	2000	1500	1000	400	200	0					
in feet	18 000	12 000	9000	6000	4500	3000	1200	600		6000	12 000	15 000	18 000	24 000	in feet
									0	200	2000	4000	5000	6000	8000	in metres

Some of the maps have different contours to highlight and clarify the principal relief features

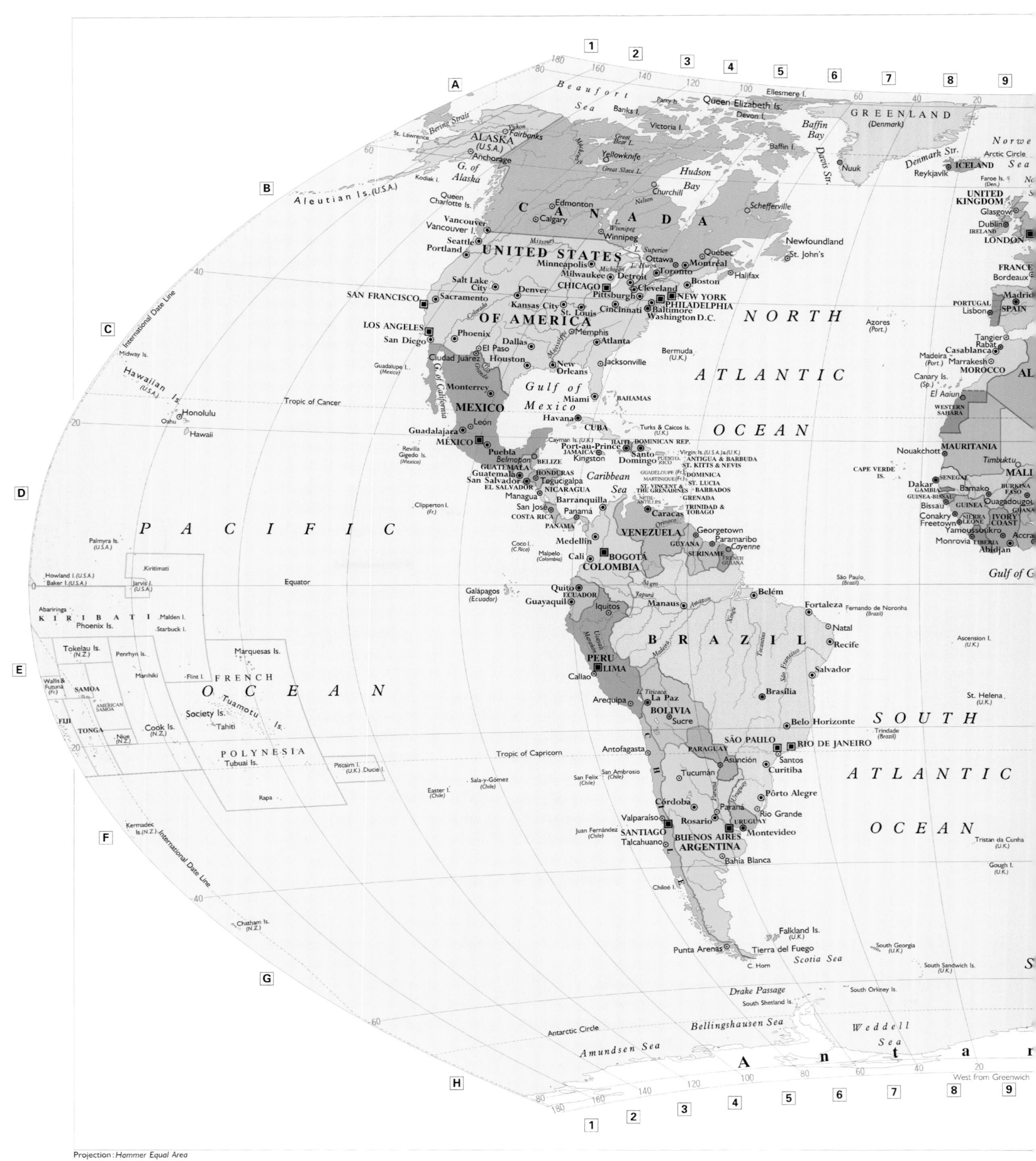

Projection: Hammer Equal Area

COPYRIGHT PHILIP'S

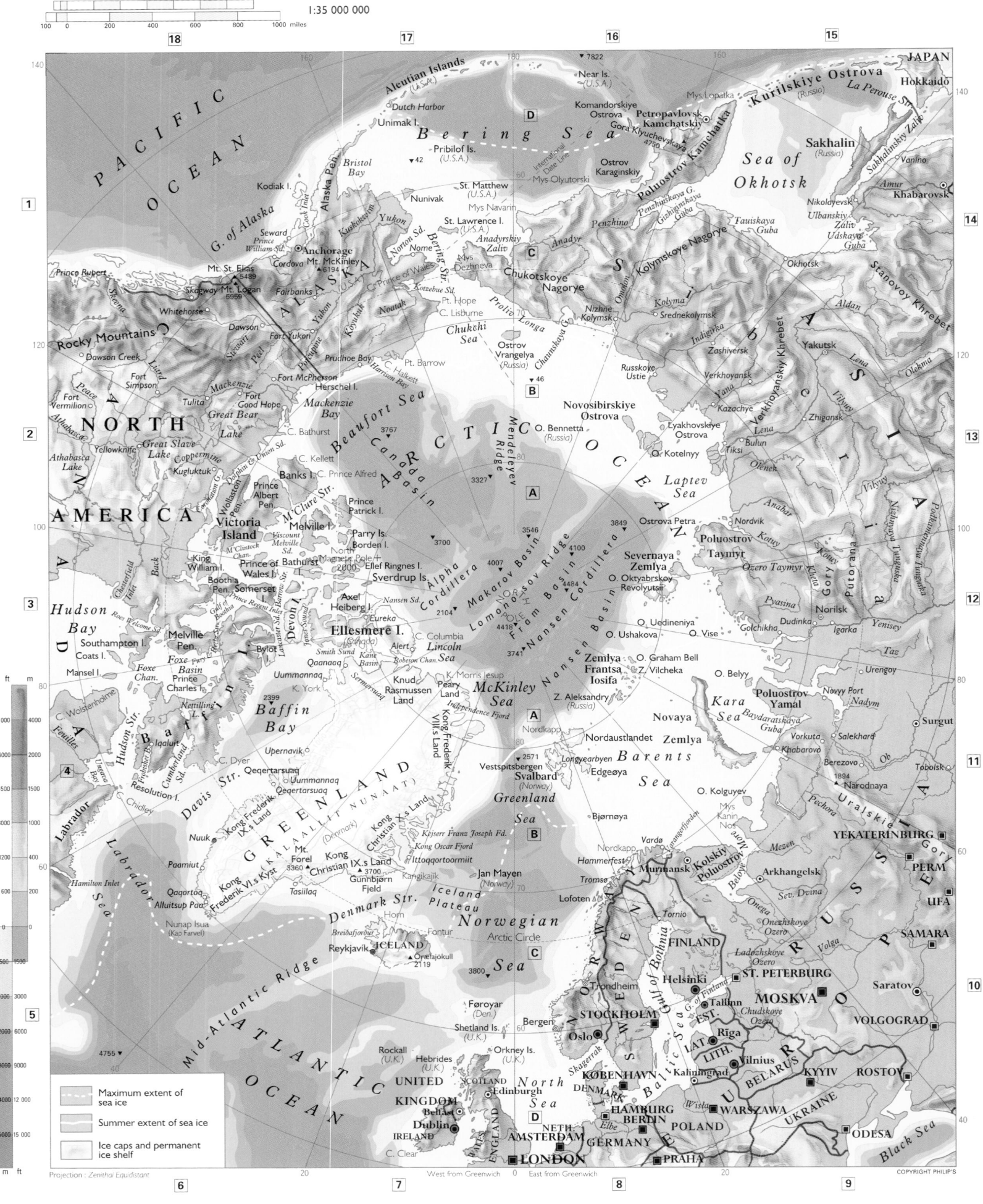

100 0 200 400 600 800 1000 1200 1400 km

1:35 000 000

100 0 200 400 600 800 1000 miles

Maximum extent of sea ice

Summer extent of sea ice

Ice caps and permanent ice shelf

Projection: Zenithal Equidistant

West from Greenwich   0   East from Greenwich

COPYRIGHT PHILIP'S

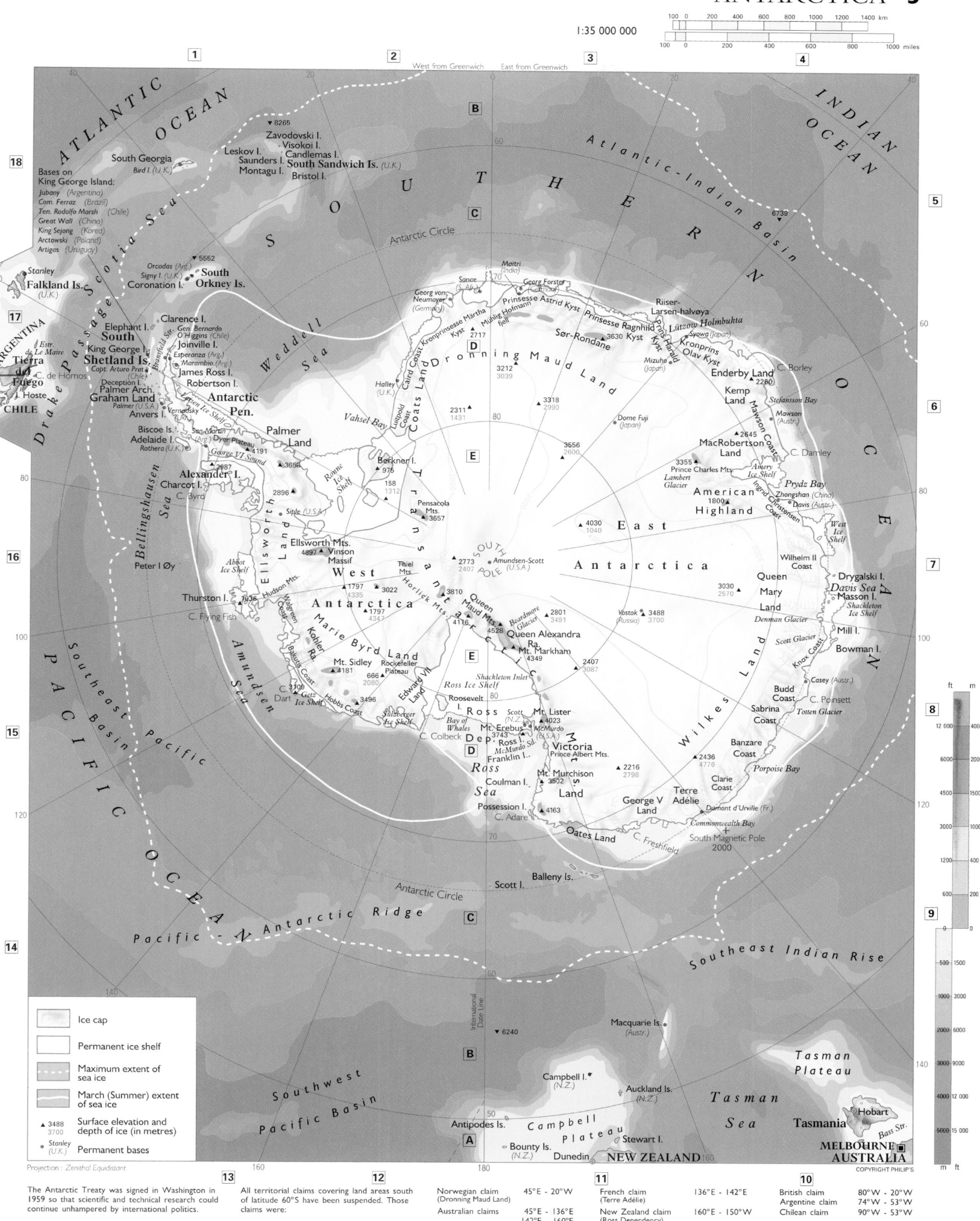

ANTARCTICA 5

1:35 000 000

|100 0 200 400 600 800 1000 1400 km|
|100 0 200 400 600 800 1000 miles|

ATLANTIC OCEAN

INDIAN OCEAN

West from Greenwich | East from Greenwich

▼ 8265

Zavodovski I.
Leskov I. • Visokoi I.
Candlemas I.
Saunders I. • South Sandwich Is. (U.K.)
Montagu I. • Bristol I.

South Georgia
Bird I. (U.K.)

S O U T H E R N

Atlantic-Indian Basin

Antarctic Circle

6739 ▼

Bases on
King George Island:
Jubany (Argentina)
Com. Ferraz (Brazil)
Ten. Rodolfo Marsh (Chile)
Great Wall (China)
King Sejong (Korea)
Arctowski (Poland)
Artigas (Uruguay)

Orcadas (Arg.) ▼ 5552
Signy I. Coronation I. • **South Orkney Is.**

• Stanley
Falkland Is.
(U.K.)

Maitri (India)
Sanae (S. Afr.)
Georg von Neumayer (Germany)
Georg Forster (German)

Prinsesse Astrid Kyst
Riiser-Larsen-halvøya

ARGENTINA

Elephant I. Clarence I.
South Shetland Is.
Gen. Bernardo O'Higgins (Chile)
Joinville I.
Esperanza (Arg.)
James Ross I.
Robertson I.

Prinsesse Martha Kyst
Kronprinsesse Märtha Kyst
Mühlig Hofmann fjell

Prinsesse Ragnhild Kyst
Sør-Rondane

Lützow Holmbukta
Kronprins Olav Kyst
Syowa (Japan)

C. Borley

Mizuho (Japan)

Enderby Land

2280 ▲

Estr. de Le Maire
C. de Hornos
Tierra del Fuego
J. Hoste
CHILE

Deception I.
Palmer Arch.
Graham Land
Palmer (U.S.A.)
Anvers I.
Vernadsky (U.K.)

Dronning Maud Land

2717 ▲
3212
3039

3318
2990

3630 Kyst

Dome Fuji (Japan)

Kemp Land

Stefansson Bay
Mawson (Austr.)

C. Damley

2645 ▲

MacRobertson Land

Biscoe Is.
Adelaide I.
Rothera (U.K.)

San Martin (Arg.)
Dyer Plateau
George VI Sound
4191

Halley (U.K.)

2311 ▲
1431

3556
2600

3355 ▲

Prince Charles Mts.
Lambert Glacier

Amery Ice Shelf

Prydz Bay

Zhongshan (China)
Davis (Austr.)

Alexander I.
Charcot I.
C. Byrd

3656

2687

Ronne Ice Shelf
975

158
1312

American Highland

1800 ▲

Ingrid Christensen Coast

West Ice Shelf

Bellingshausen Sea

2896 ▲

Siple (U.S.A.)

Pensacola Mts.
3657

4030 ▲
1040

East Antarctica

Wilhelm II Coast

Drygalski I.

Peter I Øy

Ellsworth Land

Ellsworth Mts.
4897 ▲ Vinson Massif
2773 ▲
2407

Amundsen-Scott (U.S.A.)
SOUTH POLE

Vostok (Russia) 3488
3700

3030
2570

Queen Mary Land

Davis Sea
Masson I.
Shackleton Ice Shelf

Mill I.

Southeast Pacific Basin

Thurston I.
1036

Hudson Mts.

C. Flying Fish

1797 ▲
4335
3022 ▲

Horlick Mts.
3810

Queen Maud Mts.
4116
4528

Beardmore Glacier

2801 ▲

Queen Alexandra Ra.
Mt. Markham
4349

2407
3087

2436 ▲
4776

Banzare Coast
Budd Coast
C. Poinsett

Sabrina Coast
Casey (Austr.)
Totten Glacier

West Antarctica

1797
4347

Kohler Ra.
Mt. Sidley
4181
Rockefeller Plateau
666
2080

Edward VII Land

Roosevelt I.
80

Shackleton Inlet

Ross Ice Shelf

Bowman I.

Knox Coast
Scott Glacier
Denman Glacier

W i l k e s L a n d

Porpoise Bay

Marie Byrd Land

Amundsen Sea

Getz Ice Shelf
3100
Dart
Hobbs Coast
3496

Ruppert Coast
Saunders Coast
Siple Coast

Bay of Whales
C. Colbeck

Scott
McMurdo (U.S.A.)
Ross I.
Mt. Lister
4023
Mt. Erebus
3743

McMurdo Sd.
Franklin I.

2216
2798

Clarie Coast

Dumont d'Urville (Fr.)

Terre Adélie

George V Land

Ross Sea

Salzberger Ice Shelf

Ross Dep.

Victoria
Prince Albert Mts.
Mt. Murchison
3502 ▲

Land

Coulman I.

Commonwealth Bay
South Magnetic Pole 2000

Possession I.
4163 ▲
C. Adare

Oates Land
C. Freshfield

Pacific-Antarctic Ridge

Southeast Indian Rise

Balleny Is.

Antarctic Circle

Scott I.

S O U T H W E S T

P A C I F I C

O C E A N

International Date Line

▼ 6240

Southwest Pacific Basin

Macquarie Is. (Austr.)

Campbell I. (N.Z.)

Auckland Is. (N.Z.)

Tasman Plateau

Tasman Sea

Tasmania

Hobart
Bass Str.

MELBOURNE
AUSTRALIA

COPYRIGHT PHILIP'S

Antipodes Is.
Campbell Plateau
Bounty Is. (N.Z.)
Stewart I.
Dunedin **NEW ZEALAND**

Legend:

	Ice cap
	Permanent ice shelf
	Maximum extent of sea ice
	March (Summer) extent of sea ice
▲ 3488 / 3700	Surface elevation and depth of ice (in metres)
• Stanley (U.K.)	Permanent bases

Projection: Zenithal Equidistant

ft	m
12 000	4000
9000	3000
6000	2000
4500	1500
3000	1000
1200	400
600	200
0	0
500	1500
1000	3000
2000	6000
3000	9000
4000	12 000
5000	15 000
m	ft

1:20 000 000

COPYRIGHT PHILIP'S

1:20 000 000

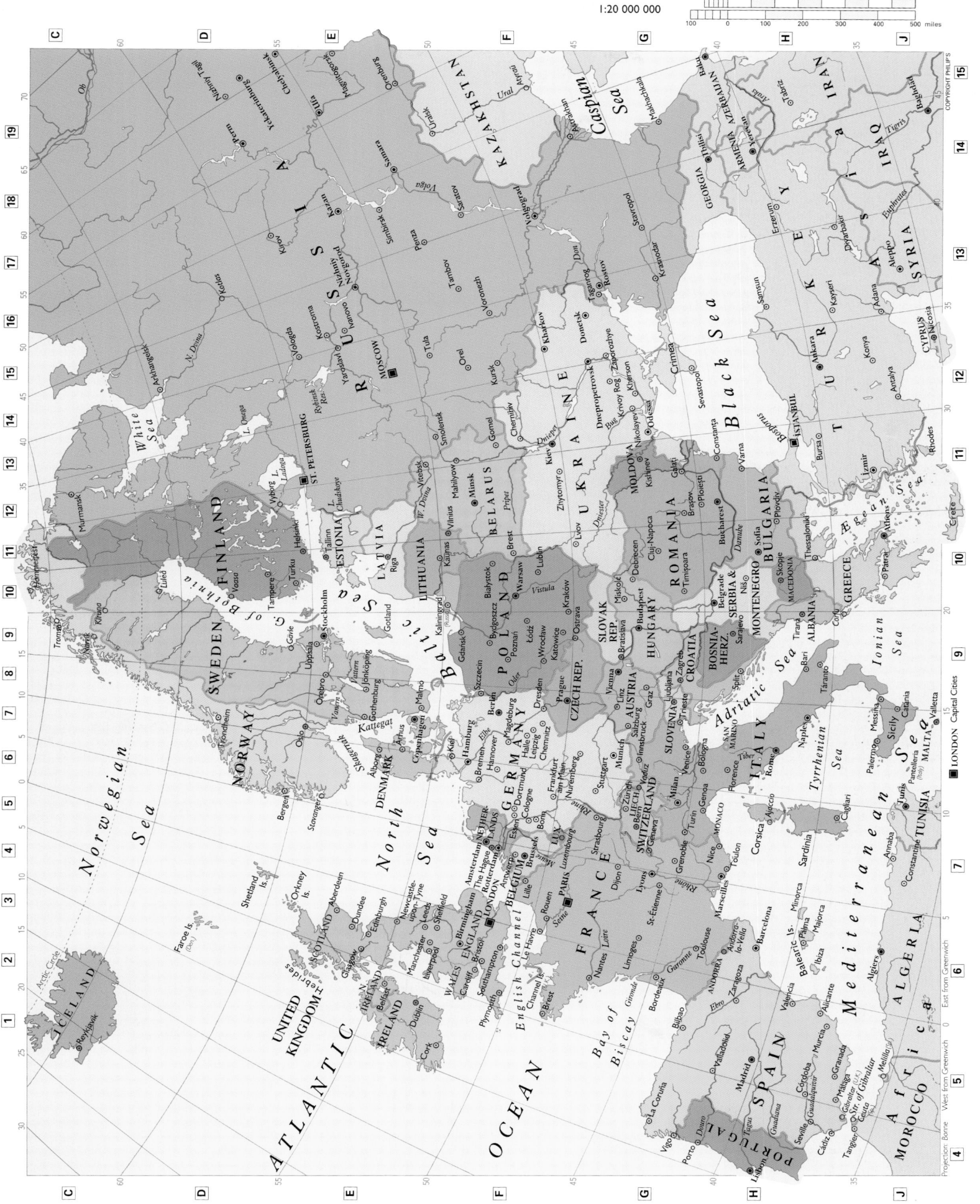

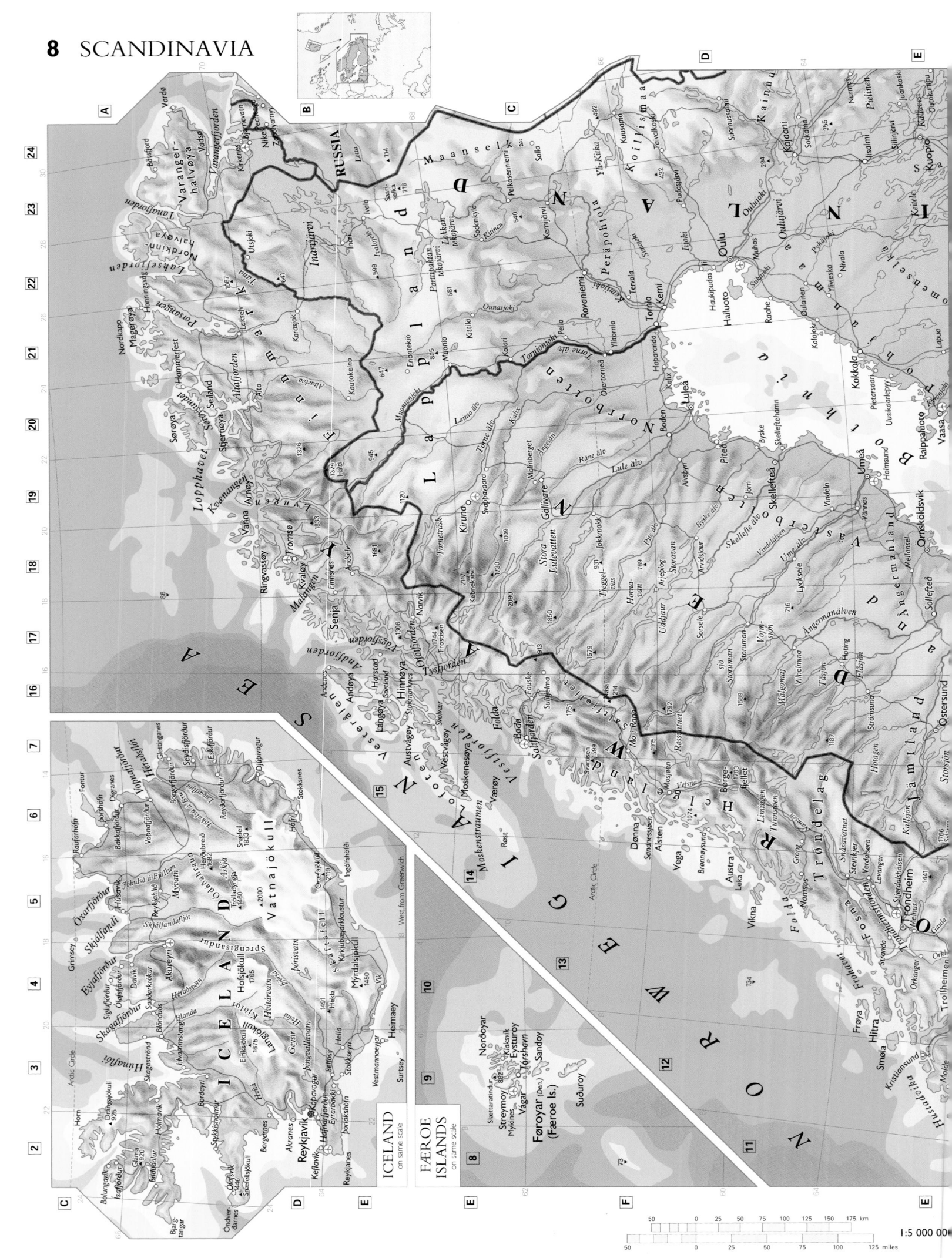

ICELAND
on same scale

FÆROE
ISLANDS
on same scale

1:5 000 000

50   0   25   50   75   100   125   150   175 km

50   0   25   50   75   100   125 miles

1:2 000 000

10 0 10 20 30 40 50 60 70 80 km
10 0 10 20 30 40 50 miles

SCOTLAND
Kintyre
Mull of Oa
Brodick
Arran
Campbeltown
Mull of Kintyre
Firth of Clyde
Ailsa Craig
Cairnryan
Stranraer
Portpatrick
L. Ryan

NORTH CHANNEL

Inishtrahull
Malin Hd.
Fanad Hd.
Malin Pen.
Carndonagh
Moville
Buncrana
Inishowen Pen.
Giants Causeway
Rathlin I.
Fair Hd.
Ballycastle
Portstewart
Portrush
Coleraine
Ballymoney
Limavady
L. Foyle
Trostan
GLENARIFF
Mts. of Antrim
ANTRIM
Garron Pt.

Tory I.
Sheep Haven
Horn Hd.
Mulroy B.
Lough Swilly
Bloody Foreland
Inishfree B.
Gweedore
Errigal 752
Rathmullen
Derryveagh Mts.
GLENVEAGH
Aran I.
The Rosses
Crohy Hd.
Gweebarra B.
Dawros Hd.
Loughros More B.
Rossan Pt.
Slieve League
Killybegs
St. John's Pt.
Donegal Bay
Ballyshannon
Bundoran

DONEGAL
Letterkenny
Lifford
Strabane
Sion Mills
Newtownstewart
Glenties
Lavagh More
Donegal
Londonderry
LONDONDERRY
Ballymena
Sawel Mt.
Sperrin Mts.
Randalstown
Ballyclare
Moneymore
Cookstown
Omagh
TYRONE
Dromore
Dungannon
Coalisland
Craigavon
Lurgan
Portadown
Banbridge
ARMAGH
Armagh
Middletown
Keady
Monaghan
Clones
Newry
Mourne Mts.
Slieve Gullion
Warrenpoint
Carlingford L.

ULSTER
NORTHERN IRELAND
Belfast
Belfast L.
Lisburn
Lough Neagh
Antrim
Newtownabbey
Carrickfergus
Bangor
Donaghadee
Newtownards
Comber
Strangford
Ards Pen.
DOWN
Portaferry
Ballyquintin Pt.
Ballynahinch
Downpatrick
St. John's Pt.
Dundrum
Dundrum B.
Newcastle
Kilkeel
Greenore

FERMANAGH
Enniskillen
Lower L. Erne
Upper L. Erne
Belturbet
MONAGHAN
Castleblaney
Cootehill
Carrickmacross
Kingscourt
CAVAN
Cavan
L. Gowna
L. Sheelin

Killala B.
Downpatrick Hd.
Killala
Ballina
Sligo Bay
Dromore West
Sligo
Colloney
S Gamph
Ballymote
SLIGO
L. Arrow
Boyle
Carrick-on-Shannon
LEITRIM
Leitrim
L. Allen
Annalee
Dundalk
LOUTH
Louth
Ardee
Dundalk Bay
Clogher Hd.
Dunleer
Drogheda
Balbriggan

Erris Hd.
Broad Haven
Mullet Pen.
Belmullet
Inishkea North
Inishkea South
Blacksod Bay
Achill Hd.
Achill I.
Clare I.
Nephin
L. Conn
806
Swinford
Charlestown
Ballaghaderreen
Knock
Castlerea
ROSCOMMON
Castlebar
MAYO
Cortaun Pen.
Newport
Westport
Clew Bay
765 Croagh Patrick
CONNACHT
Claremorris
Ballyhaunis
Castlerea
Granard
LONGFORD
Longford
Roscommon
Castlepollard
Oldcastle
Ceanannus Mor (Kells)
Blackwater
MEATH
 Athboy
Boyne
Ceanannus
Drogheda

Inishturk
Killary Harbour
Inishbofin
Inishshark
Mweelrea 819
Connemara
CONNEMARA
Clifden
Slyne Hd.
Oughterard
Lough Mask
Ballinrobe
Tuam
GALWAY
Athenry
Loughrea
Lough Corrib
IRELAND
Roscommon
Lough Ree
Athlone
Moate
WESTMEATH
Mullingar
Royal Canal
Leinster
Trim
Swords
Rush
Lambay I.
Malahide
Howth Hd.
DUBLIN
Dun Laoghaire
Bray
Greystones
Maynooth
Clondalkin

Galway
Galway Bay
Black Hd.
Aran Is.
Inishmore
Inishmaan
Inisheer
Cliffs of Moher
Hags Hd.
BURREN
Liscannor Bay
Ennistimon
Mal Bay
Mutton I.
Milltown Malbay
CLARE
Ennis
Tulla
Gort
Slieve Aughty
368
Portumna
Shannon
Birr
Mountmellick
Portlaoise
OFFALY
Tullamore
Clara
Edenderry
Bog of Allen
Grand Canal
KILDARE
Kildare
Droichead Nua
Naas
Monasterevin
Athy
Portarlington
Kinnegad
LAOIS
Mountrath
Durrow
Roscrea
Slieve Bloom
Arderin 529
Nenagh
Templemore
Thurles
Carlow
Tullow
Muine Bheag
CARLOW
Mt. Leinster 796
WICKLOW
WICKLOW MTS.
Lugnaquilla 926
Rathdrum
Avoca
Arklow
Wicklow
Wicklow Hd.
Mizen Hd.
Shillelagh
Gorey

Kilkee
Loop Hd.
Mouth of the Shannon
Ballybunion
Kilrush
Foynes
Shannon Airport
Limerick
Sixmilebridge
Keeper Hill 694
Killaloe
Lough Derg
TIPPERARY
Golden Vale
Tipperary
Cashel
Slievenamon 722
Carrick-on-Suir
Clonmel
WEXFORD
New Ross
Wexford
Enniscorthy
Wexford Harbour
Rosslare
Rosslare Harbour
Greenore Pt.
Carnsore Pt.

LIMERICK
Rathkeale
Newcastle West
Listowel
Abbeyfeale
Kilfinnane
Galtymore 920
Galty Mts.
Caher
Mitchelstown
Knockmealdown Mts. 795
Comeragh Mts. 792
Waterford
Tramore
Tramore B.
Hook Hd.
Saltee Is.

Tralee B.
Tralee
Brandon B.
Smerwick Harbour
Brandon Mt. 953
Dingle
Slieve Mish 853
Great Blasket I.
Dunmore Hd.
Inishvickillane
Dingle Bay
Killorglin
L. Leane
Killarney
KILLARNEY
Carrauntoohil 1041
Macgillycuddy's Reeks
Kenmare
KERRY
Newmarket
Kanturk
Buttevant
Mallow
Fermoy
Lismore
Dungarvan
Dungarvan Harbour
WATERFORD
Waterford Harbour
MUNSTER

Valencia I.
Puffin I.
Great Skellig
Ballinskelligs B.
Caherciveen
Kenmare River
Caha Mts. 707
Glengarriff
636
Dunmanway
Macroom
Lee
Blarney
Blackwater
CORK
Cork
Midleton
Youghal
Youghal B.
Cobh
Crosshaven
Cork Harbour
Old Head of Kinsale
Kinsale
Bandon
Clonakilty
Clonakilty B.
Passage West

Dursey I.
Castletown Bearhaven
Bear I.
Crow Hd.
Bantry Bay
Bantry
Dunmanus B.
Skull
Mizen Hd.
Long I.
Sherkin I.
Baltimore
Clear I.
C. Clear
Galley Hd.
Fastnet Rock
Skibbereen

ATLANTIC OCEAN

IRISH SEA

ST. GEORGE'S CHANNEL
St. David's Hd.
St. David's
St. Brides Bay
WALES

CELTIC SEA

Projection: Lambert's Conformal Conic
West from Greenwich
COPYRIGHT PHILIP'S

National Parks

ft m
1500 500
600 200
300 100
0 0
50 150
100 300
200 600
500 1500
1000 3000
2000 6000
m ft

SCOTLAND 11

1:2 000 000

Key to Scottish unitary authorities on map
1 CITY OF ABERDEEN
2 DUNDEE CITY
3 WEST DUNBARTONSHIRE
4 EAST DUNBARTONSHIRE
5 CITY OF GLASGOW
6 INVERCLYDE
7 RENFREWSHIRE
8 EAST RENFREWSHIRE
9 NORTH LANARKSHIRE
10 FALKIRK
11 CLACKMANNANSHIRE
12 WEST LOTHIAN
13 CITY OF EDINBURGH
14 MIDLOTHIAN

ORKNEY IS. on same scale

SHETLAND IS. on same scale

Projection : Lambert's Conformal Conic

West from Greenwich

COPYRIGHT PHILIP'S

Forest Parks in Scotland

1:2 000 000

10 0 10 20 30 40 50 60 70 80 km
10 0 10 20 30 40 50 miles

Key to English unitary authorities on map

25 HARTLEPOOL
26 DARLINGTON
27 STOCKTON-ON-TEES
28 MIDDLESBROUGH
29 REDCAR AND CLEVELAND
30 BLACKPOOL
31 BLACKBURN WITH DARWEN
32 HALTON
33 WARRINGTON
34 KINGSTON UPON HULL
35 NORTH EAST LINCOLNSHIRE
36 STOKE-ON-TRENT
37 TELFORD AND WREKIN
38 DERBY CITY
39 CITY OF NOTTINGHAM
40 LEICESTER CITY
41 RUTLAND
42 PETERBOROUGH
43 MILTON KEYNES
44 LUTON
45 NORTH SOMERSET
46 CITY OF BRISTOL
47 BATH AND NORTH EAST SOMERSET
48 SWINDON
49 READING
50 WOKINGHAM
51 WINDSOR AND MAIDENHEAD
52 SLOUGH
53 BRACKNELL FOREST
54 THURROCK
55 SOUTHEND-ON-SEA
56 MEDWAY
57 PLYMOUTH
58 TORBAY
59 POOLE
60 BOURNEMOUTH
61 SOUTHAMPTON
62 PORTSMOUTH
63 BRIGHTON AND HOVE

Key to Welsh unitary authorities on map

15 SWANSEA
16 NEATH PORT TALBOT
17 BRIDGEND
18 RHONDDA CYNON TAFF
19 MERTHYR TYDFIL
20 BLAENAU GWENT
21 CAERPHILLY
22 TORFAEN
23 CARDIFF
24 NEWPORT

NORTH SEA

IRISH SEA

North Channel

NORTHERN IRELAND

SCOTLAND

ISLE OF MAN

Edinburgh
Glasgow
Newcastle-upon-Tyne
Sunderland
Middlesbrough
Kingston upon Hull
Leeds
Bradford
Manchester
Liverpool
Sheffield
Nottingham
Derby
Stoke-on-Trent
Chester
Blackpool
Preston
Lancaster
Carlisle
Belfast
Cardiff
Swansea
York
Lincoln

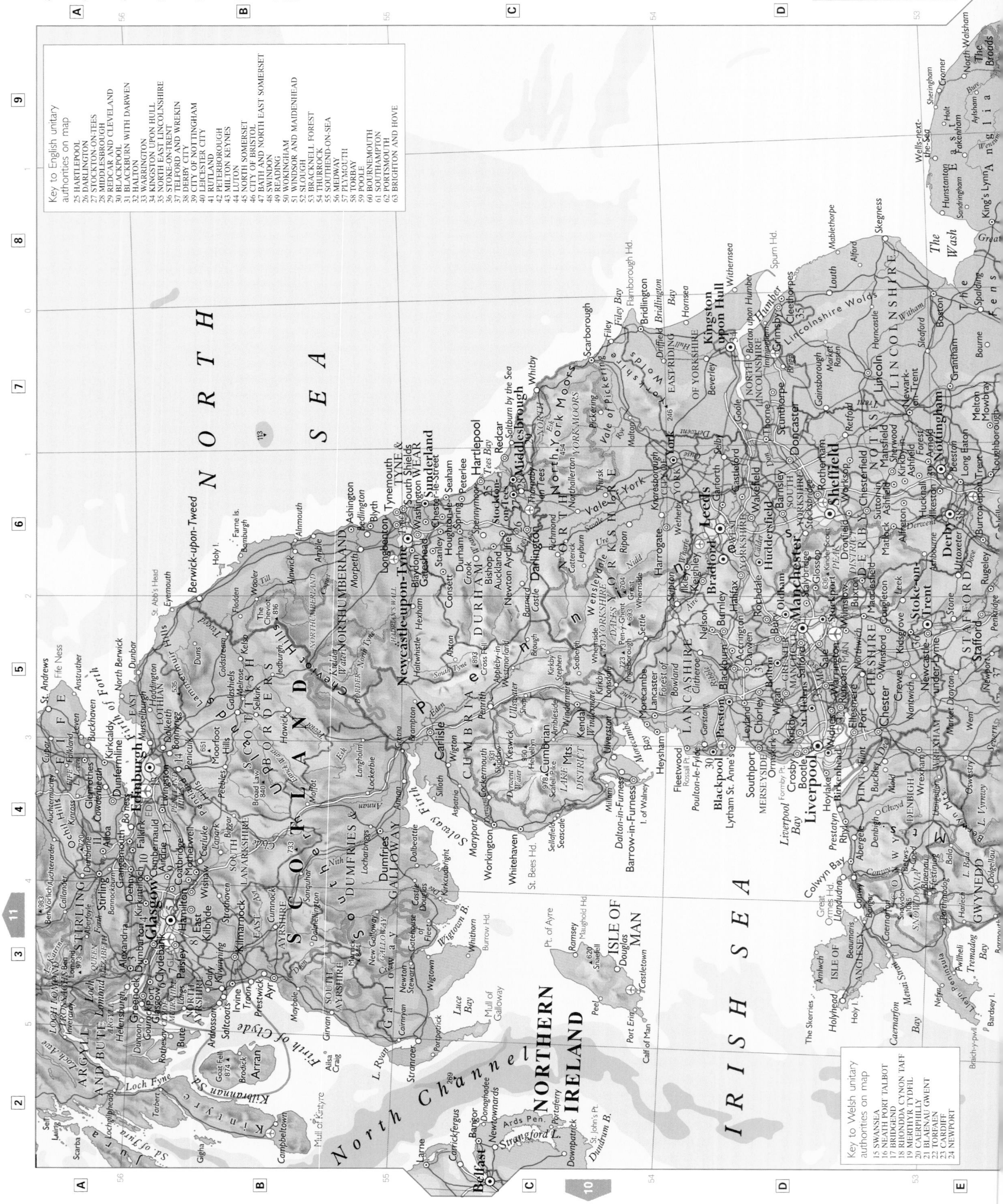

Forest Parks in Scotland

National Parks in England and Wales

Projection: Lambert's Conformal Conic

COPYRIGHT PHILIP'S

ISLES OF SCILLY
on same scale

50   0   25   50   75   100   125   150   175 km
1:5 000 000

50   0   25   50   75   100   125 miles

| 1 | 2 | 3 | 4 | 5 | 6 | 7 | 8 | 9 |

ATLANTIC OCEAN

NORWAY
Bergen
Askøy
Øsøyo
Stord
Bømlo
Leitvik
Haugesund
Kopervik
Åkrahamn
Boknafjorden
Stavanger
Sandnes
Bryne
Nærbø

Shetland Is.
Yell
Unst
Fetlar
Foula
Mainland
Lerwick
Fair Isle

Orkney Is.
Westray
Sanday
Stronsay
Mainland
Kirkwall
Hoy
South
Ronaldsay

Pentland Firth
C. Wrath
Thurso
Wick
Helmsdale

Lewis
Stornoway
Harris
St. Kilda
North Uist
Benbecula
South Uist

Outer Hebrides
North Minch
Inner Hebrides

Lairg
Golspie
Ullapool
Tain
Invergordon
Dingwall
Nairn
Elgin
Buckie
Banff
Fraserburgh
Peterhead
Inverness
Huntly
Inverurie
Aberdeen

Moray Firth
North West Highlands
Skye
Rhum
Eigg
Coll
Tobermory
Mull
Oban
Barra
Mallaig
Fort William
Ben Nevis 1342
Tiree
Colonsay

SCOTLAND
Grampian Mts.
Aviemore
Spey
Dee
Don
Ballater
Stonehaven
Forfar
Montrose
Arbroath
Dundee
St. Andrews
Perth
Stirling
L. Lomond
Glenrothes
Kirkcaldy
Dunfermline
Dunbar

Colonsay
Jura
Greenock
Glasgow
Edinburgh
Paisley
Hamilton
East Kilbride
Kilmarnock
Irvine
Arran
Ayr
Campbeltown

Berwick-upon-Tweed
Southern Uplands
Galashiels
Jedburgh
Hawick
Cheviot Hills
Alnwick

NORTH
SEA

Malin Hd.
Aran I.
Buncrana
Letterkenny
Coleraine
Ballymena
Larne
Antrim
Bangor
Belfast
Londonderry
Lifford
Donegal
NORTHERN IRELAND
Omagh
Lough Neagh
Lisburn
Lurgan
Portadown
Armagh
Newry

North Channel
Firth of Clyde
Stranraer
Kirkcudbright
Dumfries
Annan
Carlisle
Hexham
Gateshead
Durham
Newcastle-upon-Tyne
South Shields
Sunderland
Hartlepool
Redcar
Darlington
Middlesbrough
Stockton-on-Tees
Scarborough

Pennines
Cumbrian Mts.
893
Whitehaven
Workington
Barrow-in-Furness
Lancaster

Bundoran
Ballina
Sligo
Leitrim
Cavan
Castleblaney
Clones
Enniskillen
Lower L. Erne
Upper L. Erne

Douglas
I. of Man
Mull of Galloway

UNITED
KINGDOM
IRISH
SEA

Bridlington
978
Harrogate
York
Beverley
Kingston upon Hull
Blackpool
Burnley
Leeds
Bradford
Preston
Blackburn
Huddersfield
Barnsley
Doncaster
Grimsby
Bolton
Rotherham
Sheffield
Lincoln
Louth
Skegness

Achill I.
L. Conn
Castlebar
Westport
Lough Mask
Connemara
Lough Corrib
Roscommon
Longford
Athlone
Lough Ree
Mullingar
Ceanannus Mor
Boyne
Drogheda
Dundalk

Galway B.
Galway
Aran Is.
Lough Derg
Ballinasloe
Birr
Tullamore
Dublin
Dun Laoghaire
Bray

Den Helder
The Wash
King's Lynn
Cromer

Texel
Alkmaar
Haarlem
NETHERLANDS
's-Gravenhage
(Den Haag)
Hoek van Holland
ROTTERDAM
Dordrecht

Ennis
Kilrush
Nenagh
Listowel
Tralee
Dingle
953
Carrantuohill
1041
Macgillycuddy's Reeks
Valencia I.
Killarney
Mallow

IRELAND
Tipperary
Thurles
Roscrea
Carlow
Kilkenny
Carrick-on-Suir
Clonmel
Waterford
Dungarvan
Youghal
Cóbh
Cork
Bandon
Kinsale
Bantry

Anglesey
Holyhead
Bangor
Colwyn Bay
Chester
Wrexham
Crewe
Snowdon 1085
Cambrian Mts.
Welshpool
Shrewsbury

Liverpool
Warrington
Manchester
Oldham
Stockport
636
Chesterfield
Mansfield
Stoke-on-Trent
Derby
Stafford
Nottingham
Trent
Grantham
Telford
Nuneaton
Leicester
Peterborough
Corby
Thetford
Norwich
Great Yarmouth
Lowestoft

Ely
Bury St. Edmunds
Cambridge
Ipswich
Felixstowe
Harwich
Colchester
Chelmsford

Vlissingen
Zeebrugge
Oostende
Antwerpen
Brugge
Gent
Mechelen
BELGIUM
BRUSSEL
(Bruxelles)

ENGLAND
BIRMINGHAM
Wolverhampton
Redditch
Worcester
Hereford
Coventry
Rugby
Northampton
Milton Keynes
Bedford
Luton
Stevenage
Harlow
Hemel Hempstead

Pwllheli
Cardigan Bay
Aberystwyth
WALES
Carmarthen
886
Brecon
Merthyr Tydfil
Neath
Cardiff
Newport
Cheltenham
Gloucester
Cwmbran
Cotswold Hills
Oxford
High Wycombe
Watford
Slough
LONDON
Thames
Reading
Basingstoke
Chatham
Southend-on-Sea
Margate
Canterbury
Maidstone
Dover
Folkestone

Lianelli
Swansea
Port Talbot
Rhondda
Barry
Weston-super-Mare
Bath
Bristol
Swindon
Newbury
Guildford
Reigate
Crawley
Ashford
Str. of Dover

St. George's Channel
Fishguard
Haverfordwest
Milford Haven
Pembroke

Bristol Channel
Exmoor
Barnstaple
Taunton
Yeovil
Salisbury
Winchester
Fareham
Havant
Worthing
Brighton
Hastings
Eastbourne

Dunkerque
Calais
Gris Nez
Boulogne-sur-Mer
FRANCE
St-Omer
Béthune
Bruay-la-Buissière
Lens
Lille
Roubaix
Tourcoing
Villeneuve-d'Ascq
Valenciennes
Cambrai

CELTIC
SEA

Bude
Newquay
618
Dartmoor
Exeter
Exmouth
Torbay
Torquay
Plymouth
Southampton
Bournemouth
Poole
Weymouth
Newport
Isle of Wight
Portsmouth

English Channel
Le Tréport
Dieppe
Abbeville
Amiens
St-Quentin
Picardie
Pays de Caux
Fécamp
Rouen
Seine

Newquay
Truro
St. Austell
Falmouth
Penzance
Land's End
Isles of Scilly

Alderney
C. de la Hague
Pte. de Barfleur
Cherbourg
Valognes
Trouville-sur-Mer
Bolbec
Le Havre
Elbeuf
Lisieux

Guernsey
St. Peter Port
Sark
Channel Is.
(U.K.)
St. Helier
Jersey

Cotentin
Bayeux
Caen

16

20

ft   m
3000   1000
1500   500
600   200
0
0
50   150
100   300
200   600
500   1500
1000   3000
2000   6000
m   ft

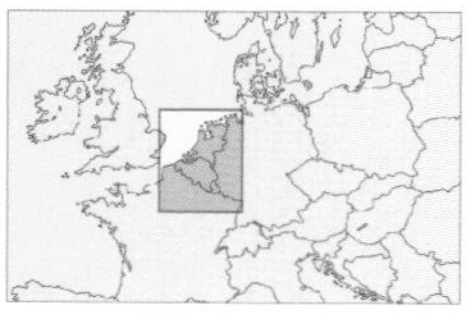

1:2 500 000

10 0 10 20 30 40 50 60 70 80 90 km
10 0 10 20 30 40 50 60 miles

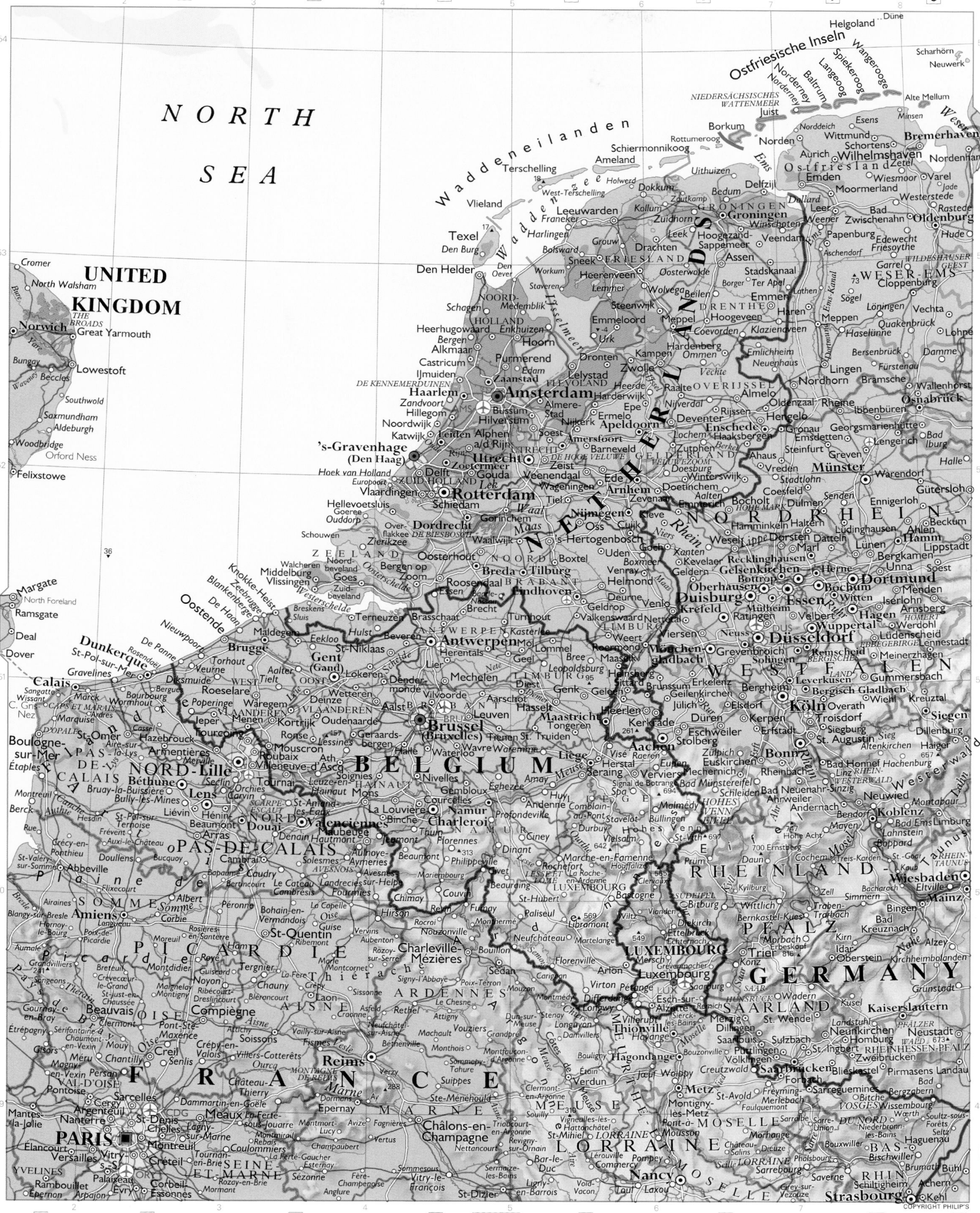

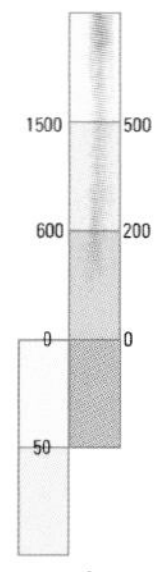

NORTH SEA

UNITED KINGDOM

Cromer · North Walsham · The Broads · Great Yarmouth · Norwich · Bungay · Beccles · Lowestoft · Southwold · Saxmundham · Aldeburgh · Woodbridge · Orford Ness · Felixstowe · Margate · North Foreland · Ramsgate · Deal · Dover

NETHERLANDS

Waddeneilanden · Terschelling · West-Terschelling · Vlieland · Texel · Den Burg · Den Helder · Schagen · Alkmaar · Haarlem · Amsterdam · Leeuwarden · Franeker · Harlingen · Bolsward · Sneek · Heerenveen · Groningen · Assen · Zwolle · Lelystad · Hoorn · Purmerend · Zaanstad · Hilversum · Utrecht · 's-Gravenhage (Den Haag) · Delft · Rotterdam · Schiedam · Dordrecht · Gouda · Leiden · Zoetermeer · Vlaardingen · Hoek van Holland · Breda · Tilburg · Eindhoven · 's-Hertogenbosch · Nijmegen · Arnhem · Apeldoorn · Deventer · Enschede · Hengelo · Almelo · Emmen · Middelburg · Vlissingen · Bergen op Zoom · Roosendaal · Oosterhout · Venlo · Roermond · Helmond · Weert · Maastricht · Heerlen

BELGIUM

Oostende · Brugge · Gent (Gand) · Antwerpen · Brussel (Bruxelles) · Mechelen · Leuven · Hasselt · Genk · Tongeren · Kortrijk · Ieper · Roeselare · Mons · Charleroi · Namur · La Louvière · Nivelles · Waterloo · Tournai · Liège · Verviers · Dinant · Bastogne · Arlon

LUXEMBOURG

Luxembourg · Esch-sur-Alzette · Diekirch · Ettelbruck

GERMANY

Bremerhaven · Oldenburg · Emden · Wilhelmshaven · Osnabrück · Münster · Dortmund · Bochum · Essen · Duisburg · Düsseldorf · Köln · Bonn · Aachen · Mönchengladbach · Krefeld · Wuppertal · Hagen · Siegen · Koblenz · Wiesbaden · Mainz · Kaiserslautern · Saarbrücken · Trier

NORDRHEIN-WESTFALEN · RHEINLAND-PFALZ · SAARLAND

FRANCE

Calais · Dunkerque · Boulogne-sur-Mer · St-Omer · Lille · Roubaix · Tourcoing · Valenciennes · Douai · Lens · Béthune · Arras · Cambrai · Amiens · Abbeville · Beauvais · Compiègne · St-Quentin · Laon · Soissons · Reims · Châlons-en-Champagne · Épernay · Charleville-Mézières · Sedan · Verdun · Metz · Thionville · Nancy · Strasbourg · Paris · Versailles · Créteil

NORD · PAS-DE-CALAIS · PICARDIE · SOMME · OISE · AISNE · ARDENNES · MARNE · MEUSE · MOSELLE · LORRAINE · VOSGES · ALSACE · SEINE-ET-MARNE · YVELINES

National Parks

Underlined towns give their name to the administrative area in which they stand.

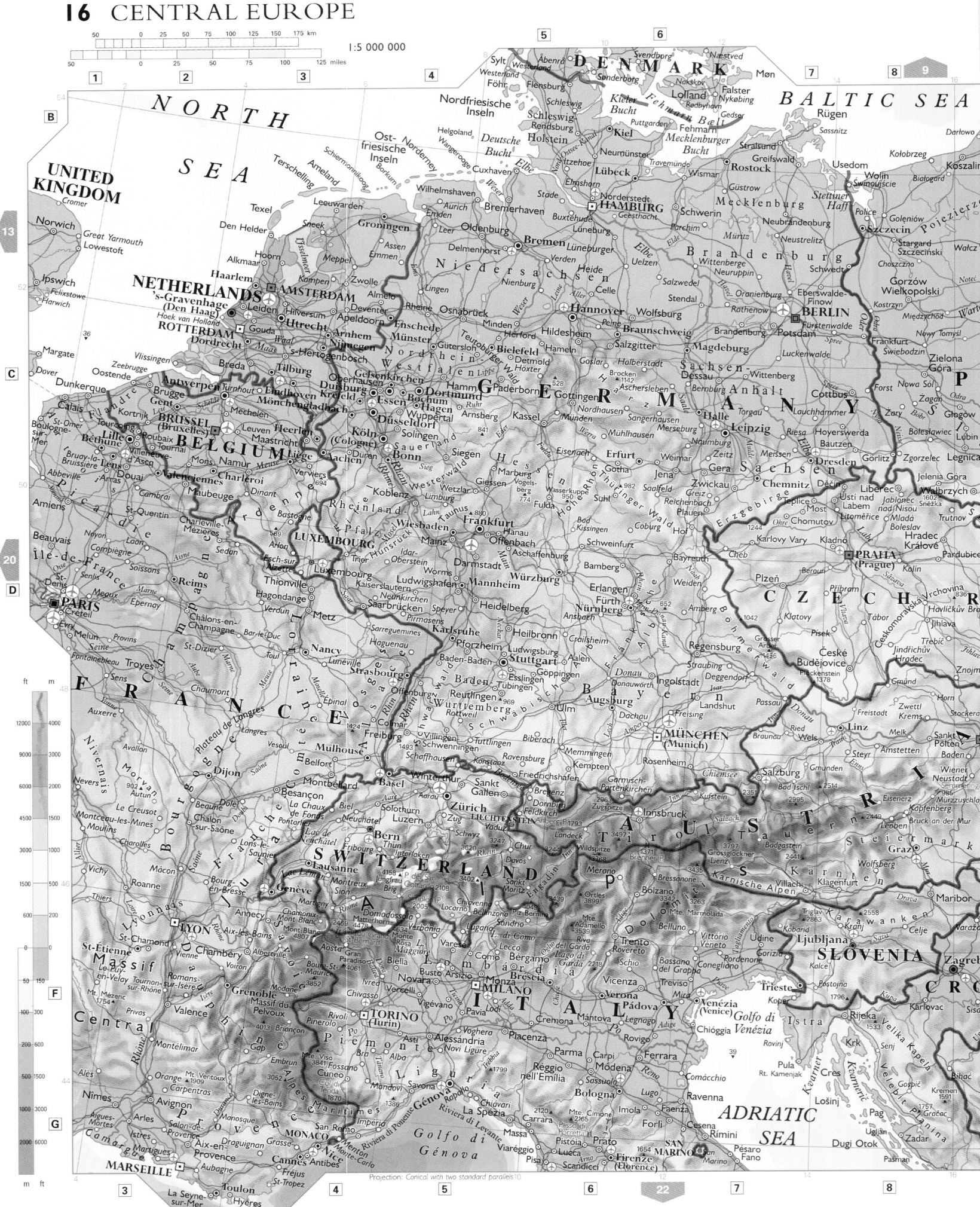

1:5 000 000

50   0   25   50   75   100   125   150   175 km
50   0   25   50   75   100   125 miles

1 **2** **3** **4** **5** **6** **7** **8** **9**

B

N O R T H

S E A

DENMARK

BALTIC SEA

UNITED
KINGDOM

13

NETHERLANDS

G E R M A N Y

C

BELGIUM

P

20

D

LUXEMBOURG

C Z E C H

F R A N C E

F

SWITZERLAND

A U S T R I A

SLOVENIA

G

I T A L Y

CRO

ADRIATIC

SEA

Projection: Conical with two standard parallels

3 **4** **5** **6** **22** **7** **8**

ft   m
12000 4000
9000   3000
6000   2000
4500   1500
3000   1000
1500   500
600   200
0   0

150
300
600
1500
3000
6000

m ft

Zatoka
Gdańska
Baltiysk
Polessk
Prienai
Vilnius
Marijampolė
LITHUANIA
Varėna
Druskininkai

Słupsk
Wejherowo
Rumia
Lębork
Gdynia
Sopot
Gdańsk
Bytów
Tczew
Elbląg
Gwardeysk
Chernyakhovsk
Gusev
Zalew
Wiślany
Kaliningrad (Russia)
Branievo
Bagrationovsk
Lyna
Kętrzyn
Giżycko Suwałki
Augustów
Sokółka
Hrodna
Marijampolė
Ashmyany Vileyka
Smarhon
Maładzyechna
Barysaw
Krupki
Shklow
Dniapro
Mstsislaw
Nyoman
342
Zhodzina
Volozhyn
MINSK
346
Cherven
Chervyen
BELARUS
Krychaw
Cherykaw
Bykhaw
Slawharad

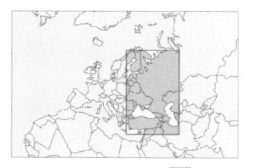

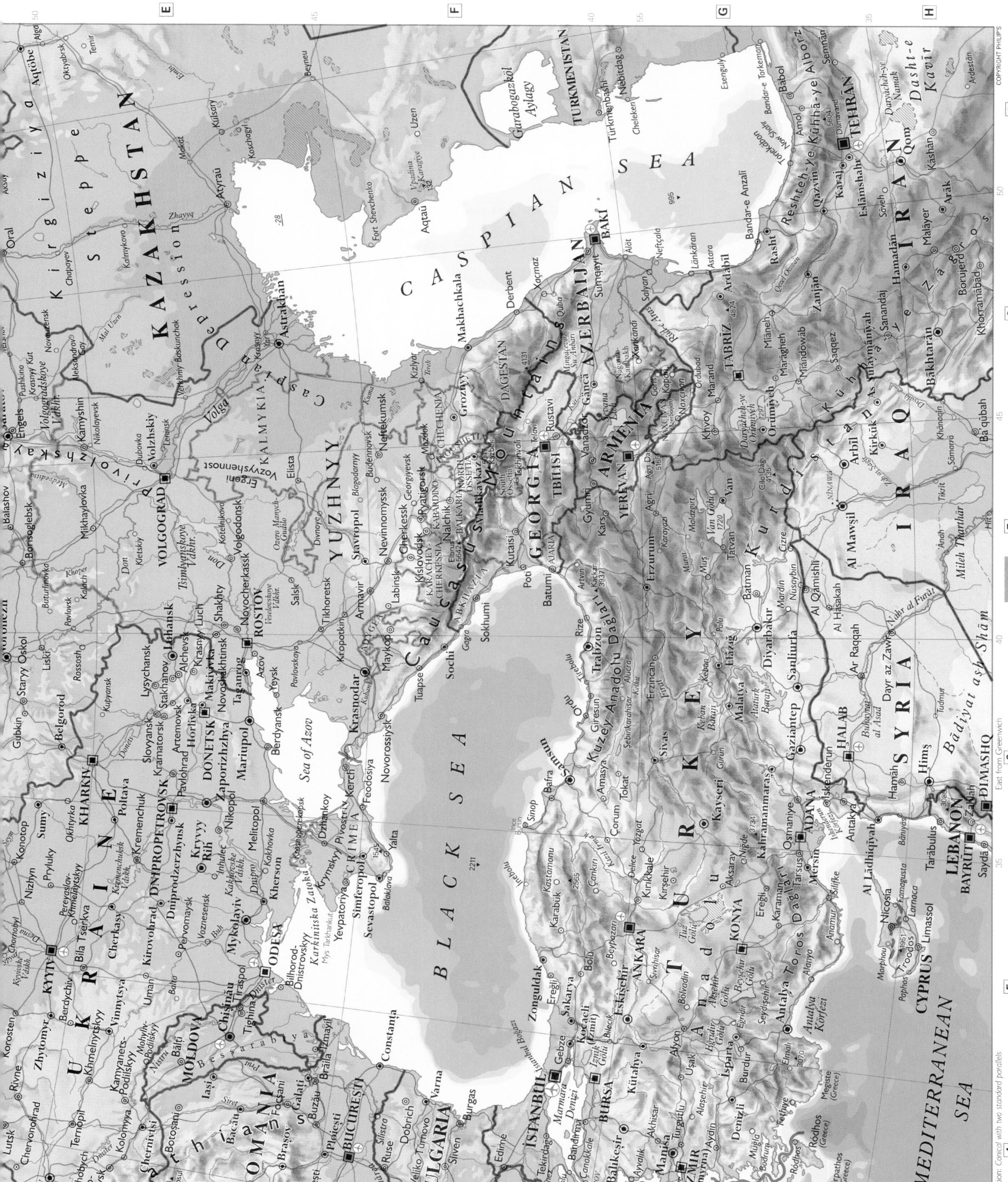
CASPIAN SEA
BLACK SEA
Sea of Azov
MEDITERRANEAN SEA
KAZAKHSTAN
UKRAINE
ROMANIA
BULGARIA
MOLDOVA
GEORGIA
ARMENIA
AZERBAIJAN
TURKEY
SYRIA
IRAQ
IRAN
CYPRUS
LEBANON
TURKMENISTAN
Caucasus Mountains
Caspian Depression
CRIMEA
KYYIV
ODESA
KHARKIV
DONETSK
DNIPROPETROVSK
VOLGOGRAD
ROSTOV
BUCUREŞTI
CHIŞINĂU
ISTANBUL
ANKARA
İZMIR
BURSA
KONYA
ADANA
TBILISI
YEREVAN
BAKI
TEHRĀN
TABRĪZ
ḤALAB
DIMASHQ
BAYRŪT
Projection: Conical with two standard parallels
East from Greenwich
COPYRIGHT PHILIP'S

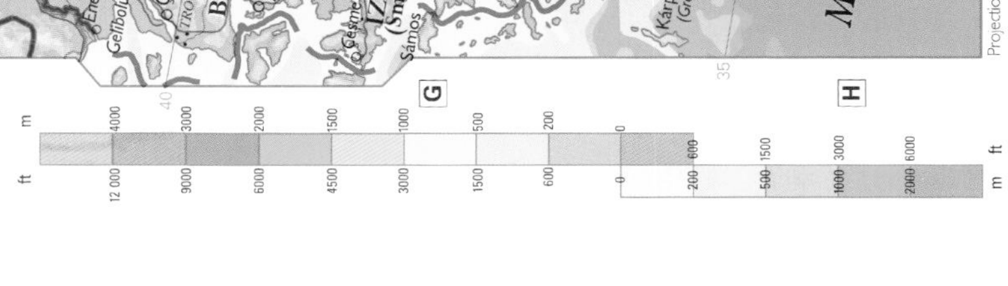
m
ft
4000
3000
2000
1500
1000
500
200
0
12 000
9000
6000
4500
3000
1500
600
0
200
600
500
1500
1000
3000
2000
6000

1:5 000 000

50 0 25 50 75 100 125 150 175 km

50 0 25 50 75 100 125 miles

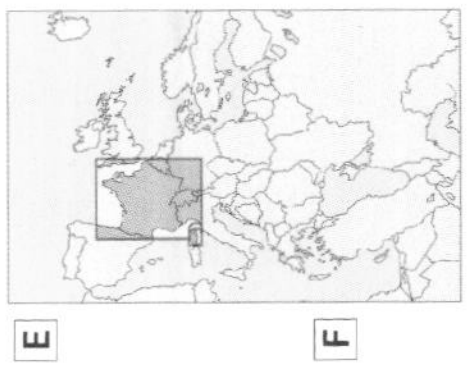

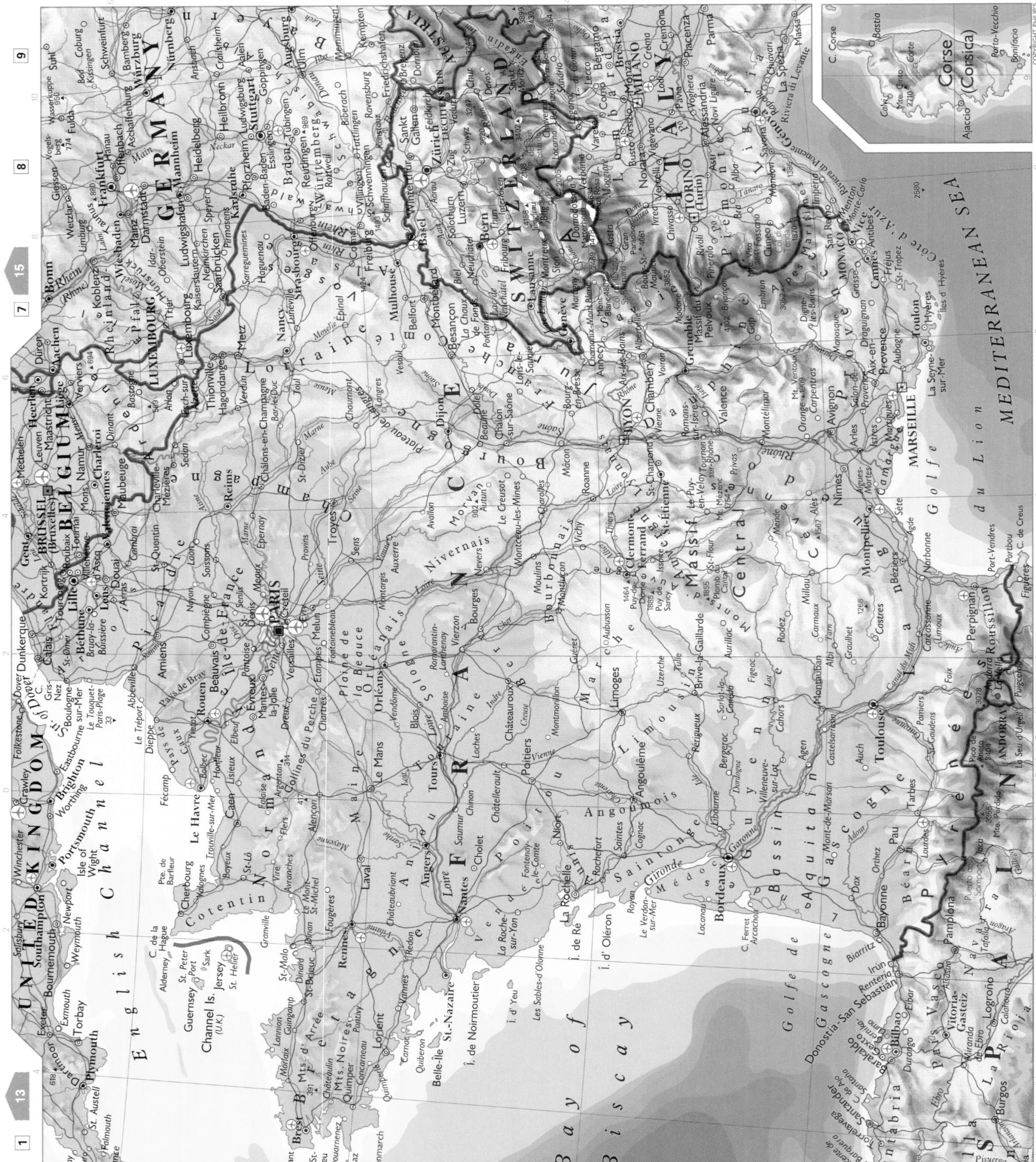

GERMANY

BELGIUM

LUXEMBOURG

SWITZERLAND

ITALY

UNITED KINGDOM

FRANCE

SPAIN

ANDORRA

MONACO

PARIS

BRUSSEL (Bruxelles)

MEDITERRANEAN SEA

Bay of Biscay

English Channel

Corse (Corsica)

East from Greenwich

West from Greenwich

Projection: Conical with two standard parallels

m ft
4000 12000
3000 9000
2000 6000
1500 4500
1000 3000
600 2000
200 600
0 0

1:5 000 000

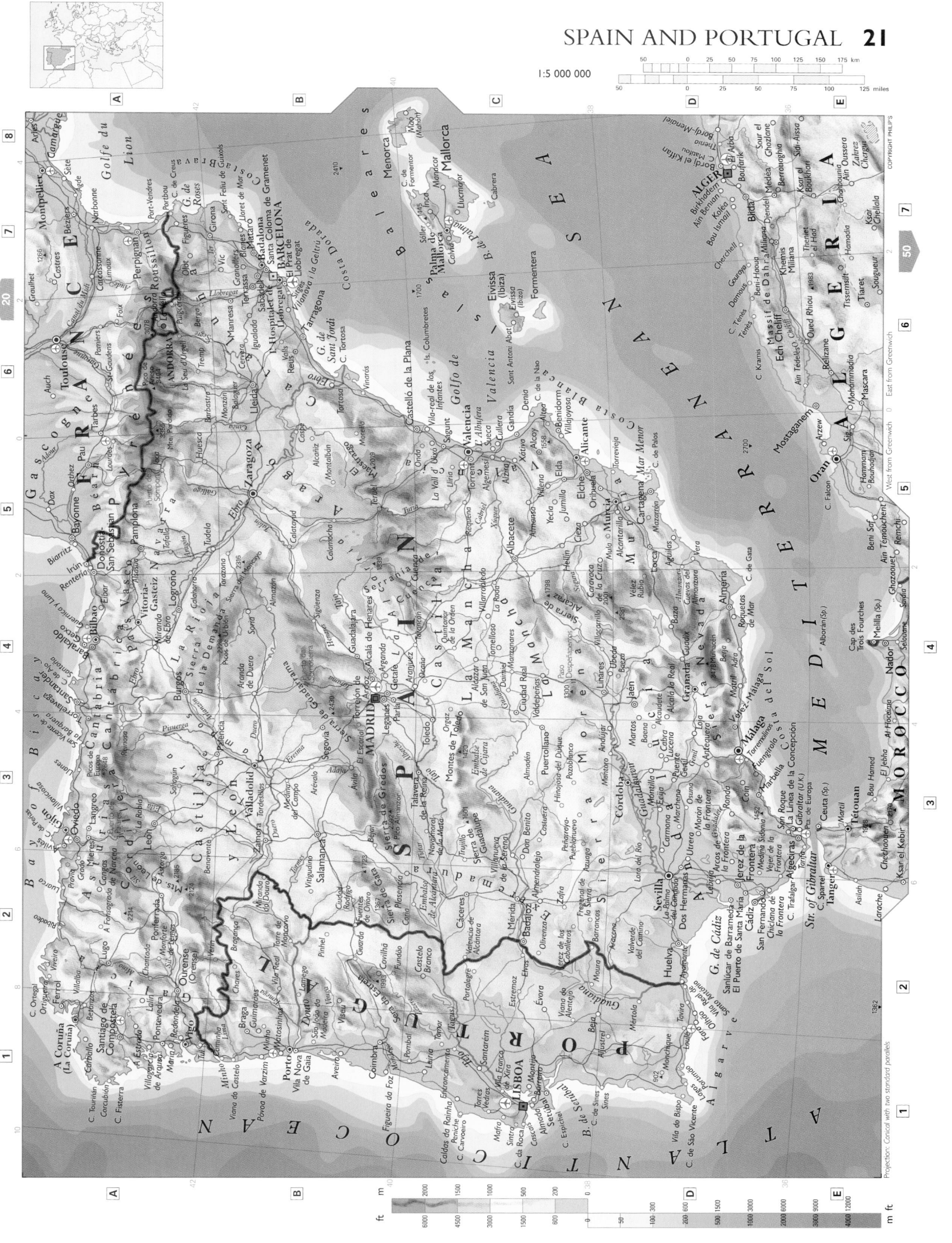

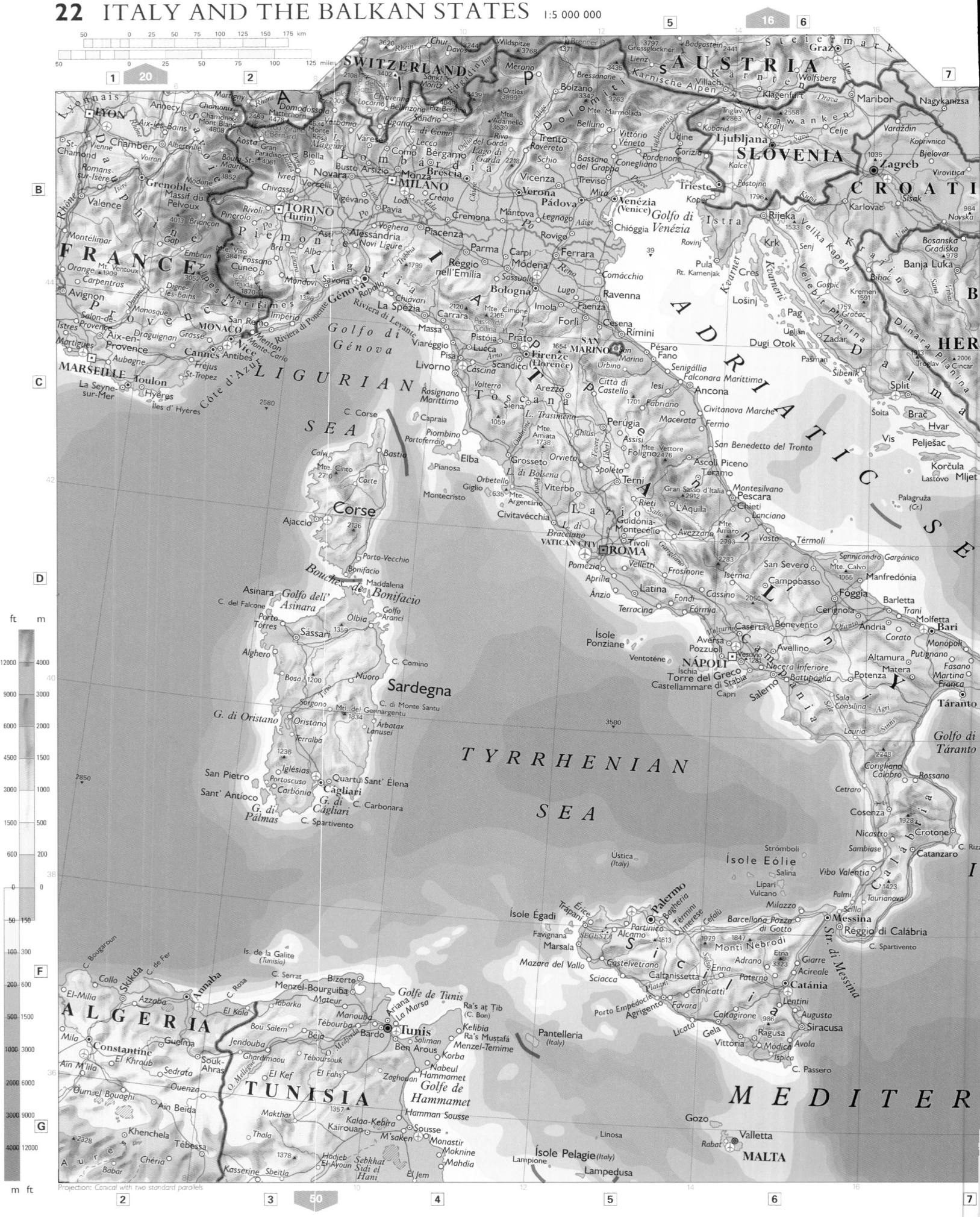

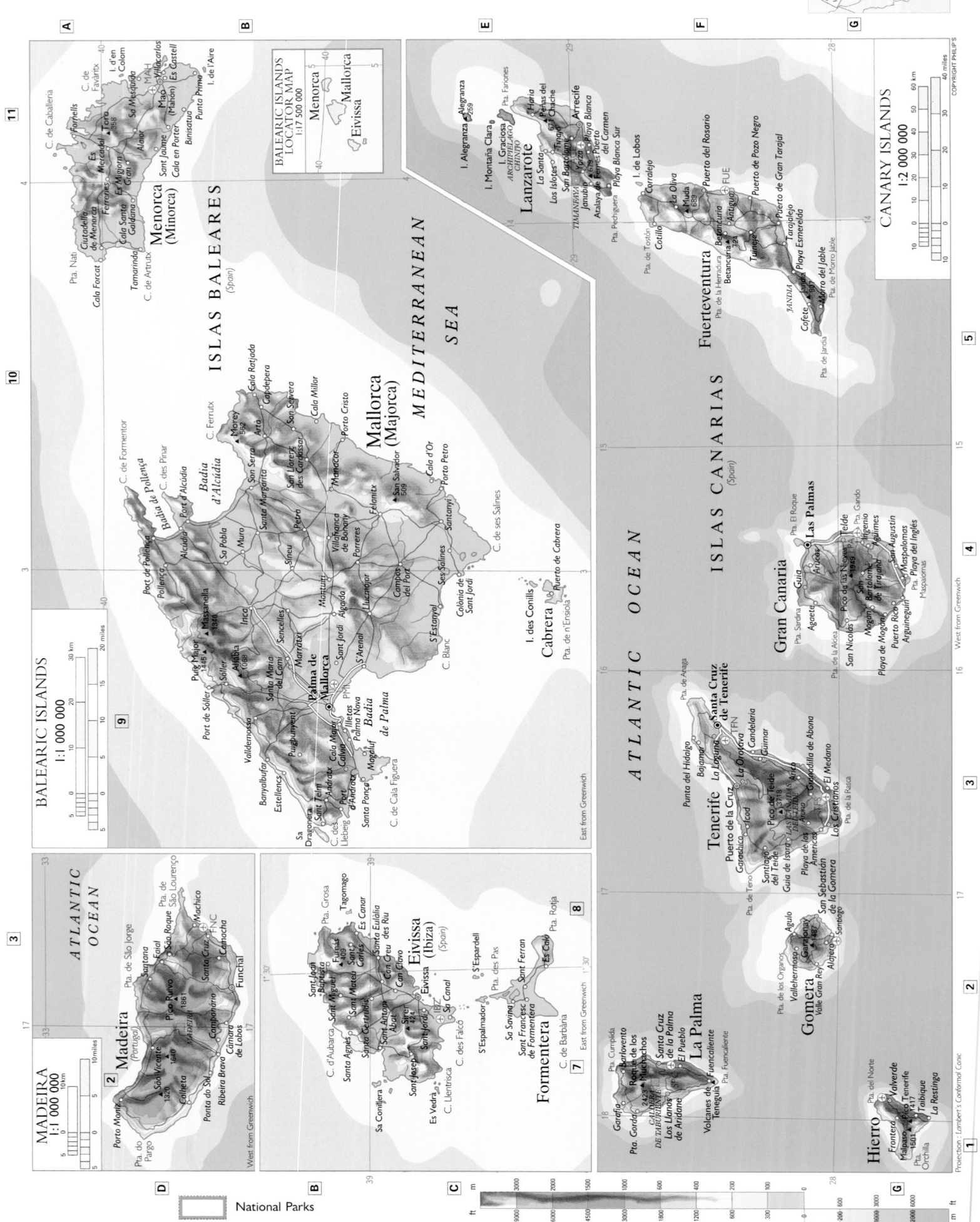

ISLAS BALEARES *(Spain)*

Menorca (Minorca)

MEDITERRANEAN SEA

Mallorca (Majorca)

Badia d'Alcúdia

Palma de Mallorca

Badia de Palma

Cabrera

ATLANTIC OCEAN

ISLAS CANARIAS *(Spain)*

Lanzarote

Fuerteventura

Gran Canaria

Las Palmas

Tenerife

Santa Cruz de Tenerife

Gomera

La Palma

Hierro

ATLANTIC OCEAN

Madeira *(Portugal)*

Funchal

Eivissa (Ibiza) *(Spain)*

Formentera

BALEARIC ISLANDS LOCATOR MAP 1:17 500 000

Menorca

Eivissa

BALEARIC ISLANDS 1:1 000 000

MADEIRA 1:1 000 000

CANARY ISLANDS 1:2 000 000

National Parks

Projection: Lambert's Conformal Conic

COPYRIGHT PHILIP'S

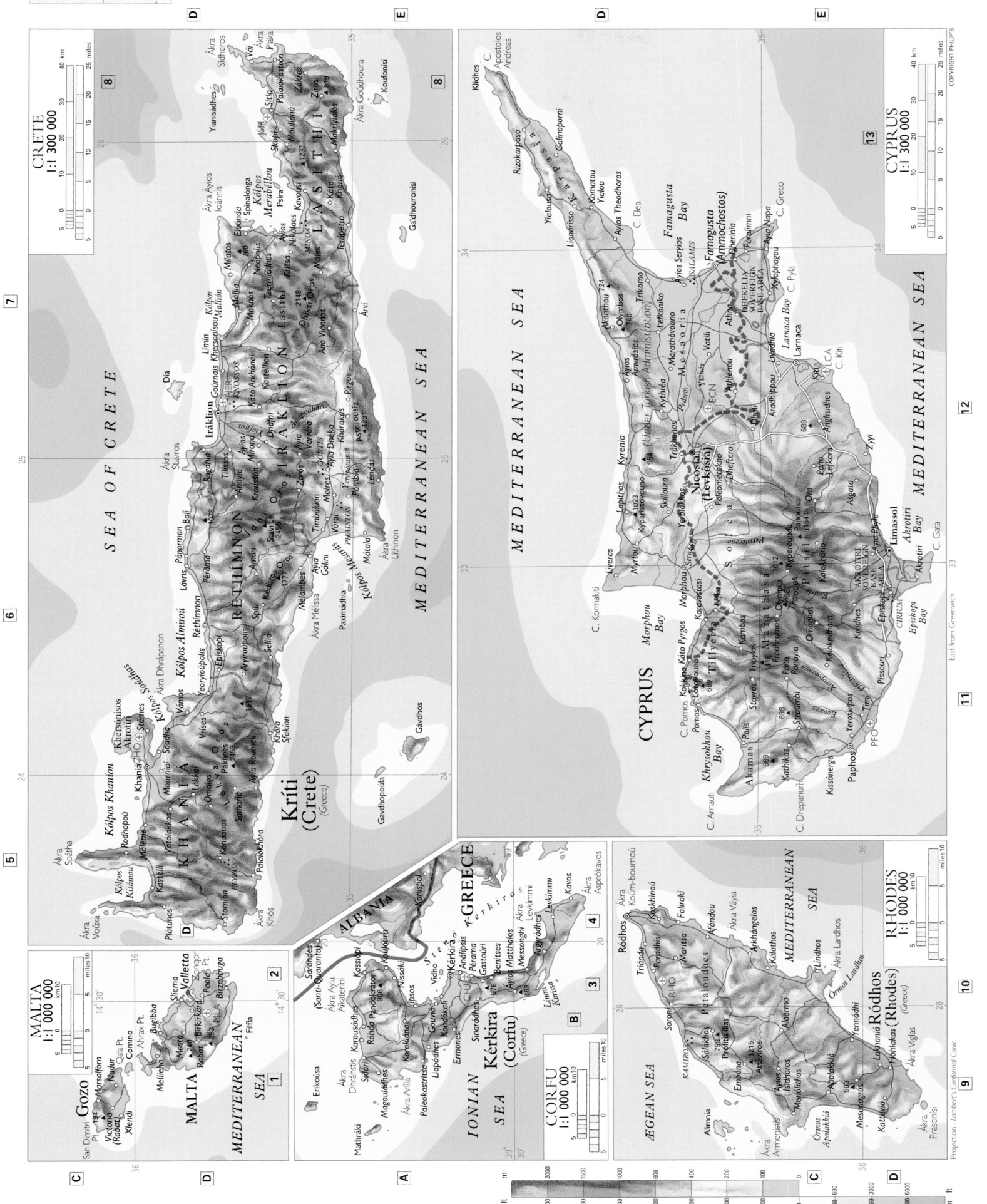

1:50 000 000

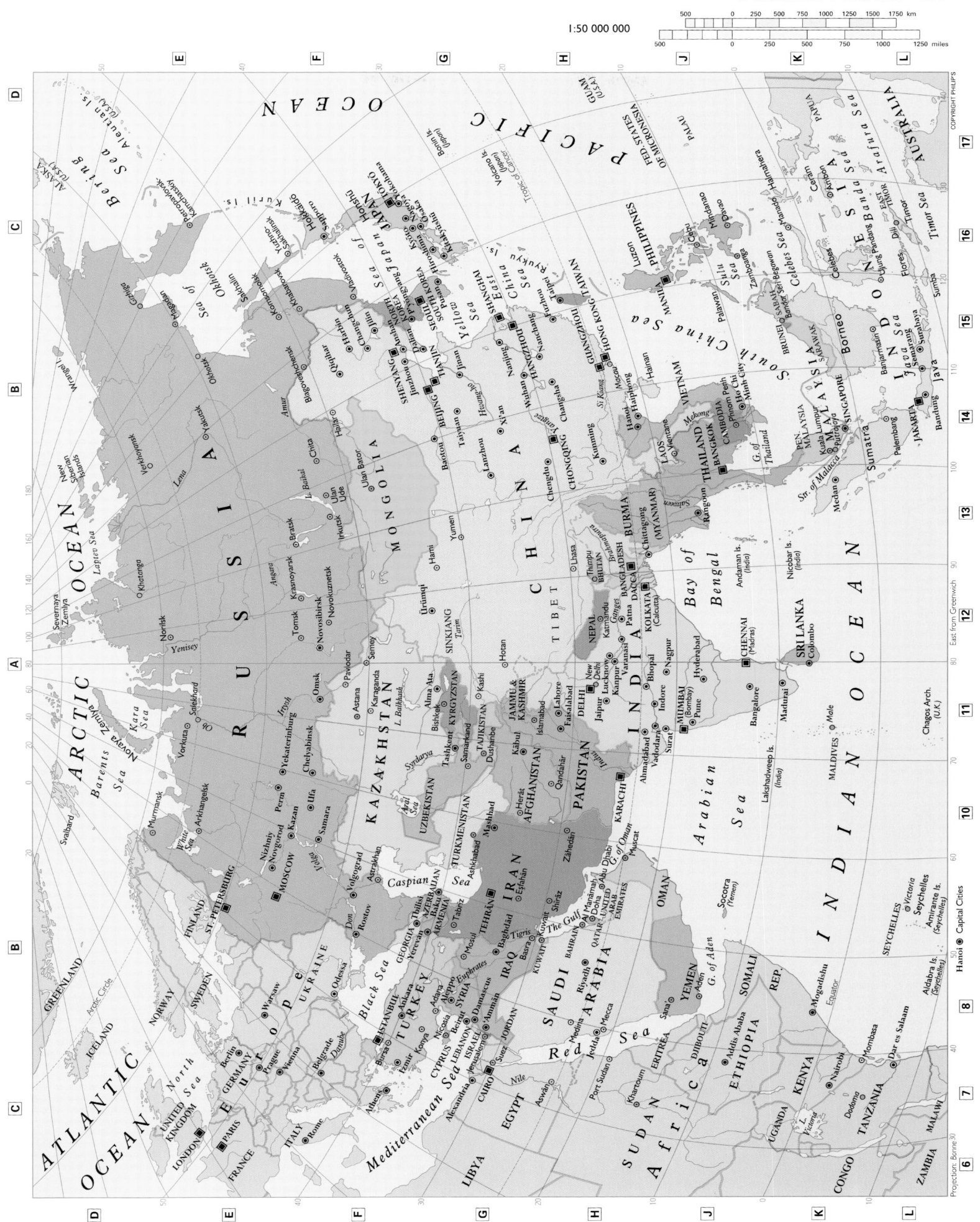

1:50 000 000

Projection Bonne

COPYRIGHT PHILIP'S

1:20 000 000

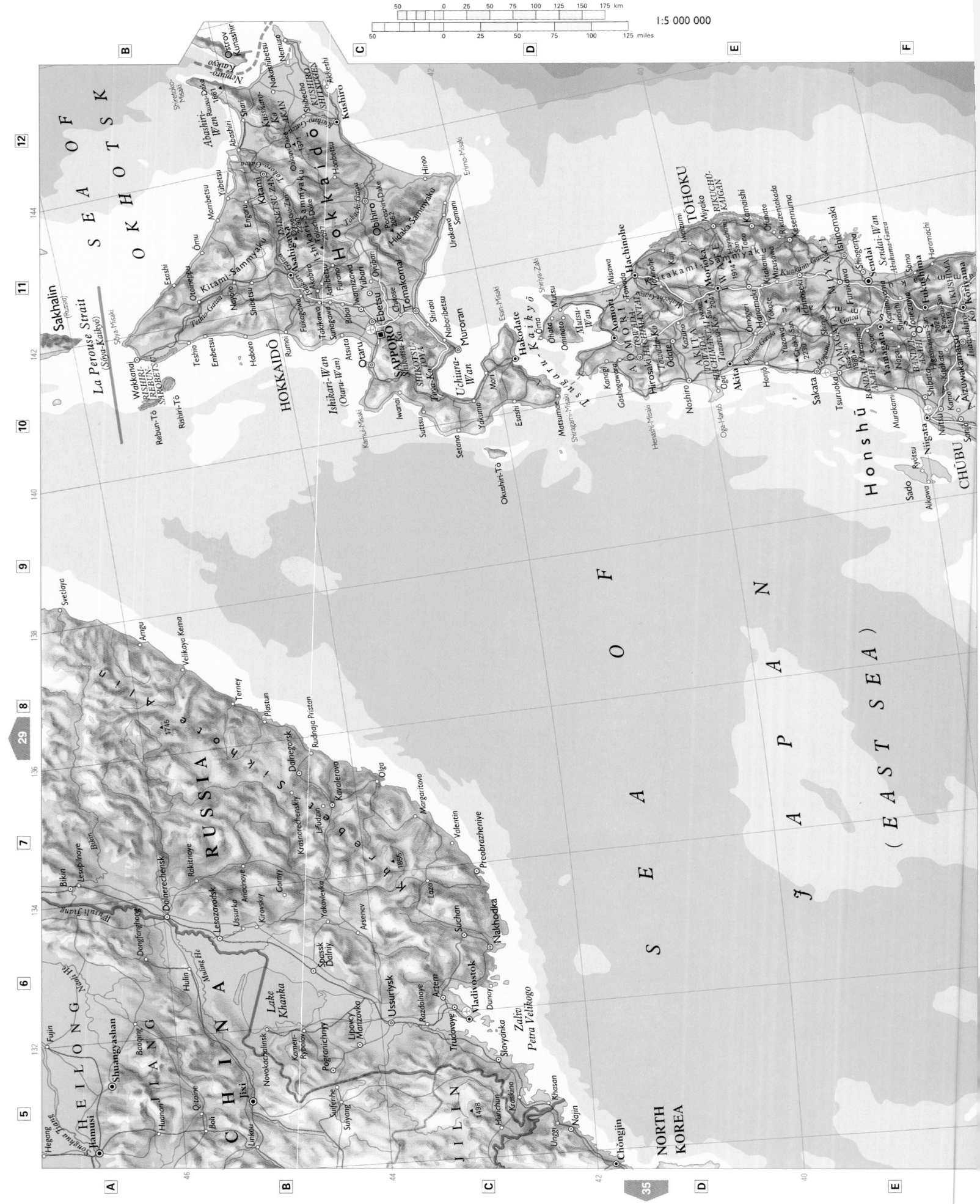

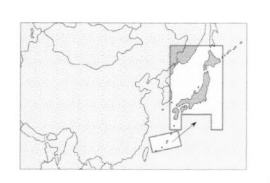

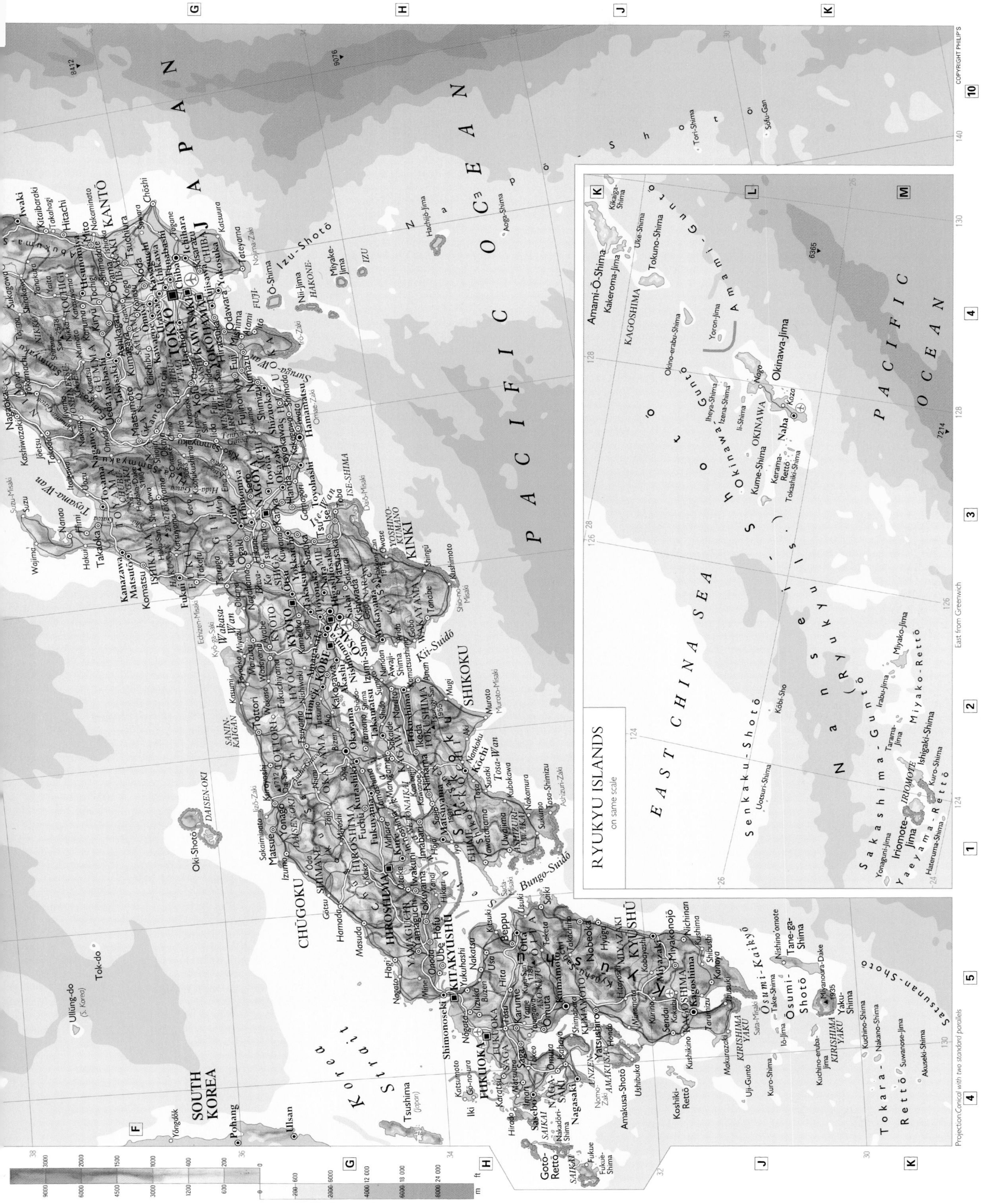

RYUKYU ISLANDS
on same scale

Projection: Conical with two standard parallels

East from Greenwich

1:15 000 000

Projection: Bonne

East from Greenwich

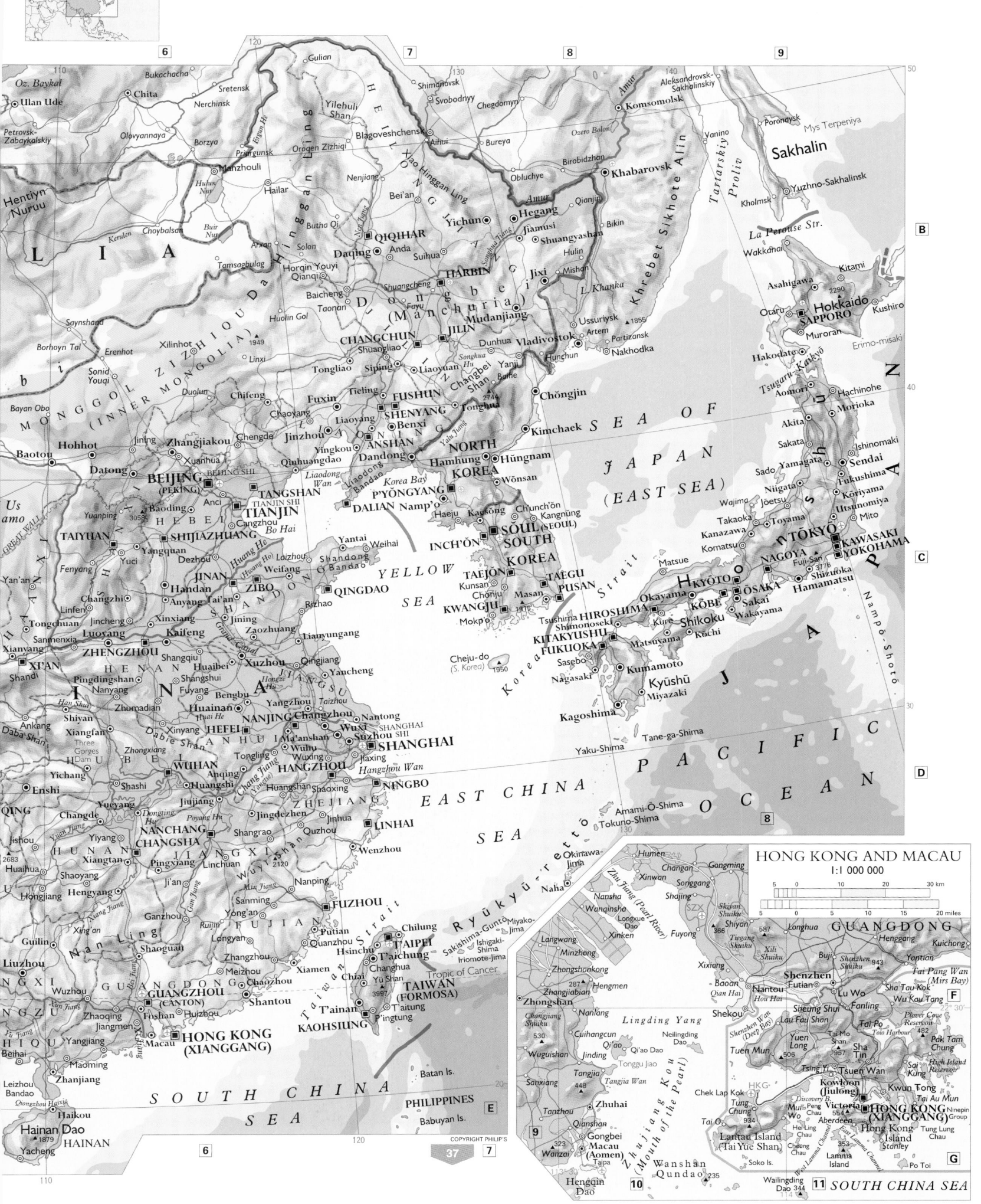

HONG KONG AND MACAU
1:1 000 000

SOUTH CHINA SEA

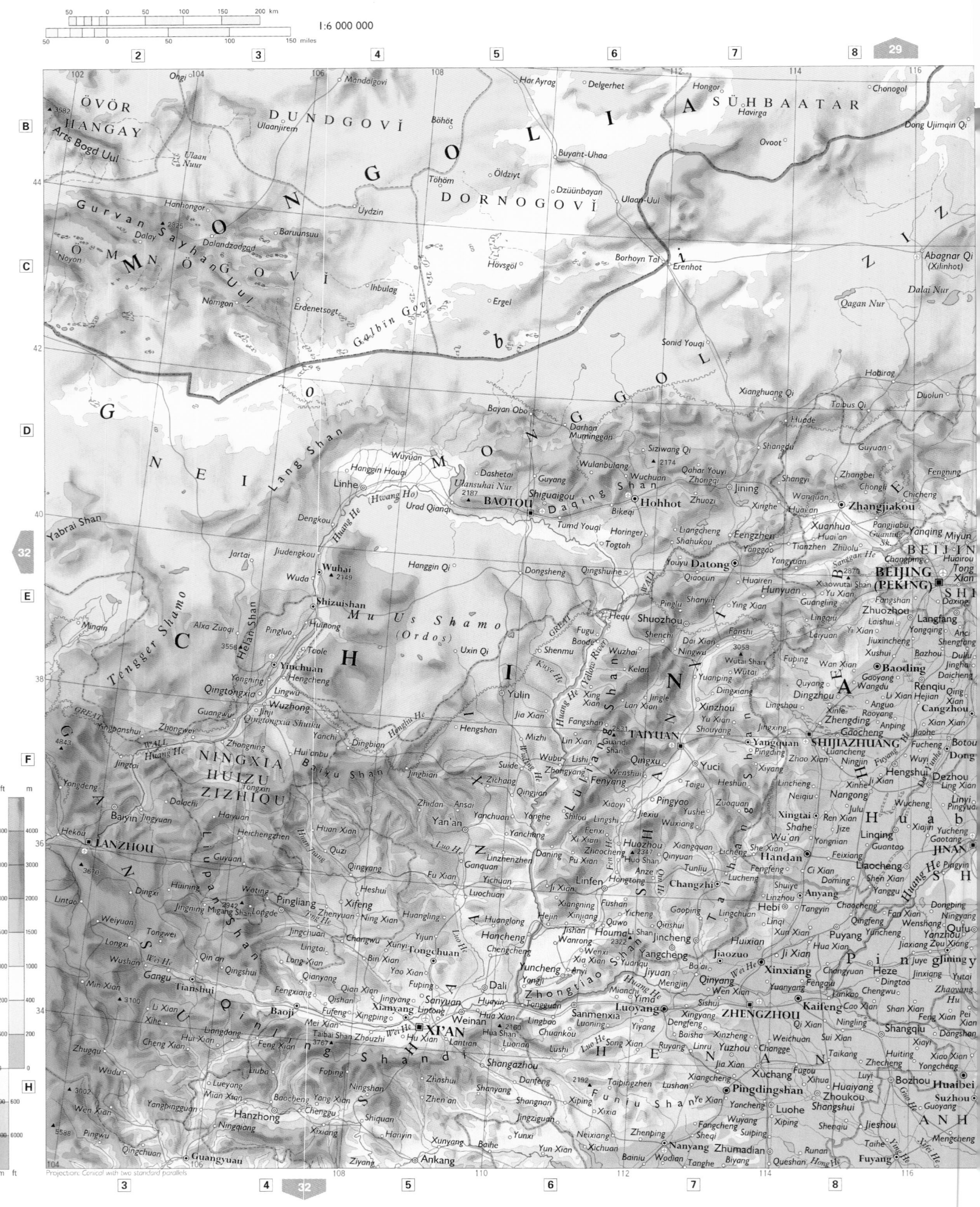

Horqin Youyi Qianqi (Ulanhot)
Baicheng
Zhenlai
HARBIN
Bin Xian
Yanshou
Linkou
Jixi
Turiy Rog
Lake Khanka

B

Hulingol
Hulin He
Da'an
Maoxing
Zhuanghe
Shuangcheng
Acheng
Shangzhi
Hengdaohezi
Maqiaohe
Pogranichnyy
Golenki

Taonan
Tuquan
Anguang
Oqan Nur Qian Gorlos
Qian an
Fuyu
Beitaolaizhao
Sanchahe
Lalin He
Wuchang
Yimianpo
Muling
Xiachengzi
Suiyang
Suifenhe

B

Jarud Qi
Shenjingzi
Tongyu
Kaoshan
Yushu
Shanhetun
Hailin
Ning'an
Dongning

Bairin Zuoqi
1949
Zhanyu
Beizhengzhen
Dehui
Fulaerji
Nong'an
Jiutai
Gangyao
Wulajie
Shulan
Dongjingcheng
Luozigou
Razdolnoye
Artem

44

Linxi
2029 Hexigten Qi
Kailu
Tongliao
Horqin Zuoyi Zhongqi
Maolin
Huaidezhen
CHANGCHUN
JILIN
Jiaohe
Jingpo Hu
Dunhua
Daxinggou
Wangqing
Mingyuegou
Yanji
Longjing
Vladivostok
Slavyanka

C

Bairin Youqi
Xar Moron He
Shuangliao
Lishu
Gongzhuling
Yitong
Shuangyang
Panshi
Huadian
Antu
Helong
Tumen
Hunchun

C

Ongniud Qi
Linhe He
Xiawa
Hure Qi
Bamiancheng
Siping
Liaoyuan
Dongfeng
Huinan
Baishan
Baihe
1677
Paektu-san 2744
Nanam
Chuuronjang

2020
Chifeng
Wutonghaolai
Kangping
Xifeng
Meihekou
Shanchengzhen
Qingyuan
Jingyu
Fusong
Changbai
Linjiang
Hoeryong
Musan
Puryong
Chŏngjin
Kyŏngsŏng

42

Heishui
Kaiyuan
Tiefa
Tieling
Liuhe
Hunjiang
Chunggang-ŭp
Ondaejin

Weichang
Fuxin
Xinlitun
Xinmin
Faku
Qingyuan
Tonghua
Irhyangdong
Musudan

1885
Beipiao
Qinghemen
Heishan
Xinbin
Huch'ang
Inpundong
Kasan-dong
Hyesan
Hapsu
Simpungdong
Kilchu

Chaoyang
Jinzhou
Liaozhong
SHENYANG
FUSHUN
Qingchengzi
Huanten
1846
Ji'an
Manp'o
Kanggye
Kapsan
Kilchu

D

Ningcheng
Beizhen
Liaoyang
Benxi
Anping Tianshifu
Kuup-tong
Ch'osan
Pungsan
2522
Ch'ail-bong
Kosŏngni
Kimch'aek (Songjin)

D

Longhua
Lingyuan
Panjin
ANSHAN
Haicheng
Lianshanguan
Pyŏktong
Koin-dong
Changjin-chosu
Kwangdaeri
Changhŭngni
Tanch'ŏn

Chengde
Pingquan
Jinxi
Niuzhuang
Kuandian
Supung Shuiku
Sakchu
Changjin
Pukch'ŏng
Sinch'ang

Luanne
Jianchang
Huludao
Xingcheng
Dashiqiao
Fengcheng
Cao He
Pyŏktong
Taegwan
Kujang
Sinhŭng
Sŏhori

30

Liugou
Shangbancheng
Kuancheng
Xingcheng
Yingkou
Gaizhou
Xiuyan
Gushan
Pukchin
Chŏngju Pakch'ŏn
Tŏkch'ŏn
Hamhŭng
Hŭngnam
Tongch'ŏn-ni

40

Mixun
Xinglong
Liaodong
Wanfu 1131
Buyun Shan
Donggou
Yongamp'o
Sinŭiju
Kusŏng
Anju
Oro
Sinp'o

G.Shuiku
Zunhua
Qinhuangdao
Wan
Dandong
Chŏngju
Chŏngju Pakch'ŏn
Sunch'ŏn
Yŏnghŭng
Sinch'ang

Sanhe
Fengrun Lulong
Funing
Liaodong Bandao
Yalu Jiang
Sŏnch'ŏn
Sukch'ŏn
Songch'ŏn
Tongch'ŏn-ni

Yutian Baodi
Luan Xian
Changli
Pikou
Sukch'ŏn
Munch'ŏn
Wŏnsan

E

TANGSHAN
Leting
Wafangdian
Zhuanghe
NORTH
Yŏnghŭng
Anbyŏn

E

TIANJIN SHI
Wuqing
Pulandian
Sunan
Kangdong
Songch'ŏn
SEA OF

Yangliuqing Hangu
Jin Xian
Lüshun
DALIAN
Korea
P'YŎNGYANG
Chunghwa
Songnim
Kowŏn
Munch'ŏn
Singosan
Kosŏng

TIANJIN
Tanggu
Bay
Namp'o
Songnim
Koksan
Sepo-ri
1638
Changdo-ri
Kansŏng

Dagu
Oikou
Miaodao Qundao
Sariwŏn
Pyŏngsan
Chiha-ri
Kŭmhwa
Hwach'ŏn
1578
Sokch'o
Yangyang

JAPAN

Huanghua
Cho-do
Chaeryŏng
Sinmak
Nam-ch'ŏn
Ch'ŏrwŏn
Hŏngsŏng
Chumunjin

38

Yanshan
Changyŏn
Haeju
Kaesŏng
Panmunjŏm
Ch'unch'ŏn
Hongch'ŏn
Kangnŭng

(EAST SEA)

guang Wudi
Zhanhua
Huang He
Penglai
Longkou
Daxindian
Paengnyŏng-do (S. Korea)
Ongjin
Yŏnan
Munsan
Ŭijŏngbu
Ch'unch'ŏn
Hongch'ŏn
Tonghae
Samch'ŏk

Deping
Huimin
Qingyun
Yantai
Ŭijŏngbu
SŎUL
Songnam
Hoengsŏng
Ullŭng-do (S. Korea)

Shanghe
Binzhou
Dongying
Laizhou Wan
Huang Xian
Fushan
Muping
Weihai
Kanghwa
Puch'ŏn
INCH'ŎN
Anyang
Wŏnju
Yŏngwol

F

Qingcheng
Gaoyuan
Guangrao
Zhaoyuan
Qixia
Wendeng
Chengshan Jiao
Ansan
Suwŏn
Osan
Ch'ungju
Chech'ŏn
Yŏngju
Ulchin

F

Zhoucun
Huantai Linzi
Shouguang
Changyi
Pingdu
Laiyang
Rushan
923
SOUTH
P'yŏngt'aek
Ch'onan
Ŭmsŏng
Koesan
Mun'gyŏng
Andong
Yŏngdŏk

ZIBO
Yidu
Weifang
Laixi
Nanhuang
Shidao
Sŏsan
KOREA
Ch'ŏngju
Yech'ŏn
Uisŏng
Chŏngha P'ohang

Tai Shan
Boshan
Fangzi
Jiaozhou
Haiyang
Anmyŏn-do
Taejŏn-ni
Nonsan
Sangju
Kimch'ŏn
Kyŏngju

36

1524
Laiwu
Zhucheng
Jimo
Chengyang
Hongsŏng
Kongju
TAEJŎN
Sŏnsan
Kumi
Changgi-Ap

Tai'an
Lingu
Anqiu
Gaomi
Lancun
Kŏnggyŏng
Yŏngdong
Waegwan
Yŏngch'ŏn
Kyŏngju

Xintai
Yishui
Wulian
Jiaozhou Wan
QINGDAO
Kunsan
Iri
Chŏnju
TAEGU
Ch'ŏngdo
Ulsan

Mengyin
Ju Xian
Liangcheng
Kochang
Koryŏng
Miryang

Pingyi
Tangtou
Puan
Chŏngŭp
Namwŏn
Chin-san
Chinju
Masan Kimhae
Tongnae

G

guan
Fei Xian
Rizhao
Shijiusuo
Sagŏ-ri
Tamyang
1915
Ch'angwŏn
PUSAN

G

Linyi
Ganyu
Andongwei
Namwŏn
Sŏngjŏng-ni
KWANGJU
Hadong
Samch'ŏnp'o
Ch'ungmu

Zaozhuang
Tancheng
Lianyungang
Haizhou Wan
Chabyŏng
Naju
Sunch'ŏn
Posŏng
Yŏsu
Tsushima

Weishan
Hanzhuang
Pizhou
YELLOW SEA
(Huang Hai)
Mokp'o
Changhŭng
Haenam
Izuhara

Tengzhou
Jiawang
Xinyi
Guanyun
Chenjiagang
Hŭksan-chedo (S. Korea)
Chindo
Korea Strait

Teng Xian
Yaowan
Xiangshui
Iki
Karatsu

34

Xuzhou
Suqian
Shuyang
Guannan
Cheju
Cheju-do (S. Korea)
Onp'yŏng-ni
JAPAN

31

Shuanggou
Suining
Lianshui
Binhai
Hallim
Halla-san 1950
Sasebo
Imari

Lingbi
Huaiyin
Huai'an
Funing
Sheyang
Taejŏng
Sŏgwipo
Mosŭlp'o
Kashima
Ōmura
Isahaya

UI
Guzhen
Suzhou
Hongze Hu
Baoying
Yancheng
Nakadōri-Shima

Huaiyuan
Bengbu
Fengyang
Gaoyou Hu
Liuzhuang
Xinghua
Dongtai
Fukue-Shima
Nagasaki
Kuchinotsu

H

East from Greenwich

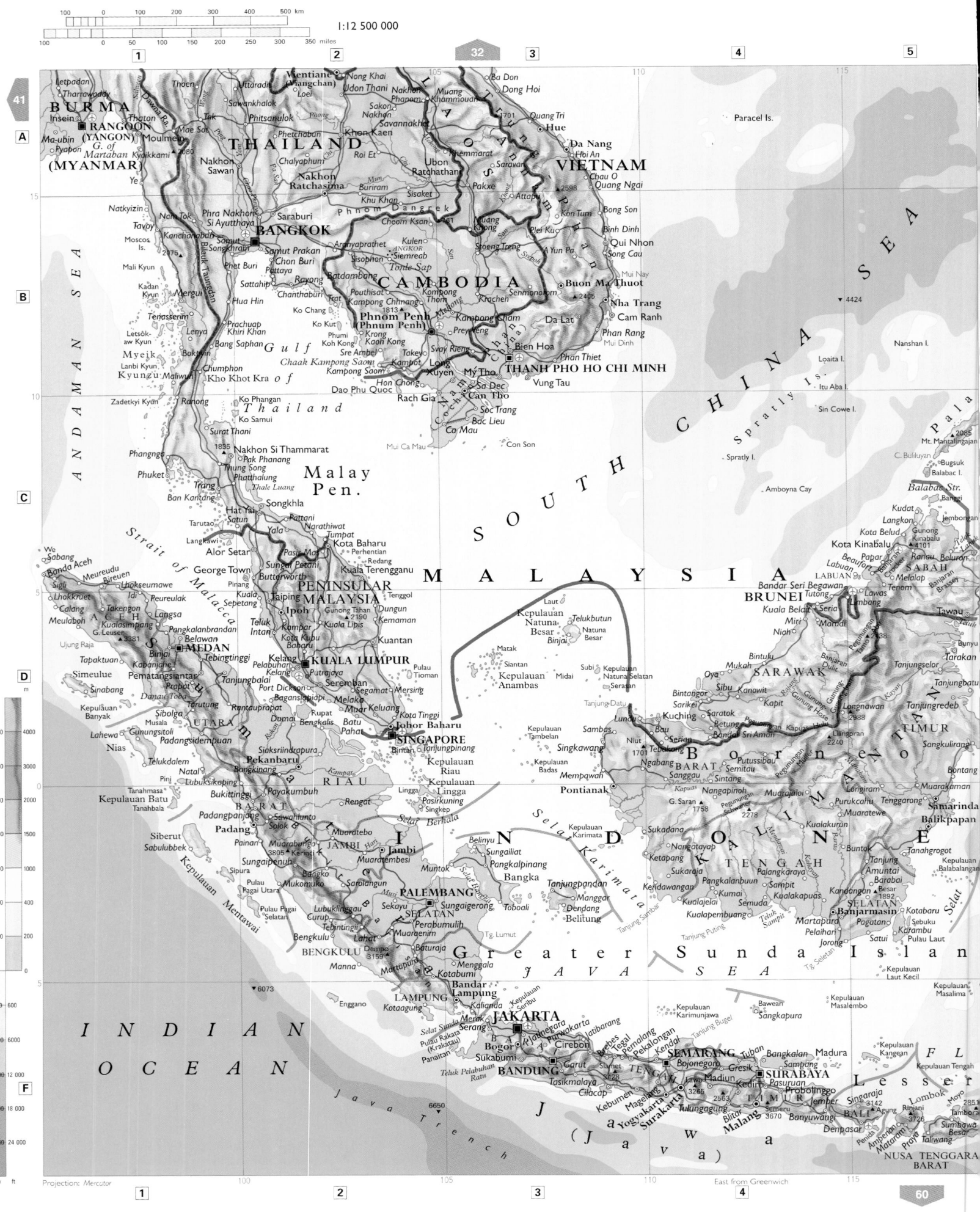

1:12 500 000

Projection: Mercator

East from Greenwich

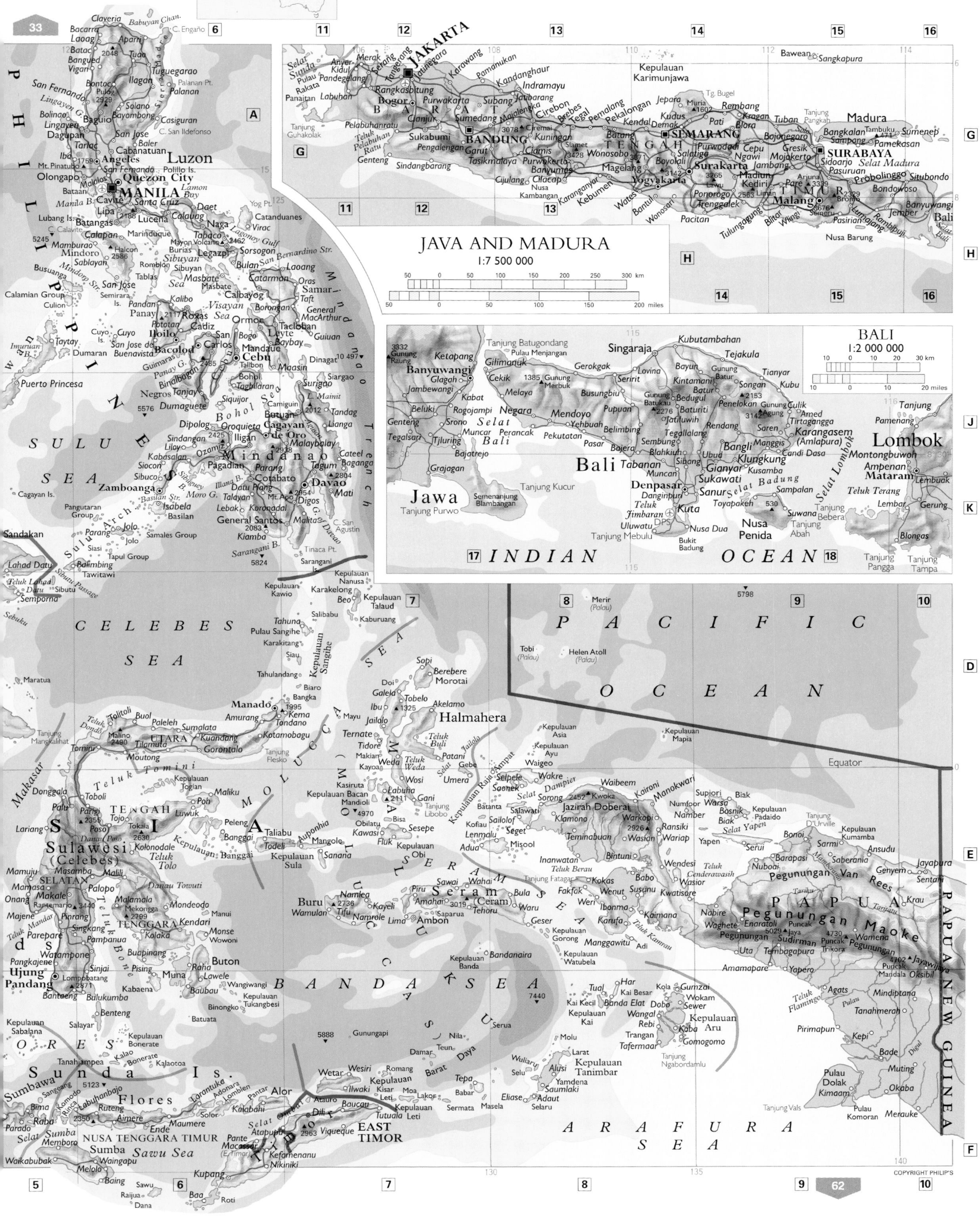

JAVA AND MADURA
1:7 500 000

50 0 50 100 150 200 250 300 km
50 0 50 100 150 200 miles

BALI
1:2 000 000

10 0 10 20 30 km
10 0 10 20 miles

JAKARTA

BANDUNG

SEMARANG

SURABAYA

Yogyakarta

Surakarta

Malang

Madura

Bali

Luzon

MANILA

Quezon City

San Fernando

Baguio

PHILIPPINE SEA

Mindoro

Panay

Negros

Cebu

Cebu

SULU SEA

Zamboanga

Mindanao

Davao

General Santos

CELEBES SEA

Manado

Halmahera

Sulawesi (Celebes)

Ujung Pandang

TENGAH

SELATAN

TENGGARA

MOLUCCA SEA

Buru

Seram (Ceram)

Ambon

BANDA SEA

Buton

Flores

Sumbawa

NUSA TENGGARA TIMUR

Sumba

Sawu Sea

EAST TIMOR

PACIFIC OCEAN

Equator

ARAFURA SEA

PAPUA NEW GUINEA

Pegunungan Maoke

Jayapura

Jayawijaya

INDIAN OCEAN

Bali

Jawa

Lombok

Denpasar

Singaraja

Mataram

Nusa Penida

Banyuwangi

COPYRIGHT PHILIP'S

1:6 000 000

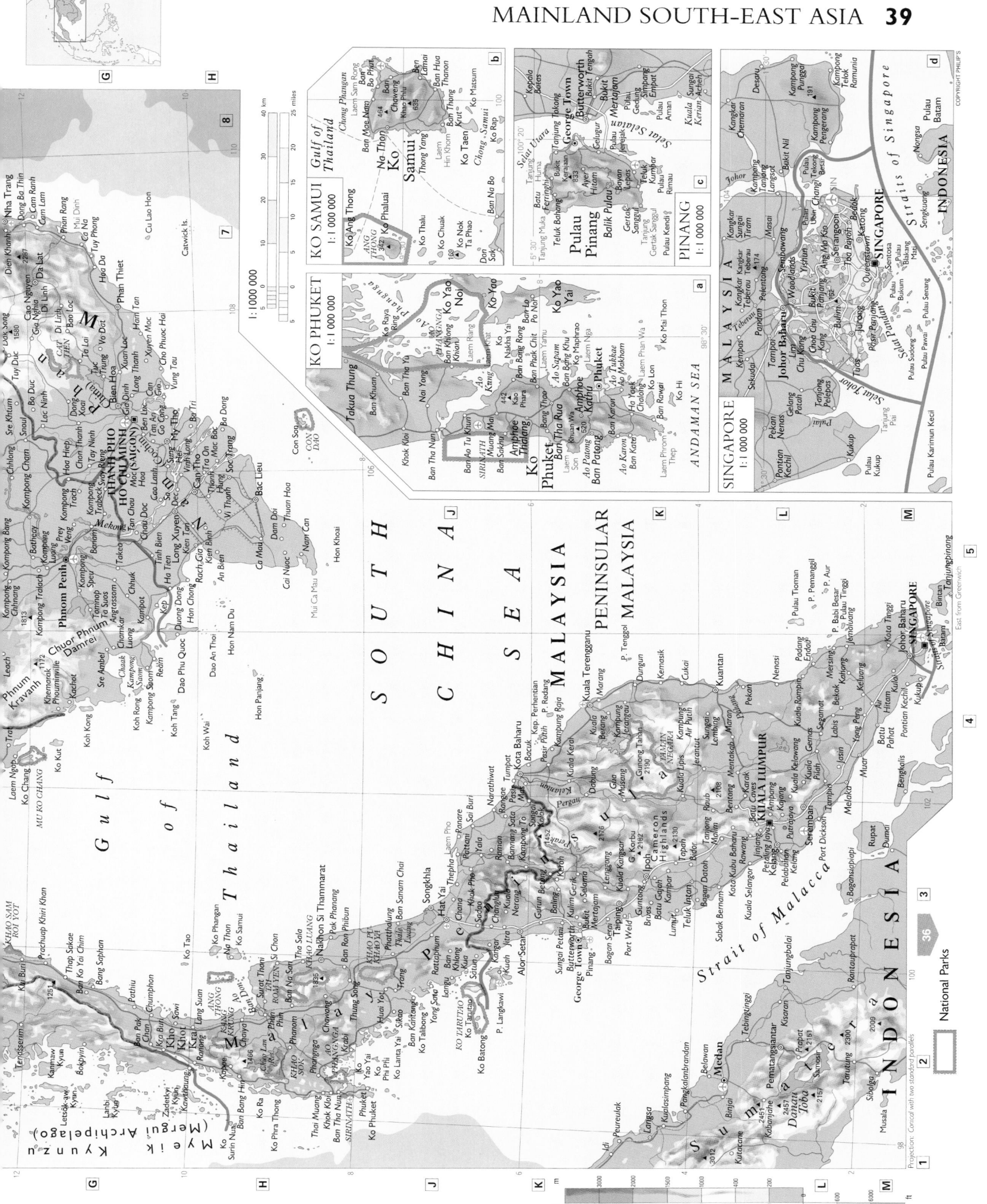

1:10 000 000

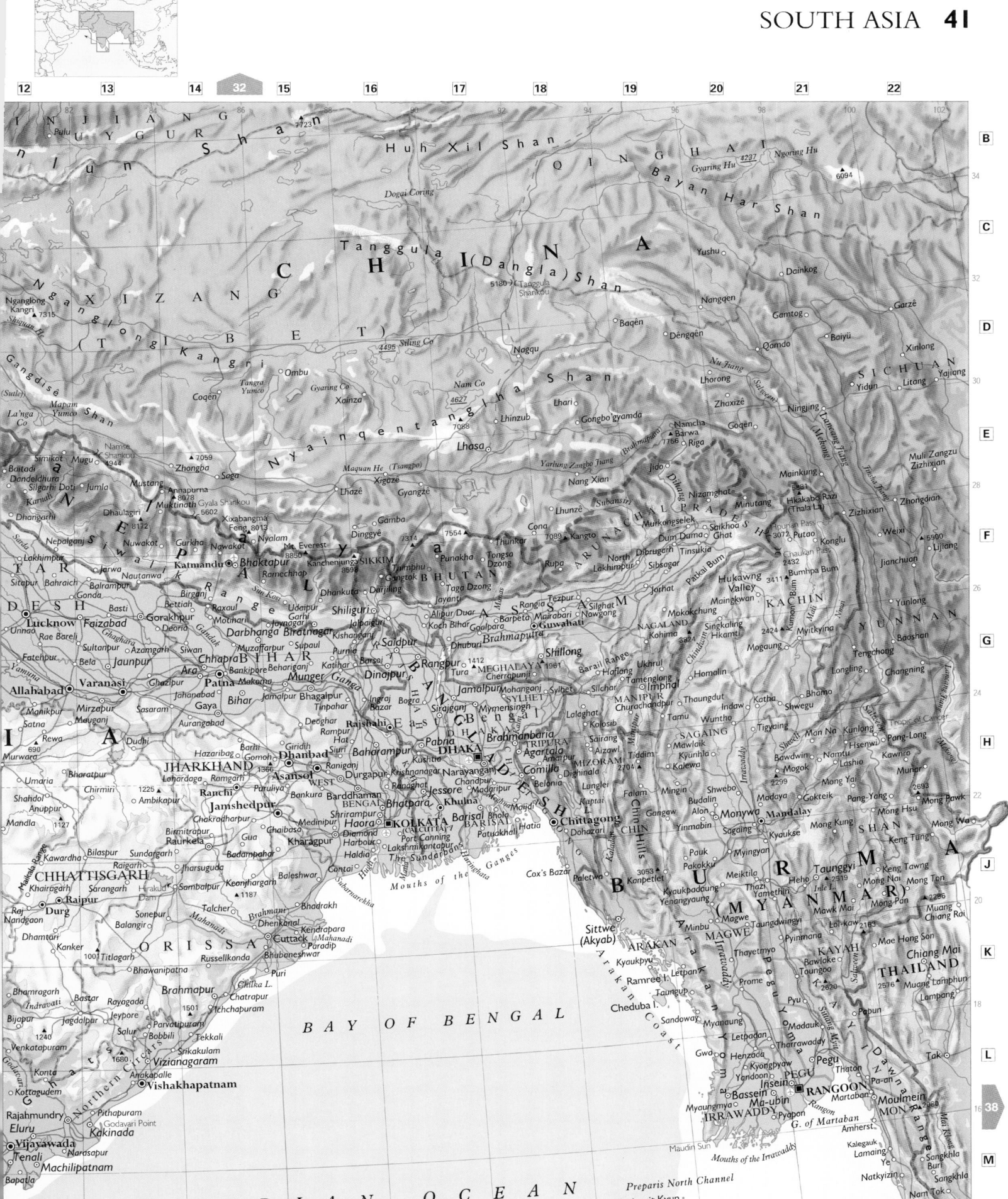

1:6 000 000

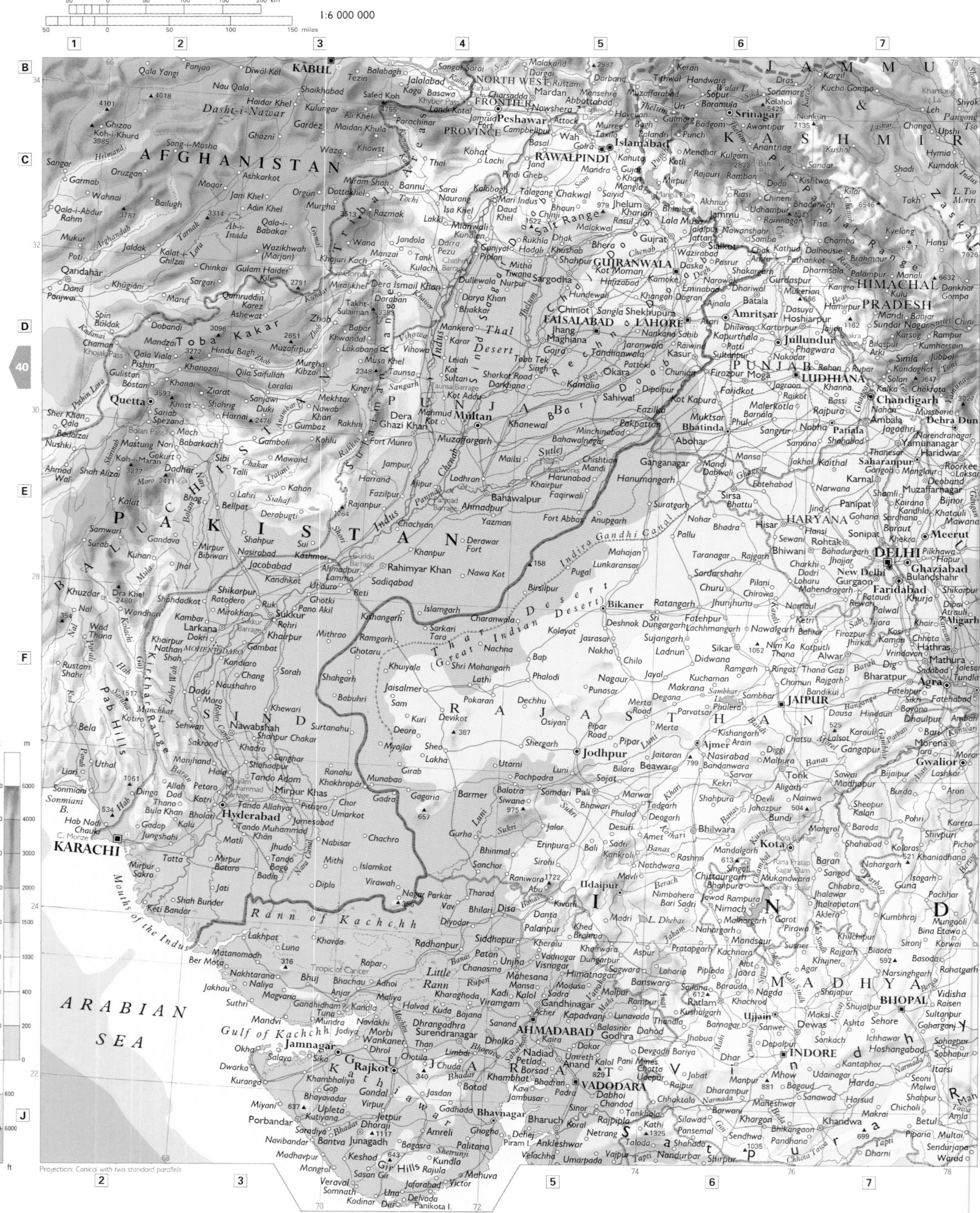

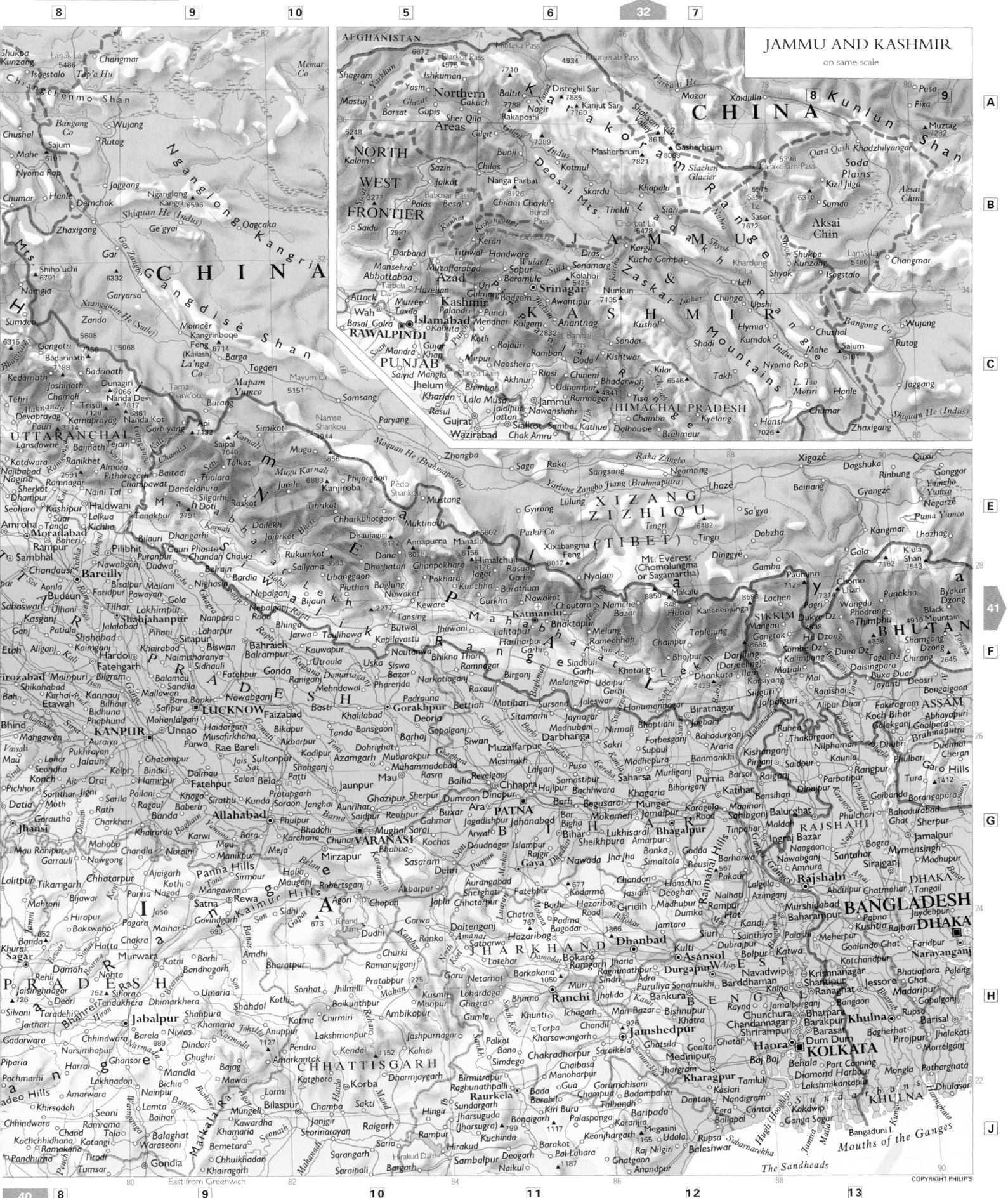

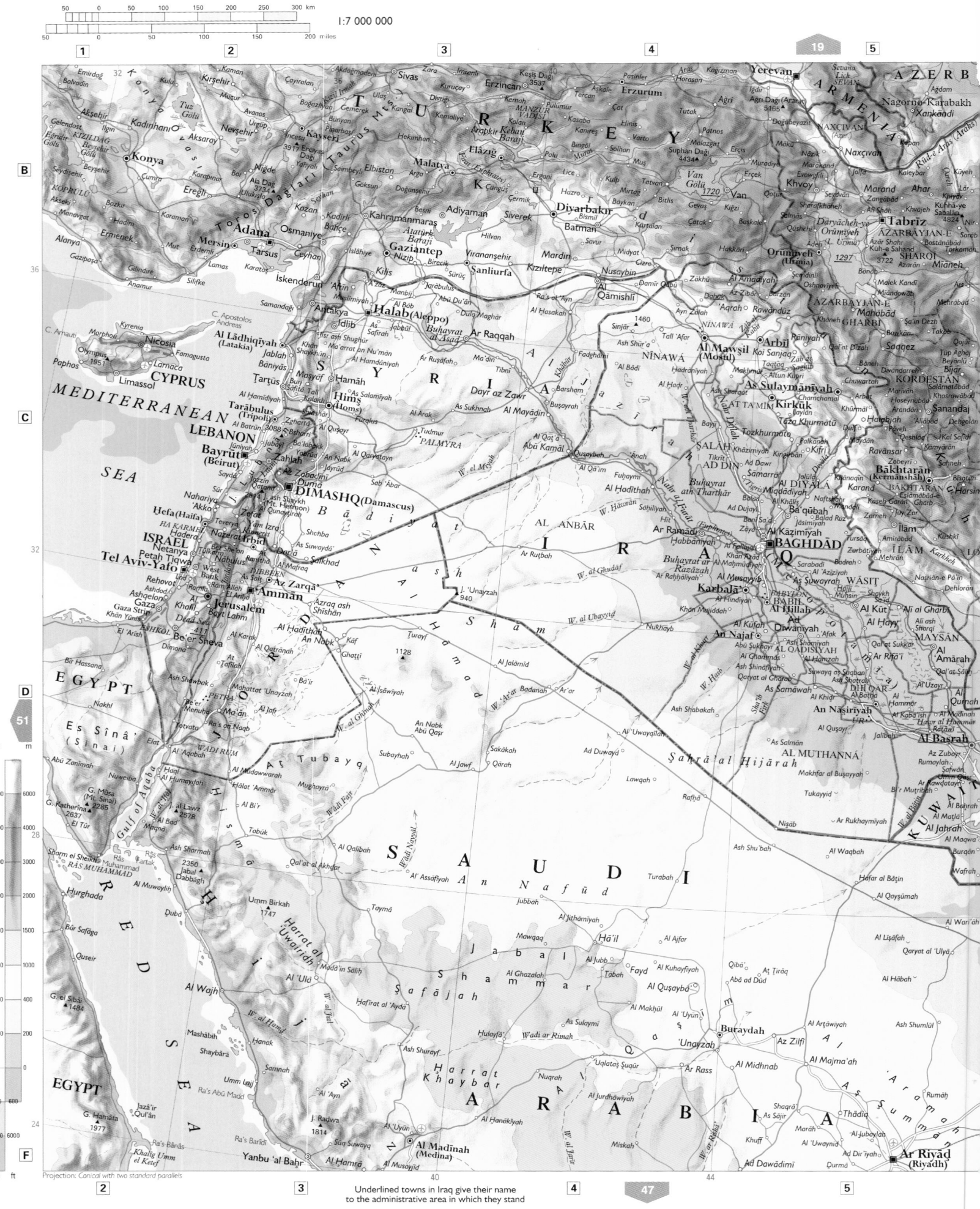

1:7 000 000

Underlined towns in Iraq give their name
to the administrative area in which they stand

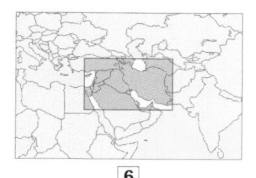

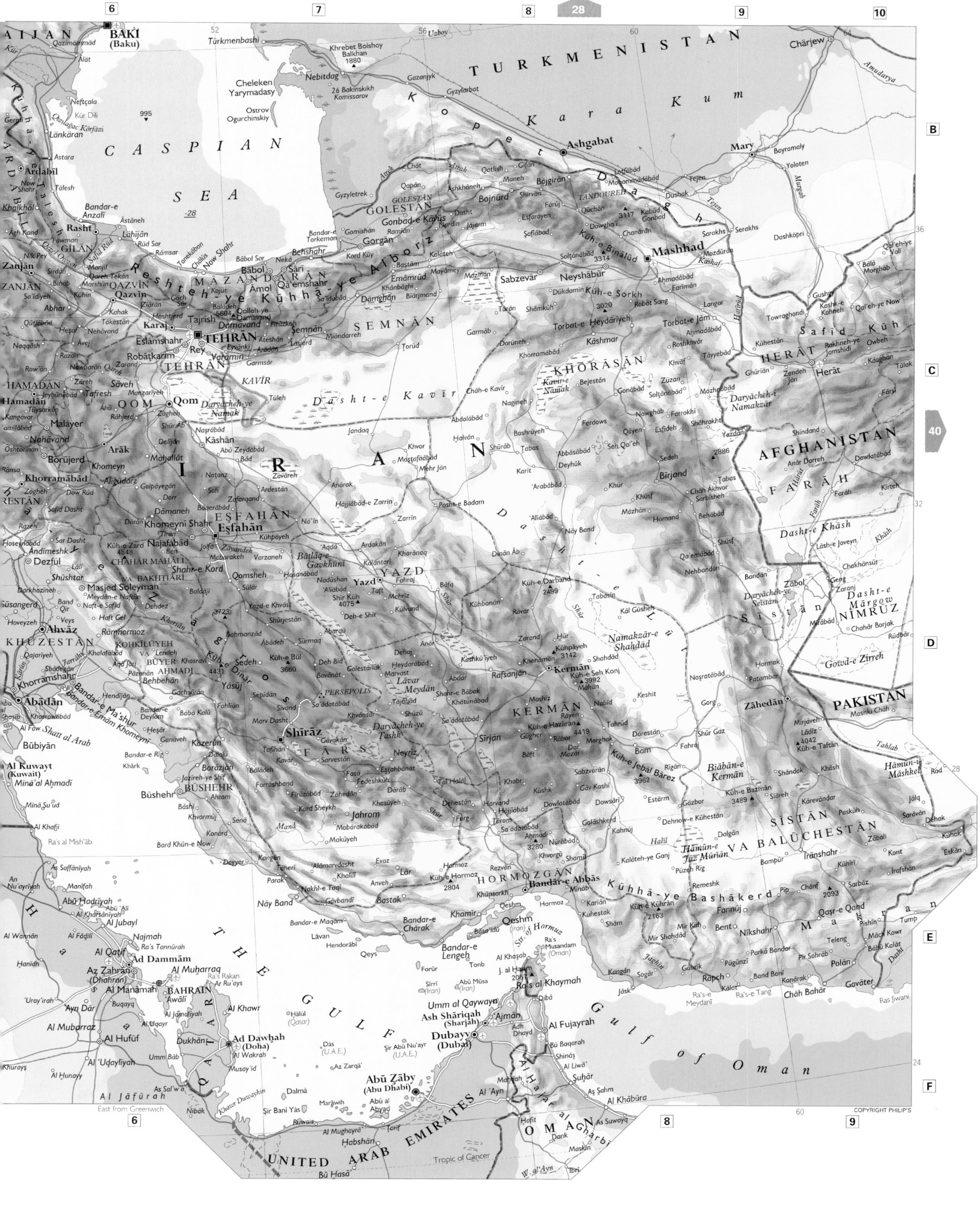

TURKMENISTAN

CASPIAN SEA

IRAN

AFGHANISTAN

PAKISTAN

UNITED ARAB EMIRATES

OMAN

QATAR

BAHRAIN

THE GULF

Gulf of Oman

Tropic of Cancer

East from Greenwich

COPYRIGHT PHILIP'S

1:2 500 000

10 0 10 20 30 40 50 60 70 80 100 km
10 0 10 20 30 40 50 60 miles

| 1 | 2 | 3 | 4 | 44 | 5 | 6 |

CYPRUS

Paphos
Episkopi
Episkopi Bay
Limassol
Akrotiri Bay
C. Gata

Al Ḥamīdīyah
Ṭall Kalakh
Halbā
Hịms (Homs)
Shinshār
Furqlus

A

Al Minā'
ASH SHAMÂL
Ṭarābulus (Tripoli)
Zgharta
Qurnat as Sawdā' 3088
Al Hirmil
Al Quṣayr
HIMṢ
Al Qaryatayn

Al Batrūn
Jubayl
Qartābā
Ibrāhīm
Al Labwah
Al Burayj 2464
Bi'r Ghadir

Jūniyah
2628 J. Sannin
Bikfayyā
Ba'labakk
2616
Yabrūd
An Nabk

M E D I T E R R A N E A N

34
BAYRŪT (Beirut)
Ash Shuwayfāt
'Alayh
Zahlah
Sirghāyā
SYRIA
Ad Dāmūr
JABAL LUBNÂN
Hawsh Mūssá
Az Zabadāni
Al Qutayfah
Dumayr
Khān Abū Shāmat

S E A
Saydā (Sidon)
Jazzin
1942 al Bārūk
(Mt Hermon) 2814
DIMASHQ
DIMASHQ (Damascus)
Dārayyā
Al Ḥājānah

LEBANON
An Nabaṭīyah at Tahta
AL JANŪB
Marj 'Uyūn
Al Khiyām
Qaṭanā
Al Kiswah
Buráq

B

Ṣūr (Tyre)
Qiryat Shemona
Qol'an Mas'ada
Golan Heights
1197
Al Qunayṭirah
As Sanamayn
DAR'Ā

Nahariyya
Me'ona
Ar Rafid
Jabal Ad Durūz
AS SUWAYDÂ

33
'Akko (Acre)
Mifraz Hefa
Hagalil
Zefat
Fiq
Shaykh Miskin
Izra
Shahbā
As Suwaydā 1600
Ṣāliḥ

Ḥefa (Haifa)
HAZAFON
Karmi'el
Yam Kinneret
Teverya (Tiberias)
Saham al Jawlān
Dar'ā
Malah

C
Qiryat Ata
Yam -210
Nazerat (Nazareth)
Afula
Ṭayiba
IRBID
Ar Ramthā
Buṣrá ash Shām
Salkhad

Dāliyat el Karmel
HA KARMEL
TEL MEGIDDO
Umm el Fahm
Jenin
Bet She'an
AJLŪN
Irbid
Al Mafraq

CAESAREA
Pardes
Hanna-Karkur
Shômrôn
Ṭulkarm
Tūbās
'Ajlūn
Umm ad Daraj
Jorash
Umm al Qittayn

Hadera
SAMARIA
1247
JARASH
ISRAEL
Netanya
HAMERKAZ
Nābulus
N. al Far'ah
Jarash
AL MAFRAQ

Herzliyya
Benē Beraq
Kefar Sava
Petah Tiqwa
SHILO
AL BALQĀ
As Salt
Wādī as Sīr

Tel Aviv-Yafo
Ramat Gan
Karama
AMMAN
Az Zarqā
Azraq ash Shishān

32
Bat Yam
Rishon le Ziyyon
Lod
West Bank
Rām Allāh
-289
Nā'ūr
AMM
AZ ZARQĀ

Yavne
Ramla
Rehovot
El Arīḥa (Jericho)
At Tunayb

Ashdod
Bet Shemesh
Jerusalem (Yerushalayim) (Al Quds)
Ma'daba
'AMMAN

Qiryat Mal'akhi
Qiryat Gat
Bayt Laḥm (Bethlehem)
MA'DABA

Ashqelon
TEL LAKHISH
Al Khalīl (Hebron)
Ma'daba

D
Gaza
N. Shiqma
Sederot
Az Ẓāhirīyah
W. al Ḥaydān
Dhibān
Al Hadithah

Gaza Strip
Khān Yūnis
Rafah
ESHKOL
Be'er Sheva (Beersheba)
Arad
-411
W. Al Mawjib
Al Qaṭrānah

Bûr Sa'îd (Port Said)
Bûr Fu'ad
Rās Burūn
N. Besor
Sedom
1305
AL KARAK
Al Karak
Al Mazār
W. al Ghadaf
W. Al Mūjib

51
Khalîg el Tîna
Sabkhet el Bardawil
El Daheir
Bor Mashash
Al Mazār

Români
Bîr el 'Abd
Dimona
-333
W. al Ḥasá
Bā'ir

31
Bîr Qaṭia
Bîr el Garārât
W. al 'Arîsh
HADAROM
JORDAN

El Qantara
Bîr el Duweidar
Bîr Kaseiba
Bîr Lahfân
Qezi'ot
Sedé Boqér
At Ṭafilah
ash Shawmari

Wāḥid
Bîr Madkûr
SHAMÂL SÎNÎ
892
-121
AT TAFILAH
1072

Ismâ'ilîya
El Malḥi
Muweilih
El Quseima
Mizpe Ramon
Nijil
Mahattat 'Unayzah

Talâta
Bîr Hasana
Hanegev
Rujm Talat al Jam'ah 1736
Al Jafr
Qa'el Jafr

ISMÂ'ILÎYA
Khamsa
G. Yi 'Allaq 1094
Bîr Beiḍa
PETRA
Wādī Mūsā
Ma'ān

El Buheirat el Murrat el Kubra (Bitter Lakes)
Bîr el Thamâda
W. el Bruk
W. Qraiya
N. Paran
MA'ĀN

Gineifa
Bîr el Thamâda
W. el Sikera
El 'Agrûd
N. Ḥiyyon
Bi'r al Mārî

E
E G Y P T
Bîr Gebeil Hisn
El Kuntilla
Ra's an Naqb

El Sueis (Suez)
Bûr Taufîq
Nakhl
W. El Ruqq
W. el Tamarând
Mahattat ash Shidīyah
SAUDI

Adabiya
Uyûn Mûsa
'Ain Sudr
E S S Î N Â' (Sinai)
El Thamad
'En 'Avrona
1592
1754
WADI RUM

Khalîg el Sueis
948 G. el Kabrît
Gebel el Tîh
Bîr Abu Muḥammad
Bîr el Butayyḥât
Bi'r al Qaṭṭâr
Batn al Ghûl

Ghubbet el Bûs
El Wabeira
Bîr el Biarât
Bîr Tâba
Al 'Aqabah
Rum

F
Bîr Abu Ṣandûq
Rās el Matarma
JANŪB SÎNÎ
Bîr el Heisi
Al 'Aqaba
At Tubayq

EL SUWEIS
1272
W. Abu Ga'da
1165
Gulf of Aqaba
W. an Nakhl
Haql
Al Mudawwarah
ARABIA

Projection: Polyconic
East from Greenwich
COPYRIGHT PHILIP'S

- - - 1974 Cease Fire Lines
National Parks

ft m
9000 3000
6000 2000
4500 1500
3000 1000
1200 400
600 200
0 0
200 600
2000 6000
m ft

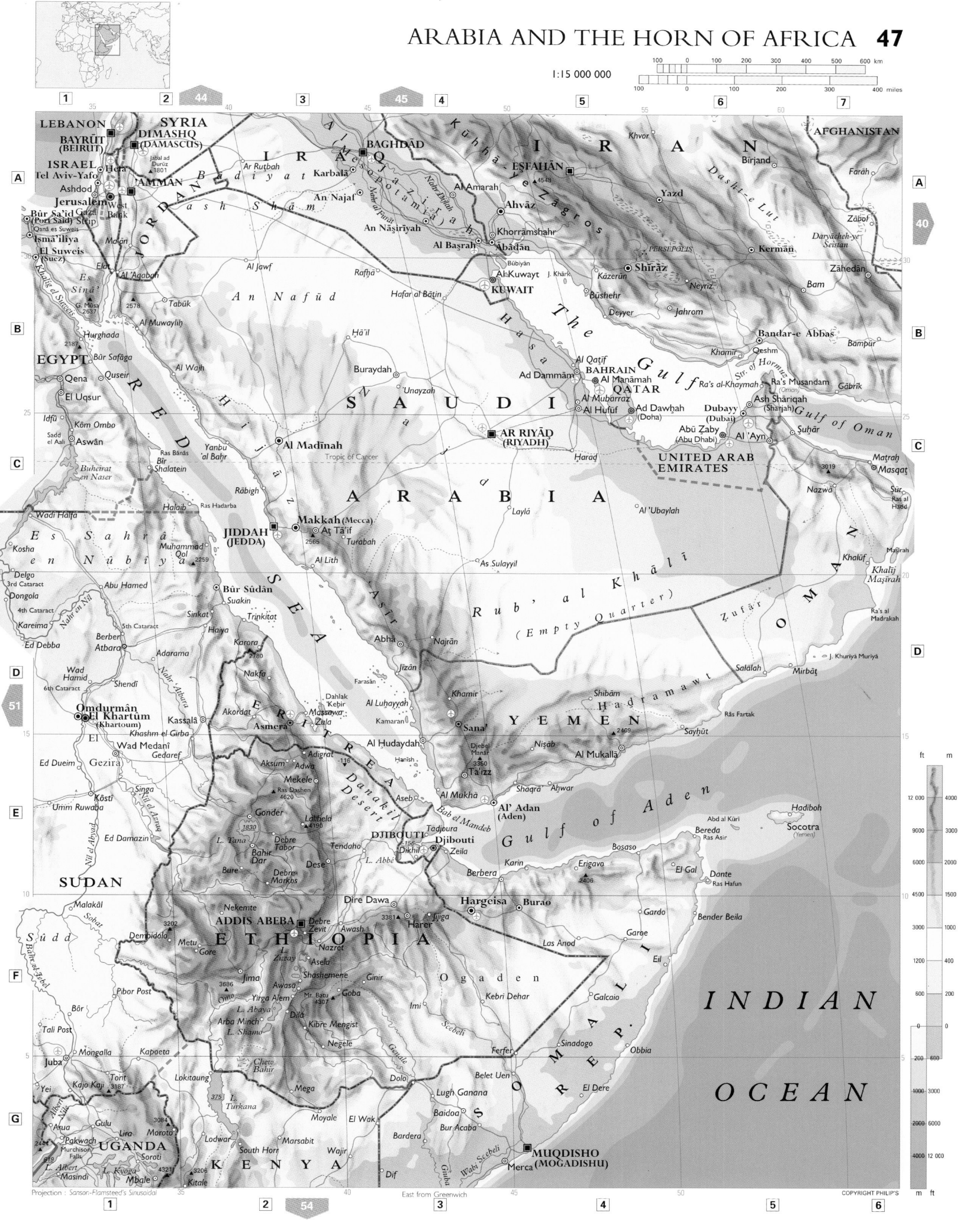

1:15 000 000

ARABIA AND THE HORN OF AFRICA

LEBANON
BAYRŪT (BEIRUT)
ISRAEL
Tel Aviv-Yafo
Ashdod
Jerusalem
Bûr Sa'id (Port Said)
Qanâ es Suweis
Ismâ'iliya
El Suweis (Suez)

SYRIA
DIMASHQ (DAMASCUS)
Jabal ad Durūz 1801
'AMMĀN
Hera
Gaza Strip
West Bank

Ma'ān
El Aqaba
Es Sinâ'
G. Mûsa 2637
2578

IRAQ
Ar Rutbah
Karbalā
An Najaf
BAGHDĀD
Nahr Dijlah
Nahr al Furāt
An Nāṣirīyah
Al Amarah
Al Başrah
Ābādān
Būbiyān
J. Khārk
Al-Kuwayt
KUWAIT
Hafar al Bāṭin

IRAN
Khvor
EṢFAHĀN
4548
Ahvāz
Khorrāmshahr
PERSEPOLIS
Būshehr
Deyyer
Kāzerūn
Shīrāz
Neyriz
Jahrom

Birjand
Farāh
AFGHANISTAN
Yazd
Dasht-e Lut
Daryācheh-ye Seistan
Zābol
Kermān
Bam
Zāhedān

EGYPT
Hurghada
2187
Bûr Safâga
Qena
Quseir
El Uqsur
Idfû
Kôm Ombo
Aswân
Sadd el Aali

Al Muwayliḥ
Tabūk
Al Wajh
Al Jawf
An Nafūd
Hā'il
Buraydah
'Unayzah
Rafḥa

SAUDI
Ad Dammām
Al Qaṭīf
BAHRAIN
Al Manāmah
Al Mubarraz
Al Hufūf
QATAR
Ad Dawḥah (Doha)
Abū Zaby (Abu Dhabi)

Bandar-e Abbas
Khamīr
Qeshm
Str. of Hormuz
Ra's al-Khaymah
Ra's Musandam (Oman)
Ash Shariqah (Sharjah)
Dubayy (Dubai)
Al 'Ayn
Ṣuḥār
Gulf of Oman
Bampūr
Gābrīk

Ras Bānās
Bîr Shalatein
Yanbu' al Baḥr
Al Madīnah
Rābigh
Ras Hadarba
Halaib

The Gulf
Hasā
AR RIYĀḌ (RIYADH)
Harad
UNITED ARAB EMIRATES
Maṭraḥ 3019
Masqaṭ
Nazwā
Ṣūr
Ras al Hadd

Tropic of Cancer

ARABIA
Najd
Laylá
Al 'Ubaylah
As Sulayyil
Masīrah
Khalūf
Khalīj Masīrah

Buheirat en Naser
Es Sahrâ en Nûbîy
Kosha
Delgo
3rd Cataract
Dongola
4th Cataract
Kareima
Ed Debba
Wad Hamid
6th Cataract
Omdurmân
El Khartûm (Khartoum)

Muhammad Qol 2259
Abu Hamed
5th Cataract
Berber
Atbara
Adarama
Shendî
Nahr 'Atbara
Khashm el Girba
El Geili
Wad Medanî
Gedaref

JIDDAH (JEDDA)
Makkah (Mecca)
Aṭ Ṭā'if
Turabah
2565

Bûr Sûdân
Suakin
Sinkat
Haiya
Karora
Akordat
Nakfa
Asmera
Kassalā
Adigrat
Aksum
Adwa

Asīr
Abha
Jīzān
Farasān
Dahlak Kebir
Massawa
Zula
Kamarān
Al Luḥayyah
Al Ḥudaydah
Danakil Desert
Hanīsh

Rub' al Khālī (Empty Quarter)
OMAN
Zufār
Salālah
Ra's al Madrakah
Mirbāṭ
J. Khuriyā Muriyā
Khamir
Shibām
Hadramawt
Rās Fartak
Sayḥūt
2469
Nişāb
Al Mukallā
Shaqrā
Aḥwar
YEMEN
Sana'
Ta'izz
Djebel Manār 3350
Aseb

Ed Dueim
Kôstî
Umm Ruwaba
El Geneina
Singa
Ed Damazin
SUDAN
Gezîra
'116
Mekele
Ras Dashen 4620
Gonder
L. Tana
Bahir Dar
Debre Tabor
Lalibela 190
Debre Markos
Dese

Bure
ADDIS ABEBA
ETHIOPIA
Nazret
Awash
Debre Zeyit
Jima 3686
Asela
Shashemene
Awasa
Mr. Batu 4307
Goba
Dilā
Kibre Mengist
Negele

Nil el Abyad
Bahr el Jebel
Sûdd
Malakâl
Nekemte
Dembidolo
3202
Metu
Gore
Omo
L. Ziway
Ginir
Yirga Alem
L. Abaya
Arba Minch
L. Shiamo
Pibor Post
Bôr
Tali Post
Juba
Yei
Kajo Kaji 3187
Mongalla
Kapoeta

Al Mukhā
Bab el Mandeb
DJIBOUTI
Djibouti
Zeila
Dikhil 156
Tadjoura
L. Abbé
Tendaho
Al' Adan (Aden)
Gulf of Aden
Abd al Kūrī
Bereda
Ras Asir
Socotra (Yemen)
Hadiboh

Dire Dawa
Harer
Jijiga 3381
Hargeisa
Burão
Berbera
Karin
Erigavo 2406
El Gal
Gardo
Bosaso
Dante
Ras Hafun
Bender Beila

Ogaden
Kebri Dehar
Imi
Scebeli
Genale
Ferfer
Garoe
Las Anod
Galcaio
Eil

Chete Bahir
Lokitaung
375 L. Turkana
Mega
Dolo
Moyale
El Wak
South Horr
Marsabit
Wajir

Lugh Ganana
Belet Uen
Sinadogo
Obbia
Baidoa
Bur Acaba
Bardera
Dif
Bur Ganana

L. Albert
Arua
Gulu
Lira
Moroto
2447
Pakwach
619
Murchison Falls
UGANDA
Masindi
L. Kyoga
Soroti
4321
Mbale
3206
Kitale
KENYA
Lodwar
Genale
Wabi Scebeli
Merca
MUQDISHO (MOGADISHU)
Gittale

SOMALI REP.

INDIAN
OCEAN

ft m
12 000 4000
9000 3000
6000 2000
4500 1500
3000 1000
1200 400
600 200
0 0
200 600
1000 3000
2000 6000
4000 12 000
m ft

COPYRIGHT PHILIP'S

Projection : Sanson-Flamsteed's Sinusoidal

East from Greenwich

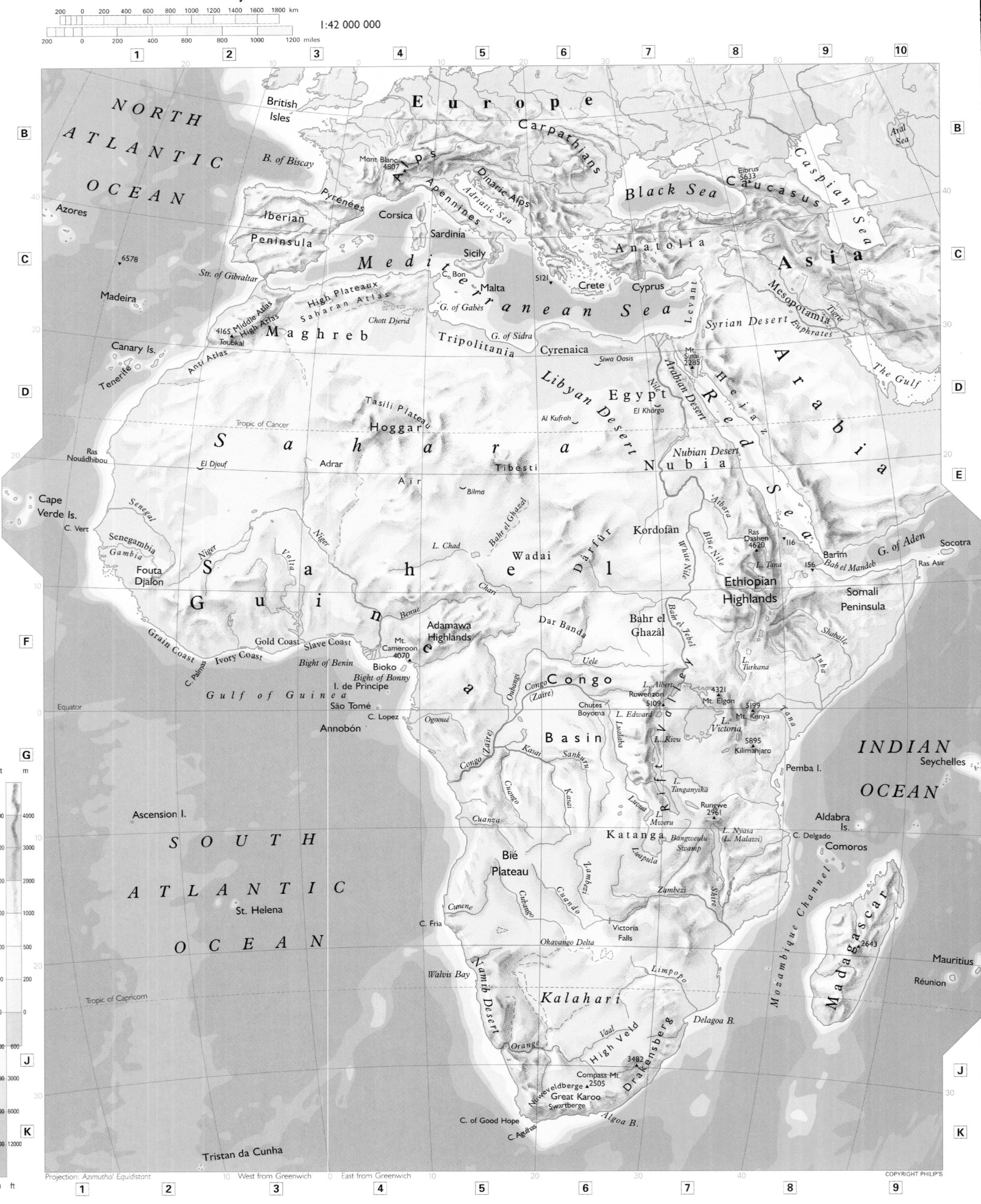

200 0 200 400 600 800 1000 1200 1400 1600 1800 km

1:42 000 000

200 0 200 400 600 800 1000 1200 miles

Projection: Azimuthal Equidistant

West from Greenwich   East from Greenwich

COPYRIGHT PHILIP'S

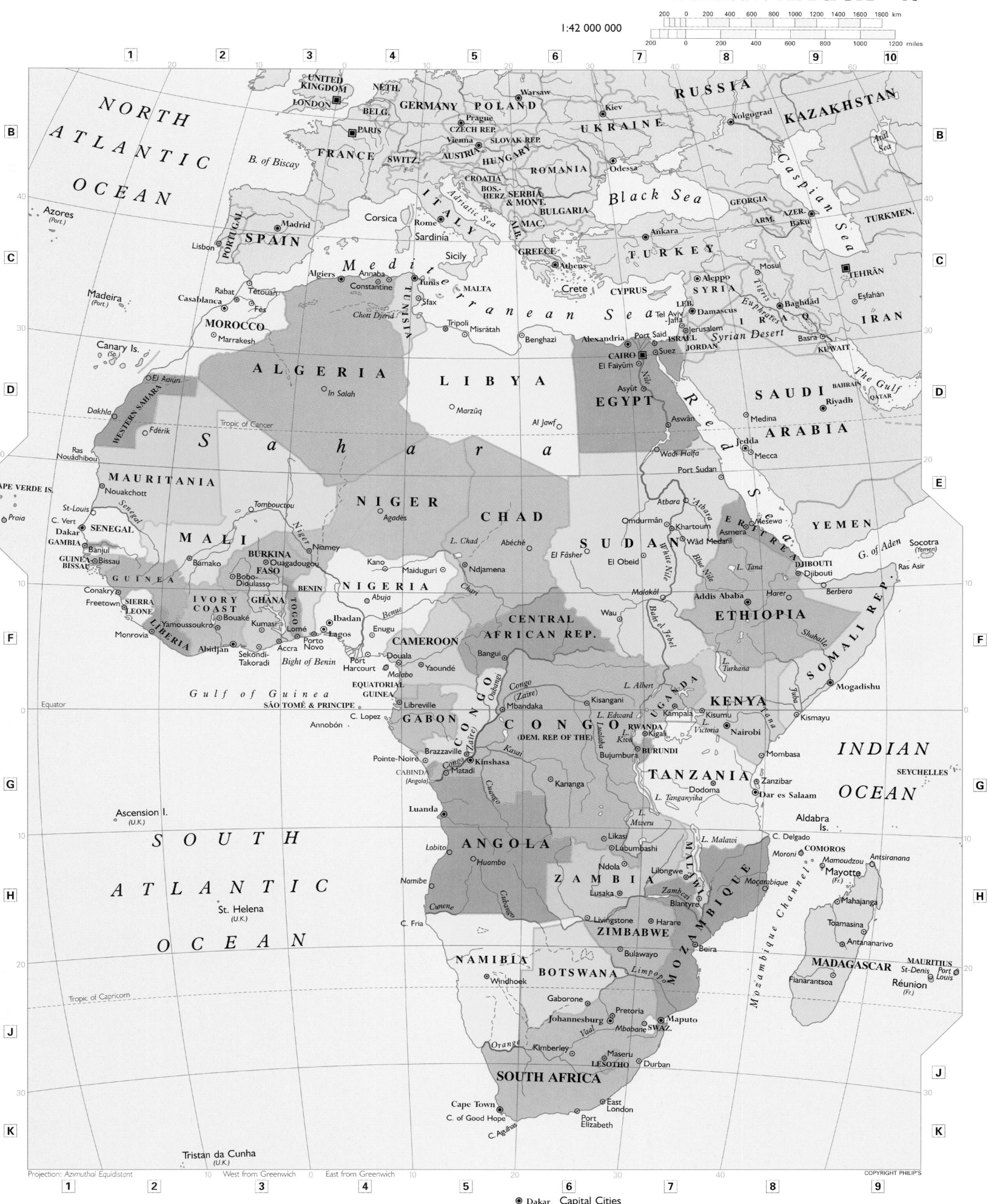

1:42 000 000

200 0 200 400 600 800 1000 1200 1400 1600 1800 km

200 0 200 400 600 800 1000 1200 miles

Projection: Azimuthal Equidistant

West from Greenwich   East from Greenwich

COPYRIGHT PHILIP'S

● Dakar   Capital Cities

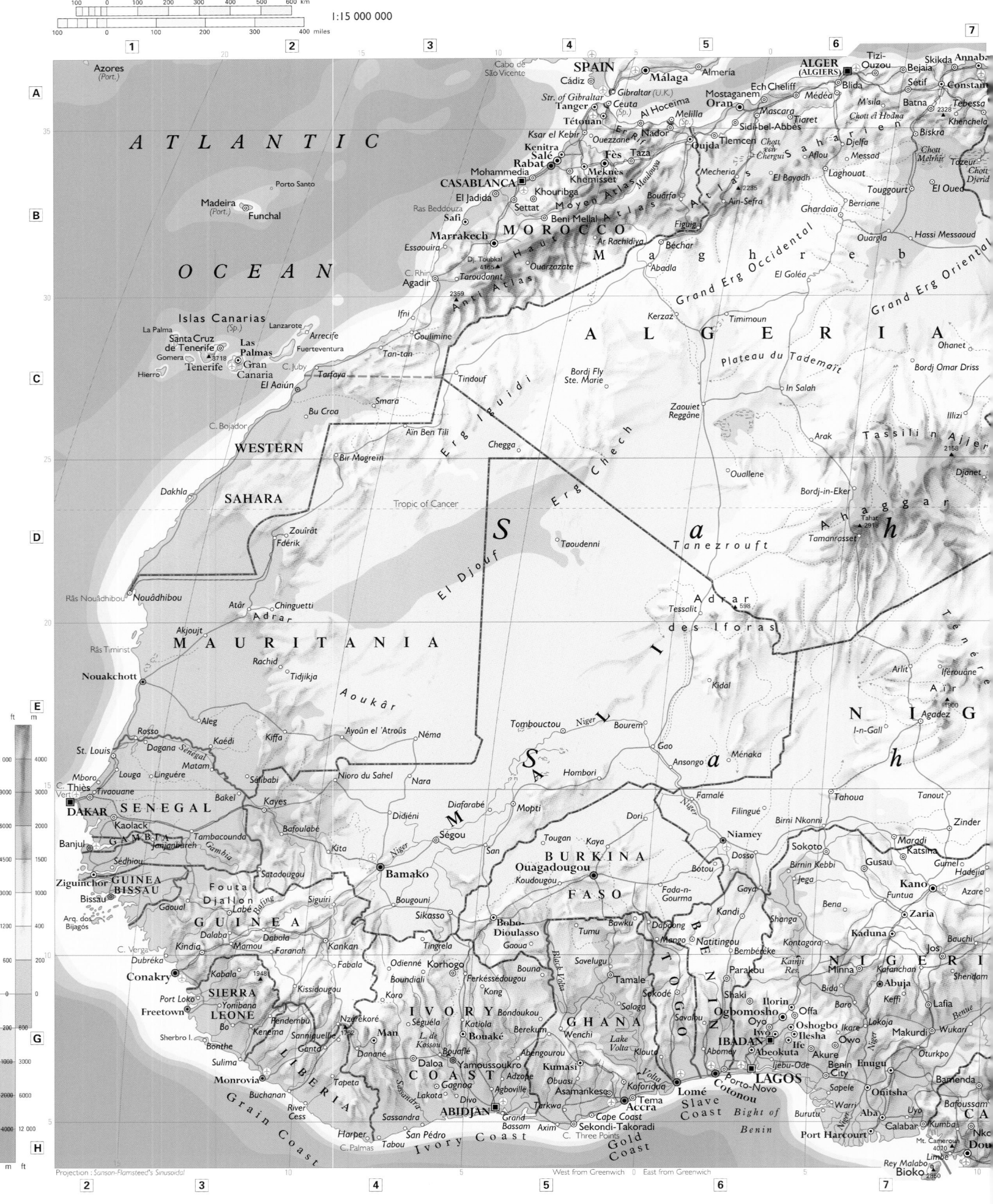

1:15 000 000

Projection : Sanson-Flamsteed's Sinusoidal

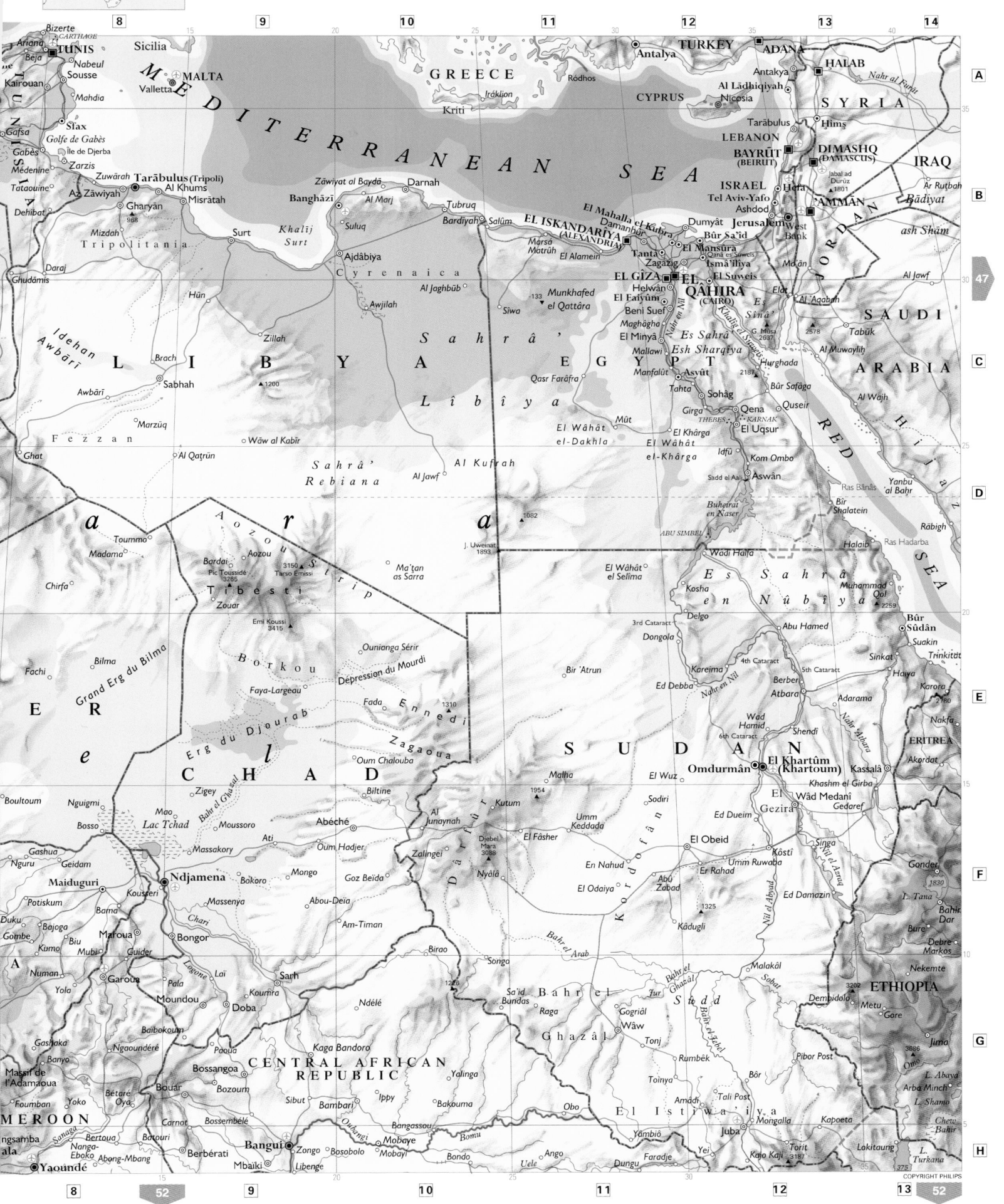

MEDITERRANEAN SEA

GREECE
TURKEY
Antalya
ADANA
HALAB
Ródhos
CYPRUS
Antakya
Iráklion
Nicosia
Al Lādhiqiyah
Kriti
SYRIA
Tarābulus
Hims
Nahr al Furāt
LEBANON
DIMASHQ (DAMASCUS)
BAYRŪT (BEIRUT)
jabal ad Dūrūz
IRAQ
ISRAEL
Ār Rutbah
Tel Aviv-Yafo
Haifa
Bādiyat
AMMĀN
ash Shām

Bizerte
CARTHAGE
Ariana
TUNIS
Beja
Nabeul
Sicilia
Sousse
MALTA
Kairouan
Mahdia
Valletta

Sfax
Golfe de Gabès
Gafsa
Gabès
Île de Djerba
Médenine
Zarzis
Zuwārah
Tarābulus (Tripoli)
Tataouine
Az Zāwiyah
Al Khums
Dehibat
Gharyān
Misrātah
968
Ghudāmis
Mizdah
Tripolitania
Surt
Daraj
Hūn
Awjilah
Zillah
Brach
Idehan Awbārī
Zāwiyat al Baydā
Darnah
Banghāzī
Al Marj
Tubruq
Suluq
Bardiyah
Salūm
EL ISKANDARĪYA (ALEXANDRIA)
El Mahalla el Kubra
Damanhūr
Dumyāt
Marsa Matrūh
El Alamein
Qanā es Suweis
Būr Sa'īd
Tanta
Zagazig
Ismā'īlīya
El Mansūra
EL GĪZA
EL QĀHIRA (CAIRO)
El Suweis
Helwān
El Faiyūm
Beni Suef
Maghāgha
El Minyā
Mallawi
Manfalūt
Asyūt
Sohâg
Girga
Qena
KARNAK
THEBES
El Uqsur

Ghat
Al Qaṭrūn
Al Kufrah
Al Jawf
El Wâhât el-Dakhla
El Wâhât el-Khârga
Idfū
Kom Ombo
Sadd el Aali
Aswān

SAHRĀ' AEGYPT Lîbîya
Munkhafed el Qattâra
Sîwa
Al Jaghbūb
Qasr Farâfra
Mût

Israel West Bank JORDAN
Ma'ān
Elat
Al 'Aqabah
Es Sinā
G. Mūsā 2637
Tabūk
SAUDI
Al Muwayliḥ
ARABIA
Hijaz
Al Wajh
RED
Quseir
Hurghada
Būr Safâga
Quser
Buheirat en Naser
Bîr Shalatein
Rābigh
Yanbu' al Bahr
Ras Bânâs
SEA

Fezzan
Sabhah
Awbārī
Marzūq
Wāw al Kabîr
Sahrā' Rebiana
Al Jawf

Toummo
Aozou Strip
Bardai
Aozou
Pic Toussidé 3285
3150 Tarso Emissi
Madama
Tibesti
Zouar
Emi Koussi 3415
Ma'tan as Sarra
J. Uweinat 1893

El Wâhât el Selîma
Wadi Halfa
Halaib
Ras Hadarba
ABU SIMBEL
Es Sahrâ en Nûbîya
Kosha
Muhammad Qol 2259
Delgo
Abu Hamed
Būr Sûdân
3rd Cataract
Suakin
Dongola
Trinkitât
Kareima
4th Cataract
5th Cataract
Berber
Haiya
Adarama
Atbara
Karora
Nafka

Chirfa
ER Ge
Grand Erg du Bilma
Bilma
Borkou
Ounianga Sérir
Dépression du Mourdi
Faya-Largeau
Fada
Ennedi
1310
Zagaoua
Erg du Djourab
Oum Chalouba
Bîr 'Atrun
SUDAN
Malha
El Khartûm (Khartoum)
Omdurmân
Kassalâ
ERITREA
Akordat

Fachi
Zigey
Biltine
1954
Sodiri
Khashm el Girba
El Wuz
Ed Dueim
Wād Medanî
Gedaref
Gonder
L. Tana
1830
Bahir Dar

Boultoum
Nguigmi
Bosso
Gashua
Nguru
Geidam
Mao
Lac Tchad
Moussoro
Ati
CHAD
Massakory
Abéché
Ôum Hadjer
Al Junaynah
Kutum
Dârfûr
El Fâsher
Umm Keddada
En Nahud
Kordofān
El Obeid
Abū Zabad
Er Rahad
Umm Ruwaba
El Gezira
Kôstî
Singa
Nîl el Azraq
Ed Damazin

Maiduguri
Potiskum
Ndjamena
Kousseri
Bokoro
Mongo
Massenya
Goz Beïda
Bahr el Ghazal
Abou-Deïa
Am-Timan
Nyâlâ
Djebel Mara 3088
Zalingei
El Odaiya
1325
Kâdugli
Nîl el Abyad

Duku
Bajoga
Gombe
Biu
Mubi
Mora
Guider
Bama
Bongor
Kournra
Sarh
Birao
Songa
Sa'îd Bundas
Bahr el Ghazâl
Raga
Wâw
Gogriâl
Tonj
Rumbek
Bôr
3202
Dembidolo
ETHIOPIA
Metu
Gore
Jima

Numan
Yola
Garoua
Pala
Laï
Moundou
Doba
Ndélé
Massif de l'Adamaoua
Gashaka
Banyo
Ngaoundéré
Baïbokoum
1226
Paoua
Bossangoa
Bouar
CENTRAL AFRICAN REPUBLIC
Bozoum
Yalinga
Bakouma
Obo
El Istiwâ'îya
Toinya
Tali Post
Kapoeta
3886
Omo
L. Abaya
Arba Minch
L. Shamo
Chew Bahir

CAMEROON
Foumban
Yoko
Oya
Bétoua
Bertoua
Nanga-Eboko
Abong-Mbang
Yaoundé
Bouar
Carnot
Bossembélé
Bambari
Sibut
Ippy
Bangui
Berbérati
Mbaïki
Zongo
Bosobolo
Mobaye
Mobayi
Uele
Bangassou
Bondo
Yambio
Dungu
Faradje
Yei
Kajo Kaji
3187
Torit
Lokitaung
L. Turkana

COPYRIGHT PHILIPS

1:15 000 000

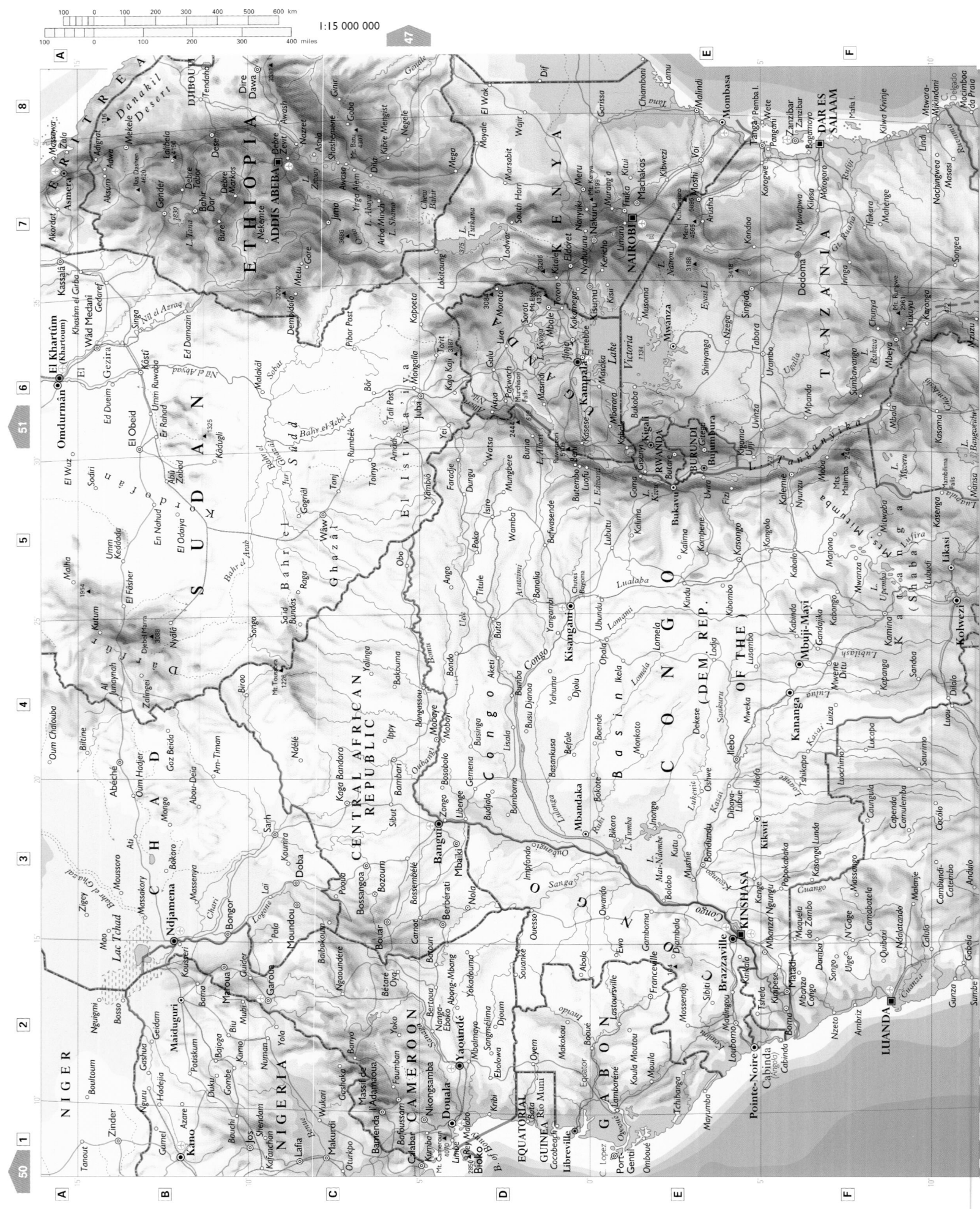

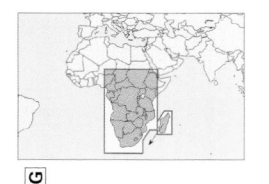

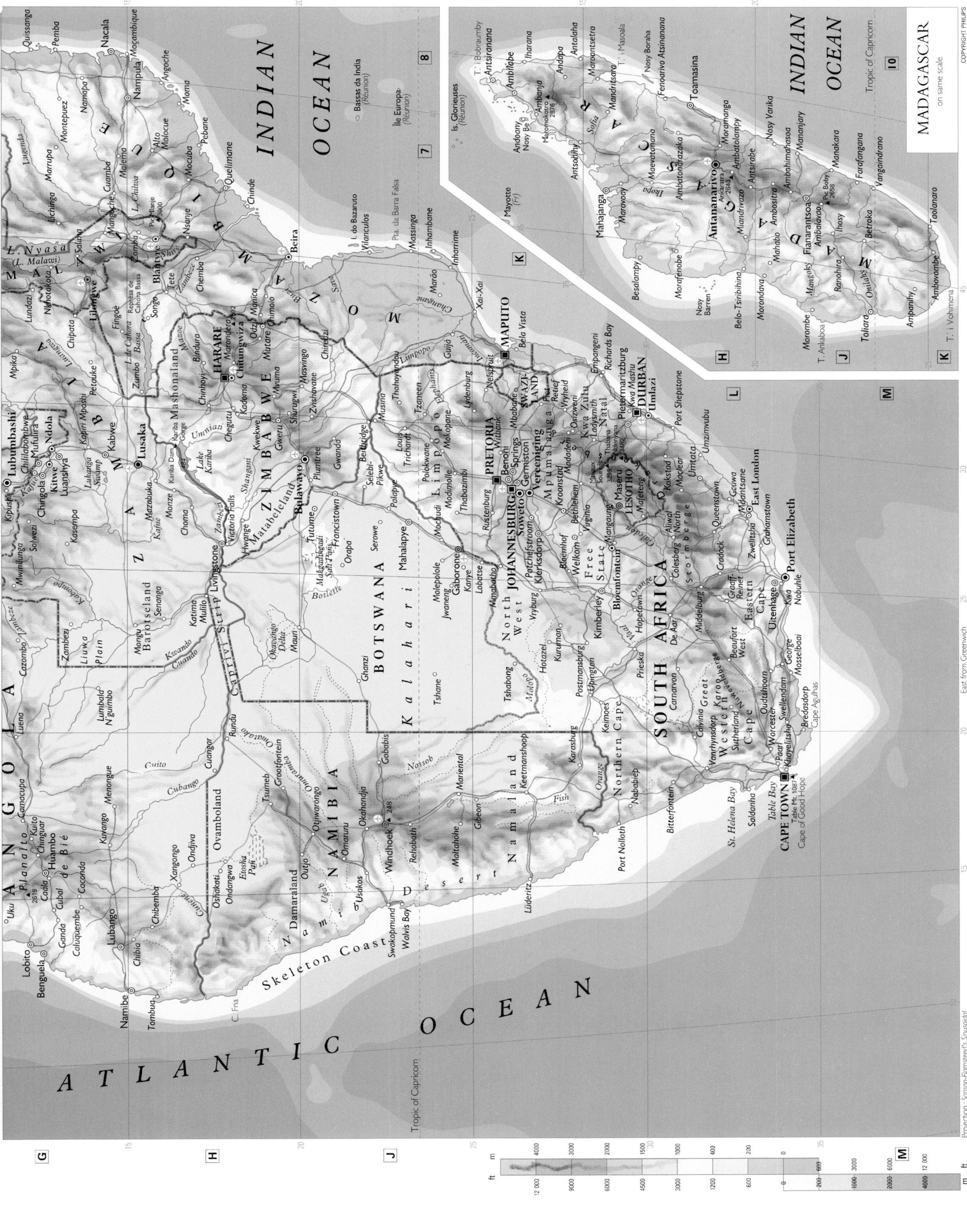
ATLANTIC OCEAN
INDIAN OCEAN
ANGOLA
ZAMBIA
MALAWI
MOZAMBIQUE
ZIMBABWE
BOTSWANA
NAMIBIA
SOUTH AFRICA
LESOTHO
SWAZILAND
MADAGASCAR
on same scale
Kalahari
Namib Desert
Skeleton Coast
Tropic of Capricorn
East from Greenwich
Projection : Sanson-Flamsteed's Sinusoidal
COPYRIGHT PHILIPS
CAPE TOWN
JOHANNESBURG
PRETORIA
HARARE
MAPUTO
DURBAN
Lusaka
Bulawayo
Windhoek
Gaborone
Antananarivo
Port Elizabeth
East London
Bloemfontein
Maseru
Beira
Lubumbashi
Ndola
Livingstone
Victoria Falls
Cape of Good Hope

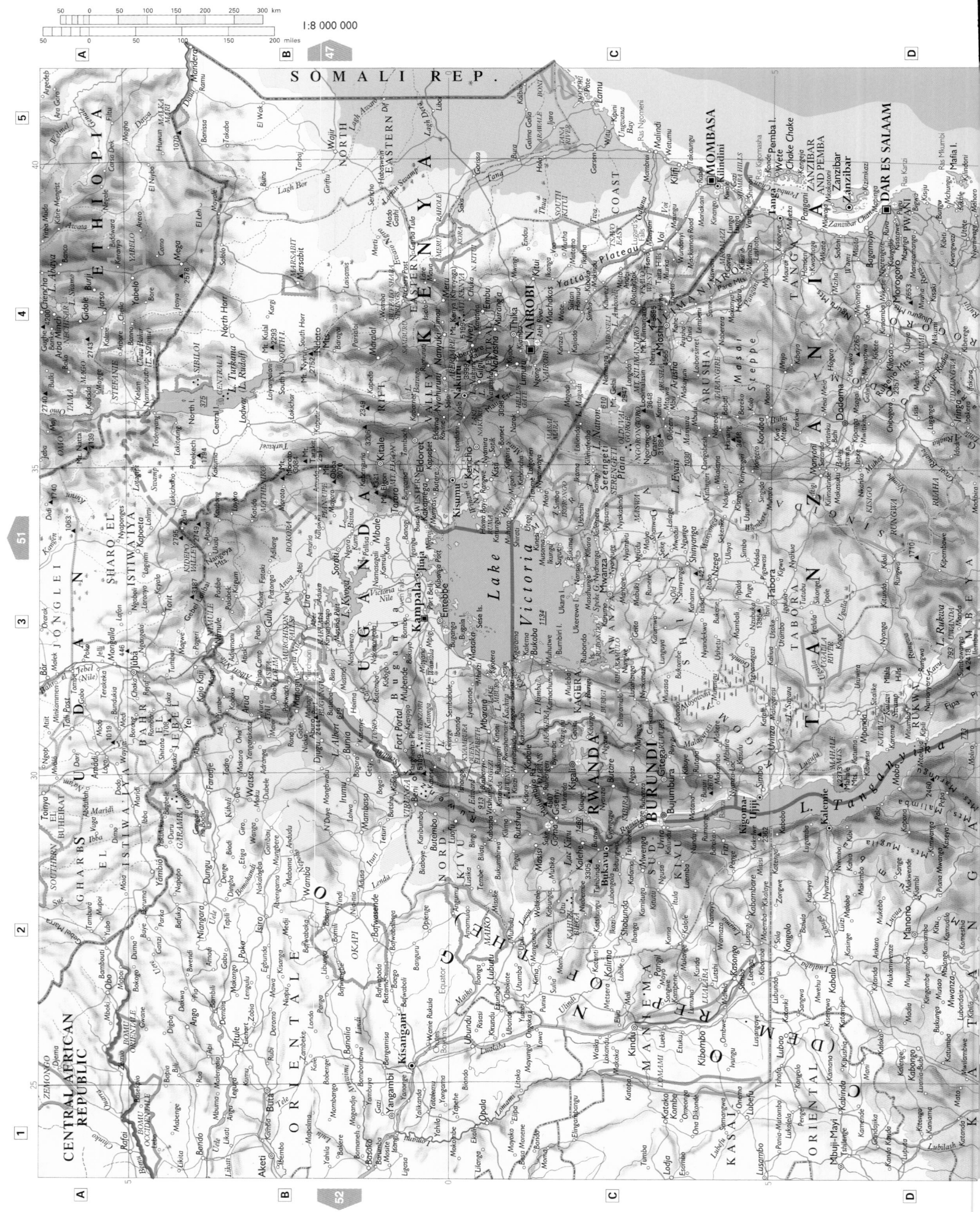

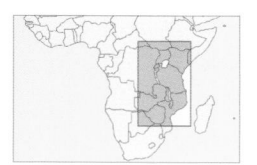

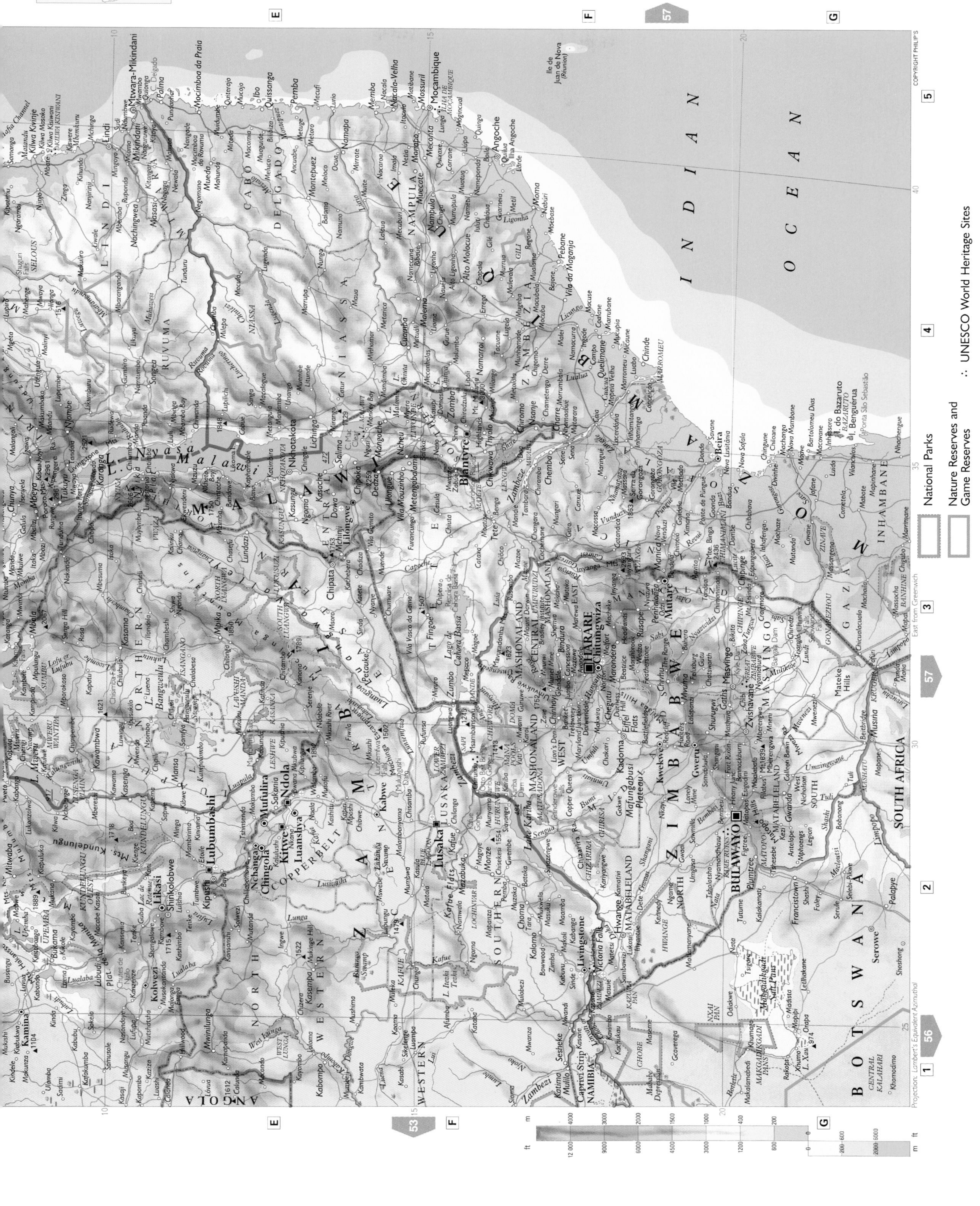
INDIAN OCEAN
MOZAMBIQUE
ZAMBIA
ZIMBABWE
MALAWI
BOTSWANA
SOUTH AFRICA
NAMIBIA
ANGOLA
L. Nyasa Malawi
HARARE
LUSAKA
Lilongwe
Blantyre
Bulawayo
Beira
Lubumbashi
National Parks
Nature Reserves and Game Reserves
UNESCO World Heritage Sites
Projection: Lambert's Equivalent Azimuthal
COPYRIGHT PHILIP'S
East from Greenwich

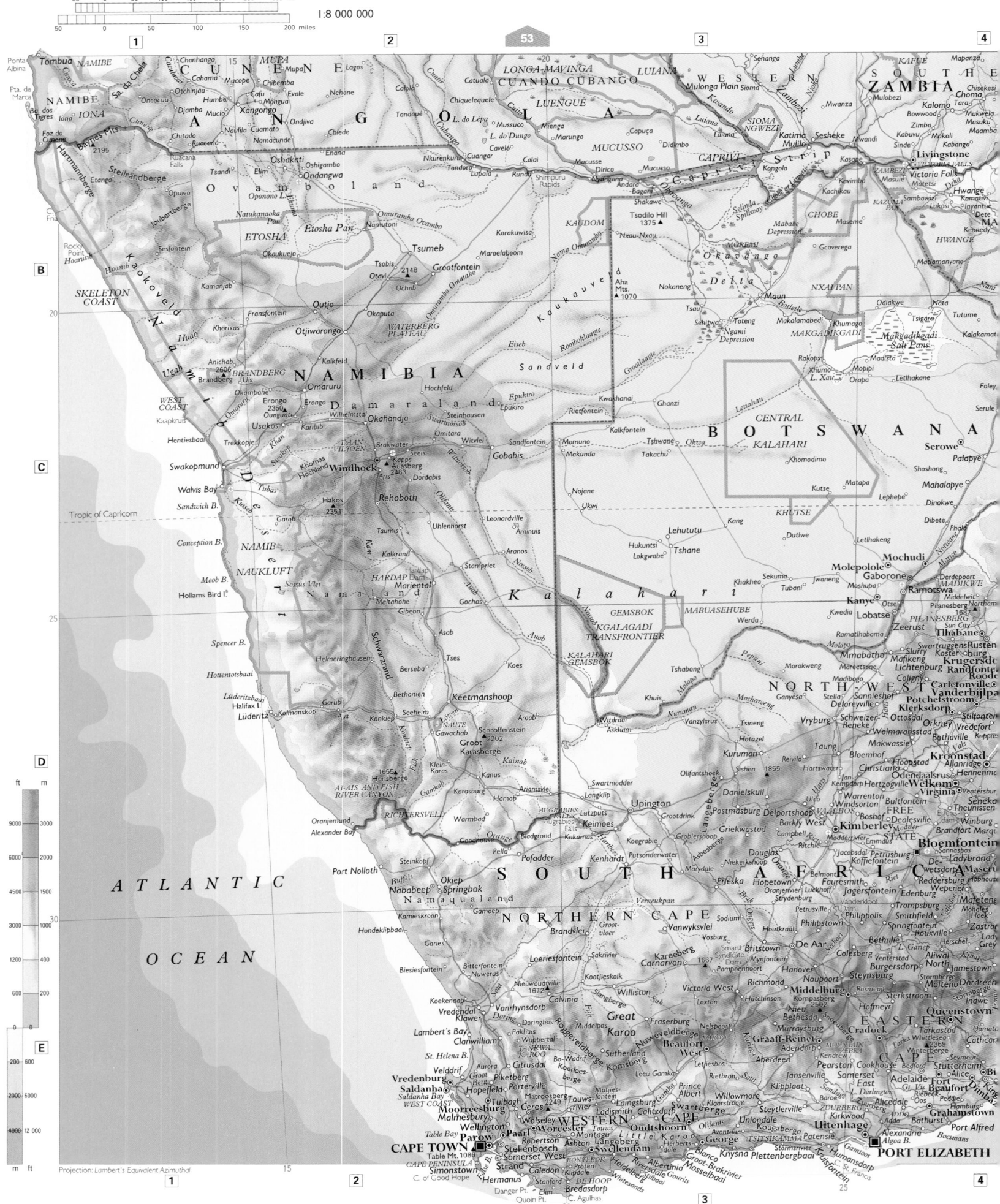

56 SOUTHERN AFRICA

50 0 50 100 150 200 250 300 km
50 0 50 100 150 200 miles

1:8 000 000

ATLANTIC

OCEAN

NAMIBIA

BOTSWANA

ANGOLA

ZAMBIA

SOUTH AFRICA

CAPE TOWN

PORT ELIZABETH

Projection: Lambert's Equivalent Azimuthal

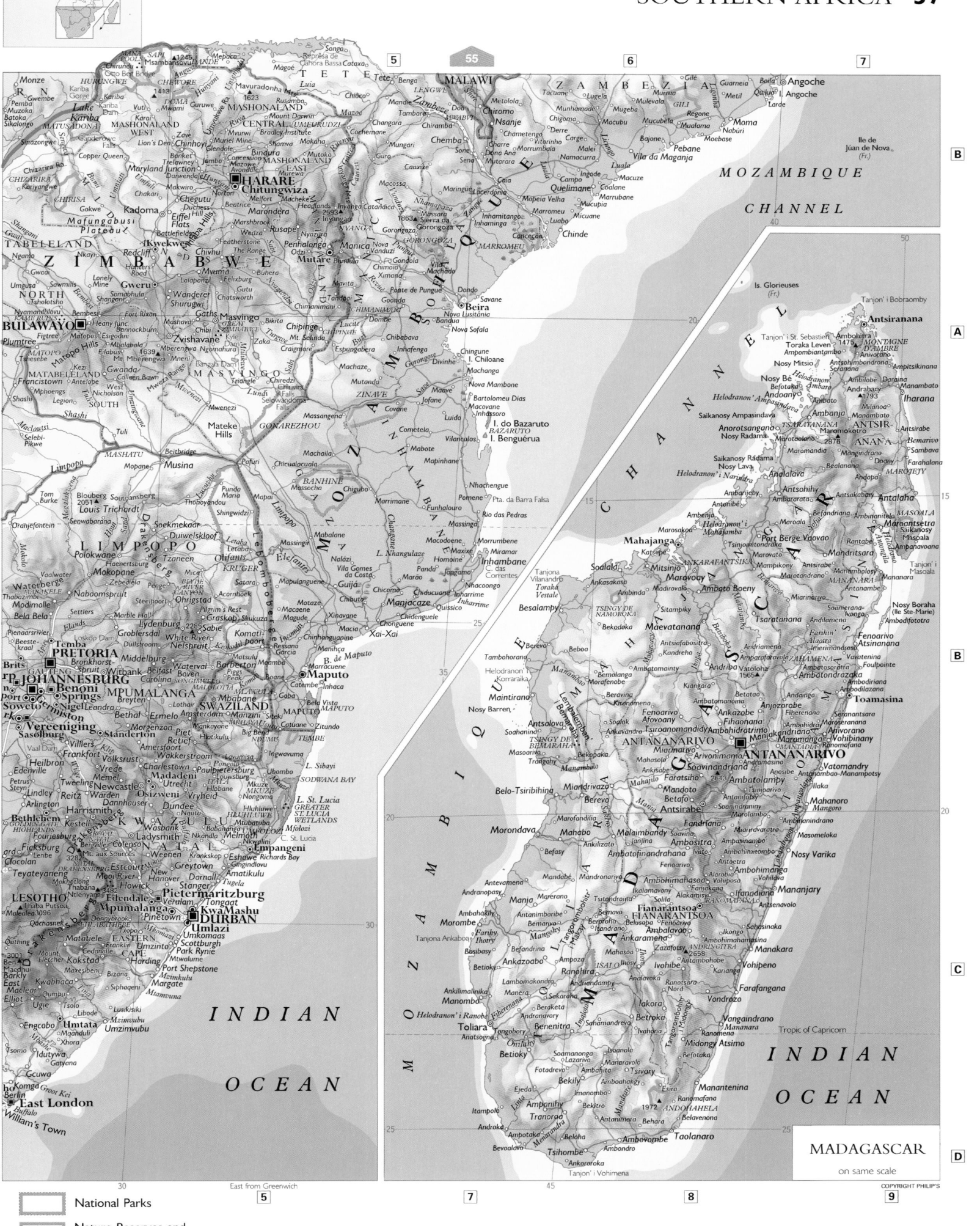

MADAGASCAR

on same scale

National Parks

Nature Reserves and
Game Reserves

∴ UNESCO World Heritage Sites

COPYRIGHT PHILIP'S

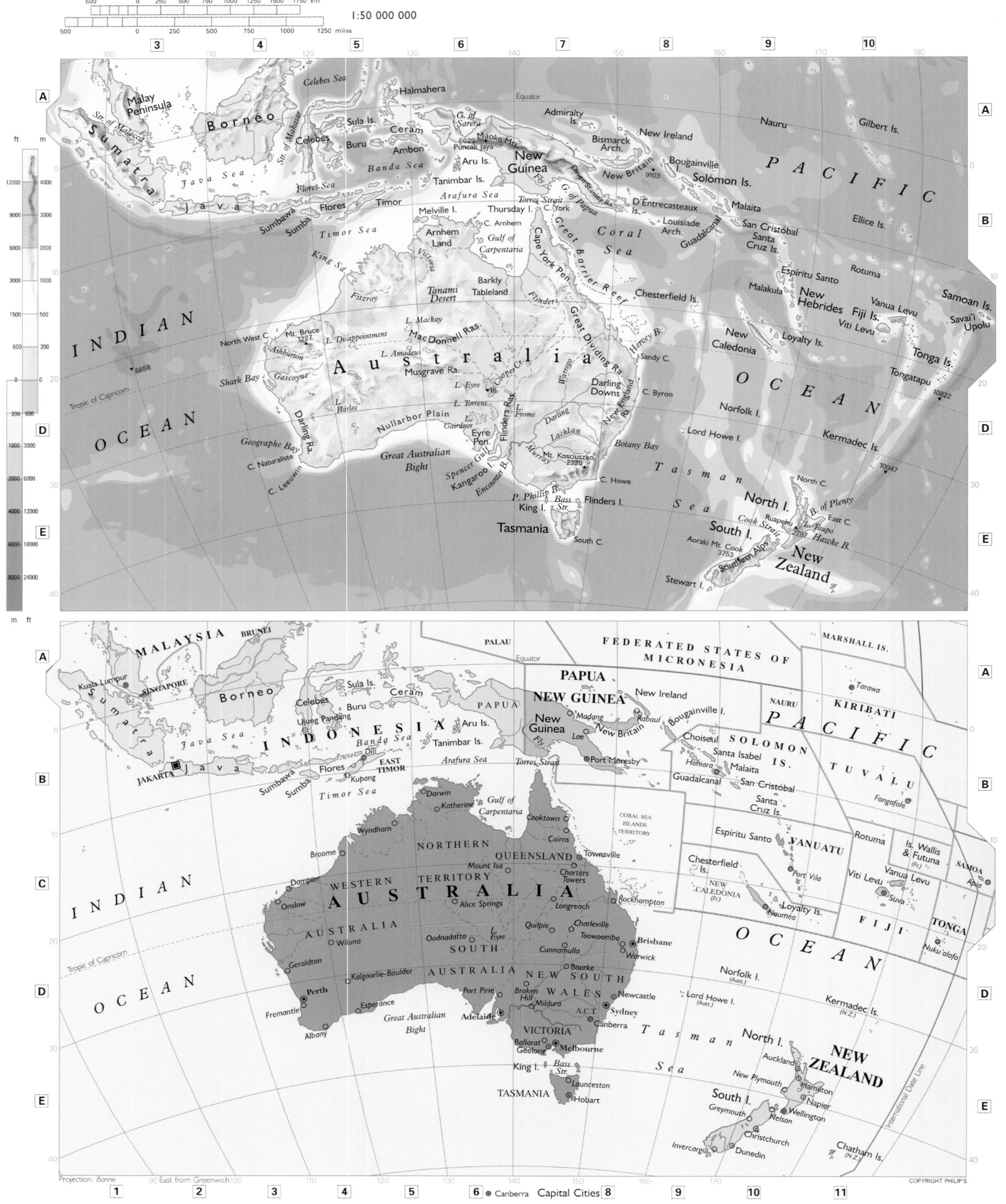

1:6 000 000

50   0   50   100   150   200 km
50   0   50   100   150 miles

TASMAN

SEA

North

Island

C. Reinga
C. Maria
van Diemen
North C.
Houhora Heads
Rangaunu B.
Doubtless B.
Mangonui
Whangaroa Harb.
Ahipara B.
Kaitaia
Okaihau
B. of Islands
Tauroa Pt.
Kaikohe
C. Brett
Rawene
Opua
Hokianga Harbour
Hikurangi
Donnelly's Crossing
Whangarei
Whangarei Harb.
Dargaville
Bream Hd.
Waipu
Bream B.
Little
Barrier I.
Great Barrier I.
Warkworth
C. Rodney
C. Colville
Helensville
Hauraki
Takapuna
Gulf
Coromandel
Whitianga
AUCKLAND
Manukau
Papakura
Thames
Pukekohe
Mayor I.
Waiuku
Mercer
Paeroa
Waihi
Tauranga Harb.
Waikato
Morrinsville
Te Aroha
Tauranga
Bay of Plenty
Huntly
White I. C. Runaway
Mount
Maunganui
Te Puke
Hamilton
Cambridge
Whakatane
Raglan
Te Awamutu
Kawerau
Opotiki
Hikurangi
Kawhia Harbour
Otorohanga
Rotorua
1753
Waipiro
Mokau
Te Kuiti
Kihikihi
L. Rotorua
Tarawera
Talaga Bay
North Taranaki
Bight
Ongarue
L. Taupo
Murupara
UREWERA
Ormond
Waitara
Taumarunui
Taupo
Gisborne
New Plymouth
WHANGANUI
Whangamomona
Waikaremoana
Poverty Bay
Inglewood
Turangi
Tarawera
Nuhaka
Mt.Taranaki
EGMONT
Ohakune
Waikokopu
C. Egmont
2518
Stratford
2797
TONGARIRO
Wairoa
Mahia Pen.
Opunake
Kapuni
Eltham
Raetihi
Waiouru
Bay Hawke Bay
Hawera
Waverley
Taihape
View
Napier
South Taranaki
Bight
Patea
Mangaweka
Ruahine
Ra.
Hastings
C. Kidnappers
Wanganui
Morton
Hunterville
Waipawa
Balls
Halcombe
Dannevirke
Waipukurau
Palmerston
North
Feilding
Woodville
C. Turnagain
Foxton
Shannon
Pahiatua
Levin
Eketahuna
Otaki
PACIFIC
C. Farewell
Paraparaumu
Masterton
Golden
D'Urville I.
Kapiti I.
Carterton
B. ABEL
Tasman Sd.
Upper Hutt
Greytown
Collingwood
TASMAN
Pelorus
Featherston
Martinborough
KAHURANGI
Takaka
Tasman
Petone
Tasman B.
Motueka
WELLINGTON
Karamea
Mts
Nelson
Havelock
OCEAN
Karamea
Bight
Picton
Lower Hutt
L. Wairarapa
Seddonville
Tadmor
Richmond
Wakefield
Eastbourne
Granity
Matiri Ra.
Murchison
Waitara
Blenheim
Cook
Westport
Lyell
Inangahua
NELSON
LAKES
Seddon
Strait
Reefton
Rotoroa
2885 Tapuaenuku
Ward
PAPAROA
Blackball
Grey
Mt Travers 2338
Spenser
Clarence
Runanga
Hanmer
Mts.
Greymouth
Stillwater
Springs
Kaikoura
Kumara
Kaikoura
Hokitika
L. Brunner
Jacksons
ARTHUR'S
Culverden
Waiau
Ross
PASS
Waikari
Hurunui
South
Arthur's
Waipara
Island
Abut Hd.
Amberley
Rangiora
Pegasus Bay
Colridge
Oxford
Kaiapoi
Whitecliffs
Springfield
New Brighton
Christchurch
Aoraki
WESTLAND
Methven
Waimakariri
Riccarton
Westland Bight
Mt Cook
Staveley
Lincoln
Lyttelton
3753
Mount
L.
Banks Pen.
COOK
Cook
Tekapo
Akaroa
Southern Alps
Fairlie
Little River
Jackson B.
Okuru
Haast
Mount
L.
Rakaia
L. Ellesmere
MOUNT
Aspiring
Pukaki
ASPIRING
Mt.
Timaru
Canterbury
Milford Sd.
Earnslaw
Wanaka
Ohau
St.
Plains
Sutherland Falls
2818
Temuka
Canterbury Bight
Bligh Sound
Milford
Wanaka
Andrews
George Sound
Sound
Arrowtown
Cromwell
Waimate
Queenstown
Waitaki
Kurow
Wakatipu
Clyde
Kakanui
Oamaru
South
Alexandra
Naseby
Mts.
Maheno
Island
Secretary I.
L.
Dunstan
Hampden
Doubtful Sd.
FIORDLAND
L. Anau
Roxburgh
Mts.
Dunback
Resolution I.
Manapouri
Waikouaiti
Palmerston
Dusky Sd.
Mossburn
Gore
Milton
Port Chalmers
Breaksea Sd.
Lumsden
Edievale
Otago Harbour
Mangapouri
Kelso
Lawrence
Saunders C.
L. South
Clinton
Tapanui
Fairfield
Dunedin
Chalky Inlet
Te Waewae B.
Ohai
Mataura
Milton
Preservation Inlet
Orepuki
Nightcaps
Gore
Balclutha
Riverton
Clifden
Hedgehope
Winton
Kaitangata
Tuatapere
Øwaka
Nugget Pt.
Invercargill
Tokanui
South Invercargill
Bluff
Ruapuke I.
Tahakopa
Halfmoon Bay
Stewart I.
Southwest C.
Port Pegasus

SAMOAN ISLANDS
1:12 000 000

SAMOA
AMERICAN
SAMOA
Savai'i
Apia
Upolu
Pago Pago
Tutuila
West from
Greenwich

Futuna
Wallis & Futuna (Fr.)
Niuafo'ou
(Tonga)
Thikombia
Labasa
Vanua Levu
Vanua Balavu
Yasawa Group
Taveuni
Koro
FIJI
Lautoka
1323
Levuka
Ovalau
Lau Group
Nandi
Viti Levu
Gau
Koro Sea
Lakeba
Suva
Moala
Vava'u
Kandavu
Vatoa
Tofua
Niuafo'ou
TONGA
(Friendly Is.)
Nuku'alofa
Tongatapu

FIJI AND TONGA
1:12 000 000

50   0   50   100   150   200 km
50   0   50   100   150 miles

West from Greenwich

National Parks

ft   m
9000   3000
6000   2000
3000   1000
1200   400
600   200
0   0
200   600
2000   6000
4000   12 000
6000   18 000
m   ft

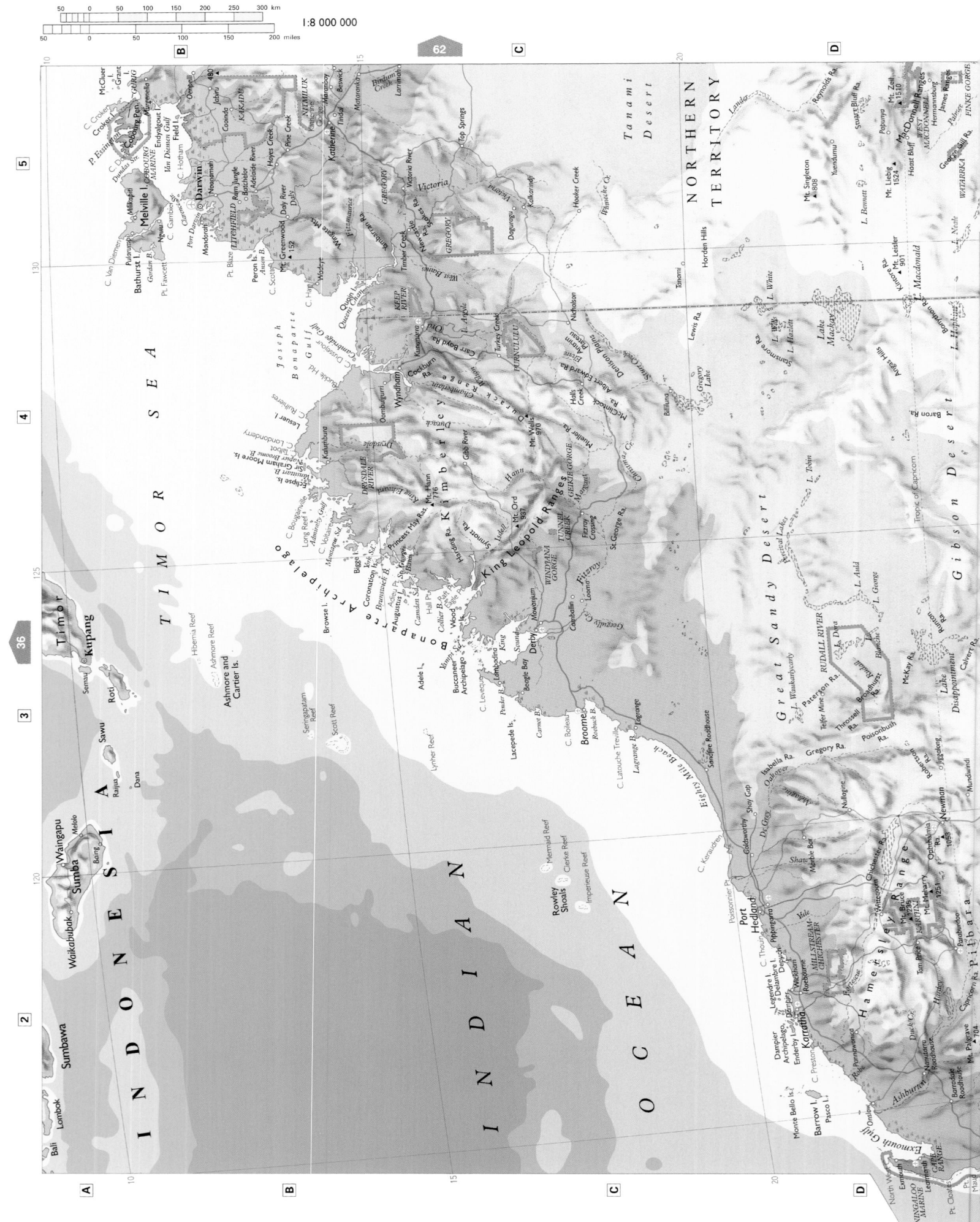

1:8 000 000

62

INDONESIA

TIMOR SEA

INDIAN OCEAN

NORTHERN TERRITORY

Tanami Desert

Great Sandy Desert

Gibson Desert

Kimberley

King Leopold Ranges

Hamersley Range

Bonaparte Archipelago

Joseph Bonaparte Gulf

Darwin

Broome

Port Hedland

Karratha

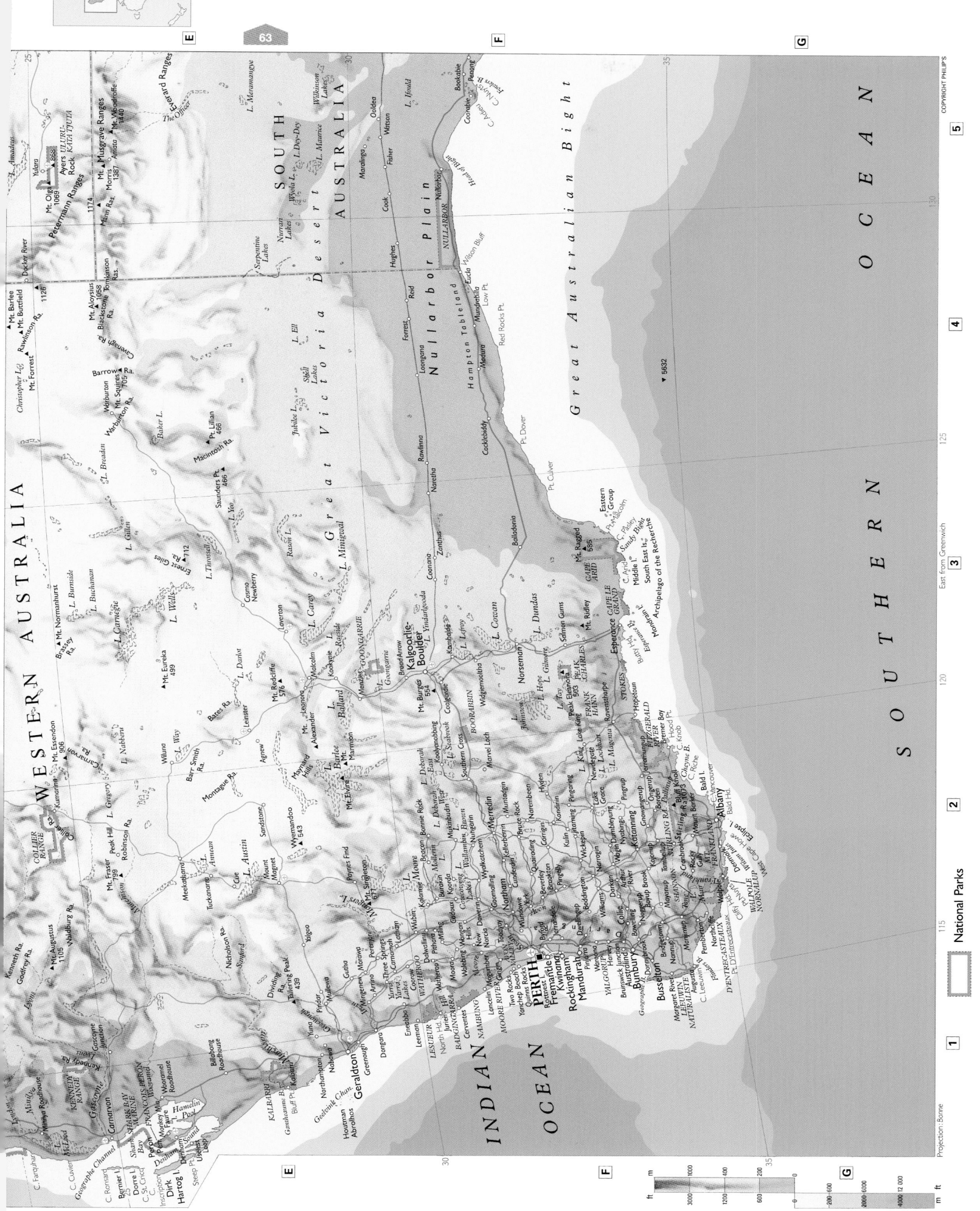

E

F

G

COPYRIGHT PHILIPS

WESTERN AUSTRALIA

SOUTH

AUSTRALIA

Great Victoria Desert

Nullarbor Plain

Hampton Tableland

NULLARBOR

Great Australian Bight

OCEAN

SOUTHERN

INDIAN

OCEAN

OCEAN

PERTH

Fremantle

Geraldton

Kalgoorlie-Boulder

Esperance

Albany

Bunbury

East from Greenwich

Projection: Bonne

National Parks

5632

1 2 3 4 5

115 120 125 130

25 30 35

m ft

3000
1200
600
0

10000
4000
2000
0

m ft

1:8 000 000

50 0 50 100 150 200 250 300 km
50 0 50 100 150 200 miles

H   J   K

CORAL SEA

149

7

Cumberland

WHITSUNDAY ISLANDS
Whitsunday I.
Hook I.
Hayman I.
GLOUCESTER I.
Gloucester Pt.
George Pt.
CONWAY
Airlie Beach
Cannonvale
Proserpine
SOUTH CUMBERLAND IS.
St. Bees I.
Carlisle I.
Brampton I.
Long I. Hamilton I.
Lindeman I.
Shaw I.
Whitsunday Pass.
Repulse Bay
C. Conway
Midge Point
Hillsborough Channel
Sarina
Seaforth
Bucasia
Kuttaboo
Farleigh
Mirani
Walkerston
Mackay

Bowen
Mt. McGuire
Foxdale
Kelsey Creek
820
738▲
Bloomsbury
Mt. Dalrymple 1259▲
Netherdale
Finch Hatton
R.3
Clarke Range
Clermont
Cullen
Kunguri
Mirani
Gargett

QUEENSLAND
EUNGELLA
Broken River Ra.

WHITSUNDAY ISLANDS
1:2 500 000

60 km 40 miles

6   58   4

CORAL SEA

Magdelane Cays
Coringa Is.
Herald Cays
Diamond Is.
Lihou Reefs and Cays
Tregrosse Is.
Abington Reef
Holmes Reefs
Flinders Reefs

Osprey Reef
Bougainville Reef

5

C

Swain Reefs
Capricorn Channel
GREAT BARRIER REEF (CAPRICORN)
Lady Elliott I.
Hervey Bay
Sandy C.
Fraser I.
Great Sandy I.
Bustard Hds.
Curtis I. Capricorn Group
Gladstone
Rockhampton
Yeppoon
C. Clinton
Port Alma
Mt. Larcom
Bundaberg
Childers
Maryborough
Gympie

GREAT BARRIER REEF
Great Barrier Reef

Great Barrier Reef
GREAT BARRIER REEF (CENTRAL)
Whitsunday I.
Cumberland Islands
Bowen
Proserpine
Mackay
Sarina
Seaforth
St. Lawrence
Marlborough
Broad Sound
Middlemount
Dysart
Blackwater
Emerald
Springsure
Rolleston
Carnarvon Gorge
Injune
Roma

GREAT BARRIER REEF (FAR NORTH)
Lizard I.
C. Bedford
Cooktown
Hopevale
Helenvale
Mt. Finnigan 1148
Daintree
Mossman
Port Douglas
Cairns
Kuranda
Edmonton
Gordonvale
Babinda
Innisfail
Tully
Cardwell
Ingham
Halifax Palm Is.
Great Palm I.
HINCHINBROOK I.
Lucinda
Cleveland Bay
Townsville
Ayr
Home Hill
Bowen

Townsville

HERBERT RIVER FALLS
WALLAMAN FALLS
UNDARA VOLCANIC

Charters Towers
Pentland
Hughenden
Prairie
Torrens Cr.
Muttaburra
Aramac
Barcaldine
Jericho
Alpha
Emerald
Blair Athol
Clermont
Capella
Rubyvale
Sapphire
Nebo
Moranbah

Great Dividing Range

GREAT BASALT WALL
WHITE MTS.
MOORRINYA
Landsborough Cr.
Aramac
Longreach
Ilfracombe
Isisford
Stonehenge
Jundah
Windorah

Cairns

C. York
Thursday I.
Horn I.
Prince of Wales I.
Port Musgrave
Cullen Pt.
Weipa
Aurukun
Archer R.
Pera Hd.
Duifken Pt.
Mapoon
Andoom

Cape York Peninsula

IRON RANGE
Temple B.
C. Grenville
Lloyd B.
Lockhart River
Claremont Pt.
Princess Charlotte Bay
C. Melville
Flinders Group
Bathurst B.
Normanby
Laura
Lakeland
Palmer
Hann R.
Walsh
Lynd
Mt. Mulgrave
Chillagoe
Almaden
Mount Garnet
Herberton
Ravenshoe
Atherton
Mareeba
Dimbulah
Mount Molloy
Mount Carbine

JARDINE RIVER
Bamaga
Turtle Head I.
Shelburne Bay
Sharp Pt.
Restoration I.

Great Dividing Range

Croydon
Georgetown
Einasleigh
Forsayth
Gilbert River
Greenvale
Mount Surprise
Kidston
Mount Coolon

Gulf of Carpentaria

Karumba
Normanton
Burketown
Gregory Downs
Camooweal
Mount Isa
Cloncurry
Julia Creek
Richmond
Maxwelton
Hughenden
Prairie
Stamford
Corfield
Winton
Jundah
Stonehenge

Mt. Isa

C. Van Diemen
Mornington I.
Wellesley Is.
Bentinck I.
Sweers I.
Leichhardt
Nicholson
LAWN HILL

NORTHERN TERRITORY

Arnhem Land
Goulburn Is.
C. Wessel
Wessel Is.
Elcho I.
C. Arnhem
Gove
Nhulunbuy
The Eighty Company
Milingimbi
Maningrida
Ramingining
Groote Eylandt
Umbakumba
Angurugu
C. Shield
Woodah I.
Bickerton I.
Caledon Bay
Blue Mud B.
Port Bradshaw
Rose R.
Numbulwar
Borroloola
Bing Bong
Wollogorang
Limmen Bight
Maria I.
C. Beatrice
Sir Edward Pellew Group
Vanderlin I.
Port McArthur
Centre I.
West I.
North I.

Roper Bar
Roper R.
Ngukurr
Mataranka
Katherine
Elliott
Newcastle Waters
Daly Waters
Dunmarra
Renner Springs
Elliott
Barkly Roadhouse

BARKLY TABLELAND

Camooweal
Barkly Tableland
Brunette Downs
Avon Downs
Ranken
Alpurrurulam

Tennant Creek
Wauchope
Murchison Ra.
Barrow Creek
Ti-Tree
Aileron
Utopia
Arltunga
Ross River
1168
Alice Springs
1128
MacDonnell Ranges
Santa Teresa
Finke
Hermannsburg

Davenport Range

SIMPSON DESERT

Diamantina
Boulia
Bedourie
Birdsville
Windorah
Betoota

L. Machattie
L. Caroline
Eyre Cr.
Georgina
Field R.
Mulligan
Toko Range
Hay R.
L. Nash

Tropic of Capricorn

Great Artesian Basin

Great Dividing Range

QUEENSLAND

1312
CARNARVON Ra.
Mt. King 868

1   2   3   4

A   B   C

135   140   145

15   20   25

60

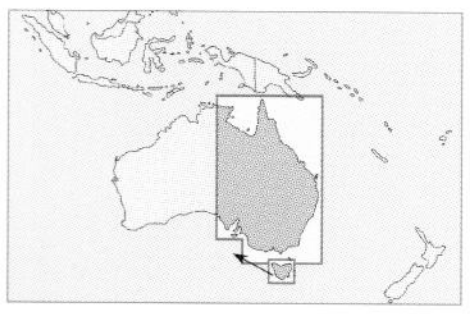

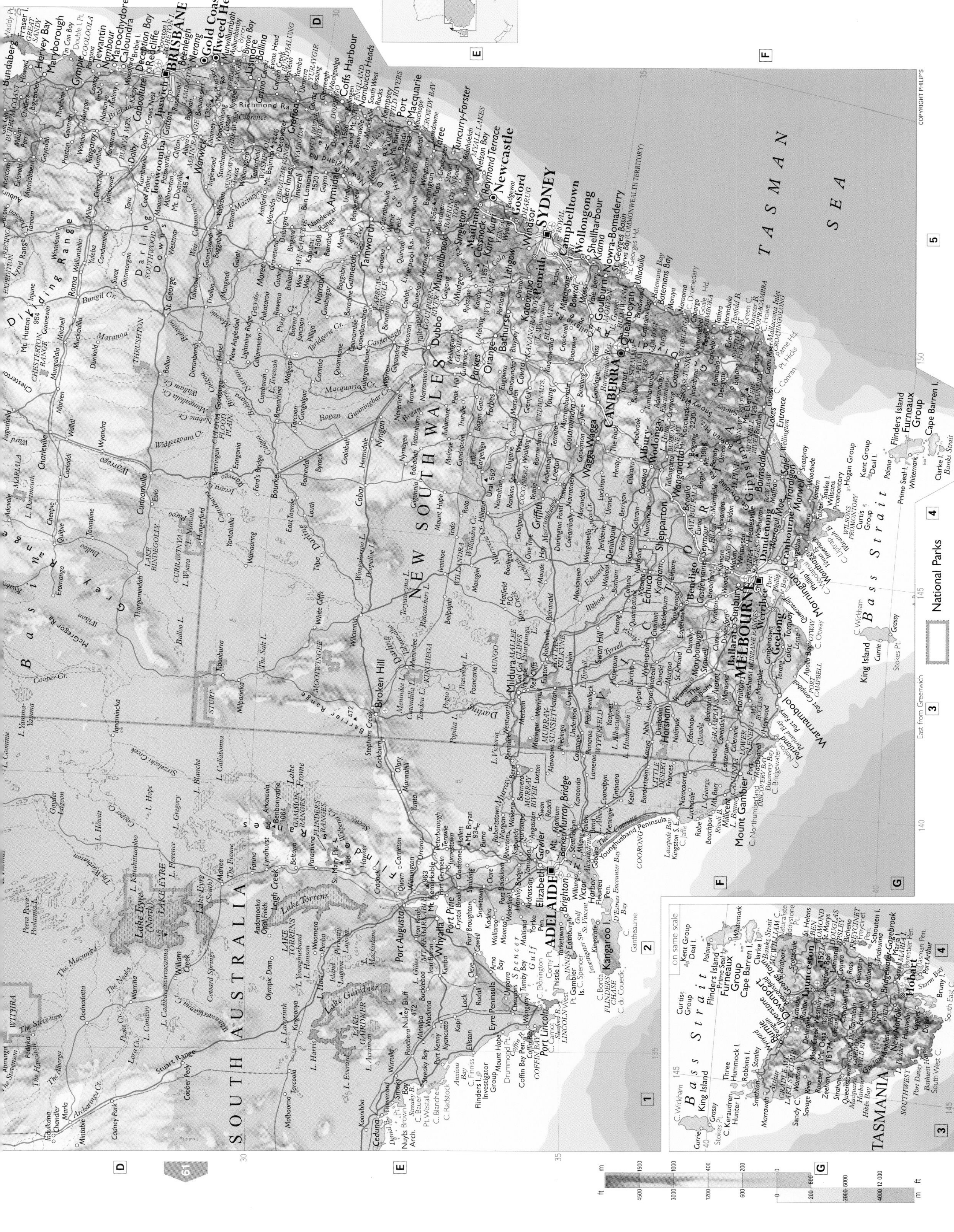

National Parks

on same scale

COPYRIGHT PHILIP'S

Projection: Bonne

TASMAN SEA

NEW SOUTH WALES

SOUTH AUSTRALIA

TASMANIA

QUEENSLAND

Great Dividing Range

Darling Downs

Lake Eyre

Lake Torrens

Lake Gairdner

Bass Strait

BRISBANE
Gold Coast
Tweed Heads
Newcastle
SYDNEY
Wollongong
CANBERRA
MELBOURNE
ADELAIDE
Hobart

m / ft
4500 / 15000
3000 / 10000
1200 / 4000
600 / 2000
400 / 1200
200 / 600
0
200 / 600
2000 / 6000
4000 / 12000
m / ft

East from Greenwich

RUSSIA

Bering Sea

Sea of Okhotsk
Okhotsk
Komandorskiye Ostrova (Russia)
Poluostrov Kamchatka
Near Is. (U.S.A.)
Andreanof Is. (U.S.A.)
Petropavlovsk-Kamchatskiy
Aleutian
Aleutian Trench
7822

Yekaterinburg
Ob'
Tomsk
Lena
Novosibirsk
Irkutsk
Oz. Baykal
Chita
Astana (Aqmola)
Semey
Blagoveshchensk
Amur
Khabarovsk
Sakhalin
La Pérouse Str.
Kurilskiye Ostrova (Russia)
Kuril Trench
10,542

MOSKVA
Volga

KAZAKHSTAN
Aral Sea
Balqash Köl
Altai
Ulaanbaatar
MONGOLIA
Changchun
Harbin
Vladivostok
Sapporo
Hakodate
Sea of Japan

Emperor Seamount Chain

Almaty
Ürümqi
SHENYANG
Kuril Trench

Toshkent
KYRGYZSTAN
BEIJING
TIANJIN
Taiyuan
NORTH KOREA
Dalian
SOUTH KOREA
SOUL
Sendai
Nagoya
TOKYO
Yokohama
JAPAN
Fuji-San 3776
10,554
Japan Trench

TAJIKISTAN
CHINA
Lanzhou
Huang He
Qingdao
Kyoto
Osaka
Shikoku
Kyūshū

AFGHANISTAN
Kabul
Srinagar
Kunlun Shan
XIZANG
Xi'an
Nanjing
Kitakyūshū
Yellow Sea

Midway Is. (U.S.A.)

PAKISTAN
Lahore
DELHI
Himalaya
8850 Mt. Everest
Lhasa
CHONGQING
Wuhan
SHANGHAI
East China Sea

Lisianski I. (U.S.A.)

Kanpur
Nepal
Ganga
Brahmaputra
Chang J.
Changsha
HANGZHOU
Ogasawara Gunto (Japan)
Minami-Tori-Shima

INDIA
Hyderabad
BANGLADESH
Kunming
Fuzhou
Taipei
Ryūkyū-rettō (Japan)
Kazan-Rettō (Japan)
South Honshu Ridge

Marcus
Necker Ridge
Wake I. (U.S.A.)

PA

KOLKATA (Calcutta)
DHAKA
Mandalay
BURMA
GUANGZHOU
Macau
HONG KONG
TAIWAN

NORTHERN MARIANAS (U.S.A.)
Saipan

International Dateline Ridge

PA

LAOS
Hanoi
Hainan
C. Engano
Luzon
Paracel Is.
MANILA

GUAM (U.S.A.)
11,022
Mariana Trench

MARSHALL IS.
Bikini Atoll
Enewetak Atoll

Bay of Bengal
Rangoon
THAILAND
BANGKOK
VIETNAM
Mekong
South China Sea
Mindoro
PHILIPPINES
Samar
Mindanao Trench
10,497

Micronesia

CHENNAI (Madras)
Andaman Is. (India)
CAMBODIA
Phnom Penh
Palawan
Yap
Caroline Is.
Truk
Dalap-Uliga-Darrit
Jaluit I.

SRI LANKA
Nicobar Is. (India)
G. of Thailand
Thanh Pho Ho Chi Minh
China
Sulu Sea
Mindanao
Koror
Pohnpei
Palikir

Colombo
MALAYSIA
Celebes Sea
4101
PALAU
FEDERATED STATES OF MICRONESIA
Butaritari
Tarawa
Gilbert Is.
Howland I. (U.S.A.)
Baker I. (U.S.A.)

Kuala Lumpur
Sea
Halmahera
Sulawesi
Buru
Seram
Maluku
Banaba
Nauru
O

SINGAPORE
BRUNEI
SABAH
Melanesia
Phoenix Is.
Abariringa
Enderbury

Sumatera
INDONESIA
Borneo
Puncak Jaya 5029
PAPUA
New Guinea
PAPUA NEW GUINEA
Admiralty Is.
Bismarck Arch.
New Ireland
Rabaul
KIR

Sunda Islands
Palembang
Ujung Pandang
Banda Sea
7440
New Britain
Bougainville
Fongafale
Tuvalu
Tokelau Is. (N.Z.)

JAKARTA
Jawa
Java Sea
Flores Sea
Flores
EAST TIMOR
Lae
Port Moresby
SOLOMON IS.
Honiara
Guadalcanal

Surabaya
Bali
Sumbawa
Sumba
Timor
Arafura Sea
Torres Strait
C. York
Santa Cruz I. 9165
Rotuma
Is. Wallis & Futuna (Fr.)
SAMOA
Apia

Java Trench
Cocos Is. (Austral.)
Christmas I. (Austral.)
C. Arnhem
Gulf of Carpentaria
Espiritu Santo
Vanua Levu
Viti Levu
Suva
FIJI
Nuku'alofa
TONGA

INDIAN
Darwin
Louisiade Arch.
Coral Sea
VANUATU
Port Vila
Is. Chesterfield

OCEAN
Broome
Cairns
Townsville
Great Barrier Reef
7570
NEW CALEDONIA (Fr.)
Nouméa
Is. Loyauté
10,822
Tonga Trench

AUSTRALIA
Mount Isa
Alice Springs
L. Eyre
Great Dividing Ra.
Rockhampton
Brisbane
Norfolk I. (Austral.)
Kermadec Is. (N.Z.)

Geraldton
Darling
Murray
Lord Howe I. (Austral.)
Kermadec Trench 10,047

Perth
Great Australian Bight
Sydney
Canberra
Mt. Kosciuszko 2237
Tasman Sea
NEW ZEALAND

Albany
Adelaide
Melbourne
Auckland

Nouvelle Amsterdam (Fr.)
I. St. Paul (Fr.)
Bass Str.
Tasmania
Hobart
Aoraki Mt. Cook 3753
Christchurch
Chatham Is. (N.Z.)

Mid-Indian Ridge
Is. Crozet (Fr.)
Dunedin
Invercargill
Bounty Is. (N.Z.)

Kerguelen (Fr.)
Auckland Is. (N.Z.)
Antipodes Is. (N.Z.)

Heard I. (Austral.)
Macquarie I. (Austral.)
Campbell I. (N.Z.)

ft m
12 000 / 4000
9000 / 3000
6000 / 2000
3000 / 1000
1500 / 500
600 / 200
0 / 0
600 / 200
3000 / 1000
6000 / 2000
12 000 / 4000
18 000 / 6000
24 000 / 8000
m ft

Arctic Circle

ALASKA
(U.S.A.)
Anchorage

Bristol Bay

Gulf of Alaska

Juneau

Is. (U.S.A.)

CANADA

Prince of Wales I.
(U.S.A.) Prince Rupert
Queen Charlotte Is.
(Canada)

Edmonton

L. Winnipeg

Newfoundland

NORTH

Vancouver
Vancouver I.
Victoria
Seattle

Calgary

Regina

Winnipeg

Québec

St. Lawrence

St. John's

Portland

Boise

L. Superior

Montréal

Ottawa

Boston

C. Mendocino

Salt Lake
City

Minneapolis

L. Michigan
L. Huron
Toronto
L. Ontario

Detroit
L. Erie
Buffalo

NEW YORK CITY
PHILADELPHIA
Baltimore
Washington D.C.

Sacramento

Denver

CHICAGO

Pittsburgh

Cincinnati

ATLANTIC

SAN FRANCISCO

Kansas City

St. Louis

UNITED STATES

Appalachian Mts.

C. Hatteras

Bermuda
(U.K.)

LOS ANGELES
San Diego

Phoenix

Oklahoma City
Memphis

Atlanta

Jacksonville

OCEAN

Ciudad
Juárez

Dallas

Houston

San Antonio

New
Orleans

Miami

BAHAMAS

Sargasso Sea

Guadalupe
(Mex.)

Monterrey

Gulf of Mexico

La Habana

CUBA

West Indies

Tropic of Cancer

C. San Lucas

MEXICO

Mérida

HAITI

DOMINICAN REP.

Leeward
Is.

Honolulu
Oahu
HAWAIIAN IS.
(U.S.A.)
Hawaii

Guadalajara

MEXICO
Puebla

JAMAICA

Kingston

PUERTO
RICO
(U.S.A.)

BARBADOS

PACIFIC

Johnston I.
(U.S.A.)

Acapulco

Is. Revilla Gigedo
(Mex.)

BELIZE

Caribbean Sea

Windward Is.

I. Clipperton
(Fr.)

GUATEMALA
Guatemala
San Salvador
EL SALVADOR

HONDURAS

NICARAGUA

Managua

Barranquilla
San José

Maracaibo

Caracas

Palmyra Is.
(U.S.A.)

North West Christmas I. Ridge

Teraina
Tabuaeran
Kiritimati

COSTA
RICA

Colón
PANAMA

Panama

VENEZUELA

I. del Coco
(Costa Rica)

Medellín

Bogotá
Cali

COLOMBIA

OCEAN

Jarvis I.
(U.S.A.)

Equator

I. de Malpelo
(Colombia)

Galápagos
(Ecuador)

Quito
ECUADOR

KIRIBATI

Malden I.
Starbuck I.

Guayaquil

Iquitos

Amazonas

BRAZIL

C. Palinas

Tongareva

Pukapuka
Manihiki

Suwarrow Is.

AMER.
SAMOA
(U.S.A.)

Vostok I.
Flint I.

Caroline I.
(Millennium I.)

Is. Marquises

Trujillo

6369
PERU

Is. de la
Société

LIMA

Cuzco

Niue
(N.Z.)

Cook Is.
(N.Z.)

Tahiti
Papeete

FRENCH POLYNESIA

Is. Tuamotu

L. Titicaca
6550

Nevada Ancohuma

Arequipa

6866

La Paz
BOLIVIA

Rarotonga

Is. Tubuai

Murúroa

Peru-

Arica

Iquique
Chile

Tropic of Capricorn

PARAGUAY

Ducie I.

Antofagasta

Pitcairn I.
(U.K.)

Asunción

Rapa

Sala-y-Gómez
(Chile)

San Felix
(Chile)

San Ambrosio
(Chile)

8050
Trench

San Miguel
de Tucumán

Porto
Alegre

I. de Pascua
(Chile)

East Pacific Ridge

Córdoba

Aconcagua
6962

Rosario

URUGUAY

Arch. de
Juan Fernández
(Chile)

Valparaíso

SANTIAGO

BUENOS
AIRES

Montevideo

Río de la Plata

Concepción

ARGENTINA

Chile Rise

SOUTH

Pacific–Antarctic Ridge

ATLANTIC

6212

OCEAN

Punta Arenas

Est. de Magallanes
Tierra del Fuego

Falkland Is.
(U.K.)

South Georgia
(U.K.)

C. de Hornos

West from Greenwich

COPYRIGHT PHILIP'S

1:35 000 000

Projection: Bonne

West from Greenwich

COPYRIGHT PHILIP'S

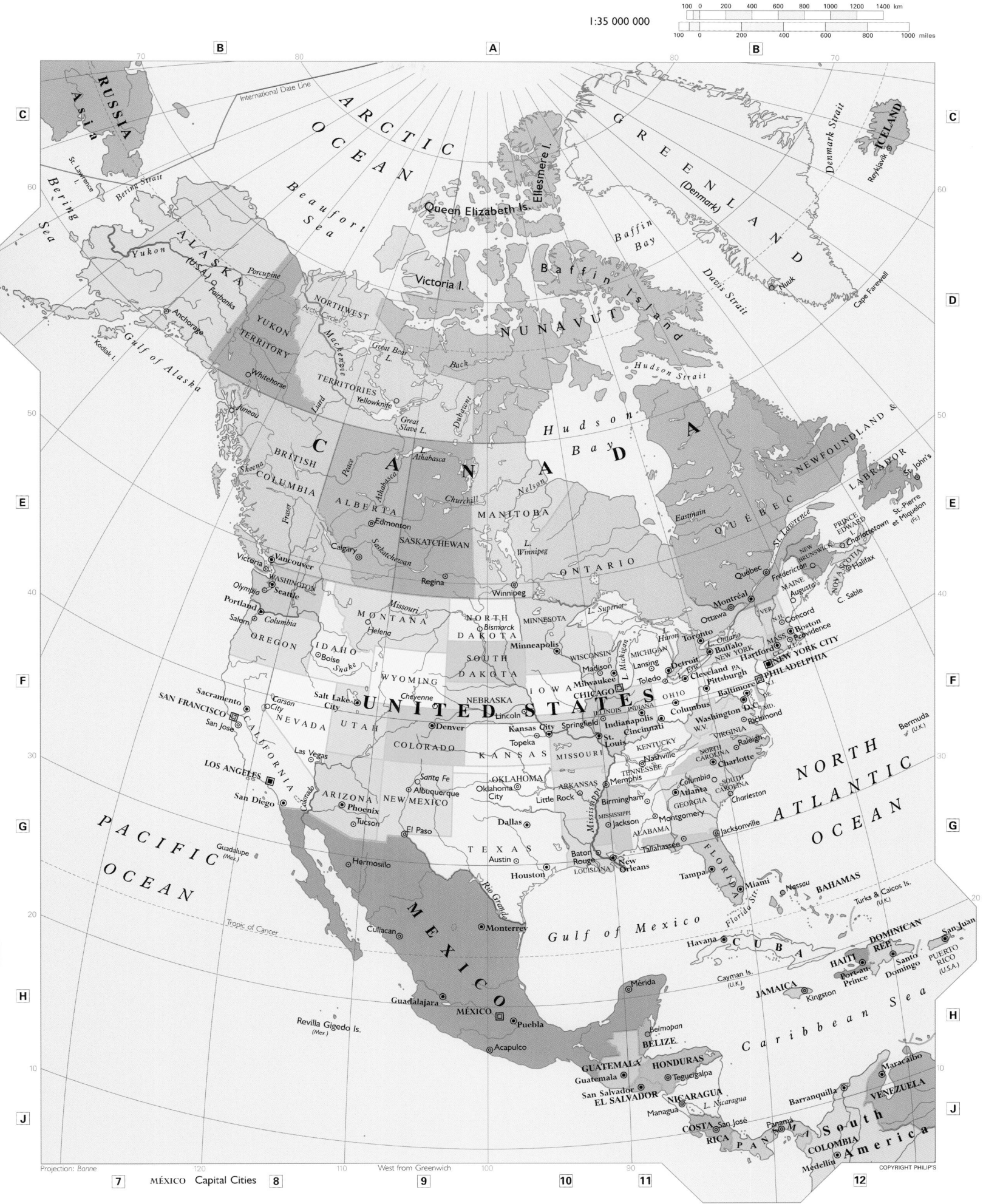

1:35 000 000

100 0   200 400   600 800   1000 1200 1400 km
100 0   200   400   600   800   1000 miles

RUSSIA
Asia

ARCTIC OCEAN

International Date Line

GREENLAND
(Denmark)

Denmark Strait

ICELAND

Reykjavik

St. Lawrence I.

Bering Strait

Bering Sea

Beaufort Sea

Queen Elizabeth Is.

Ellesmere I.

Baffin Bay

Cape Farewell

Nuuk

Yukon

ALASKA
(USA)

Porcupine

Fairbanks

Anchorage

Kodiak I.

Gulf of Alaska

YUKON TERRITORY

Whitehorse

Juneau

NORTHWEST

Arctic Circle

Mackenzie

Great Bear L.

Back

TERRITORIES

Yellowknife

Great Slave L.

Liard

Baffin Island

NUNAVUT

Hudson Strait

Davis Strait

Victoria I.

Hudson Bay

C A N A D A

BRITISH COLUMBIA

Skeena

Fraser

Peace

Athabasca

ALBERTA

Edmonton

Calgary

Athabasca L.

SASKATCHEWAN

Saskatchewan

Regina

Churchill

Nelson

MANITOBA

L. Winnipeg

ONTARIO

Winnipeg

Eastmain

QUÉBEC

NEWFOUNDLAND & LABRADOR

St. John's

St-Pierre et Miquelon (Fr.)

Québec

Fredericton

NEW BRUNSWICK

PRINCE EDWARD I.

Charlottetown

NOVA SCOTIA

Halifax

Montréal

Ottawa

L. Superior

L. Huron

MAINE

Augusta

C. Sable

Victoria

Vancouver

WASHINGTON

Olympia

Seattle

Portland

Salem

Columbia

OREGON

MONTANA

Helena

Missouri

IDAHO

Boise

Snake

NORTH DAKOTA

Bismarck

MINNESOTA

SOUTH DAKOTA

WISCONSIN

Madison

Milwaukee

Lansing

MICHIGAN

L. Michigan

Detroit

Toledo

Toronto

Buffalo

L. Erie

L. Ontario

Cleveland

PA.

Pittsburgh

NEW YORK

Hartford

MASS.

Boston

Providence

N.H.

Concord

VER.

NEW YORK CITY

PHILADELPHIA

Baltimore

N.J.

WYOMING

Cheyenne

NEBRASKA

IOWA

ILLINOIS

CHICAGO

INDIANA

OHIO

Columbus

Indianapolis

Cincinnati

Washington D.C.

W.V.

Richmond

DE.

MD.

U N I T E D   S T A T E S

Salt Lake City

UTAH

Denver

COLORADO

Lincoln

Kansas City

Topeka

KANSAS

MISSOURI

St. Louis

Springfield

KENTUCKY

VIRGINIA

Raleigh

NORTH CAROLINA

Nashville

TENNESSEE

Charlotte

SOUTH CAROLINA

Columbia

Charleston

Sacramento

SAN FRANCISCO

San Jose

Carson City

NEVADA

CALIFORNIA

Las Vegas

LOS ANGELES

San Diego

Santa Fe

ARIZONA

Phoenix

Tucson

Albuquerque

NEW MEXICO

Colorado

El Paso

OKLAHOMA

Oklahoma City

ARKANSAS

Little Rock

Memphis

MISSISSIPPI

Birmingham

Jackson

ALABAMA

Montgomery

GEORGIA

Atlanta

Jacksonville

Dallas

T E X A S

Austin

Houston

LOUISIANA

Baton Rouge

New Orleans

Mississippi

Tallahassee

FLORIDA

Tampa

Miami

Nassau

BAHAMAS

Bermuda (U.K.)

NORTH ATLANTIC OCEAN

PACIFIC OCEAN

Guadalupe (Mex.)

Hermosillo

Culiacán

Rio Grande

M E X I C O

Monterrey

Tropic of Cancer

Gulf of Mexico

Havana

CUBA

Florida Str.

Turks & Caicos Is. (U.K.)

Cayman Is. (U.K.)

JAMAICA

Kingston

HAITI

Port-au-Prince

DOMINICAN REP.

Santo Domingo

PUERTO RICO (U.S.A.)

San Juan

Caribbean Sea

Guadalajara

MÉXICO

Puebla

Revilla Gigedo Is. (Mex.)

Acapulco

Mérida

Belmopan

BELIZE

GUATEMALA

Guatemala

HONDURAS

Tegucigalpa

San Salvador

EL SALVADOR

NICARAGUA

Managua

L. Nicaragua

COSTA RICA

San José

PANAMA

Panamá

Maracaibo

VENEZUELA

Barranquilla

COLOMBIA

Medellín

South America

1:15 000 000

Projection : Bonne

ALASKA
1:30 000 000

West from Greenwich

74

COPYRIGHT PHILIP'S

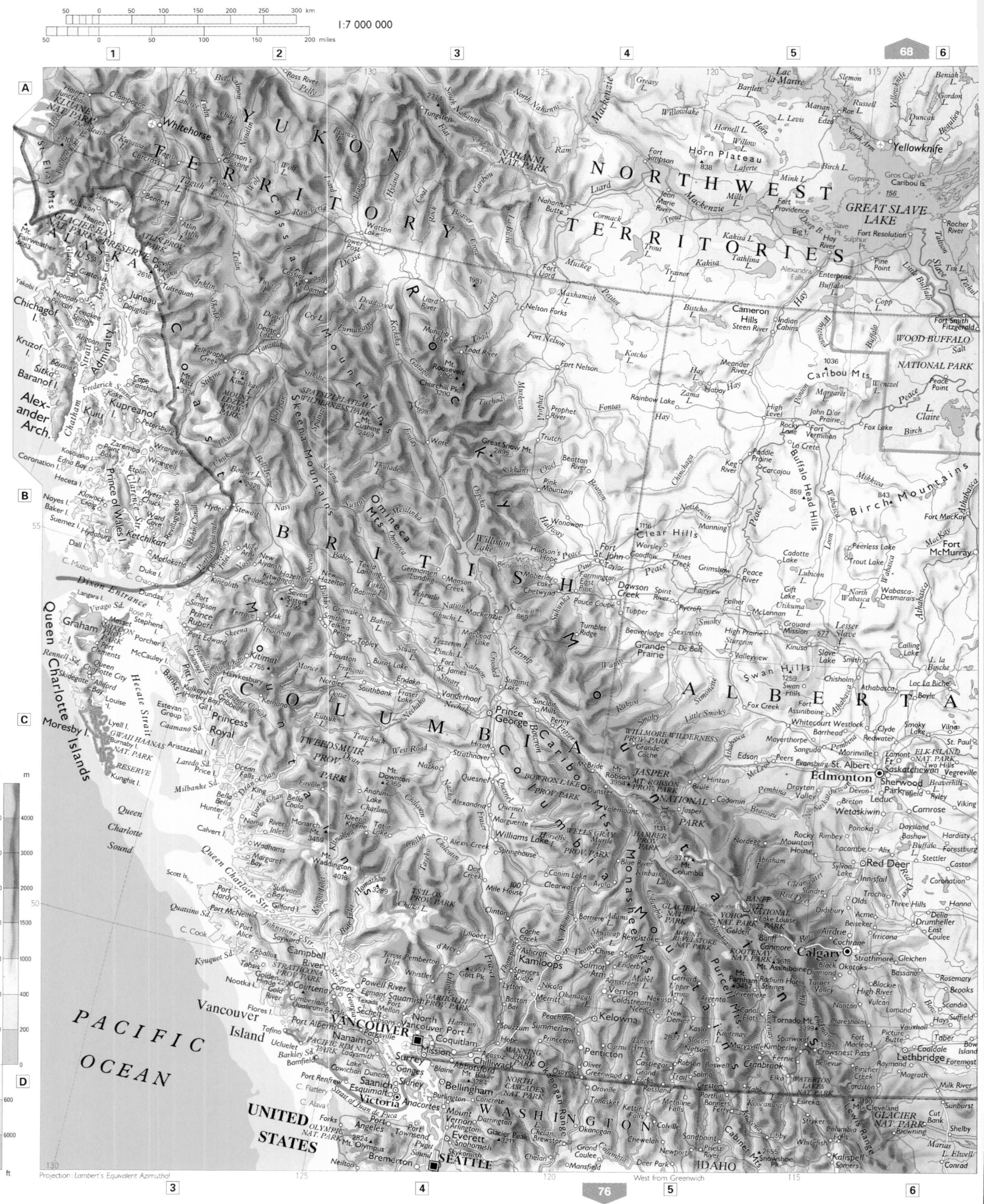

1:7 000 000

Projection: Lambert's Equivalent Azimuthal

West from Greenwich

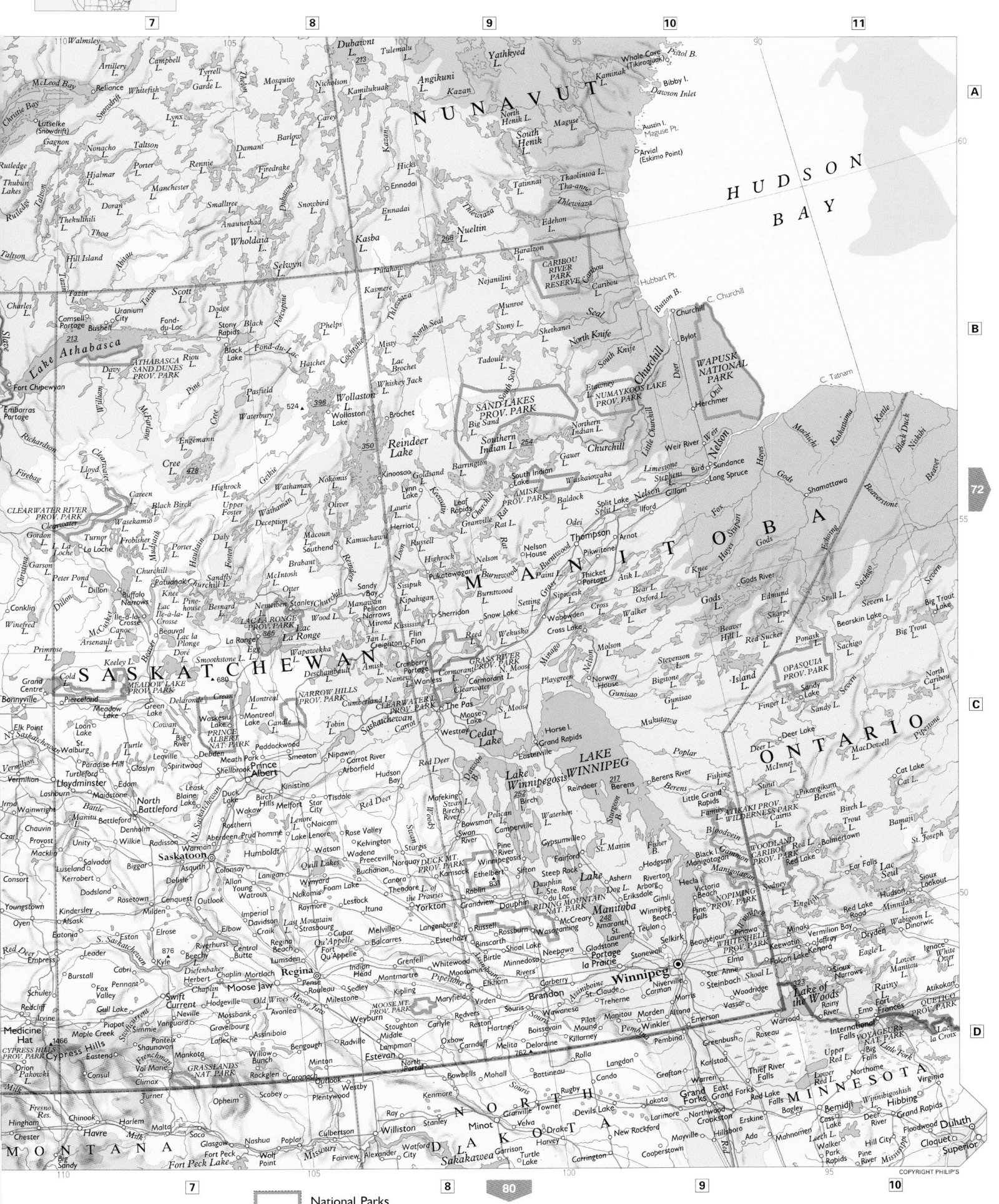

7   8   9   10   11

A   B   72   C   D

N U N A V U T

H U D S O N

B A Y

S A S K A T C H E W A N

M A N I T O B A

O N T A R I O

M O N T A N A

N O R T H   D A K O T A

M I N N E S O T A

Lake Athabasca

Reindeer Lake

LAKE WINNIPEG

Lake Winnipegosis

Saskatoon

Regina

Moose Jaw

Winnipeg

Brandon

Medicine Hat

COPYRIGHT PHILIP'S

7   8   80   9   10

☐ National Parks

National Parks

Projection: Lambert's Equivalent Azimuthal

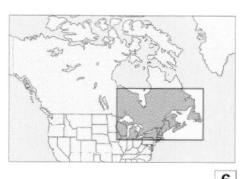

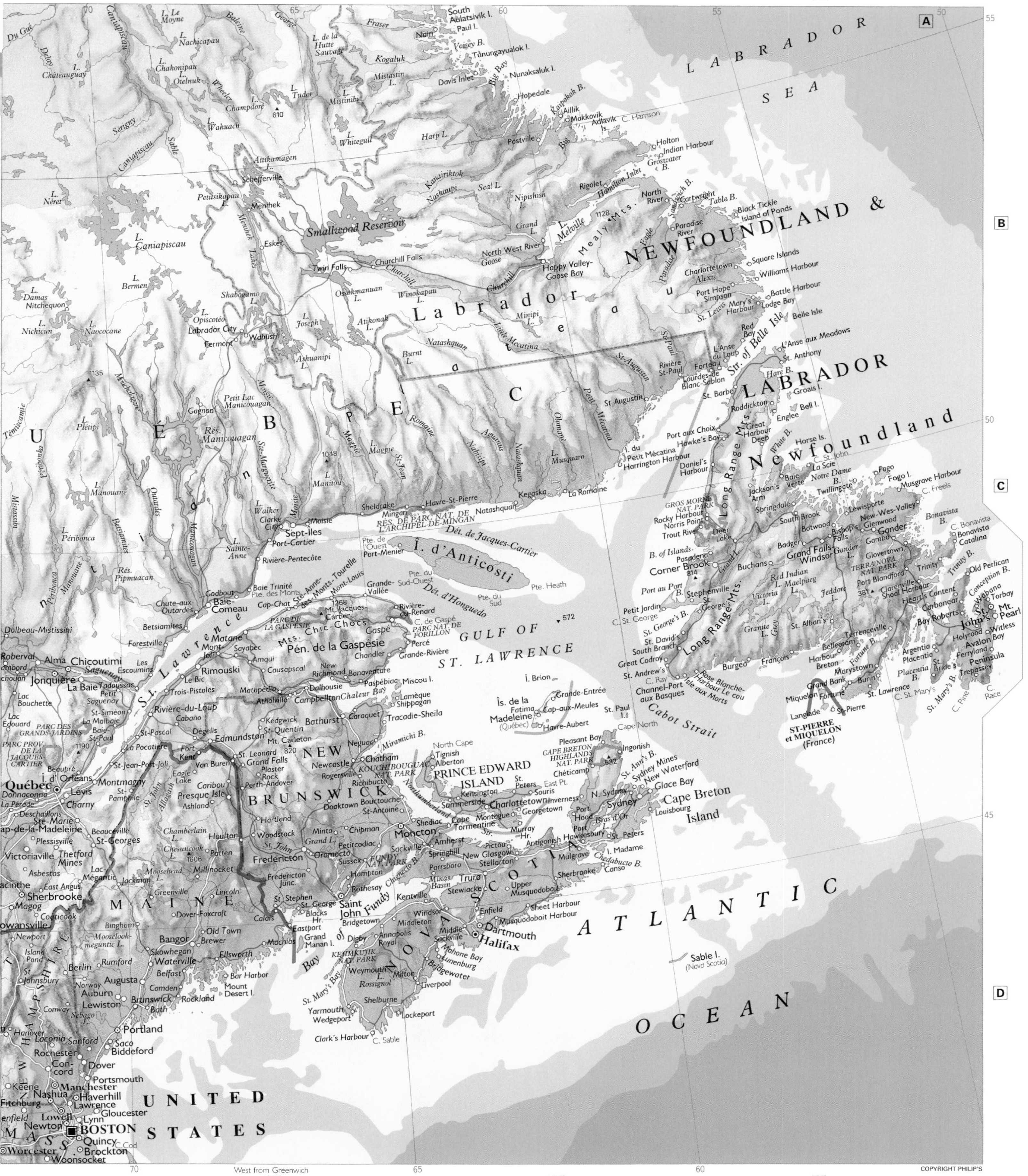

6
69
7
8
9
A
B
C
D
70
65
60
55
50
45
LABRADOR SEA
NEWFOUNDLAND &
LABRADOR
Labrador
Newfoundland
Q U É B E C
Smallwood Reservoir
Churchill Falls
Happy Valley-Goose Bay
North West River
Mealy Mts.
Labrador City
Wabush
Fermont
Schefferville
Nain
Hopedale
Makkovik
Postville
Rigolet
Cartwright
Black Tickle
Mary's Harbour
L'Anse au Loup
Forteau
Lourdes-de-Blanc-Sablon
Red Bay
L'Anse aux Meadows
St. Anthony
Str. of Belle Isle
Belle Isle
Roddickton
Port aux Choix
Hawke's Bay
Long Range Mts.
GROS MORNE NAT. PARK
Rocky Harbour
Norris Point
Trout River
Deer Lake
Corner Brook
Pasadena
Stephenville
Port au Port
St. George's B.
Channel-Port aux Basques
Cabot Strait
Grand Falls-Windsor
Gander
Lewisporte
Twillingate
Fogo I.
Bonavista
Catalina
TERRA NOVA NAT. PARK
Clarenville
Trinity
Carbonear
Conception B.
St. John's
Mt. Pearl
Holyrood
Witless
Ferryland
Avalon Peninsula
Trepassey
Placentia
Argentia
Marystown
Burin
Fortune
Grand Bank
St. Lawrence
Burgeo
Harbour Breton
ST-PIERRE et MIQUELON (France)
Miquelon
St-Pierre
Langlade
C. Race
C. Pine
C. St. Mary's
Sept-Îles
Port-Cartier
Havre-St-Pierre
Natashquan
Kegaska
La Romaine
St-Augustin
Harrington Harbour
Sheldrake
Mingan
RÉS. DE PARC NAT. DE L'ARCHIPEL-DE-MINGAN
Î. d'Anticosti
Port-Menier
Dét. de Jacques-Cartier
Dét. d'Honguedo
GULF OF ST. LAWRENCE
Baie-Comeau
Forestville
Matane
Rimouski
Trois-Pistoles
Rivière-du-Loup
Pén. de la Gaspésie
Mts. Chic-Chocs
Gaspé
Percé
Chandler
Campbellton
Chaleur Bay
Îs. de la Madeleine
Chicoutimi
Jonquière
Alma
Roberval
Dolbeau-Mistassini
St. Lawrence
Québec
Lévis
Montmagny
Edmundston
Sherbrooke
Magog
NEW BRUNSWICK
Bathurst
Miramichi
Chatham
Newcastle
Moncton
Fredericton
Saint John
Sussex
Sackville
Amherst
PRINCE EDWARD ISLAND
Charlottetown
Summerside
NOVA SCOTIA
Halifax
Dartmouth
Truro
New Glasgow
Antigonish
Yarmouth
Digby
Kentville
Windsor
Bridgewater
Liverpool
Lunenburg
Shelburne
KEJIMKUJIK NAT. PARK
Bay of Fundy
Cape Breton Island
CAPE BRETON HIGHLANDS NAT. PARK
Sydney
Glace Bay
North Sydney
Sydney Mines
New Waterford
Louisbourg
Bras d'Or L.
Sable I. (Nova Scotia)
ATLANTIC OCEAN
MAINE
UNITED STATES
Bangor
Augusta
Portland
Lewiston
Waterville
Bar Harbor
Calais
Eastport
NEW HAMPSHIRE
Manchester
Nashua
Portsmouth
Concord
Dover
Rochester
BOSTON
Lowell
Lynn
Quincy
Brockton
Worcester
Gloucester
Haverhill
West from Greenwich
COPYRIGHT PHILIP'S

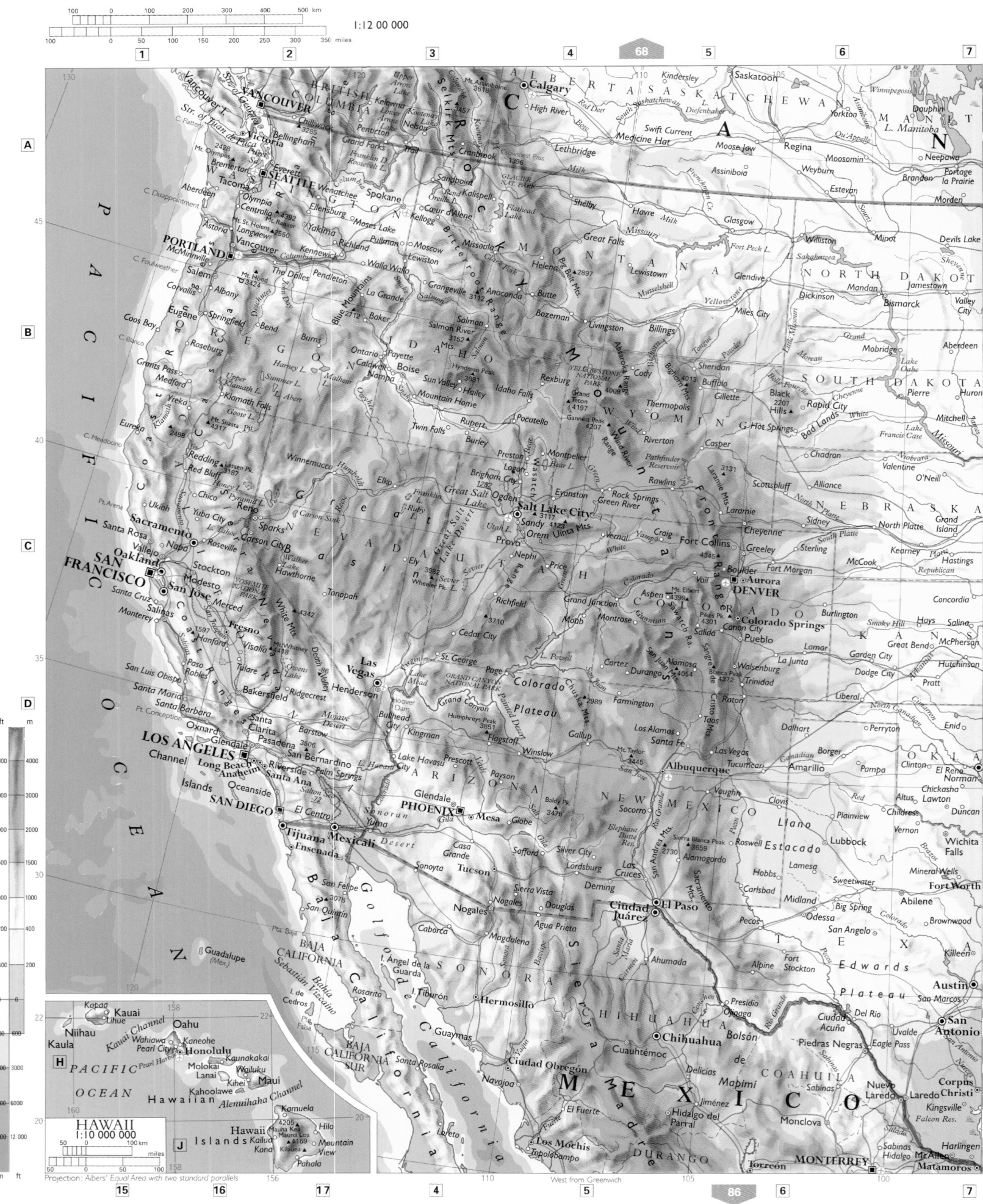

1:12 00 000

HAWAII
1:10 000 000

Projection: Albers' Equal Area with two standard parallels

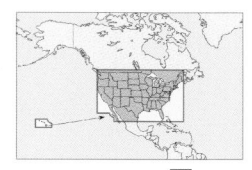

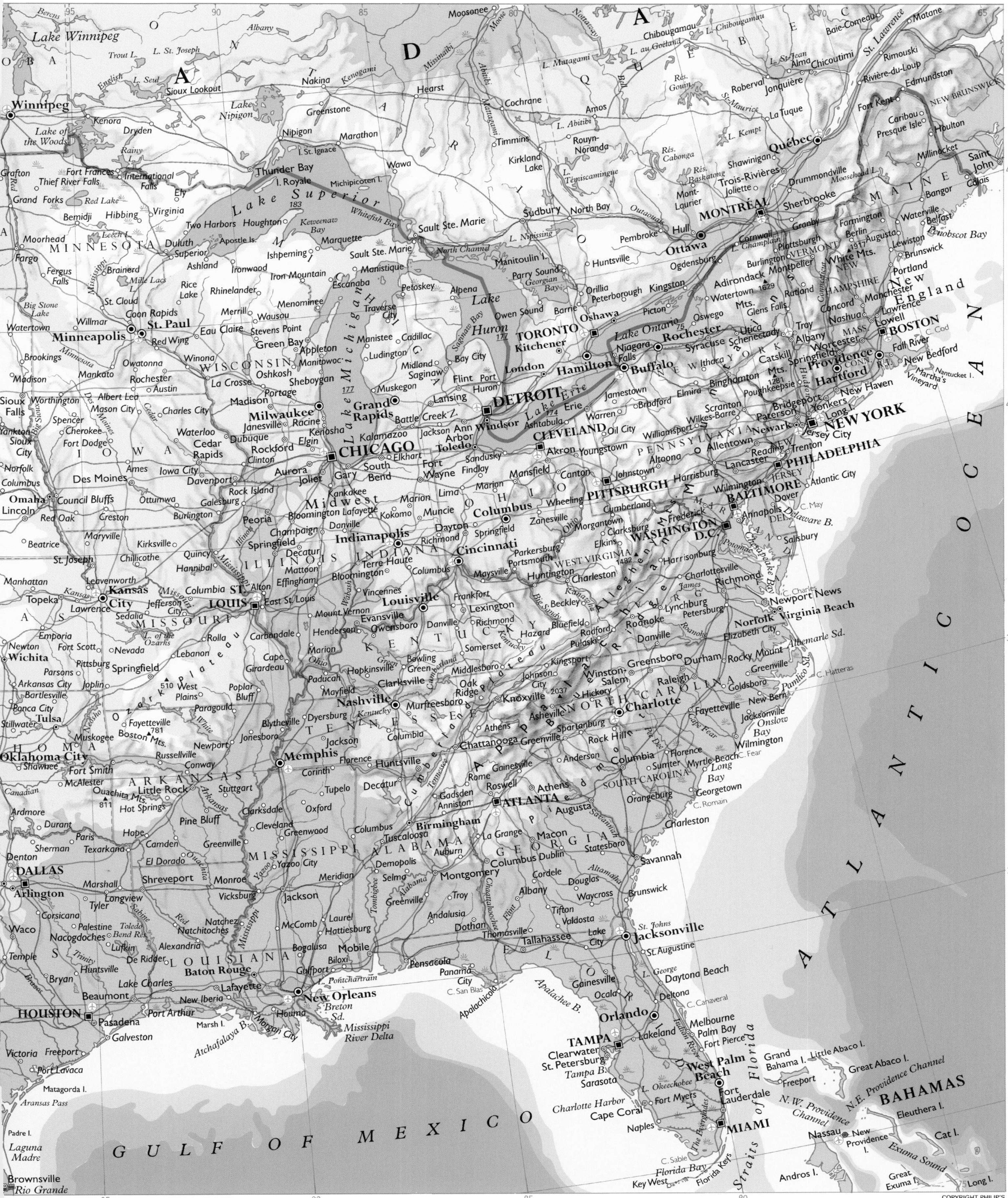
8
9
10
11
12
69
13
A
B
C
D
E
F
87
88
GULF OF MEXICO
ATLANTIC OCEAN
CANADA
ONTARIO
QUEBEC
NEW BRUNSWICK
MAINE
New England
NEW YORK
PENNSYLVANIA
NEW JERSEY
MARYLAND
DEL.
WEST VIRGINIA
VIRGINIA
NORTH CAROLINA
SOUTH CAROLINA
GEORGIA
FLORIDA
ALABAMA
MISSISSIPPI
LOUISIANA
ARKANSAS
TENNESSEE
KENTUCKY
OHIO
INDIANA
ILLINOIS
MISSOURI
IOWA
WISCONSIN
MICHIGAN
MINNESOTA
BAHAMAS
Midwest
Lake Winnipeg
Lake Superior
Lake Michigan
Lake Huron
Lake Erie
Lake Ontario
Appalachian Mts.
Ozark Plateau
Cumberland Plateau
Blue Ridge
Winnipeg
Thunder Bay
Sault Ste. Marie
Sudbury
Ottawa
MONTRÉAL
Québec
TORONTO
Hamilton
London
Windsor
Minneapolis
St. Paul
Duluth
Milwaukee
CHICAGO
DETROIT
CLEVELAND
PITTSBURGH
Buffalo
Rochester
Syracuse
Albany
BOSTON
Providence
Hartford
NEW YORK
PHILADELPHIA
BALTIMORE
WASHINGTON D.C.
Richmond
Norfolk
Virginia Beach
Columbus
Cincinnati
Indianapolis
Louisville
Nashville
Memphis
ST. LOUIS
Kansas City
Omaha
Des Moines
Tulsa
Oklahoma City
Wichita
Little Rock
DALLAS
Arlington
HOUSTON
Baton Rouge
New Orleans
Jackson
Birmingham
Montgomery
ATLANTA
Charlotte
Raleigh
Greensboro
Savannah
Jacksonville
Orlando
TAMPA
West Palm Beach
MIAMI
Key West
Nassau
Freeport
Brownsville
Straits of Florida
Florida Keys
Mississippi River Delta
COPYRIGHT PHILIP'S
95
90
85
80
75
45
40
35
30
25

50 0 50 100 150 200 km
50 0 50 100 150 miles

1:6 000 000

A B C D 80 E F

SASKATCHEWAN

ALBERTA

BRITISH COLUMBIA

MONTANA

WASHINGTON

OREGON

IDAHO

WYOMING

NEVADA

UTAH

Rocky Mountains

Bighorn Mountains

Absaroka Range

Wind River Range

Medicine Bow Mts.

Park Ra.

YELLOWSTONE NATIONAL PARK

GRAND TETON NAT. PARK

Lewis Range

Swan Range

Bitterroot Range

Salmon River Mountains

Sawtooth Range

Clearwater Mountains

Cabinet Mountains

Columbia Basin

Snake River

Columbia River

Columbia Plateau

Blue Mountains

Wallowa Mts.

Cascade Range

Olympic Mts.

Puget Sound

Great Salt Lake

Great Salt Lake Desert

Wasatch Range

Uinta Mountains

Roan Plateau

Ruby Mts.

Humboldt

Independence Mts.

Santa Rosa Range

Shoshone Mountains

Toiyabe Ra.

Warner Mts.

Harney Basin

Steens Mountain

Alvord Desert

Great Basin

Stillwater Ra.

Trinity Ra.

Coast Ranges

VANCOUVER

SEATTLE

Victoria

Nanaimo

Bellingham

Everett

Tacoma

Olympia

Spokane

Portland

Salem

Eugene

Helena

Great Falls

Billings

Missoula

Butte

Bozeman

Boise

Idaho Falls

Pocatello

Twin Falls

Salt Lake City

West Valley City

Ogden

Provo

Orem

Reno

Carson City

Casper

Sheridan

Laramie

Sacramento

Redding

Chico

Klamath Falls

Medford

Crater Lake

CRATER LAKE NAT. PARK

LASSEN VOLCANIC NAT. PARK

REDWOOD NAT. PARK

Missouri

Fort Peck Lake

Snake

Columbia

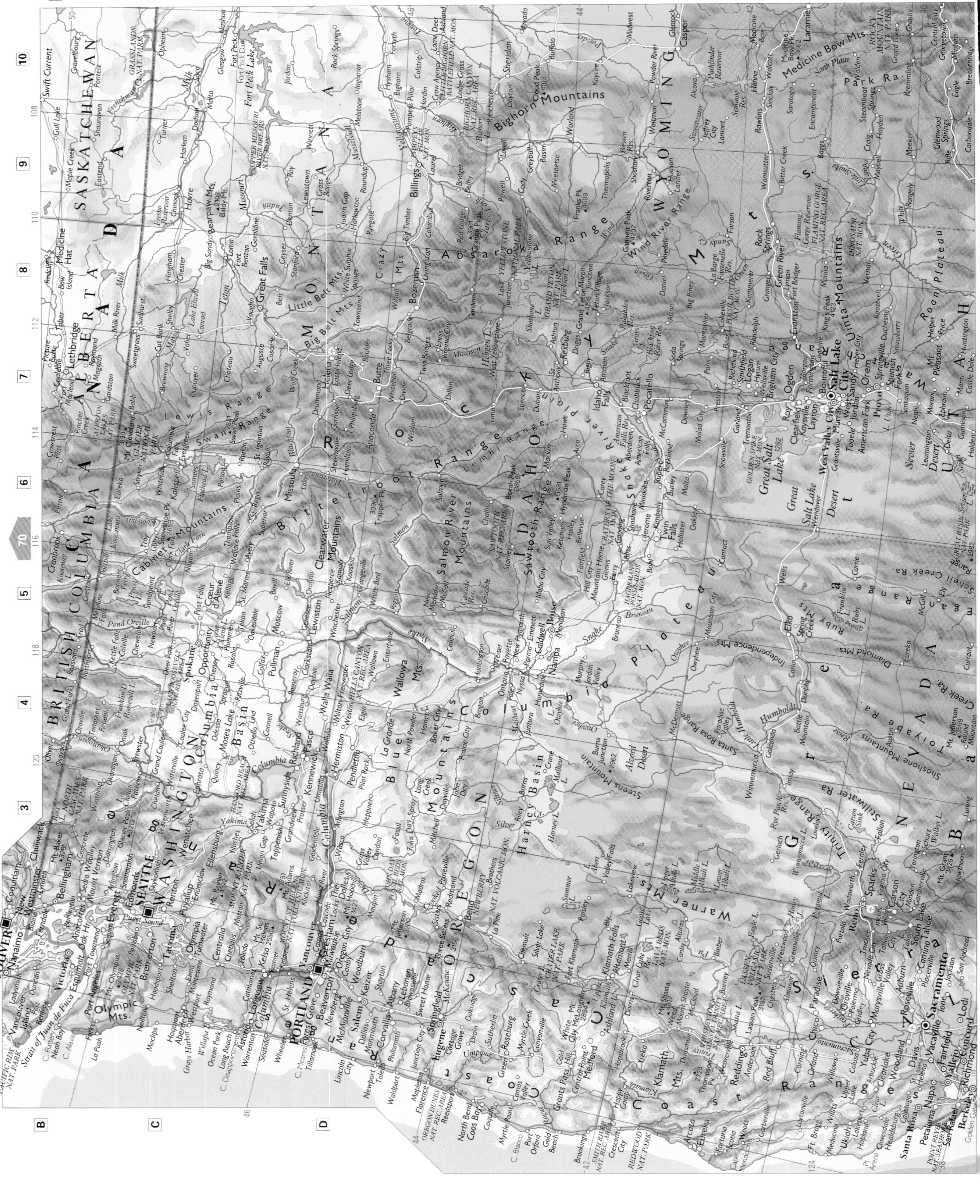

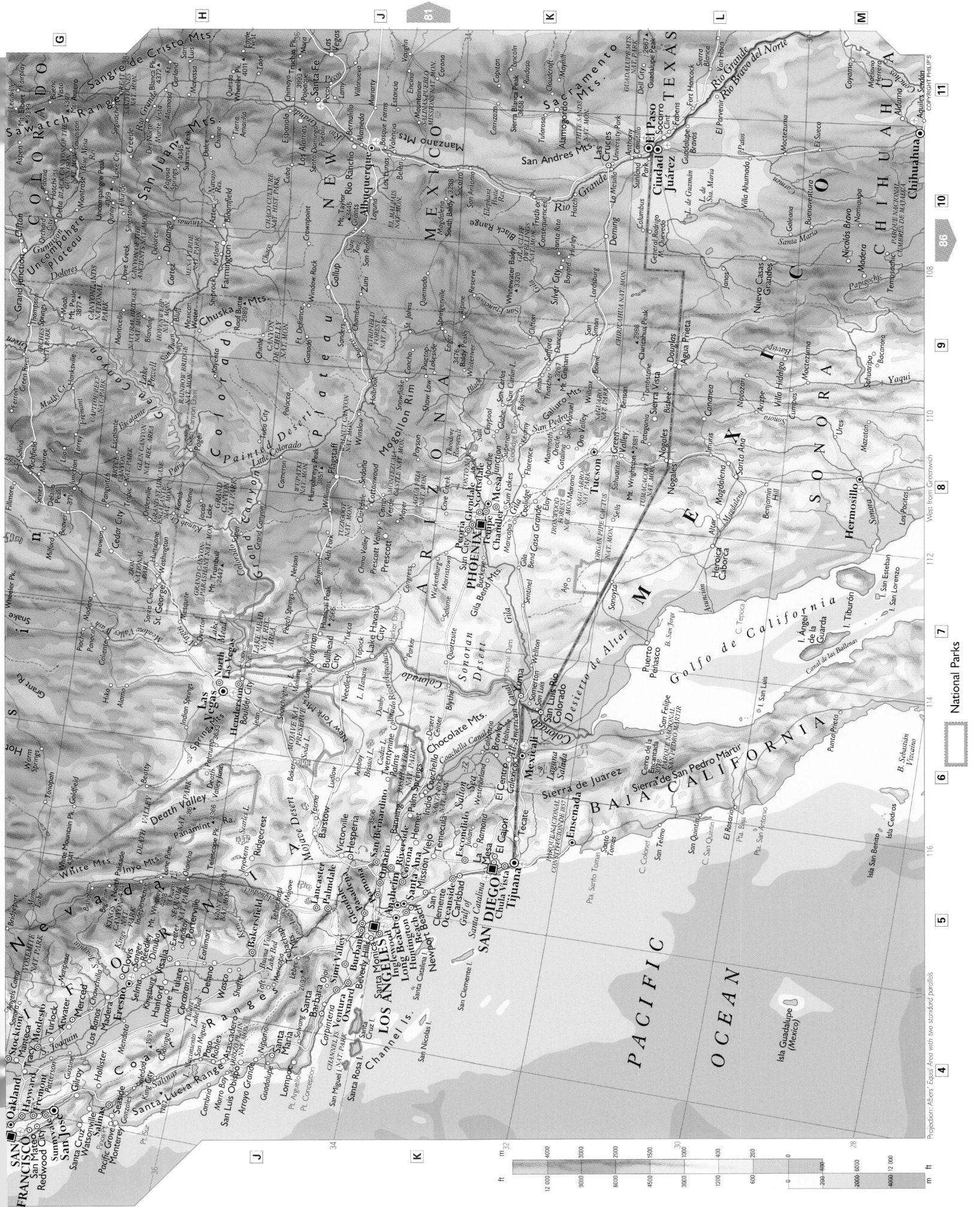

National Parks

1:2 500 000

WESTERN WASHINGTON
REGION
on same scale

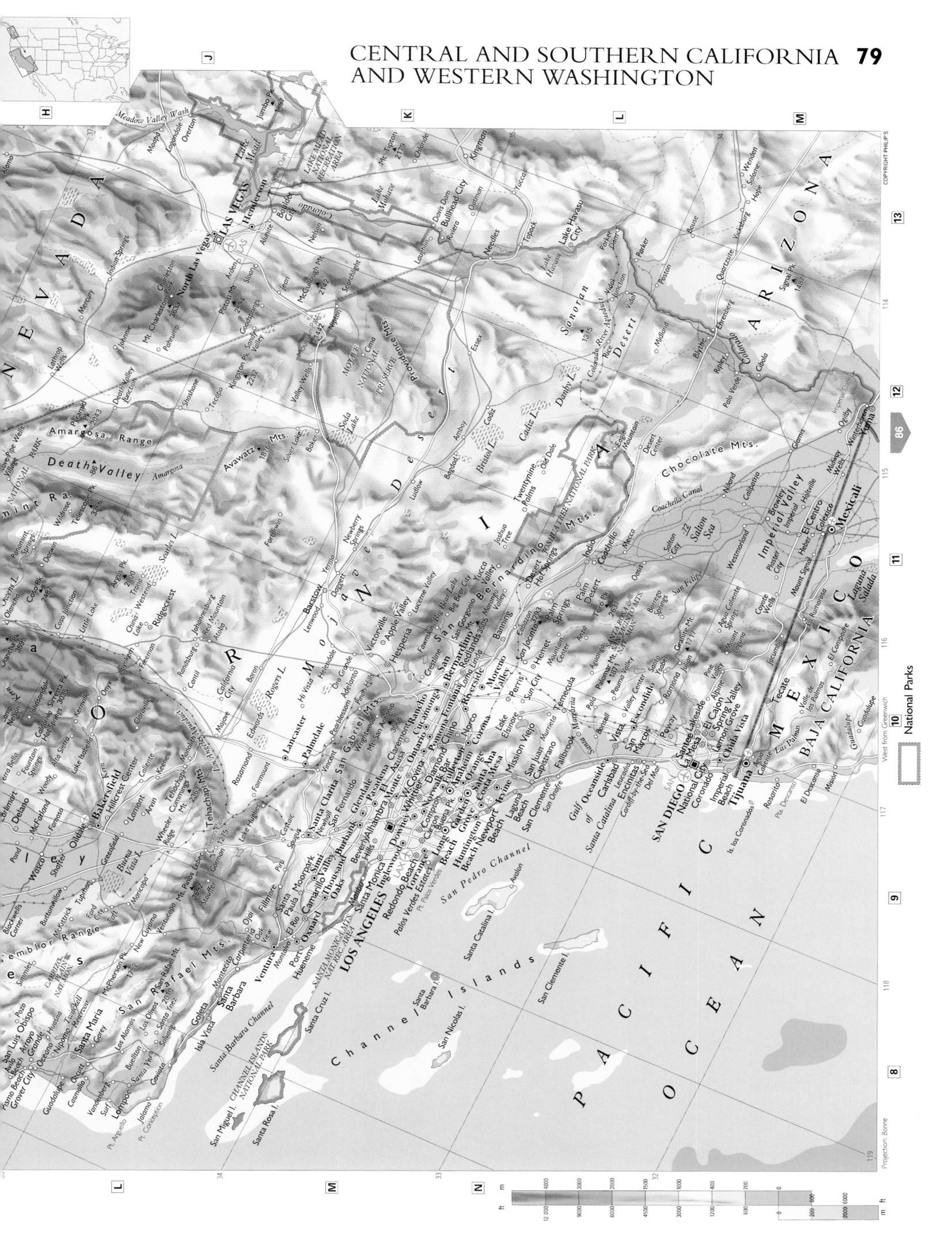

National Parks

1:6 000 000

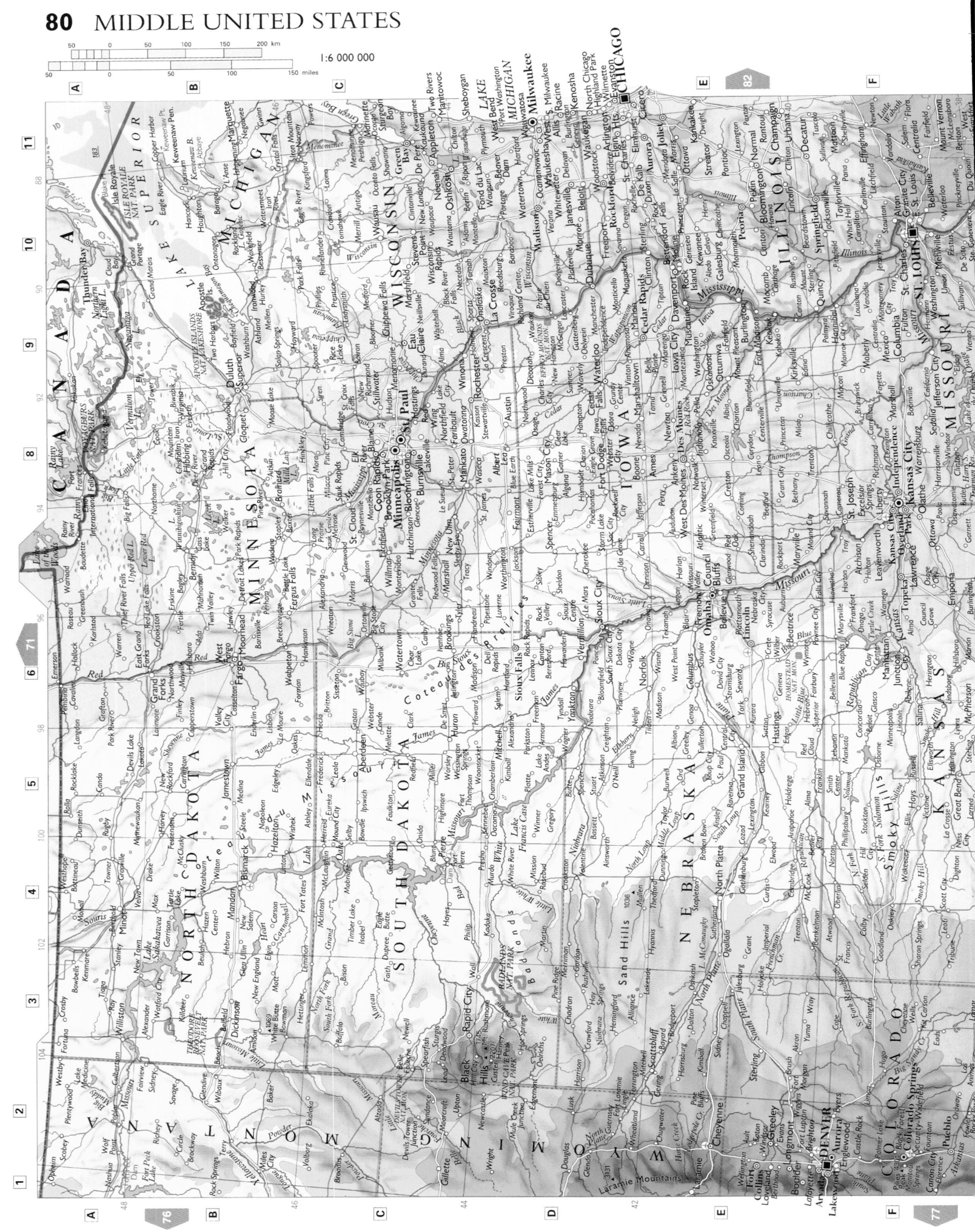

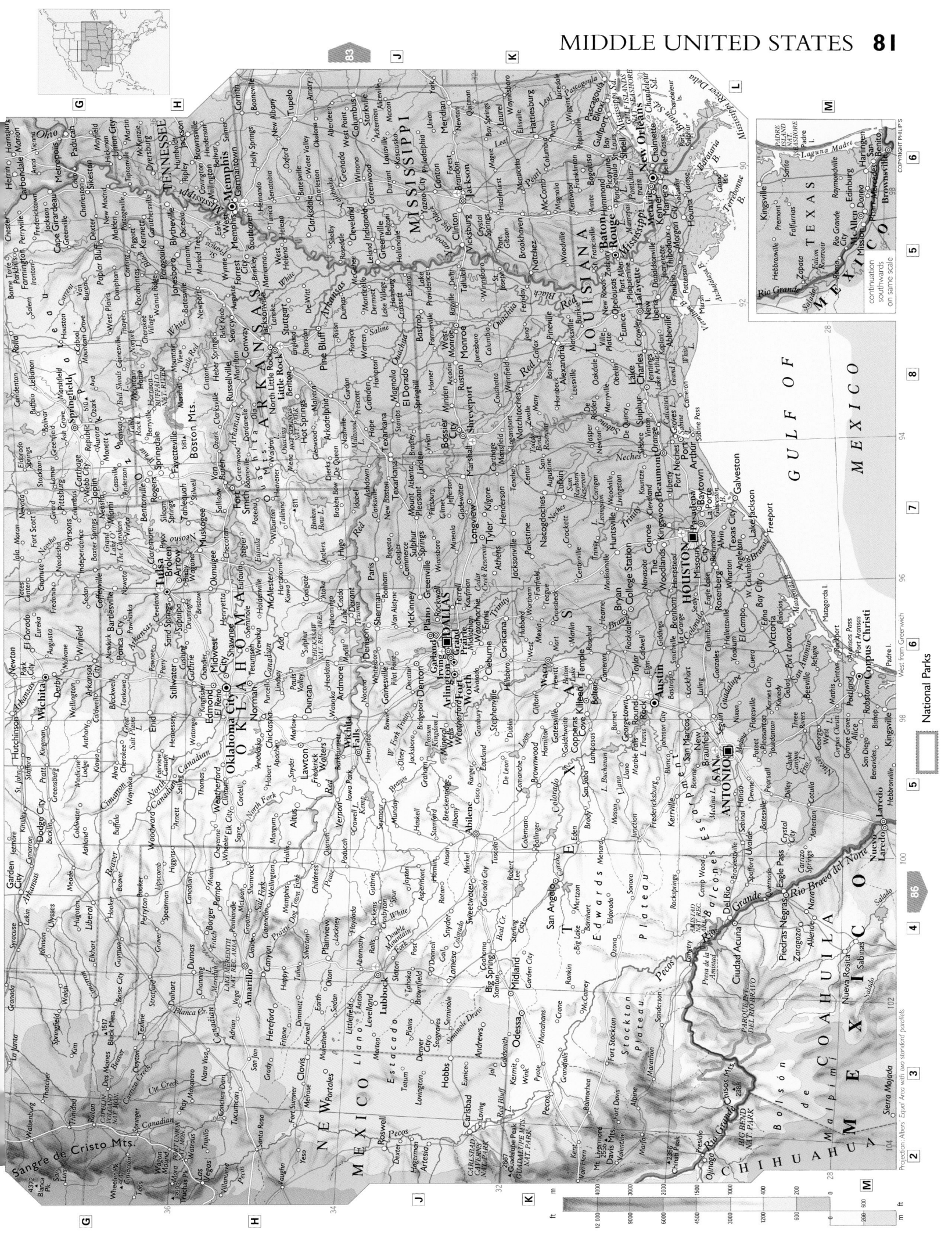

National Parks

continuation
southwards
on same scale

COPYRIGHT PHILIP'S

Projection: Albers Equal Area with two standard parallels

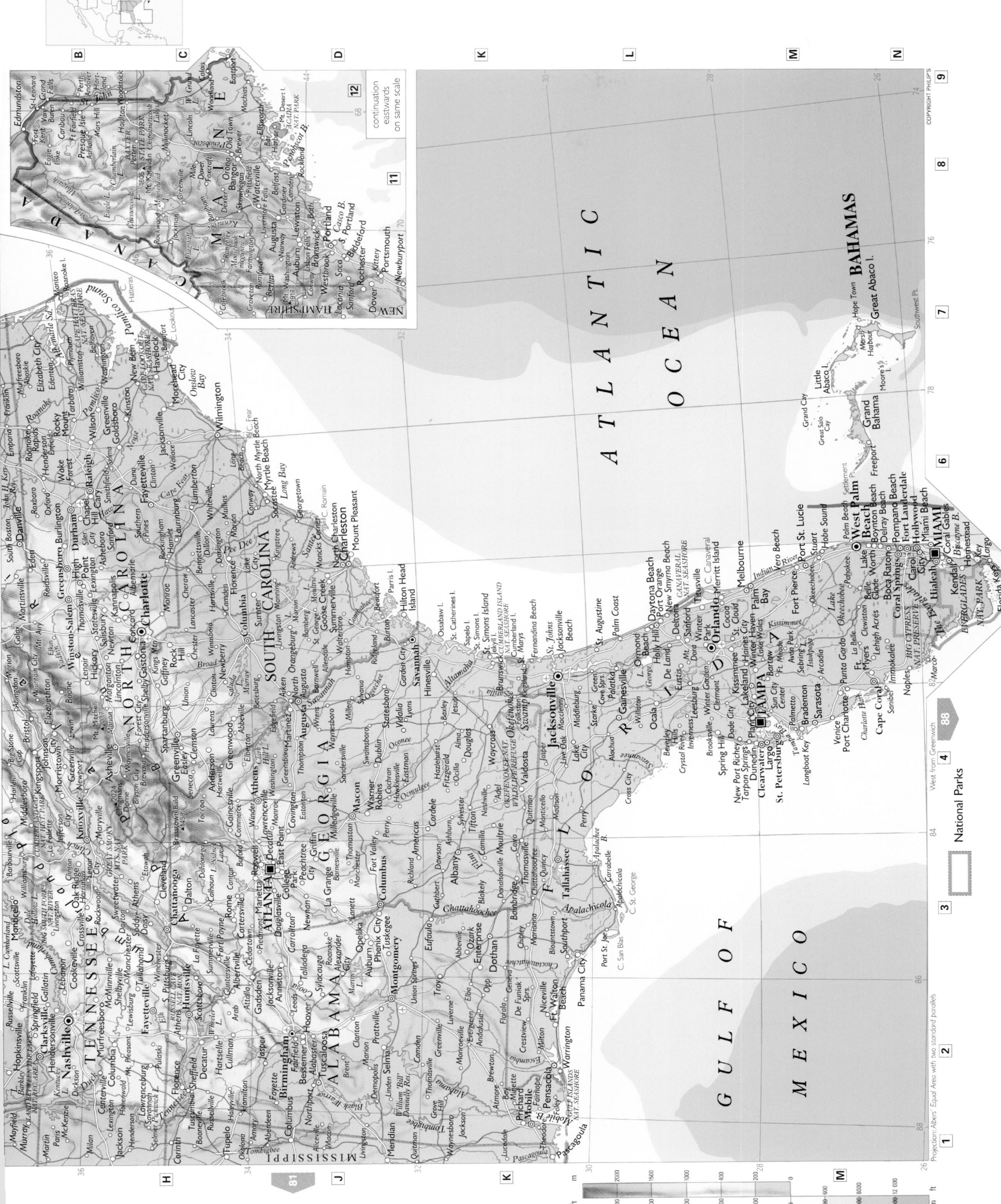

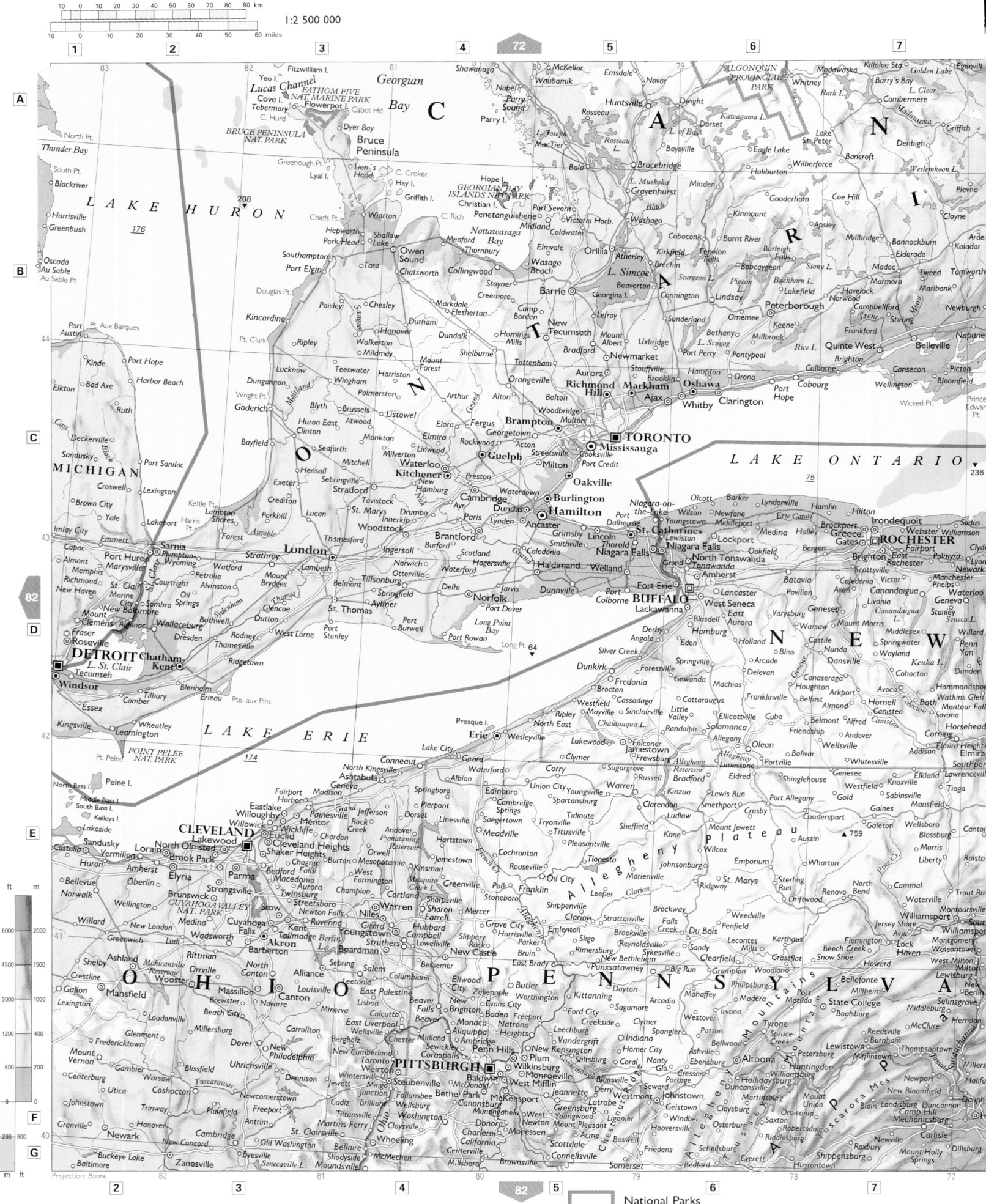

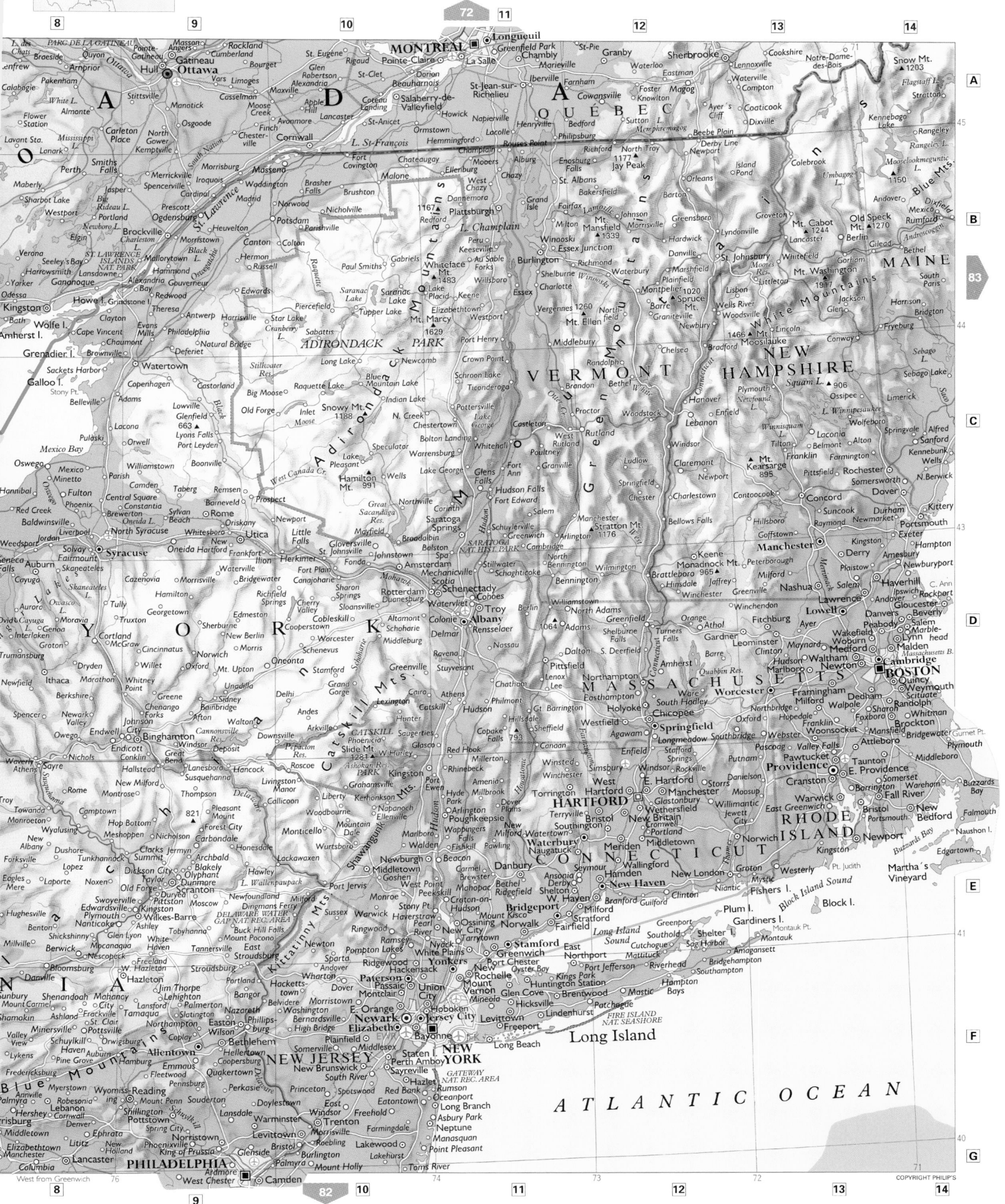

50 0 50 100 150 200 250 300 km

1:8 000 000

50   0   50   100
               150   200 miles

National Parks

State names in Central Mexico

1 DISTRITO FEDERAL   5 MÉXICO
2 AGUASCALIENTES   6 MORELOS
3 GUANAJUATO   7 QUERÉTARO
4 HIDALGO   8 TLAXCALA

Projection: Bi-polar oblique Conical Orthomorphic

West from Greenwich

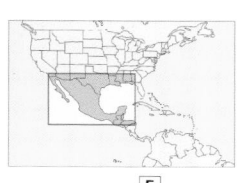

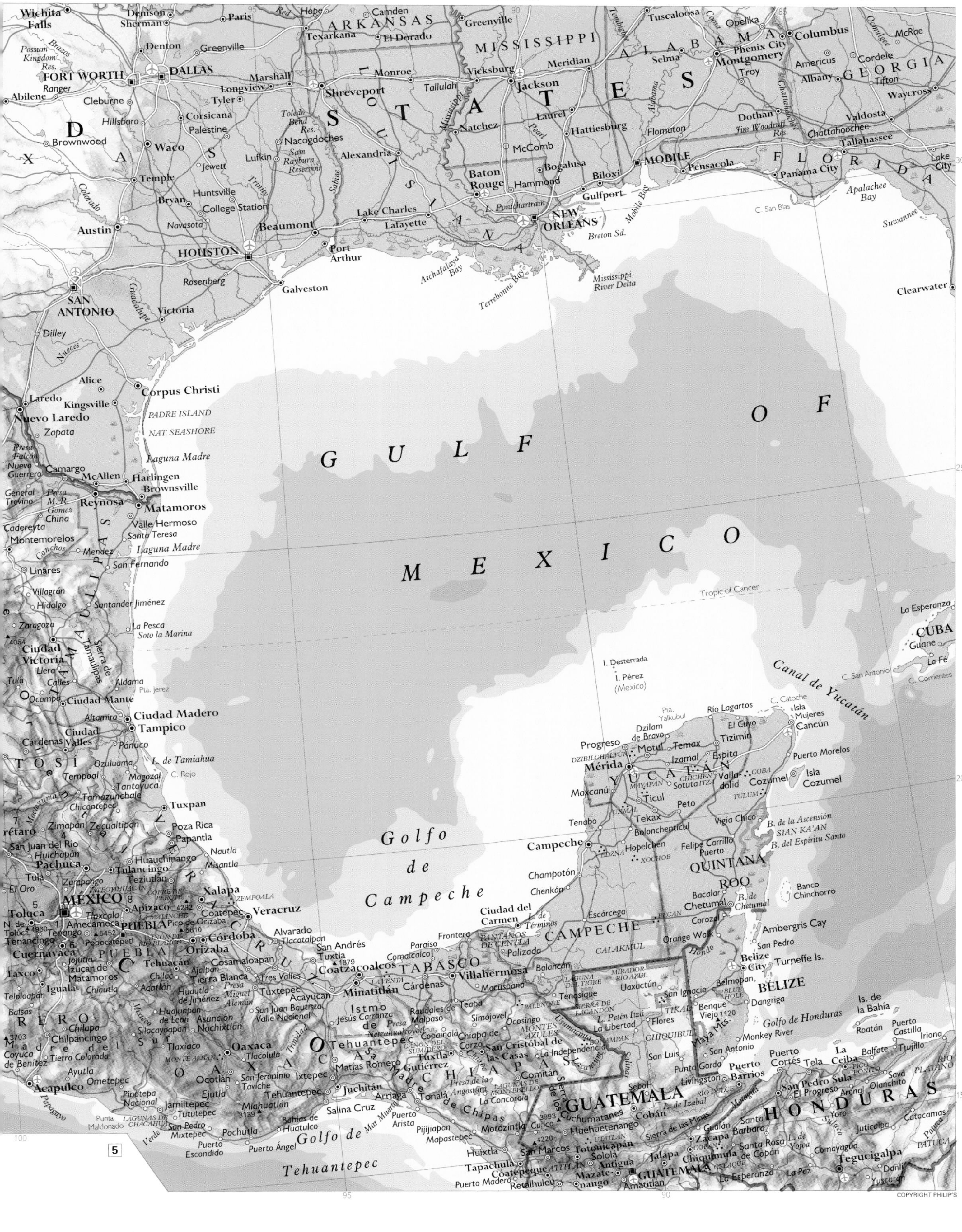

5
6
81
7
8
A
B
C
D
E
88
GULF OF MEXICO
Golfo de Campeche
Golfo de Tehuantepec
Golfo de Honduras
Canal de Yucatán
Tropic of Cancer
ARKANSAS
MISSISSIPPI
ALABAMA
GEORGIA
LOUISIANA
FLORIDA
UNITED STATES
TEXAS
TAMAULIPAS
VERACRUZ
PUEBLA
OAXACA
CHIAPAS
TABASCO
CAMPECHE
YUCATÁN
QUINTANA ROO
GUERRERO
SAN LUIS POTOSÍ
GUATEMALA
BELIZE
HONDURAS
CUBA
Wichita Falls
Denison
Sherman
Paris
Texarkana
El Dorado
Camden
Greenville
Tuscaloosa
Opelika
Columbus
McRae
Abilene
FORT WORTH
DALLAS
Denton
Marshall
Longview
Tyler
Shreveport
Monroe
Tallulah
Vicksburg
Jackson
Meridian
Selma
Montgomery
Phenix City
Troy
Americus
Albany
Cordele
Tifton
Waycross
Cleburne
Corsicana
Palestine
Waco
Nacogdoches
Lufkin
Alexandria
Natchez
Laurel
Hattiesburg
McComb
Bogalusa
Dothan
Valdosta
Tallahassee
Flomaton
Brownwood
Temple
Bryan
Huntsville
College Station
Navasota
Austin
Beaumont
Port Arthur
Lake Charles
Lafayette
Baton Rouge
Hammond
Biloxi
Gulfport
MOBILE
Pensacola
Panama City
Lake City
Apalachee Bay
NEW ORLEANS
Breton Sd.
Mississippi River Delta
Atchafalaya Bay
Terrebonne Bay
HOUSTON
Galveston
Rosenberg
Victoria
SAN ANTONIO
Dilley
Alice
Corpus Christi
Laredo
Kingsville
Nuevo Laredo
Zapata
PADRE ISLAND NAT. SEASHORE
Laguna Madre
Camargo
McAllen
Harlingen
Brownsville
Reynosa
Matamoros
Valle Hermoso
Santa Teresa
Montemorelos
Linares
San Fernando
Jiménez
Ciudad Victoria
Aldama
Ciudad Mante
Altamira
Ciudad Madero
Tampico
Pánuco
Ciudad Valles
L. de Tamiahua
Tuxpan
Poza Rica
Papantla
Nautla
Misantla
Pachuca
Tulancingo
Xalapa
Veracruz
Toluca
MÉXICO
PUEBLA
Córdoba
Orizaba
Pico de Orizaba
Popocatépetl
Cuernavaca
Alvarado
Tlacotalpan
San Andrés Tuxtla
Coatzacoalcos
Minatitlán
Cárdenas
Villahermosa
Frontera
Ciudad del Carmen
L. de Términos
Campeche
Champotón
Escárcega
Chetumal
Progreso
Mérida
Motul
Izamal
Valladolid
Tizimín
Cancún
Isla Mujeres
Puerto Morelos
Cozumel
Isla Cozumel
Ticul
Peto
Tekax
Felipe Carrillo Puerto
Bacalar
Belize City
Belmopan
Dangriga
Ambergris Cay
Turneffe Is.
I. Desterrada
I. Pérez (Mexico)
C. Catoche
Oaxaca
Tehuantepec
Juchitán
Salina Cruz
Acapulco
Chilpancingo
Iguala
Taxco
Puerto Escondido
Puerto Ángel
Tuxtla Gutiérrez
San Cristóbal de las Casas
Comitán
Tapachula
Huixtla
Tonalá
Arriaga
Flores
Cobán
Puerto Barrios
Livingston
Puerto Cortés
Tela
La Ceiba
San Pedro Sula
Tegucigalpa
Comayagua
Santa Rosa de Copán
Quetzaltenango
Huehuetenango
Antigua
Guatemala
Retalhuleu
Puerto Madero
Coatepeque
Escuintla
La Esperanza
Guane
La Fe
C. San Antonio
C. Corrientes
Clearwater
C. San Blas
Pta. Jerez
C. Rojo
Banco Chinchorro
Roatán
Trujillo
Is. de la Bahía
COPYRIGHT PHILIP'S

PUERTO RICO d
1:3 000 000

ATLANTIC OCEAN

PUERTO RICO
(U.S.A.)

Pta. Aguijereada · Isabela · Barceloneta · SAN JUAN
Aguadilla · Arecibo · Vega Baja · Bayamón · Carolina · Fajardo · Dewey
Mayagüez · San Sebastián · Utuado · Caguas · Humacao · Naguabo · Vieques · Esperanza
San German · Adjuntas · Cordillera Central 1338 Cerro de Punta · Cayey · Coamo · Yabucoa
Pta. Aguila · Yauco · Guanica · Ponce · Guayama
I. Caja de Muertos

VIRGIN ISLANDS e
1:2 000 000

Ruffling Pt. · The Settlement
Anegada · East Pt.
Virgin Islands (U.K.)
Great Camanoe
Jost Van Dyke I. · Guana I. · Beef · Virgin Gorda
Virgin Is. (U.S.A.) · Hans Lollik I. · Tortola · Road Town · Spanish Town
Charlotte Amalie · Cruz Bay · St. John I. · Peter I.
Thomas I.

ST. LUCIA f
1:2 000 000

Cap Point · Pte. Hardy · Esperance Bay
Gros Islet · Marquis
Castries · Babonneau
L'Anse la Raye · Dennery
Canaries · Millet
Soufrière · Mt. Gimie 950 · Trou Gras Pt.
Soufrière Bay · 750 Petit Piton · Micoud
Gros Piton Pt. · 796 Gros Piton · Vierge Pt.
Choiseul · **ST. LUCIA**
Laborie · Vieux Fort
C. Moule à Chique

BARBADOS g
1:2 000 000

Crabhill · North Point · ATLANTIC OCEAN
Fustic · Spring Hall
Speightstown · Portland 245 Belleplaine
Westmoreland · Mt. Hillaby 340 · **BARBADOS**
Holetown · Hillcrest
Black Rock · Bridgefield · Massiah Street · Six Cross Roads
Bridgetown · Ellerton · Ivy · Edey · The Crane
Carlisle Bay · Oistins · St. Martins
Worthing · Chancery Lane
South Point · BGI

ATLANTIC OCEAN

AMAS
ATLANTIC OCEAN

Arthur's Town · The Bight · Cat I. · San Salvador I. · Conception I. · Rum Cay
Long I. · Tropic of Cancer · Clarence Town · Samana Cay
Sandy Cay · Crooked I. · Plana Cays · Mayaguana I.
Cay Verde · Snug Corner · Acklins I.
Cay Santa Domingo · Hogsty Reef · Little Inagua I. · Turks & Caicos (U.K.) · Cockburn Town · Turks Is.
Banes · Great Inagua I.
Antilla · Lake Rose · Matthew Town
Moa · Mayari · Baracoa
Guantánamo · GUANTANAMO BAY (U.S.A.)

HAITI · **DOMINICAN REP** · PUERTO RICO (U.S.A.)
PORT-AU-PRINCE · SANTO DOMINGO
Hispaniola
A n t i l l e s

Navassa I. (U.S.A.) · Jérémie · Les Cayes

C A R I B B E A N   S E A

L e s s e r   A n t i l l e s

Leeward Islands
ANTIGUA & BARBUDA
St. Kitts & Nevis
Montserrat (U.K.)
GUADELOUPE (Fr.)
DOMINICA
MARTINIQUE (Fr.)
ST. LUCIA
ST. VINCENT & THE GRENADINES
Windward Islands
GRENADA
Barbados

Aruba (Neth.) · Curaçao · Bonaire
Oranjestad · Willemstad · **NETH. ANTILLES**

C O L O M B I A · **V E N E Z U E L A**
BARRANQUILLA · MARACAIBO · CARACAS · Trinidad & Tobago
Port of Spain

National Parks

COPYRIGHT PHILIP'S

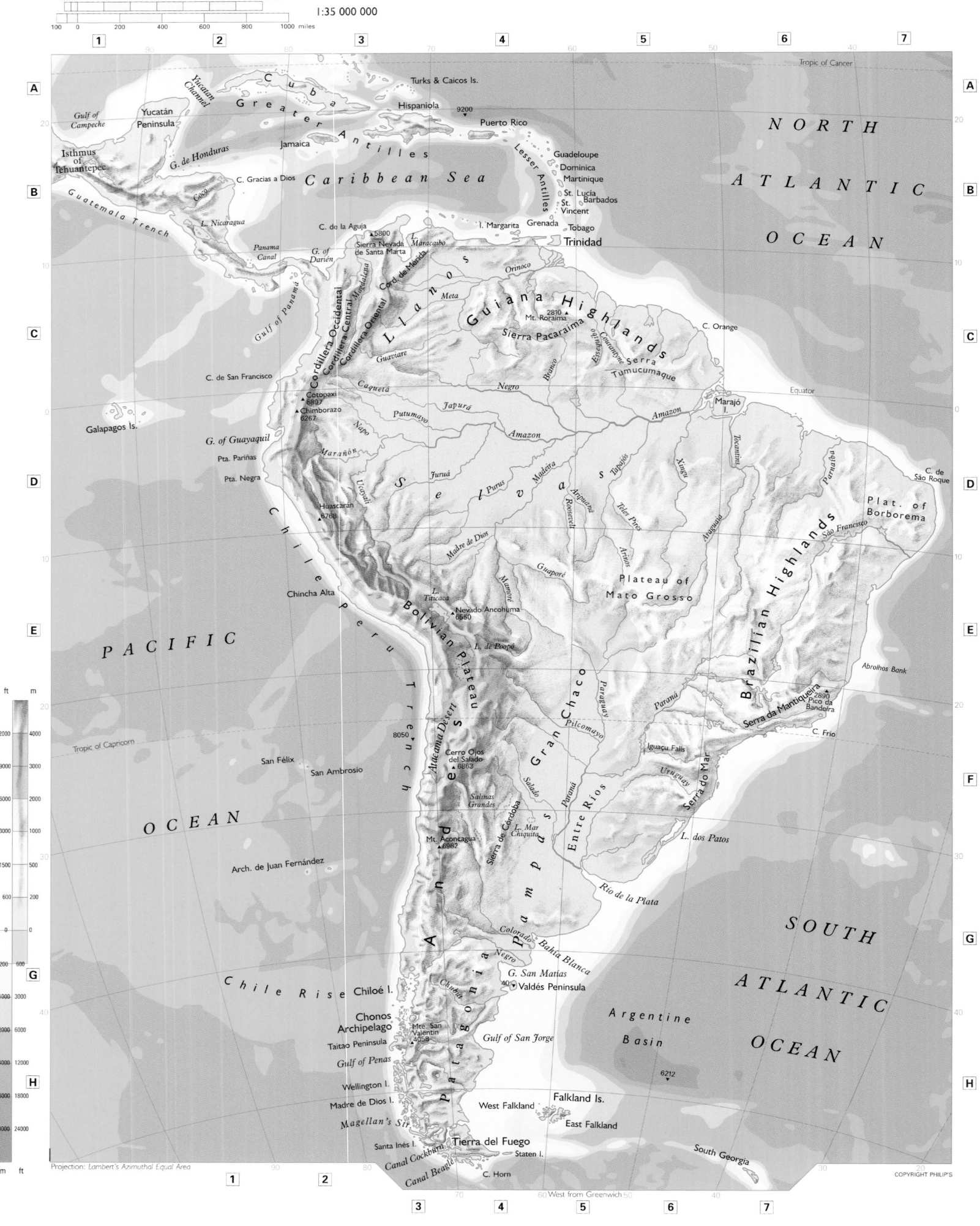

1:35 000 000

Projection: Lambert's Azimuthal Equal Area

COPYRIGHT PHILIP'S

1:35 000 000

100 0   200   400   600   800   1000 1200 1400 km

100 0   200   400   600   800   1000 miles

| | 1 | | 2 | | 3 | | 4 | | 5 | | 6 | | 7 |

A

Havana BAHAMAS
C U B A
Turks & Caicos Is.
(U.K.)
Tropic of Cancer

B
MEXICO
BELIZE
GUATEMALA HONDURAS
Guatemala Tegucigalpa
San Salvador NICARAGUA
EL SALVADOR Managua
COSTA San José
RICA P A N A M A Panamá
HAITI DOMINICAN
Port-au- REP.
Prince San Juan
JAMAICA Kingston PUERTO
RICO
(U.S.A.)
Virgin Is.
(U.K.)
ST. KITTS
& NEVIS
Basse-Terre GUADELOUPE
DOMINICA (Fr.)
Fort-de-France MARTINIQUE
(Fr.)
Castries ST. LUCIA
ST. VINCENT BARBADOS
Kingstown Bridgetown
GRENADA St. George's
ANTIGUA &
BARBUDA

N O R T H

A T L A N T I C

O C E A N

C a r i b b e a n   S e a
Barranquilla C. de
la Aguja
Cartagena
Maracaibo Caracas Port of
Barquisimeto Valencia Spain
Aruba Curaçao
TRINIDAD &
TOBAGO
Cúcuta
San Cristóbal Orinoco
Ciudad Guayana
Georgetown
Paramaribo
Cayenne
C. Orange

C
Medellín
Bucaramanga
Cali Bogotá
Magdalena
VENEZUELA
GUYANA
SURINAME
FRENCH
GUIANA
RORAIMA Essequibo
Branco
AMAPÁ
Equator
COLOMBIA
Gulf of Panamá
G. of
Darién

D
Galapagos Is.
(Ecuador)
Quito
Guayaquil
G. of Guayaquil
ECUADOR
Napo
Putumayo Japurá
Iquitos Marañón
Amazon
Manaus Santarém
AMAZONAS
Madeira
Juruá
Purus
Madre de Dios
AMAZON
Marajó
I. Belém
São Luís
Fortaleza
C. de
São Roque
Teresina Natal
MARANHÃO
RIO G.
DO NORTE Natal
CEARÁ PARAÍBA
PIAUÍ Campina
Grande
PERNAMBUCO Recife
ALAGOAS Maceió
SERGIPE
Aracaju
Salvador
Chiclayo
Trujillo
Chimbote
PERU
Ucayali
ACRE Pôrto Velho
RONDÔNIA
PARÁ
Tapajós Xingu
Tocantins
Araguaia
TOCANTINS
B R A Z I L
B A H Í A
São Francisco

E
Callao LIMA
Cuzco
L.
Titicaca BOLIVIA
La Paz
Arequipa
Cochabamba
Santa Cruz
Sucre
MATO GROSSO
Cuiabá
GOIÁS
DIS. FED. Brasília
Goiânia
MINAS GERAIS
Belo
Horizonte
ESPÍRITO
SANTO
Vitória
Ribeirão
Prêto
Juiz
de Fora
Campos
MATO GROSSO
DO SUL
SÃO PAULO Campinas R. DE J.
Niterói
SÃO
PAULO RIO DE
JANEIRO
Iquique
Antofagasta
PARAGUAY
Paraná
Pilcomayo
Asunción
PARANÁ Curitiba
P A C I F I C

F
San Félix
(Chile)
San Ambrosio
(Chile)
Tropic of Capricorn
Salta
San Miguel
de Tucumán
Resistencia
Corrientes
SANTA CATARINA
Uruguay
RIO GRANDE
DO SUL
Pôrto Alegre
O C E A N

G
Arch. de Juan Fernández
(Chile)
Viña del Mar
Valparaíso
SANTIAGO
Talca
Concepción
Valdivia
Puerto Montt
Córdoba
San Juan Santa Fe
Mendoza Paraná
Rosario
C H I L E
A R G E N T I N A
BUENOS AIRES
La Plata
Bahía
Colorado Blanca
Negro Viedma
Salado
Pelotas
URUGUAY
Montevideo
Mar del Plata
Río de la Plata
S O U T H

A T L A N T I C

O C E A N

H
Gulf of Penas
Magellan's Str.
Punta Arenas Tierra del Fuego
C. Horn
Chubut
Comodoro Rivadavia
Gulf of San Jorge
West Falkland FALKLAND IS.
(U.K.)
Stanley
East Falkland
South Georgia
(U.K.)

Projection: Lambert's Azimuthal Equal Area

COPYRIGHT PHILIP'S

| 1 | | 2 |

■ LIMA Capital Cities

1:16 000 000

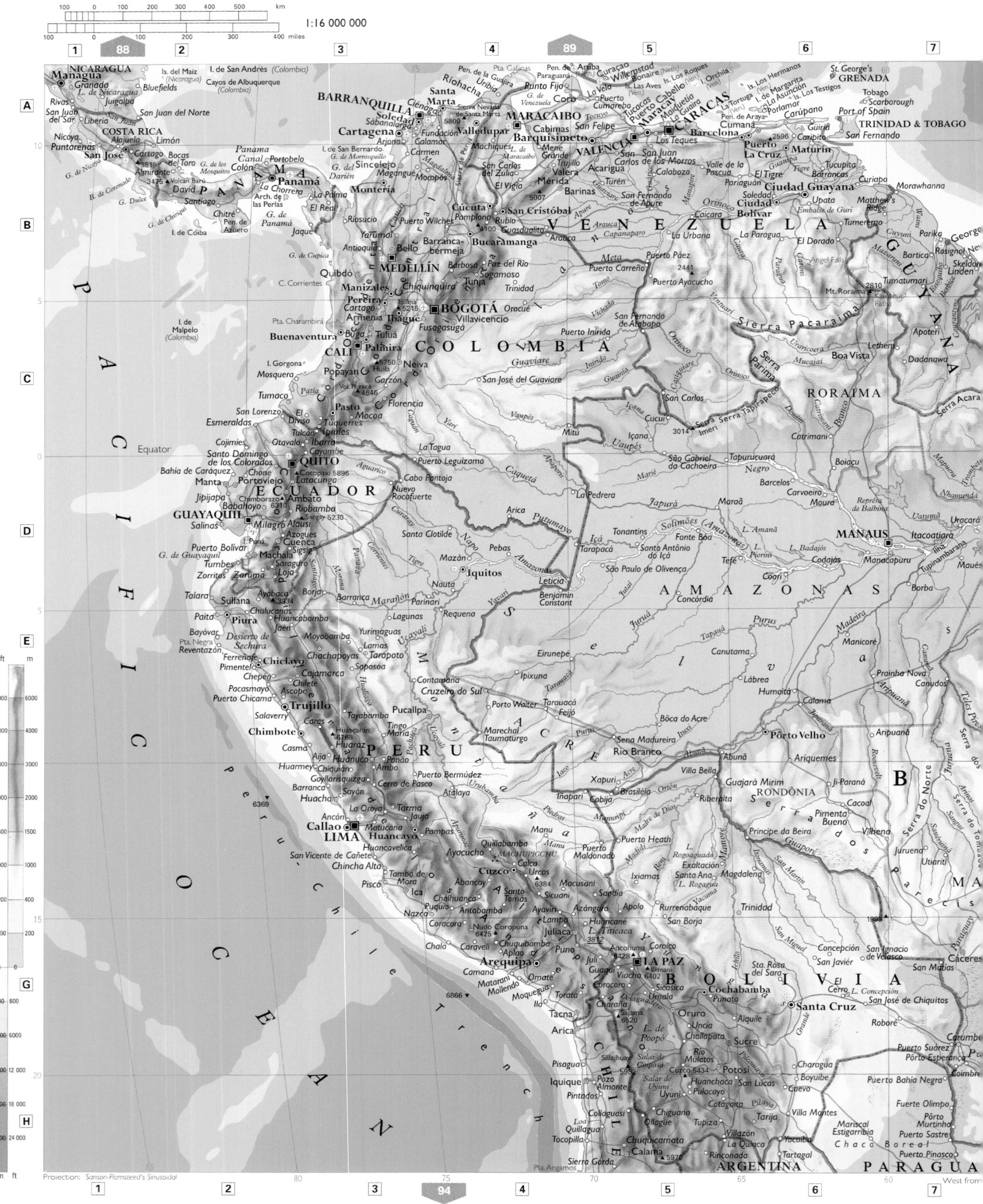

Projection: Sanson-Flamsteed's Sinusoidal

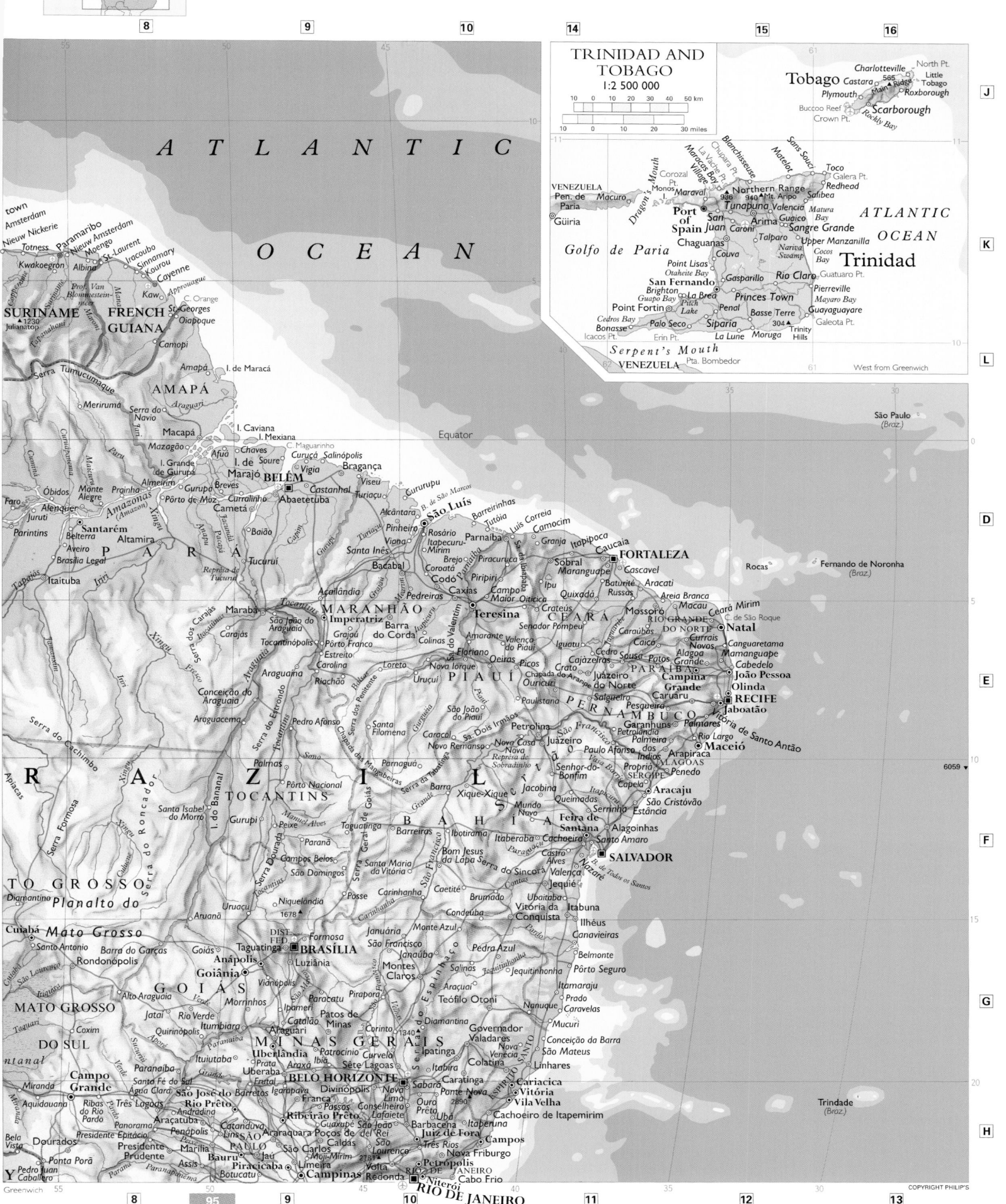

8   9   10   14   15   16

ATLANTIC

OCEAN

J

TRINIDAD AND
TOBAGO
1:2 500 000

10 0 10 20 30 40 50 km

10 0 10 20 30 miles

Tobago

North Pt.
Charlotteville
Castara 565 Little
Plymouth Main Ridge Tobago
Buccoo Reef Roxborough
Crown Pt. Scarborough
Rocky Bay

Blanchisseuse
La Vache Pt. Matelot Toco
Maracas Bay Sans Souci Galera Pt.
Corozal La Chupara Redhead
VENEZUELA Pt. Maraval Northern Range Salibea
Pen. de Monos 936 940 ▲ Mt. Aripo
Paria Macuro Tunapuna Valencia ATLANTIC
Dragon's Mouth Port San Guaico Matura
of Juan Arima Bay OCEAN
Güiria Spain Caroni Sangre Grande
Chaguanas Talparo Upper Manzanilla
Golfo de Paria Couva Nariva Cocos
Point Lisas Swamp Bay Trinidad
Otaheite Bay Gasparillo Rio Claro Guaturo Pt.
San Fernando Brighton La Brea Pierreville
Guapo Bay Pitch Penal Princes Town Mayaro Bay
Point Fortin Lake Basse Terre Guayaguayare
Cedros Bay Palo Seco Siparia 304 ▲ Galeota Pt.
Bonasse Moruga Trinity
Icacos Pt. Erin Pt. Hills
Serpent's Mouth
VENEZUELA Pta. Bombedor West from Greenwich

K

L

town
Amsterdam
Nieuw Nickerie
Totness Nieuw Amsterdam
Kwakoegron Moengo
Albina Sinnamary
Kourou
SURINAME St-Laurent Cayenne
Paramaribo Iracoubo
Prof. Van Kaw
▲1230 Blommestein- Approuague
Julianatop meer C. Orange
FRENCH St-Georges
GUIANA Oiapoque

AMAPÁ Camopi
Araguari
Serra Tumucumaque Amapá
Merirumã I. de Maracá
Serra do Macapá
Navio Mazagão Equator
Afuá Chaves C. Maguarinho
Óbidos Prainha I. Grande Soure Curuçá Salinópolis
Monte de Gurupá Vigia Bragança
Alegre Almeirim Marajó BELÉM Castanhal Viseu
Alenquer Breves Gurupá Abaetetuba Turiaçu
Juruti Pôrto-de-Móz Cametá Curuçá
Faro Santarém Cametá Barreirinhas Luís Correia
PARÁ Tucuruí Pinheiro Camocim
Belterra Baião Santa Inês Viana Itapecuru- Granja Itapipoca
Aveiro Altamira Bacabal Mirim Brejo Piracuruca Ipu Sobral Caucaia FORTALEZA
Brasília Legal Itaituba Repressa de MARANHÃO Codó Cascavel Marangugape Baturité Cascavel
Tucuruí Açailândia Pedreiras Caxias Campo Oiticica Quixadá Aracati
Serra dos Marabá Imperatriz Barra Maior CEARA Russas
Carajás São João do do Corda Teresina Crateús Mossoró RIO GRANDE Natal
Carajás Araguaia Grajaú Caraúbas DO NORTE C. de São Roque
Pôrto Franco Colinas Amarante Caicó Sousa Currais
BRAZIL Tocantinópolis Floriano Valença Iguatu Novos Canguaretama
Carolina do Piauí Oeiras Picos Cajázeiras Patos Alagoa Mamanguape
Conceição do Loreto Nova Iorque PIAUÍ Ouricuri Crato Juàzeiro Grande Cabedelo
Araguaia Riachão São João Chapada do Araripe do Norte Campina João Pessoa
Araguaína do Piauí Paulistana PERNAMBUCO Caruaru Grande Olinda
Conceição do São João São Dois Irmãos Petrolina Pesqueira RECIFE
Araguacema do Piauí Salgueiro Vitória de Jaboatão
Palmas Santa Caracol Nova Remanso São Francisco Garanhuns Santo Antão
TOCANTINS Filomena Nova Casa Juàzeiro Petrolândia Palmares
Pôrto Nacional Nova Paulo Afonso Palmeira
Santa Isabel Dianópolis Xique-Xique Jacobina dos Rio Largo
do Morro Gurupi Barra Mundo Queimadas Indios Maceió
Peixe Novo Itapicuru Propriá Arapiraca ALAGOAS
Manuel Alves Taguatinga Serrinha SERGIPE Capela Penedo
Campos Belos Barreiras Feira de Estância São Cristóvão Aracaju
Paranã Santa Maria Ibotirama Santana Alagoinhas
da Vitória Itaberaba Santo Amaro
São Domingos BAHIA Cachoeira SALVADOR
Bom Jesus Serra do Valença Nazaré B. de Todos os Santos
Carinhanha da Lápa Sincorá Jequié
Aruanã Posse Caetité Brumado Vitória da Itabuna
Niquelândia Carinhanha Condeúba Conquista Ilhéus
Januária Monte Azul Canavieiras
Formosa São Francisco Pedra Azul Belmonte
Taguatinga Janaúba Salinas Itamaraju Pôrto Seguro
DIST BRASÍLIA Montes Araçuaí Jequitinhonha Prado
FED Luziânia Claros Itamaraju
GOIÁS Viançpolis Teófilo Otoni Nanuque Caravelas
Goiânia Paracatu Pirapora Diamantina Mucuri
Alto Araguaia Ipameri Ipatinga Governador Conceição da Barra
Jataí Catalão Araguari Valadares São Mateus
Rio Verde Itumbiara Patos de Corinto Nova Linhares
MATO GROSSO Quirinópolis Minas Curvelo Venécia Colatina
DO SUL MINAS GERAIS Itabira Cariacica
Uberlândia Sabará Caratinga Vitória
Campo Prata Araxá Ibiá BELO HORIZONTE Ouro Vila Velha
Grande Uberaba Frutal Divinópolis Nova Prêto Cachoeiro de Itapemirim
Três Lagoas Santa Fé do Sul São José do Conselheiro Barbacena Campos
Rio Prêto Barretos Franca Passos Lafaiete Itaperuna
Andradina Araraquara Poços de São João Três Rios Nova Friburgo
Presidente Epitácio Penápolis Catanduva Linsu Caldas del Rei PETRÓPOLIS
Presidente Marília Jaú São Carlos Moji-Mirim São RIO DE JANEIRO
Prudente Bauru Piracicaba Lourenço Niterói
Pedro Juan Assis Limeira Volta Cabo Frio
Caballero Botucatu Campinas Redonda
Dourados

Trindade
(Braz.)

São Paulo
(Braz.)

Fernando de Noronha
(Braz.)

Rocas

6059 ▼

Greenwich 55   50   95   45   40   35   30   25

8   9   10 RIO DE JANEIRO   11   12   13

D

E

F

G

H

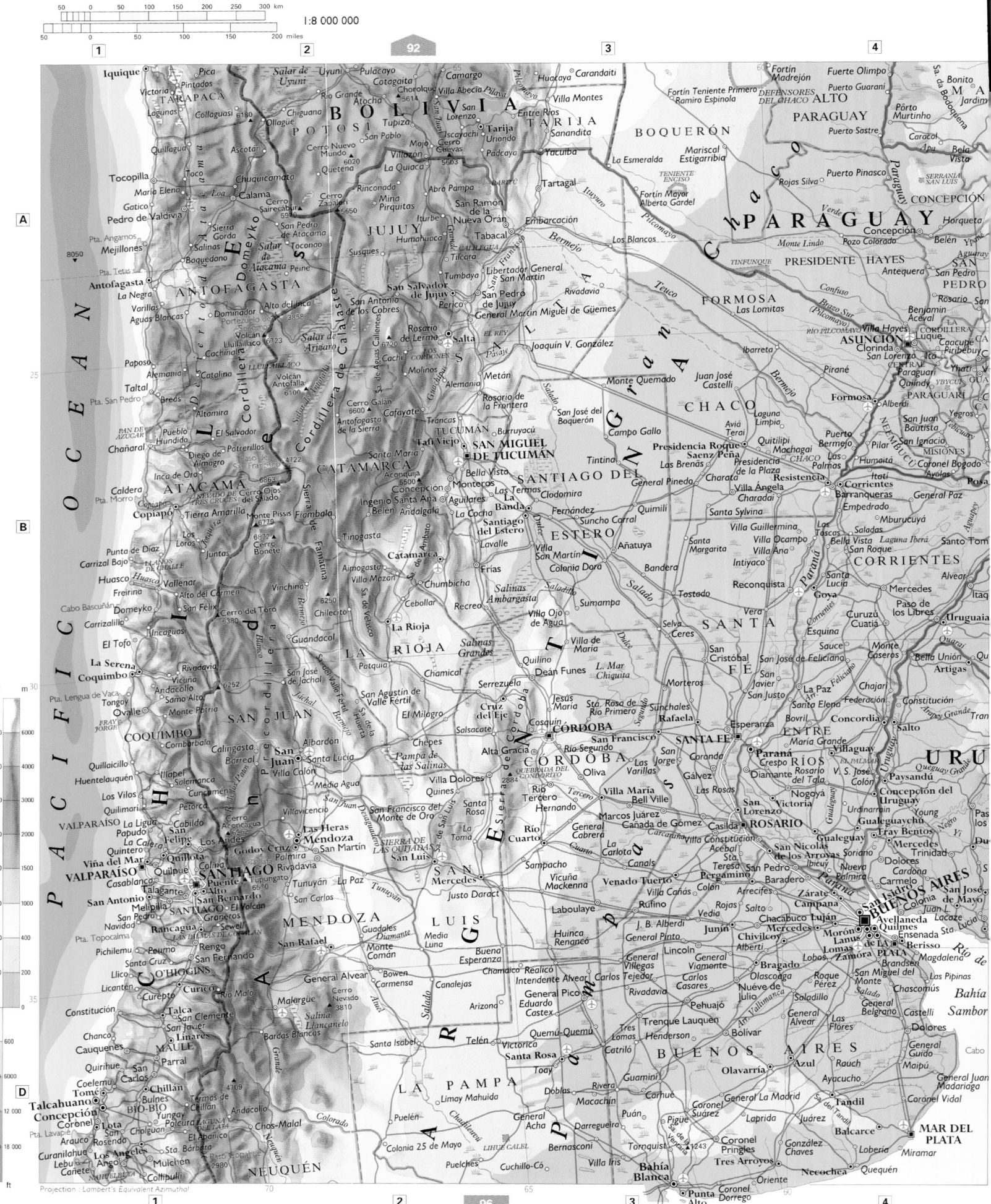

5   93   6   7

BELO
HORIZONTE
Nova Lima
Itabirito
Vitória
Itaquari
Vila
Velha
Guarapari

Congonhas
Conselheiro
Lafaiete
Ponte Nova
Carangola
Muriaé
Castelo
Cachoeiro
de Itapemirim
Pico da
Bandeira
2890

Três Lagoas
Andradina
Mirassol
Olímpia
Passos
Batatais
São Sebastião
do Paraíso
Oliveira
Campo Belo
São João
del Rei
Ouro
Prêto
Ubá
Cataguases
Cambuci
Guarus
CAMPOS
Cabo de
São Tomé

Xavantina
São José
do Rio Prêto
Ribeirão
Prêto
Guaxupé
Pocos de
Caldas
Varginha
Santos
Dumont
Lavras
Barbacena
Leopoldina
Juiz de Fora
Três
Rios
Além Paraíba
Nova Friburgo
Macaé

Panorama
Araçatuba
Catanduva
Taquaritinga
Jaboticabal
Mococa
Alfenas
Corações
São
Lourenço
Barra
do
Volta
Redonda
Barra
Mansa
Petrópolis
RIO DE JANEIRO

Presidente
Prudente
São
Carlos
Rio Claro
Ouro Fino
Mogi-Mirim
Itajubá
Pouso
Alegre
Guaratinguetá
Pirai
Nova
Iguaçu
Duque de Caxias
São Gonçalo
Cabo Frio

Maringá
CAMPINAS
Americana
Bragança
Paulista
Taubaté
São José dos C.
Angra dos Reis
Niterói
RIO DE JANEIRO

ATLANTIC

OCEAN

National Parks

1:16 000 000

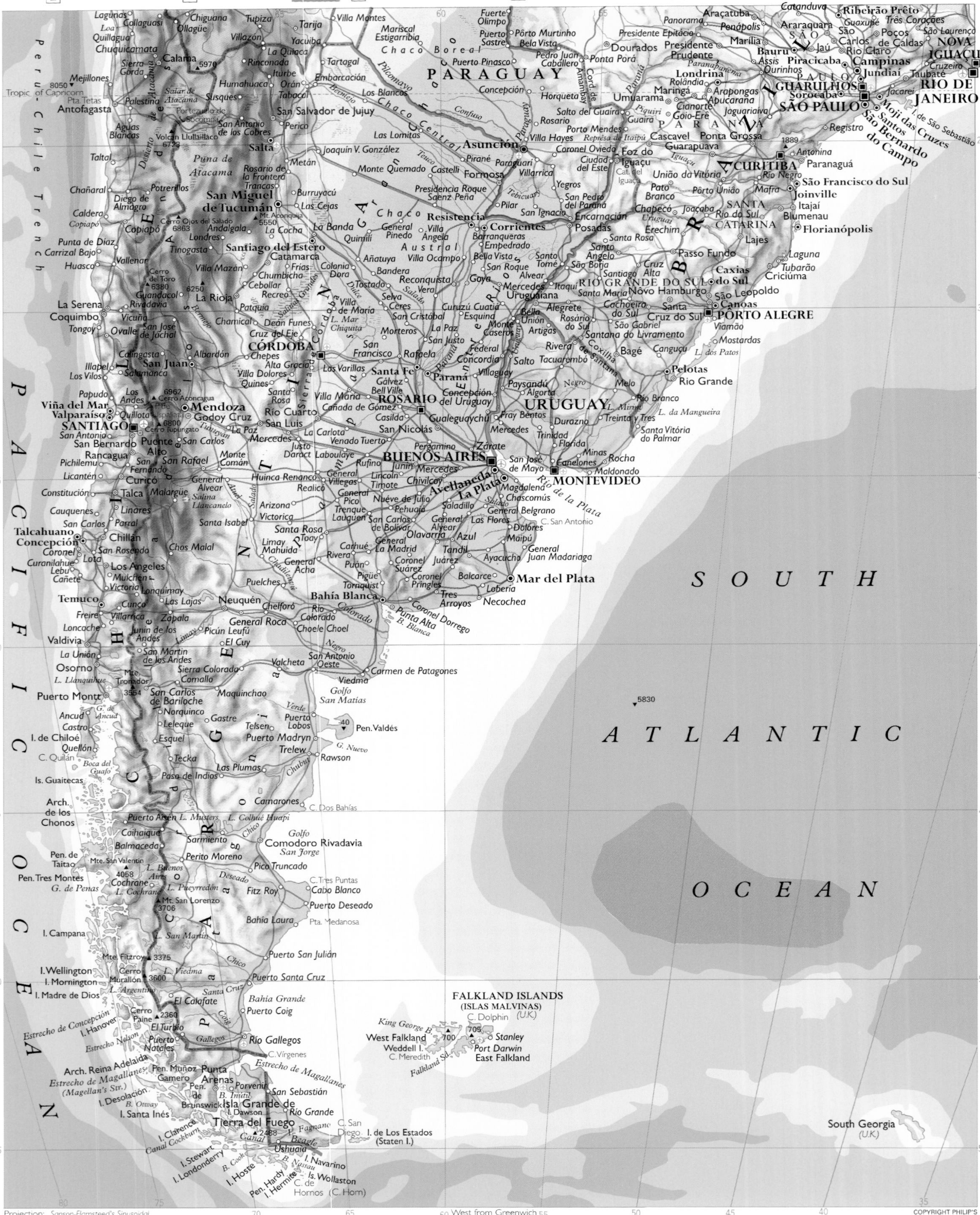

km
100 0 100 200 300 400 500

miles
100 0 100 200 300 400

PARAGUAY

BRAZIL

PARANÁ

SÃO PAULO

RIO DE JANEIRO

NOVA IGUAÇU

GUARULHOS

CURITIBA

SANTA CATARINA

Florianópolis

PORTO ALEGRE

RIO GRANDE DO SUL

URUGUAY

MONTEVIDEO

BUENOS AIRES

La Plata

Avellaneda

ROSARIO

Santa Fe

Paraná

CÓRDOBA

SANTIAGO

Valparaíso

Viña del Mar

Mendoza

Bahía Blanca

Mar del Plata

Neuquén

Concepción

Talcahuano

Temuco

Valdivia

Puerto Montt

Comodoro Rivadavia

Río Gallegos

Punta Arenas

Ushuaia

Tierra del Fuego

FALKLAND ISLANDS (ISLAS MALVINAS) (U.K.)
West Falkland
East Falkland
Stanley
Port Darwin

South Georgia (U.K.)

S O U T H   A T L A N T I C   O C E A N

P A C I F I C   O C E A N

Tropic of Capricorn

Peru-Chile Trench

Projection: Sanson-Flamsteed's Sinusoidal

West from Greenwich

COPYRIGHT PHILIP'S

ft   m
18 000 6000
12 000 4000
9000 3000
6000 2000
4500 1500
3000 1000
1200 400
600 200
0 0
200 600
2000 6000
4000 12 000
6000 18 000
8000 24 000
m ft

INDEX TO WORLD MAPS

The index contains the names of all the principal places and features shown on the World Maps. Each name is followed by an additional entry in italics giving the country or region within which it is located. The alphabetical order of names composed of two or more words is governed primarily by the first word and then by the second. This is an example of the rule:

Mīr Kūh, *Iran*	**45 E8**	26 22N	58 55 E
Mīr Shahdād, *Iran*	**45 E8**	26 15N	58 29 E
Mira, *Italy*	**22 B5**	45 26N	12 8 E
Mira por vos Cay, *Bahamas*	**89 B5**	22 9N	74 30W
Mirador-Río Azul △, *Guatemala* .	**88 C2**	17 45N	89 50W
Miraj, *India*	**40 L9**	16 50N	74 45 E

Physical features composed of a proper name (Erie) and a description (Lake) are positioned alphabetically by the proper name. The description is positioned after the proper name and is usually abbreviated:

Erie, L., *N. Amer.* **84 D4** 42 15N 81 0W

Where a description forms part of a settlement or administrative name however, it is always written in full and put in its true alphabetic position:

Mount Morris, *U.S.A.* **84 D7** 42 44N 77 52W

Names beginning with M' and Mc are indexed as if they were spelled Mac. Names beginning St. are alphabetized under Saint, but Sankt, Sint, Sant', Santa and San are all spelt in full and are alphabetized accordingly. If the same place name occurs two or more times in the index and all are in the same country, each is followed by the name of the administrative subdivision in which it is located.

The number in bold type which follows each name in the index refers to the number of the map page where that feature or place will be found. This is usually the largest scale at which the place or feature appears.

The letter and figure which are in bold type immediately after the page number give the grid square on the map page, within which the feature is situated. The letter represents the latitude and the figure the longitude. A lower case letter immediately after the page number refers to an inset map on that page.

In some cases the feature itself may fall within the specified square, while the name is outside. This is usually the case only with features which are larger than a grid square.

The geographical co-ordinates which follow the letter-figure references give the latitude and longitude of each place. The first co-ordinate indicates latitude – the distance north of the Equator. The second co-ordinate indicates longitude – the distance east or west of the Greenwich Meridian. Both latitude and longitude are measured in degrees and minutes (there are 60 minutes in a degree).

The latitude is followed by N(orth) or S(outh) and the longitude by E(ast) or W(est).

Rivers are indexed to their mouths or confluences, and carry the symbol ➔ after their names. The following symbols are also used in the index: ■ country, ☑ overseas territory or dependency, □ first order administrative area, △ national park, ⌒ other park (provincial park, nature reserve or game reserve), ✈ (LHR) principal airport (and location identifier).

Abbreviations used in the index

A.C.T. – Australian Capital Territory
A.R. – Autonomous Region
Afghan. – Afghanistan
Afr. – Africa
Ala. – Alabama
Alta. – Alberta
Amer. – America(n)
Arch. – Archipelago
Ariz. – Arizona
Ark. – Arkansas
Atl. Oc. – Atlantic Ocean
B. – Baie, Bahía, Bay, Bucht, Bugt
B.C. – British Columbia
Bangla. – Bangladesh
Barr. – Barrage
Bos.-H. – Bosnia-Herzegovina
C. – Cabo, Cap, Cape, Coast
C.A.R. – Central African Republic
C. Prov. – Cape Province
Calif. – California
Cat. – Catarata
Cent. – Central
Chan. – Channel
Colo. – Colorado
Conn. – Connecticut
Cord. – Cordillera
Cr. – Creek
Czech. – Czech Republic
D.C. – District of Columbia
Del. – Delaware
Dem. – Democratic
Dep. – Dependency
Des. – Desert
Dét. – Détroit
Dist. – District
Dj. – Djebel
Domin. – Dominica
Dom. Rep. – Dominican Republic

E. – East
E. Salv. – El Salvador
Eq. Guin. – Equatorial Guinea
Est. – Estrecho
Falk. Is. – Falkland Is.
Fd. – Fjord
Fla. – Florida
Fr. – French
G. – Golfe, Golfo, Gulf, Guba, Gebel
Ga. – Georgia
Gt. – Great, Greater
Guinea-Biss. – Guinea-Bissau
H.K. – Hong Kong
H.P. – Himachal Pradesh
Hants. – Hampshire
Harb. – Harbor, Harbour
Hd. – Head
Hts. – Heights
I.(s). – Île, Ilha, Insel, Isla, Island, Isle
Ill. – Illinois
Ind. – Indiana
Ind. Oc. – Indian Ocean
Ivory C. – Ivory Coast
J. – Jabal, Jebel
Jaz. – Jazīrah
Junc. – Junction
K. – Kap, Kapp
Kans. – Kansas
Kep. – Kepulauan
Ky. – Kentucky
L. – Lac, Lacul, Lago, Lagoa, Lake, Limni, Loch, Lough
La. – Louisiana
Ld. – Land
Liech. – Liechtenstein
Lux. – Luxembourg
Mad. P. – Madhya Pradesh
Madag. – Madagascar
Man. – Manitoba
Mass. – Massachusetts

Md. – Maryland
Me. – Maine
Medit. S. – Mediterranean Sea
Mich. – Michigan
Minn. – Minnesota
Miss. – Mississippi
Mo. – Missouri
Mont. – Montana
Mozam. – Mozambique
Mt.(s) – Mont, Montaña, Mountain
Mte. – Monte
Mti. – Monti
N. – Nord, Norte, North, Northern, Nouveau
N.B. – New Brunswick
N.C. – North Carolina
N. Cal. – New Caledonia
N. Dak. – North Dakota
N.H. – New Hampshire
N.I. – North Island
N.J. – New Jersey
N. Mex. – New Mexico
N.S. – Nova Scotia
N.S.W. – New South Wales
N.W.T. – North West Territory
N.Y. – New York
N.Z. – New Zealand
Nac. – Nacional
Nat. – National
Nebr. – Nebraska
Neths. – Netherlands
Nev. – Nevada
Nfld. – Newfoundland
Nic. – Nicaragua
O. – Oued, Ouadi
Occ. – Occidentale
Okla. – Oklahoma
Ont. – Ontario
Or. – Orientale
Oreg. – Oregon

Os. – Ostrov
Oz. – Ozero
P. – Pass, Passo, Pasul, Pulau
P.E.I. – Prince Edward Island
Pa. – Pennsylvania
Pac. Oc. – Pacific Ocean
Papua N.G. – Papua New Guinea
Pass. – Passage
Peg. – Pegunungan
Pen. – Peninsula, Péninsule
Phil. – Philippines
Pk. – Peak
Plat. – Plateau
Prov. – Province, Provincial
Pt. – Point
Pta. – Ponta, Punta
Pte. – Pointe
Qué. – Québec
Queens. – Queensland
R. – Rio, River
R.I. – Rhode Island
Ra. – Range
Raj. – Rajasthan
Recr. – Recreational, Récréatif
Reg. – Region
Rep. – Republic
Res. – Reserve, Reservoir
Rhld-Pfz. – Rheinland-Pfalz
S. – South, Southern, Sur
Si. Arabia – Saudi Arabia
S.C. – South Carolina
S. Dak. – South Dakota
S.I. – South Island
S. Leone – Sierra Leone
Sa. – Serra, Sierra
Sask. – Saskatchewan
Scot. – Scotland
Sd. – Sound
Sev. – Severnaya
Sib. – Siberia
Sprs. – Springs

St. – Saint
Sta. – Santa
Ste. – Sainte
Sto. – Santo
Str. – Strait, Stretto
Switz. – Switzerland
Tas. – Tasmania
Tenn. – Tennessee
Terr. – Territory, Territoire
Tex. – Texas
Tg. – Tanjung
Trin. & Tob. – Trinidad & Tobago
U.A.E. – United Arab Emirates
U.K. – United Kingdom
U.S.A. – United States of America
Ut. P. – Uttar Pradesh
Va. – Virginia
Vdkhr. – Vodokhranilishche
Vdskh. – Vodoskhovyshche
Vf. – Vírful
Vic. – Victoria
Vol. – Volcano
Vt. – Vermont
W. – Wadi, West
W. Va. – West Virginia
Wall. & F. Is. – Wallis and Futuna Is.
Wash. – Washington
Wis. – Wisconsin
Wlkp. – Wielkopolski
Wyo. – Wyoming
Yorks. – Yorkshire

A

A Coruña, *Spain* **21 A1** 43 20N 8 25W
A Estrada, *Spain* **21 A1** 42 43N 8 27W
A Fonsagrada, *Spain* **21 A2** 43 8N 7 4W
Aachen, *Germany* **16 C4** 50 45N 6 6 E
Aalborg = Ålborg, *Denmark* **9 H13** 57 2N 9 54 E
Aalen, *Germany* **16 D6** 48 51N 10 6 E
Aalst, *Belgium* **15 D4** 50 56N 4 2 E
Aalten, *Neths.* **15 C6** 51 56N 6 35 E
Aalter, *Belgium* **15 C3** 51 5N 3 28 E
Äänekoski, *Finland* **9 E21** 62 36N 25 44 E
Aarau, *Switz.* **20 C8** 47 23N 8 4 E
Aare →, *Switz.* **20 C8** 47 33N 8 14 E
Aarhus = Århus, *Denmark* **9 H14** 56 8N 10 11 E
Aarschot, *Belgium* **15 D4** 50 59N 4 49 E
Aba, *Dem. Rep. of the Congo* **54 B3** 3 58N 30 17 E
Aba, *Nigeria* **50 G7** 5 10N 7 19 E
Ābādān, *Iran* **45 D6** 30 22N 48 20 E
Ābādeh, *Iran* **45 D7** 31 8N 52 40 E
Abadla, *Algeria* **50 B5** 31 2N 2 45W
Abaetetuba, *Brazil* **93 D9** 1 40S 48 50W
Abagnar Qi, *China* **34 C9** 43 52N 116 2 E
Abah, Tanjung, *Indonesia* **37 K18** 8 46S 115 38 E
Abai, *Paraguay* **95 B4** 25 58S 55 54W
Abakan, *Russia* **29 D10** 53 40N 91 10 E
Abancay, *Peru* **92 F4** 13 35S 72 55W
Abariringa, *Kiribati* **64 H10** 2 50S 171 40W
Abarqū, *Iran* **45 D7** 31 10N 53 20 E
Abashiri, *Japan* **30 B12** 44 0N 144 15 E
Abashiri-Wan, *Japan* **30 C12** 44 0N 144 30 E
Ābay = Nîl el Azraq →, *Sudan* **51 E12** 15 38N 32 31 E
Abay, *Kazakhstan* **28 E8** 49 38N 72 53 E
Abaya, L., *Ethiopia* **47 F2** 6 30N 37 50 E
Abaza, *Russia* **28 D9** 52 39N 90 6 E
'Abbāsābād, *Iran* **45 C8** 33 34N 58 23 E
Abbay = Nîl el Azraq →, *Sudan* **51 E12** 15 38N 32 31 E
Abbaye, Pt., *U.S.A.* **82 B1** 46 58N 88 8W
Abbé, L., *Ethiopia* **47 E3** 11 8N 41 47 E
Abbeville, *France* **20 A4** 50 6N 1 49 E
Abbeville, *Ala., U.S.A.* **83 K3** 31 34N 85 15W
Abbeville, *La., U.S.A.* **81 L8** 29 58N 92 8W
Abbeville, *S.C., U.S.A.* **83 H4** 34 11N 82 23W
Abbot Ice Shelf, *Antarctica* **5 D16** 73 0S 92 0W
Abbottabad, *Pakistan* **42 B5** 34 10N 73 15 E
Abd al Kūrī, *Yemen* **47 E5** 12 5N 52 20 E
Ābdar, *Iran* **45 D7** 30 16N 55 19 E
'Abdolābād, *Iran* **45 C8** 34 12N 56 30 E
Abdulpur, *Bangla.* **43 G13** 24 15N 88 59 E
Abéché, *Chad* **51 F10** 13 50N 20 35 E
Abel Tasman △, *N.Z.* **59 J4** 40 59S 173 3 E
Abengourou, *Ivory C.* **50 G5** 6 42N 3 27W
Åbenrå, *Denmark* **9 J13** 55 3N 9 25 E
Abeokuta, *Nigeria* **50 G6** 7 3N 3 19 E
Aber, *Uganda* **54 B3** 2 12N 32 25 E
Aberaeron, *U.K.* **13 E3** 52 15N 4 15W
Aberayron = Aberaeron, *U.K.* **13 E3** 52 15N 4 15W
Aberchirder, *U.K.* **11 D6** 57 34N 2 37W
Abercorn, *Australia* **63 D5** 25 12S 151 5 E
Aberdare, *U.K.* **13 F4** 51 43N 3 27W
Aberdare △, *Kenya* **54 C4** 0 22S 36 44 E
Aberdare Ra., *Kenya* **54 C4** 0 15S 36 50 E
Aberdeen, *Australia* **63 E5** 32 9S 150 56 E
Aberdeen, *Canada* **71 C7** 52 20N 106 8W
Aberdeen, *China* **33 G11** 22 15N 114 9 E
Aberdeen, *S. Africa* **56 E3** 32 28S 24 2 E
Aberdeen, *U.K.* **11 D6** 57 9N 2 5W
Aberdeen, *Ala., U.S.A.* **83 J1** 33 49N 88 33W
Aberdeen, *Idaho, U.S.A.* **76 E7** 42 57N 112 50W
Aberdeen, *Md., U.S.A.* **82 F7** 39 31N 76 10W
Aberdeen, *S. Dak., U.S.A.* **80 C5** 45 28N 98 29W
Aberdeen, *Wash., U.S.A.* **78 D3** 46 59N 123 50W
Aberdeen, City of □, *U.K.* **11 D6** 57 10N 2 10W
Aberdeenshire □, *U.K.* **11 D6** 57 17N 2 36W
Aberdovey = Aberdyfi, *U.K.* **13 E3** 52 33N 4 3W
Aberdyfi, *U.K.* **13 E3** 52 33N 4 3W
Aberfeldy, *U.K.* **11 E5** 56 37N 3 51W
Aberfoyle, *U.K.* **11 E4** 56 11N 4 23W
Abergavenny, *U.K.* **13 F4** 51 49N 3 1W
Abergele, *U.K.* **12 D4** 53 17N 3 35W
Abernathy, *U.S.A.* **81 J4** 33 50N 101 51W
Abert, L., *U.S.A.* **76 E3** 42 38N 120 14W
Aberystwyth, *U.K.* **13 E3** 52 25N 4 5W
Abhā, *Si. Arabia* **47 D3** 18 0N 42 34 E
Abhar, *Iran* **45 B6** 36 9N 49 13 E
Abhayapuri, *India* **43 F14** 26 24N 90 38 E
Abidjan, *Ivory C.* **50 G5** 5 26N 3 58W
Abilene, *Kans., U.S.A.* **80 F6** 38 55N 97 13W
Abilene, *Tex., U.S.A.* **81 J5** 32 28N 99 43W
Abingdon, *U.K.* **13 F6** 51 40N 1 17W
Abingdon, *U.S.A.* **83 G5** 36 43N 81 59W
Abington Reef, *Australia* **62 B4** 18 0S 149 35 E
Abitau →, *Canada* **71 B7** 59 53N 109 3W
Abitibi →, *Canada* **72 B3** 51 3N 80 55W
Abitibi, L., *Canada* **72 C4** 48 40N 79 40W
Abkhaz Republic = Abkhazia □, *Georgia* **19 F7** 43 12N 41 5 E
Abkhazia □, *Georgia* **19 F7** 43 12N 41 5 E
Abminga, *Australia* **63 D1** 26 8S 134 51 E
Åbo = Turku, *Finland* **9 F20** 60 30N 22 19 E
Abohar, *India* **42 D6** 30 10N 74 10 E
Abomey, *Benin* **50 G6** 7 10N 2 5 E
Abong-Mbang, *Cameroon* **52 D2** 4 0N 13 8 E
Abou-Deïa, *Chad* **51 F9** 11 20N 19 20 E
Aboyne, *U.K.* **11 D6** 57 4N 2 47W
Abra Pampa, *Argentina* **94 A2** 22 43S 65 42W
Abraham L., *Canada* **70 C5** 52 15N 116 35W
Abreojos, Pta., *Mexico* **86 B2** 26 50N 113 40W
Abrud, *Romania* **17 E12** 46 19N 23 5 E
Absaroka Range, *U.S.A.* **76 D9** 44 45N 109 50W
Abu, *India* **42 G5** 24 41N 72 50 E
Abū al Abyad, *U.A.E.* **45 E7** 24 11N 53 50 E
Abū al Khaşīb, *Iraq* **45 D6** 30 25N 48 0 E
Abū 'Alī, *Si. Arabia* **45 E6** 27 20N 49 27 E
Abū 'Alī →, *Lebanon* **46 A4** 34 25N 35 50 E
Abu Dhabi = Abū Z̧āby, *U.A.E.* **45 E7** 24 28N 54 22 E
Abū Du'ān, *Syria* **44 B3** 36 25N 38 15 E
Abu el Gairi, W. →, *Egypt* **46 F2** 29 35N 33 30 E
Abu Ga'da, W. →, *Egypt* **46 F1** 29 15N 32 53 E
Abū Ḩadrīyah, *Si. Arabia* **45 E6** 27 20N 48 58 E
Abu Hamed, *Sudan* **51 E12** 19 32N 33 13 E
Abū Kamāl, *Syria* **44 C4** 34 30N 41 0 E
Abū Madd, Ra's, *Si. Arabia* **44 E3** 24 50N 37 7 E
Abū Mūsā, *U.A.E.* **45 E7** 25 52N 55 3 E
Abū Qaşr, *Si. Arabia* **44 D3** 30 21N 38 34 E
Abu Simbel, *Egypt* **51 D12** 22 18N 31 40 E
Abū Şukhayr, *Iraq* **44 D5** 31 54N 44 30 E
Abu Zabad, *Sudan* **51 F11** 12 25N 29 10 E
Abū Z̧āby, *U.A.E.* **45 E7** 24 28N 54 22 E
Abū Zeydābād, *Iran* **45 C6** 33 54N 51 45 E
Abuja, *Nigeria* **50 G7** 9 5N 7 32 E
Abukuma-Gawa →, *Japan* **30 E10** 38 6N 140 52 E
Abukuma-Sammyaku, *Japan* **30 F10** 37 30N 140 45 E
Abunã, *Brazil* **92 E5** 9 40S 65 20W
Abunã →, *Brazil* **92 E5** 9 41S 65 20W
Aburo, *Dem. Rep. of the Congo* **54 B3** 2 4N 30 53 E
Abut Hd., *N.Z.* **59 K3** 43 7S 170 15 E
Acadia △, *U.S.A.* **83 C11** 44 20N 68 13W
Açailândia, *Brazil* **93 D9** 4 57S 47 0W
Acajutla, *El Salv.* **88 D2** 13 36N 89 50W
Acámbaro, *Mexico* **86 D4** 20 0N 100 40W
Acaponeta, *Mexico* **86 C3** 22 30N 105 20W
Acapulco, *Mexico* **87 D5** 16 51N 99 56W
Acarai, Serra, *Brazil* **92 C7** 1 50N 57 50W
Acarigua, *Venezuela* **92 B5** 9 33N 69 12W
Acatlán, *Mexico* **87 D5** 18 10N 98 3W
Acayucan, *Mexico* **87 D6** 17 59N 94 58W
Accomac, *U.S.A.* **82 G8** 37 43N 75 40W
Accra, *Ghana* **50 G5** 5 35N 0 6W
Accrington, *U.K.* **12 D5** 53 45N 2 22W
Acebal, *Argentina* **94 C3** 33 20S 60 50W
Aceh □, *Indonesia* **36 D1** 4 15N 97 30 E
Achalpur, *India* **40 J10** 21 22N 77 32 E
Acheng, *China* **35 B14** 45 30N 126 58 E
Acher, *India* **42 H5** 23 10N 72 32 E
Achill Hd., *Ireland* **10 C1** 53 58N 10 15W
Achill I., *Ireland* **10 C1** 53 58N 10 1W
Achinsk, *Russia* **29 D10** 56 20N 90 20 E
Acireale, *Italy* **22 F6** 37 37N 15 10 E
Ackerman, *U.S.A.* **81 J10** 33 19N 89 11W
Acklins I., *Bahamas* **89 B5** 22 30N 74 0W
Acme, *Canada* **70 C6** 51 33N 113 30W
Acme, *U.S.A.* **84 F5** 40 8N 79 26W
Aconcagua, Cerro, *Argentina* **94 C2** 32 39S 70 0W
Aconquija, Mt., *Argentina* **94 B2** 27 0S 66 0W
Açores, Is. dos, *Atl. Oc.* **50 A1** 38 0N 27 0W
Acornhoek, *S. Africa* **57 C5** 24 37S 31 2 E
Acraman, L., *Australia* **63 E2** 32 2S 135 23 E
Acre = 'Akko, *Israel* **46 C4** 32 55N 35 4 E
Acre □, *Brazil* **92 E4** 9 1S 71 0W
Acre →, *Brazil* **92 E5** 8 45S 67 22W
Acton, *Canada* **84 C4** 43 38N 80 3W
Acuña, *Mexico* **86 B4** 29 18N 100 55W
Ad Dammām, *Si. Arabia* **45 E6** 26 20N 50 5 E
Ad Dāmūr, *Lebanon* **46 B4** 33 44N 35 27 E
Ad Dawādimī, *Si. Arabia* **44 E5** 24 35N 44 15 E
Ad Dawḩah, *Qatar* **45 E6** 25 15N 51 35 E
Ad Dawr, *Iraq* **44 C4** 34 27N 43 47 E
Ad Dir'īyah, *Si. Arabia* **44 E5** 24 44N 46 35 E
Ad Dīwānīyah, *Iraq* **44 D5** 32 0N 45 0 E
Ad Dujayl, *Iraq* **44 C5** 33 51N 44 14 E
Ad Duwayd, *Si. Arabia* **44 D4** 30 15N 42 17 E
Ada, *Minn., U.S.A.* **80 B6** 47 18N 96 31W
Ada, *Okla., U.S.A.* **81 H6** 34 46N 96 41W
Adabiya, *Egypt* **46 F1** 29 53N 32 28 E
Adair, C., *Canada* **69 A12** 71 30N 71 34W
Adaja →, *Spain* **21 B3** 41 32N 4 52W
Adak I., *U.S.A.* **68 C2** 51 45N 176 45W
Adamaoua, Massif de l', *Cameroon* **51 G7** 7 20N 12 20 E
Adamawa Highlands = Adamaoua, Massif de l', *Cameroon* **51 G7** 7 20N 12 20 E
Adamello, Mte., *Italy* **20 C9** 46 9N 10 30 E
Adaminaby, *Australia* **63 F4** 36 0S 148 45 E
Adams, *Mass., U.S.A.* **85 D11** 42 38N 73 7W
Adams, *N.Y., U.S.A.* **85 C8** 43 49N 76 1W
Adams, *Wis., U.S.A.* **80 D10** 43 57N 89 49W
Adams, Mt., *U.S.A.* **78 D5** 46 12N 121 30W
Adam's Bridge, *Sri Lanka* **40 Q11** 9 15N 79 40 E
Adams L., *Canada* **70 C5** 51 10N 119 40W
Adam's Peak, *Sri Lanka* **40 R12** 6 48N 80 30 E
Adana, *Turkey* **19 G6** 37 0N 35 16 E
Adapazarı = Sakarya, *Turkey* **19 F5** 40 48N 30 25 E
Adarama, *Sudan* **51 E12** 17 10N 34 52 E
Adare, C., *Antarctica* **5 D11** 71 0S 171 0 E
Adaut, *Indonesia* **37 F8** 8 8S 131 7 E
Adavale, *Australia* **63 D3** 25 52S 144 32 E
Adda →, *Italy* **20 D8** 45 8N 9 53 E
Addis Ababa = Addis Abeba, *Ethiopia* **47 F2** 9 2N 38 42 E
Addis Abeba, *Ethiopia* **47 F2** 9 2N 38 42 E
Addison, *U.S.A.* **84 D7** 42 1N 77 14W
Addo, *S. Africa* **56 E4** 33 32S 25 45 E
Addo △, *S. Africa* **56 E4** 33 30S 25 50 E
Ādeh, *Iran* **44 B5** 37 42N 45 11 E
Adel, *U.S.A.* **83 K4** 31 8N 83 25W
Adelaide, *Australia* **63 E2** 34 52S 138 30 E
Adelaide, *Bahamas* **88 A4** 25 4N 77 31W
Adelaide, *S. Africa* **56 E4** 32 42S 26 20 E
Adelaide I., *Antarctica* **5 C17** 67 15S 68 30W
Adelaide Pen., *Canada* **68 B10** 68 15N 97 30W
Adelaide River, *Australia* **60 B5** 13 15S 131 7 E
Adelanto, *U.S.A.* **79 L9** 34 35N 117 22W
Adele I., *Australia* **60 C3** 15 32S 123 9 E
Adélie, Terre, *Antarctica* **5 C10** 68 0S 140 0 E
Adélie Land = Adélie, Terre, *Antarctica* **5 C10** 68 0S 140 0 E
Aden = Al 'Adan, *Yemen* **47 E4** 12 45N 45 0 E
Aden, G. of, *Asia* **47 E4** 12 30N 47 30 E
Adendorp, *S. Africa* **56 E3** 32 15S 24 30 E
Adh Dhayd, *U.A.E.* **45 E7** 25 17N 55 53 E
Adhoi, *India* **42 H4** 23 26N 70 32 E
Adi, *Indonesia* **37 E8** 4 15S 133 30 E
Adieu, C., *Australia* **61 F5** 32 0S 132 10 E
Adieu Pt., *Australia* **60 C3** 15 14S 124 35 E
Adige →, *Italy* **22 B5** 45 9N 12 20 E
Adigrat, *Ethiopia* **47 E2** 14 20N 39 26 E
Adilabad, *India* **40 K11** 19 33N 78 20 E
Adirondack ⌓, *U.S.A.* **85 C10** 44 0N 74 20W
Adirondack Mts., *U.S.A.* **85 C10** 44 0N 74 0W
Adjumani, *Uganda* **54 B3** 3 20N 31 50 E
Adjuntas, *Puerto Rico* **89 d** 18 10N 66 43W
Adlavik Is., *Canada* **73 B8** 55 0N 58 40W
Admiralty G., *Australia* **60 B4** 14 20S 125 55 E
Admiralty I., *U.S.A.* **70 B2** 57 30N 134 30W
Admiralty Is., *Papua N. G.* **64 H6** 2 0S 147 0 E
Adonara, *Indonesia* **37 F6** 8 15S 123 5 E
Adoni, *India* **40 M10** 15 33N 77 18 E
Adour →, *France* **20 E3** 43 32N 1 32W
Adra, *India* **43 H12** 23 30N 86 42 E
Adra, *Spain* **21 D4** 36 43N 3 3W
Adrano, *Italy* **22 F6** 37 40N 14 50 E
Adrar, *Mauritania* **50 D3** 20 30N 7 30 E
Adrar des Iforas, *Algeria* **50 C5** 27 51N 0 11 E
Adrian, *Mich., U.S.A.* **82 E3** 41 54N 84 2W
Adrian, *Tex., U.S.A.* **81 H3** 35 16N 102 40W
Adriatic Sea, *Medit. S.* **22 C6** 43 0N 16 0 E
Adua, *Indonesia* **37 E7** 1 45S 129 50 E
Adwa, *Ethiopia* **47 E2** 14 15N 38 52 E
Adygea □, *Russia* **19 F7** 45 0N 40 0 E
Adzhar Republic = Ajaria □, *Georgia* **19 F7** 41 30N 42 0 E
Adzopé, *Ivory C.* **50 G5** 6 7N 3 49W
Ægean Sea, *Medit. S.* **23 E11** 38 30N 25 0 E
Aerhtai Shan, *Mongolia* **32 B4** 46 40N 92 45 E
'Afak, *Iraq* **44 C5** 32 4N 45 15 E
Afándou, *Greece* **25 C10** 36 18N 28 12 E
Afghanistan ■, *Asia* **40 C4** 33 0N 65 0 E
Aflou, *Algeria* **50 B6** 34 7N 2 3 E
Africa **48 E6** 10 0N 20 0 E
'Afrīn, *Syria* **44 B3** 36 32N 36 50 E
Afton, *N.Y., U.S.A.* **85 D9** 42 14N 75 32W
Afton, *Wyo., U.S.A.* **76 E8** 42 44N 110 56W
Afuá, *Brazil* **93 D8** 0 15S 50 20W
'Afula, *Israel* **46 C4** 32 37N 35 17 E
Afyon, *Turkey* **19 G5** 38 45N 30 33 E
Afyonkarahisar = Afyon, *Turkey* **19 G5** 38 45N 30 33 E
Agadès = Agadez, *Niger* **50 E7** 16 58N 7 59 E
Agadez, *Niger* **50 E7** 16 58N 7 59 E
Agadir, *Morocco* **50 B4** 30 28N 9 55W
Agaete, *Canary Is.* **24 F4** 28 6N 15 43W
Agar, *India* **42 H7** 23 40N 76 2 E
Agartala, *India* **41 H17** 23 50N 91 23 E
Agassiz, *Canada* **70 D4** 49 14N 121 46W
Agats, *Indonesia* **37 F9** 5 33S 138 0 E
Agawam, *U.S.A.* **85 D12** 42 5N 72 37W
Agboville, *Ivory C.* **50 G5** 5 55N 4 15W
Ağdam, *Azerbaijan* **44 B5** 40 0N 46 58 E
Agde, *France* **20 E5** 43 19N 3 28 E
Agen, *France* **20 D4** 44 12N 0 38 E
Āgh Kand, *Iran* **45 B6** 37 15N 48 4 E
Aginskoye, *Russia* **29 D12** 51 6N 114 32 E
Agnew, *Australia* **61 E3** 28 1S 120 31 E
Agori, *India* **43 G10** 24 33N 82 57 E
Agra, *India* **42 F7** 27 17N 77 58 E
Ağri, *Turkey* **19 G7** 39 44N 43 3 E
Agri →, *Italy* **22 D7** 40 13N 16 44 E
Ağrı Dağı, *Turkey* **19 G7** 39 50N 44 15 E
Ağri Karakose = Ağri, *Turkey* **19 G7** 39 44N 43 3 E
Agrigento, *Italy* **22 F5** 37 19N 13 34 E
Agrínion, *Greece* **23 E9** 38 37N 21 27 E
Agua Caliente, *Baja Calif., Mexico* **79 N10** 32 29N 116 59W
Agua Caliente, *Sinaloa, Mexico* **86 B3** 26 30N 108 20W
Agua Caliente Springs, *U.S.A.* **79 N10** 32 56N 116 19W
Água Clara, *Brazil* **93 H8** 20 25S 52 45W
Agua Fria ⌓, *U.S.A.* **77 J8** 34 14N 112 0W
Agua Hechicero, *Mexico* **79 N10** 32 26N 116 14W
Agua Prieta, *Mexico* **86 A3** 31 20N 109 32W
Aguadilla, *Puerto Rico* **89 d** 18 26N 67 10W
Aguadulce, *Panama* **88 E3** 8 15N 80 32W
Aguanga, *U.S.A.* **79 M10** 33 27N 116 51W
Aguanish, *Canada* **73 B7** 50 14N 62 2W
Aguanus →, *Canada* **73 B7** 50 13N 62 5W
Aguapey →, *Argentina* **94 B4** 29 7S 56 36W
Aguaray Guazú →, *Paraguay* **94 A4** 24 47S 57 19W
Aguarico →, *Ecuador* **92 D3** 0 59S 75 11W
Aguaro-Guariquito △, *Venezuela* **89 E6** 8 20N 66 35W
Aguas Blancas, *Chile* **94 A2** 24 15S 69 55W
Aguas Calientes, Sierra de, *Argentina* **94 B2** 25 26S 66 40W
Aguascalientes, *Mexico* **86 C4** 21 53N 102 12W
Aguascalientes □, *Mexico* **86 C4** 22 0N 102 20W
Aguila, Punta, *Puerto Rico* **89 d** 17 57N 67 13W
Aguilares, *Argentina* **94 B2** 27 26S 65 35W
Aguilas, *Spain* **21 D5** 37 23N 1 35W
Agüimes, *Canary Is.* **24 G4** 27 58N 15 27W
Aguja, C. de la, *Colombia* **90 B3** 11 18N 74 12W
Agujereada, Pta., *Puerto Rico* **89 d** 18 30N 67 8W
Agulhas, C., *S. Africa* **56 E3** 34 52S 20 0 E
Agulo, *Canary Is.* **24 F2** 28 11N 17 12W
Agung, Gunung, *Indonesia* **36 F5** 8 20S 115 28 E
Agur, *Uganda* **54 B3** 2 28N 32 55 E
Agusan →, *Phil.* **37 C7** 9 0N 125 30 E
Aha Mts., *Botswana* **56 B3** 19 45S 21 0 E
Ahaggar, *Algeria* **50 D7** 23 0N 6 30 E
Ahar, *Iran* **44 B5** 38 35N 47 0 E
Ahipara B., *N.Z.* **59 F4** 35 5S 173 5 E
Ahiri, *India* **40 K12** 19 30N 80 0 E
Ahmad Wal, *Pakistan* **42 E1** 29 18N 65 58 E
Ahmadabad, *India* **42 H5** 23 0N 72 40 E
Aḩmadābād, *Khorāsān, Iran* **45 C9** 35 3N 60 50 E
Aḩmadābād, *Khorāsān, Iran* **45 C8** 35 49N 59 42 E
Aḩmadī, *Iran* **45 E8** 27 56N 56 42 E
Ahmadnagar, *India* **40 K9** 19 7N 74 46 E
Ahmadpur, *Pakistan* **42 E4** 29 12N 71 10 E
Ahmadpur Lamma, *Pakistan* **42 E4** 28 19N 70 3 E
Ahmedabad = Ahmadabad, *India* **42 H5** 23 0N 72 40 E
Ahmednagar = Ahmadnagar, *India* **40 K9** 19 7N 74 46 E
Ahome, *Mexico* **86 B3** 25 55N 109 11W
Ahoskie, *U.S.A.* **83 G7** 36 17N 76 59W
Ahram, *Iran* **45 D6** 28 52N 51 16 E
Ahrax Pt., *Malta* **25 D1** 36 0N 14 22 E
Āhū, *Iran* **45 C6** 34 33N 50 2 E
Ahuachapán, *El Salv.* **88 D2** 13 54N 89 52W
Ahvāz, *Iran* **45 D6** 31 20N 48 40 E
Ahvenanmaa = Åland, *Finland* **9 F19** 60 15N 20 0 E
Aḩwar, *Yemen* **47 E4** 13 30N 46 40 E
Ai →, *India* **43 F14** 26 26N 90 44 E
Ai-Ais, *Namibia* **56 D2** 27 54S 17 59 E
Ai-Ais and Fish River Canyon △, *Namibia* **56 C2** 24 45S 17 15 E
Aichi □, *Japan* **31 G8** 35 0N 137 15 E
Aigua, *Uruguay* **95 C5** 34 13S 54 46W
Aigues-Mortes, *France* **20 E6** 43 35N 4 12 E
Aihui, *China* **33 A7** 50 10N 127 30 E
Aija, *Peru* **92 E3** 9 50S 77 45W
Aikawa, *Japan* **30 E9** 38 2N 138 15 E
Aiken, *U.S.A.* **83 J5** 33 34N 81 43W
Aileron, *Australia* **62 C1** 22 39S 133 20 E
Aillik, *Canada* **73 A8** 55 11N 59 18W
Ailsa Craig, *U.K.* **11 F3** 55 15N 5 6W
Aim, *Russia* **29 D14** 59 0N 133 55 E
Aimere, *Indonesia* **37 F6** 8 45S 121 3 E
Aimogasta, *Argentina* **94 B2** 28 33S 66 50W
Aïn Ben Tili, *Mauritania* **50 C4** 25 59N 9 27W
Aïn Sefra, *Algeria* **50 B5** 32 47N 0 37W
Ain Sudr, *Egypt* **46 F2** 29 50N 33 6 E
Ainaži, *Latvia* **9 H21** 57 50N 24 24 E
Ainsworth, *U.S.A.* **80 D5** 42 33N 99 52W
Aiquile, *Bolivia* **92 G5** 18 10S 65 10W
Aïr, *Niger* **50 E7** 18 30N 8 0 E
Air Force I., *Canada* **69 B12** 67 58N 74 5W
Air Hitam, *Malaysia* **39 M4** 1 55N 103 11 E
Airdrie, *Canada* **70 C6** 51 18N 114 2W
Airdrie, *U.K.* **11 F5** 55 52N 3 57W
Aire →, *U.K.* **12 D7** 53 43N 0 55W
Aire, I. de l', *Spain* **24 B11** 39 48N 4 16 E
Airlie Beach, *Australia* **62 J6** 20 16S 148 43 E
Aisne →, *France* **20 B5** 49 26N 2 50 E
Ait, *India* **43 G8** 25 54N 79 14 E
Aitkin, *U.S.A.* **80 B8** 46 32N 93 42W
Aiud, *Romania* **17 E12** 46 19N 23 44 E
Aix-en-Provence, *France* **20 E6** 43 32N 5 27 E
Aix-la-Chapelle = Aachen, *Germany* **16 C4** 50 45N 6 6 E
Aix-les-Bains, *France* **20 D6** 45 41N 5 53 E
Aíyion, *Greece* **23 E10** 38 15N 22 5 E
Aizawl, *India* **41 H18** 23 40N 92 44 E
Aizkraukle, *Latvia* **9 H21** 56 36N 25 11 E
Aizpute, *Latvia* **9 H19** 56 43N 21 40 E
Aizuwakamatsu, *Japan* **30 F9** 37 30N 139 56 E
Ajaccio, *France* **20 F8** 41 55N 8 40 E
Ajai ⌓, *Uganda* **54 B3** 2 52N 31 16 E
Ajaigarh, *India* **43 G9** 24 52N 80 16 E
Ajalpan, *Mexico* **87 D5** 18 22N 97 15W
Ajanta Ra., *India* **40 J9** 20 28N 75 50 E
Ajari Rep. = Ajaria □, *Georgia* **19 F7** 41 30N 42 0 E
Ajaria □, *Georgia* **19 F7** 41 30N 42 0 E
Ajax, *Canada* **84 C5** 43 50N 79 1W
Ajdābiyā, *Libya* **51 B10** 30 54N 20 4 E
Ajka, *Hungary* **17 E9** 47 4N 17 31 E
'Ajlūn, *Jordan* **46 C4** 32 18N 35 47 E
'Ajlūn □, *Jordan* **46 C4** 32 18N 35 47 E
'Ajmān, *U.A.E.* **45 E7** 25 25N 55 30 E
Ajmer, *India* **42 F6** 26 28N 74 37 E
Ajnala, *India* **42 D6** 31 50N 74 48 E
Ajo, *U.S.A.* **77 K7** 32 22N 112 52W
Ajo, C. de, *Spain* **21 A4** 43 31N 3 35W
Akabira, *Japan* **30 C11** 43 33N 142 5 E
Akagera △, *Rwanda* **54 C3** 1 31S 30 33 E
Akamas, *Cyprus* **25 D11** 35 3N 32 18 E
Akan △, *Japan* **30 C12** 43 20N 144 20 E
Akanthou, *Cyprus* **25 D12** 35 22N 33 45 E
Akaroa, *N.Z.* **59 K4** 43 49S 172 59 E
Akashi, *Japan* **31 G7** 34 45N 134 58 E
Akbarpur, *Bihar, India* **43 G10** 24 39N 83 58 E
Akbarpur, *Ut. P., India* **43 F10** 26 25N 82 32 E
Akelamo, *Indonesia* **37 D7** 1 35N 129 40 E
Aketi, *Dem. Rep. of the Congo* **52 D4** 2 38N 23 47 E
Akharnaí, *Greece* **23 E10** 38 5N 23 44 E
Akhelóös →, *Greece* **23 E9** 38 19N 21 7 E
Akhisar, *Turkey* **23 E12** 38 56N 27 48 E
Akhnur, *India* **43 C6** 32 52N 74 45 E
Akhtyrka = Okhtyrka, *Ukraine* **19 D5** 50 25N 35 0 E
Aki, *Japan* **31 H6** 33 30N 133 54 E
Akimiski I., *Canada* **72 B3** 52 50N 81 30W
Akita, *Japan* **30 E10** 39 45N 140 7 E
Akita □, *Japan* **30 E10** 39 40N 140 30 E
Akjoujt, *Mauritania* **50 E3** 19 45N 14 15W
Akkeshi, *Japan* **30 C12** 43 2N 144 51 E
'Akko, *Israel* **46 C4** 32 55N 35 4 E
Aklavik, *Canada* **68 B6** 68 12N 135 0W
Aklera, *India* **42 G7** 24 26N 76 32 E
Akō, *Japan* **31 G7** 34 45N 134 24 E
Akola, *India* **40 J10** 20 42N 77 2 E
Akordat, *Eritrea* **47 D2** 15 30N 37 40 E
Akpatok I., *Canada* **69 B13** 60 25N 68 8W
Åkrahamn, *Norway* **9 G11** 59 15N 5 10 E
Akranes, *Iceland* **8 D2** 64 19N 22 5W
Akron, *Colo., U.S.A.* **80 E3** 40 10N 103 13W
Akron, *Ohio, U.S.A.* **84 E3** 41 5N 81 31W
Akrotiri, *Cyprus* **25 E11** 34 36N 32 57 E
Akrotiri Bay, *Cyprus* **25 E12** 34 35N 33 10 E
Aksai Chin, *China* **43 B8** 35 15N 79 55 E
Aksaray, *Turkey* **19 G5** 38 25N 34 2 E
Aksay, *Kazakhstan* **19 D9** 51 11N 53 0 E
Akşehir, *Turkey* **44 B1** 38 18N 31 30 E
Akşehir Gölü, *Turkey* **19 G5** 38 30N 31 25 E
Aksu, *China* **32 B3** 41 5N 80 10 E
Aksum, *Ethiopia* **47 E2** 14 5N 38 40 E
Aktogay, *Kazakhstan* **28 E8** 46 57N 79 40 E
Aktsyabrski, *Belarus* **17 B15** 52 38N 28 53 E
Aktyubinsk = Aqtöbe, *Kazakhstan* **19 D10** 50 17N 57 10 E
Akure, *Nigeria* **50 G7** 7 15N 5 5 E
Akureyri, *Iceland* **8 D4** 65 40N 18 6W
Akuseki-Shima, *Japan* **31 K4** 29 27N 129 37 E
Akyab = Sittwe, *Burma* **41 J18** 20 18N 92 45 E
Al 'Adan, *Yemen* **47 E4** 12 45N 45 0 E
Al Aḩsā = Hasa □, *Si. Arabia* **45 E6** 25 50N 49 0 E
Al Ajfar, *Si. Arabia* **44 E4** 27 26N 43 0 E
Al Amādīyah, *Iraq* **44 B4** 37 5N 43 30 E
Al 'Amārah, *Iraq* **44 D5** 31 55N 47 15 E
Al 'Aqabah, *Jordan* **46 F4** 29 31N 35 0 E
Al 'Aqabah □, *Jordan* **46 F4** 29 30N 35 0 E
Al Arak, *Syria* **44 C3** 34 38N 38 35 E
Al 'Aramah, *Si. Arabia* **44 E5** 25 30N 46 0 E
Al 'Arţāwīyah, *Si. Arabia* **44 E5** 26 31N 45 20 E
Al 'Āşimah = 'Ammān □, *Jordan* **46 D5** 31 40N 36 30 E
Al 'Assāfīyah, *Si. Arabia* **44 D3** 28 17N 38 59 E
Al 'Ayn, *Si. Arabia* **44 E3** 25 4N 38 6 E
Al 'Ayn, *U.A.E.* **45 E7** 24 15N 55 45 E
Al 'Azīzīyah, *Iraq* **44 C5** 32 54N 45 4 E
Al Bāb, *Syria* **44 B3** 36 23N 37 29 E
Al Bad', *Si. Arabia* **44 D2** 28 28N 35 1 E
Al Bādī, *Iraq* **44 C4** 35 56N 41 32 E
Al Baḩrah, *Kuwait* **44 D5** 29 40N 47 52 E
Al Baḩral Mayyit = Dead Sea, *Asia* **46 D4** 31 30N 35 30 E
Al Balqā' □, *Jordan* **46 C4** 32 5N 35 45 E
Al Bārūk, J., *Lebanon* **46 B4** 33 39N 35 40 E
Al Başrah, *Iraq* **44 D5** 30 30N 47 50 E
Al Baţḩā, *Iraq* **44 D5** 31 6N 45 53 E
Al Batrūn, *Lebanon* **46 A4** 34 15N 35 40 E
Al Bayḑā, *Libya* **51 B10** 32 50N 21 44 E
Al Biqā, *Lebanon* **46 A5** 34 10N 36 10 E
Al Bi'r, *Si. Arabia* **44 D3** 28 51N 36 16 E
Al Burayj, *Syria* **46 A5** 34 15N 36 46 E
Al Faḑilī, *Si. Arabia* **45 E6** 26 58N 49 10 E
Al Fallūjah, *Iraq* **44 C4** 33 20N 43 55 E
Al Fāw, *Iraq* **45 D6** 30 0N 48 30 E
Al Fujayrah, *U.A.E.* **45 E8** 25 7N 56 18 E
Al Ghadaf, W. →, *Jordan* **46 D5** 31 26N 36 43 E
Al Ghammās, *Iraq* **44 D5** 31 45N 44 37 E
Al Ghazālah, *Si. Arabia* **44 E4** 26 48N 41 19 E
Al Ḩadīthah, *Iraq* **44 C4** 34 0N 41 13 E
Al Ḩadīthah, *Si. Arabia* **46 D6** 31 28N 37 8 E
Al Ḩaḑr, *Iraq* **44 C4** 35 35N 42 44 E
Al Hājānah, *Syria* **46 B5** 33 20N 36 33 E

Al Ḥajar al Gharbī, *Oman* 45 E8 24 10N 56 15 E
Al Ḥāmad, *Si. Arabia* 44 D3 31 30N 39 30 E
Al Ḥamdāniyah, *Syria* 44 C3 35 25N 36 50 E
Al Ḥammām, *Iraq* 44 D5 30 57N 46 51 E
Al Ḥamrā', *Si. Arabia* 44 E3 24 2N 38 55 E
Al Ḥamzah, *Iraq* 44 D5 31 43N 44 58 E
Al Ḥanākīyah, *Si. Arabia* 44 E4 24 51N 40 31 E
Al Harīr, W. →, *Syria* 46 C4 32 44N 35 59 E
Al Ḥasā, W. →, *Jordan* 46 D4 31 4N 35 29 E
Al Ḥasakah, *Syria* 44 B4 36 35N 40 45 E
Al Ḥaydān, W. →, *Jordan* 46 D4 31 29N 35 34 E
Al Ḥayy, *Iraq* 44 C5 32 5N 46 5 E
Al Ḥijarah, *Asia* 44 D4 30 0N 44 0 E
Al Ḥillah, *Iraq* 44 C5 32 30N 44 25 E
Al Ḥillah, *Si. Arabia* 47 B4 23 35N 46 50 E
Al Hindīyah, *Iraq* 44 C5 32 30N 44 10 E
Al Hirmil, *Lebanon* 46 A5 34 26N 36 24 E
Al Hoceïma, *Morocco* 50 A5 35 8N 3 58W
Al Ḥudaydah, *Yemen* 47 E3 14 50N 43 0 E
Al Ḥufūf, *Si. Arabia* 45 E6 25 25N 49 45 E
Al Ḥumaydah, *Si. Arabia* 44 D2 29 14N 34 56 E
Al Ḥunayy, *Si. Arabia* 45 E6 25 58N 48 45 E
Al 'Isāwīyah, *Si. Arabia* 44 D3 30 43N 37 59 E
Al Jafr, *Jordan* 46 E5 30 18N 36 14 E
Al Jāfūrah, *Si. Arabia* 45 E7 25 0N 50 15 E
Al Jaghbūb, *Libya* 51 C10 29 42N 24 38 E
Al Jahrah, *Kuwait* 44 D5 29 25N 47 40 E
Al Jalāmīd, *Si. Arabia* 44 D3 31 20N 40 6 E
Al Jamalīyah, *Qatar* 45 E6 25 37N 51 5 E
Al Janūb □, *Lebanon* 46 B4 33 20N 35 20 E
Al Jawf, *Libya* 51 D10 24 10N 23 24 E
Al Jawf, *Si. Arabia* 44 D3 29 55N 39 40 E
Al Jazirah, *Iraq* 44 C5 33 30N 44 0 E
Al Jithāmiyah, *Si. Arabia* 44 E4 27 41N 41 43 E
Al Jubayl, *Si. Arabia* 45 E6 27 0N 49 50 E
Al Jubaylah, *Si. Arabia* 44 E5 24 55N 46 25 E
Al Jubb, *Si. Arabia* 44 E4 27 11N 42 17 E
Al Junaynah, *Sudan* 51 F10 13 27N 22 45 E
Al Kaba'ish, *Iraq* 44 D5 30 58N 47 0 E
Al Karak, *Jordan* 46 D4 31 11N 35 42 E
Al Karak □, *Jordan* 46 E5 31 0N 36 0 E
Al Kāẓimīyah, *Iraq* 44 C5 33 22N 44 18 E
Al Khābūra, *Oman* 45 F8 23 57N 57 5 E
Al Khafji, *Si. Arabia* 45 E6 28 24N 48 29 E
Al Khalīl, *West Bank* 46 D4 31 32N 35 6 E
Al Khāliṣ, *Iraq* 44 C5 33 49N 44 32 E
Al Kharsānīyah, *Si. Arabia* 45 E6 27 13N 49 18 E
Al Khaṣab, *Oman* 45 E8 26 14N 56 15 E
Al Khawr, *Qatar* 45 E6 25 41N 51 30 E
Al Khiḍr, *Iraq* 44 D5 31 12N 45 33 E
Al Khiyām, *Lebanon* 46 B4 33 20N 35 36 E
Al Khums, *Libya* 51 B8 32 40N 14 17 E
Al Kiswah, *Syria* 46 B5 33 23N 36 14 E
Al Kūfah, *Iraq* 44 C5 32 2N 44 24 E
Al Kuhayfīyah, *Si. Arabia* 44 E4 27 12N 43 3 E
Al Kūt, *Iraq* 44 C5 32 30N 46 0 E
Al Kuwayt, *Kuwait* 44 D5 29 30N 48 0 E
Al Labwah, *Lebanon* 46 A5 34 11N 36 20 E
Al Lādhiqīyah, *Syria* 44 C2 35 30N 35 45 E
Al Līth, *Si. Arabia* 47 C3 20 9N 40 15 E
Al Liwā', *Oman* 45 E8 24 31N 56 36 E
Al Luḥayyah, *Yemen* 47 D3 15 45N 42 40 E
Al Madīnah, *Iraq* 44 D5 30 57N 47 16 E
Al Madīnah, *Si. Arabia* 44 E3 24 35N 39 52 E
Al Mafraq, *Jordan* 46 C5 32 17N 36 14 E
Al Mafraq □, *Jordan* 46 C5 32 17N 36 15 E
Al Maḥmūdīyah, *Iraq* 44 C5 33 3N 44 21 E
Al Majma'ah, *Si. Arabia* 44 E5 25 57N 45 22 E
Al Makhruq, W. →, *Jordan* 46 D6 31 28N 37 0 E
Al Makḥūl, *Si. Arabia* 44 E4 26 37N 42 39 E
Al Manāmah, *Bahrain* 45 E6 26 10N 50 30 E
Al Maqwa', *Kuwait* 44 D5 29 10N 47 59 E
Al Marj, *Libya* 51 B10 32 25N 20 30 E
Al Maṭlā, *Kuwait* 44 D5 29 24N 47 40 E
Al Mawjib, W. →, *Jordan* 46 D4 31 28N 35 36 E
Al Mawṣil, *Iraq* 44 B4 36 15N 43 5 E
Al Mayādin, *Syria* 44 C4 35 1N 40 27 E
Al Mazār, *Jordan* 46 D4 31 4N 35 41 E
Al Midhnab, *Si. Arabia* 44 E5 25 50N 44 18 E
Al Minā', *Lebanon* 46 A4 34 24N 35 49 E
Al Miqdādīyah, *Iraq* 44 C5 34 0N 45 0 E
Al Mubarraz, *Si. Arabia* 45 E6 25 30N 49 40 E
Al Mudawwarah, *Jordan* 46 F5 29 19N 36 0 E
Al Mughayrā', *U.A.E.* 45 E7 24 5N 53 32 E
Al Muḥarraq, *Bahrain* 45 E6 26 15N 50 40 E
Al Mukallā, *Yemen* 47 E4 14 33N 49 2 E
Al Mukhā, *Yemen* 47 E3 13 18N 43 15 E
Al Musayjid, *Si. Arabia* 44 E3 24 5N 39 5 E
Al Musayyib, *Iraq* 44 C5 32 49N 44 20 E
Al Muthanná □, *Iraq* 44 D5 30 30N 45 15 E
Al Muwayliḥ, *Si. Arabia* 44 E2 27 40N 35 30 E
Al Qādisiyah □, *Iraq* 44 D5 32 0N 45 0 E
Al Qā'im, *Iraq* 44 C4 34 21N 41 7 E
Al Qalībah, *Si. Arabia* 44 D3 28 24N 37 42 E
Al Qāmishlī, *Syria* 44 B4 37 2N 41 14 E
Al Qaryatayn, *Syria* 46 A6 34 12N 37 13 E
Al Qaṣīm, *Si. Arabia* 44 E4 26 0N 43 0 E
Al Qaṭ'ā, *Syria* 44 C4 34 40N 40 48 E
Al Qaṭīf, *Si. Arabia* 45 E6 26 35N 50 0 E
Al Qaṭrānah, *Jordan* 46 D5 31 12N 36 6 E
Al Qaṭrūn, *Libya* 51 D9 24 56N 15 3 E
Al Qayṣūmah, *Si. Arabia* 44 D5 28 20N 46 7 E
Al Quds = Jerusalem, *Israel* 46 D4 31 47N 35 10 E
Al Qunayṭirah, *Syria* 46 C3 32 55N 35 45 E
Al Qurnah, *Iraq* 44 D5 31 1N 47 25 E
Al Quṣayr, *Iraq* 44 D5 30 39N 45 50 E
Al Quṣayr, *Syria* 46 A5 34 31N 36 34 E
Al Qutayfah, *Syria* 46 B5 33 44N 36 36 E
Al 'Ubaylah, *Si. Arabia* 47 C5 21 59N 50 57 E
Al 'Uḍaylīyah, *Si. Arabia* 45 E6 25 8N 49 18 E
Al 'Ulā, *Si. Arabia* 44 E3 26 35N 38 0 E
Al 'Uqayr, *Si. Arabia* 45 E6 25 40N 50 15 E
Al 'Uwaynid, *Si. Arabia* 44 E5 24 50N 46 0 E
Al 'Uwayqīlah, *Si. Arabia* 44 D4 30 30N 42 10 E
Al 'Uyūn, Ḥijāz, *Si. Arabia* 44 E3 24 33N 39 35 E
Al 'Uyūn, Najd, *Si. Arabia* 44 E4 26 30N 43 50 E
Al 'Uzayr, *Iraq* 44 D5 31 19N 47 25 E
Al Wajh, *Si. Arabia* 44 E3 26 10N 36 30 E
Al Wakrah, *Si. Arabia* 45 E6 25 10N 51 40 E
Al Waqbah, *Si. Arabia* 44 D5 28 48N 45 33 E
Al Wari'āh, *Si. Arabia* 44 E5 27 51N 47 25 E
Ala Dağ, *Turkey* 44 B2 37 44N 35 9 E
Ala Shan Shankou = Dzungarian Gates, *Asia* 32 B3 45 0N 82 0 E
Alabama □, *U.S.A.* 83 J2 33 0N 87 0W
Alabama →, *U.S.A.* 83 K2 31 8N 87 57W

Alabaster, *U.S.A.* 83 J2 33 15N 86 49W
Alaçam Dağları, *Turkey* 23 E13 39 18N 28 49 E
Alacant = Alicante, *Spain* 21 C5 38 23N 0 30W
Alachua, *U.S.A.* 83 L4 29 47N 82 30W
Alaérma, *Greece* 25 C9 36 9N 27 57 E
Alagoa Grande, *Brazil* 93 E11 7 3S 35 35W
Alagoas □, *Brazil* 93 E11 9 0S 36 0W
Alagoinhas, *Brazil* 93 F11 12 7S 38 20W
Alaior, *Spain* 24 B11 39 57N 4 8 E
Alajero, *Canary Is.* 24 F2 28 3N 17 13W
Alajuela, *Costa Rica* 88 D3 10 2N 84 8W
Alakamisy, *Madag.* 57 C8 21 19S 47 14 E
Alaknanda →, *India* 43 D8 30 8N 78 36 E
Alakurtti, *Russia* 18 A5 67 0N 30 30 E
Alamarvdasht, *Iran* 45 E7 27 37N 52 59 E
Alameda, Calif., *U.S.A.* 78 H4 37 46N 122 15W
Alameda, N. Mex., *U.S.A.* 77 J10 35 11N 106 37W
Alamo, *U.S.A.* 79 J11 37 22N 115 10W
Alamo Crossing, *U.S.A.* 79 L13 34 16N 113 33W
Alamogordo, *U.S.A.* 77 K11 32 54N 105 57W
Alamos, *Mexico* 86 B3 27 0N 109 0W
Alamosa, *U.S.A.* 77 H11 37 28N 105 52W
Åland, *Finland* 9 F19 60 15N 20 0 E
Ålands hav, *Sweden* 9 F18 60 0N 19 30 E
Alania = North Ossetia □, *Russia* 19 F7 43 30N 44 30 E
Alanya, *Turkey* 19 G5 36 38N 32 0 E
Alaotra, Farihin', *Madag.* 57 B8 17 30S 48 30 E
Alapayevsk, *Russia* 28 D7 57 52N 61 42 E
Alappuzha = Alleppey, *India* 40 Q10 9 30N 76 28 E
Alarobia-Vohiposa, *Madag.* 57 C8 20 59S 47 9 E
Alaşehir, *Turkey* 23 E13 38 23N 28 30 E
Alaska □, *U.S.A.* 68 B5 64 0N 154 0W
Alaska, G. of, *Pac. Oc.* 68 C5 58 0N 145 0W
Alaska Peninsula, *U.S.A.* 68 C4 56 0N 159 0W
Alaska Range, *U.S.A.* 68 B4 62 50N 151 0W
Älät, *Azerbaijan* 19 G8 39 58N 49 25 E
Alatyr, *Russia* 18 D8 54 55N 46 35 E
Alausi, *Ecuador* 92 D3 2 0S 78 50W
Alava, C., *U.S.A.* 76 B1 48 10N 124 44W
Alavus, *Finland* 9 E20 62 35N 23 36 E
Alawoona, *Australia* 63 E3 34 45S 140 30 E
'Alayh, *Lebanon* 46 B4 33 46N 35 33 E
Alba, *Italy* 20 D8 44 42N 8 2 E
Alba-Iulia, *Romania* 17 E12 46 8N 23 39 E
Albacete, *Spain* 21 C5 39 0N 1 50W
Albacutya, L., *Australia* 63 F3 35 45S 141 58 E
Albanel, L., *Canada* 72 B5 50 55N 73 12W
Albania ■, *Europe* 23 D9 41 0N 20 0 E
Albany, *Australia* 61 G2 35 1S 117 58 E
Albany, Ga., *U.S.A.* 83 K3 31 35N 84 10W
Albany, N.Y., *U.S.A.* 85 D11 42 39N 73 45W
Albany, Oreg., *U.S.A.* 76 D2 44 38N 123 6W
Albany, Tex., *U.S.A.* 81 J5 32 44N 99 18W
Albany →, *Canada* 72 B3 52 17N 81 31W
Albardón, *Argentina* 94 C2 31 20S 68 30W
Albatross B., *Australia* 62 A3 12 45S 141 30 E
Albemarle, *U.S.A.* 83 H5 35 21N 80 11W
Albemarle Sd., *U.S.A.* 83 H7 36 5N 76 0W
Alberche →, *Spain* 21 C3 39 58N 4 46W
Alberdi, *Paraguay* 94 B4 26 14S 58 20W
Albert, L., *Africa* 54 B3 1 30N 31 0 E
Albert, L., *Australia* 63 F2 35 30S 139 10 E
Albert Edward Ra., *Australia* 60 C4 18 17S 127 57 E
Albert Lea, *U.S.A.* 80 D8 43 39N 93 22W
Albert Nile →, *Uganda* 54 B3 3 36N 32 2 E
Albert Town, *Bahamas* 89 B5 22 37N 74 33W
Alberta □, *Canada* 70 C6 54 40N 115 0W
Alberti, *Argentina* 94 D3 35 1S 60 16W
Albertinia, *S. Africa* 56 E3 34 11S 21 34 E
Alberton, *Canada* 73 C7 46 50N 64 0W
Albertville, *France* 20 D7 45 40N 6 22 E
Albertville, *U.S.A.* 83 H2 34 16N 86 13W
Albi, *France* 20 E5 43 56N 2 9 E
Albia, *U.S.A.* 80 E8 41 2N 92 48W
Albina, *Suriname* 93 B8 5 37N 54 15W
Albina, Ponta, *Angola* 56 B1 15 52S 11 44 E
Albion, Mich., *U.S.A.* 82 D3 42 15N 84 45W
Albion, Nebr., *U.S.A.* 80 E6 41 42N 98 0W
Albion, Pa., *U.S.A.* 84 E4 41 53N 80 22W
Alborán, *Medit. S.* 21 E4 35 57N 3 0W
Ålborg, *Denmark* 9 H13 57 2N 9 54 E
Alborz, Reshteh-ye Kūhhā-ye, *Iran* 45 C7 36 0N 52 0 E
Albuquerque, *U.S.A.* 77 J10 35 5N 106 39W
Albuquerque, Cayos de, *Caribbean* 88 D3 12 10N 81 50W
Alburg, *U.S.A.* 85 B11 44 59N 73 18W
Albury = Albury-Wodonga, *Australia* 63 F4 36 3S 146 56 E
Albury-Wodonga, *Australia* 63 F4 36 3S 146 56 E
Alcalá de Henares, *Spain* 21 B4 40 28N 3 22W
Alcalá la Real, *Spain* 21 D4 37 27N 3 57W
Álcamo, *Italy* 22 F5 37 59N 12 55 E
Alcaniz, *Spain* 21 B5 41 2N 0 8W
Alcântara, *Brazil* 93 D10 2 20S 44 30W
Alcántara, Embalse de, *Spain* 21 C2 39 44N 6 50W
Alcantarilla, *Spain* 21 D5 37 59N 1 12W
Alcaraz, Sierra de, *Spain* 21 C4 38 40N 2 20W
Alcaudete, *Spain* 21 D3 37 35N 4 5W
Alcázar de San Juan, *Spain* 21 C4 39 24N 3 12W
Alchevsk, *Ukraine* 19 E6 48 30N 38 45 E
Alcira = Alzira, *Spain* 21 C5 39 9N 0 30W
Alcova, *U.S.A.* 76 E10 42 34N 106 43W
Alcoy, *Spain* 21 C5 38 43N 0 30W
Alcúdia, *Spain* 24 B10 39 51N 3 7 E
Alcúdia, B. d', *Spain* 24 B10 39 47N 3 15 E
Aldabra Is., *Seychelles* 49 G8 9 22S 46 28 E
Aldama, *Mexico* 87 C5 23 0N 98 4W
Aldan, *Russia* 29 D13 58 40N 125 30 E
Aldan →, *Russia* 29 C13 63 28N 129 35 E
Aldea, Pta. de la, *Canary Is.* 24 G4 28 0N 15 50W
Aldeburgh, *U.K.* 13 E9 52 10N 1 37 E
Alder Pk., *U.S.A.* 78 K5 35 53N 121 22W
Alderney, *U.K.* 13 H5 49 42N 2 11W
Aldershot, *U.K.* 13 F7 51 15N 0 44W
Aledo, *U.S.A.* 80 E9 41 12N 90 45W
Aleg, *Mauritania* 50 E3 17 3N 13 55W
Alegranza, *Canary Is.* 24 E6 29 23N 13 32W
Alegranza, I., *Canary Is.* 24 E6 29 23N 13 32W
Alegre, *Brazil* 95 A7 20 50S 41 30W
Alegrete, *Brazil* 95 B4 29 40S 56 0W
Aleisk, *Russia* 28 D9 52 40N 83 0 E
Aleksandriya = Oleksandriya, *Ukraine* 17 C14 50 37N 26 19 E
Aleksandrov Gay, *Russia* 19 D8 50 9N 48 34 E
Aleksandrovsk-Sakhalinskiy, *Russia* 29 D15 50 50N 142 20 E
Aleksandry, Z., *Russia* 4 A10 80 25N 48 0 E

Além Paraíba, *Brazil* 95 A7 21 52S 42 41W
Alemania, *Argentina* 94 B2 25 40S 65 30W
Alemania, *Chile* 94 B2 25 10S 69 55W
Alençon, *France* 20 B4 48 27N 0 4 E
Alenquer, *Brazil* 93 D8 1 56S 54 46W
Alenuihaha Channel, *U.S.A.* 74 H17 20 30N 156 0W
Aleppo = Ḥalab, *Syria* 44 B3 36 10N 37 15 E
Alert, *Canada* 4 A4 83 2N 60 0W
Alessándria, *Italy* 20 D8 44 54N 8 37 E
Ålesund, *Norway* 9 E12 62 28N 6 12 E
Aleutian Is., *Pac. Oc.* 68 C2 52 0N 175 0W
Aleutian Trench, *Pac. Oc.* 64 C10 48 0N 180 0 E
Alexander, *U.S.A.* 80 B3 47 51N 103 39W
Alexander, Mt., *Australia* 61 E3 28 58S 120 16 E
Alexander Arch., *U.S.A.* 68 C6 56 0N 136 0W
Alexander Bay, *S. Africa* 56 D2 28 40S 16 30 E
Alexander City, *U.S.A.* 83 J3 32 56N 85 58W
Alexander I., *Antarctica* 5 C17 69 0S 70 0W
Alexandra, *Australia* 63 F4 37 8S 145 40 E
Alexandra, *N.Z.* 59 L2 45 14S 169 25 E
Alexandra Falls, *Canada* 70 A5 60 29N 116 18W
Alexandria = El Iskandarîya, *Egypt* 51 B11 31 13N 29 58 E
Alexandria, B.C., *Canada* 70 C4 52 35N 122 27W
Alexandria, Ont., *Canada* 85 A10 45 19N 74 38W
Alexandria, *Romania* 17 G13 43 57N 25 24 E
Alexandria, *S. Africa* 56 E4 33 38S 26 28 E
Alexandria, *U.K.* 11 F4 55 59N 4 35W
Alexandria, La., *U.S.A.* 81 K8 31 18N 92 27W
Alexandria, Minn., *U.S.A.* 80 C7 45 53N 95 22W
Alexandria, S. Dak., *U.S.A.* 80 D6 43 39N 97 47W
Alexandria, Va., *U.S.A.* 82 F7 38 48N 77 3W
Alexandria Bay, *U.S.A.* 85 B9 44 20N 75 55W
Alexandrina, L., *Australia* 63 F2 35 25S 139 10 E
Alexandroúpolis, *Greece* 23 D11 40 50N 25 54 E
Alexis →, *Canada* 73 B8 52 33N 56 8W
Alexis Creek, *Canada* 70 C4 52 10N 123 20W
Alfabia, *Spain* 24 B9 39 44N 2 44 E
Alfenas, *Brazil* 95 A6 21 20S 46 10W
Alford, Aberds., *U.K.* 11 D6 57 14N 2 41W
Alford, Lincs., *U.K.* 12 D8 53 15N 0 10 E
Alfred, Maine, *U.S.A.* 85 C14 43 29N 70 43W
Alfred, N.Y., *U.S.A.* 84 D7 42 16N 77 48W
Alfreton, *U.K.* 12 D6 53 6N 1 24W
Alga, *Kazakhstan* 19 E10 49 53N 57 20 E
Algaida, *Spain* 24 B9 39 33N 2 53 E
Ålgård, *Norway* 9 G11 58 46N 5 53 E
Algarve, *Portugal* 21 D1 36 58N 8 20W
Algeciras, *Spain* 21 D3 36 9N 5 28W
Algemesi, *Spain* 21 C5 39 11N 0 27W
Alger, *Algeria* 50 A6 36 42N 3 8 E
Algeria ■, *Africa* 50 C6 28 30N 2 0 E
Alghero, *Italy* 22 D3 40 33N 8 19 E
Algiers = Alger, *Algeria* 50 A6 36 42N 3 8 E
Algoa B., *S. Africa* 56 E4 33 50S 25 45 E
Algoma, *U.S.A.* 82 C2 44 36N 87 26W
Algona, *U.S.A.* 80 D7 43 4N 94 14W
Algonac, *U.S.A.* 84 D2 42 37N 82 32W
Algonquin □, *Canada* 72 C4 45 50N 78 30W
Algorta, *Uruguay* 96 C5 32 25S 57 23W
Alhambra, *U.S.A.* 79 L8 34 8N 118 6W
Alhucemas = Al Hoceïma, *Morocco* 50 A5 35 8N 3 58W
'Alī al Gharbī, *Iraq* 44 C5 32 30N 46 45 E
'Alī ash Sharqī, *Iraq* 44 C5 32 7N 46 44 E
'Alī Khēl, *Afghan.* 42 C3 33 57N 69 43 E
Alī Shāh, *Iran* 44 B5 38 9N 45 50 E
'Alīābād, Khorāsān, *Iran* 45 C8 32 30N 57 30 E
'Alīābād, Kordestān, *Iran* 44 C5 35 4N 46 58 E
'Alīābād, Yazd, *Iran* 45 D7 31 41N 53 49 E
Aliağa, *Turkey* 23 E12 38 47N 26 59 E
Aliákmon →, *Greece* 23 D10 40 30N 22 36 E
Alicante, *Spain* 21 C5 38 23N 0 30W
Alice, *S. Africa* 56 E4 32 48S 26 55 E
Alice, *U.S.A.* 81 M5 27 45N 98 5W
Alice →, Queens., *Australia* 62 C3 24 2S 144 50 E
Alice →, Queens., *Australia* 62 B3 15 35S 142 20 E
Alice Arm, *Canada* 70 B3 55 29N 129 31W
Alice Springs, *Australia* 62 C1 23 40S 133 50 E
Alicedale, *S. Africa* 56 E4 33 15S 26 4 E
Aliceville, *U.S.A.* 83 J1 33 8N 88 9W
Aliganj, *India* 43 F8 27 30N 79 10 E
Aligarh, Raj., *India* 42 G7 25 55N 76 15 E
Aligarh, Ut. P., *India* 42 F8 27 55N 78 10 E
Alīgūdarz, *Iran* 45 C6 33 25N 49 45 E
Alimnia, *Greece* 25 C9 36 16N 27 43 E
Alingsås, *Sweden* 9 H15 57 56N 12 31 E
Alipur, *Pakistan* 42 E4 29 25N 70 55 E
Alipur Duar, *India* 41 F16 26 30N 89 35 E
Aliquippa, *U.S.A.* 84 F4 40 37N 80 15W
Alitus = Alytus, *Lithuania* 9 J21 54 24N 24 3 E
Aliwal North, *S. Africa* 56 E4 30 45S 26 45 E
Alix, *Canada* 70 C6 52 24N 113 11W
Aljustrel, *Portugal* 21 D1 37 55N 8 10W
Alkmaar, *Neths.* 15 B4 52 37N 4 45 E
All American Canal, *U.S.A.* 77 K6 32 45N 115 15W
Allagash →, *U.S.A.* 83 B11 47 5N 69 3W
Allah Dad, *Pakistan* 42 G2 25 38N 67 34 E
Allahabad, *India* 43 G9 25 25N 81 58 E
Allan, *Canada* 71 C7 51 53N 106 4W
Allanridge, *S. Africa* 56 D4 27 45S 26 40 E
Allegany, *U.S.A.* 84 D6 42 6N 78 30W
Allegheny →, *U.S.A.* 84 F5 40 27N 80 1W
Allegheny Mts., *U.S.A.* 82 G6 38 15N 80 10W
Allegheny Reservoir, *U.S.A.* 84 E6 41 50N 79 0W
Allègre, Pte., *Guadeloupe* 88 b 16 22N 61 46W
Allen, Bog of, *Ireland* 10 C5 53 15N 7 0W
Allen, L., *Ireland* 10 B3 54 8N 8 4W
Allendale, *U.S.A.* 83 J5 33 1N 81 18W
Allende, *Mexico* 86 B4 28 20N 100 50W
Allentown, *U.S.A.* 85 F9 40 37N 75 29W
Alleppey, *India* 40 Q10 9 30N 76 28 E
Aller →, *Germany* 16 B5 52 56N 9 12 E
Alleynes B., *Barbados* 89 g 13 13N 59 39W
Alliance, Nebr., *U.S.A.* 80 D3 42 6N 102 52W
Alliance, Ohio, *U.S.A.* 84 F3 40 55N 81 6W
Allier →, *France* 20 C5 46 57N 3 4 E
Alliford Bay, *Canada* 70 C2 53 12N 131 58W
Alligator Pond, *Jamaica* 88 a 17 52N 77 34W
Alliston = New Tecumseth, *Canada* 84 B5 44 9N 79 52W
Alloa, *U.K.* 11 E5 56 7N 3 47W
Allora, *Australia* 63 D5 28 2S 152 0 E
Alluitsup Paa, *Greenland* 4 C5 60 30N 45 35W
Alma, *Canada* 73 C5 48 35N 71 40W
Alma, Ga., *U.S.A.* 83 K4 31 33N 82 28W
Alma, Kans., *U.S.A.* 80 F6 39 1N 96 17W

Alma, Mich., *U.S.A.* 82 D3 43 23N 84 39W
Alma, Nebr., *U.S.A.* 80 E5 40 6N 99 22W
Alma Ata = Almaty, *Kazakhstan* 28 E8 43 15N 76 57 E
Almada, *Portugal* 21 C1 38 40N 9 9W
Almaden, *Australia* 62 B3 17 22S 144 40 E
Almadén, *Spain* 21 C3 38 49N 4 52W
Almanor, L., *U.S.A.* 76 F3 40 14N 121 9W
Almansa, *Spain* 21 C5 38 51N 1 5W
Almanzor, Pico, *Spain* 21 B3 40 15N 5 18W
Almanzora →, *Spain* 21 D5 37 14N 1 46W
Almaty, *Kazakhstan* 28 E8 43 15N 76 57 E
Almazán, *Spain* 21 B4 41 30N 2 30W
Almeirim, *Brazil* 93 D8 1 30S 52 34W
Almelo, *Neths.* 15 B6 52 22N 6 42 E
Almendralejo, *Spain* 21 C2 38 41N 6 26W
Almere-Stad, *Neths.* 15 B5 52 20N 5 15 E
Almería, *Spain* 21 D4 36 52N 2 27W
Almirante, *Panama* 88 E3 9 10N 82 30W
Almiroú, Kólpos, *Greece* 25 D6 35 23N 24 20 E
Almond, *U.S.A.* 84 D7 42 19N 77 44W
Almont, *U.S.A.* 84 D1 43 3N 83 3W
Almonte, *Canada* 85 A8 45 14N 76 12W
Almora, *India* 43 E8 29 38N 79 40 E
Alness, *U.K.* 11 D4 57 41N 4 16W
Alnmouth, *U.K.* 12 B6 55 24N 1 37W
Alnwick, *U.K.* 12 B6 55 24N 1 42W
Aloi, *Uganda* 54 B3 2 16N 33 10 E
Alon, *Burma* 41 H19 22 12N 95 5 E
Alor, *Indonesia* 37 F6 8 15S 124 30 E
Alor Setar, *Malaysia* 39 J3 6 7N 100 22 E
Alot, *India* 42 H6 23 56N 75 40 E
Aloysius, Mt., *Australia* 61 E4 26 0S 128 38 E
Alpaugh, *U.S.A.* 78 K7 35 53N 119 29W
Alpena, *U.S.A.* 82 C4 45 4N 83 27W
Alpha, *Australia* 62 C4 23 39S 146 37 E
Alpha Cordillera, *Arctic* 4 B17 84 0N 118 0W
Alphen aan den Rijn, *Neths.* 15 B4 52 7N 4 40 E
Alpine, Ariz., *U.S.A.* 77 K9 33 51N 109 9W
Alpine, Calif., *U.S.A.* 79 N10 32 50N 116 46W
Alpine, Tex., *U.S.A.* 81 K3 30 22N 103 40W
Alps, *Europe* 20 C8 46 30N 9 30 E
Alsace □, *France* 20 B7 48 15N 7 25 E
Alsask, *Canada* 71 C7 51 21N 109 59W
Alsasua, *Spain* 21 A4 42 54N 2 10W
Alsek →, *U.S.A.* 70 B1 59 10N 138 12W
Alsten, *Norway* 8 D15 65 58N 12 40 E
Alston, *U.K.* 12 C5 54 49N 2 25W
Alta, *Norway* 8 B20 69 57N 23 10 E
Alta Gracia, *Argentina* 94 C3 31 40S 64 30W
Alta Sierra, *U.S.A.* 79 K8 35 42N 118 33W
Altaelva →, *Norway* 8 B20 69 54N 23 17 E
Altafjorden, *Norway* 8 A20 70 5N 23 5 E
Altai = Aerhtai Shan, *Mongolia* 32 B4 46 40N 92 45 E
Altamaha →, *U.S.A.* 83 K5 31 20N 81 20W
Altamira, *Brazil* 93 D8 3 12S 52 10W
Altamira, *Chile* 94 B2 25 47S 69 51W
Altamira, *Mexico* 87 C5 22 24N 97 55W
Altamont, *U.S.A.* 85 D10 42 43N 74 3W
Altamura, *Italy* 22 D7 40 49N 16 33 E
Altanbulag, *Mongolia* 32 A5 50 16N 106 30 E
Altar, *Mexico* 86 A2 30 40N 111 50W
Altar, Desierto de, *Mexico* 86 B2 30 10N 112 0W
Altata, *Mexico* 86 C3 24 30N 108 0W
Altavista, *U.S.A.* 82 G6 37 6N 79 17W
Altay, *China* 32 B3 47 48N 88 10 E
Altea, *Spain* 21 C5 38 38N 0 2W
Altiplano, *Bolivia* 90 E4 17 0S 68 0W
Alto Araguaia, *Brazil* 93 G8 17 15S 53 20W
Alto Cuchumatanes = Cuchumatanes, Sierra de los, *Guatemala* 88 C1 15 35N 91 25W
Alto del Carmen, *Chile* 94 B1 28 46S 70 30W
Alto del Inca, *Chile* 94 A2 24 10S 68 10W
Alto Ligonha, *Mozam.* 55 F4 15 30S 38 11 E
Alto Molocue, *Mozam.* 55 F4 15 50S 37 35 E
Alto Paraguay □, *Paraguay* 94 A4 21 0S 58 30W
Alto Paraná □, *Paraguay* 95 B5 25 30S 54 50W
Alton, *Canada* 84 C4 43 54N 80 5W
Alton, *U.K.* 13 F7 51 9N 0 59W
Alton, Ill., *U.S.A.* 80 F9 38 53N 90 11W
Alton, N.H., *U.S.A.* 85 C13 43 27N 71 13W
Altona, *Canada* 71 D9 49 6N 97 33W
Altoona, *U.S.A.* 84 F6 40 31N 78 24W
Altun Kupri, *Iraq* 44 C5 35 45N 44 9 E
Altun Shan, *China* 32 C3 38 30N 88 0 E
Alturas, *U.S.A.* 76 F3 41 29N 120 32W
Altus, *U.S.A.* 81 H5 34 38N 99 20W
Alucra, *Turkey* 19 F6 40 22N 38 47 E
Alūksne, *Latvia* 9 H22 57 24N 27 3 E
Alunite, *U.S.A.* 79 K12 35 59N 114 55W
Alusi, *Indonesia* 37 F8 7 35S 131 40 E
Alva, *U.S.A.* 81 G5 36 48N 98 40W
Alvarado, *Mexico* 87 D5 18 40N 95 50W
Alvarado, *U.S.A.* 81 J6 32 24N 97 13W
Alvaro Obregón, Presa, *Mexico* 86 B3 27 55N 109 52W
Alvear, *Argentina* 94 B4 29 5S 56 30W
Alvesta, *Sweden* 9 H16 56 54N 14 35 E
Alvin, *U.S.A.* 81 L7 29 26N 95 15W
Alvinston, *Canada* 84 D3 42 49N 81 52W
Älvkarleby, *Sweden* 9 F17 60 34N 17 26 E
Alvord Desert, *U.S.A.* 76 E4 42 30N 118 25W
Älvsbyn, *Sweden* 8 D19 65 40N 21 0 E
Alwar, *India* 42 F7 27 38N 76 34 E
Alxa Zuoqi, *China* 34 E3 38 50N 105 40 E
Alyangula, *Australia* 62 A2 13 55S 136 30 E
Alyata = Älät, *Azerbaijan* 19 G8 39 58N 49 25 E
Alyth, *U.K.* 11 E5 56 38N 3 13W
Alytus, *Lithuania* 9 J21 54 24N 24 3 E
Alzada, *U.S.A.* 80 C2 45 2N 104 25W
Alzira, *Spain* 21 C5 39 9N 0 30W
Am Timan, *Chad* 51 F10 11 0N 20 10 E
Amadeus, L., *Australia* 61 D5 24 54S 131 0 E
Amâdi, *Sudan* 51 G12 5 29N 30 25 E
Amadi, *Dem. Rep. of the Congo* 54 B2 3 40N 26 40 E
Amadjuak L., *Canada* 69 B12 65 0N 71 8W
Amagansett, *U.S.A.* 85 F12 40 59N 72 9W
Amagasaki, *Japan* 31 G7 34 42N 135 20 E
Amahai, *Indonesia* 37 E7 3 20S 128 55 E
Amakusa-Shotō, *Japan* 31 H5 32 15N 130 10 E
Åmål, *Sweden* 9 G15 59 3N 12 42 E
Amaliás, *Greece* 23 F9 37 47N 21 22 E
Amalner, *India* 40 J9 21 5S 75 5 E
Amamapare, *Indonesia* 37 E9 4 53S 136 38 E
Amambaí, *Brazil* 95 A4 23 5S 55 13W
Amambaí →, *Brazil* 95 A5 23 22S 53 56W
Amambay □, *Paraguay* 95 A4 23 0S 56 0W
Amambay, Cordillera de, *S. Amer.* 95 A4 23 0S 55 45W

Amami-Guntō, Japan 31 L4 27 16N 129 21 E
Amami-Ō-Shima, Japan 31 L4 28 0N 129 0 E
Aman, Pulau, Malaysia 39 c 5 16N 100 24 E
Amaná, L., Brazil 92 D6 2 35S 64 40W
Amanat →, India 43 G11 24 7N 84 4 E
Amanda Park, U.S.A. 78 C3 47 28N 123 55W
Amangeldy, Kazakhstan 28 D7 50 10N 65 10 E
Amapá, Brazil 93 C8 2 5N 50 50W
Amapá □, Brazil 93 C8 1 40N 52 0W
Amarante, Brazil 93 E10 6 14S 42 50W
Amaranth, Canada 71 C9 50 36N 98 43W
Amargosa →, U.S.A. 79 J10 36 14N 116 51W
Amargosa Range, U.S.A. 79 J10 36 20N 116 45W
Amári, Greece 25 D6 35 13N 24 40 E
Amarillo, U.S.A. 81 H4 35 13N 101 50W
Amarkantak, India 43 H9 22 40N 81 45 E
Amaro, Mte., Italy 22 C6 42 5N 14 5 E
Amarpur, India 43 G12 25 5N 87 0 E
Amarwara, India 43 H8 22 18N 79 10 E
Amasya, Turkey 19 F6 40 40N 35 50 E
Amata, Australia 61 E5 26 9S 131 9 E
Amatikulu, S. Africa 57 D5 29 3S 31 33 E
Amatitlán, Guatemala 88 D1 14 29N 90 38W
Amay, Belgium 15 D5 50 33N 5 19 E
Amazon = Amazonas →, S. Amer. 93 D9 0 5S 50 0W
Amazonas □, Brazil 92 E6 5 0S 65 0W
Amazonas →, S. Amer. 93 D9 0 5S 50 0W
Ambah, India 42 F8 26 43N 78 13 E
Ambahakily, Madag. 57 C7 21 36S 43 41 E
Ambahita, Madag. 57 C8 24 1S 45 16 E
Ambala, India 42 D7 30 23N 76 56 E
Ambalavao, Madag. 57 C8 21 50S 46 56 E
Ambanja, Madag. 57 A8 13 40S 48 27 E
Ambararata, Madag. 57 B8 15 3S 48 33 E
Ambarchik, Russia 29 C17 69 40N 162 20 E
Ambarijeby, Madag. 57 A8 14 56S 47 41 E
Ambaro, Helodranon', Madag. 57 A8 13 23S 48 38 E
Ambato, Ecuador 92 D3 1 5S 78 42W
Ambato, Madag. 57 A8 13 24S 48 29 E
Ambato, Sierra de, Argentina 94 B2 28 25S 66 10W
Ambato Boeny, Madag. 57 B8 16 28S 46 43 E
Ambatofinandrahana, Madag. 57 C8 20 33S 46 48 E
Ambatolampy, Madag. 57 B8 19 20S 47 35 E
Ambatomainty, Madag. 57 B8 17 41S 45 40 E
Ambatomanoina, Madag. 57 B8 18 18S 47 37 E
Ambatondrazaka, Madag. 57 B8 17 55S 48 28 E
Ambatosoratra, Madag. 57 B8 17 37S 48 31 E
Ambenja, Madag. 57 B8 15 17S 46 58 E
Amberg, Germany 16 D6 49 26N 11 52 E
Ambergris Cay, Belize 87 D7 18 0N 88 0W
Amberley, N.Z. 59 K4 43 9S 172 44 E
Ambikapur, India 43 H10 23 15N 83 15 E
Ambilobé, Madag. 57 A8 13 10S 49 3 E
Ambinanindrano, Madag. 57 C8 20 5S 48 23 E
Ambinanitelo, Madag. 57 B8 15 21S 49 35 E
Ambinda, Madag. 57 B8 16 25S 45 52 E
Amble, U.K. 12 B6 55 20N 1 36W
Ambleside, U.K. 12 C5 54 26N 2 58W
Ambo, Peru 92 F3 10 5S 76 10W
Amboahangy, Madag. 57 C8 24 15S 46 22 E
Ambodifototra, Madag. 57 B8 16 59S 49 52 E
Ambodilazana, Madag. 57 B8 18 6S 49 10 E
Ambodiriana, Madag. 57 B8 17 55S 49 18 E
Ambohidratrimo, Madag. 57 B8 18 50S 47 26 E
Ambohidray, Madag. 57 B8 18 36S 48 18 E
Ambohimahamasina, Madag. 57 C8 21 56S 47 11 E
Ambohimahasoa, Madag. 57 C8 21 7S 47 13 E
Ambohimanga, Madag. 57 C8 20 52S 47 36 E
Ambohimitombo, Madag. 57 C8 20 43S 47 26 E
Ambohitra, Madag. 57 A8 12 30S 49 10 E
Amboise, France 20 C4 47 24N 1 2 E
Ambon, Indonesia 37 E7 3 43S 128 12 E
Ambondro, Madag. 57 D8 25 13S 45 44 E
Amboseli △, Kenya 54 C4 2 37S 37 13 E
Amboseli, L., Kenya 54 C4 2 40S 37 10 E
Ambositra, Madag. 57 C8 20 31S 47 25 E
Ambovombe, Madag. 57 D8 25 11S 46 5 E
Amboy, U.S.A. 79 L11 34 33N 115 45W
Amboyna Cay, S. China Sea 36 C4 7 50N 112 50 E
Ambridge, U.S.A. 84 F4 40 36N 80 14W
Ambriz, Angola 52 F2 7 48S 13 8 E
Amchitka I., U.S.A. 68 C1 51 32N 179 0 E
Amderma, Russia 28 C7 69 45N 61 30 E
Amdhi, India 43 H9 23 51N 81 27 E
Ameca, Mexico 86 C4 20 30N 104 0W
Ameca →, Mexico 86 C3 20 40N 105 15W
Amecameca, Mexico 87 D5 19 7N 98 46W
Ameland, Neths. 15 A5 53 27N 5 45 E
Amenia, U.S.A. 85 E11 41 51N 73 33W
American Falls, U.S.A. 76 E7 42 47N 112 51W
American Falls Reservoir, U.S.A. 76 E7 42 47N 112 52W
American Fork, U.S.A. 76 F8 40 23N 111 48W
American Highland, Antarctica 5 D6 73 0S 75 0 E
American Samoa ☒, Pac. Oc. 59 B13 14 20S 170 40W
Americana, Brazil 95 A6 22 45S 47 20W
Americus, U.S.A. 83 K3 32 4N 84 14W
Amersfoort, Neths. 15 B5 52 9N 5 23 E
Amersfoort, S. Africa 57 D4 26 59S 29 53 E
Amery Ice Shelf, Antarctica 5 C6 69 30S 72 0 E
Ames, U.S.A. 80 E8 42 2N 93 37W
Amesbury, U.S.A. 85 D14 42 51N 70 56W
Amet, India 42 G5 25 18N 73 56 E
Amga, Russia 29 C14 60 50N 132 0 E
Amga →, Russia 29 C14 62 38N 134 32 E
Amgu, Russia 29 E14 45 45N 137 15 E
Amgun →, Russia 29 D14 52 56N 139 38 E
Amherst, Canada 73 C7 45 48N 64 8W
Amherst, Mass., U.S.A. 85 D12 42 23N 72 31W
Amherst, N.Y., U.S.A. 84 D6 42 59N 78 48W
Amherst, Ohio, U.S.A. 84 E2 41 24N 82 14W
Amherst I., Canada 85 B8 44 8N 76 43W
Amherstburg, Canada 72 D3 42 6N 83 6W
Amiata, Mte., Italy 22 C4 42 53N 11 37 E
Amidon, U.S.A. 80 B3 46 29N 103 19W
Amiens, France 20 B5 49 54N 2 16 E
Aminuis, Namibia 56 C2 23 43S 19 21 E
Amīrābād, Iran 44 C5 33 20N 46 16 E
Amirante Is., Seychelles 26 K9 6 0S 53 0 E
Amisk ⌓, Canada 71 B9 56 43N 98 0W
Amisk L., Canada 71 C8 54 35N 102 15W
Amistad ⌓, U.S.A. 81 L4 29 32N 101 12W
Amistad, Presa de la, Mexico 86 B4 29 24N 101 0W
Amite, U.S.A. 81 K9 30 44N 90 30W
Amla, India 42 J8 21 56N 78 7 E
Amlapura = Karangasem, Indonesia 37 J18 8 27S 115 37 E
Amlia I., U.S.A. 68 C2 52 4N 173 30W
Amlwch, U.K. 12 D3 53 24N 4 20W
'Ammān, Jordan 46 D4 31 57N 35 52 E
'Ammān □, Jordan 46 D5 31 40N 36 30 E
'Ammān ✕ (AMM), Jordan 46 D5 31 45N 36 2 E
Ammanford, U.K. 13 F4 51 48N 3 59W
Ammassalik = Tasiilaq, Greenland 4 C6 65 40N 37 20W
Ammochostos = Famagusta, Cyprus 25 D12 35 8N 33 55 E
Ammon, U.S.A. 76 E8 43 28N 111 58W
Amnat Charoen, Thailand 38 E5 15 51N 104 38 E
Amnura, Bangla. 43 G13 24 37N 88 25 E
Āmol, Iran 45 B7 36 23N 52 20 E
Amorgós, Greece 23 F11 36 50N 25 57 E
Amory, U.S.A. 83 J1 33 59N 88 29W
Amos, Canada 72 C4 48 35N 78 5W
Åmot, Norway 9 G13 59 57N 9 54 E
Amoy = Xiamen, China 33 D6 24 25N 118 4 E
Ampanavoana, Madag. 57 B9 15 41S 50 22 E
Ampang, Malaysia 39 L3 3 8N 101 45 E
Ampangalana, Lakandranon', Madag. 57 C8 22 48S 47 50 E
Ampanihy, Madag. 57 C7 24 40S 44 45 E
Amparafaravola, Madag. 57 B8 17 35S 48 13 E
Ampasinambo, Madag. 57 C8 20 31S 48 0 E
Ampasindava, Helodranon', Madag. 57 A8 13 40S 48 15 E
Ampasindava, Saikanosy, Madag. 57 A8 13 42S 47 55 E
Ampenan, Indonesia 36 F5 8 34S 116 4 E
Amper →, Germany 16 D6 48 29N 11 55 E
Amphoe Kathu, Thailand 39 a 7 55N 98 21 E
Amphoe Thalang, Thailand 39 a 8 1N 98 20 E
Ampitsikinana, Réunion 57 A8 12 57S 49 49 E
Ampombiantambo, Madag. 57 A8 12 42S 48 57 E
Ampotaka, Madag. 57 D7 25 3S 44 41 E
Ampoza, Madag. 57 C7 22 20S 44 44 E
Amqui, Canada 73 C6 48 28N 67 27W
Amravati, India 40 J10 20 55N 77 45 E
Amreli, India 42 J4 21 35N 71 17 E
Amritsar, India 42 D6 31 35N 74 57 E
Amroha, India 43 E8 28 53N 78 30 E
Amsterdam, Neths. 15 B4 52 23N 4 54 E
Amsterdam, U.S.A. 85 D10 42 56N 74 11W
Amsterdam ✕ (AMS), Neths. 15 B4 52 18N 4 45 E
Amsterdam, I. = Nouvelle-Amsterdam, Î., Ind. Oc. 3 F13 38 30S 77 30 E
Amstetten, Austria 16 D8 48 7N 14 51 E
Amudarya →, Uzbekistan 28 E6 43 58N 59 34 E
Amundsen Gulf, Canada 68 A7 71 0N 124 0W
Amundsen-Scott, Antarctica 5 E 90 0S 166 0 E
Amundsen Sea, Antarctica 5 D15 72 0S 115 0W
Amuntai, Indonesia 36 E5 2 28S 115 25 E
Amur →, Russia 29 D15 52 56N 141 10 E
Amurang, Indonesia 37 D6 1 5N 124 40 E
Amursk, Russia 29 D14 50 14N 136 54 E
Amyderya = Amudarya →, Uzbekistan 28 E6 43 58N 59 34 E
An Anbār □, Iraq 44 C4 33 25N 42 0 E
An Bien, Vietnam 39 H5 9 45N 105 0 E
An Hoa, Vietnam 38 E7 15 40N 108 5 E
An Nabatīyah at Tahta, Lebanon 46 B4 33 23N 35 27 E
An Nabk, Si. Arabia 44 D3 31 20N 37 20 E
An Nabk, Syria 46 A5 34 2N 36 44 E
An Nafūd, Si. Arabia 44 D4 28 15N 41 0 E
An Najaf, Iraq 44 C5 32 3N 44 15 E
An Nāṣirīyah, Iraq 44 D5 31 0N 46 15 E
An Nhon, Vietnam 38 F7 13 55N 109 7 E
An Nu'ayrīyah, Si. Arabia 45 E6 27 30N 48 30 E
An Nuwayb'ī, W. →, Si. Arabia 46 F3 29 18N 34 57 E
An Thoi, Dao, Vietnam 39 H4 9 58N 104 0 E
An Uaimh, Ireland 10 C5 53 39N 6 41W
Anabar →, Russia 29 B12 73 8N 113 36 E
'Anabtā, West Bank 46 C4 32 19N 35 7 E
Anaconda, U.S.A. 76 C7 46 8N 112 57W
Anacortes, U.S.A. 78 B4 48 30N 122 37W
Anadarko, U.S.A. 81 H5 35 4N 98 15W
Anadolu, Turkey 19 G5 39 0N 30 0 E
Anadyr, Russia 29 C18 64 35N 177 20 E
Anadyr →, Russia 29 C18 64 55N 176 5 E
Anadyrskiy Zaliv, Russia 29 C19 64 0N 180 0 E
Anaga, Pta. de, Canary Is. 24 F3 28 34N 16 9W
'Ānah, Iraq 44 C4 34 25N 42 0 E
Anaheim, U.S.A. 79 M9 33 50N 117 55W
Anahim Lake, Canada 70 C3 52 28N 125 18W
Anáhuac, Mexico 86 B4 27 14N 100 9W
Anakapalle, India 41 L13 17 42N 83 6 E
Anakie, Australia 62 C4 23 32S 147 45 E
Analalava, Madag. 57 A8 14 35S 48 0 E
Analavoka, Madag. 57 C8 22 23S 46 30 E
Análipsis, Greece 25 A3 39 36N 19 55 E
Anambar →, Pakistan 42 D3 30 15N 68 50 E
Anambas, Kepulauan, Indonesia 36 D3 3 20N 106 30 E
Anambas Is. = Anambas, Kepulauan, Indonesia 36 D3 3 20N 106 30 E
Anamosa, U.S.A. 80 D9 42 7N 91 17W
Anamur, Turkey 19 G5 36 8N 32 58 E
Anan, Japan 31 H7 33 54N 134 40 E
Anand, India 42 H5 22 32N 72 59 E
Anantapur, India 40 M10 14 39N 77 42 E
Anantnag, India 43 C6 33 45N 75 10 E
Ananyiv, Ukraine 17 E15 47 44N 29 58 E
Anapodháris →, Greece 25 E7 34 59N 25 20 E
Anápolis, Brazil 93 G9 16 15S 48 50W
Anapu →, Brazil 93 D8 1 53S 50 53W
Anār, Iran 45 D7 30 55N 55 13 E
Anārak, Iran 45 C7 33 25N 53 40 E
Anas →, India 42 H5 23 26N 74 0 E
Anatolia = Anadolu, Turkey 19 G5 39 0N 30 0 E
Anatsogno, Madag. 57 C7 23 33S 43 46 E
Añatuya, Argentina 94 B3 28 20S 62 50W
Anaunethad L., Canada 71 A8 60 55N 104 25W
Anbyŏn, N. Korea 35 E14 39 1N 127 35 E
Ancaster, Canada 84 C5 43 13N 79 59W
Anchor Bay, U.S.A. 78 G3 38 48N 123 34W
Anchorage, U.S.A. 68 B5 61 13N 149 54W
Anci, China 34 E9 39 20N 116 40 E
Ancohuma, Nevado, Bolivia 92 G5 16 0S 68 50W
Ancón, Peru 92 F3 11 50S 77 10W
Ancona, Italy 22 C5 43 38N 13 30 E
Ancud, Chile 96 E2 42 0S 73 50W
Ancud, G. de, Chile 96 E2 42 0S 73 0W
Anda, China 33 B7 46 24N 125 19 E
Andacollo, Argentina 94 D1 37 10S 70 42W
Andacollo, Chile 94 C1 30 14S 71 6W
Andaingo, Madag. 57 B8 18 12S 48 17 E
Andalgalá, Argentina 94 B2 27 40S 66 30W
Åndalsnes, Norway 9 E12 62 35N 7 43 E
Andalucía □, Spain 21 D3 37 35N 5 0W
Andalusia = Andalucía □, Spain 21 D3 37 35N 5 0W
Andalusia, U.S.A. 83 K2 31 18N 86 29W
Andaman Is., Ind. Oc. 27 H13 12 30N 92 45 E
Andaman Sea, Ind. Oc. 36 B1 13 0N 96 0 E
Andamooka Opal Fields, Australia 63 E2 30 27S 137 9 E
Andapa, Madag. 57 A8 14 39S 49 39 E
Andara, Namibia 56 B3 18 2S 21 9 E
Andenes, Norway 8 B17 69 19N 16 18 E
Andenne, Belgium 15 D5 50 28N 5 5 E
Anderson, Alaska, U.S.A. 68 B5 64 25N 149 15W
Anderson, Calif., U.S.A. 76 F2 40 27N 122 18W
Anderson, Ind., U.S.A. 82 E3 40 10N 85 41W
Anderson, Mo., U.S.A. 81 G7 36 39N 94 27W
Anderson, S.C., U.S.A. 83 H4 34 31N 82 39W
Anderson →, Canada 68 B7 69 42N 129 0W
Andes, U.S.A. 85 D10 42 12N 74 47W
Andes, Cord. de los, S. Amer. 92 H5 20 0S 68 0W
Andfjorden, Norway 8 B17 69 10N 16 20 E
Andhra Pradesh □, India 40 L11 18 0N 79 0 E
Andijon, Uzbekistan 28 E8 41 10N 72 15 E
Andikíthira, Greece 23 G10 35 52N 23 15 E
Andilamena, Madag. 57 B8 17 1S 48 35 E
Andīmeshk, Iran 45 C6 32 27N 48 21 E
Andizhan = Andijon, Uzbekistan 28 E8 41 10N 72 15 E
Andoany, Madag. 57 A8 13 25S 48 16 E
Andohahela ⌓, Madag. 57 C8 24 4S 46 44 E
Andong, S. Korea 35 F15 36 40N 128 43 E
Andongwei, China 35 G10 35 6N 119 20 E
Andoom, Australia 62 A3 12 25S 141 53 E
Andorra ■, Europe 20 E4 42 30N 1 30 E
Andorra La Vella, Andorra 20 E4 42 31N 1 32 E
Andover, U.K. 13 F6 51 12N 1 29W
Andover, Maine, U.S.A. 85 B14 44 38N 70 45W
Andover, Mass., U.S.A. 85 D13 42 40N 71 8W
Andover, N.J., U.S.A. 85 F10 40 59N 74 45W
Andover, N.Y., U.S.A. 84 D7 42 10N 77 48W
Andover, Ohio, U.S.A. 84 E4 41 36N 80 34W
Andøya, Norway 8 B16 69 10N 15 50 E
Andradina, Brazil 93 H8 20 54S 51 23W
Andrahary, Mt., Madag. 57 A8 13 37S 49 17 E
Andramasina, Madag. 57 B8 19 11S 47 35 E
Andranopasy, Madag. 57 C7 21 17S 43 44 E
Andranovory, Madag. 57 C7 23 8S 44 10 E
Andratx, Spain 24 B9 39 39N 2 25 E
Andreanof Is., U.S.A. 68 C2 51 30N 176 0W
Andrews, S.C., U.S.A. 83 J6 33 27N 79 34W
Andrews, Tex., U.S.A. 81 J3 32 19N 102 33W
Ándria, Italy 22 D7 41 13N 16 17 E
Andriamena, Madag. 57 B8 17 26S 47 30 E
Andriandampy, Madag. 57 C8 22 45S 45 41 E
Andriba, Madag. 57 B8 17 30S 46 58 E
Andringitra ⌓, Madag. 57 C8 22 13S 46 5 E
Androka, Madag. 57 C7 24 58S 44 2 E
Ándros, Greece 23 F11 37 50N 24 57 E
Andros I., Bahamas 88 B4 24 30N 78 0W
Andros Town, Bahamas 88 B4 24 43N 77 47W
Androscoggin →, U.S.A. 85 C14 43 58N 70 0W
Andselv, Norway 8 B18 69 4N 18 34 E
Andújar, Spain 21 C3 38 3N 4 5W
Andulo, Angola 52 G3 11 25S 16 45 E
Anegada I., Br. Virgin Is. 89 e 18 45N 64 20W
Anegada Passage, W. Indies 89 C7 18 15N 63 45W
Aneto, Pico de, Spain 21 A6 42 37N 0 40 E
Ang Mo Kio, Singapore 39 d 1 23N 103 50 E
Ang Thong, Thailand 38 E3 14 35N 100 31 E
Ang Thong △, Thailand 39 H2 9 40N 99 43 E
Ang Thong, Ko, Thailand 39 b 9 37N 99 41 E
Angamos, Punta, Chile 94 A1 23 1S 70 32W
Angara →, Russia 29 D10 58 5N 94 20 E
Angarsk, Russia 29 D11 52 30N 104 0 E
Angas Hills, Australia 60 D4 23 0S 127 50 E
Angaston, Australia 63 E2 34 30S 139 8 E
Ånge, Sweden 9 E16 62 31N 15 35 E
Ángel, Salto = Angel Falls, Venezuela 92 B6 5 57N 62 30W
Ángel de la Guarda, I., Mexico 86 B2 29 30N 113 30W
Angel Falls, Venezuela 92 B6 5 57N 62 30W
Angeles, Phil. 37 A6 15 9N 120 33 E
Ängelholm, Sweden 9 H15 56 15N 12 58 E
Angels Camp, U.S.A. 78 G6 38 4N 120 32W
Ångermanälven →, Sweden 8 E17 62 40N 18 0 E
Ångermanland, Sweden 8 E18 63 36N 17 45 E
Angers, Canada 85 A9 45 31N 75 29W
Angers, France 20 C3 47 30N 0 35W
Ängesån →, Sweden 8 C20 66 16N 22 47 E
Angikuni L., Canada 71 A9 62 12N 99 59W
Angkor, Cambodia 38 F4 13 22N 103 50 E
Anglesey, Isle of □, U.K. 12 D3 53 16N 4 18W
Angleton, U.S.A. 81 L7 29 10N 95 26W
Anglisidhes, Cyprus 25 E12 34 51N 33 27 E
Angmagssalik = Tasiilaq, Greenland 4 C6 65 40N 37 20W
Ango, Dem. Rep. of the Congo 54 B2 4 10N 26 5 E
Angoche, Mozam. 55 F4 16 8S 39 55 E
Angoche, I., Mozam. 55 F4 16 20S 39 50 E
Angol, Chile 94 D1 37 56S 72 45W
Angola, Ind., U.S.A. 82 E3 41 38N 85 0W
Angola, N.Y., U.S.A. 84 D5 42 38N 79 2W
Angola ■, Africa 53 G3 12 0S 18 0 E
Angoulême, France 20 D4 45 39N 0 10 E
Angoumois, France 20 D3 45 50N 0 25 E
Angra dos Reis, Brazil 95 A7 23 0S 44 10W
Angren, Uzbekistan 28 E8 41 1N 70 12 E
Angtassom, Cambodia 39 G5 11 1N 104 41 E
Angu, Dem. Rep. of the Congo 54 B1 3 23N 24 30 E
Anguang, China 35 B12 45 15N 123 45 E
Anguilla ☒, W. Indies 89 C7 18 14N 63 5W
Anguo, China 34 E8 38 28N 115 15 E
Angurugu, Australia 62 A2 14 0S 136 25 E
Angus □, U.K. 11 E6 56 46N 2 56W
Angwa →, Zimbabwe 57 B5 16 0S 30 23 E
Anhanduí →, Brazil 95 A5 21 46S 52 9W
Anholt, Denmark 9 H14 56 42N 11 33 E
Anhui □, China 33 C6 32 0N 117 0 E
Anhwei = Anhui □, China 33 C6 32 0N 117 0 E
Anichab, Namibia 56 C1 21 0S 14 46 E
Animas →, U.S.A. 77 H9 36 43N 108 13W
Anivorano, Madag. 57 B8 18 44S 48 58 E
Anjalankoski, Finland 9 F22 60 45N 26 51 E
Anjar, India 42 H4 23 6N 70 10 E
Anjou, France 20 C3 47 20N 0 15W
Anjozorobe, Madag. 57 B8 18 22S 47 52 E
Anju, N. Korea 35 E13 39 36N 125 40 E
Ankaboa, Tanjona, Madag. 57 C7 21 58S 43 20 E
Ankang, China 34 H5 32 40N 109 1 E
Ankara, Turkey 19 G5 39 57N 32 54 E
Ankarafantsika ⌓, Madag. 57 B8 16 8S 47 5 E
Ankaramena, Madag. 57 C8 21 57S 46 39 E
Ankaratra, Madag. 53 H9 19 25S 47 12 E
Ankasakasa, Madag. 57 B7 16 21S 44 52 E
Ankavandra, Madag. 57 B8 18 46S 45 18 E
Ankazoabo, Madag. 57 C7 22 18S 44 31 E
Ankazobe, Madag. 57 B8 18 20S 47 10 E
Ankeny, U.S.A. 80 E8 41 44N 93 36W
Ankilimalinika, Madag. 57 C7 22 58S 43 45 E
Ankilizato, Madag. 57 C8 20 25S 45 1 E
Ankisabe, Madag. 57 B8 19 17S 46 29 E
Ankoro, Dem. Rep. of the Congo 54 D2 6 45S 26 55 E
Ankororoka, Madag. 57 D8 25 30S 45 11 E
Anmyŏn-do, S. Korea 35 F14 36 25N 126 25 E
Ann, C., U.S.A. 85 D14 42 38N 70 35W
Ann Arbor, U.S.A. 82 D4 42 17N 83 45W
Anna, U.S.A. 81 G10 37 28N 89 15W
Annaba, Algeria 50 A7 36 50N 7 46 E
Annalee →, Ireland 10 B4 54 2N 7 24W
Annam, Vietnam 38 E7 16 0N 108 0 E
Annamitique, Chaîne, Asia 38 D6 17 0N 106 0 E
Annan, U.K. 11 G5 54 59N 3 16W
Annan →, U.K. 11 G5 54 58N 3 16W
Annapolis, U.S.A. 82 F7 38 59N 76 30W
Annapolis Royal, Canada 73 D6 44 44N 65 32W
Annapurna, Nepal 43 E10 28 34N 83 50 E
Annean, L., Australia 61 E2 26 54S 118 14 E
Annecy, France 20 D7 45 55N 6 8 E
Anning, China 32 D5 24 55N 102 26 E
Anniston, U.S.A. 83 J3 33 39N 85 50W
Annobón, Atl. Oc. 49 G4 1 25S 5 36 E
Annotto Bay, Jamaica 88 a 18 17N 76 45W
Annville, U.S.A. 85 F8 40 20N 76 31W
Áno Viánnos, Greece 25 D7 35 2N 25 21 E
Anorotsangana, Madag. 57 A8 13 56S 47 55 E
Anosibe, Madag. 57 B8 19 26S 48 13 E
Anóyia, Greece 25 D6 35 16N 24 52 E
Anping, Hebei, China 34 E8 38 15N 115 30 E
Anping, Liaoning, China 35 D12 41 5N 123 30 E
Anqing, China 33 C6 30 30N 117 3 E
Anqiu, China 35 F10 36 25N 119 10 E
Ansai, China 34 F5 36 50N 109 20 E
Ansbach, Germany 16 D6 49 28N 10 34 E
Anshan, China 35 D12 41 5N 122 58 E
Anshun, China 32 D5 26 18N 105 57 E
Ansley, U.S.A. 80 E5 41 18N 99 23W
Anson, U.S.A. 81 J5 32 45N 99 54W
Anson B., Australia 60 B5 13 20S 130 6 E
Ansongo, Mali 50 E6 15 25N 0 35 E
Ansonia, U.S.A. 85 E11 41 21N 73 5W
Anstruther, U.K. 11 E6 56 14N 2 41W
Ansudu, Indonesia 37 E9 2 11S 139 22 E
Antabamba, Peru 92 F4 14 40S 73 0W
Antakya, Turkey 19 G6 36 14N 36 10 E
Antalaha, Madag. 57 A9 14 57S 50 20 E
Antalya, Turkey 19 G5 36 52N 30 45 E
Antalya Körfezi, Turkey 19 G5 36 15N 31 30 E
Antambohobe, Madag. 57 C8 22 20S 46 47 E
Antanambao-Manampotsy, Madag. 57 B8 19 29S 48 34 E
Antanambe, Madag. 57 B8 16 26S 49 52 E
Antananarivo, Madag. 57 B8 18 55S 47 31 E
Antananarivo □, Madag. 57 B8 19 0S 47 0 E
Antanifotsy, Madag. 57 B8 19 39S 47 19 E
Antanimbaribe, Madag. 57 C7 21 30S 44 48 E
Antanimora, Madag. 57 C8 24 49S 45 40 E
Antarctic Pen., Antarctica 5 C18 67 0S 60 0W
Antarctica 5 E3 90 0S 0 0W
Antelope, Zimbabwe 55 G2 21 2S 28 31 E
Antequera, Paraguay 94 A4 24 8S 57 7W
Antequera, Spain 21 D3 37 5N 4 33W
Antero, Mt., U.S.A. 77 G10 38 41N 106 15W
Antevamena, Madag. 57 C7 21 2S 44 8 E
Anthony, Kans., U.S.A. 81 G5 37 9N 98 2W
Anthony, N. Mex., U.S.A. 77 K10 32 0N 106 36W
Anti Atlas, Morocco 50 C4 30 0N 8 30W
Anti-Lebanon = Ash Sharqi, Al Jabal, Lebanon 46 B5 33 40N 36 10 E
Antibes, France 20 E7 43 34N 7 6 E
Anticosti, Î. d', Canada 73 C7 49 30N 63 0W
Antigo, U.S.A. 80 C10 45 9N 89 9W
Antigonish, Canada 73 C7 45 38N 61 58W
Antigua, Canary Is. 24 F5 28 24N 14 1W
Antigua, Guatemala 88 D1 14 34N 90 41W
Antigua, W. Indies 89 C7 17 0N 61 50W
Antigua & Barbuda ■, W. Indies 89 C7 17 20N 61 48W
Antilla, Cuba 88 B4 20 40N 75 50W
Antilles = West Indies, Cent. Amer. 89 D7 15 0N 65 0W
Antioch, U.S.A. 78 G5 38 1N 121 48W
Antioquia, Colombia 92 B3 6 40N 75 55W
Antipodes Is., Pac. Oc. 64 M9 49 45S 178 40 E
Antlers, U.S.A. 81 H7 34 14N 95 37W
Antoetra, Madag. 57 C8 20 46S 47 20 E
Antofagasta, Chile 94 A1 23 50S 70 30W
Antofagasta □, Chile 94 A2 24 0S 69 0W
Antofagasta de la Sierra, Argentina 94 B2 26 5S 67 20W
Antofalla, Argentina 94 B2 25 30S 68 5W
Antofalla, Salar de, Argentina 94 B2 25 40S 67 45W
Anton, U.S.A. 81 J3 33 49N 102 10W
Antongila, Helodrano, Madag. 57 B8 15 30S 49 50 E
Antonibé, Madag. 57 B8 15 7S 47 24 E
Antonibé, Presqu'île d', Madag. 57 A8 14 55S 47 20 E
Antonina, Brazil 95 B6 25 26S 48 42W
Antrim, U.K. 10 B5 54 43N 6 14W
Antrim, U.S.A. 84 F3 40 7N 81 21W
Antrim □, U.K. 10 B5 54 56N 6 25W
Antrim, Mts. of, U.K. 10 A5 55 3N 6 14W
Antrim Plateau, Australia 60 C4 18 8S 128 20 E
Antsakabary, Madag. 57 B8 15 3S 48 56 E
Antsalova, Madag. 57 B7 18 40S 44 37 E
Antsenavolo, Madag. 57 C8 21 24S 48 3 E
Antsiafabositra, Madag. 57 B8 17 18S 46 57 E
Antsirabe, Antananarivo, Madag. 57 B8 19 55S 47 2 E
Antsirabe, Antsiranana, Madag. 57 A8 14 0S 49 59 E
Antsirabe, Mahajanga, Madag. 57 B8 15 57S 48 58 E
Antsiranana, Madag. 57 A8 12 25S 49 20 E
Antsiranana □, Madag. 57 A8 12 16S 49 17 E
Antsohihy, Madag. 57 A8 14 50S 47 59 E
Antsohimbondrona Seranana, Madag. 57 A8 13 7S 48 48 E
Antu, China 35 C15 42 30N 128 20 E
Antwerp = Antwerpen, Belgium 15 C4 51 13N 4 25 E
Antwerp, U.S.A. 85 B9 44 12N 75 37W
Antwerpen, Belgium 15 C4 51 13N 4 25 E
Antwerpen □, Belgium 15 C4 51 15N 4 40 E
Anupgarh, India 42 E5 29 10N 73 10 E

Anuppur, India .... 43 H9 23 6N 81 41 E
Anuradhapura, Sri Lanka ... 40 Q12 8 22N 80 28 E
Anveh, Iran .... 45 E7 27 23N 54 11 E
Anvers = Antwerpen, Belgium . 15 C4 51 13N   4 25 E
Anvers I., Antarctica 5 C17 64 30S 63 40W
Anxi, China .... 32 B4 40 30N 95 43 E
Anxious B., Australia ..... 63 E1 33 24S 134 45 E
Anyang, China .... 34 F8 36 5N 114 21 E
Anyer-Kidul, Indonesia .... 37 G11 6 4S 105 53 E
Anyi, China .... 34 G6 35 2N 111 2 E
Anza, U.S.A. 79 M10 33 35N 116 39W
Anze, China .... 34 F7 36 10N 112 12 E
Anzhero-Sudzhensk, Russia . 28 D9 56 10N 86 0 E
Ānzio, Italy .... 22 D5 41 27N 12 37 E
Ao Makham, Thailand ..... 39 a   7 50N 98 24 E
Ao Phangnga △, Thailand ... 39 a   8 10N 98 32 E
Aoga-Shima, Japan .... 31 H9 32 28N 139 46 E
Aomori, Japan .... 30 D10 40 45N 140 45 E
Aomori □, Japan .... 30 D10 40 45N 140 40 E
Aonla, India .... 43 E8 28 16N 79 11 E
Aoraki Mount Cook, N.Z. .. 59 K3 43 36S 170 9 E
Aosta, Italy .... 20 D7 45 45N   7 20 E
Aotearoa = New Zealand ■,
  Oceania .... 59 J6 40 0S 176 0 E
Aoukâr, Mauritania 50 E4 17 40N 10 0W
Aozou Strip, Chad .... 51 D9 22 0N 19 0 E
Apa →, S. Amer. 94 A4 22 6S 58 2W
Apache, U.S.A. 81 H5 34 54N 98 22W
Apache Junction, U.S.A. .. 77 K8 33 25N 111 33W
Apalachee B., U.S.A. 83 L4 30 0N 84 0W
Apalachicola, U.S.A. 83 L3 29 43N 84 59W
Apalachicola →, U.S.A. ... 83 L3 29 43N 84 58W
Apaporis →, Colombia 92 D5   1 23S 69 25W
Aparados da Serra △, Brazil . 95 B5 29 10S 50 8W
Aparri, Phil. .... 37 A6 18 22N 121 38 E
Apatity, Russia .... 18 A5 67 34N 33 22 E
Apatzingán, Mexico 86 D4 19 0N 102 20W
Apeldoorn, Neths. .... 15 B5 52 13N   5 57 E
Apennines = Appennini, Italy . 22 B4 44 30N 10 0 E
Apia, Samoa 59 A13 13 50S 171 50W
Apiacás, Serra dos, Brazil .. 92 E7   9 50S 57 0W
Apies →, S. Africa .... 57 D4 25 15S 28 8 E
Apizaco, Mexico 87 D5 19 26N 98 9W
Aplao, Peru 92 G4 16 0S 72 40W
Apo, Mt., Phil. .... 37 C7   6 53N 125 14 E
Apolakkiá, Greece .... 25 C9 36 5N 27 48 E
Apolakkiá, Órmos, Greece .. 25 C9 36 5N 27 48 E
Apolo, Bolivia 92 F5 14 30S 68 30W
Aporé →, Brazil 93 G8 19 27S 50 57W
Apostle Is., U.S.A. 80 B9 47 0N 90 40W
Apostle Islands △, U.S.A. .. 80 B9 46 57N 90 53W
Apóstoles, Argentina 95 B4 28 0S 56 0W
Apostolos Andreas, C., Cyprus . 25 D13 35 42N 34 35 E
Apoteri, Guyana 92 C7   4 2N 58 32W
Appalachian Mts., U.S.A. .. 82 G6 38 0N 80 0W
Appennini, Italy .... 22 B4 44 30N 10 0 E
Apple Hill, Canada 85 A10 45 13N 74 46W
Apple Valley, U.S.A. 79 L9 34 32N 117 14W
Appleby-in-Westmorland, U.K. . 12 C5 54 35N   2 29W
Appledore, U.K. 13 F3 51 3N   4 13W
Appleton, U.S.A. 82 C1 44 16N 88 25W
Approuague →, Fr. Guiana . 93 C8   4 30N 51 57W
Aprília, Italy .... 22 D5 41 36N 12 39 E
Apsley, Canada 84 B6 44 45N 78 6W
Apucarana, Brazil 95 A5 23 55S 51 33W
Apure →, Venezuela 92 B5   7 37N 66 25W
Apurímac →, Peru 92 F4 12 17S 73 56W
Aqâ Jarī, Iran .... 45 D6 30 42N 49 50 E
Aqaba = Al 'Aqabah, Jordan . 46 F4 29 31N 35 0 E
Aqaba, G. of, Red Sea .... 44 D2 28 15N 33 20 E
'Aqabah, Khalīj al = Aqaba, G. of,
  Red Sea .... 44 D2 28 15N 33 20 E
'Aqdā, Iran .... 45 C7 32 26N 53 37 E
'Aqrah, Iraq .... 44 B4 36 46N 43 45 E
Aqtaū, Kazakhstan ...... 28 E6 43 39N 51 12 E
Aqtöbe, Kazakhstan ...... 19 D10 50 17N 57 10 E
Aquidauana, Brazil 93 H7 20 30S 55 50W
Aquiles Serdán, Mexico ... 86 B3 28 37N 105 54W
Aquin, Haiti 89 C5 18 16N 73 24W
Aquitain, Bassin, France .. 20 D3 44 0N   0 30W
Ar Rachidiya = Er Rachidia,
  Morocco 50 B5 31 58N   4 20W
Ar Rafid, Syria .... 46 C4 32 57N 35 52 E
Ar Raḥḥāliyah, Iraq ...... 44 C4 32 44N 43 23 E
Ar Ramādī, Iraq .... 44 C4 33 25N 43 20 E
Ar Ramthā, Jordan ...... 46 C5 32 34N 36 0 E
Ar Raqqah, Syria .... 44 C3 35 59N 39 8 E
Ar Rass, Si. Arabia ...... 44 E4 25 50N 43 40 E
Ar Rifā'ī, Iraq .... 44 D5 31 50N 46 10 E
Ar Riyāḍ, Si. Arabia ..... 44 E5 24 41N 46 42 E
Ar Ru'ays, Qatar .... 45 E6 26 8N 51 12 E
Ar Rukhaymīyah, Iraq .... 44 D5 29 22N 45 38 E
Ar Ruṣāfah, Syria .... 44 C3 35 45N 38 49 E
Ar Ruṭbah, Iraq .... 44 C4 33 0N 40 15 E
Ara, India .... 43 G11 25 35N 84 32 E
Arab, U.S.A. 83 H2 34 19N 86 30W
'Arab, Bahr el →, Sudan .. 51 G11 9 0N 29 30 E
Arab, Shatt al →, Asia ... 45 D6 30 0N 48 31 E
'Arabābād, Iran .... 45 C8 33 2N 57 41 E
Arabia, Asia .... 26 G8 25 0N 45 0 E
Arabian Desert = Es Sahrâ' Esh
  Sharqîya, Egypt .... 51 C12 27 30N 32 30 E
Arabian Gulf = Gulf, The, Asia . 45 E6 27 0N 50 0 E
Arabian Sea, Ind. Oc. .... 27 H10 16 0N 65 0 E
Aracaju, Brazil 93 F11 10 55S 37 4W
Aracati, Brazil 93 D11 4 30S 37 44W
Araçatuba, Brazil 95 A5 21 10S 50 30W
Aracena, Spain 21 D2 37 53N   6 38W
Araçuaí, Brazil 93 G10 16 52S 42 4W
'Arad, Israel .... 46 D4 31 15N 35 12 E
Arad, Romania .... 17 E11 46 10N 21 20 E
Arādān, Iran .... 45 C7 35 21N 52 30 E
Aradhippou, Cyprus ...... 25 E12 34 57N 33 36 E
Arafura Sea, E. Indies .... 26 K17 9 0S 135 0 E
Aragón □, Spain 21 B5 41 25N   0 40W
Aragón →, Spain 21 A5 42 13N   1 44W
Araguacema, Brazil 93 E9 8 50S 49 20W
Araguaia →, Brazil 93 E9 5 21S 48 41W
Araguaína, Brazil 93 E9 7 12S 48 12W
Araguari, Brazil 93 G9 18 38S 48 11W
Araguari →, Brazil 93 C9 1 15N 49 55W
Arain, India .... 42 F6 26 27N 75 2 E
Arak, Algeria .... 50 C6 25 20N   3 45 E
Arāk, Iran .... 45 C6 34 0N 49 40 E
Arakan Coast, Burma .... 41 K19 19 0N 94 0 E
Arakan Yoma, Burma ..... 41 K19 20 0N 94 40 E
Araks = Aras, Rūd-e →, Asia . 44 B5 40 5N 48 29 E

Aral, Kazakhstan .... 28 E7 46 41N 61 45 E
Aral Sea, Asia .... 28 E7 44 30N 60 0 E
Aral Tengizi = Aral Sea, Asia . 28 E7 44 30N 60 0 E
Aralsk = Aral, Kazakhstan . 28 E7 46 41N 61 45 E
Aralskoye More = Aral Sea, Asia . 28 E7 44 30N 60 0 E
Aramac, Australia .... 62 C4 22 58S 145 14 E
Aran I., Ireland 10 A3 55 0N   8 30W
Aran Is., Ireland 10 C2 53 6N   9 38W
Aranda de Duero, Spain ... 21 B4 41 39N   3 42W
Arandān, Iran .... 44 C5 35 23N 46 55 E
Aranjuez, Spain 21 B4 40 1N   3 40W
Aranos, Namibia .... 56 C2 24 9S 19 7 E
Aransas Pass, U.S.A. 81 M6 27 55N 97 9W
Aranyaprathet, Thailand .. 38 F4 13 41N 102 30 E
Arapahoe, U.S.A. 80 E5 40 18N 99 54W
Arapey Grande →, Uruguay . 94 C4 30 55S 57 49W
Arapgir, Turkey .... 44 B3 39 5N 38 30 E
Arapiraca, Brazil 93 E11 9 45S 36 39W
Arapongas, Brazil 95 A5 23 29S 51 28W
Ar'ar, Si. Arabia .... 44 D4 30 59N 41 2 E
Araranguá, Brazil 95 B6 29 0S 49 30W
Araraquara, Brazil 93 H9 21 50S 48 0W
Ararás, Serra das, Brazil .. 95 B5 25 0S 53 10W
Ararat, Australia .... 63 F3 37 16S 143 0 E
Ararat, Mt. = Ağrı Dağı, Turkey . 19 F7 39 50N 44 15 E
Araria, India .... 43 F12 26 9N 87 33 E
Araripe, Chapada do, Brazil . 93 E11 7 20S 40 0W
Araruama, L. de, Brazil ... 95 A7 22 53S 42 12W
Aras, Rūd-e →, Asia ..... 44 B5 40 5N 48 29 E
Arauca, Colombia 92 B4   7 0N 70 40W
Arauca →, Venezuela 92 B5   7 24N 66 35W
Arauco, Chile 94 D1 37 16S 73 25W
Arawale ☐, Kenya .... 54 C5   1 24S 40 9 E
Araxá, Brazil 93 G9 19 35S 46 55W
Araya, Pen. de, Venezuela .. 92 A6 10 40N 64 0W
Arba Minch, Ethiopia .... 47 F2   6 0N 37 30 E
Arbat, Iraq .... 44 C5 35 25N 45 35 E
Árbatax, Italy .... 22 E3 39 56N   9 42 E
Arbil, Iraq .... 44 B5 36 15N 44 5 E
Arborfield, Canada 71 C8 53 6N 103 39W
Arborg, Canada 71 C9 50 54N 97 13W
Arbroath, U.K. 11 E6 56 34N   2 35W
Arbuckle, U.S.A. 78 F4 39 1N 122 3W
Arcachon, France 20 D3 44 40N   1 10W
Arcade, Calif., U.S.A. 84 D6 42 32N 78 25W
Arcadia, Fla., U.S.A. 83 M5 27 13N 81 52W
Arcadia, La., U.S.A. 81 J8 32 33N 92 55W
Arcadia, Pa., U.S.A. 84 F6 40 47N 78 51W
Arcata, U.S.A. 76 F1 40 52N 124 5W
Archangel = Arkhangelsk, Russia . 18 B7 64 38N 40 36 E
Archbald, U.S.A. 85 E9 41 30N 75 32W
Archer →, Australia ..... 62 A3 13 28S 141 41 E
Archer B., Australia ..... 62 A3 13 20S 141 30 E
Archer Bend = Mungkan
  Kandju △, Australia .... 62 A3 13 35S 142 52 E
Archers Post, Kenya ..... 54 B4   0 35N 37 35 E
Arches △, U.S.A. 77 G9 38 45N 109 25W
Archipel-de-Mingan △, Canada . 73 B7 50 13N 63 10W
Archipiélago Chinijo △,
  Canary Is. 24 E6 29 25N 13 40W
Archipiélago Los Roques △,
  Venezuela 89 D6 11 50N 66 44W
Arckaringa Cr. →, Australia . 63 D2 28 10S 135 22 E
Arco, U.S.A. 76 E7 43 38N 113 18W
Arcos de la Frontera, Spain . 21 D3 36 45N   5 49W
Arcot, India .... 40 N11 12 53N 79 20 E
Arctic Bay, Canada 69 A11 73 1N 85 7W
Arctic Ocean, Arctic 4 B18 78 0N 160 0W
Arctic Red River = Tsiigehtchic,
  Canada 68 B6 67 15N 134 0W
Arctowski, Antarctica 5 C18 62 30S 58 0W
Arda →, Bulgaria .... 23 D12 41 40N 26 30 E
Ardabil, Iran .... 45 B6 38 15N 48 18 E
Ardabil □, Iran .... 45 B6 38 15N 48 20 E
Ardakān = Sepīdān, Iran .. 45 D7 30 20N 52 5 E
Ardakān, Iran .... 45 C7 32 19N 53 59 E
Ardee, Ireland 10 C5 53 52N   6 33W
Arden, Canada 84 B8 44 43N 76 56W
Arden, Calif., U.S.A. 78 G5 38 36N 121 33W
Arden, Nev., U.S.A. 79 J11 36 1N 115 14W
Ardennes = Ardenne, Belgium . 15 E5 49 50N   5 5 E
Ardenne, Belgium .... 15 E5 49 50N   5 5 E
Arderin, Ireland 10 C4 53 2N   7 39W
Ardestān, Iran .... 45 C7 33 20N 52 25 E
Ardivachar Pt., U.K. 11 D1 57 23N   7 26W
Ardlethan, Australia ..... 63 E4 34 22S 146 53 E
Ardmore, Okla., U.S.A. ... 81 H6 34 10N 97 8W
Ardmore, Pa., U.S.A. 85 G9 39 58N 75 18W
Ardnamurchan, Pt. of, U.K. . 11 E2 56 43N   6 14W
Ardnave Pt., U.K. 11 F2 55 53N   6 20W
Ardrossan, Australia ..... 63 E2 34 26S 137 53 E
Ardrossan, U.K. 11 F4 55 39N   4 49W
Ards Pen., U.K. 10 B6 54 33N   5 34W
Arecibo, Puerto Rico .... 89 d 18 29N 66 43W
Areia Branca, Brazil 93 E11 5 0S 37 0W
Arena, Pt., U.S.A. 78 G3 38 57N 123 44W
Arenal, Honduras 88 C2 15 21N 86 50W
Arendal, Norway .... 9 G13 58 28N   8 46 E
Arequipa, Peru 92 G4 16 20S 71 30W
Arévalo, Spain 21 B3 41 3N   4 43W
Arezzo, Italy .... 22 C4 43 25N 11 53 E
Arga →, Turkey .... 44 B3 38 21N 37 59 E
Arganda, Spain 21 B4 40 19N   3 26W
Argentan, France 20 B3 48 45N   0 1W
Argentário, Mte., Italy .... 22 C4 42 24N 11 9 E
Argentia, Canada 73 C9 47 18N 53 58W
Argentina ■, S. Amer. ... 96 D3 35 0S 66 0W
Argentino, L., Argentina ... 96 G2 50 10S 73 0W
Argeș →, Romania ...... 17 F14 44 5N 26 38 E
Arghandab →, Afghan. ... 42 D1 31 30N 64 15 E
Argolikós Kólpos, Greece .. 23 F10 37 20N 22 52 E
Árgos, Greece .... 23 F10 37 40N 22 43 E
Argostólion, Greece ..... 23 E9 38 11N 20 29 E
Arguello, Pt., U.S.A. 79 L6 34 35N 120 39W
Arguineguín, Canary Is. ... 24 G4 27 46N 15 41W
Argus Pk., U.S.A. 79 K9 35 52N 117 26W
Argyle, L., Australia ..... 60 C4 16 20S 128 40 E
Argyll △, U.K. 11 E4 56 6N   5 0W
Argyll & Bute □, U.K. 11 E4 56 13N   5 28W
Århus, Denmark .... 9 H14 56 8N 10 11 E
Ariadnoye, Russia ...... 30 B7 45 8N 134 25 E
Ariamsvlei, Namibia ..... 56 D2 28 9S 19 51 E
Ariana, Chile 94 B3 18 32S 70 20W
Arica, Colombia 92 D4   2 0S 71 50W
Arico, Canary Is. 24 F3 28 9N 16 29W

Arid, C., Australia ...... 61 F3 34 1S 123 10 E
Arida, Japan .... 31 G7 34 5N 135 8 E
Arilla, Ákra, Greece ..... 25 A3 39 43N 19 39 E
Arima, Trin. & Tob. 89 D7 10 38N 61 17W
Arinos →, Brazil 92 F7 10 25S 58 20W
Ario de Rosales, Mexico ... 86 D4 19 12N 102 0W
Aripo, Mt., Trin. & Tob. .. 93 K15 10 45N 61 15W
Aripuanã, Brazil 92 E6   9 25S 60 30W
Aripuanã →, Brazil 92 E6   5 7S 60 25W
Ariquemes, Brazil 92 E6   9 55S 63 6W
Arisaig, U.K. 11 E3 56 55N   5 51W
Aristazabal I., Canada ... 70 C3 52 40N 129 10W
Arivonimamo, Madag. .... 57 B8 19 1S 47 11 E
Arizaro, Salar de, Argentina . 94 A2 24 40S 67 50W
Arizona, Argentina 94 D2 35 45S 65 25W
Arizona □, U.S.A. 77 J8 34 0N 112 0W
Arizpe, Mexico 86 A2 30 20N 110 11W
Arjeplog, Sweden .... 8 D18 66 3N 18 2 E
Arjona, Colombia 92 A3 10 14N 75 22W
Arjuna, Indonesia ...... 37 G15 7 49S 112 34 E
Arka, Russia .... 29 C15 60 15N 142 0 E
Arkadelphia, U.S.A. 81 H8 34 7N 93 4W
Arkaig, L., U.K. 11 E3 56 59N   5 10W
Arkalyk = Arqalyk, Kazakhstan . 28 D7 50 13N 66 50 E
Arkansas □, U.S.A. 81 H8 35 0N 92 30W
Arkansas →, U.S.A. 81 J9 33 47N 91 4W
Arkansas City, U.S.A. 81 G6 37 4N 97 2W
Arkaroola, Australia ..... 63 E2 30 20S 139 22 E
Arkhángelos, Greece ..... 25 C10 36 13N 28 7 E
Arkhangelsk, Russia ..... 18 B7 64 38N 40 36 E
Arki, India .... 42 D7 31 9N 76 58 E
Arklow, Ireland 10 D5 52 48N   6 10W
Arkport, U.S.A. 84 D7 42 24N 77 42W
Arkticheskiy, Mys, Russia .. 29 A10 81 10N 95 0 E
Arkville, U.S.A. 85 D10 42 9N 74 37W
Arlanzón →, Spain 21 A3 42 3N   4 17W
Arlbergpass, Austria ..... 16 E6 47 9N 10 12 E
Arles, France .... 20 E6 43 41N   4 40 E
Arlington, S. Africa ..... 57 D4 28 1S 27 53 E
Arlington, N.Y., U.S.A. ... 85 E11 41 42N 73 54W
Arlington, Oreg., U.S.A. .. 76 D3 45 43N 120 12W
Arlington, S. Dak., U.S.A. . 80 C6 44 22N 97 8W
Arlington, Tex., U.S.A. ... 81 J6 32 44N 97 7W
Arlington, Va., U.S.A. 82 F7 38 53N 77 7W
Arlington, Vt., U.S.A. 85 C11 43 5N 73 9W
Arlington, Wash., U.S.A. .. 78 B4 48 12N 122 8W
Arlington Heights, U.S.A. .. 82 D2 42 5N 87 59W
Arlit, Niger .... 50 E7 19 0N   7 38 E
Arlon, Belgium .... 15 E5 49 42N   5 49 E
Arltunga, Australia ...... 62 C1 23 26S 134 41 E
Armagh, U.K. 10 B5 54 21N   6 39W
Armagh □, U.K. 10 B5 54 18N   6 37W
Armando Bermudez △,
  Dom. Rep. 89 C5 19 3N 71 0W
Armavir, Russia .... 19 E7 45 2N 41 7 E
Armenia, Colombia 92 C3   4 35N 75 45W
Armenia ■, Asia .... 19 F7 40 20N 45 0 E
Armenistís, Ákra, Greece .. 25 C9 36 8N 27 42 E
Armidale, Australia ..... 63 E5 30 30S 151 40 E
Armour, U.S.A. 80 D5 43 19N 98 21W
Armstrong, B.C., Canada .. 70 C5 50 25N 119 10W
Armstrong, Ont., Canada .. 72 B2 50 18N 89 4W
Arnarfjörður, Iceland 8 D2 65 48N 23 40W
Arnaud →, Canada 69 B12 59 59N 69 46W
Arnauti, C., Cyprus ..... 25 D11 35 6N 32 17 E
Arnett, U.S.A. 81 G5 36 8N 99 46W
Arnhem, Neths. .... 15 C5 51 58N   5 55 E
Arnhem, C., Australia .... 62 A2 12 20S 137 30 E
Arnhem B., Australia .... 62 A2 12 20S 136 10 E
Arnhem Land, Australia ... 62 A1 13 10S 134 30 E
Arno →, Italy .... 22 C4 43 41N 10 17 E
Arno Bay, Australia ..... 63 E2 33 54S 136 34 E
Arnold, U.K. 12 D6 53 1N   1 7W
Arnold, U.S.A. 78 G6 38 15N 120 20W
Arnot, Canada 71 B9 55 56N 96 41W
Arnøy, Norway .... 8 A19 70 9N 20 40 E
Arnprior, Canada 85 A8 45 26N 76 21W
Arnsberg, Germany ...... 16 C5 51 24N   8 5 E
Aroab, Namibia .... 56 D2 26 41S 19 39 E
Aron, India .... 42 G6 25 57N 77 56 E
Arona, Canary Is. 24 F3 28 6N 16 40W
Arqalyk, Kazakhstan ..... 28 D7 50 13N 66 50 E
Arrah = Ara, India ...... 43 G11 25 35N 84 32 E
Arran, U.K. 11 F3 55 34N   5 12W
Arras, France .... 20 A5 50 17N   2 46 E
Arrecife, Canary Is. 24 F6 28 57N 13 37W
Arrecifes, Argentina 94 C3 34 6S 60 9W
Arrée, Mts. d', France 20 B2 48 26N   3 55W
Arriaga, Chiapas, Mexico .. 87 D6 16 15N 93 52W
Arriaga, San Luis Potosí, Mexico . 86 C4 21 55N 101 23W
Arrilalah, Australia ..... 62 C3 23 43S 143 54 E
Arrino, Australia .... 61 E2 29 30S 115 40 E
Arrow, L., Ireland 10 B3 54 3N   8 19W
Arrowhead, L., U.S.A. 79 L9 34 16N 117 10W
Arrowtown, N.Z. .... 59 L2 44 57S 168 50 E
Arroyo Grande, U.S.A. ... 79 K6 35 7N 120 35W
Ars, France .... 85 B3 37 9N 47 46 E
Arsenault L., Canada 71 B7 56 6N 108 32W
Arsenev, Russia .... 30 B6 44 10N 133 15 E
Árta, Greece .... 23 E9 39 8N 21 2 E
Artà, Spain .... 24 B10 39 41N 3 21 E
Arteaga, Mexico 86 D4 18 50N 102 20W
Artem, Russia .... 30 C6 43 22N 132 13 E
Artemovsk, Russia ...... 29 D10 54 45N 93 35 E
Artemovsk, Ukraine ...... 19 E6 48 35N 38 0 E
Artesia = Mosomane, Botswana . 56 C4 24 2S 26 19 E
Artesia, U.S.A. 81 J2 32 51N 104 24W
Arthur, Canada 84 C4 43 50N 80 32W
Arthur →, Australia ..... 63 G3 41 2S 144 40 E
Arthur Cr. →, Australia ... 62 C2 22 30S 136 25 E
Arthur Pt., Australia .... 62 C5 22 7S 150 3 E
Arthur River, Australia ... 61 F2 33 20S 117 2 E
Arthur's Pass, N.Z. ..... 59 K3 42 54S 171 35 E
Arthur's Pass △, N.Z. .... 59 K3 42 53S 171 42 E
Arthur's Town, Bahamas .. 89 B4 24 38N 75 42W
Artigas, Antarctica 5 C18 62 30S 58 0W
Artigas, Uruguay 94 C4 30 20S 56 30W
Artillery L., Canada 71 A7 63 9N 107 52W
Artois, France .... 20 A5 50 20N   2 30 E
Artrutx, C. de, Spain ..... 24 B10 39 55N   3 49 E
Artsyz, Ukraine .... 17 E15 46 4N 29 26 E
Artvin, Turkey .... 19 F7 41 14N 41 44 E
Aru, Kepulauan, Indonesia . 37 F8   6 0S 134 30 E
Aru Is. = Aru, Kepulauan,
  Indonesia .... 37 F8   6 0S 134 30 E
Arua, Uganda .... 54 B3   3 1N 30 58 E
Aruanã, Brazil 93 F8 14 54S 51 10W
Aruba ☑, W. Indies 89 D6 12 30N 70 0W

Arucas, Canary Is. 24 F4 28 7N 15 32W
Arun →, Nepal .... 43 F12 26 55N 87 10 E
Arun →, U.K. 13 G7 50 49N   0 33W
Arunachal Pradesh □, India . 41 F19 28 0N 95 0 E
Arusha, Tanzania .... 54 C4   3 20S 36 40 E
Arusha □, Tanzania ..... 54 C4   4 0S 36 30 E
Arusha △, Tanzania ..... 54 C4   3 16S 36 47 E
Arusha Chini, Tanzania ... 54 C4   3 32S 37 20 E
Aruwimi →, Dem. Rep. of
  the Congo .... 54 B1   1 13N 23 36 E
Arvada, Colo., U.S.A. 80 F2 39 48N 105 5W
Arvada, Wyo., U.S.A. 76 D10 44 39N 106 8W
Árvi, Greece .... 25 E7 34 59N 25 28 E
Arviat, Canada 71 A10 61 6N 93 59W
Arviat, Canada 71 A10 61 6N 93 59W
Arvidsjaur, Sweden ..... 8 D18 65 35N 19 10 E
Arvika, Sweden .... 9 G15 59 40N 12 36 E
Arvin, U.S.A. 79 K8 35 12N 118 50W
Arwal, India .... 43 G11 25 15N 84 41 E
Arxan, China .... 33 B6 47 11N 119 57 E
Aryirádhes, Greece ..... 25 B3 39 27N 19 58 E
Aryiroúpolis, Greece .... 25 D6 35 17N 24 20 E
Arys, Kazakhstan .... 28 E7 42 26N 68 48 E
Arzamas, Russia .... 18 C7 55 27N 43 55 E
Aş Şafā, Syria .... 46 B6 33 10N 37 0 E
As Saffānīyah, Si. Arabia .. 45 E6 27 55N 48 50 E
As Safirah, Syria .... 44 B3 36 5N 37 21 E
Aş Sahm, Oman .... 45 E8 24 10N 56 53 E
As Sājir, Si. Arabia ..... 44 E5 25 11N 44 36 E
As Salamīyah, Syria ..... 44 C3 35 1N 37 2 E
As Salmān, Iraq .... 44 D5 30 30N 44 32 E
As Salt, Jordan .... 46 C4 32 2N 35 43 E
As Sal'w'a, Qatar .... 45 E6 24 23N 50 50 E
As Samāwah, Iraq ...... 44 D5 31 15N 45 15 E
As Sanamayn, Syria ..... 46 B5 33 3N 36 10 E
As Sohar = Şuḩār, Oman .. 45 E8 24 20N 56 40 E
As Sukhnah, Syria ...... 44 C3 34 52N 38 52 E
As Sulaymānīyah, Iraq ... 44 C5 35 35N 45 29 E
As Sulaymī, Si. Arabia ... 44 E4 26 17N 41 21 E
As Sulayyil, Si. Arabia ... 47 C5 20 27N 45 34 E
As Summān, Si. Arabia ... 44 E5 25 0N 47 0 E
As Suwaydā', Syria ..... 46 C5 32 40N 36 30 E
As Suwaydā' □, Syria .... 46 C5 32 45N 36 45 E
As Suwayq, Oman ...... 45 F8 23 51N 57 26 E
Aş Şuwayrah, Iraq ...... 44 C5 32 55N 45 0 E
Asab, Namibia .... 56 D2 25 30S 18 0 E
Asad, Buḩayrat al, Syria .. 44 C3 36 0N 38 15 E
Asahi-Gawa →, Japan .... 31 G6 34 36N 133 58 E
Asahigawa, Japan ...... 30 C11 43 46N 142 22 E
Asamankese, Ghana 50 G5   5 50N   0 40W
Asan →, India .... 43 F8 29 24N 78 24 E
Asansol, India .... 43 H12 23 40N 87 1 E
Asbesberg, S. Africa .... 56 D3 29 0S 23 0 E
Asbestos, Canada 73 C5 45 47N 71 58W
Asbury Park, U.S.A. 85 F10 40 13N 74 1W
Ascension, Mexico 86 A3 31 6N 107 59W
Ascensión, B. de la, Mexico . 87 D7 19 50N 87 20W
Ascension I., Atl. Oc. 49 G2   7 57S 14 23W
Aschaffenburg, Germany .. 16 D5 49 58N   9 6 E
Aschersleben, Germany ... 16 C6 51 45N 11 29 E
Áscoli Piceno, Italy ..... 22 C5 42 51N 13 34 E
Ascope, Peru 92 E3   7 46S 79 8W
Ascotán, Chile 94 A2 21 45S 68 17W
Aseb, Eritrea .... 47 E3 13 0N 42 40 E
Asela, Ethiopia .... 47 F2   8 0N 39 0 E
Asenovgrad, Bulgaria .... 23 C11 42 1N 24 51 E
Aserradero, Mexico 86 C3 23 40N 105 43W
Asgata, Cyprus .... 25 E12 34 46N 33 15 E
Ash Fork, U.S.A. 77 J7 35 13N 112 29W
Ash Grove, U.S.A. 81 G8 37 19N 93 35W
Ash Shabab, Iraq ...... 44 D4 30 49N 43 39 E
Ash Shāmāl □, Lebanon .. 46 A5 34 25N 36 0 E
Ash Shāmiyah, Iraq ..... 44 D5 31 55N 44 35 E
Ash Shāriqah, U.A.E. .... 45 E7 25 23N 55 26 E
Ash Sharmah, Si. Arabia .. 44 D2 28 1N 35 16 E
Ash Shaṭrah, Iraq ...... 44 D5 31 30N 46 10 E
Ash Shawbak, Jordan .... 44 D2 30 32N 35 34 E
Ash Shawmari, J., Jordan .. 46 E5 30 35N 36 35 E
Ash Shināfīyah, Iraq .... 44 D5 31 35N 44 39 E
Ash Shu'bah, Si. Arabia .. 44 D5 28 54N 44 44 E
Ash Shumlūl, Si. Arabia .. 44 E5 26 31N 47 20 E
Ash Shūr'a, Iraq .... 44 C4 35 58N 43 13 E
Ash Shurayf, Si. Arabia .. 44 E3 25 43N 39 14 E
Ash Shuwayfāt, Lebanon .. 46 B4 33 45N 35 30 E
Asha, Russia .... 18 D10 55 0N 57 16 E
Ashau, Vietnam .... 38 D6 16 6N 107 22 E
Ashbourne, U.K. 12 D6 53 2N   1 43W
Ashburn, U.S.A. 83 K4 31 43N 83 39W
Ashburton, N.Z. .... 59 K3 43 53S 171 48 E
Ashburton →, Australia .. 60 D1 21 40S 114 56 E
Ashcroft, Canada 70 C4 50 40N 121 20W
Ashdod, Israel .... 46 D3 31 49N 34 35 E
Ashdown, U.S.A. 81 J7 33 40N 94 8W
Asheboro, U.S.A. 83 H6 35 43N 79 49W
Ashern, Canada 71 C9 51 11N 98 21W
Asherton, U.S.A. 81 L5 28 27N 99 46W
Asheville, U.S.A. 83 H4 35 36N 82 33W
Ashewat, Pakistan ...... 42 D3 31 22N 68 32 E
Asheweig →, Canada 72 B2 54 17N 87 12W
Ashford, Australia ...... 63 D5 29 15S 151 3 E
Ashford, U.K. .... 13 F8 51 8N   0 53 E
Ashgabat, Turkmenistan .. 28 F6 38 0N 57 50 E
Ashibetsu, Japan ...... 30 C11 43 31N 142 11 E
Ashikaga, Japan .... 31 F9 36 28N 139 29 E
Ashington, U.K. 12 B6 55 11N   1 33W
Ashizuri-Uwaki △, Japan .. 31 H6 32 56N 132 32 E
Ashizuri-Zaki, Japan .... 31 H6 32 44N 133 0 E
Ashkarkot, Afghan. ..... 42 C2 33 3N 67 58 E
Ashkhabad = Ashgabat,
  Turkmenistan .... 28 F6 38 0N 57 50 E
Āshkhāneh, Iran .... 45 B8 37 26N 56 55 E
Ashland, Kans., U.S.A. ... 81 G5 37 11N 99 46W
Ashland, Ky., U.S.A. 82 F4 38 28N 82 38W
Ashland, Mont., U.S.A. ... 76 D10 45 36N 106 16W
Ashland, Ohio, U.S.A. ... 84 F2 40 52N 82 19W
Ashland, Oreg., U.S.A. ... 76 E2 42 12N 122 43W
Ashland, Pa., U.S.A. 85 F8 40 45N 76 22W
Ashland, Va., U.S.A. 82 G7 37 46N 77 29W
Ashland, Wis., U.S.A. ... 80 B9 46 35N 90 53W
Ashley, N. Dak., U.S.A. .. 80 B5 46 2N 99 22W
Ashley, Pa., U.S.A. 85 E9 41 12N 75 55W
Ashmore and Cartier Is., Ind. Oc. . 60 B3 12 14S 123 5 E
Ashmore Reef, Australia .. 60 B3 12 14S 123 5 E
Ashmyany, Belarus ...... 9 J21 54 26N 25 52 E
Ashokan Reservoir, U.S.A. . 85 E10 41 56N 74 13W
Ashqelon, Israel .... 46 D3 31 42N 34 35 E

Ashta, India ... 42 H7 23 1N 76 43 E
Ashtabula, U.S.A. ... 84 E4 41 52N 80 47W
Ashton, S. Africa ... 56 E3 33 50S 20 5 E
Ashton, U.S.A. ... 76 D8 44 4N 111 27W
Ashuanipi, L., Canada ... 73 B6 52 45N 66 15W
Ashuapmushuan →, Canada ... 72 C5 48 37N 72 20W
Ashville, U.S.A. ... 84 F6 40 34N 78 33W
Asia ... 26 E11 45 0N 75 0 E
Asia, Kepulauan, Indonesia ... 37 D8 1 0N 131 13 E
Asifabad, India ... 40 K11 19 20N 79 24 E
Asinara, Italy ... 22 D3 41 4N 8 16 E
Asinara, G. dell', Italy ... 22 D3 41 0N 8 30 E
Asino, Russia ... 28 D9 57 0N 86 0 E
Asipovichy, Belarus ... 17 B15 53 19N 28 33 E
'Asir □, Si. Arabia ... 47 D3 18 40N 42 30 E
Asir, Ras, Somali Rep. ... 47 E5 11 55N 51 10 E
Askersund, Sweden ... 9 G16 58 53N 14 55 E
Askham, S. Africa ... 56 D3 26 59S 20 47 E
Askim, Norway ... 9 G14 59 35N 11 10 E
Askja, Iceland ... 8 D5 65 3N 16 48W
Askøy, Norway ... 9 F11 60 29N 5 10 E
Asmara = Asmera, Eritrea ... 47 D2 15 19N 38 55 E
Asmera, Eritrea ... 47 D2 15 19N 38 55 E
Åsnen, Sweden ... 9 H16 56 37N 14 45 E
Aso Kuju △, Japan ... 31 H5 32 53N 131 6 E
Aspatria, U.K. ... 12 C4 54 47N 3 19W
Aspen, U.S.A. ... 77 G10 39 11N 106 49W
Aspermont, U.S.A. ... 81 J4 33 8N 100 14W
Aspiring, Mt., N.Z. ... 59 L2 44 23S 168 46 E
Asprókavos, Ákra, Greece ... 25 B4 39 21N 20 6 E
Aspur, India ... 42 H6 23 58N 74 7 E
Asquith, Canada ... 71 C7 52 8N 107 13W
Assab = Aseb, Eritrea ... 47 E3 13 0N 42 40 E
Assam □, India ... 41 G18 26 0N 93 0 E
Assateague Island ○, U.S.A. ... 82 F8 38 15N 75 10W
Asse, Belgium ... 15 D4 50 24N 4 10 E
Assen, Neths. ... 15 A6 53 0N 6 35 E
Assiniboia, Canada ... 71 D7 49 40N 105 59W
Assiniboine →, Canada ... 71 D9 49 53N 97 8W
Assiniboine, Mt., Canada ... 70 C5 50 52N 115 39W
Assis, Brazil ... 95 A5 22 40S 50 20W
Assisi, Italy ... 22 C5 43 4N 12 37 E
Assynt, L., U.K. ... 11 C3 58 10N 5 3W
Astana, Kazakhstan ... 28 D8 51 10N 71 30 E
Āstāneh, Iran ... 45 B6 37 17N 49 59 E
Astara, Azerbaijan ... 19 G8 38 30N 48 50 E
Asteroúsia, Greece ... 25 E7 34 59N 25 3 E
Asti, Italy ... 20 D8 44 54N 8 12 E
Astipálaia, Greece ... 23 F12 36 32N 26 22 E
Astorga, Spain ... 21 A2 42 29N 6 8W
Astoria, U.S.A. ... 78 D3 46 11N 123 50W
Astrakhan, Russia ... 19 E8 46 25N 48 5 E
Asturias □, Spain ... 21 A3 43 15N 6 0W
Asunción, Paraguay ... 94 B4 25 10S 57 30W
Asunción Nochixtlán, Mexico ... 87 D5 17 28N 97 14W
Aswa →, Uganda ... 54 B3 3 43N 31 55 E
Aswa-Lolim ○, Uganda ... 54 B3 2 43N 31 35 E
Aswân, Egypt ... 51 D12 24 4N 32 57 E
Aswan Dam = Sadd el Aali, Egypt ... 51 D12 23 54N 32 54 E
Asyût, Egypt ... 51 C12 27 11N 31 4 E
At Ţafilah, Jordan ... 46 E4 30 45N 35 30 E
At Ţafilah □, Jordan ... 46 E4 30 45N 35 30 E
Aţ Ţā'if, Si. Arabia ... 47 C3 21 5N 40 27 E
At Ta'mîm □, Iraq ... 44 C5 35 30N 44 20 E
Aţ Ţirāq, Si. Arabia ... 44 E5 27 19N 44 33 E
Aţ Ţubayq, Si. Arabia ... 44 D3 29 30N 37 0 E
Atacama □, Chile ... 94 B2 27 30S 70 0W
Atacama, Desierto de, Chile ... 94 A2 24 0S 69 20W
Atacama, Salar de, Chile ... 94 A2 23 30S 68 20W
Atalaya, Peru ... 92 F4 10 45S 73 50W
Atalaya de Femes, Canary Is. ... 24 F6 28 56N 13 47W
Atami, Japan ... 31 G9 35 5N 139 4 E
Atapupu, E. Timor ... 37 F6 9 0S 124 51 E
Atâr, Mauritania ... 50 D3 20 30N 13 5W
Atari, Pakistan ... 42 D6 30 56N 74 2 E
Atascadero, U.S.A. ... 78 K6 35 29N 120 40W
Atasu, Kazakhstan ... 28 E8 48 30N 71 0 E
Atatürk Baraji, Turkey ... 19 G6 37 28N 38 30 E
Atauro, E. Timor ... 37 F7 8 10S 125 30 E
'Atbara, Sudan ... 51 E12 17 42N 33 59 E
'Atbara, Nahr →, Sudan ... 51 E12 17 40N 33 56 E
Atbasar, Kazakhstan ... 28 D7 51 48N 68 20 E
Atchafalaya B., U.S.A. ... 81 L9 29 25N 91 25W
Atchison, U.S.A. ... 80 F7 39 34N 95 7W
Āteshān, Iran ... 45 C7 35 35N 52 37 E
Ath, Belgium ... 15 D3 50 38N 3 47 E
Athabasca, Canada ... 70 C6 54 45N 113 20W
Athabasca →, Canada ... 71 B6 58 40N 110 50W
Athabasca, L., Canada ... 71 B7 59 15N 109 15W
Athabasca Sand Dunes ○, Canada ... 71 B7 59 4N 108 43W
Athboy, Ireland ... 10 C5 53 37N 6 56W
Athenry, Ireland ... 10 C3 53 18N 8 44W
Athens = Athínai, Greece ... 23 F10 37 58N 23 46 E
Athens, Ala., U.S.A. ... 83 H2 34 48N 86 58W
Athens, Ga., U.S.A. ... 83 J4 33 57N 83 23W
Athens, N.Y., U.S.A. ... 85 D11 42 16N 73 49W
Athens, Ohio, U.S.A. ... 82 F4 39 20N 82 6W
Athens, Pa., U.S.A. ... 85 E8 41 57N 76 31W
Athens, Tenn., U.S.A. ... 83 H3 35 27N 84 36W
Athens, Tex., U.S.A. ... 81 J7 32 12N 95 51W
Atherley, Canada ... 84 B5 44 37N 79 20W
Atherton, Australia ... 62 B4 17 17S 145 30 E
Athienou, Cyprus ... 25 D12 35 3N 33 32 E
Athínai, Greece ... 23 F10 37 58N 23 46 E
Athlone, Ireland ... 10 C4 53 25N 7 56W
Athna, Cyprus ... 25 D12 35 3N 33 47 E
Athol, U.S.A. ... 85 D12 42 36N 72 14W
Atholl, Forest of, U.K. ... 11 E5 56 51N 3 50W
Atholville, Canada ... 73 C6 47 59N 66 43W
Áthos, Greece ... 23 D11 40 9N 24 22 E
Athy, Ireland ... 10 C5 53 0N 7 0W
Ati, Chad ... 51 F9 13 13N 18 20 E
Atiak, Uganda ... 54 B3 3 12N 32 2 E
Atik L., Canada ... 71 B9 55 15N 96 0W
Atikaki ○, Canada ... 71 C9 51 30N 95 31W
Atikameg →, Canada ... 72 B3 52 30N 82 46W
Atikokan, Canada ... 72 C1 48 45N 91 37W
Atikonak L., Canada ... 73 B7 52 40N 64 32W
Atitlán △, Cent. Amer. ... 87 E6 14 38N 91 10W
Atka, Russia ... 29 C16 60 50N 151 48 E
Atka I., U.S.A. ... 68 C2 52 7N 174 30W
Atkinson, U.S.A. ... 80 D5 42 32N 98 59W
Atlanta, Ga., U.S.A. ... 83 J3 33 45N 84 23W
Atlanta, Tex., U.S.A. ... 81 J7 33 7N 94 10W
Atlantic, U.S.A. ... 80 E7 41 24N 95 1W
Atlantic City, U.S.A. ... 82 F8 39 21N 74 27W
Atlantic-Indian Basin, Antarctica ... 5 B4 60 0S 30 0 E

Atlantic Ocean ... 2 E9 0 0 20 0W
Atlas Mts. = Haut Atlas, Morocco ... 50 B4 32 30N 5 0W
Atlin, Canada ... 70 B2 59 31N 133 41W
Atlin →, Canada ... 70 B2 59 10N 134 30W
Atlin, L., Canada ... 70 B2 59 26N 133 45W
Atmore, U.S.A. ... 83 K2 31 2N 87 29W
Atoka, U.S.A. ... 81 H6 34 23N 96 8W
Atolia, U.S.A. ... 79 K9 35 19N 117 37W
Atrai →, Bangla. ... 43 G13 24 7N 89 22 E
Atrak = Atrek →, Turkmenistan ... 45 B8 37 35N 53 58 E
Atrauli, India ... 42 E8 28 2N 78 20 E
Atrek →, Turkmenistan ... 45 B8 37 35N 53 58 E
Atsuta, Japan ... 30 C10 43 24N 141 26 E
Attalla, U.S.A. ... 83 H2 34 1N 86 6W
Attapu, Laos ... 38 E6 14 48N 106 50 E
Attáviros, Greece ... 25 C9 36 12N 27 50 E
Attawapiskat, Canada ... 72 B3 52 56N 82 24W
Attawapiskat →, Canada ... 72 B3 52 57N 82 18W
Attawapiskat L., Canada ... 72 B2 52 18N 87 54W
Attica, Ind., U.S.A. ... 82 E2 40 18N 87 15W
Attica, Ohio, U.S.A. ... 84 E2 41 4N 82 53W
Attikamagen L., Canada ... 73 B6 55 0N 66 30W
Attleboro, U.S.A. ... 85 E13 41 57N 71 17W
Attock, Pakistan ... 42 C5 33 52N 72 20 E
Attopeu = Attapu, Laos ... 38 E6 14 48N 106 50 E
Attu I., U.S.A. ... 68 C1 52 55N 172 55 E
Attur, India ... 40 P11 11 35N 78 30 E
Atuel →, Argentina ... 94 D2 36 17S 66 50W
Åtvidaberg, Sweden ... 9 G17 58 12N 16 0 E
Atwater, U.S.A. ... 78 H6 37 21N 120 37W
Atwood, Canada ... 84 C3 43 40N 81 1W
Atwood, U.S.A. ... 80 F4 39 48N 101 3W
Atyraū, Kazakhstan ... 19 E9 47 5N 52 0 E
Au Sable →, U.S.A. ... 84 B1 44 25N 83 20W
Au Sable →, U.S.A. ... 82 C4 44 25N 83 20W
Au Sable Forks, U.S.A. ... 85 B11 44 27N 73 41W
Au Sable Pt., U.S.A. ... 84 B1 44 20N 83 20W
Aubagne, France ... 20 E6 43 17N 5 37 E
Aubarca, C. d', Spain ... 24 B7 39 4N 1 22 E
Aube →, France ... 20 B5 48 34N 3 43 E
Auberry, U.S.A. ... 78 H7 37 7N 119 29W
Auburn, Ala., U.S.A. ... 83 J3 32 36N 85 29W
Auburn, Calif., U.S.A. ... 78 G5 38 54N 121 4W
Auburn, Ind., U.S.A. ... 82 E3 41 22N 85 4W
Auburn, Maine, U.S.A. ... 83 C10 44 6N 70 14W
Auburn, N.Y., U.S.A. ... 85 D8 42 56N 76 34W
Auburn, Nebr., U.S.A. ... 80 E7 40 23N 95 51W
Auburn, Pa., U.S.A. ... 85 F8 40 36N 76 6W
Auburn, Wash., U.S.A. ... 78 C4 47 18N 122 14W
Auburn Ra., Australia ... 63 D5 25 15S 150 30 E
Auburndale, U.S.A. ... 83 L5 28 4N 81 48W
Aubusson, France ... 20 D5 45 57N 2 11 E
Auch, France ... 20 E4 43 39N 0 36 E
Auchterarder, U.K. ... 11 E5 56 18N 3 41W
Auchtermuchty, U.K. ... 11 E5 56 18N 3 13W
Auckland, N.Z. ... 59 G5 36 52S 174 46 E
Auckland Is., Pac. Oc. ... 64 N8 50 40S 166 5 E
Aude →, France ... 20 E5 43 13N 3 14 E
Auden, Canada ... 72 B2 50 14N 87 53W
Audubon, U.S.A. ... 80 E7 41 43N 94 56W
Augathella, Australia ... 63 D4 25 48S 146 35 E
Aughnacloy, U.K. ... 10 B5 54 25N 6 59W
Augrabies Falls, S. Africa ... 56 D3 28 35S 20 20 E
Augrabies Falls △, S. Africa ... 56 D3 28 40S 20 22 E
Augsburg, Germany ... 16 D6 48 25N 10 52 E
Augusta, Australia ... 61 F2 34 19S 115 9 E
Augusta, Italy ... 22 F6 37 13N 15 13 E
Augusta, Ark., U.S.A. ... 81 H9 35 17N 91 22W
Augusta, Ga., U.S.A. ... 83 J5 33 28N 81 58W
Augusta, Kans., U.S.A. ... 81 G6 37 41N 96 59W
Augusta, Maine, U.S.A. ... 69 D13 44 19N 69 47W
Augusta, Mont., U.S.A. ... 76 C7 47 30N 112 24W
Augustów, Poland ... 17 B12 53 51N 23 0 E
Augustus, Mt., Australia ... 61 D2 24 20S 116 50 E
Augustus I., Australia ... 60 C3 15 20S 124 30 E
Aukum, U.S.A. ... 78 G6 38 34N 120 43W
Auld, L., Australia ... 60 D3 22 25S 123 50 E
Ault, U.S.A. ... 80 E2 40 35N 104 44W
Aunis, France ... 20 C3 46 5N 0 50W
Auponhia, Indonesia ... 37 E7 1 58S 125 27 E
Aur, Pulau, Malaysia ... 39 L5 2 35N 104 10 E
Auraiya, India ... 43 F8 26 28N 79 33 E
Aurangabad, Bihar, India ... 43 G11 24 45N 84 18 E
Aurangabad, Maharashtra, India ... 40 K9 19 50N 75 23 E
Aurich, Germany ... 16 B4 53 28N 7 28 E
Aurillac, France ... 20 D5 44 55N 2 26 E
Aurora, Canada ... 84 C5 44 0N 79 28W
Aurora, S. Africa ... 56 E2 32 40S 18 29 E
Aurora, Colo., U.S.A. ... 80 F2 39 44N 104 52W
Aurora, Ill., U.S.A. ... 82 E1 41 45N 88 19W
Aurora, Mo., U.S.A. ... 81 G8 36 58N 93 43W
Aurora, N.Y., U.S.A. ... 85 D8 42 45N 76 42W
Aurora, Nebr., U.S.A. ... 80 E6 40 52N 98 0W
Aurora, Ohio, U.S.A. ... 84 E3 41 21N 81 20W
Aurukun, Australia ... 62 A3 13 20S 141 45 E
Aus, Namibia ... 56 D2 26 35S 16 12 E
Ausable →, Canada ... 84 C3 43 19N 81 46W
Auschwitz = Oświęcim, Poland ... 17 C10 50 2N 19 11 E
Austin, Minn., U.S.A. ... 80 D8 43 40N 92 58W
Austin, Nev., U.S.A. ... 76 G5 39 30N 117 4W
Austin, Pa., U.S.A. ... 84 E6 41 38N 78 6W
Austin, Tex., U.S.A. ... 81 K6 30 17N 97 45W
Austin, L., Australia ... 61 E2 27 40S 118 0 E
Austin I., Canada ... 71 A10 61 10N 94 0W
Austra, Norway ... 8 D14 65 8N 11 55 E
Austral Is. = Tubuai Is., French Polynesia ... 65 K13 25 0S 150 0W
Austral Seamount Chain, Pac. Oc. ... 65 K13 24 0S 150 0W
Australia ■, Oceania ... 64 K5 23 0S 135 0 E
Australian Capital Territory □, Australia ... 63 F4 35 30S 149 0 E
Australind, Australia ... 61 F2 33 17S 115 42 E
Austria ■, Europe ... 16 E8 47 0N 14 0 E
Austvågøy, Norway ... 8 B16 68 20N 14 40 E
Autlán, Mexico ... 86 D4 19 40N 104 30W
Autun, France ... 20 C6 46 58N 4 17 E
Auvergne, Mts. d', France ... 20 D5 45 20N 2 55 E
Auvergne ⊠, France ... 20 D5 45 20N 3 15 E
Auxerre, France ... 20 C5 47 48N 3 32 E
Ava, U.S.A. ... 81 G8 36 57N 92 40W
Avallon, France ... 20 C5 47 30N 3 53 E
Avalon, U.S.A. ... 79 M8 33 21N 118 20W
Avalon Pen., Canada ... 73 C9 47 30N 53 20W
Avanos, Turkey ... 44 B2 38 43N 34 51 E
Avaré, Brazil ... 95 A6 23 4S 48 58W
Avawatz Mts., U.S.A. ... 79 K10 35 40N 116 30W
Aveiro, Brazil ... 93 D7 3 10S 55 5W

Aveiro, Portugal ... 21 B1 40 37N 8 38W
Āvej, Iran ... 45 C6 35 40N 49 15 E
Avellaneda, Argentina ... 94 C4 34 50S 58 10W
Avellino, Italy ... 22 D6 40 54N 14 47 E
Avenal, U.S.A. ... 78 K6 36 0N 120 8W
Aversa, Italy ... 22 D6 40 58N 14 12 E
Avery, U.S.A. ... 76 C6 47 15N 115 49W
Aves, Is. las, Venezuela ... 89 D6 12 0N 67 30W
Avesta, Sweden ... 9 F17 60 9N 16 10 E
Avezzano, Italy ... 22 C5 42 2N 13 25 E
Aviá Terai, Argentina ... 94 B3 26 45S 60 50W
Aviemore, U.K. ... 11 D5 57 12N 3 50W
Avignon, France ... 20 E6 43 57N 4 50 E
Ávila, Spain ... 21 B3 40 39N 4 43W
Avila Beach, U.S.A. ... 79 K6 35 11N 120 44W
Avilés, Spain ... 21 A3 43 35N 5 57W
Avis, U.S.A. ... 84 E7 41 11N 77 19W
Avoca, U.S.A. ... 84 D7 42 25N 77 25W
Avoca →, Ireland ... 10 D5 52 48N 6 10W
Avola, Canada ... 70 C5 51 45N 119 19W
Avola, Italy ... 22 F6 36 56N 15 7 E
Avon, U.S.A. ... 84 D7 42 55N 77 45W
Avon →, Australia ... 61 F2 31 40S 116 7 E
Avon →, Bristol, U.K. ... 13 F5 51 29N 2 41W
Avon →, Dorset, U.K. ... 13 G6 50 44N 1 46W
Avon →, Warks., U.K. ... 13 E5 52 0N 2 8W
Avon Park, U.S.A. ... 83 M5 27 36N 81 31W
Avondale, Zimbabwe ... 55 F3 17 43S 30 58 E
Avonlea, Canada ... 71 D8 50 0N 105 0W
Avonmore, Canada ... 85 A10 45 10N 74 58W
Avonmouth, U.K. ... 13 F5 51 30N 2 42W
Avranches, France ... 20 B3 48 40N 1 20W
A'waj →, Syria ... 46 B5 33 23N 36 20 E
Awaji-Shima, Japan ... 31 G7 34 30N 134 50 E
'Awālī, Bahrain ... 45 E6 26 0N 50 30 E
Awantipur, India ... 43 C6 33 55N 75 3 E
Awasa, Ethiopia ... 47 F2 7 2N 38 28 E
Awash, Ethiopia ... 47 F3 9 1N 40 10 E
Awatere →, N.Z. ... 59 J5 41 37S 174 10 E
Awbārī, Libya ... 51 C8 26 46N 12 57 E
Awbārī, Idehan, Libya ... 51 C8 27 10N 11 30 E
Awe, L., U.K. ... 11 E3 56 17N 5 16W
Awjilah, Libya ... 51 C10 29 8N 21 7 E
Axe →, U.K. ... 13 F5 50 42N 3 4W
Axel Heiberg I., Canada ... 4 B3 80 0N 90 0W
Axim, Ghana ... 50 H5 4 51N 2 15W
Axiós →, Greece ... 23 D10 40 57N 22 35 E
Axminster, U.K. ... 13 G4 50 46N 3 0W
Ayabaca, Peru ... 92 D3 4 40S 79 53W
Ayabe, Japan ... 31 G7 35 20N 135 20 E
Ayacucho, Argentina ... 94 D4 37 5S 58 20W
Ayacucho, Peru ... 92 F4 13 0S 74 0W
Ayaguz, Kazakhstan ... 28 E9 48 10N 80 10 E
Ayamonte, Spain ... 21 D2 37 12N 7 24W
Ayan, Russia ... 29 D14 56 30N 138 16 E
Ayaviri, Peru ... 92 F4 14 50S 70 35W
Aydin, Turkey ... 23 F12 37 51N 27 51 E
Ayer, U.S.A. ... 85 D13 42 34N 71 35W
Ayer Hitam, Malaysia ... 39 c 5 24N 100 16 E
Ayer's Cliff, Canada ... 85 A12 45 10N 72 3W
Ayers Rock, Australia ... 61 E5 25 23S 131 5 E
Ayia Aikaterini, Ákra, Greece ... 25 A3 39 50N 19 50 E
Ayia Dhéka, Greece ... 25 D6 35 3N 24 58 E
Ayia Gálini, Greece ... 25 D6 35 6N 24 41 E
Ayia Napa, Cyprus ... 25 E13 34 59N 34 0 E
Ayia Phyla, Cyprus ... 25 E12 34 43N 33 1 E
Ayia Varvára, Greece ... 25 D7 35 8N 25 1 E
Ayios Amvrósios, Cyprus ... 25 D12 35 20N 33 35 E
Ayios Evstrátios, Greece ... 23 E11 39 34N 24 58 E
Ayios Ioánnis, Ákra, Greece ... 25 D7 35 20N 25 40 E
Ayios Isídhoros, Greece ... 25 C9 36 9N 27 51 E
Ayios Matthaíos, Greece ... 25 B3 39 30N 19 47 E
Ayios Nikólaos, Greece ... 25 D7 35 11N 25 41 E
Ayios Seryios, Cyprus ... 25 D12 35 12N 33 53 E
Ayios Theodhoros, Cyprus ... 25 D13 35 22N 34 1 E
Aykino, Russia ... 18 B8 62 15N 49 56 E
Aylesbury, U.K. ... 13 F7 51 49N 0 49W
Aylmer, Canada ... 84 D4 42 46N 80 59W
Aylmer, L., Canada ... 68 B8 64 0N 110 8W
'Ayn, Wādī al, Oman ... 45 F7 22 15N 55 28 E
Ayn Dār, Si. Arabia ... 45 E7 25 55N 49 10 E
Ayn Zālah, Iraq ... 44 B4 36 45N 42 35 E
Ayolas, Paraguay ... 94 B4 27 10S 56 59W
Ayon, Ostrov, Russia ... 29 C17 69 50N 169 0 E
'Ayoûn el 'Atroûs, Mauritania ... 50 E4 16 38N 9 37W
Ayr, Australia ... 62 B4 19 35S 147 25 E
Ayr, Canada ... 84 C4 43 17N 80 27W
Ayr, U.K. ... 11 F4 55 28N 4 38W
Ayr →, U.K. ... 11 F4 55 28N 4 38W
Ayre, Pt. of, U.K. ... 12 C3 54 25N 4 21W
Ayton, Australia ... 62 B4 15 56S 145 22 E
Aytos, Bulgaria ... 23 C12 42 42N 27 16 E
Ayu, Kepulauan, Indonesia ... 37 D8 0 35N 131 5 E
Ayutla, Guatemala ... 88 D1 14 40N 92 10W
Ayutla, Mexico ... 87 D5 16 58N 99 17W
Ayvacık, Turkey ... 23 E12 39 36N 26 24 E
Ayvalık, Turkey ... 23 E12 39 20N 26 46 E
Az Zabadānī, Syria ... 46 B5 33 43N 36 5 E
Az Zāhiriyah, West Bank ... 46 D3 31 25N 34 58 E
Aẓ Ẓahrān, Si. Arabia ... 45 E6 26 10N 50 7 E
Az Zarqā, Jordan ... 46 C5 32 5N 36 4 E
Az Zarqā', U.A.E. ... 45 E7 24 53N 53 4 E
Az Zarqā □, Jordan ... 46 C5 32 5N 36 4 E
Az Zāwiyah, Libya ... 51 B8 32 52N 12 56 E
Az Zibār, Iraq ... 44 B5 36 52N 44 4 E
Az Zilfi, Si. Arabia ... 44 E5 26 12N 44 52 E
Az Zubayr, Iraq ... 44 D5 30 26N 47 40 E
Azad Kashmir □, Pakistan ... 43 C5 33 50N 73 50 E
Azamgarh, India ... 43 F10 26 5N 83 13 E
Azángaro, Peru ... 92 F4 14 55S 70 13W
Āzar Shahr, Iran ... 44 B5 37 45N 45 59 E
Azaran, Iran ... 44 B5 37 25N 47 16 E
Āzarbāyjān = Azerbaijan ■, Asia ... 19 F8 40 20N 48 0 E
Āzarbāyjān-e Gharbī □, Iran ... 44 B5 37 0N 44 30 E
Āzarbāyjān-e Sharqī □, Iran ... 44 B5 37 20N 47 0 E
Azare, Nigeria ... 50 F8 11 55N 10 10 E
A'zāz, Syria ... 44 B3 36 36N 37 4 E
Azbine = Aïr, Niger ... 50 E7 18 30N 8 0 E
Azerbaijan ■, Asia ... 19 F8 40 20N 48 0 E
Azerbaijchan = Azerbaijan ■, Asia ... 19 F8 40 20N 48 0 E
Azimganj, India ... 43 G13 24 14N 88 16 E
Azogues, Ecuador ... 92 D3 2 35S 78 0W
Azores = Açores, Is. dos, Atl. Oc. ... 50 A1 38 0N 27 0W
Azov, Russia ... 19 E6 47 3N 39 25 E
Azov, Sea of, Europe ... 19 E6 46 0N 36 30 E

Azovskoye More = Azov, Sea of, Europe ... 19 E6 46 0N 36 30 E
Azraq ash Shīshān, Jordan ... 46 D5 31 50N 36 49 E
Aztec, U.S.A. ... 77 H10 36 49N 107 59W
Azúa de Compostela, Dom. Rep. ... 89 C5 18 25N 70 44W
Azuaga, Spain ... 21 C3 38 16N 5 39W
Azuero, Pen. de, Panama ... 88 E3 7 30N 80 30W
Azul, Argentina ... 94 D4 36 42S 59 43W
Azusa, U.S.A. ... 79 L9 34 8N 117 52W

B

Ba Be △, Vietnam ... 38 A5 22 25N 105 37 E
Ba Don, Vietnam ... 38 D6 17 45N 106 26 E
Ba Dong, Vietnam ... 39 H6 9 40N 106 33 E
Ba Ngoi = Cam Lam, Vietnam ... 39 G7 11 54N 109 10 E
Ba Tri, Vietnam ... 39 G6 10 2N 106 36 E
Ba Vì △, Vietnam ... 38 B5 21 1N 105 22 E
Ba Xian = Bazhou, China ... 34 E9 39 8N 116 22 E
Baa, Indonesia ... 37 F6 10 50S 123 0 E
Baardeere = Bardera, Somali Rep. ... 47 G3 2 20N 42 27 E
Baarle-Nassau, Belgium ... 15 C4 51 27N 4 56 E
Bab el Mandeb, Red Sea ... 47 E3 12 35N 43 25 E
Bābā, Koh-i-, Afghan. ... 40 B5 34 30N 67 0 E
Bābā Burnu, Turkey ... 23 E12 39 29N 26 2 E
Bābā Kalū, Iran ... 45 D6 30 7N 50 49 E
Babadag, Romania ... 17 F15 44 53N 28 44 E
Babaeski, Turkey ... 23 D12 41 26N 27 6 E
Babahoyo, Ecuador ... 92 D3 1 40S 79 30W
Babai = Sarju →, India ... 43 F9 27 21N 81 23 E
Babar, Indonesia ... 37 F7 8 0S 129 30 E
Babar, Pakistan ... 42 D3 31 7N 69 32 E
Babarkach, Pakistan ... 42 E3 29 45N 68 0 E
Babb, U.S.A. ... 76 B7 48 51N 113 27W
Baberu, India ... 43 G9 25 33N 80 43 E
Babi Besar, Pulau, Malaysia ... 39 L4 2 25N 103 59 E
Babīl □, Iraq ... 44 C5 32 30N 44 30 E
Babinda, Australia ... 62 B4 17 20S 145 56 E
Babine, Canada ... 70 B3 55 22N 126 37W
Babine →, Canada ... 70 B3 55 45N 127 44W
Babine L., Canada ... 70 C3 54 48N 126 0W
Babo, Indonesia ... 37 E8 2 30S 133 30 E
Bābol, Iran ... 45 B7 36 40N 52 50 E
Bābol Sar, Iran ... 45 B7 36 45N 52 45 E
Babruysk, Belarus ... 17 B15 53 10N 29 15 E
Babuhri, India ... 42 F3 26 49N 69 43 E
Babusar Pass, Pakistan ... 43 B5 35 12N 73 59 E
Babuyan Chan., Phil. ... 37 A6 18 40N 121 30 E
Babylon, Iraq ... 44 C5 32 34N 44 22 E
Bac Can, Vietnam ... 38 A5 22 8N 105 49 E
Bac Giang, Vietnam ... 38 B6 21 16N 106 11 E
Bac Lieu, Vietnam ... 39 H5 9 17N 105 43 E
Bac Ninh, Vietnam ... 38 B6 21 13N 106 4 E
Bac Phan, Vietnam ... 38 B5 22 0N 105 0 E
Bac Quang, Vietnam ... 38 A5 22 30N 104 48 E
Bacabal, Brazil ... 93 D10 4 15S 44 45W
Bacalar, Mexico ... 87 D7 18 50N 87 27W
Bacan, Kepulauan, Indonesia ... 37 E7 0 35S 127 30 E
Bacarra, Phil. ... 37 A6 18 15N 120 37 E
Bacău, Romania ... 17 E14 46 35N 26 55 E
Bacerac, Mexico ... 86 A3 30 18N 108 50W
Bach Long Vi, Dao, Vietnam ... 38 B6 20 10N 107 40 E
Bach Ma △, Vietnam ... 38 D6 16 11N 107 49 E
Bachhwara, India ... 43 G11 25 35N 85 54 E
Back →, Canada ... 68 B9 65 10N 104 0W
Bacolod, Phil. ... 37 B6 10 40N 122 57 E
Bacuk, Malaysia ... 39 J4 6 4N 102 25 E
Bād, Iran ... 45 C7 33 41N 52 1 E
Bad →, U.S.A. ... 80 C4 44 21N 100 22W
Bad Axe, U.S.A. ... 84 C2 43 48N 83 0W
Bad Ischl, Austria ... 16 E7 47 44N 13 38 E
Bad Kissingen, Germany ... 16 C6 50 11N 10 4 E
Bad Lands, U.S.A. ... 80 D3 43 40N 102 10W
Bada Barabil, India ... 43 H11 22 7N 85 24 E
Badajós, L., Brazil ... 92 D6 3 15S 62 50W
Badajoz, Spain ... 21 C2 38 50N 6 59W
Badakhshān □, Afghan. ... 40 A7 36 30N 71 0 E
Badalona, Spain ... 21 B7 41 26N 2 15 E
Badalzai, Afghan. ... 42 E1 29 50N 65 35 E
Badampahar, India ... 41 H15 22 10N 86 10 E
Badanah, Si. Arabia ... 44 D4 30 58N 41 30 E
Badarinath, India ... 43 D8 30 44N 79 29 E
Badas, Kepulauan, Indonesia ... 36 D3 0 45N 107 5 E
Baddo →, Pakistan ... 40 F4 28 0N 64 20 E
Bade, Indonesia ... 37 F9 7 10S 139 35 E
Baden, Austria ... 16 D9 48 1N 16 13 E
Baden, U.S.A. ... 84 F4 40 38N 80 14W
Baden-Baden, Germany ... 16 D5 48 44N 8 13 E
Baden-Württemberg □, Germany ... 16 D5 48 20N 8 40 E
Badgastein, Austria ... 16 E7 47 7N 13 9 E
Badger, Canada ... 73 C8 49 0N 56 4W
Badger, U.S.A. ... 78 J7 36 38N 119 1W
Bādghīs □, Afghan. ... 40 B3 35 0N 63 0 E
Badgingarra △, Australia ... 61 F2 30 23S 115 22 E
Badgom, India ... 43 B6 34 1N 74 45 E
Badin, Pakistan ... 42 G3 24 38N 68 54 E
Badlands △, U.S.A. ... 80 D3 43 38N 102 56W
Badrah, Iraq ... 44 C5 33 6N 45 58 E
Badrinath, India ... 43 D8 30 44N 79 29 E
Badulla, Sri Lanka ... 40 R12 7 1N 81 7 E
Badung, Selat, Indonesia ... 37 K18 8 40S 115 22 E
Baena, Spain ... 21 D3 37 37N 4 20W
Baeza, Spain ... 21 D4 37 57N 3 25W
Baffin B., Canada ... 69 A13 72 0N 64 0W
Baffin I., Canada ... 69 B12 68 0N 75 0W
Bafing →, Mali ... 50 F3 13 49N 10 50W
Bafliyún, Syria ... 44 B3 36 37N 36 59 E
Bafoulabé, Mali ... 50 F3 13 50N 10 55W
Bafoussam, Cameroon ... 52 C2 5 28N 10 25 E
Bāfq, Iran ... 45 D7 31 40N 55 25 E
Bafra, Turkey ... 19 F6 41 34N 35 54 E
Bāft, Iran ... 45 D8 29 15N 56 38 E
Bafwasende, Dem. Rep. of the Congo ... 54 B2 1 3N 27 5 E
Bagamoyo, Tanzania ... 54 D4 6 28S 38 55 E
Bagan Datoh, Malaysia ... 39 L3 3 59N 100 47 E
Bagan Serai, Malaysia ... 39 K3 5 1N 100 32 E
Baganga, Phil. ... 37 C7 7 34N 126 33 E
Bagani, Namibia ... 56 B3 18 7S 21 41 E
Bagansiapiapi, Indonesia ... 36 D2 2 12N 100 50 E
Bagasra, India ... 42 J4 21 30N 71 0 E
Bagaud, India ... 42 H6 22 19N 75 53 E
Bagdad, U.S.A. ... 79 L11 34 35N 115 53W

Bagdarin, Russia .... 29 D12 54 26N 113 36 E
Bagé, Brazil 95 C5 31 20S 54 15W
Bagenalstown = Muine Bheag,
  Ireland 10 D5 52 42N 6 58W
Baggs, U.S.A. 76 F10 41 2N 107 39W
Bagh, Pakistan .... 43 C5 33 59N 73 45 E
Baghain →, India .... 43 G9 25 32N 81 1 E
Baghdād, Iraq .... 44 C5 33 20N 44 30 E
Bagheria, Italy .... 22 E5 38 5N 13 30 E
Baghlān, Afghan. .... 40 A6 32 12N 68 46 E
Baghlān □, Afghan. .... 40 B6 36 0N 68 30 E
Bagley, U.S.A. 80 B7 47 32N 95 24W
Bago = Pegu, Burma .... 41 L20 17 20N 96 29 E
Bagodar, India .... 43 G11 24 5N 85 52 E
Bagrationovsk, Russia .... 9 J19 54 23N 20 39 E
Baguio, Phil. .... 37 A6 16 26N 120 34 E
Bah, India .... 43 F8 26 53N 78 36 E
Bahadurganj, India .... 43 F12 26 16N 87 49 E
Bahadurgarh, India .... 42 E7 28 40N 76 57 E
Bahama, Canal Viejo de,
  W. Indies 88 B4 22 10N 77 30W
Bahamas ■, N. Amer. 89 B5 24 0N 75 0W
Baharampur, India .... 43 G13 24 2N 88 27 E
Baharu Pandan = Pandan,
  Malaysia .... 39 d 1 32N 103 46 E
Bahawalnagar, Pakistan .... 42 E5 30 0N 73 15 E
Bahawalpur, Pakistan .... 42 E4 29 24N 71 40 E
Baheri, India .... 43 E8 28 45N 79 34 E
Bahgul →, India .... 43 F8 27 45N 79 36 E
Bahi, Tanzania .... 54 D4 5 58S 35 21 E
Bahi Swamp, Tanzania .... 54 D4 6 10S 35 0 E
Bahía = Salvador, Brazil 93 F11 13 0S 38 30W
Bahía □, Brazil 93 F10 12 0S 42 0W
Bahía, Is. de la, Honduras 88 C2 16 45N 86 15W
Bahía Blanca, Argentina 94 D3 38 35S 62 13W
Bahía de Caráquez, Ecuador 92 D2 0 40S 80 27W
Bahía Honda, Cuba 88 B3 22 54N 83 10W
Bahía Laura, Argentina 96 F3 48 10S 66 30W
Bahía Negra, Paraguay 92 H7 20 5S 58 5W
Bahir Dar, Ethiopia .... 47 E2 11 37N 37 10 E
Bahmanzād, Iran .... 45 D6 31 15N 51 47 E
Bahr el Ghazāl □, Sudan .... 51 G11 7 0N 28 0 E
Bahrain ■, Asia .... 45 E6 26 0N 50 35 E
Bahror, India .... 42 F7 27 51N 76 20 E
Bāhū Kalāt, Iran .... 45 E9 25 43N 61 25 E
Bai Bung, Mui = Ca Mau, Mui,
  Vietnam .... 39 H5 8 38N 104 44 E
Bai Duc, Vietnam .... 38 C5 18 3N 105 49 E
Bai Thuong, Vietnam .... 38 C5 19 54N 105 23 E
Baia Mare, Romania .... 17 E12 47 40N 23 35 E
Baião, Brazil 93 D9 2 40S 49 40W
Baïbokoum, Chad .... 51 G9 7 46N 15 43 E
Baicheng, China .... 35 B12 45 38N 122 42 E
Baidoa, Somali Rep. .... 47 G3 3 8N 43 30 E
Baie-Comeau, Canada 73 C6 49 12N 68 10W
Baie-St-Paul, Canada 73 C5 47 28N 70 32W
Baie-Trinité, Canada 73 C6 49 25N 67 20W
Baie Verte, Canada 73 C8 49 55N 56 12W
Baihar, India .... 43 H9 22 6N 80 33 E
Baihe, China .... 34 H6 32 50N 110 5 E
Baijnath, India .... 43 E8 29 55N 79 37 E
Baikal, L. = Baykal, Oz., Russia .... 29 D11 53 0N 108 0 E
Baikunthpur, India .... 43 H10 23 15N 82 33 E
Baile Atha Cliath = Dublin,
  Ireland 10 C5 53 21N 6 15W
Băilești, Romania .... 17 F12 44 1N 23 20 E
Bainbridge, Ga., U.S.A. 83 K3 30 55N 84 35W
Bainbridge, N.Y., U.S.A. 85 D9 42 18N 75 29W
Baing, Indonesia .... 37 F6 10 14S 120 34 E
Bainiu, China .... 34 H7 32 50N 112 15 E
Ba'ir, Jordan .... 46 E5 30 45N 36 55 E
Bairiki = Tarawa, Kiribati .... 64 G9 1 30N 173 0 E
Bairin Youqi, China .... 35 C10 43 30N 118 35 E
Bairin Zuoqi, China .... 35 C10 43 58N 119 15 E
Bairnsdale, Australia .... 63 F4 37 48S 147 36 E
Baisha, China .... 34 G7 34 20N 112 32 E
Baitadi, Nepal .... 43 E9 29 35N 80 25 E
Baiyu Shan, China .... 34 F5 36 45N 104 14 E
Baiyin, China .... 34 F4 37 15N 107 30 E
Baj Baj, India .... 43 H13 22 30N 88 5 E
Baja, Hungary .... 17 E10 46 12N 18 59 E
Baja, Pta., Mexico 86 B1 29 50N 116 0W
Baja California, Mexico 86 A1 31 10N 115 12W
Baja California □, Mexico 86 B2 30 0N 115 0W
Baja California Sur □, Mexico 86 B2 25 50N 111 50W
Bajag, India .... 43 H9 22 40N 81 21 E
Bajamar, Canary Is. 24 F3 28 33N 16 20W
Bajana, India .... 42 H4 23 7N 71 49 E
Bajatrejo, Indonesia .... 37 J17 8 29S 114 19 E
Bajera, Indonesia .... 37 J18 8 31S 115 2 E
Bājgīrān, Iran .... 45 B8 37 36N 58 24 E
Bajimba, Mt., Australia .... 63 D5 29 17S 152 6 E
Bajo Nuevo, Caribbean 88 C4 15 40N 78 50W
Bajoga, Nigeria .... 51 F8 10 57N 11 20 E
Bajool, Australia .... 62 C5 23 40S 150 35 E
Bakel, Senegal 50 F3 14 56N 12 20W
Baker, Calif., U.S.A. 79 K10 35 16N 116 4W
Baker, Mont., U.S.A. 80 B2 46 22N 104 17W
Baker, L., Canada 68 B10 64 0N 96 0W
Baker, Mt., U.S.A. 76 B3 48 50N 121 49W
Baker City, U.S.A. 76 D5 44 47N 117 50W
Baker I., Pac. Oc. 64 G10 0 10N 176 35W
Baker L., Australia 70 B2 52 50N 133 40W
Baker L., Canada .... 61 E4 26 54S 126 5 E
Baker Lake, Canada 68 B10 64 20N 96 3W
Bakers Creek, Australia .... 62 C4 21 13S 149 7 E
Bakers Dozen Is., Canada 72 A4 56 45N 78 45W
Bakersfield, Calif., U.S.A. 79 K8 35 23N 119 1W
Bakersfield, Vt., U.S.A. 85 B12 44 45N 72 48W
Bākhtarān, Iran .... 44 C5 34 23N 47 0 E
Bākhtarān □, Iran .... 44 C5 34 0N 46 30 E
Bakı, Azerbaijan .... 19 F8 40 29N 49 56 E
Bakkafjörður, Iceland 8 C6 66 2N 14 48W
Bakony, Hungary .... 17 E9 47 10N 17 30 E
Bakony Forest = Bakony,
  Hungary .... 17 E9 47 10N 17 30 E
Bakouma, C.A.R. .... 52 C4 5 40N 22 56 E
Bakswaho, India .... 43 G8 24 15N 79 18 E
Baku = Bakı, Azerbaijan .... 19 F8 40 29N 49 56 E
Bakutis Coast, Antarctica 5 D15 74 0S 120 0W
Baky = Bakı, Azerbaijan .... 19 F8 40 29N 49 56 E
Bala, Canada 84 A5 45 1N 79 37W
Bala, L., U.K. 12 E4 52 54N 3 36W
Bala, L., U.K. 12 E4 52 53N 3 37W
Balabac I., Phil. .... 36 C5 8 0N 117 0 E
Balabac Str., E. Indies .... 36 C5 7 53N 117 5 E
Balabagh, Afghan. .... 42 B4 34 25N 70 12 E

Ba'labakk, Lebanon .... 46 B5 34 0N 36 10 E
Balabalangan, Kepulauan,
  Indonesia .... 36 E5 2 20S 117 30 E
Balad, Iraq .... 44 C5 34 1N 44 9 E
Balad Rūz, Iraq .... 44 C5 33 42N 45 5 E
Bālādeh, Fārs, Iran .... 45 D6 29 17N 51 56 E
Bālādeh, Māzandaran, Iran .... 45 B6 36 12N 51 48 E
Balaghat, India .... 40 J12 21 49N 80 12 E
Balaghat Ra., India .... 40 K10 18 50N 76 30 E
Balaguer, Spain .... 21 B6 41 50N 0 50 E
Balaklava, Ukraine .... 19 F5 44 30N 33 30 E
Balakovo, Russia .... 18 D8 52 4N 47 55 E
Balamau, India .... 43 F9 27 10N 80 21 E
Balancán, Mexico 87 D6 17 48N 91 32W
Balashov, Russia .... 19 D7 51 30N 43 10 E
Balasinor, India .... 42 H5 22 57N 73 23 E
Balasore = Baleshwar, India .... 41 J15 21 35N 87 3 E
Balaton, Hungary .... 17 E9 46 50N 17 40 E
Balbina, Reprêsa de, Brazil 92 D7 2 0S 59 30W
Balboa, Panama 88 E4 8 57N 79 34W
Balbriggan, Ireland 10 C5 53 37N 6 11W
Balcarce, Argentina 94 D4 38 0S 58 10W
Balcarres, Canada 71 C8 50 50N 103 35W
Balchik, Bulgaria .... 23 C13 43 28N 28 11 E
Balclutha, N.Z. .... 59 M2 46 15S 169 45 E
Balcones Escarpment, U.S.A. 81 L5 29 30N 99 15W
Bald Hd., Australia .... 61 G2 35 6S 118 1 E
Bald I., Australia .... 61 F2 34 57S 118 27 E
Bald Knob, U.S.A. 81 H9 35 19N 91 34W
Baldock L., Canada 71 B9 56 33N 97 57W
Baldwin, Mich., U.S.A. 82 D3 43 54N 85 51W
Baldwin, Pa., U.S.A. 84 F5 40 23N 79 59W
Baldwinsville, U.S.A. 85 C8 43 10N 76 20W
Baldy Mt., U.S.A. 76 B9 48 9N 109 39W
Baldy Peak, U.S.A. 77 K9 33 54N 109 34W
Baleares, Is., Spain .... 24 B10 39 30N 3 0 E
Balearic Is. = Baleares, Is., Spain .... 24 B10 39 30N 3 0 E
Baleine = Whale →, Canada 73 A6 58 15N 67 40W
Baleine, Petite R. de la →,
  Canada 72 A4 56 0N 76 45W
Baler, Phil. .... 37 A6 15 46N 121 34 E
Baleshare, U.K. 11 D1 57 31N 7 22W
Baleshwar, India .... 41 J15 21 35N 87 3 E
Balfate, Honduras 88 C2 15 48N 86 25W
Bali, Greece .... 25 D6 35 25N 24 47 E
Bali, India .... 42 G5 25 11N 73 17 E
Bali, Indonesia .... 36 F4 8 20S 115 0 E
Bali □, Indonesia .... 36 F5 8 20S 115 0 E
Bali, Selat, Indonesia .... 37 J17 8 18S 114 25 E
Bali Sea, Indonesia .... 37 J17 8 0S 115 0 E
Baliapal, India .... 43 J12 21 40N 87 17 E
Balik Pulau, Malaysia .... 39 c 5 21N 100 14 E
Balikeşir, Turkey .... 23 E12 39 39N 27 53 E
Balikpapan, Indonesia .... 36 E5 1 10S 116 55 E
Balimbing, Phil. .... 37 C5 5 5N 119 58 E
Baling, Malaysia .... 39 K3 5 41N 100 55 E
Balipara, India .... 41 F18 26 50N 92 45 E
Balkan Mts. = Stara Planina,
  Bulgaria .... 23 C10 43 15N 23 0 E
Balkhash = Balqash, Kazakhstan .... 28 E8 46 50N 74 50 E
Balkhash, Ozero = Balqash Köl,
  Kazakhstan .... 28 E8 46 0N 74 50 E
Balla, Bangla. .... 41 G17 24 10N 91 35 E
Ballachulish, U.K. 11 E3 56 41N 5 8W
Balladonia, Australia .... 61 F3 32 27S 123 51 E
Ballarat, Australia .... 63 F3 37 33S 143 50 E
Ballard, L., Australia .... 61 E3 29 20S 120 40 E
Ballater, U.K. 11 D5 57 3N 3 3W
Ballena Gris = Ojo de Liebre △,
  Mexico 86 B2 27 50N 114 0W
Ballenas, Canal de, Mexico 86 B2 29 10N 113 45W
Balleny Is., Antarctica .... 5 C11 66 30S 163 0 E
Ballia, India .... 43 G11 25 46N 84 12 E
Ballina, Australia .... 63 D5 28 50S 153 31 E
Ballina, Ireland 10 B2 54 7N 9 9W
Ballinasloe, Ireland 10 C3 53 20N 8 13W
Ballinger, U.S.A. 81 K5 31 45N 99 57W
Ballinrobe, Ireland 10 C2 53 38N 9 13W
Ballinskelligs B., Ireland 10 E1 51 48N 10 13W
Ballston Spa, U.S.A. 85 D11 43 0N 73 51W
Ballybunion, Ireland 10 D2 52 31N 9 40W
Ballycastle, U.K. 10 A5 55 12N 6 15W
Ballyclare, U.K. 10 B5 54 46N 6 0W
Ballyhaunis, Ireland 10 C3 53 46N 8 46W
Ballymena, U.K. 10 B5 54 52N 6 17W
Ballymoney, U.K. 10 A5 55 5N 6 31W
Ballymote, Ireland 10 B3 54 5N 8 31W
Ballynahinch, U.K. 10 B6 54 24N 5 54W
Ballyquintin Pt., U.K. 10 B6 54 20N 5 30W
Ballyshannon, Ireland 10 B3 54 30N 8 11W
Balmaceda, Chile 96 F2 46 0S 71 50W
Balmertown, Canada 71 C10 51 4N 93 41W
Balmoral, U.K. .... 63 F3 37 15S 141 48 E
Balmorhea, U.S.A. 81 K3 30 59N 103 45W
Balochistan = Baluchistan □,
  Pakistan .... 40 F4 27 30N 65 0 E
Balonne →, Australia .... 63 D4 28 47S 147 56 E
Balotra, India .... 42 G5 25 50N 72 14 E
Balqash, Kazakhstan .... 28 E8 46 50N 74 50 E
Balqash Köl, Kazakhstan .... 28 E8 46 0N 74 50 E
Balrampur, India .... 43 F10 27 30N 82 20 E
Balranald, Australia .... 63 E3 34 38S 143 33 E
Balsas, Mexico 87 D5 18 0N 99 40W
Balsas →, Brazil 93 E9 7 15S 44 35W
Balsas →, Mexico 86 D4 17 55N 102 10W
Balston Spa, U.S.A. 85 D11 43 0N 73 52W
Balta, Ukraine .... 17 D15 48 2N 29 45 E
Bălți, Moldova .... 17 E14 47 48N 27 58 E
Baltic Sea, Europe .... 9 H18 57 0N 19 0 E
Baltimore, Ireland 10 E2 51 29N 9 22W
Baltimore, Md., U.S.A. 82 F7 39 17N 76 37W
Baltimore, Ohio, U.S.A. 84 G2 39 51N 82 36W
Baltit, Pakistan .... 43 A6 36 15N 74 40 E
Baltiysk, Russia .... 9 J18 54 41N 19 58 E
Balurghat, India .... 43 G13 25 15N 88 44 E
Balvi, Latvia .... 9 H22 57 8N 27 15 E
Balya, Turkey .... 23 E12 39 44N 27 35 E
Bam, Iran .... 45 D8 29 7N 58 14 E
Bama, Nigeria .... 51 F8 11 33N 13 41 E
Bamaga, Australia .... 62 A3 10 50S 142 25 E
Bamaji L., Canada 72 B1 51 9N 91 25W
Bamako, Mali 50 F4 12 34N 7 55W
Bambari, C.A.R. .... 52 C4 5 40N 20 35 E
Bambaroo, Australia .... 62 B4 18 50S 146 10 E
Bamberg, Germany .... 16 D6 49 54N 10 54 E
Bamberg, U.S.A. 83 J5 33 18N 81 2W

Bambili, Dem. Rep. of the Congo .... 54 B2 3 40N 26 0 E
Bamburgh, U.K. 12 B6 55 37N 1 43W
Bamenda, Cameroon .... 52 C2 5 57N 10 11 E
Bamfield, Canada 70 D3 48 45N 125 10W
Bāmīān □, Afghan. .... 40 B5 35 0N 67 0 E
Bamiancheng, China .... 35 C13 43 15N 124 2 E
Bampūr, Iran .... 45 E9 27 15N 60 21 E
Ban Ao Tu Khun, Thailand .... 39 a 8 9N 98 20 E
Ban Ban, Laos .... 38 C4 19 31N 103 30 E
Ban Bang Hin, Thailand .... 39 H2 9 32N 98 35 E
Ban Bang Khu, Thailand .... 39 a 7 57N 98 23 E
Ban Bang Rong, Thailand .... 39 a 8 3N 98 25 E
Ban Bo Phut, Thailand .... 39 b 9 33N 100 2 E
Ban Chaweng, Thailand .... 39 b 9 32N 100 3 E
Ban Chiang Klang, Thailand .... 38 C3 19 25N 100 55 E
Ban Chik, Laos .... 38 D4 17 15N 102 22 E
Ban Choho, Thailand .... 38 E4 15 2N 102 9 E
Ban Dan Lan Hoi, Thailand .... 38 D2 17 0N 99 35 E
Ban Don = Surat Thani, Thailand .... 39 H2 9 6N 99 20 E
Ban Don, Vietnam .... 38 F6 12 53N 107 48 E
Ban Don, Ao →, Thailand .... 39 H2 9 20N 99 25 E
Ban Dong, Thailand .... 38 C3 19 30N 100 59 E
Ban Hong, Thailand .... 38 C2 18 18N 98 50 E
Ban Hua Thanon, Thailand .... 39 b 9 26N 100 1 E
Ban Kaeng, Thailand .... 38 D3 17 29N 100 7 E
Ban Kantang, Thailand .... 39 J2 7 25N 99 31 E
Ban Karon, Thailand .... 39 a 7 51N 98 18 E
Ban Kata, Thailand .... 39 a 7 50N 98 18 E
Ban Keun, Laos .... 38 C4 18 22N 102 35 E
Ban Khai, Thailand .... 38 F3 12 46N 101 18 E
Ban Kheun, Laos .... 38 B3 20 13N 101 7 E
Ban Khlong Khian, Thailand .... 39 a 8 10N 98 26 E
Ban Khlong Kua, Thailand .... 39 J3 6 57N 100 8 E
Ban Khuan, Thailand .... 39 a 8 20N 98 25 E
Ban Khuan Mao, Thailand .... 39 J2 7 50N 99 37 E
Ban Ko Yai Chim, Thailand .... 39 G2 11 17N 99 26 E
Ban Kok, Thailand .... 38 D4 16 40N 103 40 E
Ban Laem, Thailand .... 38 F2 13 13N 99 59 E
Ban Lamai, Thailand .... 39 b 9 28N 100 3 E
Ban Lao Ngam, Laos .... 38 E6 15 28N 106 10 E
Ban Le Kathe, Thailand .... 38 E2 15 49N 98 53 E
Ban Lo Po Noi, Thailand .... 39 a 8 1N 98 34 E
Ban Mae Chedi, Thailand .... 38 C2 19 11N 99 31 E
Ban Mae Laeng, Thailand .... 38 B2 20 1N 99 17 E
Ban Mae Nam, Thailand .... 39 b 9 34N 100 0 E
Ban Mae Sariang, Thailand .... 38 C1 18 10N 97 56 E
Ban Mê Thuột = Buon Ma Thuot,
  Vietnam .... 38 F7 12 40N 108 3 E
Ban Mi, Thailand .... 38 E3 15 3N 100 32 E
Ban Muong Mo, Laos .... 38 C4 19 4N 103 58 E
Ban Na Bo, Thailand .... 39 b 9 19N 99 41 E
Ban Na Mo, Laos .... 38 D5 17 7N 105 40 E
Ban Na San, Thailand .... 39 H2 8 53N 99 52 E
Ban Na Tong, Laos .... 38 B3 20 56N 101 47 E
Ban Nam Bac, Laos .... 38 B4 20 38N 102 20 E
Ban Nam Ma, Laos .... 38 A3 22 2N 101 37 E
Ban Ngang, Laos .... 38 E6 15 59N 106 11 E
Ban Nong Bok, Laos .... 38 D5 17 5N 104 48 E
Ban Nong Boua, Laos .... 38 E6 15 40N 106 33 E
Ban Nong Pling, Thailand .... 38 E3 15 40N 100 10 E
Ban Pak Chan, Thailand .... 39 G2 10 32N 98 51 E
Ban Patong, Thailand .... 39 a 7 54N 98 18 E
Ban Phai, Thailand .... 38 D4 16 4N 102 44 E
Ban Phak Chit, Thailand .... 39 a 8 0N 98 24 E
Ban Pong, Thailand .... 38 F2 13 50N 99 55 E
Ban Rawai, Thailand .... 39 a 7 47N 98 20 E
Ban Ron Phibun, Thailand .... 39 H2 8 9N 99 51 E
Ban Sakhu, Thailand .... 39 a 8 4N 98 18 E
Ban Sanam Chai, Thailand .... 39 J3 7 33N 100 25 E
Ban Sangkha, Thailand .... 38 E4 14 37N 103 52 E
Ban Tak, Thailand .... 38 D2 17 2N 99 4 E
Ban Tako, Thailand .... 38 E4 14 5N 102 40 E
Ban Tha Dua, Thailand .... 38 D2 17 59N 98 39 E
Ban Tha Li, Thailand .... 38 D3 17 37N 101 25 E
Ban Tha Nun, Thailand .... 39 a 8 12N 98 18 E
Ban Tha Rua, Thailand .... 39 a 7 59N 98 22 E
Ban Tha Yu, Thailand .... 39 a 8 17N 98 22 E
Ban Thahine, Laos .... 38 E5 14 12N 105 33 E
Ban Thong Krut, Thailand .... 39 b 9 25N 99 57 E
Ban Xien Kok, Laos .... 38 B3 20 54N 100 39 E
Ban Yen Nhan, Vietnam .... 38 B6 20 57N 106 2 E
Banaba, Kiribati .... 64 H8 0 45S 169 50 E
Banalia, Dem. Rep. of the Congo .... 54 B2 1 32N 25 5 E
Banam, Cambodia .... 39 G5 11 20N 105 17 E
Banana, Australia .... 62 C5 24 28S 150 8 E
Bananal, I. do, Brazil 93 F8 11 30S 50 30W
Banaras = Varanasi, India .... 43 G10 25 22N 83 0 E
Banas →, Gujarat, India .... 42 H4 23 45N 71 25 E
Banas →, Mad. P., India .... 43 G9 24 15N 81 30 E
Bânâs, Ras, Egypt .... 51 D13 23 57N 35 59 E
Banbridge, U.K. 10 B5 54 22N 6 16W
Banbury, U.K. 13 E6 52 4N 1 20W
Banchory, U.K. 11 D6 57 3N 2 29W
Bancroft, Canada 84 A7 45 3N 77 51W
Band Boni, Iran .... 45 E8 25 30N 59 33 E
Band Qīr, Iran .... 45 D6 31 39N 48 53 E
Banda, Mad. P., India .... 43 G8 24 3N 78 57 E
Banda, Ut. P., India .... 43 G9 25 30N 80 26 E
Banda, Kepulauan, Indonesia .... 37 E7 4 37S 129 50 E
Banda Aceh, Indonesia .... 36 C1 5 35N 95 20 E
Banda Banda, Mt., Australia .... 63 E5 31 10S 152 28 E
Banda Elat, Indonesia .... 37 F8 5 40S 133 5 E
Banda Is. = Banda, Kepulauan,
  Indonesia .... 37 E7 4 37S 129 50 E
Banda Sea, Indonesia .... 37 F7 6 0S 130 0 E
Bandai-Asahi △, Japan .... 30 F10 37 38N 140 5 E
Bandan, Iran .... 45 D9 31 23N 60 44 E
Bandanaira, Indonesia .... 37 E7 4 32S 129 54 E
Bandanwara, India .... 42 F6 26 9N 74 38 E
Bandar = Machilipatnam, India .... 41 L12 16 12N 81 8 E
Bandar-e Abbās, Iran .... 45 E8 27 15N 56 15 E
Bandar-e Anzalī, Iran .... 45 B6 37 30N 49 30 E
Bandar-e Bushehr = Būshehr,
  Iran .... 45 D6 28 55N 50 55 E
Bandar-e Chārak, Iran .... 45 E7 26 45N 54 20 E
Bandar-e Deylam, Iran .... 45 D6 30 5N 50 10 E
Bandar-e Emām Khomeyni, Iran .... 45 D6 30 30N 49 5 E
Bandar-e Lengeh, Iran .... 45 E7 26 35N 54 58 E
Bandar-e Maqām, Iran .... 45 E7 26 56N 53 29 E
Bandar-e Ma'shur, Iran .... 45 D6 30 35N 49 10 E
Bandar-e Rīg, Iran .... 45 D6 29 29N 50 38 E
Bandar-e Torkeman, Iran .... 45 B7 37 0N 54 10 E
Bandar Lampung =
  Tanjungkarang Telukbetung,
  Indonesia .... 36 F3 5 20S 105 10 E
Bandar Maharani = Muar,
  Malaysia .... 39 L4 2 3N 102 34 E

Bandar Penggaram = Batu Pahat,
  Malaysia .... 39 M4 1 50N 102 56 E
Bandar Seri Begawan, Brunei .... 36 C4 4 52N 115 0 E
Bandar Sri Aman, Malaysia .... 36 D4 1 15N 111 32 E
Bandawe, Malawi .... 55 E3 11 58S 34 5 E
Bandeira, Pico da, Brazil 95 A7 20 26S 41 47W
Bandera, Argentina 94 B3 28 55S 62 20W
Banderas, B. de, Mexico 86 C3 20 40N 105 30W
Bandhogarh, India .... 43 H9 23 40N 81 2 E
Bandi →, India .... 42 F6 26 12N 75 47 E
Bandikui, India .... 42 F7 27 3N 76 34 E
Bandırma, Turkey .... 23 D13 40 20N 28 0 E
Bandjarmasin = Banjarmasin,
  Indonesia .... 36 E4 3 20S 114 35 E
Bandon, Ireland 10 E3 51 44N 8 44W
Bandon →, Ireland 10 E3 51 43N 8 37W
Bandula, Mozam. .... 55 F3 19 0S 33 7 E
Bandundu, Dem. Rep. of
  the Congo .... 52 E3 3 15S 17 22 E
Bandung, Indonesia .... 36 F3 6 54S 107 36 E
Bāneh, Iran .... 44 C5 35 59N 45 53 E
Banes, Cuba 89 B4 21 0N 75 42W
Banff, Canada 70 C5 51 10N 115 34W
Banff, U.K. 11 D6 57 40N 2 33W
Banff △, Canada 70 C5 51 30N 116 15W
Bang Fai →, Laos .... 38 D5 16 57N 104 45 E
Bang Hieng →, Laos .... 38 D5 16 10N 105 10 E
Bang Krathum, Thailand .... 38 D3 16 34N 100 18 E
Bang Lamung, Thailand .... 38 F3 13 3N 100 56 E
Bang Mun Nak, Thailand .... 38 D3 16 2N 100 23 E
Bang Pa In, Thailand .... 38 D3 16 45N 100 7 E
Bang Saphan, Thailand .... 39 G2 11 14N 99 28 E
Bang Thao, Thailand .... 39 a 7 59N 98 18 E
Bangaduni I., India .... 43 J13 21 34N 88 52 E
Bangala Dam, Zimbabwe .... 55 G3 21 7S 31 25 E
Bangalore, India .... 40 N10 12 59N 77 40 E
Banganga →, India .... 42 F6 26 7N 72 25 E
Bangaon, India .... 43 H13 23 0N 88 47 E
Bangassou, C.A.R. .... 52 D4 4 55S 23 7 E
Banggai, Indonesia .... 37 E6 1 34S 123 30 E
Banggai, Kepulauan, Indonesia .... 37 E6 1 40S 123 30 E
Banggai Arch. = Banggai,
  Kepulauan, Indonesia .... 37 E6 1 40S 123 30 E
Banggi, Malaysia .... 36 C5 7 17N 117 12 E
Banghāzī, Libya .... 51 B10 32 11N 20 3 E
Bangka, Sulawesi, Indonesia .... 37 D7 1 50N 125 5 E
Bangka, Sumatera, Indonesia .... 36 E3 2 0S 105 50 E
Bangka, Selat, Indonesia .... 36 E3 2 30S 105 30 E
Bangkalan, Indonesia .... 37 G15 7 2S 112 46 E
Bangkinang, Indonesia .... 36 D2 0 18N 101 5 E
Bangko, Indonesia .... 36 E2 2 5S 102 9 E
Bangkok, Thailand .... 38 F3 13 45N 100 35 E
Bangladesh ■, Asia .... 41 H17 24 0N 90 0 E
Bangli, Indonesia .... 37 J18 8 27S 115 21 E
Bangong Co, India .... 43 B8 35 50N 79 20 E
Bangor, Down, U.K. 10 B6 54 40N 5 40W
Bangor, Gwynedd, U.K. 12 D3 53 14N 4 8W
Bangor, Maine, U.S.A. 69 D13 44 48N 68 46W
Bangor, Pa., U.S.A. 85 F9 40 52N 75 13W
Bangued, Phil. .... 37 A6 17 40N 120 37 E
Bangui, C.A.R. .... 52 D3 4 23N 18 35 E
Banguru, Dem. Rep. of
  the Congo .... 54 B2 0 30N 27 10 E
Bangweulu, L., Zambia .... 55 E3 11 0S 30 0 E
Bangweulu Swamp, Zambia .... 55 E3 11 20S 30 15 E
Banhine △, Mozam. .... 57 C5 22 45S 32 55 E
Bani, Dom. Rep. 89 C5 18 16N 70 22W
Banī Sa'd, Iraq .... 44 C5 33 34N 44 32 E
Banihal Pass, India .... 43 C6 33 30N 75 12 E
Bāniyās, Syria .... 44 C3 35 10N 36 0 E
Banja Luka, Bos.-H. .... 22 B7 44 49N 17 11 E
Banjar, India .... 43 D7 31 38N 77 21 E
Banjar →, India .... 43 H9 22 36N 80 22 E
Banjarmasin, Indonesia .... 36 E4 3 20S 114 35 E
Banjul, Gambia 50 F2 13 28N 16 40W
Banka, India .... 43 G12 24 53N 86 55 E
Banket, Zimbabwe .... 55 F3 17 27S 30 19 E
Bankipore, India .... 41 G14 25 35N 85 10 E
Banks I., B.C., Canada 70 C3 53 20N 130 0W
Banks I., N.W.T., Canada 68 A7 73 15N 121 30W
Banks Pen., N.Z. .... 59 K4 43 45S 173 15 E
Banks Str., Australia .... 63 G4 40 40S 148 10 E
Bankura, India .... 43 H12 23 11N 87 18 E
Banmankhi, India .... 43 G12 25 53N 87 11 E
Bann →, Arm., U.K. 10 B5 54 30N 6 31W
Bann →, L'derry., U.K. 10 A5 55 8N 6 41W
Bannang Sata, Thailand .... 39 J3 6 16N 101 16 E
Banning, U.S.A. 79 M10 33 56N 116 53W
Bannockburn, Canada 84 B7 44 39N 77 33W
Bannockburn, U.K. 11 E5 56 5N 3 55W
Bannockburn, Zimbabwe .... 55 G2 20 17S 29 48 E
Bannu, Pakistan .... 40 C7 33 0N 70 18 E
Bano, India .... 43 H11 22 40N 84 55 E
Bansgaon, India .... 43 F10 26 33N 83 21 E
Banská Bystrica, Slovak Rep. .... 17 D10 48 46N 19 14 E
Banswara, India .... 42 H6 23 32N 74 24 E
Bantaeng, Indonesia .... 37 F5 5 32S 119 56 E
Bantry, Ireland 10 E2 51 41N 9 27W
Bantry B., Ireland 10 E2 51 37N 9 44W
Bantul, Indonesia .... 37 G14 7 55S 110 19 E
Bantva, India .... 42 J4 21 29N 70 12 E
Banyak, Kepulauan, Indonesia .... 36 D1 2 10N 97 10 E
Banyalbufar, Spain .... 24 B9 39 42N 2 31 E
Banyo, Cameroon .... 52 C2 6 52N 11 45 E
Banyumas, Indonesia .... 37 G13 7 32S 109 18 E
Banyuwangi, Indonesia .... 37 J17 8 13S 114 21 E
Banzare Coast, Antarctica .... 5 C9 68 0S 125 0 E
Bao Ha, Vietnam .... 38 A5 22 11N 104 21 E
Bao Lac, Vietnam .... 38 A5 22 57N 105 40 E
Bao Loc, Vietnam .... 39 G6 11 32N 107 48 E
Bao'an = Shenzhen, China .... 33 F10 22 32N 114 5 E
Baocheng, China .... 34 H4 33 12N 106 56 E
Baode, China .... 34 E6 39 1N 111 5 E
Baodi, China .... 35 E9 39 38N 117 20 E
Baoding, China .... 34 E8 38 50N 115 28 E
Baoji, China .... 34 G4 34 20N 107 5 E
Baojing, China .... 33 D8 28 45N 109 41 E
Baokang, China .... 34 D4 35 3N 98 30 E
Baoshan, China .... 32 D4 25 10N 99 5 E
Baotou, China .... 34 D6 40 32N 110 2 E
Baoying, China .... 35 H10 33 17N 119 20 E
Bap, India .... 42 F5 27 23N 72 18 E
Bapatla, India .... 41 M12 15 55N 80 30 E
Bāqerābād, Iran .... 45 C6 33 2N 51 58 E
Ba'qūbah, Iraq .... 44 C5 33 45N 44 50 E
Baquedano, Chile 94 A2 23 20S 69 52W
Bar, Ukraine .... 17 D14 49 4N 27 40 E
Bar Bigha, India .... 43 G11 25 21N 85 47 E

Bar Harbor, U.S.A. 83 C11 44 23N 68 13W
Bar-le-Duc, France .... 20 B6 48 47N 5 10 E
Bara, India .... 43 G9 25 16N 81 43 E
Bara Banki, India .... 43 F9 26 55N 81 12 E
Barabai, Indonesia .... 36 E5 2 32S 115 34 E
Baraboo, U.S.A. 80 D10 43 28N 89 45W
Baracoa, Cuba 89 B5 20 20N 74 30W
Baradá →, Syria .... 46 B5 33 33N 36 34 E
Baradero, Argentina 94 C4 33 52S 59 29W
Baraga, U.S.A. 80 B10 46 47N 88 30W
Barah →, India .... 42 F6 27 42N 77 5 E
Barahona, Dom. Rep. 89 C5 18 13N 71 7W
Barail Range, India .... 41 G18 25 15N 93 20 E
Barakaldo, Spain 21 A4 43 18N 2 59W
Barakar →, India .... 43 G12 24 7N 86 14 E
Barakhola, India .... 41 G18 25 0N 92 45 E
Barakot, India .... 43 J11 21 33N 84 59 E
Barakpur, India .... 43 H13 22 44N 88 30 E
Baralaba, Australia .... 62 C4 24 13S 149 50 E
Baralzon L., Canada 71 B9 60 0N 98 3W
Baramula, India .... 43 B6 34 15N 74 20 E
Baran, India .... 42 G7 25 9N 76 40 E
Baran →, Pakistan .... 42 G3 25 13N 68 17 E
Baranavichy, Belarus .... 17 B14 53 10N 26 0 E
Baranof, U.S.A. 70 B2 57 5N 134 50W
Baranof I., U.S.A. 68 C6 57 0N 135 0W
Barapasi, Indonesia .... 37 E9 2 15S 137 5 E
Barasat, India .... 43 H13 22 46N 88 31 E
Barat Daya, Kepulauan,
  Indonesia .... 37 F7 7 30S 128 0 E
Barataria B., U.S.A. 81 L10 29 20N 89 55W
Barauda, India .... 42 H6 23 33N 75 15 E
Baraut, India .... 42 E7 29 13N 77 7 E
Barbacena, Brazil 95 A7 21 15S 43 56W
Barbados ■, W. Indies .... 89 g 13 10N 59 30W
Barbária, C. de, Spain .... 24 C7 38 39N 1 24 E
Barbastro, Spain .... 21 A6 42 2N 0 5 E
Barberton, S. Africa .... 57 D5 25 42S 31 2 E
Barberton, U.S.A. 84 E3 41 0N 81 39W
Barbonneau, St. Lucia .... 89 f 13 59N 60 58W
Barbosa, Colombia 92 B4 5 57N 73 37W
Barbourville, U.S.A. 83 G4 36 52N 83 53W
Barbuda, W. Indies 89 C7 17 30N 61 40W
Barcaldine, Australia .... 62 C4 23 43S 145 6 E
Barcellona Pozzo di Gotto, Italy 22 E6 38 9N 15 13 E
Barcelona, Spain .... 21 B7 41 21N 2 10 E
Barcelona, Venezuela 92 A6 10 10N 64 40W
Barceloneta, Puerto Rico ...... 89 d 18 27N 66 32W
Barcelos, Brazil 92 D6 1 0S 63 0W
Barcoo →, Australia .... 62 D3 25 30S 142 50 E
Bardaï, Chad .... 51 D9 21 25N 17 0 E
Bardas Blancas, Argentina 94 D2 35 49S 69 45W
Bardawîl, Sabkhet el, Egypt ... 46 D2 31 10N 33 15 E
Barddhaman, India .... 43 H12 23 14N 87 39 E
Bardejov, Slovak Rep. .... 17 D11 49 18N 21 15 E
Bardera, Somali Rep. .... 47 G3 2 20N 42 27 E
Bardīyah, Libya .... 51 B10 31 45N 25 5 E
Bardsey I., U.K. 12 E3 52 45N 4 47W
Bardstown, U.S.A. 82 G3 37 49N 85 28W
Bareilly, India .... 43 E8 28 22N 79 27 E
Barela, India .... 43 H9 23 6N 80 3 E
Barents Sea, Arctic .... 4 B9 73 0N 39 0 E
Barfleur, Pte. de, France 20 B3 49 42N 1 16W
Bargara, Australia .... 62 C5 24 50S 152 25 E
Barguzin, Russia .... 29 D11 53 37N 109 37 E
Barh, India .... 43 G11 25 29N 85 46 E
Barhaj, India .... 43 F10 26 18N 83 44 E
Barharwa, India .... 43 G12 24 52N 87 47 E
Barhi, India .... 43 G11 24 15N 85 25 E
Bari, India .... 42 F7 26 39N 77 39 E
Bari, Italy .... 22 D7 41 8N 16 51 E
Bari Doab, Pakistan .... 42 D5 30 20N 73 0 E
Bari Sadri, India .... 42 G6 24 28N 74 30 E
Barīdī, Ra's, Si. Arabia ...... 44 E3 24 17N 37 31 E
Barim, Yemen .... 48 E8 12 39N 43 25 E
Barinas, Venezuela 92 B4 8 36N 70 15W
Baring, C., Canada 68 B8 70 0N 117 30W
Baringo, L., Kenya .... 54 B4 0 47N 36 16 E
Barisal, Bangla. .... 41 H17 22 45N 90 20 E
Barisal □, Bangla. .... 41 H17 22 40N 90 20 E
Barisan, Bukit, Indonesia ..... 36 E2 3 30S 102 15 E
Barito →, Indonesia .... 36 E4 4 0S 114 50 E
Baritú △, Argentina 94 A3 23 43S 64 40W
Bark L., Canada 84 A7 45 27N 77 51W
Barkakana, India .... 43 H11 23 37N 85 29 E
Barker, U.S.A. 84 C6 43 20N 78 33W
Barkley, L., U.S.A. 83 G2 37 1N 88 14W
Barkley Sound, Canada 70 D3 48 50N 125 10W
Barkly East, S. Africa .... 56 E4 30 58S 27 33 E
Barkly Roadhouse, Australia ... 62 B2 19 52S 135 50 E
Barkly Tableland, Australia ... 62 B2 17 50S 136 40 E
Barkly West, S. Africa .... 56 D3 28 5S 24 31 E
Barkol Kazak Zizhixian, China . 32 B4 43 37N 93 2 E
Bârlad, Romania .... 17 E14 46 15N 27 38 E
Bârlad →, Romania .... 17 F14 45 38N 27 32 E
Barlee, L., Australia .... 61 E2 29 15S 119 30 E
Barlee, Mt., Australia .... 61 D4 24 38S 128 13 E
Barletta, Italy .... 22 D7 41 19N 16 17 E
Barlovento, Canary Is. 24 F2 28 48N 17 48W
Barlow L., Canada 71 A8 62 0N 103 0W
Barmedman, Australia .... 63 E4 34 9S 147 21 E
Barmer, India .... 42 G4 25 45N 71 20 E
Barmera, Australia .... 63 E3 34 15S 140 28 E
Barmouth, U.K. 12 E3 52 44N 4 4W
Barna →, India .... 43 G10 25 21N 83 3 E
Barnagar, India .... 42 H6 23 7N 75 19 E
Barnala, India .... 42 D6 30 23N 75 33 E
Barnard Castle, U.K. 12 C6 54 33N 1 55W
Barnaul, Russia .... 28 D9 53 20N 83 40 E
Barnesville, U.S.A. 83 J3 33 3N 84 9W
Barnet □, U.K. 13 F7 51 38N 0 9W
Barneveld, Neths. .... 15 B5 52 7N 5 36 E
Barneveld, U.S.A. 85 C9 43 16N 75 14W
Barnhart, U.S.A. 81 K4 31 8N 101 10W
Barnsley, U.K. 12 D6 53 34N 1 27W
Barnstaple, U.K. 13 F3 51 5N 4 4W
Barnstaple Bay = Bideford Bay,
  U.K. 13 F3 51 5N 4 20W
Barnsville, U.S.A. 80 B6 46 43N 96 28W
Barnwell, U.S.A. 83 J5 33 15N 81 23W
Baro, Nigeria .... 50 G7 8 35N 6 18 E
Baroda = Vadodara, India ...... 42 H5 22 20N 73 10 E
Baroda, India .... 42 G7 25 29N 76 35 E
Baroe, S. Africa .... 56 E3 33 13S 24 33 E
Baron Ra., Australia .... 60 D4 23 30S 127 45 E
Barotseland, Zambia .... 53 H4 15 0S 24 0 E
Barpeta, India .... 41 F17 26 20N 91 10 E
Barques, Pt. Aux, U.S.A. 84 B2 44 4N 82 58W

Barquísimeto, Venezuela 92 A5 10 4N 69 19W
Barr Smith Range, Australia ... 61 E3 27 4S 120 20 E
Barra, Brazil 93 F10 11 5S 43 10W
Barra, U.K. 11 E1 57 0N 7 29W
Barra, Sd. of, U.K. 11 D1 57 4N 7 25W
Barra de Navidad, Mexico 86 D4 19 12N 104 41W
Barra do Corda, Brazil 93 E9 5 30S 45 10W
Barra do Piraí, Brazil 95 A7 22 30S 43 50W
Barra Falsa, Pta. da, Mozam. .. 57 C6 22 58S 35 37 E
Barra Hd., U.K. 11 E1 56 47N 7 40W
Barra Mansa, Brazil 95 A7 22 35S 44 12W
Barraba, Australia .... 63 E5 30 21S 150 35 E
Barrackpur = Barakpur, India .. 43 H13 22 44N 88 30 E
Barradale Roadhouse, Australia 60 D1 22 42S 114 58 E
Barraigh = Barra, U.K. 11 E1 57 0N 7 29W
Barranca, Lima, Peru 92 F3 10 45S 77 50W
Barranca, Loreto, Peru 92 D3 4 50S 76 50W
Barranca del Cobre △, Mexico .. 86 B3 27 18N 107 40W
Barrancabermeja, Colombia 92 B4 7 0N 73 50W
Barrancas, Venezuela 92 B6 8 55N 62 5W
Barrancos, Portugal 21 C2 38 10N 6 58W
Barranqueras, Argentina 94 B4 27 30S 59 0W
Barranquilla, Colombia 92 A4 11 0N 74 50W
Barraute, Canada 72 C4 48 26N 77 38W
Barre, Mass., U.S.A. 85 D12 42 25N 72 6W
Barre, Vt., U.S.A. 85 B12 44 12N 72 30W
Barreal, Argentina 94 C2 31 33S 69 28W
Barreiras, Brazil 93 F10 12 8S 45 0W
Barreirinhas, Brazil 93 D10 2 30S 42 50W
Barreiro, Portugal 21 C1 38 40N 9 6W
Barren, Nosy, Madag. .... 57 B7 18 25S 43 40 E
Barretos, Brazil 93 H9 20 30S 48 35W
Barrhead, Canada 70 C6 54 10N 114 24W
Barrie, Canada 84 B5 44 24N 79 40W
Barrier Ra., Australia .... 63 E3 31 0S 141 30 E
Barrière, Canada 70 C4 51 12N 120 7W
Barrington, U.S.A. 85 E13 41 44N 71 18W
Barrington L., Canada 71 B8 56 55N 100 15W
Barrington Tops, Australia .... 63 E5 32 6S 151 28 E
Barringun, Australia .... 63 D4 29 1S 145 41 E
Barro do Garças, Brazil 93 G8 15 54S 52 16W
Barron, U.S.A. 80 C9 45 24N 91 51W
Barrow, U.S.A. 68 A4 71 18N 156 47W
Barrow →, Ireland 10 D5 52 25N 6 58W
Barrow Creek, Australia .... 62 C1 21 30S 133 55 E
Barrow I., Australia .... 60 D2 20 45S 115 20 E
Barrow-in-Furness, U.K. 12 C4 54 7N 3 14W
Barrow Pt., Australia .... 62 A3 14 20S 144 40 E
Barrow Pt., U.S.A. 66 B4 71 10N 156 20W
Barrow Ra., Australia .... 61 E4 26 0S 127 40 E
Barrow Str., Canada 4 B3 74 20N 95 0W
Barry, U.K. 13 F4 51 24N 3 16W
Barry's Bay, Canada 84 A7 45 29N 77 41W
Barsat, Pakistan .... 43 A5 36 10N 72 45 E
Barsham, Syria .... 44 C4 35 21N 40 33 E
Barsi, India .... 40 K9 18 10N 75 50 E
Barsoi, India .... 41 G15 25 48N 87 57 E
Barstow, U.S.A. 79 L9 34 54N 117 1W
Barthélemy, Col, Vietnam ...... 38 C5 19 26N 104 6 E
Bartica, Guyana 92 B7 6 25N 58 40W
Bartlesville, U.S.A. 81 G7 36 45N 95 59W
Bartlett, U.S.A. 78 J8 36 29N 118 2W
Bartlett, L., Canada 70 A5 63 5N 118 20W
Bartolomeu Dias, Mozam. .... 55 G4 21 10S 35 8 E
Barton, U.S.A. 85 B12 44 45N 72 11W
Barton upon Humber, U.K. 12 D7 53 41N 0 25W
Bartow, U.S.A. 83 M5 27 54N 81 50W
Barumba, Dem. Rep. of
  the Congo .... 54 B1 1 3N 23 37 E
Baruunsuu, Mongolia .... 34 C3 43 43N 105 35 E
Barwani, India .... 42 H6 22 2N 74 57 E
Barysaw, Belarus .... 17 A15 54 17N 28 28 E
Barzān, Iraq .... 44 B5 36 55N 44 3 E
Bāsa'idū, Iran .... 45 E7 26 35N 55 20 E
Basal, Pakistan .... 42 C5 33 33N 72 13 E
Basankusa, Dem. Rep. of
  the Congo .... 52 D3 1 5N 19 50 E
Basarabeasca, Moldova .... 17 E15 46 21N 28 58 E
Basarabia = Bessarabiya,
  Moldova .... 17 E15 47 0N 28 10 E
Basawa, Afghan. .... 42 B4 34 15N 70 50 E
Bascuñán, C., Chile 94 B1 28 52S 71 35W
Basel, Switz. .... 20 C7 47 35N 7 35 E
Bashäkerd, Kühhä-ye, Iran ..... 45 E8 26 42N 58 35 E
Bashaw, Canada 70 C6 52 35N 112 58W
Bāshī, Iran .... 45 D6 28 41N 51 4 E
Bashkir Republic =
  Bashkortostan □, Russia ..... 18 D10 54 0N 57 0 E
Bashkortostan □, Russia .... 18 D10 54 0N 57 0 E
Basibasy, Madag. .... 57 C7 22 10S 43 40 E
Basilan I., Phil. .... 37 C6 6 35N 122 0 E
Basilan Str., Phil. .... 37 C6 6 50N 122 0 E
Basildon, U.K. .... 13 F8 51 34N 0 28 E
Basim = Washim, India .... 40 J10 20 3N 77 0 E
Basin, U.S.A. 76 D9 44 23N 108 2W
Basingstoke, U.K. 13 F6 51 15N 1 5W
Baskatong, Rés., Canada 72 C4 46 46N 75 50W
Basle = Basel, Switz. .... 20 C7 47 35N 7 35 E
Basoda, India .... 42 H7 23 52N 77 54 E
Basoko, Dem. Rep. of the Congo 54 B1 1 16N 23 40 E
Basque Provinces = País
  Vasco □, Spain 21 A4 42 50N 2 45W
Basra = Al Başrah, Iraq .... 44 D5 30 30N 47 50 E
Bass Str., Australia .... 63 F4 39 15S 146 30 E
Bassano, Canada 70 C6 50 48N 112 20W
Bassano del Grappa, Italy ..... 22 B4 45 46N 11 44 E
Bassas da India, Ind. Oc. ..... 53 J7 22 0S 39 0 E
Basse-Pointe, Martinique ...... 88 c 14 52N 61 8W
Basse-Terre, Guadeloupe .... 88 b 16 0N 61 44W
Basse Terre, Trin. & Tob. 93 K15 10 7N 61 19W
Bassein, Burma .... 41 L19 16 45N 94 30 E
Basses, Pte. des, Guadeloupe .. 88 b 15 52N 61 17W
Basseterre, St. Kitts & Nevis . 89 C7 17 17N 62 43W
Bassett, U.S.A. 80 D5 42 35N 99 32W
Bastak, Iran .... 45 E7 27 15N 54 25 E
Baştām, Iran .... 45 B7 36 29N 55 4 E
Bastar, India .... 41 K12 19 15N 81 40 E
Basti, India .... 43 F10 26 52N 82 55 E
Bastia, France .... 20 E8 42 40N 9 30 E
Bastogne, Belgium .... 15 D5 50 1N 5 43 E
Bastrop, La., U.S.A. 81 J9 32 47N 91 55W
Bastrop, Tex., U.S.A. 81 K6 30 7N 97 19W
Bat Yam, Israel .... 46 C3 32 2N 34 44 E
Bata, Eq. Guin. .... 52 D1 1 57N 9 50 E
Bataan □, Phil. .... 37 B6 14 40N 120 25 E
Batabanó, Cuba 88 B3 22 40N 82 20W

Batabanó, G. de, Cuba 88 B3 22 30N 82 30W
Batac, Phil. .... 37 A6 18 3N 120 34 E
Batagai, Russia .... 29 C14 67 38N 134 38 E
Batala, India .... 42 D6 31 48N 75 12 E
Batama, Dem. Rep. of the Congo 54 B2 0 58N 26 33 E
Batamay, Russia .... 29 C13 63 30N 129 15 E
Batang, Indonesia .... 37 G13 6 55S 109 45 E
Batangas, Phil. .... 37 B6 13 35N 121 10 E
Batanta, Indonesia .... 37 E8 0 55S 130 40 E
Batatais, Brazil 95 A6 20 54S 47 37W
Batavia, U.S.A. 84 D6 43 0N 78 11W
Batchelor, Australia .... 60 B5 13 4S 131 1 E
Batdambang, Cambodia .... 38 F4 13 7N 103 12 E
Batemans B., Australia .... 63 F5 35 40S 150 12 E
Batemans Bay, Australia .... 63 F5 35 44S 150 11 E
Bates Ra., Australia .... 61 E3 27 27S 121 5 E
Batesburg-Leesville, U.S.A. ... 83 J5 33 54N 81 33W
Batesville, Ark., U.S.A. 81 H9 35 46N 91 39W
Batesville, Miss., U.S.A. 81 H10 34 19N 89 57W
Batesville, Tex., U.S.A. 81 L5 28 58N 99 37W
Bath, Canada 85 B8 44 11N 76 47W
Bath, U.K. 13 F5 51 23N 2 22W
Bath, Maine, U.S.A. 83 D11 43 55N 69 49W
Bath, N.Y., U.S.A. 84 D7 42 20N 77 19W
Bath & North East Somerset □,
  U.K. 13 F5 51 21N 2 27W
Batheay, Cambodia .... 39 G5 11 59N 104 57 E
Bathsheba, Barbados .... 89 g 13 13N 59 31W
Bathurst, Australia .... 63 E4 33 25S 149 31 E
Bathurst, Canada 73 C6 47 37N 65 43W
Bathurst, S. Africa .... 56 E4 33 30S 26 50 E
Bathurst, C., Canada 68 A7 70 34N 128 0W
Bathurst B., Australia .... 62 A3 14 16S 144 25 E
Bathurst Harb., Australia ..... 63 G4 43 15S 146 10 E
Bathurst I., Australia .... 60 B5 11 30S 130 10 E
Bathurst I., Canada 4 B2 76 0N 100 30W
Bathurst Inlet, Canada 68 B9 66 50N 108 1W
Batlow, Australia .... 63 F4 35 31S 148 9 E
Batman, Turkey .... 19 G7 37 55N 41 5 E
Baţn al Ghūl, Jordan .... 46 F4 29 36N 35 56 E
Batna, Algeria .... 50 A7 35 34N 6 15 E
Batoka, Zambia .... 55 F2 16 45S 27 15 E
Baton Rouge, U.S.A. 81 K9 30 27N 91 11W
Batong, Ko, Thailand .... 39 J2 6 32N 99 12 E
Batopilas, Mexico 86 B3 27 0N 107 45W
Batouri, Cameroon .... 52 D2 4 30N 14 25 E
Båtsfjord, Norway .... 8 A23 70 38N 29 39 E
Battambang = Batdambang,
  Cambodia .... 38 F4 13 7N 103 12 E
Batticaloa, Sri Lanka .... 40 R12 7 43N 81 45 E
Battipáglia, Italy .... 22 D6 40 37N 14 58 E
Battle, U.K. .... 13 G8 50 55N 0 30 E
Battle →, Canada 71 C7 52 43N 108 15W
Battle Creek, U.S.A. 82 D3 42 19N 85 11W
Battle Ground, U.S.A. 78 E4 45 47N 122 32W
Battle Harbour, Canada 73 B8 52 16N 55 35W
Battle Lake, U.S.A. 80 B7 46 17N 95 43W
Battle Mountain, U.S.A. 76 F5 40 38N 116 56W
Battlefields, Zimbabwe .... 55 F2 18 37S 29 47 E
Battleford, Canada 71 C7 52 45N 108 15W
Batu, Ethiopia .... 47 F2 6 55N 39 45 E
Batu, Kepulauan, Indonesia .... 36 E1 0 30S 98 25 E
Batu Caves, Malaysia .... 39 L3 3 15N 101 40 E
Batu Ferringhi, Malaysia ...... 39 c 5 28N 100 15 E
Batu Gajah, Malaysia .... 39 K3 4 28N 101 3 E
Batu Is. = Batu, Kepulauan,
  Indonesia .... 36 E1 0 30S 98 25 E
Batu Pahat, Malaysia .... 39 M4 1 50N 102 56 E
Batuata, Indonesia .... 37 F6 6 12S 122 42 E
Batugondang, Tanjung,
  Indonesia .... 37 J17 8 6S 114 29 E
Batukau, Gunung, Indonesia .... 37 J18 8 20S 115 5 E
Batumi, Georgia .... 19 F7 41 39N 41 44 E
Batur, Indonesia .... 37 J18 8 15S 115 23 E
Batur, Gunung, Indonesia ...... 37 J18 8 14S 115 23 E
Baturaja, Indonesia .... 36 E2 4 11S 104 15 E
Baturité, Brazil 93 D11 4 28S 38 45W
Bau, Malaysia .... 36 D4 1 25N 110 9 E
Baubau, Indonesia .... 37 F6 5 25S 122 38 E
Bauchi, Nigeria .... 50 F7 10 22N 9 48 E
Baudette, U.S.A. 80 A7 48 43N 94 36W
Bauer, C., Australia .... 63 E1 32 44S 134 4 E
Bauhinia, Australia .... 62 C4 24 35S 149 18 E
Baukau = Baucau, E. Timor ..... 37 F7 8 27S 126 27 E
Bauld, C., Canada 69 C14 51 38N 55 26W
Bauru, Brazil 95 A6 22 10S 49 0W
Bausi, India .... 43 G12 24 48N 87 1 E
Bauska, Latvia .... 9 H21 56 24N 24 15 E
Bautzen, Germany .... 16 C8 51 10N 14 26 E
Bavānāt, Iran .... 45 D7 30 28N 53 27 E
Bavaria = Bayern □, Germany ... 16 D6 48 50N 12 0 E
Bavispe →, Mexico 86 B3 29 30N 109 11W
Bawdwin, Burma .... 41 H20 23 5N 97 20 E
Bawean, Indonesia .... 36 F4 5 46S 112 35 E
Bawku, Ghana 50 F5 11 3N 0 19W
Bawlake, Burma .... 41 K20 19 11N 97 21 E
Baxley, U.S.A. 83 K4 31 47N 82 21W
Baxter, U.S.A. 80 B7 46 21N 94 17W
Baxter Springs, U.S.A. 81 G7 37 2N 94 44W
Baxter State △, U.S.A. 83 B11 46 5N 68 57W
Bay City, Mich., U.S.A. 82 D4 43 36N 83 54W
Bay City, Tex., U.S.A. 81 L7 28 59N 95 58W
Bay Minette, U.S.A. 83 K2 30 53N 87 46W
Bay Roberts, Canada 73 C9 47 36N 53 16W
Bay St. Louis, U.S.A. 81 K10 30 19N 89 20W
Bay Springs, U.S.A. 81 K10 31 59N 89 17W
Bay View, N.Z. .... 59 H6 39 25S 176 50 E
Bayamo, Cuba 88 B4 20 20N 76 40W
Bayamón, Puerto Rico .... 89 d 18 24N 66 10W
Bayan Har Shan, China .... 32 C4 34 0N 98 0 E
Bayan Hot = Alxa Zuoqi, China . 34 E3 38 50N 105 40 E
Bayan Lepas, Malaysia .... 39 c 5 17N 100 16 E
Bayan Obo, China .... 34 D5 41 52N 109 59 E
Bayan-Ovoo = Erdenetsogt,
  Mongolia .... 34 C4 42 55N 106 5 E
Bayana, India .... 42 F7 26 55N 77 18 E
Bayanaüyl, Kazakhstan .... 28 D8 50 45N 75 45 E
Bayandalay, Mongolia .... 34 C2 43 30N 103 29 E
Bayanhongor, Mongolia .... 32 B5 46 8N 102 43 E
Bayard, N. Mex., U.S.A. 77 K9 32 46N 108 8W
Bayard, Nebr., U.S.A. 80 E3 41 45N 103 20W
Baybay, Phil. .... 37 B6 10 40N 124 55 E
Baydhabo = Baidoa, Somali Rep. 47 G3 3 8N 43 30 E
Bayern □, Germany .... 16 D6 48 50N 12 0 E
Bayeux, France 20 B3 49 17N 0 42W

Bayfield, Canada 84 C3 43 34N 81 42W
Bayfield, U.S.A. 80 B9 46 49N 90 49W
Bayındır, Turkey .... 23 E12 38 13N 27 39 E
Bayjī, Iraq .... 44 C4 35 0N 43 30 E
Baykal, Oz., Russia .... 29 D11 53 0N 108 0 E
Baykan, Turkey .... 44 B4 38 7N 41 44 E
Baykonur = Bayqongyr,
  Kazakhstan .... 28 E7 47 48N 65 50 E
Baymak, Russia .... 18 D10 52 36N 58 19 E
Baynes Mts., Namibia .... 56 B1 17 15S 13 0 E
Bayombong, Phil. .... 37 A6 16 30N 121 10 E
Bayonne, France 20 E3 43 30N 1 28W
Bayonne, U.S.A. 85 F10 40 40N 74 7W
Bayovar, Peru 92 E2 5 50S 81 0W
Bayqongyr, Kazakhstan .... 28 E7 47 48N 65 50 E
Bayram-Ali = Bayramaly,
  Turkmenistan .... 28 F7 37 37N 62 10 E
Bayramaly, Turkmenistan .... 28 F7 37 37N 62 10 E
Bayramiç, Turkey .... 23 E12 39 48N 26 36 E
Bayreuth, Germany .... 16 D6 49 56N 11 35 E
Bayrūt, Lebanon .... 46 B4 33 53N 35 31 E
Bays, L. of, Canada 84 A5 45 15N 79 4W
Baysville, Canada 84 A5 45 9N 79 7W
Bayt Lahm, West Bank .... 46 D4 31 43N 35 12 E
Baytown, U.S.A. 81 L7 29 43N 94 59W
Bayun, Indonesia .... 37 J18 8 11S 115 16 E
Baza, Spain 21 D4 37 30N 2 47W
Bazaruto △, Mozam. .... 57 C6 21 42S 35 26 E
Bazaruto, I. do, Mozam. .... 57 C6 21 40S 35 28 E
Bazhou, China .... 34 E9 39 8N 116 22 E
Bazmān, Kūh-e, Iran .... 45 D9 28 4N 60 1 E
Beach, U.S.A. 80 B3 46 58N 104 0W
Beach City, U.S.A. 84 F3 40 39N 81 35W
Beachport, Australia .... 63 F3 37 29S 140 0 E
Beachy Hd., U.K. .... 13 G8 50 44N 0 15 E
Beacon, Australia .... 61 F2 30 26S 117 52 E
Beacon, U.S.A. 85 E11 41 30N 73 58W
Beaconsfield, Australia .... 63 G4 41 11S 146 48 E
Beagle, Canal, S. Amer. 96 H3 55 0S 68 30W
Beagle Bay, Australia .... 60 C3 16 58S 122 40 E
Bealanana, Madag. .... 57 A8 14 33S 48 44 E
Beals Cr. →, U.S.A. 81 J4 32 10N 100 51W
Bear →, Calif., U.S.A. 78 G5 38 56N 121 36W
Bear →, Utah, U.S.A. 74 B4 41 30N 112 8W
Bear I., Ireland 10 E2 51 38N 9 50W
Bear L., Canada 71 B9 55 8N 96 0W
Bear L., U.S.A. 76 F8 41 59N 111 21W
Beardmore, Canada 72 C2 49 36N 87 57W
Beardmore Glacier, Antarctica 5 E11 84 30S 170 0 E
Beardstown, U.S.A. 80 F9 40 1N 90 26W
Bearma →, India .... 43 G8 24 20N 79 51 E
Béarn, France 20 E3 43 20N 0 30W
Bearpaw Mts., U.S.A. 76 B9 48 12N 109 30W
Bearskin Lake, Canada 72 B1 53 58N 91 2W
Beas →, India .... 42 D6 31 10N 74 59 E
Beata, C., Dom. Rep. 89 C5 17 40N 71 30W
Beata, I., Dom. Rep. 89 C5 17 34N 71 31W
Beatrice, U.S.A. 80 E6 40 16N 96 45W
Beatrice, Zimbabwe .... 55 F3 18 15S 30 55 E
Beatrice, C., Australia .... 62 A2 14 20S 136 55 E
Beatton →, Canada 70 B4 56 15N 120 45W
Beatton River, Canada 70 B4 57 26N 121 20W
Beatty, U.S.A. 78 J10 36 54N 116 46W
Beauce, Plaine de la, France .. 20 B4 48 10N 1 45 E
Beauceville, Canada 73 C5 46 13N 70 46W
Beaudesert, Australia .... 63 D5 27 59S 153 0 E
Beaufort, Malaysia .... 36 C5 5 30N 115 40 E
Beaufort, N.C., U.S.A. 83 H7 34 43N 76 40W
Beaufort, S.C., U.S.A. 83 J5 32 26N 80 40W
Beaufort Sea, Arctic 4 B1 72 0N 140 0W
Beaufort West, S. Africa ...... 56 E3 32 18S 22 36 E
Beaulieu →, Canada 70 A6 62 3N 113 11W
Beauly, U.K. 11 D4 57 30N 4 28W
Beauly →, U.K. 11 D4 57 29N 4 27W
Beaumaris, U.K. 12 D3 53 16N 4 6W
Beaumont, Belgium .... 15 D4 50 15N 4 14 E
Beaumont, U.S.A. 81 K7 30 5N 94 6W
Beaune, France .... 20 C6 47 2N 4 50 E
Beaupré, Canada 73 C5 47 3N 70 54W
Beauraing, Belgium .... 15 D4 50 7N 4 57 E
Beausejour, Canada 71 C9 50 5N 96 35W
Beauvais, France .... 20 B5 49 25N 2 8 E
Beauval, Canada 71 B7 55 9N 107 37W
Beaver, Okla., U.S.A. 81 G4 36 49N 100 31W
Beaver, Pa., U.S.A. 84 F4 40 42N 80 19W
Beaver, Utah, U.S.A. 77 G7 38 17N 112 38W
Beaver →, B.C., Canada 70 B4 59 52N 124 20W
Beaver →, Ont., Canada 72 A2 55 55N 87 48W
Beaver →, Sask., Canada 71 B7 55 26N 107 45W
Beaver City, U.S.A. 80 E5 40 8N 99 50W
Beaver Creek, Canada 68 B5 63 0N 141 0W
Beaver Dam, U.S.A. 80 D10 43 28N 88 50W
Beaver Falls, U.S.A. 84 F4 40 46N 80 20W
Beaver Hill L., Canada 71 C10 54 5N 94 50W
Beaver I., U.S.A. 82 C3 45 40N 85 33W
Beaverhill L., Canada 70 C6 53 27N 112 32W
Beaverlodge, Canada 70 B5 55 11N 119 29W
Beaverstone →, Canada 72 B2 54 59N 89 25W
Beaverton, Canada 84 B5 44 26N 79 9W
Beaverton, U.S.A. 78 E4 45 29N 122 48W
Beawar, India .... 42 F6 26 3N 74 18 E
Bebedouro, Brazil 95 A6 21 0S 48 25W
Bebera, Tanjung, Indonesia .... 37 K18 8 44S 115 51 E
Beboa, Madag. .... 57 B7 17 22S 44 33 E
Becan, Mexico 87 D7 18 31N 89 28W
Beccles, U.K. .... 13 E9 52 27N 1 35 E
Bečej, Serbia & M. .... 23 B9 45 36N 20 3 E
Béchar, Algeria .... 50 B5 31 38N 2 18 E
Beckley, U.S.A. 82 G5 37 47N 81 11W
Beddouza, Ras, Morocco 50 B4 32 33N 9 9W
Bedford, Canada 85 A12 45 7N 72 59W
Bedford, S. Africa .... 56 E4 32 40S 26 10 E
Bedford, U.K. 13 E7 52 8N 0 28W
Bedford, Ind., U.S.A. 82 F2 38 52N 86 29W
Bedford, Iowa, U.S.A. 80 E7 40 40N 94 44W
Bedford, Ohio, U.S.A. 84 E3 41 23N 81 32W
Bedford, Pa., U.S.A. 84 F6 40 1N 78 30W
Bedford, Va., U.S.A. 82 G6 37 20N 79 31W
Bedfordshire □, U.K. 13 E7 52 4N 0 28W
Bedok, Singapore .... 39 d 1 19N 103 56 E
Bedourie, Australia .... 62 C2 24 30S 139 30 E
Bedum, Neths. .... 15 A6 53 18N 6 36 E
Beebe Plain, Canada 85 A12 45 1N 72 9W
Beech Creek, U.S.A. 84 E7 41 5N 77 36W

Beef I., Br. Virgin Is. 89 e 18 26N 64 30W
Beenleigh, Australia 63 D5 27 43S 153 10 E
Be'er Menuha, Israel 44 D2 30 19N 35 8 E
Be'er Sheva, Israel 46 D3 31 15N 34 48 E
Beersheba = Be'er Sheva, Israel 46 D3 31 15N 34 48 E
Beestekraal, S. Africa 57 D4 25 23S 27 38 E
Beeston, U.K. 12 E6 52 56N 1 14W
Beeville, U.S.A. 81 L6 28 24N 97 45W
Befale, Dem. Rep. of the Congo 52 D4 0 25N 20 45 E
Befandriana, Mahajanga, Madag. 57 B8 15 16S 48 32 E
Befandriana, Toliara, Madag. 57 C7 21 55S 44 0 E
Befasy, Madag. 57 C7 20 33S 44 23 E
Befotaka, Antsiranana, Madag. 57 A8 13 15S 48 16 E
Befotaka, Fianarantsoa, Madag. 57 C8 23 49S 47 0 E
Bega, Australia 63 F4 36 41S 149 51 E
Begusarai, India 43 G12 25 24N 86 9 E
Behābād, Iran 45 C8 32 24N 59 47 E
Behala, India 43 H13 22 30N 88 20 E
Behara, Madag. 57 C8 24 55S 46 20 E
Behbehān, Iran 45 D6 30 30N 50 15 E
Behm Canal, U.S.A. 70 B2 55 10N 131 0W
Behshahr, Iran 45 B7 36 45N 53 35 E
Bei Jiang →, China 33 D6 23 2N 112 58 E
Bei'an, China 33 B7 48 10N 126 20 E
Beihai, China 33 D5 21 28N 109 6 E
Beijing, China 34 E9 39 55N 116 20 E
Beijing □, China 34 E9 39 55N 116 20 E
Beilen, Neths. 15 B6 52 52N 6 27 E
Beilpajah, Australia 63 E3 32 54S 143 52 E
Beinn na Faoghla = Benbecula, U.K. 11 D1 57 26N 7 21W
Beipiao, China 35 D11 41 52N 120 32 E
Beira, Mozam. 55 F3 19 50S 34 52 E
Beirut = Bayrūt, Lebanon 46 B4 33 53N 35 31 E
Beiseker, Canada 70 C6 51 23N 113 32W
Beitaolaizhao, China 35 B13 44 58N 125 58 E
Beitbridge, Zimbabwe 55 G3 22 12S 30 0 E
Beizhen = Binzhou, China 35 F10 37 20N 118 2 E
Beizhen, China 35 D11 41 38N 121 54 E
Beizhengzhen, China 35 B12 44 31N 123 30 E
Beja, Portugal 21 C2 38 2N 7 53W
Béja, Tunisia 51 A7 36 43N 9 12 E
Bejaïa, Algeria 50 A7 36 42N 5 2 E
Béjar, Spain 21 B3 40 23N 5 46W
Bejestān, Iran 45 C8 34 30N 58 5 E
Bekaa Valley = Al Biqā, Lebanon 46 A5 34 10N 36 10 E
Békéscsaba, Hungary 17 E11 46 40N 21 5 E
Bekily, Madag. 57 C8 24 13S 45 19 E
Bekisopa, Madag. 57 C8 21 40S 45 54 E
Bekitro, Madag. 57 C8 24 33S 45 18 E
Bekodoka, Madag. 57 B8 16 58S 45 7 E
Bekok, Malaysia 39 L4 2 20N 103 7 E
Bekopaka, Madag. 57 B7 19 9S 44 48 E
Bekuli, Indonesia 37 J17 8 22S 114 13 E
Bela, India 43 G10 25 50N 82 0 E
Bela, Pakistan 42 F2 26 12N 66 20 E
Bela Bela, S. Africa 57 C4 24 51S 28 19 E
Bela Crkva, Serbia & M. 23 B9 44 55N 21 27 E
Bela Vista, Brazil 94 A4 22 12S 56 20W
Bela Vista, Mozam. 57 D5 26 10S 32 44 E
Belan →, India 43 G9 24 2N 81 45 E
Belarus ■, Europe 17 B14 53 30N 27 0 E
Belau = Palau ■, Pac. Oc. 26 J17 7 30N 134 30 E
Belavenona, Madag. 57 C8 24 50S 47 4 E
Belawan, Indonesia 36 D1 3 33N 98 32 E
Belaya →, Russia 18 C9 54 40N 56 0 E
Belaya Tserkov = Bila Tserkva, Ukraine 17 D16 49 45N 30 10 E
Belcher Is., Canada 72 A3 56 15N 78 45W
Belden, U.S.A. 78 E5 40 2N 121 17W
Belebey, Russia 18 D9 54 7N 54 7 E
Beled Weyne = Belet Uen, Somali Rep. 47 G4 4 30N 45 5 E
Belém, Brazil 93 D9 1 20S 48 30W
Belén, Argentina 94 B2 27 40S 67 5W
Belén, Paraguay 94 A4 23 30S 57 6W
Belen, U.S.A. 77 J10 34 40N 106 46W
Belet Uen, Somali Rep. 47 G4 4 30N 45 5 E
Belev, Russia 18 D6 53 50N 36 5 E
Belfair, U.S.A. 78 C4 47 27N 122 50W
Belfast, S. Africa 57 D5 25 42S 30 2 E
Belfast, U.K. 10 B6 54 37N 5 56W
Belfast, Maine, U.S.A. 83 C11 44 26N 69 1W
Belfast, N.Y., U.S.A. 84 D6 42 21N 78 7W
Belfast L., U.K. 10 B6 54 40N 5 50W
Belfield, U.S.A. 80 B3 46 53N 103 12W
Belfort, France 20 C7 47 38N 6 50 E
Belfry, U.S.A. 76 D9 45 9N 109 1W
Belgaum, India 40 M9 15 55N 74 35 E
Belgium ■, Europe 15 D4 50 30N 5 0 E
Belgorod, Russia 19 D6 50 35N 36 35 E
Belgorod-Dnestrovskiy =
   Bilhorod-Dnistrovskyy, Ukraine 19 E5 46 11N 30 23 E
Belgrade = Beograd, Serbia & M. 23 B9 44 50N 20 37 E
Belgrade, U.S.A. 76 D8 45 47N 111 11W
Belhaven, U.S.A. 83 H7 35 33N 76 37W
Beli Drim →, Europe 23 C9 42 6N 20 25 E
Belimbing, Indonesia 37 J18 8 24S 115 2 E
Belinyu, Indonesia 36 E3 1 35S 105 50 E
Beliton Is. = Belitung, Indonesia 36 E3 3 10S 107 50 E
Belitung, Indonesia 36 E3 3 10S 107 50 E
Belize ■, Cent. Amer. 87 D7 17 0N 88 30W
Belize City, Belize 87 D7 17 25N 88 0W
Belkovskiy, Ostrov, Russia 29 B14 75 32N 135 44 E
Bell →, Canada 72 C4 49 48N 77 38W
Bell I., Canada 73 B8 50 46N 55 35W
Bell-Irving →, Canada 70 B3 56 12N 129 5W
Bell Peninsula, Canada 69 B11 63 50N 82 0W
Bell Ville, Argentina 94 C3 32 40S 62 40W
Bella Bella, Canada 70 C3 52 10N 128 10W
Bella Coola, Canada 70 C3 52 25N 126 40W
Bella Unión, Uruguay 94 C4 30 15S 57 40W
Bella Vista, Corrientes, Argentina 94 B4 28 33S 59 0W
Bella Vista, Tucuman, Argentina 94 B2 27 10S 65 25W
Bellaire, U.S.A. 84 F4 40 1N 80 45W
Bellary, India 40 M10 15 10N 76 56 E
Bellata, Australia 63 D4 29 53S 149 46 E
Belle-Chasse, U.S.A. 81 L10 29 51N 89 59W
Belle Fourche, U.S.A. 80 C3 44 40N 103 51W
Belle Fourche →, U.S.A. 80 C3 44 26N 102 18W
Belle Glade, U.S.A. 83 M5 26 41N 80 40W
Belle-Île, France 20 C2 47 20N 3 10W
Belle Isle, Canada 73 B8 51 57N 55 25W
Belle Isle, Str. of, Canada 73 B8 51 30N 56 30W
Belle Plaine, U.S.A. 80 E8 41 54N 92 17W
Bellefontaine, U.S.A. 82 E4 40 22N 83 46W
Bellefonte, U.S.A. 84 F7 40 55N 77 47W
Belleoram, Canada 73 C8 47 31N 55 25W

Belleplaine, Barbados 89 g 13 15N 59 34W
Belleville, Canada 84 B7 44 10N 77 23W
Belleville, Ill., U.S.A. 80 F10 38 31N 89 59W
Belleville, Kans., U.S.A. 80 F6 39 50N 97 38W
Belleville, N.Y., U.S.A. 85 C8 43 46N 76 10W
Bellevue, Canada 70 D6 49 35N 114 22W
Bellevue, Idaho, U.S.A. 76 E6 43 28N 114 16W
Bellevue, Nebr., U.S.A. 80 E7 41 8N 95 53W
Bellevue, Ohio, U.S.A. 84 E2 41 17N 82 51W
Bellevue, Wash., U.S.A. 78 C4 47 37N 122 12W
Bellin = Kangirsuk, Canada 69 B13 60 0N 70 0W
Bellingen, Australia 63 E5 30 25S 152 50 E
Bellingham, U.S.A. 68 D7 48 46N 122 29W
Bellingshausen Sea, Antarctica 5 C17 66 0S 80 0W
Bellinzona, Switz. 20 C8 46 11N 9 1 E
Bello, Colombia 92 B3 6 20N 75 33W
Bellows Falls, U.S.A. 85 C12 43 8N 72 27W
Bellpat, Pakistan 42 E3 29 0N 68 5 E
Belluno, Italy 22 A5 46 9N 12 13 E
Bellwood, U.S.A. 84 F6 40 36N 78 20W
Belmont, Canada 84 D3 42 53N 81 5W
Belmont, S. Africa 56 D3 29 28S 24 22 E
Belmont, U.S.A. 84 D6 42 14N 78 2W
Belmonte, Brazil 93 G11 16 0S 39 0W
Belmopan, Belize 87 D7 17 18N 88 30W
Belmullet, Ireland 10 B2 54 14N 9 58W
Belo Horizonte, Brazil 93 G10 19 55S 43 56W
Belo-sur-Mer, Madag. 57 C7 20 42S 44 0 E
Belo-Tsiribihina, Madag. 57 B7 19 40S 44 30 E
Belogorsk, Russia 29 D13 51 0N 128 20 E
Beloha, Madag. 57 D8 25 10S 45 3 E
Beloit, Kans., U.S.A. 80 F5 39 28N 98 6W
Beloit, Wis., U.S.A. 80 D10 42 31N 89 2W
Belokorovichi, Ukraine 17 C15 51 7N 28 2 E
Belomorsk, Russia 18 B5 64 35N 34 54 E
Belonia, India 41 H17 23 15N 91 30 E
Beloretsk, Russia 18 D10 53 58N 58 24 E
Belorussia = Belarus ■, Europe 17 B14 53 30N 27 0 E
Belovo, Russia 28 D9 54 30N 86 0 E
Beloye, Ozero, Russia 18 B6 60 10N 37 35 E
Beloye More, Russia 18 A6 66 30N 38 0 E
Belozersk, Russia 18 B6 60 1N 37 45 E
Belpre, U.S.A. 82 F5 39 17N 81 34W
Belrain, India 43 E9 28 23N 80 55 E
Belt, U.S.A. 76 C8 47 23N 110 55W
Beltana, Australia 63 E2 30 48S 138 25 E
Belterra, Brazil 93 D8 2 45S 55 0W
Belton, U.S.A. 81 K6 31 3N 97 28W
Belton L., U.S.A. 81 K6 31 8N 97 32W
Beltsy = Bălți, Moldova 17 E14 47 48N 27 58 E
Belturbet, Ireland 10 B4 54 6N 7 26W
Belukha, Russia 28 E9 49 50N 86 50 E
Beluran, Malaysia 36 C5 5 48N 117 35 E
Belvidere, Ill., U.S.A. 80 D10 42 15N 88 50W
Belvidere, N.J., U.S.A. 85 F9 40 50N 75 5W
Belyando →, Australia 62 C4 21 38S 146 50 E
Belyy, Ostrov, Russia 28 B8 73 30N 71 0 E
Belyy Yar, Russia 28 D9 58 26N 84 39 E
Belzoni, U.S.A. 81 J9 33 11N 90 29W
Bemaraha, Lembalemban' i,
   Madag. 57 B7 18 40S 44 45 E
Bemarivo, Madag. 57 C7 21 45S 44 45 E
Bemarivo →, Antsiranana,
   Madag. 57 A9 14 9S 50 9 E
Bemarivo →, Mahajanga,
   Madag. 57 B8 15 27S 47 40 E
Bemavo, Madag. 57 C8 21 33S 45 25 E
Bembéréke, Benin 50 F6 10 11N 2 43 E
Bembesi, Zimbabwe 55 G2 20 0S 28 58 E
Bembesi →, Zimbabwe 55 F2 18 57S 27 47 E
Bemetara, India 43 J9 21 42N 81 32 E
Bemidji, U.S.A. 80 B7 47 28N 94 53W
Bemolanga, Madag. 57 B8 17 44S 45 6 E
Ben, Iran 45 C6 32 32N 50 45 E
Ben Cruachan, U.K. 11 E3 56 26N 5 8W
Ben Dearg, U.K. 11 D4 57 47N 4 56W
Ben En △, Vietnam 38 C5 19 37N 105 30 E
Ben Hope, U.K. 11 C4 58 25N 4 36W
Ben Lawers, U.K. 11 E4 56 32N 4 14W
Ben Lomond, N.S.W., Australia 63 E5 30 1S 151 43 E
Ben Lomond, Tas., Australia 62 G4 41 38S 147 42 E
Ben Lomond, U.K. 11 E4 56 11N 4 38W
Ben Lomond △, Australia 63 G4 41 33S 147 39 E
Ben Luc, Vietnam 39 G6 10 39N 106 29 E
Ben Macdhui, U.K. 11 D5 57 4N 3 40W
Ben Mhor, U.K. 11 D1 57 15N 7 18W
Ben More, Arg. & Bute, U.K. 11 E2 56 26N 6 1W
Ben More, Stirl., U.K. 11 E4 56 23N 4 32W
Ben More Assynt, U.K. 11 C4 58 8N 4 52W
Ben Nevis, U.K. 11 E3 56 48N 5 1W
Ben Quang, Vietnam 38 D6 17 3N 106 55 E
Ben Vorlich, U.K. 11 E4 56 21N 4 14W
Ben Wyvis, U.K. 11 D4 57 40N 4 35W
Bena, Nigeria 50 F7 11 20N 5 50 E
Benalla, Australia 63 F4 36 30S 146 0 E
Benares = Varanasi, India 43 G10 25 22N 83 0 E
Benavente, Spain 21 A3 42 2N 5 43W
Benavides, U.S.A. 81 M5 27 36N 98 25W
Benbecula, U.K. 11 D1 57 26N 7 21W
Benbonyathe, Australia 63 E2 30 25S 139 11 E
Bend, U.S.A. 76 D3 44 4N 121 19W
Bender Beila, Somali Rep. 47 F5 9 30N 50 48 E
Bendery = Tighina, Moldova 17 E15 46 50N 29 30 E
Bendigo, Australia 63 F3 36 40S 144 15 E
Benē Beraq, Israel 46 C3 32 6N 34 51 E
Benenitra, Madag. 57 C8 23 27S 45 5 E
Benevento, Italy 22 D6 41 8N 14 45 E
Benga, Mozam. 55 F3 16 11S 33 40 E
Bengal, Bay of, Ind. Oc. 41 M17 15 0N 90 0 E
Bengalūru = Bangalore, India 40 N10 12 59N 77 40 E
Bengbu, China 35 H9 32 58N 117 20 E
Benghazi = Banghāzī, Libya 51 B10 32 11N 20 3 E
Bengkalis, Indonesia 36 D2 1 30N 102 10 E
Bengkulu, Indonesia 36 E2 3 48S 102 16 E
Bengkulu □, Indonesia 36 E2 3 48S 102 16 E
Bengough, Canada 71 D7 49 25N 105 10W
Benguela, Angola 53 G2 12 37S 13 25 E
Benguérua, I., Mozam. 57 C6 21 58S 35 28 E
Beni, Dem. Rep. of the Congo 54 B2 0 30N 29 27 E
Beni →, Bolivia 92 F5 10 23S 65 24W
Beni Mellal, Morocco 50 B4 32 21N 6 21W
Beni Suef, Egypt 51 C12 29 5N 31 6 E
Beniah L., Canada 70 A6 63 23N 112 17W
Benicia, U.S.A. 78 G4 38 3N 122 9W
Benidorm, Spain 21 C5 38 33N 0 9W
Benin ■, Africa 50 G6 10 0N 2 0 E
Benin, Bight of, W. Afr. 50 H6 5 0N 3 0 E
Benin City, Nigeria 50 G7 6 20N 5 31 E

Benitses, Greece 25 A3 39 32N 19 55 E
Benjamin Aceval, Paraguay 94 A4 24 58S 57 34W
Benjamin Constant, Brazil 92 D4 4 40S 70 15W
Benjamin Hill, Mexico 86 A2 30 10N 111 10W
Benkelman, U.S.A. 80 E4 40 3N 101 32W
Bennett, Canada 70 B2 59 56N 134 53W
Bennett, L., Australia 60 D5 22 50S 131 2 E
Bennetta, Ostrov, Russia 29 B15 76 21N 148 56 E
Bennington, N.H., U.S.A. 85 D11 43 0N 71 55W
Bennington, Vt., U.S.A. 85 D11 42 53N 73 12W
Benoni, S. Africa 57 D4 26 11S 28 18 E
Benque Viejo, Belize 87 D7 17 5N 89 8W
Benson, Ariz., U.S.A. 77 L8 31 58N 110 18W
Benson, Minn., U.S.A. 80 C7 45 19N 95 36W
Bent, Iran 45 E8 26 20N 59 31 E
Benteng, Indonesia 37 F6 6 10S 120 30 E
Bentinck I., Australia 62 B2 17 3S 139 35 E
Bento Gonçalves, Brazil 95 B5 29 10S 51 31W
Benton, Ark., U.S.A. 81 H8 34 34N 92 35W
Benton, Calif., U.S.A. 78 H8 37 48N 118 32W
Benton, Ill., U.S.A. 80 G10 38 0N 88 55W
Benton, Pa., U.S.A. 85 E8 41 12N 76 23W
Benton Harbor, U.S.A. 82 D2 42 6N 86 27W
Bentong, Malaysia 39 L3 3 31N 101 55 E
Bentonville, U.S.A. 81 G7 36 22N 94 13W
Benue →, Nigeria 50 G7 7 48N 6 46 E
Benxi, China 35 D12 41 20N 123 48 E
Beo, Indonesia 37 D7 4 25N 126 50 E
Beograd, Serbia & M. 23 B9 44 50N 20 37 E
Beppu, Japan 31 H5 33 15N 131 30 E
Beqaa Valley = Al Biqā, Lebanon 46 A5 34 10N 36 10 E
Ber Mota, India 42 H3 23 27N 68 34 E
Berach →, India 42 G6 25 15N 75 2 E
Beraketa, Madag. 57 C7 23 7S 44 25 E
Berat, Albania 23 D8 40 43N 19 59 E
Berau, Teluk, Indonesia 37 E8 2 30S 132 30 E
Beravina, Madag. 57 B8 18 10S 45 14 E
Berber, Sudan 51 E12 18 0N 34 0 E
Berbera, Somali Rep. 47 E4 10 30N 45 2 E
Berbérati, C.A.R. 52 D3 4 15N 15 40 E
Berbice →, Guyana 92 B7 6 20N 57 32W
Berdichev = Berdychiv, Ukraine 17 D15 49 57N 28 30 E
Berdsk, Russia 28 D9 54 47N 83 2 E
Berdyansk, Ukraine 19 E6 46 45N 36 50 E
Berdychiv, Ukraine 17 D15 49 57N 28 30 E
Berea, U.S.A. 82 G3 37 34N 84 17W
Berebere, Indonesia 37 D7 2 25N 128 45 E
Bereda, Somali Rep. 47 E5 11 45N 51 0 E
Berehove, Ukraine 17 D12 48 15N 22 35 E
Berekum, Ghana 50 G5 7 29N 2 34W
Berens →, Canada 71 C9 52 25N 97 2W
Berens I., Canada 71 C9 52 18N 97 18W
Berens River, Canada 71 C9 52 25N 97 0W
Beresford, U.S.A. 80 D6 43 5N 96 47W
Berestechko, Ukraine 17 C13 50 22N 25 5 E
Berevo, Mahajanga, Madag. 57 B7 17 14S 44 17 E
Berevo, Toliara, Madag. 57 B7 19 44S 44 58 E
Berezhany, Ukraine 17 D13 49 26N 24 58 E
Berezina = Byarezina →, Belarus 17 B16 52 33N 30 14 E
Bereznik, Russia 18 B7 62 51N 42 40 E
Berezniki, Russia 18 C10 59 24N 56 46 E
Berezovo, Russia 28 C7 64 0N 65 0 E
Berga, Spain 21 A6 42 6N 1 48 E
Bergama, Turkey 23 E12 39 8N 27 11 E
Bérgamo, Italy 20 D8 45 41N 9 43 E
Bergen, Neths. 15 B4 52 40N 4 43 E
Bergen, Norway 9 F11 60 20N 5 20 E
Bergen, U.S.A. 84 C7 43 5N 77 57W
Bergen op Zoom, Neths. 15 C4 51 28N 4 18 E
Bergerac, France 20 D4 44 51N 0 30 E
Bergholz, U.S.A. 84 F4 40 31N 80 53W
Bergisch Gladbach, Germany 15 D7 50 59N 7 8 E
Bergville, S. Africa 57 D4 28 52S 29 18 E
Berhala, Selat, Indonesia 36 E2 1 0S 104 15 E
Berhampore = Baharampur, India 43 G13 24 2N 88 27 E
Berhampur = Brahmapur, India 41 K14 19 15N 84 54 E
Bering Sea, Pac. Oc. 68 C1 58 0N 171 0 E
Bering Strait, Pac. Oc. 68 B3 65 30N 169 0W
Beringovskiy, Russia 29 C18 63 3N 179 19 E
Berisso, Argentina 94 C4 34 56S 57 50W
Berja, Spain 21 D4 36 50N 2 56W
Berkeley, U.S.A. 78 H4 37 52N 122 16W
Berkner I., Antarctica 5 D18 79 30S 50 0W
Berkshire, U.S.A. 85 D8 42 19N 76 11W
Berkshire Downs, U.K. 13 F6 51 33N 1 29W
Berlin, Germany 16 B7 52 30N 13 25 E
Berlin, Md., U.S.A. 85 F8 38 20N 75 13W
Berlin, N.H., U.S.A. 85 B13 44 28N 71 11W
Berlin, N.Y., U.S.A. 85 D11 42 42N 73 23W
Berlin, Wis., U.S.A. 82 D1 43 58N 88 57W
Berlin L., U.S.A. 84 E4 41 3N 81 0W
Bermejo →, Formosa, Argentina 94 B4 26 51S 58 23W
Bermejo →, San Juan, Argentina 94 C2 32 30S 67 30W
Bermen, L., Canada 73 B6 53 35N 68 55W
Bermuda ☑, Atl. Oc. 66 F13 32 45N 65 0W
Bern, Switz. 20 C7 46 57N 7 28 E
Bernalillo, U.S.A. 77 J10 35 18N 106 33W
Bernardo de Irigoyen, Argentina 95 B5 26 15S 53 40W
Bernardo O'Higgins □, Chile 94 C1 34 15S 70 45W
Bernardsville, U.S.A. 85 F10 40 43N 74 34W
Bernasconi, Argentina 94 D3 37 55S 63 44W
Bernburg, Germany 16 C6 51 47N 11 44 E
Berne = Bern, Switz. 20 C7 46 57N 7 28 E
Berneray, U.K. 11 D1 57 43N 7 11W
Bernier I., Australia 61 D1 24 50S 113 12 E
Bernina, Piz, Switz. 20 C8 46 20N 9 54 E
Beroroha, Madag. 57 C8 21 40S 45 10 E
Beroun, Czech Rep. 16 D8 49 57N 14 5 E
Berri, Australia 63 E3 34 14S 140 35 E
Berriane, Algeria 50 B6 32 50N 3 46 E
Berry, Australia 63 E5 34 46S 150 43 E
Berry, France 20 C5 46 50N 2 0 E
Berry Is., Bahamas 88 A4 25 40N 77 50W
Berryessa L., U.S.A. 78 G4 38 31N 122 6W
Berryville, U.S.A. 81 G8 36 22N 93 34W
Berseba, Namibia 56 D2 26 0S 17 46 E
Bershad, Ukraine 17 D15 48 22N 29 31 E
Berthold, U.S.A. 80 A4 48 19N 101 44W
Berthoud, U.S.A. 76 E2 40 19N 105 5W
Bertoua, Cameroon 52 D2 4 30N 13 45 E
Bertraghboy B., Ireland 10 C2 53 22N 9 54W
Berwick, U.S.A. 85 E8 41 3N 76 14W
Berwick-upon-Tweed, U.K. 12 B5 55 46N 2 0W
Berwyn Mts., U.K. 12 E4 52 54N 3 26W
Besal, Pakistan 43 B5 35 4N 73 56 E
Besalampy, Madag. 57 B7 16 43S 44 29 E
Besançon, France 20 C7 47 15N 6 2 E

Besar, Indonesia 36 E5 2 40S 116 0 E
Besnard L., Canada 71 B7 55 25N 106 0W
Besni, Turkey 44 B3 37 41N 37 52 E
Besor, N. →, Egypt 46 D3 31 28N 34 22 E
Bessarabiya = Basarabeasca,
   Moldova 17 E15 47 0N 28 10 E
Bessarabka = Basarabeasca,
   Moldova 17 E15 46 21N 28 58 E
Bessemer, Ala., U.S.A. 83 J2 33 24N 86 58W
Bessemer, Mich., U.S.A. 80 B9 46 29N 90 3W
Bessemer, Pa., U.S.A. 84 F4 40 59N 80 30W
Beswick, Australia 60 B5 14 34S 132 53 E
Bet She'an, Israel 46 C4 32 30N 35 30 E
Bet Shemesh, Israel 46 D4 31 44N 35 0 E
Betafo, Madag. 57 B8 19 50S 46 51 E
Betancuria, Canary Is. 24 F5 28 25N 14 3W
Betanzos, Spain 21 A1 43 15N 8 12W
Bétaré Oya, Cameroon 52 C2 5 40N 14 5 E
Betatao, Madag. 57 B8 18 11S 47 52 E
Bethal, S. Africa 57 D4 26 27S 29 28 E
Bethanien, Namibia 56 D2 26 31S 17 8 E
Bethany, Canada 84 B6 44 11N 78 34W
Bethany, U.S.A. 80 E7 40 16N 94 2W
Bethel, Alaska, U.S.A. 68 B3 60 48N 161 45W
Bethel, Conn., U.S.A. 85 E11 41 22N 73 25W
Bethel, Maine, U.S.A. 85 B14 44 25N 70 47W
Bethel, Vt., U.S.A. 85 C12 43 50N 72 38W
Bethel Park, U.S.A. 84 F4 40 20N 80 1W
Bethlehem = Bayt Lahm,
   West Bank 46 D4 31 43N 35 12 E
Bethlehem, S. Africa 57 D4 28 14S 28 18 E
Bethlehem, U.S.A. 85 F9 40 37N 75 23W
Bethulie, S. Africa 56 E4 30 30S 25 59 E
Béthune, France 20 A5 50 30N 2 38 E
Betioky, Madag. 57 C7 23 48S 44 20 E
Betong, Thailand 39 K3 5 45N 101 5 E
Betoota, Australia 62 D3 25 45S 140 42 E
Betroka, Madag. 57 C8 23 16S 46 0 E
Betsiamites, Canada 73 C6 48 56N 68 40W
Betsiamites →, Canada 73 C6 48 56N 68 38W
Betsiboka →, Madag. 57 B8 16 3S 46 36 E
Bettendorf, U.S.A. 80 E9 41 32N 90 30W
Bettiah, India 43 F11 26 48N 84 33 E
Betul, India 40 J10 21 58N 77 59 E
Betung, Malaysia 36 D4 1 24N 111 31 E
Betws-y-Coed, U.K. 12 D4 53 5N 3 48W
Beulah, Mich., U.S.A. 82 C2 44 38N 86 6W
Beulah, N. Dak., U.S.A. 80 B4 47 16N 101 47W
Beveren, Belgium 15 C4 51 12N 4 16 E
Beverley, Australia 61 F2 32 9S 116 56 E
Beverley, U.K. 12 D7 53 51N 0 26W
Beverly Hills, U.S.A. 85 D14 42 33N 70 53W
Beverly Hills, U.S.A. 79 L8 34 4N 118 25W
Bevoalavo, Madag. 57 D7 25 13S 45 26 E
Bewas →, India 43 H8 23 59N 79 21 E
Bexhill, U.K. 13 G8 50 51N 0 29 E
Beyānlū, Iran 44 C5 36 0N 47 51 E
Beyneu, Kazakhstan 19 E10 45 18N 55 9 E
Beypazarı, Turkey 19 F5 40 10N 31 56 E
Beyşehir Gölü, Turkey 19 G5 37 41N 31 33 E
Béziers, France 20 E5 43 20N 3 12 E
Bezwada = Vijayawada, India 41 L12 16 31N 80 39 E
Bhabua, India 43 G10 25 3N 83 37 E
Bhachau, India 40 H7 23 20N 70 16 E
Bhadar →, Gujarat, India 42 H5 22 17N 72 20 E
Bhadar →, Gujarat, India 42 J3 21 27N 69 47 E
Bhadarwah, India 43 C6 32 58N 75 46 E
Bhadgaon = Bhaktapur, Nepal 43 F11 27 38N 85 24 E
Bhadohi, India 43 G10 25 25N 82 34 E
Bhadra, India 42 E6 29 8N 75 14 E
Bhadrakh, India 41 J15 21 10N 86 30 E
Bhadran, India 42 H5 22 19N 72 6 E
Bhadravati, India 40 N9 13 49N 75 40 E
Bhag, Pakistan 42 E2 29 2N 67 49 E
Bhagalpur, India 43 G12 25 10N 87 0 E
Bhagirathi →, Uttaranchal, India 43 D8 30 8N 78 35 E
Bhagirathi →, W. Bengal, India 43 H13 23 25N 88 23 E
Bhakkar, Pakistan 42 D4 31 40N 71 5 E
Bhakra Dam, India 42 D7 31 30N 76 45 E
Bhaktapur, Nepal 43 F11 27 38N 85 24 E
Bhamo, Burma 41 G20 24 15N 97 15 E
Bhandara, India 40 J11 21 5N 79 42 E
Bhanpura, India 42 G6 24 31N 75 44 E
Bhanrer Ra., India 43 H8 23 40N 79 45 E
Bhaptiahi, India 43 F12 26 19N 86 44 E
Bharat = India ■, Asia 40 K11 20 0N 78 0 E
Bharatpur, Chhattisgarh, India 43 H9 23 44N 81 46 E
Bharatpur, Raj., India 42 F7 27 15N 77 30 E
Bharno, India 43 H11 23 14N 84 53 E
Bharuch, India 40 J8 21 47N 73 0 E
Bhatinda, India 42 D6 30 15N 74 57 E
Bhatpara, India 43 H13 22 50N 88 25 E
Bhattu, India 42 E6 29 36N 75 19 E
Bhaun, Pakistan 42 C5 32 55N 72 40 E
Bhaunagar = Bhavnagar, India 40 J8 21 45N 72 10 E
Bhawari, India 42 G5 25 42N 73 4 E
Bhayavadar, India 42 J4 21 51N 70 15 E
Bhera, Pakistan 42 C5 32 29N 72 57 E
Bhikangaon, India 42 J6 21 52N 75 57 E
Bhilsa = Vidisha, India 42 H7 23 28N 77 53 E
Bhilwara, India 42 G6 25 25N 74 38 E
Bhima →, India 40 L10 16 25N 77 17 E
Bhimbar, Pakistan 43 C6 32 59N 74 3 E
Bhind, India 43 F8 26 30N 78 46 E
Bhinga, India 43 F9 27 43N 81 56 E
Bhinmal, India 42 G5 25 0N 72 15 E
Bhiwandi, India 40 K8 19 20N 73 0 E
Bhiwani, India 42 E7 28 50N 76 9 E
Bhogava →, India 42 H5 22 26N 72 20 E
Bhola, Bangla. 41 H17 22 45N 90 35 E
Bholari, Pakistan 42 G3 25 19N 68 13 E
Bhopal, India 42 H7 23 20N 77 30 E
Bhubaneshwar, India 41 J14 20 15N 85 50 E
Bhuj, India 42 H3 23 15N 69 49 E
Bhusawal, India 40 J9 21 3N 75 46 E
Bhutan ■, Asia 41 F17 27 25N 90 30 E
Biafra, B. of = Bonny, Bight of,
   Africa 52 D1 3 30N 9 20 E
Biak, Indonesia 37 E9 1 10S 136 6 E
Biała Podlaska, Poland 17 B12 52 4N 23 6 E
Białogard, Poland 16 A8 54 2N 15 58 E
Białystok, Poland 17 B12 53 10N 23 10 E
Biaora, India 42 H7 23 56N 76 56 E
Biārjmand, Iran 45 B7 36 6N 55 53 E
Biaro, Indonesia 37 D7 2 5N 125 26 E
Biarritz, France 20 E3 43 29N 1 33W
Bias, Indonesia 37 J18 8 24S 115 36 E

Bibai, Japan .... 30 C10 43 19N 141 52 E
Bibby I., Canada 71 A10 61 55N 93 0W
Biberach, Germany .... 16 D5 48 5N 9 47 E
Bibungwa, Dem. Rep. of
   the Congo .... 54 C2 2 40S 28 15 E
Bicester, U.K. 13 F6 51 54N 1 9W
Bicheno, Australia .... 63 G4 41 52S 148 18 E
Bichia, India .... 43 H9 22 27N 80 42 E
Bickerton I., Australia .... 62 A2 13 45S 136 10 E
Bida, Nigeria .... 50 G7 9 3N 5 58 E
Bidar, India .... 40 L10 17 55N 77 35 E
Biddeford, U.S.A. 83 D10 43 30N 70 28W
Bideford, U.K. 13 F3 51 1N 4 13W
Bideford Bay, U.K. 13 F3 51 5N 4 20W
Bidhuna, India .... 43 F8 26 49N 79 31 E
Bidor, Malaysia .... 39 K3 4 6N 101 15 E
Bié, Planalto de, Angola .. 53 G3 12 0S 16 0 E
Bieber, U.S.A. 76 F3 41 7N 121 8W
Biel, Switz. .... 20 C7 47 8N 7 14 E
Bielefeld, Germany .... 16 B5 52 1N 8 33 E
Biella, Italy .... 20 D8 45 34N 8 3 E
Bielsk Podlaski, Poland ... 17 B12 52 47N 23 12 E
Bielsko-Biała, Poland ..... 17 D10 49 50N 19 2 E
Bien Hoa, Vietnam .... 39 G6 10 57N 106 49 E
Bienne = Biel, Switz. ...... 20 C7 47 8N 7 14 E
Bienville, L., Canada 72 A5 55 5N 72 40W
Biesiesfontein, S. Africa ... 56 E2 30 57S 17 58 E
Big →, Canada 73 B8 54 50N 58 55W
Big B., Canada 73 A7 55 43N 60 35W
Big Bear City, U.S.A. 79 L10 34 16N 116 51W
Big Bear Lake, U.S.A. 79 L10 34 15N 116 56W
Big Belt Mts., U.S.A. 76 C8 46 30N 111 25W
Big Bend, Swaziland ...... 57 D5 26 50S 31 58 E
Big Bend △, U.S.A. 81 L3 29 20N 103 5W
Big Black →, U.S.A. 81 K9 32 3N 91 4W
Big Blue →, U.S.A. 80 F6 39 35N 96 34W
Big Creek, U.S.A. 78 H7 37 11N 119 14W
Big Cypress △, U.S.A. 83 M5 26 0N 81 10W
Big Cypress Swamp, U.S.A. 83 M5 26 15N 81 30W
Big Falls, U.S.A. 80 A8 48 12N 93 48W
Big Fork →, U.S.A. 80 A8 48 31N 93 43W
Big Horn Mts. = Bighorn Mts.,
   U.S.A. 76 D10 44 30N 107 30W
Big I., Canada 70 A5 61 7N 116 45W
Big Lake, U.S.A. 81 K4 31 12N 101 28W
Big Moose, U.S.A. 85 C10 43 49N 74 58W
Big Muddy Cr. →, U.S.A. .. 80 A2 48 8N 104 36W
Big Pine, U.S.A. 78 H8 37 10N 118 17W
Big Piney, U.S.A. 76 E8 42 32N 110 7W
Big Rapids, U.S.A. 82 D3 43 42N 85 29W
Big Rideau L., Canada 85 B8 44 40N 76 15W
Big River, Canada 71 C7 53 50N 107 0W
Big Run, U.S.A. 84 F6 40 57N 78 55W
Big Sable Pt., U.S.A. 82 C2 44 3N 86 1W
Big Salmon →, Canada 70 A2 61 52N 134 55W
Big Sand L., Canada 71 B9 57 45N 99 45W
Big Sandy, U.S.A. 76 B8 48 11N 110 7W
Big Sandy →, U.S.A. 82 F4 38 25N 82 36W
Big Sandy Cr. →, U.S.A. ... 80 F3 38 7N 102 29W
Big Sioux →, U.S.A. 80 D6 42 29N 96 27W
Big South Fork △, U.S.A. .. 83 G3 36 27N 84 47W
Big Spring, U.S.A. 81 J4 32 15N 101 28W
Big Stone City, U.S.A. 80 C6 45 18N 96 28W
Big Stone Gap, U.S.A. 83 G4 36 52N 82 47W
Big Stone L., U.S.A. 80 C6 45 30N 96 35W
Big Sur, U.S.A. 78 J5 36 15N 121 48W
Big Timber, U.S.A. 76 D9 45 50N 109 57W
Big Trout L., Canada 72 B2 53 40N 90 0W
Big Trout Lake, Canada 72 B2 53 45N 90 0W
Biğa, Turkey .... 23 D12 40 13N 27 14 E
Bigadiç, Turkey .... 23 E13 39 22N 28 7 E
Biggar, Canada 71 C7 52 4N 108 0W
Biggar, U.K. 11 F5 55 38N 3 32W
Bigge I., Australia .... 60 B4 14 35S 125 10 E
Biggenden, Australia ...... 63 D5 25 31S 152 4 E
Biggleswade, U.K. 13 E7 52 5N 0 14W
Biggs, U.S.A. 78 F5 39 25N 121 43W
Bighorn, U.S.A. 76 C10 46 10N 107 27W
Bighorn →, U.S.A. 76 C10 46 10N 107 28W
Bighorn Canyon △, U.S.A. . 76 D9 45 10N 108 0W
Bighorn L., U.S.A. 76 D9 44 55N 108 15W
Bighorn Mts., U.S.A. 76 D10 44 30N 107 30W
Bigstone L., Canada 71 C9 53 42N 95 44W
Bigwa, Tanzania .... 54 D4 7 10S 39 10 E
Bihać, Bos.-H. .... 16 F8 44 49N 15 57 E
Bihar, India .... 43 G11 25 5N 85 40 E
Bihar □, India .... 43 G12 25 0N 86 0 E
Biharamulo, Tanzania ..... 54 C3 2 25S 31 25 E
Biharamulo △, Tanzania ... 54 C3 2 24S 31 26 E
Bihariganj, India .... 43 G12 25 44N 86 59 E
Bihor, Munții, Romania ... 17 E12 46 29N 22 47 E
Bijagós, Arquipélago dos,
   Guinea-Biss. 50 F2 11 15N 16 10W
Bijaipur, India .... 42 F7 26 2N 77 20 E
Bijapur, Chhattisgarh, India 41 K12 18 50N 80 50 E
Bijapur, Karnataka, India .. 40 L9 16 50N 75 55 E
Bījār, Iran .... 44 C5 35 52N 47 35 E
Bijawar, India .... 43 G8 24 38N 79 30 E
Bijeljina, Bos.-H. .... 23 B8 44 46N 19 14 E
Bijnor, India .... 42 E8 29 27N 78 11 E
Bikaner, India .... 42 E5 28 2N 73 18 E
Bikapur, India .... 43 F10 26 30N 82 7 E
Bikeqi, China .... 34 D6 40 43N 111 20 E
Bikfayyā, Lebanon .... 46 B4 33 55N 35 41 E
Bikin, Russia .... 29 E14 46 50N 134 20 E
Bikin →, Russia .... 30 A7 46 51N 134 2 E
Bikini Atoll, Marshall Is. .. 64 F8 12 0N 167 30 E
Bikita, Zimbabwe .... 57 C5 20 6S 31 41 E
Bila Tserkva, Ukraine ..... 17 D16 49 45N 30 10 E
Bilara, India .... 42 F5 26 14N 73 53 E
Bilaspur, Chhattisgarh, India 43 H10 22 2N 82 15 E
Bilaspur, Punjab, India .... 42 D7 31 19N 76 50 E
Bilauk Taungdan, Thailand . 38 F2 13 0N 99 0 E
Bilbao, Spain 21 A4 43 16N 2 56W
Bilbo = Bilbao, Spain 21 A4 43 16N 2 56W
Bildudalur, Iceland 8 D2 65 41N 23 36W
Bílé Karpaty, Europe ...... 17 D9 49 5N 18 0 E
Bilecik, Turkey .... 19 F5 40 5N 30 5 E
Bilgram, India .... 43 F9 27 11N 80 2 E
Bilhaur, India .... 43 F9 26 51N 80 5 E
Bilhorod-Dnistrovskyy, Ukraine 19 E5 46 11N 30 23 E
Bilibino, Russia .... 29 C17 68 3N 166 20 E
Bilibiza, Mozam. .... 55 E5 12 30S 40 20 E
Billabalong Roadhouse, Australia 61 E2 27 25S 115 49 E
Billiluna, Australia .... 60 C4 19 37S 127 41 E
Billings, U.S.A. 76 D9 45 47N 108 30W
Billiton Is. = Belitung, Indonesia 36 E3 3 10S 107 50 E
Bilma, Niger .... 51 E8 18 50N 13 30 E

Biloela, Australia .... 62 C5 24 24S 150 31 E
Biloxi, U.S.A. 81 K10 30 24N 88 53W
Bilpa Morea Claypan, Australia 62 D3 25 0S 140 0 E
Biltine, Chad .... 51 F10 14 40N 20 50 E
Bima, Indonesia .... 37 F5 8 22S 118 49 E
Bimini Is., Bahamas 88 A4 25 42N 79 25W
Bin Xian, Heilongjiang, China 35 B14 45 42N 127 32 E
Bin Xian, Shaanxi, China ... 34 G5 35 2N 108 4 E
Bina-Etawah, India .... 42 G8 24 13N 78 14 E
Bināb, Iran .... 45 B6 36 35N 48 41 E
Binalbagan, Phil. .... 37 B6 10 12N 122 50 E
Binalong, Australia .... 63 E4 34 40S 148 39 E
Bīnālūd, Kūh-e, Iran .... 45 B8 36 30N 58 30 E
Binatang = Bintangor, Malaysia 36 D4 2 10N 111 40 E
Binche, Belgium .... 15 D4 50 26N 4 10 E
Bindki, India .... 43 F9 26 2N 80 36 E
Bindura, Zimbabwe .... 55 F3 17 18S 31 18 E
Bingara, Australia .... 63 D5 29 52S 150 36 E
Bingham, U.S.A. 83 C11 45 3N 69 53W
Binghamton, U.S.A. 85 D9 42 6N 75 55W
Bingöl, Turkey .... 44 B4 38 53N 40 29 E
Binh Dinh = An Nhon, Vietnam 38 F7 13 55N 109 7 E
Binh Khe, Vietnam .... 38 F7 13 57N 108 51 E
Binh Son, Vietnam .... 38 E7 15 20N 108 40 E
Binhai, China .... 35 G10 34 2N 119 49 E
Binisatua, Spain .... 24 B11 39 50N 4 11 E
Binjai, Indonesia .... 36 D3 3 20N 98 30 E
Binnaway, Australia .... 63 E4 31 28S 149 24 E
Binongko, Indonesia ...... 37 F6 5 57S 124 2 E
Binscarth, Canada 71 C8 50 37N 101 17W
Bintan, Indonesia .... 36 D2 1 0N 104 0 E
Bintangor, Malaysia .... 36 D4 2 10N 111 40 E
Bintulu, Malaysia .... 36 D4 3 10N 113 0 E
Bintuni, Indonesia .... 37 E8 2 7S 133 32 E
Binzert = Bizerte, Tunisia .. 51 A7 37 15N 9 50 E
Binzhou, China .... 35 F10 37 20N 118 2 E
Bío Bío □, Chile 94 D1 37 35S 72 0W
Bioko, Eq. Guin. .... 52 D1 3 30N 8 40 E
Bir, India .... 40 K9 19 4N 75 46 E
Bîr Abu Muḩammad, Egypt 46 F3 29 44N 34 14 E
Bi'r ad Dabbāghāt, Jordan .. 46 E4 30 26N 35 32 E
Bi'r al Butayyiḩāt, Jordan .. 46 F4 29 47N 35 20 E
Bi'r al Mārī, Jordan .... 46 E4 30 4N 35 33 E
Bi'r al Qattār, Jordan ...... 46 F4 29 47N 35 32 E
Bîr Atrun, Sudan .... 51 E11 18 15N 26 40 E
Bîr Beïda, Egypt .... 46 E3 30 25N 34 29 E
Bîr el 'Abd, Egypt .... 46 D2 31 2N 33 0 E
Bîr el Biarât, Egypt .... 46 F3 29 30N 34 43 E
Bîr el Duweidar, Egypt .... 46 E1 30 56N 32 32 E
Bîr el Garârât, Egypt ...... 46 D2 31 3N 33 34 E
Bîr el Heisi, Egypt .... 46 F3 29 22N 34 36 E
Bîr el Jafir, Egypt .... 46 E1 30 50N 32 41 E
Bîr el Mâlḩi, Egypt .... 46 E2 30 38N 33 19 E
Bîr el Thamâda, Egypt ..... 46 E2 30 12N 33 27 E
Bîr Gebeil Ḩişn, Egypt ..... 46 E2 30 2N 33 18 E
Bi'r Ghadīr, Syria .... 46 A6 34 6N 37 3 E
Bîr Ḩasana, Egypt .... 46 E2 30 29N 33 46 E
Bîr Kaseiba, Egypt .... 46 E2 31 0N 33 17 E
Bîr Lahfân, Egypt .... 46 E2 31 0N 33 51 E
Bîr Madkûr, Egypt .... 46 E1 30 44N 32 33 E
Bîr Mogreïn, Mauritania ... 50 C3 25 10N 11 25W
Bi'r Muṭribah, Kuwait ..... 44 D5 29 54N 47 17 E
Bîr Qaṭia, Egypt .... 46 E1 30 58N 32 45 E
Bîr Shalatein, Egypt .... 51 D13 23 5N 35 25 E
Biratnagar, Nepal .... 43 F12 26 27N 87 17 E
Birawa, Dem. Rep. of the Congo 54 C2 2 20S 28 48 E
Birch →, Canada 70 B6 58 28N 112 17W
Birch Hills, Canada 71 C7 52 59N 105 25W
Birch I., Canada 71 C9 52 26N 99 54W
Birch L., N.W.T., Canada ... 70 A5 62 4N 116 33W
Birch L., Ont., Canada 72 B1 51 23N 92 18W
Birch Mts., Canada 70 B6 57 30N 113 10W
Birch River, Canada 71 C8 52 24N 101 6W
Birchip, Australia .... 63 F3 35 56S 142 55 E
Bird, Canada 71 B10 56 30N 94 13W
Bird I. = Las Aves, Is., W. Indies 89 C7 15 45N 63 55W
Bird I., Antarctica 5 B1 54 0S 38 0W
Birdsville, Australia .... 62 D2 25 51S 139 20 E
Birdum Cr. →, Australia ... 60 C5 15 14S 133 0 E
Birecik, Turkey .... 44 B3 37 2N 38 0 E
Birein, Israel .... 46 E3 30 50N 34 28 E
Bireuen, Indonesia .... 36 C1 5 14N 96 39 E
Birigui, Brazil 95 A5 21 18S 50 16W
Birjand, Iran .... 45 C8 32 53N 59 13 E
Birkenhead, U.K. 12 D4 53 23N 3 2W
Bîrlad = Bârlad, Romania .. 17 E14 46 15N 27 38 E
Birmingham, U.K. 13 E6 52 29N 1 52W
Birmingham, U.S.A. 83 J2 33 31N 86 48W
Birmingham International ✈
   (BHX), U.K. 13 E6 52 26N 1 45W
Birmitrapur, India .... 41 H14 22 24N 84 46 E
Birni Nkonni, Niger .... 50 F7 13 55N 5 15 E
Birnin Kebbi, Nigeria ..... 50 F6 12 32N 4 12 E
Birobidzhan, Russia .... 29 E14 48 50N 132 50 E
Birr, Ireland 10 C4 53 6N 7 54W
Birrie →, Australia .... 63 D4 29 43S 146 37 E
Birsilpur, India .... 42 E5 28 11N 72 15 E
Birsk, Russia .... 18 C10 55 25N 55 30 E
Birtle, Canada 71 C8 50 30N 101 5W
Birur, India .... 40 N9 13 30N 75 55 E
Biržai, Lithuania .... 9 H21 56 11N 24 45 E
Birzebbugga, Malta .... 25 D2 35 50N 14 32 E
Bisa, Indonesia .... 37 E7 1 15S 127 28 E
Bisalpur, India .... 43 E8 28 14N 79 48 E
Bisbee, U.S.A. 77 L9 31 27N 109 55W
Biscay, B. of, Atl. Oc. 20 D1 45 0N 2 0W
Biscayne B., U.S.A. 83 N5 25 40N 80 12W
Biscoe Is., Antarctica 5 C17 66 0S 67 0W
Biscostasing, Canada 72 C3 47 18N 82 9W
Bishkek, Kyrgyzstan .... 28 E8 42 54N 74 46 E
Bishnupur, India .... 43 H12 23 8N 87 20 E
Bisho, S. Africa .... 57 E4 32 50S 27 23 E
Bishop, Calif., U.S.A. 78 H8 37 22N 118 24W
Bishop, Tex., U.S.A. 81 M6 27 35N 97 48W
Bishop Auckland, U.K. 12 C6 54 39N 1 40W
Bishop's Falls, Canada 73 C8 49 2N 55 30W
Bishop's Stortford, U.K. ... 13 F8 51 52N 0 10 E
Bisina, L., Uganda .... 54 B3 1 38N 33 56 E
Biskra, Algeria .... 50 B7 34 50N 5 44 E
Bismarck, U.S.A. 80 B4 46 48N 100 47W
Bismarck Arch., Papua N. G. 64 H7 2 30S 150 0 E
Biso, Uganda .... 54 B3 1 44N 31 26 E
Bison, U.S.A. 80 C3 45 31N 102 28W
Bīsotūn, Iran .... 44 C5 34 23N 47 26 E
Bissagos = Bijagós, Arquipélago
   dos, Guinea-Biss. 50 F2 11 15N 16 10W
Bissau, Guinea-Biss. 50 F2 11 45N 15 45W
Bistcho L., Canada 70 B5 59 45N 118 50W

Bistrița, Romania .... 17 E13 47 9N 24 35 E
Bistrița →, Romania .... 17 E14 46 30N 26 57 E
Biswan, India .... 43 F9 27 29N 81 2 E
Bitlis, Turkey .... 44 B4 38 20N 42 3 E
Bitola, Macedonia .... 23 D9 41 1N 21 20 E
Bitolj = Bitola, Macedonia . 23 D9 41 1N 21 20 E
Bitter Creek, U.S.A. 76 F9 41 33N 108 33W
Bitterfontein, S. Africa .... 56 E2 31 1S 18 32 E
Bitterroot →, U.S.A. 76 C6 46 52N 114 7W
Bitterroot Range, U.S.A. ... 76 D6 46 0N 114 20W
Bitterwater, U.S.A. 78 J6 36 23N 121 0W
Biu, Nigeria .... 51 F8 10 40N 12 3 E
Biwa-Ko, Japan .... 31 G8 35 15N 136 10 E
Biwabik, U.S.A. 80 B8 47 32N 92 21W
Bixby, U.S.A. 81 H7 35 57N 95 53W
Biyang, China .... 34 H7 32 38N 113 21 E
Biysk, Russia .... 28 D9 52 40N 85 0 E
Bizana, S. Africa .... 57 E4 30 50S 29 52 E
Bizen, Japan .... 31 G7 34 43N 134 8 E
Bizerte, Tunisia .... 51 A7 37 15N 9 50 E
Bjargtangar, Iceland 8 D1 65 30N 24 30W
Bjelovar, Croatia .... 22 B7 45 56N 16 49 E
Bjørnevatn, Norway .... 8 B23 69 40N 30 0 E
Bjørnøya, Arctic .... 4 B8 74 30N 19 0 E
Black = Da →, Vietnam .... 38 B5 21 15N 105 20 E
Black →, Canada 84 B5 44 42N 79 19W
Black →, Ariz., U.S.A. 77 K8 33 44N 110 13W
Black →, Ark., U.S.A. 81 H9 35 38N 91 20W
Black →, Mich., U.S.A. 84 D2 42 59N 82 27W
Black →, N.Y., U.S.A. 85 C8 43 59N 76 4W
Black →, Wis., U.S.A. 80 D9 43 57N 91 22W
Black Bay Pen., Canada 72 C2 48 38N 88 21W
Black Birch L., Canada 71 B7 56 53N 107 45W
Black Canyon of the Gunnison △,
   U.S.A. 77 G10 38 40N 107 35W
Black Diamond, Canada 70 C6 50 45N 114 14W
Black Duck →, Canada 72 A2 56 51N 89 2W
Black Forest = Schwarzwald,
   Germany .... 16 D5 48 30N 8 20 E
Black Forest, U.S.A. 80 F2 39 0N 104 43W
Black Hd., Ireland 10 C2 53 9N 9 16W
Black Hills, U.S.A. 80 D3 44 0N 103 45W
Black I., Canada 71 C9 51 12N 96 30W
Black L., Canada 71 B7 59 12N 105 15W
Black L., Mich., U.S.A. 82 C3 45 28N 84 16W
Black L., N.Y., U.S.A. 85 B9 44 31N 75 36W
Black Lake, Canada 71 B7 59 11N 105 20W
Black Mesa, U.S.A. 81 G3 36 58N 102 58W
Black Mt. = Mynydd Du, U.K. 13 F4 51 52N 3 50W
Black Mts., U.K. 13 F4 51 55N 3 7W
Black Range, U.S.A. 77 K10 33 15N 107 50W
Black River, Jamaica ...... 88 a 18 0N 77 50W
Black River Falls, U.S.A. ... 80 C9 44 18N 90 51W
Black Rock, Barbados ...... 89 g 13 7N 59 37W
Black Sea, Eurasia .... 19 F6 43 30N 35 0 E
Black Tickle, Canada 73 B8 53 28N 55 45W
Black Volta →, Africa 50 G5 8 41N 1 33W
Black Warrior →, U.S.A. ... 83 J2 32 32N 87 51W
Blackall, Australia .... 62 C4 24 25S 145 45 E
Blackball, N.Z. .... 59 K3 42 22S 171 26 E
Blackball, Australia .... 62 B3 17 55S 141 45 E
Blackburn, U.K. 12 D5 53 45N 2 29W
Blackburn with Darwen □, U.K. 12 D5 53 45N 2 29W
Blackdown Tableland △,
   Australia .... 62 C4 23 52S 149 8 E
Blackfoot, U.S.A. 76 E7 43 11N 112 21W
Blackfoot →, U.S.A. 76 C7 46 52N 113 53W
Blackfoot River Reservoir, U.S.A. 76 E8 43 0N 111 43W
Blackpool, U.K. 12 D4 53 49N 3 3W
Blackpool □, U.K. 12 D4 53 49N 3 3W
Blackriver, U.S.A. 84 B1 44 46N 83 17W
Blacks Harbour, Canada ... 73 C6 45 3N 66 49W
Blacksburg, U.S.A. 82 G5 37 14N 80 25W
Blacksod B., Ireland 10 B1 54 6N 10 0W
Blackstone, U.S.A. 82 G7 37 4N 78 0W
Blackstone Ra., Australia .. 61 E4 26 0S 128 30 E
Blackwater = West Road →,
   Canada 70 C4 53 18N 122 53W
Blackwater, Australia ..... 62 C4 23 35S 148 53 E
Blackwater →, Meath, Ireland 10 C5 53 39N 6 41W
Blackwater →, Waterford, Ireland 10 D4 52 4N 7 52W
Blackwater →, U.K. 10 B5 54 31N 6 35W
Blackwell, U.S.A. 81 G6 36 48N 97 17W
Blackwells Corner, U.S.A. .. 79 K7 35 37N 119 47W
Bladensburg △, Australia .. 62 C3 22 30S 142 59 E
Blaenau Ffestiniog, U.K. ... 12 E4 53 0N 3 56W
Blaenau Gwent □, U.K. 13 F4 51 48N 3 12W
Blagodarnoye = Blagodarnyy,
   Russia .... 19 E7 45 7N 43 37 E
Blagodarnyy, Russia ...... 19 E7 45 7N 43 37 E
Blagoevgrad, Bulgaria ..... 23 C10 42 2N 23 5 E
Blagoveshchensk, Russia .. 29 D13 50 20N 127 30 E
Blahkiuh, Indonesia .... 37 J18 8 31S 115 12 E
Blain, U.S.A. 84 F7 40 20N 77 31W
Blaine, Minn., U.S.A. 80 C8 45 10N 93 13W
Blaine, Wash., U.S.A. 78 B4 48 59N 122 45W
Blaine Lake, Canada 71 C7 52 51N 106 52W
Blair, U.S.A. 80 E6 41 33N 96 8W
Blair Athol, Australia ...... 62 C4 22 42S 147 31 E
Blair Atholl, U.K. 11 E5 56 46N 3 50W
Blairgowrie, U.K. 11 E5 56 35N 3 21W
Blairsden, U.S.A. 78 F6 39 47N 120 37W
Blairsville, U.S.A. 84 F5 40 26N 79 16W
Blakang Mati, Pulau, Singapore 39 d 1 15N 103 50 E
Blake Pt., U.S.A. 80 A10 48 11N 88 25W
Blakely, Ga., U.S.A. 83 K3 31 23N 84 56W
Blakely, Pa., U.S.A. 85 E9 41 28N 75 37W
Blanc, C., Spain .... 24 B9 39 21N 2 51 E
Blanc, Mont, Europe ...... 20 D7 45 48N 6 50 E
Blanc-Sablon, Canada 73 B8 51 24N 57 12W
Blanca, B., Argentina 96 D4 39 10S 61 30W
Blanca Peak, U.S.A. 77 H11 37 35N 105 29W
Blanche, C., Australia ..... 63 E1 33 1S 134 9 E
Blanche, L., S. Austral., Australia 63 D2 29 15S 139 40 E
Blanche, L., W. Austral., Australia 60 D3 22 25S 123 17 E
Blanchisseuse, Trin. & Tob. . 93 K15 10 48N 61 18W
Blanco, S. Africa .... 56 E3 33 55S 22 23 E
Blanco, U.S.A. 81 K5 30 6N 98 25W
Blanco →, Argentina 94 C2 30 20S 68 42W
Blanco, C., Costa Rica 88 E2 9 34N 85 8W
Blanco, C., U.S.A. 76 E1 42 51N 124 34W
Blanda →, Iceland 8 D3 65 37N 20 9W
Blandford Forum, U.K. 13 G5 50 51N 2 9W
Blanding, U.S.A. 77 H9 37 37N 109 29W
Blanes, Spain .... 21 B7 41 40N 2 48 E
Blankenberge, Belgium .... 15 C3 51 20N 3 9 E
Blanquillo, Uruguay 95 C4 32 53S 55 37W
Blantyre, Malawi .... 55 F4 15 45S 35 0 E

Blarney, Ireland 10 E3 51 56N 8 33W
Blasdell, U.S.A. 84 D6 42 48N 78 50W
Blåvands Huk, Denmark ... 9 J13 55 33N 8 4 E
Blaydon, U.K. 12 C6 54 58N 1 42W
Blayney, Australia .... 63 E4 33 32S 149 14 E
Blaze, Pt., Australia .... 60 B5 12 56S 130 11 E
Blekinge, Sweden .... 9 H16 56 25N 15 20 E
Blenheim, Canada 84 D3 42 20N 82 0W
Blenheim, N.Z. .... 59 J4 41 38S 173 57 E
Bletchley, U.K. 13 F7 51 59N 0 44W
Blida, Algeria .... 50 A6 36 30N 2 49 E
Bligh Sound, N.Z. .... 59 L1 44 47S 167 32 E
Blind River, Canada 72 C3 46 10N 82 58W
Bliss, Idaho, U.S.A. 76 E6 42 56N 114 57W
Bliss, N.Y., U.S.A. 84 D6 42 34N 78 15W
Blissfield, U.S.A. 84 F3 40 24N 81 58W
Blitar, Indonesia .... 37 H15 8 5S 112 11 E
Block I., U.S.A. 85 E13 41 11N 71 35W
Block Island Sd., U.S.A. 85 E13 41 15N 71 40W
Bloemfontein, S. Africa .... 56 D4 29 6S 26 7 E
Bloemhof, S. Africa .... 56 D4 27 38S 25 32 E
Blois, France .... 20 C4 47 35N 1 20 E
Blönduós, Iceland 8 D3 65 40N 20 12W
Blongas, Indonesia .... 37 K19 8 53S 116 2 E
Bloodvein →, Canada 71 C9 51 47N 96 43W
Bloody Foreland, Ireland .. 10 A3 55 10N 8 17W
Bloomer, U.S.A. 80 C9 45 6N 91 29W
Bloomfield, Canada 84 C7 43 59N 77 14W
Bloomfield, Iowa, U.S.A. ... 80 E8 40 45N 92 25W
Bloomfield, N. Mex., U.S.A. 77 H10 36 43N 107 59W
Bloomfield, Nebr., U.S.A. .. 80 D6 42 36N 97 39W
Bloomington, Ill., U.S.A. ... 82 F2 39 10N 86 32W
Bloomington, Ind., U.S.A. .. 80 C8 44 50N 93 17W
Bloomington, Minn., U.S.A. 85 F8 41 0N 76 27W
Bloomsburg, U.S.A. .... 62 J6 20 48S 148 38 E
Bloomsbury, Australia ..... 37 G14 6 57S 111 25 E
Blora, Indonesia 84 E7 41 41N 77 4W
Blossburg, U.S.A. .... 57 C4 23 8S 28 59 E
Blouberg, S. Africa 83 K3 30 27N 85 3W
Blountstown, U.S.A. 80 D8 43 38N 94 6W
Blue Earth, U.S.A. 88 C2 17 24N 88 30W
Blue Hole △, Belize 85 E13 41 11N 71 35W
Blue Lagoon △, Zambia .... 55 F2 15 28S 27 26 E
Blue Mesa Reservoir, U.S.A. 77 G10 38 28N 107 20W
Blue Mountain Lake, U.S.A. 85 C10 43 52N 74 30W
Blue Mountain Pk., Jamaica 88 a 18 3N 76 36W
Blue Mts., Jamaica .... 88 a 18 3N 76 36W
Blue Mts., Maine, U.S.A. ... 85 B14 44 50N 70 35W
Blue Mts., Oreg., U.S.A. 76 D4 45 15N 119 0W
Blue Mts., Pa., U.S.A. 85 F8 40 30N 76 30W
Blue Mud B., Australia ..... 62 A2 13 30S 136 0 E
Blue Nile = Nîl el Azraq →,
   Sudan .... 51 E12 15 38N 32 31 E
Blue Rapids, U.S.A. 80 F6 39 41N 96 39W
Blue Ridge Mts., U.S.A. 83 G5 36 30N 80 15W
Blue River, Canada 70 C5 52 6N 119 18W
Bluefield, U.S.A. 82 G5 37 15N 81 17W
Bluefields, Nic. 88 D3 12 20N 83 50W
Bluff, Australia .... 62 C4 23 35S 149 4 E
Bluff, N.Z. .... 59 M2 46 37S 168 20 E
Bluff, U.S.A. 77 H9 37 17N 109 33W
Bluff Knoll, Australia ...... 61 F2 34 24S 118 15 E
Bluff Pt., Australia .... 61 E1 27 50S 114 5 E
Bluffton, U.S.A. 82 E3 40 44N 85 11W
Blumenau, Brazil 95 B6 27 0S 49 0W
Blunt, U.S.A. 80 C5 44 31N 99 59W
Bly, U.S.A. 76 E3 42 24N 121 3W
Blyde River Canyon △, S. Africa 57 C5 24 37S 31 2 E
Blyth, Canada 84 C3 43 44N 81 26W
Blyth, U.K. 12 B6 55 8N 1 31W
Blythe, U.S.A. 79 M12 33 37N 114 36W
Blytheville, U.S.A. 81 H10 35 56N 89 55W
Bo, S. Leone 50 G3 7 55N 11 50W
Bo Duc, Vietnam .... 39 G6 11 58N 106 50 E
Bo Hai, China .... 35 E10 39 0N 119 0 E
Bo Xian = Bozhou, China .. 34 H8 33 55N 115 41 E
Boa Vista, Brazil 92 C6 2 48N 60 30W
Boaco, Nic. 88 D2 12 29N 85 35W
Bo'ai, China .... 34 G7 35 10N 113 3 E
Boalsburg, U.S.A. 84 F7 40 46N 77 47W
Boane, Mozam. .... 57 D5 26 6S 32 19 E
Boardman, U.S.A. 84 E4 41 2N 80 40W
Bobadah, Australia .... 63 E4 32 19S 146 41 E
Bobbili, India .... 41 K13 18 35N 83 30 E
Bobcaygeon, Canada 84 B6 44 33N 78 33W
Bobo-Dioulasso, Burkina Faso 50 F5 11 8N 4 13W
Bóbr →, Poland .... 16 B8 52 4N 15 4 E
Bobraomby, Tanjon' i, Madag. 57 A8 12 40S 49 10 E
Bobruysk = Babruysk, Belarus 17 B15 53 10N 29 15 E
Boby, Pic, Madag. .... 53 J9 22 12S 46 55 E
Boca de Drago, Venezuela .. 93 K15 11 0N 61 50W
Bôca do Acre, Brazil 92 E5 8 50S 67 27W
Boca Raton, U.S.A. 83 M5 26 21N 80 5W
Bocas del Toro, Panama 88 E3 9 15N 82 20W
Bochnia, Poland .... 17 D11 49 58N 20 27 E
Bochum, Germany .... 16 C4 51 28N 7 13 E
Bocoyna, Mexico 86 B3 27 52N 107 35W
Bodaybo, Russia .... 29 D12 57 50N 114 0 E
Boddam, U.K. 11 B7 59 56N 1 17W
Boddington, Australia ..... 61 F2 32 50S 116 30 E
Bodega Bay, U.S.A. 78 G3 38 20N 123 3W
Boden, Sweden .... 8 D19 65 50N 21 42 E
Bodensee, Europe .... 20 C8 47 35N 9 25 E
Bodhan, India .... 40 K10 18 40N 77 44 E
Bodmin, U.K. 13 G3 50 28N 4 43W
Bodmin Moor, U.K. 13 G3 50 33N 4 36W
Bodø, Norway .... 8 C16 67 17N 14 24 E
Bodrog →, Hungary .... 17 D11 48 11N 21 22 E
Bodrum, Turkey .... 23 F12 37 3N 27 30 E
Boende, Dem. Rep. of the Congo 52 E4 0 24S 21 12 E
Boerne, U.S.A. 81 L5 29 47N 98 44W
Boesmans →, S. Africa .... 56 E4 33 42S 26 39 E
Bogalusa, U.S.A. 81 K10 30 47N 89 52W
Bogan →, Australia .... 63 D4 30 35S 146 8 E
Bogan Gate, Australia ..... 63 E4 33 7S 147 49 E
Bogantungan, Australia ... 62 C4 23 41S 147 17 E
Bogata, U.S.A. 81 J7 33 28N 95 13W
Boggabilla, Australia ...... 63 D5 28 36S 150 24 E
Boggabri, Australia .... 63 E5 30 45S 150 5 E
Boggeragh Mts., Ireland ... 10 D3 52 2N 8 55W
Boglan = Solhan, Turkey ... 44 B4 38 57N 41 3 E
Bognor Regis, U.K. 13 G7 50 47N 0 40W
Bogo, Phil. .... 37 B6 11 3N 124 0 E
Bogong, Mt., Australia .... 63 F4 36 47S 147 17 E
Bogor, Indonesia .... 36 F3 6 36S 106 48 E
Bogotá, Colombia 92 C4 4 34N 74 0W
Bogotol, Russia .... 28 D9 56 15N 89 50 E
Bogra, Bangla. .... 41 G16 24 51N 89 22 E

Boguchany, Russia .... 29 D10 58 40N 97 30 E
Bohemian Forest = Böhmerwald,
  Germany .... 16 D7 49 8N 13 14 E
Böhmerwald, Germany .... 16 D7 49 8N 13 14 E
Bohol □, Phil. .... 37 C6 9 50N 124 10 E
Bohol Sea, Phil. .... 37 C6 9 0N 124 0 E
Bohuslän, Sweden .... 9 G14 58 25N 12 0 E
Boi, Pta. de, Brazil 95 A6 23 55S 45 15W
Boiaçu, Brazil 92 D6 0 27S 61 46W
Boileau, C., Australia .... 60 C3 17 40S 122 7 E
Boise, U.S.A. 76 E5 43 37N 116 13W
Boise City, U.S.A. 81 G3 36 44N 102 31W
Boissevain, Canada 71 D8 49 15N 100 5W
Bojador, C., W. Sahara 50 C3 26 0N 14 30W
Bojana →, Albania .... 23 D8 41 52N 19 22 E
Bojnūrd, Iran .... 45 B8 37 30N 57 20 E
Bojonegoro, Indonesia .... 37 G14 7 11S 111 54 E
Bokaro, India .... 43 H11 23 46N 85 55 E
Bokhara →, Australia .... 63 D4 29 55S 146 42 E
Boknafjorden, Norway .... 9 G11 59 14N 5 40 E
Bokora ○, Uganda .... 54 B3 2 12N 31 32 E
Bokoro, Chad .... 51 F9 12 25N 17 14 E
Bokpyin, Burma .... 39 G2 11 18N 98 42 E
Bolan →, Pakistan .... 42 E2 28 38N 67 42 E
Bolan Pass, Pakistan .... 40 E5 29 50N 67 20 E
Bolaños →, Mexico 86 C4 21 14N 104 8W
Bolbec, France .... 20 B4 49 30N 0 30 E
Boldājī, Iran .... 45 D6 31 56N 51 3 E
Bole, China .... 32 B3 45 11N 81 37 E
Bolekhiv, Ukraine .... 17 D12 49 0N 23 57 E
Bolesławiec, Poland .... 16 C8 51 17N 15 37 E
Bolgrad = Bolhrad, Ukraine ... 17 F15 45 40N 28 32 E
Bolhrad, Ukraine .... 17 F15 45 40N 28 32 E
Bolívar, Argentina 94 D3 36 15S 60 53W
Bolivar, Mo., U.S.A. 81 G8 37 37N 93 25W
Bolivar, N.Y., U.S.A. 84 D6 42 4N 78 10W
Bolivar, Tenn., U.S.A. 81 H10 35 12N 89 0W
Bolivia ■, S. Amer. 92 G6 17 6S 64 0W
Bolivian Plateau = Altiplano,
  Bolivia 90 E4 17 0S 68 0W
Bollnäs, Sweden .... 9 F17 61 21N 16 24 E
Bollon, Australia .... 63 D4 28 2S 147 29 E
Bolmen, Sweden .... 9 H15 56 55N 13 40 E
Bolobo, Dem. Rep. of the Congo 52 E3 2 6S 16 20 E
Bologna, Italy .... 22 B4 44 29N 11 20 E
Bologoye, Russia .... 18 C5 57 55N 34 5 E
Bolonchenticul, Mexico 87 D7 20 0N 89 49W
Boloven, Cao Nguyen, Laos ... 38 E6 15 10N 106 30 E
Bolpur, India .... 43 H12 23 40N 87 45 E
Bolsena, L. di, Italy .... 22 C4 42 36N 11 56 E
Bolshevik, Ostrov, Russia .... 29 B11 78 30N 102 0 E
Bolshoy Anyuy →, Russia ... 29 C17 68 30N 160 49 E
Bolshoy Begichev, Ostrov,
  Russia .... 29 B12 74 20N 112 30 E
Bolshoy Kavkas = Caucasus
  Mountains, Eurasia .... 19 F7 42 50N 44 0 E
Bolshoy Lyakhovskiy, Ostrov,
  Russia .... 29 B15 73 35N 142 0 E
Bolshoy Tyuters, Ostrov, Russia 9 G22 59 51N 27 13 E
Bolsward, Neths. .... 15 A5 53 3N 5 32 E
Bolt Head, U.K. 13 G4 50 12N 3 48W
Bolton, Canada 84 C5 43 54N 79 45W
Bolton, U.K. 12 D5 53 35N 2 26W
Bolton Landing, U.S.A. 85 C11 43 32N 73 35W
Bolu, Turkey .... 19 F5 40 45N 31 35 E
Bolungavík, Iceland 8 C2 66 9N 23 15W
Bolvadin, Turkey .... 19 G5 38 45N 31 4 E
Bolzano, Italy .... 22 A4 46 31N 11 22 E
Bom Jesus da Lapa, Brazil 93 F10 13 15S 43 25W
Boma, Dem. Rep. of the Congo . 52 F2 5 50S 13 4 E
Bombala, Australia .... 63 F4 36 56S 149 15 E
Bombay = Mumbai, India ..... 40 K8 18 55N 72 50 E
Bombedor, Pta., Venezuela ... 93 L15 9 53N 61 37W
Bomboma, Dem. Rep. of
  the Congo .... 52 D3 2 25N 18 55 E
Bombombwa, Dem. Rep. of
  the Congo .... 54 B2 1 40N 25 40 E
Bomili, Dem. Rep. of the Congo . 54 B2 1 45N 27 5 E
Bømlo, Norway .... 9 G11 59 37N 5 13 E
Bomokandi →, Dem. Rep. of
  the Congo .... 54 B2 3 39N 26 8 E
Bomu →, C.A.R. .... 52 D4 4 40N 22 30 E
Bon, C., Tunisia .... 48 C5 37 1N 11 2 E
Bon Sar Pa, Vietnam .... 38 F6 12 24N 107 35 E
Bonaigarh, India .... 43 J11 21 50N 84 57 E
Bonaire, Neth. Ant. 89 D6 12 10N 68 15W
Bonampak, Mexico 87 D6 16 44N 91 5W
Bonang, Australia .... 63 F4 37 11S 148 41 E
Bonanza, Nic. 88 D3 13 54N 84 35W
Bonaparte Arch., Australia ... 60 B3 14 0S 124 30 E
Bonar Bridge, U.K. 11 D4 57 54N 4 20W
Bonasse, Trin. & Tob. 93 K15 10 5N 61 54W
Bonaventure, Canada 73 C6 48 5N 65 32W
Bonavista, Canada 73 C9 48 40N 53 5W
Bonavista, C., Canada 73 C9 48 42N 53 5W
Bonavista B., Canada 73 C9 48 45N 53 25W
Bondo, Dem. Rep. of the Congo . 54 B1 3 55N 23 53 E
Bondoukou, Ivory C. 50 G5 8 2N 2 47W
Bondowoso, Indonesia .... 37 G15 7 55S 113 49 E
Bone, Teluk, Indonesia ...... 37 E6 4 10S 120 50 E
Bonerate, Indonesia .... 37 F6 7 25S 121 5 E
Bonerate, Kepulauan, Indonesia 37 F6 6 30S 121 10 E
Bo'ness, U.K. 11 E5 56 1N 3 37W
Bonete, Cerro, Argentina 94 B2 27 55S 68 40W
Bong Son = Hoai Nhon, Vietnam 38 E7 14 28N 109 1 E
Bongor, Chad .... 51 F9 10 35N 15 20 E
Bonham, U.S.A. 81 J6 33 35N 96 11W
Boni ○, Kenya .... 54 C5 1 35S 41 18 E
Bonifacio, France .... 20 F8 41 24N 9 10 E
Bonifacio, Bouches de, Medit. S. 22 D3 41 12N 9 15 E
Bonin Is. = Ogasawara Gunto,
  Pac. Oc. .... 26 G18 27 0N 142 0 E
Bonn, Germany .... 16 C4 50 46N 7 6 E
Bonne Terre, U.S.A. 81 G9 37 55N 90 33W
Bonners Ferry, U.S.A. 76 B5 48 42N 116 19W
Bonney, L., Australia .... 63 F3 37 50S 140 20 E
Bonnie Rock, Australia ...... 61 F2 30 29S 118 22 E
Bonny, Bight of, Africa ...... 52 D1 3 30N 9 20 E
Bonnyrigg, U.K. 11 F5 55 53N 3 6W
Bonnyville, Canada 71 C6 54 20N 110 45W
Bonoi, Indonesia .... 37 E9 1 45S 137 41 E
Bonsall, U.S.A. 79 M9 33 16N 117 14W
Bontang, Indonesia .... 36 D5 0 10N 117 30 E
Bontebok ○, S. Africa .... 56 E3 34 5S 20 28 E
Bonthe, S. Leone 50 G3 7 30N 12 33W
Bontoc, Phil. .... 37 A6 17 7N 120 58 E
Bonython Ra., Australia ...... 60 D4 23 40S 128 45 E
Bookabie, Australia .... 61 F5 31 50S 132 41 E

Booker, U.S.A. 81 G4 36 27N 100 32W
Booligal, Australia .... 63 E3 33 58S 144 53 E
Boonah, Australia .... 63 D5 27 58S 152 41 E
Boone, Iowa, U.S.A. 80 D8 42 4N 93 53W
Boone, N.C., U.S.A. 83 G5 36 13N 81 41W
Booneville, Ark., U.S.A. 81 H8 35 8N 93 55W
Booneville, Miss., U.S.A. 83 H1 34 39N 88 34W
Boonville, Calif., U.S.A. 78 F3 39 1N 123 22W
Boonville, Ind., U.S.A. 82 F2 38 3N 87 16W
Boonville, Mo., U.S.A. 80 F8 38 58N 92 44W
Boonville, N.Y., U.S.A. 85 C9 43 29N 75 20W
Boorabbin, Australia .... 61 F4 31 30S 129 57 E
Boorindal, Australia .... 63 E4 30 22S 146 11 E
Boorowa, Australia .... 63 E4 34 28S 148 44 E
Boosaaso = Bosaso, Somali Rep. 47 E4 11 12N 49 18 E
Boothia, Gulf of, Canada 69 A11 71 0N 90 0W
Boothia Pen., Canada 68 A10 71 0N 94 0W
Bootle, U.K. 12 D4 53 28N 3 1W
Booué, Gabon .... 52 E2 0 5S 11 55 E
Boquete, Panama 88 E3 8 46N 82 27W
Boquilla, Presa de la, Mexico .. 86 B3 27 40N 105 30W
Boquillas del Carmen, Mexico . 86 B4 29 17N 102 53W
Bor, Serbia & M. .... 23 B10 44 5N 22 7 E
Bôr, Sudan .... 51 G12 6 10N 31 40 E
Bor Mashash, Israel .... 46 D3 31 7N 34 50 E
Borah Peak, U.S.A. 76 D7 44 8N 113 47W
Borås, Sweden .... 9 H15 57 43N 12 56 E
Borāzjān, Iran .... 45 D6 29 22N 51 10 E
Borba, Brazil 92 D7 4 12S 59 34W
Borborema, Planalto da, Brazil . 90 D7 7 0S 37 0W
Bord Khūn-e Now, Iran ...... 45 D6 28 3N 51 28 E
Borda, C., Australia .... 63 F2 35 45S 136 34 E
Bordeaux, France 20 D3 44 50N 0 36W
Borden, Australia .... 61 F2 34 3S 118 12 E
Borden-Carleton, Canada 73 C7 46 18N 63 47W
Borden I., Canada 4 B2 78 30N 111 30W
Borden Pen., Canada 69 A11 73 0N 83 0W
Border Ranges △, Australia .. 63 D5 28 24S 152 56 E
Borders = Scottish Borders □,
  U.K. 11 F6 55 35N 2 50W
Bordertown, Australia .... 63 F3 36 19S 140 45 E
Borðeyri, Iceland 8 D3 65 12N 21 6W
Bordj Fly Ste. Marie, Algeria .. 50 C5 27 19N 2 32W
Bordj-in-Eker, Algeria .... 50 D6 24 9N 5 3 E
Bordj Omar Driss, Algeria .... 50 C7 28 10N 6 40 E
Borehamwood, U.K. 13 F7 51 40N 0 15W
Borgå = Porvoo, Finland ..... 9 F21 60 24N 25 40 E
Borgarfjörður, Iceland 8 D7 65 31N 13 49W
Borgarnes, Iceland 8 D3 64 32N 21 55W
Børgefjellet, Norway .... 8 D15 65 20N 13 45 E
Borger, Neths. .... 15 B6 52 54N 6 44 E
Borger, U.S.A. 81 H4 35 39N 101 24W
Borgholm, Sweden .... 9 H17 56 52N 16 39 E
Borhoyn Tal, Mongolia ...... 34 C6 43 50N 111 58 E
Borikhane, Laos .... 38 C4 18 33N 103 43 E
Borisoglebsk, Russia .... 19 D7 51 27N 42 5 E
Borisov = Barysaw, Belarus ... 17 A15 54 17N 28 28 E
Borja, Peru 92 D3 4 20S 77 40W
Borkou, Chad .... 51 E9 18 15N 18 50 E
Borkum, Germany .... 16 B4 53 34N 6 40 E
Borley, C., Antarctica .... 5 C5 66 15S 52 30 E
Borneo, E. Indies .... 36 D5 1 0N 115 0 E
Bornholm, Denmark .... 9 J16 55 10N 15 0 E
Borogontsy, Russia .... 29 C14 62 42N 131 8 E
Boron, U.S.A. 79 L9 35 0N 117 39W
Borongan, Phil. .... 37 B7 11 37N 125 26 E
Borovichi, Russia .... 18 C5 58 25N 33 55 E
Borrego Springs, U.S.A. 79 M10 33 15N 116 23W
Borroloola, Australia .... 62 B2 16 4S 136 17 E
Borşa, Romania .... 17 E13 47 41N 24 50 E
Borsad, India .... 42 H5 22 25N 72 54 E
Borth, U.K. 13 E3 52 29N 4 2W
Borūjerd, Iran .... 45 C6 33 55N 48 50 E
Boryslav, Ukraine .... 17 D12 49 18N 23 28 E
Borzya, Russia .... 29 D12 50 24N 116 31 E
Bosa, Italy .... 22 D3 40 18N 8 30 E
Bosanska Gradiška, Bos.-H. ... 22 B7 45 10N 17 15 E
Bosaso, Somali Rep. .... 47 E4 11 12N 49 18 E
Boscastle, U.K. 13 G3 50 41N 4 42W
Boscobel, Barbados .... 89 g 13 16N 59 34W
Boshan, China .... 35 F9 36 28N 117 49 E
Boshof, S. Africa .... 56 D4 28 31S 25 13 E
Boshrūyeh, Iran .... 45 C8 33 50N 57 30 E
Bosna →, Bos.-H. .... 23 B8 45 4N 18 29 E
Bosnia i Hercegovina = Bosnia-
  Herzegovina ■, Europe .... 22 B7 44 0N 18 0 E
Bosnia-Herzegovina ■, Europe . 22 B7 44 0N 18 0 E
Bosnik, Indonesia .... 37 E9 1 5S 136 10 E
Bosobolo, Dem. Rep. of
  the Congo .... 52 D3 4 15N 19 50 E
Bosporus = İstanbul Boğazı,
  Turkey .... 23 D13 41 10N 29 10 E
Bosque Farms, U.S.A. 77 J10 34 53N 106 40W
Bossangoa, C.A.R. .... 52 C3 6 35N 17 30 E
Bossier City, U.S.A. 81 J8 32 31N 93 44W
Bosso, Niger .... 51 F8 13 43N 13 19 E
Bostan, Pakistan .... 42 D2 30 26N 67 2 E
Bostānābād, Iran .... 44 B5 37 50N 46 50 E
Bosten Hu, China .... 32 B3 41 55N 87 40 E
Boston, U.K. 12 E7 52 59N 0 2W
Boston, U.S.A. 85 D13 42 22N 71 4W
Boston Bar, Canada 70 D4 49 52N 121 30W
Boston Mts., U.S.A. 81 H8 35 42N 93 15W
Boswell, Canada 70 D5 49 28N 116 45W
Boswell, U.S.A. 84 F5 40 10N 79 2W
Botad, India .... 42 H4 22 15N 71 40 E
Botene, Laos .... 38 D3 17 35N 101 12 E
Bothaville, S. Africa .... 56 D4 27 23S 26 34 E
Bothnia, G. of, Europe ...... 8 E19 63 0N 20 0 E
Bothwell, Australia .... 63 G4 42 20S 147 1 E
Bothwell, Canada 84 D3 42 38N 81 52W
Botletle →, Botswana .... 56 C3 20 10S 23 15 E
Botoşani, Romania .... 17 E14 47 42N 26 41 E
Botou, Burkina Faso .... 50 F6 12 42N 1 59 E
Botswana ■, Africa .... 56 C3 22 0S 24 0 E
Bottineau, U.S.A. 80 A4 48 50N 100 27W
Bottrop, Germany .... 15 C6 51 31N 6 58 E
Botucatu, Brazil 95 A6 22 55S 48 30W
Botwood, Canada 73 C8 49 6N 55 23W
Bou Izakarn, Morocco 50 C4 29 12N 9 46W
Bouaké, Ivory C. 50 G4 7 40N 5 2W
Bouar, C.A.R. .... 52 C3 6 0N 15 40 E
Bouârfa, Morocco 50 B5 32 32N 1 58W
Boucaut B., Australia .... 62 A1 12 0S 134 25 E
Bouctouche, Canada 73 C7 46 30N 64 45W
Bougainville, C., Australia .... 60 B4 13 57S 126 4 E
Bougainville I., Papua N. G. ... 64 H7 6 0S 155 0 E

Bougainville Reef, Australia ... 62 B4 15 30S 147 5 E
Bougie = Bejaïa, Algeria ..... 50 A7 36 42N 5 2 E
Bougouni, Mali 50 F4 11 30N 7 20W
Bouillon, Belgium .... 15 E5 49 44N 5 3 E
Boulder, Colo., U.S.A. 80 E2 40 1N 105 17W
Boulder, Mont., U.S.A. 76 C7 46 14N 112 7W
Boulder City, U.S.A. 79 K12 35 59N 114 50W
Boulder Creek, U.S.A. 78 H4 37 7N 122 7W
Boulder Dam = Hoover Dam,
  U.S.A. 79 K12 36 1N 114 44W
Boulia, Australia .... 62 C2 22 52S 139 51 E
Boulogne-sur-Mer, France .... 20 A4 50 42N 1 36 E
Boultoum, Niger .... 51 F8 14 45N 10 25 E
Boun Neua, Laos .... 38 B3 21 38N 101 54 E
Boun Tai, Laos .... 38 B3 21 23N 101 58 E
Bouna, Ivory C. 50 G5 9 10N 3 0W
Boundary Peak, U.S.A. 78 H8 37 51N 118 21W
Boundiali, Ivory C. 50 G4 9 30N 6 20W
Bountiful, U.S.A. 76 F8 40 53N 111 53W
Bounty Is., Pac. Oc. .... 64 M9 48 0S 178 30 E
Bourbonnais, France .... 20 C5 46 28N 3 0 E
Bourdel L., Canada 72 A5 56 43N 74 10W
Bourem, Mali 50 E5 17 0N 0 24W
Bourg-en-Bresse, France ..... 20 C6 46 13N 5 12 E
Bourg-St-Maurice, France .... 20 D7 45 35N 6 46 E
Bourges, France .... 20 C5 47 9N 2 25 E
Bourget, Canada 85 A9 45 26N 75 9W
Bourgogne ⊠, France .... 20 C6 47 0N 4 50 E
Bourke, Australia .... 63 E4 30 8S 145 55 E
Bourne, U.K. 12 E7 52 47N 0 22W
Bournemouth, U.K. 13 G6 50 43N 1 52W
Bournemouth □, U.K. 13 G6 50 43N 1 52W
Bouse, U.S.A. 79 M13 33 56N 114 0W
Bouvet I. = Bouvetøya, Antarctica 3 G10 54 26S 3 24 E
Bouvetøya, Antarctica .... 3 G10 54 26S 3 24 E
Bovill, U.S.A. 76 C5 46 51N 116 24W
Bovril, Argentina 94 C4 31 21S 59 26W
Bow →, Canada 70 C6 49 57N 111 41W
Bow Island, Canada 70 D6 49 50N 111 23W
Bowbells, U.S.A. 80 A3 48 48N 102 15W
Bowdle, U.S.A. 80 C5 45 27N 99 39W
Bowelling, Australia .... 61 F2 33 25S 116 30 E
Bowen, Argentina 94 D2 35 0S 67 31W
Bowen, Australia .... 62 J6 20 0S 148 16 E
Bowen Mts., Australia .... 63 F4 37 0S 147 50 E
Bowie, Ariz., U.S.A. 77 K9 32 19N 109 29W
Bowie, Tex., U.S.A. 81 J6 33 34N 97 51W
Bowkān, Iran .... 44 B5 36 31N 46 12 E
Bowland, Forest of, U.K. 12 D5 54 0N 2 30W
Bowling Green, Ky., U.S.A. ... 82 G2 36 59N 86 27W
Bowling Green, Ohio, U.S.A. .. 82 E4 41 23N 83 39W
Bowling Green, C., Australia .. 62 B4 19 19S 147 25 E
Bowling Green Bay △, Australia 62 B4 19 15S 147 0 E
Bowman, U.S.A. 80 B3 46 11N 103 24W
Bowman I., Antarctica .... 5 C8 65 0S 104 0 E
Bowmanville = Clarington,
  Canada 84 C6 43 55N 78 41W
Bowmore, U.K. 11 F2 55 45N 6 17W
Bowral, Australia .... 63 E5 34 26S 150 27 E
Bowraville, Australia .... 63 E5 30 37S 152 52 E
Bowron →, Canada 70 C4 54 3N 121 50W
Bowron Lake ○, Canada 70 C4 53 10N 121 5W
Bowser L., Canada 70 B3 56 30N 129 30W
Bowsman, Canada 71 C8 52 14N 101 12W
Bowwood, Zambia .... 55 F2 17 5S 26 20 E
Box Cr. →, Australia .... 63 E3 34 10S 143 50 E
Boxmeer, Neths. .... 15 C5 51 38N 5 56 E
Boxtel, Neths. .... 15 C5 51 36N 5 20 E
Boyce, U.S.A. 81 K8 31 23N 92 40W
Boyd L., Canada 72 B4 52 46N 76 42W
Boyle, Canada 70 C6 54 35N 112 49W
Boyle, Ireland 10 C3 53 59N 8 18W
Boyne →, Ireland 10 C5 53 43N 6 15W
Boyne City, U.S.A. 82 C3 45 13N 85 1W
Boynton Beach, U.S.A. 83 M5 26 32N 80 4W
Boyolali, Indonesia .... 37 G14 7 32S 110 35 E
Boyoma, Chutes, Dem. Rep. of
  the Congo .... 54 B2 0 35N 25 23 E
Boysen Reservoir, U.S.A. 76 E9 43 25N 108 11W
Boyuibe, Bolivia 92 G6 20 25S 63 17W
Boyup Brook, Australia ...... 61 F2 33 50S 116 23 E
Boz Dağları, Turkey .... 23 E13 38 20N 28 0 E
Bozcaada, Turkey .... 23 E12 39 49N 26 3 E
Bozdoğan, Turkey .... 23 F13 37 40N 28 17 E
Bozeman, U.S.A. 76 D8 45 41N 111 2W
Bozen = Bolzano, Italy ...... 22 A4 46 31N 11 22 E
Bozhou, China .... 34 H8 33 55N 115 41 E
Bozoum, C.A.R. .... 52 C3 6 25N 16 35 E
Bra, Italy .... 20 D7 44 42N 7 51 E
Brabant □, Belgium .... 15 D4 50 46N 4 30 E
Brabant L., Canada 71 B8 55 58N 103 43W
Brač, Croatia .... 22 C7 43 20N 16 40 E
Bracadale, L., U.K. 11 D2 57 20N 6 30W
Bracciano, L. di, Italy .... 22 C5 42 7N 12 14 E
Bracebridge, Canada 84 A5 45 2N 79 19W
Brach, Libya .... 51 C8 27 31N 14 20 E
Bräcke, Sweden .... 9 E16 62 45N 15 26 E
Brackettville, U.S.A. 81 L4 29 19N 100 25W
Bracknell, U.K. 13 F7 51 25N 0 43W
Bracknell Forest □, U.K. 13 F7 51 25N 0 44W
Brad, Romania .... 17 E12 46 10N 22 50 E
Bradenton, U.S.A. 83 M4 27 30N 82 34W
Bradford, Canada 84 B5 44 7N 79 34W
Bradford, U.K. 12 D6 53 47N 1 45W
Bradford, Pa., U.S.A. 84 E6 41 58N 78 38W
Bradford, Vt., U.S.A. 85 C12 43 59N 72 9W
Bradley, Ark., U.S.A. 81 J8 33 6N 93 39W
Bradley, Calif., U.S.A. 78 K6 35 52N 120 48W
Bradley Institute, Zimbabwe .. 55 F3 17 7S 31 25 E
Brady, U.S.A. 81 K5 31 9N 99 20W
Braeside, Canada 85 A8 45 28N 76 24W
Braga, Portugal 21 B1 41 35N 8 25W
Bragado, Brazil 93 D9 1 0S 47 2W
Bragança, Brazil 93 D9 1 0S 47 2W
Bragança, Portugal 21 B2 41 48N 6 50W
Bragança Paulista, Brazil 95 A6 22 55S 46 32W
Brahmanbaria, Bangla. ...... 41 H17 23 58N 91 15 E
Brahmani →, India .... 41 J15 20 39N 86 46 E
Brahmapur, India .... 41 K14 19 15N 84 54 E
Brahmaputra →, Asia .... 43 J13 23 40N 90 35 E
Braich-y-pwll, U.K. 12 E3 52 47N 4 46W
Brăila, Romania .... 17 F14 45 19N 27 59 E
Brainerd, U.S.A. 80 B7 46 22N 94 12W
Braintree, U.K. .... 13 F8 51 53N 0 34 E
Braintree, U.S.A. 85 D14 42 13N 71 0W
Brak →, S. Africa .... 56 D3 29 35S 22 55 E

Brakwater, Namibia .... 56 C2 22 28S 17 3 E
Brampton, Canada 84 C5 43 45N 79 45W
Brampton, U.K. 12 C5 54 57N 2 44W
Bramton I., Australia .... 62 J7 20 50S 149 17 E
Branco →, Brazil 92 D6 1 20S 61 50W
Brandberg, Namibia .... 56 C1 21 10S 14 33 E
Brandberg ○, Namibia ...... 56 C1 21 10S 14 30 E
Brandenburg = Neubrandenburg,
  Germany .... 16 B7 53 33N 13 15 E
Brandenburg, Germany ...... 16 B7 52 25N 12 33 E
Brandenburg □, Germany .... 16 B6 52 50N 13 0 E
Brandfort, S. Africa .... 56 D4 28 40S 26 30 E
Brandon, Canada 71 D9 49 50N 99 57W
Brandon, U.S.A. 85 C11 43 48N 73 4W
Brandon B., Ireland 10 D1 52 17N 10 8W
Brandon Mt., Ireland 10 D1 52 15N 10 15W
Brandsen, Argentina 94 D4 35 10S 58 15W
Brandvlei, S. Africa .... 56 E3 30 25S 20 30 E
Branford, U.S.A. 85 E12 41 17N 72 49W
Braniewo, Poland .... 17 A10 54 25N 19 50 E
Bransfield Str., Antarctica 5 C18 63 0S 59 0W
Branson, U.S.A. 81 G8 36 39N 93 13W
Brantford, Canada 84 C4 43 10N 80 15W
Bras d'Or L., Canada 73 C7 45 50N 60 50W
Brasher Falls, U.S.A. 85 B10 44 49N 74 47W
Brasil, Planalto, Brazil 90 E6 18 0S 46 30W
Brasiléia, Brazil 92 F5 11 0S 68 45W
Brasília, Brazil 93 G9 15 47S 47 55W
Brasília Legal, Brazil 93 D7 3 49S 55 36W
Braslaw, Belarus .... 9 J22 55 38N 27 0 E
Braşov, Romania .... 17 F13 45 38N 25 35 E
Brasschaat, Belgium .... 15 C4 51 19N 4 27 E
Brassey, Banjaran, Malaysia .. 36 D5 5 0N 117 15 E
Brassey Ra., Australia ...... 61 E3 25 8S 122 15 E
Brasstown Bald, U.S.A. 83 H4 34 53N 83 49W
Brastad, Sweden .... 9 G14 58 23N 11 30 E
Bratislava, Slovak Rep. ..... 17 D9 48 10N 17 7 E
Bratsk, Russia .... 29 D11 56 10N 101 30 E
Brattleboro, U.S.A. 85 D12 42 51N 72 34W
Braunau, Austria .... 16 D7 48 15N 13 3 E
Braunschweig, Germany ..... 16 B6 52 15N 10 31 E
Braunton, U.K. 13 F3 51 7N 4 10W
Bravo del Norte, Rio = Grande,
  Rio →, U.S.A. 81 N6 25 58N 97 9W
Brawley, U.S.A. 79 N11 32 59N 115 31W
Bray, Ireland 10 C5 53 13N 6 7W
Bray, Mt., Australia .... 62 A1 14 0S 134 30 E
Bray, Pays de, France ...... 20 B4 49 46N 1 26 E
Brazeau →, Canada 70 C5 52 55N 115 14W
Brazil, U.S.A. 82 F2 39 32N 87 8W
Brazil ■, S. Amer. 93 F9 12 0S 50 0W
Brazilian Highlands = Brasil,
  Planalto, Brazil 90 E6 18 0S 46 30W
Brazo Sur →, S. Amer. 94 B4 25 21S 57 42W
Brazos →, U.S.A. 81 L7 28 53N 95 23W
Brazzaville, Congo .... 52 E3 4 9S 15 12 E
Brčko, Bos.-H. .... 23 B8 44 54N 18 46 E
Breaden, L., Australia ...... 61 E4 25 51S 125 28 E
Breaksea Sd., N.Z. .... 59 L1 45 35S 166 35 E
Bream B., N.Z. .... 59 F5 35 56S 174 28 E
Bream Hd., N.Z. .... 59 F5 35 51S 174 36 E
Breas, Chile 94 B1 25 29S 70 24W
Brebes, Indonesia .... 37 G13 6 52S 109 3 E
Brechin, Canada 84 B5 44 32N 79 10W
Brechin, U.K. 11 E6 56 44N 2 39W
Brecht, Belgium .... 15 C4 51 21N 4 38 E
Breckenridge, Colo., U.S.A. .. 76 G10 39 29N 106 3W
Breckenridge, Minn., U.S.A. .. 80 B6 46 16N 96 35W
Breckenridge, Tex., U.S.A. ... 81 J5 32 45N 98 54W
Breckland, U.K. .... 13 E8 52 30N 0 40 E
Brecon, U.K. 13 F4 51 57N 3 23W
Brecon Beacons △, U.K. 13 F4 51 50N 3 30W
Breda, Neths. .... 15 C4 51 35N 4 45 E
Bredasdorp, S. Africa .... 56 E3 34 33S 20 2 E
Bree, Belgium .... 15 C5 51 8N 5 35 E
Bregenz, Austria .... 16 E5 47 30N 9 45 E
Breiðafjörður, Iceland 8 D2 65 15N 23 15W
Brejo, Brazil 93 D10 3 41S 42 47W
Bremen, Germany .... 16 B5 53 4N 8 47 E
Bremer Bay, Australia .... 61 F2 34 21S 119 20 E
Bremer I., Australia .... 62 A2 12 5S 136 45 E
Bremerhaven, Germany ..... 16 B5 53 33N 8 36 E
Bremerton, U.S.A. 78 C4 47 34N 122 38W
Brenham, U.S.A. 81 K6 30 10N 96 24W
Brennerpass, Austria .... 16 E6 47 2N 11 30 E
Brent, U.K. 13 F8 51 33N 0 16W
Brentwood, Calif., U.S.A. 78 H5 37 56N 121 42W
Brentwood, N.Y., U.S.A. 85 F11 40 47N 73 15W
Bréscia, Italy .... 20 D9 45 33N 10 15 E
Breskens, Neths. .... 15 C3 51 23N 3 33 E
Breslau = Wrocław, Poland ... 17 C9 51 5N 17 5 E
Bressanone, Italy .... 22 A4 46 43N 11 39 E
Bressay, U.K. 11 A7 60 9N 1 6W
Brest, Belarus .... 17 B12 52 10N 23 40 E
Brest, France 20 B1 48 24N 4 31W
Brest-Litovsk = Brest, Belarus . 17 B12 52 10N 23 40 E
Bretagne ⊠, France 20 B2 48 10N 3 0W
Breton, Canada 70 C6 53 7N 114 28W
Breton Sd., U.S.A. 81 L10 29 35N 89 15W
Brett, C., N.Z. .... 59 F5 35 10S 174 20 E
Brevard, U.S.A. 83 H4 35 14N 82 44W
Breves, Brazil 93 D8 1 40S 50 29W
Brewarrina, Australia .... 63 E4 30 0S 146 51 E
Brewer, U.S.A. 83 C11 44 48N 68 46W
Brewer, Mt., U.S.A. 78 J8 36 44N 118 28W
Brewster, N.Y., U.S.A. 85 E11 41 23N 73 37W
Brewster, Ohio, U.S.A. 84 F3 40 43N 81 36W
Brewster, Wash., U.S.A. 76 B4 48 6N 119 47W
Brewster, Kap = Kangikajik,
  Greenland 4 B6 70 7N 22 0W
Brewton, U.S.A. 83 K2 31 7N 87 4W
Breyten, S. Africa .... 57 D5 26 16S 30 0 E
Briançon, France .... 20 D7 44 54N 6 39 E
Bribie I., Australia .... 63 D5 27 0S 153 10 E
Bribri, Costa Rica 88 E3 9 38N 82 50W
Bridgefield, Barbados .... 89 g 13 9N 59 36W
Bridgehampton, U.S.A. 85 F12 40 56N 72 19W
Bridgend, U.K. 13 F4 51 30N 3 34W
Bridgend □, U.K. 13 F4 51 36N 3 36W
Bridgeport, Calif., U.S.A. 78 G7 38 15N 119 14W
Bridgeport, Conn., U.S.A. 85 E11 41 11N 73 12W
Bridgeport, Nebr., U.S.A. 80 E3 41 40N 103 6W
Bridgeport, Tex., U.S.A. 81 J6 33 13N 97 45W
Bridger, U.S.A. 76 D9 45 18N 108 55W
Bridgeton, U.S.A. 82 F8 39 26N 75 14W
Bridgetown, Australia .... 61 F2 33 58S 116 7 E

108 Bridgetown INDEX TO WORLD MAPS

Bridgetown, *Barbados* **89 g** 13 5N 59 30W
Bridgetown, *Canada* **73 D6** 44 55N 65 18W
Bridgewater, *Canada* **73 D7** 44 25N 64 31W
Bridgewater, *Mass., U.S.A.* **85 E14** 41 59N 70 58W
Bridgewater, *N.Y., U.S.A.* **85 D9** 42 53N 75 15W
Bridgewater, C., *Australia* **63 F3** 38 23S 141 23 E
Bridgewater-Gagebrook, *Australia* **63 G4** 42 44S 147 14 E
Bridgnorth, *U.K.* **13 E5** 52 32N 2 25W
Bridgton, *U.S.A.* **85 B14** 44 3N 70 42W
Bridgwater, *U.K.* **13 F5** 51 8N 2 59W
Bridgwater B., *U.K.* **13 F4** 51 15N 3 15W
Bridlington, *U.K.* **12 C7** 54 5N 0 12W
Bridlington B., *U.K.* **12 C7** 54 4N 0 10W
Bridport, *Australia* **63 G4** 40 59S 147 23 E
Bridport, *U.K.* **13 G5** 50 44N 2 45W
Brig, *Switz.* **20 C7** 46 18N 7 59 E
Brigg, *U.K.* **12 D7** 53 34N 0 28W
Brigham City, *U.S.A.* **76 F7** 41 31N 112 1W
Bright, *Australia* **63 F4** 36 42S 146 56 E
Brighton, *Australia* **63 F2** 35 5S 138 30 E
Brighton, *Canada* **84 B7** 44 2N 77 44W
Brighton, *Trin. & Tob.* **93 K15** 10 13N 61 39W
Brighton, *U.K.* **13 G7** 50 49N 0 7W
Brighton, *Colo., U.S.A.* **80 F2** 39 59N 104 49W
Brighton, *N.Y., U.S.A.* **84 C7** 43 8N 77 34W
Brilliant, *U.S.A.* **84 F4** 40 15N 80 39W
Bríndisi, *Italy* **23 D7** 40 39N 17 55 E
Brinkley, *U.S.A.* **81 H9** 34 53N 91 12W
Brinnon, *U.S.A.* **78 C4** 47 41N 122 54W
Brion, Î., *Canada* **73 C7** 47 46N 61 26W
Brisbane, *Australia* **63 D5** 27 25S 153 2 E
Brisbane →, *Australia* **63 D5** 27 24S 153 9 E
Bristol, *U.K.* **13 F5** 51 26N 2 35W
Bristol, *Conn., U.S.A.* **85 E12** 41 40N 72 57W
Bristol, *Pa., U.S.A.* **85 F10** 40 6N 74 51W
Bristol, *R.I., U.S.A.* **85 E13** 41 40N 71 16W
Bristol, *Tenn., U.S.A.* **83 G4** 36 36N 82 11W
Bristol, City of □, *U.K.* **13 F5** 51 27N 2 36W
Bristol B., *U.S.A.* **68 C4** 58 0N 160 0W
Bristol Channel, *U.K.* **13 F3** 51 18N 4 30W
Bristol I., *Antarctica* **5 B1** 58 45S 28 0W
Bristol L., *U.S.A.* **77 J5** 34 23N 116 50W
Bristow, *U.S.A.* **81 H6** 35 50N 96 23W
Britain = Great Britain, *Europe* **6 E5** 54 0N 2 15W
British Columbia □, *Canada* **70 C3** 55 0N 125 15W
British Indian Ocean Terr. = Chagos Arch. ☑, *Ind. Oc.* **27 K11** 6 0S 72 0 E
British Isles, *Europe* **14 D5** 54 0N 4 0W
British Virgin Is. ☑, *W. Indies* **89 e** 18 30N 64 30W
Brits, *S. Africa* **57 D4** 25 37S 27 48 E
Britstown, *S. Africa* **56 E3** 30 37S 23 30 E
Britt, *Canada* **72 C3** 45 46N 80 34W
Brittany = Bretagne ☒, *France* **20 B2** 48 10N 3 0W
Britton, *U.S.A.* **80 C6** 45 48N 97 45W
Brive-la-Gaillarde, *France* **20 D4** 45 10N 1 32 E
Brixen = Bressanone, *Italy* **22 A4** 46 43N 11 39 E
Brixham, *U.K.* **13 G4** 50 23N 3 31W
Brno, *Czech Rep.* **17 D9** 49 10N 16 35 E
Broach = Bharuch, *India* **40 J8** 21 47N 73 0 E
Broad →, *U.S.A.* **83 J5** 34 1N 81 4W
Broad Arrow, *Australia* **61 F3** 30 23S 121 15 E
Broad B., *U.K.* **11 C2** 58 14N 6 18W
Broad Haven, *Ireland* **10 B2** 54 20N 9 55W
Broad Law, *U.K.* **11 F5** 55 30N 3 21W
Broad Sd., *Australia* **62 C4** 22 0S 149 45 E
Broadalbin, *U.S.A.* **85 C10** 43 4N 74 12W
Broadback →, *Canada* **72 B4** 51 21N 78 52W
Broadhurst Ra., *Australia* **60 D3** 22 30S 122 30 E
Broads △, *U.K.* **13 E9** 52 45N 1 30 E
Broads, The, *U.K.* **12 E9** 52 45N 1 30 E
Broadus, *U.S.A.* **80 C2** 45 27N 105 25W
Brochet, *Canada* **71 B8** 57 53N 101 40W
Brochet, L., *Canada* **71 B8** 58 36N 101 35W
Brocken, *Germany* **16 C6** 51 47N 10 37 E
Brockport, *U.S.A.* **84 C7** 43 13N 77 56W
Brockton, *U.S.A.* **85 D13** 42 5N 71 1W
Brockville, *Canada* **85 B9** 44 35N 75 41W
Brockway, *Mont., U.S.A.* **80 B2** 47 18N 105 45W
Brockway, *Pa., U.S.A.* **84 E6** 41 15N 78 47W
Brocton, *U.S.A.* **84 D5** 42 23N 79 26W
Brodeur Pen., *Canada* **69 A11** 72 30N 88 10W
Brodhead, Mt., *U.S.A.* **84 E7** 41 39N 77 47W
Brodick, *U.K.* **11 F3** 55 35N 5 9W
Brodnica, *Poland* **17 B10** 53 15N 19 25 E
Brody, *Ukraine* **17 C13** 50 5N 25 10 E
Brogan, *U.S.A.* **76 D5** 44 15N 117 31W
Broken Arrow, *U.S.A.* **81 G7** 36 3N 95 48W
Broken Bow, *Nebr., U.S.A.* **80 E5** 41 24N 99 38W
Broken Bow, *Okla., U.S.A.* **81 H7** 34 2N 94 44W
Broken Bow Lake, *U.S.A.* **81 H7** 34 9N 94 40W
Broken Hill, *Australia* **63 E3** 31 58S 141 29 E
Broken River Ra., *Australia* **62 K6** 21 0S 148 22 E
Bromley □, *U.K.* **13 F8** 51 24N 0 2 E
Bromo, *Indonesia* **37 G15** 7 55S 112 55 E
Bromsgrove, *U.K.* **13 E5** 52 21N 2 2W
Brønderslev, *Denmark* **9 H13** 57 16N 9 57 E
Bronkhorstspruit, *S. Africa* **57 D4** 25 46S 28 45 E
Brønnøysund, *Norway* **8 D15** 65 28N 12 14 E
Brook Park, *U.S.A.* **84 E4** 41 24N 81 51W
Brookhaven, *U.S.A.* **81 K9** 31 35N 90 26W
Brookings, *Oreg., U.S.A.* **76 E1** 42 3N 124 17W
Brookings, *S. Dak., U.S.A.* **80 C6** 44 19N 96 48W
Brooklin, *Canada* **84 C6** 43 55N 78 55W
Brooklyn Park, *U.S.A.* **80 C8** 45 6N 93 23W
Brooks, *Canada* **70 C6** 50 35N 111 55W
Brooks Range, *U.S.A.* **68 B5** 68 0N 152 0W
Brooksville, *U.S.A.* **83 L4** 28 33N 82 23W
Brookton, *Australia* **61 F2** 32 22S 117 0 E
Brookville, *U.S.A.* **84 E5** 41 10N 79 5W
Broom, L., *U.K.* **11 D3** 57 55N 5 15W
Broome, *Australia* **60 C3** 18 0S 122 15 E
Brora, *U.K.* **11 C5** 58 0N 3 52W
Brora →, *U.K.* **11 C5** 58 0N 3 51W
Brosna →, *Ireland* **10 C4** 53 14N 7 58W
Brothers, *U.S.A.* **76 E3** 43 49N 120 36W
Brough, *U.K.* **12 C5** 54 32N 2 18W
Brough Hd., *U.K.* **11 B5** 59 8N 3 20W
Broughton Island = Qikiqtarjuaq, *Canada* **69 B13** 67 33N 63 0W
Brown, L., *Australia* **61 F2** 31 5S 118 15 E
Brown, Pt., *Australia* **63 E1** 32 32S 133 50 E
Brown City, *U.S.A.* **84 C2** 43 13N 82 59W
Brown Willy, *U.K.* **13 G3** 50 35N 4 37W
Brownfield, *U.S.A.* **81 J3** 33 11N 102 17W
Browning, *U.S.A.* **76 B7** 48 34N 113 1W
Brownsville, *Oreg., U.S.A.* **76 D2** 44 24N 122 59W
Brownsville, *Pa., U.S.A.* **84 F5** 40 1N 79 53W
Brownsville, *Tenn., U.S.A.* **81 H10** 35 36N 89 16W
Brownsville, *Tex., U.S.A.* **81 N6** 25 54N 97 30W
Brownville, *U.S.A.* **85 C9** 44 0N 75 59W
Brownwood, *U.S.A.* **81 K5** 31 43N 98 59W
Browse I., *Australia* **60 B3** 14 7S 123 33 E
Bruas, *Malaysia* **39 K3** 4 30N 100 47 E
Bruay-la-Buissière, *France* **20 A5** 50 29N 2 33 E
Bruce, Mt., *Australia* **60 D2** 22 37S 118 8 E
Bruce Pen., *Canada* **84 B3** 45 0N 81 30W
Bruce Peninsula △, *Canada* **84 A3** 45 14N 81 36W
Bruce Rock, *Australia* **61 F2** 31 52S 118 8 E
Bruck an der Leitha, *Austria* **17 D9** 48 1N 16 47 E
Bruck an der Mur, *Austria* **16 E8** 47 24N 15 16 E
Brue →, *U.K.* **13 F5** 51 13N 2 59W
Bruges = Brugge, *Belgium* **15 C3** 51 13N 3 13 E
Brugge, *Belgium* **15 C3** 51 13N 3 13 E
Bruin, *U.S.A.* **84 E5** 41 3N 79 43W
Brûlé, *Canada* **70 C5** 53 15N 117 58W
Brumado, *Brazil* **93 F10** 14 14S 41 40W
Brumunddal, *Norway* **9 F14** 60 53N 10 56 E
Bruneau, *U.S.A.* **76 E6** 42 53N 115 48W
Bruneau →, *U.S.A.* **76 E6** 42 56N 115 57W
Brunei = Bandar Seri Begawan, *Brunei* **36 C4** 4 52N 115 0 E
Brunei ■, *Asia* **36 D4** 4 50N 115 0 E
Brunner, L., *N.Z.* **59 K3** 42 37S 171 27 E
Brunssum, *Neths.* **15 D5** 50 57N 5 59 E
Brunswick = Braunschweig, *Germany* **16 B6** 52 15N 10 31 E
Brunswick, *Ga., U.S.A.* **83 K5** 31 10N 81 30W
Brunswick, *Maine, U.S.A.* **83 D11** 43 55N 69 58W
Brunswick, *Md., U.S.A.* **82 F7** 39 19N 77 38W
Brunswick, *Mo., U.S.A.* **80 F8** 39 26N 93 8W
Brunswick, *Ohio, U.S.A.* **84 E3** 41 14N 81 51W
Brunswick, Pen. de, *Chile* **96 G2** 53 30S 71 30W
Brunswick B., *Australia* **60 C3** 15 15S 124 50 E
Brunswick Junction, *Australia* **61 F2** 33 15S 115 50 E
Bruny I., *Australia* **63 G4** 43 20S 147 15 E
Brus Laguna, *Honduras* **88 C3** 15 47N 84 35W
Brush, *U.S.A.* **80 E3** 40 15N 103 37W
Brushton, *U.S.A.* **85 B10** 44 50N 74 31W
Brusque, *Brazil* **95 B6** 27 5S 49 0W
Brussel, *Belgium* **15 D4** 50 51N 4 21 E
Brussels = Brussel, *Belgium* **15 D4** 50 51N 4 21 E
Brussels, *Canada* **84 C3** 43 44N 81 15W
Brussels Nat. ✕ (BRU), *Belgium* **15 D5** 50 54N 5 41 E
Bruthen, *Australia* **63 F4** 37 42S 147 50 E
Bruxelles = Brussel, *Belgium* **15 D4** 50 51N 4 21 E
Bryan, *Ohio, U.S.A.* **82 E3** 41 28N 84 33W
Bryan, *Tex., U.S.A.* **81 K6** 30 40N 96 22W
Bryan, Mt., *Australia* **63 E2** 33 30S 139 0 E
Bryansk, *Russia* **18 D4** 53 13N 34 25 E
Bryce Canyon △, *U.S.A.* **77 H7** 37 30N 112 10W
Bryne, *Norway* **9 G11** 58 44N 5 38 E
Bryson City, *U.S.A.* **83 H4** 35 26N 83 27W
Bsharri, *Lebanon* **46 A5** 34 15N 36 0 E
Bū Baqarah, *U.A.E.* **45 E8** 25 35N 56 25 E
Bu Craa, *W. Sahara* **50 C3** 26 45N 12 50W
Bū Ḩasā, *U.A.E.* **45 F7** 23 30N 53 20 E
Bua Yai, *Thailand* **38 E4** 15 33N 102 26 E
Buapinang, *Indonesia* **37 E6** 4 40S 121 30 E
Bubanza, *Burundi* **54 C2** 3 6S 29 23 E
Būbiyān, *Kuwait* **45 D6** 29 45N 48 15 E
Bucaramanga, *Colombia* **92 B4** 7 0N 73 0W
Bucasia, *Australia* **62 K7** 21 2S 149 10 E
Buccaneer Arch., *Australia* **60 C3** 16 7S 123 20 E
Buccoo Reef, *Trin. & Tob.* **93 J16** 11 10N 60 51W
Buchach, *Ukraine* **17 D13** 49 5N 25 25 E
Buchan, *U.K.* **11 D6** 57 32N 2 21W
Buchan Ness, *U.K.* **11 D7** 57 29N 1 46W
Buchanan, *Canada* **71 C8** 51 40N 102 45W
Buchanan, *Liberia* **50 G3** 5 57N 10 2W
Buchanan, L., *Queens., Australia* **62 C4** 21 35S 145 52 E
Buchanan, L., *W. Austral., Australia* **61 E3** 25 33S 123 2 E
Buchanan, L., *U.S.A.* **81 K5** 30 45N 98 25W
Buchanan Cr. →, *Australia* **62 B2** 19 13S 136 33 E
Buchans, *Canada* **73 C8** 48 50N 56 52W
Bucharest = Bucureşti, *Romania* **17 F14** 44 27N 26 10 E
Buchon, Pt., *U.S.A.* **78 K6** 35 15N 120 54W
Buck Hill Falls, *U.S.A.* **85 E9** 41 11N 75 16W
Buckeye, *U.S.A.* **77 K7** 33 22N 112 35W
Buckeye Lake, *U.S.A.* **84 G2** 39 55N 82 29W
Buckhannon, *U.S.A.* **82 F5** 39 0N 80 8W
Buckhaven, *U.K.* **11 E5** 56 11N 3 3W
Buckhorn L., *Canada* **84 B6** 44 29N 78 23W
Buckie, *U.K.* **11 D6** 57 41N 2 58W
Buckingham, *Canada* **72 C4** 45 37N 75 24W
Buckingham, *U.K.* **13 F7** 51 59N 0 57W
Buckingham B., *Australia* **62 A2** 12 10S 135 40 E
Buckinghamshire □, *U.K.* **13 F7** 51 53N 0 55W
Buckle Hd., *Australia* **60 B4** 14 26S 127 52 E
Buckleboo, *Australia* **63 E2** 32 54S 136 12 E
Buckley, *U.K.* **12 D4** 53 10N 3 5W
Buckley →, *Australia* **62 C2** 20 10S 138 49 E
Bucklin, *U.S.A.* **81 G5** 37 33N 99 38W
Bucks L., *U.S.A.* **78 F5** 39 54N 121 12W
Bucureşti, *Romania* **17 F14** 44 27N 26 10 E
Bucyrus, *U.S.A.* **82 E4** 40 48N 82 59W
Budalin, *Burma* **41 H19** 22 20N 95 10 E
Budapest, *Hungary* **17 E10** 47 29N 19 5 E
Budaun, *India* **43 E8** 28 5N 79 10 E
Budd Coast, *Antarctica* **5 C8** 68 0S 112 0 E
Bude, *U.K.* **13 G3** 50 49N 4 34W
Budennovsk, *Russia* **19 F7** 44 50N 44 10 E
Budge Budge = Baj Baj, *India* **43 H13** 22 30N 88 5 E
Budgewoi, *Australia* **63 E5** 33 13S 151 34 E
Budjala, *Dem. Rep. of the Congo* **52 D3** 2 50N 19 40 E
Buellton, *U.S.A.* **79 L6** 34 37N 120 12W
Buena Esperanza, *Argentina* **94 C2** 34 45S 65 15W
Buena Park, *U.S.A.* **79 M9** 33 52N 117 59W
Buena Vista, *Colo., U.S.A.* **77 G10** 38 51N 106 8W
Buena Vista, *Va., U.S.A.* **82 G6** 37 44N 79 21W
Buena Vista Lake Bed, *U.S.A.* **79 K7** 35 12N 119 18W
Buenaventura, *Colombia* **92 C3** 3 53N 77 4W
Buenaventura, *Mexico* **86 B3** 29 50N 107 30W
Buenos Aires, *Argentina* **94 C4** 34 30S 58 20W
Buenos Aires, *Costa Rica* **88 E3** 9 10N 83 20W
Buenos Aires □, *Argentina* **94 D4** 36 30S 60 0W
Buenos Aires, L., *Chile* **96 F2** 46 35S 72 30W
Buffalo, *Mo., U.S.A.* **81 G8** 37 39N 93 6W
Buffalo, *N.Y., U.S.A.* **84 D6** 42 53N 78 53W
Buffalo, *Okla., U.S.A.* **81 G5** 36 50N 99 38W
Buffalo, *S. Dak., U.S.A.* **80 C3** 45 35N 103 33W
Buffalo, *Wyo., U.S.A.* **76 D10** 44 21N 106 42W
Buffalo △, *U.S.A.* **81 G8** 36 14N 92 36W
Buffalo →, *Canada* **70 A5** 60 5N 115 5W
Buffalo →, *S. Africa* **57 D5** 28 43S 30 37 E
Buffalo Head Hills, *Canada* **70 B5** 57 25N 115 55W
Buffalo L., *Alta., Canada* **70 C6** 52 27N 112 54W
Buffalo L., *N.W.T., Canada* **70 A5** 60 12N 115 25W
Buffalo Narrows, *Canada* **71 B7** 55 51N 108 29W
Buffalo Springs ⌂, *Kenya* **54 B4** 0 32N 37 35 E
Buffels →, *S. Africa* **56 D2** 29 36S 17 3 E
Buford, *U.S.A.* **83 H4** 34 10N 84 0W
Bug = Buh →, *Ukraine* **19 E5** 46 59N 31 58 E
Bug →, *Poland* **17 B11** 52 31N 21 5 E
Buga, *Colombia* **92 C3** 4 0N 76 15W
Bugala I., *Uganda* **54 C3** 0 40S 32 20 E
Buganda, *Uganda* **54 C3** 0 0 31 30 E
Buganga, *Uganda* **54 C3** 0 3S 32 0 E
Bugel, Tanjung, *Indonesia* **37 G14** 6 26S 111 3 E
Bugibba, *Malta* **25 D1** 35 57N 14 25 E
Bugsuk, *Phil.* **36 C5** 8 15N 117 15 E
Bugulma, *Russia* **18 D9** 54 33N 52 48 E
Bugun Shara, *Mongolia* **32 B5** 49 0N 104 0 E
Bugungu ⌂, *Uganda* **54 B3** 2 17N 31 50 E
Buguruslan, *Russia* **18 D9** 53 39N 52 26 E
Buh →, *Ukraine* **19 E5** 46 59N 31 58 E
Buhera, *Zimbabwe* **57 B5** 19 18S 31 29 E
Buhl, *U.S.A.* **76 E6** 42 36N 114 46W
Builth Wells, *U.K.* **13 E4** 52 9N 3 25W
Buir Nur, *Mongolia* **33 B6** 47 50N 117 42 E
Buji, *China* **33 F11** 22 37N 114 5 E
Bujumbura, *Burundi* **54 C2** 3 16S 29 18 E
Bukachacha, *Russia* **29 D12** 52 55N 116 50 E
Bukama, *Dem. Rep. of the Congo* **55 D2** 9 10S 25 50 E
Bukavu, *Dem. Rep. of the Congo* **54 C2** 2 20S 28 52 E
Bukene, *Tanzania* **54 C3** 4 15S 32 48 E
Bukhara = Bukhoro, *Uzbekistan* **28 F7** 39 48N 64 25 E
Bukhoro, *Uzbekistan* **28 F7** 39 48N 64 25 E
Bukima, *Tanzania* **54 C3** 1 50S 33 25 E
Bukit Badung, *Indonesia* **37 K18** 8 49S 115 10 E
Bukit Kerajaan, *Malaysia* **39 c** 5 25N 100 15 E
Bukit Mertajam, *Malaysia* **39 c** 5 22N 100 28 E
Bukit Ni, *Malaysia* **39 d** 1 22N 104 12 E
Bukit Panjang, *Singapore* **39 d** 1 23N 103 46 E
Bukit Tengah, *Malaysia* **39 c** 5 22N 100 25 E
Bukittinggi, *Indonesia* **36 E2** 0 20S 100 20 E
Bukoba, *Tanzania* **54 C3** 1 20S 31 49 E
Bukum, Pulau, *Singapore* **39 d** 1 14N 103 46 E
Bukuya, *Uganda* **54 B3** 0 40N 31 52 E
Būl, Kuh-e, *Iran* **45 D7** 30 48N 52 45 E
Bula, *Indonesia* **37 E8** 3 6S 130 30 E
Bulahdelah, *Australia* **63 E5** 32 23S 152 13 E
Bulan, *Phil.* **37 B6** 12 40N 123 52 E
Bulandshahr, *India* **42 E7** 28 28N 77 51 E
Bulawayo, *Zimbabwe* **55 G2** 20 7S 28 32 E
Buldan, *Turkey* **23 E13** 38 2N 28 50 E
Bulgar, *Russia* **18 D8** 54 57N 49 4 E
Bulgaria ■, *Europe* **23 C11** 42 35N 25 30 E
Buli, Teluk, *Indonesia* **37 D7** 0 48N 128 25 E
Buliluyan, C., *Phil.* **36 C5** 8 20N 117 15 E
Bulim, *Singapore* **39 d** 1 22N 103 43 E
Bulkley →, *Canada* **70 B3** 55 15N 127 40W
Bull Shoals L., *U.S.A.* **81 G8** 36 22N 92 35W
Bulleringa △, *Australia* **62 B3** 17 39S 143 56 E
Bullhead City, *U.S.A.* **79 K12** 35 8N 114 32W
Büllingen, *Belgium* **15 D6** 50 25N 6 16 E
Bullock Creek, *Australia* **62 B3** 17 43S 144 31 E
Bulloo →, *Australia* **63 D3** 28 43S 142 30 E
Bulloo L., *Australia* **63 D3** 28 43S 142 25 E
Bulls, *N.Z.* **59 J5** 40 10S 175 24 E
Bulnes, *Chile* **94 D1** 36 42S 72 19W
Bulsar = Valsad, *India* **40 J8** 20 40N 72 58 E
Bultfontein, *S. Africa* **56 D4** 28 18S 26 10 E
Bulukumba, *Indonesia* **37 F6** 5 33S 120 11 E
Bulun, *Russia* **29 B13** 70 37N 127 30 E
Bumba, *Dem. Rep. of the Congo* **52 D4** 2 13N 22 30 E
Bumbiri I., *Tanzania* **54 C3** 1 40S 31 55 E
Bumhpa Bum, *Burma* **41 F20** 26 51N 97 14 E
Bumi →, *Zimbabwe* **55 F2** 17 0S 28 20 E
Buna, *Kenya* **54 B4** 2 58N 39 30 E
Bunazi, *Tanzania* **54 C3** 1 3S 31 23 E
Bunbury, *Australia* **61 F2** 33 20S 115 35 E
Bunclody, *Ireland* **10 D5** 52 39N 6 40W
Buncrana, *Ireland* **10 A4** 55 8N 7 27W
Bundaberg, *Australia* **63 C5** 24 54S 152 22 E
Bundey →, *Australia* **62 C2** 21 46S 135 37 E
Bundi, *India* **42 G6** 25 30N 75 35 E
Bundjalung △, *Australia* **63 D5** 29 16S 153 21 E
Bundoran, *Ireland* **10 B3** 54 28N 8 16W
Bung Kan, *Thailand* **38 C4** 18 23N 103 37 E
Bungay, *U.K.* **13 E9** 52 27N 1 28 E
Bungil Cr. →, *Australia* **63 D4** 27 5S 149 5 E
Bungo-Suidō, *Japan* **31 H6** 33 0N 132 15 E
Bungoma, *Kenya* **54 B3** 0 34N 34 34 E
Bungotakada, *Japan* **31 H5** 33 35N 131 25 E
Bungu, *Tanzania* **54 D4** 7 35S 39 0 E
Bunia, *Dem. Rep. of the Congo* **54 B3** 1 35N 30 20 E
Bunji, *Pakistan* **43 B6** 35 45N 74 40 E
Bunkie, *U.S.A.* **81 K8** 30 57N 92 11W
Bunnell, *U.S.A.* **83 L5** 29 28N 81 16W
Buntok, *Indonesia* **36 E4** 1 40S 114 58 E
Bunya Mts. △, *Australia* **63 D5** 26 51S 151 34 E
Bunyu, *Indonesia* **36 D5** 3 35N 117 50 E
Buol, *Indonesia* **37 D6** 1 15N 121 32 E
Buon Brieng, *Vietnam* **38 F7** 13 9N 108 12 E
Buon Ma Thuot, *Vietnam* **38 F7** 12 40N 108 3 E
Buong Long, *Cambodia* **38 F6** 13 44N 106 59 E
Buorkhaya, Mys, *Russia* **29 B14** 71 50N 132 40 E
Buqayq, *Si. Arabia* **45 E6** 26 0N 49 45 E
Bur Acaba, *Somali Rep.* **47 G3** 3 12N 44 20 E
Bûr Safâga, *Egypt* **44 E2** 26 43N 33 57 E
Bûr Sa'îd, *Egypt* **51 B12** 31 16N 32 18 E
Bûr Sûdân, *Sudan* **51 E13** 19 32N 37 9 E
Bura, *Kenya* **54 C4** 1 4S 39 58 E
Burakin, *Australia* **61 F2** 30 31S 117 10 E
Burao, *Somali Rep.* **47 F4** 9 32N 45 32 E
Burāq, *Syria* **46 B5** 33 11N 36 29 E
Buraydah, *Si. Arabia* **44 E4** 26 20N 43 59 E
Burbank, *U.S.A.* **79 L8** 34 11N 118 19W
Burda, *India* **42 G6** 25 50N 77 35 E
Burdekin →, *Australia* **62 B4** 19 38S 147 25 E
Burdur, *Turkey* **19 G5** 37 45N 30 17 E
Burdwan = Barddhaman, *India* **43 H12** 23 14N 87 39 E
Bure, *Ethiopia* **47 E2** 10 40N 37 4 E
Bure →, *U.K.* **12 E9** 52 38N 1 43 E
Bureya →, *Russia* **29 E13** 49 27N 129 30 E
Burford, *Canada* **84 C4** 43 7N 80 27W
Burgas, *Bulgaria* **23 C12** 42 33N 27 29 E
Burgeo, *Canada* **73 C8** 47 37N 57 38W
Burgersdorp, *S. Africa* **56 E4** 31 0S 26 20 E
Burges, Mt., *Australia* **61 F3** 30 50S 121 5 E
Burghead, *U.K.* **11 D5** 57 43N 3 30W
Burgos, *Spain* **21 A4** 42 21N 3 41W
Burgsvik, *Sweden* **9 H18** 57 3N 18 19 E
Burgundy = Bourgogne ☒, *France* **20 C6** 47 0N 4 50 E
Burhaniye, *Turkey* **23 E12** 39 30N 26 58 E
Burhanpur, *India* **40 J10** 21 18N 76 14 E
Burhi Gandak →, *India* **43 G12** 25 20N 86 37 E
Burhner →, *India* **43 H9** 22 43N 80 31 E
Burias I., *Phil.* **37 B6** 12 55N 123 5 E
Burica, Pta., *Costa Rica* **88 E3** 8 3N 82 51W
Burien, *U.S.A.* **78 C4** 47 28N 122 21W
Burigi ⌂, *Tanzania* **54 C3** 2 20S 31 6 E
Burigi, L., *Tanzania* **54 C3** 2 2S 31 22 E
Burin, *Canada* **73 C8** 47 1N 55 14W
Buriram, *Thailand* **38 E4** 15 0N 103 0 E
Burj Sāfitā, *Syria* **44 C3** 34 48N 36 7 E
Burkburnett, *U.S.A.* **81 H5** 34 6N 98 34W
Burke →, *Australia* **62 C2** 23 12S 139 33 E
Burke Chan., *Canada* **70 C3** 52 10N 127 30W
Burketown, *Australia* **62 B2** 17 45S 139 33 E
Burkina Faso ■, *Africa* **50 F5** 12 0N 1 0W
Burk's Falls, *Canada* **72 C4** 45 37N 79 24W
Burleigh Falls, *Canada* **84 B6** 44 33N 78 12W
Burley, *U.S.A.* **76 E7** 42 32N 113 48W
Burlingame, *U.S.A.* **78 H4** 37 35N 122 21W
Burlington, *Canada* **84 C5** 43 18N 79 45W
Burlington, *Colo., U.S.A.* **80 F3** 39 18N 102 16W
Burlington, *Iowa, U.S.A.* **80 E9** 40 49N 91 14W
Burlington, *Kans., U.S.A.* **80 F7** 38 12N 95 45W
Burlington, *N.C., U.S.A.* **83 G6** 36 6N 79 26W
Burlington, *N.J., U.S.A.* **85 F10** 40 4N 74 51W
Burlington, *Vt., U.S.A.* **85 B11** 44 29N 73 12W
Burlington, *Wash., U.S.A.* **78 B4** 48 28N 122 20W
Burlington, *Wis., U.S.A.* **82 D1** 42 41N 88 17W
Burlyu-Tyube, *Kazakhstan* **28 E8** 46 30N 79 10 E
Burma ■, *Asia* **41 J20** 21 0N 96 30 E
Burnaby I., *Canada* **70 C2** 52 25N 131 19W
Burnet, *U.S.A.* **81 K5** 30 45N 98 14W
Burney, *U.S.A.* **76 F3** 40 53N 121 40W
Burnham, *U.S.A.* **84 F7** 40 38N 77 34W
Burnham-on-Sea, *U.K.* **13 F5** 51 14N 3 0W
Burnie, *Australia* **63 G4** 41 4S 145 56 E
Burnley, *U.K.* **12 D5** 53 47N 2 14W
Burns, *U.S.A.* **76 E4** 43 35N 119 3W
Burns Lake, *Canada* **70 C3** 54 20N 125 45W
Burnside →, *Canada* **68 B9** 66 51N 108 4W
Burnside, L., *Australia* **61 E3** 25 22S 123 0 E
Burnsville, *U.S.A.* **80 C8** 44 47N 93 17W
Burnt, L., *Canada* **73 B7** 53 35N 64 4W
Burnt River, *Canada* **84 B6** 44 41N 78 42W
Burntwood →, *Canada* **71 B9** 56 8N 96 34W
Burntwood L., *Canada* **71 B8** 55 22N 100 26W
Burqān, *Kuwait* **44 D5** 29 0N 47 57 E
Burra, *Australia* **63 E2** 33 40S 138 55 E
Burray, *U.K.* **11 C6** 58 51N 2 54W
Burren △, *Ireland* **10 C3** 53 1N 8 58W
Burren Junction, *Australia* **63 E4** 30 7S 148 59 E
Burrinjuck Res., *Australia* **63 F4** 35 0S 148 36 E
Burro, Serranías del, *Mexico* **86 B4** 29 0N 102 0W
Burrow Hd., *U.K.* **11 G4** 54 41N 4 24W
Burrum Coast △, *Australia* **63 D5** 25 13S 152 36 E
Burruyacú, *Argentina* **94 B3** 26 30S 64 40W
Burry Port, *U.K.* **13 F3** 51 41N 4 15W
Bursa, *Turkey* **23 D13** 40 15N 29 5 E
Burstall, *Canada* **71 C7** 50 39N 109 54W
Burton, *Ohio, U.S.A.* **84 E3** 41 28N 81 8W
Burton, *S.C., U.S.A.* **83 J5** 32 25N 80 45W
Burton, L., *Canada* **72 B4** 54 45N 78 20W
Burton upon Trent, *U.K.* **12 E6** 52 48N 1 38W
Buru, *Indonesia* **37 E7** 3 30S 126 30 E
Burûn, Râs, *Egypt* **46 D2** 31 14N 33 7 E
Burundi ■, *Africa* **54 C3** 3 15S 30 0 E
Bururi, *Burundi* **54 C2** 3 57S 29 37 E
Burutu, *Nigeria* **50 G7** 5 20N 5 29 E
Burwell, *U.S.A.* **80 E5** 41 47N 99 8W
Burwick, *U.K.* **11 C5** 58 45N 2 58W
Bury, *U.K.* **12 D5** 53 35N 2 17W
Bury St. Edmunds, *U.K.* **13 E8** 52 15N 0 43 E
Buryatia □, *Russia* **29 D11** 53 0N 110 0 E
Busan = Pusan, *S. Korea* **35 G15** 35 5N 129 0 E
Busango Swamp, *Zambia* **55 E2** 14 15S 25 45 E
Buşayrah, *Syria* **44 C4** 35 9N 40 26 E
Būshehr, *Iran* **45 D6** 28 55N 50 55 E
Būshehr □, *Iran* **45 D6** 28 20N 51 45 E
Bushell, *Canada* **71 B7** 59 31N 108 45W
Bushenyi, *Uganda* **54 C3** 0 35S 30 10 E
Bushire = Būshehr, *Iran* **45 D6** 28 55N 50 55 E
Businga, *Dem. Rep. of the Congo* **52 D4** 3 16N 20 59 E
Buşra ash Shām, *Syria* **46 C5** 32 30N 36 25 E
Busselton, *Australia* **61 F2** 33 42S 115 15 E
Bussum, *Neths.* **15 B5** 52 16N 5 10 E
Busto Arsízio, *Italy* **20 D8** 45 37N 8 51 E
Busu Djanoa, *Dem. Rep. of the Congo* **52 D4** 1 43N 21 23 E
Busuanga I., *Phil.* **37 B5** 12 10N 120 0 E
Busungbiu, *Indonesia* **37 J17** 8 16S 114 58 E
Buta, *Dem. Rep. of the Congo* **54 B1** 2 50N 24 53 E
Butare, *Rwanda* **54 C2** 2 31S 29 52 E
Butaritari, *Kiribati* **64 G9** 3 30N 174 0 E
Bute, *U.K.* **11 F3** 55 48N 5 2W
Bute Inlet, *Canada* **70 C4** 50 40N 124 53W
Butemba, *Uganda* **54 B3** 1 9N 31 37 E
Butembo, *Dem. Rep. of the Congo* **54 B2** 0 9N 29 18 E
Butha Qi, *China* **33 B7** 48 0N 122 32 E
Butiaba, *Uganda* **54 B3** 1 50N 31 20 E
Butler, *Mo., U.S.A.* **80 F7** 38 16N 94 20W
Butler, *Pa., U.S.A.* **84 F5** 40 52N 79 54W
Buton, *Indonesia* **37 E6** 5 0S 122 45 E
Butte, *Mont., U.S.A.* **76 C7** 46 0N 112 32W
Butte, *Nebr., U.S.A.* **80 D5** 42 58N 98 51W
Butte Creek →, *U.S.A.* **78 F5** 39 12N 121 56W
Butterworth = Gcuwa, *S. Africa* **57 E4** 32 20S 28 11 E
Butterworth, *Malaysia* **39 c** 5 24N 100 23 E
Buttevant, *Ireland* **10 D3** 52 14N 8 40W
Buttfield, Mt., *Australia* **61 D4** 24 45S 128 9 E
Button B., *Canada* **71 B10** 58 45N 94 23W
Buttonwillow, *U.S.A.* **79 K7** 35 24N 119 28W
Butty Hd., *Australia* **61 F3** 33 54S 121 39 E
Butuan, *Phil.* **37 C7** 8 57N 125 33 E
Butung = Buton, *Indonesia* **37 E6** 5 0S 122 45 E
Buturlinovka, *Russia* **19 D7** 50 50N 40 35 E
Buur Hakaba = Bur Acaba, *Somali Rep.* **47 G3** 3 12N 44 20 E
Buxa Duar, *India* **43 F13** 27 45N 89 35 E
Buxar, *India* **43 G10** 25 34N 83 58 E
Buxtehude, *Germany* **16 B5** 53 28N 9 39 E
Buxton, *U.K.* **12 D6** 53 16N 1 54W
Buy, *Russia* **18 C7** 58 28N 41 28 E

Büyük Menderes →, Turkey ... 23 F12 37 28N 27 11 E
Büyükçekmece, Turkey ... 23 D13 41 2N 28 35 E
Buzău, Romania ... 17 F14 45 10N 26 50 E
Buzău →, Romania ... 17 F14 45 26N 27 44 E
Buzen, Japan ... 31 H5 33 35N 131 5 E
Buzi →, Mozam. ... 55 F3 19 50S 34 43 E
Buzuluk, Russia ... 18 D9 52 48N 52 12 E
Buzzards B., U.S.A. ... 85 E14 41 45N 70 37W
Buzzards Bay, U.S.A. ... 85 E14 41 44N 70 37W
Bwana Mkubwe, Dem. Rep. of the Congo ... 55 E2 13 8S 28 38 E
Bwindi △, Uganda ... 54 C2 1 2S 29 42 E
Byarezina →, Belarus ... 17 B16 52 33N 30 14 E
Bydgoszcz, Poland ... 17 B9 53 10N 18 0 E
Byelarus = Belarus ■, Europe ... 17 B14 53 30N 27 0 E
Byelorussia = Belarus ■, Europe ... 17 B14 53 30N 27 0 E
Byers, U.S.A. ... 80 F2 39 43N 104 14W
Byesville, U.S.A. ... 84 G3 39 58N 81 32W
Byfield △, Australia ... 62 C5 22 52S 150 45 E
Byford, Australia ... 61 F2 32 15S 116 0 E
Bykhaw, Belarus ... 17 B16 53 31N 30 14 E
Bykhov = Bykhaw, Belarus ... 17 B16 53 31N 30 14 E
Bylas, U.S.A. ... 77 K8 33 8N 110 7W
Bylot, Canada ... 71 B10 58 25N 94 8W
Bylot I., Canada ... 69 A12 73 13N 78 34W
Byrd, C., Antarctica ... 5 C17 69 38S 76 7W
Byrock, Australia ... 63 E4 30 40S 146 27 E
Byron, C., Australia ... 63 D5 28 43S 153 38 E
Byron Bay, Australia ... 63 D5 28 43S 153 37 E
Byrranga, Gory, Russia ... 29 B11 75 0N 100 0 E
Byrranga Mts. = Byrranga, Gory, Russia ... 29 B11 75 0N 100 0 E
Byske, Sweden ... 8 D19 64 57N 21 11 E
Byske älv →, Sweden ... 8 D19 64 57N 21 13 E
Bytom, Poland ... 17 C10 50 25N 18 54 E
Bytów, Poland ... 17 A9 54 10N 17 30 E
Byumba, Rwanda ... 54 C3 1 35S 30 4 E

C

Ca →, Vietnam ... 38 C5 18 45N 105 45 E
Ca Mau, Vietnam ... 39 H5 9 7N 105 8 E
Ca Mau, Mui, Vietnam ... 39 H5 8 38N 104 44 E
Ca Na, Vietnam ... 39 G7 11 20N 108 54 E
Caacupé, Paraguay ... 94 B4 25 23S 57 5W
Caaguazú □, Paraguay ... 95 B4 26 5S 55 31W
Caála, Angola ... 53 G3 12 46S 15 30 E
Caamaño Sd., Canada ... 70 C3 52 55N 129 25W
Caazapá, Paraguay ... 94 B4 26 8S 56 19W
Caazapá □, Paraguay ... 95 B4 26 10S 56 0W
Caballeria, C. de, Spain ... 24 A11 40 5N 4 5 E
Cabanatuan, Phil. ... 37 A6 15 30N 120 58 E
Cabano, Canada ... 73 C6 47 40N 68 56W
Cabazon, U.S.A. ... 79 M10 33 55N 116 47W
Cabedelo, Brazil ... 93 E12 7 0S 34 50W
Cabildo, Chile ... 94 C1 32 30S 71 5W
Cabimas, Venezuela ... 92 A4 10 23N 71 25W
Cabinda, Angola ... 52 F2 5 33S 12 11 E
Cabinda □, Angola ... 52 F2 5 0S 12 30 E
Cabinet Mts., U.S.A. ... 76 C6 48 0N 115 30W
Cabo Blanco, Argentina ... 96 F3 47 15S 65 47W
Cabo Frio, Brazil ... 95 A7 22 51S 42 3W
Cabo Pantoja, Peru ... 92 D3 1 0S 75 10W
Cabonga, Réservoir, Canada ... 72 C4 47 20N 76 40W
Cabool, U.S.A. ... 81 G8 37 7N 92 6W
Caboolture, Australia ... 63 D5 27 5S 152 58 E
Cabora Bassa Dam = Cahora Bassa, Reprêsa de, Mozam. ... 55 F3 15 20S 32 50 E
Caborca, Mexico ... 86 A2 30 40N 112 10W
Cabot, Mt., U.S.A. ... 85 B13 44 30N 71 25W
Cabot Hd., Canada ... 84 A3 45 14N 81 17W
Cabot Str., Canada ... 73 C8 47 15N 59 40W
Cabra, Spain ... 21 D3 37 30N 4 28W
Cabrera, Spain ... 24 B9 39 8N 2 57 E
Cabri, Canada ... 71 C7 50 35N 108 25W
Cabriel →, Spain ... 21 C5 39 14N 1 3W
Caçador, Brazil ... 95 B5 26 47S 51 0W
Čačak, Serbia & M. ... 23 C9 43 54N 20 20 E
Caçapava do Sul, Brazil ... 95 C5 30 30S 53 30W
Cáceres, Brazil ... 92 G7 16 5S 57 40W
Cáceres, Spain ... 21 C2 39 26N 6 23W
Cache Bay, Canada ... 72 C4 46 22N 80 0W
Cache Cr. →, U.S.A. ... 78 G5 38 42N 121 42W
Cache Creek, Canada ... 70 C4 50 48N 121 19W
Cachi, Argentina ... 94 B2 25 5S 66 10W
Cachimbo, Serra do, Brazil ... 93 E7 9 30S 55 30W
Cachinal de la Sierra, Chile ... 94 A2 24 58S 69 32W
Cachoeira, Brazil ... 93 F11 12 30S 39 0W
Cachoeira do Sul, Brazil ... 95 C5 30 3S 52 53W
Cachoeiro de Itapemirim, Brazil ... 95 A7 20 51S 41 7W
Cacoal, Brazil ... 92 F6 11 32S 61 18W
Cacólo, Angola ... 52 G3 10 9S 19 21 E
Caconda, Angola ... 53 G3 13 48S 15 8 E
Caddo, U.S.A. ... 81 H6 34 7N 96 16W
Cader Idris, U.K. ... 13 E4 52 42N 3 53W
Cadereyta, Mexico ... 86 B5 25 36N 100 0W
Cadibarrawirracanna, L., Australia ... 63 D2 28 52S 135 27 E
Cadillac, U.S.A. ... 82 C3 44 15N 85 24W
Cadiz, Phil. ... 37 B6 10 57N 123 15 E
Cádiz, Spain ... 21 D2 36 30N 6 20W
Cadiz, Calif., U.S.A. ... 79 L11 34 30N 115 28W
Cadiz, Ohio, U.S.A. ... 84 F4 40 22N 81 0W
Cádiz, G. de, Spain ... 21 D2 36 40N 7 0W
Cadiz L., U.S.A. ... 77 J6 34 18N 115 24W
Cadney Park, Australia ... 63 D1 27 55S 134 3 E
Cadomin, Canada ... 70 C5 53 2N 117 20W
Cadotte Lake, Canada ... 70 B5 56 26N 116 23W
Cadoux, Australia ... 61 F2 30 46S 117 7 E
Caen, France ... 20 B3 49 10N 0 22W
Caernarfon, U.K. ... 12 D3 53 8N 4 16W
Caernarfon B., U.K. ... 12 D3 53 4N 4 40W
Caernarvon = Caernarfon, U.K. ... 12 D3 53 8N 4 16W
Caerphilly, U.K. ... 13 F4 51 35N 3 13W
Caerphilly □, U.K. ... 13 F4 51 37N 3 12W
Caesarea, Israel ... 46 C3 32 30N 34 53 E
Caetité, Brazil ... 93 F10 13 50S 42 32W
Cafayate, Argentina ... 94 B2 26 2S 66 0W
Cafu, Angola ... 56 B2 16 30S 15 8 E
Cagayan de Oro, Phil. ... 37 C6 8 30N 124 40 E
Cagayan Is., Phil. ... 37 C5 9 40N 121 16 E
Cágliari, Italy ... 22 E3 39 13N 9 7 E
Cágliari, G. di, Italy ... 22 E3 39 8N 9 11 E
Caguán →, Colombia ... 92 D4 0 8S 74 18W
Caguas, Puerto Rico ... 89 d 18 14N 66 2W

Caha Mts., Ireland ... 10 E2 51 45N 9 40W
Cahama, Angola ... 56 B1 16 17S 14 19 E
Caher, Ireland ... 10 D4 52 22N 7 56W
Caherciveen, Ireland ... 10 E1 51 56N 10 14W
Cahora Bassa, L. de, Mozam. ... 55 F3 15 35S 32 0 E
Cahora Bassa, Reprêsa de, Mozam. ... 55 F3 15 20S 32 50 E
Cahore Pt., Ireland ... 10 D5 52 33N 6 12W
Cahors, France ... 20 D4 44 27N 1 27 E
Cahul, Moldova ... 17 F15 45 50N 28 15 E
Cai Bau, Dao, Vietnam ... 38 B6 21 10N 107 27 E
Cai Nuoc, Vietnam ... 39 H5 8 56N 105 1 E
Caia, Mozam. ... 55 F4 17 51S 35 24 E
Caianda, Angola ... 55 E1 11 2S 23 31 E
Caibarién, Cuba ... 88 B4 22 30N 79 30W
Caicara, Venezuela ... 92 B5 7 38N 66 10W
Caicó, Brazil ... 93 E11 6 20S 37 0W
Caicos Is., Turks & Caicos ... 89 B5 21 40N 71 40W
Caicos Passage, W. Indies ... 89 B5 22 45N 72 45W
Caird Coast, Antarctica ... 5 D1 75 0S 25 0W
Cairn Gorm, U.K. ... 11 D5 57 7N 3 39W
Cairngorm Mts., U.K. ... 11 D5 57 6N 3 42W
Cairngorms △, U.K. ... 11 D5 57 10N 3 50W
Cairnryan, U.K. ... 11 G3 54 59N 5 1W
Cairns, Australia ... 62 B4 16 57S 145 45 E
Cairns L., Canada ... 71 C10 51 42N 94 30W
Cairo = El Qâhira, Egypt ... 51 B12 30 1N 31 14 E
Cairo, Ga., U.S.A. ... 83 K3 30 52N 84 13W
Cairo, Ill., U.S.A. ... 81 G10 37 0N 89 11W
Cairo, N.Y., U.S.A. ... 85 D11 42 18N 74 0W
Caithness, U.K. ... 11 C5 58 25N 3 35W
Caithness, Ord of, U.K. ... 11 C5 58 8N 3 36W
Caja de Muertos, I., Puerto Rico ... 89 d 17 54N 66 32W
Cajamarca, Peru ... 92 E3 7 5S 78 28W
Cajàzeiras, Brazil ... 93 E11 6 52S 38 30W
Cala d'Or, Spain ... 24 B10 39 23N 3 14 E
Cala en Porter, Spain ... 24 B11 39 52N 4 8 E
Cala Figuera, C. de, Spain ... 24 B9 39 27N 2 31 E
Cala Forcat, Spain ... 24 B10 40 0N 3 47 E
Cala Major, Spain ... 24 B9 39 33N 2 37 E
Cala Mezquida = Sa Mesquida, Spain ... 24 B11 39 55N 4 16 E
Cala Millor, Spain ... 24 B10 39 35N 3 22 E
Cala Ratjada, Spain ... 24 B10 39 43N 3 27 E
Cala Santa Galdana, Spain ... 24 B10 39 56N 3 58 E
Calabar, Nigeria ... 50 H7 4 57N 8 20 E
Calabogie, Canada ... 85 A8 45 18N 76 43W
Calabozo, Venezuela ... 92 B5 9 0N 67 28W
Calàbria □, Italy ... 22 E7 39 0N 16 30 E
Calafate, Argentina ... 96 G2 50 19S 72 15W
Calahorra, Spain ... 21 A5 42 18N 1 59W
Calais, France ... 20 A4 50 57N 1 56 E
Calais, U.S.A. ... 83 C12 45 11N 67 17W
Calakmul △, Mexico ... 87 D7 18 14N 89 48W
Calalaste, Cord. de, Argentina ... 94 B2 25 0S 67 0W
Calama, Brazil ... 92 E6 8 0S 62 50W
Calama, Chile ... 94 A2 22 30S 68 55W
Calamar, Colombia ... 92 A4 10 15N 74 55W
Calamian Group, Phil. ... 37 B5 11 50N 119 55 E
Calamocha, Spain ... 21 B5 40 50N 1 17W
Calang, Indonesia ... 36 D1 4 37N 95 37 E
Calapan, Phil. ... 37 B6 13 25N 121 7 E
Calàrasi, Romania ... 17 F14 44 12N 27 20 E
Calatayud, Spain ... 21 B5 41 20N 1 40W
Calauag, Phil. ... 37 B6 13 55N 122 15 E
Calavite, C., Phil. ... 37 B6 13 26N 120 20 E
Calbayog, Phil. ... 37 B6 12 4N 124 38 E
Calca, Peru ... 92 F4 13 22S 72 0W
Calcasieu L., U.S.A. ... 81 L8 29 55N 93 18W
Calcutta = Kolkata, India ... 43 H13 22 36N 88 24 E
Calcutta, U.S.A. ... 84 F4 40 40N 80 34W
Caldas da Rainha, Portugal ... 21 C1 39 24N 9 8W
Calder →, U.K. ... 12 D6 53 44N 1 22W
Caldera, Chile ... 94 B1 27 5S 70 55W
Caldera de Taburiente △, Canary Is. ... 24 F2 28 43N 17 52W
Caldwell, Idaho, U.S.A. ... 76 E5 43 40N 116 41W
Caldwell, Kans., U.S.A. ... 81 G6 37 2N 97 37W
Caldwell, Tex., U.S.A. ... 81 K6 30 32N 96 42W
Caledon, S. Africa ... 56 E2 34 14S 19 26 E
Caledon →, S. Africa ... 56 E4 30 31S 26 5 E
Caledon B., Australia ... 62 A2 12 45S 137 0 E
Caledonia, Canada ... 84 C5 43 7N 79 58W
Caledonia, U.S.A. ... 84 D7 42 58N 77 51W
Calemba, Angola ... 56 B2 16 0S 15 44 E
Calen, Australia ... 62 J6 20 56S 148 48 E
Caletones, Chile ... 94 C1 34 6S 70 27W
Calexico, U.S.A. ... 79 N11 32 40N 115 30W
Calf of Man, U.K. ... 12 C3 54 3N 4 48W
Calgary, Canada ... 70 C6 51 0N 114 10W
Calheta, Madeira ... 24 D2 32 44N 17 11W
Calhoun, U.S.A. ... 83 H3 34 30N 84 57W
Cali, Colombia ... 92 C3 3 25N 76 35W
Calicut, India ... 40 P9 11 15N 75 43 E
Caliente, U.S.A. ... 77 H6 37 37N 114 31W
California, Mo., U.S.A. ... 80 F8 38 38N 92 34W
California, Pa., U.S.A. ... 84 F5 40 4N 79 54W
California □, U.S.A. ... 78 H7 37 30N 119 30W
California, Baja, Mexico ... 86 A1 32 10N 115 12W
California, Baja, T.N. = Baja California □, Mexico ... 86 B2 30 0N 115 0W
California, Baja, T.S. = Baja California Sur □, Mexico ... 86 B2 25 50N 111 50W
California, G. de, Mexico ... 86 B2 27 0N 111 0W
California City, U.S.A. ... 79 K9 35 10N 117 55W
California Hot Springs, U.S.A. ... 79 K8 35 51N 118 41W
Calilegua △, Argentina ... 94 B3 23 36S 64 50W
Calingasta, Argentina ... 94 C2 31 15S 69 30W
Calipatria, U.S.A. ... 79 M11 33 8N 115 31W
Calistoga, U.S.A. ... 78 G4 38 35N 122 35W
Calitzdorp, S. Africa ... 56 E3 33 33S 21 42 E
Callabonna, L., Australia ... 63 D3 29 40S 140 5 E
Callan, Ireland ... 10 D4 52 32N 7 24W
Callander, U.K. ... 11 E4 56 15N 4 13W
Callao, Peru ... 92 F3 12 0S 77 0W
Calles, Mexico ... 87 C5 23 2N 98 42W
Callicoon, U.S.A. ... 85 E9 41 46N 75 3W
Calling Lake, Canada ... 70 B6 55 15N 113 12W
Calliope, Australia ... 62 C5 24 0S 151 16 E
Calne, U.K. ... 13 F6 51 26N 2 0W
Calola, Angola ... 56 B2 16 25S 17 48 E
Caloundra, Australia ... 63 D5 26 45S 153 10 E
Calpella, U.S.A. ... 78 F3 39 14N 123 12W
Calpine, U.S.A. ... 78 F6 39 40N 120 27W
Calstock, Canada ... 72 C3 49 47N 84 9W
Caltagirone, Italy ... 22 F6 37 14N 14 31 E
Caltanissetta, Italy ... 22 F6 37 29N 14 4 E
Calulo, Angola ... 52 G2 10 1S 14 56 E

Calvert →, Australia ... 62 B2 16 17S 137 44 E
Calvert I., Canada ... 70 C3 51 30N 128 0W
Calvert Ra., Australia ... 60 D3 24 0S 122 30 E
Calvi, France ... 20 E8 42 34N 8 45 E
Calviá, Spain ... 21 C7 39 34N 2 31 E
Calvillo, Mexico ... 86 C4 21 51N 102 43W
Calvinia, S. Africa ... 56 E2 31 28S 19 45 E
Calwa, U.S.A. ... 78 J7 36 42N 119 46W
Cam →, U.K. ... 13 E8 52 21N 0 16 E
Cam Lam, Vietnam ... 39 G7 11 54N 109 10 E
Cam Pha, Vietnam ... 38 B6 21 7N 107 18 E
Cam Ranh, Vietnam ... 39 G7 11 54N 109 12 E
Cam Xuyen, Vietnam ... 38 C6 18 15N 106 0 E
Camabatela, Angola ... 52 F3 8 20S 15 26 E
Camacha, Madeira ... 24 D3 32 41N 16 49W
Camacho, Mexico ... 86 C4 24 25N 102 18W
Camacupa, Angola ... 53 G3 11 58S 17 22 E
Camagüey, Cuba ... 88 B4 21 20N 78 0W
Camaná, Peru ... 92 G4 16 30S 72 50W
Camanche Reservoir, U.S.A. ... 78 G6 38 14N 121 1W
Camaquã, Brazil ... 95 C5 30 51S 51 49W
Camaquã →, Brazil ... 95 C5 31 17S 51 47W
Câmara de Lobos, Madeira ... 24 D3 32 39N 16 59W
Camargo, Mexico ... 87 B5 26 19N 98 50W
Camarillo, U.S.A. ... 79 L7 34 13N 119 2W
Camarón, C., Honduras ... 88 C2 16 0N 85 5W
Camarones, Argentina ... 96 E3 44 50S 65 40W
Camas, U.S.A. ... 78 E4 45 35N 122 24W
Camas Valley, U.S.A. ... 76 E2 43 2N 123 40W
Camballin, Australia ... 60 C3 17 59S 124 12 E
Cambará, Brazil ... 95 A5 23 2S 50 5W
Cambay = Khambhat, India ... 42 H5 22 23N 72 33 E
Cambay, G. of = Khambhat, G. of, India ... 40 J8 20 45N 72 30 E
Cambodia ■, Asia ... 38 F5 12 15N 105 0 E
Camborne, U.K. ... 13 G2 50 12N 5 19W
Cambrai, France ... 20 A5 50 11N 3 14 E
Cambria, U.S.A. ... 78 K5 35 34N 121 5W
Cambrian Mts., U.K. ... 13 E4 52 3N 3 57W
Cambridge, Canada ... 84 C4 43 23N 80 15W
Cambridge, Jamaica ... 88 a 18 18N 77 54W
Cambridge, N.Z. ... 59 G5 37 54S 175 29 E
Cambridge, U.K. ... 13 E8 52 12N 0 8 E
Cambridge, Mass., U.S.A. ... 85 D13 42 22N 71 6W
Cambridge, Minn., U.S.A. ... 80 C8 45 34N 93 13W
Cambridge, N.Y., U.S.A. ... 85 C11 43 2N 73 22W
Cambridge, Nebr., U.S.A. ... 80 E4 40 17N 100 10W
Cambridge, Ohio, U.S.A. ... 84 F3 40 2N 81 35W
Cambridge Bay = Ikaluktutiak, Canada ... 68 B9 69 10N 105 0W
Cambridge G., Australia ... 60 B4 14 55S 128 15 E
Cambridge Springs, U.S.A. ... 84 E4 41 48N 80 4W
Cambridgeshire □, U.K. ... 13 E7 52 25N 0 7W
Cambuci, Brazil ... 95 A7 21 35S 41 55W
Cambundi-Catembo, Angola ... 52 G3 10 10S 17 35 E
Camden, Ala., U.S.A. ... 83 K2 31 59N 87 17W
Camden, Ark., U.S.A. ... 81 J8 33 35N 92 50W
Camden, Maine, U.S.A. ... 83 C11 44 13N 69 4W
Camden, N.J., U.S.A. ... 85 G9 39 56N 75 7W
Camden, N.Y., U.S.A. ... 85 C9 43 20N 75 45W
Camden, S.C., U.S.A. ... 83 H5 34 16N 80 36W
Camden Sd., Australia ... 60 C3 15 27S 124 25 E
Camdenton, U.S.A. ... 81 F8 38 1N 92 45W
Camelford, U.K. ... 13 G3 50 37N 4 42W
Cameron, Ariz., U.S.A. ... 77 J8 35 53N 111 25W
Cameron, La., U.S.A. ... 81 L8 29 48N 93 20W
Cameron, Mo., U.S.A. ... 80 F7 39 44N 94 14W
Cameron, Tex., U.S.A. ... 81 K6 30 51N 96 59W
Cameron Highlands, Malaysia ... 39 K3 4 27N 101 22 E
Cameron Hills, Canada ... 70 B5 59 48N 118 0W
Cameroun, Mt., Cameroon ... 52 D1 4 13N 9 10 E
Cameroon ■, Africa ... 51 G7 6 0N 12 30 E
Cameroun, Mt., Cameroon ... 52 D1 4 13N 9 10 E
Cametá, Brazil ... 93 D9 2 12S 49 30W
Camiguin I., Phil. ... 37 C6 18 56N 121 55 E
Camilla, U.S.A. ... 83 K3 31 14N 84 12W
Caminha, Portugal ... 21 B1 41 50N 8 50W
Camino, U.S.A. ... 78 G6 38 44N 120 41W
Camira Creek, Australia ... 63 D5 29 15S 152 58 E
Cammal, U.S.A. ... 84 E7 41 24N 77 28W
Camocim, Brazil ... 93 D10 2 55S 40 50W
Camooweal, Australia ... 62 B2 19 56S 138 7 E
Camooweal Caves △, Australia ... 62 C2 20 1S 138 11 E
Camopi, Fr. Guiana ... 93 C8 3 12N 52 17W
Camp Borden, Canada ... 84 B5 44 18N 79 56W
Camp Hill, U.S.A. ... 84 F8 40 14N 76 55W
Camp Nelson, U.S.A. ... 79 J8 36 8N 118 39W
Camp Pendleton, U.S.A. ... 79 M9 33 16N 117 23W
Camp Verde, U.S.A. ... 77 J8 34 34N 111 51W
Camp Wood, U.S.A. ... 81 L5 29 40N 100 1W
Campana, Argentina ... 94 C4 34 10S 58 55W
Campana, I., Chile ... 96 F1 48 20S 75 20W
Campanário, Madeira ... 24 D2 32 39N 17 2W
Campánia □, Italy ... 22 D6 41 0N 14 30 E
Campbell, S. Africa ... 56 D3 28 48S 23 44 E
Campbell, Calif., U.S.A. ... 78 H5 37 17N 121 57W
Campbell, Ohio, U.S.A. ... 84 E4 41 5N 80 37W
Campbell I., Pac. Oc. ... 64 N8 52 30S 169 0 E
Campbell L., Canada ... 71 A7 63 14N 106 55W
Campbell River, Canada ... 70 C3 50 5N 125 20W
Campbell Town, Australia ... 63 G4 41 52S 147 30 E
Campbellford, Canada ... 84 B7 44 18N 77 48W
Campbellpur, Pakistan ... 42 C5 33 46N 72 26 E
Campbellsville, U.S.A. ... 82 G3 37 21N 85 20W
Campbellton, Canada ... 73 C6 47 57N 66 43W
Campbelltown, Australia ... 63 E5 34 4S 150 49 E
Campbeltown, U.K. ... 11 F3 55 26N 5 36W
Campeche, Mexico ... 87 D6 19 50N 90 32W
Campeche □, Mexico ... 87 D6 19 50N 90 32W
Campeche, Golfo de, Mexico ... 87 D6 19 30N 93 0W
Camperdown, Australia ... 63 F3 38 14S 143 9 E
Camperville, Canada ... 71 C8 51 59N 100 9W
Câmpina, Romania ... 17 F13 45 10N 25 45 E
Campina Grande, Brazil ... 93 E11 7 20S 35 47W
Campinas, Brazil ... 95 A6 22 50S 47 0W
Campo Grande, Brazil ... 93 H8 20 25S 54 40W
Campo Maior, Brazil ... 93 D10 4 50S 42 12W
Campo Mourão, Brazil ... 95 A5 24 3S 52 22W
Campobasso, Italy ... 22 D6 41 34N 14 39 E
Campos, Brazil ... 95 A7 21 50S 41 20W
Campos Belos, Brazil ... 93 F9 13 10S 47 3W
Campos del Port, Spain ... 24 B10 39 26N 3 1 E
Campos Novos, Brazil ... 95 B5 27 21S 51 50W
Camptonville, U.S.A. ... 78 F5 39 27N 121 3W
Camptown, U.S.A. ... 85 E8 41 44N 76 14W
Câmpulung, Romania ... 17 F13 45 17N 25 3 E
Camrose, Canada ... 70 C6 53 0N 112 50W
Camsell Portage, Canada ... 71 B7 59 37N 109 15W
Çan, Turkey ... 23 D12 40 2N 27 3 E

Can Clavo, Spain ... 24 C7 38 57N 1 27 E
Can Creu, Spain ... 24 C7 38 58N 1 28 E
Can Gio, Vietnam ... 39 G6 10 25N 106 58 E
Can Tho, Vietnam ... 39 G5 10 2N 105 46 E
Canaan, U.S.A. ... 85 D11 42 2N 73 20W
Canada ■, N. Amer. ... 68 C10 60 0N 100 0W
Canada Basin, Arctic ... 4 B18 80 0N 145 0W
Cañada de Gómez, Argentina ... 94 C3 32 40S 61 30W
Canadian, U.S.A. ... 81 H4 35 55N 100 23W
Canadian →, U.S.A. ... 81 H7 35 28N 95 3W
Canajoharie, U.S.A. ... 85 D10 42 54N 74 35W
Çanakkale, Turkey ... 23 D12 40 8N 26 24 E
Çanakkale Boğazı, Turkey ... 23 D12 40 17N 26 32 E
Canal Flats, Canada ... 70 C5 50 10N 115 48W
Canalejas, Argentina ... 94 D2 35 15S 66 34W
Canals, Argentina ... 94 C3 33 35S 62 53W
Canandaigua, U.S.A. ... 84 D7 42 54N 77 17W
Canandaigua L., U.S.A. ... 84 D7 42 47N 77 19W
Cananea, Mexico ... 86 A2 31 0N 110 20W
Canarias, Is., Atl. Oc. ... 24 F4 28 30N 16 0W
Canaries, St. Lucia ... 89 f 13 55N 61 4W
Canarreos, Arch. de los, Cuba ... 88 B3 21 35N 81 40W
Canary Is. = Canarias, Is., Atl. Oc. ... 24 F4 28 30N 16 0W
Canaseraga, U.S.A. ... 84 D7 42 27N 77 45W
Canatlán, Mexico ... 86 C4 24 31N 104 47W
Canaveral, △, U.S.A. ... 83 L5 28 28N 80 34W
Canaveral, C., U.S.A. ... 83 L5 28 27N 80 32W
Canavieiras, Brazil ... 93 G11 15 39S 39 0W
Canberra, Australia ... 63 F4 35 15S 149 8 E
Canby, Calif., U.S.A. ... 76 F3 41 27N 120 52W
Canby, Minn., U.S.A. ... 80 C6 44 43N 96 16W
Canby, Oreg., U.S.A. ... 78 E4 45 16N 122 42W
Cancún, Mexico ... 87 C7 21 8N 86 44W
Candelaria, Argentina ... 95 B4 27 29S 55 44W
Candelaria, Canary Is. ... 24 F3 28 22N 16 22W
Candelo, Australia ... 63 F4 36 47S 149 43 E
Candi Dasa, Indonesia ... 37 J18 8 30S 115 34 E
Candia = Iráklion, Greece ... 25 D7 35 20N 25 12 E
Candle L., Canada ... 71 C7 53 50N 105 18W
Candlemas I., Antarctica ... 5 B1 57 3S 26 40W
Cando, U.S.A. ... 80 A5 48 32N 99 12W
Canea = Khaniá, Greece ... 25 D6 35 30N 24 4 E
Canelones, Uruguay ... 95 C4 34 32S 56 17W
Cañete, Chile ... 94 D1 37 50S 73 30W
Cañete, Peru ... 92 F3 13 8S 76 30W
Cangas de Narcea, Spain ... 21 A2 43 10N 6 32W
Canguaretama, Brazil ... 93 E11 6 20S 35 5W
Canguçu, Brazil ... 95 C5 31 22S 52 43W
Canguçu, Serra do, Brazil ... 95 C5 31 20S 51 53W
Cangzhou, China ... 34 E9 38 19N 116 52 E
Caniapiscau →, Canada ... 73 A6 56 40N 69 30W
Caniapiscau, L. de, Canada ... 73 B6 54 10N 69 55W
Canicattì, Italy ... 22 F5 37 21N 13 51 E
Canim Lake, Canada ... 70 C4 51 47N 120 54W
Canindeyu □, Paraguay ... 95 A5 24 10S 55 0W
Canisteo, U.S.A. ... 84 D7 42 16N 77 36W
Canisteo →, U.S.A. ... 84 D7 42 7N 77 8W
Cañitas, Mexico ... 86 C4 23 36N 102 43W
Çankırı, Turkey ... 19 F5 40 40N 33 37 E
Cankuzo, Burundi ... 54 C3 3 10S 30 31 E
Canmore, Canada ... 70 C5 51 7N 115 18W
Cann River, Australia ... 63 F4 37 35S 149 7 E
Canna, U.K. ... 11 D2 57 3N 6 33W
Cannanore, India ... 40 P9 11 53N 75 27 E
Cannes, France ... 20 E7 43 32N 7 1 E
Canning Town = Port Canning, India ... 43 H13 22 23N 88 40 E
Cannington, Canada ... 84 B5 44 20N 79 2W
Cannock, U.K. ... 13 E5 52 41N 2 1W
Cannon Ball →, U.S.A. ... 80 B4 46 20N 100 38W
Cannonsville Reservoir, U.S.A. ... 85 D9 42 4N 75 22W
Cannonvale, Australia ... 62 J6 20 17S 148 43 E
Canoas, Brazil ... 95 B5 29 56S 51 11W
Canoe L., Canada ... 71 B7 55 10N 108 15W
Canon City, U.S.A. ... 80 F2 38 27N 105 14W
Cañon de Rio Blanco △, Mexico ... 87 D5 18 43N 97 15W
Cañón del Sumidero △, Mexico ... 87 D5 19 22N 96 24W
Canora, Canada ... 71 C8 51 40N 102 30W
Canowindra, Australia ... 63 E4 33 35S 148 38 E
Canso, Canada ... 73 C7 45 20N 61 0W
Cantabria □, Spain ... 21 A4 43 10N 4 0W
Cantabrian Mts. = Cantábrica, Cordillera, Spain ... 21 A3 43 0N 5 10W
Cantábrica, Cordillera, Spain ... 21 A3 43 0N 5 10W
Cantal, Plomb du, France ... 20 D5 45 3N 2 45 E
Canterbury, Australia ... 62 D3 25 23S 141 53 E
Canterbury, U.K. ... 13 F9 51 16N 1 6 E
Canterbury Bight, N.Z. ... 59 L3 44 16S 171 55 E
Canterbury Plains, N.Z. ... 59 K3 43 55S 171 22 E
Cantil, U.S.A. ... 79 K9 35 18N 117 58W
Canton = Guangzhou, China ... 33 D6 23 5N 113 10 E
Canton, Ga., U.S.A. ... 83 H3 34 14N 84 29W
Canton, Ill., U.S.A. ... 80 E9 40 33N 90 2W
Canton, Miss., U.S.A. ... 81 J9 32 37N 90 2W
Canton, Mo., U.S.A. ... 80 E9 40 8N 91 32W
Canton, N.Y., U.S.A. ... 85 B9 44 36N 75 10W
Canton, Ohio, U.S.A. ... 84 F3 40 48N 81 23W
Canton, Pa., U.S.A. ... 84 E8 41 39N 76 51W
Canton, S. Dak., U.S.A. ... 80 D6 43 18N 96 35W
Canton L., U.S.A. ... 81 G5 36 6N 98 35W
Canudos, Brazil ... 92 E7 7 13S 58 5W
Canumã →, Brazil ... 92 D7 3 55S 59 10W
Canutama, Brazil ... 92 E6 6 30S 64 20W
Canutillo, U.S.A. ... 77 L10 31 55N 106 36W
Canvey, U.K. ... 13 F8 51 31N 0 37 E
Canyon, U.S.A. ... 81 H4 34 59N 101 55W
Canyon De Chelly △, U.S.A. ... 77 H9 36 10N 109 20W
Canyon of the Ancients △, U.S.A. ... 77 H9 37 30N 108 50W
Canyonlands △, U.S.A. ... 77 G9 38 15N 110 0W
Canyonville, U.S.A. ... 76 E2 42 56N 123 17W
Cao Bang, Vietnam ... 38 A6 22 40N 106 15 E
Cao He →, China ... 35 D13 40 10N 124 32 E
Cao Lanh, Vietnam ... 39 G5 10 27N 105 38 E
Cao Xian, China ... 34 G8 34 50N 115 35 E
Cap-aux-Meules, Canada ... 73 C7 47 23N 61 52W
Cap-Chat, Canada ... 73 C6 49 6N 66 40W
Cap-de-la-Madeleine, Canada ... 72 C5 46 22N 72 31W
Cap-Haïtien, Haiti ... 89 C5 19 40N 72 20W
Cap Pt., St. Lucia ... 89 f 14 7N 60 57W
Capac, U.S.A. ... 84 D1 43 1N 82 56W
Capanaparo →, Venezuela ... 92 B5 7 1N 67 7W
Cape →, Australia ... 62 C4 20 59S 146 51 E
Cape Arid △, Australia ... 61 F3 33 58S 123 13 E
Cape Barren I., Australia ... 63 G4 40 25S 148 15 E
Cape Breton Highlands △, Canada ... 73 C7 46 50N 60 40W
Cape Breton I., Canada ... 73 C7 46 0N 60 30W

Cape Charles, U.S.A. 82 G8 37 16N 76 1W
Cape Coast, Ghana 50 G5   5 5N   1 15W
Cape Cod ⌂, U.S.A. 82 E10 41 56N 70 6W
Cape Coral, U.S.A. 83 M5 26 33N 81 57W
Cape Dorset, Canada 69 B12 64 14N 76 32W
Cape Fear ➤, U.S.A. 83 H6 33 53N 78 1W
Cape Girardeau, U.S.A. 81 G10 37 19N 89 32W
Cape Hatteras ⌂, U.S.A. 83 H8 35 30N 75 28W
Cape Lee △, Australia .... 61 F3 33 54S 122 26 E
Cape Lookout ⌂, U.S.A. 83 H7 35 45N 76 25W
Cape May, U.S.A. 82 F8 38 56N 74 56W
Cape May Point, U.S.A. 82 F8 38 56N 74 58W
Cape Melville △, Australia .... 62 A3 14 26S 144 28 E
Cape Peninsula △, S. Africa .. 56 E2 34 20S 18 28 E
Cape Range △, Australia ..... 60 D1 22 3S 111 0 E
Cape Tormentine, Canada 73 C7 46 8N 63 47W
Cape Town, S. Africa .... 56 E2 33 55S 18 22 E
Cape Tribulation △, Australia . 62 B4 16 5S 145 25 E
Cape Verde Is. ■, Atl. Oc. 49 E1 16 0N 24 0W
Cape Vincent, U.S.A. 85 B8 44 8N 76 20W
Cape York Peninsula, Australia . 62 A3 12 0S 142 30 E
Capela, Brazil 93 F11 10 30S 37 0W
Capella, Australia .... 62 C4 23 2S 148 1 E
Capesterre, Guadeloupe ..... 88 b   16 4N 61 36W
Capesterre-Belle-Eau,
  Guadeloupe .... 88 b   16 4N 61 36W
Capim ➤, Brazil 93 D9   1 40S 47 47W
Capitan, U.S.A. 77 K11 33 35N 105 35W
Capitán Arturo Prat △, Antarctica . 5 C17 63 0S 61 0W
Capitol Reef △, U.S.A. 77 G8 38 15N 111 10W
Capitola, U.S.A. 78 J5 36 59N 121 57W
Capoche ➤, Mozam. .... 55 F3 15 35S 33 0 E
Capraia, Italy .... 20 E8 43 2N   9 50 E
Capreol, Canada 72 C3 46 43N 80 56W
Capri, Italy .... 22 D6 40 33N 14 14 E
Capricorn Group, Australia ... 62 C5 23 30S 151 55 E
Capricorn Ra., Australia ..... 60 D2 23 20S 116 50 E
Caprivi Game ⌂, Namibia .... 56 B3 17 55S 22 37 E
Caprivi Strip, Namibia .... 56 B3 18 0S 23 0 E
Captain's Flat, Australia ..... 63 F4 35 35S 149 27 E
Capulin Volcano △, U.S.A. ... 81 G3 36 47N 103 58W
Caquetá ➤, Colombia 92 D5   1 15S 69 15W
Caracal, Romania .... 17 F13 44 8N 24 22 E
Caracas, Venezuela 92 A5 10 30N 66 55W
Caracol, Mato Grosso do Sul,
  Brazil 94 A4 22 18S 57 1W
Caracol, Piauí, Brazil 93 E10 9 15S 43 22W
Carajás, Brazil 93 E8   6 5S 50 23W
Carajás, Serra dos, Brazil 93 E8   6 0S 51 30W
Carangola, Brazil 95 A7 20 44S 42 5W
Caransebeş, Romania .... 17 F12 45 28N 22 18 E
Caraquet, Canada 73 C6 47 48N 64 57W
Caras, Peru 92 E3   9 3S 77 47W
Caratasca, L., Honduras 88 C3 15 20N 83 40W
Caratinga, Brazil 93 G10 19 50S 42 10W
Caraúbas, Brazil 93 E11 5 43S 37 33W
Caravaca de la Cruz, Spain .. 21 C5 38 8N   1 52W
Caravelas, Brazil 93 G11 17 45S 39 15W
Caraveli, Peru 92 G4 15 45S 73 25W
Caravelle, Presqu'île de la,
  Martinique .... 88 c   14 46N 60 48W
Caràzinho, Brazil 95 B5 28 16S 52 46W
Carballo, Spain 21 A1 43 13N   8 41W
Carberry, Canada 71 D9 49 50N 99 25W
Carbó, Mexico 86 B2 29 42N 110 58W
Carbonara, C., Italy .... 22 E3 39 6N   9 31 E
Carbondale, Colo., U.S.A. ... 76 G10 39 24N 107 13W
Carbondale, Ill., U.S.A. 81 G10 37 44N 89 13W
Carbondale, Pa., U.S.A. 85 E9 41 35N 75 30W
Carbonear, Canada 73 C9 47 42N 53 13W
Carbónia, Italy .... 22 E3 39 10N   8 30 E
Carcajou, Canada 70 B5 57 47N 117 6W
Carcarana ➤, Argentina 94 C3 32 27S 60 48W
Carcasse, C., Haiti 89 C5 18 30N 74 28W
Carcassonne, France .... 20 E5 43 13N   2 20 E
Carcross, Canada 70 A2 60 13N 134 45W
Cardamon Hills, India .... 40 Q10 9 30N 77 15 E
Cárdenas, Cuba 88 B3 23 0N 81 30W
Cárdenas, San Luis Potosí,
  Mexico 87 C5 22 0N 99 41W
Cárdenas, Tabasco, Mexico .. 87 D6 17 59N 93 21W
Cardiff, U.K. 13 F4 51 29N   3 10W
Cardiff □, U.K. 13 F4 51 31N   3 12W
Cardiff-by-the-Sea, U.S.A. ... 79 M9 33 1N 117 17W
Cardigan, U.K. 13 E3 52 5N   4 40W
Cardigan B., U.K. 13 E3 52 30N   4 30W
Cardinal, Canada 85 B9 44 47N 75 23W
Cardona, Uruguay 94 C4 33 53S 57 18W
Cardoso, Ilha do, Brazil 95 B5 25 8S 47 58W
Cardston, Canada 70 D6 49 15N 113 20W
Cardwell, Australia .... 62 B4 18 14S 146 2 E
Careen L., Canada 71 B7 57 0N 108 11W
Carei, Romania .... 17 E12 47 40N 22 29 E
Careme = Ciremay, Indonesia . 37 G13 6 55S 108 27 E
Carey, U.S.A. 76 E7 43 19N 113 57W
Carey, L., Australia .... 61 E3 29 0S 122 15 E
Carey, L., Canada 71 A8 62 12N 102 55W
Carhué, Argentina 94 D3 37 10S 62 50W
Caria, Turkey .... 23 F13 37 20N 28 0 E
Cariacica, Brazil 93 H10 20 16S 40 25W
Caribbean Sea, W. Indies 89 D5 15 0N 75 0W
Cariboo Mts., Canada 70 C4 53 0N 121 0W
Caribou, U.S.A. 83 B12 46 52N 68 1W
Caribou ➤, Man., Canada ... 71 B10 59 20N 94 44W
Caribou ➤, N.W.T., Canada .. 70 A3 61 27N 125 45W
Caribou I., Canada 72 C2 47 22N 85 49W
Caribou Is., Canada 70 A6 61 55N 113 15W
Caribou L., Man., Canada ... 71 B9 59 21N 96 10W
Caribou L., Ont., Canada 72 B2 50 25N 89 5W
Caribou Mts., Canada 70 B5 59 12N 115 40W
Caribou River ⌂, Canada 71 B9 59 35N 96 35W
Carichic, Mexico 86 B3 27 56N 107 3W
Carillo, Mexico 86 B4 26 50N 103 55W
Carinda, Australia .... 63 E4 30 28S 147 41 E
Carinhanha, Brazil 93 F10 14 15S 44 46W
Carinhanha ➤, Brazil 93 F10 14 20S 43 47W
Carinthia = Kärnten □, Austria . 16 E8 46 52N 13 30 E
Caripito, Venezuela 92 A6 10 8N 63 6W
Carleton, Mt., Canada 73 C6 47 23N 66 53W
Carleton Place, Canada 85 A8 45 8N 76 9W
Carletonville, S. Africa ...... 56 D4 26 23S 27 22 E
Carlin, U.S.A. 76 F5 40 43N 116 7W
Carlingford L., U.K. 10 B5 54 3N   6 9W
Carlinville, U.S.A. 80 F10 39 17N 89 53W
Carlisle, U.K. 12 C5 54 54N   2 56W
Carlisle, U.S.A. 84 F7 40 12N 77 12W
Carlisle B., Barbados .... 89 g   13 5N 59 37W
Carlisle I., Australia .... 62 J7 20 49S 149 18 E

Carlos Casares, Argentina 94 D3 35 32S 61 20W
Carlos Tejedor, Argentina 94 D3 35 25S 62 25W
Carlow, Ireland 10 D5 52 50N   6 56W
Carlow □, Ireland 10 D5 52 43N   6 50W
Carlsbad, Calif., U.S.A. 79 M9 33 10N 117 21W
Carlsbad, N. Mex., U.S.A. 81 J2 32 25N 104 14W
Carlsbad Caverns △, U.S.A. .. 81 J2 32 10N 104 35W
Carluke, U.K. 11 F5 55 45N   3 50W
Carlyle, Canada 71 D8 49 40N 102 20W
Carmacks, Canada 68 B6 62 5N 136 16W
Carman, Canada 71 D9 49 30N 98 0W
Carmarthen, U.K. 13 F3 51 52N   4 19W
Carmarthen B., U.K. 13 F3 51 40N   4 30W
Carmarthenshire □, U.K. 13 F3 51 55N   4 13W
Carmaux, France .... 20 D5 44 3N   2 10 E
Carmel, U.S.A. 85 E11 41 26N 73 41W
Carmel-by-the-Sea, U.S.A. ... 78 J5 36 33N 121 55W
Carmel Valley, U.S.A. 78 J5 36 29N 121 43W
Carmelo, Uruguay 94 C4 34 0S 58 20W
Carmen, Colombia 92 B3   9 43N 75 8W
Carmen, Paraguay 95 B4 27 13S 56 12W
Carmen ➤, Mexico 86 A3 30 42N 106 29W
Carmen, I., Mexico 86 B2 26 0N 111 20W
Carmen de Patagones, Argentina . 96 E4 40 50S 63 0W
Carmensa, Argentina 94 D2 35 15S 67 40W
Carmi, U.S.A. 70 D5 49 36N 119 8W
Carmi, U.S.A. 82 F1 38 5N 88 10W
Carmichael, U.S.A. 78 G5 38 38N 121 19W
Carmila, Australia .... 62 C4 21 55S 149 24 E
Carmona, Costa Rica 88 E2 10 0N 85 15W
Carmona, Spain 21 D3 37 28N   5 42W
Carn Ban, U.K. 11 D4 57 7N   4 15W
Carn Eige, U.K. 11 D3 57 17N   5 8W
Carnac, France 20 C2 47 35N   3 6W
Carnamah, Australia .... 61 E2 29 41S 115 53 E
Carnarvon, Australia .... 61 D1 24 51S 113 42 E
Carnarvon, S. Africa .... 56 E3 30 56S 22 8 E
Carnarvon △, Australia ...... 62 C4 24 54S 148 2 E
Carnarvon Ra., Queens.,
  Australia .... 62 D4 25 15S 148 30 E
Carnarvon Ra., W. Austral.,
  Australia .... 61 E3 25 20S 120 45 E
Carnation, U.S.A. 78 C5 47 39N 121 55W
Carndonagh, Ireland 10 A4 55 16N   7 15W
Carnduff, Canada 71 D8 49 10N 101 50W
Carnegie, U.S.A. 84 F4 40 24N 80 5W
Carnegie, L., Australia ...... 61 E3 26 5S 122 30 E
Carnic Alps = Karnische Alpen,
  Europe .... 16 E7 46 36N 13 0 E
Carniche Alpi = Karnische Alpen,
  Europe .... 16 E7 46 36N 13 0 E
Carnot, C.A.R. .... 52 D3   4 59N 15 56 E
Carnot, C., Australia .... 63 E2 34 57S 135 38 E
Carnot B., Australia .... 60 C3 17 20S 122 15 E
Carnoustie, U.K. 11 E6 56 30N   2 42W
Carnsore Pt., Ireland 10 D5 52 10N   6 22W
Caro, U.S.A. 82 D4 43 29N 83 24W
Carol City, U.S.A. 83 N5 25 56N 80 16W
Carolina, Brazil 93 E9   7 10S 47 30W
Carolina, Puerto Rico .... 89 d   18 23N 65 58W
Carolina, S. Africa .... 57 D5 26 5S 30 6 E
Caroline I., Kiribati 65 H12 9 58S 150 13W
Caroline Is., Micronesia ..... 26 J17 8 0N 150 0 E
Caroni, Trin. & Tob. 93 K15 10 34N 61 23W
Caroni ➤, Venezuela 92 B6   8 21N 62 43W
Caronie = Nébrodi, Monti, Italy . 22 F6 37 54N 14 35 E
Caroona, Australia .... 63 E5 31 24S 150 26 E
Carpathians, Europe .... 17 D11 49 30N 21 0 E
Carpaţii Meridionali, Romania . 17 F13 45 30N 25 0 E
Carpentaria, G. of, Australia .. 62 A2 14 0S 139 0 E
Carpentras, France .... 20 D6 44 3N   5 2 E
Carpi, Italy .... 22 B4 44 47N 10 53 E
Carpinteria, U.S.A. 79 L7 34 24N 119 31W
Carr Boyd Ra., Australia .... 60 C4 16 15S 128 35 E
Carrabelle, U.S.A. 83 L3 29 51N 84 40W
Carranza, Presa V., Mexico .. 86 B4 27 20N 100 50W
Carrara, Italy .... 20 D9 44 5N 10 6 E
Carrauntoohill, Ireland 10 D2 52 0N   9 45W
Carrick-on-Shannon, Ireland . 10 C3 53 57N   8 5W
Carrick-on-Suir, Ireland 10 D4 52 21N   7 24W
Carrickfergus, U.K. 10 B6 54 43N   5 49W
Carrickmacross, Ireland 10 C5 53 59N   6 43W
Carrieton, Australia .... 63 E2 32 25S 138 31 E
Carrington, U.S.A. 80 B5 47 27N 99 8W
Carrizal Bajo, Chile 94 B1 28 5S 71 20W
Carrizalillo, Chile 94 B1 29 5S 71 30W
Carrizo Cr. ➤, U.S.A. 81 G3 36 55N 103 55W
Carrizo Plain ⌂, U.S.A. 78 K7 35 12N 119 48W
Carrizo Springs, U.S.A. 81 L5 28 31N 99 52W
Carrizozo, U.S.A. 77 K11 33 38N 105 53W
Carroll, U.S.A. 80 D7 42 4N 94 52W
Carrollton, Ga., U.S.A. 83 J3 33 35N 85 5W
Carrollton, Ill., U.S.A. 80 F9 39 18N 90 24W
Carrollton, Ky., U.S.A. 82 F3 38 41N 85 11W
Carrollton, Mo., U.S.A. 80 F8 39 22N 93 30W
Carrollton, Ohio, U.S.A. 84 F3 40 34N 81 5W
Carron ➤, U.K. 11 D4 57 53N   4 22W
Carron, L., U.K. 11 D3 57 22N   5 35W
Carrot ➤, Canada 71 C8 53 50N 101 17W
Carrot River, Canada 71 C7 53 17N 103 35W
Carruthers, Canada 71 C7 52 52N 109 16W
Carson ➤, U.S.A. 79 M8 33 48N 118 17W
Carson, N. Dak., U.S.A. 80 B4 46 25N 101 34W
Carson ➤, U.S.A. 78 F8 39 45N 118 40W
Carson City, U.S.A. 78 F7 39 10N 119 46W
Carson Sink, U.S.A. 76 G4 39 50N 118 25W
Cartagena, Colombia 92 A3 10 25N 75 33W
Cartagena, Spain 21 D5 37 38N   0 59W
Cartago, Colombia 92 C3   4 45N 75 55W
Cartago, Costa Rica 88 E3   9 50N 83 55W
Cartersville, U.S.A. 83 H3 34 10N 84 48W
Carterton, N.Z. .... 59 J5 41 2S 175 31 E
Carthage, Tunisia .... 51 A8 36 50N 10 21 E
Carthage, Ill., U.S.A. 80 E9 40 25N 91 8W
Carthage, Mo., U.S.A. 81 G7 37 11N 94 19W
Carthage, N.Y., U.S.A. 82 D8 43 59N 75 37W
Carthage, Tex., U.S.A. 81 J7 32 9N 94 20W
Cartier I., Australia .... 60 B3 12 31S 123 29 E
Cartwright, Canada 73 B8 53 41N 56 58W
Caruaru, Brazil 93 E11 8 15S 35 55W
Carúpano, Venezuela 92 A6 10 39N 63 15W
Caruthersville, U.S.A. 81 G10 36 11N 89 39W
Carvoeiro, Brazil 92 D6   1 30S 61 59W
Carvoeiro, C., Portugal 21 C1 39 21N   9 24W
Cary, U.S.A. 83 H6 35 47N 78 46W
Casa Grande, U.S.A. 77 K8 32 53N 111 45W
Casablanca, Chile 94 C1 33 20S 71 25W
Casablanca, Morocco 50 B4 33 36N   7 36W

Cascada de Basaseachic △,
  Mexico 86 B3 28 9N 108 15W
Cascade, Idaho, U.S.A. 76 D5 44 31N 116 2W
Cascade, Mont., U.S.A. 76 C8 47 16N 111 42W
Cascade Locks, U.S.A. 78 E5 45 40N 121 54W
Cascade Ra., U.S.A. 78 D5 47 0N 121 30W
Cascade Reservoir, U.S.A. ... 76 D5 44 32N 116 3W
Cascais, Portugal 21 C1 38 41N   9 25W
Cascavel, Brazil 95 A5 24 57S 53 28W
Cáscina, Italy .... 22 C4 43 41N 10 33 E
Casco B., U.S.A. 83 D10 43 45N 70 0W
Caserta, Italy .... 22 D6 41 4N 14 20 E
Casey, Antarctica .... 5 C8 66 0S 76 0 E
Caseyr, Raas = Asir, Ras,
  Somali Rep. .... 47 E5 11 55N 51 10 E
Cashel, Ireland 10 D4 52 30N   7 53W
Casiguran, Phil. .... 37 A6 16 22N 122 7 E
Casilda, Argentina 94 C3 33 10S 61 10W
Casino, Australia .... 63 D5 28 52S 153 3 E
Casiquiare ➤, Venezuela 92 C5   2 1N 67 7W
Casma, Peru 92 E3   9 30S 78 20W
Casmalia, U.S.A. 79 L6 34 50N 120 32W
Caspe, Spain 21 B5 41 14N   0 1W
Casper, U.S.A. 76 E10 42 51N 106 19W
Caspian Depression, Eurasia . 19 E8 47 0N 48 0 E
Caspian Sea, Eurasia .... 19 F9 43 0N 50 0 E
Cass Lake, U.S.A. 80 B7 47 23N 94 37W
Cassadaga, U.S.A. 84 D5 42 20N 79 19W
Casselman, Canada 85 A9 45 19N 75 5W
Casselton, U.S.A. 80 B6 46 54N 97 13W
Cassiar, Canada 70 B3 59 16N 129 40W
Cassiar Mts., Canada 70 B2 59 30N 130 30W
Cassino, Italy .... 22 D5 41 30N 13 49 E
Cassville, U.S.A. 81 G8 36 41N 93 52W
Castaic, U.S.A. 79 L8 34 30N 118 38W
Castalia, U.S.A. 84 E2 41 24N 82 49W
Castanhal, Brazil 93 D9   1 18S 47 55W
Castara, Trin. & Tob. 93 J16 11 17N 60 42W
Castellammare di Stábia, Italy . 22 D6 40 42N 14 29 E
Castelli, Argentina 94 D4 36 7S 57 47W
Castelló de la Plana, Spain ... 21 C5 39 58N   0 3W
Castelo, Brazil 95 A7 20 33S 41 14W
Castelo Branco, Portugal 21 C2 39 50N   7 31W
Castelsarrasin, France ...... 20 E4 44 2N   1 7 E
Castelvetrano, Italy .... 22 F5 37 41N 12 47 E
Casterton, Australia .... 63 F3 37 30S 141 30 E
Castilla-La Mancha □, Spain . 21 C4 39 30N   3 30W
Castilla y León □, Spain 21 B3 42 0N   5 0W
Castillos, Uruguay 95 C5 34 12S 53 52W
Castle Dale, U.S.A. 76 G8 39 13N 111 1W
Castle Douglas, U.K. 11 G5 54 56N   3 56W
Castle Rock, Colo., U.S.A. ... 80 F2 39 22N 104 51W
Castle Rock, Wash., U.S.A. .. 78 D4 46 17N 122 54W
Castlebar, Ireland 10 C2 53 52N   9 18W
Castlebay, U.K. 11 E1 56 57N   7 31W
Castleblaney, Ireland 10 B5 54 7N   6 44W
Castlederg, U.K. 10 B4 54 42N   7 35W
Castleford, U.K. 12 D6 53 43N   1 21W
Castlegar, Canada 70 D5 49 20N 117 40W
Castlemaine, Australia ...... 63 F3 37 2S 144 12 E
Castlepollard, Ireland 10 C4 53 41N   7 19W
Castlerea, Ireland 10 C3 53 46N   8 29W
Castlereagh ➤, Australia .... 63 E4 30 12S 147 32 E
Castlereagh B., Australia .... 62 A2 12 10S 135 10 E
Castleton, U.S.A. 85 C11 43 37N 73 11W
Castletown, U.K. 12 C3 54 5N   4 38W
Castletown Bearhaven, Ireland . 10 E2 51 39N   9 55W
Castor, Canada 70 C6 52 15N 111 50W
Castor ➤, Canada 72 B4 53 24N 78 58W
Castorland, U.S.A. 85 C9 43 53N 75 31W
Castres, France .... 20 E5 43 37N   2 13 E
Castricum, Neths. .... 15 B4 52 33N   4 40 E
Castries, St. Lucia .... 89 f   14 2N 60 58W
Castro, Brazil 95 A6 24 45S 50 0W
Castro, Chile 96 E2 42 30S 73 50W
Castro Alves, Brazil 93 F11 12 46S 39 33W
Castroville, U.S.A. 78 J5 36 46N 121 45W
Castuera, Spain 21 C3 38 43N   5 37W
Cat Ba △, Vietnam .... 38 B6 20 47N 107 3 E
Cat Ba, Dao, Vietnam ...... 38 B6 20 50N 107 0 E
Cat I., Bahamas 72 B1 51 40N 91 50W
Cat L., Canada 72 B1 51 40N 91 50W
Cat Lake, Canada 72 B1 51 40N 91 50W
Cat Tien □, Vietnam .... 39 G6 11 25N 107 17 E
Catacamas, Honduras 88 D2 14 54N 85 56W
Cataguases, Brazil 95 A7 21 23S 42 39W
Catalão, Brazil 93 G9 18 10S 47 57W
Çatalca, Turkey .... 23 D13 41 8N 28 27 E
Catalina, Canada 73 C9 48 31N 53 4W
Catalina, Chile 94 B2 25 13S 69 43W
Catalina, U.S.A. 77 K8 32 30N 110 50W
Catalonia = Cataluña □, Spain . 21 B6 41 40N   1 15 E
Cataluña □, Spain .... 21 B6 41 40N   1 15 E
Catamarca, Argentina 94 B2 28 30S 65 50W
Catamarca □, Argentina 94 B2 27 0S 65 50W
Catanduanes □, Phil. .... 37 B6 13 50N 124 20 E
Catanduva, Brazil 95 A6 21 5S 48 58W
Catánia, Italy .... 22 F6 37 30N 15 6 E
Catanzaro, Italy .... 22 E7 38 54N 16 35 E
Cataman, Phil. .... 37 B6 12 28N 124 35 E
Catatumbo-Bari △, Colombia . 89 E5   9 7S 73 3 E
Cateel, Phil. .... 37 C7   7 47N 126 24 E
Catembe, Mozam. .... 57 D5 26 0S 32 33 E
Caterham, U.K. 13 F7 51 15N   0 4W
Cathcart, S. Africa .... 56 E4 32 18S 27 10 E
Cathlamet, U.S.A. 78 D3 46 12N 123 23W
Catlettsburg, U.S.A. 82 F4 38 25N 82 36W
Catoche, C., Mexico 87 C7 21 40N 87 8W
Catril, Argentina 94 D3 36 26S 63 24W
Catrimani ➤, Brazil 92 C6   0 27N 61 41W
Catrimani, Brazil 92 C6   0 28N 61 44W
Catskill, U.S.A. 85 D11 42 14N 73 52W
Catskill ⌂, U.S.A. 85 D10 42 10N 74 25W
Catskill Mts., U.S.A. 85 D10 42 10N 74 25W
Catt, Mt., Australia .... 62 A1 13 49S 134 23 E
Cattaraugus, U.S.A. 84 D6 42 22N 78 52W
Catterick, U.K. 12 C6 54 23N   1 37W
Catuala, Angola .... 56 B2 16 25S 19 2 E
Catuane, Mozam. .... 57 D5 26 48S 32 18 E
Catur, Mozam. .... 55 E4 13 45S 35 30 E
Catwick Is., Vietnam .... 39 G7 10 0N 109 0 E
Cauca ➤, Colombia 92 B4   8 54N 74 28W
Caucaia, Brazil 93 D11 3 40S 38 35W
Caucasus Mountains, Eurasia . 19 F7 42 50N 44 0 E
Caungula, Angola .... 52 F3   8 26S 18 38 E
Cauquenes, Chile 94 D1 36 0S 72 22W
Caura ➤, Venezuela 92 B6   7 38N 64 53W

Cauresi ➤, Mozam. .... 55 F3 17 8S 33 0 E
Causapscal, Canada 73 C6 48 19N 67 12W
Cauvery ➤, India .... 40 P11 11 9N 78 52 E
Caux, Pays de, France ...... 20 B4 49 38N   0 35 E
Cavalier, U.S.A. 80 A6 48 48N 97 37W
Cavan, Ireland 10 B4 54 0N   7 22W
Cavan □, Ireland 10 C4 54 1N   7 16W
Cave Creek, U.S.A. 77 K7 33 50N 111 57W
Cavenagh Ra., Australia .... 61 E4 26 12S 127 55 E
Cavendish, Australia .... 63 F3 37 31S 142 2 E
Caviana, I., Brazil 93 C8   0 10N 50 10W
Cavite, Phil. .... 37 B6 14 29N 120 55 E
Cawndilla L., Australia ...... 63 E3 32 30S 142 15 E
Cawnpore = Kanpur, India ... 43 F9 26 28N 80 20 E
Caxias, Brazil 93 D10 4 55S 43 20W
Caxias do Sul, Brazil 95 B5 29 10S 51 10W
Cay Sal Bank, Bahamas 88 B4 23 45N 80 0W
Cayambe, Ecuador 92 C3   0 3N 78 8W
Cayenne, Fr. Guiana 93 B8   5 5N 52 18W
Cayey, Puerto Rico .... 89 d   18 7N 66 10W
Cayman Brac, Cayman Is. 88 C4 19 43N 79 49W
Cayman Is. ☑, W. Indies 88 C3 19 40N 80 30W
Cayo Romano, Cuba 88 B4 22 0N 78 0W
Cayuga, U.S.A. 85 D8 42 54N 76 44W
Cayuga L., U.S.A. 85 D8 42 41N 76 41W
Cazenovia, U.S.A. 85 D9 42 56N 75 51W
Cazombo, Angola .... 53 G4 11 54S 22 56 E
Ceanannus Mor, Ireland 10 C5 53 44N   6 53W
Ceará = Fortaleza, Brazil 93 D11 3 45S 38 35W
Ceará □, Brazil 93 E11 5 0S 40 0W
Ceará Mirim, Brazil 93 E11 5 38S 35 25W
Cebaco, I. de, Panama 88 E3   7 33N 81 9W
Cebollar, Argentina 94 B2 29 10S 66 35W
Cebu, Phil. .... 37 B6 10 18N 123 54 E
Cecil Plains, Australia ...... 63 D5 27 30S 151 11 E
Cedar ➤, U.S.A. 80 E9 41 17N 91 21W
Cedar City, U.S.A. 77 H7 37 41N 113 4W
Cedar Creek Reservoir, U.S.A. . 81 J6 32 11N 96 4W
Cedar Falls, Iowa, U.S.A. 80 D8 42 32N 92 27W
Cedar Falls, Wash., U.S.A. ... 78 C5 47 25N 121 45W
Cedar Key, U.S.A. 83 L4 29 8N 83 2W
Cedar L., Canada 71 C9 53 10N 100 0W
Cedar Rapids, U.S.A. 80 E9 41 59N 91 40W
Cedartown, U.S.A. 83 H3 34 1N 85 15W
Cedarvale, Canada 70 B3 55 1N 128 22W
Cedarville, S. Africa .... 57 E4 30 23S 29 3 E
Cedral, Mexico 86 C4 23 50N 100 42W
Cedro, Brazil 93 E11 6 34S 39 3W
Cedros, I. de, Mexico 86 B1 28 10N 115 20W
Cedros B., Trin. & Tob. 93 K15 10 16N 61 54W
Ceduna, Australia .... 63 E1 32 7S 133 46 E
Ceerigaabo = Erigavo,
  Somali Rep. .... 47 E4 10 35N 47 20 E
Cefalù, Italy .... 22 E6 38 2N 14 1 E
Cegléd, Hungary .... 17 E10 47 11N 19 47 E
Cekik, Indonesia .... 37 J17 8 12S 114 27 E
Celaque △, Honduras 88 D2 14 30N 88 43W
Celaya, Mexico 86 C4 20 31N 100 37W
Celebes Sea, Indonesia ..... 37 D6   3 0N 123 0 E
Celina, U.S.A. 82 E3 40 33N 84 35W
Celje, Slovenia .... 16 E8 46 16N 15 18 E
Celle, Germany .... 16 B6 52 37N 10 4 E
Celtic Sea, Atl. Oc. 14 F2 50 9N   9 34W
Cenderwasih, Teluk, Indonesia . 37 E9   3 0S 135 20 E
Center, N. Dak., U.S.A. 80 B4 47 7N 101 18W
Center, Tex., U.S.A. 81 K7 31 48N 94 11W
Centerburg, U.S.A. 84 F2 40 18N 82 42W
Centerville, Calif., U.S.A. 78 J7 36 44N 119 30W
Centerville, Iowa, U.S.A. 80 E8 40 44N 92 52W
Centerville, Pa., U.S.A. 84 F5 40 3N 79 59W
Centerville, Tenn., U.S.A. 83 H2 35 47N 87 28W
Centerville, Tex., U.S.A. 81 K7 31 16N 95 59W
Central = Tsentralnyy □, Russia . 28 D4 52 0N 40 0 E
Central □, Kenya .... 54 C4   0 30S 37 30 E
Central □, Malawi .... 55 E3 13 30S 33 30 E
Central □, Zambia .... 55 E2 14 25S 28 50 E
Central, Cordillera, Colombia . 92 C4   5 0N 75 0W
Central, Cordillera, Costa Rica . 88 D3 10 10N 84 5W
Central, Cordillera, Dom. Rep. . 89 C5 19 5N 71 0W
Central, Cordillera, Puerto Rico . 89 d 18 8N 66 35W
Central African Rep. ■, Africa . 51 G9   7 0N 20 0 E
Central America, America 66 H11 7 0N 85 0W
Central Butte, Canada 71 C7 50 48N 106 31W
Central City, Colo., U.S.A. ... 76 G11 39 48N 105 31W
Central City, Ky., U.S.A. 82 G2 37 18N 87 7W
Central City, Nebr., U.S.A. ... 80 E6 41 7N 98 0W
Central, I., Kenya .... 54 B4 3 30N 36 1 E
Central Island △, Kenya ..... 54 B4   2 33N 36 1 E
Central Kalahari ⌂, Botswana . 56 C3 22 36S 23 58 E
Central Makran Range, Pakistan . 40 F4 26 30N 64 15 E
Central Patricia, Canada 72 B1 51 30N 90 9W
Central Point, U.S.A. 76 E2 42 23N 122 55W
Central Russian Uplands, Europe . 6 E13 54 0N 36 0 E
Central Siberian Plateau, Russia . 26 C14 65 0N 105 0 E
Central Square, U.S.A. 85 C8 43 17N 76 9W
Centralia, Ill., U.S.A. 80 F10 38 32N 89 8W
Centralia, Mo., U.S.A. 80 F8 39 13N 92 8W
Centralia, Wash., U.S.A. 78 D4 46 43N 122 58W
Cephalonia = Kefalliní, Greece . 23 E9 38 15N 20 30 E
Cepu, Indonesia .... 37 G14 7 9S 111 35 E
Ceram = Seram, Indonesia ... 37 E7   3 10S 129 0 E
Ceram Sea = Seram Sea,
  Indonesia .... 37 E7   2 30S 128 30 E
Ceredigion □, U.K. 13 E3 52 16N   4 15W
Ceres, Argentina 94 B3 29 55S 61 55W
Ceres, S. Africa .... 56 E2 33 21S 19 18 E
Ceres, U.S.A. 78 H6 37 35N 120 57W
Cerignola, Italy .... 22 D6 41 17N 15 53 E
Cerigo = Kíthira, Greece ..... 23 F10 36 8N 23 0 E
Çerkezköy, Turkey .... 23 D12 41 17N 28 0 E
Cerralvo, I., Mexico 86 C3 24 20N 109 45W
Cerritos, Mexico 86 C4 22 27N 100 20W
Cerro Chato, Uruguay 95 C4 33 6S 55 8W
Cerro Corá △, Paraguay 95 A4 22 35S 56 2W
Cerro el Copey △, Venezuela . 89 D7 10 59N 63 53W
Cerro Hoya △, Panama 88 E3   7 17N 80 45W
Cerro Saroche △, Venezuela .. 89 D6 10 8N 69 3W
Cervantes, Australia .... 61 F2 30 31S 115 3 E
Cervera, Spain .... 21 B6 41 40N   1 5 E
Cesena, Italy .... 22 B5 44 8N 12 15 E
Cēsis, Latvia .... 9 H21 57 18N 25 15 E
České Budějovice, Czech Rep. . 16 D8 48 55N 14 25 E
Českomoravská Vrchovina,
  Czech Rep. .... 16 D8 49 30N 15 40 E
Çeşme, Turkey .... 23 E12 38 20N 26 23 E
Cessnock, Australia .... 63 E5 32 50S 151 21 E
Cetinje, Serbia & M. .... 23 C8 42 23N 18 59 E
Cetraro, Italy .... 22 E6 39 31N 15 55 E

Ceuta, N. Afr. 21 E3 35 52N 5 18W
Cévennes, France .... 20 D5 44 10N 3 50 E
Ceyhan, Turkey .... 44 B2 37 4N 35 47 E
Ceylon = Sri Lanka ■, Asia 40 R12 7 30N 80 50 E
Cha-am, Thailand .... 38 F2 12 48N 99 58 E
Cha Pa, Vietnam .... 38 A4 22 20N 103 47 E
Chacabuco, Argentina 94 C3 34 40S 60 27W
Chachapoyas, Peru 92 E3 6 15S 77 50W
Chachran, Pakistan .... 40 E7 28 55N 70 30 E
Chachoengsao, Thailand ...... 38 F3 13 42N 101 5 E
Chachro, Pakistan .... 42 G4 25 5N 70 15 E
Chaco □, Argentina 94 B4 27 0S 61 0W
Chaco □, Paraguay 94 B3 26 30S 61 0W
Chaco ➤, U.S.A. 77 H9 36 46N 108 39W
Chaco Austral, S. Amer. 96 B4 27 0S 61 30W
Chaco Boreal, S. Amer. 92 H6 22 0S 60 0W
Chaco Central, S. Amer. 96 A4 24 0S 61 0W
Chaco Culture △, U.S.A. 77 H10 36 3N 107 58W
Chacon, C., U.S.A. 70 C2 54 42N 132 0W
Chad ■, Africa .... 51 F8 15 0N 17 15 E
Chad, L. = Tchad, L., Chad 51 F8 13 30N 14 30 E
Chadan, Russia .... 29 D10 51 17N 91 35 E
Chadileuvú ➤, Argentina 94 D2 37 46S 66 0W
Chadiza, Zambia .... 55 E3 14 45S 32 27 E
Chadron, U.S.A. 80 D3 42 50N 103 0W
Chadyr-Lunga = Ciadâr-Lunga,
  Moldova .... 17 E15 46 3N 28 51 E
Chae Hom, Thailand .... 38 C2 18 43N 99 35 E
Chae Son △, Thailand .... 38 C2 18 42N 99 20 E
Chaem ➤, Thailand .... 38 C2 18 11N 98 38 E
Chaeryŏng, N. Korea .... 35 E13 38 24N 125 36 E
Chagai Hills = Châh Gay Hills,
  Afghan. .... 40 E3 29 30N 64 0 E
Chagda, Russia .... 29 D14 58 45N 130 38 E
Chaghcharán, Afghan. .... 40 B4 34 31N 65 15 E
Chagos Arch. ☑, Ind. Oc. ... 27 K11 6 0S 72 0 E
Chagres ➤, Panama 88 E4 9 33N 79 37W
Chagrin Falls, U.S.A. 84 E3 41 26N 81 24W
Chaguanas, Trin. & Tob. 93 K15 10 30N 61 26W
Châh Ákhvor, Iran .... 45 C8 32 41N 59 40 E
Châh Bahar, Iran .... 45 E9 25 20N 60 40 E
Châh-e Kavir, Iran .... 45 C8 34 29N 56 52 E
Châh Gay Hills, Afghan. .... 40 E3 29 30N 64 0 E
Chahar Burjak, Afghan. ..... 40 D3 30 15N 62 0 E
Chahár Mahäll va Bakhtíari □,
  Iran .... 45 C6 32 0N 49 0 E
Chai Wan, China .... 33 G11 22 16N 114 14 E
Chaibasa, India .... 41 H14 22 42N 85 49 E
Chainat, Thailand .... 38 E3 15 11N 100 8 E
Chaiya, Thailand .... 39 H2 9 23N 99 14 E
Chaiyaphum, Thailand ...... 38 E4 15 48N 102 2 E
Chaj Doab, Pakistan .... 42 C5 32 15N 73 0 E
Chajari, Argentina 94 C4 30 42S 58 0W
Chak Amru, Pakistan .... 42 C6 32 22N 75 11 E
Chakar ➤, Pakistan .... 42 E3 29 29N 68 2 E
Chakari, Zimbabwe .... 57 B4 18 5S 29 51 E
Chake Chake, Tanzania ..... 54 D4 5 15S 39 45 E
Chakhánsūr, Afghan. .... 40 D3 31 10N 62 0 E
Chakonipau, L., Canada 73 A6 56 18N 68 30W
Chakradharpur, India ...... 43 H11 22 45N 85 40 E
Chakrata, India .... 42 D7 30 42N 77 51 E
Chakwal, Pakistan .... 42 C5 32 56N 72 53 E
Chala, Peru 92 G4 15 48S 74 20W
Chalchihuites, Mexico 86 C4 23 29N 103 53W
Chalcis = Khalkis, Greece .. 23 E10 38 27N 23 42 E
Chaleur B., Canada 73 C6 47 55N 65 30W
Chalfant, U.S.A. 78 H8 37 32N 118 21W
Chalhuanca, Peru 92 F4 14 15S 73 15W
Chalisgaon, India .... 40 J9 20 30N 75 10 E
Chalk River, Canada 72 C4 46 1N 77 27W
Chalky Inlet, N.Z. .... 59 M1 46 3S 166 31 E
Challapata, Bolivia 92 G5 18 53S 66 50W
Challis, U.S.A. 76 D6 44 30N 114 14W
Chalmette, U.S.A. 81 L10 29 56N 89 58W
Chalon-sur-Saône, France .. 20 C6 46 48N 4 50 E
Châlons-en-Champagne, France 20 B6 48 58N 4 20 E
Chálús, Iran .... 45 B6 36 38N 51 26 E
Cham, Cu Lao, Vietnam ..... 38 E7 15 57N 108 30 E
Chama, U.S.A. 77 H10 36 54N 106 35W
Chamaicó, Argentina 94 D3 35 3S 64 58W
Chaman, Pakistan .... 40 D5 30 58N 66 25 E
Chamba, India .... 42 C7 32 35N 76 10 E
Chamba, Tanzania .... 55 E4 11 37S 37 0 E
Chambal ➤, India .... 43 F8 26 29N 79 15 E
Chamberlain, U.S.A. 80 D5 43 49N 99 20W
Chamberlain ➤, Australia .. 60 C4 15 30S 127 54 E
Chamberlain L., U.S.A. 83 B11 46 14N 69 19W
Chambers, U.S.A. 77 J9 35 11N 109 26W
Chambersburg, U.S.A. 82 F7 39 56N 77 40W
Chambéry, France .... 20 D6 45 34N 5 55 E
Chambeshi ➤, Zambia .... 52 G6 11 53S 29 48 E
Chambly, Canada 85 A11 45 27N 73 17W
Chambord, Canada 73 C5 48 25N 72 6W
Chamchamal, Iraq .... 44 C5 35 32N 44 50 E
Chamela, Mexico 86 D3 19 32N 105 5W
Chamical, Argentina 94 C2 30 22S 66 27W
Chamkar Luong, Cambodia ... 39 G4 11 0N 103 45 E
Chamoli, India .... 43 D8 30 24N 79 21 E
Chamonix-Mont Blanc, France 20 D7 45 55N 6 51 E
Champa, India .... 43 H10 22 2N 82 43 E
Champagne, Canada 70 A1 60 49N 136 30W
Champagne, France .... 20 B6 48 40N 4 20 E
Champaign, U.S.A. 82 E1 40 7N 88 15W
Champassak, Laos .... 38 E5 14 53N 105 52 E
Champawat, India .... 43 E9 29 20N 80 6 E
Champdoré, L., Canada 73 A6 55 55N 65 49W
Champion, U.S.A. 84 E4 41 19N 80 51W
Champlain, U.S.A. 85 B11 44 59N 73 27W
Champlain, L., U.S.A. 85 B11 44 40N 73 20W
Champotón, Mexico 87 D6 19 30N 90 50W
Champua, India .... 43 H11 22 5N 85 40 E
Chana, Thailand .... 39 J3 6 55N 100 44 E
Chañaral, Chile 94 B1 26 23S 70 40W
Chanárán, Iran .... 45 B8 36 39N 59 6 E
Chanasma, India .... 42 H5 23 44N 72 5 E
Chancery Lane, Barbados ... 89 g 13 4N 59 30W
Chanco, Chile 94 D1 35 44S 72 32W
Chand, India .... 43 J8 21 57N 79 7 E
Chandan, India .... 43 G12 24 38N 86 40 E
Chandan Chauki, India ..... 43 E9 28 33N 80 47 E
Chandannagar, India .... 43 H13 22 52N 88 24 E
Chandausi, India .... 43 E8 28 27N 78 49 E
Chandeleur Is., U.S.A. 81 L10 29 55N 88 57W
Chandeleur Sd., U.S.A. 81 L10 29 55N 89 0W
Chandigarh, India .... 42 D7 30 43N 76 47 E
Chandil, India .... 43 H12 22 58N 86 3 E
Chandler, Australia .... 63 D1 27 0S 133 19 E

Chandler, Canada 73 C7 48 18N 64 46W
Chandler, Ariz., U.S.A. ... 77 K8 33 18N 111 50W
Chandler, Okla., U.S.A. ... 81 H6 35 42N 96 53W
Chandod, India .... 42 J5 21 59N 73 28 E
Chandpur, Bangla. .... 41 H17 23 8N 90 45 E
Chandrapur, India .... 40 K11 19 57N 79 25 E
Chānf, Iran .... 45 E9 26 38N 60 29 E
Chang, Pakistan .... 42 F3 26 59N 68 30 E
Chang, Ko, Thailand .... 39 F4 12 0N 102 23 E
Ch'ang Chiang = Chang Jiang ➤,
  China .... 33 C7 31 48N 121 10 E
Chang Jiang ➤, China ...... 33 C7 31 48N 121 10 E
Changa, India .... 43 C7 33 53N 77 35 E
Changan, China .... 33 F10 22 48N 113 48 E
Changanacheri, India ...... 40 Q10 9 25N 76 31 E
Changane ➤, Mozam. .... 57 C5 24 30S 33 30 E
Changbai, China .... 35 D15 41 25N 128 5 E
Changbai Shan, China ...... 35 C15 42 20N 129 0 E
Changchiak'ou = Zhangjiakou,
  China .... 34 D8 40 48N 114 55 E
Ch'angchou = Changzhou, China 33 C6 31 47N 119 58 E
Changchun, China .... 35 C13 43 57N 125 17 E
Changchunling, China ...... 35 B13 45 18N 125 27 E
Changde, China .... 33 D6 29 4N 111 35 E
Changdo-ri, N. Korea ...... 35 E14 38 30N 127 40 E
Changhai = Shanghai, China 33 C7 31 15N 121 26 E
Changhua, Taiwan .... 33 D7 24 2N 120 30 E
Changhŭng, S. Korea .... 35 G14 34 41N 126 52 E
Changhŭngni, N. Korea ..... 35 D15 40 24N 128 19 E
Changi, Singapore .... 39 d 1 23N 103 59 E
Changi, Singapore ✕ (SIN),
  Singapore .... 39 M4 1 23N 103 59 E
Changjiang, China .... 38 C7 19 20N 108 55 E
Changjiang Shuiku, China .. 33 G10 22 29N 113 27 E
Changjin, N. Korea .... 35 D14 40 23N 127 15 E
Changjin-chŏsuji, N. Korea . 35 D14 40 30N 127 15 E
Changli, China .... 35 E10 39 40N 119 13 E
Changling, China .... 35 B12 44 20N 123 58 E
Changlun, Malaysia .... 39 J3 6 25N 100 26 E
Changping, China .... 34 D9 40 14N 116 12 E
Changsha, China .... 33 D6 28 12N 113 0 E
Changwu, China .... 34 G4 35 10N 107 45 E
Changyi, China .... 35 F10 36 40N 119 30 E
Changyŏn, N. Korea .... 35 E13 38 15N 125 6 E
Changyuan, China .... 34 G8 35 15N 114 42 E
Changzhi, China .... 34 F7 36 10N 113 6 E
Changzhou, China .... 33 C6 31 47N 119 58 E
Chanhanga, Angola .... 56 B1 16 0S 14 8 E
Chania = Khaniá, Greece ... 25 D6 35 30N 24 4 E
Channapatna, India .... 40 N10 12 40N 77 15 E
Channel Is., U.K. 13 H5 49 19N 2 24W
Channel Is., U.S.A. 79 M7 33 40N 119 15W
Channel Islands △, U.S.A. . 79 L7 34 0N 119 24W
Channel-Port aux Basques,
  Canada 73 C8 47 30N 59 9W
Channel Tunnel, Europe .... 13 F9 51 0N 1 30 E
Channing, U.S.A. 81 H3 35 41N 102 20W
Chantada, Spain 21 A2 42 36N 7 46W
Chanthaburi, Thailand ..... 38 F4 12 38N 102 12 E
Chantrey Inlet, Canada 68 B10 67 48N 96 20W
Chanute, U.S.A. 81 G7 37 41N 95 27W
Chao Phraya ➤, Thailand ... 38 F3 13 32N 100 36 E
Chao Phraya Lowlands, Thailand 38 E3 15 30N 100 0 E
Chaocheng, China .... 34 F8 36 4N 115 37 E
Chaoyang, China .... 35 D11 41 35N 120 22 E
Chaozhou, China .... 33 D6 23 42N 116 32 E
Chapais, Canada 72 C5 49 47N 74 51W
Chapala, Mozam. .... 55 F4 15 50S 37 35 E
Chapala, L. de, Mexico 86 C4 20 10N 103 20W
Chapayev, Kazakhstan ...... 19 D9 50 25N 51 10 E
Chapayevsk, Russia .... 18 D8 53 0N 49 40 E
Chapecó, Brazil 95 B5 27 14S 52 41W
Chapel Hill, U.S.A. 83 H6 35 55N 79 4W
Chapleau, Canada 72 C3 47 50N 83 24W
Chaplin, Canada 71 C7 50 28N 106 40W
Chaplin L., Canada 71 C7 50 22N 106 36W
Chappell, U.S.A. 80 E3 41 6N 102 28W
Chapra = Chhapra, India ... 43 G11 25 48N 84 44 E
Chara, Russia .... 29 D12 56 54N 118 20 E
Charadai, Argentina 94 B4 27 35S 59 55W
Charagua, Bolivia 92 G6 19 45S 63 10W
Charambirá, Punta, Colombia 92 C3 4 16N 77 32W
Charaña, Bolivia 92 G5 17 30S 69 25W
Charanwala, India .... 42 F5 27 51N 72 10 E
Charata, Argentina 94 B3 27 13S 61 14W
Charcas, Mexico 86 C4 23 10N 101 20W
Charcot I., Antarctica 5 C17 70 0S 70 0W
Chard, U.K. 13 G5 50 52N 2 58W
Chardon, U.S.A. 84 E3 41 35N 81 12W
Chardzhou = Chärjew,
  Turkmenistan .... 28 F7 39 6N 63 34 E
Charente ➤, France 20 D3 45 57N 1 5W
Chari ➤, Chad .... 51 F8 12 58N 14 31 E
Chârikâr, Afghan. .... 40 B6 35 0N 69 10 E
Chariton ➤, U.S.A. 80 F8 39 19N 92 58W
Chärjew, Turkmenistan ..... 28 F7 39 6N 63 34 E
Charkhari, India .... 43 G8 25 24N 79 45 E
Charkhi Dadri, India ...... 42 E7 28 37N 76 17 E
Charleroi, Belgium .... 15 D4 50 24N 4 27 E
Charleroi, U.S.A. 84 F5 40 9N 79 57W
Charles, C., U.S.A. 82 G8 37 7N 75 58W
Charles City, U.S.A. 80 D8 43 4N 92 41W
Charles L., Canada 71 B6 59 50N 110 33W
Charles Town, U.S.A. 82 F7 39 17N 77 52W
Charleston, Ill., U.S.A. .. 82 F1 39 30N 88 10W
Charleston, Miss., U.S.A. . 81 H9 34 1N 90 4W
Charleston, Mo., U.S.A. ... 81 G10 36 55N 89 21W
Charleston, S.C., U.S.A. .. 83 J6 32 46N 79 56W
Charleston, W. Va., U.S.A. 82 F5 38 21N 81 38W
Charleston L., Canada 85 B9 44 32N 76 0W
Charleston Peak, U.S.A. ... 79 J11 36 16N 115 42W
Charlestown, Ireland 10 C3 53 58N 8 48W
Charlestown, S. Africa .... 57 D4 27 26S 29 53 E
Charlestown, Ind., U.S.A. . 82 F3 38 27N 85 40W
Charlestown, N.H., U.S.A. . 85 C12 43 14N 72 25W
Charlestown of Aberlour, U.K. 11 D5 57 28N 3 14W
Charleville = Rath Luirc, Ireland 10 D3 52 21N 8 40W
Charleville, Australia .... 63 D4 26 24S 146 15 E
Charleville-Mézières, France 20 B6 49 44N 4 40 E
Charlevoix, U.S.A. 82 C3 45 19N 85 16W
Charlotte, Mich., U.S.A. .. 82 D3 42 34N 84 50W
Charlotte, N.C., U.S.A. ... 83 H5 35 13N 80 51W
Charlotte, Vt., U.S.A. 85 B11 44 19N 73 16W
Charlotte Amalie, U.S. Virgin Is. 89 e 18 21N 64 56W
Charlotte Harbor, U.S.A. .. 83 M4 26 50N 82 10W
Charlotte L., Canada 70 C3 52 12N 125 19W
Charlottesville, U.S.A. ... 82 F6 38 2N 78 30W

Charlottetown, Nfld. & L.,
  Canada 73 B8 52 46N 56 7W
Charlottetown, P.E.I., Canada 73 C7 46 14N 63 8W
Charlottetville, Trin. & Tob. 93 J16 11 20N 60 33W
Charlton, Australia .... 63 F3 36 16S 143 24 E
Charlton, U.S.A. 80 E8 40 59N 93 20W
Charlton I., Canada 72 B4 52 0N 79 20W
Charny, Canada 73 C5 46 43N 71 15W
Charolles, France .... 20 C6 46 27N 4 16 E
Charre, Mozam. .... 55 F4 17 13S 35 10 E
Charsadda, Pakistan .... 42 B4 34 7N 71 45 E
Charters Towers, Australia 62 C4 20 5S 146 13 E
Chartres, France .... 20 B4 48 29N 1 30 E
Chascomús, Argentina 94 D4 35 30S 58 0W
Chasefu, Zambia .... 55 E3 11 55S 33 8 E
Chashma Barrage, Pakistan . 42 C4 32 27N 71 20 E
Chât, Iran .... 45 B7 37 59N 55 16 E
Chatal Balkan = Udvoy Balkan,
  Bulgaria ....
Châteaubriant, France 20 C3 47 43N 1 23W
Chateaugay, U.S.A. 85 B10 44 56N 74 5W
Châteauguay, L., Canada ... 73 A5 56 26N 70 3W
Châteaulin, France 20 B1 48 11N 4 8W
Châteauroux, France .... 20 C4 46 50N 1 40 E
Châteaux, Pte. des, Guadeloupe 88 b 16 15N 61 10W
Châtellerault, France ..... 20 C4 46 50N 0 30 E
Chatham = Chatham-Kent,
  Canada 84 D2 42 24N 82 11W
Chatham = Miramichi, Canada 73 C6 47 2N 65 28W
Chatham, U.K. .... 13 F8 51 22N 0 32 E
Chatham, U.S.A. 85 D11 42 21N 73 36W
Chatham Is., Pac. Oc. 64 M10 44 0S 176 40W
Chatham-Kent, Canada 84 D2 42 24N 82 11W
Chatmohar, Bangla. .... 43 G13 24 15N 89 15 E
Chatra, India .... 43 G11 24 12N 84 56 E
Chatrapur, India .... 41 K14 19 22N 85 2 E
Chats, L. des, Canada 85 A8 45 30N 76 20W
Chatsu, India .... 42 F6 26 36N 75 57 E
Chatsworth, Canada 84 B4 44 27N 80 54W
Chatsworth, Zimbabwe ...... 55 F3 19 38S 31 13 E
Chàttagâm = Chittagong, Bangla. 41 H17 22 19N 91 48 E
Chattahoochee, U.S.A. 83 K3 30 42N 84 51W
Chattahoochee ➤, U.S.A. ... 83 K3 30 54N 84 57W
Chattanooga, U.S.A. 83 H3 35 3N 85 19W
Chatteris, U.K. .... 13 E8 52 28N 0 2 E
Chaturat, Thailand .... 38 E3 15 40N 101 51 E
Chau Doc, Vietnam .... 39 G5 10 42N 105 7 E
Chaukan Pass, Burma .... 41 F20 27 0N 97 15 E
Chaumont, France .... 20 B6 48 7N 5 8 E
Chaumont, U.S.A. 85 B8 44 4N 76 8W
Chaunskaya G., Russia ..... 4 C16 69 0N 169 0 E
Chautauqua L., U.S.A. 84 D5 42 10N 79 24W
Chauvin, Canada 71 C6 52 45N 110 10W
Chaves, Brazil 93 D9 0 15S 49 55W
Chaves, Portugal 21 B2 41 45N 7 32W
Chawang, Thailand .... 39 H2 8 25N 99 30 E
Chaykovskiy, Russia .... 18 C9 56 47N 54 9 E
Chazy, U.S.A. 85 B11 44 53N 73 26W
Cheb, Czech Rep. .... 16 C7 50 9N 12 28 E
Cheboksary, Russia .... 18 C8 56 8N 47 12 E
Cheboygan, U.S.A. 82 C3 45 39N 84 29W
Chech, Erg, Africa 50 D5 25 0N 2 15W
Chechenia □, Russia .... 19 F8 43 30N 45 29 E
Checheno-Ingush Republic =
  Chechenia □, Russia .... 19 F8 43 30N 45 29 E
Chechnya = Chechenia □, Russia 19 F8 43 30N 45 29 E
Chech'ŏn, S. Korea .... 35 F15 37 8N 128 12 E
Checotah, U.S.A. 81 H7 35 28N 95 31W
Chedabucto B., Canada 73 C7 45 25N 61 8W
Cheduba I., Burma .... 41 K18 18 45N 93 40 E
Cheepie, Australia .... 63 D4 26 33S 145 1 E
Chegdomyn, Russia .... 29 D14 51 7N 133 1 E
Chegga, Mauritania 50 C4 25 27N 5 40W
Chegutu, Zimbabwe .... 55 F3 18 10S 30 14 E
Chehalis, U.S.A. 78 D4 46 40N 122 58W
Chehalis ➤, U.S.A. 78 D3 46 57N 123 50W
Cheju do, S. Korea .... 35 H14 33 29N 126 34 E
Chekiang = Zhejiang □, China 33 D7 29 0N 120 0 E
Chela, Sa. da, Angola ..... 56 B1 16 20S 13 20 E
Chelan, U.S.A. 76 C4 47 51N 120 1W
Chelan, L., U.S.A. 76 B3 48 11N 120 30W
Cheleken, Turkmenistan .... 19 G9 39 34N 53 16 E
Cheleken Yarymadasy,
  Turkmenistan .... 45 B7 39 30N 53 15 E
Chelforó, Argentina 96 D3 39 0S 66 33W
Chelkar = Shalqar, Kazakhstan 28 E6 47 48N 59 39 E
Chelkar Tengiz, Solonchak,
  Kazakhstan .... 28 E7 48 5N 63 7 E
Chełm, Poland .... 17 C12 51 8N 23 30 E
Chełmno, Poland .... 17 B10 53 20N 18 30 E
Chelmsford, U.K. .... 13 F8 51 44N 0 29 E
Chelsea, U.S.A. 85 C12 43 59N 72 27W
Cheltenham, U.K. 13 F5 51 54N 2 4W
Chelyabinsk, Russia .... 28 D7 55 10N 61 24 E
Chelyuskin, C. = Chelyuskin, Mys,
  Russia .... 29 B11 77 30N 103 0 E
Chelyuskin, Mys, Russia ... 29 B11 77 30N 103 0 E
Chemainus, Canada 78 B3 48 55N 123 42W
Chemba, Mozam. .... 53 H6 17 9S 34 53 E
Chemnitz, Germany .... 16 C7 50 51N 12 54 E
Chemult, U.S.A. 76 E3 43 14N 121 47W
Chen, Gora, Russia .... 29 C15 65 16N 141 50 E
Chenab ➤, Pakistan .... 42 D4 30 23N 71 2 E
Chenango Forks, U.S.A. 85 D9 42 15N 75 51W
Cheney, U.S.A. 76 C5 47 30N 117 35W
Cheng Xian, China .... 34 H3 33 43N 105 42 E
Chengcheng, China .... 34 G5 35 8N 109 56 E
Chengchou = Zhengzhou, China 34 G7 34 45N 113 34 E
Chengde, China .... 35 D9 40 59N 117 58 E
Chengdu, China .... 32 C5 30 38N 104 2 E
Chenggu, China .... 34 H4 33 10N 107 21 E
Chengjiang, China .... 32 D5 24 39N 103 0 E
Chengmai, China .... 38 C7 19 50N 109 58 E
Ch'engtu = Chengdu, China . 32 C5 30 38N 104 2 E
Chengwu, China .... 34 G8 34 58N 115 50 E
Chengyang, China .... 35 F11 36 18N 120 53 E
Chenjiagang, China .... 35 G10 34 23N 119 47 E
Chenkán, Mexico 87 D6 19 8N 90 58W
Cheo Reo, Vietnam .... 38 F7 13 25N 108 28 E
Cheom Ksan, Cambodia ...... 38 E5 14 13N 104 56 E
Chepén, Peru 92 E3 7 15S 79 23W
Chepes, Argentina 94 C2 31 20S 66 35W
Chepo, Panama 88 E4 9 10N 79 6W
Chepstow, U.K. 13 F5 51 38N 2 41W
Chequamegon B., U.S.A. 80 B9 46 40N 90 30W
Cher ➤, France .... 20 C4 47 21N 0 29 E
Cheraw, U.S.A. 83 H6 34 42N 79 53W
Cherbourg, France 20 B3 49 39N 1 40W
Cherdyn, Russia .... 18 B10 60 24N 56 29 E

Cheremkhovo, Russia .... 29 D11 53 8N 103 1 E
Cherepanovo, Russia .... 28 D9 54 15N 83 30 E
Cherepovets, Russia .... 18 C6 59 5N 37 55 E
Chergui, Chott ech, Algeria 50 B6 34 21N 0 25 E
Cherikov = Cherykaw, Belarus 17 B16 53 32N 31 20 E
Cherkasy, Ukraine .... 19 E5 49 27N 32 4 E
Cherkessk, Russia .... 19 F7 44 15N 42 5 E
Cherlak, Russia .... 28 D8 54 15N 74 55 E
Chernaya, Russia .... 29 B9 70 30N 89 10 E
Chernigov = Chernihiv, Ukraine 18 D5 51 28N 31 20 E
Chernihiv, Ukraine .... 18 D5 51 28N 31 20 E
Chernivtsi, Ukraine .... 17 D13 48 15N 25 52 E
Chernobyl = Chornobyl, Ukraine 17 C16 51 20N 30 15 E
Chernogorsk, Russia .... 29 D10 53 49N 91 18 E
Chernovtsy = Chernivtsi, Ukraine 17 D13 48 15N 25 52 E
Chernyakhovsk, Russia ..... 9 J19 54 36N 21 48 E
Chernysheyskiy, Russia .... 29 C12 63 0N 112 30 E
Cherokee, Iowa, U.S.A. 80 D7 42 45N 95 33W
Cherokee, Okla., U.S.A. ... 81 G5 36 45N 98 21W
Cherokee Village, U.S.A. .. 81 G9 36 17N 91 30W
Cherokees, Grand Lake O' The,
  U.S.A. 81 G7 36 28N 95 2W
Cherrapunji, India .... 41 G17 25 17N 91 47 E
Cherry Valley, Calif., U.S.A. 79 M10 33 59N 116 57W
Cherry Valley, N.Y., U.S.A. 85 D10 42 48N 74 45W
Cherskiy, Russia .... 29 C17 68 45N 161 18 E
Cherskogo Khrebet, Russia . 29 C15 65 0N 143 0 E
Cherven, Belarus .... 17 B15 53 45N 28 28 E
Chervonohrad, Ukraine ..... 17 C13 50 25N 24 10 E
Cherwell ➤, U.K. 13 F6 51 44N 1 14W
Cherykaw, Belarus .... 17 B16 53 32N 31 20 E
Chesapeake, U.S.A. 82 G7 36 50N 76 17W
Chesapeake B., U.S.A. 82 G7 38 0N 76 10W
Cheshire □, U.K. 12 D5 53 14N 2 30W
Cheshskaya Guba, Russia ... 18 A8 67 20N 47 0 E
Cheshunt, U.K. 13 F7 51 43N 0 1W
Chesil Beach, U.K. 13 G5 50 37N 2 33W
Chesley, Canada 84 B3 44 17N 81 5W
Chester, U.K. 12 D5 53 12N 2 53W
Chester, Calif., U.S.A. ... 76 F3 40 19N 121 14W
Chester, Ill., U.S.A. 81 G10 37 55N 89 49W
Chester, Mont., U.S.A. 76 B8 48 31N 110 58W
Chester, Pa., U.S.A. 82 F8 39 51N 75 22W
Chester, S.C., U.S.A. 83 H5 34 43N 81 12W
Chester, Vt., U.S.A. 85 C12 43 16N 72 36W
Chester, W. Va., U.S.A. ... 84 F4 40 37N 80 34W
Chester-le-Street, U.K. ... 12 C6 54 51N 1 34W
Chesterfield, U.K. 12 D6 53 15N 1 25W
Chesterfield, Is., N. Cal. . 64 J7 19 52S 158 15 E
Chesterfield Inlet, Canada 68 B10 63 30N 90 45W
Chesterton Ra., Australia . 63 D4 25 30S 147 27 E
Chesterton Range △, Australia 63 D4 26 16S 147 22 E
Chestertown, U.S.A. 85 C11 43 40N 73 48W
Chesterville, Canada 85 A9 45 6N 75 14W
Chestnut Ridge, U.S.A. 84 F5 40 20N 79 10W
Chesuncook L., U.S.A. 83 C11 46 0N 69 21W
Chéticamp, Canada 73 C7 46 37N 60 59W
Chetumal, Mexico 87 D7 18 30N 88 20W
Chetumal, B. de, Mexico ... 87 D7 18 40N 88 10W
Chetwynd, Canada 70 B4 55 45N 121 36W
Cheviot, The, U.K. 12 B5 55 29N 2 9W
Cheviot Hills, U.K. 12 B5 55 20N 2 24W
Cheviot Ra., Australia .... 62 D3 25 20S 143 45 E
Chew Bahir, Ethiopia ...... 47 G2 4 40N 36 50 E
Chewelah, U.S.A. 76 B5 48 17N 117 43W
Chewore △, Zimbabwe .... 55 F2 16 0S 29 52 E
Cheyenne, Okla., U.S.A. ... 81 H5 35 37N 99 40W
Cheyenne, Wyo., U.S.A. 80 E2 41 8N 104 49W
Cheyenne ➤, U.S.A. 80 C4 44 41N 101 18W
Cheyenne Wells, U.S.A. 80 F3 38 49N 102 21W
Cheyne B., Australia ...... 61 F2 34 35S 118 50 E
Chhabra, India .... 42 G7 24 40N 76 54 E
Chhaktala, India .... 42 H6 22 6N 74 11 E
Chhapra, India .... 43 G11 25 48N 84 44 E
Chhata, India .... 42 F7 27 42N 77 30 E
Chhatarpur, Jharkhand, India 43 G11 24 23N 84 11 E
Chhatarpur, Mad. P., India 43 G8 24 55N 79 35 E
Chhattisgarh □, India ..... 43 J10 22 0N 82 0 E
Chhep, Cambodia .... 38 F5 13 45N 105 24 E
Chhindwara, Mad. P., India 43 H8 23 3N 79 29 E
Chhindwara, Mad. P., India 43 H8 22 2N 78 59 E
Chhlong, Cambodia .... 39 F5 12 15S 105 58 E
Chhota Tawa ➤, India ...... 42 H7 22 14N 76 36 E
Chhoti Kali Sindh ➤, India 42 G6 24 2N 75 31 E
Chhuikhadan, India .... 43 J9 21 32N 80 59 E
Chhuk, Cambodia .... 39 G5 10 46N 104 28 E
Chi ➤, Thailand .... 38 E5 15 11N 104 43 E
Chiai, Taiwan .... 33 D7 23 29N 120 25 E
Chiamboni, Somali Rep. .... 52 E8 1 39S 41 35 E
Chiamussu = Jiamusi, China 33 B8 46 40N 130 26 E
Chiang Dao, Thailand ...... 38 C2 19 22N 98 58 E
Chiang Kham, Thailand ..... 38 C3 19 32N 100 18 E
Chiang Khan, Thailand ..... 38 D3 17 52N 101 36 E
Chiang Khong, Thailand .... 38 B3 20 17N 100 24 E
Chiang Mai, Thailand ...... 38 C2 18 47N 98 59 E
Chiang Rai, Thailand ...... 38 C2 19 52N 99 50 E
Chiang Saen, Thailand ..... 38 B3 20 16N 100 5 E
Chiapa ➤, Mexico 87 D6 16 42N 93 0W
Chiapa de Corzo, Mexico ... 87 D6 16 42N 93 0W
Chiapas □, Mexico 87 D6 17 0N 92 45W
Chiautla, Mexico 87 D5 18 18N 98 34W
Chiávari, Italy .... 20 D8 44 19N 9 19 E
Chiavenna, Italy .... 20 C8 46 19N 9 24 E
Chiba, Japan .... 31 G10 35 30N 140 7 E
Chiba □, Japan .... 31 G10 35 30N 140 20 E
Chibabava, Mozam. .... 57 C5 20 17S 33 35 E
Chibemba, Cunene, Angola .. 53 H2 15 48S 14 8 E
Chibemba, Huila, Angola ... 56 B2 16 20S 15 20 E
Chibi, Zimbabwe .... 57 C5 20 18S 30 25 E
Chibia, Angola .... 53 H2 15 10S 13 42 E
Chibougamau, Canada 72 C5 49 56N 74 24W
Chibougamau, L., Canada ... 72 C5 49 50N 74 20W
Chibuto, Mozam. .... 57 C5 24 40S 33 33 E
Chic-Chocs, Mts., Canada .. 73 C6 48 55N 66 0W
Chicacole = Srikakulam, India 41 K13 18 14N 83 58 E
Chicago, U.S.A. 82 E2 41 52N 87 38W
Chicago Heights, U.S.A. ... 82 E2 41 30N 87 38W
Chichagof I., U.S.A. 68 C6 57 30N 135 30W
Chichén-Itzá, Mexico 87 C7 20 40N 88 36W
Chicheng, China .... 34 D8 40 55N 115 55 E
Chichester, U.K. 13 G7 50 50N 0 47W
Chichester Ra., Australia . 60 D2 22 12S 119 15 E
Chichibu, Japan .... 31 F9 36 5N 139 10 E
Chichibu-Tama △, Japan .... 31 G9 35 52N 138 42 E
Ch'ich'ihaerh = Qiqihar, China 29 E13 47 26N 124 0 E
Chicholi, India .... 42 H8 22 1N 77 40 E
Chickasaw △, U.S.A. 81 H6 34 26N 97 0W

Chickasha, U.S.A. 81 H6 35 3N 97 58W
Chiclana de la Frontera, Spain . 21 D2 36 26N 6 9W
Chiclayo, Peru ... 92 E3 6 42S 79 50W
Chico, U.S.A. ... 78 F5 39 44N 121 50W
Chico →, Chubut, Argentina . 96 E3 44 0S 67 0W
Chico →, Santa Cruz, Argentina . 96 G3 50 0S 68 30W
Chicomo, Mozam. ... 57 C5 24 31S 34 6 E
Chicomostoc, Mexico . 86 C4 22 28N 102 49W
Chicontepec, Mexico . 87 C5 20 58N 98 10W
Chicopee, U.S.A. ... 85 D12 42 9N 72 37W
Chicoutimi, Canada . 73 C5 48 28N 71 5W
Chicualacuala, Mozam. . 57 C5 22 6S 31 42 E
Chidambaram, India . 40 P11 11 20N 79 45 E
Chidenguele, Mozam. . 57 C5 24 55S 34 11 E
Chidley, C., Canada . 69 B13 60 23N 64 26W
Chiducuane, Mozam. . 57 C5 24 35S 34 25 E
Chiede, Angola . 56 B2 17 15S 16 22 E
Chiefs Pt., Canada . 84 B3 44 41N 81 18W
Chiem Hoa, Vietnam . 38 A5 22 12N 105 17 E
Chiemsee, Germany . 16 E7 47 53N 12 28 E
Chiengi, Zambia . 55 D2 8 45S 29 10 E
Chiengmai = Chiang Mai, Thailand . 38 C2 18 47N 98 59 E
Chiese →, Italy . 20 D9 45 8N 10 25 E
Chieti, Italy . 22 C6 42 21N 14 10 E
Chifeng, China . 35 C10 42 18N 118 58 E
Chignecto B., Canada . 73 C7 45 30N 64 40W
Chiguana, Bolivia . 94 A2 21 0S 67 58W
Chigwell, U.K. . 13 F8 51 37N 0 5 E
Chiha-ri, N. Korea . 35 E14 38 40N 126 30 E
Chihli, G. of = Bo Hai, China . 35 E10 39 0N 119 0 E
Chihuahua, Mexico . 86 B3 28 40N 106 3W
Chihuahua □, Mexico . 86 B3 28 40N 106 3W
Chiili = Shieli, Kazakhstan . 28 E7 44 20N 66 15 E
Chik Bollapur, India . 40 N10 13 25N 77 45 E
Chikmagalur, India . 40 N9 13 15N 75 45 E
Chikwawa, Malawi . 55 F3 16 2S 34 50 E
Chilac, Mexico . 87 D5 18 20N 97 24W
Chilam Chavki, Pakistan . 43 B6 35 5N 75 5 E
Chilanga, Zambia . 55 F2 15 33S 28 16 E
Chilapa, Mexico . 87 D5 17 40N 99 11W
Chilas, Pakistan . 43 B6 35 25N 74 5 E
Chilaw, Sri Lanka . 40 R11 7 30N 79 50 E
Chilcotin →, Canada . 70 C4 51 44N 122 23W
Childers, Australia . 63 D5 25 15S 152 17 E
Childress, U.S.A. . 81 H4 34 25N 100 13W
Chile ■, S. Amer. . 96 D2 35 0S 72 0W
Chile Rise, Pac. Oc. . 65 L18 38 0S 92 0W
Chilecito, Argentina . 94 B2 29 10S 67 30W
Chilete, Peru . 92 E3 7 10S 78 50W
Chililabombwe, Zambia . 55 E2 12 18S 27 43 E
Chilin = Jilin, China . 35 C14 43 44N 126 30 E
Chilka L., India . 41 K14 19 40N 85 25 E
Chilko →, Canada . 70 C4 52 0N 123 40W
Chilko L., Canada . 70 C4 51 20N 124 10W
Chillagoe, Australia . 62 B3 17 7S 144 33 E
Chillán, Chile . 94 D1 36 40S 72 10W
Chillicothe, Ill., U.S.A. . 80 E10 40 55N 89 29W
Chillicothe, Mo., U.S.A. . 80 F8 39 48N 93 33W
Chillicothe, Ohio, U.S.A. . 82 F4 39 20N 82 59W
Chilliwack, Canada . 70 D4 49 10N 121 54W
Chilo, India . 42 F5 27 25N 73 32 E
Chiloane, I., Mozam. . 57 C5 20 40S 34 55 E
Chiloé, I. de, Chile . 96 E2 42 30S 73 50W
Chilpancingo, Mexico . 87 D5 17 30N 99 30W
Chiltern Hills, U.K. . 13 F7 51 40N 0 53W
Chilton, U.S.A. . 82 C1 44 2N 88 10W
Chilubi, Zambia . 55 E2 11 5S 29 58 E
Chilubula, Zambia . 55 E3 10 14S 30 51 E
Chilumba, Malawi . 55 E3 10 28S 34 12 E
Chilung, Taiwan . 33 D7 25 3N 121 45 E
Chilwa, L., Malawi . 55 F4 15 15S 35 40 E
Chimaltitán, Mexico . 86 C4 21 46N 103 50W
Chimán, Panama . 88 E4 8 45N 78 40W
Chimanimani, Zimbabwe . 57 B5 19 48S 32 52 E
Chimanimani △, Zimbabwe . 57 B5 19 48S 33 0 E
Chimay, Belgium . 15 D4 50 3N 4 20 E
Chimayo, U.S.A. . 77 H11 36 0N 105 56W
Chimbay, Uzbekistan . 28 E6 42 57N 59 47 E
Chimborazo, Ecuador . 92 D3 1 29S 78 55W
Chimbote, Peru . 92 E3 9 0S 78 35W
Chimkent = Shymkent, Kazakhstan . 28 E7 42 18N 69 36 E
Chimoio, Mozam. . 55 F3 19 4S 33 30 E
Chimpembe, Zambia . 55 D2 9 31S 29 33 E
Chin □, Burma . 41 J18 22 0N 93 0 E
Chin Ling Shan = Qinling Shandi, China . 34 H5 33 50N 108 10 E
China, Mexico . 87 B5 25 40N 99 20W
China ■, Asia . 33 C6 30 0N 110 0 E
China Lake, U.S.A. . 79 K9 35 44N 117 37W
Chinan = Jinan, China . 34 F9 36 38N 117 1 E
Chinandega, Nic. . 88 D2 12 35N 87 12W
Chinati Peak, U.S.A. . 81 L2 29 57N 104 29W
Chincha Alta, Peru . 92 F3 13 25S 76 7W
Chinchaga →, Canada . 70 B5 58 53N 118 20W
Chinchilla, Australia . 63 D5 26 45S 150 38 E
Chinchorro, Banco, Mexico . 87 D7 18 35N 87 20W
Chinchou = Jinzhou, China . 35 D11 41 5N 121 3 E
Chincoteague, U.S.A. . 82 G8 37 56N 75 23W
Chinde, Mozam. . 55 F4 18 35S 36 30 E
Chindo, S. Korea . 35 G14 34 28N 126 15 E
Chindwin →, Burma . 41 J19 21 26N 95 15 E
Chineni, India . 43 C6 33 2N 75 15 E
Chinga, Mozam. . 55 F4 15 13S 38 35 E
Chingola, Zambia . 55 E2 12 31S 27 53 E
Chingole, Malawi . 55 E3 13 4S 34 17 E
Ch'ingtao = Qingdao, China . 35 F11 36 5N 120 20 E
Chinguetti, Mauritania . 50 D3 20 25N 12 24W
Chingune, Mozam. . 57 C5 20 33S 34 58 E
Chinhae, S. Korea . 35 G15 35 9N 128 47 E
Chinhanguanine, Mozam. . 57 D5 25 21S 32 30 E
Chinhoyi, Zimbabwe . 55 F3 17 20S 30 8 E
Chini, India . 42 D8 31 32N 78 15 E
Chinipas, Mexico . 86 B3 27 22N 108 32W
Chinji, Pakistan . 42 C5 32 42N 72 22 E
Chinju, S. Korea . 35 G15 35 12N 128 2 E
Chinle, U.S.A. . 77 H9 36 9N 109 33W
Chinmen = Namp'o, N. Korea . 35 E13 38 52N 125 10 E
Chino, Japan . 31 G9 35 59N 138 9 E
Chino, U.S.A. . 79 L9 34 1N 117 41W
Chino Valley, U.S.A. . 77 J7 34 45N 112 27W
Chinon, France . 20 C4 47 10N 0 15 E
Chinook, U.S.A. . 76 B9 48 35N 109 14W
Chinsali, Zambia . 55 E3 10 30S 32 2 E
Chióggia, Italy . 22 B5 45 13N 12 17 E
Chíos = Khíos, Greece . 23 E12 38 27N 26 9 E

Chipata, Zambia . 55 E3 13 38S 32 28 E
Chipinge, Zimbabwe . 55 G3 20 13S 32 28 E
Chipinge △, Zimbabwe . 55 G3 20 14S 33 0 E
Chipley, U.S.A. . 83 K3 30 47N 85 32W
Chipman, Canada . 73 C6 46 6N 65 53W
Chipoka, Malawi . 55 E3 13 57S 34 28 E
Chippenham, U.K. . 13 F5 51 27N 2 6W
Chippewa →, U.S.A. . 80 C8 44 25N 92 5W
Chippewa Falls, U.S.A. . 80 C9 44 56N 91 24W
Chipping Norton, U.K. . 13 F6 51 56N 1 32W
Chiputneticook Lakes, U.S.A. . 83 C11 45 35N 67 35W
Chiquián, Peru . 92 F3 10 10S 77 0W
Chiquibul △, Belize . 88 C2 16 49N 88 52W
Chiquimula, Guatemala . 88 D2 14 51N 89 37W
Chiquinquira, Colombia . 92 B4 5 37N 73 50W
Chirala, India . 40 M12 15 50N 80 26 E
Chiramba, Mozam. . 55 F3 16 55S 34 39 E
Chirawa, India . 42 E6 28 14N 75 42 E
Chirchiq, Uzbekistan . 28 E7 41 29N 69 35 E
Chiredzi, Zimbabwe . 57 C5 21 0S 31 38 E
Chiricahua △, U.S.A. . 77 K9 32 0N 109 20W
Chiricahua Peak, U.S.A. . 77 L9 31 51N 109 18W
Chiriquí, G. de, Panama . 88 E3 8 0N 82 10W
Chiriquí, L. de, Panama . 88 E3 9 10N 82 0W
Chirisa △, Zimbabwe . 55 F2 17 53S 28 15 E
Chirivira Falls, Zimbabwe . 55 G3 21 10S 32 12 E
Chirmiri, India . 41 H13 23 15N 82 20 E
Chirripó Grande, Cerro, Costa Rica . 88 E3 9 29N 83 29W
Chirundu, Zimbabwe . 57 B4 16 3S 28 50 E
Chisamba, Zambia . 55 E2 14 55S 28 0 E
Chisapani Garhi, Nepal . 41 F14 27 30N 84 2 E
Chisasibi, Canada . 72 B4 53 50N 79 0W
Chisholm, Canada . 70 C6 54 55N 114 10W
Chisholm, U.S.A. . 80 B8 47 29N 92 53W
Chishtian Mandi, Pakistan . 42 E5 29 50N 72 55 E
Chisimaio, Somali Rep. . 49 G8 0 22S 42 32 E
Chisimba Falls, Zambia . 55 E3 10 12S 30 56 E
Chişinău, Moldova . 17 E15 47 2N 28 50 E
Chisos Mts., U.S.A. . 81 L3 29 5N 103 15W
Chistopol, Russia . 18 C9 55 25N 50 38 E
Chita, Russia . 29 D12 52 0N 113 35 E
Chitipa, Malawi . 55 D3 9 41S 33 19 E
Chitose, Japan . 30 C10 42 49N 141 39 E
Chitral, Pakistan . 40 B7 35 50N 71 56 E
Chitré, Panama . 88 E3 7 59N 80 27W
Chittagong, Bangla. . 41 H17 22 19N 91 48 E
Chittagong □, Bangla. . 41 G17 24 5N 91 0 E
Chittaurgarh, India . 42 G6 24 52N 74 38 E
Chittoor, India . 40 N11 13 15N 79 5 E
Chitungwiza, Zimbabwe . 55 F3 18 0S 31 6 E
Chiusi, Italy . 22 C4 43 1N 11 57 E
Chivasso, Italy . 20 D7 45 11N 7 53 E
Chivhu, Zimbabwe . 55 F3 19 2S 30 52 E
Chivilcoy, Argentina . 94 C4 34 55S 60 0W
Chiwanda, Tanzania . 55 E3 11 23S 34 55 E
Chizarira, Zimbabwe . 55 F2 17 36S 27 45 E
Chizarira △, Zimbabwe . 55 F2 17 44S 27 52 E
Chizera, Zambia . 55 E2 13 10S 25 0 E
Chkalov = Orenburg, Russia . 18 D10 51 45N 55 6 E
Chloride, U.S.A. . 79 K12 35 25N 114 12W
Cho Bo, Vietnam . 38 B5 20 46N 105 10 E
Cho-do, N. Korea . 35 E13 38 30N 124 40 E
Cho Phuoc Hai, Vietnam . 39 G6 10 26N 107 18 E
Choa Chu Kang, Singapore . 39 d 1 22N 103 41 E
Choba, Kenya . 54 B4 2 30N 38 5 E
Chobe △, Botswana . 56 B4 18 37S 24 23 E
Choch'iwŏn, S. Korea . 35 F14 36 37N 127 18 E
Chocolate Mts., U.S.A. . 79 M11 33 15N 115 15W
Choctawhatchee →, U.S.A. . 83 K3 30 25N 86 8W
Choele Choel, Argentina . 96 D3 39 11S 65 40W
Choiseul, St. Lucia . 89 f 13 47N 61 3W
Choix, Mexico . 86 B3 26 40N 108 23W
Chojnice, Poland . 17 B9 53 42N 17 32 E
Chōkai-San, Japan . 30 E10 39 6N 140 3 E
Choke Canyon L., U.S.A. . 81 L5 28 30N 98 20W
Chokurdakh, Russia . 29 B15 70 38N 147 55 E
Cholame, U.S.A. . 78 K6 35 44N 120 18W
Cholet, France . 20 C3 47 4N 0 52W
Cholguan, Chile . 94 D1 37 10S 72 3W
Choluteca, Honduras . 88 D2 13 20N 87 14W
Choluteca →, Honduras . 88 D2 13 0N 87 20W
Chom Bung, Thailand . 38 F2 13 37N 99 36 E
Chom Thong, Thailand . 38 C2 18 25N 98 41 E
Choma, Zambia . 55 F2 16 48S 26 59 E
Cholomolungma = Everest, Mt., Nepal . 43 E12 28 5N 86 58 E
Chomun, India . 42 F6 27 15N 75 40 E
Chomutov, Czech Rep. . 16 C7 50 28N 13 23 E
Chon Buri, Thailand . 38 F3 13 21N 101 1 E
Chon Thanh, Vietnam . 39 G6 11 24N 106 36 E
Ch'onan, S. Korea . 35 F14 36 48N 127 9 E
Chone, Ecuador . 92 D3 0 40S 80 0W
Chong Kai, Cambodia . 38 F4 13 57N 103 35 E
Chong Mek, Thailand . 38 E5 15 10N 105 27 E
Chong Phangan, Thailand . 39 b 9 39N 100 0 E
Chong Samui, Thailand . 39 b 9 21N 99 50 E
Chŏngdo, S. Korea . 35 G15 35 38N 128 42 E
Chŏngha, S. Korea . 35 F15 36 12N 129 21 E
Chŏngjin, N. Korea . 35 D15 41 47N 129 50 E
Chŏngju, N. Korea . 35 E13 39 40N 125 5 E
Chŏngju, S. Korea . 35 E13 39 40N 125 5 E
Chongli, China . 34 D8 40 58N 115 15 E
Chongqing, China . 32 D5 29 35N 106 25 E
Chongqing Shi □, China . 32 C5 30 0N 108 0 E
Chonguene, Mozam. . 57 C5 25 3S 33 49 E
Chŏngŭp, S. Korea . 35 G14 35 35N 126 50 E
Chŏnju, S. Korea . 35 G14 35 50N 127 4 E
Chonos, Arch. de los, Chile . 96 F2 45 0S 75 0W
Chop, Ukraine . 17 D12 48 26N 22 12 E
Chopim →, Brazil . 95 B5 25 35S 53 5W
Chor, Pakistan . 42 G3 25 31N 69 46 E
Chorbat La, India . 43 B7 34 42N 76 37 E
Chorley, U.K. . 12 D5 53 39N 2 38W
Chornobyl, Ukraine . 17 C16 51 20N 30 15 E
Choroque, Cerro, Bolivia . 94 A2 20 59S 66 5W
Chorregon, Australia . 62 C3 22 40S 143 32 E
Chorro el Indio △, Venezuela . 89 E5 7 43N 72 9W
Chortkiv, Ukraine . 17 D13 49 2N 25 46 E
Ch'orwon, S. Korea . 35 E14 38 15N 127 10 E
Chorzów, Poland . 17 C10 50 18N 18 57 E
Chos-Malal, Argentina . 94 D1 37 20S 70 15W
Ch'osan, N. Korea . 35 D13 40 50N 125 47 E
Choszczno, Poland . 16 B8 53 7N 15 25 E
Choteau, U.S.A. . 76 C7 47 49N 112 11W
Chotila, India . 42 H4 22 23N 71 15 E
Chotta Udepur, India . 42 H6 22 19N 74 1 E
Chowchilla, U.S.A. . 78 H6 37 7N 120 16W

Choybalsan, Mongolia . 33 B6 48 4N 114 30 E
Christchurch, N.Z. . 59 K4 43 33S 172 47 E
Christchurch, U.K. . 13 G6 50 44N 1 47W
Christian I., Canada . 84 B4 44 50N 80 12W
Christiana, S. Africa . 56 D4 27 52S 25 8 E
Christiansted, U.S. Virgin Is. . 89 C7 17 45N 64 42W
Christie B., Canada . 71 A6 62 32N 111 10W
Christina →, Canada . 71 B6 56 40N 111 3W
Christmas Cr. →, Australia . 60 C4 18 29S 125 23 E
Christmas I. = Kiritimati, Kiribati . 65 G12 1 58N 157 27W
Christmas I., Ind. Oc. . 64 J2 10 30S 105 40 E
Christopher L., Australia . 61 D4 24 49S 127 42 E
Chtimba, Malawi . 55 E3 10 35S 34 13 E
Chū = Shū, Kazakhstan . 28 E8 43 36N 73 42 E
Chū = Shū →, Kazakhstan . 26 E10 45 0N 67 44 E
Chu →, Vietnam . 38 C5 19 53N 105 45 E
Chu Lai, Vietnam . 38 E7 15 28N 108 45 E
Chuak, Ko, Thailand . 39 b 9 28N 99 41 E
Ch'uanchou = Quanzhou, China . 33 D6 24 55N 118 34 E
Chuankou, China . 34 G6 34 20N 110 59 E
Chubbuck, U.S.A. . 76 E7 42 55N 112 28W
Chūbu □, Japan . 31 F8 36 45N 137 30 E
Chūbu-Sangaku △, Japan . 31 F8 36 30N 137 40 E
Chubut →, Argentina . 96 E3 43 20S 65 5W
Chuchi L., Canada . 70 B4 55 12N 124 30W
Chuda, India . 42 H4 22 29N 71 41 E
Chudskoye, Ozero, Russia . 9 G22 58 13N 27 30 E
Chūgoku □, Japan . 31 G6 35 0N 133 0 E
Chūgoku-Sanchi, Japan . 31 G6 35 0N 133 0 E
Chugwater, U.S.A. . 80 E2 41 46N 104 50W
Chukchi Sea, Russia . 29 C19 68 0N 175 0W
Chukotskoye Nagorye, Russia . 29 C18 68 0N 175 0 E
Chula Vista, U.S.A. . 79 N9 32 39N 117 5W
Chulucanas, Peru . 92 E2 5 8S 80 10W
Chulym →, Russia . 28 D9 57 43N 83 51 E
Chum Phae, Thailand . 38 D4 16 40N 102 6 E
Chum Saeng, Thailand . 38 E3 15 55N 100 15 E
Chumar, India . 43 C8 32 40N 78 35 E
Chumbicha, Argentina . 94 B2 29 0S 66 10W
Chumikan, Russia . 29 D14 54 40N 135 10 E
Chumphon, Thailand . 39 G2 10 35N 99 14 E
Chumuare, Mozam. . 55 E3 14 31S 31 50 E
Chumunjin, S. Korea . 35 F15 37 55N 128 54 E
Chuna →, Russia . 29 D10 57 47N 94 37 E
Chunchura, India . 43 H13 22 53N 88 27 E
Chunga, Zambia . 55 F2 15 0S 26 2 E
Chunggang-ŭp, N. Korea . 35 D14 41 48N 126 48 E
Chunghwa, N. Korea . 35 E13 38 52N 125 47 E
Ch'ungju, S. Korea . 35 F14 36 58N 127 58 E
Chungking = Chongqing, China . 32 D5 29 35N 106 25 E
Ch'ungmu, S. Korea . 35 G15 34 50N 128 20 E
Chungt'iaoshan = Zhongtiao Shan, China . 34 G6 35 0N 111 10 E
Chunian, Pakistan . 42 D6 30 57N 74 0 E
Chunya, Tanzania . 55 D3 8 30S 33 27 E
Chunyang, China . 35 C15 43 38N 129 23 E
Chupara Pt., Trin. & Tob. . 93 K15 10 49N 61 22W
Chuquibamba, Peru . 92 G4 15 47S 72 44W
Chuquicamata, Chile . 94 A2 22 15S 69 0W
Chur, Switz. . 20 C8 46 52N 9 32 E
Churachandpur, India . 41 G18 24 20N 93 40 E
Church Stretton, U.K. . 13 E5 52 32N 2 48W
Churchill, Canada . 71 B10 58 47N 94 11W
Churchill →, Man., Canada . 71 B10 58 47N 94 12W
Churchill →, Nfld. & L., Canada . 73 B7 53 19N 60 10W
Churchill, C., Canada . 71 B10 58 46N 93 12W
Churchill Falls, Canada . 73 B7 53 36N 64 19W
Churchill L., Canada . 71 B7 55 55N 108 20W
Churchill Pk., Canada . 70 B3 58 10N 125 10W
Churki, India . 43 H10 23 50N 83 12 E
Churu, India . 42 E6 28 20N 74 50 E
Churún Merú = Angel Falls, Venezuela . 92 B6 5 57N 62 30W
Chushal, India . 43 C8 33 40N 78 40 E
Chuska Mts., U.S.A. . 77 H9 36 15N 108 50W
Chusovoy, Russia . 18 C10 58 22N 57 50 E
Chute-aux-Outardes, Canada . 73 C6 49 7N 68 24W
Chuuronjang, N. Korea . 35 D15 41 35N 129 40 E
Chuvash Republic = Chuvashia □, Russia . 18 C8 55 30N 47 0 E
Chuvashia □, Russia . 18 C8 55 30N 47 0 E
Chuwārtah, Iraq . 44 C5 35 43N 45 34 E
Chuy, Uruguay . 95 C5 33 41S 53 27W
Ci Xian, China . 34 F8 36 20N 114 25 E
Ciadâr-Lunga, Moldova . 17 E15 46 3N 28 51 E
Ciamis, Indonesia . 37 G13 7 20S 108 21 E
Cianjur, Indonesia . 37 G12 6 49S 107 8 E
Cianorte, Brazil . 95 A5 23 37S 52 37W
Cibola, U.S.A. . 79 M12 33 17N 114 42W
Cicero, U.S.A. . 82 E2 41 51N 87 45W
Ciénagas del Catatumbo △, Venezuela . 89 E5 9 25N 71 54W
Ciechanów, Poland . 17 B11 52 52N 20 38 E
Ciego de Avila, Cuba . 88 B4 21 50N 78 50W
Ciénaga, Colombia . 92 A4 11 1N 74 15W
Cienfuegos, Cuba . 88 B3 22 10N 80 30W
Cieszyn, Poland . 17 D10 49 45N 18 35 E
Cieza, Spain . 21 C5 38 17N 1 23W
Cihuatlán, Mexico . 86 D4 19 14N 104 35W
Cijara, Embalse de, Spain . 21 C3 39 18N 4 52W
Cijulang, Indonesia . 37 G13 7 42S 108 27 E
Cilacap, Indonesia . 37 G13 7 43S 109 0 E
Cill Chainnigh = Kilkenny, Ireland . 10 D4 52 39N 7 15W
Cilo Dağı, Turkey . 19 G7 37 28N 43 55 E
Cima, U.S.A. . 79 K11 35 14N 115 30W
Cimarron, Kans., U.S.A. . 81 G4 37 48N 100 21W
Cimarron, N. Mex., U.S.A. . 81 G2 36 31N 104 55W
Cimarron →, U.S.A. . 81 J6 36 10N 96 17W
Cimişlia, Moldova . 17 E15 46 34N 28 44 E
Cimone, Mte., Italy . 22 B4 44 12N 10 42 E
Cinca →, Spain . 21 B6 41 26N 0 21 E
Cincar, Bos.-H. . 22 C7 43 55N 17 5 E
Cincinnati, U.S.A. . 82 F3 39 6N 84 31W
Cincinnatus, U.S.A. . 85 D9 42 33N 75 54W
Çine, Turkey . 23 F13 37 37N 28 2 E
Ciney, Belgium . 15 D5 50 18N 5 5 E
Cinto, Mte., France . 20 E8 42 24N 8 54 E
Circle, Alaska, U.S.A. . 68 B5 65 50N 144 4W
Circle, Mont., U.S.A. . 76 B2 47 25N 105 35W
Circleville, U.S.A. . 82 F4 39 36N 82 57W
Cirebon, Indonesia . 37 G13 6 45S 108 32 E
Ciremay, Indonesia . 37 G13 6 55S 108 27 E
Cirencester, U.K. . 13 F6 51 43N 1 57W
Cirium, Cyprus . 25 E11 34 40N 32 53 E
Cisco, U.S.A. . 81 J5 32 23N 98 59W
Citlaltépetl = Orizaba, Pico de, Mexico . 87 D5 19 0N 97 20W

Citrus Heights, U.S.A. . 78 G5 38 42N 121 17W
Citrusdal, S. Africa . 56 E2 32 35S 19 0 E
Città di Castello, Italy . 22 C5 43 27N 12 14 E
Ciudad Altamirano, Mexico . 86 D4 18 20N 100 40W
Ciudad Bolívar, Venezuela . 92 B6 8 5N 63 36W
Ciudad Camargo, Mexico . 86 B3 27 41N 105 10W
Ciudad de Valles, Mexico . 87 C5 22 0N 99 0W
Ciudad del Carmen, Mexico . 87 D6 18 38N 91 50W
Ciudad del Este, Paraguay . 95 B5 25 30S 54 50W
Ciudad Delicias = Delicias, Mexico . 86 B3 28 10N 105 30W
Ciudad Guayana, Venezuela . 92 B6 8 0N 62 30W
Ciudad Guerrero, Mexico . 86 B3 28 33N 107 28W
Ciudad Guzmán, Mexico . 86 D4 19 40N 103 30W
Ciudad Juárez, Mexico . 86 A3 31 40N 106 28W
Ciudad Madero, Mexico . 87 C5 22 19N 97 50W
Ciudad Mante, Mexico . 87 C5 22 50N 99 0W
Ciudad Obregón, Mexico . 86 B3 27 28N 109 59W
Ciudad Real, Spain . 21 C4 38 59N 3 55W
Ciudad Rodrigo, Spain . 21 B2 40 35N 6 32W
Ciudad Victoria, Mexico . 87 C5 23 41N 99 9W
Ciudadela, Spain . 24 B10 40 0N 3 50 E
Civitanova Marche, Italy . 22 C5 43 18N 13 44 E
Civitavécchia, Italy . 22 C4 42 6N 11 48 E
Cizre, Turkey . 19 G7 37 19N 42 10 E
Clackmannanshire □, U.K. . 11 E5 56 10N 3 43W
Clacton-on-Sea, U.K. . 13 F9 51 47N 1 11 E
Claire, L., Canada . 70 B6 58 35N 112 5W
Clairton, U.S.A. . 84 F5 40 18N 79 53W
Clallam Bay, U.S.A. . 78 B2 48 15N 124 16W
Clanton, U.S.A. . 83 J2 32 51N 86 38W
Clanwilliam, S. Africa . 56 E2 32 11S 18 52 E
Clara, Ireland . 10 C4 53 21N 7 37W
Claraville, U.S.A. . 79 K8 35 24N 118 20W
Clare, Australia . 63 E2 33 50S 138 37 E
Clare, U.S.A. . 82 D3 43 49N 84 46W
Clare □, Ireland . 10 D3 52 45N 9 0W
Clare →, Ireland . 10 C2 53 20N 9 2W
Clare I., Ireland . 10 C1 53 49N 10 0W
Claremont, Calif., U.S.A. . 79 L9 34 6N 117 43W
Claremont, N.H., U.S.A. . 85 C12 43 23N 72 20W
Claremont Pt., Australia . 62 A3 14 1S 143 41 E
Claremore, U.S.A. . 81 G7 36 19N 95 36W
Claremorris, Ireland . 10 C3 53 45N 9 0W
Clarence →, Australia . 63 D5 29 25S 153 22 E
Clarence →, N.Z. . 59 K4 42 10S 173 56 E
Clarence, I., Chile . 96 G2 54 0S 72 0W
Clarence I., Antarctica . 5 C18 61 10S 54 0W
Clarence Str., Australia . 60 B5 12 0S 131 0 E
Clarence Town, Bahamas . 89 B5 23 6N 74 59W
Clarendon, Pa., U.S.A. . 84 E5 41 47N 79 6W
Clarendon, Tex., U.S.A. . 81 H4 34 56N 100 53W
Clarenville-Shoal Harbour, Canada . 73 C9 48 10N 54 1W
Claresholm, Canada . 70 D6 50 2N 113 33W
Clarie Coast, Antarctica . 5 C9 68 0S 135 0 E
Clarinda, U.S.A. . 80 E7 40 44N 95 2W
Clarington, Canada . 84 C6 43 55N 78 41W
Clarion, Iowa, U.S.A. . 80 D8 42 44N 93 44W
Clarion, Pa., U.S.A. . 84 E5 41 13N 79 23W
Clarion →, U.S.A. . 84 E5 41 7N 79 41W
Clark, U.S.A. . 80 C6 44 53N 97 44W
Clark, Pt., Canada . 84 B3 44 4N 81 45W
Clark Fork, U.S.A. . 76 B5 48 9N 116 11W
Clark Fork →, U.S.A. . 76 B5 48 9N 116 15W
Clarkdale, U.S.A. . 77 J7 34 46N 112 3W
Clarke City, Canada . 73 B6 50 12N 66 38W
Clarke I., Australia . 63 G4 40 32S 148 10 E
Clarke Ra., Australia . 62 J6 20 40S 148 30 E
Clark's Fork →, U.S.A. . 76 D9 45 39N 108 43W
Clark's Harbour, Canada . 73 D6 43 25N 65 38W
Clarks Hill L., U.S.A. . 83 J4 33 40N 82 12W
Clarks Summit, U.S.A. . 85 E9 41 30N 75 42W
Clarksburg, U.S.A. . 82 F5 39 17N 80 30W
Clarksdale, U.S.A. . 81 H9 34 12N 90 35W
Clarksville, Ark., U.S.A. . 81 H8 35 28N 93 28W
Clarksville, Tenn., U.S.A. . 83 G2 36 32N 87 21W
Clarksville, Tex., U.S.A. . 81 J7 33 37N 95 3W
Clatskanie, U.S.A. . 78 D3 46 6N 123 12W
Claude, U.S.A. . 81 H4 35 7N 101 22W
Claveria, Phil. . 37 A6 18 37N 121 4 E
Clay, U.S.A. . 78 G5 38 17N 121 10W
Clay Center, U.S.A. . 80 F6 39 23N 97 8W
Claypool, U.S.A. . 77 K8 33 25N 110 51W
Claysburg, U.S.A. . 84 F6 40 17N 78 27W
Claysville, U.S.A. . 84 F4 40 7N 80 25W
Clayton, N. Mex., U.S.A. . 81 G3 36 27N 103 11W
Clayton, N.Y., U.S.A. . 85 B8 44 14N 76 5W
Clear, C., Ireland . 10 E2 51 25N 9 32W
Clear, L., Canada . 84 A7 45 26N 77 12W
Clear Hills, Canada . 70 B5 56 40N 119 30W
Clear I., Ireland . 10 E2 51 26N 9 30W
Clear L., U.S.A. . 78 F4 39 2N 122 47W
Clear Lake, Iowa, U.S.A. . 80 D8 43 8N 93 23W
Clear Lake, S. Dak., U.S.A. . 80 C6 44 45N 96 41W
Clear Lake Reservoir, U.S.A. . 76 F3 41 56N 121 5W
Clearfield, Pa., U.S.A. . 84 E6 41 2N 78 27W
Clearfield, Utah, U.S.A. . 76 F8 41 7N 112 2W
Clearlake, U.S.A. . 76 G2 38 57N 122 38W
Clearlake Highlands, U.S.A. . 78 G4 38 57N 122 38W
Clearwater, Canada . 70 C4 51 38N 120 2W
Clearwater →, Alta., Canada . 70 C6 52 22N 114 57W
Clearwater →, Alta., Canada . 71 B6 56 44N 111 23W
Clearwater L., Canada . 71 C9 53 34N 99 49W
Clearwater Mts., U.S.A. . 76 C6 46 5N 115 20W
Clearwater River △, Canada . 71 B7 56 55N 109 10W
Cleburne, U.S.A. . 81 J6 32 21N 97 23W
Clee Hills, U.K. . 13 E5 52 26N 2 35W
Cleethorpes, U.K. . 12 D7 53 33N 0 3W
Cleeve Cloud, U.K. . 13 F6 51 56N 2 0W
Clemson, U.S.A. . 83 H4 34 41N 82 50W
Clerke Reef, Australia . 60 C2 17 22S 119 20 E
Clermont, Australia . 62 C4 22 49S 147 39 E
Clermont, U.S.A. . 83 L5 28 33N 81 46W
Clermont-Ferrand, France . 20 D5 45 46N 3 4 E
Clervaux, Lux. . 15 D6 50 4N 6 2 E
Clevedon, U.K. . 13 F5 51 26N 2 52W
Cleveland, Miss., U.S.A. . 81 J9 33 45N 90 43W
Cleveland, Ohio, U.S.A. . 84 E3 41 30N 81 42W
Cleveland, Okla., U.S.A. . 81 G6 36 19N 96 28W
Cleveland, Tenn., U.S.A. . 83 H3 35 10N 84 53W
Cleveland, Tex., U.S.A. . 81 K7 30 21N 95 5W
Cleveland, Mt., U.S.A. . 76 B7 48 56N 113 51W
Cleveland, C., Australia . 62 B4 19 11S 147 1 E
Cleveland Heights, U.S.A. . 84 E3 41 30N 81 34W
Clevelândia, Brazil . 95 B5 26 24S 52 23W

Clew B., Ireland 10 C2   53 50N   9 49W
Clewiston, U.S.A. 83 M5   26 45N   80 56W
Clifden, Ireland 10 C1   53 29N   10 1W
Clifden, N.Z. . . . . 59 M1   46 1S 167 42 E
Cliffdell, U.S.A. 78 D5   46 56N 121 5W
Cliffy Hd., Australia . . . . 61 G2   35 1S 116 29 E
Clifton, Australia . . . . 63 D5   27 59S 151 53 E
Clifton, Ariz., U.S.A. 77 K9   33 3N 109 18W
Clifton, Colo., U.S.A. 77 G9   39 7N 108 25W
Clifton, Tex., U.S.A. 81 K6   31 47N   97 35W
Clifton Beach, Australia . . . . . 62 B4   16 46S 145 39 E
Climax, Canada 71 D7   49 10N 108 20W
Clinch →, U.S.A. 83 H3   35 53N   84 29W
Clingmans Dome, U.S.A. 83 H4   35 34N   83 30W
Clint, U.S.A. 77 L10 31 35N 106 14W
Clinton, B.C., Canada 70 C4   51 6N 121 35W
Clinton, Ont., Canada 84 C3   43 37N   81 32W
Clinton, N.Z. . . . . 59 M2   46 12S 169 23 E
Clinton, Ark., U.S.A. 81 H8   35 36N   92 28W
Clinton, Conn., U.S.A. 85 E12 41 17N   72 32W
Clinton, Ill., U.S.A. 80 E10 40 9N   88 57W
Clinton, Ind., U.S.A. 82 F2   39 40N   87 24W
Clinton, Iowa, U.S.A. 80 E9   41 51N   90 12W
Clinton, Mass., U.S.A. 85 D13 42 25N   71 41W
Clinton, Miss., U.S.A. 81 J9   32 20N   90 20W
Clinton, Mo., U.S.A. 80 F8   38 22N   93 46W
Clinton, N.C., U.S.A. 83 H6   35 0N   78 22W
Clinton, Okla., U.S.A. 81 H5   35 31N   98 58W
Clinton, S.C., U.S.A. 83 H5   34 29N   81 53W
Clinton, Tenn., U.S.A. 83 G3   36 6N   84 8W
Clinton, Wash., U.S.A. 78 C4   47 59N 122 21W
Clinton C., Australia . . . . 62 C5   22 30S 150 45 E
Clinton Colden L., Canada . . . 68 B9   63 58N 107 27W
Clintonville, U.S.A. 80 C10 44 37N   88 46W
Clipperton, I., Pac. Oc. 65 F17 10 18N 109 13W
Clisham, U.K. 11 D2   57 57N   6 49W
Clitheroe, U.K. 12 D5   53 53N   2 22W
Clo-oose, Canada 78 B2   48 39N 124 49W
Cloates, Pt., Australia . . . . 60 D1   22 43S 113 40 E
Clocolan, S. Africa . . . . 57 D4   28 55S   27 34 E
Clodomira, Argentina 94 B3   27 35S   64 14W
Clogher Hd., Ireland 10 C5   53 48N   6 14W
Clonakilty, Ireland 10 E3   51 37N   8 53W
Clonakilty B., Ireland 10 E3   51 35N   8 51W
Cloncurry, Australia . . . . 62 C3   20 40S 140 28 E
Cloncurry →, Australia . . . . . . 62 B3   18 37S 140 40 E
Clondalkin, Ireland 10 C5   53 19N   6 25W
Clones, Ireland 10 B4   54 11N   7 15W
Clonmel, Ireland 10 D4   52 21N   7 42W
Cloquet, U.S.A. 80 B8   46 43N   92 28W
Clorinda, Argentina 94 B4   25 16S   57 45W
Cloud Bay, Canada 72 C2   48 5N   89 26W
Cloud Peak, U.S.A. 76 D10 44 23N 107 11W
Cloudcroft, U.S.A. 77 K11 32 58N 105 45W
Cloverdale, U.S.A. 78 G4   38 48N 123 1W
Clovis, Calif., U.S.A. 78 J7   36 49N 119 42W
Clovis, N. Mex., U.S.A. 81 H3   34 24N 103 12W
Cloyne, Canada 84 B7   44 49N   77 11W
Cluj-Napoca, Romania . . . . 17 E12 46 47N   23 38 E
Clunes, Australia . . . . 63 F3   37 20S 143 45 E
Clutha →, N.Z. . . . . 59 M2   46 20S 169 49 E
Clwyd □, U.K. 12 D4   53 19N   3 31W
Clyde, Canada 70 C6   54 9N 113 39W
Clyde, N.Z. . . . . 59 L2   45 12S 169 20 E
Clyde, U.S.A. 84 C8   43 5N   76 52W
Clyde →, U.K. 11 F4   55 55N   4 30W
Clyde, Firth of, U.K. 11 F3   55 22N   5 1W
Clyde Muirshiel △, U.K. 11 F4   55 50N   4 40W
Clyde River, Canada 69 A13 70 30N   68 30W
Clydebank, U.K. 11 F4   55 54N   4 23W
Clymer, N.Y., U.S.A. 84 D5   42 1N   79 37W
Clymer, Pa., U.S.A. 84 D5   40 40N   79 1W
Coachella, U.S.A. 79 M10 33 41N 116 10W
Coachella Canal, U.S.A. 79 N12 32 43N 114 57W
Coahoma, U.S.A. 81 J4   32 18N 101 18W
Coahuayana →, Mexico 86 D4   18 41N 103 45W
Coahuila □, Mexico 86 B4   27 0N 103 0W
Coal →, Canada 70 B3   59 39N 126 57W
Coalane, Mozam. . . . . 55 F4   17 48S   37 2 E
Coalcomán, Mexico 86 D4   18 40N 103 10W
Coaldale, Canada 70 D6   49 45N 112 35W
Coalgate, U.S.A. 81 H6   34 32N   96 13W
Coalinga, U.S.A. 78 J6   36 9N 120 21W
Coalisland, U.K. 10 B5   54 33N   6 42W
Coalville, U.K. 12 E6   52 44N   1 23W
Coalville, U.S.A. 76 F8   40 55N 111 24W
Coamo, Puerto Rico . . . . 89 d   18 5N   66 22W
Coari, Brazil 92 D6   4 8S   63 7W
Coast □, Kenya . . . . 54 C4   2 40S   39 45 E
Coast Mts., Canada 70 C3   55 0N 129 20W
Coast Ranges, U.S.A. 78 G4   39 0N 123 0W
Coatbridge, U.K. 11 F4   55 52N   4 6W
Coatepec, Mexico 87 D5   19 27N   96 58W
Coatepeque, Guatemala 88 D1   14 46N   91 55W
Coatesville, U.S.A. 82 F8   39 59N   75 50W
Coaticook, Canada 85 A13 45 10N   71 46W
Coats I., Canada 69 B11 62 30N   83 0W
Coats Land, Antarctica 5 D1   77 0S   25 0W
Coatzacoalcos, Mexico 87 D6   18 7N   94 25W
Coba, Mexico 87 C7   20 31N   87 39W
Cobalt, Canada 72 C4   47 25N   79 42W
Cobán, Guatemala 88 C1   15 30N   90 21W
Cobar, Australia . . . . 63 E4   31 27S 145 48 E
Cóbh, Ireland 10 E3   51 51N   8 17W
Cobija, Bolivia 92 F5   11 0S   68 50W
Cobleskill, U.S.A. 85 D10 42 41N   74 29W
Coboconk, Canada 84 B6   44 39N   78 48W
Cobourg, Canada 84 C6   43 58N   78 10W
Cobourg →, Australia . . . . 60 B5   11 26S 131 58 E
Cobourg Pen., Australia . . . . . 60 B5   11 20S 132 15 E
Cobram, Australia . . . . 63 F4   35 54S 145 40 E
Cóbué, Mozam. . . . . 55 E3   12 0S   34 58 E
Coburg, Germany . . . . 16 C6   50 15N   10 58 E
Cocanada = Kakinada, India . . 41 L13 16 57N   82 11 E
Cochabamba, Bolivia 92 G5   17 26S   66 10W
Cochemane, Mozam. . . . . 55 F3   17 0S   32 54 E
Cochin, India . . . . 40 Q10 9 58N   76 20 E
Cochin China = Nam-Phan,
  Vietnam . . . . 39 G6   10 30N 106 0 E
Cochran, U.S.A. 83 J4   32 23N   83 21W
Cochrane, Alta., Canada 70 C6   51 11N 114 30W
Cochrane, Ont., Canada 72 C3   49 0N   81 0W
Cochrane, Chile 96 F2   47 15S   72 33W
Cochrane →, Canada 71 B8   59 0N 103 40W
Cochrane, L., Chile 96 F2   47 10S   72 0W
Cochranton, U.S.A. 84 E4   41 31N   80 3W
Cockburn, Australia . . . . 63 E3   32 5S 141 0 E
Cockburn, Canal, Chile 96 G2   54 30S   72 0W

Cockburn I., Canada 72 C3   45 55N   83 22W
Cockburn Ra., Australia . . . . . 60 C4   15 46S 128 0 E
Cockermouth, U.K. 12 C4   54 40N   3 22W
Cocklebiddy, Australia . . . . 61 F4   32 0S 126 3 E
Coco →, Cent. Amer. 88 D3   15 0N   83 8W
Coco, I. del, Pac. Oc. 65 G19 5 25N   87 55W
Cocoa, U.S.A. 83 L5   28 21N   80 44W
Cocobeach, Gabon . . . . 52 D1   0 59N   9 34 E
Cocos B., Trin. & Tob. 93 K15 10 25N   61 2W
Cocos Is., Ind. Oc. . . . . 64 J1   12 10S   96 55 E
Cod, C., U.S.A. 82 D10 42 5N   70 10W
Codajás, Brazil 92 D6   3 55S   62 0W
Codó, Brazil 93 D10   4 30S   43 55W
Cody, U.S.A. 76 D9   44 32N 109 3W
Coe Hill, Canada 84 B7   44 52N   77 50W
Coelemu, Chile 94 D1   36 30S   72 48W
Coen, Australia . . . . 62 A3   13 52S 143 12 E
Cœur d'Alene, U.S.A. 76 C5   47 45N 116 51W
Cœur d'Alene L., U.S.A. 76 C5   47 32N 116 48W
Coevorden, Neths. . . . . 15 B6   52 40N   6 44 E
Cofete, Canary Is. 24 F5   28 6N   14 23W
Coffeyville, U.S.A. 81 G7   37 2N   95 37W
Coffin B., Australia . . . . 63 E2   34 38S 135 28 E
Coffin Bay, Australia . . . . 63 E2   34 37S 135 29 E
Coffin Bay △, Australia . . . . . . 63 E2   34 34S 135 19 E
Coffin Bay Peninsula, Australia . 63 E2   34 32S 135 15 E
Coffs Harbour, Australia 87 D5   19 29N   97 8W
Cofre de Perote △, Mexico . . . 87 D5   19 29N   97 8W
Cognac, France 20 D3   45 41N   0 20W
Cohocton, U.S.A. 84 D7   42 30N   77 30W
Cohocton →, U.S.A. 84 D7   42 9N   77 6W
Cohoes, U.S.A. 85 D11 42 46N   73 42W
Cohuna, Australia . . . . 63 F3   35 45S 144 15 E
Coiba, I., Panama 88 E3   7 30N   81 40W
Coig →, Argentina 96 G3   51 0S   69 10W
Coigeach, Rubha, U.K. 11 C3   58 6N   5 26W
Coihaique, Chile 96 F2   45 30S   71 45W
Coimbatore, India . . . . 40 P10 11 2N   76 59 E
Coimbra, Brazil 92 G7   19 55S   57 48W
Coimbra, Portugal 21 B1   40 15N   8 27W
Coín, Spain 21 D3   36 40N   4 48W
Coipasa, Salar de, Bolivia 92 G5   19 26S   68 9W
Cojimies, Ecuador 92 C3   0 20N   80 0W
Cojutepequé, El Salv. 88 D2   13 41N   88 54W
Cokeville, U.S.A. 76 E8   42 5N 110 57W
Colac, Australia . . . . 63 F3   38 21S 143 35 E
Colatina, Brazil 93 G10 19 32S   40 37W
Colbeck, C., Antarctica 5 D13 77 6S 157 48W
Colborne, Canada 84 C7   44 0N   77 53W
Colby, U.S.A. 80 F4   39 24N 101 3W
Colchester, U.K. . . . . 13 F8   51 54N   0 55 E
Cold L., Canada 71 C7   54 33N 110 5W
Coldstream, Canada 70 C5   50 13N 119 11W
Coldstream, U.K. 11 F6   55 39N   2 15W
Coldwater, Canada 84 B5   44 42N   79 40W
Coldwater, Kans., U.S.A. 81 G5   37 16N   99 20W
Coldwater, Mich., U.S.A. 82 E3   41 57N   85 0W
Colebrook, U.S.A. 85 B13 44 54N   71 30W
Coleman, U.S.A. 81 K5   31 50N   99 26W
Coleman →, Australia . . . . 62 B3   15 6S 141 38 E
Colenso, S. Africa . . . . 57 D4   28 44S 129 52 E
Coleraine, Australia . . . . 63 F3   37 36S 141 40 E
Coleraine, U.K. 10 A5   55 8N   6 41W
Coleridge, L., N.Z. . . . . 59 K3   43 17S 171 30 E
Colesberg, S. Africa . . . . 56 E4   30 45S   25 5 E
Coleville, U.S.A. 78 G7   38 34N 119 30W
Colfax, Calif., U.S.A. 78 F6   39 6N 120 57W
Colfax, La., U.S.A. 81 K8   31 31N   92 42W
Colfax, Wash., U.S.A. 76 C5   46 53N 117 22W
Colhué Huapí, L., Argentina . . 96 F3   45 30S   69 0W
Coligny, S. Africa . . . . 57 D4   26 17S   26 15 E
Colima, Mexico 86 D4   19 14N 103 43W
Colima □, Mexico 86 D4   19 10N 103 40W
Colima, Nevado de, Mexico . . 86 D4   19 35N 103 45W
Colina, Chile 94 C1   33 13S   70 45W
Colinas, Brazil 93 E10   6 0S   44 10W
Coll, U.K. 11 E2   56 39N   6 34W
Collaguasi, Chile 94 A2   21 5S   68 45W
Collarenebri, Australia . . . . 63 D4   29 33S 148 34 E
Colleen Bawn, Zimbabwe . . . . 55 G2   21 0S   29 12 E
College Park, U.S.A. 83 J3   33 40N   84 27W
College Station, U.S.A. 81 K6   30 37N   96 21W
Collie, Australia . . . . 61 F2   33 22S 116 8 E
Collier B., Australia . . . . 60 C3   16 10S 124 15 E
Collier Ra., Australia . . . . 61 D2   24 45S 119 10 E
Collier Range △, Australia . . . 61 D2   24 39S 119 7 E
Collina, Passo di, Italy . . . . 22 B4   44 2N   10 56 E
Collingwood, Canada 84 B4   44 29N   80 13W
Collingwood, N.Z. . . . . 59 J4   40 41S 172 40 E
Collins, Canada 72 B2   50 17N   89 27W
Collinsville, Australia . . . . 62 C4   20 30S 147 56 E
Collooney, Ireland 10 B3   54 11N   8 29W
Colmar, France . . . . 20 B7   48 5N   7 20 E
Colo →, Australia . . . . 63 E5   33 25S 150 52 E
Cologne = Köln, Germany . . . . 16 C4   50 56N   6 57 E
Colom, I. d'en, Spain . . . . 24 B11 39 58N   4 16 E
Coloma, U.S.A. 78 G6   38 48N 120 53W
Colomb-Béchar = Béchar, Algeria 50 B5 31 38N   2 18W
Colombia ■, S. Amer. 92 C4   3 45N   73 0W
Colombian Basin, S. Amer. . . . 66 H12 14 0N   76 0W
Colombo, Sri Lanka . . . . 40 R11   6 56N   79 58 E
Colón, Buenos Aires, Argentina . 94 C3   33 53S   61 7W
Colón, Entre Ríos, Argentina . 94 C4   32 12S   58 10W
Colón, Cuba 88 B3   22 42N   80 54W
Colón, Panama 88 E4   9 20N   79 54W
Colón, Arch. de, Ecuador 90 D1   0 0   91 0W
Colònia de Sant Jordi, Spain . 24 B9   39 19N   2 59 E
Colonia del Sacramento,
  Uruguay 94 C4   34 25S   57 50W
Colonia Dora, Argentina 94 B3   28 34S   62 59W
Colonial Beach, U.S.A. 82 F7   38 15N   76 58W
Colonie, U.S.A. 85 D11 42 43N   73 50W
Colonsay, Canada 71 C7   51 59N 105 52W
Colonsay, U.K. 11 E2   56 5N   6 12W
Colorado □, U.S.A. 77 G10 39 30N 105 30W
Colorado →, Argentina 96 D4   39 50S   62 8W
Colorado →, N. Amer. 81 L7   31 45N 114 40W
Colorado →, U.S.A. 81 L7   28 36N   95 59W
Colorado City, U.S.A. 81 J4   32 24N 100 52W
Colorado Plateau, U.S.A. 77 H8   37 0N 111 0W
Colorado River Aqueduct, U.S.A. 79 L12 34 17N 114 10W
Colorado Springs, U.S.A. 80 F2   38 50N 104 49W
Colotlán, Mexico 86 C4   22 6N 103 16W
Colstrip, U.S.A. 76 D10 45 53N 106 38W
Colton, U.S.A. 85 B10 44 33N   74 56W
Columbia, Ky., U.S.A. 82 G3   37 6N   85 18W

Columbia, La., U.S.A. 81 J8   32 6N   92 5W
Columbia, Miss., U.S.A. 81 K10 31 15N   89 50W
Columbia, Mo., U.S.A. 80 F8   38 57N   92 20W
Columbia, Pa., U.S.A. 85 F8   40 2N   76 30W
Columbia, S.C., U.S.A. 83 J5   34 0N   81 2W
Columbia, Tenn., U.S.A. 83 H2   35 37N   87 2W
Columbia →, N. Amer. 78 D2   46 15N 124 5W
Columbia, C., Canada 4 A4   83 6N   69 57W
Columbia, District of □, U.S.A. . 82 F7   38 55N   77 0W
Columbia, Mt., Canada 70 C5   52 8N 117 20W
Columbia Basin, U.S.A. 76 C4   46 45N 119 5W
Columbia Falls, U.S.A. 76 B6   48 23N 114 11W
Columbia Mts., Canada 70 C5   52 0N 119 0W
Columbia Plateau, U.S.A. 76 D5   44 0N 117 30W
Columbiana, U.S.A. 84 F4   40 53N   80 42W
Columbretes, Is., Spain . . . . . . 21 C6   39 50N   0 50 E
Columbus, Ga., U.S.A. 83 J3   32 28N   84 59W
Columbus, Ind., U.S.A. 82 F3   39 13N   85 55W
Columbus, Kans., U.S.A. 81 G7   37 10N   94 50W
Columbus, Miss., U.S.A. 83 J1   33 30N   88 25W
Columbus, Mont., U.S.A. 76 D9   45 38N 109 15W
Columbus, N. Mex., U.S.A. . . . 77 L10 31 50N 107 38W
Columbus, Nebr., U.S.A. 80 E6   41 26N   97 22W
Columbus, Ohio, U.S.A. 82 F4   39 58N   83 0W
Columbus, Tex., U.S.A. 81 L6   29 42N   96 33W
Colusa, U.S.A. 78 F4   39 13N 122 1W
Colville, U.S.A. 76 B5   48 33N 117 54W
Colville →, U.S.A. 68 A4   70 25N 150 30W
Colville, C., N.Z. . . . . 59 G5   36 29S 175 21 E
Colwood, Canada 78 B3   48 26N 123 29W
Colwyn Bay, U.K. 12 D4   53 18N   3 44W
Comácchio, Italy . . . . 22 B5   44 42N   12 11 E
Comalcalco, Mexico 87 D6   18 16N   93 13W
Comallo, Argentina 96 E2   41 0S   70 5W
Comanche, U.S.A. 81 K5   31 54N   98 36W
Comandante Ferraz, Antarctica . 5 C18 62 30S   58 0W
Comayagua, Honduras 88 D2   14 25N   87 37W
Combahee →, U.S.A. 83 J5   32 30N   80 31W
Combarbalá, Chile 94 C1   31 11S   71 2W
Combe Martin, U.K. 13 F3   51 12N   4 3W
Comber, Canada 84 D2   42 14N   82 33W
Comber, U.K. 10 B6   54 33N   5 45W
Combermere, Canada 84 A7   45 22N   77 37W
Comblain-au-Pont, Belgium . . 15 D5   50 29N   5 35 E
Comeragh Mts., Ireland 10 D4   52 18N   7 34W
Comet, Australia . . . . 62 C4   23 36S 148 38 E
Comilla, Bangla. . . . . 41 H17 23 28N   91 10 E
Comino, Malta . . . . 25 C1   36 1N   14 20 E
Comino, C., Italy . . . . 22 D3   40 32N   9 49 E
Comitán, Mexico 87 D6   16 18N   92 9W
Commerce, Ga., U.S.A. 83 H4   34 12N   83 28W
Commerce, Tex., U.S.A. 81 J7   33 15N   95 54W
Committee B., Canada 69 B11 68 30N   86 30W
Commonwealth B., Antarctica . . 5 C10 67 0S 144 0 E
Commoron Cr. →, Australia . . 63 D5   28 22S 150 8 E
Communism Pk. = Kommunizma,
  Pik, Tajikistan . . . . 28 F8   39 0N   72 2 E
Como, Italy . . . . 20 D8   45 47N   9 5 E
Como, Lago di, Italy . . . . 20 D8   46 0N   9 11 E
Comodoro Rivadavia, Argentina . 96 F3   45 50S   67 40W
Comorin, C., India . . . . 40 Q10   8 3N   77 40 E
Comoro Is. = Comoros ■,
  Ind. Oc. . . . . 49 H8   12 10S   44 15 E
Comoros ■, Ind. Oc. . . . . 49 H8   12 10S   44 15 E
Comox, Canada 70 D4   49 42N 124 55W
Compiègne, France . . . . 20 B5   49 24N   2 50 E
Compostela, Mexico 86 C4   21 15N 104 53W
Comprida, I., Brazil 95 A6   24 50S   47 42W
Compton, Canada 85 A13 45 14N   71 49W
Compton, U.S.A. 79 M8   33 54N 118 13W
Comrat, Moldova . . . . 17 E15 46 18N   28 40 E
Con Cuong, Vietnam . . . . 38 C5   19 2N 104 54 E
Con Dao △, Vietnam . . . . 39 H6   8 42N 106 35 E
Con Son, Vietnam . . . . 39 H6   8 41N 106 37 E
Conakry, Guinea 50 G3   9 29N   13 49W
Conara, Australia . . . . 63 G4   41 50S 147 26 E
Concarneau, France 20 C2   47 52N   3 56W
Conceição, Mozam. . . . . 55 F4   18 47S   36 7 E
Conceição da Barra, Brazil . . . 93 G11 18 35S   39 45W
Conceição do Araguaia, Brazil . 93 E9   8 0S   49 2W
Concepción, Argentina 94 B2   27 20S   65 35W
Concepción, Bolivia 92 G6   16 15S   62 8W
Concepción, Chile 94 D1   36 50S   73 0W
Concepción, Mexico 87 D6   18 15N   90 5W
Concepción, Paraguay 94 A4   23 22S   57 26W
Concepción □, Chile 94 D1   37 0S   72 30W
Concepción →, Mexico 86 A2   30 32N 113 2W
Concepción, Est. de, Chile . . . 96 G2   50 30S   74 55W
Concepción B., Canada 73 C9   47 45N   53 0W
Concepción, Namibia . . . . 56 C1   23 55S   14 22 E
Concepción I., Bahamas 89 B4   23 52N   75 9W
Concession, Zimbabwe . . . . . . 55 F3   17 27S   30 56 E
Conchas Dam, U.S.A. 81 H2   35 22N 104 11W
Concho, U.S.A. 77 J9   34 28N 109 36W
Concho →, U.S.A. 81 K5   31 34N   99 43W
Conchos →, Chihuahua, Mexico . 86 B4 29 32N 105 0W
Conchos →, Tamaulipas, Mexico 87 B5   25 5N   97 32W
Concord, Calif., U.S.A. 78 H4   37 59N 122 2W
Concord, N.C., U.S.A. 83 H5   35 25N   80 35W
Concord, N.H., U.S.A. 85 C13 43 12N   71 32W
Concordia, Argentina 94 C4   31 20S   58 2W
Concórdia, Brazil 92 D5   4 36S   66 36W
Concordia, Mexico 86 C3   23 18N 106 2W
Concordia, U.S.A. 80 F6   39 34N   97 40W
Concrete, U.S.A. 76 B3   48 32N 121 45W
Condamine, Australia . . . . 63 D5   26 56S 150 9 E
Conde, U.S.A. 80 C5   45 9N   98 6W
Condeúba, Brazil 93 F10 14 52S   42 0W
Condobolin, Australia . . . . 63 E4   33 4S 147 6 E
Condon, U.S.A. 76 D3   45 14N 120 11W
Conegliano, Italy . . . . 22 B5   45 53N   12 18 E
Conejera, I. = Conills, I. des,
  Spain . . . . 24 B9   39 11N   2 58 E
Conejos, Mexico 86 B4   26 14N 103 53W
Confuso →, Paraguay 94 B4   25 9S   57 34W
Congleton, U.K. 12 D5   53 10N   2 13W
Congo (Brazzaville) = Congo ■,
  Africa . . . . 52 E3   1 0S   16 0 E
Congo (Kinshasa) = Congo, Dem.
  Rep. of the ■, Africa . . . . 52 E4   3 0S   23 0 E
Congo ■, Africa . . . . 52 E3   1 0S   16 0 E
Congo →, Africa . . . . 52 F2   6 4S   12 24 E

Congo, Dem. Rep. of the ■,
  Africa . . . . 52 E4   3 0S   23 0 E
Congo Basin, Africa . . . . 52 E4   0 10S   24 30 E
Congonhas, Brazil 95 A7   20 30S   43 52W
Congress, U.S.A. 77 J7   34 9N 112 51W
Conills, I. des, Spain . . . . 24 B9   39 11N   2 58 E
Coniston, Canada 72 C3   46 29N   80 51W
Conjeeveram = Kanchipuram,
  India . . . . 40 N11 12 52N   79 45 E
Conklin, Canada 71 B6   55 38N 111 5W
Conklin, U.S.A. 85 D9   42 2N   75 49W
Conn, L., Ireland 10 B2   54 3N   9 15W
Connacht □, Ireland 10 C2   53 43N   9 12W
Conneaut, U.S.A. 84 E4   41 57N   80 34W
Connecticut □, U.S.A. 85 E12 41 30N   72 45W
Connecticut →, U.S.A. 85 E12 41 16N   72 20W
Connell, U.S.A. 76 C4   46 40N 118 52W
Connellsville, U.S.A. 84 F5   40 1N   79 35W
Connemara □, Ireland 10 C2   53 29N   9 45W
Connemara △, Ireland 10 C2   53 32N   9 52W
Connemaugh →, U.S.A. 84 F5   40 28N   79 19W
Connersville, U.S.A. 82 F3   39 39N   85 8W
Connors Ra., Australia . . . . 62 C4   21 40S 149 10 E
Conquest, Canada 71 C7   51 32N 107 14W
Conrad, U.S.A. 76 B8   48 10N 111 57W
Conran, C., Australia . . . . 63 F4   37 49S 148 44 E
Conroe, U.S.A. 81 K7   30 19N   95 27W
Consecon, Canada 84 C7   44 0N   77 31W
Conselheiro Lafaiete, Brazil . . 95 A7   20 40S   43 48W
Consett, U.K. 12 C6   54 51N   1 50W
Consort, Canada 71 C6   52 1N 110 46W
Constance = Konstanz, Germany . 16 E5 47 40N   9 10 E
Constance, L. = Bodensee,
  Europe . . . . 20 C8   47 35N   9 25 E
Constanța, Romania . . . . 17 F15 44 14N   28 38 E
Constantia, U.S.A. 85 C8   43 15N   76 1W
Constantine, Algeria . . . . 50 A7   36 25N   6 42 E
Constitución, Chile 94 D1   35 20S   72 30W
Constitución, Uruguay 94 C4   31 0S   57 50W
Constitucion de 1857 △, Mexico . 86 A1 32 4N 115 55W
Consul, Canada 71 D7   49 20N 109 30W
Contact, U.S.A. 76 F6   41 46N 114 45W
Contai, India . . . . 43 J12 21 54N   87 46 E
Contamana, Peru 92 E4   7 19S   74 55W
Contas →, Brazil 93 F11 14 17S   39 1W
Contoocook, U.S.A. 85 C13 43 13N   71 45W
Contwoyto L., Canada 68 B8   65 42N 110 50W
Conway = Conwy, U.K. 12 D4   53 17N   3 50W
Conway = Conwy →, U.K. 12 D4   53 17N   3 50W
Conway, Australia . . . . 62 J6   20 24S 148 41 E
Conway, Ark., U.S.A. 81 H8   35 5N   92 26W
Conway, N.H., U.S.A. 85 C13 43 59N   71 7W
Conway, S.C., U.S.A. 83 J6   33 51N   79 3W
Conway, C., Australia . . . . 62 J6   20 34S 148 46 E
Conway, L., Australia . . . . 63 D2   28 17S 135 35 E
Conwy, U.K. 12 D4   53 17N   3 50W
Conwy □, U.K. 12 D4   53 10N   3 44W
Conwy →, U.K. 12 D4   53 17N   3 50W
Coober Pedy, Australia . . . . . . 63 D1   29 1S 134 43 E
Cooch Behar = Koch Bihar, India . 41 F16 26 22N 89 29 E
Cooinda, Australia . . . . 60 B5   13 15S 130 5 E
Cook, Australia . . . . 61 F5   30 37S 130 25 E
Cook, U.S.A. 80 B8   47 49N   92 39W
Cook, B., Chile 96 H3   55 10S   70 0W
Cook, C., Canada 70 C3   50 8N 127 55W
Cook, Mt. = Aoraki Mount Cook,
  N.Z. . . . . 59 K3   43 36S 170 9 E
Cook Inlet, U.S.A. 68 C4   60 0N 152 0W
Cook Is., Pac. Oc. 65 J12 17 0S 160 0W
Cook Strait, N.Z. . . . . 59 J5   41 15S 174 29 E
Cookeville, U.S.A. 83 G3   36 10N   85 30W
Cookhouse, S. Africa . . . . 56 E4   32 44S   25 47 E
Cookshire, Canada 85 A13 45 25N   71 38W
Cookstown, U.K. 10 B5   54 39N   6 45W
Cooksville, Canada 84 C5   43 36N   79 35W
Cooktown, Australia . . . . 62 B4   15 30S 145 16 E
Coolabah, Australia . . . . 63 E4   31 1S 146 43 E
Cooladdi, Australia . . . . 63 D4   26 37S 145 23 E
Coolah, Australia . . . . 63 E4   31 48S 149 41 E
Coolamon, Australia . . . . 63 E4   34 46S 147 8 E
Coolgardie, Australia . . . . 61 F3   30 55S 121 8 E
Coolidge, U.S.A. 77 K8   32 59N 111 31W
Coolidge Dam, U.S.A. 77 K8   33 0N 110 20W
Cooloola △, Australia . . . . 63 D5   26 13S 153 2 E
Cooma, Australia . . . . 63 F4   36 12S 149 8 E
Coon Rapids, U.S.A. 80 C8   45 9N   93 19W
Coonabarabran, Australia . . . . 63 E4   31 14S 149 18 E
Coonamble, Australia . . . . 63 E4   30 56S 148 27 E
Coonana, Australia . . . . 61 F3   31 0S 123 0 E
Coondapoor, India . . . . 40 N9   13 42N   74 40 E
Cooninie, L., Australia . . . . 63 D2   26 4S 139 59 E
Cooper, U.S.A. 81 J7   33 23N   95 42W
Cooper Cr. →, Australia . . . . . 63 D2   28 29S 137 46 E
Cooperstown, N. Dak., U.S.A. . 80 B5   47 27N   98 8W
Cooperstown, N.Y., U.S.A. . . . 85 D10 42 42N   74 56W
Coorabie, Australia . . . . 61 F5   31 54S 132 18 E
Coorong, The, Australia . . . . . . 63 F2   35 50S 139 20 E
Coorow, Australia . . . . 61 E2   29 53S 116 2 E
Cooroy, Australia . . . . 63 D5   26 22S 152 54 E
Coos Bay, U.S.A. 76 E1   43 22N 124 13W
Coosa →, U.S.A. 83 J2   32 30N   86 16W
Cootamundra, Australia . . . . . . 63 E4   34 36S 148 1 E
Cootehill, Ireland 10 B4   54 4N   7 5W
Copahue Paso, Argentina 94 D1   37 49S   71 8W
Copainalá, Mexico 87 D6   17 8N   93 11W
Copake Falls, U.S.A. 85 D11 42 7N   73 31W
Copán, Honduras 88 D2   14 50N   89 9W
Cope, U.S.A. 80 F3   39 40N 102 51W
Copenhagen = København,
  Denmark . . . . 9 J15   55 41N   12 34 E
Copenhagen, U.S.A. 85 C9   43 54N   75 41W
Copiapó, Chile 94 B1   27 30S   70 20W
Copiapó →, Chile 94 B1   27 19S   70 56W
Coplay, U.S.A. 85 F9   40 44N   75 29W
Copp L., Canada 70 A6   60 14N 114 40W
Coppename →, Suriname 93 B7   5 48N   55 55W
Copper Harbor, U.S.A. 82 B2   47 28N   87 53W
Copper Queen, Zimbabwe . . . 55 F2   17 29S   29 18 E
Copperas Cove, U.S.A. 81 K6   31 8N   97 54W
Copperbelt □, Zambia . . . . 55 E2   13 15S   27 30 E
Coppermine = Kugluktuk, Canada 68 B8 67 50N 115 5W
Coppermine →, Canada 68 B8   67 49N 116 4W
Copperopolis, U.S.A. 78 H6   37 58N 120 38W
Coquet →, U.K. 12 B6   55 20N   1 5W
Coquille, U.S.A. 76 E1   43 11N 124 11W
Coquimbo, Chile 94 C1   30 0S   71 20W
Coquimbo □, Chile 94 C1   31 0S   71 0W

Corabia, Romania . . . . 17 G13 43 48N 24 30 E
Coracora, Peru 92 G4 15 5S 73 45W
Coraki, Australia . . . . 63 D5 28 59S 153 17 E
Coral, U.S.A. 84 F5 40 29N 79 10W
Coral Gables, U.S.A. 83 N5 25 45N 80 16W
Coral Harbour, Canada 69 B11 64 8N 83 10W
Coral Sea, Pac. Oc. . . . . 64 J7 15 0S 150 0 E
Coral Springs, U.S.A. 83 M5 26 16N 80 13W
Coraopolis, U.S.A. 84 F4 40 31N 80 10W
Corato, Italy . . . . 22 D7 41 9N 16 25 E
Corbin, U.S.A. 82 G3 36 57N 84 6W
Corby, U.K. 13 E7 52 30N 0 41W
Corcaigh = Cork, Ireland 10 E3 51 54N 8 29W
Corcoran, U.S.A. 78 J7 36 6N 119 33W
Corcovado △, Costa Rica 88 E3 8 33N 83 35W
Corcubión, Spain 21 A1 42 56N 9 12W
Cordele, U.S.A. 83 K4 31 58N 83 47W
Cordell, U.S.A. 81 H5 35 17N 98 59W
Córdoba, Argentina 94 C3 31 20S 64 10W
Córdoba, Mexico 87 D5 18 50N 97 0W
Córdoba, Spain 21 D3 37 50N 4 50W
Córdoba □, Argentina 94 C3 31 22S 64 15W
Córdoba, Sierra de, Argentina . 94 C3 31 10S 64 25W
Cordova, U.S.A. 68 B5 60 33N 145 45W
Corella →, Australia . . . . 62 B3 19 34S 140 47 E
Corfield, Australia . . . . 62 C3 21 40S 143 21 E
Corfu = Kérkira, Greece . . . . . 25 A3 39 38N 19 50 E
Corfu, Str. of, Greece . . . . 25 A4 39 34N 20 0 E
Coria, Spain 21 C2 39 58N 6 33W
Corigliano Cálabro, Italy . . . . . 22 E7 39 36N 16 31 E
Coringa Is., Australia . . . . 62 B4 16 58S 149 58 E
Corinth = Kórinthos, Greece . . 23 F10 37 56N 22 55 E
Corinth, Miss., U.S.A. 83 H1 34 56N 88 31W
Corinth, N.Y., U.S.A. 85 C11 43 15N 73 49W
Corinth, G. of = Korinthiakós
   Kólpos, Greece . . . . 23 E10 38 16N 22 30 E
Corinto, Brazil 93 G10 18 20S 44 30W
Corinto, Nic. 88 D2 12 30N 87 10W
Cork, Ireland 10 E3 51 54N 8 29W
Cork □, Ireland 10 E3 51 57N 8 40W
Cork Harbour, Ireland 10 E3 51 47N 8 16W
Çorlu, Turkey . . . . 23 D12 41 11N 27 49 E
Cormack L., Canada 70 A4 60 56N 121 37W
Cormorant, Canada 71 C8 54 14N 100 35W
Cormorant L., Canada 71 C8 54 15N 100 50W
Corn Is. = Maíz, Is. del, Nic. . . 88 D3 12 15N 83 4W
Cornélio Procópio, Brazil 95 A5 23 7S 50 40W
Corner Brook, Canada 73 C8 48 57N 57 58W
Corneşti, Moldova . . . . 17 E15 47 21N 28 1 E
Corning, Ark., U.S.A. 81 G9 36 25N 90 35W
Corning, Calif., U.S.A. 76 G2 39 56N 122 11W
Corning, Iowa, U.S.A. 80 E7 40 59N 94 44W
Corning, N.Y., U.S.A. 84 D7 42 9N 77 3W
Cornwall, Canada 85 A10 45 2N 74 44W
Cornwall, U.S.A. 85 F8 40 17N 76 25W
Cornwall □, U.K. 13 G3 50 26N 4 40W
Corny Pt., Australia . . . . 63 E2 34 55S 137 0 E
Coro, Venezuela 92 A5 11 25N 69 41W
Coroatá, Brazil 93 D10 4 8S 44 0W
Corocoro, Bolivia 92 G5 17 15S 68 28W
Coroico, Bolivia 92 G5 16 0S 67 50W
Coromandel, N.Z. . . . . 59 G5 36 45S 175 31 E
Coromandel Coast, India . . . . 40 N12 12 30N 81 0 E
Corona, Calif., U.S.A. 79 M9 33 53N 117 34W
Corona, N. Mex., U.S.A. 77 J11 34 15N 105 36W
Coronach, Canada 71 D7 49 7N 105 31W
Coronado, U.S.A. 79 N9 32 41N 117 11W
Coronado, B. de, Costa Rica . . 88 E3 9 0N 83 40W
Coronados, Is. los, U.S.A. 79 N9 32 25N 117 15W
Coronation, Canada 70 C6 52 5N 111 27W
Coronation Gulf, Canada 68 B8 68 25N 110 0W
Coronation I., Antarctica 5 C18 60 45S 46 0W
Coronation Is., Australia . . . . . 60 B3 14 57S 124 55 E
Coronda, Argentina 94 C3 31 58S 60 56W
Coronel, Chile 94 D1 37 0S 73 10W
Coronel Bogado, Paraguay . . . 94 B4 27 11S 56 18W
Coronel Dorrego, Argentina . . 94 D3 38 40S 61 10W
Coronel Oviedo, Paraguay . . . 94 B4 25 24S 56 30W
Coronel Pringles, Argentina . . 94 D3 38 0S 61 30W
Coronel Suárez, Argentina . . . 94 D3 37 30S 61 52W
Coronel Vidal, Argentina 94 D4 37 28S 57 45W
Coropuna, Nevado, Peru 92 G4 15 30S 72 41W
Corowa, Australia . . . . 63 F4 35 58S 146 21 E
Corozal, Belize 87 D7 18 23N 88 23W
Corozal Pt., Trin. & Tob. 93 K15 10 44N 61 40W
Corpus, Argentina 95 B4 27 10S 55 30W
Corpus Christi, U.S.A. 81 M6 27 47N 97 24W
Corpus Christi, L., U.S.A. 81 L6 28 2N 97 52W
Corralejo, Canary Is. 24 F6 28 43N 13 53W
Corraun Pen., Ireland 10 C2 53 54N 9 54W
Correntes, C. das, Mozam. . . . 57 C6 24 6S 35 34 E
Corrib, L., Ireland 10 C2 53 27N 9 16W
Corrientes, Argentina 94 B4 27 30S 58 45W
Corrientes □, Argentina 94 B4 28 0S 57 0W
Corrientes →, Argentina 94 C4 30 42S 59 38W
Corrientes →, Peru 92 D4 3 43S 74 35W
Corrientes, C., Colombia 92 B3 5 30N 77 34W
Corrientes, C., Cuba 88 B3 21 43N 84 30W
Corrientes, C., Mexico 86 C3 20 25N 105 42W
Corrigan, U.S.A. 81 K7 31 0N 94 52W
Corrigin, Australia . . . . 61 F2 32 20S 117 53 E
Corry, U.S.A. 84 E5 41 55N 79 39W
Corse, C., France . . . . 20 E8 43 1N 9 25 E
Corse ⊠, France . . . . 20 F8 42 0N 9 0 E
Corsica = Corse ⊠, France . . . 20 F8 42 0N 9 0 E
Corsicana, U.S.A. 81 J6 32 6N 96 28W
Corte, France . . . . 20 E8 42 19N 9 11 E
Cortez, U.S.A. 77 H9 37 21N 108 35W
Cortland, N.Y., U.S.A. 85 D8 42 36N 76 11W
Cortland, Ohio, U.S.A. 84 E4 41 20N 80 44W
Çorum, Turkey . . . . 19 F5 40 30N 34 57 E
Corumbá, Brazil 92 G7 19 0S 57 30W
Corunna = A Coruña, Spain . . 21 A1 43 20N 8 25W
Corvallis, U.S.A. 76 D2 44 34N 123 16W
Corvette, L. de la, Canada . . . 72 B5 53 25N 74 3W
Corydon, U.S.A. 80 E8 40 46N 93 19W
Cosalá, Mexico 86 C3 24 28N 106 40W
Cosamaloapan, Mexico 87 D5 18 23N 95 50W
Cosenza, Italy . . . . 22 E7 39 18N 16 15 E
Coshocton, U.S.A. 84 F3 40 16N 81 51W
Cosmo Newberry, Australia . . 61 E3 28 0S 122 54 E
Coso Junction, U.S.A. 79 J9 36 3N 117 57W
Coso Pk., U.S.A. 79 J9 36 13N 117 44W
Cosquín, Argentina 94 C3 31 15S 64 30W
Costa Blanca, Spain 21 C5 38 25N 0 10W
Costa Brava, Spain . . . . 21 B7 41 30N 3 0 E
Costa del Sol, Spain 21 D3 36 30N 4 30W
Costa Dorada, Spain . . . . 21 B6 41 12N 1 15 E

Costa Mesa, U.S.A. 79 M9 33 38N 117 55W
Costa Rica ■, Cent. Amer. . . . 88 E3 10 0N 84 0W
Cosumnes →, U.S.A. 78 G5 38 16N 121 26W
Cotabato, Phil. . . . . 37 C6 7 14N 124 15 E
Cotagaita, Bolivia 94 A2 20 45S 65 40W
Côte-d'Ivoire = Ivory Coast ■,
   Africa 50 G4 7 30N 5 0W
Coteau des Prairies, U.S.A. . . . 80 C6 45 20N 97 50W
Coteau du Missouri, U.S.A. . . . 80 B4 47 0N 100 0W
Cotentin, France 20 B3 49 15N 1 30W
Cotillo, Canary Is. 24 F5 28 41N 14 1W
Cotonou, Benin . . . . 50 G6 6 20N 2 25 E
Cotopaxi, Ecuador 92 D3 0 40S 78 30W
Cotswold Hills, U.K. 13 F5 51 42N 2 10W
Cottage Grove, U.S.A. 76 E2 43 48N 123 3W
Cottbus, Germany . . . . 16 C8 51 45N 14 20 E
Cottonwood, U.S.A. 77 J7 34 45N 112 1W
Cotulla, U.S.A. 81 L5 28 26N 99 14W
Coudersport, U.S.A. 84 E6 41 46N 78 1W
Couedic, C. du, Australia . . . . 63 F2 36 5S 136 40 E
Coulee City, U.S.A. 76 C4 47 37N 119 17W
Coulman I., Antarctica . . . . . . 5 D11 73 35S 170 0 E
Coulonge →, Canada 72 C4 45 52N 76 46W
Coulterville, U.S.A. 78 H6 37 43N 120 12W
Council, U.S.A. 76 D5 44 44N 116 26W
Council Bluffs, U.S.A. 80 E7 41 16N 95 52W
Council Grove, U.S.A. 80 F6 38 40N 96 29W
Coupeville, U.S.A. 78 B4 48 13N 122 41W
Courantyne →, S. Amer. 92 B7 5 55N 57 5W
Courcelles, Belgium . . . . 15 D4 50 28N 4 22 E
Courtenay, Canada 70 D4 49 45N 125 0W
Courtland, U.S.A. 78 G5 38 20N 121 34W
Courtrai = Kortrijk, Belgium . . . 15 D3 50 50N 3 17 E
Courtright, Canada 84 D2 42 49N 82 28W
Coushatta, U.S.A. 81 J8 32 1N 93 21W
Coutts Crossing, Australia . . . 63 D5 29 49S 152 55 E
Couva, Trin. & Tob. 93 K15 10 24N 61 30W
Couvin, Belgium . . . . 15 D4 50 3N 4 29 E
Cove I., Canada 84 A3 45 17N 81 44W
Coventry, U.K. 13 E6 52 25N 1 28W
Covilhã, Portugal 21 B2 40 17N 7 31W
Covington, Ga., U.S.A. 83 J4 33 36N 83 51W
Covington, Ky., U.S.A. 82 F3 39 5N 84 31W
Covington, Okla., U.S.A. 81 G6 36 18N 97 35W
Covington, Tenn., U.S.A. 81 H10 35 34N 89 39W
Covington, Va., U.S.A. 82 G5 37 47N 79 59W
Cowal, L., Australia . . . . 63 E4 33 40S 147 25 E
Cowan, L., Australia . . . . 61 F3 31 45S 121 45 E
Cowan L., Canada 71 C7 54 0N 107 15W
Cowangie, Australia . . . . 63 F3 35 12S 141 26 E
Cowansville, Canada 85 A12 45 14N 72 46W
Coward Springs, Australia . . . 63 D2 29 24S 136 49 E
Cowcowing Lakes, Australia . . 61 F2 30 55S 117 20 E
Cowdenbeath, U.K. 11 E5 56 7N 3 21W
Cowell, Australia . . . . 63 E2 33 39S 136 56 E
Cowes, U.K. 13 G6 50 45N 1 18W
Cowichan L., Canada 78 B2 48 53N 124 17W
Cowlitz →, U.S.A. 78 D4 46 6N 122 55W
Cowra, Australia . . . . 63 E4 33 49S 148 42 E
Coxilha Grande, Brazil 95 B5 28 18S 51 30W
Coxim, Brazil 93 G8 18 30S 54 55W
Cox's Bazar, Bangla. . . . . 41 J17 21 26N 91 59 E
Coyote Wells, U.S.A. 79 N11 32 44N 115 58W
Coyuca de Benítez, Mexico . . 87 D4 17 1N 100 8W
Coyuca de Catalan, Mexico . . 86 D4 18 18N 100 41W
Cozad, U.S.A. 80 E5 40 52N 99 59W
Cozumel, Mexico 87 C7 20 31N 86 55W
Cozumel, Isla, Mexico 87 C7 20 30N 86 40W
Crabhill, Barbados . . . . 89 g 13 19N 59 38W
Cracow = Kraków, Poland . . . . 17 C10 50 4N 19 57 E
Cracow, Australia . . . . 63 D5 25 17S 150 17 E
Cradle Mt.-Lake St. Clair △,
   Australia . . . . 63 G4 41 49S 147 56 E
Cradock, Australia . . . . 63 E2 32 6S 138 31 E
Cradock, S. Africa . . . . 56 E4 32 8S 25 36 E
Craig, U.S.A. 76 F10 40 31N 107 33W
Craigavon, U.K. 10 B5 54 27N 6 23W
Craigmore, Zimbabwe . . . . . . 55 G3 20 28S 32 50 E
Craik, Canada 71 C7 51 3N 105 49W
Crailsheim, Germany . . . . 16 D6 49 8N 10 5 E
Craiova, Romania . . . . 17 F12 44 21N 23 48 E
Cramsie, Australia . . . . 62 C3 23 20S 144 15 E
Cranberry L., U.S.A. 85 B10 44 11N 74 50W
Cranberry Portage, Canada . . 71 C8 54 35N 101 23W
Cranbrook, Australia . . . . 61 F2 34 18S 117 33 E
Cranbrook, Canada 70 D5 49 30N 115 46W
Crandon, U.S.A. 80 C10 45 34N 88 54W
Crane, Oreg., U.S.A. 76 E4 43 25N 118 35W
Crane, Tex., U.S.A. 81 K3 31 24N 102 21W
Cranston, U.S.A. 85 E13 41 47N 71 26W
Crater L., U.S.A. 76 E2 42 56N 122 6W
Crater Lake △, U.S.A. 76 E2 42 55N 122 10W
Craters of the Moon △, U.S.A. . 76 E7 43 25N 113 30W
Crateús, Brazil 93 E10 5 10S 40 39W
Crato, Brazil 93 E11 7 10S 39 25W
Craven, L., Canada 72 B4 54 20N 76 56W
Crawford, U.S.A. 80 D3 42 41N 103 25W
Crawfordsville, U.S.A. 82 E2 40 2N 86 54W
Crawley, U.K. 13 F7 51 7N 0 11W
Crazy Mts., U.S.A. 76 C8 46 12N 110 20W
Crean L., Canada 71 C7 54 5N 106 9W
Crediton, Canada 84 C3 43 17N 81 33W
Crediton, U.K. 13 G4 50 47N 3 40W
Cree →, Canada 71 B7 58 57N 105 47W
Cree →, U.K. 11 G4 54 55N 4 25W
Cree L., Canada 71 B7 57 30N 106 30W
Creede, U.S.A. 77 H10 37 51N 106 56W
Creekside, U.S.A. 84 F5 40 40N 79 11W
Creel, Mexico 86 B3 27 45N 107 38W
Creemore, Canada 84 B4 44 19N 80 6W
Creighton, Canada 71 C8 54 45N 101 54W
Creighton, U.S.A. 80 D6 42 28N 97 54W
Crema, Italy . . . . 20 D8 45 22N 9 41 E
Cremona, Italy . . . . 20 D9 45 7N 10 2 E
Cres, Croatia . . . . 16 F8 44 58N 14 25 E
Crescent City, U.S.A. 76 F1 41 45N 124 12W
Crespo, Argentina 94 C3 32 2S 60 19W
Cresson, U.S.A. 84 F6 40 28N 78 36W
Crestline, Calif., U.S.A. 79 L9 34 14N 117 18W
Crestline, Ohio, U.S.A. 84 F2 40 47N 82 44W
Creston, Canada 70 D5 49 10N 116 31W
Creston, Calif., U.S.A. 78 K6 35 32N 120 33W
Creston, Iowa, U.S.A. 80 E7 41 4N 94 22W
Crestview, Calif., U.S.A. 78 H8 37 46N 118 58W
Crestview, Fla., U.S.A. 83 K2 30 46N 86 34W
Crete = Kríti, Greece . . . . 25 D7 35 15N 25 0 E

Crete, U.S.A. 80 E6 40 38N 96 58W
Créteil, France . . . . 20 B5 48 47N 2 28 E
Creus, C. de, Spain . . . . 21 A7 42 20N 3 19 E
Creuse →, France . . . . 20 C4 47 0N 0 34 E
Crewe, U.K. 12 D5 53 6N 2 26W
Crewkerne, U.K. 13 G5 50 53N 2 48W
Crianlarich, U.K. 11 E4 56 24N 4 37W
Criciúma, Brazil 95 B6 28 40S 49 23W
Crieff, U.K. 11 E5 56 22N 3 50W
Crimea □, Ukraine . . . . 19 E5 45 30N 33 10 E
Crimean Pen. = Krymskyy
   Pivostriv, Ukraine . . . . 19 F5 45 0N 34 0 E
Crişul Alb →, Romania . . . . . . 17 E11 46 42N 21 17 E
Crişul Negru →, Romania . . . . 17 E11 46 42N 21 16 E
Crna →, Macedonia . . . . 23 D9 41 33N 21 59 E
Crna Gora = Montenegro □,
   Serbia & M. . . . . 23 C8 42 40N 19 20 E
Crna Gora, Macedonia . . . . . . 23 C9 42 10N 21 30 E
Crna Reka = Crna →, Macedonia 23 D9 41 33N 21 59 E
Croagh Patrick, Ireland 10 C2 53 46N 9 40W
Croatia ■, Europe . . . . 16 F9 45 20N 16 0 E
Crocker, Banjaran, Malaysia . . 36 C5 5 40N 116 30 E
Crockett, U.S.A. 81 K7 31 19N 95 27W
Crocodile = Krokodil →, Mozam. 57 D5 25 14S 32 18 E
Crocodile Is., Australia . . . . . . 62 A1 12 3S 134 58 E
Crohy Hd., Ireland 10 B3 54 55N 8 26W
Croix, L. La, Canada 72 C1 48 20N 92 15W
Croker, C., Australia . . . . 60 B5 10 58S 132 35 E
Croker, C., Canada 84 B4 44 58N 80 59W
Croker I., Australia . . . . 60 B5 11 12S 132 32 E
Cromarty, U.K. 11 D4 57 40N 4 2W
Cromer, U.K. . . . . 12 E9 52 56N 1 17 E
Cromwell, N.Z. . . . . 59 L2 45 3S 169 14 E
Cromwell, U.S.A. 85 E12 41 36N 72 39W
Crook, U.K. 12 C6 54 43N 1 45W
Crooked →, Canada 70 C4 54 50N 122 54W
Crooked →, U.S.A. 76 D3 44 32N 121 16W
Crooked I., Bahamas 89 B5 22 50N 74 10W
Crooked Island Passage,
   Bahamas 89 B5 23 0N 74 30W
Crookston, Minn., U.S.A. 80 B6 47 47N 96 37W
Crookston, Nebr., U.S.A. 80 D4 42 56N 100 45W
Crookwell, Australia . . . . 63 E4 34 28S 149 24 E
Crosby, U.K. 12 D4 53 30N 3 3W
Crosby, N. Dak., U.S.A. 80 A3 48 55N 103 18W
Crosby, Pa., U.S.A. 84 E6 41 45N 78 23W
Crosbyton, U.S.A. 81 J4 33 40N 101 14W
Cross City, U.S.A. 83 L4 29 38N 83 7W
Cross Fell, U.K. 12 C5 54 43N 2 28W
Cross L., Canada 71 C9 54 45N 97 30W
Cross Lake, Canada 71 C9 54 37N 97 47W
Cross Sound, U.S.A. 68 C6 58 0N 135 0W
Crossett, U.S.A. 81 J9 33 8N 91 58W
Crosshaven, Ireland 10 E3 51 47N 8 17W
Crossville, U.S.A. 83 G3 35 57N 85 2W
Croswell, U.S.A. 84 C2 43 16N 82 37W
Croton-on-Hudson, U.S.A. . . . 85 E11 41 12N 73 55W
Crotone, Italy . . . . 22 E7 39 5N 17 8 E
Crow →, Canada 70 B4 59 41N 124 20W
Crow Agency, U.S.A. 76 D10 45 36N 107 28W
Crow Hd., Ireland 10 E1 51 35N 10 9W
Crowell, U.S.A. 81 J5 33 59N 99 43W
Crowley, U.S.A. 81 K8 30 13N 92 22W
Crowley, L., U.S.A. 78 H8 37 35N 118 42W
Crown Point, Ind., U.S.A. 82 E2 41 25N 87 22W
Crown Point, N.Y., U.S.A. 85 C11 43 57N 73 26W
Crown Pt., Trin. & Tob. 93 J16 11 18N 60 51W
Crownpoint, U.S.A. 77 J9 35 41N 108 9W
Crows Landing, U.S.A. 78 H5 37 23N 121 6W
Crows Nest, Australia . . . . 63 D5 27 16S 152 4 E
Crowsnest Pass, Canada 70 D6 49 40N 114 40W
Croydon, Australia . . . . 62 B3 18 13S 142 14 E
Croydon □, U.K. 13 F7 51 22N 0 5W
Crozet, Is., Ind. Oc. . . . . 3 G12 46 27S 52 0 E
Cruz, C., Cuba 88 C4 19 50N 77 50W
Cruz Alta, Brazil 95 B5 28 45S 53 40W
Cruz Bay, U.S. Virgin Is. . . . . . 89 e 18 20N 64 48W
Cruz del Eje, Argentina 94 C3 30 45S 64 50W
Cruzeiro, Brazil 95 A7 22 33S 45 0W
Cruzeiro do Oeste, Brazil 95 A5 23 46S 53 4W
Cruzeiro do Sul, Brazil 92 E4 7 35S 72 35W
Cry L., Canada 70 B3 58 45N 129 0W
Crystal Bay, U.S.A. 78 F7 39 15N 120 0W
Crystal Brook, Australia . . . . . 63 E2 33 21S 138 12 E
Crystal City, U.S.A. 81 L5 28 41N 99 50W
Crystal Falls, U.S.A. 82 B1 46 5N 88 20W
Crystal River, U.S.A. 83 L4 28 54N 82 35W
Crystal Springs, U.S.A. 81 K9 31 59N 90 21W
Csongrád, Hungary . . . . 17 E11 46 43N 20 12 E
Cu Lao Hon, Vietnam . . . . 39 G7 10 54N 108 18 E
Cua Rao, Vietnam . . . . 38 C5 19 16N 104 27 E
Cuácua →, Mozam. . . . . 55 F4 17 54S 37 0 E
Cuamato, Angola . . . . 56 B2 17 2S 15 7 E
Cuamba, Mozam. . . . . 55 E4 14 45S 36 22 E
Cuando →, Angola . . . . 53 H4 17 30S 23 15 E
Cuando Cubango □, Angola . . 56 B3 16 25S 20 0 E
Cuangar, Angola . . . . 56 B2 17 36S 18 39 E
Cuango = Kwango →, Dem. Rep.
   of the Congo . . . . 52 E3 3 14S 17 22 E
Cuanza →, Angola . . . . 52 F2 9 21S 13 9 E
Cuarto →, Argentina 94 C3 33 25S 63 2W
Cuatrociénegas, Mexico 86 B4 26 59N 102 5W
Cuauhtémoc, Mexico 86 B3 28 25N 106 52W
Cuba, N. Mex., U.S.A. 77 J10 36 1N 107 4W
Cuba, N.Y., U.S.A. 84 D6 42 13N 78 17W
Cuba ■, W. Indies 88 B4 22 0N 79 0W
Cubango →, Africa . . . . 56 B3 18 50S 22 25 E
Cuc Phuong △, Vietnam . . . . . 38 B5 20 17N 105 38 E
Cuchumatanes, Sierra de los,
   Guatemala 88 C1 15 35N 91 25W
Cuckfield, U.K. 13 F7 51 1N 0 8W
Cucuí, Brazil 92 C5 1 12N 66 50W
Cucurpe, Mexico 86 A2 30 20N 110 43W
Cúcuta, Colombia 92 B4 7 54N 72 31W
Cuddalore, India . . . . 40 P11 11 46N 79 45 E
Cuddapah, India . . . . 40 M11 14 30N 78 47 E
Cudgewa, L., Australia . . . . . . 62 D3 25 45S 141 26 E
Cue, Australia . . . . 61 E2 27 25S 117 54 E
Cuenca, Ecuador 92 D3 2 50S 79 9W
Cuenca, Spain 21 B4 40 5N 2 10W
Cuenca, Serranía de, Spain . . 21 C5 39 55N 1 50W
Cuernavaca, Mexico 87 D5 18 55N 99 15W
Cuero, U.S.A. 81 L6 29 6N 97 17W
Cueva de la Quebrada del
   Toro △, Venezuela 89 D6 10 46N 69 3W
Cuevas del Almanzora, Spain . 21 D5 37 18N 1 58W
Cuevo, Bolivia 92 H6 20 15S 63 30W

Cuiabá, Brazil 93 G7 15 30S 56 0W
Cuiabá →, Brazil 93 G7 17 5S 56 36W
Cuihangcun, China . . . . 33 G10 22 27N 113 32 E
Cuijk, Neths. . . . . 15 C5 51 44N 5 50 E
Cuilco, Guatemala 88 C1 15 24N 91 58W
Cuillin Hills, U.K. 11 D2 57 13N 6 15W
Cuillin Sd., U.K. 11 D2 57 4N 6 20W
Cuito →, Angola . . . . 56 B3 18 1S 20 48 E
Cuitzeo, L. de, Mexico 86 D4 19 55N 101 5W
Cukai, Malaysia . . . . 39 K4 4 13N 103 25 E
Culbertson, U.S.A. 80 A2 48 9N 104 31W
Culcairn, Australia . . . . 63 F4 35 41S 147 3 E
Culebra, Isla de, Puerto Rico . . 89 d 18 19N 65 18W
Culgoa →, Australia . . . . 63 D4 29 56S 146 20 E
Culgoa Flood Plain △, Australia 63 D4 28 58S 147 5 E
Culiacán, Mexico 86 C3 24 50N 107 23W
Culiacán →, Mexico 86 C3 24 30N 107 42W
Culik, Indonesia . . . . 37 J18 8 21S 115 37 E
Culion, Phil. . . . . 37 B6 11 54N 119 58 E
Cullarin Ra., Australia . . . . . . 63 E4 34 30S 149 30 E
Cullen, U.K. 11 D6 57 42N 2 49W
Cullen Pt., Australia . . . . 62 A3 11 57S 141 54 E
Cullera, Spain 21 C5 39 9N 0 17W
Cullman, U.S.A. 83 H2 34 11N 86 51W
Culloden, U.K. 13 G4 50 51N 3 24W
Culpeper, U.S.A. 82 F7 38 30N 78 0W
Culuene →, Brazil 93 F8 12 56S 52 51W
Culver, Pt., Australia . . . . 61 F3 32 54S 124 43 E
Culverden, N.Z. . . . . 59 K4 42 47S 172 49 E
Cumaná, Venezuela 92 A6 10 30N 64 5W
Cumberland, B.C., Canada . . . 70 D4 49 40N 125 0W
Cumberland, Ont., Canada . . . 85 A9 45 29N 75 24W
Cumberland, U.S.A. 82 F6 39 39N 78 46W
Cumberland →, U.S.A. 83 G2 36 15N 87 0W
Cumberland, L., U.S.A. 83 G3 36 57N 84 55W
Cumberland Gap △, U.S.A. . . 83 G4 36 36N 83 40W
Cumberland I., U.S.A. 83 K5 30 50N 81 25W
Cumberland Is., Australia . . . . 62 J7 20 35S 149 10 E
Cumberland Island △, U.S.A. . 83 K5 30 12N 81 24W
Cumberland L., Canada 71 C8 54 3N 102 18W
Cumberland Pen., Canada . . . 69 B13 67 0N 64 0W
Cumberland Plateau, U.S.A. . . 83 H3 36 0N 85 0W
Cumberland Sd., Canada 69 B13 65 30N 66 0W
Cumbernauld, U.K. 11 F5 55 57N 3 58W
Cumborah, Australia . . . . 63 D4 29 40S 147 45 E
Cumbres de Majalca △, Mexico 86 B3 28 52N 106 24W
Cumbres de Monterrey △,
   Mexico 86 B4 25 40N 100 35W
Cumbria □, U.K. 12 C5 54 42N 2 52W
Cumbrian Mts., U.K. 12 C5 54 30N 3 0W
Cumbum, India . . . . 40 M11 15 40N 79 10 E
Cuminá →, Brazil 93 D7 1 30S 56 0W
Cummings Mt., U.S.A. 79 K8 35 2N 118 34W
Cummins, Australia . . . . 63 E2 34 16S 135 43 E
Cumnock, Australia . . . . 63 E4 32 59S 148 46 E
Cumnock, U.K. 11 F4 55 28N 4 17W
Cumpas, Mexico 86 B3 30 0N 109 48W
Cumplida, Pta., Canary Is. . . . 24 F2 28 50N 17 48W
Cunco, Chile 96 D2 38 55S 72 2W
Cuncumén, Chile 94 C1 31 53S 70 38W
Cunderdin, Australia . . . . 61 F2 31 37S 117 12 E
Cunene →, Angola . . . . 56 B1 17 20S 11 50 E
Cúneo, Italy . . . . 20 D7 44 23N 7 32 E
Çüngüş, Turkey . . . . 44 B3 38 13N 39 17 E
Cunillera, I. = Sa Conillera, Spain 24 C7 38 59N 1 13 E
Cunnamulla, Australia . . . . . . 63 D4 28 2S 145 38 E
Cupar, Canada 71 C8 50 57N 104 10W
Cupar, U.K. 11 E5 56 19N 3 1W
Cupica, G. de, Colombia 92 B3 6 25N 77 30W
Curaçao, Neth. Ant. 89 D6 12 10N 69 0W
Curanilahue, Chile 94 D1 37 29S 73 28W
Curaray →, Peru 92 D4 2 20S 74 5W
Curepto, Chile 94 D1 35 8S 72 1W
Curiapo, Venezuela 92 B6 8 33N 61 5W
Curicó, Chile 94 C1 34 55S 71 20W
Curitiba, Brazil 95 B6 25 20S 49 10W
Curitibanos, Brazil 95 B5 27 18S 50 36W
Currabubula, Australia . . . . . . 63 E5 31 16S 150 44 E
Currais Novos, Brazil 93 E11 6 13S 36 30W
Curralinho, Brazil 93 D9 1 45S 49 46W
Currant, U.S.A. 76 G6 38 51N 115 32W
Currawinya △, Australia . . . . . 63 D3 28 55S 144 27 E
Current →, U.S.A. 81 G9 36 15S 90 55W
Currie, Australia . . . . 63 F3 39 56S 143 53 E
Currie, U.S.A. 76 F6 40 16N 114 45W
Curtea de Argeş, Romania . . . 17 F13 45 12N 24 42 E
Curtis, U.S.A. 80 E4 40 38N 100 31W
Curtis Group, Australia . . . . . . 63 F4 39 30S 146 37 E
Curtis I., Australia . . . . 62 C5 23 35S 151 10 E
Curuápanema →, Brazil 93 D7 2 25S 55 2W
Curuçá, Brazil 93 D9 0 43S 47 50W
Curuguaty, Paraguay 95 A4 24 31S 55 42W
Curup, Indonesia . . . . 36 E2 4 26S 102 13 E
Cururupu, Brazil 93 D10 1 50S 44 50W
Curuzú Cuatiá, Argentina 94 B4 29 50S 58 5W
Curvelo, Brazil 93 G10 18 45S 44 27W
Cushing, U.S.A. 81 H6 35 59N 96 46W
Cushing, Mt., Canada 70 B3 57 35N 126 57W
Cusihuiriáchic, Mexico 86 B3 28 10N 106 50W
Custer, U.S.A. 80 D3 43 46N 103 36W
Cut Bank, U.S.A. 76 B7 48 38N 112 20W
Cutchogue, U.S.A. 85 E12 41 1N 72 30W
Cuthbert, U.S.A. 83 K3 31 46N 84 48W
Cutler, U.S.A. 78 J7 36 31N 119 17W
Cuttaburra →, Australia . . . . . 63 D3 29 43S 144 22 E
Cuttack, India . . . . 41 J14 20 25N 85 57 E
Cuvier, C., Australia . . . . 61 D1 23 14S 113 22 E
Cuvier I., N.Z. . . . . 59 G5 36 27S 175 50 E
Cuxhaven, Germany . . . . 16 B5 53 51N 8 41 E
Cuyahoga Falls, U.S.A. 84 E3 41 8N 81 29W
Cuyahoga Valley △, U.S.A. . . . 84 E3 41 15N 81 33W
Cuyo, Phil. . . . . 37 B6 10 50N 121 5 E
Cuyuni →, Guyana 92 B7 6 23N 58 41W
Cuzco, Bolivia 92 H5 20 0S 66 50W
Cuzco, Peru 92 F4 13 32S 72 0W
Cwmbran, U.K. 13 F4 51 39N 3 2W
Cyangugu, Rwanda . . . . 54 C2 2 29S 28 54 E
Cyclades = Kikládhes, Greece . 23 F11 37 0N 24 30 E
Cygnet, Australia . . . . 63 G4 43 8S 147 1 E
Cynthiana, U.S.A. 82 F3 38 23N 84 18W
Cypress Hills, Canada 71 D7 49 40N 109 30W
Cypress Hills △, Canada 71 D7 49 40N 109 30W
Cyprus ■, Asia . . . . 25 E12 35 0N 33 0 E
Cyrenaica, Libya . . . . 51 C10 27 0N 23 0 E
Czar, Canada 71 C6 52 27N 110 50W
Czech Rep. ■, Europe . . . . . . 16 D8 50 0N 15 0 E
Częstochowa, Poland . . . . . . 17 C10 50 49N 19 7 E

D

Da →, Vietnam 38 B5 21 15N 105 20 E
Da Hinggan Ling, China 33 B7 48 0N 121 0 E
Da Lat, Vietnam 39 G7 11 56N 108 25 E
Da Nang, Vietnam 38 D7 16 4N 108 13 E
Da Qaidam, China 32 C4 37 50N 95 15 E
Da Yunhe →, China 35 G11 34 25N 120 5 E
Da'an, China 35 B13 45 30N 124 7 E
Daan Viljoen ⌓, Namibia 56 C2 22 2S 16 45 E
Daba Shan, China 33 C5 32 0N 109 0 E
Dabbagh, Jabal, Si. Arabia 44 E2 27 52N 35 45 E
Dabhoi, India 42 H5 22 10N 73 20 E
Dabo = Pasirkuning, Indonesia 36 E2 0 30S 104 33 E
Dabola, Guinea 50 F3 10 50N 11 5W
Dabung, Malaysia 39 K4 5 23N 102 1 E
Dacca = Dhaka, Bangla. 43 H14 23 43N 90 26 E
Dacca = Dhaka □, Bangla. 43 G14 24 25N 90 25 E
Dachau, Germany 16 D6 48 15N 11 26 E
Dadanawa, Guyana 92 C7 2 50N 59 30W
Dade City, U.S.A. 83 L4 28 22N 82 11W
Dadhar, Pakistan 42 E2 29 28N 67 39 E
Dadra & Nagar Haveli □, India 40 J8 20 5N 73 0 E
Dadri = Charkhi Dadri, India 42 E7 28 37N 76 17 E
Dadu, Pakistan 42 F2 26 45N 67 45 E
Daet, Phil. 37 B6 14 2N 122 55 E
Dagana, Senegal 50 E2 16 30N 15 35W
Dagestan □, Russia 19 F8 42 30N 47 0 E
Daggett, U.S.A. 79 L10 34 52N 116 52W
Daghestan Republic = Dagestan □, Russia 19 F8 42 30N 47 0 E
Dağlıq Qarabağ = Nagorno-Karabakh □, Azerbaijan 19 F8 39 55N 46 45 E
Dagö = Hiiumaa, Estonia 9 G20 58 50N 22 45 E
Dagu, China 35 E9 38 59N 117 40 E
Dagupan, Phil. 37 A6 16 3N 120 20 E
Daguragu, Australia 60 C5 17 33S 130 30 E
Dahlak Kebir, Eritrea 47 D3 15 50N 40 10 E
Dahlonega, U.S.A. 83 H4 34 32N 83 59W
Dahod, India 42 H6 22 50N 74 15 E
Dahūk, Iraq 44 B3 36 50N 43 1 E
Dai Hao, Vietnam 38 C6 18 1N 106 25 E
Dai-Sen, Japan 31 G6 35 22N 133 32 E
Dai Xian, China 34 E7 39 4N 112 58 E
Daicheng, China 34 E9 38 42N 116 38 E
Daingean, Ireland 10 C4 53 18N 7 17W
Daintree, Australia 62 B4 16 20S 145 20 E
Daintree △, Australia 62 B4 16 8S 145 2 E
Daiō-Misaki, Japan 31 G8 34 15N 136 45 E
Daisen-Oki △, Japan 31 G6 35 23N 133 34 E
Daisetsu-Zan, Japan 30 C11 43 30N 142 57 E
Daisetsu-Zan △, Japan 30 C11 43 30N 142 55 E
Dajarra, Australia 62 C2 21 42S 139 30 E
Dak Dam, Cambodia 38 F6 12 20N 107 21 E
Dak Nhe, Vietnam 38 E6 15 28N 107 48 E
Dak Pek, Vietnam 38 E6 15 4N 107 44 E
Dak Song, Vietnam 39 F6 12 19N 107 35 E
Dak Sui, Vietnam 38 E6 14 55N 107 43 E
Dakar, Senegal 50 F2 14 34N 17 29W
Dakhla, W. Sahara 50 D2 23 50N 15 53W
Dakhla, El Wâhât el-, Egypt 51 C11 25 30N 28 50 E
Dakor, India 42 H5 22 45N 73 11 E
Dakota City, U.S.A. 80 D6 42 25N 96 25W
Đakovica, Serbia & M. 23 C9 42 22N 20 26 E
Dalachi, China 34 F3 36 48N 105 0 E
Dalai Nur, China 34 C9 43 20N 116 45 E
Dālaki, Iran 45 D6 29 26N 51 17 E
Dalälven →, Sweden 9 F17 60 12N 16 43 E
Dalaman →, Turkey 23 F13 36 41N 28 43 E
Dalandzadgad, Mongolia 34 C3 43 27N 104 30 E
Dalap-Uliga-Darrit, Marshall Is. 64 G9 7 7N 171 24 E
Dalarna, Sweden 9 F16 61 0N 14 0 E
Dālbandīn, Pakistan 40 E4 29 0N 64 23 E
Dalbeattie, U.K. 11 G5 54 56N 3 50W
Dalbeg, Australia 62 C4 20 16S 147 18 E
Dalby, Australia 63 D5 27 10S 151 17 E
Dale City, U.S.A. 82 F7 38 38N 77 18W
Dale Hollow L., U.S.A. 83 G3 36 32N 85 27W
Dalgān, Iran 45 E8 27 31N 59 19 E
Dalhart, U.S.A. 81 G3 36 4N 102 31W
Dalhousie, Canada 73 C6 48 5N 66 26W
Dalhousie, India 42 C6 32 38N 75 58 E
Dali, Shaanxi, China 34 G5 34 48N 109 58 E
Dali, Yunnan, China 32 D5 25 40N 100 10 E
Dalian, China 35 E11 38 50N 121 40 E
Daliang Shan, China 32 D5 28 0N 102 45 E
Daling He →, China 35 D11 40 55N 121 40 E
Dāliyat el Karmel, Israel 46 C4 32 43N 35 2 E
Dalkeith, U.K. 11 F5 55 54N 3 4W
Dallas, Oreg., U.S.A. 76 D2 44 55N 123 19W
Dallas, Tex., U.S.A. 81 J6 32 47N 96 49W
Dalmā, U.A.E. 45 E7 24 30N 52 20 E
Dalmacija, Croatia 22 C7 43 20N 17 0 E
Dalmas, L., Canada 73 B5 53 30N 71 50W
Dalmatia = Dalmacija, Croatia 22 C7 43 20N 17 0 E
Dalmau, India 43 F9 26 4N 81 2 E
Dalmellington, U.K. 11 F4 55 19N 4 23W
Dalnegorsk, Russia 29 E14 44 32N 135 33 E
Dalnerechensk, Russia 29 E14 45 50N 133 40 E
Dalnevostochnyy □, Russia 29 C14 67 0N 140 0 E
Daloa, Ivory C. 50 G4 7 0N 6 30W
Dalry, U.K. 11 F4 55 42N 4 43W
Dalrymple, L., Australia 62 C4 20 40S 147 0 E
Dalrymple, Mt., Australia 62 K6 21 1S 148 39 E
Dalsland, Sweden 9 G14 58 50N 12 15 E
Daltenganj, India 43 H11 24 0N 84 4 E
Dalton, Ga., U.S.A. 83 H3 34 46N 84 58W
Dalton, Mass., U.S.A. 85 D11 42 28N 73 11W
Dalton, Nebr., U.S.A. 80 E3 41 25N 102 58W
Dalton-in-Furness, U.K. 12 C4 54 10N 3 11W
Dalvík, Iceland 8 D4 65 58N 18 32W
Dalwallinu, Australia 61 F2 30 17S 116 40 E
Daly →, Australia 60 B5 13 35S 130 19 E
Daly City, U.S.A. 78 H4 37 42N 122 28W
Daly L., Canada 71 B7 56 32N 105 39W
Daly River, Australia 60 B5 13 46S 130 42 E
Daly Waters, Australia 62 B1 16 15S 133 24 E
Dam Doi, Vietnam 39 H5 8 50N 105 12 E
Dam Ha, Vietnam 38 B6 21 21N 107 36 E
Daman, India 40 J8 20 25N 72 57 E
Dāmaneh, Iran 45 C6 33 1N 50 29 E
Damanhûr, Egypt 51 B12 31 0N 30 30 E
Damant L., Canada 71 A7 61 45N 105 5W
Damanzhuang, China 34 E9 38 5N 116 35 E
Damar, Indonesia 37 F7 7 7S 128 40 E
Damaraland, Namibia 56 C2 20 0S 15 0 E
Damascus = Dimashq, Syria 46 B5 33 30N 36 18 E
Damāvand, Iran 45 C7 35 47N 52 0 E
Damāvand, Qolleh-ye, Iran 45 C7 35 56N 52 10 E
Damba, Angola 52 F3 6 44S 15 20 E
Dâmboviţa →, Romania 17 F14 44 12N 26 26 E
Dame Marie, Haiti 89 C5 18 36N 74 26W
Dāmghān, Iran 45 B7 36 10N 54 17 E
Damiel, Spain 21 C4 39 4N 3 37W
Damietta = Dumyât, Egypt 51 B12 31 24N 31 48 E
Daming, China 34 F8 36 15N 115 6 E
Damīr Qābū, Syria 44 B4 36 58N 41 51 E
Dammam = Ad Dammām, Si. Arabia 45 E6 26 20N 50 5 E
Damodar →, India 43 H12 23 17N 87 35 E
Damoh, India 43 H8 23 50N 79 28 E
Dampier, Australia 60 D2 20 41S 116 42 E
Dampier, Selat, Indonesia 37 E8 0 40S 131 0 E
Dampier Arch., Australia 60 D2 20 38S 116 32 E
Damrei, Chuor Phnum, Cambodia 39 G4 11 30N 103 0 E
Dan Xian, China 38 C7 19 31N 109 33 E
Dana, Indonesia 37 F6 11 0S 122 52 E
Dana, L., Canada 72 B4 50 53N 77 20W
Dana, Mt., U.S.A. 78 H7 37 54N 119 12W
Danakil Desert, Ethiopia 47 E3 12 45N 41 0 E
Danané, Ivory C. 50 G4 7 16N 8 9W
Danau Poso, Indonesia 37 E6 1 52S 120 35 E
Danbury, U.S.A. 85 E11 41 24N 73 28W
Danby L., U.S.A. 77 J6 34 13N 115 5W
Dand, Afghan. 42 D1 31 28N 65 32 E
Dande ⌓, Zimbabwe 55 F3 15 56S 30 16 E
Dandeldhura, Nepal 43 E9 29 20N 80 35 E
Dandeli, India 40 M9 15 5N 74 30 E
Dandenong, Australia 63 F4 38 0S 145 15 E
Dandong, China 35 D13 40 10N 124 20 E
Danfeng, China 34 H6 33 45N 110 25 E
Danger Is. = Pukapuka, Cook Is. 65 J11 10 53S 165 49W
Danger Pt., S. Africa 56 E2 34 40S 19 17 E
Danginpuri, Indonesia 37 K18 8 40S 115 13 E
Dangla Shan = Tanggula Shan, China 32 C4 32 40N 92 10 E
Dangrek, Phnom, Thailand 38 E5 14 15N 105 0 E
Dangriga, Belize 87 D7 17 0N 88 13W
Dangshan, China 34 G9 34 27N 116 22 E
Daniel, U.S.A. 76 E8 42 52N 110 4W
Daniel's Harbour, Canada 73 B8 50 13N 57 35W
Danielskuil, S. Africa 56 D3 28 11S 23 33 E
Danielson, U.S.A. 85 E13 41 48N 71 53W
Danilov, Russia 18 C7 58 16N 40 13 E
Daning, China 34 F6 36 28N 110 45 E
Ḑank, Oman 45 F8 23 33N 56 16 E
Dankhar Gompa, India 40 C11 32 10N 78 10 E
Danlí, Honduras 88 D2 14 4N 86 35W
Dannemora, U.S.A. 85 B11 44 43N 73 44W
Dannevirke, N.Z. 59 J6 40 12S 176 8 E
Dannhauser, S. Africa 57 D5 28 0S 30 3 E
Dansville, U.S.A. 84 D7 42 34N 77 42W
Danta, India 42 G5 24 11N 72 46 E
Dantan, India 43 J12 21 57N 87 20 E
Danube = Dunărea →, Europe 17 F15 45 20N 29 40 E
Danvers, U.S.A. 85 D14 42 34N 70 56W
Danville, Ill., U.S.A. 82 E2 40 8N 87 37W
Danville, Ky., U.S.A. 82 G3 37 39N 84 46W
Danville, Pa., U.S.A. 85 F8 40 58N 76 37W
Danville, Va., U.S.A. 83 G6 36 36N 79 23W
Danville, Vt., U.S.A. 85 B12 44 25N 72 9W
Danzig = Gdańsk, Poland 17 A10 54 22N 18 40 E
Dapaong, Togo 50 F6 10 55N 0 16 E
Daqing Shan, China 34 D6 40 40N 111 0 E
Dar Banda, Africa 48 F6 8 0N 23 0 E
Dar el Beida = Casablanca, Morocco 50 B4 33 36N 7 36W
Dar es Salaam, Tanzania 54 D4 6 50S 39 12 E
Dar Mazār, Iran 45 D8 29 14N 57 20 E
Darʻā, Syria 46 C5 32 36N 36 7 E
Darʻā □, Syria 46 C5 32 55N 36 10 E
Dārāb, Iran 45 D7 28 50N 54 30 E
Daraban, Pakistan 42 D4 31 44N 70 20 E
Daraina, Madag. 57 A8 13 12S 49 40 E
Daraj, Libya 51 B8 30 10N 10 28 E
Dārān, Iran 45 C6 32 59N 50 24 E
Dārayyā, Syria 46 B5 33 28N 36 15 E
Darband, Pakistan 42 B5 34 20N 72 50 E
Darband, Kūh-e, Iran 45 D8 31 34N 57 8 E
Darbhanga, India 43 F11 26 15N 85 55 E
D'Arcy, Canada 70 C4 50 27N 122 35W
Dardanelle, Ark., U.S.A. 81 H8 35 13N 93 9W
Dardanelle, Calif., U.S.A. 78 G7 38 20N 119 50W
Dardanelles = Çanakkale Boğazı, Turkey 23 D12 40 17N 26 32 E
Dārestān, Iran 45 D8 29 9N 58 42 E
Dârfûr, Sudan 51 F10 13 40N 24 0 E
Dargai, Pakistan 42 B4 34 25N 71 55 E
Dargan Ata, Turkmenistan 28 E7 40 29N 62 10 E
Dargaville, N.Z. 59 F4 35 57S 173 52 E
Darhan, Mongolia 32 B5 49 37N 106 21 E
Darhan Muminggan Lianheqi, China 34 D6 41 40N 110 28 E
Darıca, Turkey 23 D13 40 45N 29 23 E
Darién △, Panama 88 E4 7 36N 77 57W
Darién, G. del, Colombia 92 B3 9 0N 77 0W
Dariganga = Ovoot, Mongolia 34 B7 45 21N 113 45 E
Darjeeling = Darjiling, India 43 F13 27 3N 88 18 E
Darjiling, India 43 F13 27 3N 88 18 E
Darkan, Australia 61 F2 33 20S 116 43 E
Darkhana, Pakistan 42 D5 30 39N 72 11 E
Darkhazīneh, Iran 45 D6 31 54N 48 39 E
Darkot Pass, Pakistan 43 A5 36 45N 73 26 E
Darling →, Australia 63 E3 34 4S 141 54 E
Darling Downs, Australia 63 D5 27 30S 150 30 E
Darling Ra., Australia 61 F2 32 30S 116 0 E
Darlington, U.K. 12 C6 54 32N 1 33W
Darlington, U.S.A. 83 H6 34 18N 79 52W
Darlington □, U.K. 12 C6 54 32N 1 33W
Darlington, L., S. Africa 56 E4 33 10S 25 9 E
Darlot, L., Australia 61 E3 27 48S 121 35 E
Darłowo, Poland 16 A9 54 25N 16 25 E
Darmstadt, Germany 16 D5 49 51N 8 39 E
Darnah, Libya 51 B10 32 45N 22 45 E
Darnall, S. Africa 57 D5 29 23S 31 18 E
Darnley, C., Antarctica 5 C6 68 0S 69 0 E
Darnley B., Canada 68 B7 69 30N 123 30W
Darr →, Australia 62 C3 23 39S 143 50 E
Darra Pezu, Pakistan 42 C4 32 19N 70 44 E
Darrequeira, Argentina 94 D3 37 42S 63 10W
Darrington, U.S.A. 76 B3 48 15N 121 36W
Dart →, U.K. 13 G4 50 24N 3 39W
Dart, C., Antarctica 5 D14 73 6S 126 20W
Dartford, U.K. 13 F8 51 26N 0 13 E
Dartmoor, U.K. 13 G4 50 38N 3 57W
Dartmoor △, U.K. 13 G4 50 37N 3 59W
Dartmouth, Canada 73 D7 44 40N 63 30W
Dartmouth, U.K. 13 G4 50 21N 3 36W
Dartmouth Res., Australia 63 D4 26 4S 145 18 E
Dartuch, C. = Artrutx, C. de, Spain 24 B10 39 55N 3 49 E
Darvaza, Turkmenistan 28 E6 40 11N 58 24 E
Darvel, Teluk = Lahad Datu, Teluk, Malaysia 37 D5 4 50N 118 20 E
Darwen, U.K. 12 D5 53 42N 2 29W
Darwendale, Zimbabwe 57 B5 17 41S 30 33 E
Darwha, India 40 J10 20 15N 77 45 E
Darwin, Australia 60 B5 12 25S 130 51 E
Darwin, U.S.A. 79 J9 36 15N 117 35W
Darya Khan, Pakistan 42 D4 31 48N 71 6 E
Daryoi Amu = Amudarya →, Uzbekistan 28 E6 43 58N 59 34 E
Dās, U.A.E. 45 E7 25 20N 53 30 E
Dashen, Ras, Ethiopia 47 E2 13 8N 38 26 E
Dashetai, China 34 D5 41 0N 109 5 E
Dashhowuz, Turkmenistan 28 E6 41 49N 59 58 E
Dashköpri, Turkmenistan 45 B9 36 16N 62 8 E
Dasht, Iran 45 B8 37 17N 56 7 E
Dasht →, Pakistan 40 G2 25 10N 61 40 E
Daska, Pakistan 42 C6 32 20N 74 20 E
Dasuya, India 42 D6 31 49N 75 38 E
Datça, Turkey 23 F12 36 46N 27 40 E
Datia, India 43 G8 25 39N 78 27 E
Datong, China 34 D7 40 6N 113 18 E
Dattakhel, Pakistan 42 C3 32 54N 69 46 E
Datu, Tanjung, Indonesia 36 D3 2 5N 109 39 E
Datu Piang, Phil. 37 C6 7 2N 124 30 E
Datuk, Tanjong = Datu, Tanjung, Indonesia 36 D3 2 5N 109 39 E
Daud Khel, Pakistan 42 C4 32 53N 71 34 E
Daudnagar, India 43 G11 25 2N 84 24 E
Daugava →, Latvia 9 H21 57 4N 24 3 E
Daugavpils, Latvia 9 J22 55 53N 26 32 E
Daulpur, India 42 F7 26 45N 77 59 E
Dauphin, Canada 71 C8 51 9N 100 5W
Dauphin, U.S.A. 84 F8 40 22N 76 56W
Dauphin L., Canada 71 C9 51 20N 99 45W
Dauphiné, France 20 D6 45 15N 5 25 E
Dausa, India 42 F7 26 52N 76 20 E
Davangere, India 40 M9 14 25N 75 55 E
Davao, Phil. 37 C7 7 0N 125 40 E
Davao G., Phil. 37 C7 6 30N 125 48 E
Dāvar Panāh = Sarāvān, Iran 45 E9 27 25N 62 15 E
Davenport, Calif., U.S.A. 78 H4 37 1N 122 12W
Davenport, Iowa, U.S.A. 80 E9 41 32N 90 35W
Davenport, Wash., U.S.A. 76 C4 47 39N 118 9W
Davenport Ra., Australia 62 C1 20 28S 134 0 E
Daventry, U.K. 13 E6 52 16N 1 10W
David, Panama 88 E3 8 30N 82 30W
David City, U.S.A. 80 E6 41 15N 97 8W
David Gorodok = Davyd Haradok, Belarus 17 B14 52 4N 27 8 E
Davidson, Canada 71 C7 51 16N 105 59W
Davis, Antarctica 5 C6 68 34S 77 55 E
Davis, U.S.A. 78 G5 38 33N 121 44W
Davis Dam, U.S.A. 79 K12 35 11N 114 34W
Davis Inlet, Canada 73 A7 55 50N 60 59W
Davis Mts., U.S.A. 81 K2 30 50N 103 55W
Davis Sea, Antarctica 5 C7 66 0S 92 0 E
Davis Str., N. Amer. 69 B14 65 0N 58 0W
Davos, Switz. 20 C8 46 48N 9 49 E
Davy L., Canada 71 B7 58 53N 108 18W
Davyd Haradok, Belarus 17 B14 52 4N 27 8 E
Dawei = Tavoy, Burma 38 E2 14 2N 98 12 E
Dawes Ra., Australia 62 C5 24 40S 150 40 E
Dawlish, U.K. 13 G4 50 35N 3 28W
Dawna Ra., Burma 38 D2 16 30N 98 30 E
Dawros Hd., Ireland 10 B3 54 50N 8 33W
Dawson, Canada 68 B6 64 10N 139 30W
Dawson, U.S.A. 83 K3 31 46N 84 27W
Dawson, I., Chile 96 G2 53 50S 70 50W
Dawson B., Canada 71 C8 52 53N 100 49W
Dawson Creek, Canada 70 B4 55 45N 120 15W
Dawson Inlet, Canada 71 A10 61 50N 93 25W
Dawson Ra., Australia 62 C4 24 30S 149 48 E
Dax, France 20 E3 43 44N 1 3W
Daxian, China 32 C5 31 15N 107 23 E
Daxindian, China 35 F11 37 30N 120 50 E
Daxinggou, China 35 C15 43 25N 129 40 E
Daxue Shan, China 32 C5 30 30N 101 30 E
Daylesford, Australia 63 F3 37 21S 144 9 E
Dayr az Zawr, Syria 44 C4 35 20N 40 5 E
Daysland, Canada 70 C6 52 50N 112 20W
Dayton, Nev., U.S.A. 78 F7 39 14N 119 36W
Dayton, Ohio, U.S.A. 82 F3 39 45N 84 12W
Dayton, Pa., U.S.A. 84 F5 40 53N 79 15W
Dayton, Tenn., U.S.A. 83 H3 35 30N 85 1W
Dayton, Wash., U.S.A. 76 C4 46 19N 117 59W
Dayton, Wyo., U.S.A. 76 D10 44 53N 107 16W
Daytona Beach, U.S.A. 83 L5 29 13N 81 1W
Dayville, U.S.A. 76 D4 44 28N 119 32W
De Aar, S. Africa 56 E3 30 39S 24 0 E
De Biesbosch △, Neths. 15 C4 51 45N 4 48 E
De Funiak Springs, U.S.A. 83 K2 30 43N 86 7W
De Grey →, Australia 60 D2 20 12S 119 13 E
De Haan, Belgium 15 C3 51 16N 3 2 E
De Hoge Veluwe △, Neths. 15 B5 52 5N 5 46 E
De Hoop ⌓, S. Africa 56 E3 34 30S 20 28 E
De Kalb, U.S.A. 80 E10 41 56N 88 46W
De Kennemerduinen △, Neths. 15 B4 52 27N 4 33 E
De Land, U.S.A. 83 L5 29 2N 81 18W
De Leon, U.S.A. 81 J5 32 7N 98 32W
De Panne, Belgium 15 C2 51 6N 2 34 E
De Pere, U.S.A. 82 C1 44 27N 88 4W
De Queen, U.S.A. 81 H7 34 2N 94 21W
De Quincy, U.S.A. 81 K8 30 27N 93 26W
De Ridder, U.S.A. 81 K8 30 51N 93 17W
De Smet, U.S.A. 80 C6 44 23N 97 33W
De Soto, U.S.A. 80 F9 38 8N 90 34W
De Tour Village, U.S.A. 82 C4 46 0N 83 56W
De Witt, U.S.A. 81 H9 34 18N 91 20W
Dead Sea, Asia 46 D4 31 30N 35 30 E
Deadwood, U.S.A. 80 C3 44 23N 103 44W
Deadwood L., Canada 70 B3 59 10N 128 30W
Deal, U.K. 13 F9 51 13N 1 25 E
Deal I., Australia 63 F4 39 30S 147 20 E
Dealesville, S. Africa 56 D4 28 41S 25 44 E
Dean →, Canada 70 C3 52 49N 126 58W
Dean, Forest of, U.K. 13 F5 51 45N 2 33W
Dean Chan., Canada 70 C3 52 30N 127 15W
Deán Funes, Argentina 94 C3 30 20S 64 20W
Dease →, Canada 70 B3 59 56N 128 32W
Dease L., Canada 70 B2 58 40N 130 5W
Dease Lake, Canada 70 B2 58 25N 130 6W
Death Valley, U.S.A. 79 J10 36 15N 116 50W
Death Valley △, U.S.A. 79 J10 36 45N 117 15W
Death Valley Junction, U.S.A. 79 J10 36 20N 116 25W
Debar, Macedonia 23 D9 41 31N 20 30 E
Debden, Canada 71 C7 53 30N 106 50W
Dębica, Poland 17 C11 50 2N 21 25 E
DeBolt, Canada 70 B5 55 12N 118 1W
Deborah East, L., Australia 61 F2 30 45S 119 0 E
Deborah West, L., Australia 61 F2 30 45S 118 50 E
Debre Markos, Ethiopia 47 E2 10 20N 37 40 E
Debre Tabor, Ethiopia 47 E2 11 50N 38 26 E
Debre Zeyit, Ethiopia 47 F2 11 48N 38 30 E
Debrecen, Hungary 17 E11 47 33N 21 42 E
Decatur, Ala., U.S.A. 83 H2 34 36N 86 59W
Decatur, Ga., U.S.A. 83 J3 33 47N 84 18W
Decatur, Ill., U.S.A. 80 F10 39 51N 88 57W
Decatur, Ind., U.S.A. 82 E3 40 50N 84 56W
Decatur, Tex., U.S.A. 81 J6 33 14N 97 35W
Deccan, India 40 L11 18 0N 79 0 E
Deception Bay, Australia 63 D5 27 10S 153 5 E
Deception I., Antarctica 5 C17 63 0S 60 15W
Deception L., Canada 71 B8 56 33N 104 13W
Dechhu, India 42 F5 26 46N 72 20 E
Děčín, Czech Rep. 16 C8 50 47N 14 12 E
Deckerville, U.S.A. 84 C2 43 32N 82 44W
Decorah, U.S.A. 80 D9 43 18N 91 48W
Dedéagach = Alexandroúpolis, Greece 23 D11 40 50N 25 54 E
Dedham, U.S.A. 85 D13 42 15N 71 10W
Dedza, Malawi 55 E3 14 20S 34 20 E
Dee →, Aberds., U.K. 11 D6 57 9N 2 5W
Dee →, Dumf. & Gall., U.K. 11 G4 54 51N 4 3W
Dee →, Wales, U.K. 12 D4 53 22N 3 17W
Deep B., Canada 70 A5 61 15N 116 35W
Deep Bay = Shenzhen Wan, China 33 G10 22 27N 113 55 E
Deepwater, Australia 63 D5 29 25S 151 51 E
Deer →, Canada 71 B10 58 23N 94 13W
Deer L., Canada 71 C10 52 40N 94 20W
Deer Lake, Nfld. & L., Canada 73 C8 49 11N 57 27W
Deer Lake, Ont., Canada 71 C10 52 36N 94 20W
Deer Lodge, U.S.A. 76 C7 46 24N 112 44W
Deer Park, U.S.A. 76 C5 47 57N 117 28W
Deer River, U.S.A. 80 B8 47 20N 93 48W
Deeragun, Australia 62 B4 19 16S 146 33 E
Deerdepoort, S. Africa 56 C4 24 37S 26 27 E
Deferiet, U.S.A. 85 B9 44 2N 75 41W
Defiance, U.S.A. 82 E3 41 17N 84 22W
Degana, India 42 F6 26 50N 74 20 E
Dégelis, Canada 73 C6 47 30N 68 35W
Deggendorf, Germany 16 D7 48 50N 12 57 E
Degh →, Pakistan 42 D5 31 3N 73 21 E
Deh Bīd, Iran 45 D7 30 39N 53 11 E
Deh-e Shīr, Iran 45 D7 31 29N 53 45 E
Dehaj, Iran 45 D7 30 42N 54 53 E
Dehak, Iran 45 E9 27 11N 62 37 E
Dehdez, Iran 45 D6 31 43N 50 17 E
Dehej, India 42 J5 21 44N 72 40 E
Dehestān, Iran 45 D7 28 30N 55 35 E
Dehgolān, Iran 44 C5 35 17N 47 25 E
Dehibat, Tunisia 51 B8 32 0N 10 47 E
Dehlorān, Iran 44 C5 32 41N 47 16 E
Dehnow-e Kühestān, Iran 45 E8 27 58N 58 32 E
Dehra Dun, India 42 D8 30 20N 78 4 E
Dehri, India 43 G11 24 50N 84 15 E
Dehui, China 35 B13 44 30N 125 40 E
Deinze, Belgium 15 D3 50 59N 3 32 E
Dej, Romania 17 E12 47 10N 23 52 E
Deka →, Zimbabwe 56 B4 18 4S 26 42 E
Dekese, Dem. Rep. of the Congo 52 E4 3 24S 21 24 E
Del Mar, U.S.A. 79 N9 32 58N 117 16W
Del Norte, U.S.A. 77 H10 37 41N 106 21W
Del Rio, U.S.A. 81 L4 29 22N 100 54W
Delambre I., Australia 60 D2 20 26S 117 5 E
Delano, U.S.A. 79 K7 35 46N 119 15W
Delano Peak, U.S.A. 77 G7 38 22N 112 22W
Delareyville, S. Africa 56 D4 26 41S 25 26 E
Delaronde L., Canada 71 C7 54 3N 107 3W
Delavan, U.S.A. 80 D10 42 38N 88 39W
Delaware, U.S.A. 82 E4 40 18N 83 4W
Delaware □, U.S.A. 82 F8 39 0N 75 20W
Delaware →, U.S.A. 85 G9 39 15N 75 20W
Delaware B., U.S.A. 82 F8 39 0N 75 10W
Delaware Water Gap ⌓, U.S.A. 85 E10 41 10N 74 55W
Delay →, Canada 73 A5 56 56N 71 28W
Delegate, Australia 63 F4 37 4S 148 56 E
Delevan, U.S.A. 84 D6 42 29N 78 29W
Delft, Neths. 15 B4 52 1N 4 22 E
Delfzijl, Neths. 15 A6 53 20N 6 55 E
Delgado, C., Mozam. 55 E5 10 45S 40 40 E
Delgerhet, Mongolia 34 B6 45 50N 110 30 E
Delgo, Sudan 51 D12 20 6N 30 40 E
Delhi, Canada 84 D4 42 51N 80 30W
Delhi, India 42 E7 28 38N 77 17 E
Delhi, La., U.S.A. 81 J9 32 28N 91 30W
Delhi, N.Y., U.S.A. 85 D10 42 17N 74 55W
Delia, Canada 70 C6 51 38N 112 23W
Delice, Turkey 19 G5 39 54N 34 2 E
Delicias, Mexico 86 B3 28 10N 105 30W
Delījān, Iran 45 C6 33 59N 50 40 E
Déline, Canada 68 B7 65 11N 123 25W
Delisle, Canada 71 C7 51 55N 107 8W
Dell City, U.S.A. 77 L11 31 56N 105 12W
Dell Rapids, U.S.A. 80 D6 43 50N 96 43W
Delmar, U.S.A. 85 D11 42 37N 73 47W
Delmenhorst, Germany 16 B5 53 3N 8 37 E
Delonga, Ostrova, Russia 29 B15 76 40N 149 20 E
Deloraine, Australia 63 G4 41 30S 146 40 E
Deloraine, Canada 71 D8 49 15N 100 29W
Delphi, U.S.A. 82 E2 40 36N 86 41W
Delphos, U.S.A. 82 E3 40 51N 84 21W
Delportshoop, S. Africa 56 D3 28 22S 24 20 E
Delray Beach, U.S.A. 83 M5 26 28N 80 4W
Delta, Colo., U.S.A. 77 G9 38 44N 108 4W
Delta, Utah, U.S.A. 76 G7 39 21N 112 35W
Delta Junction, U.S.A. 68 B5 64 2N 145 44W
Deltona, U.S.A. 83 L5 28 54N 81 16W
Delungra, Australia 63 D5 29 39S 150 51 E
Delvada, India 42 J4 20 46N 71 2 E
Delvinë, Albania 23 E9 39 59N 20 6 E
Demak, Indonesia 37 G14 6 53S 110 38 E
Demanda, Sierra de la, Spain 21 A4 42 15N 3 0W
Demavend = Damāvand, Qolleh-ye, Iran 45 C7 35 56N 52 10 E
Dembia, Dem. Rep. of the Congo 54 B2 3 33N 25 48 E
Dembidolo, Ethiopia 47 F1 8 34N 34 50 E

Demchok, *India* . . . . **43 C8** 32 42N 79 29 E
Demer ➤, *Belgium* . . . . **15 D4** 50 57N 4 42 E
Deming, *N. Mex., U.S.A.* . . . **77 K10** 32 16N 107 46W
Deming, *Wash., U.S.A.* **78 B4** 48 50N 122 13W
Demini ➤, *Brazil* **92 D6** 0 46S 62 56W
Demirci, *Turkey* . . . . **23 E13** 39 2N 28 38 E
Demirköy, *Turkey* . . . . **23 D12** 41 49N 27 45 E
Demopolis, *U.S.A.* **83 J2** 32 31N 87 50W
Dempo, *Indonesia* . . . . **36 E2** 4 2S 103 15 E
Den Burg, *Neths.* . . . . **15 A4** 53 3N 4 47 E
Den Chai, *Thailand* . . . . **38 D3** 17 59N 100 4 E
Den Haag = 's-Gravenhage,
　Neths. . . . . **15 B4** 52 7N 4 17 E
Den Helder, *Neths.* . . . . **15 B4** 52 57N 4 45 E
Den Oever, *Neths.* . . . . **15 B5** 52 56N 5 2 E
Denair, *U.S.A.* **78 H6** 37 32N 120 48W
Denau, *Uzbekistan* . . . . **28 F7** 38 16N 67 54 E
Denbigh, *Canada* **84 A7** 45 8N 77 15W
Denbigh, *U.K.* **12 D4** 53 12N 3 25W
Denbighshire □, *U.K.* **12 D4** 53 8N 3 22W
Dendang, *Indonesia* . . . . **36 E3** 3 7S 107 56 E
Dendermonde, *Belgium* . . . . **15 C4** 51 2N 4 5 E
Dengfeng, *China* . . . . **34 G7** 34 25N 113 2 E
Dengkou, *China* . . . . **34 D4** 40 18N 106 55 E
Denham, *Australia* . . . . **61 E1** 25 56S 113 31 E
Denham, Mt., *Jamaica* . . . . . **88 a** 18 13N 77 32W
Denham Ra., *Australia* . . . . . **62 C4** 21 55S 147 46 E
Denham Sd., *Australia* . . . . . **61 E1** 25 45S 113 15 E
Denholm, *Canada* **71 C7** 52 39N 108 1W
Denia, *Spain* . . . . **21 C6** 38 49N 0 8 E
Denial B., *Australia* . . . . **63 E1** 32 14S 133 32 E
Deniliquin, *Australia* . . . . . . **63 F3** 35 30S 144 58 E
Denison, *Iowa, U.S.A.* **80 E7** 42 1N 95 21W
Denison, *Tex., U.S.A.* **81 J6** 33 45N 96 33W
Denison Plains, *Australia* . . . **60 C4** 18 35S 128 0 E
Denizli, *Turkey* . . . . **19 G4** 37 42N 29 2 E
Denman Glacier, *Antarctica* . . **5 C7** 66 45S 99 25 E
Denmark, *Australia* . . . . **61 F2** 34 59S 117 25 E
Denmark ■, *Europe* . . . . **9 J13** 55 45N 10 0 E
Denmark Str., *Atl. Oc.* **4 C6** 66 0N 30 0W
Dennery, *St. Lucia* . . . . **89 f** 13 55N 60 54W
Dennison, *U.S.A.* **84 F3** 40 24N 81 19W
Denny, *U.K.* **11 E5** 56 1N 3 55W
Denpasar, *Indonesia* . . . . . . **36 F5** 8 39S 115 13 E
Denpasar ✈ (DPS), *Indonesia* . **37 K18** 8 44S 115 10 E
Denton, *Mont., U.S.A.* **76 C9** 47 19N 109 57W
Denton, *Tex., U.S.A.* **81 J6** 33 13N 97 8W
D'Entrecasteaux △, *Australia* . . **61 F2** 34 20S 115 33 E
D'Entrecasteaux, Pt., *Australia* . **61 F2** 34 50S 115 57 E
Denver, *Colo., U.S.A.* **80 F2** 39 44N 104 59W
Denver, *Pa., U.S.A.* **85 F8** 40 14N 76 8W
Denver City, *U.S.A.* **81 J3** 32 58N 102 50W
Deoband, *India* . . . . **42 E7** 29 42N 77 43 E
Deogarh, *India* . . . . **42 G5** 25 32N 73 54 E
Deoghar, *India* . . . . **43 G12** 24 30N 86 42 E
Deolali, *India* . . . . **40 K8** 19 58N 73 50 E
Deoli = Devli, *India* . . . . **42 G6** 25 50N 75 20 E
Deora, *India* . . . . **42 F4** 26 22N 70 55 E
Deori, *India* . . . . **43 H8** 23 24N 79 1 E
Deoria, *India* . . . . **43 F10** 26 31N 83 48 E
Deosai Mts., *Pakistan* . . . . . **43 B6** 35 40N 75 0 E
Deosri, *India* . . . . **43 F14** 26 46N 90 29 E
Depalpur, *India* . . . . **42 H6** 22 51N 75 33 E
Deping, *China* . . . . **35 F9** 37 25N 116 58 E
Deposit, *U.S.A.* **85 D9** 42 4N 75 25W
Depuch I., *Australia* . . . . **60 D2** 20 37S 117 44 E
Deputatskiy, *Russia* . . . . **29 C14** 69 18N 139 54 E
Dera Ghazi Khan, *Pakistan* . . **42 D4** 30 5N 70 43 E
Dera Ismail Khan, *Pakistan* . . **42 D4** 31 50N 70 50 E
Derabugti, *Pakistan* . . . . **42 E3** 29 2N 69 9 E
Derawar Fort, *Pakistan* . . . . . **42 E4** 28 46N 71 20 E
Derbent, *Russia* . . . . **19 F8** 42 5N 48 15 E
Derby, *Australia* . . . . **60 C3** 17 18S 123 38 E
Derby, *U.K.* **12 E6** 52 56N 1 28W
Derby, *Conn., U.S.A.* **85 E11** 41 19N 73 5W
Derby, *Kans., U.S.A.* **81 G6** 37 33N 97 16W
Derby, *N.Y., U.S.A.* **84 D6** 42 41N 78 58W
Derby City □, *U.K.* **12 E6** 52 56N 1 28W
Derby Line, *U.S.A.* **85 B12** 45 0N 72 6W
Derbyshire □, *U.K.* **12 D6** 53 11N 1 38W
Derdepoort, *S. Africa* . . . . . . **56 C4** 24 38S 26 24 E
Dereham, *U.K.* . . . . **13 E8** 52 41N 0 57 E
Derg ➤, *U.K.* **10 B4** 54 44N 7 26W
Derg, L., *Ireland* **10 D3** 53 0N 8 20W
Dergaon, *India* . . . . **41 F19** 26 45N 94 0 E
Dermott, *U.S.A.* **81 J9** 33 32N 91 26W
Derry = Londonderry, *U.K.* . . **10 B4** 55 0N 7 20W
Derry = Londonderry □, *U.K.* . **10 B4** 55 0N 7 20W
Derry, *N.H., U.S.A.* **85 D13** 42 53N 71 19W
Derry, *Pa., U.S.A.* **84 F5** 40 20N 79 18W
Derryveagh Mts., *Ireland* . . . **10 B3** 54 56N 8 11W
Derwent ➤, *Cumb., U.K.* . . . **12 C4** 54 39N 3 33W
Derwent ➤, *Derby, U.K.* **12 E6** 52 57N 1 28W
Derwent ➤, *N. Yorks., U.K.* . . **12 D7** 53 45N 0 58W
Derwent Water, *U.K.* **12 C4** 54 35N 3 9W
Des Moines, *Iowa, U.S.A.* . . . **80 E8** 41 35N 93 37W
Des Moines, *N. Mex., U.S.A.* . **81 G3** 36 46N 103 50W
Des Moines ➤, *U.S.A.* **80 E9** 40 23N 91 25W
Desaguadero ➤, *Argentina* . . **94 C2** 34 30S 66 46W
Desaguadero ➤, *Bolivia* **92 G5** 16 35S 69 5W
Desar, *Malaysia* . . . . **39 d** 1 31N 104 17 E
Descanso, Pta., *Mexico* **79 N9** 32 21N 117 3W
Deschaillons-sur-St-Laurent,
　Canada **73 C5** 46 32N 72 7W
Deschambault L., *Canada* . . . **71 C8** 54 50N 103 30W
Deschutes ➤, *U.S.A.* **76 D3** 45 38N 120 55W
Dese, *Ethiopia* . . . . **47 E2** 11 5N 39 40 E
Deseado ➤, *Argentina* **96 F3** 47 45S 65 54W
Desert Center, *U.S.A.* **79 M11** 33 43N 115 24W
Desert Hot Springs, *U.S.A.* . . **79 M10** 33 58N 116 30W
Deshnok, *India* . . . . **42 F5** 27 48N 73 21 E
Desierto Central de Baja
　California △, *Mexico* **86 B2** 29 40N 114 43W
Desna ➤, *Ukraine* . . . . **17 C16** 50 33N 30 32 E
Desolación, I., *Chile* **96 G2** 53 0S 74 0W
Despeñaperros, Paso, *Spain* . **21 C4** 38 24N 3 30W
Dessau, *Germany* . . . . **16 C7** 51 51N 12 14 E
Dessye = Dese, *Ethiopia* . . . . **47 E2** 11 5N 39 40 E
D'Estrees B., *Australia* . . . . . **63 F2** 35 55S 137 45 E
Desuri, *India* . . . . **42 G5** 25 18N 73 35 E
Det Udom, *Thailand* . . . . **38 E5** 14 54N 105 5 E
Dete, *Zimbabwe* . . . . **56 B4** 18 38S 26 50 E
Detmold, *Germany* . . . . **16 C5** 51 56N 8 52 E
Detour, Pt., *U.S.A.* **82 C2** 45 40N 86 40W
Detroit, *U.S.A.* **84 D1** 42 20N 83 3W
Detroit Lakes, *U.S.A.* **80 B7** 46 49N 95 51W
Deurne, *Neths.* . . . . **15 C5** 51 27N 5 49 E
Deutsche Bucht, *Germany* . . . **16 A5** 54 15N 8 0 E

Deva, *Romania* . . . . **17 F12** 45 53N 22 55 E
Devakottai, *India* . . . . **40 Q11** 9 55N 78 45 E
Devaprayag, *India* . . . . **43 D8** 30 13N 78 35 E
Deventer, *Neths.* . . . . **15 B6** 52 15N 6 10 E
Deveron ➤, *U.K.* **11 D6** 57 41N 2 32W
Devgadh Bariya, *India* . . . . . **42 H5** 22 40N 73 55 E
Devikot, *India* . . . . **42 F4** 26 42N 71 12 E
Devils Den, *U.S.A.* **78 K7** 35 46N 119 58W
Devils Lake, *U.S.A.* **80 A5** 48 7N 98 52W
Devils Paw, *Canada* **70 B2** 58 47N 134 0W
Devils Postpile △, *U.S.A.* . . . **78 H7** 37 37N 119 5W
Devils Tower △, *U.S.A.* **80 C2** 44 35N 104 57W
Devils Tower Junction, *U.S.A.* . **80 C2** 44 31N 104 57W
Devine, *U.S.A.* **81 L5** 29 8N 98 54W
Devizes, *U.K.* **13 F6** 51 22N 1 58W
Devli, *India* . . . . **42 G6** 25 50N 75 20 E
Devon, *Canada* **70 C6** 53 24N 113 44W
Devon □, *U.K.* **13 G4** 50 50N 3 40W
Devon I., *Canada* **4 B3** 75 10N 85 0W
Devonport, *Australia* . . . . . . **63 G4** 41 10S 146 22 E
Devonport, *N.Z.* . . . . **59 G5** 36 49S 174 49 E
Dewas, *India* . . . . **42 H7** 22 59N 76 3 E
Dewetsdorp, *S. Africa* . . . . . **56 D4** 29 33S 26 39 E
Dewey, *Puerto Rico* . . . . **89 d** 18 18N 65 18W
Dexter, *Maine, U.S.A.* **83 C11** 45 1N 69 18W
Dexter, *Mo., U.S.A.* **81 G10** 36 48N 89 57W
Dexter, *N. Mex., U.S.A.* **81 J2** 33 12N 104 22W
Dey-Dey, L., *Australia* . . . . . **61 E5** 29 12S 131 4 E
Deyhūk, *Iran* . . . . **45 C8** 33 15N 57 30 E
Deyyer, *Iran* . . . . **45 E6** 27 55N 51 55 E
Dezadeash L., *Canada* **70 A1** 60 28N 136 58W
Dezfūl, *Iran* . . . . **45 C6** 32 20N 48 30 E
Dezhneva, Mys, *Russia* **29 C19** 66 5N 169 40W
Dezhou, *China* . . . . **34 F9** 37 26N 116 18 E
Dhadhar ➤, *India* . . . . **43 G11** 24 56N 85 24 E
Dháfni, *Greece* . . . . **25 D7** 35 13N 25 3 E
Dhahiriya = Az Zāhirīyah,
　West Bank . . . . **46 D3** 31 25N 34 58 E
Dhahran = Az Zahrān, *Si. Arabia* . **45 E6** 26 10N 50 7 E
Dhak, *Pakistan* . . . . **42 C5** 32 25N 72 33 E
Dhaka, *Bangla.* . . . . **43 H14** 23 43N 90 26 E
Dhaka □, *Bangla.* . . . . **43 G14** 24 25N 90 25 E
Dhali, *Cyprus* . . . . **25 D12** 35 1N 33 25 E
Dhampur, *India* . . . . **43 E8** 29 19N 78 33 E
Dhamtari, *India* . . . . **41 J12** 20 42N 81 35 E
Dhanbad, *India* . . . . **43 H12** 23 50N 86 30 E
Dhangarhi, *Nepal* . . . . **41 E12** 28 55N 80 40 E
Dhankuta, *Nepal* . . . . **43 F12** 26 55N 87 40 E
Dhar, *India* . . . . **42 H6** 22 35N 75 26 E
Dharampur, *India* . . . . **42 H6** 22 13N 75 18 E
Dharamsala = Dharmsala, *India* . **42 C7** 32 16N 76 23 E
Dhariwal, *India* . . . . **42 D6** 31 57N 75 19 E
Dharla ➤, *Bangla.* . . . . **43 G13** 25 46N 89 42 E
Dharmapuri, *India* . . . . **40 N11** 12 10N 78 10 E
Dharmjaygarh, *India* . . . . **43 H10** 22 28N 83 13 E
Dharmsala, *India* . . . . **42 C7** 32 16N 76 23 E
Dharni, *India* . . . . **42 J7** 21 33N 76 53 E
Dharwad, *India* . . . . **40 M9** 15 30N 75 4 E
Dhasan ➤, *India* . . . . **43 G8** 25 48N 79 24 E
Dhaulagiri, *Nepal* . . . . **43 E10** 28 39N 83 28 E
Dhebar, L., *India* . . . . **42 G6** 24 10N 74 0 E
Dheftera, *Cyprus* . . . . **25 D12** 35 5N 33 16 E
Dhenkanal, *India* . . . . **41 J14** 20 45N 85 35 E
Dherinia, *Cyprus* . . . . **25 D12** 35 3N 33 57 E
Dhī Qār □, *Iraq* . . . . **44 D5** 31 0N 46 15 E
Dhiarrizos ➤, *Cyprus* . . . . . . **25 E11** 34 41N 32 34 E
Dhībān, *Jordan* . . . . **46 D4** 31 30N 35 46 E
Dhikti Óros, *Greece* . . . . **25 D7** 35 8N 25 30 E
Dhilwan, *India* . . . . **42 D6** 31 31N 75 21 E
Dhimarkhera, *India* . . . . **43 H9** 23 28N 80 22 E
Dhírfis Óros, *Greece* . . . . . . **23 E10** 38 40N 23 54 E
Dholka, *India* . . . . **42 H5** 22 44N 72 29 E
Dhoraji, *India* . . . . **42 J4** 21 45N 70 37 E
Dhráhstis, Ákra, *Greece* . . . . **25 A3** 39 48N 19 40 E
Dhrangadhra, *India* . . . . **42 H4** 22 59N 71 31 E
Dhrápanon, Ákra, *Greece* . . . **25 D6** 35 28N 24 14 E
Dhrol, *India* . . . . **42 H4** 22 33N 70 25 E
Dhuburi, *India* . . . . **41 F16** 26 2N 89 59 E
Dhule, *India* . . . . **40 J9** 20 58N 74 50 E
Di Linh, *Vietnam* . . . . **39 G7** 11 35N 108 4 E
Di Linh, Cao Nguyen, *Vietnam* . **39 G7** 11 30N 108 0 E
Día, *Greece* . . . . **25 D7** 35 28N 25 14 E
Diablo, Mt., *U.S.A.* **78 H5** 37 53N 121 56W
Diablo Range, *U.S.A.* **78 J5** 37 20N 121 25W
Diafarabé, *Mali* **50 F5** 14 9N 4 57W
Diamante, *Argentina* **94 C3** 32 5S 60 40W
Diamante ➤, *Argentina* **94 C2** 34 30S 66 46W
Diamantina, *Brazil* **93 G10** 18 17S 43 40W
Diamantina △, *Australia* . . . . **62 C3** 23 33S 141 23 E
Diamantina ➤, *Australia* . . . . **63 D2** 26 45S 139 10 E
Diamantino, *Brazil* **93 F7** 14 30S 56 30W
Diamond Bar, *U.S.A.* **79 L9** 34 1N 117 48W
Diamond Harbour, *India* . . . . **43 H13** 22 11N 88 14 E
Diamond Is., *Australia* . . . . . . **62 B5** 17 25S 151 5 E
Diamond Mts., *U.S.A.* **76 G6** 39 55N 115 58W
Diamond Springs, *U.S.A.* . . . **78 G6** 38 42N 120 49W
Dībā, *Oman* . . . . **45 E8** 25 45N 56 16 E
Dibai, *India* . . . . **42 E8** 28 13N 78 15 E
Dibaya-Lubue, *Dem. Rep. of
　the Congo* . . . . **52 E3** 4 12S 19 54 E
Dibbeen △, *Jordan* . . . . **46 C4** 32 20N 35 45 E
Dibete, *Botswana* . . . . **56 C4** 23 45S 26 32 E
Dibrugarh, *India* . . . . **41 F19** 27 29N 94 55 E
Dickens, *U.S.A.* **81 J4** 33 37N 100 50W
Dickinson, *U.S.A.* **80 B3** 46 53N 102 47W
Dickson, *U.S.A.* **83 G2** 36 5N 87 23W
Dickson City, *U.S.A.* **85 E9** 41 29N 75 40W
Didiéni, *Mali* **50 F4** 13 53N 8 6W
Didsbury, *Canada* **70 C6** 51 35N 114 10W
Didwana, *India* . . . . **42 F6** 27 23N 74 33 E
Diefenbaker, L., *Canada* **71 C7** 51 0N 106 55W
Diego de Almagro, *Chile* **94 B1** 26 22S 70 3W
Diego Garcia, *Ind. Oc.* . . . . . **3 E13** 7 50S 72 50 E
Diekirch, *Lux.* . . . . **15 E6** 49 52N 6 10 E
Dien Ban, *Vietnam* . . . . **38 E7** 15 53N 108 16 E
Dien Bien, *Vietnam* . . . . **38 B4** 21 20N 103 0 E
Dien Khanh, *Vietnam* . . . . . . **39 F7** 12 15N 109 6 E
Dieppe, *France* . . . . **20 B4** 49 54N 1 4 E
Dierks, *U.S.A.* **81 H8** 34 7N 94 1W
Diest, *Belgium* . . . . **15 D5** 50 58N 5 4 E
Dif, *Somali Rep.* . . . . **47 G3** 0 59N 40 58 E
Differdange, *Lux.* . . . . **15 E5** 49 31N 5 54 E
Dig, *India* . . . . **42 F7** 27 28N 77 20 E
Digba, *Dem. Rep. of the Congo* . **54 B2** 4 25N 25 48 E
Digby, *Canada* **73 D6** 44 38N 65 50W
Diggi, *India* . . . . **42 F6** 26 22N 75 26 E
Dighinala, *Bangla.* . . . . **41 H18** 23 15N 92 5 E

Dighton, *U.S.A.* **80 F4** 38 29N 100 28W
Digne-les-Bains, *France* . . . . **20 D7** 44 5N 6 12 E
Digos, *Phil.* . . . . **37 C7** 6 45N 125 20 E
Digranes, *Iceland* **8 C6** 66 4N 14 44W
Digul ➤, *Indonesia* . . . . **37 F9** 7 7S 138 42 E
Dihang = Brahmaputra ➤, *Asia* . **32 D3** 23 40N 90 35 E
Dijlah, Nahr ➤, *Asia* . . . . **44 D5** 31 0N 47 25 E
Dijon, *France* . . . . **20 C6** 47 20N 5 3 E
Dikhil, *Djibouti* . . . . **47 E3** 11 8N 42 20 E
Dikkil = Dikhil, *Djibouti* . . . . **47 E3** 11 8N 42 20 E
Diksmuide, *Belgium* . . . . **15 C2** 51 2N 2 52 E
Dikson, *Russia* . . . . **28 B9** 73 40N 80 5 E
Dila, *Ethiopia* . . . . **47 F2** 6 21N 38 22 E
Dili, *E. Timor* . . . . **37 F7** 8 39S 125 34 E
Dilley, *U.S.A.* **81 L5** 28 40N 99 10W
Dilli = Delhi, *India* . . . . **42 E7** 28 38N 77 17 E
Dillingham, *U.S.A.* **68 C4** 59 3N 158 28W
Dillon, *Canada* **71 B7** 55 56N 108 35W
Dillon, *Mont., U.S.A.* **76 D7** 45 13N 112 38W
Dillon, *S.C., U.S.A.* **83 H6** 34 25N 79 22W
Dillon ➤, *Canada* **71 B7** 55 56N 108 56W
Dillsburg, *U.S.A.* **84 F7** 40 7N 77 2W
Dilolo, *Dem. Rep. of the Congo* . **52 G4** 10 28S 22 18 E
Dimas, *Mexico* **86 C3** 23 43N 106 47W
Dimashq, *Syria* . . . . **46 B5** 33 30N 36 18 E
Dimashq □, *Syria* . . . . **46 B5** 33 30N 36 30 E
Dimbaza, *S. Africa* . . . . **57 E4** 32 50S 27 14 E
Dimboola, *Australia* . . . . **63 F3** 36 28S 142 7 E
Dîmbovita = Dâmbovița ➤,
　Romania . . . . **17 F14** 44 12N 26 26 E
Dimbulah, *Australia* . . . . **62 B4** 17 8S 145 4 E
Dimitrovgrad, *Bulgaria* . . . . . **23 C11** 42 5N 25 35 E
Dimitrovgrad, *Russia* . . . . . . **18 D8** 54 14N 49 39 E
Dimitrovo = Pernik, *Bulgaria* . **23 C10** 42 35N 23 2 E
Dimmitt, *U.S.A.* **81 H3** 34 33N 102 19W
Dimona, *Israel* . . . . **46 D4** 31 2N 35 1 E
Dinagat, *Phil.* . . . . **37 B7** 10 10N 125 40 E
Dinajpur, *Bangla.* . . . . **41 G16** 25 33N 88 43 E
Dinan, *France* **20 B2** 48 28N 2 2W
Dīnān Āb, *Iran* . . . . **45 C8** 32 4N 56 49 E
Dinant, *Belgium* . . . . **15 D4** 50 16N 4 55 E
Dinapur, *India* . . . . **43 G11** 25 38N 85 5 E
Dinār, Kūh-e, *Iran* . . . . **45 D6** 30 42N 51 46 E
Dinard, *France* **20 B2** 48 38N 2 6W
Dinaric Alps = Dinara Planina,
　Croatia . . . . **22 C7** 44 0N 16 30 E
Dindigul, *India* . . . . **40 P11** 10 25N 78 0 E
Dindori, *India* . . . . **43 H9** 22 57N 81 5 E
Ding Xian = Dingzhou, *China* . **34 E8** 38 30N 114 59 E
Dinga, *Pakistan* . . . . **42 G2** 25 26N 67 10 E
Dingbian, *China* . . . . **34 F4** 37 35N 107 32 E
Dingle, *Ireland* **10 D1** 52 9N 10 17W
Dingle B., *Ireland* **10 D1** 52 3N 10 20W
Dingmans Ferry, *U.S.A.* **85 E10** 41 13N 74 55W
Dingo, *Australia* . . . . **62 C4** 23 38S 149 19 E
Dingtao, *China* . . . . **34 G8** 35 5N 115 35 E
Dingwall, *U.K.* **11 D4** 57 36N 4 26W
Dingxi, *China* . . . . **34 G3** 35 30N 104 33 E
Dingxiang, *China* . . . . **34 E7** 38 30N 112 58 E
Dingzhou, *China* . . . . **34 E8** 38 30N 114 59 E
Dinh, Mui, *Vietnam* . . . . **39 G7** 11 22N 109 1 E
Dinh Lap, *Vietnam* . . . . **38 B6** 21 33N 107 6 E
Dinira △, *Venezuela* **89 E6** 9 57N 70 6W
Dinokwe, *Botswana* . . . . **56 C4** 23 29S 26 37 E
Dinorwic, *Canada* **71 D10** 49 41N 92 30W
Dinosaur △, *U.S.A.* **76 F9** 40 47N 111 30W
Dinosaur △, *U.S.A.* **76 F9** 40 30N 108 45W
Dinuba, *U.S.A.* **78 J7** 36 32N 119 23W
Dipalpur, *Pakistan* . . . . **42 D5** 30 40N 73 39 E
Diplo, *Pakistan* . . . . **42 G3** 24 35N 69 35 E
Dipolog, *Phil.* . . . . **37 C6** 8 36N 123 20 E
Dipperu △, *Australia* . . . . **62 C4** 21 56S 148 42 E
Dir, *Pakistan* . . . . **40 B7** 35 8N 71 59 E
Dire Dawa, *Ethiopia* . . . . **47 F3** 9 35N 41 45 E
Diriamba, *Nic.* **88 D2** 11 51N 86 19W
Dirk Hartog I., *Australia* . . . . **61 E1** 25 50S 113 5 E
Dirranbandi, *Australia* . . . . . . **63 D4** 28 33S 148 17 E
Disa, *India* . . . . **42 G5** 24 18N 72 10 E
Disappointment, C., *U.S.A.* . . **76 C2** 46 18N 124 5W
Disappointment, L., *Australia* . **60 D3** 23 20S 122 40 E
Disaster B., *Australia* . . . . . . **63 F4** 37 15S 149 58 E
Discovery B., *Australia* . . . . . **63 F3** 38 10S 140 40 E
Discovery B., *China* . . . . **33 G11** 22 18N 114 1 E
Disko = Qeqertarsuaq, *Greenland* . **69 B5** 69 45N 53 30W
Diss, *U.K.* . . . . **13 E9** 52 23N 1 7 E
Disteghil Sar, *Pakistan* . . . . . **43 A6** 36 20N 75 12 E
Distrito Federal □, *Brazil* **93 G9** 15 45S 47 45W
Distrito Federal □, *Mexico* . . . **87 D5** 19 15N 99 10W
Diu, *India* . . . . **42 J4** 20 45N 70 58 E
Divändarreh, *Iran* . . . . **44 C5** 35 55N 47 2 E
Divide, *U.S.A.* **76 D7** 45 45N 112 45W
Dividing Ra., *Australia* . . . . . **61 E2** 27 45S 116 0 E
Divinópolis, *Brazil* **93 H10** 20 10S 44 54W
Divnoye, *Russia* . . . . **19 E7** 45 55N 43 21 E
Divo, *Ivory C.* **50 G4** 5 48N 5 15W
Diwāl Kol, *Afghan.* . . . . **42 B2** 34 23N 67 52 E
Dixie Mt., *U.S.A.* **78 F6** 39 55N 120 16W
Dixon, *Calif., U.S.A.* **78 G5** 38 27N 121 49W
Dixon, *Ill., U.S.A.* **80 E10** 41 50N 89 29W
Dixon Entrance, *U.S.A.* **68 C6** 54 30N 132 0W
Dixville, *Canada* **85 A13** 45 4N 71 46W
Diyālā □, *Iraq* . . . . **44 C5** 33 45N 45 0 E
Diyālā ➤, *Iraq* . . . . **44 C5** 33 14N 44 31 E
Diyarbakır, *Turkey* . . . . **19 G7** 37 55N 40 18 E
Diyodar, *India* . . . . **42 G4** 24 8N 71 50 E
Djakarta = Jakarta, *Indonesia* . **36 F3** 6 9S 106 49 E
Djamba, *Angola* . . . . **56 B1** 16 45S 13 58 E
Djambala, *Congo* . . . . **52 E2** 2 32S 14 30 E
Djanet, *Algeria* . . . . **50 D7** 24 35N 9 32 E
Djawa = Jawa, *Indonesia* . . . . **36 F3** 7 0S 110 0 E
Djelfa, *Algeria* . . . . **50 B6** 34 40N 3 15 E
Djema, *C.A.R.* . . . . **54 A2** 6 3N 25 15 E
Djerba, I. de, *Tunisia* . . . . . . **51 B8** 33 50N 10 48 E
Djerid, Chott, *Tunisia* . . . . . . **50 B7** 33 42N 8 30 E
Djibouti, *Djibouti* . . . . **47 E3** 11 30N 43 5 E
Djibouti ■, *Africa* . . . . **47 E3** 12 0N 43 0 E
Djolu, *Dem. Rep. of the Congo* . **52 D4** 0 35N 22 5 E
Djoum, *Cameroon* . . . . **52 D2** 2 41N 12 35 E
Djourab, Erg du, *Chad* . . . . . **51 E9** 16 40N 18 50 E
Djugu, *Dem. Rep. of the Congo* . **54 B3** 1 55N 30 35 E
Djúpivogur, *Iceland* **8 D6** 64 39N 14 17W
Dmitriya Lapteva, Proliv, *Russia* . **29 B15** 73 0N 140 0 E
Dnepr = Dnipro ➤, *Ukraine* . . **19 E5** 46 30N 32 18 E
Dneprodzerzhinsk =
　Dniprodzerzhynsk, *Ukraine* . **19 E5** 48 32N 34 37 E
Dnepropetrovsk =
　Dnipropetrovsk, *Ukraine* . . **19 E5** 48 30N 35 0 E

Dnestr = Dnister ➤, *Europe* . . **17 E16** 46 18N 30 17 E
Dnieper = Dnipro ➤, *Ukraine* . **19 E5** 46 30N 32 18 E
Dniester = Dnister ➤, *Europe* . **17 E16** 46 18N 30 17 E
Dnipro ➤, *Ukraine* . . . . **19 E5** 46 30N 32 18 E
Dniprodzerzhynsk, *Ukraine* . . **19 E5** 48 32N 34 37 E
Dnipropetrovsk, *Ukraine* . . . . **19 E6** 48 30N 35 0 E
Dnister ➤, *Europe* . . . . **17 E16** 46 18N 30 17 E
Dno, *Russia* . . . . **18 C4** 57 50N 29 58 E
Dnyapro = Dnipro ➤, *Ukraine* . **19 E5** 46 30N 32 18 E
Doaktown, *Canada* **73 C6** 46 33N 66 8W
Doan Hung, *Vietnam* . . . . . . **38 B5** 21 30N 105 10 E
Doany, *Madag.* . . . . **57 A8** 14 21S 49 30 E
Doba, *Chad* . . . . **51 G9** 8 40N 16 50 E
Dobandi, *Pakistan* . . . . **42 D2** 31 13N 66 50 E
Dobbyn, *Australia* . . . . **62 B3** 19 44S 140 2 E
Dobele, *Latvia* . . . . **9 H20** 56 37N 23 16 E
Doberai, Jazirah, *Indonesia* . . **37 E8** 1 25S 133 0 E
Doblas, *Argentina* **94 D3** 37 5S 64 0W
Dobo, *Indonesia* . . . . **37 F8** 5 45S 134 15 E
Doboj, *Bos.-H.* . . . . **23 B8** 44 46N 18 4 E
Dobrich, *Bulgaria* . . . . **23 C12** 43 37N 27 49 E
Dobruja, *Europe* . . . . **17 F15** 44 30N 28 15 E
Dobrush, *Belarus* . . . . **17 B16** 52 25N 31 22 E
Doc, Mui, *Vietnam* . . . . **38 D6** 17 58N 106 30 E
Docker River, *Australia* . . . . . **61 D4** 24 52S 129 5 E
Doctor Arroyo, *Mexico* **86 C4** 23 40N 100 11W
Doda, *India* . . . . **43 C6** 33 10N 75 34 E
Doda, L., *Canada* **72 C4** 49 25N 75 13W
Dodecanese = Dhodhekánisos,
　Greece . . . . **23 F12** 36 35N 27 0 E
Dodge City, *U.S.A.* **81 G5** 37 45N 100 1W
Dodge L., *Canada* **71 B7** 59 50N 105 36W
Dodgeville, *U.S.A.* **80 D9** 42 58N 90 8W
Dodoma, *Tanzania* . . . . **54 D4** 6 8S 35 45 E
Dodoma □, *Tanzania* . . . . . . **54 D4** 6 0S 36 0 E
Dodori △, *Kenya* . . . . **54 C5** 1 55S 41 7 E
Dodsland, *Canada* **71 C7** 51 50N 108 45W
Dodson, *U.S.A.* **76 B9** 48 24N 108 15W
Doesburg, *Neths.* . . . . **15 B6** 52 1N 6 9 E
Doetinchem, *Neths.* . . . . **15 C6** 51 59N 6 18 E
Dog Creek, *Canada* **70 C4** 51 35N 122 14W
Dog L., *Man., Canada* **71 C9** 51 2N 98 31W
Dog L., *Ont., Canada* **72 C2** 48 48N 89 30W
Dogran, *Pakistan* . . . . **42 D5** 31 48N 73 35 E
Doğubayazıt, *Turkey* . . . . **44 B5** 39 31N 44 5 E
Doha = Ad Dawḥah, *Qatar* . . **45 E6** 25 15N 51 35 E
Dohazari, *Bangla.* . . . . **41 H18** 22 10N 92 5 E
Dohrighat, *India* . . . . **43 F10** 26 16N 83 31 E
Doi, *Indonesia* . . . . **37 D7** 2 14N 127 49 E
Doi Inthanon △, *Thailand* . . . **38 C2** 18 33N 98 34 E
Doi Khuntan △, *Thailand* . . . . **38 C2** 18 33N 99 14 E
Doi Luang, *Thailand* . . . . **38 C3** 18 30N 101 0 E
Doi Luang △, *Thailand* . . . . . **38 C2** 19 22N 99 35 E
Doi Saket, *Thailand* . . . . **38 C2** 18 52N 99 9 E
Doi Suthep △, *Thailand* . . . . . **38 C2** 18 49N 98 53 E
Dois Irmãos, Sa., *Brazil* **93 E10** 9 0S 42 30W
Dokkum, *Neths.* . . . . **15 A5** 53 20N 5 59 E
Dokri, *Pakistan* . . . . **42 F3** 27 25N 68 7 E
Dolak, Pulau, *Indonesia* . . . . **37 F9** 8 0S 138 30 E
Dolbeau-Mistassini, *Canada* . . **73 C5** 48 53N 72 14W
Dole, *France* . . . . **20 C6** 47 7N 5 31 E
Dolgellau, *U.K.* **12 E4** 52 45N 3 53W
Dolgelley = Dolgellau, *U.K.* . . **12 E4** 52 45N 3 53W
Dollard, *Neths.* . . . . **15 A7** 53 20N 7 10 E
Dolo, *Ethiopia* . . . . **47 G3** 4 11N 42 3 E
Dolomites = Dolomiti, *Italy* . . **22 A4** 46 23N 11 51 E
Dolomiti, *Italy* . . . . **22 A4** 46 23N 11 51 E
Dolores, *Argentina* **94 D4** 36 20S 57 40W
Dolores, *Uruguay* **94 C4** 33 34S 58 15W
Dolores, *U.S.A.* **77 H9** 37 28N 108 30W
Dolores ➤, *U.S.A.* **77 G9** 38 49N 109 17W
Dolphin, C., *Falk. Is.* **96 G5** 51 10S 59 0W
Dolphin and Union Str., *Canada* . **68 B8** 69 5N 114 45W
Dom Pedrito, *Brazil* **95 C5** 31 0S 54 40W
Doma, Zimbabwe . . . . **55 F3** 16 28S 30 12 E
Domariaganj ➤, *India* . . . . . . **43 F10** 26 17N 83 44 E
Domasi, *Malawi* . . . . **55 F4** 15 15S 35 22 E
Dombarovskiy, *Russia* . . . . . . **28 D6** 50 46N 59 32 E
Dombås, *Norway* . . . . **9 E13** 62 4N 9 8 E
Dome Fuji, *Antarctica* . . . . . . **5 D5** 77 20S 39 45 E
Domel I. = Letsôk-aw Kyun,
　Burma . . . . **39 G2** 11 30N 98 25 E
Domeyko, *Chile* **94 B1** 29 0S 71 0W
Domeyko, Cordillera, *Chile* . . **94 A2** 24 30S 69 0W
Dominador, *Chile* **94 A2** 24 21S 69 20W
Dominica ■, *W. Indies* **89 C7** 15 20N 61 20W
Dominica Passage, *W. Indies* . **89 C7** 15 10N 61 20W
Dominican Rep. ■, *W. Indies* . **89 C5** 19 0N 70 30W
Domodóssola, *Italy* . . . . **20 C8** 46 7N 8 17 E
Domville, Mt., *Australia* . . . . . **63 D5** 28 1S 151 15 E
Don ➤, *Russia* . . . . **19 E6** 47 4N 39 18 E
Don ➤, *Aberds., U.K.* **11 D6** 57 11N 2 5W
Don ➤, *S. Yorks., U.K.* **12 D7** 53 41N 0 52W
Don, C., *Australia* . . . . **60 B5** 11 18S 131 46 E
Don Benito, *Spain* **21 C3** 38 53N 5 51W
Don Figuero Mts., *Jamaica* . . **88 a** 18 5N 77 36W
Don Sak, *Thailand* . . . . **39 b** 9 18N 99 41 E
Dona Ana = Nhamaabué,
　Mozam. . . . . **55 F4** 17 25S 35 5 E
Donaghadee, *U.K.* **10 B6** 54 39N 5 33W
Donald, *Australia* . . . . **63 F3** 36 23S 143 0 E
Donaldsonville, *U.S.A.* **81 K9** 30 6N 90 59W
Donalsonville, *U.S.A.* **83 K3** 31 3N 84 53W
Donau = Dunărea ➤, *Europe* . **17 F15** 45 20N 29 40 E
Donauwörth, *Germany* . . . . . **16 D6** 48 43N 10 47 E
Doncaster, *U.K.* **12 D6** 53 32N 1 6W
Dondo, *Mozam.* . . . . **55 F3** 19 33S 34 46 E
Dondo, Teluk, *Indonesia* . . . . **37 D6** 0 50N 120 30 E
Dondra Head, *Sri Lanka* . . . . **40 S12** 5 55N 80 40 E
Donegal, *Ireland* **10 B3** 54 39N 8 5W
Donegal □, *Ireland* **10 B4** 54 53N 8 0W
Donegal B., *Ireland* **10 B3** 54 31N 8 49W
Donets ➤, *Russia* . . . . **19 E7** 47 33N 40 55 E
Donetsk, *Ukraine* . . . . **19 E6** 48 0N 37 45 E
Dong Ba Thin, *Vietnam* . . . . . **39 F7** 12 8N 109 13 E
Dong Dang, *Vietnam* . . . . **38 B6** 21 54N 106 42 E
Dong Giam, *Vietnam* . . . . . . **38 C5** 19 25N 105 31 E
Dong Ha, *Vietnam* . . . . **38 D6** 16 55N 107 8 E
Dong Hene, *Laos* . . . . **38 D5** 16 40N 105 18 E
Dong Hoi, *Vietnam* . . . . **38 D6** 17 29N 106 36 E
Dong Khe, *Vietnam* . . . . **38 A6** 22 26N 106 27 E
Dong Ujimqin Qi, *China* . . . . **34 B9** 45 32N 116 55 E
Dong Van, *Vietnam* . . . . **38 A5** 23 16N 105 22 E
Dong Xoai, *Vietnam* . . . . **39 G6** 11 32N 106 55 E
Dongara, *Australia* . . . . **61 E1** 29 14S 114 57 E
Dongbei, *China* . . . . **29 E13** 45 0N 125 0 E
Dongchuan, *China* . . . . **32 D5** 26 8N 103 1 E

Dongfang, China .... 38 C7 18 50N 108 33 E
Dongfeng, China .... 35 C13 42 40N 125 34 E
Donggala, Indonesia ...... 37 E5 0 30S 119 40 E
Donggou, China .... 35 E13 39 52N 124 10 E
Dongguang, China .... 34 F9 37 50N 116 30 E
Dongjingcheng, China ..... 35 B15 44 5N 129 10 E
Dongning, China .... 35 B16 44 2N 131 5 E
Dongola, Sudan .... 51 E12 19 9N 30 22 E
Dongping, China .... 34 G9 35 55N 116 20 E
Dongsheng, China .... 34 E6 39 50N 110 0 E
Dongtai, China .... 35 H11 32 51N 120 21 E
Dongting Hu, China .... 33 D6 29 18N 112 45 E
Donington, C., Australia . 63 E2 34 45S 136 0 E
Doniphan, U.S.A. 81 G9 36 37N 90 50W
Dønna, Norway .... 8 C15 66 6N 12 30 E
Donna, U.S.A. 81 M5 26 9N 98 4W
Donnacona, Canada 73 C5 46 41N 71 41W
Donnelly's Crossing, N.Z. 59 F4 35 42S 173 38 E
Donnybrook, Australia .... 61 F2 33 34S 115 48 E
Donnybrook, S. Africa .... 57 D4 29 59S 29 48 E
Donora, U.S.A. 84 F5 40 11N 79 52W
Donostia = Donostia-San
  Sebastián, Spain 21 A5 43 17N 1 58W
Donostia-San Sebastián, Spain 21 A5 43 17N 1 58W
Doon →, U.K. 11 F4 55 27N 4 39W
Dora, L., Australia ...... 60 D3 22 0S 123 0 E
Dora Báltea →, Italy ..... 20 D8 45 11N 8 3 E
Doran L., Canada 71 A7 61 13N 108 6W
Dorchester, U.K. 13 G5 50 42N 2 27W
Dorchester, C., Canada ... 69 B12 65 27N 77 27W
Dordabis, Namibia .... 56 C2 22 52S 17 38 E
Dordogne →, France 20 D3 45 2N 0 36W
Dordrecht, Neths. .... 15 C4 51 48N 4 39 E
Dordrecht, S. Africa ..... 56 E4 31 20S 27 3 E
Doré L., Canada 71 C7 54 46N 107 17W
Doré Lake, Canada 71 C7 54 38N 107 36W
Dori, Burkina Faso 50 F5 14 3N 0 2W
Doring →, S. Africa ...... 56 E2 31 54S 18 39 E
Doringbos, S. Africa ..... 56 E2 31 59S 19 16 E
Dorking, U.K. 13 F7 51 14N 0 19W
Dornbirn, Austria .... 16 E5 47 25N 9 45 E
Dornie, U.K. 11 D3 57 17N 5 31W
Dornoch, U.K. 11 D4 57 53N 4 2W
Dornoch Firth, U.K. 11 D4 57 51N 4 4W
Dornogovĭ □, Mongolia .... 34 C6 44 0N 110 0 E
Dorohoi, Romania .... 17 E14 47 56N 26 23 E
Döröö Nuur, Mongolia ..... 32 B4 48 0N 93 0 E
Dorr, Iran .... 45 C6 33 17N 50 38 E
Dorre I., Australia ...... 61 E1 25 13S 113 12 E
Dorrigo, Australia .... 63 E5 30 20S 152 44 E
Dorris, U.S.A. 76 F3 41 58N 121 55W
Dorset, Canada 84 A6 45 14N 78 54W
Dorset, U.S.A. 84 E4 41 40N 80 40W
Dorset □, U.K. 13 G5 50 45N 2 26W
Dortmund, Germany .... 16 C4 51 30N 7 28 E
Doruma, Dem. Rep. of the Congo 54 B2 4 42N 27 33 E
Dorūneh, Iran .... 45 C8 35 10N 57 18 E
Dos Bahías, C., Argentina 96 E3 44 58S 65 32W
Dos Hermanas, Spain 21 D3 37 16N 5 55W
Dos Palos, U.S.A. 78 J6 36 59N 120 37W
Dosso, Niger .... 50 F6 13 0N 3 13 E
Dothan, U.S.A. 83 K3 31 13N 85 24W
Doty, U.S.A. 78 D3 46 38N 123 17W
Douai, France .... 20 A5 50 21N 3 4 E
Douala, Cameroon .... 52 D1 4 0N 9 45 E
Douarnenez, France 20 B1 48 6N 4 21W
Double Island Pt., Australia 63 D5 25 56S 153 11 E
Double Mountain Fork →, U.S.A. 81 J4 33 16N 100 0W
Doubs →, France .... 20 C6 46 53N 5 1 E
Doubtful Sd., N.Z. .... 59 L1 45 20S 166 49 E
Doubtless B., N.Z. .... 59 F4 34 55S 173 26 E
Douglas, S. Africa .... 56 D3 29 4S 23 46 E
Douglas, U.K. 12 C3 54 10N 4 28W
Douglas, Ariz., U.S.A. ... 77 L9 31 21N 109 33W
Douglas, Ga., U.S.A. 83 K4 31 31N 82 51W
Douglas, Wyo., U.S.A. 80 D2 42 45N 105 24W
Douglas Apsley △, Australia 63 G4 41 45S 148 11 E
Douglas Chan., Canada 70 C3 53 40N 129 20W
Douglas Pt., Canada 84 B3 44 19N 81 37W
Douglasville, U.S.A. 83 J3 33 45N 84 45W
Dounreay, U.K. 11 C5 58 35N 3 44W
Dourada, Serra, Brazil ... 93 F9 13 10S 48 45W
Dourados, Brazil 95 A5 22 9S 54 50W
Dourados →, Brazil 95 A5 21 58S 54 18W
Dourados, Serra dos, Brazil 95 A5 23 30S 53 30W
Douro →, Europe 21 B1 41 8N 8 40W
Dove →, U.K. 12 E6 52 51N 1 36W
Dove Creek, U.S.A. 77 H9 37 46N 108 54W
Dover, Australia .... 63 G4 43 18S 147 2 E
Dover, U.K. .... 13 F9 51 7N 1 19 E
Dover, Del., U.S.A. 82 F8 39 10N 75 32W
Dover, N.H., U.S.A. 85 C14 43 12N 70 56W
Dover, N.J., U.S.A. 85 F10 40 53N 74 34W
Dover, Ohio, U.S.A. 84 F3 40 32N 81 29W
Dover, Pt., Canada .... 61 F4 32 32S 125 32 E
Dover, Str. of, Europe ... 13 G9 51 0N 1 30 E
Dover-Foxcroft, U.S.A. ... 85 C11 45 11N 69 13W
Dover Plains, U.S.A. 85 E11 41 43N 73 35W
Dovey = Dyfi →, U.K. 13 E3 52 32N 4 3W
Dovrefjell, Norway .... 9 E13 62 15N 9 33 E
Dow Rūd, Iran .... 45 C6 33 28N 49 4 E
Dowa, Malawi .... 55 E3 13 38S 33 58 E
Dowagiac, U.S.A. 82 E2 41 59N 86 6W
Dowerin, Australia .... 61 F2 31 12S 117 2 E
Dowghā'i, Iran .... 45 B8 36 54N 58 32 E
Dowlatābād, Iran .... 45 D8 28 20N 56 40 E
Down □, U.K. 10 B5 54 23N 6 2W
Downey, Calif., U.S.A. ... 79 M8 33 56N 118 7W
Downey, Idaho, U.S.A. 76 E7 42 26N 112 7W
Downham Market, U.K. ..... 13 E8 52 37N 0 23 E
Downieville, U.S.A. 78 F6 39 34N 120 50W
Downpatrick, U.K. 10 B6 54 20N 5 43W
Downpatrick Hd., Ireland . 10 B2 54 20N 9 21W
Downs, U.S.A. 85 D10 42 5N 74 50W
Downton, Mt., Canada 70 C4 52 42N 124 52W
Dowsāri, Iran .... 45 D8 28 25N 57 59 E
Doyle, U.S.A. 78 E6 40 2N 120 6W
Doylestown, U.S.A. 85 F9 40 21N 75 10W
Dozois, Rés., Canada 72 C4 47 30N 77 5W
Dra Khel, Pakistan .... 42 F2 27 58N 66 45 E
Drachten, Neths. .... 15 A6 53 7N 6 5 E
Drăgăşani, Romania .... 17 F13 44 39N 24 17 E
Dragichyn, Belarus .... 17 B13 52 15N 25 8 E
Dragoman, Prokhod, Bulgaria 23 C10 42 58N 22 53 E
Dragon's Mouth = Boca de
  Drago, Venezuela 93 K15 11 0N 61 50W
Draguignan, France .... 20 E7 43 32N 6 27 E
Drain, U.S.A. 76 E2 43 40N 123 19W

Drake, U.S.A. 80 B4 47 55N 100 23W
Drake Passage, S. Ocean .. 5 B17 58 0S 68 0W
Drakensberg, S. Africa ... 57 D4 31 0S 28 0 E
Dráma, Greece .... 23 D11 41 9N 24 10 E
Drammen, Norway .... 9 G14 59 42N 10 12 E
Drangajökull, Iceland 8 C2 66 9N 22 15W
Dras, India .... 43 B6 34 25N 75 48 E
Drau = Drava →, Croatia .. 23 B8 45 33N 18 55 E
Drava →, Croatia .... 23 B8 45 33N 18 55 E
Drayton Valley, Canada ... 70 C6 53 12N 114 58W
Drenthe □, Neths. .... 15 B6 52 52N 6 40 E
Drepanum, C., Cyprus ..... 25 E11 34 54N 32 19 E
Dresden, Canada 84 D2 42 35N 82 11W
Dresden, Germany .... 16 C7 51 3N 13 44 E
Dreux, France .... 20 B4 48 44N 1 23 E
Driffield, U.K. 12 C7 54 0N 0 26W
Driftwood, U.S.A. 84 E6 41 20N 78 8W
Driggs, U.S.A. 76 E8 43 44N 111 6W
Drin →, Albania .... 23 C8 42 1N 19 38 E
Drina →, Bos.-H. .... 23 B8 44 53N 19 21 E
Drøbak, Norway .... 9 G14 59 39N 10 39 E
Drobeta-Turnu Severin, Romania 17 F12 44 39N 22 41 E
Drochia, Moldova .... 17 D14 48 2N 27 48 E
Drogheda, Ireland 10 C5 53 43N 6 22W
Drogichin = Dragichyn, Belarus 17 B13 52 15N 25 8 E
Drogobych = Drohobych, Ukraine 17 D12 49 20N 23 30 E
Drohobych, Ukraine .... 17 D12 49 20N 23 30 E
Droichead Atha = Drogheda,
  Ireland 10 C5 53 43N 6 22W
Droichead Nua, Ireland ... 10 C5 53 11N 6 48W
Droitwich, U.K. 13 E5 52 16N 2 8W
Dromedary, C., Australia . 63 F5 36 17S 150 10 E
Dromore, U.K. 10 B4 54 31N 7 28W
Dromore West, Ireland 10 B3 54 15N 8 52W
Dronfield, U.K. 12 D6 53 19N 1 27W
Dronning Maud Land, Antarctica 5 D3 72 30S 12 0 E
Dronten, Neths. .... 15 B5 52 32N 5 43 E
Drumbo, Canada 84 C4 43 16N 80 35W
Drumheller, Canada 70 C6 51 25N 112 40W
Drummond, U.S.A. 76 C7 46 40N 113 9W
Drummond I., U.S.A. 82 C4 46 1N 83 39W
Drummond Pt., Australia .. 63 E2 34 9S 135 16 E
Drummond Ra., Australia .. 62 C4 23 45S 147 10 E
Drummondville, Canada 72 C5 45 55N 72 25W
Drumright, U.S.A. 81 H6 35 59N 96 36W
Druskininkai, Lithuania .. 9 J20 54 3N 23 58 E
Drut →, Belarus .... 17 B16 53 8N 30 5 E
Druzhina, Russia .... 29 C15 68 14N 145 18 E
Dry Harbour Mts., Jamaica a 18 19N 77 24W
Dry Tortugas, U.S.A. 88 B3 24 38N 82 55W
Dryden, Canada 71 D10 49 47N 92 50W
Dryden, U.S.A. 85 D8 42 30N 76 18W
Drygalski I., Antarctica . 5 C7 66 0S 92 0 E
Drysdale →, Australia .... 60 B4 13 59S 126 51 E
Drysdale I., Australia ... 62 A2 11 41S 136 0 E
Drysdale River △, Australia 60 B4 14 56S 127 2 E
Du Bois, U.S.A. 84 E6 41 8N 78 46W
Du Gué →, Canada 72 A5 57 21N 70 45W
Du Quoin, U.S.A. 80 G10 38 1N 89 14W
Duanesburg, U.S.A. 85 D10 42 45N 74 11W
Duaringa, Australia ...... 62 C4 23 42S 149 42 E
Duarte, Pico, Dom. Rep. .. 89 C5 19 2N 70 59W
Dubā, Si. Arabia .... 44 E2 27 10N 35 40 E
Dubai = Dubayy, U.A.E. ... 45 E7 25 18N 55 20 E
Dubāsari, Moldova .... 17 E15 47 15N 29 10 E
Dubāsari Vdkhr., Moldova . 17 E15 47 30N 29 0 E
Dubawnt →, Canada 71 A8 64 33N 100 6W
Dubawnt, L., Canada 71 A8 63 8N 101 28W
Dubayy, U.A.E. .... 5 E7 25 18N 55 20 E
Dubbo, Australia .... 63 E4 32 11S 148 35 E
Dubele, Dem. Rep. of the Congo 54 B2 2 56N 29 35 E
Dublin, Ireland 10 C5 53 21N 6 15W
Dublin, Ga., U.S.A. 83 J4 32 32N 82 54W
Dublin, Tex., U.S.A. 81 J5 32 5N 98 21W
Dublin □, Ireland 10 C5 53 24N 6 20W
Dublin ✈ (DUB), Ireland .. 10 C5 53 26N 6 15W
Dubno, Ukraine .... 17 C13 50 25N 25 45 E
Dubois, U.S.A. 76 D7 44 10N 112 14W
Dubossary = Dubāsari, Moldova 17 E15 47 15N 29 10 E
Dubossary Vdkhr. = Dubāsari
  Vdkhr., Moldova .... 17 E15 47 30N 29 0 E
Dubovka, Russia .... 19 E7 49 5N 44 50 E
Dubrajpur, India .... 43 H12 23 48N 87 25 E
Dubréka, Guinea 50 G3 9 46N 13 31W
Dubrovitsa = Dubrovytsya,
  Ukraine .... 17 C14 51 31N 26 35 E
Dubrovnik, Croatia .... 23 C8 42 39N 18 6 E
Dubrovytsya, Ukraine ..... 17 C14 51 31N 26 35 E
Dubuque, U.S.A. 80 D9 42 30N 90 41W
Duchesne, U.S.A. 76 F8 40 10N 110 24W
Duchess, Australia .... 62 C2 21 20S 139 50 E
Ducie I., Pac. Oc. 65 K15 24 40S 124 48W
Duck →, U.S.A. 83 G2 36 2N 87 52W
Duck Cr. →, Australia .... 60 D2 22 37S 116 53 E
Duck Lake, Canada 71 C7 52 50N 106 16W
Duck Mountain △, Canada .. 71 C8 51 45N 101 0W
Duckwall, Mt., U.S.A. 78 H6 37 58N 120 7W
Dudhi, India .... 41 G13 24 15N 83 10 E
Dudinka, Russia .... 29 C9 69 30N 86 13 E
Dudley, U.K. 13 E5 52 31N 2 5W
Dudwa, India .... 43 E9 28 30N 80 41 E
Duero = Douro →, Europe .. 21 B1 41 8N 8 40W
Dufftown, U.K. 11 D5 57 27N 3 8W
Dūghī Kalā, Afghan. ...... 40 C3 32 20N 62 50 E
Dugi Otok, Croatia .... 16 G8 44 0N 15 3 E
Duifken Pt., Australia ... 62 A3 12 33S 141 38 E
Duisburg, Germany .... 16 C4 51 26N 6 45 E
Duiwelskloof, S. Africa .. 57 C5 23 42S 30 10 E
Dūkdamin, Iran .... 45 C8 35 59N 57 43 E
Dukelský Průsmyk, Slovak Rep. 17 D11 49 25N 21 42 E
Dukhān, Qatar .... 45 E6 25 25N 50 50 E
Duki, Pakistan .... 40 D6 30 14N 68 25 E
Duku, Nigeria .... 51 F8 10 43N 10 43 E
Dulce, U.S.A. 77 H10 36 56N 107 0W
Dulce →, Argentina 94 C3 30 32S 62 33W
Dulce, G., Costa Rica 88 E3 8 40N 83 20W
Dulf, Iraq .... 44 C5 35 7N 45 51 E
Dulit, Banjaran, Malaysia 36 D4 3 15N 114 30 E
Duliu, China .... 34 E9 39 2N 116 55 E
Dullewala, Pakistan ...... 42 D4 31 50N 71 25 E
Dullstroom, S. Africa .... 57 D5 25 27S 30 7 E
Dulq Maghār, Syria .... 44 B3 36 22N 38 39 E
Duluth, U.S.A. 80 B8 46 47N 92 6W
Dum Dum, India .... 43 H13 22 39N 88 33 E
Dum Duma, India .... 41 F19 27 40N 95 40 E
Dūmā, Syria .... 46 B5 33 34N 36 24 E
Dumaguete, Phil. .... 37 C6 9 17N 123 15 E
Dumai, Indonesia .... 36 D2 1 35N 101 28 E

Dumaran, Phil. .... 37 B5 10 33N 119 50 E
Dumas, Ark., U.S.A. 81 J9 33 53N 91 29W
Dumas, Tex., U.S.A. 81 H4 35 52N 101 58W
Dumayr, Syria .... 46 B5 33 39N 36 42 E
Dumbarton, U.K. 11 F4 55 57N 4 33W
Dumbleyung, Australia .... 61 F2 33 17S 117 42 E
Dumfries, U.K. 11 F5 55 4N 3 37W
Dumfries & Galloway □, U.K. 11 F5 55 9N 3 58W
Dumka, India .... 43 G12 24 12N 87 15 E
Dumoine →, Canada 72 C4 46 13N 77 51W
Dumoine, L., Canada 72 C4 46 55N 77 55W
Dumont d'Urville, Antarctica 5 C10 67 0S 110 0 E
Dumraon, India .... 43 G11 25 33N 84 8 E
Dumyāt, Egypt .... 51 B12 31 24N 31 48 E
Dún Dealgan = Dundalk, Ireland 10 B5 54 1N 6 24W
Dún Laoghaire, Ireland ... 10 C5 53 17N 6 8W
Duna = Dunărea →, Europe . 17 F15 45 20N 29 40 E
Dunagiri, India .... 43 D8 30 31N 79 52 E
Dunaj = Dunărea →, Europe 17 F15 45 20N 29 40 E
Dunakeszi, Hungary .... 17 E10 47 37N 19 8 E
Dunărea →, Europe .... 17 F15 45 20N 29 40 E
Dunaújváros, Hungary ..... 17 E10 46 58N 18 57 E
Dunav = Dunărea →, Europe 17 F15 45 20N 29 40 E
Dunay, Russia .... 30 C6 42 52N 132 22 E
Dunback, N.Z. .... 59 L3 45 23S 170 36 E
Dunbar, U.K. 11 E6 56 0N 2 31W
Dunblane, U.K. 11 E5 56 11N 3 58W
Duncan, Canada 70 D4 48 45N 123 40W
Duncan, Ariz., U.S.A. 77 K9 32 43N 109 6W
Duncan, Okla., U.S.A. 81 H6 34 30N 97 57W
Duncan, L., Canada 72 B4 53 29N 77 58W
Duncan L., Canada 70 A6 62 51N 113 58W
Duncan Town, Bahamas 88 B4 22 15N 75 45W
Duncannon, U.S.A. 84 F7 40 23N 77 2W
Duncansby Head, U.K. 11 C5 58 38N 3 1W
Duncansville, U.S.A. 84 F6 40 25N 78 26W
Dundalk, Canada 84 B4 44 10N 80 24W
Dundalk, Ireland 10 B5 54 1N 6 24W
Dundalk, U.S.A. 82 F7 39 16N 76 32W
Dundalk Bay, Ireland 10 C5 53 55N 6 15W
Dundas = Uummannaq,
  Greenland 4 B4 77 0N 69 0W
Dundas = Uummannaq,
  Greenland 4 B5 70 58N 52 0W
Dundas, Canada 84 C5 43 17N 79 59W
Dundas, L., Australia .... 61 F3 32 35S 121 50 E
Dundas I., Canada 70 C2 54 30N 130 50W
Dundas Str., Australia ... 60 B5 11 15S 131 35 E
Dundee, S. Africa .... 57 D5 28 11S 30 15 E
Dundee, U.K. 11 E6 56 28N 2 59W
Dundee, U.S.A. 84 D8 42 32N 76 59W
Dundee City □, U.K. 11 E6 56 30N 2 58W
Dundgovĭ □, Mongolia ..... 34 B4 45 10N 106 0 E
Dundrum, U.K. 10 B6 54 16N 5 52W
Dundrum B., U.K. 10 B6 54 13N 5 47W
Dunedin, N.Z. .... 59 L3 45 50S 170 33 E
Dunedin, U.S.A. 83 L4 28 1N 82 47W
Dunfermline, U.K. 11 E5 56 5N 3 27W
Dungannon, Canada 84 C3 43 51N 81 36W
Dungannon, U.K. 10 B5 54 31N 6 46W
Dungarpur, India .... 42 H5 23 52N 73 45 E
Dungarvan, Ireland 10 D4 52 5N 7 37W
Dungarvan Harbour, Ireland 10 D4 52 4N 7 35W
Dungeness, U.K. .... 13 G8 50 54N 0 59 E
Dungo, L. do, Angola ..... 56 B2 17 15S 19 0 E
Dungog, Australia .... 63 E5 32 22S 151 46 E
Dungu, Dem. Rep. of the Congo 54 B2 3 40N 28 32 E
Dungun, Malaysia .... 39 K4 4 45N 103 25 E
Dunhua, China .... 35 C15 43 20N 128 14 E
Dunhuang, China .... 32 B4 40 8N 94 36 E
Dunk I., Australia .... 62 B4 17 59S 146 29 E
Dunkeld, Australia .... 63 F3 37 40S 142 22 E
Dunkeld, U.K. 11 E5 56 34N 3 35W
Dunkerque, France .... 20 A5 51 2N 2 20 E
Dunkery Beacon, U.K. 13 F4 51 9N 3 36W
Dunkirk = Dunkerque, France 20 A5 51 2N 2 20 E
Dunkirk, U.S.A. 84 D5 42 29N 79 20W
Dúnleary = Dún Laoghaire,
  Ireland 10 C5 53 17N 6 8W
Dunleer, Ireland 10 C5 53 50N 6 24W
Dunmanus B., Ireland 10 E2 51 31N 9 50W
Dunmanway, Ireland 10 E2 51 43N 9 6W
Dunmara, Australia .... 62 B1 16 42S 133 25 E
Dunmore, U.S.A. 85 E9 41 25N 75 38W
Dunmore Hd., Ireland 10 D1 52 10N 10 35W
Dunmore Town, Bahamas 88 A4 25 30N 76 39W
Dunn, U.S.A. 83 H6 35 19N 78 37W
Dunnellon, U.S.A. 83 L4 29 3N 82 28W
Dunnet Hd., U.K. 11 C5 58 40N 3 21W
Dunning, U.S.A. 80 E4 41 50N 100 6W
Dunnville, Canada 84 D5 42 54N 79 36W
Dunolly, Australia .... 63 F3 36 51S 143 44 E
Dunoon, U.K. 11 F4 55 57N 4 56W
Dunphy, U.S.A. 76 F5 40 42N 116 31W
Duns, U.K. 11 F6 55 47N 2 20W
Dunseith, U.S.A. 80 A4 48 50N 100 3W
Dunsmuir, U.S.A. 76 F2 41 13N 122 16W
Dunstable, U.K. 13 F7 51 53N 0 32W
Dunstan Mts., N.Z. .... 59 L2 44 53S 169 35 E
Dunster, Canada 70 C5 53 8N 119 50W
Dunvegan, U.K. 11 D2 57 27N 6 35W
Dunvegan L., Canada 71 A7 60 8N 107 10W
Duolun, China .... 34 C9 42 12N 116 28 E
Duong Dong, Vietnam ...... 39 G4 10 13N 103 58 E
Dupree, U.S.A. 80 C4 45 4N 101 35W
Dupuyer, U.S.A. 76 B7 48 13N 112 30W
Duque de Caxias, Brazil .. 95 A7 22 45S 43 19W
Durack →, Australia ...... 60 C4 15 33S 127 52 E
Durack Ra., Australia .... 60 C4 16 50S 127 40 E
Durance →, France .... 20 E6 43 55N 4 45 E
Durand, U.S.A. 80 C9 44 38N 91 58W
Durango, Mexico 86 C4 24 3N 104 39W
Durango, U.S.A. 77 H10 37 16N 107 53W
Durango □, Mexico 86 C4 25 0N 105 0W
Durant, Miss., U.S.A. 81 J10 33 4N 89 51W
Durant, Okla., U.S.A. 81 J6 33 59N 96 25W
Durazno, Uruguay 94 C4 33 25S 56 31W
Durazzo = Durrës, Albania 23 D8 41 19N 19 28 E
Durban, S. Africa .... 57 D5 29 49S 31 1 E
Durbuy, Belgium .... 15 D5 50 21N 5 28 E
Düren, Germany .... 16 C4 50 48N 6 29 E
Durg, India .... 41 J12 21 15N 81 22 E
Durgapur, India .... 43 H12 23 30N 87 20 E
Durham, Canada 84 B4 44 10N 80 49W
Durham, U.K. 12 C6 54 47N 1 34W
Durham, Calif., U.S.A. ... 78 F5 39 39N 121 48W
Durham, N.C., U.S.A. 83 H6 35 59N 78 54W
Durham, N.H., U.S.A. 85 C14 43 8N 70 56W

Durham □, U.K. 12 C6 54 42N 1 45W
Qurmā, Si. Arabia .... 44 E5 24 37N 46 8 E
Durmitor, Serbia & M. .... 23 C8 43 10N 19 0 E
Durness, U.K. 11 C4 58 34N 4 45W
Durrës, Albania .... 23 D8 41 19N 19 28 E
Durrow, Ireland 10 D4 52 51N 7 24W
Dursey I., Ireland 10 E1 51 36N 10 12W
Dursley, U.K. 13 F5 51 40N 2 21W
Dursunbey, Turkey .... 23 E13 39 35N 28 37 E
Duru, Dem. Rep. of the Congo 54 B2 4 14N 28 50 E
Durūz, Jabal ad, Jordan .. 46 C5 32 35N 36 40 E
D'Urville, Tanjung, Indonesia 37 E9 1 28S 137 54 E
D'Urville I., N.Z. .... 59 J4 40 50S 173 55 E
Duryea, U.S.A. 85 E9 41 20N 75 45W
Dushak, Turkmenistan ..... 28 F7 37 13N 60 1 E
Dushanbe, Tajikistan ..... 28 F7 38 33N 68 48 E
Dushore, U.S.A. 85 E8 41 31N 76 24W
Dusky Sd., N.Z. .... 59 L1 45 47S 166 30 E
Dussejour, C., Australia . 60 B4 14 45S 128 13 E
Düsseldorf, Germany ...... 16 C4 51 14N 6 47 E
Dutch Harbor, U.S.A. 68 C3 53 53N 166 32W
Dutlwe, Botswana .... 56 C3 23 58S 23 46 E
Dutton, Canada 84 D3 42 39N 81 30W
Dutton →, Australia ...... 62 C3 20 44S 143 10 E
Duwayhin, Khawr, U.A.E. .. 45 E6 24 20N 51 25 E
Duyun, China .... 32 D5 26 18N 107 29 E
Dvina, Severnaya →, Russia 18 B7 64 32N 40 30 E
Dvinsk = Daugavpils, Latvia 9 J22 55 53N 26 32 E
Dvinskaya Guba, Russia ... 18 B6 65 0N 39 0 E
Dwarka, India .... 42 H3 22 18N 69 8 E
Dwellingup, Australia .... 61 F2 32 43S 116 4 E
Dwight, Canada 84 A5 45 20N 79 1W
Dwight, U.S.A. 82 E1 41 5N 88 26W
Dyatlovo = Dzyatlava, Belarus 17 B13 53 28N 25 28 E
Dyce, U.K. 11 D6 57 13N 2 12W
Dyer, C., Canada 69 B13 66 37N 61 16W
Dyer Bay, Canada 84 A3 45 10N 81 20W
Dyer Plateau, Antarctica . 5 D17 70 45S 65 30W
Dyersburg, U.S.A. 81 G10 36 3N 89 23W
Dyfi →, U.K. 13 E3 52 32N 4 3W
Dymer, Ukraine .... 17 C16 50 47N 30 18 E
Dysart, Australia .... 62 C4 22 32S 148 23 E
Dzamin Üüd = Borhoyn Tal,
  Mongolia .... 34 C6 43 50N 111 58 E
Dzerzhinsk, Russia .... 18 C7 56 14N 43 30 E
Dzhalinda, Russia .... 29 D13 53 26N 124 0 E
Dzhambul = Taraz, Kazakhstan 28 E8 42 54N 71 22 E
Dzhankoy, Ukraine .... 19 E5 45 40N 34 20 E
Dzhezkazgan = Zhezqazghan,
  Kazakhstan .... 28 E7 47 44N 67 40 E
Dzhizak = Jizzakh, Uzbekistan 28 E7 40 6N 67 50 E
Dzhugdzur, Khrebet, Russia 29 D14 57 30N 138 0 E
Dzhungarskiye Vorota =
  Dzungarian Gates, Asia . 32 B3 45 0N 82 0 E
Działdowo, Poland .... 17 B11 53 15N 20 15 E
Dzibilchaltún, Mexico 87 C7 21 5N 89 36W
Dzibilchaltun, Yucatán, Mexico 87 C7 21 5N 89 36W
Dzierżoniów, Poland ...... 17 C9 50 45N 16 39 E
Dzilam de Bravo, Mexico .. 87 C7 21 24N 88 53W
Dzungaria = Junggar Pendi,
  China .... 32 B3 44 30N 86 0 E
Dzungarian Gates, Asia ... 32 B3 45 0N 82 0 E
Dzuumod, Mongolia .... 32 B5 47 45N 106 58 E
Dzyarzhynsk, Belarus ..... 17 B14 53 40N 27 1 E
Dzyatlava, Belarus .... 17 B13 53 28N 25 28 E

E

E.C. Manning △, Canada ... 70 D4 49 5N 120 45W
Eabamet L., Canada 72 B2 51 30N 87 46W
Eads, U.S.A. 80 F3 38 29N 102 47W
Eagar, U.S.A. 77 J9 34 6N 109 17W
Eagle, Alaska, U.S.A. 68 B5 64 47N 141 12W
Eagle, Colo., U.S.A. 76 G10 39 39N 106 50W
Eagle →, Canada 73 B8 53 36N 57 26W
Eagle Butte, U.S.A. 80 C4 45 0N 101 10W
Eagle Grove, U.S.A. 80 D8 42 40N 93 54W
Eagle L., Canada 71 D10 49 42N 93 13W
Eagle L., Calif., U.S.A. . 76 F3 40 39N 120 45W
Eagle L., Maine, U.S.A. .. 83 B11 46 20N 69 22W
Eagle Lake, Canada 84 A6 45 8N 78 29W
Eagle Lake, Maine, U.S.A. 83 B11 47 3N 68 36W
Eagle Lake, Tex., U.S.A. . 81 L6 29 35N 96 20W
Eagle Mountain, U.S.A. ... 79 M11 33 49N 115 27W
Eagle Nest, U.S.A. 77 H11 36 33N 105 16W
Eagle Pass, U.S.A. 81 L4 28 43N 100 30W
Eagle Pk., U.S.A. 78 G7 38 10N 119 25W
Eagle Pt., Australia ..... 60 C3 16 11S 124 23 E
Eagle River, Mich., U.S.A. 82 B1 47 24N 88 18W
Eagle River, Wis., U.S.A. 80 C10 45 55N 89 15W
Eaglehawk, Australia ..... 63 F3 36 44S 144 15 E
Eagles Mere, U.S.A. 85 E8 41 25N 76 33W
Ealing □, U.K. 13 F7 51 31N 0 20W
Ear Falls, Canada 71 C10 50 38N 93 13W
Earle, U.S.A. 81 H9 35 16N 90 28W
Earlimart, U.S.A. 79 K7 35 53N 119 16W
Earn →, U.K. 11 E5 56 21N 3 18W
Earn, L., U.K. 11 E4 56 23N 4 13W
Earnslaw, Mt., N.Z. ...... 59 L2 44 32S 168 27 E
Earth, U.S.A. 81 H3 34 14N 102 24W
Easley, U.S.A. 83 H4 34 50N 82 36W
East Anglia, U.K. .... 12 E9 52 30N 1 0 E
East Angus, Canada 73 C5 45 30N 71 40W
East Antarctica, Antarctica 5 D7 80 0S 90 0 E
East Aurora, U.S.A. 84 D6 42 46N 78 37W
East Ayrshire □, U.K. 11 F4 55 26N 4 11W
East Bengal, Bangla. ..... 41 H17 24 0N 90 0 E
East Beskids = Vychodné
  Beskydy, Europe .... 17 D11 49 20N 22 0 E
East Brady, U.S.A. 84 F5 40 59N 79 36W
East C., N.Z. .... 59 G7 37 42S 178 35 E
East Chicago, U.S.A. 82 E2 41 38N 87 27W
East China Sea, Asia ..... 33 D7 30 0N 126 0 E
East Coulee, Canada 70 C6 51 23N 112 27W
East Dereham = Dereham, U.K. 13 E8 52 41N 0 57 E
East Dunbartonshire □, U.K. 11 F4 55 57N 4 13W
East Falkland, Falk. Is. . 96 G5 51 30S 58 30W
East Grand Forks, U.S.A. . 80 B6 47 56N 97 1W
East Greenwich, U.S.A. ... 85 E13 41 40N 71 27W
East Grinstead, U.K. 13 F8 51 7N 0 0W
East Hartford, U.S.A. 85 E12 41 46N 72 39W
East Helena, U.S.A. 76 C8 46 35N 111 56W
East Indies, Asia .... 26 K15 0 0N 120 0 E
East Kilbride, U.K. 11 F4 55 47N 4 11W
East Lamma Channel, China 33 G11 22 14N 114 9 E
East Lansing, U.S.A. 82 D3 42 44N 84 29W
East Liverpool, U.S.A. ... 84 F4 40 37N 80 35W

East London, S. Africa . . . . 57 E4   33 0S 27 55 E
East Lothian □, U.K. 11 F6   55 58N   2 44W
East Main = Eastmain, Canada . 72 B4   52 10N 78 30W
East Northport, U.S.A. 85 F11 40 53N 73 20W
East Orange, U.S.A. 85 F10 40 46N 74 13W
East Pacific Ridge, Pac. Oc. . . . 65 J17 15 0S 110 0W
East Palestine, U.S.A. 84 F4   40 50N 80 33W
East Pine, Canada 70 B4   55 48N 120 12W
East Point, U.S.A. 83 J3   33 41N 84 27W
East Providence, U.S.A. 85 E13 41 49N 71 23W
East Pt., Br. Virgin Is. . . . . 89 e   18 40N 64 18W
East Pt., Canada 73 C7   46 27N 61 58W
East Renfrewshire □, U.K. 11 F4   55 46N   4 21W
East Retford = Retford, U.K. . . 12 D7   53 19N   0 56W
East Riding of Yorkshire □, U.K. 12 D7   53 55N   0 30W
East Rochester, U.S.A. 84 C7   43 7N 77 29W
East St. Louis, U.S.A. 80 F9   38 37N 90 9W
East Schelde = Oosterschelde →,
   Neths. . . . . 15 C4   51 33N   4 0 E
East Sea = Japan, Sea of, Asia . 30 E7   40 0N 135 0 E
East Siberian Sea, Russia . . . . . 29 B17 73 0N 160 0 E
East Stroudsburg, U.S.A. 85 E9   41 1N 75 11W
East Sussex □, U.K. . . . . 13 G8   50 56N   0 19 E
East Tawas, U.S.A. 82 C4   44 17N 83 29W
East Timor ■, Asia . . . . 37 F7   8 50S 126 0 E
East Toorale, Australia . . . . 63 E4   30 27S 145 28 E
East Walker →, U.S.A. 78 G7   38 52N 119 10W
East Windsor, U.S.A. 85 F10 40 17N 74 34W
Eastbourne, N.Z. . . . . 59 J5   41 19S 174 55 E
Eastbourne, U.K. . . . . 13 G8   50 46N   0 18 E
Eastend, Canada 71 D7   49 32N 108 50W
Easter I. = Pascua, I. de, Chile . 65 K17 27 7S 109 23W
Eastern □, Kenya . . . . 54 C4   0 0   38 30 E
Eastern Cape □, S. Africa . . . . . 56 E4   32 0S 26 0 E
Eastern Cr. →, Australia . . . . . . 62 C3   20 40S 141 35 E
Eastern Ghats, India . . . . 40 N11 14 0N 78 50 E
Eastern Group = Lau Group, Fiji 59 C9   17 0S 178 30W
Eastern Group, Australia . . . . . . 61 F3   33 30S 124 30 E
Eastern Transvaal =
   Mpumalanga □, S. Africa . . . . 57 D5   26 0S 30 0 E
Easterville, Canada 71 C9   53 8N 99 49W
Easthampton, U.S.A. 85 D12 42 16N 72 40W
Eastlake, U.S.A. 84 E3   41 40N 81 26W
Eastland, U.S.A. 81 J5   32 24N 98 49W
Eastleigh, U.K. 13 G6   50 58N   1 21W
Eastmain, Canada 72 B4   52 10N 78 30W
Eastmain →, Canada 72 B4   52 27N 78 26W
Eastman, Canada 85 A12 45 18N 72 19W
Eastman, U.S.A. 83 J4   32 12N 83 11W
Easton, Md., U.S.A. 82 F7   38 47N 76 5W
Easton, Pa., U.S.A. 85 F9   40 41N 75 13W
Easton, Wash., U.S.A. 78 C5   47 14N 121 11W
Eastpointe, U.S.A. 84 D2   42 28N 82 56W
Eastport, U.S.A. 83 C12 44 56N 67 0W
Eastsound, U.S.A. 78 B4   48 42N 122 55W
Eaton, U.S.A. 80 E2   40 32N 104 42W
Eatonia, Canada 71 C7   51 13N 109 25W
Eatonton, U.S.A. 83 J4   33 20N 83 23W
Eatontown, U.S.A. 85 F10 40 19N 74 4W
Eatonville, U.S.A. 78 D4   46 52N 122 16W
Eau Claire, U.S.A. 80 C9   44 49N 91 30W
Eau Claire, L. à l', Canada 72 A5   56 10N 74 25W
Ebbw Vale, U.K. 13 F4   51 46N   3 12W
Ebeltoft, Denmark . . . . 9 H14   56 12N 10 41 E
Ebensburg, U.S.A. 84 F6   40 29N 78 44W
Eberswalde-Finow, Germany . . 16 B7   52 50N 13 49 E
Ebetsu, Japan . . . . 30 C10 43 7N 141 34 E
Ebey's Landing △, U.S.A. 78 B4   48 13N 122 41W
Ebolowa, Cameroon . . . . 52 D2   2 55N 11 10 E
Ebro →, Spain . . . . 21 B6   40 43N   0 54 E
Eceabat, Turkey . . . . 23 D12 40 11N 26 21 E
Ech Chélif, Algeria . . . . 50 A6   36 10N   1 20 E
Echigo-Sammyaku, Japan . . . . . 31 F9   36 50N 139 50 E
Echizen-Misaki, Japan . . . . 31 G7   35 59N 135 57 E
Echo Bay, N.W.T., Canada 68 B8   66 5N 117 55W
Echo Bay, Ont., Canada 72 C3   46 29N 84 4W
Echoing →, Canada 72 B1   55 51N 92 5W
Echternach, Lux. . . . . 15 E6   49 49N   6 25 E
Echuca, Australia . . . . 63 F3   36 10S 144 45 E
Ecija, Spain 21 D3   37 30N   5 10W
Eclipse I., Australia . . . . 61 G2   35 5S 117 58 E
Eclipse Is., Australia . . . . 60 B4   13 54S 126 19 E
Eclipse Sd., Canada 69 A11 72 38N 79 0W
Ecuador ■, S. Amer. 92 D3   2 0S 78 0W
Ed Damazin, Sudan . . . . 51 F12 11 46N 34 21 E
Ed Dar el Beida = Casablanca,
   Morocco 50 B4   33 36N   7 36W
Ed Debba, Sudan . . . . 51 E12 18 0N 30 51 E
Ed Dueim, Sudan . . . . 51 F12 14 0N 32 10 E
Edam, Canada 71 C7   53 11N 108 46W
Edam, Neths. . . . . 15 B5   52 31N   5 3 E
Eday, U.K. 11 B6   59 11N   2 47W
Eddrachillis B., U.K. 11 C3   58 17N   5 14W
Eddystone, U.K. 13 G3   50 11N   4 16W
Eddystone Pt., Australia . . . . . . 63 G4   40 59S 148 20 E
Ede, Neths. . . . . 15 B5   52 4N   5 40 E
Edehon L., Canada 71 A9   60 25N 97 15W
Eden, Australia . . . . 63 F4   37 3S 149 55 E
Eden, N.C., U.S.A. 83 G6   36 29N 79 53W
Eden, N.Y., U.S.A. 84 D6   42 39N 78 55W
Eden, Tex., U.S.A. 81 K5   31 13N 99 51W
Eden →, U.K. 12 C4   54 57N   3 1W
Edenburg, S. Africa . . . . 56 D4   29 43S 25 58 E
Edendale, S. Africa . . . . 57 D5   29 39S 30 18 E
Edenderry, Ireland 10 C4   53 21N   7 4W
Edenton, U.S.A. 83 G7   36 4N 76 39W
Edenville, S. Africa . . . . 57 D4   27 37S 27 34 E
Eder →, Germany . . . . 16 C5   51 12N   9 28 E
Edgar, U.S.A. 80 E6   40 22N 97 58W
Edgartown, U.S.A. 85 E14 41 23N 70 31W
Edge Hill, U.K. 13 E6   52 8N   1 26W
Edgefield, U.S.A. 83 J5   33 47N 81 56W
Edgeley, U.S.A. 80 B5   46 22N 98 43W
Edgemont, U.S.A. 80 D3   43 18N 103 50W
Edgeøya, Svalbard . . . . 4 B9   77 45N 22 30 E
Édhessa, Greece . . . . 23 D10 40 48N 22 5 E
Edievale, N.Z. . . . . 59 L2   45 49S 169 22 E
Edina, U.S.A. 80 E8   40 10N 92 11W
Edinboro, U.S.A. 84 E4   41 52N 80 8W
Edinburg, U.S.A. 81 M5   26 18N 98 10W
Edinburgh, U.K. 11 F5   55 57N   3 13W
Edinburgh ✈ (EDI), U.K. 11 F5   55 54N   3 22W
Edinburgh, City of □, U.K. 11 F5   55 57N   3 17W
Edineţ, Moldova . . . . 17 D14 48 9N 27 18 E
Edirne, Turkey . . . . 23 D12 41 40N 26 34 E
Edison, U.S.A. 78 B4   48 33N 122 27W
Edithburgh, Australia . . . . 63 F2   35 5S 137 43 E
Edmeston, U.S.A. 85 D9   42 42N 75 15W

Edmond, U.S.A. 81 H6   35 39N 97 29W
Edmonds, U.S.A. 78 C4   47 49N 122 23W
Edmonton, Australia . . . . 62 B4   17 2S 145 46 E
Edmonton, Canada 70 C6   53 30N 113 30W
Edmund L., Canada 72 B1   54 45N 93 17W
Edmundston, Canada 73 C6   47 23N 68 20W
Edna, U.S.A. 81 L6   28 59N 96 39W
Edremit, Turkey . . . . 23 E12 39 34N 27 0 E
Edremit Körfezi, Turkey . . . . . . 23 E12 39 30N 26 45 E
Edson, Canada 70 C5   53 35N 116 28W
Eduardo Castex, Argentina . . . 94 D3   35 50S 64 18W
Edward →, Australia . . . . 63 F3   35 5S 143 30 E
Edward, L., Africa . . . . 54 C2   0 25S 29 40 E
Edward River, Australia . . . . 62 A3   14 59S 141 26 E
Edward VII Land, Antarctica . . 5 E13   80 0S 150 0 E
Edwards, Calif., U.S.A. 79 L9   34 55N 117 51W
Edwards, N.Y., U.S.A. 85 B9   44 20N 75 15W
Edwards Air Force Base, U.S.A. 79 L9   34 50N 117 40W
Edwards Plateau, U.S.A. 81 K4   30 45N 101 20W
Edwardsville, U.S.A. 85 E9   41 15N 75 56W
Edxná, Mexico 87 D6   19 35N 90 15W
Edzo, Canada 70 A5   62 49N 116 4W
Eeklo, Belgium . . . . 15 C3   51 11N   3 33 E
Effigy Mounds △, U.S.A. 80 D9   43 5N 91 11W
Effingham, U.S.A. 82 F1   39 7N 88 33W
Égadi, Ìsole, Italy . . . . 22 F5   37 55N 12 16 E
Egan Range, U.S.A. 76 G6   39 35N 114 55W
Eganville, Canada 84 A7   45 32N 77 5W
Eger = Cheb, Czech Rep. . . . . . 16 C7   50 9N 12 28 E
Eger, Hungary . . . . 17 E11 47 53N 20 27 E
Egersund, Norway . . . . 9 G12   58 26N   6 1 E
Egg L., Canada 71 B7   55 5N 105 30W
Éghezée, Belgium . . . . 15 D4   50 35N   4 55 E
Egmont, Canada 70 D4   49 45N 123 56W
Egmont, N.Z. . . . . 59 H5   39 17S 174 4 E
Egmont, C., N.Z. . . . . 59 H4   39 16S 173 45 E
Egmont, Mt. = Taranaki, Mt., N.Z. 59 H5   39 17S 174 5 E
Egra, India . . . . 43 J12 21 54N 87 32 E
Eğridir, Turkey . . . . 19 G5   37 52N 30 51 E
Eğridir Gölü, Turkey . . . . 19 G5   37 53N 30 50 E
Egvekinot, Russia 29 C19 66 19N 179 50W
Egypt ■, Africa . . . . 51 C12 28 0N 31 0 E
Ehime □, Japan . . . . 31 H6   33 30N 132 40 E
Ehrenberg, U.S.A. 79 M12 33 36N 114 31W
Eibar, Spain 21 A4   43 11N   2 28W
Eidsvold, Australia . . . . 63 D5   25 25S 151 12 E
Eidsvoll, Norway . . . . 9 F14   60 19N 11 14 E
Eifel, Germany . . . . 16 C4   50 15N   6 50 E
Eiffel Flats, Zimbabwe . . . . 55 F3   18 20S 30 0 E
Eigg, U.K. 11 E2   56 54N   6 10W
Eighty Mile Beach, Australia . . . 60 C3   19 30S 120 40 E
Eil, Somali Rep. . . . . 47 F4   8 0N 49 50 E
Eil, L., U.K. 11 E3   56 51N   5 16W
Eildon, Australia . . . . 63 F4   37 10S 146 0 E
Eildon, L., Australia . . . . 63 F4   37 10S 146 0 E
Einasleigh, Australia . . . . 62 B3   18 32S 144 5 E
Einasleigh →, Australia . . . . 62 B3   17 30S 142 17 E
Eindhoven, Neths. . . . . 15 C5   51 26N   5 28 E
Eire = Europe 10 C4   53 50N   7 52W
Eiríksjökull, Iceland 8 D3   64 46N 20 24W
Eirunepé, Brazil 92 E5   6 35S 69 53W
Eiseb →, Namibia . . . . 56 C2   20 33S 20 59 E
Eisenach, Germany . . . . 16 C6   50 58N 10 19 E
Eisenerz, Austria . . . . 16 E8   47 32N 14 54 E
Eivissa, Spain . . . . 24 C7   38 54N   1 26 E
Ejeda, Madag. . . . . 57 C7   24 20S 44 31 E
Ejutla, Mexico 87 D5   16 34N 96 44W
Ekalaka, U.S.A. 80 C2   45 53N 104 33W
Eketahuna, N.Z. . . . . 59 J5   40 38S 175 43 E
Ekibastuz, Kazakhstan . . . . 28 D8   51 50N 75 10 E
Ekoli, Dem. Rep. of the Congo . 54 C1   0 23S 24 13 E
Eksjö, Sweden . . . . 9 H16   57 40N 14 58 E
Ekuma →, Namibia . . . . 56 B2   18 40S 16 2 E
Ekwan →, Canada 72 B3   53 12N 82 15W
Ekwan Pt., Canada 72 B3   53 16N 82 7W
El Aaiún, W. Sahara 50 C3   27 9N 13 12W
El 'Agrûd, Egypt . . . . 46 E3   30 14N 34 24 E
El 'Alamein, Egypt . . . . 51 B11 30 48N 28 58 E
El 'Aqaba, W. →, Egypt . . . . . . 46 E2   30 7N 33 54 E
El Ariha, West Bank . . . . 46 D4   31 52N 35 27 E
El 'Arîsh, Egypt . . . . 46 D2   31 8N 33 50 E
El 'Arîsh, W. →, Egypt . . . . 46 D2   31 8N 33 47 E
El Asnam = Ech Chélif, Algeria . 50 A6   36 10N   1 20 E
El Bayadh, Algeria . . . . 50 B6   33 40N   1 1 E
El Bluff, Nic. 88 D3   11 59N 83 40W
El Brûk, W. →, Egypt . . . . 46 E2   30 15N 33 50 E
El Cajon, U.S.A. 79 N10 32 48N 116 58W
El Campo, U.S.A. 81 L6   29 12N 96 16W
El Centro, U.S.A. 79 N11 32 48N 115 34W
El Cerro, Bolivia 92 G6   17 30S 61 40W
El Compadre, Mexico 79 N10 32 20N 116 14W
El Cuy, Argentina 96 D3   39 55S 68 25W
El Cuyo, Mexico 87 C7   21 30N 87 40W
El Daheir, Egypt . . . . 46 D3   31 13N 34 10 E
El Dátil, Mexico 86 B2   30 7N 112 15W
El Dere, Somali Rep. . . . . 47 G4   3 50N 47 8 E
El Descanso, Mexico 79 N10 32 12N 116 58W
El Desemboque, Mexico 86 A2   30 30N 112 57W
El Diviso, Colombia 92 C3   1 22N 78 14W
El Djouf, Mauritania 50 D4   20 0N   9 0W
El Dorado, Ark., U.S.A. 81 J8   33 12N 92 40W
El Dorado, Kans., U.S.A. 81 G6   37 49N 96 52W
El Dorado, Venezuela 92 B6   6 55N 61 37W
El Escorial, Spain 21 B3   40 35N   4 7W
El Faiyûm, Egypt . . . . 51 C12 29 19N 30 50 E
El Fâsher, Sudan . . . . 51 F11 13 33N 25 26 E
El Ferrol = Ferrol, Spain 21 A1   43 29N   8 15W
El Fuerte, Mexico 86 B3   26 30N 108 40W
El Gal, Somali Rep. . . . . 47 E5   10 58N 50 20 E
El Geneina = Al Junaynah, Sudan 51 F10 13 27N 22 45 E
El Gîza, Egypt . . . . 51 C12 30 0N 31 10 E
El Gogorrón △, Mexico 86 C4   21 50N 100 50W
El Goléa, Algeria . . . . 50 B6   30 30N   2 50 E
El Guácharo △, Venezuela 89 D7   10 8N 63 21W
El Guaviare, Venezuela 89 E6   9 45N 69 30W
El Iskandarîya, Egypt . . . . 51 B11 31 13N 29 58 E
El Istiwa'iya, Sudan . . . . 51 G11   5 0N 28 0 E
El Jadida, Morocco 50 B4   33 11N   8 17W
El Jardal, Honduras 88 D2   14 54N 88 50W
El Kabrît, G., Egypt . . . . 46 E2   29 42N 33 16 E
El Khârga, Egypt . . . . 51 C12 25 30N 30 33 E
El Khartûm, Sudan . . . . 51 E12 15 31N 32 35 E
El Kuntilla, Egypt . . . . 46 E3   30 1N 34 45 E
El Maestrazgo, Spain 21 B5   40 30N   0 25W
El Mahalla el Kubra, Egypt . . . . 51 B12 31 0N 31 0 E
El Mansûra, Egypt . . . . 51 B12 31 0N 31 19 E
El Medano, Canary Is. 24 F3   28 3N 16 32W

El Milagro, Argentina 94 C2   30 59S 65 59W
El Minyâ, Egypt . . . . 51 C12 28 7N 30 33 E
El Monte, U.S.A. 79 L8   34 4N 118 1W
El Obeid, Sudan . . . . 51 F12 13 8N 30 10 E
El Odaiya, Sudan . . . . 51 F11 12 8N 28 12 E
El Oro, Mexico 87 D4   19 48N 100 8W
El Oued, Algeria . . . . 50 B7   33 20N   6 58 E
El Palmar △, Argentina 94 C4   32 10S 58 31W
El Palmito, Presa, Mexico 86 B3   25 40N 105 30W
El Paso, U.S.A. 77 L10 31 45N 106 29W
El Paso Robles, U.S.A. 78 K6   35 38N 120 41W
El Pinacate y Gran Desierto de
   Altar = Gran Desierto del
   Pinacate △, Mexico 86 A2   31 51N 113 32W
El Portal, U.S.A. 78 H7   37 41N 119 47W
El Porvenir, Mexico 86 A3   31 15N 105 51W
El Prat de Llobregat, Spain . . . 21 B7   41 18N   2 3 E
El Progreso, Honduras 88 C2   15 26N 87 51W
El Pueblito, Mexico 86 B3   29 3N 105 4W
El Pueblo, Canary Is. 24 F2   28 36N 17 47W
El Puerto de Santa María, Spain 21 D2   36 36N   6 13W
El Qâhira, Egypt . . . . 51 B12 30 1N 31 14 E
El Qantara, Egypt . . . . 46 E1   30 51N 32 20 E
El Quseima, Egypt . . . . 46 E3   30 40N 34 15 E
El Real, Panama 92 B3   8 0N 77 40W
El Reno, U.S.A. 81 H6   35 32N 97 57W
El Rey △, Argentina 94 A3   24 40S 64 34W
El Rio, U.S.A. 79 L7   34 14N 119 10W
El Roque, Pta., Canary Is. 24 F4   28 10N 15 25W
El Rosarito, Mexico 86 B2   28 38N 114 4W
El Saheira, W. →, Egypt . . . . . . 46 E2   30 5N 33 25 E
El Salto, Mexico 86 C3   23 47N 105 22W
El Salvador ■, Cent. Amer. 88 D2   13 50N 89 0W
El Sauce, Nic. 88 D2   13 0N 86 40W
El Sueco, Mexico 86 B3   29 54N 106 24W
El Suweis, Egypt . . . . 51 C12 29 58N 32 31 E
El Tamarâni, W. →, Egypt . . . . . 46 E3   30 7N 34 43 E
El Thamad, Egypt . . . . 46 F3   29 40N 34 28 E
El Tigre, Venezuela 92 B6   8 44N 64 15W
El Tîh, Gebal, Egypt . . . . 46 F2   29 40N 33 50 E
El Tîna, Khalîg, Egypt . . . . 46 D1   31 10N 32 40 E
El Tofo, Chile 94 B1   29 22S 71 18W
El Tránsito, Chile 94 B1   28 52S 70 17W
El Tûr, Egypt . . . . 44 D2   28 14N 33 36 E
El Turbio, Argentina 96 G2   51 45S 72 5W
El Uqsur, Egypt . . . . 51 C12 25 41N 32 38 E
El Venado, Mexico 86 C4   22 56N 101 10W
El Vergel, Mexico 86 B3   26 28N 106 22W
El Vigía, Venezuela 92 B4   8 38N 71 39W
El Wabeira, Egypt . . . . 46 F2   29 34N 33 6 E
El Wak, Kenya . . . . 54 B5   2 49N 40 56 E
El Wuz, Sudan . . . . 51 E12 15 5N 30 10 E
Elat, Israel . . . . 46 F3   29 30N 34 56 E
Elâzığ, Turkey . . . . 19 G6   38 37N 39 14 E
Elba, Italy . . . . 22 C4   42 46N 10 17 E
Elba, U.S.A. 83 K2   31 25N 86 4W
Elbasan, Albania . . . . 23 D9   41 9N 20 9 E
Elbe →, Europe . . . . 16 B5   53 50N   9 0 E
Elbert, Mt., U.S.A. 77 G10 39 7N 106 27W
Elberton, U.S.A. 83 H4   34 7N 82 52W
Elbeuf, France . . . . 20 B4   49 17N   1 2 E
Elbidtan, Turkey . . . . 44 B3   38 13N 37 12 E
Elbing = Elbląg, Poland . . . . . . 17 A10 54 10N 19 25 E
Elbląg, Poland . . . . 17 A10 54 10N 19 25 E
Elbow, Canada 71 C7   51 7N 106 35W
Elbrus, Asia . . . . 19 F7   43 21N 42 30 E
Elburz Mts. = Alborz, Reshteh-ye
   Kühhâ-ye, Iran . . . . 45 C7   36 0N 52 0 E
Elche, Spain 21 C5   38 15N   0 42W
Elcho I., Australia . . . . 62 A2   11 55S 135 45 E
Elda, Spain 21 C5   38 29N   0 47W
Elde →, Germany . . . . 16 B6   53 7N 11 15 E
Eldon, Mo., U.S.A. 80 F8   38 21N 92 35W
Eldon, Wash., U.S.A. 78 C3   47 33N 123 3W
Eldora, U.S.A. 80 D8   42 22N 93 5W
Eldorado, Argentina 95 B5   26 28S 54 43W
Eldorado, Canada 84 B7   44 35N 77 31W
Eldorado, Mexico 86 C3   24 20N 107 22W
Eldorado, Ill., U.S.A. 82 G1   37 49N 88 26W
Eldorado, Tex., U.S.A. 81 K4   30 52N 100 36W
Eldorado Springs, U.S.A. 81 G8   37 52N 94 1W
Eldoret, Kenya . . . . 54 B4   0 30N 35 17 E
Eldred, U.S.A. 84 E6   41 58N 78 23W
Elea, C., Cyprus . . . . 25 D13 35 19N 34 4 E
Eleanora, Pk., Australia . . . . . . 61 F3   32 57S 121 9 E
Elefantes →, Africa . . . . 57 C5   24 10S 32 40 E
Elektrostal, Russia . . . . 18 C6   55 41N 38 32 E
Elephant Butte Reservoir, U.S.A. 77 K10 33 9N 107 11W
Elephant I., Antarctica 5 C18   61 0S 55 0W
Eleuthera, Bahamas 88 B4   25 0N 76 20W
Elgin, Canada 85 B8   44 36N 76 13W
Elgin, U.K. 11 D5   57 39N   3 19W
Elgin, Ill., U.S.A. 82 D1   42 2N 88 17W
Elgin, N. Dak., U.S.A. 80 B4   46 24N 101 51W
Elgin, Oreg., U.S.A. 76 D5   45 34N 117 55W
Elgin, Tex., U.S.A. 81 K6   30 21N 97 22W
Elgon, Mt., Africa . . . . 54 B3   1 10N 34 30 E
Eliase, Indonesia . . . . 37 F8   8 21S 130 48 E
Elim, Namibia . . . . 56 B2   17 48S 15 31 E
Elim, S. Africa . . . . 56 E2   34 35S 19 45 E
Elista, Russia . . . . 19 E7   46 16N 44 14 E
Elizabeth, Australia . . . . 63 E2   34 42S 138 41 E
Elizabeth, U.S.A. 85 F10 40 40N 74 13W
Elizabeth City, U.S.A. 83 G7   36 18N 76 14W
Elizabethton, U.S.A. 83 G4   36 21N 82 13W
Elizabethtown, Ky., U.S.A. 82 G3   37 42N 85 52W
Elizabethtown, N.Y., U.S.A. . . . 85 B11 44 13N 73 36W
Elizabethtown, Pa., U.S.A. 85 F8   40 9N 76 36W
Elk, Poland . . . . 17 B12 53 50N 22 21 E
Elk →, U.S.A. 70 D5   49 11N 115 14W
Elk →, U.S.A. 83 H2   34 46N 87 16W
Elk City, U.S.A. 81 H5   35 25N 99 25W
Elk Creek, U.S.A. 78 F4   39 36N 122 32W
Elk Grove, U.S.A. 78 G5   38 25N 121 22W
Elk Island △, Canada 70 C6   53 35N 112 59W
Elk Lake, Canada 72 C3   47 40N 80 25W
Elk Point, Canada 71 C6   53 54N 110 55W
Elk River, Idaho, U.S.A. 76 C5   46 47N 116 11W
Elk River, Minn., U.S.A. 80 C8   45 18N 93 35W
Elkedra →, Australia . . . . 62 C2   21 8S 136 22 E
Elkhart, Ind., U.S.A. 82 E3   41 41N 85 58W
Elkhart, Kans., U.S.A. 81 G4   37 0N 101 54W
Elkhorn, Canada 71 D8   49 59N 101 14W
Elkhorn →, U.S.A. 80 E6   41 8N 96 19W
Elkhovo, Bulgaria . . . . 23 C12 42 10N 26 40 E
Elkin, U.S.A. 83 G5   36 15N 80 51W
Elkins, U.S.A. 82 F6   38 55N 79 51W

Elkland, U.S.A. 84 E7   41 59N 77 19W
Elko, Canada 70 D5   49 20N 115 10W
Elko, U.S.A. 76 F6   40 50N 115 46W
Elkton, U.S.A. 84 C1   43 49N 83 11W
Ell, L., Australia . . . . 61 E4   29 13S 127 46 E
Ellef Ringnes I., Canada 4 B2   78 30N 102 2W
Ellen, Mt., U.S.A. 85 B12 44 9N 72 56W
Ellenburg, U.S.A. 85 B11 44 54N 73 48W
Ellendale, U.S.A. 80 B5   46 0N 98 32W
Ellensburg, U.S.A. 76 C3   46 59N 120 34W
Ellenville, U.S.A. 85 E10 41 43N 74 24W
Ellerton, Barbados . . . . 89 g   13 9N 59 33W
Ellery, Mt., Australia . . . . 63 F4   37 28S 148 47 E
Ellesmere, L., N.Z. . . . . 59 M4   43 47S 172 28 E
Ellesmere I., Canada 4 B4   79 30N 80 0W
Ellesmere Port, U.K. 12 D5   53 17N   2 54W
Ellice Is. = Tuvalu ■, Pac. Oc. . 64 H9   8 0S 178 0 E
Ellicottville, U.S.A. 84 D6   42 17N 78 40W
Elliot, Australia . . . . 62 B1   17 33S 133 32 E
Elliot, S. Africa . . . . 57 E4   31 22S 27 48 E
Elliot Lake, Canada 72 C3   46 25N 82 35W
Elliotdale = Xhora, S. Africa . . . 57 E4   31 55S 28 38 E
Ellis, U.S.A. 80 F5   38 56N 99 34W
Elliston, Australia . . . . 63 E1   33 39S 134 53 E
Ellisville, U.S.A. 81 K10 31 36N 89 12W
Ellon, U.K. 11 D6   57 22N   2 4W
Ellore = Eluru, India . . . . 41 L12 16 48N 81 8 E
Ellsworth, Kans., U.S.A. 80 F5   38 44N 98 14W
Ellsworth, Maine, U.S.A. 83 C11 44 33N 68 25W
Ellsworth Land, Antarctica 5 D16   76 0S 89 0W
Ellsworth Mts., Antarctica 5 D16   78 30S 85 0W
Ellwood City, U.S.A. 84 F4   40 52N 80 17W
Elma, Canada 71 D9   49 52N 95 55W
Elma, U.S.A. 78 D3   47 0N 123 25W
Elmalı, Turkey . . . . 19 G4   36 44N 29 56 E
Elmhurst, U.S.A. 82 E2   41 53N 87 56W
Elmira, Canada 84 C4   43 36N 80 33W
Elmira, U.S.A. 84 D8   42 6N 76 48W
Elmira Heights, U.S.A. 84 D8   42 8N 76 50W
Elmore, Australia . . . . 63 F3   36 30S 144 37 E
Elmore, U.S.A. 79 M11 33 7N 115 49W
Elmshorn, Germany . . . . 16 B5   53 43N   9 40 E
Elmvale, Canada 84 B5   44 35N 79 52W
Elora, Canada 84 C4   43 41N 80 26W
Eloúnda, Greece . . . . 25 D7   35 16N 25 42 E
Eloy, U.S.A. 77 K8   32 45N 111 33W
Elrose, Canada 71 C7   51 12N 108 0W
Elsie, U.S.A. 78 E3   45 52N 123 36W
Elsinore = Helsingør, Denmark . 9 H15   56 2N 12 35 E
Eltham, N.Z. . . . . 59 H5   39 26S 174 19 E
Eluru, India . . . . 41 L12 16 48N 81 8 E
Elvas, Portugal 21 C2   38 50N   7 10W
Elverum, Norway . . . . 9 F14   60 53N 11 34 E
Elvire →, Australia . . . . 60 C4   17 51S 128 11 E
Elvire, Mt., Australia . . . . 61 E2   29 22S 119 36 E
Elwell, L., U.S.A. 76 B8   48 22N 111 17W
Elwood, Ind., U.S.A. 82 E3   40 17N 85 50W
Elwood, Nebr., U.S.A. 80 E5   40 36N 99 52W
Elx = Elche, Spain 21 C5   38 15N   0 42W
Ely, U.K. . . . . 13 E8   52 24N   0 16 E
Ely, Minn., U.S.A. 80 B9   47 55N 91 51W
Ely, Nev., U.S.A. 76 G6   39 15N 114 54W
Elyria, U.S.A. 84 E2   41 22N 82 7W
Emâmrûd, Iran . . . . 45 B7   36 30N 55 0 E
Emba, Kazakhstan . . . . 28 E6   48 50N 58 8 E
Emba →, Kazakhstan . . . . 19 E9   46 55N 53 28 E
Embarcación, Argentina 94 A3   23 10S 64 0W
Embarras Portage, Canada 71 B6   58 27N 111 28W
Embetsu, Japan . . . . 30 B10 44 44N 141 47 E
Embi = Emba, Kazakhstan . . . . 28 E6   48 50N 58 8 E
Embi →= Emba →, Kazakhstan . 19 E9   46 55N 53 28 E
Embóna, Greece . . . . 25 C9   36 13N 27 51 E
Embrun, France . . . . 20 D7   44 34N   6 30 E
Embu, Kenya . . . . 54 C4   0 32S 37 38 E
Emden, Germany . . . . 16 B4   53 21N   7 12 E
Emerald, Australia . . . . 62 C4   23 32S 148 10 E
Emerson, Canada 71 D9   49 0N 97 10W
Emet, Turkey . . . . 23 E13 39 20N 29 15 E
Emi Koussi, Chad . . . . 51 E9   19 45N 18 55 E
Eminabad, Pakistan . . . . 42 C6   32 2N 74 8 E
Emine, Nos, Bulgaria . . . . 23 C12 42 40N 27 56 E
Emissi, Tarso, Chad . . . . 51 D9   21 27N 18 36 E
Emlenton, U.S.A. 84 E5   41 11N 79 43W
Emmaus, S. Africa . . . . 56 D4   29 2S 25 15 E
Emmaus, U.S.A. 85 F9   40 32N 75 30W
Emmeloord, Neths. . . . . 15 B5   52 44N   5 46 E
Emmen, Neths. . . . . 15 B6   52 48N   6 57 E
Emmet, Australia . . . . 62 C3   24 45S 144 30 E
Emmetsburg, U.S.A. 80 D7   43 7N 94 41W
Emmett, Idaho, U.S.A. 76 E5   43 52N 116 30W
Emmett, Mich., U.S.A. 84 D2   42 59N 82 46W
Emmonak, U.S.A. 68 B3   62 46N 164 30W
Emo, Canada 71 D10 48 38N 93 50W
Empalme, Mexico 86 B2   28 1N 110 49W
Empangeni, S. Africa . . . . 57 D5   28 50S 31 52 E
Empedrado, Argentina 94 B4   28 0S 58 46W
Emperor Seamount Chain,
   Pac. Oc. . . . . 64 D9   40 0N 170 0 E
Emporia, Kans., U.S.A. 80 F6   38 25N 96 11W
Emporia, Va., U.S.A. 83 G7   36 42N 77 32W
Emporium, U.S.A. 84 E6   41 31N 78 14W
Empress, Canada 71 C7   50 57N 110 0W
Empty Quarter = Rub' al Khâli,
   Si. Arabia . . . . 47 D4   19 0N 48 0 E
Ems →, Germany . . . . 16 B4   53 20N   7 12 E
Emsdale, Canada 84 A5   45 32N 79 19W
Emu, China . . . . 35 C15 43 40N 128 21 E
Emu Park, Australia . . . . 62 C5   23 13S 150 50 E
'En 'Avrona, Israel . . . . 46 F4   29 43N 35 0 E
Ena, Japan . . . . 31 G8   35 25N 137 25 E
Enana, Namibia . . . . 56 B2   17 30S 16 23 E
Enard B., U.K. 11 C3   58 5N   5 20W
Enare = Inarijärvi, Finland . . . . 8 B22   69 0N 28 0 E
Enarotali, Indonesia . . . . 37 E9   3 55S 136 21 E
Encampment, U.S.A. 76 F10 41 12N 106 47W
Encantadas, Serra, Brazil 95 C5   30 40S 53 0W
Encarnación, Paraguay 95 B4   27 15S 55 50W
Encarnación de Diaz, Mexico . . 86 C4   21 30N 102 13W
Encinitas, U.S.A. 79 M9   33 3N 117 17W
Encino, U.S.A. 77 J11 34 39N 105 28W
Encounter B., Australia . . . . 63 F2   35 45S 138 45 E
Endako, Canada 70 C3   54 6N 125 2W
Ende, Indonesia . . . . 37 F6   8 45S 121 40 E
Endeavour Str., Australia . . . . . 62 A3   10 45S 142 0 E
Enderbury I., Kiribati 64 H10   3 8S 171 05W
Enderby, Canada 70 C5   50 35N 119 10W
Enderby I., Australia . . . . 60 D2   20 35S 116 30 E

Enderby Land, Antarctica ... 5 C5 66 0S 53 0 E
Enderlin, U.S.A. ... 80 B6 46 38N 97 36W
Endicott, U.S.A. ... 85 D8 42 6N 76 4W
Endwell, U.S.A. ... 85 D8 42 6N 76 2W
Endyalgout I., Australia ... 60 B5 11 40S 132 35 E
Eneabba, Australia ... 61 E2 29 49S 115 16 E
Enewetak Atoll, Marshall Is. ... 64 F8 11 30N 162 15 E
Enez, Turkey ... 23 D12 40 45N 26 5 E
Enfer, Pte. d', Martinique ... 88 c 14 22N 60 54W
Enfield, Canada ... 73 D7 44 56N 63 32W
Enfield, Conn., U.S.A. ... 85 E12 41 58N 72 36W
Enfield, N.H., U.S.A. ... 85 C12 43 59N 72 9W
Engadin, Switz. ... 20 C9 46 45N 10 10 E
Engaño, C., Dom. Rep. ... 89 C6 18 30N 68 20W
Engaño, C., Phil. ... 37 A6 18 35N 122 23 E
Engaru, Japan ... 30 B11 44 3N 143 31 E
Engcobo, S. Africa ... 57 E4 31 37S 28 0 E
Engels, Russia ... 19 D8 51 28N 46 6 E
Engemann L., Canada ... 71 B7 58 0N 106 55W
Enggano, Indonesia ... 36 F2 5 20S 102 40 E
England, U.S.A. ... 81 H9 34 33N 91 58W
England □, U.K. ... 13 E5 53 0N 2 0W
Englee, Canada ... 73 B8 50 45N 56 5W
Englehart, Canada ... 72 C4 47 49N 79 52W
Englewood, U.S.A. ... 80 F2 39 39N 104 59W
English →, Canada ... 71 C10 49 12N 91 5W
English Bazar = Ingraj Bazar,
  India ... 43 G13 24 58N 88 10 E
English Channel, Europe ... 13 G6 50 0N 2 0W
English River, Canada ... 72 C1 49 14N 91 0W
Enid, U.S.A. ... 81 G6 36 24N 97 53W
Enkhuizen, Neths. ... 15 B5 52 42N 5 17 E
Enna, Italy ... 22 F6 37 34N 14 16 E
Ennadai, Canada ... 71 A8 61 8N 100 53W
Ennadai L., Canada ... 71 A8 60 58N 101 20W
Ennedi, Chad ... 51 E10 17 15N 22 0 E
Enngonia, Australia ... 63 D4 29 21S 145 50 E
Ennis, Ireland ... 10 D3 52 51N 8 59W
Ennis, Mont., U.S.A. ... 76 D8 45 21N 111 44W
Ennis, Tex., U.S.A. ... 81 J6 32 20N 96 38W
Enniscorthy, Ireland ... 10 D5 52 30N 6 34W
Enniskillen, Ireland ... 10 B4 54 21N 7 39W
Ennistimon, Ireland ... 10 D2 52 57N 9 17W
Enns →, Austria ... 16 D8 48 14N 14 32 E
Enontekiö, Finland ... 8 B20 68 23N 23 37 E
Enosburg Falls, U.S.A. ... 85 B12 44 55N 72 48W
Enriquillo, L., Dom. Rep. ... 89 C5 18 20N 72 5W
Enschede, Neths. ... 15 B6 52 13N 6 53 E
Ensenada, Argentina ... 94 C4 34 55S 57 55W
Ensenada, Mexico ... 86 A1 31 50N 116 50W
Ensenada de los Muertos,
  Mexico ... 86 C2 23 59N 109 50W
Ensiola, Pta. de n', Spain ... 24 B9 39 7N 2 55 E
Entebbe, Uganda ... 54 B3 0 4N 32 28 E
Enterprise, Canada ... 70 A5 60 47N 115 45W
Enterprise, Ala., U.S.A. ... 83 K3 31 19N 85 51W
Enterprise, Oreg., U.S.A. ... 76 D5 45 25N 117 17W
Entre Ríos, Bolivia ... 94 A3 21 30S 64 25W
Entre Ríos □, Argentina ... 94 C4 30 30S 58 30W
Entroncamento, Portugal ... 21 C1 39 28N 8 28W
Enugu, Nigeria ... 50 G7 6 30N 7 30 E
Enumclaw, U.S.A. ... 78 C5 47 12N 121 59W
Eólie, Ís., Italy ... 22 E6 38 30N 14 57 E
Epe, Neths. ... 15 B5 52 21N 5 59 E
Épernay, France ... 20 B5 49 3N 3 56 E
Ephesus, Turkey ... 23 F12 37 55N 27 22 E
Ephraim, U.S.A. ... 76 G8 39 22N 111 35W
Ephrata, Pa., U.S.A. ... 85 F8 40 11N 76 11W
Ephrata, Wash., U.S.A. ... 76 C4 47 19N 119 33W
Épinal, France ... 20 B7 48 10N 6 27 E
Episkopí, Cyprus ... 25 E11 34 40N 32 54 E
Episkopí, Greece ... 25 D6 35 20N 24 20 E
Episkopí Bay, Cyprus ... 25 E11 34 35N 32 50 E
Epsom, U.K. ... 13 F7 51 19N 0 16W
Epukiro, Namibia ... 56 C2 21 40S 19 9 E
Equatorial Guinea ■, Africa ... 52 D1 2 0N 8 0 E
Er Rachidia, Morocco ... 50 B5 31 58N 4 20W
Er Rahad, Sudan ... 51 F12 12 45N 30 32 E
Er Rif, Morocco ... 50 A5 35 1N 4 1W
Erāwadi Myit = Irrawaddy →,
  Burma ... 41 M19 15 50N 95 6 E
Erāwadi Myitwanya = Irrawaddy,
  Mouths of the, Burma ... 41 M19 15 30N 95 0 E
Erbil = Arbīl, Iraq ... 44 B5 36 15N 44 5 E
Erçek, Turkey ... 44 B4 38 39N 43 36 E
Erçiyaş Dağı, Turkey ... 44 B2 38 30N 35 30 E
Érd, Hungary ... 17 E10 47 22N 18 56 E
Erdao Jiang →, China ... 35 C14 43 0N 127 0 E
Erdek, Turkey ... 23 D12 40 23N 27 47 E
Erdene = Ulaan-Uul, Mongolia ... 34 B6 44 13N 111 10 E
Erdenet, Mongolia ... 32 B5 49 2N 104 5 E
Erdenetsogt, Mongolia ... 34 C4 42 55N 106 5 E
Erebus, Mt., Antarctica ... 5 D11 77 35S 167 0 E
Erechim, Brazil ... 95 B5 27 35S 52 15W
Ereğli, Konya, Turkey ... 19 G5 37 31N 34 4 E
Ereğli, Zonguldak, Turkey ... 19 F5 41 15N 31 24 E
Erenhot, China ... 34 C7 43 48N 112 2 E
Eresma →, Spain ... 21 B3 41 26N 4 45W
Erfenisdam, S. Africa ... 56 D4 28 30S 26 50 E
Erfurt, Germany ... 16 C6 50 58N 11 2 E
Ergani, Turkey ... 44 B3 38 17N 39 49 E
Ergel, Mongolia ... 34 C5 43 8N 109 5 E
Ergeni Vozvyshennost, Russia ... 19 E7 47 0N 44 0 E
Érgli, Latvia ... 9 H21 56 54N 25 38 E
Eriboll, L., U.K. ... 11 C4 58 30N 4 42W
Érice, Italy ... 22 E5 38 2N 12 35 E
Erie, U.S.A. ... 84 D4 42 8N 80 5W
Erie, L., N. Amer. ... 84 D4 42 15N 81 0W
Erie Canal, U.S.A. ... 84 C7 43 5N 78 43W
Erieau, Canada ... 84 D3 42 16N 81 57W
Erigavo, Somali Rep. ... 47 E4 10 35N 47 20 E
Erikoúsa, Greece ... 25 A3 39 53N 19 34 E
Eriksdale, Canada ... 71 C9 50 52N 98 7W
Erimanthos, Greece ... 23 F9 37 57N 21 50 E
Erimo-misaki, Japan ... 30 D11 41 50N 143 15 E
Erin Pt., Trin. & Tob. ... 93 K15 10 13N 61 40W
Erinpura, India ... 42 G5 25 9N 73 3 E
Eriskay, U.K. ... 11 D1 57 4N 7 18W
Eritrea ■, Africa ... 47 D2 14 0N 38 30 E
Erlangen, Germany ... 16 D6 49 36N 11 0 E
Erldunda, Australia ... 62 D1 25 14S 133 12 E
Ermelo, Neths. ... 15 B5 52 18N 5 35 E
Ermelo, S. Africa ... 57 D4 26 31S 29 59 E
Ermenek, Turkey ... 44 B2 36 38N 33 0 E
Ermones, Greece ... 25 A3 39 37N 19 46 E
Ernakulam, India ... 40 Q10 9 59N 76 22 E
Erne →, Ireland ... 10 B3 54 30N 8 16W
Erne, Lower L., U.K. ... 10 B4 54 28N 7 47W

Erne, Upper L., U.K. ... 10 B4 54 14N 7 32W
Ernest Giles Ra., Australia ... 61 E3 27 0S 123 45 E
Erode, India ... 40 P10 11 24N 77 45 E
Eromanga, Australia ... 63 D3 26 40S 143 11 E
Erongo, Namibia ... 56 C2 21 39S 15 58 E
Erramala Hills, India ... 40 M11 15 30N 78 15 E
Errigal, Ireland ... 10 A3 55 2N 8 6W
Erris Hd., Ireland ... 10 B1 54 19N 10 0W
Erskine, U.S.A. ... 80 B7 47 40N 96 0W
Ertis = Irtysh →, Russia ... 28 C7 61 4N 68 52 E
Erwin, U.S.A. ... 83 G4 36 9N 82 25W
Erzgebirge, Germany ... 16 C7 50 27N 12 55 E
Erzin, Russia ... 29 D10 50 15N 95 10 E
Erzincan, Turkey ... 19 G6 39 46N 39 30 E
Erzurum, Turkey ... 19 G7 39 57N 41 15 E
Es Caló, Spain ... 24 C8 38 40N 1 30 E
Es Canar, Spain ... 24 B8 39 2N 1 36 E
Es Mercadal, Spain ... 24 B11 39 59N 4 5 E
Es Migjorn Gran, Spain ... 24 B11 39 57N 4 3 E
Es Sahrâ' Esh Sharqîya, Egypt ... 51 C12 27 30N 32 30 E
Es Sînâ', Egypt ... 46 F3 29 0N 34 0 E
Es Vedrà, Spain ... 24 C7 38 52N 1 12 E
Esambo, Dem. Rep. of the Congo ... 54 C1 3 48S 23 30 E
Esan-Misaki, Japan ... 30 D10 41 40N 141 10 E
Esashi, Hokkaidō, Japan ... 30 B11 44 56N 142 35 E
Esashi, Hokkaidō, Japan ... 30 D10 41 52N 140 7 E
Esbjerg, Denmark ... 9 J13 55 29N 8 29 E
Escalante, U.S.A. ... 77 H8 37 47N 111 36W
Escalante →, U.S.A. ... 77 H8 37 24N 110 57W
Escalón, Mexico ... 86 B4 26 46N 104 20W
Escambia →, U.S.A. ... 83 K2 30 32N 87 11W
Escanaba, U.S.A. ... 82 C2 45 45N 87 4W
Esch-sur-Alzette, Lux. ... 15 E6 49 32N 6 0 E
Escondido, U.S.A. ... 79 M9 33 7N 117 5W
Escuinapa, Mexico ... 86 C3 22 50N 105 50W
Escuintla, Guatemala ... 88 D1 14 20N 90 48W
Esenguly, Turkmenistan ... 28 F6 37 37N 53 59 E
Eşfahān, Iran ... 45 C6 32 39N 51 43 E
Eşfahān □, Iran ... 45 C6 32 50N 51 50 E
Esfarāyen, Iran ... 45 B8 37 4N 57 30 E
Esfideh, Iran ... 45 C8 33 39N 59 46 E
Esh Sham = Dimashq, Syria ... 46 B5 33 30N 36 18 E
Esha Ness, U.K. ... 11 A7 60 29N 1 38W
Esher, U.K. ... 13 F7 51 21N 0 20W
Eshkol △, Israel ... 46 D3 31 20N 34 30 E
Eshowe, S. Africa ... 57 D5 28 50S 31 30 E
Esigodini, Zimbabwe ... 57 C4 20 18S 28 56 E
Esil = Ishim →, Russia ... 28 D8 57 45N 71 10 E
Esira, Madag. ... 57 C8 24 20S 46 42 E
Esk →, Cumb., U.K. ... 12 C4 54 58N 3 2W
Esk →, N. Yorks., U.K. ... 12 C7 54 30N 0 37W
Eskān, Iran ... 45 E9 26 48N 63 9 E
Esker, Canada ... 73 B6 53 53N 66 25W
Eskifjörður, Iceland ... 8 D7 65 3N 13 55W
Eskilstuna, Sweden ... 9 G17 59 22N 16 32 E
Eskimo Point = Arviat, Canada ... 71 A10 61 6N 93 59W
Eskişehir, Turkey ... 19 G5 39 50N 30 30 E
Esla →, Spain ... 21 B2 41 29N 6 3W
Eslāmābād-e Gharb, Iran ... 44 C5 34 10N 46 30 E
Eslāmshahr, Iran ... 45 C6 35 40N 51 10 E
Esme, Turkey ... 23 E13 38 23N 28 58 E
Esmeraldas, Ecuador ... 92 C3 1 0N 79 40W
Esnagi L., Canada ... 72 C3 48 36N 84 33W
Espanola, Canada ... 72 C3 46 15N 81 46W
Espanola, U.S.A. ... 77 H10 35 59N 106 5W
Esparta, Costa Rica ... 88 E3 9 59N 84 40W
Esperance, Australia ... 61 F3 33 45S 121 55 E
Esperance B., Australia ... 61 F3 33 48S 121 55 E
Esperance B., St. Lucia ... 89 f 14 4N 60 55W
Esperanza, Antarctica ... 5 C18 65 0S 55 0W
Esperanza, Argentina ... 94 C3 31 29S 61 3W
Esperanza, Puerto Rico ... 89 d 18 6N 65 28W
Espichel, C., Portugal ... 21 C1 38 22N 9 16W
Espigão, Serra do, Brazil ... 95 B5 26 35S 50 30W
Espinazo, Serra del = Espinhaço,
  Serra do, Brazil ... 93 G10 17 30S 43 30W
Espinhaço, Serra do, Brazil ... 93 G10 17 30S 43 30W
Espinilho, Serra do, Brazil ... 95 B5 28 30S 55 0W
Espírito Santo □, Brazil ... 93 H10 20 0S 40 45W
Espíritu Santo, Vanuatu ... 64 J8 15 15S 166 50 E
Espíritu Santo, B. del, Mexico ... 87 D7 19 15N 87 0W
Espíritu Santo, I., Mexico ... 86 C2 24 30N 110 23W
Espita, Mexico ... 87 C7 21 1N 88 19W
Espoo, Finland ... 9 F21 60 12N 24 40 E
Espungabera, Mozam. ... 57 C5 20 29S 32 45 E
Esquel, Argentina ... 96 E2 42 55S 71 20W
Esquimalt, Canada ... 70 D4 48 26N 123 25W
Esquina, Argentina ... 94 C4 30 0S 59 30W
Essaouira, Morocco ... 50 B4 31 32N 9 42W
Essebie, Dem. Rep. of the Congo ... 54 B3 2 58N 30 40 E
Essen, Belgium ... 15 C4 51 28N 4 28 E
Essen, Germany ... 16 C4 51 28N 7 2 E
Essendon, Mt., Australia ... 61 E3 25 0S 120 29 E
Essequibo →, Guyana ... 92 B7 6 50N 58 30W
Essex, Canada ... 84 D2 42 10N 82 49W
Essex, Calif., U.S.A. ... 79 L11 34 44N 115 15W
Essex, N.Y., U.S.A. ... 85 B11 44 19N 73 21W
Essex □, U.K. ... 13 F8 51 54N 0 27 E
Essex Junction, U.S.A. ... 85 B11 44 29N 73 7W
Esslingen, Germany ... 16 D5 48 44N 9 18 E
Estados, I. de Los, Argentina ... 96 G4 54 40S 64 30W
Eştahbānāt, Iran ... 45 D7 29 8N 54 4 E
Estância, Brazil ... 93 F11 11 16S 37 26W
Estancia, U.S.A. ... 77 J10 34 46N 106 4W
Estārm, Iran ... 45 D8 28 21N 58 21 E
Estcourt, S. Africa ... 57 D4 29 0S 29 53 E
Este △, Dom. Rep. ... 89 C6 18 14N 68 42W
Estelí, Nic. ... 88 D2 13 9N 86 22W
Estellencs, Spain ... 24 B9 39 39N 2 29 E
Esterhazy, Canada ... 71 C8 50 37N 102 5W
Estevan, Canada ... 71 D8 49 10N 102 59W
Estevan Group, Canada ... 70 C3 53 3N 129 38W
Estherville, U.S.A. ... 80 D7 43 24N 94 50W
Eston, Canada ... 71 C7 51 8N 108 40W
Estonia ■, Europe ... 9 G21 58 30N 25 30 E
Estreito, Brazil ... 93 E9 6 32S 47 25W
Estrela, Serra da, Portugal ... 21 B2 40 10N 7 45W
Estremoz, Portugal ... 21 C2 38 51N 7 39W
Estrondo, Serra do, Brazil ... 93 E9 7 20S 48 0W
Esztergom, Hungary ... 17 E10 47 47N 18 44 E
Etah, India ... 43 F8 27 35N 78 40 E
Étampes, France ... 20 B5 48 26N 2 10 E
Etanga, Namibia ... 56 B1 17 55S 13 0 E
Etawah, India ... 43 F8 26 48N 79 6 E
Etawney L., Canada ... 71 B9 57 50N 96 50W
Ethel, U.S.A. ... 78 D4 46 32N 122 46W
Ethelbert, Canada ... 71 C8 51 32N 100 25W
Ethiopia ■, Africa ... 47 F3 8 0N 40 0 E

Ethiopian Highlands, Ethiopia ... 26 J7 10 0N 37 0 E
Etive, L., U.K. ... 11 E3 56 29N 5 10W
Etna, Italy ... 22 F6 37 50N 14 55 E
Etoile, Dem. Rep. of the Congo ... 55 E2 11 33S 27 30 E
Etosha △, Namibia ... 56 B2 19 0S 16 0 E
Etosha Pan, Namibia ... 56 B2 18 40S 16 30 E
Etowah, U.S.A. ... 83 H3 35 20N 84 32W
Ettelbruck, Lux. ... 15 E6 49 51N 6 5 E
Ettrick Water →, U.K. ... 11 F6 55 31N 2 55W
Etuku, Dem. Rep. of the Congo ... 54 C2 3 42S 25 45 E
Etzatlán, Mexico ... 86 C4 20 48N 104 5W
Etzná, Mexico ... 87 D6 19 35N 90 15W
Etzná-Tixmucuy = Edxná, Mexico ... 87 D6 19 35N 90 15W
Eubenangee Swamp △, Australia ... 62 B4 16 25S 146 1 E
Euboea = Évvoia, Greece ... 23 E11 38 30N 24 0 E
Eucla, Australia ... 61 F4 31 41S 128 52 E
Euclid, U.S.A. ... 84 E3 41 34N 81 32W
Eucumbene, L., Australia ... 63 F4 36 2S 148 40 E
Eudora, U.S.A. ... 81 J9 33 7N 91 16W
Eufaula, Ala., U.S.A. ... 83 K3 31 54N 85 9W
Eufaula, Okla., U.S.A. ... 81 H7 35 17N 95 35W
Eufaula L., U.S.A. ... 81 H7 35 18N 95 21W
Eugene, U.S.A. ... 76 E2 44 5N 123 4W
Eugowra, Australia ... 63 E4 33 22S 148 24 E
Eulo, Australia ... 63 D4 28 10S 145 3 E
Eungella △, Australia ... 62 C4 20 57S 148 40 E
Eunice, La., U.S.A. ... 81 K8 30 30N 92 25W
Eunice, N. Mex., U.S.A. ... 81 J3 32 26N 103 10W
Eupen, Belgium ... 15 D6 50 37N 6 3 E
Euphrates = Furāt, Nahr al →,
  Asia ... 44 D5 31 0N 47 25 E
Eureka, Canada ... 4 B3 80 0N 85 56W
Eureka, Calif., U.S.A. ... 76 F1 40 47N 124 9W
Eureka, Kans., U.S.A. ... 81 G6 37 49N 96 17W
Eureka, Mont., U.S.A. ... 76 B6 48 53N 115 3W
Eureka, Nev., U.S.A. ... 76 G5 39 31N 115 58W
Eureka, S. Dak., U.S.A. ... 80 C5 45 46N 99 38W
Eureka, Mt., Australia ... 61 E3 26 35S 121 35 E
Euroa, Australia ... 63 F4 36 44S 145 35 E
Europa, Île, Ind. Oc. ... 53 J8 22 20S 40 22 E
Europa, Picos de, Spain ... 21 A3 43 10N 4 49W
Europa, Pta. de, Gib. ... 21 D3 36 3N 5 21W
Europe ... 6 E10 50 0N 20 0 E
Europoort, Neths. ... 15 C4 51 57N 4 10 E
Eustis, U.S.A. ... 83 L5 28 51N 81 41W
Eutsuk L., Canada ... 70 C3 53 20N 126 45W
Evale, Angola ... 56 B2 16 33S 15 44 E
Evans, U.S.A. ... 80 E2 40 23N 104 41W
Evans, L., Canada ... 72 B4 50 50N 77 0W
Evans City, U.S.A. ... 84 F4 40 46N 80 4W
Evans Head, Australia ... 63 D5 29 7S 153 27 E
Evans Mills, U.S.A. ... 85 B9 44 6N 75 48W
Evansburg, Canada ... 70 C5 53 36N 114 59W
Evanston, Ill., U.S.A. ... 82 E2 42 3N 87 41W
Evanston, Wyo., U.S.A. ... 76 F8 41 16N 110 58W
Evansville, U.S.A. ... 82 G2 37 58N 87 35W
Evaz, Iran ... 45 E7 27 46N 53 59 E
Eveleth, U.S.A. ... 80 B8 47 28N 92 32W
Evensk, Russia ... 29 C16 62 12N 159 30 E
Everard, L., Australia ... 63 E2 31 30S 135 0 E
Everard Ranges, Australia ... 61 E5 27 5S 132 28 E
Everest, Mt., Nepal ... 43 E12 28 5N 86 58 E
Everett, Pa., U.S.A. ... 84 F6 40 1N 78 23W
Everett, Wash., U.S.A. ... 78 C4 47 59N 122 12W
Everglades △, U.S.A. ... 83 N5 25 30N 81 0W
Everglades, The, U.S.A. ... 83 N5 25 50N 81 0W
Everglades City, U.S.A. ... 83 N5 25 52N 81 23W
Evergreen, Ala., U.S.A. ... 83 K2 31 26N 86 57W
Evergreen, Mont., U.S.A. ... 76 B6 48 9N 114 13W
Evesham, U.K. ... 13 E6 52 6N 1 56W
Evje, Norway ... 9 G12 58 36N 7 51 E
Évora, Portugal ... 21 C2 38 33N 7 57W
Evowghli, Iran ... 44 B5 38 43N 45 13 E
Évreux, France ... 20 B4 49 3N 1 8 E
Évros →, Greece ... 23 D12 41 40N 26 34 E
Évry, France ... 20 B5 48 38N 2 27 E
Évvoia, Greece ... 23 E11 38 30N 24 0 E
Ewe, L., U.K. ... 11 D3 57 49N 5 38W
Ewing, U.S.A. ... 80 D5 42 16N 98 21W
Ewo, Congo ... 52 E2 0 48S 14 45 E
Exaltación, Bolivia ... 92 F5 13 10S 65 20W
Excelsior Springs, U.S.A. ... 80 F7 39 20N 94 13W
Exe →, U.K. ... 13 G4 50 41N 3 29W
Exeter, Canada ... 84 C3 43 21N 81 29W
Exeter, U.K. ... 13 G4 50 43N 3 31W
Exeter, Calif., U.S.A. ... 78 J7 36 18N 119 9W
Exeter, N.H., U.S.A. ... 85 D14 42 59N 70 57W
Exmoor, U.K. ... 13 F4 51 12N 3 45W
Exmoor △, U.K. ... 13 F4 51 8N 3 42W
Exmouth, Australia ... 60 D1 21 54S 114 10 E
Exmouth, U.K. ... 13 G4 50 37N 3 25W
Exmouth G., Australia ... 60 D1 22 15S 114 15 E
Expedition △, Australia ... 63 D4 25 41S 149 7 E
Expedition Ra., Australia ... 62 C4 24 30S 149 12 E
Extremadura □, Spain ... 21 C2 39 30N 6 5W
Exuma Sound, Bahamas ... 88 B4 24 30N 76 20W
Eyasi, L., Tanzania ... 54 C4 3 30S 35 0 E
Eye Pen., U.K. ... 11 C2 58 13N 6 10W
Eyemouth, U.K. ... 11 F6 55 52N 2 5W
Eyjafjörður, Iceland ... 8 C4 66 15N 18 30W
Eyre (North), Australia ... 63 D2 28 30S 137 20 E
Eyre (South), Australia ... 63 D2 29 18S 137 25 E
Eyre Mts., N.Z. ... 59 L2 45 25S 168 25 E
Eyre Pen., Australia ... 63 E2 33 30S 136 17 E
Eysturoy, Færoe Is. ... 8 E9 62 13N 6 54W
Ezine, Turkey ... 23 E12 39 48N 26 20 E
Ezouza →, Cyprus ... 25 E11 34 44N 32 27 E

F

F.Y.R.O.M. = Macedonia ■,
  Europe ... 23 D9 41 53N 21 40 E
Fabala, Guinea ... 50 G4 9 44N 9 5W
Fabens, U.S.A. ... 77 L10 31 30N 106 10W
Fabriano, Italy ... 22 C5 43 20N 12 54 E
Fachi, Niger ... 51 E8 18 6N 11 34 E
Fada, Chad ... 51 E10 17 13N 21 34 E
Fada-n-Gourma, Burkina Faso ... 50 F6 12 10N 0 30 E
Faddeyevskiy, Ostrov, Russia ... 29 B15 76 0N 144 0 E
Fadghāmī, Syria ... 44 C4 35 53N 40 52 E
Faenza, Italy ... 22 B4 44 17N 11 53 E
Færoe Is. = Føroyar, Atl. Oc. ... 8 F9 62 0N 7 0W
Făgăras, Romania ... 17 F13 45 48N 24 58 E
Fagersta, Sweden ... 9 F16 60 1N 15 46 E

Fagnano, L., Argentina ... 96 G3 54 30S 68 0W
Fahlīan, Iran ... 45 D6 30 11N 51 28 E
Fahraj, Kermān, Iran ... 45 D8 29 0N 59 0 E
Fahraj, Yazd, Iran ... 45 D7 31 46N 54 36 E
Faial, Madeira ... 24 D3 32 47N 16 53W
Fair Haven, U.S.A. ... 82 D9 43 36N 73 16W
Fair Hd., U.K. ... 10 A5 55 14N 6 9W
Fair Isle, U.K. ... 14 B6 59 30N 1 40W
Fair Oaks, U.S.A. ... 78 G5 38 39N 121 16W
Fairbanks, U.S.A. ... 68 B5 64 51N 147 43W
Fairbury, U.S.A. ... 80 E6 40 8N 97 11W
Fairfax, U.S.A. ... 85 B11 44 40N 73 1W
Fairfield, Ala., U.S.A. ... 83 J2 33 29N 86 55W
Fairfield, Calif., U.S.A. ... 78 G4 38 15N 122 3W
Fairfield, Conn., U.S.A. ... 85 E11 41 9N 73 16W
Fairfield, Idaho, U.S.A. ... 76 E6 43 21N 114 44W
Fairfield, Ill., U.S.A. ... 82 F1 38 23N 88 22W
Fairfield, Iowa, U.S.A. ... 80 E9 40 56N 91 57W
Fairfield, Tex., U.S.A. ... 81 K7 31 44N 96 10W
Fairford, Canada ... 71 C9 51 37N 98 38W
Fairhope, U.S.A. ... 83 K2 30 31N 87 54W
Fairlie, N.Z. ... 59 L3 44 5S 170 49 E
Fairmead, U.S.A. ... 78 H6 37 5N 120 10W
Fairmont, Minn., U.S.A. ... 80 D7 43 39N 94 28W
Fairmont, W. Va., U.S.A. ... 82 F5 39 29N 80 9W
Fairmount, Calif., U.S.A. ... 79 L8 34 45N 118 26W
Fairmount, N.Y., U.S.A. ... 85 C8 43 5N 76 12W
Fairplay, U.S.A. ... 77 G11 39 15N 106 2W
Fairport, U.S.A. ... 84 C7 43 6N 77 27W
Fairport Harbor, U.S.A. ... 84 E3 41 45N 81 17W
Fairview, Canada ... 70 B5 56 5N 118 25W
Fairview, Mont., U.S.A. ... 80 B2 47 51N 104 3W
Fairview, Okla., U.S.A. ... 81 G5 36 16N 98 29W
Fairweather, Mt., U.S.A. ... 70 B1 58 55N 137 32W
Faisalabad, Pakistan ... 42 D5 31 30N 73 5 E
Faith, U.S.A. ... 80 C3 45 2N 102 2W
Faizabad, India ... 43 F10 26 45N 82 10 E
Fajardo, Puerto Rico ... 89 d 18 20N 65 39W
Fajr, W. →, Si. Arabia ... 44 D3 29 10N 38 10 E
Fakenham, U.K. ... 12 E8 52 51N 0 51 E
Fakfak, Indonesia ... 37 E8 2 55S 132 18 E
Faku, China ... 35 C12 42 32N 123 21 E
Falaise, France ... 20 B3 48 54N 0 12W
Falaise, Mui, Vietnam ... 38 C5 19 6N 105 45 E
Falam, Burma ... 41 H18 23 0N 93 45 E
Falcó, C. des, Spain ... 24 C7 38 50N 1 23 E
Falcón, Presa, Mexico ... 87 B5 26 35N 99 10W
Falcon Lake, Canada ... 71 D9 49 42N 95 15W
Falcon Reservoir, U.S.A. ... 81 M5 26 34N 99 10W
Falconara Marittima, Italy ... 22 C5 43 37N 13 24 E
Falcone, C. del, Italy ... 22 D3 40 58N 8 12 E
Falconer, U.S.A. ... 84 D5 42 7N 79 13W
Faleshty = Fălești, Moldova ... 17 E14 47 32N 27 44 E
Fălești, Moldova ... 17 E14 47 32N 27 44 E
Falfurrias, U.S.A. ... 81 M5 27 14N 98 9W
Falher, Canada ... 70 B5 55 44N 117 15W
Faliraki, Greece ... 25 C10 36 22N 28 12 E
Falkenberg, Sweden ... 9 H15 56 54N 12 30 E
Falkirk, U.K. ... 11 F5 56 0N 3 47W
Falkirk □, U.K. ... 11 F5 55 58N 3 49W
Falkland, U.K. ... 11 E5 56 16N 3 12W
Falkland Is. ☑, Atl. Oc. ... 96 G5 51 30S 59 0W
Falkland Sd., Falk. Is. ... 96 G5 52 0S 60 0W
Falköping, Sweden ... 9 G15 58 12N 13 33 E
Fall River, U.S.A. ... 85 E13 41 43N 71 10W
Fallbrook, U.S.A. ... 79 M9 33 23N 117 15W
Fallon, U.S.A. ... 76 G4 39 28N 118 47W
Falls City, U.S.A. ... 80 E7 40 3N 95 36W
Falls Creek, U.S.A. ... 84 E6 41 9N 78 48W
Falmouth, Jamaica ... 88 a 18 30N 77 40W
Falmouth, U.K. ... 13 G2 50 9N 5 5W
Falmouth, U.S.A. ... 85 E14 41 33N 70 37W
Falsa, Pta., Mexico ... 86 B1 27 51N 115 3W
False B., S. Africa ... 56 E2 34 15S 18 40 E
Falso, C., Honduras ... 88 C3 15 12N 83 21W
Falster, Denmark ... 9 J14 54 45N 11 55 E
Falsterbo, Sweden ... 9 J15 55 23N 12 50 E
Fălticeni, Romania ... 17 E14 47 21N 26 20 E
Falun, Sweden ... 9 F16 60 37N 15 37 E
Famagusta, Cyprus ... 25 D12 35 8N 33 55 E
Famagusta Bay, Cyprus ... 25 D13 35 15N 34 0 E
Famalé, Niger ... 50 F6 14 33N 1 5 E
Famatina, Sierra de, Argentina ... 94 B2 27 30S 68 0W
Family L., Canada ... 71 C9 51 54N 95 27W
Famoso, U.S.A. ... 79 K7 35 37N 119 12W
Fan Xian, China ... 34 G8 35 55N 115 38 E
Fanad Hd., Ireland ... 10 A4 55 17N 7 38W
Fandriana, Madag. ... 57 C8 20 14S 47 21 E
Fang, Thailand ... 38 C2 19 55N 99 13 E
Fangcheng, China ... 34 H7 33 18N 112 59 E
Fangshan, China ... 34 E6 38 3N 111 25 E
Fangzi, China ... 35 F10 36 33N 119 10 E
Fanjakana, Madag. ... 57 C8 21 10S 46 53 E
Fanjiatun, China ... 35 C13 43 40N 125 15 E
Fanling, China ... 33 F11 22 30N 114 8 E
Fannich, L., U.K. ... 11 D4 57 38N 4 59W
Fannūj, Iran ... 45 E8 26 35N 59 38 E
Fanø, Denmark ... 9 J13 55 25N 8 25 E
Fano, Italy ... 22 C5 43 50N 13 1 E
Fanshi, China ... 34 E7 39 12N 113 20 E
Fao = Al Fāw, Iraq ... 45 D6 30 0N 48 30 E
Faqirwali, Pakistan ... 42 E5 29 27N 73 0 E
Far East = Dalnevostochnyy □,
  Russia ... 29 C14 67 0N 140 0 E
Far East, Asia ... 26 E16 40 0N 130 0 E
Faradje, Dem. Rep. of the Congo ... 54 B2 3 50N 29 45 E
Farafangana, Madag. ... 57 C8 22 49S 47 50 E
Farāh, Afghan. ... 40 C3 32 20N 62 7 E
Farāh □, Afghan. ... 40 C3 32 25N 62 10 E
Farahalana, Madag. ... 57 A9 14 26S 50 10 E
Faranah, Guinea ... 50 F3 10 3N 10 45W
Farasān, Jazā'ir, Si. Arabia ... 47 D3 16 45N 41 55 E
Farasan Is. = Farasān, Jazā'ir,
  Si. Arabia ... 47 D3 16 45N 41 55 E
Faratsiho, Madag. ... 57 B8 19 24S 46 57 E
Fareham, U.K. ... 13 G6 50 51N 1 11W
Farewell, C., N.Z. ... 59 J4 40 29S 172 43 E
Farewell C. = Nunap Isua,
  Greenland ... 69 C15 59 48N 43 55W
Farghona, Uzbekistan ... 28 E8 40 23N 71 19 E
Fargo, U.S.A. ... 80 B6 46 53N 96 48W
Fār'iah, W. al →, West Bank ... 46 C4 32 12N 35 27 E
Faribault, U.S.A. ... 80 C8 44 18N 93 16W
Faridabad, India ... 42 E6 28 26N 77 19 E
Faridkot, India ... 42 D6 30 44N 74 45 E
Faridpur, Bangla. ... 43 H13 23 15N 89 55 E
Faridpur, India ... 43 E8 28 13N 79 33 E
Farīmān, Iran ... 45 C8 35 40N 59 49 E

Farina, Australia 63 E2 30 3S 138 15 E
Fariones, Pta., Canary Is. 24 E6 29 13N 13 28W
Farleigh, Australia 62 K7 21 4S 149 8 E
Farmerville, U.S.A. 81 J8 32 47N 92 24W
Farmingdale, U.S.A. 85 F10 40 12N 74 10W
Farmington, Canada 70 B4 55 54N 120 30W
Farmington, Calif., U.S.A. 78 H6 37 55N 120 59W
Farmington, Maine, U.S.A. 83 C10 44 40N 70 9W
Farmington, Mo., U.S.A. 81 G9 37 47N 90 25W
Farmington, N.H., U.S.A. 85 C13 43 24N 71 4W
Farmington, N. Mex., U.S.A. 77 H9 36 44N 108 12W
Farmington, Utah, U.S.A. 76 F8 41 0N 111 12W
Farmington →, U.S.A. 85 E12 41 51N 72 38W
Farmville, U.S.A. 82 G6 37 18N 78 24W
Farne Is., U.K. 12 B6 55 38N 1 37W
Farnham, Canada 85 A12 45 17N 72 59W
Farnham, Mt., Canada 70 C5 50 29N 116 30W
Faro, Brazil 93 D7 2 10S 56 39W
Faro, Canada 68 B6 62 11N 133 22W
Faro, Portugal 21 D2 37 2N 7 55W
Fårö, Sweden 9 H18 57 55N 19 5 E
Farquhar, C., Australia 61 D1 23 50S 113 36 E
Farrars Cr. →, Australia 62 D3 25 35S 140 43 E
Farrāshband, Iran 45 D7 28 57N 52 5 E
Farrell, U.S.A. 84 E4 41 13N 80 30W
Farrokhī, Iran 45 C8 33 50N 59 31 E
Farruch, C. = Ferrutx, C., Spain 24 B10 39 47N 3 21 E
Fārs □, Iran 45 D7 29 30N 55 0 E
Fársala, Greece 23 E10 39 17N 22 23 E
Farson, U.S.A. 76 E9 42 6N 109 27W
Farsund, Norway 9 G12 58 5N 6 55 E
Fartak, Râs, Si. Arabia 44 D2 28 5N 34 34 E
Fartak, Ra's, Yemen 47 D5 15 38N 52 15 E
Fartura, Serra da, Brazil 95 B5 26 21S 52 52W
Fārūj, Iran 45 B8 37 14N 58 14 E
Farvel, Kap = Nunap Isua, Greenland 69 C15 59 48N 43 55W
Farwell, U.S.A. 81 H3 34 23N 103 2W
Fāryāb □, Afghan. 40 B4 36 0N 65 0 E
Fasā, Iran 45 D7 29 0N 53 39 E
Fasano, Italy 22 D7 40 50N 17 22 E
Fastiv, Ukraine 17 C15 50 7N 29 57 E
Fastnet Rock, Ireland 10 E2 51 22N 9 37W
Fastov = Fastiv, Ukraine 17 C15 50 7N 29 57 E
Fatagar, Tanjung, Indonesia 37 E8 2 46S 131 57 E
Fatehabad, Haryana, India 42 E6 29 31N 75 27 E
Fatehabad, Ut. P., India 42 F8 27 1N 78 19 E
Fatehgarh, India 43 F8 27 25N 79 35 E
Fatehpur, Bihar, India 43 G11 24 38N 85 14 E
Fatehpur, Raj., India 42 F6 28 0N 74 40 E
Fatehpur, Ut. P., India 43 G9 25 56N 81 13 E
Fatehpur, Ut. P., India 43 F9 27 10N 81 13 E
Fatehpur Sikri, India 42 F6 27 6N 77 40 E
Fathom Five ⌂, Canada 84 A3 45 17N 81 40W
Fatima, Canada 73 C7 47 24N 61 53W
Faulkton, U.S.A. 80 C5 45 2N 99 8W
Faure I., Australia 61 E1 25 52S 113 50 E
Fauresmith, S. Africa 56 D4 29 44S 25 17 E
Fauske, Norway 8 C16 67 17N 15 25 E
Favara, Italy 22 F5 37 19N 13 39 E
Faváritx, C. de, Spain 24 B11 40 0N 4 15 E
Favignana, Italy 22 F5 37 56N 12 20 E
Fawcett, Pt., Australia 60 B5 11 46S 130 2 E
Fawn →, Canada 72 A2 55 20N 87 35W
Fawnskin, U.S.A. 79 L10 34 16N 116 56W
Faxaflói, Iceland 8 D2 64 29N 23 0W
Faya-Largeau, Chad 51 E9 17 58N 19 6 E
Fayd, Si. Arabia 44 E4 27 1N 42 52 E
Fayette, Ala., U.S.A. 83 J2 33 41N 87 50W
Fayette, Mo., U.S.A. 80 F8 39 9N 92 41W
Fayetteville, Ark., U.S.A. 81 G7 36 4N 94 10W
Fayetteville, N.C., U.S.A. 83 H6 35 3N 78 53W
Fayetteville, Tenn., U.S.A. 83 H2 35 9N 86 34W
Fazilka, India 42 D6 30 27N 74 2 E
Fazilpur, Pakistan 42 E4 29 18N 70 29 E
Fdérik, Mauritania 50 D3 22 40N 12 45W
Feale →, Ireland 10 D2 52 27N 9 37W
Fear, C., U.S.A. 83 J7 33 50N 77 58W
Feather →, U.S.A. 76 G3 38 47N 121 36W
Feather Falls, U.S.A. 78 F5 39 36N 121 16W
Featherston, N.Z. 59 J5 41 6S 175 20 E
Featherstone, Zimbabwe 55 F3 18 42S 30 55 E
Fécamp, France 20 B4 49 45N 0 22 E
Fedala = Mohammedia, Morocco 50 B4 33 44N 7 21W
Federación, Argentina 94 C4 31 0S 57 55W
Féderal, Argentina 96 C5 30 57S 58 48W
Federal Way, U.S.A. 78 C4 47 18N 122 19W
Fedeshkūh, Iran 45 D7 28 49N 53 50 E
Fehmarn, Germany 16 A6 54 27N 11 7 E
Fehmarn Bælt, Europe 9 J14 54 35N 11 20 E
Fehmarn Belt = Fehmarn Bælt, Europe 9 J14 54 35N 11 20 E
Fei Xian, China 35 G9 35 18N 117 59 E
Feijó, Brazil 92 E4 8 9S 70 21W
Feilding, N.Z. 59 J5 40 13S 175 35 E
Feira de Santana, Brazil 93 F11 12 15S 38 57W
Feixiang, China 34 F8 36 30N 114 45 E
Felanitx, Spain 24 B10 39 28N 3 9 E
Feldkirch, Austria 16 E5 47 15N 9 37 E
Felipe Carrillo Puerto, Mexico 87 D7 19 38N 88 3W
Felixburg, Zimbabwe 57 B5 19 29S 30 51 E
Felixstowe, U.K. 13 F9 51 58N 1 23 E
Felton, U.S.A. 78 H4 37 3N 122 4W
Femer Bælt = Fehmarn Bælt, Europe 9 J14 54 35N 11 20 E
Femunden, Norway 9 E14 62 10N 11 53 E
Fen He →, China 34 G6 35 36N 110 42 E
Fenelon Falls, Canada 84 B6 44 32N 78 45W
Feng Xian, Jiangsu, China 34 G9 34 43N 116 35 E
Feng Xian, Shaanxi, China 34 H4 33 54N 106 40 E
Fengcheng, China 35 D13 40 28N 124 5 E
Fengfeng, China 34 F8 36 28N 114 8 E
Fengning, China 34 D9 41 10N 116 33 E
Fengqiu, China 34 G8 35 2N 114 25 E
Fengrun, China 35 E10 39 48N 118 8 E
Fengtai, China 34 E9 39 50N 116 18 E
Fengxiang, China 34 G4 34 29N 107 25 E
Fengyang, China 35 H9 32 51N 117 29 E
Fengzhen, China 34 D7 40 25N 113 2 E
Fenoarivo, Fianarantsoa, Madag. 57 C8 21 43S 46 24 E
Fenoarivo, Fianarantsoa, Madag. 57 C8 20 52S 46 53 E
Fenoarivo Afovoany, Madag. 57 B8 18 26S 46 34 E
Fenoarivo Atsinanana, Madag. 57 B8 17 22S 49 25 E
Fens, The, U.K. 12 E7 52 38N 0 2W
Fenton, U.S.A. 82 D4 42 48N 83 42W
Fenxi, China 34 F6 36 40N 111 31 E
Fenyang, China 34 F6 37 18N 111 48 E
Feodosiya, Ukraine 19 E6 45 2N 35 16 E
Ferdows, Iran 45 C8 33 58N 58 2 E
Ferfer, Somali Rep. 47 F4 5 4N 45 9 E
Fergana = Farghona, Uzbekistan 28 E8 40 23N 71 19 E
Fergus, Canada 84 C4 43 43N 80 24W
Fergus Falls, U.S.A. 80 B6 46 17N 96 4W
Ferkéssédougou, Ivory C. 50 G4 9 35N 5 6W
Ferland, Canada 72 B2 50 19N 88 27W
Fermanagh □, U.K. 10 B4 54 21N 7 40W
Fermo, Italy 22 C5 43 9N 13 43 E
Fermont, Canada 73 B6 52 47N 67 5W
Fermoy, Ireland 10 D3 52 9N 8 16W
Fernández, Argentina 94 B3 27 55S 63 50W
Fernandina Beach, U.S.A. 83 K5 30 40N 81 27W
Fernando de Noronha, Brazil 93 D12 4 0S 33 10W
Fernando Póo = Bioko, Eq. Guin. 52 D1 3 30N 8 40 E
Ferndale, U.S.A. 78 B4 48 51N 122 36W
Fernie, Canada 70 D5 49 30N 115 5W
Fernlees, Australia 62 C4 23 51S 148 7 E
Fernley, U.S.A. 76 G4 39 36N 119 15W
Ferozepore = Firozpur, India 42 D6 30 55N 74 40 E
Ferrara, Italy 22 B4 44 50N 11 35 E
Ferreñafe, Peru 92 E3 6 42S 79 50W
Ferrerías, Spain 24 B11 39 59N 4 1 E
Ferret, C., France 20 D3 44 38N 1 15W
Ferriday, U.S.A. 81 K9 31 38N 91 33W
Ferrol, Spain 21 A1 43 29N 8 15W
Ferron, U.S.A. 77 G8 39 5N 111 8W
Ferrutx, C., Spain 24 B10 39 47N 3 21 E
Ferryland, Canada 73 C9 47 2N 52 53W
Fertile, U.S.A. 80 B6 47 32N 96 17W
Fès, Morocco 50 B5 34 0N 5 0W
Fessenden, U.S.A. 80 B5 47 39N 99 38W
Festus, U.S.A. 80 F9 38 13N 90 24W
Feteşti, Romania 17 F14 44 22N 27 51 E
Fethiye, Turkey 19 G4 36 36N 29 6 E
Fetlar, U.K. 11 A8 60 36N 0 52W
Feuilles →, Canada 69 C12 58 47N 70 4W
Fez = Fès, Morocco 50 B5 34 0N 5 0W
Fezzan, Libya 51 C8 27 0N 13 0 E
Fiambalá, Argentina 94 B2 27 45S 67 37W
Fianarantsoa, Madag. 57 C8 21 26S 47 5 E
Fianarantsoa □, Madag. 57 B8 19 30S 47 0 E
Ficksburg, S. Africa 57 D4 28 51S 27 53 E
Field →, Australia 62 C2 23 48S 138 0 E
Field I., Australia 60 B5 12 5S 132 23 E
Fier, Albania 23 D8 40 43N 19 33 E
Fife ⌂, U.K. 11 E5 56 15N 3 15W
Fife □, U.K. 11 E5 56 16N 3 1W
Fife Ness, U.K. 11 E6 56 17N 2 35W
Fifth Cataract, Sudan 51 E12 18 22N 33 50 E
Figeac, France 20 D5 44 37N 2 2 E
Figtree, Zimbabwe 55 G2 20 22S 28 20 E
Figueira da Foz, Portugal 21 B1 40 7N 8 54W
Figueres, Spain 21 A7 42 18N 2 58 E
Figuig, Morocco 50 B5 32 5N 1 11W
Fihaonana, Madag. 57 B8 18 36S 47 12 E
Fiherenana, Madag. 57 B8 18 29S 48 24 E
Fiherenana →, Madag. 57 C7 23 19S 43 37 E
Fiji ■, Pac. Oc. 59 C8 17 20S 179 0 E
Filabusi, Zimbabwe 57 C4 20 34S 29 20 E
Filey, U.K. 12 C7 54 12N 0 18W
Filey B., U.K. 12 C7 54 12N 0 15W
Filfla, Malta 25 D1 35 47N 14 24 E
Filiatrá, Greece 23 F9 37 9N 21 35 E
Filingué, Niger 50 F6 14 21N 3 22 E
Filipstad, Sweden 9 G16 59 43N 14 9 E
Fillmore, Calif., U.S.A. 79 L8 34 24N 118 55W
Fillmore, Utah, U.S.A. 77 G7 38 58N 112 20W
Finch, Canada 85 A9 45 11N 75 7W
Finch Hatton, Australia 62 K6 20 25S 148 39 E
Findhorn →, U.K. 11 D5 57 38N 3 38W
Findlay, U.S.A. 82 E4 41 2N 83 39W
Finger L., Canada 72 B1 53 33N 93 30W
Finger Lakes, U.S.A. 85 D8 42 40N 76 30W
Fingoè, Mozam. 55 E3 14 55S 31 50 E
Finisterre, C. = Fisterra, C., Spain 21 A1 42 50N 9 19W
Finke, Australia 62 D1 25 34S 134 35 E
Finke Gorge △, Australia 60 D5 24 8S 132 49 E
Finland ■, Europe 8 E22 63 0N 27 0 E
Finland, G. of, Europe 9 G21 60 0N 26 0 E
Finlay →, Canada 70 B3 57 0N 125 10W
Finley, Australia 63 F4 35 38S 145 35 E
Finley, U.S.A. 80 B6 47 31N 97 50W
Finn →, Ireland 10 B4 54 51N 7 28W
Finnigan, Mt., Australia 62 B4 15 49S 145 17 E
Finniss, C., Australia 63 E1 33 8S 134 51 E
Finnmark, Norway 8 B20 69 37N 23 57 E
Finnsnes, Norway 8 B18 69 14N 18 0 E
Finspång, Sweden 9 G16 58 43N 15 47 E
Fiora →, Italy 22 C4 42 20N 11 34 E
Fiordland △, N.Z. 59 L1 45 46S 167 0 E
Fiq, Syria 46 C4 32 46N 35 41 E
Firat = Furāt, Nahr al →, Asia 44 D5 31 0N 47 25 E
Fire Island ⌂, U.S.A. 85 F11 40 38N 73 8W
Firebag →, Canada 71 B6 57 45N 111 21W
Firebaugh, U.S.A. 78 J6 36 52N 120 27W
Firedrake L., Canada 71 A8 61 25N 104 30W
Firenze, Italy 22 C4 43 46N 11 15 E
Firk, Sha'ib →, Iraq 44 D5 30 59N 44 34 E
Firozabad, India 43 F8 27 10N 78 25 E
Firozpur, India 42 D6 30 55N 74 40 E
Firozpur-Jhirka, India 42 F7 27 48N 76 57 E
Fīrūzābād, Iran 45 D7 28 52N 52 35 E
Fīrūzkūh, Iran 45 C7 35 50N 52 50 E
Firvale, Canada 70 C3 52 27N 126 13W
Fish →, Namibia 56 D2 28 7S 17 10 E
Fish →, S. Africa 56 E3 31 30S 20 16 E
Fish River Canyon, Namibia 56 D2 27 40S 17 35 E
Fisher, Australia 61 F5 30 30S 131 0 E
Fisher B., Canada 71 C9 51 35N 97 13W
Fishers I., U.S.A. 85 E13 41 15N 72 0W
Fishguard, U.K. 13 E3 52 0N 4 58W
Fishing L., Canada 71 C9 52 10N 95 24W
Fishkill, U.S.A. 85 E11 41 32N 73 53W
Fisterra, C., Spain 21 A1 42 50N 9 19W
Fitchburg, U.S.A. 85 D13 42 35N 71 48W
Fitz Roy, Argentina 96 F3 47 0S 67 0W
Fitzgerald, Canada 70 B6 59 51N 111 36W
Fitzgerald, U.S.A. 83 K4 31 43N 83 15W
Fitzgerald River △, Australia 61 F3 33 53S 120 3 E
Fitzmaurice →, Australia 60 B5 14 45S 130 5 E
Fitzroy →, Queens., Australia 62 C5 23 32S 150 52 E
Fitzroy →, W. Austral., Australia 60 C3 17 31S 123 35 E
Fitzroy, Mte., Argentina 96 F2 49 17S 73 5W
Fitzroy Crossing, Australia 60 C4 18 9S 125 38 E
Fitzwilliam I., Canada 84 A3 45 30N 81 45W
Fiume = Rijeka, Croatia 16 F8 45 20N 14 21 E
Five Points, U.S.A. 78 J6 36 26N 120 6W
Fizi, Dem. Rep. of the Congo 54 C2 4 17S 28 55 E
Flagstaff, U.S.A. 77 J8 35 12N 111 39W
Flagstaff L., U.S.A. 83 C10 45 12N 70 18W
Flaherty I., Canada 72 A4 56 15N 79 15W
Flåm, Norway 9 F12 60 50N 7 7 E
Flambeau →, U.S.A. 80 C9 45 18N 91 14W
Flamborough Hd., U.K. 12 C7 54 7N 0 5W
Flaming Gorge ⌂, U.S.A. 76 F9 41 10N 109 25W
Flaming Gorge Reservoir, U.S.A. 76 F9 41 10N 109 25W
Flamingo, Teluk, Indonesia 37 F9 5 30S 138 0 E
Flanders = Flandre, Europe 14 F8 50 50N 2 30 E
Flandre, Europe 14 F8 50 50N 2 30 E
Flandre-Occidentale = West-Vlaanderen □, Belgium 15 D2 51 0N 3 0 E
Flandre-Orientale = Oost-Vlaanderen □, Belgium 15 C3 51 5N 3 50 E
Flandreau, U.S.A. 80 C6 44 3N 96 36W
Flanigan, U.S.A. 78 E7 40 10N 119 53W
Flannan Is., U.K. 11 C1 58 9N 7 52W
Flåsjön, Sweden 8 D16 64 5N 15 40 E
Flat →, Canada 70 A3 61 33N 125 18W
Flathead L., U.S.A. 76 C7 47 51N 114 8W
Flattery, C., Australia 62 A4 14 58S 145 21 E
Flattery, C., U.S.A. 78 B2 48 23N 124 29W
Flatwoods, U.S.A. 82 F4 38 31N 82 43W
Fleetwood, U.K. 12 D4 53 55N 3 1W
Fleetwood, U.S.A. 85 F9 40 27N 75 49W
Flekkefjord, Norway 9 G12 58 18N 6 39 E
Flemington, U.S.A. 84 E7 41 7N 77 28W
Flensburg, Germany 16 A5 54 47N 9 27 E
Flers, France 20 B3 48 47N 0 33W
Flesherton, Canada 84 B4 44 16N 80 33W
Flesko, Tanjung, Indonesia 37 D6 0 29N 124 30 E
Fleurieu Pen., Australia 63 F2 35 40S 138 5 E
Flevoland □, Neths. 15 B5 52 30N 5 30 E
Flin Flon, Canada 71 C8 54 46N 101 53W
Flinders →, Australia 62 B3 17 36S 140 36 E
Flinders B., Australia 61 F2 34 19S 115 19 E
Flinders Group, Australia 62 A3 14 11S 144 15 E
Flinders I., S. Austral., Australia 63 E1 33 44S 134 41 E
Flinders I., Tas., Australia 63 G4 40 0S 148 0 E
Flinders Ranges, Australia 63 E2 31 30S 138 30 E
Flinders Reefs, Australia 62 B4 17 37S 148 31 E
Flint, U.K. 12 D4 53 15N 3 8W
Flint, U.S.A. 82 D4 43 1N 83 41W
Flint →, U.S.A. 83 K3 30 57N 84 34W
Flint I., Kiribati 65 J12 11 26S 151 48W
Flintshire □, U.K. 12 D4 53 17N 3 17W
Flodden, U.K. 12 B5 55 37N 2 8W
Floodwood, U.S.A. 80 B8 46 55N 92 55W
Flora, U.S.A. 82 F1 38 40N 88 29W
Florala, U.S.A. 83 K2 31 0N 86 20W
Florence = Firenze, Italy 22 C4 43 46N 11 15 E
Florence, Ala., U.S.A. 83 H2 34 48N 87 41W
Florence, Ariz., U.S.A. 77 K8 33 2N 111 23W
Florence, Colo., U.S.A. 80 F2 38 23N 105 8W
Florence, Oreg., U.S.A. 76 E1 43 58N 124 7W
Florence, S.C., U.S.A. 83 H6 34 12N 79 46W
Florence, L., Australia 63 D2 28 53S 138 9 E
Florencia, Colombia 92 C3 1 36N 75 36W
Florennes, Belgium 15 D4 50 15N 4 35 E
Florenville, Belgium 15 E5 49 40N 5 19 E
Flores, Guatemala 88 C2 16 59N 89 50W
Flores, Indonesia 37 F6 8 35S 121 0 E
Flores I., Canada 70 D3 49 20N 126 10W
Flores Sea, Indonesia 37 F6 6 30S 120 0 E
Floreşti, Moldova 17 E15 47 53N 28 17 E
Floresville, U.S.A. 81 L5 29 8N 98 10W
Floriano, Brazil 93 E10 6 50S 43 0W
Florianópolis, Brazil 95 B6 27 30S 48 30W
Florida, Cuba 88 B4 21 32N 78 14W
Florida, Uruguay 95 C4 34 7S 56 10W
Florida □, U.S.A. 83 L5 28 0N 82 0W
Florida, Straits of, U.S.A. 88 B4 25 0N 80 0W
Florida B., U.S.A. 88 B3 25 0N 80 45W
Florida Keys, U.S.A. 83 N5 24 40N 81 0W
Flórina, Greece 23 D9 40 48N 21 26 E
Florø, Norway 9 F11 61 35N 5 1 E
Flower Station, Canada 85 A8 45 10N 76 41W
Flowerpot I., Canada 84 A3 45 18N 81 38W
Floydada, U.S.A. 81 J4 33 59N 101 20W
Fluk, Indonesia 37 E7 1 42S 127 44 E
Flushing = Vlissingen, Neths. 15 C3 51 26N 3 34 E
Flying Fish, C., Antarctica 5 D15 72 6S 102 29W
Foam Lake, Canada 71 C8 51 40N 103 32W
Foça, Turkey 23 E12 38 39N 26 46 E
Fochabers, U.K. 11 D5 57 37N 3 6W
Focşani, Romania 17 F14 45 41N 27 15 E
Fóggia, Italy 22 D6 41 27N 15 34 E
Fogo, Canada 73 C9 49 43N 54 17W
Fogo I., Canada 73 C9 49 40N 54 5W
Föhr, Germany 16 A5 54 43N 8 30 E
Foix, France 20 E4 42 58N 1 38 E
Folda, Nord-Trøndelag, Norway 8 D14 64 32N 10 30 E
Folda, Nordland, Norway 8 C16 67 38N 14 50 E
Foley, Botswana 56 C4 21 34S 27 21 E
Foley, U.S.A. 83 K2 30 24N 87 41W
Foleyet, Canada 72 C3 48 15N 82 25W
Folgefonni, Norway 9 F12 60 3N 6 23 E
Foligno, Italy 22 C5 42 57N 12 42 E
Folkestone, U.K. 13 F9 51 5N 1 12 E
Folkston, U.S.A. 83 K5 30 50N 82 0W
Follansbee, U.S.A. 84 F4 40 19N 80 35W
Folsom L., U.S.A. 78 G5 38 42N 121 9W
Fond-du-Lac, Canada 71 B7 59 19N 107 12W
Fond du Lac, U.S.A. 80 D10 43 47N 88 27W
Fond-du-Lac →, Canada 71 B7 59 17N 106 0W
Fonda, U.S.A. 85 D10 42 57N 74 22W
Fondi, Italy 22 D5 41 21N 13 25 E
Fongafale, Tuvalu 64 H9 8 31S 179 13 E
Fonsagrada = A Fonsagrada, Spain 21 A2 43 8N 7 4W
Fonseca, G. de, Cent. Amer. 88 D2 13 10N 87 40W
Fontainebleau, France 20 B5 48 24N 2 40 E
Fontana, U.S.A. 79 L9 34 6N 117 26W
Fontas →, Canada 70 B4 58 14N 121 48W
Fonte Boa, Brazil 92 D5 2 33S 66 0W
Fontenay-le-Comte, France 20 C3 46 28N 0 48W
Fontenelle Reservoir, U.S.A. 76 E8 42 1N 110 3W
Fontur, Iceland 8 C6 66 23N 14 32W
Foochow = Fuzhou, China 33 D6 26 5N 119 16 E
Foping, China 34 H5 33 41N 108 0 E
Forbes, Australia 63 E4 33 22S 148 5 E
Forbesganj, India 43 F12 26 17N 87 18 E
Ford City, Calif., U.S.A. 79 K7 35 9N 119 27W
Ford City, Pa., U.S.A. 84 F5 40 46N 79 32W
Førde, Norway 9 F11 61 27N 5 53 E
Ford's Bridge, Australia 63 D4 29 41S 145 29 E
Fordyce, U.S.A. 81 J8 33 49N 92 25W
Forel, Mt., Greenland 4 C6 66 52N 36 55W
Foremost, Canada 70 D6 49 26N 111 34W
Forest, Canada 84 C3 43 6N 82 0W
Forest, U.S.A. 81 J10 32 22N 89 29W
Forest City, Iowa, U.S.A. 80 D8 43 16N 93 39W
Forest City, N.C., U.S.A. 83 H5 35 20N 81 52W
Forest City, Pa., U.S.A. 85 E9 41 39N 75 28W
Forest Grove, U.S.A. 78 E3 45 31N 123 7W
Forestburg, Canada 70 C6 52 35N 112 1W
Foresthill, U.S.A. 78 F6 39 1N 120 49W
Forestier Pen., Australia 63 G4 43 0S 148 0 E
Forestville, Canada 73 C6 48 48N 69 2W
Forestville, Calif., U.S.A. 78 G4 38 28N 122 54W
Forestville, N.Y., U.S.A. 84 D5 42 28N 79 10W
Forfar, U.K. 11 E6 56 39N 2 53W
Forillon △, Canada 73 C7 48 46N 64 12W
Forks, U.S.A. 78 C2 47 57N 124 23W
Forksville, U.S.A. 85 E8 41 29N 76 35W
Forlì, Italy 22 B5 44 13N 12 3 E
Forman, U.S.A. 80 B6 46 7N 97 38W
Formby Pt., U.K. 12 D4 53 33N 3 6W
Formentera, Spain 24 C7 38 43N 1 27 E
Formentor, C. de, Spain 24 B10 39 58N 3 13 E
Former Yugoslav Republic of Macedonia = Macedonia ■, Europe 23 D9 41 53N 21 40 E
Fórmia, Italy 22 D5 41 15N 13 37 E
Formosa = Taiwan ■, Asia 33 D7 23 30N 121 0 E
Formosa, Argentina 94 B4 26 15S 58 10W
Formosa, Brazil 93 G9 15 32S 47 20W
Formosa □, Argentina 94 B4 25 0S 60 0W
Formosa, Serra, Brazil 93 F8 12 0S 55 0W
Formosa B. = Ungwana B., Kenya 54 C5 2 40S 40 20 E
Fornells, Spain 24 A11 40 3N 4 7 E
Føroyar, Atl. Oc. 8 F9 62 0N 7 0W
Forres, U.K. 11 D5 57 37N 3 37W
Forrest, Australia 61 F4 30 51S 128 6 E
Forrest, Mt., Australia 61 D4 24 48S 127 45 E
Forrest City, U.S.A. 81 H9 35 1N 90 47W
Forsayth, Australia 62 B3 18 33S 143 34 E
Forssa, Finland 9 F20 60 49N 23 38 E
Forst, Germany 16 C8 51 45N 14 37 E
Forsyth, U.S.A. 76 C10 46 16N 106 41W
Fort Abbas, Pakistan 42 E5 29 12N 72 52 E
Fort Albany, Canada 72 B3 52 15N 81 35W
Fort Ann, U.S.A. 85 C11 43 25N 73 30W
Fort Assiniboine, Canada 70 C6 54 20N 114 45W
Fort Augustus, U.K. 11 D4 57 9N 4 42W
Fort Beaufort, S. Africa 56 E4 32 46S 26 40 E
Fort Benton, U.S.A. 76 C8 47 49N 110 40W
Fort Bragg, U.S.A. 76 G2 39 26N 123 48W
Fort Bridger, U.S.A. 76 F8 41 19N 110 23W
Fort Chipewyan, Canada 71 B6 58 42N 111 8W
Fort Clatsop ⌂, U.S.A. 78 D3 46 8N 123 53W
Fort Collins, U.S.A. 80 E2 40 35N 105 5W
Fort-Coulonge, Canada 72 C4 45 50N 76 45W
Fort Covington, U.S.A. 85 B10 44 59N 74 29W
Fort Davis, U.S.A. 81 K3 30 35N 103 54W
Fort-de-France, Martinique 88 c 14 36N 61 2W
Fort Defiance, U.S.A. 77 J9 35 45N 109 5W
Fort Dodge, U.S.A. 80 D7 42 30N 94 11W
Fort Edward, U.S.A. 85 C11 43 16N 73 35W
Fort Erie, Canada 84 D6 42 54N 78 56W
Fort Fairfield, U.S.A. 83 B12 46 46N 67 50W
Fort Frances, Canada 71 D10 48 36N 93 24W
Fort Franklin = Déline, Canada 68 B7 65 11N 123 25W
Fort Garland, U.S.A. 77 H11 37 26N 105 26W
Fort George = Chisasibi, Canada 72 B4 53 50N 79 0W
Fort Good Hope, Canada 68 B7 66 14N 128 40W
Fort Hancock, U.S.A. 77 L11 31 18N 105 51W
Fort Hope, Canada 72 B2 51 30N 88 0W
Fort Irwin, U.S.A. 79 K10 35 16N 116 34W
Fort Kent, U.S.A. 83 B11 47 15N 68 36W
Fort Klamath, U.S.A. 76 E3 42 42N 122 0W
Fort Laramie, U.S.A. 80 D2 42 13N 104 31W
Fort Lauderdale, U.S.A. 83 M5 26 7N 80 8W
Fort Liard, Canada 70 A4 60 14N 123 30W
Fort Liberté, Haiti 89 C5 19 42N 71 51W
Fort Lupton, U.S.A. 80 E2 40 5N 104 49W
Fort MacKay, Canada 70 B6 57 12N 111 41W
Fort Macleod, Canada 70 D6 49 45N 113 30W
Fort McMurray, Canada 70 B6 56 44N 111 7W
Fort McPherson, Canada 68 B6 67 30N 134 55W
Fort Madison, U.S.A. 80 E9 40 38N 91 27W
Fort Meade, U.S.A. 83 M5 27 45N 81 48W
Fort Morgan, U.S.A. 80 E3 40 15N 103 48W
Fort Myers, U.S.A. 83 M5 26 39N 81 52W
Fort Nelson, Canada 70 B4 58 50N 122 44W
Fort Nelson →, Canada 70 B4 59 32N 124 0W
Fort Norman = Tulita, Canada 68 B7 64 57N 125 30W
Fort Payne, U.S.A. 83 H3 34 26N 85 43W
Fort Peck, U.S.A. 76 B10 48 1N 106 27W
Fort Peck Dam, U.S.A. 76 C10 48 0N 106 26W
Fort Peck L., U.S.A. 76 C10 48 0N 106 26W
Fort Pierce, U.S.A. 83 M5 27 27N 80 20W
Fort Pierre, U.S.A. 80 C4 44 21N 100 22W
Fort Plain, U.S.A. 85 D10 42 56N 74 37W
Fort Portal, Uganda 54 B3 0 40N 30 20 E
Fort Providence, Canada 70 A5 61 3N 117 40W
Fort Qu'Appelle, Canada 71 C8 50 45N 103 50W
Fort Resolution, Canada 70 A6 61 10N 113 40W
Fort Rixon, Zimbabwe 55 G2 20 2S 29 17 E
Fort Ross, U.S.A. 78 G3 38 32N 123 13W
Fort Rupert = Waskaganish, Canada 72 B4 51 30N 78 40W
Fort St. James, Canada 70 C4 54 30N 124 10W
Fort St. John, Canada 70 B4 56 15N 120 50W
Fort Saskatchewan, Canada 70 C6 53 40N 113 15W
Fort Scott, U.S.A. 81 G7 37 50N 94 42W
Fort Severn, Canada 72 A2 56 0N 87 40W
Fort Shevchenko, Kazakhstan 19 F9 44 35N 50 23 E
Fort Simpson, Canada 70 A4 61 45N 121 15W
Fort Smith, Canada 70 B6 60 0N 111 51W
Fort Smith, U.S.A. 81 H7 35 23N 94 25W
Fort Stockton, U.S.A. 81 K3 30 53N 102 53W
Fort Sumner, U.S.A. 81 H2 34 28N 104 15W
Fort Thompson, U.S.A. 80 C5 44 3N 99 26W
Fort Union ⌂, U.S.A. 81 H2 35 54N 105 1W
Fort Valley, U.S.A. 83 J4 32 33N 83 53W
Fort Vermilion, Canada 70 B5 58 24N 116 0W
Fort Walton Beach, U.S.A. 83 K2 30 25N 86 36W
Fort Wayne, U.S.A. 82 E3 41 4N 85 9W
Fort William, U.K. 11 E3 56 49N 5 7W
Fort Worth, U.S.A. 81 J6 32 45N 97 18W
Fort Yates, U.S.A. 80 B4 46 5N 100 38W
Fort Yukon, U.S.A. 68 B5 66 34N 145 16W
Fortaleza, Brazil 93 D11 3 45S 38 35W

Forteau, Canada 73 B8 51 28N 56 58W
Fortescue →, Australia ...... 60 D2 21 0S 116 4 E
Forth →, U.K. 11 E5 56 9N 3 50W
Forth, Firth of, U.K. 11 E6 56 5N 2 55W
Fortrose, U.K. 11 D4 57 35N 4 9W
Fortuna, Calif., U.S.A. 76 F1 40 36N 124 9W
Fortuna, N. Dak., U.S.A. 80 A3 48 55N 103 47W
Fortune, Canada 73 C8 47 4N 55 50W
Fortune B., Canada 73 C8 47 30N 55 22W
Forūr, Iran .... 45 E7 26 17N 54 32 E
Foshan, China .... 33 D6 23 4N 113 5 E
Fosna, Norway .... 8 E14 63 50N 10 20 E
Fosnavåg, Norway .... 9 E11 62 22N 5 38 E
Fossano, Italy .... 20 D7 44 33N 7 43 E
Fossil, U.S.A. 76 D3 45 0N 120 9W
Fossil Butte △, U.S.A. 76 F8 41 50N 110 27W
Foster, Canada 85 A12 45 17N 72 30W
Foster →, Canada 71 B7 55 47N 105 49W
Fosters Ra., Australia ...... 62 C1 21 35S 133 48 E
Fostoria, U.S.A. 82 E4 41 10N 83 25W
Fotadrevo, Madag. .... 57 C8 24 3S 45 1 E
Fougères, France 20 B3 48 21N 1 14W
Foul Pt., Sri Lanka .... 40 Q12 8 35N 81 18 E
Foula, U.K. 11 A6 60 10N 2 5W
Foulness I., U.K. .... 13 F8 51 36N 0 55 E
Foulpointe, Madag. .... 57 B8 17 41S 49 31 E
Foulweather, C., U.S.A. 74 B2 44 50N 124 5W
Fouman, Cameroon .... 52 C2 5 45N 10 50 E
Fountain, U.S.A. 80 F2 38 41N 104 42W
Fountain Springs, U.S.A. 79 K8 35 54N 118 51W
Fouriesburg, S. Africa ...... 56 D4 28 38S 28 14 E
Foúrnoi, Greece .... 23 F12 37 36N 26 32 E
Fourth Cataract, Sudan ...... 51 E12 18 47N 32 3 E
Fouta Djallon, Guinea 50 F3 11 20N 12 10W
Foux, Cap-à-, Haiti 89 C5 19 43N 73 27W
Foveaux Str., N.Z. .... 59 M2 46 42S 168 10 E
Fowey, U.K. 13 G3 50 20N 4 39W
Fowler, Calif., U.S.A. 78 J7 36 38N 119 41W
Fowler, Colo., U.S.A. 80 F3 38 8N 104 2W
Fowlers B., Australia .... 61 F5 31 59S 132 34 E
Fowman, Iran .... 45 B6 37 13N 49 19 E
Fox →, Canada 71 B10 56 3N 93 18W
Fox Creek, Canada 70 C5 54 24N 116 48W
Fox Lake, Canada 70 B6 58 28N 114 31W
Fox Valley, Canada 71 C7 50 30N 109 25W
Foxboro, U.S.A. 85 D13 42 4N 71 16W
Foxdale, Australia .... 62 J6 20 22S 148 35 E
Foxe Basin, Canada 69 B12 66 0N 77 0W
Foxe Chan., Canada 69 B11 65 0N 80 0W
Foxe Pen., Canada 69 B12 65 0N 76 0W
Foxton, N.Z. .... 59 J5 40 29S 175 18 E
Foyle, Lough, U.K. 10 A4 55 7N 7 4W
Foynes, Ireland 10 D2 52 37N 9 7W
Foz do Cunene, Angola ...... 56 B1 17 15S 11 48 E
Foz do Iguaçu, Brazil 95 B5 25 30S 54 30W
Frackville, U.S.A. 85 F8 40 47N 76 14W
Fraile Muerto, Uruguay 95 C5 32 31S 54 32W
Fram Basin, Arctic .... 4 A 87 30N 80 0 E
Framingham, U.S.A. 85 D13 42 17N 71 25W
Franca, Brazil 93 H9 20 33S 47 30W
Francavilla Fontana, Italy .... 23 D7 40 32N 17 35 E
France ■, Europe .... 20 C5 47 0N 3 0 E
Frances, Australia .... 63 F3 36 41S 140 55 E
Frances →, Canada 70 A3 60 16N 129 10W
Frances L., Canada 70 A3 61 23N 129 30W
Franceville, Gabon .... 52 E2 1 40S 13 32 E
Franche-Comté ▣, France .... 20 C6 46 50N 5 55 E
Francis Case, L., U.S.A. 80 D5 43 4N 98 34W
Francisco Beltrão, Brazil 95 B5 26 5S 53 4W
Francisco I. Madero, Coahuila,
    Mexico 86 B4 25 48N 103 18W
Francisco I. Madero, Durango,
    Mexico 86 C4 24 32N 104 22W
Francistown, Botswana ...... 57 C4 21 7S 27 33 E
François, Canada 73 C8 47 35N 56 45W
François L., Canada 70 C3 54 0N 125 30W
Francois Peron △, Australia .. 61 E1 25 42S 113 33 E
Franeker, Neths. .... 15 A5 53 12N 5 33 E
Frank Hann △, Australia .... 61 F3 32 52S 120 19 E
Frankford, Canada 84 B7 44 12N 77 36W
Frankfort, S. Africa .... 57 D4 27 17S 28 30 E
Frankfort, Ind., U.S.A. 82 E2 40 17N 86 31W
Frankfort, Kans., U.S.A. 80 F6 39 42N 96 25W
Frankfort, Ky., U.S.A. 82 F3 38 12N 84 52W
Frankfort, N.Y., U.S.A. 85 C9 43 2N 75 4W
Frankfurt, Brandenburg,
    Germany .... 16 B8 52 20N 14 32 E
Frankfurt, Hessen, Germany .. 16 C5 50 7N 8 41 E
Fränkische Alb, Germany .... 16 D6 49 10N 11 23 E
Frankland →, Australia ...... 61 G2 35 0S 116 48 E
Franklin, Ky., U.S.A. 83 G2 36 43N 86 35W
Franklin, La., U.S.A. 81 L9 29 48N 91 30W
Franklin, Mass., U.S.A. 85 D13 42 5N 71 24W
Franklin, N.H., U.S.A. 85 C13 43 27N 71 39W
Franklin, Nebr., U.S.A. 80 E5 40 6N 98 57W
Franklin, Pa., U.S.A. 84 E5 41 24N 79 50W
Franklin, Va., U.S.A. 83 G7 36 41N 76 56W
Franklin, W. Va., U.S.A. 82 F6 38 39N 79 20W
Franklin B., Canada 68 B7 69 45N 126 0W
Franklin D. Roosevelt L., U.S.A. 76 B4 48 18N 118 9W
Franklin-Gordon Wild Rivers △,
    Australia .... 63 G4 42 19S 145 51 E
Franklin I., Antarctica ...... 5 D11 76 10S 168 30 E
Franklin Mts., Canada 76 F6 48 26N 115 22W
Franklin Str., Canada 68 A10 72 0N 96 0W
Franklinton, U.S.A. 81 K9 30 51N 90 9W
Franklinville, U.S.A. 84 D6 42 20N 78 27W
Franks Pk., U.S.A. 76 E9 43 58N 109 18W
Frankston, Australia .... 63 F4 38 8S 145 8 E
Fransfontein, Namibia ...... 56 C2 20 12S 15 1 E
Frantsa Iosifa, Zemlya, Russia 28 A6 82 0N 55 0 E
Franz, Canada 72 C3 48 25N 84 30W
Franz Josef Land = Frantsa Iosifa,
    Zemlya, Russia .... 28 A6 82 0N 55 0 E
Fraser →, B.C., Canada 84 D2 52 30N 82 0W
Fraser →, Nfld. & L., Canada 70 D4 49 7N 123 11W
Fraser, Mt., Australia ...... 61 E2 25 35S 118 20 E
Fraser I., Australia .... 63 D5 25 15S 153 10 E
Fraser Lake, Canada 70 C4 54 0N 124 50W
Fraserburg, S. Africa .... 56 E3 31 55S 21 30 E
Fraserburgh, U.K. 11 D6 57 42N 2 1W
Fraserdale, Canada 72 C3 49 55N 81 37W
Fray Bentos, Uruguay 94 C4 33 10S 58 15W
Fray Jorge △, Chile 94 C1 30 42S 71 40W
Fredericia, Denmark .... 9 J13 55 34N 9 45 E
Frederick, Md., U.S.A. 82 F7 39 25N 77 25W

Frederick, Okla., U.S.A. 81 H5 34 23N 99 1W
Frederick, S. Dak., U.S.A. 80 C5 45 50N 98 31W
Fredericksburg, Pa., U.S.A. .. 85 F8 40 27N 76 26W
Fredericksburg, Tex., U.S.A. .. 81 K5 30 16N 98 52W
Fredericksburg, Va., U.S.A. .. 82 F7 38 18N 77 28W
Fredericktown, Mo., U.S.A. .. 81 G9 37 34N 90 18W
Fredericktown, Ohio, U.S.A. .. 84 F2 40 29N 82 33W
Frederico I. Madero, Presa,
    Mexico 86 B3 28 7N 105 40W
Frederico Westphalen, Brazil .. 95 B5 27 22S 53 24W
Fredericton, Canada 73 C6 45 57N 66 40W
Fredericton Junction, Canada 73 C6 45 41N 66 40W
Frederikshåb = Paamiut,
    Greenland 69 B15 62 0N 49 43W
Frederikshavn, Denmark .... 9 H14 57 28N 10 31 E
Frederiksted, U.S. Virgin Is. .. 89 C7 17 43N 64 53W
Fredonia, Ariz., U.S.A. 77 H7 36 57N 112 32W
Fredonia, Kans., U.S.A. 81 G7 37 32N 95 49W
Fredonia, N.Y., U.S.A. 84 D5 42 26N 79 20W
Fredrikstad, Norway .... 9 G14 59 13N 10 57 E
Free State ▣, S. Africa ...... 56 D4 28 30S 27 0 E
Freehold, U.S.A. 85 F10 40 16N 74 17W
Freel Peak, U.S.A. 78 G7 38 52N 119 54W
Freeland, U.S.A. 85 E9 41 1N 75 54W
Freels, C., Canada 73 C9 49 15N 53 30W
Freeman, Calif., U.S.A. 79 K9 35 35N 117 53W
Freeman, S. Dak., U.S.A. 80 D6 43 21N 97 26W
Freeport, Bahamas 88 A4 26 30N 78 47W
Freeport, Ill., U.S.A. 80 D10 42 17N 89 36W
Freeport, N.Y., U.S.A. 85 F11 40 39N 73 35W
Freeport, Ohio, U.S.A. 84 F3 40 12N 81 15W
Freeport, Pa., U.S.A. 84 F5 40 41N 79 41W
Freeport, Tex., U.S.A. 81 L7 28 57N 95 21W
Freetown, S. Leone 50 G3 8 30N 13 17W
Frégate, L. de la, Canada 72 B5 53 15N 74 45W
Fregenal de la Sierra, Spain .. 21 C2 38 10N 6 39W
Freibourg = Fribourg, Switz. .. 20 C7 46 49N 7 9 E
Freiburg, Germany .... 16 E4 47 59N 7 51 E
Freire, Chile 96 D2 38 54S 72 38W
Freirina, Chile 94 B1 28 30S 71 10W
Freising, Germany .... 16 D6 48 24N 11 45 E
Freistadt, Austria .... 16 D8 48 30N 14 30 E
Fréjus, France .... 20 E7 43 25N 6 44 E
Fremantle, Australia .... 61 F2 32 7S 115 47 E
Fremont, Calif., U.S.A. 78 H4 37 32N 121 57W
Fremont, Mich., U.S.A. 82 D3 43 28N 85 57W
Fremont, Nebr., U.S.A. 80 E6 41 26N 96 30W
Fremont, Ohio, U.S.A. 82 E4 41 21N 83 7W
Fremont →, U.S.A. 77 G8 38 24N 110 42W
French Camp, U.S.A. 78 H5 37 53N 121 16W
French Creek →, U.S.A. 84 E5 41 24N 79 50W
French Guiana ☑, S. Amer. .. 93 C8 4 0N 53 0W
French Polynesia ☑, Pac. Oc. 65 K13 20 0S 145 0W
Frenchman Cr. →, N. Amer. .. 76 B10 48 31N 107 10W
Frenchman Cr. →, U.S.A. 80 E4 40 14N 100 50W
Fresco →, Brazil 93 E8 7 15S 51 30W
Freshfield, C., Antarctica .... 5 C10 68 25S 151 10 E
Fresnillo, Mexico 86 C4 23 10N 103 0W
Fresno, U.S.A. 78 J7 36 44N 119 47W
Fresno Reservoir, U.S.A. 76 B9 48 36N 109 57W
Frew →, Australia .... 62 C2 20 0S 135 38 E
Frewsburg, U.S.A. 84 D5 42 3N 79 10W
Freycinet △, Australia ...... 63 G4 42 11S 148 19 E
Freycinet Pen., Australia .... 63 G4 42 10S 148 25 E
Fria, C., Namibia .... 56 B1 18 0S 12 0 E
Friant, U.S.A. 78 J7 36 59N 119 43W
Frias, Argentina 94 B2 28 40S 65 5W
Fribourg, Switz. .... 20 C7 46 49N 7 9 E
Friday Harbor, U.S.A. 78 B3 48 32N 123 1W
Friedens, U.S.A. 84 F6 40 3N 78 59W
Friedrichshafen, Germany .... 16 E5 47 39N 9 30 E
Friendly Is. = Tonga ■, Pac. Oc. 59 D11 19 50S 174 30W
Friendship, U.S.A. 84 D6 42 12N 78 8W
Friesland ▣, Neths. .... 15 A5 53 5N 5 50 E
Frio →, U.S.A. 81 L5 28 26N 98 11W
Frio, C., Brazil 90 F6 22 50S 41 50W
Friona, U.S.A. 81 H3 34 38N 102 43W
Fritch, U.S.A. 81 H4 35 38N 101 36W
Frobisher B., Canada 69 B13 62 30N 66 0W
Frobisher Bay = Iqaluit, Canada 69 B13 63 44N 68 31W
Frobisher L., Canada 71 B7 56 20N 108 15W
Frohavet, Norway .... 8 E13 64 0N 9 30 E
Frome →, U.K. 13 F5 51 14N 2 19W
Frome, U.K. 13 G5 50 41N 2 6W
Frome, L., Australia .... 63 E2 30 45S 139 45 E
Front Range, U.S.A. 74 C5 40 25N 105 45W
Front Royal, U.S.A. 82 F6 38 55N 78 12W
Frontera, Canary Is. 24 G2 27 47N 17 59W
Frontera, Mexico 87 D6 18 30N 92 40W
Fronteras, Mexico 86 A3 30 56N 109 31W
Frosinone, Italy .... 22 D5 41 38N 13 19 E
Frostburg, U.S.A. 82 F6 39 39N 78 56W
Frostisen, Norway .... 8 B17 68 14N 17 10 E
Frøya, Norway .... 8 E13 63 43N 8 40 E
Frunze = Bishkek, Kyrgyzstan 28 E8 42 54N 74 46 E
Frutal, Brazil 93 H9 20 0S 49 0W
Frýdek-Místek, Czech Rep. .. 17 D10 49 40N 18 20 E
Fryeburg, U.S.A. 85 B14 44 1N 70 59W
Fu Xian = Wafangdian, China 35 E11 39 38N 121 58 E
Fu Xian, China .... 34 G5 36 0N 109 20 E
Fucheng, China .... 34 F9 37 50N 116 10 E
Fuchou = Fuzhou, China .... 33 D6 26 5N 119 16 E
Fuchū, Japan .... 31 G6 34 34N 133 14 E
Fuencaliente, Canary Is. 24 F2 28 28N 17 50W
Fuencaliente, Pta., Canary Is. .. 24 F2 28 27N 17 51W
Fuengirola, Spain 21 D3 36 32N 4 41W
Fuentes de Oñoro, Spain 21 B2 40 33N 6 52W
Fuerte →, Mexico 86 B3 25 50N 109 25W
Fuerte Olimpo, Paraguay 94 A4 21 0S 57 51W
Fuerteventura, Canary Is. 24 F6 28 30N 14 0W
Fuerteventura ✕ (FUE), Canary Is. 24 F6 28 24N 13 52W
Fufeng, China .... 34 G5 34 22N 108 0 E
Fugou, China .... 34 G8 34 3N 114 25 E
Fugu, China .... 34 E6 39 2N 111 3 E
Fuhai, China .... 32 B3 47 2N 87 25 E
Fuḥaymī, Iraq .... 44 C4 34 16N 42 10 E
Fuji, Japan .... 31 G9 35 9N 138 39 E
Fuji-Hakone △, Japan ...... 31 G9 35 15N 138 45 E
Fuji-San, Japan .... 31 G9 35 22N 138 44 E
Fuji-Yoshida, Japan .... 31 G9 35 30N 138 46 E
Fujian ▣, China .... 33 D6 26 0N 118 0 E
Fujinomiya, Japan .... 31 G9 35 10N 138 40 E
Fujisawa, Japan .... 31 G9 35 22N 139 29 E
Fujiyama, Mt. = Fuji-San, Japan 31 G9 35 22N 138 44 E
Fukagawa, Japan .... 30 C11 43 43N 142 2 E
Fukien = Fujian ▣, China .... 33 D6 26 0N 118 0 E
Fukuchiyama, Japan .... 31 G7 35 19N 135 9 E
Fukue-Shima, Japan .... 31 H4 32 40N 128 45 E

Fukui, Japan .... 31 F8 36 5N 136 10 E
Fukui ▣, Japan .... 31 G8 36 0N 136 12 E
Fukuoka, Japan .... 31 H5 33 39N 130 21 E
Fukuoka ▣, Japan .... 31 H5 33 30N 131 0 E
Fukushima, Japan .... 30 F10 37 44N 140 28 E
Fukushima ▣, Japan .... 30 F10 37 30N 140 15 E
Fukuyama, Japan .... 31 G6 34 35N 133 20 E
Fulda, Germany .... 16 C5 50 32N 9 40 E
Fulda →, Germany .... 16 C5 51 25N 9 39 E
Fulford Harbour, Canada 78 B3 48 47N 123 27W
Fullerton, Calif., U.S.A. 79 M9 33 53N 117 56W
Fullerton, Nebr., U.S.A. 80 E6 41 22N 97 58W
Fulongquan, China .... 35 B13 44 20N 124 42 E
Fulton, Mo., U.S.A. 80 F9 38 52N 91 57W
Fulton, N.Y., U.S.A. 85 C8 43 19N 76 25W
Funabashi, Japan .... 31 G10 35 45N 140 0 E
Funafuti = Fongafale, Tuvalu 64 H9 8 31S 179 13 E
Funchal, Madeira 24 D3 32 38N 16 54W
Funchal ✕ (FNC), Madeira .. 24 D3 32 42N 16 45W
Fundación, Colombia 92 A4 10 31N 74 11W
Fundão, Portugal 21 B2 40 8N 7 30W
Fundy →, Canada 73 C6 45 35N 65 10W
Fundy, B. of, Canada 73 D6 45 0N 66 0W
Funhalouro, Mozam. .... 57 C5 23 3S 34 25 E
Funing, Hebei, China .... 35 E10 39 53N 119 12 E
Funing, Jiangsu, China ...... 35 H10 33 45N 119 50 E
Funiu Shan, China .... 34 H7 33 30N 112 20 E
Funtua, Nigeria .... 50 F7 11 30N 7 18 E
Fuping, Hebei, China .... 34 E8 38 48N 114 12 E
Fuping, Shaanxi, China ...... 34 G5 34 42N 109 10 E
Furano, Japan .... 30 C11 43 21N 142 23 E
Furāt, Nahr al →, Asia ...... 44 D5 31 0N 47 25 E
Fürg, Iran .... 45 D7 28 18N 55 13 E
Furnás, Spain .... 24 B8 39 3N 1 32 E
Furnas, Reprêsa de, Brazil .. 95 A6 20 50S 45 30W
Furneaux Group, Australia .. 63 G4 40 10S 147 50 E
Furqlus, Syria .... 46 A6 34 36N 37 8 E
Fürstenwalde, Germany ...... 16 B8 52 22N 14 3 E
Fürth, Germany .... 16 D6 49 28N 10 59 E
Furukawa, Japan .... 30 E10 38 34N 140 58 E
Fury and Hecla Str., Canada .. 69 B11 69 56N 84 0W
Fusagasuga, Colombia 92 C4 4 21N 74 22W
Fushan, Shandong, China .... 35 F11 37 30N 121 15 E
Fushan, Shanxi, China ...... 34 G6 35 58N 111 51 E
Fushun, China .... 35 D12 41 50N 123 56 E
Fusong, China .... 35 C14 42 20N 127 15 E
Fustic, Barbados .... 89 g 13 16N 59 38W
Futian, China .... 33 F11 22 32N 114 4 E
Futuna, Wall. & F. Is. 59 B8 14 25S 178 20W
Fuxin, China .... 35 C11 42 5N 121 48 E
Fuyang, China .... 34 H8 33 0N 115 48 E
Fuyang, China .... 33 F10 22 40N 113 49 E
Fuyang He →, China .... 34 E9 38 12N 117 0 E
Fuyong, China .... 33 F10 22 40N 113 49 E
Fuyu, China .... 35 B13 45 12N 124 43 E
Fuzhou, China .... 33 D6 26 5N 119 16 E
Fylde, U.K. 12 D5 53 50N 2 58W
Fyn, Denmark .... 9 J14 55 20N 10 30 E
Fyne, L., U.K. 11 F3 55 59N 5 23W

G

Gabela, Angola .... 52 G2 11 0S 14 24 E
Gabès, Tunisia .... 51 B8 33 53N 10 2 E
Gabès, G. de, Tunisia .... 51 B8 34 0N 10 30 E
Gabon ■, Africa .... 52 E2 0 10S 10 0 E
Gaborone, Botswana .... 56 C4 24 45S 25 57 E
Gabriels, U.S.A. 85 B10 44 26N 74 12W
Gābrīk, Iran .... 45 E8 25 44N 58 28 E
Gabrovo, Bulgaria .... 23 C11 42 52N 25 19 E
Gāch Sār, Iran .... 45 B6 36 7N 51 19 E
Gachsārān, Iran .... 45 D6 30 15N 50 45 E
Gadag, India .... 40 M9 15 30N 75 45 E
Gadap, Pakistan .... 42 G2 25 5N 67 28 E
Gadarwara, India .... 43 H8 22 50N 78 50 E
Gadhada, India .... 42 J4 22 0N 71 35 E
Gadra, Pakistan .... 42 G4 25 40N 70 38 E
Gadsden, U.S.A. 83 H3 34 1N 86 1W
Gadwal, India .... 40 L10 16 10N 77 50 E
Gaffney, U.S.A. 83 H5 35 5N 81 39W
Gafsa, Tunisia .... 50 B7 34 24N 8 43 E
Gagaria, India .... 42 G4 25 43N 70 46 E
Gagnoa, Ivory C. 50 G4 6 56N 5 16W
Gagnon, Canada 73 B6 51 50N 68 5W
Gagnon, L., Canada 71 A6 62 3N 110 27W
Gahini, Rwanda .... 54 C3 1 50S 30 30 E
Gahmar, India .... 43 G10 25 27N 83 49 E
Gai Xian = Gaizhou, China .. 35 D12 40 22N 122 20 E
Gaïdhouronísi, Greece ...... 25 E7 34 53N 25 41 E
Gail, U.S.A. 81 J4 32 46N 101 27W
Gaillimh = Galway, Ireland .. 10 C2 53 17N 9 3W
Gaines, U.S.A. 84 E7 41 46N 77 35W
Gainesville, Fla., U.S.A. 83 L4 29 40N 82 20W
Gainesville, Ga., U.S.A. 83 H4 34 18N 83 50W
Gainesville, Mo., U.S.A. 81 G8 36 36N 92 26W
Gainesville, Tex., U.S.A. 81 J6 33 38N 97 8W
Gainsborough, U.K. 12 D7 53 24N 0 46W
Gairdner, L., Australia ...... 63 E2 31 30S 136 0 E
Gairloch, U.K. 11 D3 57 43N 5 41W
Gairloch, L., U.K. 11 D3 57 43N 5 45W
Gaizhou, China .... 35 D12 40 22N 122 20 E
Gaj →, Pakistan .... 42 F2 26 26N 67 21 E
Galán, Cerro, Argentina 94 B2 25 55S 66 52W
Galana →, Kenya .... 54 C5 3 9S 40 8 E
Galápagos = Colón, Arch. de,
    Ecuador 90 D1 0 0 91 0W
Galashiels, U.K. 11 F6 55 37N 2 49W
Galați, Romania .... 17 F15 45 27N 28 2 E
Galatina, Italy .... 23 D8 40 10N 18 10 E
Galcaio, Somali Rep. .... 47 F4 6 30N 47 30 E
Galdhøpiggen, Norway ...... 9 F12 61 38N 8 18 E
Galeana, Chihuahua, Mexico .. 86 A3 30 7N 107 38W
Galeana, Nuevo León, Mexico 86 C4 24 50S 100 4W
Galela, Indonesia .... 37 D7 1 50N 127 49 E
Galena, U.S.A. 68 B4 64 44N 156 56W
Galeota Pt., Trin. & Tob. 93 K16 10 8N 60 59W
Galera Pt., Trin. & Tob. 89 D7 10 49N 60 54W
Galesburg, U.S.A. 80 E9 40 57N 90 22W
Galeton, U.S.A. 84 E7 41 44N 77 39W
Galich, Russia .... 18 C7 58 22N 42 24 E
Galicia ▣, Spain 21 A2 42 43N 7 45W
Galilee = Hagalil, Israel .... 46 C4 32 53N 35 18 E
Galilee, L., Australia .... 62 C4 22 20S 145 50 E

Galilee, Sea of = Yam Kinneret,
    Israel .... 46 C4 32 45N 35 35 E
Galina Pt., Jamaica .... 88 a 18 24N 76 58W
Galinoporni, Cyprus .... 25 D13 35 31N 34 18 E
Galion, U.S.A. 84 F2 40 44N 82 47W
Galiuro Mts., U.S.A. 77 K8 32 30N 110 20W
Galiwinku, Australia .... 62 A2 12 2S 135 34 E
Gallan Hd., U.K. 11 C1 58 15N 7 2W
Gallatin, U.S.A. 83 G2 36 24N 86 27W
Galle, Sri Lanka .... 40 R12 6 5N 80 10 E
Gállego →, Spain 21 B5 41 39N 0 51W
Gallegos →, Argentina 96 G3 51 35S 69 0W
Galley Hd., Ireland 10 E3 51 32N 8 55W
Gallinas, Pta., Colombia 92 A4 12 28N 71 40W
Gallipoli = Gelibolu, Turkey .. 23 D12 40 28N 26 43 E
Gallipoli, Italy .... 23 D8 40 3N 17 58 E
Gallipolis, U.S.A. 82 F4 38 49N 82 12W
Gällivare, Sweden .... 8 C19 67 9N 20 40 E
Galloo I., U.S.A. 85 C8 43 55N 76 25W
Galloway, U.K. 11 F4 55 1N 4 29W
Galloway, Mull of, U.K. 11 F4 54 39N 4 51W
Gallup, U.S.A. 77 J9 35 32N 108 45W
Galoya, Sri Lanka .... 40 Q12 8 10N 80 55 E
Galt, U.S.A. 78 G5 38 15N 121 18W
Galty Mts., Ireland 10 D3 52 22N 8 10W
Galtymore, Ireland 10 D3 52 21N 8 11W
Galva, U.S.A. 80 E9 41 10N 90 3W
Galveston, U.S.A. 81 L7 29 18N 94 48W
Galveston B., U.S.A. 81 L7 29 36N 94 50W
Gálvez, Argentina 94 C3 32 0S 61 14W
Galway, Ireland 10 C2 53 17N 9 3W
Galway ▣, Ireland 10 C2 53 22N 9 1W
Galway B., Ireland 10 C2 53 13N 9 10W
Gam →, Vietnam .... 38 B5 21 55N 105 12 E
Gamagōri, Japan .... 31 G8 34 50N 137 14 E
Gambat, Pakistan .... 42 F3 27 17N 68 26 E
Gambhir →, India .... 42 F6 26 58N 77 27 E
Gambia ■, W. Afr. 50 F2 13 25N 16 0W
Gambia →, W. Afr. 50 F2 13 28N 16 34W
Gambier, U.S.A. 84 F2 40 22N 82 23W
Gambier, C., Australia ...... 60 B5 11 56S 130 57 E
Gambier Is., Australia ...... 63 F2 35 3S 136 30 E
Gambo, Canada 73 C9 48 47N 54 13W
Gamboli, Pakistan .... 42 E3 29 53N 68 24 E
Gamboma, Congo .... 52 E3 1 55S 15 52 E
Gamka →, S. Africa .... 56 E3 33 18S 21 39 E
Gamkab →, Namibia .... 56 D2 28 4S 17 54 E
Gammon →, Canada 71 C9 51 24N 95 44W
Gammon Ranges △, Australia 63 E2 30 38S 139 8 E
Gamtoos →, S. Africa ...... 56 E4 33 58S 25 1 E
Gan Jiang →, China .... 33 D6 29 15N 116 0 E
Ganado, U.S.A. 77 J9 35 43N 109 33W
Gananoque, Canada 85 B8 44 20N 76 10W
Ganāveh, Iran .... 45 D6 29 35N 50 35 E
Gäncä, Azerbaijan .... 19 F8 40 45N 46 20 E
Gancheng, China .... 38 C7 18 51N 108 37 E
Gand = Gent, Belgium ...... 15 C3 51 2N 3 42 E
Ganda, Angola .... 53 G2 13 3S 14 35 E
Gandajika, Dem. Rep. of
    the Congo .... 52 F4 6 45S 23 57 E
Gandak →, India .... 43 G11 25 39N 85 13 E
Gandava, Pakistan .... 42 E2 28 32N 67 32 E
Gander, Canada 73 C9 48 58N 54 35W
Gander L., Canada 73 C9 48 58N 54 35W
Ganderowe Falls, Zimbabwe 55 F2 17 20S 29 10 E
Gandhi Sagar, India .... 42 G6 24 40N 75 40 E
Gandhinagar, India .... 42 H5 23 15N 72 45 E
Gandia, Spain 21 C5 38 58N 0 9W
Gando, Pta., Canary Is. 24 G4 27 55N 15 22W
Ganedidalem = Gani, Indonesia 37 E7 0 48S 128 14 E
Ganga →, India .... 43 H14 23 20N 90 30 E
Ganga Sagar, India .... 43 J13 21 38N 88 5 E
Gangan →, India .... 43 E8 28 38N 78 58 E
Ganganagar, India .... 42 E5 29 56N 73 56 E
Gangapur, India .... 42 F7 26 32N 76 49 E
Gangaw, Burma .... 41 H19 22 5N 94 5 E
Gangdisê Shan, China ...... 41 D12 31 20N 81 0 E
Ganges = Ganga →, India .. 43 H14 23 20N 90 30 E
Ganges, Canada 70 D4 48 51N 123 31W
Ganges, Mouths of the, India 43 J14 21 30N 90 0 E
Gangoh, India .... 42 E7 29 46N 77 18 E
Gangotri, India .... 43 D8 30 50N 79 10 E
Gangtok, India .... 41 F16 27 20N 88 37 E
Gangu, China .... 34 G3 34 40N 105 15 E
Gangyao, China .... 35 B14 44 12N 126 37 E
Gani, Indonesia .... 37 E7 0 48S 128 14 E
Ganj, India .... 43 F8 27 45N 78 57 E
Gannett Peak, U.S.A. 76 E9 43 11N 109 39W
Ganquan, China .... 34 F5 36 20N 109 20 E
Gansu ▣, China .... 34 G3 36 0N 104 0 E
Ganta, Liberia 50 G4 7 15N 8 59W
Gantheaume, C., Australia .. 63 F2 36 4S 137 32 E
Gantheaume B., Australia .. 61 E1 27 40S 114 10 E
Gantsevichi = Hantsavichy,
    Belarus .... 17 B14 52 49N 26 30 E
Ganyem = Genyem, Indonesia 37 E10 2 46S 140 12 E
Ganyu, China .... 35 G10 34 50N 119 8 E
Ganzhou, China .... 33 D6 25 51N 114 56 E
Gao, Mali 50 E5 16 15N 0 5W
Gaomi, China .... 35 F10 36 20N 119 42 E
Gaoping, China .... 34 G7 35 45N 112 55 E
Gaotang, China .... 34 F9 36 50N 116 15 E
Gaoua, Burkina Faso 50 F5 10 20N 3 8W
Gaoual, Guinea 50 F3 11 45N 13 25W
Gaoxiong = Kaohsiung, Taiwan 33 D7 22 35N 120 16 E
Gaoyang, China .... 34 E8 38 40N 115 45 E
Gaoyou Hu, China .... 35 H10 32 45N 119 20 E
Gaoyuan, China .... 35 F9 37 8N 117 58 E
Gap, France .... 20 D7 44 33N 6 5 E
Gapat →, India .... 43 G10 24 30N 82 28 E
Gapuwiyak, Australia ...... 62 A2 12 25S 135 43 E
Gar, China .... 32 C2 32 10N 79 58 E
Garabogazköl Aylagy,
    Turkmenistan .... 19 F9 41 0N 53 30 E
Garachico, Canary Is. 24 F3 28 22N 16 46W
Garachiné, Panama 88 E4 8 0N 78 12W
Garafia, Canary Is. 24 F2 28 48N 17 57W
Garah, Australia .... 63 D4 29 5S 149 38 E
Garajonay, Canary Is. 24 F2 28 7N 17 14W
Garamba →, Dem. Rep. of
    the Congo .... 54 B2 4 10N 29 40 E
Garanhuns, Brazil 93 E11 8 50S 36 30W
Garautha, India .... 43 G8 25 34N 79 18 E
Garba Tula, Kenya .... 54 B4 0 30N 38 32 E
Garberville, U.S.A. 76 F2 40 6N 123 48W
Garbiyang, India .... 43 D9 30 8N 80 54 E

Garda, L. di, Italy . . . . **22 B4** 45 40N 10 41 E
Garde L., Canada **71 A7** 62 50N 106 13W
Garden City, Ga., U.S.A. . . . **83 J5** 32 6N 81 9W
Garden City, Kans., U.S.A. . . **81 G4** 37 58N 100 53W
Garden City, Tex., U.S.A. . . . **81 K4** 31 52N 101 29W
Garden Grove, U.S.A. **79 M9** 33 47N 117 55W
Gardēz, Afghan. . . . . **42 C3** 33 37N 69 9 E
Gardiner, Maine, U.S.A. . . . **83 C11** 44 14N 69 47W
Gardiner, Mont., U.S.A. **76 D8** 45 2N 110 22W
Gardiners I., U.S.A. **85 E12** 41 6N 72 6W
Gardner, U.S.A. **85 D13** 42 34N 71 59W
Gardner Canal, Canada **70 C3** 53 27N 128 8W
Gardnerville, U.S.A. **78 G7** 38 56N 119 45W
Gardo, Somali Rep. . . . . **47 F4** 9 30N 49 6 E
Garey, U.S.A. **79 L6** 34 53N 120 19W
Garfield, U.S.A. **76 C5** 47 1N 117 9W
Garforth, U.K. **12 D6** 53 47N 1 24W
Gargett, Australia . . . . **62 K6** 21 9S 148 46 E
Garibaldi △, Canada **70 D4** 49 50N 123 0W
Gariep, L., S. Africa . . . . **56 E4** 30 40S 25 40 E
Garies, S. Africa . . . . **56 E2** 30 32S 17 59 E
Garigliano →, Italy . . . . **22 D5** 41 13N 13 45 E
Garissa, Kenya . . . . **54 C4** 0 25S 39 40 E
Garland, Tex., U.S.A. **81 J6** 32 55N 96 38W
Garland, Utah, U.S.A. **76 F7** 41 47N 112 10W
Garm, Tajikistan . . . . **28 F8** 39 0N 70 20 E
Garmāb, Iran . . . . **45 C8** 35 25N 56 45 E
Garmisch-Partenkirchen, Germany . . . **16 E6** 47 30N 11 6 E
Garmo, Qullai = Kommunizma, Pik, Tajikistan . . . **28 F8** 39 0N 72 2 E
Garmsār, Iran . . . . **45 C7** 35 20N 52 25 E
Garner, U.S.A. **80 D8** 43 6N 93 36W
Garnett, U.S.A. **80 F7** 38 17N 95 14W
Garo Hills, India . . . . **43 G14** 25 30N 90 30 E
Garoe, Somali Rep. . . . . **47 F4** 8 25N 48 33 E
Garonne →, France **20 D3** 45 2N 0 36W
Garoowe = Garoe, Somali Rep. . . . **47 F4** 8 25N 48 33 E
Garot, India . . . . **42 G6** 24 19N 75 41 E
Garoua, Cameroon . . . . **51 G8** 9 19N 13 21 E
Garrauli, India . . . . **43 G8** 25 5N 79 22 E
Garrison, Mont., U.S.A. **76 C7** 46 31N 112 49W
Garrison, N. Dak., U.S.A. . . . **80 B4** 47 40N 101 25W
Garrison Res. = Sakakawea, L., U.S.A. . . . **80 B4** 47 30N 101 25W
Garron Pt., U.K. **10 A6** 55 3N 5 59W
Garry →, U.K. **11 E5** 56 44N 3 47W
Garry, L., Canada **68 B9** 65 58N 100 18W
Garsen, Kenya . . . . **54 C5** 2 20S 40 5 E
Garson L., Canada **71 B6** 56 19N 110 2W
Garstang, U.K. **12 D5** 53 55N 2 46W
Garu, India . . . . **43 H11** 23 40N 84 14 E
Garub, Namibia . . . . **56 D2** 26 37S 16 0 E
Garut, Indonesia . . . . **37 G12** 7 14S 107 53 E
Garvie Mts., N.Z. . . . . **59 L2** 45 30S 168 50 E
Garwa = Garoua, Cameroon . . . **51 G8** 9 19N 13 21 E
Garwa, India . . . . **43 G10** 24 11N 83 47 E
Gary, U.S.A. **82 E2** 41 36N 87 20W
Garzê, China . . . . **32 C5** 31 38N 100 1 E
Garzón, Colombia **92 C3** 2 10N 75 40W
Gas-San, Japan . . . . **30 E10** 38 32N 140 1 E
Gasan Kuli = Esenguly, Turkmenistan . . . **28 F6** 37 37N 53 59 E
Gascogne, France . . . . **20 E4** 43 45N 0 20 E
Gascogne, G. de, Europe **20 D2** 44 0N 2 0W
Gascony = Gascogne, France . . . **20 E4** 43 45N 0 20 E
Gascoyne →, Australia . . . . . **61 D1** 24 52S 113 37 E
Gascoyne Junction, Australia . . . **61 E2** 25 2S 115 17 E
Gashaka, Nigeria . . . . **51 G8** 7 20N 11 29 E
Gasherbrum, Pakistan . . . . . . **43 B7** 35 40N 76 40 E
Gashua, Nigeria . . . . **51 F8** 12 54N 11 0 E
Gasparillo, Trin. & Tob. **93 K15** 10 18N 61 26W
Gaspé, Canada **73 C7** 48 52N 64 30W
Gaspé, C. de, Canada **73 C7** 48 48N 64 7W
Gaspé Pen. = Gaspésie, Pén. de la, Canada . . . **73 C6** 48 45N 65 40W
Gaspésie △, Canada **73 C6** 48 55N 66 10W
Gaspésie, Pén. de la, Canada . . . **73 C6** 48 45N 65 40W
Gasteiz = Vitoria-Gasteiz, Spain . . . **21 A4** 42 50N 2 41W
Gastonia, U.S.A. **83 H5** 35 16N 81 11W
Gastre, Argentina **96 E3** 42 20S 69 15W
Gata, C., Cyprus . . . . **25 E12** 34 34N 33 2 E
Gata, C. de, Spain **21 D4** 36 41N 2 13W
Gata, Sierra de, Spain **21 B2** 40 20N 6 45W
Gataga →, Canada **70 B3** 58 35N 126 59W
Gatehouse of Fleet, U.K. **11 G4** 54 53N 4 12W
Gates, U.S.A. **84 C7** 43 9N 77 42W
Gateshead, U.K. **12 C6** 54 57N 1 35W
Gatesville, U.S.A. **81 K6** 31 26N 97 45W
Gateway, U.S.A. **85 F11** 40 26S 73 30W
Gaths, Zimbabwe . . . . **55 G3** 20 2S 30 32 E
Gatico, Chile **94 A1** 22 29S 70 20W
Gatineau, Canada **85 A9** 45 29N 75 38W
Gatineau △, Canada **72 C4** 45 40N 76 0W
Gatineau →, Canada **72 C4** 45 27N 75 42W
Gatton, Australia . . . . **63 D5** 27 32S 152 17 E
Gatun, L., Panama **88 E4** 9 7N 79 56W
Gatwick, London ✈ (LGW), U.K. . . . **13 F7** 51 10N 0 11W
Gatyana, S. Africa . . . . **57 E4** 32 16S 28 31 E
Gau, Fiji . . . . **59 D8** 18 2S 179 18 E
Gauer L., Canada **71 B9** 57 0N 97 50W
Gauhati = Guwahati, India . . . **41 F17** 26 10N 91 45 E
Gauja →, Latvia . . . . **9 H21** 57 10N 24 16 E
Gaula →, Norway . . . . **8 E14** 63 21N 10 14 E
Gauri Phanta, India . . . . **43 E9** 28 41N 80 36 E
Gausta, Norway . . . . **9 G13** 59 48N 8 40 E
Gauteng □, S. Africa . . . . **57 D4** 26 0S 28 0 E
Gāv Koshī, Iran . . . . **45 D8** 28 38N 57 12 E
Gāvakān, Iran . . . . **45 D7** 29 37N 53 10 E
Gāvāter, Iran . . . . **45 E9** 25 10N 61 31 E
Gāvbandī, Iran . . . . **45 E7** 27 12N 53 4 E
Gavdopoúla, Greece . . . . **25 E6** 34 56N 24 0 E
Gávdhos, Greece . . . . **25 E6** 34 50N 24 5 E
Gaviota, U.S.A. **79 L6** 34 29N 120 13W
Gāvkhūni, Bāţlāq-e, Iran . . . . **45 C7** 32 6N 52 52 E
Gävle, Sweden . . . . **9 F17** 60 40N 17 9 E
Gawachab, Namibia . . . . **56 D2** 27 4S 17 55 E
Gawilgarh Hills, India . . . . . . **40 J10** 21 15N 76 45 E
Gawler, Australia . . . . **63 E2** 34 30S 138 42 E
Gaxun Nur, China . . . . **32 B5** 42 22N 100 30 E
Gay, Russia . . . . **18 D10** 51 27N 58 27 E
Gaya, India . . . . **43 G11** 24 47N 85 4 E
Gaya, Niger . . . . **50 F6** 11 52N 3 28 E
Gaylord, U.S.A. **82 C3** 45 2N 84 41W
Gayndah, Australia . . . . **63 D5** 25 35S 151 32 E
Gaysin = Haysyn, Ukraine . . . **17 D15** 48 57N 29 25 E
Gayvoron = Hayvoron, Ukraine . . . **17 D15** 48 22N 29 52 E
Gaza, Gaza Strip . . . . **46 D3** 31 30N 34 28 E

Gaza □, Mozam. . . . . **57 C5** 23 10S 32 45 E
Gaza Strip ☑, Asia . . . . **46 D3** 31 29N 34 25 E
Gazanjyk, Turkmenistan . . . . **45 B7** 39 16N 55 32 E
Gāzbor, Iran . . . . **45 D8** 28 5N 58 51 E
Gazi, Dem. Rep. of the Congo . . . **54 B1** 1 3N 24 30 E
Gaziantep, Turkey . . . . **19 G6** 37 6N 37 23 E
Gazimağosa = Famagusta, Cyprus . . . **25 D12** 35 8N 33 55 E
Gcoverega, Botswana . . . . **56 B3** 19 8S 24 18 E
Gcuwa, S. Africa . . . . **57 E4** 32 20S 28 11 E
Gdańsk, Poland . . . . **17 A10** 54 22N 18 40 E
Gdańska, Zatoka, Poland . . . . **17 A10** 54 30N 19 20 E
Gdov, Russia . . . . **9 G22** 58 48N 27 55 E
Gdynia, Poland . . . . **17 A10** 54 35N 18 33 E
Gebe, Indonesia . . . . **37 D7** 0 5N 129 25 E
Gebze, Turkey . . . . **23 D13** 40 47N 29 25 E
Gedaref, Sudan . . . . **51 F13** 14 2N 35 28 E
Gedser, Denmark . . . . **9 J14** 54 35N 11 55 E
Gediz →, Turkey . . . . **23 E12** 38 35N 26 48 E
Gedung, Pulau, Malaysia . . . . **39 c** 5 17N 100 23 E
Geegully Cr. →, Australia . . . . **60 C3** 18 32S 123 41 E
Geel, Belgium . . . . **15 C4** 51 10N 4 59 E
Geelong, Australia . . . . **63 F3** 38 10S 144 22 E
Geelvink B. = Cenderwasih, Teluk, Indonesia . . . **37 E9** 3 0S 135 20 E
Geelvink Chan., Australia . . . . **61 E1** 28 30S 114 0 E
Geesthacht, Germany . . . . **16 B6** 53 26N 10 22 E
Geidam, Nigeria . . . . **51 F8** 12 57N 11 57 E
Geikie →, Canada **71 B8** 57 45N 103 52W
Geikie Gorge △, Australia . . . . **60 C4** 18 3S 125 41 E
Geistown, U.S.A. **84 F6** 40 18N 78 52W
Geita, Tanzania . . . . **54 C3** 2 48S 32 12 E
Gejiu, China . . . . **32 D5** 23 20N 103 10 E
Gel, Meydān-e, Iran . . . . **45 D7** 29 4N 54 50 E
Gela, Italy . . . . **22 F6** 37 4N 14 15 E
Gelang Patah, Malaysia . . . . . **39 d** 1 27N 103 35 E
Gelderland □, Neths. . . . . **15 B6** 52 5N 6 10 E
Geldrop, Neths. . . . . **15 C5** 51 25N 5 32 E
Geleen, Neths. . . . . **15 D5** 50 57N 5 49 E
Gelibolu, Turkey . . . . **23 D12** 40 28N 26 43 E
Gelsenkirchen, Germany . . . . **16 C4** 51 32N 7 6 E
Gelugur, Malaysia . . . . **39 c** 5 22N 100 18 E
Gemas, Malaysia . . . . **39 L4** 2 37N 102 36 E
Gembloux, Belgium . . . . **15 D4** 50 34N 4 43 E
Gemena, Dem. Rep. of the Congo . . . **52 D3** 3 13N 19 48 E
Gemerek, Turkey . . . . **44 B3** 39 15N 36 10 E
Gemlik, Turkey . . . . **23 D13** 40 26N 29 9 E
Gemsbok △, Botswana . . . . . . **56 D3** 25 5S 21 1 E
Genale →, Ethiopia . . . . **47 F2** 6 2N 39 1 E
General Acha, Argentina **94 D3** 37 20S 64 38W
General Alvear, Buenos Aires, Argentina . . . **94 D4** 36 0S 60 0W
General Alvear, Mendoza, Argentina . . . **94 D2** 35 0S 67 40W
General Artigas, Paraguay **94 B4** 26 52S 56 16W
General Belgrano, Argentina . . . **94 D4** 36 35S 58 47W
General Bernardo O'Higgins, Antarctica . . . **5 C18** 63 0S 58 3W
General Cabrera, Argentina . . . **94 C3** 32 53S 63 52W
General Cepeda, Mexico **86 B4** 25 23N 101 27W
General Guido, Argentina **94 D4** 36 40S 57 50W
General Juan Madariaga, Argentina . . . **94 D4** 37 0S 57 0W
General La Madrid, Argentina . . . **94 D3** 37 17S 61 20W
General MacArthur, Phil. . . . . **37 B7** 11 18N 125 28 E
General Martín Miguel de Güemes, Argentina . . . **94 A3** 24 50S 65 0W
General Paz, Argentina **94 B4** 27 45S 57 36W
General Pico, Argentina **94 D3** 35 45S 63 50W
General Pinedo, Argentina . . . **94 B3** 27 15S 61 20W
General Pinto, Argentina **94 C3** 34 45S 61 50W
General Roca, Argentina **96 D3** 39 2S 67 35W
General Santos, Phil. . . . . **37 C7** 6 5N 125 14 E
General Trevino, Mexico **87 B5** 26 14N 99 29W
General Trías, Mexico **86 B3** 28 21N 106 22W
General Viamonte, Argentina . . . **94 D3** 35 1S 61 3W
General Villegas, Argentina . . . **94 D3** 35 5S 63 0W
Genesee, Idaho, U.S.A. **76 C5** 46 33N 116 56W
Genesee, Pa., U.S.A. **84 E7** 41 59N 77 54W
Genesee →, U.S.A. **84 C7** 43 16N 77 36W
Geneseo, Ill., U.S.A. **80 E9** 41 27N 90 9W
Geneseo, N.Y., U.S.A. **84 D7** 42 48N 77 49W
Geneva = Genève, Switz. . . . . **20 C7** 46 12N 6 9 E
Geneva, Ala., U.S.A. **83 K3** 31 2N 85 52W
Geneva, N.Y., U.S.A. **84 D8** 42 52N 76 59W
Geneva, Nebr., U.S.A. **80 E6** 40 32N 97 36W
Geneva, Ohio, U.S.A. **84 E4** 41 48N 80 57W
Geneva, L. = Léman, L., Europe . . . **20 C7** 46 26N 6 30 E
Geneva, L., U.S.A. **82 D1** 42 38N 88 30W
Genève, Switz. . . . . **20 C7** 46 12N 6 9 E
Genil →, Spain **21 D3** 37 42N 5 19W
Genk, Belgium . . . . **15 D5** 50 58N 5 32 E
Gennargentu, Mti. del, Italy . . . **22 D3** 40 1N 9 19 E
Genoa = Génova, Italy . . . . . . **20 D8** 44 25N 8 57 E
Genoa, Australia . . . . **63 F4** 37 29S 149 35 E
Genoa, N.Y., U.S.A. **85 D8** 42 40N 76 32W
Genoa, Nebr., U.S.A. **80 E6** 41 27N 97 44W
Genoa, Nev., U.S.A. **78 F7** 39 2N 119 50W
Génova, Italy . . . . **20 D8** 44 25N 8 57 E
Génova, G. di, Italy . . . . **22 C3** 44 0N 9 0 E
Genriyetty, Ostrov, Russia . . . **29 B16** 77 6N 156 30 E
Gent, Belgium . . . . **15 C3** 51 2N 3 42 E
Genteng, Bali, Indonesia . . . . **37 J17** 8 22S 114 9 E
Genteng, Jawa, Indonesia . . . . **37 G12** 7 22S 106 24 E
Genyem, Indonesia . . . . **37 E10** 2 46S 140 12 E
Geographe B., Australia . . . . . **61 F2** 33 30S 115 15 E
Geographe Chan., Australia . . . **61 D1** 24 30S 113 0 E
Georg Forster, Antarctica . . . . **5 D3** 71 0S 12 0 E
Georg von Neumayer, Antarctica . . . **5 D17** 71 0S 68 30W
Georga, Zemlya, Russia . . . . . **28 A5** 80 30N 49 0 E
George, S. Africa . . . . **56 E3** 33 58S 22 29 E
George →, Canada **73 A6** 58 49N 66 10W
George, L., N.S.W., Australia . . . **63 F4** 35 10S 149 25 E
George, L., S. Austral., Australia . . . **63 F3** 37 25S 140 0 E
George, L., W. Austral., Australia . . . **60 D3** 22 45S 123 40 E
George, L., Uganda . . . . **54 B3** 0 5N 30 10 E
George, L., Fla., U.S.A. **83 L5** 29 17N 81 36W
George, L., N.Y., U.S.A. **85 C11** 43 37N 73 33W
George Gill Ra., Australia . . . . **60 D5** 24 22S 131 45 E
George Pt., Australia . . . . **62 J6** 20 6S 148 36 E
George River = Kangiqsualujjuaq, Canada . . . **69 C13** 58 30N 65 59W
George Sound, N.Z. . . . . **59 L1** 44 52S 167 25 E
George Town, Australia . . . . . **63 G4** 41 6S 146 49 E
George Town, Bahamas **88 B4** 23 33N 75 47W
George Town, Cayman Is. **88 C3** 19 20N 81 24W
George Town, Malaysia . . . . . **39 c** 5 25N 100 20 E

George V Land, Antarctica . . . **5 C10** 69 0S 148 0 E
George VI Sound, Antarctica . . . **5 D17** 71 0S 68 0W
George West, U.S.A. **81 L5** 28 20N 98 7W
Georgetown = Janjanbureh, Gambia . . . **50 F3** 13 30N 14 47W
Georgetown, Australia . . . . . . **62 B3** 18 17S 143 33 E
Georgetown, Ont., Canada . . . **84 C5** 43 40N 79 56W
Georgetown, P.E.I., Canada . . . **73 C7** 46 13N 62 24W
Georgetown, Guyana **92 B7** 6 50N 58 12W
Georgetown, Calif., U.S.A. . . . **78 G6** 38 54N 120 50W
Georgetown, Colo., U.S.A. . . . **76 G11** 39 42N 105 42W
Georgetown, Ky., U.S.A. **82 F3** 38 13N 84 33W
Georgetown, N.Y., U.S.A. . . . **85 D9** 42 46N 75 44W
Georgetown, Ohio, U.S.A. . . . **82 F4** 38 52N 83 54W
Georgetown, S.C., U.S.A. **83 J6** 33 23N 79 17W
Georgetown, Tex., U.S.A. **81 K6** 30 38N 97 41W
Georgia □, U.S.A. **83 K5** 32 50N 83 15W
Georgia ■, Asia . . . . **19 F7** 42 0N 43 0 E
Georgia, Str. of, Canada **70 D4** 49 25N 124 0W
Georgian B., Canada **84 A4** 45 15N 81 0W
Georgian Bay Islands △, Canada . . . **84 B5** 44 53N 79 52W
Georgina →, Australia . . . . . . **62 C2** 23 30S 139 47 E
Georgina I., Canada **84 B5** 44 22N 79 17W
Georgiyevsk, Russia . . . . **19 F7** 44 12N 43 28 E
Gera, Germany . . . . **16 C7** 50 53N 12 4 E
Geraardsbergen, Belgium . . . . **15 D3** 50 45N 3 53 E
Geral, Serra, Brazil **95 B6** 26 25S 50 0W
Geral de Goiás, Serra, Brazil . . . **93 F9** 12 0S 46 0W
Geraldine, U.S.A. **76 C8** 47 36N 110 16W
Geraldton, Australia . . . . **61 E1** 28 48S 114 32 E
Geraldton, Canada **72 C2** 49 44N 86 59W
Gereshk, Afghan. . . . . **40 D4** 31 47N 64 35 E
Gerik, Malaysia . . . . **39 K3** 5 50N 101 15 E
Gering, U.S.A. **80 E3** 41 50N 103 40W
Gerlach, U.S.A. **76 F4** 40 39N 119 21W
Germansen Landing, Canada . . . **70 B4** 55 43N 124 40W
Germantown, U.S.A. **81 M10** 35 5N 89 49W
Germany ■, Europe . . . . **16 C6** 51 0N 10 0 E
Germī, Iran . . . . **45 B6** 39 1N 48 3 E
Germiston, S. Africa . . . . **57 D4** 26 15S 28 10 E
Gernika-Lumo, Spain **21 A4** 43 19N 2 40W
Gero, Japan . . . . **31 G8** 35 48N 137 14 E
Gerokgak, Indonesia . . . . **37 J17** 8 11S 114 27 E
Gerona = Girona, Spain . . . . . **21 B7** 41 58N 2 46 E
Gerrard, Canada **70 C5** 50 30N 117 17W
Gertak Sanggul, Malaysia . . . . **39 c** 5 17N 100 12 E
Gertak Sanggul, Tanjung, Malaysia . . . **39 c** 5 16N 100 11 E
Gerung, Indonesia . . . . **37 K19** 8 43S 116 7 E
Geser, Indonesia . . . . **37 E8** 3 50S 130 54 E
Getafe, Spain **21 B4** 40 18N 3 44W
Gettysburg, Pa., U.S.A. **82 F7** 39 50N 77 14W
Gettysburg, S. Dak., U.S.A. . . . **80 C5** 45 1N 99 57W
Getxo, Spain **21 A4** 43 21N 2 59W
Getz Ice Shelf, Antarctica **5 D14** 75 0S 130 0W
Geyser, U.S.A. **76 C8** 47 16N 110 30W
Geyserville, U.S.A. **78 G4** 38 42N 122 54W
Ghaggar →, India . . . . **42 E6** 29 30N 74 53 E
Ghaghara →, India . . . . **43 G11** 25 45N 84 40 E
Ghaghat →, Bangla. . . . . **43 G13** 25 19N 89 38 E
Ghagra, India . . . . **43 H11** 23 17N 84 33 E
Ghagra →, India . . . . **43 F9** 27 29N 81 9 E
Ghana ■, W. Afr. **50 G5** 8 0N 1 0W
Ghansor, India . . . . **43 H9** 22 39N 80 1 E
Ghanzi, Botswana . . . . **56 C3** 21 50S 21 34 E
Ghardaïa, Algeria . . . . **50 B6** 32 20N 3 37 E
Gharyān, Libya . . . . **51 B8** 32 10N 13 0 E
Ghat, Libya . . . . **51 D8** 24 59N 10 11 E
Ghatal, India . . . . **43 H12** 22 40N 87 46 E
Ghatampur, India . . . . **43 F9** 26 8N 80 13 E
Ghats, Eastern, India . . . . **40 N11** 14 0N 78 50 E
Ghats, Western, India . . . . . . **40 N9** 14 0N 75 0 E
Ghatsila, India . . . . **43 H12** 22 36N 86 29 E
Ghaṭṭī, Si. Arabia . . . . **44 D3** 31 16N 37 31 E
Ghawdex = Gozo, Malta . . . . . **25 C1** 36 3N 14 15 E
Ghazal, Bahr el →, Chad . . . . **51 F9** 13 0N 15 47 E
Ghazâl, Bahr el →, Sudan . . . . **51 G12** 9 31N 30 25 E
Ghaziabad, India . . . . **42 E7** 28 42N 77 26 E
Ghazipur, India . . . . **43 G10** 25 38N 83 35 E
Ghazni, Afghan. . . . . **42 C3** 33 30N 68 28 E
Ghazni □, Afghan. . . . . **40 C6** 32 10N 68 20 E
Ghent = Gent, Belgium . . . . . **15 C3** 51 2N 3 42 E
Gheorghe Gheorghiu-Dej = Oneşti, Romania . . . **17 E14** 46 17N 26 47 E
Ghinah, Wādī al →, Si. Arabia . . . **44 D3** 30 27N 38 14 E
Ghizao, Afghan. . . . . **42 C1** 33 20N 65 44 E
Ghizar →, Pakistan . . . . **43 A5** 36 15N 73 43 E
Ghotaru, India . . . . **42 F4** 27 20N 70 1 E
Ghotki, Pakistan . . . . **42 E3** 28 5N 69 21 E
Ghowr □, Afghan. . . . . **40 C4** 34 0N 64 20 E
Ghudāf, W. al →, Iraq . . . . . . **44 C4** 32 56N 43 30 E
Ghudāmis, Libya . . . . **49 C4** 30 11N 9 29 E
Ghūdāmis □, Libya . . . . **51 B8** 30 25N 10 25 E
Ghughri, India . . . . **43 H9** 22 39N 80 41 E
Ghugus, India . . . . **40 K11** 19 58N 79 12 E
Ghulam Mohammad Barrage, Pakistan . . . **42 G3** 25 30N 68 20 E
Ghūrīān, Afghan. . . . . **40 B2** 34 17N 61 25 E
Gia Dinh, Vietnam . . . . **39 G6** 10 49N 106 42 E
Gia Lai = Plei Ku, Vietnam . . . **38 F7** 13 57N 108 0 E
Gia Nghia, Vietnam . . . . **39 G6** 11 58N 107 42 E
Gia Ngoc, Vietnam . . . . **38 E7** 14 50N 108 58 E
Gia Vuc, Vietnam . . . . **38 E7** 14 42N 108 34 E
Giant Forest, U.S.A. **78 J8** 36 36N 118 43W
Giant Sequoia △, U.S.A. **78 K8** 36 0N 118 32W
Giants Causeway, U.K. **10 A5** 55 16N 6 29W
Gianyar, Indonesia . . . . **37 K18** 8 32S 115 20 E
Giarabub = Al Jaghbūb, Libya . . . **51 C10** 29 42N 24 38 E
Giarre, Italy . . . . **22 F6** 37 43N 15 11 E
Gibara, Cuba **88 B4** 21 9N 76 11W
Gibb River, Australia . . . . **60 C4** 16 26S 126 26 E
Gibbon, U.S.A. **80 E5** 40 45N 98 51W
Gibeon, Namibia . . . . **56 C2** 25 9S 17 43 E
Gibraltar ☑, Europe **21 D3** 36 7N 5 22W
Gibraltar, Str. of, Medit. S. . . . **21 E3** 35 55N 5 40W
Gibraltar Range △, Australia . . . **63 D5** 29 31S 152 19 E
Gibson Desert, Australia . . . . **60 D4** 24 0S 126 0 E
Gibsons, Canada **70 D4** 49 24N 123 32W
Gibsonville, U.S.A. **78 F6** 39 46N 120 54W
Giddings, U.S.A. **81 K6** 30 11N 96 56W
Giebnegáisi = Kebnekaise, Sweden . . . **8 C18** 67 53N 18 33 E
Giessen, Germany . . . . **16 C5** 50 34N 8 41 E
Gīfān, Iran . . . . **45 B8** 37 54N 57 28 E
Gift Lake, Canada **70 B5** 55 53N 115 49W
Gifu, Japan . . . . **31 G8** 35 30N 136 45 E
Gifu □, Japan . . . . **31 G8** 35 40N 137 0 E
Giganta, Sa. de la, Mexico . . . **86 B2** 25 30N 111 30W

Gigha, U.K. **11 F3** 55 42N 5 44W
Giglio, Italy . . . . **22 C4** 42 20N 10 52 E
Gil I., Canada **70 C3** 53 12N 129 15W
Gila →, U.S.A. **77 K6** 32 43N 114 33W
Gila Bend, U.S.A. **77 K7** 32 57N 112 43W
Gila Bend Mts., U.S.A. **77 K7** 33 10N 113 0W
Gila Cliff Dwellings △, U.S.A. . . . **77 K9** 33 2N 108 16W
Gīlān □, Iran . . . . **45 B6** 37 0N 50 0 E
Gilbert →, Australia . . . . **62 B3** 16 35S 141 15 E
Gilbert Is., Kiribati . . . . **64 G9** 1 0N 172 0 E
Gilbert River, Australia . . . . . **62 B3** 18 9S 142 52 E
Gilead, U.S.A. **85 B14** 44 24N 70 59W
Gilgandra, Australia . . . . **63 E4** 31 43S 148 39 E
Gilgil, Kenya . . . . **54 C4** 0 30S 36 20 E
Gilgit, India . . . . **43 B6** 35 50N 74 15 E
Gilgit →, Pakistan . . . . **43 B6** 35 44N 74 37 E
Gili □, Mozam. . . . . **55 F4** 16 39S 38 27 E
Gilimanuk, Indonesia . . . . . . **37 J17** 8 10S 114 26 E
Gillam, Canada **71 B10** 56 20N 94 40W
Gillen, L., Australia . . . . **61 E3** 26 11S 124 38 E
Gilles, L., Australia . . . . **63 E2** 32 50S 136 45 E
Gillette, U.S.A. **80 C2** 44 18N 105 30W
Gilliat, Australia . . . . **62 C3** 20 40S 141 28 E
Gillingham, U.K. . . . . **13 F8** 51 23N 0 33 E
Gilmer, U.S.A. **81 J7** 32 44N 94 57W
Gilmore, L., Australia . . . . . . **61 F3** 32 29S 121 37 E
Gilroy, U.S.A. **78 H5** 37 1N 121 34W
Gimie, Mt, St. Lucia . . . . **89 f** 13 54N 61 0W
Gimli, Canada **71 C9** 50 40N 97 0W
Gin Gin, Australia . . . . **63 D5** 25 0S 151 58 E
Gingin, Australia . . . . **61 F2** 31 22S 115 54 E
Gingindlovu, S. Africa . . . . . . **57 D5** 29 2S 31 30 E
Ginir, Ethiopia . . . . **47 F3** 7 6N 40 40 E
Gióna, Óros, Greece . . . . **23 E10** 38 38N 22 14 E
Gir Hills, India . . . . **42 J4** 21 0N 71 0 E
Girab, India . . . . **42 F4** 26 2N 70 38 E
Girāfi, W. →, Egypt . . . . **46 F3** 29 58N 34 39 E
Girard, Kans., U.S.A. **81 G7** 37 31N 94 51W
Girard, Ohio, U.S.A. **84 E4** 41 9N 80 42W
Girard, Pa., U.S.A. **84 E4** 42 0N 80 19W
Girdle Ness, U.K. **11 D6** 57 9N 2 3W
Giresun, Turkey . . . . **19 F6** 40 55N 38 30 E
Girga, Egypt . . . . **51 C12** 26 17N 31 55 E
Giri →, India . . . . **42 D7** 30 28N 77 41 E
Giridih, India . . . . **43 G12** 24 10N 86 21 E
Girne = Kyrenia, Cyprus . . . . **25 D12** 35 20N 33 20 E
Girona, Spain . . . . **21 B7** 41 58N 2 46 E
Gironde →, France **20 D3** 45 32N 1 7W
Girraween △, Australia . . . . . **63 D5** 28 46S 151 54 E
Giru, Australia . . . . **62 B4** 19 30S 147 5 E
Girvan, U.K. **11 F4** 55 14N 4 51W
Gisborne, N.Z. . . . . **59 H7** 38 39S 178 5 E
Gisenyi, Rwanda . . . . **54 C2** 1 41S 29 15 E
Gislaved, Sweden . . . . **9 H15** 57 19N 13 32 E
Gitega, Burundi . . . . **54 C2** 3 26S 29 56 E
Giuba →, Somali Rep. . . . . . . **47 G3** 1 30N 42 35 E
Giurgiu, Romania . . . . **17 G13** 43 52N 25 57 E
Giza = El Gîza, Egypt . . . . . . **51 C12** 30 0N 31 10 E
Gizhiga, Russia . . . . **29 C17** 62 3N 160 30 E
Gizhiginskaya Guba, Russia . . . **29 C16** 61 0N 158 0 E
Giżycko, Poland . . . . **17 A11** 54 2N 21 48 E
Gjirokastër, Albania . . . . **23 D9** 40 7N 20 10 E
Gjoa Haven, Canada **68 B10** 68 38N 95 53W
Gjøvik, Norway . . . . **9 F14** 60 47N 10 43 E
Glace Bay, Canada **73 C8** 46 11N 59 58W
Glacier △, Canada **70 C5** 51 15N 117 30W
Glacier △, U.S.A. **76 B7** 48 30N 113 18W
Glacier Bay △, U.S.A. **70 B1** 58 45N 136 30W
Glacier Peak, U.S.A. **76 B3** 48 7N 121 7W
Gladewater, U.S.A. **81 J7** 32 33N 94 56W
Gladstone, Queens., Australia . . . **62 C5** 23 52S 151 16 E
Gladstone, S. Austral., Australia . . . **63 E2** 33 15S 138 22 E
Gladstone, Canada **71 C9** 50 13N 98 57W
Gladstone, U.S.A. **82 C2** 45 51N 87 1W
Gladwin, U.S.A. **82 D3** 43 59N 84 29W
Glagah, Indonesia . . . . **37 J17** 8 13S 114 18 E
Gláma = Glomma →, Norway . . . **9 G14** 59 12N 10 57 E
Gláma, Iceland **8 D2** 65 48N 23 0W
Glamis, U.S.A. **79 N11** 32 55N 115 5W
Glamorgan, Vale of □, U.K. . . . **13 F4** 51 28N 3 25W
Glasco, Kans., U.S.A. **80 F6** 39 22N 97 50W
Glasco, N.Y., U.S.A. **85 D11** 42 3N 73 57W
Glasgow, U.K. **11 F4** 55 51N 4 15W
Glasgow, Ky., U.S.A. **82 G3** 37 0N 85 55W
Glasgow, Mont., U.S.A. **76 B10** 48 12N 106 38W
Glasgow, City of □, U.K. **11 F4** 55 51N 4 12W
Glasgow International ✈ (GLA), U.K. . . . **11 F4** 55 51N 4 21W
Glaslyn, Canada **71 C7** 53 22N 108 21W
Glastonbury, U.K. **13 F5** 51 9N 2 43W
Glastonbury, U.S.A. **85 E12** 41 43N 72 37W
Glazov, Russia . . . . **18 C9** 58 9N 52 40 E
Gleichen, Canada **70 C6** 50 52N 113 3W
Gleiwitz = Gliwice, Poland . . . **17 C10** 50 22N 18 41 E
Glen, U.S.A. **85 B13** 44 7N 71 11W
Glen Affric, U.K. **11 D3** 57 17N 5 1W
Glen Canyon, U.S.A. **77 H8** 37 10N 110 40W
Glen Canyon △, U.S.A. **77 H8** 37 15N 111 0W
Glen Canyon Dam, U.S.A. . . . **77 H8** 36 57N 111 29W
Glen Coe, U.K. **11 E3** 56 40N 5 0W
Glen Cove, U.S.A. **85 F11** 40 52N 73 38W
Glen Garry, U.K. **11 D3** 57 3N 5 7W
Glen Innes, Australia . . . . **63 D5** 29 44S 151 44 E
Glen Lyon, U.S.A. **85 E8** 41 10N 76 5W
Glen Mor, U.K. **11 D4** 57 9N 4 37W
Glen Moriston, U.K. **11 D4** 57 11N 4 52W
Glen More △, U.K. **11 D5** 57 8N 3 40W
Glen Robertson, Canada **85 A10** 45 22N 74 30W
Glen Spean, U.K. **11 E4** 56 53N 4 40W
Glen Ullin, U.S.A. **80 B4** 46 49N 101 50W
Glenariff △, Ireland **10 A5** 55 2N 6 0W
Glencoe, Canada **84 D3** 42 45N 81 43W
Glencoe, S. Africa . . . . **57 D5** 28 11S 30 11 E
Glencoe, U.S.A. **80 C7** 44 46N 94 9W
Glendale, Ariz., U.S.A. **77 K7** 33 32N 112 11W
Glendale, Calif., U.S.A. **79 L8** 34 9N 118 15W
Glendale, Zimbabwe . . . . **55 F3** 17 22S 31 5 E
Glendive, U.S.A. **80 B2** 47 7N 104 43W
Glendo, U.S.A. **80 D2** 42 30N 105 2W
Glenelg →, Australia . . . . **63 F3** 38 4S 140 59 E
Glenfield, U.S.A. **85 C9** 43 43N 75 24W
Glengarriff, Ireland **10 E2** 51 45N 9 34W
Glenmont, U.S.A. **84 F2** 40 31N 82 6W
Glenmorgan, Australia . . . . . . **63 D4** 27 14S 149 42 E
Glennallen, U.S.A. **68 B5** 62 7N 145 33W

Glennamaddy, Ireland 10 C3   53 37N   8 33W
Glenns Ferry, U.S.A. 76 E6   42 57N 115 18W
Glenore, Australia .... 62 B3   17 50S 141 12 E
Glenreagh, Australia .... 63 E5   30 2S 153 1 E
Glenrock, U.S.A. 76 E11   42 52N 105 52W
Glenrothes, U.K. 11 E5   56 12N   3 10W
Glens Falls, U.S.A. 85 C11   43 19N   73 39W
Glenside, U.S.A. 85 F9   40 6N   75 9W
Glenties, Ireland 10 B3   54 49N   8 16W
Glenveagh △, Ireland 10 A3   55 3N   8 1W
Glenville, U.S.A. 82 F5   38 56N   80 50W
Glenwood, Canada 73 C9   49 0N   54 58W
Glenwood, Ark., U.S.A. 81 H8   34 20N   93 33W
Glenwood, Iowa, U.S.A. 80 E7   41 3N   95 45W
Glenwood, Minn., U.S.A. 80 C7   45 39N   95 23W
Glenwood, Wash., U.S.A. 78 D5   46 1N 121 17W
Glenwood Springs, U.S.A. ... 76 G10   39 33N 107 19W
Glettinganes, Iceland 8 D7   65 30N   13 37W
Gliwice, Poland .... 17 C10   50 22N   18 41 E
Globe, U.S.A. 77 K8   33 24N 110 47W
Głogów, Poland .... 16 C9   51 37N   16 5 E
Glomma →, Norway .... 9 G14   59 12N   10 57 E
Glorieuses, Is., Ind. Oc. .. 57 A8   11 30S   47 20 E
Glossop, U.K. 12 D6   53 27N   1 56W
Gloucester, Australia ...... 63 E5   32 0S 151 59 E
Gloucester, U.K. 13 F5   51 53N   2 15W
Gloucester, U.S.A. 85 D14   42 37N   70 40W
Gloucester I., Australia ... 62 J6   20 0S 148 30 E
Gloucester Island △, Australia 62 J6   20 2S 148 30 E
Gloucester Point, U.S.A. ... 82 G7   37 15N   76 29W
Gloucestershire □, U.K. 13 F5   51 46N   2 15W
Gloversville, U.S.A. 85 C10   43 3N   74 21W
Glovertown, Canada 73 C9   48 40N   54 3W
Glusk, Belarus .... 17 B15   52 53N   28 41 E
Gmünd, Austria .... 16 D8   48 45N   15 0 E
Gmunden, Austria .... 16 E7   47 55N   13 48 E
Gniezno, Poland .... 17 B9   52 30N   17 35 E
Gnowangerup, Australia ..... 61 F2   33 58S 117 59 E
Go Cong, Vietnam .... 39 G6   10 22N 106 40 E
Gō-no-ura, Japan .... 31 H4   33 44N 129 40 E
Goa, India .... 40 M8   15 33N   73 59 E
Goa □, India .... 40 M8   15 33N   73 59 E
Goalen Hd., Australia ...... 63 F5   36 33S 150 4 E
Goalpara, India .... 41 F17   26 10N   90 40 E
Goaltor, India .... 43 H12   22 43N   87 10 E
Goalundo Ghat, Bangla. ..... 43 H13   23 50N   89 47 E
Goat Fell, U.K. 11 F3   55 38N   5 11W
Goba, Ethiopia .... 47 F2   7 1N   39 59 E
Goba, Mozam. .... 57 D5   26 15S   32 13 E
Gobabis, Namibia .... 56 C2   22 30S   19 0 E
Gobi, Asia .... 34 C6   44 0N 110 0 E
Gobō, Japan .... 31 H7   33 53N 135 10 E
Gochas, Namibia .... 56 C2   24 59S   18 55 E
Godalming, U.K. 13 F7   51 11N   0 36W
Godavari →, India .... 41 L13   16 25N   82 18 E
Godavari Pt., India .... 41 L13   17 0N   82 20 E
Godbout, Canada 73 C6   49 20N   67 38W
Godda, India .... 43 G12   24 50N   87 13 E
Goderich, Canada 84 C3   43 45N   81 41W
Godfrey Ra., Australia ..... 61 D2   24 0S 117 6 E
Godhavn = Qeqertarsuaq,
   Greenland 69 B14   69 15N   53 38W
Godhra, India .... 42 H5   22 49N   73 40 E
Godoy Cruz, Argentina 94 C2   32 56S   68 52W
Gods →, Canada 72 A1   56 22N   92 51W
Gods L., Canada 72 B1   54 40N   94 15W
Gods River, Canada 71 C10   54 50N   94 5W
Godthåb = Nuuk, Greenland .. 69 B14   64 10N   51 35W
Goeie Hoop, Kaap die = Good
   Hope, C. of, S. Africa .. 56 E2   34 24S   18 30 E
Goéland, L. au, Canada 72 C4   49 50N   76 48W
Goélands, L. aux, Canada ... 73 A7   55 27N   64 17W
Goeree, Neths. .... 15 C3   51 50N   4 0 E
Goes, Neths. .... 15 C3   51 30N   3 55 E
Goffstown, U.S.A. 85 C13   43 1N   71 36W
Gogama, Canada 72 C3   47 35N   81 43W
Gogebic, L., U.S.A. 80 B10   46 30N   89 35W
Gogra = Ghaghara →, India .. 43 G11   25 45N   84 40 E
Gogriâl, Sudan .... 51 G11   8 30N   28 8 E
Gohana, India .... 42 E7   29 8N   76 42 E
Goharganj, India .... 42 H7   23 1N   77 41 E
Goi →, India .... 42 H6   22 4N   74 46 E
Goiânia, Brazil 93 G9   16 43S   49 20W
Goiás, Brazil 93 G8   15 55S   50 10W
Goiás □, Brazil 93 F9   12 10S   48 0W
Goio-Erê, Brazil 95 A5   24 12S   53 1W
Gojō, Japan .... 31 G7   34 21N 135 42 E
Gojra, Pakistan .... 42 D5   31 10N   72 40 E
Gökçeada, Turkey .... 23 D11   40 10N   25 50 E
Gökova Körfezi, Turkey ..... 23 F12   36 55N   27 50 E
Gokteik, Burma .... 41 H20   22 26N   97 0 E
Gokurt, Pakistan .... 42 E2   29 40N   67 26 E
Gokwe, Zimbabwe .... 57 B4   18 7S   28 58 E
Gola, India .... 43 E9   28 3N   80 32 E
Golakganj, India .... 43 F13   26 8N   89 52 E
Golan Heights = Hagolan, Syria 46 C4   33 0N   35 45 E
Goläshkerd, Iran .... 45 E8   27 59N   57 16 E
Golchikha, Russia .... 4 B12   71 45N   83 30 E
Golconda, U.S.A. 76 F5   40 58N 117 30W
Gold, U.S.A. 84 E7   41 52N   77 50W
Gold Beach, U.S.A. 76 E1   42 25N 124 25W
Gold Coast, W. Afr. 50 H5   4 0N   1 40W
Gold Hill, U.S.A. 76 E2   42 26N 123 3W
Gold River, Canada 70 D3   49 46N 126 3W
Golden, Canada 70 C5   51 20N 116 59W
Golden B., N.Z. .... 59 J4   40 40S 172 50 E
Golden Gate, U.S.A. 76 H2   37 54N 122 30W
Golden Gate Highlands △,
   S. Africa .... 57 D4   28 40S   28 40 E
Golden Hinde, Canada 70 D3   49 40N 125 44W
Golden Lake, Canada 84 A7   45 34N   77 21W
Golden Spike △, U.S.A. 76 F7   41 37N 112 33W
Golden Vale, Ireland 10 D3   52 33N   8 17W
Goldendale, U.S.A. 76 D3   45 49N 120 50W
Goldfield, U.S.A. 77 H5   37 42N 117 14W
Goldsand L., Canada 71 B8   57 2N 101 8W
Goldsboro, U.S.A. 83 H7   35 23N   77 59W
Goldsmith, U.S.A. 81 K3   31 59N 102 37W
Goldsworthy, Australia ..... 60 D2   20 21S 119 30 E
Goldthwaite, U.S.A. 81 K5   31 27N   98 34W
Goleniów, Poland .... 16 B8   53 35N   14 50 E
Golestãn □, Iran .... 45 B7   37 20N   55 25 E
Golestãnak, Iran .... 45 D7   30 36N   54 14 E
Goleta, U.S.A. 79 L7   34 27N 119 50W
Golfito, Costa Rica 88 E3   8 41N   83 5W
Golfo Aranci, Italy .... 22 D3   40 59N   9 38 E
Goliad, U.S.A. 81 L6   28 40N   97 23W

Golpāyegān, Iran .... 45 C6   33 27N   50 18 E
Golra, Pakistan .... 42 C5   33 37N   72 56 E
Golspie, U.K. 11 D5   57 58N   3 59W
Goma, Dem. Rep. of the Congo 54 C2   1 37S   29 10 E
Gomal Pass, Pakistan .... 42 D3   31 56N   69 20 E
Gomati →, India .... 43 G10   25 32N   83 11 E
Gombari, Dem. Rep. of
   the Congo .... 54 B2   2 45N   29 3 E
Gombe, Nigeria .... 51 F8   10 19N   11 2 E
Gombe →, Tanzania .... 54 C3   4 38S   31 40 E
Gomel = Homyel, Belarus .... 17 B16   52 28N   31 0 E
Gomera, Canary Is. 24 F2   28 7N   17 14W
Gómez Palacio, Mexico 86 B4   25 40N 104 0W
Gomīshān, Iran .... 45 B7   37 4N   54 6 E
Gomogomo, Indonesia .... 37 F8   6 39S 134 43 E
Gomoh, India .... 41 H15   23 52N   86 10 E
Gompa = Ganta, Liberia 50 G4   7 15N   8 59W
Gonābād, Iran .... 45 C8   34 15N   58 45 E
Gonaïves, Haiti 89 C5   19 20N   72 42W
Gonarezhou △, Zimbabwe ..... 55 G3   21 32S   31 55 E
Gonâve, G. de la, Haiti 89 C5   19 29N   72 42W
Gonâve, I. de la, Haiti 89 C5   18 45N   73 0W
Gonbad-e Kāvūs, Iran .... 45 B7   37 20N   55 25 E
Gonda, India .... 43 F9   27 9N   81 58 E
Gondal, India .... 42 J4   21 58N   70 52 E
Gonder, Ethiopia .... 47 E2   12 39N   37 30 E
Gondia, India .... 40 J12   21 23N   80 10 E
Gondola, Mozam. .... 55 F3   19 10S   33 37 E
Gönen, Turkey .... 23 D12   40 6N   27 39 E
Gongbei, China .... 33 G10   22 12N 113 32 E
Gonghe, China .... 32 C5   36 18N 100 32 E
Gongming, China .... 33 F10   22 47N 113 53 E
Gongolgon, Australia .... 63 E4   30 21S 146 54 E
Gongzhuling, China .... 35 C13   43 30N 124 40 E
Gonzales, Calif., U.S.A. ... 78 J5   36 30N 121 26W
Gonzales, Tex., U.S.A. 81 L6   29 30N   97 27W
González Chaves, Argentina . 94 D3   38 2S   60 5W
Good Hope, C. of, S. Africa . 56 E2   34 24S   18 30 E
Gooderham, Canada 84 B6   44 54N   78 21W
Goodhouse, S. Africa .... 56 D2   28 57S   18 13 E
Gooding, U.S.A. 76 E6   42 56N 114 43W
Goodland, U.S.A. 80 F4   39 21N 101 43W
Goodlow, Canada 70 B4   56 20N 120 8W
Goodooga, Australia .... 63 D4   29 3S 147 28 E
Goodsprings, U.S.A. 79 K11   35 49N 115 27W
Goole, U.K. 12 D7   53 42N   0 53W
Goolgowi, Australia .... 63 E4   33 58S 145 41 E
Goomalling, Australia ...... 61 F2   31 15S 116 49 E
Goomeri, Australia .... 63 D5   26 12S 152 6 E
Goonda, Mozam. .... 55 F3   19 48S   33 57 E
Goondiwindi, Australia ..... 63 D5   28 30S 150 21 E
Goongarrie, Australia ...... 61 F3   30 7S 121 30 E
Goongarrie, L., Australia .. 61 F3   30 3S 121 9 E
Goonyella, Australia .... 62 C4   21 47S 147 58 E
Goose →, Canada 73 B7   53 20N   60 35W
Goose Creek, U.S.A. 83 J5   32 59N   80 2W
Goose L., U.S.A. 76 F3   41 56N 120 26W
Gop, India .... 40 H6   22 5N   69 50 E
Gopalganj, India .... 43 F11   26 28N   84 30 E
Göppingen, Germany .... 16 D5   48 42N   9 39 E
Gorakhpur, India .... 43 F10   26 47N   83 23 E
Goražde, Bos.-H. .... 23 C8   43 38N   18 58 E
Gorda, U.S.A. 78 K5   35 53N 121 26W
Gorda, Pta., Canary Is. 24 F2   28 45N   18 0W
Gorda, Pta., Nic. 88 D3   14 20N   83 10W
Gordan B., Australia .... 60 B5   11 35S 130 10 E
Gordon, U.S.A. 80 D3   42 48N 102 12W
Gordon →, Australia .... 63 G4   42 27N 145 30 E
Gordon L., Alta., Canada ... 71 B6   56 30N 110 25W
Gordon L., N.W.T., Canada .. 70 A6   63 5N 113 11W
Gordonvale, Australia ...... 62 B4   17 5S 145 50 E
Gore, Ethiopia .... 47 F2   8 12N   35 32 E
Gore, N.Z. .... 59 M2   46 5S 168 58 E
Gore Bay, Canada 72 C3   45 57N   82 28W
Gorey, Ireland 10 D5   52 41N   6 18W
Gorg, Iran .... 45 D8   29 29N   59 43 E
Gorgān, Iran .... 45 B7   36 50N   54 29 E
Gorgona, I., Colombia 92 C3   3 0N   78 10W
Gorham, U.S.A. 85 B13   44 23N   71 10W
Goriganga →, India .... 43 E9   29 45N   80 23 E
Gorinchem, Neths. .... 15 C4   51 50N   4 59 E
Goris, Armenia .... 19 G8   39 31N   46 22 E
Gorízia, Italy .... 22 B5   45 56N   13 37 E
Gorkiy = Nizhniy Novgorod,
   Russia .... 18 C7   56 20N   44 0 E
Gorkovskoye Vdkhr., Russia . 18 C7   57 2N   43 4 E
Gorleston, U.K. .... 13 E9   52 35N   1 44 E
Görlitz, Germany .... 16 C8   51 9N   14 58 E
Gorlovka = Horlivka, Ukraine 19 E6   48 19N   38 5 E
Gorman, U.S.A. 79 L8   34 47N 118 51W
Gorna Dzhumayo = Blagoevgrad,
   Bulgaria .... 23 C10   42 2N   23 5 E
Gorna Oryakhovitsa, Bulgaria 23 C11   43 7N   25 40 E
Gorno-Altay □, Russia ...... 28 D9   51 0N   86 0 E
Gorno-Altaysk, Russia ...... 28 D9   51 50N   86 5 E
Gornyatski, Russia .... 18 A11   67 32N   64 3 E
Gornyy, Russia .... 30 B6   44 57N 133 59 E
Gorodenka = Horodenka, Ukraine 17 D13   48 41N   25 29 E
Gorodok = Horodok, Ukraine . 17 D12   49 46N   23 32 E
Gorokhov = Horokhiv, Ukraine 17 C13   50 30N   24 45 E
Goromonzi, Zimbabwe .... 55 F3   17 52S   31 22 E
Gorong, Kepulauan, Indonesia 37 E8   3 59S 131 25 E
Gorongosa △, Mozam. .... 57 B5   18 50S   34 29 E
Gorongose →, Mozam. .... 57 C5   20 30S   34 40 E
Gorongoza, Mozam. .... 55 F3   18 44S   34 2 E
Gorongoza, Sa. da, Mozam. .. 55 F3   18 27S   34 2 E
Gorontalo, Indonesia .... 37 D6   0 35N 123 5 E
Gort, Ireland 10 C3   53 3N   8 49W
Gortis, Greece .... 25 D6   35 4N   24 58 E
Gorzów Wielkopolski, Poland 16 B8   52 43N   15 15 E
Gosford, Australia .... 63 E5   33 23S 151 18 E
Goshen, Calif., U.S.A. 78 J7   36 21N 119 25W
Goshen, Ind., U.S.A. 82 E3   41 35N   85 50W
Goshen, N.Y., U.S.A. 85 E10   41 24N   74 20W
Goshogawara, Japan .... 30 D10   40 48N 140 27 E
Gosier, Guadeloupe .... 88 b   16 12N   61 30W
Goslar, Germany .... 16 C6   51 54N   10 25 E
Gospič, Croatia .... 16 F8   44 35N   15 23 E
Gosport, U.K. 13 G6   50 48N   1 9W
Gosse →, Australia .... 62 B1   19 32S 134 37 E
Göta älv →, Sweden .... 9 H14   57 42N   11 54 E
Göta kanal, Sweden .... 9 G16   58 30N   15 58 E
Götaland, Sweden .... 9 G15   57 30N   14 30 E
Göteborg, Sweden .... 9 H14   57 43N   11 59 E
Gotha, Germany .... 16 C6   50 56N   10 42 E
Grand-Vigie, Pte. de la,
   Guadeloupe .... 88 b   16 32N   61 27W
Gothenburg = Göteborg, Sweden 9 H14   57 43N   11 59 E
Gothenburg, U.S.A. 80 E4   40 56N 100 10W

Gotland, Sweden .... 9 H18   57 30N   18 33 E
Gotō-Rettō, Japan .... 31 H4   32 55N 129 5 E
Gotska Sandön, Sweden ...... 9 G18   58 24N   19 15 E
Götsu, Japan .... 31 G6   35 0N 132 14 E
Gott Pk., Canada 70 C4   50 18N 122 16W
Göttingen, Germany .... 16 C5   51 31N   9 55 E
Gottwaldov = Zlín, Czech Rep. 17 D9   49 14N   17 40 E
Goubangzi, China .... 35 D11   41 20N 121 52 E
Gouda, Neths. .... 15 B4   52 1N   4 42 E
Goúdhoura, Ákra, Greece .... 25 E8   34 59N   26 6 E
Gough I., Atl. Oc. 2 G9   40 10S   9 45W
Gouin, Rés., Canada 72 C5   48 35N   74 40W
Goulburn, Australia .... 63 E4   34 44S 149 44 E
Goulburn Is., Australia .... 62 A1   11 40S 133 20 E
Goulimine, Morocco 50 C3   28 56N   10 0W
Gourits →, S. Africa .... 56 E3   34 21S   21 52 E
Goúrnais, Greece .... 25 D7   35 19N   25 16 E
Gourock, U.K. 11 F4   55 57N   4 49W
Gouverneur, U.S.A. 85 B9   44 20N   75 28W
Gouviá, Greece .... 25 A3   39 39N   19 50 E
Governador Valadares, Brazil 93 G10   18 15S   41 57W
Governor's Harbour, Bahamas 88 A4   25 10N   76 14W
Govindgarh, India .... 43 G9   24 23N   81 18 E
Gowan Ra., Australia .... 62 D4   25 0S 145 0 E
Gowanda, U.S.A. 84 D6   42 28N   78 56W
Gower, U.K. 13 F3   51 35N   4 10W
Gowna, L., Ireland 10 C4   53 51N   7 34W
Goya, Argentina 94 B4   29 10S   59 10W
Goyder Lagoon, Australia ... 63 D2   27 3S 138 58 E
Goyllarisquisga, Peru 92 F3   10 31S   76 24W
Goz Beïda, Chad .... 51 F10   12 10N   21 20 E
Gozo, Malta .... 25 C1   36 3N   14 15 E
Graaff-Reinet, S. Africa ... 56 E3   32 13S   24 32 E
Gračac, Croatia .... 16 F8   44 18N   15 57 E
Gracias a Dios, C., Honduras 88 D3   15 0N   83 10W
Graciosa, I., Canary Is. ... 24 E6   29 15N   13 32W
Grado, Spain 21 A2   43 23N   6 4W
Grady, U.S.A. 81 H3   34 49N 103 19W
Grafham Water, U.K. 13 E7   52 19N   0 18W
Grafton, Australia .... 63 D5   29 38S 152 58 E
Grafton, N. Dak., U.S.A. ... 80 A6   48 25N   97 25W
Grafton, W. Va., U.S.A. 82 F5   39 21N   80 2W
Graham, Canada 72 C1   49 20N   90 30W
Graham, U.S.A. 81 J5   33 6N   98 35W
Graham, Mt., U.S.A. 77 K9   32 42N 109 52W
Graham Bell, Ostrov = Greem-
   Bell, Ostrov, Russia .... 28 A7   81 0N   62 0 E
Graham I., Canada 70 C2   53 40N 132 30W
Graham Land, Antarctica 5 C17   65 0S   64 0W
Grahamstown, S. Africa ..... 56 E4   33 19S   26 31 E
Grahamsville, U.S.A. 85 E10   41 51N   74 33W
Grain Coast, W. Afr. 50 H3   4 20N   10 0W
Grajagan, Indonesia .... 37 K17   8 35S 114 13 E
Grajagan, Teluk, Indonesia . 37 K17   8 40S 114 18 E
Grajaú, Brazil 93 E9   5 50S   46 4W
Grajaú →, Brazil 93 D10   3 41S   44 48W
Grampian, U.S.A. 84 F6   40 58N   78 37W
Grampian Highlands = Grampian
   Mts., U.K. 11 E5   56 50N   4 0W
Grampian Mts., U.K. 11 E5   56 50N   4 0W
Grampians, The, Australia .. 63 F3   37 0S 142 20 E
Gran Canaria, Canary Is. ... 24 G4   27 55N   15 35W
Gran Chaco, S. Amer. 94 B3   25 0S   61 0W
Gran Desierto del Pinacate △,
   Mexico 86 A2   31 51N 113 32W
Gran Paradiso, Italy .... 20 D7   45 33N   7 17 E
Gran Sasso d'Itália, Italy . 22 C5   42 27N   13 42 E
Granada, Nic. 88 D2   11 58N   86 0W
Granada, Spain 21 D4   37 10N   3 35W
Granada, U.S.A. 81 F3   38 4N 102 19W
Granadilla de Abona, Canary Is. 24 F3   28 7N   16 33W
Granard, Ireland 10 C4   53 47N   7 30W
Granbury, U.S.A. 81 J6   32 27N   97 47W
Granby, Canada 85 A12   45 25N   72 45W
Granby, U.S.A. 76 F11   40 5N 105 56W
Grand →, Canada 84 D5   42 51N   79 34W
Grand →, Mo., U.S.A. 80 F8   39 23N   93 7W
Grand →, S. Dak., U.S.A. ... 80 C4   45 40N 100 45W
Grand Bahama, Bahamas 88 A4   26 40N   78 30W
Grand Bank, Canada 73 C8   47 6N   55 48W
Grand Bassam, Ivory C. 50 G5   5 10N   3 49W
Grand-Bourg, Guadeloupe .... 88 b   15 53N   61 19W
Grand Canal = Yun Ho →, China 35 E9   39 10N 117 10 E
Grand Canyon, U.S.A. 77 H7   36 3N 112 9W
Grand Canyon △, U.S.A. 77 H7   36 15N 112 30W
Grand Canyon-Parashant △,
   U.S.A. 77 H7   36 30N 113 20W
Grand Cayman, Cayman Is. ... 88 C3   19 20N   81 20W
Grand Centre, Canada 71 C6   54 25N 110 13W
Grand Coulee, U.S.A. 76 C4   47 57N 119 0W
Grand Coulee Dam, U.S.A. ... 76 C4   47 57N 118 59W
Grand Falls, Canada 73 C6   47 3N   67 44W
Grand Falls-Windsor, Canada 73 C8   48 56N   55 40W
Grand Forks, Canada 70 D5   49 0N 118 30W
Grand Forks, U.S.A. 80 B6   47 55N   97 3W
Grand Gorge, U.S.A. 85 D10   42 21N   74 29W
Grand Haven, U.S.A. 82 D2   43 4N   86 13W
Grand I., Mich., U.S.A. 82 B2   46 31N   86 40W
Grand I., N.Y., U.S.A. 84 D6   43 0N   78 58W
Grand Island, U.S.A. 80 E5   40 55N   98 21W
Grand Isle, La., U.S.A. 81 L9   29 14N   90 0W
Grand Isle, Vt., U.S.A. 85 B11   44 43N   73 18W
Grand Junction, U.S.A. 77 G9   39 4N 108 33W
Grand L., Canada 73 C6   45 57N   66 7W
Grand L., Nfld. & L., Canada 73 C8   49 0N   57 30W
Grand L., Nfld. & L., Canada 73 B7   53 40N   60 30W
Grand L., U.S.A. 81 L8   29 55N   92 47W
Grand Lake, U.S.A. 76 F11   40 15N 105 49W
Grand Manan I., Canada 73 D6   44 45N   66 52W
Grand Marais, Canada 80 B9   47 45N   90 25W
Grand Marais, U.S.A. 82 B3   46 40N   85 59W
Grand-Mère, Canada 72 C5   46 36N   72 40W
Grand Portage, U.S.A. 80 B10   47 58N   89 41W
Grand Prairie, U.S.A. 81 J6   32 47N   97 0W
Grand Rapids, Canada 71 C9   53 12N   99 19W
Grand Rapids, Mich., U.S.A. 82 D2   42 58N   85 40W
Grand Rapids, Minn., U.S.A. 80 B8   47 14N   93 31W
Grand St-Bernard, Col du,
   Europe .... 20 D7   45 50N   7 10 E
Grand Staircase-Escalante △,
   U.S.A. 77 H8   37 5N 111 20W
Grand Teton, U.S.A. 76 E8   43 54N 111 50W
Grand Union Canal, U.K. 13 E7   52 7N   0 53W

Grande →, Mendoza, Argentina 94 D2   36 52S   69 45W
Grande →, Bolivia 92 G6   15 51S   64 39W
Grande →, Bahia, Brazil 93 F10   11 30S   44 30W
Grande →, Minas Gerais, Brazil 93 H8   20 6S   51 4W
Grande, Rio →, U.S.A. 81 N6   25 58N   97 9W
Grande Baleine, R. de la →,
   Canada 72 A4   55 16N   77 47W
Grande Cache, Canada 70 C5   53 53N 119 8W
Grande-Entrée, Canada 73 C7   47 30N   61 40W
Grande Prairie, Canada 70 B5   55 10N 118 50W
Grande-Rivière, Canada 73 C7   48 26N   64 30W
Grande-Terre, Guadeloupe ... 88 b   16 20N   61 25W
Grande-Vallée, Canada 73 C6   49 14N   65 8W
Grandfalls, U.S.A. 81 K3   31 20N 102 51W
Grands-Jardins △, Canada ... 73 C5   47 41N   70 51W
Grandview, Canada 71 C8   51 10N 100 42W
Grandview, U.S.A. 76 C4   46 15N 119 54W
Graneros, Chile 94 C1   34 5S   70 45W
Grangemouth, U.K. 11 E5   56 1N   3 42W
Granger, U.S.A. 76 F9   41 35N 109 58W
Grangeville, U.S.A. 76 D5   45 56N 116 7W
Granisle, Canada 70 C3   54 53N 126 13W
Granite City, U.S.A. 80 F9   38 42N   90 9W
Granite Falls, U.S.A. 80 C7   44 49N   95 33W
Granite L., Canada 73 C8   48 8N   57 5W
Granite Mt., U.S.A. 79 M10   33 5N 116 28W
Granite Pk., U.S.A. 76 D9   45 10N 109 48W
Graniteville, U.S.A. 85 B12   44 8N   72 29W
Granity, N.Z. .... 59 J3   41 39S 171 51 E
Granja, Brazil 93 D10   3 7S   40 50W
Granollers, Spain .... 21 B7   41 39N   2 18 E
Grant, U.S.A. 80 E4   40 53N 101 42W
Grant, Mt., U.S.A. 76 G4   38 34N 118 48W
Grant City, U.S.A. 80 E7   40 29N   94 25W
Grant I., Australia .... 60 B5   11 10S 132 52 E
Grant Range, U.S.A. 77 G6   38 30N 115 25W
Grantham, U.K. 12 E7   52 55N   0 38W
Grantown-on-Spey, U.K. 11 D5   57 20N   3 36W
Grants, U.S.A. 77 J10   35 9N 107 52W
Grants Pass, U.S.A. 76 E2   42 26N 123 19W
Grantsville, U.S.A. 76 F7   40 36N 112 28W
Granville, France 20 B3   48 50N   1 35W
Granville, N. Dak., U.S.A. . 80 A4   48 16N 100 47W
Granville, N.Y., U.S.A. 85 C11   43 24N   73 16W
Granville, Ohio, U.S.A. 84 F2   40 4N   82 31W
Granville L., Canada 71 B8   56 18N 100 30W
Graskop, S. Africa .... 57 C5   24 56S   30 49 E
Grass →, Canada 71 B9   56 3N   96 33W
Grass Range, U.S.A. 76 C9   47 0N 109 0W
Grass River △, Canada 71 C8   54 40N 100 50W
Grass Valley, Calif., U.S.A. 78 F6   39 13N 121 4W
Grass Valley, Oreg., U.S.A. 76 D3   45 22N 120 47W
Grasse, France .... 20 E7   43 38N   6 56 E
Grassflat, U.S.A. 84 F6   41 0N   78 6W
Grasslands △, Canada 71 D7   49 11N 107 38W
Grassy, Australia .... 63 G3   40 3S 144 5 E
Graulhet, France .... 20 E4   43 45N   1 59 E
Gravelbourg, Canada 71 D7   49 50N 106 35W
's-Gravenhage, Neths. ...... 15 B4   52 7N   4 17 E
Gravenhurst, Canada 84 B5   44 52N   79 20W
Gravesend, Australia .... 63 D5   29 35S 150 20 E
Gravesend, U.K. .... 13 F8   51 26N   0 22 E
Gravois, Pointe-à-, Haiti .. 89 C5   18 15N   73 56W
Grayling, U.S.A. 82 C3   44 40N   84 43W
Grays, U.K. .... 13 F8   51 28N   0 21 E
Grays Harbor, U.S.A. 76 C1   46 59N 124 1W
Grays L., U.S.A. 76 E8   43 4N 111 26W
Grays River, U.S.A. 78 D3   46 21N 123 37W
Graz, Austria .... 16 E8   47 4N   15 27 E
Greasy L., Canada 70 A4   62 55N 122 12W
Great Abaco I., Bahamas 88 A4   26 25N   77 10W
Great Artesian Basin, Australia 62 C3   23 0S 144 0 E
Great Australian Bight, Australia 61 F5   33 30S 130 0 E
Great Bahama Bank, Bahamas 88 B4   23 15N   78 0W
Great Barrier I., N.Z. ..... 59 G5   36 11S 175 25 E
Great Barrier Reef, Australia 62 B4   18 0S 146 50 E
Great Barrington, U.S.A. ... 85 D11   42 12N   73 22W
Great Basalt Wall △, Australia 62 B4   19 52S 145 43 E
Great Basin, U.S.A. 76 G5   40 0N 117 0W
Great Basin △, U.S.A. 76 G6   38 55N 114 14W
Great Bear →, Canada 68 B7   65 0N 124 0W
Great Bear L., Canada 68 B7   65 30N 120 0W
Great Belt = Store Bælt, Denmark 9 J14   55 20N   11 0 E
Great Bend, Kans., U.S.A. .. 80 F5   38 22N   98 46W
Great Bend, Pa., U.S.A. 85 E9   41 58N   75 45W
Great Blasket I., Ireland .. 10 D1   52 6N   10 32W
Great Britain, Europe 6 E5   54 0N   2 15W
Great Camanoe, Br. Virgin Is. 89 e   18 30N   64 35W
Great Codroy, Canada 73 C8   47 51N   59 16W
Great Dividing Ra., Australia 62 C4   23 0S 146 0 E
Great Driffield = Driffield, U.K. 12 C7   54 0N   0 26W
Great Exuma I., Bahamas 88 B4   23 30N   75 50W
Great Falls, U.S.A. 76 C8   47 30N 111 17W
Great Fish = Groot Vis →,
   S. Africa .... 56 E4   33 28S   27 5 E
Great Guana Cay, Bahamas ... 88 B4   24 0N   76 20W
Great Inagua I., Bahamas ... 89 B5   21 0N   73 20W
Great Indian Desert = Thar
   Desert, India .... 42 F5   28 0N   72 0 E
Great Karoo, S. Africa ..... 56 E3   31 55S   21 0 E
Great Lake, Australia ...... 63 G4   41 50S 146 40 E
Great Lakes, N. Amer. 66 E11   46 0N   84 0W
Great Malvern, U.K. 13 E5   52 7N   2 18W
Great Miami →, U.S.A. 82 F3   39 20N   84 40W
Great Ormes Head, U.K. 12 D4   53 20N   3 52W
Great Ouse →, U.K. .... 12 E8   52 48N   0 21 E
Great Palm I., Australia ... 62 B4   18 45S 146 40 E
Great Pedro Bluff, Jamaica . 88 a   17 51N   77 44W
Great Plains, N. Amer. 66 E9   47 0N 105 0W
Great Ruaha →, Tanzania .... 54 D4   7 56S   37 52 E
Great Sacandaga Res., U.S.A. 85 C10   43 6N   74 16W
Great Saint Bernard Pass =
   Grand St-Bernard, Col du,
   Europe .... 20 D7   45 50N   7 10 E
Great Salt L., U.S.A. 76 F7   41 15N 112 40W
Great Salt Lake Desert, U.S.A. 76 F7   40 50N 113 30W
Great Salt Plains L., U.S.A. 81 G5   36 45N   98 8W
Great Sand Dunes △, U.S.A. . 77 H11   37 48N 105 45W
Great Sandy, Australia ..... 63 D5   26 13S 153 2 E
Great Sandy Desert, Australia 60 D3   21 0S 124 0 E
Great Sangi = Sangihe, Pulau,
   Indonesia .... 37 D7   3 35N 125 30 E
Great Skellig, Ireland 10 E1   51 47N   10 33W
Great Slave L., Canada 70 A5   61 23N 115 38W
Great Smoky Mts. △, U.S.A. . 83 H4   35 40N   83 40W

Great Snow Mt., Canada 70 B4 57 26N 124 0W
Great Stour = Stour →, U.K. .. 13 F9 51 18N 1 22 E
Great Victoria Desert, Australia 61 E4 29 30S 126 30 E
Great Wall, Antarctica 5 C18 62 30S 58 0W
Great Wall, China .... 34 E5 38 30N 109 30 E
Great Whernside, U.K. 12 C6 54 10N 1 58W
Great Yarmouth, U.K. .... 13 E9 52 37N 1 44 E
Great Zab = Zāb al Kabir →, Iraq 44 C4 36 1N 43 24 E
Great Zimbabwe, Zimbabwe .... 55 G3 20 16S 30 54 E
Greater Antilles, W. Indies 89 C5 17 40N 74 0W
Greater London □, U.K. 13 F7 51 31N 0 6W
Greater Manchester □, U.K. ... 12 D5 53 30N 2 15W
Greater St. Lucia Wetlands △,
  S. Africa .... 57 D5 28 6S 32 27 E
Greater Sudbury = Sudbury,
  Canada 72 C3 46 30N 81 0W
Greco, C., Cyprus .... 25 E13 34 57N 34 5 E
Gredos, Sierra de, Spain 21 B3 40 20N 5 0W
Greece, U.S.A. 84 C7 43 13N 77 41W
Greece ■, Europe .... 23 E9 40 0N 23 0 E
Greeley, Colo., U.S.A. 80 E2 40 25N 104 42W
Greeley, Nebr., U.S.A. 80 E5 41 33N 98 32W
Greem-Bell, Ostrov, Russia .... 28 A7 81 0N 62 0 E
Green →, Ky., U.S.A. 82 G2 37 54N 87 30W
Green →, Utah, U.S.A. 77 G9 38 11N 109 53W
Green B., U.S.A. 82 C2 45 0N 87 30W
Green Bay, U.S.A. 82 C2 44 31N 88 0W
Green C., Australia .... 63 F5 37 13S 150 1 E
Green Cove Springs, U.S.A. 83 L5 29 59N 81 42W
Green Lake, Canada 71 C7 54 17N 107 47W
Green Mts., U.S.A. 85 B12 43 45N 72 45W
Green River, Utah, U.S.A. 77 G8 38 59N 110 10W
Green River, Wyo., U.S.A. 76 F9 41 32N 109 28W
Green Valley, U.S.A. 77 L8 31 52N 110 56W
Greenbank, U.S.A. 78 B4 48 6N 122 34W
Greenbush, Mich., U.S.A. 84 B1 44 35N 83 19W
Greenbush, Minn., U.S.A. 80 A6 48 42N 96 11W
Greencastle, U.S.A. 82 F2 39 38N 86 52W
Greene, U.S.A. 85 D9 42 20N 75 46W
Greenfield, Calif., U.S.A. 78 J5 36 19N 121 15W
Greenfield, Calif., U.S.A. 79 K8 35 15N 119 0W
Greenfield, Ind., U.S.A. 82 F3 39 47N 85 46W
Greenfield, Iowa, U.S.A. 80 E7 41 18N 94 28W
Greenfield, Mass., U.S.A. 85 D12 42 35N 72 36W
Greenfield, Mo., U.S.A. 81 G8 37 25N 93 51W
Greenfield Park, Canada 85 A11 45 29N 73 29W
Greenland ☒, N. Amer. 4 C5 66 0N 45 0W
Greenland Sea, Arctic 4 B7 73 0N 10 0W
Greenock, U.K. 11 F4 55 57N 4 46W
Greenore, Ireland 10 B5 54 2N 6 8W
Greenore Pt., Ireland 10 D5 52 14N 6 19W
Greenough, Australia .... 61 E1 28 58S 114 43 E
Greenough →, Australia ...... 61 E1 28 51S 114 38 E
Greenough Pt., Canada 84 B3 44 58N 81 26W
Greenport, U.S.A. 85 E12 41 6N 72 22W
Greensboro, Ga., U.S.A. 83 J4 33 35N 83 11W
Greensboro, N.C., U.S.A. 83 G6 36 4N 79 48W
Greensboro, Vt., U.S.A. 85 B12 44 36N 72 18W
Greensburg, Ind., U.S.A. 82 F3 39 20N 85 29W
Greensburg, Kans., U.S.A. 81 G5 37 36N 99 18W
Greensburg, Pa., U.S.A. 84 F5 40 18N 79 33W
Greenstone Pt., U.K. 11 D3 57 55N 5 37W
Greenvale, Australia .... 62 B4 18 59S 145 7 E
Greenville, Ala., U.S.A. 83 K2 31 50N 86 38W
Greenville, Calif., U.S.A. 78 E6 40 8N 120 57W
Greenville, Maine, U.S.A. 83 C11 45 28N 69 35W
Greenville, Mich., U.S.A. 81 D3 43 11N 85 15W
Greenville, Miss., U.S.A. 81 J9 33 24N 91 4W
Greenville, Mo., U.S.A. 81 G9 37 8N 90 27W
Greenville, N.C., U.S.A. 83 H7 35 37N 77 23W
Greenville, N.H., U.S.A. 85 D13 42 46N 71 49W
Greenville, N.Y., U.S.A. 85 D10 42 25N 74 1W
Greenville, Ohio, U.S.A. 82 E3 40 6N 84 38W
Greenville, Pa., U.S.A. 84 E4 41 24N 80 23W
Greenville, S.C., U.S.A. 83 H4 34 51N 82 24W
Greenville, Tenn., U.S.A. 83 G4 36 13N 82 51W
Greenville, Tex., U.S.A. 81 J6 33 8N 96 7W
Greenwater Lake △, Canada .. 71 C8 52 32N 103 30W
Greenwich, Conn., U.S.A. 85 E11 41 2N 73 38W
Greenwich, N.Y., U.S.A. 85 C11 43 5N 73 30W
Greenwich, Ohio, U.S.A. 84 E2 41 2N 82 31W
Greenwich □, U.K. .... 13 F8 51 29N 0 1 E
Greenwood, Canada 70 D5 49 10N 118 40W
Greenwood, Ark., U.S.A. 81 H7 35 13N 94 16W
Greenwood, Ind., U.S.A. 82 F2 39 37N 86 7W
Greenwood, Miss., U.S.A. 81 J9 33 31N 90 11W
Greenwood, S.C., U.S.A. 83 H4 34 12N 82 10W
Greenwood, Mt., Australia .... 60 B5 13 48S 130 4 E
Gregory, U.S.A. 80 D5 43 14N 99 20W
Gregory △, Australia .... 60 C5 15 38S 131 15 E
Gregory →, Australia .... 62 B2 17 53S 139 17 E
Gregory, L., S. Austral., Australia 63 D2 28 55S 139 0 E
Gregory, L., W. Austral.,
  Australia .... 61 E2 25 38S 119 58 E
Gregory Downs, Australia ..... 62 B2 18 35S 138 45 E
Gregory L., Australia .... 60 D4 20 0S 127 40 E
Gregory Ra., Queens., Australia 62 B3 19 30S 143 40 E
Gregory Ra., W. Austral.,
  Australia .... 60 D3 21 20S 121 12 E
Greifswald, Germany .... 16 A7 54 5N 13 23 E
Greiz, Germany .... 16 C7 50 39N 12 10 E
Gremikha, Russia .... 18 A6 67 59N 39 47 E
Grenå, Denmark .... 9 H14 56 25N 10 53 E
Grenada, U.S.A. 81 J10 33 47N 89 49W
Grenada ■, W. Indies 89 D7 12 10N 61 40W
Grenadier I., U.S.A. 85 B8 44 3N 76 22W
Grenadines, St. Vincent 89 D7 12 40N 61 20W
Grenen, Denmark .... 9 H14 57 44N 10 40 E
Grenfell, Australia .... 63 E4 33 52S 148 8 E
Grenfell, Canada 71 C8 50 30N 102 56W
Grenoble, France .... 20 D6 45 12N 5 42 E
Grenville, C., Australia .... 62 A3 12 0S 143 13 E
Grenville Chan., Canada 70 C3 53 40N 129 46W
Gresham, U.S.A. 78 E4 45 30N 122 26W
Gresik, Indonesia .... 37 G15 7 13S 112 38 E
Gretna, U.K. 11 F5 55 0N 3 3W
Grevenmacher, Lux. .... 15 E6 49 41N 6 26 E
Grey →, N.Z. .... 59 K3 42 27S 171 12 E
Grey, C., Australia .... 62 A2 13 0S 136 35 E
Grey Ra., Australia .... 63 D3 27 0S 143 30 E
Greybull, U.S.A. 76 D9 44 30N 108 3W
Greymouth, N.Z. .... 59 K3 42 29S 171 13 E
Greystones, Ireland 10 C5 53 9N 6 5W
Greytown, N.Z. .... 59 J5 41 5S 175 29 E

Greytown, S. Africa .... 57 D5 29 1S 30 36 E
Gribbell I., Canada 70 C3 53 23N 129 0W
Gridley, U.S.A. 78 F5 39 22N 121 42W
Griekwastad, S. Africa .... 56 D3 28 49S 23 15 E
Griffin, U.S.A. 83 J3 33 15N 84 16W
Griffith, Australia .... 63 E4 34 18S 146 2 E
Griffith, Canada 84 A7 45 15N 77 10W
Griffith I., Canada 84 B4 44 50N 80 55W
Grimaylov = Hrymayliv, Ukraine 17 D14 49 20N 26 5 E
Grimes, U.S.A. 78 F5 39 4N 121 54W
Grimsay, U.K. 11 D1 57 29N 7 14W
Grimsby, Canada 84 C5 43 12N 79 34W
Grimsby, U.K. 12 D7 53 34N 0 5W
Grimsey, Iceland 8 C5 66 33N 17 58W
Grimshaw, Canada 70 B5 56 10N 117 40W
Grimstad, Norway .... 9 G13 58 20N 8 35 E
Grindstone I., Canada 85 B8 44 43N 76 14W
Grinnell, U.S.A. 80 E8 41 45N 92 43W
Gris-Nez, C., France .... 20 A4 50 52N 1 35 E
Groais I., Canada 73 B8 50 55N 55 35W
Groblersdal, S. Africa .... 57 D4 25 15S 29 25 E
Grodno = Hrodna, Belarus .... 17 B12 53 42N 23 52 E
Grodzyanka = Hrodzyanka,
  Belarus .... 17 B15 53 31N 28 42 E
Groesbeck, U.S.A. 81 K6 31 32N 96 31W
Grójec, Poland .... 17 C11 51 50N 20 58 E
Grong, Norway .... 8 D15 64 25N 12 8 E
Groningen, Neths. .... 15 A6 53 15N 6 35 E
Groningen □, Neths. .... 15 A6 53 16N 6 40 E
Groom, U.S.A. 81 H4 35 12N 101 6W
Groot →, S. Africa .... 56 E3 33 45S 24 36 E
Groot Berg →, S. Africa ..... 56 E2 32 47S 18 8 E
Groot-Brakrivier, S. Africa .... 56 E3 34 2S 22 18 E
Groot Karasberge, Namibia .... 56 D2 27 20S 18 40 E
Groot-Kei →, S. Africa .... 57 E4 32 41S 28 22 E
Groot Vis →, S. Africa .... 56 E4 33 28S 27 5 E
Grootdrink, S. Africa .... 56 D3 28 33S 21 42 E
Groote Eylandt, Australia ..... 62 A2 14 0S 136 40 E
Grootfontein, Namibia .... 56 B2 19 31S 18 6 E
Grootlaagte →, Africa .... 56 C3 20 55S 21 27 E
Grootvloer →, S. Africa .... 56 E3 30 0S 20 40 E
Gros C., Canada 70 A6 61 59N 113 32W
Gros Islet, St. Lucia .... 89 f 14 5N 60 58W
Gros Morne △, Canada 73 C8 49 40N 57 50W
Gros Piton, St. Lucia .... 89 f 13 49N 61 5W
Gros Piton Pt., St. Lucia ..... 89 f 13 49N 61 5W
Grossa, Pta., Spain .... 24 B8 39 6N 1 36 E
Grosser Arber, Germany ...... 16 D7 49 6N 13 8 E
Grosseto, Italy .... 22 C4 42 46N 11 8 E
Grossglockner, Austria .... 16 E7 47 5N 12 40 E
Groswater B., Canada 73 B8 54 20N 57 40W
Groton, Conn., U.S.A. 85 E12 41 21N 72 5W
Groton, N.Y., U.S.A. 85 D8 42 36N 76 22W
Groton, S. Dak., U.S.A. 80 C5 45 27N 98 6W
Grouard Mission, Canada 70 B5 55 33N 116 9W
Groundhog →, Canada 72 C3 48 45N 82 58W
Grouw, Neths. .... 15 A5 53 5N 5 51 E
Grove City, U.S.A. 84 E4 41 10N 80 5W
Grove Hill, U.S.A. 83 K2 31 42N 87 47W
Groveland, U.S.A. 78 H6 37 50N 120 14W
Grover City, U.S.A. 79 K6 35 7N 120 37W
Groves, U.S.A. 81 L8 29 57N 93 54W
Groveton, U.S.A. 85 B13 44 36N 71 31W
Groznyy, Russia .... 19 F8 43 20N 45 45 E
Grudziądz, Poland .... 17 B10 53 30N 18 47 E
Gruinard B., U.K. 11 D3 57 56N 5 35W
Grundy Center, U.S.A. 80 D8 42 22N 92 47W
Gruver, U.S.A. 81 G4 36 16N 101 24W
Gryazi, Russia .... 18 D6 52 30N 39 58 E
Gryazovets, Russia .... 18 C7 58 50N 40 10 E
Gua, India .... 41 H14 22 18N 85 20 E
Gua Musang, Malaysia .... 39 K3 4 53N 101 58 E
Guacanayabo, G. de, Cuba ... 88 B4 20 40N 77 20W
Guachipas →, Argentina 94 B2 25 40S 65 30W
Guadalajara, Mexico 86 C4 20 40N 103 20W
Guadalajara, Spain 21 B4 40 37N 3 12W
Guadalcanal, Solomon Is. .... 64 H8 9 32S 160 12 E
Guadales, Argentina 94 C2 34 30S 67 55W
Guadalete →, Spain 21 D2 36 35N 6 13W
Guadalquivir →, Spain 21 D2 36 47N 6 22W
Guadalupe = Guadeloupe ☒,
  W. Indies .... 88 b 16 20N 61 40W
Guadalupe, Mexico 79 N10 32 4N 116 32W
Guadalupe, U.S.A. 79 L6 34 59N 120 33W
Guadalupe →, Mexico 79 N10 32 6N 116 51W
Guadalupe →, U.S.A. 81 L6 28 27N 96 47W
Guadalupe, Sierra de, Spain .. 21 C3 39 28N 5 30W
Guadalupe Bravos, Mexico ... 86 A3 31 20N 106 10W
Guadalupe I., Pac. Oc. 66 G8 29 0N 118 50W
Guadalupe Mts. △, U.S.A. ... 81 K2 31 40N 104 30W
Guadalupe Peak, U.S.A. 81 K2 31 50N 104 52W
Guadalupe y Calvo, Mexico ... 86 B3 26 6N 106 58W
Guadarrama, Sierra de, Spain . 21 B4 41 0N 4 0W
Guadeloupe ☒, Guadeloupe ... 88 b 16 10N 61 40W
Guadeloupe ☒, W. Indies ..... 88 b 16 20N 61 40W
Guadeloupe Passage, W. Indies 89 C7 16 50N 62 15W
Guadiana →, Portugal 21 D2 37 14N 7 22W
Guadix, Spain 21 D4 37 18N 3 11W
Guafo, Boca del, Chile 96 E2 43 35S 74 0W
Guaico, Trin. & Tob. 93 K15 10 35N 61 9W
Guainía →, Colombia 92 C5 2 1N 67 7W
Guaíra, Brazil 95 A5 24 5S 54 10W
Guaíra □, Paraguay 94 B4 25 45S 56 30W
Guaitecas, Is., Chile 96 E2 44 0S 74 30W
Guajará-Mirim, Brazil 92 F5 10 50S 65 20W
Guajira, Pen. de la, Colombia . 92 A4 12 0N 72 0W
Gualán, Guatemala 88 C2 15 8N 89 22W
Gualeguay, Argentina 94 C4 33 10S 59 14W
Gualeguaychú, Argentina 94 C4 33 3S 59 31W
Gualequay →, Argentina 94 C4 33 19S 59 39W
Guam ☒, Pac. Oc. .... 64 F6 13 27N 144 45 E
Guamini, Argentina 94 D3 37 1S 62 28W
Guamúchil, Mexico 86 B3 25 25N 108 3W
Guana I., Br. Virgin Is. ...... 89 e 18 30N 64 30W
Guanabacoa, Cuba 88 B3 23 8N 82 18W
Guanacaste △, Costa Rica ... 88 D2 10 57N 85 30W
Guanacaste, Cordillera del,
  Costa Rica 88 D2 10 40N 85 4W
Guanaceví, Mexico 86 B3 25 40N 106 0W
Guanahani = San Salvador I.,
  Bahamas 89 B5 24 0N 74 40W
Guanajay, Cuba 88 B3 22 56N 82 42W
Guanajuato, Mexico 86 C4 21 0N 101 20W
Guanajuato □, Mexico 86 C4 20 40N 101 20W
Guandacol, Argentina 94 B2 29 30S 68 40W
Guane, Cuba 88 B3 22 10N 84 7W
Guangdong □, China .... 33 D6 23 0N 113 0 E

Guangling, China .... 34 E8 39 47N 114 22 E
Guangrao, China .... 35 F10 37 5N 118 25 E
Guangwu, China .... 34 F3 37 48N 105 57 E
Guangxi Zhuangzu Zizhiqu □,
  China .... 33 D5 24 0N 109 0 E
Guangzhou, China .... 33 D6 23 5N 113 10 E
Guanica, Puerto Rico .... 89 d 17 59N 66 55W
Guanipa →, Venezuela 92 B6 9 56N 62 26W
Guannan, China .... 35 G10 34 8N 119 21 E
Guantánamo, Cuba 89 B4 20 10N 75 14W
Guantánamo B., Cuba 89 C4 19 59N 75 10W
Guantao, China .... 34 F8 36 42N 115 25 E
Guanyun, China .... 35 G10 34 20N 119 18 E
Guápiles, Costa Rica 88 D3 10 10N 83 46W
Guapo B., Trin. & Tob. 93 K15 10 12N 61 41W
Guaporé, Brazil 95 B5 28 51S 51 54W
Guaporé →, Brazil 92 F5 11 55S 65 4W
Guaqui, Bolivia 92 G5 16 41S 68 54W
Guaramacal △, Venezuela 89 E5 9 13N 70 12W
Guarapari, Brazil 95 A7 20 40S 40 30W
Guarapuava, Brazil 95 B5 25 20S 51 30W
Guaratinguetá, Brazil 95 A6 22 49S 45 9W
Guaratuba, Brazil 95 B6 25 53S 48 38W
Guarda, Portugal 21 B2 40 32N 7 20W
Guardafui, C. = Asir, Ras,
  Somali Rep. .... 47 E5 11 55N 51 10 E
Guárico □, Venezuela 92 B5 8 40N 66 35W
Guarujá, Brazil 95 A6 24 2S 46 25W
Guarulhos, Brazil 95 A6 23 29S 46 33W
Guarus, Brazil 95 A7 21 44S 41 20W
Guasave, Mexico 86 B3 25 34N 108 27W
Guasdualito, Venezuela 92 B4 7 15N 70 44W
Guatemala, Guatemala 88 D1 14 40N 90 22W
Guatemala ■, Cent. Amer. ... 88 C1 15 40N 90 30W
Guatopo △, Venezuela 89 D6 10 5N 66 30W
Guatuaro Pt., Trin. & Tob. ... 93 K16 10 19N 60 59W
Guaviare →, Colombia 92 C5 4 3N 67 44W
Guaxupé, Brazil 95 A6 21 10S 46 50W
Guayaguayare, Trin. & Tob. .. 93 K15 10 12N 61 3W
Guayama, Puerto Rico .... 89 d 17 59N 66 7W
Guayaquil, Ecuador 92 D3 2 15S 79 52W
Guayaquil, G. de, Ecuador ... 92 D2 3 10S 81 0W
Guaymas, Mexico 86 B2 27 59N 110 54W
Guba, Dem. Rep. of the Congo 55 E2 10 38S 26 27 E
Gubkin, Russia .... 19 D6 51 17N 37 32 E
Gudbrandsdalen, Norway .... 9 F14 61 33N 10 10 E
Gudur, India .... 40 M11 14 12N 79 55 E
Guecho = Getxo, Spain 21 A4 43 21N 2 59W
Guelmine = Goulimine, Morocco 50 C3 28 56N 10 0W
Guelph, Canada 84 C4 43 35N 80 20W
Guéret, France .... 20 C4 46 11N 1 51 E
Guerneville, U.S.A. 78 G4 38 30N 123 0W
Guernica = Gernika-Lumo, Spain 21 A4 43 19N 2 40W
Guernsey, U.K. 13 H5 49 26N 2 35W
Guernsey, U.S.A. 80 D2 42 19N 104 45W
Guerrero □, Mexico 87 D5 17 30N 100 0W
Gügher, Iran .... 45 D8 29 28N 56 27 E
Guhakolak, Tanjung, Indonesia 37 G11 6 50S 105 14 E
Guia, Canary Is. 24 F4 28 8N 15 38W
Guia de Isora, Canary Is. 24 F3 28 12N 16 46W
Guia Lopes da Laguna, Brazil . 95 A4 21 26S 56 7W
Guiana Highlands, S. Amer. .. 90 C4 5 10N 60 40W
Guidónia-Montecélio, Italy .... 22 C5 42 1N 12 45 E
Guiją, Mozam. .... 57 C5 24 27S 33 0 E
Guildford, U.K. 13 F7 51 14N 0 34W
Guilford, U.S.A. 85 E12 41 17N 72 41W
Guilin, China .... 33 D6 25 18N 110 15 E
Guillaume-Delisle, L., Canada . 72 A4 56 15N 76 17W
Güimar, Canary Is. 24 F3 28 18N 16 24W
Guimarães, Portugal 21 B1 41 28N 8 24W
Guimaras □, Phil. .... 37 B6 10 35N 122 37 E
Guinda, U.S.A. 78 G4 38 50N 122 12W
Guinea, Africa .... 48 F4 8 0N 8 0 E
Guinea ■, W. Afr. 50 F3 10 20N 11 30W
Guinea, Gulf of, Atl. Oc. ..... 49 F4 3 0N 2 30 E
Guinea-Bissau ■, Africa 50 F3 12 0N 15 0W
Güines, Cuba 88 B3 22 50N 82 0W
Guingamp, France 20 B2 48 34N 3 10W
Güiria, Venezuela 92 A6 10 32N 62 18W
Guiuan, Phil. .... 37 B7 11 5N 125 55 E
Guiyang, China .... 32 D5 26 32N 106 40 E
Guizhou □, China .... 32 D5 27 0N 107 0 E
Gujar Khan, Pakistan .... 42 C5 33 16N 73 19 E
Gujarat □, India .... 42 H4 23 20N 71 0 E
Gujranwala, Pakistan .... 42 C6 32 10N 74 12 E
Gujrat, Pakistan .... 42 C6 32 40N 74 2 E
Gulbarga, India .... 40 L10 17 20N 76 50 E
Gulbene, Latvia .... 9 H22 57 8N 26 52 E
Gulf, The, Asia .... 45 E6 27 0N 50 0 E
Gulf Islands △, U.S.A. 83 C2 30 10N 87 10W
Gulfport, U.S.A. 81 K10 30 22N 89 6W
Gulgong, Australia .... 63 E4 32 20S 149 49 E
Gulistan, Pakistan .... 42 D2 30 30N 66 35 E
Gull Lake, Canada 71 C7 50 10N 108 29W
Güllük, Turkey .... 23 F12 37 14N 27 35 E
Gulmarg, India .... 43 B6 34 3N 74 25 E
Gulshad, Kazakhstan .... 28 E8 46 45N 74 25 E
Gulu, Uganda .... 54 B3 2 48N 32 17 E
Gulwe, Tanzania .... 54 D4 6 30S 36 25 E
Gumal →, Pakistan .... 42 D3 31 40N 71 50 E
Gumbaz, Pakistan .... 42 D3 30 2N 69 0 E
Gumel, Nigeria .... 50 F7 12 39N 9 22 E
Gumla, India .... 43 H11 23 3N 84 33 E
Gumlu, Australia .... 62 B4 19 53S 147 41 E
Gumma □, Japan .... 31 F9 36 30N 138 20 E
Gumzai, Indonesia .... 37 F8 5 28S 134 42 E
Guna, India .... 42 G7 24 40N 77 19 E
Gunisao →, Canada 71 C9 53 56N 97 53W
Gunisao L., Canada 71 C9 53 33N 96 15W
Gunjyal, Pakistan .... 42 C4 32 20N 71 55 E
Gunnedah, Australia .... 63 E5 30 59S 150 15 E
Gunnewin, Australia .... 63 D4 25 59S 148 33 E
Gunningbar Cr. →, Australia . 63 E4 31 14S 147 6 E
Gunnison, Colo., U.S.A. 77 G10 38 33N 106 56W
Gunnison, Utah, U.S.A. 76 G8 39 9N 111 49W
Gunnison →, U.S.A. 76 G9 39 4N 108 35W
Gunpowder, Australia .... 62 B2 19 42S 139 22 E
Guntakal, India .... 40 M10 15 11N 77 27 E
Guntersville, U.S.A. 83 H2 34 21N 86 18W
Guntong, Malaysia .... 39 K3 4 36N 101 3 E
Guntur, India .... 41 L12 16 23N 80 30 E
Gunungapi, Indonesia .... 37 F7 6 45S 126 30 E
Gunungsitoli, Indonesia ..... 36 D1 1 15N 97 30 E
Gunza, Angola .... 52 G2 10 50S 13 50 E
Guo He →, China .... 35 H9 32 59N 117 10 E

Guoyang, China .... 34 H9 33 32N 116 12 E
Gupis, Pakistan .... 43 A5 36 15N 73 20 E
Gurdaspur, India .... 42 C6 32 5N 75 31 E
Gurdon, U.S.A. 81 J8 33 55N 93 9W
Gurgaon, India .... 42 E7 28 27N 77 1 E
Gurgueia →, Brazil 93 E10 6 50S 43 24W
Gurha, India .... 42 G4 25 12N 71 39 E
Guri, Embalse de, Venezuela .. 92 B6 7 50N 62 52W
Gurig △, Australia .... 60 B5 11 36S 132 17 E
Gurkha, Nepal .... 43 E11 28 5N 84 40 E
Gurley, Australia .... 63 D4 29 45S 149 48 E
Gurnet Point, U.S.A. 85 D14 42 1N 70 34W
Guro, Mozam. .... 55 F3 17 26S 32 30 E
Gurué, Mozam. .... 55 F4 15 25S 36 58 E
Gurun, Malaysia .... 39 K3 5 49N 100 27 E
Gürün, Turkey .... 19 G6 38 43N 37 15 E
Gurupá, Brazil 93 D8 1 25S 51 35W
Gurupá, I. Grande de, Brazil .. 93 D8 1 25S 51 45W
Gurupi, Brazil 93 F9 11 43S 49 4W
Gurupi →, Brazil 93 D9 1 13S 46 6W
Guruwe, Zimbabwe .... 57 B5 16 40S 30 42 E
Guryev = Atyraū, Kazakhstan . 19 E9 47 5N 52 0 E
Gusau, Nigeria .... 50 F7 12 12N 6 40 E
Gusev, Russia .... 9 J20 54 35N 22 10 E
Gushan, China .... 35 E12 39 50N 123 35 E
Gushgy, Turkmenistan .... 28 F7 35 20N 62 18 E
Gusinoozersk, Russia .... 29 D11 51 16N 106 27 E
Gustavus, U.S.A. 70 B1 58 25N 135 44W
Gustine, U.S.A. 78 H6 37 16N 121 0W
Güstrow, Germany .... 16 B7 53 47N 12 10 E
Gütersloh, Germany .... 16 C5 51 54N 8 24 E
Gutha, Australia .... 61 E2 28 58S 115 55 E
Guthalungra, Australia ...... 62 B4 19 52S 147 50 E
Guthrie, Okla., U.S.A. 81 H6 35 53N 97 25W
Guthrie, Tex., U.S.A. 81 J4 33 37N 100 19W
Guttenberg, U.S.A. 80 D9 42 47N 91 6W
Gutu, Zimbabwe .... 57 B5 19 41S 31 9 E
Guwahati, India .... 41 F17 26 10N 91 45 E
Guy Fawkes River △, Australia . 63 D5 30 0S 152 20 E
Guyana ■, S. Amer. 92 C7 5 0N 59 0W
Guyane française = French
  Guiana ☒, S. Amer. 93 C8 4 0N 53 0W
Guyang, China .... 34 D6 41 0N 110 5 E
Guyenne, France .... 20 D4 44 30N 0 40 E
Guymon, U.S.A. 81 G4 36 41N 101 29W
Guyra, Australia .... 63 E5 30 15S 151 40 E
Guyuan, Hebei, China .... 34 D8 41 37N 115 40 E
Guyuan, Ningxia Huizu, China . 34 G4 36 0N 106 20 E
Güzelyurt = Morphou, Cyprus . 25 D11 35 12N 32 59 E
Guzhen, China .... 35 H9 33 22N 117 18 E
Guzmán, L. de, Mexico 86 A3 31 25N 107 25W
Gvardeysk, Russia .... 9 J19 54 39N 21 5 E
Gwa, Burma .... 41 L19 17 36N 94 34 E
Gwaai, Zimbabwe .... 55 F2 19 15S 27 45 E
Gwaai →, Zimbabwe .... 55 F2 17 59S 26 52 E
Gwabegar, Australia .... 63 E4 30 31S 149 0 E
Gwādar, Pakistan .... 40 G3 25 10N 62 18 E
Gwaii Haanas △, Canada 70 C2 52 21N 131 26W
Gwalior, India .... 42 F8 26 12N 78 10 E
Gwanda, Zimbabwe .... 55 G2 20 55S 29 0 E
Gwane, Dem. Rep. of the Congo 54 B2 4 45N 25 48 E
Gweebarra B., Ireland 10 B3 54 51N 8 23W
Gweedore, Ireland 10 A3 55 3N 8 13W
Gweru, Zimbabwe .... 55 F2 19 28S 29 45 E
Gwinn, U.S.A. 82 B2 46 19N 87 27W
Gwydir →, Australia .... 63 D4 29 27S 149 48 E
Gwynedd □, U.K. 12 E3 52 52N 4 10W
Gyandzha = Gäncä, Azerbaijan . 19 F8 40 45N 46 20 E
Gyaring Hu, China .... 32 C4 34 50N 97 40 E
Gydanskiy Poluostrov, Russia . 28 C8 70 0N 78 0 E
Gympie, Australia .... 63 D5 26 11S 152 38 E
Gyöngyös, Hungary .... 17 E10 47 48N 19 56 E
Győr, Hungary .... 17 E9 47 41N 17 40 E
Gypsum Pt., Canada 70 A6 61 53N 114 35W
Gypsumville, Canada 71 C9 51 45N 98 40W
Gyula, Hungary .... 17 E11 46 38N 21 17 E
Gyumri, Armenia .... 19 F7 40 47N 43 50 E
Gyzylarbat, Turkmenistan .... 28 F6 39 4N 56 23 E
Gyzyletrek, Turkmenistan .... 45 B7 37 36N 54 46 E

H

Ha 'Arava →, Israel .... 46 E4 30 50N 35 20 E
Ha Coi, Vietnam .... 38 B6 21 26N 107 46 E
Ha Dong, Vietnam .... 38 B5 20 58N 105 46 E
Ha Giang, Vietnam .... 38 A5 22 50N 104 59 E
Ha Karmel △, Israel .... 46 C4 32 45N 35 3 E
Ha Tien, Vietnam .... 39 G5 10 23N 104 29 E
Ha Tinh, Vietnam .... 38 C5 18 20N 105 54 E
Ha Trung, Vietnam .... 38 C5 19 58N 105 50 E
Ha Yaek Chalong, Thailand .. 39 a 7 50N 98 22 E
Haaksbergen, Neths. .... 15 B6 52 9N 6 45 E
Haapsalu, Estonia .... 9 G20 58 56N 23 30 E
Haarlem, Neths. .... 15 B4 52 23N 4 39 E
Haast →, N.Z. .... 59 K2 43 50S 169 2 E
Haast Bluff, Australia .... 60 D5 23 22S 132 0 E
Hab →, Pakistan .... 42 G3 24 53N 66 41 E
Hab Nadi Chauki, Pakistan .. 42 G2 25 0N 66 50 E
Habaswein, Kenya .... 54 B4 1 2N 39 30 E
Habay, Canada 70 B5 58 50N 118 44W
Ḥabbānīyah, Iraq .... 44 C4 33 17N 43 29 E
Haboro, Japan .... 30 B10 44 22N 141 42 E
Habshān, U.A.E. .... 45 F7 23 50N 53 37 E
Hachijō-Jima, Japan .... 31 H9 33 5N 139 45 E
Hachinohe, Japan .... 30 D10 40 30N 141 29 E
Hachiōji, Japan .... 31 G9 35 40N 139 20 E
Hachŏn, N. Korea .... 35 D15 41 29N 129 2 E
Hackensack, U.S.A. 85 F10 40 53N 74 3W
Hackettstown, U.S.A. 85 F10 40 51N 74 50W
Hadali, Pakistan .... 42 C5 32 16N 72 11 E
Hadarba, Ras, Sudan .... 51 D13 22 4N 36 51 E
Hadarom □, Israel .... 46 E4 31 0N 35 0 E
Hadd, Ra's al, Oman .... 47 C6 22 35N 59 50 E
Haddington, U.K. 11 F6 55 57N 2 47W
Hadejia, Nigeria .... 50 F7 12 30N 10 5 E
Hadera, Israel .... 46 C3 32 27N 34 55 E
Hadera, N. →, Israel .... 46 C3 32 28N 34 52 E
Haderslev, Denmark .... 9 J13 55 15N 9 30 E
Hadhramaut = Ḥaḑramawt,
  Yemen .... 47 D4 15 30N 49 30 E
Hadiboh, Yemen .... 47 E5 12 39N 54 2 E
Hadong, S. Korea .... 35 G14 35 5N 127 44 E
Ḥaḑramawt, Yemen .... 47 D4 15 30N 49 30 E
Ḥaḑrāniyah, Iraq .... 44 C4 35 38N 43 14 E

Hadrian's Wall, U.K. **12 B5** 55 0N 2 30W
Haeju, N. Korea .... **35 E13** 38 3N 125 45 E
Haenam, S. Korea .... **35 G14** 34 34N 126 35 E
Haenertsburg, S. Africa ...... **57 C4** 24 0S 29 50 E
Haerhpin = Harbin, China .... **35 B14** 45 48N 126 40 E
Hafar al Bāṭin, Si. Arabia .... **44 D5** 28 32N 45 52 E
Hafirat al 'Aydā, Si. Arabia ... **44 E3** 26 26N 39 12 E
Hafit, Oman .... **45 F7** 23 59N 55 49 E
Hafizabad, Pakistan .... **42 C5** 32 5N 73 40 E
Haflong, India .... **41 G18** 25 10N 93 5 E
Hafnarfjörður, Iceland **8 D3** 64 4N 21 57W
Haft Gel, Iran .... **45 D6** 31 30N 49 32 E
Hafun, Ras, Somali Rep. ...... **47 E5** 10 29N 51 30 E
Hagalil, Israel .... **46 C4** 32 53N 35 18 E
Hagen, Germany .... **16 C4** 51 21N 7 27 E
Hagerman, U.S.A. **81 J2** 33 7N 104 20W
Hagerman Fossil Beds △, U.S.A. **76 E6** 42 48N 114 57W
Hagerstown, U.S.A. **82 F7** 39 39N 77 43W
Hagersville, Canada **84 D4** 42 58N 80 3W
Hagfors, Sweden .... **9 F15** 60 3N 13 45 E
Hagi, Japan .... **31 G5** 34 30N 131 22 E
Hagolan, Syria .... **46 C4** 33 0N 35 45 E
Hagondange, France .... **20 B7** 49 16N 6 11 E
Hags Hd., Ireland **10 D2** 52 57N 9 28W
Hague, C. de la, France **20 B3** 49 44N 1 56W
Hague, The = 's-Gravenhage,
 Neths. .... **15 B4** 52 7N 4 17 E
Haguenau, France .... **20 B7** 48 49N 7 47 E
Hai Duong, Vietnam .... **38 B6** 20 56N 106 19 E
Haicheng, China .... **35 D12** 40 50N 122 45 E
Haidar Khel, Afghan. .... **42 C3** 33 58N 68 38 E
Haidarābād = Hyderabad, India **40 L11** 17 22N 78 29 E
Haidargarh, India .... **43 F9** 26 37N 81 22 E
Haifa = Ḥefa, Israel .... **46 C4** 32 46N 35 0 E
Haikou, China .... **33 D6** 20 1N 110 16 E
Ḥā'il, Si. Arabia .... **44 E4** 27 28N 41 45 E
Hailar, China .... **33 B6** 49 10N 119 38 E
Hailey, U.S.A. **76 E6** 43 31N 114 19W
Haileybury, Canada **72 C4** 47 30N 79 38W
Hailin, China .... **35 B15** 44 37N 129 30 E
Hailong, China .... **35 C13** 42 32N 125 40 E
Hailuoto, Finland .... **8 D21** 65 3N 24 45 E
Hainan □, China .... **33 E5** 19 0N 109 30 E
Hainaut □, Belgium .... **15 D4** 50 30N 4 0 E
Haines, Alaska, U.S.A. **70 B1** 59 14N 135 26W
Haines, Oreg., U.S.A. **76 D5** 44 55N 117 56W
Haines City, U.S.A. **83 L5** 28 7N 81 38W
Haines Junction, Canada **70 A1** 60 45N 137 30W
Haiphong, Vietnam .... **32 D5** 20 47N 106 41 E
Haiti ■, W. Indies **89 C5** 19 0N 72 30W
Haiya, Sudan .... **51 E13** 18 20N 36 21 E
Haiyang, China .... **35 F11** 36 47N 121 9 E
Haiyuan, China .... **34 F3** 36 35N 105 52 E
Haizhou, China .... **35 G10** 34 37N 119 7 E
Haizhou Wan, China .... **35 G10** 34 50N 119 20 E
Hajdúböszörmény, Hungary .. **17 E11** 47 40N 21 30 E
Hajipur, India .... **43 G11** 25 45N 85 13 E
Ḥājjī Muḥsin, Iraq .... **44 C5** 32 35N 45 29 E
Ḥājjīābād, Iran .... **45 D7** 28 19N 55 55 E
Ḥājjīābād-e Zarrīn, Iran ..... **45 C7** 33 9N 54 51 E
Hajnówka, Poland .... **17 B12** 52 47N 23 35 E
Hakansson, Mts., Dem. Rep. of
 the Congo .... **55 D2** 8 40S 25 45 E
Hakkâri, Turkey .... **44 B4** 37 34N 43 44 E
Hakken-Zan, Japan .... **31 G7** 34 10N 135 54 E
Hakodate, Japan .... **30 D10** 41 45N 140 44 E
Hakos, Namibia .... **56 C2** 23 13S 16 21 E
Haku-San, Japan .... **31 F8** 36 9N 136 46 E
Haku-San △, Japan .... **31 F8** 36 15N 136 45 E
Hakui, Japan .... **31 F8** 36 53N 136 47 E
Hala, Pakistan .... **40 G6** 25 43N 68 20 E
Halab, Syria .... **44 B3** 36 10N 37 15 E
Ḥalabjah, Iraq .... **44 C5** 35 10N 45 58 E
Halaib, Sudan .... **51 D13** 22 12N 36 30 E
Ḥālat 'Ammār, Si. Arabia .... **44 D3** 29 10N 36 4 E
Halba, Lebanon .... **46 A5** 34 34N 36 6 E
Halberstadt, Germany .... **16 C6** 51 54N 11 3 E
Halcombe, N.Z. .... **59 J5** 40 8S 175 30 E
Halcon, Phil. .... **37 B6** 13 0N 121 30 E
Halden, Norway .... **9 G14** 59 9N 11 23 E
Haldia, India .... **41 H16** 22 5N 88 3 E
Haldimand, Canada **84 D5** 42 59N 79 52W
Haldwani, India .... **43 E8** 29 31N 79 30 E
Hale →, Australia .... **62 C2** 24 56S 135 53 E
Halesowen, U.K. **13 E5** 52 27N 2 3W
Halesworth, U.K. .... **13 E9** 52 20N 1 31 E
Haleyville, U.S.A. **83 H2** 34 14N 87 37W
Halfmoon Bay, N.Z. .... **59 M2** 46 50S 168 5 E
Halfway →, Canada **70 B4** 56 12N 121 32W
Halia, India .... **43 G10** 24 50N 82 19 E
Haliburton, Canada **84 A6** 45 3N 78 30W
Halifax, Australia .... **62 B4** 18 32S 146 22 E
Halifax, Canada **73 D7** 44 38N 63 35W
Halifax, U.K. **12 D6** 53 43N 1 52W
Halifax, U.S.A. **84 F8** 40 25N 76 55W
Halifax B., Australia .... **62 B4** 18 50S 147 0 E
Halifax I., Namibia .... **56 D2** 26 38S 15 4 E
Ḥalīl →, Iran .... **45 E8** 27 40N 58 30 E
Halkirk, U.K. **11 C5** 58 30N 3 29W
Hall Beach = Sanirajak, Canada **69 B11** 68 46N 81 12W
Hall Pen., Canada **69 B13** 63 30N 66 0W
Hall Pt., Australia .... **60 C3** 15 40S 124 23 E
Halland, Sweden .... **9 H15** 57 8N 12 47 E
Halle, Belgium .... **15 D4** 50 44N 4 13 E
Halle, Germany .... **16 C6** 51 30N 11 56 E
Hällefors, Sweden .... **9 G16** 59 47N 14 31 E
Hallett, Australia .... **63 E2** 33 25S 138 55 E
Hallettsville, U.S.A. **81 L6** 29 27N 96 57W
Hallim, S. Korea .... **35 H14** 33 24N 126 15 E
Hallingdalselvi →, Norway ... **9 F13** 60 23N 9 35 E
Hallock, U.S.A. **80 A6** 48 47N 96 57W
Halls Creek, Australia .... **60 C4** 18 16S 127 38 E
Hallsberg, Sweden .... **9 G16** 59 5N 15 7 E
Hallstead, U.S.A. **85 E9** 41 58N 75 45W
Halmahera, Indonesia .... **37 D7** 0 40N 128 0 E
Halmstad, Sweden .... **9 H15** 56 41N 12 52 E
Hälsingborg = Helsingborg,
 Sweden .... **9 H15** 56 3N 12 42 E
Hälsingland, Sweden .... **9 F16** 61 40N 16 5 E
Halstad, U.K. .... **13 F8** 51 57N 0 40 E
Halti, Finland .... **8 B19** 69 17N 21 18 E
Halton □, U.K. **12 D5** 53 22N 2 45W
Haltwhistle, U.K. **12 C5** 54 58N 2 26W
Ḥālūl, Qatar .... **45 E7** 25 40N 52 40 E
Halvad, India .... **42 H4** 23 1N 71 11 E
Ḥalvān, Iran .... **45 C8** 33 57N 56 15 E
Ham Tan, Vietnam .... **39 G6** 10 40N 107 45 E

Ham Yen, Vietnam .... **38 A5** 22 4N 105 3 E
Hamab, Namibia .... **56 D2** 28 7S 19 16 E
Hamada, Japan .... **31 G6** 34 56N 132 4 E
Hamadān, Iran .... **45 C6** 34 52N 48 32 E
Hamadān □, Iran .... **45 C6** 35 0N 49 0 E
Hamāh, Syria .... **44 C3** 35 5N 36 40 E
Hamamatsu, Japan .... **31 G8** 34 45N 137 45 E
Hamar, Norway .... **9 F14** 60 48N 11 7 E
Hamāta, Gebel, Egypt .... **44 E2** 24 17N 35 0 E
Hambantota, Sri Lanka ...... **40 R12** 6 10N 81 10 E
Hamber △, Canada **70 C5** 52 20N 118 0W
Hamburg, Germany .... **16 B5** 53 33N 9 59 E
Hamburg, Ark., U.S.A. **81 J9** 33 14N 91 48W
Hamburg, N.Y., U.S.A. **84 D6** 42 43N 78 50W
Hamburg, Pa., U.S.A. **85 F9** 40 33N 75 59W
Hamd, W. al →, Si. Arabia ... **44 E3** 24 55N 36 20 E
Hamden, U.S.A. **85 E12** 41 23N 72 54W
Häme, Finland .... **9 F20** 61 38N 25 10 E
Hämeenlinna, Finland .... **9 F21** 61 0N 24 28 E
Hamelin Pool, Australia ..... **61 E1** 26 22S 114 20 E
Hameln, Germany .... **16 B5** 52 6N 9 21 E
Hamerkaz □, Israel .... **46 C3** 32 15N 34 55 E
Hamersley Ra., Australia .... **60 D2** 22 0S 117 45 E
Hamhung, N. Korea .... **35 E14** 39 54N 127 30 E
Hami, China .... **32 B4** 42 55N 93 25 E
Hamilton, Australia .... **63 F3** 37 45S 142 2 E
Hamilton, Canada **84 C5** 43 15N 79 50W
Hamilton, N.Z. .... **59 G5** 37 47S 175 19 E
Hamilton, U.K. **11 F4** 55 46N 4 2W
Hamilton, Ala., U.S.A. **83 H1** 34 9N 87 59W
Hamilton, Mont., U.S.A. **76 C6** 46 15N 114 10W
Hamilton, N.Y., U.S.A. **85 D9** 42 50N 75 33W
Hamilton, Ohio, U.S.A. **82 F3** 39 24N 84 34W
Hamilton, Tex., U.S.A. **81 K5** 31 42N 98 7W
Hamilton →, Australia .... **62 C2** 23 30S 139 47 E
Hamilton City, U.S.A. **78 F4** 39 45N 122 1W
Hamilton I., Australia .... **62 J6** 20 21S 148 56 E
Hamilton Inlet, Canada **73 B8** 54 0N 57 30W
Hamilton Mt., U.S.A. **85 C10** 43 25N 74 22W
Hamina, Finland .... **9 F22** 60 34N 27 12 E
Hamirpur, H.P., India .... **42 D7** 31 41N 76 31 E
Hamirpur, Ut. P., India ...... **43 G9** 25 57N 80 9 E
Hamlet, U.S.A. **83 H6** 34 53N 79 42W
Hamley Bridge, Australia .... **63 E2** 34 17S 138 35 E
Hamlin = Hameln, Germany .. **16 B5** 52 6N 9 21 E
Hamlin, N.Y., U.S.A. **84 C7** 43 17N 77 55W
Hamlin, Tex., U.S.A. **81 J4** 32 53N 100 8W
Hamm, Germany .... **16 C4** 51 40N 7 50 E
Ḥammār, Hawr al, Iraq ...... **44 D5** 30 50N 47 10 E
Hammerfest, Norway .... **8 A20** 70 39N 23 41 E
Hammond, Ind., U.S.A. **82 E2** 41 38N 87 30W
Hammond, La., U.S.A. **81 K9** 30 30N 90 28W
Hammond, N.Y., U.S.A. **85 B9** 44 27N 75 42W
Hammondsport, U.S.A. **84 D7** 42 25N 77 13W
Hammonton, U.S.A. **82 F8** 39 39N 74 48W
Hampden, N.Z. .... **59 L3** 45 18S 170 50 E
Hampshire □, U.K. **13 F6** 51 7N 1 23W
Hampshire Downs, U.K. **13 F6** 51 15N 1 10W
Hampton, N.B., Canada **73 C6** 45 32N 65 51W
Hampton, Ont., Canada **84 C6** 43 58N 78 45W
Hampton, Ark., U.S.A. **81 J8** 33 32N 92 28W
Hampton, Iowa, U.S.A. **80 D8** 42 45N 93 13W
Hampton, N.H., U.S.A. **85 D14** 42 57N 70 50W
Hampton, S.C., U.S.A. **83 J5** 32 52N 81 7W
Hampton, Va., U.S.A. **82 G7** 37 2N 76 21W
Hampton Bays, U.S.A. **85 F12** 40 53N 72 30W
Hampton Tableland, Australia **61 F4** 32 0S 127 0 E
Hamyang, S. Korea .... **35 G14** 35 32N 127 42 E
Han Pijesak, Bos.-H. .... **23 B8** 44 5N 18 57 E
Hanak, Si. Arabia .... **44 E3** 25 32N 37 0 E
Hanamaki, Japan .... **30 E10** 39 23N 141 7 E
Hanang, Tanzania .... **54 C4** 4 30S 35 25 E
Hanau, Germany .... **16 C5** 50 7N 8 56 E
Hanbogd = Ihbulag, Mongolia **34 C4** 43 11N 107 10 E
Hancheng, China .... **34 G6** 35 31N 110 25 E
Hancock, Mich., U.S.A. **80 B10** 47 8N 88 35W
Hancock, N.Y., U.S.A. **85 E9** 41 57N 75 17W
Handa, Japan .... **31 G8** 34 53N 136 55 E
Handan, China .... **34 F8** 36 35N 114 28 E
Handeni, Tanzania .... **54 D4** 5 25S 38 2 E
Handwara, India .... **43 B6** 34 21N 74 20 E
Hanegev, Israel .... **46 E4** 30 50N 35 0 E
Hanford, U.S.A. **78 J7** 36 20N 119 39W
Hanford Reach △, U.S.A. **76 C4** 46 40N 119 28W
Hang Chat, Thailand .... **38 C2** 18 20N 99 21 E
Hang Dong, Thailand .... **38 C2** 18 41N 98 55 E
Hangang →, S. Korea .... **35 F14** 37 50N 126 30 E
Hangayn Nuruu, Mongolia ... **32 B4** 47 30N 99 0 E
Hangchou = Hangzhou, China **33 C7** 30 18N 120 11 E
Hanggin Houqi, China .... **34 D4** 40 58N 107 4 E
Hanggin Qi, China .... **34 E5** 39 52N 108 50 E
Hangu, China .... **35 E9** 39 18N 117 53 E
Hangzhou, China .... **33 C7** 30 18N 120 11 E
Hangzhou Wan, China .... **33 C7** 30 15N 120 45 E
Hanhongor, Mongolia .... **34 C3** 43 55N 104 28 E
Ḥanīdḥ, Si. Arabia .... **45 E6** 26 35N 48 38 E
Ḥanīsh, Yemen .... **47 E3** 13 45N 42 46 E
Hankinson, U.S.A. **80 B6** 46 4N 96 54W
Hanko, Finland .... **9 G20** 59 50N 22 57 E
Hanksville, U.S.A. **77 G8** 38 22N 110 43W
Hanle, India .... **43 C8** 32 42N 79 4 E
Hanmer Springs, N.Z. .... **59 K4** 42 32S 172 50 E
Hann →, Australia .... **60 C4** 17 26S 126 17 E
Hann, Mt., Australia .... **60 C4** 15 45S 126 0 E
Hanna, Canada **70 C6** 51 40N 111 54W
Hannah B., Canada **72 B4** 51 40N 80 0W
Hannibal, Mo., U.S.A. **80 F9** 39 42N 91 22W
Hannibal, N.Y., U.S.A. **85 C8** 43 19N 76 35W
Hannover, Germany .... **16 B5** 52 22N 9 46 E
Hanoi, Vietnam .... **32 D5** 21 5N 105 55 E
Hanover = Hannover, Germany **16 B5** 52 22N 9 46 E
Hanover, Canada **84 B3** 44 9N 81 2W
Hanover, S. Africa .... **56 E3** 31 4S 24 29 E
Hanover, N.H., U.S.A. **85 C12** 43 42N 72 17W
Hanover, Ohio, U.S.A. **84 F2** 40 4N 82 16W
Hanover, Pa., U.S.A. **82 F7** 39 48N 76 59W
Hanover, I., Chile **96 G2** 51 0S 74 50W
Hans Lollik I., U.S. Virgin Is. . **89 e** 18 24N 64 53W
Hansdiha, India .... **43 G12** 24 36N 87 5 E
Hansi, India .... **42 E6** 29 10N 75 57 E
Hanson, L., Australia .... **63 E2** 31 0S 136 15 E
Hantsavichy, Belarus .... **17 B14** 52 49N 26 30 E
Hanumangarh, India .... **42 E6** 29 35N 74 19 E
Hanzhong, China .... **34 H4** 33 10N 107 1 E
Hanzhuang, China .... **35 G9** 34 33N 117 23 E
Haora, India .... **43 H13** 22 37N 88 20 E

Haparanda, Sweden .... **8 D21** 65 52N 24 8 E
Happy, U.S.A. **81 H4** 34 45N 101 52W
Happy Camp, U.S.A. **76 F2** 41 48N 123 23W
Happy Valley-Goose Bay, Canada **73 B7** 53 15N 60 20W
Hapsu, N. Korea .... **35 D15** 41 13N 128 51 E
Hapur, India .... **42 E7** 28 45N 77 45 E
Har, Indonesia .... **37 F8** 5 16S 133 14 E
Har-Ayrag, Mongolia .... **34 B5** 45 47N 109 16 E
Har Hu, China .... **32 C4** 38 20N 97 38 E
Har Us Nuur, Mongolia ...... **32 B4** 48 0N 92 0 E
Har Yehuda, Israel .... **46 D3** 31 35N 34 57 E
Ḥaraḍ, Si. Arabia .... **47 C4** 24 22N 49 0 E
Haranomachi, Japan .... **30 F10** 37 38N 140 58 E
Harare, Zimbabwe .... **55 F3** 17 43S 31 2 E
Harbin, China .... **35 B14** 45 48N 126 40 E
Harbor Beach, U.S.A. **84 C2** 43 51N 82 39W
Harbour Breton, Canada **73 C8** 47 29N 55 50W
Harbour Deep, Canada **73 B8** 50 25N 56 32W
Harda, India .... **42 H7** 22 27N 77 5 E
Hardangerfjorden, Norway ... **9 F12** 60 5N 6 0 E
Hardangervidda, Norway .... **9 F12** 60 7N 7 20 E
Hardap □, Namibia .... **56 C2** 24 29S 17 45 E
Hardap Dam, Namibia .... **56 C2** 24 32S 17 50 E
Hardenberg, Neths. .... **15 B6** 52 34N 6 37 E
Harderwijk, Neths. .... **15 B5** 52 21N 5 38 E
Hardey →, Australia .... **60 D2** 22 45S 116 8 E
Hardin, U.S.A. **76 D10** 45 44N 107 37W
Harding, S. Africa .... **57 E4** 30 35S 29 55 E
Harding Ra., Australia .... **60 C3** 16 17S 124 55 E
Hardisty, Canada **70 C6** 52 40N 111 18W
Hardoi, India .... **43 F9** 27 26N 80 6 E
Hardwar = Haridwar, India .. **42 E8** 29 58N 78 9 E
Hardwick, U.S.A. **85 B12** 44 30N 72 22W
Hardy, Pen., Chile **96 H3** 55 30S 68 20W
Hardy, Pte., St. Lucia .... **89 f** 14 6N 60 56W
Hare B., Canada **73 B8** 51 15N 55 45W
Hareid, Norway .... **9 E12** 62 22N 6 1 E
Harer, Ethiopia .... **47 F3** 9 20N 42 8 E
Hargeisa, Somali Rep. .... **47 F3** 9 30N 44 2 E
Hari →, Indonesia .... **36 E2** 1 16S 104 5 E
Haria, Canary Is. **24 E6** 29 8N 13 32W
Haridwar, India .... **42 E8** 29 58N 78 9 E
Harim, Jabal al, Oman ...... **45 E8** 25 58N 56 14 E
Haringhata →, Bangla. ...... **41 J16** 22 0N 89 58 E
Harīrūd →, Asia .... **40 A2** 37 24N 60 38 E
Härjedalen, Sweden .... **9 E15** 62 22N 13 5 E
Harlan, Iowa, U.S.A. **80 E7** 41 39N 95 19W
Harlan, Ky., U.S.A. **83 G4** 36 51N 83 19W
Harlech, U.K. **12 E3** 52 52N 4 6W
Harlem, U.S.A. **76 B9** 48 32N 108 47W
Harlingen, Neths. .... **15 A5** 53 11N 5 25 E
Harlingen, U.S.A. **81 M6** 26 12N 97 42W
Harlow, U.K. .... **13 F8** 51 46N 0 8 E
Harlowton, U.S.A. **76 C9** 46 26N 109 50W
Harnai, Pakistan .... **42 D2** 30 6N 67 56 E
Harney Basin, U.S.A. **76 E4** 43 30N 119 0W
Harney L., U.S.A. **76 E4** 43 14N 119 8W
Harney Peak, U.S.A. **80 D3** 43 52N 103 32W
Härnösand, Sweden .... **9 E17** 62 38N 17 55 E
Harp L., Canada **73 A7** 55 5N 61 50W
Harper, Liberia **50 H4** 4 25N 7 43W
Harrai, India .... **43 H8** 22 37N 79 13 E
Harrand, Pakistan .... **42 E4** 29 28N 70 3 E
Harricana →, Canada **72 B4** 50 56N 79 32W
Harriman, U.S.A. **83 H3** 35 56N 84 33W
Harrington Harbour, Canada . **73 B8** 50 31N 59 30W
Harris, U.K. **11 D2** 57 50N 6 55W
Harris, L., Australia .... **63 E2** 31 10S 135 10 E
Harris, Sd. of, U.K. **11 D1** 57 44N 7 6W
Harris Pt., Canada **84 C2** 43 6N 82 9W
Harrisburg, Ill., U.S.A. **81 G10** 37 44N 88 32W
Harrisburg, Nebr., U.S.A. **80 E3** 41 33N 103 44W
Harrisburg, Pa., U.S.A. **84 F8** 40 16N 76 53W
Harrismith, S. Africa .... **57 D4** 28 15S 29 8 E
Harrison, Ark., U.S.A. **81 G8** 36 14N 93 7W
Harrison, Maine, U.S.A. **85 B14** 44 7N 70 39W
Harrison, Nebr., U.S.A. **80 D3** 42 41N 103 53W
Harrison, C., Canada **73 B8** 54 55N 57 55W
Harrison L., Canada **70 D4** 49 33N 121 50W
Harrisonburg, U.S.A. **82 F6** 38 27N 78 52W
Harrisonville, U.S.A. **80 F7** 38 39N 94 21W
Harriston, Canada **84 C4** 43 57N 80 53W
Harrisville, Mich., U.S.A. **84 B1** 44 39N 83 17W
Harrisville, N.Y., U.S.A. **85 B9** 44 9N 75 19W
Harrisville, Pa., U.S.A. **84 E5** 41 8N 80 0W
Harrodsburg, U.S.A. **82 G3** 37 46N 84 51W
Harrogate, U.K. **12 C6** 54 0N 1 33W
Harrow □, U.K. **13 F7** 51 35N 0 21W
Harrowsmith, Canada **85 B8** 44 24N 76 40W
Harry S. Truman Reservoir,
 U.S.A. **80 F7** 38 16N 93 24W
Harsin, Iran .... **44 C5** 34 18N 47 33 E
Harstad, Norway .... **8 B17** 68 48N 16 30 E
Harsud, India .... **42 H7** 22 6N 76 44 E
Hart, U.S.A. **82 D2** 43 42N 86 22W
Hart, L., Australia .... **63 E2** 31 10S 136 25 E
Hartbees →, S. Africa .... **56 D3** 28 45S 20 32 E
Hartford, Conn., U.S.A. **85 E12** 41 46N 72 41W
Hartford, Ky., U.S.A. **82 G2** 37 27N 86 55W
Hartford, S. Dak., U.S.A. **80 D6** 43 38N 96 57W
Hartford, Wis., U.S.A. **80 D10** 43 19N 88 22W
Hartford City, U.S.A. **82 E3** 40 27N 85 22W
Hartland, Canada **73 C6** 46 20N 67 32W
Hartland Pt., U.K. **13 F3** 51 1N 4 32W
Hartlepool, U.K. **12 C6** 54 42N 1 13W
Hartlepool □, U.K. **12 C6** 54 42N 1 17W
Hartley Bay, Canada **70 C3** 53 25N 129 15W
Hartmannberge, Namibia .... **56 B1** 17 0S 13 0 E
Hartney, Canada **71 D8** 49 30N 100 35W
Harts →, S. Africa .... **56 D3** 28 24S 24 17 E
Hartselle, U.S.A. **83 H2** 34 27N 86 56W
Hartshorne, U.S.A. **81 H7** 34 51N 95 34W
Hartstown, U.S.A. **84 E4** 41 33N 80 23W
Hartsville, U.S.A. **83 H5** 34 23N 80 4W
Hartswater, S. Africa .... **56 D3** 27 34S 24 43 E
Hartwell, U.S.A. **83 H4** 34 21N 82 56W
Harunabad, Pakistan .... **42 E5** 29 35N 73 8 E
Harvand, Iran .... **45 D7** 28 25N 55 43 E
Harvey, Australia .... **61 F2** 33 5S 115 54 E
Harvey, Ill., U.S.A. **82 E2** 41 36N 87 50W
Harvey, N. Dak., U.S.A. **80 B5** 47 47N 99 56W
Harwich, U.K. .... **13 F9** 51 56N 1 17 E
Haryana □, India .... **42 E7** 29 0N 76 10 E
Haryn →, Belarus .... **17 B14** 52 7N 27 17 E
Harz, Germany .... **16 C6** 51 38N 10 44 E

Hasa □, Si. Arabia .... **45 E6** 25 50N 49 0 E
Ḥasanābād, Iran .... **45 C7** 32 8N 52 44 E
Ḥasb, W. →, Iraq .... **44 D5** 31 45N 44 17 E
Hasdo →, India .... **43 J10** 21 44N 82 44 E
Hashimoto, Japan .... **31 G7** 34 19N 135 37 E
Hashtjerd, Iran .... **45 C6** 35 52N 50 40 E
Haskell, U.S.A. **81 J5** 33 10N 99 44W
Haslemere, U.K. **13 F7** 51 5N 0 43W
Hasselt, Belgium .... **15 D5** 50 56N 5 21 E
Hassi Messaoud, Algeria .... **50 B7** 31 51N 6 1 E
Hässleholm, Sweden .... **9 H15** 56 10N 13 46 E
Hastings, N.Z. .... **59 H6** 39 39S 176 52 E
Hastings, U.K. .... **13 G8** 50 51N 0 35 E
Hastings, Mich., U.S.A. **82 D3** 42 39N 85 17W
Hastings, Minn., U.S.A. **80 C8** 44 44N 92 51W
Hastings, Nebr., U.S.A. **80 E5** 40 35N 98 23W
Hastings Ra., Australia ...... **63 E5** 31 15S 152 14 E
Hat Yai, Thailand .... **39 J3** 7 1N 100 27 E
Hatanbulag = Ergel, Mongolia **34 C5** 43 8N 109 5 E
Hatay = Antalya, Turkey ..... **19 G5** 36 52N 30 45 E
Hatch, U.S.A. **77 K10** 32 40N 107 9W
Hatchet L., Canada **71 B8** 58 36N 103 40W
Hateruma-Shima, Japan ..... **31 M1** 24 3N 123 47 E
Hatfield P.O., Australia ...... **63 E3** 33 54S 143 49 E
Hatgal, Mongolia .... **32 A5** 50 26N 100 9 E
Hathras, India .... **42 F8** 27 36N 78 6 E
Hatia, Bangla. .... **41 H17** 22 30N 91 5 E
Hato Mayor, Dom. Rep. **89 C6** 18 46N 69 15W
Hatta, India .... **43 G8** 24 7N 79 36 E
Hattah, Australia .... **63 E3** 34 48S 142 17 E
Hatteras, C., U.S.A. **83 H8** 35 14N 75 32W
Hattiesburg, U.S.A. **81 K10** 31 20N 89 17W
Hatvan, Hungary .... **17 E10** 47 40N 19 45 E
Hau Bon = Cheo Reo, Vietnam **38 B3** 13 25N 108 28 E
Hau Duc, Vietnam .... **38 E7** 15 20N 108 13 E
Haugesund, Norway .... **9 G11** 59 23N 5 13 E
Haukipudas, Finland .... **8 D21** 65 12N 25 20 E
Haultain →, Canada **71 B7** 55 51N 106 46W
Hauraki G., N.Z. .... **59 G5** 36 35S 175 5 E
Haut Atlas, Morocco **50 B4** 32 30N 5 0W
Hautes Fagnes = Hohe Venn,
 Belgium .... **15 D6** 50 30N 6 5 E
Hauts Plateaux, Algeria ..... **48 C4** 35 0N 1 0 E
Havana = La Habana, Cuba .. **88 B3** 23 8N 82 22W
Havana, U.S.A. **80 E9** 40 18N 90 4W
Havant, U.K. **13 G7** 50 51N 0 58W
Havasor = Kiğzi, Turkey ..... **44 B4** 38 18N 43 25 E
Havasu, L., U.S.A. **79 L12** 34 18N 114 28W
Havel →, Germany .... **16 B7** 52 50N 12 3 E
Havelian, Pakistan .... **42 B5** 34 2N 73 10 E
Havelock, Canada **84 B7** 44 26N 77 53W
Havelock, N.Z. .... **59 J4** 41 17S 173 48 E
Havelock, U.S.A. **83 H7** 34 53N 76 54W
Haverfordwest, U.K. **13 F3** 51 48N 4 58W
Haverhill, U.K. .... **13 E8** 52 5N 0 28 E
Haverhill, U.S.A. **85 D13** 42 47N 71 5W
Haverstraw, U.S.A. **85 E11** 41 12N 73 58W
Havirga, Mongolia .... **34 B7** 45 41N 113 5 E
Havířov, Czech Rep. .... **17 D10** 49 46N 18 20 E
Havlíčkův Brod, Czech Rep. .. **16 D8** 49 36N 15 33 E
Havre, U.S.A. **76 B9** 48 33N 109 41W
Havre-Aubert, Canada **73 C7** 47 12N 61 56W
Havre-St.-Pierre, Canada **73 B7** 50 18N 63 33W
Haw →, U.S.A. **83 H6** 35 36N 79 3W
Hawaii □, U.S.A. **74 H16** 19 30N 156 30W
Hawaii I., Pac. Oc. **74 J17** 20 0N 155 0W
Hawaiian Is., Pac. Oc. **74 H17** 20 30N 156 0W
Hawaiian Ridge, Pac. Oc. ... **65 E11** 24 0N 165 0W
Hawarden, U.S.A. **80 D6** 43 0N 96 29W
Hawea, L., N.Z. .... **59 L2** 44 28S 169 19 E
Hawera, N.Z. .... **59 H5** 39 35S 174 19 E
Hawick, U.K. **11 F6** 55 26N 2 47W
Hawk Junction, Canada **72 C3** 48 5N 84 38W
Hawke B., N.Z. .... **59 H6** 39 25S 177 20 E
Hawker, Australia .... **63 E2** 31 59S 138 22 E
Hawkesbury, Canada **72 C5** 45 37N 74 37W
Hawkesbury I., Canada **70 C3** 53 37N 129 3W
Hawkesbury Pt., Australia ... **62 A1** 11 55S 134 5 E
Hawkinsville, U.S.A. **83 J4** 32 17N 83 28W
Hawley, Minn., U.S.A. **80 B6** 46 53N 96 19W
Hawley, Pa., U.S.A. **85 E9** 41 28N 75 11W
Ḥawrān, W. →, Iraq .... **44 C4** 33 58N 42 34 E
Hawsh Mūssá, Lebanon ..... **46 B4** 33 45N 35 55 E
Hawthorne, U.S.A. **76 G4** 38 32N 118 38W
Hay, Australia .... **63 E3** 34 30S 144 51 E
Hay →, Australia .... **62 C2** 24 50S 138 0 E
Hay →, Canada **70 A5** 60 50N 116 26W
Hay, C., Australia .... **60 B4** 14 5S 129 29 E
Hay I., Canada **84 B4** 44 53N 80 58W
Hay L., Canada **70 B5** 58 50N 118 50W
Hay-on-Wye, U.K. **13 E4** 52 5N 3 8W
Hay River, Canada **70 A5** 60 51N 115 44W
Hay Springs, U.S.A. **80 D3** 42 41N 102 41W
Haya = Tehoru, Indonesia ... **37 E7** 3 23S 129 30 E
Hayachine-San, Japan ...... **30 E10** 39 34N 141 29 E
Hayden, Australia **76 F10** 40 30N 107 16W
Haydon, Australia **80 C4** 44 23N 101 1W
Hayes, U.S.A. **72 A1** 57 3N 92 12W
Hayes →, U.S.A. .... **80 B5** 13 43S 131 22 E
Hayle, U.K. **13 G2** 50 11N 5 26W
Hayling I., U.K. **13 G7** 50 48N 0 59W
Haymen I., Australia .... **62 J6** 20 3S 148 52 E
Hayrabolu, Turkey .... **23 D12** 41 12N 27 5 E
Hays, Canada **70 C6** 50 6N 111 48W
Hays, U.S.A. **80 F5** 38 53N 99 20W
Haysyn, Ukraine .... **17 D15** 48 57N 29 25 E
Hayvoron, Ukraine .... **17 D15** 48 22N 29 52 E
Hayward, Calif., U.S.A. **78 H4** 37 40N 122 5W
Hayward, Wis., U.S.A. **80 B9** 46 1N 91 29W
Haywards Heath, U.K. **13 G7** 51 0N 0 5W
Ḥazafon □, Israel .... **46 C4** 32 40N 35 20 E
Hāzārān, Kūh-e, Iran .... **45 D8** 29 35N 57 20 E
Hazaribag, India .... **43 H11** 23 58N 85 26 E
Hazaribag Road, India ...... **43 G11** 24 12N 85 57 E
Hazelton, Canada **70 B3** 55 20N 127 42W
Hazelton, U.S.A. **80 B4** 46 29N 100 17W
Hazen, U.S.A. **80 B4** 47 18N 101 38W
Hazlehurst, Ga., U.S.A. **83 K4** 31 52N 82 36W
Hazlehurst, Miss., U.S.A. ... **81 K9** 31 52N 90 24W
Hazlet, U.S.A. **85 F10** 40 25N 74 12W
Hazleton, U.S.A. **85 F9** 40 57N 75 59W
Hazlett, L., Australia .... **60 D4** 21 30S 128 48 E
Hazro, Turkey .... **44 B4** 38 15N 40 47 E
Head of Bight, Australia .... **61 F5** 31 30S 131 25 E
Headlands, Zimbabwe ...... **55 F3** 18 15S 32 2 E

Healdsburg, U.S.A. 78 G4 38 37N 122 52W
Healdton, U.S.A. 81 H6 34 14N 97 29W
Healesville, Australia 63 F4 37 35S 145 30 E
Heany Junction, Zimbabwe 57 C4 20 6S 28 54 E
Heard I., Ind. Oc. 3 G13 53 0S 74 0 E
Hearne, U.S.A. 81 K6 30 53N 96 36W
Hearst, Canada 72 C3 49 40N 83 41W
Heart →, U.S.A. 80 B4 46 46N 100 50W
Heart's Content, Canada 73 C9 47 54N 53 27W
Heath, Pte., Canada 73 C7 49 8N 61 40W
Heathrow, London ✈ (LHR), U.K. 13 F7 51 28N 0 27W
Heavener, U.S.A. 81 H7 34 53N 94 36W
Hebbronville, U.S.A. 81 M5 27 18N 98 41W
Hebei □, China 34 E9 39 0N 116 0 E
Hebel, Australia 63 D4 28 58S 147 47 E
Heber, U.S.A. 79 N11 32 44N 115 32W
Heber City, U.S.A. 76 F8 40 31N 111 25W
Heber Springs, U.S.A. 81 H9 35 30N 92 2W
Hebert, Canada 71 C7 50 30N 107 10W
Hebgen L., U.S.A. 76 D8 44 52N 111 20W
Hebi, China 34 G8 35 57N 114 7 E
Hebrides, U.K. 6 D4 57 30N 7 0W
Hebrides, Sea of the, U.K. 11 D2 57 5N 7 0W
Hebron = Al Khalīl, West Bank 46 D4 31 32N 35 6 E
Hebron, Canada 69 C13 58 5N 62 30W
Hebron, N. Dak., U.S.A. 80 B3 46 54N 102 3W
Hebron, Nebr., U.S.A. 80 E6 40 10N 97 35W
Hecate Str., Canada 70 C2 53 10N 130 30W
Heceta I., U.S.A. 70 B2 55 46N 133 40W
Hechi, China 32 D5 24 40N 108 2 E
Hechuan, China 32 C5 30 2N 106 12 E
Hecla, U.S.A. 80 C5 45 53N 98 9W
Hecla I., Canada 71 C9 51 10N 96 43W
Hede, Sweden 9 E15 62 23N 13 30 E
Hedemora, Sweden 9 F16 60 18N 15 58 E
Heerde, Neths. 15 B6 52 24N 6 2 E
Heerenveen, Neths. 15 B5 52 57N 5 55 E
Heerhugowaard, Neths. 15 B4 52 40N 4 51 E
Heerlen, Neths. 15 D5 50 55N 5 58 E
Ḥefa, Israel 46 C4 32 46N 35 0 E
Ḥefa □, Israel 46 C4 32 40N 35 0 E
Hefei, China 33 C6 31 52N 117 18 E
Hegang, China 33 B8 47 20N 130 19 E
Hei Ling Chau, China 33 G11 22 15N 114 2 E
Heichengzhen, China 34 F4 36 24N 106 3 E
Heidelberg, Germany 16 D5 49 24N 8 42 E
Heidelberg, S. Africa 56 E3 34 6S 20 59 E
Heilbron, S. Africa 57 D4 27 16S 27 59 E
Heilbronn, Germany 16 D5 49 9N 9 13 E
Heilongjiang □, China 33 B7 48 0N 126 0 E
Heilunkiang = Heilongjiang □, China 33 B7 48 0N 126 0 E
Heimaey, Iceland 8 E3 63 26N 20 17W
Heinola, Finland 9 F22 61 13N 26 2 E
Heinze Kyun, Burma 38 E1 14 25N 97 45 E
Heishan, China 35 D12 41 40N 122 5 E
Heishui, China 35 C10 42 8N 119 30 E
Hejaz = Ḥijāz □, Si. Arabia 44 E3 24 0N 40 0 E
Hejian, China 34 E9 38 25N 116 5 E
Hejin, China 34 G6 35 35N 110 42 E
Hekımhan, Turkey 44 B3 38 50N 37 55 E
Hekla, Iceland 8 E4 63 56N 19 35W
Hekou, China 32 D5 22 30N 103 59 E
Helan Shan, China 34 E3 38 30N 105 55 E
Helen Atoll, Pac. Oc. 37 D8 2 40N 132 0 E
Helena, Ark., U.S.A. 81 H9 34 32N 90 36W
Helena, Mont., U.S.A. 76 C7 46 36N 112 2W
Helendale, U.S.A. 79 L9 34 44N 117 19W
Helensburgh, U.K. 11 E4 56 1N 4 43W
Helensville, N.Z. 59 G5 36 41S 174 29 E
Helenvale, Australia 62 B4 15 43S 145 14 E
Helgeland, Norway 8 C15 66 7N 13 29 E
Helgoland, Germany 16 A4 54 10N 7 53 E
Heligoland = Helgoland, Germany 16 A4 54 10N 7 53 E
Heligoland B. = Deutsche Bucht, Germany 16 A5 54 15N 8 0 E
Hella, Iceland 8 E3 63 50N 20 24W
Hellertown, U.S.A. 85 F9 40 35N 75 21W
Hellespont = Çanakkale Boğazı, Turkey 23 D12 40 17N 26 32 E
Hellevoetsluis, Neths. 15 C4 51 50N 4 8 E
Hellhole Gorge △, Australia 62 D3 25 31S 144 12 E
Hellín, Spain 21 C5 38 31N 1 40W
Hells Canyon ⌓, U.S.A. 76 D5 45 30N 117 45W
Hell's Gate △, Kenya 54 C4 0 54S 36 19 E
Helmand □, Afghan. 40 D4 31 20N 64 0 E
Helmand →, Afghan. 40 D2 31 12N 61 34 E
Helmeringhausen, Namibia 56 D2 25 54S 16 57 E
Helmond, Neths. 15 C5 51 29N 5 41 E
Helmsdale, U.K. 11 C5 58 7N 3 39W
Helmsdale →, U.K. 11 C5 58 7N 3 40W
Helong, China 35 C15 42 40N 129 0 E
Helper, U.S.A. 76 G8 39 41N 110 51W
Helsingborg, Sweden 9 H15 56 3N 12 42 E
Helsingfors = Helsinki, Finland 9 F21 60 15N 25 3 E
Helsingør, Denmark 9 H15 56 2N 12 35 E
Helsinki, Finland 9 F21 60 15N 25 3 E
Helston, U.K. 13 G2 50 6N 5 17W
Helvellyn, U.K. 12 C4 54 32N 3 1W
Helwân, Egypt 51 C12 29 50N 31 20 E
Hemel Hempstead, U.K. 13 F7 51 44N 0 28W
Hemet, U.S.A. 79 M10 33 45N 116 58W
Hemingford, U.S.A. 80 D3 42 19N 103 4W
Hemmingford, Canada 85 A11 45 3N 73 35W
Hempstead, U.S.A. 81 K6 30 6N 96 5W
Hemse, Sweden 9 H18 57 15N 18 22 E
Henan □, China 34 H8 34 0N 114 0 E
Henares →, Spain 21 B4 40 24N 3 30W
Henashi-Misaki, Japan 30 D9 40 37N 139 51 E
Henderson, Argentina 94 D3 36 18S 61 43W
Henderson, Ky., U.S.A. 82 G2 37 50N 87 35W
Henderson, N.C., U.S.A. 83 G6 36 20N 78 25W
Henderson, Nev., U.S.A. 79 J12 36 2N 114 59W
Henderson, Tenn., U.S.A. 83 H1 35 26N 88 38W
Henderson, Tex., U.S.A. 81 J7 32 9N 94 48W
Hendersonville, N.C., U.S.A. 83 H4 35 19N 82 28W
Hendersonville, Tenn., U.S.A. 83 G2 36 18N 86 37W
Hendījān, Iran 45 D6 30 14N 49 43 E
Hendorābī, Iran 45 E7 26 40N 53 37 E
Hengcheng, China 34 E4 38 18N 106 28 E
Hengdaohezi, China 35 B15 44 52N 129 0 E
Hengelo, Neths. 15 B6 52 16N 6 48 E
Henggang, China 33 F11 22 39N 114 12 E
Hengmen, China 33 F10 22 33N 113 35 E
Hengqin Dao, China 33 G10 22 7N 113 34 E
Hengshan, China 34 F5 37 58N 109 5 E
Hengshui, China 34 F8 37 41N 115 40 E
Hengyang, China 33 D6 26 59N 112 22 E
Henley-on-Thames, U.K. 13 F7 51 32N 0 54W
Henlopen, C., U.S.A. 82 F8 38 48N 75 6W
Hennenman, S. Africa 56 D4 27 59S 27 1 E
Hennessey, U.S.A. 81 G6 36 6N 97 54W
Henri Pittier △, Venezuela 89 D6 10 26N 67 37W
Henrietta, U.S.A. 81 J5 33 49N 98 12W
Henrietta, Ostrov = Genriyetty, Ostrov, Russia 29 B16 77 6N 156 30 E
Henrietta Maria, C., Canada 72 A3 55 9N 82 20W
Henry, U.S.A. 80 E10 41 7N 89 22W
Henryetta, U.S.A. 81 H7 35 27N 95 59W
Henryville, Canada 85 A11 45 8N 73 11W
Hensall, Canada 84 C3 43 26N 81 30W
Hentiesbaai, Namibia 56 C1 22 8S 14 18 E
Hentiyn Nuruu, Mongolia 33 B5 48 30N 108 30 E
Henty, Australia 63 F4 35 30S 147 0 E
Henzada, Burma 41 L19 17 38N 95 26 E
Heppner, U.S.A. 76 D4 45 21N 119 33W
Hepworth, Canada 84 B3 44 37N 81 9W
Hequ, China 34 E6 39 20N 111 15 E
Héraðsflói, Iceland 8 D6 65 42N 14 12W
Héraðsvötn →, Iceland 8 D4 65 45N 19 25W
Heraklion = Iráklion, Greece 25 D7 35 20N 25 12 E
Herald Cays, Australia 62 B4 16 58S 149 9 E
Herāt, Afghan. 40 B3 34 20N 62 7 E
Herāt □, Afghan. 40 B3 35 0N 62 0 E
Herbert →, Australia 62 B4 18 31S 146 17 E
Herbert River Falls △, Australia 62 B4 18 15S 145 32 E
Herberton, Australia 62 B4 17 20S 145 25 E
Herbertsdale, S. Africa 56 E3 34 1S 21 46 E
Herceg-Novi, Serbia & M. 23 C8 42 30N 18 33 E
Herchmer, Canada 71 B10 57 22N 94 10W
Herðubreið, Iceland 8 D5 65 11N 16 21W
Hereford, U.K. 13 E5 52 4N 2 43W
Hereford, U.S.A. 81 H3 34 49N 102 24W
Herefordshire □, U.K. 13 E5 52 8N 2 40W
Herentals, Belgium 15 C4 51 12N 4 51 E
Herford, Germany 16 B5 52 7N 8 39 E
Herington, U.S.A. 80 F6 38 40N 96 57W
Herkimer, U.S.A. 85 D10 43 0N 74 59W
Herlong, U.S.A. 78 E6 40 8N 120 8W
Herm, U.K. 13 H5 49 30N 2 28W
Hermann, U.S.A. 80 F9 38 42N 91 27W
Hermannsburg, Australia 60 D5 23 57S 132 45 E
Hermanus, S. Africa 56 E2 34 27S 19 12 E
Hermidale, Australia 63 E4 31 30S 146 42 E
Hermiston, U.S.A. 76 D4 45 51N 119 17W
Hermite, I., Chile 96 H3 55 50S 68 0W
Hermon, U.S.A. 85 B9 44 28N 75 14W
Hermon, Mt. = Shaykh, J. ash, Lebanon 46 B4 33 25N 35 50 E
Hermosillo, Mexico 86 B2 29 10N 111 0W
Hernád →, Hungary 17 D11 47 56N 21 8 E
Hernandarias, Paraguay 95 B5 25 20S 54 40W
Hernandez, U.S.A. 78 J6 36 24N 120 46W
Hernando, Argentina 94 C3 32 28S 63 40W
Hernando, U.S.A. 81 H10 34 50N 90 0W
Herndon, U.S.A. 84 F8 40 43N 76 51W
Herne, Germany 15 C7 51 32N 7 14 E
Herne Bay, U.K. 13 F9 51 21N 1 8 E
Herning, Denmark 9 H13 56 8N 8 58 E
Heroica = Caborca, Mexico 86 A2 30 40N 112 10W
Heroica Nogales = Nogales, Mexico 86 A2 31 20N 110 56W
Heron Bay, Canada 72 C2 48 40N 86 25W
Herradura, Pta. de la, Canary Is. 24 F5 28 26N 14 8W
Herreid, U.S.A. 80 C4 45 50N 100 4W
Herrin, U.S.A. 81 G10 37 48N 89 2W
Herriot, Canada 71 B8 56 22N 101 16W
Herschel I., Canada 4 C1 69 35N 139 5W
Hershey, U.S.A. 85 F8 40 17N 76 39W
Hersonissos, Greece 25 D7 35 18N 25 22 E
Herstal, Belgium 15 D5 50 40N 5 38 E
Hertford, U.K. 13 F7 51 48N 0 4W
Hertfordshire □, U.K. 13 F7 51 51N 0 5W
's-Hertogenbosch, Neths. 15 C5 51 42N 5 17 E
Hertzogville, S. Africa 56 D4 28 9S 25 30 E
Hervey B., Australia 62 C5 25 0S 152 52 E
Herzliyya, Israel 46 C3 32 10N 34 50 E
Ḥeṣār, Fārs, Iran 45 D6 29 52N 50 16 E
Ḥeṣār, Markazī, Iran 45 C6 35 50N 49 12 E
Heshui, China 34 G5 35 48N 108 0 E
Heshun, China 34 F7 37 22N 113 32 E
Hesperia, U.S.A. 79 L9 34 25N 117 18W
Hesse = Hessen □, Germany 16 C5 50 30N 9 0 E
Hessen □, Germany 16 C5 50 30N 9 0 E
Hetch Hetchy Aqueduct, U.S.A. 78 H5 37 29N 122 19W
Hettinger, U.S.A. 80 C3 46 0N 102 42W
Heuvelton, U.S.A. 85 B9 44 37N 75 25W
Hewitt, U.S.A. 81 K6 31 27N 97 11W
Hexham, U.K. 12 C5 54 58N 2 4W
Hexigten Qi, China 35 C9 43 18N 117 30 E
Ḥeydarābād, Iran 45 D7 30 33N 55 38 E
Heysham, U.K. 12 C5 54 3N 2 53W
Heywood, Australia 63 F3 38 8S 141 37 E
Heze, China 34 G8 35 14N 115 20 E
Hi, Ko, Thailand 39 a 7 44N 98 22 E
Hi Vista, U.S.A. 79 L9 34 45N 117 46W
Hialeah, U.S.A. 83 N5 25 50N 80 17W
Hiawatha, U.S.A. 80 F7 39 51N 95 32W
Hibbing, U.S.A. 80 B8 47 25N 92 56W
Hibbs B., Australia 63 G4 42 35S 145 15 E
Hibernia Reef, Australia 60 B3 12 0S 123 23 E
Hickman, U.S.A. 81 G10 36 34N 89 11W
Hickory, U.S.A. 83 H5 35 44N 81 21W
Hicks, Pt., Australia 63 F4 37 49S 149 17 E
Hicks L., Canada 71 A9 61 25N 100 0W
Hicksville, U.S.A. 85 F11 40 46N 73 32W
Hida-Gawa →, Japan 31 G8 35 26N 137 3 E
Hida-Sammyaku, Japan 31 F8 36 30N 137 40 E
Hidaka-Sammyaku, Japan 30 C11 42 35N 142 45 E
Hidalgo, Mexico 87 C5 24 15N 99 26W
Hidalgo □, Mexico 87 C5 20 30N 99 10W
Hidalgo, Presa M., Mexico 86 B3 26 30N 108 35W
Hidalgo del Parral, Mexico 86 B3 26 58N 105 40W
Hierro, Canary Is. 24 G1 27 44N 18 0W
Higashiajima-San, Japan 30 F10 37 40N 140 10 E
Higashiōsaka, Japan 31 G7 34 40N 135 37 E
Higgins, U.S.A. 81 G4 36 7N 100 2W
Higgins Corner, U.S.A. 78 F5 39 2N 121 5W
High Bridge, U.S.A. 85 F10 40 40N 74 54W
High Island Res., China 33 G11 22 22N 114 21 E
High Level, Canada 70 B5 58 31N 117 8W
High Point, U.S.A. 83 H6 35 57N 80 0W
High Prairie, Canada 70 B5 55 30N 116 30W
High River, Canada 70 C6 50 30N 113 50W
High Tatra = Tatry, Slovak Rep. 17 D11 49 20N 20 0 E
High Veld, Africa 48 J6 27 0S 27 0 E
High Wycombe, U.K. 13 F7 51 37N 0 45W
Highland □, U.K. 11 D4 57 17N 4 21W
Highland Park, U.S.A. 82 D2 42 11N 87 48W
Highmore, U.S.A. 80 C5 44 31N 99 27W
Highrock L., Man., Canada 71 B8 55 45N 100 30W
Highrock L., Sask., Canada 71 B7 57 5N 105 32W
Higüey, Dom. Rep. 89 C6 18 37N 68 42W
Hiiumaa, Estonia 9 G20 58 50N 22 45 E
Ḥijāz □, Si. Arabia 44 E3 24 0N 40 0 E
Hijo = Tagum, Phil. 37 C7 7 33N 125 53 E
Hikari, Japan 31 H5 33 58N 131 58 E
Hiko, U.S.A. 78 H11 37 32N 115 14W
Hikone, Japan 31 G8 35 15N 136 10 E
Hikurangi, Gisborne, N.Z. 59 H6 37 55S 178 4 E
Hikurangi, Northland, N.Z. 59 F5 35 36S 174 17 E
Hildesheim, Germany 16 B5 52 9N 9 56 E
Hill →, Australia 61 F2 30 23S 115 3 E
Hill City, Idaho, U.S.A. 76 E6 43 18N 115 3W
Hill City, Kans., U.S.A. 80 F5 39 22N 99 51W
Hill City, S. Dak., U.S.A. 80 D3 43 56N 103 35W
Hill Island L., Canada 71 A7 60 30N 109 50W
Hillaby, Mt., Barbados 89 g 13 12N 59 35W
Hillcrest, Barbados 89 g 13 13N 59 32W
Hillcrest Center, U.S.A. 79 K8 35 23N 118 57W
Hillegom, Neths. 15 B4 52 18N 4 35 E
Hillerød, Denmark 9 J15 55 56N 12 19 E
Hillsboro, Kans., U.S.A. 80 F6 38 21N 97 12W
Hillsboro, N. Dak., U.S.A. 80 B6 47 26N 97 3W
Hillsboro, N.H., U.S.A. 85 C13 43 7N 71 54W
Hillsboro, Ohio, U.S.A. 82 F4 39 12N 83 37W
Hillsboro, Oreg., U.S.A. 78 E4 45 31N 122 59W
Hillsboro, Tex., U.S.A. 81 J6 32 1N 97 8W
Hillsborough, Grenada 89 D7 12 28N 61 28W
Hillsborough Channel, Australia 62 J7 20 56S 149 15 E
Hillsdale, Mich., U.S.A. 82 E3 41 56N 84 38W
Hillsdale, N.Y., U.S.A. 85 D11 42 11N 73 30W
Hillsport, Canada 72 C2 49 27N 85 34W
Hillston, Australia 63 E4 33 30S 145 31 E
Hilo, U.S.A. 74 J17 19 44N 155 5W
Hilton, U.S.A. 84 C7 43 17N 77 48W
Hilton Head Island, U.S.A. 83 J5 32 13N 80 45W
Hilversum, Neths. 15 B5 52 14N 5 10 E
Himachal Pradesh □, India 42 D7 31 30N 77 0 E
Himalaya, Asia 43 E11 29 0N 84 0 E
Himatnagar, India 40 H8 23 37N 72 57 E
Himeji, Japan 31 G7 34 50N 134 40 E
Himi, Japan 31 F8 36 50N 136 55 E
Ḥimş, Syria 46 A5 34 40N 36 45 E
Ḥimş □, Syria 46 A6 34 30N 37 0 E
Hinche, Haiti 89 C5 19 9N 72 1W
Hinchinbrook I., Australia 62 B4 18 20S 146 15 E
Hinchinbrook Island △, Australia 62 B4 18 14S 146 6 E
Hinckley, U.K. 13 E6 52 33N 1 22W
Hinckley, U.S.A. 80 B8 46 1N 92 56W
Hindaun, India 42 F7 26 44N 77 5 E
Hindmarsh, L., Australia 63 F3 36 5S 141 55 E
Hindu Bagh, Pakistan 42 D2 30 56N 67 50 E
Hindu Kush, Asia 40 B7 36 0N 71 0 E
Hindupur, India 40 N10 13 49N 77 32 E
Hines Creek, Canada 70 B5 56 20N 118 40W
Hinesville, U.S.A. 83 K5 31 51N 81 36W
Hinganghat, India 40 J11 20 30N 78 52 E
Hingham, U.S.A. 76 B8 48 33N 110 25W
Hingir, India 43 J10 21 57N 83 41 E
Hingoli, India 40 K10 19 41N 77 15 E
Hinna = Imi, Ethiopia 47 F3 6 28N 42 10 E
Hinnøya, Norway 8 B16 68 35N 15 50 E
Hinojosa del Duque, Spain 21 C3 38 30N 5 9W
Hinsdale, U.S.A. 85 D12 42 47N 72 29W
Hinton, Canada 70 C5 53 26N 117 34W
Hinton, U.S.A. 82 G5 37 40N 80 54W
Hirado, Japan 31 H4 33 22N 129 33 E
Hirakud Dam, India 41 J13 21 32N 83 45 E
Hiran →, India 43 H8 23 6N 79 21 E
Hirapur, India 43 G8 24 22N 79 13 E
Hiratsuka, Japan 31 G9 35 19N 139 21 E
Hiroo, Japan 30 C11 42 17N 143 19 E
Hirosaki, Japan 30 D10 40 34N 140 28 E
Hiroshima, Japan 31 G6 34 24N 132 30 E
Hiroshima □, Japan 31 G6 34 50N 133 0 E
Hisar, India 42 E6 29 12N 75 45 E
Hisb, Sha'ib = Ḥasb, W. →, Iraq 44 D5 31 45N 44 17 E
Ḥismá, Si. Arabia 44 D3 28 30N 36 0 E
Hispaniola, W. Indies 89 C5 19 0N 71 0W
Hīt, Iraq 44 C4 33 38N 42 49 E
Hita, Japan 31 H5 33 20N 130 58 E
Hitachi, Japan 31 F10 36 36N 140 39 E
Hitchin, U.K. 13 F7 51 58N 0 16W
Hitoyoshi, Japan 31 H5 32 13N 130 45 E
Hitra, Norway 8 E13 63 30N 8 45 E
Hixon, Canada 70 C4 53 25N 122 35W
Ḥiyyon, N. →, Israel 46 E4 30 25N 35 10 E
Hjalmar L., Canada 71 A7 61 33N 109 25W
Hjälmaren, Sweden 9 G16 59 18N 15 40 E
Hjørring, Denmark 9 H13 57 29N 9 59 E
Hkakabo Razi, Burma 41 E20 28 25N 97 23 E
Hlobane, S. Africa 57 D5 27 42S 31 0 E
Hluhluwe, S. Africa 57 D5 28 1S 32 15 E
Hluhluwe ⌓, S. Africa 57 C5 22 10S 32 5 E
Hlyboka, Ukraine 17 D13 48 5N 25 56 E
Ho Chi Minh City = Thanh Pho Ho Chi Minh, Vietnam 39 G6 10 58N 106 40 E
Ho Thuong, Vietnam 38 C5 19 32N 105 48 E
Hoa Binh, Vietnam 38 B5 20 50N 105 20 E
Hoa Da, Vietnam 39 G7 11 16N 108 40 E
Hoa Hiep, Vietnam 39 G5 11 34N 105 51 E
Hoai Nhon, Vietnam 38 E7 14 28N 109 1 E
Hoang Lien Son, Vietnam 38 A4 22 0N 104 0 E
Hoanib →, Namibia 56 B2 19 27S 12 46 E
Hoare B., Canada 69 B13 65 17N 62 30W
Hoarusib →, Namibia 56 B2 19 3S 12 36 E
Hobart, Australia 63 G4 42 50S 147 21 E
Hobart, U.S.A. 81 H5 35 1N 99 6W
Hobbs, U.S.A. 81 J3 32 42N 103 8W
Hobbs Coast, Antarctica 5 D14 74 50S 131 0W
Hobe Sound, U.S.A. 83 M5 27 4N 80 8W
Hoboken, U.S.A. 85 F10 40 45N 74 4W
Hobro, Denmark 9 H13 56 39N 9 46 E
Hoburgen, Sweden 9 H18 56 55N 18 7 E
Hochfeld, Namibia 56 C2 21 28S 17 58 E
Hodaka-Dake, Japan 31 F8 36 17N 137 39 E
Hodeida = Al Ḥudaydah, Yemen 47 E3 14 50N 43 0 E
Hodgeville, Canada 71 C7 50 7N 106 58W
Hodgson, Canada 71 C9 51 13N 97 36W
Hódmezővásárhely, Hungary 17 E11 46 28N 20 22 E
Hodna, Chott el, Algeria 50 A6 35 26N 4 43 E
Hodonín, Czech Rep. 17 D9 48 50N 17 10 E
Hoeamdong, N. Korea 35 C16 42 30N 130 16 E
Hoek van Holland, Neths. 15 C4 52 0N 4 7 E
Hoengsŏng, S. Korea 35 F14 37 29N 127 59 E
Hoeryong, N. Korea 35 C15 42 30N 129 45 E
Hoeyang, N. Korea 35 E14 38 43N 127 36 E
Hof, Germany 16 C6 50 19N 11 55 E
Hofmeyr, S. Africa 56 E4 31 39S 25 50 E
Höfn, Iceland 8 D6 64 15N 15 13W
Hofors, Sweden 9 F17 60 31N 16 15 E
Hofsjökull, Iceland 8 D4 64 49N 18 48W
Hōfu, Japan 31 G5 34 3N 131 34 E
Hogan Group, Australia 63 F4 39 13S 147 1 E
Hogarth, Mt., Australia 62 C2 21 48S 136 58 E
Hoggar = Ahaggar, Algeria 50 D7 23 0N 6 30 E
Hogsty Reef, Bahamas 89 B5 21 41N 73 48W
Hoh →, U.S.A. 78 C2 47 45N 124 29W
Hohe Venn, Belgium 15 D6 50 30N 6 5 E
Hohenwald, U.S.A. 83 H2 35 33N 87 33W
Hoher Rhön = Rhön, Germany 16 C5 50 24N 9 58 E
Hohhot, China 34 D6 40 52N 111 40 E
Hóhlakas, Greece 25 D9 35 57N 27 53 E
Hoi An, Vietnam 38 E7 15 30N 108 19 E
Hoi Xuan, Vietnam 38 B5 20 25N 105 9 E
Hoisington, U.S.A. 80 F5 38 31N 98 47W
Hōjō, Japan 31 H6 33 58N 132 46 E
Hokianga Harbour, N.Z. 59 F4 35 31S 173 22 E
Hokitika, N.Z. 59 K3 42 42S 171 0 E
Hokkaidō □, Japan 30 C11 43 30N 143 0 E
Holbrook, Australia 63 F4 35 42S 147 18 E
Holbrook, U.S.A. 77 J8 34 54N 110 10W
Holden, U.S.A. 76 G7 39 6N 112 16W
Holdenville, U.S.A. 81 H6 35 5N 96 24W
Holdrege, U.S.A. 80 E5 40 26N 99 23W
Holetown, Barbados 89 g 13 11N 59 38W
Holguín, Cuba 88 B4 20 50N 76 20W
Hollams Bird I., Namibia 56 C1 24 40S 14 30 E
Holland, Mich., U.S.A. 82 D2 42 47N 86 7W
Holland, N.Y., U.S.A. 84 D6 42 38N 78 32W
Hollandale, U.S.A. 81 J9 33 10N 90 51W
Holley, U.S.A. 84 C6 43 14N 78 2W
Hollidaysburg, U.S.A. 84 F6 40 26N 78 24W
Hollis, U.S.A. 81 H5 34 41N 99 55W
Hollister, Calif., U.S.A. 78 J5 36 51N 121 24W
Hollister, Idaho, U.S.A. 76 E6 42 21N 114 35W
Holly Hill, U.S.A. 83 L5 29 16N 81 3W
Holly Springs, U.S.A. 81 H10 34 46N 89 27W
Hollywood, U.S.A. 83 N5 26 1N 80 9W
Holman, Canada 68 A8 70 44N 117 44W
Hólmavík, Iceland 8 D3 65 42N 21 40W
Holmen, U.S.A. 80 D9 43 58N 91 15W
Holmes Reefs, Australia 62 B4 16 27S 148 0 E
Holmsund, Sweden 8 E19 63 41N 20 20 E
Holroyd →, Australia 62 A3 14 10S 141 36 E
Holstebro, Denmark 9 H13 56 22N 8 37 E
Holsworthy, U.K. 13 G3 50 48N 4 22W
Holton, Canada 73 B8 54 31N 57 12W
Holton, U.S.A. 80 F7 39 28N 95 44W
Holtville, U.S.A. 79 N11 32 49N 115 23W
Holwerd, Neths. 15 A5 53 22N 5 54 E
Holy I., Angl., U.K. 12 D3 53 17N 4 37W
Holy I., Northumberland, U.K. 12 B6 55 40N 1 47W
Holyhead, U.K. 12 D3 53 18N 4 38W
Holyoke, Colo., U.S.A. 80 E3 40 35N 102 18W
Holyoke, Mass., U.S.A. 85 D12 42 12N 72 37W
Holyrood, Canada 73 C9 47 27N 53 8W
Homa Bay, Kenya 54 C3 0 36S 34 30 E
Homalin, Burma 41 G19 24 55N 95 0 E
Homand, Iran 45 C8 32 28N 59 37 E
Homathko →, Canada 70 C4 51 0N 124 56W
Hombori, Mali 50 E5 15 20N 1 38W
Home B., Canada 69 B13 68 40N 67 10W
Home Hill, Australia 62 B4 19 43S 147 25 E
Homedale, U.S.A. 76 E5 43 37N 116 56W
Homer, Alaska, U.S.A. 68 C4 59 39N 151 33W
Homer, La., U.S.A. 81 J8 32 48N 93 4W
Homer City, U.S.A. 84 F5 40 32N 79 10W
Homestead, Australia 62 C4 20 20S 145 40 E
Homestead, U.S.A. 83 N5 25 28N 80 29W
Homestead ⌓, U.S.A. 80 E6 40 17N 96 50W
Homewood, U.S.A. 78 F6 39 4N 120 8W
Homoine, Mozam. 57 C6 23 55S 35 8 E
Homs = Ḥimş, Syria 46 A5 34 40N 36 45 E
Homyel, Belarus 17 B16 52 28N 31 0 E
Hon Chong, Vietnam 39 G5 10 25N 104 30 E
Hon Me, Vietnam 38 C5 19 23N 105 56 E
Honan = Henan □, China 34 H8 34 0N 114 0 E
Honbetsu, Japan 30 C11 43 7N 143 37 E
Honcut, U.S.A. 78 F5 39 20N 121 32W
Hondeklipbaai, S. Africa 56 E2 30 19S 17 17 E
Hondo, Japan 31 H5 32 27N 130 12 E
Hondo, U.S.A. 81 L5 29 21N 99 9W
Hondo →, Belize 87 D7 18 25N 88 21W
Honduras ■, Cent. Amer. 88 D2 14 40N 86 30W
Honduras, G. de, Caribbean 88 C2 16 50N 87 0W
Hønefoss, Norway 9 F14 60 10N 10 18 E
Honesdale, U.S.A. 85 E9 41 34N 75 16W
Honey L., U.S.A. 78 E6 40 15N 120 19W
Honfleur, France 20 B4 49 25N 0 13 E
Hong →, Vietnam 32 D5 22 0N 104 0 E
Hong Gai, Vietnam 38 B6 20 57N 107 5 E
Hong He →, China 34 H8 32 25N 115 35 E
Hong Kong □, China 33 G11 22 11N 114 14 E
Hong Kong I., China 33 G11 22 16N 114 12 E
Hong Kong International ✈ (HKG), China 33 G10 22 19N 113 57 E
Hongch'ŏn, S. Korea 35 F14 37 44N 127 53 E
Hongjiang, China 33 D5 27 7N 109 59 E
Hongliu He →, China 34 F5 38 0N 109 50 E
Hongor, Mongolia 34 B7 45 45N 112 50 E
Hongsa, Laos 38 C3 19 43N 101 20 E
Hongshui He →, China 33 D5 23 48N 109 30 E
Hongsŏng, S. Korea 35 F14 36 37N 126 38 E
Hongtong, China 34 F6 36 16N 111 40 E
Honguedo, Détroit d', Canada 73 C7 49 15N 64 0W
Hongwon, N. Korea 35 E14 40 0N 127 56 E
Hongze Hu, China 35 H10 33 15N 118 35 E
Honiara, Solomon Is. 64 H7 9 27S 159 57 E
Honiton, U.K. 13 G4 50 47N 3 11W
Honjō, Japan 30 E10 39 23N 140 3 E
Honningsvåg, Norway 8 A21 70 59N 25 59 E
Honolulu, U.S.A. 74 H16 21 19N 157 52W
Honshū, Japan 33 C8 36 0N 138 0 E
Hood, Mt., U.S.A. 76 D3 45 23N 121 42W
Hood, Pt., Australia 61 F2 34 23S 119 34 E

Hood River, U.S.A. 76 D3 45 43N 121 31W
Hoodsport, U.S.A. 78 C3 47 24N 123 9W
Hoogeveen, Neths. 15 B6 52 44N 6 28 E
Hoogezand-Sappemeer, Neths. 15 A6 53 9N 6 45 E
Hooghly = Hugli →, India 43 J13 21 56N 88 4 E
Hooghly-Chinsura = Chunchura, India 43 H13 22 53N 88 27 E
Hook Hd., Ireland 10 D5 52 7N 6 56W
Hook I., Australia 62 J6 20 4S 149 0 E
Hook of Holland = Hoek van Holland, Neths. 15 C4 52 0N 4 7 E
Hooker, U.S.A. 81 G4 36 52N 101 13W
Hooker Creek, Australia 60 C5 18 23S 130 38 E
Hoonah, U.S.A. 70 B1 58 7N 135 27W
Hooper Bay, U.S.A. 68 B3 61 32N 166 6W
Hoopeston, U.S.A. 82 E2 40 28N 87 40W
Hoopstad, S. Africa 56 D4 27 50S 25 55 E
Hoorn, Neths. 15 B5 52 38N 5 4 E
Hoover, U.S.A. 83 J2 33 20N 86 11W
Hoover Dam, U.S.A. 79 K12 36 1N 114 44W
Hooversville, U.S.A. 84 F6 40 9N 78 55W
Hop Bottom, U.S.A. 85 E9 41 42N 75 46W
Hope, Canada 70 D4 49 25N 121 25W
Hope, Ariz., U.S.A. 79 M13 33 43N 113 42W
Hope, Ark., U.S.A. 81 J8 33 40N 93 36W
Hope, L., S. Austral., Australia 63 D2 28 24S 139 18 E
Hope, L., W. Austral., Australia 61 F3 32 35S 120 15 E
Hope, Pt., Canada 4 C17 68 20N 166 50W
Hope I., Canada 84 B4 44 55N 80 11W
Hope Town, Bahamas 88 A4 26 35N 76 57W
Hopedale, Canada 73 A7 55 28N 60 13W
Hopedale, U.S.A. 85 D13 42 8N 71 33W
Hopefield, S. Africa 56 E2 33 3S 18 22 E
Hopei = Hebei □, China 34 E9 39 0N 116 0 E
Hopelchén, Mexico 87 D7 19 46N 89 50W
Hopetoun, Vic., Australia 63 F3 35 42S 142 22 E
Hopetoun, W. Austral., Australia 61 F3 33 57S 120 7 E
Hopetown, S. Africa 56 D3 29 34S 24 3 E
Hopevale, Australia 62 B4 15 16S 145 20 E
Hopewell, U.S.A. 82 G7 37 18N 77 17W
Hopkins, L., Australia 60 D4 24 15S 128 35 E
Hopkinsville, U.S.A. 83 G2 36 52N 87 29W
Hopland, U.S.A. 78 G3 38 58N 123 7W
Hoquiam, U.S.A. 78 D3 46 59N 123 53W
Horden Hills, Australia 60 D5 20 15S 130 0 E
Horinger, China 34 D6 40 28N 111 48 E
Horlick Mts., Antarctica 5 E15 84 0S 102 0W
Hormak, Iran 45 D9 29 58N 60 51 E
Hormoz, Iran 45 E7 27 35N 55 0 E
Hormoz, Jaz.-ye, Iran 45 E8 27 8N 56 28 E
Hormozgān □, Iran 45 E8 27 30N 56 0 E
Hormuz, Küh-e, Iran 45 E7 27 27N 55 10 E
Hormuz, Str. of, The Gulf 45 E8 26 30N 56 30 E
Horn, Austria 16 D8 48 39N 15 40 E
Horn, Iceland 8 C2 66 28N 22 28W
Horn →, Canada 70 A5 61 30N 118 1W
Horn, Cape = Hornos, C. de, Chile 96 H3 55 50S 67 30W
Horn Head, Ireland 10 A3 55 14N 8 0W
Horn I., Australia 62 A3 10 37S 142 17 E
Horn Plateau, Canada 70 A5 62 15N 119 15W
Hornavan, Sweden 8 C17 66 15N 17 30 E
Hornbeck, U.S.A. 81 K8 31 20N 93 24W
Hornbrook, U.S.A. 76 F2 41 55N 122 33W
Horncastle, U.K. 12 D7 53 13N 0 7W
Hornell, U.S.A. 84 D7 42 20N 77 40W
Hornell L., Canada 70 A5 62 20N 119 25W
Hornepayne, Canada 72 C3 49 14N 84 48W
Hornings Mills, Canada 84 B4 44 9N 80 12W
Hornitos, U.S.A. 78 H6 37 30N 120 14W
Hornos, C. de, Chile 96 H3 55 50S 67 30W
Hornsea, U.K. 12 D7 53 55N 0 11W
Horobetsu = Noboribetsu, Japan 30 C10 42 24N 141 6 E
Horodenka, Ukraine 17 D13 48 41N 25 29 E
Horodok, Khmelnytskyy, Ukraine 17 D14 49 10N 26 34 E
Horodok, Lviv, Ukraine 17 D12 49 46N 23 32 E
Horokhiv, Ukraine 17 C13 50 30N 24 45 E
Horqin Youyi Qianqi, China 35 A12 46 5N 122 3 E
Horqueta, Paraguay 94 A4 23 15S 56 55W
Horse Creek, U.S.A. 80 E3 41 57N 105 10W
Horse I., Canada 71 C9 53 20N 99 6W
Horse Is., Canada 73 B8 50 15N 55 50W
Horsefly L., Canada 70 C4 52 25N 121 0W
Horseheads, U.S.A. 84 D8 42 10N 76 49W
Horsens, Denmark 9 J13 55 52N 9 51 E
Horsham, Australia 63 F3 36 44S 142 13 E
Horsham, U.K. 13 F7 51 4N 0 20W
Horten, Norway 9 G14 59 25N 10 32 E
Horton, U.S.A. 80 F7 39 40N 95 32W
Horton →, Canada 68 B7 69 56N 126 52W
Horwood L., Canada 72 C3 48 5N 82 20W
Hose, Gunung-Gunung, Malaysia 36 D4 2 5N 114 6 E
Hoseynābād, Khuzestān, Iran 45 C6 32 45N 48 20 E
Hoseynābād, Kordestān, Iran 44 C5 35 33N 47 8 E
Hoshangabad, India 42 H7 22 45N 77 45 E
Hoshiarpur, India 42 D6 31 30N 75 58 E
Hospet, India 40 M10 15 15N 76 20 E
Hoste, I., Chile 96 H3 55 0S 69 0W
Hot, Thailand 38 C2 18 8N 98 29 E
Hot Creek Range, U.S.A. 76 G6 38 40N 116 20W
Hot Springs, Ark., U.S.A. 81 H8 34 31N 93 3W
Hot Springs, S. Dak., U.S.A. 80 D3 43 26N 103 29W
Hot Springs △, U.S.A. 81 H8 34 32N 93 4W
Hotagen, Sweden 8 E16 63 50N 14 30 E
Hotan, China 32 C2 37 25N 79 55 E
Hotazel, S. Africa 56 D3 27 17S 22 58 E
Hotchkiss, U.S.A. 77 G10 38 48N 107 43W
Hotham, C., Australia 60 B5 12 2S 131 18 E
Hoting, Sweden 8 D17 64 8N 16 15 E
Hotte, Massif de la, Haiti 89 C5 18 30N 73 45W
Hottentotsbaai, Namibia 56 D1 26 8S 14 59 E
Hou Hai, China 33 F10 22 32N 113 56 E
Houei Sai, Laos 38 B3 20 18N 100 26 E
Houffalize, Belgium 15 D5 50 8N 5 48 E
Houghton, Mich., U.S.A. 80 B10 47 7N 88 34W
Houghton, N.Y., U.S.A. 84 D6 42 25N 78 10W
Houghton L., U.S.A. 82 C3 44 21N 84 44W
Houghton-le-Spring, U.K. 12 C6 54 51N 1 28W
Houhora Heads, N.Z. 59 F4 34 49S 173 9 E
Houlton, U.S.A. 83 B12 46 8N 67 51W
Houma, U.S.A. 81 L9 29 36N 90 43W
Housatonic →, U.S.A. 85 E11 41 10N 73 7W
Houston, Canada 70 C3 54 25N 126 39W
Houston, Mo., U.S.A. 81 G9 37 22N 91 58W
Houston, Tex., U.S.A. 81 L7 29 46N 95 22W
Hout →, S. Africa 57 C4 23 4S 29 36 E
Houtkraal, S. Africa 56 E3 30 23S 24 5 E

Houtman Abrolhos, Australia 61 E1 28 43S 113 48 E
Hovd, Mongolia 32 B4 48 2N 91 37 E
Hove, U.K. 13 G7 50 50N 0 10W
Hovenweep △, U.S.A. 77 H9 37 20N 109 0W
Hoveyzeh, Iran 45 D6 31 27N 48 4 E
Hövsgöl, Mongolia 34 C5 43 37N 109 39 E
Hövsgöl Nuur, Mongolia 32 A5 51 0N 100 30 E
Howard, Australia 63 D5 25 16S 152 32 E
Howard, Pa., U.S.A. 84 F7 41 1N 77 40W
Howard, S. Dak., U.S.A. 80 C6 44 1N 97 32W
Howe, U.S.A. 76 E7 43 48N 113 0W
Howe, C., Australia 63 F5 37 30S 150 0 E
Howe I., Canada 85 B8 44 16N 76 17W
Howell, U.S.A. 82 D4 42 36N 83 56W
Howick, Canada 85 A11 45 11N 73 51W
Howick, S. Africa 57 D5 29 28S 30 14 E
Howick Group, Australia 62 A4 14 20S 145 30 E
Howitt, L., Australia 63 D2 27 40S 138 40 E
Howland I., Pac. Oc. 64 G10 0 48N 176 38W
Howrah = Haora, India 43 H13 22 37N 88 20 E
Howth Hd., Ireland 10 C5 53 22N 6 3W
Höxter, Germany 16 C5 51 46N 9 22 E
Hoy, U.K. 11 C5 58 50N 3 15W
Høyanger, Norway 9 F12 61 13N 6 4 E
Hoyerswerda, Germany 16 C8 51 26N 14 14 E
Hoylake, U.K. 12 D4 53 24N 3 10W
Hpa-an = Pa-an, Burma 41 L20 16 51N 97 40 E
Hpungan Pass, Burma 41 F20 27 30N 96 55 E
Hradec Králové, Czech Rep. 16 C8 50 15N 15 50 E
Hrodna, Belarus 17 B12 53 42N 23 52 E
Hrodzyanka, Belarus 17 B15 53 31N 28 42 E
Hron →, Slovak Rep. 17 E10 47 49N 18 45 E
Hrvatska = Croatia ■, Europe 16 F9 45 20N 16 0 E
Hrymayliv, Ukraine 17 D14 49 20N 26 5 E
Hsenwi, Burma 41 H20 23 22N 97 55 E
Hsiamen = Xiamen, China 33 D6 24 25N 118 4 E
Hsian = Xi'an, China 34 G5 34 15N 109 0 E
Hsinchu, Taiwan 33 D7 24 48N 120 58 E
Hsinhailien = Lianyungang, China 35 G10 34 40N 119 11 E
Hsüchou = Xuzhou, China 35 G9 34 18N 117 10 E
Hu Xian, China 34 G5 34 8N 108 42 E
Hua Hin, Thailand 38 F2 12 34N 99 58 E
Hua Xian, Henan, China 34 G8 35 30N 114 30 E
Hua Xian, Shaanxi, China 34 G5 34 30N 109 48 E
Huab →, Namibia 56 B2 20 52S 13 25 E
Huachinera, Mexico 86 A3 30 9N 108 55W
Huacho, Peru 92 F3 11 10S 77 35W
Huade, China 34 D7 41 55N 113 59 E
Huadian, China 35 C14 43 0N 126 40 E
Huai Had △, Thailand 38 D5 16 52N 104 17 E
Huai He →, China 33 C6 33 0N 118 30 E
Huai Nam Dang △, Thailand 38 C2 19 30N 98 30 E
Huai Yot, Thailand 39 J2 7 45N 99 37 E
Huai'an, Hebei, China 34 D8 40 30N 114 20 E
Huai'an, Jiangsu, China 35 H10 33 30N 119 10 E
Huaibei, China 34 G9 34 0N 116 48 E
Huaide = Gongzhuling, China 35 C13 43 30N 124 40 E
Huaidezhen, China 35 C13 43 48N 124 50 E
Huainan, China 33 C6 32 38N 116 58 E
Huairen, China 34 E7 39 48N 113 20 E
Huairou, China 34 D9 40 20N 116 35 E
Huaiyang, China 34 H8 33 40N 114 52 E
Huaiyin, China 35 H10 33 30N 119 2 E
Huaiyuan, China 35 H9 32 55N 117 10 E
Huajianzi, China 35 D13 41 23N 125 20 E
Huajuapan de Leon, Mexico 87 D5 17 50N 97 48W
Hualapai Peak, U.S.A. 77 J7 35 5N 113 54W
Huallaga →, Peru 92 E3 5 15S 75 30W
Huambo, Angola 53 G3 12 42S 15 54 E
Huan Jiang →, China 34 G5 34 28N 109 0 E
Huan Xian, China 34 F4 36 33N 107 7 E
Huancabamba, Peru 92 E3 5 10S 79 15W
Huancane, Peru 92 G5 15 10S 69 44W
Huancavelica, Peru 92 F3 12 50S 75 5W
Huancayo, Peru 92 F3 12 5S 75 12W
Huanchaca, Bolivia 92 H5 20 15S 66 40W
Huang Hai = Yellow Sea, China 35 G12 35 0N 123 0 E
Huang He →, China 35 F10 37 55N 118 50 E
Huang Xian, China 35 F11 37 38N 120 30 E
Huangling, China 34 G5 35 34N 109 15 E
Huanglong, China 34 G5 35 30N 109 59 E
Huangshan, China 33 D6 29 42N 118 25 E
Huangshi, China 33 C6 30 10N 115 3 E
Huangsongdian, China 35 C14 43 45N 127 25 E
Huantai, China 35 F9 36 58N 117 56 E
Huánuco, Peru 92 E3 9 55S 76 15W
Huaraz, Peru 92 E3 9 30S 77 32W
Huarmey, Peru 92 F3 10 5S 78 5W
Huascarán, Peru 92 E3 9 8S 77 36W
Huasco, Chile 94 B1 28 30S 71 15W
Huasco →, Chile 94 B1 28 27S 71 13W
Huasna, U.S.A. 79 K6 35 6N 120 24W
Huatabampo, Mexico 86 B3 26 50N 109 50W
Huauchinango, Mexico 87 C5 20 11N 98 3W
Huautla de Jiménez, Mexico 87 D5 18 8N 96 51W
Huay Namota, Mexico 86 C4 21 56N 104 30W
Huayin, China 34 G6 34 35N 110 5 E
Hubbard, Ohio, U.S.A. 84 E4 41 9N 80 34W
Hubbard, Tex., U.S.A. 81 K6 31 51N 96 48W
Hubbart Pt., Canada 71 B10 59 21N 94 41W
Hubei □, China 33 C6 31 0N 112 0 E
Hubli, India 40 M9 15 22N 75 15 E
Huch'ang, N. Korea 35 D14 41 25N 127 2 E
Hucknall, U.K. 12 D6 53 3N 1 13W
Huddersfield, U.K. 12 D6 53 39N 1 47W
Hudiksvall, Sweden 9 F17 61 43N 17 10 E
Hudson, Canada 72 B1 50 6N 92 9W
Hudson, Mass., U.S.A. 85 D13 42 23N 71 34W
Hudson, N.Y., U.S.A. 85 D11 42 15N 73 46W
Hudson, Wis., U.S.A. 80 C8 44 58N 92 45W
Hudson, Wyo., U.S.A. 76 E9 42 54N 108 35W
Hudson →, U.S.A. 85 F10 40 42N 74 2W
Hudson Bay, Nunavut, Canada 69 C11 60 0N 86 0W
Hudson Bay, Sask., Canada 71 C8 52 51N 102 23W
Hudson Falls, U.S.A. 85 C11 43 18N 73 35W
Hudson Mts., Antarctica 5 D16 74 32S 99 20W
Hudson Str., Canada 69 B13 62 0N 70 0W
Hudson's Hope, Canada 70 B4 56 0N 121 54W
Hue, Vietnam 38 D6 16 30N 107 35 E
Huehuetenango, Guatemala 88 C1 15 20N 91 28W
Huejúcar, Mexico 86 C4 22 21N 103 13W
Huelva, Spain 21 D2 37 18N 6 57W
Huentelauquén, Chile 94 C1 31 38S 71 33W
Huerta, Sa. de la, Argentina 94 C2 31 10S 67 30W
Huesca, Spain 21 A5 42 8N 0 25W
Huetamo, Mexico 86 D4 18 36N 100 54W

Hugh →, Australia 62 D1 25 1S 134 1 E
Hughenden, Australia 62 C3 20 52S 144 10 E
Hughes, Australia 61 F4 30 42S 129 31 E
Hughesville, U.S.A. 85 E8 41 14N 76 44W
Hugli →, India 43 J13 21 56N 88 4 E
Hugo, Colo., U.S.A. 80 F3 39 8N 103 28W
Hugo, Okla., U.S.A. 81 H7 34 1N 95 31W
Hugoton, U.S.A. 81 G4 37 11N 101 21W
Hui Xian = Huixian, China 34 G7 35 27N 113 12 E
Hui Xian, China 34 H4 33 50N 106 4 E
Hui'anbu, China 34 F4 37 28N 106 38 E
Huichapán, Mexico 87 C5 20 24N 99 40W
Huifa He →, China 35 C14 43 0N 127 50 E
Huila, Nevado del, Colombia 92 C3 3 0N 76 0W
Huimin, China 35 F9 37 27N 117 28 E
Huinan, China 35 C14 42 40N 126 2 E
Huinca Renancó, Argentina 94 C3 34 51S 64 22W
Huining, China 34 G3 35 38N 105 0 E
Huinong, China 34 E4 39 5N 106 35 E
Huisache, Mexico 86 C4 22 55N 100 25W
Huiting, China 34 G9 34 5N 116 5 E
Huixian, China 34 G7 35 27N 113 12 E
Huixtla, Mexico 87 D6 15 9N 92 28W
Huize, China 32 D5 26 24N 103 15 E
Hukawng Valley, Burma 41 F20 26 30N 96 30 E
Hüksan-chedo, S. Korea 35 G13 34 40N 125 30 E
Hukuntsi, Botswana 56 C3 23 58S 21 45 E
Ḩulayfā', Si. Arabia 44 E4 25 58N 40 45 E
Hulin He →, China 35 B12 45 0N 122 10 E
Hull = Kingston upon Hull, U.K. 12 D7 53 45N 0 21W
Hull, Canada 85 A9 45 25N 75 44W
Hull →, U.K. 12 D7 53 44N 0 20W
Hulst, Neths. 15 C4 51 17N 4 2 E
Hulun Nur, China 33 B6 49 0N 117 30 E
Huma, Tanjung, Malaysia 39 c 5 29N 100 16 E
Humacao, Puerto Rico 89 d 18 9N 65 50W
Humahuaca, Argentina 94 A2 23 10S 65 25W
Humaitá, Brazil 92 E6 7 35S 63 1W
Humaitá, Paraguay 94 B4 27 2S 58 31W
Humansdorp, S. Africa 56 E3 34 2S 24 46 E
Humbe, Angola 56 B1 16 40S 14 55 E
Humber →, U.K. 12 D7 53 42N 0 27W
Humboldt, Canada 71 C7 52 15N 105 9W
Humboldt, Iowa, U.S.A. 80 D7 42 44N 94 13W
Humboldt, Tenn., U.S.A. 81 H10 35 50N 88 55W
Humboldt →, U.S.A. 76 F4 39 59N 118 36W
Humboldt Gletscher = Sermersuaq, Greenland 4 B4 79 30N 62 0W
Hume, U.S.A. 78 J8 36 48N 118 54W
Hume, L., Australia 63 F4 36 0S 147 5 E
Humen, China 33 F10 22 50N 113 40 E
Humenné, Slovak Rep. 17 D11 48 55N 21 50 E
Humphreys, Mt., U.S.A. 78 H8 37 17N 118 40W
Humphreys Peak, U.S.A. 77 J8 35 21N 111 41W
Humptulips, U.S.A. 78 C3 47 14N 123 57W
Hūn, Libya 51 C9 29 2N 16 0 E
Hun Jiang →, China 35 D13 40 50N 125 38 E
Húnaflói, Iceland 8 D3 65 50N 20 50W
Hunan □, China 33 D6 27 30N 112 0 E
Hunchun, China 35 C16 42 52N 130 28 E
Hundewali, Pakistan 42 D5 31 55N 72 38 E
Hundred Mile House, Canada 70 C4 51 38N 121 18W
Hunedoara, Romania 17 F12 45 40N 22 50 E
Hung Yen, Vietnam 38 B6 20 39N 106 4 E
Hungary ■, Europe 17 E10 47 20N 19 20 E
Hungary, Plain of, Europe 6 F10 47 0N 20 0 E
Hungerford, Australia 63 D3 28 58S 144 24 E
Hŭngnam, N. Korea 35 E14 39 49N 127 45 E
Hunsberge, Namibia 56 D2 27 45S 17 12 E
Hunsrück, Germany 16 D4 49 56N 7 27 E
Hunstanton, U.K. 12 E8 52 56N 0 29 E
Hunter I., Australia 63 G3 40 30S 144 45 E
Hunter I., Canada 70 C3 51 55N 128 0W
Hunter Ra., Australia 63 E5 32 45S 150 15 E
Hunters Road, Zimbabwe 55 F2 19 9S 29 49 E
Hunterville, N.Z. 59 H5 39 56S 175 35 E
Huntingburg, U.S.A. 82 F2 38 18N 86 57W
Huntingdon, Canada 72 C5 45 6N 74 10W
Huntingdon, U.K. 13 E7 52 20N 0 11W
Huntington, Ind., U.S.A. 82 E3 40 53N 85 30W
Huntington, Oreg., U.S.A. 76 D5 44 21N 117 16W
Huntington, Utah, U.S.A. 76 G8 39 20N 110 58W
Huntington, W. Va., U.S.A. 82 F4 38 25N 82 27W
Huntington Beach, U.S.A. 79 M9 33 40N 118 5W
Huntington Station, U.S.A. 85 F11 40 52N 73 26W
Huntly, N.Z. 59 G5 37 34S 175 11 E
Huntly, U.K. 11 D6 57 27N 2 47W
Huntsville, Canada 84 A5 45 20N 79 14W
Huntsville, Ala., U.S.A. 83 H2 34 44N 86 35W
Huntsville, Tex., U.S.A. 81 K7 30 43N 95 33W
Hunyani →, Zimbabwe 55 F3 15 57S 30 39 E
Hunyuan, China 34 E7 39 42N 113 42 E
Hunza →, India 43 B6 35 54N 74 20 E
Huo Xian = Huozhou, China 34 F6 36 36N 111 42 E
Huong Khe, Vietnam 38 C5 18 13N 105 41 E
Huonville, Australia 63 G4 43 0S 147 5 E
Huozhou, China 34 F6 36 36N 111 42 E
Hupeh = Hubei □, China 33 C6 31 0N 112 0 E
Ḩūr, Iran 45 D8 30 50N 57 7 E
Hurd, C., Canada 84 A3 45 13N 81 44W
Hure Qi, China 35 C11 42 45N 121 45 E
Hurghada, Egypt 51 C12 27 15N 33 50 E
Hurley, N. Mex., U.S.A. 77 K9 32 42N 108 8W
Hurley, Wis., U.S.A. 80 B9 46 27N 90 11W
Huron, Calif., U.S.A. 78 J6 36 12N 120 6W
Huron, Ohio, U.S.A. 84 E2 41 24N 82 33W
Huron, S. Dak., U.S.A. 80 C5 44 22N 98 13W
Huron, L., U.S.A. 84 B2 44 30N 82 40W
Huron East, Canada 84 C3 43 37N 81 18W
Hurricane, U.S.A. 77 H7 37 11N 113 17W
Hurunui →, N.Z. 59 K4 42 54S 173 18 E
Húsavík, Iceland 8 C5 66 3N 17 21W
Huşi, Romania 17 E15 46 41N 28 7 E
Huskvarna, Sweden 9 H16 57 47N 14 15 E
Hustadvika, Norway 8 E12 63 0N 7 0 E
Hustontown, U.S.A. 84 F6 40 3N 78 2W
Hutchinson, Kans., U.S.A. 81 F6 38 5N 97 56W
Hutchinson, Minn., U.S.A. 80 C7 44 54N 94 22W
Hutte Sauvage, L. de la, Canada 73 A7 56 15N 64 45W
Hutton, Mt., Australia 63 D4 25 51S 148 20 E
Huy, Belgium 15 D5 50 31N 5 15 E
Huzhou, China 33 C7 30 51N 120 8 E
Hvammstangi, Iceland 8 D3 65 24N 20 57W
Hvar, Croatia 22 C7 43 11N 16 28 E

Hvítá →, Iceland 8 D3 64 30N 21 58W
Hwachŏn-chŏsuji, S. Korea 35 E14 38 5N 127 50 E
Hwang Ho = Huang He →, China 35 F10 37 55N 118 50 E
Hwange, Zimbabwe 55 F2 18 18S 26 30 E
Hwange △, Zimbabwe 56 B4 19 0S 26 30 E
Hyannis, Mass., U.S.A. 82 E10 41 39N 70 17W
Hyannis, Nebr., U.S.A. 80 E4 42 0N 101 46W
Hyargas Nuur, Mongolia 32 B4 49 0N 93 0 E
Hydaburg, U.S.A. 70 B2 55 15N 132 50W
Hyde Park, U.S.A. 85 E11 41 47N 73 56W
Hyden, Australia 61 F2 32 24S 118 53 E
Hyder, U.S.A. 70 B2 55 55N 130 5W
Hyderabad, India 40 L11 17 22N 78 29 E
Hyderabad, Pakistan 42 G3 25 23N 68 24 E
Hyères, France 20 E7 43 8N 6 9 E
Hyères, Îs. d', France 20 E7 43 0N 6 20 E
Hyesan, N. Korea 35 D15 41 20N 128 10 E
Hyland →, Canada 70 B3 59 52N 128 12W
Hymia, India 43 C8 33 40N 78 2 E
Hyndman Peak, U.S.A. 76 E6 43 45N 114 8W
Hyōgo □, Japan 31 G7 35 15N 134 50 E
Hyrum, U.S.A. 76 F8 41 38N 111 51W
Hysham, U.S.A. 76 C10 46 18N 107 14W
Hythe, U.K. 13 F9 51 4N 1 5 E
Hyūga, Japan 31 H5 32 25N 131 35 E
Hyvinge = Hyvinkää, Finland 9 F21 60 38N 24 50 E
Hyvinkää, Finland 9 F21 60 38N 24 50 E

I

I-n-Gall, Niger 50 E7 16 51N 7 1 E
Iaco →, Brazil 92 E5 9 3S 68 34W
Iakora, Madag. 57 C8 23 6S 46 40 E
Ialomița →, Romania 17 F14 44 42N 27 51 E
Ib →, India 43 J10 21 34N 83 48 E
Iba, Phil. 37 A6 15 22N 120 0 E
Ibadan, Nigeria 50 G6 7 22N 3 58 E
Ibagué, Colombia 92 C3 4 20N 75 20W
Ibar →, Serbia & M. 23 C9 43 43N 20 45 E
Ibaraki □, Japan 31 F10 36 10N 140 10 E
Ibarra, Ecuador 92 C3 0 21N 78 7W
Ibembo, Dem. Rep. of the Congo 54 B1 2 35N 23 35 E
Ibera, L., Argentina 94 B4 28 30S 57 9W
Iberian Peninsula, Europe 6 H5 40 0N 5 0W
Iberville, Canada 85 A11 45 19N 73 17W
Iberville, Lac d', Canada 72 A5 55 55N 73 15W
Ibiá, Brazil 93 G9 19 30S 46 30W
Ibiapaba, Sa. da, Brazil 93 D10 4 0S 41 30W
Ibicuí →, Brazil 95 B4 29 25S 56 47W
Ibicuy, Argentina 94 C4 33 55S 59 10W
Ibiza = Eivissa, Spain 24 C7 38 54N 1 26 E
Ibo, Mozam. 55 E5 12 22S 40 40 E
Ibonma, Indonesia 37 E8 3 29S 133 31 E
Ibotirama, Brazil 93 F10 12 13S 43 12W
Ibrāhīm →, Lebanon 46 A4 34 4N 35 38 E
'Ibri, Oman 47 F8 23 14N 56 30 E
Ibu, Indonesia 37 D7 1 35N 127 33 E
Ibusuki, Japan 31 J5 31 12N 130 40 E
Ica, Peru 92 F3 14 0S 75 48W
Iça →, Brazil 92 D5 2 55S 67 58W
Icacos Pt., Trin. & Tob. 93 K15 10 3N 61 57W
Içana, Brazil 92 C5 0 21N 67 19W
Içana →, Brazil 92 C5 0 26N 67 19W
İçel = Mersin, Turkey 19 G5 36 51N 34 36 E
Iceland ■, Europe 8 D4 64 45N 19 0W
Iceland Plateau, Arctic 4 C7 64 0N 10 0W
Ich'ang = Yichang, China 33 C6 30 40N 111 20 E
Ichchapuram, India 41 K14 19 10N 84 40 E
Ichhawar, India 42 H7 23 1N 77 1 E
Ichihara, Japan 31 G10 35 28N 140 5 E
Ichikawa, Japan 31 G9 35 44N 139 55 E
Ichilo →, Bolivia 92 G6 15 57S 64 50W
Ichinohe, Japan 30 D10 40 13N 141 17 E
Ichinomiya, Japan 31 G8 35 18N 136 48 E
Ichinoseki, Japan 30 E10 38 55N 141 8 E
Icod, Canary Is. 24 F3 28 22N 16 43W
Ida Grove, U.S.A. 80 D7 42 21N 95 28W
Idabel, U.S.A. 81 J7 33 54N 94 50W
Idaho □, U.S.A. 76 D7 45 0N 115 0W
Idaho City, U.S.A. 76 E6 43 50N 115 50W
Idaho Falls, U.S.A. 76 E7 43 30N 112 2W
Idalia △, Australia 62 C3 24 49S 144 36 E
Idar-Oberstein, Germany 16 D4 49 43N 7 16 E
Idfû, Egypt 51 D12 24 55N 32 49 E
Ídhi Óros, Greece 25 D6 35 15N 24 45 E
Ídhra, Greece 23 F10 37 20N 23 28 E
Idi, Indonesia 36 C1 5 2N 97 37 E
Idiofa, Dem. Rep. of the Congo 52 E3 4 55S 19 42 E
Idlib, Syria 44 C3 35 55N 36 36 E
Idria, U.S.A. 78 J6 36 25N 120 41W
Idutywa, S. Africa 57 E4 32 8S 28 18 E
Ieper, Belgium 15 D2 50 51N 2 53 E
Ierápetra, Greece 25 E7 35 1N 25 44 E
Iesi, Italy 22 C5 43 31N 13 14 E
Ifakara, Tanzania 52 F7 8 8S 36 41 E
'Ifāl, W. al →, Si. Arabia 44 D2 28 7N 35 3 E
Ifanadiana, Madag. 57 C8 21 19S 47 39 E
Ife, Nigeria 50 G6 7 30N 4 31 E
Iffley, Australia 62 B3 18 53S 141 12 E
Iforas, Adrar des, Africa 50 E6 19 40N 1 40 E
Ifould, L., Australia 61 F5 30 52S 132 6 E
Iganga, Uganda 54 B3 0 37N 33 28 E
Igarapava, Brazil 93 H9 20 3S 47 47W
Igarka, Russia 28 C9 67 30N 86 33 E
Igatimi, Paraguay 95 A4 24 5S 55 40W
Iggesund, Sweden 9 F17 61 39N 17 10 E
Iglésias, Italy 22 E3 39 19N 8 32 E
Igloolik, Canada 69 B11 69 20N 81 49W
Igluligaarjuk = Chesterfield Inlet, Canada 68 B10 63 30N 90 45W
Iglulik = Igloolik, Canada 69 B11 69 20N 81 49W
Ignace, Canada 72 C1 49 30N 91 40W
Iğneada Burnu, Turkey 23 D13 41 53N 28 2 E
Igoumenitsa, Greece 23 E9 39 32N 20 18 E
Iguaçu →, Brazil 95 B5 25 36S 54 36W
Iguaçu △, Brazil 95 B5 25 41S 53 40W
Iguaçu, Cat. del, Brazil 95 B5 25 41S 54 26W
Iguaçu Falls = Iguaçu, Cat. del, Brazil 95 B5 25 41S 54 26W
Iguala, Mexico 87 D5 18 20N 99 40W
Igualada, Spain 21 B6 41 37N 1 37 E
Iguassu = Iguaçu →, Brazil 95 B5 25 36S 54 36W
Iguatu, Brazil 93 E11 6 20S 39 18W

Iguazú △, Argentina ... 95 B5 25 42S 54 22W
Iguidi, Erg, Africa ... 50 C4 27 0N 7 0 E
Iharana, Madag. ... 57 A9 13 25S 50 0 E
Ihbulag, Mongolia ... 34 C4 43 11N 107 10 E
Iheya-Shima, Japan ... 31 L3 27 4N 127 58 E
Ihosy, Madag. ... 57 C8 22 24S 46 8 E
Ihotry, Farihy, Madag. ... 57 C7 21 56S 43 41 E
Ii, Finland ... 8 D21 65 19N 25 22 E
Ii-Shima, Japan ... 31 L3 26 43N 127 47 E
Iida, Japan ... 31 G8 35 35N 137 50 E
Iijoki →, Finland ... 8 D21 65 20N 25 20 E
Iisalmi, Finland ... 8 E22 63 32N 27 10 E
Iiyama, Japan ... 31 F9 36 51N 138 22 E
Iizuka, Japan ... 31 H5 33 38N 130 42 E
Ijebu-Ode, Nigeria ... 50 G6 6 47N 3 58 E
IJmuiden, Neths. ... 15 B4 52 28N 4 35 E
IJssel →, Neths. ... 15 B5 52 35N 5 50 E
IJsselmeer, Neths. ... 15 B5 52 45N 5 20 E
Ijuí, Brazil ... 95 B5 28 23S 53 55W
Ijuí →, Brazil ... 95 B4 27 58S 55 20W
Ikalamavony, Madag. ... 57 C8 21 9S 46 35 E
Ikaluktutiak, Canada ... 68 B9 69 10N 105 0W
Ikare, Nigeria ... 50 G7 7 32N 5 40 E
Ikeda, Japan ... 31 G6 34 1N 133 48 E
Ikela, Dem. Rep. of the Congo ... 52 E4 1 6S 23 6 E
Iki, Japan ... 31 H4 33 45N 129 42 E
Ikimba L., Tanzania ... 54 C3 1 30S 31 20 E
Ikongo, Madag. ... 57 C8 21 52S 47 27 E
Ikopa →, Madag. ... 57 B8 16 45S 46 40 E
Ikorongo △, Tanzania ... 54 C3 1 50S 34 53 E
Ikparjuk = Arctic Bay, Canada ... 69 A11 73 1N 85 7W
Ikungu, Tanzania ... 54 C3 1 33S 33 42 E
Ilagan, Phil. ... 37 A6 17 7N 121 53 E
Ilaka, Madag. ... 57 B8 19 33S 48 52 E
Īlām, Iran ... 44 C5 33 36N 46 36 E
Ilam, Nepal ... 43 F12 26 58N 87 58 E
Ilam □, Iran ... 44 C5 33 0N 47 0 E
Ilanskiy, Russia ... 29 D10 56 14N 96 3 E
Iława, Poland ... 17 B10 53 36N 19 34 E
Ile →, Kazakhstan ... 28 E8 45 53N 77 10 E
Île-à-la-Crosse, Canada ... 71 B7 55 27N 107 53W
Île-à-la-Crosse, Lac, Canada ... 71 B7 55 40N 107 45W
Île-de-France ☒, France ... 20 B5 49 0N 2 20 E
Ilebo, Dem. Rep. of the Congo ... 52 E4 4 17S 20 55 E
Ilek, Russia ... 28 D6 51 32N 53 21 E
Ilek →, Russia ... 18 D9 51 30N 53 22 E
Ilesha, Nigeria ... 50 G6 7 37N 4 40 E
Ilford, Canada ... 71 B9 56 4N 95 35W
Ilfracombe, Australia ... 62 C3 23 30S 144 30 E
Ilfracombe, U.K. ... 13 F3 51 12N 4 8W
Ilha de Moçambique, Mozam. ... 55 F5 15 4S 40 52 E
Ilhéus, Brazil ... 93 F11 14 49S 39 2W
Ili = Ile →, Kazakhstan ... 28 E8 45 53N 77 10 E
Iliamna L., U.S.A. ... 68 C4 59 30N 155 0W
Iligan, Phil. ... 37 C6 8 12N 124 13 E
Ilion, U.S.A. ... 85 D9 43 1N 75 2W
Ilkeston, U.K. ... 12 E6 52 58N 1 19W
Ilkley, U.K. ... 12 D6 53 56N 1 48W
Illampu = Ancohuma, Nevado, Bolivia ... 92 G5 16 0S 68 50W
Illana B., Phil. ... 37 C6 7 35N 123 45 E
Illapel, Chile ... 94 C1 32 0S 71 10W
Iller →, Germany ... 16 D6 48 23N 9 58 E
Illetas, Spain ... 24 B9 39 32N 2 35 E
Illimani, Nevado, Bolivia ... 92 G5 16 30S 67 50W
Illinois □, U.S.A. ... 80 E10 40 15N 89 30W
Illinois →, U.S.A. ... 80 F9 38 58N 90 28W
Illizi, Algeria ... 50 C7 26 31N 8 32 E
Ilmajoki, Finland ... 9 E20 62 44N 22 34 E
Ilmen, Ozero, Russia ... 18 C5 58 15N 31 10 E
Ilo, Peru ... 92 G4 17 40S 71 20W
Iloilo, Phil. ... 37 B6 10 45N 122 33 E
Ilorin, Nigeria ... 50 G6 8 30N 4 35 E
Ilwaco, U.S.A. ... 78 D2 46 19N 124 3W
Ilwaki, Indonesia ... 37 F7 7 55S 126 30 E
Imabari, Japan ... 31 G6 34 4N 133 0 E
Imaloto →, Madag. ... 57 C8 23 27S 45 13 E
Imandra, Ozero, Russia ... 18 A5 67 30N 33 0 E
Imanombo, Madag. ... 57 C8 24 26S 45 49 E
Imari, Japan ... 31 H4 33 15N 129 52 E
Imatra, Finland ... 18 B4 61 12N 28 48 E
Imbil, Australia ... 63 D5 26 22S 152 32 E
imeni 26 Bakinskikh Komissarov = Neftçala, Azerbaijan ... 19 G8 39 19N 49 12 E
imeni 26 Bakinskikh Komissarov, Turkmenistan ... 45 B7 39 22N 54 10 E
Imeri, Serra, Brazil ... 92 C5 0 50N 65 25W
Imerimandroso, Madag. ... 57 B8 17 26S 48 35 E
Imi, Ethiopia ... 47 F3 6 28N 42 10 E
Imlay, U.S.A. ... 76 F4 40 40N 118 9W
Imlay City, U.S.A. ... 84 D1 43 2N 83 5W
Immingham, U.K. ... 12 D7 53 37N 0 13W
Immokalee, U.S.A. ... 83 M5 26 25N 81 25W
Imola, Italy ... 22 B4 44 20N 11 42 E
Imperatriz, Brazil ... 93 E9 5 30S 47 29W
Impéria, Italy ... 20 E8 43 53N 8 3 E
Imperial, Canada ... 71 C7 51 21N 105 28W
Imperial, Calif., U.S.A. ... 79 N11 32 51N 115 34W
Imperial, Nebr., U.S.A. ... 80 E4 40 31N 101 39W
Imperial Beach, U.S.A. ... 79 N9 32 35N 117 8W
Imperial Dam, U.S.A. ... 79 N12 32 55N 114 25W
Imperial Reservoir, U.S.A. ... 79 N12 32 53N 114 28W
Imperial Valley, U.S.A. ... 79 N11 33 0N 115 30W
Imperieuse Reef, Australia ... 60 C2 17 36S 118 50 E
Impfondo, Congo ... 52 D3 1 40N 18 0 E
Imphal, India ... 41 G18 24 48N 93 56 E
Imroz = Gökçeada, Turkey ... 23 D11 40 10N 25 50 E
Imuris, Mexico ... 86 A2 30 47N 110 52W
Imuruan B., Phil. ... 37 B5 10 40N 119 10 E
In Salah, Algeria ... 50 C6 27 10N 2 32 E
Ina, Japan ... 31 G8 35 50N 137 55 E
Inagua □, Bahamas ... 89 B5 21 0N 73 24W
Inangahua, N.Z. ... 59 J3 41 52S 171 59 E
Inanwatan, Indonesia ... 37 E8 2 8S 132 10 E
Iñapari, Peru ... 92 F5 11 0S 69 40W
Inari, Finland ... 8 B22 68 54N 27 5 E
Inarijärvi, Finland ... 8 B22 69 0N 28 0 E
Inawashiro-Ko, Japan ... 30 F10 37 29N 140 6 E
Inca, Spain ... 24 B9 39 43N 2 54 E
Inca de Oro, Chile ... 94 B2 26 45S 69 54W
Incaguasi, Chile ... 94 B1 29 12S 71 5W
Ince Burun, Turkey ... 19 F5 42 7N 34 56 E
İncesu, Turkey ... 44 B2 38 38N 35 11 E
Inch'ŏn, S. Korea ... 35 F14 37 27N 126 40 E
İncirliova, Turkey ... 23 F12 37 50N 27 41 E

Incline Village, U.S.A. ... 76 G4 39 10N 119 58W
Incomáti →, Mozam. ... 57 D5 25 46S 32 43 E
Indalsälven →, Sweden ... 9 E17 62 36N 17 30 E
Indaw, Burma ... 41 G20 24 15N 96 5 E
Independence, Calif., U.S.A. ... 78 J8 36 48N 118 12W
Independence, Iowa, U.S.A. ... 80 D9 42 28N 91 54W
Independence, Kans., U.S.A. ... 81 G7 37 14N 95 42W
Independence, Ky., U.S.A. ... 82 F3 38 57N 84 33W
Independence, Mo., U.S.A. ... 80 F7 39 6N 94 25W
Independence Fjord, Greenland ... 4 A6 82 10N 29 0W
Independence Mts., U.S.A. ... 76 F5 41 20N 116 0W
Index, U.S.A. ... 78 C5 47 50N 121 33W
India ■, Asia ... 40 K11 20 0N 78 0 E
Indian →, U.S.A. ... 83 M5 27 59N 80 34W
Indian Cabins, Canada ... 70 B5 59 52N 117 40W
Indian Harbour, Canada ... 73 B8 54 27N 57 13W
Indian Head, Canada ... 71 C8 50 30N 103 41W
Indian Lake, Canada ... 85 C10 43 47N 74 16W
Indian Ocean ... 26 K11 5 0S 75 0 E
Indian Springs, U.S.A. ... 79 J11 36 35N 115 40W
Indiana, U.S.A. ... 84 F5 40 37N 79 9W
Indiana □, U.S.A. ... 82 F3 40 0N 86 0W
Indianapolis, U.S.A. ... 82 F2 39 46N 86 9W
Indianola, Iowa, U.S.A. ... 80 E8 41 22N 93 34W
Indianola, Miss., U.S.A. ... 81 J9 33 27N 90 39W
Indiga, Russia ... 18 A8 67 38N 49 9 E
Indigirka →, Russia ... 29 B15 70 48N 148 54 E
Indio, U.S.A. ... 79 M10 33 43N 116 13W
Indira Gandhi Canal, India ... 42 F5 28 0N 72 0 E
Indo-China, Asia ... 26 H14 15 0N 102 0 E
Indonesia ■, Asia ... 36 F5 5 0S 115 0 E
Indore, India ... 42 H6 22 42N 75 53 E
Indramayu, Indonesia ... 37 G13 6 20S 108 19 E
Indravati →, India ... 41 K12 19 20N 80 20 E
Indre →, France ... 20 C4 47 16N 0 11 E
Indulkana, Australia ... 63 D1 26 58S 133 5 E
Indus →, Pakistan ... 42 G2 24 20N 67 47 E
Indus, Mouths of the, Pakistan ... 42 H3 24 0N 68 0 E
Inebolu, Turkey ... 19 F5 41 55N 33 40 E
Infiernillo, Presa del, Mexico ... 86 D4 18 9N 102 0W
Ingenio, Canary Is. ... 24 G4 27 55N 15 26W
Ingenio Santa Ana, Argentina ... 94 B2 27 25S 65 40W
Ingersoll, Canada ... 84 C4 43 4N 80 55W
Ingham, Australia ... 62 B4 18 43S 146 10 E
Ingleborough, U.K. ... 12 C5 54 10N 2 22W
Inglewood, Queens., Australia ... 63 D5 28 25S 151 2 E
Inglewood, Vic., Australia ... 63 F3 36 29S 143 53 E
Inglewood, N.Z. ... 59 H5 39 9S 174 14 E
Inglewood, U.S.A. ... 79 M8 33 58N 118 21W
Ingólfshöfði, Iceland ... 8 E5 63 48N 16 39W
Ingolstadt, Germany ... 16 D6 48 46N 11 26 E
Ingomar, U.S.A. ... 76 C10 46 35N 107 23W
Ingonish, Canada ... 73 C7 46 42N 60 18W
Ingraj Bazar, India ... 43 G13 24 58N 88 10 E
Ingrid Christensen Coast, Antarctica ... 5 C6 69 30S 76 0 E
Ingulec = Inhulec, Ukraine ... 19 E5 47 42N 33 14 E
Ingushetia □, Russia ... 19 F8 43 20N 44 50 E
Ingwavuma, S. Africa ... 57 D5 27 9S 31 59 E
Inhaca, Mozam. ... 57 D5 26 1S 32 57 E
Inhafenga, Mozam. ... 57 C5 20 36S 33 53 E
Inhambane, Mozam. ... 57 C6 23 54S 35 30 E
Inhambane □, Mozam. ... 57 C5 22 30S 34 20 E
Inhaminga, Mozam. ... 55 F4 18 26S 35 0 E
Inharrime, Mozam. ... 57 C6 24 30S 35 0 E
Inharrime →, Mozam. ... 57 C6 24 30S 35 0 E
Inhulec, Ukraine ... 19 E5 47 42N 33 14 E
Ining = Yining, China ... 28 E9 43 58N 81 10 E
Inírida →, Colombia ... 92 C5 3 55N 67 52W
Inishbofin, Ireland ... 10 C1 53 37N 10 13W
Inisheer, Ireland ... 10 C2 53 3N 9 32W
Inishfree B., Ireland ... 10 A3 55 4N 8 23W
Inishkea North, Ireland ... 10 B1 54 9N 10 11W
Inishkea South, Ireland ... 10 B1 54 7N 10 12W
Inishmaan, Ireland ... 10 C2 53 5N 9 35W
Inishmore, Ireland ... 10 C2 53 8N 9 45W
Inishowen Pen., Ireland ... 10 A4 55 14N 7 15W
Inishshark, Ireland ... 10 C1 53 37N 10 16W
Inishturk, Ireland ... 10 C1 53 42N 10 7W
Inishvickillane, Ireland ... 10 D1 52 3N 10 37W
Injune, Australia ... 63 D4 25 53S 148 32 E
Inklin →, Canada ... 70 B2 58 50N 133 10W
Inland Kaikoura Ra., N.Z. ... 59 J4 41 59S 173 41 E
Inland Sea = Setonaikai, Japan ... 31 G6 34 20N 133 30 E
Inle L., Burma ... 41 J20 20 30N 96 58 E
Inlet, U.S.A. ... 85 C10 43 45N 74 48W
Inn →, Austria ... 16 D7 48 35N 13 28 E
Innamincka, Australia ... 63 D3 27 44S 140 46 E
Inner Hebrides, U.K. ... 11 E2 57 0N 6 30W
Inner Mongolia = Nei Monggol Zizhiqu □, China ... 34 D7 42 0N 112 0 E
Inner Sound, U.K. ... 11 D3 57 30N 5 55W
Innerkip, Canada ... 84 C4 43 13N 80 42W
Innetalling I., Canada ... 72 A4 56 0N 79 0W
Innisfail, Australia ... 62 B4 17 33S 146 5 E
Innisfail, Canada ... 70 C6 52 2N 113 57W
In'noshima, Japan ... 31 G6 34 19N 133 10 E
Innsbruck, Austria ... 16 E6 47 16N 11 23 E
Inny →, Ireland ... 10 C4 53 30N 7 50W
Inongo, Dem. Rep. of the Congo ... 52 E3 1 55S 18 30 E
Inoucdjouac = Inukjuak, Canada ... 69 C12 58 25N 78 15W
Inowrocław, Poland ... 17 B10 52 50N 18 12 E
Inpundong, N. Korea ... 35 D14 41 25N 126 34 E
Inscription, C., Australia ... 61 E1 25 29S 112 59 E
Insein, Burma ... 41 L20 16 50N 96 5 E
Inta, Russia ... 18 A11 66 5N 60 8 E
Intendente Alvear, Argentina ... 94 D3 35 12S 63 32W
Interlaken, Switz. ... 20 C7 46 41N 7 50 E
Interlaken, U.S.A. ... 85 D8 42 37N 76 44W
International Falls, U.S.A. ... 80 A8 48 36N 93 25W
Intiyaco, Argentina ... 94 B3 28 43S 60 5W
Inukjuak, Canada ... 69 C12 58 25N 78 15W
Inútil, B., Chile ... 96 G2 53 30S 70 15W
Inuvik, Canada ... 68 B6 68 16N 133 40W
Inveraray, U.K. ... 11 E3 56 14N 5 5W
Inverbervie, U.K. ... 11 E6 56 51N 2 17W
Invercargill, N.Z. ... 59 M2 46 24S 168 24 E
Inverclyde □, U.K. ... 11 F4 55 55N 4 49W
Inverell, Australia ... 63 D5 29 45S 151 8 E
Invergordon, U.K. ... 11 D4 57 41N 4 10W
Inverloch, Australia ... 63 F4 38 38S 145 45 E
Invermere, Canada ... 70 C5 50 30N 116 2W
Inverness, Canada ... 73 C7 46 15N 61 19W
Inverness, U.K. ... 11 D4 57 29N 4 13W
Inverness, U.S.A. ... 83 L4 28 50N 82 20W
Inverurie, U.K. ... 11 D6 57 17N 2 23W
Investigator Group, Australia ... 63 E1 34 45S 134 20 E

Investigator Str., Australia ... 63 F2 35 30S 137 0 E
Inya, Russia ... 28 D9 50 28N 86 37 E
Inyanga, Zimbabwe ... 55 F3 18 12S 32 40 E
Inyangani, Zimbabwe ... 55 F3 18 5S 32 50 E
Inyantue, Zimbabwe ... 56 B4 18 33S 26 39 E
Inyo Mts., U.S.A. ... 78 J9 36 40N 118 0W
Inyokern, U.S.A. ... 79 K9 35 39N 117 49W
Inza, Russia ... 18 D8 53 55N 46 25 E
Iō-Jima, Japan ... 31 J5 30 48N 130 18 E
Ioánnina, Greece ... 23 E9 39 42N 20 47 E
Iola, U.S.A. ... 81 G7 37 55N 95 24W
Iona, U.K. ... 11 E2 56 20N 6 25W
Ione, U.S.A. ... 78 G6 38 21N 120 56W
Ionia, U.S.A. ... 82 D3 42 59N 85 4W
Ionian Is. = Iónioi Nísoi, Greece ... 23 E9 38 40N 20 0 E
Ionian Sea, Medit. S. ... 23 E7 37 30N 17 30 E
Iónioi Nísoi, Greece ... 23 E9 38 40N 20 0 E
Íos, Greece ... 23 F11 36 41N 25 20 E
Iowa □, U.S.A. ... 80 D8 42 18N 93 30W
Iowa →, U.S.A. ... 80 E9 41 10N 91 1W
Iowa City, U.S.A. ... 80 E9 41 40N 91 32W
Iowa Falls, U.S.A. ... 80 D8 42 31N 93 16W
Iowa Park, U.S.A. ... 81 J5 33 57N 98 40W
Ipala, Tanzania ... 54 C3 4 30S 32 52 E
Ipameri, Brazil ... 93 G9 17 44S 48 9W
Ipatinga, Brazil ... 93 G10 19 32S 42 30W
Ipiales, Colombia ... 92 C3 0 50N 77 37W
Ipin = Yibin, China ... 32 D5 28 45N 104 32 E
Ipixuna, Brazil ... 92 E4 7 0S 71 40W
Ipoh, Malaysia ... 39 K3 4 35N 101 5 E
Ippy, C.A.R. ... 52 C4 6 5N 21 7 E
Ipsala, Turkey ... 23 D12 40 55N 26 23 E
Ipswich, Australia ... 63 D5 27 35S 152 40 E
Ipswich, U.K. ... 13 E9 52 4N 1 10 E
Ipswich, Mass., U.S.A. ... 85 D14 42 41N 70 50W
Ipswich, S. Dak., U.S.A. ... 80 C5 45 27N 99 2W
Ipu, Brazil ... 93 D10 4 23S 40 44W
Iqaluit, Canada ... 69 B13 63 44N 68 31W
Iquique, Chile ... 92 H4 20 19S 70 5W
Iquitos, Peru ... 92 D4 3 45S 73 10W
Irabu-Jima, Japan ... 31 M2 24 50N 125 10 E
Iracoubo, Fr. Guiana ... 93 B8 5 30N 53 10W
Īrafshān, Iran ... 45 E9 26 42N 61 56 E
Iráklion, Greece ... 25 D7 35 20N 25 12 E
Iráklion □, Greece ... 25 D7 35 10N 25 10 E
Irala, Paraguay ... 95 B5 25 55S 54 35W
Iran ■, Asia ... 45 C7 33 0N 53 0 E
Iran, Gunung-Gunung, Malaysia ... 36 D4 2 20N 114 50 E
Iran, Plateau of, Asia ... 26 F9 32 0N 55 0 E
Iran Ra. = Iran, Gunung-Gunung, Malaysia ... 36 D4 2 20N 114 50 E
Īrānshahr, Iran ... 45 E9 27 15N 60 40 E
Irapuato, Mexico ... 86 C4 20 40N 101 30W
Iraq ■, Asia ... 44 C5 33 0N 44 0 E
Irati, Brazil ... 95 B5 25 25S 50 38W
Irbid, Jordan ... 46 C4 32 35N 35 48 E
Irbid □, Jordan ... 46 C5 32 15N 36 35 E
Ireland ■, Europe ... 10 C4 53 50N 7 52W
Irhyangdong, N. Korea ... 35 D15 41 15N 129 30 E
Iri, S. Korea ... 35 G14 35 59N 127 0 E
Irian Jaya = Papua □, Indonesia ... 37 E9 4 0S 137 0 E
Iringa, Tanzania ... 54 D4 7 48S 35 43 E
Iringa □, Tanzania ... 54 D4 7 48S 35 43 E
Iriomote △, Japan ... 31 M1 24 29N 123 53 E
Iriomote-Jima, Japan ... 31 M1 24 19N 123 48 E
Iriona, Honduras ... 88 C2 15 57N 85 11W
Iriri →, Brazil ... 93 D8 3 52S 52 37W
Irish Republic ■, Europe ... 10 C4 53 50N 7 52W
Irish Sea, U.K. ... 12 D3 53 38N 4 48W
Irkutsk, Russia ... 29 D11 52 18N 104 20 E
Irma, Canada ... 71 C6 52 55N 111 14W
Iró-Zaki, Japan ... 31 G9 34 36N 138 51 E
Iron Baron, Australia ... 63 E2 32 58S 137 11 E
Iron Gate = Portile de Fier, Europe ... 17 F12 44 44N 22 30 E
Iron Knob, Australia ... 63 E2 32 46S 137 8 E
Iron Mountain, U.S.A. ... 82 C1 45 49N 88 4W
Iron Range △, Australia ... 62 A3 12 34S 143 18 E
Iron River, U.S.A. ... 80 B10 46 6N 88 39W
Irondequoit, U.S.A. ... 84 C7 43 13N 77 35W
Ironton, Mo., U.S.A. ... 81 G9 37 36N 90 38W
Ironton, Ohio, U.S.A. ... 82 F4 38 32N 82 41W
Ironwood, U.S.A. ... 80 B9 46 27N 90 9W
Ironwood Forest △, U.S.A. ... 77 K8 32 25N 111 23W
Iroquois, Canada ... 85 B9 44 51N 75 19W
Iroquois Falls, Canada ... 72 C3 48 46N 80 41W
Irpin, Ukraine ... 17 C16 50 30N 30 15 E
Irrara Cr. →, Australia ... 63 D4 29 35S 145 31 E
Irrawaddy □, Burma ... 41 L19 17 0N 95 0 E
Irrawaddy →, Burma ... 41 M19 15 50N 95 6 E
Irrawaddy, Mouths of the, Burma ... 41 M19 15 30N 95 0 E
Irricana, Canada ... 70 C6 51 19N 113 37W
Irtysh →, Russia ... 28 C7 61 4N 68 52 E
Irumu, Dem. Rep. of the Congo ... 54 B2 1 32N 29 53 E
Irún, Spain ... 21 A5 43 20N 1 52W
Irunea = Pamplona, Spain ... 21 A5 42 48N 1 38W
Irvine, U.K. ... 11 F4 55 37N 4 41W
Irvine, Calif., U.S.A. ... 79 M9 33 41N 117 46W
Irvine, Ky., U.S.A. ... 82 G4 37 42N 83 58W
Irvinestown, U.K. ... 10 B4 54 28N 7 39W
Irving, U.S.A. ... 81 J6 32 49N 96 56W
Irvona, U.S.A. ... 84 F6 40 46N 78 33W
Irwin →, Australia ... 61 E1 29 15S 114 54 E
Irymple, Australia ... 63 E3 34 14S 142 8 E
Isa Khel, Pakistan ... 42 C4 32 41N 71 17 E
Isaac →, Australia ... 62 C4 22 55S 149 20 E
Isabel, U.S.A. ... 80 C4 45 24N 101 26W
Isabela, Phil. ... 37 C6 6 40N 121 59 E
Isabela, Puerto Rico ... 89 d 18 30N 67 2W
Isabela, I., Mexico ... 86 C3 21 51N 105 55W
Isabella, Cord., Nic. ... 88 D2 13 30N 85 25W
Isabella Ra., Australia ... 60 D3 21 0S 121 4 E
Ísafjarðardjúp, Iceland ... 8 C2 66 10N 23 0W
Ísafjörður, Iceland ... 8 C2 66 5N 23 9W
Isagarh, India ... 42 G7 24 48N 77 51 E
Isahaya, Japan ... 31 H5 32 52N 130 2 E
Isaka, Tanzania ... 54 C3 3 56S 32 59 E
Isalo △, Madag. ... 57 C8 22 23S 45 16 E
Isana →, Brazil ... 92 C5 0 26N 67 19W
Isangano △, Zambia ... 55 E3 11 8S 30 35 E
Isar →, Germany ... 16 D7 48 48N 12 57 E
Íschia, Italy ... 22 D5 40 44N 13 57 E
Isdell →, Australia ... 60 C3 16 27S 124 51 E
Ise, Japan ... 31 G8 34 25N 136 45 E
Ise-Shima △, Japan ... 31 G8 34 25N 136 48 E
Ise-Wan, Japan ... 31 G8 34 43N 136 43 E

Iseramagazi, Tanzania ... 54 C3 4 37S 32 10 E
Isère □, France ... 20 D6 44 59N 4 51 E
Isère →, France ... 20 D6 44 59N 4 51 E
Isérnia, Italy ... 22 D6 41 36N 14 14 E
Isfahan = Eşfahān, Iran ... 45 C6 32 39N 51 43 E
Ishigaki-Shima, Japan ... 31 M2 24 20N 124 10 E
Ishikari-Gawa →, Japan ... 30 C10 43 15N 141 23 E
Ishikari-Sammyaku, Japan ... 30 C11 43 30N 143 0 E
Ishikari-Wan, Japan ... 30 C10 43 25N 141 1 E
Ishikawa □, Japan ... 31 F8 36 30N 136 30 E
Ishim, Russia ... 28 D7 56 10N 69 30 E
Ishim →, Russia ... 28 D8 57 45N 71 10 E
Ishinomaki, Japan ... 30 E10 38 32N 141 20 E
Ishioka, Japan ... 31 F10 36 11N 140 16 E
Ishkuman, Pakistan ... 43 A5 36 30N 73 50 E
Ishpeming, U.S.A. ... 82 B2 46 29N 87 40W
Isil Kul, Russia ... 28 D8 54 55N 71 16 E
Isiolo, Kenya ... 54 B4 0 24N 37 33 E
Isiro, Dem. Rep. of the Congo ... 54 B2 2 53N 27 40 E
Isisford, Australia ... 62 C3 24 15S 144 21 E
İskenderun, Turkey ... 19 G6 36 32N 36 10 E
İskenderun Körfezi, Turkey ... 19 G6 36 40N 35 50 E
İskůr →, Bulgaria ... 23 C11 43 45N 24 25 E
Iskut →, Canada ... 70 B2 56 45N 131 49W
Isla →, U.K. ... 11 E5 56 32N 3 20W
Isla Coiba △, Panama ... 88 E3 7 33N 81 36W
Isla de Salamanca △, Colombia ... 89 D5 10 59N 74 40W
Isla Gorge △, Australia ... 62 D4 25 10S 149 57 E
Isla Tiburón y San Esteban △, Mexico ... 86 B2 29 0N 112 20W
Isla Vista, U.S.A. ... 79 L7 34 25N 119 53W
Islam Headworks, Pakistan ... 42 E5 29 49N 72 33 E
Islamabad, Pakistan ... 42 C5 33 40N 73 10 E
Islamgarh, Pakistan ... 42 F4 27 51N 70 48 E
Islamkot, Pakistan ... 42 G4 24 42N 70 13 E
Islampur, India ... 43 G11 25 9N 85 12 E
Island L., Canada ... 71 C10 53 47N 94 25W
Island Lagoon, Australia ... 63 E2 31 30S 136 40 E
Island Pond, U.S.A. ... 85 B13 44 49N 71 53W
Islands, B. of, Canada ... 73 C8 49 11N 58 15W
Islands, B. of, N.Z. ... 59 F5 35 15S 174 6 E
Islay, U.K. ... 11 F2 55 46N 6 10W
Isle →, France ... 20 D3 44 55N 0 15W
Isle aux Morts, Canada ... 73 C8 47 35N 59 0W
Isle of Wight □, U.K. ... 13 G6 50 41N 1 17W
Isle Royale △, U.S.A. ... 82 B1 48 0N 88 55W
Isleton, U.S.A. ... 78 G5 38 10N 121 37W
Ismail = Izmayil, Ukraine ... 17 F15 45 22N 28 46 E
Ismâ'ilîya, Egypt ... 51 B12 30 37N 32 18 E
Isoanala, Madag. ... 57 C8 23 50S 45 44 E
Isogstalo, India ... 43 B8 34 15N 78 46 E
Ísparta, Turkey ... 19 G5 37 47N 30 30 E
Íspica, Italy ... 22 F6 36 47N 14 55 E
Israel ■, Asia ... 46 D3 32 0N 34 50 E
Issoire, France ... 20 D5 45 32N 3 15 E
Issyk-Kul, Ozero = Ysyk-Köl, Kyrgyzstan ... 28 E8 42 25N 77 15 E
İstanbul, Turkey ... 23 D13 41 0N 29 0 E
İstanbul Boğazı, Turkey ... 23 D13 41 10N 29 10 E
Istiaía, Greece ... 23 E10 38 57N 23 9 E
Istokpoga, L., U.S.A. ... 83 M5 27 23N 81 17W
Istra, Croatia ... 16 F7 45 10N 14 0 E
Istres, France ... 20 E6 43 31N 4 59 E
Istria = Istra, Croatia ... 16 F7 45 10N 14 0 E
Itá, Paraguay ... 94 B4 25 29S 57 21W
Itaberaba, Brazil ... 93 F10 12 32S 40 18W
Itabira, Brazil ... 93 G10 19 37S 43 13W
Itabirito, Brazil ... 95 A7 20 15S 43 48W
Itabuna, Brazil ... 93 F11 14 48S 39 16W
Itacaunas →, Brazil ... 93 E9 5 21S 49 8W
Itacoatiara, Brazil ... 92 D7 3 8S 58 25W
Itaipú, Represa de, Brazil ... 95 B5 25 30S 54 30W
Itaituba, Brazil ... 93 D7 4 10S 55 50W
Itajaí, Brazil ... 95 B6 27 50S 48 39W
Itajubá, Brazil ... 95 A6 22 24S 45 30W
Itaka, Tanzania ... 55 D3 8 50S 32 49 E
Itala △, S. Africa ... 57 D5 27 30S 31 7 E
Italy ■, Europe ... 22 C5 42 0N 13 0 E
Itamaraju, Brazil ... 93 G11 17 5S 39 31W
Itampolo, Madag. ... 57 C7 24 41S 43 57 E
Itandrano, Madag. ... 57 C8 21 47S 45 17 E
Itapecuru-Mirim, Brazil ... 93 D10 3 24S 44 20W
Itaperuna, Brazil ... 95 A7 21 10S 41 54W
Itapetininga, Brazil ... 95 A6 23 36S 48 7W
Itapeva, Brazil ... 95 A6 23 59S 48 59W
Itapicuru →, Bahia, Brazil ... 93 F11 11 47S 37 32W
Itapicuru →, Maranhão, Brazil ... 93 D10 2 52S 44 12W
Itapipoca, Brazil ... 93 D11 3 30S 39 35W
Itapuá □, Paraguay ... 95 B4 26 40S 55 40W
Itaquari, Brazil ... 95 A7 20 20S 40 25W
Itaqui, Brazil ... 94 B4 29 8S 56 30W
Itararé, Brazil ... 95 A6 24 6S 49 23W
Itarsi, India ... 42 H7 22 36N 77 51 E
Itati, Argentina ... 94 B4 27 16S 58 15W
Itatiaia △, Brazil ... 95 A7 22 25S 44 38W
Itchen →, U.K. ... 13 G6 50 55N 1 22W
Itezhi Tezhi, L., Zambia ... 55 F2 15 30S 25 30 E
Ithaca = Itháki, Greece ... 23 E9 38 25N 20 40 E
Ithaca, U.S.A. ... 85 D8 42 27N 76 30W
Itháki, Greece ... 23 E9 38 25N 20 40 E
Itiquira →, Brazil ... 93 G7 17 18S 56 44W
Itō, Japan ... 31 G9 34 58N 139 5 E
Itoigawa, Japan ... 31 F8 37 2N 137 51 E
Itonamas →, Bolivia ... 92 F6 12 28S 64 24W
Ittoqqortoormiit, Greenland ... 4 B6 70 20N 23 0W
Itu, Brazil ... 95 A6 23 17S 47 15W
Itu Aba I., S. China Sea ... 36 B4 10 23N 114 21 E
Ituiutaba, Brazil ... 93 G9 19 0S 49 25W
Itumbiara, Brazil ... 93 G9 18 20S 49 10W
Ituna, Canada ... 71 C8 51 10N 103 24W
Itunge Port, Tanzania ... 55 D3 9 40S 33 55 E
Iturbe, Argentina ... 94 A2 23 0S 65 25W
Ituri →, Dem. Rep. of the Congo ... 54 B2 1 40N 27 1 E
Iturup, Ostrov, Russia ... 29 E15 45 0N 148 0 E
Ituxi →, Brazil ... 92 E6 7 18S 64 51W
Ituyuro →, Argentina ... 94 A3 22 40S 63 50W
Itzehoe, Germany ... 16 B5 53 55N 9 31 E
Ivaí →, Brazil ... 95 A5 23 18S 53 42W
Ivalo, Finland ... 8 B22 68 38N 27 35 E
Ivalojoki →, Finland ... 8 B22 68 40N 27 40 E
Ivanava, Belarus ... 17 B13 52 7N 25 29 E
Ivanhoe, Australia ... 63 E3 32 56S 144 20 E
Ivanhoe, Calif., U.S.A. ... 78 J7 36 23N 119 13W
Ivanhoe, Minn., U.S.A. ... 80 C6 44 28N 96 15W
Ivano-Frankivsk, Ukraine ... 17 D13 48 40N 24 40 E
Ivanovo = Ivanava, Belarus ... 17 B13 52 7N 25 29 E
Ivanovo, Russia ... 18 C7 57 5N 41 0 E

INDEX TO WORLD MAPS
John Day Fossil Beds 129

Ivato, *Madag.* **57 C8** 20 37S 47 10 E
Ivatsevichy, *Belarus* **17 B13** 52 43N 25 21 E
Ivdel, *Russia* **18 B11** 60 42N 60 24 E
Ivinheima →, *Brazil* **95 A5** 23 14S 53 42W
Ivinhema, *Brazil* **95 A5** 22 10S 53 37W
Ivohibe, *Madag.* **57 C8** 22 31S 46 57 E
Ivory Coast, *W. Afr.* **50 H4** 4 20N 5 0W
Ivory Coast ■, *Africa* **50 G4** 7 30N 5 0W
Ivrea, *Italy* **20 D7** 45 28N 7 52 E
Ivujivik, *Canada* **69 B12** 62 24N 77 55W
Ivybridge, *U.K.* **13 G4** 50 23N 3 56W
Iwaizumi, *Japan* **30 E10** 39 50N 141 45 E
Iwaki, *Japan* **31 F10** 37 3N 140 55 E
Iwakuni, *Japan* **31 G6** 34 15N 132 8 E
Iwamizawa, *Japan* **30 C10** 43 12N 141 46 E
Iwanai, *Japan* **30 C10** 42 58N 140 30 E
Iwata, *Japan* **31 G8** 34 42N 137 51 E
Iwate □, *Japan* **30 E10** 39 30N 141 30 E
Iwate-San, *Japan* **30 E10** 39 51N 141 0 E
Iwo, *Nigeria* **50 G6** 7 39N 4 9 E
Ixiamas, *Bolivia* **92 F5** 13 50S 68 5W
Ixopo, *S. Africa* **57 E5** 30 11S 30 5 E
Ixtepec, *Mexico* **87 D5** 16 32N 95 10W
Ixtlán del Río, *Mexico* **86 C4** 21 5N 104 21W
Iyo, *Japan* **31 H6** 33 45N 132 45 E
Izabal, L. de, *Guatemala* **88 C2** 15 30N 89 10W
Izamal, *Mexico* **87 C7** 20 56N 89 1W
Izena-Shima, *Japan* **31 L3** 26 56N 127 56 E
Izhevsk, *Russia* **18 C9** 56 51N 53 14 E
Izhma →, *Russia* **18 A9** 65 19N 52 54 E
Izmayil, *Ukraine* **17 F15** 45 22N 28 46 E
İzmir, *Turkey* **23 E12** 38 25N 27 8 E
İzmit = Kocaeli, *Turkey* **19 F4** 40 45N 29 50 E
İznik Gölü, *Turkey* **23 D13** 40 27N 29 30 E
Izra, *Syria* **46 C5** 32 51N 36 15 E
Izu-Shotō, *Japan* **31 G10** 34 30N 140 0 E
Izúcar de Matamoros, *Mexico* **87 D5** 18 36N 98 28W
Izumi-Sano, *Japan* **31 G7** 34 23N 135 18 E
Izumo, *Japan* **31 G6** 35 20N 132 46 E
Izyaslav, *Ukraine* **17 C14** 50 5N 26 50 E

J

Jabalpur, *India* **43 H8** 23 9N 79 58 E
Jabbūl, *Syria* **44 B3** 36 4N 37 30 E
Jabiru, *Australia* **60 B5** 12 40S 132 53 E
Jablah, *Syria* **44 C3** 35 20N 36 0 E
Jablonec nad Nisou, *Czech Rep.* **16 C8** 50 43N 15 10 E
Jaboatão, *Brazil* **93 E11** 8 7S 35 1W
Jaboticabal, *Brazil* **95 A6** 21 15S 48 17W
Jaca, *Spain* **21 A5** 42 35N 0 33W
Jacareí, *Brazil* **95 A6** 23 20S 46 0W
Jacarèzinho, *Brazil* **95 A6** 23 5S 49 58W
Jackman, *U.S.A.* **83 C10** 45 35N 70 17W
Jacksboro, *U.S.A.* **81 J5** 33 14N 98 15W
Jackson, *Barbados* **89 g** 13 7N 59 36W
Jackson, *Ala., U.S.A.* **83 K2** 31 31N 87 53W
Jackson, *Calif., U.S.A.* **78 G6** 38 21N 120 46W
Jackson, *Ky., U.S.A.* **82 G4** 37 33N 83 23W
Jackson, *Mich., U.S.A.* **82 D3** 42 15N 84 24W
Jackson, *Minn., U.S.A.* **80 D7** 43 37N 95 1W
Jackson, *Miss., U.S.A.* **81 J9** 32 18N 90 12W
Jackson, *Mo., U.S.A.* **81 G10** 37 23N 89 40W
Jackson, *N.H., U.S.A.* **85 B13** 44 10N 71 11W
Jackson, *Ohio, U.S.A.* **82 F4** 39 3N 82 39W
Jackson, *Tenn., U.S.A.* **83 H1** 35 37N 88 49W
Jackson, *Wyo., U.S.A.* **76 E8** 43 29N 110 46W
Jackson B., *N.Z.* **59 K2** 43 58S 168 42 E
Jackson L., *U.S.A.* **76 E8** 43 52N 110 36W
Jacksons, *N.Z.* **59 K3** 42 46S 171 32 E
Jackson's Arm, *Canada* **73 C8** 49 52N 56 47W
Jacksonville, *Ala., U.S.A.* **83 J3** 33 49N 85 46W
Jacksonville, *Ark., U.S.A.* **81 H8** 34 52N 92 7W
Jacksonville, *Calif., U.S.A.* **78 H6** 37 52N 120 24W
Jacksonville, *Fla., U.S.A.* **83 K5** 30 20N 81 39W
Jacksonville, *Ill., U.S.A.* **80 F9** 39 44N 90 14W
Jacksonville, *N.C., U.S.A.* **83 H7** 34 45N 77 26W
Jacksonville, *Tex., U.S.A.* **81 K7** 31 58N 95 17W
Jacksonville Beach, *U.S.A.* **83 K5** 30 17N 81 24W
Jacmel, *Haiti* **89 C5** 18 14N 72 32W
Jacob Lake, *U.S.A.* **77 H7** 36 43N 112 13W
Jacobabad, *Pakistan* **42 E3** 28 20N 68 29 E
Jacobina, *Brazil* **93 F10** 11 11S 40 30W
Jacques-Cartier ⌓, *Canada* **73 C5** 47 15N 71 33W
Jacques-Cartier, Dét. de, *Canada* **73 C7** 50 0N 63 30W
Jacques-Cartier, Mt., *Canada* **73 C6** 48 57N 66 0W
Jacuí →, *Brazil* **95 C5** 30 2S 51 15W
Jacumba, *U.S.A.* **79 N10** 32 37N 116 11W
Jacundá →, *Brazil* **93 D8** 1 57S 50 26W
Jaén, *Peru* **92 E3** 5 25S 78 40W
Jaén, *Spain* **21 D4** 37 44N 3 43W
Jafarabad, *India* **42 J4** 20 52N 71 22 E
Jaffa = Tel Aviv-Yafo, *Israel* **46 C3** 32 4N 34 48 E
Jaffa, C., *Australia* **63 F2** 36 58S 139 40 E
Jaffna, *Sri Lanka* **40 Q12** 9 45N 80 2 E
Jaffray, *Canada* **71 D10** 49 47N 94 26W
Jaffrey, *U.S.A.* **85 D12** 42 49N 72 2W
Jagadhri, *India* **42 D7** 30 10N 77 20 E
Jagadishpur, *India* **43 G11** 25 30N 84 21 E
Jagdalpur, *India* **41 K13** 19 3N 82 0 E
Jagersfontein, *S. Africa* **56 D4** 29 44S 25 27 E
Jaghīn →, *Iran* **45 E8** 27 17N 57 13 E
Jagodina, *Serbia & M.* **23 C9** 44 5N 21 15 E
Jagraon, *India* **40 D9** 30 50N 75 25 E
Jagtial, *India* **40 K11** 18 50N 79 0 E
Jaguariaíva, *Brazil* **95 A6** 24 10S 49 50W
Jaguaribe →, *Brazil* **93 D11** 4 25S 37 45W
Jagüey Grande, *Cuba* **88 B3** 22 35N 81 7W
Jahanabad, *India* **43 G11** 25 13N 84 59 E
Jahazpur, *India* **42 G6** 25 37N 75 17 E
Jahrom, *Iran* **45 D7** 28 30N 53 31 E
Jaijon, *India* **42 D7** 31 21N 76 9 E
Jailolo, *Indonesia* **37 D7** 1 5N 127 30 E
Jailolo, Selat, *Indonesia* **37 D7** 0 5N 129 5 E
Jaipur, *India* **42 F6** 27 0N 75 50 E
Jais, *India* **43 F9** 26 15N 81 32 E
Jaisalmer, *India* **42 F4** 26 55N 70 54 E
Jaisinghnagar, *India* **43 H8** 23 38N 78 34 E
Jaitaran, *India* **42 F5** 26 12N 73 56 E
Jaithari, *India* **43 H8** 23 14N 78 37 E
Jājarm, *Iran* **45 B8** 36 58N 56 27 E
Jakam →, *India* **42 H6** 23 54N 74 13 E
Jakarta, *Indonesia* **36 F3** 6 9S 106 49 E
Jakhal, *India* **42 E6** 29 48N 75 50 E
Jakhau, *India* **42 H3** 23 13N 68 43 E
Jakobstad = Pietarsaari, *Finland* **8 E20** 63 40N 22 43 E
Jal, *U.S.A.* **81 J3** 32 7N 103 12W
Jalālābād, *Afghan.* **42 B4** 34 30N 70 29 E
Jalalabad, *India* **43 F8** 27 41N 79 42 E
Jalalpur Jattan, *Pakistan* **42 C6** 32 38N 74 11 E
Jalama, *U.S.A.* **79 L6** 34 29N 120 29W
Jalapa, *Guatemala* **88 D2** 14 39N 89 59W
Jalapa Enríquez = Xalapa, *Mexico* **87 D5** 19 32N 96 55W
Jalasjärvi, *Finland* **9 E20** 62 29N 22 47 E
Jalaun, *India* **43 F8** 26 8N 79 25 E
Jaldhaka →, *Bangla.* **43 F13** 26 16N 89 16 E
Jalesar, *India* **42 F8** 27 29N 78 19 E
Jaleswar, *Nepal* **43 F11** 26 38N 85 48 E
Jalgaon, *India* **40 J9** 21 0N 75 42 E
Jalībah, *Iraq* **44 D5** 30 35N 46 32 E
Jalisco □, *Mexico* **86 D4** 20 0N 104 0W
Jalkot, *Pakistan* **43 B5** 35 14N 73 24 E
Jalna, *India* **40 K9** 19 48N 75 38 E
Jalón →, *Spain* **21 B5** 41 47N 1 4W
Jalor, *India* **42 G5** 25 21N 72 37 E
Jalpa, *Mexico* **86 C4** 21 38N 102 58W
Jalpaiguri, *India* **41 F16** 26 32N 88 46 E
Jaluit I., *Marshall Is.* **64 G8** 6 0N 169 30 E
Jalūlā, *Iraq* **44 C5** 34 16N 45 10 E
Jamaica ■, *W. Indies* **88 a** 18 10N 77 30W
Jamalpur, *Bangla.* **41 G16** 24 52N 89 56 E
Jamalpur, *India* **43 G12** 25 18N 86 28 E
Jamalpurganj, *India* **43 H13** 23 2N 87 59 E
Jamanxim →, *Brazil* **93 D7** 4 43S 56 18W
Jambewangi, *Indonesia* **37 J17** 8 17S 114 7 E
Jambi, *Indonesia* **36 E2** 1 38S 103 30 E
Jambi □, *Indonesia* **36 E2** 1 30S 102 30 E
Jambusar, *India* **42 H5** 22 3N 72 51 E
James →, *S. Dak., U.S.A.* **80 D6** 42 52N 97 18W
James →, *Va., U.S.A.* **82 G7** 36 56N 76 27W
James B., *Canada* **72 B3** 54 0N 80 0W
James Ranges, *Australia* **60 D5** 24 10S 132 30 E
James Ross I., *Antarctica* **5 C18** 63 58S 57 50W
Jamesabad, *Pakistan* **42 G3** 25 17N 69 15 E
Jamestown, *Australia* **63 E2** 33 10S 138 32 E
Jamestown, *S. Africa* **56 E4** 31 6S 26 45 E
Jamestown, *N. Dak., U.S.A.* **80 B5** 46 54N 98 42W
Jamestown, *N.Y., U.S.A.* **84 D5** 42 6N 79 14W
Jamestown, *Pa., U.S.A.* **84 E4** 41 29N 80 27W
Jamīlābād, *Iran* **45 C6** 34 24N 48 28 E
Jamiltepec, *Mexico* **87 D5** 16 17N 97 49W
Jamira →, *India* **43 J13** 21 35N 88 28 E
Jamkhandi, *India* **40 L9** 16 30N 75 15 E
Jammu, *India* **42 C6** 32 43N 74 54 E
Jammu & Kashmir □, *India* **43 B7** 34 25N 77 0 E
Jamnagar, *India* **42 H4** 22 30N 70 6 E
Jamni →, *India* **43 G8** 25 13N 78 35 E
Jampur, *Pakistan* **42 E4** 29 39N 70 40 E
Jamrud, *Pakistan* **42 C4** 33 59N 71 24 E
Jämsä, *Finland* **9 F21** 61 53N 25 10 E
Jamshedpur, *India* **43 H12** 22 44N 86 12 E
Jamtara, *India* **43 H12** 23 59N 86 49 E
Jämtland, *Sweden* **8 E15** 63 31N 14 0 E
Jan L., *Canada* **71 C8** 54 56N 102 55W
Jan Mayen, *Arctic* **4 B7** 71 0N 9 0W
Janakkala, *Finland* **9 F21** 60 54N 24 36 E
Janaúba, *Brazil* **93 G10** 15 48S 43 19W
Jand, *Pakistan* **42 C5** 33 30N 72 6 E
Jandaq, *Iran* **45 C7** 34 3N 54 22 E
Jandía, *Canary Is.* **24 F5** 28 6N 14 21W
Jandía △, *Canary Is.* **24 F5** 28 4N 14 19W
Jandía, Pta. de, *Canary Is.* **24 F5** 28 3N 14 31W
Jandola, *Pakistan* **42 C4** 32 20N 70 9 E
Jandowae, *Australia* **63 D5** 26 45S 151 7 E
Janesville, *U.S.A.* **80 D10** 42 41N 89 1W
Jangamo, *Mozam.* **57 C6** 24 6S 35 21 E
Janghai, *India* **43 G10** 25 33N 82 19 E
Janjanbureh, *Gambia* **50 F3** 13 30N 14 47W
Janjgir, *India* **43 J10** 22 1N 82 34 E
Janjina, *Madag.* **57 C8** 20 30S 45 50 E
Janos, *Mexico* **86 A3** 30 45N 108 10W
Januária, *Brazil* **93 G10** 15 25S 44 25W
Janûb Sînî □, *Egypt* **46 F2** 29 30N 33 50 E
Janubio, *Canary Is.* **24 F6** 28 56N 13 50W
Jaora, *India* **42 H6** 23 40N 75 10 E
Japan ■, *Asia* **31 G8** 36 0N 136 0 E
Japan, Sea of, *Asia* **30 E7** 40 0N 135 0 E
Japan Trench, *Pac. Oc.* **26 F18** 32 0N 142 0 E
Japen = Yapen, *Indonesia* **37 E9** 1 50S 136 0 E
Japla, *India* **43 G11** 24 33N 84 1 E
Japurá →, *Brazil* **92 D5** 3 8S 65 46W
Jaquarão, *Brazil* **95 C5** 32 34S 53 23W
Jaqué, *Panama* **88 E4** 7 27N 78 8W
Jarābulus, *Syria* **44 B3** 36 49N 38 1 E
Jarama →, *Spain* **21 B4** 40 24N 3 32W
Jaranwala, *Pakistan* **42 D5** 31 15N 73 26 E
Jarash, *Jordan* **46 C4** 32 17N 35 54 E
Jarash □, *Jordan* **46 C4** 32 17N 35 54 E
Jardim, *Brazil* **94 A4** 21 28S 56 2W
Jardine River △, *Australia* **62 A3** 11 9S 142 21 E
Jardines de la Reina, Arch. de los, *Cuba* **88 B4** 20 50N 78 50W
Jargalang, *China* **35 C12** 43 5N 122 55 E
Jari →, *Brazil* **93 D8** 1 9S 51 54W
Jarīr, W. al →, *Si. Arabia* **44 E4** 25 38N 42 30 E
Jarosław, *Poland* **17 C12** 50 2N 22 42 E
Jarrahdale, *Australia* **61 F2** 32 24S 116 5 E
Jarrahi →, *Iran* **45 D6** 30 49N 48 48 E
Jarres, Plaine des, *Laos* **38 C4** 19 27N 103 10 E
Jartai, *China* **34 E3** 39 45N 105 48 E
Jarud Qi, *China* **35 B11** 44 28N 120 50 E
Järvenpää, *Finland* **9 F21** 60 29N 25 5 E
Jarvis, *Canada* **84 D4** 42 53N 80 6W
Jarvis I., *Pac. Oc.* **65 H12** 0 15S 160 5W
Jarwa, *India* **43 F10** 27 38N 82 30 E
Jasdan, *India* **42 H4** 22 2N 71 12 E
Jashpurnagar, *India* **43 H11** 22 54N 84 9 E
Jasidih, *India* **43 G12** 24 31N 86 39 E
Jāsimīyah, *Iraq* **44 C5** 33 45N 44 41 E
Jasin, *Malaysia* **39 L4** 2 20N 102 26 E
Jāsk, *Iran* **45 E8** 25 38N 57 45 E
Jasło, *Poland* **17 D11** 49 45N 21 30 E
Jaso, *India* **43 G9** 24 30N 80 29 E
Jasper, *Alta., Canada* **70 C5** 52 55N 118 5W
Jasper, *Ont., Canada* **85 B9** 44 52N 75 57W
Jasper, *Ala., U.S.A.* **83 J2** 33 50N 87 17W
Jasper, *Fla., U.S.A.* **83 K4** 30 31N 82 57W
Jasper, *Ind., U.S.A.* **82 F2** 38 24N 86 56W
Jasper, *Tex., U.S.A.* **81 K8** 30 56N 94 1W
Jasper △, *Canada* **70 C5** 52 50N 118 8W
Jasrasar, *India* **42 F5** 27 43N 73 49 E
Jászberény, *Hungary* **17 E10** 47 30N 19 55 E
Jataí, *Brazil* **93 G8** 17 58S 51 48W
Jati, *Pakistan* **42 G3** 24 20N 68 19 E
Jatibarang, *Indonesia* **37 G13** 6 28S 108 18 E
Jatiluwih, *Indonesia* **37 J18** 8 23S 115 8 E
Jatinegara, *Indonesia* **37 G12** 6 13S 106 52 E
Játiva = Xàtiva, *Spain* **21 C5** 38 59N 0 32W
Jaú, *Brazil* **95 A6** 22 10S 48 30W
Jauja, *Peru* **92 F3** 11 45S 75 15W
Jaunpur, *India* **43 G10** 25 46N 82 44 E
Java = Jawa, *Indonesia* **36 F3** 7 0S 110 0 E
Java Barat □, *Indonesia* **37 G12** 7 0S 107 0 E
Java Sea, *Indonesia* **36 E3** 4 35S 107 15 E
Java Tengah □, *Indonesia* **37 G14** 7 0S 110 0 E
Java Timur □, *Indonesia* **37 G15** 8 0S 113 0 E
Java Trench, *Ind. Oc.* **36 F3** 9 0S 105 0 E
Jawa, *Indonesia* **36 F3** 7 0S 110 0 E
Jawad, *India* **42 G6** 24 36N 74 51 E
Jay Peak, *U.S.A.* **85 B12** 44 55N 72 32W
Jaya, Puncak, *Indonesia* **37 E9** 3 57S 137 17 E
Jayanti, *India* **41 F16** 26 45N 89 40 E
Jayapura, *Indonesia* **37 E10** 2 28S 140 38 E
Jayawijaya, Pegunungan, *Indonesia* **37 E9** 5 0S 139 0 E
Jaynagar, *India* **41 F15** 26 43N 86 9 E
Jayrūd, *Syria* **44 C3** 33 49N 36 44 E
Jayton, *U.S.A.* **81 J4** 33 15N 100 34W
Jāz Mūrīān, Hāmūn-e, *Iran* **45 E8** 27 20N 58 55 E
Jazīreh-ye Shīf, *Iran* **45 D6** 29 4N 50 54 E
Jazminal, *Mexico* **86 C4** 24 56N 101 25W
Jazzin, *Lebanon* **46 B4** 33 31N 35 35 E
Jean, *U.S.A.* **79 K11** 35 47N 115 20W
Jean Marie River, *Canada* **70 A4** 61 32N 120 38W
Jean Rabel, *Haiti* **89 C5** 19 50N 73 5W
Jeanerette, *U.S.A.* **81 L9** 29 55N 91 40W
Jeanette, Ostrov = Zhannetty, Ostrov, *Russia* **29 B16** 76 43N 158 0 E
Jeannette, *U.S.A.* **84 F5** 40 20N 79 36W
Jebāl Bārez, Kūh-e, *Iran* **45 D8** 28 30N 58 20 E
Jebel, Bahr el →, *Sudan* **51 G12** 9 30N 30 25 E
Jedburgh, *U.K.* **11 F6** 55 29N 2 33W
Jedda = Jiddah, *Si. Arabia* **47 C2** 21 29N 39 10 E
Jeddore L., *Canada* **73 C8** 48 3N 55 55W
Jędrzejów, *Poland* **17 C11** 50 35N 20 15 E
Jefferson, *Iowa, U.S.A.* **80 D7** 42 1N 94 23W
Jefferson, *Ohio, U.S.A.* **84 E4** 41 44N 80 46W
Jefferson, *Tex., U.S.A.* **81 J7** 32 46N 94 21W
Jefferson, Mt., *Nev., U.S.A.* **76 G5** 38 51N 117 0W
Jefferson, Mt., *Oreg., U.S.A.* **76 D3** 44 41N 121 48W
Jefferson City, *Mo., U.S.A.* **80 F8** 38 34N 92 10W
Jefferson City, *Tenn., U.S.A.* **83 G4** 36 7N 83 30W
Jeffersontown, *U.S.A.* **82 F3** 38 12N 85 35W
Jeffersonville, *U.S.A.* **82 F3** 38 17N 85 44W
Jeffrey City, *U.S.A.* **76 E10** 42 30N 107 49W
Jega, *Nigeria* **50 F6** 12 15N 4 23 E
Jeju = Cheju do, *S. Korea* **35 H14** 33 29N 126 34 E
Jēkabpils, *Latvia* **9 H21** 56 29N 25 57 E
Jekyll I., *U.S.A.* **83 K5** 31 4N 81 25W
Jelenia Góra, *Poland* **16 C8** 50 50N 15 45 E
Jelgava, *Latvia* **9 H20** 56 41N 23 49 E
Jemaja, *Indonesia* **39 L5** 3 5N 105 45 E
Jemaluang, *Malaysia* **39 L4** 2 16N 103 52 E
Jember, *Indonesia* **37 H15** 8 11S 113 41 E
Jembongan, *Malaysia* **36 C5** 6 45N 117 20 E
Jena, *Germany* **16 C6** 50 54N 11 35 E
Jena, *U.S.A.* **81 K8** 31 41N 92 8W
Jenin, *West Bank* **46 C4** 32 28N 35 18 E
Jenkins, *U.S.A.* **82 G4** 37 10N 82 38W
Jenner, *U.S.A.* **78 G3** 38 27N 123 7W
Jennings, *U.S.A.* **81 K8** 30 13N 92 40W
Jepara, *Indonesia* **37 G14** 7 40S 109 14 E
Jeparit, *Australia* **63 F3** 36 8S 142 1 E
Jequié, *Brazil* **93 F10** 13 51S 40 5W
Jequitinhonha, *Brazil* **93 G10** 16 30S 41 0W
Jequitinhonha →, *Brazil* **93 G11** 15 51S 38 53W
Jerantut, *Malaysia* **39 L4** 3 56N 102 22 E
Jerejak, Pulau, *Malaysia* **39 c** 5 19N 100 19 E
Jérémie, *Haiti* **89 C5** 18 40N 74 10W
Jerez, Punta, *Mexico* **87 C5** 22 58N 97 40W
Jerez de García Salinas, *Mexico* **86 C4** 22 39N 103 0W
Jerez de la Frontera, *Spain* **21 D2** 36 41N 6 7W
Jerez de los Caballeros, *Spain* **21 C2** 38 20N 6 45W
Jericho = El Arīḥā, *West Bank* **46 D4** 31 52N 35 27 E
Jericho, *Australia* **62 C4** 23 38S 146 6 E
Jerid, Chott el = Djerid, Chott, *Tunisia* **50 B7** 33 42N 8 30 E
Jerilderie, *Australia* **63 F4** 35 20S 145 41 E
Jermyn, *U.S.A.* **85 E9** 41 31N 75 31W
Jerome, *U.S.A.* **76 E6** 42 44N 114 31W
Jerramungup, *Australia* **61 F2** 33 55S 118 55 E
Jersey, *U.K.* **13 H5** 49 11N 2 7W
Jersey City, *U.S.A.* **85 F10** 40 44N 74 4W
Jersey Shore, *U.S.A.* **84 E7** 41 12N 77 15W
Jerseyville, *U.S.A.* **80 F9** 39 7N 90 20W
Jerusalem, *Israel* **46 D4** 31 47N 35 10 E
Jervis B., *Australia* **63 F5** 35 8S 150 46 E
Jervis Inlet, *Canada* **70 C4** 50 0N 123 57W
Jesi = Iesi, *Italy* **22 C5** 43 31N 13 14 E
Jessore, *Bangla.* **41 H16** 23 10N 89 10 E
Jesup, *U.S.A.* **83 K5** 31 36N 81 53W
Jesús Carranza, *Mexico* **87 D5** 17 28N 95 1W
Jesús María, *Argentina* **94 C3** 30 59S 64 5W
Jetmore, *U.S.A.* **81 F5** 38 4N 99 54W
Jetpur, *India* **42 J4** 21 45N 70 10 E
Jevnaker, *Norway* **9 F14** 60 15N 10 26 E
Jewett, *U.S.A.* **84 F3** 40 22N 81 2W
Jewett City, *U.S.A.* **85 E13** 41 36N 72 0W
Jeyḥūnābād, *Iran* **45 C6** 34 58N 48 59 E
Jeypore, *India* **41 K13** 18 50N 82 38 E
Jha Jha, *India* **43 G12** 24 46N 86 22 E
Jhaarkand = Jharkhand □, *India* **43 H11** 24 0N 85 50 E
Jhabua, *India* **42 H6** 22 46N 74 36 E
Jhajjar, *India* **42 E7** 28 37N 76 42 E
Jhal, *Pakistan* **42 E2** 28 17N 67 27 E
Jhal Jhao, *Pakistan* **40 F4** 26 20N 65 35 E
Jhalawar, *India* **42 G7** 24 40N 76 10 E
Jhalida, *India* **43 H11** 23 22N 85 58 E
Jhalrapatan, *India* **42 G7** 24 33N 76 10 E
Jhang Maghiana, *Pakistan* **42 D5** 31 15N 72 22 E
Jhansi, *India* **43 G8** 25 30N 78 36 E
Jhargram, *India* **43 H12** 22 27N 86 59 E
Jharia, *India* **43 H12** 23 45N 86 26 E
Jharkhand □, *India* **43 H11** 24 0N 85 50 E
Jharsuguda, *India* **41 J14** 21 56N 84 5 E
Jhelum, *Pakistan* **42 C5** 33 0N 73 45 E
Jhelum →, *Pakistan* **42 D5** 31 20N 72 10 E
Jhilmilli, *India* **43 H10** 23 24N 82 51 E
Jhudo, *Pakistan* **42 G3** 24 58N 69 18 E
Jhunjhunu, *India* **42 E6** 28 10N 75 30 E
Ji-Paraná, *Brazil* **92 F6** 10 52S 62 57W
Ji Xian, *Hebei, China* **34 F8** 37 35N 115 30 E
Ji Xian, *Henan, China* **34 G8** 35 22N 114 5 E
Ji Xian, *Shanxi, China* **34 F6** 36 7N 110 40 E
Jia Xian, *Henan, China* **34 H7** 33 59N 113 12 E
Jia Xian, *Shaanxi, China* **34 E6** 38 12N 110 28 E
Jiamusi, *China* **33 B8** 46 40N 130 26 E
Ji'an, *Jiangxi, China* **33 D6** 27 6N 114 59 E
Ji'an, *Jilin, China* **35 D14** 41 5N 126 10 E
Jianchang, *China* **35 D11** 40 55N 120 35 E
Jianchangying, *China* **35 D10** 40 10N 118 50 E
Jiangcheng, *China* **32 D5** 22 36N 101 52 E
Jiangmen, *China* **33 D6** 22 32N 113 0 E
Jiangsu □, *China* **35 H11** 33 0N 120 0 E
Jiangxi □, *China* **33 D6** 27 30N 116 0 E
Jiao Xian = Jiaozhou, *China* **35 F11** 36 18N 120 1 E
Jiaohe, *Hebei, China* **34 E9** 38 2N 116 20 E
Jiaohe, *Jilin, China* **35 C14** 43 40N 127 22 E
Jiaozhou, *China* **35 F11** 36 18N 120 1 E
Jiaozhou Wan, *China* **35 F11** 36 5N 120 10 E
Jiaozuo, *China* **34 G7** 35 16N 113 12 E
Jiawang, *China* **35 G9** 34 28N 117 26 E
Jiaxiang, *China* **34 G9** 35 25N 116 20 E
Jiaxing, *China* **33 C7** 30 49N 120 45 E
Jiayi = Chiai, *Taiwan* **33 D7** 23 29N 120 25 E
Jibuti = Djibouti ■, *Africa* **47 E3** 12 0N 43 0 E
Jicarón, I., *Panama* **88 E3** 7 10N 81 50W
Jiddah, *Si. Arabia* **47 C2** 21 29N 39 10 E
Jido, *India* **41 E19** 29 2N 94 58 E
Jieshou, *China* **34 H8** 33 18N 115 22 E
Jiexiu, *China* **34 F6** 37 2N 111 55 E
Jiggalong, *Australia* **60 D3** 23 21S 120 47 E
Jigni, *India* **43 G8** 25 45N 79 25 E
Jihlava, *Czech Rep.* **16 D8** 49 28N 15 35 E
Jihlava →, *Czech Rep.* **17 D9** 48 55N 16 36 E
Jijiga, *Ethiopia* **47 F3** 9 20N 42 50 E
Jilin, *China* **35 C14** 43 44N 126 30 E
Jilin □, *China* **35 C14** 44 0N 127 0 E
Jilong = Chilung, *Taiwan* **33 D7** 25 3N 121 45 E
Jim Thorpe, *U.S.A.* **85 F9** 40 52N 75 44W
Jima, *Ethiopia* **47 F2** 7 40N 36 47 E
Jimbaran, Teluk, *Indonesia* **37 K18** 8 46S 115 9 E
Jiménez, *Mexico* **86 B4** 27 10N 104 54W
Jimo, *China* **35 F11** 36 23N 120 30 E
Jin Xian = Jinzhou, *China* **34 E8** 38 2N 115 2 E
Jin Xian, *China* **35 E11** 38 55N 121 42 E
Jinan, *China* **34 F9** 36 38N 117 1 E
Jinchang, *China* **32 C5** 38 30N 102 10 E
Jincheng, *China* **34 G7** 35 29N 112 50 E
Jind, *India* **42 E7** 29 19N 76 22 E
Jindabyne, *Australia* **63 F4** 36 25S 148 35 E
Jinding, *China* **33 G10** 22 22N 113 33 E
Jindřichův Hradec, *Czech Rep.* **16 D8** 49 10N 15 2 E
Jing He →, *China* **34 G5** 34 27N 109 4 E
Jingbian, *China* **34 F5** 37 20N 108 30 E
Jingchuan, *China* **34 G4** 35 20N 107 20 E
Jingdezhen, *China* **33 D6** 29 20N 117 11 E
Jinggu, *China* **32 D5** 23 35N 100 41 E
Jinghai, *China* **34 E9** 38 55N 116 55 E
Jingle, *China* **34 E6** 38 20N 111 55 E
Jingning, *China* **34 G3** 35 30N 105 43 E
Jingpo Hu, *China* **35 C15** 43 55N 128 55 E
Jingtai, *China* **34 F3** 37 10N 104 6 E
Jingxing, *China* **34 E8** 38 2N 114 8 E
Jingyang, *China* **34 G5** 34 30N 108 50 E
Jingyu, *China* **35 C14** 42 25N 126 45 E
Jingyuan, *China* **34 F3** 36 30N 104 40 E
Jingziguan, *China* **34 H6** 33 15N 111 0 E
Jinhua, *China* **33 D6** 29 8N 119 38 E
Jining, *Nei Monggol Zizhiqu, China* **34 D7** 41 5N 113 0 E
Jining, *Shandong, China* **34 G9** 35 22N 116 34 E
Jinja, *Uganda* **54 B3** 0 25N 33 12 E
Jinjang, *Malaysia* **39 L3** 3 13N 101 39 E
Jinji, *China* **34 F4** 37 58N 106 8 E
Jinnah Barrage, *Pakistan* **40 C7** 32 58N 71 33 E
Jinotega, *Nic.* **88 D2** 13 6N 85 59W
Jinotepe, *Nic.* **88 D2** 11 50N 86 10W
Jinsha Jiang →, *China* **32 D5** 28 50N 104 36 E
Jinxi, *China* **35 D11** 40 52N 120 50 E
Jinxiang, *China* **34 G9** 35 5N 116 22 E
Jinzhou, *Hebei, China* **34 E8** 38 2N 115 2 E
Jinzhou, *Liaoning, China* **35 D11** 41 5N 121 3 E
Jiparaná →, *Brazil* **92 E6** 8 3S 62 52W
Jipijapa, *Ecuador* **92 D2** 1 0S 80 40W
Jiquilpan, *Mexico* **86 D4** 19 57N 102 42W
Jishan, *China* **34 G6** 35 34N 110 58 E
Jisr ash Shughūr, *Syria* **44 C3** 35 49N 36 18 E
Jitarning, *Australia* **61 F2** 32 48S 117 57 E
Jitra, *Malaysia* **39 J3** 6 16N 100 25 E
Jiu →, *Romania* **17 F12** 43 47N 23 48 E
Jiudengkou, *China* **34 E4** 39 56N 106 40 E
Jiujiang, *China* **33 D6** 29 42N 115 58 E
Jiulong = Kowloon, *China* **33 G11** 22 19N 114 11 E
Jiutai, *China* **35 B13** 44 10N 125 50 E
Jiuxincheng, *China* **34 E8** 39 17N 115 59 E
Jixi, *China* **35 B16** 45 20N 130 50 E
Jiyang, *China* **35 F9** 37 0N 117 12 E
Jiyuan, *China* **34 G7** 35 7N 112 57 E
Jīzān, *Si. Arabia* **47 D3** 17 0N 42 20 E
Jize, *China* **34 F8** 36 54N 114 56 E
Jizl, Wādī al →, *Si. Arabia* **44 E3** 25 39N 38 25 E
Jizō-Zaki, *Japan* **31 G6** 35 34N 133 20 E
Jizzakh, *Uzbekistan* **28 E7** 40 6N 67 50 E
Joaçaba, *Brazil* **95 B5** 27 5S 51 31W
João Pessoa, *Brazil* **93 E12** 7 10S 34 52W
Joaquín V. González, *Argentina* **94 B3** 25 10S 64 0W
Jobat, *India* **42 H6** 22 25N 74 34 E
Jodhpur, *India* **42 F5** 26 23N 73 8 E
Jodiya, *India* **42 H4** 22 42N 70 18 E
Joensuu, *Finland* **18 B4** 62 37N 29 49 E
Jōetsu, *Japan* **31 F9** 37 12N 138 10 E
Jofane, *Mozam.* **57 C5** 21 15S 34 18 E
Jogbani, *India* **43 F12** 26 25N 87 15 E
Jõgeva, *Estonia* **9 G22** 58 45N 26 24 E
Jogjakarta = Yogyakarta, *Indonesia* **36 F4** 7 49S 110 22 E
Johannesburg, *S. Africa* **57 D4** 26 10S 28 2 E
Johannesburg, *U.S.A.* **79 K9** 35 22N 117 38W
Johilla →, *India* **43 H9** 23 37N 81 14 E
John Crow Mts., *Jamaica* **88 a** 18 5N 76 25W
John Day, *U.S.A.* **76 D4** 44 25N 118 57W
John Day →, *U.S.A.* **76 D3** 45 44N 120 39W
John Day Fossil Beds ⌓, *U.S.A.* **76 D4** 44 33N 119 38W

John D'Or Prairie, Canada 70 B5 58 30N 115 8W
John F. Kennedy International,
  New York ✈ (JFK), U.S.A. .. 85 F11 40 38N 73 47W
John H. Kerr Reservoir, U.S.A. . 83 G6 36 36N 78 18W
John o' Groats, U.K. 11 C5 58 38N   3 4W
Johnnie, U.S.A. 79 J10 36 25N 116 5W
John's Ra., Australia .... 62 C1 21 55S 133 23 E
Johnson, Kans., U.S.A. 81 G4 37 34N 101 45W
Johnson, Vt., U.S.A. 85 B12 44 38N 72 41W
Johnson City, N.Y., U.S.A. 85 D9 42 7N 75 58W
Johnson City, Tenn., U.S.A. ... 83 G4 36 19N 82 21W
Johnson City, Tex., U.S.A. 81 K5 30 17N 98 25W
Johnsonburg, U.S.A. 84 E6 41 29N 78 41W
Johnsondale, U.S.A. 79 K8 35 58N 118 32W
Johnsons Crossing, Canada ... 70 A2 60 29N 133 18W
Johnston, L., Australia .... 61 F3 32 25S 120 30 E
Johnston Falls = Mambilima
  Falls, Zambia .... 55 E2 10 31S 28 45 E
Johnston I., Pac. Oc. 65 F11 17 10N 169 8W
Johnstone Str., Canada 70 C3 50 28N 126 0W
Johnstown, N.Y., U.S.A. 85 C10 43 0N 74 22W
Johnstown, Ohio, U.S.A. 84 F2 40 9N 82 41W
Johnstown, Pa., U.S.A. 84 F6 40 20N 78 55W
Johor, Selat, Asia .... 39 d   1 28N 103 47 E
Johor Baharu, Malaysia ...... 39 d   1 28N 103 46 E
Jõhvi, Estonia .... 9 G22 59 22N 27 27 E
Joinville, Brazil 95 B6 26 15S 48 55W
Joinville I., Antarctica 5 C18 65 0S 55 30W
Jojutla, Mexico 87 D5 18 37N 99 11W
Jokkmokk, Sweden .... 8 C18 66 5N 19 50 E
Jökulsá á Bru →, Iceland 8 D6 65 40N 14 16W
Jökulsá á Fjöllum →, Iceland .. 8 C5 66 10N 16 30W
Jolfā, Āzarbāijān-e Sharqī, Iran 44 B5 38 57N 45 38 E
Jolfā, Eşfahan, Iran .... 45 C6 32 58N 51 37 E
Joliet, U.S.A. 82 E1 41 32N 88 5W
Joliette, Canada 72 C5 46 3N 73 24W
Jolo, Phil. .... 37 C6 6 0N 121 0 E
Jolon, U.S.A. 78 K5 35 58N 121 9W
Jombang, Indonesia .... 37 G15 7 33S 112 14 E
Jonava, Lithuania .... 9 J21 55 8N 24 12 E
Jones Sound, Canada 4 B3 76 0N 85 0W
Jonesboro, Ark., U.S.A. 81 H9 35 50N 90 42W
Jonesboro, La., U.S.A. 81 J8 32 15N 92 43W
Joniškis, Lithuania .... 9 H20 56 13N 23 35 E
Jönköping, Sweden .... 9 H16 57 45N 14 8 E
Jonquière, Canada 73 C5 48 27N 71 14W
Joplin, U.S.A. 81 G7 37 6N 94 31W
Jora, India .... 42 F6 26 20N 77 49 E
Jordan, Mont., U.S.A. 76 C10 47 19N 106 55W
Jordan, N.Y., U.S.A. 85 C8 43 4N 76 29W
Jordan ■, Asia .... 46 E5 31 0N 36 0 E
Jordan →, Asia .... 46 D4 31 48N 35 32 E
Jordan Valley, U.S.A. 76 E5 42 59N 117 3W
Jorhat, India .... 41 F19 26 45N 94 12 E
Jörn, Sweden .... 8 D19 65 4N 20 1 E
Jorong, Indonesia .... 36 E4 3 58S 114 56 E
Jørpeland, Norway .... 9 G11 59 3N   6 1 E
Jorquera →, Chile 94 B2 28 3S 69 58W
Jos, Nigeria .... 50 G7 9 53N   8 51 E
José Battle y Ordóñez, Uruguay 95 C4 33 20S 55 10W
Joseph, L., Nfld. & L., Canada . 73 B6 52 45N 65 18W
Joseph, L., Ont., Canada 84 A5 45 10N 79 44W
Joseph Bonaparte G., Australia 60 B4 14 35S 128 50 E
Joshinath, India .... 43 D8 30 34N 79 34 E
Joshinetsu-Kōgen △, Japan .. 31 F9 36 42N 138 32 E
Joshua Tree, U.S.A. 79 L10 34 8N 116 19W
Joshua Tree △, U.S.A. 79 M10 33 55N 116 0W
Jost Van Dyke, Br. Virgin Is. .. 89 e 18 29N 64 47W
Jostedalsbreen, Norway ..... 9 F12 61 40N   6 59 E
Jotunheimen, Norway .... 9 F13 61 35N   8 25 E
Joubertberge, Namibia ...... 56 B1 18 30S 12 25 E
Jourdanton, U.S.A. 81 L5 28 55N 98 33W
Jovellanos, Cuba 88 B3 22 40N 81 10W
Ju Xian, China .... 35 F10 36 35N 118 20 E
Juan Aldama, Mexico 86 C4 24 20N 103 23W
Juan Bautista Alberdi, Argentina 94 C3 34 26S 61 48W
Juan de Fuca Str., Canada 78 B2 48 15N 124 0W
Juan de Nova, Ind. Oc. ...... 57 B7 17 3S 43 45 E
Juan Fernández, Arch. de,
  Pac. Oc. 90 G2 33 50S 80 0W
Juan José Castelli, Argentina .. 94 B3 25 27S 60 57W
Juan L. Lacaze, Uruguay 94 C4 34 0S 57 25W
Juankoski, Finland .... 8 E23 63 3N 28 19 E
Juárez, Argentina 94 D4 37 40S 59 43W
Juárez, Mexico 79 N11 32 20N 115 57W
Juárez, Sierra de, Mexico 86 A1 32 0N 116 0W
Juàzeiro, Brazil 93 E10 9 30S 40 30W
Juàzeiro do Norte, Brazil 93 E11 7 10S 39 18W
Juba = Giuba →, Somali Rep. . 47 G3 1 30N 42 35 E
Juba, Sudan .... 51 H12 4 50N 31 35 E
Jubany, Antarctica 5 C18 62 30S 58 0W
Jubayl, Lebanon .... 46 A4 34 5N 35 39 E
Jubbah, Si. Arabia .... 44 D4 28 2N 40 56 E
Jubbal, India .... 42 D7 31 5N 77 40 E
Jubbulpore = Jabalpur, India . 43 H8 23 9N 79 58 E
Jubilee L., Australia .... 61 E4 29 0S 126 50 E
Juby, C., Morocco 50 C3 28 0N 12 59W
Júcar = Xúquer →, Spain 21 C5 39 5N   0 10W
Júcaro, Cuba 88 B4 21 37N 78 51W
Juchitán, Mexico 87 D5 16 27N 95 5W
Judaea = Har Yehuda, Israel .. 46 D3 31 35N 34 57 E
Judith →, U.S.A. 76 C9 47 44N 109 39W
Judith, Pt., U.S.A. 85 E13 41 22N 71 29W
Judith Gap, U.S.A. 76 C9 46 41N 109 45W
Jugoslavia = Serbia &
  Montenegro ■, Europe .... 23 B9 43 20N 20 0 E
Juigalpa, Nic. 88 D2 12 6N 85 26W
Juiz de Fora, Brazil 95 A7 21 43S 43 19W
Jujuy □, Argentina 94 A2 23 20S 65 40W
Julesburg, U.S.A. 80 E3 40 59N 102 16W
Juli, Peru 92 G5 16 10S 69 25W
Julia Cr. →, Australia .... 62 C3 20 0S 141 11 E
Julia Creek, Australia .... 62 C3 20 39S 141 44 E
Juliaca, Peru 92 G4 15 25S 70 10W
Julian, U.S.A. 79 M10 33 4N 116 38W
Julian, L., Canada 72 B4 54 25N 77 57W
Julianatop, Suriname 93 C7   3 40N 56 30W
Julianehåb = Qaqortoq,
  Greenland 69 B6 60 43N 46 0W
Julimes, Mexico 86 B3 28 25N 105 27W
Jullundur, India .... 42 D6 31 20N 75 40 E
Julu, China .... 34 F8 37 15N 115 2 E
Jumbo, Zimbabwe .... 55 F3 17 30S 30 58 E
Jumbo Pk., U.S.A. 79 J12 36 12N 114 11W
Jumentos Cays, Bahamas ... 88 B4 23 0N 75 40W
Jumilla, Spain 21 C5 38 28N   1 19W
Jumla, Nepal .... 43 E10 29 15N 82 13 E

Jumna = Yamuna →, India ... 43 G9 25 30N 81 53 E
Junagadh, India .... 42 J4 21 30N 70 30 E
Junction, Tex., U.S.A. 81 K5 30 29N 99 46W
Junction, Utah, U.S.A. 77 G7 38 14N 112 13W
Junction B., Australia .... 62 A1 11 52S 133 55 E
Junction City, Kans., U.S.A. .. 80 F6 39 2N 96 50W
Junction City, Oreg., U.S.A. .. 76 D2 44 13N 123 12W
Junction Pt., Australia ...... 62 A1 11 45S 133 50 E
Jundah, Australia .... 62 C3 24 46S 143 2 E
Jundiaí, Brazil 95 A6 24 30S 47 0W
Juneau, U.S.A. 70 B2 58 18N 134 25W
Junee, Australia .... 63 E4 34 53S 147 35 E
Jungfrau, Switz. .... 20 C7 46 32N   7 58 E
Junggar Pendi, China .... 32 B3 44 30N 86 0 E
Jungshahi, Pakistan .... 42 G2 24 52N 67 44 E
Juniata →, U.S.A. 84 F7 40 30N 77 40W
Junín, Argentina 94 C3 34 33S 60 57W
Junín de los Andes, Argentina 96 D2 39 45S 71 0W
Jūniyah, Lebanon .... 46 B4 33 59N 35 38 E
Juntas, Chile 94 B2 28 24S 69 58W
Juntura, U.S.A. 76 E4 43 45N 118 5W
Jur, Nahr el →, Sudan ...... 51 G11 8 45N 29 15 E
Jura = Jura, Mts. du, Europe .. 20 C7 46 40N   6 5 E
Jura = Schwäbische Alb,
  Germany .... 16 D5 48 20N   9 30 E
Jura, U.K. 11 F3 56 0N   5 50W
Jura, Mts. du, Europe .... 20 C7 46 40N   6 5 E
Jura, Sd. of, U.K. 11 F3 55 57N   5 45W
Jurbarkas, Lithuania .... 9 J20 55 4N 22 46 E
Jurien, Australia .... 61 F2 30 18S 115 2 E
Jūrmala, Latvia .... 9 H20 56 58N 23 34 E
Jurong, Singapore .... 39 d   1 19N 103 42 E
Juruá →, Brazil 92 D5 2 37S 65 44W
Juruena, Brazil 92 F7 13 0S 58 10W
Juruena →, Brazil 92 E7   7 20S 58 3W
Juruti, Brazil 93 D7   2 9S 56 4W
Justo Daract, Argentina 94 C2 33 52S 65 12W
Jutaí →, Brazil 92 D5   2 43S 66 57W
Juticalpa, Honduras 88 D2 14 40N 86 12W
Jutland = Jylland, Denmark ... 9 H13 56 25N   9 30 E
Juventud, I. de la, Cuba 88 B3 21 40N 82 40W
Jüy Zar, Iran .... 44 C5 33 50N 46 18 E
Juye, China .... 34 G9 35 22N 116 5 E
Jwaneng, Botswana .... 53 J4 24 45S 24 50 E
Jylland, Denmark .... 9 H13 56 25N   9 30 E
Jyväskylä, Finland .... 9 E21 62 14N 25 50 E

K

K2, Pakistan .... 43 B7 35 58N 76 32 E
Kaap Plateau, S. Africa ...... 56 D3 28 30S 24 0 E
Kaapkruis, Namibia .... 56 C1 21 55S 13 57 E
Kaapstad = Cape Town, S. Africa 56 E2 33 55S 18 22 E
Kabaena, Indonesia .... 37 F6   5 15S 122 0 E
Kabala, S. Leone 50 G3   9 38N 11 37W
Kabale, Uganda .... 54 C3   1 15S 30 0 E
Kabalo, Dem. Rep. of the Congo 54 D2 6 0S 27 0 E
Kabambare, Dem. Rep. of
  the Congo .... 54 C2   4 41S 27 39 E
Kabango, Dem. Rep. of
  the Congo .... 55 D2   8 35S 28 30 E
Kabanjahe, Indonesia .... 36 D1   3 6N 98 30 E
Kabardino-Balkar Republic =
  Kabardino-Balkaria □, Russia 19 F7 43 30N 43 30 E
Kabardino-Balkaria □, Russia . 19 F7 43 30N 43 30 E
Kabarega Falls = Murchison
  Falls, Uganda .... 54 B3   2 15N 31 30 E
Kabasalan, Phil. .... 37 C6   7 47N 122 44 E
Kabat, Indonesia .... 37 J17   8 16S 114 19 E
Kabetogama, U.S.A. 80 A8 48 28N 92 59W
Kabin Buri, Thailand .... 38 F3 13 57N 101 43 E
Kabinakagami L., Canada 72 C3 48 54N 84 25W
Kabinda, Dem. Rep. of the Congo 52 F4 6 19S 24 0 E
Kabompo, Zambia .... 55 E1 13 36S 24 14 E
Kabompo →, Zambia .... 53 G4 14 10S 23 11 E
Kabondo, Dem. Rep. of
  the Congo .... 55 D2   8 58S 25 40 E
Kabongo, Dem. Rep. of
  the Congo .... 54 D2   7 22S 25 33 E
Kabūd Gonbad, Iran .... 45 B8 37 5N 59 45 E
Kābul, Afghan. .... 42 B3 34 28N 69 11 E
Kābul □, Afghan. .... 40 B6 34 30N 69 0 E
Kābul →, Pakistan .... 42 C5 33 55N 72 14 E
Kabunga, Dem. Rep. of
  the Congo .... 54 C2   1 38S 28 3 E
Kaburuang, Indonesia ...... 37 D7   3 50N 126 30 E
Kabwe, Zambia .... 55 E2 14 30S 28 29 E
Kachchh, Gulf of, India ..... 42 H3 22 50N 69 15 E
Kachchh, Rann of, India ..... 42 H4 24 0N 70 0 E
Kachchhidhana, India ...... 43 J8 21 44N 78 46 E
Kachebera, Zambia .... 55 E3 13 50S 32 50 E
Kachikau, Botswana .... 56 B3 18 8S 24 26 E
Kachin □, Burma .... 41 G20 26 0N 97 30 E
Kachira, L., Uganda .... 54 C3   0 40S 31 7 E
Kachiry, Kazakhstan .... 28 D8 53 10N 75 50 E
Kachnara, India .... 42 H6 23 50N 75 6 E
Kachot, Cambodia .... 39 G4 11 30N 103 3 E
Kaçkar, Turkey .... 19 F7 40 45N 41 10 E
Kadan Kyun, Burma .... 38 F2 12 30N 98 20 E
Kadanai →, Afghan. .... 42 D1 31 22N 65 45 E
Kadavu, Fiji .... 59 D8 19 0S 178 15 E
Kadhimain = Al Kāẓimīyah, Iraq 44 C5 33 22N 44 18 E
Kadi, India .... 42 H5 23 18N 72 23 E
Kadina, Australia .... 63 E2 33 55S 137 43 E
Kadipur, India .... 43 F10 26 10N 82 23 E
Kadirli, Turkey .... 44 B3 37 23N 36 5 E
Kadiyevka = Stakhanov, Ukraine 19 E6 48 35N 38 40 E
Kadoka, U.S.A. 80 D4 43 50N 101 31W
Kadoma, Zimbabwe .... 55 F2 18 20S 29 52 E
Kadugli, Sudan .... 51 F11 11 0N 29 45 E
Kaduna, Nigeria .... 50 F7 10 30N   7 21 E
Kaédi, Mauritania 50 F3 16 9N 13 28W
Kaeng Khoï, Thailand ...... 38 E3 14 35N 101 0 E
Kaeng Krachan △, Thailand .. 38 F2 12 57N 99 23 E
Kaeng Tana △, Thailand ..... 38 E5 15 25N 105 32 E
Kaesŏng, N. Korea .... 35 F14 37 58N 126 35 E
Kāf, Si. Arabia .... 44 D3 31 25N 37 29 E
Kafan = Kapan, Armenia .... 19 G8 39 18N 46 27 E
Kafanchan, Nigeria .... 50 G7 9 40N   8 20 E
Kafinda, Zambia .... 55 E3 12 32S 30 20 E
Kafirévs, Ákra, Greece ...... 23 E11 38 9N 24 38 E
Kafue, Zambia .... 55 F2 15 46S 28 9 E
Kafue △, Zambia .... 55 F2 15 12S 25 38 E
Kafue →, Zambia .... 53 H5 15 30S 29 0 E

Kafue Flats, Zambia .... 55 F2 15 40S 27 25 E
Kafulwe, Zambia .... 55 D2   9 0S 29 1 E
Kaga, Afghan. .... 42 B4 34 14N 70 10 E
Kaga Bandoro, C.A.R. .... 52 C3   7 0N 19 10 E
Kagan, Uzbekistan .... 28 F7 39 43N 64 33 E
Kagawa □, Japan .... 31 G7 34 15N 134 0 E
Kagera □, Tanzania .... 54 C3   2 0S 31 30 E
Kagera →, Uganda .... 54 C3   0 57S 31 47 E
Kağızman, Turkey .... 44 B4 40 5N 43 10 E
Kagoshima, Japan .... 31 J5 31 35N 130 33 E
Kagoshima □, Japan .... 31 J5 31 30N 130 30 E
Kagul = Cahul, Moldova ..... 17 F15 45 50N 28 15 E
Kahak, Iran .... 45 B6 36 6N 49 46 E
Kahama, Tanzania .... 54 C3   4 8S 32 30 E
Kahan, Pakistan .... 42 E3 29 18N 68 54 E
Kahang, Malaysia .... 39 L4   2 12N 103 32 E
Kahayan →, Indonesia ...... 36 E4 3 40S 114 0 E
Kahe, Tanzania .... 54 C4   3 30S 37 25 E
Kahnūj, Iran .... 45 E8 27 55N 57 40 E
Kahoka, U.S.A. 80 E9 40 25N 91 44W
Kahoolawe, U.S.A. 74 H16 20 33N 156 37W
Kahramanmaraş, Turkey .... 19 G6 37 37N 36 53 E
Kahurangi △, N.Z. .... 59 J4 41 10S 172 32 E
Kahuta, Pakistan .... 42 C5 33 35N 73 24 E
Kai, Kepulauan, Indonesia ... 37 F8 5 55S 132 45 E
Kai Besar, Indonesia .... 37 F8 5 35S 133 0 E
Kai Is. = Kai, Kepulauan,
  Indonesia .... 37 F8   5 55S 132 45 E
Kai Kecil, Indonesia .... 37 F8 5 45S 132 40 E
Kaiapoi, N.Z. .... 59 K4 43 24S 172 40 E
Kaieteur Falls, Guyana 92 B7   5 1N 59 10W
Kaifeng, China .... 34 G8 34 48N 114 21 E
Kaikohe, N.Z. .... 59 F4 35 25S 173 49 E
Kaikoura, N.Z. .... 59 K4 42 25S 173 43 E
Kailash = Kangrinboqe Feng,
  China .... 43 D9 31 0N 81 25 E
Kailu, China .... 35 C11 43 38N 121 18 E
Kailua Kona, U.S.A. 74 J17 19 39N 155 59W
Kaimana, Indonesia .... 37 E8 3 39S 133 45 E
Kaimanawa Mts., N.Z. ...... 59 H5 39 15S 175 56 E
Kaimganj, India .... 43 F8 27 33N 79 24 E
Kaimur Hills, India .... 43 G10 24 30N 82 0 E
Kainab →, Namibia .... 56 D2 28 32S 19 34 E
Kainji Res., Nigeria .... 50 F6 10 1N   4 40 E
Kainuu, Finland .... 8 D23 64 30N 29 7 E
Kaipara Harbour, N.Z. ...... 59 G5 36 25S 174 14 E
Kaipokok B., Canada 73 B8 54 54N 59 47W
Kaira, India .... 42 H5 22 45N 72 50 E
Kairana, India .... 42 E7 29 24N 77 15 E
Kaironi, Indonesia .... 37 E8 0 47S 133 40 E
Kairouan, Tunisia .... 51 A8 35 45N 10 5 E
Kaiserslautern, Germany .... 16 D4 49 26N   7 45 E
Kaitaia, N.Z. .... 59 F4 35 8S 173 17 E
Kaitangata, N.Z. .... 59 M2 46 17S 169 51 E
Kaithal, India .... 42 E7 29 48N 76 26 E
Kaitu →, Pakistan .... 42 C4 33 10N 70 30 E
Kaiyuan, China .... 35 C13 42 28N 124 1 E
Kajaani, Finland .... 8 D22 64 17N 27 46 E
Kajabbi, Australia .... 62 C3 20 0S 140 1 E
Kajana = Kajaani, Finland .... 8 D22 64 17N 27 46 E
Kajang, Malaysia .... 39 L3   2 59N 101 48 E
Kajiado, Kenya .... 54 C4   1 53S 36 48 E
Kajo Kaji, Sudan .... 51 H12 3 58N 31 40 E
Kakabeka Falls, Canada 72 C2 48 24N 89 37W
Kakadu △, Australia .... 60 B5 12 0S 132 3 E
Kakamas, S. Africa .... 56 D3 28 45S 20 33 E
Kakamega, Kenya .... 54 B3   0 20N 34 46 E
Kakanui Mts., N.Z. .... 59 L3 45 10S 170 30 E
Kakdwip, India .... 43 J13 21 53N 88 11 E
Kake, Japan .... 31 G6 34 36N 132 19 E
Kake, U.S.A. 70 B2 56 59N 133 57W
Kakegawa, Japan .... 31 G9 34 45N 138 1 E
Kakeroma-Jima, Japan ...... 31 K4 28 8N 129 14 E
Kakhovka, Ukraine .... 19 E5 46 45N 33 30 E
Kakhovske Vdskh., Ukraine .. 19 E5 47 5N 34 0 E
Kakinada, India .... 41 L13 16 57N 82 11 E
Kakisa →, Canada 70 A5 61 3N 118 10W
Kakisa L., Canada 70 A5 60 56N 117 43W
Kakogawa, Japan .... 31 G7 34 46N 134 51 E
Kakwa →, Canada 70 C5 54 37N 118 28W
Kāl Gūsheh, Iran .... 45 D8 30 59N 58 12 E
Kal Safid, Iran .... 44 C5 34 52N 47 23 E
Kalaallit Nunaat = Greenland ☑,
  N. Amer. 4 C5 66 0N 45 0W
Kalabagh, Pakistan .... 42 C4 33 0N 71 28 E
Kalabahi, Indonesia .... 37 F6   8 13S 124 31 E
Kalach, Russia .... 19 D7 50 22N 41 0 E
Kaladan →, Burma .... 41 J18 20 20N 93 5 E
Kaladar, Canada 84 B7 44 37N 77 5W
Kalahari, Africa .... 56 C3 24 0S 21 30 E
Kalahari Gemsbok △, S. Africa 56 D3 25 30S 20 30 E
Kalajoki, Finland .... 8 D20 64 12N 24 0 E
Kalakamati, Botswana ...... 57 C4 20 40S 27 25 E
Kalakan, Russia .... 29 D12 55 15N 116 45 E
K'alak'unlun Shank'ou =
  Karakoram Pass, Asia ..... 43 B7 35 33N 77 50 E
Kalam, Pakistan .... 43 B5 35 34N 72 30 E
Kalama, Dem. Rep. of the Congo 54 C2 2 52S 28 35 E
Kalama, U.S.A. 78 E4 46 1N 122 51W
Kalámai, Greece .... 23 F10 37 3N 22 10 E
Kalamata = Kalámai, Greece .. 23 F10 37 3N 22 10 E
Kalamazoo, U.S.A. 82 D3 42 17N 85 35W
Kalamazoo →, U.S.A. 82 D2 42 40N 86 10W
Kalambo Falls, Tanzania .... 55 D3   8 37S 31 35 E
Kalan, Turkey .... 44 B3 39 7N 39 32 E
Kalannie, Australia .... 61 F2 30 22S 117 5 E
Kalāntarī, Iran .... 45 C7 32 10N 54 10 E
Kalao, Indonesia .... 37 F6   7 21S 121 0 E
Kalaotoa, Indonesia .... 37 F6   7 20S 121 50 E
Kalasin, Thailand .... 38 D4 16 26N 103 30 E
Kalat, Pakistan .... 40 E5 29 8N 66 31 E
Kalāteh, Iran .... 45 B7 36 33N 55 41 E
Kalāteh-ye Ganj, Iran ...... 45 E8 27 31N 57 55 E
Kalbarri, Australia .... 61 E1 27 51S 114 30 E
Kalbarri △, Australia .... 61 E1 27 51S 114 30 E
Kalce, Slovenia .... 16 F8 45 54N 14 13 E
Kale, Turkey .... 23 F13 37 27N 28 49 E
Kalegauk Kyun, Burma ..... 41 M20 15 33N 97 35 E
Kalehe, Dem. Rep. of the Congo 54 C2 2 6S 28 50 E
Kalema, Tanzania .... 54 C3   1 12S 31 55 E
Kalemie, Dem. Rep. of the Congo 54 D2 5 55S 29 9 E
Kalewa, Burma .... 41 H19 23 10N 94 15 E
Kaleybar, Iran .... 44 B5 38 47N 47 2 E
Kalgoorlie-Boulder, Australia . 61 F3 30 40S 121 22 E

Kali →, India .... 43 F8 27 6N 79 55 E
Kali Sindh →, India .... 42 G6 25 32N 76 17 E
Kaliakra, Nos, Bulgaria ..... 23 C13 43 21N 28 30 E
Kalianda, Indonesia .... 36 F3 5 50S 105 45 E
Kalibo, Phil. .... 37 B6 11 43N 122 22 E
Kalima, Dem. Rep. of the Congo 54 C2 2 33S 26 32 E
Kalimantan, Indonesia ...... 36 E4 0 0 114 0 E
Kalimantan Barat □, Indonesia . 36 E4 0 0 110 30 E
Kalimantan Selatan □, Indonesia 36 E5 2 30S 115 30 E
Kalimantan Tengah □, Indonesia 36 E4 2 0S 113 30 E
Kalimantan Timur □, Indonesia 36 D5 1 30N 116 30 E
Kálimnos, Greece .... 23 F12 37 0N 27 0 E
Kalimpong, India .... 43 F13 27 4N 88 35 E
Kaliningrad, Russia .... 9 J19 54 42N 20 32 E
Kalinkavichy, Belarus ...... 17 B15 52 12N 29 20 E
Kalinkovichi = Kalinkavichy,
  Belarus .... 17 B15 52 12N 29 20 E
Kaliro, Uganda .... 54 B3   0 56N 33 30 E
Kalispell, U.S.A. 76 B6 48 12N 114 19W
Kalisz, Poland .... 17 C10 51 45N 18 8 E
Kaliua, Tanzania .... 54 D3   5 5S 31 48 E
Kalix, Sweden .... 8 D20 65 53N 23 12 E
Kalix →, Sweden .... 8 D20 65 50N 23 11 E
Kalka, India .... 42 D7 30 46N 76 57 E
Kalkarindji, Australia ...... 60 C5 17 30S 130 47 E
Kalkaska, U.S.A. 82 C3 44 44N 85 11W
Kalkfeld, Namibia .... 56 C2 20 57S 16 14 E
Kalkfontein, Botswana ..... 56 C3 22 4S 20 57 E
Kalkrand, Namibia .... 56 C2 24 1S 17 35 E
Kallavesi, Finland .... 8 E22 62 58N 27 30 E
Kallsjön, Sweden .... 8 E15 63 38N 13 0 E
Kalmar, Sweden .... 9 H17 56 40N 16 20 E
Kalmyk Republic = Kalmykia □,
  Russia .... 19 E8 46 5N 46 1 E
Kalmykia □, Russia .... 19 E8 46 5N 46 1 E
Kalmykovo, Kazakhstan .... 19 E9 49 0N 51 47 E
Kalna, India .... 43 H13 23 13N 88 25 E
Kalnai, India .... 43 H10 22 46N 83 30 E
Kalocsa, Hungary .... 17 E10 46 32N 19 0 E
Kalokhorio, Cyprus .... 25 E12 34 51N 33 2 E
Kaloko, Dem. Rep. of the Congo 54 D2 6 47S 25 48 E
Kalol, Gujarat, India .... 42 H5 22 37N 73 31 E
Kalol, Gujarat, India .... 42 H5 23 15N 72 33 E
Kalomo, Zambia .... 55 F2 17 0S 26 30 E
Kalpi, India .... 43 F8 26 8N 79 47 E
Kalu, Pakistan .... 42 G2 25 5N 67 39 E
Kaluga, Russia .... 18 D6 54 35N 36 10 E
Kalulushi, Zambia .... 55 E2 12 50S 28 3 E
Kalundborg, Denmark ...... 9 J14 55 41N 11 5 E
Kalush, Ukraine .... 17 D13 49 3N 24 23 E
Kalutara, Sri Lanka .... 40 R12 6 35N 80 0 E
Kalya, Russia .... 18 B10 60 15N 59 59 E
Kalyan, India .... 40 K8 19 15N 73 9 E
Kama, Dem. Rep. of the Congo 54 C2 3 30S 27 5 E
Kama →, Russia .... 18 C9 55 45N 52 0 E
Kamachumu, Tanzania ..... 54 C3   1 37S 31 37 E
Kamaishi, Japan .... 30 E10 39 16N 141 53 E
Kamalia, Pakistan .... 42 D5 30 44N 72 42 E
Kaman, India .... 42 F6 27 39N 77 16 E
Kamanjab, Namibia .... 56 B2 19 35S 14 51 E
Kamapanda, Zambia .... 55 E1 12 5S 24 0 E
Kamarán, Yemen .... 47 D3 15 21N 42 35 E
Kamativi, Zimbabwe .... 56 B4 18 20S 27 6 E
Kambalda, Australia .... 61 F3 31 10S 121 37 E
Kambar, Pakistan .... 42 F3 27 37N 68 1 E
Kambarka, Russia .... 18 C9 56 15N 54 11 E
Kambolé, Zambia .... 55 D3   8 47S 30 48 E
Kambos, Cyprus .... 25 D11 35 2N 32 44 E
Kambove, Dem. Rep. of
  the Congo .... 55 E2 10 51S 26 33 E
Kamchatka, Poluostrov, Russia 29 D16 57 0N 160 0 E
Kamchatka Pen. = Kamchatka,
  Poluostrov, Russia .... 29 D16 57 0N 160 0 E
Kamchiya →, Bulgaria ...... 23 C12 43 4N 27 44 E
Kame Ruins, Zimbabwe ..... 55 G2 20 7S 28 25 E
Kamen, Russia .... 28 D9 53 50N 81 30 E
Kamen-Rybolov, Russia ..... 30 B6 44 46N 132 2 E
Kamenjak, Rt, Croatia ...... 16 F7 44 47N 13 55 E
Kamenka, Russia .... 18 A7 65 58N 44 0 E
Kamenka Bugskaya = Kamyanka-
  Buzka, Ukraine .... 17 C13 50 8N 24 16 E
Kamensk Uralskiy, Russia ... 28 D7 56 25N 62 2 E
Kamenskoye, Russia .... 29 C17 62 45N 165 30 E
Kameoka, Japan .... 31 G7 35 0N 135 35 E
Kamiah, U.S.A. 76 C5 46 14N 116 2W
Kamieskroon, S. Africa ..... 56 E2 30 9S 17 56 E
Kamilukuak L., Canada 71 A8 62 22N 101 40W
Kamin-Kashyrskyy, Ukraine .. 17 C13 51 39N 24 56 E
Kamina, Dem. Rep. of the Congo 55 D2 8 45S 25 0 E
Kaminak L., Canada 71 A10 62 10N 95 0W
Kaministiquia, Canada 72 C1 48 32N 89 35W
Kaminoyama, Japan .... 30 E10 38 9N 140 17 E
Kamiros, Greece .... 25 C9 36 20N 27 56 E
Kamituga, Dem. Rep. of
  the Congo .... 54 C2 3 2S 28 10 E
Kamla →, India .... 43 G12 25 35N 86 36 E
Kamloops, Canada 70 C4 50 40N 120 20W
Kamo, Japan .... 30 F9 37 39N 139 3 E
Kamoke, Pakistan .... 42 C6 32 4N 74 4 E
Kampala, Uganda .... 54 B3   0 20N 32 30 E
Kampar, Malaysia .... 39 K3   4 18N 101 9 E
Kampar →, Indonesia ...... 36 D2 0 30N 103 8 E
Kampen, Neths. .... 15 B5 52 33N   5 53 E
Kampene, Dem. Rep. of
  the Congo .... 54 C2 3 36S 26 40 E
Kamphaeng Phet, Thailand .. 38 D2 16 28N 99 30 E
Kampolombo, L., Zambia .... 55 E2 11 37S 29 42 E
Kampong Chhnang, Cambodia 39 F5 12 20N 104 35 E
Kampong Pengerang, Malaysia 39 d 1 22N 104 7 E
Kampong Punggai, Malaysia . 39 d 1 27N 104 18 E
Kampong Saom, Cambodia .. 39 G4 10 38N 103 30 E
Kampong Saom, Chaak,
  Cambodia .... 39 G4 10 50N 103 32 E
Kampong Tanjong Langsat,
  Malaysia .... 39 d 1 28N 104 1 E
Kampong Telok Ramunia,
  Malaysia .... 39 d 1 22N 104 15 E
Kampong To, Thailand ...... 39 J3 6 3N 101 13 E
Kampot, Cambodia .... 39 G5 10 36N 104 10 E
Kampuchea = Cambodia ■, Asia 38 F5 12 15N 105 0 E
Kampung Air Putih, Malaysia . 39 K4 4 15N 103 10 E
Kampung Jerangau, Malaysia . 39 K4 4 50N 103 10 E
Kampung Raja, Malaysia .... 39 K4 5 45N 102 35 E
Kampungbaru = Tolitoli,
  Indonesia .... 37 D6   1 5N 120 50 E
Kamrau, Teluk, Indonesia ... 37 E8 3 30S 133 36 E
Kamsack, Canada 71 C8 51 34N 101 54W

Kamskoye Vdkhr., Russia ...... 18 C10 58 41N 56 7 E
Kamuchawie L., Canada 71 B8 56 18N 101 59W
Kamui-Misaki, Japan ...... 30 C10 43 20N 140 21 E
Kamyanets-Podilskyy, Ukraine .. 17 D14 48 45N 26 40 E
Kamyanka-Buzka, Ukraine ...... 17 C13 50 8N 24 16 E
Kāmyārān, Iran ...... 44 C5 34 47N 46 56 E
Kamyshin, Russia ...... 19 D8 50 10N 45 24 E
Kanaaupscow, Canada 69 C12 53 39N 77 9W
Kanaaupscow →, Canada 72 B4 54 2N 76 30W
Kanab, U.S.A. 77 H7 37 3N 112 32W
Kanab →, U.S.A. 77 H7 36 24N 112 38W
Kanagi, Japan ...... 30 D10 40 54N 140 27 E
Kanairiktok →, Canada 73 A7 55 2N 60 18W
Kananga, Dem. Rep. of
the Congo ...... 52 F4 5 55S 22 18 E
Kanash, Russia ...... 18 C8 55 30N 47 32 E
Kanaskat, U.S.A. 78 C5 47 19N 121 54W
Kanastraíon, Ákra = Palioúrion,
Ákra, Greece ...... 23 E10 39 57N 23 45 E
Kanawha →, U.S.A. 82 F4 38 50N 82 9W
Kanazawa, Japan ...... 31 F8 36 30N 136 38 E
Kanchanaburi, Thailand ...... 38 E2 14 2N 99 31 E
Kanchenjunga, Nepal ...... 43 F13 27 50N 88 10 E
Kanchipuram, India ...... 40 N11 12 52N 79 45 E
Kandaghat, India ...... 42 D7 30 59N 77 7 E
Kandahar = Qandahār, Afghan. .. 40 D4 31 32N 65 43 E
Kandalaksha, Russia ...... 18 A5 67 9N 32 30 E
Kandalakshskiy Zaliv, Russia .. 18 A6 66 0N 35 0 E
Kandangan, Indonesia ...... 36 E5 2 50S 115 20 E
Kandanghaur, Indonesia ...... 37 G13 6 21S 108 6 E
Kandanos, Greece ...... 25 D5 35 19N 23 44 E
Kandavu = Kadavu, Fiji ...... 59 D8 19 0S 178 15 E
Kandhkot, Pakistan ...... 42 E3 28 16N 69 8 E
Kandhla, India ...... 42 E7 29 18N 77 19 E
Kandi, Benin ...... 50 F6 11 7N 2 55 E
Kandi, India ...... 43 H13 23 58N 88 5 E
Kandiaro, Pakistan ...... 42 F3 27 4N 68 13 E
Kandla, India ...... 42 H4 23 0N 70 10 E
Kandos, Australia ...... 63 E4 32 45S 149 58 E
Kandreho, Madag. ...... 57 B8 17 29S 46 6 E
Kandy, Sri Lanka ...... 40 R12 7 18N 80 43 E
Kane, U.S.A. 84 E6 41 40N 78 49W
Kane Basin, Greenland 4 B4 79 1N 70 0W
Kaneohe, U.S.A. 74 H16 21 25N 157 48W
Kang, Botswana ...... 56 C3 23 41S 22 50 E
Kang Krung △, Thailand ...... 39 H2 9 30N 98 50 E
Kangān, Fārs, Iran ...... 45 E7 27 50N 52 3 E
Kangān, Hormozgān, Iran ...... 45 E8 25 48N 57 28 E
Kangar, Malaysia ...... 39 J3 6 27N 100 12 E
Kangaroo I., Australia ...... 63 F2 35 45S 137 0 E
Kangaroo Mts., Australia ...... 62 C3 23 29S 141 51 E
Kangasala, Finland ...... 9 F21 61 28N 24 4 E
Kangāvar, Iran ...... 45 C6 34 40N 48 0 E
Kangdong, N. Korea ...... 35 E14 39 9N 126 5 E
Kangean, Kepulauan, Indonesia 36 F5 6 55S 115 23 E
Kangean Is. = Kangean,
Kepulauan, Indonesia ...... 36 F5 6 55S 115 23 E
Kanggye, N. Korea ...... 35 D14 41 0N 126 35 E
Kanggyŏng, S. Korea ...... 35 F14 36 10N 127 0 E
Kanghwa, S. Korea ...... 35 F14 37 45N 126 30 E
Kangikajik, Greenland 4 B6 70 7N 22 0W
Kangiqliniq = Rankin Inlet,
Canada 68 B10 62 30N 93 0W
Kangiqsualujjuaq, Canada 69 C13 58 30N 65 59W
Kangiqsujuaq, Canada 69 B12 61 30N 72 0W
Kangiqtugaapik = Clyde River,
Canada 69 A13 70 30N 68 30W
Kangirsuk, Canada 69 B13 60 0N 70 0W
Kangkar Chemaran, Malaysia .. 39 d 1 34N 104 12 E
Kangkar Sungai Tiram, Malaysia 39 d 1 35N 103 55 E
Kangkar Teberau, Malaysia .... 39 d 1 32N 103 51 E
Kangnŭng, S. Korea ...... 35 F15 37 45N 128 54 E
Kangping, China ...... 35 C12 42 43N 123 18 E
Kangra, India ...... 42 C7 32 6N 76 16 E
Kangrinboqe Feng, China ...... 43 D9 31 0N 81 25 E
Kangto, India ...... 41 F18 27 50N 92 35 E
Kanhar →, India ...... 43 G10 24 28N 83 8 E
Kaniama, Dem. Rep. of
the Congo ...... 54 D1 7 30S 24 12 E
Kaniapiskau = Caniapiscau →,
Canada 73 A6 56 40N 69 30W
Kaniapiskau, L. = Caniapiscau, L.
de, Canada 73 B6 54 10N 69 55W
Kanin, Poluostrov, Russia ...... 18 A8 68 0N 45 0 E
Kanin Nos, Mys, Russia ...... 18 A7 68 39N 43 32 E
Kanin Pen. = Kanin, Poluostrov,
Russia ...... 18 A8 68 0N 45 0 E
Kaniva, Australia ...... 63 F3 36 22S 141 18 E
Kanjut Sar, Pakistan ...... 43 A6 36 7N 75 25 E
Kankaanpää, Finland ...... 9 F20 61 44N 22 50 E
Kankakee, U.S.A. 82 E2 41 7N 87 52W
Kankakee →, U.S.A. 82 E1 41 23N 88 15W
Kankan, Guinea 50 F4 10 23N 9 15W
Kankendy = Xankändi, Azerbaijan 19 G8 39 52N 46 49 E
Kanker, India ...... 41 J12 20 10N 81 40 E
Kankroli, India ...... 42 G5 25 4N 73 53 E
Kannapolis, U.S.A. 83 H5 35 30N 80 37W
Kannauj, India ...... 43 F8 27 3N 79 56 E
Kannod, India ...... 40 H10 22 45N 76 40 E
Kano, Nigeria ...... 50 F7 12 2N 8 30 E
Kan'onji, Japan ...... 31 G6 34 7N 133 39 E
Kanowit, Malaysia ...... 36 D4 2 14N 112 20 E
Kanoya, Japan ...... 31 J5 31 25N 130 50 E
Kanpetlet, Burma ...... 41 J18 21 10N 93 59 E
Kanpur, India ...... 43 F9 26 28N 80 20 E
Kansas □, U.S.A. 80 F6 38 30N 99 0W
Kansas →, U.S.A. 80 F7 39 7N 94 37W
Kansas City, Kans., U.S.A. 80 F7 39 7N 94 38W
Kansas City, Mo., U.S.A. 80 F7 39 6N 94 35W
Kansenia, Dem. Rep. of
the Congo ...... 55 E2 10 20S 26 0 E
Kansk, Russia ...... 29 D10 56 20N 95 37 E
Kansŏng, S. Korea ...... 35 E15 38 24N 128 30 E
Kansu = Gansu □, China ...... 34 G3 36 0N 104 0 E
Kantaphor, India ...... 42 H7 22 35N 76 34 E
Kantharalak, Thailand ...... 38 E5 14 39N 104 39 E
Kantli →, India ...... 42 E6 28 20N 75 30 E
Kantō □, Japan ...... 31 F9 36 15N 139 30 E
Kantō-Sanchi, Japan ...... 31 G9 35 59N 138 50 E
Kanuma, Japan ...... 31 F9 36 34N 139 42 E
Kanus, Namibia ...... 56 D2 27 50S 18 39 E
Kanye, Botswana ...... 56 C4 24 55S 25 28 E
Kanzenze, Dem. Rep. of
the Congo ...... 55 E2 10 30S 25 12 E
Kanzi, Ras, Tanzania ...... 54 D4 7 1S 39 33 E
Kao Phara, Thailand ...... 39 a 8 3N 98 22 E

Kaohsiung, Taiwan ...... 33 D7 22 35N 120 16 E
Kaokoveld, Namibia ...... 56 B1 19 15S 14 30 E
Kaolack, Senegal 50 F2 14 5N 16 8W
Kaoshan, China ...... 35 B13 44 38N 124 50 E
Kapaa, U.S.A. 74 G15 22 5N 159 19W
Kapadvanj, India ...... 42 H5 23 5N 73 0 E
Kapan, Armenia ...... 19 G8 39 18N 46 27 E
Kapanga, Dem. Rep. of
the Congo ...... 52 F4 8 30S 22 40 E
Kapchagai = Qapshaghay,
Kazakhstan ...... 28 E8 43 51N 77 14 E
Kapela = Velika Kapela, Croatia . 16 F8 45 10N 15 5 E
Kapema, Dem. Rep. of the Congo 55 E2 10 45S 28 22 E
Kapfenberg, Austria ...... 16 E8 47 26N 15 18 E
Kapiri Mposhi, Zambia ...... 55 E2 13 59S 28 43 E
Kāpīsā □, Afghan. ...... 40 B6 35 0N 69 20 E
Kapiskau →, Canada 72 B3 52 47N 81 55W
Kapit, Malaysia ...... 36 D4 2 0N 112 55 E
Kapiti I., N.Z. ...... 59 J5 40 50S 174 56 E
Kaplan, U.S.A. 81 K8 30 0N 92 17W
Kapoe, Thailand ...... 39 H2 9 34N 98 32 E
Kapoeta, Sudan ...... 51 H12 4 50N 33 35 E
Kaposvár, Hungary ...... 17 E9 46 25N 17 47 E
Kapowsin, U.S.A. 78 D4 46 59N 122 13W
Kapps, Namibia ...... 56 C2 22 32S 17 18 E
Kapsan, N. Korea ...... 35 D15 41 4N 128 19 E
Kapsukas = Marijampolė,
Lithuania ...... 9 J20 54 33N 23 19 E
Kaptai L., Bangla. ...... 41 H18 22 40N 92 20 E
Kapuas →, Indonesia ...... 36 E3 0 25S 109 20 E
Kapuas Hulu, Pegunungan,
Malaysia ...... 36 D4 1 30N 113 30 E
Kapuas Hulu Ra. = Kapuas Hulu,
Pegunungan, Malaysia ...... 36 D4 1 30N 113 30 E
Kapulo, Dem. Rep. of the Congo 55 D2 8 18S 29 15 E
Kapunda, Australia ...... 63 E2 34 20S 138 56 E
Kapuni, N.Z. ...... 59 H5 39 29S 174 8 E
Kapurthala, India ...... 42 D6 31 23N 75 25 E
Kapuskasing, Canada 72 C3 49 25N 82 30W
Kapuskasing →, Canada 72 C3 49 49N 82 0W
Kaputar, Australia ...... 63 E5 30 15S 150 10 E
Kaputir, Kenya ...... 54 B4 2 5N 35 28 E
Kara, Russia ...... 28 C7 69 10N 65 0 E
Kara Bogaz Gol, Zaliv =
Garabogazköl Aylagy,
Turkmenistan ...... 19 F9 41 0N 53 30 E
Kara Kalpak Republic =
Qoraqalpoghistan □,
Uzbekistan ...... 28 E6 43 0N 58 0 E
Kara Kum, Turkmenistan ...... 28 F6 39 30N 60 0 E
Kara Sea, Russia ...... 28 B7 75 0N 70 0 E
Karabiğa, Turkey ...... 23 D12 40 23N 27 17 E
Karabük, Turkey ...... 19 F5 41 12N 32 37 E
Karaburun, Turkey ...... 23 E12 38 41N 26 28 E
Karabutaq = Qarabutaq,
Kazakhstan ...... 28 E7 49 59N 60 14 E
Karacabey, Turkey ...... 23 D13 40 12N 28 21 E
Karacasu, Turkey ...... 23 F13 37 43N 28 35 E
Karachey-Cherkessia □, Russia . 19 F7 43 40N 41 30 E
Karachi, Pakistan ...... 42 G2 24 53N 67 0 E
Karad, India ...... 40 L9 17 15N 74 10 E
Karaganda = Qaraghandy,
Kazakhstan ...... 28 E8 49 50N 73 10 E
Karagayly, Kazakhstan ...... 28 E8 49 26N 76 0 E
Karaginskiy, Ostrov, Russia .... 29 D17 58 45N 164 0 E
Karagiye, Vpadina, Kazakhstan . 19 F9 43 27N 51 45 E
Karagiye Depression = Karagiye,
Vpadina, Kazakhstan ...... 19 F9 43 27N 51 45 E
Karagola Road, India ...... 43 G12 25 29N 87 23 E
Karaikal, India ...... 40 P11 10 59N 79 50 E
Karaikkudi, India ...... 40 P11 10 5N 78 45 E
Karaj, Iran ...... 45 C6 35 48N 51 0 E
Karak, Malaysia ...... 39 L4 3 25N 102 2 E
Karakalpakstan =
Qoraqalpoghistan □,
Uzbekistan ...... 28 E6 43 0N 58 0 E
Karakelong, Indonesia ...... 37 D7 4 35N 126 50 E
Karakitang, Indonesia ...... 37 D7 3 14N 125 28 E
Karakol, Kyrgyzstan ...... 28 E8 42 30N 78 20 E
Karakoram Pass, Asia ...... 43 B7 35 33N 77 50 E
Karakoram Ra., Pakistan ...... 43 B7 35 30N 77 0 E
Karakuwisa, Namibia ...... 56 B2 18 56S 19 40 E
Karalon, Russia ...... 29 D12 57 5N 115 50 E
Karama, Jordan ...... 46 D4 31 57N 35 35 E
Karaman, Turkey ...... 19 G5 37 14N 33 13 E
Karamay, China ...... 32 B3 45 30N 84 58 E
Karambu, Indonesia ...... 36 E5 3 53S 116 6 E
Karamea Bight, N.Z. ...... 59 J3 41 22S 171 40 E
Karamnasa →, India ...... 43 G10 25 31N 83 52 E
Karand, Iran ...... 44 C5 34 16N 46 15 E
Karanganyar, Indonesia ...... 37 G13 7 38S 109 37 E
Karangasem, Indonesia ...... 37 J18 8 27S 115 37 E
Karanjia, India ...... 43 J11 21 47N 85 58 E
Karasburg, Namibia ...... 56 D2 28 0S 18 44 E
Karasino, Russia ...... 28 C9 66 50N 86 50 E
Karasjok, Norway ...... 8 B21 69 27N 25 30 E
Karasuk, Russia ...... 28 D8 53 44N 78 2 E
Karasuyama, Japan ...... 31 F10 36 39N 140 9 E
Karatau, Khrebet = Qarataū,
Kazakhstan ...... 28 E7 43 30N 69 30 E
Karatsu, Japan ...... 31 H5 33 26N 129 58 E
Karaul, Russia ...... 28 B9 70 6N 82 15 E
Karauli, India ...... 42 F7 26 30N 77 4 E
Karavostasi, Cyprus ...... 25 D11 35 8N 32 50 E
Karawang, Indonesia ...... 37 G12 6 30S 107 15 E
Karawanken, Europe ...... 16 E8 46 30N 14 40 E
Karayazı, Turkey ...... 19 G7 39 41N 42 9 E
Karazhal, Kazakhstan ...... 28 E8 48 2N 70 49 E
Karbalā', Iraq ...... 44 C5 32 36N 44 3 E
Karcag, Hungary ...... 17 E11 47 19N 20 57 E
Karcha →, Pakistan ...... 43 B7 34 45N 76 10 E
Karchana, India ...... 43 G9 25 17N 81 56 E
Kardhitsa, Greece ...... 23 E9 39 23N 21 54 E
Kärdla, Estonia ...... 9 G20 58 50N 22 40 E
Kareeberge, S. Africa ...... 56 E3 30 59S 21 50 E
Kareha →, India ...... 43 G12 25 44N 86 21 E
Kareima, Sudan ...... 51 E12 18 30N 31 49 E
Karelia □, Russia ...... 18 A5 65 30N 32 30 E
Karelian Republic = Karelia □,
Russia ...... 18 A5 65 30N 32 30 E
Karera, India ...... 42 G8 25 32N 78 9 E
Kārevāndar, Iran ...... 45 E9 27 53N 60 44 E
Kargasok, Russia ...... 28 D9 59 3N 80 53 E
Kargat, Russia ...... 28 D9 55 10N 80 15 E
Kargil, India ...... 43 B7 34 32N 76 12 E
Kargopol, Russia ...... 18 B6 61 30N 38 58 E
Karhal, India ...... 43 F8 27 1N 78 57 E

Kariān, Iran ...... 45 E8 26 57N 57 14 E
Karianga, Madag. ...... 57 C8 22 25S 47 22 E
Kariba, Zimbabwe ...... 55 F2 16 28S 28 50 E
Kariba, L., Zimbabwe ...... 55 F2 16 40S 28 25 E
Kariba Dam, Zimbabwe ...... 55 F2 16 30S 28 35 E
Kariba Gorge, Zambia ...... 55 F2 16 30S 28 50 E
Karibib, Namibia ...... 56 C2 22 0S 15 56 E
Karijini △, Australia ...... 60 D2 23 8S 118 15 E
Karimata, Kepulauan, Indonesia 36 E3 1 25S 109 0 E
Karimata, Selat, Indonesia ...... 36 E3 2 0S 108 40 E
Karimata Is. = Karimata,
Kepulauan, Indonesia ...... 36 E3 1 25S 109 0 E
Karimnagar, India ...... 40 K11 18 26N 79 10 E
Karimun Kecil, Pulau, Indonesia 39 d 1 8N 103 22 E
Karimunjawa, Kepulauan,
Indonesia ...... 36 F4 5 50S 110 30 E
Karin, Somali Rep. ...... 47 E4 10 50N 45 52 E
Karīt, Iran ...... 45 C8 33 29N 56 55 E
Kariya, Japan ...... 31 G8 34 58N 137 1 E
Kariyangwe, Zimbabwe ...... 57 B4 18 0S 27 38 E
Karkaralinsk = Qarqaraly,
Kazakhstan ...... 28 E8 49 26N 75 30 E
Karkheh →, Iran ...... 44 D5 31 2N 47 29 E
Karkinitska Zatoka, Ukraine .... 19 E5 45 56N 33 0 E
Karkinitskiy Zaliv = Karkinitska
Zatoka, Ukraine ...... 19 E5 45 56N 33 0 E
Karlovac, Croatia ...... 16 F8 45 31N 15 36 E
Karlovo, Bulgaria ...... 23 C11 42 38N 24 47 E
Karlovy Vary, Czech Rep. ...... 16 C7 50 13N 12 51 E
Karlsbad = Karlovy Vary,
Czech Rep. ...... 16 C7 50 13N 12 51 E
Karlsborg, Sweden ...... 9 G16 58 33N 14 33 E
Karlshamn, Sweden ...... 9 H16 56 10N 14 51 E
Karlskoga, Sweden ...... 9 G16 59 28N 14 33 E
Karlskrona, Sweden ...... 9 H16 56 10N 15 35 E
Karlsruhe, Germany ...... 16 D5 49 0N 8 23 E
Karlstad, Sweden ...... 9 G15 59 23N 13 30 E
Karlstad, U.S.A. 80 A6 48 35N 96 31W
Karmi'el, Israel ...... 46 C4 32 55N 35 18 E
Karnak, Egypt ...... 51 C12 25 43N 32 39 E
Karnal, India ...... 42 E7 29 42N 77 2 E
Karnali →, Nepal ...... 43 E9 28 45N 81 16 E
Karnaphuli Res. = Kaptai L.,
Bangla. ...... 41 H18 22 40N 92 20 E
Karnaprayag, India ...... 43 D8 30 16N 79 15 E
Karnataka □, India ...... 40 N10 13 15N 77 0 E
Karnes City, U.S.A. 81 L6 28 53N 97 54W
Karnische Alpen, Europe ...... 16 E7 46 36N 13 0 E
Kärnten □, Austria ...... 16 E8 46 52N 13 30 E
Karoi, Zimbabwe ...... 55 F2 16 48S 29 45 E
Karon, Ao, Thailand ...... 39 a 7 51N 98 17 E
Karonga, Malawi ...... 55 D3 9 57S 33 55 E
Karoo △, S. Africa ...... 56 E3 32 18S 22 27 E
Karoonda, Australia ...... 63 F2 35 1S 139 59 E
Karor, Pakistan ...... 42 D4 31 15N 70 59 E
Karora, Sudan ...... 51 E13 17 44N 38 15 E
Karpasia, Cyprus ...... 25 D13 35 32N 34 15 E
Kárpathos, Greece ...... 23 G12 35 37N 27 10 E
Karpinsk, Russia ...... 18 B7 59 45N 60 1 E
Karpogory, Russia ...... 18 B7 64 0N 44 27 E
Karpuz Burnu = Apostolos
Andreas, C., Cyprus ...... 25 D13 35 42N 34 35 E
Karratha, Australia ...... 60 D2 20 53S 116 40 E
Kars, Turkey ...... 19 F7 40 40N 43 5 E
Karsakpay, Kazakhstan ...... 28 E7 47 55N 66 40 E
Karshi = Qarshi, Uzbekistan .... 28 F7 38 53N 65 48 E
Karsiyang, India ...... 43 F13 26 56N 88 18 E
Karsog, India ...... 42 D7 31 23N 77 12 E
Kartaly, Russia ...... 28 D7 53 3N 60 40 E
Kartapur, India ...... 42 D6 31 27N 75 32 E
Karthaus, U.S.A. 84 E6 41 8N 78 9W
Karufa, Indonesia ...... 37 E8 3 50S 133 20 E
Karuma △, Uganda ...... 54 B3 2 5N 32 15 E
Karumba, Australia ...... 62 B3 17 31S 140 50 E
Karumo, Tanzania ...... 54 C3 2 25S 32 50 E
Karumwa, Tanzania ...... 54 C3 3 12S 32 38 E
Kārūn →, Iran ...... 45 D6 30 26N 48 10 E
Karungu, Kenya ...... 54 C3 0 50S 34 10 E
Karviná, Czech Rep. ...... 17 D10 49 53N 18 31 E
Karwan →, India ...... 42 F8 27 26N 78 4 E
Karwar, India ...... 40 M9 14 55N 74 13 E
Karwi, India ...... 43 G9 25 12N 80 57 E
Kasache, Malawi ...... 55 E3 13 25S 34 20 E
Kasai →, Dem. Rep. of
the Congo ...... 52 E3 3 30S 16 10 E
Kasai-Oriental □, Dem. Rep. of
the Congo ...... 54 D1 5 0S 24 30 E
Kasaji, Dem. Rep. of the Congo . 55 E1 10 25S 23 27 E
Kasama, Zambia ...... 55 E3 10 16S 31 9 E
Kasan-dong, N. Korea ...... 35 D14 41 18N 126 55 E
Kasane, Namibia ...... 56 B3 17 34S 24 50 E
Kasanga, Tanzania ...... 55 D3 8 30S 31 10 E
Kasanka △, Zambia ...... 55 E3 11 34S 30 15 E
Kasaragod, India ...... 40 N9 12 30N 74 58 E
Kasba L., Canada 71 A8 60 20N 102 10W
Kāseh Garān, Iran ...... 44 C5 34 5N 46 2 E
Kasempa, Zambia ...... 55 E2 13 30S 25 44 E
Kasenga, Dem. Rep. of
the Congo ...... 55 E2 10 20S 28 45 E
Kasese, Uganda ...... 54 B3 0 13N 30 3 E
Kasewa, Zambia ...... 55 E2 14 28S 28 53 E
Kasganj, India ...... 43 F8 27 48N 78 42 E
Kashabowie, Canada 72 C1 48 40N 90 26W
Kashaf, Iran ...... 45 C9 35 58N 61 7 E
Kāshān, Iran ...... 45 C6 34 5N 51 30 E
Kashechewan, Canada 72 B3 52 18N 81 37W
Kashgar = Kashi, China ...... 32 C2 39 30N 76 2 E
Kashi, China ...... 32 C2 39 30N 76 2 E
Kashimbo, Dem. Rep. of
the Congo ...... 55 E2 11 12S 26 19 E
Kashipur, India ...... 43 E8 29 15N 79 0 E
Kashiwazaki, Japan ...... 31 F9 37 22N 138 33 E
Kashk-e Kohneh, Afghan. ...... 40 B3 34 55N 62 30 E
Kashkū'īyeh, Iran ...... 45 D7 30 31N 55 40 E
Kashmir, Asia ...... 43 C7 34 0N 76 0 E
Kashmor, Pakistan ...... 42 E3 28 28N 69 32 E
Kasiari, India ...... 43 H12 22 8N 87 14 E
Kasimov, Russia ...... 18 D7 54 55N 41 20 E
Kasinge, Dem. Rep. of the Congo 54 D2 6 15S 26 58 E
Kasiruta, Indonesia ...... 37 E7 0 25S 127 12 E
Kaskaskia →, U.S.A. 80 G10 37 58N 89 57W
Kaskattama →, Canada 71 B10 57 3N 90 4W
Kaskinen, Finland ...... 9 E19 62 22N 21 15 E
Kaslo, Canada 70 D5 49 55N 116 55W

Kasmere L., Canada 71 B8 59 34N 101 10W
Kasongo, Dem. Rep. of
the Congo ...... 54 C2 4 30S 26 33 E
Kasongo Lunda, Dem. Rep. of
the Congo ...... 52 F3 6 35S 16 49 E
Kásos, Greece ...... 23 G12 35 20N 26 55 E
Kassalâ, Sudan ...... 51 E13 15 30N 36 0 E
Kassel, Germany ...... 16 C5 51 18N 9 26 E
Kassiópi, Greece ...... 25 A3 39 48N 19 53 E
Kasson, U.S.A. 80 C8 44 2N 92 45W
Kastamonu, Turkey ...... 19 F5 41 25N 33 43 E
Kastélli, Greece ...... 25 D5 35 29N 23 38 E
Kastéllion, Greece ...... 25 D7 35 12N 25 20 E
Kasterlee, Belgium ...... 15 C4 51 15N 4 59 E
Kastoria, Greece ...... 23 D9 40 30N 21 19 E
Kasulu, Tanzania ...... 54 C3 4 37S 30 5 E
Kasumi, Japan ...... 31 G7 35 38N 134 38 E
Kasungu, Malawi ...... 55 E3 13 0S 33 29 E
Kasungu △, Malawi ...... 55 E3 12 53S 33 9 E
Kasur, Pakistan ...... 42 D6 31 5N 74 25 E
Kataba, Zambia ...... 55 F2 16 5S 25 10 E
Katahdin, Mt., U.S.A. 83 C11 45 54N 68 56W
Katako Kombe, Dem. Rep. of
the Congo ...... 54 C1 3 25S 24 20 E
Katale, Tanzania ...... 54 C3 4 52S 31 7 E
Katanda, Katanga, Dem. Rep. of
the Congo ...... 54 D1 7 52S 24 13 E
Katanda, Nord-Kivu, Dem. Rep.
of the Congo ...... 54 C2 0 55S 29 21 E
Katanga □, Dem. Rep. of
the Congo ...... 54 D2 8 0S 25 0 E
Katangi, India ...... 40 J11 21 56N 79 50 E
Katanning, Australia ...... 61 F2 33 40S 117 33 E
Katavi △, Tanzania ...... 54 D3 6 51S 31 3 E
Katavi Swamp, Tanzania ...... 54 D3 6 50S 31 10 E
Katerini, Greece ...... 23 D10 40 18N 22 37 E
Katghora, India ...... 43 H10 22 30N 82 33 E
Katha, Burma ...... 41 G20 24 10N 96 30 E
Katherîna, Gebel, Egypt ...... 44 D2 28 30N 33 57 E
Katherine, Australia ...... 60 B5 14 27S 132 20 E
Katherine Gorge, Australia .... 60 B5 14 18S 132 28 E
Kathi, India ...... 42 J6 21 47N 74 3 E
Kathiawar, India ...... 42 H4 22 20N 71 0 E
Kathikas, Cyprus ...... 25 E11 34 55N 32 25 E
Kathmandu = Katmandu, Nepal 43 F11 27 45N 85 20 E
Kathua, India ...... 42 C6 32 23N 75 34 E
Katihar, India ...... 43 G12 25 34N 87 36 E
Katima Mulilo, Zambia ...... 56 B3 17 28S 24 13 E
Katimbira, Malawi ...... 55 E3 12 53S 33 9 E
Katingan = Mendawai →,
Indonesia ...... 36 E4 3 30S 113 0 E
Katiola, Ivory C. 50 G4 8 10N 5 10W
Katmandu, Nepal ...... 43 F11 27 45N 85 20 E
Katni, India ...... 43 H9 23 51N 80 24 E
Káto Arkhánai, Greece ...... 25 D7 35 15N 25 10 E
Káto Khorió, Greece ...... 25 D7 35 3N 25 47 E
Káto Pyrgos, Cyprus ...... 25 D11 35 11N 32 41 E
Katompe, Dem. Rep. of
the Congo ...... 54 D2 6 2S 26 23 E
Katong, Singapore ...... 39 d 1 18N 103 53 E
Katonga →, Uganda ...... 54 B3 0 34N 31 50 E
Katoomba, Australia ...... 63 E5 33 41S 150 19 E
Katowice, Poland ...... 17 C10 50 17N 19 5 E
Katrine, L., U.K. 11 E4 56 15N 4 30W
Katrineholm, Sweden ...... 9 G17 59 9N 16 12 E
Katsepe, Madag. ...... 57 B8 15 45S 46 15 E
Katsina, Nigeria ...... 50 F7 13 0N 7 32 E
Katsumoto, Japan ...... 31 H4 33 51N 129 42 E
Katsuura, Japan ...... 31 G10 35 10N 140 20 E
Katsuyama, Japan ...... 31 F8 36 3N 136 30 E
Kattavía, Greece ...... 25 D9 35 57N 27 46 E
Kattegat, Denmark ...... 9 H14 56 40N 11 20 E
Katumba, Dem. Rep. of
the Congo ...... 54 D2 7 40S 25 17 E
Katwa, India ...... 43 H13 23 30N 88 5 E
Katwijk, Neths. ...... 15 B4 52 12N 4 24 E
Kauai, U.S.A. 74 H15 22 3N 159 30W
Kauai Channel, U.S.A. 74 H15 21 45N 158 50W
Kaudom △, Namibia ...... 56 B3 18 45S 20 51 E
Kaufman, U.S.A. 81 J6 32 35N 96 19W
Kauhajoki, Finland ...... 9 E20 62 25N 22 10 E
Kaukauna, U.S.A. 82 C1 44 17N 88 17W
Kaukauveld, Namibia ...... 56 C3 20 0S 20 15 E
Kaunakakai, U.S.A. 74 H16 21 6N 157 1W
Kaunas, Lithuania ...... 9 J20 54 54N 23 54 E
Kaunia, Bangla. ...... 43 G13 25 46N 89 26 E
Kautokeino, Norway ...... 8 B20 69 0N 23 4 E
Kauwapur, India ...... 43 F10 27 31N 82 18 E
Kavacha, Russia ...... 29 C17 60 16N 169 51 E
Kavalerovo, Russia ...... 30 B7 44 15N 135 4 E
Kavali, India ...... 40 M12 14 55N 80 1 E
Kaválla, Greece ...... 23 D11 40 57N 24 28 E
Kavār, Iran ...... 45 D7 29 11N 52 44 E
Kavi, India ...... 42 H5 22 12N 72 38 E
Kavimba, Botswana ...... 56 B3 18 2S 24 38 E
Kavīr, Dasht-e, Iran ...... 45 C7 34 30N 55 0 E
Kavos, Greece ...... 25 B4 39 23N 20 3 E
Kaw, Fr. Guiana 93 C8 4 30N 52 15W
Kawagama L., Canada 84 A6 45 18N 78 45W
Kawagoe, Japan ...... 31 G9 35 55N 139 29 E
Kawaguchi, Japan ...... 31 G9 35 52N 139 45 E
Kawambwa, Zambia ...... 55 D2 9 48S 29 3 E
Kawanoe, Japan ...... 31 G6 34 1N 133 34 E
Kawardha, India ...... 43 J9 22 0N 81 17 E
Kawasaki, Japan ...... 31 G9 35 31N 139 43 E
Kawasi, Indonesia ...... 37 E7 1 38S 127 28 E
Kawerau, N.Z. ...... 59 H6 38 7S 176 42 E
Kawhia Harbour, N.Z. ...... 59 H5 38 5S 174 51 E
Kawio, Kepulauan, Indonesia .. 37 D7 4 30N 125 30 E
Kawnro, Burma ...... 41 H21 22 48N 99 8 E
Kawthaung, Burma ...... 39 H2 10 5N 98 36 E
Kawthoolei = Kayin □, Burma .. 41 L20 18 0N 97 30 E
Kawthule = Kayin □, Burma .... 41 L20 18 0N 97 30 E
Kaya, Burkina Faso 50 F5 13 4N 1 10W
Kayah □, Burma ...... 41 K20 19 15N 97 15 E
Kayan →, Indonesia ...... 36 D5 2 55N 117 35 E
Kaycee, U.S.A. 76 E10 43 43N 106 38W
Kayeli, Indonesia ...... 37 E7 3 20S 127 10 E
Kayenta, U.S.A. 77 H8 36 44N 110 15W
Kayes, Mali 50 F3 14 25N 11 30W
Kayin □, Burma ...... 41 L20 18 0N 97 30 E
Kayoa, Indonesia ...... 37 D7 0 1N 127 28 E
Kayomba, Zambia ...... 55 E1 13 11S 24 2 E
Kayseri, Turkey ...... 19 G6 38 45N 35 30 E
Kaysville, U.S.A. 76 F8 41 2N 111 56W
Kazachye, Russia ...... 29 B14 70 52N 135 58 E
Kazakhstan ■, Asia ...... 28 E7 50 0N 70 0 E

Kazan, *Russia* .... **18 C8** 55 50N 49 10 E
Kazan ➤, *Canada* **71 A9** 64 2N 95 29W
Kazan-Rettō, *Pac. Oc.* .... **64 E6** 25 0N 141 0 E
Kazanlŭk, *Bulgaria* .... **23 C11** 42 38N 25 20 E
Kazatin = Kozyatyn, *Ukraine* ... **17 D15** 49 45N 28 50 E
Kāzerūn, *Iran* .... **45 D6** 29 38N 51 40 E
Kazi Magomed = Qazimämmäd,
  Azerbaijan .... **45 A6** 40 3N 49 0 E
Kazuma Pan △, *Zimbabwe* .... **55 F2** 18 20S 25 48 E
Kazuno, *Japan* .... **30 D10** 40 10N 140 45 E
Kazym ➤, *Russia* .... **28 C7** 63 54N 65 50 E
Kéa, *Greece* .... **23 F11** 37 35N 24 22 E
Keady, *U.K.* **10 B5** 54 15N 6 42W
Kearney, *U.S.A.* **80 E5** 40 42N 99 5W
Kearny, *U.S.A.* **77 K8** 33 3N 110 55W
Kearsarge, Mt., *U.S.A.* **85 C13** 43 22N 71 50W
Keban, *Turkey* .... **19 G6** 38 50N 38 50 E
Keban Barajı, *Turkey* .... **19 G6** 38 41N 38 33 E
Kebnekaise, *Sweden* .... **8 C18** 67 53N 18 33 E
Kebri Dehar, *Ethiopia* .... **47 F3** 6 45N 44 17 E
Kebumen, *Indonesia* .... **37 G13** 7 42S 109 40 E
Kechika ➤, *Canada* **70 B3** 59 41N 127 12W
Kecskemét, *Hungary* .... **17 E10** 46 57N 19 42 E
Kėdainiai, *Lithuania* .... **9 J21** 55 15N 24 2 E
Kedarnath, *India* .... **43 D8** 30 44N 79 4 E
Kedgwick, *Canada* **73 C6** 47 40N 67 20W
Kédhros Óros, *Greece* .... **25 D6** 35 11N 24 37 E
Kediri, *Indonesia* .... **36 F4** 7 51S 112 1 E
Keeler, *U.S.A.* **78 J9** 36 29N 117 52W
Keeley L., *Canada* **71 C7** 54 54N 108 8W
Keeling Is. = Cocos Is., *Ind. Oc.* **64 J1** 12 10S 96 55 E
Keelung = Chilung, *Taiwan* ... **33 D7** 25 3N 121 45 E
Keene, *Canada* **84 B6** 44 15N 78 10W
Keene, *Calif., U.S.A.* **79 K8** 35 13N 118 33W
Keene, *N.H., U.S.A.* **85 D12** 42 56N 72 17W
Keene, *N.Y., U.S.A.* **85 B11** 44 16N 73 46W
Keep River △, *Australia* ...... **60 C4** 15 49S 129 8 E
Keeper Hill, *Ireland* **10 D3** 52 45N 8 16W
Keer-Weer, C., *Australia* ..... **62 A3** 14 0S 141 32 E
Keeseville, *U.S.A.* **85 B11** 44 29N 73 30W
Keetmanshoop, *Namibia* ..... **56 D2** 26 35S 18 8 E
Keewatin, *Canada* **71 D10** 49 46N 94 34W
Keewatin ➤, *Canada* **71 B8** 56 29N 100 46W
Kefallinía, *Greece* .... **23 E9** 38 15N 20 30 E
Kefamenanu, *Indonesia* ...... **37 F6** 9 28S 124 29 E
Kefar Sava, *Israel* .... **46 C3** 32 11N 34 54 E
Keffi, *Nigeria* .... **50 G7** 8 55N 7 43 E
Keflavík, *Iceland* **8 D2** 64 2N 22 35W
Keg River, *Canada* **70 B5** 57 54N 117 55W
Kegaska, *Canada* **73 B7** 50 9N 61 18W
Keighley, *U.K.* **12 D6** 53 52N 1 54W
Keila, *Estonia* .... **9 G21** 59 18N 24 25 E
Keimoes, *S. Africa* .... **56 D3** 28 41S 20 59 E
Keitele, *Finland* .... **8 E22** 63 10N 26 20 E
Keith, *Australia* .... **63 F3** 36 6S 140 20 E
Keith, *U.K.* **11 D6** 57 32N 2 57W
Keizer, *U.S.A.* **76 D2** 44 57N 123 1W
Kejimkujik △, *Canada* **73 D6** 44 25N 65 25W
Kejserr Franz Joseph Fd.,
  Greenland **4 B6** 73 30N 24 30W
Kekri, *India* .... **42 G6** 26 0N 75 10 E
Kelan, *China* .... **34 E6** 38 43N 111 31 E
Kelang, *Malaysia* .... **39 L3** 3 2N 101 26 E
Kelantan ➤, *Malaysia* .... **39 J4** 6 13N 102 14 E
Kelkit ➤, *Turkey* .... **19 F6** 40 45N 36 32 E
Kellerberrin, *Australia* .... **61 F2** 31 36S 117 38 E
Kellett, C., *Canada* **4 B1** 72 0N 126 0W
Kelleys I., *U.S.A.* **84 E2** 41 36N 82 42W
Kellogg, *U.S.A.* **76 C5** 47 32N 116 7W
Kells = Ceanannus Mor, *Ireland* **10 C5** 53 44N 6 53W
Kelokedhara, *Cyprus* .... **25 E11** 34 48N 32 39 E
Kelowna, *Canada* **70 D5** 49 50N 119 25W
Kelsey Creek, *Australia* ...... **62 J6** 20 26S 148 31 E
Kelseyville, *U.S.A.* **78 G4** 38 59N 122 50W
Kelso, *N.Z.* .... **59 L2** 45 54S 169 15 E
Kelso, *U.K.* **11 F6** 55 36N 2 26W
Kelso, *U.S.A.* **78 D4** 46 9N 122 54W
Keluang, *Malaysia* .... **39 L4** 2 3N 103 18 E
Kelvington, *Canada* **71 C8** 52 10N 103 30W
Kem, *Russia* .... **18 B5** 65 0N 34 38 E
Kem ➤, *Russia* .... **18 B5** 64 57N 34 41 E
Kema, *Indonesia* .... **37 D7** 1 22N 125 8 E
Kemah, *Turkey* .... **44 B3** 39 32N 39 5 E
Kemaman, *Malaysia* .... **36 D2** 4 12N 103 18 E
Kemano, *Canada* **70 C3** 53 35N 128 0W
Kemasik, *Malaysia* .... **39 K4** 4 25N 103 27 E
Kemerovo, *Russia* .... **28 D9** 55 20N 86 5 E
Kemi, *Finland* .... **8 D21** 65 44N 24 34 E
Kemi älv = Kemijoki ➤, *Finland* **8 D21** 65 47N 24 32 E
Kemijärvi, *Finland* .... **8 C22** 66 43N 27 22 E
Kemijoki ➤, *Finland* .... **8 D21** 65 47N 24 32 E
Kemmerer, *U.S.A.* **76 F8** 41 48N 110 32W
Kemmuna = Comino, *Malta* .. **25 C1** 36 1N 14 20 E
Kemp, L., *U.S.A.* **81 J5** 33 46N 99 9W
Kemp Land, *Antarctica* ...... **5 C5** 69 0S 55 0 E
Kempas, *Malaysia* .... **39 d** 1 33N 103 42 E
Kempsey, *Australia* .... **63 E5** 31 1S 152 50 E
Kempt, L., *Canada* **72 C5** 47 25N 74 22W
Kempten, *Germany* .... **16 E6** 47 45N 10 17 E
Kempton, *Australia* .... **63 G4** 42 31S 147 12 E
Kemptville, *Canada* **85 B9** 45 0N 75 38W
Ken ➤, *India* .... **43 G9** 25 13N 80 27 E
Kenai, *U.S.A.* **68 B4** 60 33N 151 16W
Kendal, *India* .... **43 H10** 22 45N 82 37 E
Kendal, *Indonesia* .... **37 G14** 6 56S 110 14 E
Kendal, *U.K.* **12 C5** 54 20N 2 44W
Kendall, *Australia* .... **63 E5** 31 35S 152 44 E
Kendall, *U.S.A.* **83 N5** 25 41N 80 19W
Kendall ➤, *Australia* .... **62 A3** 14 4S 141 35 E
Kendallville, *U.S.A.* **82 E3** 41 27N 85 16W
Kendari, *Indonesia* .... **37 E6** 3 50S 122 30 E
Kendawangan, *Indonesia* .... **36 E4** 2 32S 110 17 E
Kendi, Pulau, *Malaysia* ...... **39 c** 5 13N 100 11 E
Kendrapara, *India* .... **41 J15** 20 35N 86 30 E
Kendrew, *S. Africa* .... **56 E3** 32 32S 24 30 E
Kene Thao, *Laos* .... **38 D3** 17 44N 101 10 E
Kenedy, *U.S.A.* **81 L6** 28 49N 97 51W
Kenema, *S. Leone* **50 G3** 7 50N 11 14W
Keng Kok, *Laos* .... **38 D5** 16 26N 105 12 E
Keng Tawng, *Burma* .... **41 J21** 20 45N 98 18 E
Keng Tung, *Burma* .... **41 J21** 21 0N 99 30 E
Kengeja, *Tanzania* .... **54 D4** 5 26S 39 45 E
Kenhardt, *S. Africa* .... **56 D3** 29 19S 21 12 E
Kenitra, *Morocco* **50 B4** 34 15N 6 40W
Kenli, *China* .... **35 F10** 37 30N 118 20 E
Kenmare, *Ireland* **10 E2** 51 53N 9 36W
Kenmare, *U.S.A.* **80 A3** 48 41N 102 5W

Kenmare River, *Ireland* **10 E2** 51 48N 9 51W
Kennebago Lake, *U.S.A.* **85 A14** 45 4N 70 40W
Kennebec, *U.S.A.* **80 D5** 43 54N 99 52W
Kennebec ➤, *U.S.A.* **83 D11** 43 45N 69 46W
Kennebunk, *U.S.A.* **85 C14** 43 23N 70 33W
Kennedy, *Zimbabwe* .... **56 B4** 18 52S 27 10 E
Kennedy Ra., *Australia* ...... **61 D2** 24 45S 115 10 E
Kennedy Range △, *Australia* . **61 D2** 24 34S 115 2 E
Kenner, *U.S.A.* **81 L9** 29 59N 90 15W
Kenneth Ra., *Australia* ...... **61 D2** 23 50S 117 8 E
Kennett, *U.S.A.* **81 G9** 36 14N 90 3W
Kennewick, *U.S.A.* **76 C4** 46 12N 119 7W
Kenogami ➤, *Canada* **72 B3** 51 6N 84 28W
Kenora, *Canada* **71 D10** 49 47N 94 29W
Kenosha, *U.S.A.* **82 D2** 42 35N 87 49W
Kensington, *Canada* **73 C7** 46 28N 63 34W
Kent, *Ohio, U.S.A.* **84 E3** 41 9N 81 22W
Kent, *Tex., U.S.A.* **81 K2** 31 4N 104 13W
Kent, *Wash., U.S.A.* **78 C4** 47 23N 122 14W
Kent □, *U.K.* .... **13 F8** 51 12N 0 40 E
Kent Group, *Australia* .... **63 F4** 39 30S 147 20 E
Kent Pen., *Canada* **68 B9** 68 30N 107 0W
Kentaū, *Kazakhstan* .... **28 E7** 43 32N 68 36 E
Kentland, *U.S.A.* **82 E2** 40 46N 87 27W
Kenton, *U.S.A.* **82 E4** 40 39N 83 37W
Kentucky □, *U.S.A.* **82 G3** 37 0N 84 0W
Kentucky ➤, *U.S.A.* **82 F3** 38 41N 85 11W
Kentucky L., *U.S.A.* **83 G2** 37 1N 88 16W
Kentville, *Canada* **73 C7** 45 6N 64 29W
Kentwood, *U.S.A.* **81 K9** 30 56N 90 31W
Kenya ■, *Africa* .... **54 B4** 1 0N 38 0 E
Kenya, Mt., *Kenya* .... **54 C4** 0 10S 37 18 E
Keo Neua, Deo, *Vietnam* .... **38 C5** 18 23N 105 10 E
Keokuk, *U.S.A.* **80 E9** 40 24N 91 24W
Keonjhargarh, *India* .... **43 J11** 21 28N 85 35 E
Kep, *Cambodia* .... **39 G5** 10 29N 104 19 E
Kep, *Vietnam* .... **38 B6** 21 24N 106 16 E
Kepala Batas, *Malaysia* ...... **39 c** 5 31N 100 26 E
Kepi, *Indonesia* .... **37 F9** 6 32S 139 19 E
Kerala □, *India* .... **40 P10** 11 0N 76 15 E
Kerama-Rettō, *Japan* .... **31 L3** 26 5N 127 15 E
Keran, *Pakistan* .... **43 B5** 34 35N 73 59 E
Kerang, *Australia* .... **63 F3** 35 40S 143 55 E
Keraudren, C., *Australia* ..... **60 C2** 19 58S 119 45 E
Kerava, *Finland* .... **9 F21** 60 25N 25 5 E
Kerch, *Ukraine* .... **19 E6** 45 20N 36 20 E
Kerguelen, *Ind. Oc.* .... **3 G13** 49 15S 69 10 E
Kericho, *Kenya* .... **54 C4** 0 22S 35 15 E
Kerinci, *Indonesia* .... **36 E2** 1 40S 101 15 E
Kerki, *Turkmenistan* .... **28 F7** 37 50N 65 12 E
Kérkira, *Greece* .... **25 A3** 39 38N 19 50 E
Kerkrade, *Neths.* .... **15 D6** 50 53N 6 4 E
Kermadec Is., *Pac. Oc.* **64 L10** 30 0S 178 15W
Kermadec Trench, *Pac. Oc.* .. **64 L10** 30 30S 176 0W
Kermān, *Iran* .... **45 D8** 30 15N 57 1 E
Kerman, *U.S.A.* **78 J6** 36 43N 120 4W
Kermān □, *Iran* .... **45 D8** 30 0N 57 0 E
Kermān, Biābān-e, *Iran* ...... **45 D8** 28 45N 59 45 E
Kermānshāh = Bākhtarān, *Iran* **44 C5** 34 23N 47 0 E
Kermit, *U.S.A.* **81 K3** 31 52N 103 6W
Kern ➤, *U.S.A.* **79 K7** 35 16N 119 18W
Kernow = Cornwall □, *U.K.* .. **13 G3** 50 26N 4 40W
Kernville, *U.S.A.* **79 K8** 35 45N 118 26W
Keroh, *Malaysia* .... **39 K3** 5 43N 101 1 E
Kerrera, *U.K.* **11 E3** 56 24N 5 33W
Kerrobert, *Canada* **71 C7** 51 56N 109 8W
Kerrville, *U.S.A.* **81 K5** 30 3N 99 8W
Kerry □, *Ireland* **10 D2** 52 7N 9 35W
Kerry Hd., *Ireland* **10 D2** 52 25N 9 56W
Kerulen ➤, *Asia* .... **33 B6** 48 48N 117 0 E
Kerzaz, *Algeria* **50 C5** 29 29N 1 37W
Kesagami ➤, *Canada* **72 B4** 51 40N 79 45W
Kesagami L., *Canada* **72 B3** 50 23N 80 15W
Keşan, *Turkey* .... **23 D12** 40 49N 26 38 E
Kesennuma, *Japan* .... **30 E10** 38 54N 141 35 E
Keshit, *Iran* .... **45 D8** 29 43N 58 17 E
Kestell, *S. Africa* .... **57 D4** 28 17S 28 42 E
Kestenga, *Russia* .... **18 A5** 65 50N 31 45 E
Keswick, *U.K.* **12 C4** 54 36N 3 8W
Ket ➤, *Russia* .... **28 D9** 58 55N 81 32 E
Ketapang, *Bali, Indonesia* ... **37 J17** 8 9S 114 23 E
Ketapang, *Kalimantan, Indonesia* **36 E4** 1 55S 110 0 E
Ketchikan, *U.S.A.* **70 B2** 55 21N 131 39W
Ketchum, *U.S.A.* **76 E6** 43 41N 114 22W
Ketef, Khalîg Umm el, *Egypt* . **44 F2** 23 40N 35 35 E
Keti Bandar, *Pakistan* .... **42 G2** 24 8N 67 27 E
Ketri, *India* .... **42 E6** 28 1N 75 50 E
Kętrzyn, *Poland* .... **17 A11** 54 7N 21 22 E
Kettering, *U.K.* **13 E7** 52 24N 0 43W
Kettering, *U.S.A.* **82 F3** 39 41N 84 10W
Kettle ➤, *Canada* **71 B11** 56 40N 89 34W
Kettle Falls, *U.S.A.* **76 B4** 48 37N 118 3W
Kettle Pt., *Canada* **84 C2** 43 13N 82 1W
Kettleman City, *U.S.A.* **78 J7** 36 1N 119 58W
Keuka L., *U.S.A.* **84 D7** 42 30N 77 9W
Keuruu, *Finland* .... **9 E21** 62 16N 24 41 E
Kewanee, *U.S.A.* **80 E10** 41 14N 89 56W
Kewaunee, *U.S.A.* **82 C2** 44 27N 87 31W
Keweenaw B., *U.S.A.* **82 B1** 47 0N 88 15W
Keweenaw Pen., *U.S.A.* **82 B2** 47 30N 88 0W
Keweenaw Pt., *U.S.A.* **82 B2** 47 25N 87 43W
Key Largo, *U.S.A.* **83 N5** 25 5N 80 27W
Key West, *U.S.A.* **75 F10** 24 33N 81 48W
Keynsham, *U.K.* **13 F5** 51 24N 2 29W
Keyser, *U.S.A.* **82 F6** 39 26N 78 59W
Kezhma, *Russia* .... **29 D11** 58 59N 101 9 E
Kezi, *Zimbabwe* .... **57 C4** 20 58S 28 32 E
Kgalagadi Transfrontier △, *Africa* **56 D3** 25 10S 21 0 E
Khabarovsk, *Russia* .... **29 E14** 48 30N 135 5 E
Khabr, *Iran* .... **45 D8** 28 51N 56 22 E
Khābūr ➤, *Syria* .... **44 C4** 35 17N 40 35 E
Khachmas = Xaçmaz, *Azerbaijan* **19 F8** 41 31N 48 42 E
Khadro, *India* .... **42 H2** 23 25N 73 50 E
Khadzhilyangar, *China* .... **43 B8** 35 45N 79 20 E
Khaga, *India* .... **43 G9** 25 47N 81 7 E
Khagaria, *India* .... **43 G12** 25 30N 86 32 E
Khaipur, *Pakistan* .... **42 E5** 29 34N 72 17 E
Khair, *India* .... **42 F7** 27 57N 77 46 E
Khairabad, *India* .... **43 F9** 27 33N 80 47 E
Khairagarh, *India* .... **43 J9** 21 27N 81 2 E
Khairpur, *Pakistan* .... **42 F3** 27 32N 68 49 E
Khairpur Nathan Shah, *Pakistan* **42 F2** 27 6N 67 44 E
Khairwara, *India* .... **42 H5** 23 58N 73 38 E
Khaisor ➤, *Pakistan* .... **42 D3** 31 17N 68 59 E
Khajuri Kach, *Pakistan* ...... **42 C3** 32 4N 69 51 E

Khakassia □, *Russia* .... **28 D9** 53 0N 90 0 E
Khakhea, *Botswana* .... **56 C3** 24 48S 23 22 E
Khalafābād, *Iran* .... **45 D6** 30 54N 49 24 E
Khalilabad, *India* .... **43 F10** 26 48N 83 5 E
Khalīlī, *Iran* .... **45 E7** 27 38N 53 17 E
Khalkhāl, *Iran* .... **45 B6** 37 37N 48 32 E
Khalkis, *Greece* .... **23 E10** 38 27N 23 42 E
Khalmer Yu, *Russia* .... **28 C7** 67 58N 65 1 E
Khalturin, *Russia* .... **18 C8** 58 40N 48 50 E
Khalūf, *Oman* .... **47 C6** 20 30N 58 13 E
Kham Keut, *Laos* .... **38 C5** 18 15N 104 43 E
Khamaria, *India* .... **43 H9** 23 5N 80 48 E
Khambhaliya, *India* .... **42 H3** 22 14N 69 41 E
Khambhat, *India* .... **42 H5** 22 23N 72 33 E
Khambhat, G. of, *India* ...... **40 J8** 20 45N 72 30 E
Khamir, *Iran* .... **45 E7** 26 57N 55 36 E
Khamir, *Yemen* .... **46 E1** 30 27N 32 23 E
Khān ➤, *Namibia* .... **56 C2** 22 37S 14 56 E
Khān Abū Shāmat, *Syria* .... **46 B5** 33 39N 36 53 E
Khān Azād, *Iraq* .... **44 C5** 33 7N 44 22 E
Khān Mujiddah, *Iraq* .... **44 C4** 32 21N 43 48 E
Khān Shaykhūn, *Syria* ...... **44 C3** 35 26N 36 38 E
Khān Yūnis, *Gaza Strip* ...... **46 D3** 31 21N 34 18 E
Khanai, *Pakistan* .... **42 D2** 30 30N 67 8 E
Khānaqin, *Iraq* .... **44 C5** 34 23N 45 25 E
Khānbāghī, *Iran* .... **45 B7** 36 10N 55 25 E
Khandwa, *India* .... **40 J10** 21 49N 76 22 E
Khandyga, *Russia* .... **29 C14** 62 42N 135 35 E
Khāneh, *Iran* .... **44 B5** 36 41N 45 8 E
Khanewal, *Pakistan* .... **42 D4** 30 20N 71 55 E
Khangah Dogran, *Pakistan* ... **42 D5** 31 50N 73 37 E
Khanh Duong, *Vietnam* ...... **38 F7** 12 44N 108 44 E
Khaniá, *Greece* .... **25 D6** 35 30N 24 4 E
Khaniá □, *Greece* .... **25 D6** 35 30N 24 0 E
Khaniadhana, *India* .... **42 G8** 25 1N 78 8 E
Khanion, Kólpos, *Greece* ..... **25 D5** 35 33N 23 55 E
Khanka, L., *Asia* .... **29 E14** 45 0N 132 24 E
Khankendy = Xankändi,
  Azerbaijan .... **19 G8** 39 52N 46 49 E
Khanna, *India* .... **42 D7** 30 42N 76 16 E
Khanozai, *Pakistan* .... **42 D2** 30 37N 67 19 E
Khanpur, *Pakistan* .... **42 E4** 28 42N 70 35 E
Khanty-Mansiysk, *Russia* .... **28 C7** 61 0N 69 0 E
Khao Laem △, *Thailand* ..... **38 E2** 14 56N 98 31 E
Khao Luang △, *Thailand* ..... **39 H2** 8 34N 99 42 E
Khao Phlu, *Thailand* .... **39 b** 9 29N 99 59 E
Khao Pu-Khao Ya △, *Thailand* **39 J2** 7 26N 99 57 E
Khao Sam Roi Yot △, *Thailand* **39 F2** 12 13N 99 57 E
Khao Sok △, *Thailand* ...... **39 H2** 8 55N 98 38 E
Khao Yai △, *Thailand* .... **38 E3** 14 21N 101 29 E
Khaoen Si Nakharin △, *Thailand* **38 E2** 14 47N 99 0 E
Khapalu, *Pakistan* .... **43 B7** 35 10N 76 20 E
Khapcheranga, *Russia* ...... **29 E12** 49 42N 112 24 E
Kharagoda, *India* .... **42 H4** 23 11N 71 46 E
Kharagpur, *India* .... **43 H12** 22 20N 87 25 E
Khárakas, *Greece* .... **25 D7** 35 1N 25 7 E
Kharan Kalat, *Pakistan* ...... **40 E4** 28 34N 65 21 E
Kharānaq, *Iran* .... **45 C7** 32 20N 54 45 E
Kharda, *India* .... **40 K9** 18 40N 75 34 E
Khardung La, *India* .... **43 B7** 34 20N 77 43 E
Kharg = Khārk, Jazireh-ye, *Iran* **45 D6** 29 15N 50 28 E
Khârga, El Wâhât-el, *Egypt* ... **51 C12** 25 10N 30 35 E
Khargon, *India* .... **40 J9** 21 45N 75 40 E
Khari ➤, *India* .... **42 G6** 25 54N 74 31 E
Kharian, *Pakistan* .... **42 C5** 32 49N 73 52 E
Khārk, Jazireh-ye, *Iran* ...... **45 D6** 29 15N 50 28 E
Kharkiv, *Ukraine* .... **19 E6** 49 58N 36 20 E
Kharkov = Kharkiv, *Ukraine* .. **19 E6** 49 58N 36 20 E
Kharovsk, *Russia* .... **18 C7** 59 56N 40 13 E
Kharsawangarh, *India* .... **43 H11** 22 48N 85 50 E
Kharta, *Turkey* .... **23 D13** 40 55N 29 7 E
Khartoum = El Khartûm, *Sudan* **51 E12** 15 31N 32 35 E
Khasan, *Russia* .... **30 C5** 42 25N 130 40 E
Khāsh, *Iran* .... **40 E2** 28 15N 61 15 E
Khashm el Girba, *Sudan* ..... **51 F13** 14 59N 35 58 E
Khaskovo, *Bulgaria* .... **23 D11** 41 56N 25 30 E
Khatanga, *Russia* .... **29 B11** 72 0N 102 20 E
Khatanga ➤, *Russia* .... **29 B11** 72 55N 106 0 E
Khatauli, *India* .... **42 E7** 29 17N 77 43 E
Khatra, *India* .... **43 H12** 22 59N 86 51 E
Khātūnābād, *Iran* .... **45 D7** 30 1N 55 25 E
Khatyrka, *Russia* .... **29 C18** 62 3N 175 15 E
Khavda, *India* .... **42 H3** 23 51N 69 43 E
Khaybar, Harrat, *Si. Arabia* ... **44 E4** 25 45N 40 0 E
Khayelitsha, *S. Africa* .... **53 L3** 34 5S 18 42 E
Khāzimiyah, *Iraq* .... **44 C4** 34 46N 43 37 E
Khe Bo, *Vietnam* .... **38 C5** 19 8N 104 41 E
Khe Long, *Vietnam* .... **38 B5** 21 29N 104 46 E
Khe Sanh, *Vietnam* .... **38 D6** 16 37N 106 45 E
Khed Brahma, *India* .... **40 G8** 24 7N 73 5 E
Khekra, *India* .... **42 E7** 28 52N 77 20 E
Khemarak Phouminville,
  Cambodia .... **39 G4** 11 37N 102 59 E
Khemisset, *Morocco* **50 B4** 33 50N 6 1W
Khemmarat, *Thailand* .... **38 D5** 16 10N 105 15 E
Khenāmān, *Iran* .... **45 D8** 30 27N 56 29 E
Khenchela, *Algeria* .... **50 A7** 35 28N 7 11 E
Khersān ➤, *Iran* .... **45 D6** 31 33N 50 22 E
Khersónisos Akrotíri, *Greece* .. **25 D6** 35 30N 24 10 E
Kheta ➤, *Russia* .... **29 B11** 71 54N 102 6 E
Khewari, *Pakistan* .... **42 F3** 26 36N 68 52 E
Khilchipur, *India* .... **42 G7** 24 2N 76 34 E
Khilok, *Russia* .... **29 D12** 51 30N 110 45 E
Khíos, *Greece* .... **23 E12** 38 27N 26 9 E
Khirsadoh, *India* .... **43 H8** 22 11N 78 47 E
Khiuma = Hiiumaa, *Estonia* .. **9 G20** 58 50N 22 45 E
Khiva, *Uzbekistan* .... **28 E7** 41 30N 60 18 E
Khiyāv, *Iran* .... **44 B5** 38 30N 47 45 E
Khlong Khlung, *Thailand* ..... **38 D2** 16 12N 99 43 E
Khmelnik, *Ukraine* .... **17 D14** 49 33N 27 58 E
Khmelnitskiy = Khmelnytskyy,
  Ukraine .... **17 D14** 49 23N 27 0 E
Khmelnytskyy, *Ukraine* ...... **17 D14** 49 23N 27 0 E
Khmer Rep. = Cambodia ■, *Asia* **38 F5** 12 15N 105 0 E
Khoai, Hon, *Vietnam* .... **39 H5** 8 26N 104 50 E
Khodoriv, *Ukraine* .... **17 D13** 49 24N 24 19 E
Khodzent = Khŭjand, *Tajikistan* **28 E7** 40 17N 69 37 E
Khojak Pass, *Afghan.* .... **42 D2** 30 51N 66 34 E
Khok Kloi, *Thailand* .... **39 a** 8 43N 98 19 E
Khok Pho, *Thailand* .... **39 J3** 6 43N 101 6 E
Kholm, *Russia* .... **18 C5** 57 10N 31 15 E
Kholmsk, *Russia* .... **29 E15** 47 40N 142 5 E
Khomas Hochland, *Namibia* .. **56 C2** 22 40S 16 0 E
Khomeyn, *Iran* .... **45 C6** 33 40N 50 7 E
Khomeynī Shahr, *Iran* .... **45 C6** 32 41N 51 31 E

Khomodino, *Botswana* .... **56 C3** 22 46S 23 52 E
Khon Kaen, *Thailand* .... **38 D4** 16 30N 102 47 E
Khong, *Cambodia* .... **38 F5** 13 32N 105 58 E
Khong Sedone, *Laos* .... **38 E5** 15 34N 105 49 E
Khonuu, *Russia* .... **29 C15** 66 30N 143 12 E
Khoper ➤, *Russia* .... **19 D6** 49 30N 42 20 E
Khóra Sfakíon, *Greece* .... **25 D6** 35 15N 24 9 E
Khorāsān □, *Iran* .... **45 C8** 34 0N 58 0 E
Khorat = Nakhon Ratchasima,
  Thailand .... **38 E4** 14 59N 102 12 E
Khorat, Cao Nguyen, *Thailand* **38 E4** 15 30N 102 50 E
Khorixas, *Namibia* .... **56 C1** 20 16S 14 59 E
Khorramābād, *Khorāsān, Iran* . **45 C8** 35 6N 57 57 E
Khorramābād, *Lorestān, Iran* .. **45 C6** 33 30N 48 25 E
Khorrāmshahr, *Iran* .... **45 D6** 30 29N 48 15 E
Khorugh, *Tajikistan* .... **28 F8** 37 30N 71 36 E
Khosravī, *Iran* .... **45 D6** 30 48N 51 28 E
Khosrowābād, *Khuzestān, Iran* . **45 D6** 30 10N 48 25 E
Khosrowābād, *Kordestān, Iran* . **44 C5** 35 31N 47 38 E
Khost, *Pakistan* .... **42 D2** 30 13N 67 35 E
Khosūyeh, *Iran* .... **45 D7** 28 32N 54 26 E
Khotyn, *Ukraine* .... **17 D14** 48 31N 26 27 E
Khouribga, *Morocco* **50 B4** 32 58N 6 57W
Khowst, *Afghan.* .... **42 C3** 33 22N 69 58 E
Khowst □, *Afghan.* .... **40 C6** 33 20N 70 0 E
Khoyniki, *Belarus* .... **17 C15** 51 54N 29 55 E
Khrysokhou B., *Cyprus* ...... **25 D11** 35 6N 32 25 E
Khu Khan, *Thailand* .... **38 E5** 14 42N 104 12 E
Khuan Wa, *Thailand* .... **39 a** 7 53N 98 17 E
Khudzhand = Khŭjand, *Tajikistan* **28 E7** 40 17N 69 37 E
Khuff, *Si. Arabia* .... **44 E5** 24 55N 44 53 E
Khūgiānī, *Afghan.* .... **42 D2** 31 34N 66 32 E
Khuis, *Botswana* .... **56 D3** 26 40S 21 49 E
Khuiyala, *India* .... **42 F4** 27 9N 70 25 E
Khŭjand, *Tajikistan* .... **28 E7** 40 17N 69 37 E
Khujner, *India* .... **42 H7** 23 47N 76 36 E
Khulna, *Bangla.* .... **41 H16** 22 45N 89 34 E
Khulna □, *Bangla.* .... **41 H16** 22 25N 89 35 E
Khumago, *Botswana* .... **56 C3** 20 26S 24 32 E
Khŭnsorkh, *Iran* .... **45 E8** 27 9N 56 7 E
Khunti, *India* .... **43 H11** 23 5N 85 17 E
Khūr, *Iran* .... **45 C8** 32 55N 58 18 E
Khurai, *India* .... **42 G8** 24 3N 78 23 E
Khurayş, *Si. Arabia* .... **45 E6** 25 6N 48 2 E
Khuriyā Muriyā, Jazā'ir, *Oman* . **47 D6** 17 30N 55 58 E
Khurja, *India* .... **42 E7** 28 15N 77 58 E
Khūrmāl, *Iraq* .... **44 C5** 35 18N 46 2 E
Khurr, Wādī al, *Iraq* .... **44 C4** 32 3N 43 52 E
Khūsf, *Iran* .... **45 C8** 32 46N 58 53 E
Khush, *Afghan.* .... **40 C3** 32 55N 62 10 E
Khushab, *Pakistan* .... **42 C5** 32 20N 72 20 E
Khust, *Ukraine* .... **17 D12** 48 10N 23 18 E
Khutse △, *Botswana* .... **56 C3** 23 31S 24 12 E
Khuzdar, *Pakistan* .... **42 F2** 27 52N 66 30 E
Khūzestān □, *Iran* .... **45 D6** 31 0N 49 0 E
Khvāf, *Iran* .... **45 C9** 34 33N 60 8 E
Khvājeh, *Iran* .... **44 B5** 38 9N 46 35 E
Khvānsār, *Iran* .... **45 D7** 29 56N 54 8 E
Khvor, *Iran* .... **45 C7** 33 45N 55 0 E
Khvorgū, *Iran* .... **45 E8** 27 34N 56 27 E
Khvormūj, *Iran* .... **45 D6** 28 40N 51 30 E
Khvoy, *Iran* .... **44 B5** 38 35N 45 0 E
Khyber Pass, *Afghan.* .... **42 B4** 34 10N 71 8 E
Kiabukwa, *Dem. Rep. of
  the Congo* .... **55 D1** 8 40S 24 48 E
Kiama, *Australia* .... **63 E5** 34 40S 150 50 E
Kiamba, *Phil.* .... **37 C6** 6 2N 124 46 E
Kiambi, *Dem. Rep. of the Congo* **54 D2** 7 15S 28 0 E
Kiambu, *Kenya* .... **54 C4** 1 8S 36 50 E
Kiangara, *Madag.* .... **57 B8** 17 58S 47 2 E
Kiangsi = Jiangxi □, *China* ... **33 D6** 27 30N 116 0 E
Kiangsu = Jiangsu □, *China* .. **35 H11** 33 0N 120 0 E
Kibale △, *Uganda* .... **54 B3** 0 16N 30 18 E
Kibanga Port, *Uganda* .... **54 B3** 0 10N 32 58 E
Kibara, *Tanzania* .... **54 C3** 2 8S 33 30 E
Kibare, Mts., *Dem. Rep. of
  the Congo* .... **54 D2** 8 25S 27 10 E
Kibira △, *Burundi* .... **54 C3** 3 6S 30 24 E
Kibombo, *Dem. Rep. of
  the Congo* .... **54 C2** 3 57S 25 53 E
Kibondo, *Tanzania* .... **54 C3** 3 35S 30 45 E
Kibre Mengist, *Ethiopia* ...... **47 F2** 5 54N 38 59 E
Kibumbu, *Burundi* .... **54 C2** 3 32S 29 45 E
Kibungo, *Rwanda* .... **54 C3** 2 10S 30 32 E
Kibuye, *Burundi* .... **54 C2** 3 39S 29 59 E
Kibuye, *Rwanda* .... **54 C2** 2 3S 29 21 E
Kibwesa, *Tanzania* .... **54 D2** 6 30S 29 58 E
Kibwezi, *Kenya* .... **54 C4** 2 27S 37 57 E
Kichha, *India* .... **43 E8** 28 53N 79 30 E
Kichha ➤, *India* .... **43 E8** 28 41N 79 18 E
Kichmengskiy Gorodok, *Russia* **18 B8** 59 59N 45 48 E
Kicking Horse Pass, *Canada* .. **70 C5** 51 28N 116 16W
Kidal, *Mali* .... **50 E6** 18 26N 1 22 E
Kidderminster, *U.K.* **13 E5** 52 24N 2 15W
Kidepo Valley △, *Uganda* .... **54 B3** 3 52N 33 50 E
Kidete, *Tanzania* .... **54 D4** 6 25S 37 17 E
Kidnappers, C., *N.Z.* .... **59 H6** 39 38S 177 5 E
Kidsgrove, *U.K.* **12 D5** 53 5N 2 14W
Kidston, *Australia* .... **62 B3** 18 52S 144 8 E
Kidugallo, *Tanzania* .... **54 D4** 6 49S 38 15 E
Kiel, *Germany* .... **16 A6** 54 19N 10 8 E
Kiel Canal = Nord-Ostsee-Kanal,
  Germany .... **16 A5** 54 12N 9 32 E
Kielce, *Poland* .... **17 C11** 50 52N 20 42 E
Kielder Water, *U.K.* **12 B5** 55 11N 2 31W
Kieler Bucht, *Germany* ...... **16 A6** 54 35N 10 25 E
Kien Binh, *Vietnam* .... **39 H5** 9 55N 105 19 E
Kien Tan, *Vietnam* .... **39 G5** 10 7N 105 17 E
Kienge, *Dem. Rep. of the Congo* **55 E2** 10 30S 27 30 E
Kiev = Kyyiv, *Ukraine* .... **17 C16** 50 30N 30 28 E
Kiffa, *Mauritania* **50 E3** 16 37N 11 24W
Kifrī, *Iraq* .... **44 C5** 34 45N 45 0 E
Kigali, *Rwanda* .... **54 C3** 1 59S 30 4 E
Kigarama, *Tanzania* .... **54 C3** 1 1S 31 50 E
Kigezi □, *Uganda* .... **54 C3** 0 34S 29 55 E
Kigoma □, *Tanzania* .... **54 D3** 5 0S 30 0 E
Kigoma-Ujiji, *Tanzania* ...... **54 C2** 4 55S 29 36 E
Kigomasha, Ras, *Tanzania* ... **54 C4** 4 58S 38 58 E
Kığzı, *Turkey* .... **44 B4** 38 18N 43 25 E
Kihei, *U.S.A.* **74 H16** 20 47N 156 28W
Kihnu, *Estonia* .... **9 G21** 58 9N 24 1 E
Kii-Sanchi, *Japan* .... **31 G8** 34 20N 136 0 E
Kii-Suidō, *Japan* .... **31 H7** 33 40N 134 45 E
Kikaiga-Shima, *Japan* .... **31 K4** 28 19N 129 59 E
Kikinda, *Serbia & M.* .... **23 B9** 45 50N 20 30 E
Kikládhes, *Greece* .... **23 F11** 37 0N 24 30 E
Kikwit, *Dem. Rep. of the Congo* **52 E3** 5 0S 18 45 E

Kilar, *India* .... 42 C7   33 6N 76 25 E
Kilauea Crater, *U.S.A.* 74 J17 19 25N 155 17W
Kilbrannan Sd., *U.K.* 11 F3 55 37N 5 26W
Kilchu, *N. Korea* .... 35 D15 40 57N 129 25 E
Kilcoy, *Australia* .... 63 D5 26 59S 152 30 E
Kildare, *Ireland* 10 C5 53 9N 6 55W
Kildare □, *Ireland* 10 C5 53 10N 6 50W
Kilfinnane, *Ireland* 10 D3 52 21N 8 28W
Kilgore, *U.S.A.* 81 J7 32 23N 94 53W
Kilifi, *Kenya* .... 54 C4   3 40S 39 48 E
Kilimanjaro, *Tanzania* ...... 54 C4   3 7S 37 20 E
Kilimanjaro □, *Tanzania* .... 54 C4   4 0S 38 0 E
Kilindini, *Kenya* .... 54 C4   4 4S 39 40 E
Kilis, *Turkey* .... 44 B3 36 42N 37 6 E
Kiliya, *Ukraine* .... 17 F15 45 28N 29 16 E
Kilkee, *Ireland* 10 D2 52 41N 9 39W
Kilkeel, *U.K.* 10 B5 54 4N 6 0W
Kilkenny, *Ireland* 10 D4 52 39N 7 15W
Kilkenny □, *Ireland* 10 D4 52 35N 7 15W
Kilkieran B., *Ireland* 10 C2 53 20N 9 41W
Kilkis, *Greece* .... 23 D10 40 58N 22 57 E
Killala, *Ireland* 10 B2 54 13N 9 12W
Killala B., *Ireland* 10 B2 54 16N 9 8W
Killaloe, *Canada* 84 A7 45 33N 77 25W
Killaloe, *Ireland* 10 D3 52 48N 8 28W
Killarney, *Australia* .... 63 D5 28 20S 152 18 E
Killarney, *Canada* 71 D9 49 10N 99 40W
Killarney, *Ireland* 10 D2 52 4N 9 30W
Killarney △, *Ireland* 10 D2 52 0N 9 33W
Killary Harbour, *Ireland* ... 10 C2 53 38N 9 52W
Killdeer, *U.S.A.* 80 B3 47 26N 102 48W
Killeen, *U.S.A.* 81 K6 31 7N 97 44W
Killin, *U.K.* 11 E4 56 28N 4 19W
Killíni, *Greece* .... 23 F10 37 54N 22 25 E
Killorglin, *Ireland* 10 D2 52 6N 9 47W
Killybegs, *Ireland* 10 B3 54 38N 8 26W
Kilmarnock, *U.K.* 11 F4 55 37N 4 29W
Kilmore, *Australia* .... 63 F3 37 25S 144 53 E
Kilondo, *Tanzania* .... 55 D3   9 45S 34 20 E
Kilosa, *Tanzania* .... 54 D4   6 48S 37 0 E
Kilrush, *Ireland* 10 D2 52 38N 9 29W
Kilwa Kisiwani, *Tanzania* .. 55 D4   8 58S 39 32 E
Kilwa Kivinje, *Tanzania* ... 55 D4   8 45S 39 25 E
Kilwa Masoko, *Tanzania* ... 55 D4   8 55S 39 30 E
Kilwinning, *U.K.* 11 F4 55 39N 4 43W
Kim, *U.S.A.* 81 G3 37 15N 103 21W
Kimaam, *Indonesia* .... 37 F9   7 58S 138 53 E
Kimamba, *Tanzania* .... 54 D4   6 45S 37 10 E
Kimba, *Australia* .... 63 E2 33 8S 136 23 E
Kimball, *Nebr., U.S.A.* 80 E3 41 14N 103 40W
Kimball, *S. Dak., U.S.A.* ... 80 D5 43 45N 98 57W
Kimberley, *Australia* ...... 60 C4 16 20S 127 0 E
Kimberley, *Canada* 70 D5 49 40N 115 59W
Kimberley, *S. Africa* ...... 56 D3 28 43S 24 46 E
Kimberly, *U.S.A.* 76 E6 42 32N 114 22W
Kimch'aek, *N. Korea* ...... 35 D15 40 40N 129 10 E
Kimch'ŏn, *S. Korea* ...... 35 F15 36 11N 128 4 E
Kimje, *S. Korea* .... 35 G14 35 48N 126 45 E
Kimmirut, *Canada* 69 B13 62 50N 69 50W
Kimpese, *Dem. Rep. of*
 the Congo .... 52 F2   5 35S 14 26 E
Kimry, *Russia* .... 18 C6 56 55N 37 15 E
Kinabalu, Gunong, *Malaysia* . 36 C5   6 3N 116 14 E
Kinaskan L., *Canada* 70 B2 57 38N 130 8W
Kinbasket L., *Canada* 70 C5 52 0N 118 10W
Kincardine, *Canada* 84 B3 44 10N 81 40W
Kincolith, *Canada* 70 C3 55 0N 129 57W
Kinda, *Dem. Rep. of the Congo* . 55 D2   9 18S 25 4 E
Kinde, *U.S.A.* 84 C2 43 56N 83 0W
Kinder Scout, *U.K.* 12 D6 53 24N 1 52W
Kindersley, *Canada* 71 C7 51 30N 109 10W
Kindia, *Guinea* 50 F3 10 0N 12 52W
Kindu, *Dem. Rep. of the Congo* . 54 C2   2 55S 25 50 E
Kineshma, *Russia* .... 18 C7 57 30N 42 5 E
Kinesi, *Tanzania* .... 54 C3   1 25S 33 50 E
King, L., *Australia* .... 61 F2 33 10S 119 35 E
King, Mt., *Australia* .... 62 D4 25 10S 147 30 E
King City, *U.S.A.* 78 J5 36 13N 121 8W
King Cr. ➤, *Australia* ..... 62 C2 24 35S 139 30 E
King Edward ➤, *Australia* .. 60 B4 14 14S 126 35 E
King Frederick VI Land = Kong
 Frederik VI Kyst, *Greenland* .. 69 B15 63 0N 43 0W
King George B., *Falk. Is.* ... 96 G4 51 30S 60 30W
King George I., *Antarctica* .. 5 C18 60 0S 60 0W
King George Is., *Canada* ... 69 C11 57 20N 80 30W
King I. = Kadan Kyun, *Burma* . 38 F2 12 30N 98 20 E
King I., *Australia* .... 62 F3 39 50S 144 0 E
King I., *Canada* 70 C3 52 10N 127 40W
King Leopold Ranges, *Australia* . 60 C4 17 30S 125 45 E
King of Prussia, *U.S.A.* 85 F9 40 5N 75 23W
King Sd., *Australia* .... 60 C3 16 50S 123 20 E
King Sejong, *Antarctica* 5 C18 62 30S 58 0W
King William I., *Canada* 68 B10 69 10N 97 25W
King William's Town, *S. Africa* . 56 E4 32 51S 27 22 E
Kingait = Cape Dorset, *Canada* . 69 B12 64 14N 76 32W
Kingaok = Bathurst Inlet, *Canada* 68 B9 66 50N 108 1W
Kingaroy, *Australia* .... 63 D5 26 32S 151 51 E
Kingfisher, *U.S.A.* 81 H6 35 52N 97 56W
Kingirbān, *Iraq* .... 44 C5 34 40N 44 54 E
Kingisepp = Kuressaare, *Estonia* . 9 G20 58 15N 22 30 E
Kingman, *Ariz., U.S.A.* 79 K12 35 12N 114 4W
Kingman, *Kans., U.S.A.* 81 G5 37 39N 98 7W
Kingoonya, *Australia* ...... 63 E2 30 55S 135 19 E
Kingri, *Pakistan* .... 42 D3 30 27N 69 49 E
Kings ➤, *U.S.A.* 78 J7 36 3N 119 50W
Kings Canyon △, *U.S.A.* ... 78 J8 36 50N 118 40W
King's Lynn, *U.K.* .... 12 E8 52 45N 0 24 E
Kings Mountain, *U.S.A.* 83 H5 35 15N 81 20W
Kings Park, *U.S.A.* 85 F11 40 53N 73 16W
King's Peak, *U.S.A.* 76 F8 40 46N 110 27W
Kingsbridge, *U.K.* 13 G4 50 17N 3 47W
Kingsburg, *U.S.A.* 78 J7 36 31N 119 33W
Kingscote, *Australia* ...... 63 F2 35 40S 137 38 E
Kingscourt, *Ireland* 10 C5 53 55N 6 48W
Kingsford, *U.S.A.* 82 C1 45 48N 88 4W
Kingsland, *U.S.A.* 83 K5 30 48N 81 41W
Kingsport, *U.S.A.* 80 D7 42 35N 95 58W
Kingsport, *U.S.A.* 83 G4 36 33N 82 33W
Kingston, *Canada* 85 B8 44 14N 76 30W
Kingston, *Jamaica* .... 88 a 18 0N 76 50W
Kingston, *N.Z.* .... 59 L2 45 20S 168 43 E
Kingston, *N.H., U.S.A.* 85 D13 42 56N 71 3W
Kingston, *N.Y., U.S.A.* 85 E11 41 56N 73 59W
Kingston, *Pa., U.S.A.* 85 E9 41 16N 75 54W
Kingston, *R.I., U.S.A.* 85 E13 41 29N 71 30W
Kingston Pk., *U.S.A.* 79 K11 35 45N 115 54W
Kingston South East, *Australia* . 63 F2 36 51S 139 55 E

Kingston upon Hull, *U.K.* 12 D7 53 45N 0 21W
Kingston upon Hull □, *U.K.* .. 12 D7 53 45N 0 21W
Kingston-upon-Thames □, *U.K.* . 13 F7 51 24N 0 17W
Kingstown, *St. Vincent* 89 D7 13 10N 61 10W
Kingstree, *U.S.A.* 83 J6 33 40N 79 50W
Kingsville, *Canada* 84 D2 42 2N 82 45W
Kingsville, *U.S.A.* 81 M6 27 31N 97 52W
Kingussie, *U.K.* 11 D4 57 6N 4 2W
Kingwood, *U.S.A.* 81 K7 29 54N 95 18W
Kınık, *Turkey* .... 23 E12 39 6N 27 24 E
Kinistino, *Canada* 71 C7 52 57N 105 2W
Kinkala, *Congo* .... 52 E2   4 18S 14 49 E
Kinki □, *Japan* .... 31 H8 33 45N 136 0 E
Kinleith, *N.Z.* .... 59 H5 38 20S 175 56 E
Kinlochleven, *U.K.* 11 E4 56 43N 5 0W
Kinmount, *Canada* 84 B6 44 48N 78 45W
Kinna, *Sweden* .... 9 H15 57 32N 12 42 E
Kinnairds Hd., *U.K.* 11 D6 57 43N 2 1W
Kino, *Mexico* 86 B2 28 45N 111 59W
Kinoje ➤, *Canada* 72 B3 52 8N 81 25W
Kinomoto, *Japan* .... 31 G8 35 30N 136 13 E
Kinoni, *Uganda* .... 54 C3   0 41S 30 28 E
Kinoosao, *Canada* 71 B8 57 5N 102 1W
Kinross, *U.K.* 11 E5 56 13N 3 25W
Kinsale, *Ireland* 10 E3 51 42N 8 31W
Kinsale, Old Hd. of, *Ireland* . 10 E3 51 37N 8 33W
Kinshasa = Chang Jiang ➤, *China* . 33 C7 31 48N 121 10 E
Kinshasa, *Dem. Rep. of*
 the Congo .... 52 E3   4 20S 15 15 E
Kinsley, *U.S.A.* 81 G5 37 55N 99 25W
Kinsman, *U.S.A.* 84 E4 41 26N 80 35W
Kinston, *U.S.A.* 83 H7 35 16N 77 35W
Kintamani, *Indonesia* ..... 37 J18   8 14S 115 19 E
Kintore, *U.K.* 11 D6 57 14N 2 20W
Kintore Ra., *Australia* ..... 60 D4 23 15S 128 47 E
Kintyre, *U.K.* 11 F3 55 30N 5 35W
Kintyre, Mull of, *U.K.* 11 F3 55 17N 5 47W
Kinushseo ➤, *Canada* 72 A3 55 15N 83 45W
Kinuso, *Canada* 70 B5 55 20N 115 25W
Kinyangiri, *Tanzania* ...... 54 C3   4 25S 34 37 E
Kinzua, *U.S.A.* 84 E6 41 52N 78 58W
Kinzua Dam, *U.S.A.* 84 E6 41 53N 79 0W
Kiosk, *Canada* 72 C4 46 6N 78 53W
Kiowa, *Kans., U.S.A.* 81 G5 37 1N 98 29W
Kiowa, *Okla., U.S.A.* 81 H7 34 43N 95 54W
Kipahigan L., *Canada* 71 B8 55 20N 101 55W
Kipanga, *Tanzania* .... 54 D4   6 15S 35 20 E
Kiparissía, *Greece* .... 23 F9 37 15N 21 40 E
Kiparissiakós Kólpos, *Greece* . 23 F9 37 25N 21 25 E
Kipawa, L., *Canada* 72 C4 46 50N 79 0W
Kipembawe, *Tanzania* ..... 54 D3   7 38S 33 27 E
Kipengere Ra., *Tanzania* ... 55 D3   9 12S 34 15 E
Kipili, *Tanzania* .... 54 D3   7 28S 30 32 E
Kipini, *Kenya* .... 54 C5   2 30S 40 32 E
Kipling, *Canada* 71 C8 50 6N 102 38W
Kippure, *Ireland* 10 C5 53 11N 6 21W
Kipushi, *Dem. Rep. of the Congo* . 55 E2 11 48S 27 12 E
Kiranomena, *Madag.* ...... 57 B8 18 17S 46 2 E
Kirensk, *Russia* .... 29 D11 57 50N 107 55 E
Kirghizia = Kyrgyzstan ■, *Asia* . 28 E8 42 0N 75 0 E
Kirghizstan = Kyrgyzstan ■, *Asia* 28 E8 42 0N 75 0 E
Kirgiziya Steppe, *Eurasia* ... 19 E10 50 0N 55 0 E
Kiribati ■, *Pac. Oc.* .... 64 H10 5 0S 180 0 E
Kırıkkale, *Turkey* .... 19 G5 39 51N 33 32 E
Kirillov, *Russia* .... 18 C6 59 49N 38 24 E
Kirin = Jilin, *China* .... 35 C14 43 44N 126 30 E
Kirinyaga = Kenya, Mt., *Kenya* . 54 C4   0 10S 37 18 E
Kirishima Yaku △, *Japan* ... 31 J5 31 24N 130 50 E
Kiritimati, *Kiribati* 65 G12 1 58N 157 27W
Kirkby, *U.K.* 12 D5 53 30N 2 54W
Kirkby-in-Ashfield, *U.K.* 12 D6 53 6N 1 14W
Kirkby Lonsdale, *U.K.* 12 C5 54 12N 2 36W
Kirkby Stephen, *U.K.* 12 C5 54 29N 2 21W
Kirkcaldy, *U.K.* 11 E5 56 7N 3 9W
Kirkcudbright, *U.K.* 11 G4 54 50N 4 2W
Kirkee, *India* .... 40 K8 18 34N 73 56 E
Kirkenes, *Norway* .... 8 B23 69 40N 30 5 E
Kirkfield, *Canada* 84 B6 44 34N 78 59W
Kirkintilloch, *U.K.* 11 F4 55 56N 4 8W
Kirkjubæjarklaustur, *Iceland* . 8 E4 63 47N 18 4W
Kirkkonummi, *Finland* ..... 9 F21 60 8N 24 26 E
Kirkland Lake, *Canada* 72 C3 48 9N 80 2W
Kırklareli, *Turkey* .... 23 D12 41 44N 27 15 E
Kirksville, *U.S.A.* 80 E8 40 12N 92 35W
Kirkūk, *Iraq* .... 44 C5 35 30N 44 21 E
Kirkwall, *U.K.* 11 C6 58 59N 2 58W
Kirkwood, *S. Africa* ...... 56 E4 33 22S 25 15 E
Kirov, *Russia* .... 18 C8 58 35N 49 40 E
Kirovabad = Gäncä, *Azerbaijan* . 19 F8 40 45N 46 20 E
Kirovograd = Kirovohrad,
 Ukraine .... 19 E5 48 35N 32 20 E
Kirovohrad, *Ukraine* ...... 19 E5 48 35N 32 20 E
Kirovsk, *Russia* .... 18 A5 67 32N 33 41 E
Kirovskiy, *Kamchatka, Russia* . 29 D16 54 27N 155 42 E
Kirovskiy, *Primorsk, Russia* .. 30 B7 45 7N 133 30 E
Kirriemuir, *U.K.* 11 E5 56 41N 3 1W
Kirsanov, *Russia* .... 18 D7 52 35N 42 40 E
Kırşehir, *Turkey* .... 19 G5 39 14N 34 5 E
Kirthar Range, *Pakistan* .... 42 F2 27 0N 67 0 E
Kirtland, *U.S.A.* 77 H9 36 44N 108 21W
Kiruna, *Sweden* .... 8 C19 67 52N 20 15 E
Kirundu, *Dem. Rep. of the Congo* . 54 C2   0 50S 25 35 E
Kiryū, *Japan* .... 31 F9 36 24N 139 20 E
Kisalaya, *Nic.* 88 D3 14 40N 84 3W
Kisámou, Kólpos, *Greece* ... 25 D5 35 30N 23 38 E
Kisanga, *Dem. Rep. of the Congo* 54 B2   2 30N 26 35 E
Kisangani, *Dem. Rep. of*
 the Congo .... 54 B2   0 35N 25 15 E
Kisar, *Indonesia* .... 37 F7   8 5S 127 10 E
Kisarawe, *Tanzania* .... 54 D4   6 53S 39 0 E
Kisarazu, *Japan* .... 31 G9 35 23N 139 55 E
Kishanganga ➤, *Pakistan* .. 43 B5 34 18N 73 28 E
Kishangarh, *Raj., India* .... 42 F6 26 34N 74 52 E
Kishangarh, *Raj., India* .... 42 F4 27 50N 70 30 E
Kishinev = Chişinău, *Moldova* . 17 E15 47 2N 28 50 E
Kishiwada, *Japan* .... 31 G7 34 28N 135 22 E
Kishtwar, *India* .... 43 C6 33 20N 75 48 E
Kisigo ➤, *Tanzania* .... 54 D3   6 27S 34 17 E
Kisii, *Kenya* .... 54 C3   0 40S 34 45 E
Kisiju, *Tanzania* .... 54 D4   7 23S 39 19 E
Kisizi, *Uganda* .... 54 C2   1 0S 29 58 E
Kiskőrös, *Hungary* .... 17 E10 46 37N 19 20 E
Kiskunfélegyháza, *Hungary* . 17 E10 46 42N 19 53 E
Kiskunhalas, *Hungary* ..... 17 E10 46 28N 19 37 E
Kislovodsk, *Russia* .... 19 F7 43 50N 42 45 E

Kismayu = Chisimaio,
 Somali Rep. .... 49 G8   0 22S 42 32 E
Kiso-Gawa ➤, *Japan* ...... 31 G8 35 20N 136 45 E
Kiso-Sammyaku, *Japan* .... 31 G8 35 45N 137 45 E
Kisofukushima, *Japan* ..... 31 G8 35 52N 137 43 E
Kisoro, *Uganda* .... 54 C2   1 17S 29 48 E
Kissidougou, *Guinea* 50 G3   9 5N 10 5W
Kissimmee, *U.S.A.* 83 L5 28 18N 81 24W
Kissimmee ➤, *U.S.A.* 83 M5 27 9N 80 52W
Kississing L., *Canada* 71 B8 55 10N 101 20W
Kisumu, *Kenya* .... 54 C3   0 3S 34 45 E
Kiswere, *Tanzania* .... 55 D4   9 27S 39 30 E
Kit Carson, *U.S.A.* 80 F3 38 46N 102 48W
Kita, *Mali* 50 F4 13 5N 9 25W
Kitaibaraki, *Japan* .... 31 F10 36 50N 140 45 E
Kitakami-Gawa ➤, *Japan* ... 30 E10 38 25N 141 19 E
Kitakami, *Japan* .... 30 E10 39 20N 141 10 E
Kitakami-Sammyaku, *Japan* . 30 E10 39 30N 141 30 E
Kitakata, *Japan* .... 30 F9 37 39N 139 52 E
Kitakyūshū, *Japan* .... 31 H5 33 50N 130 50 E
Kitale, *Kenya* .... 54 B4   1 0N 35 0 E
Kitami, *Japan* .... 30 C11 43 48N 143 54 E
Kitami-Sammyaku, *Japan* ... 30 B11 44 22N 142 43 E
Kitangiri, L., *Tanzania* ..... 54 C3   4 5S 34 20 E
Kitaya, *Tanzania* .... 55 E5 10 38S 40 8 E
Kitchener, *Canada* 84 C4 43 27N 80 29W
Kitega = Gitega, *Burundi* ... 54 C2   3 26S 29 56 E
Kitengo, *Dem. Rep. of the Congo* 54 D1   7 26S 24 8 E
Kitgum, *Uganda* .... 54 B3   3 17N 32 52 E
Kíthira, *Greece* .... 23 F10 36 8N 23 0 E
Kíthnos, *Greece* .... 23 F11 37 26N 24 27 E
Kiti, *Cyprus* .... 25 E12 34 50N 33 34 E
Kiti, C., *Cyprus* .... 25 E12 34 48N 33 36 E
Kitimat, *Canada* 70 C3 54 3N 128 38W
Kitinen ➤, *Finland* .... 8 C22 67 14N 27 27 E
Kitsuki, *Japan* .... 31 H5 33 25N 131 37 E
Kittakittaooloo, L., *Australia* . 63 D2 28 3S 138 14 E
Kittanning, *U.S.A.* 84 F5 40 49N 79 31W
Kittatinny Mts., *U.S.A.* 85 F10 41 0N 75 0W
Kittery, *U.S.A.* 83 D10 43 5N 70 45W
Kittilä, *Finland* .... 8 C21 67 40N 24 51 E
Kitui, *Kenya* .... 54 C4   1 17S 38 0 E
Kitwanga, *Canada* 70 B3 55 6N 128 4W
Kitwe, *Zambia* .... 55 E2 12 54S 28 13 E
Kivarli, *India* .... 42 G5 24 33N 72 46 E
Kivertsi, *Ukraine* .... 17 C13 50 50N 25 28 E
Kividhes, *Cyprus* .... 25 E11 34 46N 32 51 E
Kivu, L., *Dem. Rep. of the Congo* . 54 C2   1 48S 29 0 E
Kiyev = Kyyiv, *Ukraine* .... 17 C16 50 30N 30 28 E
Kiyevskoye Vdkhr. = Kyyivske
 Vdskh., *Ukraine* .... 17 C16 51 0N 30 25 E
Kizel, *Russia* .... 18 C10 59 3N 57 40 E
Kiziguru, *Rwanda* .... 54 C3   1 46S 30 23 E
Kızıl Irmak ➤, *Turkey* ..... 19 F6 41 44N 35 58 E
Kizil Jilga, *China* .... 43 B8 35 26N 78 50 E
Kızıltepe, *Turkey* .... 44 B4 37 12N 40 35 E
Kizimkazi, *Tanzania* ...... 54 D4   6 28S 39 30 E
Kizlyar, *Russia* .... 19 F8 43 51N 46 40 E
Kizyl-Arvat = Gyzylarbat,
 Turkmenistan .... 28 F6 39 4N 56 23 E
Kjölur, *Iceland* 8 D4 64 50N 19 25W
Kladno, *Czech Rep.* ...... 16 C8 50 10N 14 7 E
Klaeng, *Thailand* .... 38 F3 12 47N 101 39 E
Klagenfurt, *Austria* .... 16 E8 46 38N 14 20 E
Klaipėda, *Lithuania* ...... 9 J19 55 43N 21 10 E
Klaksvík, *Færoe Is.* 8 E9 62 14N 6 35W
Klamath ➤, *U.S.A.* 76 F1 41 33N 124 5W
Klamath Falls, *U.S.A.* 76 E3 42 13N 121 46W
Klamath Mts., *U.S.A.* 76 F2 41 20N 123 0W
Klamono, *Indonesia* ...... 37 E8   1 8S 131 30 E
Klappan ➤, *Canada* 70 B3 58 0N 129 43W
Klarälven ➤, *Sweden* ..... 9 G15 59 23N 13 32 E
Klatovy, *Czech Rep.* ...... 16 D7 49 23N 13 18 E
Klawer, *S. Africa* .... 56 E2 31 44S 18 36 E
Klazienaveen, *Neths.* ..... 15 B6 52 44N 7 0 E
Kleena Kleene, *Canada* 70 C4 52 0N 124 59W
Klein-Karas, *Namibia* ..... 56 D2 27 33S 18 7 E
Klerksdorp, *S. Africa* ..... 56 D4 26 53S 26 38 E
Kletsk = Klyetsk, *Belarus* .. 17 B14 53 5N 26 45 E
Kletskiy, *Russia* .... 19 E7 49 16N 43 11 E
Klickitat, *U.S.A.* 78 E5 45 49N 121 9W
Klickitat ➤, *U.S.A.* 78 E5 45 42N 121 17W
Klidhes, *Cyprus* .... 25 D13 35 42N 34 36 E
Klinaklini ➤, *Canada* 70 C3 51 21N 125 40W
Klip ➤, *S. Africa* .... 57 D4 27 3S 29 3 E
Klipdale, *S. Africa* .... 56 E2 34 19S 19 57 E
Klipplaat, *S. Africa* ...... 56 E3 33 1S 24 22 E
Kłodzko, *Poland* .... 17 C9 50 28N 16 38 E
Klong Wang Chao △, *Thailand* . 38 D2 16 20N 99 9 E
Klouto, *Togo* .... 50 G6   6 57N 0 44 E
Kluane △, *Canada* 70 A1 60 45N 139 30W
Kluane L., *Canada* 68 B6 61 15N 138 40W
Kluczbork, *Poland* .... 17 C10 50 58N 18 12 E
Klukwan, *U.S.A.* 70 B1 59 24N 135 54W
Klungkung, *Indonesia* ..... 37 K18 8 32S 115 24 E
Klyetsk, *Belarus* .... 17 B14 53 5N 26 45 E
Klyuchevskaya, Gora, *Russia* . 29 D17 55 50N 160 30 E
Knaresborough, *U.K.* 12 C6 54 1N 1 28W
Knee L., *Man., Canada* 72 A1 55 3N 94 45W
Knee L., *Sask., Canada* 71 B7 55 51N 107 0W
Knight Inlet, *Canada* 70 C3 50 45N 125 40W
Knighton, *U.K.* 13 E4 52 21N 3 3W
Knights Ferry, *U.S.A.* 78 H6 37 50N 120 40W
Knights Landing, *U.S.A.* ... 78 G5 38 48N 121 43W
Knob, C., *Australia* .... 61 F2 34 32S 119 16 E
Knock, *Ireland* 10 C3 53 48N 8 55W
Knockmealdown Mts., *Ireland* . 10 D4 52 14N 7 56W
Knokke-Heist, *Belgium* .... 15 C3 51 21N 3 17 E
Knossós, *Greece* .... 25 D7 35 16N 25 10 E
Knowlton, *Canada* 85 A12 45 13N 72 31W
Knox, *U.S.A.* 82 E2 41 18N 86 37W
Knox Coast, *Antarctica* .... 5 C8 66 30S 108 0 E
Knoxville, *Iowa, U.S.A.* 80 E8 41 19N 93 6W
Knoxville, *Pa., U.S.A.* 84 E7 41 57N 77 27W
Knoxville, *Tenn., U.S.A.* ... 83 H4 35 58N 83 55W
Knud Rasmussen Land,
 Greenland 4 A5 79 0N 60 0W
Knysna, *S. Africa* .... 56 E3 34 2S 23 2 E
Ko Kha, *Thailand* .... 38 C2 18 11N 99 24 E
Ko Tarutao △, *Thailand* ... 39 J2   6 31N 99 26 E
Ko Yao, *Thailand* .... 39 a   8 7N 98 35 E
Koartac = Quaqtaq, *Canada* . 69 B13 60 55N 69 40W
Koba, *Indonesia* .... 37 F8   6 37S 134 37 E
Kobarid, *Slovenia* .... 16 E7 46 15N 13 30 E
Kobayashi, *Japan* .... 31 J5 31 56N 130 59 E
Kōbe, *Japan* .... 31 G7 34 45N 135 10 E

København, *Denmark* ..... 9 J15 55 41N 12 34 E
Kōbi-Sho, *Japan* .... 31 M1 25 56N 123 41 E
Koblenz, *Germany* .... 16 C4 50 21N 7 36 E
Kobryn, *Belarus* .... 17 B13 52 15N 24 22 E
Kocaeli, *Turkey* .... 19 F4 40 45N 29 50 E
Kočani, *Macedonia* ...... 23 D10 41 55N 22 25 E
Koch Bihar, *India* .... 41 F16 26 22N 89 29 E
Kochang, *S. Korea* .... 35 G14 35 41N 127 55 E
Kochas, *India* .... 43 G10 25 15N 83 56 E
Kochi = Cochin, *India* .... 40 Q10 9 58N 76 20 E
Kōchi, *Japan* .... 31 H6 33 30N 133 35 E
Kōchi □, *Japan* .... 31 H6 33 40N 133 30 E
Kochiu = Gejiu, *China* .... 32 D5 23 20N 103 10 E
Kodarma, *India* .... 43 G11 24 28N 85 36 E
Kodiak, *U.S.A.* 68 C4 57 47N 152 24W
Kodiak I., *U.S.A.* 68 C4 57 30N 152 45W
Kodinar, *India* .... 42 J4 20 46N 70 46 E
Koedoesberge, *S. Africa* ... 56 E3 32 40S 20 11 E
Koes, *Namibia* .... 56 D2 26 0S 19 15 E
Koffiefontein, *S. Africa* .... 56 D4 29 30S 25 0 E
Kofiau, *Indonesia* .... 37 E7   1 11S 129 50 E
Koforidua, *Ghana* 50 G5   6 3N 0 17W
Kōfu, *Japan* .... 31 G9 35 40N 138 30 E
Koga, *Japan* .... 31 F9 36 11N 139 43 E
Kogaluc ➤, *Canada* 73 A7 56 12N 61 44W
Køge, *Denmark* .... 9 J15 55 27N 12 11 E
Koh-i-Khurd, *Afghan.* ..... 42 C1 33 30N 65 59 E
Koh-i-Maran, *Pakistan* .... 42 E2 29 18N 66 50 E
Kohat, *Pakistan* .... 42 C4 33 40N 71 29 E
Kohima, *India* .... 41 G19 25 35N 94 10 E
Kohkīlūyeh va Būyer Aḥmadī □,
 Iran .... 45 D6 31 30N 50 30 E
Kohler Ra., *Antarctica* 5 D15 77 0S 110 0W
Kohlu, *Pakistan* .... 42 E3 29 54N 69 15 E
Kohtla-Järve, *Estonia* ..... 9 G22 59 20N 27 20 E
Koi Sanjaq, *Iraq* .... 44 B5 36 5N 44 38 E
Koillismaa, *Finland* ...... 8 D23 65 44N 28 36 E
Koin-dong, *N. Korea* ..... 35 D14 40 28N 126 18 E
Kojŏ, *N. Korea* .... 35 E14 38 58N 127 58 E
Kojonup, *Australia* .... 61 F2 33 48S 117 10 E
Kojūr, *Iran* .... 45 B6 36 23N 51 43 E
Kokand = Qŭqon, *Uzbekistan* . 28 E8 40 30N 70 57 E
Kokas, *Indonesia* .... 37 E8   2 42S 132 26 E
Kokchetav = Kökshetaū,
 Kazakhstan .... 28 D7 53 20N 69 25 E
Kokemäenjoki ➤, *Finland* .. 9 F19 61 32N 21 44 E
Kokkola, *Finland* .... 8 E20 63 50N 23 8 E
Koko Kyunzu, *Burma* ..... 41 M18 14 10N 93 25 E
Kokomo, *U.S.A.* 82 E2 40 29N 86 8W
Koksan, *N. Korea* .... 35 E14 38 46N 126 40 E
Kökshetaū, *Kazakhstan* ... 28 D7 53 20N 69 25 E
Koksoak ➤, *Canada* 69 C13 58 30N 68 10W
Kokstad, *S. Africa* .... 57 E4 30 32S 29 29 E
Kokubu, *Japan* .... 31 J5 31 44N 130 46 E
Kola, *Indonesia* .... 37 F8   5 35S 134 30 E
Kola, *Russia* .... 18 A5 68 45N 33 8 E
Kola Pen. = Kolskiy Poluostrov,
 Russia .... 18 A6 67 30N 38 0 E
Kolachi ➤, *Pakistan* ...... 42 F2 27 8N 67 2 E
Kolahoi, *India* .... 43 B6 34 12N 75 22 E
Kolaka, *Indonesia* .... 37 E6   4 3S 121 46 E
Kolar, *India* .... 40 N11 13 12N 78 15 E
Kolar Gold Fields, *India* ... 40 N11 12 58N 78 16 E
Kolaras, *India* .... 42 G6 25 14N 77 36 E
Kolari, *Finland* .... 8 C20 67 20N 23 48 E
Kolayat, *India* .... 40 F8 27 50N 72 50 E
Kolding, *Denmark* .... 9 J13 55 30N 9 29 E
Kolepom = Dolak, Pulau,
 Indonesia .... 37 F9   8 0S 138 30 E
Kolguyev, Ostrov, *Russia* .. 18 A8 69 20N 48 30 E
Kolhapur, *India* .... 40 L9 16 43N 74 15 E
Kolín, *Czech Rep.* .... 16 C8 50 2N 15 9 E
Kolkas rags, *Latvia* ...... 9 H20 57 46N 22 37 E
Kolkata, *India* .... 43 H13 22 36N 88 24 E
Kollam = Quilon, *India* .... 40 Q10 8 50N 76 38 E
Kollum, *Neths.* .... 15 A6 53 17N 6 10 E
Kolmanskop, *Namibia* .... 56 D2 26 45S 15 14 E
Köln, *Germany* .... 16 C4 50 56N 6 57 E
Koło, *Poland* .... 17 B10 52 14N 18 40 E
Kołobrzeg, *Poland* .... 16 A8 54 10N 15 35 E
Kolomna, *Russia* .... 18 C6 55 8N 38 45 E
Kolomyya, *Ukraine* ...... 17 D13 48 31N 25 2 E
Kolonodale, *Indonesia* .... 37 E6   2 0S 121 19 E
Kolosib, *India* .... 41 G18 24 15N 92 45 E
Kolpashevo, *Russia* ...... 28 D9 58 20N 83 5 E
Kolpino, *Russia* .... 18 C5 59 44N 30 39 E
Kolskiy Poluostrov, *Russia* .. 18 A6 67 30N 38 0 E
Kolskiy Zaliv, *Russia* ..... 18 A5 69 23N 34 0 E
Kolwezi, *Dem. Rep. of the Congo* 55 E2 10 40S 25 25 E
Kolyma ➤, *Russia* .... 29 C17 69 30N 161 0 E
Kolymskoye Nagorye, *Russia* . 29 C16 63 0N 157 0 E
Kôm Ombo, *Egypt* .... 51 D12 24 25N 32 52 E
Komandorskiye Is. =
 Komandorskiye Ostrova,
 Russia .... 29 D17 55 0N 167 0 E
Komandorskiye Ostrova, *Russia* 29 D17 55 0N 167 0 E
Komárno, *Slovak Rep.* .... 17 E10 47 49N 18 5 E
Komatipoort, *S. Africa* .... 57 D5 25 25S 31 55 E
Komatou Yialou, *Cyprus* ... 25 D13 35 25N 34 8 E
Komatsu, *Japan* .... 31 F8 36 25N 136 30 E
Komatsushima, *Japan* .... 31 H7 34 0N 134 35 E
Komi □, *Russia* .... 18 B10 64 0N 55 0 E
Kommunizma, Pik, *Tajikistan* . 28 F8 39 0N 72 2 E
Komodo, *Indonesia* ...... 37 F5   8 37S 119 20 E
Komoran, Pulau, *Indonesia* . 37 F9   8 18S 138 45 E
Komoro, *Japan* .... 31 F9 36 19N 138 26 E
Komotini, *Greece* .... 23 D11 41 9N 25 26 E
Kompasberg, *S. Africa* .... 56 E3 31 45S 24 32 E
Kompong Bang, *Cambodia* . 38 F5 12 24N 104 40 E
Kompong Cham, *Cambodia* . 39 F5 12 0N 105 30 E
Kompong Chhnang = Kompong
 Chhnang, *Cambodia* ..... 38 F5 12 20N 104 35 E
Kompong Chikreng, *Cambodia* . 38 F5 13 5N 104 18 E
Kompong Kleang, *Cambodia* . 38 F5 13 6N 104 8 E
Kompong Luong, *Cambodia* . 39 G5 11 49N 104 48 E
Kompong Pranak, *Cambodia* . 38 F5 13 35N 104 55 E
Kompong Som = Kompong
 Saom, *Cambodia* .... 39 G4 10 38N 103 30 E
Kompong Som, Chhung =
 Kampong Saom, Chaak,
 Cambodia .... 39 G4 10 50N 103 32 E
Kompong Speu, *Cambodia* . 39 G5 11 26N 104 32 E
Kompong Sralao, *Cambodia* . 38 E5 14 5N 105 46 E
Kompong Thom, *Cambodia* . 38 F5 12 35N 104 51 E
Kompong Trabeck, *Cambodia* . 38 F5 13 6N 105 14 E
Kompong Trabeck, *Cambodia* . 39 G5 11 9N 105 28 E
Kompong Trach, *Cambodia* . 39 G5 11 25N 105 48 E
Kompong Tralach, *Cambodia* . 39 G5 11 54N 104 47 E

Komrat = Comrat, *Moldova* .... **17 E15** 46 18N 28 40 E
Komsberg, *S. Africa* .... **56 E3** 32 40S 20 45 E
Komsomolets, Ostrov, *Russia* . **29 A10** 80 30N 95 0 E
Komsomolsk, *Russia* .... **29 D14** 50 30N 137 0 E
Kon Tum, *Vietnam* .... **38 E7** 14 24N 108 0 E
Kon Tum, Plateau du, *Vietnam* . **38 E7** 14 30N 108 30 E
Konarhã □, *Afghan.* .... **40 B7** 34 30N 71 3 E
Konári, *Iran* .... **45 D6** 28 13N 51 36 E
Konch, *India* .... **43 G8** 26 0N 79 10 E
Konde, *Tanzania* .... **54 C4** 4 57S 39 45 E
Kondinin, *Australia* .... **61 F2** 32 34S 118 8 E
Kondoa, *Tanzania* .... **54 C4** 4 55S 35 50 E
Kondókali, *Greece* .... **25 A3** 39 38N 19 51 E
Kondopaga, *Russia* .... **18 B5** 62 12N 34 17 E
Kondratyevo, *Russia* .... **29 D10** 57 22N 98 15 E
Konevo, *Russia* .... **18 B6** 62 8N 39 20 E
Kong = Khong ➤, *Cambodia* . **38 F5** 13 32N 105 58 E
Kong, *Ivory C.* **50 G5** 8 54N 4 36W
Kong, Koh, *Cambodia* ...... **39 G4** 11 20N 103 0 E
Kong Christian IX Land,
  Greenland **4 C6** 68 0N 36 0W
Kong Christian X Land,
  Greenland **4 B6** 74 0N 29 0W
Kong Frederik IX Land,
  Greenland **4 C5** 67 0N 52 0W
Kong Frederik VI Kyst, *Greenland* **69 B15** 63 0N 43 0W
Kong Frederik VIII Land,
  Greenland **4 B6** 78 30N 26 0W
Kong Oscar Fjord, *Greenland* . **4 B6** 72 20N 24 0W
Kongju, *S. Korea* .... **35 F14** 36 30N 127 0 E
Konglu, *Burma* .... **41 F20** 27 13N 97 57 E
Kongola, *Namibia* .... **56 B3** 17 45S 23 20 E
Kongolo, Kasai-Or., *Dem. Rep. of*
  the Congo .... **54 D1** 5 26S 24 49 E
Kongolo, Katanga, *Dem. Rep. of*
  the Congo .... **54 D2** 5 22S 27 0 E
Kongsberg, *Norway* .... **9 G13** 59 39N 9 39 E
Kongsvinger, *Norway* ...... **9 F15** 60 12N 12 2 E
Kongwa, *Tanzania* .... **54 D4** 6 11S 36 26 E
Koni, *Dem. Rep. of the Congo* . **55 E2** 10 40S 27 11 E
Koni, Mts., *Dem. Rep. of*
  the Congo .... **55 E2** 10 36S 27 10 E
Konin, *Poland* .... **17 B10** 52 12N 18 15 E
Konjic, *Bos.-H.* .... **23 C7** 43 42N 17 58 E
Konkiep, *Namibia* .... **56 D2** 26 49S 17 15 E
Konosha, *Russia* .... **18 B7** 61 0N 40 5 E
Kōnosu, *Japan* .... **31 F9** 36 3N 139 31 E
Konotop, *Ukraine* .... **19 D5** 51 12N 33 7 E
Końskie, *Poland* .... **17 C11** 51 15N 20 23 E
Konstanz, *Germany* .... **16 E5** 47 40N 9 10 E
Kont, *Iran* .... **45 E9** 26 55N 61 50 E
Kontagora, *Nigeria* .... **50 F7** 10 23N 5 27 E
Konya, *Turkey* .... **19 G5** 37 52N 32 35 E
Konza, *Kenya* .... **54 C4** 1 45S 37 7 E
Koocanusa, L., *Canada* **76 B6** 49 20N 115 15W
Kookynie, *Australia* .... **61 E3** 29 17S 121 22 E
Koolyanobbing, *Australia* ... **61 F2** 30 48S 119 36 E
Koonibba, *Australia* .... **63 E1** 31 54S 133 25 E
Koorawatha, *Australia* ..... **63 E4** 34 2S 148 33 E
Koorda, *Australia* .... **61 F2** 30 48S 117 35 E
Kooskia, *U.S.A.* **76 C6** 46 9N 115 59W
Kootenay △, *Canada* **70 C5** 51 0N 116 0W
Kootenay L., *U.S.A.* **70 D5** 49 19N 117 39W
Kootenay L., *Canada* **70 D5** 49 45N 116 50W
Kootjieskolk, *S. Africa* .... **56 E3** 31 15S 20 21 E
Kopaonik, *Serbia & M.* .... **23 C9** 43 10N 20 50 E
Kópavogur, *Iceland* **8 D3** 64 6N 21 55W
Koper, *Slovenia* .... **16 F7** 45 31N 13 44 E
Kopervik, *Norway* .... **9 G11** 59 17N 5 17 E
Kopet Dagh, *Asia* .... **45 B8** 38 0N 58 0 E
Kopi, *Australia* .... **63 E2** 33 24S 135 40 E
Köping, *Sweden* .... **9 G17** 59 31N 16 3 E
Koppeh Dāgh = Kopet Dagh, *Asia* **45 B8** 38 0N 58 0 E
Koppies, *S. Africa* .... **57 D4** 27 20S 27 30 E
Koprivnica, *Croatia* .... **22 A7** 46 12N 16 45 E
Kopychyntsi, *Ukraine* ...... **17 D13** 49 7N 25 58 E
Kora △, *Kenya* .... **54 C4** 0 14S 38 44 E
Korab, *Macedonia* .... **23 D9** 41 44N 20 40 E
Korakiána, *Greece* .... **25 A3** 39 42N 19 45 E
Koral, *India* .... **42 J5** 21 50N 73 12 E
Korba, *India* .... **43 H10** 22 20N 82 45 E
Korbu, G., *Malaysia* ...... **39 K3** 4 41N 101 18 E
Korçë, *Albania* .... **23 D9** 40 37N 20 50 E
Korčula, *Croatia* .... **22 C7** 42 56N 16 57 E
Kord Kūy, *Iran* .... **45 B7** 36 48N 54 7 E
Kord Sheykh, *Iran* .... **45 D7** 28 31N 52 53 E
Kordestān □, *Iran* .... **44 C5** 36 0N 47 0 E
Kordofân, *Sudan* .... **51 F11** 13 0N 29 0 E
Korea, North ■, *Asia* ..... **35 E14** 40 0N 127 0 E
Korea, South ■, *Asia* ..... **35 G15** 36 0N 128 0 E
Korea Bay, *Korea* .... **35 E13** 39 0N 124 0 E
Korea Strait, *Asia* .... **35 H15** 34 0N 129 30 E
Korets, *Ukraine* .... **17 C14** 50 40N 27 5 E
Korhogo, *Ivory C.* **50 G4** 9 29N 5 28W
Korinthiakós Kólpos, *Greece* . **23 E10** 38 16N 22 30 E
Kórinthos, *Greece* .... **23 F10** 37 56N 22 55 E
Korissa, Límni, *Greece* .... **25 B3** 39 27N 19 53 E
Kōriyama, *Japan* .... **30 F10** 37 24N 140 23 E
Korla, *China* .... **32 B3** 41 45N 86 4 E
Kormakiti, C., *Cyprus* ..... **25 D11** 35 23N 32 56 E
Kornat, *Croatia* .... **22 C6** 43 50N 15 20 E
Korneshty = Corneşti, *Moldova* **17 E15** 47 21N 28 1 E
Koro, *Fiji* .... **59 C8** 17 19S 179 23 E
Koro, *Ivory C.* **50 G4** 8 32N 7 30W
Koro Sea, *Fiji* **59 C9** 17 30S 179 45W
Korogwe, *Tanzania* .... **54 D4** 5 5S 38 25 E
Koronadal, *Phil.* .... **37 C6** 6 12N 125 1 E
Körös ➤, *Hungary* .... **17 E11** 46 43N 20 12 E
Korosten, *Ukraine* .... **17 C15** 50 54N 28 36 E
Korostyshev, *Ukraine* ..... **17 C15** 50 19N 29 4 E
Korraraika, Helodranon' i,
  Madag. .... **57 B7** 17 45S 43 57 E
Korsakov, *Russia* .... **29 E15** 46 36N 142 42 E
Korshunovo, *Russia* .... **29 D12** 58 37N 110 10 E
Korsør, *Denmark* .... **9 J14** 55 20N 11 9 E
Kortrijk, *Belgium* .... **15 D3** 50 50N 3 17 E
Korwai, *India* .... **42 G8** 24 7N 78 5 E
Koryakskoye Nagorye, *Russia* . **29 C18** 61 0N 171 0 E
Koryŏng, *S. Korea* .... **35 G15** 35 44N 128 15 E
Kos, *Greece* .... **23 F12** 36 50N 27 15 E
Koschagyl, *Kazakhstan* .... **19 E9** 46 40N 54 0 E
Kościan, *Poland* .... **17 B9** 52 5N 16 40 E
Kosciusko, *U.S.A.* **81 J10** 33 4N 89 35W
Kosciuszko, Mt., *Australia* . **63 F4** 36 27S 148 16 E
Kosha, *Sudan* .... **51 D12** 20 50N 30 30 E
K'oshih = Kashi, *China* .... **32 C2** 39 30N 76 2 E
Koshiki-Rettō, *Japan* ...... **31 J4** 31 45N 129 49 E

Kosi, *India* .... **42 F7** 27 48N 77 29 E
Kosi ➤, *India* .... **43 E8** 26 43N 78 57 E
Košice, *Slovak Rep.* ...... **17 D11** 48 42N 21 15 E
Koskinoú, *Greece* .... **25 C10** 36 23N 28 13 E
Koslan, *Russia* .... **18 B8** 63 34N 49 14 E
Kosŏng, *N. Korea* .... **35 E15** 38 40N 128 22 E
Kosovo □, *Serbia & M.* .... **23 C9** 42 30N 21 0 E
Kosovska Mitrovica, *Serbia & M.* **23 C9** 42 54N 20 52 E
Kossou, L. de, *Ivory C.* **50 G4** 6 59N 5 31W
Koster, *S. Africa* .... **56 D4** 25 52S 26 54 E
Kôstî, *Sudan* .... **51 F12** 13 8N 32 43 E
Kostopil, *Ukraine* .... **17 C14** 50 51N 26 22 E
Kostroma, *Russia* .... **18 C7** 57 50N 40 58 E
Kostrzyn, *Poland* .... **16 B8** 52 35N 14 39 E
Koszalin, *Poland* .... **16 A9** 54 11N 16 8 E
Kot Addu, *Pakistan* .... **42 D4** 30 30N 71 0 E
Kot Kapura, *India* .... **42 D6** 30 35N 74 50 E
Kot Moman, *Pakistan* ..... **42 C5** 32 13N 73 0 E
Kot Sultan, *Pakistan* ...... **42 D4** 30 46N 70 56 E
Kota, *India* .... **42 G6** 25 14N 75 49 E
Kota Baharu, *Malaysia* .... **39 J4** 6 7N 102 14 E
Kota Barrage, *India* ...... **42 G6** 25 6N 75 51 E
Kota Belud, *Malaysia* ..... **36 C5** 6 21N 116 26 E
Kota Kinabalu, *Malaysia* ... **36 C5** 6 0N 116 4 E
Kota Kubu Baharu, *Malaysia* . **39 L3** 3 34N 101 39 E
Kota Tinggi, *Malaysia* ..... **39 M4** 1 44N 103 53 E
Kotaagung, *Indonesia* ..... **36 F2** 5 38S 104 29 E
Kotabaru, *Indonesia* ...... **36 E5** 3 20S 116 20 E
Kotabumi, *Indonesia* ...... **36 E2** 4 49S 104 54 E
Kotamobagu, *Indonesia* .... **37 D6** 0 57N 124 31 E
Kotcho L., *Canada* **70 B4** 59 7N 121 12W
Kotdwara, *India* .... **43 E8** 29 45N 78 32 E
Kotelnich, *Russia* .... **18 C8** 58 22N 48 24 E
Kotelnikovo, *Russia* .... **19 E7** 47 38N 43 8 E
Kotelnyy, Ostrov, *Russia* ... **29 B14** 75 10N 139 0 E
Kothari ➤, *India* .... **42 G6** 25 20N 75 4 E
Kothi, *Chhattisgarh, India* .. **43 H10** 23 21N 82 3 E
Kothi, *Mad. P., India* ..... **43 G9** 24 45N 80 40 E
Kotiro, *Pakistan* .... **42 F2** 26 17N 67 13 E
Kotka, *Finland* .... **9 F22** 60 28N 26 58 E
Kotlas, *Russia* .... **18 B8** 61 17N 46 43 E
Kotli, *Pakistan* .... **42 C5** 33 30N 73 55 E
Kotma, *India* .... **43 H9** 23 12N 81 58 E
Kotmul, *Pakistan* .... **43 B6** 36 32N 75 10 E
Kotor, *Serbia & M.* .... **23 C8** 42 25N 18 47 E
Kotovsk, *Ukraine* .... **17 E15** 47 45N 29 35 E
Kotputli, *India* .... **42 F7** 27 43N 76 12 E
Kotri, *Pakistan* .... **42 G3** 25 22N 68 22 E
Kotturu, *India* .... **40 M10** 14 45N 76 10 E
Kotuy ➤, *Russia* .... **29 B11** 71 54N 102 6 E
Kotzebue, *U.S.A.* **68 B3** 66 53N 162 39W
Kouchibouguac △, *Canada* . **73 C6** 46 50N 65 0W
Koudougou, *Burkina Faso* .. **50 F5** 12 10N 2 20W
Koufonísi, *Greece* .... **25 E8** 34 56N 26 8 E
Kougaberge, *S. Africa* ..... **56 E3** 33 48S 23 50 E
Kouilou ➤, *Congo* .... **52 E2** 4 10S 12 5 E
Koula Moutou, *Gabon* ..... **52 E2** 1 15S 12 25 E
Koulen = Kulen, *Cambodia* . **38 F5** 13 50N 104 40 E
Kouloúra, *Greece* .... **25 A3** 39 42N 19 54 E
Koúm-bournoú, Ákra, *Greece* **25 C10** 36 15N 28 11 E
Koumala, *Australia* .... **62 C4** 21 38S 149 15 E
Koumra, *Chad* .... **51 G9** 8 50N 17 35 E
Kounradskiy, *Kazakhstan* .. **28 E8** 46 59N 75 0 E
Kountze, *U.S.A.* **81 K7** 30 22N 94 19W
Kouris ➤, *Cyprus* .... **25 E11** 34 38N 32 54 E
Kourou, *Fr. Guiana* **93 B8** 5 9N 52 39W
Kousséri, *Cameroon* .... **51 F8** 12 0N 14 55 E
Kouvola, *Finland* .... **9 F22** 60 52N 26 43 E
Kovdor, *Russia* .... **18 A5** 67 34N 30 24 E
Kovel, *Ukraine* .... **17 C13** 51 11N 24 38 E
Kovrov, *Russia* .... **18 C7** 56 25N 41 25 E
Kowanyama, *Australia* ..... **62 B3** 15 29S 141 44 E
Kowloon, *China* .... **33 G11** 22 19N 114 11 E
Kowŏn, *N. Korea* .... **35 E14** 39 26N 127 14 E
Koyampattur = Coimbatore, *India* **40 P10** 11 2N 76 59 E
Köyceğiz, *Turkey* .... **23 F13** 36 57N 28 40 E
Koza, *Japan* .... **31 L3** 26 19N 127 46 E
Kozan, *Turkey* .... **44 B2** 37 26N 35 50 E
Kozáni, *Greece* .... **23 D9** 40 19N 21 47 E
Kozhikode = Calicut, *India* .. **40 P9** 11 15N 75 43 E
Kozhva, *Russia* .... **18 A10** 65 10N 57 0 E
Kozyatyn, *Ukraine* .... **17 D15** 49 45N 28 50 E
Kra, Isthmus of = Kra, Kho Khot,
  Thailand .... **39 G2** 10 15N 99 30 E
Kra, Kho Khot, *Thailand* ... **39 G2** 10 15N 99 30 E
Kra Buri, *Thailand* .... **39 G2** 10 22N 98 46 E
Kraai ➤, *S. Africa* .... **56 E4** 30 40S 26 45 E
Krabi, *Thailand* .... **39 H2** 8 4N 98 55 E
Kracheh, *Cambodia* .... **38 F6** 12 32N 106 10 E
Kragan, *Indonesia* .... **37 G14** 6 43S 111 38 E
Kragerø, *Norway* .... **9 G13** 58 52N 9 25 E
Kragujevac, *Serbia & M.* ... **23 B9** 44 2N 20 56 E
Krakatau = Rakata, Pulau,
  Indonesia .... **36 F3** 6 10S 105 20 E
Krakatoa = Rakata, Pulau,
  Indonesia .... **36 F3** 6 10S 105 20 E
Krakor, *Cambodia* .... **38 F5** 12 32N 104 12 E
Kraków, *Poland* .... **17 C10** 50 4N 19 57 E
Kralanh, *Cambodia* .... **38 F4** 13 35N 103 25 E
Kraljevo, *Serbia & M.* ..... **23 C9** 43 44N 20 41 E
Kramatorsk, *Ukraine* ...... **19 E6** 48 50N 37 30 E
Kramfors, *Sweden* .... **9 E17** 62 55N 17 48 E
Kranj, *Slovenia* .... **16 E8** 46 16N 14 22 E
Krankskop, *S. Africa* ...... **57 D5** 28 0S 30 47 E
Krasavino, *Russia* .... **18 B8** 60 58N 46 29 E
Kraskino, *Russia* .... **29 E14** 42 44N 130 48 E
Krasník, *Poland* .... **17 C12** 50 55N 22 15 E
Krasnoarmeysk, *Russia* .... **28 D5** 51 0N 45 42 E
Krasnodar, *Russia* .... **19 E6** 45 5N 39 0 E
Krasnokamsk, *Russia* ...... **18 C10** 58 4N 55 48 E
Krasnoperekopsk, *Ukraine* . **19 E5** 46 0N 33 54 E
Krasnorechenskiy, *Russia* .. **30 B7** 44 41N 135 14 E
Krasnoselkup, *Russia* ..... **28 C9** 65 20N 82 10 E
Krasnoturinsk, *Russia* ..... **18 C11** 59 46N 60 12 E
Krasnoufimsk, *Russia* ..... **18 C10** 56 36N 57 38 E
Krasnouralsk, *Russia* ...... **18 C11** 58 21N 60 3 E
Krasnovishersk, *Russia* .... **18 B10** 60 23N 57 3 E
Krasnoyarsk, *Russia* ...... **29 D10** 56 8N 93 0 E
Krasnyy Kut, *Russia* ...... **19 D8** 50 50N 47 0 E
Krasnyy Luch, *Ukraine* .... **19 E6** 48 13N 39 0 E
Krasnyy Yar, *Russia* .... **19 E8** 46 43N 48 23 E
Kratie = Kracheh, *Cambodia* . **38 F6** 12 32N 106 10 E
Krau, *Indonesia* .... **37 E10** 3 19S 140 5 E
Kravanh, Chuor Phnum,
  Cambodia .... **39 G4** 12 0N 103 32 E
Krefeld, *Germany* .... **16 C4** 51 20N 6 33 E
Kremen, *Croatia* .... **16 F8** 44 28N 15 53 E
Kremenchuk, *Ukraine* ..... **19 E5** 49 5N 33 25 E

Kremenchuksk Vdskh., *Ukraine* . **19 E5** 49 20N 32 30 E
Kremenets, *Ukraine* .... **17 C13** 50 8N 25 43 E
Kremmling, *U.S.A.* **76 F10** 40 4N 106 24W
Krems, *Austria* .... **16 D8** 48 25N 15 36 E
Kribi, *Cameroon* .... **52 D1** 2 57N 9 56 E
Krichev = Krychaw, *Belarus* . **17 B16** 53 40N 31 41 E
Kriós, Ákra, *Greece* .... **25 D5** 35 13N 23 34 E
Krishna ➤, *India* .... **41 M12** 15 57N 80 59 E
Krishnanagar, *India* .... **43 H13** 23 24N 88 33 E
Kristiansand, *Norway* ..... **9 G13** 58 8N 8 1 E
Kristianstad, *Sweden* ...... **9 H16** 56 2N 14 9 E
Kristiansund, *Norway* ..... **8 E12** 63 7N 7 45 E
Kristiinankaupunki, *Finland* . **9 E19** 62 16N 21 21 E
Kristinehamn, *Sweden* ..... **9 G16** 59 18N 14 7 E
Kristinestad = Kristiinankaupunki,
  Finland .... **9 E19** 62 16N 21 21 E
Kríti, *Greece* .... **25 D7** 35 15N 25 0 E
Kritsá, *Greece* .... **25 D7** 35 10N 25 41 E
Krivoy Rog = Kryvyy Rih, *Ukraine* **19 E5** 47 51N 33 20 E
Krk, *Croatia* .... **16 F8** 45 8N 14 40 E
Krokodil ➤, *Mozam.* .... **57 D5** 25 14S 32 18 E
Krong Kaoh Kong, *Cambodia* . **36 B2** 11 35N 103 0 E
Kronprins Olav Kyst, *Antarctica* **5 C5** 69 0S 42 0 E
Kronprinsesse Märtha Kyst,
  Antarctica **5 D2** 73 30S 10 0W
Kronshtadt, *Russia* .... **18 B4** 59 57N 29 51 E
Kroonstad, *S. Africa* ...... **56 D4** 27 43S 27 19 E
Kropotkin, *Russia* .... **19 E7** 45 28N 40 28 E
Krosno, *Poland* .... **17 D11** 49 42N 21 46 E
Krotoszyn, *Poland* .... **17 C9** 51 42N 17 23 E
Kroussón, *Greece* .... **25 D6** 35 13N 24 59 E
Kruger △, *S. Africa* .... **57 C5** 24 50S 26 10 E
Krugersdorp, *S. Africa* ..... **57 D4** 26 5S 27 46 E
Kruisfontein, *S. Africa* ..... **56 E3** 33 59S 24 43 E
Krung Thep = Bangkok, *Thailand* **38 F3** 13 45N 100 35 E
Krupki, *Belarus* .... **17 A15** 54 19N 29 8 E
Kruševac, *Serbia & M.* ..... **23 C9** 43 35N 21 28 E
Krychaw, *Belarus* .... **17 B16** 53 40N 31 41 E
Krymskyi Poluostrov = Krymskyy
  Pivostriv, *Ukraine* ...... **19 F5** 45 0N 34 0 E
Krymskyy Pivostriv, *Ukraine* . **19 F5** 45 0N 34 0 E
Kryvyy Rih, *Ukraine* .... **19 E5** 47 51N 33 20 E
Ksar el Kebir, *Morocco* **50 B4** 35 0N 6 0W
Ksar es Souk = Er Rachidia,
  Morocco **50 B5** 31 58N 4 20W
Kuah, *Malaysia* .... **39 J2** 6 19N 99 51 E
Kuala Belait, *Malaysia* .... **36 D4** 4 35N 114 11 E
Kuala Berang, *Malaysia* ... **39 K4** 5 5N 103 1 E
Kuala Dungun = Dungun,
  Malaysia .... **39 K4** 4 45N 103 25 E
Kuala Kangsar, *Malaysia* ... **39 K3** 4 46N 100 56 E
Kuala Kelawang, *Malaysia* . **39 L4** 2 56N 102 5 E
Kuala Kerai, *Malaysia* ..... **39 K4** 5 30N 102 12 E
Kuala Kerian, *Malaysia* .... **39 c** 4 10N 100 2 3 E
Kuala Lipis, *Malaysia* ..... **39 L3** 4 10N 102 3 E
Kuala Lumpur, *Malaysia* ... **39 L3** 3 9N 101 41 E
Kuala Nerang, *Malaysia* ... **39 J3** 6 16N 100 37 E
Kuala Pilah, *Malaysia* ..... **39 L4** 2 45N 102 15 E
Kuala Rompin, *Malaysia* ... **39 L4** 2 49N 103 29 E
Kuala Selangor, *Malaysia* .. **39 L3** 3 20N 101 15 E
Kuala Sepetang, *Malaysia* . **39 K3** 4 49N 100 28 E
Kuala Terengganu, *Malaysia* . **39 K4** 5 20N 103 8 E
Kualajelai, *Indonesia* ..... **36 E4** 2 58S 110 46 E
Kualakapuas, *Indonesia* ... **36 E4** 2 55S 114 20 E
Kualakurun, *Indonesia* .... **36 E4** 1 10S 113 50 E
Kualapembuang, *Indonesia* . **36 E4** 3 14S 112 38 E
Kualasimpang, *Indonesia* .. **36 D1** 4 17N 98 3 E
Kuancheng, *China* .... **35 D10** 40 37N 118 30 E
Kuandang, *Indonesia* ..... **37 D6** 0 56N 123 1 E
Kuandian, *China* .... **35 D13** 40 45N 124 45 E
Kuangchou = Guangzhou, *China* **33 D6** 23 5N 113 10 E
Kuantan, *Malaysia* .... **39 L4** 3 49N 103 20 E
Kuba = Quba, *Azerbaijan* .. **19 F8** 41 21N 48 32 E
Kuban ➤, *Russia* .... **19 E6** 45 20N 37 30 E
Kubokawa, *Japan* .... **31 H6** 33 12N 133 8 E
Kubu, *Indonesia* .... **37 J18** 8 16S 115 35 E
Kubutambahan, *Indonesia* . **37 J18** 8 5S 115 10 E
Kucar, Tanjung, *Indonesia* . **37 K18** 8 39S 114 34 E
Kucha Gompa, *India* ...... **43 B7** 34 25N 76 56 E
Kuchinda, *India* .... **43 J11** 21 44N 84 21 E
Kuching, *Malaysia* .... **36 D4** 1 33N 110 25 E
Kuchino-eruba-Jima, *Japan* . **31 J5** 30 28N 130 12 E
Kuchino-Shima, *Japan* .... **31 K4** 29 57N 129 55 E
Kuchinotsu, *Japan* .... **31 H5** 32 36N 130 11 E
Kucing = Kuching, *Malaysia* . **36 D4** 1 33N 110 25 E
Kud ➤, *Pakistan* .... **42 F2** 26 5N 66 20 E
Kuda, *India* .... **40 H7** 23 10N 71 15 E
Kudat, *Malaysia* .... **36 C5** 6 55N 116 55 E
Kudus, *Indonesia* .... **37 G14** 6 48S 110 51 E
Kudymkar, *Russia* .... **18 C9** 59 1N 54 39 E
Kueiyang = Guiyang, *China* . **33 D5** 26 32N 106 40 E
Kufra Oasis = Al Kufrah, *Libya* . **51 D10** 24 17N 23 15 E
Kufstein, *Austria* .... **16 E7** 47 35N 12 11 E
Kugaaruk = Pelly Bay, *Canada* . **69 B11** 68 38N 89 50W
Kugluktuk, *Canada* **68 B8** 67 50N 115 5W
Kugong I., *Canada* **72 A4** 56 18N 79 50W
Kūhak, *Iran* .... **40 F3** 27 12N 63 10 E
Kuhan, *Pakistan* .... **42 E2** 28 19N 67 14 E
Kühbonān, *Iran* .... **45 D8** 31 23N 56 19 E
Kuhin, *Iran* .... **45 B6** 36 22N 49 40 E
Kūhīrī, *Iran* .... **45 E9** 26 55N 61 2 E
Kūhpāyeh, Eşfahan, *Iran* ... **45 C7** 32 44N 52 20 E
Kūhpāyeh, Kermān, *Iran* ... **45 D8** 30 35N 57 15 E
Kūhrān, Kūh-e, *Iran* .... **45 E8** 26 46N 58 12 E
Kui Buri, *Thailand* .... **39 F2** 12 3N 99 52 E
Kuichong, *China* .... **33 F11** 22 38N 114 25 E
Kuiseb ➤, *Namibia* .... **56 C1** 22 59S 14 31 E
Kuito, *Angola* .... **53 G3** 12 22S 16 55 E
Kuiu I., *U.S.A.* **70 B2** 57 45N 134 10W
Kujang, *N. Korea* .... **35 E14** 39 57N 126 1 E
Kuji, *Japan* .... **30 D10** 40 11N 141 46 E
Kujū-San, *Japan* .... **31 H5** 33 5N 131 15 E
Kukës, *Albania* .... **23 C9** 42 5N 20 27 E
Kukup, *Malaysia* .... **39 d** 1 20N 103 27 E
Kukup, Pulau, *Malaysia* ... **39 d** 1 18N 103 27 E
Kula, *Turkey* .... **23 E13** 38 32N 28 40 E
Kulachi, *Pakistan* .... **42 D4** 31 56N 70 27 E
Kulai, *Malaysia* .... **39 M4** 1 44N 103 35 E
Kulasekarappattinam, *India* . **40 Q11** 8 20N 78 0 E
Kuldīga, *Latvia* .... **9 H19** 56 58N 21 59 E
Kulgam, *India* .... **43 C6** 33 36N 75 2 E
Kulgera, *Australia* .... **62 D1** 25 50S 133 18 E
Kulim, *Malaysia* .... **39 K3** 5 22N 100 34 E
Kulin, *Australia* .... **61 F2** 32 40S 118 2 E

Kulkayu = Hartley Bay, *Canada* . **70 C3** 53 25N 129 15W
Kŭlob, *Tajikistan* .... **28 F7** 37 55N 69 50 E
Kulsary, *Kazakhstan* ...... **19 E9** 46 59N 54 1 E
Kulti, *India* .... **43 H12** 23 43N 86 50 E
Kulu, *India* .... **42 D7** 31 58N 77 6 E
Kulumbura, *Australia* ..... **60 B4** 13 55S 126 35 E
Kulunda, *Russia* .... **28 D8** 52 35N 78 57 E
Kulungar, *Afghan.* .... **42 C3** 34 0N 69 2 E
Kŭlvand, *Iran* .... **45 D7** 31 21N 54 35 E
Kulwin, *Australia* .... **63 F3** 35 0S 142 42 E
Kulyab = Kŭlob, *Tajikistan* . **28 F7** 37 55N 69 50 E
Kuma ➤, *Russia* .... **19 F8** 44 55N 47 0 E
Kumagaya, *Japan* .... **31 F9** 36 9N 139 22 E
Kumai, *Indonesia* .... **36 E4** 2 44S 111 43 E
Kumamba, Kepulauan, *Indonesia* **37 E9** 1 36S 138 45 E
Kumamoto, *Japan* .... **31 H5** 32 45N 130 45 E
Kumamoto □, *Japan* ...... **31 H5** 32 55N 130 55 E
Kumanovo, *Macedonia* .... **23 C9** 42 9N 21 42 E
Kumara, *N.Z.* .... **59 K3** 42 37S 171 12 E
Kumarina, *Australia* ...... **61 D2** 24 41S 119 32 E
Kumasi, *Ghana* **50 G5** 6 41N 1 38W
Kumba, *Cameroon* .... **52 D1** 4 36N 9 24 E
Kumbakonam, *India* ...... **40 P11** 10 58N 79 25 E
Kumbarilla, *Australia* ..... **63 D5** 27 15S 150 55 E
Kumbhraj, *India* .... **42 G7** 24 22N 77 3 E
Kumbia, *Australia* .... **63 D5** 26 41S 151 39 E
Kümch'ŏn, *N. Korea* ...... **35 E14** 38 10N 126 29 E
Kumdok, *India* .... **43 C8** 33 32N 78 10 E
Kume-Shima, *Japan* ...... **31 L3** 26 20N 126 47 E
Kumertau, *Russia* .... **18 D10** 52 45N 55 57 E
Kumharsain, *India* .... **42 D7** 31 19N 77 27 E
Kümhwa, *S. Korea* .... **35 E14** 38 17N 127 28 E
Kumi, *Uganda* .... **54 B3** 1 30N 33 58 E
Kumla, *Sweden* .... **9 G16** 59 8N 15 10 E
Kumo, *Nigeria* .... **51 F8** 10 1N 11 12 E
Kumon Bum, *Burma* ...... **41 F20** 26 30N 97 15 E
Kunashir, Ostrov, *Russia* ... **29 E15** 44 0N 146 0 E
Kunda, *Estonia* .... **9 G22** 59 30N 26 34 E
Kunda, *India* .... **43 G9** 25 43N 81 31 E
Kundar ➤, *Pakistan* .... **42 D3** 31 56N 69 19 E
Kundelungu △, *Dem. Rep. of*
  the Congo .... **55 E2** 10 30S 27 40 E
Kundelungu Ouest △, *Dem. Rep.*
  of the Congo .... **55 E2** 9 55S 27 17 E
Kundian, *Pakistan* .... **42 C4** 32 27N 71 28 E
Kundla, *India* .... **42 J4** 21 21N 71 25 E
Kung, Ao, *Thailand* .... **39 a** 8 5N 98 24 E
Kunga ➤, *Bangla.* .... **43 J13** 21 46N 89 30 E
Kunghit I., *Canada* **70 C2** 52 6N 131 3W
Kungrad = Qünghirot, *Uzbekistan* **28 E6** 43 6N 58 54 E
Kungsbacka, *Sweden* ..... **9 H15** 57 30N 12 5 E
Kungur, *Russia* .... **18 C10** 57 25N 56 57 E
Kungurri, *Australia* .... **62 K6** 21 4S 148 45 E
Kunhar ➤, *Pakistan* .... **43 B5** 34 20N 73 30 E
Kuningan, *Indonesia* ...... **37 G13** 6 59S 108 29 E
Kunlong, *Burma* .... **41 H21** 23 20N 98 50 E
Kunlun Shan, *Asia* .... **32 C3** 36 0N 86 30 E
Kunming, *China* .... **32 D5** 25 1N 102 41 E
Kunsan, *S. Korea* .... **35 G14** 35 59N 126 45 E
Kununurra, *Australia* ...... **60 C4** 15 40S 128 50 E
Kunwari ➤, *India* .... **43 F8** 26 26N 79 11 E
Kunya-Urgench = Köneürgench,
  Turkmenistan .... **28 E6** 42 19N 59 10 E
Kuopio, *Finland* .... **8 E22** 62 53N 27 35 E
Kupa ➤, *Croatia* .... **16 F9** 45 28N 16 24 E
Kupang, *Indonesia* .... **37 F6** 10 19S 123 39 E
Kupreanof I., *U.S.A.* **70 B2** 56 50N 133 30W
Kupyansk-Uzlovoi, *Ukraine* . **19 E6** 49 40N 37 43 E
Kuqa, *China* .... **32 B3** 41 35N 82 30 E
Kür ➤, *Azerbaijan* .... **19 G8** 39 29N 49 15 E
Kür Dili, *Azerbaijan* ...... **45 B6** 39 29N 49 13 E
Kura = Kür ➤, *Azerbaijan* .. **19 G8** 39 29N 49 15 E
Kuranda, *Australia* .... **62 B4** 16 48S 145 35 E
Kuranga, *India* .... **42 H3** 22 4N 69 10 E
Kurashiki, *Japan* .... **31 G6** 34 40N 133 50 E
Kurayoshi, *Japan* .... **31 G6** 35 26N 133 50 E
Kürdzhali, *Bulgaria* .... **23 D11** 41 38N 25 21 E
Kure, *Japan* .... **31 G6** 34 14N 132 32 E
Kuressaare, *Estonia* ...... **9 G20** 58 15N 22 30 E
Kurgan, *Russia* .... **28 D7** 55 26N 65 18 E
Kuri, *India* .... **42 F4** 26 37N 70 43 E
Kuria Maria Is. = Khuriyā Muriyā,
  Jazā'ir, *Oman* .... **47 D6** 17 30N 55 58 E
Kuridala, *Australia* .... **62 C3** 21 16S 140 29 E
Kurigram, *Bangla.* .... **41 G16** 25 49N 89 39 E
Kurikka, *Finland* .... **9 E20** 62 36N 22 24 E
Kuril Is. = Kurilskiye Ostrova,
  Russia .... **29 E15** 45 0N 150 0 E
Kuril Trench, *Pac. Oc.* .... **26 E19** 44 0N 153 0 E
Kurilsk, *Russia* .... **29 E15** 45 14N 147 53 E
Kurilskiye Ostrova, *Russia* . **29 E15** 45 0N 150 0 E
Kurino, *Japan* .... **31 J5** 31 57N 130 43 E
Kurinskaya Kosa = Kür Dili,
  Azerbaijan .... **45 B6** 39 3N 49 13 E
Kurnool, *India* .... **40 M11** 15 45N 78 0 E
Kuro-Shima, Kagoshima, *Japan* . **31 J4** 30 50N 129 57 E
Kuro-Shima, Okinawa, *Japan* . **31 M2** 24 14N 124 1 E
Kurow, *N.Z.* .... **59 L3** 44 44S 170 29 E
Kurram ➤, *Pakistan* ...... **42 C4** 32 36N 71 20 E
Kurri Kurri, *Australia* ..... **63 E5** 32 50S 151 28 E
Kurrimine, *Australia* ...... **62 B4** 17 47S 146 6 E
Kurshskiy Zaliv, *Russia* .... **9 J19** 55 9N 21 6 E
Kursk, *Russia* .... **18 D6** 51 42N 36 11 E
Kuruçay, *Turkey* .... **44 B3** 39 39N 38 29 E
Kuruktag, *China* .... **32 B3** 41 0N 89 0 E
Kuruman, *S. Africa* .... **56 D3** 27 28S 23 28 E
Kuruman ➤, *S. Africa* ..... **56 D3** 26 56S 20 39 E
Kurume, *Japan* .... **31 H5** 33 15N 130 30 E
Kurunegala, *Sri Lanka* .... **40 R12** 7 30N 80 23 E
Kurya, *Russia* .... **18 B10** 61 42N 57 9 E
Kus Gölü, *Turkey* .... **23 D12** 40 10N 27 55 E
Kuşadası, *Turkey* .... **23 F12** 37 52N 27 15 E
Kusamba, *Indonesia* ...... **37 K18** 8 34S 115 27 E
Kusatsu, *Japan* .... **31 F9** 36 37N 138 36 E
Kusawa L., *Canada* **70 A1** 60 20N 136 13W
Kushalgarh, *India* .... **42 H6** 23 10N 74 27 E
Kushikino, *Japan* .... **31 J5** 31 44N 130 16 E
Kushimoto, *Japan* .... **31 H7** 33 28N 135 47 E
Kushiro, *Japan* .... **30 C12** 42 59N 144 23 E
Kushiro-Gawa ➤, *Japan* ... **30 C12** 42 59N 144 23 E
Kushiro Shitsugen △, *Japan* . **30 C12** 43 9N 144 26 E
Kūshk, *Iran* .... **45 D8** 28 46N 56 51 E
Kushka = Gushgy, *Turkmenistan* **28 F7** 35 20N 62 18 E
Kūshki, *Iran* .... **44 C5** 33 31N 47 13 E
Kushol, *India* .... **43 C7** 33 40N 76 36 E
Kushtia, *Bangla.* .... **41 H16** 23 55N 89 5 E
Kushva, *Russia* .... **18 C10** 58 18N 59 45 E

Kuskokwim B., U.S.A. 68 C3 59 45N 162 25W
Kusmi, India .... 43 H10 23 17N 83 55 E
Kussharo-Ko, Japan .... 30 C12 43 38N 144 21 E
Kustanay = Qostanay,
  Kazakhstan .... 28 D7 53 10N 63 35 E
Kut, Ko, Thailand .... 39 G4 11 40N 102 35 E
Kuta, Indonesia .... 37 K18 8 43S 115 11 E
Kütahya, Turkey .... 19 G5 39 30N 30 2 E
Kutaisi, Georgia .... 19 F7 42 19N 42 40 E
Kutaraja = Banda Aceh,
  Indonesia .... 36 C1 5 35N 95 20 E
Kutch, Gulf of = Kachchh, Gulf of,
  India .... 42 H3 22 50N 69 15 E
Kutch, Rann of = Kachchh, Rann
  of, India .... 42 H4 24 0N 70 0 E
Kutiyana, India .... 42 J4 21 36N 70 2 E
Kutno, Poland .... 17 B10 52 15N 19 23 E
Kutse, Botswana .... 56 C3 21 7S 22 16 E
Kuttabul, Australia .... 62 K6 21 1S 148 54 E
Kutu, Dem. Rep. of the Congo 52 E3 2 40S 18 11 E
Kutum, Sudan .... 51 F10 14 10N 24 40 E
Kuujjuaq, Canada 69 C13 58 6N 68 15W
Kuujjuarapik, Canada 72 A4 55 20N 77 35W
Kuŭp-tong, N. Korea ...... 35 D14 40 45N 126 1 E
Kuusamo, Finland .... 8 D23 65 57N 29 8 E
Kuusankoski, Finland ..... 9 F22 60 55N 26 38 E
Kuwait = Al Kuwayt, Kuwait . 44 D5 29 30N 48 0 E
Kuwait ■, Asia .... 44 D5 29 30N 47 30 E
Kuwana, Japan .... 31 G8 35 5N 136 43 E
Kuwana ➤, India .... 43 F10 26 25N 83 15 E
Kuybyshev = Samara, Russia 18 D9 53 8N 50 6 E
Kuybyshev, Russia .... 28 D8 55 27N 78 19 E
Kuybyshevskoye Vdkhr., Russia 18 C8 55 2N 49 30 E
Kuye He ➤, China .... 34 E6 38 23N 110 46 E
Küyeh, Iran .... 44 B5 38 45N 47 57 E
Kuyto, Ozero, Russia ..... 18 B5 65 6N 31 20 E
Kuyumba, Russia .... 29 C10 60 58N 96 59 E
Kuzey Anadolu Dağları, Turkey 19 F6 41 30N 35 0 E
Kuznetsk, Russia .... 18 D8 53 12N 46 40 E
Kuzomen, Russia .... 18 A6 66 22N 36 50 E
Kvænangen, Norway ...... 8 A19 70 5N 21 15 E
Kvaløy, Norway .... 8 B18 69 40N 18 30 E
Kvarner, Croatia .... 16 F8 44 50N 14 10 E
Kvarnerič, Croatia .... 16 F8 44 43N 14 37 E
Kwa-Nobuhle, S. Africa ... 53 L5 33 50S 25 22 E
Kwabhaca, S. Africa ...... 57 E4 30 51S 29 0 E
Kwakhanai, Botswana ..... 56 C3 21 39S 21 16 E
Kwakoegron, Suriname 93 B7 5 12N 55 25W
Kwale, Kenya .... 54 C4 4 15S 39 31 E
KwaMashu, S. Africa ...... 57 D5 29 45S 30 58 E
Kwando ➤, Africa .... 56 B3 18 27S 23 32 E
Kwangchow = Guangzhou, China 33 D6 23 5N 113 10 E
Kwangdaeri, N. Korea ..... 35 D14 40 31N 127 32 E
Kwangju, S. Korea .... 35 G14 35 9N 126 54 E
Kwango ➤, Dem. Rep. of
  the Congo .... 52 E3 3 14S 17 22 E
Kwangsi-Chuang = Guangxi
  Zhuangzu Zizhiqu □, China 33 D5 24 0N 109 0 E
Kwangtung = Guangdong □,
  China .... 33 D6 23 0N 113 0 E
Kwataboahegan ➤, Canada . 72 B3 51 9N 80 50W
Kwatisore, Indonesia ..... 37 E8 3 18S 134 50 E
KwaZulu Natal □, S. Africa .. 57 D5 29 0S 30 0 E
Kweichow = Guizhou □, China 32 D5 27 0N 107 0 E
Kwekwe, Zimbabwe .... 55 F2 18 58S 29 48 E
Kwidzyn, Poland .... 17 B10 53 44N 18 55 E
Kwinana New Town, Australia 61 F2 32 15S 115 47 E
Kwoka, Indonesia .... 37 E8 0 31S 132 27 E
Kwun Tong, China .... 33 G11 22 19N 114 13 E
Kyabra Cr. ➤, Australia ... 63 D3 25 36S 142 55 E
Kyabram, Australia ...... 63 F4 36 19S 145 4 E
Kyaikto, Burma .... 38 D1 17 20N 97 3 E
Kyakhta, Russia .... 29 D11 50 30N 106 25 E
Kyambura ➤, Uganda ..... 54 C3 0 7S 30 9 E
Kyancutta, Australia ...... 63 E2 33 8S 135 33 E
Kyaukpadaung, Burma ..... 41 J19 20 52N 95 8 E
Kyaukpyu, Burma .... 41 K18 19 28N 93 30 E
Kyaukse, Burma .... 41 J20 21 36N 96 10 E
Kyburz, U.S.A. 78 G6 38 47N 120 18W
Kyelang, India .... 42 C7 32 35N 77 2 E
Kyenjojo, Uganda .... 54 B3 0 40N 30 37 E
Kyle, Canada 71 C7 50 50N 108 2W
Kyle Dam, Zimbabwe ..... 55 G3 20 15S 31 0 E
Kyle of Lochalsh, U.K. 11 D3 57 17N 5 44W
Kymijoki ➤, Finland ...... 9 F22 60 30N 26 55 E
Kyneton, Australia .... 63 F3 37 10S 144 29 E
Kynuna, Australia .... 62 C3 21 37S 141 55 E
Kyō-ga-Saki, Japan .... 31 G7 35 45N 135 15 E
Kyoga, L., Uganda .... 54 B3 1 35N 33 0 E
Kyogle, Australia .... 63 D5 28 40S 153 0 E
Kyongju, S. Korea .... 35 G15 35 51N 129 14 E
Kyongpyaw, Burma .... 41 L19 17 12N 95 10 E
Kyŏngsŏng, N. Korea ..... 35 D15 41 35N 129 36 E
Kyōto, Japan .... 31 G7 35 0N 135 45 E
Kyōto □, Japan .... 31 G7 35 15N 135 45 E
Kyparissovouno, Cyprus ... 25 D12 35 19N 33 10 E
Kyperounda, Cyprus ...... 25 E11 34 56N 32 58 E
Kyrenia, Cyprus .... 25 D12 35 20N 33 20 E
Kyrgyzstan ■, Asia .... 28 E8 42 0N 75 0 E
Kyrönjoki ➤, Finland ..... 8 E19 63 14N 21 45 E
Kystatyam, Russia .... 29 C13 67 20N 123 10 E
Kythira, Greece .... 23 F10 36 8N 23 0 E
Kythréa, Cyprus .... 25 D12 35 15N 33 29 E
Kyunhla, Burma .... 41 H19 23 25N 95 15 E
Kyuquot Sound, Canada ... 70 D3 50 2N 127 22W
Kyūshū, Japan .... 31 H5 33 0N 131 0 E
Kyūshū □, Japan .... 31 H5 33 0N 131 0 E
Kyūshū-Sanchi, Japan ..... 31 H5 32 35N 131 17 E
Kyustendil, Bulgaria ...... 23 C10 42 16N 22 41 E
Kyusyur, Russia .... 29 B13 70 19N 127 30 E
Kyyiv, Ukraine .... 17 C16 50 30N 30 28 E
Kyyivske Vdskh., Ukraine .. 17 C16 51 0N 30 25 E
Kyzyl, Russia .... 29 D10 51 50N 94 30 E
Kyzyl Kum, Uzbekistan .... 28 E7 42 30N 65 0 E
Kyzyl-Kyya, Kyrgyzstan .... 28 E8 40 16N 72 8 E
Kyzyl-Orda = Qyzylorda,
  Kazakhstan .... 28 E7 44 48N 65 28 E

L

La Alcarria, Spain 21 B4 40 31N 2 45W
La Amistad △, Cent. Amer. . 88 E3 9 28N 83 18W
La Asunción, Venezuela ... 92 A6 11 2N 63 53W
La Baie, Canada 73 C5 48 19N 70 53W
La Banda, Argentina 94 B3 27 45S 64 10W
La Barca, Mexico 86 C4 20 20N 102 40W

La Barge, U.S.A. 76 E8 42 16N 110 12W
La Belle, U.S.A. 83 M5 26 46N 81 26W
La Biche ➤, Canada 70 B4 59 57N 123 50W
La Biche, L., Canada 70 C6 54 50N 112 5W
La Blanquilla, Venezuela ... 89 D7 11 51N 64 37W
La Bomba, Mexico 86 A1 31 53N 115 2W
La Brea, Trin. & Tob. 93 K15 10 15N 61 37W
La Calera, Chile 94 C1 32 50S 71 10W
La Campana △, Chile 94 C1 32 58S 71 14W
La Canal = Sa Canal, Spain . 24 C7 38 51N 1 23 E
La Carlota, Argentina 94 C3 33 30S 63 20W
La Ceiba, Honduras 88 C2 15 40N 86 50W
La Chaux-de-Fonds, Switz. .. 20 C7 47 7N 6 50 E
La Chorrera, Panama 88 E4 8 53N 79 47W
La Cocha, Argentina 94 B2 27 50S 65 40W
La Concepción, Panama ... 88 E3 8 31N 82 37W
La Concordia, Mexico 87 D6 16 8N 92 38W
La Coruña = A Coruña, Spain 21 A1 43 20N 8 25W
La Crescent, U.S.A. 80 D9 43 50N 91 18W
La Crete, Canada 70 B5 58 11N 116 24W
La Crosse, Kans., U.S.A. .. 80 F5 38 32N 99 18W
La Crosse, Wis., U.S.A. 80 D9 43 48N 91 15W
La Cruz, Costa Rica 88 D2 11 4N 85 39W
La Cruz, Mexico 86 C3 23 55N 106 54W
La Désirade, Guadeloupe .. 88 b 16 18N 61 3W
La Escondida, Mexico 86 C5 24 6N 99 55W
La Esmeralda, Paraguay ... 94 A3 22 16S 62 33W
La Esperanza, Cuba 88 B3 22 46N 83 44W
La Esperanza, Honduras ... 88 D2 14 15N 88 10W
La Estrada = A Estrada, Spain 21 A1 42 43N 8 27W
La Fayette, U.S.A. 83 H3 34 42N 85 17W
La Fé, Cuba 88 B3 22 2N 84 15W
La Follette, U.S.A. 83 G3 36 23N 84 7W
La Grande, U.S.A. 76 D4 45 20N 118 5W
La Grande ➤, Canada 72 B5 53 50N 79 0W
La Grande Deux, Rés., Canada 72 B4 53 40N 76 55W
La Grande Quatre, Rés., Canada 72 B5 54 0N 73 15W
La Grande Trois, Rés., Canada 72 B4 53 40N 75 10W
La Grange, Calif., U.S.A. .. 78 H6 37 42N 120 27W
La Grange, Ga., U.S.A. 83 J3 33 2N 85 2W
La Grange, Ky., U.S.A. 82 F3 38 25N 85 23W
La Grange, Tex., U.S.A. 81 L6 29 54N 96 52W
La Guaira, Venezuela 92 A5 10 36N 66 56W
La Habana, Cuba 88 B3 23 8N 82 22W
La Independencia, Mexico .. 87 D6 16 31N 91 47W
La Isabela, Dom. Rep. 89 C5 19 58N 71 2W
La Junta, U.S.A. 81 F3 37 59N 103 33W
La Laguna, Canary Is. 24 F3 28 28N 16 18W
La Libertad, Guatemala 88 C1 16 47N 90 7W
La Libertad, Mexico 86 B2 29 55N 112 41W
La Ligua, Chile 94 C1 32 30S 71 16W
La Línea de la Concepción, Spain 21 D3 36 15N 5 23W
La Loche, Canada 71 B7 56 29N 109 26W
La Louvière, Belgium ..... 15 D4 50 27N 4 10 E
La Lune, Trin. & Tob. 93 K15 10 3N 61 22W
La Malbaie, Canada 73 C5 47 40N 70 10W
La Malinche △, Mexico 87 D5 19 15N 98 3W
La Mancha, Spain 21 C4 39 10N 2 54W
La Martre, L., Canada 70 A5 63 15N 117 55W
La Mesa, U.S.A. 79 N9 32 46N 117 3W
La Misión, Mexico 86 A1 32 5N 116 50W
La Moure, U.S.A. 80 B5 46 21N 98 18W
La Negra, Chile 94 A1 23 46S 70 18W
La Oliva, Canary Is. 24 F6 28 36N 13 57W
La Orotava, Canary Is. 24 F3 28 22N 16 31W
La Oroya, Peru 92 F3 11 32S 75 54W
La Palma, Canary Is. 24 F2 28 40N 17 50W
La Palma, Panama 88 E4 8 15N 78 0W
La Palma del Condado, Spain 21 D2 37 21N 6 38W
La Paloma, Chile 94 C1 30 35S 71 0W
La Pampa □, Argentina 94 D2 36 50S 66 0W
La Paragua, Venezuela 92 B6 6 50N 63 20W
La Paz, Entre Rios, Argentina 94 C4 30 50S 59 45W
La Paz, San Luis, Argentina . 94 C2 33 30S 67 20W
La Paz, Bolivia 92 G5 16 20S 68 10W
La Paz, Honduras 88 D2 14 20N 87 47W
La Paz, Mexico 86 C2 24 10N 110 20W
La Paz Centro, Nic. 88 D2 12 20N 86 41W
La Pedrera, Colombia 92 D5 1 18S 69 43W
La Pérade, Canada 73 C5 46 35N 72 12W
La Perouse Str., Asia ..... 30 B11 45 40N 142 0 E
La Pesca, Mexico 87 C5 23 46N 97 47W
La Piedad, Mexico 86 C4 20 20N 102 1W
La Pine, U.S.A. 76 E3 43 40N 121 30W
La Plata, U.S.A. 94 D4 35 0S 57 55W
La Pocatière, Canada 73 C5 47 22N 70 2W
La Porte, Ind., U.S.A. 82 E2 41 36N 86 43W
La Porte, Tex., U.S.A. 81 L7 29 39N 95 1W
La Purísima, Mexico 86 B2 26 10N 112 4W
La Push, U.S.A. 78 C2 47 55N 124 38W
La Quiaca, Argentina 94 A2 22 5S 65 35W
La Restinga, Canary Is. 24 G2 27 38N 17 59W
La Rioja, Argentina 94 B2 29 20S 67 0W
La Rioja □, Argentina 94 B2 29 30S 67 0W
La Rioja □, Spain 21 A4 42 20N 2 20W
La Robla, Spain 21 A3 42 50N 5 41W
La Roche-en-Ardenne, Belgium 15 D5 50 11N 5 35 E
La Roche-sur-Yon, France .. 20 C3 46 40N 1 25W
La Rochelle, France 20 C3 46 10N 1 9W
La Roda, Spain 21 C4 39 13N 2 15W
La Romana, Dom. Rep. 89 C6 18 27N 68 57W
La Ronge, Canada 71 B7 55 5N 105 20W
La Rumorosa, Mexico 79 N10 32 33N 116 4W
La Sabina = Sa Savina, Spain 24 C7 38 44N 1 25 E
La Salle, U.S.A. 80 E10 41 20N 89 6W
La Santa, Canary Is. 24 E6 29 5N 13 40W
La Sarre, Canada 72 C4 48 45N 79 15W
La Scie, Canada 73 C8 49 57N 55 36W
La Selva Beach, U.S.A. 78 J5 36 56N 121 51W
La Serena, Chile 94 B1 29 55S 71 10W
La Seu d'Urgell, Spain .... 21 A6 42 22N 1 23 E
La Seyne-sur-Mer, France .. 20 E6 43 7N 5 52 E
La Soufrière, St. Vincent ... 89 D7 13 20N 61 11W
La Spézia, Italy .... 20 D8 44 7N 9 50 E
La Tagua, Colombia 92 C4 0 3N 74 40W
La Tortuga, Venezuela 89 D6 11 0N 65 22W
La Trinité, Martinique .... 88 c 14 43N 60 58W
La Tuque, Canada 72 C5 47 30N 72 50W
La Unión, Chile 96 E2 40 10S 73 0W
La Unión, El Salv. 88 D2 13 20N 87 50W
La Unión, Mexico 86 D4 17 58N 101 49W
La Urbana, Venezuela 92 B5 7 8N 66 56W
La Vache Pt., Trin. & Tob. .. 93 K15 10 47N 61 37W
La Vall d'Uixó, Spain 21 C5 39 49N 0 15W
La Vega, Dom. Rep. 89 C5 19 20N 70 30W
La Vela de Coro, Venezuela 92 A5 11 27N 69 34W
La Venta, Mexico 87 D6 18 8N 94 3W

La Ventura, Mexico 86 C4 24 38N 100 54W
Laas Caanood = Las Anod,
  Somali Rep. .... 47 F4 8 26N 47 19 E
Labasa, Fiji .... 59 C8 16 30S 179 27 E
Labe = Elbe ➤, Europe .... 16 B5 53 50N 9 0 E
Labé, Guinea 50 F3 11 24N 12 16W
Laberge, L., Canada 70 A1 61 11N 135 12W
Labinsk, Russia .... 19 F7 44 40N 40 48 E
Labis, Malaysia .... 39 L4 2 22N 103 2 E
Laborie, St. Lucia .... 89 f 13 45N 61 2W
Labrador, Canada 73 B7 53 20N 61 0W
Labrador City, Canada 73 B6 52 57N 66 55W
Labrador Sea, Atl. Oc. 69 C14 57 0N 54 0W
Lábrea, Brazil 92 E6 7 15S 64 51W
Labuan, Malaysia .... 36 C5 5 20N 115 14 E
Labuan, Pulau, Malaysia ... 36 C5 5 21N 115 13 E
Labuha, Indonesia .... 37 E7 0 30S 127 30 E
Labuhan, Indonesia ...... 37 G11 6 22S 105 50 E
Labuhanbajo, Indonesia ... 37 F6 8 28S 119 54 E
Labuk, Telok, Malaysia .... 36 C5 6 10N 117 50 E
Labyrinth, L., Australia ... 63 E2 30 40S 135 11 E
Labytnangi, Russia ...... 28 C7 66 39N 66 21 E
Lac-Bouchette, Canada ... 73 C5 48 16N 72 11W
Lac Édouard, Canada 72 C5 47 40N 72 16W
Lac La Biche, Canada 70 C6 54 45N 111 58W
Lac la Martre = Wha Ti, Canada 68 B8 63 8N 117 16W
Lac La Ronge △, Canada .. 71 B7 55 9N 104 41W
Lac-Mégantic, Canada 73 C5 45 35N 70 53W
Lac Thien, Vietnam ...... 38 F7 12 25N 108 11 E
Lacanau, France 20 D3 44 58N 1 5W
Lacantún ➤, Mexico 87 D6 16 36N 90 40W
Laccadive Is. = Lakshadweep Is.,
  India .... 27 H11 10 0N 72 30 E
Lacepede B., Australia .... 63 F2 36 40S 139 40 E
Lacepede Is., Australia .... 60 C3 16 55S 122 0 E
Lacerdónia, Mozam. ...... 55 F4 18 3S 35 35 E
Lacey, U.S.A. 78 C4 47 7N 122 49W
Lachhmangarh, India ..... 42 F6 27 50N 75 4 E
Lachi, Pakistan .... 42 C4 33 25N 71 20 E
Lachine, Canada 72 C5 45 30N 73 40W
Lachlan ➤, Australia ..... 63 E3 34 22S 143 55 E
Lachute, Canada 72 C5 45 39N 74 21W
Lackawanna, U.S.A. 84 D6 42 50N 78 50W
Lackawaxen, U.S.A. 85 E10 41 29N 74 59W
Lacolle, Canada 85 A11 45 5N 73 22W
Lacombe, Canada 70 C6 52 30N 113 44W
Lacona, U.S.A. 85 C8 43 39N 76 10W
Laconia, U.S.A. 85 C13 43 32N 71 28W
Ladakh Ra., India .... 43 C8 34 0N 78 0 E
Ladismith, S. Africa ...... 56 E3 33 28S 21 15 E
Lādiz, Iran .... 45 D9 28 55N 61 15 E
Ladnun, India .... 42 F6 27 38N 74 25 E
Ladoga, L. = Ladozhskoye Ozero,
  Russia .... 18 B5 61 15N 30 30 E
Ladozhskoye Ozero, Russia 18 B5 61 15N 30 30 E
Lady Elliott I., Australia ... 62 C5 24 7S 152 42 E
Lady Grey, S. Africa ...... 56 E4 30 43S 27 13 E
Ladybrand, S. Africa ...... 56 D4 29 9S 27 29 E
Ladysmith, Canada 70 D4 49 0N 123 49W
Ladysmith, S. Africa ...... 57 D4 28 32S 29 46 E
Ladysmith, U.S.A. 80 C9 45 28N 91 12W
Lae, Papua N. G. .... 64 H6 6 40S 147 2 E
Laem Khat, Thailand ..... 39 a 9 25N 99 56 E
Laem Nga, Thailand ...... 39 a 7 55N 98 27 E
Laem Ngop, Thailand ..... 39 F4 12 10N 102 26 E
Laem Phan Wa, Thailand .. 39 a 7 47N 98 25 E
Laem Pho, Thailand ...... 39 J3 6 55N 101 19 E
Laem Phrom Thep, Thailand 39 a 7 45N 98 19 E
Laem Riang, Thailand .... 39 a 8 7N 98 27 E
Laem Sam Rong, Thailand .. 39 a 9 35N 100 4 E
Laem Son, Thailand ...... 39 b 7 59N 98 16 E
Laem Yamu, Thailand ..... 39 a 7 59N 98 26 E
Læsø, Denmark .... 9 H14 57 15N 11 5 E
Lafayette, Colo., U.S.A. ... 76 F2 39 58N 105 12W
Lafayette, Ind., U.S.A. 82 E2 40 25N 86 54W
Lafayette, La., U.S.A. 81 K9 30 14N 92 1W
Lafayette, Tenn., U.S.A. ... 83 G2 36 31N 86 2W
Laferte ➤, Canada 70 A5 61 53N 117 44W
Lafia, Nigeria .... 50 G7 8 30N 8 34 E
Lafleche, Canada 71 D7 49 45N 106 40W
Lagan ➤, U.K. 10 B6 54 36N 5 55W
Lagarfljót ➤, Iceland 8 D6 65 40N 14 18W
Lågen ➤, Oppland, Norway . 9 F14 61 8N 10 25 E
Lågen ➤, Vestfold, Norway . 9 G14 59 3N 10 3 E
Laghouat, Algeria .... 50 B6 33 50N 2 59 E
Lagoa do Peixe △, Brazil .. 95 C5 31 12S 50 55W
Lagoa Vermelha, Brazil 95 B5 28 13S 51 32W
Lagonoy G., Phil. .... 37 B6 13 50N 123 50 E
Lagos, Nigeria .... 50 G6 6 25N 3 27 E
Lagos, Portugal 21 D1 37 5N 8 41W
Lagos de Moreno, Mexico .. 86 C4 21 21N 101 55W
Lagrange, Australia ...... 60 C3 18 45S 121 43 E
Lagrange B., Australia .... 60 C3 18 38S 121 42 E
Laguna, Brazil 95 B6 28 30S 48 50W
Laguna, U.S.A. 77 J10 35 2N 107 25W
Laguna Beach, U.S.A. 79 M9 33 33N 117 47W
Laguna de la Restinga △,
  Venezuela 89 D6 10 58N 64 0W
Laguna del Laja △, Chile ... 94 D1 37 27S 71 20W
Laguna del Tigre △, Guatemala 88 C1 17 32N 90 56W
Laguna Limpia, Argentina .. 94 B4 26 32S 59 45W
Lagunas, Chile 94 A2 21 0S 69 45W
Lagunas, Peru 92 E3 5 10S 75 35W
Lagunas de Chacahua △, Mexico 87 D5 16 0N 97 43W
Lagunas de Montebello △,
  Mexico 87 D6 16 8N 91 41W
Lahad Datu, Malaysia ..... 37 C5 5 0N 118 20 E
Lahad Datu, Teluk, Malaysia 37 D5 4 50N 118 20 E
Lahan Sai, Thailand ...... 38 E4 14 25N 102 52 E
Lahanam, Laos .... 38 D5 16 16N 105 16 E
Lahar, India .... 43 F8 26 12N 78 57 E
Laharpur, India .... 43 F9 27 43N 80 56 E
Lahat, Indonesia .... 36 E2 3 45S 103 30 E
Lahewa, Indonesia .... 36 D1 1 22N 97 12 E
Lāhījān, Iran .... 45 B6 37 10N 50 6 E
Lahn ➤, Germany .... 16 C4 50 19N 7 37 E
Laholm, Sweden .... 9 H15 56 30N 13 2 E
Lahore, Pakistan .... 42 D6 31 32N 74 22 E
Lahri, Pakistan .... 42 E3 29 11N 68 13 E
Lahti, Finland .... 9 F21 60 58N 25 40 E
Lahtis = Lahti, Finland .... 9 F21 60 58N 25 40 E
Laï, Chad .... 51 G9 9 25N 16 18 E
Lai Chau, Vietnam .... 38 A4 22 5N 103 3 E
Laila = Layla, Si. Arabia ... 47 C4 22 10N 46 40 E
Laingsburg, S. Africa ..... 56 E3 33 9S 20 52 E

Lainio älv ➤, Sweden ..... 8 C20 67 35N 22 40 E
Lairg, U.K. 11 C4 58 2N 4 24W
Laishui, China .... 34 E8 39 23N 115 45 E
Laiwu, China .... 35 F9 36 15N 117 40 E
Laixi, China .... 35 F11 36 50N 120 31 E
Laiyang, China .... 35 F11 36 59N 120 45 E
Laiyuan, China .... 34 E8 39 20N 114 40 E
Laizhou, China .... 35 F10 37 8N 119 57 E
Laizhou Wan, China ...... 35 F10 37 30N 119 30 E
Laja ➤, Mexico 86 C4 20 55N 100 46W
Lajes, Brazil 95 B5 27 48S 50 20W
Lak Sao, Laos .... 38 C5 18 11N 104 59 E
Lakaband, Pakistan ...... 42 D3 31 2N 69 15 E
Lake Alpine, U.S.A. 78 G7 38 29N 120 0W
Lake Andes, U.S.A. 80 D5 43 9N 98 32W
Lake Arthur, U.S.A. 81 K8 30 5N 92 41W
Lake Bindegolly △, Australia 63 D3 28 0S 144 12 E
Lake Cargelligo, Australia .. 63 E4 33 15S 146 22 E
Lake Charles, U.S.A. 81 K8 30 14N 93 13W
Lake City, Colo., U.S.A. ... 77 G10 38 2N 107 19W
Lake City, Fla., U.S.A. 83 K4 30 11N 82 38W
Lake City, Mich., U.S.A. ... 82 C3 44 20N 85 13W
Lake City, Minn., U.S.A. ... 80 C8 44 27N 92 16W
Lake City, Pa., U.S.A. 84 D4 42 1N 80 21W
Lake City, S.C., U.S.A. 83 J6 33 52N 79 45W
Lake Cowichan, Canada ... 70 D4 48 49N 124 3W
Lake District △, U.K. 12 C4 54 30N 3 21W
Lake Elsinore, U.S.A. 79 M9 33 38N 117 20W
Lake Eyre △, Australia .... 63 D2 28 40S 137 10 E
Lake Gairdner △, Australia . 63 E2 31 41S 135 51 E
Lake George, U.S.A. 85 C11 43 26N 73 43W
Lake Grace, Australia ..... 61 F2 33 7S 118 28 E
Lake Harbour = Kimmirut,
  Canada 69 B13 62 50N 69 50W
Lake Havasu City, U.S.A. .. 79 L12 34 27N 114 22W
Lake Hughes, U.S.A. 79 L8 34 41N 118 26W
Lake Isabella, U.S.A. 79 K8 35 38N 118 28W
Lake Jackson, U.S.A. 81 L7 29 3N 95 27W
Lake Junction, U.S.A. 76 D8 44 35N 110 28W
Lake King, Australia ...... 61 F2 33 5S 119 45 E
Lake Lenore, Canada 71 C8 52 24N 104 59W
Lake Louise, Canada 70 C5 51 30N 116 10W
Lake Malawi △, Malawi ... 55 E3 14 2S 34 53 E
Lake Mburo △, Uganda ... 54 C3 0 33S 30 56 E
Lake Mead △, U.S.A. 79 K12 36 15N 114 30W
Lake Meredith △, U.S.A. .. 81 H4 35 50N 101 50W
Lake Mills, U.S.A. 80 D8 43 25N 93 32W
Lake Nakuru △, Kenya .... 54 C4 0 21S 36 8 E
Lake Placid, U.S.A. 85 B11 44 17N 73 59W
Lake Pleasant, U.S.A. 85 C10 43 28N 74 25W
Lake Providence, U.S.A. ... 81 J9 32 48N 91 10W
Lake Roosevelt △, U.S.A. .. 76 C4 47 57N 118 59W
Lake St. Peter, Canada 84 A6 45 18N 78 2W
Lake Superior △, Canada .. 72 C3 47 45N 84 45W
Lake Torrens △, Australia .. 63 E2 30 55S 137 40 E
Lake Village, U.S.A. 81 J9 33 20N 91 17W
Lake Wales, U.S.A. 83 M5 27 54N 81 35W
Lake Worth, U.S.A. 83 M5 26 37N 80 3W
Lakeba, Fiji 59 D9 18 13S 178 47W
Lakefield, Canada 84 B6 44 25N 78 16W
Lakefield △, Australia ..... 62 B3 15 24S 144 26 E
Lakehurst, U.S.A. 85 F10 40 1N 74 19W
Lakeland, Australia ...... 62 B3 15 49S 144 57 E
Lakeland, U.S.A. 83 M5 28 3N 81 57W
Lakemba = Lakeba, Fiji 59 D9 18 13S 178 47W
Lakeport, Calif., U.S.A. 78 F4 39 3N 122 55W
Lakeport, Mich., U.S.A. ... 84 C2 43 7N 82 30W
Lakes Entrance, Australia .. 63 F4 37 50S 148 0 E
Lakeside, Ariz., U.S.A. 77 J9 34 9N 109 58W
Lakeside, Calif., U.S.A. 79 N10 32 52N 116 55W
Lakeside, Nebr., U.S.A. ... 80 D3 42 3N 102 26W
Lakeside, Ohio, U.S.A. 84 E2 41 32N 82 46W
Lakeview, U.S.A. 76 E3 42 11N 120 21W
Lakeville, U.S.A. 80 C8 44 39N 93 14W
Lakewood, Colo., U.S.A. ... 80 F2 39 44N 105 5W
Lakewood, N.J., U.S.A. 85 F10 40 6N 74 13W
Lakewood, N.Y., U.S.A. 84 D5 42 6N 79 19W
Lakewood, Ohio, U.S.A. ... 84 E3 41 29N 81 48W
Lakewood, Wash., U.S.A. .. 78 C4 47 11N 122 32W
Lakha, India .... 42 F4 26 9N 70 54 E
Lakhaniá, Greece .... 25 D9 35 58N 27 54 E
Lakhimpur, India .... 43 F9 27 57N 80 46 E
Lakhnadon, India .... 43 H8 22 58N 79 36 E
Lakhnau = Lucknow, India . 43 F9 26 50N 81 0 E
Lakhonpheng, Laos ...... 38 E5 15 54N 105 34 E
Lakhpat, India .... 42 H3 23 48N 68 47 E
Lakin, U.S.A. 81 G4 37 57N 101 15W
Lakitusaki ➤, Canada 72 B3 54 21N 82 25W
Lakki, Pakistan .... 42 C4 32 36N 70 55 E
Lákkoi, Greece .... 25 D5 35 24N 23 57 E
Lakonikós Kólpos, Greece .. 23 F10 36 40N 22 40 E
Lakota, Ivory C. 50 G4 5 50N 5 30W
Lakota, U.S.A. 80 A5 48 2N 98 21W
Laksar, India .... 42 E8 29 46N 78 3 E
Laksefjorden, Norway .... 8 A21 70 45N 26 50 E
Lakselv, Norway .... 8 A21 70 2N 25 0 E
Lakshadweep Is., India .... 27 H11 10 0N 72 30 E
Lakshmanpur, India ...... 43 H10 22 58N 83 3 E
Lakshmikantapur, India ... 43 H13 22 5N 88 20 E
Lala Musa, Pakistan ..... 42 C5 32 40N 73 57 E
Lalaghat, India .... 41 H18 24 30N 92 40 E
Lalago, Tanzania .... 54 C3 3 28S 33 58 E
Lalapanzi, Zimbabwe ..... 55 F3 19 20S 30 15 E
L'Albufera, Spain 21 C5 39 20N 0 27W
Lalganj, India .... 43 G11 25 52N 85 13 E
Lalgola, India .... 43 G13 24 25N 88 15 E
Lāli, Iran .... 45 C6 32 21N 49 6 E
Lalibela, Ethiopia .... 47 E2 12 3N 39 0 E
Lalín, China .... 35 B14 45 12N 127 0 E
Lalín, Spain 21 A1 42 40N 8 5W
Lalín He ➤, China .... 35 B13 45 32N 125 40 E
Lalitapur, Nepal .... 43 F11 27 40N 85 20 E
Lalitpur, India .... 43 G8 24 42N 78 28 E
Lalkua, India .... 43 E8 29 5N 79 31 E
Lalsot, India .... 42 F7 26 34N 76 20 E
Lam, Vietnam .... 38 B6 21 21N 106 31 E
Lam Pao Res., Thailand ... 38 D4 16 50N 103 15 E
Lamaing, Burma .... 41 M20 15 25N 97 53 E
Lamar, Colo., U.S.A. 80 F3 38 5N 102 37W
Lamar, Mo., U.S.A. 81 G7 37 30N 94 16W
Lamas, Peru 92 E3 6 28S 76 31W
Lambaréné, Gabon ...... 52 E2 0 41S 10 12 E
Lambasa = Labasa, Fiji .... 59 C8 16 30S 179 27 E
Lambay I., Ireland 10 C5 53 29N 6 1W
Lambert Glacier, Antarctica 5 D6 71 0S 70 0 E
Lambert's Bay, S. Africa ... 56 E2 32 5S 18 17 E

Lambeth, *Canada*	84 D3	42 54N 81 18W
Lambomakondro, *Madag.*	57 C7	22 41S 44 44 E
Lambton Shores, *Canada*	84 C3	43 10N 81 56W
Lame Deer, *U.S.A.*	76 D10	45 37N 106 40W
Lamego, *Portugal*	21 B2	41 5N 7 52W
Lamèque, *Canada*	73 C7	47 45N 64 38W
Lameroo, *Australia*	63 F3	35 19S 140 33 E
Lamesa, *U.S.A.*	81 J4	32 44N 101 58W
Lamia, *Greece*	23 E10	38 55N 22 26 E
Lamington △, *Australia*	63 D5	28 13S 153 12 E
Lamma I., *China*	33 G11	22 12N 114 8 E
Lammermuir Hills, *U.K.*	11 F6	55 50N 2 40W
Lamoille ➤, *U.S.A.*	85 B11	44 38N 73 13W
Lamon B., *Phil.*	37 B6	14 30N 122 20 E
Lamont, *Canada*	70 C6	53 46N 112 50W
Lamont, *Calif., U.S.A.*	79 K8	35 15N 118 55W
Lamont, *Wyo., U.S.A.*	76 E10	42 13N 107 29W
Lampa, *Peru*	92 G4	15 22S 70 22W
Lampang, *Thailand*	38 C2	18 16N 99 32 E
Lampasas, *U.S.A.*	81 K5	31 4N 98 11W
Lampazos de Naranjo, *Mexico*	86 B4	27 2N 100 32W
Lampedusa, *Medit. S.*	22 G5	35 36N 12 40 E
Lampeter, *U.K.*	13 E3	52 7N 4 4W
Lampione, *Medit. S.*	22 G5	35 33N 12 20 E
Lampman, *Canada*	71 D8	49 25N 102 50W
Lampung □, *Indonesia*	36 F2	5 30S 104 30 E
Lamta, *India*	43 H9	22 8N 80 7 E
Lamu, *Kenya*	54 C5	2 16S 40 55 E
Lamy, *U.S.A.*	77 J11	35 29N 105 53W
Lanak La, *China*	43 B8	34 27N 79 32 E
Lanak'o Shank'ou = Lanak La, *China*	43 B8	34 27N 79 32 E
Lanark, *Canada*	85 A8	45 1N 76 22W
Lanark, *U.K.*	11 F5	55 40N 3 47W
Lanbi Kyun, *Burma*	39 G2	10 50N 98 20 E
Lancang Jiang ➤, *China*	32 D5	21 40N 101 10 E
Lancashire □, *U.K.*	12 D5	53 50N 2 48W
Lancaster, *Canada*	85 A10	45 10N 74 30W
Lancaster, *U.K.*	12 C5	54 3N 2 48W
Lancaster, *Calif., U.S.A.*	79 L8	34 42N 118 8W
Lancaster, *Ky., U.S.A.*	82 G3	37 37N 84 35W
Lancaster, *N.H., U.S.A.*	85 B13	44 29N 71 34W
Lancaster, *N.Y., U.S.A.*	84 D6	42 54N 78 40W
Lancaster, *Ohio, U.S.A.*	82 F4	39 43N 82 36W
Lancaster, *Pa., U.S.A.*	85 F8	40 2N 76 19W
Lancaster, *S.C., U.S.A.*	83 H5	34 43N 80 46W
Lancaster, *Wis., U.S.A.*	80 D9	42 51N 90 43W
Lancaster Sd., *Canada*	69 A11	74 13N 84 0W
Lancelin, *Australia*	61 F2	31 0S 115 18 E
Lanchow = Lanzhou, *China*	34 F2	36 1N 103 52 E
Lanciano, *Italy*	22 C6	42 14N 14 23 E
Lancun, *China*	35 F11	36 25N 120 10 E
Land Between the Lakes △, *U.S.A.*	83 G1	36 55N 88 7W
Landeck, *Austria*	16 E6	47 9N 10 34 E
Lander, *U.S.A.*	76 E9	42 50N 108 44W
Lander ➤, *Australia*	60 D5	22 0S 132 0 E
Landes, *France*	20 D3	44 0N 1 0W
Landi Kotal, *Pakistan*	42 B4	34 7N 71 6 E
Landisburg, *U.S.A.*	84 F7	40 21N 77 19W
Land's End, *U.K.*	13 G2	50 4N 5 44W
Landsborough Cr. ➤, *Australia*	62 C3	22 28S 144 35 E
Landshut, *Germany*	16 D7	48 34N 12 8 E
Landskrona, *Sweden*	9 J15	55 53N 12 50 E
Lanesboro, *U.S.A.*	85 E9	41 57N 75 34W
Lanett, *U.S.A.*	83 J3	32 52N 85 12W
Lang Qua, *Vietnam*	38 A5	22 16N 104 27 E
Lang Shan, *China*	34 D4	41 0N 106 30 E
Lang Son, *Vietnam*	38 B6	21 52N 106 42 E
Lang Suan, *Thailand*	39 H2	9 57N 99 4 E
La'nga Co, *China*	41 D12	30 45N 81 15 E
Langar, *Iran*	45 C9	35 23N 60 25 E
Langara I., *Canada*	70 C2	54 14N 133 1W
Langdon, *U.S.A.*	80 A5	48 45N 98 22W
Langeberg, *S. Africa*	56 E3	33 55S 21 0 E
Langeberge, *S. Africa*	56 D3	28 15S 22 33 E
Langeland, *Denmark*	9 J14	54 56N 10 48 E
Langenburg, *Canada*	71 C8	50 51N 101 43W
Langholm, *U.K.*	11 F5	55 9N 3 0W
Langjökull, *Iceland*	8 D3	64 39N 20 12W
Langkawi, Pulau, *Malaysia*	39 J2	6 25N 99 45 E
Langklip, *S. Africa*	56 D3	28 12S 20 20 E
Langkon, *Malaysia*	36 C5	6 30N 116 40 E
Langlade, *St-P. & M.*	73 C8	46 50N 56 20W
Langley, *Canada*	78 A4	49 7N 122 39W
Langøya, *Norway*	8 B16	68 45N 14 50 E
Langreo, *Spain*	21 A3	43 18N 5 40W
Langres, *France*	20 C6	47 52N 5 20 E
Langres, Plateau de, *France*	20 C6	47 45N 5 3 E
Langsa, *Indonesia*	36 D1	4 30N 97 57 E
Langtry, *U.S.A.*	81 L4	29 49N 101 34W
Langu, *Thailand*	39 J2	6 53N 99 47 E
Languedoc, *France*	20 E5	43 58N 3 55 E
Langwang, *China*	33 F9	22 38N 113 27 E
Langxiangzhen, *China*	34 E9	39 43N 116 8 E
Lanigan, *Canada*	71 C7	51 51N 105 2W
Lankao, *China*	34 G8	34 48N 114 50 E
Länkäran, *Azerbaijan*	19 G8	38 48N 48 52 E
Lannion, *France*	20 B2	48 46N 3 29W
L'Annonciation, *Canada*	72 C5	46 25N 74 55W
Lansdale, *U.S.A.*	85 F9	40 14N 75 17W
Lansdowne, *Australia*	63 E5	31 48S 152 30 E
Lansdowne, *Canada*	85 B8	44 24N 76 1W
Lansdowne, *India*	43 E8	29 50N 78 41 E
Lansdowne House, *Canada*	72 B2	52 14N 87 53W
L'Anse, *U.S.A.*	82 B1	46 45N 88 27W
L'Anse au Loup, *Canada*	73 B8	51 32N 56 50W
L'Anse aux Meadows, *Canada*	73 B8	51 36N 55 32W
L'Anse la Raye, *St. Lucia*	89 f	13 55N 61 19W
Lansford, *U.S.A.*	85 F9	40 50N 75 53W
Lansing, *U.S.A.*	82 D3	42 44N 84 33W
Lanta Yai, Ko, *Thailand*	39 J2	7 35N 99 3 E
Lantau I., *China*	33 G10	22 15N 113 56 E
Lantian, *China*	34 G5	34 11N 109 20 E
Lanus, *Argentina*	94 C4	34 44S 58 27W
Lanusei, *Italy*	22 E3	39 52N 9 34 E
Lanzarote, *Canary Is.*	24 F6	29 0N 13 40W
Lanzarote ✕ (ACE), *Canary Is.*	24 F6	28 57N 13 40W
Lanzhou, *China*	34 F2	36 1N 103 52 E
Lao Bao, *Laos*	38 D6	16 35N 106 30 E
Lao Cai, *Vietnam*	38 A4	22 30N 103 57 E
Laoag, *Phil.*	37 A6	18 7N 120 34 E
Laoang, *Phil.*	37 B7	12 32N 125 8 E
Laoha He ➤, *China*	35 C11	43 25N 120 35 E
Laois □, *Ireland*	10 D4	52 57N 7 36W
Laon, *France*	20 B5	49 33N 3 35 E

Laona, *U.S.A.*	82 C1	45 34N 88 40W
Laos ■, *Asia*	38 D5	17 45N 105 0 E
Lapa, *Brazil*	95 B6	25 46S 49 44W
Lapeer, *U.S.A.*	82 D4	43 3N 83 19W
Lapithos, *Cyprus*	25 D12	35 21N 33 11 E
Lapland = Lappland, *Europe*	8 B21	68 7N 24 0 E
Laporte, *U.S.A.*	85 E8	41 25N 76 30W
Lappeenranta, *Finland*	9 F23	61 3N 28 12 E
Lappland, *Europe*	8 B21	68 7N 24 0 E
Laprida, *Argentina*	94 D3	37 34S 60 45W
Lapseki, *Turkey*	23 D12	40 20N 26 41 E
Laptev Sea, *Russia*	29 B13	76 0N 125 0 E
Lapua, *Finland*	8 E20	62 58N 23 0 E
L'Áquila, *Italy*	22 C5	42 22N 13 22 E
Lár, *Ázarbájān-e Sharqí, Iran*	44 B5	38 30N 47 52 E
Lár, *Fárs, Iran*	45 E7	27 40N 54 14 E
Laramie, *U.S.A.*	80 E2	41 19N 105 35W
Laramie ➤, *U.S.A.*	76 F11	42 13N 104 33W
Laramie Mts., *U.S.A.*	80 E2	42 0N 105 30W
Laranjeiras do Sul, *Brazil*	95 B5	25 23S 52 23W
Larantuka, *Indonesia*	37 F6	8 21S 122 55 E
Larat, *Indonesia*	37 F8	7 0S 132 0 E
Larde, *Mozam.*	55 F4	16 28S 39 43 E
Larder Lake, *Canada*	72 C4	48 5N 79 40W
Lardhos, Ákra = Líndhos, Ákra, *Greece*	25 C10	36 4N 28 10 E
Lardhos, Órmos, *Greece*	25 C10	36 4N 28 2 E
Laredo, *U.S.A.*	81 M5	27 30N 99 30W
Laredo Sd., *Canada*	70 C3	52 30N 128 53W
Largo, *U.S.A.*	83 M4	27 55N 82 47W
Largs, *U.K.*	11 F4	55 47N 4 52W
Lariang, *Indonesia*	37 E5	1 26S 119 17 E
Larimore, *U.S.A.*	80 B6	47 54N 97 38W
Lárisa, *Greece*	23 E10	39 36N 22 27 E
Larkana, *Pakistan*	42 F3	27 32N 68 18 E
Larnaca, *Cyprus*	25 E12	34 55N 33 38 E
Larnaca Bay, *Cyprus*	25 E12	34 53N 33 45 E
Larne, *U.K.*	10 B6	54 51N 5 51W
Larned, *U.S.A.*	80 F5	38 11N 99 6W
Larose, *U.S.A.*	81 L9	29 34N 90 23W
Larrimah, *Australia*	60 C5	15 35S 133 12 E
Larsen Ice Shelf, *Antarctica*	5 C17	67 0S 62 0W
Larvik, *Norway*	9 G14	59 4N 10 2 E
Las Animas, *U.S.A.*	80 F3	38 4N 103 13W
Las Anod, *Somali Rep.*	47 F4	8 26N 47 19 E
Las Aves, Is., *W. Indies*	89 C7	15 45N 63 55W
Las Breñas, *Argentina*	94 B3	27 5S 61 7W
Las Cañadas del Teide △, *Canary Is.*	24 F3	28 15N 16 37W
Las Cejas, *Argentina*	96 B4	26 53S 64 44W
Las Chimeneas, *Mexico*	79 N10	32 8N 116 5W
Las Cruces, *U.S.A.*	77 K10	32 19N 106 47W
Las Flores, *Argentina*	94 D4	36 10S 59 7W
Las Heras, *Argentina*	94 C2	32 51S 68 49W
Las Lajas, *Argentina*	96 D2	38 30S 70 25W
Las Lomitas, *Argentina*	94 A3	24 43S 60 35W
Las Palmas, *Argentina*	94 B4	27 8S 58 45W
Las Palmas, *Canary Is.*	24 F4	28 7N 15 26W
Las Palmas ➤, *Mexico*	79 N10	32 26N 116 54W
Las Palmas ✕ (LPA), *Canary Is.*	24 G4	27 55N 15 25W
Las Palmas de Cocalán △, *Chile*	94 C1	34 18S 71 4W
Las Piedras, *Uruguay*	95 C4	34 44S 56 14W
Las Pipinas, *Argentina*	94 D4	35 30S 57 19W
Las Plumas, *Argentina*	96 E3	43 40S 67 15W
Las Rosas, *Argentina*	94 C3	32 30S 61 35W
Las Tablas, *Panama*	88 E3	7 49N 80 14W
Las Termas, *Argentina*	94 B3	27 29S 64 52W
Las Toscas, *Argentina*	94 B4	28 21S 59 18W
Las Truchas, *Mexico*	86 D4	17 57N 102 13W
Las Varillas, *Argentina*	94 C3	31 50S 62 50W
Las Vegas, *N. Mex., U.S.A.*	77 J11	35 36N 105 13W
Las Vegas, *Nev., U.S.A.*	79 J11	36 10N 115 9W
Las Vegas McCarran International ✕ (LAS), *U.S.A.*	79 J11	36 5N 115 9W
Lascano, *Uruguay*	95 C5	33 35S 54 12W
Lash-e Joveyn, *Afghan.*	40 D2	31 45N 61 30 E
Lashburn, *Canada*	71 C7	53 10N 109 40W
Lashio, *Burma*	41 H20	22 56N 97 45 E
Lashkar, *India*	42 F8	26 10N 78 10 E
Lasithi, *Greece*	25 D7	35 11N 25 31 E
Lasithi □, *Greece*	25 D7	35 5N 25 50 E
Lāsjerd, *Iran*	45 C7	35 24N 53 4 E
Lassen Pk., *U.S.A.*	76 F3	40 29N 121 31W
Lassen Volcanic △, *U.S.A.*	76 F3	40 30N 121 20W
Last Mountain L., *Canada*	71 C7	51 5N 105 14W
Lastchance Cr. ➤, *U.S.A.*	78 E5	40 2N 121 15W
Lastoursville, *Gabon*	52 E2	0 55S 12 38 E
Lastovo, *Croatia*	22 C7	42 46N 16 55 E
Lat Yao, *Thailand*	38 E2	15 45N 99 48 E
Latacunga, *Ecuador*	92 D3	0 50S 78 35W
Latakia = Al Lādhiqīyah, *Syria*	44 C2	35 30N 35 45 E
Latchford, *Canada*	72 C4	47 20N 79 50W
Latehar, *India*	43 H11	23 45N 84 30 E
Latham, *Australia*	61 E2	29 44S 116 20 E
Lathi, *India*	42 F4	27 43N 71 23 E
Lathrop Wells, *U.S.A.*	79 J10	36 39N 116 24W
Latina, *Italy*	22 D5	41 28N 12 52 E
Latium = Lazio □, *Italy*	22 C5	42 10N 12 30 E
Laton, *U.S.A.*	78 J7	36 26N 119 41W
Latouche Treville, C., *Australia*	60 C3	18 27S 121 49 E
Latrobe, *Australia*	63 G4	41 14S 146 30 E
Latrobe, *U.S.A.*	84 F5	40 19N 79 23W
Latvia ■, *Europe*	9 H20	56 50N 24 0 E
Lau Fau Shan, *China*	33 G10	22 28N 113 59 E
Lau Group, *Fiji*	59 C9	17 0S 178 30W
Lauchhammer, *Germany*	16 C7	51 29N 13 47 E
Laughlin, *U.S.A.*	77 J6	35 8N 114 35W
Laukaa, *Finland*	9 E21	62 24N 25 56 E
Launceston, *Australia*	63 G4	41 24S 147 8 E
Launceston, *U.K.*	13 G3	50 38N 4 22W
Laune ➤, *Ireland*	10 D2	52 7N 9 47W
Launglon Bok, *Burma*	38 F1	13 50N 97 54 E
Laura, *Australia*	62 B3	15 32S 144 32 E
Laurel, *Miss., U.S.A.*	81 K10	31 41N 89 8W
Laurel, *Mont., U.S.A.*	76 D9	45 40N 108 46W
Laurencekirk, *U.K.*	11 E6	56 50N 2 28W
Laurens, *U.S.A.*	83 H4	34 30N 82 1W
Laurentian Plateau, *Canada*	73 B6	52 0N 70 0W
Lauria, *Italy*	22 E6	40 2N 15 50 E
Laurie L., *Canada*	71 B8	56 35N 101 57W
Laurinburg, *U.S.A.*	83 H6	34 47N 79 28W
Laurium, *U.S.A.*	82 B1	47 14N 88 27W
Lausanne, *Switz.*	20 C7	46 32N 6 38 E
Laut, *Indonesia*	36 D3	4 45N 108 0 E
Laut, Pulau, *Indonesia*	36 E5	3 40S 116 10 E
Laut Kecil, Kepulauan, *Indonesia*	36 E5	4 45S 115 40 E
Lautoka, *Fiji*	59 C7	17 37S 177 27 E

Lava Beds △, *U.S.A.*	76 F3	41 40N 121 30W
Lavagh More, *Ireland*	10 B3	54 46N 8 6W
Laval, *France*	20 B3	48 4N 0 48W
Lavalle, *Argentina*	94 B2	28 15S 65 15W
Lavant Station, *Canada*	85 A8	45 3N 76 42W
Lāvar Meydān, *Iran*	45 D7	30 20N 54 30 E
Laverton, *Australia*	61 E3	28 44S 122 29 E
Lavras, *Brazil*	95 A7	21 20S 45 0W
Lávrion, *Greece*	23 F11	37 40N 24 4 E
Lávris, *Greece*	25 D6	35 25N 24 40 E
Lavumisa, *Swaziland*	57 D5	27 20S 31 55 E
Lavushi Manda △, *Zambia*	55 E3	12 45S 31 0 E
Lawas, *Malaysia*	36 D5	4 55N 115 25 E
Lawele, *Indonesia*	37 F6	5 13S 122 57 E
Lawn Hill △, *Australia*	62 B2	18 15S 138 6 E
Lawng Pit, *Burma*	41 G20	25 30N 97 25 E
Lawqah, *Si. Arabia*	44 D4	29 49N 42 45 E
Lawrence, *N.Z.*	59 L2	45 55S 169 41 E
Lawrence, *Kans., U.S.A.*	80 F7	38 58N 95 14W
Lawrence, *Mass., U.S.A.*	85 D13	42 43N 71 10W
Lawrenceburg, *Ind., U.S.A.*	82 F3	39 6N 84 52W
Lawrenceburg, *Tenn., U.S.A.*	83 H2	35 14N 87 20W
Lawrenceville, *Ga., U.S.A.*	83 J4	33 57N 83 59W
Lawrenceville, *Pa., U.S.A.*	84 E7	41 59N 77 8W
Laws, *U.S.A.*	78 H8	37 24N 118 20W
Lawton, *U.S.A.*	81 H5	34 37N 98 25W
Lawu, *Indonesia*	37 G14	7 40S 111 13 E
Laxford, L., *U.K.*	11 C3	58 24N 5 6W
Layla, *Si. Arabia*	47 C4	22 10N 46 40 E
Laylān, *Iraq*	44 C5	35 18N 44 31 E
Layton, *U.S.A.*	76 F7	41 4N 111 58W
Laytonville, *U.S.A.*	76 G2	39 41N 123 29W
Lazarivo, *Madag.*	57 C8	23 54S 44 59 E
Lazio □, *Italy*	22 C5	42 10N 12 30 E
Lazo, *Russia*	30 C6	43 25N 133 55 E
Le Bic, *Canada*	73 C6	48 20N 68 41W
Le Creusot, *France*	20 C6	46 48N 4 24 E
Le François, *Martinique*	88 c	14 38N 60 57W
Le Havre, *France*	20 B4	49 30N 0 5 E
Le Lamentin, *Martinique*	88 c	14 35N 61 2W
Le Mans, *France*	20 C4	48 0N 0 10 E
Le Marin, *Martinique*	88 c	14 27N 60 55W
Le Mars, *U.S.A.*	80 D6	42 47N 96 10W
Le Mont-St-Michel, *France*	20 B3	48 40N 1 30W
Le Prêcheur, *Martinique*	88 c	14 50N 61 12W
Le Puy-en-Velay, *France*	20 D5	45 3N 3 52 E
Le Robert, *Martinique*	88 c	14 40N 60 56W
Le St-Esprit, *Martinique*	88 c	14 34N 60 56W
Le Sueur, *U.S.A.*	80 C8	44 28N 93 55W
Le Thuy, *Vietnam*	38 D6	17 14N 106 49 E
Le Touquet-Paris-Plage, *France*	20 A4	50 30N 1 36 E
Le Tréport, *France*	20 A4	50 3N 1 20 E
Le Verdon-sur-Mer, *France*	20 D3	45 33N 1 4W
Lea ➤, *U.K.*	13 F8	51 31N 0 1 E
Leach, *Cambodia*	39 F4	12 21N 103 46 E
Lead, *U.S.A.*	80 C3	44 21N 103 46W
Leader, *Canada*	71 C7	50 50N 109 30W
Leadville, *U.S.A.*	77 G10	39 15N 106 18W
Leaf ➤, *U.S.A.*	81 K10	30 59N 88 44W
Leaf Rapids, *Canada*	71 B9	56 30N 99 59W
Leamington, *Canada*	84 D2	42 3N 82 36W
Leamington, *U.S.A.*	76 G7	39 32N 112 17W
Leamington Spa = Royal Leamington Spa, *U.K.*	13 E6	52 18N 1 31W
Leandro Norte Alem, *Argentina*	95 B4	27 34S 55 15W
Leane, L., *Ireland*	10 D2	52 2N 9 32W
Learmonth, *Australia*	60 D1	22 13S 114 10 E
Leask, *Canada*	71 C7	53 5N 106 45W
Leatherhead, *U.K.*	13 F7	51 18N 0 20W
Leavenworth, *Kans., U.S.A.*	80 F7	39 19N 94 55W
Leavenworth, *Wash., U.S.A.*	76 C3	47 36N 120 40W
Lebak, *Phil.*	37 C6	6 32N 124 5 E
Lebam, *U.S.A.*	78 D3	46 34N 123 33W
Lebanon, *Ind., U.S.A.*	82 E2	40 3N 86 28W
Lebanon, *Kans., U.S.A.*	80 F5	39 49N 98 33W
Lebanon, *Ky., U.S.A.*	82 G3	37 34N 85 15W
Lebanon, *Mo., U.S.A.*	81 G8	37 41N 92 40W
Lebanon, *N.H., U.S.A.*	85 C12	43 39N 72 15W
Lebanon, *Oreg., U.S.A.*	76 D2	44 32N 122 55W
Lebanon, *Pa., U.S.A.*	85 F8	40 20N 76 26W
Lebanon, *Tenn., U.S.A.*	83 G2	36 12N 86 18W
Lebanon ■, *Asia*	46 B5	34 0N 36 0 E
Lebec, *U.S.A.*	79 L8	34 50N 118 52W
Lebel-sur-Quévillon, *Canada*	72 C4	49 3N 76 59W
Lebombo-berge, *S. Africa*	57 C5	24 30S 32 0 E
Lębork, *Poland*	17 A9	54 33N 17 46 E
Lebrija, *Spain*	21 D2	36 53N 6 5W
Lebu, *Chile*	94 D1	37 40S 73 47W
Lecce, *Italy*	23 D8	40 23N 18 11 E
Lecco, *Italy*	20 D8	45 51N 9 23 E
Lech ➤, *Germany*	16 D6	48 43N 10 56 E
Lecontes Mills, *U.S.A.*	84 E6	41 5N 78 17W
Łęczyca, *Poland*	17 B10	52 5N 19 15 E
Ledong, *China*	38 C7	18 41N 109 5 E
Leduc, *Canada*	70 C6	53 15N 113 30W
Lee, *U.S.A.*	85 D11	42 19N 73 15W
Lee ➤, *Ireland*	10 E3	51 53N 8 56W
Lee Vining, *U.S.A.*	78 H7	37 58N 119 7W
Leech L., *U.S.A.*	80 B7	47 10N 94 24W
Leechburg, *U.S.A.*	84 F5	40 37N 79 36W
Leeds, *U.K.*	12 D6	53 48N 1 33W
Leeds, *U.S.A.*	83 J2	33 33N 86 33W
Leek, *Neths.*	15 A6	53 10N 6 24 E
Leek, *U.K.*	12 D5	53 7N 2 1W
Leeman, *Australia*	61 E1	29 57S 114 58 E
Leeper, *U.S.A.*	84 E5	41 22N 79 18W
Leer, *Germany*	16 B4	53 13N 7 26 E
Leesburg, *U.S.A.*	83 L5	28 49N 81 53W
Leeton, *Australia*	63 E4	34 33S 146 23 E
Leetonia, *U.S.A.*	84 F4	40 53N 80 45W
Leeu Gamka, *S. Africa*	56 E3	32 47S 21 59 E
Leeuwarden, *Neths.*	15 A5	53 15N 5 48 E
Leeuwin, C., *Australia*	61 F2	34 20S 115 9 E
Leeuwin Naturaliste △, *Australia*	61 F2	34 23S 115 9 E
Leeward Is., *Atl. Oc.*	89 C7	16 30N 63 30W
Lefka, *Cyprus*	25 D11	35 6N 32 51 E
Lefkoniko, *Cyprus*	25 D12	35 18N 33 44 E
Lefroy, *Canada*	84 B5	44 16N 79 34W
Lefroy, L., *Australia*	61 F3	31 21S 121 40 E
Leganés, *Spain*	21 B4	40 19N 3 45W
Legazpi, *Phil.*	37 B6	13 10N 123 45 E
Legendre I., *Australia*	60 D2	20 22S 116 55 E
Legionowo, *Poland*	17 B11	52 25N 20 50 E
Legnago, *Italy*	22 B4	45 11N 11 18 E
Legnica, *Poland*	16 C9	51 12N 16 10 E

Leh, *India*	43 B7	34 9N 77 35 E
Lehigh Acres, *U.S.A.*	83 M5	26 36N 81 39W
Lehighton, *U.S.A.*	85 F9	40 50N 75 43W
Lehututu, *Botswana*	56 C3	23 54S 21 55 E
Leiah, *Pakistan*	42 D4	30 58N 70 58 E
Leicester, *U.K.*	13 E6	52 38N 1 8W
Leicester City □, *U.K.*	13 E6	52 38N 1 8W
Leicestershire □, *U.K.*	13 E6	52 41N 1 17W
Leichhardt ➤, *Australia*	62 B2	17 35S 139 48 E
Leichhardt Ra., *Australia*	62 C4	20 46S 147 40 E
Leiden, *Neths.*	15 B4	52 9N 4 30 E
Leie ➤, *Belgium*	15 C3	51 2N 3 45 E
Leine ➤, *Germany*	16 B5	52 43N 9 36 E
Leinster, *Australia*	61 E3	27 51S 120 36 E
Leinster □, *Ireland*	10 C4	53 3N 7 8W
Leinster, Mt., *Ireland*	10 D5	52 37N 6 46W
Leipzig, *Germany*	16 C7	51 18N 12 22 E
Leiria, *Portugal*	21 C1	39 46N 8 53W
Leirvik, *Norway*	9 G11	59 47N 5 28 E
Leisler, Mt., *Australia*	60 D4	23 23S 129 20 E
Leith, *U.K.*	11 F5	55 59N 3 11W
Leith Hill, *U.K.*	13 F7	51 11N 0 22W
Leitrim, *Ireland*	10 B3	54 0N 8 5W
Leitrim □, *Ireland*	10 B4	54 8N 8 0W
Leizhou Bandao, *China*	33 D6	21 0N 110 0 E
Lek ➤, *Neths.*	15 C4	51 54N 4 35 E
Leka, *Norway*	8 D14	65 5N 11 35 E
Lékva Óros, *Greece*	25 D6	35 18N 24 3 E
Leland, *Mich., U.S.A.*	82 C3	45 1N 85 45W
Leland, *Miss., U.S.A.*	81 J9	33 24N 90 54W
Léman, L., *Europe*	20 C7	46 26N 6 30 E
Lembar, *Indonesia*	37 K19	8 45S 116 4 E
Lembuak, *Indonesia*	37 K19	8 36S 116 11 E
Lemera, *Dem. Rep. of the Congo*	54 C2	3 0S 28 55 E
Lemhi Ra., *U.S.A.*	76 D7	44 30N 113 30W
Lemmer, *Neths.*	15 B5	52 51N 5 43 E
Lemmon, *U.S.A.*	80 C3	45 57N 102 10W
Lemon Grove, *U.S.A.*	79 N9	32 45N 117 2W
Lemoore, *U.S.A.*	78 J7	36 18N 119 46W
Lemvig, *Denmark*	9 H13	56 33N 8 20 E
Lena ➤, *Russia*	29 B13	72 52N 126 40 E
Léndas, *Greece*	25 E6	34 56N 24 56 E
Lendeh, *Iran*	45 D6	30 58N 50 25 E
Lenggong, *Malaysia*	39 K3	5 6N 100 58 E
Lengua de Vaca, Pta., *Chile*	94 C1	30 14S 71 38W
Lengwe △, *Malawi*	55 F3	16 14S 34 45 E
Leninogorsk, *Kazakhstan*	28 D9	50 20N 83 30 E
Leninsk, *Russia*	19 E8	48 40N 45 15 E
Leninsk-Kuznetskiy, *Russia*	28 D9	54 44N 86 10 E
Lenkoran = Länkäran, *Azerbaijan*	19 G8	38 48N 48 52 E
Lenmalu, *Indonesia*	37 E8	1 45S 130 15 E
Lennox, *U.S.A.*	80 D6	43 21N 96 53W
Lennoxville, *Canada*	85 A13	45 22N 71 51W
Lenoir, *U.S.A.*	83 H5	35 55N 81 32W
Lenoir City, *U.S.A.*	83 H3	35 48N 84 16W
Lenore L., *Canada*	71 C8	52 30N 104 59W
Lenox, *U.S.A.*	85 D11	42 22N 73 17W
Lens, *France*	20 A5	50 26N 2 50 E
Lensk, *Russia*	29 C12	60 48N 114 55 E
Lentini, *Italy*	22 F6	37 17N 15 0 E
Lenwood, *U.S.A.*	79 L9	34 53N 117 7W
Lenya, *Burma*	36 B1	11 33N 98 57 E
Leoben, *Austria*	16 E8	47 22N 15 5 E
Leodhas = Lewis, *U.K.*	11 C2	58 9N 6 40W
Leola, *U.S.A.*	80 C5	45 43N 98 56W
Leominster, *U.K.*	13 E5	52 14N 2 43W
Leominster, *U.S.A.*	85 D13	42 32N 71 46W
León, *Mexico*	86 C4	21 7N 101 40W
León, *Nic.*	88 D2	12 20N 86 51W
León, *Spain*	21 A3	42 38N 5 34W
Leon, *U.S.A.*	80 E8	40 44N 93 45W
León ➤, *U.S.A.*	81 K6	31 14N 97 28W
León, Montes de, *Spain*	21 A2	42 30N 6 18W
Leonardtown, *U.S.A.*	82 F7	38 17N 76 38W
Leonardville, *Namibia*	56 C2	23 29S 18 49 E
Leongatha, *Australia*	63 F4	38 30S 145 58 E
Leonora, *Australia*	61 E3	28 49S 121 19 E
Leopoldina, *Brazil*	95 A7	21 28S 42 40W
Leopoldsburg, *Belgium*	15 C5	51 7N 5 13 E
Leoti, *U.S.A.*	80 F4	38 29N 101 21W
Leova, *Moldova*	17 E15	46 28N 28 15 E
Leoville, *Canada*	71 C7	53 39N 107 33W
Lepel = Lyepyel, *Belarus*	18 D4	54 50N 28 40 E
Lépo, L. do, *Angola*	56 B2	17 0S 19 0 E
Leppävirta, *Finland*	9 E22	62 29N 27 46 E
Lerdo, *Mexico*	86 B4	25 32N 103 32W
Leribe, *Lesotho*	57 D4	28 51S 28 3 E
Lérida = Lleida, *Spain*	21 B6	41 37N 0 39 E
Lerwick, *U.K.*	11 A7	60 9N 1 9W
Les Cayes, *Haiti*	89 C5	18 15N 73 46W
Les Coteaux, *Canada*	85 A10	45 15N 74 13W
Les Sables-d'Olonne, *France*	20 C3	46 30N 1 45W
Lesbos = Lésvos, *Greece*	23 E12	39 10N 26 20 E
Leshan, *China*	32 D5	29 33N 103 41 E
Leshukonskoye, *Russia*	18 B8	64 54N 45 46 E
Leshwe △, *Dem. Rep. of the Congo*	55 E2	12 45S 29 30 E
Leskov I., *Antarctica*	5 B1	56 0S 28 0W
Leskovac, *Serbia & M.*	23 C9	43 0N 21 58 E
Lesopilnoye, *Russia*	30 A7	46 44N 134 20 E
Lesotho ■, *Africa*	57 D4	29 40S 28 0 E
Lesozavodsk, *Russia*	29 E14	45 30N 133 29 E
Lesse ➤, *Belgium*	15 D4	50 15N 4 54 E
Lesse et Lomme △, *Belgium*	15 D5	50 8N 5 9 E
Lesser Antilles, *W. Indies*	89 D7	15 0N 61 0W
Lesser Slave L., *Canada*	70 B5	55 30N 115 25W
Lesser Sunda Is., *Indonesia*	37 F6	8 0S 120 0 E
Lessines, *Belgium*	15 D3	50 42N 3 50 E
Lester, *U.S.A.*	78 C5	47 12N 121 29W
Lester B. Pearson International, Toronto ✕ (YYZ), *Canada*	84 C5	43 46N 79 37W
Lestock, *Canada*	71 C8	51 19N 103 59W
Lesuer I., *Australia*	60 B4	13 50S 127 17 E
Lesueur △, *Australia*	61 F2	30 11S 115 10 E
Lésvos, *Greece*	23 E12	39 10N 26 20 E
Leszno, *Poland*	17 C9	51 50N 16 30 E
Letaba, *S. Africa*	57 C5	23 59S 31 50 E
Letchworth, *U.K.*	13 F7	51 59N 0 13W
Lethbridge, *Canada*	70 D6	49 45N 112 45W
Lethem, *Guyana*	92 C7	3 20N 59 50W
Leti, Kepulauan, *Indonesia*	37 F7	8 10S 128 0 E
Leti Is. = Leti, Kepulauan, *Indonesia*	37 F7	8 10S 128 0 E
Letiahau ➤, *Botswana*	56 C3	21 16S 24 0 E
Leticia, *Colombia*	92 D5	4 9S 70 0W

Leting, China . . . . 35 E10 39 23N 118 55 E
Letjiesbos, S. Africa . . . . 56 E3 32 34S 22 16 E
Letlhakane, Botswana . . . . . . 56 C4 21 27S 25 30 E
Letlhakeng, Botswana . . . . . . 56 C3 24 0S 24 59 E
Letong, Indonesia . . . . 36 D3 2 58N 105 42 E
Letpadan, Burma . . . . 41 L19 17 45N 95 45 E
Letpan, Burma . . . . 41 K19 19 28N 94 10 E
Letsôk-aw Kyun, Burma . . . . . 39 G2 11 30N 98 25 E
Letterkenny, Ireland 10 B4 54 57N 7 45W
Leucadia, U.S.A. 79 M9 33 4N 117 18W
Leuchars, U.K. 11 E6 56 24N 2 53W
Leuser, G., Indonesia . . . . 36 D1 3 46N 97 12 E
Leuven, Belgium . . . . 15 D4 50 52N 4 42 E
Leuze-en-Hainaut, Belgium . . 15 D3 50 36N 3 37 E
Levádhia, Greece . . . . 23 E10 38 27N 22 54 E
Levanger, Norway . . . . 8 E14 63 45N 11 19 E
Levelland, U.S.A. 81 J3 33 35N 102 23W
Leven, U.K. 11 E6 56 12N 3 0W
Leven, L., U.K. 11 E5 56 12N 3 22W
Leven, Toraka, Madag. . . . . . . 57 A8 12 30S 47 45 E
Leveque, C., Australia . . . . . . 60 C3 16 20S 123 0 E
Levice, Slovak Rep. . . . . 17 D10 48 13N 18 35 E
Levin, N.Z. . . . . 59 J5 40 37S 175 18 E
Lévis, Canada 73 C5 46 48N 71 9W
Levis, L., Canada 70 A5 62 37N 117 58W
Levittown, N.Y., U.S.A. 85 F11 40 44N 73 31W
Levittown, Pa., U.S.A. 85 F10 40 9N 74 51W
Levkás, Greece . . . . 23 E9 38 40N 20 43 E
Levkímmi, Greece . . . . 25 B4 39 25N 20 3 E
Levkímmi, Ákra, Greece . . . . . 25 B4 39 29N 20 4 E
Levkôsia = Nicosia, Cyprus . . 25 D12 35 10N 33 25 E
Levskigrad = Karlovo, Bulgaria . 23 C11 42 38N 24 47 E
Lewes, U.K. . . . . 13 G8 50 52N 0 1 E
Lewes, U.S.A. 82 F8 38 46N 75 9W
Lewis, U.K. 11 C2 58 9N 6 40W
Lewis →, U.S.A. 78 E4 45 51N 122 48W
Lewis, Butt of, U.K. 11 C2 58 31N 6 16W
Lewis Ra., Australia . . . . 60 D4 20 3S 128 50 E
Lewis Range, U.S.A. 76 C7 48 5N 113 5W
Lewis Run, U.S.A. 84 E6 41 52N 78 40W
Lewisburg, Pa., U.S.A. 84 F8 40 58N 76 54W
Lewisburg, Tenn., U.S.A. 83 H2 35 27N 86 48W
Lewisburg, W. Va., U.S.A. 82 G5 37 48N 80 27W
Lewisporte, Canada 73 C8 49 15N 55 3W
Lewiston, Idaho, U.S.A. 76 C5 46 25N 117 1W
Lewiston, Maine, U.S.A. 83 C11 44 6N 70 13W
Lewiston, N.Y., U.S.A. 84 C5 43 11N 79 3W
Lewistown, Mont., U.S.A. 76 C9 47 4N 109 26W
Lewistown, Pa., U.S.A. 84 F7 40 36N 77 34W
Lexington, Ill., U.S.A. 80 E10 40 39N 88 47W
Lexington, Ky., U.S.A. 82 F3 38 3N 84 30W
Lexington, Mich., U.S.A. 84 C2 43 16N 82 32W
Lexington, Mo., U.S.A. 80 F8 39 11N 93 52W
Lexington, N.C., U.S.A. 83 H5 35 49N 80 15W
Lexington, N.Y., U.S.A. 85 D10 42 15N 74 22W
Lexington, Nebr., U.S.A. 80 E5 40 47N 99 45W
Lexington, Ohio, U.S.A. 84 F2 40 41N 82 35W
Lexington, Tenn., U.S.A. 83 H1 35 39N 88 24W
Lexington, Va., U.S.A. 82 G6 37 47N 79 27W
Lexington Park, U.S.A. 82 F7 38 16N 76 27W
Leyburn, U.K. 12 C6 54 19N 1 48W
Leyland, U.K. 12 D5 53 42N 2 43W
Leyte □, Phil. . . . . 37 B6 11 0N 125 0 E
Lezhë, Albania . . . . 23 D8 41 47N 19 39 E
Lhasa, China . . . . 32 D4 29 25N 90 58 E
Lhazê, China . . . . 32 D3 29 5N 87 38 E
Lhokkruet, Indonesia . . . . . . 36 D1 4 55N 95 24 E
Lhokseumawe, Indonesia . . . . 36 C1 5 10N 97 10 E
L'Hospitalet de Llobregat, Spain . 21 B7 41 21N 2 6 E
Li, Thailand . . . . 38 D2 17 48N 98 57 E
Li Xian, Gansu, China . . . . 34 G3 34 10N 105 5 E
Li Xian, Hebei, China . . . . 34 E8 38 30N 115 35 E
Liancourt Rocks = Tok-do, Asia . 31 F5 37 15N 131 52 E
Lianga, Phil. . . . . 37 C7 8 38N 126 6 E
Liangcheng,
   Nei Monggol Zizhiqu, China . 34 D7 40 28N 112 25 E
Liangcheng, Shandong, China . 35 G10 35 32N 119 37 E
Liangdang, China . . . . 34 H4 33 56N 106 18 E
Liangpran, Indonesia . . . . 36 D4 1 4N 114 23 E
Lianshanguan, China . . . . 35 D12 40 53N 123 43 E
Lianshui, China . . . . 35 H10 33 42N 119 20 E
Lianyungang, China . . . . 35 G10 34 40N 119 11 E
Liao He →, China . . . . 35 D11 41 0N 121 50 E
Liaocheng, China . . . . 34 F8 36 28N 115 58 E
Liaodong Bandao, China . . . . 35 E12 40 0N 122 30 E
Liaodong Wan, China . . . . 35 D11 40 20N 121 10 E
Liaoning □, China . . . . 35 D12 41 40N 122 30 E
Liaoyang, China . . . . 35 D12 41 15N 122 58 E
Liaoyuan, China . . . . 35 C13 42 58N 125 2 E
Liaozhong, China . . . . 35 D12 41 23N 122 50 E
Liard →, Canada 70 A4 61 51N 121 18W
Liard River, Canada 70 B3 59 25N 126 5W
Liari, Pakistan . . . . 42 G2 25 37N 66 30 E
Libau = Liepāja, Latvia . . . . . . 9 H19 56 30N 21 0 E
Libby, U.S.A. 76 B6 48 23N 115 33W
Libenge, Dem. Rep. of the Congo 52 D3 3 40N 18 55 E
Liberal, U.S.A. 81 G4 37 3N 100 55W
Liberec, Czech Rep. . . . . 16 C8 50 47N 15 7 E
Liberia, Costa Rica 88 D2 10 40N 85 30W
Liberia ■, W. Afr. 50 G4 6 30N 9 30W
Liberty, Mo., U.S.A. 80 F7 39 15N 94 25W
Liberty, N.Y., U.S.A. 85 E10 41 48N 74 45W
Liberty, Pa., U.S.A. 84 E7 41 34N 77 6W
Liberty, Tex., U.S.A. 81 K7 30 3N 94 48W
Lībiya, Sahrā', Africa . . . . 51 C10 25 0N 25 0 E
Libobo, Tanjung, Indonesia . . 37 E7 0 54S 128 28 E
Libode, S. Africa . . . . 57 E4 31 33S 29 2 E
Libourne, France 20 D3 44 55N 0 14W
Libramont, Belgium . . . . 15 E5 49 55N 5 23 E
Libreville, Gabon . . . . 52 D1 0 25N 9 26 E
Libya ■, N. Afr. . . . . 51 C9 27 0N 17 0 E
Libyan Desert = Lībiya, Sahrā',
   Africa . . . . 51 C10 25 0N 25 0 E
Licantén, Chile 94 D1 35 55S 72 0W
Licata, Italy . . . . 22 F5 37 6N 13 56 E
Licheng, China . . . . 34 F7 36 28N 113 20 E
Lichfield, U.K. 13 E6 52 41N 1 49W
Lichinga, Mozam. . . . . 55 E4 13 13S 35 11 E
Lichtenburg, S. Africa . . . . . . 56 D4 26 8S 26 8 E
Licking →, U.S.A. . . . . 81 F9 36 N 84 30W
Licungo →, Mozam. . . . . 55 F4 17 40S 37 15 E
Lida, Belarus . . . . 9 K21 53 53N 25 15 E
Lidköping, Sweden . . . . 9 G15 58 31N 13 6 E
Liebig, Mt., Australia . . . . 60 D5 23 18S 131 22 E
Liechtenstein ■, Europe . . . . . 20 C8 47 8N 9 35 E
Liège, Belgium . . . . 15 D5 50 38N 5 35 E
Liège □, Belgium . . . . 15 D5 50 32N 5 35 E

Liegnitz = Legnica, Poland . . . 16 C9 51 12N 16 10 E
Lienart, Dem. Rep. of the Congo 54 B2 3 3N 25 31 E
Lienyunchiangshih =
   Lianyungang, China . . . . . . 35 G10 34 40N 119 11 E
Lienz, Austria . . . . 16 E7 46 50N 12 46 E
Liepāja, Latvia . . . . 9 H19 56 30N 21 0 E
Lier, Belgium . . . . 15 C4 51 7N 4 34 E
Lièvre →, Canada 72 C4 45 31N 75 26W
Liffey →, Ireland 10 C5 53 21N 6 13W
Lifford, Ireland 10 B4 54 51N 7 29W
Lifudzin, Russia . . . . 30 B7 44 21N 134 58 E
Lightning Ridge, Australia . . . 63 D4 29 22S 148 0 E
Ligonha →, Mozam. . . . . 55 F4 16 54S 39 9 E
Ligonier, U.S.A. 84 F5 40 15N 79 14W
Liguria □, Italy . . . . 20 D8 44 30N 8 50 E
Ligurian Sea, Medit. S. . . . . . . 22 C3 43 20N 9 0 E
Lihou Reefs and Cays, Australia 62 B5 17 25S 151 40 E
Lihue, U.S.A. 74 H15 21 59N 159 23W
Lihué Calel △, Argentina 94 D2 38 0S 65 10W
Lijiang, China . . . . 32 D5 26 55N 100 20 E
Likasi, Dem. Rep. of the Congo 55 E2 10 55S 26 48 E
Likoma I., Malawi . . . . 55 E3 12 3S 34 45 E
Likumburu, Tanzania . . . . 55 D4 9 43S 35 8 E
Lille, France . . . . 20 A5 50 38N 3 3 E
Lille Bælt, Denmark . . . . 9 J13 55 20N 9 45 E
Lillehammer, Norway . . . . 9 F14 61 8N 10 30 E
Lillesand, Norway . . . . 9 G13 58 15N 8 23 E
Lillian Pt., Australia . . . . 61 E4 27 40S 126 6 E
Lillooet, Canada 70 C4 50 44N 121 57W
Lillooet →, Canada 70 D4 49 15N 121 57W
Lilongwe, Malawi . . . . 55 E3 14 0S 33 48 E
Liloy, Phil. . . . . 37 C6 8 4N 122 39 E
Lim →, Bos.-H. . . . . 23 C8 43 45N 19 15 E
Lim Chu Kang, Singapore . . . . 39 d 1 26N 103 43 E
Lima, Indonesia . . . . 37 E7 3 39S 127 58 E
Lima, Mont., U.S.A. 76 D7 44 38N 112 36W
Lima, Ohio, U.S.A. 82 E3 40 44N 84 6W
Lima →, Portugal 21 B1 41 41N 8 50W
Liman, Indonesia . . . . 37 G14 7 48S 111 45 E
Limassol, Cyprus . . . . 25 E12 34 42N 33 1 E
Limavady, U.K. 10 A5 55 3N 6 56W
Limay →, Argentina 94 D2 39 0S 68 0W
Limay Mahuida, Argentina . . . 94 D2 37 10S 66 45W
Limbang, Brunei . . . . 36 D5 4 42N 115 6 E
Limbaži, Latvia . . . . 9 H21 57 31N 24 42 E
Limbdi, India . . . . 42 H4 22 34N 71 51 E
Limbe, Cameroon . . . . 52 D1 4 1N 9 10 E
Limburg, Germany . . . . 16 C5 50 22N 8 4 E
Limburg □, Belgium . . . . 15 C5 51 2N 5 25 E
Limburg □, Neths. . . . . 15 C5 51 20N 5 55 E
Limeira, Brazil 95 A6 22 35S 47 28W
Limerick, Ireland 10 D3 52 40N 8 37W
Limerick, U.S.A. 85 C14 43 41N 70 48W
Limerick □, Ireland 10 D3 52 30N 8 50W
Limestone, U.S.A. 84 D6 42 2N 78 38W
Limestone →, Canada 71 B10 56 31N 94 7W
Limfjorden, Denmark . . . . 9 H13 56 55N 9 0 E
Limia = Lima →, Portugal . . . 21 B1 41 41N 8 50W
Limingen, Norway . . . . 8 D15 64 48N 13 35 E
Limmen Bight, Australia . . . . 62 A2 14 40S 135 35 E
Limmen Bight →, Australia . . 62 B2 15 7S 135 44 E
Límnos, Greece . . . . 23 E11 39 50N 25 5 E
Limoges, Canada 85 A9 45 20N 75 16W
Limoges, France . . . . 20 D4 45 50N 1 15 E
Limón, Costa Rica 88 E3 10 0N 83 2W
Limon, U.S.A. 80 F3 39 16N 103 41W
Limousin □, France . . . . 20 D4 45 30N 1 30 E
Limoux, France . . . . 20 E5 43 4N 2 12 E
Limpopo →, S. Africa . . . . . . 57 C4 24 5S 29 0 E
Limpopo →, Africa . . . . 57 D5 25 5S 33 30 E
Limuru, Kenya . . . . 54 C4 1 2S 36 35 E
Lin Xian, China . . . . 34 F6 37 57N 110 58 E
Linares, Chile 94 D1 35 50S 71 40W
Linares, Mexico 87 C5 24 50N 99 40W
Linares, Spain 21 C4 38 10N 3 40W
Lincheng, China . . . . 34 F8 37 25N 114 30 E
Lincoln = Beamsville, Canada . 84 C5 43 12N 79 28W
Lincoln, Argentina 94 C3 34 55S 61 30W
Lincoln, N.Z. . . . . 59 K4 43 38S 172 30 E
Lincoln, U.K. 12 D7 53 14N 0 32W
Lincoln, Calif., U.S.A. 78 G5 38 54N 121 17W
Lincoln, Ill., U.S.A. 80 E10 40 9N 89 22W
Lincoln, Kans., U.S.A. 80 F5 39 3N 98 9W
Lincoln, Maine, U.S.A. 83 C11 45 22N 68 30W
Lincoln, N.H., U.S.A. 85 B13 44 3N 71 40W
Lincoln, N. Mex., U.S.A. 77 K11 33 30N 105 23W
Lincoln, Nebr., U.S.A. 80 E6 40 49N 96 41W
Lincoln City, U.S.A. 76 D1 44 57N 124 1W
Lincoln Hav = Lincoln Sea, Arctic 4 A5 84 0N 55 0W
Lincoln Sea, Arctic 4 A5 84 0N 55 0W
Lincolnshire □, U.K. 12 D7 53 14N 0 32W
Lincolnshire Wolds, U.K. 12 D7 53 26N 0 13W
Lincolnton, U.S.A. 83 H5 35 29N 81 16W
Lind, U.S.A. 76 C4 46 58N 118 37W
Linda, U.S.A. 78 F5 39 8N 121 34W
Lindeman I., Australia . . . . . . 62 J7 20 27S 149 3 E
Linden, Guyana 92 B7 6 0N 58 10W
Linden, Ala., U.S.A. 83 J2 32 18N 87 48W
Linden, Calif., U.S.A. 78 G5 38 1N 121 5W
Linden, Tex., U.S.A. 81 J7 33 1N 94 22W
Lindenhurst, U.S.A. 85 F11 40 41N 73 23W
Lindesnes, Norway . . . . 9 H12 57 58N 7 3 E
Líndhos, Greece . . . . 25 C10 36 6N 28 4 E
Líndhos, Ákra, Greece . . . . . . 25 C10 36 4N 28 10 E
Lindi, Tanzania . . . . 55 D4 9 58S 39 38 E
Lindi □, Tanzania . . . . 55 D4 9 40S 38 30 E
Lindi →, Dem. Rep. of the Congo 54 B2 0 33N 25 5 E
Lindsay, Canada 84 B6 44 22N 78 43W
Lindsay, Calif., U.S.A. 78 J7 36 12N 119 5W
Lindsay, Okla., U.S.A. 81 H6 34 50N 97 38W
Lindsborg, U.S.A. 80 F6 38 35N 97 40W
Linesville, U.S.A. 84 E4 41 39N 80 26W
Linfen, China . . . . 34 F6 36 3N 111 30 E
Ling Xian, China . . . . 34 F9 37 22N 116 30 E
Lingao, China . . . . 38 C7 19 56N 109 42 E
Lingayen, Phil. . . . . 37 A6 16 1N 120 14 E
Lingayen G., Phil. . . . . 37 A6 16 10N 120 15 E
Lingbi, China . . . . 35 H9 33 33N 117 33 E
Lingchuan, China . . . . 34 G7 35 45N 113 12 E
Lingding Yang, China . . . . 33 G10 22 25N 113 45 E
Lingen, Germany . . . . 16 B4 52 31N 7 19 E
Lingga, Indonesia . . . . 36 E2 0 12S 104 37 E
Lingga, Kepulauan, Indonesia . 36 E2 0 10S 104 30 E
Lingga Arch. = Lingga,
   Kepulauan, Indonesia . . . . . 36 E2 0 10S 104 30 E
Lingle, U.S.A. 80 D2 42 8N 104 21W

Lingqiu, China . . . . 34 E8 39 28N 114 22 E
Lingshi, China . . . . 34 F6 36 48N 111 48 E
Lingshou, China . . . . 34 E8 38 20N 114 20 E
Lingshui, China . . . . 38 C8 18 27N 110 0 E
Lingtai, China . . . . 34 G4 35 0N 107 40 E
Linguère, Senegal 50 E2 15 25N 15 5W
Lingwu, China . . . . 34 E4 38 6N 106 20 E
Lingyuan, China . . . . 35 D10 41 10N 119 15 E
Linhai, China . . . . 33 D7 28 50N 121 8 E
Linhares, Brazil 93 G10 19 25S 40 4W
Linhe, China . . . . 34 D4 40 48N 107 20 E
Linjiang, China . . . . 35 D14 41 50N 127 0 E
Linköping, Sweden . . . . 9 G16 58 28N 15 36 E
Linkou, China . . . . 35 B16 45 15N 130 18 E
Linnhe, L., U.K. 11 E3 56 36N 5 25W
Linosa, Medit. S. . . . . 22 G5 35 51N 12 50 E
Linqi, China . . . . 34 G7 35 45N 113 52 E
Linqing, China . . . . 34 F8 36 50N 115 42 E
Linqu, China . . . . 35 F10 36 25N 118 30 E
Linru, China . . . . 34 G7 34 11N 112 52 E
Lins, Brazil 95 A6 21 40S 49 44W
Linstead, Jamaica . . . . 88 a 18 8N 77 2W
Linta →, Madag. . . . . 57 D7 25 2S 44 5 E
Linton, Ind., U.S.A. 82 F2 39 2N 87 10W
Linton, N. Dak., U.S.A. 80 B4 46 16N 100 14W
Lintong, China . . . . 34 G5 34 20N 109 10 E
Linwood, Canada 84 C4 43 35N 80 43W
Linxi, China . . . . 35 C10 43 36N 118 2 E
Linxia, China . . . . 32 C5 35 36N 103 10 E
Linyanti →, Africa . . . . 56 B4 17 50S 25 5 E
Linyi, China . . . . 35 G10 35 5N 118 21 E
Linz, Austria . . . . 16 D8 48 18N 14 18 E
Linzhenzhen, China . . . . 34 F5 36 30N 109 59 E
Linzi, China . . . . 35 F10 36 50N 118 20 E
Lion, G. du, France . . . . 20 E6 43 10N 4 0 E
Lionárisso, Cyprus . . . . 25 D13 35 28N 34 8 E
Lions, G. of = Lion, G. du, France 20 E6 43 10N 4 0 E
Lion's Den, Zimbabwe . . . . . . 55 F3 17 15S 30 5 E
Lion's Head, Canada 84 B3 44 58N 81 15W
Lipa, Phil. . . . . 37 B6 13 57N 121 10 E
Lipali, Mozam. . . . . 55 F4 15 50S 35 50 E
Lípari, Italy . . . . 22 E6 38 26N 14 58 E
Lípari, Is. = Eólie, Ís., Italy . . . 22 E6 38 30N 14 57 E
Lipcani, Moldova . . . . 17 D14 48 14N 26 48 E
Lipetsk, Russia . . . . 18 D6 52 37N 39 35 E
Lipkany = Lipcani, Moldova . . 17 D14 48 14N 26 48 E
Lipovcy Manzovka, Russia . . . 30 B5 44 12N 132 26 E
Lipovets, Ukraine . . . . 17 D15 49 12N 29 1 E
Lippe →, Germany . . . . 16 C4 51 39N 6 36 E
Lipscomb, U.S.A. 81 G4 36 14N 100 16W
Liptrap, C., Australia . . . . 63 F4 38 50S 145 55 E
Liquillo, Sierra de, Puerto Rico . 89 d 18 20N 65 47W
Lira, Uganda . . . . 54 B3 2 17N 32 57 E
Liria = Lliria, Spain 21 C5 39 37N 0 35W
Lisala, Dem. Rep. of the Congo 52 D4 2 12N 21 38 E
Lisboa, Portugal 21 C1 38 42N 9 10W
Lisbon = Lisboa, Portugal . . . 21 C1 38 42N 9 10W
Lisbon, N. Dak., U.S.A. 80 B6 46 27N 97 41W
Lisbon, N.H., U.S.A. 85 B13 44 13N 71 55W
Lisbon, Ohio, U.S.A. 84 F4 40 46N 80 46W
Lisbon Falls, U.S.A. 83 D10 44 0N 70 4W
Lisburn, U.K. 10 B5 54 31N 6 3W
Lisburne, C., U.S.A. 4 C17 68 53N 166 13W
Liscannor B., Ireland 10 D2 52 55N 9 24W
Lishi, China . . . . 34 F6 37 31N 111 8 E
Lishu, China . . . . 35 C13 43 20N 124 18 E
Lisianski I., Pac. Oc. 64 E10 26 2N 174 0W
Lisichansk = Lysychansk, Ukraine 19 E6 48 55N 38 30 E
Lisieux, France . . . . 20 B4 49 10N 0 12 E
Liski, Russia . . . . 19 D6 51 3N 39 30 E
Lismore, Australia . . . . 63 D5 28 44S 153 21 E
Lismore, Ireland 10 D4 52 8N 7 55W
Lista, Norway . . . . 9 G12 58 7N 6 39 E
Lister, Mt., Antarctica . . . . . . 5 D11 78 0S 162 0 E
Liston, Australia . . . . 63 D5 28 39S 152 6 E
Listowel, Canada 84 C4 43 44N 80 58W
Listowel, Ireland 10 D2 52 27N 9 29W
Litani →, Lebanon . . . . 46 B4 33 20N 35 15 E
Litchfield, Calif., U.S.A. 78 E6 40 24N 120 23W
Litchfield, Conn., U.S.A. 85 E11 41 45N 73 11W
Litchfield, Ill., U.S.A. 80 F10 39 11N 89 39W
Litchfield, Minn., U.S.A. 80 C7 45 8N 94 32W
Litchfield △, Australia . . . . . . 60 B5 13 14S 131 1 E
Lithgow, Australia . . . . 63 E5 33 25S 150 8 E
Líthinon, Ákra, Greece . . . . . . 25 E6 34 55N 24 44 E
Lithuania ■, Europe . . . . 9 J20 55 30N 24 0 E
Lititz, U.S.A. 85 F8 40 9N 76 18W
Litoměřice, Czech Rep. . . . . . 16 C8 50 33N 14 10 E
Little Abaco I., Bahamas 88 A4 26 50N 77 30W
Little Barrier I., N.Z. . . . . 59 G5 36 12S 175 8 E
Little Belt Mts., U.S.A. 76 C8 46 40N 110 45W
Little Bighorn Battlefield △,
   U.S.A. 76 D10 45 34N 107 26W
Little Blue →, U.S.A. 80 F6 39 42N 96 41W
Little Buffalo →, U.S.A. 70 A6 61 0N 113 46W
Little Cayman, Cayman Is. . . . 88 C3 19 41N 80 3W
Little Churchill →, Canada . . 71 B9 57 30N 95 22W
Little Colorado →, U.S.A. . . . 77 H8 36 12N 111 48W
Little Current, Canada 72 C3 45 55N 82 0W
Little Current →, Canada . . . 72 B3 50 57N 84 36W
Little Falls, Minn., U.S.A. 80 C7 45 59N 94 22W
Little Falls, N.Y., U.S.A. 85 C10 43 3N 74 51W
Little Fork →, U.S.A. 80 A8 48 31N 93 35W
Little Grand Rapids, Canada . 71 C9 52 0N 95 29W
Little Humboldt →, U.S.A. . . . 76 F5 41 1N 117 43W
Little Inagua I., Bahamas 89 B5 21 40N 73 50W
Little Karoo, S. Africa . . . . . . 56 E3 33 45S 21 0 E
Little Lake, U.S.A. 79 K9 35 56N 117 55W
Little Laut Is. = Laut Kecil,
   Kepulauan, Indonesia . . . . . 36 E5 4 45S 115 40 E
Little Mecatina = Petit-
   Mécatina →, Canada 73 B8 50 40N 59 30W
Little Minch, U.K. 11 D2 57 35N 6 45W
Little Missouri →, U.S.A. 80 B3 47 36N 102 25W
Little Ouse →, U.K. . . . . 13 E9 52 22N 1 12 E
Little Rann, India . . . . 42 H4 23 25N 71 25 E
Little Red →, U.S.A. 81 H9 35 11N 91 27W
Little River, N.Z. . . . . 59 K4 43 45S 172 49 E
Little Rock, U.S.A. 81 H8 34 45N 92 17W
Little Ruaha →, Tanzania . . . 54 D4 7 57S 37 53 E
Little Sable Pt., U.S.A. 82 D2 43 38N 86 33W
Little Sioux →, U.S.A. 80 E6 41 48N 96 4W
Little Smoky →, Canada 70 C5 54 44N 117 11W
Little Snake →, U.S.A. 76 F9 40 27N 108 26W
Little Tobago, Trin. & Tob. . . . 93 J16 11 18N 60 30W
Little Valley, U.S.A. 84 D6 42 15N 78 48W
Little Wabash →, U.S.A. 82 G1 37 55N 88 5W

Little White →, U.S.A. 80 D4 43 40N 100 40W
Little Zab = Zāb aş Şaghīr →,
   Iraq . . . . 44 C4 35 17N 43 29 E
Littlefield, U.S.A. 81 J3 33 55N 102 20W
Littlehampton, U.K. 13 G7 50 49N 0 32W
Littleton, U.S.A. 85 B13 44 18N 71 46W
Liu He →, China . . . . 35 D11 40 55N 121 35 E
Liuba, China . . . . 34 H4 33 38N 106 55 E
Liugou, China . . . . 35 D10 40 57N 118 15 E
Liuhe, China . . . . 35 C13 42 17N 125 43 E
Liukang Tenggaja = Sabalana,
   Kepulauan, Indonesia . . . . . 37 F5 6 45S 118 50 E
Liuli, Tanzania . . . . 55 E3 11 3S 34 38 E
Liuwa Plain, Zambia . . . . 53 G4 14 20S 22 30 E
Liuzhou, China . . . . 33 D5 24 22N 109 22 E
Liuzhuang, China . . . . 35 H11 33 12N 120 18 E
Livadhia, Cyprus . . . . 25 E12 34 57N 33 38 E
Live Oak, Calif., U.S.A. 78 F5 39 17N 121 40W
Live Oak, Fla., U.S.A. 83 K4 30 18N 82 59W
Liveras, Cyprus . . . . 25 D11 35 23N 32 57 E
Livermore, U.S.A. 78 H5 37 41N 121 47W
Livermore, Mt., U.S.A. 81 K2 30 38N 104 11W
Livermore Falls, U.S.A. 83 C11 44 29N 70 11W
Liverpool, Canada 73 D7 44 5N 64 41W
Liverpool, U.K. 12 D4 53 25N 3 0W
Liverpool, U.S.A. 85 C8 43 6N 76 13W
Liverpool Bay, U.K. 12 D4 53 30N 3 20W
Liverpool Ra., Australia . . . . . 63 E5 31 50S 150 30 E
Livingston, Guatemala 88 C2 15 50N 88 50W
Livingston, U.K. 11 F5 55 54N 3 30W
Livingston, Ala., U.S.A. 83 J1 32 35N 88 11W
Livingston, Calif., U.S.A. 78 H6 37 23N 120 43W
Livingston, Mont., U.S.A. 76 D8 45 40N 110 34W
Livingston, S.C., U.S.A. 83 J5 33 32N 80 53W
Livingston, Tenn., U.S.A. 83 G3 36 23N 85 19W
Livingston, Tex., U.S.A. 81 K7 30 43N 94 56W
Livingston, L., U.S.A. 81 K7 30 50N 95 10W
Livingston Manor, U.S.A. 85 E10 41 54N 74 50W
Livingstone, Zambia . . . . 55 F2 17 46S 25 52 E
Livingstone Mts., Tanzania . . 55 D3 9 40S 34 20 E
Livingstonia, Malawi . . . . 55 E3 10 38S 34 5 E
Livny, Russia . . . . 18 D6 52 30N 37 30 E
Livonia, Mich., U.S.A. 82 D4 42 23N 83 23W
Livonia, N.Y., U.S.A. 84 D7 42 49N 77 40W
Livorno, Italy . . . . 22 C4 43 33N 10 19 E
Livramento, Brazil 95 C4 30 55S 55 30W
Liwale, Tanzania . . . . 55 D4 9 48S 37 58 E
Liwonde △, Malawi . . . . 55 E4 14 48S 35 20 E
Lizard I., Australia . . . . 62 A4 14 42S 145 30 E
Lizard Pt., U.K. 13 H2 49 57N 5 13W
Ljubljana, Slovenia . . . . 16 E8 46 4N 14 33 E
Ljungan →, Sweden . . . . 9 E17 62 18N 17 23 E
Ljungby, Sweden . . . . 9 H15 56 49N 13 55 E
Ljusdal, Sweden . . . . 9 F17 61 46N 16 3 E
Ljusnan →, Sweden . . . . 9 F17 61 12N 17 8 E
Ljusne, Sweden . . . . 9 F17 61 13N 17 7 E
Llancanelo, Salina, Argentina . 94 D2 35 40S 69 8W
Llandeilo, U.K. 13 F4 51 53N 3 59W
Llandovery, U.K. 13 F4 51 59N 3 48W
Llandrindod Wells, U.K. 13 E4 52 14N 3 22W
Llandudno, U.K. 12 D4 53 19N 3 50W
Llanelli, U.K. 13 F3 51 41N 4 10W
Llanes, Spain 21 A3 43 25N 4 50W
Llangollen, U.K. 12 E4 52 58N 3 11W
Llanidloes, U.K. 13 E4 52 27N 3 31W
Llano, U.S.A. 81 K5 30 45N 98 41W
Llano →, U.S.A. 81 K5 30 39N 98 26W
Llano Estacado, U.S.A. 81 J3 33 30N 103 0W
Llanos, S. Amer. 92 C4 5 0N 71 35W
Llanos de Challe △, Chile . . . 94 B1 28 8S 71 1W
Llanquihue, L., Chile 96 E1 41 10S 72 50W
Llanwrtyd Wells, U.K. 13 E4 52 7N 3 38W
Llebeig, C. des, Spain . . . . . . 24 B9 39 33N 2 18 E
Lleida, Spain . . . . 21 B6 41 37N 0 39 E
Llentrisca, C., Spain . . . . 24 C7 38 52N 1 15 E
Llera, Mexico 87 C5 23 19N 99 1W
Lleyn Peninsula, U.K. 12 E3 52 51N 4 36W
Llico, Chile 94 C1 34 46S 72 5W
Lliria, Spain 21 C5 39 37N 0 35W
Llobregat →, Spain . . . . 21 B7 41 19N 2 9 E
Lloret de Mar, Spain . . . . 21 B7 41 41N 2 53 E
Lloyd B., Australia . . . . 62 A3 12 45S 143 27 E
Lloyd L., Canada 71 B7 57 22N 108 57W
Lloydminster, Canada 71 C7 53 17N 110 0W
Llucmajor, Spain . . . . 24 B9 39 29N 2 53 E
Llullaillaco △, Chile 94 A2 24 50S 68 51W
Llullaillaco, Volcán, S. Amer. . 94 A2 24 43S 68 30W
Lo →, Vietnam . . . . 38 B5 21 18N 105 25 E
Loa, U.S.A. 77 G8 38 24N 111 39W
Loa →, Chile 94 A1 21 26S 70 41W
Loaita I., S. China Sea . . . . . . 36 B4 10 41N 114 25 E
Loange →, Dem. Rep. of
   the Congo . . . . 52 E4 4 17S 20 2 E
Lobatse, Botswana . . . . 56 D4 25 12S 25 40 E
Lobería, Argentina 94 D4 38 10S 58 40W
Lobito, Angola . . . . 53 G2 12 18S 13 35 E
Lobos, Argentina 94 D4 35 10S 59 0W
Lobos, I., Mexico 86 B2 27 15N 110 30W
Lobos, I. de, Canary Is. 24 F6 28 45N 13 50W
Loc Binh, Vietnam . . . . 38 B6 21 46N 106 54 E
Loc Ninh, Vietnam . . . . 39 G6 11 50N 106 34 E
Locarno, Switz. . . . . 20 C8 46 10N 8 47 E
Loch Baghasdail = Lochboisdale,
   U.K. 11 D1 57 9N 7 20W
Loch Garman = Wexford, Ireland 10 D5 52 20N 6 28W
Loch Lomond and the
   Trossachs △, U.K. 11 E4 56 10N 4 40W
Loch Nam Madadh =
   Lochmaddy, U.K. 11 D1 57 36N 7 10W
Lochaber, U.K. 11 E3 56 59N 5 1W
Locharbriggs, U.K. 11 F5 55 7N 3 35W
Lochboisdale, U.K. 11 D1 57 9N 7 20W
Loche, L. La, Canada 71 B7 56 30N 109 30W
Lochem, Neths. . . . . 15 B6 52 9N 6 26 E
Loches, France . . . . 20 C4 47 7N 1 0 E
Lochgilphead, U.K. 11 E3 56 2N 5 26W
Lochinvar △, Zambia . . . . 55 F2 15 55S 27 15 E
Lochinver, U.K. 11 C3 58 9N 5 14W
Lochmaddy, U.K. 11 D1 57 36N 7 10W
Lochnagar, Australia . . . . 62 C4 23 33S 145 38 E
Lochnagar, U.K. 11 E5 56 57N 3 15W
Lochy, L., U.K. 11 E4 57 0N 4 53W
Lock, Australia . . . . 63 E2 33 34S 135 46 E
Lock Haven, U.S.A. 84 E7 41 8N 77 28W
Lockeford, U.S.A. 78 G5 38 10N 121 9W
Lockeport, Canada 73 D6 43 47N 65 4W
Lockerbie, U.K. 11 F5 55 7N 3 21W

Lockhart, U.S.A. .... 81 L6　29 53N　97 40W
Lockhart, L., Australia .... 61 F2　33 15S 119　3 E
Lockhart River, Australia ..... 62 A3　12 58S 143 30 E
Lockney, U.S.A. .... 81 H4　34　7N 101 27W
Lockport, U.S.A. .... 84 C6　43 10N　78 42W
Lod, Israel .... 46 D3　31 57N　34 54 E
Lodeinoye Pole, Russia .... 18 B5　60 44N　33 33 E
Lodge Bay, Canada .... 73 B8　52 14N　55 51W
Lodge Grass, U.S.A. 76 D10 45 19N 107 22W
Lodgepole Cr. ➤, U.S.A. ...... 80 E2　41 20N 104 30W
Lodhran, Pakistan .... 42 E4　29 32N　71 30 E
Lodi, Italy .... 20 D8　45 19N　9 30 E
Lodi, Calif., U.S.A. .... 78 G5　38　8N 121 16W
Lodi, Ohio, U.S.A. .... 84 E3　41　2N　82　0W
Lodja, Dem. Rep. of the Congo 54 C1　3 30S　23 23 E
Lodwar, Kenya .... 54 B4　3 10N　35 40 E
Łódź, Poland .... 17 C10 51 45N 19 27 E
Loei, Thailand .... 38 D3　17 29N 101 35 E
Loengo, Dem. Rep. of the Congo 54 C2　4 48S　26 30 E
Loeriesfontein, S. Africa ...... 56 E2　31　0S　19 26 E
Lofoten, Norway .... 8 B15　68 30N　14　0 E
Logan, Iowa, U.S.A. .... 80 E7　41 39N　95 47W
Logan, Ohio, U.S.A. .... 82 F4　39 32N　82 25W
Logan, Utah, U.S.A. .... 76 F8　41 44N 111 50W
Logan, W. Va., U.S.A. .... 82 G5　37 51N　81 59W
Logan, Mt., Canada .... 68 B5　60 34N 140 23W
Logandale, U.S.A. .... 79 J12　36 36N 114 29W
Logansport, Ind., U.S.A. ...... 82 E2　40 45N　86 22W
Logansport, La., U.S.A. ...... 81 K8　31 58N　94　0W
Logone ➤, Chad .... 51 F9　12　6N　15　2 E
Logroño, Spain .... 21 A4　42 28N　2 27W
Lohardaga, India .... 43 H11 23 27N　84 45 E
Loharia, India .... 42 H6　23 45N　74 14 E
Loharu, India .... 42 E6　28 27N　75 49 E
Lohja, Finland .... 9 F21　60 12N　24　5 E
Lohri Wah ➤, Pakistan .... 42 F2　27 27N　67 37 E
Loi-kaw, Burma .... 41 K20 19 40N　97 17 E
Loimaa, Finland .... 9 F20　60 50N　23　5 E
Loir ➤, France .... 20 C3　47 33N　0 32W
Loire ➤, France .... 20 C2　47 16N　2 10W
Loja, Ecuador .... 92 D3　3 59S　79 16W
Loja, Spain .... 21 D3　37 10N　4 10W
Loji = Kawasi, Indonesia ...... 37 E7　1 38S 127 28 E
Lokandu, Dem. Rep. of
  the Congo .... 54 C2　2 30S　25 45 E
Lokeren, Belgium .... 15 C3　51　6N　3 59 E
Lokgwabe, Botswana .... 56 C3　24 10S　21 50 E
Lokichokio, Kenya .... 54 B3　4 19N　34 13 E
Lokitaung, Kenya .... 54 B4　4 12N　35 48 E
Lokkan tekojärvi, Finland ..... 8 C22　67 55N　27　35 E
Lokoja, Nigeria .... 50 G7　7 47N　6 45 E
Lola, Mt., U.S.A. .... 78 F6　39 26N 120 22W
Loliondo, Tanzania .... 54 C4　2　2S　35 39 E
Lolland, Denmark .... 9 J14　54 45N　11 30 E
Lolo, U.S.A. .... 76 C6　46 45N 114　5W
Lom, Bulgaria .... 23 C10 43 48N　23 12 E
Lom Kao, Thailand .... 38 D3　16 53N 101 14 E
Lom Sak, Thailand .... 38 D3　16 47N 101 15 E
Loma, U.S.A. .... 76 C8　47 56N 110 30W
Loma Linda, U.S.A. .... 79 L9　34　3N 117 16W
Lomami ➤, Dem. Rep. of
  the Congo .... 54 B1　0 46N　24 16 E
Lomas de Zamóra, Argentina .. 94 C4　34 45S　58 25W
Lombadina, Australia .... 60 C3　16 31S 122 54 E
Lombárdia □, Italy .... 20 D8　45 40N　9 30 E
Lombardy = Lombárdia □, Italy 20 D8　45 40N　9 30 E
Lomblen, Indonesia .... 37 F6　8 30S 123 32 E
Lombok, Indonesia .... 36 F5　8 45S 116 30 E
Lombok, Selat, Indonesia ..... 37 K18　8 30S 115 50 E
Lomé, Togo .... 50 G6　6 9N　1 20 E
Lomela, Dem. Rep. of the Congo 52 E4　2 19S　23 15 E
Lomela ➤, Dem. Rep. of
  the Congo .... 52 E4　0 15S　20 40 E
Lommel, Belgium .... 15 C5　51 14N　5 19 E
Lomond, Canada .... 70 C6　50 24N 112 36W
Lomond, L., U.K. .... 11 E4　56　8N　4 38W
Lomphat, Cambodia .... 38 F6　13 30N 106 59 E
Lompobatang, Indonesia ...... 37 F5　5 24S 119 56 E
Lompoc, U.S.A. .... 79 L6　34 38N 120 28W
Łomża, Poland .... 17 B12 53 10N　22　2 E
Lon, Ko, Thailand .... 39 a　7 47N　98 23 E
Loncoche, Chile .... 96 D2　39 20S　72 50W
Londa, India .... 40 M9　15 30N　74 30 E
Londiani, Kenya .... 54 C4　0 10S　35 33 E
London, Canada .... 84 D3　42 59N　81 15W
London, U.K. .... 13 F7　51 30N　0　3W
London, Ky., U.S.A. .... 82 G3　37　8N　84　5W
London, Ohio, U.S.A. .... 82 F4　39 53N　83 27W
London, Greater □, U.K. ..... 13 F7　51 36N　0　5W
London Gatwick ✈ (LGW), U.K. 13 F7　51 10N　0 11W
London Heathrow ✈ (LHR), U.K. 13 F7　51 28N　0 27W
London Stansted ✈ (STN), U.K. 13 F8　51 54N　0 14 E
Londonderry, U.K. .... 10 B4　55　0N　7 20W
Londonderry □, U.K. .... 10 B4　55　0N　7 20W
Londonderry, C., Australia .... 60 B4　13 45S 126 55 E
Londonderry, I., Chile .... 96 H2　55　0S　71　0W
Londres, Argentina .... 96 B3　27 43S　67　7W
Londrina, Brazil .... 95 A5　23 18S　51 10W
Lone Pine, U.S.A. .... 78 J8　36 36N 118　4W
Lonely Mine, Zimbabwe ...... 57 B4　19 30S　28 49 E
Long B., U.S.A. .... 83 J6　33 35N　78 45W
Long Beach, Calif., U.S.A. .... 79 M8　33 47N 118 11W
Long Beach, N.Y., U.S.A. ..... 85 F11　40 35N　73 39W
Long Beach, Wash., U.S.A. .... 78 D2　46 21N 124　3W
Long Branch, U.S.A. .... 85 F11　40 18N　74　0W
Long Creek, U.S.A. .... 76 D4　44 43N 119　6W
Long Eaton, U.K. .... 12 E6　52 53N　1 15W
Long I., Australia .... 62 J6　20 22S 148 51 E
Long I., Bahamas .... 89 B4　23 20N　75 10W
Long I., Canada .... 72 B4　54 50N　79 20W
Long I., Ireland .... 10 E2　51 30N　9 34W
Long I., U.S.A. .... 85 F11　40 45N　73 30W
Long Island Sd., U.S.A. ...... 85 E12　41 10N　73　0W
Long L., Canada .... 72 C2　49 30N　86 50W
Loimaa, U.S.A. .... 85 C10 43 58N　75　0W
Long Point B., Canada .... 84 D4　42 40N　80 10W
Long Prairie ➤, U.S.A. .... 80 C7　46 20N　94 36W
Long Pt., Canada .... 84 D4　42 35N　80　2W
Long Range Mts., Canada .... 73 C8　49 30N　57 30W
Long Reef, Australia .... 60 B4　14　1S 125 48 E
Long Spruce, Canada .... 71 B10 56 24N　94 21W
Long Str. = Longa, Proliv, Russia 4 C16　70　0N 175　0 E
Long Thanh, Vietnam .... 39 G6　10 47N 106 57 E
Long Xian, China .... 34 G4　34 55N 106 55 E
Long Xuyen, Vietnam .... 39 G5　10 19N 105 28 E
Longa, Proliv, Russia .... 4 C16　70　0N 175　0 E
Longbenton, U.K. .... 12 B6　55　1N　1 31W

Longboat Key, U.S.A. .... 83 M4　27 23N　82 39W
Longde, China .... 34 G4　35 30N 106 20 E
Longford, Australia .... 63 G4　41 32S 147　3 E
Longford, Ireland .... 10 C4　53 43N　7 49W
Longford □, Ireland .... 10 C4　53 42N　7 45W
Longhua, Guangdong, China .. 33 F11 22 39N 114　0 E
Longhua, Hebei, China .... 35 D9　41 18N 117 45 E
Longido, Tanzania .... 54 C4　2 43S　36 42 E
Longiram, Indonesia .... 36 E5　0　5S 115 45 E
Longkou, China .... 35 F11 37 40N 120 18 E
Longlac, Canada .... 72 C2　49 45N　86 25W
Longmeadow, U.S.A. .... 85 D12 42　3N　72 34W
Longmont, U.S.A. .... 80 E2　40 10N 105　6W
Longnawan, Indonesia .... 36 D4　1 51N 114 55 E
Longreach, Australia .... 62 C3　23 28S 144 14 E
Longueuil, Canada .... 85 A11 45 32N　73 28W
Longview, Tex., U.S.A. .... 81 J7　32 30N　94 44W
Longview, Wash., U.S.A. ..... 78 D4　46　8N 122 57W
Longxi, China .... 34 G3　34 53N 104 40 E
Longxue Dao, China .... 33 F10 22 41N 113 38 E
Longyearbyen, Norway .... 4 B8　78 13N　5 38 E
Lonoke, U.S.A. .... 81 H9　34 47N　91 54W
Lonquimay, Chile .... 96 D2　38 26S　71 14W
Lons-le-Saunier, France ...... 20 C6　46 40N　5 31 E
Looe, U.K. .... 13 G3　50 22N　4 28W
Lookout, C., Canada .... 72 A3　55 18N　83 56W
Lookout, C., U.S.A. .... 83 H7　34 35N　76 32W
Loolmalasin, Tanzania .... 54 C4　3　0S　35 53 E
Loon ➤, Alta., Canada .... 70 B5　57　8N 115　3W
Loon ➤, Man., Canada .... 71 B8　55 53N 101 59W
Loon Lake, Canada .... 71 C7　54　2N 109 10W
Loongana, Australia .... 61 F4　30 52S 127　5 E
Loop Hd., Ireland .... 10 D2　52 34N　9 56W
Lop Buri, Thailand .... 38 E3　14 48N 100 37 E
Lop Nor = Lop Nur, China ... 32 B4　40 20N　90 10 E
Lop Nur, China .... 32 B4　40 20N　90 10 E
Lopatina, Gora, Russia .... 29 D15 50 47N 143 10 E
Lopez, U.S.A. .... 85 E8　41 27N　76 20W
Lopez, C., Gabon .... 52 E1　0 47S　8 40 E
Lopphavet, Norway .... 8 A19　70 27N　21 15 E
Lora ➤, Afghan. .... 40 D4　31 35N　66 32 E
Lora, Hámün-i-, Pakistan ..... 40 E4　29 38N　64 58 E
Lora Cr. ➤, Australia .... 63 D2　28 10S 135 22 E
Lora del Río, Spain .... 21 D3　37 39N　5 33W
Lorain, U.S.A. .... 84 E2　41 28N　82 11W
Loralai, Pakistan .... 42 D3　30 20N　68 41 E
Lorca, Spain .... 21 D5　37 41N　1 42W
Lord Howe I., Pac. Oc. .... 64 L7　31 33S 159　6 E
Lord Howe Ridge, Pac. Oc. ... 64 L8　30　0S 162 30 E
Lordsburg, U.S.A. .... 77 K9　32 21N 108 43W
Lorestan □, Iran .... 45 C6　33 30N　48 40 E
Loreto, Brazil .... 93 E9　7　5S　45 10W
Loreto, Mexico .... 86 B2　26　1N 111 21W
Lorient, France .... 20 C2　47 45N　3 23W
Lormi, India .... 43 H9　22 17N　81 41 E
Lorn, U.K. .... 11 E3　56 26N　5 10W
Lorn, Firth of, U.K. .... 11 E3　56 20N　5 40W
Lorne, Australia .... 63 F3　38 33S 143 59 E
Lorovouni, Cyprus .... 25 D11 35　8N　32　36 E
Lorraine ⊠, France .... 20 B7　48 53N　6　0 E
Los Alamos, Calif., U.S.A. .... 79 L6　34 44N 120 17W
Los Alamos, N. Mex., U.S.A. .. 77 J10　35 53N 106 19W
Los Altos, U.S.A. .... 78 H4　37 23N 122　7W
Los Andes, Chile .... 94 C1　32 50S　70 40W
Los Angeles, Chile .... 94 D1　37 28S　72 23W
Los Angeles, U.S.A. .... 79 M8　34　4N 118 15W
Los Angeles, Bahia de, Mexico 86 B2　28 56N 113 34W
Los Angeles Aqueduct, U.S.A. . 79 K9　35 22N 118　5W
Los Angeles International ✈
  (LAX), U.S.A. .... 79 M8　33 57N 118 25W
Los Banos, U.S.A. .... 78 H6　37　4N 120 51W
Los Blancos, Argentina .... 94 A3　23 40S　62 30W
Los Cardones △, Argentina ... 94 B2　25　8S　65 55W
Los Chiles, Costa Rica .... 88 D3　11　3N　84 43W
Los Cristianos, Canary Is. .... 24 F3　28　3N　16 42W
Los Gatos, U.S.A. .... 78 H5　37 14N 121 59W
Los Haïtises △, Dom. Rep. ... 89 C6　19　4N　69 36W
Los Hermanos Is., Venezuela .. 89 D7　11 45N　64 25W
Los Islotes, Canary Is. .... 24 E6　29　4N　13 44W
Los Llanos de Aridane, Canary Is. 24 F2　28 38N　17 54W
Los Loros, Chile .... 94 B1　27 50S　70　6W
Los Lunas, U.S.A. .... 77 J10　34 48N 106 44W
Los Mochis, Mexico .... 86 B3　25 45N 108 57W
Los Olivos, U.S.A. .... 79 L6　34 40N 120　7W
Los Palacios, Cuba .... 88 B3　22 35N　83 15W
Los Reyes, Mexico .... 86 D4　19 34N 102 30W
Los Roques Is., Venezuela .... 89 D6　11 50N　66 45W
Los Teques, Venezuela .... 92 A5　10 21N　67　2W
Los Testigos, Is., Venezuela .. 92 A6　11 23N　63　6W
Los Vilos, Chile .... 94 C1　32 10S　71 30W
Lošinj, Croatia .... 16 F8　44 30N　14 30 E
Loskop Dam, S. Africa .... 57 D4　25 23S　29 20 E
Lossiemouth, U.K. .... 11 D5　57 42N　3 17W
Lostwithiel, U.K. .... 13 G3　50 24N　4 41W
Lot ➤, France .... 20 D4　44 18N　0 20 E
Lota, Chile .... 94 D1　37　5S　73 10W
Lotfābād, Iran .... 45 B8　37 32N　59 20 E
Lothair, S. Africa .... 57 D5　26 22S　30 27 E
Loubomo, Congo .... 52 E2　4　9S　12 47 E
Loudonville, U.S.A. .... 84 F2　40 38N　82 14W
Louga, Senegal .... 50 E2　15 45N　16　5W
Loughborough, U.K. .... 12 E6　52 47N　1 11W
Loughrea, Ireland .... 10 C3　53 12N　8 33W
Loughros More B., Ireland .... 10 B3　54 48N　8 32W
Louis Trichardt, S. Africa .... 57 C4　23　1S　29 43 E
Louis XIV, Pte., Canada ...... 72 B4　54 37N　79 45W
Louisa, U.S.A. .... 82 F4　38　7N　82 36W
Louisbourg, Canada .... 73 C8　45 55N　60　0W
Louise I., Canada .... 70 C2　52 55N 131 50W
Louiseville, Canada .... 72 C5　46 20N　72 56W
Louisiade Arch., Papua N. G. .. 64 J7　11 10S 153　0 E
Louisiana, U.S.A. .... 80 F9　39 27N　91 3W
Louisiana □, U.S.A. .... 81 K9　30 50N　92　0W
Louisville, Ky., U.S.A. .... 82 F3　38 15N　85 46W
Louisville, Miss., U.S.A. ...... 81 J10　33　7N　89 3W
Louisville, Ohio, U.S.A. ...... 84 F3　40 50N　81 16W
Loulé, Portugal .... 21 D1　37　9N　8　0W
Loup City, U.S.A. .... 80 E5　41 17N　98 58W
Loups Marins, Lacs des, Canada 72 A5　56 30N　73 45W
Lourdes, France .... 20 E3　43　6N　0　3W
Louth, Australia .... 63 E4　30 30S 145　8 E
Louth, Ireland .... 10 C5　53 58N　6 32W
Louth, U.K. .... 12 D7　53 22N　0　1W
Louth □, Ireland .... 10 C5　53 56N　6 34W
Louvain = Leuven, Belgium ... 15 D4　50 52N　4 42 E
Louwsburg, S. Africa .... 57 D5　27 37S　31 7 E
Lovech, Bulgaria .... 23 C11 43　8N　24 42 E
Loveland, U.S.A. .... 80 E2　40 24N 105　5W

Lovell, U.S.A. .... 76 D9　44 50N 108 24W
Lovelock, U.S.A. .... 76 F4　40 11N 118 28W
Loviisa, Finland .... 9 F22　60 28N　26 12 E
Loving, U.S.A. .... 81 J2　32 17N 104　6W
Lovington, U.S.A. .... 81 J3　32 57N 103 21W
Lovisa = Loviisa, Finland ..... 9 F22　60 28N　26 12 E
Low, L., Canada .... 72 B4　52 29N　76 17W
Low Pt., Australia .... 61 F4　32 25S 127 25 E
Low Tatra = Nízké Tatry,
  Slovak Rep. .... 17 D10 48 55N　19 30 E
Lowa, Dem. Rep. of the Congo . 54 C2　1 25S　25 47 E
Lowa ➤, Dem. Rep. of
  the Congo .... 54 C2　1 24S　25 51 E
Lowell, U.S.A. .... 85 D13 42 38N　71 19W
Lowellville, U.S.A. .... 84 E4　41　2N　80 32W
Löwen ➤, Namibia .... 56 D2　26 51S　18 17 E
Lower Alkali L., U.S.A. .... 76 F3　41 16N 120　2W
Lower Arrow L., Canada ...... 70 D5　49 40N 118　5W
Lower California = Baja
  California, Mexico .... 86 A1　31 10N 115 12W
Lower Hutt, N.Z. .... 59 J5　41 10S 174 55 E
Lower Lake, U.S.A. .... 78 G4　38 55N 122 37W
Lower Manitou L., Canada .... 71 D10 49 15N　93　0W
Lower Post, Canada .... 70 B3　59 58N 128 30W
Lower Red L., U.S.A. .... 80 B7　47 58N　95　0W
Lower Saxony =
  Niedersachsen □, Germany .. 16 B5　52 50N　9　0 E
Lower Tunguska = Tunguska,
  Nizhnyaya ➤, Russia .... 29 C9　65 48N　88　4 E
Lower Zambezi △, Zambia .... 55 F2　15 25S　29 40 E
Lowestoft, U.K. .... 13 E9　52 29N　1 45 E
Lowgar □, Afghan. .... 40 B6　34　0N　69　0 E
Łowicz, Poland .... 17 B10 52　6N　19 55 E
Lowville, U.S.A. .... 85 C9　43 47N　75 29W
Loxton, Australia .... 63 E3　34 28S 140 31 E
Loxton, S. Africa .... 56 E3　31 30S　22 22 E
Loyalton, U.S.A. .... 78 F6　39 41N 120 14W
Loyalty Is. = Loyauté, Îs., N. Cal. 64 K8　20 50S 166 30 E
Loyang = Luoyang, China .... 34 G7　34 40N 112 26 E
Loyauté, Îs., N. Cal. .... 64 K8　20 50S 166 30 E
Loyev = Loyew, Belarus ...... 17 C16 51 56N　30 46 E
Loyew, Belarus .... 17 C16 51 56N　30 46 E
Loyoro, Uganda .... 54 B3　3 22N　34 14 E
Lu Wo, China .... 33 F11 22 33N 114　6 E
Luachimo, Angola .... 52 F4　7 23S　20 48 E
Luajan ➤, India .... 43 G11 24 44N　85　1 E
Lualaba ➤, Dem. Rep. of
  the Congo .... 54 B2　0 26N　25 20 E
Luampa, Zambia .... 55 F1　15　4S　24 20 E
Luan Chau, Vietnam .... 38 B4　21 38N 103 24 E
Luan He ➤, China .... 35 E10 39 20N 119　5 E
Luan Xian, China .... 35 E10 39 40N 118 40 E
Luancheng, China .... 34 F8　37 53N 114 40 E
Luanda, Angola .... 52 F2　8 50S　13 15 E
Luang, Thale, Thailand .... 39 J3　7 30N 100 15 E
Luang Prabang, Laos .... 38 C4　19 52N 102 10 E
Luangwa, Zambia .... 55 F3　15 35S　30 16 E
Luangwa ➤, Zambia .... 55 E3　14 25S　30 25 E
Luangwa Valley, Zambia ..... 55 E3　13 30S　31 30 E
Luanne, China .... 35 D9　40 55N 117 40 E
Luanping, China .... 35 D9　40 53N 117 23 E
Luanshya, Zambia .... 55 E2　13　3S　28 28 E
Luapula □, Zambia .... 55 E2　11　0S　29　0 E
Luapula ➤, Africa .... 55 D2　9 26S　28 33 E
Luarca, Spain .... 21 A2　43 32N　6 32W
Luashi, Dem. Rep. of the Congo 55 E1　10 50S　23 36 E
Luau, Angola .... 52 G4　10 40S　22 10 E
Lubana, Ozero = Lubānas Ezers,
  Latvia .... 9 H22　56 45N　27　0 E
Lubānas Ezers, Latvia .... 9 H22　56 45N　27　0 E
Lubang Is., Phil. .... 37 B6　13 50N 120 12 E
Lubango, Angola .... 53 G2　14 55S　13 30 E
Lubao, Dem. Rep. of the Congo 54 D2　5 17S　25 42 E
Lubbock, U.S.A. .... 81 J4　33 35N 101 51W
Lübeck, Germany .... 16 B6　53 52N　10 40 E
Lubefu, Dem. Rep. of the Congo 54 C1　4 47S　24 27 E
Lubefu ➤, Dem. Rep. of
  the Congo .... 54 C1　4 10S　23　0 E
Lubero = Luofu, Dem. Rep. of
  the Congo .... 54 C2　0 10S　29 15 E
Lubicon L., Canada .... 70 B5　56 23N 115 56W
Lubilash ➤, Dem. Rep. of
  the Congo .... 52 F4　6　2S　23 45 E
Lubin, Poland .... 16 C9　51 24N　16 11 E
Lublin, Poland .... 17 C12 51 12N　22 38 E
Lubnän, Jabal, Lebanon ...... 46 B4　34　0N　35 40 E
Lubny, Ukraine .... 28 D4　50　3N　32 58 E
Lubongola, Dem. Rep. of
  the Congo .... 54 C2　2 35S　27 50 E
Lububu, Dem. Rep. of the Congo 52 F5　9 57S　25 58 E
Lubudi ➤, Dem. Rep. of
  the Congo .... 55 D2　9　0S　25 35 E
Lubuklinggau, Indonesia ..... 36 E2　3 15S 102 55 E
Lubuksikaping, Indonesia ..... 36 D2　0 10N 100 15 E
Lubumbashi, Dem. Rep. of
  the Congo .... 55 E2　11 40S　27 28 E
Lubunda, Dem. Rep. of
  the Congo .... 54 D2　5 12S　26 41 E
Lubungu, Zambia .... 55 E2　14 35S　26 24 E
Lubutu, Dem. Rep. of the Congo 54 C2　0 45S　26 30 E
Luc An Chau, Vietnam .... 38 A5　22　6N 104 43 E
Lucan, Canada .... 84 C3　43 11N　81 24W
Lucania, Canada .... 68 B5　61　1N 140 27W
Lucas Channel, Canada .... 84 A3　45 21N　81 45W
Lucca, Italy .... 22 C4　43 50N　10 29 E
Luce Bay, U.K. .... 11 G4　54 45N　4 48W
Lucea, Jamaica .... 88 a　18 25N　78 10W
Lucedale, U.S.A. .... 83 K1　30 56N　88 35W
Lucena, Phil. .... 37 B6　13 56N 121 37 E
Lucena, Spain .... 21 D3　37 27N　4 31W
Lučenec, Slovak Rep. .... 17 D10 48 18N　19 42 E
Lucerne = Luzern, Switz. ..... 20 C8　47　3N　8 18 E
Lucerne, U.S.A. .... 78 F4　39　6N 122 48W
Lucerne Valley, U.S.A. .... 79 L10　34 27N 116 57W
Lucero, Mexico .... 86 A3　30 49N 106 30W
Lucheng, China .... 34 F7　36 20N 113 11 E
Lucheringo ➤, Mozam. .... 55 E4　11 43S　36 17 E
Lucia, U.S.A. .... 78 J5　36　2N 121 33W
Lucinda, Australia .... 62 B4　18 32S 146 20 E
Luckenwalde, Germany .... 16 B7　52　5N　13 10 E
Luckhoff, S. Africa .... 56 D3　29 44S　24 43 E
Lucknow, Canada .... 84 C3　43 57N　81 31W
Lucknow, India .... 43 F9　26 50N　81　0 E
Lüda = Dalian, China .... 35 E11 38 50N 121 40 E
Lüderitz, Namibia .... 56 D2　26 41S　15　8 E
Lüderitzbaai, Namibia .... 56 D2　26 36S　15　8 E
Ludhiana, India .... 42 D6　30 57N　75 56 E
Ludington, U.S.A. .... 82 D2　43 57N　86 27W

Ludlow, U.K. .... 13 E5　52 22N　2 42W
Ludlow, Calif., U.S.A. .... 79 L10　34 43N 116 10W
Ludlow, Pa., U.S.A. .... 84 E6　41 43N　78 56W
Ludlow, Vt., U.S.A. .... 85 C12 43 24N　72 42W
Ludvika, Sweden .... 9 F16　60　8N　15 14 E
Ludwigsburg, Germany .... 16 D5　48 53N　9 11 E
Ludwigshafen, Germany ...... 16 D5　49 29N　8 26 E
Lueki, Dem. Rep. of the Congo 54 C2　3 20S　25 48 E
Luena, Dem. Rep. of the Congo 55 D2　9 28S　25 43 E
Luena, Zambia .... 55 E3　10 40S　30 25 E
Lüeyang, China .... 34 H4　33 22N 106 10 E
Lufira ➤, Dem. Rep. of
  the Congo .... 55 D2　9 30S　27　0 E
Lufkin, U.S.A. .... 81 K7　31 21N　94 44W
Lufupa, Dem. Rep. of the Congo 55 E1　10 37S　24 56 E
Luga, Russia .... 18 C4　58 40N　29 55 E
Lugano, Switz. .... 20 C8　46　1N　8 57 E
Lugansk = Luhansk, Ukraine .. 19 E6　48 38N　39 15 E
Lugard's Falls, Kenya .... 54 C4　3　6S　38 41 E
Lugela, Mozam. .... 55 F4　16 25S　36 43 E
Lugenda ➤, Mozam. .... 55 E4　11 25S　38 33 E
Lugh Ganana, Somali Rep. .... 47 G3　3 48N　42 34 E
Lugnaquillia, Ireland .... 10 D5　52 58N　6 28W
Lugo, Italy .... 22 B4　44 25N　11 54 E
Lugo, Spain .... 21 A2　43　2N　7 35W
Lugoj, Romania .... 17 F11 45 42N　21 57 E
Lugovoy = Qulan, Kazakhstan . 28 E8　42 55N　72 43 E
Luhansk, Ukraine .... 19 E6　48 38N　39 15 E
Luiana, Angola .... 56 B3　17 25S　22 59 E
Luimneach = Limerick, Ireland 10 D3　52 40N　8 37W
Luing, U.K. .... 11 E3　56 14N　5 39W
Luís Correia, Brazil .... 93 D10　3　0S　41 35W
Luitpold Coast, Antarctica .... 5 D1　78 30S　32　0W
Luiza, Dem. Rep. of the Congo 52 F4　7 40S　22 30 E
Luizi, Dem. Rep. of the Congo 54 D2　6　0S　27 25 E
Luján, Argentina .... 94 C4　34 45S　59　5W
Lukanga Swamp, Zambia ..... 55 E2　14 30S　27 40 E
Lukenie ➤, Dem. Rep. of
  the Congo .... 52 E3　3　0S　18 50 E
Lukhisaral, India .... 43 G12 25 11N　86　5 E
Lukolela, Dem. Rep. of the Congo 54 D1　5 23S　24 32 E
Lukosi, Zimbabwe .... 55 F2　18 30S　26 30 E
Łuków, Poland .... 17 C12 51 55N　22 23 E
Lukusuzi △, Zambia .... 55 E3　12 43S　32 36 E
Lule älv ➤, Sweden .... 8 D19　65 35N　22 10 E
Luleå, Sweden .... 8 D20　65 35N　22 10 E
Lüleburgaz, Turkey .... 23 D12 41 23N　27 22 E
Luling, U.S.A. .... 81 L6　29 41N　97 39W
Lulong, China .... 35 E10 39 53N 118 51 E
Lulonga ➤, Dem. Rep. of
  the Congo .... 52 D3　1　0N　18 10 E
Lulua ➤, Dem. Rep. of
  the Congo .... 52 E4　4 30S　20 30 E
Lumajang, Indonesia .... 37 H15　8　8S 113 13 E
Lumbala N'guimbo, Angola ... 53 G4　14 18S　21 18 E
Lumberton, U.S.A. .... 83 H6　34 37N　79　0W
Lumsden, Canada .... 71 C8　50 39N 104 52W
Lumsden, N.Z. .... 59 L2　45 44S 168 27 E
Lumut, Malaysia .... 39 K3　4 13N 100 37 E
Lumut, Tanjung, Indonesia ... 36 E3　3 50S 105 58 E
Luna, India .... 42 H3　23 43N　69 16 E
Lunavada, India .... 42 H5　23　8N　73 37 E
Lund, Sweden .... 9 J15　55 44N　13 12 E
Lundazi, Zambia .... 55 E3　12 20S　33　7 E
Lundi ➤, Zimbabwe .... 55 G3　21 43S　32 34 E
Lundu, Malaysia .... 36 D3　1 40N 109 50 E
Lundy, U.K. .... 13 F3　51 10N　4 41W
Lune ➤, U.K. .... 12 C5　54　0N　2 51W
Lüneburg, Germany .... 16 B6　53 15N　10 24 E
Lüneburg Heath = Lüneburger
  Heide, Germany .... 16 B6　53 10N　10 12 E
Lüneburger Heide, Germany .. 16 B6　53 10N　10 12 E
Lunenburg, Canada .... 73 D7　44 22N　64 18W
Lunéville, France .... 20 B7　48 36N　6 30 E
Lunga ➤, Zambia .... 55 E2　14 34S　26 25 E
Lunglei, India .... 41 H18 22 55N　92 45 E
Luni, India .... 42 G5　26　0N　73　6 E
Luni ➤, India .... 42 G4　24 41N　71 14 E
Luninets = Luninyets, Belarus . 17 B14 52 15N　26 50 E
Luning, U.S.A. .... 76 G4　38 30N 118 11W
Luninyets, Belarus .... 17 B14 52 15N　26 50 E
Lunkaransar, India .... 42 E5　28 29N　73 44 E
Lunsemfwa ➤, Zambia .... 55 E3　14 54S　30 12 E
Lunsemfwa Falls, Zambia .... 55 E2　14 30S　29　6 E
Luo He ➤, China .... 34 G6　34 35N 110 20 E
Luochuan, China .... 34 G5　35 45N 109 26 E
Luofu, China .... 54 C2　0 10S　29 15 E
Luohe, China .... 34 H8　33 32N 114　2 E
Luoning, China .... 34 G6　34 35N 111 40 E
Luoyang, China .... 34 G7　34 40N 112 26 E
Luozigou, China .... 35 C16 43 42N 130 18 E
Lupanshui, China .... 32 D5　26 38N 104 48 E
Lupilichi, Mozam. .... 55 E4　11 47S　35 13 E
Luque, Paraguay .... 94 B4　25 19S　57 25W
Luray, U.S.A. .... 82 F6　38 40N　78 28W
Lurgan, U.K. .... 10 B5　54 28N　6 19W
Lusaka, Zambia .... 55 F2　15 28S　28 16 E
Lusambo, Dem. Rep. of
  the Congo .... 54 C1　4 58S　23 28 E
Lusangaye, Dem. Rep. of
  the Congo .... 54 C2　4 54S　26　0 E
Luseland, Canada .... 71 C7　52　5N 109 24W
Lusenga Plain △, Zambia ..... 55 D2　9 22S　29 14 E
Lushan, China .... 34 H7　33 45N 112 55 E
Lushi, China .... 34 G6　34　3N 111　3 E
Lushnjë, Albania .... 23 D8　40 55N　19 41 E
Lushoto, Tanzania .... 54 C4　4 47S　38 20 E
Lüshun, China .... 35 E11 38 45N 121 15 E
Lusk, U.S.A. .... 80 D2　42 46N 104 27W
Lüt, Dasht-e, Iran .... 45 D8　31 30N　58　0 E
Lutherstadt Wittenberg,
  Germany .... 16 C7　51 53N　12 39 E
Luton, U.K. .... 13 F7　51 53N　0 24W
Luton □, U.K. .... 13 F7　51 53N　0 24W
Lutselk'e, Canada .... 71 A6　62 24N 110 44W
Lutsk, Ukraine .... 17 C13 50 50N　25 15 E
Lützow Holmbukta, Antarctica . 5 C4　69 10S　37 30 E
Lutzputs, S. Africa .... 56 D3　28　3S　20 40 E
Luuq = Lugh Ganana,
  Somali Rep. .... 47 G3　3 48N　42 34 E
Luverne, Ala., U.S.A. .... 83 K2　31 43N　86 16W
Luverne, Minn., U.S.A. .... 80 D6　43 39N　96 13W
Luvua, Dem. Rep. of the Congo 55 D2　8 48S　25 17 E
Luvua ➤, Dem. Rep. of
  the Congo .... 54 D2　6 50S　27 30 E

Luvuvhu →, S. Africa .... 57 C5   22 25S   31 18 E
Luwegu →, Tanzania .... 55 D4   8 31S   37 23 E
Luwuk, Indonesia .... 37 E6   0 56S 122 47 E
Luxembourg, Lux. .... 15 E6   49 37N   6 9 E
Luxembourg □, Belgium .... 15 E5   49 58N   5 30 E
Luxembourg ■, Europe .... 20 B7   49 45N   6 0 E
Luxembourg ✈ (LUX), Lux. .... 15 E6   49 37N   6 10 E
Luxi, China .... 32 D4   24 27N   98 36 E
Luxor = El Uqsur, Egypt .... 51 C12   25 41N   32 38 E
Luyi, China .... 34 H8   33 50N 115 35 E
Luza, Russia .... 18 B8   60 39N   47 10 E
Luzern, Switz. .... 20 C8   47 3N   8 18 E
Luzhou, China .... 32 D5   28 52N 105 20 E
Luziânia, Brazil 93 G9   16 20S   48 0W
Luzon, Phil. .... 37 A6   16 0N 121 0 E
Lviv, Ukraine .... 17 D13   49 50N   24 0 E
Lvov = Lviv, Ukraine .... 17 D13   49 50N   24 0 E
Lyakhavichy, Belarus .... 17 B14   53 2N   26 32 E
Lyakhovskiye, Ostrova, Russia ... 29 B15   73 40N 141 0 E
Lyal I., Canada 84 B3   44 57N   81 24W
Lybster, U.K. 11 C5   58 18N   3 15W
Lycksele, Sweden .... 8 D18   64 38N   18 40 E
Lydda = Lod, Israel .... 46 D3   31 57N   34 54 E
Lydenburg, S. Africa .... 57 D5   25 10S   30 29 E
Lydia, Turkey .... 23 E13   38 48N   28 19 E
Lyell, N.Z. .... 59 J4   41 48S 172 4 E
Lyell I., Canada 70 C2   52 40N 131 35W
Lyepyel, Belarus .... 18 D4   54 50N   28 40 E
Lykens, U.S.A. 85 F8   40 34N   76 42W
Lyman, U.S.A. 76 F8   41 20N 110 18W
Lyme B., U.K. 13 G4   50 42N   2 53W
Lyme Regis, U.K. 13 G5   50 43N   2 57W
Lymington, U.K. 13 G6   50 45N   1 32W
Łyna →, Poland .... 9 J19   54 37N   21 14 E
Lynchburg, U.S.A. 82 G6   37 25N   79 9W
Lynd →, Australia .... 62 B3   16 28S 143 18 E
Lynd Ra., Australia .... 63 D4   25 30S 149 20 E
Lynden, Canada 84 C4   43 14N   80 9W
Lynden, U.S.A. 78 B4   48 57N 122 27W
Lyndhurst, Australia .... 63 E2   30 15S 138 18 E
Lyndon →, Australia .... 61 D1   23 29S 114 6 E
Lyndonville, N.Y., U.S.A. 84 C6   43 20N   78 23W
Lyndonville, Vt., U.S.A. 85 B12   44 31N   72 1W
Lyngen, Norway .... 8 B19   69 45N   20 30 E
Lynher Reef, Australia .... 60 C3   15 27S 121 55 E
Lynn, U.S.A. 85 D14   42 28N   70 57W
Lynn Lake, Canada 71 B8   56 51N 101 3W
Lynnwood, U.S.A. 78 C4   47 49N 122 19W
Lynton, U.K. 13 F4   51 13N   3 50W
Lyntupy, Belarus .... 9 J22   55 4N   26 23 E
Lynx L., Canada 71 A7   62 25N 106 15W
Lyon, France .... 20 D6   45 46N   4 50 E
Lyonnais, France .... 20 D6   45 45N   4 15 E
Lyons = Lyon, France .... 20 D6   45 46N   4 50 E
Lyons, Ga., U.S.A. 83 J4   32 12N   82 19W
Lyons, Kans., U.S.A. 80 F5   38 21N   98 12W
Lyons, N.Y., U.S.A. 84 C8   43 5N   77 0W
Lyons →, Australia .... 61 E2   25 2S 115 9 E
Lyons Falls, U.S.A. 85 C9   43 37N   75 22W
Lys = Leie →, Belgium .... 15 C3   51 2N   3 45 E
Lysva, Russia .... 18 C10   58 7N   57 49 E
Lysychansk, Ukraine .... 19 E6   48 55N   38 30 E
Lytham St. Anne's, U.K. 12 D4   53 45N   3 0W
Lyttelton, N.Z. .... 59 K4   43 35S 172 44 E
Lytton, Canada 70 C4   50 13N 121 31W
Lyubertsy, Russia .... 18 C6   55 39N   37 50 E
Lyuboml, Ukraine .... 17 C13   51 11N   24 4 E

M

M.R. Gomez, Presa, Mexico 87 B5   26 10N   99 0W
Ma →, Vietnam .... 38 C5   19 47N 105 56 E
Ma'adaba, Jordan .... 46 E4   30 43N   35 47 E
Maamba, Zambia .... 56 B4   17 17S   26 28 E
Ma'ān, Jordan .... 46 E4   30 12N   35 44 E
Ma'ān □, Jordan .... 46 F5   30 0N   36 0 E
Maanselkä, Finland .... 8 C23   63 52N   28 32 E
Ma'anshan, China .... 33 C6   31 44N 118 29 E
Maarianhamina, Finland .... 9 F18   60 5N   19 55 E
Ma'arrat an Nu'mān, Syria ... 44 C3   35 43N   36 43 E
Maas →, Neths. .... 15 C4   51 45N   4 32 E
Maaseik, Belgium .... 15 C5   51 6N   5 45 E
Maasin, Phil. .... 37 B6   10 8N 124 50 E
Maastricht, Neths. .... 15 D5   50 50N   5 40 E
Maave, Mozam. .... 57 C5   21 4S   34 47 E
Mababe Depression, Botswana . 56 B3   18 50S   24 15 E
Mabalane, Mozam. .... 57 C5   23 37S   32 31 E
Mabel L., Canada 70 C5   50 35N 118 43W
Mabenge, Dem. Rep. of
   the Congo .... 54 B1   4 15N   24 12 E
Maberly, Canada 85 B8   44 50N   76 32W
Mablethorpe, U.K. .... 12 D8   53 20N   0 15 E
Maboma, Dem. Rep. of
   the Congo .... 54 B2   2 30N   28 10 E
Mabuasehube △, Botswana ..... 56 D3   25 5S   21 10 E
Mac Bac, Vietnam .... 39 H6   9 46N 106 7 E
Macachín, Argentina 94 D3   37 10S   63 43W
Macaé, Brazil 95 A7   22 20S   41 43W
McAlester, U.S.A. 81 H7   34 56N   95 46W
McAllen, U.S.A. 81 M5   26 12N   98 14W
MacAlpine L., Canada 68 B9   66 32N 102 45W
Macamic, Canada 72 C4   48 45N   79 0W
Macao = Macau, China .... 33 G10   22 12N 113 33 E
Macapá, Brazil 93 C8   0 5N   51 4W
Macarao △, Venezuela 89 D6   10 22N   67 7W
McArthur →, Australia .... 62 B2   15 54S 136 40 E
McArthur, Port, Australia ..... 62 B2   16 4S 136 23 E
Macau, Brazil 93 E11   5 15S   36 40W
Macau, China .... 33 G10   22 12N 113 33 E
McBride, Canada 70 C4   53 20N 120 19W
McCall, U.S.A. 76 D5   44 55N 116 6W
McCamey, U.S.A. 81 K3   31 8N 102 14W
McCammon, U.S.A. 76 E7   42 39N 112 12W
McCauley I., Canada 70 C2   53 40N 130 15W
McCleary, U.S.A. 78 C3   47 3N 123 16W
Macclenny, U.S.A. 83 K4   30 17N   82 7W
Macclesfield, U.K. 12 D5   53 15N   2 8W
M'Clintock Chan., Canada 68 A9   72 0N 102 0W
McClintock Ra., Australia ..... 60 C4   18 44S 127 38 E
McCloud, U.S.A. 76 F2   41 15N 122 8W
McClure, U.S.A. 84 F7   40 42N   77 19W
McClure, L., U.S.A. 78 H6   37 35N 120 16W
M'Clure Str., Canada 4 B2   75 0N 119 0W
McClusky, U.S.A. 80 B4   47 29N 100 27W

McComb, U.S.A. 81 K9   31 15N   90 27W
McConaughy, L., U.S.A. 80 E4   41 14N 101 40W
McCook, U.S.A. 80 E4   40 12N 100 38W
McCreary, Canada 71 C9   50 47N   99 29W
McCullough Mt., U.S.A. 79 K11   35 35N 115 13W
McCusker →, Canada 71 B7   55 32N 108 39W
McDame, Canada 70 B3   59 44N 128 59W
McDermitt, U.S.A. 76 F5   41 59N 117 43W
McDonald, U.S.A. 84 F4   40 22N   80 14W
Macdonald, L., Australia .... 60 D4   23 30S 129 0 E
McDonald Is., Ind. Oc. .... 3 G13   53 0S   73 0 E
MacDonnell Ranges, Australia . 60 D5   23 40S 133 0 E
MacDowell L., Canada 72 B1   52 15N   92 45W
Macduff, U.K. 11 D6   57 40N   2 31W
Macedonia = Makedhonía □,
   Greece .... 23 D10   40 39N   22 0 E
Macedonia, U.S.A. 84 E3   41 19N   81 31W
Macedonia ■, Europe .... 23 D9   41 53N   21 40 E
Maceió, Brazil 93 E11   9 40S   35 41W
Macerata, Italy .... 22 C5   43 18N   13 27 E
McFarland, U.S.A. 79 K7   35 41N 119 14W
McFarlane →, Canada 71 B7   59 12N 107 58W
Macfarlane, L., Australia .... 63 E2   32 0S 136 40 E
McGehee, U.S.A. 81 J9   33 38N   91 24W
McGill, U.S.A. 76 G6   39 23N 114 47W
Macgillycuddy's Reeks, Ireland . 10 E2   51 58N   9 45W
McGraw, U.S.A. 85 D8   42 36N   76 8W
McGregor, U.S.A. 80 D9   43 1N   91 11W
McGregor Ra., Australia .... 63 D3   27 0S 142 45 E
McGuire, Mt., Australia .... 62 J6   20 18S 148 23 E
Mach, Pakistan .... 40 E5   29 50N   67 20 E
Māch Kowr, Iran .... 45 E9   25 48N   61 28 E
Machado = Jiparaná →, Brazil . 92 E6   8 3S   62 52W
Machagai, Argentina 94 B3   26 56S   60 2W
Machakos, Kenya .... 54 C4   1 30S   37 15 E
Machala, Ecuador 92 D3   3 20S   79 57W
Machanga, Mozam. .... 57 C6   20 59S   35 0 E
Machattie, L., Australia .... 62 C2   24 50S 139 48 E
Machava, Mozam. .... 57 D5   25 54S   32 28 E
Macheke, Zimbabwe .... 57 B5   18 5S   31 51 E
Machhu →, India .... 42 H4   23 6N   70 46 E
Machias, Maine, U.S.A. 83 C12   44 43N   67 28W
Machias, N.Y., U.S.A. 84 D6   42 25N   78 30W
Machichi →, Canada 71 B10   57 3N   92 6W
Machico, Madeira 24 D3   32 43N   16 44W
Machilipatnam, India .... 41 L12   16 12N   81 8 E
Machiques, Venezuela 92 A4   10 4N   72 34W
Machupicchu, Peru 92 F4   13 8S   72 30W
Machynlleth, U.K. 13 E4   52 35N   3 50W
Macia, Mozam. .... 57 D5   25 2S   33 8 E
McIlwraith Ra., Australia .... 62 A3   13 50S 143 20 E
McInnes L., Canada 71 C10   52 13N   93 45W
McIntosh, U.S.A. 80 C4   45 55N 101 21W
McIntosh L., Canada 71 B8   55 45N 105 0W
Macintosh Ra., Australia .... 61 E4   27 39S 125 32 E
Macintyre →, Australia .... 63 D5   28 37S 150 47 E
Mackay, Australia .... 62 K7   21 8S 149 11 E
Mackay, U.S.A. 76 E7   43 55N 113 37W
McKay →, Canada 70 B6   57 10N 111 38W
Mackay, L., Australia .... 60 D4   22 30S 129 0 E
McKay Ra., Australia .... 60 D3   23 0S 122 30 E
McKeesport, U.S.A. 84 F5   40 21N   79 52W
McKellar, Canada 84 A5   45 30N   79 55W
McKenna, U.S.A. 78 D4   46 56N 122 33W
Mackenzie, Canada 70 B4   55 20N 123 5W
Mackenzie, U.S.A. 83 G1   36 8N   88 31W
Mackenzie →, Australia .... 62 C4   23 38S 149 46 E
Mackenzie →, Canada 68 B6   69 10N 134 20W
McKenzie →, U.S.A. 76 D2   44 7N 123 6W
Mackenzie Bay, Canada 4 B1   69 0N 137 30W
Mackenzie City = Linden, Guyana 92 B7   6 0N   58 10W
Mackenzie Mts., Canada 68 B6   64 0N 130 0W
Mackinaw City, U.S.A. 81 C11   45 47N   84 44W
McKinlay, Australia .... 62 C3   21 16S 141 18 E
McKinlay →, Australia .... 62 C3   20 50S 141 28 E
McKinley, Mt., U.S.A. 68 B4   63 4N 151 0W
McKinley Sea, Arctic 4 A7   82 0N   0 0W
McKinney, U.S.A. 81 J6   33 12N   96 37W
Mackinnon Road, Kenya .... 54 C4   3 40S   39 1 E
McKittrick, U.S.A. 79 K7   35 18N 119 37W
Macklin, Canada 71 C7   52 20N 109 56W
Macksville, Australia .... 63 E5   30 40S 152 56 E
McLaughlin, U.S.A. 80 C4   45 49N 100 49W
Maclean, Australia .... 63 D5   29 26S 153 16 E
McLean, U.S.A. 81 H4   35 14N 100 36W
McLeansboro, U.S.A. 80 F10   38 6N   88 32W
Maclear, S. Africa .... 57 E4   31 2S   28 23 E
Maclear, C., Malawi .... 55 E3   13 58S   34 49 E
Macleay →, Australia .... 63 E5   30 56S 153 0 E
McLennan, Canada 70 B5   55 42N 116 50W
McLeod →, Canada 70 C5   54 9N 115 44W
MacLeod, B., Canada 71 A7   62 53N 110 0W
MacLeod, L., Australia .... 61 D1   24 9S 113 47 E
MacLeod Lake, Canada 70 C4   54 58N 123 0W
McLoughlin, Mt., U.S.A. 76 E2   42 27N 122 19W
McMechen, U.S.A. 84 G4   39 57N   80 44W
McMinnville, Oreg., U.S.A. 76 D2   45 13N 123 12W
McMinnville, Tenn., U.S.A. 83 H3   35 41N   85 46W
McMurdo Sd., Antarctica ...... 5 D11   77 0S 170 0 E
McMurray = Fort McMurray,
   Canada 70 B6   56 44N 111 7W
McMurray, U.S.A. 78 B4   48 19N 122 14W
Macodoene, Mozam. .... 57 C6   23 32S   35 5 E
Macomb, U.S.A. 80 E9   40 27N   90 40W
Mâcon, France .... 20 C6   46 19N   4 50 E
Macon, Ga., U.S.A. 83 J4   32 51N   83 38W
Macon, Miss., U.S.A. 83 J1   33 7N   88 34W
Macon, Mo., U.S.A. 80 F8   39 44N   92 28W
Macossa, Mozam. .... 55 F3   17 55S   33 56 E
Macoun L., Canada 71 B8   56 32N 103 40W
Macovane, Mozam. .... 57 C6   21 30S   35 2 E
McPherson, U.S.A. 80 F6   38 22N   97 40W
McPherson Pk., U.S.A. 79 L7   34 53N 119 53W
McPherson Ra., Australia ...... 63 D5   28 15S 153 15 E
Macquarie →, Australia .... 63 E4   30 7S 147 24 E
Macquarie Harbour, Australia . 63 G4   42 15S 145 23 E
Macquarie Is., Pac. Oc. .... 64 N7   54 36S 158 55 E
MacRobertson Land, Antarctica . 5 D6   71 0S   64 0 E
Macroom, Ireland 10 E3   51 54N   8 57W
MacTier, Canada 84 A5   45 9N   79 46W
Macubela, Mozam. .... 55 F4   16 53S   37 49 E
Macuira △, Colombia 89 D5   12 9N   71 21W
Macuiza, Mozam. .... 55 F3   18 7S   34 29 E
Macuro, Venezuela 93 K15   10 42N   61 55W
Macusani, Peru 92 F4   14 4S   70 29W
Macuse, Mozam. .... 55 F4   17 45S   37 10 E
Macuspana, Mexico 87 D6   17 46N   92 36W

Macusse, Angola .... 56 B3   17 48S   20 23 E
Ma'dabā □, Jordan .... 46 D4   31 43N   35 47 E
Madadeni, S. Africa .... 57 D5   27 43S   30 3 E
Madagascar ■, Africa .... 57 C8   20 0S   47 0 E
Madama, Niger .... 51 D8   22 0N   13 40 E
Madame, I., Canada 73 C7   45 30N   60 58W
Madaripur, Bangla. .... 41 H17   23 19N   90 15 E
Madauk, Burma .... 41 L20   17 56N   96 52 E
Madawaska, Canada 84 A7   45 30N   78 0W
Madawaska →, Canada 84 A8   45 27N   76 21W
Madaya, Burma .... 41 H20   22 12N   96 10 E
Maddalena, Italy .... 22 D3   41 16N   9 23 E
Madeira, Atl. Oc. 24 D3   32 50N   17 0W
Madeira →, Brazil 92 D7   3 22S   58 45W
Madeleine, Îs. de la, Canada ... 73 C7   47 30N   61 40W
Madera, Mexico 86 B3   29 12N 108 7W
Madera, Calif., U.S.A. 78 J6   36 57N 120 3W
Madera, Pa., U.S.A. 84 F6   40 49N   78 26W
Madha, India .... 40 L9   18 0N   75 30 E
Madhavpur, India .... 42 J3   21 15N   69 58 E
Madhepura, India .... 43 F12   26 11N   86 23 E
Madhubani, India .... 43 F12   26 21N   86 7 E
Madhupur, India .... 43 G12   24 16N   86 39 E
Madhya Pradesh □, India ...... 42 J8   22 50N   78 0 E
Madidi →, Bolivia 92 F5   12 32S   66 52W
Madikeri, India .... 40 N9   12 30N   75 45 E
Madikwe △, S. Africa .... 57 D5   27 38S   32 15 E
Madill, U.S.A. 81 H6   34 6N   96 46W
Madimba, Dem. Rep. of
   the Congo .... 52 E3   4 58S   15 5 E
Ma'din, Syria .... 44 C3   35 45N   39 36 E
Madingou, Congo .... 52 E2   4 10S   13 33 E
Madirovalo, Madag. .... 57 B8   16 26S   46 32 E
Madison, Calif., U.S.A. 78 G5   38 41N 121 59W
Madison, Fla., U.S.A. 83 K4   30 28N   83 25W
Madison, Ind., U.S.A. 82 F3   38 44N   85 23W
Madison, Nebr., U.S.A. 80 E6   41 50N   97 27W
Madison, Ohio, U.S.A. 84 E3   41 46N   81 3W
Madison, S. Dak., U.S.A. 80 D6   44 0N   97 7W
Madison, Wis., U.S.A. 80 D10   43 4N   89 24W
Madison →, U.S.A. 76 D8   45 56N 111 31W
Madison Heights, U.S.A. 82 G6   37 25N   79 8W
Madisonville, Ky., U.S.A. 82 G2   37 20N   87 30W
Madisonville, Tex., U.S.A. 81 K7   30 57N   95 55W
Madista, Botswana .... 56 C4   21 15S   25 6 E
Madiun, Indonesia .... 36 F4   7 38S 111 32 E
Madoc, Canada 84 B7   44 30N   77 28W
Madona, Latvia .... 9 H22   56 53N   26 5 E
Madrakah, Ra's al, Oman ...... 47 D6   19 0N   57 50 E
Madras = Chennai, India ...... 40 N12   13 8N   80 19 E
Madras = Tamil Nadu □, India . 40 P10   11 0N   77 0 E
Madras, U.S.A. 76 D3   44 38N 121 8W
Madre, Laguna, U.S.A. 81 M6   27 0N   97 30W
Madre, Sierra, Phil. .... 37 A6   17 0N 122 0 E
Madre de Dios →, Bolivia 92 F5   10 59S   66 8W
Madre de Dios, I., Chile 96 G1   50 20S   75 10W
Madre del Sur, Sierra, Mexico . 87 D5   17 30N 100 0W
Madre Occidental, Sierra, Mexico 86 B3   27 0N 107 0W
Madre Oriental, Sierra, Mexico . 86 C5   25 0N 100 0W
Madri, India .... 42 G5   24 16N   73 32 E
Madrid, Spain 21 B4   40 25N   3 45W
Madrid, U.S.A. 85 B9   44 45N   75 8W
Madura, Australia .... 61 F4   31 55S 127 0 E
Madura, Indonesia .... 37 G15   7 30S 114 0 E
Madura, Selat, Indonesia ...... 37 G15   7 30S 113 20 E
Madurai, India .... 40 Q11   9 55N   78 10 E
Madurantakam, India .... 40 N11   12 30N   79 50 E
Mae Chan, Thailand .... 38 B2   20 9N   99 52 E
Mae Hong Son, Thailand ...... 38 C2   19 16N   97 56 E
Mae Khlong →, Thailand ...... 38 F3   13 24N 100 0 E
Mae Phrik, Thailand .... 38 D2   17 27N   99 7 E
Mae Ping △, Thailand .... 38 D2   17 37N   98 51 E
Mae Ramat, Thailand .... 38 D2   16 58N   98 31 E
Mae Rim, Thailand .... 38 C2   18 54N   98 57 E
Mae Sot, Thailand .... 38 D2   16 43N   98 34 E
Mae Suai, Thailand .... 38 C2   19 39N   99 33 E
Mae Tha, Thailand .... 38 C2   18 28N   99 8 E
Mae Wong △, Thailand .... 38 E2   15 54N   99 12 E
Mae Yom △, Thailand .... 38 C3   18 43N 100 15 E
Maebashi, Japan .... 31 F9   36 24N 139 4 E
Maesteg, U.K. 13 F4   51 36N   3 40W
Maestra, Sierra, Cuba 88 B4   20 15N   77 0W
Maevatanana, Madag. .... 57 B8   16 56S   46 49 E
Mafeking = Mafikeng, S. Africa . 56 D4   25 50S   25 38 E
Mafeking, Canada 71 C8   52 40N 101 10W
Mafeteng, Lesotho .... 56 D4   29 51S   27 15 E
Maffra, Australia .... 63 F4   37 53S 146 58 E
Mafia I., Tanzania .... 54 D4   7 45S   39 50 E
Mafikeng, S. Africa .... 56 D4   25 50S   25 38 E
Mafra, Brazil 95 B6   26 10S   49 55W
Mafra, Portugal 21 C1   38 55N   9 20W
Mafungbusi Plateau, Zimbabwe 55 F2   18 30S   29 8 E
Magadan, Russia .... 29 D16   59 38N 150 50 E
Magadi, Kenya .... 54 C4   1 54S   36 19 E
Magadi, L., Kenya .... 54 C4   1 54S   36 19 E
Magaliesburg, S. Africa .... 57 D4   26 0S   27 32 E
Magallanes, Estrecho de, Chile . 96 G2   52 30S   75 0W
Magangué, Colombia 92 B4   9 14N   74 45W
Magdalen Is. = Madeleine, Îs. de
   la, Canada 73 C7   47 30N   61 40W
Magdalena, Argentina 94 D4   35 5S   57 30W
Magdalena, Bolivia 92 F6   13 13S   63 57W
Magdalena, U.S.A. 77 J10   34 7N 107 15W
Magdalena →, Colombia 92 A4   11 6N   74 51W
Magdalena →, Mexico 86 A2   30 40N 112 25W
Magdalena, B., Mexico 86 C2   24 30N 112 10W
Magdalena, Llano de la, Mexico 86 C2   25 0N 111 30W
Magdeburg, Germany .... 16 B6   52 7N   11 38 E
Magdelaine Cays, Australia .... 62 B5   16 33S 150 18 E
Magee, U.S.A. 81 K10   31 52N   89 44W
Magelang, Indonesia .... 36 F4   7 29S 110 13 E
Magellan's Str. = Magallanes,
   Estrecho de, Chile 96 G2   52 30S   75 0W
Magenta, L., Australia .... 61 F2   33 30S 119 2 E
Magerøya, Norway .... 8 A21   71 3N   25 40 E
Maggiore, Lago, Italy .... 20 D8   45 57N   8 39 E
Maggotty, Jamaica .... 88 a   18 9N   77 46W
Maghâgha, Egypt .... 51 C12   28 38N   30 50 E
Magherafelt, U.K. 10 B5   54 45N   6 37W
Maghreb, N. Afr. 48 B4   32 0N   4 0W
Magistralnyy, Russia .... 29 D11   56 16N 107 36 E
Magnetic Pole (North), Canada . 4 A2   88 30N 107 0W
Magnetic Pole (South),
   Antarctica .... 5 C9   64 8S 138 8 E
Magnitogorsk, Russia .... 18 D10   53 27N   59 4 E
Magnolia, Ark., U.S.A. 81 J8   33 16N   93 14W

Magnolia, Miss., U.S.A. 81 K9   31 9N   90 28W
Magog, Canada 85 A12   45 18N   72 9W
Magoro, Uganda .... 54 B3   1 45N   34 12 E
Magoša = Famagusta, Cyprus . 25 D12   35 8N   33 55 E
Magoye, Zambia .... 55 F2   16 1S   27 30 E
Magozal, Mexico 87 C5   21 34N   97 59W
Magpie, L., Canada 73 B7   51 0N   64 41W
Magrath, Canada 70 D6   49 25N 112 50W
Maguarinho, C., Brazil 93 D9   0 15S   48 30W
Magude, Mozam. .... 57 D5   25 2S   32 40 E
Maguse = Famagusta, Cyprus . 25 D12   35 8N   33 55 E
Magvana, India .... 42 H3   23 13N   69 22 E
Magwe, Burma .... 41 J19   20 10N   95 0 E
Maha Sarakham, Thailand ..... 38 D4   16 12N 103 16 E
Mahābād, Iran .... 44 B5   36 50N   45 45 E
Mahabharat Lekh, Nepal ...... 43 E10   28 30N   82 0 E
Mahabo, Madag. .... 57 C7   20 23S   44 40 E
Mahadeo Hills, India .... 43 H8   22 20N   78 30 E
Mahaffey, U.S.A. 84 F6   40 53N   78 44W
Mahagi, Dem. Rep. of the Congo 54 B3   2 20N   31 0 E
Mahajamba →, Madag. .... 57 B8   15 33S   47 8 E
Mahajamba, Helodranon' i,
   Madag. .... 57 B8   15 24S   47 5 E
Mahajan, India .... 42 E5   28 48N   73 56 E
Mahajanga, Madag. .... 57 B8   15 40S   46 25 E
Mahajanga □, Madag. .... 57 B8   17 0S   47 0 E
Mahajilo →, Madag. .... 57 B8   19 42S   45 22 E
Mahakam →, Indonesia .... 36 E5   0 35S 117 17 E
Mahalapye, Botswana .... 56 C4   23 1S   26 51 E
Mahale Mts., Tanzania .... 54 D3   6 20S   30 0 E
Mahale Mts. △, Tanzania ...... 54 D2   6 10S   29 50 E
Maḥallāt, Iran .... 45 C6   33 55N   50 30 E
Māhān, Iran .... 45 D8   30 5N   57 18 E
Mahan →, India .... 43 H10   23 30N   82 50 E
Mahanadi →, India .... 41 J15   20 20N   86 25 E
Mahananda →, India .... 43 G12   25 12N   87 52 E
Mahanoro, Madag. .... 57 B8   19 54S   48 48 E
Mahanoy City, U.S.A. 85 F8   40 49N   76 9W
Maharashtra □, India .... 40 J9   20 30N   75 30 E
Mahasham, W. →, Egypt ...... 46 E3   30 15N   34 10 E
Mahasoa, Madag. .... 57 C8   22 12S   46 6 E
Mahasolo, Madag. .... 57 B8   19 7S   46 22 E
Mahattat ash Shidīyah, Jordan . 46 F4   29 55S   35 55 E
Mahattat 'Unayzah, Jordan .... 46 E4   30 30N   35 47 E
Mahavavy →, Madag. .... 57 B8   15 57S   45 54 E
Mahaxay, Laos .... 38 D5   17 22N 105 12 E
Mahbubnagar, India .... 40 L10   16 45N   77 59 E
Maḥdah, Oman .... 45 E7   24 24N   55 59 E
Mahdia, Tunisia .... 51 A8   35 28N   11 0 E
Mahe, India .... 43 C8   33 10N   78 32 E
Mahendragarh, India .... 42 E7   28 17N   76 14 E
Mahenge, Tanzania .... 55 D4   8 45S   36 41 E
Maheno, N.Z. .... 59 L3   45 10S 170 50 E
Mahesana, India .... 42 H5   23 39N   72 26 E
Maheshwar, India .... 42 H6   22 11N   75 35 E
Mahgawan, India .... 43 F8   26 29N   78 37 E
Mahi →, India .... 42 H5   22 15N   72 55 E
Mahia Pen., N.Z. .... 59 H6   39 9S 177 55 E
Mahilyow, Belarus .... 17 B16   53 55N   30 18 E
Mahmud Kot, Pakistan .... 42 D4   30 16N   71 0 E
Mahnomen, U.S.A. 80 B7   47 19N   95 58W
Mahoba, India .... 43 G8   25 15N   79 55 E
Mahón = Maó, Spain .... 24 B11   39 53N   4 16 E
Mahone Bay, Canada 73 D7   44 30N   64 20W
Mahopac, U.S.A. 85 E11   41 22N   73 45W
Mahuva, India .... 42 J4   21 5N   71 48 E
Mai-Ndombe, L., Dem. Rep. of
   the Congo .... 52 E3   2 0S   18 20 E
Mai-Sai, Thailand .... 38 B2   20 20N   99 55 E
Mai Thon, Ko, Thailand ...... 39 a   7 40N   98 28 E
Maicurú →, Brazil 93 D8   2 14S   54 17W
Maidan Khula, Afghan. .... 42 C3   33 36N   69 50 E
Maidenhead, U.K. 13 F7   51 31N   0 42W
Maidstone, Canada 71 C7   53 5N 109 20W
Maidstone, U.K. .... 13 F8   51 16N   0 32 E
Maiduguri, Nigeria .... 51 F8   12 0N   13 20 E
Maihar, India .... 43 G9   24 16N   80 45 E
Maijdi, Bangla. .... 41 H17   22 48N   91 10 E
Maikala Ra., India .... 41 J12   22 0N   81 0 E
Maiko, Dem. Rep. of
   the Congo .... 54 C2   0 30S   27 50 E
Mailani, India .... 43 E9   28 17N   80 21 E
Mailsi, Pakistan .... 42 E5   29 48N   72 15 E
Main →, Germany .... 16 C5   50 0N   8 18 E
Main →, U.K. 10 B5   54 48N   6 18W
Main Range △, Australia ...... 63 D5   28 11S 152 27 E
Main Ridge, Trin. & Tob. 93 J16   11 16N   60 40W
Maine, France 20 C3   48 20N   0 15W
Maine □, U.S.A. 83 C11   45 20N   69 0W
Maine →, Ireland 10 D2   52 9N   9 45W
Maingkwan, Burma .... 41 F20   26 15N   96 37 E
Mainit, L., Phil. .... 37 C7   9 31N 125 30 E
Mainland, Orkney, U.K. 11 C5   58 59N   3 8W
Mainland, Shet., U.K. 11 A7   60 15N   1 22W
Mainoru, Australia .... 62 A1   14 0S 134 6 E
Mainpuri, India .... 43 F8   27 18N   79 4 E
Maintirano, Madag. .... 57 B7   18 3S   44 1 E
Mainz, Germany .... 16 C5   50 1N   8 14 E
Maipú, Argentina 94 D4   36 52S   57 50W
Maiquetía, Venezuela 92 A5   10 36N   66 57W
Mairabari, India .... 41 F18   26 30N   92 22 E
Maisí, Cuba 89 B5   20 17N   74 9W
Maisí, Pta. de, Cuba 89 B5   20 10N   74 10W
Maitland, N.S.W., Australia ... 63 E5   32 33S 151 36 E
Maitland, S. Austral., Australia . 63 E2   34 23S 137 40 E
Maitland →, Canada 84 C3   43 45N   81 43W
Maitri, Antarctica 5 D3   70 0S   3 0W
Maiz, Is. del, Nic. 88 D3   12 15N   83 4W
Maizuru, Japan .... 31 G7   35 25N 135 22 E
Majalengka, Indonesia .... 37 G13   6 50S 108 13 E
Majene, Indonesia .... 37 E5   3 38S 118 57 E
Majete △, Malawi .... 55 F3   15 54S   34 34 E
Majorca = Mallorca, Spain .... 24 B10   39 30N   3 0 E
Makaha, Zimbabwe .... 57 B5   17 20S   32 39 E
Makalamabedi, Botswana ...... 56 C3   20 19S   23 51 E
Makale, Indonesia .... 37 E5   3 6S 119 51 E
Makamba, Burundi .... 54 C2   4 8S   29 49 E
Makarikari = Makgadikgadi Salt
   Pans, Botswana .... 56 C4   20 40S   25 45 E
Makarov Basin, Arctic .... 4 A   87 0N 150 0W
Makarovo, Russia .... 29 D11   57 40N 107 45 E
Makasar = Ujung Pandang,
   Indonesia .... 37 F5   5 10S 119 20 E
Makasar, Selat, Indonesia ..... 37 E5   1 0S 118 20 E

Makasar, Str. of = Makasar, Selat,
  Indonesia .... 37 E5   1 0S 118 20 E
Makat, Kazakhstan .... 19 E9   47 39N 53 19 E
Makedhonía □, Greece ..... 23 D10 40 39N 22 0 E
Makedonija = Macedonia ■,
  Europe .... 23 D9   41 53N 21 40 E
Makeyevka = Makiyivka, Ukraine 19 E6 48 0N 38 0 E
Makgadikgadi △, Botswana .. 56 C3 20 27S 24 47 E
Makgadikgadi Salt Pans,
  Botswana .... 56 C4   20 40S 25 45 E
Makhachkala, Russia .... 19 F8   43 0N 47 30 E
Makhfar al Buşayyah, Iraq .. 44 D5   30 0N 46 10 E
Makhmūr, Iraq .... 44 C4   35 46N 43 35 E
Makian, Indonesia .... 37 D7   0 20N 127 20 E
Makindu, Kenya .... 54 C4   2 18S 37 50 E
Makinsk, Kazakhstan .... 28 D8   52 37N 70 26 E
Makiyivka, Ukraine .... 19 E6   48 0N 38 0 E
Makkah, Si. Arabia .... 47 C2   21 30N 39 54 E
Makkovik, Canada 73 A8   55 10N 59 10W
Makó, Hungary .... 17 E11 46 14N 20 33 E
Makokou, Gabon .... 52 D2   0 40N 12 50 E
Makongo, Dem. Rep. of
  the Congo .... 54 B2   3 25N 26 17 E
Makoro, Dem. Rep. of the Congo 54 B2   3 10N 29 59 E
Makrai, India .... 40 H10 22 2N 77 0 E
Makran Coast Range, Pakistan 40 G4 25 40N 64 0 E
Makrana, India .... 42 F6   27 2N 74 46 E
Makriyialos, Greece .... 25 D7   35 2N 25 59 E
Mākū, Iran .... 44 B5   39 15N 44 31 E
Makunda, Botswana .... 56 C3   22 30S 20 7 E
Makurazaki, Japan .... 31 J5   31 15N 130 20 E
Makurdi, Nigeria .... 50 G7   7 43N   8 35 E
Makūyeh, Iran .... 45 D7   28 7N 53 9 E
Makwassie, S. Africa .... 56 D4   27 17S 26 0 E
Makwiro, Zimbabwe .... 57 B5   17 58S 30 25 E
Mal B., Ireland 10 D2   52 50N   9 30W
Mala, Pta., Panama 88 E3   7 28N 80 2W
Malabar Coast, India .... 40 P9   11 0N 75 0 E
Malacca, Str. of, Indonesia .. 39 L3   3 0N 101 0 E
Malad City, U.S.A. 76 E7   42 12N 112 15W
Maladzyechna, Belarus ..... 17 A14 54 20N 26 50 E
Málaga, Spain 21 D3   36 43N   4 23W
Malagarasi, Tanzania .... 54 D3   5 5S 30 50 E
Malagarasi ➤, Tanzania .... 54 D2   5 12S 29 47 E
Malagasy Rep. = Madagascar ■,
  Africa .... 57 C8   20 0S 47 0 E
Malahide, Ireland 10 C5   53 26N   6 9W
Malaimbandy, Madag. ...... 57 C8   20 20S 45 36 E
Malakâl, Sudan .... 51 G12   9 33N 31 40 E
Malakand, Pakistan .... 42 B4   34 40N 71 55 E
Malakwal, Pakistan .... 42 C5   32 34N 73 13 E
Malamala, Indonesia .... 37 E6   3 21S 120 55 E
Malanda, Australia .... 62 B4   17 22S 145 35 E
Malang, Indonesia .... 36 F4   7 59S 112 45 E
Malangen, Norway .... 8 B18   69 24N 18 37 E
Malanje, Angola .... 52 F3   9 36S 16 17 E
Mälaren, Sweden .... 9 G17   59 30N 17 10 E
Malargüe, Argentina 94 D2   35 32S 69 30W
Malartic, Canada 72 C4   48 9N 78 9W
Malaryta, Belarus .... 17 C13 51 50N 24 3 E
Malatya, Turkey .... 19 G6   38 25N 38 20 E
Malawi ■, Africa .... 55 E3   11 55S 34 0 E
Malawi, L. = Nyasa, L., Africa 55 E3 12 30S 34 30 E
Malay Pen., Asia .... 39 J3   7 25N 100 0 E
Malaya Vishera, Russia ..... 18 C5   58 55N 32 25 E
Malaybalay, Phil. .... 37 C7   8 5N 125 7 E
Malāyer, Iran .... 45 C6   34 19N 48 51 E
Malaysia ■, Asia .... 39 K4   5 0N 110 0 E
Malazgirt, Turkey .... 19 G7   39 10N 42 33 E
Malbon, Australia .... 62 C3   21 5S 140 17 E
Malbooma, Australia .... 63 E1   30 41S 134 11 E
Malbork, Poland .... 17 B10 54 3N 19 1 E
Malcolm, Australia .... 61 E3   28 51S 121 25 E
Malcolm, Pt., Australia ..... 61 F3   33 48S 123 45 E
Maldah, India .... 43 G13 25 2N 88 9 E
Maldegem, Belgium .... 15 C3   51 14N   3 26 E
Malden, Mass., U.S.A. 85 D13 42 26N 71 4W
Malden, Mo., U.S.A. 81 G10 36 34N 89 57W
Malden I., Kiribati 65 H12   4 3S 155 1W
Maldives ■, Ind. Oc. .... 27 J11   5 0N 73 0 E
Maldon, U.K. .... 13 F8   51 44N   0 42 E
Maldonado, Uruguay 95 C5   34 59S 55 0W
Maldonado, Punta, Mexico .. 87 D5   16 19N 98 35W
Male, Maldives .... 27 J11   4 0N 73 28 E
Malé Karpaty, Slovak Rep. .. 17 D9   48 30N 17 20 E
Maléa, Ákra, Greece .... 23 F10 36 28N 23 7 E
Malegaon, India .... 40 J9   20 30N 74 38 E
Malei, Mozam. .... 55 F4   17 12S 36 58 E
Malek Kandī, Iran .... 44 B5   37 9N 46 6 E
Malela, Dem. Rep. of the Congo 54 C2   4 22S 26 8 E
Malema, Mozam. .... 55 E4   14 57S 37 20 E
Máleme, Greece .... 25 D5   35 31N 23 49 E
Malenga, Australia .... 63 D5   26 45S 152 52 E
Malerkotla, India .... 42 D6   30 32N 75 58 E
Máles, Greece .... 25 D7   35 6N 25 35 E
Malgomaj, Sweden .... 8 D17   64 40N 16 30 E
Malha, Sudan .... 51 E11 15 8N 25 10 E
Malhargarh, India .... 42 G6   24 17N 74 59 E
Malheur ➤, U.S.A. 76 D5   44 4N 116 59W
Malheur L., U.S.A. 76 E4   43 20N 118 48W
Mali ■, Africa 50 E5   17 0N   3 0W
Mali ➤, Burma .... 41 G20 25 40N 97 40 E
Mali Kyun, Burma .... 38 F2   13 0N 98 20 E
Malibu, U.S.A. 79 L8   34 2N 118 41W
Maliku, Indonesia .... 37 E6   0 39S 123 16 E
Malili, Indonesia .... 37 E6   2 42S 121 6 E
Malimba, Mts., Dem. Rep. of
  the Congo .... 54 D2   7 30S 29 30 E
Malin Hd., Ireland 10 A4   55 23N   7 23W
Malin Pen., Ireland 10 A4   55 20N   7 17W
Malindi, Kenya .... 54 C5   3 12S 40 5 E
Malines = Mechelen, Belgium 15 C4   51 2N   4 29 E
Malino, Indonesia .... 37 D6   1 0N 121 0 E
Malinyi, Tanzania .... 55 D4   8 56S 36 0 E
Malita, Phil. .... 37 C7   6 19N 125 39 E
Maliwun, Burma .... 36 B1   10 17N 98 40 E
Maliya, India .... 42 H4   23 5N 70 46 E
Malka Mari △, Kenya ...... 54 B5   11 41N 40 46 E
Malkara, Turkey .... 23 D12 40 53N 26 53 E
Mallacoota Inlet, Australia .. 63 F4   37 34S 149 40 E
Mallaig, U.K. 11 D3   57 0N   5 50W
Mallawan, India .... 43 F9   27 4N 80 12 E
Mallawi, Egypt .... 51 C12 27 44N 30 44 E
Mállia, Greece .... 25 D7   35 17N 25 32 E
Mallión, Kólpos, Greece .... 25 D7   35 19N 25 27 E
Mallorca, Spain .... 24 B10 39 30N   3 0 E
Mallorytown, Canada 85 B9   44 29N 75 53W
Mallow, Ireland 10 D3   52 8N   8 39W

Malmberget, Sweden .... 8 C19   67 11N 20 40 E
Malmédy, Belgium .... 15 D6   50 25N   6 2 E
Malmesbury, S. Africa ..... 56 E2   33 28S 18 41 E
Malmö, Sweden .... 9 J15   55 36N 12 59 E
Malolos, Phil. .... 37 B6   14 50N 120 49 E
Malolotja △, Swaziland ..... 57 D5   26 4S 31 6 E
Malombe L., Malawi .... 55 E4   14 40S 35 15 E
Malone, U.S.A. 85 B10 44 51N 74 18W
Måløy, Norway .... 9 F11   61 57N   5 6 E
Malpaso, Canary Is. 24 G1   27 43N 18 3W
Malpelo, I. de, Colombia ... 92 C2   4 3N 81 35W
Malpur, India .... 42 H5   23 21N 73 27 E
Malpura, India .... 42 F6   26 17N 75 23 E
Malta, Idaho, U.S.A. 76 E7   42 18N 113 22W
Malta, Mont., U.S.A. 76 B10 48 21N 107 52W
Malta ■, Europe .... 25 D2   35 55N 14 26 E
Maltahöhe, Namibia .... 56 C2   24 55S 17 0 E
Malton, Canada 84 C5   43 42N 79 38W
Malton, U.K. 12 C7   54 8N   0 49W
Maluku, Indonesia .... 37 E7   1 0S 127 0 E
Maluku □, Indonesia .... 37 E7   3 0S 128 0 E
Maluku Sea = Molucca Sea,
  Indonesia .... 37 E6   0 0 125 0 E
Malvan, India .... 40 L8   16 2N 73 30 E
Malvern, U.S.A. 81 H8   34 22N 92 49W
Malvern Hills, U.K. 13 E5   52 0N   2 19W
Malvinas, Is. = Falkland Is. ☑,
  Atl. Oc. 96 G5   51 30S 59 0W
Malya, Tanzania .... 54 C3   3 5S 33 38 E
Malyn, Ukraine .... 17 C15 50 46N 29 3 E
Malyy Lyakhovskiy, Ostrov,
  Russia .... 29 B15 74 7N 140 36 E
Mama, Russia .... 29 D12 58 18N 112 54 E
Mamanguape, Brazil 93 E11   6 50S 35 4W
Mamarr Mitlā, Egypt .... 46 E1   30 2N 32 54 E
Mamasa, Indonesia .... 37 E5   2 55S 119 20 E
Mambasa, Dem. Rep. of
  the Congo .... 54 B2   1 22N 29 3 E
Mamberamo ➤, Indonesia .. 37 E9   2 0S 137 50 E
Mambilima Falls, Zambia ... 55 E2   10 31S 28 45 E
Mambirima, Dem. Rep. of
  the Congo .... 55 E2   11 25S 27 33 E
Mambo, Tanzania .... 54 C4   4 52S 38 22 E
Mambrui, Kenya .... 54 C5   3 30S 40 5 E
Mamburao, Phil. .... 37 B6   13 13N 120 39 E
Mameigwess L., Canada 72 B2   52 35N 87 50W
Mammoth, U.S.A. 77 K8   32 43N 110 39W
Mammoth Cave △, U.S.A. .. 82 G3   37 8N 86 13W
Mamoré ➤, Bolivia 92 F5   10 23S 65 53W
Mamou, Guinea 50 F3   10 15N 12 0W
Mamoudzou, Mayotte ...... 53 a   12 48S 45 14 E
Mampikony, Madag. .... 57 B8   16 6S 47 38 E
Mamuju, Indonesia .... 37 E5   2 41S 118 50 E
Mamuno, Botswana .... 56 C3   22 16S 20 1 E
Man, Ivory C. 50 G4   7 30N   7 40W
Man, I. of, U.K. 12 C3   54 5N   4 30W
Man-Bazar, India .... 43 H12 23 4N 86 39 E
Man Na, Burma .... 41 H20 23 27N 97 19 E
Mana ➤, Fr. Guiana 93 B8   5 45N 53 55W
Mana Pools △, Zimbabwe ... 55 F2   15 56S 29 25 E
Manaar, G. of = Mannar, G. of,
  Asia .... 40 Q11   8 30N 79 0 E
Manacapuru, Brazil 92 D6   3 16S 60 37W
Manacor, Spain .... 24 B10 39 34N   3 13 E
Manado, Indonesia .... 37 D6   1 29N 124 51 E
Managua, Nic. 88 D2   12 6N 86 20W
Managua, L. de, Nic. 88 D2   12 20N 86 30W
Manakara, Madag. .... 57 C8   22 8S 48 1 E
Manali, India .... 42 C7   32 16N 77 10 E
Manama = Al Manāmah, Bahrain 45 E6 26 10N 50 30 E
Manambao ➤, Madag. ..... 57 B7   17 35S 44 0 E
Manambato, Madag. .... 57 A8   13 43S 49 7 E
Manambolo ➤, Madag. .... 57 B7   19 18S 44 22 E
Manambolosy, Madag. ..... 57 B8   16 2S 49 40 E
Mananara, Madag. .... 57 B8   16 10S 49 46 E
Mananara △, Madag. ...... 57 B8   16 14S 49 45 E
Mananara ➤, Madag. ...... 57 C8   23 21S 47 42 E
Mananjary, Madag. .... 57 C8   21 13S 48 20 E
Manantenina, Madag. ...... 57 C8   24 17S 47 19 E
Manaos = Manaus, Brazil ... 92 D7   3 0S 60 0W
Manapire ➤, Venezuela 92 B5   7 42N 66 7W
Manapouri, N.Z. .... 59 L1   45 34S 167 39 E
Manapouri, L., N.Z. .... 59 L1   45 32S 167 32 E
Manār, Jabal, Yemen ...... 47 E3   14 2N 44 17 E
Manaravolo, Madag. .... 57 C8   23 59S 45 39 E
Manas, China .... 32 B3   44 17N 85 56 E
Manas ➤, India .... 41 F17 26 12N 90 40 E
Manaslu, Nepal .... 43 E11 28 33N 84 33 E
Manasquan, U.S.A. 85 F10 40 8N 74 3W
Manassa, U.S.A. 77 H11 37 11N 105 56W
Manatí, Puerto Rico .... 89 d   18 26N 66 29W
Manaung, Burma .... 41 K18 18 45N 93 40 E
Manaus, Brazil 92 D7   3 0S 60 0W
Manawan L., Canada 71 B8   55 24N 103 14W
Manbij, Syria .... 44 B3   36 31N 37 57 E
Manchegorsk, Russia ...... 28 C4   67 54N 32 58 E
Manchester, U.K. 12 D5   53 29N   2 12W
Manchester, Calif., U.S.A. .. 78 G3   38 58N 123 41W
Manchester, Conn., U.S.A. . 85 E12 41 47N 72 31W
Manchester, Ga., U.S.A. ... 83 J3   32 51N 84 37W
Manchester, Iowa, U.S.A. .. 80 D9   42 29N 91 27W
Manchester, Ky., U.S.A. 82 G4   37 9N 83 46W
Manchester, N.H., U.S.A. ... 85 D13 42 59N 71 28W
Manchester, N.Y., U.S.A. ... 84 D7   42 56N 77 16W
Manchester, Pa., U.S.A. 85 F8   40 4N 76 43W
Manchester, Tenn., U.S.A. .. 83 H2   35 29N 86 5W
Manchester, Vt., U.S.A. 85 C11 43 10N 73 5W
Manchester International ✈
  (MAN), U.K. 12 D5   53 21N   2 17W
Manchester L., Canada 71 A7   61 28N 107 29W
Manchhar L., Pakistan ..... 42 F2   26 25N 67 39 E
Manchuria = Dongbei, China 29 E13 45 0N 125 0 E
Manchurian Plain, China ... 26 E16 47 0N 124 0 E
Mand ➤, India .... 43 J10 21 42N 83 15 E
Mand ➤, Iran .... 45 D7   28 20N 52 30 E
Manda, Ludewe, Tanzania .. 55 E3   10 30S 34 40 E
Manda, Mbeya, Tanzania ... 54 D3   7 58S 32 29 E
Manda, Mbeya, Tanzania ... 55 D3   8 30S 32 49 E
Mandabé, Madag. .... 57 C7   21 0S 44 55 E
Mandaguari, Brazil 95 A5   23 32S 51 42W
Mandah = Töhöm, Mongolia 34 B5   44 27N 108 2 E
Mandal, Norway .... 9 G12   58 2N   7 25 E
Mandala, Puncak, Indonesia 37 E10   4 44S 140 20 E
Mandalay, Burma .... 41 J20 22 0N 96 4 E
Mandale = Mandalay, Burma 41 J20 22 0N 96 4 E
Mandalgarh, India .... 42 G6   25 12N 75 6 E
Mandalgovĭ, Mongolia ..... 34 B4   45 45N 106 10 E
Mandalī, Iraq .... 44 C5   33 43N 45 28 E

Mandan, U.S.A. 80 B4   46 50N 100 54W
Mandar, Teluk, Indonesia ... 37 E5   3 35S 119 15 E
Mandaue, Phil. .... 37 B6   10 20N 123 56 E
Mandera, Kenya .... 54 B5   3 55N 41 53 E
Mandeville, Jamaica .... 88 a   18 2N 77 31W
Mandi, India .... 42 D7   31 39N 76 58 E
Mandi Dabwali, India ...... 42 E6   29 58N 74 42 E
Mandimba, Mozam. .... 55 E4   14 20S 35 40 E
Mandioli, Indonesia .... 37 E7   0 40S 127 20 E
Mandla, India .... 43 H9   22 39N 80 30 E
Mandorah, Australia ...... 60 B5   12 32S 130 42 E
Mandoto, Madag. .... 57 B8   19 34S 46 17 E
Mandra, Pakistan .... 42 C5   33 23N 73 12 E
Mandrare ➤, Madag. ...... 57 D8   25 10S 46 30 E
Mandritsara, Madag. ...... 57 B8   15 50S 48 49 E
Mandurah, Australia ...... 61 F2   32 36S 115 48 E
Mandvi, India .... 42 H3   22 51N 69 22 E
Mandya, India .... 40 N10 12 30N 77 0 E
Mandzai, Pakistan .... 42 D2   30 55N 67 6 E
Maneh, Iran .... 45 B8   37 39N 57 7 E
Manera, Madag. .... 57 C7   22 55S 44 20 E
Maneroo Cr. ➤, Australia .. 62 C3   23 21S 143 53 E
Manfalût, Egypt .... 51 C12 27 20N 30 52 E
Manfredónia, Italy .... 22 D6   41 38N 15 55 E
Mangabeiras, Chapada das,
  Brazil 93 F9   10 0S 46 30W
Mangalia, Romania .... 17 G15 43 50N 28 35 E
Mangalore, India .... 40 N9   12 55N 74 47 E
Mangan, India .... 43 F13 27 31N 88 32 E
Mangaung, S. Africa ...... 53 K5   29 10S 26 12 E
Mangawan, India .... 43 G9   24 41N 81 33 E
Mangaweka, N.Z. .... 59 H5   39 48S 175 47 E
Manggar, Indonesia .... 36 E3   2 50S 108 10 E
Manggawitu, Indonesia .... 37 J18   8 29S 115 31 E
Manggis, Indonesia .... 57 A8   14 17S 48 58 E
Mangindrano, Madag. ..... 57 A8   14 17S 48 58 E
Mangla, Pakistan .... 42 C5   33 7N 73 39 E
Mangla Dam, Pakistan .... 43 C5   33 9N 73 44 E
Manglaur, India .... 42 E7   29 44N 77 49 E
Mangnai, China .... 32 C4   37 52N 91 43 E
Mango, Togo .... 50 F6   10 20N   0 30 E
Mangoche, Malawi .... 55 E4   14 25S 35 16 E
Mangoky ➤, Madag. .... 57 C7   21 29S 43 41 E
Mangole, Indonesia .... 37 E6   1 50S 125 55 E
Mangombe, Dem. Rep. of
  the Congo .... 54 C2   1 20S 26 48 E
Mangonui, N.Z. .... 59 F4   35 1S 173 32 E
Mangoro ➤, Madag. .... 57 B8   20 0S 48 45 E
Mangrol, Mad. P., India ... 42 J4   21 7N 70 7 E
Mangrol, Raj., India ...... 42 G6   25 20N 76 31 E
Mangueira, L. da, Brazil ... 95 C5   33 0S 52 50W
Mangum, U.S.A. 81 H5   34 53N 99 30W
Mangyshlak, Poluostrov,
  Kazakhstan .... 28 E6   44 30N 52 30 E
Manhattan, U.S.A. 80 F6   39 11N 96 35W
Manhiça, Mozam. .... 57 D5   25 23S 32 49 E
Mania ➤, Madag. .... 57 B8   19 42S 45 22 E
Manica, Mozam. .... 57 B5   18 58S 32 59 E
Manica □, Mozam. .... 57 B5   19 10S 33 45 E
Manicaland □, Zimbabwe .. 55 F3   19 0S 32 30 E
Manicoré, Brazil 92 E6   5 48S 61 16W
Manicouagan ➤, Canada .. 73 C6   49 30N 68 30W
Manicouagan, Rés., Canada 73 B6   51 5N 68 40W
Maniema □, Dem. Rep. of
  the Congo .... 54 C2   3 0S 26 0 E
Manifah, Si. Arabia .... 45 E6   27 44N 49 0 E
Manifold, C., Australia ..... 62 C5   22 41S 150 50 E
Manigotagan, Canada 71 C9   51 6N 96 18W
Manigotagan ➤, Canada ... 71 C9   51 7N 96 20W
Manihari, India .... 43 G12 25 21N 87 38 E
Manihiki, Cook Is. 65 J11 10 24S 161 1W
Manika, Plateau de la, Dem. Rep.
  of the Congo .... 55 E2   10 0S 25 5 E
Manikpur, India .... 43 G9   25 4N 81 7 E
Manila, Phil. .... 37 B6   14 40N 121 3 E
Manila, U.S.A. 76 F9   40 59N 109 43W
Manila B., Phil. .... 37 B6   14 40N 120 35 E
Manilla, Australia .... 63 E5   30 45S 150 43 E
Maningrida, Australia ..... 62 A1   12 3S 134 13 E
Manipur □, India .... 41 G19 25 0N 94 0 E
Manipur ➤, Burma .... 41 H19 23 45N 94 20 E
Manisa, Turkey .... 23 E12 38 38N 27 30 E
Manistee, U.S.A. 82 C2   44 15N 86 19W
Manistee ➤, U.S.A. 82 C2   44 15N 86 21W
Manistique, U.S.A. 82 C2   45 57N 86 15W
Manitoba □, Canada 71 B9   53 30N 97 0W
Manitoba, L., Canada 71 C9   51 0N 98 45W
Manitou, Canada 71 D9   49 15N 98 32W
Manitou ➤, U.S.A. 73 B6   50 55N 65 17W
Manitou Is., U.S.A. 82 C3   45 8N 86 0W
Manitou L., Canada 71 C7   52 43N 109 43W
Manitou Springs, U.S.A. ... 80 F2   38 52N 104 55W
Manitoulin I., Canada 72 C3   45 40N 82 30W
Manitouwadge, Canada 72 C2   49 8N 85 48W
Manitowoc, U.S.A. 82 C2   44 5N 87 40W
Manizales, Colombia 92 B3   5 5N 75 32W
Manja, Madag. .... 57 C5   21 26S 44 20 E
Manjacaze, Mozam. .... 57 C5   24 45S 34 0 E
Manjakandriana, Madag. ... 57 B8   18 55S 47 47 E
Manjhand, Pakistan ...... 42 G3   25 50N 68 10 E
Manjil, Iran .... 45 B6   36 46N 49 30 E
Manjimup, Australia ...... 61 F2   34 15S 116 6 E
Manjra ➤, India .... 40 K10 18 49N 77 52 E
Mankato, Kans., U.S.A. 80 F5   39 47N 98 13W
Mankato, Minn., U.S.A. 80 C8   44 10N 94 0W
Mankayane, Swaziland .... 57 D5   26 40S 31 4 E
Mankera, Pakistan .... 42 D4   31 23N 71 26 E
Mankota, Canada 71 D7   49 25N 107 5W
Manlay = Üydzin, Mongolia 34 B4   44 9N 107 0 E
Manmad, India .... 40 J9   20 18N 74 28 E
Mann Ranges, Australia ... 61 E5   26 6S 130 5 E
Manna, Indonesia .... 36 E2   4 25S 102 55 E
Mannahill, Australia ...... 63 E3   32 25S 139 59 E
Mannar, Sri Lanka .... 40 Q11   9 1N 79 54 E
Mannar, G. of, Asia .... 40 Q11   8 30N 79 0 E
Mannar I., Sri Lanka ...... 40 Q11   9 5N 79 45 E
Mannheim, Germany ...... 16 D5   49 29N   8 29 E
Manning, Canada 70 B5   56 53N 117 39W
Manning, Oreg., U.S.A. 78 E3   45 45N 123 13W
Manning, S.C., U.S.A. 83 J5   33 42N 80 13W
Mannum, Australia .... 63 E2   34 50S 139 20 E
Manoharpur, India .... 43 H11 22 23N 85 12 E
Manokwari, Indonesia .... 37 E8   0 54S 134 0 E
Manombo, Madag. .... 57 C7   22 57S 43 28 E
Manono, Dem. Rep. of the Congo 54 D2   7 15S 27 25 E

Manosque, France .... 20 E6   43 49N   5 47 E
Manotick, Canada 85 A9   45 13N 75 41W
Manouane ➤, Canada 73 C5   49 30N 71 10W
Manouane, L., Canada 73 B5   50 45N 70 45W
Manp'o, N. Korea .... 35 D14 41 6N 126 24 E
Manpojin = Manp'o, N. Korea 35 D14 41 6N 126 24 E
Manpur, Chhattisgarh, India 43 H10 23 17N 83 35 E
Manpur, Mad. P., India .... 42 H6   22 26N 75 37 E
Manresa, Spain .... 21 B6   41 48N   1 50 E
Mansa, Gujarat, India ...... 42 H5   23 27N 72 45 E
Mansa, Punjab, India ...... 42 E6   30 0N 75 27 E
Mansa, Zambia .... 55 E2   11 13S 28 55 E
Mansehra, Pakistan .... 42 B5   34 20N 73 15 E
Mansel I., Canada 69 B11 62 0N 80 0W
Mansfield, Australia ...... 63 F4   37 4S 146 6 E
Mansfield, U.K. 12 D6   53 9N   1 11W
Mansfield, La., U.S.A. 81 J8   32 2N 93 43W
Mansfield, Mass., U.S.A. ... 85 D13 42 2N 71 13W
Mansfield, Ohio, U.S.A. 84 F2   40 45N 82 31W
Mansfield, Pa., U.S.A. 84 E7   41 48N 77 5W
Mansfield, Mt., U.S.A. 85 B12 44 33N 72 49W
Manson Creek, Canada 70 B4   55 37N 124 32W
Manta, Ecuador 92 D2   1 0S 80 40W
Mantadia △, Madag. ...... 57 B8   18 54S 48 21 E
Mantalingajan, Mt., Phil. .. 36 C5   8 55N 117 45 E
Mantare, Tanzania .... 54 C3   2 42S 33 13 E
Manteca, U.S.A. 78 H5   37 48N 121 13W
Manteo, U.S.A. 83 H8   35 55N 75 40W
Mantes-la-Jolie, France ... 20 B4   48 58N   1 41 E
Manthani, India .... 40 K11 18 40N 79 35 E
Manti, U.S.A. 76 G8   39 16N 111 38W
Mantiqueira, Serra da, Brazil 95 A7 22 0S 44 0W
Manton, U.S.A. 82 C3   44 25N 85 24W
Mántova, Italy .... 22 B4   45 9N 10 48 E
Mänttä, Finland .... 9 E21 62 0N 24 40 E
Mantua = Mántova, Italy ... 22 B4   45 9N 10 48 E
Manu, Peru 92 F4   12 10S 70 51W
Manu ➤, Peru 92 F4   12 16S 70 55W
Manu'a Is., Amer. Samoa .. 59 B14 14 13S 169 35W
Manuel Alves ➤, Brazil 93 F9   11 19S 48 28W
Manui, Indonesia .... 37 E6   3 35S 123 5 E
Manukau, N.Z. .... 59 G5   40 43S 175 13 E
Manuripi ➤, Bolivia 92 F5   11 6S 67 36W
Many, U.S.A. 81 K8   31 34N 93 29W
Manyara, L., Tanzania ..... 54 C4   3 40S 35 50 E
Manych-Gudilo, Ozero, Russia 19 E7 46 24N 42 38 E
Manyonga ➤, Tanzania .... 54 C3   4 10S 34 15 E
Manyoni, Tanzania .... 54 D3   5 45S 34 55 E
Manzai, Pakistan .... 42 C4   32 12N 70 15 E
Manzanar △, U.S.A. 78 J7   36 44N 118 9W
Manzanares, Spain 21 C4   39 2N   3 22W
Manzanillo, Cuba 88 B4   20 20N 77 31W
Manzanillo, Mexico 86 D4   19 0N 104 20W
Manzanillo, Pta., Panama .. 88 E4   9 30N 79 40W
Manzano Mts., U.S.A. 77 J10 34 40N 106 20W
Manzariyeh, Iran .... 45 C6   34 53N 50 50 E
Manzini, Swaziland .... 57 D5   26 30S 31 18 E
Mao, Chad .... 51 F9   14 4N 15 19 E
Maó, Spain .... 24 B11 39 53N   4 16 E
Maoke, Pegunungan, Indonesia 37 E9   3 40S 137 30 E
Maolin, China .... 35 C12 43 58N 123 30 E
Maoming, China .... 33 D6   21 50N 110 54 E
Maoxing, China .... 35 B13 45 28N 124 40 E
Mapam Yumco, China ..... 32 C3   30 45N 81 28 E
Mapastepec, Mexico 87 D6   15 26N 92 54W
Maphrao, Ko, Thailand .... 39 a   7 56N 98 26 E
Mapia, Kepulauan, Indonesia 37 D8   0 50N 134 20 E
Mapimí, Mexico 86 B4   25 50N 103 50W
Mapimí, Bolsón de, Mexico 86 B4   27 30N 104 15W
Mapinga, Tanzania .... 54 D4   6 40S 39 12 E
Mapinhane, Mozam. ...... 57 C6   22 20S 35 0 E
Maple Creek, Canada 71 D7   49 55N 109 29W
Maple Valley, U.S.A. 78 C4   47 25N 122 3W
Mapleton, U.S.A. 76 D2   44 2N 123 52W
Mapuera ➤, Brazil 92 D7   1 5S 57 2W
Mapulanguene, Mozam. ... 57 C5   24 29S 32 6 E
Maputo, Mozam. .... 57 D5   25 58S 32 32 E
Maputo □, Mozam. .... 57 D5   26 23S 32 48 E
Maputo □, Mozam. .... 57 D5   26 0S 32 25 E
Maputo, B. de, Mozam. .... 57 D5   25 50S 32 45 E
Maqiaohe, China .... 35 B16 44 40N 130 30 E
Maqnā, Si. Arabia .... 44 D2   28 25N 34 50 E
Maquan He = Brahmaputra ➤,
  Asia .... 32 D3   23 40N 90 35 E
Maquela do Zombo, Angola 52 F3   6 0S 15 15 E
Maquinchao, Argentina 96 E3   41 15S 68 50W
Maquoketa, U.S.A. 80 D9   42 4N 90 40W
Mar, Serra do, Brazil 95 B6   25 30S 49 0W
Mar Chiquita, L., Argentina 94 C3   30 40S 62 50W
Mar del Plata, Argentina ... 94 D4   38 0S 57 30W
Mar Menor, Spain 21 D5   37 40N   0 45W
Mara, Tanzania .... 54 C3   1 30S 34 32 E
Mara □, Tanzania .... 54 C3   1 45S 34 20 E
Maraã, Brazil 92 D5   1 52S 65 25W
Marabá, Brazil 93 E9   5 20S 49 5W
Maracá, I. de, Brazil 93 C8   2 10N 50 30W
Maracaibo, Venezuela 92 A4   10 40N 71 37W
Maracaibo, L. de, Venezuela 92 B4   9 40N 71 30W
Maracaju, Brazil 95 A4   21 38S 55 9W
Maracas Bay Village, Trin. & Tob. 93 K15 10 46N 61 28W
Maracay, Venezuela 92 A5   10 15N 67 28W
Maradi, Niger .... 50 F7   13 29N   7 20 E
Marāgheh, Iran .... 44 B5   37 30N 46 12 E
Marāh, Si. Arabia .... 44 E5   25 0N 45 35 E
Marajó, I. de, Brazil 93 D9   1 0S 49 30W
Marākand, Iran .... 44 B5   38 51N 45 16 E
Marakele △, S. Africa ...... 57 C4   32 14S 25 27 E
Maralal, Kenya .... 54 B4   1 0N 36 38 E
Maralinga, Australia ...... 61 F5   30 13S 131 32 E
Marama, Malaysia .... 39 L4   3 35N 102 45 E
Maran, Malaysia .... 39 L4   3 35N 102 45 E
Marana, U.S.A. 77 K8   32 27N 111 13W
Maranboy, Australia ...... 60 B5   14 40S 132 39 E
Marand, Iran .... 44 B5   38 30N 45 45 E
Marang, Malaysia .... 39 K4   5 12N 103 13 E
Maranguape, Brazil 93 D11   3 55S 38 50W
Maranhão = São Luís, Brazil 93 D10   2 39S 44 15W
Maranhão □, Brazil 93 E9   5 0S 46 0W
Maranoa ➤, Australia ..... 63 D4   27 50S 148 37 E
Marañón ➤, Peru 92 D4   4 30S 73 35W
Marão, Mozam. .... 57 C5   24 18S 34 2 E
Maraş = Kahramanmaraş, Turkey 19 G6 37 37N 36 53 E
Marathasa, Cyprus .... 25 E11 34 59N 32 51 E
Marathon, Australia ...... 62 C3   20 51S 143 32 E
Marathon, Canada 72 C2   48 44N 86 23W
Marathon, N.Y., U.S.A. 85 D8   42 27N 76 2W
Marathon, Tex., U.S.A. 81 K3   30 12N 103 15W

Marathóvouno, Cyprus .... 25 D12 35 13N 33 37 E
Maratua, Indonesia .... 37 D5 2 10N 118 35 E
Maraval, Trin. & Tob. 93 K15 10 43N 61 32W
Maravatío, Mexico 86 D4 19 51N 100 25W
Marāwih, U.A.E. .... 45 E7 24 18N 53 18 E
Marbella, Spain 21 D3 36 30N 4 57W
Marble Bar, Australia .... 60 D2 21 9S 119 44 E
Marble Falls, U.S.A. 81 K5 30 35N 98 16W
Marblehead, U.S.A. 85 D14 42 30N 70 51W
Marburg, Germany .... 16 C5 50 47N 8 46 E
March, U.K. .... 13 E8 52 33N 0 5 E
Marche, France .... 20 C4 46 5N 1 20 E
Marche-en-Famenne, Belgium . 15 D5 50 14N 5 19 E
Marchena, Spain 21 D3 37 18N 5 23W
Marco, U.S.A. 83 N5 25 58N 81 44W
Marcos Juárez, Argentina 94 C3 32 42S 62 5W
Marcus I. = Minami-Tori-Shima,
  Pac. Oc. .... 64 E7 24 20N 153 58 E
Marcus Necker Ridge, Pac. Oc. . 64 F9 20 0N 175 0 E
Marcy, Mt., U.S.A. 85 B11 44 7N 73 56W
Mardan, Pakistan .... 42 B5 34 20N 72 0 E
Mardin, Turkey .... 19 G7 37 20N 40 43 E
Maree, L., U.K. 11 D3 57 40N 5 26W
Mareeba, Australia .... 62 B4 16 59S 145 28 E
Mareetsane, S. Africa .... 56 D4 26 9S 25 25 E
Marek = Stanke Dimitrov,
  Bulgaria .... 23 C10 42 17N 23 9 E
Marengo, U.S.A. 80 E8 41 48N 92 4W
Marerano, Madag. .... 57 C7 21 23S 44 52 E
Marfa, U.S.A. 81 K2 30 19N 104 1W
Marfa Pt., Malta .... 25 D1 35 59N 14 19 E
Margaret →, Australia .... 60 C4 18 9S 125 41 E
Margaret Bay, Canada 70 C3 51 20N 127 35W
Margaret L., Canada 70 B5 58 56N 115 25W
Margarita, I. de, Venezuela 92 A6 11 0N 64 0W
Margaret River, Australia ..... 61 F2 33 57S 115 4 E
Margaritovo, Russia .... 30 C7 43 25N 134 45 E
Margate, S. Africa .... 57 E5 30 50S 30 20 E
Margate, U.K. .... 13 F9 51 23N 1 23 E
Margherita Pk., Uganda ...... 54 B3 0 22N 29 51 E
Mārgow, Dasht-e, Afghan. .... 40 D3 30 40N 62 30 E
Marguerite, Canada 70 C4 52 30N 122 25W
Mari El □, Russia .... 18 C8 56 30N 48 0 E
Mari Indus, Pakistan .... 42 C4 32 57N 71 34 E
Mari Republic = Mari El □, Russia 18 C8 56 30N 48 0 E
María Elena, Chile 94 A2 22 18S 69 40W
María Grande, Argentina 94 C4 31 45S 59 55W
Maria I., N. Terr., Australia .... 62 A2 14 52S 135 45 E
Maria I., Tas., Australia ...... 63 G4 42 35S 148 0 E
Maria Island △, Australia ..... 63 G4 42 38S 148 5 E
Maria van Diemen, C., N.Z. .... 59 F4 34 29S 172 40 E
Mariakani, Kenya .... 54 C4 3 50S 39 27 E
Mariala △, Australia .... 63 D4 25 57S 145 2 E
Marian, Australia .... 62 K6 21 9S 148 57 E
Marian L., Canada 70 A5 63 0N 116 15W
Mariana Trench, Pac. Oc. ..... 26 H18 13 0N 145 0 E
Marianao, Cuba 88 B3 23 8N 82 24W
Marianna, Ark., U.S.A. 81 H9 34 46N 90 46W
Marianna, Fla., U.S.A. 83 K3 30 46N 85 14W
Marias →, U.S.A. 76 C8 47 56N 110 30W
Mariato, Punta, Panama 88 E3 7 12N 80 52W
Maribor, Slovenia .... 16 E8 46 36N 15 40 E
Marico →, Africa .... 56 C4 23 35S 26 57 E
Maricopa, Ariz., U.S.A. 77 K7 33 4N 112 3W
Maricopa, Calif., U.S.A. 79 K7 35 4N 119 24W
Marié →, Brazil 92 D5 0 27S 66 26W
Marie Byrd Land, Antarctica ... 5 D14 79 30S 125 0W
Marie-Galante, Guadeloupe .... 88 b 15 56N 61 16W
Mariecourt = Kangiqsujuaq,
  Canada 69 B12 61 30N 72 0W
Mariembourg, Belgium .... 15 D4 50 6N 4 31 E
Mariental, Namibia .... 56 C2 24 36S 18 0 E
Marienville, U.S.A. 84 E5 41 28N 79 8W
Mariestad, Sweden .... 9 G15 58 43N 13 50 E
Marietta, Ga., U.S.A. 83 J3 33 57N 84 33W
Marietta, Ohio, U.S.A. 82 F5 39 25N 81 27W
Marieville, Canada 85 A11 45 26N 73 10W
Mariinsk, Russia .... 28 D9 56 10N 87 20 E
Marijampolė, Lithuania .... 9 J20 54 33N 23 19 E
Marília, Brazil 95 A6 22 13S 50 0W
Marín, Spain 21 A1 42 23N 8 42W
Marina, U.S.A. 78 J5 36 41N 121 48W
Marinduque, Phil. .... 37 B6 13 25N 122 0 E
Marine City, U.S.A. 84 D2 42 43N 82 30W
Marinette, U.S.A. 82 C2 45 6N 87 38W
Maringá, Brazil 95 A5 23 26S 52 2W
Marion, Ala., U.S.A. 83 J2 32 38N 87 19W
Marion, Ill., U.S.A. 81 G10 37 44N 88 56W
Marion, Ind., U.S.A. 82 E3 40 32N 85 40W
Marion, Iowa, U.S.A. 80 D9 42 2N 91 36W
Marion, Kans., U.S.A. 80 F6 38 21N 97 1W
Marion, N.C., U.S.A. 83 H5 35 41N 82 1W
Marion, Ohio, U.S.A. 82 E4 40 35N 83 8W
Marion, S.C., U.S.A. 83 H6 34 11N 79 24W
Marion, Va., U.S.A. 83 G5 36 50N 81 31W
Marion, L., U.S.A. 83 J5 33 28N 80 10W
Mariposa, U.S.A. 78 H7 37 29N 119 58W
Mariscal Estigarribia, Paraguay 94 A3 22 3S 60 40W
Maritime Alps = Maritimes,
  Alpes, Europe .... 20 D7 44 10N 7 10 E
Maritimes, Alpes, Europe ..... 20 D7 44 10N 7 10 E
Maritsa = Évros →, Greece .... 23 D12 41 40N 26 34 E
Maritsá, Greece .... 25 C10 36 22N 28 8 E
Mariupol, Ukraine .... 19 E6 47 5N 37 31 E
Mariusa △, Venezuela 89 E7 9 24N 61 27W
Marīvān, Iran .... 44 C5 35 30N 46 25 E
Marj 'Uyūn, Lebanon .... 46 B4 33 20N 35 35 E
Marka = Merca, Somali Rep. ... 47 G3 1 48N 44 50 E
Markdale, Canada 84 B4 44 19N 80 39W
Marked Tree, U.S.A. 81 H9 35 32N 90 25W
Market Drayton, U.K. 12 E5 52 54N 2 29W
Market Harborough, U.K. 13 E7 52 29N 0 55W
Market Rasen, U.K. 12 D7 53 24N 0 20W
Markham, Canada 84 C5 43 52N 79 16W
Markham, Mt., Antarctica ..... 5 E11 83 0S 164 0 E
Markleeville, U.S.A. 78 G7 38 42N 119 47W
Markovo, Russia .... 29 C17 64 40N 170 24 E
Marks, Russia .... 18 D8 51 45N 46 50 E
Marksville, U.S.A. 81 K8 31 8N 92 4W
Marla, Australia .... 63 D1 27 19S 133 33 E
Marlbank, Canada 84 B7 44 26N 77 6W
Marlboro, Mass., U.S.A. 85 D13 42 19N 71 33W
Marlboro, N.Y., U.S.A. 85 E11 41 36N 73 59W
Marlborough, Australia .... 62 C4 22 46S 149 52 E
Marlborough, U.K. 13 F6 51 25N 1 43W
Marlborough Downs, U.K. 13 F6 51 27N 1 53W
Marlin, U.S.A. 81 K6 31 18N 96 54W
Marlow, U.K. 13 F7 51 34N 0 46W

Marlow, U.S.A. 81 H6 34 39N 97 58W
Marmagao, India .... 40 M8 15 25N 73 56 E
Marmara, Turkey .... 23 D12 40 35N 27 34 E
Marmara, Sea of = Marmara
  Denizi, Turkey .... 23 D13 40 45N 28 15 E
Marmara Denizi, Turkey ...... 23 D13 40 45N 28 15 E
Marmaris, Turkey .... 23 F13 36 50N 28 14 E
Marmion, Mt., Australia ...... 61 E2 29 16S 119 50 E
Marmion L., Canada 72 C1 48 55N 91 20W
Marmolada, Mte., Italy .... 22 A4 46 26N 11 51 E
Marmora, Canada 84 B7 44 28N 77 41W
Marne →, France .... 20 B5 48 48N 2 24 E
Maroala, Madag. .... 57 B8 15 23S 47 59 E
Maroantsetra, Madag. .... 57 B8 15 26S 49 44 E
Maroelaboom, Namibia .... 56 B2 19 15S 18 53 E
Marofandilia, Madag. .... 57 C7 20 7S 44 34 E
Marojejy △, Madag. .... 57 A8 14 26S 49 21 E
Marolambo, Madag. .... 57 C8 20 2S 48 7 E
Maromandia, Madag. .... 57 A8 14 13S 48 5 E
Maromokotro, Madag. .... 57 A8 14 0S 49 0 E
Marondera, Zimbabwe .... 55 F3 18 5S 31 42 E
Maroni →, Fr. Guiana 93 B8 5 30N 54 0W
Maroochydore, Australia ...... 63 D5 26 29S 153 5 E
Maroona, Australia .... 63 F3 37 27S 142 54 E
Marosakoa, Madag. .... 57 B8 15 26S 46 38 E
Maroseranana, Madag. .... 57 B8 18 32S 48 51 E
Marotandrano, Madag. .... 57 B8 16 10S 48 50 E
Marotaolano, Madag. .... 57 A8 12 47S 49 15 E
Maroua, Cameroon .... 51 F8 10 40N 14 20 E
Marovato, Madag. .... 57 B8 15 48S 48 5 E
Marovoay, Madag. .... 57 B8 16 6S 46 39 E
Marquard, S. Africa .... 56 D4 28 40S 27 28 E
Marquesas Is. = Marquises, Ìs.,
  French Polynesia 65 H14 9 30S 140 0W
Marquette, U.S.A. 82 B2 46 33N 87 24W
Marquis, St. Lucia .... 89 f 14 2N 60 54W
Marquises, Ìs., French Polynesia 65 H14 9 30S 140 0W
Marra, Djebel, Sudan .... 51 F10 13 10N 24 22 E
Marracuene, Mozam. .... 57 D5 25 45S 32 35 E
Marrakech, Morocco 50 B4 31 9N 8 0W
Marrawah, Australia .... 63 G3 40 55S 144 42 E
Marree, Australia .... 63 D2 29 39S 138 1 E
Marrero, U.S.A. 81 L9 29 54N 90 6W
Marrimane, Mozam. .... 57 C5 22 58S 33 34 E
Marromeu, Mozam. .... 57 B6 18 15S 36 25 E
Marromeu △, Mozam. .... 57 B6 19 0S 36 0 E
Marrowie Cr. →, Australia .... 63 E4 33 23S 145 40 E
Marrubane, Mozam. .... 55 F4 18 0S 37 0 E
Marrupa, Mozam. .... 55 E4 13 8S 37 30 E
Mars Hill, U.S.A. 83 B12 46 31N 67 52W
Marsá Matrûh, Egypt .... 51 B11 31 19N 27 9 E
Marsabit, Kenya .... 54 B4 2 18N 38 0 E
Marsabit △, Kenya .... 54 B4 2 23N 37 56 E
Marsala, Italy .... 22 F5 37 48N 12 26 E
Marsalforn, Malta .... 25 C1 36 4N 14 16 E
Marsden, Australia .... 63 E4 33 47S 147 32 E
Marseille, France .... 20 E6 43 18N 5 23 E
Marseilles = Marseille, France . 20 E6 43 18N 5 23 E
Marsh I., U.S.A. 81 L9 29 34N 91 53W
Marshall, Ark., U.S.A. 81 H8 35 55N 92 38W
Marshall, Mich., U.S.A. 82 D3 42 16N 84 58W
Marshall, Minn., U.S.A. 80 C7 44 25N 95 45W
Marshall, Mo., U.S.A. 80 F8 39 7N 93 12W
Marshall, Tex., U.S.A. 81 J7 32 33N 94 23W
Marshall →, Australia .... 62 C2 22 59S 136 59 E
Marshall Is. ■, Pac. Oc. ...... 64 G9 9 0N 171 0 E
Marshalltown, U.S.A. 80 D8 42 3N 92 55W
Marshbrook, Zimbabwe ...... 57 B5 18 33S 31 9 E
Marshfield, Mo., U.S.A. 81 G8 37 15N 92 54W
Marshfield, Vt., U.S.A. 85 B12 44 20N 72 20W
Marshfield, Wis., U.S.A. 80 C9 44 40N 90 10W
Marshūn, Iran .... 45 B6 36 19N 49 23 E
Märsta, Sweden .... 9 G17 59 37N 17 52 E
Mart, U.S.A. 81 K6 31 33N 96 50W
Martaban, Burma .... 41 L20 16 30N 97 35 E
Martaban, G. of, Burma ...... 41 L20 16 5N 96 30 E
Martapura, Kalimantan,
  Indonesia .... 36 E4 3 22S 114 47 E
Martapura, Sumatera, Indonesia 36 E2 4 19S 104 22 E
Martelange, Belgium .... 15 E5 49 49N 5 43 E
Martha's Vineyard, U.S.A. 85 E14 41 25N 70 38W
Martigny, Switz. .... 20 C7 46 6N 7 3 E
Martigues, France .... 20 E6 43 24N 5 4 E
Martin, Slovak Rep. .... 17 D10 49 6N 18 58 E
Martin, S. Dak., U.S.A. 80 D4 43 11N 101 44W
Martin, Tenn., U.S.A. 81 G10 36 21N 88 51W
Martin, L., U.S.A. 83 J3 32 41N 85 55W
Martina Franca, Italy .... 22 D7 40 42N 17 20 E
Martinborough, N.Z. .... 59 J5 41 14S 175 29 E
Martinez, Calif., U.S.A. 78 G4 38 1N 122 8W
Martinez, Ga., U.S.A. 83 J4 33 31N 82 4W
Martinique ☑, W. Indies ..... 88 c 14 40N 61 0W
Martinique Passage, W. Indies . 89 C7 15 15N 61 0W
Martinópolis, Brazil 95 A5 22 11S 51 12W
Martin's Bay, Barbados ...... 89 g 13 12N 59 29W
Martins Ferry, U.S.A. 84 F4 40 6N 80 44W
Martinsburg, Pa., U.S.A. 84 F6 40 19N 78 20W
Martinsburg, W. Va., U.S.A. ... 82 F7 39 27N 77 58W
Martinsville, Ind., U.S.A. 82 F2 39 26N 86 25W
Martinsville, Va., U.S.A. 83 G6 36 41N 79 52W
Marton, N.Z. .... 59 J5 40 4S 175 23 E
Martos, Spain 21 D4 37 44N 3 58W
Marudi, Malaysia .... 36 D4 4 11N 114 19 E
Maruf, Afghan. .... 40 D5 31 30N 67 6 E
Marugame, Japan .... 31 G6 34 15N 133 40 E
Marunga, Angola .... 56 B3 17 28S 20 2 E
Marungu, Mts., Dem. Rep. of
  the Congo .... 54 D3 7 30S 30 0 E
Marv Dasht, Iran .... 45 D7 29 50N 52 40 E
Marvast, Iran .... 45 D7 30 30N 54 15 E
Marvel Loch, Australia .... 61 F2 31 28S 119 29 E
Marwar, India .... 42 G5 25 43N 73 45 E
Mary, Turkmenistan .... 28 F7 37 40N 61 50 E
Maryborough = Port Laoise,
  Ireland 10 C4 53 2N 7 18W
Maryborough, Queens., Australia 63 D5 25 31S 152 37 E
Maryborough, Vic., Australia .. 63 F3 37 0S 143 44 E
Maryfield, Canada 71 D8 49 50N 101 35W
Maryland □, U.S.A. 82 F7 39 0N 76 30W
Maryland Junction, Zimbabwe . 55 F3 17 45S 30 31 E
Maryport, U.K. 12 C4 54 44N 3 28W
Mary's Harbour, Canada 73 B8 52 18N 55 51W
Marystown, Canada 73 C8 47 10N 55 10W
Marysville, Canada 70 D5 49 35N 116 0W
Marysville, Calif., U.S.A. 78 F5 39 9N 121 35W
Marysville, Kans., U.S.A. 80 F6 39 51N 96 39W
Marysville, Mich., U.S.A. 84 D2 42 54N 82 29W
Marysville, Ohio, U.S.A. 82 E4 40 14N 83 22W

Marysville, Wash., U.S.A. 78 B4 48 3N 122 11W
Maryville, Mo., U.S.A. 80 E7 40 21N 94 52W
Maryville, Tenn., U.S.A. 83 H4 35 46N 83 58W
Marzūq, Libya .... 51 C8 25 53N 13 57 E
Masahunga, Tanzania .... 54 C3 2 6S 33 18 E
Masai, Malaysia .... 39 d 1 29N 103 53 E
Masai Mara △, Kenya .... 54 C4 1 25S 35 5 E
Masai Steppe, Tanzania ...... 54 C4 4 30S 36 30 E
Masaka, Uganda .... 54 C3 0 21S 31 45 E
Masalembo, Kepulauan,
  Indonesia .... 36 F4 5 35S 114 30 E
Masalima, Kepulauan, Indonesia 36 F5 5 4S 117 5 E
Masamba, Indonesia .... 37 E6 2 30S 120 15 E
Masan, S. Korea .... 35 G15 35 11N 128 32 E
Masandam, Ra's, Oman ...... 45 E8 26 30N 56 30 E
Masasi, Tanzania .... 55 E4 10 45S 38 52 E
Masaya, Nic. 88 D2 12 0N 86 7W
Masbate, Phil. .... 37 B6 12 21N 123 36 E
Mascara, Algeria .... 50 A6 35 26N 0 6 E
Mascota, Mexico 86 C4 20 30N 104 50W
Masela, Indonesia .... 37 F7 8 9S 129 51 E
Maseru, Lesotho .... 56 D4 29 18S 27 30 E
Mashaba, Zimbabwe .... 55 G3 20 2S 30 29 E
Mashābih, Si. Arabia .... 44 E3 25 35N 36 30 E
Mashatu △, Botswana .... 57 C4 22 5S 29 5 E
Masherbrum, Pakistan .... 43 B7 35 38N 76 18 E
Mashhad, Iran .... 45 B8 36 20N 59 35 E
Mashiz, Iran .... 45 D8 29 56N 56 37 E
Mashonaland, Zimbabwe ..... 53 H6 16 30S 31 0 E
Mashonaland Central □,
  Zimbabwe .... 57 B5 17 30S 31 0 E
Mashonaland East □, Zimbabwe 57 B5 18 0S 32 0 E
Mashonaland West □, Zimbabwe 57 B4 17 30S 29 30 E
Mashrakh, India .... 43 F11 26 7N 84 48 E
Masi Manimba,
  Dem. Rep. of the Congo .... 52 E3 4 40S 17 54 E
Masindi, Uganda .... 54 B3 1 40N 31 43 E
Masindi Port, Uganda .... 54 B3 1 43N 32 2 E
Maşīrah, Oman .... 47 C6 21 0N 58 50 E
Maşīrah, Khalīj, Oman .... 47 C6 20 10N 58 10 E
Masisi, Dem. Rep. of the Congo 54 C2 1 23S 28 49 E
Masjed Soleyman, Iran ...... 45 D6 31 55N 49 18 E
Mask, L., Ireland 10 C2 53 36N 9 22W
Maskin, Oman .... 45 F8 23 30N 56 50 E
Masoala, Tanjon' i, Madag. ... 57 B9 15 59S 50 13 E
Masoarivo, Madag. .... 57 B7 19 3S 44 19 E
Masohi = Amahai, Indonesia .. 37 E7 3 20S 128 55 E
Masomeloka, Madag. .... 57 C8 20 17S 48 37 E
Mason, Nev., U.S.A. 78 G7 38 56N 119 8W
Mason, Tex., U.S.A. 81 K5 30 45N 99 14W
Mason City, U.S.A. 80 D8 43 9N 93 12W
Maspalomas, Canary Is. 24 G4 27 46N 15 35W
Maspalomas, Pta., Canary Is. .. 24 G4 27 43N 15 36W
Masqat, Oman .... 47 C6 23 37N 58 36 E
Massa, Italy .... 20 D9 44 1N 10 9 E
Massachusetts □, U.S.A. 85 D13 42 30N 72 0W
Massachusetts B., U.S.A. 85 D14 42 20N 70 50W
Massakory, Chad .... 51 F9 13 0N 15 49 E
Massanella, Spain .... 24 B9 39 48N 2 51 E
Massangena, Mozam. .... 57 C5 21 34S 33 0 E
Massango, Angola .... 52 F3 8 2S 16 21 E
Massawa = Mitsiwa, Eritrea .. 47 D2 15 35N 39 25 E
Massena, U.S.A. 85 B10 44 56N 74 54W
Massénya, Chad .... 51 F9 11 21N 16 9 E
Masset, Canada 70 C2 54 2N 132 10W
Massiah Street, Barbados .... 89 g 13 9N 59 29W
Massif Central, France .... 20 D5 44 55N 3 0 E
Massillon, U.S.A. 84 F3 40 48N 81 32W
Massinga, Mozam. .... 57 C6 23 15S 35 22 E
Massingir, Mozam. .... 57 C5 23 51S 32 4 E
Masson-Angers, Canada 85 A9 45 32N 75 25W
Masson I., Antarctica .... 5 C7 66 10S 93 20 E
Mastanli = Momchilgrad,
  Bulgaria .... 23 D11 41 33N 25 23 E
Masterton, N.Z. .... 59 J5 40 56S 175 39 E
Mastic, U.S.A. 85 F12 40 47N 72 54W
Mastuj, Pakistan .... 43 A5 36 20N 72 36 E
Mastung, Pakistan .... 40 E5 29 50N 66 56 E
Masty, Belarus .... 17 B13 53 27N 24 38 E
Masuda, Japan .... 31 G5 34 40N 131 51 E
Masvingo, Zimbabwe .... 55 G3 20 8S 30 49 E
Masvingo □, Zimbabwe ...... 55 G3 21 0S 31 30 E
Maswa □, Tanzania .... 54 C3 2 58S 34 19 E
Maşyāf, Syria .... 44 C3 35 4N 36 20 E
Matabeleland, Zimbabwe ..... 53 H5 18 0S 27 0 E
Matabeleland North □,
  Zimbabwe .... 55 F2 19 0S 28 0 E
Matabeleland South □,
  Zimbabwe .... 55 G2 21 0S 29 0 E
Matachewan, Canada 72 C3 47 56N 80 39W
Matadi, Dem. Rep. of the Congo 52 F2 5 52S 13 31 E
Matagalpa, Nic. 88 D2 13 0N 85 58W
Matagami, Canada 72 C4 49 45N 77 34W
Matagami, L., Canada 72 C4 49 50N 77 40W
Matagorda B., U.S.A. 81 L6 28 40N 96 0W
Matagorda I., U.S.A. 81 L6 28 15N 96 30W
Matak, Indonesia .... 36 D3 3 18N 106 16 E
Mátala, Greece .... 25 E6 34 59N 24 45 E
Matam, Senegal 50 E3 15 34N 13 17W
Matamoros, Campeche, Mexico 87 D6 18 50N 90 50W
Matamoros, Coahuila, Mexico . 86 B4 25 33N 103 15W
Matamoros, Tamaulipas, Mexico 87 B5 25 50N 97 30W
Ma'ţan as Sarra, Libya ...... 51 D10 21 45N 22 0 E
Matandu →, Tanzania .... 55 D3 8 45S 34 19 E
Matane, Canada 73 C6 48 50N 67 33W
Matanomadh, India .... 42 H3 23 33N 68 57 E
Matanzas, Cuba 88 B3 23 0N 81 40W
Matapa, Botswana .... 56 C3 23 11S 24 39 E
Matapan, C. = Taínaron, Ákra,
  Greece .... 23 F10 36 22N 22 27 E
Matapédia, Canada 73 C6 48 0N 66 59W
Matapo △, Zimbabwe .... 55 G2 20 30S 29 40 E
Matara, Sri Lanka .... 40 S12 5 58N 80 30 E
Mataram, Indonesia .... 36 F5 8 35S 116 7 E
Matarani, Peru 92 G4 17 0S 72 10W
Mataranka, Australia .... 60 B5 14 55S 133 4 E
Matarma, Râs, Egypt .... 46 E1 30 27N 32 44 E
Mataró, Spain .... 21 B7 41 32N 2 29 E
Matatiele, S. Africa .... 57 E4 30 20S 28 49 E
Mataura, N.Z. .... 59 M2 46 11S 168 51 E
Matehuala, Mexico 86 C4 23 40N 100 40W
Mateke Hills, Zimbabwe ..... 55 G3 21 48S 31 0 E
Matelot, Trin. & Tob. 93 K15 10 50N 61 7W
Matera, Italy .... 22 D7 40 40N 16 36 E
Matetsi, Zimbabwe .... 55 F2 18 12S 26 0 E
Matheniko △, Uganda .... 54 B3 2 49N 34 27 E
Mathis, U.S.A. 81 L6 28 6N 97 50W

Mathráki, Greece .... 25 A3 39 48N 19 31 E
Mathura, India .... 42 F7 27 30N 77 40 E
Mati, Phil. .... 37 C7 6 55N 126 15 E
Matiali, India .... 43 F13 26 56N 88 49 E
Matías Romero, Mexico 87 D5 16 53N 95 2W
Matibane, Mozam. .... 55 E5 14 49S 40 45 E
Matiri Na., N.Z. .... 59 J4 41 38S 172 20 E
Matjiesfontein, S. Africa ..... 56 E3 33 14S 20 35 E
Matla →, India .... 43 J13 21 40N 88 40 E
Matlamanyane, Botswana .... 56 B4 19 33S 25 57 E
Matli, Pakistan .... 42 G3 25 2N 68 39 E
Matlock, U.K. 12 D6 53 9N 1 33W
Mato Grosso □, Brazil 93 F8 14 0S 55 0W
Mato Grosso, Planalto do, Brazil 93 G8 15 0S 55 0W
Mato Grosso do Sul □, Brazil .. 93 G8 18 0S 55 0W
Matobo = Matapo △, Zimbabwe 55 G2 20 30S 29 40 E
Matochkin Shar, Russia ...... 28 B6 73 10N 56 40 E
Matopo Hills, Zimbabwe ..... 55 G2 20 36S 28 20 E
Matopos, Zimbabwe .... 55 G2 20 20S 28 29 E
Matosinhos, Portugal 21 B1 41 11N 8 42W
Matroosberg, S. Africa ...... 56 E2 33 23S 19 40 E
Maṭruḥ, Oman .... 47 C6 23 37N 58 30 E
Matsue, Japan .... 31 G6 35 25N 133 10 E
Matsum, Ko, Thailand .... 39 b 9 22N 99 59 E
Matsumae, Japan .... 30 D10 41 26N 140 7 E
Matsumoto, Japan .... 31 F9 36 15N 138 0 E
Matsusaka, Japan .... 31 H4 33 20N 129 49 E
Matsuura, Japan .... 31 H4 33 20N 129 49 E
Matsuyama, Japan .... 31 H6 33 45N 132 45 E
Mattagami →, Canada 72 B3 50 43N 81 29W
Mattancheri, India .... 40 Q10 9 50N 76 15 E
Mattawa, Canada 72 C4 46 20N 78 45W
Matterhorn, Switz. .... 20 D7 45 58N 7 39 E
Matthew Town, Bahamas 89 B5 20 57N 73 40W
Matthew's Ridge, Guyana 92 B6 7 37N 60 10W
Mattice, Canada 72 C3 49 40N 83 20W
Mattituck, U.S.A. 85 F12 40 59N 72 32W
Mattō, Japan .... 31 F8 36 31N 136 34 E
Mattoon, U.S.A. 82 F1 39 29N 88 23W
Matuba, Mozam. .... 57 C5 24 28S 32 49 E
Matucana, Peru 92 F3 11 55S 76 25W
Matūn = Khowst, Afghan. .... 42 C3 33 22N 69 58 E
Matura B., Trin. & Tob. 93 K15 10 39N 61 1W
Maturín, Venezuela 92 B6 9 45N 63 11W
Matusadona △, Zimbabwe .... 55 F2 16 58S 28 42 E
Mau, Mad. P., India .... 43 F8 26 17N 78 41 E
Mau, Ut. P., India .... 43 G10 25 56N 83 33 E
Mau, Ut. P., India .... 43 G9 25 17N 81 23 E
Mau Escarpment, Kenya ..... 54 C4 0 40S 36 0 E
Mau Ranipur, India .... 43 G8 25 16N 79 8 E
Maubeuge, France .... 20 A6 50 17N 3 57 E
Maud, Pt., Australia .... 60 D1 23 6S 113 45 E
Maude, Australia .... 63 E3 34 29S 144 18 E
Maudin Sun, Burma .... 41 M19 16 0N 94 30 E
Maués, Brazil 92 D7 3 20S 57 45W
Mauganj, India .... 43 G12 24 50N 81 55 E
Maughold Hd., U.K. 12 C3 54 18N 4 18W
Maui, U.S.A. 74 H16 20 48N 156 20W
Maulamyaing = Moulmein,
  Burma .... 41 L20 16 30N 97 40 E
Maule □, Chile 94 D1 36 5S 72 30W
Maumee, U.S.A. 82 E4 41 34N 83 39W
Maumee →, U.S.A. 82 E4 41 42N 83 28W
Maumere, Indonesia .... 37 F6 8 38S 122 13 E
Maun, Botswana .... 56 C3 20 0S 23 26 E
Mauna Kea, U.S.A. 74 J17 19 50N 155 28W
Mauna Loa, U.S.A. 74 J17 19 30N 155 35W
Maungmagan Kyunzu, Burma . 38 E1 14 0N 97 48 E
Maupin, U.S.A. 76 D3 45 11N 121 5W
Maurepas, L., U.S.A. 81 K9 30 15N 90 30W
Maurice, L., Australia .... 61 E5 29 30S 131 0 E
Mauricie △, Canada 72 C5 46 45N 73 0W
Mauritania ■, Africa 50 E3 20 50N 10 0W
Mauritius ■, Ind. Oc. .... 49 J9 20 0S 57 0 E
Mauston, U.S.A. 80 D9 43 48N 90 5W
Mavli, India .... 42 G5 24 45N 73 55 E
Mavuradonha Mts., Zimbabwe 55 F3 16 30S 31 30 E
Mawa, Dem. Rep. of the Congo 54 B2 2 45N 26 40 E
Mawai, India .... 43 H9 22 30N 81 4 E
Mawana, India .... 42 E7 29 6N 77 58 E
Mawand, Pakistan .... 42 E3 29 33N 68 38 E
Mawk Mai, Burma .... 41 J20 20 14N 97 37 E
Mawlaik, Burma .... 41 H19 23 40N 94 26 E
Mawlamyine = Moulmein, Burma 41 L20 16 30N 97 40 E
Mawqaq, Si. Arabia .... 44 E4 27 25N 41 8 E
Mawson Base, Antarctica .... 5 C6 67 30S 62 53 E
Mawson Coast, Antarctica ... 5 C6 68 30S 63 0 E
Max, U.S.A. 80 B4 47 49N 101 18W
Maxcanú, Mexico 87 C6 20 40N 92 0W
Maxesibeni, S. Africa .... 57 E4 30 49S 29 23 E
Maxhamish L., Canada 70 B4 59 50N 123 17W
Maxixe, Mozam. .... 57 C6 23 54S 35 17 E
Maxville, Canada 85 A10 45 17N 74 51W
Maxwell, U.S.A. 78 F4 39 17N 122 11W
Maxwelton, Australia .... 62 C3 20 43S 142 41 E
May, C., U.S.A. 82 F8 38 56N 74 58W
May Pen, Jamaica .... 88 a 17 58N 77 15W
Maya →, Russia .... 29 D14 60 28N 134 28 E
Maya Mts., Belize 87 D7 16 30N 89 0W
Mayaguana, Bahamas 89 B5 22 30N 72 44W
Mayagüez, Puerto Rico ...... 89 d 18 12N 67 9W
Mayanup, Australia .... 61 F2 33 57S 116 27 E
Mayapan, Mexico 87 C7 20 28N 89 11W
Mayapan, Yucatán, Mexico ... 87 C7 20 30N 89 25W
Mayari, Cuba 89 B4 20 40N 75 41W
Mayaro B., Trin. & Tob. 93 K16 10 14N 61 0W
Maybell, U.S.A. 76 F9 40 31N 108 5W
Maybole, U.K. 11 F4 55 21N 4 42W
Maydān, Iraq .... 44 C5 34 55N 45 37 E
Maydena, Australia .... 63 G4 42 45S 146 30 E
Mayenne →, France 20 C3 47 30N 0 32W
Mayer, U.S.A. 77 J7 34 24N 112 14W
Mayerthorpe, Canada 70 C5 53 57N 115 8W
Mayfield, Ky., U.S.A. 83 G1 36 44N 88 38W
Mayfield, N.Y., U.S.A. 85 C10 43 6N 74 16W
Mayhill, U.S.A. 77 K11 32 53N 105 29W
Maykop, Russia .... 19 F7 44 35N 40 10 E
Maymyo, Burma .... 38 A1 22 2N 96 28 E
Maynard, Mass., U.S.A. 85 D13 42 26N 71 27W
Maynard, Wash., U.S.A. 78 C4 47 59N 122 55W
Maynard Hills, Australia ..... 61 E2 28 28S 119 49 E
Mayne →, Australia .... 62 C3 23 40S 141 55 E
Maynooth, Ireland 10 C5 53 23N 6 34W
Mayo □, Ireland 10 C2 53 53N 9 3W
Mayon Volcano, Phil. .... 37 B6 13 15N 123 41 E
Mayor I., N.Z. .... 59 G6 37 16S 176 17 E

Mayotte ☑, Ind. Oc. .... 53 G9   12 50S   45 10 E
Maysān ☐, Iraq .... 44 D5   31 55N   47 15 E
Maysville, U.S.A. 82 F4   38 39N   83 46W
Mayu, Indonesia .... 37 D7   1 30N 126 30 E
Mayville, N. Dak., U.S.A. 80 B6   47 30N   97 20W
Mayville, N.Y., U.S.A. 84 D5   42 15N   79 30W
Mayya, Russia .... 29 C14 61 44N 130 18 E
Mazabuka, Zambia .... 55 F2   15 52S   27 44 E
Mazagān = El Jadida, Morocco . 50 B4   33 11N   8 17W
Mazagão, Brazil 93 D8   0 7S   51 16W
Mazán, Peru 92 D4   3 30S   73 0W
Māzandarān ☐, Iran .... 45 B7   36 30N   52 0 E
Mazapil, Mexico 86 C4   24 38N 101 34W
Mazara del Vallo, Italy .... 22 F5   37 39N   12 35 E
Mazarrón, Spain 21 D5   37 38N   1 19W
Mazaruni ➔, Guyana 92 B7   6 25N   58 35W
Mazatán, Mexico 86 B2   29 0N 110 8W
Mazatenango, Guatemala 88 D1   14 35N   91 30W
Mazatlán, Mexico 86 C3   23 13N 106 25W
Mažeikiai, Lithuania .... 9 H20 56 20N   22 20 E
Māzhān, Iran .... 45 C8   32 30N   59 0 E
Mazinān, Iran .... 45 B8   36 19N   56 56 E
Mazoe, Mozam. .... 55 F3   16 42S   33 7 E
Mazoe ➔, Mozam. .... 55 F3   16 20S   33 30 E
Mazowe, Zimbabwe .... 55 F3   17 28S   30 58 E
Mazurian Lakes = Mazurski,
    Pojezierze, Poland .... 17 B11 53 50N   21 0 E
Mazurski, Pojezierze, Poland .. 17 B11 53 50N   21 0 E
Mazyr, Belarus .... 17 B15 51 59N   29 15 E
Mazzarrón, Spain 52 B7   6 25N   58 35W
Mbabane, Swaziland .... 57 D5   26 18S   31 6 E
Mbaïki, C.A.R. .... 52 D3   3 53N   18 1 E
Mbala, Zambia .... 55 D3   8 46S   31 24 E
Mbalabala, Zimbabwe .... 57 C4   20 27S   29 3 E
Mbale, Uganda .... 54 B3   1 8N   34 12 E
Mbalmayo, Cameroon .... 52 D2   3 33N   11 33 E
Mbamba Bay, Tanzania ...... 55 E3   11 13S   34 49 E
Mbandaka, Dem. Rep. of
    the Congo .... 52 D3   0 1N   18 18 E
Mbanza Congo, Angola ...... 52 F2   6 18S   14 16 E
Mbanza Ngungu, Dem. Rep. of
    the Congo .... 52 F2   5 12S   14 53 E
Mbarangandu, Tanzania ..... 55 D4   10 11S   36 48 E
Mbarara, Uganda .... 54 C3   0 35S   30 40 E
Mbashe ➔, S. Africa .... 57 E4   32 15S   28 54 E
Mbenkuru ➔, Tanzania ...... 55 D4   9 25S   39 50 E
Mberengwa, Zimbabwe ...... 55 G2   20 29S   29 57 E
Mberengwa, Mt., Zimbabwe .. 55 G2   20 37S   29 55 E
Mbesuma, Zambia .... 55 E3   10 0S   32 2 E
Mbeya, Tanzania .... 55 D3   8 54S   33 29 E
Mbeya ☐, Tanzania .... 54 D3   8 15S   33 30 E
Mbinga, Tanzania .... 55 E4   10 50S   35 0 E
Mbini = Río Muni ☐, Eq. Guin. . 52 D2   1 30N   10 0 E
Mbour, Senegal 50 F2   14 22N   16 54W
Mbuji-Mayi, Dem. Rep. of
    the Congo .... 54 D1   6 9S   23 40 E
Mbulu, Tanzania .... 54 C4   3 45S   35 30 E
Mburucuyá, Argentina 94 B4   28 1S   58 14W
McCarran International, Las
    Vegas ✈ (LAS), U.S.A. 79 J11 36 5N 115 9W
Mchinja, Tanzania .... 55 D4   9 44S   39 45 E
Mchinji, Malawi .... 55 E3   13 47S   32 58 E
McMurdo, Antarctica .... 5 D11 77 0S 140 0 E
Mdantsane, S. Africa .... 53 L5   32 56S   27 46 E
Mead, L., U.S.A. 79 J12 36 1N 114 44W
Meade, U.S.A. 81 G4   37 17N 100 20W
Meadow Lake, Canada 71 C7   54 10N 108 26W
Meadow Lake △, Canada 71 C7   54 27N 109 0W
Meadow Valley Wash ➔, U.S.A. . 79 J12 36 40N 114 34W
Meadville, U.S.A. 84 E4   41 39N   80 9W
Meaford, Canada 84 B4   44 36N   80 35W
Mealy Mts., Canada 73 B8   53 10N   58 0W
Meander River, Canada 70 B5   59 2N 117 42W
Meares, C., U.S.A. 76 D2   45 37N 124 0W
Mearim ➔, Brazil 93 D10   3 4S   44 35W
Meath ☐, Ireland 10 C5   53 40N   6 57W
Meath Park, Canada 71 C7   53 27N 105 22W
Meaux, France .... 20 B5   48 58N   2 50 E
Mebechi-Gawa ➔, Japan ..... 30 D10 40 31N 141 31 E
Mebulu, Tanjung, Indonesia .. 37 K18   8 50S 115 5 E
Mecanhelas, Mozam. .... 55 F4   15 12S   35 54 E
Mecca = Makkah, Si. Arabia .. 47 C2   21 30N   39 54 E
Mecca, U.S.A. 79 M10 33 34N 116 5W
Mechanicsburg, U.S.A. 84 F8   40 13N   77 1W
Mechanicville, U.S.A. 85 D11 42 54N   73 41W
Mechelen, Belgium .... 15 C4   51 2N   4 29 E
Mecheria, Algeria 50 B5   33 35N   0 18W
Mecklenburg, Germany ...... 16 B6   53 33N   11 40 E
Mecklenburger Bucht, Germany 16 A6   54 20N   11 40 E
Meconta, Mozam. .... 55 E4   14 59S   39 50 E
Medan, Indonesia .... 36 D1   3 40N   98 38 E
Médanos de Coro △, Venezuela 89 D6   11 35N   69 44W
Medanosa, Pta., Argentina ... 96 F3   48 8S   66 0W
Médéa, Algeria .... 50 A6   36 12N   2 50 E
Medellín, Colombia 92 B3   6 15N   75 35W
Medelpad, Sweden .... 9 E17 62 33N   16 30 E
Medemblik, Neths. .... 15 B5   52 46N   5 8 E
Medford, Mass., U.S.A. 85 D13 42 25N   71 7W
Medford, Oreg., U.S.A. 76 E2   42 9N 122 52W
Medford, Wis., U.S.A. 80 C9   45 9N   90 20W
Medgidia, Romania .... 17 F15 44 15N   28 19 E
Media Agua, Argentina 94 C2   31 58S   68 25W
Media Luna, Argentina 94 C2   34 45S   66 44W
Medianeira, Brazil 95 B5   25 17S   54 5W
Mediaş, Romania .... 17 E13 46 9N   24 22 E
Medicine Bow, U.S.A. 76 F10 41 54N 106 12W
Medicine Bow Pk., U.S.A. 76 F10 41 21N 106 19W
Medicine Bow Ra., U.S.A. 76 F10 41 10N 106 25W
Medicine Hat, Canada 71 D6   50 0N 110 45W
Medicine Lake, U.S.A. 80 A2   48 30N 104 30W
Medicine Lodge, U.S.A. 81 G5   37 17N   98 35W
Medina = Al Madīnah, Si. Arabia 44 E3   24 35N   39 52 E
Medina, N. Dak., U.S.A. 80 B5   46 54N   99 18W
Medina, N.Y., U.S.A. 84 C6   43 13N   78 23W
Medina, Ohio, U.S.A. 84 E3   41 8N   81 52W
Medina ➔, U.S.A. 81 L5   29 16N   98 29W
Medina del Campo, Spain 21 B3   41 18N   4 55W
Medina L., U.S.A. 81 L5   29 32N   98 56W
Medina Sidonia, Spain 21 D3   36 28N   5 57W
Medinipur, India .... 43 H12 22 25N   87 21 E
Mediterranean Sea, Europe ... 49 C5   35 0N   15 0 E
Médoc, France 20 D3   45 0N   0 50W
Medveditsa ➔, Russia .... 19 E7   49 35N   42 41 E
Medvezhi, Ostrava, Russia ... 29 B17 71 0N 161 0 E
Medvezhyegorsk, Russia ..... 18 B5   63 0N   34 25 E
Medway ☐, U.K. .... 13 F8   51 25N   0 32 E
Medway ➔, U.K. .... 13 F8   51 27N   0 46 E
Meekatharra, Australia ...... 61 E2   26 32S 118 29 E
Meeker, U.S.A. 76 F10 40 2N 107 55W

Meelpaeg Res., Canada 73 C8   48 15N   56 33W
Meerut, India .... 42 E7   29 1N   77 42 E
Meeteetse, U.S.A. 76 D9   44 9N 108 52W
Mega, Ethiopia .... 47 G2   3 57N   38 19 E
Mégara, Greece .... 23 F10 37 58N   23 22 E
Megasini, India .... 43 J12 21 38N   86 21 E
Meghalaya ☐, India .... 41 G17 25 50N   91 0 E
Meghna ➔, Bangla. 72 C4   48 35N   75 55W
Meharry, Mt., Australia ..... 60 D2   22 59S 118 35 E
Mehlville, U.S.A. 80 F9   38 30N   90 19W
Mehndawal, India .... 43 F10 26 58N   83 5 E
Mehr Jān, Iran .... 45 C7   33 50N   55 6 E
Mehrābād, Iran .... 44 B5   36 53N   47 55 E
Mehrān, Iran .... 44 C5   33 7N   46 10 E
Mehrīz, Iran .... 45 D7   31 35N   54 28 E
Mei Xian, China .... 34 G4   34 18N 107 55 E
Meiktila, Burma .... 41 J19 20 53N   95 54 E
Meissen, Germany .... 16 C7   51 9N   13 29 E
Meizhou, China .... 33 D6   24 16N 116 6 E
Meja, India .... 43 G10 25 9N   82 7 E
Mejillones, Chile 94 A1   23 10S   70 30W
Mekele, Ethiopia .... 47 E2   13 33N   39 30 E
Mekhtar, Pakistan .... 40 D6   30 30N   69 15 E
Meknès, Morocco 50 B4   33 57N   5 33W
Mekong ➔, Asia .... 39 H6   9 30N 106 15 E
Mekongga, Indonesia .... 37 E6   3 39S 121 15 E
Mekvari = Kür ➔, Azerbaijan . 19 G8   39 29N   49 15 E
Melagiri Hills, India .... 40 N10 12 20N   77 30 E
Melaka, Malaysia .... 39 L4   2 15N 102 15 E
Melalap, Malaysia .... 36 C5   5 10N 116 5 E
Mélambes, Greece .... 25 D6   35 8N   24 40 E
Melanesia, Pac. Oc. .... 64 H7   4 0S 155 0 E
Melaya, Indonesia .... 37 J17   8 17S 114 30 E
Melbourne, Australia .... 63 F4   37 50S 145 0 E
Melbourne, U.S.A. 83 L5   28 5N   80 37W
Melchor Múzquiz, Mexico 86 B4   27 50N 101 30W
Melchor Ocampo, Mexico 86 C4   24 52N 101 40W
Mélèzes ➔, Canada 72 A5   57 40N   69 29W
Melfort, Canada 71 C8   52 50N 104 37W
Melfort, Zimbabwe .... 55 F3   18 0S   31 25 E
Melhus, Norway .... 8 E14 63 17N   10 18 E
Melilla, N. Afr. 21 E4   35 21N   2 57W
Melipilla, Chile 94 C1   33 42S   71 15W
Mélissa, Ákra, Greece ...... 25 D6   35 6N   24 33 E
Melita, Canada 71 D8   49 15N 101 0W
Melitopol, Ukraine .... 19 E6   46 50N   35 22 E
Melk, Austria .... 16 D8   48 13N   15 20 E
Mellansel, Sweden .... 8 E18 63 25N   18 17 E
Mellen, U.S.A. 80 B9   46 20N   90 40W
Mellerud, Sweden .... 9 G15 58 41N   12 28 E
Mellette, U.S.A. 80 C5   45 9N   98 30W
Mellieha, Malta .... 25 D1   35 57N   14 22 E
Melo, Uruguay 95 C5   32 20S   54 10W
Melolo, Indonesia .... 37 F6   9 53S 120 40 E
Melouprey, Cambodia ...... 38 F5   13 48N 105 16 E
Melrose, Australia .... 63 E4   32 42S 146 57 E
Melrose, U.K. 11 F6   55 36N   2 43W
Melrose, Minn., U.S.A. 80 C7   45 40N   94 49W
Melrose, N. Mex., U.S.A. 81 H3   34 26N 103 38W
Melstone, U.S.A. 76 C10 46 36N 107 52W
Melton Mowbray, U.K. 12 E7   52 47N   0 54W
Melun, France .... 20 B5   48 32N   2 39 E
Melville, Canada 71 C8   50 55N 102 50W
Melville, C., Australia ...... 62 A3   14 11S 144 30 E
Melville, L., Canada 73 B8   53 30N   60 0W
Melville B., Australia ...... 62 A2   12 0S 136 45 E
Melville I., Australia ...... 60 B5   11 30S 131 0 E
Melville I., Canada 4 B2   75 30N 112 0W
Melville Pen., Canada 69 B11 68 0N   84 0W
Memba, Mozam. .... 55 E5   14 11S   40 30 E
Memboro, Indonesia .... 37 F5   9 30S 119 30 E
Memel = Klaipėda, Lithuania . 9 J19 55 43N   21 10 E
Memel, S. Africa .... 57 D4   27 38S   29 36 E
Memmingen, Germany ...... 16 E6   47 58N   10 10 E
Mempawah, Indonesia ...... 36 D3   0 30N 109 5 E
Memphis, Mich., U.S.A. 84 D2   42 54N   82 46W
Memphis, Tenn., U.S.A. 81 H10 35 8N   90 3W
Memphis, Tex., U.S.A. 81 H4   34 44N 100 33W
Memphremagog, L., U.S.A. ... 85 B12 45 0N   72 12W
Mena, U.S.A. 81 H7   34 35N   94 15W
Menai Strait, U.K. 12 D3   53 11N   4 13W
Ménaka, Mali .... 50 E6   15 59N   2 18 E
Menan = Chao Phraya ➔,
    Thailand .... 38 F3   13 32N 100 36 E
Menarandra ➔, Madag. ..... 57 D7   25 17S   44 30 E
Menard, U.S.A. 81 K5   30 55N   99 47W
Mendawai ➔, Indonesia .... 36 E4   3 30S 113 0 E
Mende, France .... 20 D5   44 31N   3 30 E
Mendeleyev Ridge, Arctic 4 B17 80 0N 178 0W
Mendez, Mexico 87 B5   25 7N   98 34W
Mendhar, India .... 43 C6   33 35N   74 10 E
Mendip Hills, U.K. 13 F5   51 17N   2 40W
Mendocino, U.S.A. 76 G2   39 19N 123 48W
Mendocino, C., U.S.A. 76 F1   40 26N 124 25W
Mendota, Calif., U.S.A. 78 J6   36 45N 120 23W
Mendota, Ill., U.S.A. 80 E10 41 33N   89 7W
Mendoyo, Indonesia .... 37 J17   8 23S 114 42 E
Mendoza, Argentina 94 C2   32 50S   68 52W
Mendoza ☐, Argentina 94 C2   33 0S   69 0W
Mene Grande, Venezuela 92 B4   9 49N   70 56W
Menemen, Turkey .... 23 E12 38 34N   27 3 E
Menen, Belgium .... 15 D3   50 47N   3 7 E
Menggala, Indonesia .... 36 E3   4 30S 105 15 E
Mengjin, China .... 34 G7   34 55N 112 45 E
Mengyin, China .... 35 G9   35 40N 117 58 E
Mengzi, China .... 32 D5   23 20N 103 22 E
Menihek, Canada 73 B6   54 28N   56 36W
Menihek L., Canada 73 B6   54 0N   67 0W
Menin = Menen, Belgium .... 15 D3   50 47N   3 7 E
Menindee, Australia .... 63 E3   32 20S 142 25 E
Menindee L., Australia ...... 63 E3   32 20S 142 25 E
Meningie, Australia .... 63 F2   35 50S 139 18 E
Menjangan, Pulau, Indonesia . 37 J17   8 7S 114 31 E
Menlo Park, U.S.A. 78 H4   37 27N 122 12W
Menominee, U.S.A. 82 C2   45 6N   87 37W
Menominee ➔, U.S.A. 82 C2   45 6N   87 36W
Menomonie, U.S.A. 80 C9   44 53N   91 55W
Menongue, Angola .... 53 G3   14 48S   17 52 E
Menorca, Spain .... 24 B11 40 0N   4 0 E
Mentakab, Malaysia .... 39 L4   3 29N 102 21 E
Mentawai, Kepulauan, Indonesia 36 E1   2 0S   99 0 E
Menton, France .... 20 E7   43 50N   7 29 E
Mentor, U.S.A. 84 E3   41 40N   81 21W
Menzelinsk, Russia .... 18 C9   55 53N   53 1 E
Menzies, Australia .... 61 E3   29 40S 121 2 E
Meob B., Namibia .... 56 C1   24 25S   14 34 E
Me'ona, Israel .... 46 B4   33 1N   35 15 E

Meoqui, Mexico 86 B3   28 17N 105 29W
Mepaco, Mozam. .... 55 F3   15 57S   30 48 E
Meppel, Neths. .... 15 B6   52 42N   6 12 E
Merabéllou, Kólpos, Greece .. 25 D7   35 10N   25 50 E
Merak, Indonesia .... 37 F12   6 10N 106 26 E
Meramangye, L., Australia ... 61 E5   28 25S 132 13 E
Meran = Merano, Italy ...... 22 A4   46 40N   11 9 E
Merano, Italy .... 22 A4   46 40N   11 9 E
Merauke, Indonesia .... 37 F10   8 29S 140 24 E
Merbein, Australia .... 63 E3   34 10S 142 2 E
Merbuk, Gunung, Indonesia . 37 J17   8 13S 114 39 E
Merca, Somali Rep. .... 47 G3   1 48N   44 50 E
Merced, U.S.A. 78 H6   37 18N 120 29W
Merced ➔, U.S.A. 78 H6   37 21N 120 59W
Merced Pk., U.S.A. 78 H7   37 36N 119 24W
Mercedes, Buenos Aires,
    Argentina 94 C4   34 40S   59 30W
Mercedes, Corrientes, Argentina 94 B4   29 10S   58 5W
Mercedes, San Luis, Argentina . 94 C2   33 40S   65 21W
Mercedes, Uruguay 94 C4   33 12S   58 0W
Mercedita, Chile 81 M6   26 9N   97 55W
Merceditas, Chile 94 B1   28 20S   70 35W
Mercer, N.Z. .... 59 G5   37 16S 175 5 E
Mercer, U.S.A. 84 E4   41 14N   80 15W
Mercer Island, U.S.A. 78 C4   47 35N 122 15W
Mercury, U.S.A. 79 J11 36 40N 115 58W
Mercy, C., Canada 69 B13 65 0N   63 30W
Mere, U.K. 13 F5   51 6N   2 16W
Meredith, C., Falk. Is. 96 G4   52 15S   60 40W
Meredith, L., U.S.A. 81 H4   35 43N 101 33W
Mergui, Burma .... 38 F2   12 26N   98 34 E
Mergui Arch. = Myeik Kyunzu,
    Burma .... 39 G1   11 30N   97 30 E
Mérida, Mexico 87 C7   20 58N   89 37W
Mérida, Spain 21 C2   38 55N   6 25W
Mérida, Venezuela 92 B4   8 24N   71 8W
Mérida, Cord. de, Venezuela . 92 B4   9 0N   71 0W
Meriden, U.K. 13 E6   52 26N   1 38W
Meriden, U.S.A. 85 E12 41 32N   72 48W
Meridian, Calif., U.S.A. 78 F5   39 9N 121 55W
Meridian, Idaho, U.S.A. 76 E5   43 37N 116 24W
Meridian, Miss., U.S.A. 83 J1   32 22N   88 42W
Merinda, Australia .... 62 C4   20 2S 148 11 E
Merir, Pac. Oc. .... 37 D8   4 10N 132 30 E
Merirumã, Brazil 93 C8   1 5N   54 40W
Merkel, U.S.A. 81 J5   32 28N 100 1W
Mermaid Reef, Australia .... 60 C2   17 6S 119 36 E
Merredin, Australia .... 61 F2   31 28S 118 18 E
Merrick, U.K. 11 F4   55 8N   4 28W
Merrickville, Canada 85 B9   44 55N   75 50W
Merrill, Oreg., U.S.A. 76 E3   42 1N 121 36W
Merrill, Wis., U.S.A. 80 C10 45 11N   89 41W
Merrimack ➔, U.S.A. 85 D14 42 49N   70 49W
Merriman, U.S.A. 80 D4   42 55N 101 42W
Merritt, Canada 70 C4   50 10N 120 45W
Merritt Island, U.S.A. 83 L5   28 21N   80 42W
Merriwa, Australia .... 63 E5   32 6S 150 22 E
Merry I., Canada 72 A4   55 29N   77 31W
Merryville, U.S.A. 81 K8   30 45N   93 33W
Mersch, Lux. .... 15 E6   49 44N   6 7 E
Mersea I., U.K. .... 13 F8   51 47N   0 58 E
Merseburg, Germany .... 16 C6   51 22N   11 59 E
Mersey ➔, U.K. 12 D4   53 25N   3 1W
Merseyside ☐, U.K. 12 D4   53 31N   3 2W
Mersin, Turkey .... 19 G5   36 51N   34 36 E
Mersing, Malaysia .... 39 L4   2 25N 103 50 E
Merta, India .... 42 F6   26 39N   74 4 E
Merta Road, India .... 42 F5   26 43N   73 55 E
Merthyr Tydfil, U.K. 13 F4   51 45N   3 22W
Merthyr Tydfil ☐, U.K. 13 F4   51 46N   3 21W
Mértola, Portugal 21 D2   37 40N   7 40W
Mertzon, U.S.A. 81 K4   31 16N 100 49W
Meru, Kenya .... 54 B4   0 3N   37 40 E
Meru, Tanzania .... 54 C4   3 15S   36 46 E
Meru △, Kenya .... 54 B4   0 5N   38 10 E
Mesa, U.S.A. 77 K8   33 25N 111 50W
Mesa Verde △, U.S.A. 77 H9   37 11N 108 29W
Mesanagrós, Greece .... 25 C9   36 1N   27 49 E
Mesaoria, Cyprus .... 25 D12 35 12N   33 14 E
Mesarás, Kólpos, Greece .... 25 D6   35 6N   24 47 E
Mesgouez, L., Canada 72 B5   51 20N   75 0W
Meshed = Mashhad, Iran .... 45 B8   36 20N   59 35 E
Meshoppen, U.S.A. 85 E8   41 36N   76 3W
Mesilinka ➔, Canada 70 B4   56 6N 124 30W
Mesilla, U.S.A. 77 K10 32 16N 106 48W
Mesolóngion, Greece ...... 23 E9   38 21N   21 28 E
Mesopotamia = Al Jazirah, Iraq . 44 C5   33 30N   44 0 E
Mesopotamia, U.S.A. 84 E4   41 27N   80 57W
Mesquite, U.S.A. 77 H6   36 47N 114 6W
Messaad, Algeria .... 50 B6   34 8N   3 30 E
Messalo ➔, Mozam. .... 55 E4   12 25S   39 15 E
Messina = Musina, S. Africa .. 57 C5   22 20S   30 5 E
Messina, Italy .... 22 E6   38 11N   15 34 E
Messina, Str. di, Italy ...... 22 F6   38 15N   15 35 E
Messíni, Greece .... 23 F10 37 4N   22 1 E
Messiniakós Kólpos, Greece .. 23 F10 36 45N   22 5 E
Messonghi, Greece .... 25 B3   39 29N   19 56 E
Mesta ➔, Bulgaria .... 23 D11 40 54N   24 49 E
Meta ➔, S. Amer. 92 B5   6 12N   67 28W
Meta Incognita Pen., Canada . 69 B13 62 45N   68 30W
Metabetchouan, Canada 73 C5   48 26N   71 52W
Metairie, U.S.A. 81 L9   29 58N   90 10W
Metaline Falls, U.S.A. 76 B5   48 52N 117 22W
Metán, Argentina 94 B3   25 30S   65 0W
Metangula, Mozam. .... 55 E3   12 40S   34 50 E
Metengobalame, Mozam. .... 55 E3   14 49S   34 30 E
Methven, N.Z. .... 59 K3   43 38S 171 40 E
Metil, Mozam. .... 55 F4   16 24S   39 0 E
Metlakatla, U.S.A. 68 C6   55 8N 131 35W
Metropolis, U.S.A. 81 G10 37 9N   88 44W
Metu, Ethiopia .... 47 F2   8 18N   35 35 E
Metz, France .... 20 B7   49 8N   6 10 E
Meulaboh, Indonesia ...... 36 D1   4 11N   96 3 E
Meureudu, Indonesia ...... 36 C1   5 19N   96 10 E
Meuse ➔, Europe .... 15 D5   50 45N   5 41 E
Mexia, U.S.A. 81 K6   31 41N   96 29W
Mexiana, I., Brazil 93 D9   0 0N   49 30W
Mexicali, Mexico 79 N11 32 40N 115 30W
Mexican Plateau, Mexico 66 G9   25 0N 105 0W
Mexican Water, U.S.A. 77 H9   36 57N 109 32W
México, Mexico 87 D5   19 20N   99 10W
Mexico, Maine, U.S.A. 85 B14 44 34N   70 33W
Mexico, Mo., U.S.A. 80 F9   39 10N   91 53W
Mexico, N.Y., U.S.A. 85 C8   43 28N   76 18W
Mexico ■, Cent. Amer. 86 C4   25 0N 105 0W
Mexico, G. of, Cent. Amer. ... 87 C7   25 0N   90 0W
Mexico B., U.S.A. 85 C8   43 35N   76 20W

Meydān-e Naftūn, Iran ...... 45 D6   31 56N   49 18 E
Meydani, Ra's-e, Iran .... 45 E8   25 24N   59 6 E
Meymaneh, Afghan. .... 40 B4   35 53N   64 38 E
Mezen, Russia .... 18 A7   65 50N   44 20 E
Mezen ➔, Russia .... 18 A7   65 44N   44 22 E
Mézenc, Mt., France .... 20 D6   44 54N   4 11 E
Mezhdurechenskiy, Russia ... 28 D7   59 36N   65 56 E
Mezőkövesd, Hungary ...... 17 E11 47 49N   20 35 E
Mezőtúr, Hungary .... 17 E11 47 1N   20 41 E
Mezquital, Mexico 86 C4   23 29N 104 23W
Mfolozi ➔, S. Africa .... 57 D5   28 25S   32 26 E
Mgeta, Tanzania .... 55 D4   8 22S   36 6 E
Mhlaba Hills, Zimbabwe .... 55 F3   18 30S   30 30 E
Mhow, India .... 42 H6   22 33N   75 50 E
Miahuatlán, Mexico 87 D5   16 21N   96 36W
Miami, Fla., U.S.A. 83 N5   25 47N   80 11W
Miami, Okla., U.S.A. 81 G7   36 53N   94 53W
Miami, Tex., U.S.A. 81 H4   35 42N 100 38W
Miami Beach, U.S.A. 83 N5   25 47N   80 8W
Mian Xian, China .... 34 H4   33 10N 106 32 E
Miandarreh, Iran .... 45 C7   35 37N   53 39 E
Miāndowāb, Iran .... 44 B5   37 0N   46 5 E
Miandrivazo, Madag. .... 57 B8   19 31S   45 29 E
Miāneh, Iran .... 44 B5   37 30N   47 40 E
Mianwali, Pakistan .... 42 C4   32 38N   71 28 E
Miarinarivo, Antananarivo,
    Madag. .... 57 B8   18 57S   46 55 E
Miarinarivo, Toamasina, Madag. 57 B8   16 38S   48 15 E
Miarravaratra, Madag. ...... 57 C8   20 13S   47 31 E
Miass, Russia .... 18 D11 54 59N   60 6 E
Mica, S. Africa .... 57 C5   24 10S   30 48 E
Michalovce, Slovak Rep. .... 17 D11 48 47N   21 58 E
Michigan ☐, U.S.A. 82 C3   44 0N   85 0W
Michigan, L., U.S.A. 82 D2   44 0N   87 0W
Michigan City, U.S.A. 82 E2   41 43N   86 54W
Michipicoten I., Canada 72 C2   47 40N   85 40W
Michoacan ☐, Mexico 86 D4   19 0N 102 0W
Michurin, Bulgaria .... 23 C12 42 9N   27 51 E
Michurinsk, Russia .... 18 D7   52 58N   40 27 E
Mico, Pta., Nic. 88 D3   12 0N   83 30W
Micoud, St. Lucia .... 89 f   13 49N   60 54W
Micronesia, Pac. Oc. .... 64 G7   11 0N 160 0 E
Micronesia, Federated States
    of ■, Pac. Oc. .... 64 G7   9 0N 150 0 E
Midai, Indonesia .... 36 D3   3 0N 107 47 E
Midale, Canada 71 D8   49 25N 103 20W
Middelburg, Neths. .... 15 C3   51 30N   3 36 E
Middelburg, Eastern Cape,
    S. Africa .... 56 E4   31 30S   25 0 E
Middelburg, Mpumalanga,
    S. Africa .... 57 D4   25 49S   29 28 E
Middelpos, S. Africa .... 56 E3   31 55S   20 13 E
Middelwit, S. Africa .... 56 C4   24 51S   27 3 E
Middle Alkali L., U.S.A. 76 F3   41 27N 120 5W
Middle Bass I., U.S.A. 84 E2   41 41N   82 49W
Middle East, Asia .... 26 F7   38 0N   40 0 E
Middle Fork Feather ➔, U.S.A. . 78 F5   39 38N 121 30W
Middle I., Australia .... 61 F3   34 6S 123 11 E
Middle Loup ➔, U.S.A. 80 E5   41 17N   98 24W
Middle Sackville, Canada ... 73 D7   44 47N   63 42W
Middleboro, U.S.A. 85 E14 41 54N   70 55W
Middleburg, Fla., U.S.A. 83 K5   30 4N   81 52W
Middleburg, N.Y., U.S.A. 85 D10 42 36N   74 20W
Middleburg, Pa., U.S.A. 84 F7   40 47N   77 3W
Middlebury, U.S.A. 85 B11 44 1N   73 10W
Middlemount, Australia .... 62 C4   22 50S 148 40 E
Middleport, N.Y., U.S.A. 84 C6   43 13N   78 29W
Middleport, Ohio, U.S.A. 82 F4   39 0N   82 3W
Middlesboro, U.S.A. 83 G4   36 36N   83 43W
Middlesbrough, U.K. 12 C6   54 35N   1 13W
Middlesbrough ☐, U.K. 12 C6   54 28N   1 13W
Middlesex, Belize 88 C2   17 2N   88 31W
Middlesex, N.J., U.S.A. 85 F10 40 36N   74 30W
Middlesex, N.Y., U.S.A. 84 D7   42 42N   77 16W
Middleton, Australia .... 62 C3   22 22S 141 32 E
Middleton, Canada 73 D6   44 57N   65 4W
Middleton Cr. ➔, Australia .. 62 C3   22 35S 141 51 E
Middletown, U.K. 10 B5   54 17N   6 51W
Middletown, Calif., U.S.A. ... 78 G4   38 45N 122 37W
Middletown, Conn., U.S.A. .. 85 E12 41 34N   72 39W
Middletown, N.Y., U.S.A. 85 E10 41 27N   74 25W
Middletown, Ohio, U.S.A. ... 82 F3   39 31N   84 24W
Middletown, Pa., U.S.A. 85 F8   40 12N   76 44W
Midge Point, Australia ..... 62 J6   20 39S 148 43 E
Midhurst, U.K. 13 G7   50 59N   0 44W
Midi, Canal du ➔, France ... 20 E4   43 45N   1 21 E
Midland, Canada 84 B5   44 45N   79 50W
Midland, Calif., U.S.A. 79 M12 33 52N 114 48W
Midland, Mich., U.S.A. 82 D3   43 37N   84 14W
Midland, Pa., U.S.A. 84 F4   40 39N   80 27W
Midland, Tex., U.S.A. 81 K3   32 0N 102 3W
Midlands ☐, Zimbabwe ..... 55 F2   19 40S   29 0 E
Midleton, Ireland 10 E3   51 55N   8 10W
Midlothian, U.S.A. 81 J6   32 30N   97 0W
Midlothian ☐, U.K. 11 F5   55 51N   3 5W
Midongy, Tangorombohitr' i,
    Madag. .... 57 C8   23 30S   47 0 E
Midongy Atsimo, Madag. .... 57 C8   23 35S   47 1 E
Midway Is., Pac. Oc. 64 E10 28 13N 177 22W
Midway Wells, U.S.A. 79 N11 32 41N 115 7W
Midwest, U.S.A. 75 B9   42 0N   90 0W
Midwest, Wyo., U.S.A. 76 E10 43 25N 106 16W
Midwest City, U.S.A. 81 H6   35 27N   97 24W
Midyat, Turkey .... 44 B4   37 25N   41 23 E
Midzŏr, Bulgaria .... 23 C10 43 24N   22 40 E
Mie ☐, Japan .... 31 G8   34 30N 136 10 E
Międzychód, Poland .... 16 B8   52 35N   15 53 E
Międzyrzec Podlaski, Poland . 17 C12 51 58N   22 45 E
Mielec, Poland .... 17 C11 50 15N   21 25 E
Mienga, Angola .... 56 B2   17 12S   19 48 E
Miercurea-Ciuc, Romania .... 17 E13 46 21N   25 48 E
Mieres, Spain 21 A3   43 18N   5 48W
Mifflintown, U.S.A. 84 F7   40 34N   77 24W
Mifraz Hefa, Israel .... 46 C4   32 52N   35 0 E
Miguel Alemán, Presa, Mexico 87 D5   18 15N   96 40W
Mihara, Japan .... 31 G6   34 24N 133 5 E
Mikese, Tanzania .... 54 D4   6 48S   37 55 E
Mikhaylovgrad = Montana,
    Bulgaria .... 23 C10 43 27N   23 16 E
Mikhaylovka, Russia .... 19 D7   50 3N   43 5 E
Mikkeli, Finland .... 9 F22 61 43N   27 15 E
Mikkwa ➔, Canada 70 B6   58 25N 114 46W
Mikonos, Greece .... 23 F11 37 30N   25 25 E
Mikumi, Tanzania .... 54 D4   7 26S   37 0 E
Mikumi △, Tanzania .... 54 D4   7 35S   37 15 E
Mikun, Russia .... 18 B9   62 20N   50 0 E

Milaca, *U.S.A.* **80 C8** 45 45N 93 39W
Milagro, *Ecuador* **92 D3** 2 11S 79 36W
Milan = Milano, *Italy* .... **20 D8** 45 28N 9 12 E
Milan, *Mo., U.S.A.* **80 E8** 40 12N 93 7W
Milan, *Tenn., U.S.A.* **83 H1** 35 55N 88 46W
Milange, *Mozam.* .... **55 F4** 16 3S 35 45 E
Milano, *Italy* .... **20 D8** 45 28N 9 12 E
Milanoa, *Madag.* .... **57 A8** 13 35S 49 47 E
Milâs, *Turkey* .... **23 F12** 37 20N 27 50 E
Milatos, *Greece* .... **25 D7** 35 18N 25 34 E
Milazzo, *Italy* .... **22 E6** 38 13N 15 15 E
Milbank, *U.S.A.* **80 C6** 45 13N 96 38W
Milbanke Sd., *Canada* **70 C3** 52 15N 128 35W
Milden, *Canada* **71 C7** 51 29N 107 32W
Mildenhall, *U.K.* .... **13 E8** 52 21N 0 32 E
Mildmay, *Canada* **84 B3** 44 3N 81 7W
Mildura, *Australia* .... **63 E3** 34 13S 142 9 E
Miles, *Australia* .... **63 D5** 26 40S 150 9 E
Miles City, *U.S.A.* **80 B2** 46 25N 105 51W
Milestone, *Canada* **71 D8** 49 59N 104 31W
Miletus, *Turkey* .... **23 F12** 37 30N 27 18 E
Milford, *Calif., U.S.A.* **78 E6** 40 10N 120 22W
Milford, *Conn., U.S.A.* **85 E11** 41 14N 73 3W
Milford, *Del., U.S.A.* **82 F8** 38 55N 75 26W
Milford, *Mass., U.S.A.* **85 D13** 42 8N 71 31W
Milford, *N.H., U.S.A.* **85 D13** 42 50N 71 39W
Milford, *Pa., U.S.A.* **85 E10** 41 19N 74 48W
Milford, *Utah, U.S.A.* **77 G7** 38 24N 113 1W
Milford Haven, *U.K.* **13 F2** 51 42N 5 7W
Milford Sd., *N.Z.* .... **59 L1** 44 41S 167 47 E
Milford Sound, *N.Z.* .... **59 L1** 44 41S 167 55 E
Milḩ, Baḩr al = Razāzah, Buḩayrat ar, *Iraq* .... **44 C4** 32 40N 43 35 E
Milikapiti, *Australia* .... **60 B5** 11 26S 130 40 E
Miling, *Australia* .... **61 F2** 30 30S 116 17 E
Milk ➤, *U.S.A.* **76 B10** 48 4N 106 19W
Milk River, *Canada* **70 D6** 49 10N 112 5W
Mill I., *Antarctica* .... **5 C8** 66 0S 101 30 E
Mill Valley, *U.S.A.* **78 H4** 37 54N 122 32W
Millau, *France* .... **20 D5** 44 8N 3 4 E
Millbridge, *Canada* **84 B7** 44 41N 77 36W
Millbrook, *Canada* **84 B6** 44 10N 78 29W
Millbrook, *U.S.A.* **85 E11** 41 47N 73 42W
Mille Lacs, L. des, *Canada* **72 C1** 48 45N 90 35W
Mille Lacs L., *U.S.A.* **80 B8** 46 15N 93 39W
Milledgeville, *U.S.A.* **83 J4** 33 5N 83 14W
Millen, *U.S.A.* **83 J5** 32 48N 81 57W
Millennium I. = Caroline I., *Kiribati* **65 H12** 9 58S 150 13W
Miller, *U.S.A.* **80 C5** 44 31N 98 59W
Millersburg, *Ohio, U.S.A.* **84 F3** 40 33N 81 55W
Millersburg, *Pa., U.S.A.* **84 F8** 40 32N 76 58W
Millerton, *U.S.A.* **85 E11** 41 57N 73 31W
Millerton L., *U.S.A.* **78 J7** 37 1N 119 41W
Millet, *St. Lucia* .... **89 f** 13 55N 60 59W
Millheim, *U.S.A.* **84 F7** 40 54N 77 29W
Millicent, *Australia* .... **63 F3** 37 34S 140 21 E
Millington, *U.S.A.* **81 H10** 35 20N 89 53W
Millinocket, *U.S.A.* **83 C11** 45 39N 68 43W
Millmerran, *Australia* .... **63 D5** 27 53S 151 16 E
Millom, *U.K.* **12 C4** 54 13N 3 16W
Mills L., *Canada* **70 A5** 61 30N 118 20W
Millsboro, *U.S.A.* **84 G5** 40 0N 80 0W
Millstream-Chichester △, *Australia* .... **60 D2** 21 35S 117 6 E
Milltown Malbay, *Ireland* **10 D2** 52 52N 9 24W
Millville, *N.J., U.S.A.* **82 F8** 39 24N 75 2W
Millville, *Pa., U.S.A.* **85 E8** 41 7N 76 32W
Millwood L., *U.S.A.* **81 J8** 33 42N 93 58W
Milne ➤, *Australia* .... **62 C2** 21 10S 137 33 E
Milo, *U.S.A.* **83 C11** 45 15N 68 59W
Milos, *Greece* .... **23 F11** 36 44N 24 25 E
Milparinka, *Australia* .... **63 D3** 29 46S 141 57 E
Milton, *N.S., Canada* **73 D7** 44 4N 64 45W
Milton, *Ont., Canada* **84 C5** 43 31N 79 53W
Milton, *N.Z.* .... **59 M2** 46 7S 169 59 E
Milton, *Calif., U.S.A.* **78 G6** 38 3N 120 51W
Milton, *Fla., U.S.A.* **83 K2** 30 38N 87 3W
Milton, *Pa., U.S.A.* **84 F8** 41 1N 76 51W
Milton, *Vt., U.S.A.* **85 B11** 44 38N 73 7W
Milton-Freewater, *U.S.A.* **76 D4** 45 56N 118 23W
Milton Keynes, *U.K.* **13 E7** 52 1N 0 44W
Milton Keynes □, *U.K.* **13 E7** 52 1N 0 44W
Milverton, *Canada* **84 C4** 43 34N 80 55W
Milwaukee, *U.S.A.* **82 D2** 43 2N 87 55W
Milwaukee Deep, *Atl. Oc.* **89 C6** 19 50N 68 0W
Milwaukie, *U.S.A.* **78 E4** 45 27N 122 38W
Min Jiang ➤, *Fujian, China* .... **33 D6** 26 0N 119 35 E
Min Jiang ➤, *Sichuan, China* .... **32 D5** 28 45N 104 40 E
Min Xian, *China* .... **34 G3** 34 25N 104 5 E
Mina Pirquitas, *Argentina* **94 A2** 22 40S 66 30W
Minā Su'ud, *Si. Arabia* .... **45 D6** 28 45N 48 28 E
Mīnā' al Aḩmadī, *Kuwait* .... **45 D6** 29 5N 48 10 E
Minago ➤, *Canada* **71 C9** 54 33N 98 59W
Minaki, *Canada* **71 D10** 49 59N 94 40W
Minamata, *Japan* .... **31 H5** 32 10N 130 30 E
Minami-Arapusa △, *Japan* .... **31 G9** 35 30N 138 5 E
Minami-Tori-Shima, *Pac. Oc.* .... **64 E7** 24 20N 153 58 E
Minas, *Uruguay* **95 C4** 34 20S 55 10W
Minas, Sierra de las, *Guatemala* **88 C2** 15 9N 89 31W
Minas Basin, *Canada* **73 C7** 45 20N 64 12W
Minas Gerais □, *Brazil* **93 G9** 18 50S 46 0W
Minatitlán, *Mexico* **87 D6** 17 59N 94 31W
Minbu, *Burma* .... **41 J19** 20 10N 94 52 E
Minchinabad, *Pakistan* .... **42 D5** 30 10N 73 34 E
Mindanao, *Phil.* .... **37 C6** 8 0N 125 0 E
Mindanao Sea = Bohol Sea, *Phil.* .... **37 C6** 9 0N 124 0 E
Mindanao Trench, *Pac. Oc.* .... **37 B7** 12 0N 126 6 E
Minden, *Canada* **84 B6** 44 55N 78 43W
Minden, *Germany* .... **16 B5** 52 17N 8 55 E
Minden, *La., U.S.A.* **81 J8** 32 37N 93 17W
Minden, *Nev., U.S.A.* **78 G7** 38 57N 119 46W
Mindiptana, *Indonesia* .... **37 F10** 5 55S 140 22 E
Mindoro, *Phil.* .... **37 B6** 13 0N 121 0 E
Mindoro Str., *Phil.* .... **37 B6** 12 30N 120 30 E
Mine, *Japan* .... **31 G5** 34 12N 131 7 E
Minehead, *U.K.* **13 F4** 51 12N 3 29W
Mineola, *N.Y., U.S.A.* **85 F11** 40 45N 73 39W
Mineola, *Tex., U.S.A.* **81 J7** 32 40N 95 29W
Mineral King, *U.S.A.* **78 J8** 36 27N 118 36W
Mineral Wells, *U.S.A.* **81 J5** 32 48N 98 7W
Minersville, *U.S.A.* **85 F8** 40 41N 76 16W
Minerva, *U.S.A.* **84 F3** 40 44N 81 6W
Minetto, *U.S.A.* **85 C8** 43 24N 76 28W
Mingäçevir Su Anbarı, *Azerbaijan* .... **19 F8** 40 57N 46 50 E
Mingan, *Canada* **73 B7** 50 20N 64 0W

Mingechaurskoye Vdkhr. = Mingäçevir Su Anbarı, *Azerbaijan* .... **19 F8** 40 57N 46 50 E
Mingela, *Australia* .... **62 B4** 19 52S 146 38 E
Mingenew, *Australia* .... **61 E2** 29 12S 115 21 E
Mingera Cr. ➤, *Australia* .... **62 C2** 20 38S 137 45 E
Mingin, *Burma* .... **41 H19** 22 50N 94 30 E
Mingo Junction, *U.S.A.* **84 F4** 40 19N 80 37W
Mingteke Daban = Mintaka Pass, *Pakistan* .... **43 A6** 37 0N 74 58 E
Mingyuegue, *China* .... **35 C15** 43 2N 128 50 E
Minho = Miño ➤, *Spain* **21 A2** 41 52N 8 40W
Minho, *Portugal* **21 B1** 41 25N 8 20W
Minidoka, *U.S.A.* **76 E7** 42 45N 113 29W
Minigwal, L., *Australia* .... **61 E3** 29 31S 123 14 E
Minilya ➤, *Australia* .... **61 D1** 23 45S 114 0 E
Minilya Roadhouse, *Australia* .... **61 D1** 23 55S 114 0 E
Minipi L., *Canada* **73 B7** 52 25N 60 45W
Mink L., *Canada* **70 A5** 61 54N 117 40W
Minna, *Nigeria* .... **50 G7** 9 37N 6 30 E
Minneapolis, *Kans., U.S.A.* **80 F6** 39 8N 97 42W
Minneapolis, *Minn., U.S.A.* **80 C8** 44 59N 93 16W
Minnedosa, *Canada* **71 C9** 50 14N 99 50W
Minnesota □, *U.S.A.* **80 B8** 46 0N 94 15W
Minnesota ➤, *U.S.A.* **80 C8** 44 54N 93 9W
Minnewaukan, *U.S.A.* **80 A5** 48 4N 99 15W
Minnipa, *Australia* .... **63 E2** 32 51S 135 9 E
Minnitaki L., *Canada* **72 C1** 49 57N 92 10W
Mino, *Japan* .... **31 G8** 35 32N 136 55 E
Miño ➤, *Spain* **21 A2** 41 52N 8 40W
Minorca = Menorca, *Spain* .... **24 B11** 40 0N 4 0 E
Minot, *U.S.A.* **80 A4** 48 14N 101 18W
Minqin, *China* .... **34 E2** 38 38N 103 20 E
Minsk, *Belarus* .... **17 B14** 53 52N 27 30 E
Mińsk Mazowiecki, *Poland* .... **17 B11** 52 10N 21 33 E
Mintabie, *Australia* .... **63 D1** 27 15S 133 7 E
Mintaka Pass, *Pakistan* .... **43 A6** 37 0N 74 58 E
Minto, *Canada* **73 C6** 46 5N 66 5W
Minto, L., *Canada* **72 A5** 57 13N 75 0W
Minton, *Canada* **71 D8** 49 10N 104 35W
Minturn, *U.S.A.* **76 G10** 39 35N 106 26W
Minusinsk, *Russia* .... **29 D10** 53 43N 91 20 E
Minutang, *India* .... **41 E20** 28 15N 96 30 E
Minzhong, *China* .... **33 F10** 22 37N 113 30 E
Miquelon, *Canada* **72 C4** 49 25N 76 27W
Miquelon, St-P. & M. **73 C8** 47 8N 56 22W
Mir Kūh, *Iran* .... **45 E8** 26 22N 58 55 E
Mir Shahdād, *Iran* .... **45 E8** 26 15N 58 29 E
Mira, *Italy* .... **22 B5** 45 26N 12 8 E
Mira por vos Cay, *Bahamas* **89 B5** 22 9N 74 30W
Mirador-Río Azul △, *Guatemala* **88 C2** 17 45N 89 50W
Miraj, *India* .... **40 L9** 16 50N 74 45 E
Miram Shah, *Pakistan* .... **42 C4** 33 0N 70 2 E
Miramar, *Argentina* **94 D4** 38 15S 57 50W
Miramar, *Mozam.* .... **57 C6** 23 50S 35 35 E
Miramichi, *Canada* **73 C6** 47 2N 65 28W
Miramichi B., *Canada* **73 C7** 47 15N 65 0W
Miranda, *Brazil* **93 H7** 20 10S 56 15W
Miranda ➤, *Brazil* **92 G7** 19 25S 57 20W
Miranda de Ebro, *Spain* **21 A4** 42 41N 2 57W
Miranda do Douro, *Portugal* **21 B2** 41 30N 6 16W
Mirandópolis, *Brazil* **95 A5** 21 9S 51 6W
Mirango, *Malawi* .... **55 E3** 13 32S 34 58 E
Mirani, *Australia* .... **62 K6** 21 8S 148 53 E
Mirassol, *Brazil* **95 A6** 20 46S 49 28W
Mirbāṭ, *Oman* .... **47 D5** 17 0N 54 45 E
Miri, *Malaysia* .... **36 D4** 4 23N 113 59 E
Miriam Vale, *Australia* .... **62 C5** 24 20S 151 33 E
Mirim, L., *S. Amer.* **95 C5** 32 45S 52 50W
Mirnyy, *Russia* .... **29 C12** 62 33N 113 53 E
Mirokhan, *Pakistan* .... **42 F3** 27 46N 68 6 E
Mirond L., *Canada* **71 B8** 55 6N 102 47W
Mirpur, *Pakistan* .... **43 C5** 33 32N 73 56 E
Mirpur Batoro, *Pakistan* .... **42 G3** 24 44N 68 16 E
Mirpur Bibiwari, *Pakistan* .... **42 E2** 28 33N 67 44 E
Mirpur Khas, *Pakistan* .... **42 G3** 25 30N 69 0 E
Mirpur Sakro, *Pakistan* .... **42 G2** 24 33N 67 41 E
Mirs Bay = Tai Pang Wan, *H.K.* .... **33 F11** 22 33N 114 24 E
Mirtağ, *Turkey* .... **44 B4** 38 23N 41 56 E
Miryang, *S. Korea* .... **35 G15** 35 31N 128 44 E
Mirzapur, *India* .... **43 G10** 25 10N 82 34 E
Mirzapur-cum-Vindhyachal = Mirzapur, *India* .... **43 G10** 25 10N 82 34 E
Misantla, *Mexico* **87 D5** 19 56N 96 50W
Misawa, *Japan* .... **30 D10** 40 41N 141 24 E
Miscou I., *Canada* **73 C7** 47 57N 64 31W
Mish'āb, Ra's al, *Si. Arabia* .... **45 D6** 28 15N 48 43 E
Mishan, *China* .... **33 B8** 45 37N 131 48 E
Mishawaka, *U.S.A.* **82 E2** 41 40N 86 11W
Mishima, *Japan* .... **31 G9** 35 10N 138 52 E
Misión, *Mexico* **79 N10** 32 6N 116 53W
Misiones □, *Argentina* **95 B5** 27 0S 55 0W
Misiones □, *Paraguay* **94 B4** 27 0S 56 0W
Miskah, *Si. Arabia* .... **44 E4** 24 49N 42 56 E
Miskitos, Cayos, *Nic.* **88 D3** 14 26N 82 50W
Miskolc, *Hungary* .... **17 D11** 48 7N 20 50 E
Misoke, *Dem. Rep. of the Congo* .... **54 C2** 0 42S 28 2 E
Misool, *Indonesia* .... **37 E8** 1 52S 130 10 E
Miṣrātah, *Libya* .... **51 B9** 32 24N 15 3 E
Missanabie, *Canada* **72 C3** 48 20N 84 6W
Missinaibi ➤, *Canada* **72 B3** 50 43N 81 29W
Missinaibi L., *Canada* **72 C3** 48 23N 83 40W
Mission, *Canada* **70 D4** 49 10N 122 15W
Mission, *S. Dak., U.S.A.* **80 D4** 43 18N 100 39W
Mission, *Tex., U.S.A.* **81 M5** 26 13N 98 20W
Mission Beach, *Australia* .... **62 B4** 17 53S 146 6 E
Mission Viejo, *U.S.A.* **79 M9** 33 36N 117 40W
Missisa L., *Canada* **72 B2** 52 20N 85 7W
Mississagi ➤, *Canada* **72 C3** 46 15N 83 9W
Mississippi □, *U.S.A.* **84 C3** 43 32N 79 35W
Mississippi □, *U.S.A.* **81 J10** 33 0N 90 0W
Mississippi ➤, *U.S.A.* **81 L10** 29 9N 89 15W
Mississippi L., *Canada* **85 A8** 45 5N 76 10W
Mississippi River Delta, *U.S.A.* **81 L9** 29 10N 89 15W
Mississippi River Delta, *U.S.A.* **81 K10** 30 20N 89 0W
Missoula, *U.S.A.* **76 C7** 46 52N 114 1W
Missouri □, *U.S.A.* **80 F8** 38 25N 92 30W
Missouri ➤, *U.S.A.* **80 F9** 38 49N 90 7W
Missouri City, *U.S.A.* **81 L7** 29 37N 95 32W
Missouri Valley, *U.S.A.* **80 E7** 41 34N 95 53W
Mist, *U.S.A.* **78 E3** 45 59N 123 15W
Mistassibi ➤, *Canada* **73 B5** 48 53N 72 13W
Mistassini, *Canada* **73 C5** 48 42N 72 20W
Mistassini ➤, *Canada* **73 B5** 48 42N 72 20W
Mistassini, L., *Canada* **72 B5** 51 0N 73 30W
Mistastin L., *Canada* **73 A7** 55 57N 63 20W
Mistinibi, L., *Canada* **73 A7** 55 56N 64 17W
Mistissini, *Canada* **73 C5** 48 53N 72 12W

Misty L., *Canada* **71 B8** 58 53N 101 40W
Misurata = Miṣrātah, *Libya* .... **51 B9** 32 24N 15 3 E
Mitchell, *Australia* .... **63 D4** 26 29S 147 58 E
Mitchell, *Canada* **84 C3** 43 28N 81 12W
Mitchell, *Nebr., U.S.A.* **80 E3** 41 57N 103 49W
Mitchell, *Oreg., U.S.A.* **76 D3** 44 34N 120 9W
Mitchell, *S. Dak., U.S.A.* **80 D6** 43 43N 98 2W
Mitchell ➤, *Australia* .... **62 B3** 15 12S 141 35 E
Mitchell, Mt., *U.S.A.* **83 H4** 35 46N 82 16W
Mitchell and Alice Rivers △, *Australia* .... **62 B3** 15 28S 142 5 E
Mitchell Ranges, *Australia* .... **62 A2** 12 49S 135 36 E
Mitchelstown, *Ireland* **10 D3** 52 15N 8 16W
Mitha Tiwana, *Pakistan* .... **42 C5** 32 13N 72 6 E
Mithi, *Pakistan* .... **42 G3** 24 44N 69 48 E
Mithrao, *Pakistan* .... **42 F3** 27 28N 69 40 E
Mitilíni, *Greece* .... **23 E12** 39 6N 26 35 E
Mito, *Japan* .... **31 F10** 36 20N 140 30 E
Mitrovica = Kosovska Mitrovica, *Serbia & M.* .... **23 C9** 42 54N 20 52 E
Mitsinjo, *Madag.* .... **57 B8** 16 1S 45 52 E
Mitsiwa, *Eritrea* .... **47 D2** 15 35N 39 25 E
Mitsukaidō, *Japan* .... **31 F9** 36 1N 139 59 E
Mittagong, *Australia* .... **63 E5** 34 28S 150 29 E
Mittimatalik = Pond Inlet, *Canada* **69 A12** 72 40N 77 0W
Mitú, *Colombia* **92 C4** 1 15N 70 13W
Mitumba, *Tanzania* .... **54 D3** 7 8S 31 2 E
Mitumba, Mts. of the Congo .... **54 D2** 7 0S 27 30 E
Mitwaba, *Dem. Rep. of the Congo* .... **55 D2** 8 2S 27 17 E
Mityana, *Uganda* .... **54 B3** 0 23N 32 2 E
Mixteco ➤, *Mexico* **87 D5** 18 11N 98 30W
Miyagi □, *Japan* .... **30 E10** 38 15N 140 45 E
Miyah, W. el ➤, *Syria* .... **44 C3** 34 44N 39 57 E
Miyake-Jima, *Japan* .... **31 G9** 34 5N 139 30 E
Miyako, *Japan* .... **30 E10** 39 40N 141 59 E
Miyako-Jima, *Japan* .... **31 M2** 24 45N 125 20 E
Miyako-Jima, *Japan* .... **31 M2** 24 24N 125 0 E
Miyako-Rettō, *Japan* .... **31 M2** 24 24N 125 0 E
Miyakonojō, *Japan* .... **31 J5** 31 40N 131 5 E
Miyani, *India* .... **42 J3** 21 50N 69 26 E
Miyanoura-Dake, *Japan* .... **31 J5** 30 20N 130 31 E
Miyazaki, *Japan* .... **31 J5** 31 56N 131 30 E
Miyazaki □, *Japan* .... **31 H5** 32 30N 131 30 E
Miyazu, *Japan* .... **31 G7** 35 35N 135 10 E
Miyet, Bahr el = Dead Sea, *Asia* .... **46 D4** 31 30N 35 30 E
Miyoshi, *Japan* .... **31 G6** 34 48N 132 51 E
Miyun, *China* .... **34 D9** 40 28N 116 50 E
Miyun Shuiku, *China* .... **35 D9** 40 30N 117 0 E
Mizdah, *Libya* .... **51 B8** 31 30N 13 0 E
Mizen Hd., *Cork, Ireland* **10 E2** 51 27N 9 50W
Mizen Hd., *Wicklow, Ireland* **10 D5** 52 51N 6 4W
Mizhi, *China* .... **34 F6** 37 47N 110 12 E
Mizoram □, *India* .... **41 H18** 23 30N 92 40 E
Mizpe Ramon, *Israel* .... **46 E3** 30 34N 34 49 E
Mizuho, *Antarctica* .... **5 D5** 70 30S 41 0 E
Mizusawa, *Japan* .... **30 E10** 39 8N 141 8 E
Mjölby, *Sweden* .... **9 G16** 58 20N 15 10 E
Mjøsa, *Norway* .... **9 F14** 60 40N 11 0 E
Mkata, *Tanzania* .... **54 D4** 5 45S 38 20 E
Mkhaya △, *Swaziland* .... **57 D5** 26 34S 31 45 E
Mkokotoni, *Tanzania* .... **54 D4** 5 55S 39 15 E
Mkomazi, *Tanzania* .... **54 C4** 4 40S 38 7 E
Mkomazi ➤, *S. Africa* .... **57 E5** 30 12S 30 50 E
Mkomazi △, *Tanzania* .... **54 C4** 4 4S 38 7 E
Mkulwe, *Tanzania* .... **55 D3** 8 37S 32 20 E
Mkumbi, Ras, *Tanzania* .... **54 D4** 7 38S 39 55 E
Mkushi, *Zambia* .... **55 E2** 14 25S 29 15 E
Mkushi River, *Zambia* .... **55 E2** 13 32S 29 45 E
Mkuze, *S. Africa* .... **57 D5** 27 10S 32 0 E
Mkuze ➤, *S. Africa* .... **57 D5** 29 27S 29 30 E
Mladá Boleslav, *Czech Rep.* .... **16 C8** 50 27N 14 53 E
Mlala Hills, *Tanzania* .... **54 D3** 6 50S 31 40 E
Mlange = Mulanje, *Malawi* .... **55 F4** 16 2S 35 33 E
Mlanje, Pic, *Malawi* .... **53 H7** 15 57S 35 38 E
Mława, *Poland* .... **17 B11** 53 9N 20 25 E
Mlawula △, *Swaziland* .... **57 D5** 26 12S 32 2 E
Mljet, *Croatia* .... **22 C7** 42 43N 17 30 E
Mmabatho, *S. Africa* .... **56 D4** 25 49S 25 30 E
Mo i Rana, *Norway* .... **8 C16** 66 20N 14 7 E
Moa, *Cuba* **89 B4** 20 40N 74 56W
Moa, *Indonesia* .... **37 F7** 8 0S 128 0 E
Moab, *U.S.A.* **77 G9** 38 35N 109 33W
Moala, *Fiji* .... **59 D8** 18 36S 179 53 E
Moama, *Australia* .... **63 F3** 36 7S 144 46 E
Moamba, *Mozam.* .... **57 D5** 25 36S 32 15 E
Moapa, *U.S.A.* **79 J12** 36 40N 114 37W
Moate, *Ireland* **10 C4** 53 24N 7 44W
Moba, *Dem. Rep. of the Congo* .... **54 D2** 7 0S 29 48 E
Mobārakābād, *Iran* .... **45 D7** 28 24N 53 20 E
Mobaye, *C.A.R.* .... **52 D4** 4 25N 21 5 E
Mobayi, *Dem. Rep. of the Congo* .... **52 D4** 4 15N 21 8 E
Moberly Lake, *Canada* **70 B4** 55 50N 121 44W
Moberly, *U.S.A.* **80 F8** 39 25N 92 26W
Mobile, *U.S.A.* **83 K1** 30 41N 88 3W
Mobile B., *U.S.A.* **83 K2** 30 30N 88 0W
Mobridge, *U.S.A.* **80 C4** 45 32N 100 26W
Moc Chau, *Vietnam* .... **38 B5** 20 50N 104 38 E
Moc Hoa, *Vietnam* .... **39 G5** 10 46N 105 56 E
Mocabe Kasari, *Dem. Rep. of the Congo* .... **55 D2** 9 58S 26 12 E
Moçambique, *Mozam.* .... **55 F5** 15 3S 40 42 E
Mocanaqua, *U.S.A.* **85 E8** 41 9N 76 8W
Mochima △, *Venezuela* **89 D7** 10 30N 64 5W
Mochudi, *Botswana* .... **56 C4** 24 27S 26 7 E
Mocimboa da Praia, *Mozam.* .... **55 E5** 11 25S 40 20 E
Moclips, *U.S.A.* **78 C2** 47 14N 124 13W
Mocoa, *Colombia* **92 C3** 1 7N 76 35W
Mococa, *Brazil* **95 A6** 21 28S 47 0W
Mocorito, *Mexico* **86 B3** 25 30N 107 53W
Moctezuma, *Mexico* **86 B3** 29 50N 109 0W
Moctezuma ➤, *Mexico* **87 C5** 21 59N 98 34W
Mocúzari, Presa, *Mexico* **86 B3** 27 10N 109 10W
Modane, *France* .... **20 D7** 45 12N 6 40 E
Modasa, *India* .... **42 H5** 23 30N 73 21 E
Modder ➤, *S. Africa* .... **56 D3** 29 2S 24 38 E
Modderrivier, *S. Africa* .... **56 D3** 29 2S 24 38 E
Módena, *Italy* .... **22 B4** 44 40N 10 55 E
Modena, *U.S.A.* **77 H7** 37 48N 113 56W
Modesto, *U.S.A.* **78 H6** 37 39N 121 0W
Módica, *Italy* .... **22 F6** 36 52N 14 46 E
Modimolle, *S. Africa* .... **57 C4** 24 42S 28 22 E
Moe, *Australia* .... **63 F4** 38 12S 146 19 E
Moebase, *Mozam.* .... **55 F4** 17 3S 38 41 E
Moengo, *Suriname* **93 B8** 5 45N 54 20W
Moffat, *U.K.* **11 F5** 55 21N 3 27W
Moga, *India* .... **42 D6** 30 48N 75 8 E

Mogadishu = Muqdisho, *Somali Rep.* .... **47 G4** 2 2N 45 25 E
Mogador = Essaouira, *Morocco* **50 B4** 31 32N 9 42W
Mogalakwena ➤, *S. Africa* .... **57 C4** 22 38S 28 40 E
Mogami-Gawa ➤, *Japan* .... **30 E10** 38 45N 140 0 E
Mogán, *Canary Is.* **24 G4** 27 53N 15 43W
Mogaung, *Burma* .... **41 G20** 25 20N 97 0 E
Mogi das Cruzes, *Brazil* **95 A6** 23 31S 46 11W
Mogi-Guaçu ➤, *Brazil* **95 A6** 20 53S 48 10W
Mogi-Mirim, *Brazil* **95 A6** 22 29S 47 0W
Mogilev = Mahilyow, *Belarus* .... **17 B16** 53 55N 30 18 E
Mogilev-Podolskiy = Mohyliv-Podilskyy, *Ukraine* .... **17 D14** 48 26N 27 48 E
Mogincual, *Mozam.* .... **55 F5** 15 35S 40 25 E
Mogocha, *Russia* .... **29 D12** 53 40N 119 50 E
Mogok, *Burma* .... **41 H20** 23 0N 96 40 E
Mogollon Rim, *U.S.A.* **77 J8** 34 10N 110 50W
Mogumber, *Australia* .... **61 F2** 31 2S 116 3 E
Mohács, *Hungary* .... **17 F10** 45 58N 18 41 E
Mohales Hoek, *Lesotho* .... **56 E4** 30 7S 27 26 E
Mohall, *U.S.A.* **80 A4** 48 46N 101 31W
Mohall, *U.S.A.* .... **45 B8** 37 52N 59 5 E
Moḩammadābād, *Iran* **50 B4** 33 44N 7 21W
Mohammedia, *Morocco* .... **43 G11** 24 43N 85 0 E
Mohana ➤, *India* .... **43 F9** 26 41N 80 58 E
Mohanlalganj, *India* **79 K12** 35 12N 114 34W
Mohave, L., *U.S.A.* **85 D11** 42 47N 73 41W
Mohawk ➤, *U.S.A.* .... **42 F3** 27 19N 68 7 E
Mohenjodaro, *Pakistan* **10 D2** 52 58N 9 27W
Moher, Cliffs of, *Ireland* **84 F3** 40 45N 82 0W
Mohicanville Reservoir, *U.S.A.* .... **54 D4** 6 8S 39 8 E
Mohoro, *Tanzania* .... **17 D14** 48 26N 27 48 E
Mohyliv-Podilskyy, *Ukraine* **11 E3** 56 47N 5 52W
Moidart, L., *U.K.* **84 B7** 44 21N 77 24W
Moira ➤, *Canada* .... **25 D6** 35 4N 24 56 E
Moires, *Greece* .... **9 G21** 58 3N 25 12 E
Moisaküla, *Estonia* **73 B6** 50 12N 66 1W
Moisie, *Canada* **73 B6** 50 14N 66 5W
Moisie ➤, *Canada* **79 K8** 35 3N 118 10W
Mojave, *U.S.A.* **79 K11** 35 7N 115 30W
Mojave ➤, *U.S.A.* **79 L10** 35 0N 116 30W
Mojave Desert, *U.S.A.* **94 A2** 21 48S 65 33W
Mojo, *Bolivia* .... **37 G15** 7 28S 112 26 E
Mojokerto, *Indonesia* .... **59 H5** 38 52S 175 56 E
Mokai, *N.Z.* .... **55 E2** 12 25S 28 20 E
Mokambo, *Dem. Rep. of the Congo* .... **43 G11** 25 24N 85 55 E
Mokameh, *India* .... **59 H5** 38 42S 174 39 E
Mokau, *N.Z.* **78 G5** 38 13N 121 28W
Mokelumne ➤, *U.S.A.* **78 G6** 38 18N 120 43W
Mokelumne Hill, *U.S.A.* .... **25 D7** 35 16N 25 27 E
Mokhós, *Greece* .... **57 D4** 29 22S 29 2 E
Mokhotlong, *Lesotho* .... **41 F19** 26 15N 94 30 E
Mokokchung, *India* .... **57 C4** 23 14S 27 43 E
Mokolo ➤, *S. Africa* .... **57 C4** 24 10S 28 55 E
Mokopane, *S. Africa* .... **35 G14** 34 50N 126 25 E
Mokp'o, *S. Korea* .... **23 C9** 42 50N 20 30 E
Mokra Gora, *Serbia & M.* .... **15 C5** 51 11N 5 5 E
Mol, *Belgium* .... **28 D9** 57 40N 83 50 E
Molchanovo, *Russia* **12 D4** 53 9N 3 8W
Mold, *U.K.* .... **17 E15** 47 0N 28 0 E
Moldavia = Moldova ■, *Europe* .... **8 E12** 62 45N 7 9 E
Molde, *Norway* .... **17 E15** 47 0N 28 0 E
Moldova ■, *Europe* .... **17 F13** 45 36N 24 45 E
Moldoveanu, Vf., *Romania* **13 F7** 51 24N 0 21W
Mole ➤, *U.K.* .... **63 G4** 41 34S 146 24 E
Mole Creek, *Australia* .... **56 C4** 24 28S 25 28 E
Molepolole, *Botswana* .... **22 D7** 41 12N 16 36 E
Molfetta, *Italy* **80 E9** 41 30N 90 31W
Moline, *U.S.A.* **94 B2** 35 28S 66 15W
Molinos, *Argentina* .... **54 D2** 8 12S 30 30 E
Moliro, *Dem. Rep. of the Congo* **92 G4** 17 0S 72 0W
Mollendo, *Peru* .... **61 F2** 30 30S 117 35 E
Mollerin, L., *Australia* .... **17 A14** 54 20N 26 50 E
Molodechno = Maladzyechna, *Belarus* **74 H16** 21 8N 157 0W
Molokai, *U.S.A.* .... **63 E4** 33 5S 148 54 E
Molong, *Australia* .... **56 D3** 28 30S 20 12 E
Molopo ➤, *Africa* **71 C9** 54 22N 96 40W
Molson L., *Canada* .... **56 E4** 31 22S 26 22 E
Molteno, *S. Africa* .... **37 F8** 6 45S 131 40 E
Molu, *Indonesia* .... **37 E6** 0 0 125 0 E
Molucca Sea, *Indonesia* .... **37 E7** 1 0S 127 0 E
Moluccas = Maluku, *Indonesia* .... **54 C1** 1 35S 23 52 E
Moma, *Dem. Rep. of the Congo* .... **55 F4** 16 47S 39 4 E
Moma, *Mozam.* .... **54 C4** 2 3S 38 43 E
Mombasa, *Kenya* .... **30 B11** 44 21N 143 22 E
Mombetsu, *Japan* .... **23 D11** 41 33N 25 23 E
Momchilgrad, *Bulgaria* .... **54 C2** 1 42S 27 0 E
Momi, *Dem. Rep. of the Congo* **92 C4** 9 14N 74 26W
Mompós, *Colombia* .... **9 J15** 54 57N 12 20 E
Møn, *Denmark* .... **41 L20** 16 0N 97 30 E
Mon □, *Burma* **89 C6** 18 30N 67 45W
Mona, Canal de la = Mona Passage, *W. Indies* **89 C6** 18 5N 67 54W
Mona, Isla, *Puerto Rico* **88 E3** 9 37N 82 36W
Mona, Pta., *Costa Rica* **89 C6** 18 30N 67 45W
Mona Passage, *W. Indies* **84 F4** 40 41N 80 17W
Monaca, *U.S.A.* .... **20 E7** 43 46N 7 23 E
Monaco ■, *Europe* **11 D4** 57 10N 4 4W
Monadhliath Mts., *U.K.* **85 D12** 42 52N 72 7W
Monadnock, Mt., *U.S.A.* **10 B5** 54 15N 6 57W
Monaghan, *Ireland* **10 B5** 54 11N 6 56W
Monaghan □, *Ireland* **81 K3** 31 36N 102 54W
Monahans, *U.S.A.* .... **55 E5** 14 56S 40 19 E
Monapo, *Mozam.* **11 D3** 57 26N 5 8W
Monar, L., *U.K.* **70 C5** 51 55N 125 57W
Monarch Mt., *Canada* **70 C5** 51 0N 118 43W
Monashee Mts., *Canada* **10 C4** 53 8N 7 4W
Monasterevin, *Ireland* .... **23 D9** 41 2N 21 20 E
Monastir = Bitola, *Macedonia* **21 B5** 41 48N 1 50W
Moncayo, Sierra del, *Spain* .... **18 A5** 67 54N 32 58 E
Monchegorsk, *Russia* .... **16 C4** 51 11N 6 27 E
Mönchengladbach, *Germany* **21 D1** 37 19N 8 38W
Monchique, *Portugal* **83 J5** 33 12N 80 1W
Moncks Corner, *U.S.A.* **86 B4** 26 50N 101 30W
Monclova, *Mexico* **73 C7** 46 24N 64 51W
Moncton, *Canada* **21 B1** 41 9N 8 52W
Mondego ➤, *Portugal* .... **37 E6** 3 34S 122 9 E
Mondeodo, *Indonesia* .... **20 D8** 45 23N 7 49 E
Mondovì, *Italy* .... **61 F3** 34 9S 122 14 E
Mondrain I., *Australia* .... **88 a** 18 16N 77 7W
Moneague, *Jamaica* **81 G8** 36 55N 93 55W
Monett, *U.S.A.* **10 B5** 54 41N 6 40W
Moneymore, *U.K.* **21 A2** 42 31N 7 33W
Monforte de Lemos, *Spain* .... **38 B6** 21 27N 107 54 E
Mong Cai, *Vietnam* .... **41 J21** 21 54N 98 30 E
Mong Hsu, *Burma*

Mong Kung, *Burma* **41 J20** 21 35N 97 35 E
Mong Nai, *Burma* **41 J20** 20 32N 97 46 E
Mong Pawk, *Burma* **41 H21** 22 4N 99 16 E
Mong Ton, *Burma* **41 J21** 20 17N 98 45 E
Mong Wa, *Burma* **41 J22** 21 26N 100 27 E
Mong Yai, *Burma* **41 H21** 22 21N 98 3 E
Mongalla, *Sudan* **51 G12** 5 8N 31 42 E
Mongers, L., *Australia* **61 E2** 29 25S 117 5 E
Monghyr = Munger, *India* **43 G12** 25 23N 86 30 E
Mongibello = Etna, *Italy* **22 F6** 37 50N 14 55 E
Mongo, *Chad* **51 F9** 12 14N 18 43 E
Mongolia ■, *Asia* **29 E10** 47 0N 103 0 E
Mongu, *Zambia* **53 H4** 15 16S 23 12 E
Mônguá, *Angola* **56 B2** 16 43S 15 20 E
Monifieth, *U.K.* **11 E6** 56 30N 2 48W
Monkey Bay, *Malawi* **55 E4** 14 7S 35 1 E
Monkey Mia, *Australia* **61 E1** 25 48S 113 43 E
Monkey River, *Belize* **87 D7** 16 22N 88 29W
Monkoto, *Dem. Rep. of the Congo* **52 E4** 1 38S 20 35 E
Monkton, *Canada* **84 C3** 43 35N 81 5W
Monmouth, *U.K.* **13 F5** 51 48N 2 42W
Monmouth, *Ill., U.S.A.* **80 E9** 40 55N 90 39W
Monmouth, *Oreg., U.S.A.* **76 D2** 44 51N 123 14W
Monmouthshire □, *U.K.* **13 F5** 51 48N 2 54W
Mono L., *U.S.A.* **78 H7** 38 1N 119 1W
Monolith, *U.S.A.* **79 K8** 35 7N 118 22W
Monólithos, *Greece* **25 C9** 36 7N 27 45 E
Monongahela, *U.S.A.* **84 F5** 40 12N 79 56W
Monópoli, *Italy* **22 D7** 40 57N 17 18 E
Monos I., *Trin. & Tob.* **93 K15** 10 42N 61 44W
Monroe, *Ga., U.S.A.* **83 J4** 33 47N 83 43W
Monroe, *La., U.S.A.* **81 J8** 32 30N 92 7W
Monroe, *Mich., U.S.A.* **82 E4** 41 55N 83 24W
Monroe, *N.C., U.S.A.* **83 H5** 34 59N 80 33W
Monroe, *N.Y., U.S.A.* **85 E10** 41 20N 74 11W
Monroe, *Utah, U.S.A.* **77 G7** 38 38N 112 7W
Monroe, *Wash., U.S.A.* **78 C5** 47 51N 121 58W
Monroe, *Wis., U.S.A.* **80 D10** 42 36N 89 38W
Monroe City, *U.S.A.* **80 F9** 39 39N 91 44W
Monroeton, *U.S.A.* **85 E8** 41 43N 76 29W
Monroeville, *Ala., U.S.A.* **83 K2** 31 31N 87 20W
Monroeville, *Pa., U.S.A.* **84 F5** 40 26N 79 45W
Monrovia, *Liberia* **50 G3** 6 18N 10 47W
Mons, *Belgium* **15 D3** 50 27N 3 58 E
Monse, *Indonesia* **37 E6** 4 7S 123 15 E
Mont-de-Marsan, *France* **20 E3** 43 54N 0 31W
Mont-Joli, *Canada* **73 C6** 48 37N 68 10W
Mont-Laurier, *Canada* **72 C4** 46 35N 75 30W
Mont-Louis, *Canada* **73 C6** 49 15N 65 44W
Mont-St-Michel, Le, *France* **20 B3** 48 40N 1 30W
Mont-Tremblant ⌂, *Canada* **72 C5** 46 30N 74 30W
Montagne d'Ambre △, *Madag.* **57 A8** 12 37S 49 8 E
Montagu, *S. Africa* **56 E3** 33 45S 20 8 E
Montagu I., *Antarctica* **5 B1** 58 25S 26 20W
Montague, *Canada* **73 C7** 46 10N 62 39W
Montague, I., *Mexico* **86 A2** 31 40N 114 56W
Montague Ra., *Australia* **61 E2** 27 15S 119 30 E
Montague Sd., *Australia* **60 B4** 14 28S 125 20 E
Montalbán, *Spain* **21 B5** 40 50N 0 45W
Montalvo, *U.S.A.* **79 L7** 34 15N 119 12W
Montana, *Bulgaria* **23 C10** 43 27N 23 16 E
Montaña, *Peru* **92 E4** 6 0S 73 0W
Montana □, *U.S.A.* **76 C9** 47 0N 110 0W
Montaña Clara, I., *Canary Is.* **24 E6** 29 17N 13 33W
Montargis, *France* **20 C5** 47 59N 2 43 E
Montauban, *France* **20 D4** 44 2N 1 21 E
Montauk, *U.S.A.* **85 E13** 41 3N 71 57W
Montauk Pt., *U.S.A.* **85 E13** 41 4N 71 52W
Montbéliard, *France* **20 C7** 47 31N 6 48 E
Montceau-les-Mines, *France* **20 C6** 46 40N 4 23 E
Montclair, *U.S.A.* **85 F10** 40 49N 74 13W
Monte Albán, *Mexico* **87 D5** 17 2N 96 45W
Monte Alegre, *Brazil* **93 D8** 2 0S 54 0W
Monte Azul, *Brazil* **93 G10** 15 9S 42 53W
Monte Bello Is., *Australia* **60 D2** 20 30S 115 45 E
Monte-Carlo, *Monaco* **20 E7** 43 44N 7 25 E
Monte Caseros, *Argentina* **94 C4** 30 10S 57 50W
Monte Comán, *Argentina* **94 C2** 34 40S 67 53W
Monte Cristi, *Dom. Rep.* **89 C5** 19 52N 71 39W
Monte Lindo →, *Paraguay* **94 A4** 23 56S 57 12W
Monte Patria, *Chile* **94 C1** 30 42S 70 58W
Monte Quemado, *Argentina* **94 B3** 25 53S 62 41W
Monte Rio, *U.S.A.* **78 G4** 38 28N 123 0W
Monte Santu, C. di, *Italy* **22 D3** 40 5N 9 44 E
Monte Vista, *U.S.A.* **77 H10** 37 35N 106 9W
Monteagudo, *Argentina* **95 B5** 27 14S 54 8W
Montebello, *Canada* **72 C5** 45 40N 74 55W
Montecito, *U.S.A.* **79 L7** 34 26N 119 40W
Montecristo, *Italy* **22 C4** 42 20N 10 19 E
Montego Bay, *Jamaica* **88 a** 18 30N 78 0W
Montélimar, *France* **20 D6** 44 33N 4 45 E
Montello, *U.S.A.* **80 D10** 43 48N 89 20W
Montemorelos, *Mexico* **87 B5** 25 11N 99 42W
Montenegro, *Brazil* **95 B5** 29 39S 51 29W
Montenegro □, *Serbia & M.* **23 C8** 42 40N 19 20 E
Montepuez, *Mozam.* **55 E4** 13 8S 38 59 E
Montepuez →, *Mozam.* **55 E5** 12 32S 40 27 E
Monterey, *U.S.A.* **78 J5** 36 37N 121 55W
Monterey B., *U.S.A.* **78 J5** 36 45N 122 0W
Montería, *Colombia* **92 B3** 8 46N 75 53W
Monteros, *Argentina* **94 B2** 27 11S 65 30W
Monterrey, *Mexico* **86 B4** 25 40N 100 30W
Montes Azules ⌂, *Mexico* **87 D6** 16 21N 91 3W
Montes Claros, *Brazil* **93 G10** 16 30S 43 50W
Montesano, *U.S.A.* **78 D3** 46 59N 123 36W
Montesilvano, *Italy* **22 C6** 42 29N 14 8 E
Montevideo, *Uruguay* **95 C4** 34 50S 56 11W
Montevideo, *U.S.A.* **80 C7** 44 57N 95 43W
Montezuma, *U.S.A.* **80 E8** 41 35N 92 32W
Montezuma Castle ⌂, *U.S.A.* **77 J8** 34 34N 111 45W
Montgomery, *U.K.* **13 E4** 52 34N 3 8W
Montgomery, *Ala., U.S.A.* **83 J2** 32 23N 86 19W
Montgomery, *Pa., U.S.A.* **84 E8** 41 10N 76 53W
Montgomery, *W. Va., U.S.A.* **82 F5** 38 11N 81 19W
Montgomery City, *U.S.A.* **80 F9** 38 59N 91 30W
Monticello, *Ark., U.S.A.* **81 J9** 33 38N 91 47W
Monticello, *Fla., U.S.A.* **83 K4** 30 33N 83 52W
Monticello, *Ind., U.S.A.* **82 E2** 40 45N 86 46W
Monticello, *Iowa, U.S.A.* **80 D9** 42 15N 91 12W
Monticello, *Ky., U.S.A.* **83 G3** 36 50N 84 51W
Monticello, *Minn., U.S.A.* **80 C8** 45 18N 93 48W
Monticello, *Miss., U.S.A.* **81 K9** 31 33N 90 7W
Monticello, *N.Y., U.S.A.* **85 E10** 41 39N 74 42W
Monticello, *Utah, U.S.A.* **77 H9** 37 52N 109 21W
Montijo, *Portugal* **21 C1** 38 41N 8 54W
Montilla, *Spain* **21 D3** 37 36N 4 40W
Montluçon, *France* **20 C5** 46 22N 2 36 E
Montmagny, *Canada* **73 C5** 46 58N 70 34W
Montmartre, *Canada* **71 C8** 50 14N 103 27W
Montmorillon, *France* **20 C4** 46 26N 0 50 E
Monto, *Australia* **62 C5** 24 52S 151 6 E
Montongbuwoh, *Indonesia* **37 K19** 8 33S 116 4 E
Montoro, *Spain* **21 C3** 38 1N 4 27W
Montour Falls, *U.S.A.* **84 D8** 42 21N 76 51W
Montoursville, *U.S.A.* **84 E8** 41 15N 76 55W
Montpelier, *Idaho, U.S.A.* **76 E8** 42 19N 111 18W
Montpelier, *Vt., U.S.A.* **85 B12** 44 16N 72 35W
Montpellier, *France* **20 E5** 43 37N 3 52 E
Montréal, *Canada* **85 A11** 45 31N 73 34W
Montreal →, *Canada* **72 C3** 47 14N 84 39W
Montreal L., *Canada* **71 C7** 54 20N 105 45W
Montreal Lake, *Canada* **71 C7** 54 3N 105 46W
Montreux, *Switz.* **20 C7** 46 26N 6 55 E
Montrose, *U.K.* **11 E6** 56 44N 2 27W
Montrose, *Colo., U.S.A.* **77 G10** 38 29N 107 53W
Montrose, *Pa., U.S.A.* **85 E9** 41 50N 75 53W
Monts, Pte. des, *Canada* **73 C6** 49 20N 67 12W
Montserrat ☒, *W. Indies* **89 C7** 16 40N 62 10W
Montuiri, *Spain* **24 B9** 39 34N 2 59 E
Monywa, *Burma* **41 H19** 22 7N 95 11 E
Monza, *Italy* **20 D8** 45 35N 9 16 E
Monze, *Zambia* **55 F2** 16 17S 27 29 E
Monze, C., *Pakistan* **42 G2** 24 47N 66 37 E
Monzón, *Spain* **21 B6** 41 52N 0 10 E
Mooers, *U.S.A.* **85 B11** 44 58N 73 35W
Mooi →, *S. Africa* **57 D5** 28 45S 30 34 E
Mooi River, *S. Africa* **57 D4** 29 13S 29 50 E
Moonah →, *Australia* **62 C2** 22 3S 138 33 E
Moonda, L., *Australia* **62 D3** 25 52S 140 25 E
Moonie, *Australia* **63 D5** 27 46S 150 20 E
Moonie →, *Australia* **63 D4** 29 19S 148 43 E
Moonta, *Australia* **63 E2** 34 6S 137 32 E
Moora, *Australia* **61 F2** 30 37S 115 58 E
Moorcroft, *U.S.A.* **80 C2** 44 16N 104 57W
Moore →, *Australia* **61 F2** 31 22S 115 30 E
Moore, L., *Australia* **61 E2** 29 50S 117 35 E
Moore Park, *Australia* **62 C5** 24 43S 152 17 E
Moore River △, *Australia* **61 F2** 31 7S 115 39 E
Moorefield, *U.S.A.* **82 F6** 39 5N 78 59W
Moores Res., *U.S.A.* **85 B13** 44 45N 71 50W
Moorfoot Hills, *U.K.* **11 F5** 55 44N 3 8W
Moorhead, *U.S.A.* **80 B6** 46 53N 96 45W
Moorpark, *U.S.A.* **79 L8** 34 17N 118 53W
Moorreesburg, *S. Africa* **56 E2** 33 6S 18 38 E
Moorrinya △, *Australia* **62 C3** 21 42S 144 58 E
Moose →, *Canada* **72 B3** 51 20N 80 25W
Moose →, *U.S.A.* **85 C9** 43 38N 75 24W
Moose Creek, *Canada* **85 A10** 45 15N 74 58W
Moose Factory, *Canada* **72 B3** 51 16N 80 32W
Moose Jaw, *Canada* **71 C7** 50 24N 105 30W
Moose Jaw →, *Canada* **71 C7** 50 34N 105 18W
Moose Lake, *U.S.A.* **80 B8** 46 27N 92 46W
Moose Mountain ⌂, *Canada* **71 D8** 49 48N 102 25W
Moosehead L., *U.S.A.* **83 C11** 45 38N 69 40W
Mooselookmeguntic L., *U.S.A.* **83 C10** 44 55N 70 49W
Moosilauke, Mt., *U.S.A.* **85 B13** 44 3N 71 40W
Moosomin, *Canada* **71 C8** 50 9N 101 40W
Moosonee, *Canada* **72 B3** 51 17N 80 39W
Moosup, *U.S.A.* **85 E13** 41 43N 71 53W
Mopane, *S. Africa* **57 C4** 22 37S 29 52 E
Mopeia Velha, *Mozam.* **55 F4** 17 30S 35 40 E
Mopipi, *Botswana* **56 C3** 21 6S 24 55 E
Mopoi, *C.A.R.* **54 A2** 5 6N 26 54 E
Mopti, *Mali* **50 F5** 14 30N 4 0W
Moqor, *Afghan.* **42 C2** 32 50N 67 42 E
Moquegua, *Peru* **92 G4** 17 15S 70 46W
Mora, *Sweden* **9 F16** 61 2N 14 38 E
Mora, *Minn., U.S.A.* **80 C8** 45 53N 93 18W
Mora, *N. Mex., U.S.A.* **77 J11** 35 58N 105 20W
Mora →, *U.S.A.* **81 H2** 35 35N 104 25W
Moradabad, *India* **43 E8** 28 50N 78 50 E
Morafenobe, *Madag.* **57 B7** 17 50S 44 53 E
Moramanga, *Madag.* **57 B8** 18 56S 48 12 E
Moran, *Kans., U.S.A.* **81 G7** 37 55N 95 10W
Moran, *Wyo., U.S.A.* **76 E8** 43 53N 110 37W
Moranbah, *Australia* **62 C4** 22 1S 148 6 E
Morant Bay, *Jamaica* **88 a** 17 53N 76 25W
Morant Cays, *Jamaica* **88 C4** 17 22N 76 0W
Morant Pt., *Jamaica* **88 a** 17 55N 76 12W
Morar, *India* **42 F8** 26 14N 78 14 E
Morar, L., *U.K.* **11 E3** 56 57N 5 40W
Moratuwa, *Sri Lanka* **40 R11** 6 45N 79 55 E
Morava →, *Serbia & M.* **23 B9** 44 36N 21 4 E
Morava →, *Slovak Rep.* **17 D9** 48 10N 16 59 E
Moravia, *U.S.A.* **85 D8** 42 43N 76 25W
Moravian Hts. = Českomoravská Vrchovina, *Czech Rep.* **16 D8** 49 30N 15 40 E
Morawa, *Australia* **61 E2** 29 13S 116 0 E
Morawhanna, *Guyana* **92 B7** 8 30N 59 40W
Moray □, *U.K.* **11 D5** 57 31N 3 18W
Moray Firth, *U.K.* **11 D5** 57 40N 3 52W
Morbi, *India* **42 H4** 22 50N 70 42 E
Morden, *Canada* **71 D9** 49 15N 98 10W
Mordovian Republic = Mordvinia □, *Russia* **18 D7** 54 20N 44 30 E
Mordvinia □, *Russia* **18 D7** 54 20N 44 30 E
Morea, *Greece* **6 H10** 37 45N 22 10 E
Moreau →, *U.S.A.* **80 C4** 45 18N 100 43W
Morecambe, *U.K.* **12 C5** 54 5N 2 52W
Morecambe B., *U.K.* **12 C5** 54 7N 3 0W
Moree, *Australia* **63 D4** 29 28S 149 54 E
Morehead, *U.S.A.* **82 F4** 38 11N 83 26W
Morehead City, *U.S.A.* **83 H7** 34 43N 76 43W
Morel →, *India* **42 F7** 26 13N 76 36 E
Morelia, *Mexico* **86 D4** 19 42N 101 7W
Morella, *Australia* **62 C3** 23 0S 143 52 E
Morella, *Spain* **21 B5** 40 35N 0 5W
Morelos, *Mexico* **86 B3** 26 42N 107 40W
Morelos □, *Mexico* **87 D5** 18 40N 99 10W
Moremi ⌂, *Botswana* **56 B3** 19 18S 23 10 E
Morena, *India* **42 F8** 26 30N 78 4 E
Morena, Sierra, *Spain* **21 C3** 38 20N 4 0W
Moreno Valley, *U.S.A.* **79 M10** 33 56N 117 15W
Moresby I., *Canada* **70 C2** 52 30N 131 40W
Moreton I., *Australia* **63 D5** 27 10S 153 25 E
Moreton Island △, *Australia* **63 D5** 27 2S 153 24 E
Morey, *Spain* **24 B10** 39 44N 3 20 E
Morgan, *U.S.A.* **76 F8** 41 2N 111 41W
Morgan City, *U.S.A.* **81 L9** 29 42N 91 12W
Morgan Hill, *U.S.A.* **78 H5** 37 8N 121 39W
Morganfield, *U.S.A.* **82 G2** 37 41N 87 55W
Morganton, *U.S.A.* **83 H5** 35 45N 81 41W
Morgantown, *U.S.A.* **82 F6** 39 38N 79 57W
Morgenzon, *S. Africa* **57 D4** 26 45S 29 36 E
Morghak, *Iran* **45 D8** 29 7N 57 54 E
Morhar →, *India* **43 G11** 25 29N 85 11 E
Mori, *Japan* **30 C10** 42 6N 140 35 E
Moriarty, *U.S.A.* **77 J10** 34 59N 106 3W
Morice L., *Canada* **70 C3** 53 50N 127 40W
Morinville, *Canada* **70 C6** 53 49N 113 41W
Morioka, *Japan* **30 E10** 39 45N 141 8 E
Moris, *Mexico* **86 B3** 28 8N 108 32W
Morlaix, *France* **20 B2** 48 36N 3 52W
Mornington, *Australia* **63 F4** 38 15S 145 5 E
Mornington, I., *Chile* **96 F1** 49 50S 75 30W
Mornington I., *Australia* **62 B2** 16 30S 139 30 E
Moro, *Pakistan* **42 F2** 26 40N 68 0 E
Moro →, *Pakistan* **42 E2** 29 42N 67 22 E
Moro G., *Phil.* **37 C6** 6 30N 123 0 E
Morocco ■, *N. Afr.* **50 B4** 32 0N 5 50W
Morogoro, *Tanzania* **54 D4** 6 50S 37 40 E
Morogoro □, *Tanzania* **54 D4** 8 0S 37 0 E
Moroleón, *Mexico* **86 C4** 20 8N 101 32W
Morombe, *Madag.* **57 C7** 21 45S 43 22 E
Moron, *Argentina* **94 C4** 34 39S 58 37W
Morón, *Cuba* **88 B4** 22 8N 78 39W
Morón de la Frontera, *Spain* **21 D3** 37 6N 5 28W
Morona →, *Peru* **92 D3** 4 40S 77 10W
Morondava, *Madag.* **57 C7** 20 17S 44 17 E
Morongo Valley, *U.S.A.* **79 L10** 34 3N 116 37W
Moroni, *Comoros Is.* **49 H8** 11 40S 43 16 E
Moroni, *U.S.A.* **76 G8** 39 32N 111 35W
Morotai, *Indonesia* **37 D7** 2 10N 128 30 E
Moroto, *Uganda* **54 B3** 2 28N 34 42 E
Moroto, Mt., *Uganda* **54 B3** 2 30N 34 43 E
Morpeth, *U.K.* **12 B6** 55 10N 1 41W
Morphou, *Cyprus* **25 D11** 35 12N 32 59 E
Morphou Bay, *Cyprus* **25 D11** 35 15N 32 50 E
Morrilton, *U.S.A.* **81 H8** 35 9N 92 44W
Morrinhos, *Brazil* **93 G9** 17 45S 49 10W
Morrinsville, *N.Z.* **59 G5** 37 40S 175 32 E
Morris, *Canada* **71 D9** 49 25N 97 22W
Morris, *Ill., U.S.A.* **80 E10** 41 22N 88 26W
Morris, *Minn., U.S.A.* **80 C7** 45 35N 95 55W
Morris, *N.Y., U.S.A.* **85 D9** 42 33N 75 15W
Morris, *Pa., U.S.A.* **84 E7** 41 35N 77 17W
Morris, Mt., *Australia* **61 E5** 26 9S 131 4 E
Morris Jesup, Kap, *Greenland* **4 A5** 83 40N 34 0W
Morrisburg, *Canada* **85 B9** 44 55N 75 7W
Morristown, *Ariz., U.S.A.* **77 K7** 33 51N 112 37W
Morristown, *N.J., U.S.A.* **85 F10** 40 48N 74 29W
Morristown, *N.Y., U.S.A.* **85 B9** 44 35N 75 39W
Morristown, *Tenn., U.S.A.* **83 G4** 36 13N 83 18W
Morrisville, *N.Y., U.S.A.* **85 D9** 42 53N 75 35W
Morrisville, *Pa., U.S.A.* **85 F10** 40 13N 74 47W
Morrisville, *Vt., U.S.A.* **85 B12** 44 34N 72 36W
Morro, Pta., *Chile* **94 B1** 27 6S 71 0W
Morro Bay, *U.S.A.* **78 K6** 35 22N 120 51W
Morro del Jable, *Canary Is.* **24 F5** 28 3N 14 23W
Morro Jable, Pta. de, *Canary Is.* **24 F5** 28 2N 14 20W
Morrocoy △, *Venezuela* **89 D6** 10 48N 68 13W
Morrosquillo, G. de, *Colombia* **88 E4** 9 35N 75 40W
Morrumbene, *Mozam.* **57 C6** 23 31S 35 16 E
Morshansk, *Russia* **18 D7** 53 28N 41 50 E
Morteros, *Argentina* **94 C3** 30 50S 62 0W
Mortlach, *Canada* **71 C7** 50 27N 106 4W
Mortlake, *Australia* **63 F3** 38 5S 142 50 E
Morton, *Tex., U.S.A.* **81 J3** 33 44N 102 46W
Morton, *Wash., U.S.A.* **78 D4** 46 34N 122 17W
Moruga, *Trin. & Tob.* **93 K15** 10 4N 61 16W
Morundah, *Australia* **63 E4** 34 57S 146 19 E
Moruya, *Australia* **63 F5** 35 58S 150 3 E
Morvan, *France* **20 C6** 47 5N 4 3 E
Morven, *Australia* **63 D4** 26 22S 147 5 E
Morvern, *U.K.* **11 E3** 56 38N 5 44W
Morwell, *Australia* **63 F4** 38 10S 146 22 E
Morzhovets, Ostrov, *Russia* **18 A7** 66 44N 42 35 E
Moscos Is., *Burma* **38 E1** 14 0N 97 30 E
Moscow = Moskva, *Russia* **18 C6** 55 45N 37 35 E
Moscow, *Idaho, U.S.A.* **76 C5** 46 44N 117 0W
Moscow, *Pa., U.S.A.* **85 E9** 41 20N 75 31W
Mosel →, *Europe* **20 A7** 50 22N 7 36 E
Moselle = Mosel →, *Europe* **20 A7** 50 22N 7 36 E
Moses Lake, *U.S.A.* **76 C4** 47 8N 119 17W
Mosgiel, *N.Z.* **59 L3** 45 53S 170 21 E
Moshaweng →, *S. Africa* **56 D3** 26 35S 22 50 E
Moshi, *Tanzania* **54 C4** 3 22S 37 18 E
Moshupa, *Botswana* **56 C4** 24 46S 25 29 E
Mosjøen, *Norway* **8 D15** 65 51N 13 12 E
Moskenesøya, *Norway* **8 C15** 67 58N 13 0 E
Moskenstraumen, *Norway* **8 C15** 67 47N 12 45 E
Moskva, *Russia* **18 C6** 55 45N 37 35 E
Mosomane, *Botswana* **56 C4** 24 2S 26 19 E
Mosonmagyaróvár, *Hungary* **17 E9** 47 52N 17 18 E
Mosquera, *Colombia* **92 C3** 2 35N 78 24W
Mosquero, *U.S.A.* **81 H3** 35 47N 103 58W
Mosquitia, *Honduras* **88 C3** 15 20N 84 10W
Mosquito Coast = Mosquitia, *Honduras* **88 C3** 15 20N 84 10W
Mosquito Creek L., *U.S.A.* **84 E4** 41 18N 80 46W
Mosquito L., *Canada* **71 A8** 62 35N 103 20W
Mosquitos, G. de los, *Panama* **88 E3** 9 15N 81 10W
Moss, *Norway* **9 G14** 59 27N 10 40 E
Moss Vale, *Australia* **63 E5** 34 32S 150 25 E
Mossbank, *Canada* **71 D7** 49 56N 105 56W
Mossburn, *N.Z.* **59 L2** 45 41S 168 15 E
Mosselbaai, *S. Africa* **56 E3** 34 11S 22 8 E
Mossendjo, *Congo* **52 E2** 2 55S 12 42 E
Mossgiel, *Australia* **63 E3** 33 15S 144 5 E
Mossman, *Australia* **62 B4** 16 21S 145 15 E
Mossoró, *Brazil* **93 E11** 5 10S 37 15W
Mossuril, *Mozam.* **55 E5** 14 58S 40 42 E
Most, *Czech Rep.* **16 C7** 50 31N 13 38 E
Mosta, *Malta* **25 D1** 35 55N 14 26 E
Mostaganem, *Algeria* **50 A6** 35 54N 0 5 E
Mostar, *Bos.-H.* **23 C7** 43 22N 17 50 E
Mostardas, *Brazil* **95 C5** 31 2S 50 51W
Mostiska = Mostyska, *Ukraine* **17 D12** 49 48N 23 4 E
Mosty = Masty, *Belarus* **17 B13** 53 27N 24 38 E
Mostyska, *Ukraine* **17 D12** 49 48N 23 4 E
Mosul = Al Mawşil, *Iraq* **44 B4** 36 15N 43 5 E
Mosŭlpo, *S. Korea* **35 H14** 33 20N 126 17 E
Motagua →, *Guatemala* **88 C2** 15 44N 88 14W
Motala, *Sweden* **9 G16** 58 32N 15 1 E
Motaze, *Mozam.* **57 C5** 24 48S 32 52 E
Moth, *India* **43 G8** 25 43N 78 57 E
Motherwell, *U.K.* **11 F5** 55 47N 3 58W
Motihari, *India* **43 F11** 26 30N 84 55 E
Motozintla de Mendoza, *Mexico* **87 D6** 15 21N 92 14W
Motril, *Spain* **21 D4** 36 31N 3 37W
Mott, *U.S.A.* **80 B3** 46 23N 102 20W
Motueka, *N.Z.* **59 J4** 41 7S 173 1 E
Motueka →, *N.Z.* **59 J4** 41 5S 173 1 E
Motul, *Mexico* **87 C7** 21 0N 89 20W
Mouchalagane →, *Canada* **73 B6** 50 56N 68 41W
Moúdhros, *Greece* **23 E11** 39 50N 25 18 E
Mouila, *Gabon* **52 E2** 1 50S 11 0 E
Moulamein, *Australia* **63 F3** 35 3S 144 1 E
Moule, *Guadeloupe* **88 b** 16 20N 61 21W
Moule à Chique, C., *St. Lucia* **89 f** 13 43N 60 57W
Mouliana, *Greece* **25 D7** 35 10N 25 59 E
Moulins, *France* **20 C5** 46 35N 3 19 E
Moulmein, *Burma* **41 L20** 16 30N 97 40 E
Moulouya, O. →, *Morocco* **50 B5** 35 5N 2 25W
Moultrie, *U.S.A.* **83 K4** 31 11N 83 47W
Moultrie, L., *U.S.A.* **83 J5** 33 20N 80 5W
Mound City, *Mo., U.S.A.* **80 E7** 40 7N 95 14W
Mound City, *S. Dak., U.S.A.* **80 C4** 45 44N 100 4W
Moundou, *Chad* **51 G9** 8 40N 16 10 E
Moundsville, *U.S.A.* **84 G4** 39 55N 80 44W
Moung, *Cambodia* **38 F4** 12 46N 103 27 E
Mount Airy, *U.S.A.* **83 G5** 36 31N 80 37W
Mount Albert, *Canada* **84 B5** 44 8N 79 19W
Mount Aspiring △, *N.Z.* **59 L2** 44 19S 168 47 E
Mount Barker, *S. Austral., Australia* **63 F2** 35 5S 138 52 E
Mount Barker, *W. Austral., Australia* **61 F2** 34 38S 117 40 E
Mount Brydges, *Canada* **84 D3** 42 54N 81 29W
Mount Burr, *Australia* **63 F3** 37 34S 140 26 E
Mount Carmel = Ha Karmel △, *Israel* **46 C4** 32 45N 35 5 E
Mount Carmel, *Ill., U.S.A.* **82 F2** 38 25N 87 46W
Mount Carmel, *Pa., U.S.A.* **85 F8** 40 47N 76 24W
Mount Charleston, *U.S.A.* **79 J11** 36 16N 115 37W
Mount Clemens, *U.S.A.* **84 D2** 42 35N 82 53W
Mount Coolon, *Australia* **62 C4** 21 25S 147 25 E
Mount Darwin, *Zimbabwe* **55 F3** 16 47S 31 38 E
Mount Desert I., *U.S.A.* **83 C11** 44 21N 68 20W
Mount Dora, *U.S.A.* **83 L5** 28 48N 81 38W
Mount Edziza ⌂, *Canada* **70 B2** 57 30N 130 45W
Mount Elgon △, *E. Afr.* **54 B3** 1 4N 34 42 E
Mount Field △, *Australia* **63 G4** 42 39S 146 35 E
Mount Fletcher, *S. Africa* **57 E4** 30 40S 28 30 E
Mount Forest, *Canada* **84 C4** 43 59N 80 43W
Mount Gambier, *Australia* **63 F3** 37 50S 140 46 E
Mount Garnet, *Australia* **62 B4** 17 37S 145 6 E
Mount Holly, *U.S.A.* **85 G10** 39 59N 74 47W
Mount Holly Springs, *U.S.A.* **84 F7** 40 7N 77 12W
Mount Hope, *N.S.W., Australia* **63 E4** 32 51S 145 51 E
Mount Hope, *S. Austral., Australia* **63 E2** 34 7S 135 23 E
Mount Isa, *Australia* **62 C2** 20 42S 139 26 E
Mount Jewett, *U.S.A.* **84 E6** 41 44N 78 39W
Mount Kaputar △, *Australia* **63 E5** 30 16S 150 10 E
Mount Kenya △, *Kenya* **54 C4** 0 7S 37 21 E
Mount Kilimanjaro △, *Tanzania* **54 C4** 3 2S 37 19 E
Mount Kisco, *U.S.A.* **85 E11** 41 12N 73 44W
Mount Laguna, *U.S.A.* **79 N10** 32 52N 116 25W
Mount Larcom, *Australia* **62 C5** 23 48S 150 59 E
Mount Lofty Ra., *Australia* **63 E2** 34 35S 139 5 E
Mount Magnet, *Australia* **61 E2** 28 2S 117 47 E
Mount Maunganui, *N.Z.* **59 G6** 37 40S 176 14 E
Mount Molloy, *Australia* **62 B4** 16 42S 145 20 E
Mount Morgan, *Australia* **62 C5** 23 40S 150 25 E
Mount Morris, *U.S.A.* **84 D7** 42 44N 77 52W
Mount Pearl, *Canada* **73 C9** 47 31N 52 47W
Mount Penn, *U.S.A.* **85 F9** 40 20N 75 54W
Mount Perry, *Australia* **63 D5** 25 13S 151 42 E
Mount Pleasant, *Iowa, U.S.A.* **80 E9** 40 58N 91 33W
Mount Pleasant, *Mich., U.S.A.* **82 D3** 43 36N 84 46W
Mount Pleasant, *Pa., U.S.A.* **84 F5** 40 9N 79 33W
Mount Pleasant, *S.C., U.S.A.* **83 J6** 32 47N 79 52W
Mount Pleasant, *Tenn., U.S.A.* **83 H2** 35 32N 87 12W
Mount Pleasant, *Tex., U.S.A.* **81 J7** 33 9N 94 58W
Mount Pleasant, *Utah, U.S.A.* **76 G8** 39 33N 111 27W
Mount Pocono, *U.S.A.* **85 E9** 41 7N 75 22W
Mount Rainier △, *U.S.A.* **78 D5** 46 55N 121 50W
Mount Revelstoke △, *Canada* **70 C5** 51 5N 118 30W
Mount Robson ⌂, *Canada* **70 C5** 53 0N 119 0W
Mount St. Helens ⌂, *U.S.A.* **78 D4** 46 14N 122 11W
Mount Selinda, *Zimbabwe* **57 C5** 20 24S 32 43 E
Mount Shasta, *U.S.A.* **76 F2** 41 19N 122 19W
Mount Signal, *U.S.A.* **79 N11** 32 39N 115 37W
Mount Sterling, *Ill., U.S.A.* **80 F9** 39 59N 90 45W
Mount Sterling, *Ky., U.S.A.* **82 F4** 38 4N 83 56W
Mount Surprise, *Australia* **62 B3** 18 10S 144 17 E
Mount Union, *U.S.A.* **84 F7** 40 23N 77 53W
Mount Upton, *U.S.A.* **85 D9** 42 26N 75 23W
Mount Vernon, *Ill., U.S.A.* **82 F1** 38 19N 88 55W
Mount Vernon, *Ind., U.S.A.* **80 F10** 38 17N 88 57W
Mount Vernon, *N.Y., U.S.A.* **85 F11** 40 55N 73 50W
Mount Vernon, *Ohio, U.S.A.* **84 F2** 40 23N 82 29W
Mount Vernon, *Wash., U.S.A.* **78 B4** 48 25N 122 20W
Mount William △, *Australia* **63 G4** 40 56S 148 14 E
Mountain Ash, *U.K.* **13 F4** 51 40N 3 23W
Mountain Center, *U.S.A.* **79 M10** 33 42N 116 44W
Mountain City, *Nev., U.S.A.* **76 F6** 41 50N 115 58W
Mountain City, *Tenn., U.S.A.* **83 G5** 36 29N 81 48W
Mountain Dale, *U.S.A.* **85 E10** 41 41N 74 32W
Mountain Grove, *U.S.A.* **81 G8** 37 8N 92 16W
Mountain Home, *Ark., U.S.A.* **81 G8** 36 20N 92 23W
Mountain Home, *Idaho, U.S.A.* **76 E6** 43 8N 115 41W
Mountain Iron, *U.S.A.* **80 B8** 47 32N 92 37W
Mountain Pass, *U.S.A.* **79 K11** 35 29N 115 35W
Mountain View, *Ark., U.S.A.* **81 H8** 35 52N 92 7W
Mountain View, *Calif., U.S.A.* **78 H4** 37 23N 122 5W
Mountain View, *Hawaii, U.S.A.* **74 J17** 19 33N 155 7W
Mountain Zebra △, *S. Africa* **56 E4** 32 14S 25 27 E
Mountainair, *U.S.A.* **77 J10** 34 31N 106 15W
Mountlake Terrace, *U.S.A.* **78 C4** 47 47N 122 19W
Mountmellick, *Ireland* **10 C4** 53 7N 7 20W
Mountrath, *Ireland* **10 D4** 53 0N 7 28W
Moura, *Australia* **62 C4** 24 35S 149 58 E
Moura, *Brazil* **92 D6** 1 32S 61 38W
Moura, *Portugal* **21 C2** 38 7N 7 30W
Mourdi, Dépression du, *Chad* **51 E10** 18 10N 23 0 E
Mourilyan, *Australia* **62 B4** 17 35S 146 3 E
Mourne →, *U.K.* **10 B4** 54 52N 7 26W
Mourne Mts., *U.K.* **10 B5** 54 10N 6 0W
Mourniai, *Greece* **25 D6** 35 29N 24 1 E
Mournies = Mourniai, *Greece* **25 D6** 35 29N 24 1 E
Mouscron, *Belgium* **15 D3** 50 45N 3 12 E
Moussoro, *Chad* **51 F9** 13 41N 16 35 E
Moutong, *Indonesia* **37 D6** 0 28N 121 13 E
Movas, *Mexico* **86 B3** 28 10N 109 25W
Moville, *Ireland* **10 A4** 55 11N 7 3W
Mowandjum, *Australia* **60 C3** 17 22S 123 40 E
Moy →, *Ireland* **10 B2** 54 8N 9 8W
Moyale, *Kenya* **54 B4** 3 30N 39 0 E
Moyen Atlas, *Morocco* **50 B4** 33 0N 5 0W

Moyne, L. le, *Canada* **73 A6**   56 45N   68 47W
Moyo, *Indonesia* .... **36 F5**   8 10S 117 40 E
Moyobamba, *Peru* **92 E3**   6 0S   77 0W
Moyyero ➛, *Russia* .... **29 C11** 68 44N 103 42 E
Moyynty, *Kazakhstan* .... **28 E8**   47 10N   73 18 E
Mozambique = Moçambique,
   Mozam. .... **55 F5**   15 3S   40 42 E
Mozambique ■, *Africa* .... **55 F4**   19 0S   35 0 E
Mozambique Chan., *Africa* ... **57 B7**   17 30S   42 30 E
Mozdok, *Russia* .... **19 F7**   43 45N   44 48 E
Mozdūrān, *Iran* .... **45 B9**   36 9N   60 35 E
Mozhnābād, *Iran* .... **45 C9**   34 7N   60 6 E
Mozyr = Mazyr, *Belarus* ..... **17 B15** 51 59N   29 15 E
Mpanda, *Tanzania* .... **54 D3**   6 23S   31 1 E
Mphoengs, *Zimbabwe* .... **57 C4**   21 10S   27 51 E
Mpika, *Zambia* .... **55 E3**   11 51S   31 25 E
Mpulungu, *Zambia* .... **55 D3**   8 51S   31 5 E
Mpumalanga, *S. Africa* ...... **57 D5**   29 50S   30 33 E
Mpumalanga □, *S. Africa* .... **57 D5**   26 0S   30 0 E
Mpwapwa, *Tanzania* .... **54 D4**   6 23S   36 30 E
Mqanduli, *S. Africa* .... **57 E4**   31 49S   28 45 E
Msambansovu, *Zimbabwe* ... **55 F3**   15 50S   30 3 E
M'sila, *Algeria* .... **50 A6**   35 30N   4 29 E
Msoro, *Zambia* .... **55 E3**   13 35S   31 50 E
Mstislavl = Mstsislaw, *Belarus* . **17 A16** 54 0N   31 50 E
Mstsislaw, *Belarus* .... **17 A16** 54 0N   31 50 E
Mtama, *Tanzania* .... **55 E4**   10 17S   39 21 E
Mtamvuna ➛, *S. Africa* ..... **57 E5**   31 6S   30 12 E
Mtilikwe ➛, *Zimbabwe* ..... **55 G3**   21 9S   31 30 E
Mtubatuba, *S. Africa* .... **57 D5**   28 30S   32 8 E
Mtwalume, *S. Africa* .... **57 E5**   30 30S   30 38 E
Mtwara-Mikindani, *Tanzania* . **55 E5**   10 20S   40 20 E
Mu Gia, Deo, *Vietnam* ...... **38 D5**   17 40N 105 47 E
Mu Ko Chang △, *Thailand* ... **39 G4**   11 59N 102 22 E
Mu Us Shamo, *China* .... **34 E5**   39 0N 109 0 E
Muang Chiang Rai = Chiang Rai,
   Thailand .... **38 C2**   19 52N   99 50 E
Muang Khong, *Laos* .... **38 E5**   14 7N 105 51 E
Muang Lamphun, *Thailand* ... **38 C2**   18 40N   99 2 E
Muang Mai, *Thailand* .... **39 a**   9 5N   98 21 E
Muang Pak Beng, *Laos* ...... **38 C3**   19 54N 101 8 E
Muar, *Malaysia* .... **39 L4**   2 3N 102 34 E
Muarabungo, *Indonesia* ..... **36 E2**   1 28S 102 52 E
Muaraenim, *Indonesia* ...... **36 E2**   3 40S 103 50 E
Muarajuloi, *Indonesia* .... **36 E4**   0 12S 114 3 E
Muarakaman, *Indonesia* ..... **36 E5**   0 2S 116 45 E
Muaratebo, *Indonesia* .... **36 E2**   1 30S 102 26 E
Muaratembesi, *Indonesia* .... **36 E2**   1 42S 103 8 E
Muaratewe, *Indonesia* .... **36 E4**   0 58S 114 52 E
Mubarakpur, *India* .... **43 F10** 26 6N   83 18 E
Mubarraz = Al Mubarraz,
   Si. Arabia .... **45 E6**   25 30N   49 40 E
Mubende, *Uganda* .... **54 B3**   0 33N   31 22 E
Mubi, *Nigeria* .... **51 F8**   10 18N   13 16 E
Mucajaí ➛, *Brazil* **92 C6**   2 25N   60 52W
Muchachos, Roque de los,
   Canary Is. **24 F2**   28 44N   17 52W
Muchinga Mts., *Zambia* ..... **55 E3**   11 30S   31 30 E
Muck, *U.K.* **11 E2**   56 50N   6 15W
Muckadilla, *Australia* .... **63 D4**   26 35S 148 23 E
Muckle Flugga, *U.K.* **11 A8**   60 51N   0 54W
Mucuri, *Brazil* **93 G11** 18 0S   39 36W
Mucusso, *Angola* .... **56 B3**   18 1S   21 25 E
Muda, *Canary Is.* **24 F6**   28 34N   13 57W
Mudanjiang, *China* .... **35 B15** 44 38N 129 30 E
Mudanya, *Turkey* .... **23 D13** 40 25N   28 50 E
Muddy Cr. ➛, *U.S.A.* **77 H8**   38 24N 110 42W
Mudgee, *Australia* .... **63 E4**   32 32S 149 31 E
Mudjatik ➛, *Canada* **71 B7**   56 1N 107 36W
Muecate, *Mozam.* .... **55 E4**   14 55S   39 40 E
Mueda, *Mozam.* .... **55 E4**   11 36S   39 28 E
Mueller Ra., *Australia* .... **60 C4**   18 18S 126 46 E
Muende, *Mozam.* .... **55 E3**   14 28S   33 0 E
Muerto, Mar, *Mexico* **87 D6**   16 10N   94 10W
Mufulira, *Zambia* .... **55 E2**   12 32S   28 15 E
Mughal Sarai, *India* .... **43 G10** 25 18N   83 7 E
Mughayrā', *Si. Arabia* ...... **44 D3**   29 17N   37 41 E
Mugi, *Japan* .... **31 H7**   33 40N 134 25 E
Mugila, Mts., *Dem. Rep. of
   the Congo* .... **54 D2**   7 0S   28 50 E
Muğla, *Turkey* .... **23 F13** 37 15N   28 22 E
Mugu, *Nepal* .... **43 E10** 29 45N   82 30 E
Muhammad, Râs, *Egypt* ..... **44 E2**   27 44N   34 16 E
Muhammad Qol, *Sudan* ..... **51 D13** 20 53N   37 9 E
Muhammadabad, *India* ...... **43 F10** 26 4N   83 25 E
Muhesi ➛, *Tanzania* .... **54 D4**   7 0S   35 20 E
Mühlhausen, *Germany* ...... **16 C6**   51 12N   10 27 E
Mühlig Hofmann fjell, *Antarctica* **5 D3**   72 30S   5 0 E
Muhos, *Finland* .... **8 D22** 64 47N   25 59 E
Muhu, *Estonia* .... **9 G20** 58 36N   23 11 E
Muhutwe, *Tanzania* .... **54 C3**   1 35S   31 45 E
Mui Wo, *China* .... **33 G10** 22 16N 113 59 E
Muine Bheag, *Ireland* **10 D5**   52 42N   6 58W
Muir, L., *Australia* .... **61 F2**   34 30S 116 40 E
Muir of Ord, *U.K.* **11 D4**   57 32N   4 28W
Mujnak = Muynak, *Uzbekistan* . **28 E6**   43 44N   59 10 E
Muka, Tanjung, *Malaysia* .... **39 c**   5 28N 100 11 E
Mukacheve, *Ukraine* .... **17 D12** 48 27N   22 45 E
Mukachevo = Mukacheve,
   Ukraine .... **17 D12** 48 27N   22 45 E
Mukah, *Malaysia* .... **36 D4**   2 55N 112 5 E
Mukandwara, *India* .... **42 G6**   24 49N   75 59 E
Mukdahan, *Thailand* .... **38 D5**   16 32N 104 43 E
Mukden = Shenyang, *China* .. **35 D12** 41 48N 123 27 E
Mukerian, *India* .... **42 D6**   31 57N   75 37 E
Mukinbudin, *Australia* .... **61 F2**   30 55S 118 5 E
Mukishi, *Dem. Rep. of the Congo* **55 D1**   8 30S   24 44 E
Mukomuko, *Indonesia* .... **36 E2**   2 30S 101 10 E
Mukomwenze, *Dem. Rep. of
   the Congo* .... **54 D2**   6 49S   27 15 E
Muktsar, *India* .... **42 D6**   30 30N   74 30 E
Mukur = Moqor, *Afghan.* .... **42 C2**   32 50N   67 42 E
Mukwela, *Zambia* .... **55 F2**   17 0S   26 40 E
Mula, *Spain* **21 C5**   38 3N   1 33W
Mula ➛, *Pakistan* .... **42 F2**   27 57N   67 36 E
Mulange, *Dem. Rep. of
   the Congo* .... **54 C2**   3 40S   27 10 E
Mulanje, *Malawi* .... **55 F4**   16 2S   35 33 E
Mulanje, Mt., *Malawi* .... **55 F4**   16 0S   35 30 E
Mulchén, *Chile* **94 D1**   37 45S   72 20W
Mulde ➛, *Germany* .... **16 C7**   51 53N   12 15 E
Mule Creek Junction, *U.S.A.* .. **80 D2**   43 19N 104 8W
Muleba, *Tanzania* .... **54 C3**   1 50S   31 37 E
Mulejé, *Mexico* **86 B2**   26 53N 112 1W
Muleshoe, *U.S.A.* **81 H3**   34 13N 102 43W
Mulgrave, *Canada* **73 C7**   45 38N   61 31W

Mulhacén, *Spain* **21 D4**   37 4N   3 20W
Mülheim, *Germany* .... **33 C6**   51 25N   6 54 E
Mulhouse, *France* .... **20 C7**   47 40N   7 20 E
Muling, *China* .... **35 B16** 44 35N 130 10 E
Mull, *U.K.* **11 E3**   56 25N   5 56W
Mull, Sound of, *U.K.* **11 E3**   56 30N   5 50W
Mullaittivu, *Sri Lanka* .... **40 Q12** 9 15N   80 49 E
Mullen, *U.S.A.* **80 D4**   42 3N 101 1W
Mullens, *U.S.A.* **82 G5**   37 35N   81 23W
Muller, Pegunungan, *Indonesia* . **36 D4**   0 30N 113 30 E
Mullet Pen., *Ireland* **10 B1**   54 13N   10 2W
Mullewa, *Australia* .... **61 E2**   28 29S 115 30 E
Mulligan ➛, *Australia* .... **62 D2**   25 0S 139 0 E
Mullingar, *Ireland* **10 C4**   53 31N   7 21W
Mullins, *U.S.A.* **83 H6**   34 12N   79 15W
Mullumbimby, *Australia* ..... **63 D5**   28 30S 153 30 E
Mulobezi, *Zambia* .... **55 F2**   16 45S   25 7 E
Mulroy B., *Ireland* **10 A4**   55 15N   7 46W
Multan, *Pakistan* .... **42 D4**   30 15N   71 36 E
Mulumbe, Mts., *Dem. Rep. of
   the Congo* .... **55 D2**   8 40S   27 30 E
Mulungushi Dam, *Zambia* ... **55 E2**   14 48S   28 48 E
Mulvane, *U.S.A.* **81 G6**   37 29N   97 15W
Mumbai, *India* .... **40 K8**   18 55N   72 50 E
Mumbwa, *Zambia* .... **55 F2**   15 0S   27 0 E
Mun ➛, *Thailand* .... **38 E5**   15 19N 105 30 E
Muna, *Indonesia* .... **37 F6**   5 0S 122 30 E
Munabao, *India* .... **42 G4**   25 45N   70 17 E
Munamagi, *Estonia* .... **9 H22** 57 43N   27 4 E
Muncan, *Indonesia* .... **37 K18** 8 34S 115 11 E
Muncar, *Indonesia* .... **37 J17** 8 26S 114 20 E
München, *Germany* .... **16 D6**   48 8N   11 34 E
München-Gladbach =
   Mönchengladbach, *Germany* **16 C4**   51 11N   6 27 E
Muncho Lake, *Canada* **70 B3**   59 0N 125 50W
Munch'ŏn, *N. Korea* .... **35 E14** 39 14N 127 19 E
Muncie, *U.S.A.* **82 E3**   40 12N   85 23W
Muncoonie, L., *Australia* ..... **62 D2**   25 12S 138 40 E
Mundabbera, *Australia* ...... **63 D5**   25 36S 151 18 E
Munday, *U.S.A.* **81 J5**   33 27N   99 38W
Münden, *Germany* .... **16 C5**   51 25N   9 38 E
Mundiwindi, *Australia* .... **60 D3**   23 47S 120 9 E
Mundo Novo, *Brazil* **93 F10** 11 50S   40 29W
Mundra, *India* .... **42 H3**   22 54N   69 48 E
Mundrabilla, *Australia* .... **61 F4**   31 52S 127 51 E
Mungallala, *Australia* .... **63 D4**   26 28S 147 34 E
Mungallala Cr. ➛, *Australia* .. **63 D4**   28 53S 147 5 E
Mungana, *Australia* .... **62 B3**   17 8S 144 27 E
Mungaoli, *India* .... **42 G8**   24 24N   78 7 E
Mungari, *Mozam.* .... **55 F3**   17 12S   33 30 E
Mungbere, *Dem. Rep. of
   the Congo* .... **54 B2**   2 36N   28 28 E
Mungeli, *India* .... **43 H9**   22 4N   81 41 E
Munger, *India* .... **43 G12** 25 23N   86 30 E
Mungkan Kandju △, *Australia* . **62 A3**   13 35S 142 52 E
Munich = München, *Germany* . **16 D6**   48 8N   11 34 E
Munising, *U.S.A.* **82 B2**   46 25N   86 40W
Munku-Sardyk, *Russia* ...... **29 D11** 51 45N 100 20 E
Muñoz Gamero, Pen., *Chile* .. **96 G2**   52 30S   73 5W
Munroe L., *Canada* **71 B9**   59 13N   98 35W
Munsan, *S. Korea* .... **35 F14** 37 51N 126 48 E
Münster, *Germany* .... **16 C4**   51 58N   7 37 E
Munster □, *Ireland* **10 D3**   52 18N   8 44W
Muntadgin, *Australia* .... **61 F2**   31 45S 118 33 E
Muntok, *Indonesia* .... **36 E3**   2 5S 105 10 E
Munyama, *Zambia* .... **55 F2**   16 5S   28 31 E
Muong Beng, *Laos* .... **38 B3**   20 23N 101 46 E
Muong Boum, *Vietnam* ...... **38 A4**   22 24N 102 49 E
Muong Et, *Laos* .... **38 B5**   20 49N 104 1 E
Muong Hai, *Laos* .... **38 B3**   21 3N 101 49 E
Muong Hiem, *Laos* .... **38 B4**   20 5N 103 22 E
Muong Houn, *Laos* .... **38 B3**   20 8N 101 23 E
Muong Hung, *Vietnam* ...... **38 B4**   20 56N 103 53 E
Muong Kau, *Laos* .... **38 E5**   15 6N 105 47 E
Muong Khao, *Laos* .... **38 C4**   19 38N 103 32 E
Muong Khoua, *Laos* .... **38 B4**   21 5N 102 31 E
Muong Liep, *Laos* .... **38 C3**   18 29N 101 40 E
Muong May, *Laos* .... **38 E6**   14 49N 106 56 E
Muong Ngeun, *Laos* .... **38 B3**   20 36N 101 3 E
Muong Ngoi, *Laos* .... **38 B4**   20 43N 102 41 E
Muong Nhie, *Vietnam* .... **38 A4**   22 12N 102 28 E
Muong Nong, *Laos* .... **38 D6**   16 22N 106 30 E
Muong Ou Tay, *Laos* .... **38 A3**   22 7N 101 48 E
Muong Oua, *Laos* .... **38 C3**   18 18N 101 20 E
Muong Peun, *Laos* .... **38 B4**   20 13N 103 52 E
Muong Phalane, *Laos* .... **38 D5**   16 39N 105 34 E
Muong Phieng, *Laos* .... **38 C3**   19 6N 101 32 E
Muong Phine, *Laos* .... **38 D6**   16 32N 106 2 E
Muong Sai, *Laos* .... **38 B3**   20 42N 101 59 E
Muong Saiapoun, *Laos* ...... **38 C3**   18 24N 101 31 E
Muong Sen, *Vietnam* .... **38 C5**   19 24N 104 8 E
Muong Sing, *Laos* .... **38 B3**   21 11N 101 9 E
Muong Son, *Laos* .... **38 B4**   20 27N 103 19 E
Muong Soui, *Laos* .... **38 C4**   19 33N 102 52 E
Muong Va, *Laos* .... **38 B4**   21 53N 102 19 E
Muong Xia, *Vietnam* .... **38 B5**   20 19N 104 50 E
Muonio, *Finland* .... **8 C20** 67 57N   23 34 E
Muonionjoki ➛, *Finland* ..... **8 C20** 67 11N   23 34 E
Muping, *China* .... **35 F11** 37 22N 121 36 E
Muqdisho, *Somali Rep.* ...... **47 G4**   2 2N   45 25 E
Mur ➛, *Austria* .... **17 E9**   46 18N   16 52 E
Murakami, *Japan* .... **30 E9**   38 14N 139 29 E
Murallón, Cerro, *Chile* **96 F2**   49 48S   73 30W
Muranda, *Rwanda* .... **54 C2**   1 52S   29 20 E
Murang'a, *Kenya* .... **54 C4**   0 45S   37 9 E
Murashi, *Russia* .... **18 C8**   59 30N   49 0 E
Murat ➛, *Turkey* .... **19 G7**   38 46N   40 0 E
Muratlı, *Turkey* .... **23 D12** 41 10N   27 29 E
Murayama, *Japan* .... **30 E10** 38 30N 140 25 E
Murchison ➛, *Australia* ..... **61 E1**   27 45S 114 0 E
Murchison, Mt., *Antarctica* ... **5 D11** 73 0S 168 0 E
Murchison Falls, *Uganda* .... **54 B3**   2 15N   31 30 E
Murchison Falls △, *Uganda* .. **54 B3**   2 17N   31 48 E
Murchison Ra., *Australia* .... **62 C1**   20 0S 134 10 E
Murchison Rapids, *Malawi* ... **55 F3**   15 55S   34 35 E
Murcia, *Spain* **21 D5**   38 5N   1 10W
Murcia □, *Spain* **21 D5**   37 50N   1 30W
Murdo, *U.S.A.* **80 D4**   43 53N 100 43W
Murdoch Pt., *Australia* ...... **62 A3**   14 37S 144 55 E
Mureş ➛, *Romania* .... **17 E11** 46 15N   20 13 E
Mureşul = Mureş ➛, *Romania* **17 E11** 46 15N   20 13 E
Murewa, *Zimbabwe* .... **57 B5**   17 39S   31 47 E
Murfreesboro, N.C., *U.S.A.* .. **83 G7**   36 27N   77 6W
Murfreesboro, Tenn., *U.S.A.* .. **83 H2**   35 51N   86 24W
Murgab = Murghob, *Tajikistan* . **28 F8**   38 10N   74 2 E
Murgab ➛, *Turkmenistan* .... **45 B9**   38 18N   61 10 E
Murgenella, *Australia* .... **60 B5**   11 34S 132 56 E
Murgha Kibzai, *Pakistan* .... **42 D3**   30 44N   69 25 E

Murghob, *Tajikistan* .... **28 F8**   38 10N   74 2 E
Murgon, *Australia* .... **63 D5**   26 15S 151 54 E
Muri, *India* .... **43 H11** 23 22N   85 52 E
Muria, *Indonesia* .... **37 G14** 6 36S 110 53 E
Muriaé, *Brazil* **95 A7**   21 8S   42 23W
Muriel Mine, *Zimbabwe* ..... **55 F3**   17 14S   30 40 E
Müritz, *Germany* .... **16 B7**   53 25N   12 42 E
Murliganj, *India* .... **43 G12** 25 54N   86 59 E
Murmansk, *Russia* .... **18 A5**   68 57N   33 10 E
Muro, *Spain* .... **24 B10** 39 44N   3 3 E
Murom, *Russia* .... **18 C7**   55 35N   42 3 E
Muroran, *Japan* .... **30 C10** 42 25N 141 0 E
Muroto, *Japan* .... **31 H7**   33 18N 134 9 E
Muroto-Misaki, *Japan* .... **31 H7**   33 15N 134 10 E
Murphy, *U.S.A.* **76 E5**   43 13N 116 33W
Murphys, *U.S.A.* **78 G6**   38 8N 120 28W
Murray, Ky., *U.S.A.* **83 G1**   36 37N   88 19W
Murray, Utah, *U.S.A.* **76 F8**   40 40N 111 53W
Murray ➛, *Australia* .... **63 F2**   35 20S 139 22 E
Murray, L., *U.S.A.* **83 H5**   34 3N   81 13W
Murray Bridge, *Australia* .... **63 F2**   35 6S 139 14 E
Murray Harbour, *Canada* ... **73 C7**   46 0N   62 28W
Murray River △, *Australia* ... **63 E3**   34 23S 140 32 E
Murraysburg, *S. Africa* ...... **56 E3**   31 58S   23 47 E
Murree, *Pakistan* .... **42 C5**   33 56N   73 28 E
Murrieta, *U.S.A.* **79 M9** 33 33N 117 13W
Murrumbidgee ➛, *Australia* .. **63 E3**   34 43S 143 12 E
Murrumburrah, *Australia* .... **63 E4**   34 32S 148 22 E
Murrurundi, *Australia* .... **63 E5**   31 42S 150 51 E
Murshidabad, *India* .... **43 G13** 24 11N   88 19 E
Murtle L., *Canada* **70 C5**   52 8N 119 38W
Murtoa, *Australia* .... **63 F3**   36 35S 142 28 E
Murungu, *Tanzania* .... **54 C3**   4 12S   31 10 E
Mururoa, *French Polynesia* ... **65 K14** 21 52S 138 55W
Murwara, *India* .... **43 H9**   23 46N   80 28 E
Murwillumbah, *Australia* ..... **63 D5**   28 18S 153 27 E
Mürzzuschlag, *Austria* ...... **16 E8**   47 36N   15 41 E
Muş, *Turkey* .... **19 G7**   38 45N   41 30 E
Mûsa, Gebel, *Egypt* .... **44 D2**   28 33N   33 59 E
Musa Khel, *Pakistan* .... **42 D3**   30 59N   69 52 E
Mûsa Qal'eh, *Afghan.* .... **40 C4**   32 20N   64 50 E
Musafirkhana, *India* .... **43 F9**   26 22N   81 48 E
Musala, *Bulgaria* .... **23 C10** 42 13N   23 37 E
Musala, *Indonesia* .... **36 D1**   1 41N   98 28 E
Musan, *N. Korea* .... **35 C15** 42 12N 129 12 E
Musangu, *Dem. Rep. of
   the Congo* .... **55 E1**   10 28S   23 55 E
Musasa, *Tanzania* .... **54 C3**   3 25S   31 30 E
Musay'īd, *Qatar* .... **45 E6**   25 0N   51 33 E
Muscat = Masqaṭ, *Oman* .... **47 C6**   23 37N   58 36 E
Muscatine, *U.S.A.* **80 E9**   41 25N   91 3W
Musgrave Harbour, *Canada* .. **73 C9**   49 27N   53 58W
Musgrave Ranges, *Australia* .. **61 E5**   26 0S 132 0 E
Mushie, *Dem. Rep. of the Congo* **52 E3**   2 56S   16 55 E
Musi ➛, *Indonesia* .... **36 E2**   2 20S 104 56 E
Musina, *S. Africa* .... **57 C5**   22 20S   30 5 E
Muskeg ➛, *Canada* **70 A4**   60 20N 123 20W
Muskegon, *U.S.A.* **82 D2**   43 14N   86 16W
Muskegon ➛, *U.S.A.* **82 D2**   43 14N   86 21W
Muskegon Heights, *U.S.A.* ... **82 D2**   43 12N   86 16W
Muskogee, *U.S.A.* **81 H7**   35 45N   95 22W
Muskoka, L., *Canada* **84 B5**   45 0N   79 25W
Muskwa ➛, *Canada* **70 B4**   58 47N 122 48W
Muslimiyah, *Syria* .... **44 B3**   36 19N   37 12 E
Musofu, *Zambia* .... **55 E2**   13 30S   29 0 E
Musoma, *Tanzania* .... **54 C3**   1 30S   33 48 E
Musquaro, L., *Canada* **73 B7**   50 38N   61 5W
Musquodoboit Harbour, *Canada* **73 D7**   44 50N   63 9W
Musselburgh, *U.K.* **11 F5**   55 57N   3 2W
Musselshell ➛, *U.S.A.* **76 C10** 47 21N 107 57W
Mussoorie, *India* .... **42 D8**   30 27N   78 6 E
Mussuco, *Angola* .... **56 B2**   17 2S   19 3 E
Mustafakemalpaşa, *Turkey* ... **23 D13** 40 2N   28 24 E
Mustang, *Nepal* .... **43 E10** 29 10N   83 55 E
Musters, L., *Argentina* **96 F3**   45 20S   69 25W
Musudan, *N. Korea* .... **35 D15** 40 50N 129 43 E
Muswellbrook, *Australia* ..... **63 E5**   32 16S 150 56 E
Mût, *Egypt* .... **51 C11** 25 28N   28 58 E
Mut, *Turkey* .... **44 B2**   36 40N   33 28 E
Mutanda, *Mozam.* .... **57 C5**   21 0S   33 34 E
Mutanda, *Zambia* .... **55 E2**   12 24S   26 13 E
Mutare, *Zimbabwe* .... **55 F3**   18 58S   32 38 E
Muting, *Indonesia* .... **37 F10** 7 23S 140 20 E
Mutki = Mirtağ, *Turkey* ..... **44 B4**   38 23N   41 56 E
Mutoko, *Zimbabwe* .... **57 B5**   17 24S   32 13 E
Mutoray, *Russia* .... **29 C11** 60 56N 101 0 E
Mutshatsha, *Dem. Rep. of
   the Congo* .... **55 E1**   10 35S   24 20 E
Mutsu, *Japan* .... **30 D10** 41 5N 140 55 E
Mutsu-Wan, *Japan* .... **30 D10** 41 5N 140 55 E
Muttaburra, *Australia* .... **62 C3**   22 38S 144 29 E
Mutton I., *Ireland* **10 D2**   52 49N   9 32W
Mutuáli, *Mozam.* .... **55 E4**   14 55S   37 0 E
Muweilih, *Egypt* .... **46 E3**   30 42N   34 19 E
Muy Muy, *Nic.* **88 D2**   12 39N   85 36W
Muyinga, *Burundi* .... **54 C3**   3 14S   30 33 E
Muynak, *Uzbekistan* .... **28 E6**   43 44N   59 10 E
Muzaffarabad, *Pakistan* ..... **43 B5**   34 25N   73 30 E
Muzaffargarh, *Pakistan* ..... **42 D4**   30 5N   71 14 E
Muzaffarnagar, *India* .... **42 E7**   29 26N   77 40 E
Muzaffarpur, *India* .... **43 F11** 26 7N   85 23 E
Muzafirpur, *Pakistan* .... **42 D3**   30 58N   69 9 E
Muzhi, *Russia* .... **18 A11** 65 25N   64 40 E
Mvuma, *Zimbabwe* .... **55 F3**   19 16S   30 30 E
Mvurwi, *Zimbabwe* .... **55 F3**   17 0S   30 57 E
Mwabvi △, *Malawi* .... **55 F3**   16 42S   35 0 E
Mwadui, *Tanzania* .... **54 C3**   3 26S   33 32 E
Mwambo, *Tanzania* .... **55 E5**   10 30S   40 22 E
Mwandi, *Zambia* .... **55 F1**   17 30S   24 51 E
Mwanza, *Dem. Rep. of the Congo* **54 D2**   7 55S   26 43 E
Mwanza, *Tanzania* .... **54 C3**   2 30S   32 58 E
Mwanza, *Zambia* .... **55 F1**   16 58S   24 28 E
Mwanza □, *Tanzania* .... **54 C3**   2 0S   33 0 E
Mwaya, *Tanzania* .... **55 D3**   9 32S   33 55 E
Mweelrea, *Ireland* **10 C2**   53 39N   9 49W
Mweka, *Dem. Rep. of the Congo* **52 E4**   4 50S   21 34 E
Mwenezi, *Zimbabwe* .... **55 G3**   21 15S   30 48 E
Mwenezi ➛, *Mozam.* .... **55 G3**   22 40S   31 50 E
Mwenga, *Dem. Rep. of
   the Congo* .... **54 C2**   3 1S   28 28 E
Mweru, L., *Zambia* .... **55 D2**   9 0S   28 40 E
Mweru Wantipa △, *Zambia* .. **55 D2**   8 38S   29 10 E
Mweza Range, *Zimbabwe* ... **55 G3**   21 0S   30 0 E
Mwilambwe, *Dem. Rep. of
   the Congo* .... **54 D2**   8 7S   25 5 E
Mwimbi, *Tanzania* .... **55 D3**   8 38S   31 39 E

Mwinilunga, *Zambia* .... **55 E1**   11 43S   24 25 E
My Tho, *Vietnam* .... **39 G6**   10 29N 106 23 E
Myajlar, *India* .... **42 F4**   26 15N   70 20 E
Myanaung, *Burma* .... **41 K19** 18 18N   95 22 E
Myanmar = Burma ■, *Asia* ... **41 J20** 21 0N   96 30 E
Myaungmya, *Burma* .... **41 L19** 16 30N   94 40 E
Mycenæ, *Greece* .... **23 F10** 37 39N   22 52 E
Myeik Kyunzu, *Burma* .... **39 G1**   11 30N   97 30 E
Myers Chuck, *U.S.A.* **70 B2**   55 44N 132 17W
Myerstown, *U.S.A.* **85 F8**   40 22N   76 19W
Myingyan, *Burma* .... **41 J19** 21 30N   95 20 E
Myitkyina, *Burma* .... **41 G20** 25 24N   97 26 E
Mykines, *Færoe Is.* **8 E9**   62 7N   7 35W
Mykolayiv, *Ukraine* .... **19 E5**   46 58N   32 0 E
Mymensingh, *Bangla.* .... **41 G17** 24 45N   90 24 E
Mynydd Du, *U.K.* **13 F4**   51 52N   3 50W
Mýrdalsjökull, *Iceland* **8 E4**   63 40N   19 6W
Myrtle Beach, *U.S.A.* **83 J6**   33 42N   78 53W
Myrtle Creek, *U.S.A.* **76 E2**   43 1N 123 17W
Myrtle Point, *U.S.A.* **76 E1**   43 4N 124 8W
Myrtou, *Cyprus* .... **25 D12** 35 18N   33 4 E
Mysia, *Turkey* .... **23 E12** 39 50N   27 0 E
Mysore = Karnataka □, *India* . **40 N10** 13 15N   77 0 E
Mysore, *India* .... **40 N10** 12 17N   76 41 E
Mystic, *U.S.A.* **85 E13** 41 21N   71 58W
Myszków, *Poland* .... **17 C10** 50 45N   19 22 E
Mytishchi, *Russia* .... **18 C6**   55 50N   37 50 E
Mývatn, *Iceland* **8 D5**   65 36N   17 0W
Mzimba, *Malawi* .... **55 E3**   11 55S   33 39 E
Mzimkulu ➛, *S. Africa* ...... **57 E5**   30 44S   30 28 E
Mzimvubu ➛, *S. Africa* ..... **57 E4**   31 38S   29 33 E
Mzuzu, *Malawi* .... **55 E3**   11 30S   33 55 E

N

Na Hearadh = Harris, *U.K.* ... **11 D2**   57 50N   6 55W
Na Noi, *Thailand* .... **38 C3**   18 19N 100 43 E
Na Phao, *Laos* .... **38 D5**   17 35N 105 44 E
Na Sam, *Vietnam* .... **38 A6**   22 3N 106 37 E
Na San, *Vietnam* .... **38 B5**   21 12N 104 2 E
Na Thon, *Thailand* .... **39 b**   9 32N   99 56 E
Naab ➛, *Germany* .... **16 D6**   49 1N   12 2 E
Naantali, *Finland* .... **9 F19** 60 29N   22 2 E
Naas, *Ireland* **10 C5**   53 12N   6 40W
Nababeep, *S. Africa* .... **56 D2**   29 36S   17 46 E
Nabadwip = Navadwip, *India* . **43 H13** 23 34N   88 20 E
Nabawa, *Australia* .... **61 E1**   28 30S 114 48 E
Nabberu, L., *Australia* ...... **61 E3**   25 50S 120 30 E
Naberezhnyye Chelny, *Russia* . **18 C9**   55 42N   52 19 E
Nabeul, *Tunisia* .... **51 A8**   36 30N   10 44 E
Nabha, *India* .... **42 D7**   30 26N   76 14 E
Nabīd, *Iran* .... **45 D8**   29 40N   57 38 E
Nabire, *Indonesia* .... **37 E9**   3 15S 135 26 E
Nabisar, *Pakistan* .... **42 G3**   25 8N   69 40 E
Nabisipi ➛, *Canada* **73 B7**   50 14N   62 13W
Nabiswera, *Uganda* .... **54 B3**   1 27N   32 15 E
Nâblus = Nābulus, *West Bank* . **46 C4**   32 14N   35 15 E
Naboomspruit, *S. Africa* ..... **57 C4**   24 32S   28 40 E
Nābulus, *West Bank* .... **46 C4**   32 14N   35 15 E
Nacala, *Mozam.* .... **55 E5**   14 31S   40 34 E
Nacala-Velha, *Mozam.* ...... **55 E5**   14 32S   40 34 E
Nacaome, *Honduras* **88 D2**   13 31N   87 30W
Nacaroa, *Mozam.* .... **55 E4**   14 22S   39 56 E
Naches, *U.S.A.* **76 C3**   46 44N 120 42W
Naches ➛, *U.S.A.* **78 D6**   46 38N 120 31W
Nachicapau, L., *Canada* **73 A6**   56 40N   68 5W
Nachingwea, *Tanzania* ...... **55 E4**   10 23S   38 49 E
Nachna, *India* .... **42 F4**   27 34N   71 41 E
Nacimiento L., *U.S.A.* **78 K6**   35 46N 120 53W
Naco, *Mexico* **86 A3**   31 20N 109 56W
Nacogdoches, *U.S.A.* **81 K7**   31 36N   94 39W
Nácori Chico, *Mexico* **86 B3**   29 39N 109 1W
Nacozari, *Mexico* **86 A3**   30 24N 109 39W
Nadi, *Fiji* .... **59 C7**   17 42S 177 20 E
Nadiad, *India* .... **42 H5**   22 41N   72 56 E
Nador, *Morocco* **50 B5**   35 14N   2 58W
Nadur, *Malta* .... **25 C1**   36 2N   14 18 E
Nadūshan, *Iran* .... **45 C7**   32 2N   53 35 E
Nadvirna, *Ukraine* .... **17 D13** 48 37N   24 30 E
Nadvoitsy, *Russia* .... **18 B5**   63 52N   34 14 E
Nadvornaya = Nadvirna, *Ukraine* **17 D13** 48 37N   24 30 E
Nadym, *Russia* .... **28 C8**   65 35N   72 42 E
Nadym ➛, *Russia* .... **28 C8**   66 12N   72 0 E
Nærbø, *Norway* .... **9 G11** 58 40N   5 39 E
Næstved, *Denmark* .... **9 J14** 55 13N   11 44 E
Naft-e Safid, *Iran* .... **45 D6**   31 40N   49 17 E
Naftshahr, *Iran* .... **44 C5**   34 0N   45 30 E
Nafud Desert = An Nafūd,
   Si. Arabia .... **44 D4**   28 15N   41 0 E
Naga, *Phil.* .... **37 B6**   13 38N 123 15 E
Nagahama, *Japan* .... **31 G8**   35 23N 136 16 E
Nagai, *Japan* .... **30 E10** 38 6N 140 2 E
Nagaland □, *India* .... **41 G19** 26 0N   94 30 E
Nagano, *Japan* .... **31 F9**   36 40N 138 10 E
Nagano □, *Japan* .... **31 F9**   36 15N 138 0 E
Nagaoka, *Japan* .... **31 F9**   37 27N 138 51 E
Nagappattinam, *India* .... **40 P11** 10 46N   79 51 E
Nagar ➛, *Bangla.* .... **43 G13** 24 27N   89 12 E
Nagar Parkar, *Pakistan* ..... **42 G4**   24 28N   70 46 E
Nagasaki, *Japan* .... **31 H4**   32 47N 129 50 E
Nagasaki □, *Japan* .... **31 H4**   32 50N 129 40 E
Nagato, *Japan* .... **31 G5**   34 19N 131 5 E
Nagaur, *India* .... **42 F5**   27 15N   73 45 E
Nagda, *India* .... **42 H6**   23 27N   75 25 E
Nagercoil, *India* .... **40 Q10** 8 12N   77 26 E
Nagina, *India* .... **43 E8**   29 30N   78 30 E
Nagineh, *Iran* .... **45 C8**   34 20N   57 15 E
Nagir, *Pakistan* .... **43 A6**   36 12N   74 42 E
Nagod, *India* .... **43 G9**   24 34N   80 36 E
Nagoorin, *Australia* .... **62 C5**   24 17S 151 15 E
Nagorno-Karabakh □, *Azerbaijan* **19 F8**   39 55N   46 45 E
Nagornyy, *Russia* .... **29 D13** 55 58N 124 57 E
Nagoya, *Japan* .... **31 G8**   35 10N 136 50 E
Nagpur, *India* .... **40 J11** 21 8N   79 10 E
Nagua, *Dom. Rep.* **89 C6**   19 23N   69 50W
Naguabo, *Puerto Rico* ...... **89 d**   18 13N   65 44W
Nagykanizsa, *Hungary* ...... **17 E9**   46 28N   17 0 E
Nagykörös, *Hungary* .... **17 E10** 47 5N   19 48 E
Naha, *Japan* .... **31 L3**   26 13N 127 42 E
Nahan, *India* .... **42 D7**   30 33N   77 18 E
Nahanni Butte, *Canada* **70 A4**   61 2N 123 31W
Nahanni △, *Canada* **70 A4**   61 15N 125 0W
Nahargarh, Mad. P., *India* ... **42 G6**   24 10N   75 14 E
Nahargarh, Raj., *India* ...... **42 G7**   24 55N   76 50 E
Nahariyya, *Israel* .... **44 C2**   33 1N   35 5 E

Nahāvand, Iran .... 45 C6   34 10N 48 22 E
Nahuelbuta △, Chile 94 D1   37 44S 72 57W
Nai Yong, Thailand .... 39 a   8 14N 98 22 E
Naicá, Mexico 86 B3   27 53N 105 31W
Naicam, Canada 71 C8   52 30N 104 30W
Naikoon △, Canada 70 C2   53 55N 131 55W
Naimisharanya, India .... 43 F9   27 21N 80 30 E
Nain, Canada 73 A7   56 34N 61 40W
Nā'īn, Iran .... 45 C7   32 54N 53 0 E
Naini Tal, India .... 43 E8   29 30N 79 30 E
Nainpur, India .... 40 H12 22 30N 80 10 E
Nainwa, India .... 42 G6   25 46N 75 51 E
Nairn, U.K. 11 D5   57 35N   3 53W
Nairobi, Kenya .... 54 C4   1 17S 36 48 E
Nairobi △, Kenya .... 54 C4   1 22S 36 50 E
Naissaar, Estonia .... 9 G21 59 34N 24 29 E
Naivasha, Kenya .... 54 C4   0 40S 36 30 E
Naivasha, L., Kenya .... 54 C4   0 48S 36 20 E
Najaf = An Najaf, Iraq .... 44 C5   32 3N 44 15 E
Najafābād, Iran .... 45 C6   32 40N 51 15 E
Najd, Si. Arabia .... 47 B3   26 30N 42 0 E
Najibabad, India .... 42 E8   29 40N 78 20 E
Najin, N. Korea .... 35 C16 42 12N 130 15 E
Najmah, Si. Arabia .... 45 E6   26 42N 50 6 E
Najrān, Si. Arabia .... 47 D3   17 34N 44 18 E
Naju, S. Korea .... 35 G14 35 3N 126 43 E
Nakadōri-Shima, Japan ...... 31 H4   32 57N 129 4 E
Nakalagba, Dem. Rep. of
  the Congo .... 54 B2   2 50N 27 58 E
Nakaminato, Japan .... 31 F10 36 21N 140 36 E
Nakamura, Japan .... 31 H6   32 59N 132 56 E
Nakano, Japan .... 31 F9   36 45N 138 22 E
Nakano-Shima, Japan .... 31 K4   29 51N 129 52 E
Nakashibetsu, Japan .... 30 C12 43 33N 144 59 E
Nakfa, Eritrea .... 47 D2   16 40N 38 32 E
Nakha Yai, Ko, Thailand ..... 39 a   8 3N 98 28 E
Nakhichevan = Naxçivan,
  Azerbaijan .... 19 G8   39 12N 45 15 E
Nakhichevan Rep. = Naxçıvan □,
  Azerbaijan .... 19 G8   39 25N 45 26 E
Nakhl, Egypt .... 46 F2   29 55N 33 43 E
Nakhl-e Taqī, Iran .... 45 E7   27 28N 52 36 E
Nakhodka, Russia .... 29 E14 42 53N 132 54 E
Nakhon Nayok, Thailand ..... 38 E3   14 12N 101 13 E
Nakhon Pathom, Thailand .... 38 F3   13 49N 100 3 E
Nakhon Phanom, Thailand .... 38 D5   17 23N 104 43 E
Nakhon Ratchasima, Thailand . 38 E4   14 59N 102 12 E
Nakhon Sawan, Thailand ..... 38 E3   15 35N 100 10 E
Nakhon Si Thammarat, Thailand 39 H3   8 29N 100 0 E
Nakhon Thai, Thailand .... 38 D3   17 5N 100 44 E
Nakhtarana, India .... 42 H3   23 20N 69 15 E
Nakina, Canada 72 B2   50 10N 86 40W
Nakodar, India .... 42 D6   31 8N 75 31 E
Nakskov, Denmark .... 9 J14   54 50N 11 8 E
Naktong →, S. Korea .... 35 G15 35 7N 128 57 E
Nakuru, Kenya .... 54 C4   0 15S 36 4 E
Nakuru, L., Kenya .... 54 C4   0 23S 36 5 E
Nakusp, Canada 70 C5   50 20N 117 45W
Nal, Pakistan .... 42 F2   27 40N 66 12 E
Nal →, Pakistan .... 42 G1   25 20N 65 30 E
Nalázi, Mozam. .... 57 C5   24 3S 33 20 E
Nalchik, Russia .... 19 F7   43 30N 43 33 E
Nalgonda, India .... 40 L11 17 6N 79 15 E
Nalhati, India .... 43 G12 24 17N 87 52 E
Naliya, India .... 42 H3   23 16N 68 50 E
Nallamalai Hills, India .... 40 M11 15 30N 78 50 E
Nam Can, Vietnam .... 39 H5   8 46N 104 59 E
Nam-ch'on, N. Korea .... 35 E14 38 15N 126 26 E
Nam Co, China .... 32 C4   30 30N 90 45 E
Nam Dinh, Vietnam .... 38 B6   20 25N 106 5 E
Nam Du, Hon, Vietnam ...... 39 H5   9 41N 104 21 E
Nam Nao △, Thailand .... 38 D3   16 44N 101 32 E
Nam Ngum Dam, Laos .... 38 C4   18 35N 102 34 E
Nam-Phan, Vietnam .... 39 G6   10 30N 106 0 E
Nam Phong, Thailand .... 38 D4   16 42N 102 52 E
Nam Tha, Laos .... 38 B3   20 58N 101 30 E
Nam Tok, Thailand .... 38 E2   14 21N 99 4 E
Namacunde, Angola .... 56 B2   17 18S 15 50 E
Namacurra, Mozam. .... 57 B6   17 30S 36 50 E
Namak, Daryācheh-ye, Iran .. 45 C7   34 30N 52 0 E
Namak, Kavir-e, Iran .... 45 C8   34 30N 57 30 E
Namakzār, Daryācheh-ye, Iran . 45 C9   34 0N 60 30 E
Namaland, Namibia .... 56 C2   26 0S 17 0 E
Namangan, Uzbekistan .... 28 E8   41 0N 71 40 E
Namapa, Mozam. .... 55 E4   13 43S 39 50 E
Namaqualand, S. Africa ...... 56 E2   30 0S 17 0 E
Namasagali, Uganda .... 54 B3   1 2N 33 0 E
Namber, Indonesia .... 37 E8   1 2S 134 49 E
Nambour, Australia .... 63 D5   26 32S 152 58 E
Nambucca Heads, Australia .. 63 E5   30 37S 153 0 E
Nambung △, Australia .... 61 F2   30 30S 115 5 E
Namcha Barwa, China .... 32 D4   29 40N 95 10 E
Namche Bazar, Nepal .... 43 F12 27 51N 86 47 E
Namchonjŏm = Nam-ch'on,
  N. Korea .... 35 E14 38 15N 126 26 E
Namecunda, Mozam. .... 55 E4   14 54S 37 37 E
Nameponda, Mozam. .... 55 F4   15 50S 39 50 E
Nametil, Mozam. .... 55 F4   15 40S 39 21 E
Namew L., Canada 71 C8   54 14N 101 56W
Namgia, India .... 43 D8   31 48N 78 40 E
Namib Desert, Namibia ...... 56 C2   22 30S 15 0 E
Namib-Naukluft △, Namibia .. 56 C2   24 40S 15 16 E
Namibe, Angola .... 53 H2   15 7S 12 11 E
Namibe □, Angola .... 56 B1   16 35S 12 30 E
Namibia ■, Africa .... 56 C2   22 0S 18 9 E
Namibwoestyn = Namib Desert,
  Namibia .... 56 C2   22 30S 15 0 E
Namlea, Indonesia .... 37 E7   3 18S 127 5 E
Namoi →, Australia .... 63 E4   30 12S 149 30 E
Nampa, U.S.A. 76 E5   43 34N 116 34W
Namp'o, N. Korea .... 35 E13 38 52N 125 10 E
Nampō-Shotō, Japan .... 31 J10 32 0N 140 0 E
Nampula, Mozam. .... 55 F4   15 6S 39 15 E
Namrole, Indonesia .... 37 E7   3 46S 126 46 E
Namse Shankou, China ...... 41 E13 30 0N 82 25 E
Namsen →, Norway .... 8 D14 64 28N 11 37 E
Namsos, Norway .... 8 D14 64 29N 11 30 E
Namtok Chat Trakan △, Thailand 38 D3   17 17N 100 40 E
Namtok Mae Surin △, Thailand 38 C2   18 55N 98 2 E
Namtsy, Russia .... 29 C13 62 43N 129 37 E
Namtu, Burma .... 41 H20 23 5N 97 28 E
Namtumbo, Tanzania .... 55 E4   10 30S 36 4 E
Namu, Canada 70 C3   51 49N 127 50W
Namur, Belgium .... 15 D4   50 27N   4 52 E
Namur □, Belgium .... 15 D4   50 17N   5 0 E
Namutoni, Namibia .... 56 B2   18 49S 16 55 E
Namwala, Zambia .... 55 F2   15 44S 26 30 E

Namwŏn, S. Korea .... 35 G14 35 23N 127 23 E
Nan, Thailand .... 38 C3   18 48N 100 46 E
Nan →, Thailand .... 38 E3   15 42N 100 9 E
Nan-ch'ang = Nanchang, China 33 D6   28 42N 115 55 E
Nanaimo, Canada 70 D4   49 10N 124 0W
Nanam, N. Korea .... 35 D15 41 44N 129 40 E
Nanango, Australia .... 63 D5   26 40S 152 0 E
Nanao, Japan .... 31 F8   37 0N 137 0 E
Nanchang, China .... 33 D6   28 42N 115 55 E
Nanching = Nanjing, China ... 33 C6   32 2N 118 47 E
Nanchong, China .... 32 C5   30 43N 106 2 E
Nancy, France .... 20 B7   48 42N   6 12 E
Nanda Devi, India .... 43 D8   30 23N 79 59 E
Nanda Kot, India .... 43 D9   30 17N 80 5 E
Nandan, Japan .... 31 G7   34 10N 134 42 E
Nanded, India .... 40 K10 19 10N 77 20 E
Nandewar Ra., Australia ..... 63 E5   30 15S 150 35 E
Nandi = Nadi, Fiji .... 59 C7   17 42S 177 20 E
Nandigram, India .... 43 H12 22 1N 87 58 E
Nandurbar, India .... 40 J9   21 20N 74 15 E
Nandyal, India .... 40 M11 15 30N 78 30 E
Nanga-Eboko, Cameroon .... 52 D2   4 41N 12 22 E
Nanga Parbat, Pakistan ..... 43 B6   35 10N 74 35 E
Nangade, Mozam. .... 55 E4   11 5S 39 36 E
Nangapinoh, Indonesia ...... 36 E4   0 20S 111 44 E
Nangarhār □, Afghan. .... 40 B7   34 20N 70 0 E
Nangatayap, Indonesia ...... 36 E4   1 32S 110 34 E
Nangeya Mts., Uganda ...... 54 B3   3 30N 33 30 E
Nangong, China .... 34 F8   37 23N 115 22 E
Nanhuang, China .... 35 F11 36 58N 121 48 E
Nanjeko, Zambia .... 55 F1   15 31S 23 30 E
Nanjing, China .... 33 C6   32 2N 118 47 E
Nanjirinji, Tanzania .... 55 D4   9 41S 39 5 E
Nanking = Nanjing, China .... 33 C6   32 2N 118 47 E
Nankoku, Japan .... 31 H6   33 39N 133 44 E
Nanlang, China .... 33 G10 22 30N 113 32 E
Nanning, China .... 32 D5   22 48N 108 20 E
Nannup, Australia .... 61 F2   33 59S 115 48 E
Nanpara, India .... 43 F9   27 52N 81 33 E
Nanpi, China .... 34 E9   38 2N 116 45 E
Nanping, China .... 33 D6   26 38N 118 10 E
Nanripe, Mozam. .... 55 E4   13 52S 38 52 E
Nansei-Shotō = Ryūkyū-rettō,
  Japan .... 31 M3   26 0N 126 0 E
Nansen Basin, Arctic .... 4 A10 84 0N 50 0 E
Nansen Cordillera, Arctic .... 4 A   87 0N 90 0 E
Nansen Sd., Canada 4 A3   81 0N 91 0W
Nansha, China .... 33 F10 22 45N 113 34 E
Nanshan I., S. China Sea .... 36 B5   10 45N 115 49 E
Nansio, Tanzania .... 54 C3   2 3S 33 4 E
Nantes, France 20 C3   47 12N   1 33W
Nanticoke, U.S.A. 85 E8   41 12N 76 0W
Nanton, Canada 70 C6   50 21N 113 46W
Nantong, China .... 33 C7   32 1N 120 52 E
Nantou, China .... 33 F10 22 32N 113 55 E
Nantucket I., U.S.A. 82 E10 41 16N 70 5W
Nantwich, U.K. 12 D5   53 4N   2 31W
Nanty Glo, U.S.A. 84 F6   40 28N 78 50W
Nanuque, Brazil 93 G10 17 50S 40 21W
Nanusa, Kepulauan, Indonesia 37 D7   4 45N 127 1 E
Nanutarra Roadhouse, Australia 60 D2   22 32S 115 30 E
Nanyang, China .... 34 H7   33 11N 112 30 E
Nanyuki, Kenya .... 54 B4   0 2N   37 4 E
Nao, C. de la, Spain .... 21 C6   38 44N   0 14 E
Naococane, L., Canada 73 B5   52 50N 70 45W
Napa, U.S.A. 78 G4   38 18N 122 17W
Napa →, U.S.A. 78 G4   38 10N 122 19W
Napanee, Canada 84 B8   44 15N 77 0W
Napanoch, U.S.A. 85 E10 41 44N 74 22W
Nape, Laos .... 38 C5   18 18N 105 6 E
Nape Pass = Keo Neua, Deo,
  Vietnam .... 38 C5   18 23N 105 10 E
Napier, N.Z. .... 59 H6   39 30S 176 56 E
Napier Broome B., Australia .. 60 B4   14 2S 126 37 E
Napier Pen., Australia .... 62 A2   12 4S 135 43 E
Napierville, Canada 85 A11 45 11N 73 25W
Naples = Nápoli, Italy .... 22 D6   40 50N 14 15 E
Naples, U.S.A. 83 M5   26 8N 81 48W
Napo →, Peru 92 D4   3 20S 72 40W
Napoleon, N. Dak., U.S.A. ... 80 B5   46 30N 99 46W
Napoleon, Ohio, U.S.A. 82 E3   41 23N 84 8W
Nápoli, Italy .... 22 D6   40 50N 14 15 E
Napopo, Dem. Rep. of the Congo 54 B2   4 15N 28 0 E
Naqb, Ra's an, Jordan ...... 46 F4   30 0N 35 29 E
Naqqāsh, Iran .... 45 C6   35 40N 49 6 E
Nara, Japan .... 31 G7   34 40N 135 49 E
Nara, Mali 50 E4   15 10N   7 20W
Nara □, Japan .... 31 G8   34 30N 136 0 E
Nara Canal, Pakistan .... 42 G3   24 30N 69 20 E
Nara Visa, U.S.A. 81 H3   35 37N 103 6W
Naracoorte, Australia .... 63 F3   36 58S 140 45 E
Naradhan, Australia .... 63 E4   33 34S 146 17 E
Naraini, India .... 43 G9   25 11N 80 29 E
Narasapur, India .... 41 L12 16 26N 81 40 E
Narathiwat, Thailand .... 39 J3   6 30N 101 48 E
Narayanganj, Bangla. .... 41 H17 23 40N 90 33 E
Narayanpet, India .... 40 L10 16 45N 77 30 E
Narberth, U.K. 13 F3   51 47N   4 44W
Narbonne, France .... 20 E5   43 11N   3 0 E
Nardin, Iran .... 45 B7   37 3N 55 59 E
Nardò, Italy .... 23 D8   40 11N 18 2 E
Narembeen, Australia .... 61 F2   32 7S 118 24 E
Narendranagar, India .... 42 D8   30 10N 78 18 E
Nares Str., Arctic 66 A13 80 0N 70 0W
Naretha, Australia .... 61 F3   31 0S 124 45 E
Narew →, Poland .... 17 B11 52 26N 20 41 E
Nari →, Pakistan .... 42 F2   28 0N 67 40 E
Narin, Afghan. .... 40 A6   36 5N 69 0 E
Narindra, Helodranon' i, Madag. 57 A8   14 55S 47 30 E
Narita, Japan .... 31 G10 35 47N 140 19 E
Nariva Swamp, Trin. & Tob. .. 93 K15 10 26N 61 4W
Narmada →, India .... 42 J5   21 38N 72 36 E
Narmland, Sweden .... 9 F15 60 0N 13 30 E
Narnaul, India .... 42 E7   28 5N 76 11 E
Narodnaya, Russia .... 18 A10 65 5N 59 58 E
Narok, Kenya .... 54 C4   1 55S 35 52 E
Narooma, Australia .... 63 F5   36 14S 150 4 E
Narowal, Pakistan .... 42 C6   32 6N 74 52 E
Narrabri, Australia .... 63 E4   30 19S 149 46 E
Narran →, Australia .... 63 D4   29 45S 147 20 E
Narrandera, Australia .... 63 E4   34 42S 146 31 E
Narrogin, Australia .... 61 F2   32 58S 117 14 E
Narromine, Australia .... 63 E4   32 12S 148 12 E
Narrow Hills △, Canada 71 C8   54 0N 104 37W
Narsimhapur, India .... 43 H8   22 54N 79 14 E
Narsinghgarh, India .... 42 H7   23 45N 76 40 E

Naruto, Japan .... 31 G7   34 11N 134 37 E
Narva, Estonia .... 18 C4   59 23N 28 12 E
Narva →, Russia .... 9 G22 59 27N 28 2 E
Narva Bay, Estonia .... 9 G19 59 35N 27 35 E
Narvik, Norway .... 8 B17 68 28N 17 26 E
Narwana, India .... 42 E7   29 39N 76 6 E
Naryan-Mar, Russia .... 18 A9   67 42N 53 12 E
Narym, Russia .... 28 D9   59 0N 81 30 E
Naryn, Kyrgyzstan .... 28 E8   41 26N 75 58 E
Nasa, Norway .... 8 C16 66 29N 15 23 E
Naseby, N.Z. .... 59 L3   45 1S 170 10 E
Naselle, U.S.A. 78 D3   46 22N 123 49W
Naser, Buheirat en, Egypt .... 51 D12 23 0N 32 30 E
Nashua, Mont., U.S.A. 76 B10 48 8N 106 22W
Nashua, N.H., U.S.A. 85 D13 42 45N 71 28W
Nashville, Ark., U.S.A. 81 J8   33 57N 93 51W
Nashville, Ga., U.S.A. 83 K4   31 12N 83 15W
Nashville, Tenn., U.S.A. 83 G2   36 10N 86 47W
Nasik, India .... 40 K8   19 58N 73 50 E
Nasirabad, India .... 42 F6   26 15N 74 45 E
Nasirabad, Pakistan .... 42 E3   28 23N 68 24 E
Nasiriyah = An Nāşiriyah, Iraq . 44 D5   31 0N 46 15 E
Naskaupi →, Canada 73 B7   53 47N 60 51W
Naşrābād, Iran .... 45 C6   34 8N 51 26 E
Naşrīān-e Pa'īn, Iran .... 44 C5   32 52N 46 52 E
Nass →, Canada 70 C3   55 0N 129 40W
Nassau, Bahamas 88 A4   25 5N 77 20W
Nassau, U.S.A. 85 D11 42 31N 73 37W
Nassau, B., Chile 96 H3   55 20S 68 0W
Nasser, L. = Naser, Buheirat en,
  Egypt .... 51 D12 23 0N 32 30 E
Nässjö, Sweden .... 9 H16 57 39N 14 42 E
Nastapoka →, Canada 72 A4   56 55N 76 33W
Nastapoka, Is., Canada 72 A4   56 55N 76 50W
Nata, Botswana .... 56 C4   20 12S 26 12 E
Nata →, Botswana .... 56 C4   20 14S 26 10 E
Natal, Brazil 93 E11   5 47S 35 13W
Natal, Indonesia .... 36 D1   0 35N 99 7 E
Natal, S. Africa .... 53 K6   28 30S 30 30 E
Natal Drakensberg △, S. Africa 57 D4   29 27S 29 30 E
Naţanz, Iran .... 45 C6   33 30N 51 55 E
Natashquan, Canada 73 B7   50 14N 61 46W
Natashquan →, Canada 73 B7   50 7N 61 50W
Natchez, U.S.A. 81 K9   31 34N 91 24W
Natchitoches, U.S.A. 81 K8   31 46N 93 5W
Nathalia, Australia .... 63 F4   36 1S 145 13 E
Nathdwara, India .... 42 G5   24 55N 73 50 E
Nati, Pta., Spain .... 24 A10 40 3N   3 50 E
Natimuk, Australia .... 63 F3   36 42S 142 0 E
Nation →, Canada 70 B4   55 30N 123 32W
National City, U.S.A. 79 N9   32 41N 117 6W
Natitingou, Benin .... 50 F6   10 20N   1 26 E
Natividad, I., Mexico 86 B1   27 50N 115 10W
Natkyizin, Burma .... 38 E1   14 57N 97 59 E
Natron, L., Tanzania .... 54 C4   2 20S 36 0 E
Natrona Heights, U.S.A. 84 F5   40 37N 79 44W
Natukanaoka Pan, Namibia ... 56 B2   18 40S 15 45 E
Natuna Besar, Kepulauan,
  Indonesia .... 36 D3   4 0N 108 15 E
Natuna Is. = Natuna Besar,
  Kepulauan, Indonesia ..... 36 D3   4 0N 108 15 E
Natuna Selatan, Kepulauan,
  Indonesia .... 36 D3   2 45N 109 0 E
Natural Bridge, U.S.A. 85 B9   44 5N 75 30W
Natural Bridges △, U.S.A. ... 77 H8   37 36N 110 1W
Naturaliste, C., Australia .... 63 G4   40 50S 148 15 E
Nau Qala, Afghan. .... 42 B3   34 5N 68 5 E
Naugatuck, U.S.A. 85 E11 41 30N 73 3W
Naujaat = Repulse Bay, Canada 69 B11 66 30N 86 30W
Naumburg, Germany .... 16 C6   51 9N 11 47 E
Nā'ūr at Tunayb, Jordan ..... 46 D4   31 48N 35 57 E
Nauru ■, Pac. Oc. .... 64 H8   1 0S 166 0 E
Naushahra = Nowshera, Pakistan 40 C8   34 0N 72 0 E
Naushahro, Pakistan .... 42 F3   26 50N 68 7 E
Naushon I., U.S.A. 85 E14 41 29N 70 45W
Nauta, Peru 92 D4   4 31S 73 35W
Nautanwa, India .... 41 F13 27 20N 83 25 E
Naute △, Namibia .... 56 D2   26 55S 17 57 E
Nautla, Mexico 87 C5   20 20N 96 50W
Nava, Mexico 86 B4   28 25N 100 46W
Navadwip, India .... 43 H13 23 34N 88 20 E
Navahrudak, Belarus .... 17 B13 53 40N 25 50 E
Navajo Reservoir, U.S.A. 77 H10 36 48N 107 36W
Navalmoral de la Mata, Spain . 21 C3   39 52N   5 33W
Navan = An Uaimh, Ireland .. 10 C5   53 39N   6 41W
Navarin, Mys, Russia .... 4 C16 62 15N 179 5 E
Navarino, I., Chile 96 H3   55 0S 67 40W
Navarra □, Spain 21 A5   42 40N   1 40W
Navarre, U.S.A. 84 F3   40 43N 81 31W
Navarro →, U.S.A. 78 F3   39 11N 123 45W
Navasota, U.S.A. 81 K6   30 23N 96 5W
Navassa I., W. Indies 89 C5   18 30N 75 0W
Naver →, U.K. 11 C4   58 32N   4 14W
Navibandar, India .... 42 J3   21 26N 69 48 E
Navidad, Chile 94 C1   33 57S 171 50W
Navirai, Brazil 95 A5   23 8S 54 13W
Navlakhi, India .... 42 H4   22 58N 70 28 E
Năvodari, Romania .... 17 F15 44 19N 28 36 E
Navoi = Nawoiy, Uzbekistan .. 28 E7   40 9N 65 22 E
Navojoa, Mexico 86 B3   27 0N 109 30W
Navolato, Mexico 86 C3   24 47N 107 42W
Návpaktos, Greece .... 23 E9   38 24N 21 50 E
Návplion, Greece .... 23 F10 37 33N 22 50 E
Navsari, India .... 40 J8   20 57N 72 59 E
Nawa Kot, Pakistan .... 42 E4   28 21N 71 24 E
Nawab Khan, Pakistan ...... 42 D3   30 17N 69 12 E
Nawabganj, Ut. P., India .... 43 F9   26 56N 81 14 E
Nawabganj, Ut. P., India .... 43 E8   28 32N 79 40 E
Nawabshah, Pakistan .... 42 F3   26 15N 68 25 E
Nawada, India .... 43 G11 24 50N 85 33 E
Nawakot, Nepal .... 43 F11 27 55N 85 10 E
Nawalgarh, India .... 42 F6   27 50N 75 15 E
Nawanshahr, India .... 43 C6   32 33N 74 48 E
Nawar, Dasht-i-, Afghan. .... 42 C3   33 52N 68 0 E
Nawoiy, Uzbekistan .... 28 E7   40 9N 65 22 E
Naxçivan, Azerbaijan .... 19 G8   39 12N 45 15 E
Naxçıvan □, Azerbaijan ..... 19 G8   39 25N 45 26 E
Náxos, Greece .... 23 F11 37 8N 25 25 E
Nay, Mui, Vietnam .... 38 F7   12 55N 109 23 E
Nāy Band, Būshehr, Iran ..... 45 E7   27 20N 52 40 E
Nāy Band, Khorāsān, Iran .... 45 C8   32 20N 57 34 E
Nayakhan, Russia .... 29 C16 61 56N 159 0 E
Nayarit □, Mexico 86 C4   22 0N 105 0W
Nayoro, Japan .... 30 B11 44 21N 142 28 E
Nayyāl, W. →, Si. Arabia .... 44 D3   28 35N 39 4 E
Nazaré, Brazil 93 F11 13 2S 39 0W
Nazareth = Nazerat, Israel ... 46 C4   32 42N 35 17 E

Nazareth, U.S.A. 85 F9   40 44N 75 19W
Nazas, Mexico 86 B4   25 10N 104 6W
Nazas →, Mexico 86 B4   25 35N 103 25W
Nazca, Peru 92 F4   14 50S 74 57W
Naze, The, U.K. .... 13 F9   51 53N   1 18 E
Nazerat, Israel .... 46 C4   32 42N 35 17 E
Năzik, Iran .... 44 B5   39 1N 45 4 E
Nazilli, Turkey .... 23 F13 37 55N 28 15 E
Nazko, Canada 70 C4   53 1N 123 37W
Nazko →, Canada 70 C4   53 7N 123 34W
Nazret, Ethiopia .... 47 F2   8 32N 39 22 E
Nazwa, Oman .... 47 C6   22 56N 57 32 E
Nchanga, Zambia .... 55 E2   12 30S 27 49 E
Ncheu, Malawi .... 55 E3   14 50S 34 47 E
Ndala, Tanzania .... 54 C3   4 45S 33 15 E
Ndalatando, Angola .... 52 F2   9 12S 14 48 E
Ndareda, Tanzania .... 54 C4   4 12S 35 30 E
Ndélé, C.A.R. .... 52 C4   8 25N 20 36 E
Ndjamena, Chad .... 51 F8   12 10N 14 59 E
Ndola, Zambia .... 55 E2   13 0S 28 34 E
Ndoto Mts., Kenya .... 54 B4   2 0N 37 0 E
Nduguti, Tanzania .... 54 C3   4 18S 34 41 E
Ndumu △, S. Africa .... 57 D5   26 52S 32 15 E
Neagh, Lough, U.K. 10 B5   54 37N   6 25W
Neah Bay, U.S.A. 78 B2   48 22N 124 37W
Neale, L., Australia .... 60 D5   24 15S 130 0 E
Neápolis, Greece .... 23 D5   35 15N 25 37 E
Near Is., U.S.A. .... 68 C1   52 30N 174 0 E
Neath, U.K. 13 F4   51 39N   3 48W
Neath Port Talbot □, U.K. ... 13 F4   51 42N   3 45W
Nebine Cr. →, Australia ..... 63 D4   29 27S 146 56 E
Nebitdag, Turkmenistan ..... 19 G9   39 30N 54 2 E
Nebo, Australia .... 62 C4   21 42S 148 42 E
Nebraska □, U.S.A. 80 E5   41 30N 99 30W
Nebraska City, U.S.A. 80 E7   40 41N 95 52W
Nébrodi, Monti, Italy .... 22 F6   37 54N 14 35 E
Necedah, U.S.A. 80 C9   44 2N   90 4W
Nechako →, Canada 70 C4   53 55N 122 42W
Neches →, U.S.A. 81 L8   29 58N 93 51W
Neckar →, Germany .... 16 D5   49 27N   8 29 E
Necochea, Argentina 94 D4   38 30S 58 50W
Needles, Canada 70 D5   49 53N 118 7W
Needles, U.S.A. 79 L12 34 51N 114 37W
Needles, The, U.K. 13 G6   50 39N   1 35W
Ñeembucú □, Paraguay 94 B4   27 0S 58 0W
Neemuch = Nimach, India ... 42 G6   24 30N 74 56 E
Neenah, U.S.A. 82 C1   44 11N 88 28W
Neepawa, Canada 71 C9   50 15N 99 30W
Neftçala, Azerbaijan .... 19 G8   39 19N 49 12 E
Neftekumsk, Russia .... 19 F7   44 46N 44 50 E
Nefyn, U.K. 12 E3   52 56N   4 31W
Negapatam = Nagappattinam,
  India .... 40 P11 10 46N 79 51 E
Negara, Indonesia .... 37 J17   8 22S 114 37 E
Negaunee, U.S.A. 82 B2   46 30N 87 36W
Negele, Ethiopia .... 47 F2   5 20N 39 36 E
Negev Desert = Hanegev, Israel 46 E4   30 50N 35 0 E
Negombo, Sri Lanka .... 40 R11   7 12N 79 50 E
Negotin, Serbia & M. .... 23 B10 44 16N 22 37 E
Negra, Peru 92 E2   6 6S 81 10W
Negrais, C. = Maudin Sun, Burma 41 M19 16 0N 94 30 E
Negril, Jamaica .... 88 a   18 22N 78 20W
Negro →, Argentina 96 E4   2 1S 62 47W
Negro →, Brazil 92 D7   3 0S 60 0W
Negro →, Uruguay 95 C4   33 24S 58 22W
Negros, Phil. .... 37 C6   9 30N 122 40 E
Neguac, Canada 73 C6   47 15N 65 5W
Nehalem →, U.S.A. 78 E3   45 40N 123 56W
Nehāvand, Iran .... 45 C6   35 56N 49 31 E
Nehbandān, Iran .... 45 D9   31 35N 60 5 E
Nei Monggol Zizhiqu □, China 34 D7   42 0N 112 0 E
Neijiang, China .... 32 D5   29 35N 104 55 E
Neilingding Dao, China ..... 33 G10 22 25N 113 48 E
Neillsville, U.S.A. 80 C9   44 34N 90 36W
Neilton, U.S.A. 76 C2   47 25N 123 53W
Neiqiu, China .... 34 F8   37 15N 114 30 E
Neiva, Colombia 92 C3   2 56N 75 18W
Neixiang, China .... 34 H6   33 10N 111 52 E
Nejanilini L., Canada 71 B9   59 33N 97 48W
Nejd = Najd, Si. Arabia ..... 47 B3   26 30N 42 0 E
Nekā, Iran .... 45 B7   36 39N 53 19 E
Nekemte, Ethiopia .... 47 F2   9 4N 36 30 E
Neksø, Denmark .... 9 J16   55 4N 15 12 E
Nelia, Australia .... 62 C3   20 39S 142 12 E
Neligh, U.S.A. 80 D5   42 8N 98 2W
Nelkan, Russia .... 29 D14 57 40N 136 4 E
Nellore, India .... 40 M11 14 27N 79 59 E
Nelson, Canada 70 D5   49 30N 117 20W
Nelson, N.Z. .... 59 J4   41 18S 173 16 E
Nelson, U.K. 12 D5   53 50N   2 13W
Nelson, Ariz., U.S.A. 77 J7   35 31N 113 19W
Nelson, Nev., U.S.A. 79 K12 35 42N 114 50W
Nelson →, Canada 71 C9   54 33N 98 2W
Nelson, C., Australia .... 63 F3   38 26S 141 32 E
Nelson, Estrecho, Chile 96 G2   51 30S 75 0W
Nelson Forks, Canada 70 B4   59 30N 124 0W
Nelson House, Canada 71 B9   55 47N 98 51W
Nelson L., Canada 71 B8   55 48N 100 7W
Nelson Lakes △, N.Z. ...... 59 J4   41 55S 172 44 E
Nelspoort, S. Africa .... 56 E3   32 7S 23 0 E
Nelspruit, S. Africa .... 57 D5   25 29S 30 59 E
Néma, Mauritania 50 E4   16 40N   7 15W
Neman = Nemunas →, Lithuania 9 J19 55 25N 21 10 E
Neman, Russia .... 9 J20   55 2N 22 2 E
Nemeiben L., Canada 71 B7   55 20N 105 20W
Nemiscau, Canada 72 B4   51 18N 76 54W
Nemiscau, L., Canada 72 B4   51 25N 76 40W
Nemunas →, Lithuania ...... 9 J19   55 25N 21 10 E
Nemuro, Japan .... 30 C12 43 20N 145 35 E
Nemuro-Kaikyō, Japan ...... 30 C12 43 30N 145 30 E
Nen Jiang →, China .... 35 B13 45 28N 124 30 E
Nenagh, Ireland 10 D3   52 52N   8 11W
Nenasi, Malaysia .... 39 L4   3 9N 103 23 E
Nene →, U.K. .... 12 E8   52 49N   0 11 E
Nenjiang, China .... 33 B7   49 10N 125 10 E
Neno, Malawi .... 55 F3   15 25S 34 40 E
Neodesha, U.S.A. 81 G7   37 25N 95 41W
Neosho, U.S.A. 81 G7   36 52N 94 22W
Neosho →, U.S.A. 81 H7   36 48N 95 18W
Nepal ■, Asia .... 43 F11 28 0N 84 30 E
Nepalganj, Nepal .... 43 E9   28 5N 81 40 E
Nepalganj Road, India ...... 43 E9   28 1N 81 41 E
Nephi, U.S.A. 76 G8   39 43N 111 50W
Nephin, Ireland 10 B2   54 1N   9 22W
Neptune, U.S.A. 85 F10 40 13N 74 2W
Nerang, Australia .... 63 D5   27 58S 153 20 E
Nerchinsk, Russia .... 29 D12 52 0N 116 39 E

Néret, L., Canada 73 B5 54 45N 70 44W
Neretva →, Croatia .... 23 C7 43 1N 17 27 E
Neringa, Lithuania .... 9 J19 55 20N 21 5 E
Neris →, Lithuania .... 9 J21 55 8N 24 16 E
Neryungri, Russia .... 29 D13 57 38N 124 28 E
Nescopeck, U.S.A. 85 E8 41 3N 76 12W
Ness, L., U.K. 11 D4 57 15N 4 32W
Ness City, U.S.A. 80 F5 38 27N 99 54W
Nesterov, Ukraine .... 17 C12 50 4N 23 58 E
Nesvizh = Nyasvizh, Belarus . 17 B14 53 14N 26 38 E
Netanya, Israel .... 46 C3 32 20N 34 51 E
Netarhat, India .... 43 H11 23 29N 84 16 E
Nete →, Belgium .... 15 C4 51 7N 4 14 E
Netherdale, Australia ...... 62 K6 21 10S 148 33 E
Netherlands ■, Europe ...... 15 C5 52 0N 5 30 E
Netherlands Antilles ☑, W. Indies 92 A5 12 15N 69 0W
Netrang, India .... 42 J5 21 39N 73 21 E
Nettilling L., Canada 69 B12 66 30N 71 0W
Netzahualcoyotl, Presa, Mexico 87 D6 17 10N 93 30W
Neubrandenburg, Germany .. 16 B7 53 33N 13 15 E
Neuchâtel, Switz. .... 20 C7 47 0N 6 55 E
Neuchâtel, Lac de, Switz. ... 20 C7 46 53N 6 50 E
Neufchâteau, Belgium ...... 15 E5 49 50N 5 25 E
Neumünster, Germany ...... 16 A5 54 4N 9 58 E
Neunkirchen, Germany ..... 16 D4 49 20N 7 9 E
Neuquén, Argentina 96 D3 38 55S 68 0W
Neuquén ☐, Argentina 94 D2 38 0S 69 50W
Neuruppin, Germany .... 16 B7 52 55N 12 48 E
Neuse →, U.S.A. 83 H7 35 6N 76 29W
Neusiedler See, Austria .... 17 E9 47 50N 16 47 E
Neustrelitz, Germany ...... 16 B7 53 21N 13 4 E
Neva →, Russia .... 18 C5 59 50N 30 30 E
Nevada, Iowa, U.S.A. 80 D8 42 1N 93 27W
Nevada, Mo., U.S.A. 81 G7 37 51N 94 22W
Nevada ☐, U.S.A. 76 G5 39 0N 117 0W
Nevada City, U.S.A. 78 F6 39 16N 121 1W
Nevado, Cerro, Argentina ... 94 D2 35 30S 68 32W
Nevado de Colima = Volcán de
  Colima △, Mexico 86 D4 19 30N 103 40W
Nevado de Tres Cruces △, Chile 94 B2 27 13S 69 5W
Nevel, Russia .... 18 C4 56 0N 29 55 E
Nevers, France .... 20 C5 47 0N 3 9 E
Nevertire, Australia .... 63 E4 31 50S 147 44 E
Neville, Canada 71 D7 49 58N 107 39W
Nevinnomyssk, Russia ..... 19 F7 44 40N 42 0 E
Nevis, St. Kitts & Nevis 89 C7 17 0N 62 30W
Nevşehir, Turkey .... 44 B2 38 33N 34 40 E
Nevyansk, Russia .... 18 C11 57 30N 60 13 E
New →, U.S.A. 82 F5 38 10N 81 12W
New Aiyansh, Canada 70 B3 55 12N 129 4W
New Albany, Ind., U.S.A. ... 82 F3 38 18N 85 49W
New Albany, Miss., U.S.A. .. 81 H10 34 29N 89 0W
New Albany, Pa., U.S.A. 85 E8 41 36N 76 27W
New Amsterdam, Guyana ... 92 B7 6 15N 57 36W
New Angledool, Australia ... 63 D4 29 5S 147 55 E
New Baltimore, U.S.A. 84 D2 42 41N 82 44W
New Bedford, U.S.A. 85 E14 41 38N 70 56W
New Berlin, N.Y., U.S.A. ... 85 D9 42 37N 75 20W
New Berlin, Pa., U.S.A. 84 F8 40 50N 76 57W
New Bern, U.S.A. 83 H7 35 7N 77 3W
New Bethlehem, U.S.A. 84 F5 41 0N 79 20W
New Bloomfield, U.S.A. 84 F7 40 25N 77 11W
New Boston, U.S.A. 81 J7 33 28N 94 25W
New Braunfels, U.S.A. 81 L5 29 42N 98 8W
New Brighton, N.Z. .... 59 K4 43 29S 172 43 E
New Brighton, U.S.A. 84 F4 40 42N 80 19W
New Britain, Papua N. G. ... 64 H7 5 50S 150 20 E
New Britain, U.S.A. 85 E12 41 40N 72 47W
New Brunswick, U.S.A. 85 F10 40 30N 74 27W
New Brunswick ☐, Canada .. 73 C6 46 50N 66 30W
New Caledonia ☑, Pac. Oc. .. 64 K8 21 0S 165 0 E
New Castile = Castilla-La
  Mancha ☐, Spain 21 C4 39 30N 3 30W
New Castle, Ind., U.S.A. 82 F3 39 55N 85 22W
New Castle, Pa., U.S.A. 84 F4 41 0N 80 21W
New City, U.S.A. 85 E11 41 9N 73 59W
New Concord, U.S.A. 84 G3 39 59N 81 54W
New Cumberland, U.S.A. ... 84 F4 40 30N 80 36W
New Cuyama, U.S.A. 79 L7 34 57N 119 38W
New Delhi, India .... 42 E7 28 37N 77 13 E
New Denver, Canada 70 D5 50 0N 117 25W
New Don Pedro Reservoir, U.S.A. 78 H6 37 43N 120 24W
New England, U.S.A. 80 B3 46 32N 102 52W
New England Ra., Australia .. 63 E5 30 20S 151 45 E
New Forest, U.K. 13 G6 50 53N 1 34W
New Galloway, U.K. 11 F4 55 5N 4 9W
New Glasgow, Canada 73 C7 45 35N 62 36W
New Guinea, Oceania ...... 26 K17 4 0S 136 0 E
New Hamburg, Canada 84 C4 43 23N 80 42W
New Hampshire ☐, U.S.A. .. 85 C13 44 0N 71 30W
New Hampton, U.S.A. 80 D8 43 3N 92 19W
New Hanover, S. Africa .... 57 D5 29 22S 30 31 E
New Hartford, U.S.A. 85 C9 43 4N 75 18W
New Haven, Conn., U.S.A. .. 85 E12 41 18N 72 55W
New Haven, Mich., U.S.A. .. 84 D2 42 44N 82 48W
New Hazelton, Canada 70 B3 55 20N 127 30W
New Hebrides = Vanuatu ■,
  Pac. Oc. .... 64 J8 15 0S 168 0 E
New Holland, U.S.A. 85 F8 40 6N 76 5W
New Iberia, U.S.A. 81 K9 30 1N 91 49W
New Ireland, Papua N. G. ... 64 H7 3 20S 151 50 E
New Jersey ☐, U.S.A. 82 E8 40 0N 74 30W
New Kensington, U.S.A. 84 F5 40 34N 79 46W
New Lexington, U.S.A. 82 F4 39 43N 82 13W
New Liskeard, Canada 72 C4 47 31N 79 41W
New London, Conn., U.S.A. . 85 E12 41 22N 72 6W
New London, Ohio, U.S.A. .. 84 E2 41 5N 82 24W
New London, Wis., U.S.A. .. 80 C10 44 23N 88 45W
New Madrid, U.S.A. 81 G10 36 36N 89 32W
New Martinsville, U.S.A. ... 82 F5 39 39N 80 52W
New Meadows, U.S.A. 76 D5 44 58N 116 18W
New Melones L., U.S.A. 78 H6 37 57N 120 31W
New Mexico ☐, U.S.A. 77 J10 34 30N 106 0W
New Milford, Conn., U.S.A. . 85 E11 41 35N 73 25W
New Milford, Pa., U.S.A. 85 E9 41 52N 75 44W
New Norcia, Australia ...... 61 F2 30 57S 116 13 E
New Norfolk, Australia ..... 63 G4 42 46S 147 2 E
New Orleans, U.S.A. 81 L9 29 58N 90 4W
New Philadelphia, U.S.A. ... 84 F3 40 30N 81 27W
New Plymouth, N.Z. .... 59 H5 39 4S 174 5 E
New Plymouth, U.S.A. 76 E5 43 58N 116 49W
New Port Richey, U.S.A. 83 L4 28 16N 82 43W
New Providence I., Bahamas 88 A4 25 25N 78 35W
New Quay, U.K. 13 E3 52 13N 4 21W
New Radnor, U.K. 13 E4 52 15N 3 9W
New Richmond, Canada 73 C6 48 15N 65 45W
New Richmond, U.S.A. 80 C8 45 7N 92 32W

New River Gorge △, U.S.A. .. 82 G5 37 53N 81 5W
New Roads, U.S.A. 81 K9 30 42N 91 26W
New Rochelle, U.S.A. 85 F11 40 55N 73 47W
New Rockford, U.S.A. 80 B5 47 41N 99 8W
New Romney, U.K. .... 13 G8 50 59N 0 57 E
New Ross, Ireland 10 D5 52 23N 6 57W
New Salem, U.S.A. 80 B4 46 51N 101 25W
New Scone = Scone, U.K. 11 E5 56 25N 3 24W
New Siberian I. = Novaya Sibir,
  Ostrov, Russia .... 29 B16 75 10N 150 0 E
New Siberian Is. =
  Novosibirskiye Ostrova, Russia 29 B15 75 0N 142 0 E
New Smyrna Beach, U.S.A. .. 83 L5 29 1N 80 56W
New South Wales ☐, Australia 63 E4 33 0S 146 0 E
New Tecumseth, Canada 84 B5 44 9N 79 52W
New Town, U.S.A. 80 B3 47 59N 102 30W
New Tredegar, U.K. 13 F4 51 44N 3 16W
New Ulm, U.S.A. 80 C7 44 19N 94 28W
New Waterford, Canada 73 C7 46 13N 60 4W
New-Wes-Valley, Canada ... 73 C9 49 8N 53 36W
New Westminster, Canada .. 78 A4 49 13N 122 55W
New York, U.S.A. 85 F11 40 45N 74 0W
New York ☐, U.S.A. 85 D9 43 0N 75 0W
New York J.F. Kennedy
  International ✈ (JFK), U.S.A. 85 F11 40 38N 73 47W
New York Mts., U.S.A. 77 J6 35 0N 115 20W
New Zealand ■, Oceania ... 59 J6 40 0S 176 0 E
Newaj →, India .... 42 G7 24 24N 76 49 E
Newala, Tanzania .... 55 E4 10 58S 39 18 E
Newark, Del., U.S.A. 82 F8 39 41N 75 46W
Newark, N.J., U.S.A. 85 F10 40 44N 74 10W
Newark, N.Y., U.S.A. 84 C7 43 3N 77 6W
Newark, Ohio, U.S.A. 84 F2 40 3N 82 24W
Newark International ✈ (EWR),
  U.S.A. 85 F10 40 42N 74 10W
Newark-on-Trent, U.K. 12 D7 53 5N 0 48W
Newark Valley, U.S.A. 85 D8 42 14N 76 11W
Newberg, U.S.A. 76 D2 45 18N 122 58W
Newberry, Mich., U.S.A. ... 82 B3 46 21N 85 30W
Newberry, S.C., U.S.A. 83 H5 34 17N 81 37W
Newberry ⌒, U.S.A. 76 E2 43 42N 122 43W
Newberry Springs, U.S.A. .. 79 L10 34 50N 116 41W
Newboro L., Canada 85 B8 44 38N 76 20W
Newbridge = Droichead Nua,
  Ireland 10 C5 53 11N 6 48W
Newburgh, Canada 84 B8 44 19N 76 52W
Newburgh, U.S.A. 85 E10 41 30N 74 1W
Newbury, U.K. 13 F6 51 24N 1 20W
Newbury, N.H., U.S.A. 85 B12 43 19N 72 3W
Newbury, Vt., U.S.A. 85 B12 44 5N 72 4W
Newburyport, U.S.A. 83 D10 42 49N 70 53W
Newcastle, Australia ...... 63 E5 33 0S 151 46 E
Newcastle, N.B., Canada ... 73 C6 47 1N 65 38W
Newcastle, Ont., Canada ... 72 D4 43 55N 78 35W
Newcastle, S. Africa ...... 57 D4 27 45S 29 58 E
Newcastle, U.K. 10 B6 54 13N 5 54W
Newcastle, Calif., U.S.A. ... 78 G5 38 53N 121 8W
Newcastle, Wyo., U.S.A. ... 80 D2 43 50N 104 11W
Newcastle Emlyn, U.K. 13 E3 52 2N 4 28W
Newcastle Ra., Australia ... 60 C5 15 45S 130 15 E
Newcastle-under-Lyme, U.K. . 12 D5 53 1N 2 14W
Newcastle-upon-Tyne, U.K. . 12 C6 54 58N 1 36W
Newcastle Waters, Australia . 62 B1 17 30S 133 28 E
Newcastle West, Ireland ... 10 D2 52 27N 9 3W
Newcomb, U.S.A. 85 C10 43 58N 74 10W
Newcomerstown, U.S.A. ... 84 F3 40 16N 81 36W
Newdegate, Australia ...... 61 F2 33 6S 119 0 E
Newell, Australia .... 62 B4 16 20S 145 16 E
Newell, U.S.A. 80 C3 44 43N 103 25W
Newfane, U.S.A. 84 C6 43 17N 78 43W
Newfield, U.S.A. 85 D8 42 18N 76 33W
Newfound L., U.S.A. 85 C13 43 40N 71 47W
Newfoundland, Canada 73 C8 49 0N 55 0W
Newfoundland, U.S.A. 85 E9 41 18N 75 19W
Newfoundland & Labrador ☐,
  Canada 73 B8 53 0N 58 0W
Newhall, U.S.A. 79 L8 34 23N 118 32W
Newhaven, U.K. .... 13 G8 50 47N 0 3 E
Newkirk, U.S.A. 81 G6 36 53N 97 3W
Newlyn, U.K. 13 G2 50 6N 5 34W
Newman, Australia .... 60 D2 23 18S 119 45 E
Newman, U.S.A. 78 H5 37 19N 121 1W
Newmarket, Canada 84 B5 44 3N 79 28W
Newmarket, Ireland 10 D2 52 13N 9 0W
Newmarket, U.K. .... 13 E8 52 15N 0 25 E
Newmarket, U.S.A. 85 C14 43 4N 70 56W
Newnan, U.S.A. 83 J3 33 23N 84 48W
Newport, Ireland 10 C2 53 53N 9 33W
Newport, I. of W., U.K. 13 G6 50 42N 1 17W
Newport, Newp., U.K. 13 F5 51 35N 3 0W
Newport, Ark., U.S.A. 81 H9 35 37N 91 16W
Newport, Ky., U.S.A. 82 F3 39 5N 84 30W
Newport, N.H., U.S.A. 85 C12 43 22N 72 10W
Newport, N.Y., U.S.A. 85 C9 43 11N 75 1W
Newport, Oreg., U.S.A. 76 D1 44 39N 124 3W
Newport, Pa., U.S.A. 84 F7 40 29N 77 8W
Newport, R.I., U.S.A. 85 E13 41 29N 71 19W
Newport, Tenn., U.S.A. 83 H4 35 58N 83 11W
Newport, Vt., U.S.A. 85 B12 44 56N 72 13W
Newport, Wash., U.S.A. 76 B5 48 11N 117 3W
Newport ☐, U.K. 13 F4 51 33N 3 1W
Newport Beach, U.S.A. 79 M9 33 37N 117 56W
Newport News, U.S.A. 82 G7 36 59N 76 25W
Newport Pagnell, U.K. 13 E7 52 5N 0 43W
Newquay, U.K. 13 G2 50 25N 5 6W
Newry, U.K. 10 B5 54 11N 6 21W
Newton, Ill., U.S.A. 80 F10 38 59N 88 10W
Newton, Iowa, U.S.A. 80 E8 41 42N 93 3W
Newton, Kans., U.S.A. 81 F6 38 3N 97 21W
Newton, Mass., U.S.A. 85 D13 42 21N 71 12W
Newton, Miss., U.S.A. 81 J10 32 19N 89 10W
Newton, N.C., U.S.A. 83 H5 35 40N 81 13W
Newton, N.J., U.S.A. 85 E10 41 3N 74 45W
Newton, Tex., U.S.A. 81 K8 30 51N 93 46W
Newton Abbot, U.K. 13 G4 50 32N 3 37W
Newton Aycliffe, U.K. 12 C6 54 37N 1 34W
Newton Falls, U.S.A. 84 E4 41 11N 80 59W
Newton Stewart, U.K. 11 G4 54 57N 4 30W
Newtown, U.K. 13 E4 52 31N 3 19W
Newtownabbey, U.K. 10 B6 54 40N 5 56W
Newtownards, U.K. 10 B6 54 36N 5 42W
Newtownbarry = Bunclody,
  Ireland 10 D5 52 39N 6 40W
Newtownstewart, U.K. 10 B4 54 43N 7 23W
Newville, U.S.A. 84 F7 40 10N 77 24W
Neya, Russia .... 18 C7 58 21N 43 49 E

Neyriz, Iran .... 45 D7 29 15N 54 19 E
Neyshâbûr, Iran .... 45 B8 36 10N 58 50 E
Nezhin = Nizhyn, Ukraine .. 19 D5 51 5N 31 55 E
Nezperce, U.S.A. 76 C5 46 14N 116 14W
Ngabang, Indonesia .... 36 D3 0 23N 109 55 E
Ngabordamlu, Tanjung,
  Indonesia .... 37 F8 6 56S 134 11 E
N'Gage, Angola .... 52 F3 7 46S 15 16 E
Ngami Depression, Botswana 56 C3 20 30S 22 46 E
Ngamo, Zimbabwe .... 55 F2 19 3S 27 32 E
Nganglong Kangri, China ... 41 C12 33 0N 81 0 E
Ngao, Thailand .... 38 C2 18 46N 99 59 E
Ngaoundéré, Cameroon .... 52 C2 7 15N 13 35 E
Ngapara, N.Z. .... 59 L3 44 57S 170 46 E
Ngara, Tanzania .... 54 C3 2 29S 30 40 E
Ngawi, Indonesia .... 37 G14 7 24S 111 26 E
Nghia Lo, Vietnam .... 38 B5 21 33N 104 28 E
Ngoma, Malawi .... 55 E3 13 8S 33 45 E
Ngomahura, Zimbabwe .... 55 G3 20 26S 30 43 E
Ngomba, Tanzania .... 55 D3 8 20S 32 53 E
Ngoring Hu, China .... 32 C4 34 55N 97 5 E
Ngorongoro, Tanzania ..... 54 C4 3 11S 35 32 E
Ngorongoro ⌒, Tanzania ... 54 C4 2 40S 35 30 E
Ngozi, Burundi .... 54 C2 2 54S 29 50 E
Ngudu, Tanzania .... 54 C3 2 58S 33 25 E
Nguigmi, Niger .... 51 F8 14 20N 13 20 E
Nguiu, Australia .... 60 B5 11 46S 130 38 E
Ngukurr, Australia .... 62 A1 14 44S 134 44 E
Ngunga, Tanzania .... 54 C3 3 37S 33 37 E
Nguru, Nigeria .... 51 F8 12 56N 10 29 E
Nguru Mts., Tanzania ...... 54 D4 6 0S 37 30 E
Ngusi, Malawi .... 55 E3 14 0S 34 50 E
Nguyen Binh, Vietnam ..... 38 A5 22 39N 105 56 E
Nha Trang, Vietnam .... 39 F7 12 16N 109 10 E
Nhacoongo, Mozam. ...... 57 C6 24 18S 35 14 E
Nhamaabué, Mozam. ...... 55 F4 17 25S 35 5 E
Nhamundá →, Brazil 93 D7 2 12S 56 41W
Nhangulaze, L., Mozam. ... 57 C5 24 0S 34 30 E
Nhill, Australia .... 63 F3 36 18S 141 40 E
Nho Quan, Vietnam .... 38 B5 20 18N 105 45 E
Nhulunbuy, Australia ...... 62 A2 12 10S 137 20 E
Nia-nia, Dem. Rep. of the Congo 54 B2 1 30N 27 40 E
Niagara Falls, Canada 84 C5 43 7N 79 5W
Niagara Falls, U.S.A. 84 C5 43 5N 79 4W
Niagara-on-the-Lake, Canada 84 C5 43 15N 79 4W
Niah, Malaysia .... 36 D4 3 58N 113 46 E
Niamey, Niger .... 50 F6 13 27N 2 6 E
Niangara, Dem. Rep. of
  the Congo .... 54 B2 3 42N 27 50 E
Niantic, U.S.A. 85 E12 41 20N 72 11W
Nias, Indonesia .... 36 D1 1 0N 97 30 E
Niassa ⌒, Mozam. .... 55 E4 12 4S 36 57 E
Niassa ☐, Mozam. .... 55 E4 13 30S 36 0 E
Nibâk, Si. Arabia .... 45 E7 24 25N 50 50 E
Nicaragua ■, Cent. Amer. .. 88 D2 11 40N 85 30W
Nicaragua, L. de, Nic. 88 D2 12 0N 85 30W
Nicastro, Italy .... 22 E7 38 59N 16 19 E
Nice, France .... 20 E7 43 42N 7 14 E
Niceville, U.S.A. 83 K2 30 31N 86 30W
Nichicun, L., Canada 73 B5 53 5N 71 0W
Nichinan, Japan .... 31 J5 31 38N 131 23 E
Nicholás, Canal, W. Indies .. 88 B3 23 30N 80 5W
Nicholasville, U.S.A. 82 G3 37 53N 84 34W
Nichols, U.S.A. 85 D8 42 1N 76 22W
Nicholson, Australia ...... 60 C4 18 2S 128 54 E
Nicholson, U.S.A. 85 E9 41 37N 75 47W
Nicholson →, Australia .... 62 B2 17 31S 139 36 E
Nicholson L., Canada 71 A8 62 40N 102 40W
Nicholson Ra., Australia ... 61 E2 27 15S 116 45 E
Nickol B., Australia 85 B10 44 41N 74 39W
Nicobar Is., Ind. Oc. ...... 27 J13 9 0N 93 30 E
Nicola, Canada 70 C4 50 12N 120 40W
Nicolls Town, Bahamas 88 A4 25 8N 78 0W
Nicosia, Cyprus .... 25 D12 35 10N 33 25 E
Nicoya, Costa Rica 88 D2 10 9N 85 27W
Nicoya, G. de, Costa Rica .. 88 E3 10 0N 85 0W
Nicoya, Pen. de, Costa Rica . 88 E2 9 45N 85 40W
Nidd →, U.K. 12 D6 53 59N 1 23W
Niedersachsen ☐, Germany . 16 B5 52 50N 9 0 E
Niekerkshoop, S. Africa .... 56 D3 29 19S 22 51 E
Niemba, Dem. Rep. of the Congo 54 D2 5 58S 28 24 E
Niemen = Nemunas →,
  Lithuania .... 9 J19 55 25N 21 10 E
Nienburg, Germany .... 16 B5 52 39N 9 13 E
Nieu Bethesda, S. Africa ... 56 E3 31 51S 24 34 E
Nieuw Amsterdam, Suriname 93 B7 5 53N 55 5W
Nieuw Nickerie, Suriname .. 93 B7 6 0N 56 59W
Nieuwoudtville, S. Africa ... 56 E2 31 23S 19 7 E
Nieuwpoort, Belgium ...... 15 C2 51 8N 2 45 E
Nieves, Pico de las, Canary Is. 24 G4 27 57N 15 35W
Niğde, Turkey .... 19 G5 37 58N 34 40 E
Nigel, S. Africa .... 57 D4 26 27S 28 25 E
Niger ■, W. Afr. .... 50 E7 17 30N 10 0 E
Niger →, W. Afr. .... 50 G7 5 33N 6 33 E
Nigeria ■, W. Afr. .... 50 G7 8 30N 8 0 E
Nighasin, India .... 43 E9 28 14N 80 52 E
Nightcaps, N.Z. .... 59 L2 45 57S 168 2 E
Nii-Jima, Japan .... 31 G9 34 20N 139 15 E
Niigata, Japan .... 30 F9 37 58N 139 0 E
Niigata ☐, Japan .... 31 F9 37 15N 138 45 E
Niihama, Japan .... 31 H6 33 55N 133 16 E
Niihau, U.S.A. 74 H14 21 54N 160 9W
Niimi, Japan .... 31 G6 34 59N 133 28 E
Niitsu, Japan .... 30 F9 37 48N 139 7 E
Nijil, Jordan .... 46 E4 30 32N 35 33 E
Nijkerk, Neths. .... 15 B5 52 13N 5 30 E
Nijmegen, Neths. .... 15 C5 51 50N 5 52 E
Nijverdal, Neths. .... 15 B6 52 22N 6 28 E
Nik Pey, Iran .... 45 B6 36 50N 48 10 E
Nikiniki, Indonesia .... 37 F6 9 49S 124 30 E
Nikkō, Japan .... 31 F9 36 45N 139 35 E
Nikkō ☐, Japan .... 31 F9 36 56N 139 37 E
Nikolayev = Mykolayiv, Ukraine 19 E5 46 58N 32 0 E
Nikolayevsk, Russia ...... 19 D8 50 0N 45 35 E
Nikolayevsk-na-Amur, Russia 29 D15 53 8N 140 44 E
Nikolskoye, Russia .... 29 D17 55 12N 166 0 E
Nikopol, Ukraine .... 19 E5 47 35N 34 25 E
Nikshahr, Iran .... 45 E9 26 15N 60 10 E
Nikšić, Serbia & M. .... 23 C8 42 50N 18 57 E
Nîl, Nahr en →, Africa .... 51 B12 30 10N 31 6 E
Nîl el Abyad →, Sudan ..... 51 E12 15 38N 32 31 E
Nîl el Azraq →, Sudan ..... 51 E12 15 38N 32 31 E
Nila, Indonesia .... 37 F7 6 44S 129 31 E
Niland, U.S.A. 79 M11 33 14N 115 31W
Nile = Nîl, Nahr en →, Africa 51 B12 30 10N 31 6 E
Niles, Mich., U.S.A. 82 E2 41 50N 86 15W
Niles, Ohio, U.S.A. 84 E4 41 11N 80 46W

Nim Ka Thana, India ...... 42 F6 27 44N 75 48 E
Nimach, India .... 42 G6 24 30N 74 56 E
Nimbahera, India .... 42 G6 24 37N 74 45 E
Nîmes, France .... 20 E6 43 50N 4 23 E
Nimfaion, Ákra = Pinnes, Ákra,
  Greece .... 23 D11 40 5N 24 20 E
Nimmitabel, Australia ..... 63 F4 36 29S 149 15 E
Ninawá, Iraq .... 44 B4 36 25N 43 10 E
Ninawá ☐, Iraq .... 44 B4 36 15N 43 0 E
Nindigully, Australia ...... 63 D4 28 21S 148 50 E
Ninepin Group, China ..... 33 G11 22 16N 114 21 E
Nineveh = Ninawá, Iraq ... 44 B4 36 25N 43 10 E
Ning Xian, China .... 34 G4 35 30N 107 58 E
Ningaloo ⌒, Australia ..... 60 D1 22 23S 113 32 E
Ning'an, China .... 35 B15 44 22N 129 20 E
Ningbo, China .... 33 D7 29 51N 121 28 E
Ningcheng, China .... 35 D10 41 32N 119 53 E
Ningjing Shan, China ..... 32 D4 30 0N 98 20 E
Ningjin, China .... 34 F8 37 35N 114 57 E
Ningling, China .... 34 G8 34 25N 115 22 E
Ningpo = Ningbo, China ... 33 D7 29 51N 121 28 E
Ningqiang, China .... 34 H4 32 47N 106 15 E
Ningshan, China .... 34 H5 33 21N 108 21 E
Ningsia Hui A.R. = Ningxia Huizu
  Zizhiqu ☐, China .... 34 F4 38 0N 106 0 E
Ningwu, China .... 34 E7 39 0N 112 18 E
Ningxia Huizu Zizhiqu ☐, China 34 F4 38 0N 106 0 E
Ningyang, China .... 34 G9 35 47N 116 45 E
Ninh Binh, Vietnam .... 38 B5 20 15N 105 55 E
Ninh Giang, Vietnam ...... 38 B6 20 44N 106 24 E
Ninh Hoa, Vietnam .... 38 F7 12 30N 109 7 E
Ninh Ma, Vietnam .... 38 F7 12 48N 109 21 E
Ninove, Belgium .... 15 D4 50 51N 4 2 E
Nioaque, Brazil 95 A4 21 5S 55 50W
Niobrara, U.S.A. 80 D6 42 45N 98 2W
Niobrara →, U.S.A. 80 D6 42 46N 98 3W
Nioro du Sahel, Mali 50 E4 15 15N 9 30W
Niort, France 20 C3 46 19N 0 29W
Nipawin, Canada 71 C8 53 20N 104 0W
Nipigon, Canada 72 C2 49 0N 88 17W
Nipigon, L., Canada 72 C2 49 50N 88 30W
Nipishish L., Canada 73 B7 54 12N 60 45W
Nipissing, L., Canada 72 C4 46 20N 80 0W
Nipomo, U.S.A. 79 K6 35 3N 120 29W
Nipton, U.S.A. 79 K11 35 28N 115 16W
Niquelândia, Brazil 93 F9 14 33S 48 23W
Nīr, Iran .... 44 B5 38 2N 47 59 E
Nirasaki, Japan .... 31 G9 35 42N 138 27 E
Nirmal, India .... 40 K11 19 3N 78 20 E
Nirmali, India .... 43 F12 26 20N 86 35 E
Niš, Serbia & M. .... 23 C9 43 19N 21 58 E
Nişāb, Si. Arabia .... 44 D5 29 11N 44 43 E
Nişāb, Yemen .... 47 E4 14 25N 46 29 E
Nishinomiya, Japan .... 31 G7 34 45N 135 20 E
Nishino'omote, Japan ..... 31 J5 30 43N 130 59 E
Nishiwaki, Japan .... 31 G7 34 59N 134 58 E
Niskibi →, Canada 72 A2 56 29N 88 9W
Nisqually →, U.S.A. 78 C4 47 6N 122 42W
Nissáki, Greece .... 25 A3 39 43N 19 52 E
Nissum Bredning, Denmark . 9 H13 56 40N 8 20 E
Nistru = Dnister →, Europe . 17 E16 46 18N 30 17 E
Nisutlin →, Canada 70 A2 60 14N 132 34W
Nitchequon, Canada 73 B5 53 10N 70 58W
Niterói, Brazil 95 A7 22 52S 43 0W
Nith →, Canada 84 C4 43 12N 80 23W
Nith →, U.K. 11 F5 55 14N 3 33W
Nitmiluk △, Australia ...... 60 B5 14 6S 132 15 E
Nitra, Slovak Rep. .... 17 D10 48 19N 18 4 E
Nitra →, Slovak Rep. ...... 17 E10 47 46N 18 10 E
Niuafo'ou, Tonga 59 B11 15 30S 175 58W
Niue, Cook Is. 65 J11 19 2S 169 54W
Niut, Indonesia .... 36 D4 0 55N 110 6 E
Niuzhuang, China .... 35 D12 40 58N 122 28 E
Nivala, Finland .... 8 E21 63 56N 24 57 E
Nivelles, Belgium .... 15 D4 50 35N 4 20 E
Nivernais, France .... 20 C5 47 15N 3 30 E
Niwas, India .... 43 H9 23 3N 80 26 E
Nixon, U.S.A. 81 L6 29 16N 97 46W
Nizamabad, India .... 40 K11 18 45N 78 7 E
Nizamghat, India .... 41 E19 28 20N 95 45 E
Nizhne Kolymsk, Russia ... 29 C17 68 34N 160 55 E
Nizhneangarsk, Russia .... 29 D11 55 47N 109 30 E
Nizhnekamsk, Russia ..... 18 C9 55 38N 51 49 E
Nizhneudinsk, Russia ..... 29 D10 54 54N 99 3 E
Nizhnevartovsk, Russia .... 28 C8 60 56N 76 38 E
Nizhniy Novgorod, Russia .. 18 C7 56 20N 44 0 E
Nizhniy Tagil, Russia ..... 18 C10 57 55N 59 57 E
Nizhyn, Ukraine .... 19 D5 51 5N 31 55 E
Nizip, Turkey .... 44 B3 37 5N 37 50 E
Nízké Tatry, Slovak Rep. ... 17 D10 48 55N 19 30 E
Njakwa, Malawi .... 55 E3 11 1S 33 56 E
Njanji, Zambia .... 55 E3 14 25S 31 46 E
Njinjo, Tanzania .... 55 D4 8 48S 38 54 E
Njombe, Tanzania .... 55 D3 9 20S 34 50 E
Njombe →, Tanzania ...... 54 D4 6 56S 35 6 E
Nkana, Zambia .... 55 E2 12 50S 28 8 E
Nkandla, S. Africa .... 57 D5 28 37S 31 5 E
Nkayi, Zimbabwe .... 55 F2 19 41S 29 20 E
Nkhotakota, Malawi ...... 55 E3 12 56S 34 15 E
Nkhotakota ⌒, Malawi .... 55 E3 12 50S 34 0 E
Nkongsamba, Cameroon ... 52 D1 4 55N 9 55 E
Nkurenkuru, Namibia ..... 56 B2 17 42S 18 32 E
Nmai →, Burma .... 41 G20 25 30N 97 25 E
Noakhali = Maijdi, Bangla. .. 41 H17 22 48N 91 10 E
Nobel, Canada 84 A4 45 25N 80 6W
Nobeoka, Japan .... 31 H5 32 36N 131 41 E
Noblesville, U.S.A. 82 E3 40 3N 86 1W
Noboribetsu, Japan .... 30 C10 42 24N 141 6 E
Nocera Inferiore, Italy .... 22 D6 40 44N 14 38 E
Nocona, U.S.A. 81 J6 33 47N 97 44W
Nogales, Mexico 86 A2 31 20N 110 56W
Nogales, U.S.A. 77 L8 31 20N 110 56W
Nōgata, Japan .... 31 H5 33 48N 130 44 E
Noggerup, Australia ...... 61 F2 33 32S 116 5 E
Noginsk, Russia .... 29 C10 64 30N 90 50 E
Nogoa →, Australia ...... 62 C4 23 40S 147 55 E
Nogoyá, Argentina 94 C4 32 24S 59 48W
Nohar, India .... 42 E6 29 11N 74 49 E
Nohta, India .... 43 H8 23 40N 79 34 E
Noires, Mts., France 20 B2 48 11N 3 40W
Noirmoutier, Î. de, France .. 20 C2 46 58N 2 10W
Nojane, Botswana .... 56 C3 23 15S 20 14 E
Nojima-Zaki, Japan .... 31 G9 34 54N 139 53 E
Nok Kundi, Pakistan ...... 40 E3 28 50N 62 45 E
Nok Ta Phao, Ko, Thailand . 39 b 9 23N 99 40 E
Nokaneng, Botswana ...... 56 B3 19 40S 22 17 E

Nokia, *Finland* ... 9 F20 61 30N 23 30 E
Nokomis, *Canada* ... 71 C8 51 35N 105 0W
Nokomis L., *Canada* ... 71 B8 57 0N 103 0W
Nola, *C.A.R.* ... 52 D3 3 35N 16 4 E
Noma Omuramba →, *Namibia* ... 56 B3 18 52S 20 53 E
Nombre de Dios, *Panama* ... 88 E4 9 34N 79 28W
Nome, *U.S.A.* ... 68 B3 64 30N 165 25W
Nomo-Zaki, *Japan* ... 31 H4 32 35N 129 44 E
Nonacho L., *Canada* ... 71 A7 61 42N 109 40W
Nonda, *Australia* ... 62 C3 20 40S 142 28 E
Nong Chang, *Thailand* ... 38 E2 15 23N 99 51 E
Nong Het, *Laos* ... 38 C4 19 29N 103 59 E
Nong Khai, *Thailand* ... 38 D4 17 50N 102 46 E
Nong'an, *China* ... 35 B13 44 25N 125 5 E
Nongoma, *S. Africa* ... 57 D5 27 58S 31 35 E
Nongsa, *Indonesia* ... 39 d 1 11N 104 8 E
Nonoava, *Mexico* ... 86 B3 27 28N 106 44W
Nonoava →, *Mexico* ... 86 B3 27 29N 106 45W
Nonthaburi, *Thailand* ... 38 F3 13 51N 100 34 E
Noonamah, *Australia* ... 60 B5 12 40S 131 4 E
Noord Brabant □, *Neths.* ... 15 C5 51 40N 5 0 E
Noord Holland □, *Neths.* ... 15 B4 52 30N 4 45 E
Noordbeveland, *Neths.* ... 15 C3 51 35N 3 50 E
Noordoostpolder, *Neths.* ... 15 B5 52 45N 5 45 E
Noordwijk, *Neths.* ... 15 B4 52 14N 4 26 E
Nootka I., *Canada* ... 70 D3 49 32N 126 42W
Nopiming △, *Canada* ... 71 C9 50 30N 95 37W
Noralee, *Canada* ... 70 C3 53 59N 126 26W
Noranda = Rouyn-Noranda, *Canada* ... 72 C4 48 20N 79 0W
Norco, *U.S.A.* ... 79 M9 33 56N 117 33W
Nord-Kivu □, *Dem. Rep. of the Congo* ... 54 C2 1 0S 29 0 E
Nord-Ostsee-Kanal, *Germany* ... 16 A5 54 12N 9 32 E
Nordaustlandet, *Svalbard* ... 4 B9 79 14N 23 0 E
Nordegg, *Canada* ... 70 C5 52 29N 116 5W
Norderney, *Germany* ... 16 B4 53 42N 7 9 E
Norderstedt, *Germany* ... 16 B5 53 42N 10 1 E
Nordfjord, *Norway* ... 9 F11 61 55N 5 30 E
Nordfriesische Inseln, *Germany* ... 16 A5 54 40N 8 20 E
Nordhausen, *Germany* ... 16 C6 51 30N 10 47 E
Norðoyar, *Færoe Is.* ... 8 E9 62 17N 6 35W
Nordkapp, *Norway* ... 8 A21 71 10N 25 50 E
Nordkapp, *Svalbard* ... 4 A9 80 31N 20 0 E
Nordkinn-halvøya, *Norway* ... 8 A22 70 55N 27 40 E
Nordrhein-Westfalen □, *Germany* ... 16 C4 51 45N 7 30 E
Nordvik, *Russia* ... 29 B12 74 2N 111 32 E
Nore →, *Ireland* ... 10 D4 52 25N 6 58W
Norfolk, *Canada* ... 84 D4 42 50N 80 23W
Norfolk, *Nebr., U.S.A.* ... 80 D6 42 2N 97 25W
Norfolk, *Va., U.S.A.* ... 82 G7 36 51N 76 17W
Norfolk □, *U.K.* ... 13 E8 52 39N 0 54 E
Norfolk I., *Pac. Oc.* ... 64 K8 28 58S 168 3 E
Norfork L., *U.S.A.* ... 81 G8 36 15N 92 14W
Norilsk, *Russia* ... 29 C9 69 20N 88 6 E
Norma, Mt., *Australia* ... 62 C3 20 55S 140 42 E
Normal, *U.S.A.* ... 80 E10 40 31N 88 59W
Norman, *U.S.A.* ... 81 H6 35 13N 97 26W
Norman →, *Australia* ... 62 B3 19 18S 141 51 E
Norman Wells, *Canada* ... 68 B7 65 17N 126 51W
Normanby →, *Australia* ... 62 A3 14 23S 144 10 E
Normandie, *France* ... 20 B4 48 45N 0 10 E
Normandin, *Canada* ... 72 C5 48 49N 72 31W
Normandy = Normandie, *France* ... 20 B4 48 45N 0 10 E
Normanhurst, Mt., *Australia* ... 61 E3 25 4S 122 30 E
Normanton, *Australia* ... 62 B3 17 40S 141 10 E
Normétal, *Canada* ... 72 C4 49 0N 79 22W
Norquay, *Canada* ... 71 C8 51 53N 102 5W
Norquinco, *Argentina* ... 96 E2 41 51S 70 55W
Norrbotten □, *Sweden* ... 8 C19 66 30N 22 30 E
Norris Point, *Canada* ... 73 C8 49 31N 57 53W
Norristown, *U.S.A.* ... 85 F9 40 7N 75 21W
Norrköping, *Sweden* ... 9 G17 58 37N 16 11 E
Norrland, *Sweden* ... 9 E16 62 15N 15 45 E
Norrtälje, *Sweden* ... 9 G18 59 46N 18 42 E
Norseman, *Australia* ... 61 F3 32 8S 121 43 E
Norsk, *Russia* ... 29 D14 52 30N 130 5 E
Norte, Pta. del, *Canary Is.* ... 24 G2 27 51N 17 57W
Norte, Serra do, *Brazil* ... 92 F7 11 20S 59 0W
North, C., *Canada* ... 73 C7 47 2N 60 20W
North Adams, *U.S.A.* ... 85 D11 42 42N 73 7W
North America ... 66 F10 40 0N 100 0W
North Arm, *Canada* ... 70 A5 62 0N 114 30W
North Augusta, *U.S.A.* ... 83 J5 33 30N 81 59W
North Ayrshire □, *U.K.* ... 11 F4 55 45N 4 44W
North Bass I., *U.S.A.* ... 84 E2 41 44N 82 53W
North Battleford, *Canada* ... 71 C7 52 50N 108 17W
North Bay, *Canada* ... 72 C4 46 20N 79 30W
North Belcher Is., *Canada* ... 72 A4 56 50N 79 50W
North Bend, *Oreg., U.S.A.* ... 76 E1 43 24N 124 14W
North Bend, *Pa., U.S.A.* ... 84 E7 41 20N 77 42W
North Bend, *Wash., U.S.A.* ... 78 C5 47 30N 121 47W
North Bennington, *U.S.A.* ... 85 D11 42 56N 73 15W
North Berwick, *U.K.* ... 11 E6 56 4N 2 42W
North Berwick, *U.S.A.* ... 85 C14 43 18N 70 44W
North C., *Canada* ... 73 C7 47 5N 64 0W
North C., *N.Z.* ... 59 F4 34 23S 173 4 E
North Canadian →, *U.S.A.* ... 81 H7 35 16N 95 31W
North Canton, *U.S.A.* ... 84 F3 40 53N 81 24W
North Cape = Nordkapp, *Norway* ... 8 A21 71 10N 25 50 E
North Cape = Nordkapp, *Svalbard* ... 4 A9 80 31N 20 0 E
North Caribou L., *Canada* ... 72 B1 52 50N 90 40W
North Carolina □, *U.S.A.* ... 83 H6 35 30N 80 0W
North Cascades △, *U.S.A.* ... 76 B3 48 45N 121 10W
North Channel, *Canada* ... 72 C3 46 0N 83 0W
North Channel, *U.K.* ... 11 F3 55 13N 5 52W
North Charleston, *U.S.A.* ... 83 J6 32 53N 79 58W
North Chicago, *U.S.A.* ... 82 D2 42 19N 87 51W
North Creek, *U.S.A.* ... 85 C11 43 41N 73 59W
North Dakota □, *U.S.A.* ... 80 B5 47 30N 100 15W
North Downs, *U.K.* ... 13 F8 51 19N 0 21 E
North East, *U.S.A.* ... 84 D5 42 13N 79 50W
North East Frontier Agency = Arunachal Pradesh □, *India* ... 41 F19 28 0N 95 0 E
North East Lincolnshire □, *U.K.* ... 12 D7 53 34N 0 2W
North Eastern □, *Kenya* ... 54 B5 1 30N 40 0 E
North Esk →, *U.K.* ... 11 E6 56 46N 2 24W
North European Plain, *Europe* ... 6 E10 55 0N 25 0 E
North Foreland, *U.K.* ... 13 F9 51 22N 1 28 E
North Fork, *U.S.A.* ... 78 H7 37 14N 119 21W
North Fork American →, *U.S.A.* ... 78 G5 38 57N 120 59W
North Fork Feather →, *U.S.A.* ... 78 F5 38 33N 121 30W
North Fork Grand →, *U.S.A.* ... 80 C3 45 47N 102 16W
North Fork Red →, *U.S.A.* ... 81 H5 34 24N 99 14W
North Frisian Is. = Nordfriesische Inseln, *Germany* ... 16 A5 54 40N 8 20 E

North Gower, *Canada* ... 85 A9 45 8N 75 43W
North Hd., *Australia* ... 61 F1 30 14S 114 59 E
North Henik L., *Canada* ... 71 A9 61 45N 97 40W
North Highlands, *U.S.A.* ... 78 G5 38 40N 121 23W
North Horr, *Kenya* ... 54 B4 3 20N 37 8 E
North I., *Kenya* ... 54 B4 4 5N 36 5 E
North I., *N.Z.* ... 59 H5 38 0S 175 0 E
North Kingsville, *U.S.A.* ... 84 E4 41 54N 80 42W
North Kitui △, *Kenya* ... 54 C4 0 15S 38 29 E
North Knife →, *Canada* ... 71 B10 58 53N 94 45W
North Koel →, *India* ... 43 G10 24 45N 83 50 E
North Korea ■, *Asia* ... 35 E14 40 0N 127 0 E
North Lakhimpur, *India* ... 41 F19 27 14N 94 7 E
North Las Vegas, *U.S.A.* ... 79 J11 36 12N 115 7W
North Lincolnshire □, *U.K.* ... 12 D7 53 36N 0 30W
North Little Rock, *U.S.A.* ... 81 H8 34 45N 92 16W
North Loup →, *U.S.A.* ... 80 E5 41 17N 98 24W
North Luangwa △, *Zambia* ... 55 E3 11 49S 32 9 E
North Magnetic Pole, *Canada* ... 4 A2 88 30N 107 0W
North Minch, *U.K.* ... 11 C3 58 5N 5 55W
North Moose L., *Canada* ... 71 C8 54 11N 100 6W
North Moose L., *Man., Canada* ... 71 C8 54 4N 100 12W
North Myrtle Beach, *U.S.A.* ... 83 J6 33 48N 78 42W
North Nahanni →, *Canada* ... 70 A4 62 15N 123 20W
North Olmsted, *U.S.A.* ... 84 E3 41 25N 81 56W
North Ossetia □, *Russia* ... 19 F7 43 30N 44 30 E
North Pagai, I. = Pagai Utara, Pulau, *Indonesia* ... 36 E2 2 35S 100 0 E
North Palisade, *U.S.A.* ... 78 H8 37 6N 118 31W
North Platte, *U.S.A.* ... 80 E4 41 8N 100 46W
North Platte →, *U.S.A.* ... 80 E4 41 7N 100 42W
North Pole, *Arctic* ... 4 A 90 0N 0 0W
North Portal, *Canada* ... 71 D8 49 0N 102 33W
North Powder, *U.S.A.* ... 76 D5 45 2N 117 55W
North Pt., *Barbados* ... 89 g 13 20N 59 37W
North Pt., *Trin. & Tob.* ... 93 J16 11 21N 60 31W
North Pt., *U.S.A.* ... 84 A1 45 2N 83 16W
North Rhine Westphalia = Nordrhein-Westfalen □, *Germany* ... 16 C4 51 45N 7 30 E
North River, *Canada* ... 73 B8 53 49N 57 6W
North Ronaldsay, *U.K.* ... 11 B6 59 22N 2 26W
North Saskatchewan →, *Canada* ... 71 C7 53 15N 105 5W
North Sea, *Europe* ... 14 C7 56 0N 4 0 E
North Seal →, *Canada* ... 71 B9 58 50N 98 7W
North Somerset □, *U.K.* ... 13 F5 51 24N 2 45W
North Sporades = Vóriai Sporádhes, *Greece* ... 23 E10 39 15N 23 30 E
North Sydney, *Canada* ... 73 C7 46 12N 60 15W
North Syracuse, *U.S.A.* ... 85 C8 43 8N 76 7W
North Taranaki Bight, *N.Z.* ... 59 H5 38 50S 174 15 E
North Thompson →, *Canada* ... 70 C4 50 40N 120 20W
North Tonawanda, *U.S.A.* ... 84 C6 43 2N 78 53W
North Troy, *U.S.A.* ... 85 B12 45 0N 72 24W
North Truchas Pk., *U.S.A.* ... 77 J11 36 0N 105 30W
North Twin I., *Canada* ... 72 B4 53 20N 80 0W
North Tyne →, *U.K.* ... 12 B5 55 0N 2 8W
North Uist, *U.K.* ... 11 D1 57 40N 7 15W
North Vancouver, *Canada* ... 70 D4 49 19N 123 4W
North Vernon, *U.S.A.* ... 82 F3 39 0N 85 38W
North Wabasca L., *Canada* ... 70 B6 56 0N 113 55W
North Walsham, *U.K.* ... 12 E9 52 50N 1 22 E
North West = Severo-Zapadnyy □, *Russia* ... 28 C4 65 0N 40 0 E
North-West □, *S. Africa* ... 56 D4 27 0S 25 0 E
North West C., *Australia* ... 60 D1 21 45S 114 9 E
North West Christmas I. Ridge, *Pac. Oc.* ... 65 G11 6 30N 165 0W
North West Frontier □, *Pakistan* ... 42 C4 34 0N 72 0 E
North West Highlands, *U.K.* ... 11 D4 57 33N 4 58W
North West River, *Canada* ... 73 B7 53 30N 60 10W
North Western □, *Zambia* ... 55 E2 13 30S 25 30 E
North Wildwood, *U.S.A.* ... 82 F8 39 0N 74 48W
North York Moors, *U.K.* ... 12 C7 54 23N 0 53W
North York Moors △, *U.K.* ... 12 C7 54 27N 0 51W
North Yorkshire □, *U.K.* ... 12 C6 54 15N 1 25W
Northallerton, *U.K.* ... 12 C6 54 20N 1 26W
Northam, *Australia* ... 61 F2 31 35S 116 42 E
Northam, *S. Africa* ... 56 C4 24 56S 27 18 E
Northampton, *Australia* ... 61 E1 28 27S 114 33 E
Northampton, *U.K.* ... 13 E7 52 15N 0 53W
Northampton, *Mass., U.S.A.* ... 85 D12 42 19N 72 38W
Northampton, *Pa., U.S.A.* ... 85 F9 40 41N 75 30W
Northamptonshire □, *U.K.* ... 13 E7 52 16N 0 55W
Northbridge, *U.S.A.* ... 85 D13 42 9N 71 39W
Northcliffe, *Australia* ... 61 F2 34 39S 116 7 E
Northeast Providence Chan., *W. Indies* ... 88 A4 26 0N 76 0W
Northern = Limpopo □, *S. Africa* ... 57 C4 24 5S 29 0 E
Northern □, *Malawi* ... 55 E3 11 0S 34 0 E
Northern □, *Zambia* ... 55 E3 10 30S 31 0 E
Northern Areas □, *Pakistan* ... 43 A5 36 30N 73 0 E
Northern Cape □, *S. Africa* ... 56 D3 30 0S 20 0 E
Northern Circars, *India* ... 41 L13 17 30N 82 30 E
Northern Indian L., *Canada* ... 71 B9 57 20N 97 20W
Northern Ireland □, *U.K.* ... 10 B5 54 45N 7 0W
Northern Light L., *Canada* ... 72 C1 48 15N 90 39W
Northern Marianas ☑, *Pac. Oc.* ... 64 F6 17 0N 145 0 E
Northern Province □, *S. Africa* ... 57 C4 24 0S 29 0 E
Northern Range, *Trin. & Tob.* ... 93 K15 10 46N 61 15W
Northern Territory □, *Australia* ... 60 D5 20 0S 133 0 E
Northfield, *Minn., U.S.A.* ... 80 C8 44 27N 93 9W
Northfield, *Vt., U.S.A.* ... 85 B12 44 9N 72 40W
Northland □, *N.Z.* ... 59 F4 35 30S 173 30 E
Northome, *U.S.A.* ... 80 B7 47 52N 94 17W
Northport, *Ala., U.S.A.* ... 83 J2 33 14N 87 35W
Northport, *Wash., U.S.A.* ... 76 B5 48 55N 117 48W
Northumberland □, *U.K.* ... 12 B6 55 12N 2 0W
Northumberland, C., *Australia* ... 63 F3 38 5S 140 40 E
Northumberland Is., *Australia* ... 62 C4 21 30S 149 50 E
Northumberland Str., *Canada* ... 73 C7 46 20N 64 0W
Northville, *U.S.A.* ... 85 C10 43 13N 74 11W
Northwest Providence Channel, *W. Indies* ... 88 A4 26 0N 78 0W
Northwest Territories □, *Canada* ... 68 B9 63 0N 118 0W
Northwich, *U.K.* ... 12 D5 53 15N 2 31W
Northwood, *Iowa, U.S.A.* ... 80 D8 43 27N 93 13W
Northwood, *N. Dak., U.S.A.* ... 80 B6 47 44N 97 34W
Norton, *U.S.A.* ... 80 F5 39 50N 99 53W
Norton, *Zimbabwe* ... 55 F3 17 52S 30 40 E
Norton Sd., *U.S.A.* ... 68 B3 63 50N 164 0W
Norwalk, *Calif., U.S.A.* ... 79 M8 33 54N 118 5W
Norwalk, *Conn., U.S.A.* ... 85 E11 41 7N 73 22W
Norwalk, *Iowa, U.S.A.* ... 80 E8 41 29N 93 41W
Norwalk, *Ohio, U.S.A.* ... 84 E2 41 15N 82 37W
Norway, *Maine, U.S.A.* ... 83 C10 44 13N 70 32W

Norway, *Mich., U.S.A.* ... 82 C2 45 47N 87 55W
Norway ■, *Europe* ... 8 E14 63 0N 11 0 E
Norway House, *Canada* ... 71 C9 53 59N 97 50W
Norwegian Sea, *Atl. Oc.* ... 4 C8 66 0N 1 0 E
Norwich, *Canada* ... 84 D4 42 59N 80 36W
Norwich, *U.K.* ... 13 E9 52 38N 1 18 E
Norwich, *Conn., U.S.A.* ... 85 E12 41 31N 72 5W
Norwich, *N.Y., U.S.A.* ... 85 D9 42 32N 75 32W
Norwood, *Canada* ... 84 B7 44 23N 77 59W
Norwood, *U.S.A.* ... 85 B10 44 45N 75 0W
Noshiro, *Japan* ... 30 D10 40 12N 140 0 E
Noṣratābād, *Iran* ... 45 D8 29 55N 60 0 E
Noss Hd., *U.K.* ... 11 C5 58 28N 3 3W
Nossob →, *S. Africa* ... 56 D3 26 55S 20 45 E
Nosy Barren, *Madag.* ... 53 H8 18 25S 43 40 E
Nosy Be, *Madag.* ... 53 G9 13 25S 48 15 E
Nosy Boraha, *Madag.* ... 57 B8 16 50S 49 55 E
Nosy Lava, *Madag.* ... 57 A8 14 33S 47 36 E
Nosy Varika, *Madag.* ... 57 C8 20 35S 48 32 E
Noteć →, *Poland* ... 16 B8 52 44N 15 26 E
Notikewin →, *Canada* ... 70 B5 57 2N 117 38W
Notodden, *Norway* ... 9 G13 59 35N 9 17 E
Notre Dame B., *Canada* ... 73 C8 49 45N 55 30W
Notre-Dame-de-Koartac = Quaqtaq, *Canada* ... 69 B13 60 55N 69 40W
Notre-Dame-des-Bois, *Canada* ... 85 A13 45 24N 71 4W
Notre-Dame-d'Ivugivic = Ivujivik, *Canada* ... 69 B12 62 24N 77 55W
Notre-Dame-du-Nord, *Canada* ... 72 C4 47 36N 79 30W
Nottawasaga B., *Canada* ... 84 B4 44 35N 80 15W
Nottaway →, *Canada* ... 72 B4 51 22N 78 55W
Nottingham, *U.K.* ... 12 E6 52 58N 1 10W
Nottingham, City of □, *U.K.* ... 12 E6 52 58N 1 10W
Nottingham I., *Canada* ... 69 B12 63 20N 77 55W
Nottinghamshire □, *U.K.* ... 12 D6 53 10N 1 3W
Nottoway →, *U.S.A.* ... 82 G7 36 33N 76 55W
Notwane →, *Botswana* ... 56 C4 23 35S 26 58 E
Nouâdhibou, *Mauritania* ... 50 D2 20 54N 17 0W
Nouâdhibou, Ras, *Mauritania* ... 50 D2 20 50N 17 0W
Nouakchott, *Mauritania* ... 50 E2 18 9N 15 58W
Nouméa, *N. Cal.* ... 64 K8 22 17S 166 30 E
Noupoort, *S. Africa* ... 56 E3 31 10S 24 57 E
Nouveau Comptoir = Wemindji, *Canada* ... 72 B4 53 0N 78 49W
Nouvelle-Amsterdam, Î., *Ind. Oc.* ... 3 F13 38 30S 77 30 E
Nouvelle-Calédonie = New Caledonia ☑, *Pac. Oc.* ... 64 K8 21 0S 165 0 E
Nova Casa Nova, *Brazil* ... 93 E10 9 25S 41 5W
Nova Esperança, *Brazil* ... 95 A5 23 8S 52 24W
Nova Friburgo, *Brazil* ... 95 A7 22 16S 42 30W
Nova Iguaçu, *Brazil* ... 95 A7 22 45S 43 28W
Nova Iorque, *Brazil* ... 93 E10 7 0S 44 5W
Nova Lima, *Brazil* ... 95 A7 19 59S 43 51W
Nova Lusitânia, *Mozam.* ... 55 F3 19 50S 34 34 E
Nova Mambone, *Mozam.* ... 57 C6 21 0S 35 3 E
Nova Scotia □, *Canada* ... 73 C7 45 10N 63 0W
Nova Sofala, *Mozam.* ... 57 C5 20 7S 34 42 E
Nova Venécia, *Brazil* ... 93 G10 18 45S 40 24W
Nova Zagora, *Bulgaria* ... 23 C11 42 32N 26 1 E
Novar, *Canada* ... 84 A5 45 27N 79 15W
Novara, *Italy* ... 20 B8 45 28N 8 38 E
Novato, *U.S.A.* ... 78 G4 38 6N 122 35W
Novaya Lyalya, *Russia* ... 18 B5 60 7N 32 16 E
Novaya Sibir, Ostrov, *Russia* ... 29 B16 75 10N 150 0 E
Novaya Zemlya, *Russia* ... 28 B6 75 0N 56 0 E
Nové Zámky, *Slovak Rep.* ... 17 D10 48 2N 18 8 E
Novgorod, *Russia* ... 18 C5 58 30N 31 25 E
Novgorod-Seversky = Novhorod-Siverskyy, *Ukraine* ... 18 D5 52 2N 33 10 E
Novhorod-Siverskyy, *Ukraine* ... 18 D5 52 2N 33 10 E
Novi Ligure, *Italy* ... 20 B8 44 46N 8 47 E
Novi Pazar, *Serbia & M.* ... 23 C9 43 12N 20 28 E
Novi Sad, *Serbia & M.* ... 23 B8 45 18N 19 52 E
Novo Hamburgo, *Brazil* ... 95 B5 29 37S 51 7W
Novo Mesto, *Slovenia* ... 22 B6 45 47N 15 12 E
Novo Remanso, *Brazil* ... 93 E10 9 41S 42 4W
Novoaltaysk, *Russia* ... 28 D9 53 30N 84 0 E
Novocherkassk, *Russia* ... 19 E7 47 27N 40 15 E
Novogrudok = Navahrudak, *Belarus* ... 17 B13 53 40N 25 50 E
Novohrad-Volynskyy, *Ukraine* ... 17 C14 50 34N 27 35 E
Novokachalinsk, *Russia* ... 30 B6 45 5N 132 0 E
Novokuybyshevsk, *Russia* ... 18 D8 53 7N 49 58 E
Novokuznetsk, *Russia* ... 28 D9 53 45N 87 10 E
Novomoskovsk, *Russia* ... 18 D6 54 5N 38 15 E
Novorossiysk, *Russia* ... 19 F6 44 43N 37 46 E
Novorybnoye, *Russia* ... 29 B11 72 50N 105 50 E
Novoselytsya, *Ukraine* ... 17 D14 48 14N 26 15 E
Novoshakhtinsk, *Russia* ... 19 E6 47 46N 39 58 E
Novosibirsk, *Russia* ... 28 D9 55 0N 83 5 E
Novosibirskiye Ostrova, *Russia* ... 29 B15 75 0N 142 0 E
Novotroitsk, *Russia* ... 18 D10 51 10N 58 15 E
Novouzensk, *Russia* ... 19 D8 50 32N 48 17 E
Novovolynsk, *Ukraine* ... 17 C13 50 45N 24 4 E
Novska, *Croatia* ... 22 B7 45 19N 17 0 E
Novvy Urengoy, *Russia* ... 28 C8 65 48N 76 52 E
Novyy Bor, *Russia* ... 18 A9 66 43N 52 19 E
Novyy Port, *Russia* ... 28 C8 67 40N 72 30 E
Now Shahr, *Iran* ... 45 B6 36 40N 51 30 E
Nowa Sól, *Poland* ... 16 C8 51 48N 15 44 E
Nowata, *U.S.A.* ... 81 G7 36 42N 95 38W
Nowbarān, *Iran* ... 45 C6 35 8N 49 42 E
Nowghāb, *Iran* ... 45 C8 33 53N 59 4 E
Nowgong, *Assam, India* ... 41 F18 26 20N 92 50 E
Nowgong, *Mad. P., India* ... 43 G8 25 4N 79 27 E
Nowra, *Australia* ... 63 E5 34 53S 150 35 E
Nowshera, *Pakistan* ... 40 C8 34 0N 72 0 E
Nowy Sącz, *Poland* ... 17 D11 49 40N 20 41 E
Nowy Targ, *Poland* ... 17 D11 49 29N 20 2 E
Nowy Tomyśl, *Poland* ... 16 B9 52 19N 16 10 E
Noxen, *U.S.A.* ... 85 E8 41 25N 76 4W
Noxon, *U.S.A.* ... 76 C6 48 0N 115 43W
Noyabr'sk, *Russia* ... 28 C8 64 34N 76 21 E
Noyon, *France* ... 20 B5 49 34N 2 59 E
Noyon, *Mongolia* ... 34 C2 43 2N 102 4 E
Nqutu, *S. Africa* ... 57 D5 28 13S 30 32 E
Nsanje, *Malawi* ... 55 F4 16 55S 35 12 E
Nsomba, *Zambia* ... 55 E2 10 45S 29 51 E
Nu Jiang →, *China* ... 32 D4 29 58N 97 25 E
Nu Shan, *China* ... 32 D4 26 0N 99 20 E
Nubia, *Africa* ... 48 D7 21 0N 32 0 E
Nubian Desert = Nûbîya, Es Sahrâ en, *Sudan* ... 51 D12 21 30N 33 30 E
Nûbîya, Es Sahrâ en, *Sudan* ... 51 D12 21 30N 33 30 E
Nuboai, *Indonesia* ... 37 E9 2 10S 136 30 E
Nubra →, *India* ... 43 B7 34 35N 77 35 E
Nueces →, *U.S.A.* ... 81 M6 27 51N 97 30W

Nueltin L., *Canada* ... 71 A9 60 30N 99 30W
Nueva Gerona, *Cuba* ... 88 B3 21 53N 82 49W
Nueva Palmira, *Uruguay* ... 94 C4 33 52S 58 20W
Nueva Rosita, *Mexico* ... 86 B4 28 0N 101 11W
Nueva San Salvador, *El Salv.* ... 88 D2 13 40N 89 18W
Nuéve de Julio, *Argentina* ... 94 D3 35 30S 61 0W
Nuevitas, *Cuba* ... 88 B4 21 30N 77 20W
Nuevo, G., *Argentina* ... 96 E4 43 0S 64 30W
Nuevo Casas Grandes, *Mexico* ... 86 A3 30 22N 108 0W
Nuevo Guerrero, *Mexico* ... 87 B5 26 34N 99 15W
Nuevo Laredo, *Mexico* ... 87 B5 27 30N 99 30W
Nuevo León □, *Mexico* ... 86 C5 25 0N 100 0W
Nuevo Rocafuerte, *Ecuador* ... 92 D3 0 55S 75 27W
Nugget Pt., *N.Z.* ... 59 M2 46 27S 169 50 E
Nuhaka, *N.Z.* ... 59 H6 39 3S 177 45 E
Nukey Bluff, *Australia* ... 63 E2 32 26S 135 29 E
Nukhayb, *Iraq* ... 44 C4 32 4N 42 3 E
Nuku'alofa, *Tonga* ... 59 E12 21 10S 174 0W
Nukus, *Uzbekistan* ... 28 E6 42 27N 59 41 E
Nullagine, *Australia* ... 60 D3 21 53S 120 7 E
Nullagine →, *Australia* ... 60 D3 21 20S 120 20 E
Nullarbor, *Australia* ... 61 F5 31 28S 130 55 E
Nullarbor △, *Australia* ... 61 F2 32 39S 115 37 E
Nullarbor Plain, *Australia* ... 61 F4 31 10S 129 0 E
Numalla, L., *Australia* ... 63 D3 28 43S 144 20 E
Numan, *Nigeria* ... 51 G8 9 29N 12 3 E
Numata, *Japan* ... 31 F9 36 45N 139 4 E
Numazu, *Japan* ... 31 G9 35 7N 138 51 E
Numbulwar, *Australia* ... 62 A2 14 15S 135 45 E
Numfoor, *Indonesia* ... 37 E8 1 0S 134 50 E
Numurkah, *Australia* ... 63 F4 36 5S 145 26 E
Nunaksaluk I., *Canada* ... 73 A7 55 49N 60 20W
Nunap Isua, *Greenland* ... 69 C15 59 48N 43 55W
Nunavut □, *Canada* ... 69 B11 66 0N 85 0W
Nunda, *U.S.A.* ... 84 D7 42 35N 77 56W
Nuneaton, *U.K.* ... 13 E6 52 32N 1 27W
Nungarin, *Australia* ... 61 F2 31 12S 118 6 E
Nungo, *Mozam.* ... 55 E4 13 23S 37 43 E
Nungwe, *Tanzania* ... 54 C3 2 48S 32 2 E
Nunivak I., *U.S.A.* ... 68 B3 60 10N 166 30W
Nunkun, *India* ... 43 C7 33 57N 76 2 E
Núoro, *Italy* ... 22 D3 40 20N 9 20 E
Nūrābād, *Iran* ... 45 E8 27 47N 57 12 E
Nuremberg = Nürnberg, *Germany* ... 16 D6 49 27N 11 3 E
Nuri, *Mexico* ... 86 B3 28 2N 109 22W
Nuriootpa, *Australia* ... 63 E2 34 27S 139 0 E
Nuristan □, *Afghan.* ... 40 B7 35 20N 71 0 E
Nurmes, *Finland* ... 8 E23 63 33N 29 10 E
Nürnberg, *Germany* ... 16 D6 49 27N 11 3 E
Nurpur, *Pakistan* ... 42 D4 31 53N 71 54 E
Nurran, L. = Terewah, L., *Australia* ... 63 D4 29 52S 147 35 E
Nurrari Lakes, *Australia* ... 61 E5 29 1S 130 5 E
Nusa Barung, *Indonesia* ... 37 H15 8 30S 113 30 E
Nusa Dua, *Indonesia* ... 37 K18 8 48S 115 14 E
Nusa Kambangan, *Indonesia* ... 37 G13 7 40S 108 10 E
Nusa Tenggara Barat □, *Indonesia* ... 36 F5 8 50S 117 30 E
Nusa Tenggara Timur □, *Indonesia* ... 37 F6 9 30S 122 0 E
Nusaybin, *Turkey* ... 19 G7 37 3N 41 10 E
Nushki, *Pakistan* ... 42 E2 29 35N 66 0 E
Nuuk, *Greenland* ... 69 B14 64 10N 51 35W
Nuwakot, *Nepal* ... 43 E10 28 10N 83 55 E
Nuweiba', *Egypt* ... 44 D2 28 59N 34 39 E
Nuwerus, *S. Africa* ... 56 E2 31 8S 18 24 E
Nuweveldberge, *S. Africa* ... 56 E3 32 10S 21 45 E
Nuyts, C., *Australia* ... 61 F5 32 2S 132 21 E
Nuyts, Pt., *Australia* ... 61 G2 35 4S 116 38 E
Nuyts Arch., *Australia* ... 63 E1 32 35S 133 20 E
Nxai Pan △, *Botswana* ... 56 B3 19 50S 24 46 E
Nxau-Nxau, *Botswana* ... 56 B3 18 57S 21 4 E
Nyabing, *Australia* ... 61 F2 33 33S 118 9 E
Nyack, *U.S.A.* ... 85 E11 41 5N 73 55W
Nyagan, *Russia* ... 28 C7 62 30N 65 38 E
Nyahanga, *Tanzania* ... 54 C3 2 20S 33 37 E
Nyahua, *Tanzania* ... 54 D3 5 25S 33 23 E
Nyahururu, *Kenya* ... 54 B4 0 2N 36 27 E
Nyainqentanglha Shan, *China* ... 32 D4 30 0N 90 0 E
Nyakanazi, *Tanzania* ... 54 C3 3 2S 31 10 E
Nyâlâ, *Sudan* ... 51 F10 12 2N 24 58 E
Nyamandhlovu, *Zimbabwe* ... 55 F2 19 55S 28 16 E
Nyambiti, *Tanzania* ... 54 C3 2 48S 33 27 E
Nyamwaga, *Tanzania* ... 54 C3 1 27S 34 33 E
Nyandekwa, *Tanzania* ... 54 C3 3 57S 32 32 E
Nyandoma, *Russia* ... 18 B7 61 40N 40 12 E
Nyanga △, *Zimbabwe* ... 55 F3 18 17S 32 46 E
Nyangana, *Namibia* ... 56 B3 18 0S 20 40 E
Nyanguge, *Tanzania* ... 54 C3 2 30S 33 12 E
Nyanza, *Rwanda* ... 54 C2 2 20S 29 42 E
Nyanza □, *Kenya* ... 54 C3 0 10S 34 15 E
Nyanza-Lac, *Burundi* ... 54 C2 4 21S 29 36 E
Nyasa, L., *Africa* ... 55 E3 12 30S 34 30 E
Nyasvizh, *Belarus* ... 17 B14 53 14N 26 38 E
Nyazepetrovsk, *Russia* ... 18 C10 56 3N 59 36 E
Nyazura, *Zimbabwe* ... 55 F3 18 40S 32 16 E
Nyazwidzi →, *Zimbabwe* ... 55 G3 20 0S 31 17 E
Nybro, *Sweden* ... 9 H16 56 44N 15 55 E
Nyda, *Russia* ... 28 C8 66 40N 72 58 E
Nyeri, *Kenya* ... 54 C4 0 23S 36 56 E
Nyika △, *Malawi* ... 55 E3 10 30S 33 53 E
Nyíregyháza, *Hungary* ... 17 E11 47 58N 21 47 E
Nykøbing, *Storstrøm, Denmark* ... 9 J14 54 56N 11 52 E
Nykøbing, *Vestsjælland, Denmark* ... 9 J14 55 55N 11 40 E
Nykøbing, *Viborg, Denmark* ... 9 H13 56 48N 8 51 E
Nyköping, *Sweden* ... 9 G17 58 45N 17 1 E
Nylstroom = Modimolle, *S. Africa* ... 57 C4 24 42N 28 22 E
Nymagee, *Australia* ... 63 E4 32 7S 146 20 E
Nymboida △, *Australia* ... 63 D5 29 38S 152 26 E
Nynäshamn, *Sweden* ... 9 G17 58 54N 17 57 E
Nyngan, *Australia* ... 63 E4 31 30S 147 8 E
Nyoman = Nemunas →, *Lithuania* ... 9 J19 55 25N 21 10 E
Nysa, *Poland* ... 17 C9 50 30N 17 22 E
Nysa →, *Europe* ... 16 B8 52 4N 14 46 E
Nyssa, *U.S.A.* ... 76 E5 43 53N 117 0W
Nyunzu, *Dem. Rep. of the Congo* ... 54 D2 5 57S 27 58 E
Nyurba, *Russia* ... 29 C12 63 17N 118 28 E
Nzega, *Tanzania* ... 54 C3 4 10S 33 12 E
Nzérékoré, *Guinea* ... 50 G4 7 49N 8 48W
Nzeto, *Angola* ... 52 F2 7 10S 12 52 E
Nzilo, Chutes de, *Dem. Rep. of the Congo* ... 55 E2 10 18S 25 27 E
Nzubuka, *Tanzania* ... 54 C3 4 45S 32 50 E

O

Ō-Shima, Japan 31 G9 34 44N 139 24 E
Oa, Mull of, U.K. 11 F2 55 35N 6 20W
Oacoma, U.S.A. 80 D5 43 48N 99 24W
Oahe, L., U.S.A. 80 C4 44 27N 100 24W
Oahe Dam, U.S.A. 80 C4 44 27N 100 24W
Oahu, U.S.A. 74 H16 21 28N 157 58W
Oak Harbor, U.S.A. 78 B4 48 18N 122 39W
Oak Hill, U.S.A. 82 G5 37 59N 81 9W
Oak Ridge, U.S.A. 83 G3 36 1N 84 16W
Oak View, U.S.A. 79 L7 34 24N 119 18W
Oakan-Dake, Japan 30 C12 43 27N 144 10 E
Oakdale, Calif., U.S.A. 78 H6 37 46N 120 51W
Oakdale, La., U.S.A. 81 K8 30 49N 92 40W
Oakes, U.S.A. 80 B5 46 8N 98 6W
Oakesdale, U.S.A. 76 C5 47 8N 117 15W
Oakey, Australia 63 D5 27 25S 151 43 E
Oakfield, U.S.A. 84 C6 43 4N 78 16W
Oakham, U.K. 13 E7 52 40N 0 43W
Oakhurst, U.S.A. 78 H7 37 19N 119 40W
Oakland, U.S.A. 78 H4 37 49N 122 16W
Oakley, Idaho, U.S.A. 76 E7 42 15N 113 53W
Oakley, Kans., U.S.A. 80 F4 39 8N 100 51W
Oakover →, Australia 60 D3 21 0S 120 40 E
Oakridge, U.S.A. 76 E2 43 45N 122 28W
Oakville, Canada 84 C5 43 27N 79 41W
Oakville, U.S.A. 78 D3 46 51N 123 14W
Oamaru, N.Z. 59 L3 45 5S 170 59 E
Oasis, Calif., U.S.A. 79 M10 33 28N 116 6W
Oasis, Nev., U.S.A. 78 H9 37 29N 117 55W
Oates Land, Antarctica 5 C11 69 0S 160 0 E
Oatlands, Australia 63 G4 42 17S 147 21 E
Oatman, U.S.A. 79 K12 35 1N 114 19W
Oaxaca, Mexico 87 D5 17 2N 96 40W
Oaxaca □, Mexico 87 D5 17 0N 97 0W
Ob →, Russia 28 C7 66 45N 69 30 E
Oba, Canada 72 C3 49 4N 84 7W
Obama, Japan 31 G7 35 30N 135 45 E
Oban, U.K. 11 E3 56 25N 5 29W
Obbia, Somali Rep. 47 F4 5 25N 48 30 E
Obera, Argentina 95 B4 27 21S 55 2W
Oberhausen, Germany 16 C4 51 28N 6 51 E
Oberlin, Kans., U.S.A. 80 F4 39 49N 100 32W
Oberlin, La., U.S.A. 81 K8 30 37N 92 46W
Oberlin, Ohio, U.S.A. 84 E2 41 18N 82 13W
Oberon, Australia 63 E4 33 45S 149 52 E
Obi, Indonesia 37 E7 1 23S 127 45 E
Óbidos, Brazil 93 D7 1 50S 55 30W
Obihiro, Japan 30 C11 42 56N 143 12 E
Obilatu, Indonesia 37 E7 1 25S 127 20 E
Obluchye, Russia 29 E14 49 1N 131 4 E
Obo, C.A.R. 54 A2 5 20N 26 32 E
Oboa, Mt., Uganda 54 B3 1 45N 34 45 E
Oboyan, Russia 28 D4 51 15N 36 21 E
Obozerskaya = Obozerskiy, Russia 18 B7 63 34N 40 21 E
Obozerskiy, Russia 18 B7 63 34N 40 21 E
Observatory Inlet, Canada 70 B3 55 10N 129 54W
Obshchi Syrt, Russia 6 E16 52 0N 53 0 E
Obskaya Guba, Russia 28 C8 69 0N 73 0 E
Obuasi, Ghana 50 G5 6 17N 1 40W
Ocala, U.S.A. 83 L4 29 11N 82 8W
Ocampo, Chihuahua, Mexico 86 B3 28 9N 108 24W
Ocampo, Tamaulipas, Mexico 87 C5 22 50N 99 20W
Ocaña, Spain 21 C4 39 55N 3 30W
Oconomowoc, U.S.A. 80 D10 43 7N 88 30W
Occidental, Cordillera, Colombia 92 C3 5 0N 76 0W
Occidental, Grand Erg, Algeria 50 B6 30 20N 1 0 E
Ocean City, Md., U.S.A. 82 F8 38 20N 75 5W
Ocean City, N.J., U.S.A. 82 F8 39 17N 74 35W
Ocean City, Wash., U.S.A. 78 C2 47 4N 124 10W
Ocean Falls, Canada 70 C3 52 18N 127 48W
Ocean I. = Banaba, Kiribati 64 H8 0 45S 169 50 E
Ocean Park, U.S.A. 78 D2 46 30N 124 3W
Oceano, U.S.A. 79 K6 35 6N 120 37W
Oceanport, U.S.A. 85 F10 40 19N 74 3W
Oceanside, U.S.A. 79 M9 33 12N 117 23W
Ochil Hills, U.K. 11 E5 56 14N 3 40W
Ocho Rios, Jamaica 88 a 18 24N 77 6W
Ocilla, U.S.A. 83 K4 31 36N 83 15W
Ocmulgee →, U.S.A. 83 K4 31 58N 82 33W
Ocniţa, Moldova 17 D14 48 25N 27 30 E
Oconee →, U.S.A. 83 K4 31 58N 82 33W
Oconto, U.S.A. 82 C2 44 53N 87 52W
Oconto Falls, U.S.A. 82 C1 44 52N 88 9W
Ocosingo, Mexico 87 D6 17 10N 92 15W
Ocotal, Nic. 88 D2 13 41N 86 31W
Ocotlán, Mexico 86 C4 20 21N 102 42W
Ocotlán de Morelos, Mexico 87 D5 16 48N 96 40W
Ōda, Japan 31 G6 35 11N 132 30 E
Ódáðahraun, Iceland 8 D5 65 5N 17 0W
Odate, Japan 30 D10 40 16N 140 34 E
Odawara, Japan 31 G9 35 20N 139 6 E
Odda, Norway 9 F12 60 3N 6 35 E
Odei →, Canada 71 B9 56 6N 96 54W
Ödemiş, Turkey 23 E13 38 15N 28 0 E
Odendaalsrus, S. Africa 56 D4 27 48S 26 45 E
Odense, Denmark 9 J14 55 22N 10 23 E
Oder →, Europe 16 B8 53 33N 14 38 E
Odesa, Ukraine 19 E5 46 30N 30 45 E
Odessa = Odesa, Ukraine 19 E5 46 30N 30 45 E
Odessa, Canada 85 B8 44 17N 76 43W
Odessa, Tex., U.S.A. 81 K3 31 52N 102 23W
Odessa, Wash., U.S.A. 76 C4 47 20N 118 41W
Odiakwe, Botswana 56 C4 20 12S 25 17 E
Odienné, Ivory C. 50 G4 9 30N 7 34W
Odintsovo, Russia 18 C6 55 39N 37 15 E
O'Donnell, U.S.A. 81 J4 32 58N 101 50W
Odorheiu Secuiesc, Romania 17 E13 46 21N 25 21 E
Odra = Oder →, Europe 16 B8 53 33N 14 38 E
Odzi, Zimbabwe 57 B5 19 0S 32 20 E
Odzi →, Zimbabwe 57 B5 19 45S 32 23 E
Oeiras, Brazil 93 E10 7 0S 42 8W
Oelrichs, U.S.A. 80 D3 43 11N 103 14W
Oelwein, U.S.A. 80 D9 42 41N 91 55W
Oenpelli, Australia 60 B5 12 20S 133 4 E
Ofanto →, Italy 22 D7 41 22N 16 13 E
Offa, Nigeria 50 G6 8 13N 4 42 E
Offaly □, Ireland 10 C4 53 15N 7 30W
Offenbach, Germany 16 C5 50 6N 8 44 E
Offenburg, Germany 16 D4 48 28N 7 56 E
Ofotfjorden, Norway 8 B17 68 27N 17 0 E
Ōfunato, Japan 30 E10 39 4N 141 43 E
Oga, Japan 30 E9 39 55N 139 50 E
Oga-Hantō, Japan 30 E9 39 58N 139 47 E
Ogaden, Ethiopia 47 F3 7 30N 45 30 E
Ōgaki, Japan 31 G8 35 21N 136 37 E
Ogallala, U.S.A. 80 E4 41 8N 101 43W
Ogasawara Gunto, Pac. Oc. 26 G18 27 0N 142 0 E
Ogbomosho, Nigeria 50 G6 8 1N 4 11 E
Ogden, U.S.A. 76 F7 41 13N 111 58W
Ogdensburg, U.S.A. 85 B9 44 42N 75 30W
Ogeechee →, U.S.A. 83 K5 31 50N 81 3W
Ogilby, U.S.A. 79 N12 32 49N 114 50W
Oglio →, Italy 22 B4 45 2N 10 39 E
Ogmore, Australia 62 C4 22 37S 149 35 E
Ogoki, Canada 72 B2 51 38N 85 58W
Ogoki →, Canada 72 B2 51 38N 85 57W
Ogoki L., Canada 72 B2 50 50N 87 10W
Ogoki Res., Canada 72 B2 50 45N 88 15W
Ogooué →, Gabon 52 E1 1 0S 9 0 E
Ogowe = Ogooué →, Gabon 52 E1 1 0S 9 0 E
Ogre, Latvia 9 H21 56 49N 24 36 E
Ogurchinskiy, Ostrov, Turkmenistan 45 B7 38 55N 53 2 E
Ohai, N.Z. 59 L2 45 55S 168 0 E
Ohakune, N.Z. 59 H5 39 24S 175 24 E
Ohata, Japan 30 D10 41 24N 141 10 E
Ohau, L., N.Z. 59 L2 44 15S 169 53 E
Ohio □, U.S.A. 84 F2 40 15N 82 45W
Ohio →, U.S.A. 82 G1 36 59N 89 8W
Ohře →, Czech Rep. 16 C8 50 30N 14 10 E
Ohrid, Macedonia 23 D9 41 8N 20 52 E
Ohridsko Jezero, Macedonia 23 D9 41 8N 20 52 E
Ohrigstad, S. Africa 57 C5 24 39S 30 36 E
Oiapoque, Brazil 93 3 50N 51 50W
Oikou, China 35 E9 38 35N 117 42 E
Oil City, U.S.A. 84 E5 41 26N 79 42W
Oil Springs, Canada 84 D2 42 47N 82 7W
Oildale, U.S.A. 79 K7 35 25N 119 1W
Oise →, France 20 B5 49 0N 2 4 E
Oistins, Barbados 89 g 13 4N 59 33W
Oistins B., Barbados 89 g 13 4N 59 33W
Ōita, Japan 31 H5 33 14N 131 36 E
Ōita □, Japan 31 H5 33 15N 131 30 E
Oiticica, Brazil 93 E10 5 3S 41 5W
Ojacaliente, Mexico 86 C4 22 34N 102 15W
Ojai, U.S.A. 79 L7 34 27N 119 15W
Ojinaga, Mexico 86 B4 29 34N 104 25W
Ojiya, Japan 31 F9 37 18N 138 48 E
Ojo de Liebre ⌓, Mexico 86 B2 27 50N 114 0W
Ojos del Salado, Cerro, Argentina 94 B2 27 0S 68 40W
Oka →, Russia 18 C7 56 20N 43 59 E
Okaba, Indonesia 37 F9 8 6S 139 42 E
Okahandja, Namibia 56 C2 22 0S 16 59 E
Okanagan L., Canada 70 D5 50 0N 119 30W
Okanogan, U.S.A. 76 B4 48 22N 119 35W
Okanogan →, U.S.A. 76 B4 48 6N 119 44W
Okapi △, Dem. Rep. of the Congo 54 B2 2 30N 27 20 E
Okaputa, Namibia 56 C2 20 5S 17 0 E
Okara, Pakistan 42 D5 30 50N 73 31 E
Okaukuejo, Namibia 56 B2 19 10S 16 0 E
Okavango Delta, Botswana 56 B3 18 45S 22 45 E
Okavango Swamp = Okavango Delta, Botswana 56 B3 18 45S 22 45 E
Okaya, Japan 31 F9 36 5N 138 10 E
Okayama, Japan 31 G6 34 40N 133 54 E
Okayama □, Japan 31 G6 35 0N 133 50 E
Okazaki, Japan 31 G8 34 57N 137 10 E
Okeechobee, U.S.A. 83 M5 27 15N 80 50W
Okeechobee, L., U.S.A. 83 M5 27 0N 80 50W
Okefenokee ⌓, U.S.A. 83 K4 30 44N 82 7W
Okefenokee Swamp, U.S.A. 83 K4 30 40N 82 20W
Okehampton, U.K. 13 G4 50 44N 4 0W
Okha, India 42 H3 22 27N 69 4 E
Okha, Russia 29 D15 53 40N 143 0 E
Okhotsk, Russia 29 D15 59 20N 143 10 E
Okhotsk, Sea of, Asia 29 D15 55 0N 145 0 E
Okhotskiy Perevoz, Russia 29 C14 61 52N 135 35 E
Okhtyrka, Ukraine 19 D5 50 25N 35 0 E
Oki-Shotō, Japan 31 F6 36 5N 133 15 E
Okiep, S. Africa 56 D2 29 39S 17 53 E
Okinawa □, Japan 31 L4 26 40N 128 0 E
Okinawa-Guntō, Japan 31 L4 26 40N 128 0 E
Okinawa-Jima, Japan 31 L4 26 32N 128 0 E
Okino-erabu-Shima, Japan 31 L4 27 21N 128 33 E
Oklahoma □, U.S.A. 81 H6 35 20N 97 30W
Oklahoma City, U.S.A. 81 H6 35 30N 97 30W
Okmulgee, U.S.A. 81 H7 35 37N 95 58W
Oknitsa = Ocniţa, Moldova 17 D14 48 25N 27 30 E
Okolo, Uganda 54 B3 2 37N 31 8 E
Okolona, U.S.A. 81 J10 34 0N 88 45W
Okombahe, Namibia 56 C2 21 23S 15 22 E
Okotoks, Canada 70 C6 50 43N 113 58W
Oksibil, Indonesia 37 E10 4 59S 140 35 E
Oksovskiy, Russia 18 B6 62 33N 39 57 E
Oktabrsk = Oktyabrsk, Kazakhstan 19 E10 49 28N 57 25 E
Oktyabrsk, Kazakhstan 19 E10 49 28N 57 25 E
Oktyabrskiy = Aktsyabrski, Belarus 17 B15 52 38N 28 53 E
Oktyabrskiy, Russia 18 D9 54 28N 53 28 E
Oktyabrskoy Revolyutsii, Ostrov, Russia 29 B10 79 30N 97 0 E
Okuru, N.Z. 59 K2 43 55S 168 55 E
Okushiri-Tō, Japan 30 C9 42 15N 139 30 E
Okwa →, Botswana 56 C3 22 30S 23 0 E
Ola, U.S.A. 81 H8 35 2N 93 13W
Ólafsfjörður, Iceland 8 C4 66 4N 18 39W
Ólafsvík, Iceland 8 D2 64 53N 23 43W
Olancha, U.S.A. 79 J8 36 17N 118 1W
Olancha Pk., U.S.A. 79 J8 36 15N 118 7W
Olanchito, Honduras 88 C2 15 30N 86 30W
Öland, Sweden 9 H17 56 45N 16 38 E
Olary, Australia 63 E3 32 18S 140 19 E
Olascoaga, Argentina 94 D3 35 15S 60 39W
Olathe, U.S.A. 80 F7 38 53N 94 49W
Olavarría, Argentina 94 D3 36 55S 60 20W
Oława, Poland 17 C9 50 57N 17 20 E
Ólbia, Italy 22 D3 40 55N 9 31 E
Olcott, U.S.A. 84 C6 43 20N 78 42W
Old Bahama Chan. = Bahama, Canal Viejo de, W. Indies 88 B4 22 10N 77 30W
Old Baldy Pk. = San Antonio, Mt., U.S.A. 79 L9 34 17N 117 38W
Old Castile = Castilla y Leon □, Spain 21 B3 42 0N 5 0W
Old Crow, Canada 68 B6 67 30N 139 55W
Old Dale, U.S.A. 79 L11 34 8N 115 47W
Old Forge, N.Y., U.S.A. 85 C10 43 43N 74 58W
Old Forge, Pa., U.S.A. 85 E9 41 22N 75 45W
Old Perlican, Canada 73 C9 48 5N 53 1W
Old Shinyanga, Tanzania 54 C3 3 33S 33 27 E
Old Speck Mt., U.S.A. 85 B14 44 34N 70 57W
Old Town, U.S.A. 83 C11 44 56N 68 39W
Old Washington, U.S.A. 84 F3 40 2N 81 27W
Old Wives L., Canada 71 C7 50 5N 106 0W
Oldbury, U.K. 13 F5 51 38N 2 33W
Oldcastle, Ireland 10 C4 53 46N 7 10W
Oldeani, Tanzania 54 C4 3 22S 35 35 E
Oldenburg, Germany 16 B5 53 9N 8 13 E
Oldenzaal, Neths. 15 B6 52 19N 6 53 E
Oldham, U.K. 12 D5 53 33N 2 7W
Oldman →, Canada 70 D6 49 57N 111 42W
Oldmeldrum, U.K. 11 D6 57 20N 2 19W
Olds, Canada 70 C6 51 50N 114 10W
Olduvai Gorge, Tanzania 54 C4 2 57S 35 23 E
Oldziyt, Mongolia 34 B5 44 40N 109 1 E
Olean, U.S.A. 84 D6 42 5N 78 26W
Olekma →, Russia 29 C13 60 22N 120 42 E
Olekminsk, Russia 29 C13 60 25N 120 30 E
Oleksandriya, Ukraine 17 C14 50 37N 26 19 E
Olema, U.S.A. 78 G4 38 3N 122 47W
Olenegorsk, Russia 18 A5 68 9N 33 18 E
Olenek, Russia 29 C12 68 28N 112 18 E
Olenek →, Russia 29 B13 73 0N 120 10 E
Oléron, Î. d', France 20 D3 45 55N 1 15W
Oleśnica, Poland 17 C9 51 13N 17 22 E
Olevsk, Ukraine 17 C14 51 12N 27 39 E
Olga, Russia 29 E14 43 50N 135 14 E
Olga, L., Canada 72 C4 49 47N 77 15W
Olga, Mt., Australia 61 E5 25 20S 130 50 E
Ölgiy, Mongolia 32 B3 48 56N 89 57 E
Olhão, Portugal 21 D2 37 3N 7 48W
Olifants = Elefantes →, Africa 57 C5 24 10S 32 40 E
Olifants →, Namibia 56 C2 25 30S 19 30 E
Olifantshoek, S. Africa 56 D3 27 57S 22 42 E
Ólimbos, Óros, Greece 23 D10 40 6N 22 23 E
Olímpia, Brazil 95 A6 20 44S 48 54W
Olinda, Brazil 93 E12 8 1S 34 51W
Oliva, Argentina 94 C3 32 0S 63 38W
Olivehurst, U.S.A. 78 F5 39 6N 121 34W
Olivenza, Spain 21 C2 38 41N 7 9W
Oliver, Canada 70 D5 49 13N 119 37W
Oliver L., Canada 71 B8 56 56N 103 22W
Ollagüe, Chile 94 A2 21 15S 68 10W
Olney, Ill., U.S.A. 82 F1 38 44N 88 5W
Olney, Tex., U.S.A. 81 J5 33 22N 98 45W
Olomane →, Canada 73 B7 50 14N 60 37W
Olomouc, Czech Rep. 17 D9 49 38N 17 12 E
Olonets, Russia 18 B5 61 0N 32 54 E
Olongapo, Phil. 37 B6 14 50N 120 18 E
Olot, Spain 21 A7 42 11N 2 30 E
Olovyannaya, Russia 29 D12 50 58N 115 35 E
Oloy →, Russia 29 C16 66 29N 159 29 E
Olsztyn, Poland 17 B11 53 48N 20 29 E
Olt →, Romania 17 G13 43 43N 24 51 E
Olteniţa, Romania 17 F14 44 7N 26 42 E
Olton, U.S.A. 81 H3 34 11N 102 8W
Olymbos, Cyprus 25 D12 35 21N 33 45 E
Olympia, Greece 23 F9 37 39N 21 39 E
Olympia, U.S.A. 78 D4 47 3N 122 53W
Olympic △, U.S.A. 78 C3 47 48N 123 30W
Olympic Dam, Australia 63 E2 30 30S 136 55 E
Olympic Mts., U.S.A. 78 C3 47 55N 123 45W
Olympus, Cyprus 25 E11 34 56N 32 52 E
Olympus, Mt. = Ólimbos, Óros, Greece 23 D10 40 6N 22 23 E
Olympus, Mt. = Uludağ, Turkey 23 D13 40 4N 29 13 E
Olympus, Mt., U.S.A. 78 C3 47 48N 123 43W
Olyphant, U.S.A. 85 E9 41 27N 75 36W
Om →, Russia 28 D8 54 59N 73 22 E
Om Koi, Thailand 38 D2 17 48N 98 22 E
Ōma, Japan 30 D10 41 45N 141 5 E
Ōmachi, Japan 31 F8 36 30N 137 50 E
Omae-Zaki, Japan 31 G9 34 36N 138 14 E
Ōmagari, Japan 30 E10 39 27N 140 29 E
Omagh, U.K. 10 B4 54 36N 7 19W
Omagh □, U.K. 10 B4 54 35N 7 15W
Omaha, U.S.A. 80 E7 41 17N 95 58W
Omak, U.S.A. 76 B4 48 25N 119 31W
Omalos, Greece 25 D5 35 19N 23 55 E
Oman ■, Asia 47 C6 23 0N 58 0 E
Oman, G. of, Asia 45 E8 24 30N 58 30 E
Omaruru, Namibia 56 C2 21 26S 16 0 E
Omaruru →, Namibia 56 C1 22 7S 14 15 E
Omate, Peru 92 G4 16 45S 71 0W
Ombai, Selat, Indonesia 37 F6 8 30S 124 50 E
Omboué, Gabon 52 E1 1 35S 9 15 E
Ombrone →, Italy 22 C4 42 42N 11 5 E
Omdurmân, Sudan 51 E12 15 40N 32 28 E
Omemee, Canada 84 B6 44 18N 78 33W
Omeonga, Dem. Rep. of the Congo 54 C1 3 40S 24 22 E
Ometepe, I. de, Nic. 88 D2 11 32N 85 35W
Ometepec, Mexico 87 D5 16 39N 98 23W
Ominato, Japan 30 D10 41 17N 141 10 E
Omineca →, Canada 70 B4 56 3N 124 16W
Omitara, Namibia 56 C2 22 16S 18 2 E
Ōmiya, Japan 31 G9 35 54N 139 38 E
Ommen, Neths. 15 B6 52 31N 6 26 E
Ömnögovĭ □, Mongolia 34 C3 43 15N 104 0 E
Omo →, Ethiopia 47 F2 6 25N 36 10 E
Omodhos, Cyprus 25 E11 34 51N 32 48 E
Omolon →, Russia 29 C16 68 42N 158 36 E
Omono-Gawa →, Japan 30 E10 39 46N 140 3 E
Omsk, Russia 28 D8 55 0N 73 12 E
Omsukchan, Russia 29 C16 62 32N 155 48 E
Ōmu, Japan 30 B11 44 34N 142 58 E
Omul, Vf., Romania 17 F13 45 27N 25 29 E
Ōmura, Japan 31 H4 32 56N 129 57 E
Omuramba Omatako →, Namibia 56 B2 17 45S 20 25 E
Omuramba Ovambo →, Namibia 56 B2 18 45S 16 59 E
Ōmuta, Japan 31 H5 33 5N 130 26 E
Onaga, U.S.A. 80 F6 39 29N 96 10W
Onalaska, U.S.A. 80 D9 43 53N 91 14W
Onancock, U.S.A. 82 G8 37 43N 75 45W
Onang, Indonesia 37 E5 3 2S 118 49 E
Onaping L., Canada 72 C3 47 3N 81 30W
Onavas, Mexico 86 B3 28 28N 109 30W
Onawa, U.S.A. 80 D6 42 2N 96 6W
Oncócua, Angola 56 B1 16 30S 13 25 E
Onda, Spain 21 C5 39 55N 0 17W
Ondaejin, N. Korea 35 D15 41 34N 129 40 E
Ondangwa, Namibia 56 B2 17 57S 16 4 E
Ondjiva, Angola 56 B2 16 48S 15 50 E
Öndörshil, Mongolia 34 B5 45 13N 108 5 E
Öndverðarnes, Iceland 8 D1 64 52N 24 0W
One Tree, Australia 63 E3 34 11S 144 43 E
Onega, Russia 18 B6 64 0N 38 10 E
Onega →, Russia 18 B6 63 58N 38 2 E
Onega, G. of = Onezhskaya Guba, Russia 18 B6 64 24N 36 38 E
Onega, L. = Onezhskoye Ozero, Russia 18 B6 61 44N 35 22 E
Oneida, U.S.A. 85 C9 43 6N 75 39W
Oneida L., U.S.A. 85 C9 43 12N 75 54W
O'Neill, U.S.A. 80 D5 42 27N 98 39W
Onekotan, Ostrov, Russia 29 E16 49 25N 154 45 E
Onema, Dem. Rep. of the Congo 54 C1 4 35S 24 30 E
Oneonta, U.S.A. 85 D9 42 27N 75 4W
Oneşti, Romania 17 E14 46 17N 26 47 E
Onezhskaya Guba, Russia 18 B6 64 24N 36 38 E
Onezhskoye Ozero, Russia 18 B6 61 44N 35 22 E
Ongarue, N.Z. 59 H5 38 42S 175 19 E
Ongers →, S. Africa 56 E3 31 4S 23 13 E
Ongerup, Australia 61 F2 33 58S 118 28 E
Ongjin, N. Korea 35 F13 37 56N 125 21 E
Ongkharak, Thailand 38 E3 14 8N 101 1 E
Ongniud Qi, China 35 C10 43 0N 118 38 E
Ongoka, Dem. Rep. of the Congo 54 C2 1 20S 26 0 E
Ongole, India 40 M12 15 33N 80 2 E
Ongon = Havirga, Mongolia 34 B7 45 41N 113 5 E
Onida, U.S.A. 80 C4 44 42N 100 4W
Onilahy →, Madag. 57 C7 23 34S 43 45 E
Onitsha, Nigeria 50 G7 6 6N 6 42 E
Onoda, Japan 31 G5 33 59N 131 11 E
Onpyŏng-ni, S. Korea 35 H14 33 25N 126 55 E
Onslow, Australia 60 D2 21 40S 115 12 E
Onslow B., U.S.A. 83 H7 34 20N 77 15W
Ontake-San, Japan 31 G8 35 53N 137 29 E
Ontario, Calif., U.S.A. 79 L9 34 4N 117 39W
Ontario, Oreg., U.S.A. 76 D5 44 2N 116 58W
Ontario □, Canada 72 B2 48 0N 83 0W
Ontario, L., N. Amer. 84 C7 43 20N 78 0W
Ontonagon, U.S.A. 80 B10 46 52N 89 19W
Onyx, U.S.A. 79 K8 35 41N 118 14W
Oodnadatta, Australia 63 D2 27 33S 135 30 E
Ooldea, Australia 61 F5 30 27S 131 50 E
Oombulgurri, Australia 60 C4 15 15S 127 45 E
Oorindi, Australia 62 C3 20 40S 141 1 E
Oost-Vlaanderen □, Belgium 15 C3 51 5N 3 50 E
Oostende, Belgium 15 C2 51 15N 2 54 E
Oosterhout, Neths. 15 C4 51 39N 4 47 E
Oosterschelde →, Neths. 15 C4 51 33N 4 0 E
Oosterwolde, Neths. 15 B6 53 0N 6 17 E
Ootacamund = Udagamandalam, India 40 P10 11 30N 76 44 E
Ootsa L., Canada 70 C3 53 50N 126 2W
Op Luang △, Thailand 38 C2 18 12N 98 32 E
Opala, Dem. Rep. of the Congo 54 C1 0 40S 24 20 E
Opanake, Sri Lanka 40 R12 6 35N 80 40 E
Opasatika, Canada 72 C3 49 30N 82 50W
Opasquia ⌓, Canada 72 B1 53 33N 93 5W
Opava, Czech Rep. 17 D9 49 57N 17 58 E
Opelika, U.S.A. 83 J3 32 39N 85 23W
Opelousas, U.S.A. 81 K8 30 32N 92 5W
Opémisca, L., Canada 72 C5 49 56N 74 52W
Opheim, U.S.A. 76 B10 48 51N 106 24W
Ophthalmia Ra., Australia 60 D2 23 15S 119 30 E
Opinaca →, Canada 72 B4 52 15N 78 2W
Opinaca, Rés., Canada 72 B4 52 39N 76 20W
Opinnagau →, Canada 72 B3 54 12N 82 25W
Opiscotéo, L., Canada 73 B6 53 10N 68 10W
Opole, Poland 17 C9 50 42N 17 58 E
Oponono L., Namibia 56 B2 18 8S 15 45 E
Oporto = Porto, Portugal 21 B1 41 8N 8 40W
Opotiki, N.Z. 59 H6 38 1S 177 19 E
Opp, U.S.A. 83 K2 31 17N 86 16W
Oppdal, Norway 9 E13 62 35N 9 41 E
Opportunity, U.S.A. 76 C5 47 39N 117 15W
Opua, N.Z. 59 F5 35 19S 174 9 E
Opunake, N.Z. 59 H4 39 26S 173 52 E
Opuwo, Namibia 56 B1 18 3S 13 45 E
Ora, Cyprus 25 E12 34 51N 33 12 E
Oracle, U.S.A. 77 K8 32 37N 110 46W
Oradea, Romania 17 E11 47 2N 21 58 E
Öræfajökull, Iceland 8 D5 64 2N 16 39W
Orai, India 43 G8 25 58N 79 30 E
Oral = Zhayyq →, Kazakhstan 19 E9 47 0N 51 48 E
Oral, Kazakhstan 19 D9 51 20N 51 20 E
Oran, Algeria 50 A5 35 45N 0 39W
Orange, Australia 63 E4 33 15S 149 7 E
Orange, France 20 D6 44 8N 4 47 E
Orange, Calif., U.S.A. 79 M9 33 47N 117 51W
Orange, Mass., U.S.A. 85 D12 42 35N 72 19W
Orange, Tex., U.S.A. 81 K8 30 6N 93 44W
Orange, Va., U.S.A. 82 F6 38 15N 78 7W
Orange →, S. Africa 56 D2 28 41S 16 28 E
Orange, C., Brazil 93 C8 4 20N 51 30W
Orange Cove, U.S.A. 78 J7 36 38N 119 19W
Orange Free State = Free State □, S. Africa 56 D4 28 30S 27 0 E
Orange Grove, U.S.A. 81 M6 27 58N 97 56W
Orange Walk, Belize 87 D7 18 6N 88 33W
Orangeburg, U.S.A. 83 J5 33 30N 80 52W
Orangeville, Canada 84 C4 43 55N 80 5W
Oranienburg, Germany 16 B7 52 45N 13 14 E
Oranje = Orange →, S. Africa 56 D2 28 41S 16 28 E
Oranjemund, Namibia 56 D2 28 38S 16 29 E
Oranjerivier, S. Africa 56 D3 29 40S 24 12 E
Oranjestad, Aruba 89 D6 12 32N 70 2W
Orapa, Botswana 53 J5 21 15S 25 30 E
Oras, Phil. 37 B7 12 9N 125 28 E
Orbetello, Italy 22 C4 42 27N 11 13 E
Orbisonia, U.S.A. 84 F7 40 15N 77 54W
Orbost, Australia 63 F4 37 40S 148 29 E
Orcadas, Antarctica 5 C18 60 44S 44 37W
Orcas I., U.S.A. 78 B4 48 42N 122 56W
Orchard City, U.S.A. 77 G10 38 50N 107 58W
Orchila, I., Venezuela 89 D6 11 48N 66 10W
Orchilla, Pta., Canary Is. 24 G1 27 42N 18 10W
Orcutt, U.S.A. 79 L6 34 52N 120 27W
Ord, U.S.A. 80 E5 41 36N 98 56W
Ord →, Australia 60 C4 15 33S 128 15 E
Ord, Mt., Australia 60 C4 17 20S 125 34 E
Orderville, U.S.A. 77 H7 37 17N 112 38W
Ordos = Mu Us Shamo, China 34 E5 39 0N 109 0 E
Ordu, Turkey 19 F6 40 55N 37 53 E
Ordway, U.S.A. 80 F3 38 13N 103 46W
Ore, Dem. Rep. of the Congo 54 B2 3 17N 29 30 E
Ore Mts. = Erzgebirge, Germany 16 C7 50 27N 12 55 E
Örebro, Sweden 9 G16 59 20N 15 18 E
Oregon, U.S.A. 80 D10 42 1N 89 20W
Oregon □, U.S.A. 76 E3 44 0N 121 0W
Oregon City, U.S.A. 78 E4 45 21N 122 36W
Oregon Dunes ⌓, U.S.A. 76 E1 42 3N 123 26W
Orekhovo-Zuyevo, Russia 18 C6 55 50N 38 55 E

Orel, Russia ... 18 D6 52 57N 36 3 E
Orem, U.S.A. ... 76 F8 40 19N 111 42W
Ören, Turkey ... 23 F12 37 3N 27 57 E
Orenburg, Russia ... 18 D10 51 45N 55 6 E
Orense = Ourense, Spain ... 21 A2 42 19N 7 55W
Orepuki, N.Z. ... 59 M1 46 19S 167 46 E
Orestiás, Greece ... 23 D12 41 30N 26 33 E
Orestos Pereyra, Mexico ... 86 B3 26 31N 105 40W
Orford Ness, U.K. ... 13 E9 52 5N 1 35 E
Organ Pipe Cactus △, U.S.A. ... 77 K7 32 0N 113 10W
Organos, Pta. de los, Canary Is. ... 24 F2 28 12N 17 17W
Orgaz, Spain ... 21 C4 39 39N 3 53W
Orgeyev = Orhei, Moldova ... 17 E15 47 24N 28 50 E
Orhaneli, Turkey ... 23 E13 39 54N 28 59 E
Orhangazi, Turkey ... 23 D13 40 29N 29 18 E
Orhei, Moldova ... 17 E15 47 24N 28 50 E
Orhon Gol →, Mongolia ... 32 A5 50 21N 106 0 E
Oriental, Cordillera, Colombia ... 92 B4 6 0N 73 0W
Oriental, Grand Erg, Algeria ... 50 B7 30 0N 6 30 E
Orientale □, Dem. Rep. of
the Congo ... 54 B2 2 20N 26 0 E
Oriente, Argentina ... 94 D3 38 44S 60 37W
Orihuela, Spain ... 21 C5 38 7N 0 55W
Orillia, Canada ... 84 B5 44 40N 79 24W
Orinoco →, Venezuela ... 92 B6 9 15N 61 30W
Orion, Canada ... 71 D6 49 27N 110 49W
Oriskany, U.S.A. ... 85 C9 43 10N 75 20W
Orissa □, India ... 41 K14 20 0N 84 0 E
Orissaare, Estonia ... 9 G20 58 34N 23 5 E
Oristano, Italy ... 22 E3 39 54N 8 36 E
Oristano, G. di, Italy ... 22 E3 39 50N 8 29 E
Orizaba, Mexico ... 87 D5 18 51N 97 6W
Orizaba, Pico de, Mexico ... 87 D5 19 0N 97 20W
Orkanger, Norway ... 8 E13 63 18N 9 52 E
Orkla →, Norway ... 8 E13 63 18N 9 51 E
Orkney, S. Africa ... 56 D4 26 58S 26 40 E
Orkney □, U.K. ... 11 B5 59 2N 3 13W
Orkney Is., U.K. ... 11 B6 59 0N 3 0W
Orland, U.S.A. ... 78 F4 39 45N 122 12W
Orlando, U.S.A. ... 83 L5 28 33N 81 23W
Orléanais, France ... 20 C5 48 0N 2 0 E
Orléans, France ... 20 C4 47 54N 1 52 E
Orleans, U.S.A. ... 85 B12 44 49N 72 12W
Orléans, Î. d', Canada ... 73 C5 46 54N 70 58W
Ormara, Pakistan ... 40 G4 25 16N 64 33 E
Ormoc, Phil. ... 37 B6 11 0N 124 37 E
Ormond, N.Z. ... 59 H6 38 33S 177 56 E
Ormond Beach, U.S.A. ... 83 L5 29 17N 81 3W
Ormskirk, U.K. ... 12 D5 53 35N 2 54W
Ormstown, Canada ... 85 A11 45 8N 74 0W
Örnsköldsvik, Sweden ... 8 E18 63 17N 18 40 E
Oro, N. Korea ... 35 D14 40 1N 127 27 E
Oro →, Mexico ... 86 B3 25 35N 105 2W
Oro Grande, U.S.A. ... 79 L9 34 36N 117 20W
Oro Valley, U.S.A. ... 77 K8 32 26N 110 58W
Orocué, Colombia ... 92 C4 4 48N 71 20W
Orofino, U.S.A. ... 76 C5 46 29N 116 15W
Orol Dengizi = Aral Sea, Asia ... 28 E7 44 30N 60 0 E
Oromocto, Canada ... 73 C6 45 54N 66 29W
Orono, Canada ... 84 C6 43 59N 78 37W
Orono, U.S.A. ... 83 C11 44 53N 68 40W
Oronsay, U.K. ... 11 E2 56 1N 6 15W
Oroqen Zizhiqi, China ... 33 A7 50 34N 123 43 E
Oroquieta, Phil. ... 37 C6 8 32N 123 44 E
Orosháza, Hungary ... 17 E11 46 32N 20 42 E
Orotukan, Russia ... 29 C16 62 16N 151 42 E
Oroville, Calif., U.S.A. ... 78 F5 39 31N 121 33W
Oroville, Wash., U.S.A. ... 76 B4 48 56N 119 26W
Oroville, L., U.S.A. ... 78 F5 39 33N 121 29W
Orroroo, Australia ... 63 E2 32 43S 138 38 E
Orrville, U.S.A. ... 84 F3 40 50N 81 46W
Orsha, Belarus ... 18 D5 54 30N 30 25 E
Orsk, Russia ... 18 D10 51 12N 58 34 E
Orşova, Romania ... 17 F12 44 41N 22 25 E
Ortaca, Turkey ... 23 F13 36 49N 28 45 E
Ortegal, C., Spain ... 21 A2 43 43N 7 52W
Orthez, France ... 20 E3 43 29N 0 48W
Ortigueira, Spain ... 21 A2 43 40N 7 50W
Orting, U.S.A. ... 78 C4 47 6N 122 12W
Ortles, Italy ... 20 C9 46 31N 10 33 E
Ortón →, Bolivia ... 92 F5 10 50S 67 0W
Ortonville, U.S.A. ... 80 C6 45 19N 96 27W
Orūmīyeh, Iran ... 44 B5 37 40N 45 0 E
Orūmīyeh, Daryācheh-ye, Iran ... 44 B5 37 50N 45 30 E
Oruro, Bolivia ... 92 G5 18 0S 67 9W
Orust, Sweden ... 9 G14 58 10N 11 40 E
Oruzgān □, Afghan. ... 40 C5 33 30N 66 0 E
Orvieto, Italy ... 22 C5 42 43N 12 7 E
Orwell, N.Y., U.S.A. ... 85 C9 43 35N 75 50W
Orwell, Ohio, U.S.A. ... 84 E4 41 32N 80 52W
Orwell →, U.K. ... 13 F9 51 59N 1 18 E
Orwigsburg, U.S.A. ... 85 F8 40 38N 76 6W
Oryakhovo, Bulgaria ... 23 C10 43 40N 23 57 E
Osa, Russia ... 18 C10 57 17N 55 26 E
Osa, Pen. de, Costa Rica ... 88 E3 8 0N 84 0W
Osage, U.S.A. ... 80 D8 43 17N 92 49W
Osage →, U.S.A. ... 80 F9 38 35N 91 57W
Osage City, U.S.A. ... 80 F7 38 38N 95 50W
Ōsaka, Japan ... 31 G7 34 40N 135 30 E
Osan, S. Korea ... 35 F14 37 11N 127 4 E
Osawatomie, U.S.A. ... 80 F7 38 31N 94 57W
Osborne, U.S.A. ... 80 F5 39 26N 98 42W
Osceola, Ark., U.S.A. ... 81 H10 35 42N 89 58W
Osceola, Iowa, U.S.A. ... 80 E8 41 2N 93 46W
Oscoda, U.S.A. ... 84 B1 44 26N 83 20W
Ösel = Saaremaa, Estonia ... 9 G20 58 30N 22 30 E
Osgoode, Canada ... 85 A9 45 8N 75 36W
Osh, Kyrgyzstan ... 28 E8 40 37N 72 49 E
Oshakati, Namibia ... 53 H3 17 45S 15 40 E
Oshawa, Canada ... 84 C6 43 50N 78 50W
Oshigambo, Namibia ... 56 B2 17 45S 16 5 E
Oshkosh, Nebr., U.S.A. ... 80 E3 41 24N 102 21W
Oshkosh, Wis., U.S.A. ... 80 C10 44 1N 88 33W
Oshmyany = Ashmyany, Belarus ... 9 J21 54 26N 25 52 E
Oshnovīyeh, Iran ... 44 B5 37 2N 45 6 E
Oshogbo, Nigeria ... 50 G6 7 48N 4 37 E
Oshtorīnān, Iran ... 45 C6 34 1N 48 38 E
Oshwe, Dem. Rep. of the Congo ... 52 E3 3 25S 19 28 E
Osijek, Croatia ... 23 B8 45 34N 18 41 E
Osipovichi = Asipovichy, Belarus ... 17 B15 53 19N 28 33 E
Osiyan, India ... 42 F5 26 43N 72 55 E
Osizweni, S. Africa ... 57 D5 27 49S 30 7 E
Oskaloosa, U.S.A. ... 80 E8 41 18N 92 39W
Oskarshamn, Sweden ... 9 H17 57 15N 16 27 E
Oskélanéo, Canada ... 72 C4 48 5N 75 15W
Öskemen, Kazakhstan ... 28 E9 50 0N 82 36 E
Oslo, Norway ... 9 G14 59 55N 10 45 E
Oslofjorden, Norway ... 9 G14 59 20N 10 35 E

Osmanabad, India ... 40 K10 18 5N 76 10 E
Osmaniye, Turkey ... 19 G6 37 5N 36 10 E
Osnabrück, Germany ... 16 B5 52 17N 8 3 E
Osorio, Brazil ... 95 B5 29 53S 50 17W
Osorno, Chile ... 96 E2 40 25S 73 0W
Osoyoos, Canada ... 70 D5 49 0N 119 30W
Ospika →, Canada ... 70 B4 56 20N 124 0W
Osprey Reef, Australia ... 62 A4 13 52S 146 36 E
Oss, Neths. ... 15 C5 51 46N 5 32 E
Óssa, Óros, Greece ... 23 E10 39 47N 22 42 E
Ossabaw I., U.S.A. ... 83 K5 31 50N 81 5W
Ossining, U.S.A. ... 85 E11 41 10N 73 55W
Ossipee, U.S.A. ... 85 C13 43 41N 71 7W
Ossokmanuan L., Canada ... 73 B7 53 25N 65 0W
Ossora, Russia ... 29 D17 59 20N 163 13 E
Ostend = Oostende, Belgium ... 15 C2 51 15N 2 54 E
Oster, Ukraine ... 17 C16 50 57N 30 53 E
Osterburg, U.S.A. ... 84 F6 40 16N 78 31W
Österdalälven, Sweden ... 9 F16 61 30N 13 45 E
Østerdalen, Norway ... 9 F14 61 40N 10 50 E
Östersund, Sweden ... 8 E16 63 10N 14 38 E
Ostfriesische Inseln, Germany ... 16 B4 53 42N 7 0 E
Ostrava, Czech Rep. ... 17 D10 49 51N 18 18 E
Ostróda, Poland ... 17 B10 53 42N 19 58 E
Ostroh, Ukraine ... 17 C14 50 20N 26 30 E
Ostrołęka, Poland ... 17 B11 53 4N 21 32 E
Ostrów Mazowiecka, Poland ... 17 B11 52 50N 21 51 E
Ostrów Wielkopolski, Poland ... 17 C9 51 36N 17 44 E
Ostrowiec-Świętokrzyski, Poland ... 17 C11 50 55N 21 22 E
Ostuni, Italy ... 23 D7 40 44N 17 35 E
Ōsumi-Kaikyō, Japan ... 31 J5 30 55N 131 0 E
Ōsumi-Shotō, Japan ... 31 J5 30 30N 130 0 E
Osuna, Spain ... 21 D3 37 14N 5 8W
Oswegatchie →, U.S.A. ... 85 B9 44 42N 75 30W
Oswego, U.S.A. ... 85 C8 43 27N 76 31W
Oswego →, U.S.A. ... 85 C8 43 27N 76 30W
Oswestry, U.K. ... 12 E4 52 52N 3 3W
Oświęcim, Poland ... 17 C10 50 2N 19 11 E
Otago □, N.Z. ... 59 L2 45 15S 170 0 E
Otago Harbour, N.Z. ... 59 L3 45 47S 170 42 E
Otaheite B., Trin. & Tob. ... 93 K15 10 20N 61 30W
Ōtake, Japan ... 31 G6 34 12N 132 13 E
Otaki, N.Z. ... 59 J5 40 45S 175 10 E
Otaru, Japan ... 30 C10 43 10N 141 0 E
Otaru-Wan = Ishikari-Wan, Japan ... 30 C10 43 25N 141 1 E
Otavalo, Ecuador ... 92 C3 0 13N 78 20W
Otavi, Namibia ... 56 B2 19 40S 17 24 E
Otchinjau, Angola ... 56 B1 16 30S 13 56 E
Otelnuk, L., Canada ... 73 A6 56 9N 68 12W
Othello, U.S.A. ... 76 C4 46 50N 119 10W
Otjiwarongo, Namibia ... 56 C2 20 30S 16 33 E
Otoineppu, Japan ... 30 B11 44 44N 142 16 E
Otorohanga, N.Z. ... 59 H5 38 12S 175 14 E
Otoskwin →, Canada ... 72 B2 52 13N 88 6W
Otra →, Norway ... 9 G13 58 9N 8 1 E
Otranto, Italy ... 23 D8 40 9N 18 28 E
Otranto, C. d', Italy ... 23 D8 40 7N 18 30 E
Otranto, Str. of, Italy ... 23 D8 40 15N 18 40 E
Otse, S. Africa ... 56 D4 25 2S 25 45 E
Ōtsu, Japan ... 31 G7 35 0N 135 50 E
Ōtsuki, Japan ... 31 G9 35 36N 138 57 E
Ottawa = Outaouais →, Canada ... 72 C5 45 27N 74 8W
Ottawa, Canada ... 85 A9 45 27N 75 42W
Ottawa, Ill., U.S.A. ... 80 E10 41 21N 88 51W
Ottawa, Kans., U.S.A. ... 80 F7 38 37N 95 16W
Ottawa Is., Canada ... 69 C11 59 35N 80 10W
Otter Cr. →, U.S.A. ... 85 B11 44 13N 73 17W
Otter L., Canada ... 71 B8 55 35N 104 39W
Otterville, Canada ... 84 D4 42 55N 80 36W
Ottery St. Mary, U.K. ... 13 G4 50 44N 3 17W
Otto Beit Bridge, Zimbabwe ... 55 F2 15 59S 28 56 E
Ottosdal, S. Africa ... 56 D4 26 46S 25 59 E
Ottumwa, U.S.A. ... 80 E8 41 1N 92 25W
Oturkpo, Nigeria ... 50 G7 7 16N 8 8 E
Otway, B., Chile ... 96 G2 53 30S 74 0W
Otway, C., Australia ... 63 F3 38 52S 143 30 E
Otwock, Poland ... 17 B11 52 5N 21 20 E
Ou →, Laos ... 38 B4 20 4N 102 13 E
Ou Neua, Laos ... 38 A3 22 18N 101 48 E
Ou-Sammyaku, Japan ... 30 E10 39 20N 140 35 E
Ouachita →, U.S.A. ... 81 K9 31 38N 91 49W
Ouachita, L., U.S.A. ... 81 H8 34 34N 93 12W
Ouachita Mts., U.S.A. ... 81 H7 34 40N 94 25W
Ouagadougou, Burkina Faso ... 50 F5 12 25N 1 30W
Ouahran = Oran, Algeria ... 50 A5 35 45N 0 39W
Ouallene, Algeria ... 50 D6 24 41N 1 11 E
Ouargla, Algeria ... 50 B7 31 59N 5 16 E
Ouarzazate, Morocco ... 50 B4 30 55N 6 50W
Oubangi →, Dem. Rep. of
the Congo ... 52 E3 0 30S 17 50 E
Ouddorp, Neths. ... 15 C3 51 50N 3 57 E
Oude Rijn →, Neths. ... 15 B4 52 12N 4 24 E
Oudenaarde, Belgium ... 15 D3 50 50N 3 37 E
Oudtshoorn, S. Africa ... 56 E3 33 35S 22 14 E
Ouessant, Î. d', France ... 20 B1 48 28N 5 6W
Ouesso, Congo ... 52 D3 1 37N 16 5 E
Ouest, Pte. de l', Canada ... 73 C7 49 52N 64 40W
Ouezzane, Morocco ... 50 B4 34 51N 5 35W
Oughterard, Ireland ... 10 C2 53 26N 9 18W
Oujda, Morocco ... 50 B5 34 41N 1 55W
Oulainen, Finland ... 8 D21 64 17N 24 47 E
Oulu, Finland ... 8 D21 65 1N 25 29 E
Oulujärvi, Finland ... 8 D22 64 25N 27 15 E
Oulujoki →, Finland ... 8 D21 65 1N 25 30 E
Oum Chalouba, Chad ... 51 E10 15 48N 20 46 E
Oum Hadjer, Chad ... 51 F9 13 18N 19 41 E
Ounasjoki →, Finland ... 8 C21 66 31N 25 40 E
Ounguati, Namibia ... 56 C2 22 0S 15 46 E
Ounianga Sérir, Chad ... 51 E10 18 54N 20 51 E
Our →, Lux. ... 15 E6 49 55N 6 5 E
Ouray, U.S.A. ... 77 G10 38 1N 107 40W
Ourense, Spain ... 21 A2 42 19N 7 55W
Ouricuri, Brazil ... 93 E10 7 53S 40 5W
Ourinhos, Brazil ... 95 A6 23 0S 49 54W
Ouro Fino, Brazil ... 95 A6 22 16S 46 25W
Ouro Prêto, Brazil ... 95 A7 20 20S 43 30W
Ourthe →, Belgium ... 15 D5 50 29N 5 35 E
Ouse →, E. Susx., U.K. ... 13 G8 50 47N 0 4 E
Ouse →, N. Yorks., U.K. ... 12 D7 53 44N 0 55W
Outaouais →, Canada ... 72 C5 45 27N 74 8W
Outardes →, Canada ... 73 C6 49 24N 69 30W
Outer Hebrides, U.K. ... 11 D1 57 30N 7 40W
Outjo, Namibia ... 56 C2 20 5S 16 7 E
Outlook, Canada ... 71 C7 51 30N 107 0W
Outokumpu, Finland ... 8 E23 62 43N 29 1 E
Ouyen, Australia ... 63 F3 35 1S 142 22 E

Ovalau, Fiji ... 59 C8 17 40S 178 48 E
Ovalle, Chile ... 94 C1 30 33S 71 18W
Ovamboland, Namibia ... 56 B2 18 30S 16 0 E
Overflakkee, Neths. ... 15 C4 51 44N 4 10 E
Overijssel □, Neths. ... 15 B6 52 25N 6 35 E
Overland Park, U.S.A. ... 80 F7 38 55N 94 50W
Overton, U.S.A. ... 79 J12 36 33N 114 27W
Övertorneå, Sweden ... 8 C20 66 23N 23 38 E
Ovid, U.S.A. ... 85 D8 42 41N 76 49W
Oviedo, Spain ... 21 A3 43 25N 5 50W
Oviši, Latvia ... 9 H19 57 33N 21 44 E
Ovoot, Mongolia ... 34 B7 45 21N 113 45 E
Övör Hangay □, Mongolia ... 34 B2 45 0N 102 30 E
Ovruch, Ukraine ... 17 C15 51 25N 28 45 E
Owaka, N.Z. ... 59 M2 46 27S 169 40 E
Owambo = Ovamboland,
Namibia ... 56 B2 18 30S 16 0 E
Owasco L., U.S.A. ... 85 D8 42 50N 76 31W
Owase, Japan ... 31 G8 34 7N 136 12 E
Owatonna, U.S.A. ... 80 C8 44 5N 93 14W
Owbeh, Afghan. ... 40 B3 34 28N 63 10 E
Owego, U.S.A. ... 85 D8 42 6N 76 16W
Owen Falls Dam, Uganda ... 54 B3 0 30N 33 5 E
Owen Sound, Canada ... 84 B4 44 35N 80 55W
Owens →, U.S.A. ... 78 J9 36 32N 117 59W
Owens L., U.S.A. ... 79 J9 36 26N 117 57W
Owensboro, U.S.A. ... 82 G2 37 46N 87 7W
Owl →, Canada ... 71 B10 57 51N 92 44W
Owo, Nigeria ... 50 G7 7 10N 5 39 E
Owosso, U.S.A. ... 82 D3 43 0N 84 10W
Owyhee, U.S.A. ... 76 F5 41 57N 116 6W
Owyhee →, U.S.A. ... 76 E5 43 49N 117 2W
Owyhee, L., U.S.A. ... 76 E5 43 38N 117 14W
Ox Mts. = Slieve Gamph, Ireland ... 10 B3 54 6N 9 0W
Öxarfjörður, Iceland ... 8 C5 66 15N 16 45W
Oxbow, Canada ... 71 D8 49 14N 102 10W
Oxelösund, Sweden ... 9 G17 58 43N 17 5 E
Oxford, N.Z. ... 59 K4 43 18S 172 11 E
Oxford, U.K. ... 13 F6 51 46N 1 15W
Oxford, Mass., U.S.A. ... 85 D13 42 7N 71 52W
Oxford, Miss., U.S.A. ... 81 H10 34 22N 89 31W
Oxford, N.C., U.S.A. ... 83 G6 36 19N 78 35W
Oxford, N.Y., U.S.A. ... 85 D9 42 27N 75 36W
Oxford, Ohio, U.S.A. ... 82 F3 39 31N 84 45W
Oxford L., Canada ... 71 C9 54 51N 95 37W
Oxfordshire □, U.K. ... 13 F6 51 48N 1 16W
Oxnard, U.S.A. ... 79 L7 34 12N 119 11W
Oxus = Amudarya →, Uzbekistan ... 28 E6 43 58N 59 34 E
Oya, Malaysia ... 36 D4 2 55N 111 55 E
Oyama, Japan ... 31 F9 36 18N 139 48 E
Oyem, Gabon ... 52 D2 1 34N 11 31 E
Oyen, Canada ... 71 C6 51 22N 110 28W
Oykel →, U.K. ... 11 D4 57 56N 4 26W
Oymyakon, Russia ... 29 C15 63 25N 142 44 E
Oyo, Nigeria ... 50 G6 7 46N 3 56 E
Oyster Bay, U.S.A. ... 85 F11 40 52N 73 32W
Ōyūbari, Japan ... 30 C11 43 1N 142 5 E
Ozamiz, Phil. ... 37 C6 8 15N 123 50 E
Ozark, Ala., U.S.A. ... 83 K3 31 28N 85 39W
Ozark, Ark., U.S.A. ... 81 H8 35 29N 93 50W
Ozark, Mo., U.S.A. ... 81 G8 37 1N 93 12W
Ozark Plateau, U.S.A. ... 81 G9 37 20N 91 40W
Ozarks, L. of the, U.S.A. ... 80 F8 38 12N 92 38W
Ózd, Hungary ... 17 D11 48 14N 20 15 E
Ozette L., U.S.A. ... 78 B2 48 6N 124 38W
Ozona, U.S.A. ... 81 K4 30 43N 101 12W
Ozuluama, Mexico ... 87 C5 21 40N 97 50W

P

Pa-an, Burma ... 41 L20 16 51N 97 40 E
Pa Mong Dam, Thailand ... 38 D4 18 0N 102 22 E
Pa Sak →, Thailand ... 36 B2 15 30N 101 0 E
Paamiut, Greenland ... 69 B15 62 0N 49 43W
Paarl, S. Africa ... 56 E2 33 45S 18 56 E
Pab Hills, Pakistan ... 42 F2 26 30N 66 45 E
Pabbay, U.K. ... 11 D1 57 46N 7 14W
Pabianice, Poland ... 17 C10 51 40N 19 20 E
Pabna, Bangla. ... 41 G16 24 1N 89 18 E
Pabo, Uganda ... 54 B3 3 1N 32 10 E
Pacaja →, Brazil ... 93 D8 1 56S 50 50W
Pacaraima, Sa., S. Amer. ... 92 C6 4 0N 62 30W
Pacasmayo, Peru ... 92 E3 7 20S 79 35W
Pachhar, India ... 42 G7 24 40N 77 42 E
Pachitea →, Peru ... 92 E4 8 46S 74 33W
Pachmarhi, India ... 43 H8 22 28N 78 26 E
Pachpadra, India ... 40 G8 25 58N 72 10 E
Pachuca, Mexico ... 87 C5 20 10N 98 40W
Pacific, Canada ... 70 C3 54 48N 128 28W
Pacific-Antarctic Ridge, Pac. Oc. ... 5 B13 43 0S 115 0W
Pacific Grove, U.S.A. ... 78 J5 36 38N 121 56W
Pacific Ocean ... 65 G14 10 0N 140 0W
Pacific Rim △, Canada ... 70 D4 48 40N 124 45W
Pacifica, U.S.A. ... 78 H4 37 36N 122 30W
Pacitan, Indonesia ... 37 H14 8 12S 111 7 E
Packwood, U.S.A. ... 78 D5 46 36N 121 40W
Padaido, Kepulauan, Indonesia ... 37 E9 1 15S 136 30 E
Padang, Indonesia ... 36 E2 1 0S 100 20 E
Padang Endau, Malaysia ... 39 L4 2 40N 103 38 E
Padangpanjang, Indonesia ... 36 E2 0 40S 100 20 E
Padangsidempuan, Indonesia ... 36 D1 1 30N 99 15 E
Paddle Prairie, Canada ... 70 B5 57 57N 117 29W
Paddockwood, Canada ... 71 C7 53 30N 105 30W
Paderborn, Germany ... 16 C5 51 42N 8 45 E
Padma, India ... 43 G11 24 12N 85 22 E
Pádova, Italy ... 22 B4 45 25N 11 53 E
Padra, India ... 42 H5 22 15N 73 7 E
Padrauna, India ... 43 F10 26 54N 83 59 E
Padre I., U.S.A. ... 81 M6 27 10N 97 25W
Padre Island △, U.S.A. ... 81 M6 26 36N 97 10W
Padstow, U.K. ... 13 G3 50 33N 4 58W
Padua = Pádova, Italy ... 22 B4 45 25N 11 53 E
Paducah, Ky., U.S.A. ... 82 G1 37 5N 88 37W
Paducah, Tex., U.S.A. ... 81 H4 34 1N 100 18W
Paengnyŏng-do, S. Korea ... 35 F13 37 57N 124 40 E
Paeroa, N.Z. ... 59 G5 37 23S 175 41 E
Pafúri, Mozam. ... 57 C5 22 28S 31 17 E
Pag, Croatia ... 16 F8 44 25N 15 3 E
Pagadian, Phil. ... 37 C6 7 55N 123 30 E
Pagai Selatan, Pulau, Indonesia ... 36 E2 3 0S 100 15 E
Pagai Utara, Pulau, Indonesia ... 36 E2 2 35S 100 0 E
Pagalu = Annobón, Atl. Oc. ... 49 G4 1 25S 5 36 E
Pagara, India ... 43 G9 24 22N 80 1 E
Pagastikós Kólpos, Greece ... 23 E10 39 15N 23 0 E

Pagatan, Indonesia ... 36 E5 3 33S 115 59 E
Page, U.S.A. ... 77 H8 36 57N 111 27W
Pago Pago, Amer. Samoa ... 59 B13 14 16S 170 43W
Pagosa Springs, U.S.A. ... 77 H10 37 16N 107 1W
Pagwa River, Canada ... 72 B2 50 2N 85 14W
Pahala, U.S.A. ... 74 J17 19 12N 155 29W
Pahang →, Malaysia ... 39 L4 3 30N 103 9 E
Pahiatua, N.Z. ... 59 J5 40 27S 175 50 E
Pahokee, U.S.A. ... 83 M5 26 50N 80 40W
Pahrump, U.S.A. ... 79 J11 36 12N 115 59W
Pahute Mesa, U.S.A. ... 78 H10 37 20N 116 45W
Pai, Thailand ... 38 C2 19 19N 98 27 E
Paicines, U.S.A. ... 78 J5 36 44N 121 17W
Paide, Estonia ... 9 G21 58 57N 25 31 E
Paignton, U.K. ... 13 G4 50 26N 3 35W
Päijänne, Finland ... 9 F21 61 30N 25 30 E
Pailani, India ... 43 G9 25 45N 80 26 E
Pailin, Cambodia ... 38 F4 12 46N 102 36 E
Painan, Indonesia ... 36 E2 1 21S 100 34 E
Painesville, U.S.A. ... 84 E3 41 43N 81 15W
Paint Hills = Wemindji, Canada ... 72 B4 53 0N 78 49W
Painted Desert, U.S.A. ... 77 J8 36 0N 111 0W
Paintsville, U.S.A. ... 82 G4 37 49N 82 48W
País Vasco □, Spain ... 21 A4 42 50N 2 45W
Paisley, Canada ... 84 B3 44 18N 81 16W
Paisley, U.K. ... 11 F4 55 50N 4 25W
Paisley, U.S.A. ... 76 E3 42 42N 120 32W
Paita, Peru ... 92 E2 5 11S 81 9W
Pajares, Puerto de, Spain ... 21 A3 42 58N 5 46W
Pak Lay, Laos ... 38 C3 18 15N 101 27 E
Pak Phanang, Thailand ... 39 H3 8 21N 100 12 E
Pak Sane, Laos ... 38 C4 18 22N 103 39 E
Pak Song, Laos ... 38 E6 15 11N 106 14 E
Pak Suong, Laos ... 38 C4 19 58N 102 15 E
Pak Tam Chung, China ... 33 G11 22 24N 114 19 E
Pakaur, India ... 43 G12 24 38N 87 51 E
Pakenham, Canada ... 85 A8 45 18N 76 18W
Pákhnes, Greece ... 25 D6 35 16N 24 4 E
Pakhuis, S. Africa ... 56 E2 32 9S 19 5 E
Pakistan ■, Asia ... 42 E4 30 0N 70 0 E
Pakkading, Laos ... 38 C4 18 19N 103 59 E
Pakokku, Burma ... 41 J19 21 20N 95 0 E
Pakowki L., Canada ... 71 D6 49 20N 111 0W
Pakpattan, Pakistan ... 42 D5 30 25N 73 27 E
Paktīā □, Afghan. ... 40 C6 33 30N 69 15 E
Paktīkā □, Afghan. ... 40 C6 32 30N 69 0 E
Pakwach, Uganda ... 54 B3 2 28N 31 27 E
Pakxe, Laos ... 38 E5 15 5N 105 52 E
Pal Lahara, India ... 43 J11 21 27N 85 11 E
Pala, Chad ... 51 G9 9 25N 15 5 E
Pala, Dem. Rep. of the Congo ... 54 D2 6 45S 29 30 E
Palabek, Uganda ... 54 B3 3 22N 32 33 E
Palacios, U.S.A. ... 81 L6 28 42N 96 13W
Palagruža, Croatia ... 22 C7 42 24N 16 15 E
Palaiókastron, Greece ... 25 D8 35 12N 26 15 E
Palaiokhóra, Greece ... 25 D5 35 16N 23 39 E
Palam, India ... 40 K10 19 0N 77 0 E
Palampur, India ... 42 C7 32 10N 76 30 E
Palana, Australia ... 63 F4 39 45S 147 55 E
Palana, Russia ... 29 D16 59 10N 159 59 E
Palanan, Phil. ... 37 A6 17 8N 122 29 E
Palanan Pt., Phil. ... 37 A6 17 17N 122 30 E
Palandri, Pakistan ... 43 C5 33 42N 73 40 E
Palanga, Lithuania ... 9 J19 55 58N 21 3 E
Palangkaraya, Indonesia ... 36 E4 2 16S 113 56 E
Palani Hills, India ... 40 P10 10 14N 77 33 E
Palanpur, India ... 42 G5 24 10N 72 25 E
Palapye, Botswana ... 56 C4 22 30S 27 7 E
Palas, Pakistan ... 43 B5 35 4N 73 14 E
Palashi, India ... 43 H13 23 47N 88 15 E
Palasponga, India ... 43 J11 21 47N 85 34 E
Palatka, Russia ... 29 C16 60 6N 150 54 E
Palatka, U.S.A. ... 83 L5 29 39N 81 38W
Palau ■, Pac. Oc. ... 26 J17 7 30N 134 30 E
Palauk, Burma ... 38 F2 13 10N 98 40 E
Palawan, Phil. ... 36 C5 9 30N 118 30 E
Palayankottai, India ... 40 Q10 8 45N 77 45 E
Paldiski, Estonia ... 9 G21 59 23N 24 9 E
Paleleh, Indonesia ... 37 D6 1 10N 121 50 E
Palembang, Indonesia ... 36 E2 3 0S 104 50 E
Palencia, Spain ... 21 A3 42 1N 4 34W
Palenque, Mexico ... 87 D6 17 31N 91 58W
Palenque, Ruinas de, Mexico ... 87 D6 17 29N 92 1W
Paleokastrítsa, Greece ... 25 A3 39 40N 19 41 E
Paleometokho, Cyprus ... 25 D12 35 7N 33 11 E
Palermo, Italy ... 22 E5 38 7N 13 22 E
Palermo, U.S.A. ... 76 G3 39 26N 121 33W
Palestina, Chile ... 96 A3 23 50S 69 47W
Palestine, Asia ... 46 D4 32 0N 35 0 E
Palestine, U.S.A. ... 81 K7 31 46N 95 38W
Paletwa, Burma ... 41 J18 21 10N 92 50 E
Palghat, India ... 40 P10 10 46N 76 42 E
Palgrave, Mt., Australia ... 60 D2 23 22S 115 58 E
Pali, India ... 42 G5 25 50N 73 20 E
Palikir, Micronesia ... 64 G7 6 55N 158 9 E
Paliouri, Ákra, Greece ... 23 E10 39 57N 23 45 E
Palisades Reservoir, U.S.A. ... 76 E8 43 20N 111 12W
Paliseul, Belgium ... 15 E5 49 54N 5 8 E
Palitana, India ... 42 J4 21 32N 71 49 E
Palizada, Mexico ... 87 D6 18 18N 92 8W
Palk Bay, Asia ... 40 Q11 9 30N 79 15 E
Palk Strait, Asia ... 40 Q11 10 0N 79 45 E
Palkānah, Iraq ... 44 C5 35 49N 44 26 E
Palkot, India ... 43 H11 22 53N 84 39 E
Pallanza = Verbánia, Italy ... 20 D8 45 56N 8 33 E
Pallarenda, Australia ... 62 B4 19 12S 146 46 E
Pallinup →, Australia ... 61 F2 34 27S 118 50 E
Pallisa, Uganda ... 54 B3 1 12N 33 43 E
Pallu, India ... 42 E6 28 59N 74 14 E
Palm Bay, U.S.A. ... 83 L5 28 2N 80 35W
Palm Beach, U.S.A. ... 83 M6 26 43N 80 2W
Palm Coast, U.S.A. ... 83 L5 29 32N 81 10W
Palm Desert, U.S.A. ... 79 M10 33 43N 116 22W
Palm Is., Australia ... 62 B4 18 40S 146 35 E
Palm Springs, U.S.A. ... 79 M10 33 50N 116 33W
Palma, Mozam. ... 55 E5 10 46S 40 29 E
Palma →, Brazil ... 93 F9 12 33S 47 52W
Palma, B. de, Spain ... 24 B9 39 30N 2 39 E
Palma de Mallorca, Spain ... 24 B9 39 35N 2 39 E
Palma Soriano, Cuba ... 88 B4 20 15N 76 0W
Palmares, Brazil ... 93 E11 8 41S 35 28W
Palmas, Brazil ... 95 B5 26 29S 52 0W
Palmas, C., Liberia ... 50 H4 4 27N 7 46W
Pálmas, G. di, Italy ... 22 E3 39 0N 8 30 E
Palmdale, U.S.A. ... 79 L8 34 35N 118 7W
Palmeira das Missões, Brazil ... 95 B5 27 55S 53 17W
Palmeira dos Índios, Brazil ... 93 E11 9 25S 36 37W

Palmer, Antarctica 5 C17 64 35S 60 0W
Palmer, U.S.A. 68 B5 61 36N 149 7W
Palmer →, Australia .... 62 B3 16 0S 142 26 E
Palmer Arch., Antarctica 5 C17 64 15S 65 0W
Palmer Lake, U.S.A. 80 F2 39 7N 104 55W
Palmer Land, Antarctica 5 D18 73 0S 63 0W
Palmerston, Canada 84 C4 43 50N 80 51W
Palmerston, N.Z. .... 59 L3 45 29S 170 43 E
Palmerston North, N.Z. ..... 59 J5 40 21S 175 39 E
Palmerton, U.S.A. 85 F9 40 48N 75 37W
Palmetto, U.S.A. 83 M4 27 31N 82 34W
Palmi, Italy .... 22 E6 38 21N 15 51 E
Palmira, Argentina 94 C2 32 59S 68 34W
Palmira, Colombia 92 C3 3 32N 76 16W
Palmyra = Tudmur, Syria .... 44 C3 34 36N 38 15 E
Palmyra, Mo., U.S.A. 80 F9 39 48N 91 32W
Palmyra, N.J., U.S.A. 85 F9 40 1N 75 1W
Palmyra, N.Y., U.S.A. 84 C7 43 5N 77 18W
Palmyra, Pa., U.S.A. 85 F8 40 18N 76 36W
Palmyra Is., Pac. Oc. 65 G11 5 52N 162 5W
Palo Alto, U.S.A. 78 H4 37 27N 122 10W
Palo Seco, Trin. & Tob. 93 K15 10 4N 61 36W
Palo Verde, U.S.A. 79 M12 33 26N 114 44W
Palo Verde △, Costa Rica ... 88 D2 10 21N 85 21W
Palomar Mt., U.S.A. 79 M10 33 22N 116 50W
Palopo, Indonesia .... 37 E6   3 0S 120 16 E
Palos, C. de, Spain 21 D5 37 38N   0 40W
Palos Verdes, U.S.A. 79 M8 33 48N 118 23W
Palos Verdes, Pt., U.S.A. ... 79 M8 33 43N 118 26W
Palu, Indonesia .... 37 E5   1 0S 119 52 E
Palu, Turkey .... 19 G7 38 45N 40 0 E
Palwal, India .... 42 E7 28 8N 77 0 E
Pamanukan, Indonesia ...... 37 G12 6 16S 107 49 E
Pamekasan, Indonesia ...... 37 G15 7 10S 113 28 E
Pamenang, Indonesia .... 37 J19 8 24S 116 6 E
Pamiers, France .... 20 E4 43 7N   1 39 E
Pamir, Tajikistan .... 28 F8 37 40N 73 0 E
Pamlico →, U.S.A. 83 H7 35 20N 76 28W
Pamlico Sd., U.S.A. 83 H8 35 20N 76 0W
Pampa, U.S.A. 81 H4 35 32N 100 58W
Pampa de las Salinas, Argentina 94 C2 32 1S 66 58W
Pampanua, Indonesia .... 37 E6   4 16S 120 8 E
Pampas, Argentina 94 D3 35 0S 63 0W
Pampas, Peru 92 F4 12 20S 74 50W
Pamplona, Colombia 92 B4   7 23N 72 39W
Pamplona, Spain 21 A5 42 48N   1 38W
Pampoenpoort, S. Africa .... 56 E3 31 3S 22 40 E
Pan de Azúcar △, Chile 94 B1 26 0S 70 40W
Pana, U.S.A. 80 F10 39 23N 89 05W
Panaca, U.S.A. 77 H6 37 47N 114 23W
Panaitan, Indonesia .... 37 G11 6 36S 105 12 E
Panaji, India .... 40 M8 15 25N 73 50 E
Panamá, Panama 88 E4   9 0N 79 25W
Panama ■, Cent. Amer. 88 E4   8 48N 79 55W
Panamá, G. de, Panama 88 E4   8 4N 79 20W
Panama Canal, Panama 88 E4   9 10N 79 37W
Panama City, U.S.A. 83 K3 30 5N 85 40W
Panamint Range, U.S.A. 79 J9 36 20N 117 20W
Panamint Springs, U.S.A. ... 79 J9 36 20N 117 28W
Panão, Peru 92 E3   9 55S 75 55W
Panare, Thailand .... 39 J3   6 51N 101 30 E
Panay, Phil. .... 37 B6 11 10N 122 30 E
Panay, G., Phil. .... 37 B6 11 0N 122 30 E
Pančevo, Serbia & M. ...... 23 B9 44 52N 20 41 E
Panda, Mozam. .... 57 C5 24 2S 34 45 E
Pandan, Malaysia .... 39 d   1 32N 103 46 E
Pandan, Phil. .... 37 B6 11 45N 122 10 E
Pandan, Selat, Singapore ... 39 d   1 15N 103 44 E
Pandan Tampoi = Tampoi,
  Malaysia .... 39 d   1 30N 103 39 E
Pandegelang, Indonesia .... 37 G12 6 25S 106 5 E
Pandhana, India .... 42 J7 21 42N 76 13 E
Pandharpur, India .... 40 L9 17 41N 75 20 E
Pando, Uruguay 95 C4 34 44S 56 0W
Pando, L. = Hope, L., Australia 63 D2 28 24S 139 18 E
Pandokrátor, Greece .... 25 A3 39 45N 19 50 E
Pandora, Costa Rica 88 E3   9 43N 83 3W
Panevėžys, Lithuania .... 9 J21 55 42N 24 25 E
Panfilov, Kazakhstan .... 28 E8 44 10N 80 0 E
Pang-Long, Burma .... 41 H21 23 11N 98 45 E
Pang Sida △, Thailand ..... 38 E4 14 5N 102 17 E
Pang-Yang, Burma .... 41 H21 22 7N 98 48 E
Panga, Dem. Rep. of the Congo 54 B2 1 52N 26 18 E
Pangalanes, Canal des =
  Ampangalana, Lakandranon',
  Madag. .... 57 C8 22 48S 47 50 E
Pangani, Tanzania .... 54 D4   5 25S 38 58 E
Pangani →, Tanzania .... 54 D4   5 26S 38 58 E
Pangfou = Bengbu, China ... 35 H9 32 58N 117 20 E
Pangil, Dem. Rep. of the Congo 54 C2 3 10S 26 35 E
Pangkah, Tanjung, Indonesia 37 G15 6 51S 112 33 E
Pangkajene, Indonesia ...... 37 E5   4 46S 119 34 E
Pangkalanbrandan, Indonesia 36 D1   4 1N 98 20 E
Pangkalanbuun, Indonesia .. 36 E4   2 41S 111 37 E
Pangkalpinang, Indonesia ... 36 E3   2 0S 106 0 E
Pangnirtung, Canada 69 B13 66 8N 65 43W
Pangong Tso, India .... 42 B8 34 40N 78 40 E
Panguitch, U.S.A. 77 H7 37 50N 112 26W
Pangutaran Group, Phil. .... 37 C6   6 18N 120 34 E
Panhandle, U.S.A. 81 H4 35 21N 101 23W
Pani Mines, India .... 42 H5 22 29N 73 50 E
Pania-Mutombo, Dem. Rep. of
  the Congo .... 54 D1   5 11S 23 51 E
Panikota I., India .... 42 J4 20 46N 71 21 E
Panipat, India .... 42 E7 29 25N 77 2 E
Panjal Range = Pir Panjal Range,
  India .... 42 C7 32 30N 76 50 E
Panjang, Hon, Vietnam ..... 39 H4   9 20N 103 28 E
Panjgur, Pakistan .... 40 F4 27 0N 64 5 E
Panjim = Panaji, India ..... 40 M8 15 25N 73 50 E
Panjin, China .... 35 D12 41 3N 122 2 E
Panjinad Barrage, Pakistan .. 40 E7 29 22N 71 15 E
Panjnad →, Pakistan .... 42 E4 28 57N 70 30 E
Panjwai, Afghan. .... 42 D1 31 6N 126 38 E
Panmunjŏm, N. Korea ...... 35 F14 37 59N 126 38 E
Panna, India .... 43 G9 24 40N 80 15 E
Panna Hills, India .... 43 G9 24 40N 81 15 E
Pannawonica, Australia ..... 60 D2 21 39S 116 19 E
Pannga, Tanjung, Indonesia . 37 K19 8 54S 116 2 E
Pannirtuuq = Pangnirtung,
  Canada 69 B13 66 8N 65 43W
Pano Akil, Pakistan .... 42 F3 27 51N 69 7 E
Pano Lefkara, Cyprus ...... 25 E12 34 53N 33 20 E
Pano Panayia, Cyprus ...... 25 E11 34 55N 32 38 E
Panorama, Brazil 95 A5 21 21S 51 51W
Pánormon, Greece .... 25 D6 35 25N 24 41 E
Pansemal, India .... 42 J6 21 39N 74 42 E
Panshan = Panjin, China .... 35 D12 41 3N 122 2 E

Panshi, China .... 35 C14 42 58N 126 5 E
Pantanal, Brazil 92 H7 17 30S 57 40W
Pantanos de Centla △, Mexico 87 D6 18 25N 92 25W
Pantar, Indonesia .... 37 F6   8 28S 124 10 E
Pante Macassar, E. Timor .... 37 F6   9 30S 123 58 E
Pante Makasar = Pante Macassar,
  E. Timor .... 37 F6   9 30S 123 58 E
Pantelleria, Italy .... 22 F4 36 50N 11 57 E
Pánuco, Mexico 87 C5 22 0N 98 15W
Paola, Malta .... 25 D2 35 52N 14 30 E
Paola, U.S.A. 80 F7 38 35N 94 53W
Paonia, U.S.A. 77 G10 38 52N 107 36W
Paoting = Baoding, China ... 34 E8 38 50N 115 28 E
Paot'ou = Baotou, China .... 34 D6 40 32N 110 2 E
Paoua, C.A.R. .... 52 C3   7 9N 16 20 E
Pápa, Hungary .... 17 E9 47 22N 17 30 E
Papa Stour, U.K. 11 A7 60 20N   1 42W
Papa Westray, U.K. 11 B6 59 20N   2 55W
Papagayo →, Mexico 87 D5 16 36N 99 43W
Papagayo, G. de, Costa Rica . 88 D2 10 30N 85 50W
Papakura, N.Z. .... 59 G5 37 4S 174 59 E
Papantla, Mexico 87 C5 20 30N 97 30W
Papar, Malaysia .... 36 C5   5 45N 116 0 E
Paparoa △, N.Z. .... 59 K3 42 7S 171 26 E
Papeete, Tahiti 65 J13 17 32S 149 34W
Paphos, Cyprus .... 25 E11 34 46N 32 25 E
Papigochic →, Mexico 86 B3 29 9N 109 40W
Paposo, Chile 94 B1 25 0S 70 30W
Papoutsa, Cyprus .... 25 E12 34 54N 33 4 E
Papua □, Indonesia .... 37 E9   4 0S 137 0 E
Papua New Guinea ■, Oceania 64 H6 8 0S 145 0 E
Papudo, Chile 94 C1 32 29S 71 27W
Papun, Burma .... 41 K20 18 2N 97 30 E
Papunya, Australia .... 60 D5 23 15S 131 54 E
Pará = Belém, Brazil 93 D9   1 20S 48 30W
Pará □, Brazil 93 D8   3 20S 52 0W
Paraburdoo, Australia ...... 60 D2 23 14S 117 32 E
Paracatu, Brazil 93 G9 17 10S 46 50W
Paracel Is., S. China Sea .... 36 A4 15 50N 112 0 E
Parachilna, Australia .... 63 E2 31 10S 138 21 E
Parachinar, Pakistan .... 42 C4 33 55N 70 5 E
Paradhísi, Greece .... 25 C10 36 18N 28 7 E
Paradip, India .... 41 J15 20 15N 86 35 E
Paradise, Calif., U.S.A. 78 F5 39 46N 121 37W
Paradise, Nev., U.S.A. 79 J11 36 9N 115 10W
Paradise →, Canada 73 B8 53 27N 57 19W
Paradise Hill, Canada 71 C7 53 32N 109 28W
Paradise River, Canada 73 B8 53 27N 57 17W
Paradise Valley, U.S.A. 76 F5 41 30N 117 32W
Parado, Indonesia .... 37 F5   8 42S 118 30 E
Paragould, U.S.A. 81 G9 36 3N 90 29W
Paragua →, Venezuela 92 B6   6 55N 62 55W
Paraguaçu →, Brazil 93 F11 12 45S 38 54W
Paraguaçu Paulista, Brazil .. 95 A5 22 22S 50 35W
Paraguaná, Pen. de, Venezuela 92 A5 12 0N 70 0W
Paraguarí, Paraguay 94 B4 25 36S 57 0W
Paraguarí □, Paraguay 94 B4 26 0S 57 0W
Paraguay ■, S. Amer. 94 A4 23 0S 57 0W
Paraguay →, Paraguay 94 B4 27 18S 58 38W
Paraíba = João Pessoa, Brazil 93 E12 7 10S 34 52W
Paraíba □, Brazil 93 E11 7 0S 36 0W
Paraíba do Sul →, Brazil 95 A7 21 37S 41 3W
Parainen, Finland .... 9 F20 60 18N 22 18 E
Paraiso, Mexico 87 D6 18 24N 93 14W
Parak, Iran .... 45 E7 27 38N 52 5 E
Parakou, Benin .... 50 G6   9 25N   2 40 E
Paralimni, Cyprus .... 25 D12 35 2N 33 58 E
Paramaribo, Suriname 93 B7   5 50N 55 10W
Páramos del Batallón y La
  Negra △, Venezuela 89 E5   8 2N 71 55W
Paramushir, Ostrov, Russia .. 29 D16 50 24N 156 0 E
Paran →, Israel .... 46 E4 30 20N 35 10 E
Paraná, Argentina 94 C3 31 45S 60 30W
Paraná, Brazil 93 F9 12 30S 47 48W
Paraná □, Brazil 95 A5 24 30S 51 0W
Paraná →, Argentina 94 C4 33 43S 59 15W
Paranaguá, Brazil 95 B6 25 30S 48 30W
Paranaíba, Brazil 93 G8 19 40S 51 11W
Paranaíba →, Brazil 93 H8 20 6S 51 4W
Paranapanema →, Brazil ... 95 A5 22 40S 53 9W
Paranapiacaba, Serra do, Brazil 95 A6 24 31S 48 35W
Paranavaí, Brazil 95 A5 23 4S 52 56W
Parang, Maguindanao, Phil. .. 37 C6   7 23N 124 16 E
Parang, Sulu, Phil. .... 37 C6   5 55N 120 54 E
Parângul Mare, Vf., Romania 17 F12 45 20N 23 37 E
Paraparaumu, N.Z. .... 59 J5 40 57S 175 3 E
Parbati →, Mad. P., India ... 42 G7 25 50N 76 30 E
Parbati →, Raj., India ...... 42 F7 26 54N 77 53 E
Parbhani, India .... 40 K10 19 8N 76 52 E
Parchim, Germany .... 16 B6 53 26N 11 52 E
Pardes Hanna-Karkur, Israel 46 C3 32 28N 34 57 E
Pardo →, Bahia, Brazil 93 G11 15 40S 39 0W
Pardo →, Mato Grosso, Brazil 95 A5 21 46S 52 9W
Pardubice, Czech Rep. ..... 16 C8 50 3N 15 45 E
Pare, Indonesia .... 37 G15 7 43S 112 12 E
Pare Mts., Tanzania .... 54 C4   4 0S 37 45 E
Parecis, Serra dos, Brazil ... 92 F7 13 0S 60 0W
Paren, Russia .... 29 C17 62 30N 163 15 E
Parent, Canada 72 C5 47 55N 74 35W
Parent, L., Canada 72 C4 48 31N 77 1W
Parepare, Indonesia .... 37 E5   4 0S 119 40 E
Párga, Greece .... 23 E9 39 15N 20 29 E
Pargo, Pta. do, Madeira 24 D2 32 49N 17 17W
Paria, G. de, Venezuela 93 K14 10 20N 62 0W
Pariaguán, Venezuela 92 B6   8 51N 64 34W
Paricutín, Cerro, Mexico 86 D4 19 28N 102 15W
Parigi, Indonesia .... 37 E6   0 50S 120 5 E
Parika, Guyana 92 B7   6 50N 58 20W
Parima, Serra, Brazil 92 C6   2 30N 64 0W
Parinari, Peru 92 D4   4 35S 74 25W
Pariñas, Pta., S. Amer. 90 D2   4 30S 82 0W
Parintins, Brazil 93 D7   2 40S 56 50W
Pariparit Kyun, Burma ..... 41 M18 14 55N 93 45 E
Paris, Canada 84 D4 43 12N 80 25W
Paris, France .... 20 B5 48 50N   2 20 E
Paris, Idaho, U.S.A. 76 E8 42 14N 111 24W
Paris, Ky., U.S.A. 82 F3 38 13N 84 15W
Paris, Tenn., U.S.A. 83 G1 36 18N 88 19W
Paris, Tex., U.S.A. 81 J7 33 40N 95 33W
Parish, U.S.A. 85 C8 43 25N 76 8W
Parishville, U.S.A. 85 B10 44 38N 74 49W
Park, U.S.A. 78 B4 48 45N 122 18W
Park →, U.S.A. 81 G6 37 48N 97 20W
Park City, U.S.A. 80 C9 36 56N 90 27W
Park Falls, U.S.A. 84 B3 44 36N 91 45W
Park Head, Canada 81 G9 37 53N 90 28W
Park Hills, U.S.A. 84 B3 44 36N 91 45W
Park Range, U.S.A. 76 G10 40 0N 106 30W
Park Rapids, U.S.A. 80 B7 46 55N 95 4W

Park River, U.S.A. 80 A6 48 24N 97 45W
Park Rynie, S. Africa .... 57 E5 30 25S 30 45 E
Parkā Bandar, Iran .... 45 E8 25 55N 59 35 E
Parkano, Finland .... 9 E20 62 1N 23 0 E
Parker, Ariz., U.S.A. 79 L12 34 9N 114 17W
Parker, Pa., U.S.A. 84 E5 41 5N 79 41W
Parker Dam, U.S.A. 79 L12 34 18N 114 8W
Parkersburg, U.S.A. 82 F5 39 16N 81 34W
Parkes, Australia .... 63 E4 33 9S 148 11 E
Parkfield, U.S.A. 78 K6 35 54N 120 26W
Parkhill, Canada 84 C3 43 15N 81 38W
Parkland, U.S.A. 78 C4 47 19N 122 26W
Parkston, U.S.A. 80 D6 43 24N 97 59W
Parksville, Canada 70 D4 49 20N 124 21W
Parla, Spain 21 B4 40 14N   3 46W
Parma, Italy .... 20 D9 44 48N 10 20 E
Parma, Idaho, U.S.A. 76 E5 43 47N 116 57W
Parma, Ohio, U.S.A. 84 E3 41 23N 81 43W
Parnaguá, Brazil 93 F10 10 10S 44 38W
Parnaíba, Brazil 93 D10 2 54S 41 47W
Parnaíba →, Brazil 93 D10 3 0S 41 50W
Parnassós, Greece .... 23 E10 38 35N 22 30 E
Pärnu, Estonia .... 9 G21 58 28N 24 33 E
Paroo →, Australia .... 63 E3 31 28S 143 32 E
Páros, Greece .... 23 F11 37 5N 25 12 E
Parowan, U.S.A. 77 H7 37 51N 112 50W
Parral, Chile 94 D1 36 10S 71 52W
Parras, Mexico 86 B4 25 30N 102 20W
Parrett →, U.K. 13 F4 51 12N   3 1W
Parris I., U.S.A. 83 J5 32 20N 80 41W
Parrsboro, Canada 73 C7 45 30N 64 25W
Parry I., Canada 84 A4 45 18N 80 10W
Parry Is., Canada 4 B2 77 0N 110 0W
Parry Sound, Canada 84 A5 45 20N 80 0W
Parsnip →, Canada 70 B4 55 10N 123 2W
Parsons, U.S.A. 81 G7 37 20N 95 16W
Parsons Ra., Australia ...... 62 A2 13 30S 135 15 E
Partinico, Italy .... 22 E5 38 3N 13 7 E
Partridge I., Canada 72 A2 55 59N 87 37W
Paru →, Brazil 93 D8   1 33S 52 38W
Parvān □, Afghan. .... 40 B6 35 0N 69 0 E
Parvatipuram, India .... 41 K13 18 50N 83 25 E
Parvatsar, India .... 42 F6 26 52N 74 49 E
Parys, S. Africa .... 56 D4 26 52S 27 29 E
Pas, Pta. des, Spain .... 24 C7 38 46N   1 26 E
Pasadena, Canada 73 C8 49 1N 57 36W
Pasadena, Calif., U.S.A. 79 L8 34 9N 118 8W
Pasadena, Tex., U.S.A. 81 L7 29 43N 95 13W
Pasaje →, Argentina 94 B3 25 39S 63 56W
Pasar, Indonesia .... 37 J17 8 27S 114 54 E
Pascagoula, U.S.A. 81 K10 30 21N 88 33W
Pascagoula →, U.S.A. 81 K10 30 23N 88 37W
Pașcani, Romania .... 17 E14 47 14N 26 45 E
Pasco, U.S.A. 76 C4 46 14N 119 6W
Pasco, Cerro de, Peru 92 F3 10 45S 76 10W
Pasco I., Australia .... 60 D2 20 57S 115 20 E
Pascoag, U.S.A. 85 E13 41 57N 71 42W
Pascua, I. de, Chile 65 K17 27 7S 109 23W
Pasfield L., Canada 71 B7 58 24N 105 20W
Pashmakli = Smolyan, Bulgaria 23 D11 41 36N 24 38 E
Pasir Mas, Malaysia .... 39 J4   6 2N 102 8 E
Pasir Panjang, Singapore ... 39 d   1 18N 103 46 E
Pasir Putih, Malaysia ...... 39 K4   5 50N 102 24 E
Pasirian, Indonesia .... 37 H15 8 13S 113 8 E
Pasirkuning, Indonesia ..... 36 E2   0 30S 104 33 E
Paskūh, Iran .... 45 E9 27 34N 63 58 E
Pasley, C., Australia .... 61 F3 33 52S 123 35 E
Pašman, Croatia .... 16 G8 43 58N 15 20 E
Pasni, Pakistan .... 40 G3 25 5N 63 27 E
Paso Cantinela, Mexico 79 N11 32 33N 115 47W
Paso de Indios, Argentina ... 96 E3 43 55S 69 0W
Paso de los Libres, Argentina 94 B4 29 44S 57 10W
Paso de los Toros, Uruguay .. 94 C4 32 45S 56 30W
Paso Robles, U.S.A. 77 J3 35 38N 120 41W
Paspébiac, Canada 73 C6 48 3N 65 17W
Pasrur, Pakistan .... 42 C6 32 16N 74 43 E
Passage West, Ireland 10 E3 51 52N   8 21W
Passaic, U.S.A. 85 F10 40 51N 74 7W
Passau, Germany .... 16 D7 48 34N 13 28 E
Passero, C., Italy .... 22 F6 36 41N 15 10 E
Passo Fundo, Brazil 95 B5 28 10S 52 20W
Passos, Brazil 93 H9 20 45S 46 37W
Pastavy, Belarus .... 9 J22 55 4N 26 50 E
Pastaza →, Peru 92 D3   4 50S 76 52W
Pasto, Colombia 92 C3   1 13N 77 17W
Pasuruan, Indonesia .... 37 G15 7 40S 112 44 E
Patagonia, Argentina 96 F3 45 0S 69 0W
Patagonia, U.S.A. 77 L8 31 33N 110 45W
Patambar, Iran .... 45 D9 29 45N 60 17 E
Patan = Lalitapur, Nepal .... 43 F11 27 40N 85 20 E
Patan, Gujarat, India .... 40 H8 23 54N 72 14 E
Patan, Maharashtra, India ... 40 K9 17 22N 73 57 E
Patani, Indonesia .... 37 D7   0 20N 128 50 E
Pataudi, India .... 42 E7 28 18N 76 48 E
Patchewollock, Australia .... 63 F3 35 22S 142 12 E
Patchogue, U.S.A. 85 F11 40 46N 73 1W
Pate, Kenya .... 54 C5   2 10S 41 0 E
Patea, N.Z. .... 59 H5 39 45S 174 30 E
Patensie, S. Africa .... 56 E3 33 46S 24 49 E
Paternò, Italy .... 22 F6 37 34N 14 54 E
Pateros, U.S.A. 76 B4 48 3N 119 54W
Paterson, U.S.A. 85 F10 40 55N 74 11W
Paterson Ra., Australia ..... 60 D3 21 45S 122 10 E
Pathankot, India .... 42 C6 32 18N 75 45 E
Pathein = Bassein, Burma ... 41 L19 16 45N 94 30 E
Pathfinder Reservoir, U.S.A. 76 E10 42 28N 106 51W
Pathiu, Thailand .... 39 G2 10 42N 99 19 E
Pathum Thani, Thailand .... 38 E3 14 1N 100 32 E
Pati, Indonesia .... 37 G14 6 45S 111 1 E
Patía →, Colombia 92 C3   2 13N 78 40W
Patiala, Punjab, India ...... 42 D7 30 23N 76 26 E
Patiala, Ut. P., India .... 43 F8 27 43N 79 1 E
Patkai Bum, India .... 41 F19 27 0N 95 30 E
Pátmos, Greece .... 23 F12 37 21N 26 36 E
Patna, India .... 43 G11 25 35N 85 12 E
Pato Branco, Brazil 95 B5 26 13S 52 40W
Patong, Ao, Thailand ...... 39 a   7 54N 98 17 E
Patonga, Uganda .... 54 B3   2 45N 33 15 E
Patos, Brazil 93 E11 6 55S 37 16W
Patos, L. dos, Brazil 95 C5 31 20S 51 0W
Patos, Rio de los →, Argentina 94 C2 31 18S 69 25W
Patos de Minas, Brazil 93 G9 18 35S 46 32W
Patquía, Argentina 94 C2 30 2S 66 55W
Pátrai, Greece .... 23 E9 38 14N 21 47 E
Pátraïkós Kólpos, Greece ... 23 E9 38 17N 21 30 E
Patras = Pátrai, Greece ..... 23 E9 38 14N 21 47 E
Patrocínio, Brazil 93 G9 18 57S 47 0W
Pattani, Thailand .... 39 J3   6 48N 101 15 E

Pattaya, Thailand .... 36 B2 12 52N 100 55 E
Patten, U.S.A. 83 C11 46 0N 68 38W
Patterson, Calif., U.S.A. 78 H5 37 28N 121 8W
Patterson, La., U.S.A. 81 L9 29 42N 91 18W
Patterson, Mt., U.S.A. 78 G7 38 29N 119 20W
Patti, Punjab, India .... 42 D6 31 17N 74 54 E
Patti, Ut. P., India .... 43 G10 25 55N 82 12 E
Patton, U.S.A. 84 F6 40 38N 78 39W
Patuakhali, Bangla. .... 41 H17 22 20N 90 25 E
Patuanak, Canada 71 B7 55 55N 107 43W
Patuca →, Honduras 88 C3 15 50N 84 18W
Patuca, Punta, Honduras ... 88 C3 15 49N 84 14W
Pátzcuaro, Mexico 86 D4 19 30N 101 40W
Pau, France 20 E3 43 19N   0 25W
Pauk, Burma .... 41 J19 21 27N 94 30 E
Paul I., Canada 73 A7 56 30N 61 20W
Paul Smiths, U.S.A. 85 B10 44 26N 74 15W
Paulatuk, Canada 68 B7 69 25N 124 0W
Paulista, Brazil 93 E10 8 9S 41 9W
Paulo Afonso, Brazil 93 E11 9 21S 38 15W
Paulo de Valdivia, Chile 94 A2 22 30S 55 40W
Pauls Valley, U.S.A. 81 H6 34 44N 97 13W
Pauma Valley, U.S.A. 79 M10 33 16N 116 58W
Pauri, India .... 43 D8 30 9N 78 47 E
Pāveh, Iran .... 44 C5 35 3N 46 22 E
Pavia, Italy .... 20 D8 45 7N   9 8 E
Pavilion, U.S.A. 84 D6 42 52N 78 1W
Pävilosta, Latvia .... 9 H19 56 53N 21 14 E
Pavlodar, Kazakhstan ...... 28 D8 52 33N 77 0 E
Pavlograd = Pavlohrad, Ukraine 19 E6 48 30N 35 52 E
Pavlohrad, Ukraine .... 19 E6 48 30N 35 52 E
Pavlovo, Russia .... 18 C7 55 58N 43 5 E
Pavlovsk, Russia .... 19 D7 50 26N 40 5 E
Pavlovskaya, Russia .... 19 E6 46 17N 39 47 E
Pawai, Pulau, Singapore .... 39 d   1 11N 103 44 E
Pawayan, India .... 43 E9 28 4N 80 6 E
Pawhuska, U.S.A. 81 G6 36 40N 96 20W
Pawling, U.S.A. 85 E11 41 34N 73 36W
Pawnee, U.S.A. 81 G6 36 20N 96 48W
Pawnee City, U.S.A. 80 E6 40 7N 96 9W
Pawtucket, U.S.A. 85 E13 41 53N 71 23W
Paximádhia, Greece .... 25 E6 35 0N 24 35 E
Paxoí, Greece .... 23 E9 39 14N 20 12 E
Paxton, Ill., U.S.A. 82 E1 40 27N 88 6W
Paxton, Nebr., U.S.A. 80 E4 41 7N 101 21W
Payakumbuh, Indonesia .... 36 E2   0 20S 100 35 E
Payette, U.S.A. 76 D5 44 5N 116 56W
Payne Bay = Kangirsuk, Canada 69 B13 60 0N 70 0W
Payne L., Canada 69 C12 59 30N 74 30W
Paynes Find, Australia ..... 61 E2 29 15S 117 42 E
Paynesville, U.S.A. 80 C7 45 23N 94 43W
Paysandú, Uruguay 94 C4 32 19S 58 8W
Payson, U.S.A. 77 J8 34 14N 111 20W
Paz →, Guatemala 88 D1 13 44N 90 10W
Paz, B. de la, Mexico 86 C2 24 15N 110 25W
Pāzanān, Iran .... 45 D6 30 35N 49 59 E
Pazardzhik, Bulgaria .... 23 C11 42 12N 24 20 E
Pe Ell, U.S.A. 78 D3 46 34N 123 18W
Peabody, U.S.A. 85 D14 42 31N 70 56W
Peace →, Canada 70 B6 59 0N 111 25W
Peace Point, Canada 70 B6 59 7N 112 27W
Peace River, Canada 70 B5 56 15N 117 18W
Peach Springs, U.S.A. 77 J7 35 32N 113 25W
Peachland, Canada 70 D5 49 47N 119 45W
Peachtree City, U.S.A. 83 J3 33 25N 84 35W
Peak, The = Kinder Scout, U.K. 12 D6 53 24N 1 52W
Peak Charles △, Australia .. 12 D6 53 24N   1 52W
Peak District △, U.K. ...... 63 E4 32 47S 148 11 E
Peak Hill, N.S.W., Australia . 63 E4 32 47S 148 11 E
Peak Hill, W. Austral., Australia 61 E2 25 35S 118 43 E
Peak Ra., Australia .... 62 C4 22 50S 148 20 E
Peake Cr. →, Australia ..... 63 D2 28 2S 136 7 E
Peale, Mt., U.S.A. 77 G9 38 26N 109 14W
Pearblossom, U.S.A. 79 L9 34 30N 117 55W
Pearl →, U.S.A. 81 K10 30 11N 89 32W
Pearl City, U.S.A. 74 H16 21 24N 157 59W
Pearl Harbor, U.S.A. 74 H16 21 21N 157 57W
Pearl River, U.S.A. 85 E10 41 4N 74 2W
Pearsall, U.S.A. 81 L5 28 54N 99 6W
Peary Land, Greenland 4 A6 82 40N 33 0W
Pease →, U.S.A. 81 H5 34 12N 99 2W
Peawanuck, Canada 69 C11 55 15N 85 12W
Pebane, Mozam. .... 55 F4 17 10S 38 8 E
Pebas, Peru 92 D4   3 10S 71 46W
Pebble Beach, U.S.A. 78 J5 36 34N 121 57W
Peç, Serbia & M. .... 23 C9 42 40N 20 17 E
Pechenga, Russia .... 18 A5 69 29N 31 4 E
Pechenizhyn, Ukraine ...... 17 D13 48 30N 24 48 E
Pechiguera, Pta., Canary Is. . 24 F6 28 51N 13 53W
Pechora, Russia .... 18 A10 65 10N 57 11 E
Pechora →, Russia .... 18 A9 68 13N 54 15 E
Pechorskaya Guba, Russia .. 18 A9 68 40N 54 0 E
Pečory, Russia .... 9 H22 57 48N 27 40 E
Pecos, U.S.A. 81 K3 31 26N 103 30W
Pecos →, U.S.A. 81 L3 29 42N 101 22W
Pécs, Hungary .... 17 E10 46 5N 18 15 E
Pedder, L., Australia .... 63 G4 42 55S 146 10 E
Peddie, S. Africa .... 57 E4 33 14S 27 7 E
Pedernales, Dom. Rep. 89 C5 18 2N 71 44W
Pédieos →, Cyprus .... 25 D12 35 10N 33 54 E
Pedirka, Australia .... 63 D2 26 40S 135 14 E
Pedra Azul, Brazil 93 G10 16 2S 41 17W
Pedreiras, Brazil 93 D10 4 32S 44 40W
Pedro Afonso, Brazil 93 E9   9 0S 48 10W
Pedro Cays, Jamaica 88 C4 17 5N 77 48W
Pedro de Valdivia, Chile 94 A2 22 55S 69 38W
Pedro Juan Caballero, Paraguay 95 A4 22 30S 55 40W
Pee Dee →, U.S.A. 83 J6 33 22N 79 16W
Peebinga, Australia .... 63 E3 34 52S 140 57 E
Peebles, U.K. 11 F5 55 40N   3 11W
Peekskill, U.S.A. 85 E11 41 17N 73 55W
Peel, U.K. 12 C3 54 13N   4 40W
Peel →, Australia .... 63 E5 30 50S 150 29 E
Peel →, Canada 68 B6 67 0N 135 0W
Peel Sd., Canada 68 A10 73 0N 96 0W
Peera Peera Poolanna L.,
  Australia .... 63 D2 26 30S 138 0 E
Peerless Lake, Canada 70 B6 56 37N 114 40W
Peers, Canada 70 C5 53 40N 116 0W
Pegasus Bay, N.Z. .... 59 K4 43 20S 173 10 E
Pegu, Burma .... 41 L20 17 20N 96 29 E
Pegu Yoma, Burma .... 41 K20 19 0N 96 0 E
Pehuajó, Argentina 94 D3 35 45S 62 0W
Pei Xian = Pizhou, China ... 34 G9 34 44N 116 55 E
Peine, Chile 94 A2 23 45S 68 8W
Peine, Germany .... 16 B6 52 19N 10 14 E

Peip'ing = Beijing, China ...... 34 E9　39 55N 116 20 E
Peipus, L. = Chudskoye, Ozero,
　Russia .... 9 G22 58 13N　27 30 E
Peixe, Brazil .... 93 F9　12　0S　48 40W
Peixe →, Brazil .... 93 H8　21 31S　51 58W
Pekalongan, Indonesia .... 36 F3　6 53S 109 40 E
Pekan, Malaysia .... 39 L4　3 30N 103 25 E
Pekan Nenas, Malaysia .... 39 d　1 31N 103 31 E
Pekanbaru, Indonesia .... 36 D2　0 30N 101 15 E
Pekin, U.S.A. .... 80 E10 40 35N　89 40W
Peking = Beijing, China ..... 34 E9　39 55N 116 20 E
Pekutatan, Indonesia .... 37 J17　8 25S 114 48 E
Pelabuhan Kelang, Malaysia .. 39 L3　3　0N 101 23 E
Pelabuhan Ratu, Teluk, Indonesia 37 G12　7 5S 106 30 E
Pelabuhanratu, Indonesia .... 37 G12　7　0S 106 32 E
Pelagie, Is., Italy .... 22 G5 35 39N　12 33 E
Pelaihari, Indonesia .... 36 E4　3 55S 114 45 E
Peleaga, Vf., Romania .... 17 F12 45 22N　22 55 E
Pelée, Mt., Martinique ...... 88 c　14 48N　61 10W
Pelee, Pt., Canada .... 72 D3　41 54N　82 31W
Pelee I., Canada .... 84 E2　41 47N　82 40W
Pelekech, Kenya .... 54 B4　3 52N　35　8 E
Peleng, Indonesia .... 37 E6　1 20S 123 30 E
Pelentong, Malaysia .... 39 d　1 32N 103 49 E
Pelican, U.S.A. .... 70 B1　57 58N 136 14W
Pelican L., Canada .... 71 C8　52 28N 100 20W
Pelican Narrows, Canada ..... 71 B8　55 10N 102 56W
Peljesac, Croatia .... 22 C7　42 55N　17 25 E
Pelkosenniemi, Finland ...... 8 C22 67　6N　27 28 E
Pella, S. Africa .... 56 D2　29　1S　19　6 E
Pella, U.S.A. .... 80 E8　41 25N　92 55W
Pello, Finland .... 8 C21 66 47N　23 59 E
Pelly →, Canada .... 68 B6　62 47N 137 19W
Pelly Bay, Canada .... 69 B11 68 38N　89 50W
Peloponnese = Pelopónnisos □,
　Greece .... 23 F10 37 10N　22　0 E
Pelopónnisos □, Greece ...... 23 F10 37 10N　22　0 E
Pelorus Sd., N.Z. .... 59 J4　40 59S 173 59 E
Pelotas, Brazil .... 95 C5　31 42S　52 23W
Pelotas →, Brazil .... 95 B5　27 28S　51 55W
Pelvoux, Massif du, France .. 20 D7　44 52N　6 20 E
Pemalang, Indonesia .... 37 G13　6 53S 109 23 E
Pemanggil, Pulau, Malaysia .. 39 L5　2 37N 104 21 E
Pematangsiantar, Indonesia .. 36 D1　2 57N　99　5 E
Pemba, Mozam. .... 55 E5　12 58S　40 30 E
Pemba, Zambia .... 55 F2　16 30S　27 28 E
Pemba Channel, Tanzania ..... 54 D4　5　0S　39 37 E
Pemba I., Tanzania .... 54 D4　5　0S　39 45 E
Pemberton, Australia .... 61 F2　34 30S 116　0 E
Pemberton, Canada .... 70 C4　50 25N 122 50W
Pembina, Canada .... 80 A6　48 58N　97 15W
Pembroke, Canada .... 72 C4　45 50N　77　7W
Pembroke, U.K. .... 13 F3　51 41N　4 55W
Pembrokeshire □, U.K. .... 13 F3　51 52N　4 56W
Pembrokeshire Coast △, U.K. . 13 F2　51 50N　5　2W
Pen-y-Ghent, U.K. .... 12 C5　54 10N　2 14W
Penal, Trin. & Tob. .... 93 K15 10　9N　61 29W
Penang = Pinang, Malaysia ... 39 c　5 25N 100 15 E
Penápolis, Brazil .... 95 A6　21 30S　50　0W
Peñarroya-Pueblonuevo, Spain 21 C3　38 19N　5 16W
Penarth, U.K. .... 13 F4　51 26N　3 11W
Peñas, C. de, Spain .... 21 A3　43 42N　5 52W
Peñas, G. de, Chile .... 96 F2　47　0S　75　0W
Peñas del Chache, Canary Is. . 24 E6　29　6N　13 33W
Pench'i = Benxi, China ...... 35 D12 41 20N 123 48 E
Pend Oreille →, U.S.A. ...... 76 B5　49　4N 117 37W
Pend Oreille, L., U.S.A. .... 76 C5　48 10N 116 21W
Pendembu, S. Leone .... 50 G3　9　7N　11 14W
Pender B., Australia .... 60 C3　16 45S 122 42 E
Pendleton, U.S.A. .... 76 D4　45 40N 118 47W
Pendra, India .... 43 H9　22 46N　81 57 E
Penedo, Brazil .... 93 F11 10 15S　36 36W
Penelokan, Indonesia .... 37 J18　8 17S 115 22 E
Penetanguishene, Canada ..... 84 B5　44 50N　79 55W
Penfield, U.S.A. .... 84 E6　41 13N　78 35W
Peng Chau, China .... 33 G11 22 17N 114　2 E
Pengalengan, Indonesia ...... 37 G12　7　9S 107 30 E
Penge, Kasai-Or., Dem. Rep. of
　the Congo .... 54 D1　5 30S　24 33 E
Penge, Sud-Kivu, Dem. Rep. of
　the Congo .... 54 C2　4 27S　28 25 E
Penglai, China .... 35 F11 37 48N 120 42 E
Penguin, Australia .... 63 G4　41　8S 146　6 E
Penhalonga, Zimbabwe .... 55 F3　18 52S　32 40 E
Peniche, Portugal .... 21 C1　39 19N　9 22W
Penicuik, U.K. .... 11 F5　55 50N　3 13W
Penida, Nusa, Indonesia ..... 36 F5　8 45S 115 30 E
Peninsular Malaysia □, Malaysia 39 L4　4　0N 102　0 E
Penitente, Serra do, Brazil . 93 E9　8 45S　46 20W
Penkridge, U.K. .... 12 E5　52 44N　2　6W
Penmarch, Pte. de, France ... 20 C1　47 48N　4 22W
Penn Hills, U.S.A. .... 84 F5　40 28N　79 52W
Penn Yan, U.S.A. .... 84 D7　42 40N　77　3W
Pennant, Canada .... 71 C7　50 32N 108 14W
Penner →, India .... 40 M12 14 35N　80 10 E
Pennines, U.K. .... 12 C5　54 45N　2 27W
Pennington, U.S.A. .... 78 F5　39 15N 121 47W
Pennsburg, U.S.A. .... 85 F9　40 23N　75 29W
Pennsylvania □, U.S.A. ...... 82 E7　40 45N　77 30W
Penny, Canada .... 70 C4　53 51N 121 20W
Penobscot →, U.S.A. .... 83 C11 44 30N　68 48W
Penobscot B., U.S.A. .... 83 C11 44 35N　68 50W
Penola, Australia .... 63 F3　37 25S 140 48 E
Penong, Australia .... 61 F5　31 56S 133　1 E
Penonomé, Panama .... 88 E3　8 31N　80 21W
Penrith, Australia .... 63 E5　33 43S 150 38 E
Penrith, U.K. .... 12 C5　54 40N　2 45W
Penryn, U.K. .... 13 G2　50　9N　5　7W
Pensacola, U.S.A. .... 83 K2　30 25N　87 13W
Pensacola Mts., Antarctica .. 5 E1　84　0S　40　0W
Pense, Canada .... 71 C8　50 25N 104 59W
Penshurst, Australia .... 63 F3　37 49S 142 20 E
Penticton, Canada .... 70 D5　49 30N 119 38W
Pentland, Australia .... 62 C4　20 32S 145 25 E
Pentland Firth, U.K. .... 11 C5　58 43N　3 10W
Pentland Hills, U.K. .... 11 F5　55 48N　3 25W
Pentland Hills △, U.K. ...... 11 F5　55 50N　3 20W
Penza, Russia .... 18 D8　53 15N　45　5 E
Penzance, U.K. .... 13 G2　50　7N　5 33W
Penzhino, Russia .... 29 C17 63 30N 167 55 E
Penzhinskaya Guba, Russia ... 29 C17 61 30N 163　0 E
Peoria, Ariz., U.S.A. .... 77 K7　33 35N 112 14W
Peoria, Ill., U.S.A. .... 80 E10 40 42N　89 36W
Pepacton Reservoir, U.S.A. .. 85 D10 42　5N　74 58W
Pepani →, S. Africa .... 56 D3　25 49S　22 47 E
Pera Hd., Australia .... 62 A3　12 55S 141 37 E
Perabumulih, Indonesia ...... 36 E2　3 27S 104 15 E
Perak →, Malaysia .... 39 K3　4　0N 100 50 E

Pérama, Kérkira, Greece ..... 25 A3　39 34N　19 54 E
Pérama, Kríti, Greece .... 25 D6　35 20N　24 40 E
Perancak, Indonesia .... 37 J17　8 24S 114 37 E
Peräpohjola, Finland .... 8 C22 66 16N　26 10 E
Percé, Canada .... 73 C7　48 31N　64 13W
Perche, Collines du, France . 20 B4　48 30N　0 40 E
Percival Lakes, Australia ... 60 D4　21 25S 125　0 E
Percy Is., Australia .... 62 C5　21 39S 150 16 E
Perdido, Mte., Spain .... 21 A6　42 40N　0　5 E
Perdu, Mt. = Perdido, Mte., Spain 21 A6　42 40N　0　5 E
Pereira, Colombia .... 92 C3　4 49N　75 43W
Perenjori, Australia .... 61 E2　29 26S 116 16 E
Pereyaslav-Khmelnytskyy,
　Ukraine .... 19 D5　50　3N　31 28 E
Pérez, I., Mexico .... 87 C7　22 24N　89 42W
Pergamino, Argentina .... 94 C3　33 52S　60 30W
Pergau →, Malaysia .... 39 K3　5 23N 102　2 E
Perham, U.S.A. .... 80 B7　46 36N　95 34W
Perhentian, Kepulauan, Malaysia 39 K4　5 54N 102 42 E
Péribonka →, Canada .... 73 C5　48 45N　72　5W
Péribonka, L., Canada .... 73 B5　50 1N　71 10W
Perico, Argentina .... 94 A2　24 20S　65　5W
Perico, Mexico .... 86 B3　25　3N 107 42W
Périgueux, France .... 20 D4　45 10N　0 42 E
Perijá, Venezuela .... 89 E5　9 30N　72 55W
Perijá, Sierra de, Colombia . 92 B4　9 30N　73　3W
Peristerona →, Cyprus .... 25 D12 35　8N　33　5 E
Perito Moreno, Argentina .... 96 F2　46 36S　70 56W
Perkasie, U.S.A. .... 85 F9　40 22N　75 18W
Perlas, Arch. de las, Panama 88 E4　8 41N　79　7W
Perlas, Punta de, Nic. ...... 88 D3　12 30N　83 30W
Perm, Russia .... 18 C10 58　0N　56 10 E
Pernambuco = Recife, Brazil . 93 E12　8　0S　35　0W
Pernambuco □, Brazil .... 93 E11　8　0S　37　0W
Pernatty Lagoon, Australia .. 63 E2　31 30S 137 12 E
Pernik, Bulgaria .... 23 C10 42 35N　23　2 E
Peron Is., Australia .... 60 B5　13　9S 130　4 E
Peron Pen., Australia .... 61 E1　26　0S 113 10 E
Perow, Canada .... 70 C3　54 35N 126 10W
Perpignan, France .... 20 E5　42 42N　2 53 E
Perris, U.S.A. .... 79 M9　33 47N 117 14W
Perry, Fla., U.S.A. .... 83 K4　30　7N　83 35W
Perry, Ga., U.S.A. .... 83 J4　32 28N　83 44W
Perry, Iowa, U.S.A. .... 80 E7　41 51N　94　6W
Perry, Okla., U.S.A. .... 81 G6　36 17N　97 14W
Perryton, U.S.A. .... 81 G4　36 24N 100 48W
Perryville, U.S.A. .... 81 G10 37 43N　89 52W
Persepolis, Iran .... 45 D7　29 55N　52 50 E
Pershotravensk, Ukraine ..... 17 C14 50 13N　27 40 E
Persia = Iran ■, Asia .... 45 C7　33　0N　53　0 E
Persian Gulf = Gulf, The, Asia 45 E6　27　0N　50　0 E
Perth, Australia .... 61 F2　31 57S 115 52 E
Perth, Canada .... 85 B8　44 55N　76 15W
Perth, U.K. .... 11 E5　56 24N　3 26W
Perth & Kinross □, U.K. ..... 11 E5　56 45N　3 55W
Perth Amboy, U.S.A. .... 85 F10 40 31N　74 16W
Perth-Andover, Canada .... 73 C6　46 44N　67 42W
Peru, Ind., U.S.A. .... 82 E2　40 45N　86　4W
Peru, N.Y., U.S.A. .... 85 B11 44 35N　73 32W
Peru ■, S. Amer. .... 92 D4　4　0S　75　0W
Peru Basin, Pac. Oc. .... 65 J18 20　0S　95　0W
Peru-Chile Trench, Pac. Oc. . 92 G3　20　0S　72　0W
Perúgia, Italy .... 22 C5　43　7N　12 23 E
Pervomaysk, Ukraine .... 19 E5　48 10N　30 46 E
Pervouralsk, Russia .... 18 C10 56 59N　59 59 E
Pésaro, Italy .... 22 C5　43 54N　12 55 E
Pescara, Italy .... 22 C6　42 28N　14 13 E
Peshawar, Pakistan .... 42 B4　34　2N　71 37 E
Peshkopi, Albania .... 23 D9　41 41N　20 25 E
Peshtigo, U.S.A. .... 82 C2　45　4N　87 46W
Pesqueira, Brazil .... 93 E11　8 20S　36 42W
Petah Tiqwa, Israel .... 46 C3　32　6N　34 53 E
Petaling Jaya, Malaysia ..... 39 L3　3　4N 101 42 E
Petaloudhes, Greece .... 25 C10 36 18N　28　5 E
Petaluma, U.S.A. .... 78 G4　38 14N 122 39W
Pétange, Lux. .... 15 E5　49 33N　5 55 E
Petaro, Pakistan .... 42 G3　25 31N　68 18 E
Petatlán, Mexico .... 86 D4　17 31N 101 16W
Petauke, Zambia .... 55 E3　14 14S　31 20 E
Petawawa, Canada .... 72 C4　45 54N　77 17W
Petén Itzá, L., Guatemala ... 88 C2　16 58N　89 50W
Peter I. Br. Virgin Is. ..... 89 e　18 22N　64 35W
Peter I.s Øy, Antarctica .... 5 C16 69　0S　91　0W
Peter Pond L., Canada .... 71 B7　55 55N 108 44W
Peterbell, Canada .... 72 C3　48 36N　83 21W
Peterborough, Australia ..... 63 E2　32 58S 138 51 E
Peterborough, Canada .... 84 B6　44 20N　78 20W
Peterborough, U.K. .... 13 E7　52 35N　0 15W
Peterborough □, U.K. .... 13 E7　52 35N　0 15W
Peterculter, U.K. .... 11 D6　57　6N　2 16W
Peterhead, U.K. .... 11 D7　57 31N　1 48W
Peterlee, U.K. .... 12 C6　54 47N　1 20W
Petermann Ranges, Australia . 60 E5　26　0S 130 30 E
Petersburg, Alaska, U.S.A. .. 68 C6　56 48N 132 58W
Petersburg, Pa., U.S.A. ..... 84 F6　40 34N　78　3W
Petersburg, Va., U.S.A. ..... 82 G7　37 14N　77 24W
Petersburg, W. Va., U.S.A. .. 82 F6　39　1N　79　5W
Petersfield, U.K. .... 13 F7　51　1N　0 56W
Petit-Canal, Guadeloupe ..... 88 b　16 25N　61 31W
Petit Jardin, Canada .... 89 C5　18 27N　72 51W
Petit Jardin, Canada .... 73 C8　48 28N　59 14W
Petit Lac Manicouagan, Canada 73 B6　51 25N　67 40W
Petit-Mécatina →, Canada .... 73 B8　50 40N　59　30W
Petit-Mécatina, Î. du, Canada 73 B8　50 30N　59 25W
Petit Piton, St. Lucia ...... 89 f　13 51N　61　5W
Petit-Saguenay, Canada ...... 73 C5　47 59N　70　1W
Petitcodiac, Canada .... 73 C6　45 57N　65 11W
Petite Terre, Iles de la,
　Guadeloupe .... 88 b　16 13N　61　9W
Petitot →, Canada .... 70 A4　60 14N 123 29W
Petitsikapau L., Canada ..... 73 B6　54 37N　66 25W
Petlad, India .... 42 H5　22 30N　72 45 E
Peto, Mexico .... 87 C7　20 10N　88 53W
Petone, N.Z. .... 59 J5　41 13S 174 53 E
Petorca, Chile .... 94 C1　32 15S　70 56W
Petoskey, U.S.A. .... 82 C3　45 22N　84 57W
Petra, Jordan .... 46 E4　30 20N　35 22 E
Petra, Spain .... 24 B10 39 37N　3　6 E
Petra, Ostrova, Russia ...... 4 B13 76 15N 118 30 E
Petra Velikogo, Zaliv, Russia 30 C6　42 40N 132　0 E
Petrich, Bulgaria .... 23 D10 41 24N　23 13 E
Petrified Forest △, U.S.A. .. 77 J9　35　0N 109 30W
Petrikov = Pyetrikaw, Belarus 17 B15 52　11N　28 29 E
Petrolândia, Brazil .... 93 E11　9　5S　38 20W
Petrolia, Canada .... 84 D2　42 54N　82　9W
Petrolina, Brazil .... 93 E10　9 24S　40 30W
Petropavl, Kazakhstan .... 28 D7　54 53N　69 13 E

Petropavlovsk = Petropavl,
　Kazakhstan .... 28 D7　54 53N　69 13 E
Petropavlovsk-Kamchatskiy,
　Russia .... 29 D16 53　3N 158 43 E
Petrópolis, Brazil .... 95 A7　22 33S　43　9W
Petrosani, Romania .... 17 F12 45 28N　23 20 E
Petrovaradin, Serbia & M. ... 23 B8　45 16N　19 55 E
Petrovsk, Russia .... 18 D8　52 22N　45 19 E
Petrovsk-Zabaykalskiy, Russia 29 D11 51 20N 108 55 E
Petrozavodsk, Russia .... 18 B5　61 41N　34 20 E
Petrus Steyn, S. Africa ..... 57 D4　27 38S　28　8 E
Petrusburg, S. Africa .... 56 D4　29　4S　25 26 E
Peumo, Chile .... 94 C1　34 21S　71 12W
Peureulak, Indonesia .... 36 D1　4 48N　97 45 E
Pevek, Russia .... 29 C18 69 41N 171 19 E
Pforzheim, Germany .... 16 D5　48 52N　8 41 E
Phagwara, India .... 40 D9　31 10N　75 40 E
Phaistós, Greece .... 25 D6　35　2N　24 50 E
Phala, Botswana .... 56 C4　23 45S　26 50 E
Phalera = Phulera, India .... 42 F6　26 52N　75 16 E
Phalodi, India .... 42 F5　27 12N　72 24 E
Phaluai, Ko, Thailand .... 39 b　9 32N　99 41 E
Phan, Thailand .... 38 C2　19 28N　99 43 E
Phan Rang, Vietnam .... 39 G7　11 34N 109　0 E
Phan Ri = Hoa Da, Vietnam ... 39 G7　11 16N 108 40 E
Phan Thiet, Vietnam .... 39 G7　11　1N 108　9 E
Phanat Nikhom, Thailand ..... 38 F3　13 27N 101 11 E
Phangan, Ko, Thailand .... 39 H3　9 45N 100　0 E
Phangnga, Thailand .... 39 a　8 28N　98 30 E
Phangnga, Ao, Thailand ...... 39 a　8 16N　98 33 E
Phanom Sarakham, Thailand ... 38 F3　13 45N 101 21 E
Phaphund, India .... 43 F8　26 36N　79 28 E
Pharenda, India .... 43 F10 27　5N　83 17 E
Pharr, U.S.A. .... 81 M5　26 12N　98 11W
Phatthalung, Thailand .... 39 J3　7 39N 100　6 E
Phayao, Thailand .... 38 C2　19 11N　99 55 E
Phelps, U.S.A. .... 84 D7　42 58N　77　3W
Phelps L., Canada .... 71 B8　59 15N 103 15W
Phenix City, U.S.A. .... 83 J3　32 28N　85　0W
Phet Buri, Thailand .... 38 F2　13　1N　99 55 E
Phetchabun, Thailand .... 38 D3　16 25N 101　8 E
Phetchabun, Thiu Khao, Thailand 38 E3　16　0N 101 20 E
Phetchaburi = Phet Buri, Thailand 38 F2　13　1N　99 55 E
Phi Phi, Ko, Thailand .... 39 J2　7 45N　98 46 E
Phiafay, Laos .... 38 E6　14 48N 106　0 E
Phibun Mangsahan, Thailand .. 38 E5　15 14N 105 14 E
Phichai, Thailand .... 38 D3　17 22N 100 10 E
Phichit, Thailand .... 38 D3　16 26N 100 22 E
Philadelphia, Miss., U.S.A. . 81 J10 32 46N　89　7W
Philadelphia, N.Y., U.S.A. .. 85 B9　44　9N　75 43W
Philadelphia, Pa., U.S.A. ... 85 G9　39 57N　75 10W
Philip, U.S.A. .... 80 C4　44　2N 101 40W
Philippeville, Belgium ...... 15 D4　50 12N　4 33 E
Philippi, U.S.A. .... 82 F5　39　9N　80　3W
Philippi L., Australia ...... 62 C2　24 20S 138 55 E
Philippine Sea, Pac. Oc. .... 26 H16 18　0N 125　0 E
Philippines ■, Asia .... 37 B6　12　0N 123　0 E
Philippolis, S. Africa ...... 56 E4　30 15S　25 16 E
Philippopolis = Plovdiv, Bulgaria 23 C11 42 8N　24 44 E
Philipsburg, Canada .... 85 A11 45　2N　73　5W
Philipsburg, Mont., U.S.A. .. 76 C7　46 20N 113 18W
Philipsburg, Pa., U.S.A. .... 84 F6　40 54N　78 13W
Philipstown = Daingean, Ireland 10 C4　53 18N　7 17W
Philipstown, S. Africa ...... 56 E3　30 28S　24 30 E
Phillip I., Australia .... 63 F4　38 30S 145 12 E
Phillips, U.S.A. .... 80 C9　45 42N　90 24W
Phillipsburg, Kans., U.S.A. . 80 F5　39 45N　99 19W
Phillipsburg, N.J., U.S.A. .. 85 F9　40 42N　75 12W
Philmont, U.S.A. .... 85 D11 42 15N　73 39W
Philomath, U.S.A. .... 76 D2　44 32N 123 22W
Phimai, Thailand .... 38 E4　15 13N 102 30 E
Phitsanulok, Thailand .... 38 D3　16 50N 100 12 E
Phnom Dangrek, Thailand ..... 36 B2　14　0N 104　0 E
Phnom Penh, Cambodia .... 39 G5　11 33N 104 55 E
Phnom Penh = Phnom Penh,
　Cambodia .... 39 G5　11 33N 104 55 E
Phoenicia, U.S.A. .... 85 D10 42　5N　74 14W
Phoenix, Ariz., U.S.A. ...... 77 K7　33 27N 112　4W
Phoenix, N.Y., U.S.A. .... 85 C8　43 14N　76 18W
Phoenix Is., Kiribati .... 64 H10　3 30S 172　0W
Phoenixville, U.S.A. .... 85 F9　40　8N　75 31W
Phon, Thailand .... 38 E4　15 49N 102 36 E
Phon Tiou, Laos .... 38 D5　17 53N 104 37 E
Phong →, Thailand .... 38 D4　16 23N 102 56 E
Phong Saly, Laos .... 38 B4　21 42N 102　9 E
Phong Tho, Vietnam .... 38 A4　22 32N 103 21 E
Phonhong, Laos .... 38 C4　18 30N 102 25 E
Phonum, Thailand .... 39 H2　8 49N　98 48 E
Phosphate Hill, Australia ... 62 C2　21 53S 139 58 E
Photharam, Thailand .... 38 F2　13 41N　99 51 E
Phra Nakhon Si Ayutthaya,
　Thailand .... 38 E3　14 25N 100 30 E
Phra Thong, Ko, Thailand .... 39 H2　9　5N　98 17 E
Phrae, Thailand .... 38 C3　18　7N 100　9 E
Phrom Phiram, Thailand ...... 38 D3　17　2N 100 12 E
Phu Dien, Vietnam .... 38 C5　18 58N 105 31 E
Phu Hin Rang Kla △, Thailand 38 D3　17　0N 100 59 E
Phu Kradung △, Thailand ..... 38 D3　17　0N 101 44 E
Phu Loi, Laos .... 38 B4　20 14N 103 14 E
Phu Luang △, Thailand .... 38 D3　17 15N 101 29 E
Phu Ly, Vietnam .... 38 B5　20 35N 105 50 E
Phu Phan △, Thailand .... 38 D4　17　0N 103 56 E
Phu Quoc, Dao, Vietnam ...... 39 G4　10 20N 104　0 E
Phuc Tho, Vietnam .... 38 B5　21 24N 105 13 E
Phuc Yen, Vietnam .... 38 B5　21 16N 105 45 E
Phuket, Thailand .... 39 a　7 53N　98 24 E
Phuket, Ko, Thailand .... 39 a　8　0N　98 22 E
Phul, India .... 42 D6　30 19N　75 14 E
Phulad, India .... 42 G5　25 38N　73 49 E
Phulchari, Bangla. .... 43 G13 25 11N　89 37 E
Phulera, India .... 42 F6　26 52N　75 16 E
Phulpur, India .... 43 G10 25 31N　82 49 E
Phun Phin, Thailand .... 39 H2　9　7N　99 12 E
Piacenza, Italy .... 20 D8　45　1N　9 40 E
Piai, Tanjung, Malaysia ..... 39 d　1 17N 103 30 E
Pian Cr. →, Australia .... 63 E4　30　2S 148 12 E
Pian-Upe △, Uganda .... 54 B3　1 44N　34 20 E
Pianosa, Italy .... 22 C4　42 35N　10　5 E
Piapot, Canada .... 71 D7　49 59N 109　8W
Piatra Neamţ, Romania .... 17 E14 46 56N　26 21 E
Piauí □, Brazil .... 93 E10　7　0S　43　0W
Piauí →, Brazil .... 93 E10　6 38S　42 42W
Piave →, Italy .... 22 B5　45 32N　12 44 E
Pibor Post, Sudan .... 51 G12　6 47N　33　3 E
Picardie ▨, France .... 20 B5　49 50N　3　0 E
Picardy = Picardie ▨, France 20 B5　49 50N　3　0 E

Picayune, U.S.A. .... 81 K10 30 32N　89 41W
Pichhor, India .... 43 G8　25 58N　78 20 E
Pichilemu, Chile .... 94 C1　34 22S　72　0W
Pichor, India .... 42 G8　25 11N　78 11 E
Pickerel L., Canada .... 72 C1　48 40N　91 25W
Pickering, U.K. .... 12 C7　54 15N　0 46W
Pickering, Vale of, U.K. .... 12 C7　54 14N　0 45W
Pickle Lake, Canada .... 72 B1　51 30N　90 12W
Pickwick L., U.S.A. .... 83 H1　35　4N　88 15W
Pico Bonito △, Honduras ..... 88 C2　15 34N　86 48W
Pico Truncado, Argentina .... 96 F3　46 40S　68　0W
Picos, Brazil .... 93 E10　7　5S　41 28W
Picton, Australia .... 63 E5　34 12S 150 34 E
Picton, Canada .... 84 B7　44　1N　77 9W
Picton, N.Z. .... 59 J5　41 18S 174　3 E
Pictou, Canada .... 73 C7　45 41N　62 42W
Picture Butte, Canada .... 70 D6　49 55N 112 45W
Pictured Rocks △, U.S.A. .... 82 B2　46 30N　86 30W
Picún Leufú, Argentina ...... 96 D3　39 30S　69　5W
Pidurutalagala, Sri Lanka ... 40 R12　7 10N　80 50 E
Piedmont = Piemonte □, Italy 20 D7　45　0N　8　0 E
Piedmont, Ala., U.S.A. ...... 83 J3　33 55N　85 37W
Piedmont, S.C., U.S.A. ...... 75 D10 34　0N　81 30W
Piedras Negras, Mexico ...... 86 B4　28 42N 100 31W
Pieksämäki, Finland .... 9 E22 62 18N　27 10 E
Piemonte □, Italy .... 20 D7　45　0N　8　0 E
Pienaarsrivier, S. Africa ... 57 D4　25 15S　28 18 E
Piercefield, U.S.A. .... 85 B10 44 13N　74 35W
Pierceland, Canada .... 71 C7　54 20N 109 46W
Pierpont, U.S.A. .... 84 E4　41 45N　80 34W
Pierre, U.S.A. .... 80 C4　44 22N 100 21W
Pierreville, Trin. & Tob. ... 93 K16 10 16N　61　0W
Piet Retief, S. Africa ...... 57 D5　27　1S　30 50 E
Pietarsaari, Finland .... 8 E20 63 40N　22 43 E
Pietermaritzburg, S. Africa . 57 D5　29 35S　30 15 E
Pietersburg = Polokwane,
　S. Africa .... 57 C4　23 54S　29 25 E
Pietrosul, Vf., Maramureş,
　Romania .... 17 E13 47 35N　24 43 E
Pietrosul, Vf., Suceava, Romania 17 E13 47 12N　25 18 E
Pigeon L., Canada .... 84 B6　44 27N　78 30W
Piggott, U.S.A. .... 81 G9　36 23N　90 11W
Pigüe, Argentina .... 94 D3　37 36S　62 25W
Pihani, India .... 43 F9　27 36N　80 15 E
Pihlajavesi, Finland .... 9 F23 61 45N　28 45 E
Pijijiapan, Mexico .... 87 D6　15 42N　93 14W
Pikangikum Berens, Canada ... 71 C10 51 49N　94　0W
Pikes Peak, U.S.A. .... 80 F2　38 50N 105　3W
Piketberg, S. Africa .... 56 E2　32 55S　18 40 E
Pikeville, U.S.A. .... 82 G4　37 29N　82 31W
Pikou, China .... 35 E12 39 18N 122 22 E
Pikwitonei, Canada .... 71 B9　55 35N　97　9W
Piła, Poland .... 16 B9　53 10N　16 48 E
Pilanesberg △, S. Africa .... 56 D4　25 15S　27　4 E
Pilani, India .... 42 E6　28 22N　75 33 E
Pilar, Paraguay .... 94 B4　26 50S　58 20W
Pilaya →, Bolivia .... 92 H6　20 55S　64 4W
Pilbara, Australia .... 60 D2　23 35S 117 25 E
Pilcomayo →, Paraguay .... 94 B4　25 21S　57 42W
Pilgrim's Rest, S. Africa ... 57 C5　24 55S　30 44 E
Pilibhit, India .... 43 E8　28 40N　79 50 E
Pilica →, Poland .... 17 C11 51 52N　21 17 E
Pilkhawa, India .... 42 E7　28 43N　77 42 E
Pilliga, Australia .... 63 E4　30 21S 148 54 E
Pílos, Greece .... 23 F9　36 55N　21 42 E
Pilot Mound, Canada .... 71 D9　49 15N　98 54W
Pilot Point, U.S.A. .... 81 J6　33 24N　96 58W
Pilot Rock, U.S.A. .... 76 D4　45 29N 118 50W
Pilsen = Plzeň, Czech Rep. .. 16 D7　49 45N　13 22 E
Pima, U.S.A. .... 77 K9　32 54N 109 50W
Pimba, Australia .... 63 E2　31 18S 136 46 E
Pimenta Bueno, Brazil .... 92 F6　11 35S　61 10W
Pimentel, Peru .... 92 E3　6 45S　79 55W
Pinang, Malaysia .... 39 c　5 25N 100 15 E
Pinar, C. des, Spain .... 24 B10 39 53N　3 12 E
Pinar del Río, Cuba .... 88 B3　22 26N　83 40W
Pınarhisar, Turkey .... 23 D12 41 37N　27 30 E
Pinatubo, Mt., Phil. .... 37 A6　15　8N 120 21 E
Pincher Creek, Canada .... 70 D6　49 30N 113 57W
Pinchi L., Canada .... 70 C4　54 38N 124 30W
Pinckneyville, U.S.A. .... 80 F10 38　5N　89 23W
Pińczów, Poland .... 17 C11 50 32N　20 32 E
Pindar, Australia .... 61 E2　28 30S 115 47 E
Pindi Gheb, Pakistan .... 42 C5　33 14N　72 21 E
Pindos Óros, Greece .... 23 E9　40　0N　21　0 E
Pindus Mts. = Pindos Óros,
　Greece .... 23 E9　40　0N　21　0 E
Pine →, B.C., Canada .... 70 B4　56　8N 120 43W
Pine →, Sask., Canada .... 71 B7　58 50N 105 38W
Pine, C., Canada .... 73 C9　46 37N　53 32W
Pine Bluff, U.S.A. .... 81 H9　34 13N　92 1W
Pine Bluffs, U.S.A. .... 80 E2　41 11N 104　4W
Pine City, U.S.A. .... 80 C8　45 50N　92 59W
Pine Cr. →, U.S.A. .... 84 E7　41 10N　77 16W
Pine Creek, Australia .... 60 B5　13 50S 131 50 E
Pine Falls, Canada .... 71 C9　50 34N　96 11W
Pine Flat Res., U.S.A. ...... 78 J7　36 50N 119 20W
Pine Grove, U.S.A. .... 85 F8　40 33N　76 23W
Pine Pass, Canada .... 70 B4　55 25N 122 42W
Pine Point, Canada .... 70 A6　60 50N 114 28W
Pine Ridge, U.S.A. .... 80 D3　43　2N 102 33W
Pine River, Canada .... 71 C8　51 45N 100 30W
Pine River, U.S.A. .... 80 B7　46 43N　94 24W
Pine Valley, U.S.A. 79 N10 32 50N 116 32W
Pinecrest, U.S.A. .... 78 G6　38 12N 120　1W
Pinedale, Calif., U.S.A. .... 78 J7　36 50N 119 48W
Pinedale, Wyo., U.S.A. ...... 76 E9　42 52N 109 52W
Pinega →, Russia .... 18 B8　64 30N　44 19 E
Pinehill, Australia .... 62 C4　23 38S 146 57 E
Pinehouse L., Canada .... 71 B7　55 32N 106 35W
Pineimuta →, Canada .... 72 B1　52　8N　88 33W
Pinerolo, Italy .... 20 D7　44 53N　7 21 E
Pinetop, U.S.A. .... 77 J9　34　8N 109 56W
Pinetown, S. Africa .... 57 D5　29 48S　30 54 E
Pineville, U.S.A. .... 81 K8　31 19N　92 26W
Ping →, Thailand .... 38 E3　15 42N 100　9 E
Pingaring, Australia .... 61 F2　32 40S 118 32 E
Pingding, China .... 34 F7　37 47N 113 38 E
Pingdingshan, China .... 34 H7　33 43N 113 27 E
Pingdong, Taiwan .... 33 D7　22 39N 120 30 E
Pingdu, China .... 35 F10 36 42N 119 59 E
Pingelly, Australia .... 61 F2　32 32S 117　5 E
Pingguo, China .... 34 G5　23 35S 106 31 E
Pingliang, China .... 34 G4　35 35N 106 31 E
Pinglu, China .... 34 E7　39 31N 112 30 E
Pingquan, China .... 35 D10 41　1N 118 37 E
Pingrup, Australia .... 61 F2　33 32S 118 29 E
P'ingtung, Taiwan .... 33 D7　22 38N 120 30 E

Pingwu, China .... 34 H3 32 25N 104 30 E
Pingxiang, China .... 32 D5 22 6N 106 46 E
Pingyao, China .... 34 F7 37 12N 112 10 E
Pingyi, China .... 35 G9 35 30N 117 35 E
Pingyuan, China .... 34 F9 37 10N 116 22 E
Pinhal, Brazil 95 A6 22 10S 46 46W
Pinheiro, Brazil 93 D9   2 31S 45 5W
Pinheiro Machado, Brazil 95 C5 31 34S 53 23W
Pinhel, Portugal 21 B2 40 50N   7 1W
Pini, Indonesia .... 36 D1   0 10N 98 40 E
Piniós →, Greece .... 23 E10 39 55N 22 41 E
Pinjarra, Australia .... 61 F2 32 37S 115 52 E
Pink Mountain, Canada 70 B4   57 3N 122 52W
Pinnacles, U.S.A. 78 J5 36 33N 121 19W
Pinnacles △, U.S.A. 78 J5 36 25N 121 12W
Pinnaroo, Australia .... 63 F3 35 17S 140 53 E
Pínnes, Ákra, Greece .... 23 D11 40 5N 24 20 E
Pinon Hills, U.S.A. 79 L9 34 26N 117 39W
Pinos, Mexico 86 C4 22 20N 101 40W
Pinos, Mt., U.S.A. 79 L7 34 49N 119 8W
Pinos Pt., U.S.A. 77 H3 36 38N 121 57W
Pinotepa Nacional, Mexico ... 87 D5 16 19N 98 3W
Pinrang, Indonesia .... 37 E5   3 46S 119 41 E
Pins, Pte. aux, Canada 84 D3 42 15N 81 51W
Pinsk, Belarus .... 17 B14 52 10N 26 1 E
Pintados, Chile 92 H5 20 35S 69 40W
Pinyug, Russia .... 18 B8 60 5N 48 0 E
Pioche, U.S.A. 77 H6 37 56N 114 27W
Piombino, Italy .... 22 C4 42 55N 10 32 E
Pioner, Ostrov, Russia ...... 29 B10 79 50N 92 0 E
Piorini, L., Brazil 92 D6   3 15S 62 35W
Piotrków Trybunalski, Poland . 17 C10 51 23N 19 43 E
Pīp, Iran .... 45 E9 26 45N 60 10 E
Pipar, India .... 42 F5 26 25N 73 31 E
Pipar Road, India .... 42 F5 26 27N 73 27 E
Piparia, Mad. P., India ..... 42 H8 22 45N 78 23 E
Piparia, Mad. P., India ..... 42 J7 21 49N 77 37 E
Pipestone, U.S.A. 80 D6 44 0N 96 19W
Pipestone →, Canada 72 B2 52 53N 89 23W
Pipestone Cr. →, Canada 71 D8 49 38N 100 15W
Piplan, Pakistan .... 42 C4 32 17N 71 21 E
Piploda, India .... 42 H6 23 37N 74 56 E
Pipmuacan, Rés., Canada 73 C5 49 45N 70 30W
Pippingarra, Australia ...... 60 D2 20 27S 118 42 E
Piqua, U.S.A. 82 E3 40 9N 84 15W
Piquiri →, Brazil 95 A5 24 3S 54 14W
Pir Panjal Range, India ..... 42 C7 32 30N 76 50 E
Pir Sohrāb, Iran .... 45 E9 25 44N 60 54 E
Piracicaba, Brazil 95 A6 22 45S 47 40W
Piracuruca, Brazil 93 D10 3 50S 41 50W
Piræus = Piraiévs, Greece ... 23 F10 37 57N 23 42 E
Piraiévs, Greece .... 23 F10 37 57N 23 42 E
Pirajuí, Brazil 95 A6 21 59S 49 29W
Piram I., India .... 42 J5 21 36N 72 21 E
Pirané, Argentina 94 B4 25 42S 59 6W
Pirapora, Brazil 93 G10 17 20S 44 56W
Pirawa, India .... 42 G7 24 10N 76 2 E
Pírgos, Greece .... 23 F9 37 40N 21 27 E
Piribebuy, Paraguay 94 B4 25 26S 57 2W
Pirimapun, Indonesia .... 37 F9 6 20S 138 24 E
Pirin Planina, Bulgaria ..... 23 D10 41 40N 23 30 E
Pirineos = Pyrénées, Europe . 20 E4 42 45N   0 18 E
Piripiri, Brazil 93 D10 4 15S 41 46W
Pirmasens, Germany .... 16 D4 49 12N   7 36 E
Pirot, Serbia & M. .... 23 C10 43 9N 22 33 E
Piru, Indonesia .... 37 E7   3 4S 128 12 E
Piru, U.S.A. 79 L8 34 25N 118 48W
Pisa, Italy .... 22 C4 43 43N 10 23 E
Pisagua, Chile 92 G4 19 40S 70 15W
Pisco, Peru 92 F3 13 50S 76 12W
Písek, Czech Rep. .... 16 D8 49 19N 14 10 E
Pishan, China .... 32 C2 37 30N 78 33 E
Pīshīn, Iran .... 45 E9 26 6N 61 47 E
Pishin, Pakistan .... 42 D2 30 35N 67 0 E
Pishin Lora →, Pakistan ..... 42 E1 29 9N 64 5 E
Pising, Indonesia .... 37 F6   5 8S 121 53 E
Pismo Beach, U.S.A. 79 K6 35 9N 120 38W
Pissis, Cerro, Argentina 94 B2 27 45S 68 48W
Pissouri, Cyprus .... 25 E11 34 40N 32 42 E
Pistóia, Italy .... 22 C4 43 55N 10 54 E
Pistol B., Canada 71 A10 62 25N 92 37W
Pisuerga →, Spain 21 B3 41 33N   4 52W
Pit →, U.S.A. 76 F2 40 47N 122 6W
Pitarpunga, L., Australia ... 63 E3 34 24S 143 30 E
Pitcairn I., Pac. Oc. 65 K14 25 5S 130 5W
Pitch L., Trin. & Tob. 93 K15 10 12N 61 39W
Pite älv →, Sweden .... 8 D19 65 20N 21 25 E
Piteå, Sweden .... 8 D19 65 20N 21 25 E
Piteşti, Romania .... 17 F13 44 52N 24 54 E
Pithapuram, India .... 41 L13 17 10N 82 15 E
Pithara, Australia .... 61 F2 30 20S 116 35 E
Pithoragarh, India .... 43 E9 29 35N 80 13 E
Pithoro, Pakistan .... 42 G3 25 31N 69 23 E
Pitlochry, U.K. 11 E5 56 42N   3 44W
Pitsilia, Cyprus .... 25 E12 34 55N 33 0 E
Pitt I., Canada 70 C3 53 30N 129 50W
Pittsburg, Calif., U.S.A. ... 78 G5 38 2N 121 53W
Pittsburg, Kans., U.S.A. 81 G7 37 25N 94 42W
Pittsburg, Tex., U.S.A. 81 J7 33 0N 94 59W
Pittsburgh, U.S.A. 84 F5 40 26N 80 1W
Pittsfield, Ill., U.S.A. 80 F9 39 36N 90 49W
Pittsfield, Maine, U.S.A. ... 83 C11 44 47N 69 23W
Pittsfield, Mass., U.S.A. ... 85 D11 42 27N 73 15W
Pittsfield, N.H., U.S.A. 85 C13 43 18N 71 20W
Pittston, U.S.A. 85 E9 41 19N 75 47W
Pittsworth, Australia .... 63 D5 27 41S 151 37 E
Pituri →, Australia .... 62 C2 22 35S 138 30 E
Piura, Peru 92 E2   5 15S 80 38W
Pixley, U.S.A. 78 K7 35 58N 119 18W
Pizhou, China .... 34 G9 34 44N 116 55 E
Placentia, Canada 73 C9 47 0N 54 40W
Placentia B., Canada 73 C9 47 0N 54 40W
Placerville, U.S.A. 78 G6 38 44N 120 48W
Placetas, Cuba 88 B4 22 15N 79 44W
Plainfield, N.J., U.S.A. 85 F10 40 37N 74 25W
Plainfield, Ohio, U.S.A. 84 F3 40 13N 81 43W
Plainfield, Vt., U.S.A. 85 B12 44 17N 72 26W
Plains, Mont., U.S.A. 76 C6 47 28N 114 53W
Plains, Tex., U.S.A. 81 J3 33 11N 102 50W
Plainview, Nebr., U.S.A. 80 D6 42 21N 97 47W
Plainview, Tex., U.S.A. 81 H4 34 11N 101 43W
Plainwell, U.S.A. 82 D3 42 27N 85 38W
Plaistow, U.S.A. 85 D13 42 50N 71 6W
Pláka, Ákra, Greece .... 25 D8 35 11N 26 19 E
Plana Cays, Bahamas 89 B5 22 38N 73 30W
Planada, U.S.A. 78 H6 37 16N 120 19W
Plano, U.S.A. 81 J6 33 1N 96 42W

Plant City, U.S.A. 83 M4 28 1N 82 7W
Plaquemine, U.S.A. 81 K9 30 17N 91 14W
Plasencia, Spain 21 B2 40 3N   6 8W
Plaster City, U.S.A. 79 N11 32 47N 115 51W
Plaster Rock, Canada 73 C6 46 53N 67 22W
Plastun, Russia .... 30 B8 44 45N 136 19 E
Plata, Río de la, S. Amer. .. 94 C4 34 45S 57 30W
Plátani →, Italy .... 22 F5 37 23N 13 16 E
Plátanos, Greece .... 25 D5 35 28N 23 33 E
Platte, U.S.A. 80 D5 43 23N 98 51W
Platte →, Mo., U.S.A. 80 F7 39 16N 94 50W
Platte →, Nebr., U.S.A. 80 E7 41 4N 95 53W
Platteville, U.S.A. 80 D9 42 44N 90 29W
Plattsburgh, U.S.A. 85 B11 44 42N 73 28W
Plattsmouth, U.S.A. 80 E7 41 1N 95 53W
Plauen, Germany .... 16 C7 50 30N 12 8 E
Plavinas, Latvia .... 9 H21 56 35N 25 46 E
Playa Blanca, Canary Is. 24 F6 28 55N 13 37W
Playa Blanca Sur, Canary Is. . 24 F6 28 51N 13 50W
Playa de las Americas, Canary Is. 24 F3 28 5N 16 43W
Playa de Mogán, Canary Is. .. 24 G4 27 48N 15 47W
Playa del Inglés, Canary Is. . 24 G4 27 45N 15 33W
Playa Esmeralda, Canary Is. .. 24 F5 28 8N 14 16W
Playgreen L., Canada 71 C9 54 0N 98 15W
Pleasant Bay, Canada 73 C7 46 51N 60 48W
Pleasant Hill, U.S.A. 78 H4 37 57N 122 4W
Pleasant Mount, U.S.A. 85 E9 41 44N 75 26W
Pleasanton, Calif., U.S.A. .. 78 H5 37 39N 121 52W
Pleasanton, Tex., U.S.A. 81 L5 28 58N 98 29W
Pleasantville, N.J., U.S.A. .. 82 F8 39 24N 74 32W
Pleasantville, Pa., U.S.A. .. 84 E5 41 35N 79 34W
Plei Ku, Vietnam .... 38 F7 13 57N 108 0 E
Plenty →, Australia .... 62 C2 23 25S 136 31 E
Plenty, B. of, N.Z. .... 59 G6 37 45S 177 0 E
Plentywood, U.S.A. 80 A2 48 47N 104 34W
Plesetsk, Russia .... 18 B7 62 43N 40 20 E
Plessisville, Canada 73 C5 46 14N 71 47W
Plétipi, L., Canada 73 B5 51 44N 70 6W
Pleven, Bulgaria .... 23 C11 43 26N 24 37 E
Plevlja, Serbia & M. .... 23 C8 43 21N 19 21 E
Plevna, Canada 84 B8 44 58N 76 59W
Płock, Poland .... 17 B10 52 32N 19 40 E
Plöckenstein, Germany .... 16 D7 48 46N 13 51 E
Ploiești, Romania .... 17 F14 44 57N 26 5 E
Plonge, Lac la, Canada 71 B7 55 8N 107 20W
Plovdiv, Bulgaria .... 23 C11 42 8N 24 44 E
Plover Cove Res., China ..... 33 G11 22 28N 114 15 E
Plum, U.S.A. 84 F5 40 29N 79 47W
Plum I., U.S.A. 85 E12 41 11N 72 12W
Plumas, U.S.A. 78 F7 39 45N 120 4W
Plummer, U.S.A. 76 C5 47 20N 116 53W
Plumtree, Zimbabwe .... 55 G2 20 27S 27 55 E
Plungė, Lithuania .... 9 J19 55 53N 21 59 E
Plymouth, Trin. & Tob. 93 J16 11 14N 60 48W
Plymouth, U.K. 13 G3 50 22N   4 10W
Plymouth, Calif., U.S.A. 78 G6 38 29N 120 51W
Plymouth, Ind., U.S.A. 82 E2 41 21N 86 19W
Plymouth, Mass., U.S.A. 85 E14 41 57N 70 40W
Plymouth, N.C., U.S.A. 83 H7 35 52N 76 43W
Plymouth, N.H., U.S.A. 85 C13 43 46N 71 41W
Plymouth, Pa., U.S.A. 85 E9 41 14N 75 57W
Plymouth, Wis., U.S.A. 82 D2 43 45N 87 59W
Plympton-Wyoming, Canada 84 D2 42 57N 82 7W
Plynlimon = Pumlumon Fawr,
  U.K. 13 E4 52 28N   3 46W
Plzeň, Czech Rep. .... 16 D7 49 45N 13 22 E
Po →, Italy .... 22 B5 44 57N 12 4 E
Po Hai = Bo Hai, China ...... 35 E10 39 0N 119 0 E
Po Toi, China .... 33 G11 22 10N 114 16 E
Pobeda, Russia .... 29 C15 65 12N 146 12 E
Pobedy, Pik, Kyrgyzstan ..... 28 E8 42 0N 79 58 E
Pocahontas, Ark., U.S.A. 81 G9 36 16N 90 58W
Pocahontas, Iowa, U.S.A. 80 D7 42 44N 94 40W
Pocatello, U.S.A. 76 E7 42 52N 112 27W
Pochutla, Mexico 87 D5 15 50N 96 31W
Pocito Casas, Mexico 86 B2 28 32N 111 6W
Pocomoke City, U.S.A. 82 F8 38 5N 75 34W
Poços de Caldas, Brazil 95 A6 21 50S 46 33W
Podgorica, Serbia & M. ...... 23 C8 42 30N 19 19 E
Podílska Vysochyna, Ukraine . 17 D14 49 0N 28 0 E
Podolsk, Russia .... 18 C6 55 25N 37 30 E
Podporozhye, Russia .... 18 B5 60 55N 34 2 E
Pofadder, S. Africa .... 56 D2 29 10S 19 22 E
Pogranichnyy, Russia .... 30 B5 44 25N 131 24 E
Poh, Indonesia .... 37 E6   0 46S 122 51 E
P'ohang, S. Korea .... 35 F15 36 1N 129 23 E
Pohjanmaa, Finland .... 8 E20 62 58N 22 50 E
Pohnpei, Micronesia .... 64 G7   6 55N 158 10 E
Pohri, India .... 42 G6 25 32N 77 22 E
Poinsett, C., Antarctica .... 5 C8 65 42S 113 18 E
Point Arena, U.S.A. 78 G3 38 55N 123 41W
Point Baker, U.S.A. 70 B2 56 21N 133 37W
Point Edward, Canada 72 D3 43 0N 82 30W
Point Fortin, Trin. & Tob. .. 93 K15 10 10N 61 42W
Point Hope, U.S.A. 68 B3 68 21N 166 47W
Point L., Canada 68 B8 65 15N 113 4W
Point Lisas, Trin. & Tob. ... 93 K15 10 32N 61 30W
Point Pedro, Sri Lanka ...... 40 Q12 9 50N 80 15 E
Point Pelee △, Canada 84 E2 41 57N 82 31W
Point Pleasant, N.J., U.S.A. . 85 F10 40 5N 74 4W
Point Pleasant, W. Va., U.S.A. 82 F4 38 51N 82 8W
Point Reyes △, U.S.A. 78 G2 38 0N 122 55W
Pointe-à-Pitre, Guadeloupe .. 88 b 16 10N 61 32W
Pointe-au-Pic = La Malbaie,
  Canada 73 C5 47 40N 70 10W
Pointe-Claire, Canada 85 A11 45 26N 73 50W
Pointe-Gatineau, Canada 85 A9 45 28N 75 42W
Pointe-Noire, Congo .... 52 E2   4 48S 11 53 E
Pointe Noire, Guadeloupe .... 88 b 16 14N 61 47W
Poisonbush Ra., Australia ... 60 D3 22 30S 121 30 E
Poissonnier Pt., Australia .. 60 C2 19 57S 119 10 E
Poitiers, France .... 20 C4 46 35N   0 20 E
Poitou, France 20 C3 46 40N   0 10W
Pojoaque, U.S.A. 77 J11 35 54N 106 1W
Pokaran, India .... 40 F7 27 0N 71 50 E
Pokataroo, Australia .... 63 D4 29 30S 148 36 E
Pokhara, Nepal .... 43 E10 28 14N 83 58 E
Poko, Dem. Rep. of the Congo . 54 B2   3 7N 26 52 E
Pokrovsk, Russia .... 29 C13 61 29N 129 0 E
Pola = Pula, Croatia .... 16 F7 44 54N 13 57 E
Polacca, U.S.A. 77 J8 35 50N 110 23W
Polan, Iran .... 45 E9 25 30N 61 10 E
Poland ■, Europe .... 17 C10 52 0N 20 0 E
Polar Bear △, Canada 72 A2 55 0N 83 45W
Polatsk, Belarus .... 18 C4 55 30N 28 50 E
Polcura, Chile 94 D1 37 17S 71 43W
Polessk, Russia .... 9 J19 54 50N 21 8 E

Polesye = Pripet Marshes,
  Europe .... 17 B15 52 10N 28 10 E
Polevskoy, Russia .... 18 C11 56 26N 60 11 E
Pŏlgyo-ri, S. Korea .... 35 G14 34 51N 127 21 E
Police, Poland .... 16 B8 53 33N 14 33 E
Polillo Is., Phil. .... 37 B6 14 56N 122 0 E
Polis, Cyprus .... 25 D11 35 2N 32 26 E
Políyiros, Greece .... 23 D10 40 23N 23 25 E
Polk, U.S.A. 84 E5 41 22N 79 56W
Pollachi, India .... 40 P10 10 35N 77 0 E
Pollença, Spain .... 24 B10 39 53N   3 1 E
Pollença, B. de, Spain ...... 24 B10 39 53N   3 8 E
Polnovat, Russia .... 28 C7 63 50N 65 54 E
Polokwane, S. Africa .... 57 C4 23 54S 29 25 E
Polonne, Ukraine .... 17 C14 50 6N 27 30 E
Polonnoye = Polonne, Ukraine . 17 C14 50 6N 27 30 E
Polson, U.S.A. 76 C6 47 41N 114 9W
Poltava, Ukraine .... 19 E5 49 35N 34 35 E
Põltsamaa, Estonia .... 9 G21 58 41N 25 58 E
Polunochnoye, Russia .... 28 C7 60 52N 60 25 E
Põlva, Estonia .... 9 G22 58 3N 27 3 E
Polyarny, Russia .... 18 A5 69 8N 33 20 E
Polynesia, Pac. Oc. 65 F11 10 0S 162 0W
Polynésie française = French
  Polynesia ☑, Pac. Oc. 65 K12 20 0S 145 0W
Pomaro, Mexico 86 D4 18 20N 103 18W
Pombal, Portugal 21 C1 39 55N   8 40W
Pómbia, Greece .... 25 E6 35 0N 24 51 E
Pomene, Mozam. .... 57 C6 22 53S 35 33 E
Pomeroy, Ohio, U.S.A. 82 F4 39 2N 82 2W
Pomeroy, Wash., U.S.A. 76 C5 46 28N 117 36W
Pomézia, Italy .... 22 D5 41 40N 12 30 E
Pomona, Australia .... 63 D5 26 22S 152 52 E
Pomona, U.S.A. 79 L9 34 4N 117 45W
Pomorskie, Pojezierze, Poland . 17 B9 53 40N 16 37 E
Pomos, Cyprus .... 25 D11 35 9N 32 33 E
Pomos, C., Cyprus .... 25 D11 35 10N 32 33 E
Pompano Beach, U.S.A. 83 M5 26 14N 80 8W
Pompeys Pillar, U.S.A. 76 D10 45 59N 107 57W
Pompeys Pillar △, U.S.A. 76 D10 46 0N 108 0W
Pompton Lakes, U.S.A. 85 F10 41 0N 74 17W
Ponape = Pohnpei, Micronesia . 64 G7   6 55N 158 10 E
Ponask L., Canada 72 B1 54 0N 92 41W
Ponca, U.S.A. 80 D6 42 34N 96 43W
Ponca City, U.S.A. 81 G6 36 42N 97 5W
Ponce, Puerto Rico .... 89 d 18 1N 66 37W
Ponchatoula, U.S.A. 81 K9 30 26N 90 26W
Poncheville, L., Canada 72 B4 50 10N 76 55W
Pond, U.S.A. 79 K7 35 43N 119 20W
Pond Inlet, Canada 69 A12 72 40N 77 0W
Ponds, I. of, Canada 73 B8 53 27N 55 52W
Pondicherry, India .... 40 P11 11 59N 79 50 E
Ponferrada, Spain 21 A2 42 32N   6 35W
Ponnani, India .... 40 P9 10 45N 75 59 E
Ponoka, Canada 70 C6 52 42N 113 40W
Ponorogo, Indonesia .... 37 G14 7 52S 111 27 E
Ponoy, Russia .... 18 A7 67 0N 41 13 E
Ponoy →, Russia .... 18 A7 66 59N 41 17 E
Ponta do Sol, Madeira 24 D2 32 42N 17 7W
Ponta Grossa, Brazil 95 B5 25 7S 50 10W
Ponta Porã, Brazil 95 A4 22 20S 55 35W
Pontarlier, France .... 20 C7 46 54N   6 20 E
Pontchartrain L., U.S.A. 81 K10 30 5N 90 5W
Ponte do Pungué, Mozam. ..... 55 F3 19 30S 34 33 E
Ponte Nova, Brazil 95 A7 20 25S 42 54W
Ponteix, Canada 71 D7 49 46N 107 29W
Pontevedra, Spain 21 A1 42 26N   8 40W
Pontiac, Ill., U.S.A. 80 E10 40 53N 88 38W
Pontiac, Mich., U.S.A. 82 D4 42 38N 83 18W
Pontian Kechil, Malaysia .... 39 d   1 29N 103 23 E
Pontianak, Indonesia .... 36 E3   0 3S 109 15 E
Pontine Is. = Ponziane, Ísole, Italy 22 D5 40 55N 12 57 E
Pontine Mts. = Kuzey Anadolu
  Dağları, Turkey .... 19 F6 41 30N 35 0 E
Pontivy, France 20 B2 48 5N   2 58W
Pontoise, France .... 20 B5 49 3N   2 5 E
Ponton →, Canada 70 B5 58 27N 116 11W
Pontypool, Canada 84 B6 44 6N 78 38W
Pontypool, U.K. 13 F4 51 42N   3 2W
Ponziane, Ísole, Italy ...... 22 D5 40 55N 12 57 E
Poochera, Australia .... 63 E1 32 43S 134 51 E
Poole, U.K. 13 G6 50 43N   1 59W
Poole □, U.K. 13 G6 50 43N   1 59W
Poona = Pune, India .... 40 K8 18 29N 73 57 E
Pooncarie, Australia .... 63 E3 33 22S 142 31 E
Poopelloe L., Australia ..... 63 E3 31 40S 144 0 E
Poopó, L. de, Bolivia 92 G5 18 30S 67 35W
Popayán, Colombia 92 C3   2 27N 76 36W
Poperinge, Belgium .... 15 D2 50 51N   2 42 E
Popilta L., Australia .... 63 E3 33 10S 141 42 E
Popio L., Australia .... 63 E3 33 10S 141 52 E
Poplar, U.S.A. 80 A2 48 7N 105 12W
Poplar →, Canada 71 C9 53 0N 97 19W
Poplar Bluff, U.S.A. 81 G9 36 46N 90 24W
Poplarville, U.S.A. 81 K10 30 51N 89 32W
Popocatépetl, Volcán, Mexico . 87 D5 19 2N 98 38W
Popokabaka, Dem. Rep. of
  the Congo .... 52 F3   5 41S 16 40 E
Poprad, Slovak Rep. .... 17 D11 49 3N 20 18 E
Porali →, Pakistan .... 42 G2 25 58N 66 26 E
Porbandar, India .... 42 J3 21 44N 69 43 E
Porcher I., Canada 70 C2 53 50N 130 30W
Porcupine →, Canada 71 B8 59 11N 104 46W
Porcupine →, U.S.A. 68 B5 66 34N 145 19W
Porcupine Gorge △, Australia . 62 C3 20 22S 144 26 E
Pordenone, Italy .... 22 B5 45 57N 12 39 E
Pori, Finland .... 9 F19 61 29N 21 48 E
Porlamar, Venezuela 92 A6 10 57N 63 51W
Poronaysk, Russia .... 29 E15 49 13N 143 0 E
Poroshiri-Dake, Japan .... 30 C11 42 41N 142 52 E
Poroto Mts., Tanzania .... 55 D3   9 0S 33 30 E
Porpoise B., Antarctica ..... 5 C9 66 0S 127 0 E
Porreres, Spain .... 24 B10 39 31N   3 2 E
Porsangen, Norway .... 8 A21 70 40N 25 40 E
Porsgrunn, Norway .... 9 G13 59 10N   9 40 E
Port Alberni, Canada 70 D4 49 14N 124 50W
Port Alfred, S. Africa ...... 56 E4 33 36S 26 55 E
Port Alice, Canada 70 C3 50 20N 127 25W
Port Allegany, U.S.A. 84 E6 41 48N 78 17W
Port Allen, U.S.A. 81 K9 30 27N 91 12W
Port Alma, Australia .... 62 C5 23 38S 150 53 E
Port Angeles, U.S.A. 78 B3 48 7N 123 27W
Port Antonio, Jamaica .... 88 a 18 10N 76 30W
Port Aransas, U.S.A. 81 M6 27 50N 97 4W
Port Arthur, Australia ...... 63 G4 43 7S 147 50 E
Port Arthur, U.S.A. 81 L8 29 54N 93 56W
Port au Choix, Canada 73 B8 50 43N 57 22W
Port au Port B., Canada 73 C8 48 40N 58 50W

Port-au-Prince, Haiti 89 C5 18 40N 72 20W
Port Augusta, Australia ..... 63 E2 32 30S 137 50 E
Port Austin, U.S.A. 84 B2 44 3N 83 1W
Port Bell, Uganda .... 54 B3   0 18N 32 35 E
Port Bergé Vaovao, Madag. ... 57 B8 15 33S 47 40 E
Port Blandford, Canada 73 C9 48 20N 54 10W
Port Bradshaw, Australia .... 62 A2 12 30S 137 20 E
Port Broughton, Australia ... 63 E2 33 37S 137 56 E
Port Burwell, Canada 84 D4 42 40N 80 48W
Port Canning, India .... 43 H13 22 23N 88 40 E
Port-Cartier, Canada 73 B6 50 2N 66 50W
Port Chalmers, N.Z. .... 59 L3 45 49S 170 30 E
Port Charlotte, U.S.A. 83 M4 26 59N 82 6W
Port Chester, U.S.A. 85 F11 41 0N 73 40W
Port Clements, Canada 70 C2 53 40N 132 10W
Port Clinton, U.S.A. 82 E4 41 31N 82 56W
Port Colborne, Canada 84 D4 42 50N 79 10W
Port Coquitlam, Canada 70 D4 49 15N 122 45W
Port Credit, Canada 84 C5 43 33N 79 35W
Port Curtis, Australia ...... 62 C5 23 57S 151 20 E
Port d'Alcúdia, Spain .... 24 B10 39 50N   3 7 E
Port Dalhousie, Canada 84 C5 43 13N 79 16W
Port Darwin, Australia ...... 60 B5 12 24S 130 45 E
Port Darwin, Falk. Is. 96 G5 51 50S 59 0W
Port Davey, Australia .... 63 G4 43 16S 145 55 E
Port-de-Paix, Haiti 89 C5 19 50N 72 50W
Port de Pollença, Spain ..... 24 B10 39 54N   3 4 E
Port de Sóller, Spain .... 24 B9 39 48N   2 42 E
Port Dickson, Malaysia ...... 39 L3   2 30N 101 49 E
Port Douglas, Australia ..... 62 B4 16 30S 145 30 E
Port Dover, Canada 84 D4 42 47N 80 12W
Port Edward, Canada 70 C2 54 12N 130 10W
Port Elgin, Canada 84 B3 44 25N 81 25W
Port Elizabeth, S. Africa ... 56 E4 33 58S 25 40 E
Port Ellen, U.K. 11 F2 55 38N   6 11W
Port Erin, U.K. 12 C3 54 5N   4 45W
Port Essington, Australia ... 60 B5 11 15S 132 10 E
Port Ewen, U.S.A. 85 E11 41 54N 73 59W
Port Fairy, Australia .... 63 F3 38 22S 142 12 E
Port Gamble, U.S.A. 78 C4 47 51N 122 35W
Port-Gentil, Gabon .... 52 E1   0 40S   8 50 E
Port Germein, Australia ..... 63 E2 33 1S 138 1 E
Port Gibson, U.S.A. 81 K9 31 58N 90 59W
Port Glasgow, U.K. 11 F4 55 56N   4 41W
Port Harcourt, Nigeria ...... 50 H7   4 40N   7 10 E
Port Hardy, Canada 70 C3 50 41N 127 30W
Port Harrison = Inukjuak, Canada 69 C12 58 25N 78 5W
Port Hawkesbury, Canada 73 C7 45 36N 61 22W
Port Hedland, Australia ..... 60 D2 20 25S 118 35 E
Port Henry, U.S.A. 85 B11 44 3N 73 28W
Port Hood, Canada 73 C7 46 0N 61 32W
Port Hope, Canada 84 C6 43 56N 78 20W
Port Hope, U.S.A. 84 C2 43 57N 82 43W
Port Hope Simpson, Canada ... 73 B8 52 33N 56 18W
Port Hueneme, U.S.A. 79 L7 34 7N 119 12W
Port Huron, U.S.A. 84 D2 42 58N 82 26W
Port Jefferson, U.S.A. 85 F11 40 57N 73 3W
Port Jervis, U.S.A. 85 E10 41 22N 74 41W
Port Kelang = Pelabuhan Kelang,
  Malaysia .... 39 L3   3 0N 101 23 E
Port Kenny, Australia .... 63 E1 33 10S 134 41 E
Port Lairge = Waterford, Ireland 10 D4 52 15N   7 8W
Port Laoise, Ireland 10 C4 53 2N   7 18W
Port Lavaca, U.S.A. 81 L6 28 37N 96 38W
Port Leyden, U.S.A. 85 C9 43 35N 75 21W
Port Lincoln, Australia ..... 63 E2 34 42S 135 52 E
Port Loko, S. Leone 50 G3   8 48N 12 46W
Port-Louis, Guadeloupe ...... 88 b 16 28N 61 32W
Port Louis, Mauritius .... 49 H9 20 10S 57 30 E
Port MacDonnell, Australia .. 63 F3 38 5S 140 48 E
Port McNeill, Canada 70 C3 50 35N 127 6W
Port Macquarie, Australia ... 63 E5 31 25S 152 25 E
Port Maria, Jamaica .... 88 a 18 25N 76 55W
Port Matilda, U.S.A. 84 F6 40 48N 78 3W
Port Mellon, Canada 70 D4 49 32N 123 31W
Port-Menier, Canada 73 C7 49 51N 64 15W
Port Moody, Canada 78 A4 49 17N 122 51W
Port Morant, Jamaica .... 88 a 17 54N 76 19W
Port Moresby, Papua N. G. ... 64 H6   9 24S 147 8 E
Port Musgrave, Australia .... 62 A3 11 55S 141 50 E
Port Neches, U.S.A. 81 L8 30 0N 93 59W
Port Nolloth, S. Africa ..... 56 D2 29 17S 16 52 E
Port Nouveau-Québec =
  Kangiqsualujjuaq, Canada .. 69 C13 58 30N 65 59W
Port of Spain, Trin. & Tob. . 89 D7 10 40N 61 31W
Port Orange, U.S.A. 83 L5 29 9N 80 59W
Port Orchard, U.S.A. 78 C4 47 32N 122 38W
Port Orford, U.S.A. 76 E1 42 45N 124 30W
Port Pegasus, N.Z. .... 59 M1 47 12S 167 41 E
Port Perry, Canada 84 B6 44 6N 78 56W
Port Phillip B., Australia .. 63 F3 38 10S 144 50 E
Port Pirie, Australia .... 63 E2 33 10S 138 1 E
Port Renfrew, Canada 70 D4 48 30N 124 20W
Port Roper, Australia .... 62 A2 14 45S 135 25 E
Port Rowan, Canada 84 D4 42 40N 80 30W
Port Safaga = Bûr Safâga, Egypt 44 E2 26 43N 33 57 E
Port Said = Bûr Sa'îd, Egypt . 51 B12 31 16N 32 18 E
Port St. Joe, U.S.A. 83 L3 29 49N 85 18W
Port St. Johns = Umzimvubu,
  S. Africa .... 57 E4 31 38S 29 33 E
Port St. Lucie, U.S.A. 83 M5 27 20N 80 20W
Port Sanilac, U.S.A. 84 C2 43 26N 82 33W
Port Severn, Canada 84 B5 44 48N 79 43W
Port Shepstone, S. Africa ... 57 E5 30 44S 30 28 E
Port Simpson, Canada 70 C2 54 30N 130 20W
Port Stanley = Stanley, Falk. Is. 96 G5 51 40S 59 51W
Port Stanley, Canada 84 D3 42 40N 81 10W
Port Sudan = Bûr Sûdân, Sudan 51 E13 19 32N 37 9 E
Port Sulphur, U.S.A. 81 L10 29 29N 89 42W
Port Talbot, U.K. 13 F4 51 35N   3 47W
Port Townsend, U.S.A. 78 B4 48 7N 122 45W
Port-Vendres, France .... 20 E5 42 32N   3 8 E
Port Vila, Vanuatu .... 64 J8 17 45S 168 18 E
Port Vladimir, Russia .... 18 A5 69 25N 33 6 E
Port Wakefield, Australia ... 63 E2 34 12S 138 10 E
Port Washington, U.S.A. 82 D2 43 23N 87 53W
Porta Orientalis, Romania ... 17 F12 45 0N 22 18 E
Portadown, U.K. 10 B5 54 25N   6 27W
Portaferry, U.K. 10 B6 54 23N   5 33W
Portage, Pa., U.S.A. 84 F6 40 23N 78 41W
Portage, Wis., U.S.A. 80 D10 43 33N 89 28W
Portage la Prairie, Canada .. 71 D9 49 58N 98 18W
Portageville, U.S.A. 81 G10 36 26N 89 42W
Portalegre, Portugal 21 C2 39 19N   7 25W
Portales, U.S.A. 81 H3 34 11N 103 20W
Portarlington, Ireland 10 C4 53 9N   7 14W
Portbou, Spain .... 21 A7 42 25N   3 9 E

Porter L., N.W.T., Canada 71 A7 61 41N 108 5W
Porter L., Sask., Canada 71 B7 56 20N 107 20W
Porterville, S. Africa ..... 56 E2 33 0S 19 0 E
Porterville, U.S.A. 78 J8 36 4N 119 1W
Porthcawl, U.K. 13 F4 51 29N 3 42W
Porthill, U.S.A. 76 B5 48 59N 116 30W
Porthmadog, U.K. 12 E3 52 55N 4 8W
Portile de Fier, Europe ..... 17 F12 44 44N 22 30 E
Portimão, Portugal 21 D1 37 8N 8 32W
Portishead, U.K. 13 F5 51 29N 2 46W
Portknockie, U.K. 11 D6 57 42N 2 51W
Portland, N.S.W., Australia ..... 63 E5 33 20S 150 0 E
Portland, Vic., Australia ..... 63 F3 38 20S 141 35 E
Portland, Canada 85 B8 44 42N 76 12W
Portland, Conn., U.S.A. 85 E12 41 34N 72 38W
Portland, Maine, U.S.A. 69 D12 43 39N 70 16W
Portland, Mich., U.S.A. 82 D3 42 52N 84 54W
Portland, Oreg., U.S.A. 78 E4 45 32N 122 37W
Portland, Pa., U.S.A. 85 F9 40 55N 75 6W
Portland ✕ (PDX), U.S.A. 78 E4 45 35N 122 36W
Portland, I. of, U.K. 13 G5 50 33N 2 26W
Portland B., Australia ..... 63 F3 38 15S 141 45 E
Portland Bight, Jamaica ..... 88 a 17 52N 77 5W
Portland Bill, U.K. 13 G5 50 31N 2 28W
Portland Canal, U.S.A. 70 B2 55 56N 130 0W
Portland Pt., Jamaica ..... 88 a 17 42N 77 11W
Portmadoc = Porthmadog, U.K. 12 E3 52 55N 4 8W
Portmore, Jamaica ..... 88 a 17 53N 77 33W
Porto, Portugal 21 B1 41 8N 8 40W
Pôrto Alegre, Brazil 95 C5 30 5S 51 10W
Porto Cristo, Spain ..... 24 B10 39 33N 3 20 E
Pôrto de Móz, Brazil 93 D8 1 41S 52 13W
Porto Empédocle, Italy ..... 22 F5 37 17N 13 32 E
Pôrto Esperança, Brazil 92 G7 19 37S 57 29W
Pôrto Franco, Brazil 93 E9 6 20S 47 24W
Pôrto Mendes, Brazil 95 A5 24 30S 54 15W
Porto Moniz, Madeira 24 D2 32 52N 17 11W
Pôrto Murtinho, Brazil 92 H7 21 45S 57 55W
Pôrto Nacional, Brazil 93 F9 10 40S 48 30W
Porto-Novo, Benin ..... 50 G6 6 23N 2 42 E
Porto Petro, Spain ..... 24 B10 39 22N 3 13 E
Porto Santo, I. de, Madeira 50 B2 33 45N 16 25W
Pôrto Seguro, Brazil 93 G11 16 26S 39 5W
Porto Tórres, Italy ..... 22 D3 40 50N 8 24 E
Pôrto União, Brazil 95 B5 26 10S 51 10W
Pôrto Válter, Brazil 92 E4 8 15S 72 40W
Porto-Vecchio, France ..... 20 F8 41 35N 9 16 E
Pôrto Velho, Brazil 92 E6 8 46S 63 54W
Portobelo, Panama 88 E4 9 35N 79 42W
Portoferráio, Italy ..... 22 C4 42 48N 10 20 E
Portola, U.S.A. 78 F6 39 49N 120 28W
Portoscuso, Italy ..... 22 E3 39 12N 8 24 E
Portoviejo, Ecuador 92 D2 1 7S 80 28W
Portpatrick, U.K. 11 G3 54 51N 5 7W
Portree, U.K. 11 D2 57 25N 6 12W
Portrush, U.K. 10 A5 55 12N 6 40W
Portsmouth, Domin. 89 C7 15 34N 61 27W
Portsmouth, U.K. 13 G6 50 48N 1 6W
Portsmouth, N.H., U.S.A. 83 D10 43 5N 70 45W
Portsmouth, Ohio, U.S.A. 82 F4 38 44N 82 57W
Portsmouth, R.I., U.S.A. 85 E13 41 36N 71 15W
Portsmouth, Va., U.S.A. 82 G7 36 50N 76 18W
Portsmouth □, U.K. 13 G6 50 48N 1 6W
Portsoy, U.K. 11 D6 57 41N 2 41W
Portstewart, U.K. 10 A5 55 11N 6 43W
Porttipahtan tekojärvi, Finland ..... 8 B22 68 5N 26 40 E
Portugal ■, Europe 21 C1 40 0N 8 0W
Portumna, Ireland 10 C3 53 6N 8 14W
Portville, U.S.A. 84 D6 42 3N 78 20W
Porvenir, Chile 96 G2 53 10S 70 16W
Porvoo, Finland ..... 9 F21 60 24N 25 40 E
Posadas, Argentina 95 B4 27 30S 55 50W
Poshan = Boshan, China ..... 35 F9 36 28N 117 49 E
Posht-e Badam, Iran ..... 45 C7 33 2N 58 40 E
Poso, Indonesia ..... 37 E6 1 20S 120 55 E
Posong, S. Korea ..... 35 G14 34 46N 127 5 E
Posse, Brazil 93 F9 14 4S 46 18W
Possession I., Antarctica ..... 5 D11 72 4S 172 0 E
Possum Kingdom L., U.S.A. 81 J5 32 52N 98 26W
Post, U.S.A. 81 J4 33 12N 101 23W
Post Falls, U.S.A. 76 C5 47 43N 116 57W
Postavy = Pastavy, Belarus ..... 9 J22 55 4N 26 50 E
Poste-de-la-Baleine = Kuujjuarapik, Canada 72 A4 55 20N 77 35W
Postmasburg, S. Africa ..... 56 D3 28 18S 23 5 E
Postojna, Slovenia ..... 16 F8 45 46N 14 12 E
Poston, U.S.A. 79 M12 34 0N 114 24W
Postville, Canada 73 B8 54 54N 59 47W
Potchefstroom, S. Africa ..... 56 D4 26 41S 27 7 E
Poteau, U.S.A. 81 H7 35 3N 94 37W
Poteet, U.S.A. 81 L5 29 2N 98 35W
Potenza, Italy ..... 22 D6 40 38N 15 48 E
Poteriteri, L., N.Z. ..... 59 M1 46 5S 167 10 E
Potgietersrus = Mokopane, S. Africa ..... 57 C4 24 10S 28 55 E
Poti, Georgia ..... 19 F7 42 10N 41 38 E
Potiskum, Nigeria ..... 51 F8 11 39N 11 2 E
Potomac →, U.S.A. 82 G7 38 0N 76 23W
Potosí, Bolivia 92 G5 19 38S 65 50W
Potosi Mt., U.S.A. 79 K11 35 57N 115 29W
Pototan, Phil. ..... 37 B6 10 54N 122 38 E
Potrerillos, Chile 94 B2 26 30S 69 30W
Potsdam, Germany ..... 16 B7 52 25N 13 4 E
Potsdam, U.S.A. 85 B10 44 40N 74 59W
Pottersville, U.S.A. 85 C11 43 43N 73 50W
Pottstown, U.S.A. 85 F9 40 15N 75 39W
Pottsville, U.S.A. 85 F8 40 41N 76 12W
Pottuvil, Sri Lanka ..... 40 R12 6 55N 81 50 E
Pouce Coupé, Canada 70 B4 55 40N 120 10W
Poughkeepsie, U.S.A. 85 E11 41 42N 73 56W
Poulaphouca Res., Ireland 10 C5 53 8N 6 30W
Poulsbo, U.S.A. 78 C4 47 44N 122 38W
Poultney, U.S.A. 85 C11 43 31N 73 14W
Poulton-le-Fylde, U.K. 12 D5 53 51N 2 58W
Pouso Alegre, Brazil 95 A6 22 14S 45 57W
Pouthisat, Cambodia ..... 38 F4 12 34N 103 50 E
Považská Bystrica, Slovak Rep. ..... 17 D10 49 8N 18 27 E
Povenets, Russia ..... 18 B5 62 50N 34 50 E
Poverty B., N.Z. ..... 59 H7 38 43S 178 2 E
Póvoa de Varzim, Portugal 21 B1 41 25N 8 46W
Povungnituk = Puvirnituq, Canada 69 B12 60 2N 77 10W
Powassan, Canada 72 C4 46 5N 79 25W
Poway, U.S.A. 79 N9 32 58N 117 2W
Powder →, U.S.A. 80 B2 46 45N 105 26W
Powder River, U.S.A. 76 E10 43 2N 106 59W

Powell, U.S.A. 76 D9 44 45N 108 46W
Powell, L., U.S.A. 77 H8 36 57N 111 29W
Powell River, Canada 70 D4 49 50N 124 35W
Powers, U.S.A. 82 C2 45 41N 87 32W
Powys □, U.K. 13 E4 52 20N 3 20W
Poyang Hu, China ..... 33 D6 29 5N 116 20 E
Poyarkovo, Russia ..... 29 E13 49 36N 128 41 E
Poza Rica, Mexico 87 C5 20 33N 97 27W
Požarevac, Serbia & M. ..... 23 B9 44 35N 21 18 E
Poznań, Poland ..... 17 B9 52 25N 16 55 E
Pozo, U.S.A. 79 K6 35 20N 120 24W
Pozo Almonte, Chile 92 H5 20 10S 69 50W
Pozo Colorado, Paraguay 94 A4 23 30S 58 45W
Pozoblanco, Spain 21 C3 38 23N 4 51W
Pozzuoli, Italy ..... 22 D6 40 49N 14 7 E
Prachin Buri, Thailand ..... 38 E3 14 0N 101 25 E
Prachuap Khiri Khan, Thailand ..... 39 G2 11 49N 99 48 E
Prado, Brazil 93 G11 17 20S 39 13W
Prague = Praha, Czech Rep. ..... 16 C8 50 5N 14 22 E
Praha, Czech Rep. ..... 16 C8 50 5N 14 22 E
Praia, C. Verde Is. 49 E1 15 2N 23 34W
Prainha, Amazonas, Brazil 92 E6 7 10S 60 30W
Prainha, Pará, Brazil 93 D8 1 45S 53 30W
Prairie, Australia ..... 62 C3 20 50S 144 35 E
Prairie City, U.S.A. 76 D4 44 28N 118 43W
Prairie Dog Town Fork →, U.S.A. 81 H5 34 30N 99 23W
Prairie du Chien, U.S.A. 80 D9 43 3N 91 9W
Prairies, L. of the, Canada 71 C8 51 16N 101 32W
Pran Buri, Thailand ..... 38 F2 12 23N 99 55 E
Prapat, Indonesia ..... 36 D1 2 41N 98 58 E
Prasonísi, Ákra, Greece ..... 25 D9 35 42N 27 46 E
Prata, Brazil 93 G9 19 25S 48 54W
Pratabpur, India ..... 43 H10 23 28N 83 15 E
Pratapgarh, Raj., India ..... 42 G6 24 2N 74 40 E
Pratapgarh, Ut. P., India ..... 43 G9 25 56N 81 59 E
Prato, Italy ..... 22 C4 43 53N 11 6 E
Pratt, U.S.A. 81 G5 37 39N 98 44W
Prattville, U.S.A. 83 J2 32 28N 86 29W
Pravia, Spain 21 A2 43 30N 6 12W
Praya, Indonesia ..... 36 F5 8 39S 116 17 E
Precipice △, Australia ..... 63 D5 25 18S 150 5 E
Precordillera, Argentina 94 C2 30 0S 69 1W
Preeceville, Canada 71 C8 51 57N 102 40W
Preiļi, Latvia ..... 9 H22 56 18N 26 43 E
Premont, U.S.A. 81 M5 27 22N 98 7W
Prentice, U.S.A. 80 C9 45 33N 90 17W
Preobrazheniye, Russia ..... 30 C6 42 54N 133 54 E
Preparis North Channel, Ind. Oc. ..... 41 M18 15 12N 93 40 E
Preparis South Channel, Ind. Oc. ..... 41 M18 14 36N 93 40 E
Přerov, Czech Rep. ..... 17 D9 49 28N 17 27 E
Prescott, Canada 85 B9 44 45N 75 30W
Prescott, Ariz., U.S.A. 77 J7 34 33N 112 28W
Prescott, Ark., U.S.A. 81 J8 33 48N 93 23W
Prescott Valley, U.S.A. 77 J7 34 40N 112 18W
Preservation Inlet, N.Z. ..... 59 M1 46 8S 166 35 E
Presho, U.S.A. 80 D4 43 54N 100 3W
Presidencia de la Plaza, Argentina 94 B4 27 0S 59 50W
Presidencia Roque Saenz Peña, Argentina 94 B3 26 45S 60 30W
Presidente Epitácio, Brazil 93 H8 21 56S 52 6W
Presidente Hayes □, Paraguay 94 A4 24 0S 59 0W
Presidente Prudente, Brazil 95 A5 22 5S 51 25W
Presidio, Mexico 86 B4 29 29N 104 23W
Presidio, U.S.A. 81 L2 29 34N 104 22W
Prešov, Slovak Rep. ..... 17 D11 49 0N 21 15 E
Prespa, L. = Prespansko Jezero, Macedonia ..... 23 D9 40 55N 21 0 E
Prespansko Jezero, Macedonia ..... 23 D9 40 55N 21 0 E
Presque I., U.S.A. 84 D4 42 9N 80 6W
Presque Isle, U.S.A. 83 B12 46 41N 68 1W
Prestatyn, U.K. 12 D4 53 20N 3 24W
Presteigne, U.K. 13 E5 52 17N 3 0W
Preston, Canada 84 C4 43 23N 80 21W
Preston, U.K. 12 D5 53 46N 2 42W
Preston, Idaho, U.S.A. 76 E8 42 6N 111 53W
Preston, Minn., U.S.A. 80 D8 43 40N 92 5W
Preston, C., Australia ..... 60 D2 20 51S 116 12 E
Prestonburg, U.S.A. 82 G4 37 39N 82 46W
Prestwick, U.K. 11 F4 55 29N 4 37W
Pretoria, S. Africa ..... 57 D4 25 44S 28 12 E
Préveza, Greece ..... 23 E9 38 57N 20 45 E
Prey Veng, Cambodia ..... 39 G5 11 35N 105 29 E
Pribilof Is., U.S.A. 68 C2 57 0N 170 0W
Příbram, Czech Rep. ..... 16 D8 49 41N 14 2 E
Price, U.S.A. 76 G8 39 36N 110 49W
Price I., Canada 70 C3 52 23N 128 41W
Prichard, U.S.A. 83 K1 30 44N 88 5W
Priekule, Latvia ..... 9 H19 56 26N 21 35 E
Prienai, Lithuania ..... 9 J20 54 38N 23 57 E
Prieska, S. Africa ..... 56 D3 29 40S 22 42 E
Priest L., U.S.A. 76 B5 48 35N 116 52W
Priest River, U.S.A. 76 B5 48 10N 116 54W
Priest Valley, U.S.A. 78 J6 36 10N 120 39W
Prievidza, Slovak Rep. ..... 17 D10 48 46N 18 36 E
Prikaspiyskaya Nizmennost = Caspian Depression, Eurasia ..... 19 E8 47 0N 48 0 E
Prilep, Macedonia ..... 23 D9 41 21N 21 32 E
Priluki = Pryluky, Ukraine ..... 19 D5 50 30N 32 24 E
Prime Seal I., Australia ..... 63 G4 40 3S 147 43 E
Primrose L., Canada 71 C7 54 55N 109 45W
Prince Albert, Canada 71 C7 53 15N 105 50W
Prince Albert, S. Africa ..... 56 E3 33 12S 22 2 E
Prince Albert △, Canada 71 C7 54 0N 106 25W
Prince Albert Mts., Antarctica ..... 5 D11 76 0S 161 30 E
Prince Albert Pen., Canada 68 A8 72 30N 116 0W
Prince Albert Sd., Canada 68 A8 70 25N 115 0W
Prince Alfred, C., Canada 4 B1 74 20N 124 40W
Prince Charles I., Canada 69 B12 67 47N 76 12W
Prince Charles Mts., Antarctica ..... 5 D6 72 0S 67 0 E
Prince Edward I. □, Canada 73 C7 46 20N 63 20W
Prince Edward Is., Ind. Oc. ..... 3 G11 46 35S 38 0 E
Prince Edward Pt., Canada 84 C8 43 56N 76 52W
Prince George, Canada 70 C4 53 55N 122 50W
Prince of Wales, C., U.S.A. 66 C3 65 36N 168 5W
Prince of Wales I., Australia ..... 62 A3 10 40S 142 10 E
Prince of Wales I., Canada 68 A10 73 0N 99 0W
Prince of Wales I., U.S.A. 68 C6 55 47N 132 50W
Prince Patrick I., Canada 4 B2 77 0N 120 0W
Prince Regent Inlet, Canada 4 B3 73 0N 90 0W
Prince Rupert, Canada 70 C2 54 20N 130 20W
Princes Town, Trin. & Tob. 93 K15 10 16N 61 23W
Princess Charlotte B., Australia ..... 62 A3 14 25S 144 0 E
Princess May Ranges, Australia ..... 60 C4 15 30S 125 30 E
Princess Royal I., Canada 70 C3 53 0N 128 40W
Princeton, Canada 70 D4 49 27N 120 30W
Princeton, Calif., U.S.A. 78 F4 39 24N 122 1W
Princeton, Ill., U.S.A. 80 E10 41 23N 89 28W

Princeton, Ind., U.S.A. 82 F2 38 21N 87 34W
Princeton, Ky., U.S.A. 82 G2 37 7N 87 53W
Princeton, Mo., U.S.A. 80 E8 40 24N 93 35W
Princeton, N.J., U.S.A. 85 F10 40 21N 74 39W
Princeton, W. Va., U.S.A. 82 G5 37 22N 81 6W
Principe, I. de, Atl. Oc. ..... 48 F4 1 37N 7 27 E
Principe da Beira, Brazil 92 F6 12 20S 64 30W
Prineville, U.S.A. 76 D3 44 18N 120 51W
Prins Harald Kyst, Antarctica ..... 5 D4 70 0S 35 1 E
Prinsesse Astrid Kyst, Antarctica ..... 5 D3 70 45S 12 30 E
Prinsesse Ragnhild Kyst, Antarctica ..... 5 D4 70 15S 27 30 E
Prinzapolca, Nic. 88 D3 13 20N 83 35W
Priozersk, Russia ..... 18 B5 61 2N 30 7 E
Pripet = Prypyat →, Europe ..... 17 C16 51 20N 30 15 E
Pripet Marshes, Europe ..... 17 B15 52 10N 28 10 E
Pripyats = Pripet Marshes, Europe ..... 17 B15 52 10N 28 10 E
Pripyats = Prypyat →, Europe ..... 17 C16 51 20N 30 15 E
Priština, Serbia & M. ..... 23 C9 42 40N 21 13 E
Privas, France ..... 20 D6 44 45N 4 37 E
Privolzhskaya Vozvyshennost, Russia ..... 19 D8 51 0N 46 0 E
Privolzhskiy □, Russia ..... 28 D6 56 0N 50 0 E
Prizren, Serbia & M. ..... 23 C9 42 13N 20 45 E
Probolinggo, Indonesia ..... 37 G15 7 46S 113 13 E
Proctor, U.S.A. 85 C11 43 40N 73 2W
Proddatur, India ..... 40 M11 14 45N 78 30 E
Prodhromos, Cyprus ..... 25 E11 34 57N 32 50 E
Profítis Ilías, Greece ..... 25 C9 36 17N 27 56 E
Profondeville, Belgium ..... 15 D4 50 23N 4 52 E
Progreso, Coahuila, Mexico 86 B4 27 28N 101 4W
Progreso, Yucatán, Mexico 87 C7 21 20N 89 40W
Prokopyevsk, Russia ..... 28 D9 54 0N 86 45 E
Prokuplje, Serbia & M. ..... 23 C9 43 16N 21 36 E
Prome, Burma ..... 41 K19 18 49N 95 13 E
Prophet →, Canada 70 B4 58 48N 122 40W
Prophet River, Canada 70 B4 58 6N 122 43W
Propriá, Brazil 93 F11 10 13S 36 51W
Proserpine, Australia ..... 62 J6 20 21S 148 36 E
Prosna →, Poland ..... 17 B9 52 6N 17 44 E
Prospect, U.S.A. 85 C9 43 18N 75 9W
Prosser, U.S.A. 76 C4 46 12N 119 46W
Prostějov, Czech Rep. ..... 17 D9 49 30N 17 9 E
Proston, Australia ..... 63 D5 26 8S 151 32 E
Provence, France ..... 20 E6 43 40N 5 46 E
Providence, Ky., U.S.A. 82 G2 37 24N 87 46W
Providence, R.I., U.S.A. 85 E13 41 49N 71 24W
Providence Bay, Canada 72 C3 45 41N 82 15W
Providence Mts., U.S.A. 79 K11 35 10N 115 15W
Providencia, I. de, Colombia 88 D3 13 25N 81 26W
Provideniya, Russia 29 C19 64 23N 173 18W
Provins, France ..... 20 B5 48 33N 3 15 E
Provo, U.S.A. 76 F8 40 14N 111 39W
Provost, Canada 71 C6 52 25N 110 20W
Prudhoe Bay, U.S.A. 68 A5 70 18N 148 22W
Prudhoe I., Australia ..... 62 C4 21 19S 149 41 E
Prud'homme, Canada 71 C7 52 20N 105 54W
Pruszków, Poland ..... 17 B11 52 9N 20 49 E
Prut →, Romania ..... 17 F15 45 28N 28 10 E
Pruzhany, Belarus ..... 17 B13 52 33N 24 28 E
Prydz B., Antarctica ..... 5 C6 69 0S 74 0 E
Pryluky, Ukraine ..... 19 D5 50 30N 32 24 E
Pryor, U.S.A. 81 G7 36 19N 95 19W
Prypyat →, Europe ..... 17 C16 51 20N 30 15 E
Przemyśl, Poland ..... 17 D12 49 50N 22 45 E
Przhevalsk = Karakol, Kyrgyzstan ..... 28 E8 42 30N 78 20 E
Psará, Greece ..... 23 E11 38 37N 25 38 E
Psira, Greece ..... 25 D7 35 12N 25 52 E
Pskov, Russia ..... 18 C4 57 50N 28 25 E
Ptich = Ptsich →, Belarus ..... 17 B15 52 9N 28 52 E
Ptolemaís, Greece ..... 23 D9 40 30N 21 43 E
Ptsich →, Belarus ..... 17 B15 52 9N 28 52 E
Pu Xian, China ..... 34 F6 36 24N 111 6 E
Pua, Thailand ..... 38 C3 19 11N 100 55 E
Puán, Argentina 94 D3 37 30S 62 45W
Puan, S. Korea ..... 35 G14 35 44N 126 44 E
Pucallpa, Peru 92 E4 8 25S 74 30W
Pudasjärvi, Finland ..... 8 D22 65 23N 26 53 E
Pudozh, Russia ..... 18 B6 61 48N 36 32 E
Puducherry = Pondicherry, India ..... 40 P11 11 59N 79 50 E
Pudukkottai, India ..... 40 P11 10 28N 78 47 E
Puebla, Mexico 87 D5 19 3N 98 12W
Puebla □, Mexico 87 D5 18 30N 98 0W
Pueblo, U.S.A. 80 F2 38 16N 104 37W
Pueblo Hundido, Chile 94 B1 26 20S 70 5W
Puelches, Argentina 94 D2 38 5S 65 51W
Puelén, Argentina 94 D2 37 32S 67 38W
Puente Alto, Chile 94 C1 33 32S 70 35W
Puente-Genil, Spain 21 D3 37 22N 4 47W
Puerca, Pta., Puerto Rico ..... 89 d 18 13N 65 36W
Puerco →, U.S.A. 77 J10 34 22N 107 50W
Puerto Aisén, Chile 96 F2 45 27S 73 0W
Puerto Arista, Mexico 87 D6 15 56N 93 48W
Puerto Armuelles, Panama 88 E3 8 20N 82 51W
Puerto Ayacucho, Venezuela 92 B5 5 40N 67 35W
Puerto Barrios, Guatemala 88 C2 15 40N 88 32W
Puerto Bermejo, Argentina 94 B4 26 55S 58 34W
Puerto Bermúdez, Peru 92 F4 10 20S 74 58W
Puerto Bolívar, Ecuador 92 D3 3 19S 79 55W
Puerto Cabello, Venezuela 92 A5 10 28N 68 1W
Puerto Cabezas, Nic. 88 D3 14 0N 83 30W
Puerto Cabo Gracias á Dios, Nic. 88 D3 15 0N 83 10W
Puerto Carreño, Colombia 92 B5 6 12N 67 22W
Puerto Castilla, Honduras 88 C2 16 0N 86 0W
Puerto Chicama, Peru 92 E3 7 45S 79 20W
Puerto Coig, Argentina 96 G3 50 54S 69 15W
Puerto Cortés, Costa Rica 88 E3 8 55N 84 0W
Puerto Cortés, Honduras 88 C2 15 51N 88 0W
Puerto Cumarebo, Venezuela 92 A5 11 29N 69 30W
Puerto de Alcudia = Port d'Alcúdia, Spain ..... 24 B10 39 50N 3 7 E
Puerto de Cabrera, Spain ..... 24 B9 39 8N 2 56 E
Puerto de Gran Tarajal, Canary Is. 24 F5 28 13N 14 1W
Puerto de la Cruz, Canary Is. 24 F3 28 24N 16 32W
Puerto de los Angeles △, Mexico 86 B3 23 29N 105 45W
Puerto de Pozo Negro, Canary Is. 24 F6 28 19N 13 55W
Puerto de Sóller = Port de Sóller, Spain ..... 24 B9 39 48N 2 42 E
Puerto del Carmen, Canary Is. 24 F6 28 55N 13 38W
Puerto del Rosario, Canary Is. 24 F6 28 30N 13 52W
Puerto Deseado, Argentina 96 F3 47 55S 66 0W
Puerto Escondido, Mexico 87 D5 15 50N 97 3W
Puerto Inírida, Colombia 92 C5 3 53N 67 52W
Puerto Juárez, Mexico 87 C7 21 11N 86 49W

Puerto La Cruz, Venezuela 92 A6 10 13N 64 38W
Puerto Leguízamo, Colombia 92 D4 0 12S 74 46W
Puerto Limón, Colombia 92 C4 3 23N 73 30W
Puerto Lobos, Argentina 96 E3 42 0S 65 3W
Puerto Madryn, Argentina 96 E3 42 48S 65 4W
Puerto Maldonado, Peru 92 F5 12 30S 69 10W
Puerto Manotí, Cuba 88 B4 21 22N 76 50W
Puerto Montt, Chile 96 E2 41 28S 73 0W
Puerto Morazán, Nic. 88 D2 12 51N 87 11W
Puerto Morelos, Mexico 87 C7 20 49N 86 52W
Puerto Natales, Chile 96 G2 51 45S 72 15W
Puerto Padre, Cuba 88 B4 21 13N 76 35W
Puerto Páez, Venezuela 92 B5 6 13N 67 28W
Puerto Peñasco, Mexico 86 A2 31 20N 113 33W
Puerto Pinasco, Paraguay 94 A4 22 36S 57 50W
Puerto Plata, Dom. Rep. 89 C5 19 48N 70 45W
Puerto Pollensa = Port de Pollença, Spain ..... 24 B10 39 54N 3 4 E
Puerto Princesa, Phil. ..... 37 C5 9 46N 118 45 E
Puerto Rico, Canary Is. 24 G4 27 47N 15 42W
Puerto Rico ☑, W. Indies ..... 89 d 18 15N 66 45W
Puerto Rico Trench, Atl. Oc. 89 C6 19 50N 66 0W
Puerto San Julián, Argentina 96 F3 49 18S 67 43W
Puerto Sastre, Paraguay 94 A4 22 2S 57 55W
Puerto Suárez, Bolivia 92 G7 18 58S 57 52W
Puerto Vallarta, Mexico 86 C3 20 36N 105 15W
Puerto Wilches, Colombia 92 B4 7 21N 73 54W
Puertollano, Spain 21 C3 38 43N 4 7W
Pueyrredón, L., Argentina 96 F2 47 20S 72 0W
Puffin I., Ireland 10 E1 51 50N 10 24W
Pugachev, Russia ..... 18 D8 52 0N 48 49 E
Pugal, India ..... 42 E5 28 30N 72 48 E
Puge, Tanzania ..... 54 C3 4 45S 33 11 E
Puget Sound, U.S.A. 76 C2 47 50N 122 30W
Pugŏdong, N. Korea ..... 35 C16 42 5N 130 0 E
Pugu, Tanzania ..... 54 D4 6 55S 39 4 E
Pûgûnzi, Iran ..... 45 E8 25 49N 59 10 E
Puig Major, Spain ..... 24 B9 39 48N 2 47 E
Puigcerdà, Spain ..... 21 A6 42 24N 1 50 E
Puigpunyent, Spain ..... 24 B9 39 38N 2 32 E
Pujon-chösuji, N. Korea ..... 35 D14 40 35N 127 35 E
Pukaki, L., N.Z. ..... 59 L3 44 4S 170 1 E
Pukapuka, Cook Is. 65 J11 10 53S 165 49W
Pukaskwa △, Canada 72 C2 48 20N 86 0W
Pukatawagan, Canada 71 B8 55 45N 101 20W
Pukchin, N. Korea ..... 35 D13 40 12N 125 45 E
Pukch'ŏng, N. Korea ..... 35 D15 40 14N 128 10 E
Pukekohe, N.Z. ..... 59 G5 37 12S 174 55 E
Pukhrayan, India ..... 43 F8 26 14N 79 51 E
Pula, Croatia ..... 16 F7 44 54N 13 57 E
Pulacayo, Bolivia 92 H5 20 25S 66 41W
Pulai, Malaysia ..... 39 d 1 20N 103 31 E
Pulandian, China ..... 35 E11 39 25N 121 58 E
Pularumpi, Australia ..... 60 B5 11 24S 130 26 E
Pulaski, N.Y., U.S.A. 85 C8 43 34N 76 8W
Pulaski, Tenn., U.S.A. 83 H2 35 12N 87 2W
Pulaski, Va., U.S.A. 82 G5 37 3N 80 47W
Pulau →, Indonesia ..... 37 F9 5 50S 138 15 E
Puławy, Poland ..... 17 C11 51 23N 21 59 E
Pulga, U.S.A. 78 F5 39 48N 121 29W
Pulicat L., India ..... 40 N12 13 40N 80 15 E
Pullman, U.S.A. 76 C5 46 44N 117 10W
Pulog, Mt., Phil. ..... 37 A6 16 40N 120 50 E
Pultusk, Poland ..... 17 B11 52 43N 21 6 E
Pumlumon Fawr, U.K. 13 E4 52 28N 3 46W
Puná, I., Ecuador 92 D2 2 55S 80 5W
Punakha, Bhutan ..... 41 F16 27 42N 89 52 E
Punasar, India ..... 42 F5 27 6N 73 6 E
Punata, Bolivia 92 G5 17 32S 65 50W
Punch, India ..... 43 C6 33 48N 74 4 E
Punch →, Pakistan ..... 42 C5 33 12N 73 40 E
Punda Maria, S. Africa ..... 57 C5 22 40S 31 5 E
Pune, India ..... 40 K8 18 29N 73 57 E
P'ungsan, N. Korea ..... 35 D15 40 50N 128 9 E
Pungue, Ponte de, Mozam. ..... 55 F3 19 0S 34 0 E
Punjab □, India ..... 42 D7 31 0N 76 0 E
Punjab □, Pakistan ..... 42 E6 32 0N 72 30 E
Puno, Peru 92 G4 15 55S 70 3W
Punpun →, India ..... 43 G11 25 31N 85 18 E
Punta, Cerro de, Puerto Rico ..... 89 d 18 10N 66 37W
Punta Alta, Argentina 96 D4 38 53S 62 4W
Punta Arenas, Chile 96 G2 53 10S 71 0W
Punta de Díaz, Chile 94 B1 28 0S 70 45W
Punta del Hidalgo, Canary Is. 24 F3 28 33N 16 19W
Punta Gorda, Belize 87 D7 16 10N 88 45W
Punta Gorda, U.S.A. 83 M5 26 56N 82 3W
Punta Prieta, Mexico 86 B2 28 58N 114 17W
Punta Prima, Spain ..... 24 B11 39 48N 4 16 E
Puntarenas, Costa Rica 88 E3 10 0N 84 50W
Punto Fijo, Venezuela 92 A4 11 50N 70 13W
Punxsatawney, U.S.A. 84 F6 40 57N 78 59W
Pupuan, Indonesia ..... 37 J18 8 19S 115 0 E
Puquio, Peru 92 F4 14 45S 74 10W
Pur →, Russia ..... 28 C8 67 31N 77 55 E
Purace, Vol., Colombia 92 C3 2 21N 76 23W
Puralia = Puruliya, India ..... 43 H12 23 17N 86 24 E
Puranpur, India ..... 43 E9 28 31N 80 9 E
Purbeck, Isle of, U.K. 13 G5 50 39N 1 59W
Purcell, U.S.A. 81 H6 35 1N 97 22W
Purcell Mts., Canada 70 D5 49 55N 116 15W
Puri, India ..... 41 K14 19 50N 85 58 E
Purmerend, Neths. ..... 15 B4 52 32N 4 58 E
Purnia, India ..... 43 G12 25 45N 87 31 E
Pursat = Pouthisat, Cambodia ..... 38 F4 12 34N 103 50 E
Puruliya, India ..... 43 H12 23 17N 86 24 E
Purus →, Brazil 92 D6 3 42S 61 28W
Purvis, U.S.A. 81 K10 31 9N 89 25W
Purwa, India ..... 43 F9 26 28N 80 47 E
Purwakarta, Indonesia ..... 37 G12 6 35S 107 29 E
Purwodadi, Indonesia ..... 37 G14 7 7S 110 55 E
Purwokerto, Indonesia ..... 37 G13 7 25S 109 14 E
Puryŏng, N. Korea ..... 35 C15 42 5N 129 43 E
Pusan, S. Korea ..... 35 G15 35 5N 129 0 E
Pushkino, Russia ..... 19 D8 51 16N 47 0 E
Putahow L., Canada 71 B8 59 54N 100 40W
Putao, Burma ..... 41 F20 27 28N 97 30 E
Putaruru, N.Z. ..... 59 H5 38 2S 175 50 E
Putignano, Italy ..... 22 D7 40 51N 17 7 E
Puting, Tanjung, Indonesia ..... 36 E4 3 31S 111 46 E
Putnam, U.S.A. 85 E13 41 55N 71 55W
Putorana, Gory, Russia ..... 29 C10 69 0N 95 0 E
Putrajaya, Malaysia ..... 39 L3 2 55N 101 40 E
Puttalam, Sri Lanka ..... 40 Q11 8 1N 79 55 E
Puttgarden, Germany ..... 16 A6 54 30N 11 10 E

Putumayo →, S. Amer. 92 D5 3 7S 67 58W
Putussibau, Indonesia 36 D4 0 50N 112 56 E
Puvirnituq, Canada 69 B12 60 2N 77 10W
Puy-de-Dôme, France 20 D5 45 46N 2 57 E
Puyallup, U.S.A. 78 C4 47 12N 122 18W
Puyang, China 34 G8 35 40N 115 1 E
Pūzeh Rīg, Iran 45 E8 27 20N 58 40 E
Pwani □, Tanzania 54 D4 7 0S 39 0 E
Pweto, Dem. Rep. of the Congo 55 D2 8 25S 28 51 E
Pwllheli, U.K. 12 E3 52 53N 4 25W
Pya-ozero, Russia 18 A5 66 5N 30 58 E
Pyapon, Burma 41 L19 16 20N 95 40 E
Pyasina →, Russia 29 B9 73 30N 87 0 E
Pyatigorsk, Russia 19 F7 44 2N 43 6 E
Pyè = Prome, Burma 41 K19 18 49N 95 13 E
Pyetrikaw, Belarus 17 B15 52 11N 28 29 E
Pyhäjoki, Finland 8 D21 64 28N 24 14 E
Pyinmana, Burma 41 K20 19 45N 96 12 E
Pyla, C., Cyprus 25 E12 34 56N 33 51 E
Pymatuning Reservoir, U.S.A. 84 E4 41 30N 80 28W
Pyŏktong, N. Korea 35 D13 40 50N 125 50 E
Pyŏnggang, N. Korea 35 E14 38 24N 127 17 E
P'yŏngt'aek, S. Korea 35 F14 37 1N 127 4 E
P'yŏngyang, N. Korea 35 E13 39 0N 125 30 E
Pyote, U.S.A. 81 K3 31 32N 103 8W
Pyramid L., U.S.A. 76 G4 40 1N 119 35W
Pyramid Pk., U.S.A. 79 J10 36 25N 116 37W
Pyrénées, Europe 20 E4 42 45N 0 18 E
Pyu, Burma 41 K20 18 30N 96 28 E

Q

Qaanaaq, Greenland 4 B4 77 40N 69 0W
Qachasnek, S. Africa 57 E4 30 6S 28 42 E
Qa'el Jafr, Jordan 46 E5 30 20N 36 25 E
Qa'emābād, Iran 45 D9 31 44N 60 2 E
Qā'emshahr, Iran 45 B7 36 30N 52 53 E
Qagan Nur, China 34 C8 43 30N 114 55 E
Qahar Youyi Zhongqi, China 34 D7 41 12N 112 40 E
Qahremānshahr = Bākhtarān, Iran 44 C5 34 23N 47 0 E
Qaidam Pendi, China 32 C4 37 0N 95 0 E
Qajarīyeh, Iran 45 D6 31 1N 48 22 E
Qala, Ras il, Malta 25 C1 36 2N 14 20 E
Qala-i-Jadid = Spīn Būldak, Afghan. 42 D2 31 1N 66 25 E
Qala Point = Qala, Ras il, Malta 25 C1 36 2N 14 20 E
Qala Viala, Pakistan 42 D2 30 49N 67 17 E
Qala Yangi, Afghan. 42 B2 34 20N 66 30 E
Qal'at al Akhḑar, Si. Arabia 44 E3 28 0N 37 10 E
Qal'at Dīzah, Iraq 44 B5 36 11N 45 7 E
Qal'at Şāliḩ, Iraq 44 D5 31 31N 47 16 E
Qal'at Sukkar, Iraq 44 D5 31 51N 46 5 E
Qamani'tuaq = Baker Lake, Canada 68 B10 64 20N 96 3W
Qamdo, China 32 C4 31 15N 97 6 E
Qamruddin Karez, Pakistan 42 D3 31 45N 68 20 E
Qandahār, Afghan. 40 D4 31 32N 65 43 E
Qandahār □, Afghan. 40 D4 31 0N 65 0 E
Qapān, Iran 45 B7 37 40N 55 47 E
Qapshaghay, Kazakhstan 28 E8 43 51N 77 14 E
Qaqortoq, Greenland 69 B6 60 43N 46 0W
Qara Qash →, China 43 B8 35 0N 78 30 E
Qarabutaq, Kazakhstan 28 E7 49 59N 60 14 E
Qaraghandy, Kazakhstan 28 E8 49 50N 73 10 E
Qārah, Si. Arabia 44 D4 29 55N 40 3 E
Qarataū, Kazakhstan 28 E8 43 10N 70 28 E
Qarataū, Kazakhstan 28 E7 43 30N 69 30 E
Qardho = Gardo, Somali Rep. 47 F4 9 30N 49 6 E
Qareh →, Iran 44 B5 39 25N 47 22 E
Qareh Tekān, Iran 45 B6 36 38N 49 29 E
Qarqan He →, China 32 C3 39 30N 88 30 E
Qarqaraly, Kazakhstan 28 E8 49 26N 75 30 E
Qarshi, Uzbekistan 28 F7 38 53N 65 48 E
Qartabā, Lebanon 46 A4 34 4N 35 50 E
Qaryat al Gharab, Iraq 44 D5 31 27N 44 48 E
Qaryat al 'Ulyā, Si. Arabia 44 E5 27 33N 47 42 E
Qasr 'Amra, Jordan 44 D3 31 48N 36 35 E
Qaşr-e Qand, Iran 45 E9 26 15N 60 45 E
Qasr Farâfra, Egypt 51 C11 27 0N 28 1 E
Qatanā, Syria 46 B5 33 26N 36 4 E
Qatar ■, Asia 45 E6 25 30N 51 15 E
Qatlīsh, Iran 45 B8 37 50N 57 19 E
Qattâra, Munkhafed el, Egypt 51 C11 29 30N 27 30 E
Qattâra Depression = Qattâra, Munkhafed el, Egypt 51 C11 29 30N 27 30 E
Qawām al Ḩamzah = Al Ḩamzah, Iraq 44 D5 31 43N 44 58 E
Qāyen, Iran 45 C8 33 40N 59 10 E
Qazaqstan = Kazakhstan ■, Asia 28 E7 50 0N 70 0 E
Qazimämmäd, Azerbaijan 45 A6 40 3N 49 0 E
Qazvin, Iran 45 B6 36 15N 50 0 E
Qazvin □, Iran 45 B6 36 20N 50 0 E
Qena, Egypt 51 C12 26 10N 32 43 E
Qeqertarsuaq, Greenland 69 B5 69 45N 53 30W
Qeqertarsuaq, Greenland 69 B14 69 15N 53 38W
Qeshlāq, Iran 44 C5 34 55N 46 28 E
Qeshm, Iran 45 E8 26 55N 56 10 E
Qeys, Iran 45 E7 26 32N 53 58 E
Qezel Owzen →, Iran 45 B6 36 45N 49 22 E
Qezi'ot, Israel 46 E3 30 52N 34 26 E
Qi Xian, China 34 G8 34 40N 114 48 E
Qian Gorlos, China 35 B13 45 5N 124 42 E
Qian Hai, China 33 F10 22 32N 113 54 E
Qian Xian, China 34 G5 34 31N 108 15 E
Qianshan, China 33 G10 22 15N 113 31 E
Qianyang, China 34 G4 34 40N 107 8 E
Qi'ao, China 33 G10 22 25N 113 39 E
Qi'ao Dao, China 33 G10 22 25N 113 38 E
Qikiqtarjuaq, Canada 69 B13 67 33N 63 0W
Qila Safed, Pakistan 40 E2 29 0N 61 30 E
Qila Saifullāh, Pakistan 42 D3 30 45N 68 17 E
Qilian Shan, China 32 C4 38 30N 96 0 E
Qin He →, China 34 G7 35 1N 113 22 E
Qin Ling = Qinling Shandi, China 34 H5 33 50N 108 10 E
Qin'an, China 34 G3 34 48N 105 40 E
Qing Xian, China 34 E9 38 35N 116 45 E
Qingcheng, China 35 F9 37 15N 117 40 E
Qingdao, China 35 F11 36 5N 120 20 E
Qingfeng, China 34 G8 35 52N 115 8 E
Qinghai □, China 32 C4 36 0N 98 0 E
Qinghai Hu, China 32 C5 36 40N 100 10 E
Qinghecheng, China 35 D13 41 28N 124 15 E
Qinghemen, China 35 D11 41 48N 121 25 E
Qingjian, China 34 F6 37 8N 110 8 E
Qingjiang = Huaiyin, China 35 H10 33 30N 119 2 E
Qingshui, China 34 G4 34 48N 106 8 E
Qingshuihe, China 34 E6 39 55N 111 35 E
Qingtongxia Shuiku, China 34 F3 37 50N 105 58 E
Qingxu, China 34 F7 37 34N 112 22 E
Qingyang, China 34 F4 36 2N 107 55 E
Qingyuan, China 35 C13 42 10N 124 55 E
Qingyun, China 35 F9 37 45N 117 20 E
Qinhuangdao, China 35 E10 39 56N 119 30 E
Qinling Shandi, China 34 H5 33 50N 108 10 E
Qinshui, China 34 G7 35 40N 112 8 E
Qinyang = Jiyuan, China 34 G7 35 7N 112 57 E
Qinyuan, China 34 F7 36 29N 112 20 E
Qinzhou, China 32 D5 21 58N 108 38 E
Qionghai, China 38 C8 19 15N 110 26 E
Qiongzhou Haixia, China 38 B8 20 10N 110 15 E
Qiqihar, China 29 E13 47 26N 124 0 E
Qirāīya, W. →, Egypt 46 E3 30 27N 34 0 E
Qiryat Ata, Israel 46 C4 32 47N 35 6 E
Qiryat Gat, Israel 46 D3 31 32N 34 46 E
Qiryat Mal'akhi, Israel 46 D3 31 44N 34 44 E
Qiryat Shemona, Israel 46 B4 33 13N 35 35 E
Qiryat Yam, Israel 46 C4 32 51N 35 4 E
Qishan, China 34 G4 34 25N 107 38 E
Qitai, China 32 B3 44 2N 89 35 E
Qixia, China 35 F11 37 17N 120 52 E
Qızılağac Körfäzi, Azerbaijan 45 B6 39 9N 49 0 E
Qojūr, Iran 44 B5 36 12N 47 55 E
Qom, Iran 45 C6 34 40N 51 0 E
Qom □, Iran 45 C6 34 40N 51 0 E
Qomolangma Feng = Everest, Mt., Nepal 43 E12 28 5N 86 58 E
Qomsheh, Iran 45 D6 32 0N 51 55 E
Qoraqalpoghistan □, Uzbekistan 28 E6 43 0N 58 0 E
Qostanay, Kazakhstan 28 D7 53 10N 63 35 E
Quabbin Reservoir, U.S.A. 85 D12 42 20N 72 20W
Quairading, Australia 61 F2 32 0S 117 21 E
Quakertown, U.S.A. 85 F9 40 26N 75 21W
Qualicum Beach, Canada 70 D4 49 22N 124 26W
Quambatook, Australia 63 F3 35 49S 143 34 E
Quambone, Australia 63 E4 30 57S 147 53 E
Quamby, Australia 62 C3 20 22S 140 17 E
Quan Long = Ca Mau, Vietnam 39 H5 9 7N 105 8 E
Quanah, U.S.A. 81 H5 34 18N 99 44W
Quang Ngai, Vietnam 38 E7 15 13N 108 58 E
Quang Tri, Vietnam 38 D6 16 45N 107 13 E
Quang Yen, Vietnam 38 B6 20 56N 106 52 E
Quantock Hills, U.K. 13 F4 51 8N 3 10W
Quanzhou, China 33 D6 24 55N 118 34 E
Qu'Appelle, Canada 71 C8 50 33N 103 53W
Quaqtaq, Canada 69 B13 60 55N 69 40W
Quaraí, Brazil 94 C4 30 15S 56 20W
Quartu Sant'Élena, Italy 22 E3 39 15N 9 10 E
Quartzsite, U.S.A. 79 M12 33 40N 114 13W
Quatsino Sd., Canada 70 C3 50 25N 127 58W
Quba, Azerbaijan 19 F8 41 21N 48 32 E
Qūchān, Iran 45 B8 37 10N 58 27 E
Queanbeyan, Australia 63 F4 35 17S 149 14 E
Québec, Canada 73 C5 46 52N 71 13W
Québec □, Canada 73 C6 48 0N 74 0W
Quebrada del Condorito △, Argentina 94 C3 31 49S 64 40W
Queen Alexandra Ra., Antarctica 5 E11 85 0S 170 0 E
Queen Charlotte City, Canada 70 C2 53 15N 132 2W
Queen Charlotte Is., Canada 70 C2 53 20N 132 10W
Queen Charlotte Sd., Canada 70 C3 51 0N 128 0W
Queen Charlotte Strait, Canada 70 C3 50 45N 127 10W
Queen Elizabeth ⌓, U.K. 11 E4 56 7N 4 30W
Queen Elizabeth △, Uganda 54 C3 0 0 30 0 E
Queen Elizabeth Is., Canada 66 B10 76 0N 95 0W
Queen Mary Land, Antarctica 5 D7 70 0S 95 0 E
Queen Maud G., Canada 68 B9 68 15N 102 30W
Queen Maud Land = Dronning Maud Land, Antarctica 5 D3 72 30S 12 0 E
Queen Maud Mts., Antarctica 5 E13 86 0S 160 0W
Queens Chan., Australia 60 C4 15 0S 129 30 E
Queenscliff, Australia 63 F3 38 16S 144 39 E
Queensland □, Australia 62 C3 22 0S 142 0 E
Queenstown, Australia 63 G4 42 4S 145 35 E
Queenstown, N.Z. 59 L2 45 1S 168 40 E
Queenstown, Singapore 39 d 1 18N 103 48 E
Queenstown, S. Africa 56 E4 31 52S 26 52 E
Queets, U.S.A. 78 C2 47 32N 124 20W
Queguay Grande →, Uruguay 94 C4 32 9S 58 9W
Queimadas, Brazil 93 F11 11 0S 39 38W
Quelimane, Mozam. 55 F4 17 53S 36 58 E
Quellón, Chile 96 E2 43 7S 73 37W
Quelpart = Cheju do, S. Korea 35 H14 33 29N 126 34 E
Quemado, N. Mex., U.S.A. 77 J9 34 20N 108 30W
Quemado, Tex., U.S.A. 81 L4 28 58N 100 35W
Quemú-Quemú, Argentina 94 D3 36 3S 63 36W
Quequén, Argentina 94 D4 38 30S 58 30W
Querétaro, Mexico 86 C4 20 36N 100 23W
Querétaro □, Mexico 86 C5 20 30N 100 0W
Queshan, China 34 H8 32 55N 114 2 E
Quesnel, Canada 70 C4 53 0N 122 30W
Quesnel →, Canada 70 C4 52 58N 122 29W
Quesnel L., Canada 70 C4 52 30N 121 20W
Questa, U.S.A. 77 H11 36 42N 105 36W
Quetico ⌓, Canada 72 C1 48 30N 91 45W
Quetta, Pakistan 42 D2 30 15N 66 55 E
Quezaltenango, Guatemala 88 D1 14 50N 91 30W
Quezon City, Phil. 37 B6 14 38N 121 0 E
Qufār, Si. Arabia 44 E4 27 26N 41 37 E
Qui Nhon, Vietnam 38 F7 13 40N 109 13 E
Quibaxe, Angola 52 F2 8 24S 14 27 E
Quibdo, Colombia 92 B3 5 42N 76 40W
Quiberon, France 20 C2 47 29N 3 9W
Quiet L., Canada 70 A2 61 5N 133 5W
Quiindy, Paraguay 94 B4 25 58S 57 14W
Quila, Mexico 86 C3 24 23N 107 13W
Quilán, C., Chile 96 E2 43 15S 74 30W
Quilcene, U.S.A. 78 C4 47 49N 122 53W
Quilimarí, Chile 94 C1 32 5S 71 30W
Quilino, Argentina 94 C3 30 14S 64 29W
Quill Lakes, Canada 71 C8 51 55N 104 13W
Quillabamba, Peru 92 F4 12 50S 72 50W
Quillagua, Chile 94 A2 21 40S 69 40W
Quillaicillo, Chile 94 C1 31 17S 71 40W
Quillota, Chile 94 C1 32 54S 71 16W
Quilmes, Argentina 94 C4 34 43S 58 15W
Quilon, India 40 Q10 8 50N 76 38 E
Quilpie, Australia 63 D3 26 35S 144 11 E
Quilpué, Chile 94 C1 33 5S 71 33W
Quilua, Mozam. 55 F4 16 17S 39 54 E
Quimili, Argentina 94 B3 27 40S 62 30W
Quimper, France 20 B1 48 0N 4 9W
Quimperlé, France 20 C2 47 53N 3 33W
Quinault →, U.S.A. 78 C2 47 21N 124 18W
Quincy, Calif., U.S.A. 78 F6 39 56N 120 57W
Quincy, Fla., U.S.A. 83 K3 30 35N 84 34W
Quincy, Ill., U.S.A. 80 F9 39 56N 91 23W
Quincy, Mass., U.S.A. 85 D14 42 15N 71 0W
Quincy, Wash., U.S.A. 76 C4 47 22N 119 56W
Quines, Argentina 94 C2 32 13S 65 48W
Quinga, Mozam. 55 F5 15 49S 40 15 E
Quinns Rocks, Australia 61 F2 31 40S 115 42 E
Quintana Roo □, Mexico 87 D7 19 0N 88 0W
Quintanar de la Orden, Spain 21 C4 39 36N 3 5W
Quinte West, Canada 84 B7 44 10N 77 34W
Quintero, Chile 94 C1 32 45S 71 30W
Quirihue, Chile 94 D1 36 15S 72 35W
Quirindi, Australia 63 E5 31 28S 150 40 E
Quirinópolis, Brazil 93 G8 18 32S 50 30W
Quissanga, Mozam. 55 E5 12 24S 40 28 E
Quissico, Mozam. 57 C5 24 42S 34 44 E
Quitilipi, Argentina 94 B3 26 50S 60 13W
Quitman, U.S.A. 83 K4 30 47N 83 34W
Quito, Ecuador 92 D3 0 15S 78 35W
Quixadá, Brazil 93 D11 4 55S 39 0W
Quixaxe, Mozam. 55 F5 15 17S 40 4 E
Qulan, Kazakhstan 28 E8 42 55N 72 43 E
Qul'ân, Jazâ'ir, Egypt 44 E2 24 22N 35 31 E
Qumbu, S. Africa 57 E4 31 10S 28 48 E
Quneitra, Syria 46 B4 33 7N 35 48 E
Qŭnghirot, Uzbekistan 28 E6 43 6N 58 54 E
Quoin I., Australia 60 B4 14 54S 129 32 E
Quoin Pt., S. Africa 56 E2 34 46S 19 37 E
Quorn, Australia 63 E2 32 25S 138 5 E
Qŭqon, Uzbekistan 28 E8 40 30N 70 57 E
Qurnat as Sawdā', Lebanon 46 A5 34 18N 36 6 E
Quşaybā', Si. Arabia 44 E4 26 53N 43 35 E
Qusaybah, Iraq 44 C4 34 24N 40 59 E
Quseir, Egypt 44 E2 26 7N 34 16 E
Qūshchī, Iran 44 B5 37 59N 45 3 E
Quthing, Lesotho 57 E4 30 25S 27 36 E
Qūţīābād, Iran 45 C6 35 47N 48 30 E
Quwo, China 34 G6 35 38N 111 25 E
Quyang, China 34 E8 38 35N 114 40 E
Quynh Nhai, Vietnam 38 B4 21 49N 103 33 E
Quyon, Canada 85 A8 45 31N 76 14W
Quzhou, China 33 D6 28 57N 118 54 E
Quzi, China 34 F4 36 20N 107 20 E
Qyzylorda, Kazakhstan 28 E7 44 48N 65 28 E

R

Ra, Ko, Thailand 39 H2 9 13N 98 16 E
Raahe, Finland 8 D21 64 40N 24 28 E
Raalte, Neths. 15 B6 52 23N 6 16 E
Raasay, U.K. 11 D2 57 25N 6 4W
Raasay, Sd. of, U.K. 11 D2 57 30N 6 8W
Raba, Indonesia 37 F5 8 36S 118 55 E
Rába →, Hungary 17 E9 47 38N 17 38 E
Rabai, Kenya 54 C4 3 50S 39 31 E
Rabat = Victoria, Malta 25 C1 36 3N 14 14 E
Rabat, Malta 25 D1 35 53N 14 24 E
Rabat, Morocco 50 B4 34 2N 6 48W
Rabaul, Papua N. G. 64 H7 4 24S 152 18 E
Rābigh, Si. Arabia 47 C2 22 50N 39 5 E
Râbniţa, Moldova 17 E15 47 45N 29 0 E
Rābor, Iran 45 D8 29 17N 56 55 E
Race, C., Canada 73 C9 46 40N 53 5W
Rach Gia, Vietnam 39 G5 10 5N 105 5 E
Rachid, Mauritania 50 E3 18 45N 11 35W
Racibórz, Poland 17 C10 50 7N 18 18 E
Racine, U.S.A. 82 D2 42 41N 87 51W
Rackerby, U.S.A. 78 F5 39 26N 121 22W
Radama, Nosy, Madag. 57 A8 14 0S 47 47 E
Radama, Saikanosy, Madag. 57 A8 14 16S 47 53 E
Rădăuţi, Romania 17 E13 47 50N 25 59 E
Radcliff, U.S.A. 82 G3 37 51N 85 57W
Radekhiv, Ukraine 17 C13 50 25N 24 32 E
Radekhov = Radekhiv, Ukraine 17 C13 50 25N 24 32 E
Radford, U.S.A. 82 G5 37 8N 80 34W
Radhanpur, India 42 H4 23 50N 71 38 E
Radhwa, Jabal, Si. Arabia 44 E3 24 34N 38 18 E
Radisson, Qué., Canada 72 B4 53 47N 77 37W
Radisson, Sask., Canada 71 C7 52 30N 107 20W
Radium Hot Springs, Canada 70 C5 50 35N 116 2W
Radnor Forest, U.K. 13 E4 52 17N 3 10W
Radom, Poland 17 C11 51 23N 21 12 E
Radomsko, Poland 17 C10 51 5N 19 28 E
Radomyshl, Ukraine 17 C15 50 30N 29 12 E
Radstock, C., Australia 63 E1 33 12S 134 20 E
Radviliškis, Lithuania 9 J20 55 49N 23 33 E
Radville, Canada 71 D8 49 30N 104 15W
Rae, Canada 70 A5 62 50N 116 3W
Rae Bareli, India 43 F9 26 18N 81 20 E
Rae Isthmus, Canada 69 B11 66 40N 87 30W
Raeren, Belgium 15 D6 50 41N 6 7 E
Raeside, L., Australia 61 E3 29 20S 122 0 E
Raetihi, N.Z. 59 H5 39 25S 175 17 E
Rafaela, Argentina 94 C3 31 10S 61 30W
Rafah, Gaza Strip 46 D3 31 18N 34 14 E
Rafai, C.A.R. 54 B1 4 59N 23 58 E
Rafḩā, Si. Arabia 44 D4 29 35N 43 35 E
Rafsanjān, Iran 45 D8 30 30N 56 5 E
Raft Pt., Australia 60 C3 16 4S 124 26 E
Rāgâ, Sudan 51 G11 8 28N 25 41 E
Ragachow, Belarus 17 B16 53 8N 30 5 E
Ragama, Sri Lanka 40 R11 7 0N 79 50 E
Ragged, Mt., Australia 61 F3 33 27S 123 25 E
Ragged Pt., Barbados 89 g 13 10N 59 10W
Raghunathpalli, India 43 H11 22 14N 84 48 E
Raghunathpur, India 43 H12 23 33N 86 40 E
Raglan, N.Z. 59 G5 37 55S 174 55 E
Ragusa, Italy 22 F6 36 55N 14 44 E
Raha, Indonesia 37 E6 4 55S 123 0 E
Rahaeng = Tak, Thailand 38 D2 16 52N 99 8 E
Rahatgarh, India 43 H8 23 47N 78 22 E
Rahimyar Khan, Pakistan 42 E4 28 30N 70 25 E
Rāhjerd, Iran 45 C6 34 22N 50 22 E
Rahole ⌓, Kenya 54 B4 0 5N 38 57 E
Rahon, India 42 D7 31 3N 76 7 E
Raichur, India 40 L10 16 10N 77 20 E
Raiganj, India 43 G13 25 37N 88 10 E
Raigarh, India 41 J13 21 56N 83 25 E
Raijua, Indonesia 37 F6 10 37S 121 36 E
Raikot, India 42 D6 30 41N 75 42 E
Railton, Australia 63 G4 41 25S 146 28 E
Rainbow Bridge ⌓, U.S.A. 77 H8 37 5N 110 58W
Rainbow Lake, Canada 70 B5 58 30N 119 23W
Rainier, U.S.A. 78 D4 46 53N 122 41W
Rainier, Mt., U.S.A. 78 D5 46 52N 121 46W
Rainy L., Canada 71 D10 48 42N 93 10W
Rainy River, Canada 71 D10 48 43N 94 29W
Raippaluoto, Finland 8 E19 63 13N 21 14 E
Raipur, India 41 J12 21 17N 81 45 E
Raisen, India 42 H8 23 20N 77 48 E
Raisio, Finland 9 F20 60 28N 22 11 E
Raj Nandgaon, India 41 J12 21 5N 81 5 E
Raj Nilgiri, India 43 J12 21 28N 86 46 E
Raja, Ujung, Indonesia 36 D1 3 40N 96 25 E
Raja Ampat, Kepulauan, Indonesia 37 E7 0 30S 130 0 E
Rajahmundry, India 41 L12 17 1N 81 48 E
Rajang →, Malaysia 36 D4 2 30N 112 0 E
Rajanpur, Pakistan 42 E4 29 6N 70 19 E
Rajapalaiyam, India 40 Q10 9 25N 77 35 E
Rajasthan □, India 42 F5 26 45N 73 30 E
Rajasthan Canal = Indira Gandhi Canal, India 42 F5 28 0N 72 0 E
Rajauri, India 43 C6 33 25N 74 21 E
Rajgarh, Mad. P., India 42 G7 24 2N 76 45 E
Rajgarh, Raj., India 42 F7 27 14N 76 38 E
Rajgarh, Raj., India 42 E6 28 40N 75 25 E
Rajgir, India 43 G11 25 2N 85 25 E
Rajkot, India 42 H4 22 15N 70 56 E
Rajmahal Hills, India 43 G12 24 30N 87 30 E
Rajpipla, India 40 J8 21 50N 73 30 E
Rajpur, India 42 H6 22 18N 74 21 E
Rajpura, India 42 D7 30 25N 76 32 E
Rajshahi, Bangla. 41 G16 24 22N 88 39 E
Rajshahi □, Bangla. 43 G13 25 0N 89 0 E
Rajula, India 42 J4 21 3N 71 26 E
Rakaia, N.Z. 59 K4 43 45S 172 1 E
Rakaia →, N.Z. 59 K4 43 36S 172 15 E
Rakan, Ra's, Qatar 45 E6 26 10N 51 20 E
Rakaposhi, Pakistan 43 A6 36 10N 74 25 E
Rakata, Pulau, Indonesia 36 F3 6 10S 105 20 E
Rakhiv, Ukraine 17 D13 48 3N 24 12 E
Rakhni, Pakistan 42 D3 30 4N 69 56 E
Rakhni →, Pakistan 42 E3 29 31N 69 36 E
Rakitnoye, Russia 30 B7 45 36N 134 17 E
Rakops, Botswana 56 C3 21 1S 24 28 E
Rakvere, Estonia 9 G22 59 20N 26 25 E
Raleigh, U.S.A. 83 H6 35 47N 78 39W
Ralls, U.S.A. 81 J4 33 41N 101 24W
Ralston, U.S.A. 84 E8 41 30N 76 57W
Ram →, Canada 70 A4 62 1N 123 41W
Râm Allâh, West Bank 46 D4 31 55N 35 10 E
Rama, Nic. 88 D3 12 9N 84 15W
Ramakona, India 43 J8 21 43N 78 50 E
Rāmallāh = Râm Allâh, West Bank 46 D4 31 55N 35 10 E
Raman, Thailand 39 J3 6 29N 101 18 E
Ramanathapuram, India 40 Q11 9 25N 78 55 E
Ramanetaka, B. de, Madag. 57 A8 14 13S 47 52 E
Ramanujganj, India 43 H10 23 48N 83 42 E
Ramat Gan, Israel 46 C3 32 4N 34 48 E
Ramatlhabama, S. Africa 56 D4 25 37S 25 33 E
Ramban, India 43 C6 33 14N 75 12 E
Rambipuji, Indonesia 37 H15 8 12S 113 37 E
Rame Hd., Australia 63 F4 37 47S 149 30 E
Ramechhap, Nepal 43 F12 27 25N 86 10 E
Ramganga →, India 43 F8 27 5N 79 58 E
Ramgarh, Jharkhand, India 43 H11 23 40N 85 35 E
Ramgarh, Raj., India 42 F6 27 16N 75 14 E
Ramgarh, Raj., India 42 F4 27 30N 70 36 E
Rāmhormoz, Iran 45 D6 31 15N 49 35 E
Ramīān, Iran 45 B7 37 3N 55 16 E
Ramingining, Australia 62 A2 12 19S 135 3 E
Ramla, Israel 46 D3 31 55N 34 52 E
Ramm = Rum, Jordan 46 F4 29 39N 35 26 E
Ramm, Jabal, Jordan 46 F4 29 35N 35 24 E
Ramnad = Ramanathapuram, India 40 Q11 9 25N 78 55 E
Ramnagar, Jammu & Kashmir, India 43 C6 32 47N 75 18 E
Ramnagar, Uttaranchal, India 43 E8 29 24N 79 7 E
Râmnicu Sărat, Romania 17 F14 45 26N 27 3 E
Râmnicu Vâlcea, Romania 17 F13 45 9N 24 21 E
Ramona, U.S.A. 79 M10 33 2N 116 52W
Ramore, Canada 72 C3 48 30N 80 25W
Ramotswa, Botswana 56 C4 24 50S 25 52 E
Rampur, H.P., India 42 D7 31 26N 77 43 E
Rampur, Mad. P., India 42 H5 23 25N 73 53 E
Rampur, Ut. P., India 43 E8 28 50N 79 5 E
Rampur Hat, India 43 G12 24 10N 87 50 E
Rampura, India 42 G6 24 30N 75 27 E
Ramrama Tola, India 43 J8 21 52N 79 55 E
Ramree I., Burma 41 K19 19 0N 93 40 E
Rāmsar, Iran 45 B6 36 53N 50 41 E
Ramsey, U.K. 12 C3 54 20N 4 22W
Ramsey, U.S.A. 85 E10 41 4N 74 9W
Ramsey L., Canada 72 C3 47 13N 82 15W
Ramsgate, U.K. 13 F9 51 20N 1 25 E
Ramtek, India 40 J11 21 20N 79 15 E
Rana Pratap Sagar Dam, India 42 G6 24 58N 75 38 E
Ranaghat, India 43 H13 23 15N 88 35 E
Ranahu, Pakistan 42 G3 25 55N 69 45 E
Ranau, Malaysia 36 C5 6 2N 116 40 E
Rancagua, Chile 94 C1 34 10S 70 50W
Rancheria →, Canada 70 A3 60 13N 129 7W
Ranchester, U.S.A. 76 D10 44 54N 107 10W
Ranchi, India 43 H11 23 19N 85 27 E
Rancho Cucamonga, U.S.A. 79 L9 34 10N 117 30W
Randalstown, U.K. 10 B5 54 45N 6 19W
Randers, Denmark 9 H14 56 29N 10 1 E
Randfontein, S. Africa 57 D4 26 8S 27 45 E
Randle, U.S.A. 78 D5 46 32N 121 57W
Randolph, Mass., U.S.A. 85 D13 42 10N 71 2W
Randolph, N.Y., U.S.A. 84 D6 42 10N 78 59W
Randolph, Utah, U.S.A. 76 F8 41 40N 111 11W
Randolph, Vt., U.S.A. 85 C12 43 55N 72 40W
Randsburg, U.S.A. 79 K9 35 22N 117 39W
Råne älv →, Sweden 8 D20 65 50N 22 20 E
Rangae, Thailand 39 J3 6 19N 101 44 E
Rangaunu B., N.Z. 59 F4 34 51S 173 15 E
Rangeley, U.S.A. 85 B14 44 58N 70 39W
Rangeley L., U.S.A. 85 B14 44 55N 70 43W
Rangely, U.S.A. 76 F9 40 5N 108 48W
Ranger, U.S.A. 81 J5 32 28N 98 41W
Rangia, India 41 F17 26 28N 91 38 E
Rangiora, N.Z. 59 K4 43 19S 172 36 E
Rangitaiki →, N.Z. 59 G6 37 54S 176 49 E
Rangitata →, N.Z. 59 K3 43 45S 171 15 E
Rangkasbitung, Indonesia 37 G12 6 21S 106 15 E
Rangon →, Burma 41 L20 16 28N 96 40 E
Rangoon, Burma 41 L20 16 45N 96 20 E

Rangpur, Bangla. 41 G16 25 42N 89 22 E
Rangsit, Thailand 38 F3 13 59N 100 37 E
Ranibennur, India 40 M9 14 35N 75 30 E
Raniganj, Ut. P., India 43 F9 27 3N 82 13 E
Raniganj, W. Bengal, India 41 H15 23 40N 87 5 E
Raniwara, India 40 G8 24 50N 72 10 E
Ranikhet, India 43 E8 29 39N 79 25 E
Ranka, India 43 H10 23 59N 83 47 E
Ranken →, Australia 62 C2 20 31S 137 36 E
Rankin, U.S.A. 81 K4 31 13N 101 56W
Rankin Inlet, Canada 68 B10 62 30N 93 0W
Rankins Springs, Australia 63 E4 33 49S 146 14 E
Rannoch, L., U.K. 11 E4 56 41N 4 20W
Rannoch Moor, U.K. 11 E4 56 38N 4 48W
Ranobe, Helodranon' i, Madag. 57 C7 23 3S 43 33 E
Ranohira, Madag. 57 C8 22 29S 45 24 E
Ranomafana, Toamasina,
Madag. 57 B8 18 57S 48 50 E
Ranomafana, Toliara, Madag. 57 C8 24 34S 47 0 E
Ranomafana △, Madag. 57 C8 21 16S 47 25 E
Ranomena, Madag. 57 C8 23 25S 47 17 E
Ranong, Thailand 39 H2 9 56N 98 40 E
Ranotsara Nord, Madag. 57 C8 22 48S 46 36 E
Ransa, Iran 45 C6 33 39N 48 18 E
Ransiki, Indonesia 37 E8 1 30S 134 10 E
Rantabe, Madag. 57 B8 15 42S 49 39 E
Rantauprapat, Indonesia 36 D1 2 15N 99 50 E
Rantemario, Indonesia 37 E5 3 15S 119 57 E
Rantoul, U.S.A. 82 E1 40 19N 88 9W
Raoyang, China 34 E8 38 15N 115 45 E
Rap, Ko, Thailand 39 b 9 59 57 E
Rapa, French Polynesia 65 K13 27 35S 144 20W
Rapa Nui = Pascua, I. de, Chile 65 K17 27 7S 109 23W
Rapallo, Italy 20 D8 44 21N 9 14 E
Rapar, India 42 H4 23 34N 70 38 E
Rāpch, Iran 45 E8 25 40N 59 15 E
Raper, C., Canada 69 B13 69 44N 67 6W
Rapid City, U.S.A. 80 D3 44 5N 103 14W
Rapid River, U.S.A. 82 C2 45 55N 86 58W
Rapla, Estonia 9 G21 59 1N 24 52 E
Rapti →, India 43 F10 26 18N 83 41 E
Raquette →, U.S.A. 85 B10 45 0N 74 42W
Raquette Lake, U.S.A. 85 C10 43 49N 74 40W
Rarotonga, Cook Is. 65 K12 21 30S 160 0W
Ra's al ʿAyn, Syria 44 B4 36 45N 40 12 E
Ra's al Khaymah, U.A.E. 45 E7 25 50N 55 59 E
Rasca, Pta. de la, Canary Is. 24 G3 27 59N 16 41W
Raseiniai, Lithuania 9 J20 55 25N 23 5 E
Rashmi, India 42 G6 25 4N 74 22 E
Rasht, Iran 45 B6 37 20N 49 40 E
Rasi Salai, Thailand 38 E5 15 20N 104 9 E
Rason L., Australia 61 E3 28 45S 124 25 E
Rasra, India 43 G10 25 50N 83 50 E
Rasul, Pakistan 42 C5 32 42N 73 34 E
Rat Buri, Thailand 38 F2 13 30N 99 54 E
Rat Islands, U.S.A. 68 C1 52 0N 178 0 E
Rat L., Canada 71 B9 56 10N 99 40W
Ratangarh, India 42 E6 28 5N 74 35 E
Raţāwi, Iraq 44 D5 30 38N 47 13 E
Rath, India 43 G8 25 36N 79 37 E
Rath Luirc, Ireland 10 D3 52 21N 8 40W
Rathdrum, Ireland 10 D5 52 56N 6 14W
Rathenow, Germany 16 B7 52 37N 12 19 E
Rathkeale, Ireland 10 D3 52 32N 8 56W
Rathlin I., U.K. 10 A5 55 18N 6 14W
Rathmelton, Ireland 10 A4 55 2N 7 38W
Ratibor = Racibórz, Poland 17 C10 50 7N 18 18 E
Ratlam, India 42 H6 23 20N 75 0 E
Ratnagiri, India 40 L8 16 57N 73 18 E
Ratodero, Pakistan 42 F3 27 48N 68 18 E
Raton, U.S.A. 81 G2 36 54N 104 24W
Rattaphum, Thailand 39 J3 7 8N 100 16 E
Rattray Hd., U.K. 11 D7 57 38N 1 50W
Ratz, Mt., Canada 70 B2 57 23N 132 12W
Raub, Malaysia 39 L3 3 47N 101 52 E
Rauch, Argentina 94 D4 36 45S 59 5W
Raudales de Malpaso, Mexico 87 D6 17 30N 23 30W
Raufarhöfn, Iceland 8 C6 66 27N 15 57W
Raufoss, Norway 9 F14 60 44N 10 37 E
Raukumara Ra., N.Z. 59 H6 38 5S 177 55 E
Rauma, Finland 9 F19 61 10N 21 30 E
Raung, Gunung, Indonesia 37 J17 8 8S 114 3 E
Raurkela, India 43 H11 22 14N 84 50 E
Rausu-Dake, Japan 30 B12 44 4N 145 7 E
Rava-Ruska, Ukraine 17 C12 50 15N 23 42 E
Rava Russkaya = Rava-Ruska,
Ukraine 17 C12 50 15N 23 42 E
Ravalli, U.S.A. 76 C6 47 17N 114 11W
Ravānsar, Iran 44 C5 34 43N 46 40 E
Rāvar, Iran 45 D8 31 20N 56 51 E
Ravena, U.S.A. 85 D11 42 28N 73 49W
Ravenna, Italy 22 B5 44 25N 12 12 E
Ravenna, Nebr., U.S.A. 80 E5 41 1N 98 55W
Ravenna, Ohio, U.S.A. 84 E3 41 9N 81 15W
Ravensburg, Germany 16 E5 47 46N 9 36 E
Ravenshoe, Australia 62 B4 17 37S 145 29 E
Ravensthorpe, Australia 61 F3 33 35S 120 2 E
Ravenswood, Australia 62 C4 20 6S 146 54 E
Ravenswood, U.S.A. 82 F5 38 57N 81 46W
Ravi →, Pakistan 42 D4 30 35N 71 49 E
Rawalpindi, Pakistan 42 C5 33 38N 73 8 E
Rawāndūz, Iraq 44 B5 36 40N 44 30 E
Rawang, Malaysia 39 L3 3 20N 101 35 E
Rawene, N.Z. 59 F4 35 25S 173 32 E
Rawlinna, Australia 61 F4 30 58S 125 28 E
Rawlins, U.S.A. 76 F10 41 47N 107 14W
Rawlinson Ra., Australia 61 D4 24 40S 128 30 E
Rawson, Argentina 96 E3 43 15S 65 5W
Raxaul, India 43 F11 26 59N 84 51 E
Ray, U.S.A. 80 A3 48 21N 103 10W
Ray, C., Canada 73 C8 47 33N 59 15W
Raya Ring, Ko, Thailand 39 a 8 18N 98 29 E
Rayadurg, India 40 M10 14 40N 76 50 E
Rayagada, India 41 K13 19 15N 83 20 E
Raychikhinsk, Russia 29 E13 49 46N 129 25 E
Rāyen, Iran 45 D8 29 34N 57 26 E
Rayleigh, U.K. 13 F8 51 36N 0 37 E
Raymond, Canada 70 D6 49 30N 112 35W
Raymond, Calif., U.S.A. 78 H7 37 13N 119 54W
Raymond, N.H., U.S.A. 85 C13 43 2N 71 11W
Raymond, Wash., U.S.A. 78 D3 46 41N 123 44W
Raymondville, U.S.A. 81 M6 26 29N 97 47W
Raymore, Canada 71 C8 51 25N 104 31W
Rayón, Mexico 86 B2 29 43N 110 35W
Rayong, Thailand 38 F3 12 40N 101 5 E
Rayville, U.S.A. 81 J9 32 29N 91 46W
Raz, Pte. du, France 20 C1 48 2N 4 47W

Razan, Iran 45 C6 35 23N 49 2 E
Razāzah, Buḩayrat ar, Iraq 44 C4 32 40N 43 35 E
Razāzah, L. = Razāzah, Buḩayrat
ar, Iraq 44 C4 32 40N 43 35 E
Razdel'naya = Rozdilna, Ukraine 17 E16 46 50N 30 2 E
Razdolnoye, Russia 30 C5 43 30N 131 52 E
Razeh, Iran 45 C6 32 47N 49 59 E
Razgrad, Bulgaria 23 C12 43 33N 26 34 E
Razim, Lacul, Romania 17 F15 44 50N 29 0 E
Razmak, Pakistan 42 C3 32 45N 69 50 E
Ré, Î. de, France 20 C3 46 12N 1 30W
Reading, U.K. 13 F7 51 27N 0 58W
Reading, U.S.A. 85 F9 40 20N 75 56W
Reading □, U.K. 13 F7 51 27N 0 58W
Realicó, Argentina 94 D3 35 0S 64 15W
Ream, Cambodia 39 G4 10 34N 103 39 E
Reata, Mexico 86 B4 26 8N 101 5W
Reay Forest, U.K. 11 C4 58 22N 4 55W
Rebi, Indonesia 37 F8 6 23S 134 7 E
Rebiana, Libya 51 D10 24 12N 22 10 E
Rebiana, Sahrâ', Libya 51 D10 24 30N 21 0 E
Rebun-Tō, Japan 30 B10 45 23N 141 2 E
Recherche, Arch. of the, Australia 61 F3 34 15S 122 50 E
Rechna Doab, Pakistan 42 D5 31 35N 73 30 E
Rechytsa, Belarus 17 B16 52 21N 30 24 E
Recife, Brazil 93 E12 8 0S 35 0W
Recklinghausen, Germany 15 C7 51 37N 7 12 E
Reconquista, Argentina 94 B4 29 10S 59 45W
Recreo, Argentina 94 B2 29 25S 65 10W
Red →, La., U.S.A. 81 K9 31 1N 91 45W
Red →, N. Dak., U.S.A. 68 C10 49 0N 97 15W
Red Bank, U.S.A. 85 F10 40 21N 74 5W
Red Bay, Canada 73 B8 51 44N 56 25W
Red Bluff, U.S.A. 76 F2 40 11N 122 15W
Red Bluff L., U.S.A. 81 K3 31 54N 103 55W
Red Cliffs, Australia 63 E3 34 19S 142 11 E
Red Cloud, U.S.A. 80 E5 40 5N 98 32W
Red Creek, U.S.A. 85 C8 43 14N 76 45W
Red Deer, Canada 70 C6 52 20N 113 50W
Red Deer →, Alta., Canada 71 C7 50 58N 110 0W
Red Deer →, Man., Canada 71 C8 52 53N 101 1W
Red Deer L., Canada 71 C8 52 55N 101 20W
Red Hook, U.S.A. 85 E11 41 55N 73 53W
Red Indian L., Canada 73 C8 48 35N 57 0W
Red L., Canada 71 C10 51 3N 93 49W
Red Lake, Canada 71 C10 51 3N 93 49W
Red Lake Falls, U.S.A. 80 B6 47 53N 96 16W
Red Lake Road, Canada 71 C10 49 59N 93 25W
Red Lodge, U.S.A. 76 D9 45 11N 109 15W
Red Mountain, U.S.A. 79 K9 35 37N 117 38W
Red Oak, U.S.A. 80 E7 41 1N 95 14W
Red Rock, Canada 72 C2 48 55N 88 15W
Red Rock, L., U.S.A. 80 E8 41 22N 92 59W
Red Rocks Pt., Australia 61 F4 32 13S 127 32 E
Red Sea, Asia 47 C2 25 0N 36 0 E
Red Slate Mt., U.S.A. 78 H8 37 31N 118 52W
Red Sucker L., Canada 72 B1 54 9N 93 40W
Red Tower Pass = Turnu Roşu,
P., Romania 17 F13 45 33N 24 17 E
Red Wing, U.S.A. 80 C8 44 34N 92 31W
Redang, Malaysia 39 K4 5 49N 103 2 E
Redange, Lux. 15 E5 49 46N 5 52 E
Redcar, U.K. 12 C6 54 37N 1 4W
Redcar & Cleveland □, U.K. 12 C7 54 29N 1 0W
Redcliff, Canada 71 C6 50 10N 110 50W
Redcliffe, Australia 63 D5 27 12S 153 0 E
Redcliffe, Mt., Australia 61 E3 28 30S 121 30 E
Reddersburg, S. Africa 56 D4 29 41S 26 10 E
Redding, U.S.A. 76 F2 40 35N 122 24W
Redditch, U.K. 13 E6 52 18N 1 56W
Redfield, U.S.A. 80 C5 44 53N 98 31W
Redford, U.S.A. 85 B11 44 38N 73 48W
Redhead, Trin. & Tob. 93 K16 10 48N 60 3W
Redlands, U.S.A. 79 M9 34 4N 117 11W
Redmond, Oreg., U.S.A. 76 D3 44 17N 121 11W
Redmond, Wash., U.S.A. 78 C4 47 41N 122 7W
Redon, France 20 C2 47 40N 2 6W
Redonda, Antigua & B. 89 C7 16 58N 62 19W
Redondela, Spain 21 A1 42 15N 8 38W
Redondo Beach, U.S.A. 79 M8 33 50N 118 23W
Redruth, U.K. 13 G2 50 14N 5 14W
Redvers, Canada 71 D8 49 35N 101 40W
Redwater, Canada 70 C6 53 55N 113 6W
Redwood, U.S.A. 85 B9 44 18N 75 48W
Redwood △, U.S.A. 76 F1 41 40N 124 5W
Redwood City, U.S.A. 78 H4 37 30N 122 15W
Redwood Falls, U.S.A. 80 C7 44 32N 95 7W
Ree, L., Ireland 10 C3 53 35N 8 0W
Reed, L., Canada 71 C8 54 38N 100 30W
Reed City, U.S.A. 82 D3 43 53N 85 31W
Reedley, U.S.A. 78 J7 36 36N 119 27W
Reedsburg, U.S.A. 80 D9 43 32N 90 0W
Reedsport, U.S.A. 76 E1 43 42N 124 6W
Reedsville, U.S.A. 84 F7 40 39N 77 35W
Reefton, N.Z. 59 K3 42 6S 171 51 E
Refugio, U.S.A. 81 L6 28 18N 97 17W
Regensburg, Germany 16 D7 49 1N 12 6 E
Reggâne = Zaouiet Reggâne,
Algeria 50 C6 26 32N 0 3 E
Réggio di Calábria, Italy 22 E6 38 6N 15 39 E
Réggio nell'Emília, Italy 22 B4 44 43N 10 36 E
Reghin, Romania 17 E13 46 46N 24 42 E
Regina, Canada 71 C8 50 27N 104 35W
Regina Beach, Canada 71 C8 50 47N 105 0W
Registro, Brazil 95 A6 24 29S 47 49W
Rehar →, India 43 H10 23 55N 82 40 E
Rehli, India 43 H8 23 38N 79 5 E
Rehoboth, Namibia 56 C2 23 15S 17 4 E
Rehovot, Israel 46 D3 31 54N 34 48 E
Reichenbach, Germany 16 C7 50 37N 12 17 E
Reid, Australia 61 F4 30 49S 128 26 E
Reidsville, U.S.A. 83 G6 36 21N 79 40W
Reigate, U.K. 13 F7 51 14N 0 12W
Reims, France 20 B6 49 15N 4 1 E
Reina Adelaida, Arch., Chile 96 G2 52 20S 74 0W
Reina Sofía, Tenerife ✈ (TFS),
Canary Is. 24 F3 28 3N 16 33W
Reindeer →, Canada 71 B8 55 36N 103 11W
Reindeer I., Canada 71 C9 52 30N 98 0W
Reindeer L., Canada 71 B8 57 15N 102 15W
Reinga, C., N.Z. 59 F4 34 25S 172 43 E
Reinosa, Spain 21 A3 43 2N 4 15W
Reitz, S. Africa 57 D4 27 48S 28 29 E
Reivilo, S. Africa 56 D3 27 36S 24 8 E
Reliance, Canada 71 A7 63 0N 109 20W
Remarkable, Mt., Australia 63 E2 32 48S 138 10 E
Rembang, Indonesia 37 G14 6 42S 111 21 E

Remedios, Panama 88 E3 8 15N 81 50W
Remeshk, Iran 45 E8 26 55N 58 50 E
Remich, Lux. 15 E6 49 32N 6 22 E
Remscheid, Germany 15 C7 51 11N 7 12 E
Ren Xian, China 34 F8 37 8N 114 40 E
Rendang, Indonesia 37 J18 8 26S 115 25 E
Rendsburg, Germany 16 A5 54 17N 9 39 E
Renfrew, Canada 85 A8 45 30N 76 40W
Renfrewshire □, U.K. 11 F4 55 49N 4 38W
Rengat, Indonesia 36 E2 0 30S 102 45 E
Rengo, Chile 94 C1 34 24S 70 50W
Reni, Ukraine 17 F15 45 28N 28 15 E
Renmark, Australia 63 E3 34 11S 140 43 E
Rennell Sd., Canada 70 C2 53 23N 132 35W
Renner Springs, Australia 62 B1 18 20S 133 47 E
Rennes, France 20 B3 48 7N 1 41W
Reno, U.S.A. 78 F7 39 31N 119 48W
Reno →, Italy 22 B5 44 38N 12 16 E
Renovo, U.S.A. 84 E7 41 20N 77 45W
Renqiu, China 34 E9 38 43N 116 5 E
Rensselaer, Ind., U.S.A. 82 E2 40 57N 87 9W
Rensselaer, N.Y., U.S.A. 85 D11 42 38N 73 45W
Renton, U.S.A. 78 C4 47 29N 122 12W
Reotipur, India 43 G10 25 33N 83 45 E
Republic, Mo., U.S.A. 81 G8 37 7N 93 29W
Republic, Wash., U.S.A. 76 B4 48 39N 118 44W
Republican →, U.S.A. 80 F6 39 4N 96 48W
Repulse B., Australia 62 J6 20 35S 148 46 E
Repulse Bay, Canada 69 B11 66 30N 86 30W
Requena, Peru 92 E4 5 5S 73 52W
Requena, Spain 21 C5 39 30N 1 4W
Reşadiye = Datça, Turkey 23 F12 36 46N 27 40 E
Reserve, U.S.A. 77 K9 33 43N 108 45W
Resht = Rasht, Iran 45 B6 37 20N 49 40 E
Resistencia, Argentina 94 B4 27 30S 59 0W
Reşiţa, Romania 17 F11 45 18N 21 53 E
Resolution I., Canada 69 B13 61 30N 65 0W
Resolution I., N.Z. 59 L1 45 40S 166 40 E
Ressano Garcia, Mozam. 57 D5 25 25S 32 0 E
Reston, Canada 71 D8 49 33N 101 6W
Retalhuleu, Guatemala 88 D1 14 33N 91 46W
Retenue, L. de, Dem. Rep. of
the Congo 55 E2 11 0S 27 0 E
Retford, U.K. 12 D7 53 19N 0 56W
Réthímnon, Greece 25 D6 35 18N 24 30 E
Réthímnon □, Greece 25 D6 35 23N 24 28 E
Reti, Pakistan 42 E3 28 5N 69 48 E
Réunion ✉, Ind. Oc. 49 J9 21 0S 56 0 E
Reus, Spain 21 B6 41 10N 1 5 E
Reutlingen, Germany 16 D5 48 29N 9 12 E
Reval = Tallinn, Estonia 9 G21 59 22N 24 48 E
Revda, Russia 18 C10 56 48N 59 57 E
Revelganj, India 43 G11 25 50N 84 40 E
Revelstoke, Canada 70 C5 51 0N 118 10W
Reventazón, Peru 92 E2 6 10S 80 58W
Revillagigedo, Is. de, Pac. Oc. 86 D2 18 40N 112 0W
Revúè →, Mozam. 55 F3 19 50S 34 0 E
Rewa, India 43 G9 24 33N 81 25 E
Rewari, India 42 E7 28 15N 76 40 E
Rexburg, U.S.A. 76 E8 43 49N 111 47W
Rey, Iran 45 C6 35 35N 51 25 E
Rey, I. del, Panama 88 E4 8 20N 78 30W
Rey Malabo, Eq. Guin. 52 D1 3 45N 8 50 E
Reyes, Pt., U.S.A. 78 H3 38 0N 123 0W
Reyðarfjörður, Iceland 8 D6 65 2N 14 13W
Reykjahlíð, Iceland 8 D5 65 40N 16 55W
Reykjanes, Iceland 8 E2 63 48N 22 40W
Reykjavík, Iceland 8 D3 64 10N 21 57W
Reynolds Ra., Australia 60 D5 22 30S 133 0 E
Reynoldsville, U.S.A. 84 E6 41 5N 78 58W
Reynosa, Mexico 87 B5 26 5N 98 18W
Rēzekne, Latvia 9 H22 56 30N 27 17 E
Rezvān, Iran 45 E8 27 34N 56 6 E
Rhayader, U.K. 13 E4 52 18N 3 29W
Rhein →, Europe 15 C6 51 52N 6 2 E
Rhein-Main-Donau-Kanal,
Germany 16 D6 49 1N 11 27 E
Rheine, Germany 16 B4 52 17N 7 26 E
Rheinland-Pfalz □, Germany 16 C4 50 0N 7 0 E
Rhin = Rhein →, Europe 15 C6 51 52N 6 2 E
Rhine = Rhein →, Europe 15 C6 51 52N 6 2 E
Rhinelander, U.S.A. 85 E11 41 56N 73 55W
Rhineland-Palatinate =
Rheinland-Pfalz □, Germany 16 C4 50 0N 7 0 E
Rhinelander, U.S.A. 80 C10 45 38N 89 25W
Rhinns Pt., U.K. 11 F2 55 40N 6 29W
Rhino Camp, Uganda 54 B3 3 0N 31 22 E
Rhir, Cap, Morocco 50 B4 30 38N 9 54W
Rhode Island □, U.S.A. 85 E13 41 40N 71 30W
Rhodes, Greece 25 C10 36 15N 28 10 E
Rhodope Mts. = Rhodopi Planina,
Bulgaria 23 D11 41 40N 24 20 E
Rhodopi Planina, Bulgaria 23 D11 41 40N 24 20 E
Rhön, Germany 16 C5 50 24N 9 58 E
Rhondda, U.K. 13 F4 51 39N 3 31W
Rhondda Cynon Taff □, U.K. 13 F4 51 42N 3 27W
Rhône →, France 20 E6 43 28N 4 42 E
Rhum, U.K. 11 E2 57 0N 6 20W
Rhyl, U.K. 12 D4 53 20N 3 29W
Riachão, Brazil 93 E9 7 20S 46 37W
Riasi, India 43 C6 33 10N 74 50 E
Riau □, Indonesia 36 D2 0 0 102 35 E
Riau, Kepulauan, Indonesia 36 D2 0 30N 104 20 E
Riau Arch. = Riau, Kepulauan,
Indonesia 36 D2 0 30N 104 20 E
Ribadeo, Spain 21 A2 43 35N 7 5W
Ribas do Rio Pardo, Brazil 93 H8 20 27S 53 46W
Ribauè, Mozam. 55 E4 14 57S 38 17 E
Ribble →, U.K. 12 D5 53 52N 2 25W
Ribe, Denmark 9 J13 55 19N 8 44 E
Ribeira Brava, Madeira 24 D2 32 41N 17 4W
Ribeirão Prêto, Brazil 95 A6 21 10S 47 50W
Riberalta, Bolivia 92 F5 11 0S 66 0W
Riccarton, N.Z. 59 K4 43 32S 172 37 E
Rice, U.S.A. 79 L12 34 5N 114 51W
Rice L., U.S.A. 84 B6 44 12N 78 10W
Rice Lake, U.S.A. 80 C9 45 30N 91 44W
Rich, C., Canada 84 B4 44 43N 80 38W
Richards Bay, S. Africa 57 D5 28 48S 32 6 E
Richardson →, Canada 71 B6 58 25N 111 14W
Richardson Lakes, U.S.A. 82 C10 44 46N 70 58W
Richardson Springs, U.S.A. 78 F5 39 51N 121 46W
Riche, C., Australia 61 F2 34 36S 118 47 E
Richey, U.S.A. 80 B2 47 39N 105 4W
Richfield, U.S.A. 77 G8 38 46N 112 5W
Richfield Springs, U.S.A. 85 D10 42 51N 74 59W

Richford, U.S.A. 85 B12 45 0N 72 40W
Richibucto, Canada 73 C7 46 42N 64 54W
Richland, Ga., U.S.A. 83 J3 32 5N 84 40W
Richland, Wash., U.S.A. 76 C4 46 17N 119 18W
Richland Center, U.S.A. 80 D9 43 21N 90 23W
Richlands, U.S.A. 82 G5 37 6N 81 48W
Richmond, Australia 62 C3 20 43S 143 8 E
Richmond, N.Z. 59 J4 41 20S 173 12 E
Richmond, U.K. 12 C6 54 25N 1 43W
Richmond, Calif., U.S.A. 78 H4 37 56N 122 21W
Richmond, Ind., U.S.A. 82 F3 39 50N 84 53W
Richmond, Ky., U.S.A. 82 G3 37 45N 84 18W
Richmond, Mich., U.S.A. 84 D2 42 49N 82 45W
Richmond, Mo., U.S.A. 80 F8 39 17N 93 58W
Richmond, Tex., U.S.A. 81 L7 29 35N 95 46W
Richmond, Utah, U.S.A. 76 F8 41 56N 111 48W
Richmond, Va., U.S.A. 82 G7 37 33N 77 27W
Richmond, Vt., U.S.A. 85 B12 44 24N 72 59W
Richmond Hill, Canada 84 C5 43 52N 79 27W
Richmond Ra., Australia 63 D5 29 0S 152 45 E
Richtersveld △, S. Africa 56 D2 28 15S 17 10 E
Richwood, U.S.A. 82 F5 38 14N 80 32W
Ridder = Leninogorsk,
Kazakhstan 28 D9 50 20N 83 30 E
Riddlesburg, U.S.A. 84 F6 40 9N 78 15W
Ridgecrest, U.S.A. 79 K9 35 38N 117 40W
Ridgefield, Conn., U.S.A. 85 E11 41 17N 73 30W
Ridgefield, Wash., U.S.A. 78 E4 45 49N 122 45W
Ridgeland, U.S.A. 83 J5 32 29N 80 59W
Ridgetown, Canada 84 D3 42 26N 81 52W
Ridgewood, U.S.A. 85 F10 40 59N 74 7W
Ridgway, U.S.A. 84 E6 41 25N 78 44W
Riding Mountain △, Canada 71 C9 50 50N 100 0W
Ridley, Mt., Australia 61 F3 33 12S 122 7 E
Riebeek-Oos, S. Africa 56 E4 33 10S 26 10 E
Ried, Austria 16 D7 48 14N 13 30 E
Riesa, Germany 16 C7 51 17N 13 17 E
Riet →, S. Africa 56 D3 29 0S 23 54 E
Rietbron, S. Africa 56 E3 32 54S 23 10 E
Rietfontein, Namibia 56 C3 21 58S 20 58 E
Rieti, Italy 22 C5 42 24N 12 51 E
Rif = Er Rif, Morocco 50 A5 35 1N 4 1W
Riffe L., U.S.A. 78 D4 46 32N 122 26W
Rifle, U.S.A. 76 G10 39 32N 107 47W
Rift Valley, Africa 48 G7 7 0N 30 0 E
Rift Valley □, Kenya 54 B4 0 20N 36 0 E
Rīga, Latvia 9 H21 56 53N 24 8 E
Riga, G. of, Latvia 9 H20 57 40N 23 45 E
Rīgān, Iran 45 D8 28 37N 58 58 E
Rīgas Jūras Līcis = Riga, G. of,
Latvia 9 H20 57 40N 23 45 E
Rigaud, Canada 85 A10 45 29N 74 18W
Rigby, U.S.A. 76 E8 43 40N 111 55W
Rigestān, Afghan. 40 D4 30 15N 65 0 E
Riggins, U.S.A. 76 D5 45 25N 116 19W
Rigolet, Canada 73 B8 54 10N 58 23W
Rihand Dam, India 43 G10 24 9N 83 2 E
Riihimäki, Finland 9 F21 60 45N 24 48 E
Riiser-Larsen-halvøya, Antarctica 5 C4 68 0S 35 0 E
Rijeka, Croatia 16 F8 45 20N 14 21 E
Rijssen, Neths. 15 B6 52 19N 6 31 E
Rikuchū-Kaigan △, Japan 30 E11 39 20N 142 0 E
Rikuzentakada, Japan 30 E10 39 0N 141 40 E
Riley, U.S.A. 76 E4 43 32N 119 28W
Rimah, Wadi ar →, Si. Arabia 44 E4 26 5N 41 30 E
Rimau, Pulau, Malaysia 39 c 5 15N 100 16 E
Rimbey, Canada 70 C6 52 35N 114 15W
Rimersburg, U.S.A. 84 E5 41 3N 79 30W
Rímini, Italy 22 B5 44 3N 12 33 E
Rimouski, Canada 73 C6 48 27N 68 30W
Rimrock, U.S.A. 78 D5 46 38N 121 10W
Rinca, Indonesia 37 F5 8 45S 119 35 E
Rincón de Romos, Mexico 86 C4 22 14N 102 18W
Rinconada, Argentina 94 A2 22 26S 66 10W
Rind →, India 43 G9 25 53N 80 33 E
Ringas, India 42 F6 27 21N 75 34 E
Ringkøbing, Denmark 9 H13 56 5N 8 15 E
Ringvassøy, Norway 8 B18 69 56N 19 15 E
Ringwood, U.S.A. 85 E10 41 7N 74 15W
Rinjani, Indonesia 36 F5 8 24S 116 28 E
Rio Branco, Brazil 92 E5 9 58S 67 49W
Río Branco, Uruguay 95 C5 32 40S 53 40W
Río Bravo →, N. Amer. 86 B4 29 2N 102 45W
Río Bravo del Norte →, Mexico 87 B5 25 57N 97 9W
Rio Brilhante, Brazil 95 A5 21 48S 54 33W
Rio Claro, Brazil 95 A6 22 19S 47 35W
Rio Claro, Trin. & Tob. 89 D7 10 20N 61 25W
Río Colorado, Argentina 96 D4 39 0S 64 0W
Río Cuarto, Argentina 94 C3 33 10S 64 25W
Rio das Pedras, Mozam. 57 C6 23 8S 35 28 E
Rio de Janeiro, Brazil 95 A7 23 0S 43 12W
Rio de Janeiro □, Brazil 95 A7 22 50S 43 0W
Rio do Sul, Brazil 95 B6 27 13S 49 37W
Río Dulce △, Guatemala 88 C2 15 43N 88 50W
Río Gallegos, Argentina 96 G3 51 35S 69 15W
Río Grande, Argentina 96 G3 53 50S 67 45W
Río Grande, Brazil 95 C5 32 0S 52 20W
Río Grande, Mexico 86 C4 23 50N 103 2W
Río Grande, Nic. 88 D3 12 54N 83 33W
Río Grande, Puerto Rico 89 d 18 23N 65 50W
Rio Grande City, U.S.A. 81 M5 26 23N 98 49W
Río Grande de Santiago →,
Mexico 86 C3 21 36N 105 26W
Río Grande do Norte □, Brazil 93 E11 5 40S 36 0W
Río Grande do Sul □, Brazil 95 C5 30 0S 53 0W
Río Hato, Panama 88 E3 8 22N 80 10W
Río Lagartos, Mexico 87 C7 21 36N 88 10W
Río Largo, Brazil 93 E11 9 28S 35 50W
Río Mulatos, Bolivia 92 G5 19 40S 66 50W
Río Muni □, Eq. Guin. 52 D2 1 30N 10 0 E
Río Negro, Brazil 95 B6 26 0S 49 55W
Río Pardo, Brazil 95 C5 30 0S 52 30W
Río Pilcomayo △, Argentina 94 B4 25 5S 58 5W
Río Platano △, Honduras 88 C3 15 45N 84 45W
Río Rancho, U.S.A. 77 J10 35 14N 106 38W
Río Segundo, Argentina 94 C3 31 40S 63 59W
Río Tercero, Argentina 94 C3 32 15S 64 8W
Rio Verde, Brazil 93 G8 17 50S 51 0W
Río Verde, Mexico 87 C5 21 56N 100 0W
Rio Vista, U.S.A. 78 G5 38 10N 121 42W
Ríobamba, Ecuador 92 D3 1 50S 78 45W
Ríohacha, Colombia 92 A4 11 33N 72 55W
Ríosucio, Colombia 92 B3 7 27N 77 7W
Riou L., Canada 71 B7 59 7N 106 25W
Ripley, Canada 84 B3 44 4N 81 35W
Ripley, Calif., U.S.A. 79 M12 33 32N 114 39W
Ripley, N.Y., U.S.A. 84 D5 42 16N 79 43W

Ripley, Tenn., U.S.A. 81 H10 35 45N 89 32W
Ripley, W. Va., U.S.A. 82 F5 38 49N 81 43W
Ripon, U.K. 12 C6 54 9N 1 31W
Ripon, Calif., U.S.A. 78 H5 37 44N 121 7W
Ripon, Wis., U.S.A. 82 D1 43 51N 88 50W
Rishā', W. ar →, Si. Arabia ... 44 E5 25 33N 44 5 E
Rishiri-Rebun-Sarobetsu △, Japan ... 30 B10 45 26N 141 30 E
Rishiri-Tō, Japan .... 30 B10 45 11N 141 15 E
Rishon le Ẕiyyon, Israel ..... 46 D3 31 58N 34 48 E
Rison, U.S.A. 81 J8 33 58N 92 11W
Risør, Norway .... 9 G13 58 43N 9 13 E
Rita Blanca Cr. →, U.S.A. ... 81 H3 35 40N 102 29W
Ritter, Mt., U.S.A. 78 H7 37 41N 119 12W
Rittman, U.S.A. 84 F3 40 58N 81 47W
Ritzville, U.S.A. 76 C4 47 8N 118 23W
Riva del Garda, Italy ...... 22 B4 45 53N 10 50 E
Rivadavia, Buenos Aires, Argentina ... 94 D3 35 29S 62 59W
Rivadavia, Mendoza, Argentina 94 C2 33 13S 68 30W
Rivadavia, Salta, Argentina .. 94 A3 24 5S 62 54W
Rivadavia, Chile 94 B1 29 57S 70 35W
Rivas, Nic. 88 D2 11 30N 85 50W
River Cess, Liberia 50 G4 5 30N 9 32W
River Jordan, Canada 78 B2 48 26N 124 3W
Rivera, Argentina 94 D3 37 12S 63 14W
Rivera, Uruguay 95 C4 31 0S 55 50W
Riverbank, U.S.A. 78 H6 37 44N 120 56W
Riverdale, U.S.A. 78 J7 36 26N 119 52W
Riverhead, U.S.A. 85 F12 40 55N 72 40W
Riverhurst, Canada 71 C7 50 55N 106 50W
Rivers, Canada 71 C8 50 2N 100 14W
Rivers Inlet, Canada 70 C3 51 42N 127 15W
Riverside, S. Africa .... 56 E3 34 7S 21 15 E
Riverside, U.S.A. 79 M9 33 59N 117 22W
Riverton, Australia .... 63 E2 34 10S 138 46 E
Riverton, Canada 71 C9 51 1N 97 0W
Riverton, N.Z. .... 59 M2 46 21S 168 0 E
Riverton, U.S.A. 76 E9 43 2N 108 23W
Riverton Heights, U.S.A. ... 78 C4 47 28N 122 17W
Riviera, U.S.A. 79 K12 35 4N 114 35W
Riviera di Levante, Italy .... 20 D8 44 15N 9 30 E
Riviera di Ponente, Italy .... 20 D8 44 10N 8 20 E
Rivière-au-Renard, Canada .. 73 C7 48 59N 64 23W
Rivière-du-Loup, Canada ... 73 C6 47 50N 69 30W
Rivière-Pentecôte, Canada .. 73 C6 49 57N 67 1W
Rivière-Pilote, Martinique ... 88 c 14 26N 60 53W
Rivière St-Paul, Canada 73 B8 51 28N 57 45W
Rivière-Salée, Martinique ... 88 c 14 31N 61 0W
Rivne, Ukraine .... 17 C14 50 40N 26 10 E
Rivoli, Italy .... 20 D7 45 3N 7 31 E
Rivoli B., Australia .... 63 F3 37 32S 140 3 E
Riyadh = Ar Riyāḍ, Si. Arabia 44 E5 24 41N 46 42 E
Rize, Turkey .... 19 F7 41 0N 40 30 E
Rizhao, China .... 35 G10 35 25N 119 30 E
Rizokarpaso, Cyprus ...... 25 D13 35 36N 34 23 E
Rizzuto, C., Italy .... 22 E7 38 53N 17 5 E
Rjukan, Norway .... 9 G13 59 54N 8 33 E
Road Town, Br. Virgin Is. ... 89 e 18 27N 64 37W
Roan Plateau, U.S.A. 76 G9 39 20N 109 20W
Roanne, France .... 20 C6 46 3N 4 4 E
Roanoke, Ala., U.S.A. 83 J3 33 9N 85 22W
Roanoke, Va., U.S.A. 82 G6 37 16N 79 56W
Roanoke →, U.S.A. 83 H7 35 57N 76 42W
Roanoke I., U.S.A. 83 H8 35 55N 75 40W
Roanoke Rapids, U.S.A. ... 83 G7 36 28N 77 40W
Roatán, Honduras 88 C2 16 18N 86 35W
Robāt Sang, Iran .... 45 C8 35 35N 59 10 E
Robāṭkarim, Iran .... 45 C6 35 25N 50 59 E
Robāṭkarim □, Iran .... 45 B6 35 26N 50 59 E
Robbins I., Australia ...... 63 G4 40 42S 145 0 E
Robe →, Australia .... 60 D2 21 42S 116 15 E
Robert Lee, U.S.A. 81 K4 31 54N 100 29W
Robertsdale, U.S.A. 84 F6 40 11N 78 6W
Robertsganj, India .... 43 G10 24 44N 83 4 E
Robertson, S. Africa ...... 56 E2 33 46S 19 50 E
Robertson I., Antarctica ... 5 C18 65 15S 59 30W
Robertson Ra., Australia ... 60 D3 23 15S 121 0 E
Robertstown, Australia .... 63 E2 33 58S 139 5 E
Roberval, Canada 73 C5 48 32N 72 15W
Robeson Chan., N. Amer. .. 4 A4 82 0N 61 30W
Robesonia, U.S.A. 85 F8 40 21N 76 8W
Robinson, U.S.A. 82 F2 39 0N 87 44W
Robinson →, Australia .... 62 B2 16 3S 137 16 E
Robinson Ra., Australia .... 61 E2 25 40S 119 0 E
Robinvale, Australia ...... 63 E3 34 40S 142 45 E
Roblin, Canada 71 C8 51 14N 101 21W
Roboré, Bolivia 92 G7 18 10S 59 45W
Robson, Canada 70 D5 49 20N 117 41W
Robson, Mt., Canada 70 C5 53 10N 119 10W
Robstown, U.S.A. 81 M6 27 47N 97 40W
Roca, C. da, Portugal 21 C1 38 40N 9 31W
Roca Partida, I., Mexico ... 86 D2 19 1N 112 2W
Rocas, I., Brazil 93 D12 4 0S 34 1W
Rocha, Uruguay 95 C5 34 30S 54 25W
Rochdale, U.K. 12 D5 53 38N 2 9W
Rochefort, Belgium ...... 15 D5 50 9N 5 12 E
Rochefort, France 20 D3 45 56N 0 57W
Rochelle, U.S.A. 80 E10 41 56N 89 4W
Rocher River, Canada 70 A6 61 23N 112 44W
Rochester, U.K. .... 13 F8 51 23N 0 31 E
Rochester, Ind., U.S.A. 82 E2 41 4N 86 13W
Rochester, Minn., U.S.A. ... 80 C8 44 1N 92 28W
Rochester, N.H., U.S.A. ... 85 C14 43 18N 70 59W
Rochester, N.Y., U.S.A. ... 84 C7 43 10N 77 37W
Rock →, Canada 70 A3 60 7N 127 7W
Rock Creek, U.S.A. 84 E4 41 40N 80 52W
Rock Falls, U.S.A. 80 E10 41 47N 89 41W
Rock Hill, U.S.A. 83 H5 34 56N 81 1W
Rock Island, U.S.A. 80 E9 41 30N 90 34W
Rock Rapids, U.S.A. 80 D6 43 26N 96 10W
Rock Sound, Bahamas 88 B4 24 54N 76 12W
Rock Springs, Mont., U.S.A. 76 C10 46 49N 106 15W
Rock Springs, Wyo., U.S.A. 76 F9 41 35N 109 14W
Rock Valley, U.S.A. 80 D6 43 12N 96 18W
Rockall, Atl. Oc. 6 D3 57 37N 13 42W
Rockdale, Tex., U.S.A. 81 K6 30 39N 97 0W
Rockdale, Wash., U.S.A. ... 78 C5 47 22N 121 28W
Rockeby = Mungkan Kandju △, Australia ... 62 A3 13 35S 142 52 E
Rockefeller Plateau, Antarctica 5 E14 80 0S 140 0W
Rockford, U.S.A. 80 D10 42 16N 89 6W
Rockglen, Canada 71 D7 49 11N 105 57W
Rockhampton, Australia ... 62 C5 23 22S 150 32 E
Rockingham, Australia .... 61 F2 32 15S 115 38 E
Rockingham, U.S.A. 83 H6 34 57N 79 46W
Rockingham B., Australia .. 62 B4 18 5S 146 10 E
Rocklake, U.S.A. 80 A5 48 47N 99 15W

Rockland, Canada 85 A9 45 33N 75 17W
Rockland, Idaho, U.S.A. ... 76 E7 42 34N 112 53W
Rockland, Maine, U.S.A. ... 83 C11 44 6N 69 7W
Rockland, Mich., U.S.A. ... 80 B10 46 44N 89 11W
Rocklin, U.S.A. 78 G5 38 48N 121 14W
Rockmart, U.S.A. 83 H3 34 0N 85 3W
Rockport, Mass., U.S.A. ... 85 D14 42 39N 70 37W
Rockport, Mo., U.S.A. 80 E7 40 25N 95 31W
Rockport, Tex., U.S.A. 81 L6 28 2N 97 3W
Rocksprings, U.S.A. 81 K4 30 1N 100 13W
Rockville, Conn., U.S.A. ... 85 E12 41 52N 72 28W
Rockville, Md., U.S.A. 82 F7 39 5N 77 9W
Rockwall, U.S.A. 81 J6 32 56N 96 28W
Rockwell City, U.S.A. 80 D7 42 24N 94 38W
Rockwood, Canada 84 C4 43 37N 80 8W
Rockwood, Maine, U.S.A. .. 83 C11 45 41N 69 45W
Rockwood, Tenn., U.S.A. .. 83 H3 35 52N 84 41W
Rocky Ford, U.S.A. 80 F3 38 3N 103 43W
Rocky Gully, Australia .... 61 F2 34 30S 116 57 E
Rocky Harbour, Canada ... 73 C8 49 36N 57 55W
Rocky Island L., Canada ... 72 C3 46 55N 83 0W
Rocky Lane, Canada 70 B5 58 31N 116 22W
Rocky Mount, U.S.A. 83 H7 35 57N 77 48W
Rocky Mountain △, U.S.A. . 76 F11 40 25N 105 45W
Rocky Mountain House, Canada 70 C6 52 22N 114 55W
Rocky Mts., N. Amer. 76 G10 49 0N 115 0W
Rocky Point, Namibia ..... 56 B2 19 3S 12 30 E
Rod, Pakistan .... 40 E3 28 10N 63 5 E
Rødbyhavn, Denmark ..... 9 J14 54 39N 11 22 E
Roddickton, Canada 73 B8 50 51N 56 8W
Rodez, France .... 20 D5 44 21N 2 33 E
Rodhopoú, Greece .... 25 D5 35 34N 23 45 E
Ródhos, Greece .... 25 C10 36 15N 28 10 E
Rodney, Canada 84 D3 42 34N 81 41W
Rodney, C., N.Z. .... 59 G5 36 17S 174 50 E
Rodriguez, Ind. Oc. ...... 3 E13 19 45S 63 20 E
Roe →, U.K. 10 A5 55 6N 6 59W
Roebling, U.S.A. 85 F10 40 7N 74 47W
Roebourne, Australia ..... 60 D2 20 44S 117 9 E
Roebuck B., Australia ..... 60 C3 18 5S 122 20 E
Roermond, Neths. .... 15 C6 51 12N 6 0 E
Roes Welcome Sd., Canada . 69 B11 65 0N 87 0W
Roeselare, Belgium ...... 15 D3 50 57N 3 7 E
Rogachev = Ragachow, Belarus 17 B16 53 8N 30 5 E
Rogagua, L., Bolivia 92 F5 13 43S 66 50W
Rogatyn, Ukraine .... 17 D13 49 24N 24 36 E
Rogdhia, Greece .... 25 D7 35 22N 25 1 E
Rogers, U.S.A. 81 G7 36 20N 94 7W
Rogers City, U.S.A. 82 C4 45 25N 83 49W
Rogersville, Canada 73 C6 46 44N 65 26W
Roggan →, Canada 72 B4 54 24N 79 25W
Roggan L., Canada 72 B4 54 8N 77 50W
Roggeveldberge, S. Africa .. 56 E3 32 10S 20 10 E
Rogoaguado, L., Bolivia ... 92 F5 13 0S 65 30W
Rogojampi, Indonesia ..... 37 J17 8 19S 114 17 E
Rogue →, U.S.A. 76 E1 42 26N 124 26W
Róhda, Greece .... 25 A3 39 48N 19 46 E
Rohnert Park, U.S.A. 78 G4 38 16N 122 40W
Rohri, Pakistan .... 42 F3 27 45N 68 51 E
Rohri Canal, Pakistan ..... 42 F3 26 15N 68 27 E
Rohtak, India .... 42 E7 28 55N 76 43 E
Roi Et, Thailand .... 38 D4 16 4N 103 40 E
Roja, Latvia .... 9 H20 57 29N 22 43 E
Rojas, Argentina 94 C3 34 10S 60 45W
Rojo, C., Mexico 87 C5 21 33N 97 20W
Rokan →, Indonesia ..... 36 D2 2 0N 100 50 E
Rokiškis, Lithuania ...... 9 J21 55 55N 25 35 E
Rolândia, Brazil 95 A5 23 18S 51 23W
Rolla, U.S.A. 81 G9 37 57N 91 46W
Rolleston, Australia ...... 62 C4 24 28S 148 35 E
Rollingstone, Australia .... 62 B4 19 2S 146 24 E
Roma, Australia .... 63 D4 26 32S 148 49 E
Roma, Italy .... 22 D5 41 54N 12 29 E
Roma, Sweden .... 9 H18 57 32N 18 26 E
Romain, C., U.S.A. 83 J6 33 0N 79 22W
Romaine, Canada 73 B7 50 13N 60 40W
Romaine →, Canada 73 B7 50 18N 63 47W
Roman, Romania .... 17 E14 46 57N 26 55 E
Romang, Indonesia ...... 37 F7 7 30S 127 20 E
Români, Egypt .... 46 E1 30 59N 32 38 E
Romania ■, Europe ...... 17 F12 46 0N 25 0 E
Romano, Cayo, Cuba 88 B4 22 0N 77 30W
Romans-sur-Isère, France .. 20 D6 45 3N 5 3 E
Romblon, Phil. .... 37 B6 12 33N 122 17 E
Rome = Roma, Italy ...... 22 D5 41 54N 12 29 E
Rome, Ga., U.S.A. 83 H3 34 15N 85 10W
Rome, N.Y., U.S.A. 85 C9 43 13N 75 27W
Rome, Pa., U.S.A. 85 E8 41 51N 76 21W
Romney, U.S.A. 82 F6 39 21N 78 45W
Romney Marsh, U.K. ..... 13 F8 51 2N 0 54 E
Rømø, Denmark .... 9 J13 55 10N 8 30 E
Romorantin-Lanthenay, France 20 C4 47 21N 1 45 E
Romsdalen, Norway ..... 9 E12 62 25N 7 52 E
Romsey, U.K. 13 G6 51 0N 1 29W
Ron, Vietnam .... 38 D6 17 53N 106 27 E
Rona, U.K. 11 D3 57 34N 5 59W
Ronan, U.S.A. 76 C6 47 32N 114 6W
Roncador, Cayos, Colombia . 88 D3 13 32N 80 4W
Roncador, Serra do, Brazil . 93 F8 12 30S 52 30W
Ronda, Spain 21 D3 36 46N 5 12W
Rondane, Norway .... 9 F13 61 57N 9 50 E
Rondônia □, Brazil 92 F6 11 0S 63 0W
Rondonópolis, Brazil 93 G8 16 28S 54 38W
Rong, Koh, Cambodia .... 39 G4 10 45N 103 15 E
Ronge, L. la, Canada 71 B7 55 6N 105 17W
Rønne, Denmark .... 9 J16 55 6N 14 43 E
Ronne Ice Shelf, Antarctica . 5 D18 78 0S 60 0W
Ronsard, C., Australia .... 61 D1 24 46S 113 10 E
Ronse, Belgium .... 15 D3 50 45N 3 35 E
Roodepoort, S. Africa .... 57 D4 26 11S 27 54 E
Roof Butte, U.S.A. 77 H9 36 28N 109 5W
Rooiboklaagte →, Namibia . 56 C3 20 50S 21 0 E
Roorkee, India .... 42 E7 29 52N 77 59 E
Roosendaal, Neths. ...... 15 C4 51 32N 4 29 E
Roosevelt, U.S.A. 76 F8 40 18N 109 59W
Roosevelt →, Brazil 92 E6 7 35S 60 20W
Roosevelt, Mt., Canada ... 70 B3 58 26N 125 20W
Roosevelt I., Antarctica ... 5 D12 79 30S 162 0W
Roper →, Australia ...... 62 A2 14 43S 135 27 E
Roper Bar, Australia ..... 62 A1 14 44S 134 44 E
Roque Pérez, Argentina ... 94 D4 35 25S 59 24W
Roquetas de Mar, Spain ... 21 D4 36 46N 2 36W
Roraima □, Brazil 92 C6 2 0N 61 30W
Roraima, Mt., Venezuela ... 92 B6 5 10N 60 40W
Røros, Norway .... 9 E14 62 35N 11 23 E
Rosa, Zambia .... 55 D3 9 33S 31 15 E

Rosa, L., Bahamas 89 B5 21 0N 73 30W
Rosa, Monte, Europe ..... 20 D7 45 57N 7 53 E
Rosalia, U.S.A. 76 C5 47 14N 117 22W
Rosamond, U.S.A. 79 L8 34 52N 118 10W
Rosario, Argentina 94 C3 33 0S 60 40W
Rosário, Brazil 93 D10 3 0S 44 15W
Rosario, Baja Calif., Mexico . 86 B1 30 0N 115 50W
Rosario, Sinaloa, Mexico ... 86 C3 23 0N 105 52W
Rosario, Paraguay 94 A4 24 30S 57 35W
Rosario de la Frontera, Argentina 94 B3 25 50S 65 0W
Rosario de Lerma, Argentina 94 A2 24 59S 65 35W
Rosário do Sul, Brazil 95 C5 30 15S 54 55W
Rosarito, Mexico 79 N9 32 18N 117 4W
Roscoe, U.S.A. 85 E10 41 56N 74 55W
Roscommon, Ireland 10 C3 53 38N 8 11W
Roscommon □, Ireland ... 10 C3 53 49N 8 23W
Roscrea, Ireland 10 D4 52 57N 7 49W
Rose →, Australia .... 62 A2 14 16S 135 45 E
Rose Blanche-Harbour Le Cou, Canada ... 73 C8 47 38N 58 45W
Rose Pt., Canada 70 C2 54 11N 131 39W
Rose Valley, Canada 71 C8 52 19N 103 49W
Roseau, Domin. 89 C7 15 20N 61 24W
Roseau, U.S.A. 80 A7 48 51N 95 46W
Rosebery, Australia ...... 63 G4 41 46S 145 33 E
Rosebud, S. Dak., U.S.A. .. 80 D4 43 14N 100 51W
Rosebud, Tex., U.S.A. 81 K6 31 4N 96 59W
Roseburg, U.S.A. 76 E2 43 13N 123 20W
Rosedale, U.S.A. 81 J9 33 51N 91 2W
Rosehearty, U.K. 11 D6 57 42N 2 7W
Roseland, U.S.A. 78 G4 38 25N 122 43W
Rosemary, Canada 70 C6 50 46N 112 5W
Rosenberg, U.S.A. 81 L7 29 34N 95 49W
Rosenheim, Germany .... 16 E7 47 51N 12 7 E
Roses, G. de, Spain ...... 21 A7 42 10N 3 15 E
Rosetown, Canada 71 C7 51 35N 107 59W
Roseville, Calif., U.S.A. ... 78 G5 38 45N 121 17W
Roseville, Mich., U.S.A. ... 84 D2 42 30N 82 56W
Rosewood, Australia ..... 63 D5 27 38S 152 36 E
Roshkhvār, Iran .... 45 C8 34 58N 59 37 E
Rosignano Marittimo, Italy . 22 C4 43 24N 10 28 E
Rosignol, Guyana 92 B7 6 15N 57 30W
Roşiori de Vede, Romania .. 17 F13 44 9N 25 0 E
Roskilde, Denmark ...... 9 J15 55 38N 12 3 E
Roslavl, Russia .... 18 D5 53 57N 32 55 E
Rosmead, S. Africa ...... 56 E4 31 29S 25 8 E
Ross, Australia .... 63 G4 42 2S 147 30 E
Ross, N.Z. .... 59 K3 42 53S 170 49 E
Ross Dependency, Antarctica 5 D12 76 0S 170 0W
Ross I., Antarctica ...... 5 D11 77 30S 168 0 E
Ross Ice Shelf, Antarctica .. 5 E12 80 0S 180 0 E
Ross L., U.S.A. 76 B3 48 44N 121 4W
Ross-on-Wye, U.K. 13 F5 51 54N 2 34W
Ross River, Australia ..... 62 C1 23 44S 134 30 E
Ross River, Canada 70 A2 62 30N 131 30W
Ross Sea, Antarctica ..... 5 D11 74 0S 178 0 E
Rossall Pt., U.K. 12 D4 53 55N 3 3W
Rossan Pt., Ireland 10 B3 54 42N 8 47W
Rossano, Italy .... 22 E7 39 36N 16 39 E
Rossburn, Canada 71 C8 50 40N 100 49W
Rosseau, Canada 84 A5 45 16N 79 39W
Rosseau, L., Canada 84 A5 45 10N 79 35W
Rosses, The, Ireland 10 A3 55 2N 8 20W
Rossignol, L., Canada 72 B5 52 43N 73 40W
Rossignol L., Canada 73 D6 44 12N 65 10W
Rossland, Canada 70 D5 49 6N 117 50W
Rosslare, Ireland 10 D5 52 17N 6 24W
Rosslare Harbour, Ireland . 10 D5 52 15N 6 20W
Rosso, Mauritania 50 E2 16 40N 15 45W
Rossosh, Russia .... 19 D6 50 15N 39 28 E
Røssvatnet, Norway ..... 8 D16 65 45N 14 5 E
Rosthern, Canada 71 C7 52 40N 106 20W
Rostock, Germany ...... 16 A7 54 5N 12 8 E
Rostov, Don, Russia ..... 19 E6 47 15N 39 45 E
Rostov, Yaroslavl, Russia .. 18 C6 57 14N 39 25 E
Roswell, Ga., U.S.A. 83 H3 34 2N 84 22W
Roswell, N. Mex., U.S.A. .. 81 J4 33 24N 104 32W
Rotan, U.S.A. 81 J4 32 51N 100 28W
Rother →, U.K. .... 13 G8 50 59N 0 45 E
Rothera, Antarctica 5 C17 67 20S 68 0W
Rotherham, U.K. 12 D6 53 26N 1 20W
Rothes, U.K. 11 D5 57 32N 3 13W
Rothesay, Canada 73 C6 45 23N 66 0W
Rothesay, U.K. 11 F3 55 50N 5 3W
Roti, Indonesia .... 37 F6 10 50S 123 0 E
Roto, Australia .... 63 E4 33 0S 145 30 E
Rotondo, Mte., France .... 20 E8 42 14N 9 8 E
Rotoiti, L., N.Z. .... 59 J4 41 55S 172 39 E
Rotorua, N.Z. .... 59 H6 38 9S 176 16 E
Rotorua, L., N.Z. .... 59 H6 38 5S 176 18 E
Rotterdam, Neths. ...... 15 C4 51 55N 4 30 E
Rotterdam, U.S.A. 85 D10 42 48N 74 1W
Rottnest I., Australia ..... 61 F2 32 0S 115 27 E
Rottumeroog, Neths. .... 15 A6 53 33N 6 34 E
Rottweil, Germany ...... 16 D5 48 9N 8 37 E
Rotuma, Fiji .... 64 J9 12 25S 177 5 E
Roubaix, France .... 20 A5 50 40N 3 10 E
Rouen, France .... 20 B4 49 27N 1 4 E
Rouleau, Canada 71 C8 50 10N 104 56W
Round Mountain, U.S.A. .. 76 G5 38 43N 117 4W
Round Mt., Australia ..... 63 E5 30 26S 152 16 E
Round Rock, U.S.A. 81 K6 30 31N 97 41W
Roundup, U.S.A. 76 C9 46 27N 108 33W
Rousay, U.K. 11 B5 59 10N 3 2W
Rouses Point, U.S.A. 85 B11 44 59N 73 22W
Rouseville, U.S.A. 84 E5 41 28N 79 42W
Roussillon, France ...... 20 E5 42 30N 2 35 E
Rouxville, S. Africa ...... 56 E4 30 25S 26 50 E
Rouyn-Noranda, Canada .. 72 C4 48 20N 79 0W
Rovaniemi, Finland ...... 8 C21 66 29N 25 41 E
Rovereto, Italy .... 22 B4 45 53N 11 3 E
Rovigo, Italy .... 22 B4 45 4N 11 47 E
Rovinj, Croatia .... 16 F7 45 5N 13 40 E
Rovno = Rivne, Ukraine ... 17 C14 50 40N 26 10 E
Rovuma = Ruvuma →, Tanzania 55 E5 10 29S 40 28 E
Row'ān, Iran .... 45 C6 35 8N 48 51 E
Rowena, Australia ...... 63 D4 29 48S 148 55 E
Rowley Shoals, Australia .. 60 C2 17 30S 119 0 E
Roxas, Phil. .... 37 B6 11 36N 122 49 E
Roxboro, U.S.A. 83 G6 36 24N 78 59W
Roxborough, Trin. & Tob. .. 93 J16 11 16N 60 36W
Roxburgh, N.Z. .... 59 L2 45 33S 169 19 E
Roxbury, U.S.A. 84 F7 40 6N 78 5W
Roy, Mont., U.S.A. 76 C9 47 20N 108 58W
Roy, N. Mex., U.S.A. 81 H2 35 57N 104 12W
Roy, Utah, U.S.A. 76 F7 41 10N 112 2W

Royal Canal, Ireland 10 C4 53 30N 7 13W
Royal Leamington Spa, U.K. 13 E6 52 18N 1 31W
Royal Natal △, S. Africa ... 57 D4 28 43S 28 51 E
Royal Tunbridge Wells, U.K. 13 F8 51 7N 0 16 E
Royale, Isle, U.S.A. 80 B10 48 0N 88 54W
Royan, France 20 D3 45 37N 1 2W
Royston, U.K. 13 E7 52 3N 0 0W
Rozdilna, Ukraine .... 17 E16 46 50N 30 2 E
Rozhyshche, Ukraine .... 17 C13 50 54N 25 15 E
Rtishchevo, Russia ...... 18 D7 52 18N 43 46 E
Ruacaná, Namibia ...... 56 B1 17 27S 14 21 E
Ruaha △, Tanzania ...... 54 D3 7 41S 34 30 E
Ruahine Ra., N.Z. .... 59 H6 39 55S 176 2 E
Ruapehu, N.Z. .... 59 H5 39 17S 175 35 E
Ruapuke I., N.Z. .... 59 M2 46 46S 168 31 E
Ruâq, W. →, Egypt ...... 46 F2 30 0N 33 49 E
Rub' al Khālī, Si. Arabia ... 47 D4 19 0N 48 0 E
Rubeho Mts., Tanzania ... 54 D4 6 50S 36 25 E
Rubh a' Mhail, U.K. 11 F2 55 56N 6 8W
Rubha Hunish, U.K. 11 D2 57 42N 6 20W
Rubha Robhanais = Lewis, Butt of., U.K. ... 11 C2 58 31N 6 16W
Rubicon →, U.S.A. 78 G5 38 53N 121 4W
Rubio, Venezuela 92 B4 7 43N 72 22W
Rubondo △, Tanzania .... 54 C3 2 18S 31 58 E
Rubtsovsk, Russia ...... 28 D9 51 30N 81 10 E
Ruby L., U.S.A. 76 F6 40 10N 115 28W
Ruby Mts., U.S.A. 76 F6 40 30N 115 20W
Rubyvale, Australia ..... 62 C4 23 25S 147 42 E
Rúd Sar, Iran .... 45 B6 37 8N 50 18 E
Rudall, Australia .... 63 E2 33 43S 136 17 E
Rudall →, Australia ..... 60 D3 22 34S 122 13 E
Rudall River △, Australia .. 60 D3 22 38S 122 30 E
Rudewa, Tanzania ...... 55 E3 10 7S 34 40 E
Rudnyy, Kazakhstan ..... 28 D7 52 57N 63 7 E
Rudolfa, Ostrov, Russia ... 28 A6 81 45N 58 30 E
Rudyard, U.S.A. 82 B3 46 14N 84 36W
Ruenya →, Africa .... 55 F3 16 24S 33 48 E
Rufiji →, Tanzania ...... 54 D4 7 50S 39 15 E
Rufino, Argentina 94 C3 34 20S 62 50W
Rufling Pt., Br. Virgin Is. .. 89 e 18 44N 64 27W
Rufunsa, Zambia .... 55 F2 15 4S 29 34 E
Rugby, U.K. 13 E6 52 23N 1 16W
Rugby, U.S.A. 80 A5 48 22N 100 0W
Rügen, Germany .... 16 A7 54 22N 13 24 E
Ruhengeri, Rwanda ..... 54 C2 1 30S 29 36 E
Ruhnu, Estonia .... 9 H20 57 48N 23 15 E
Ruhr →, Germany ...... 16 C4 51 27N 6 43 E
Ruhuhu →, Tanzania .... 55 E3 10 31S 34 34 E
Ruidoso, U.S.A. 77 K11 33 20N 105 41W
Ruivo, Pico, Madeira 24 D3 32 45N 16 56W
Rujm Tal'at al Jamā'ah, Jordan 46 E4 30 24N 35 30 E
Ruk, Pakistan .... 42 F3 27 50N 68 42 E
Rukhla, Pakistan .... 42 C4 32 27N 71 57 E
Ruki →, Dem. Rep. of the Congo 52 E3 0 5N 18 17 E
Rukwa □, Tanzania ...... 54 D3 7 0S 31 30 E
Rukwa, L., Tanzania ..... 54 D3 8 0S 32 20 E
Rulhieres, C., Australia ... 60 B4 13 56S 127 22 E
Rum = Rhum, U.K. 11 E2 57 0N 6 20W
Rum, Jordan .... 46 F4 29 39N 35 26 E
Rum Cay, Bahamas 89 B5 23 40N 74 58W
Rum Jungle, Australia ... 60 B5 13 0S 130 59 E
Ruma △, Kenya .... 54 C3 0 39S 34 18 E
Rumāḥ, Si. Arabia ...... 44 E5 25 29N 47 10 E
Rumania = Romania ■, Europe 17 F12 46 0N 25 0 E
Rumaylah, Iraq .... 44 D5 30 47N 47 37 E
Rumbêk, Sudan .... 51 G11 6 54N 29 37 E
Rumford, U.S.A. 83 C10 44 33N 70 33W
Rumia, Poland .... 17 A10 54 37N 18 25 E
Rumoi, Japan .... 30 C10 43 56N 141 39 E
Rumonge, Burundi ..... 54 C2 3 59S 29 26 E
Rumuruti, Kenya .... 54 B4 0 17N 36 32 E
Runan, China .... 34 H8 33 0N 114 30 E
Runanga, N.Z. .... 59 K3 42 25S 171 15 E
Runaway, C., N.Z. ...... 59 G6 37 32S 177 59 E
Runaway Bay, Jamaica ... 88 a 18 27N 77 20W
Runcorn, U.K. 12 D5 53 21N 2 44W
Rundu, Namibia .... 56 B2 17 52S 19 43 E
Rungwa, Tanzania ...... 54 D3 6 55S 33 32 E
Rungwa →, Tanzania .... 54 D3 7 36S 31 50 E
Rungwe, Tanzania ...... 55 D3 9 11S 33 32 E
Rungwe, Mt., Tanzania ... 52 F6 9 8S 33 40 E
Runton Ra., Australia .... 60 D3 23 31S 123 6 E
Ruoqiang, China .... 32 C3 38 55N 88 10 E
Rupa, India .... 41 F18 27 15N 92 21 E
Rupar, India .... 42 D7 31 2N 76 38 E
Rupat, Indonesia .... 36 D2 1 45N 101 40 E
Rupen →, India .... 42 H4 23 28N 71 31 E
Rupert, U.S.A. 76 E7 42 37N 113 41W
Rupert →, Canada 72 B4 51 29N 78 45W
Rupert B., Canada 72 B4 51 35N 79 0W
Rupert House = Waskaganish, Canada ... 72 B4 51 30N 78 40W
Rupsa, India .... 43 J12 21 37N 87 1 E
Rurrenabaque, Bolivia ... 92 F5 14 30S 67 32W
Rusambo, Zimbabwe .... 55 F3 16 30S 32 4 E
Rusape, Zimbabwe ..... 55 F3 18 35S 32 8 E
Ruschuk = Ruse, Bulgaria . 23 C12 43 48N 25 59 E
Ruse, Bulgaria .... 23 C12 43 48N 25 59 E
Rush, Ireland 10 C5 53 31N 6 6W
Rushan, China .... 35 F11 36 56N 121 30 E
Rushden, U.K. 13 E7 52 18N 0 35W
Rushmore, Mt., U.S.A. ... 80 D3 43 53N 103 28W
Rushville, Ill., U.S.A. 80 E9 40 7N 90 34W
Rushville, Ind., U.S.A. 82 F3 39 37N 85 27W
Rushville, Nebr., U.S.A. ... 80 D3 42 43N 102 28W
Russas, Brazil 93 D11 4 55S 37 50W
Russell, Canada 71 C8 50 50N 101 20W
Russell, Kans., U.S.A. 80 F5 38 54N 98 52W
Russell, N.Y., U.S.A. 85 B9 44 27N 75 9W
Russell, Pa., U.S.A. 84 E5 41 56N 79 8W
Russell Cave △, U.S.A. ... 83 H3 34 59N 85 49W
Russell L., Man., Canada .. 71 B8 56 15N 101 30W
Russell L., N.W.T., Canada . 70 A5 63 5N 115 44W
Russellkonda, India ..... 41 K14 19 57N 84 42 E
Russellville, Ala., U.S.A. .. 83 H2 34 30N 87 44W
Russellville, Ark., U.S.A. .. 81 H8 35 17N 93 8W
Russellville, Ky., U.S.A. ... 83 G2 36 51N 86 53W
Russia ■, Eurasia ...... 29 C11 62 0N 105 0 E
Russian →, U.S.A. 78 G3 38 27N 123 8W
Russkoye Ustie, Russia ... 4 B15 71 0N 149 0 E
Rustam, Pakistan .... 42 B5 34 25N 72 13 E
Rustam Shahr, Pakistan .. 42 F2 26 58N 66 6 E
Rustavi, Georgia .... 19 F8 41 30N 45 0 E
Rustenburg, S. Africa .... 56 D4 25 41S 27 14 E
Ruston, U.S.A. 81 J8 32 32N 92 38W

Rutana, Burundi .... 54 C3   3 55S 30 0 E
Ruteng, Indonesia .... 37 F6   8 35S 120 30 E
Ruth, U.S.A. 84 C2   43 42N 82 45W
Rutherford, U.S.A. 78 G4   38 26N 122 24W
Rutland, U.S.A. 85 C12 43 37N 72 58W
Rutland □, U.K. 13 E7   52 38N   0 40W
Rutland Water, U.K. 13 E7   52 39N   0 38W
Rutledge →, Canada 71 A6   61 4N 112 0W
Rutledge L., Canada 71 A6   61 33N 110 47W
Rutshuru, Dem. Rep. of
  the Congo .... 54 C2   1 13S 29 25 E
Ruvu, Tanzania .... 54 D4   6 49S 38 43 E
Ruvu →, Tanzania .... 54 D4   6 23S 38 52 E
Ruvuba △, Burundi .... 54 C2   3 3S 29 33 E
Ruvuma □, Tanzania .... 55 E4   10 20S 36 0 E
Ruvuma →, Tanzania .... 55 E5   10 29S 40 28 E
Ruwais, U.A.E. .... 45 E7   24 5N 52 50 E
Ruwenzori, Africa .... 54 B2   0 30N 29 55 E
Ruwenzori △, Uganda ...... 54 B2   0 20S 30 0 E
Ruya →, Zimbabwe .... 57 B5   16 27S 32 5 E
Ruyigi, Burundi .... 54 C3   3 29S 30 15 E
Ružomberok, Slovak Rep. .. 17 D10 49 3N 19 17 E
Rwanda ■, Africa .... 54 C3   2 0S 30 0 E
Ryan, L., U.K. 11 G3   55 0N   5 2W
Ryazan, Russia .... 18 D6   54 40N 39 40 E
Ryazhsk, Russia .... 18 D6   53 45N 40 3 E
Rybache = Rybachye, Kazakhstan 28 E9 46 40N 81 20 E
Rybachiy Poluostrov, Russia 18 A5 69 43N 32 0 E
Rybachye, Kazakhstan ..... 28 E9   46 40N 81 20 E
Rybinsk, Russia .... 18 C6   58 5N 38 50 E
Rybinskoye Vdkhr., Russia . 18 C6   58 30N 38 25 E
Rybnitsa = Râbniţa, Moldova 17 E15 47 45N 29 0 E
Rycroft, Canada 70 B5   55 45N 118 40W
Ryde, U.K. 13 G6   50 43N   1 9W
Ryderwood, U.S.A. 78 D3   46 23N 123 3W
Rye, U.K. .... 13 G8   50 57N   0 45 E
Rye →, U.K. 12 C7   54 11N   0 44W
Rye Bay, U.K. .... 13 G8   50 52N   0 49 E
Rye Patch Reservoir, U.S.A. 76 F4 40 28N 118 19W
Ryegate, U.S.A. 76 C9   46 18N 109 15W
Ryley, Canada 70 C6   53 17N 112 26W
Rylstone, Australia .... 63 E4   32 46S 149 58 E
Ryōtsu, Japan .... 30 E9   38 5N 138 26 E
Rypin, Poland .... 17 B10 53 3N 19 25 E
Ryūgasaki, Japan .... 31 G10 35 54N 140 11 E
Ryūkyū Is. = Ryūkyū-rettō, Japan 31 M3 26 0N 126 0 E
Ryūkyū-rettō, Japan ...... 31 M3 26 0N 126 0 E
Rzeszów, Poland .... 17 C11 50 5N 21 58 E
Rzhev, Russia .... 18 C5   56 20N 34 20 E

S

Sa, Thailand .... 38 C3   18 34N 100 45 E
Sa Canal, Spain .... 24 C7   38 51N   1 23 E
Sa Conillera, Spain .... 24 C7   38 59N   1 13 E
Sa Dec, Vietnam .... 39 G5   10 20N 105 46 E
Sa Dragonera, Spain ...... 24 B9   39 35N   2 19 E
Sa Mesquida, Spain .... 24 B11 39 55N   4 16 E
Sa Savina, Spain .... 24 C7   38 44N   1 25 E
Sa'ādatābād, Fārs, Iran ... 45 D7   30 10N 53 5 E
Sa'ādatābād, Hormozgān, Iran 45 D7 28 3N 55 53 E
Sa'ādatābād, Kermān, Iran . 45 D7   29 40N 55 51 E
Saale →, Germany .... 16 C6   51 56N 11 54 E
Saalfeld, Germany .... 16 C6   50 38N 11 21 E
Saanich, Canada 78 B3   48 29N 123 26W
Saar →, Europe .... 15 E6   49 41N   6 32 E
Saarbrücken, Germany ..... 16 D4   49 14N   6 59 E
Saaremaa, Estonia .... 9 G20   58 30N 22 30 E
Saarijärvi, Finland .... 9 E21   62 43N 25 16 E
Saariselkä, Finland .... 8 B23   68 16N 28 15 E
Sab 'Ābar, Syria .... 44 C3   33 46N 37 41 E
Saba, W. Indies 89 C7   17 42N 63 26W
Šabac, Serbia & M. .... 23 B8   44 48N 19 42 E
Sabadell, Spain .... 21 B7   41 28N   2 7 E
Sabah □, Malaysia .... 36 C5   6 0N 117 0 E
Sabak Bernam, Malaysia ... 39 L3   3 46N 100 58 E
Sabalana, Kepulauan, Indonesia 37 F5 6 45S 118 50 E
Sábana de la Mar, Dom. Rep. 89 C6 19 7N 69 24W
Sábanalarga, Colombia 92 A4   10 38N 74 55W
Sabang, Indonesia .... 36 C1   5 50N 95 15 E
Sabará, Brazil 93 G10 19 55S 43 46W
Sabarmati →, India .... 42 H5   22 18N 72 22 E
Sabattis, U.S.A. 85 B10 44 6N 74 40W
Sabhah, Libya .... 51 C8   27 9N 14 29 E
Sabi →, India .... 42 E7   28 29N 76 44 E
Sabie, S. Africa .... 57 D5   25 10S 30 48 E
Sabinal, Mexico 86 A3   30 58N 107 25W
Sabinal, U.S.A. 81 L5   29 19N 99 28W
Sabinas, Mexico 86 B4   27 50N 101 10W
Sabinas →, Mexico 86 B4   27 37N 100 42W
Sabinas Hidalgo, Mexico .. 86 B4   26 33N 100 10W
Sabine →, U.S.A. 81 L8   29 59N 93 47W
Sabine L., U.S.A. 81 L8   29 53N 93 51W
Sabine Pass, U.S.A. 81 L8   29 44N 93 54W
Sabinsville, U.S.A. 84 E7   41 52N 77 31W
Sablayan, Phil. .... 37 B6   12 50N 120 50 E
Sable, Canada 73 A6   55 30N 68 21W
Sable, C., Canada 73 D6   43 29N 65 38W
Sable, C., U.S.A. 75 E10 25 9N 81 8W
Sable I., Canada 73 D8   44 0N 60 0W
Sabrina Coast, Antarctica . 5 C9   68 0S 120 0 E
Sabulubbek, Indonesia .... 36 E1   1 36S 98 40 E
Sabzevār, Iran .... 45 B8   36 15N 57 40 E
Sabzvārān, Iran .... 45 D8   28 45N 57 50 E
Sac City, U.S.A. 80 D7   42 25N 95 0W
Săcele, Romania .... 17 F13 45 37N 25 41 E
Sachigo →, Canada 72 A2   55 6N 88 58W
Sachigo, L., Canada 72 B1   53 50N 92 12W
Sachsen □, Germany .... 16 C7   50 55N 13 10 E
Sachsen-Anhalt □, Germany 16 C7   52 0N 12 0 E
Sackets Harbor, U.S.A. ... 85 C8   43 57N 76 7W
Sackville, Canada 73 C7   45 54N 64 22W
Saco, Maine, U.S.A. 83 D10 43 30N 70 27W
Saco, Mont., U.S.A. 76 B10 48 28N 107 21W
Sacramento, U.S.A. 78 G5   38 35N 121 29W
Sacramento →, U.S.A. 78 G5   38 3N 121 56W
Sacramento Mts., U.S.A. .. 77 K11 32 30N 105 30W
Sacramento Valley, U.S.A. . 78 G5   39 30N 122 0W
Sada-Misaki, Japan .... 31 H6   33 20N 132 1 E
Sadabad, India .... 42 F8   27 27N 78 3 E
Sadani, Tanzania .... 54 D4   5 58S 38 35 E
Sadao, Thailand .... 39 J3   6 38N 100 26 E
Sadd el Aali, Egypt .... 51 D12 23 54N 32 54 E

Saddle Mt., U.S.A. 78 E3   45 58N 123 41W
Sadimi, Dem. Rep. of the Congo 55 D1 9 25S 23 32 E
Sado, Japan .... 30 F9   38 0N 138 25 E
Sadon, Burma .... 41 G20 25 28N 97 55 E
Sadra, India .... 42 H5   23 21N 72 43 E
Sadri, India .... 42 G5   25 11N 73 26 E
Sæby, Denmark .... 9 H14   57 21N 10 30 E
Saegertown, U.S.A. 84 E4   41 43N 80 9W
Şafājah, Si. Arabia .... 44 E3   26 25N 39 0 E
Saffle, Sweden .... 9 G15   59 8N 12 55 E
Safford, U.S.A. 77 K9   32 50N 109 43W
Saffron Walden, U.K. ..... 13 E8   52 1N   0 16 E
Safi, Morocco 50 B4   32 18N   9 20W
Şafiābād, Iran .... 45 B8   36 45N 57 58 E
Safid Dasht, Iran .... 45 C6   33 27N 48 11 E
Safid Kūh, Afghan. .... 40 B3   34 45N 63 0 E
Safid Rūd →, Iran .... 45 B6   37 23N 50 11 E
Safipur, India .... 43 F9   26 44N 80 21 E
Sag Harbor, U.S.A. 85 F12 41 0N 72 18W
Saga, Japan .... 31 H5   33 15N 130 16 E
Saga □, Japan .... 31 H5   33 15N 130 20 E
Sagae, Japan .... 30 E10 38 22N 140 17 E
Sagamartha = Everest, Mt.,
  Nepal .... 43 E12 28 5N 86 58 E
Sagamore, U.S.A. 84 F5   40 46N 79 14W
Sagar, Karnataka, India ... 40 M9   14 14N 75 6 E
Sagar, Mad. P., India ..... 43 H8   23 50N 78 44 E
Sagara, L., Tanzania ...... 54 D3   5 20S 31 0 E
Saginaw, U.S.A. 82 D4   43 26N 83 56W
Saginaw →, U.S.A. 82 D4   43 39N 83 51W
Saginaw B., U.S.A. 82 D4   43 50N 83 40W
Saglouc = Salluit, Canada . 69 B12 62 14N 75 38W
Sagō-ri, S. Korea .... 35 G14 35 25N 126 49 E
Sagua la Grande, Cuba 88 B3   22 50N 80 10W
Saguache, U.S.A. 77 G10 38 5N 106 8W
Saguaro △, U.S.A. 77 K8   32 12N 110 38W
Saguenay →, Canada 73 C5   48 22N 71 0W
Sagunt, Spain 21 C5   39 42N   0 18W
Sagunto = Sagunt, Spain .. 21 C5   39 42N   0 18W
Sagwara, India .... 42 H6   23 41N 74 1 E
Sahagún, Spain 21 A3   42 18N   5 2W
Saham al Jawlān, Syria .... 46 C4   32 45N 35 55 E
Sahamandrevo, Madag. .... 57 C8   23 15S 45 35 E
Sahand, Kūh-e, Iran ...... 44 B5   37 44N 46 27 E
Sahara, Africa .... 50 D6   23 0N   5 0 E
Saharan Atlas = Saharien, Atlas,
  Algeria .... 50 B6   33 30N   1 0 E
Saharanpur, India .... 42 E7   29 58N 77 33 E
Saharien, Atlas, Algeria ... 50 B6   33 30N   1 0 E
Saharsa, India .... 43 G12 25 53N 86 36 E
Sahasinaka, Madag. .... 57 C8   21 49S 47 49 E
Sahaswan, India .... 43 E8   28 5N 78 45 E
Sahel, Africa .... 50 E5   16 0N   5 0 E
Sahibganj, India .... 43 G12 25 12N 87 40 E
Sāhiliyah, Iraq .... 44 C4   33 43N 42 42 E
Sahiwal, Pakistan .... 42 D5   30 45N 73 8 E
Şahneh, Iran .... 44 C5   34 29N 47 41 E
Sahrawi = Western Sahara ■,
  Africa 50 D3   25 0N 13 0W
Sahuaripa, Mexico 86 B3   29 0N 109 13W
Sahuarita, U.S.A. 77 L8   31 57N 110 58W
Sahuayo, Mexico 86 C4   20 4N 102 43W
Sai →, India .... 43 G10 25 39N 82 47 E
Sai Buri, Thailand .... 39 J3   6 43N 101 45 E
Sai Kung, China .... 33 G11 22 23N 114 16 E
Sa'id Bundas, Sudan ...... 51 G10   8 24N 24 48 E
Sa'īdābād = Sīrjān, Iran .. 45 D7   29 30N 55 45 E
Sa'īdābād, Iran .... 45 B7   36 8N 54 11 E
Sa'īdīyeh, Iran .... 45 B6   36 20N 48 55 E
Saidpur, Bangla. .... 41 G16 25 48N 89 0 E
Saidpur, India .... 43 G10 25 33N 83 11 E
Saidu, Pakistan .... 43 B5   34 43N 72 24 E
Saigon = Thanh Pho Ho Chi
  Minh, Vietnam .... 39 G6   10 58N 106 40 E
Saijō, Japan .... 31 H6   33 55N 133 11 E
Saikai △, Japan .... 31 H4   32 58N 129 36 E
Saikanosy Masoala, Madag. 57 B9   15 45S 50 10 E
Saikhoa Ghat, India ...... 41 F19 27 50N 95 40 E
Saiki, Japan .... 31 H5   32 58N 131 51 E
Sailana, India .... 42 H6   23 28N 74 55 E
Sailolof, Indonesia ...... 37 E8   1 15S 130 46 E
Saimaa, Finland .... 9 F23   61 15N 28 15 E
Sa'in Dezh, Iran .... 44 B5   36 40N 46 25 E
St. Abb's Head, U.K. 11 F6   55 55N   2 8W
St. Alban's, Canada 73 C8   47 51N 55 50W
St. Albans, U.K. 13 F7   51 45N   0 19W
St. Albans, Vt., U.S.A. ... 85 B11 44 49N 73 5W
St. Albans, W. Va., U.S.A. . 82 F5   38 23N 81 50W
St. Alban's Head, U.K. 13 G5   50 34N   2 4W
St. Albert, Canada 70 C6   53 37N 113 32W
St. Andrew's, Canada 73 C8   47 45N 59 15W
St. Andrews, U.K. 11 E6   56 20N   2 47W
St-Anicet, Canada 85 A10 45 8N 74 22W
St. Anns B., Canada 73 C7   46 22N 60 25W
St. Ann's Bay, Jamaica ... 88 a   18 26N 77 15W
St. Anthony, Canada 73 B8   51 22N 55 35W
St. Anthony, U.S.A. 76 E8   43 58N 111 41W
St-Antoine, Canada 73 C7   46 22N 64 45W
St. Arnaud, Australia ..... 63 F3   36 40S 143 16 E
St-Augustin, Canada 73 B8   51 13N 58 38W
St-Augustin →, Canada 73 B8   51 16N 58 40W
St. Augustine, U.S.A. 83 L5   29 54N 81 19W
St. Austell, U.K. 13 G3   50 20N   4 47W
St. Barbe, Canada 73 B8   51 12N 56 46W
St-Barthélemy, W. Indies .. 89 C7   17 50N 62 50W
St. Bees Hd., U.K. 12 C4   54 31N   3 38W
St. Bee's I., Australia .... 62 J7   20 56S 149 26 E
St. Bride's, Canada 73 C9   46 56N 54 10W
St. Brides B., U.K. 13 F2   51 49N   5 9W
St-Brieuc, France 20 B2   48 30N   2 46W
St. Catharines, Canada ... 84 C5   43 10N 79 15W
St. Catherines I., U.S.A. .. 83 K5   31 40N 81 10W
St. Catherine's Pt., U.K. .. 13 G6   50 34N   1 18W
St-Chamond, France ...... 20 D6   45 28N   4 31 E
St. Charles, Ill., U.S.A. ... 82 E1   41 54N 88 19W
St. Charles, Mo., U.S.A. ... 80 F9   38 47N 90 29W
St. Charles, Va., U.S.A. ... 82 F7   36 48N 83 4W
St. Christopher-Nevis = St. Kitts
  & Nevis ■, W. Indies ... 89 C7   17 20N 62 40W
St. Clair, Mich., U.S.A. ... 84 D2   42 50N 82 30W
St. Clair, Pa., U.S.A. 85 F8   40 43N 76 12W
St. Clair →, U.S.A. 84 D2   42 38N 82 31W
St. Clair, L., Canada 72 D3   42 30N 82 45W
St. Clair, L., U.S.A. 84 D2   42 27N 82 39W
St. Clairsville, U.S.A. 84 F4   40 5N 80 54W
St. Claude, Canada 71 D9   49 40N 98 20W
St. Clears, U.K. 13 F3   51 49N   4 31W

St-Clet, Canada 85 A10 45 21N 74 13W
St. Cloud, Fla., U.S.A. 83 L5   28 15N 81 17W
St. Cloud, Minn., U.S.A. .. 80 C7   45 34N 94 10W
St. Cricq, C., Australia ... 61 E1   25 17S 113 6 E
St. Croix, U.S. Virgin Is. .. 89 C7   17 45N 64 45W
St. Croix →, U.S.A. 80 C8   44 45N 92 48W
St. Croix Falls, U.S.A. 80 C8   45 24N 92 38W
St. David's, Canada 73 C8   48 12N 58 52W
St. David's, U.K. 13 F2   51 53N   5 16W
St. David's Head, U.K. 13 F2   51 54N   5 19W
St-Denis, France .... 20 B5   48 56N   2 22 E
St-Dizier, France .... 20 B6   48 38N   4 56 E
St. Elias, Mt., U.S.A. 68 B5   60 18N 140 56W
St. Elias Mts., N. Amer. ... 70 A1   60 33N 139 28W
St-Étienne, France .... 20 D6   45 27N   4 22 E
St. Eugène, Canada 85 A10 45 30N 74 28W
St-Eustatius, W. Indies ... 89 C7   17 20N 63 0W
St-Félicien, Canada 72 C5   48 40N 72 25W
St-Flour, France .... 20 D5   45 2N   3 6 E
St. Francis, U.S.A. 80 F4   39 47N 101 48W
St. Francis →, U.S.A. 81 H9   34 38N 90 36W
St. Francis, C., S. Africa .. 56 E3   34 14S 24 49 E
St. Francisville, U.S.A. 81 K9   30 47N 91 23W
St-François, L., Canada ... 85 A10 45 10N 74 22W
St. Gabriel, Canada 72 C5   46 17N 73 24W
St. Gallen = Sankt Gallen, Switz. 20 C8 47 26N   9 22 E
St-Gaudens, France ...... 20 E4   43 6N   0 44 E
St. George, Australia ..... 63 D4   28 1S 148 30 E
St. George, Canada 73 C6   45 11N 66 50W
St. George, S.C., U.S.A. ... 83 J5   33 11N 80 35W
St. George, Utah, U.S.A. .. 77 H7   37 6N 113 35W
St. George, C., Canada 73 C8   48 30N 59 16W
St. George, C., U.S.A. 83 L3   29 40N 85 5W
St. George Ra., Australia .. 60 C4   18 40S 125 0 E
St. George's, Canada 73 C8   48 26N 58 31W
St. George's, Grenada 89 D7   12 5N 61 43W
St. George's B., Canada ... 73 C8   48 24N 58 53W
St. Georges Basin, N.S.W.,
  Australia .... 63 F5   35 7S 150 36 E
St. Georges Basin, W. Austral.,
  Australia .... 60 C4   15 23S 125 2 E
St. George's Channel, Europe 10 E6 52 0N   6 0W
St. Georges Hd., Australia . 63 F5   35 12S 150 42 E
St. Gotthard P. = San Gottardo,
  P. del, Switz. .... 20 C8   46 33N   8 33 E
St. Helena, Atl. Oc. 48 H3   15 58S   5 42W
St. Helena, U.S.A. 76 G2   38 30N 122 28W
St. Helena, Mt., U.S.A. ... 78 G4   38 40N 122 36W
St. Helena B., S. Africa ... 56 E2   32 40S 18 10 E
St. Helens, Australia ..... 63 G4   41 20S 148 15 E
St. Helens, U.K. 12 D5   53 27N   2 44W
St. Helens, U.S.A. 78 E4   45 52N 122 48W
St. Helens, Mt., U.S.A. ... 78 D4   46 12N 122 12W
St. Helier, U.K. 13 H5   49 10N   2 7W
St-Hubert, Belgium .... 15 D5   50 2N   5 23 E
St-Hyacinthe, Canada 72 C5   45 40N 72 58W
St. Ignace, U.S.A. 82 C3   45 52N 84 44W
St. Ignace I., Canada 72 C2   48 45N 88 0W
St. Ignatius, U.S.A. 76 C6   47 19N 114 6W
St. Ives, Cambs., U.K. 13 E7   52 20N   0 4W
St. Ives, Corn., U.K. 13 G2   50 12N   5 30W
St. James, U.S.A. 80 D7   43 59N 94 38W
St-Jean →, Canada 73 B7   50 17N 64 20W
St-Jean, L., Canada 73 C5   48 40N 72 0W
St-Jean-Port-Joli, Canada . 73 C5   47 15N 70 13W
St-Jean-sur-Richelieu, Canada 85 A11 45 20N 73 20W
St-Jérôme, Canada 72 C5   45 47N 74 0W
St. John, U.S.A. 81 G5   38 0N 98 46W
St. John →, U.S.A. 83 C12 45 12N 66 5W
St. John, C., Canada 73 C8   50 0N 55 32W
St. John, U.S. Virgin Is. ... 89 e   18 20N 64 42W
St. John's, Antigua & B. .. 89 C7   17 6N 61 51W
St. John's, Canada 73 C9   47 35N 52 40W
St. Johns, Ariz., U.S.A. ... 77 J9   34 30N 109 22W
St. Johns, Mich., U.S.A. .. 82 D3   43 0N 84 33W
St. Johns →, U.S.A. 83 K5   30 24N 81 24W
St. John's Pt., Ireland 10 B3   54 34N   8 27W
St. Johnsbury, U.S.A. 85 B12 44 25N 72 1W
St. Johnsville, U.S.A. 85 D10 43 0N 74 43W
St-Joseph, Martinique .... 88 c   14 39N 61 4W
St-Joseph, L., U.S.A. 81 K9   31 55N 91 14W
St. Joseph, Mo., U.S.A. ... 80 F7   39 46N 94 50W
St. Joseph →, U.S.A. 82 D2   42 7N 86 29W
St. Joseph, I., Canada 72 C3   46 12N 83 58W
St. Joseph, L., Canada 72 B1   51 10N 90 35W
St-Jovite, Canada 72 C5   46 8N 74 38W
St. Kilda, U.K. 14 C2   57 49N   8 34W
St. Kitts & Nevis ■, W. Indies 89 C7 17 20N 62 40W
St. Laurent, Canada 71 C9   50 25N 97 58W
St. Lawrence, Australia ... 62 C4   22 16S 149 31 E
St. Lawrence, Canada 73 C8   46 54N 55 23W
St. Lawrence →, Canada ... 73 C6   49 30N 66 0W
St. Lawrence, Gulf of, Canada 73 C7 48 25N 62 0W
St. Lawrence I., U.S.A. 68 B3   63 30N 170 30W
St. Lawrence Islands △, Canada 85 B9 44 27N 75 52W
St. Leonard, Canada 73 C6   47 12N 67 58W
St. Lewis →, Canada 73 B8   52 26N 56 11W
St-Lô, France 20 B3   49 7N   1 5W
St-Louis, Guadeloupe ..... 88 b   15 56N 61 19W
St. Louis, Senegal 50 E2   16 8N 16 27W
St. Louis, U.S.A. 80 F9   38 37N 90 12W
St. Louis →, U.S.A. 80 B8   47 15N 92 45W
St. Lucia ■, W. Indies .... 89 f   14 0N 60 50W
St. Lucia, L., S. Africa .... 57 D5   28 5S 32 30 E
St. Lucia Channel, W. Indies 89 D7 14 15N 61 0W
St. Maarten, W. Indies 89 C7   18 0N 63 5W
St. Magnus B., U.K. 11 A7   60 25N   1 35W
St-Malo, France 20 B2   48 39N   2 1W
St-Marc, Haiti 89 C5   19 10N 72 41W
St. Maries, U.S.A. 76 C5   47 19N 116 35W
St-Martin, C., Martinique . 88 c   14 52N 61 14W
St. Martin, L., Canada 71 C9   51 40N 98 30W
St. Martins, Barbados ..... 89 g   13 5N 59 28W
St. Mary Pk., Australia ... 63 E2   31 32S 138 34 E
St. Marys, Australia ...... 63 G4   41 35S 148 11 E
St. Marys, Canada 84 C3   43 20N 81 10W
St. Mary's, Corn., U.K. ... 13 H1   49 55N   6 18W
St. Mary's, Orkney, U.K. .. 11 C6   58 54N   2 54W
St. Marys, Ga., U.S.A. 83 K5   30 44N 81 33W
St. Marys, Pa., U.S.A. 84 E6   41 26N 78 34W
St. Mary's, C., Canada 73 C9   46 50N 53 50W
St. Mary's B., Canada 73 C9   46 50N 53 50W
St. Marys Bay, Canada 73 D6   44 25N 66 10W
St-Mathieu, Pte., France .. 20 B1   48 20N   4 45W
St. Matthew I., U.S.A. 68 B2   60 24N 172 42W

St-Maurice →, Canada 72 C5   46 21N 72 31W
St. Mawes, U.K. 13 G2   50 10N   5 2W
St-Nazaire, France 20 C2   47 17N   2 12W
St. Neots, U.K. 13 E7   52 14N   0 15W
St-Niklaas, Belgium ...... 15 C4   51 10N   4 8 E
St-Omer, France .... 20 A5   50 45N   2 15 E
St-Pamphile, Canada 73 C6   46 58N 69 48W
St-Pascal, Canada 73 C6   47 32N 69 48W
St. Paul, Canada 70 C6   54 0N 111 17W
St. Paul, Minn., U.S.A. ... 80 C8   44 57N 93 6W
St. Paul, Nebr., U.S.A. ... 80 E5   41 13N 98 27W
St-Paul →, Canada 73 B8   51 27N 57 42W
St. Paul, I., Ind. Oc. ..... 3 F13   38 55S 77 34 E
St. Paul I., Canada 73 C7   47 12N 60 9W
St. Peter, U.S.A. 80 C8   44 20N 93 57W
St. Peter Port, U.K. 13 H5   49 26N   2 33W
St. Peter's, N.S., Canada .. 73 C7   45 40N 60 53W
St. Peter's, P.E.I., Canada . 73 C7   46 25N 62 35W
St. Petersburg = Sankt-Peterburg,
  Russia .... 18 C5   59 55N 30 20 E
St. Petersburg, U.S.A. 83 M4   27 46N 82 39W
St-Pie, Canada 85 A12 45 30N 72 54W
St-Pierre, Martinique ..... 88 c   14 45N 61 10W
St-Pierre, St-P. & M. 73 C8   46 46N 56 12W
St-Pierre, L., Canada 72 C5   46 40N 72 40W
St-Pierre-et-Miquelon ☑,
  N. Amer. 73 C8   46 55N 56 10W
St-Quentin, Canada 73 C6   47 30N 67 23W
St-Quentin, France .... 20 B5   49 50N   3 16 E
St. Regis, U.S.A. 76 C6   47 18N 115 6W
St. Sebastien, Tanjon' i, Madag. 57 A8 12 26S 48 44 E
St-Siméon, Canada 73 C5   47 51N 69 54W
St. Simons I., Canada 83 K5   31 12N 81 15W
St. Simons Island, U.S.A. .. 83 K5   31 9N 81 22W
St. Stephen, Canada 73 C6   45 16N 67 17W
St. Thomas, Canada 84 D3   42 45N 81 10W
St. Thomas I., U.S. Virgin Is. 89 e 18 20N 64 55W
St-Tite, Canada 72 C5   46 45N 72 34W
St-Tropez, France .... 20 E7   43 17N   6 38 E
St-Troud = St. Truiden, Belgium 15 D5 50 48N   5 10 E
St. Truiden, Belgium ...... 15 D5   50 48N   5 10 E
St. Vincent, G., Australia . 63 F2   35 0S 138 0 E
St. Vincent & the Grenadines ■,
  W. Indies 89 D7   13 0N 61 10W
St. Vincent Passage, W. Indies 89 D7 13 30N 61 0W
St-Vith, Belgium .... 15 D6   50 17N   6 9 E
St. Walburg, Canada 71 C7   53 39N 109 12W
Ste-Agathe-des-Monts, Canada 72 C5 46 3N 74 17W
Ste-Anne, Guadeloupe .... 88 b   16 13N 61 24W
Ste-Anne, L., Canada 73 B6   50 0N 67 42W
Ste-Anne-des-Monts-Tourelle,
  Canada 73 C6   49 8N 66 30W
Ste. Genevieve, U.S.A. 80 G9   37 59N 90 2W
Ste-Marguerite →, Canada . 73 B6   50 9N 66 36W
Ste-Marie, Canada 73 C5   46 26N 71 0W
Ste-Marie, Martinique .... 88 c   14 48N 61 1W
Ste-Rose, Guadeloupe .... 88 b   16 20N 61 45W
Ste. Rose du Lac, Canada .. 71 C9   51 4N 99 30W
Saintes, France 20 D3   45 45N   0 37W
Saintes, Îs. des, Guadeloupe 88 b 15 50N 61 35W
Saintfield, U.K. 10 B6   54 28N   5 49W
Saintonge, France 20 D3   45 40N   0 50W
Saipan, Pac. Oc. .... 64 F6   15 12N 145 45 E
Sairang, India .... 41 H18 23 50N 92 45 E
Sairecábur, Cerro, Bolivia . 94 A2   22 43S 67 54W
Saitama □, Japan .... 31 F9   36 25N 139 30 E
Saiyid, Pakistan .... 42 C5   33 7N 73 2 E
Sajama, Bolivia 92 G5   18 7S 69 0W
Sajószentpéter, Hungary ... 17 D11 48 12N 20 44 E
Sajum, India .... 43 C8   33 20N 79 0 E
Sak →, S. Africa .... 56 E3   30 52S 20 25 E
Sakai, Japan .... 31 G7   34 30N 135 30 E
Sakaide, Japan .... 31 G6   34 19N 133 50 E
Sakaiminato, Japan .... 31 G6   35 38N 133 11 E
Sakākah, Si. Arabia ...... 44 D4   30 0N 40 8 E
Sakakawea, L., U.S.A. 80 B4   47 30N 101 25W
Sakami →, Canada 72 B4   53 40N 76 40W
Sakami, L., Canada 72 B4   53 15N 77 0W
Sakania, Dem. Rep. of the Congo 55 E2 12 43S 28 30 E
Sakaraha, Madag. .... 57 C7   22 55S 44 32 E
Sakarya, Turkey .... 19 F5   40 48N 30 25 E
Sakashima-Guntō, Japan .. 31 M2   24 46N 124 0 E
Sakata, Japan .... 30 E9   38 55N 139 50 E
Sakchu, N. Korea .... 35 D13 40 23N 125 2 E
Sakeny →, Madag. .... 57 C8   20 0S 45 25 E
Sakha □, Russia .... 29 C13 66 0N 130 0 E
Sakhalin, Russia .... 29 D15 51 0N 143 0 E
Sakhalinskiy Zaliv, Russia . 29 D15 54 0N 141 0 E
Šakiai, Lithuania .... 9 J20   54 59N 23 2 E
Sakon Nakhon, Thailand .. 38 D5   17 10N 104 9 E
Sakrand, Pakistan .... 42 F3   26 10N 68 15 E
Sakri, India .... 43 F12 26 13N 86 5 E
Sakrivier, S. Africa ...... 56 E3   30 54S 20 28 E
Sakti, India .... 43 H10 22 2N 82 58 E
Sakuma, Japan .... 31 G8   35 3N 137 49 E
Sakurai, Japan .... 31 G7   34 30N 135 51 E
Sala, Sweden .... 9 G17   59 58N 16 35 E
Sala Consilina, Italy ..... 22 D6   40 23N 15 36 E
Sala-y-Gómez, Pac. Oc. ... 65 K17 26 28S 105 28W
Salaberry-de-Valleyfield, Canada 85 A10 45 15N 74 8W
Salada, L., Mexico 77 K6   32 20N 115 40W
Saladas, Argentina 94 B4   28 15S 58 40W
Saladillo, Argentina 94 D4   35 40S 59 55W
Salado →, Buenos Aires,
  Argentina 94 D4   35 44S 57 22W
Salado →, La Pampa, Argentina 96 D3 37 30S 67 0W
Salado →, Santa Fe, Argentina 94 C3 31 40S 60 41W
Salado →, Mexico 81 M5   26 52N 99 19W
Salaga, Ghana 50 G5   8 31N   0 31W
Sālah, Syria .... 46 C5   32 40N 36 45 E
Şalāḩ ad Din □, Iraq ...... 44 C4   34 35N 43 35 E
Salakhos, Greece .... 25 C9   36 17N 27 57 E
Salālah, Oman .... 47 D5   16 56N 53 59 E
Salamanca, Chile 94 C1   31 46S 70 59W
Salamanca, Spain 21 B3   40 58N   5 39W
Salamanca, U.S.A. 84 D6   42 10N 78 43W
Salāmatābād, Iran .... 44 C5   35 39N 47 50 E
Salamís, Greece .... 23 D12 35 13N 48 55 E
Salamis, Greece .... 23 F10 37 56N 23 30 E
Salar de Atacama, Chile ... 94 A2   23 30S 68 25W
Salar de Uyuni, Bolivia ... 92 H5   20 30S 67 45W
Salatiga, Indonesia ...... 37 G14 7 19S 110 30 E
Salavat, Russia .... 18 D10 53 21N 55 55 E
Salaverry, Peru 92 E3   8 15S 79 0W
Salawati, Indonesia ...... 37 E8   1 7S 130 52 E
Salaya, India .... 42 H3   22 19N 69 35 E
Salayar, Indonesia .... 37 F6   6 7S 120 30 E
Salcombe, U.K. 13 G4   50 14N   3 47W

Saldanha, S. Africa .... 56 E2 33 0S 17 58 E
Saldanha B., S. Africa .... 56 E2 33 6S 18 0 E
Saldus, Latvia .... 9 H20 56 38N 22 30 E
Sale, Australia .... 63 F4 38 6S 147 6 E
Salé, Morocco 50 B4 34 3N   6 48W
Sale, U.K. 12 D5 53 26N   2 19W
Salekhard, Russia .... 28 C7 66 30N 66 35 E
Salem, India .... 40 P11 11 40N 78 11 E
Salem, Ill., U.S.A. 82 F1 38 38N 88 57W
Salem, Ind., U.S.A. 82 F2 38 36N 86 6W
Salem, Mass., U.S.A. 85 D14 42 31N 70 53W
Salem, Mo., U.S.A. 81 G9 37 39N 91 32W
Salem, N.H., U.S.A. 85 D13 42 45N 71 12W
Salem, N.J., U.S.A. 82 F8 39 34N 75 28W
Salem, N.Y., U.S.A. 85 C11 43 10N 73 20W
Salem, Ohio, U.S.A. 84 F4 40 54N 80 52W
Salem, Oreg., U.S.A. 76 D2 44 56N 123 2W
Salem, S. Dak., U.S.A. 80 D6 43 44N 97 23W
Salem, Va., U.S.A. 82 G5 37 18N 80 3W
Salerno, Italy .... 22 D6 40 41N 14 47 E
Salford, U.K. 12 D5 53 30N   2 18W
Salgótarján, Hungary .... 17 D10 48 5N 19 47 E
Salgueiro, Brazil 93 E11   8 4S 39 6W
Salibabu, Indonesia .... 37 D7   3 51N 126 40 E
Salibea, Trin. & Tob. 93 K15 10 43N 61 2W
Salida, U.S.A. 74 C5 38 32N 106 0W
Salihli, Turkey .... 23 E13 38 28N 28 8 E
Salihorsk, Belarus .... 17 B14 52 51N 27 27 E
Salima, Malawi .... 53 G6 13 47S 34 28 E
Salina, Italy .... 22 E6 38 34N 14 50 E
Salina, Kans., U.S.A. 80 F6 38 50N 97 37W
Salina, Utah, U.S.A. 77 G8 38 58N 111 51W
Salina Cruz, Mexico 87 D5 16 10N 95 10W
Salinas, Brazil 93 G10 16 10S 42 10W
Salinas, Chile 94 A2 23 31S 69 29W
Salinas, Ecuador 92 D2   2 10S 80 58W
Salinas, U.S.A. 78 J5 36 40N 121 39W
Salinas →, Guatemala 87 D6 16 28N 90 31W
Salinas →, U.S.A. 78 J5 36 45N 121 48W
Salinas, B. de, Nic. 88 D2 11 4N 85 45W
Salinas, Pampa de las, Argentina 94 C2 31 58S 66 42W
Salinas Ambargasta, Argentina 94 B3 29 0S 65 0W
Salinas de Hidalgo, Mexico .. 86 C4 22 30N 101 40W
Salinas Grandes, Argentina .. 94 C3 30 0S 65 0W
Salinas Pueblo Missions △,
  U.S.A. 77 J10 34 16N 106 5W
Saline →, Ark., U.S.A. 81 J8 33 10N 92 8W
Saline →, Kans., U.S.A. 80 F6 38 52N 97 30W
Salines, C. de ses, Spain .... 24 B10 39 16N   3 4 E
Salinópolis, Brazil 93 D9   0 40S 47 20W
Salisbury, U.K. 13 F6 51 4N   1 47W
Salisbury, Md., U.S.A. 82 F8 38 22N 75 36W
Salisbury, N.C., U.S.A. 83 H5 35 40N 80 29W
Salisbury I., Canada 69 B12 63 30N 77 0W
Salisbury Plain, U.K. 13 F6 51 14N   1 55W
Şalkhad, Syria .... 8 C23 55 50N 28 49 E
Salla, Finland .... 8 C23 66 50N 28 49 E
Salliq = Coral Harbour, Canada 69 B11 64 8N 83 10W
Sallisaw, U.S.A. 81 H7 35 28N 94 47W
Salluit, Canada 69 B12 62 14N 75 38W
Salmās, Iran .... 44 B5 38 11N 44 47 E
Salmo, Canada 70 D5 49 10N 117 20W
Salmon, U.S.A. 76 D7 45 11N 113 54W
Salmon →, Canada 70 C4 54 3N 122 40W
Salmon →, U.S.A. 76 D5 45 51N 116 47W
Salmon Arm, Canada 70 C5 50 40N 119 15W
Salmon Gums, Australia ..... 61 F3 32 59S 121 38 E
Salmon River Mts., U.S.A. ... 76 D6 45 0N 114 30W
Salo, Finland .... 9 F20 60 22N 23 10 E
Salome, U.S.A. 79 M13 33 47N 113 37W
Salon, India .... 43 F9 26 2N 81 27 E
Salon-de-Provence, France ... 20 E6 43 39N   5 6 E
Salonica = Thessaloníki, Greece 23 D10 40 38N 22 58 E
Salonta, Romania .... 17 E11 46 49N 21 42 E
Salpausselkä, Finland .... 9 F22 61 0N 27 0 E
Salsacate, Argentina 94 C2 31 20S 65 5W
Salsk, Russia .... 19 E7 46 28N 41 30 E
Salso →, Italy .... 22 F5 37 6N 13 57 E
Salt →, Canada 70 B6 60 0N 112 25W
Salt →, U.S.A. 77 K7 33 23N 112 19W
Salt Lake City, U.S.A. 76 F8 40 45N 111 53W
Salt Range, Pakistan .... 42 C5 32 30N 72 25 E
Salta, Argentina 94 A2 24 57S 65 25W
Salta □, Argentina 94 A2 24 48S 65 30W
Saltash, U.K. 13 G3 50 24N   4 14W
Saltburn by the Sea, U.K. ... 12 C7 54 35N   0 58W
Saltcoats, U.K. 11 F4 55 38N   4 47W
Saltee Is., Ireland 10 D5 52 7N   6 37W
Saltfjellet, Norway .... 8 C16 66 40N 15 15 E
Saltfjorden, Norway .... 8 C16 67 15N 14 10 E
Saltillo, Mexico 86 B4 25 25N 101 0W
Salto, Argentina 94 C3 34 20S 60 15W
Salto, Uruguay 94 C4 31 27S 57 50W
Salto →, Italy .... 22 C5 42 26N 12 25 E
Salto del Guaira, Paraguay ... 95 A5 24 3S 54 17W
Salton City, U.S.A. 79 M11 33 29N 115 51W
Salton Sea, U.S.A. 79 M11 33 15N 115 45W
Saltsburg, U.S.A. 84 F5 40 29N 79 27W
Saluda →, U.S.A. 83 J5 34 1N 81 4W
Salûm, Egypt .... 51 B11 31 31N 25 7 E
Salur, India .... 41 K13 18 27N 83 18 E
Salvador, Brazil 93 F11 13 0S 38 30W
Salvador, Canada 71 C7 52 10N 109 32W
Salvador, El ■, Cent. Amer. .. 88 D2 13 50N 89 0W
Salvador, L., U.S.A. 81 L9 29 43N 90 15W
Salween →, Burma .... 41 L20 16 31N 97 37 E
Salyan, Azerbaijan .... 19 G8 39 33N 48 59 E
Salzach →, Austria .... 16 D7 48 12N 12 56 E
Salzburg, Austria .... 16 E7 47 48N 13 2 E
Salzgitter, Germany .... 16 B6 52 9N 10 19 E
Salzwedel, Germany .... 16 B6 52 52N 11 10 E
Sam, India .... 42 F4 26 50N 70 31 E
Sam Ngao, Thailand .... 38 D2 17 18N 99 0 E
Sam Rayburn Reservoir, U.S.A. 81 K7 31 4N 94 5W
Sam Son, Vietnam .... 38 C5 19 44N 105 54 E
Sam Teu, Laos .... 38 C5 19 59N 104 38 E
Sama de Langreo = Langreo,
  Spain 21 A3 43 18N   5 40W
Samagaltay, Russia .... 29 D10 50 36N 95 3 E
Samales Group, Phil. .... 37 C6   6 0N 122 0 E
Samana, India .... 42 D7 30 10N 76 13 E
Samana Cay, Bahamas 89 B5 23 3N 73 45W
Samanga, Tanzania .... 55 D4   8 20S 39 13 E
Samangān □, Afghan. .... 40 B5 36 15N 68 3 E
Samangwa, Dem. Rep. of
  the Congo .... 54 C1   4 23S 24 10 E
Samani, Japan .... 30 C11 42 7N 142 56 E

Samar, Phil. .... 37 B7 12 0N 125 0 E
Samara, Russia .... 18 D9 53 8N 50 6 E
Samaria = Shōmrōn, West Bank 46 C4 32 15N 35 13 E
Samariá, Greece .... 25 D5 35 17N 23 58 E
Samarinda, Indonesia .... 36 E5   0 30S 117 9 E
Samarkand = Samarqand,
  Uzbekistan .... 28 F7 39 40N 66 55 E
Samarqand, Uzbekistan ...... 28 F7 39 40N 66 55 E
Sāmarrā', Iraq .... 44 C4 34 12N 43 52 E
Samastipur, India .... 43 G11 25 50N 85 50 E
Samba, Dem. Rep. of the Congo 54 C2   4 38S 26 22 E
Samba, India .... 43 C6 32 32N 75 10 E
Sambalpur, India .... 41 J14 21 28N 84 4 E
Sambar, Tanjung, Indonesia .. 36 E4   2 59S 110 19 E
Sambas, Indonesia .... 36 D3   1 20N 109 20 E
Sambava, Madag. .... 57 A9 14 16S 50 10 E
Sambawizi, Zimbabwe .... 55 F2 18 24S 26 13 E
Sambhal, India .... 43 E8 28 35N 78 37 E
Sambhar, India .... 42 F6 26 52N 75 6 E
Sambhar L., India .... 42 F6 26 55N 75 12 E
Sambiase, Italy .... 22 E7 38 58N 16 17 E
Sambir, Ukraine .... 17 D12 49 30N 23 10 E
Sambor, Cambodia .... 38 F6 12 46N 106 0 E
Samborombón, B., Argentina . 94 D4 36 5S 57 20W
Samburu □, Kenya .... 54 B4   0 37N 37 31 E
Samch'ŏk, S. Korea .... 35 F15 37 30N 129 10 E
Samch'onp'o, S. Korea ...... 35 G15 35 0N 128 6 E
Same, Tanzania .... 54 C4   4 2S 37 38 E
Samfya, Zambia .... 55 E2 11 22S 29 31 E
Samnah, Si. Arabia .... 44 E3 25 10N 37 15 E
Samo Alto, Chile 94 C1 30 22S 71 0W
Samoa ■, Pac. Oc. 59 B13 14 0S 172 0W
Samokov, Bulgaria .... 23 C10 42 18N 23 35 E
Sámos, Greece .... 23 F12 37 45N 26 50 E
Samothráki = Mathráki, Greece 25 A3 39 48N 119 31 E
Samothráki, Greece .... 23 D11 40 28N 25 28 E
Sampacho, Argentina 94 C3 33 20S 64 50W
Sampalan, Indonesia .... 37 K18   8 41S 115 34 E
Sampang, Indonesia .... 37 G15   7 11S 113 13 E
Sampit, Indonesia .... 36 E4   2 34S 113 0 E
Sampit, Teluk, Indonesia ..... 36 E4   3 5S 113 3 E
Samrong, Cambodia .... 38 E4 14 15N 103 30 E
Samrong, Thailand .... 38 E3 15 10N 100 40 E
Samsø, Denmark .... 9 J14 55 50N 10 35 E
Samsun, Turkey .... 19 F6 41 15N 36 22 E
Samui, Ko, Thailand .... 39 b   9 30N 100 0 E
Samusole, Dem. Rep. of
  the Congo .... 55 E1 10 2S 24 0 E
Samut Prakan, Thailand ..... 38 F3 13 32N 100 40 E
Samut Songkhram →, Thailand 36 B1 13 24N 100 1 E
Samwari, Pakistan .... 42 E2 28 30N 66 46 E
San, Mali 50 F5 13 15N   4 57W
San →, Cambodia .... 38 F5 13 32N 105 57 E
San →, Poland .... 17 C11 50 45N 21 51 E
San Agustín, C., Phil. .... 37 C7   6 20N 126 13 E
San Agustín de Valle Fértil,
  Argentina 94 C2 30 35S 67 30W
San Ambrosio, Pac. Oc. 90 F3 26 28S 79 53W
San Andreas, U.S.A. 78 G6 38 12N 120 41W
San Andrés, I. de, Caribbean .. 88 D3 12 42N 81 46W
San Andres Mts., U.S.A. 77 K10 33 0N 106 30W
San Andrés Tuxtla, Mexico ... 87 D5 18 30N 95 20W
San Angelo, U.S.A. 81 K4 31 28N 100 26W
San Anselmo, U.S.A. 78 H4 37 59N 122 34W
San Antonio, Belize 87 D7 16 15N 89 2W
San Antonio, Chile 94 C1 33 40S 71 40W
San Antonio, N. Mex., U.S.A. . 77 K10 33 55N 106 52W
San Antonio, Tex., U.S.A. 81 L5 29 25N 98 30W
San Antonio →, U.S.A. 81 L6 28 30N 96 54W
San Antonio, C., Argentina ... 94 D4 36 15S 56 40W
San Antonio, C., Cuba 88 B3 21 50N 84 57W
San Antonio, Mt., U.S.A. 79 L9 34 17N 117 38W
San Antonio de los Baños, Cuba 88 B3 22 54N 82 31W
San Antonio de los Cobres,
  Argentina 94 A2 24 10S 66 17W
San Antonio Oeste, Argentina . 96 E4 40 40S 65 0W
San Ardo, U.S.A. 78 J6 36 1N 120 54W
San Agustín, Canary Is. 24 G4 27 47N 15 32W
San Augustine, U.S.A. 81 K7 31 30N 94 7W
San Bartolomé, Canary Is. 24 F6 28 59N 13 37W
San Bartolomé de Tirajana,
  Canary Is. 24 G4 27 54N 15 34W
San Benedetto del Tronto, Italy 22 C5 42 57N 13 53 E
San Benedicto, I., Mexico 86 D2 19 18N 110 49W
San Benito, U.S.A. 81 M6 26 8N 97 38W
San Benito →, U.S.A. 78 J5 36 53N 121 34W
San Benito Mt., U.S.A. 78 J6 36 22N 120 37W
San Bernardino, U.S.A. 79 L9 34 7N 117 19W
San Bernardino Mts., U.S.A. .. 79 L10 34 10N 116 45W
San Bernardino Str., Phil. .... 37 B6 13 0N 125 0 E
San Bernardo, Chile 94 C1 33 40S 70 50W
San Bernardo, I. de, Colombia . 92 B3   9 45N 75 50W
San Blas, Mexico 86 B3 26 4N 108 46W
San Blas, Arch. de, Panama ... 88 E4   9 50N 78 31W
San Blas, C., U.S.A. 83 L3 29 40N 85 21W
San Borja, Bolivia 92 F5 14 50S 66 52W
San Buenaventura = Ventura,
  U.S.A. 79 L7 34 17N 119 18W
San Buenaventura, Mexico ... 86 B4 27 5N 101 32W
San Carlos = Sant Carles, Spain 24 B8 39 3N   1 34 E
San Carlos, Argentina 94 C2 33 50S 69 0W
San Carlos, Chile 94 D1 36 10S 72 0W
San Carlos, Baja Calif. S., Mexico 86 C2 24 47N 112 6W
San Carlos, Coahuila, Mexico . 86 B4 29 0N 100 54W
San Carlos, Nic. 88 D3 11 12N 84 50W
San Carlos, Phil. .... 37 B6 10 29N 123 25 E
San Carlos, Uruguay 95 C5 34 46S 54 58W
San Carlos, U.S.A. 77 K8 33 21N 110 27W
San Carlos, Venezuela 92 B5   9 40N 68 36W
San Carlos de Bariloche,
  Argentina 96 E2 41 10S 71 25W
San Carlos de Bolívar, Argentina 94 D3 36 15S 61 6W
San Carlos del Zulia, Venezuela 92 B4   9 1N 71 55W
San Carlos L., U.S.A. 77 K8 33 11N 110 32W
San Clemente, Chile 94 D1 35 30S 71 29W
San Clemente, U.S.A. 79 M9 33 26N 117 37W
San Clemente I., U.S.A. 79 N8 32 53N 118 29W
San Cristóbal = Es Migjorn Gran,
  Spain .... 24 B11 39 57N   4 3 E
San Cristóbal, Argentina 94 C3 30 20S 61 10W
San Cristóbal, Dom. Rep. 89 C5 18 25N 70 6W
San Cristóbal, Venezuela 92 B4   7 46N 72 14W
San Cristóbal de la Casas,
  Mexico 87 D6 16 50N 92 33W
San Diego, Calif., U.S.A. 79 N9 32 43N 117 9W
San Diego, Tex., U.S.A. 81 M5 27 46N 98 14W
San Diego, C., Argentina 96 G3 54 40S 65 10W
San Diego de la Unión, Mexico 86 C4 21 28N 100 52W

San Diego International ✈ (SAN),
  U.S.A. 79 N9 32 44N 117 11W
San Dimitri, Ras, Malta ...... 25 C1 36 4N 14 11 E
San Dimitri Point = San Dimitri,
  Ras, Malta .... 25 C1 36 4N 14 11 E
San Estanislao, Paraguay 94 A4 24 39S 56 26W
San Felipe, Chile 94 C1 32 43S 70 42W
San Felipe, Mexico 86 A2 31 0N 114 52W
San Felipe, Venezuela 92 A5 10 20N 68 44W
San Felipe →, U.S.A. 79 M11 33 12N 115 49W
San Félix, Chile 94 B1 28 56S 70 28W
San Félix, Pac. Oc. 90 F2 26 23S 80 0W
San Fernando = Sant Ferran,
  Spain .... 24 C7 38 42N   1 28 E
San Fernando, Chile 94 C1 34 30S 71 0W
San Fernando, Baja Calif.,
  Mexico 86 B1 29 55N 115 10W
San Fernando, Tamaulipas,
  Mexico 87 C5 24 51N 98 10W
San Fernando, La Union, Phil. . 37 A6 16 40N 120 23 E
San Fernando, Pampanga, Phil. 37 A6 15 5N 120 37 E
San Fernando, Spain 21 D2 36 28N   6 17W
San Fernando, Trin. & Tob. ... 89 D7 10 20N 61 30W
San Fernando, U.S.A. 79 L8 34 17N 118 26W
San Fernando de Apure,
  Venezuela 92 B5   7 54N 67 15W
San Fernando de Atabapo,
  Venezuela 92 C5   4 3N 67 42W
San Francisco, Argentina 94 C3 31 30S 62 5W
San Francisco, U.S.A. 78 H4 37 47N 122 25W
San Francisco →, U.S.A. 77 K9 32 59N 109 22W
San Francisco, C. de, Colombia 90 C3   6 18N 77 29W
San Francisco, Paso de, S. Amer. 94 B2 27 0S 68 0W
San Francisco de Macorís,
  Dom. Rep. 89 C5 19 19N 70 15W
San Francisco del Monte de Oro,
  Argentina 94 C2 32 36S 66 8W
San Francisco del Oro, Mexico 86 B3 26 52N 105 50W
San Francisco International ✈
  (SFO), U.S.A. 78 H4 37 37N 122 22W
San Francisco Javier = Sant
  Francesc de Formentera, Spain 24 C7 38 42N   1 26 E
San Gabriel, Chile 94 C1 33 47S 70 15W
San Gabriel Mts., U.S.A. 79 L9 34 20N 118 0W
San German, Puerto Rico ..... 89 d 18 4N 67 4W
San Gorgonio Mt., U.S.A. 79 L10 34 7N 116 51W
San Gottardo, P. del, Switz. ... 20 C8 46 33N   8 33 E
San Gregorio, Uruguay 95 C4 32 37S 55 40W
San Gregorio, U.S.A. 78 H4 37 20N 122 23W
San Ignacio, Belize 87 D7 17 10N 89 0W
San Ignacio, Bolivia 92 G6 16 20S 60 55W
San Ignacio, Mexico 86 B2 27 27N 113 0W
San Ignacio, Paraguay 88 C2 26 52S 57 3W
San Ignacio, Mexico 86 B2 27 0N 113 10W
San Ignacio, L., Mexico 86 B2 26 50N 113 11W
San Ildefonso, C., Phil. ...... 37 A6 16 0N 122 1 E
San Isidro, Argentina 94 C4 34 29S 58 31W
San Jacinto, U.S.A. 79 M10 33 47N 116 57W
San Jaime = Sant Jaume, Spain 24 B11 39 54N   4 4 E
San Javier, Misiones, Argentina 95 B4 27 55S 55 5W
San Javier, Santa Fe, Argentina 94 C4 30 40S 59 55W
San Javier, Bolivia 92 G6 16 18S 62 30W
San Javier, Chile 94 D1 35 40S 71 45W
San Jeronimo Taviche, Mexico 87 D5 16 38N 96 32W
San Joaquin, U.S.A. 78 J6 36 36N 120 11W
San Joaquin →, U.S.A. 78 G5 38 4N 121 51W
San Joaquin Valley, U.S.A. ... 78 J6 37 20N 121 0W
San Jon, U.S.A. 81 H3 35 6N 103 20W
San Jordi = Sant Jordi, Spain . 24 B9 39 33N   2 46 E
San Jorge, Argentina 94 C3 31 54S 61 50W
San Jorge, B. de, Mexico 86 A2 31 20N 113 20W
San Jorge, G., Argentina 96 F3 46 0S 66 0W
San José = San Josep, Spain .. 24 C7 38 55N   1 18 E
San José, Costa Rica 88 D1   9 55N 84 2W
San José, Guatemala 88 D1 14 0N 90 50W
San José, Mexico 86 C2 25 0N 110 50W
San José, Mind. Occ., Phil. ... 37 B6 12 27N 121 4 E
San Jose, Nueva Ecija, Phil. .. 37 A6 15 45N 120 55 E
San Jose, U.S.A. 78 H5 37 20N 121 53W
San Jose →, U.S.A. 77 J10 34 25N 106 45W
San Jose de Buenavista, Phil. . 37 B6 10 45N 121 56 E
San José de Chiquitos, Bolivia 92 G6 17 53S 60 50W
San José de Feliciano, Argentina 94 C4 30 26S 58 46W
San José de Jáchal, Argentina . 94 C2 30 15S 68 46W
San José de Mayo, Uruguay ... 94 C4 34 27S 56 40W
San José del Cabo, Mexico 86 C3 23 0N 109 40W
San José del Guaviare, Colombia 92 C4   2 35N 72 38W
San Josep, Spain .... 24 C7 38 55N   1 18 E
San Juan, Argentina 94 C2 31 30S 68 30W
San Juan, Mexico 86 C4 21 20N 102 50W
San Juan, Puerto Rico .... 89 d 18 28N 66 7W
San Juan, Trin. & Tob. 93 K15 10 39N 61 29W
San Juan □, Argentina 94 C2 31 9S 69 0W
San Juan →, Argentina 94 C2 32 0S 67 25W
San Juan →, Nic. 88 D3 10 56N 83 42W
San Juan →, U.S.A. 77 H8 37 16N 110 26W
San Juan Bautista = Sant Joan
  Baptista, Spain .... 24 B8 39 5N   1 31 E
San Juan Bautista, Paraguay .. 94 B4 26 37S 57 6W
San Juan Bautista, U.S.A. 78 J5 36 51N 121 32W
San Juan Bautista Valle
  Nacional, Mexico 87 D5 17 47N 96 19W
San Juan Capistrano, U.S.A. .. 79 M9 33 30N 117 40W
San Juan Cr. →, U.S.A. 78 J5 35 40N 120 22W
San Juan de Guadalupe, Mexico 86 C4 24 38N 102 44W
San Juan de los Morros,
  Venezuela 92 B5   9 55N 67 21W
San Juan del Norte, Nic. 88 D3 10 58N 83 40W
San Juan del Norte, B. de, Nic. 88 D3 11 0N 83 40W
San Juan del Río, Mexico 87 C5 20 25N 100 0W
San Juan del Sur, Nic. 88 D2 11 20N 85 51W
San Juan I., U.S.A. 78 B3 48 32N 123 5W
San Juan Mts., U.S.A. 77 H10 37 30N 107 0W
San Justo, Argentina 94 C3 30 47S 60 30W
San Kamphaeng, Thailand ... 38 C2 18 45N 99 8 E
San Lázaro, C., Mexico 86 C2 24 50N 112 18W
San Lázaro, Sa., Mexico 86 C3 23 25N 110 0W
San Leandro, U.S.A. 78 H4 37 44N 122 9W
San Lorenzo = Sant Llorenç de
  Cardassar, Spain .... 24 B10 39 37N   3 17 E
San Lorenzo, Argentina 94 C3 32 45S 60 45W
San Lorenzo, Ecuador 92 C3   1 15N 78 50W
San Lorenzo, Paraguay 94 B4 25 20S 57 32W
San Lorenzo →, Mexico 86 C3 24 15N 107 24W
San Lorenzo, I., Mexico 86 B2 28 35N 112 50W
San Lorenzo, Mte., Argentina . 96 F2 47 40S 72 20W

San Lucas, Bolivia 92 H5 20 5S 65 7W
San Lucas, Baja Calif. S., Mexico 86 C3 22 53N 109 54W
San Lucas, Baja Calif. S., Mexico 86 B2 27 10N 112 14W
San Lucas, U.S.A. 78 J5 36 8N 121 1W
San Lucas, C., Mexico 86 C3 22 50N 110 0W
San Luis, Argentina 94 C2 33 20S 66 0W
San Luis, Cuba 88 B3 22 17N 83 46W
San Luis, Guatemala 88 C2 16 14N 89 27W
San Luis, Ariz., U.S.A. 77 K6 32 29N 114 47W
San Luis, Colo., U.S.A. 77 H11 37 12N 105 25W
San Luis □, Argentina 94 C2 34 0S 66 0W
San Luis, I., Mexico 86 B2 29 58N 114 26W
San Luis, Sierra de, Argentina 94 C2 32 30S 66 10W
San Luis de la Paz, Mexico ... 86 C4 21 19N 100 32W
San Luis Obispo, U.S.A. 79 K6 35 17N 120 40W
San Luis Potosí, Mexico 86 C4 22 9N 100 59W
San Luis Potosí □, Mexico ... 86 C4 22 10N 101 0W
San Luis Reservoir, U.S.A. ... 78 H5 37 4N 121 5W
San Luis Río Colorado, Mexico 86 A2 32 29N 114 58W
San Manuel, U.S.A. 77 K8 32 36N 110 38W
San Marcos, Guatemala 88 D1 14 59N 91 52W
San Marcos, Mexico 86 B2 27 13N 112 6W
San Marcos, Calif., U.S.A. ... 79 M9 33 9N 117 10W
San Marcos, Tex., U.S.A. 81 L6 29 53N 97 56W
San Marino, San Marino ..... 16 G7 43 55N 12 30 E
San Marino ■, Europe .... 22 C5 43 56N 12 25 E
San Martín, Antarctica 5 C17 68 11S 67 0W
San Martín, Argentina 94 C2 33 5S 68 28W
San Martín →, Bolivia 92 F6 13 8S 63 43W
San Martín, L., Argentina 96 F2 48 50S 72 50W
San Martín de los Andes,
  Argentina 96 E2 40 10S 71 20W
San Mateo = Sant Mateu, Spain 24 B7 40 28N   0 0 E
San Mateo, U.S.A. 78 H4 37 34N 122 19W
San Matías, Bolivia 92 G7 16 25S 58 20W
San Matías, G., Argentina 96 E4 41 30S 64 0W
San Miguel = Sant Miguel, Spain 24 B7 39 3N   1 26 E
San Miguel, El Salv. 88 D2 13 30N 88 12W
San Miguel, Panama 88 E4   8 27N 78 55W
San Miguel, U.S.A. 78 K6 35 45N 120 42W
San Miguel →, Bolivia 92 F6 13 52S 63 56W
San Miguel de Tucumán,
  Argentina 94 B2 26 50S 65 20W
San Miguel del Monte, Argentina 94 D4 35 23S 58 50W
San Miguel I., U.S.A. 79 L6 34 2N 120 23W
San Nicolás, Canary Is. 24 G4 27 58N 15 47W
San Nicolás de los Arroyas,
  Argentina 94 C3 33 25S 60 10W
San Nicolas I., U.S.A. 79 M7 33 15N 119 30W
San Onofre, U.S.A. 79 M9 33 22N 117 34W
San Pablo, Bolivia 94 A2 21 43S 66 38W
San Pablo, U.S.A. 78 H4 37 58N 122 21W
San Pedro, Buenos Aires,
  Argentina 94 C4 33 40S 59 40W
San Pedro, Misiones, Argentina 95 B5 26 30S 54 10W
San Pedro, Chile 94 C1 33 54S 71 28W
San Pédro, Ivory C. 50 H4   4 50N   6 33W
San Pedro, Mexico 86 C2 23 55N 110 17W
San Pedro □, Paraguay 94 A4 24 0S 57 0W
San Pedro →, Chihuahua,
  Mexico 86 B3 28 20N 106 10W
San Pedro →, Nayarit, Mexico 86 C3 21 45N 105 30W
San Pedro →, U.S.A. 77 K8 32 59N 110 47W
San Pedro, Pta., Chile 94 B1 25 30S 70 38W
San Pedro Channel, U.S.A. ... 79 M8 33 30N 118 25W
San Pedro de Atacama, Chile . 94 A2 22 55S 68 15W
San Pedro de Jujuy, Argentina 94 A3 24 12S 64 55W
San Pedro de las Colonias,
  Mexico 86 B4 25 50N 102 59W
San Pedro de Macorís,
  Dom. Rep. 89 C6 18 30N 69 18W
San Pedro del Norte, Nic. 88 D3 13 4N 84 33W
San Pedro del Paraná, Paraguay 94 B4 26 43S 56 13W
San Pedro Mártir, Sierra, Mexico 86 A1 31 0N 115 30W
San Pedro Mixtepec, Mexico .. 87 D5 16 2N 97 7W
San Pedro Ocampo = Melchor
  Ocampo, Mexico 86 C4 24 52N 101 40W
San Pedro Sula, Honduras 88 C2 15 30N 88 0W
San Pietro, Italy .... 22 E3 39 8N   8 17 E
San Quintín, Mexico 86 A1 30 29N 115 57W
San Rafael, Argentina 94 C2 34 40S 68 21W
San Rafael, Calif., U.S.A. 78 H4 37 58N 122 32W
San Rafael, N. Mex., U.S.A. .. 77 J10 35 7N 107 53W
San Rafael Mt., U.S.A. 79 L7 34 41N 119 52W
San Rafael Mts., U.S.A. 79 L7 34 40N 119 50W
San Ramón de la Nueva Orán,
  Argentina 94 A3 23 10S 64 20W
San Remo, Italy .... 20 E7 43 49N   7 46 E
San Roque, Argentina 94 B4 28 25S 58 45W
San Roque, Spain 21 D3 36 17N   5 21W
San Rosendo, Chile 94 D1 37 16S 72 43W
San Saba, U.S.A. 81 K5 31 2N 98 43W
San Salvador, El Salv. 88 D2 13 40N 89 10W
San Salvador de Jujuy,
  Argentina 94 A3 24 10S 64 48W
San Salvador I., Bahamas 89 B5 24 0N 74 40W
San Sebastián = Donostia-San
  Sebastián, Spain 21 A5 43 17N   1 58W
San Sebastián, Argentina 96 G3 53 10S 68 30W
San Sebastián, Puerto Rico ... 89 d 18 20N 66 59W
San Sebastián de la Gomera,
  Canary Is. 24 F2 28 5N 17 7W
San Serra = Son Serra, Spain . 24 B10 39 43N   3 13 E
San Severo, Italy .... 22 D6 41 41N 15 23 E
San Simeon, U.S.A. 78 K5 35 39N 121 11W
San Simon, U.S.A. 77 K9 32 16N 109 14W
San Telmo = Sant Telm, Spain 24 B9 39 35N   2 21 E
San Telmo, Mexico 86 A1 30 58N 116 6W
San Tiburcio, Mexico 86 C4 24 8N 101 32W
San Valentín, Mte., Chile 96 F2 46 30S 73 30W
San Vicente de la Barquera,
  Spain 21 A3 43 23N   4 29W
San Vito, Costa Rica 88 E3   8 50N 82 58W
Sana', Yemen .... 47 D3 15 27N 44 12 E
Sana →, Bos.-H. .... 16 F9 45 3N 16 23 E
Sanaga →, Cameroon .... 52 D1   3 35N   9 38 E
Sanaloa, Presa, Mexico 86 C3 24 50N 107 20W
Sanana, Indonesia .... 37 E7   2 4S 125 58 E
Sanand, India .... 42 H5 22 59N 72 25 E
Sanandaj, Iran .... 44 C5 35 18N 47 1 E
Sanandita, Bolivia 94 A3 21 40S 63 45W
Sanawad, India .... 42 H7 22 11N 76 5 E
Sancellas = Sencelles, Spain .. 24 B9 39 39N   2 54 E
Sanchahe, China .... 35 B14 44 50N 126 2 E
Sánchez, Dom. Rep. 89 C6 19 15N 69 36W
Sanchor, India .... 42 G4 24 45N 71 55 E

Sancti Spíritus, *Cuba* 88 B4   21 52N   79 33W
Sancy, Puy de, *France* .... 20 D5   45 32N   2 50 E
Sand →, *S. Africa* .... 57 C5   22 25S   30 5 E
Sand Hills, *U.S.A.* 80 D4   42 10N   101 30W
Sand Lakes ⌂, *Canada* 71 B9   57 51N   98 32W
Sand Springs, *U.S.A.* 81 G6   36 9N   96 7W
Sanda, *Japan* .... 31 G7   34 53N   135 14 E
Sandakan, *Malaysia* .... 36 C5   5 53N   118 4 E
Sandan = Sambor, *Cambodia* .. 38 F6   12 46N   106 0 E
Sandanski, *Bulgaria* .... 23 D10   41 35N   23 16 E
Sanday, *U.K.* 11 B6   59 16N   2 31W
Sandefjord, *Norway* .... 9 G14   59 10N   10 15 E
Sanders, *U.S.A.* 77 J9   35 13N   109 20W
Sanderson, *U.S.A.* 81 K3   30 9N   102 24W
Sandersville, *U.S.A.* 83 J4   32 59N   82 48W
Sandfire Roadhouse, *Australia* . 60 C3   19 45S   121 15 E
Sandfly L., *Canada* 71 B7   55 43N   106 6W
Sandfontein, *Namibia* .... 56 C2   23 48S   29 1 E
Sandia, *Peru* 92 F5   14 10S   69 30W
Sandila, *India* .... 43 F9   27 5N   80 31 E
Sandnes, *Norway* .... 9 G11   58 50N   5 45 E
Sandnessjøen, *Norway* .... 8 C15   66 2N   12 38 E
Sandoa, *Dem. Rep. of the Congo* 52 F4   9 41S   23 0 E
Sandomierz, *Poland* .... 17 C11   50 40N   21 43 E
Sandover →, *Australia* .... 62 C2   21 43S   136 32 E
Sandoway, *Burma* .... 41 K19   18 20N   94 30 E
Sandoy, *Færoe Is.* 8 F9   61 52N   6 46W
Sandpoint, *U.S.A.* 76 B5   48 17N   116 33W
Sandray, *U.K.* 11 E1   56 53N   7 31W
Sandringham, *U.K.* .... 12 E8   52 51N   0 31 E
Sandstone, *Australia* .... 61 E2   27 59S   119 16 E
Sandusky, Mich., *U.S.A.* 84 C2   43 25N   82 50W
Sandusky, Ohio, *U.S.A.* 84 E2   41 27N   82 42W
Sandviken, *Sweden* .... 9 F17   60 38N   16 46 E
Sandwich, C., *Australia* .... 62 B4   18 14S   146 18 E
Sandwich B., *Canada* 73 B8   53 40N   57 15W
Sandwich B., *Namibia* .... 56 C1   23 25S   14 20 E
Sandy, Oreg., *U.S.A.* 78 E4   45 24N   122 16W
Sandy, Pa., *U.S.A.* 84 E6   41 6N   78 46W
Sandy, Utah, *U.S.A.* 76 F8   40 35N   111 50W
Sandy Bay, *Canada* 71 B8   55 31N   102 19W
Sandy Bight, *Australia* .... 61 F3   33 50S   123 20 E
Sandy C., Queens., *Australia* ... 62 C5   24 42S   153 15 E
Sandy C., Tas., *Australia* ...... 63 G3   41 25S   144 45 E
Sandy Cay, *Bahamas* 89 B4   23 13N   75 18W
Sandy Cr. →, *U.S.A.* 76 F9   41 51N   109 47W
Sandy L., *Canada* 72 B1   53 2N   93 0W
Sandy Lake, *Canada* 72 B1   53 0N   93 15W
Sandy Valley, *U.S.A.* 79 K11   35 49N   115 36W
Sanford, Fla., *U.S.A.* 83 L5   28 48N   81 16W
Sanford, Maine, *U.S.A.* 83 D10   43 27N   70 47W
Sanford, N.C., *U.S.A.* 83 H6   35 29N   79 10W
Sanford →, *Australia* .... 61 E2   27 22S   115 53 E
Sanford, Mt., *U.S.A.* 68 B5   62 13N   144 8W
Sang-i-Masha, *Afghan.* .... 42 C2   33 8N   67 27 E
Sanga, *Mozam.* .... 55 E4   12 22S   35 21 E
Sanga →, *Congo* .... 52 E3   1 5S   17 0 E
Sangamner, *India* .... 40 K9   19 37N   74 15 E
Sangar, *Afghan.* .... 42 C1   32 56N   65 30 E
Sangar, *Russia* .... 29 C13   64 2N   127 31 E
Sangar Sarai, *Afghan.* .... 42 B4   34 27N   70 35 E
Sangarh →, *Pakistan* .... 42 D4   30 43N   70 44 E
Sangay, *Ecuador* 92 D3   2 0S   78 20W
Sange, *Dem. Rep. of the Congo* 54 D2   6 58S   28 21 E
Sangeang, *Indonesia* .... 37 F5   8 12S   119 6 E
Sanger, *U.S.A.* 78 J7   36 42N   119 33W
Sangerhausen, *Germany* ...... 16 C6   51 28N   11 18 E
Sanggau, *Indonesia* .... 36 D4   0 5N   110 30 E
Sanggau, *Indonesia* .... 36 D4   0 5N   110 30 E
Sanghar, *Pakistan* .... 42 F3   26 2N   68 57 E
Sangihe, Kepulauan, *Indonesia* . 37 D7   3 0N   125 30 E
Sangihe, Pulau, *Indonesia* ..... 37 D7   3 35N   125 30 E
Sangju, S. Korea .... 35 F15   36 25N   128 10 E
Sangkapura, *Indonesia* .... 36 F4   5 52S   112 40 E
Sangkhla, *Thailand* .... 38 E2   14 57N   98 28 E
Sangkulirang, *Indonesia* .... 36 D5   0 59N   117 58 E
Sangla, *Pakistan* .... 42 D5   31 43N   73 23 E
Sangli, *India* .... 40 L9   16 55N   74 33 E
Sangmélima, *Cameroon* .... 52 D2   2 57N   12 1 E
Sangod, *India* .... 42 G7   24 55N   76 17 E
Sangre de Cristo Mts., *U.S.A.* .. 81 G2   37 30N   105 20W
Sangre Grande, *Trin. & Tob.* ... 93 K15   10 35N   61 8W
Sangrur, *India* .... 42 D6   30 14N   75 50 E
Sangudo, *Canada* 70 C6   53 50N   114 54W
Sangue →, *Brazil* 92 F7   11 1S   58 39W
Sanibel, *U.S.A.* 83 M4   26 26N   82 1W
Sanikiluaq, *Canada* 69 C12   56 32N   79 14W
Sanin-Kaigan △, *Japan* .... 31 G7   35 39N   134 37 E
Sanirajak, *Canada* 69 B11   68 46N   81 12W
Sanjawi, *Pakistan* .... 42 D3   30 17N   68 21 E
Sanje, *Uganda* .... 54 C3   0 49S   31 30 E
Sanjo, *Japan* .... 30 F9   37 37N   138 57 E
Sankh →, *India* .... 43 H11   22 15N   84 48 E
Sankt Gallen, *Switz.* .... 20 C8   47 26N   9 22 E
Sankt Moritz, *Switz.* .... 20 C8   46 30N   9 50 E
Sankt-Peterburg, *Russia* ...... 18 C5   59 55N   30 20 E
Sankt Pölten, *Austria* .... 16 D8   48 12N   15 38 E
Sankuru →, *Dem. Rep. of
   the Congo* .... 52 E4   4 17S   20 25 E
Sanliurfa, *Turkey* .... 19 G6   37 12N   38 50 E
Sanlúcar de Barrameda, *Spain* . 21 D2   36 46N   6 21W
Sanmenxia, *China* .... 34 G6   34 47N   111 12 E
Sanming, *China* .... 33 D6   26 15N   117 40 E
Sannaspos, *S. Africa* .... 56 D4   29 6S   26 34 E
Sannicandro Gargánico, *Italy* .. 22 D6   41 50N   15 34 E
Sânnicolau Mare, *Romania* .... 17 E11   46 5N   20 39 E
Sannieshof, *S. Africa* .... 56 D4   26 30S   25 47 E
Sannin, J., *Lebanon* .... 46 B4   33 57N   35 52 E
Sanniquellie, *Liberia* 50 G4   7 19N   8 38W
Sanoe, *Antarctica* 5 D2   70 20S   9 0W
Sanok, *Poland* .... 17 D12   49 35N   22 10 E
Sanquhar, *U.K.* 11 F5   55 22N   3 54W
Sans Souci, Trin. & Tob. 93 K16   10 50N   61 0W
Sant Antoni Abat, *Spain* ...... 24 C7   38 59N   1 19 E
Sant Carles, *Spain* .... 24 B8   39 3N   1 34 E
Sant Feliu de Guíxols, *Spain* ... 21 B7   41 45N   3 1 E
Sant Ferran, *Spain* .... 24 C7   38 42N   1 28 E
Sant Francesc de Formentera,
   Spain .... 24 C7   38 42N   1 26 E
Sant Jaume, *Spain* .... 24 B11   39 54N   4 4 E
Sant Joan Baptista, *Spain* ..... 24 B8   39 5N   1 31 E
Sant Jordi, Ibiza, *Spain* .... 24 C7   38 53N   1 24 E
Sant Jordi, Mallorca, *Spain* .... 24 B9   39 33N   2 46 E
Sant Jordi, G. de, *Spain* .... 21 B6   40 53N   1 2 E
Sant Llorenç des Cardassar,
   Spain .... 24 B10   39 37N   3 17 E
Sant Mateu, *Spain* .... 24 B7   39 3N   1 23 E
Sant Miguel, *Spain* .... 24 B7   39 3N   1 26 E

Sant Telm, *Spain* .... 24 B9   39 35N   2 21 E
Santa Agnès, *Spain* .... 24 B7   39 3N   1 21 E
Santa Ana, *Bolivia* 92 F5   13 50S   65 40W
Santa Ana, El Salv. 88 D2   14 0N   89 31W
Santa Ana, *Mexico* 86 A2   30 31N   111 8W
Santa Ana, *U.S.A.* 79 M9   33 46N   117 52W
Sant' Antíoco, *Italy* .... 22 E3   39 4N   8 27 E
Santa Bárbara, Chile 94 D1   37 40S   72 1W
Santa Bárbara, Honduras 88 D2   14 53N   88 14W
Santa Bárbara, Mexico 86 B3   26 48N   105 50W
Santa Barbara, U.S.A. 79 L7   34 25N   119 42W
Santa Barbara Channel, U.S.A. .. 79 L7   34 15N   120 0W
Santa Barbara I., U.S.A. 79 M7   33 29N   119 2W
Santa Catalina, Gulf of, U.S.A. .. 79 N9   33 10N   117 50W
Santa Catalina, I., Mexico 86 B2   25 40N   110 50W
Santa Catalina I., U.S.A. 79 M8   33 23N   118 25W
Santa Catarina ☐, *Brazil* 95 B6   27 25S   48 30W
Santa Catarina, I. de, *Brazil* ... 95 B6   27 30S   48 40W
Santa Cecília, *Brazil* 95 B5   26 56S   50 18W
Santa Clara, Cuba 88 B4   22 20N   80 0W
Santa Clara, Calif., U.S.A. 78 H5   37 21N   121 57W
Santa Clara, Utah, U.S.A. 77 H7   37 8N   113 39W
Santa Clara, El Golfo de, Mexico 86 A2   31 42N   114 30W
Santa Clara de Olimar, Uruguay . 95 C5   32 54S   54 54W
Santa Clarita, U.S.A. 79 L8   34 24N   118 30W
Santa Clotilde, Peru 92 D4   2 33S   73 45W
Santa Coloma de Gramenet,
   Spain .... 21 B7   41 27N   2 13 E
Santa Cruz, Argentina 96 G3   50 0S   68 32W
Santa Cruz, Bolivia 92 G6   17 43S   63 10W
Santa Cruz, Chile 94 C1   34 38S   71 27W
Santa Cruz, Costa Rica 88 D2   10 15N   85 35W
Santa Cruz, Madeira 24 D3   32 42N   16 46W
Santa Cruz, Phil. .... 37 B6   14 20N   121 24 E
Santa Cruz, U.S.A. 78 J4   36 58N   122 1W
Santa Cruz →, Argentina 96 G3   50 10S   68 20W
Santa Cruz de la Palma,
   Canary Is. 24 F2   28 41N   17 46W
Santa Cruz de la Palma ✗ (SPC),
   Canary Is. 24 F2   28 40N   17 45W
Santa Cruz de Tenerife,
   Canary Is. 24 F3   28 28N   16 15W
Santa Cruz del Norte, Cuba 88 B3   23 9N   81 55W
Santa Cruz del Sur, Cuba 88 B4   20 44N   78 0W
Santa Cruz do Rio Pardo, Brazil . 95 A6   22 54S   49 37W
Santa Cruz do Sul, Brazil 95 B5   29 42S   52 25W
Santa Cruz Is., Solomon Is. ..... 64 J8   10 30S   166 0 E
Santa Cruz Mts., *U.S.A.* .... 88 a   17 58N   77 43W
Santa Domingo, Cay, Bahamas .. 88 B4   21 25N   75 15W
Santa Elena, Argentina 94 C4   30 58S   59 47W
Santa Elena, C., Costa Rica 88 D2   10 54N   85 56W
Santa Eulàlia des Riu, Spain .... 24 C8   38 59N   1 32 E
Santa Fe, Argentina 94 C3   31 35S   60 41W
Santa Fe, U.S.A. 77 J11   35 41N   105 57W
Santa Fé ☐, Argentina 94 C3   31 50S   60 55W
Santa Fé do Sul, Brazil 93 H8   20 13S   50 56W
Santa Filomena, Brazil 93 E9   9 6S   45 50W
Santa Gertrudis, Spain .... 24 C7   39 0N   1 26 E
Santa Inés, Brazil 93 F11   13 17S   39 48W
Santa Inés, I., Chile 96 G2   54 0S   73 0W
Santa Isabel, Argentina 94 D2   36 10S   66 54W
Santa Isabel do Morro, Brazil ... 93 F8   11 34S   50 40W
Santa Lucía, Corrientes,
   Argentina 94 B4   28 58S   59 5W
Santa Lucía, San Juan, Argentina 94 C2   31 30S   68 30W
Santa Lucia, Uruguay 94 C4   34 27S   56 24W
Santa Lucia Range, U.S.A. 78 K5   36 0N   121 20W
Santa Magdalena, I., Mexico 86 C2   24 40N   112 15W
Santa Margarita, Argentina 94 D3   38 28S   61 35W
Santa Margarita, U.S.A. 78 K6   35 23N   120 37W
Santa Margarita →, U.S.A. 79 M9   33 13N   117 23W
Santa Margarita, I., Mexico 86 C2   24 30N   111 50W
Santa María, Argentina 94 B2   26 40S   66 0W
Santa Maria, Brazil 95 B5   29 40S   53 48W
Santa María →, Mexico 86 A3   31 0N   107 14W
Santa Maria, B. de, Mexico 86 B3   25 10N   108 40W
Santa Maria da Vitória, Brazil ... 93 F10   13 24S   44 12W
Santa Maria del Camí, Spain .... 24 B9   39 38N   2 47 E
Santa Maria di Léuca, C., Italy .. 23 E8   39 47N   18 22 E
Santa Marta, Colombia 92 A4   11 15N   74 13W
Santa Marta, Sierra Nevada de,
   Colombia 92 A4   10 55N   73 50W
Santa Marta Grande, C., Brazil .. 95 B6   28 43S   48 50W
Santa Maura = Levkás, Greece .. 23 E9   38 40N   20 43 E
Santa Monica, U.S.A. 79 M8   34 1N   118 29W
Santa Monica Mts. ⌂, U.S.A. ... 79 L8   34 4N   118 44W
Santa Paula, U.S.A. 79 L7   34 21N   119 4W
Santa Ponça, Spain .... 24 B9   39 30N   2 28 E
Santa Rita, U.S.A. 77 K10   32 48N   108 4W
Santa Rosa, La Pampa, Argentina 94 D3   36 40S   64 17W
Santa Rosa, San Luis, Argentina . 94 C2   32 21S   65 10W
Santa Rosa, Brazil 95 B5   27 52S   54 29W
Santa Rosa, Calif., U.S.A. 78 G4   38 26N   122 43W
Santa Rosa, N. Mex., U.S.A. 81 H2   34 57N   104 41W
Santa Rosa and San Jacinto
   Mts. ⌂, U.S.A. 79 M10   33 28N   116 20W
Santa Rosa de Copán, Honduras 88 D2   14 47N   88 46W
Santa Rosa de Río Primero,
   Argentina 94 C3   31 8S   63 20W
Santa Rosa del Sara, Bolivia 92 G6   17 7S   63 35W
Santa Rosa I., Calif., U.S.A. 79 M6   33 58N   120 6W
Santa Rosa I., Fla., U.S.A. 83 K2   30 20N   86 50W
Santa Rosa Range, U.S.A. 76 F5   41 45N   117 40W
Santa Rosalía, Mexico 86 B2   27 20N   112 20W
Santa Sylvina, Argentina 94 B3   27 50S   61 10W
Santa Tecla = Nueva San
   Salvador, El Salv. 88 D2   13 40N   89 18W
Santa Teresa, Argentina 94 C3   33 25S   60 47W
Santa Teresa, Australia .... 62 C1   24 8S   134 22 E
Santa Teresa, Mexico 87 B5   25 17N   97 51W
Santa Teresa △, Uruguay 95 C5   33 57S   53 31W
Santa Vitória do Palmar, Brazil . 95 C5   33 32S   53 25W
Santa Ynez →, U.S.A. 79 L6   35 41N   120 36W
Santa Ynez Mts., U.S.A. 79 L6   34 30N   120 0W
Santa Ysabel, U.S.A. 79 M10   33 7N   116 40W
Santai, China .... 32 C5   31 5N   104 58 E
Santana, Madeira 24 D3   32 48N   16 52W
Santana, Coxilha de, Brazil 95 C4   30 50S   55 35W
Santana do Livramento, Brazil .. 95 C4   30 55S   55 30W
Santander, Spain 21 A4   43 27N   3 51W
Santander Jiménez, Mexico 87 C5   24 11N   98 29W
Santanilla, Is., Honduras 88 C3   17 22N   83 57W
Santanyí, Spain .... 24 B10   39 20N   3 5 E
Santaquin, U.S.A. 76 G8   39 59N   111 47W
Santarém, Brazil 93 D8   2 25S   54 42W

Santarém, Portugal 21 C1   39 12N   8 42W
Santaren Channel, W. Indies 88 B4   24 0N   79 30W
Santee, U.S.A. 79 N10   32 50N   116 58W
Santee →, U.S.A. 83 J6   33 7N   79 17W
Santiago, Brazil 95 B5   29 11S   54 52W
Santiago, Canary Is. 24 F2   28 2N   17 12W
Santiago, Chile 94 C1   33 24S   70 40W
Santiago, Panama 88 E3   8 0N   81 0W
Santiago ☐, Chile 94 C1   33 30S   70 50W
Santiago →, Mexico 66 G9   25 11N   105 26W
Santiago →, Peru 92 D3   4 27S   77 38W
Santiago de Compostela, Spain . 21 A1   42 52N   8 37W
Santiago de Cuba, Cuba 88 C4   20 0N   75 49W
Santiago de los Cabelleros,
   Dom. Rep. 89 C5   19 30N   70 40W
Santiago del Estero, Argentina .. 94 B3   27 50S   64 15W
Santiago del Estero ☐, Argentina 94 B3   27 40S   63 15W
Santiago del Teide, Canary Is. ... 24 F3   28 17N   16 48W
Santiago Ixcuintla, Mexico 86 C3   21 50N   105 11W
Santiago Papasquiaro, Mexico .. 86 C3   25 0N   105 20W
Santiaguillo, L. de, Mexico 86 C4   24 50N   104 50W
Santo Amaro, Brazil 93 F11   12 30S   38 43W
Santo Anastácio, Brazil 95 A5   21 58S   51 39W
Santo André, Brazil 95 A6   23 39S   46 29W
Santo Ângelo, Brazil 95 B5   28 15S   54 15W
Santo Antônio do Içá, Brazil 92 D5   3 5S   67 57W
Santo Antônio do Leverger,
   Brazil 93 G7   15 52S   56 5W
Santo Domingo, Dom. Rep. 89 C6   18 30N   69 59W
Santo Domingo, Baja Calif.,
   Mexico 86 A1   30 43N   116 2W
Santo Domingo, Baja Calif. S.,
   Mexico 86 B2   25 32N   112 2W
Santo Domingo, Nic. 88 D3   12 14N   84 59W
Santo Domingo de los
   Colorados, Ecuador 92 D3   0 15S   79 9W
Santo Domingo Pueblo, U.S.A. .. 77 J10   35 31N   106 22W
Santo Tomás, Mexico 86 A1   31 33N   116 24W
Santo Tomás, Peru 92 F4   14 26S   72 8W
Santo Tomé, Argentina 95 B4   28 40S   56 5W
Santo Tomé de Guayana =
   Ciudad Guayana, Venezuela .. 92 B6   8 0N   62 30W
Santoña, Spain 21 A4   43 29N   3 27W
Santorini = Thira, Greece .... 23 F11   36 23N   25 27 E
Santos, Brazil 95 A6   24 0S   46 20W
Santos Dumont, Brazil 95 A7   22 55S   43 10W
Sanur, Indonesia .... 37 K18   8 41S   115 15 E
Sanwer, India .... 42 H6   22 59N   75 50 E
Sanxiang, China .... 33 G9   22 21N   113 25 E
Sanyuan, China .... 34 G5   34 35N   108 58 E
São Bernardo do Campo, Brazil . 95 A6   23 45S   46 34W
São Borja, Brazil 95 B4   28 39S   56 0W
São Carlos, Brazil 95 A6   22 0S   47 50W
São Cristóvão, Brazil 93 F11   11 1S   37 15W
São Domingos, Brazil 93 F9   13 25S   46 19W
São Francisco, Brazil 93 G10   16 0S   44 50W
São Francisco →, Brazil 93 F11   10 30S   36 24W
São Francisco do Sul, Brazil 95 B6   26 15S   48 36W
São Gabriel, Brazil 95 C5   30 20S   54 20W
São Gonçalo, Brazil 95 A7   22 48S   43 5W
Sao Hill, Tanzania .... 55 D4   8 20S   35 12 E
São João da Boa Vista, Brazil ... 95 A6   22 0S   46 52W
São João da Madeira, Portugal .. 21 B1   40 54N   8 30W
São João do Araguaia, Brazil ... 93 E9   5 23S   48 46W
São João do Piauí, Brazil 93 E10   8 21S   42 15W
São João do Rei, Brazil 95 A7   21 8S   44 15W
São Joaquim, Brazil 95 B6   28 18S   49 56W
São Joaquim △, Brazil 95 B6   28 15S   49 37W
São Jorge, Pta. de, Madeira 24 D3   32 50N   16 53W
São José, Brazil 95 B5   27 38S   48 39W
São José do Norte, Brazil 95 C5   32 1S   52 3W
São José do Rio Prêto, Brazil 95 A6   20 50S   49 20W
São José dos Campos, Brazil 95 A6   23 7S   45 52W
São Leopoldo, Brazil 95 B5   29 50S   51 10W
São Lourenço, Brazil 95 A6   22 7S   45 3W
São Lourenço →, Brazil 93 G7   17 53S   57 27W
São Lourenço, Pta. de, Madeira . 24 D3   32 44N   16 39W
São Lourenço do Sul, Brazil 95 C5   31 22S   51 58W
São Luís, Brazil 93 D10   2 39S   44 15W
São Luís Gonzaga, Brazil 95 B5   28 25S   55 0W
São Marcos →, Brazil 93 G9   18 15S   47 37W
São Marcos, B. de, Brazil 93 D10   2 0S   44 0W
São Mateus, Brazil 93 G11   18 44S   39 50W
São Mateus do Sul, Brazil 95 B5   25 52S   50 23W
São Miguel do Oeste, Brazil 95 B5   26 45S   53 34W
São Paulo, Brazil 95 A6   23 32S   46 37W
São Paulo ☐, Brazil 95 A6   22 0S   49 0W
São Paulo, I., Atl. Oc. 2 D8   0 50N   31 40W
São Paulo de Olivença, Brazil ... 92 D5   3 27S   68 48W
São Roque, Madeira 24 D3   32 46N   16 48W
São Roque, C. de, Brazil 93 E11   5 30S   35 16W
São Sebastião, I. de, Brazil 95 A6   23 50S   45 18W
São Sebastião do Paraíso, Brazil 95 A6   20 54S   46 59W
São Tomé, Brazil 93 E11   5 23S   35 20W
São Tomé, São Tomé & Príncipe 48 F4   0 10N   6 39 E
São Tomé, C. de, Brazil 95 A7   22 0S   40 59W
São Tomé & Príncipe ■, Africa .. 49 F4   0 12N   6 39 E
São Vicente, Brazil 95 A6   23 57S   46 23W
São Vicente, C. de, Portugal 21 D1   37 0N   9 0W
Saona, I., Dom. Rep. 89 C6   18 10N   68 40W
Saône →, France .... 20 D6   45 44N   4 50 E
Saonek, Indonesia .... 37 E8   0 22S   130 55 E
Sapam, Ao, Thailand .... 39 a   8 2N   98 26 E
Saparua, Indonesia .... 37 E7   3 33S   128 40 E
Sapele, Nigeria .... 50 G7   5 50N   5 40 E
Sapelo I., U.S.A. 83 K5   31 25N   81 12W
Sapi ⌂, Zimbabwe .... 55 F2   15 48S   29 42 E
Saposoa, Peru 92 E3   6 55S   76 45W
Sapphire, Australia .... 62 C4   23 28S   147 43 E
Sappho, U.S.A. 78 B2   48 4N   124 16W
Sapporo, Japan .... 30 C10   43 0N   141 21 E
Sapulpa, U.S.A. 81 H6   35 59N   96 5W
Saqqez, Iran .... 44 B5   36 15N   46 20 E
Sar Dasht, Iran .... 45 C6   32 32N   48 52 E
Sar-e Pol ☐, Afghan. .... 40 B4   36 20N   65 50 E
Sar Gachineh = Yāsūj, Iran ..... 45 D6   30 31N   51 31 E
Sar Planina, Macedonia .... 23 C9   42 10N   21 0 E
Sara Buri = Saraburi, Thailand .. 38 E3   14 30N   100 55 E
Sarāb, Iran .... 44 B5   37 55N   47 40 E
Sarabadi, Iraq .... 44 C5   33 1N   44 48 E
Saraburi, Thailand .... 38 E3   14 30N   100 55 E
Saradiya, India .... 42 J4   21 34N   70 2 E
Saraikela, India .... 43 H11   22 42N   85 56 E
Sarajevo, Bos.-H. .... 23 C8   43 52N   18 26 E
Sarakhs, Turkmenistan .... 45 B9   36 32N   61 13 E

Saran, Gunung, Indonesia ...... 36 E4   0 30S   111 25 E
Saranac L., U.S.A. 85 B10   44 20N   74 10W
Saranac Lake, U.S.A. 85 B10   44 20N   74 8W
Saranda, Tanzania .... 54 D3   5 45S   34 59 E
Sarandí del Yi, Uruguay 95 C4   33 18S   55 38W
Sarandí Grande, Uruguay 94 C4   33 44S   56 20W
Sarangani B., Phil. .... 37 C7   6 0N   125 13 E
Sarangani Is., Phil. .... 37 C7   5 25N   125 25 E
Sarangarh, India .... 41 J13   21 30N   83 5 E
Saransk, Russia .... 18 D8   54 10N   45 10 E
Sarapul, Russia .... 18 C9   56 28N   53 48 E
Sarasota, U.S.A. 83 M4   27 20N   82 32W
Saratoga, Calif., U.S.A. 78 H4   37 16N   122 2W
Saratoga, Wyo., U.S.A. 76 F10   41 27N   106 49W
Saratoga △, U.S.A. 85 D11   43 0N   73 37W
Saratoga Springs, U.S.A. 85 C11   43 5N   73 47W
Saratok, Malaysia .... 36 D4   1 55N   111 17 E
Saratov, Russia .... 19 D8   51 30N   46 2 E
Sarāvān, Iran .... 45 E9   27 25N   62 15 E
Saravane, Laos .... 38 E6   15 43N   106 25 E
Sarawak ☐, Malaysia .... 36 D4   2 0N   113 0 E
Saray, Turkey .... 23 D12   41 26N   27 55 E
Sarayköy, Turkey .... 23 F13   37 55N   28 54 E
Sarbāz, Iran .... 45 E9   26 38N   61 19 E
Sarbīsheh, Iran .... 45 C8   32 30N   59 40 E
Sarda →, India .... 41 F12   27 21N   81 23 E
Sardarshahr, India .... 42 E6   28 30N   74 29 E
Sardegna ☐, Italy .... 22 D3   40 0N   9 0 E
Sardhana, India .... 42 E7   29 9N   77 39 E
Sardina, Pta., Canary Is. 24 F4   28 9N   15 44W
Sardinia = Sardegna ☐, Italy ... 22 D3   40 0N   9 0 E
Sardis, Turkey .... 23 E12   38 28N   28 2 E
Sārdūīyeh = Dar Mazār, Iran ... 45 D8   29 14N   57 20 E
Saren, Indonesia .... 37 J18   8 26S   115 34 E
Sargasso Sea, Atl. Oc. 66 G13   27 0N   72 0W
Sargodha, Pakistan .... 42 C5   32 10N   72 40 E
Sarh, Chad .... 51 G9   9 5N   18 23 E
Sārī, Iran .... 45 B7   36 30N   53 4 E
Saria, India .... 43 J10   21 38N   83 22 E
Sariab, Pakistan .... 42 D2   30 6N   66 59 E
Sarıgöl, Turkey .... 23 E13   38 14N   28 41 E
Sarikei, Malaysia .... 36 D4   2 8N   111 30 E
Sarila, India .... 43 G8   25 46N   79 41 E
Sarina, Australia .... 62 C4   21 22S   149 13 E
Sarita, U.S.A. 81 M6   27 13N   97 47W
Sariwŏn, N. Korea .... 35 E13   38 31N   125 46 E
Sarju →, India .... 43 F9   27 21N   81 23 E
Sark, U.K. 13 H5   49 25N   2 22W
Sarkari Tala, India .... 42 F4   27 39N   70 52 E
Şarköy, Turkey .... 23 D12   40 36N   27 6 E
Sarlat-la-Canéda, France .... 20 D4   44 54N   1 13 E
Sarmi, Indonesia .... 37 E9   1 49S   138 44 E
Sarmiento, Argentina 96 F3   45 35S   69 5W
Särna, Sweden .... 9 F15   61 41N   13 8 E
Sarnia, Canada 84 D2   42 58N   82 23W
Sarolangun, Indonesia .... 36 E2   2 19S   102 42 E
Saronikós Kólpos, Greece ...... 23 F10   37 45N   23 45 E
Saros Körfezi, Turkey .... 23 D12   40 30N   26 15 E
Sarpsborg, Norway .... 9 G14   59 16N   11 7 E
Sarre = Saar →, Europe .... 15 E6   49 41N   6 32 E
Sarreguemines, France .... 20 B7   49 5N   7 4 E
Sarthe →, France 20 C3   47 33N   0 31W
Saruna →, Pakistan .... 42 F2   26 31N   67 7 E
Sarvar, India .... 42 F6   26 4N   75 0 E
Sarvestān, Iran .... 45 D7   29 20N   53 10 E
Sary-Tash, Kyrgyzstan .... 28 F8   39 44N   73 15 E
Saryshagan, Kazakhstan .... 28 E8   46 12N   73 38 E
Sasan Gir, India .... 42 J4   21 10N   70 36 E
Sasaram, India .... 43 G11   24 57N   84 5 E
Sasebo, Japan .... 31 H4   33 10N   129 43 E
Saser, India .... 43 B7   34 50N   77 50 E
Saskatchewan ☐, Canada 71 C8   54 40N   106 0W
Saskatchewan →, Canada 71 C8   53 37N   100 40W
Saskatoon, Canada 71 C7   52 10N   106 38W
Saskylakh, Russia .... 29 B12   71 55N   114 1 E
Saslaya △, Nic. 88 D3   13 45N   85 4W
Sasolburg, S. Africa .... 57 D4   26 46S   27 49 E
Sasovo, Russia .... 18 D7   54 25N   41 55 E
Sassandra, Ivory C. 50 H4   4 55N   6 8W
Sassandra →, Ivory C. 50 H4   4 58N   6 5W
Sássari, Italy .... 22 D3   40 43N   8 34 E
Sassnitz, Germany .... 16 A7   54 29N   13 39 E
Sassuolo, Italy .... 22 B4   44 33N   10 47 E
Sasyk, Ozero, Ukraine .... 17 F15   45 45N   29 20 E
Sata-Misaki, Japan .... 31 J5   31 0N   130 40 E
Satadougou, Mali 50 F3   12 25N   11 25W
Satakunta, Finland .... 9 F20   61 45N   23 0 E
Satara, India .... 40 L8   17 44N   73 58 E
Satara, S. Africa .... 57 C5   24 29S   31 47 E
Satbarwa, India .... 43 H11   23 55N   84 16 E
Satevó, Mexico 86 B3   27 57N   106 7W
Satilla →, U.S.A. 83 K5   30 59N   81 29W
Satka, Russia .... 18 C10   55 3N   59 1 E
Satmala Hills, India .... 40 J9   20 15N   74 40 E
Satna, India .... 43 G9   24 35N   80 50 E
Sátoraljaújhely, Hungary .... 17 D11   48 25N   21 41 E
Satpura Ra., India .... 42 J10   21 25N   76 10 E
Satsuna-Shotō, Japan .... 31 K5   30 0N   130 0 E
Sattahip, Thailand .... 38 F3   12 41N   100 54 E
Satu Mare, Romania .... 17 E12   47 46N   22 55 E
Satui, Indonesia .... 36 E5   3 50S   115 27 E
Satun, Thailand .... 39 J3   6 43N   100 2 E
Saturnina →, Brazil 92 F7   12 15S   58 10W
Sauce, Argentina 94 C4   30 5S   58 46W
Sauceda, Mexico 86 B4   25 55N   101 18W
Saucillo, Mexico 86 B3   28 1N   105 17W
Sauda, Norway .... 9 G12   59 40N   6 20 E
Sauðarkrókur, Iceland 8 D4   65 45N   19 40W
Saudi Arabia ■, Asia .... 44 B3   26 0N   44 0 E
Sauerland, Germany .... 16 C4   51 12N   7 59 E
Saugeen →, Canada 84 B3   44 30N   81 22W
Saugerties, U.S.A. 85 D11   42 5N   73 57W
Saugus, U.S.A. 79 L8   34 25N   118 32W
Sauk Centre, U.S.A. 80 C7   45 44N   94 57W
Sauk Rapids, U.S.A. 80 C7   45 35N   94 10W
Sault Ste. Marie, Canada 72 C3   46 30N   84 20W
Sault Ste. Marie, U.S.A. 69 D11   46 30N   84 21W
Saumlaki, Indonesia .... 37 F8   7 55S   131 20 E
Saumur, France 20 C3   47 15N   0 5W
Saunders, C., N.Z. .... 59 L3   45 53S   170 45 E
Saunders I., Antarctica 5 B1   57 48S   26 28W
Saunders Point, Australia ...... 61 E4   27 52S   125 38 E
Saurimo, Angola .... 52 F4   9 40S   20 12 E
Sausalito, U.S.A. 78 H4   37 51N   122 29W
Sava →, Serbia & M. .... 23 B9   44 50N   20 26 E
Savá, Honduras 88 C2   15 32N   86 15W
Savage, U.S.A. 80 B2   47 27N   104 21W

Savage I. = Niue, Cook Is. 65 J11 19 2S 169 54W
Savage River, Australia ...... 63 G4 41 31S 145 14 E
Savai'i, Samoa 59 A12 13 28S 172 24W
Savalou, Benin .... 50 G6 7 57N 1 58 E
Savane, Mozam. .... 55 F4 19 37S 35 8 E
Savanna, U.S.A. 80 D9 42 5N 90 8W
Savanna-la-Mar, Jamaica .... 88 a 18 10N 78 10W
Savannah, Ga., U.S.A. 83 J5 32 5N 81 6W
Savannah, Mo., U.S.A. 80 F7 39 56N 94 50W
Savannah, Tenn., U.S.A. 83 H1 35 14N 88 15W
Savannah →, U.S.A. 83 J5 32 2N 80 53W
Savannakhet, Laos .... 38 D5 16 30N 104 49 E
Savant L., Canada 72 B1 50 16N 90 44W
Savant Lake, Canada 72 B1 50 14N 90 40W
Save →, Mozam. .... 57 C5 21 16S 34 0 E
Săveh, Iran .... 45 C6 35 2N 50 20 E
Savelugu, Ghana 50 G5 9 38N 0 54W
Savo, Finland .... 8 E22 62 45N 27 30 E
Savoie □, France .... 20 D7 45 26N 6 25 E
Savona, Italy .... 20 D8 44 17N 8 30 E
Savona, U.S.A. 84 D7 42 17N 77 13W
Savonlinna, Finland .... 18 B4 61 52N 28 53 E
Savoy = Savoie □, France ... 20 D7 45 26N 6 25 E
Savur, Turkey .... 44 B4 37 34N 40 53 E
Sawahlunto, Indonesia ..... 36 E2 0 40S 100 52 E
Sawai, Indonesia .... 37 E7 3 0S 129 5 E
Sawai Madhopur, India ..... 42 G7 26 0N 76 25 E
Sawang Daen Din, Thailand .. 38 D4 17 28N 103 28 E
Sawankhalok, Thailand ..... 38 D2 17 19N 99 50 E
Sawara, Japan .... 31 G10 35 55N 140 30 E
Sawatch Range, U.S.A. 77 G10 38 30N 106 30W
Sawel Mt., U.K. 10 B4 54 50N 7 2W
Sawi, Thailand .... 39 G2 10 14N 99 5 E
Sawmills, Zimbabwe .... 55 F2 19 30S 28 2 E
Sawtooth △, U.S.A. 76 D6 44 0N 114 50W
Sawtooth Range, U.S.A. 76 E6 44 3N 114 58W
Sawu, Indonesia .... 37 F6 10 35S 121 50 E
Sawu Sea, Indonesia ...... 37 F6 9 30S 121 50 E
Saxby →, Australia .... 62 B3 18 25S 140 53 E
Saxmundham, U.K. .... 13 E9 52 13N 1 30 E
Saxony = Sachsen □, Germany 16 C7 50 55N 13 10 E
Saxony, Lower =
  Niedersachsen □, Germany . 16 B5 52 50N 9 0 E
Saxton, U.S.A. 84 F6 40 13N 78 15W
Sayabec, Canada 73 C6 48 35N 67 41W
Sayaboury, Laos .... 38 C3 19 15N 101 45 E
Sayán, Peru 92 F3 11 8S 77 12W
Sayan, Vostochnyy, Russia .. 29 D10 54 0N 96 0 E
Sayan, Zapadnyy, Russia .... 29 D10 52 30N 94 0 E
Saydā, Lebanon .... 46 B4 33 35N 35 25 E
Sayhandulaan = Oldziyt,
  Mongolia .... 34 B5 44 40N 109 1 E
Sayḩūt, Yemen .... 47 D5 15 12N 51 10 E
Saylac = Zeila, Somali Rep. .. 47 E3 11 21N 43 30 E
Saynshand, Mongolia ...... 33 B6 44 55N 110 11 E
Sayre, Okla., U.S.A. 81 H5 35 18N 99 38W
Sayre, Pa., U.S.A. 85 E8 41 59N 76 32W
Sayreville, U.S.A. 85 F10 40 28N 74 22W
Sayula, Mexico 86 D4 19 50N 103 40W
Sayward, Canada 70 C3 50 21N 125 55W
Sazanit, Albania .... 23 D8 40 30N 19 20 E
Sázava →, Czech Rep. ...... 16 D8 49 53N 14 24 E
Sazin, Pakistan .... 43 B5 35 35N 73 30 E
Scafell Pike, U.K. 12 C4 54 27N 3 14W
Scalloway, U.K. 11 A7 60 9N 1 17W
Scalpay, U.K. 11 D3 57 18N 6 0W
Scandia, Canada 70 C6 50 20N 112 2W
Scandicci, Italy .... 22 C4 43 45N 11 11 E
Scandinavia, Europe ...... 8 E16 64 0N 12 0 E
Scapa Flow, U.K. 11 C5 58 53N 3 3W
Scappoose, U.S.A. 78 E4 45 45N 122 53W
Scarba, U.K. 11 E3 56 11N 5 43W
Scarborough, Trin. & Tob. ... 89 D7 11 11N 60 42W
Scarborough, U.K. 12 C7 54 17N 0 24W
Scariff I., Ireland 10 E1 51 44N 10 15W
Scarp, U.K. 11 C1 58 1N 7 8W
Scebeli, Wabi →, Somali Rep. . 47 G3 2 0N 44 0 E
Schaffhausen, Switz. ...... 20 C8 47 42N 8 39 E
Schagen, Neths. .... 15 B4 52 49N 4 48 E
Schaghticoke, U.S.A. 85 D11 42 54N 73 35W
Schefferville, Canada 73 B6 54 48N 66 50W
Schelde →, Belgium .... 15 C4 51 15N 4 16 E
Schell Creek Ra., U.S.A. 76 G6 39 15N 114 30W
Schellsburg, U.S.A. 84 F6 40 3N 78 39W
Schenectady, U.S.A. 85 D11 42 49N 73 57W
Schenevus, U.S.A. 85 D10 42 33N 74 50W
Schiedam, Neths. .... 15 C4 51 55N 4 25 E
Schiermonnikoog, Neths. ... 15 A6 53 30N 6 15 E
Schio, Italy .... 22 B4 45 43N 11 21 E
Schiphol, Amsterdam ✈ (AMS),
  Neths. .... 15 B4 52 18N 4 45 E
Schleswig, Germany .... 16 A5 54 31N 9 34 E
Schleswig-Holstein □, Germany 16 A5 54 30N 9 30 E
Schœlcher, Martinique ..... 88 c 14 36N 61 7W
Schoharie, U.S.A. 85 D10 42 40N 74 19W
Schoharie →, U.S.A. 85 D10 42 57N 74 18W
Scholls, U.S.A. 78 E4 45 24N 122 56W
Schouten I., Australia ..... 63 G4 42 20S 148 20 E
Schouten Is. = Supiori, Indonesia 37 E9 1 0S 136 0 E
Schouwen, Neths. .... 15 C3 51 43N 3 45 E
Schreiber, Canada 72 C2 48 45N 87 20W
Schroffenstein, Namibia .... 56 D2 27 11S 18 42 E
Schroon Lake, U.S.A. 85 C11 43 50N 73 46W
Schuler, Canada 71 C6 50 20N 110 6W
Schumacher, Canada 72 C3 48 30N 81 16W
Schurz, U.S.A. 76 G4 38 57N 118 49W
Schuyler, U.S.A. 80 E6 41 27N 97 4W
Schuylerville, U.S.A. 85 C11 43 6N 73 35W
Schuylkill →, U.S.A. 85 G9 39 53N 75 12W
Schuylkill Haven, U.S.A. 85 F8 40 37N 76 11W
Schwäbische Alb, Germany .. 16 D5 48 20N 9 30 E
Schwaner, Pegunungan,
  Indonesia .... 36 E4 1 0S 112 30 E
Schwarzrand, Namibia ..... 56 D2 25 37S 16 50 E
Schwarzwald, Germany ..... 16 D5 48 30N 8 20 E
Schwedt, Germany .... 16 B8 53 3N 14 16 E
Schweinfurt, Germany ..... 16 C6 50 3N 10 14 E
Schweizer-Reneke, S. Africa . 56 D4 27 11S 25 18 E
Schwenningen = Villingen-
  Schwenningen, Germany .. 16 D5 48 3N 8 26 E
Schwerin, Germany .... 16 B6 53 36N 11 22 E
Schwyz, Switz. .... 20 C8 47 2N 8 39 E
Sciacca, Italy .... 22 F5 37 31N 13 3 E
Scilla, Italy .... 22 E6 38 15N 15 43 E
Scilly, Isles of, U.K. 13 H1 49 56N 6 22W
Scioto →, U.S.A. 82 F4 38 44N 83 1W
Scituate, U.S.A. 85 D14 42 12N 70 44W
Scobey, U.S.A. 80 A2 48 47N 105 25W

Scone, Australia .... 63 E5 32 5S 150 52 E
Scone, U.K. 11 E5 56 25N 3 24W
Scoresbysund = Ittoqqortoormiit,
  Greenland 4 B6 70 20N 23 0W
Scotia, Calif., U.S.A. 76 F1 40 29N 124 6W
Scotia, N.Y., U.S.A. 85 D11 42 50N 73 58W
Scotia Sea, Antarctica 5 B18 56 5S 56 0W
Scotland, Canada 84 C4 43 1N 80 22W
Scotland □, U.K. 11 E5 57 0N 4 0W
Scott, Antarctica .... 5 D11 77 0S 165 0 E
Scott, C., Australia .... 60 B4 13 30S 129 49 E
Scott City, U.S.A. 80 F4 38 29N 100 54W
Scott Glacier, Antarctica ... 5 C8 66 15S 100 5 E
Scott I., Antarctica .... 5 C11 67 0S 179 0 E
Scott Is., Canada 70 C3 50 48N 128 40W
Scott L., Canada 71 B7 59 55N 106 18W
Scott Reef, Australia ...... 60 B3 14 0S 121 50 E
Scottburgh, S. Africa ...... 57 E5 30 15S 30 47 E
Scottdale, U.S.A. 84 F5 40 6N 79 35W
Scottish Borders □, U.K. ... 11 F6 55 35N 2 50W
Scottsbluff, U.S.A. 80 E3 41 52N 103 40W
Scottsboro, U.S.A. 83 H3 34 40N 86 2W
Scottsburg, U.S.A. 82 F3 38 41N 85 47W
Scottsdale, Australia ...... 63 G4 41 9S 147 31 E
Scottsdale, U.S.A. 77 K7 33 29N 111 56W
Scottsville, Ky., U.S.A. 83 G2 36 45N 86 11W
Scottsville, N.Y., U.S.A. 84 C7 43 2N 77 47W
Scottville, U.S.A. 82 D2 43 58N 86 17W
Scranton, U.S.A. 85 E9 41 25N 75 40W
Scugog, L., Canada 84 B6 44 10N 78 55W
Scunthorpe, U.K. 12 D7 53 36N 0 39W
Scusciuban, Somali Rep. .... 47 E5 10 18N 50 12 E
Seabrook, L., Australia ..... 61 F2 30 55S 119 40 E
Seaford, U.K. .... 13 G8 50 47N 0 7 E
Seaford, U.S.A. 82 F8 38 39N 75 37W
Seaforth, Australia .... 62 J6 20 55S 148 57 E
Seaforth, Canada 84 C3 43 35N 81 25W
Seaforth, L., U.K. 11 D2 57 52N 6 36W
Seagraves, U.S.A. 81 J3 32 57N 102 34W
Seaham, U.K. 12 C6 54 50N 1 20W
Seal →, Canada 71 B10 59 4N 94 48W
Seal L., Canada 73 B7 54 20N 61 30W
Sealy, U.S.A. 81 L6 29 47N 96 9W
Searchlight, U.S.A. 79 K12 35 28N 114 55W
Searcy, U.S.A. 81 H9 35 15N 91 44W
Searles L., U.S.A. 79 K9 35 44N 117 21W
Seascale, U.K. 12 C4 54 24N 3 29W
Seaside, Calif., U.S.A. 78 J5 36 37N 121 50W
Seaside, Oreg., U.S.A. 78 E3 46 0N 123 56W
Seaspray, Australia .... 63 F4 38 25S 147 15 E
Seattle, U.S.A. 78 C4 47 36N 122 20W
Seattle-Tacoma International ✈
  (SEA), U.S.A. 78 C4 47 27N 122 18W
Seaview Ra., Australia ..... 62 B4 18 40S 145 45 E
Sebago L., U.S.A. 85 C14 43 52N 70 34W
Sebago L., U.S.A. 85 C14 43 51N 70 34W
Sebastián Vizcaíno, B., Mexico 86 B2 28 0N 114 30W
Sebastopol = Sevastopol,
  Ukraine .... 19 F5 44 35N 33 30 E
Sebastopol, U.S.A. 78 G4 38 24N 122 49W
Sebewaing, U.S.A. 82 D4 43 44N 83 27W
Sebha = Sabhah, Libya ..... 51 C8 27 9N 14 29 E
Şebinkarahisar, Turkey ..... 19 F6 40 22N 38 28 E
Sebring, Fla., U.S.A. 83 M5 27 30N 81 27W
Sebring, Ohio, U.S.A. 84 F3 40 55N 81 2W
Sebringville, Canada 84 C3 43 24N 81 4W
Sebta = Ceuta, N. Afr. 21 E3 35 52N 5 18W
Sebuku, Indonesia .... 36 E5 3 30S 116 25 E
Sebuku, Teluk, Malaysia .... 36 D5 4 0N 118 10 E
Sechelt, Canada 70 D4 49 25N 123 42W
Sechura, Desierto de, Peru .. 92 E2 6 0S 80 30W
Secretary I., N.Z. .... 59 L1 45 15S 166 56 E
Secunderabad, India ...... 40 L11 17 28N 78 30 E
Security-Widefield, U.S.A. .. 80 F2 38 45N 104 45W
Sedalia, U.S.A. 80 F8 38 42N 93 14W
Sedan, France .... 20 C6 49 43N 4 57 E
Sedan, U.S.A. 81 G6 37 8N 96 11W
Sedbergh, U.K. 12 C5 54 20N 2 31W
Seddon, N.Z. .... 59 J5 41 40S 174 7 E
Seddonville, N.Z. .... 59 J4 41 33S 172 1 E
Sedé Boqér, Israel .... 46 E3 30 52N 34 47 E
Sedeh, Fārs, Iran .... 45 D7 30 45N 52 11 E
Sedeh, Khorāsān, Iran ..... 45 C8 33 20N 59 14 E
Sederot, Israel .... 46 D3 31 32N 34 37 E
Sédhiou, Senegal 50 F2 12 44N 15 30W
Sedley, Canada 71 C8 50 10N 104 0W
Sedom, Israel .... 46 D4 31 5N 35 20 E
Sedona, U.S.A. 77 J8 34 52N 111 46W
Sedova, Pik, Russia .... 28 B6 73 29N 54 58 E
Sedro Woolley, U.S.A. 78 B4 48 30N 122 14W
Seeheim, Namibia .... 56 D2 26 50S 17 45 E
Seeis, Namibia .... 56 C2 22 29S 17 39 E
Seekoei →, S. Africa ...... 56 E4 30 18S 25 1 E
Seeley's Bay, Canada 85 B8 44 29N 76 14W
Seferihisar, Turkey .... 23 E12 38 10N 26 50 E
Seg-ozero, Russia .... 18 B5 63 20N 33 46 E
Segamat, Malaysia .... 39 L4 2 30N 102 50 E
Segesta, Italy .... 22 F5 37 56N 12 50 E
Seget, Indonesia .... 37 E8 1 24S 130 58 E
Segezha, Russia .... 18 B5 63 44N 34 19 E
Ségou, Mali 50 F4 13 30N 6 16W
Segovia = Coco →, Cent. Amer. 88 D3 15 0N 83 8W
Segovia, Spain 21 B3 40 57N 4 10W
Segre →, Spain .... 21 B6 41 40N 0 43 E
Séguéla, Ivory C. 50 G4 7 55N 6 40W
Seguin, U.S.A. 81 L6 29 34N 97 58W
Segundo →, Argentina 94 C3 30 53S 62 44W
Segura →, Spain 21 C5 38 3N 0 44W
Seh Konj, Kūh-e, Iran ..... 45 D8 30 6N 57 30 E
Seh Qal'eh, Iran .... 45 C8 33 40N 58 24 E
Sehitwa, Botswana .... 56 C3 20 30S 22 30 E
Sehlabathebe △, Lesotho ... 57 D4 29 53S 29 7 E
Sehore, India .... 42 H7 23 10N 77 5 E
Sehwan, Pakistan .... 42 F2 26 28N 67 53 E
Seil, U.K. 11 E3 56 18N 5 38W
Seiland, Norway .... 8 A20 70 25N 23 15 E
Seiling, U.S.A. 81 G5 36 9N 98 56W
Seinäjoki, Finland .... 9 E20 62 40N 22 51 E
Seine →, France .... 20 B4 49 26N 0 26 E
Seistan = Sīstān, Asia ..... 45 D9 30 50N 61 0 E
Seistan, Daryācheh-ye = Sīstān,
  Daryācheh-ye, Iran ...... 45 D9 31 0N 61 0 E
Sekayu, Indonesia .... 36 E2 2 51S 103 51 E
Seke, Tanzania .... 54 C3 3 20S 33 31 E
Sekenke, Tanzania .... 54 C3 4 18S 34 11 E
Sekondi-Takoradi, Ghana ... 50 H5 4 58N 1 45W
Sekudai, Malaysia .... 39 d 1 32N 103 39 E
Sekuma, Botswana .... 56 C3 24 36S 23 50 E
Selah, U.S.A. 76 C3 46 39N 120 32W

Selama, Malaysia .... 39 K3 5 12N 100 42 E
Selaru, Indonesia .... 37 F8 8 9S 131 0 E
Selatan, Selat, Malaysia .... 39 c 5 15N 100 20 E
Selby, U.K. 12 D6 53 47N 1 5W
Selby, U.S.A. 80 C4 45 31N 100 2W
Selçuk, Turkey .... 23 F12 37 56N 27 22 E
Selden, U.S.A. 80 F4 39 33N 100 34W
Sele →, Italy .... 22 D6 40 29N 14 56 E
Selebi-Pikwe, Botswana .... 57 C4 21 58S 27 48 E
Selemdzha →, Russia ..... 29 D13 51 42N 128 53 E
Selenga = Selenge Mörön →,
  Asia .... 32 A5 52 16N 106 16 E
Selenge Mörön →, Asia .... 32 A5 52 16N 106 16 E
Seletan, Tanjung, Indonesia . 36 E4 4 10S 114 40 E
Sélibabi, Mauritania 50 E3 15 10N 12 15W
Seligman, U.S.A. 77 J7 35 20N 112 53W
Selíma, El Wâhât el, Sudan .. 51 D11 21 22N 29 19 E
Selinda Spillway →, Botswana 56 B3 18 35S 23 10 E
Selinsgrove, U.S.A. 84 F8 40 48N 76 52W
Selkirk, Canada 71 C9 50 10N 96 55W
Selkirk, U.K. 11 F6 55 33N 2 50W
Selkirk I. = Horse I., Canada . 71 C9 53 20N 99 6W
Selkirk Mts., Canada 68 C8 51 15N 117 40W
Sellafield, U.K. 12 C4 54 25N 3 29W
Selliá, Greece .... 25 D6 35 12N 24 23 E
Sells, U.S.A. 77 L8 31 55N 111 53W
Selma, Ala., U.S.A. 83 J2 32 25N 87 1W
Selma, Calif., U.S.A. 78 J7 36 34N 119 37W
Selma, N.C., U.S.A. 83 H6 35 32N 78 17W
Selmer, U.S.A. 83 H1 35 10N 88 36W
Selous △, Tanzania .... 54 D4 8 37S 37 42 E
Selowandoma Falls, Zimbabwe 55 G3 21 15S 31 50 E
Selpele, Indonesia .... 37 E8 0 1S 130 5 E
Selsey Bill, U.K. 13 G7 50 43N 0 47W
Seltso, Russia .... 18 D5 53 22N 34 4 E
Selu, Indonesia .... 37 F8 7 32S 130 55 E
Selva, Argentina 94 B3 29 50S 62 0W
Selva Lancandona = Montes
  Azules △, Mexico 87 D6 16 21N 91 3W
Selvas, Brazil 92 E5 6 30S 67 0W
Selwyn L., Canada 71 B8 60 0N 104 30W
Selwyn Mts., Canada 68 B6 63 0N 130 0W
Selwyn Ra., Australia ..... 62 C3 21 10S 140 0 E
Seman →, Albania .... 23 D8 40 47N 19 30 E
Semarang, Indonesia ..... 36 F4 7 0S 110 26 E
Sembabule, Uganda ...... 54 C3 0 4S 31 25 E
Sembawang, Singapore .... 39 d 1 27N 103 50 E
Sembung, Indonesia ...... 37 J18 8 28S 115 11 E
Semenanjung Blambangan,
  Indonesia .... 37 K17 8 42S 114 29 E
Semeru, Indonesia .... 37 H15 8 4S 112 55 E
Semey, Kazakhstan .... 28 D9 50 30N 80 10 E
Seminoe Reservoir, U.S.A. .. 76 F10 42 9N 106 55W
Seminole, Okla., U.S.A. 81 H6 35 14N 96 41W
Seminole, Tex., U.S.A. 81 J3 32 43N 102 39W
Seminole Draw →, U.S.A. .. 81 J3 32 27N 102 20W
Semipalatinsk = Semey,
  Kazakhstan .... 28 D9 50 30N 80 10 E
Semirara Is., Phil. .... 37 B6 12 0N 121 20 E
Semitau, Indonesia .... 36 D4 0 29N 111 57 E
Semiyarka, Kazakhstan .... 28 D8 50 55N 78 23 E
Semiyarskoye = Semiyarka,
  Kazakhstan .... 28 D8 50 55N 78 23 E
Semmering P., Austria ..... 16 E8 47 41N 15 45 E
Semnān, Iran .... 45 C7 35 40N 53 23 E
Semnān □, Iran .... 45 C7 36 0N 54 0 E
Semporna, Malaysia ...... 37 D5 4 30N 118 33 E
Semuda, Indonesia .... 36 E4 2 51S 112 58 E
Sen →, Cambodia .... 36 B3 13 45N 105 12 E
Senā, Iran .... 45 D6 28 27N 51 36 E
Sena, Mozam. .... 55 F4 17 25S 35 0 E
Sena Madureira, Brazil 92 E5 9 5S 68 45W
Senador Pompeu, Brazil ... 93 E11 5 40S 39 20W
Senang, Pulau, Singapore .. 39 d 1 10N 103 44 E
Senanga, Zambia .... 53 H4 16 7S 23 16 E
Senatobia, U.S.A. 81 H10 34 37N 89 58W
Sencelles, Spain .... 24 B9 39 39N 2 54 E
Sendai, Kagoshima, Japan .. 31 J5 31 50N 130 20 E
Sendai, Miyagi, Japan ..... 30 E10 38 15N 140 53 E
Sendai-Wan, Japan .... 30 E10 38 15N 141 0 E
Sendhwa, India .... 42 J6 21 41N 75 6 E
Seneca, U.S.A. 83 H4 34 41N 82 57W
Seneca Falls, U.S.A. 85 D8 42 55N 76 48W
Seneca L., U.S.A. 84 D8 42 40N 76 54W
Senecaville L., U.S.A. 84 G3 39 55N 81 25W
Senegal ■, W. Afr. 50 F3 14 30N 14 30W
Sénégal →, W. Afr. 50 E2 15 48N 16 32W
Senegambia, Africa 48 E2 12 45N 12 0W
Senekal, S. Africa .... 57 D4 28 20S 27 36 E
Senga Hill, Zambia .... 55 D3 9 19S 31 11 E
Senge Khambab = Indus →,
  Pakistan .... 42 G2 24 20N 67 47 E
Sengua →, Zimbabwe ..... 55 F2 17 7S 28 5 E
Senhor-do-Bonfim, Brazil ... 93 F10 10 30S 40 10W
Senigállia, Italy .... 22 C5 43 43N 13 13 E
Senj, Croatia .... 16 F8 45 0N 14 58 E
Senja, Norway .... 8 B17 69 25N 17 30 E
Senkaku-Shotō, Japan ..... 31 L1 25 45N 124 0 E
Senkuang, Indonesia ...... 39 d 1 11N 104 2 E
Senlis, France .... 20 B5 49 13N 2 35 E
Senmonorom, Cambodia ... 38 F6 12 27N 107 12 E
Senneterre, Canada 72 C4 48 25N 77 15W
Seno, Laos .... 38 D5 16 35N 104 50 E
Sens, France .... 20 B5 48 11N 3 15 E
Senta, Serbia & M. .... 23 B9 45 55N 20 3 E
Sentani, Indonesia .... 37 E10 2 36S 140 37 E
Sentery = Lubao, Dem. Rep. of
  the Congo .... 54 D2 5 17S 25 42 E
Sentinel, U.S.A. 77 K7 32 52N 113 13W
Sentosa, Singapore ...... 39 d 1 15N 103 50 E
Seo de Urgel = La Seu d'Urgell,
  Spain .... 21 A6 42 22N 1 23 E
Seohara, India .... 43 E8 29 15N 78 33 E
Seonath →, India .... 43 J10 21 44N 82 28 E
Seondha, India .... 43 F8 26 9N 78 48 E
Seoni, India .... 43 H8 22 5N 79 30 E
Seoni Malwa, India .... 42 H8 22 27N 77 28 E
Seoul = Sŏul, S. Korea .... 35 F14 37 31N 126 58 E
Sepīdān, Iran .... 45 D7 30 20N 52 5 E
Sepo-ri, N. Korea .... 35 E14 38 57N 127 25 E
Sepone, Laos .... 38 D6 16 45N 106 13 E
Sept-Îles, Canada 73 B6 50 13N 66 22W
Sequim, U.S.A. 78 B3 48 5N 123 6W
Sequoia △, U.S.A. 78 J8 36 30N 118 30W
Seraing, Belgium .... 15 D5 50 35N 5 32 E
Serakhis →, Cyprus ...... 25 D11 35 13N 32 55 E
Seram, Indonesia .... 37 E7 3 10S 129 0 E
Seram Sea, Indonesia ..... 37 E7 2 30S 130 30 E

Seranantsara, Madag. ...... 57 B8 18 30S 49 5 E
Serang, Indonesia .... 37 G12 6 8S 106 10 E
Serangoon, Singapore ..... 39 d 1 23N 103 54 E
Serasan, Indonesia .... 36 D3 2 29N 109 4 E
Serbia □, Serbia & M. ..... 23 C9 43 30N 21 0 E
Serbia & Montenegro ■, Europe 23 B9 43 20N 20 0 E
Serdobsk, Russia .... 18 D7 52 28N 44 10 E
Seremban, Malaysia ...... 39 L3 2 43N 101 53 E
Serengeti △, Tanzania .... 54 C3 2 11S 35 0 E
Serengeti Plain, Tanzania .. 54 C4 2 40S 35 0 E
Serenje, Zambia .... 55 E3 13 14S 30 15 E
Sereth = Siret →, Romania . 17 F14 45 24N 28 1 E
Sergino, Russia .... 28 C7 62 25N 65 12 E
Sergipe □, Brazil 93 F11 10 30S 37 30W
Sergiyev Posad, Russia .... 18 C6 56 20N 38 10 E
Seria, Brunei .... 36 D4 4 37N 114 23 E
Serian, Malaysia .... 36 D4 1 10N 110 31 E
Seribu, Kepulauan, Indonesia 36 F3 5 36S 106 33 E
Sérifos, Greece .... 23 F11 37 9N 24 30 E
Sérigny →, Canada 73 A6 56 47N 66 0W
Seringapatam Reef, Australia 60 B3 13 38S 122 5 E
Seririt, Indonesia .... 37 J17 8 12S 114 56 E
Sermata, Indonesia .... 37 F7 8 15S 128 50 E
Sermersuaq, Greenland 4 B4 79 30N 62 0W
Serov, Russia .... 18 C11 59 29N 60 35 E
Serowe, Botswana .... 56 C4 22 25S 26 43 E
Serpentine Lakes, Australia . 61 E4 28 30S 129 10 E
Serpent's Mouth = Sierpe, Bocas
  de la, Venezuela 93 L15 10 0N 61 30W
Serpukhov, Russia .... 18 D6 54 55N 37 28 E
Serra do Navio, Brazil 93 C8 0 59N 52 3W
Sérrai, Greece .... 23 D10 41 5N 23 31 E
Serranía San Luís □, Paraguay 94 A4 22 35S 57 22W
Serrezuela, Argentina 94 C2 30 40S 65 20W
Serrinha, Brazil 93 F11 11 39S 39 0W
Sertanópolis, Brazil 95 A5 23 4S 51 2W
Serua, Indonesia .... 37 F8 6 18S 130 1 E
Serui, Indonesia .... 37 E9 1 53S 136 10 E
Serule, Botswana .... 56 C4 21 57S 27 20 E
Ses Salines, Spain .... 24 B10 39 21N 3 3 E
Sese Is., Uganda .... 54 C3 0 20S 32 20 E
Sesepe, Indonesia .... 37 E7 1 30S 127 59 E
Sesfontein, Namibia ...... 56 B1 19 7S 13 39 E
Sesheke, Zambia .... 56 B3 17 29S 24 13 E
S'Espalmador, Spain ...... 24 C7 38 47N 1 26 E
S'Espardell, Spain .... 24 C7 38 48N 1 29 E
S'Estanyol, Spain .... 24 B9 39 22N 2 54 E
Setana, Japan .... 30 C9 42 26N 139 51 E
Sète, France .... 20 E5 43 25N 3 42 E
Sete Lagôas, Brazil 93 G10 19 27S 44 16W
Sétif, Algeria .... 50 A7 36 9N 5 26 E
Seto, Japan .... 31 G8 35 14N 137 6 E
Setonaikai, Japan .... 31 G6 34 20N 133 30 E
Setonaikai △, Japan ...... 31 G6 34 15N 133 15 E
Settat, Morocco 50 B4 33 0N 7 40W
Setting L., Canada 71 C9 55 0N 98 38W
Settle, U.K. 12 C5 54 5N 2 16W
Settlement Pt., Bahamas ... 83 M6 26 40N 79 0W
Settlers, S. Africa .... 57 C4 25 2S 28 30 E
Setúbal, Portugal 21 C1 38 30N 8 58W
Setúbal, B. de, Portugal ... 21 C1 38 40N 8 56W
Seul, Lac, Canada 72 B1 50 20N 92 30W
Sevan, Ozero = Sevana Lich,
  Armenia .... 19 F8 40 30N 45 20 E
Sevana Lich, Armenia ..... 19 F8 40 30N 45 20 E
Sevastopol, Ukraine ...... 19 F5 44 35N 33 30 E
Seven Sisters, Canada 70 C3 54 56N 128 10W
Severn →, Canada 72 A2 56 2N 87 36W
Severn →, U.K. 13 F5 51 35N 2 40W
Severn L., Canada 72 B1 53 54N 90 48W
Severnaya Zemlya, Russia .. 29 B10 79 0N 100 0 E
Severnyye Uvaly, Russia ... 18 C8 60 0N 50 0 E
Severo-Kurilsk, Russia .... 29 D16 50 40N 156 8 E
Severo-Yenisevskiy, Russia . 29 C10 60 22N 93 1 E
Severo-Zapadnyy □, Russia . 28 C4 65 0N 40 0 E
Severodvinsk, Russia ..... 18 B6 64 27N 39 58 E
Severomorsk, Russia ...... 18 A5 69 5N 33 27 E
Severouralsk, Russia ..... 18 B10 60 9N 59 57 E
Sevier, U.S.A. 77 G7 38 39N 112 11W
Sevier →, U.S.A. 77 G7 39 4N 113 6W
Sevier Desert, U.S.A. 76 G7 39 40N 112 45W
Sevier L., U.S.A. 76 G7 38 54N 113 9W
Sevilla, Spain 21 D2 37 23N 5 58W
Seville = Sevilla, Spain 21 D2 37 23N 5 58W
Sevlievo, Bulgaria .... 23 C11 43 2N 25 6 E
Sewani, India .... 42 E6 28 58N 75 39 E
Seward, Alaska, U.S.A. 68 B5 60 7N 149 27W
Seward, Nebr., U.S.A. 80 E6 40 55N 97 6W
Seward, Pa., U.S.A. 84 F5 40 25N 79 1W
Seward Peninsula, U.S.A. .. 68 B3 65 30N 166 0W
Sewell, Chile 94 C1 34 10S 70 23W
Sewer, Indonesia .... 37 F8 5 53S 134 40 E
Sewickley, U.S.A. 84 F4 40 32N 80 12W
Sexsmith, Canada 70 B5 55 21N 118 47W
Seychelles ■, Ind. Oc. .... 27 K9 5 0S 56 0 E
Seyðisfjörður, Iceland 8 D6 65 16N 13 57W
Seydişehir, Turkey .... 19 G5 37 25N 31 51 E
Seydvān, Iran .... 44 B5 38 34N 45 2 E
Seyhan →, Turkey .... 44 B2 36 43N 34 53 E
Seym →, Ukraine .... 19 D5 51 27N 32 34 E
Seymour, Australia ...... 63 F4 37 0S 145 10 E
Seymour, S. Africa .... 57 E4 32 33S 26 46 E
Seymour, Conn., U.S.A. ... 85 E11 41 24N 73 4W
Seymour, Ind., U.S.A. 82 F3 38 58N 85 53W
Seymour, Tex., U.S.A. 81 J5 33 35N 99 16W
Sfântu Gheorghe, Romania . 17 F13 45 52N 25 48 E
Sfax, Tunisia .... 51 B8 34 49N 10 48 E
Sha Tau Kok, China ...... 33 F11 22 33N 114 13 E
Sha Tin, China .... 33 G11 22 23N 114 12 E
Shaanxi □, China .... 34 G5 35 0N 109 0 E
Shaba = Katanga □, Dem. Rep. of
  the Congo .... 54 D2 8 0S 25 0 E
Shaba △, Kenya .... 54 B4 0 38N 37 48 E
Shaballe = Scebeli, Wabi →,
  Somali Rep. .... 47 G3 2 0N 44 0 E
Shabogamo L., Canada 73 B6 53 15N 66 30W
Shabunda, Dem. Rep. of
  the Congo .... 54 C2 2 40S 27 16 E
Shache, China .... 32 C2 38 20N 77 10 E
Shackleton Ice Shelf, Antarctica 5 C8 66 0S 100 0 E
Shackleton Inlet, Antarctica . 5 E11 83 0S 160 0 E
Shādegān, Iran .... 45 D6 30 40N 48 38 E
Shadi, India .... 43 C7 33 24N 77 14 E
Shadrinsk, Russia .... 28 D7 56 5N 63 32 E
Shady side, U.S.A. 84 G4 39 58N 80 45W
Shafter, U.S.A. 79 K7 35 30N 119 16W
Shaftesbury, U.K. 13 F5 51 0N 2 11W

Shagram, Pakistan .... 43 A5 36 24N 72 20 E
Shah Alizai, Pakistan ...... 42 E2 29 25N 66 33 E
Shah Bunder, Pakistan ..... 42 G2 24 13N 67 56 E
Shahabad, Punjab, India ... 42 D7 30 10N 76 55 E
Shahabad, Raj., India ...... 42 G7 25 15N 77 11 E
Shahabad, Ut. P., India .... 43 F8 27 36N 79 56 E
Shahadpur, Pakistan .... 42 G3 25 55N 68 35 E
Shahba, Syria .... 46 C5 32 52N 36 38 E
Shahdad, Iran .... 45 D8 30 30N 57 40 E
Shahdad, Namakzār-e, Iran . 45 D8 30 20N 58 20 E
Shahdadkot, Pakistan ...... 42 F2 27 50N 67 55 E
Shahdol, India .... 43 H9 23 19N 81 26 E
Shahe, China .... 34 F8 37 0N 114 32 E
Shahganj, India .... 43 F10 26 3N 82 44 E
Shahgarh, India .... 40 F6 27 15N 69 50 E
Shahjahanpur, India .... 43 F8 27 54N 79 57 E
Shahpur, India .... 42 H7 22 12N 77 58 E
Shahpur, Baluchistan, Pakistan . 42 E3 28 46N 68 27 E
Shahpur, Punjab, Pakistan . 42 C5 32 17N 72 26 E
Shahpur Chakar, Pakistan .. 42 F3 26 9N 68 39 E
Shahpura, Mad. P., India ... 43 H9 23 10N 80 45 E
Shahpura, Raj., India ...... 42 G6 25 38N 74 56 E
Shahr-e Bābak, Iran .... 45 D7 30 7N 55 9 E
Shahr-e Kord, Iran .... 45 C6 32 15N 50 55 E
Shāhrakht, Iran .... 45 C9 33 38N 60 16 E
Shahrig, Pakistan .... 42 D2 30 15N 67 40 E
Shahukou, China .... 34 D7 40 20N 112 18 E
Shaikhabad, Afghan. .... 42 B3 34 2N 68 45 E
Shajapur, India .... 42 H7 23 27N 76 21 E
Shajing, China .... 33 F10 22 44N 113 48 E
Shakargarh, Pakistan ...... 42 C6 32 17N 75 10 E
Shakawe, Botswana .... 56 B3 18 28S 21 49 E
Shaker Heights, U.S.A. 84 E3 41 29N 81 32W
Shakhty, Russia .... 19 E7 47 40N 40 16 E
Shakhunya, Russia .... 18 C8 57 40N 46 46 E
Shaki, Nigeria .... 50 G6   8 41N   3 21 E
Shaksam Valley, Asia .... 43 A7 36 0N 76 20 E
Shallow Lake, Canada 84 B3 44 36N 81 5W
Shalqar, Kazakhstan .... 28 E6 47 48N 59 39 E
Shaluli Shan, China .... 32 C4 30 40N 99 55 E
Shām, Iran .... 45 E8 26 39N 57 21 E
Shām, Bādiyat ash, Asia .... 44 C3 32 0N 40 0 E
Shamāl Sīnî □, Egypt .... 46 E2 30 30N 33 30 E
Shamattawa, Canada 72 A1 55 51N 92 5W
Shamattawa →, Canada 72 A2 55 1N 85 23W
Shamil, Iran .... 45 E8 27 30N 56 55 E
Shāmkūh, Iran .... 45 C8 35 47N 57 50 E
Shamli, India .... 42 E7 29 32N 77 18 E
Shammar, Jabal, Si. Arabia .. 44 E4 27 40N 41 0 E
Shamo = Gobi, Asia .... 34 C6 44 0N 110 0 E
Shamo, L., Ethiopia .... 47 F2   5 45N 37 30 E
Shamokin, U.S.A. 85 F8 40 47N 76 34W
Shamrock, U.S.A. 81 H4 35 13N 100 15W
Shamva, Zimbabwe .... 55 F3 17 20S 31 32 E
Shan □, Burma .... 41 J21 21 30N 98 30 E
Shan Xian, China .... 34 G9 34 50N 116 5 E
Shanchengzhen, China ..... 35 C13 42 20N 125 20 E
Shāndak, Iran .... 45 D9 28 28N 60 27 E
Shandon, U.S.A. 78 K6 35 39N 120 23W
Shandong □, China .... 35 G10 36 0N 118 0 E
Shandong Bandao, China ... 35 F11 37 0N 121 0 E
Shang Xian = Shangzhou, China . 34 H5 33 50N 109 58 E
Shanga, Nigeria .... 50 F6 11 12N   4 33 E
Shangalowe, Dem. Rep. of
  the Congo .... 55 E2 10 50S 26 30 E
Shangani, Zimbabwe .... 57 B4 19 41S 29 20 E
Shangani →, Zimbabwe ..... 55 F2 18 41S 27 10 E
Shangbancheng, China ..... 35 D10 40 50N 118 1 E
Shangdu, China .... 34 D7 41 30N 113 30 E
Shanghai, China .... 33 C7 31 15N 121 26 E
Shanghe, China .... 35 F9 37 20N 117 10 E
Shangnan, China .... 34 H6 33 32N 110 50 E
Shangqiu, China .... 34 G8 34 26N 115 36 E
Shangrao, China .... 33 D6 28 25N 117 59 E
Shangshui, China .... 33 C6 33 42N 114 35 E
Shangzhi, China .... 35 B14 45 22N 127 56 E
Shangzhou, China .... 34 H5 33 50N 109 58 E
Shanhetun, China .... 35 B14 44 33N 127 15 E
Shanklin, U.K. 13 G6 50 38N   1 11W
Shannon, N.Z. .... 59 J5 40 33S 175 25 E
Shannon △, Australia ...... 61 F2 31 55S 117 51 E
Shannon →, Ireland 10 D2 52 35N   9 30W
Shannon, Mouth of the, Ireland . 10 D2 52 30N   9 55W
Shannon Airport, Ireland ... 10 D3 52 42N   8 57W
Shansi = Shanxi □, China ... 34 F7 37 0N 112 0 E
Shantar, Ostrov Bolshoy, Russia . 29 D14 55 9N 137 40 E
Shantipur, India .... 43 H13 23 17N 88 25 E
Shantou, China .... 33 D6 23 18N 116 40 E
Shantung = Shandong □, China . 35 G10 36 0N 118 0 E
Shanxi □, China .... 34 F7 37 0N 112 0 E
Shanyang, China .... 34 H5 33 31N 109 55 E
Shanyin, China .... 34 E7 39 25N 112 56 E
Shaoguan, China .... 33 D6 24 48N 113 35 E
Shaoxing, China .... 33 D7 30 0N 120 35 E
Shaoyang, China .... 33 D6 27 14N 111 25 E
Shap, U.K. 12 C5 54 32N   2 40W
Shapinsay, U.K. 11 B6 59 3N   2 51W
Shaqra', Si. Arabia .... 44 E5 25 15N 45 16 E
Shaqrā', Yemen .... 47 E4 13 22N 45 44 E
Sharafkhāneh, Iran .... 44 B5 38 11N 45 35 E
Sharbot Lake, Canada 85 B8 44 46N 76 41W
Shari, Japan .... 30 C12 43 55N 144 40 E
Sharjah = Ash Shāriqah, U.A.E. . 45 E7 25 23N 55 26 E
Shark B., Australia .... 61 E1 25 30S 113 32 E
Shark Bay △, Australia ..... 61 F2 32 49S 118 49 E
Sharon, Mass., U.S.A. 85 D13 42 7N 71 11W
Sharon, Pa., U.S.A. 84 E4 41 14N 80 31W
Sharon Springs, Kans., U.S.A. . 80 F4 38 54N 101 45W
Sharon Springs, N.Y., U.S.A. . 85 D10 42 48N 74 37W
Sharp Pt., Australia .... 62 A3 10 58S 142 43 E
Sharpe L., Canada 72 B1 54 24N 93 40W
Sharpsville, U.S.A. 84 E4 41 15N 80 29W
Sharya, Russia .... 18 C8 58 22N 45 20 E
Shashemene, Ethiopia ...... 47 F2   7 13N 38 33 E
Shashi, Botswana .... 57 C4 21 15S 27 27 E
Shashi, China .... 33 C6 30 25N 112 14 E
Shashi →, Africa .... 55 G2 21 14S 29 20 E
Shasta, Mt., U.S.A. 76 F2 41 25N 122 12W
Shasta L., U.S.A. 76 F2 40 43N 122 25W
Shatt al Arab = Arab, Shatt al →,
  Asia .... 45 D6 30 0N 48 31 E
Shaunavon, Canada 71 D7 49 35N 108 25W
Shaver L., U.S.A. 78 H7 37 9N 119 18W
Shaw →, Australia .... 60 D2 20 21S 119 17 E
Shaw I., Australia .... 62 J7 20 30S 149 2 E
Shawanaga, Canada 84 A4 45 31N 80 17W
Shawangunk Mts., U.S.A. ... 85 E10 41 35N 74 30W

Shawano, U.S.A. 82 C1 44 47N 88 36W
Shawinigan, Canada 72 C5 46 35N 72 50W
Shawnee, U.S.A. 81 H6 35 20N 96 55W
Shay Gap, Australia .... 60 D3 20 30S 120 10 E
Shaybārā, Si. Arabia .... 44 E3 25 26N 36 47 E
Shaykh, J. ash, Lebanon .... 46 B4 33 25N 35 50 E
Shaykh Miskin, Syria .... 46 C5 32 49N 36 9 E
Shaykh Sa'īd, Iraq .... 44 C5 32 34N 46 17 E
Shchuchinsk, Kazakhstan ... 28 D8 52 56N 70 12 E
She Xian, China .... 34 F7 36 30N 113 40 E
Shebele = Scebeli, Wabi →,
  Somali Rep. .... 47 G3   2 0N 44 0 E
Sheboygan, U.S.A. 82 D2 43 46N 87 45W
Shediac, Canada 73 C7 46 14N 64 32W
Sheelin, L., Ireland 10 C4 53 48N   7 20W
Sheep Haven, Ireland 10 A4 55 11N   7 52W
Sheerness, U.K. .... 13 F8 51 26N   0 47 E
Sheet Harbour, Canada 73 D7 44 56N 62 31W
Sheffield, U.K. 12 D6 53 23N   1 28W
Sheffield, Ala., U.S.A. 83 H2 34 46N 87 41W
Sheffield, Mass., U.S.A. 85 D11 42 5N 73 21W
Sheffield, Pa., U.S.A. 84 E5 41 42N 79 3W
Sheikhpura, India .... 43 G11 25 9N 85 53 E
Shekhupura, Pakistan ...... 42 D5 31 42N 73 58 E
Shekou, China .... 33 G10 22 30N 113 55 E
Shelburne, N.S., Canada ... 73 D6 43 47N 65 20W
Shelburne, Ont., Canada ... 84 B4 44 4N 80 15W
Shelburne, U.S.A. 85 B11 44 23N 73 14W
Shelburne B., Australia ..... 62 A3 11 50S 142 50 E
Shelburne Falls, U.S.A. 85 D12 42 36N 72 45W
Shelby, Mich., U.S.A. 82 D2 43 37N 86 22W
Shelby, Miss., U.S.A. 81 J9 33 57N 90 46W
Shelby, Mont., U.S.A. 76 B8 48 30N 111 51W
Shelby, N.C., U.S.A. 83 H5 35 17N 81 32W
Shelby, Ohio, U.S.A. 84 F2 40 53N 82 40W
Shelbyville, Ill., U.S.A. 80 F10 39 24N 88 48W
Shelbyville, Ind., U.S.A. 82 F3 39 31N 85 47W
Shelbyville, Ky., U.S.A. 82 F3 38 13N 85 14W
Shelbyville, Tenn., U.S.A. ... 83 H2 35 29N 86 28W
Sheldon, U.S.A. 80 D7 43 11N 95 51W
Sheldrake, Canada 73 B7 50 20N 64 51W
Shelikhova, Zaliv, Russia ... 29 D16 59 30N 157 0 E
Shell Lakes, Australia ...... 61 E4 29 20S 127 30 E
Shellbrook, Canada 71 C7 53 13N 106 24W
Shellharbour, Australia ..... 63 E5 34 31S 150 51 E
Shelter I., U.S.A. 85 E12 41 5N 72 21W
Shelton, Conn., U.S.A. 85 E11 41 19N 73 5W
Shelton, Wash., U.S.A. 78 C3 47 13N 123 6W
Shen Xian, China .... 34 F8 36 15N 115 40 E
Shenandoah, Iowa, U.S.A. .. 80 E7 40 46N 95 22W
Shenandoah, Pa., U.S.A. ... 85 F8 40 49N 76 12W
Shenandoah, Va., U.S.A. ... 82 F6 38 29N 78 37W
Shenandoah △, U.S.A. 82 F6 38 35N 78 22W
Shenandoah →, U.S.A. 82 F7 39 19N 77 44W
Shenchi, China .... 34 E7 39 8N 112 10 E
Shendam, Nigeria .... 50 G7   8 49N   9 30 E
Shendī, Sudan .... 51 E12 16 46N 33 22 E
Shengfang, China .... 34 E9 39 3N 116 42 E
Shenjingzi, China .... 35 B13 44 40N 124 30 E
Shenmu, China .... 34 E6 38 50N 110 29 E
Shenqiu, China .... 34 H8 33 25N 115 5 E
Shensi = Shaanxi □, China .. 34 G5 35 0N 109 0 E
Shenyang, China .... 35 D12 41 48N 123 27 E
Shenzhen, China .... 33 F10 22 32N 114 5 E
Shenzhen ✈ (SZX), China .. 33 F10 22 41N 113 49 E
Shenzhen Shuiku, China .... 33 F11 22 34N 114 8 E
Shenzhen Wan, China ...... 33 G10 22 27N 113 55 E
Sheo, India .... 42 F4 26 11N 71 15 E
Sheopur Kalan, India .... 40 G10 25 40N 76 40 E
Shepetivka, Ukraine .... 17 C14 50 10N 27 10 E
Shepetovka = Shepetivka,
  Ukraine .... 17 C14 50 10N 27 10 E
Shepparton, Australia ...... 63 F4 36 23S 145 26 E
Sheppey, I. of, U.K. .... 13 F8 51 25N   0 48 E
Shepton Mallet, U.K. 13 F5 51 11N   2 33W
Sheqi, China .... 34 H7 33 12N 112 57 E
Sher Qila, Pakistan .... 43 A6 36 7N 74 2 E
Sherborne, U.K. 13 G5 50 57N   2 31W
Sherbro I., S. Leone 50 G3   7 30N 12 40W
Sherbrooke, N.S., Canada .. 73 C7 45 8N 61 59W
Sherbrooke, Qué., Canada .. 85 A13 45 28N 71 57W
Sherburne, U.S.A. 85 D9 42 41N 75 30W
Shergarh, India .... 42 F5 26 20N 72 18 E
Sherghati, India .... 43 G11 24 34N 84 47 E
Sheridan, Ark., U.S.A. 81 H8 34 19N 92 24W
Sheridan, Wyo., U.S.A. 76 D10 44 48N 106 58W
Sheringham, U.K. .... 12 E9 52 56N   1 13 E
Sherkin I., Ireland 10 E2 51 28N   9 26W
Sherkot, India .... 43 E8 29 22N 78 35 E
Sherman, U.S.A. 81 J6 33 40N 96 35W
Sherpur, India .... 43 G10 25 34N 83 47 E
Sherridon, Canada 71 B8 55 8N 101 5W
Sherwood Forest, U.K. 12 D6 53 6N   1 7W
Sherwood Park, Canada 70 C6 53 31N 113 19W
Sheslay →, Canada 70 B2 58 48N 132 5W
Shethanei L., Canada 71 B9 58 48N 97 50W
Shetland □, U.K. 11 A7 60 30N   1 30W
Shetland Is., U.K. 11 A7 60 30N   1 30W
Shetrunji →, India .... 42 J5 21 19N 72 7 E
Sheung Shui, China .... 33 F11 22 31N 114 7 E
Sheyenne →, U.S.A. 80 B6 47 2N 96 50W
Shibām, Yemen .... 47 D4 15 59N 48 36 E
Shibata, Japan .... 30 F9 37 57N 139 20 E
Shibecha, Japan .... 30 C12 43 17N 144 36 E
Shibetsu, Japan .... 30 B11 44 10N 142 23 E
Shibogama L., Canada 72 B2 53 35N 88 15W
Shibushi, Japan .... 31 J5 31 25N 131 8 E
Shickshinny, U.S.A. 85 E8 41 9N 76 9W
Shickshock Mts. = Chic-Chocs,
  Mts., Canada 73 C6 48 55N 66 0W
Shidao, China .... 35 F12 36 50N 122 25 E
Shido, Japan .... 31 G7 34 19N 134 10 E
Shiel, L., U.K. 11 E3 56 48N   5 34W
Shield, C., Australia .... 62 A2 13 20S 136 20 E
Shieli, Kazakhstan .... 28 E7 44 20N 66 15 E
Shiga □, Japan .... 31 G8 35 20N 136 0 E
Shiguaigou, China .... 34 D6 40 52N 110 15 E
Shihchiachuangi = Shijiazhuang,
  China .... 34 E8 38 2N 114 28 E
Shihezi, China .... 32 B3 44 15N 86 2 E
Shijiazhuang, China .... 34 E8 38 2N 114 28 E
Shikarpur, India .... 42 E8 28 17N 78 7 E
Shikarpur, Pakistan .... 42 F3 27 57N 68 39 E
Shikohabad, India .... 43 F8 27 6N 78 36 E
Shikoku □, Japan .... 31 H6 33 30N 133 30 E
Shikoku-Sanchi, Japan ..... 31 H6 33 30N 133 30 E
Shikotsu-Ko, Japan .... 30 C10 42 45N 141 25 E

Shikotsu-Tôya △, Japan .... 30 C10 44 4N 145 8 E
Shiliguri, India .... 41 F16 26 45N 88 25 E
Shilka, Russia .... 29 D12 52 0N 115 55 E
Shilka →, Russia .... 29 D13 53 20N 121 26 E
Shillelagh, Ireland 10 D5 52 45N   6 32W
Shillington, U.S.A. 85 F9 40 18N 75 58W
Shillong, India .... 41 G17 25 35N 91 53 E
Shilo, West Bank .... 46 C4 32 4N 35 18 E
Shilou, China .... 34 F6 37 0N 110 48 E
Shimabara, Japan .... 31 H5 32 48N 130 20 E
Shimada, Japan .... 31 G9 34 49N 138 10 E
Shimane □, Japan .... 31 G6 35 0N 132 30 E
Shimanovsk, Russia .... 29 D13 52 15N 127 30 E
Shimba Hills △, Kenya ...... 54 C4   4 14S 39 25 E
Shimizu, Japan .... 31 G9 35 0N 138 30 E
Shimodate, Japan .... 31 F9 36 20N 139 55 E
Shimoga, India .... 40 N9 13 57N 75 32 E
Shimoni, Kenya .... 54 C4   4 38S 39 20 E
Shimonoseki, Japan .... 31 H5 33 58N 130 55 E
Shimpuru Rapids, Namibia .. 56 B2 17 45S 19 55 E
Shin, L., U.K. 11 C4 58 5N   4 30W
Shinano-Gawa →, Japan .... 31 F9 36 50N 138 30 E
Shināş, Oman .... 45 E8 24 46N 56 28 E
Shindand, Afghan. .... 40 C3 33 12N 62 8 E
Shinglehouse, U.S.A. 84 E6 41 58N 78 12W
Shingū, Japan .... 31 H7 33 40N 135 55 E
Shingwidzi, S. Africa .... 57 C5 23 5S 31 25 E
Shinjō, Japan .... 30 E10 38 46N 140 18 E
Shinshār, Syria .... 46 A5 34 36N 36 43 E
Shinyanga, Tanzania .... 54 C3   3 45S 33 27 E
Shinyanga □, Tanzania ..... 54 C3   3 50S 34 0 E
Shio-no-Misaki, Japan ...... 31 H7 33 25N 135 45 E
Shiogama, Japan .... 30 E10 38 19N 141 1 E
Shiojiri, Japan .... 31 F8 36 6N 137 58 E
Shipchenski Prokhod, Bulgaria . 23 C11 42 45N 25 15 E
Shiping, China .... 32 D5 23 45N 102 23 E
Shippagan, Canada 73 C7 47 45N 64 45W
Shippensburg, U.S.A. 84 F7 40 3N 77 31W
Shippenville, U.S.A. 84 E5 41 15N 79 28W
Shiprock, U.S.A. 77 H9 36 47N 108 41W
Shiqma, N. →, Israel .... 46 D3 31 37N 34 30 E
Shiquan, China .... 34 H5 33 5N 108 15 E
Shiquan He = Indus →, Pakistan . 42 G2 24 20N 67 47 E
Shīr Kūh, Iran .... 45 D7 31 39N 54 3 E
Shiragami-Misaki, Japan .... 30 D10 41 24N 140 12 E
Shirakawa, Fukushima, Japan . 31 F10 37 7N 140 13 E
Shirakawa, Gifu, Japan ..... 31 F8 36 17N 136 56 E
Shirane-San, Gumma, Japan . 31 F9 36 48N 139 22 E
Shirane-San, Yamanashi, Japan . 31 G9 35 42N 138 9 E
Shiraoi, Japan .... 30 C10 42 33N 141 21 E
Shīrāz, Iran .... 45 D7 29 42N 52 30 E
Shire →, Africa .... 55 F4 17 42S 35 19 E
Shiretoko-Misaki, Japan .... 30 B12 44 21N 145 20 E
Shirinab →, Pakistan .... 42 D2 30 15N 66 28 E
Shiriya-Zaki, Japan .... 30 D10 41 25N 141 30 E
Shiroishi, Japan .... 30 F10 38 0N 140 37 E
Shīrvān, Iran .... 45 B8 37 30N 57 50 E
Shirwa, L. = Chilwa, L., Malawi . 55 F4 15 15S 35 40 E
Shivpuri, India .... 42 G7 25 26N 77 42 E
Shixian, China .... 35 C15 43 5N 129 50 E
Shiyan, China .... 33 F10 22 42N 113 56 E
Shiyan Shuiku, China .... 33 F10 22 42N 113 54 E
Shizuishan, China .... 34 E4 39 15N 106 50 E
Shizuoka, Japan .... 31 G9 34 57N 138 24 E
Shizuoka □, Japan .... 31 G9 35 15N 138 40 E
Shklov = Shklow, Belarus ... 17 A16 54 16N 30 15 E
Shklow, Belarus .... 17 A16 54 16N 30 15 E
Shkodër, Albania .... 23 C8 42 4N 19 32 E
Shkumbini →, Albania ...... 23 D8 41 2N 19 31 E
Shmidta, Ostrov, Russia .... 29 A10 81 0N 91 0 E
Shō-Gawa →, Japan .... 31 F8 36 47N 137 4 E
Shoal L., Canada 71 D9 49 33N 95 1W
Shoal Lake, Canada 71 C8 50 30N 100 35W
Shōdo-Shima, Japan .... 31 G7 34 30N 134 15 E
Sholapur = Solapur, India .. 40 L9 17 43N 75 56 E
Shōmrōn, West Bank .... 46 C4 32 15N 35 13 E
Shoreham by Sea, U.K. 13 G7 50 50N   0 16W
Shori →, Pakistan .... 42 E3 28 29N 69 44 E
Shorkot Road, Pakistan .... 42 D5 30 47N 72 15 E
Shoshone, Calif., U.S.A. 79 K10 35 58N 116 16W
Shoshone, Idaho, U.S.A. ... 76 E6 42 56N 114 25W
Shoshone L., U.S.A. 76 D8 44 22N 110 43W
Shoshone Mts., U.S.A. 76 G5 39 20N 117 25W
Shoshong, Botswana .... 56 C4 22 56S 26 31 E
Shoshoni, U.S.A. 76 E9 43 14N 108 7W
Shouguang, China .... 35 F10 37 52N 118 45 E
Shouyang, China .... 34 F7 37 54N 113 8 E
Show Low, U.S.A. 77 J9 34 15N 110 2W
Shreveport, U.S.A. 81 J8 32 31N 93 45W
Shrewsbury, U.K. 13 E5 52 43N   2 45W
Shri Mohangarh, India ..... 42 F4 27 17N 71 18 E
Shrirampur, India .... 43 H13 22 44N 88 21 E
Shropshire □, U.K. 13 E5 52 36N   2 45W
Shū, Kazakhstan .... 28 E8 43 36N 73 42 E
Shū →, Kazakhstan .... 26 E10 45 0N 67 44 E
Shuangcheng, China .... 35 B14 45 20N 126 15 E
Shuanggou, China .... 35 G9 34 2N 117 30 E
Shuangliao, China .... 35 C12 43 29N 123 30 E
Shuangshanzi, China .... 35 D10 40 20N 119 8 E
Shuangyang, China .... 35 C13 43 28N 125 40 E
Shuangyashan, China ...... 33 B8 46 28N 131 5 E
Shuguri Falls, Tanzania .... 55 D4   8 33S 37 22 E
Shuiye, China .... 34 F8 36 7N 114 8 E
Shujalpur, India .... 42 H7 23 18N 76 46 E
Shukpa Kunzang, India .... 43 B8 34 22N 78 22 E
Shulan, China .... 35 B14 44 28N 127 0 E
Shule, China .... 32 C2 39 25N 76 3 E
Shumagin Is., U.S.A. 68 C4 55 7N 160 30W
Shumen, Bulgaria .... 23 C12 43 18N 26 55 E
Shumikha, Russia .... 28 D7 55 10N 63 15 E
Shuo Xian = Shuozhou, China . 34 E7 39 20N 112 33 E
Shuozhou, China .... 34 E7 39 20N 112 33 E
Shūr →, Fārs, Iran .... 45 D7 28 30N 55 0 E
Shūr →, Kermān, Iran ...... 45 D8 30 52N 57 37 E
Shūr →, Yazd, Iran .... 45 D7 31 45N 55 15 E
Shūr Āb, Iran .... 45 C6 34 23N 51 11 E
Shūr Gaz, Iran .... 45 D8 29 10N 59 20 E
Shūrāb, Iran .... 45 C8 33 43N 56 29 E
Shūrjestān, Iran .... 45 D7 31 24N 52 25 E
Shurugwi, Zimbabwe .... 55 F3 19 40S 30 0 E
Shūsf, Iran .... 45 D9 31 50N 60 5 E
Shūshtar, Iran .... 45 D6 32 0N 48 50 E
Shuswap L., Canada 70 C5 50 55N 119 3W
Shwebo, Burma .... 41 H19 22 30N 95 45 E
Shwegu, Burma .... 41 G20 24 15N 96 26 E

Shweli →, Burma .... 41 H20 23 45N 96 45 E
Shymkent, Kazakhstan ..... 28 E7 42 18N 69 36 E
Shyok, India .... 43 B8 34 13N 78 12 E
Shyok →, Pakistan .... 43 B6 35 13N 75 53 E
Si Chon, Thailand .... 39 H2   9 0N 99 54 E
Si Kiang = Xi Jiang →, China . 33 D6 22 5N 113 20 E
Si Lanna △, Thailand .... 38 C2 19 17N 99 12 E
Si-ngan = Xi'an, China ...... 34 G5 34 15N 109 0 E
Si Prachan, Thailand .... 38 E3 14 37N 100 9 E
Si Racha, Thailand .... 38 F3 13 10N 100 48 E
Si Xian, China .... 35 H9 33 30N 117 50 E
Siachen Glacier, Asia .... 43 B7 35 20N 77 30 E
Siahaf →, Pakistan .... 42 E3 29 3N 68 57 E
Siahan Range, Pakistan .... 40 F4 27 30N 64 40 E
Siaksriindrapura, Indonesia . 36 D2   0 51N 102 0 E
Sialkot, Pakistan .... 42 C6 32 32N 74 30 E
Siam = Thailand ■, Asia .... 38 E4 16 0N 102 0 E
Sian = Xi'an, China .... 34 G5 34 15N 109 0 E
Sian Ka'an, Mexico 87 D7 19 35N 87 40W
Siantan, Indonesia .... 36 D3   3 10N 106 15 E
Sīāreh, Iran .... 45 D9 28 5N 60 14 E
Siargao I., Phil. .... 37 C7   9 52N 126 3 E
Siari, Pakistan .... 43 B7 34 55N 76 40 E
Siasi, Phil. .... 37 C6   5 34N 120 50 E
Siau, Indonesia .... 37 D7   2 50N 125 25 E
Šiauliai, Lithuania .... 9 J20 55 56N 23 15 E
Sibâi, Gebel el, Egypt ...... 44 E2 25 45N 34 10 E
Sibang, Indonesia .... 37 K18   8 34S 115 13 E
Sibay, Russia .... 18 D10 52 42N 58 39 E
Sibayi, L., S. Africa .... 57 D5 27 20S 32 45 E
Šibenik, Croatia .... 22 C6 43 48N 15 54 E
Siberia = Sibirskiy □, Russia . 4 D13 60 0N 100 0 E
Siberia, Russia .... 36 E1   1 30S 99 0 E
Siberut, Indonesia .... 36 E1   1 30S 99 0 E
Sibi, Pakistan .... 42 E2 29 30N 67 54 E
Sibil = Oksibil, Indonesia ... 37 E10 4 59S 140 35 E
Sibiloi △, Kenya .... 54 B4   4 0N 36 20 E
Sibirskiy □, Russia .... 29 D10 58 0N 90 0 E
Sibiti, Congo .... 52 E2   3 38S 13 19 E
Sibiu, Romania .... 17 F13 45 45N 24 9 E
Sibley, U.S.A. 80 D7 43 24N 95 45W
Sibolga, Indonesia .... 36 D1   1 42N 98 45 E
Sibsagar, India .... 41 F19 27 0N 94 36 E
Sibu, Malaysia .... 36 D4   2 18N 111 49 E
Sibuco, Phil. .... 37 C6   7 20N 122 10 E
Sibuguey B., Phil. .... 37 C6   7 50N 122 45 E
Sibut, C.A.R. .... 52 C3   5 46N 19 10 E
Sibutu, Phil. .... 37 D5   4 45N 119 30 E
Sibutu Passage, E. Indies ... 37 D5   4 50N 120 0 E
Sibuyan I., Phil. .... 37 B6 12 25N 122 40 E
Sibuyan Sea, Phil. .... 37 B6 12 30N 122 20 E
Sicamous, Canada 70 C5 50 49N 119 0W
Siccus →, Australia .... 63 E2 31 55S 139 17 E
Sichuan □, China .... 32 C5 30 30N 103 0 E
Sicilia, Italy .... 22 F6 37 30N 14 30 E
Sicily = Sicilia, Italy .... 22 F6 37 30N 14 30 E
Sicuani, Peru 92 F4 14 21S 71 10W
Sidári, Greece .... 25 A3 39 47N 19 41 E
Siddhapur, India .... 42 H5 23 56N 72 25 E
Siddipet, India .... 40 K11 18 5N 78 51 E
Sidhauli, India .... 43 F9 27 17N 80 50 E
Sidheros, Ákra, Greece .... 25 D8 35 19N 26 19 E
Sidhi, India .... 43 G9 24 25N 81 53 E
Sidi-bel-Abbès, Algeria 50 A5 35 13N   0 39W
Sidi Ifni, Morocco 50 C3 29 29N 10 12W
Sidlaw Hills, U.K. 11 E5 56 32N   3 2W
Sidley, Mt., Antarctica 5 D14 77 2S 126 2W
Sidmouth, U.K. 13 G4 50 40N   3 15W
Sidmouth, C., Australia .... 62 A3 13 25S 143 36 E
Sidney, Canada 70 D4 48 39N 123 24W
Sidney, Mont., U.S.A. 80 B2 47 43N 104 9W
Sidney, N.Y., U.S.A. 85 D9 42 19N 75 24W
Sidney, Nebr., U.S.A. 80 E3 41 8N 102 59W
Sidney, Ohio, U.S.A. 82 E3 40 17N 84 9W
Sidney Lanier, L., U.S.A. ... 83 H4 34 10N 84 4W
Sidoarjo, Indonesia .... 37 G15   7 27S 112 43 E
Sidon = Saydā, Lebanon .... 46 B4 33 35N 35 25 E
Sidra, G. of = Surt, Khalij, Libya . 51 B9 31 40N 18 30 E
Siedlce, Poland .... 17 B12 52 10N 22 20 E
Sieg →, Germany .... 16 C4 50 46N   7 6 E
Siegen, Germany .... 16 C5 50 51N   8 0 E
Siem Pang, Cambodia ...... 38 E6 14 7N 106 23 E
Siem Reap = Siemreab,
  Cambodia .... 38 F4 13 20N 103 52 E
Siemreab, Cambodia .... 38 F4 13 20N 103 52 E
Siena, Italy .... 22 C4 43 19N 11 21 E
Sieradz, Poland .... 17 C10 51 37N 18 41 E
Sierpe, Bocas de la, Venezuela . 93 L15 10 0N 61 30W
Sierra Blanca, U.S.A. 77 L11 31 11N 105 22W
Sierra Blanca Peak, U.S.A. .. 77 K11 33 23N 105 49W
Sierra City, U.S.A. 78 F6 39 34N 120 38W
Sierra Colorada, Argentina . 96 E3 40 35S 67 50W
Sierra de Bahoruco △, Dom. Rep. . 89 C5 18 10N 71 25W
Sierra de La Culata △, Venezuela . 89 E5   8 45N 71 10W
Sierra de Lancandón △,
  Guatemala 88 C1 16 59N 90 23W
Sierra de las Quijadas △,
  Argentina 94 C2 32 29S 67 5W
Sierra de San Luis △, Venezuela . 89 D6 11 20N 69 43W
Sierra Gorda, Chile .... 94 A2 22 50S 69 15 E
Sierra Leone ■, W. Afr. 50 G3   9 0N 12 0W
Sierra Madre, Mexico 87 D6 16 0N 93 0W
Sierra Mojada, Mexico 86 B4 27 19N 103 42W
Sierra Nevada, Spain 21 D4 37 3N   3 15W
Sierra Nevada, U.S.A. 78 H8 39 0N 120 30W
Sierra Nevada □, Venezuela . 89 E5   8 35N 70 45W
Sierra Nevada de Santa Marta △,
  Colombia 89 D5 10 56N 73 36W
Sierra Vista, U.S.A. 77 L8 31 33N 110 18W
Sierraville, U.S.A. 78 F6 39 36N 120 22W
Sifnos, Greece .... 23 F11 37 0N 24 45 E
Sifton, Canada 71 C8 51 21N 100 8W
Sifton Pass, Canada 70 B3 57 52N 126 15W
Sighetu-Marmației, Romania . 17 E12 47 57N 23 52 E
Sighișoara, Romania .... 17 E13 46 12N 24 50 E
Sigli, Indonesia .... 36 C1   5 25N 96 0 E
Siglufjörður, Iceland 8 C4 66 12N 18 55W
Signal, U.S.A. 79 L13 34 30N 113 38W
Signal de Botrang, Belgium . 15 D6 50 29N   6 4 E
Signal Pk., U.S.A. 79 M12 33 20N 114 2W
Signy I., Antarctica 5 C18 60 45S 45 56W
Sigsig, Ecuador 92 D3 3 0S 78 50W
Sigüenza, Spain 21 B4 41 3N   2 40W
Siguiri, Guinea 50 F4 11 31N   9 10W
Sigulda, Latvia .... 9 H21 57 10N 24 55 E
Sihora, India .... 43 H9 23 29N 80 6 E
Siikajoki →, Finland .... 8 D21 64 50N 24 43 E

Siilinjärvi, Finland .... 8 E22 63 4N 27 39 E
Sijarira Ra. = Chizarira,
  Zimbabwe .... 55 F2 17 36S 27 45 E
Sika, India .... 42 H3 22 26N 69 47 E
Sikani Chief ➤, Canada 70 B4 57 47N 122 15W
Sikao, Thailand .... 39 J2 7 34N 99 21 E
Sikar, India .... 42 F6 27 33N 75 10 E
Sikasso, Mali 50 F4 11 18N 5 35W
Sikeston, U.S.A. 81 G10 36 53N 89 35W
Sikhote Alin, Khrebet, Russia 29 E14 45 0N 136 0 E
Sikhote Alin Ra. = Sikhote Alin,
  Khrebet, Russia .... 29 E14 45 0N 136 0 E
Sikinos, Greece .... 23 F11 36 40N 25 8 E
Sikkim □, India .... 41 F16 27 50N 88 30 E
Sil ➤, Spain 21 A2 42 27N 7 43W
Silacayoapan, Mexico 87 D5 17 30N 98 9W
Silawad, India .... 42 J6 21 54N 74 54 E
Silchar, India .... 41 G18 24 49N 92 48 E
Siler City, U.S.A. 83 H6 35 44N 79 28W
Silesia = Śląsk, Poland .... 16 C9 51 0N 16 30 E
Silgarhi Doti, Nepal .... 43 E9 29 15N 81 0 E
Silghat, India .... 41 F18 26 35N 93 0 E
Silifke, Turkey .... 19 G5 36 22N 33 58 E
Siliguri = Shiliguri, India . 41 F16 26 45N 88 25 E
Siling Co, China .... 32 C3 31 50N 89 20 E
Silistra, Bulgaria .... 23 B12 44 6N 27 19 E
Silivri, Turkey .... 23 D13 41 4N 28 14 E
Siljan, Sweden .... 9 F16 60 55N 14 45 E
Silkeborg, Denmark .... 9 H13 56 10N 9 32 E
Silkwood, Australia .... 62 B4 17 45S 146 2 E
Sillajhuay, Cordillera, Chile 92 G5 19 46S 68 40W
Sillamäe, Estonia .... 9 G22 59 24N 27 45 E
Silloth, U.K. 12 C4 54 52N 3 23W
Siloam Springs, U.S.A. 81 G7 36 11N 94 32W
Silsbee, U.S.A. 81 K7 30 21N 94 11W
Šilutė, Lithuania .... 9 J19 55 21N 21 33 E
Silvani, India .... 43 H8 23 18N 78 25 E
Silver City, U.S.A. 77 K9 32 46N 108 17W
Silver Cr. ➤, U.S.A. 76 E4 43 16N 119 13W
Silver Creek, U.S.A. 84 D5 42 33N 79 10W
Silver L., U.S.A. 78 G6 38 39N 120 6W
Silver Lake, Calif., U.S.A. . 79 K10 35 21N 116 7W
Silver Lake, Oreg., U.S.A. . 76 E3 43 8N 121 3W
Silverton, Colo., U.S.A. ... 77 H10 37 49N 107 40W
Silverton, Tex., U.S.A. 81 H4 34 28N 101 19W
Silvies ➤, U.S.A. 76 E4 43 34N 119 2W
Simaltala, India .... 43 G12 24 43N 86 33 E
Simanggang = Bandar Sri Aman,
  Malaysia .... 36 D4 1 15N 111 32 E
Simard, L., Canada 72 C4 47 40N 78 40W
Simav, Turkey .... 23 E13 39 4N 28 58 E
Simba, Tanzania .... 18 D8 54 20N 48 25 E
Simbirsk, Russia .... 54 C2 4 51S 29 41 E
Simbo, Tanzania .... 54 C2 4 51S 29 41 E
Simcoe, Canada 84 D4 42 50N 80 20W
Simcoe, L., Canada 84 B5 44 25N 79 20W
Simdega, India .... 43 H11 22 37N 84 31 E
Simeria, Romania .... 17 F12 45 51N 23 1 E
Simeulue, Indonesia .... 36 D1 2 45N 95 45 E
Simferopol, Ukraine .... 19 F5 44 55N 34 3 E
Sími, Greece .... 23 F12 36 35N 27 50 E
Simi Valley, U.S.A. 79 L8 34 16N 118 47W
Simikot, Nepal .... 43 E9 30 0N 81 50 E
Simla, India .... 42 D7 31 2N 77 9 E
Simmie, Canada 71 D7 49 56N 108 6W
Simmler, U.S.A. 79 K7 35 21N 119 59W
Simojoki ➤, Finland .... 8 D21 65 35N 25 1 E
Simojovel, Mexico 87 D6 17 12N 92 38W
Simonette ➤, Canada 70 B5 55 9N 118 15W
Simonstown, S. Africa ..... 56 E2 34 14S 18 26 E
Simpang Empat, Malaysia .. 39 c 5 27N 100 29 E
Simplonpass, Switz. .... 20 C8 46 15N 8 3 E
Simpson Desert, Australia . 62 D2 25 0S 137 0 E
Simpson Desert △, Australia 62 C2 24 59S 138 21 E
Simpson Pen., Canada 69 B11 68 34N 88 45W
Simpungdong, N. Korea .... 35 D15 40 56N 129 29 E
Simrishamn, Sweden .... 9 J16 55 33N 14 22 E
Simsbury, U.S.A. 85 E12 41 53N 72 48W
Simushir, Ostrov, Russia ... 29 E16 46 50N 152 30 E
Sin Cowe I., S. China Sea .. 36 C4 9 53N 114 19 E
Sinabang, Indonesia .... 36 D1 2 30N 96 24 E
Sinadogo, Somali Rep. ..... 47 F4 5 50N 47 0 E
Sinai = Es Sînâ', Egypt .... 46 F3 29 0N 34 0 E
Sinai, Mt. = Mûsa, Gebel, Egypt 44 D2 28 33N 33 59 E
Sinai Peninsula, Egypt ..... 26 G7 29 30N 34 0 E
Sinaloa □, Mexico 86 C3 25 0N 107 30W
Sinaloa de Leyva, Mexico .. 86 B3 25 50N 108 20W
Sinarádhes, Greece 92 B3 19 51N 73 0W
Sincelejo, Colombia 92 B3 9 18N 75 24W
Sinch'ang, N. Korea .... 35 D15 40 7N 128 28 E
Sinchang-ni, N. Korea ..... 35 E14 39 24N 126 8 E
Sinclair, U.S.A. 76 F10 41 47N 107 7W
Sinclair Mills, Canada 70 C4 54 5N 121 40W
Sinclair's B., U.K. 11 C5 58 31N 3 5W
Sinclairville, U.S.A. 84 D5 42 16N 79 16W
Sincorá, Serra do, Brazil ... 93 F10 13 30S 41 0W
Sind, Pakistan .... 42 G3 26 0N 68 30 E
Sind □, Pakistan .... 42 G3 26 0N 69 0 E
Sind ➤, Jammu & Kashmir,
  India .... 43 B6 34 18N 74 45 E
Sind ➤, Mad. P., India ..... 43 F8 26 26N 79 13 E
Sind Sagar Doab, Pakistan . 42 D4 32 0N 71 30 E
Sindangan, Phil. .... 37 C6 8 10N 123 5 E
Sindangbarang, Indonesia . 37 G12 7 27S 107 1 E
Sinde, Zambia .... 55 F2 17 28S 25 51 E
Sindh = Sind □, Pakistan .. 42 G3 26 0N 69 0 E
Sindri, India .... 43 H12 23 45N 86 42 E
Sines, Portugal 21 D1 37 56N 8 51W
Sines, C. de, Portugal 21 D1 37 58N 8 53W
Sineu, Spain .... 24 B10 39 38N 3 1 E
Sing Buri, Thailand .... 38 E3 14 53N 100 25 E
Singa, Sudan .... 51 F12 13 10N 33 57 E
Singapore ■, Asia .... 39 d 1 17N 103 51 E
Singapore, Straits of, Asia . 39 d 1 15N 104 0 E
Singapore Changi ✈ (SIN),
  Singapore .... 39 M4 1 23N 103 59 E
Singaraja, Indonesia ...... 36 F5 8 7S 115 6 E
Singida, Tanzania .... 54 C3 4 49S 34 48 E
Singida □, Tanzania .... 54 D3 6 0S 34 30 E
Singitikós Kólpos, Greece .. 23 D11 40 6N 24 0 E
Singkaling Hkamti, Burma . 41 G19 26 0N 95 39 E
Singkang, Indonesia .... 37 E6 4 8S 120 1 E
Singkawang, Indonesia .... 36 D3 1 0N 108 57 E
Singkep, Indonesia .... 36 E2 0 30S 104 25 E
Singleton, Australia .... 63 E5 32 33S 151 0 E
Singleton, Mt., N. Terr., Australia 60 D5 22 0S 130 46 E
Singleton, Mt., W. Austral.,
  Australia .... 61 E2 29 27S 117 15 E

Singoli, India .... 42 G6 25 0N 75 22 E
Singora = Songkhla, Thailand 39 J3 7 13N 100 37 E
Singosan, N. Korea .... 35 E14 38 52N 127 25 E
Sinhung, N. Korea .... 35 D14 40 11N 127 34 E
Sinjai, Indonesia .... 37 F6 5 7S 120 20 E
Sinjär, Iraq .... 44 B4 36 19N 41 52 E
Sinkat, Sudan .... 51 E13 18 55N 36 49 E
Sinkiang Uighur = Xinjiang
  Uygur Zizhiqu □, China .. 32 C3 42 0N 86 0 E
Sinmak, N. Korea .... 35 E14 38 25N 126 14 E
Sinnamary, Fr. Guiana 93 B8 5 25N 53 0W
Sinni ➤, Italy .... 22 D7 40 8N 16 41 E
Sinop, Turkey .... 19 F6 42 1N 35 11 E
Sinor, India .... 42 J5 21 55N 73 20 E
Sinp'o, N. Korea .... 35 E15 40 0N 128 13 E
Sinsk, Russia .... 29 C13 61 8N 126 48 E
Sintang, Indonesia .... 36 D4 0 5N 111 35 E
Sinton, U.S.A. 81 L6 28 2N 97 31W
Sintra, Portugal 21 C1 38 47N 9 25W
Sinüiju, N. Korea .... 35 D13 40 5N 124 24 E
Siocon, Phil. .... 37 C6 7 40N 122 10 E
Siófok, Hungary .... 17 E10 46 54N 18 3 E
Sion, Switz. .... 20 C7 46 14N 7 20 E
Sion Mills, U.K. 10 B4 54 48N 7 29W
Sioux City, U.S.A. 80 D6 42 30N 96 24W
Sioux Falls, U.S.A. 80 D6 43 33N 96 44W
Sioux Lookout, Canada 72 B1 50 10N 91 50W
Sioux Narrows, Canada 71 D10 49 25N 94 10W
Siparia, Trin. & Tob. 93 K15 10 8N 61 31W
Siping, China .... 35 C13 43 8N 124 21 E
Sipiwesk L., Canada 71 B9 55 5N 97 35W
Siple, Antarctica .... 5 D7 75 0S 74 0 E
Sipra ➤, India .... 42 H6 23 55N 75 28 E
Sipura, Indonesia .... 36 E1 2 18S 99 40 E
Siquia ➤, Nic. 88 D3 12 10N 84 20W
Siquijor, Phil. 88 D3 10 6N 83 30W
Siquirres, Costa Rica ...... 37 C6 9 12N 123 35 E
Şır Abū Nu'ayr, U.A.E. ... 45 E7 25 20N 54 20 E
Sir Banī Yās, U.A.E. ...... 45 E7 24 19N 52 37 E
Sir Edward Pellew Group,
  Australia .... 62 B2 15 40S 137 10 E
Sir Graham Moore Is., Australia 60 B4 13 53S 126 36 E
Sir James MacBrien, Mt., Canada 68 B7 62 7N 127 41W
Sira ➤, Norway .... 9 G12 58 23N 6 34 E
Siracusa, Italy .... 22 F6 37 4N 15 17 E
Sirajganj, Bangla. .... 43 G13 24 25N 89 47 E
Sirathu, India .... 43 G9 25 39N 81 19 E
Sirdän, Iran .... 45 B6 36 39N 49 12 E
Sirdaryo = Syrdarya ➤,
  Kazakhstan .... 28 E7 46 3N 61 0 E
Siren, U.S.A. 80 C8 45 47N 92 24W
Sirer, U.S.A. .... 24 C7 38 56N 1 22 E
Siret ➤, Romania .... 17 F14 45 24N 28 1 E
Sirghāyā, Syria .... 46 B5 33 51N 36 8 E
Sirinath △, Thailand ...... 39 a 8 30N 98 17 E
Sírjan, Iran .... 45 D7 29 30N 55 45 E
Sirmaur, India .... 43 G9 24 51N 81 23 E
Sirohi, India .... 42 G5 24 52N 72 53 E
Sironj, India .... 42 G7 24 5N 77 39 E
Siros, Greece .... 23 F11 37 28N 24 57 E
Sirretta Pk., U.S.A. 79 K8 35 56N 118 19W
Sirsi, Iran .... 45 E7 25 55N 54 32 E
Sirsa, India .... 42 E6 29 33N 75 4 E
Sirsa ➤, India .... 43 F8 26 51N 79 4 E
Sisak, Croatia .... 16 F9 45 30N 16 21 E
Sisaket, Thailand .... 38 E5 15 8N 104 23 E
Sishen, S. Africa .... 56 D3 27 47S 22 59 E
Sishui, Henan, China ...... 34 G7 34 48N 113 15 E
Sishui, Shandong, China .. 35 G9 35 42N 117 18 E
Sisipuk L., Canada 71 B8 55 45N 101 50W
Sisophon, Cambodia ...... 38 F4 13 38N 102 59 E
Sisseton, U.S.A. 80 C6 45 40N 97 3W
Sīstān, Asia .... 45 D9 30 50N 61 0 E
Sīstān, Daryācheh-ye, Iran . 45 D9 31 0N 61 0 E
Sīstān va Balūchestān □, Iran 45 E9 27 0N 62 0 E
Sisters, U.S.A. 76 D3 44 18N 121 33W
Siswa Bazar, India .... 43 F10 27 9N 83 46 E
Sitamarhi, India .... 43 F11 26 37N 85 30 E
Sitampiky, Madag. .... 57 B8 16 41S 46 6 E
Sitapur, India .... 43 F9 27 38N 80 45 E
Siteki, Swaziland .... 57 D5 26 32S 31 58 E
Sitges, Spain .... 21 B6 41 17N 1 47 E
Sitia, Greece .... 23 D8 35 13S 23 40 E
Sitka, U.S.A. 70 B1 57 3N 135 20W
Sitoti, Botswana .... 56 C3 23 15S 23 40 E
Sittang Myit ➤, Burma .... 41 L20 17 20N 96 45 E
Sittard, Neths. .... 15 C5 51 0N 5 52 E
Sittingbourne, U.K. .... 13 F8 51 21N 0 45 E
Sittoung = Sittang Myit ➤,
  Burma .... 41 L20 17 20N 96 45 E
Sittwe, Burma .... 41 J18 20 18N 92 45 E
Situbondo, Indonesia ..... 37 G16 7 42S 114 0 E
Siuna, Nic. 88 D3 13 37N 84 45W
Siuri, India .... 43 H12 23 50N 87 34 E
Sivand, Iran .... 45 D7 30 5N 52 55 E
Sivas, Turkey .... 19 G6 39 43N 36 58 E
Siverek, Turkey .... 44 B3 37 50N 39 19 E
Sivomaskinskiy, Russia .... 18 A11 66 40N 62 35 E
Sivrihisar, Turkey .... 19 G5 39 30N 31 35 E
Sîwa, Egypt .... 51 C11 29 11N 25 31 E
Siwa, El Wâhât es, Egypt .. 51 C11 29 10N 25 30 E
Siwa Oasis = Siwa, El Wâhât es,
  Egypt .... 48 D6 29 10N 25 30 E
Siwalik Range, Nepal ..... 43 F10 28 0N 83 0 E
Siwan, India .... 43 F11 26 13N 84 21 E
Siwana, India .... 42 G5 25 38N 72 25 E
Six Cross Roads, Barbados . 89 g 13 10N 59 28W
Sixmilebridge, Ireland 10 D3 52 44N 8 46W
Sixth Cataract, Sudan ..... 51 E12 16 20N 32 42 E
Siziwang Qi, China .... 34 D6 41 25N 111 40 E
Sjælland, Denmark .... 9 J14 55 30N 11 30 E
Sjumen = Shumen, Bulgaria 23 C12 43 18N 26 55 E
Skadarsko Jezero, Serbia & M. 23 C8 42 10N 19 20 E
Skaftafell, Iceland 8 D5 64 1N 17 0W
Skagafjörður, Iceland 8 D4 65 54N 19 35W
Skagastølstindane, Norway 9 F12 61 28N 7 52 E
Skagaströnd, Iceland 8 D3 65 50N 20 19W
Skagen, Denmark .... 9 H14 57 43N 10 35 E
Skagerrak, Denmark ...... 9 H13 57 30N 9 0 E
Skagit ➤, U.S.A. 78 B4 48 23N 122 22W
Skagway, U.S.A. 68 C6 59 28N 135 19W
Skala-Podilska = Skala
  Podilska, Ukraine .... 17 D14 48 50N 26 15 E
Skala Podolskaya = Skala-
  Podilska, Ukraine .... 17 D14 48 50N 26 15 E
Skalat, Ukraine .... 17 D13 49 23N 25 55 E
Skåne, Sweden .... 9 J15 55 59N 13 30 E
Skaneateles, U.S.A. 85 D8 42 57N 76 26W

Skaneateles L., U.S.A. 85 D8 42 51N 76 22W
Skara, Sweden .... 9 G15 58 25N 13 30 E
Skardu, Pakistan .... 43 B6 35 20N 75 44 E
Skarżysko-Kamienna, Poland 17 C11 51 7N 20 52 E
Skeena ➤, Canada 70 C2 54 9N 130 5W
Skeena Mts., Canada 70 B3 56 40N 128 30W
Skegness, U.K. .... 12 D8 53 9N 0 20 E
Skeldon, Guyana 92 B7 5 55N 57 20W
Skeleton Coast △, Namibia 56 C1 20 0S 13 0 E
Skellefte älv ➤, Sweden .... 8 D19 64 45N 21 10 E
Skellefteå, Sweden .... 8 D19 64 45N 20 50 E
Skelleftehamn, Sweden .... 8 D19 64 40N 21 9 E
Skerries, The, U.K. 12 D3 53 25N 4 36W
Ski, Norway .... 9 G14 59 43N 10 52 E
Skíathos, Greece .... 23 E10 39 12N 23 30 E
Skibbereen, Ireland 10 E2 51 33N 9 16W
Skiddaw, U.K. 12 C4 54 39N 3 9W
Skidegate, Canada 70 C2 53 15N 132 1W
Skien, Norway .... 9 G13 59 12N 9 35 E
Skierniewice, Poland ...... 17 C11 51 58N 20 10 E
Skikda, Algeria .... 50 A7 36 50N 6 58 E
Skilloura, Cyprus .... 25 D12 35 14N 33 10 E
Skipton, U.K. 12 D5 53 58N 2 3W
Skírmish Pt., Australia .... 62 A1 11 59S 134 17 E
Skíros, Greece .... 23 E11 38 55N 24 34 E
Skive, Denmark .... 9 H13 56 33N 9 2 E
Skjálfandafljót ➤, Iceland . 8 D5 65 59N 17 25W
Skjálfandi, Iceland 8 C5 66 5N 17 30W
Skoghall, Sweden .... 9 G15 59 20N 13 30 E
Skole, Ukraine .... 17 D12 49 3N 23 30 E
Skópelos, Greece .... 23 E10 39 9N 23 47 E
Skopi, Greece .... 25 D8 35 11N 26 2 E
Skopje, Macedonia .... 23 C9 42 1N 21 26 E
Skövde, Sweden .... 9 G15 58 24N 13 50 E
Skovorodino, Russia ...... 29 D13 54 0N 124 0 E
Skowhegan, U.S.A. 83 C11 44 46N 69 43W
Skull, Ireland 10 E2 51 32N 9 34W
Skunk ➤, U.S.A. 80 E9 40 42N 91 7W
Skuodas, Lithuania .... 9 H19 56 16N 21 33 E
Skvyra, Ukraine .... 17 D15 49 44N 29 40 E
Skye, U.K. 11 D2 57 15N 6 10W
Skykomish, U.S.A. 76 C3 47 42N 121 22W
Skyros, Greece .... 23 E11 38 55N 24 34 E
Slade Pt., Australia .... 62 K7 21 5S 149 13 E
Slættaratindur, Færoe Is. .. 8 E9 62 18N 7 1W
Slagelse, Denmark .... 9 J14 55 23N 11 19 E
Slamet, Indonesia .... 37 G13 7 16S 109 8 E
Slaney ➤, Ireland 10 D5 52 26N 6 33W
Slangberge, S. Africa ...... 56 E3 31 32S 20 48 E
Slate Is., Canada 72 C2 48 40N 87 0W
Slatina, Romania .... 17 F13 44 28N 24 22 E
Slatington, U.S.A. 85 F9 40 45N 75 37W
Slaton, U.S.A. 81 J4 33 26N 101 39W
Slave ➤, Canada 70 A6 61 18N 113 39W
Slave Coast, W. Afr. ...... 50 G6 6 0N 2 30 E
Slave Lake, Canada 70 B6 55 17N 114 43W
Slave Pt., Canada 70 A5 61 11N 115 56W
Slavgorod, Russia .... 28 D8 53 1N 78 37 E
Slavonski Brod, Croatia ... 17 C14 50 15N 27 2 E
Slavuta, Ukraine .... 30 C5 42 53N 131 21 E
Slavyanka, Russia .... 19 E6 48 55N 37 36 E
Slavyansk = Slovyansk, Ukraine 17 B16 53 27N 31 0 E
Slawharad, Belarus 12 D7 53 0N 0 24W
Sleaford, U.K. .... 63 E2 34 55S 135 45 E
Sleaford B., Australia 11 D3 57 5N 5 47W
Sleat, Sd. of, U.K. 69 C11 58 30N 81 0W
Sleeper Is., Canada 82 C2 44 50N 86 5W
Sleeping Bear Dunes △, U.S.A. 80 C7 44 18N 94 43W
Sleepy Eye, U.S.A. 70 A5 63 13N 116 4W
Slemon L., Canada 85 E10 41 9N 78 25W
Slide Mt., U.S.A. 85 E10 41 9N 78 25W
Slidell, U.S.A. 81 K10 30 17N 89 47W
Sliema, Malta .... 25 D2 35 54N 14 30 E
Slieve Aughty, Ireland 10 C3 53 4N 8 30W
Slieve Bloom, Ireland 10 C4 53 4N 7 40W
Slieve Donard, U.K. 10 B6 54 11N 5 55W
Slieve Gamph, Ireland 10 B3 54 6N 9 0W
Slieve Gullion, U.K. 10 B5 54 7N 6 26W
Slieve League, Ireland 10 B3 54 40N 8 42W
Slieve Mish, Ireland 10 D2 52 12N 9 50W
Slievenamon, Ireland 10 D4 52 25N 7 34W
Sligeach = Sligo, Ireland .. 10 B3 54 16N 8 28W
Sligo, Ireland 10 B3 54 16N 8 28W
Sligo, U.S.A. 84 E5 41 6N 79 29W
Sligo □, Ireland 10 B3 54 8N 8 42W
Sligo B., Ireland 10 B3 54 18N 8 40W
Slippery Rock, U.S.A. 84 E4 41 3N 80 3W
Slite, Sweden .... 9 H18 57 42N 18 48 E
Sliven, Bulgaria .... 23 C12 42 42N 26 19 E
Sloan, U.S.A. 79 K11 35 57N 115 13W
Sloansville, U.S.A. 85 D10 42 45N 74 22W
Slobodskoy, Russia .... 18 C9 58 40N 50 6 E
Slobozia, Romania .... 17 F14 44 34N 27 23 E
Slocan, Canada 70 D5 49 48N 117 28W
Slonim, Belarus .... 17 B13 53 4N 25 19 E
Slough, U.K. 13 F7 51 30N 0 36W
Slough □, U.K. 13 F7 51 30N 0 36W
Sloughhouse, U.S.A. 78 G5 38 26N 121 12W
Slovak Rep. ■, Europe ... 17 D10 48 30N 20 0 E
Slovakia = Slovak Rep. ■, Europe 17 D10 48 30N 20 0 E
Slovakian Ore Mts. = Slovenské
  Rudohorie, Slovak Rep. .. 17 D10 48 45N 20 0 E
Slovenia ■, Europe .... 16 F8 45 58N 14 30 E
Slovenija = Slovenia ■, Europe 16 F8 45 58N 14 30 E
Slovenské Rudohorie,
  Slovak Rep. .... 17 D10 48 45N 20 0 E
Slovyansk, Ukraine .... 19 E6 48 55N 37 36 E
Sluch ➤, Ukraine .... 17 C14 51 37N 26 38 E
Sluis, Neths. .... 15 C3 51 18N 3 23 E
Słupsk, Poland .... 17 A9 54 30N 17 3 E
Slurry, S. Africa .... 56 D4 25 49S 25 42 E
Slutsk, Belarus .... 17 B14 53 2N 27 31 E
Slyne Hd., Ireland 10 C1 53 25N 10 10W
Slyudyanka, Russia .... 29 D11 51 40N 103 40 E
Småland, Sweden .... 9 H16 57 15N 15 25 E
Smalltree L., Canada 71 A8 61 0N 105 0W
Smallwood Res., Canada .. 73 B7 54 5N 64 30W
Smarhon, Belarus .... 17 A14 54 20N 26 24 E
Smartt Syndicate Dam, S. Africa 56 E3 30 45S 23 10 E
Smartville, U.S.A. 78 F5 39 13N 121 18W
Smeaton, Canada 71 C8 53 30N 104 49W
Smederevo, Serbia & M. ... 23 B9 44 40N 20 57 E
Smerwick Harbour, Ireland 10 D1 52 12N 10 23W
Smethport, U.S.A. 84 E6 41 49N 78 27W
Smidovich, Russia .... 29 E14 48 36N 133 49 E
Smith, Canada 70 B6 55 10N 114 0W

Smith Center, U.S.A. 80 F5 39 47N 98 47W
Smith River ◌, U.S.A. 76 F2 41 55N 124 0W
Smith Sd., N. Amer. 4 B4 78 25N 74 0W
Smithburne ➤, Australia .. 70 C3 54 45N 127 10W
Smithers, Canada .... 57 E4 30 9S 26 30 E
Smithfield, S. Africa 83 H6 35 31N 78 21W
Smithfield, N.C., U.S.A. ... 76 F8 41 50N 111 50W
Smithfield, Utah, U.S.A. .. 85 B9 44 55N 76 0W
Smiths Falls, Canada ...... 63 G4 40 53S 145 6 E
Smithton, Australia 81 K6 50 10N 117 21W
Smithville, Canada 80 F6 39 4N 96 48W
Smithville, U.S.A. 80 F6 39 15N 99 30W
Smoky ➤, Canada 70 C6 54 10N 112 30W
Smoky Bay, Australia ..... 18 D5 54 45N 32 5 E
Smoky Hill ➤, U.S.A. ...... 23 D9 49 9N 20 58 E
Smoky Hills, U.S.A. .... 23 D11 41 36N 24 38 E
Smoky Lake, Canada 72 C3 49 17N 81 37W
Smøla, Norway .... 8 E13 63 23N 8 3 E
Smolensk, Russia 71 C7 54 40N 106 50W
Smolikas, Óros, Greece .... 9 F17 58 15N 11 0 E
Smolyan, Bulgaria .... 17 A14 54 20N 26 24 E
Smooth Rock Falls, Canada 82 F8 39 18N 75 36W
Smoothstone L., Canada .. 8 B6 64 48N 15 34W
Smorgon = Smarhon, Belarus 12 C3 54 16N 4 27W
Smyrna = İzmir, Turkey ... 8 D2 64 49N 23 46W
Smyrna, U.S.A. 76 C4 46 12N 119 20W
Snæfell, Iceland .... 63 F4 38 47S 146 33 E
Snæfell, U.K. 76 G6 39 0N 114 20W
Snæfellsjökull, Iceland 76 E7 42 50N 114 0W
Snake ➤, U.S.A. .... 8 D14 64 12N 12 0 E
Snake I., Australia .... 15 A5 53 2N 5 40 E
Snake Range, U.S.A. ...... 56 E3 31 46S 24 20 E
Snake River Plain, U.S.A. . 78 H6 31 10N 120 26W
Snåsavatnet, Norway ..... 16 C8 50 41N 15 50 E
Sneek, Neths. 11 D2 57 33N 6 28W
Sneeuberge, S. Africa ..... 9 E13 62 19N 9 16 E
Snelling, U.S.A. 78 C4 47 55N 122 6W
Snežka, Europe .... 39 F6 12 4N 106 26 E
Snizort, L., U.K. 82 F8 38 11N 75 24W
Snøhetta, Norway 71 C8 54 52N 100 3W
Snohomish, U.S.A. 78 H4 39 23N 122 45W
Snow Hill, U.S.A. 85 A14 45 38N 70 48W
Snow Lake, Canada 84 E7 41 2N 77 57W
Snow Mt., Calif., U.S.A. .. 71 A8 60 45N 103 0W
Snow Mt., Maine, U.S.A. . 12 D3 53 4N 4 5W
Snow Shoe, U.S.A. 12 D4 53 7N 3 59W
Snowbird L., Canada 71 A6 62 24N 110 44W
Snowdon, U.K. 71 A6 62 24N 110 44W
Snowdonia △, U.K. 77 J8 34 30N 110 5W
Snowdrift = Łutselk'e, Canada 76 B6 48 13N 115 41W
Snowdrift ➤, Canada ...... 63 E2 33 46S 138 14 E
Snowflake, U.S.A. 76 F7 41 58N 112 43W
Snowshoe Pk., U.S.A. .... 63 F4 38 30S 145 30 E
Snowtown, Australia 85 C10 43 42N 74 23W
Snowville, U.S.A. .... 63 F4 36 45S 148 30 E
Snowy ➤, Australia 89 B5 22 33N 73 52W
Snowy Mt., U.S.A. .... 17 D13 48 27N 25 38 E
Snowy Mts., Australia 81 H5 34 40N 98 57W
Snug Corner, Bahamas 81 J4 32 44N 100 55W
Snyatyn, Ukraine .... 57 B7 18 42S 44 13 E
Snyder, Okla., U.S.A. ..... 57 B8 16 6S 45 20 E
Snyder, Tex., U.S.A. ...... 57 B8 18 32S 45 15 E
Soahanina, Madag. .... 57 C7 23 52S 44 47 E
Soalala, Madag. .... 42 C4 33 1N 71 44 E
Soaloka, Madag. .... 57 B8 16 6S 45 20 E
Soamanonga, Madag. ..... 57 B8 18 32S 45 15 E
Soan ➤, Pakistan .... 16 B5 52 9N 5 19 E
Soanierana-Ivongo, Madag. 57 B8 16 55S 49 35 E
Soanindraniny, Madag. ... 57 C8 19 54S 47 14 E
Soavina, Madag. .... 57 C8 20 23S 46 56 E
Soavinandriana, Madag. ... 57 B8 19 9S 46 45 E
Sobat, Nahr ➤, Sudan .... 51 G12 9 22N 31 33 E
Sobhapur, India .... 42 H8 22 47N 78 17 E
Sobradinho, Reprêsa de, Brazil 93 E10 9 30S 42 0W
Sobral, Brazil 93 D10 3 50S 40 20W
Soc Giang, Vietnam .... 38 A6 22 54N 106 1 E
Soc Trang, Vietnam .... 39 H5 9 37N 105 50 E
Socastee, U.S.A. 83 J6 33 41N 79 1W
Soch'e = Shache, China ... 32 C2 38 0N 77 16 E
Sochi, Russia .... 19 F6 43 35N 39 40 E
Société, Is. de la,
  French Polynesia 65 J12 17 0S 151 0W
Society Is. = Société, Is. de la,
  French Polynesia 65 J12 17 0S 151 0W
Socompa, Portezuelo de, Chile 94 A2 24 27S 68 18W
Socorro, N. Mex., U.S.A. . 77 J10 34 4N 106 54W
Socorro, Tex., U.S.A. 77 L10 31 39N 106 18W
Socorro, I., Mexico 86 D2 18 45N 110 58W
Socotra, Yemen .... 47 E5 12 30N 54 0 E
Soda L., U.S.A. 77 J5 35 10N 116 4W
Soda Plains, India .... 43 B8 35 30N 79 0 E
Soda Springs, U.S.A. 76 E8 42 39N 111 36W
Sodankylä, Finland .... 8 C22 67 29N 26 40 E
Soddy-Daisy, U.S.A. 83 H3 35 17N 85 10W
Söderhamn, Sweden ...... 9 F17 61 18N 17 10 E
Söderköping, Sweden ..... 9 G17 58 31N 16 20 E
Södermanland, Sweden ... 9 G17 58 56N 16 55 E
Södertälje, Sweden .... 9 G17 59 12N 17 39 E
Sodiri, Sudan .... 51 F11 14 27N 29 0 E
Sodus, U.S.A. 84 C7 43 14N 77 4W
Sodwana Bay △, S. Africa . 57 D5 27 35S 32 43 E
Soekmekaar, S. Africa ..... 57 C4 23 30S 29 55 E
Soest, Neths. .... 15 B5 52 9N 5 19 E
Sofala □, Mozam. .... 57 B5 19 30S 34 30 E
Sofia ➤, Madag. .... 23 C10 42 45N 23 20 E
Sofiya, Bulgaria .... 23 C10 42 45N 23 20 E
Sōfu-Gan, Japan .... 31 K10 29 49N 140 21 E
Sogamoso, Colombia 92 B4 5 43N 72 56W
Sogār, Iran .... 45 E8 25 53N 58 6 E
Sogndalsfjøra, Norway ... 9 F12 61 14N 7 5 E
Sognefjorden, Norway .... 9 G12 58 5N 7 48 E
Sogwipo, S. Korea .... 9 F11 61 10N 5 50 E
Soh, Iran .... 35 H14 33 13N 126 34 E
Sohâg, Egypt .... 45 C6 33 26N 51 27 E
Sohagpur, India .... 51 C12 26 33N 31 43 E
Sōhori, N. Korea .... 42 H8 22 42N 78 12 E
Soignies, Belgium .... 15 D4 50 35N 4 5 E
Soissons, France .... 20 B5 49 25N 3 19 E
Sōja, Japan .... 31 G6 34 40N 133 45 E
Sojat, India .... 42 G5 25 55N 73 45 E
Sokal, Ukraine .... 17 C13 50 31N 24 15 E
Söke, Turkey .... 23 F12 37 48N 27 28 E
Sokelo, Dem. Rep. of the Congo 55 D1 9 55S 24 36 E
Sokhumi, Georgia .... 19 F7 43 0N 41 0 E

Soko Islands, China .... 33 G10 22 10N 113 54 E
Sokodé, Togo .... 50 G6 9 0N 1 11 E
Sokol, Russia .... 18 C7 59 30N 40 5 E
Sokółka, Poland .... 17 B12 53 25N 23 30 E
Sokołów Podlaski, Poland .. 17 B12 52 25N 22 15 E
Sokoto, Nigeria .... 50 F7 13 2N 5 16 E
Sol Iletsk, Russia .... 18 D10 51 10N 55 0 E
Solai, Kenya .... 54 B4 0 2N 36 12 E
Solan, India .... 42 D7 30 55N 77 7 E
Solano, Phil. .... 37 A6 16 31N 121 15 E
Solapur, India .... 40 L9 17 43N 75 56 E
Soldotna, U.S.A. 68 B4 60 29N 151 3W
Soléa, Cyprus .... 25 D12 35 5N 33 4 E
Soledad, Colombia 92 A4 10 55N 74 46W
Soledad, U.S.A. 78 J5 36 26N 121 20W
Soledad, Venezuela 92 B6 8 10N 63 34W
Solent, The, U.K. 13 G6 50 45N 1 25W
Solfonn, Norway .... 9 F12 60 2N 6 57 E
Solhan, Turkey .... 44 B4 38 57N 41 3 E
Soligalich, Russia .... 18 C7 59 5N 42 10 E
Soligorsk = Salihorsk, Belarus . 17 B14 52 51N 27 27 E
Solihull, U.K. 13 E6 52 26N 1 47W
Solikamsk, Russia .... 18 C10 59 38N 56 50 E
Solila, Madag. .... 57 C8 21 25S 46 37 E
Solimões = Amazonas →,
   S. Amer. 93 D9 0 5S 50 0W
Solingen, Germany .... 16 C4 51 10N 7 5 E
Sollefteå, Sweden .... 8 E17 63 12N 17 20 E
Sóller, Spain .... 24 B9 39 46N 2 43 E
Solo →, Indonesia .... 37 G15 6 47S 112 22 E
Sologne, France .... 20 C4 47 40N 1 45 E
Solok, Indonesia .... 36 E2 0 45S 100 40 E
Sololá, Guatemala 88 D1 14 49N 91 10W
Solomon, N. Fork →, U.S.A. . 80 F5 39 29N 98 26W
Solomon, S. Fork →, U.S.A. . 80 F5 39 25N 99 12W
Solomon Is. ■, Pac. Oc. .... 64 H7 6 0S 155 0 E
Solon, China .... 33 B7 46 32N 121 10 E
Solon Springs, U.S.A. 80 B9 46 22N 91 49W
Solor, Indonesia .... 37 F6 8 27S 123 0 E
Solothurn, Switz. .... 20 C7 47 13N 7 32 E
Šolta, Croatia .... 22 C7 43 24N 16 15 E
Solṭānābād, Khorāsān, Iran .. 45 C8 34 13N 59 58 E
Solṭānābād, Khorāsān, Iran .. 45 B8 36 29N 58 5 E
Solunska Glava, Macedonia .. 23 D9 41 44N 21 31 E
Solvang, U.S.A. 79 L6 34 36N 120 8W
Solvay, U.S.A. 85 C8 43 3N 76 13W
Sölvesborg, Sweden .... 9 H16 56 5N 14 35 E
Solvychegodsk, Russia .... 18 B8 61 21N 46 56 E
Solway Firth, U.K. 12 C4 54 49N 3 35W
Solwezi, Zambia .... 55 E2 12 11S 26 21 E
Sōma, Japan .... 30 F10 37 40N 140 50 E
Soma, Turkey .... 23 E12 39 10N 27 35 E
Somabhula, Zimbabwe .... 57 B4 19 42S 29 40 E
Somali Pen., Africa .... 48 F8 7 0N 46 0 E
Somali Rep. ■, Africa .... 47 F4 7 0N 47 0 E
Somalia = Somali Rep. ■, Africa 47 F4 7 0N 47 0 E
Sombor, Serbia & M. .... 23 B8 45 46N 19 9 E
Sombra, Canada 84 D2 42 43N 82 29W
Sombrerete, Mexico 86 C4 23 40N 103 40W
Sombrero, Anguilla 89 C7 18 37N 63 30W
Somdari, India .... 42 G5 25 47N 72 38 E
Somers, U.S.A. 76 B6 48 5N 114 13W
Somerset, Ky., U.S.A. 82 G3 37 5N 84 36W
Somerset, Mass., U.S.A. .. 85 E13 41 47N 71 8W
Somerset, Pa., U.S.A. 84 F5 40 1N 79 5W
Somerset □, U.K. 13 F5 51 9N 3 0W
Somerset East, S. Africa .... 56 E4 32 42S 25 35 E
Somerset I., Canada 68 A10 73 30N 93 0W
Somerset West, S. Africa .. 56 E2 34 8S 18 50 E
Somersworth, U.S.A. 85 C14 43 16N 70 52W
Somerton, U.S.A. 77 K6 32 36N 114 43W
Somerville, U.S.A. 85 F10 40 35N 74 38W
Someş →, Romania .... 17 D12 47 49N 22 43 E
Somme →, France .... 20 A4 50 11N 1 38 E
Somnath, India .... 42 J4 20 53N 70 22 E
Somosierra, Puerto de, Spain 21 B4 41 4N 3 35W
Somoto, Nic. 88 D2 13 28N 86 37W
Somport, Puerto de, Spain .. 20 E3 42 48N 0 31W
Son →, India .... 43 G11 25 42N 84 52 E
Son Ha, Vietnam .... 38 E7 15 3N 108 34 E
Son Hoa, Vietnam .... 38 F7 13 2N 108 58 E
Son La, Vietnam .... 38 B4 21 20N 103 50 E
Son Serra, Spain .... 24 B10 39 43N 3 13 E
Son Tay, Vietnam .... 38 B5 21 8N 105 30 E
Soná, Panama 88 E3 8 0N 81 20W
Sonamarg, India .... 43 B6 34 18N 75 21 E
Sonamukhi, India .... 43 H12 23 18N 87 27 E
Sonar →, India .... 43 G8 24 24N 79 56 E
Sŏnch'ŏn, N. Korea .... 35 E13 39 48N 124 55 E
Sondags →, S. Africa .... 56 E4 33 44S 25 51 E
Sondar, India .... 43 C6 33 28N 75 56 E
Sønderborg, Denmark .... 9 J13 54 55N 9 49 E
Sóndrio, Italy .... 20 C8 46 10N 9 52 E
Sone, Mozam. .... 55 F3 17 23S 34 55 E
Sonepur, India .... 41 J13 20 55N 83 50 E
Song Cau, Vietnam .... 38 F7 13 27N 109 18 E
Song Xian, China .... 34 G7 34 12N 112 8 E
Songan, Indonesia .... 37 J18 8 13S 115 24 E
Songch'ŏn, N. Korea .... 35 E14 39 12N 126 15 E
Songea, Tanzania .... 55 E4 10 40S 35 40 E
Songgang, China .... 33 F10 22 46N 113 50 E
Songhua Hu, China .... 35 C14 43 35N 126 50 E
Songhua Jiang →, China .... 33 B8 47 45N 132 30 E
Songimvelo △, S. Africa .... 57 D5 25 50S 31 2 E
Songjin, N. Korea .... 35 D15 40 40N 129 10 E
Songjŏng-ni, S. Korea .... 35 G14 35 8N 126 47 E
Songkhla, Thailand .... 39 J3 7 13N 100 37 E
Songnim, N. Korea .... 35 E13 38 45N 125 39 E
Songo, Mozam. .... 53 H6 15 34S 32 38 E
Songo, Sudan .... 51 G10 9 47N 24 21 E
Songpan, China .... 32 C5 32 40N 103 30 E
Songwe, Dem. Rep. of the Congo 54 C2 3 20S 26 16 E
Songwe →, Africa .... 55 D3 9 44S 33 58 E
Sonhat, India .... 43 H10 23 29N 82 31 E
Sonid Youqi, China .... 34 C7 42 45N 112 48 E
Sonipat, India .... 42 E7 29 0N 77 5 E
Sonkach, India .... 42 H7 22 59N 76 21 E
Sonmiani, Pakistan .... 42 G2 25 25N 66 26 E
Sonmiani B., Pakistan .... 42 G2 25 15N 66 30 E
Sono →, Brazil 93 E9 9 58S 48 11W
Sonoma, U.S.A. 78 G4 38 18N 122 28W
Sonora, U.S.A. 78 H6 37 59N 120 23W
Sonora, Tex., U.S.A. 81 K4 30 34N 100 39W
Sonora □, Mexico 86 B2 29 0N 111 0W
Sonora →, Mexico 86 B2 28 50N 111 33W
Sonoran Desert, U.S.A. 79 L12 33 40N 114 15W

Sonoyta, Mexico 86 A2 31 51N 112 50W
Sŏnsan, S. Korea .... 35 F15 36 14N 128 17 E
Sonsonate, El Salv. 88 D2 13 43N 89 44W
Soochow = Suzhou, China .. 33 C7 31 19N 120 38 E
Sooke, Canada 78 B3 48 13N 123 43W
Sop Hao, Laos .... 38 B5 20 33N 104 27 E
Sop Prap, Thailand .... 38 D2 17 53N 99 20 E
Sopi, Indonesia .... 37 D7 2 34N 128 28 E
Sopot, Poland .... 17 A10 54 27N 18 31 E
Sopron, Hungary .... 17 E9 47 45N 16 32 E
Sopur, India .... 43 B6 34 18N 74 27 E
Sør-Rondane, Antarctica .... 5 D4 72 0S 25 0 E
Sorah, Pakistan .... 42 F3 27 13N 68 56 E
Soraon, India .... 43 G9 25 37N 81 51 E
Sorel-Tracy, Canada 72 C5 46 0N 73 10W
Sórgono, Italy .... 22 D3 40 1N 9 6 E
Soria, Spain 21 B4 41 43N 2 32W
Soriano, Uruguay 94 C4 33 24S 58 19W
Sorkh, Kuh-e, Iran .... 45 C8 35 40N 58 30 E
Soroca, Moldova .... 17 D15 48 8N 28 12 E
Sorocaba, Brazil 95 A6 23 31S 47 27W
Sorochinsk, Russia .... 18 D9 52 26N 53 10 E
Soroki = Soroca, Moldova .. 17 D15 48 8N 28 12 E
Sorong, Indonesia .... 37 E8 0 55S 131 15 E
Soroni, Greece .... 25 C10 36 21N 28 1 E
Soroti, Uganda .... 54 B3 1 43N 33 35 E
Sørøya, Norway .... 8 A20 70 40N 22 30 E
Sørøysundet, Norway .... 8 A20 70 25N 23 0 E
Sorrell, Australia .... 63 G4 42 47S 147 34 E
Sorsele, Sweden .... 8 D17 65 31N 17 30 E
Sorsogon, Phil. .... 37 B6 13 0N 124 0 E
Sortavala, Russia .... 18 B5 61 42N 30 41 E
Sortland, Norway .... 8 B16 68 42N 15 25 E
Sŏsan, S. Korea .... 35 F14 36 47N 126 27 E
Soscumica, L., Canada 72 B4 50 15N 77 27W
Sosnogorsk, Russia .... 18 B9 63 37N 53 51 E
Sosnowiec, Poland .... 17 C10 50 20N 19 10 E
Sossus Vlei, Namibia .... 56 C2 24 40S 15 23 E
Sōsura, N. Korea .... 35 C16 42 16N 130 36 E
Sot →, India .... 43 F8 27 27N 79 37 E
Sotkamo, Finland .... 8 D23 64 8N 28 23 E
Soto la Marina →, Mexico .. 87 C5 23 40N 97 40W
Sotuta, Mexico 87 C7 20 29N 89 43W
Souanké, Congo .... 52 D2 2 10N 14 3 E
Souderton, U.S.A. 85 F9 40 19N 75 19W
Soúdha, Greece .... 25 D6 35 29N 24 4 E
Soúdhas, Kólpos, Greece .... 25 D6 35 25N 24 10 E
Soufrière, Guadeloupe .... 88 b 16 5N 61 40W
Soufrière, St. Lucia .... 89 f 13 51N 61 3W
Soufrière Bay, Domin. .... 89 f 15 53N 61 6W
Soukhouma, Laos .... 38 E5 14 38N 105 48 E
Sŏul, S. Korea .... 35 F14 37 31N 126 58 E
Sound, The, U.K. 13 G3 50 20N 4 10W
Sources, Mt. aux, Lesotho .. 57 D4 28 45S 28 50 E
Soure, Brazil 93 D9 0 35S 48 30W
Souris, Man., Canada 71 D8 49 40N 100 20W
Souris, P.E.I., Canada 73 C7 46 21N 62 15W
Souris →, Canada 80 A5 49 40N 99 34W
Sousa, Brazil 93 E11 6 45S 38 10W
Sousse, Tunisia .... 51 A8 35 50N 10 38 E
Sout →, S. Africa .... 56 E3 31 35S 18 24 E
South Africa ■, Africa .... 56 E3 32 0S 23 0 E
South America 90 E5 10 0S 60 0W
South Aulatsivik I., Canada .. 73 A7 56 45N 61 30W
South Australia □, Australia 63 E2 32 0S 139 0 E
South Ayrshire □, U.K. 11 F4 55 18N 4 41W
South Baldy, U.S.A. 77 J10 33 59N 107 11W
South Bass I., U.S.A. 84 E2 41 38N 82 53W
South Bend, Ind., U.S.A. .. 82 E2 41 41N 86 15W
South Bend, Wash., U.S.A. . 78 D3 46 40N 123 48W
South Boston, U.S.A. 83 G6 36 42N 78 54W
South Branch, Canada 73 C8 47 55N 59 2W
South Brook, Canada 73 C8 49 26N 56 5W
South Carolina □, U.S.A. .. 83 J5 34 0N 81 0W
South Charleston, U.S.A. .. 82 F5 38 22N 81 44W
South China Sea, Asia .... 36 C4 10 0N 113 0 E
South Cumberland Is. △,
   Australia .... 62 J7 20 42S 149 11 E
South Dakota □, U.S.A. 80 C5 44 15N 100 0W
South Deerfield, U.S.A. 85 D12 42 29N 72 37W
South Downs, U.K. 13 G7 50 52N 0 25W
South East C., Australia .... 63 G4 43 40S 146 50 E
South-East Indian Rise, Ind. Oc. 5 B10 43 0S 80 0 E
South East Is., Australia .... 61 F3 34 17S 123 30 E
South Esk →, U.K. 11 E6 56 43N 2 31W
South Foreland, U.K. .... 13 F9 51 8N 1 24 E
South Fork American →, U.S.A. 78 G5 38 45N 121 5W
South Fork Feather →, U.S.A. 78 F5 39 17N 121 36W
South Fork Grand →, U.S.A. 80 C3 45 43N 102 17W
South Fork Republican →, U.S.A. 80 E4 40 3N 101 31W
South Georgia, Antarctica .. 96 G9 54 30S 37 0W
South Gloucestershire □, U.K. 13 F5 51 32N 2 28W
South Hadley, U.S.A. 85 D12 42 16N 72 35W
South Haven, U.S.A. 82 D2 42 24N 86 16W
South Henik L., Canada 71 A9 61 30N 97 20W
South Honshu Ridge, Pac. Oc. 64 E6 23 0N 143 0 E
South Horr, Kenya .... 54 B4 2 12N 36 56 E
South I., Kenya .... 54 B4 2 35N 36 35 E
South I., N.Z. .... 59 L3 44 0S 170 0 E
South Indian Lake, Canada . 71 B9 56 47N 98 56W
South Invercargill, N.Z. .... 59 M2 46 26S 168 23 E
South Island △, Kenya .... 54 B4 2 39N 36 35 E
South Kitui △, Kenya .... 54 C4 1 48S 38 46 E
South Knife →, Canada 71 B10 58 55N 94 37W
South Koel →, India .... 43 H11 22 32N 85 14 E
South Korea ■, Asia .... 35 G15 36 0N 128 0 E
South Lake Tahoe, U.S.A. .. 78 G6 38 57N 119 59W
South Lanarkshire □, U.K. . 11 F5 55 37N 3 53W
South Loup →, U.S.A. 80 E5 41 4N 98 39W
South Luangwa △, Zambia . 55 E3 13 0S 31 20 E
South Magnetic Pole, Antarctica 5 C9 64 8S 138 8 E
South Milwaukee, U.S.A. .. 82 D2 42 55N 87 52W
South Molton, U.K. 13 F4 51 1N 3 51W
South Moose L., Canada 71 C8 53 46N 100 8W
South Nahanni →, Canada . 70 A4 61 3N 123 21W
South Nation →, Canada .. 85 A9 45 34N 75 6W
South Natuna Is. = Natuna
   Selatan, Kepulauan, Indonesia 36 D3 2 45N 109 0 E
South Negril Pt., Jamaica .. 88 a 18 14N 78 30W
South Orkney Is., Antarctica 5 C18 63 0S 45 0W
South Ossetia □, Georgia .. 19 F7 42 21N 44 2 E
South Pagai, I. = Pagai Selatan,
   Pulau, Indonesia .... 36 E2 3 0S 100 15 E
South Paris, U.S.A. 85 B14 44 14N 70 31W
South Pittsburg, U.S.A. 83 H3 35 1N 85 42W
South Platte →, U.S.A. 80 E4 41 7N 100 42W
South Pole, Antarctica .... 5 E 90 0S 0 0 E

South Porcupine, Canada 72 C3 48 30N 81 12W
South Portland, U.S.A. 83 D10 43 38N 70 15W
South Pt., U.S.A. 84 B1 44 52N 83 19W
South Pt., Barbados .... 89 g 13 2N 59 32W
South River, Canada 72 C4 45 52N 79 23W
South River, U.S.A. 85 F10 40 27N 74 23W
South Ronaldsay, U.K. 11 C6 58 48N 2 58W
South Sandwich Is., Antarctica 5 B1 57 0S 27 0W
South Saskatchewan →, Canada 71 C7 53 15N 105 5W
South Seal →, Canada 71 B9 58 48N 98 8W
South Shetland Is., Antarctica 5 C18 62 0S 59 0W
South Shields, U.K. 12 C6 55 0N 1 25W
South Sioux City, U.S.A. .. 80 D6 42 28N 96 24W
South Taranaki Bight, N.Z. 59 H5 39 40S 174 5 E
South Thompson →, Canada 70 C4 50 40N 120 20W
South Twin I., Canada 72 B4 53 7N 79 52W
South Tyne →, U.K. 12 C5 54 59N 2 8W
South Uist, U.K. 11 D1 57 20N 7 15W
South West Africa = Namibia ■,
   Africa .... 56 C2 22 0S 18 9 E
South West C., Australia .... 63 G4 43 34S 146 3 E
South Williamsport, U.S.A. 84 E8 41 13N 77 0W
South Yorkshire □, U.K. .. 12 D6 53 27N 1 36W
Southampton, U.K. 13 G6 50 54N 1 23W
Southampton, U.S.A. 85 F12 40 53N 72 23W
Southampton □, U.K. 13 G6 50 54N 1 23W
Southampton I., Canada 69 B11 64 30N 84 0W
Southaven, U.S.A. 81 H9 34 59N 90 2W
Southbank, Canada 70 C3 54 2N 125 46W
Southbridge, N.Z. .... 59 K4 43 48S 172 16 E
Southbridge, U.S.A. 85 D12 42 5N 72 2W
Southeast Pacific Basin, Pac. Oc. 5 C15 16 30S 92 0W
Southend, Canada 71 B8 56 19N 103 22W
Southend-on-Sea, U.K. .... 13 F8 51 32N 0 44 E
Southend-on-Sea □, U.K. .. 13 F8 51 32N 0 44 E
Southern = Yuzhnyy □, Russia 28 E5 44 0N 40 0 E
Southern □, Malawi .... 55 F4 15 0S 35 0 E
Southern □, Zambia .... 55 F2 16 20S 26 20 E
Southern Alps, N.Z. .... 59 K3 43 41S 170 11 E
Southern Cross, Australia .. 61 F2 31 12S 119 15 E
Southern Indian L., Canada . 71 B9 57 10N 98 30W
Southern Ocean, Antarctica 5 C6 62 0S 60 0 E
Southern Pines, U.S.A. 83 H6 35 11N 79 24W
Southern Uplands, U.K. 11 F5 55 28N 3 52W
Southington, U.S.A. 85 E12 41 36N 72 53W
Southland □, N.Z. .... 59 L1 45 30S 168 0 E
Southold, U.S.A. 85 E12 41 4N 72 26W
Southport, Australia .... 63 D5 27 58S 153 25 E
Southport, Fla., U.S.A. 83 K3 30 17N 85 38W
Southport, N.Y., U.S.A. 84 D8 42 3N 76 49W
Southport, U.K. 12 D4 53 39N 3 0W
Southwest →, Australia .... 63 G4 43 8S 146 5 E
Southwest C., N.Z. .... 59 M1 47 17S 167 28 E
Southwold, U.K. .... 13 E9 52 20N 1 41 E
Southwood △, Australia .... 63 D5 27 48S 150 8 E
Soutpansberg, S. Africa .... 57 C4 23 0S 29 30 E
Sovetsk, Kaliningrad, Russia . 9 J19 55 6N 21 50 E
Sovetsk, Kirov, Russia .... 18 C8 57 38N 48 53 E
Sovetskaya Gavan = Vanino,
   Russia .... 29 E15 48 50N 140 5 E
Soweto, S. Africa .... 57 D4 26 14S 27 54 E
Sōya-Kaikyō = La Perouse Str.,
   Asia .... 30 B11 45 40N 142 0 E
Sōya-Misaki, Japan .... 30 B10 45 30N 141 55 E
Sozh →, Belarus .... 17 B16 51 57N 30 48 E
Spa, Belgium .... 15 D5 50 29N 5 53 E
Spain ■, Europe 21 B4 39 0N 4 0W
Spalding, Australia .... 63 E2 33 30S 138 37 E
Spalding, U.K. 12 E7 52 48N 0 9W
Spangler, U.S.A. 84 F6 40 39N 78 48W
Spanish, Canada 72 C3 46 12N 82 20W
Spanish Fork, U.S.A. 76 F8 40 7N 111 39W
Spanish Town, Br. Virgin Is. 89 e 17 43N 64 26W
Spanish Town, Jamaica .... 88 a 18 0N 76 57W
Sparks, U.S.A. 78 F7 39 32N 119 45W
Sparta = Spárti, Greece .... 23 F10 37 5N 22 25 E
Sparta, Mich., U.S.A. 82 D3 43 10N 85 42W
Sparta, N.J., U.S.A. 85 E10 41 2N 74 38W
Sparta, Wis., U.S.A. 80 D9 43 56N 90 49W
Spartanburg, U.S.A. 84 E5 41 49N 79 41W
Spárti, Greece .... 23 F10 37 5N 22 25 E
Spartivento, C., Calabria, Italy 22 F7 37 55N 16 4 E
Spartivento, C., Sard., Italy 22 E3 38 53N 8 50 E
Sparwood, Canada 70 D6 49 44N 114 53W
Spassk Dalniy, Russia .... 29 E14 44 40N 132 48 E
Spátha, Ákra, Greece .... 25 D5 35 42N 23 43 E
Spatsizi →, Canada 70 B3 57 42N 128 7W
Spatsizi Plateau Wilderness △,
   Canada 70 B3 57 40N 128 0W
Spean →, U.K. 11 E4 56 55N 4 59W
Spearfish, U.S.A. 80 C3 44 30N 103 52W
Spearman, U.S.A. 81 G4 36 12N 101 12W
Speculator, U.S.A. 85 C10 43 30N 74 25W
Speightstown, Barbados .... 89 g 13 15N 59 39W
Spence Bay = Taloyoak, Canada 68 B10 69 32N 93 32W
Spencer, Idaho, U.S.A. 76 D7 44 22N 112 11W
Spencer, Iowa, U.S.A. 80 D7 43 9N 95 9W
Spencer, N.Y., U.S.A. 85 D8 42 13N 76 30W
Spencer, Nebr., U.S.A. 80 D5 42 53N 98 42W
Spencer, C., Australia .... 63 F2 35 20S 136 53 E
Spencer B., Namibia .... 56 D1 25 30S 14 47 E
Spencer G., Australia .... 63 E2 34 0S 137 20 E
Spencerville, Canada 85 B9 44 51N 75 33W
Spences Bridge, Canada 70 C4 50 25N 121 20W
Spennymoor, U.K. 12 C6 54 42N 1 36W
Spenser Mts., N.Z. .... 59 K4 42 15S 172 45 E
Sperrin Mts., U.K. 10 B5 54 50N 7 0W
Spey →, U.K. 11 D5 57 40N 3 6W
Speyer, Germany .... 16 D5 49 29N 8 25 E
Spezand, Pakistan .... 42 E2 29 59N 67 0 E
Spili, Greece .... 25 D6 35 13N 24 31 E
Spīn Būldak, Afghan. .... 42 D2 31 1N 66 25 E
Spinalónga, Greece .... 25 D7 35 18N 25 44 E
Spirit Lake, U.S.A. 78 D4 46 15N 122 9W
Spirit River, Canada 70 B5 55 45N 118 50W
Spiritwood, Canada 71 C7 53 24N 107 33W
Spithead, U.K. 13 G6 50 45N 1 10W
Spitzbergen = Svalbard, Arctic 4 B8 78 0N 17 0 E
Spjelkavik, Norway .... 9 E12 62 28N 6 22 E
Split, Croatia .... 22 C7 43 31N 16 26 E
Split L., Canada 71 B9 56 8N 96 15W
Split Lake, Canada 71 B9 56 8N 96 15W
Spofford, U.S.A. 81 L4 29 10N 100 25W
Spokane, U.S.A. 76 C5 47 40N 117 24W

Spoleto, Italy .... 22 C5 42 44N 12 44 E
Spooner, U.S.A. 80 C9 45 50N 91 53W
Sporyy Navolok, Mys, Russia 28 B7 75 50N 68 40 E
Sprague, U.S.A. 76 C5 47 18N 117 59W
Spratly I., S. China Sea .... 36 C4 8 38N 111 55 E
Spratly Is., S. China Sea .... 36 C4 8 20N 112 0 E
Spray, U.S.A. 76 D4 44 50N 119 48W
Spree →, Germany .... 16 B7 52 32N 13 13 E
Sprengisandur, Iceland 8 D5 64 52N 18 7W
Spring City, U.S.A. 85 F9 40 11N 75 33W
Spring Creek, U.S.A. 76 F6 40 45N 115 38W
Spring Garden, U.S.A. 78 F6 39 52N 120 47W
Spring Hall, Barbados .... 89 g 13 18N 59 36W
Spring Hill, U.S.A. 83 L4 28 27N 82 41W
Spring Mts., U.S.A. 77 H6 36 0N 115 45W
Spring Valley, U.S.A. 79 N10 32 45N 117 5W
Springbok, S. Africa .... 56 D2 29 42S 17 54 E
Springboro, U.S.A. 84 E4 41 48N 80 22W
Springdale, Canada 73 C8 49 30N 56 6W
Springdale, U.S.A. 81 G7 36 11N 94 8W
Springer, U.S.A. 81 G2 36 22N 104 36W
Springerville, U.S.A. 77 J9 34 8N 109 17W
Springfield, Canada 84 D4 42 50N 80 56W
Springfield, N.Z. .... 59 K3 43 19S 171 56 E
Springfield, Colo., U.S.A. . 81 G3 37 24N 102 37W
Springfield, Ill., U.S.A. 80 F10 39 48N 89 39W
Springfield, Mass., U.S.A. . 85 D12 42 6N 72 35W
Springfield, Mo., U.S.A. .. 81 G8 37 13N 93 17W
Springfield, Ohio, U.S.A. .. 82 F4 39 55N 83 49W
Springfield, Oreg., U.S.A. . 76 D2 44 3N 123 1W
Springfield, Tenn., U.S.A. . 83 G2 36 31N 86 53W
Springfield, Vt., U.S.A. 85 C12 43 18N 72 29W
Springfontein, S. Africa .... 56 E4 30 15S 25 40 E
Springhill, Canada 73 C7 45 40N 64 4W
Springhill, U.S.A. 81 J8 33 0N 93 28W
Springhouse, Canada 70 C4 51 56N 122 7W
Springs, S. Africa .... 57 D4 26 13S 28 25 E
Springsure, Australia .... 62 C4 24 8S 148 6 E
Springvale, U.S.A. 85 C14 43 28N 70 48W
Springville, Calif., U.S.A. . 78 J8 36 8N 118 49W
Springville, N.Y., U.S.A. .. 84 D6 42 31N 78 40W
Springville, Utah, U.S.A. .. 76 F8 40 10N 111 37W
Springwater, U.S.A. 84 D7 42 38N 77 35W
Spruce-Creek, U.S.A. 84 F6 40 36N 78 9W
Spruce Knob-Seneca Rocks △,
   U.S.A. 82 F6 38 50N 79 30W
Spruce Mt., U.S.A. 85 B12 44 12N 72 19W
Spur, U.S.A. 81 J4 33 28N 100 52W
Spurn Hd., U.K. .... 12 D8 53 35N 0 8 E
Spuzzum, Canada 70 D4 49 37N 121 23W
Squam L., U.S.A. 85 C13 43 45N 71 32W
Squamish, Canada 70 D4 49 45N 123 10W
Square Islands, Canada 73 B8 52 47N 55 47W
Squires, Mt., Australia .... 61 E4 26 14S 127 28 E
Srbija = Serbia □, Serbia & M. 23 C9 43 30N 21 0 E
Sre Ambel, Cambodia .... 39 G4 11 8N 103 46 E
Sre Khtum, Cambodia .... 39 F6 12 10N 106 52 E
Sre Umbell = Sre Ambel,
   Cambodia .... 39 G4 11 8N 103 46 E
Srebrenica, Bos.-H. .... 23 B8 44 6N 19 18 E
Sredinny Ra. = Sredinnyy
   Khrebet, Russia .... 29 D16 57 0N 160 0 E
Sredinnyy Khrebet, Russia . 29 D16 57 0N 160 0 E
Srednekolymsk, Russia .... 29 C16 67 27N 153 40 E
Srem, Poland .... 17 B9 52 6N 17 2 E
Sremska Mitrovica, Serbia & M. 23 B8 44 59N 19 38 E
Srepok →, Cambodia .... 38 F6 13 33N 106 16 E
Sretensk, Russia .... 29 D12 52 10N 117 40 E
Sri Lanka ■, Asia .... 40 R12 7 30N 80 50 E
Srikakulam, India .... 41 K13 18 14N 83 58 E
Srinagar, India .... 43 B6 34 5N 74 50 E
Srono, Indonesia .... 37 J17 8 24S 114 16 E
Staaten →, Australia .... 62 B3 16 24S 141 17 E
Staaten River △, Australia . 62 B3 16 15S 142 40 E
Stade, Germany .... 16 B5 53 35N 9 29 E
Stadskanaal, Neths. .... 15 A6 53 4N 6 55 E
Staffa, U.K. 11 E2 56 27N 6 21W
Stafford, U.K. 12 E5 52 49N 2 7W
Stafford, U.S.A. 81 G5 37 58N 98 36W
Stafford Springs, U.S.A. .. 85 E12 41 57N 72 18W
Staffordshire □, U.K. 12 E5 52 53N 2 10W
Staines, U.K. 13 F7 51 26N 0 29W
Stakhanov, Ukraine .... 19 E6 48 35N 38 40 E
Stalis, Greece .... 25 D7 35 17N 25 25 E
Stalowa Wola, Poland .... 17 C12 50 34N 22 3 E
Stalybridge, U.K. 12 D5 53 28N 2 3W
Stamford, Australia .... 62 C3 21 15S 143 46 E
Stamford, U.K. 12 E7 52 39N 0 29W
Stamford, Conn., U.S.A. .. 85 E11 41 3N 73 32W
Stamford, N.Y., U.S.A. 85 D10 42 25N 74 38W
Stamford, Tex., U.S.A. 81 J5 32 57N 99 48W
Stampriet, Namibia .... 56 C2 24 20S 18 28 E
Stamps, U.S.A. 81 J8 33 22N 93 30W
Standerton, S. Africa .... 57 D4 26 55S 29 7 E
Standish, U.S.A. 82 D4 43 59N 83 57W
Stanford, S. Africa .... 56 E2 34 26S 19 29 E
Stanger, S. Africa .... 57 D5 29 27S 31 14 E
Stanislaus →, U.S.A. 78 H5 37 40N 121 14W
Stanke Dimitrov, Bulgaria . 23 C10 42 17N 23 9 E
Stanley, Australia .... 63 G4 40 46S 145 19 E
Stanley, China .... 33 G11 22 13N 114 12 E
Stanley, Falk. Is. 96 G5 51 40S 59 51W
Stanley, U.K. 12 C6 54 53N 1 41W
Stanley, Idaho, U.S.A. 76 D6 44 13N 114 56W
Stanley, N. Dak., U.S.A. .. 80 A3 48 19N 102 23W
Stanley, N.Y., U.S.A. 84 D7 42 48N 77 6W
Stanley Mission, Canada .. 71 B8 55 25N 104 33W
Stanovoy Khrebet, Russia . 29 D13 55 0N 130 0 E
Stanovoy Ra. = Stanovoy
   Khrebet, Russia .... 29 D13 55 0N 130 0 E
Stansmore Ra., Australia .. 60 D4 21 23S 128 33 E
Stansted, London ✈ (STN), U.K. 13 F8 51 54N 0 14 E
Stanthorpe, Australia .... 63 D5 28 36S 151 59 E
Stanton, U.S.A. 81 J4 32 8N 101 48W
Stanwood, U.S.A. 78 B4 48 15N 122 23W
Staples, U.S.A. 80 B7 46 21N 94 48W
Star City, Canada 71 C8 52 50N 104 20W
Star Lake, U.S.A. 85 B9 44 10N 75 2W
Stara Planina, Bulgaria .... 23 C10 43 15N 23 0 E
Stara Zagora, Bulgaria .... 23 C11 42 26N 25 39 E
Starachowice, Poland .... 17 C11 51 3N 21 2 E
Staraya Russa, Russia .... 18 C5 57 58N 31 23 E
Starbuck I., Kiribati 65 H12 5 37S 155 55W
Starcke △, Australia .... 62 A3 14 56S 145 2 E
Stargard Szczeciński, Poland 16 B8 53 20N 15 0 E
Staritsa, Russia .... 18 C5 56 33N 34 55 E

Starke, U.S.A. 83 L4 29 57N 82 7W
Starogard Gdański, Poland .. 17 B10 53 59N 18 30 E
Starokonstantinov =
  Starokonstyantyniv, Ukraine 17 D14 49 48N 27 10 E
Starokonstyantyniv, Ukraine 17 D14 49 48N 27 10 E
Start Pt., U.K. 13 G4 50 13N 3 39W
Staryy Chartoriysk, Ukraine 17 C13 51 15N 25 54 E
Staryy Oskol, Russia .... 19 D6 51 19N 37 55 E
State College, U.S.A. 84 F7 40 48N 77 52W
Stateline, U.S.A. 78 G7 38 57N 119 56W
Staten, I. = Estados, I. de Los,
  Argentina 96 G4 54 40S 64 30W
Staten I., U.S.A. 85 F10 40 35N 74 9W
Statesboro, U.S.A. 83 J5 32 27N 81 47W
Statesville, U.S.A. 83 H5 35 47N 80 53W
Stauffer, U.S.A. 79 L7 34 45N 119 3W
Staunton, Ill., U.S.A. 80 F10 39 1N 89 47W
Staunton, Va., U.S.A. 82 F6 38 9N 79 4W
Stavanger, Norway .... 9 G11 58 57N 5 40 E
Staveley, N.Z. .... 59 K3 43 40S 171 32 E
Stavelot, Belgium .... 15 D5 50 23N 5 55 E
Stavern, Norway .... 9 G14 59 0N 10 1 E
Stavoren, Neths. .... 15 B5 52 53N 5 22 E
Stavropol, Russia .... 19 E7 45 5N 42 0 E
Stavros, Cyprus .... 25 D11 35 1N 32 38 E
Stavrós, Greece .... 25 D6 35 12N 24 45 E
Stavros, Ákra, Greece .... 25 D6 35 26N 24 58 E
Stawell, Australia .... 63 F3 37 5S 142 47 E
Stawell →, Australia .... 62 C3 20 20S 142 55 E
Stayner, Canada 84 B4 44 25N 80 5W
Stayton, U.S.A. 76 D2 44 48N 122 48W
Steamboat Springs, U.S.A. 76 F10 40 29N 106 50W
Steele, U.S.A. 80 B5 46 51N 99 55W
Steelton, U.S.A. 84 F8 40 14N 76 50W
Steen River, Canada 70 B5 59 40N 117 12W
Steens Mt., U.S.A. 76 E4 42 35N 118 40W
Steenwijk, Neths. .... 15 B6 52 47N 6 7 E
Steep Pt., Australia .... 61 E1 26 8S 113 8 E
Steep Rock, Canada 71 C9 51 30N 98 48W
Stefanie L. = Chew Bahir,
  Ethiopia .... 47 G2 4 40N 36 50 E
Stefansson Bay, Antarctica 5 C5 67 20S 59 8 E
Steiermark □, Austria .... 16 E8 47 26N 15 0 E
Steilacoom, U.S.A. 78 C4 47 10N 122 36W
Steilrandberge, Namibia 56 B1 45 15S 13 20 E
Steinbach, Canada 71 D9 49 32N 96 40W
Steinhausen, Namibia .... 56 C2 21 49S 18 20 E
Steinkjer, Norway .... 8 D14 64 1N 11 31 E
Steinkopf, S. Africa .... 56 D2 29 18S 17 43 E
Stellarton, Canada 73 C7 45 32N 62 30W
Stellenbosch, S. Africa .... 56 E2 33 58S 18 50 E
Stendal, Germany .... 16 B6 52 36N 11 53 E
Steornabhaigh = Stornoway,
  U.K. 11 C2 58 13N 6 23W
Stepanakert = Xankändi,
  Azerbaijan .... 19 G8 39 52N 46 49 E
Stephens Creek, Australia 63 E3 31 50S 141 30 E
Stephens I., Canada 70 C2 54 10N 130 45W
Stephens L., Canada 71 B9 56 32N 95 0W
Stephenville, Canada 73 C8 48 31N 58 35W
Stephenville, U.S.A. 81 J5 32 13N 98 12W
Steppe, Asia .... 26 D9 50 0N 50 0 E
Sterkstroom, S. Africa .... 56 E4 31 32S 26 32 E
Sterling, Colo., U.S.A. 80 E3 40 37N 103 13W
Sterling, Ill., U.S.A. 80 E10 41 48N 89 42W
Sterling, Kans., U.S.A. 80 F5 38 13N 98 12W
Sterling City, U.S.A. 81 K4 31 51N 101 0W
Sterling Heights, U.S.A. 82 D4 42 35N 83 0W
Sterling Run, U.S.A. 84 E6 41 25N 78 12W
Sterlitamak, Russia .... 18 D10 53 40N 56 0 E
Stérnes, Greece .... 25 D6 35 30N 24 9 E
Stettin = Szczecin, Poland 16 B8 53 27N 14 27 E
Stettiner Haff, Germany .. 16 B8 53 47N 14 15 E
Stettler, Canada 70 C6 52 19N 112 40W
Steubenville, U.S.A. 84 F4 40 22N 80 37W
Stevenage, U.K. 13 F7 51 55N 0 13W
Stevens Point, U.S.A. 80 C10 44 31N 89 34W
Stevenson, U.S.A. 78 E5 45 42N 121 53W
Stevenson L., Canada 71 C9 53 55N 96 0W
Stevensville, U.S.A. 76 C6 46 30N 114 5W
Stewart, Canada 70 B3 55 56N 129 57W
Stewart, U.S.A. 78 F7 39 5N 119 46W
Stewart →, Canada 68 B6 63 19N 139 26W
Stewart, C., Canada .... 62 A1 11 57S 134 56 E
Stewart, I., Chile 96 G2 54 50S 71 15W
Stewart I., N.Z. .... 59 M1 46 58S 167 54 E
Stewarts Point, U.S.A. 78 G3 38 39N 123 24W
Stewartville, U.S.A. 80 D8 43 51N 92 29W
Stewiacke, Canada 73 C7 45 9N 63 22W
Steynsburg, S. Africa .... 56 E4 31 15S 25 49 E
Steyr, Austria .... 16 D8 48 3N 14 25 E
Steytlerville, S. Africa .... 56 E3 33 17S 24 19 E
Stigler, U.S.A. 81 H7 35 15N 95 8W
Stikine →, Canada 70 B2 56 40N 132 30W
Stilfontein, S. Africa .... 56 D4 26 51S 26 50 E
Stillwater, N.Z. .... 59 K3 42 27S 171 20 E
Stillwater, Minn., U.S.A. 80 C8 45 3N 92 49W
Stillwater, N.Y., U.S.A. 85 D11 42 55N 73 41W
Stillwater, Okla., U.S.A. 81 G6 36 7N 97 4W
Stillwater Range, U.S.A. 76 G4 39 50N 118 5W
Stillwater Reservoir, U.S.A. 85 C9 43 54N 75 3W
Stilwell, U.S.A. 81 H7 35 49N 94 38W
Štip, Macedonia .... 23 D10 41 42N 22 10 E
Stirling, Canada 84 B7 44 18N 77 33W
Stirling, U.K. 11 E5 56 8N 3 57W
Stirling □, U.K. 11 E4 56 12N 4 18W
Stirling Ra., Australia .... 61 F2 34 23S 118 0 E
Stirling Range △, Australia 61 F2 34 26S 118 20 E
Stittsville, Canada 85 A9 45 15N 75 55W
Stjernøya, Norway .... 8 A20 70 20N 22 40 E
Stjørdalshalsen, Norway .. 8 E14 63 29N 10 51 E
Stockerau, Austria .... 16 D9 48 24N 16 12 E
Stockholm, Sweden .... 9 G18 59 20N 18 3 E
Stockport, U.K. 12 D5 53 25N 2 9W
Stocksbridge, U.K. 12 D6 53 29N 1 35W
Stockton, Calif., U.S.A. 78 H5 37 58N 121 17W
Stockton, Kans., U.S.A. 80 F5 39 26N 99 16W
Stockton, Mo., U.S.A. 81 G8 37 42N 93 48W
Stockton-on-Tees, U.K. .. 12 C6 54 35N 1 19W
Stockton-on-Tees □, U.K. 12 C6 54 35N 1 19W
Stockton Plateau, U.S.A. 81 K3 30 30N 102 30W
Stoeng Treng, Cambodia 38 F5 13 31N 105 58 E
Stoer, Pt. of, U.K. 11 C3 58 16N 5 23W
Stoke-on-Trent, U.K. 12 D5 53 1N 2 11W
Stoke-on-Trent □, U.K. .. 12 D5 53 1N 2 11W
Stokes △, Australia .... 61 E2 29 55S 115 6 E
Stokes Pt., Australia .... 63 G3 40 10S 143 56 E

Stokes Ra., Australia .... 60 C5 15 50S 130 50 E
Stokksnes, Iceland 8 D6 64 14N 14 58W
Stokmarknes, Norway .... 8 B16 68 34N 14 54 E
Stolac, Bos.-H. .... 23 C7 43 5N 17 59 E
Stolbovoy, Ostrov, Russia 29 B14 74 44N 135 14 E
Stolbtsy = Stowbtsy, Belarus 17 B14 53 30N 26 43 E
Stolin, Belarus .... 17 C14 51 53N 26 50 E
Stómion, Greece .... 25 D5 35 21N 23 32 E
Stone, U.K. 12 E5 52 55N 2 9W
Stoneboro, U.S.A. 84 E4 41 20N 80 7W
Stonehaven, U.K. 11 E6 56 59N 2 12W
Stonehenge, Australia .... 62 C3 24 22S 143 17 E
Stonehenge, U.K. 13 F6 51 9N 1 45W
Stonewall, Canada 71 C9 50 10N 97 19W
Stony L., Man., Canada .. 71 B9 58 51N 98 40W
Stony L., Ont., Canada .. 84 B6 44 30N 78 5W
Stony Point, U.S.A. 85 E11 41 14N 73 59W
Stony Pt., U.S.A. 85 C8 43 50N 76 18W
Stony Rapids, Canada .. 71 B7 59 16N 105 50W
Stony Tunguska = Tunguska,
  Podkamennaya →, Russia 29 C10 61 50N 90 13 E
Stonyford, U.S.A. 78 F4 39 23N 122 33W
Stora Lulevatten, Sweden 8 C18 67 10N 19 30 E
Storavan, Sweden .... 8 D18 65 45N 18 10 E
Stord, Norway .... 9 G11 59 52N 5 23 E
Store Bælt, Denmark .... 9 J14 55 20N 11 0 E
Storm B., Australia .... 63 G4 43 10S 147 30 E
Storm Lake, U.S.A. 80 D7 42 39N 95 13W
Stormberge, S. Africa .... 56 E4 31 16S 26 17 E
Stormsrivier, S. Africa .... 56 E3 33 59S 23 52 E
Stornoway, U.K. 11 C2 58 13N 6 23W
Storozhinets = Storozhynets,
  Ukraine .... 17 D13 48 14N 25 45 E
Storozhynets, Ukraine .. 17 D13 48 14N 25 45 E
Storrs, U.S.A. 85 E12 41 49N 72 15W
Storsjön, Sweden .... 8 E16 63 9N 14 30 E
Storuman, Sweden .... 8 D17 65 5N 17 10 E
Storuman, sjö, Sweden .. 8 D17 65 13N 16 50 E
Stouffville, Canada 84 C5 43 58N 79 15W
Stoughton, Canada 71 D8 49 40N 103 0W
Stour →, Dorset, U.K. .. 13 G6 50 43N 1 47W
Stour →, Kent, U.K. .... 13 F9 51 18N 1 22 E
Stour →, Suffolk, U.K. .. 13 F9 51 57N 1 4 E
Stourbridge, U.K. 13 E5 52 28N 2 8W
Stout L., Canada 71 C10 52 0N 94 40W
Stove Pipe Wells Village, U.S.A. 79 J9 36 35N 117 11W
Stow, U.S.A. 84 E3 41 10N 81 27W
Stowbtsy, Belarus .... 17 B14 53 30N 26 43 E
Stowmarket, U.K. .... 13 E9 52 12N 1 0 E
Strabane, U.K. 10 B4 54 50N 7 27W
Strahan, Australia .... 63 G4 42 9S 145 20 E
Stralsund, Germany .... 16 A7 54 18N 13 4 E
Strand, S. Africa .... 56 E2 34 9S 18 48 E
Stranda, Møre og Romsdal,
  Norway .... 9 E12 62 19N 6 58 E
Stranda, Nord-Trøndelag,
  Norway .... 8 E14 63 33N 10 14 E
Strangford L., U.K. 10 B6 54 30N 5 37W
Stranraer, U.K. 11 G3 54 54N 5 1W
Strasbourg, Canada 71 C8 51 4N 104 55W
Strasbourg, France .... 20 B7 48 35N 7 42 E
Stratford, Canada 84 C4 43 23N 81 0W
Stratford, N.Z. .... 59 H5 39 20S 174 19 E
Stratford, Calif., U.S.A. 78 J7 36 11N 119 49W
Stratford, Conn., U.S.A. 85 E11 41 12N 73 8W
Stratford, Tex., U.S.A. 81 G3 36 20N 102 4W
Stratford-upon-Avon, U.K. 13 E6 52 12N 1 42W
Strath Spey, U.K. 11 D5 57 9N 3 49W
Strathalbyn, Australia .... 63 F2 35 13S 138 53 E
Strathaven, U.K. 11 F4 55 40N 4 5W
Strathcona △, Canada .. 70 D3 49 38N 125 40W
Strathmore, Canada 70 C6 51 5N 113 18W
Strathmore, U.K. 11 E5 56 37N 3 7W
Strathmore, U.S.A. 78 J7 36 9N 119 4W
Strathnaver, Canada 70 C4 53 20N 122 33W
Strathpeffer, U.K. 11 D4 57 35N 4 32W
Strathroy, Canada 84 D3 42 58N 81 38W
Strathy Pt., U.K. 11 C4 58 36N 4 1W
Strattanville, U.S.A. 84 E5 41 12N 79 19W
Stratton, U.S.A. 85 A14 45 8N 70 26W
Stratton Mt., U.S.A. 85 C12 43 4N 72 55W
Straubing, Germany .... 16 D7 48 52N 12 34 E
Straumnes, Iceland 8 C2 66 26N 23 8W
Strawberry →, U.S.A. 76 F8 40 10N 110 24W
Streaky B., Australia .... 63 E1 32 48S 134 13 E
Streaky Bay, Australia .... 63 E1 32 51S 134 18 E
Streator, U.S.A. 80 E10 41 8N 88 50W
Streetsboro, U.S.A. 84 E3 41 14N 81 21W
Streetsville, Canada 84 C5 43 35N 79 42W
Strelka, Russia .... 29 D10 58 5N 93 3 E
Streng →, Cambodia .... 38 F4 13 12N 103 37 E
Streymoy, Færoe Is. 8 E9 62 8N 7 5W
Strezhevoy, Russia .... 28 C8 60 42N 77 34 E
Strímón →, Greece .... 23 D10 40 46N 23 51 E
Strimonikós Kólpos, Greece 23 D11 40 33N 24 0 E
Stroma, U.K. 11 C5 58 41N 3 7W
Strómboli, Italy .... 22 E6 38 47N 15 13 E
Stromeferry, U.K. 11 D3 57 21N 5 33W
Stromness, U.K. 11 C5 58 58N 3 17W
Stromsburg, U.S.A. 80 E6 41 7N 97 36W
Strömstad, Sweden .... 9 G14 58 56N 11 10 E
Strömsund, Sweden .... 8 E16 63 51N 15 33 E
Strongsville, U.S.A. 84 E3 41 19N 81 50W
Stronsay, U.K. 11 B6 59 7N 2 35W
Stroud, U.K. 13 F5 51 45N 2 13W
Stroud Road, Australia .. 63 E5 32 18S 151 57 E
Stroudsburg, U.S.A. 85 F9 40 59N 75 12W
Stroumbi, Cyprus .... 25 E11 34 53N 32 29 E
Struer, Denmark .... 9 H13 56 30N 8 35 E
Strumica, Macedonia .... 23 D10 41 28N 22 41 E
Struthers, Canada 72 C2 48 41N 85 51W
Struthers, U.S.A. 84 E4 41 4N 80 39W
Stryker, U.S.A. 76 B6 48 41N 114 46W
Stryy, Ukraine .... 17 D12 49 16N 23 48 E
Strzelecki Cr. →, Australia 63 D2 29 37S 139 59 E
Stuart, Fla., U.S.A. 83 M5 27 12N 80 15W
Stuart, Nebr., U.S.A. 80 D5 42 36N 99 8W
Stuart →, Canada 70 C4 54 0N 123 35W
Stuart Bluff Ra., Australia 60 D5 22 50S 131 52 E
Stuart L., Canada 70 C4 54 30N 124 30W
Stuart Ra., Australia .... 63 D1 29 10S 134 56 E
Stull L., Canada 72 B1 54 24N 92 34W
Stung Treng = Stoeng Treng,
  Cambodia .... 38 F5 13 31N 105 58 E
Stupart →, Canada 72 A1 56 0N 93 25W
Sturgeon B., Canada 71 C9 52 0N 97 50W
Sturgeon Bay, U.S.A. 82 C2 44 50N 87 23W

Sturgeon Falls, Canada .. 72 C4 46 25N 79 57W
Sturgeon L., Alta., Canada 70 B5 55 6N 117 32W
Sturgeon L., Ont., Canada 72 C1 50 0N 90 45W
Sturgeon L., Ont., Canada 84 B6 44 28N 78 43W
Sturgis, Canada 71 C8 51 56N 102 36W
Sturgis, Mich., U.S.A. 82 E3 41 48N 85 25W
Sturgis, S. Dak., U.S.A. 80 C3 44 25N 103 31W
Sturt △, Australia .... 63 D3 27 17S 141 37 E
Sturt Cr. →, Australia .. 60 C4 19 8S 127 50 E
Stutterheim, S. Africa .... 56 E4 32 33S 27 28 E
Stuttgart, Germany .... 16 D5 48 48N 9 11 E
Stuttgart, U.S.A. 81 H9 34 30N 91 33W
Stuyvesant, U.S.A. 85 D11 42 23N 73 45W
Stykkishólmur, Iceland .. 8 D2 65 2N 22 40W
Styria = Steiermark □, Austria 16 E8 47 26N 15 0 E
Su Xian = Suzhou, China 34 H9 33 41N 116 59 E
Suakin, Sudan .... 51 E13 19 8N 37 20 E
Suan, N. Korea .... 33 E14 38 42N 126 22 E
Suaqui, Mexico 86 B3 29 12N 109 41W
Suar, India .... 43 E8 29 2N 79 3 E
Subang, Indonesia .... 37 G12 6 34S 107 45 E
Subansiri →, India .... 41 F18 26 48N 93 50 E
Subarnarekha →, India .. 43 H12 22 34N 87 24 E
Subayhah, Si. Arabia .... 44 D3 30 2N 38 50 E
Subi, Indonesia .... 36 D3 2 58N 108 50 E
Subotica, Serbia & M. .... 23 A8 46 6N 19 39 E
Suceava, Romania .... 17 E14 47 38N 26 16 E
Suchitoto, El Salv. 88 D2 13 56N 89 0W
Suchou = Suzhou, China 33 C7 31 19N 120 38 E
Süchow = Xuzhou, China 35 G9 34 18N 117 10 E
Suck →, Ireland 10 C3 53 17N 8 3W
Sucre, Bolivia 92 G5 19 0S 65 15W
Sucuriú →, Brazil 93 H8 20 47S 51 38W
Sud, Pte. du, Canada 73 C7 49 3N 62 14W
Sud-Kivu □, Dem. Rep. of
  the Congo .... 54 C2 3 0S 28 30 E
Sud-Ouest, Pte., Canada 73 C7 49 23N 63 36W
Sudan, U.S.A. 81 H3 34 4N 102 32W
Sudan ■, Africa .... 51 E11 15 0N 30 0 E
Sudbury, Canada 72 C3 46 30N 81 0W
Sudbury, U.K. .... 13 E8 52 2N 0 45 E
Sûdd, Sudan .... 51 G12 8 20N 30 0 E
Sudeten Mts. = Sudety, Europe 17 C9 50 20N 16 45 E
Sudety, Europe .... 17 C9 50 20N 16 45 E
Suðuroy, Færoe Is. 8 F9 61 32N 6 50W
Sudi, Tanzania .... 55 E4 10 11S 39 57 E
Sudirman, Pegunungan,
  Indonesia .... 37 E9 4 30S 137 0 E
Sudong, Pulau, Singapore 39 d 1 12N 103 43 E
Sueca, Spain 21 C5 39 12N 0 21W
Suemez I., U.S.A. 70 B2 55 15N 133 20W
Suez = El Suweis, Egypt 51 C12 29 58N 32 31 E
Suez, G. of = Suweis, Khalîg el,
  Egypt .... 51 C12 28 40N 33 0 E
Suez Canal = Suweis, Qanâ es,
  Egypt .... 51 B12 31 0N 32 20 E
Suffield, Canada 70 C6 50 12N 111 10W
Suffolk, U.S.A. 82 G7 36 44N 76 35W
Suffolk □, U.K. .... 13 E9 52 16N 1 0 E
Sugarcreek, U.S.A. 84 E5 41 59N 79 21W
Sugarive →, India .... 43 F12 26 16N 86 24 E
Sugluk = Salluit, Canada 69 B12 62 14N 75 38W
Suhār, Oman .... 45 E8 24 20N 56 40 E
Sühbaatar □, Mongolia .. 34 B8 45 30N 114 0 E
Suhl, Germany .... 16 C6 50 36N 10 42 E
Sui, Pakistan .... 42 E3 28 37N 69 19 E
Sui Xian, China .... 34 H6 33 30N 110 12 E ... 34 F6 37 30N 110 12 E
Suide, China .... 34 F6 37 30N 110 12 E
Suifenhe, China .... 35 B16 44 32N 131 10 E
Suihua, China .... 33 B7 46 32N 126 55 E
Suining, China .... 35 H9 33 56N 117 58 E
Suiping, China .... 34 H7 33 10N 113 59 E
Suir →, Ireland 10 D4 52 16N 7 9W
Suisun City, U.S.A. 78 G4 38 15N 122 2W
Suiyang, China .... 35 B16 44 30N 130 56 E
Suizhong, China .... 35 D11 40 21N 120 20 E
Sujangarh, India .... 42 F6 27 42N 74 31 E
Sukabumi, Indonesia .... 37 G12 6 56S 106 50 E
Sukadana, Indonesia .... 36 E3 1 10S 110 0 E
Sukagawa, Japan .... 31 F10 37 17N 140 23 E
Sukaraja, Indonesia .... 36 E4 2 28S 110 25 E
Sukawati, Indonesia .... 37 K18 8 35S 115 17 E
Sukch'ŏn, N. Korea .... 35 E13 39 22N 125 35 E
Sukhona →, Russia .... 18 C6 61 15N 46 39 E
Sukhothai, Thailand .... 38 D2 17 1N 99 49 E
Sukhumi = Sokhumi, Georgia 19 F7 43 0N 41 0 E
Sukkur, Pakistan .... 42 F3 27 42N 68 54 E
Sukkur Barrage, Pakistan 42 F3 27 40N 68 50 E
Sukri →, India .... 42 G4 25 4N 71 43 E
Sukumo, Japan .... 31 H6 32 56N 132 44 E
Sukunka →, Canada 70 B4 55 45N 121 15W
Sula, Kepulauan, Indonesia 37 E7 1 45S 125 0 E
Sulaco →, Honduras 88 C2 15 2N 87 44W
Sulaiman Range, Pakistan 42 D3 30 30N 69 50 E
Sūlār, Iran .... 45 D6 31 53N 51 54 E
Sulawesi Sea = Celebes Sea,
  Indonesia .... 37 D6 3 0N 123 0 E
Sulawesi Selatan □, Indonesia 37 E6 2 30S 120 0 E
Sulawesi Utara □, Indonesia 37 D6 1 0N 122 30 E
Sulima, S. Leone 50 G3 6 58N 11 32W
Sulina, Romania .... 17 F15 45 10N 29 40 E
Sulitjelma, Norway .... 8 C17 67 9N 16 3 E
Sullana, Peru 92 D2 4 52S 80 39W
Sullivan, Ill., U.S.A. 80 F10 39 36N 88 37W
Sullivan, Ind., U.S.A. 82 F2 39 6N 87 24W
Sullivan, Mo., U.S.A. 80 F9 38 13N 91 10W
Sullivan Bay, Canada 70 C3 50 55N 126 50W
Sullivan I. = Lanbi Kyun, Burma 39 G2 10 50N 98 20 E
Sullom Voe, U.K. 11 A7 60 27N 1 20W
Sulphur, La., U.S.A. 81 K8 30 14N 93 23W
Sulphur, Okla., U.S.A. 81 H6 34 31N 96 58W
Sulphur Pt., Canada 70 A6 60 56N 114 48W
Sulphur Springs, U.S.A. 81 J7 33 8N 95 36W
Sultan, Canada 72 C3 47 36N 82 47W
Sultan, U.S.A. 78 C5 47 52N 121 49W
Sultanpur, Mad. P., India 42 H8 23 9N 77 56 E
Sultanpur, Punjab, India 42 D6 31 13N 75 11 E
Sultanpur, Ut. P., India 43 F10 26 18N 82 4 E
Sulu Arch., Phil. .... 37 C6 6 0N 121 0 E
Sulu Sea, E. Indies .... 37 C6 8 0N 120 0 E
Suluq, Libya .... 51 B10 31 44N 20 14 E
Sulzberger Ice Shelf, Antarctica 5 E13 78 0S 150 0W
Sumalata, Indonesia .... 37 D6 1 0N 122 31 E
Sumampa, Argentina 94 B3 29 25S 63 29W
Sumatera □, Indonesia .. 36 D2 0 40N 100 20 E
Sumatera Barat □, Indonesia 36 E2 1 0S 101 0 E

Sumatera Utara □, Indonesia 36 D1 2 30N 98 0 E
Sumatra = Sumatera □,
  Indonesia .... 36 D2 0 40N 100 20 E
Sumba, Indonesia .... 37 F5 9 45S 119 35 E
Sumba, Selat, Indonesia 37 F5 9 0S 118 40 E
Sumbawa, Indonesia .... 36 F5 8 26S 117 30 E
Sumbawa Besar, Indonesia 36 F5 8 30S 117 26 E
Sumbawanga □, Tanzania 52 F6 8 0S 31 30 E
Sumbe, Angola .... 52 G2 11 10S 13 48 E
Sumbu □, Zambia .... 55 D3 8 43S 30 22 E
Sumburgh Hd., U.K. 11 B7 59 52N 1 17W
Sumdeo, India .... 43 D8 31 26N 78 44 E
Sumdo, China .... 43 B8 35 6N 78 41 E
Sumedang, Indonesia .. 37 G12 6 52S 107 55 E
Sumen = Shumen, Bulgaria 23 C12 43 18N 26 55 E
Sumenep, Indonesia .... 37 G15 7 1S 113 52 E
Sumgait = Sumqayıt, Azerbaijan 19 F8 40 34N 49 38 E
Summer, L., U.S.A. 76 E3 42 50N 120 45W
Summerland, Canada 70 D5 49 32N 119 41W
Summerside, Canada 73 C7 46 24N 63 47W
Summersville, U.S.A. 82 F5 38 17N 80 51W
Summerville, Ga., U.S.A. 83 H3 34 29N 85 21W
Summerville, S.C., U.S.A. 83 J5 33 1N 80 11W
Summit Lake, Canada .. 70 C4 54 20N 122 40W
Summit Peak, U.S.A. 76 H10 37 21N 106 42W
Sumner, Iowa, U.S.A. 80 D8 42 51N 92 6W
Sumner, Wash., U.S.A. .. 78 C4 47 12N 122 14W
Sumoto, Japan .... 31 G7 34 21N 134 54 E
Šumperk, Czech Rep. .... 17 D9 49 59N 16 59 E
Sumqayıt, Azerbaijan .. 19 F8 40 34N 49 38 E
Sumter, U.S.A. 83 J5 33 55N 80 21W
Sumy, Ukraine .... 19 D5 50 57N 34 50 E
Sun City, S. Africa .... 56 D4 25 17S 27 3 E
Sun City, Ariz., U.S.A. 77 K7 33 36N 112 17W
Sun City, Calif., U.S.A. 79 M9 33 42N 117 11W
Sun City Center, U.S.A. 83 M4 27 43N 82 18W
Sun Lakes, U.S.A. 77 K8 33 10N 111 52W
Sun Valley, U.S.A. 76 E6 43 42N 114 21W
Sunagawa, Japan .... 30 C10 43 29N 141 55 E
Sunan, N. Korea .... 35 E13 39 15N 125 40 E
Sunart, L., U.K. 11 E3 56 42N 5 43W
Sunburst, U.S.A. 76 B8 48 53N 111 55W
Sunbury, Australia .... 63 F3 37 35S 144 44 E
Sunbury, U.S.A. 85 F8 40 52N 76 48W
Sunchales, Argentina .. 94 C3 30 58S 61 35W
Suncho Corral, Argentina 94 B3 27 55S 63 27W
Sunch'ŏn, S. Korea .... 35 G14 34 52N 127 31 E
Suncook, U.S.A. 85 C13 43 8N 71 27W
Sunda, Selat, Indonesia 36 F3 6 20S 105 30 E
Sunda Is., Indonesia .... 26 K14 5 0S 105 0 E
Sunda Str. = Sunda, Selat,
  Indonesia .... 36 F3 6 20S 105 30 E
Sundance, Canada 71 B10 56 32N 94 4W
Sundance, U.S.A. 80 C2 44 24N 104 23W
Sundar Nagar, India .... 42 D7 31 32N 76 53 E
Sundarbans, Asia .... 41 J16 22 0N 89 0 E
Sundargarh, India .... 41 H14 22 4N 84 5 E
Sundays = Sondags →, S. Africa 56 E4 33 44S 25 51 E
Sunderland, Canada 84 B5 44 16N 79 4W
Sunderland, U.K. 12 C6 54 55N 1 23W
Sundown △, Australia .. 63 D5 28 49S 151 38 E
Sundre, Canada 70 C6 51 49N 114 38W
Sundsvall, Sweden .... 9 E17 62 23N 17 17 E
Sung Hei, Vietnam .... 39 G6 10 20N 106 2 E
Sungai Acheh, Malaysia 39 c 5 8N 100 30 E
Sungai Kolok, Thailand .. 39 J3 6 2N 101 58 E
Sungai Lembing, Malaysia 39 L4 3 55S 103 3 E
Sungai Petani, Malaysia 39 K3 5 37N 100 30 E
Sungaigerong, Indonesia 36 E2 2 59S 104 52 E
Sungailiat, Indonesia .... 36 E3 1 51S 106 8 E
Sungaipenuh, Indonesia 36 E2 2 1S 101 20 E
Sungari = Songhua Jiang →,
  China .... 33 B8 47 45N 132 30 E
Sunghua Chiang = Songhua
  Jiang →, China .... 33 B8 47 45N 132 30 E
Sunland Park, U.S.A. 77 L10 31 50N 106 40W
Sunndalsøra, Norway .. 9 E13 62 40N 8 33 E
Sunnyside, U.S.A. 76 C3 46 20N 120 0W
Sunnyvale, U.S.A. 78 H4 37 23N 122 2W
Suntar, Russia .... 29 C12 62 15N 117 30 E
Suomenselkä, Finland .. 8 E21 62 52N 24 0 E
Suomussalmi, Finland .. 8 D23 64 54N 29 10 E
Suoyarvi, Russia .... 18 B5 62 3N 32 20 E
Supai, U.S.A. 77 H7 36 15N 112 41W
Supaul, India .... 43 F12 26 10N 86 40 E
Superior, Ariz., U.S.A. 77 K8 33 18N 111 6W
Superior, Mont., U.S.A. 76 C6 47 12N 114 53W
Superior, Nebr., U.S.A. 80 E5 40 1N 98 4W
Superior, Wis., U.S.A. 80 B8 46 44N 92 6W
Superior, L., N. Amer. .. 72 C2 47 0N 87 0W
Suphan Buri, Thailand .. 38 E3 14 14N 100 10 E
Suphan Dağı, Turkey .. 44 B4 38 54N 42 48 E
Supiori, Indonesia .... 37 E9 1 0S 136 0 E
Supung Shuiku, China .. 35 D13 40 35N 124 50 E
Süq Suwayq, Si. Arabia 44 E3 24 23N 38 27 E
Suqian, China .... 35 H10 33 54N 118 8 E
Suqutra = Socotra, Yemen 47 E5 12 30N 54 0 E
Şūr, Lebanon .... 46 B4 33 19N 35 16 E
Şür, Oman .... 47 C6 22 34N 59 32 E
Sur, Pt., U.S.A. 78 J5 36 18N 121 54W
Sura →, Russia .... 18 C8 56 6N 46 0 E
Surab, Pakistan .... 42 E2 28 25N 66 15 E
Surabaja = Surabaya, Indonesia 37 G15 7 17S 112 45 E
Surabaya, Indonesia .... 37 G15 7 17S 112 45 E
Surakarta, Indonesia .... 37 G14 7 35S 110 48 E
Surat, Australia .... 63 D4 27 10S 149 6 E
Surat, India .... 40 J8 21 12N 72 55 E
Surat Thani, Thailand .. 39 H2 9 6N 99 20 E
Suratgarh, India .... 42 E5 29 18N 73 55 E
Surendranagar, India .. 42 H4 22 45N 71 40 E
Surf, U.S.A. 79 L6 34 41N 120 36W
Surgut, Russia .... 28 C8 61 14N 73 20 E
Suriapet, India .... 40 L11 17 10N 79 40 E
Surigao, Phil. .... 37 C7 9 47N 125 29 E
Surin, Thailand .... 38 E4 14 50N 103 34 E
Surin Nua, Ko, Thailand 39 H1 9 30N 97 55 E
Surinam ■, S. Amer. 93 C7 4 0N 56 0W
Suriname ■ = Surinam ■, S. Amer. 93 C7 4 0N 56 0W
Suriname →, Surinam .. 93 B7 5 50N 55 15W
Sürmaq, Iran .... 45 D7 31 3N 52 48 E
Surrey □, U.K. 13 F7 51 15N 0 31W
Sursand, India .... 43 F11 26 39N 85 43 E
Sursar →, India .... 43 F12 26 14N 87 3 E
Surt, Libya .... 51 B9 31 11N 16 39 E
Surt, Khalīj, Libya .... 51 B9 31 40N 18 30 E
Surtanahu, Pakistan .... 42 F4 26 22N 70 0 E

Surtsey, Iceland 8 E3 63 20N 20 30W
Suruga-Wan, Japan ...... 31 G9 34 45N 138 30 E
Susaki, Japan .... 31 H6 33 22N 133 17 E
Süsangerd, Iran .... 45 D6 31 35N 48 6 E
Susanville, U.S.A. 76 F3 40 25N 120 39W
Susner, India .... 42 H7 23 57N 76 5 E
Susquehanna, U.S.A. 85 E9 41 57N 75 36W
Susquehanna →, U.S.A. ... 85 G8 39 33N 76 5W
Susques, Argentina 94 A2 23 35S 66 25W
Sussex, Canada 73 C6 45 45N 65 37W
Sussex, U.S.A. 85 E10 41 13N 74 37W
Sussex, E. □, U.K. .... 13 G8 51 0N   0 20 E
Sussex, W. □, U.K. 13 G7 51 0N   0 30W
Sustut →, Canada 70 B3 56 20N 127 30W
Susuman, Russia .... 29 C15 62 47N 148 10 E
Susunu, Indonesia .... 37 E8   3 7S 133 39 E
Susurluk, Turkey .... 23 E13 39 54N 28 8 E
Sutherland, S. Africa ..... 56 E3 32 24S 20 40 E
Sutherland, U.K. 11 C4 58 12N   4 50W
Sutherland, U.S.A. 80 E4 41 10N 101 8W
Sutherland Falls, N.Z. .... 59 L1 44 48S 167 46 E
Sutherlin, U.S.A. 76 E2 43 23N 123 19W
Suthri, India .... 42 H3 23 3N 68 55 E
Sutlej →, Pakistan .... 42 E4 29 23N 71 3 E
Sutter, U.S.A. 78 F5 39 10N 121 45W
Sutter Creek, U.S.A. 78 G6 38 24N 120 48W
Sutton, Canada 85 A12 45 6N 72 37W
Sutton, Nebr., U.S.A. 80 E6 40 36N 97 52W
Sutton, W. Va., U.S.A. 82 F5 38 40N 80 43W
Sutton →, Canada 72 A3 55 15N 83 45W
Sutton Coldfield, U.K. 13 E6 52 35N   1 49W
Sutton in Ashfield, U.K. .. 12 D6 53 8N   1 16W
Sutton L., Canada 72 B3 54 15N 84 42W
Suttor →, Australia ...... 62 C4 21 36S 147 2 E
Suttsu, Japan .... 30 C10 42 48N 140 14 E
Suva, Fiji .... 59 D8 18 6S 178 30 E
Suva Planina, Serbia & M. . 23 C10 43 10N 22 5 E
Suvorov Is. = Suwarrow Is.,
  Cook Is. 65 J11 15 0S 163 0W
Suwałki, Poland .... 17 A12 54 8N 22 59 E
Suwana, Indonesia .... 37 K18 8 44S 115 36 E
Suwannaphum, Thailand ... 38 E4 15 33N 103 47 E
Suwannee →, U.S.A. 83 L4 29 17N 83 10W
Suwanose-Jima, Japan .... 31 K4 29 38N 129 43 E
Suwarrow Is., Cook Is. 65 J11 15 0S 163 0W
Suwayq aş Şuqban, Iraq ... 44 D5 31 32N 46 7 E
Suweis, Khalîg el, Egypt .. 51 C12 28 40N 33 0 E
Suweis, Qanâ es, Egypt ... 51 B12 31 0N 32 20 E
Suwŏn, S. Korea .... 35 F14 37 17N 127 1 E
Suzdal, Russia .... 18 C7 56 29N 40 26 E
Suzhou, Anhui, China .... 34 H9 33 41N 116 59 E
Suzhou, Jiangsu, China ... 33 C7 31 19N 120 38 E
Suzu, Japan .... 31 F8 37 25N 137 17 E
Suzu-Misaki, Japan ...... 31 F8 37 31N 137 21 E
Suzuka, Japan .... 31 G8 34 55N 136 36 E
Svalbard, Arctic .... 4 B8 78 0N 17 0 E
Svappavaara, Sweden ..... 8 C19 67 40N 21 3 E
Svartisen, Norway .... 8 C15 66 40N 13 50 E
Svay Chek, Cambodia ..... 38 F4 13 48N 102 58 E
Svay Rieng, Cambodia .... 39 G5 11 9N 105 45 E
Svealand □, Sweden ...... 9 G16 60 20N 15 0 E
Sveg, Sweden .... 9 E16 62 2N 14 21 E
Svendborg, Denmark ..... 9 J14 55 4N 10 35 E
Sverdrup Is., Canada 4 B3 79 0N 97 0W
Svetlaya, Russia .... 30 A9 46 33N 138 18 E
Svetlogorsk = Svyetlahorsk,
  Belarus .... 17 B15 52 38N 29 46 E
Svir →, Russia .... 18 B5 60 30N 32 48 E
Svishtov, Bulgaria .... 23 C11 43 36N 25 23 E
Svislach, Belarus .... 17 B13 53 3N 24 2 E
Svobodnyy, Russia .... 29 D13 51 20N 128 0 E
Svolvær, Norway .... 8 B16 68 15N 14 34 E
Svyetlahorsk, Belarus .... 17 B15 52 38N 29 46 E
Swabian Alps = Schwäbische
  Alb, Germany .... 16 D5 48 20N   9 30 E
Swaffham, U.K. .... 13 E8 52 39N   0 42 E
Swainsboro, U.S.A. 83 J4 32 36N 82 20W
Swakop →, Namibia ...... 56 C2 22 38S 14 36 E
Swakopmund, Namibia ... 56 C1 22 37S 14 30 E
Swale →, U.K. 12 C6 54 5N   1 20W
Swan →, Australia .... 61 F2 32 3S 115 45 E
Swan →, Canada 71 C8 52 30N 100 45W
Swan Hill, Australia ..... 63 F3 35 20S 143 33 E
Swan Hills, Canada 70 C5 54 43N 115 24W
Swan Is. = Santanilla, Is.,
  Honduras 88 C3 17 22N 83 57W
Swan L., Canada 71 C8 52 30N 100 40W
Swan Peak, U.S.A. 76 C7 47 43N 113 38W
Swan River, Canada 76 C7 48 0N 101 49W
Swan River, Canada 71 C8 52 10N 101 16W
Swanage, U.K. 13 G6 50 36N   1 58W
Swansea, Australia ...... 63 G4 42 8S 148 4 E
Swansea, Canada 84 C5 43 38N 79 28W
Swansea, U.K. 13 F4 51 37N   3 57W
Swansea □, U.K. 13 F3 51 38N   4 3W
Swar →, Pakistan .... 43 B5 34 40N 72 5 E
Swartberge, S. Africa ..... 56 E3 33 20S 22 0 E
Swartmodder, S. Africa ... 56 D3 28 1S 20 32 E
Swartnossob →, Namibia .. 56 C2 23 8S 18 42 E
Swartruggens, S. Africa ... 56 D4 25 39S 26 42 E
Swastika, Canada 72 C3 48 7N 80 6W
Swatow = Shantou, China . 33 D6 23 18N 116 40 E
Swaziland ■, Africa ...... 57 D5 26 30S 31 30 E
Sweden ■, Europe .... 9 G16 57 0N 15 0 E
Sweet Home, U.S.A. 76 D2 44 24N 122 44W
Sweetgrass, U.S.A. 76 B8 48 59N 111 58W
Sweetwater, Nev., U.S.A. .. 78 G7 38 27N 119 9W
Sweetwater, Tenn., U.S.A. . 83 H3 35 36N 84 28W
Sweetwater, Tex., U.S.A. .. 81 J4 32 28N 100 25W
Sweetwater →, U.S.A. 76 E10 42 31N 107 2W
Swellendam, S. Africa .... 56 E3 34 1S 20 26 E
Świdnica, Poland .... 17 C9 50 50N 16 30 E
Świdnik, Poland .... 17 C12 51 13N 22 39 E
Świebodzin, Poland ...... 16 B8 52 15N 15 31 E
Świecie, Poland .... 17 B10 53 25N 18 30 E
Swift Current, Canada 71 C7 50 20N 107 45W
Swift Current →, Canada .. 71 C7 50 38N 107 44W
Swilly, L., Ireland 10 A4 55 12N   7 33W
Swindon, U.K. 13 F6 51 34N   1 46W
Swindon □, U.K. 13 F6 51 34N   1 46W
Swinemünde = Świnoujście,
  Poland .... 16 B8 53 54N 14 16 E
Swinford, Ireland 10 C3 53 57N   8 58W
Świnoujście, Poland ..... 16 B8 53 54N 14 16 E
Switzerland ■, Europe .... 20 C8 46 30N   8 0 E
Swords, Ireland 10 C5 53 28N   6 13W
Swoyerville, U.S.A. 85 E9 41 18N 75 53W

Sydenham →, Canada 84 D2 42 33N 82 25W
Sydney, Australia .... 63 E5 33 53S 151 10 E
Sydney, Canada 73 C7 46 7N 60 7W
Sydney L., Canada 71 C10 50 41N 94 25W
Sydney Mines, Canada 73 C7 46 18N 60 15W
Sydprøven = Alluitsup Paa,
  Greenland 69 B15 60 30N 45 35W
Sydra, G. of = Surt, Khalīj, Libya 51 B9 31 40N 18 30 E
Sykesville, U.S.A. 84 E6 41 3N 78 50W
Syktyvkar, Russia .... 18 B9 61 45N 50 40 E
Sylacauga, U.S.A. 83 J2 33 10N 86 15W
Sylarna, Sweden .... 8 E15 63 2N 12 13 E
Sylhet, Bangla. .... 41 G17 24 54N 91 52 E
Sylhet □, Bangla. .... 41 G17 24 50N 91 50 E
Sylt, Germany .... 16 A5 54 54N   8 22 E
Sylvan Beach, U.S.A. 85 C9 43 12N 75 44W
Sylvan Lake, Canada 70 C6 52 20N 114 3W
Sylvania, U.S.A. 83 J5 32 45N 81 38W
Sylvester, U.S.A. 83 K4 31 32N 83 50W
Sym, Russia .... 28 C9 60 20N 88 18 E
Symón, Mexico 86 C4 24 42N 102 35W
Synnott Ra., Australia .... 60 C4 16 30S 125 20 E
Syowa, Antarctica .... 5 C5 69 0S 39 35 E
Syracuse, Kans., U.S.A. ... 81 G4 37 59N 101 45W
Syracuse, N.Y., U.S.A. 85 C8 43 3N 76 9W
Syracuse, Nebr., U.S.A. ... 80 E6 40 39N 96 11W
Syrdarya →, Kazakhstan .. 28 E7 46 3N 61 0 E
Syria ■, Asia .... 44 C3 35 0N 38 0 E
Syrian Desert = Shām, Bādiyat
  ash, Asia .... 44 C3 32 0N 40 0 E
Syzran, Russia .... 18 D8 53 12N 48 30 E
Szczecin, Poland .... 16 B8 53 27N 14 27 E
Szczecinek, Poland ...... 17 B9 53 43N 16 41 E
Szczeciński, Zalew = Stettiner
  Haff, Germany .... 16 B8 53 47N 14 15 E
Szczytno, Poland .... 17 B11 53 33N 21 0 E
Szechwan = Sichuan □, China 32 C5 30 30N 103 0 E
Szeged, Hungary .... 17 E11 46 16N 20 10 E
Székesfehérvár, Hungary .. 17 E10 47 15N 18 25 E
Szekszárd, Hungary ...... 17 E10 46 22N 18 42 E
Szentes, Hungary .... 17 E11 46 39N 20 21 E
Szolnok, Hungary .... 17 E11 47 10N 20 15 E
Szombathely, Hungary ... 17 E9 47 14N 16 38 E

T

Ta Khli Khok, Thailand ... 38 E3 15 18N 100 20 E
Ta Lai, Vietnam .... 39 G6 11 24N 107 23 E
Tabacal, Argentina 94 A3 23 15S 64 15W
Tabaco, Phil. .... 37 B6 13 22N 123 44 E
Tābah, Si. Arabia .... 44 E4 26 55N 42 38 E
Tabanan, Indonesia ...... 37 K18 8 32S 115 8 E
Tabas, Khorāsān, Iran .... 45 C9 32 48N 60 12 E
Tabas, Khorāsān, Iran .... 45 C8 33 35N 56 55 E
Tabasará, Serranía de, Panama 88 E3 8 35N 81 40W
Tabasco □, Mexico 87 D6 17 45N 93 30W
Tabāsīn, Iran .... 45 D8 31 12N 57 54 E
Tabatinga, Serra da, Brazil . 93 F10 10 30S 44 0W
Taber, Canada 70 D6 49 47N 112 8W
Taberg, U.S.A. 85 C9 43 18N 75 37W
Tablas I., Phil. .... 37 B6 12 25N 122 2 E
Table B., Canada 73 B8 53 40N 56 25W
Table B., S. Africa .... 56 E2 33 35S 18 25 E
Table Mt., S. Africa ...... 56 E2 34 0S 18 22 E
Table Rock L., U.S.A. 81 G8 36 36N 93 19W
Tabletop, Mt., Australia ... 62 C4 23 24S 147 11 E
Tábor, Czech Rep. .... 16 D8 49 25N 14 39 E
Tabora, Tanzania .... 54 D3 5 2S 32 50 E
Tabora □, Tanzania ...... 54 D3 5 0S 33 0 E
Tabou, Ivory C. 50 H4 4 30N   7 20W
Tabrīz, Iran .... 44 B5 38 7N 46 20 E
Tabuaeran, Kiribati 65 G12 3 51N 159 22W
Tabūk, Si. Arabia .... 44 D3 28 23N 36 36 E
Tacámbaro de Codallos, Mexico 86 D4 19 14N 101 28W
Tacheng, China .... 32 B3 46 40N 82 58 E
Tach'ing Shan = Daqing Shan,
  China .... 34 D6 40 40N 111 0 E
Tacloban, Phil. .... 37 B6 11 15N 124 58 E
Tacna, Peru 92 G4 18 0S 70 20W
Tacoma, U.S.A. 78 C4 47 14N 122 26W
Tacuarembó, Uruguay 95 C4 31 45S 56 0W
Tademaït, Plateau du, Algeria 50 C6 28 30N 2 30 E
Tadjoura, Djibouti ...... 47 E3 11 50N 42 55 E
Tadmor, N.Z. .... 59 J4 41 27S 172 45 E
Tadoule L., Canada 71 B9 58 36N 98 20W
Tadoussac, Canada 73 C6 48 11N 69 42W
Tadzhikistan = Tajikistan ■, Asia 28 F8 38 30N 70 0 E
Taechŏn-ni, S. Korea ..... 35 F14 36 21N 126 36 E
Taegu, S. Korea .... 35 G15 35 50N 128 37 E
Taegwan, N. Korea ...... 35 D13 40 13N 125 12 E
Taejŏn, S. Korea .... 35 F14 36 20N 127 28 E
Taen, Ko, Thailand ...... 39 b 9 22N 99 57 E
Tafalla, Spain 21 A5 42 30N   1 41W
Tafelbaai = Table B., S. Africa 56 E2 33 35S 18 25 E
Tafermaar, Indonesia .... 37 F8 6 47S 134 10 E
Tafí Viejo, Argentina 94 B2 26 43S 65 17W
Tafīhān, Iran .... 45 D7 29 25N 52 39 E
Tafresh, Iran .... 45 C6 34 45N 49 57 E
Taft, Iran .... 45 D7 31 45N 54 14 E
Taft, Phil. .... 37 B7 11 57N 125 30 E
Taft, U.S.A. 79 K7 35 8N 119 28W
Taftān, Kūh-e, Iran ..... 45 D9 28 40N 61 0 E
Taga Dzong, Bhutan ..... 41 F16 27 5N 89 55 E
Taganrog, Russia .... 19 E6 47 12N 38 50 E
Tagbilaran, Phil. .... 37 C6 9 39N 123 51 E
Tagish, Canada 70 A2 60 19N 134 16W
Tagish L., Canada 70 A2 60 10N 134 20W
Tagliamento →, Italy .... 22 B5 45 38N 13 6 E
Tagomago, Spain .... 24 B8 39 2N   1 39 E
Taguatinga, Brazil 93 F10 12 16S 42 26W
Tagum, Phil. .... 37 C7 7 33N 125 53 E
Tagus = Tejo →, Europe .. 21 C1 38 40N   9 24W
Tahakopa, N.Z. .... 59 M2 46 30S 169 23 E
Tahan, Gunong, Malaysia . 39 K4 4 34N 102 17 E
Tahat, Algeria .... 50 D7 23 18N   5 33 E
Tāherī, Iran .... 45 E7 27 43N 52 20 E
Tahiti, French Polynesia .. 65 J13 17 37S 149 27W
Tahlequah, U.S.A. 81 H7 35 55N 94 58W
Tahoe, L., U.S.A. 78 G6 39 6N 120 2W
Tahoe City, U.S.A. 78 F6 39 10N 120 9W
Tahoka, U.S.A. 81 J4 33 10N 101 48W
Taholah, U.S.A. 78 C2 47 21N 124 17W
Tahoua, Niger .... 50 F7 14 57N   5 16 E
Tahrūd, Iran .... 45 D8 29 26N 57 49 E
Tahsis, Canada 70 D3 49 55N 126 40W

Tahta, Egypt .... 51 C12 26 44N 31 32 E
Tahulandang, Indonesia .. 37 D7 2 27N 125 23 E
Tahuna, Indonesia ...... 37 D7 3 38N 125 30 E
Tai Au Mun, China ...... 33 G11 22 18N 114 17 E
Tai Mo Shan, China ..... 33 G11 22 25N 114 7 E
Tai O, China .... 33 G10 22 15N 113 52 E
Tai Pang Wan, H.K. ...... 33 F11 22 33N 114 24 E
Tai Po, China .... 33 G11 22 27N 114 10 E
Tai Rom Yen △, Thailand .. 39 H2 8 45N 99 30 E
Tai Shan, China .... 35 F9 36 25N 117 20 E
Tai Yue Shan = Lantau I., China 33 G10 22 15N 113 56 E
Tai'an, China .... 35 F9 36 12N 117 8 E
Taibei = T'aipei, Taiwan .. 33 D7 25 4N 121 29 E
Taibique, Canary Is. 24 G2 27 42N 17 58W
Taibus Qi, China .... 34 D8 41 54N 115 22 E
T'aichung, Taiwan ...... 33 D7 24 9N 120 37 E
Taieri →, N.Z. .... 59 M3 46 3S 170 12 E
Taigu, China .... 34 F7 37 28N 112 30 E
Taihang Shan, China .... 34 G7 36 0N 113 30 E
Taihape, N.Z. .... 59 H5 39 41S 175 48 E
Taihe, China .... 34 H8 33 20N 115 42 E
Taikang, China .... 34 G8 34 5N 114 50 E
Tailem Bend, Australia ... 63 F2 35 12S 139 29 E
Taimyr Peninsula = Taymyr,
  Poluostrov, Russia ..... 29 B11 75 0N 100 0 E
Tain, U.K. 11 D4 57 49N   4 4W
T'ainan, Taiwan .... 33 D7 23 0N 120 10 E
Tainaron, Ákra, Greece ... 23 F10 36 22N 22 27 E
Taipa, China .... 33 G10 22 10N 113 35 E
T'aipei, Taiwan .... 33 D7 25 4N 121 29 E
Taiping, Malaysia .... 39 K3 4 51N 100 44 E
Taipingzhen, China ...... 34 H6 33 35N 111 42 E
Tairbeart = Tarbert, U.K. .. 11 D2 57 54N   6 49W
Taita Hills, Kenya ...... 54 C4 3 25S 38 15 E
Taitao, Pen. de, Chile 96 F2 46 30S 75 0W
T'aitung, Taiwan .... 33 D7 22 43N 121 4 E
Taivalkoski, Finland ..... 8 D23 65 33N 28 12 E
Taiwan ■, Asia .... 33 D7 23 30N 121 0 E
Taíyetos Óros, Greece .... 23 F10 37 0N 22 23 E
Taiyiba, Israel .... 46 C4 32 36N 35 27 E
Taiyuan, China .... 34 F7 37 52N 112 33 E
Taizhong = T'aichung, Taiwan 33 D7 24 9N 120 37 E
Ta'izz, Yemen .... 47 E3 13 35N 44 2 E
Tājābād, Iran .... 45 D7 30 2N 54 24 E
Tajikistan ■, Asia .... 28 F8 38 30N 70 0 E
Tajima, Japan .... 31 F9 37 12N 139 46 E
Tajo = Tejo →, Europe 21 C1 38 40N   9 24W
Tajrīsh, Iran .... 45 C6 35 48N 51 25 E
Tak, Thailand .... 38 D2 16 52N 99 8 E
Takāb, Iran .... 44 B5 36 24N 47 7 E
Takachiho, Japan .... 31 H5 32 42N 131 18 E
Takachu, Botswana ...... 56 C3 22 37S 21 58 E
Takada, Japan .... 31 F9 37 7N 138 15 E
Takahagi, Japan .... 31 F10 36 43N 140 45 E
Takaka, N.Z. .... 59 J4 40 51S 172 50 E
Takamatsu, Japan ...... 31 G7 34 20N 134 5 E
Takaoka, Japan .... 31 F8 36 47N 137 0 E
Takapuna, N.Z. .... 59 G5 36 47S 174 47 E
Takasaki, Japan .... 31 F9 36 20N 139 0 E
Takatsuki, Japan .... 31 G7 34 51N 135 37 E
Takaungu, Kenya .... 54 C4 3 38S 39 52 E
Takayama, Japan .... 31 F8 36 18N 137 11 E
Take-Shima, Japan ...... 31 J5 30 49N 130 26 E
Takefu, Japan .... 31 G8 35 50N 136 10 E
Takengon, Indonesia .... 36 D1 4 45N 96 50 E
Takeo, Japan .... 31 H5 33 12N 130 1 E
Takeshima = Tok-do, Asia . 31 F5 37 15N 131 52 E
Tākestān, Iran .... 45 C6 36 0N 49 40 E
Taketa, Japan .... 31 H5 32 58N 131 24 E
Takev, Cambodia .... 39 G5 10 59N 104 47 E
Takh, India .... 43 C7 33 6N 77 32 E
Takht-Sulaiman, Pakistan . 42 D3 31 40N 69 58 E
Takikawa, Japan .... 30 C10 43 33N 141 54 E
Takla L., Canada 70 B3 55 15N 125 45W
Takla Landing, Canada ... 70 B3 55 30N 125 50W
Takla Makan = Taklamakan
  Shamo, China .... 32 C3 38 0N 83 0 E
Taklamakan Shamo, China 32 C3 38 0N 83 0 E
Taku →, Canada 70 B2 58 30N 133 50W
Takua Thung, Thailand ... 39 a 8 24N 98 27 E
Tal Halāl, Iran .... 45 D7 28 54N 55 1 E
Tala, Uruguay 95 C4 34 21S 55 46W
Talagang, Pakistan ...... 42 C5 32 55N 72 25 E
Talagante, Chile 94 C1 33 40S 70 50W
Talamanca, Cordillera de,
  Cent. Amer. 88 E3 9 20N 83 20W
Talara, Peru 92 D2 4 38S 81 18W
Talas, Kyrgyzstan ...... 28 E8 42 30N 72 13 E
Talāta, Egypt .... 46 E1 30 36N 32 20 E
Talaud, Kepulauan, Indonesia 37 D7 4 30N 126 50 E
Talaud Is. = Talaud, Kepulauan,
  Indonesia .... 37 D7 4 30N 126 50 E
Talavera de la Reina, Spain . 21 C3 39 55N   4 46W
Talayan, Phil. .... 37 C6 6 52N 124 24 E
Talbandh, India .... 43 H12 22 3N 86 20 E
Talbot, C., Australia ..... 60 B4 13 48S 126 43 E
Talbragar →, Australia ... 63 E4 32 12S 148 37 E
Talca, Chile 94 D1 35 28S 71 40W
Talcahuano, Chile 94 D1 36 40S 73 10W
Talcher, India .... 41 J14 21 0N 85 18 E
Taldy Kurgan = Taldyqorghan,
  Kazakhstan .... 28 E8 45 10N 78 45 E
Taldyqorghan, Kazakhstan 28 E8 45 10N 78 45 E
Tālesh, Iran .... 45 B6 37 58N 48 58 E
Tālesh, Kūhhā-ye, Iran ... 45 B6 37 42N 48 55 E
Tali Post, Sudan .... 51 G12 5 55N 30 44 E
Taliabu, Indonesia ...... 37 E6 1 50S 125 0 E
Talibon, Phil. .... 37 B6 10 9N 124 20 E
Talibong, Ko, Thailand ... 39 J2 7 15N 99 23 E
Talihina, U.S.A. 81 H7 34 45N 95 3W
Taliwang, Indonesia ..... 36 F5 8 50S 116 55 E
Tall 'Afar, Iraq .... 44 B4 36 22N 42 27 E
Tall Kalakh, Syria ...... 46 A5 34 41N 36 15 E
Talladega, U.S.A. 83 J2 33 26N 86 6W
Tallahassee, U.S.A. 83 K3 30 27N 84 17W
Tallangatta, Australia ... 63 F4 36 15S 147 19 E
Tallering Pk., Australia ... 61 E2 28 6S 115 37 E
Talli, Pakistan .... 42 E3 29 32N 68 8 E
Tallinn, Estonia .... 9 G21 59 22N 24 48 E
Tallmadge, U.S.A. 84 E3 41 6N 81 27W
Tallulah, U.S.A. 81 J9 32 25N 91 11W
Taloyoak, Canada 68 B10 69 32N 93 32W
Talpa de Allende, Mexico . 86 C4 20 23N 104 51W
Talparo, Trin. & Tob. 93 K15 10 30N 61 17W
Talsi, Latvia .... 9 H20 57 10N 22 30 E
Taltal, Chile 94 B1 25 23S 70 33W
Taltson →, Canada 70 A6 61 24N 112 46W

Talwood, Australia ...... 63 D4 28 29S 149 29 E
Talyawalka Cr. →, Australia 63 E3 32 28S 142 22 E
Tam Ky, Vietnam .... 38 E7 15 34N 108 29 E
Tam Quan, Vietnam ..... 38 E7 14 35N 109 3 E
Tama, Japan 80 E8 41 58N 92 35W
Tamale, Ghana 50 G5 9 22N   0 50W
Taman Negara △, Malaysia . 39 K4 4 38N 102 26 E
Tamano, Japan .... 31 G6 34 29N 133 59 E
Tamanrasset, Algeria .... 50 D7 22 50N   5 30 E
Tamaqua, U.S.A. 85 F9 40 48N 75 58W
Tamar →, U.K. 13 G3 50 27N   4 15W
Tamarinda, Spain .... 24 B10 39 55N   3 49 E
Tamashima, Japan ...... 31 G6 34 32N 133 40 E
Tamaulipas □, Mexico ... 87 C5 24 0N 99 0W
Tamaulipas, Sierra de, Mexico 87 C5 23 30N 98 20W
Tamazula, Mexico 86 C3 24 55N 106 58W
Tamazunchale, Mexico ... 87 C5 21 16N 98 47W
Tambacounda, Senegal ... 50 F3 13 45N 13 40W
Tambelan, Kepulauan, Indonesia 36 D3 1 0N 107 30 E
Tambo, Australia .... 62 C4 24 54S 146 14 E
Tambo de Mora, Peru 92 F3 13 30S 76 8W
Tambohorano, Madag. ... 57 B7 17 30S 43 58 E
Tambora, Indonesia ..... 36 F5 8 12S 118 5 E
Tambov, Russia .... 18 D7 52 45N 41 28 E
Tambuku, Indonesia ..... 37 G15 7 8S 113 40 E
Tâmega →, Portugal 21 B1 41 5N   8 21W
Tamenglong, India ...... 41 G18 25 0N 93 35 E
Tamiahua, L. de, Mexico .. 87 C5 21 30N 97 30W
Tamil Nadu □, India ..... 40 P10 11 0N   7 0 E
Tamluk, India .... 43 H12 22 18N 87 58 E
Tammerfors = Tampere, Finland 9 F20 61 30N 23 50 E
Tammisaari, Finland ..... 9 F20 60 0N 23 26 E
Tamo Abu, Pegunungan,
  Malaysia .... 36 D5 3 10N 115 5 E
Tampa, U.S.A. 83 M4 27 57N 82 27W
Tampa, Tanjung, Indonesia 37 K19 8 55S 116 12 E
Tampa B., U.S.A. 83 M4 27 50N 82 30W
Tampere, Finland .... 9 F20 61 30N 23 50 E
Tampico, Mexico 87 C5 22 20N 97 50W
Tampin, Malaysia ...... 39 L4 2 28N 102 13 E
Tampoi, Malaysia ...... 39 d 1 30N 103 39 E
Tamu, Burma .... 41 G19 24 13N 94 6 E
Tamworth, Australia .... 63 E5 31 7S 150 58 E
Tamworth, Canada 84 B8 44 29N 77 0W
Tamworth, U.K. 13 E6 52 39N   1 41W
Tamyang, S. Korea ...... 35 G14 35 19N 126 59 E
Tan An, Vietnam .... 39 G6 10 32N 106 25 E
Tan Chau, Vietnam ...... 39 G5 10 48N 105 12 E
Tan-Tan, Morocco 50 C3 28 29N 11 1W
Tana →, Kenya .... 54 C5 2 32S 40 31 E
Tana →, Norway .... 8 A23 70 30N 28 2 E
Tana, L., Ethiopia .... 47 E2 13 5N 37 30 E
Tana River Primate △, Kenya 54 C5 1 55S 40 7 E
Tanabe, Japan .... 31 H7 33 44N 135 22 E
Tanafjorden, Norway .... 8 A23 70 45N 28 25 E
Tanahbala, Indonesia .... 36 E1 0 30S 98 30 E
Tanahgrogot, Indonesia .. 36 E5 1 55S 116 15 E
Tanahjampea, Indonesia . 37 F6 7 10S 120 35 E
Tanahmasa, Indonesia ... 36 E1 0 12S 98 39 E
Tanahmerah, Indonesia .. 37 F10 6 5S 140 16 E
Tanakpur, India .... 43 E9 29 5N 80 7 E
Tanakura, Japan .... 31 F10 37 10N 140 20 E
Tanami, Australia ...... 60 C4 19 59S 129 43 E
Tanami Desert, Australia . 60 C5 18 50S 132 0 E
Tanana →, U.S.A. 68 B4 65 10N 151 58W
Tananarive = Antananarivo,
  Madag. .... 57 B8 18 55S 47 31 E
Tánaro →, Italy .... 20 D8 44 55N   8 40 E
Tancheng, China .... 35 G10 34 25N 118 20 E
Tanch'ŏn, N. Korea ..... 35 D15 40 27N 128 54 E
Tanda, Ut. P., India ..... 43 F10 26 33N 82 35 E
Tanda, Ut. P., India ..... 43 E8 28 57N 78 56 E
Tandag, Phil. .... 37 C7 9 4N 126 9 E
Tandaia, Tanzania ...... 55 D3 9 25S 34 15 E
Tandaué, Angola .... 56 B2 16 58S 18 5 E
Tandil, Argentina 94 D4 37 15S 59 6W
Tandil, Sa. del, Argentina . 94 D4 37 30S 59 0W
Tandlianwala, Pakistan .. 42 D5 31 3N 73 9 E
Tando Adam, Pakistan ... 42 G3 25 45N 68 40 E
Tando Allahyar, Pakistan . 42 G3 25 28N 68 43 E
Tando Bago, Pakistan .... 42 G3 24 47N 68 58 E
Tando Mohommed Khan,
  Pakistan .... 42 G3 25 8N 68 32 E
Tandou L., Australia ..... 63 E3 32 40S 142 5 E
Tandragee, U.K. 10 B5 54 21N   6 24W
Tane-ga-Shima, Japan ... 31 J5 30 30N 131 0 E
Taneatua, N.Z. .... 59 H6 38 4S 177 1 E
Tanen Tong Dan = Dawna Ra.,
  Burma .... 38 D2 16 30N 98 30 E
Tanezrouft, Algeria ..... 50 D6 23 9N   0 11 E
Tang, Koh, Cambodia .... 39 G4 10 16N 103 7 E
Tang, Ra's-e, Iran ...... 45 E8 25 21N 59 52 E
Tang Krasang, Cambodia . 38 F5 12 34N 105 3 E
Tanga, Tanzania .... 54 D4 5 5S 39 2 E
Tanga □, Tanzania ...... 54 D4 5 20S 38 0 E
Tanganyika, L., Africa .... 54 D3 6 40S 30 0 E
Tanger, Morocco 50 A4 35 50N   5 49W
Tangerang, Indonesia .... 37 G12 6 11S 106 37 E
Tanggu, China .... 35 E9 39 2N 117 40 E
Tanggula Shan, China ... 32 C4 32 40N 92 10 E
Tanghe, China .... 34 H7 32 47N 112 50 E
Tangier = Tanger, Morocco 50 A4 35 50N   5 49W
Tangjia, China .... 33 G10 22 22N 113 35 E
Tangjia Wan, China ..... 33 G10 22 21N 113 36 E
Tangorin, Australia ..... 62 C3 21 47S 144 12 E
Tangorombohitr'i Makay,
  Madag. .... 57 C8 21 0S 45 15 E
Tangshan, China .... 35 E10 39 38N 118 10 E
Tangtou, China .... 35 G10 35 28N 118 30 E
Tanimbar, Kepulauan, Indonesia 37 F8 7 30S 131 30 E
Tanimbar Is. = Tanimbar,
  Kepulauan, Indonesia .. 37 F8 7 30S 131 30 E
Taninthari = Tenasserim, Burma 39 F2 12 6N 99 3 E
Tanjay, Phil. .... 37 C6 9 30N 123 5 E
Tanjong Malim, Malaysia . 39 L3 3 42N 101 31 E
Tanjong Pelepas, Malaysia 39 d 1 21N 103 33 E
Tanjore = Thanjavur, India 40 P11 10 48N 79 12 E
Tanjung, Indonesia ..... 37 J19 8 21S 116 9 E
Tanjung, Phil. .... 36 E5 2 10S 115 25 E
Tanjung Tokong, Malaysia 39 c 5 28N 100 18 E
Tanjungbalai, Indonesia .. 36 D1 2 55N 99 44 E
Tanjungbatu, Indonesia .. 36 D5 2 23N 118 3 E
Tanjungkarang Telukbetung,
  Indonesia .... 36 F3 5 20S 105 10 E
Tanjungpandan, Indonesia 36 E3 2 43S 107 38 E
Tanjungpinang, Indonesia 36 D2 1 5N 104 30 E

Tanjungredeb, *Indonesia* ...... **36 D5**   2 9N 117 29 E
Tanjungselor, *Indonesia* ...... **36 D5**   2 55N 117 25 E
Tank, *Pakistan* .... **42 C4**   32 14N 70 25 E
Tankhala, *India* .... **42 J5**   21 58N 73 47 E
Tankwa-Karoo △, *S. Africa* .... **56 E2**   32 14S 19 50 E
Tannersville, *U.S.A.* **85 E9**   41 3N 75 18W
Tannu-Ola, *Russia* .... **29 D10** 51 0N 94 0 E
Tannum Sands, *Australia* ..... **62 C5**   23 57S 151 22 E
Tanout, *Niger* .... **50 F7**   14 50N 8 55 E
Tanta, *Egypt* .... **51 B12** 30 45N 30 57 E
Tantoyuca, *Mexico* **87 C5**   21 21N 98 10W
Tantung = Dandong, *China* .... **35 D13** 40 10N 124 20 E
Tanunda, *Australia* .... **63 E2**   34 30S 139 0 E
Tanzania ■, *Africa* .... **54 D3**   6 0S 34 0 E
Tanzhou, *China* .... **33 G9**   22 16N 113 28 E
Tao, Ko, *Thailand* .... **39 G2**   10 5N 99 52 E
Tao'an = Taonan, *China* ...... **35 B12** 45 22N 122 40 E
Tao'er He →, *China* .... **35 B13** 45 45N 124 5 E
Taolanaro, *Madag.* .... **57 D8**   25 2S 47 0 E
Taole, *China* .... **34 E4**   38 48N 106 40 E
Taonan, *China* .... **35 B12** 45 22N 122 40 E
Taos, *U.S.A.* **77 H11** 36 24N 105 35W
Taoudenni, *Mali* **50 D5**   22 40N 3 55W
Tapa, *Estonia* .... **9 G21** 59 15N 25 50 E
Tapa Shan = Daba Shan, *China* . **33 C5**   32 0N 109 0 E
Tapachula, *Mexico* **87 E6**   14 54N 92 17W
Tapah, *Malaysia* .... **39 K3**   4 12N 101 15 E
Tapajós →, *Brazil* **93 D8**   2 24S 54 41W
Tapaktuan, *Indonesia* .... **36 D1**   3 15N 97 10 E
Tapanahoni →, *Suriname* **93 C8**   4 20N 54 25W
Tapanui, *N.Z.* .... **59 L2**   45 56S 169 18 E
Tapauá →, *Brazil* **92 E6**   5 40S 64 21W
Tapes, *Brazil* **95 C5**   30 40S 51 23W
Tapeta, *Liberia* **50 G4**   6 29N 8 52W
Taphan Hin, *Thailand* .... **38 D3**   16 13N 100 26 E
Tapi →, *India* .... **40 J8**   21 8N 72 41 E
Tapirapecó, Serra, *Venezuela* . **92 C5**   1 10N 65 0W
Tapo-Capara △, *Venezuela* ... **89 E5**   7 55N 71 15W
Tapuaenuku, *N.Z.* .... **59 K4**   42 0S 173 39 E
Tapul Group, *Phil.* .... **37 C6**   5 35N 120 50 E
Tapurucuará, *Brazil* **92 D5**   0 24S 65 2W
Taquara, *Brazil* **95 B5**   29 36S 50 46W
Taquari →, *Brazil* **92 G7**   19 15S 57 17W
Tara, *Australia* .... **63 D5**   27 17S 150 31 E
Tara, *Canada* **84 B3**   44 28N 81 9W
Tara, *Russia* .... **28 D8**   56 55N 74 24 E
Tara, *Zambia* .... **55 F2**   16 58S 26 45 E
Tara →, *Serbia & M.* .... **23 C8**   43 21N 18 51 E
Tarābulus, *Lebanon* .... **46 A4**   34 31N 35 50 E
Tarābulus, *Libya* .... **51 B8**   32 49N 13 7 E
Taradehi, *India* .... **43 H8**   23 18N 79 21 E
Tarajalejo, *Canary Is.* **24 F5**   28 12N 14 7W
Tarakan, *Indonesia* .... **36 D5**   3 20N 117 35 E
Tarakit, Mt., *Kenya* .... **54 B4**   2 2N 35 10 E
Tarama-Jima, *Japan* .... **31 M2** 24 39N 124 42 E
Taran, Mys, *Russia* .... **9 J18** 54 56N 19 59 E
Taranagar, *India* .... **42 E6** 28 43N 74 50 E
Taranaki □, *N.Z.* .... **59 H5** 39 25S 174 30 E
Taranaki, Mt., *N.Z.* .... **59 H5** 39 17S 174 5 E
Tarancón, *Spain* **21 B4** 40 1N 3 0W
Tarangire △, *Tanzania* ...... **54 C4**   4 21S 36 7 E
Taransay, *U.K.* **11 D1** 57 54N 7 0W
Táranto, *Italy* .... **22 D7** 40 28N 17 14 E
Táranto, G. di, *Italy* ...... **22 D7** 40 8N 17 20 E
Tarapacá, *Colombia* **92 D5**   2 56S 69 46W
Tarapacá □, *Chile* **94 A2** 20 45S 69 30W
Tarapoto, *Peru* **92 E3**   6 30S 76 20W
Tararua Ra., *N.Z.* .... **59 J5** 40 45S 175 25 E
Tarashcha, *Ukraine* .... **17 D16** 49 30N 30 31 E
Tarauacá, *Brazil* **92 E4**   8 6S 70 48W
Tarauacá →, *Brazil* **92 E5**   6 42S 69 48W
Tarawa, *Kiribati* .... **64 G9**   1 30N 173 0 E
Tarawera, *N.Z.* .... **59 H6** 39 2S 176 36 E
Tarawera, L., *N.Z.* .... **59 H6** 38 13S 176 27 E
Taraz, *Kazakhstan* .... **28 E8** 42 54N 71 22 E
Tarazona, *Spain* **21 B5** 41 55N 1 43W
Tarbagatay, Khrebet, *Kazakhstan* **28 E9** 48 0N 83 0 E
Tarbat Ness, *U.K.* **11 D5** 57 52N 3 47W
Tarbela Dam, *Pakistan* ...... **42 B5** 34 8N 72 52 E
Tarbert, Arg. & Bute, *U.K.* .. **11 F3** 55 52N 5 25W
Tarbert, W. Isles, *U.K.* **11 D2** 57 54N 6 49W
Tarbes, *France* .... **20 E4** 43 15N 0 3 E
Tarboro, *U.S.A.* **83 H7** 35 54N 77 32W
Tarcoola, *Australia* .... **63 E1** 30 44S 134 36 E
Tarcoon, *Australia* .... **63 E4** 30 15S 146 43 E
Taree, *Australia* .... **63 E5** 31 50S 152 30 E
Tarfaya, *Morocco* **50 C3** 27 55N 12 55W
Tărgoviște, *Romania* .... **17 F13** 44 55N 25 27 E
Târgu-Jiu, *Romania* .... **17 F12** 45 5N 23 19 E
Târgu Mureş, *Romania* ...... **17 E13** 46 31N 24 38 E
Ţarif, *U.A.E.* .... **45 E7** 24 3N 53 46 E
Tarifa, *Spain* **21 D3** 36 1N 5 36W
Tarija, *Bolivia* **94 A3** 21 30S 64 40W
Tarija □, *Bolivia* **94 A3** 21 30S 63 30W
Tariku →, *Indonesia* .... **37 E9**   2 55S 138 26 E
Tarim Basin = Tarim Pendi, *China* **32 B3** 40 0N 84 0 E
Tarim He →, *China* .... **32 C3** 39 30N 88 30 E
Tarim Pendi, *China* .... **32 B3** 40 0N 84 0 E
Taritatu →, *Indonesia* ...... **37 E9**   2 54S 138 27 E
Tarka →, *S. Africa* .... **56 E4** 32 10S 26 0 E
Tarkastad, *S. Africa* ...... **56 E4** 32 0S 26 16 E
Tarkhankut, Mys, *Ukraine* ... **19 E5** 45 25N 32 30 E
Tarko Sale, *Russia* .... **28 C8** 64 55N 77 50 E
Tarkwa, *Ghana* **50 G5**   5 20N 2 0W
Tarlac, *Phil.* .... **37 A6** 15 29N 120 35 E
Tarma, *Peru* **92 F3** 11 25S 75 45W
Tarn →, *France* .... **20 E4** 44 5N 1 6 E
Târnăveni, *Romania* .... **17 E13** 46 19N 24 13 E
Tarnobrzeg, *Poland* .... **17 C11** 50 35N 21 41 E
Tarnów, *Poland* .... **17 C11** 50 3N 21 0 E
Tarnowskie Góry, *Poland* .... **17 C10** 50 27N 18 54 E
Ţārom, *Iran* .... **45 D7** 28 11N 55 46 E
Taroom, *Australia* .... **63 D4** 25 36S 149 48 E
Taroudannt, *Morocco* **50 B4** 30 30N 8 52W
Tarpon Springs, *U.S.A.* **83 L4** 28 9N 82 45W
Tarragona, *Spain* .... **21 B6** 41 5N 1 17 E
Tarraleah, *Australia* .... **63 G4** 42 17S 146 26 E
Tàrrega = Terrassa, *Spain* ... **21 B7** 41 34N 2 1 E
Tarrytown, *U.S.A.* **85 E11** 41 4N 73 52W
Tarshiha = Me'ona, *Israel* ... **46 B4** 33 1N 35 15 E
Tarsus, *Turkey* .... **19 G5** 36 58N 34 55 E
Tartagal, *Argentina* **94 A3** 22 30S 63 50W
Tartu, *Estonia* .... **9 G22** 58 20N 26 44 E
Ţarţūs, *Syria* .... **44 C2** 34 55N 35 55 E
Tarumizu, *Japan* .... **31 J5** 31 29N 130 42 E

Tarutao = Ko Tarutao △, *Thailand* **39 J2**   6 31N 99 26 E
Tarutao, Ko, *Thailand* ...... **39 J2**   6 33N 99 40 E
Tarutung, *Indonesia* .... **36 D1**   2 0N 98 54 E
Taseko →, *Canada* **70 C4** 52 8N 123 45W
Tash-Kömür, *Kyrgyzstan* ..... **28 E8** 41 40N 72 10 E
Tash-Kumyr = Tash-Kömür,
  Kyrgyzstan .... **28 E8** 41 40N 72 10 E
Tashauz = Dashhowuz,
  Turkmenistan .... **28 E6** 41 49N 59 58 E
Tashi Chho Dzong = Thimphu,
  Bhutan .... **41 F16** 27 31N 89 45 E
Ţashk, Daryācheh-ye, *Iran* ... **45 D7** 29 45N 53 35 E
Tashkent = Toshkent, *Uzbekistan* **28 E7** 41 20N 69 10 E
Tashtagol, *Russia* .... **28 D9** 52 47N 87 53 E
Tasiilaq, *Greenland* **4 C6** 65 40N 37 20W
Tasikmalaya, *Indonesia* ..... **37 G13** 7 18S 108 12 E
Tåsjön, *Sweden* .... **8 D16** 64 15N 15 40 E
Taskan, *Russia* .... **29 C16** 62 59N 150 20 E
Tasman B., *N.Z.* .... **59 J4** 40 59S 173 25 E
Tasman Mts., *N.Z.* .... **59 J4** 41 3S 172 25 E
Tasman Pen., *Australia* .... **63 G4** 43 10S 148 0 E
Tasman Sea, *Pac. Oc.* ...... **64 L8** 36 0S 160 0 E
Tasmania □, *Australia* ..... **63 G4** 42 0S 146 30 E
Tassili n'Ajjer, *Algeria* .... **50 C7** 25 47N 8 1 E
Tatabánya, *Hungary* .... **17 E10** 47 32N 18 25 E
Tatahouine, *Tunisia* .... **51 B8** 32 56N 10 27 E
Tataouine, *Tunisia* .... **51 B8** 32 57N 10 29 E
Tatar Republic = Tatarstan □,
  Russia .... **18 C5** 55 30N 51 30 E
Tatarbunary, *Ukraine* .... **17 F15** 45 50N 29 39 E
Tatarsk, *Russia* .... **28 D8** 55 14N 76 0 E
Tatarstan □, *Russia* .... **18 C5** 55 30N 51 30 E
Tateyama, *Japan* .... **31 G9** 35 0N 139 50 E
Tathlina L., *Canada* **70 A5** 60 33N 117 39W
Tathra, *Australia* .... **63 F4** 36 44S 149 59 E
Tatinnai L., *Canada* .... **71 A9** 60 55N 97 40 E
Tatla L., *Canada* **70 C4** 52 0N 124 20W
Tatnam, C., *Canada* **71 B10** 57 16N 91 0W
Tatra = Tatry, *Slovak Rep.* .. **17 D11** 49 20N 20 0 E
Tatry, *Slovak Rep.* .... **17 D11** 49 20N 20 0 E
Tatshenshini →, *Canada* **70 B1** 59 28N 137 45W
Tatsuno, *Japan* .... **31 G7** 34 52N 134 33 E
Tatta, *Pakistan* .... **42 G2** 24 42N 67 55 E
Tatuí, *Brazil* **95 A6** 23 25S 47 53W
Tatum, *U.S.A.* **81 J3** 33 16N 103 19W
Tat'ung = Datong, *China* .... **34 D7** 40 6N 113 18 E
Tatvan, *Turkey* .... **19 G7** 38 31N 42 15 E
Taubaté, *Brazil* **95 A6** 23 0S 45 36W
Tauern, *Austria* .... **16 E7** 47 15N 12 40 E
Taumarunui, *N.Z.* .... **59 H5** 38 53S 175 15 E
Taumaturgo, *Brazil* **92 E4** 8 54S 72 51W
Taung, *S. Africa* .... **56 D3** 27 33S 24 47 E
Taungdwingyi, *Burma* .... **41 J19** 20 1N 95 40 E
Taunggyi, *Burma* .... **41 J20** 20 50N 97 0 E
Taungup, *Burma* .... **41 K19** 18 51N 94 14 E
Taungup Taunggya, *Burma* .... **41 K18** 18 20N 93 40 E
Taunsa, *Pakistan* .... **42 D4** 30 42N 70 39 E
Taunsa Barrage, *Pakistan* ... **42 D4** 30 42N 70 50 E
Taunton, *U.K.* **13 F4** 51 1N 3 5W
Taunton, *U.S.A.* **85 E13** 41 54N 71 6W
Taunus, *Germany* .... **16 C5** 50 13N 8 34 E
Taupo, *N.Z.* .... **59 H6** 38 41S 176 7 E
Taupo, L., *N.Z.* .... **59 H5** 38 46S 175 55 E
Tauragė, *Lithuania* .... **9 J20** 55 14N 22 16 E
Tauranga, *N.Z.* .... **59 G6** 37 42S 176 11 E
Tauranga Harb., *N.Z.* ...... **59 G6** 37 30S 176 5 E
Taureau, Rés., *Canada* **72 C5** 46 46N 73 50W
Taurianova, *Italy* .... **22 E7** 38 21N 16 1 E
Taurus Mts. = Toros Dağları,
  Turkey .... **19 G5** 37 0N 32 30 E
Tavda, *Russia* .... **28 D7** 58 7N 65 8 E
Tavda →, *Russia* .... **28 D7** 57 47N 67 18 E
Taveta, *Tanzania* .... **54 C4** 3 23S 37 37 E
Taveuni, *Fiji* **59 C9** 16 51S 179 58W
Tavira, *Portugal* **21 D2** 37 8N 7 40W
Tavistock, *Canada* **84 C4** 43 19N 80 50W
Tavistock, *U.K.* **13 G3** 50 33N 4 9W
Tavoy, *Burma* .... **38 E2** 14 2N 98 12 E
Taw →, *U.K.* **13 F3** 51 4N 4 4W
Tawa →, *India* .... **42 H8** 22 48N 77 48 E
Tawas City, *U.S.A.* **82 C4** 44 16N 83 31W
Tawau, *Malaysia* .... **36 D5** 4 20N 117 55 E
Tawitawi, *Phil.* .... **37 B6** 5 10N 120 0 E
Taxco de Alarcón, *Mexico* ... **87 D5** 18 33N 99 36W
Taxila, *Pakistan* .... **42 C5** 33 42N 72 52 E
Tay →, *U.K.* **11 E5** 56 43N 3 59W
Tay, Firth of, *U.K.* **11 E5** 56 37N 3 38W
Tay, L., *Australia* .... **61 F3** 32 55S 120 48 E
Tay, L., *U.K.* **11 E4** 56 32N 4 8W
Tay Ninh, *Vietnam* .... **39 G6** 11 20N 106 5 E
Tayabamba, *Peru* **92 E3** 8 15S 77 16W
Taylakova, *Russia* .... **28 D8** 59 13N 74 0 E
Taylakovy = Taylakova, *Russia* . **28 D8** 59 13N 74 0 E
Taylor, *Canada* **70 B4** 56 13N 120 40W
Taylor, *Nebr., U.S.A.* **80 E5** 41 46N 99 23W
Taylor, *Pa., U.S.A.* **85 E9** 41 23N 75 43W
Taylor, *Tex., U.S.A.* **81 K6** 30 34N 97 25W
Taylor, Mt., *U.S.A.* **77 J10** 35 14N 107 37W
Taylorville, *U.S.A.* **80 F10** 39 33N 89 18W
Taymā, *Si. Arabia* .... **44 E3** 27 35N 38 45 E
Taymyr, Oz., *Russia* .... **29 B11** 74 20N 102 0 E
Taymyr, Poluostrov, *Russia* .. **29 B11** 75 0N 100 0 E
Tayport, *U.K.* **11 E6** 56 27N 2 52W
Tayrona △, *Colombia* **89 D5** 11 20N 74 2W
Tayshet, *Russia* .... **29 D10** 55 58N 98 1 E
Taytay, *Phil.* .... **37 B5** 10 45N 119 30 E
Tāyyebād, *Iran* .... **45 C9** 34 45N 60 45 E
Tāyyebād □, *Iran* .... **45 C9** 34 44N 60 44 E
Taz →, *Russia* .... **28 C8** 67 32N 78 40 E
Taza, *Morocco* **50 B5** 34 16N 4 6W
Tāza Khurmātū, *Iraq* .... **44 C5** 35 18N 44 20 E
Tazawa-Ko, *Japan* .... **30 E10** 39 43N 140 40 E
Tazin, *Canada* **71 B7** 59 48N 109 55W
Tazin L., *Canada* **71 B7** 59 44N 108 42W
Tazovskiy, *Russia* .... **28 C8** 67 30N 78 44 E
Tbilisi, *Georgia* .... **19 F7** 41 43N 44 50 E
Tchad = Chad ■, *Africa* .... **51 F8** 15 0N 17 15 E
Tchad, L., *Chad* .... **51 F8** 13 30N 14 30 E
Tch'eng-tou = Chengdu, *China* . **32 C5** 30 38N 104 2 E
Tchentlo L., *Canada* **70 B4** 55 15N 125 0W
Tchibanga, *Gabon* .... **52 E2** 2 45S 11 0 E
Tch'ong-k'ing = Chongqing,
  China .... **32 D5** 29 35N 106 25 E
Tczew, *Poland* .... **17 A10** 54 8N 18 50 E
Te Anau, L., *N.Z.* .... **59 L1** 45 15S 167 45 E
Te Aroha, *N.Z.* .... **59 G5** 37 32S 175 44 E

Te Awamutu, *N.Z.* .... **59 H5** 38 1S 175 20 E
Te Kuiti, *N.Z.* .... **59 H5** 38 20S 175 11 E
Te Puke, *N.Z.* .... **59 G6** 37 46S 176 22 E
Te Waewae B., *N.Z.* .... **59 M1** 46 13S 167 33 E
Teague, *U.S.A.* **81 K6** 31 38N 96 17W
Teapa, *Mexico* **87 D6** 18 35N 92 56W
Tebakang, *Malaysia* .... **36 D4** 1 6N 110 30 E
Teberu, *Malaysia* .... **39 d** 1 30N 103 42 E
Tébessa, *Algeria* .... **50 A7** 35 22N 8 8 E
Tebicuary →, *Paraguay* **94 B4** 26 36S 58 16W
Tebingtinggi, Riau, *Indonesia* . **36 E2** 1 0N 102 45 E
Tebingtinggi, Sumatera Utara,
  Indonesia .... **36 D1** 3 20N 9 9 E
Tecate, *Mexico* **79 N10** 32 34N 116 38W
Tecka, *Argentina* **96 E2** 43 29S 70 48W
Tecomán, *Mexico* **86 D4** 18 55N 103 53W
Tecopa, *U.S.A.* **79 K10** 35 51N 116 13W
Tecuala, *Mexico* **86 C3** 22 23N 105 27W
Tecuci, *Romania* .... **17 F14** 45 51N 27 27 E
Tecumseh, *Canada* **84 D2** 42 19N 82 54W
Tecumseh, *Mich., U.S.A.* **82 D4** 42 0N 83 57W
Tecumseh, *Okla., U.S.A.* **81 H6** 35 15N 96 56W
Tedzhen = Tejen, *Turkmenistan* . **28 F7** 37 23N 60 31 E
Tees →, *U.K.* **12 C6** 54 37N 1 10W
Tees B., *U.K.* **12 C6** 54 40N 1 9W
Teeswater, *Canada* **84 C3** 43 59N 81 17W
Tefé, *Brazil* **92 D6** 3 25S 64 50W
Tegal, *Indonesia* .... **36 F3** 6 52S 109 8 E
Tegallalang, *Indonesia* .... **37 J18** 8 27S 115 17 E
Tegalsari, *Indonesia* ...... **37 J17** 8 25S 114 8 E
Tegid, L. = Bala, L., *U.K.* .. **12 E4** 52 53N 3 37W
Tegucigalpa, *Honduras* **88 D2** 14 5N 87 14W
Tehachapi, *U.S.A.* **79 K8** 35 8N 118 27W
Tehachapi Mts., *U.S.A.* **79 L8** 35 0N 118 30W
Teheran = Tehrān, *Iran* .... **45 C6** 35 44N 51 30 E
Tehoru, *Indonesia* .... **37 E7** 3 23S 129 30 E
Tehrān, *Iran* .... **45 C6** 35 44N 51 30 E
Tehrān □, *Iran* .... **45 C6** 35 30N 51 30 E
Tehri, *India* .... **43 D8** 30 23N 78 29 E
Tehuacán, *Mexico* **87 D5** 18 30N 97 30W
Tehuantepec, *Mexico* **87 D5** 16 21N 95 13W
Tehuantepec, G. de, *Mexico* .. **87 D5** 15 50N 95 12W
Tehuantepec, Istmo de, *Mexico* **87 D6** 17 0N 94 30W
Teide, Pico de, *Canary Is.* .. **24 F3** 28 15N 16 38W
Teifi →, *U.K.* **13 E3** 52 5N 4 41W
Teign →, *U.K.* **13 G4** 50 32N 3 32W
Teignmouth, *U.K.* **13 G4** 50 33N 3 31W
Tejakula, *Indonesia* ...... **37 J18** 8 8S 115 20 E
Tejam, *India* .... **43 E9** 29 57N 80 11 E
Tejen, *Turkmenistan* .... **28 F7** 37 23N 60 31 E
Tejen →, *Turkmenistan* ..... **45 B9** 37 24N 60 38 E
Tejo →, *Europe* **21 C1** 38 40N 9 24W
Tejon Pass, *U.S.A.* **79 L8** 34 49N 118 53W
Tekamah, *U.S.A.* **80 E6** 41 47N 96 13W
Tekapo, L., *N.Z.* .... **59 K3** 43 53S 170 33 E
Tekax, *Mexico* **87 C7** 20 11N 89 18W
Tekeli, *Kazakhstan* .... **28 E8** 44 50N 79 0 E
Tekirdağ, *Turkey* .... **23 D12** 40 58N 27 30 E
Tekkali, *India* .... **41 K14** 18 37N 84 15 E
Tekoa, *U.S.A.* **76 C5** 47 14N 117 4W
Tekong Besar, Pulau, *Singapore* **39 d** 1 25N 104 3 E
Tel Aviv ✈ (TLV), *Israel* ... **46 C3** 32 5N 34 49 E
Tel Aviv-Yafo, *Israel* ..... **46 C3** 32 4N 34 48 E
Tel Lakhish, *Israel* .... **46 D3** 31 34N 34 51 E
Tel Megiddo, *Israel* .... **46 C4** 32 35N 35 11 E
Tela, *Honduras* **88 C2** 15 40N 87 28W
Telanaipura = Jambi, *Indonesia* **36 E2** 1 38S 103 30 E
Telavi, *Georgia* .... **19 F8** 42 0N 45 30 E
Telde, *Canary Is.* **24 G4** 27 59N 15 25W
Telegraph Creek, *Canada* **70 B2** 58 0N 131 10W
Telekhany = Tsyelyakhany,
  Belarus .... **17 B13** 52 30N 25 46 E
Telemark, *Norway* .... **9 G12** 59 15N 7 40 E
Telén, *Argentina* **94 D2** 36 15S 65 31W
Teleng, *Iran* .... **45 E9** 25 47N 61 3 E
Teles Pires →, *Brazil* **92 E7** 7 21S 58 3W
Telescope Pk., *U.S.A.* **79 J9** 36 10N 117 5W
Telfer Mine, *Australia* .... **60 C3** 21 40S 122 12 E
Telford, *U.K.* **13 E5** 52 40N 2 27W
Telford and Wrekin □, *U.K.* .. **12 E5** 52 45N 2 27W
Telkwa, *Canada* **70 C3** 54 41N 127 5W
Tell City, *U.S.A.* **82 G2** 37 57N 86 46W
Tellicherry, *India* .... **40 P9** 11 45N 75 30 E
Telluride, *U.S.A.* **77 H10** 37 56N 107 49W
Teloloapán, *Mexico* **87 D5** 18 21N 99 51W
Telpos Iz, *Russia* .... **18 B10** 63 16N 59 13 E
Telsen, *Argentina* **96 E3** 42 30S 66 50W
Telšiai, *Lithuania* .... **9 H20** 55 59N 22 14 E
Teluk Anson = Teluk Intan,
  Malaysia .... **39 K3** 4 3N 101 0 E
Teluk Bahang, *Malaysia* .... **39 c** 5 28N 100 13 E
Teluk Betung = Tanjungkarang
  Telukbetung, *Indonesia* ... **36 F3** 5 20S 105 10 E
Teluk Intan, *Malaysia* ..... **39 K3** 4 3N 101 0 E
Teluk Kumbar, *Malaysia* .... **39 c** 5 18N 100 14 E
Telukbutun, *Indonesia* ..... **36 D3** 4 13N 108 12 E
Telukdalem, *Indonesia* ..... **36 D1** 0 33N 97 50 E
Tema, *Ghana* **50 G5** 5 41N 0 0W
Temax, *Mexico* **87 C7** 21 10N 88 50W
Temba, *S. Africa* .... **57 D4** 25 20S 28 17 E
Tembagapura, *Indonesia* .... **37 E9** 4 20S 137 0 E
Tembe, Dem. Rep. of the Congo . **54 C2** 0 16S 28 14 E
Tembe △, *S. Africa* .... **57 D5** 26 51S 32 24 E
Temblor Range, *U.S.A.* **79 K7** 35 20N 119 50W
Teme →, *U.K.* **13 E5** 52 11N 2 13W
Temecula, *U.S.A.* **79 M9** 33 30N 117 9W
Temerloh, *Malaysia* .... **36 D2** 3 27N 102 25 E
Teminabuan, *Indonesia* ..... **37 E8** 1 26S 132 1 E
Temir, *Kazakhstan* .... **19 E10** 49 1N 57 14 E
Temirtau, *Kazakhstan* ...... **28 D8** 50 5N 72 56 E
Temirtau, *Russia* .... **28 D9** 53 10N 87 30 E
Temiscamie →, *Canada* **73 B5** 50 59N 73 5W
Témiscamie →, *Canada* **72 C4** 46 44N 79 5W
Témiscamingue, L., *Canada* .. **72 C4** 47 10N 79 25W
Temosachic, *Mexico* **86 B3** 28 58N 107 50W
Tempe, *U.S.A.* **77 K8** 33 25N 111 56W
Tempiute, *U.S.A.* **78 H11** 37 39N 115 38W
Temple, *U.S.A.* **81 K6** 31 6N 97 21W
Temple B., *Australia* ...... **62 A3** 12 15S 143 3 E
Templemore, *Ireland* **10 D4** 52 47N 7 51W
Templeton, *U.S.A.* **78 K6** 35 33N 120 42W
Templeton →, *Australia* ... **62 C2** 21 0S 138 40 E
Tempoal, *Mexico* **87 C5** 21 31N 98 23W
Temuco, *Chile* **96 D2** 38 45S 72 40W
Temuka, *N.Z.* .... **59 L3** 44 14S 171 17 E

Tenabo, *Mexico* **87 C6** 20 2N 90 12W
Tenaha, *U.S.A.* **81 K7** 31 57N 94 15W
Tenakee Springs, *U.S.A.* **70 B1** 57 47N 135 13W
Tenali, *India* .... **41 L12** 16 15N 80 35 E
Tenancingo, *Mexico* **87 D5** 19 0N 99 33W
Tenango, *Mexico* **87 D5** 19 7N 99 33W
Tenasserim, *Burma* .... **39 F2** 12 6N 99 3 E
Tenasserim □, *Burma* ...... **38 F2** 14 0N 98 30 E
Tenby, *U.K.* **13 F3** 51 40N 4 42W
Tenda, Colle di, *France* .... **20 D7** 44 7N 7 36 E
Tendaho, *Ethiopia* .... **47 E3** 11 48N 40 54 E
Tendukhera, *India* .... **43 H8** 23 24N 79 33 E
Teneguía, Volcanes de,
  Canary Is. **24 F2** 28 28N 17 51W
Tenerife, *Canary Is.* **24 F3** 28 15N 16 35W
Tenerife, Pico, *Canary Is.* .. **24 G1** 27 43N 18 1W
Tenerife Norte ✈ (TFN),
  Canary Is. **24 F3** 28 28N 16 17W
Tenerife Sur ✈ (TFS), *Canary Is.* **24 F3** 28 3N 16 33W
Teng Xian, *China* .... **35 G9** 35 5N 117 10 E
Tengah □, *Indonesia* ...... **37 E6** 1 30S 121 0 E
Tengah, Kepulauan, *Indonesia* . **36 F5** 7 5S 118 15 E
Tengchong, *China* .... **34 D1** 25 0N 98 28 E
Tengchowfu = Penglai, *China* . **35 F11** 37 48N 120 42 E
Tenggara □, *Indonesia* ..... **37 E6** 3 50S 122 0 E
Tenggarong, *Indonesia* ..... **36 E5** 0 24S 116 58 E
Tenggol, Pulau, *Malaysia* ... **39 K4** 4 48N 103 41 E
Tengiz, Ozero, *Kazakhstan* ... **28 D7** 50 30N 69 0 E
Teniente Enciso △, *Paraguay* . **94 A3** 21 5S 61 8W
Teniente Rodolfo Marsh,
  Antarctica **5 C18** 62 30S 58 0W
Tenino, *U.S.A.* **78 D4** 46 51N 122 51W
Tenkasi, *India* .... **40 Q10** 8 55N 77 20 E
Tenke, Katanga, Dem. Rep. of
  the Congo .... **55 E2** 11 22S 26 40 E
Tenke, Katanga, Dem. Rep. of
  the Congo .... **55 E2** 10 32S 26 7 E
Tennant Creek, *Australia* ... **62 B1** 19 30S 134 15 E
Tennessee □, *U.S.A.* **83 H2** 36 0N 86 30W
Tennessee →, *U.S.A.* **82 G1** 37 4N 88 34W
Teno, Pta. de, *Canary Is.* ... **24 F3** 28 21N 16 55W
Tenom, *Malaysia* .... **36 C5** 5 4N 115 57 E
Tenosique, *Mexico* **87 D6** 17 30N 91 24W
Tenryū-Gawa →, *Japan* ..... **31 G8** 35 39N 137 48 E
Tenterden, *U.K.* .... **13 F8** 51 4N 0 42 E
Tenterfield, *Australia* .... **63 D5** 29 0S 152 0 E
Teófilo Otoni, *Brazil* **93 G10** 17 50S 41 30W
Tepa, *Indonesia* .... **37 F7** 7 52S 129 31 E
Tepalcatepec →, *Mexico* **86 D4** 18 35N 101 59W
Tepehuanes, *Mexico* **86 B3** 25 21N 105 44W
Tepetongo, *Mexico* **86 C4** 22 28N 103 9W
Tepic, *Mexico* **86 C4** 21 30N 104 54W
Teplice, *Czech Rep.* ...... **16 C7** 50 40N 13 48 E
Tepoca, C., *Mexico* **86 A2** 30 20N 112 25W
Tequila, *Mexico* **86 C4** 20 54N 103 47W
Ter →, *Spain* .... **21 A7** 42 2N 3 12 E
Ter Apel, *Neths.* .... **15 B7** 52 53N 7 5 E
Teraina, *Kiribati* **65 G11** 4 43N 160 25W
Téramo, *Italy* .... **22 C5** 42 39N 13 42 E
Terang, *Australia* .... **63 F3** 38 15S 142 55 E
Terang, Teluk, *Indonesia* ... **37 K19** 8 44S 116 0 E
Tercero →, *Argentina* **94 C3** 32 58S 61 47W
Terebovlya, *Ukraine* ...... **17 D13** 49 18N 25 44 E
Terek →, *Russia* .... **19 F8** 44 0N 47 30 E
Terepaima △, *Venezuela* **89 E6** 9 58N 69 17W
Teresina, *Brazil* **93 E10** 5 9S 42 45W
Terewah, L., *Australia* .... **63 D4** 29 52S 147 35 E
Teridgerie Cr. →, *Australia* . **63 E4** 30 25S 148 50 E
Termez = Termiz, *Uzbekistan* . **28 F7** 37 15N 67 15 E
Términi Imerese, *Italy* ..... **22 F5** 37 59N 13 42 E
Términos, L. de, *Mexico* **87 D6** 18 35N 91 30W
Termiz, *Uzbekistan* .... **28 F7** 37 15N 67 15 E
Térmoli, *Italy* .... **22 C6** 42 0N 15 0 E
Ternate, *Indonesia* .... **37 D7** 0 45N 127 25 E
Terneuzen, *Neths.* .... **15 C3** 51 20N 3 50 E
Terney, *Russia* .... **29 E14** 45 3N 136 37 E
Terni, *Italy* .... **22 C5** 42 34N 12 37 E
Ternopil, *Ukraine* .... **17 D13** 49 30N 25 40 E
Ternopol = Ternopil, *Ukraine* . **17 D13** 49 30N 25 40 E
Terowie, *Australia* .... **63 E2** 33 8S 138 55 E
Terra Bella, *U.S.A.* **79 K7** 35 58N 119 3W
Terra Nova △, *Canada* **73 C9** 48 33N 53 55W
Terrace, *Canada* **70 C3** 54 30N 128 35W
Terrace Bay, *Canada* **72 C2** 48 47N 87 5W
Terracina, *Italy* .... **22 D5** 41 17N 13 15 E
Terralba, *Italy* .... **22 E3** 39 43N 8 39 E
Terranova = Ólbia, *Italy* .... **22 D3** 40 55N 9 31 E
Terrassa, *Spain* .... **21 B7** 41 34N 2 1 E
Terre Haute, *U.S.A.* **82 F2** 39 28N 87 25W
Terrebonne B., *U.S.A.* **81 L9** 29 5N 90 35W
Terrell, *U.S.A.* **81 J6** 32 44N 96 17W
Terrenceville, *Canada* **73 C9** 47 40N 54 44W
Terry, *U.S.A.* **80 B2** 46 47N 105 19W
Terryville, *U.S.A.* **85 E11** 41 41N 73 3W
Terschelling, *Neths.* ...... **15 A5** 53 25N 5 20 E
Teruel, *Spain* **21 B5** 40 22N 1 8W
Tervola, *Finland* .... **8 C21** 66 6N 24 49 E
Teryaweyna L., *Australia* ... **63 E3** 32 18S 143 22 E
Teshio, *Japan* .... **30 B10** 44 53N 141 44 E
Teshio-Gawa →, *Japan* ..... **30 B10** 44 53N 141 45 E
Tesiyn Gol →, *Mongolia* .... **32 A4** 50 40N 93 20 E
Teslin, *Canada* **70 A2** 60 10N 132 43W
Teslin →, *Canada* **70 A2** 61 34N 134 35W
Teslin L., *Canada* **70 A2** 60 15N 132 57W
Tessalit, *Mali* .... **50 D6** 20 12N 1 0 E
Test →, *U.K.* **13 G6** 50 56N 1 29W
Testigos, Is. Las, *Venezuela* . **89 D7** 11 23N 63 7W
Tetachuck L., *Canada* **70 C3** 53 18N 125 55W
Tetas, Pta., *Chile* **94 A1** 23 31S 70 38W
Tete, *Mozam.* .... **55 F3** 16 13S 33 33 E
Tete □, *Mozam.* .... **55 F3** 15 15S 32 40 E
Teterev →, *Ukraine* .... **17 C16** 51 1N 30 5 E
Teteven, *Bulgaria* .... **23 C11** 42 58N 24 17 E
Tethul →, *Canada* **70 A6** 60 35N 112 12W
Tetiyev, *Ukraine* .... **17 D15** 49 22N 29 38 E
Teton →, *U.S.A.* **76 C8** 47 56N 110 31W
Tétouan, *Morocco* **50 A4** 35 35N 5 21W
Tetovo, *Macedonia* .... **23 C9** 42 1N 20 59 E
Teuco →, *Argentina* **94 B3** 25 35S 60 11W
Teulon, *Canada* **71 C9** 50 23N 97 16W
Teun, *Indonesia* .... **37 F7** 6 59S 129 8 E
Teutoburger Wald, *Germany* .. **16 B5** 52 5N 8 22 E
Tevere →, *Italy* .... **22 D5** 41 44N 12 14 E
Teverya, *Israel* .... **46 C4** 32 47N 35 32 E
Teviot →, *U.K.* **11 F6** 55 29N 2 38W
Tewantin, *Australia* ...... **63 D5** 26 27S 153 3 E
Tewkesbury, *U.K.* **13 F5** 51 59N 2 9W

Texada I., Canada 70 D4   49 40N 124 25W
Texarkana, Ark., U.S.A. 81 J8   33 26N 94 2W
Texarkana, Tex., U.S.A. 81 J7   33 26N 94 3W
Texas, Australia . . . . 63 D5   28 49S 151 9 E
Texas □, U.S.A. 81 K5   31 40N 98 30W
Texas City, U.S.A. 81 L7   29 24N 94 54W
Texel, Neths. . . . . 15 A4   53 5N   4 50 E
Texline, U.S.A. 81 G3   36 23N 103 2W
Texoma, L., U.S.A. 81 J6   33 50N 96 34W
Tezin, Afghan. . . . . 42 B3   34 24N 69 30 E
Teziutlán, Mexico 87 D5   19 50N 97 22W
Tezpur, India . . . . 41 F18 26 40N 92 45 E
Tezzeron L., Canada 70 C4   54 43N 124 30W
Tha-anne →, Canada 71 A10 60 31N 94 37W
Tha Deua, Laos . . . . 38 D4   17 57N 102 53 E
Tha Deua, Laos . . . . 38 C3   19 26N 101 50 E
Tha Pla, Thailand . . . . 38 D3   17 48N 100 32 E
Tha Rua, Thailand . . . . 38 E3   14 34N 100 44 E
Tha Sala, Thailand . . . . 39 H2   8 40N 99 56 E
Tha Song Yang, Thailand . . . . 38 D1   17 34N 97 55 E
Thaba Putsoa, Lesotho . . . . . . 57 D4   29 45S 28 0 E
Thabana Ntlenyana, Lesotho . . 57 D4   29 30S 29 16 E
Thabazimbi, S. Africa . . . . 57 C4   24 40S 27 21 E
Thādiq, Si. Arabia . . . . 44 E5   25 18N 45 52 E
Thai Binh, Vietnam . . . . 38 B6   20 35N 106 1 E
Thai Muang, Thailand . . . . . . 39 H2   8 24N 98 16 E
Thai Nguyen, Vietnam . . . . . . 38 B5   21 35N 105 55 E
Thailand ■, Asia . . . . 38 E4   16 0N 102 0 E
Thailand, G. of, Asia . . . . 39 G3   11 30N 101 0 E
Thakhek, Laos . . . . 38 D5   17 25N 104 45 E
Thal, Pakistan . . . . 42 C4   33 28N 70 33 E
Thal Desert, Pakistan . . . . 42 D4   31 10N 71 30 E
Thala La = Hkakabo Razi, Burma 41 E20 28 25N 97 23 E
Thalabarivat, Cambodia . . . . . 38 F5   13 33N 105 57 E
Thallon, Australia . . . . 63 D4   28 39S 148 49 E
Thalu, Ko, Thailand . . . . 39 b   9 26N 99 54 E
Thames, N.Z. . . . . 59 G5   37 7S 175 34 E
Thames →, Canada 84 D2   42 20N 82 25W
Thames →, U.K. . . . . 13 F8   51 29N   0 34 E
Thames →, U.S.A. 85 E12 41 18N 72 5W
Thames Estuary, U.K. . . . . 13 F8   51 29N   0 52 E
Thamesford, Canada 84 C4   43 4N 81 0W
Thamesville, Canada 84 D3   42 33N 81 59W
Than, India . . . . 42 H4   22 34N 71 11 E
Than Uyen, Vietnam . . . . 38 B4   22 0N 103 54 E
Thana Gazi, India . . . . 42 F7   27 25N 76 19 E
Thandla, India . . . . 42 H6   23 0N 74 34 E
Thane, India . . . . 40 K8   19 12N 72 59 E
Thanesar, India . . . . 42 D7   30 1N 76 52 E
Thanet, I. of, U.K. . . . . 13 F9   51 21N   1 20 E
Thangool, Australia . . . . 62 C5   24 38S 150 42 E
Thanh Hoa, Vietnam . . . . 38 C5   19 48N 105 46 E
Thanh Pho Ho Chi Minh, Vietnam 39 G6 10 58N 106 40 E
Thanh Thuy, Vietnam . . . . 38 A5   22 55N 104 51 E
Thanjavur, India . . . . 40 P11 10 48N 79 12 E
Thano Bula Khan, Pakistan . . . 42 G2   25 22N 67 50 E
Thaolinta L., Canada 71 A9   61 30N 96 25W
Thap Lan △, Thailand . . . . . . 38 E4   14 15N 102 16 E
Thap Sakae, Thailand . . . . 39 G2   11 30N 99 37 E
Thap Than, Thailand . . . . 38 E2   15 27N 99 54 E
Thar Desert, India . . . . 42 F5   28 0N 72 0 E
Tharad, India . . . . 42 G4   24 30N 71 44 E
Thargomindah, Australia . . . . . 63 D3   27 58S 143 46 E
Tharrawaddy, Burma . . . . 41 L19 17 38N 95 48 E
Tharthār, Buḩayrat ath, Iraq . . 44 C4   34 0N 43 15 E
Tharthar, L. = Tharthār, Buḩayrat
  ath, Iraq . . . . 44 C4   34 0N 43 15 E
Tharthār, W. ath →, Iraq . . . . 44 C4   33 59N 43 12 E
Thásos, Greece . . . . 23 D11 40 40N 24 40 E
That Khe, Vietnam . . . . 38 A6   22 16N 106 28 E
Thatcher, Ariz., U.S.A. 77 K9   32 51N 109 46W
Thatcher, Colo., U.S.A. 81 G2   37 33N 104 7W
Thaton, Burma . . . . 41 L20 16 55N 97 22 E
Thaungdut, Burma . . . . 41 G19 24 30N 94 40 E
Thayer, U.S.A. 81 G9   36 31N 91 33W
Thayetmyo, Burma . . . . 41 K19 19 20N 95 10 E
Thazi, Burma . . . . 41 J20 21 0N 96 5 E
The Alberga →, Australia . . . . 63 D2   27 6S 135 33 E
The Bight, Bahamas 89 B4   24 19N 75 24W
The Crane, Barbados . . . . 89 g   13 6N 59 27W
The Dalles, U.S.A. 76 D3   45 36N 121 10W
The English Company's Is.,
  Australia . . . . 62 A2   11 50S 136 32 E
The Frome →, Australia . . . . . 63 D2   29 8S 137 54 E
The Great Divide = Great
  Dividing Ra., Australia . . . . 62 C4   23 0S 146 0 E
The Hague = 's-Gravenhage,
  Neths. . . . . 15 B4   52 7N   4 17 E
The Hamilton →, Australia . . . 63 D2   26 40S 135 19 E
The Macumba →, Australia . . . 63 D2   27 52S 137 12 E
The Neales →, Australia . . . . . 63 D2   28 8S 136 47 E
The Officer →, Australia . . . . . 61 E5   27 46S 132 30 E
The Pas, Canada 71 C8   53 45N 101 15W
The Range, Zimbabwe . . . . . . 55 F3   19 2S 31 2 E
The Rock, Australia . . . . 63 F4   35 15S 147 2 E
The Salt L., Australia . . . . 63 E3   30 6S 142 8 E
The Sandheads, India . . . . 43 J13 21 10N 88 20 E
The Settlement, Br. Virgin Is. . 89 e   18 43N 64 22W
The Stevenson →, Australia . . . 63 D2   27 6S 135 33 E
The Warburton →, Australia . . . 63 D2   28 4S 137 28 E
The Woodlands, U.S.A. 81 K7   30 9N 95 27W
Thebes = Thívai, Greece . . . . . 23 E10 38 19N 23 19 E
Thebes, Egypt . . . . 51 C12 25 40N 32 35 E
Thedford, U.S.A. 80 E4   41 59N 100 35W
Theebine, Australia . . . . 63 D5   25 57S 152 34 E
Thekulthili L., Canada 71 A7   61 3N 110 0W
Thelon →, Canada 71 A8   64 16N 96 4W
Theodore, Australia . . . . 62 C5   24 55S 150 3 E
Theodore, Canada 71 C8   51 26N 102 55W
Theodore, U.S.A. 83 K1   30 33N 88 10W
Theodore Roosevelt △, U.S.A. . 80 B3   47 0N 103 25W
Theodore Roosevelt L., U.S.A. . 77 K8   33 40N 111 10W
Thepha, Thailand . . . . 39 J3   6 52N 100 58 E
Theresa, U.S.A. 85 B9   44 13N 75 48W
Thermaïkós Kólpos, Greece . . . 23 D10 40 15N 22 45 E
Thermopolis, U.S.A. 76 E9   43 39N 108 13W
Thermopylae P., Greece . . . . . 23 E10 38 48N 22 35 E
Thessalon, Canada 72 C3   46 20N 83 30W
Thessaloníki, Greece . . . . 23 D10 40 38N 22 58 E
Thessaloníki, Gulf of =
  Thermaïkós Kólpos, Greece . 23 D10 40 15N 22 45 E
Thetford, U.K. . . . . 13 E8   52 25N   0 45 E
Thetford Mines, Canada 73 C5   46 8N 71 18W
Theun →, Laos . . . . 38 C5   18 19N 104 0 E
Theunissen, S. Africa . . . . 56 D4   28 26S 26 43 E
Thevenard, Australia . . . . 63 E1   32 9S 133 38 E

Thibodaux, U.S.A. 81 L9   29 48N 90 49W
Thicket Portage, Canada 71 B9   55 19N 97 42W
Thief River Falls, U.S.A. 80 A6   48 7N 96 10W
Thiel Mts., Antarctica 5 E16   85 15S 91 0W
Thiers, France . . . . 20 D5   45 52N   3 33 E
Thiès, Senegal 50 F2   14 50N 16 51W
Thika, Kenya . . . . 54 C4   1 1S 37 5 E
Thikombia, Fiji 59 B9   15 44S 179 55W
Thimphu, Bhutan . . . . 41 F16 27 31N 89 45 E
Þingvallavatn, Iceland 8 D3   64 11N 21 9W
Thionville, France . . . . 20 B7   49 20N   6 10 E
Thíra, Greece . . . . 23 F11 36 23N 25 27 E
Third Cataract, Sudan . . . . 51 E12 19 42N 30 20 E
Thirsk, U.K. 12 C6   54 14N   1 19W
Thiruvananthapuram =
  Trivandrum, India . . . . 40 Q10 8 41N 77 0 E
Thisted, Denmark . . . . 9 H13 56 58N 8 40 E
Thistle I., Australia . . . . 63 F2   35 0S 136 8 E
Thívai, Greece . . . . 23 E10 38 19N 23 19 E
Þjórsá →, Iceland 8 E3   63 47N 20 48W
Thlewiaza →, Canada 71 A10 60 29N 94 40W
Thmar Puok, Cambodia . . . . . 38 F4   13 57N 103 4 E
Tho Vinh, Vietnam . . . . 38 C5   19 16N 105 42 E
Thoa →, Canada 71 A7   60 31N 109 47W
Thoen, Thailand . . . . 38 D2   17 43N 99 12 E
Thoeng, Thailand . . . . 38 C3   19 41N 100 12 E
Thohoyandou, S. Africa . . . . . 53 J6   22 58S 30 29 E
Tholdi, Pakistan . . . . 43 B7   35 5N 76 6 E
Thomas, U.S.A. 81 H5   35 45N 98 45W
Thomas, L., Australia . . . . 63 D2   26 4S 137 58 E
Thomaston, U.S.A. 83 J3   32 53N 84 20W
Thomasville, Ala., U.S.A. 83 K2   31 55N 87 44W
Thomasville, Ga., U.S.A. 83 K4   30 50N 83 59W
Thomasville, N.C., U.S.A. 83 H5   35 53N 80 5W
Thompson, Canada 71 B9   55 45N 97 52W
Thompson, U.S.A. 85 E9   41 52N 75 31W
Thompson →, Canada 70 C4   50 15N 121 24W
Thompson →, U.S.A. 80 F8   39 46N 93 37W
Thompson Falls, U.S.A. 76 C6   47 36N 115 21W
Thompson Pk., U.S.A. 76 F2   41 0N 123 0W
Thompson Springs, U.S.A. 77 G9   38 58N 109 43W
Thompsontown, U.S.A. 84 F7   40 33N 77 14W
Thomson, U.S.A. 83 J4   33 28N 82 30W
Thomson →, Australia . . . . . . 62 C3   25 11S 142 53 E
Thong Yang, Thailand . . . . . . 39 b   9 28N 99 56 E
Þórisvatn, Iceland 8 D4   64 20N 18 55W
Thornaby on Tees, U.K. 12 C6   54 33N   1 18W
Thornbury, Canada 84 B4   44 34N 80 26W
Thorne, U.S.A. 12 D7   53 37N   0 57W
Thornhill, Canada 70 C3   54 31N 128 32W
Thorold, Canada 84 C5   43 7N 79 12W
Þórshöfn, Iceland 8 C6   66 12N 15 20W
Thouin, C., Australia . . . . 60 D2   20 20S 118 10 E
Thousand Oaks, U.S.A. 79 L8   34 10N 118 50W
Thrace, Turkey . . . . 23 D12 41 0N 27 0 E
Three Forks, U.S.A. 76 D8   45 54N 111 33W
Three Hills, Canada 70 C6   51 43N 113 15W
Three Hummock I., Australia . . 63 G3   40 25S 144 55 E
Three Points, C., Ghana 50 H5   4 42N   2 6W
Three Rivers, Calif., U.S.A. . . . 78 J8   36 26N 118 54W
Three Rivers, Tex., U.S.A. 81 L5   28 28N 98 11W
Three Sisters, U.S.A. 76 D3   44 4N 121 51W
Three Springs, Australia . . . . . 61 E2   29 32S 115 45 E
Throssell, L., Australia . . . . . . 61 E3   27 33S 124 10 E
Throssell Ra., Australia . . . . . . 60 D3   22 3S 121 43 E
Thrushton △, Australia . . . . . . 63 D4   27 47S 147 40 E
Thuan Hoa, Vietnam . . . . 39 H5   8 58N 105 30 E
Thubun Lakes, Canada 71 A6   61 30N 112 0W
Thuin, Belgium . . . . 15 D4   50 20N   4 17 E
Thule = Qaanaaq, Greenland . 4 B4   77 40N 69 0W
Thule Air Base = Uummannaq,
  Greenland 4 B5   70 58N 52 0W
Thun, Switz. . . . . 20 C7   46 45N   7 38 E
Thunder B., U.S.A. 84 B1   45 0N 83 20W
Thunder Bay, Canada 72 C2   48 20N 89 15W
Thung Salaeng Luang △,
  Thailand . . . . 38 D3   16 43N 100 50 E
Thung Song, Thailand . . . . 39 H2   8 10N 99 40 E
Thunkar, Bhutan . . . . 41 F17 27 55N 91 0 E
Thuong Tra, Vietnam . . . . 38 D6   16 2N 107 42 E
Thüringer Wald, Germany . . . . 16 C6   50 35N 11 0 E
Thurles, Ireland 10 D4   52 41N   7 49W
Thurrock □, U.K. . . . . 13 F8   51 31N   0 23 E
Thursday I., Australia . . . . 62 A3   10 30S 142 3 E
Thurso, Canada 72 C4   45 36N 75 15W
Thurso, U.K. 11 C5   58 36N   3 32W
Thurso →, U.K. 11 C5   58 36N   3 32W
Thurston I., Antarctica 5 D16   72 0S 100 0W
Thutade L., Canada 70 B3   57 0N 126 55W
Thyolo, Malawi . . . . 55 F4   16 7S 35 5 E
Ti Tree, Australia . . . . 62 C1   22 5S 133 22 E
Tian Shan, Asia . . . . 32 B3   40 30N 76 0 E
Tianjin, China . . . . 35 E9   39 8N 117 10 E
Tianshui, China . . . . 34 G3   34 32N 105 40 E
Tianyar, Indonesia . . . . 37 J18   8 12S 115 30 E
Tianzhen, China . . . . 34 D8   40 24N 114 5 E
Tianzhuangtai, China . . . . 35 D12 40 43N 122 5 E
Tiaret, Algeria . . . . 50 A6   35 20N   1 21 E
Tibagi, Brazil 95 A5   24 30S 50 24W
Tibagi →, Brazil 95 A5   22 47S 51 1W
Tiber = Tevere →, Italy . . . . . 22 D5   41 44N 12 14 E
Tiberias = Teverya, Israel . . . . 46 C4   32 47N 35 32 E
Tiberias, L. = Yam Kinneret,
  Israel . . . . 46 C4   32 45N 35 35 E
Tibesti, Chad . . . . 51 D9   21 0N 17 30 E
Tibet = Xizang Zizhiqu □, China 32 C3   32 0N 88 0 E
Tibet, Plateau of, Asia . . . . . . 26 F12 32 0N 86 0 E
Tibooburra, Australia . . . . 63 D3   29 26S 142 1 E
Tibro, Sweden . . . . 9 G15 58 17N 14 4 E
Tiburón, I., Mexico 86 B2   29 0N 112 30W
Ticino →, Italy . . . . 20 D8   45 9N   9 14 E
Ticonderoga, U.S.A. 85 C11 43 51N 73 26W
Ticul, Mexico 87 C7   20 20N 89 31W
Tidaholm, Sweden . . . . 9 G15 58 12N 13 58 E
Tidioute, U.S.A. 84 E5   41 41N 79 24W
Tidjikja, Mauritania 50 E3   18 29N 11 35W
Tidore, Indonesia . . . . 37 D7   0 40N 127 25 E
Tieyang Shuiku, China . . . . . . 33 F10 22 37N 113 53 E
Tiel, Neths. . . . . 15 C5   51 53N   5 26 E
Tieling, China . . . . 35 C12 42 20N 123 55 E
Tielt, Belgium . . . . 15 C3   51 0N   3 20 E
Tien Shan = Tian Shan, Asia . . 32 B3   40 30N 76 0 E
Tien-tsin = Tianjin, China . . . . 35 E9   39 8N 117 10 E
Tien Yen, Vietnam . . . . 38 B6   21 20N 107 24 E
T'ienching = Tianjin, China . . . 35 E9   39 8N 117 10 E
Tienen, Belgium . . . . 15 D4   50 48N   4 57 E

Tientsin = Tianjin, China . . . . 35 E9   39 8N 117 10 E
Tieri, Australia . . . . 62 C4   23 2S 148 21 E
Tierra Amarilla, Chile 94 B1   27 28S 70 18W
Tierra Amarilla, U.S.A. 77 H10 36 42N 106 33W
Tierra Colorada, Mexico 87 D5   17 10N 99 35W
Tierra de Campos, Spain 21 A3   42 10N   4 50W
Tierra del Fuego, I. Gr. de,
  Argentina 96 G3   54 0S 69 0W
Tiétar →, Spain 21 C3   39 50N   6 1W
Tietê →, Brazil 95 A5   20 40S 51 35W
Tiffin, U.S.A. 82 E4   41 7N 83 11W
Tifton, U.S.A. 83 K4   31 27N 83 31W
Tifu, Indonesia . . . . 37 E7   3 39S 126 24 E
Tighina, Moldova . . . . 17 E15 46 50N 29 30 E
Tigil, Russia . . . . 29 D16 57 49N 158 40 E
Tignish, Canada 73 C7   46 58N 64 2W
Tigre →, Peru 92 D4   4 30S 74 10W
Tigre →, Venezuela 92 B6   9 20N 62 30W
Tigris = Dijlah, Nahr →, Asia . 44 D5   31 0N 47 25 E
Tigyaing, Burma . . . . 41 H20 23 45N 96 10 E
Tijara, India . . . . 42 F7   27 56N 76 31 E
Tijuana, Mexico 79 N9   32 30N 117 10W
Tikal, Guatemala 88 C2   17 13N 89 24W
Tikal △, Guatemala 88 C2   17 23N 89 34W
Tikamgarh, India . . . . 43 G8   24 44N 78 50 E
Tikhoretsk, Russia . . . . 19 E7   45 56N 40 5 E
Tikhvin, Russia . . . . 18 C5   59 35N 33 30 E
Tikiraqjuaq = Whale Cove,
  Canada 71 A10 62 10N 92 34W
Tikrīt, Iraq . . . . 44 C4   34 35N 43 37 E
Tiksi, Russia . . . . 29 B13 71 40N 128 45 E
Tilamuta, Indonesia . . . . 37 D6   0 32N 122 23 E
Tilburg, Neths. . . . . 15 C5   51 31N   5 6 E
Tilbury, Canada 84 D2   42 17N 82 23W
Tilbury, U.K. . . . . 13 F8   51 27N   0 22 E
Tilcara, Argentina 94 A2   23 36S 65 23W
Tilden, U.S.A. 80 D6   42 3N 97 50W
Tilhar, India . . . . 43 F8   28 0N 79 45 E
Tilichiki, Russia . . . . 29 C17 60 27N 166 5 E
Tilissos, Greece . . . . 25 D7   35 20N 25 1 E
Till →, U.K. 12 B5   55 41N   2 13W
Tillamook, U.S.A. 76 D2   45 27N 123 51W
Tillsonburg, Canada 84 D4   42 53N 80 44W
Tillyeria, Cyprus . . . . 25 D11 35 6N 32 40 E
Tílos, Greece . . . . 23 F12 36 27N 27 27 E
Tilpa, Australia . . . . 63 E3   30 57S 144 24 E
Tilt →, U.K. 11 E5   56 46N   3 51W
Tilton, U.S.A. 85 C13 43 27N 71 36W
Tiltonsville, U.S.A. 84 F4   40 10N 80 41W
Timagami, Canada 72 C3   47 0N 80 10W
Timagami, L., Canada 72 C3   47 0N 80 10W
Timanfaya △, Canary Is. 24 F6   29 0N 13 46W
Timanskiy Kryazh, Russia . . . . 18 A9   65 58N 50 5 E
Timaru, N.Z. . . . . 59 L3   44 23S 171 14 E
Timau, Kenya . . . . 54 B4   0 4N 37 15 E
Timbákion, Greece . . . . 25 D6   35 4N 24 45 E
Timber Creek, Australia . . . . . 60 C5   15 40S 130 29 E
Timber Lake, U.S.A. 80 C4   45 26N 101 5W
Timber Mt., U.S.A. 78 H10 37 6N 116 28W
Timbuktu = Tombouctou, Mali . 50 E5   16 50N   3 0W
Timi, Cyprus . . . . 25 E11 34 44N 32 31 E
Timimoun, Algeria . . . . 50 C6   29 14N   0 16 E
Timirist, Rās, Mauritania 50 E2   19 21N 16 30W
Timiskaming, L. =
  Témiscamingue, L., Canada . 72 C4   47 10N 79 25W
Timișoara, Romania . . . . 17 F11 45 43N 21 15 E
Timmins, Canada 72 C3   48 28N 81 25W
Timok →, Serbia & M. . . . . . . 23 B10 44 10N 22 40 E
Timor, Asia . . . . 37 F7   9 0S 125 0 E
Timor Leste = East Timor ■, Asia 37 F7   8 50S 126 0 E
Timor Sea, Ind. Oc. . . . . 60 B4   12 0S 127 0 E
Tin Can Bay, Australia . . . . . . 63 D5   25 56S 153 0 E
Tin Mt., U.S.A. 78 J9   36 50N 117 10W
Tina →, S. Africa . . . . 57 E4   31 18S 29 13 E
Tinaca Pt., Phil. . . . . 37 C7   5 30N 125 25 E
Tinajo, Canary Is. 24 E6   29 4N 13 42W
Tindal, Australia . . . . 60 B5   14 31S 132 22 E
Tindouf, Algeria 50 C4   27 42N   8 10W
Tinfunque △, Paraguay 94 A3   23 55S 60 17W
Tinggi, Pulau, Malaysia . . . . . 39 L5   2 18N 104 7 E
Tingo Maria, Peru 92 E3   9 10S 75 54W
Tingrela, Ivory C. 50 F4   10 27N   6 25W
Tinh Bien, Vietnam . . . . 39 G5   10 36N 104 57 E
Tinnevelly = Tirunelveli, India . 40 Q10 8 45N 77 45 E
Tinogasta, Argentina 94 B2   28 5S 67 32W
Tínos, Greece . . . . 23 F11 37 33N 25 8 E
Tinpahar, India . . . . 43 G12 24 59N 87 44 E
Tintina, Argentina 94 B3   27 2S 62 45W
Tintinara, Australia . . . . 63 F3   35 48S 140 2 E
Tioga, N. Dak., U.S.A. 80 A3   48 23N 102 56W
Tioga, Pa., U.S.A. 84 E7   41 55N 77 8W
Tioman, Pulau, Malaysia . . . . 39 L5   2 50N 104 10 E
Tionesta, U.S.A. 84 E5   41 30N 79 28W
Tipongpani, India . . . . 41 F19 27 20N 95 55 E
Tipperary, Ireland 10 D3   52 28N   8 10W
Tipperary □, Ireland 10 D4   52 37N   7 55W
Tipton, Calif., U.S.A. 78 J7   36 4N 119 19W
Tipton, Iowa, U.S.A. 80 E9   41 46N 91 8W
Tipton Mt., U.S.A. 79 K12 35 32N 114 12W
Tiptonville, U.S.A. 81 G10 36 23N 89 29W
Tīrān, Iran . . . . 45 C6   32 45N 51 8 E
Tiranë, Albania . . . . 23 D8   41 18N 19 49 E
Tiraspol, Moldova . . . . 17 E15 46 55N 29 35 E
Tire, Turkey . . . . 23 E12 38 5N 27 50 E
Tirebolu, Turkey . . . . 19 F6   40 58N 38 45 E
Tiree, U.K. 11 E2   56 31N   6 55W
Tiree, Passage of, U.K. 11 E2   56 30N   6 30W
Tîrgovişte = Târgovişte, Romania 17 F13 44 55N 25 27 E
Tîrgu-Jiu = Târgu-Jiu, Romania 17 F12 45 5N 23 19 E
Tîrgu Mureş = Târgu Mureş,
  Romania . . . . 17 E13 46 31N 24 38 E
Tirich Mir, Pakistan . . . . 40 A7   36 15N 71 55 E
Tírnavos, Greece . . . . 23 E10 39 45N 22 18 E
Tirodi, India . . . . 40 J11 21 40N 79 44 E
Tirol □, Austria . . . . 16 E6   47 3N 10 43 E
Tirso →, Italy . . . . 22 E3   39 53N   8 32 E
Tiruchchirappalli, India . . . . . 40 P11 10 45N 78 45 E
Tirunelveli, India . . . . 40 Q10 8 45N 77 45 E
Tirupati, India . . . . 40 N11 13 39N 79 25 E
Tiruppur, India . . . . 40 P10 11 5N 77 22 E
Tiruvannamalai, India . . . . . . 40 N11 12 15N 79 9 E
Tisa, India . . . . 42 C7   32 50N 76 9 E
Tisa →, Serbia & M. . . . . 23 B9   45 15N 20 17 E
Tisdale, Canada 71 C8   52 50N 104 0W
Tishomingo, U.S.A. 81 H6   34 14N 96 41W
Tisza = Tisa →, Serbia & M. . . 23 B9   45 15N 20 17 E
Tit-Ary, Russia . . . . 29 B13 71 55N 127 2 E
Tithwal, Pakistan . . . . 43 B5   34 21N 73 50 E

Titicaca, L., S. Amer. 92 G5   15 30S 69 30W
Titule, Dem. Rep. of the Congo 54 B2   3 15N 25 31 E
Titusville, Fla., U.S.A. 83 L5   28 37N 80 49W
Titusville, Pa., U.S.A. 84 E5   41 38N 79 41W
Tivaouane, Senegal 50 F2   14 56N 16 45W
Tiverton, U.K. 13 G4   50 54N   3 29W
Tívoli, Italy . . . . 22 D5   41 58N 12 45 E
Tizi-Ouzou, Algeria . . . . 50 A6   36 42N   4 3 E
Tizimín, Mexico 87 C7   21 0N 88 1W
Tjeggelvas, Sweden . . . . 8 C17 66 37N 17 45 E
Tjirebon = Cirebon, Indonesia . 36 F3   6 45S 108 32 E
Tjluring, Indonesia . . . . 37 J17   8 25S 114 13 E
Tjörn, Sweden . . . . 9 G14 58 0N 11 35 E
Tlacotalpan, Mexico 87 D5   18 37N 95 40W
Tlahualilo, Mexico 86 B4   26 20N 103 30W
Tlaquepaque, Mexico 86 C4   20 39N 103 19W
Tlaxcala, Mexico 87 D5   19 20N 98 14W
Tlaxcala □, Mexico 87 D5   19 30N 98 20W
Tlaxiaco, Mexico 87 D5   17 18N 97 40W
Tlemcen, Algeria 50 B5   34 52N   1 21W
To Bong, Vietnam . . . . 38 F7   12 45N 109 16 E
Toa Payoh, Singapore . . . . 39 d   1 20N 103 51 E
Toad →, Canada 70 B4   59 25N 124 57W
Toad River, Canada 70 B3   58 51N 125 14W
Toamasina, Madag. . . . . 57 B8   18 10S 49 25 E
Toamasina □, Madag. . . . . . . 57 B8   18 0S 49 0 E
Toay, Argentina 94 D3   36 43S 64 38W
Toba, Japan . . . . 31 G8   34 30N 136 51 E
Toba, Danau, Indonesia . . . . . 36 D1   2 30N 97 30 E
Toba Kakar, Pakistan . . . . 42 D3   31 30N 69 0 E
Toba Tek Singh, Pakistan . . . . 42 D5   30 55N 72 25 E
Tobago, Trin. & Tob. 89 D7   11 10N 60 30W
Tobelo, Indonesia . . . . 37 D7   1 45N 127 56 E
Tobermory, Canada 84 A3   45 12N 81 40W
Tobermory, U.K. 11 E2   56 38N   6 5W
Tobi, Pac. Oc. . . . . 37 D8   2 40N 131 10 E
Tobin, U.S.A. 78 F5   39 55N 121 19W
Tobin, L., Australia . . . . 60 D4   21 45S 125 49 E
Tobin L., Canada 71 C8   53 35N 103 30W
Toboali, Indonesia . . . . 36 E3   3 0S 106 25 E
Tobol →, Russia . . . . 28 D7   58 10N 68 12 E
Toboli, Indonesia . . . . 37 E6   0 38S 120 5 E
Tobolsk, Russia . . . . 28 D7   58 15N 68 10 E
Tobruk = Tubruq, Libya . . . . . 51 B10 32 7N 23 55 E
Tobyhanna, U.S.A. 85 E9   41 11N 75 25W
Tobyl = Tobol →, Russia . . . . 28 D7   58 10N 68 12 E
Tocantinópolis, Brazil 93 E9   6 20S 47 25W
Tocantins □, Brazil 93 F9   10 0S 48 0W
Tocantins →, Brazil 93 D9   1 45S 49 10W
Toccoa, U.S.A. 83 H4   34 35N 83 19W
Tochi →, Pakistan . . . . 42 C4   32 49N 70 41 E
Tochigi, Japan . . . . 31 F9   36 25N 139 45 E
Tochigi □, Japan . . . . 31 F9   36 45N 139 45 E
Toco, Trin. & Tob. 93 K16 10 50N 60 57W
Toconao, Chile 94 A2   23 11S 68 1W
Tocopilla, Chile 94 A1   22 5S 70 10W
Tocumwal, Australia . . . . 63 F4   35 51S 145 31 E
Tocuyo →, Venezuela 92 A5   11 3N 68 23W
Todd →, Australia . . . . 62 C2   24 52S 135 48 E
Todeli, Indonesia . . . . 37 E6   1 40S 124 29 E
Todenyang, Kenya . . . . 54 B4   4 35N 35 56 E
Todgarh, India . . . . 42 G5   25 42N 73 58 E
Todos os Santos, B. de, Brazil . 93 F11 12 48S 38 38W
Todos Santos, Mexico 86 C2   23 27N 110 13W
Toe Hd., U.K. 11 D1   57 50N   7 8W
Tofield, Canada 70 C6   53 25N 112 40W
Tofino, Canada 70 D3   49 11N 125 55W
Tofua, Tonga 59 D11 19 45S 175 5W
Tōgane, Japan . . . . 31 G10 35 33N 140 22 E
Togian, Kepulauan, Indonesia . 37 E6   0 20S 121 50 E
Togliatti, Russia . . . . 18 D8   53 32N 49 24 E
Togo ■, W. Afr. . . . . 50 G6   8 30N   1 35 E
Togtoh, China . . . . 34 D6   40 15N 111 10 E
Tōhoku □, Japan . . . . 30 E10 39 50N 141 45 E
Töhöm, Mongolia . . . . 34 B5   44 27N 108 2 E
Toinya, Sudan . . . . 51 G11   6 17N 29 46 E
Toiyabe Range, U.S.A. 76 G5   39 30N 117 0W
Tojikiston = Tajikistan ■, Asia . 28 F8   38 30N 70 0 E
Tojo, Indonesia . . . . 37 E6   1 20S 121 15 E
Tōjō, Japan . . . . 31 G6   34 53N 133 16 E
Tok, U.S.A. 68 B5   63 20N 142 59W
Tok-do, Asia . . . . 31 F5   37 15N 131 52 E
Tokachi-Dake, Japan . . . . 30 C11 43 17N 142 5 E
Tokachi-Gawa →, Japan . . . . 30 C11 42 44N 143 42 E
Tokala, Indonesia . . . . 37 E6   1 30S 121 40 E
Tōkamachi, Japan . . . . 31 F9   37 8N 138 43 E
Tokanui, N.Z. . . . . 59 M2   46 34S 168 56 E
Tokara-Rettō, Japan . . . . 31 K4   29 37N 129 43 E
Tokarahi, N.Z. . . . . 59 L3   44 56S 170 39 E
Tokashiki-Shima, Japan . . . . . 31 L3   26 11N 127 21 E
Tokat, Turkey . . . . 19 F6   40 22N 36 35 E
Tŏkch'ŏn, N. Korea . . . . 35 E14 39 45N 126 18 E
Tokelau Is., Pac. Oc. 78 D3   46 42N 123 59W
Tokelau Is., Pac. Oc. 64 H10 9 0S 171 45W
Tokmak, Kyrgyzstan . . . . 28 E8   42 49N 75 15 E
Toko Ra., Australia . . . . 62 C2   23 5S 138 20 E
Tokoro-Gawa →, Japan . . . . . 30 B12 44 7N 144 5 E
Tokuno-Shima, Japan . . . . 31 L4   27 56N 128 55 E
Tokushima, Japan . . . . 31 G7   34 4N 134 34 E
Tokushima □, Japan . . . . 31 H7   33 55N 134 0 E
Tokuyama, Japan . . . . 31 G5   34 3N 131 50 E
Tōkyō, Japan . . . . 31 G9   35 45N 139 45 E
Tolaga Bay, N.Z. . . . . 59 H7   38 21S 178 20 E
Tolbukhin = Dobrich, Bulgaria . 23 C12 43 37N 27 49 E
Toledo, Brazil 95 A5   24 44S 53 45W
Toledo, Spain 21 C3   39 50N   4 2W
Toledo, Ohio, U.S.A. 82 E4   41 39N 83 33W
Toledo, Oreg., U.S.A. 76 D2   44 37N 123 56W
Toledo, Wash., U.S.A. 76 C2   46 26N 122 51W
Toledo, Montes de, Spain 21 C3   39 33N   4 20W
Toledo Bend Reservoir, U.S.A. . 81 K8   31 11N 93 34W
Tolga, Australia . . . . 62 B4   17 15S 145 29 E
Toliara, Madag. . . . . 57 C7   23 21S 43 40 E
Toliara □, Madag. . . . . 57 C8   21 0S 45 0 E
Tolima, Colombia 92 C3   4 40N 75 19W
Tolitoli, Indonesia . . . . 37 D6   1 5N 120 50 E
Tollhouse, U.S.A. 78 H7   37 1N 119 24W
Tolo, Teluk, Indonesia . . . . . . 37 E6   2 20S 122 10 E
Tolo Harbour, China . . . . 33 G11 22 27N 114 12 E
Toluca, Mexico 87 D5   19 20N 99 40W
Tom Burke, S. Africa . . . . 57 C4   23 5S 28 0 E
Tom Price, Australia . . . . 60 D2   22 40S 117 48 E
Tomah, U.S.A. 80 D9   43 59N 90 30W
Tomahawk, U.S.A. 80 C10 45 28N 89 44W
Tomakomai, Japan . . . . 30 C10 42 38N 141 36 E
Tomales, U.S.A. 78 G4   38 15N 122 53W
Tomales B., U.S.A. 78 G3   38 15N 123 58W

Tomar, Portugal 21 C1 39 36N 8 25W
Tomaszów Mazowiecki, Poland 17 C10 51 30N 20 2 E
Tomatlán, Mexico 86 D3 19 56N 105 15W
Tombador, Serra do, Brazil .. 92 F7 12 0S 58 0W
Tombigbee →, U.S.A. 83 K2 31 8N 87 57W
Tombouctou, Mali 50 E5 16 50N 3 0W
Tombstone, U.S.A. 77 L8 31 43N 110 4W
Tombua, Angola .... 56 B1 15 55S 11 55 E
Tomé, Chile 94 D1 36 36S 72 57W
Tomelloso, Spain 21 C4 39 10N 3 2W
Tomini, Indonesia .... 37 D6 0 30N 120 30 E
Tomini, Teluk, Indonesia .... 37 E6 0 10S 121 0 E
Tomintoul, U.K. 11 D5 57 15N 3 23W
Tomkinson Ranges, Australia . 61 E4 26 11S 129 5 E
Tommot, Russia .... 29 D13 59 4N 126 20 E
Tomnop Ta Suos, Cambodia . 39 G5 11 20N 104 15 E
Tomo →, Colombia 92 B5 5 20N 67 48W
Toms Place, U.S.A. 78 H8 37 34N 118 41W
Toms River, U.S.A. 85 G10 39 58N 74 12W
Tomsk, Russia .... 28 D9 56 30N 85 5 E
Tonalá, Mexico 87 D6 16 8N 93 41W
Tonantins, Brazil 92 D5 2 45S 67 45W
Tonasket, U.S.A. 76 B4 48 42N 119 26W
Tonawanda, U.S.A. 84 D6 43 1N 78 53W
Tonb, Iran .... 45 E7 26 15N 55 15 E
Tonbridge, U.K. .... 13 F8 51 11N 0 17 E
Tondano, Indonesia .... 37 D6 1 35N 124 54 E
Tondoro, Namibia .... 56 B2 17 45S 18 50 E
Tone →, Australia .... 61 F2 34 25S 116 25 E
Tone-Gawa →, Japan .... 31 F9 35 44N 140 51 E
Tonekābon, Iran .... 45 B6 36 45N 51 12 E
Tong Xian, China .... 34 E9 39 55N 116 35 E
Tonga ■, Pac. Oc. 59 D11 19 50S 174 30W
Tonga Trench, Pac. Oc. 64 J10 18 0S 173 0W
Tongaat, S. Africa .... 57 D5 29 33S 31 9 E
Tongareva, Cook Is. 65 H12 9 0S 158 0W
Tongariro △, N.Z. .... 59 H5 39 8S 175 33 E
Tongatapu Group, Tonga 59 E12 21 0S 175 0W
Tongchŏn-ni, N. Korea ...... 35 E14 39 50N 127 25 E
Tongchuan, China .... 34 G5 35 6N 109 3 E
Tongeren, Belgium .... 15 D5 50 47N 5 28 E
Tonggu Jiao, China .... 33 G10 22 22N 113 37 E
Tongguan, China .... 34 G6 34 40N 110 25 E
Tonghae, S. Korea .... 35 F15 37 29N 129 7 E
Tonghua, China .... 35 D13 41 42N 125 58 E
Tongjosŏn Man, N. Korea .... 35 E15 39 30N 128 0 E
Tongking, G. of = Tonkin, G. of,
    Asia .... 32 E5 20 0N 108 0 E
Tongliao, China .... 35 C12 43 38N 122 18 E
Tongling, China .... 33 C6 30 55N 117 48 E
Tongnae, S. Korea .... 35 G15 35 12N 129 5 E
Tongobory, Madag. .... 57 C7 23 32S 44 20 E
Tongoy, Chile 94 C1 30 16S 71 31W
Tongres = Tongeren, Belgium . 15 D5 50 47N 5 28 E
Tongsa Dzong, Bhutan .... 41 F17 27 31N 90 31 E
Tongue, U.K. 11 C4 58 29N 4 25W
Tongue →, U.S.A. 80 B2 46 25N 105 52W
Tongwei, China .... 34 G3 35 0N 105 5 E
Tongxin, China .... 34 F3 36 59N 105 58 E
Tongyang, N. Korea .... 35 E14 39 9N 126 53 E
Tongyu, China .... 35 B12 44 45N 123 4 E
Tonj, Sudan .... 51 G11 7 20N 28 44 E
Tonk, India .... 42 F6 26 6N 75 54 E
Tonkawa, U.S.A. 81 G6 36 41N 97 18W
Tonkin = Bac Phan, Vietnam . 38 B5 22 0N 105 0 E
Tonkin, G. of, Asia .... 32 E5 20 0N 108 0 E
Tonle Sap, Cambodia .... 38 F4 13 0N 104 0 E
Tono, Japan .... 30 E10 39 19N 141 32 E
Tonopah, U.S.A. 77 G5 38 4N 117 14W
Tonosí, Panama 88 E3 7 20N 80 20W
Tons →, Haryana, India .... 42 D7 30 30N 77 39 E
Tons →, Ut. P., India ..... 43 F10 26 1N 83 33 E
Tønsberg, Norway .... 9 G14 59 19N 10 25 E
Tonto △, U.S.A. 77 K8 33 39N 111 7W
Toobanna, Australia .... 62 B4 18 42S 146 9 E
Toodyay, Australia .... 61 F2 31 34S 116 28 E
Tooele, U.S.A. 76 F7 40 32N 112 18W
Toompine, Australia .... 63 D3 27 15S 144 19 E
Toora, Australia .... 63 F4 38 39S 146 23 E
Toora-Khem, Russia .... 29 D10 52 28N 96 17 E
Toowoomba, Australia .... 63 D5 27 32S 151 56 E
Top-ozero, Russia .... 18 A5 65 35N 32 0 E
Top Springs, Australia ...... 60 C5 16 37S 131 51 E
Topaz, U.S.A. 78 G7 38 41N 119 30W
Topeka, U.S.A. 80 F7 39 3N 95 40W
Topley, Canada 70 C3 54 49N 126 18W
Topocalma, Pta., Chile 94 C1 34 10S 72 2W
Topock, U.S.A. 79 L12 34 46N 114 29W
Topol'čany, Slovak Rep. .... 17 D10 48 35N 18 12 E
Topolobampo, Mexico 86 B3 25 40N 109 4W
Toppenish, U.S.A. 76 C3 46 23N 120 19W
Toraka Vestale, Madag. ..... 57 B7 16 20S 43 58 E
Torata, Peru 92 G4 17 23S 70 1W
Torbalı, Turkey .... 23 E12 38 10N 27 21 E
Torbat-e Heydārīyeh, Iran .. 45 C8 35 15N 59 12 E
Torbat-e Jām, Iran .... 45 C9 35 16N 60 35 E
Torbay, Canada 73 C9 47 40N 52 42W
Torbay □, U.K. 13 G4 50 26N 3 31W
Tordesillas, Spain 21 B3 41 30N 5 0W
Torfaen □, U.K. 13 F4 51 43N 3 3W
Torgau, Germany .... 16 C7 51 34N 13 0 E
Torhout, Belgium .... 15 C3 51 5N 3 7 E
Tori-Shima, Japan .... 31 J10 30 29N 140 19 E
Torin, Mexico 86 B2 27 33N 110 15W
Torino, Italy .... 20 D7 45 3N 7 40 E
Torit, Sudan .... 51 H12 4 27N 32 31 E
Torkamān, Iran .... 44 B5 37 35N 47 23 E
Tormes →, Spain 21 B2 41 18N 6 29W
Tornado Mt., Canada 70 D6 49 55N 114 40W
Torne älv →, Sweden .... 8 D21 65 50N 24 12 E
Torneå = Tornio, Finland .... 8 D21 65 50N 24 12 E
Torneträsk, Sweden .... 8 B18 68 24N 19 15 E
Tornio, Finland .... 8 D21 65 50N 24 12 E
Tornionjoki →, Finland ..... 8 D21 65 50N 24 12 E
Tornquist, Argentina 94 D3 38 8S 62 15W
Toro, Spain .... 24 B11 39 59N 4 8 E
Toro △, Uganda .... 54 C3 0 5S 30 22 E
Toro, Cerro del, Chile 94 B2 29 10S 69 50W
Toro Pk., U.S.A. 79 M10 33 34N 116 24W
Toroníios Kólpos, Greece .... 23 D10 40 5S 23 30 E
Toronto, Canada 84 C5 43 39N 79 20W
Toronto, U.S.A. 84 F4 40 28N 80 36W
Toronto Lester B. Pearson
    International ✈ (YYZ), Canada 84 C5 43 40N 79 34W
Toropets, Russia .... 18 C5 56 30N 31 40 E
Tororo, Uganda .... 54 B3 0 45N 34 12 E
Toros Dağları, Turkey ...... 19 G5 37 0N 32 30 E

Torpa, India .... 43 H11 22 57N 85 6 E
Torquay, U.K. 13 G4 50 27N 3 32W
Torrance, U.S.A. 79 M8 33 50N 118 19W
Torre de Moncorvo, Portugal . 21 B2 41 12N 7 8W
Torre del Greco, Italy ...... 22 D6 40 47N 14 22 E
Torrejón de Ardoz, Spain .. 21 B4 40 27N 3 29W
Torrelavega, Spain 21 A3 43 20N 4 5W
Torremolinos, Spain 21 D3 36 38N 4 30W
Torrens →, Australia ...... 63 E2 31 0S 137 50 E
Torrens Cr. →, Australia ... 62 C4 22 23S 145 9 E
Torrens Creek, Australia .... 62 C4 20 48S 145 3 E
Torrent, Spain 21 C5 39 27N 0 28W
Torreón, Mexico 86 B4 25 33N 103 26W
Torres, Brazil 95 B5 29 21S 49 44W
Torres, Mexico 86 B2 28 46N 110 47W
Torres Strait, Australia .... 64 H6 9 50S 142 20 E
Torres Vedras, Portugal 21 C1 39 5N 9 15W
Torrevieja, Spain 21 D5 37 59N 0 42W
Torrey, U.S.A. 77 G8 38 18N 111 25W
Torridge →, U.K. 13 G3 51 0N 4 13W
Torridon, L., U.K. 11 D3 57 35N 5 50W
Torrington, Conn., U.S.A. .. 85 E11 41 48N 73 7W
Torrington, Wyo., U.S.A. .. 80 D2 42 4N 104 11W
Tórshavn, Færoe Is. 8 E9 62 5N 6 56W
Tortola, Br. Virgin Is. ..... 89 e 18 19N 64 45W
Tortosa, Spain .... 21 B6 40 49N 0 31 E
Tortosa, C., Spain .... 21 B6 40 41N 0 52 E
Tortue, I. de la, Haiti 89 B5 20 5N 72 57W
Tortuguero △, Costa Rica .. 88 D3 10 31N 83 29W
Torūd, Iran .... 45 C7 35 25N 55 5 E
Toruń, Poland .... 17 B10 53 0N 18 39 E
Tory I., Ireland 10 A3 55 16N 8 14W
Tosa, Japan .... 31 H6 33 24N 133 23 E
Tosa-Shimizu, Japan .... 31 H6 32 52N 132 58 E
Tosa-Wan, Japan .... 31 H6 33 15N 133 30 E
Toscana □, Italy .... 22 C4 43 25N 11 0 E
Toshkent, Uzbekistan .... 28 E7 41 20N 69 10 E
Tostado, Argentina 94 B3 29 15S 61 50W
Tostón, Pta. de, Canary Is. .. 24 F5 28 42N 14 2W
Tosu, Japan .... 31 H5 33 22N 130 31 E
Toteng, Botswana .... 56 C3 20 22S 22 58 E
Totma, Russia .... 18 C7 60 0N 42 40 E
Totnes, U.K. 13 G4 50 26N 3 42W
Totness, Suriname 93 B7 5 53N 56 19W
Totonicapán, Guatemala 88 D1 14 58N 91 12W
Totten Glacier, Antarctica .. 5 C8 66 45S 116 10 E
Tottenham, Australia .... 63 E4 32 14S 147 21 E
Tottenham, Canada 84 B5 44 1N 79 49W
Tottori, Japan .... 31 G7 35 30N 134 15 E
Tottori □, Japan .... 31 G7 35 30N 134 12 E
Toubkal, Djebel, Morocco .. 50 B4 31 0N 8 0W
Tougan, Burkina Faso 50 F5 13 11N 2 58W
Touggourt, Algeria .... 50 B7 33 6N 6 4 E
Toul, France .... 20 B6 48 40N 5 53 E
Toulon, France .... 20 E6 43 10N 5 55 E
Toulouse, France .... 20 E4 43 37N 1 27 E
Toummo, Niger .... 51 D8 22 45N 14 8 E
Toungoo, Burma .... 41 K20 19 0N 96 30 E
Touraine, France .... 20 C4 47 20N 0 30 E
Tourcoing, France .... 20 A5 50 42N 3 10 E
Touriñán, C., Spain 21 A1 43 3N 9 18W
Tournai, Belgium .... 15 D3 50 35N 3 25 E
Tournon-sur-Rhône, France . 20 D6 45 4N 4 50 E
Tours, France .... 20 C4 47 22N 0 40 E
Toussora, Mt., C.A.R. ...... 52 C4 9 7N 23 14 E
Touws →, S. Africa .... 56 E3 33 45S 21 11 E
Touwsrivier, S. Africa ...... 56 E3 33 20S 20 2 E
Towada, Japan .... 30 D10 40 37N 141 13 E
Towada-Hachimantai △, Japan 30 D10 40 27N 140 55 E
Towada-Ko, Japan .... 30 D10 40 28N 140 55 E
Towanda, U.S.A. 85 E8 41 46N 76 27W
Towang, India .... 41 F17 27 37N 91 50 E
Tower, U.S.A. 80 B8 47 48N 92 17W
Towerhill Cr. →, Australia .. 62 C3 22 28S 144 35 E
Towner, U.S.A. 80 A4 48 21N 100 25W
Townsend, U.S.A. 76 C8 46 19N 111 31W
Townshend I., Australia ..... 62 C5 22 10S 150 31 E
Townsville, Australia .... 62 B4 19 15S 146 45 E
Towraghondi, Afghan. .... 40 B3 35 13N 62 16 E
Towson, U.S.A. 82 F7 39 24N 76 36W
Towuti, Danau, Indonesia .... 37 E6 2 45S 121 32 E
Toya-Ko, Japan .... 30 C10 42 35N 140 51 E
Toyama, Japan .... 31 F8 36 40N 137 15 E
Toyama □, Japan .... 31 F8 36 45N 137 30 E
Toyama-Wan, Japan .... 31 F8 37 0N 137 30 E
Toyapakeh, Indonesia .... 37 K18 8 41S 115 29 E
Toyohashi, Japan .... 31 G8 34 45N 137 25 E
Toyokawa, Japan .... 31 G8 34 48N 137 27 E
Toyonaka, Japan .... 31 G7 34 50N 135 28 E
Toyooka, Japan .... 31 G7 35 35N 134 48 E
Toyota, Japan .... 31 G8 35 3N 137 7 E
Tozeur, Tunisia .... 50 B7 33 56N 8 0 E
Tozkhurmato, Iraq .... 44 C5 34 56N 44 38 E
Trá Lí = Tralee, Ireland 10 D2 52 16N 9 42W
Tra On, Vietnam .... 39 H5 9 58N 105 55 E
Trabzon, Turkey .... 19 F6 41 0N 39 45 E
Tracadie-Sheila, Canada 73 C7 47 30N 64 55W
Tracy, Calif., U.S.A. 78 H5 37 44N 121 26W
Tracy, Minn., U.S.A. 80 C7 44 14N 95 37W
Trafalgar, C., Spain 21 D2 36 10N 6 2W
Trail, Canada 70 D5 49 5N 117 40W
Trainor L., Canada 70 A4 60 24N 120 17W
Trákhonas, Cyprus .... 25 D12 35 12N 33 21 E
Tralee, Ireland 10 D2 52 16N 9 42W
Tralee B., Ireland 10 D2 52 17N 9 55W
Tramore, Ireland 10 D4 52 10N 7 10W
Tramore B., Ireland 10 D4 52 9N 7 10W
Tran Ninh, Cao Nguyen, Laos . 38 C4 19 30N 103 10 E
Tranås, Sweden .... 9 G16 58 3N 14 59 E
Trancas, Argentina 94 B2 26 11S 65 20W
Trang, Thailand .... 39 J2 7 33N 99 38 E
Trangahy, Madag. .... 57 B7 19 7S 44 31 E
Trangan, Indonesia .... 37 F8 6 40S 134 20 E
Trangie, Australia .... 63 E4 32 4S 148 0 E
Trani, Italy .... 22 D7 41 17N 16 25 E
Tranoroa, Madag. .... 57 C8 24 42S 45 4 E
Tranqueras, Uruguay 95 C4 31 13S 55 45W
Transantarctic Mts., Antarctica 5 E12 85 0S 170 0W
Transilvania, Romania ...... 17 E12 46 30N 24 0 E
Transilvanian Alps = Carpaţii
    Meridionali, Romania ..... 17 F13 45 30N 25 0 E
Transylvania = Transilvania,
    Romania .... 17 E12 46 30N 24 0 E
Trápani, Italy .... 22 E5 38 1N 12 29 E
Trapper Pk., U.S.A. 76 D6 45 54N 114 18W
Traralgon, Australia .... 63 F4 38 12S 146 34 E
Trasimeno, L., Italy .... 22 C5 43 8N 12 6 E
Trat, Thailand .... 39 F4 12 14N 102 33 E

Tratani →, Pakistan .... 42 E3 29 19N 68 20 E
Traun, Austria .... 16 D8 48 14N 14 15 E
Traveller's L., Australia .... 63 E3 33 20S 142 0 E
Travemünde, Germany .... 16 B6 53 57N 10 52 E
Travers, Mt., N.Z. .... 59 K4 42 1S 172 45 E
Traverse City, U.S.A. 82 C3 44 46N 85 38W
Travis, L., U.S.A. 81 K5 30 24N 97 55W
Travnik, Bos.-H. .... 23 B7 44 17N 17 39 E
Trébbia →, Italy .... 20 D8 45 4N 9 41 E
Trebič, Czech Rep. .... 16 D8 49 14N 15 55 E
Trebinje, Bos.-H. .... 23 C8 42 44N 18 22 E
Trebonne, Australia .... 62 B4 18 37S 146 5 E
Tregaron, U.K. 13 E4 52 14N 3 56W
Tregrosse Is., Australia .... 62 B5 17 41S 150 43 E
Treherne, Canada 71 D9 49 38N 98 42W
Treinta y Tres, Uruguay 95 C5 33 16S 54 17W
Trelawney, Zimbabwe .... 57 B5 17 30S 30 30 E
Trelew, Argentina 96 E3 43 10S 65 20W
Trelleborg, Sweden .... 9 J15 55 20N 13 10 E
Tremadog Bay, U.K. 12 E3 52 51N 4 18W
Tremonton, U.S.A. 76 F7 41 43N 112 10W
Tremp, Spain .... 21 A6 42 10N 0 52 E
Trenche →, Canada 72 C5 47 46N 72 53W
Trenčín, Slovak Rep. .... 17 D10 48 52N 18 4 E
Trenggalek, Indonesia ...... 37 H14 8 3S 111 43 E
Trenque Lauquen, Argentina . 94 D3 36 5S 62 45W
Trent →, Canada 84 B7 44 6N 77 34W
Trent →, U.K. 12 D7 53 41N 0 42W
Trento, Italy .... 22 A4 46 4N 11 8 E
Trenton = Quinte West, Canada 84 B7 44 10N 77 34W
Trenton, Mo., U.S.A. 80 E8 40 5N 93 37W
Trenton, N.J., U.S.A. 85 F10 40 14N 74 46W
Trenton, Nebr., U.S.A. 80 E4 40 11N 101 1W
Trepassey, Canada 73 C9 46 43S 53 25W
Tres Arroyos, Argentina 94 D3 38 26S 60 20W
Três Corações, Brazil 95 A6 21 44S 45 15W
Tres Lagoas, Brazil 93 H8 20 50S 51 43W
Tres Lomas, Argentina 94 D3 36 27S 62 51W
Tres Marías, Islas, Mexico .. 86 C3 21 25N 106 28W
Tres Montes, C., Chile 96 F1 46 50S 75 30W
Três Pinos, U.S.A. 78 J5 36 48N 121 19W
Três Pontas, Brazil 95 A6 21 23S 45 29W
Tres Puentes, Chile 94 B1 27 50S 70 15W
Três Puntas, C., Argentina .. 96 F3 47 0S 66 0W
Três Rios, Brazil 95 A7 22 6S 43 15W
Tres Valles, Mexico 87 D5 18 15N 96 8W
Tresco, U.K. 13 H1 49 57N 6 20W
Treviso, Italy .... 22 B5 45 40N 12 15 E
Triabunna, Australia .... 63 G4 42 30S 147 55 E
Triánda, Greece .... 25 C10 36 25N 28 10 E
Triangle, Zimbabwe .... 57 C5 21 2S 31 28 E
Tribal Areas □, Pakistan ... 42 C4 33 0N 70 0 E
Tribulation, C., Australia ... 62 B4 16 5S 145 29 E
Tribune, U.S.A. 80 F4 38 28N 101 45W
Trichinopoly = Tiruchchirappalli,
    India .... 40 P11 10 45N 78 45 E
Trichur, India .... 40 P10 10 30N 76 18 E
Trida, Australia .... 63 E4 33 1S 145 1 E
Trier, Germany .... 16 D4 49 45N 6 38 E
Trieste, Italy .... 22 B5 45 40N 13 46 E
Triglav, Slovenia .... 16 E7 46 21N 13 50 E
Trikkala, Greece .... 23 E9 39 34N 21 47 E
Trikomo, Cyprus .... 25 D12 35 17N 33 52 E
Trikora, Puncak, Indonesia .. 37 E9 4 15S 138 45 E
Trim, Ireland 10 C5 53 33N 6 48W
Trincomalee, Sri Lanka ..... 40 Q12 8 38N 81 15 E
Trindade, Brazil 93 G9 16 40S 49 30W
Trindade, I., Atl. Oc. 2 F8 20 20S 29 50W
Trinidad, Bolivia 92 F6 14 46S 64 50W
Trinidad, Cuba 88 B4 21 48N 80 0W
Trinidad, Uruguay 94 C4 33 30S 56 50W
Trinidad →, Mexico 87 D5 17 49N 95 9W
Trinidad, U.S.A. 81 G2 37 10N 104 31W
Trinidad, Trin. & Tob. 89 D7 10 30N 61 15W
Trinidad & Tobago ■, W. Indies 89 D7 10 30N 61 20W
Trinity, Canada 73 C9 48 59N 53 55W
Trinity, U.S.A. 81 K7 30 57N 95 22W
Trinity →, Calif., U.S.A. .. 76 F2 41 11N 123 42W
Trinity →, Tex., U.S.A. ... 81 L7 29 45N 94 43W
Trinity B., Canada 73 C9 48 20N 53 10W
Trinity Hills, Trin. & Tob. .. 93 K15 10 16N 61 6W
Trinity Is., U.S.A. 68 C4 56 33N 154 25W
Trinity Range, U.S.A. 76 F4 40 15N 118 45W
Trinkitat, Sudan .... 51 E13 18 45N 37 51 E
Trinway, U.S.A. 84 F2 40 9N 82 1W
Tripoli = Tarābulus, Lebanon . 46 A4 34 31N 35 50 E
Tripoli = Tarābulus, Libya .. 51 B8 32 49N 13 7 E
Tripolis, Greece .... 23 F10 37 31N 22 25 E
Tripolitania, N. Afr. .... 51 B8 31 0N 13 0 E
Tripura □, India .... 41 H18 24 0N 92 0 E
Tripylos, Cyprus .... 25 E11 34 59N 32 41 E
Tristan da Cunha, Atl. Oc. .. 49 K2 37 6S 12 20W
Trisul, India .... 43 D8 30 19N 79 47 E
Trivandrum, India .... 40 Q10 8 41N 77 0 E
Trnava, Slovak Rep. .... 17 D9 48 23N 17 35 E
Trochu, Canada 70 C6 51 50N 113 13W
Trodely I., Canada 72 B4 52 15N 79 26W
Troglav, Croatia .... 22 C7 43 56N 16 36 E
Troilus, L., Canada 72 B5 50 50N 74 35W
Trois-Pistoles, Canada 73 C6 48 5N 69 10W
Trois-Rivières, Canada 72 C5 46 25N 72 34W
Trois-Rivières, Guadeloupe .. 88 b 15 57N 61 40W
Troitsk, Russia .... 28 D7 54 10N 61 35 E
Troitsko Pechorsk, Russia .. 18 B10 62 40N 56 10 E
Trölladyngja, Iceland 8 D5 64 54N 17 16W
Trollhättan, Sweden .... 9 G15 58 17N 12 20 E
Trollheimen, Norway .... 8 E13 62 46N 9 1 E
Trombetas →, Brazil 93 D7 1 55S 55 35W
Tromsø, Norway .... 8 B18 69 40N 18 56 E
Trona, U.S.A. 79 K9 35 46N 117 23W
Tronador, Mte., Argentina .. 96 E2 41 10S 71 50W
Trøndelag, Norway .... 8 D14 64 17N 11 50 E
Trondheim, Norway .... 8 E14 63 36N 10 25 E
Trondheimsfjorden, Norway . 8 E14 63 35N 10 30 E
Troodos, Cyprus .... 25 E11 34 55N 32 52 E
Troon, U.K. 11 F4 55 33N 4 39W
Tropic, U.S.A. 77 H7 37 37N 112 5W
Trostan, U.K. 10 A5 55 3N 6 10W
Trou Gras Pt., St. Lucia .... 89 f 13 51N 60 53W
Trout →, Canada 70 A5 61 19N 119 51W
Trout L., N.W.T., Canada .. 70 A4 60 40N 121 14W
Trout L., Ont., Canada 71 C10 51 20N 93 15W
Trout Lake, Canada 70 B6 56 30N 114 32W
Trout Lake, U.S.A. 78 E5 46 0N 121 32W
Trout River, Canada 73 C8 49 29N 58 8W
Trout Run, U.S.A. 84 E7 41 23N 77 3W
Trouville-sur-Mer, France .. 20 B4 49 21N 0 5 E
Trowbridge, U.K. 13 F5 51 18N 2 12W

Troy, Turkey .... 23 E12 39 57N 26 12 E
Troy, Ala., U.S.A. 83 K3 31 48N 85 58W
Troy, Kans., U.S.A. 80 F7 39 47N 95 5W
Troy, Mo., U.S.A. 80 F9 38 59N 90 59W
Troy, Mont., U.S.A. 76 B6 48 28N 115 53W
Troy, N.Y., U.S.A. 85 D11 42 44N 73 41W
Troy, Ohio, U.S.A. 82 E3 40 2N 84 12W
Troy, Pa., U.S.A. 85 E8 41 47N 76 47W
Troyes, France .... 20 B6 48 19N 4 3 E
Truchas Peak, U.S.A. 81 H2 35 58N 105 39W
Trucial States = United Arab
    Emirates ■, Asia .... 45 F7 23 50N 54 0 E
Truckee, U.S.A. 78 F6 39 20N 120 11W
Trudovoye, Russia .... 30 C6 43 17N 132 5 E
Trujillo, Honduras 88 C2 16 0N 86 0W
Trujillo, Peru 92 E3 8 6S 79 0W
Trujillo, Spain 21 C3 39 28N 5 55W
Trujillo, U.S.A. 81 H2 35 32N 104 42W
Trujillo, Venezuela 92 B4 9 22N 70 38W
Truk, Micronesia .... 64 G7 7 25N 151 46 E
Truman, U.S.A. 80 D7 43 50N 94 26W
Trumann, U.S.A. 81 H9 35 41N 90 31W
Trumansburg, U.S.A. 85 D8 42 33N 76 40W
Trumbull, Mt., U.S.A. 77 H7 36 25N 113 8W
Trundle, Australia .... 63 E4 32 53S 147 35 E
Trung-Phan = Annam, Vietnam 38 E7 16 0N 108 0 E
Truro, Canada 73 C7 45 21N 63 14W
Truro, U.K. 13 G2 50 16N 5 4W
Truskavets, Ukraine .... 17 D12 49 17N 23 30 E
Trutch, Canada 70 B4 57 44N 122 57W
Truth or Consequences, U.S.A. 77 K10 33 8N 107 15W
Trutnov, Czech Rep. .... 16 C8 50 37N 15 54 E
Truxton, U.S.A. 85 D8 42 45N 76 2W
Tryonville, U.S.A. 84 E5 41 42N 79 48W
Tsandi, Namibia .... 56 B1 17 42S 14 50 E
Tsangpo = Brahmaputra →, Asia 32 D3 23 40N 90 35 E
Tsaratanana, Madag. .... 57 B8 16 47S 47 39 E
Tsaratanana △, Madag. ..... 57 A8 13 57S 48 52 E
Tsaratanana, Mt. de =
    Maromokotro, Madag. ..... 57 A8 14 0S 49 0 E
Tsarevo = Michurin, Bulgaria . 23 C12 42 9N 27 51 E
Tsau, Botswana .... 56 C3 20 8S 22 22 E
Tsavo East △, Kenya .... 54 C4 2 44S 38 47 E
Tsavo West △, Kenya .... 54 C4 3 19S 37 57 E
Tsentralnyy □, Russia ...... 28 D4 52 0N 40 0 E
Tses, Namibia .... 56 D2 25 58S 18 8 E
Tsetserleg, Mongolia .... 32 B5 47 36N 101 32 E
Tshabong, Botswana .... 56 D3 26 2S 22 29 E
Tshane, Botswana .... 56 C3 24 5S 21 54 E
Tshela, Dem. Rep. of the Congo 52 E2 4 57S 13 4 E
Tshesebe, Botswana .... 57 C4 21 51S 27 32 E
Tshibeke, Dem. Rep. of
    the Congo .... 54 C2 2 40S 28 35 E
Tshikapa, Dem. Rep. of
    the Congo .... 54 C2 2 23S 28 43 E
Tshikapa, Dem. Rep. of
    the Congo .... 52 F4 6 28S 20 48 E
Tshilenge, Dem. Rep. of
    the Congo .... 54 D1 6 17S 23 48 E
Tshinsenda, Dem. Rep. of
    the Congo .... 55 E2 12 20S 28 0 E
Tshofa, Dem. Rep. of the Congo 54 D2 5 13S 25 16 E
Tshwane, Botswana .... 56 C3 22 24S 22 1 E
Tsigara, Botswana .... 56 C4 20 22S 25 54 E
Tsihombe, Madag. .... 57 D8 25 10S 45 41 E
Tsiigehtchic, Canada 68 B6 67 15N 134 0W
Tsimlyansk Res. = Tsimlyanskoye
    Vdkhr., Russia .... 19 E7 48 0N 43 0 E
Tsimlyanskoye Vdkhr., Russia . 19 E7 48 0N 43 0 E
Tsinan = Jinan, China ...... 34 F9 36 38N 117 1 E
Tsineng, S. Africa .... 56 D3 27 5S 23 5 E
Tsing Yi, China .... 33 G11 22 21N 114 6 E
Tsinghai = Qinghai □, China . 32 C4 36 0N 98 0 E
Tsingtao = Qingdao, China .. 35 F11 36 5N 120 20 E
Tsingy de Bemaraha △, Madag. 57 B8 18 35S 45 25 E
Tsingy de Namoraka △, Madag. 57 B8 16 29S 45 25 E
Tsinjoarivo, Madag. .... 57 B8 19 37S 47 40 E
Tsinjomitondraka, Madag. .... 57 B8 15 40S 47 8 E
Tsiroanomandidy, Madag. .... 57 B8 18 46S 46 2 E
Tsitondroina, Madag. .... 57 C8 21 19S 46 0 E
Tsitsikamma △, S. Africa ... 56 E3 34 3S 23 40 E
Tsivory, Madag. .... 57 C8 24 4S 46 5 E
Tskhinvali, Georgia .... 19 F7 42 14N 44 1 E
Tsnori, Namibia .... 18 D7 54 55N 41 58 E
Tsobis, Namibia .... 56 B2 19 27N 17 30 E
Tsodilo Hill, Botswana ..... 56 B3 18 49S 21 43 E
Tsogttsetsiy = Baruunsuu,
    Mongolia .... 34 C3 43 43N 105 35 E
Tsolo, S. Africa .... 57 E4 31 18S 28 37 E
Tsomo, S. Africa .... 57 E4 32 0S 27 42 E
Tsu, Japan .... 31 G8 34 45N 136 25 E
Tsu L., Canada 70 A6 60 40N 111 52W
Tsuchiura, Japan .... 31 F10 36 5N 140 15 E
Tsuen Wan, China .... 33 G11 22 22N 114 6 E
Tsugaru-Kaikyō, Japan ..... 30 D10 41 35N 141 0 E
Tsumeb, Namibia .... 56 B2 19 9S 17 44 E
Tsumis, Namibia .... 56 C2 23 39S 17 29 E
Tsuruga, Japan .... 31 G8 35 45N 136 2 E
Tsurugi-San, Japan .... 31 H7 33 51N 134 6 E
Tsuruoka, Japan .... 30 E9 38 44N 139 50 E
Tsushima, Gifu, Japan ...... 31 G8 35 10N 136 43 E
Tsushima, Nagasaki, Japan .. 31 G4 34 20N 129 20 E
Tsuyama, Japan .... 31 G7 35 3N 134 0 E
Tsyelyakhany, Belarus ...... 17 B13 52 30N 25 46 E
Tual, Indonesia .... 37 F8 5 38S 132 44 E
Tuam, Ireland 10 C3 53 31N 8 51W
Tuamotu Arch. = Tuamotu Is.,
    French Polynesia 65 J13 17 0S 144 0W
Tuamotu Is., French Polynesia 65 J13 17 0S 144 0W
Tuamotu Ridge, Pac. Oc. 65 K14 20 0S 138 0W
Tuao, Phil. .... 37 A6 17 55N 121 22 E
Tuapse, Russia .... 19 F6 44 5N 39 10 E
Tuas, Singapore .... 39 d 1 19N 103 39 E
Tuatapere, N.Z. .... 59 M1 46 8S 167 41 E
Tuba City, U.S.A. 77 H8 36 8N 111 14W
Tuban, Indonesia .... 37 G15 6 54S 112 3 E
Tubarão, Brazil 95 B6 28 30S 49 0W
Tūbās, West Bank .... 46 C4 32 19N 35 22 E
Tubas →, Namibia .... 56 C2 22 54S 14 35 E
Tübingen, Germany .... 16 D5 48 31N 9 4 E
Tubruq, Libya .... 51 B10 32 7N 23 55 E
Tubuai Is., French Polynesia . 65 K13 25 0S 150 0W
Tuc Trung, Vietnam .... 39 G6 11 1N 107 12 E
Tucacas, Venezuela 92 A5 10 48N 68 19W
Tuchodi →, Canada 70 B4 58 17N 123 42W
Tuckanarra, Australia ...... 61 E2 27 7S 118 5 E
Tucson, U.S.A. 77 K8 32 13N 110 58W

Tucumán □, *Argentina* **94 B2** 26 48S 66 2W
Tucumcari, *U.S.A.* **81 H3** 35 10N 103 44W
Tucupita, *Venezuela* **92 B6** 9 2N 62 3W
Tucuruí, *Brazil* **93 D9** 3 42S 49 44W
Tucuruí, Reprêsa de, *Brazil* **93 D9** 4 0S 49 30W
Tudela, *Spain* **21 A5** 42 4N 1 39W
Tudmur, *Syria* **44 C3** 34 36N 38 15 E
Tudor, L., *Canada* **73 A6** 55 50N 65 25W
Tuen Mun, *China* **33 G10** 22 24N 113 59 E
Tugela →, *S. Africa* **57 D5** 29 14S 31 30 E
Tuguegarao, *Phil.* **37 A6** 17 35N 121 42 E
Tugur, *Russia* **29 D14** 53 44N 136 45 E
Tui, *Spain* **21 A1** 42 3N 8 39W
Tuineje, *Canary Is.* **24 F5** 28 19N 14 3W
Tukangbesi, Kepulauan, *Indonesia* **37 F6** 6 0S 124 0 E
Tukarak I., *Canada* **72 A4** 56 15N 78 45W
Tukayyid, *Iraq* **44 D5** 29 47N 45 36 E
Tukkae, Ao, *Thailand* **39 a** 7 51N 98 25 E
Tuktoyaktuk, *Canada* **68 B6** 69 27N 133 2W
Tukums, *Latvia* **9 H20** 56 58N 23 10 E
Tukuyu, *Tanzania* **55 D3** 9 17S 33 35 E
Tula, *Hidalgo, Mexico* **87 C5** 20 5N 99 20W
Tula, *Tamaulipas, Mexico* **87 C5** 23 0N 99 40W
Tula, *Russia* **18 D6** 54 13N 37 38 E
Tulancingo, *Mexico* **87 C5** 20 5N 99 22W
Tulare, *U.S.A.* **78 J7** 36 13N 119 21W
Tulare Lake Bed, *U.S.A.* **78 K7** 36 0N 119 48W
Tularosa, *U.S.A.* **77 K10** 33 5N 106 1W
Tulbagh, *S. Africa* **56 E2** 33 16S 19 6 E
Tulcán, *Ecuador* **92 C3** 0 48N 77 43W
Tulcea, *Romania* **17 F15** 45 13N 28 46 E
Tulchyn, *Ukraine* **17 D15** 48 41N 28 49 E
Tūleh, *Iran* **45 C7** 34 35N 52 33 E
Tulemalu L., *Canada* **71 A9** 62 58N 99 25W
Tuli, *Zimbabwe* **55 G2** 21 58S 29 13 E
Tulia, *U.S.A.* **81 H4** 34 32N 101 46W
Tulita, *Canada* **68 B7** 64 57N 125 30W
Ṭūlkarm, *West Bank* **46 C4** 32 19N 35 2 E
Tulla, *Ireland* **10 D3** 52 53N 8 46W
Tullahoma, *U.S.A.* **83 H2** 35 22N 86 13W
Tullamore, *Australia* **63 E4** 32 39S 147 36 E
Tullamore, *Ireland* **10 C4** 53 16N 7 31W
Tulle, *France* **20 D4** 45 16N 1 46 E
Tullow, *Ireland* **10 D5** 52 49N 6 45W
Tully, *Australia* **62 B4** 17 56S 145 55 E
Tully, *U.S.A.* **85 D8** 42 48N 76 7W
Tulsa, *U.S.A.* **81 G7** 36 10N 95 55W
Tulsequah, *Canada* **70 B2** 58 39N 133 35W
Tulua, *Colombia* **92 C3** 4 6N 76 11W
Tulun, *Russia* **29 D11** 54 32N 100 35 E
Tulungagung, *Indonesia* **37 H14** 8 5S 111 54 E
Tuma →, *Nic.* **88 D3** 13 6N 84 35W
Tumacacori ⌓, *U.S.A.* **77 L8** 31 34N 111 3W
Tumaco, *Colombia* **92 C3** 1 50N 78 45W
Tumatumari, *Guyana* **92 B7** 5 20N 58 55W
Tumba, *Sweden* **9 G17** 59 12N 17 48 E
Tumba, L., *Dem. Rep. of the Congo* **52 E3** 0 50S 18 0 E
Tumbarumba, *Australia* **63 F4** 35 44S 148 0 E
Tumbaya, *Argentina* **94 A2** 23 50S 65 26W
Tumbes, *Peru* **92 D2** 3 37S 80 27W
Tumbwe, *Dem. Rep. of the Congo* **55 E2** 11 25S 27 15 E
Tumby Bay, *Australia* **63 E2** 34 21S 136 8 E
Tumd Youqi, *China* **34 D6** 40 30N 110 30 E
Tumen, *China* **35 C15** 43 0N 129 50 E
Tumen Jiang →, *China* **35 C16** 42 20N 130 35 E
Tumeremo, *Venezuela* **92 B6** 7 18N 61 30W
Tumkur, *India* **40 N10** 13 18N 77 6 E
Tump, *Pakistan* **40 F3** 26 7N 62 16 E
Tumpat, *Malaysia* **39 J4** 6 11N 102 10 E
Tumu, *Ghana* **50 F5** 10 56N 1 56W
Tumucumaque, Serra, *Brazil* **93 C8** 2 0N 55 0W
Tumut, *Australia* **63 F4** 35 16S 148 13 E
Tumwater, *U.S.A.* **78 C4** 47 1N 122 54W
Tuna, *India* **42 H4** 22 59N 70 5 E
Tunapuna, *Trin. & Tob.* **93 K15** 10 38N 61 24W
Tunas de Zaza, *Cuba* **88 B4** 21 39N 79 34W
Tunbridge Wells = Royal Tunbridge Wells, *U.K.* **13 F8** 51 7N 0 16 E
Tuncurry, *Australia* **63 E5** 32 17S 152 29 E
Tundla, *India* **42 F8** 27 12N 78 17 E
Tunduru, *Tanzania* **55 E4** 11 8S 37 25 E
Tundzha →, *Bulgaria* **23 C11** 41 40N 26 35 E
Tung Chung, *China* **33 G10** 22 17N 113 57 E
Tung Lung Chau, *China* **33 G11** 22 15N 114 17 E
Tungabhadra →, *India* **40 M11** 15 57N 78 15 E
Tungla, *Nic.* **88 D3** 13 24N 84 21W
Tungsten, *Canada* **70 A3** 61 57N 128 16W
Tunguska, Nizhnyaya →, *Russia* **29 C9** 65 48N 88 4 E
Tunguska, Podkamennaya →, *Russia* **29 C10** 61 50N 90 13 E
Tunica, *U.S.A.* **81 H9** 34 41N 90 23W
Tunis, *Tunisia* **50 A7** 36 50N 10 11 E
Tunisia ■, *Africa* **50 B6** 33 30N 9 10 E
Tunja, *Colombia* **92 B4** 5 33N 73 25W
Tunkhannock, *U.S.A.* **85 E9** 41 32N 75 57W
Tunliu, *China* **34 F7** 36 13N 112 52 E
Tunnel Creek △, *Australia* **60 C4** 17 41S 125 18 E
Tunnsjøen, *Norway* **8 D15** 64 45N 13 25 E
Tunungayualok I., *Canada* **73 A7** 56 0N 61 0W
Tunuyán, *Argentina* **94 C2** 33 35S 69 0W
Tunuyán →, *Argentina* **94 C2** 33 33S 67 30W
Tuolumne, *U.S.A.* **78 H6** 37 58N 120 15W
Tuolumne →, *U.S.A.* **78 H5** 37 36N 121 13W
Tūp Āghāj, *Iran* **44 B5** 36 3N 47 50 E
Tupã, *Brazil* **95 A5** 21 57S 50 28W
Tupelo, *U.S.A.* **83 H1** 34 16N 88 43W
Tupinambaranas, *Brazil* **92 D7** 3 0S 58 0W
Tupiza, *Bolivia* **94 A2** 21 30S 65 40W
Tupman, *U.S.A.* **79 K7** 35 18N 119 21W
Tupper, *Canada* **70 B4** 55 32N 120 1W
Tupper Lake, *U.S.A.* **85 B10** 44 14N 74 28W
Tupungato, Cerro, *S. Amer.* **94 C2** 33 15S 69 50W
Tuquan, *China* **35 B11** 45 18N 121 38 E
Túquerres, *Colombia* **92 C3** 1 5N 77 37W
Tura, *Russia* **29 C11** 64 20N 100 17 E
Turabah, *Si. Arabia* **44 D4** 28 20N 43 15 E
Tūrān, *Iran* **45 C8** 35 39N 56 42 E
Turan, *Russia* **29 D10** 51 55N 95 0 E
Ṭurayf, *Si. Arabia* **44 D3** 31 41N 38 39 E
Turda, *Romania* **17 E12** 46 34N 23 47 E
Turek, *Poland* **17 B10** 52 3N 18 30 E
Turen, *Venezuela* **92 B5** 9 17N 69 6W
Turfan = Turpan, *China* **32 B3** 43 58N 89 10 E
Turfan Depression = Turpan Hami, *China* **26 E12** 42 40N 89 25 E
Turgeon →, *Canada* **72 C4** 50 0N 78 56W
Tŭrgovishte, *Bulgaria* **23 C12** 43 17N 26 38 E
Turgutlu, *Turkey* **23 E12** 38 30N 27 43 E
Turgwe →, *Zimbabwe* **57 C5** 21 31S 32 15 E
Turia →, *Spain* **21 C5** 39 27N 0 19W
Turiaçu, *Brazil* **93 D9** 1 40S 45 19W
Turiaçu →, *Brazil* **93 D9** 1 36S 45 19W
Turin = Torino, *Italy* **20 D7** 45 3N 7 40 E
Turkana, L., *Africa* **54 B4** 3 30N 36 5 E
Turkestan = Türkistan, *Kazakhstan* **28 E7** 43 17N 68 16 E
Turkey ■, *Eurasia* **19 G6** 39 0N 36 0 E
Turkey Creek, *Australia* **60 C4** 17 2S 128 12 E
Türkistan, *Kazakhstan* **28 E7** 43 17N 68 16 E
Türkmenbashi, *Turkmenistan* **19 G9** 40 5N 53 5 E
Turkmenistan ■, *Asia* **28 F6** 39 0N 59 0 E
Turks & Caicos Is. ⊘, *W. Indies* **89 B5** 21 20N 71 20W
Turks Island Passage, *W. Indies* **89 B5** 21 30N 71 30W
Turku, *Finland* **9 F20** 60 30N 22 19 E
Turkwel →, *Kenya* **54 B4** 3 6N 36 6 E
Turlock, *U.S.A.* **78 H6** 37 30N 120 51W
Turnagain →, *Canada* **70 B3** 59 12N 127 35W
Turnagain, C., *N.Z.* **59 J6** 40 28S 176 38 E
Turneffe Is., *Belize* **87 D7** 17 20N 87 50W
Turner, *U.S.A.* **76 B9** 48 51N 108 24W
Turner Pt., *Australia* **62 A1** 11 47S 133 32 E
Turner Valley, *Canada* **70 C6** 50 40N 114 17W
Turners Falls, *U.S.A.* **85 D12** 42 36N 72 33W
Turnhout, *Belgium* **15 C4** 51 19N 4 57 E
Turnor L., *Canada* **71 B7** 56 35N 108 35W
Tŭrnovo = Veliko Tŭrnovo, *Bulgaria* **23 C11** 43 5N 25 41 E
Turnu Măgurele, *Romania* **17 G13** 43 46N 24 56 E
Turnu Roşu, P., *Romania* **17 F13** 45 33N 24 17 E
Turpan, *China* **32 B3** 43 58N 89 10 E
Turpan Hami, *China* **26 E12** 42 40N 89 25 E
Turriff, *U.K.* **11 D6** 57 32N 2 27W
Tursāq, *Iraq* **44 C5** 33 27N 45 47 E
Turtle Head I., *Australia* **62 A3** 10 56S 142 37 E
Turtle L., *Canada* **71 C7** 53 36N 108 38W
Turtle Lake, *U.S.A.* **80 B4** 47 31N 100 53W
Turtleford, *Canada* **71 C7** 53 23N 108 57W
Turuépano △, *Venezuela* **89 D7** 10 34N 62 43W
Turukhansk, *Russia* **29 C9** 65 21N 88 5 E
Tuscaloosa, *U.S.A.* **83 J2** 33 12N 87 34W
Tuscany = Toscana □, *Italy* **22 C4** 43 25N 11 0 E
Tuscarawas →, *U.S.A.* **84 F3** 40 24N 81 25W
Tuscarora Mt., *U.S.A.* **84 F7** 40 55N 77 55W
Tuscola, *Ill., U.S.A.* **82 F1** 39 48N 88 17W
Tuscola, *Tex., U.S.A.* **81 J5** 32 12N 99 48W
Tuscumbia, *U.S.A.* **83 H2** 34 44N 87 42W
Tuskegee, *U.S.A.* **83 J3** 32 25N 85 42W
Tustin, *U.S.A.* **79 M9** 33 44N 117 49W
Tuticorin, *India* **40 Q11** 8 50N 78 12 E
Tutóia, *Brazil* **93 D10** 2 45S 42 20W
Tutong, *Brunei* **36 D4** 4 47N 114 40 E
Tutrakan, *Bulgaria* **23 B12** 44 2N 26 40 E
Tuttle Creek L., *U.S.A.* **80 F6** 39 22N 96 40W
Tuttlingen, *Germany* **16 E5** 47 58N 8 48 E
Tutuala, *E. Timor* **37 F7** 8 25S 127 15 E
Tutuila, *Amer. Samoa* **59 B13** 14 19S 170 50W
Tutume, *Botswana* **53 J5** 20 30S 27 5 E
Tututepec, *Mexico* **87 D5** 16 9N 97 38W
Tuva □, *Russia* **29 D10** 51 30N 95 0 E
Tuvalu ■, *Pac. Oc.* **64 H9** 8 0S 178 0 E
Tuxpan, *Mexico* **87 C5** 20 58N 97 23W
Tuxtla Gutiérrez, *Mexico* **87 D6** 16 50N 93 10W
Tuy = Tui, *Spain* **21 A1** 42 3N 8 39W
Tuy An, *Vietnam* **38 F7** 13 17N 109 16 E
Tuy Duc, *Vietnam* **39 F6** 12 15N 107 27 E
Tuy Hoa, *Vietnam* **38 F7** 13 5N 109 10 E
Tuy Phong, *Vietnam* **39 G7** 11 14N 108 43 E
Tuya L., *Canada* **70 B2** 59 7N 130 35W
Tuyen Hoa, *Vietnam* **38 D6** 17 50N 106 10 E
Tuyen Quang, *Vietnam* **38 B5** 21 50N 105 10 E
Tūysarkān, *Iran* **45 C6** 34 33N 48 27 E
Tuz Gölü, *Turkey* **19 G5** 38 42N 33 18 E
Ṭūz Khurmātū = Tozkhurmato, *Iraq* **44 C5** 34 56N 44 38 E
Tuzigoot ⌓, *U.S.A.* **77 J7** 34 46N 112 2W
Tuzla, *Bos.-H.* **23 B8** 44 34N 18 41 E
Tver, *Russia* **18 C6** 56 55N 35 55 E
Twain, *U.S.A.* **78 E5** 40 1N 121 3W
Twain Harte, *U.S.A.* **78 G6** 38 2N 120 14W
Tweed, *Canada* **84 B7** 44 29N 77 19W
Tweed →, *U.K.* **11 F6** 55 45N 2 0W
Tweed Heads, *Australia* **63 D5** 28 10S 153 31 E
Tweedsmuir ⌓, *Canada* **70 C3** 53 0N 126 20W
Twentynine Palms, *U.S.A.* **79 L10** 34 8N 116 3W
Twillingate, *Canada* **73 C9** 49 42N 54 45W
Twin Bridges, *U.S.A.* **76 D7** 45 33N 112 20W
Twin Falls, *Canada* **73 B7** 53 30N 64 32W
Twin Falls, *U.S.A.* **76 E6** 42 34N 114 28W
Twin Valley, *U.S.A.* **80 B6** 47 16N 96 16W
Twinsburg, *U.S.A.* **84 E3** 41 18N 81 26W
Twitchell Reservoir, *U.S.A.* **79 L6** 34 59N 120 19W
Two Harbors, *U.S.A.* **80 B9** 47 2N 91 40W
Two Hills, *Canada* **70 C6** 53 43N 111 52W
Two Rivers, *U.S.A.* **82 C2** 44 9N 87 34W
Two Rocks, *Australia* **61 F2** 31 30S 115 35 E
Twofold B., *Australia* **63 F4** 37 8S 149 59 E
Tyachiv, *Ukraine* **17 D12** 48 1N 23 35 E
Tychy, *Poland* **17 C10** 50 9N 18 59 E
Tyler, *Minn., U.S.A.* **80 C6** 44 18N 96 8W
Tyler, *Tex., U.S.A.* **81 J7** 32 21N 95 18W
Tynda, *Russia* **29 D13** 55 10N 124 43 E
Tyndall, *U.S.A.* **80 D6** 43 0N 97 50W
Tyne →, *U.K.* **12 C6** 54 59N 1 32W
Tyne & Wear □, *U.K.* **12 B6** 55 6N 1 17W
Tynemouth, *U.K.* **12 B6** 55 1N 1 26W
Tyre = Sūr, *Lebanon* **46 B4** 33 19N 35 16 E
Tyrifjorden, *Norway* **9 F14** 60 2N 10 8 E
Tyrol = Tirol □, *Austria* **16 E6** 47 3N 10 43 E
Tyrone, *U.S.A.* **84 F6** 40 40N 78 14W
Tyrone □, *U.K.* **10 B4** 54 38N 7 11W
Tyrrell →, *Australia* **63 F3** 35 26S 142 51 E
Tyrrell, L., *Australia* **63 F3** 35 20S 142 50 E
Tyrrell L., *Canada* **71 A7** 63 7N 105 27W
Tyrrhenian Sea, *Medit. S.* **22 E5** 40 0N 12 30 E
Tysfjorden, *Norway* **8 B17** 68 7N 16 25 E
Tyulgan, *Russia* **18 D10** 52 22N 56 12 E
Tyumen, *Russia* **28 D7** 57 11N 65 29 E
Tywi →, *U.K.* **13 F3** 51 48N 4 21W
Tywyn, *U.K.* **13 E3** 52 35N 4 5W
Tzaneen, *S. Africa* **57 C5** 23 47S 30 9 E
Tzermiádhes, *Greece* **25 D7** 35 12N 25 29 E
Tzukong = Zigong, *China* **32 D5** 29 15N 104 48 E

U

U Taphao, *Thailand* **38 F3** 12 35N 101 0 E
U.S.A. = United States of America ■, *N. Amer.* **74 C7** 37 0N 96 0W
U.S. Virgin Is. ⊘, *W. Indies* **89 e** 18 20N 65 0W
Uatumã →, *Brazil* **92 D7** 2 26S 57 37W
Uaupés, *Brazil* **92 D5** 0 8S 67 5W
Uaupés →, *Brazil* **92 C5** 0 2N 67 16W
Uaxactún, *Guatemala* **88 C2** 17 25N 89 29W
Ubá, *Brazil* **95 A7** 21 8S 43 0W
Ubaitaba, *Brazil* **93 F11** 14 18S 39 20W
Ubangi = Oubangi →, *Dem. Rep. of the Congo* **52 E3** 0 30S 17 50 E
Ubauro, *Pakistan* **42 E3** 28 15N 69 45 E
Ubayyiḍ, W. al →, *Iraq* **44 C4** 32 34N 43 48 E
Ube, *Japan* **31 H5** 33 56N 131 15 E
Úbeda, *Spain* **21 C4** 38 3N 3 23W
Uberaba, *Brazil* **93 G9** 19 50S 47 55W
Uberlândia, *Brazil* **93 G9** 19 0S 48 20W
Ubin, Pulau, *Singapore* **39 d** 1 25N 103 56 E
Ubolratna Res., *Thailand* **38 D4** 16 45N 102 30 E
Ubombo, *S. Africa* **57 D5** 27 31S 32 4 E
Ubon Ratchathani, *Thailand* **38 E5** 15 15N 104 50 E
Ubondo, *Dem. Rep. of the Congo* **54 C2** 0 55S 25 42 E
Ubort →, *Belarus* **17 B15** 52 6N 28 30 E
Ubud, *Indonesia* **37 J18** 8 30S 115 16 E
Ubundu, *Dem. Rep. of the Congo* **54 C2** 0 22S 25 30 E
Ucayali →, *Peru* **92 D4** 4 30S 73 30W
Uchab, *Namibia* **56 B2** 19 47S 17 42 E
Uchiura-Wan, *Japan* **30 C10** 42 25N 140 40 E
Uchquduq, *Uzbekistan* **28 E7** 41 50N 62 50 E
Uchur →, *Russia* **29 D14** 58 48N 130 35 E
Ucluelet, *Canada* **70 D3** 48 57N 125 32W
Uda →, *Russia* **29 D14** 54 42N 135 14 E
Udagamandalam, *India* **40 P10** 11 30N 76 44 E
Udainagar, *India* **42 H7** 22 33N 76 13 E
Udaipur, *India* **42 G5** 24 36N 73 44 E
Udaipur Garhi, *Nepal* **43 F12** 27 0N 86 35 E
Udala, *India* **43 J12** 21 35N 86 34 E
Uddevalla, *Sweden* **9 G14** 58 21N 11 55 E
Uddjaur, *Sweden* **8 D17** 65 56N 17 49 E
Uden, *Neths.* **15 C5** 51 40N 5 37 E
Udgir, *India* **40 K10** 18 25N 77 5 E
Udhampur, *India* **43 C6** 33 0N 75 5 E
Údine, *Italy* **22 A5** 46 3N 13 14 E
Udmurtia □, *Russia* **18 C9** 57 30N 52 30 E
Udon Thani, *Thailand* **38 D4** 17 29N 102 46 E
Udupi, *India* **40 N9** 13 25N 74 42 E
Udzungwa △, *Tanzania* **54 D4** 7 52S 36 35 E
Udzungwa Range, *Tanzania* **55 D4** 9 30S 35 10 E
Ueda, *Japan* **31 F9** 36 24N 138 16 E
Uedineniya, Os., *Russia* **4 B12** 78 0N 85 0 E
Uele →, *Dem. Rep. of the Congo* **52 D4** 3 45N 24 45 E
Uelen, *Russia* **29 C19** 66 10N 170 0W
Uelzen, *Germany* **16 B6** 52 57N 10 32 E
Ufa, *Russia* **18 D10** 54 45N 55 55 E
Ufa →, *Russia* **18 D10** 54 40N 56 0 E
Ugab →, *Namibia* **56 C1** 20 55S 13 30 E
Ugalla →, *Tanzania* **54 D3** 5 8S 30 42 E
Ugalla River ⌓, *Tanzania* **54 D3** 5 50S 31 54 E
Uganda ■, *Africa* **54 B3** 2 0N 32 0 E
Ugie, *S. Africa* **57 E4** 31 10S 28 13 E
Uglegorsk, *Russia* **29 E15** 49 5N 142 2 E
Ugljan, *Croatia* **16 F8** 44 12N 15 10 E
Uhlenhorst, *Namibia* **56 C2** 23 45S 17 55 E
Uhrichsville, *U.S.A.* **84 F3** 40 24N 81 21W
Uibhist a Deas = South Uist, *U.K.* **11 D1** 57 20N 7 15W
Uibhist a Tuath = North Uist, *U.K.* **11 D1** 57 40N 7 15W
Uig, *U.K.* **11 D2** 57 35N 6 21W
Uíge, *Angola* **52 F2** 7 30S 14 40 E
Uijŏngbu, *S. Korea* **35 F14** 37 48N 127 0 E
Ŭiju, *N. Korea* **35 D13** 40 15N 124 35 E
Uinta Mts., *U.S.A.* **76 F8** 40 45N 110 30W
Uis, *Namibia* **56 C1** 21 8S 14 49 E
Uitenhage, *S. Africa* **56 E4** 33 40S 25 28 E
Uithuizen, *Neths.* **15 A6** 53 24N 6 41 E
Ujh →, *India* **42 C6** 32 10N 75 18 E
Ujhani, *India* **43 F8** 28 0N 79 6 E
Uji-guntō, *Japan* **31 J4** 31 15N 129 25 E
Ujjain, *India* **42 H6** 23 9N 75 43 E
Ujung Pandang, *Indonesia* **37 F5** 5 10S 119 20 E
Uka, *Russia* **29 D17** 57 50N 162 0 E
Ukara I., *Tanzania* **54 C3** 1 50S 33 0 E
Uke-Shima, *Japan* **31 K4** 28 2N 129 14 E
Ukerewe I., *Tanzania* **54 C3** 2 0S 33 0 E
Ukhrul, *India* **41 G19** 25 10N 94 25 E
Ukhta, *Russia* **18 B9** 63 34N 53 41 E
Ukiah, *U.S.A.* **78 F3** 39 9N 123 13W
Ukmergė, *Lithuania* **9 J21** 55 15N 24 45 E
Ukraine ■, *Europe* **19 E5** 49 0N 32 0 E
Ukwi, *Botswana* **56 C3** 23 29S 20 30 E
Ulaan-Uul, *Mongolia* **34 B6** 44 13N 111 10 E
Ulaanbaatar, *Mongolia* **29 E11** 47 55N 106 53 E
Ulaangom, *Mongolia* **32 A4** 50 5N 92 10 E
Ulaanjirem, *Mongolia* **34 B3** 45 5N 105 30 E
Ulamba, *Dem. Rep. of the Congo* **55 D1** 9 3S 23 38 E
Ulan Bator = Ulaanbaatar, *Mongolia* **29 E11** 47 55N 106 53 E
Ulan Ude, *Russia* **29 D11** 51 45N 107 40 E
Ulaya, *Morogoro, Tanzania* **54 D4** 7 3S 36 55 E
Ulaya, *Tabora, Tanzania* **54 C3** 4 25S 33 30 E
Ulcinj, *Serbia & M.* **23 D8** 41 58N 19 10 E
Ulco, *S. Africa* **56 D3** 28 21S 24 15 E
Ulefoss, *Norway* **9 G13** 59 17N 9 16 E
Ulhasnagar, *India* **40 K8** 19 15N 73 10 E
Uliastay, *Mongolia* **32 B4** 47 56N 97 28 E
Ulladulla, *Australia* **63 F5** 35 21S 150 29 E
Ullapool, *U.K.* **11 D3** 57 54N 5 9W
Ullswater, *U.K.* **12 C5** 54 34N 2 52W
Ullŭng-do, *S. Korea* **31 F5** 37 30N 130 30 E
Ulm, *Germany* **16 D5** 48 23N 9 58 E
Ulmarra, *Australia* **63 D5** 29 37S 153 4 E
Ulonguè, *Mozam.* **55 E3** 14 37S 34 19 E
Ulricehamn, *Sweden* **9 H15** 57 46N 13 26 E
Ulsan, *S. Korea* **35 G15** 35 20N 129 15 E
Ulsta, *U.K.* **11 A7** 60 30N 1 9W
Ulster □, *U.K.* **10 B5** 54 35N 6 30W
Ulubat Gölü, *Turkey* **23 D13** 40 9N 28 35 E
Uludağ, *Turkey* **23 D13** 40 4N 29 13 E
Uluguru Mts., *Tanzania* **54 D4** 7 15S 37 40 E
Ulungur He →, *China* **32 B3** 47 1N 87 24 E
Uluru = Ayers Rock, *Australia* **61 E5** 25 23S 131 5 E
Uluru-Kata Tjuta △, *Australia* **61 E5** 25 19S 131 1 E
Ulutau, *Kazakhstan* **28 E7** 48 39N 67 1 E
Uluwatu, *Indonesia* **37 K18** 8 50S 115 5 E
Ulva, *U.K.* **11 E2** 56 29N 6 13W
Ulverston, *U.K.* **12 C4** 54 13N 3 5W
Ulverstone, *Australia* **63 G4** 41 11S 146 11 E
Ulya, *Russia* **29 D15** 59 10N 142 0 E
Ulyanovsk = Simbirsk, *Russia* **18 D8** 54 20N 48 25 E
Ulyasutay = Uliastay, *Mongolia* **32 B4** 47 56N 97 28 E
Ulysses, *U.S.A.* **81 G4** 37 35N 101 22W
Umala, *Bolivia* **92 G5** 17 25S 68 5W
Uman, *Ukraine* **17 D16** 48 40N 30 12 E
Umaria, *India* **41 H12** 23 35N 80 50 E
Umarkot, *Pakistan* **40 G6** 25 15N 69 40 E
Umarpada, *India* **42 J5** 21 27N 73 30 E
Umatilla, *U.S.A.* **76 D4** 45 55N 119 21W
Umba, *Russia* **18 A5** 66 42N 34 11 E
Umbagog L., *U.S.A.* **85 B13** 44 46N 71 3W
Umbakumba, *Australia* **62 A2** 13 47S 136 50 E
Umbrella Mts., *N.Z.* **59 L2** 45 35S 169 5 E
Ume älv →, *Sweden* **8 E19** 63 45N 20 20 E
Umeå, *Sweden* **8 E19** 63 45N 20 20 E
Umera, *Indonesia* **37 E7** 0 12S 129 37 E
Umfolozi ⌓, *S. Africa* **57 D5** 28 18S 31 50 E
Umfuli →, *Zimbabwe* **55 F2** 17 30S 29 23 E
Umfurudzi ⌓, *Zimbabwe* **55 F3** 17 6S 31 40 E
Umgusa, *Zimbabwe* **55 F2** 19 29S 27 52 E
Umkomaas, *S. Africa* **57 E5** 30 13S 30 48 E
Umlazi, *S. Africa* **53 L6** 29 59S 30 54 E
Umm ad Daraj, J., *Jordan* **46 C4** 32 18N 35 48 E
Umm al Qaywayn, *U.A.E.* **45 E7** 25 30N 55 35 E
Umm al Qittayn, *Jordan* **46 C5** 32 18N 36 40 E
Umm Bāb, *Qatar* **45 E6** 25 12N 50 48 E
Umm Durman = Omdurmân, *Sudan* **51 E12** 15 40N 32 28 E
Umm el Fahm, *Israel* **46 C4** 32 31N 35 9 E
Umm Keddada, *Sudan* **51 F11** 13 33N 26 35 E
Umm Lajj, *Si. Arabia* **44 E3** 25 0N 37 23 E
Umm Ruwaba, *Sudan* **51 F12** 12 50N 31 20 E
Umnak I., *U.S.A.* **68 C3** 53 15N 168 20W
Umniati →, *Zimbabwe* **55 F2** 16 49S 28 45 E
Umpqua →, *U.S.A.* **76 E1** 43 40N 124 12W
Umreth, *India* **42 H5** 22 41N 73 4 E
Umtata, *S. Africa* **57 E4** 31 36S 28 49 E
Umuarama, *Brazil* **95 A5** 23 45S 53 20W
Umvukwe Ra., *Zimbabwe* **55 F3** 16 45S 30 45 E
Umzimvubu, *S. Africa* **57 E4** 31 38S 29 33 E
Umzingwane →, *Zimbabwe* **55 G2** 22 12S 29 56 E
Umzinto, *S. Africa* **57 E5** 30 15S 30 45 E
Una, *India* **42 J4** 20 46N 71 8 E
Una →, *Bos.-H.* **16 F9** 45 0N 16 20 E
Unadilla, *U.S.A.* **85 D9** 42 20N 75 19W
Unalakleet, *U.S.A.* **68 B3** 63 52N 160 47W
Unalaska, *U.S.A.* **68 C3** 53 53N 166 32W
Unalaska I., *U.S.A.* **68 C3** 53 35N 166 50W
'Unayzah, *Si. Arabia* **44 E4** 26 6N 43 58 E
'Unayzah, J., *Asia* **44 C3** 32 12N 39 18 E
Uncía, *Bolivia* **92 G5** 18 25S 66 40W
Uncompahgre Peak, *U.S.A.* **77 G10** 38 4N 107 28W
Uncompahgre Plateau, *U.S.A.* **77 G9** 38 20N 108 15W
Undara Volcanic △, *Australia* **62 B3** 18 14S 144 41 E
Underbool, *Australia* **63 F3** 35 10S 141 51 E
Ungarie, *Australia* **63 E4** 33 38S 146 56 E
Ungarra, *Australia* **63 E2** 34 12S 136 2 E
Ungava, Pén. d', *Canada* **69 C12** 60 0N 74 0W
Ungava B., *Canada* **69 C13** 59 30N 67 30W
Ungeny = Ungheni, *Moldova* **17 E14** 47 11N 27 51 E
Unggi, *N. Korea* **35 C16** 42 16N 130 28 E
Ungheni, *Moldova* **17 E14** 47 11N 27 51 E
Ungwana B., *Kenya* **54 C5** 2 40S 40 20 E
União da Vitória, *Brazil* **95 B5** 26 13S 51 5W
Unimak I., *U.S.A.* **68 C3** 54 45N 164 0W
Union, *Miss., U.S.A.* **81 J10** 32 34N 89 7W
Union, *Mo., U.S.A.* **80 F9** 38 27N 91 0W
Union, *S.C., U.S.A.* **83 H5** 34 43N 81 37W
Union City, *Calif., U.S.A.* **78 H4** 37 36N 122 1W
Union City, *N.J., U.S.A.* **85 F10** 40 45N 74 2W
Union City, *Pa., U.S.A.* **84 E5** 41 54N 79 51W
Union City, *Tenn., U.S.A.* **81 G10** 36 26N 89 3W
Union Gap, *U.S.A.* **76 C3** 46 33N 120 28W
Union Springs, *U.S.A.* **83 J3** 32 9N 85 43W
Uniondale, *S. Africa* **56 E3** 33 39S 23 7 E
Uniontown, *U.S.A.* **82 F6** 39 54N 79 44W
Unionville, *U.S.A.* **80 E8** 40 29N 93 1W
United Arab Emirates ■, *Asia* **45 F7** 23 50N 54 0 E
United Kingdom ■, *Europe* **14 E6** 53 0N 2 0W
United States of America ■, *N. Amer.* **74 C7** 37 0N 96 0W
Unity, *Canada* **71 C7** 52 30N 109 5W
University Park, *U.S.A.* **77 K10** 32 17N 106 45W
Unjha, *India* **42 H5** 23 46N 72 24 E
Unnao, *India* **43 F9** 26 35N 80 30 E
Unsengedsi →, *Zimbabwe* **55 F3** 15 43S 31 14 E
Unst, *U.K.* **11 A8** 60 44N 0 53W
Unuk →, *Canada* **70 B2** 56 5N 131 3W
Unzen-Amakusa △, *Japan* **31 H5** 32 15N 130 10 E
Uozu, *Japan* **31 F8** 36 48N 137 24 E
Upata, *Venezuela* **92 B6** 8 1N 62 24W
Upemba △, *Dem. Rep. of the Congo* **55 D2** 9 0S 26 35 E
Upemba, L., *Dem. Rep. of the Congo* **55 D2** 8 30S 26 20 E
Upernavik, *Greenland* **4 B5** 72 49N 56 20W
Upington, *S. Africa* **56 D3** 28 25S 21 15 E
Upleta, *India* **42 J4** 21 46N 70 16 E
'Upolu, *Samoa* **59 A13** 13 58S 172 0W
Upper Alkali L., *U.S.A.* **76 F3** 41 47N 120 8W
Upper Arrow L., *Canada* **70 C5** 50 30N 117 50W
Upper Foster L., *Canada* **71 B7** 56 47N 105 20W
Upper Hutt, *N.Z.* **59 J5** 41 8S 175 5 E
Upper Klamath L., *U.S.A.* **76 E3** 42 25N 121 55W
Upper Lake, *U.S.A.* **78 F4** 39 10N 122 54W
Upper Manzanilla, *Trin. & Tob.* **93 K15** 10 31N 61 4W
Upper Missouri River Breaks ⌓, *U.S.A.* **76 C9** 47 50N 108 55W
Upper Musquodoboit, *Canada* **73 C7** 45 10N 62 58W
Upper Red L., *U.S.A.* **80 A7** 48 8N 94 45W
Upper Sandusky, *U.S.A.* **82 E4** 40 50N 83 17W
Upper Volta = Burkina Faso ■, *Africa* **50 F5** 12 0N 1 0W
Uppland, *Sweden* **9 F17** 59 59N 17 48 E
Uppsala, *Sweden* **9 G17** 59 53N 17 38 E
Upshi, *India* **43 C7** 33 48N 77 52 E
Upstart, C., *Australia* **62 B4** 19 41S 147 45 E
Upton, *U.S.A.* **80 C2** 44 6N 104 38W
Uqsuqtuuq = Gjoa Haven, *Canada* **68 B10** 68 38N 95 53W
Ur, *Iraq* **44 D5** 30 55N 46 25 E
Urad Qianqi, *China* **34 D5** 40 40N 108 30 E
Urakawa, *Japan* **30 C11** 42 9N 142 47 E

Ural = Uralskiy □, Russia .... 28 C7   64 0N 70 0 E
Ural = Zhayyq ⇒, Kazakhstan ... 19 E9   47 0N 51 48 E
Ural, Australia .... 63 E4   33 21S 146 12 E
Ural Mts. = Uralskie Gory,
  Eurasia .... 18 C10   60 0N 59 0 E
Uralla, Australia .... 63 E5   30 37S 151 29 E
Uralsk = Oral, Kazakhstan ...... 19 D9   51 20N 51 20 E
Uralskie Gory, Eurasia .... 18 C10   60 0N 59 0 E
Uralskiy □, Russia .... 28 C7   64 0N 70 0 E
Urambo, Tanzania .... 54 D3   5 4S 32 0 E
Urandangi, Australia .... 62 C2   21 32S 138 14 E
Uranium City, Canada 71 B7   59 34N 108 37W
Uraricoera ⇒, Brazil 92 C6   3 2N 60 30W
Urawa, Japan .... 31 G9   35 50N 139 40 E
Uray, Russia .... 28 C7   60 5N 65 15 E
'Uray'irah, Si. Arabia .... 45 E6   25 57N 48 53 E
Urbana, Ill., U.S.A. 82 E1   40 7N 88 12W
Urbana, Ohio, U.S.A. 82 E4   40 7N 83 45W
Urbino, Italy .... 22 C5   43 43N 12 38 E
Urbión, Picos de, Spain 21 A4   42 1N   2 52W
Urcos, Peru 92 F4   13 40S 71 38W
Urdinarrain, Argentina 94 C4   32 37S 58 52W
Urdzhar, Kazakhstan .... 28 E9   47 5N 81 38 E
Ure ⇒, U.K. 12 C6   54 5N   1 20W
Ures, Mexico 86 B2   29 30N 110 30W
Urewera △, N.Z. .... 59 H6   38 29S 177 7 E
Urfa = Şanlıurfa, Turkey .... 19 G6   37 12N 38 50 E
Urganch, Uzbekistan .... 28 E7   41 40N 60 41 E
Urgench = Urganch, Uzbekistan . 28 E7   41 40N 60 41 E
Ürgüp, Turkey .... 44 B2   38 38N 34 56 E
Uri, India .... 43 B6   34 8N 74 2 E
Uribia, Colombia 92 A4   11 43N 72 16W
Uriondo, Bolivia 94 A3   21 41S 64 41W
Urique, Mexico 86 B3   27 13N 107 55W
Urique ⇒, Mexico 86 B3   26 29N 107 58W
Urk, Neths. .... 15 B5   52 39N   5 36 E
Urla, Turkey .... 23 E12   38 20N 26 47 E
Urmia = Orūmīyeh, Iran .... 44 B5   37 40N 45 0 E
Urmia, L. = Orūmīyeh,
  Daryācheh-ye, Iran .... 44 B5   37 50N 45 30 E
Uroševac, Serbia & M. .... 23 C9   42 23N 21 10 E
Uroyan, Montanas de,
  Puerto Rico .... 89 d   18 12N 67 0W
Uruaçu, Brazil 93 F9   14 30S 49 10W
Uruapan, Mexico 86 D4   19 30N 102 0W
Urubamba ⇒, Peru 92 F4   10 43S 73 48W
Uruçara, Brazil 92 D7   2 32S 57 45W
Uruçuí, Brazil 93 E10   7 20S 44 28W
Uruguai ⇒, Brazil 95 B5   26 0S 53 30W
Uruguaiana, Brazil 94 B4   29 50S 57 0W
Uruguay ■, S. Amer. 94 C4   32 30S 56 30W
Uruguay ⇒, S. Amer. 94 C4   34 12S 58 18W
Urumchi = Ürümqi, China ...... 28 E9   43 45N 87 45 E
Ürümqi, China .... 28 E9   43 45N 87 45 E
Urup, Ostrov, Russia .... 29 E16   46 0N 151 0 E
Usa ⇒, Russia .... 18 A10   66 16N 59 49 E
Uşak, Turkey .... 19 G4   38 43N 29 28 E
Usakos, Namibia .... 56 C2   21 54S 15 31 E
Usedom, Germany .... 16 B8   53 55N 14 2 E
Useless Loop, Australia .... 61 E1   26 8S 113 23 E
Ush-Tobe, Kazakhstan .... 28 E8   45 16N 78 0 E
Ushakova, Ostrov, Russia ...... 4 A12   82 0N 80 0 E
Ushant = Ouessant, Î. d', France 20 B1   48 28N   5 6W
Ushashi, Tanzania .... 54 C3   1 59S 33 57 E
Ushibuka, Japan .... 31 H5   32 11N 130 1 E
Ushuaia, Argentina 96 G3   54 50S 68 23W
Ushumun, Russia .... 29 D13   52 47N 126 32 E
Usk, Canada 70 C3   54 38N 128 26W
Usk ⇒, U.K. 13 F5   51 33N   2 58W
Uska, India .... 43 F10   27 12N 83 7 E
Usman, Russia .... 18 D6   52 5N 39 48 E
Usoke, Tanzania .... 54 D3   5 8S 32 24 E
Usolye Sibirskoye, Russia ...... 29 D11   52 48N 103 40 E
Uspallata, P. de, Argentina 94 C2   32 37S 69 22W
Uspenskiy, Kazakhstan .... 28 E8   48 41N 72 43 E
Ussuri ⇒, Asia .... 30 A7   48 27N 135 0 E
Ussuriysk, Russia .... 29 E14   43 48N 131 59 E
Ussurka, Russia .... 30 B6   45 12N 133 31 E
Ust-Bolsheretsk, Russia .... 29 D16   52 50N 156 15 E
Ust-Chaun, Russia .... 29 C18   68 47N 170 30 E
Ust-Ilimsk, Russia .... 29 D11   58 3N 102 39 E
Ust-Ishim, Russia .... 28 D8   57 45N 71 10 E
Ust-Kamchatsk, Russia .... 29 D17   56 10N 162 28 E
Ust-Kamenogorsk = Öskemen,
  Kazakhstan .... 28 E9   50 0N 82 36 E
Ust-Khayryuzovo, Russia .... 29 D16   57 15N 156 45 E
Ust-Kut, Russia .... 29 D11   56 50N 105 42 E
Ust-Kuyga, Russia .... 29 B14   70 1N 135 43 E
Ust-Maya, Russia .... 29 C14   60 30N 134 28 E
Ust-Mil, Russia .... 29 D14   59 40N 133 11 E
Ust-Nera, Russia .... 29 C15   64 35N 143 15 E
Ust-Nyukzha, Russia .... 29 D13   56 34N 121 37 E
Ust-Olenek, Russia .... 29 B12   73 0N 120 5 E
Ust-Omchug, Russia .... 29 C15   61 9N 149 38 E
Ust-Port, Russia .... 28 C9   69 40N 84 26 E
Ust-Tsilma, Russia .... 18 A9   65 28N 52 11 E
Ust Urt = Ustyurt Plateau, Asia . 28 E6   44 0N 55 0 E
Ust-Usa, Russia .... 18 A10   66 2N 56 57 E
Ust-Vorkuta, Russia .... 18 A11   67 24N 64 0 E
Ústí nad Labem, Czech Rep. ... 16 C8   50 41N 14 3 E
Ústica, Italy .... 22 E5   38 42N 13 11 E
Ustinov = Izhevsk, Russia ...... 18 C9   56 51N 53 14 E
Ustyurt Plateau, Asia .... 28 E6   44 0N 55 0 E
Usu, China .... 32 B3   44 27N 84 40 E
Usuki, Japan .... 31 H5   33 8N 131 49 E
Usulután, El Salv. 88 D2   13 25N 88 28W
Usumacinta ⇒, Mexico 87 D6   17 0N 91 0W
Usumbura = Bujumbura, Burundi 54 C2   3 16S 29 18 E
Usure, Tanzania .... 54 C3   4 40S 34 22 E
Usutu ⇒, Mozam. .... 57 D5   26 48S 32 7 E
Uta, Indonesia .... 37 E9   4 33S 136 0 E
Utah □, U.S.A. 76 G8   39 20N 111 30W
Utah L., U.S.A. 76 F8   40 10N 111 58W
Utara, Selat, Malaysia .... 39 c   5 28N 100 20 E
Utarni, India .... 42 F4   26 5N 71 58 E
Utatlan, Guatemala 88 C1   15 2N 91 11W
Ute Creek ⇒, U.S.A. 81 H3   35 21N 103 50W
Utena, Lithuania .... 9 J21   55 27N 25 40 E
Utete, Tanzania .... 54 D4   8 0S 38 45 E
Uthai Thani, Thailand .... 38 E3   15 22N 100 3 E
Uthal, Pakistan .... 42 G2   25 44N 66 40 E
Utiariti, Brazil 92 F7   13 0S 58 10W
Utica, N.Y., U.S.A. 85 C9   43 6N 75 14W
Utica, Ohio, U.S.A. 84 F2   40 14N 82 27W
Utikuma L., Canada 70 B5   55 50N 115 30W
Utopia, Australia .... 62 C1   22 14S 134 33 E
Utraula, India .... 43 F10   27 19N 82 25 E

Utrecht, Neths. .... 15 B5   52 5N   5 8 E
Utrecht, S. Africa .... 57 D5   27 38S 30 20 E
Utrecht □, Neths. .... 15 B5   52 6N   5 7 E
Utrera, Spain 21 D3   37 12N   5 48W
Utsjoki, Finland .... 8 B22   69 51N 26 59 E
Utsunomiya, Japan .... 31 F9   36 30N 139 50 E
Uttar Pradesh □, India .... 43 F9   27 0N 80 0 E
Uttaradit, Thailand .... 38 D3   17 36N 100 5 E
Uttaranchal □, India .... 43 D8   30 0N 79 30 E
Uttoxeter, U.K. 12 E6   52 54N   1 52W
Utuado, Puerto Rico .... 89 d   18 16N 66 42W
Uummannaq, Greenland 4 B4   77 0N 69 0W
Uummannaq, Greenland 4 B5   70 58N 52 0W
Uummannarsuaq = Nunap Isua,
  Greenland 69 C15   59 48N 43 55W
Uusikaarlepyy, Finland .... 8 E20   63 32N 22 31 E
Uusikaupunki, Finland .... 9 F19   60 47N 21 25 E
Uva, Russia .... 18 C9   56 59N 52 13 E
Uvalde, U.S.A. 81 L5   29 13N 99 47W
Uvat, Russia .... 28 D7   59 5N 68 50 E
Uvinza, Tanzania .... 54 D3   5 5S 30 24 E
Uvira, Dem. Rep. of the Congo . 54 C2   3 22S 29 3 E
Uvs Nuur, Mongolia .... 32 A4   50 20N 92 30 E
'Uwairidh, Ḥarrat al, Si. Arabia . 44 E3   26 50N 38 0 E
Uwajima, Japan .... 31 H6   33 10N 132 35 E
Uwanda △, Tanzania .... 54 D3   7 46S 32 0 E
Uweinat, Jebel, Sudan .... 51 D10   21 54N 24 58 E
Uxbridge, Canada 84 B5   44 6N 79 7W
Uxin Qi, China .... 34 E5   38 50N 109 5 E
Uxmal, Mexico 87 C7   20 22N 89 46W
Uxmal, Ruinas, Mexico 87 C7   20 22N 89 46W
Üydzin, Mongolia .... 34 B4   44 9N 107 0 E
Uyo, Nigeria .... 50 G7   5 1N 7 53 E
Uyûn Mûsa, Egypt .... 46 F1   29 53N 32 40 E
Uyuni, Bolivia 92 H5   20 28S 66 47W
Uzbekistan ■, Asia .... 28 E7   41 30N 65 0 E
Uzen, Kazakhstan .... 19 F9   43 29N 52 54 E
Uzen, Mal ⇒, Kazakhstan ...... 19 E9   49 4N 49 44 E
Uzerche, France .... 20 D4   45 25N   1 34 E
Uzh ⇒, Ukraine .... 17 C16   51 15N 30 12 E
Uzhgorod = Uzhhorod, Ukraine . 17 D12   48 36N 22 18 E
Uzhhorod, Ukraine .... 17 D12   48 36N 22 18 E
Užice, Serbia & M. .... 23 C8   43 55N 19 50 E
Uzunköprü, Turkey .... 23 D12   41 16N 26 43 E

V

Vaal ⇒, S. Africa .... 56 D3   29 4S 23 38 E
Vaal Dam, S. Africa .... 57 D4   27 0S 28 14 E
Vaalbos △, S. Africa .... 56 D3   28 22S 24 20 E
Vaalwater, S. Africa .... 57 C4   24 15S 28 8 E
Vaasa, Finland .... 8 E19   63 6N 21 38 E
Vác, Hungary .... 17 E10   47 49N 19 10 E
Vacaria, Brazil 95 B5   28 31S 50 52W
Vacaville, U.S.A. 78 G5   38 21N 121 59W
Vach = Vakh ⇒, Russia .... 28 C8   60 45N 76 45 E
Vache, Î. à, Haiti 89 C5   18 2N 73 35W
Vadnagar, India .... 42 H5   23 47N 72 40 E
Vadodara, India .... 42 H5   22 20N 73 10 E
Vadsø, Norway .... 8 A23   70 3N 29 50 E
Vaduz, Liech. .... 20 C8   47 8N   9 31 E
Værøy, Norway .... 8 C15   67 40N 12 40 E
Vágar, Færoe Is. 8 E9   62 5N   7 15W
Vágsfjorden, Norway .... 8 B17   68 50N 16 50 E
Váh ⇒, Slovak Rep. .... 17 D9   47 43N 18 7 E
Vahsel B., Antarctica 5 D1   75 0S 35 0W
Vái, Greece .... 25 D8   35 15N 26 18 E
Vaigach, Russia .... 28 B6   70 10N 59 0 E
Vail, U.S.A. 74 C5   39 40N 106 20W
Vaisali ⇒, India .... 43 F8   26 28N 78 53 E
Vakh ⇒, Russia .... 28 C8   60 45N 76 45 E
Val-d'Or, Canada 72 C4   48 7N 77 47W
Val Marie, Canada 71 D7   49 15N 107 45W
Valahia, Romania .... 17 F13   44 35N 25 0 E
Valandovo, Macedonia .... 23 D10   41 19N 22 34 E
Valcheta, Argentina 96 E3   40 40S 66 8W
Valdai Hills = Valdayskaya
  Vozvyshennost, Russia ...... 18 C5   57 0N 33 30 E
Valdayskaya Vozvyshennost,
  Russia .... 18 C5   57 0N 33 30 E
Valdepeñas, Spain 21 C4   38 43N   3 25W
Valdés, Pen., Argentina 96 E4   42 30S 63 45W
Valdez, U.S.A. 68 B5   61 7N 146 16W
Valdivia, Chile 96 D2   39 50S 73 14W
Valdosta, U.S.A. 83 K4   30 50N 83 17W
Valdres, Norway .... 9 F13   61 5N   9 5 E
Vale, U.S.A. 76 E5   43 59N 117 15W
Vale of Glamorgan □, U.K. 13 F4   51 28N   3 25W
Valemount, Canada 70 C5   52 50N 119 15W
Valença, Brazil 93 F11   13 20S 39 5W
Valença do Piauí, Brazil 93 E10   6 20S 41 45W
Valence, France .... 20 D6   44 57N   4 54 E
Valencia, Spain 21 C5   39 27N   0 23W
Valencia, Trin. & Tob. 93 K15   10 39N 61 11W
Valencia, U.S.A. 77 J10   34 48N 106 43W
Valencia, Venezuela 92 A5   10 11N 68 0W
Valencia □, Spain 21 C5   39 20N   0 40W
Valencia, G. de, Spain .... 21 C6   39 30N   0 0 E
Valencia de Alcántara, Spain ... 21 C2   39 25N   7 14W
Valencia I., Ireland 10 E1   51 54N 10 22W
Valenciennes, France .... 20 A5   50 20N   3 34 E
Valentim, Sa. do, Brazil 93 E10   6 0S 43 30W
Valentin, Russia .... 30 C7   43 8N 134 17 E
Valentine, U.S.A. 81 K2   30 35N 104 30W
Valera, Venezuela 92 B4   9 19N 70 37W
Valga, Estonia .... 9 H22   57 47N 26 2 E
Valier, U.S.A. 76 B7   48 18N 112 16W
Valjevo, Serbia & M. .... 23 B8   44 18N 19 53 E
Valka, Latvia .... 9 H21   57 42N 25 57 E
Valkeakoski, Finland .... 9 F20   61 16N 24 2 E
Valkenswaard, Neths. .... 15 C5   51 21N   5 29 E
Vall de Uxó = La Vall d'Uixó,
  Spain 21 C5   39 49N   0 15W
Valladolid, Mexico 87 C7   20 40N 88 11W
Valladolid, Spain 21 B3   41 38N   4 43W
Valldemossa, Spain .... 24 B9   39 43N   2 37 E
Valle de la Pascua, Venezuela .. 92 B5   9 13N 66 0W
Valle de las Palmas, Mexico 79 N10   32 20N 116 43W
Valle de Santiago, Mexico 86 C4   20 25N 101 15W
Valle de Suchil, Mexico 86 C4   23 38N 103 55W
Valle de Zaragoza, Mexico 86 B3   27 28N 105 49W
Valle Fértil, Sierra del, Argentina 94 C2   30 20S 68 0W
Valle Gran Rey, Canary Is. 24 F2   28 5N 17 20W
Valle Hermoso, Mexico 87 B5   25 35N 97 40W
Valledupar, Colombia 92 A4   10 29N 73 15W

Vallehermoso, Canary Is. 24 F2   28 10N 17 15W
Vallejo, U.S.A. 78 G4   38 7N 122 14W
Vallenar, Chile 94 B1   28 30S 70 50W
Valletta, Malta .... 25 D2   35 54N 14 31 E
Valley Center, U.S.A. 79 M9   33 13N 117 2W
Valley City, U.S.A. 80 B6   46 55N 98 0W
Valley Falls, Oreg., U.S.A. 76 E3   42 29N 120 17W
Valley Falls, R.I., U.S.A. 85 E13   41 54N 71 24W
Valley Springs, U.S.A. 78 G6   38 12N 120 50W
Valley View, U.S.A. 85 F8   40 39N 76 33W
Valley Wells, U.S.A. 79 K11   35 27N 115 46W
Valleyview, Canada 70 B5   55 5N 117 17W
Vallimanca, Arroyo, Argentina .. 94 D4   35 40S 59 10W
Valls, Spain .... 21 B6   41 18N   1 15 E
Valmiera, Latvia .... 9 H21   57 37N 25 29 E
Valognes, France 20 B3   49 30N   1 28W
Valona = Vlorë, Albania .... 23 D8   40 32N 19 28 E
Valozhyn, Belarus .... 17 A14   54 3N 26 30 E
Valparaíso, Chile 94 C1   33 2S 71 40W
Valparaíso, Mexico 86 C4   22 50N 103 32W
Valparaíso, U.S.A. 82 E2   41 28N 87 4W
Valparaíso □, Chile 94 C1   33 2S 71 40W
Vals ⇒, S. Africa .... 56 D4   27 23S 26 30 E
Vals, Tanjung, Indonesia .... 37 F9   8 26S 137 25 E
Valsad, India .... 40 J8   20 40N 72 58 E
Valverde, Canary Is. 24 G2   27 48N 17 55W
Valverde del Camino, Spain 21 D2   37 35N   6 47W
Vammala, Finland .... 9 F20   61 20N 22 54 E
Vámos, Greece .... 25 D6   35 24N 24 13 E
Van, Turkey .... 19 G7   38 30N 43 20 E
Van, L. = Van Gölü, Turkey .... 19 G7   38 30N 43 0 E
Van Alstyne, U.S.A. 81 J6   33 25N 96 35W
Van Blommestein Meer,
  Suriname 93 C7   4 45N 55 0W
Van Buren, Canada 73 C6   47 10N 67 55W
Van Buren, Ark., U.S.A. 81 H7   35 26N 94 21W
Van Buren, Maine, U.S.A. 83 B11   47 10N 67 58W
Van Buren, Mo., U.S.A. 81 G9   37 0N 91 1W
Van Canh, Vietnam .... 38 F7   13 37N 109 0 E
Van Diemen, C., N. Terr.,
  Australia .... 60 B5   11 9S 130 24 E
Van Diemen, C., Queens.,
  Australia .... 62 B2   16 30S 139 46 E
Van Diemen G., Australia ...... 60 B5   11 45S 132 0 E
Van Gölü, Turkey .... 19 G7   38 30N 43 0 E
Van Horn, U.S.A. 81 K2   31 3N 104 50W
Van Ninh, Vietnam .... 38 F7   12 42N 109 14 E
Van Rees, Pegunungan,
  Indonesia .... 37 E9   2 35S 138 15 E
Van Wert, U.S.A. 82 E3   40 52N 84 35W
Van Yen, Vietnam .... 38 B5   21 4N 104 42 E
Vanadzor, Armenia .... 19 F7   40 48N 44 30 E
Vanavara, Russia .... 29 C11   60 22N 102 16 E
Vancouver, Canada 70 D4   49 15N 123 10W
Vancouver, U.S.A. 78 E4   45 38N 122 40W
Vancouver, C., Australia .... 61 G2   35 2S 118 11 E
Vancouver I., Canada 70 D3   49 50N 126 0W
Vancouver International ✈ (YVR),
  U.S.A. 78 A3   49 10N 123 10W
Vandalia, Ill., U.S.A. 80 F10   38 58N 89 6W
Vandalia, Mo., U.S.A. 80 F9   39 19N 91 29W
Vandenburg, U.S.A. 79 L6   34 35N 120 33W
Vanderbijlpark, S. Africa .... 57 D4   26 42S 27 54 E
Vanderhoof, Canada 70 C4   54 0N 124 0W
Vanderkloof Dam, S. Africa .... 56 E3   30 4S 24 40 E
Vanderlin I., Australia .... 62 B2   15 44S 137 2 E
Vänern, Sweden .... 9 G15   58 47N 13 30 E
Vänersborg, Sweden .... 9 G15   58 26N 12 19 E
Vang Vieng, Laos .... 38 C4   18 58N 102 32 E
Vanga, Kenya .... 54 C4   4 35S 39 12 E
Vangaindrano, Madag. .... 57 C8   23 21S 47 36 E
Vanguard, Canada 71 D7   49 55N 107 20W
Vanino, Russia .... 29 E15   48 50N 140 5 E
Vanna, Norway .... 8 A18   70 6N 19 50 E
Vännäs, Sweden .... 8 E18   63 58N 19 48 E
Vannes, France 20 C2   47 40N   2 47W
Vanrhynsdorp, S. Africa .... 56 E2   31 36S 18 44 E
Vansbro, Sweden .... 9 F16   60 32N 14 15 E
Vansittart B., Australia .... 60 B4   14 3S 126 17 E
Vantaa, Finland .... 9 F21   60 18N 24 58 E
Vanua Balavu, Fiji 59 C9   17 40S 178 57W
Vanua Levu, Fiji .... 59 C8   16 33S 179 15 E
Vanuatu ■, Pac. Oc. .... 64 J8   15 0S 168 0 E
Vanwyksvlei, S. Africa .... 56 E3   30 18S 21 49 E
Vanzylsrus, S. Africa .... 56 D3   26 52S 22 4 E
Vapnyarka, Ukraine .... 17 D15   48 32N 28 45 E
Varāmīn, Iran .... 45 C6   35 20N 51 39 E
Varāmīn □, Iran .... 45 C6   35 18N 51 35 E
Varanasi, India .... 43 G10   25 22N 83 0 E
Varangerfjorden, Norway ...... 8 A23   70 3N 29 25 E
Varangerhalvøya, Norway ...... 8 A23   70 25N 29 30 E
Varaždin, Croatia .... 16 E9   46 20N 16 20 E
Varberg, Sweden .... 9 H15   57 6N 12 20 E
Vardak □, Afghan. .... 40 B6   34 0N 68 0 E
Vardar = Axiós ⇒, Greece ...... 23 D10   40 57N 22 35 E
Varde, Denmark .... 9 J13   55 38N   8 29 E
Vardø, Norway .... 8 A24   70 23N 31 5 E
Varella, Mui, Vietnam .... 38 F7   12 54N 109 26 E
Varēna, Lithuania .... 9 J21   54 12N 24 30 E
Varese, Italy .... 20 D8   45 48N   8 50 E
Varginha, Brazil 95 A6   21 33S 45 25W
Varillas, Chile 94 A1   24 0S 70 10W
Varkaus, Finland .... 9 E22   62 19N 27 50 E
Varna, Bulgaria .... 23 C12   43 13N 27 50 E
Värnamo, Sweden .... 9 H16   57 10N 14 3 E
Vars, Canada 85 A9   45 21N 75 21W
Varysburg, U.S.A. 84 D6   42 46N 78 19W
Varzaneh, Iran .... 45 C7   32 25N 52 40 E
Vasa Barris ⇒, Brazil 93 F11   11 10S 37 10W
Vascongadas = País Vasco □,
  Spain 21 A4   42 50N   2 45W
Vasht = Khāsh, Iran .... 40 E2   28 15N 61 15 E
Vasilevichi, Belarus .... 17 B15   52 15N 29 50 E
Vasilkov = Vasylkiv, Ukraine ... 17 C16   50 7N 30 15 E
Vaslui, Romania .... 17 E14   46 38N 27 42 E
Vassar, Canada 71 D9   49 6N 95 55W
Vassar, U.S.A. 82 D4   43 22N 83 35W
Västerås, Sweden .... 9 G17   59 37N 16 38 E
Västerbotten, Sweden .... 8 D18   64 36N 20 4 E
Västerdalälven ⇒, Sweden ..... 9 F16   60 30N 14 7 E
Västervik, Sweden .... 9 H17   57 43N 16 33 E
Västmanland, Sweden .... 9 G16   59 45N 16 20 E
Vasto, Italy .... 22 C6   42 8N 14 40 E
Vasylkiv, Ukraine .... 17 C16   50 7N 30 15 E
Vatersay, U.K. 11 E1   56 55N   7 32W
Vatican City ■, Europe .... 22 D5   41 54N 12 27 E

Vatili, Cyprus .... 25 D12   35 6N 33 40 E
Vatnajökull, Iceland 8 D5   64 30N 16 48W
Vatoa, Fiji 59 D9   19 50S 178 13W
Vatólakkos, Greece .... 25 D5   35 27N 23 53 E
Vatoloha, Madag. .... 57 B8   17 52S 47 48 E
Vatomandry, Madag. .... 57 B8   19 20S 48 59 E
Vatra-Dornei, Romania .... 17 E13   47 22N 25 22 E
Vatrak ⇒, India .... 42 H5   23 9N 73 2 E
Vättern, Sweden .... 9 G16   58 25N 14 30 E
Vaudreuil-Dorion, Canada 85 A10   45 23N 74 3W
Vaughn, Mont., U.S.A. 76 C8   47 33N 111 33W
Vaughn, N. Mex., U.S.A. 77 J11   34 36N 105 13W
Vaujours L., Canada 72 A5   55 27N 74 15W
Vaupés = Uaupés ⇒, Brazil 92 C5   0 2N 67 16W
Vaupes □, Colombia 92 C4   1 0N 71 0W
Vauxhall, Canada 70 C6   50 5N 112 9W
Vav, India .... 42 G4   24 22N 71 31 E
Vavatenina, Madag. .... 57 B8   17 28S 49 12 E
Vava'u, Tonga 59 D12   18 36S 174 0W
Vawkavysk, Belarus .... 17 B13   53 9N 24 30 E
Växjö, Sweden .... 9 H16   56 52N 14 50 E
Vaygach, Ostrov, Russia .... 28 C6   70 0N 60 0 E
Váyia, Ákra, Greece .... 25 C10   36 15N 28 11 E
Vechte ⇒, Neths. .... 15 B6   52 34N   6 6 E
Vedea ⇒, Romania .... 17 G13   43 42N 25 41 E
Vedia, Argentina 94 C3   34 30S 61 31W
Veendam, Neths. .... 15 A6   53 5N   6 52 E
Veenendaal, Neths. .... 15 B5   52 2N   5 34 E
Vefsna ⇒, Norway .... 8 D15   65 48N 13 10 E
Vega, Norway .... 8 D14   65 40N 11 55 E
Vega, U.S.A. 81 H3   35 15N 102 26W
Vega Baja, Puerto Rico .... 89 d   18 27N 66 23W
Vegreville, Canada 70 C6   53 30N 112 5W
Vejer de la Frontera, Spain 21 D3   36 15N   5 59W
Vejle, Denmark .... 9 J13   55 43N   9 30 E
Velas, C., Costa Rica 88 D2   10 21N 85 52W
Velasco, Sierra de, Argentina ... 94 B2   29 20S 67 10W
Velddrif, S. Africa .... 56 E2   32 42S 18 11 E
Velebit Planina, Croatia .... 16 F8   44 50N 15 20 E
Veles, Macedonia .... 23 D9   41 46N 21 47 E
Vélez-Málaga, Spain 21 D3   36 48N   4 5W
Vélez Rubio, Spain 21 D4   37 41N   2 5W
Velhas ⇒, Brazil 93 G10   17 13S 44 49W
Velika Kapela, Croatia .... 16 F8   45 10N 15 5 E
Velikaya ⇒, Russia .... 18 C4   57 48N 28 10 E
Velikaya Kema, Russia .... 30 B8   45 30N 137 12 E
Veliki Ustyug, Russia .... 18 B8   60 47N 46 20 E
Velikiye Luki, Russia .... 18 C5   56 25N 30 32 E
Veliko Tŭrnovo, Bulgaria ...... 23 C11   43 5N 25 41 E
Velikonda Range, India .... 40 M11   14 45N 79 10 E
Velletri, Italy .... 22 D5   41 41N 12 47 E
Vellore, India .... 40 N11   12 57N 79 10 E
Velsk, Russia .... 18 B7   61 10N 42 5 E
Veluwezoom △, Neths. .... 15 B6   52 5N   6 0 E
Velva, U.S.A. 80 A4   48 4N 100 56W
Venado Tuerto, Argentina 94 C3   33 50S 62 0W
Vendée □, France 20 C3   46 50N   1 35W
Vendôme, France .... 20 C4   47 47N   1 3 E
Venézia, Italy .... 22 B5   45 27N 12 21 E
Venézia, G. di, Italy .... 22 B5   45 15N 13 0 E
Venezuela ■, S. Amer. 92 B5   8 0N 66 0W
Venezuela, G. de, Venezuela 92 A4   11 30N 71 0W
Vengurla, India .... 40 M8   15 53N 73 45 E
Venice = Venézia, Italy .... 22 B5   45 27N 12 21 E
Venice, U.S.A. 83 M4   27 6N 82 27W
Venkatapuram, India .... 41 K12   18 20N 80 30 E
Venlo, Neths. .... 15 C6   51 22N   6 11 E
Vennesla, Norway .... 9 G12   58 15N   7 59 E
Venray, Neths. .... 15 C6   51 31N   6 0 E
Ventana, Punta de la, Mexico .. 86 C3   24 4N 109 48W
Ventana, Sa. de la, Argentina .. 94 D3   38 0S 62 30W
Ventersburg, S. Africa .... 56 D4   28 7S 27 9 E
Venterstad, S. Africa .... 56 E4   30 47S 25 48 E
Ventnor, U.K. 13 G6   50 36N   1 12W
Ventoténe, Italy .... 22 D5   40 47N 13 25 E
Ventoux, Mt., France .... 20 D6   44 10N   5 17 E
Ventspils, Latvia .... 9 H19   57 25N 21 32 E
Ventuarí ⇒, Venezuela 92 C5   3 58N 67 2W
Ventucopa, U.S.A. 79 L7   34 50N 119 29W
Ventura, U.S.A. 79 L7   34 17N 119 18W
Venus B., Australia .... 63 F4   38 40S 145 42 E
Vera, Argentina 94 B3   29 30S 60 20W
Vera, Spain 21 D5   37 15N   1 51W
Veracruz, Mexico 87 D5   19 0N 96 15W
Veracruz □, Mexico 87 D5   19 0N 96 15W
Veraval, India .... 42 J4   20 53N 70 27 E
Verbánia, Italy .... 20 D8   45 56N   8 33 E
Vercelli, Italy .... 20 D8   45 19N   8 25 E
Verdalsøra, Norway .... 8 E14   63 48N 11 30 E
Verde ⇒, Argentina 96 E3   41 56N 65 5W
Verde ⇒, Goiás, Brazil 93 G8   18 1S 50 14W
Verde ⇒, Mato Grosso do Sul,
  Brazil 93 H8   21 25S 52 20W
Verde ⇒, Chihuahua, Mexico .. 86 B3   26 29N 107 58W
Verde ⇒, Oaxaca, Mexico 87 D5   15 59N 97 50W
Verde ⇒, Veracruz, Mexico 86 C4   21 10N 102 50W
Verde ⇒, Paraguay 94 A4   23 9S 57 37W
Verde ⇒, U.S.A. 74 D4   33 33N 111 40W
Verde, Cay, Bahamas 88 B4   23 0N 75 5W
Verden, Germany .... 16 B5   52 55N   9 14 E
Verdi, U.S.A. 78 F7   39 31N 119 59W
Verdun, France .... 20 B6   49 9N   5 24 E
Vereeniging, S. Africa .... 57 D4   26 38S 27 57 E
Verga, C., Guinea 50 F3   10 30N 14 10W
Vergara, Uruguay 95 C5   32 56S 53 57W
Vergemont Cr. ⇒, Australia .... 62 C3   24 16S 143 16 E
Vergennes, U.S.A. 85 B11   44 10N 73 15W
Verín, Spain 21 B2   41 57N   7 27W
Verkhnevilyuysk, Russia .... 29 C13   63 27N 120 18 E
Verkhniy Baskunchak, Russia .. 19 E8   48 14N 46 44 E
Verkhoyansk, Russia .... 29 C14   67 35N 133 25 E
Verkhoyansk Ra. =
  Verkhoyanskiy Khrebet, Russia 29 C13   66 0N 129 0 E
Verkhoyanskiy Khrebet, Russia . 29 C13   66 0N 129 0 E
Vermilion, Canada 71 C6   53 20N 110 50W
Vermilion, U.S.A. 84 E2   41 25N 82 22W
Vermilion ⇒, Canada 71 C6   53 22N 110 51W
Vermilion ⇒, U.S.A. 81 L9   29 45N 91 55W
Vermilion Bay, Canada 71 D10   49 51N 93 34W
Vermilion L., U.S.A. 80 B8   47 53N 92 26W
Vermillion, U.S.A. 80 D6   42 47N 96 56W
Vermillion ⇒, Canada 72 C5   47 38N 72 56W
Vermont □, U.S.A. 85 C12   44 0N 73 0W
Vernadsky, Antarctica 5 C17   65 0S 64 0W
Vernal, U.S.A. 76 F9   40 27N 109 32W
Vernalis, U.S.A. 78 H5   37 36N 121 17W
Verner, Canada 72 C3   46 25N 80 8W

Verneukpan, S. Africa .... 56 E3   30 0S   21 0 E
Vernon, Canada 70 C5   50 20N 119 15W
Vernon, U.S.A. 81 H5   34 9N   99 17W
Vernonia, U.S.A. 78 E3   45 52N 123 11W
Vero Beach, U.S.A. 83 M5   27 38N   80 24W
Véroia, Greece .... 23 D10 40 34N   22 12 E
Verona, Canada 85 B8   44 29N   76 42W
Verona, Italy .... 22 B4   45 27N   10 59 E
Verona, U.S.A. 80 D10 42 59N   89 32W
Versailles, France .... 20 B5   48 48N   2 8 E
Vert, C., Senegal 50 F2   14 45N   17 30W
Verulam, S. Africa .... 57 D5   29 38S   31 2 E
Verviers, Belgium .... 15 D5   50 37N   5 52 E
Veselovskoye Vdkhr., Russia .. 19 E7   46 58N   41 25 E
Vesoul, France .... 20 C7   47 40N   6 11 E
Vesterålen, Norway .... 8 B16   68 45N   15 0 E
Vestfjorden, Norway .... 8 C15   67 55N   14 0 E
Vestmannaeyjar, Iceland 8 E3   63 27N   20 15W
Vestspitsbergen, Svalbard .... 4 B8   78 40N   17 0 E
Vestvågøy, Norway .... 8 B15 68 18N   13 50 E
Vesuvio, Italy .... 22 D6   40 49N   14 26 E
Vesuvius, Mt. = Vesuvio, Italy . 22 D6   40 49N   14 26 E
Veszprém, Hungary .... 17 E9   47 8N   17 57 E
Vetlanda, Sweden .... 9 H16 57 24N   15 3 E
Vetlugu →, Russia .... 18 C8   56 36N   46 4 E
Vettore, Mte., Italy .... 22 C5   42 49N   13 16 E
Veurne, Belgium .... 15 C2   51 5N   2 40 E
Veys, Iran .... 45 D6   31 30N   49 0 E
Vezhen, Bulgaria .... 23 C11 42 50N   24 20 E
Vi Thanh, Vietnam .... 39 H5   9 42N 105 26 E
Viacha, Bolivia 92 G5   16 39S   68 18W
Viamão, Brazil 95 C5   30 5S   51 0W
Viana, Brazil 93 D10   3 13S   44 55W
Viana do Alentejo, Portugal .. 21 C2   38 17N   7 59W
Viana do Castelo, Portugal ... 21 B1   41 42N   8 50W
Vianden, Lux. .... 15 E6   49 56N   6 12 E
Viangchan = Vientiane, Laos .. 38 D4   17 58N 102 36 E
Vianópolis, Brazil 93 G9   16 40S   48 35W
Viaréggio, Italy .... 22 C4   43 52N   10 14 E
Vibo Valéntia, Italy .... 22 E7   38 40N   16 6 E
Viborg, Denmark .... 9 H13 56 27N   9 23 E
Vic, Spain .... 21 B7   41 58N   2 19 E
Vicenza, Italy .... 22 B4   45 33N   11 33 E
Vich = Vic, Spain .... 21 B7   41 58N   2 19 E
Vichada →, Colombia 92 C5   4 55N   67 50W
Vichy, France .... 20 C5   46 9N   3 26 E
Vicksburg, Ariz., U.S.A. 79 M13 33 45N 113 45W
Vicksburg, Miss., U.S.A. 81 J9   32 21N   90 53W
Victor, India .... 42 J4   21 0N   71 30 E
Victor, U.S.A. 84 D7   42 58N   77 24W
Victor Harbor, Australia ..... 63 F2   35 30S 138 37 E
Victoria, Argentina 94 C3   32 40S   60 10W
Victoria, Canada 70 D4   48 30N 123 25W
Victoria, Chile 96 D2   38 13S   72 20W
Victoria, China .... 33 G1   22 17N 114 9 E
Victoria, Malta .... 25 C1   36 3N   14 14 E
Victoria, Kans., U.S.A. 80 F5   38 52N   99 9W
Victoria, Tex., U.S.A. 81 L6   28 48N   97 0W
Victoria □, Australia .... 63 F3   37 0S 144 0 E
Victoria →, Australia .... 60 C4   15 10S 129 40 E
Victoria, Grand L., Canada ... 72 C4   47 31N   77 30W
Victoria, L., Africa .... 54 C3   1 0S   33 0 E
Victoria, L., Australia .... 63 E3   33 57S 141 15 E
Victoria, Mt., Burma .... 41 J18 21 15N   93 55 E
Victoria Beach, Canada 71 C9   50 40N   96 35W
Victoria de Durango = Durango,
   Mexico 86 C4   24 3N 104 39W
Victoria de las Tunas, Cuba .. 88 B4   20 58N   76 59W
Victoria Falls, Zimbabwe ..... 55 F2   17 58S   25 52 E
Victoria Harbour, Canada 84 B5   44 45N   79 45W
Victoria I., Canada 68 A8   71 0N 111 0W
Victoria L., Canada 73 C8   48 20N   57 27W
Victoria Ld., Antarctica ...... 5 D11   75 0S 160 0 E
Victoria Nile →, Uganda ..... 54 B3   2 14N   31 26 E
Victoria River, Australia ..... 60 C5   16 25S 131 0 E
Victoria Str., Canada 68 B9   69 31N 100 30W
Victoria West, S. Africa ...... 56 E3   31 25S   23 4 E
Victoriaville, Canada 73 C5   46 4N   71 56W
Victorica, Argentina 94 D2   36 20S   65 30W
Victorville, U.S.A. 79 L9   34 32N 117 18W
Vicuña, Chile 94 C1   30 0S   70 50W
Vicuña Mackenna, Argentina . 94 C3   33 53S   64 25W
Vidal, U.S.A. 79 L12 34 7N 114 31W
Vidal Junction, U.S.A. 79 L12 34 11N 114 34W
Vidalia, U.S.A. 83 J4   32 13N   82 25W
Vidho, Greece .... 25 A3   39 38N   19 55 E
Vidin, Bulgaria .... 23 C10 43 59N   22 50 E
Vidisha, India .... 42 H7   23 28N   77 53 E
Vidzy, Belarus .... 9 J22   55 23N   26 37 E
Viedma, Argentina 96 E4   40 50S   63 0W
Viedma, L., Argentina 96 F2   49 30S   72 30W
Vielsalm, Belgium .... 15 D5   50 17N   5 54 E
Vieng Pou Kha, Laos .... 38 B3   20 41N 101 4 E
Vienna = Wien, Austria ...... 16 D9   48 12N   16 22 E
Vienna, Ill., U.S.A. 81 G10 37 25N   88 54W
Vienna, Mo., U.S.A. 80 F9   38 11N   91 57W
Vienne, France .... 20 D6   45 31N   4 53 E
Vienne →, France .... 20 C4   47 13N   0 5 E
Vientiane, Laos .... 38 D4   17 58N 102 36 E
Vientos, Paso de los, Caribbean 89 C5   20 0N   74 0W
Vieques, Isla de, Puerto Rico .. 89 d   18 8N   65 25W
Vierge Pt., St. Lucia .... 89 f   13 49N   60 53W
Vierzon, France .... 20 C5   47 13N   2 5 E
Vietnam ■, Asia .... 38 C6   19 0N 106 0 E
Vieux Fort, St. Lucia .... 89 f   13 46N   60 58W
Vigan, Phil. .... 37 A6   17 35N 120 28 E
Vigévano, Italy .... 20 D8   45 19N   8 51 E
Vigia, Brazil 93 D9   0 50S   48 5W
Vigia Chico, Mexico 87 D7   19 46N   87 35W
Viglas, Ákra, Greece .... 25 D9   35 54N   27 51 E
Vigo, Spain 21 A1   42 12N   8 41W
Vihowa, Pakistan .... 42 D4   31 8N   70 30 E
Vihowa →, Pakistan .... 42 D4   31 8N   70 41 E
Vijayawada, India .... 41 L12 16 31N   80 39 E
Vijosë →, Albania .... 23 D8   40 37N   19 24 E
Vik, Iceland 8 E4   63 25N   19 1W
Vikeke = Viqueque, E. Timor . 37 F7   8 52S 126 23 E
Viking, Canada 70 C6   53 7N 111 50W
Vikna, Norway .... 8 D14 64 55N   10 58 E
Vila da Maganja, Mozam. .... 55 F4   17 18S   37 30 E
Vila do Bispo, Portugal 21 D1   37 5N   8 53W
Vila Franca de Xira, Portugal . 21 C1   38 57N   8 59W
Vila Gamito, Mozam. .... 55 E3   14 12S   33 0 E
Vila Gomes da Costa, Mozam. . 57 C5   24 20S   33 37 E
Vila Machado, Mozam. .... 55 F3   19 15S   34 14 E
Vila Mouzinho, Mozam. ...... 55 E3   14 48S   34 25 E
Vila Nova de Gaia, Portugal .. 21 B1   41 8N   8 37W

Vila Real, Portugal 21 B2   41 17N   7 48W
Vila-real de los Infantes, Spain . 21 C5   39 55N   0 3W
Vila Real de Santo António,
   Portugal 21 D2   37 10N   7 28W
Vila Vasco da Gama, Mozam. .. 55 E3   14 54S   32 14 E
Vila Velha, Brazil 95 A7   20 20S   40 17W
Vilagarcía de Arousa, Spain .. 21 A1   42 34N   8 46W
Vilaine →, France 20 C2   47 30N   2 27W
Vilanandro, Tanjona, Madag. .. 57 B7   16 11S   44 27 E
Vilanculos, Mozam. .... 57 C6   22 1S   35 17 E
Vilanova i la Geltrú, Spain ... 21 B6   41 13N   1 40 E
Vilcheka, Z., Russia .... 4 A11   80 30N   60 30 E
Vileyka, Belarus .... 17 A14 54 30N   26 53 E
Vilhelmina, Sweden .... 8 D17 64 35N   16 39 E
Vilhena, Brazil 92 F6   12 40S   60 5W
Viliga, Russia .... 29 C16 61 36N 156 56 E
Viliya = Neris →, Lithuania .. 9 J21   55 8N   24 16 E
Viljandi, Estonia .... 9 G21 58 28N   25 30 E
Vilkitskogo, Proliv, Russia .... 29 B11 78 0N 103 0 E
Vilkovo = Vylkove, Ukraine ... 17 F15 45 28N   29 32 E
Villa Abecia, Bolivia 94 A2   21 0S   68 18W
Villa Ahumada, Mexico 86 A3   30 38N 106 30W
Villa Ana, Argentina 94 B4   28 28S   59 40W
Villa Ángela, Argentina 94 B3   27 34S   60 45W
Villa Bella, Bolivia 92 F5   10 25S   65 22W
Villa Cañás, Argentina 94 C3   34 0S   61 35W
Villa Colón, Argentina 94 C2   31 38S   68 20W
Villa Constitución, Argentina . 94 C3   33 15S   60 20W
Villa de María, Argentina 94 B3   29 55S   63 43W
Villa Dolores, Argentina 94 C2   31 58S   65 15W
Villa Frontera, Mexico 86 B4   26 56N 101 27W
Villa Guillermina, Argentina .. 94 B4   28 15S   59 29W
Villa Hayes, Paraguay 94 B4   25 5S   57 20W
Villa Iris, Argentina 94 D3   38 12S   63 12W
Villa Juárez, Mexico 86 B4   27 37N 100 44W
Villa María, Argentina 94 C3   32 20S   63 10W
Villa Mazán, Argentina 94 B2   28 40S   66 30W
Villa Montes, Bolivia 94 A3   21 10S   63 30W
Villa Ocampo, Argentina 94 B4   28 30S   59 20W
Villa Ocampo, Mexico 86 B3   26 29N 105 30W
Villa Ojo de Agua, Argentina . 94 B3   29 30S   63 44W
Villa San José, Argentina 94 C4   32 12S   58 15W
Villa San Martín, Argentina .. 94 B3   28 15S   64 9W
Villa Unión, Mexico 86 C3   23 12N 106 14W
Villacarlos, Spain .... 24 B11 39 53N   4 17 E
Villacarrillo, Spain 21 C4   38 7N   3 3W
Villach, Austria .... 16 E7   46 37N   13 51 E
Villafranca de los Caballeros,
   Spain .... 24 B10 39 34N   3 25 E
Villagrán, Mexico 87 C5   24 29N   99 29W
Villaguay, Argentina 94 C4   32 0S   59 0W
Villahermosa, Mexico 87 D6   17 59N   92 55W
Villajoyosa, Spain 21 C5   38 30N   0 12W
Villalba, Spain 21 A2   43 26N   7 40W
Villanueva, U.S.A. 81 H2   35 16N 105 22W
Villanueva de la Serena, Spain 21 C3   38 59N   5 50W
Villanueva y Geltrú = Vilanova i
   la Geltrú, Spain .... 21 B6   41 13N   1 40 E
Villarreal = Vila-real de los
   Infantes, Spain 21 C5   39 55N   0 3W
Villarrica, Chile 96 D2   39 15S   72 15W
Villarrica, Paraguay 94 B4   25 40S   56 30W
Villarrobledo, Spain 21 C4   39 18N   2 36W
Villavicencio, Argentina 94 C2   32 28S   69 0W
Villavicencio, Colombia 92 C4   4 9N   73 37W
Villaviciosa, Spain 21 A3   43 32N   5 27W
Villazón, Bolivia 94 A2   22 0S   65 35W
Ville-Marie, Canada 72 C4   47 20N   79 30W
Ville Platte, U.S.A. 81 K8   30 41N   92 17W
Villena, Spain 21 C5   38 39N   0 52W
Villeneuve-d'Ascq, France .... 20 A5   50 38N   3 9 E
Villeneuve-sur-Lot, France ... 20 D4   44 24N   0 42 E
Villiers, S. Africa .... 57 D4   27 2S   28 36 E
Villingen-Schwenningen,
   Germany .... 16 D5   48 3N   8 26 E
Vilna, Canada 70 C6   54 7N 111 55W
Vilnius, Lithuania .... 9 J21   54 38N   25 19 E
Vilvoorde, Belgium .... 15 D4   50 56N   4 26 E
Vilyuy →, Russia .... 29 C13 64 24N 126 26 E
Vilyuysk, Russia .... 29 C13 63 40N 121 35 E
Viña del Mar, Chile 94 C1   33 0S   71 30W
Vinaròs, Spain .... 21 B6   40 30N   0 27 E
Vincennes, U.S.A. 82 F2   38 41N   87 32W
Vincent, U.S.A. 79 L8   34 33N 118 11W
Vinchina, Argentina 94 B2   28 45S   68 15W
Vindelälven →, Sweden ..... 8 E18 63 55N   19 50 E
Vindeln, Sweden .... 8 D18 64 12N   19 43 E
Vindhya Ra., India .... 42 H7   22 50N   77 0 E
Vineland, U.S.A. 82 F8   39 29N   75 2W
Vinh, Vietnam .... 38 C5   18 45N 105 38 E
Vinh Linh, Vietnam .... 38 D6   17 4N 107 2 E
Vinh Long, Vietnam .... 39 G5   10 16N 105 57 E
Vinh Yen, Vietnam .... 38 B5   21 21N 105 35 E
Vinita, U.S.A. 81 G7   36 39N   95 9W
Vinkovci, Croatia .... 23 B8   45 19N   18 48 E
Vinnitsa = Vinnytsya, Ukraine . 17 D15 49 15N   28 30 E
Vinnytsya, Ukraine .... 17 D15 49 15N   28 30 E
Vinson Massif, Antarctica ... 5 D16 78 35S   85 25W
Vinton, Calif., U.S.A. 78 F6   39 48N 120 10W
Vinton, Iowa, U.S.A. 80 D8   42 10N   92 1W
Vinton, La., U.S.A. 81 K8   30 11N   93 35W
Viqueque, E. Timor .... 37 F7   8 52S 126 23 E
Virac, Phil. .... 37 B6   13 30N 124 20 E
Virachey, Cambodia .... 38 F6   13 59N 106 49 E
Virachey △, Cambodia ...... 38 E6   14 14N 106 55 E
Virago Sd., Canada 70 C2   54 0N 132 30W
Viramgam, India .... 42 H5   23 5N   72 0 E
Viranşehir, Turkey .... 44 B3   37 13N   39 45 E
Virawah, Pakistan .... 42 G4   24 31N   70 46 E
Virden, Canada 71 D8   49 50N 100 56W
Vire, France 20 B3   48 50N   0 53W
Virgenes, C., Argentina 96 G3   52 19S   68 21W
Virgin →, U.S.A. 77 H6   36 28N 114 21W
Virgin Gorda, Br. Virgin Is. .. 89 e   18 30N   64 26W
Virgin Is. (British) ☑, W. Indies 89 e   18 30N   64 30W
Virgin Is. (U.S.) ☑, W. Indies . 89 e   18 20N   65 0W
Virgin Islands △, Virgin Is. .. 89 C7   18 20N   64 42W
Virginia, S. Africa .... 56 D4   28 8S   26 55 E
Virginia, U.S.A. 80 B8   47 31N   92 32W
Virginia □, U.S.A. 82 G7   37 30N   78 45W
Virginia Beach, U.S.A. 82 G8   36 51N   75 59W
Virginia City, Mont., U.S.A. .. 76 D8   45 18N 111 56W
Virginia City, Nev., U.S.A. ... 78 F7   39 19N 119 39W
Virginia Falls, Canada 70 A3   61 38N 125 42W
Virginiatown, Canada 72 C4   48 9N   79 36W
Viroqua, U.S.A. 80 D9   43 34N   90 53W
Virovitica, Croatia .... 23 B7   45 51N   17 21 E

Virpur, India .... 42 J4   21 51N   70 42 E
Virton, Belgium .... 15 E5   49 35N   5 32 E
Virudunagar, India .... 40 Q10 9 30N   77 58 E
Virunga △, Dem. Rep. of
   the Congo .... 54 B2   0 5N   29 38 E
Vis, Croatia .... 22 C7   43 4N   16 10 E
Visalia, U.S.A. 78 J7   36 20N 119 18W
Visayan Sea, Phil. .... 37 B6   11 30N 123 30 E
Visby, Sweden .... 9 H18 57 37N   18 18 E
Viscount Melville Sd., Canada . 4 B2   74 10N 108 0W
Visé, Belgium .... 15 D5   50 44N   5 41 E
Višegrad, Bos.-H. .... 23 C8   43 47N   19 17 E
Viseu, Brazil 93 D9   1 10S   46 5W
Viseu, Portugal 21 B2   40 40N   7 55W
Vishakhapatnam, India ...... 41 L13 17 45N   83 20 E
Visnagar, India .... 42 H5   23 45N   72 32 E
Viso, Mte., Italy .... 20 D7   44 38N   7 5 E
Visokoi I., Antarctica 5 B1   56 43S   27 15W
Vista, U.S.A. 79 M9 33 12N 117 14W
Vistula = Wisła →, Poland ... 17 A10 54 22N   18 55 E
Vitebsk = Vitsyebsk, Belarus . 18 C5   55 10N   30 15 E
Viterbo, Italy .... 22 C5   42 25N   12 6 E
Viti Levu, Fiji .... 59 C7   17 30S 177 30 E
Vitigudino, Spain 21 B2   41 1N   6 26W
Vitim, Russia .... 29 D12 59 28N 112 35 E
Vitim →, Russia .... 29 D12 59 26N 112 34 E
Vitória, Brazil 93 H10 20 20S   40 22W
Vitória da Conquista, Brazil .. 93 F10 14 51S   40 51W
Vitória de São Antão, Brazil .. 93 E11   8 10S   35 20W
Vitoria-Gasteiz, Spain 21 A4   42 50N   2 41W
Vitsyebsk, Belarus .... 18 C5   55 10N   30 15 E
Vittória, Italy .... 22 F6   36 57N   14 32 E
Vittório Véneto, Italy .... 22 B5   45 59N   12 18 E
Viveiro, Spain 21 A2   43 39N   7 38W
Vivian, U.S.A. 81 J8   32 53N   93 59W
Vizcaíno, Desierto de, Mexico . 86 B2   27 40N 113 50W
Vizcaíno, Sierra, Mexico 86 B2   27 30N 114 0W
Vize, Turkey .... 23 D12 41 34N   27 45 E
Vizianagaram, India .... 41 K13 18 6N   83 30 E
Vjosë →, Albania .... 23 D8   40 37N   19 24 E
Vladikavkaz, Russia .... 19 F7   43 0N   44 35 E
Vladimir, Russia .... 18 C7   56 15N   40 30 E
Vladimir Volynskiy = Volodymyr-
   Volynskyy, Ukraine ...... 17 C13 50 50N   24 18 E
Vladivostok, Russia .... 29 E14 43 10N 131 53 E
Vlieland, Neths. .... 15 A4   53 16N   4 55 E
Vlissingen, Neths. .... 15 C3   51 26N   3 34 E
Vlorë, Albania .... 23 D8   40 32N   19 28 E
Vltava →, Czech Rep. ...... 16 D8   50 21N   14 30 E
Vo Dat, Vietnam .... 39 G6   11 9N 107 31 E
Voe, U.K. 11 A7   60 21N   1 16W
Vogelkop = Doberai, Jazirah,
   Indonesia .... 37 E8   1 25S 133 0 E
Vogelsberg, Germany .... 16 C5   50 31N   9 12 E
Voghera, Italy .... 20 D8   44 59N   9 1 E
Vohibinany, Madag. .... 57 B8   18 49S   49 4 E
Vohilava, Madag. .... 57 C8   21 4S   48 0 E
Vohimarina = Iharana, Madag. . 57 A9   13 25S   50 0 E
Vohimena, Tanjon' i, Madag. .. 57 D8   25 36S   45 8 E
Vohipeno, Madag. .... 57 C8   22 22S   47 51 E
Voi, Kenya .... 54 C4   3 25S   38 32 E
Voiron, France .... 20 D6   45 22N   5 35 E
Voisey B., Canada 73 A7   56 15N   61 50W
Vojmsjön, Sweden .... 8 D17 64 55N   16 40 E
Vojvodina □, Serbia & M. .... 23 B9   45 20N   20 0 E
Volborg, U.S.A. 80 C2   45 51N 105 41W
Volcán de Colima △, Mexico . 86 D4   19 30N 103 40W
Volcano Is. = Kazan-Rettō,
   Pac. Oc. .... 64 E6   25 0N 141 0 E
Volcans △, Rwanda .... 54 C2   1 30S   29 26 E
Volda, Norway .... 9 E12 62 9N   6 5 E
Volga = Privolzhskiy □, Russia 18 D8   56 0N   50 0 E
Volga →, Russia .... 19 E8   46 0N   48 30 E
Volga Hts. = Privolzhskaya
   Vozvyshennost, Russia ... 19 D8   51 0N   46 0 E
Volgodonsk, Russia .... 19 E7   47 33N   42 5 E
Volgograd, Russia .... 19 E7   48 40N   44 25 E
Volgogradskoye Vdkhr., Russia 19 D8   50 0N   45 20 E
Volkhov →, Russia .... 18 B5   60 8N   32 20 E
Volkovysk = Vawkavysk, Belarus 17 B13 53 9N   24 30 E
Volksrust, S. Africa .... 57 D4   27 24S   29 53 E
Volochanka, Russia .... 29 B10 71 0N   94 28 E
Volodymyr-Volynskyy, Ukraine . 17 C13 50 50N   24 18 E
Vologda, Russia .... 18 C6   59 10N   39 45 E
Vólos, Greece .... 23 E10 39 24N   22 59 E
Volovets, Ukraine .... 17 D12 48 43N   23 11 E
Volozhin = Valozhyn, Belarus . 17 A14 54 3N   26 30 E
Volsk, Russia .... 18 D8   52 5N   47 22 E
Volta →, Ghana .... 48 F4   5 46N   0 41 E
Volta, L., Ghana .... 50 G6   7 30N   0 0 E
Volta Redonda, Brazil 95 A7   22 31S   44 5W
Voltaire, C., Australia .... 60 B4   14 16S 125 35 E
Volterra, Italy .... 22 C4   43 24N   10 51 E
Volturno →, Italy .... 22 D5   41 1N   13 55 E
Volzhskiy, Russia .... 19 E7   48 56N   44 46 E
Vondrozo, Madag. .... 57 C8   22 49S   47 20 E
Vopnafjörður, Iceland 8 D6   65 45N   14 50W
Vóriai Sporádhes, Greece .... 23 E10 39 15N   23 30 E
Vorkuta, Russia .... 18 A11 67 48N   64 20 E
Vormsi, Estonia .... 9 G20 59 1N   23 13 E
Voronezh, Russia .... 19 D6   51 40N   39 10 E
Võrts Järv, Estonia .... 9 G22 58 16N   26 3 E
Võru, Estonia .... 9 H22 57 48N   26 54 E
Vosges, France .... 20 B7   48 20N   7 10 E
Voss, Norway .... 9 F12 60 38N   6 26 E
Vostok, Antarctica .... 5 D8   78 30S 106 50 E
Vostok I., Kiribati 65 J12 10 5S 152 23W
Votkinsk, Russia .... 18 C9   57 0N   53 55 E
Votkinskoye Vdkhr., Russia ... 18 C10 57 22N   55 12 E
Votsuri-Shima, Japan .... 31 M1 25 45N 123 29 E
Vouga →, Portugal 21 B1   40 41N   8 40W
Voúxa, Ákra, Greece .... 25 D5   35 37N   23 32 E
Voyageurs △, U.S.A. 80 A8   48 32N   93 0W
Vozhe, Ozero, Russia .... 18 B6   60 45N   39 0 E
Voznesensk, Ukraine .... 19 E5   47 35N   31 21 E
Vrangelya, Ostrov, Russia ... 29 B19 71 0N 180 0 E
Vranje, Serbia & M. .... 23 C9   42 34N   21 54 E
Vratsa, Bulgaria .... 23 C10 43 15N   23 30 E
Vrbas →, Bos.-H. .... 22 B7   45 8N   17 29 E
Vrede, S. Africa .... 57 D4   27 24S   29 6 E
Vredefort, S. Africa .... 56 D4   27 0S   27 22 E
Vredenburg, S. Africa .... 56 E2   32 56S   18 0 E
Vredendal, S. Africa .... 56 E2   31 41S   18 35 E
Vrindavan, India .... 42 F7   27 37N   77 40 E
Vríses, Greece .... 25 D6   35 23N   24 13 E
Vršac, Serbia & M. .... 23 B9   45 8N   21 20 E

Vryburg, S. Africa .... 56 D3   26 55S   24 45 E
Vryheid, S. Africa .... 57 D5   27 45S   30 47 E
Vu Liet, Vietnam .... 38 C5   18 43N 105 23 E
Vukovar, Croatia .... 23 B8   45 21N   18 59 E
Vulcan, Canada 70 C6   50 25N 113 15W
Vulcan, Romania .... 17 F12 45 23N   23 17 E
Vulcaneşti, Moldova .... 17 F15 45 41N   28 18 E
Vulcano, Italy .... 22 E6   38 24N   14 58 E
Vulkaneshty = Vulcaneşti,
   Moldova .... 17 F15 45 41N   28 18 E
Vunduzi →, Mozam. .... 55 F3   18 56S   34 1 E
Vung Tau, Vietnam .... 39 G6   10 21N 107 4 E
Vwaza △, Malawi .... 55 E3   10 58S   33 25 E
Vyatka = Kirov, Russia ...... 18 C8   58 35N   49 40 E
Vyatka →, Russia .... 18 C9   55 37N   51 5 E
Vyatskiye Polyany, Russia ... 18 C9   56 14N   51 5 E
Vyazemskiy, Russia .... 29 E14 47 32N 134 45 E
Vyazma, Russia .... 18 C5   55 10N   34 15 E
Vyborg, Russia .... 18 B4   60 43N   28 47 E
Vychegda →, Russia .... 18 B8   61 18N   46 36 E
Vychodné Beskydy, Europe ... 17 D11 49 20N   22 0 E
Vyg-ozero, Russia .... 18 B5   63 47N   34 29 E
Vylkove, Ukraine .... 17 F15 45 28N   29 32 E
Vynohradiv, Ukraine .... 17 D12 48 9N   23 2 E
Vyrnwy, L., U.K. 12 E4   52 48N   3 31W
Vyshniy Volochek, Russia ... 18 C5   57 30N   34 30 E
Vyshzha = imeni 26 Bakinskikh
   Komissarov, Turkmenistan . 45 B7   39 22N   54 10 E
Vyškov, Czech Rep. .... 17 D9   49 17N   17 0 E
Vytegra, Russia .... 18 B6   61 0N   36 27 E

W

W.A.C. Bennett Dam, Canada .. 70 B4   56 2N 122 6W
Waal →, Neths. .... 15 C5   51 37N   5 0 E
Waalwijk, Neths. .... 15 C5   51 42N   5 4 E
Wabakimi △, Canada 72 B2   50 43N   89 29W
Wabana, Canada 73 C9   47 40N   53 0W
Wabasca →, Canada 70 B5   58 22N 115 20W
Wabasca-Desmarais, Canada . 70 B6   55 57N 113 56W
Wabash, U.S.A. 82 E3   40 48N   85 49W
Wabigoon L., Canada 71 D10 49 44N   92 44W
Wabowden, Canada 71 C9   54 55N   98 38W
Wabuk Pt., Canada 72 A2   55 20N   85 5W
Wabush, Canada 73 B6   52 55N   66 52W
Waco, U.S.A. 81 K6   31 33N   97 9W
Waconichi, L., Canada 72 B5   50 8N   74 0W
Wad Hamid, Sudan .... 51 E12 16 30N   32 45 E
Wad Medanî, Sudan .... 51 F12 14 28N   33 30 E
Wad Thana, Pakistan .... 42 F2   27 22N   66 23 E
Wadai, Africa .... 48 E5   12 0N   19 0 E
Wadayama, Japan .... 31 G7   35 19N 134 52 E
Waddeneilanden, Neths. .... 15 A5   53 20N   5 10 E
Waddenzee, Neths. .... 15 A5   53 6N   5 10 E
Waddington, Canada 85 B9   44 52N   75 12W
Waddington, Mt., Canada ... 70 C3   51 23N 125 15W
Waddy Pt., Australia .... 63 C5   24 58S 153 21 E
Wadebridge, U.K. 13 G3   50 31N   4 51W
Wadena, Canada 71 C8   51 57N 103 47W
Wadena, U.S.A. 80 B7   46 26N   95 8W
Wadeye, Australia .... 60 B4   14 28S 129 52 E
Wadhams, Canada 70 C3   51 30N 127 30W
Wādī as Sīr, Jordan .... 46 D4   31 56N   35 49 E
Wadi Halfa, Sudan .... 51 D12 21 53N   31 19 E
Wadi Ram △, Jordan .... 46 F4   29 30N   35 20 E
Wadsworth, Nev., U.S.A. 76 G4   39 38N 119 17W
Wadsworth, Ohio, U.S.A. 84 E3   41 2N   81 44W
Waegwan, S. Korea .... 35 G15 35 59N 128 23 E
Wafangdian, China .... 35 E11 39 38N 121 58 E
Wafrah, Si. Arabia .... 44 D5   28 33N   47 56 E
Wageningen, Neths. .... 15 C5   51 58N   5 40 E
Wager B., Canada 69 B11 65 26N   88 40W
Wagga Wagga, Australia .... 63 F4   35 7S 147 24 E
Waghete, Indonesia .... 37 E9   4 10S 135 50 E
Wagin, Australia .... 61 F2   33 17S 117 25 E
Wagner, U.S.A. 80 D5   43 5N   98 18W
Wagon Mound, U.S.A. 81 G2   36 1N 104 42W
Wagoner, U.S.A. 81 H7   35 58N   95 22W
Wah, Pakistan .... 42 C5   33 45N   72 40 E
Wahai, Indonesia .... 37 E7   2 48S 129 35 E
Wahiawa, U.S.A. 74 H15 21 30N 158 2W
Wāhid, Egypt .... 46 E1   30 48N   32 21 E
Wahnai, Afghan. .... 42 C1   32 40N   65 50 E
Wahoo, U.S.A. 80 E6   41 13N   96 37W
Wahpeton, U.S.A. 80 B6   46 16N   96 36W
Waiau →, N.Z. .... 59 K4   42 47S 173 22 E
Waibeem, Indonesia .... 37 E8   0 30S 132 59 E
Waigeo, Indonesia .... 37 E8   0 20S 130 40 E
Waihi, N.Z. .... 59 G5   37 23S 175 52 E
Waihou →, N.Z. .... 59 G5   37 15S 175 40 E
Waika, Dem. Rep. of the Congo 54 C2   2 22S   25 42 E
Waikabubak, Indonesia ..... 37 F5   9 45S 119 25 E
Waikaremoana, L., N.Z. ..... 59 H6   38 49S 177 9 E
Waikari, N.Z. .... 59 K4   42 58S 172 41 E
Waikato →, N.Z. .... 59 G5   37 23S 174 43 E
Waikerie, Australia .... 63 E3   34 9S 140 0 E
Waikokopu, N.Z. .... 59 H6   39 3S 177 52 E
Waikouaiti, N.Z. .... 59 L3   45 36S 170 41 E
Wailingding Dao, China ..... 33 G11 22 6N 114 2 E
Wailuku, U.S.A. 74 H16 20 53N 156 30W
Waimakariri →, N.Z. .... 59 K4   43 24S 172 42 E
Waimate, N.Z. .... 59 L3   44 45S 171 3 E
Wainganga →, India .... 40 K11 18 50N   79 55 E
Waingapu, Indonesia .... 37 F6   9 35S 120 11 E
Waini →, Guyana 92 B7   8 20N   59 50W
Wainwright, Canada 71 C6   52 50N 110 50W
Waiouru, N.Z. .... 59 H5   39 28S 175 41 E
Waipara, N.Z. .... 59 K4   43 3S 172 46 E
Waipawa, N.Z. .... 59 H6   39 56S 176 38 E
Waipiro, N.Z. .... 59 H7   38 2S 178 22 E
Waipu, N.Z. .... 59 F5   35 59S 174 29 E
Waipukurau, N.Z. .... 59 H6   40 1S 176 33 E
Wairakei, N.Z. .... 59 H6   38 37S 176 6 E
Wairarapa, L., N.Z. .... 59 J5   41 14S 175 15 E
Wairoa, N.Z. .... 59 H6   39 3S 177 25 E
Waitaki →, N.Z. .... 59 L3   44 56S 171 7 E
Waitara, N.Z. .... 59 H5   38 59S 174 15 E
Waitsburg, U.S.A. 76 C5   46 16N 118 9W
Waiuku, N.Z. .... 59 G5   37 15S 174 45 E
Wajima, Japan .... 31 F8   37 30N 137 0 E
Wajir, Kenya .... 54 B5   1 42N   40 5 E
Wakasa, Japan .... 31 G7   35 20N 134 24 E
Wakasa-Wan, Japan .... 31 G7   35 40N 135 30 E
Wakatipu, L., N.Z. .... 59 L2   45 5S 168 33 E

Wakaw, Canada ... 71 C7 52 39N 105 44W
Wakayama, Japan ... 31 G7 34 15N 135 15 E
Wakayama □, Japan ... 31 H7 33 50N 135 30 E
Wake Forest, U.S.A. ... 83 H6 35 59N 78 30W
Wake I., Pac. Oc. ... 64 F8 19 18N 166 36 E
WaKeeney, U.S.A. ... 80 F5 39 1N 99 53W
Wakefield, Jamaica ... 88 a 18 26N 77 42W
Wakefield, N.Z. ... 59 J4 41 24S 173 5 E
Wakefield, U.K. ... 12 D6 53 41N 1 29W
Wakefield, Mass., U.S.A. ... 85 D13 42 30N 71 4W
Wakefield, Mich., U.S.A. ... 80 B10 46 29N 89 56W
Wakkanai, Japan ... 30 B10 45 28N 141 35 E
Wakkerstroom, S. Africa ... 57 D5 27 24S 30 10 E
Wakool, Australia ... 63 F3 35 28S 144 23 E
Wakool ➤, Australia ... 63 F3 35 5S 143 33 E
Wakre, Indonesia ... 37 E8 0 19S 131 5 E
Wakuach, L., Canada ... 73 A6 55 34N 67 32W
Walamba, Zambia ... 55 E2 13 30S 28 42 E
Wałbrzych, Poland ... 16 C9 50 45N 16 18 E
Walbury Hill, U.K. ... 13 F6 51 21N 1 28W
Walcha, Australia ... 63 E5 30 55S 151 31 E
Walcheren, Neths. ... 15 C3 51 30N 3 35 E
Walcott, U.S.A. ... 76 F10 41 46N 106 51W
Wałcz, Poland ... 16 B9 53 17N 16 27 E
Waldburg Ra., Australia ... 61 D2 24 40S 117 35 E
Walden, Colo., U.S.A. ... 76 F10 40 44N 106 17W
Walden, N.Y., U.S.A. ... 85 E10 41 34N 74 11W
Waldport, U.S.A. ... 76 D1 44 26N 124 4W
Waldron, U.S.A. ... 81 H7 34 54N 94 5W
Walebing, Australia ... 61 F2 30 41S 116 13 E
Wales □, U.K. ... 13 E3 52 19N 4 43W
Walgett, Australia ... 63 E4 30 0S 148 5 E
Walgreen Coast, Antarctica ... 5 D15 75 15S 105 0W
Walker, U.S.A. ... 80 B7 47 6N 94 35W
Walker, L., Canada ... 73 B6 50 20N 67 11W
Walker L., Canada ... 71 C9 54 42N 95 57W
Walker L., U.S.A. ... 76 G4 38 42N 118 43W
Walkerston, Australia ... 62 K7 21 11S 149 8 E
Walkerton, Canada ... 84 B3 44 10N 81 10W
Wall, U.S.A. ... 80 D3 44 0N 102 8W
Walla Walla, U.S.A. ... 76 C4 46 4N 118 20W
Wallace, Idaho, U.S.A. ... 76 C6 47 28N 115 56W
Wallace, N.C., U.S.A. ... 83 H7 34 44N 77 59W
Wallaceburg, Canada ... 84 D2 42 34N 82 23W
Wallachia = Valahia, Romania ... 17 F13 44 35N 25 0 E
Wallal, Australia ... 63 D4 26 32S 146 7 E
Wallam Cr. ➤, Australia ... 63 D4 28 40S 147 20 E
Wallambin, L., Australia ... 61 F2 30 57S 117 35 E
Wallangarra, Australia ... 63 D5 28 56S 151 58 E
Wallaroo, Australia ... 63 E2 33 56S 137 39 E
Wallenpaupack, L., U.S.A. ... 85 E9 41 25N 75 15W
Wallingford, U.S.A. ... 85 E12 41 27N 72 50W
Wallis & Futuna, Is., Pac. Oc. ... 64 J10 13 18S 176 10W
Wallowa, U.S.A. ... 76 D5 45 34N 117 32W
Wallowa Mts., U.S.A. ... 76 D5 45 20N 117 30W
Walls, U.K. ... 11 A7 60 14N 1 33W
Walls of Jerusalem △, Australia ... 63 G4 41 56S 146 15 E
Wallula, U.S.A. ... 76 C4 46 5N 118 54W
Wallumbilla, Australia ... 63 D4 26 33S 149 9 E
Walmsley, L., Canada ... 71 A7 63 25N 108 36W
Walney, I. of, U.K. ... 12 C4 54 6N 3 15W
Walnut Canyon △, U.S.A. ... 77 J8 35 15N 111 20W
Walnut Creek, U.S.A. ... 78 H4 37 54N 122 4W
Walnut Ridge, U.S.A. ... 81 G9 36 4N 90 57W
Walpole, Australia ... 61 F2 34 58S 116 44 E
Walpole, U.S.A. ... 85 D13 42 9N 71 15W
Walsall, U.K. ... 13 E6 52 35N 1 58W
Walsenburg, U.S.A. ... 81 G2 37 38N 104 47W
Walsh, U.S.A. ... 81 G3 37 23N 102 17W
Walsh ➤, Australia ... 62 B3 16 31S 143 42 E
Walterboro, U.S.A. ... 83 J5 32 55N 80 40W
Walters, U.S.A. ... 81 H5 34 22N 98 19W
Waltham, U.S.A. ... 85 D13 42 23N 71 14W
Waltman, U.S.A. ... 76 E10 43 4N 107 12W
Walton, U.S.A. ... 85 D9 42 10N 75 8W
Walton-on-the-Naze, U.K. ... 13 F9 51 51N 1 17 E
Walvis Bay, Namibia ... 56 C1 23 0S 14 28 E
Walvisbaai = Walvis Bay, Namibia ... 56 C1 23 0S 14 28 E
Wamba, Dem. Rep. of the Congo ... 54 B2 2 10N 27 57 E
Wamba, Kenya ... 54 B4 0 58N 37 19 E
Wamego, U.S.A. ... 80 F6 39 12N 96 18W
Wamena, Indonesia ... 37 E9 4 4S 138 57 E
Wamsutter, U.S.A. ... 76 F9 41 40N 107 58W
Wamulan, Indonesia ... 37 E7 3 27S 126 7 E
Wan Xian, China ... 34 E8 38 47N 115 7 E
Wana, Pakistan ... 42 C3 32 20N 69 32 E
Wanaaring, Australia ... 63 D3 29 38S 144 9 E
Wanaka, N.Z. ... 59 L2 44 42S 169 9 E
Wanaka, L., N.Z. ... 59 L2 44 33S 169 7 E
Wanapitei L., Canada ... 72 C3 46 45N 80 40W
Wandel Sea = McKinley Sea, Arctic ... 4 A7 82 0N 0 0W
Wanderer, Zimbabwe ... 55 F3 19 36S 30 1 E
Wandhari, Pakistan ... 42 F2 27 42N 66 48 E
Wandoan, Australia ... 63 D4 26 5S 149 55 E
Wanfu, China ... 35 D12 40 8N 122 38 E
Wang ➤, Thailand ... 38 D2 17 8N 99 2 E
Wang Noi, Thailand ... 38 E3 14 13N 100 44 E
Wang Saphung, Thailand ... 38 D3 17 18N 101 46 E
Wang Thong, Thailand ... 38 D3 16 50N 100 26 E
Wanga, Dem. Rep. of the Congo ... 54 B2 2 58N 29 12 E
Wangal, Indonesia ... 37 F8 6 8S 134 9 E
Wanganella, Australia ... 63 F3 35 6S 144 49 E
Wanganui, N.Z. ... 59 H5 39 56S 175 3 E
Wangaratta, Australia ... 63 F4 36 21S 146 19 E
Wangary, Australia ... 63 E2 34 35S 135 29 E
Wangdu, China ... 34 E8 38 40N 115 7 E
Wangerooge, Germany ... 16 B4 53 47N 7 54 E
Wangiwangi, Indonesia ... 37 F6 5 22S 123 37 E
Wangqing, China ... 35 C15 43 12N 129 42 E
Wankaner, India ... 42 H4 22 35N 71 0 E
Wanless, Canada ... 71 C8 54 11N 101 21W
Wanning, China ... 38 C8 18 48N 110 22 E
Wanon Niwat, Thailand ... 38 D4 17 38N 103 46 E
Wanqinsha, China ... 33 F10 22 43N 113 33 E
Wanquan, China ... 34 D8 40 50N 114 40 E
Wanrong, China ... 34 G6 35 25N 110 50 E
Wanshan Qundao, China ... 33 G10 21 57N 113 45 E
Wantage, U.K. ... 13 F6 51 35N 1 25W
Wanzai, China ... 33 G10 22 12N 113 31 E
Wapakoneta, U.S.A. ... 82 E3 40 34N 84 12W
Wapato, U.S.A. ... 76 C3 46 27N 120 25W
Wapawekka L., Canada ... 71 C8 54 55N 104 40W
Wapikopa L., Canada ... 72 B2 52 56N 87 53W
Wapiti ➤, Canada ... 70 B5 55 5N 118 18W
Wappingers Falls, U.S.A. ... 85 E11 41 36N 73 55W

Wapsipinicon ➤, U.S.A. ... 80 E9 41 44N 90 19W
Wapusk △, Canada ... 71 B10 57 46N 93 22W
Wapusk Nat. Park △ ... 71 B10 90 0S 180 0 E
Warangal, India ... 40 L11 17 58N 79 35 E
Waraseoni, India ... 43 J9 21 45N 80 2 E
Waratah, Australia ... 63 G4 41 30S 145 30 E
Waratah B., Australia ... 63 F4 38 54S 146 5 E
Warburton, Vic., Australia ... 63 F4 37 47S 145 42 E
Warburton, W. Austral., Australia ... 61 E4 26 8S 126 35 E
Warburton Ra., Australia ... 61 E4 25 55S 126 28 E
Ward, N.Z. ... 59 J5 41 49S 174 11 E
Ward ➤, Australia ... 63 D4 26 28S 146 6 E
Ward Mt., U.S.A. ... 78 H8 37 12N 118 54W
Warden, S. Africa ... 57 D4 27 50S 29 0 E
Wardha, India ... 40 J11 20 45N 78 39 E
Wardha ➤, India ... 40 K11 19 57N 79 11 E
Ware, Canada ... 70 B3 57 26N 125 41W
Ware, U.K. ... 13 F8 51 49N 0 0W
Ware, U.S.A. ... 85 D12 42 16N 72 14W
Waregem, Belgium ... 15 D3 50 53N 3 27 E
Wareham, U.S.A. ... 85 E14 41 46N 70 43W
Waremme, Belgium ... 15 D5 50 43N 5 15 E
Warialda, Australia ... 63 D5 29 29S 150 33 E
Wariap, Indonesia ... 37 E8 1 30S 134 5 E
Warin Chamrap, Thailand ... 38 E5 15 12N 104 53 E
Warkopi, Indonesia ... 37 E8 1 12S 134 9 E
Warm Springs, U.S.A. ... 77 G5 38 10N 116 20W
Warman, Canada ... 71 C7 52 19N 106 30W
Warmbad = Bela Bela, S. Africa ... 57 C4 24 51S 28 19 E
Warmbad, Namibia ... 56 D2 28 25S 18 42 E
Warminster, U.K. ... 13 F5 51 12N 2 10W
Warminster, U.S.A. ... 85 F9 40 12N 75 6W
Warner Mts., U.S.A. ... 76 F3 41 40N 120 15W
Warner Robins, U.S.A. ... 83 J4 32 37N 83 36W
Waroona, Australia ... 61 F2 32 50S 115 58 E
Warracknabeal, Australia ... 63 F3 36 9S 142 26 E
Warragul, Australia ... 63 F4 38 10S 145 58 E
Warrego ➤, Australia ... 63 E4 30 24S 145 21 E
Warrego Ra., Australia ... 62 C4 24 58S 146 0 E
Warren, Australia ... 63 E4 31 42S 147 51 E
Warren, Ark., U.S.A. ... 81 J8 33 37N 92 4W
Warren, Mich., U.S.A. ... 82 D4 42 30N 83 0W
Warren, Minn., U.S.A. ... 80 A6 48 12N 96 46W
Warren, Ohio, U.S.A. ... 84 E4 41 14N 80 49W
Warren, Pa., U.S.A. ... 84 E5 41 51N 79 9W
Warrenpoint, U.K. ... 10 B5 54 6N 6 15W
Warrensburg, Mo., U.S.A. ... 80 F8 38 46N 93 44W
Warrensburg, N.Y., U.S.A. ... 85 C11 43 29N 73 46W
Warrenton, S. Africa ... 56 D3 28 9S 24 47 E
Warrenton, U.S.A. ... 78 D3 46 10N 123 56W
Warri, Nigeria ... 50 G7 5 30N 5 41 E
Warrina, Australia ... 63 D2 28 12S 135 50 E
Warrington, U.K. ... 12 D5 53 24N 2 35W
Warrington, U.S.A. ... 83 K2 30 23N 87 17W
Warrington □, U.K. ... 12 D5 53 24N 2 35W
Warrnambool, Australia ... 63 F3 38 25S 142 30 E
Warroad, U.S.A. ... 80 A7 48 54N 95 19W
Warruwi, Australia ... 62 A1 11 36S 133 20 E
Warsa, Indonesia ... 37 E9 0 47S 135 55 E
Warsak Dam, Pakistan ... 42 B4 34 11N 71 19 E
Warsaw = Warszawa, Poland ... 17 B11 52 13N 21 0 E
Warsaw, Ind., U.S.A. ... 82 E3 41 14N 85 51W
Warsaw, N.Y., U.S.A. ... 84 D6 42 45N 78 8W
Warsaw, Ohio, U.S.A. ... 84 F3 40 20N 82 0W
Warszawa, Poland ... 17 B11 52 13N 21 0 E
Warta ➤, Poland ... 16 B8 52 35N 14 39 E
Warthe = Warta ➤, Poland ... 16 B8 52 35N 14 39 E
Waru, Indonesia ... 37 E8 3 30S 130 36 E
Warwick, Australia ... 63 D5 28 10S 152 1 E
Warwick, U.K. ... 13 E6 52 18N 1 35W
Warwick, N.Y., U.S.A. ... 85 E10 41 16N 74 22W
Warwick, R.I., U.S.A. ... 85 E13 41 42N 71 28W
Warwickshire □, U.K. ... 13 E6 52 14N 1 38W
Wasaga Beach, Canada ... 84 B4 44 31N 80 1W
Wasagaming, Canada ... 71 C9 50 39N 99 58W
Wasatch Ra., U.S.A. ... 76 F8 40 30N 111 15W
Wasbank, S. Africa ... 57 D5 28 15S 30 9 E
Wasco, Calif., U.S.A. ... 79 K7 35 36N 119 20W
Wasco, Oreg., U.S.A. ... 76 D3 45 36N 120 42W
Waseca, U.S.A. ... 80 C8 44 5N 93 30W
Wasekamio L., Canada ... 71 B7 56 45N 108 45W
Wash, The, U.K. ... 12 E8 52 58N 0 20 E
Washago, Canada ... 84 B5 44 45N 79 20W
Washburn, N. Dak., U.S.A. ... 80 B4 47 17N 101 2W
Washburn, Wis., U.S.A. ... 80 B9 46 40N 90 54W
Washim, India ... 40 J10 20 3N 77 0 E
Washington, U.K. ... 12 C6 54 55N 1 30W
Washington, D.C., U.S.A. ... 82 F7 38 54N 77 2W
Washington, Ga., U.S.A. ... 83 J4 33 44N 82 44W
Washington, Ind., U.S.A. ... 82 F2 38 40N 87 10W
Washington, Iowa, U.S.A. ... 80 E9 41 18N 91 42W
Washington, Mo., U.S.A. ... 80 F9 38 33N 91 1W
Washington, N.C., U.S.A. ... 83 H7 35 33N 77 3W
Washington, N.J., U.S.A. ... 85 F10 40 46N 74 59W
Washington, Pa., U.S.A. ... 84 F4 40 10N 80 15W
Washington, Utah, U.S.A. ... 77 H7 37 8N 113 31W
Washington □, U.S.A. ... 76 C3 47 30N 120 30W
Washington, Mt., U.S.A. ... 85 B13 44 16N 71 18W
Washington Court House, U.S.A. ... 82 F4 39 32N 83 26W
Washington I., U.S.A. ... 82 C2 45 23N 86 54W
Washougal, U.S.A. ... 78 E4 45 35N 122 21W
Washpool △, Australia ... 63 D5 29 22S 152 20 E
Wasian, Indonesia ... 37 E8 1 47S 133 19 E
Wasilla, U.S.A. ... 68 B5 61 35N 149 26W
Wasior, Indonesia ... 37 E8 2 43S 134 30 E
Wāsiṭ □, Iraq ... 44 C5 32 30N 46 0 E
Waskaganish, Canada ... 72 B4 51 30N 78 40W
Waskaiowaka, L., Canada ... 71 B9 56 33N 96 23W
Waskesiu Lake, Canada ... 71 C7 53 55N 106 5W
Wasserkuppe, Germany ... 16 C5 50 29N 9 55 E
Waswanipi, Canada ... 72 C4 49 40N 76 29W
Waswanipi, L., Canada ... 72 C4 49 35N 76 40W
Watampone, Indonesia ... 37 E6 4 29S 120 25 E
Watamu, Kenya ... 54 C5 3 23S 40 0 E
Watarrka △, Australia ... 60 D5 24 20S 131 30 E
Water Park Pt., Australia ... 62 C5 22 56S 150 47 E
Water Valley, U.S.A. ... 81 H10 34 10N 89 38W
Waterberg Plateau △, Namibia ... 56 C2 20 25S 17 18 E
Waterberge, S. Africa ... 57 C4 24 10S 28 0 E
Waterbury, Conn., U.S.A. ... 85 E11 41 33N 73 3W
Waterbury, Vt., U.S.A. ... 85 B12 44 20N 72 46W
Waterdown, Canada ... 84 C5 43 20N 79 53W
Waterford, Ireland ... 10 D4 52 15N 7 8W
Waterford, Calif., U.S.A. ... 78 H6 37 38N 120 46W
Waterford, Pa., U.S.A. ... 84 E5 41 57N 79 59W

Waterford □, Ireland ... 10 D4 52 10N 7 40W
Waterford Harbour, Ireland ... 10 D5 52 8N 6 58W
Waterhen L., Canada ... 71 C9 52 10N 99 40W
Waterloo, Belgium ... 15 D4 50 43N 4 25 E
Waterloo, Ont., Canada ... 84 C4 43 30N 80 32W
Waterloo, Qué., Canada ... 85 A12 45 22N 72 32W
Waterloo, Ill., U.S.A. ... 80 F9 38 20N 90 9W
Waterloo, Iowa, U.S.A. ... 80 D8 42 30N 92 21W
Waterloo, N.Y., U.S.A. ... 84 D8 42 54N 76 52W
Watersmeet, U.S.A. ... 80 B10 46 16N 89 11W
Waterton Lakes △, Canada ... 70 D6 48 45N 115 0W
Watertown, Conn., U.S.A. ... 85 E11 41 36N 73 7W
Watertown, N.Y., U.S.A. ... 85 C9 43 59N 75 55W
Watertown, S. Dak., U.S.A. ... 80 C6 44 54N 97 7W
Watertown, Wis., U.S.A. ... 80 D10 43 12N 88 43W
Waterval-Boven, S. Africa ... 57 D5 25 40S 30 18 E
Waterville, Canada ... 85 A13 45 16N 71 54W
Waterville, Maine, U.S.A. ... 83 C11 44 33N 69 38W
Waterville, N.Y., U.S.A. ... 85 D9 42 56N 75 23W
Waterville, Pa., U.S.A. ... 84 E7 41 19N 77 21W
Waterville, Wash., U.S.A. ... 76 C3 47 39N 120 4W
Watervliet, U.S.A. ... 85 D11 42 44N 73 42W
Wates, Indonesia ... 37 G14 7 51S 110 10 E
Watford, Canada ... 84 D3 42 57N 81 53W
Watford, U.K. ... 13 F7 51 40N 0 24W
Watford City, U.S.A. ... 80 B3 47 48N 103 17W
Wathaman ➤, Canada ... 71 B8 57 16N 102 59W
Wathaman L., Canada ... 71 B8 56 58N 103 44W
Watheroo, Australia ... 61 F2 30 15S 116 0 E
Watheroo △, Australia ... 61 F2 30 19S 115 48 E
Wating, China ... 34 G4 35 40N 106 38 E
Watkins Glen, U.S.A. ... 84 D8 42 23N 76 52W
Watling I. = San Salvador I., Bahamas ... 89 B5 24 0N 74 40W
Watonga, U.S.A. ... 81 H5 35 51N 98 25W
Watrous, Canada ... 71 C7 51 40N 105 25W
Watrous, U.S.A. ... 81 H2 35 48N 104 59W
Watsa, Dem. Rep. of the Congo ... 54 B2 3 4N 29 30 E
Watseka, U.S.A. ... 82 E2 40 47N 87 44W
Watson, Australia ... 61 F5 30 29S 131 31 E
Watson, Canada ... 71 C8 52 10N 104 30W
Watson Lake, Canada ... 70 A3 60 6N 128 49W
Watsontown, U.S.A. ... 84 E8 41 5N 76 52W
Watsonville, U.S.A. ... 78 J5 36 55N 121 45W
Wattiwarriganna Cr. ➤, Australia ... 63 D2 28 57S 136 10 E
Watuata = Batuata, Indonesia ... 37 F6 6 12S 122 42 E
Watubela, Kepulauan, Indonesia ... 37 E8 4 28S 131 35 E
Watubela Is. = Watubela, Kepulauan, Indonesia ... 37 E8 4 28S 131 35 E
Wau = Wâw, Sudan ... 51 G11 7 45N 28 1 E
Waubamik, Canada ... 84 A4 45 27N 80 1W
Waubay, U.S.A. ... 80 C6 45 20N 97 18W
Wauchope, N.S.W., Australia ... 63 E5 31 28S 152 45 E
Wauchope, N. Terr., Australia ... 62 C1 20 36S 134 15 E
Wauchula, U.S.A. ... 83 M5 27 33N 81 49W
Waukarlycarly, L., Australia ... 60 D3 21 18S 121 56 E
Waukegan, U.S.A. ... 82 D2 42 22N 87 50W
Waukesha, U.S.A. ... 82 D1 43 1N 88 14W
Waukon, U.S.A. ... 80 D9 43 16N 91 29W
Waupaca, U.S.A. ... 80 C10 44 21N 89 5W
Waupun, U.S.A. ... 80 D10 43 38N 88 44W
Waurika, U.S.A. ... 81 H6 34 10N 98 0W
Wausau, U.S.A. ... 80 C10 44 58N 89 38W
Wautoma, U.S.A. ... 80 C10 44 4N 89 18W
Wauwatosa, U.S.A. ... 82 D2 43 3N 88 0W
Waveney ➤, U.K. ... 13 E9 52 35N 1 39 E
Waverley, N.Z. ... 59 H5 39 46S 174 37 E
Waverly, Iowa, U.S.A. ... 80 D8 42 44N 92 29W
Waverly, N.Y., U.S.A. ... 85 E8 42 1N 76 32W
Wavre, Belgium ... 15 D4 50 43N 4 38 E
Wâw, Sudan ... 51 G11 7 45N 28 1 E
Wāw al Kabir, Libya ... 51 C9 25 20N 16 43 E
Wawa, Canada ... 72 C3 47 59N 84 47W
Wawanesa, Canada ... 71 D9 49 36N 99 40W
Wawona, U.S.A. ... 78 H7 37 32N 119 39W
Waxahachie, U.S.A. ... 81 J6 32 24N 96 51W
Way, L., Australia ... 61 E3 26 45S 120 16 E
Waycross, U.S.A. ... 83 K4 31 13N 82 21W
Wayland, U.S.A. ... 84 D7 42 34N 77 35W
Wayne, Nebr., U.S.A. ... 80 D6 42 14N 97 1W
Wayne, W. Va., U.S.A. ... 82 F4 38 13N 82 27W
Waynesboro, Ga., U.S.A. ... 83 J4 33 6N 82 1W
Waynesboro, Miss., U.S.A. ... 83 K1 31 40N 88 39W
Waynesboro, Pa., U.S.A. ... 82 F7 39 45N 77 35W
Waynesboro, Va., U.S.A. ... 82 F6 38 4N 78 53W
Waynesburg, U.S.A. ... 82 F5 39 54N 80 11W
Waynesville, U.S.A. ... 83 H4 35 28N 82 58W
Waynoka, U.S.A. ... 81 G5 36 35N 98 53W
Wazirabad, Pakistan ... 42 C6 32 30N 74 8 E
We, Indonesia ... 36 C1 5 51N 95 18 E
Weald, The, U.K. ... 13 F8 51 4N 0 20 E
Wear ➤, U.K. ... 12 C6 54 55N 1 23W
Weatherford, Okla., U.S.A. ... 81 H5 35 32N 98 43W
Weatherford, Tex., U.S.A. ... 81 J6 32 46N 97 48W
Weaverville, U.S.A. ... 76 F2 40 44N 122 56W
Webb City, U.S.A. ... 81 G7 37 9N 94 28W
Webequie, Canada ... 72 B2 52 59N 87 21W
Webster, Mass., U.S.A. ... 85 D13 42 3N 71 53W
Webster, N.Y., U.S.A. ... 84 C7 43 13N 77 26W
Webster, S. Dak., U.S.A. ... 80 C6 45 20N 97 31W
Webster City, U.S.A. ... 80 D8 42 28N 93 49W
Webster Springs, U.S.A. ... 82 F5 38 29N 80 25W
Weda, Indonesia ... 37 D7 0 21N 127 50 E
Weda, Teluk, Indonesia ... 37 D7 0 20N 128 0 E
Weddell I., Falk. Is. ... 96 G4 51 50S 61 0W
Weddell Sea, Antarctica ... 5 D1 72 30S 40 0W
Wedderburn, Australia ... 63 F3 36 26S 143 33 E
Wedgeport, Canada ... 73 D6 43 44N 65 59W
Wedza, Zimbabwe ... 55 F3 18 40S 31 33 E
Wee Waa, Australia ... 63 E4 30 11S 149 26 E
Weed, U.S.A. ... 76 F2 41 25N 122 23W
Weed Heights, U.S.A. ... 78 G7 38 59N 119 13W
Weedsport, U.S.A. ... 85 C8 43 3N 76 35W
Weedville, U.S.A. ... 84 E6 41 17N 78 30W
Weenen, S. Africa ... 57 D5 28 48S 30 7 E
Weert, Neths. ... 15 C5 51 15N 5 43 E
Wei He ➤, Hebei, China ... 34 F8 36 10N 115 45 E
Wei He ➤, Shaanxi, China ... 34 G6 34 38N 110 15 E
Weichang, China ... 35 D9 41 58N 117 49 E
Weichuan, China ... 34 G7 34 20N 113 59 E
Weiden, Germany ... 16 D7 49 41N 12 10 E
Weifang, China ... 35 F10 36 44N 119 7 E
Weihai, China ... 35 F12 37 30N 122 6 E
Weimar, Germany ... 16 C6 50 58N 11 19 E
Weinan, China ... 34 G5 34 31N 109 29 E
Weipa, Australia ... 62 A3 12 40S 141 50 E
Weir ➤, Australia ... 63 D4 28 20S 149 50 E

Weir ➤, Canada ... 71 B10 56 54N 93 21W
Weir River, Canada ... 71 B10 56 49N 94 6W
Weirton, U.S.A. ... 84 F4 40 24N 80 35W
Weiser, U.S.A. ... 76 D5 44 10N 117 0W
Weishan, China ... 35 G9 34 47N 117 5 E
Weiyuan, China ... 34 G3 35 7N 104 10 E
Wejherowo, Poland ... 17 A10 54 35N 18 12 E
Wekusko L., Canada ... 71 C9 54 40N 99 50W
Welch, U.S.A. ... 82 G5 37 26N 81 35W
Welford △, Australia ... 62 D3 25 5S 143 16 E
Welkom, S. Africa ... 56 D4 28 0S 26 46 E
Welland, Canada ... 84 D5 43 0N 79 15W
Welland ➤, U.K. ... 13 E7 52 51N 0 5W
Wellesley Is., Australia ... 62 B2 16 42S 139 30 E
Wellingborough, U.K. ... 13 E7 52 19N 0 41W
Wellington, Australia ... 63 E4 32 35S 148 59 E
Wellington, Canada ... 84 C7 43 57N 77 20W
Wellington, N.Z. ... 59 J5 41 19S 174 46 E
Wellington, S. Africa ... 56 E2 33 38S 19 1 E
Wellington, Somst., U.K. ... 13 G4 50 58N 3 13W
Wellington, Telford & Wrekin, U.K. ... 13 E5 52 42N 2 30W
Wellington, Colo., U.S.A. ... 80 E2 40 42N 105 0W
Wellington, Kans., U.S.A. ... 81 G6 37 16N 97 24W
Wellington, Nev., U.S.A. ... 78 G7 38 45N 119 23W
Wellington, Ohio, U.S.A. ... 84 E2 41 10N 82 13W
Wellington, Tex., U.S.A. ... 81 H4 34 51N 100 13W
Wellington, I., Chile ... 96 F2 49 30S 75 0W
Wellington, L., Australia ... 63 F4 38 6S 147 20 E
Wells, U.K. ... 13 F5 51 13N 2 39W
Wells, Maine, U.S.A. ... 85 C14 43 20N 70 35W
Wells, N.Y., U.S.A. ... 85 C10 43 24N 74 17W
Wells, Nev., U.S.A. ... 76 F6 41 7N 114 58W
Wells, L., Australia ... 61 E3 26 44S 123 15 E
Wells, Mt., Australia ... 60 C4 17 25S 127 8 E
Wells Gray △, Canada ... 70 C4 52 30N 120 15W
Wells-next-the-Sea, U.K. ... 12 E8 52 57N 0 51 E
Wells River, U.S.A. ... 85 B12 44 9N 72 4W
Wellsboro, U.S.A. ... 84 E7 41 45N 77 18W
Wellsburg, U.S.A. ... 84 F4 40 16N 80 37W
Wellsville, N.Y., U.S.A. ... 84 D7 42 7N 77 57W
Wellsville, Ohio, U.S.A. ... 84 F4 40 36N 80 39W
Wellsville, Utah, U.S.A. ... 76 F8 41 38N 111 56W
Wellton, U.S.A. ... 77 K6 32 40N 114 8W
Wels, Austria ... 16 D8 48 9N 14 1 E
Welshpool, U.K. ... 13 E4 52 39N 3 8W
Welwyn Garden City, U.K. ... 13 F7 51 48N 0 12W
Wem, U.K. ... 12 E5 52 52N 2 44W
Wembere ➤, Tanzania ... 54 C3 4 10S 34 15 E
Wemindji, Canada ... 72 B4 53 0N 78 49W
Wen Xian, China ... 34 G7 34 55N 113 5 E
Wenatchee, U.S.A. ... 76 C3 47 25N 120 19W
Wenchang, China ... 38 C8 19 38N 110 42 E
Wenchi, Ghana ... 50 G5 7 46N 2 8W
Wenchow = Wenzhou, China ... 33 D7 28 0N 120 38 E
Wenden, U.S.A. ... 79 M13 33 49N 113 33W
Wendeng, China ... 35 F12 37 15N 122 5 E
Wendesi, Indonesia ... 37 E8 2 30S 134 17 E
Wendover, U.S.A. ... 76 F6 40 44N 114 2W
Wenlock ➤, Australia ... 62 A3 12 2S 141 55 E
Wenshan, China ... 32 D5 23 20N 104 18 E
Wenshang, China ... 34 G9 35 45N 116 30 E
Wenshui, China ... 34 F7 37 26N 112 1 E
Wensleydale, U.K. ... 12 C6 54 17N 2 0W
Wensu, China ... 32 B3 41 15N 80 10 E
Wensum ➤, U.K. ... 12 E8 52 40N 1 15 E
Wentworth, Australia ... 63 E3 34 2S 141 54 E
Wentzel L., Canada ... 70 B6 59 2N 114 28W
Wenut, Indonesia ... 37 E8 3 11S 133 19 E
Wenxi, China ... 34 G6 35 20N 111 10 E
Wenxian, China ... 34 H3 32 43N 104 36 E
Wenzhou, China ... 33 D7 28 0N 120 38 E
Weott, U.S.A. ... 76 F2 40 20N 123 55W
Wepener, S. Africa ... 56 D4 29 42S 27 3 E
Werda, Botswana ... 56 D3 25 24S 23 15 E
Weri, Indonesia ... 37 E8 3 10S 132 38 E
Werra ➤, Germany ... 16 C5 51 24N 9 39 E
Werrimull, Australia ... 63 E3 34 25S 141 38 E
Werris Creek, Australia ... 63 E5 31 18S 150 38 E
Weser ➤, Germany ... 16 B5 53 36N 8 28 E
Wesiri, Indonesia ... 37 F7 7 30S 126 30 E
Weslemkoon L., Canada ... 84 A7 45 2N 77 25W
Wesleyville, Canada ... 84 D4 42 9N 80 0W
Wessel, C., Australia ... 62 A2 10 59S 136 46 E
Wessel Is., Australia ... 62 A2 11 10S 136 45 E
Wessington Springs, U.S.A. ... 80 C5 44 5N 98 34W
West, U.S.A. ... 81 K6 31 48N 97 6W
West ➤, U.S.A. ... 85 D12 42 52N 72 33W
West Antarctica, Antarctica ... 5 D15 80 0S 90 0W
West Baines ➤, Australia ... 60 C4 15 38S 129 59 E
West Bank ☑, Asia ... 46 C4 32 6N 35 13 E
West Bend, U.S.A. ... 82 D1 43 25N 88 11W
West Bengal □, India ... 43 H13 23 0N 88 0 E
West Berkshire □, U.K. ... 13 F6 51 25N 1 17W
West Beskids = Západné Beskydy, Europe ... 17 D10 49 30N 19 0 E
West Branch, U.S.A. ... 82 C3 44 17N 84 14W
West Branch Susquehanna ➤, U.S.A. ... 85 F8 40 53N 76 48W
West Bromwich, U.K. ... 13 E6 52 32N 1 59W
West Burra, U.K. ... 11 A7 60 5N 1 21W
West Canada Cr. ➤, U.S.A. ... 85 C10 43 1N 74 58W
West Cape Howe, Australia ... 61 G2 35 8S 117 36 E
West Chazy, U.S.A. ... 85 B11 44 49N 73 28W
West Chester, U.S.A. ... 85 G9 39 58N 75 36W
West Coast △, Namibia ... 56 C1 21 53S 14 14 E
West Coast △, S. Africa ... 56 E2 33 13S 18 0 E
West Columbia, U.S.A. ... 81 L7 29 9N 95 39W
West Covina, U.S.A. ... 79 L9 34 4N 117 54W
West Des Moines, U.S.A. ... 80 E8 41 35N 93 43W
West Dunbartonshire □, U.K. ... 11 F4 55 59N 4 30W
West End, Bahamas ... 88 A4 26 41N 78 58W
West Falkland, Falk. Is. ... 96 G5 51 40S 60 0W
West Fargo, U.S.A. ... 80 B6 46 52N 96 54W
West Farmington, U.S.A. ... 84 E4 41 23N 80 58W
West Fjord = Vestfjorden, Norway ... 8 C15 67 55N 14 0 E
West Fork Trinity ➤, U.S.A. ... 81 J6 32 48N 96 54W
West Frankfort, U.S.A. ... 80 G10 37 54N 88 55W
West Hartford, U.S.A. ... 85 E12 41 45N 72 44W
West Haven, U.S.A. ... 85 E12 41 17N 72 57W
West Hazleton, U.S.A. ... 85 F9 40 58N 76 0W
West Helena, U.S.A. ... 81 H9 34 33N 90 38W
West Hurley, U.S.A. ... 85 E10 41 59N 74 7W
West Ice Shelf, Antarctica ... 5 C7 67 0S 85 0 E
West Indies, Cent. Amer. ... 89 D7 15 0N 65 0W
West Jordan, U.S.A. ... 76 F8 40 36N 111 56W

West Lamma Channel, China .. 33 G11 22 13N 114 4 E
West Lorne, Canada 84 D3 42 36N 81 36W
West Lothian □, U.K. 11 F5 55 54N 3 36W
West Lunga ➤, Zambia ...... 55 E1 13 6S 24 39 E
West MacDonnell △, Australia . 60 D5 23 38S 132 59 E
West Memphis, U.S.A. 81 H9 35 9N 90 11W
West Midlands □, U.K. 13 E6 52 26N 2 0W
West Mifflin, U.S.A. 84 F5 40 22N 79 52W
West Milton, U.S.A. 84 E8 41 1N 76 50W
West Monroe, U.S.A. 81 J8 32 31N 92 9W
West Newton, U.S.A. 84 F5 40 14N 79 46W
West Nicholson, Zimbabwe .. 55 G2 21 2S 29 20 E
West Palm Beach, U.S.A. 83 M5 26 43N 80 3W
West Plains, U.S.A. 81 G9 36 44N 91 51W
West Point, N.Y., U.S.A. 85 E11 41 24N 73 58W
West Point, Nebr., U.S.A. 80 E6 41 51N 96 43W
West Point, Va., U.S.A. 82 G7 37 32N 76 48W
West Pt. = Ouest, Pte. de l',
   Canada 73 C7 49 52N 64 40W
West Pt., Australia ...... 63 F2 35 1S 135 56 E
West Road ➤, Canada 70 C4 53 18N 122 53W
West Rutland, U.S.A. 85 C11 43 38N 73 5W
West Schelde =
   Westerschelde ➤, Neths. .... 15 C3 51 25N 3 25 E
West Seneca, U.S.A. 84 D6 42 51N 78 48W
West Siberian Plain, Russia .. 26 C11 62 0N 75 0 E
West Sussex □, U.K. 13 G7 50 55N 0 30W
West-Terschelling, Neths. .... 15 A5 53 22N 5 13 E
West Valley City, U.S.A. 76 F8 40 42N 111 57W
West Virginia □, U.S.A. 82 F5 38 45N 80 30W
West-Vlaanderen □, Belgium . 15 D2 51 0N 3 0 E
West Walker ➤, U.S.A. 78 G7 38 54N 119 9W
West Wyalong, Australia .... 63 E4 33 56S 147 10 E
West Yellowstone, U.S.A. 76 D8 44 40N 111 6W
West Yorkshire □, U.K. 12 D6 53 45N 1 40W
Westall, Pt., Australia ...... 63 E1 32 55S 134 4 E
Westbrook, U.S.A. 83 D10 43 41N 70 22W
Westbury, Australia ...... 63 G4 41 30S 146 51 E
Westby, U.S.A. 80 A2 48 52N 104 3W
Westend, U.S.A. 79 K9 35 42N 117 24W
Westerland, Germany ...... 9 J13 54 54N 8 17 E
Westerly, U.S.A. 85 E13 41 22N 71 50W
Western □, Kenya ...... 54 B3 0 30N 34 30 E
Western □, Zambia ...... 55 F1 15 0S 24 4 E
Western Australia □, Australia . 61 E2 25 0S 118 0 E
Western Cape □, S. Africa ... 56 E3 34 0S 20 0 E
Western Dvina = Daugava ➤,
   Latvia .... 9 H21 57 4N 24 3 E
Western Ghats, India ...... 40 N9 14 0N 75 0 E
Western Isles □, U.K. 11 D1 57 30N 7 10W
Western Sahara ■, Africa 50 D3 25 0N 13 0W
Western Samoa = Samoa ■,
   Pac. Oc. 59 B13 14 0S 172 0W
Westernport, U.S.A. 82 F6 39 29N 79 3W
Westerschelde ➤, Neths. .... 15 C3 51 25N 3 25 E
Westerwald, Germany ...... 16 C4 50 38N 7 56 E
Westfield, Mass., U.S.A. 85 D12 42 7N 72 45W
Westfield, N.Y., U.S.A. 84 D5 42 20N 79 35W
Westfield, Pa., U.S.A. 84 E7 41 55N 77 32W
Westhill, U.K. 11 D6 57 9N 2 19W
Westhope, U.S.A. 80 A4 48 55N 101 1W
Westland △, N.Z. ...... 59 K2 43 16S 170 16 E
Westland Bight, N.Z. ...... 59 K3 42 55S 170 5 E
Westlock, Canada 70 C6 54 9N 113 55W
Westmar, Australia ...... 63 D4 27 55S 149 44 E
Westmeath □, Ireland 10 C4 53 33N 7 34W
Westminster, U.S.A. 82 F7 39 34N 76 59W
Westmont, U.S.A. 84 F6 40 19N 78 58W
Westmoreland, Barbados .... 89 g 13 13N 59 37W
Westmorland, U.S.A. 79 M11 33 2N 115 37W
Weston, Oreg., U.S.A. 76 D4 45 49N 118 26W
Weston, W. Va., U.S.A. 82 F5 39 2N 80 28W
Weston I., Canada 72 B4 52 33N 79 36W
Weston-super-Mare, U.K. 13 F5 51 21N 2 58W
Westover, U.S.A. 84 F6 40 45N 78 40W
Westport, Canada 85 B8 44 40N 76 25W
Westport, Ireland 10 C2 53 48N 9 31W
Westport, N.Z. ...... 59 J3 41 46S 171 37 E
Westport, N.Y., U.S.A. 85 B11 44 11N 73 26W
Westport, Oreg., U.S.A. 78 D3 46 8N 123 23W
Westport, Wash., U.S.A. 78 D2 46 53N 124 6W
Westray, Canada 71 C8 53 36N 101 24W
Westray, U.K. 11 B5 59 18N 3 0W
Westree, Canada 72 C3 47 26N 81 34W
Westville, U.S.A. 78 F6 39 8N 120 42W
Westwood, U.S.A. 76 F3 40 18N 121 0W
Wetar, Indonesia ...... 37 F7 7 48S 126 30 E
Wetaskiwin, Canada 70 C6 52 55N 113 24W
Wete, Tanzania ...... 52 F7 5 4S 39 43 E
Wetherby, U.K. 12 D6 53 56N 1 23W
Wethersfield, U.S.A. 85 E12 41 42N 72 40W
Wetteren, Belgium ...... 15 D3 51 0N 3 53 E
Wetzlar, Germany ...... 16 C5 50 32N 8 31 E
Wewoka, U.S.A. 81 H6 35 9N 96 30W
Wexford, Ireland 10 D5 52 20N 6 28W
Wexford □, Ireland 10 D5 52 20N 6 25W
Wexford Harbour, Ireland 10 D5 52 20N 6 25W
Weyburn, Canada 71 D8 49 40N 103 50W
Weymouth, Canada 73 D6 44 30N 66 1W
Weymouth, U.K. 13 G5 50 37N 2 28W
Weymouth, U.S.A. 85 D14 42 13N 70 58W
Weymouth, C., Australia .... 62 A3 12 37S 143 27 E
Wha Ti, Canada 68 B8 63 8N 117 16W
Whakatane, N.Z. ...... 59 G6 37 57S 177 1 E
Whale ➤, Canada 73 A6 58 15N 67 40W
Whale Cove, Canada 71 A10 62 10N 92 34W
Whales, B. of, Antarctica 5 D12 78 0S 165 0W
Whalsay, U.K. 11 A8 60 22N 0 59W
Whangamomona, N.Z. ...... 59 H5 39 8S 174 44 E
Whanganui △, N.Z. ...... 59 H5 39 17S 174 53 E
Whangarei, N.Z. ...... 59 F5 35 43S 174 21 E
Whangarei Harb., N.Z. .... 59 F5 35 45S 174 28 E
Wharfe ➤, U.K. 12 D6 53 51N 1 9W
Wharfedale, U.K. 12 C5 54 6N 2 1W
Wharton, N.J., U.S.A. 85 F10 40 54N 74 35W
Wharton, Pa., U.S.A. 84 E6 41 31N 78 1W
Wharton, Tex., U.S.A. 81 L6 29 9N 96 6W
Wheatland, Calif., U.S.A. 78 F5 39 1N 121 25W
Wheatland, Wyo., U.S.A. 80 D2 42 3N 104 58W
Wheatley, Canada 84 D2 42 6N 82 27W
Wheaton, Md., U.S.A. 82 F7 39 3N 77 3W
Wheaton, Minn., U.S.A. 80 C6 45 48N 96 30W
Wheelbarrow Pk., U.S.A. 78 H10 37 26N 116 5W
Wheeler, Oreg., U.S.A. 76 D2 45 41N 123 53W
Wheeler, Tex., U.S.A. 81 H4 35 27N 100 16W
Wheeler ➤, Canada 73 A6 57 2N 67 13W
Wheeler L., U.S.A. 83 H2 34 48N 87 23W

Wheeler Pk., N. Mex., U.S.A. ... 77 H11 36 34N 105 25W
Wheeler Pk., Nev., U.S.A. ... 77 G6 38 57N 114 15W
Wheeler Ridge, U.S.A. 79 L8 35 0N 118 57W
Wheeling, U.S.A. 84 F4 40 4N 80 43W
Whernside, U.K. 12 C5 54 14N 2 24W
Whiskey Jack L., Canada 71 B8 58 23N 101 55W
Whiskeytown-Shasta-Trinity ⌓,
   U.S.A. 76 F2 40 45N 122 15W
Whistleduck Cr. ➤, Australia . 62 C2 20 15S 135 18 E
Whistler, Canada 70 C4 50 7N 122 58W
Whitby, Canada 84 C6 43 52N 78 56W
Whitby, U.K. 12 C7 54 29N 0 37W
White ➤, Ark., U.S.A. 81 J9 33 57N 91 5W
White ➤, Ind., U.S.A. 82 F2 38 25N 87 45W
White ➤, S. Dak., U.S.A. 80 D5 43 42N 99 27W
White ➤, Tex., U.S.A. 81 J4 33 14N 100 56W
White ➤, Utah, U.S.A. 76 F9 40 4N 109 41W
White ➤, Vt., U.S.A. 85 C12 43 37N 72 20W
White ➤, Wash., U.S.A. 78 C4 47 12N 122 15W
White, L., Australia ...... 60 D4 21 9S 128 56 E
White B., Canada 73 C8 50 0N 56 35W
White Bird, U.S.A. 76 D5 45 46N 116 18W
White Butte, U.S.A. 80 B3 46 23N 103 18W
White City, U.S.A. 76 E2 42 26N 122 51W
White Cliffs, Australia .... 63 E3 30 50S 143 10 E
White Hall, U.S.A. 80 F9 39 26N 90 24W
White Haven, U.S.A. 85 E9 41 4N 75 47W
White Horse, Vale of, U.K. .. 13 F6 51 37N 1 30W
White I., N.Z. ...... 59 G6 37 30S 177 13 E
White L., Canada 85 A8 45 18N 76 31W
White L., U.S.A. 81 L8 29 44N 92 30W
White Mountain Peak, U.S.A. .. 77 G4 37 38N 118 15W
White Mts., Calif., U.S.A. 78 H8 37 30N 118 15W
White Mts., N.H., U.S.A. 85 B13 44 15N 71 15W
White Mts. △, Australia .... 62 C4 20 43S 145 12 E
White Nile = Nîl el Abyad ➤,
   Sudan .... 51 E12 15 38N 32 31 E
White Otter L., Canada 72 C1 49 5N 91 55W
White Pass, Canada 78 D5 46 38N 121 24W
White Plains, U.S.A. 85 E11 41 2N 73 46W
White River, Canada 72 C2 48 35N 85 20W
White River, S. Africa .... 57 D5 25 20S 31 0 E
White River, U.S.A. 80 D4 43 34N 100 45W
White Rock, Canada 78 A4 49 2N 122 48W
White Russia = Belarus ■,
   Europe .... 17 B14 53 30N 27 0 E
White Sands △, U.S.A. 77 K10 32 46N 106 20W
White Sea = Beloye More, Russia 18 A6 66 30N 38 0 E
White Sulphur Springs, Mont.,
   U.S.A. 76 C8 46 33N 110 54W
White Sulphur Springs, W. Va.,
   U.S.A. 82 G5 37 48N 80 18W
White Swan, U.S.A. 78 D6 46 23N 120 44W
Whitecliffs, N.Z. ...... 59 K3 43 26S 171 55 E
Whitecourt, Canada 70 C5 54 10N 115 45W
Whiteface Mt., U.S.A. 85 B11 44 22N 73 54W
Whitefield, U.S.A. 85 B13 44 23N 71 37W
Whitefish, U.S.A. 76 B6 48 25N 114 20W
Whitefish L., Canada 71 A7 62 41N 106 48W
Whitefish Point, U.S.A. 82 B3 46 45N 84 59W
Whitegull, L. = Goélands, L. aux,
   Canada 73 A7 55 27N 64 17W
Whitehall, Mich., U.S.A. 82 D2 43 24N 86 21W
Whitehall, Mont., U.S.A. 76 D7 45 52N 112 6W
Whitehall, N.Y., U.S.A. 85 C11 43 33N 73 24W
Whitehall, Wis., U.S.A. 80 C9 44 22N 91 19W
Whitehaven, U.K. 12 C4 54 33N 3 35W
Whitehorse, Canada 70 A1 60 43N 135 3W
Whitemark, Australia ...... 63 G4 40 7S 148 3 E
Whiteriver, U.S.A. 77 K9 33 50N 109 58W
Whitesand ➤, Canada 70 A5 60 9N 115 45W
Whitesands, S. Africa .... 56 E3 34 23S 20 50 E
Whitesboro, N.Y., U.S.A. 85 C9 43 7N 75 18W
Whitesboro, Tex., U.S.A. 81 J6 33 39N 96 54W
Whiteshell ⌓, Canada 71 D9 50 0N 95 40W
Whitesville, U.S.A. 84 D7 42 2N 77 46W
Whiteville, U.S.A. 83 H6 34 20N 78 42W
Whitewater, U.S.A. 82 D1 42 50N 88 44W
Whitewater Baldy, U.S.A. 77 K9 33 20N 108 39W
Whitewater L., Canada 72 B2 50 50N 89 10W
Whitewood, Australia ...... 62 C3 21 28S 143 30 E
Whitewood, Canada 71 C8 50 20N 102 20W
Whithorn, U.K. 11 G4 54 44N 4 26W
Whitianga, N.Z. ...... 59 G5 36 47S 175 41 E
Whitman, U.S.A. 85 D14 42 5N 70 56W
Whitney, Canada 84 A6 45 31N 78 14W
Whitney, Mt., U.S.A. 78 J8 36 35N 118 18W
Whitney Point, U.S.A. 85 D9 42 20N 75 58W
Whitstable, U.K. ...... 13 F9 51 21N 1 3 E
Whitsunday I., Australia .... 62 J7 20 15S 149 4 E
Whitsunday Islands △, Australia 62 J7 20 15S 149 0 E
Whitsunday Passage, Australia . 62 J6 20 16S 148 51 E
Whittier, U.S.A. 79 M8 33 58N 118 3W
Whittlesea, Australia ...... 63 F4 37 27S 145 9 E
Wholdaia L., Canada 71 A8 60 43N 104 20W
Whyalla, Australia ...... 63 E2 33 2S 137 30 E
Wiang Kosai △, Thailand .... 38 D2 17 54N 99 29 E
Wiarton, Canada 84 B3 44 40N 81 10W
Wiay, U.K. 11 D1 57 24N 7 13W
Wibaux, U.S.A. 80 B2 46 59N 104 11W
Wichian Buri, Thailand .... 38 E3 15 39N 101 7 E
Wichita, U.S.A. 81 G6 37 42N 97 20W
Wichita Falls, U.S.A. 81 J5 33 54N 98 30W
Wick, U.K. 11 C5 58 26N 3 5W
Wicked Pt., Canada 84 C7 43 52N 77 15W
Wickenburg, U.S.A. 77 K7 33 58N 112 44W
Wickepin, Australia ...... 61 F2 32 50S 117 30 E
Wickham, Australia ...... 60 D2 20 42S 117 11 E
Wickham, C., Australia .... 63 F3 39 35S 143 57 E
Wicklewood, Australia 84 E3 41 36N 81 28W
Wicklow, Ireland 10 D5 52 59N 6 3W
Wicklow □, Ireland 10 D5 52 57N 6 25W
Wicklow Hd., Ireland 10 D6 52 58N 6 0W
Wicklow Mts., Ireland 10 C5 52 58N 6 26W
Wicklow Mts. △, Ireland 10 C5 53 6N 6 21W
Widgiegoara Cr. ➤, Australia . 63 D4 28 51S 146 8 E
Widgiemooltha, Australia .... 61 F3 31 30S 121 34 E
Widnes, U.K. 12 D5 53 23N 2 45W
Wieluń, Poland ...... 17 C10 51 15N 18 34 E
Wien, Austria ...... 16 D9 48 12N 16 22 E
Wiener Neustadt, Austria .... 16 E9 47 49N 16 16 E
Wiesbaden, Germany ...... 16 C5 50 4N 8 14 E
Wigan, U.K. 12 D5 53 33N 2 38W
Wiggins, Colo., U.S.A. 80 E2 40 14N 104 4W
Wiggins, Miss., U.S.A. 81 K10 30 51N 89 8W
Wight, I. of □, U.K. 13 G6 50 40N 1 20W
Wigston, U.K. 13 E6 52 35N 1 6W
Wigton, U.K. 12 C4 54 50N 3 10W

Wigtown, U.K. 11 G4 54 53N 4 27W
Wigtown B., U.K. 11 G4 54 46N 4 15W
Wilber, U.S.A. 80 E6 40 29N 96 58W
Wilberforce, Canada 84 A6 45 2N 78 13W
Wilberforce, C., Australia .... 62 A2 11 54S 136 35 E
Wilburton, U.S.A. 81 H7 34 55N 95 19W
Wilcannia, Australia ...... 63 E3 31 30S 143 26 E
Wilcox, U.S.A. 84 E6 41 35N 78 41W
Wildrose, U.S.A. 79 J9 36 14N 117 11W
Wildspitze, Austria ...... 16 E6 46 53N 10 53 E
Wilge ➤, S. Africa ...... 57 D4 27 3S 28 20 E
Wilhelm II Coast, Antarctica .. 5 C7 68 0S 90 0 E
Wilhelmshaven, Germany .... 16 B5 53 31N 8 7 E
Wilhelmstal, Namibia ...... 56 C2 21 58S 16 21 E
Wilkes-Barre, U.S.A. 85 E9 41 15N 75 53W
Wilkie, Canada 71 C7 52 27N 108 42W
Wilkinsburg, U.S.A. 84 F5 40 26N 79 53W
Wilkinson Lakes, Australia .. 61 E5 29 40S 132 39 E
Willandra Creek ➤, Australia . 63 E4 33 22S 145 52 E
Willapa B., U.S.A. 76 C2 46 40N 124 0W
Willapa Hills, U.S.A. 78 D3 46 35N 123 25W
Willard, N.Y., U.S.A. 84 D8 42 40N 76 50W
Willard, Ohio, U.S.A. 84 E2 41 3N 82 44W
Willcox, U.S.A. 77 K9 32 15N 109 50W
Willemstad, Neth. Ant. 89 D6 12 5N 69 0W
Willet, U.S.A. 85 D9 42 28N 75 55W
William ➤, Canada 71 B7 59 8N 109 19W
William 'Bill' Dannely Res.,
   U.S.A. 83 J2 32 10N 87 10W
William Creek, Australia .... 63 D2 28 58S 136 22 E
Williams, Australia ...... 61 F2 33 2S 116 52 E
Williams, Ariz., U.S.A. 77 J7 35 15N 112 11W
Williams, Calif., U.S.A. 78 F4 39 9N 122 9W
Williams Harbour, Canada .. 73 B8 52 33N 55 47W
Williams Lake, Canada 70 C4 52 10N 122 10W
Williamsburg, Ky., U.S.A. .. 83 G3 36 44N 84 10W
Williamsburg, Pa., U.S.A. .. 84 F6 40 28N 78 12W
Williamsburg, Va., U.S.A. .. 82 G7 37 17N 76 44W
Williamson, N.Y., U.S.A. .. 84 C7 43 14N 77 11W
Williamson, W. Va., U.S.A. .. 82 G4 37 41N 82 17W
Williamsport, U.S.A. 84 E7 41 15N 77 0W
Williamston, U.S.A. 83 H7 35 51N 77 4W
Williamstown, Australia .... 63 F3 37 51S 144 52 E
Williamstown, Ky., U.S.A. .. 82 F3 38 38N 84 34W
Williamstown, Mass., U.S.A. . 85 D11 42 41N 73 12W
Williamstown, N.Y., U.S.A. . 85 C9 43 26N 75 53W
Willimantic, U.S.A. 85 E12 41 43N 72 13W
Willingboro, U.S.A. 82 E8 40 3N 74 54W
Williston, S. Africa ...... 56 E3 31 20S 20 53 E
Williston, Fla., U.S.A. 83 L4 29 23N 82 27W
Williston, N. Dak., U.S.A. .. 80 A3 48 9N 103 37W
Williston L., Canada 70 B4 56 0N 124 0W
Willits, U.S.A. 76 G2 39 25N 123 21W
Willmar, U.S.A. 80 C7 45 7N 95 3W
Willmore Wilderness ⌓, Canada 70 C5 53 45N 119 30W
Willoughby, U.S.A. 84 E3 41 39N 81 24W
Willow Bunch, Canada 71 D7 49 20N 105 35W
Willow L., Canada 70 A5 62 10N 119 8W
Willow Wall, The, China .... 35 C12 42 10N 122 0 E
Willowick, U.S.A. 84 E3 41 38N 81 28W
Willowlake ➤, Canada 70 A4 62 42N 123 8W
Willowmore, S. Africa .... 56 E3 33 15S 23 30 E
Willows, U.S.A. 78 F4 39 31N 122 12W
Willowvale = Gatyana, S. Africa 57 E4 32 16S 28 31 E
Wills, L., Australia ...... 60 D4 21 25S 128 51 E
Wills Cr. ➤, Australia .... 62 C3 22 43S 140 2 E
Willsboro, U.S.A. 85 B11 44 21N 73 24W
Willunga, Australia ...... 63 F2 35 15S 138 30 E
Wilmette, U.S.A. 82 D2 42 5N 87 42W
Wilmington, Australia .... 63 E2 32 39S 138 7 E
Wilmington, Del., U.S.A. .. 82 F8 39 45N 75 33W
Wilmington, N.C., U.S.A. .. 83 H7 34 14N 77 55W
Wilmington, Ohio, U.S.A. .. 82 F4 39 27N 83 50W
Wilmington, Vt., U.S.A. 85 D12 42 52N 72 52W
Wilmslow, U.K. 12 D5 53 19N 2 13W
Wilpena Cr. ➤, Australia .... 63 E2 31 25S 139 29 E
Wilsall, U.S.A. 76 D8 45 59N 110 38W
Wilson, N.C., U.S.A. 83 H7 35 44N 77 55W
Wilson, N.Y., U.S.A. 84 C6 43 19N 78 50W
Wilson, Pa., U.S.A. 85 F9 40 41N 75 15W
Wilson ➤, Australia ...... 60 C4 16 48S 128 16 E
Wilson Bluff, Australia .... 61 F4 31 41S 129 0 E
Wilson Inlet, Australia .... 61 G2 35 0S 117 22 E
Wilsons Promontory, Australia . 63 F4 38 55S 146 25 E
Wilton, U.S.A. 80 B4 47 10N 100 47W
Wilton ➤, Australia ...... 62 A1 14 45S 134 33 E
Wiltshire □, U.K. 13 F6 51 18N 1 53W
Wiltz, Lux. ...... 15 E5 49 57N 5 55 E
Wiluna, Australia ...... 61 E3 26 36S 120 14 E
Wimborne Minster, U.K. .. 13 G6 50 48N 1 59W
Wimmera ➤, Australia .... 63 F3 36 8S 141 56 E
Winam G., Kenya ...... 54 C3 0 20S 34 15 E
Winburg, S. Africa ...... 56 D4 28 30S 27 2 E
Winchendon, U.S.A. 85 D12 42 41N 72 3W
Winchester, U.K. 13 F6 51 4N 1 18W
Winchester, Conn., U.S.A. .. 85 E11 41 53N 73 9W
Winchester, Idaho, U.S.A. .. 76 C5 46 14N 116 38W
Winchester, Ind., U.S.A. .. 82 E3 40 10N 84 59W
Winchester, Ky., U.S.A. .. 82 G3 38 0N 84 11W
Winchester, N.H., U.S.A. .. 85 D12 42 46N 72 23W
Winchester, Nev., U.S.A. .. 79 J11 36 6N 115 10W
Winchester, Tenn., U.S.A. .. 83 H2 35 1N 86 7W
Winchester, Va., U.S.A. .. 82 F6 39 11N 78 10W
Wind ➤, U.S.A. 76 E9 43 12N 108 12W
Wind Cave ⌓, U.S.A. 80 D3 43 32N 103 17W
Wind River Range, U.S.A. .. 76 E9 43 0N 109 30W
Windau = Ventspils, Latvia .. 9 H19 57 25N 21 32 E
Windber, U.S.A. 84 F6 40 14N 78 50W
Winder, U.S.A. 83 J4 34 0N 83 45W
Windermere, U.K. 12 C5 54 23N 2 55W
Windhoek, Namibia ...... 56 C2 22 35S 17 4 E
Windom, U.S.A. 80 D7 43 52N 95 7W
Windorah, Australia ...... 62 D3 25 24S 142 36 E
Window Rock, U.S.A. 77 J9 35 41N 109 3W
Windrush ➤, U.K. 13 F6 51 43N 1 24W
Windsor, Australia ...... 63 E5 33 37S 150 50 E
Windsor, N.S., Canada 73 D7 44 59N 64 5W
Windsor, Ont., Canada 84 D2 42 18N 83 0W
Windsor, U.K. 13 F7 51 29N 0 36W
Windsor, Colo., U.S.A. 80 E2 40 29N 104 54W
Windsor, Conn., U.S.A. 85 E12 41 50N 72 39W
Windsor, Mo., U.S.A. 80 F8 38 32N 93 31W
Windsor, N.Y., U.S.A. 85 D9 42 5N 75 37W
Windsor, Vt., U.S.A. 85 C12 43 29N 72 24W
Windsor & Maidenhead □, U.K. 13 F7 51 29N 0 40W
Windsorton, S. Africa .... 56 D3 28 16S 24 44 E
Windward Is., W. Indies 89 D7 13 0N 61 0W

Windward Passage = Vientos,
   Paso de los, Caribbean 89 C5 20 0N 74 0W
Winefred L., Canada 71 B6 55 30N 110 30W
Winfield, U.S.A. 81 G6 37 15N 96 59W
Wingate Mts., Australia .... 60 B5 14 25S 130 40 E
Wingham, Australia ...... 63 E5 31 48S 152 22 E
Wingham, Canada 84 C3 43 55N 81 20W
Winisk, Canada 72 A2 55 20N 85 15W
Winisk ➤, Canada 72 A2 55 17N 85 5W
Winisk L., Canada 72 B2 52 55N 87 22W
Wink, U.S.A. 81 K3 31 45N 103 9W
Winkler, Canada 71 D9 49 10N 97 56W
Winlock, U.S.A. 78 D4 46 30N 122 56W
Winnebago, L., U.S.A. 82 D1 44 0N 88 26W
Winnecke Cr. ➤, Australia .. 60 C5 18 35S 131 34 E
Winnemucca, U.S.A. 76 F5 40 58N 117 44W
Winnemucca L., U.S.A. 76 F4 40 7N 119 21W
Winnett, U.S.A. 76 C9 47 0N 108 21W
Winnfield, U.S.A. 81 K8 31 56N 92 38W
Winnibigoshish, L., U.S.A. .. 80 B7 47 27N 94 13W
Winnipeg, Canada 71 D9 49 54N 97 9W
Winnipeg ➤, Canada 71 C9 50 38N 96 19W
Winnipeg, L., Canada 71 C9 52 0N 97 0W
Winnipeg Beach, Canada .. 71 C9 50 30N 96 58W
Winnipegosis, Canada 71 C9 51 39N 99 55W
Winnipegosis L., Canada .. 71 C9 52 30N 100 0W
Winnipesaukee, L., U.S.A. .. 85 C13 43 38N 71 21W
Winnsboro, La., U.S.A. 81 J9 32 10N 91 43W
Winnsboro, S.C., U.S.A. .. 83 H5 34 23N 81 5W
Winnsboro, Tex., U.S.A. .. 81 J7 32 58N 95 17W
Winokapau, L., Canada 73 B7 53 15N 62 50W
Winona, Minn., U.S.A. 80 C9 44 3N 91 39W
Winona, Miss., U.S.A. 81 J10 33 29N 89 44W
Winooski, U.S.A. 85 B11 44 29N 73 11W
Winooski ➤, U.S.A. 85 B11 44 32N 73 17W
Winschoten, Neths. ...... 15 A7 53 9N 7 3 E
Winsford, U.K. 12 D5 53 12N 2 31W
Winslow, Ariz., U.S.A. 77 J8 35 2N 110 42W
Winslow, Wash., U.S.A. .. 78 C4 47 38N 122 31W
Winsted, U.S.A. 85 E11 41 55N 73 4W
Winston-Salem, U.S.A. 83 G5 36 6N 80 15W
Winter Garden, U.S.A. 83 L5 28 34N 81 35W
Winter Haven, U.S.A. 83 M5 28 1N 81 44W
Winter Park, U.S.A. 83 L5 28 36N 81 20W
Winterhaven, U.S.A. 79 N12 32 47N 114 39W
Winters, U.S.A. 78 G5 38 32N 121 58W
Wintersville, U.S.A. 84 F4 40 23N 80 42W
Winterswijk, Neths. ...... 15 C6 51 58N 6 43 E
Winterthur, Switz. ...... 20 C8 47 30N 8 44 E
Winthrop, U.S.A. 76 B3 48 28N 120 10W
Winton, Australia ...... 62 C3 22 24S 143 3 E
Winton, N.Z. ...... 59 M2 46 8S 168 20 E
Wirrulla, Australia ...... 63 E1 32 24S 134 31 E
Wisbech, U.K. ...... 13 E8 52 41N 0 9 E
Wisconsin □, U.S.A. 80 C10 44 45N 89 30W
Wisconsin ➤, U.S.A. 80 D9 43 0N 91 15W
Wisconsin Rapids, U.S.A. .. 80 C10 44 23N 89 49W
Wisdom, U.S.A. 76 D7 45 37N 113 27W
Wishaw, U.K. 11 F5 55 46N 3 54W
Wishek, U.S.A. 80 B5 46 16N 99 33W
Wisła ➤, Poland ...... 17 A10 54 22N 18 55 E
Wismar, Germany ...... 16 B6 53 54N 11 29 E
Wisner, U.S.A. 80 E6 41 59N 96 55W
Witbank, S. Africa ...... 57 D4 25 51S 29 14 E
Witdraai, S. Africa ...... 56 D3 26 58S 20 48 E
Witham, U.K. ...... 13 F8 51 48N 0 40 E
Witham ➤, U.K. 12 E7 52 59N 0 2W
Withernsea, U.K. ...... 12 D8 53 44N 0 1 E
Witjira △, Australia ...... 63 D2 26 22S 135 37 E
Witney, U.K. 13 F6 51 48N 1 28W
Witnossob ➤, Namibia .... 56 D3 23 55S 18 45 E
Wittenberge, Germany .... 16 B6 53 0N 11 45 E
Wittenoom, Australia .... 60 D2 22 15S 118 20 E
Witvlei, Namibia ...... 56 C2 22 23S 18 32 E
Wkra ➤, Poland ...... 17 B11 52 27N 20 44 E
Wlingi, Indonesia ...... 37 H15 8 5S 112 25 E
Włocławek, Poland ...... 17 B10 52 40N 19 3 E
Włodawa, Poland ...... 17 C12 51 33N 23 31 E
Woburn, U.S.A. 85 D13 42 29N 71 9W
Wodian, China ...... 34 H7 32 50N 112 35 E
Wodonga = Albury-Wodonga,
   Australia .... 63 F4 36 3S 146 56 E
Wokam, Indonesia ...... 37 F8 5 45S 134 28 E
Woking, U.K. 13 F7 51 19N 0 34W
Wokingham, U.K. 13 F7 51 24N 0 49W
Wokingham □, U.K. 13 F7 51 25N 0 51W
Wolf ➤, Canada 70 A2 60 17N 132 33W
Wolf Creek, U.S.A. 76 C7 47 0N 112 4W
Wolf L., Canada 70 A2 60 24N 131 40W
Wolf Point, U.S.A. 80 A2 48 5N 105 39W
Wolfe I., Canada 85 B8 44 7N 76 20W
Wolfeboro, U.S.A. 85 C13 43 35N 71 13W
Wolfsberg, Austria ...... 16 E8 46 50N 14 52 E
Wolfsburg, Germany ...... 16 B6 52 25N 10 48 E
Wolin, Poland ...... 16 B8 53 50N 14 37 E
Wollaston, Is., Chile 96 H3 55 40S 67 30W
Wollaston L., Canada 71 B8 58 7N 103 10W
Wollaston Lake, Canada .. 71 B8 58 3N 103 33W
Wollaston Pen., Canada .. 68 B8 69 30N 115 0W
Wollongong, Australia .... 63 E5 34 25S 150 54 E
Wolmaransstad, S. Africa .. 56 D4 27 12S 25 59 E
Wolseley, S. Africa ...... 56 E2 33 26S 19 7 E
Wolsey, U.S.A. 80 C5 44 24N 98 28W
Wolstenholme, C., Canada .. 66 C12 62 35N 77 30W
Wolvega, Neths. ...... 15 B6 52 52N 6 0 E
Wolverhampton, U.K. 13 E5 52 35N 2 7W
Wondai, Australia ...... 63 D5 26 20S 151 49 E
Wongalarroo L., Australia .. 63 E3 31 32S 144 0 E
Wongan Hills, Australia .. 61 F2 30 51S 116 37 E
Wŏnju, S. Korea ...... 35 F14 37 22N 127 58 E
Wonosari, Indonesia ...... 37 G14 7 58S 110 36 E
Wonosobo, Indonesia .... 37 G13 7 22S 109 54 E
Wonowon, Canada 70 B4 56 44N 121 48W
Wŏnsan, N. Korea ...... 35 E14 39 11N 127 27 E
Wonthaggi, Australia .... 63 F4 38 37S 145 37 E
Wood Buffalo △, Canada .. 70 B6 59 0N 113 41W
Wood Is., Australia ...... 60 C3 16 24S 123 19 E
Wood L., Canada 71 B8 55 17N 103 17W
Woodah, I., Australia .... 62 A2 13 27S 136 10 E
Woodbourne, U.S.A. 85 E10 41 46N 74 36W
Woodbridge, Canada 84 C5 43 47N 79 36W
Woodbridge, U.K. ...... 13 E9 52 6N 1 20 E
Woodburn, U.S.A. 76 D2 45 9N 122 51W
Woodenbong, Australia .. 63 D5 28 24S 152 39 E
Woodend, Australia ...... 63 F3 37 20S 144 33 E
Woodford, Australia ...... 63 D5 26 58S 152 47 E
Woodfords, U.S.A. 78 G7 38 47N 119 50W

odlake, U.S.A. 78 J7 36 25N 119 6W
odroffe, Calif., U.S.A. 78 G5 38 41N 121 46W
odland, Maine, U.S.A. 83 C12 45 9N 67 25W
odland, Pa., U.S.A. 84 F6 40 59N 78 21W
odland, Wash., U.S.A. 78 E4 45 54N 122 45W
odland Caribou △, Canada 71 C10 51 0N 94 45W
odlands, Singapore 39 d 1 27N 103 47 E
odridge, Mt., Australia 61 E5 26 20S 131 45 E
ods, L. of the, Canada 71 D10 49 15N 94 45W
odstock, Australia 62 B4 19 35S 146 50 E
odstock, N.B., Canada 73 C6 46 11N 67 37W
odstock, Ont., Canada 84 C4 43 10N 80 45W
odstock, U.K. 13 F6 51 51N 1 20W
odstock, Vt., U.S.A. 85 C12 43 37N 72 31W
odsville, U.S.A. 85 B13 44 9N 72 2W
odville, N.Z. 59 J5 40 20S 175 53 E
odville, Miss., U.S.A. 81 K9 31 6N 91 18W
odville, Tex., U.S.A. 81 K7 30 47N 94 25W
odward, U.S.A. 81 G5 36 26N 99 24W
ody, U.S.A. 79 K8 35 42N 118 50W
ody →, Canada 71 C8 52 31N 100 51W
olacombe, U.K. 13 F3 51 10N 4 13W
olamai, C., Australia 63 F4 38 30S 145 23 E
ooler, U.S.A. 12 B5 55 33N 2 1W
oolgoolga, Australia 63 E5 30 6S 153 11 E
oomera, Australia 63 E2 31 5S 136 50 E
oonsocket, R.I., U.S.A. 85 E13 42 0N 71 31W
oonsocket, S. Dak., U.S.A. 80 C5 44 3N 98 17W
ooramel, Australia 61 E1 25 47S 114 10 E
ooramel Roadhouse, Australia 61 E1 25 45S 114 17 E
ooster, U.S.A. 84 F3 40 48N 81 56W
orcester, S. Africa 56 E2 33 39S 19 27 E
orcester, U.K. 13 E5 52 11N 2 12W
orcester, Mass., U.S.A. 85 D13 42 16N 71 48W
orcester, N.Y., U.S.A. 85 D10 42 36N 74 45W
orcestershire □, U.K. 13 E5 52 13N 2 10W
orkington, U.K. 12 C4 54 39N 3 33W
orksop, U.K. 12 D6 53 18N 1 7W
orkum, Neths. 15 B5 52 59N 5 26 E
orland, U.S.A. 76 D10 44 1N 107 57W
orms, Germany 16 D5 49 37N 8 21 E
orsley, Canada 70 B5 56 31N 119 8W
ortham, U.S.A. 81 K6 31 47N 96 28W
orthing, Barbados 89 g 13 5N 59 35W
orthing, U.K. 13 G7 50 49N 0 21W
orthington, Minn., U.S.A. 80 D7 43 37N 95 36W
orthington, Pa., U.S.A. 84 F5 40 50N 79 38W
osi, Indonesia 37 E7 0 15S 128 0 E
ou-han = Wuhan, China 33 C6 30 31N 114 18 E
ousi = Wuxi, China 33 C7 31 33N 120 18 E
owoni, Indonesia 37 E6 4 5S 123 5 E
rangel I. = Vrangelya, Ostrov,
Russia 29 B19 71 0N 180 0 E
rangell, U.S.A. 70 B2 56 28N 132 23W
rangell Mts., U.S.A. 68 B5 61 30N 142 0W
rath, C., U.K. 11 C3 58 38N 5 1W
ray, U.S.A. 80 E3 40 5N 102 13W
rekin, The, U.K. 13 E5 52 41N 2 32W
rens, U.S.A. 83 J4 33 12N 82 23W
rexham, U.K. 12 D4 53 3N 3 0W
rexham □, U.K. 12 D5 53 1N 2 58W
right, U.S.A. 80 D2 43 47N 105 30W
rightson, Mt., U.S.A. 77 L8 31 42N 110 51W
rightwood, U.S.A. 79 L9 34 21N 117 38W
rigley, Canada 68 B7 63 16N 123 37W
rocław, Poland 17 C9 51 5N 17 5 E
rześnia, Poland 17 B9 52 21N 17 36 E
u Jiang →, China 32 D5 29 40N 107 20 E
u Kau Tang, China 33 F11 22 30N 114 14 E
u'an, China 34 F8 36 40N 114 15 E
ubin, Australia 61 F2 30 6S 116 37 E
ubu, China 34 F6 37 28N 110 42 E
uchang, China 34 F9 37 12N 116 20 E
uchuan, China 34 D6 41 5N 111 28 E
udi, China 35 F9 37 40N 117 35 E
uding He →, China 34 F6 37 2N 110 23 E
udinna, Australia 63 E2 33 0S 135 22 E
udu, China 34 H3 33 22N 104 54 E
uguishan, China 33 G9 22 25N 113 25 E
uhan, China 33 C6 30 31N 114 18 E
uhe, China 35 H9 33 10N 117 50 E
uhsi = Wuxi, China 33 C7 31 33N 120 18 E
uhu, China 33 C6 31 22N 118 21 E
ukari, Nigeria 50 G7 7 51N 9 42 E
ulajie, China 35 B14 46 5N 126 33 E
ulanbulang, China 34 D6 41 5N 110 55 E
ular L., India 43 B6 34 20N 74 30 E
ulian, China 35 G10 35 40N 119 12 E
uliaru, Indonesia 37 F8 7 27S 131 0 E
uluk'omushih Ling, China 32 C3 36 25N 87 25 E
ulumuchi = Ürümqi, China 28 E9 43 45N 87 45 E
undowie, Australia 61 F2 31 47S 116 23 E
untho, Burma 41 H19 23 55N 95 45 E
upatki △, U.S.A. 77 J8 35 35N 111 20W
uppertal, Germany 16 C4 51 16N 7 12 E
uppertal, S. Africa 56 E2 32 13S 19 12 E
uqing, China 35 E9 39 23N 117 4 E
urtsboro, U.S.A. 85 E10 41 35N 74 29W
ürzburg, Germany 16 D5 49 46N 9 55 E
ushan, China 34 G3 34 43N 104 53 E
usuli Jiang = Ussuri →, Asia 30 A7 48 27N 135 0 E
utai, China 34 E7 38 40N 113 12 E
uting = Huimin, China 35 F9 37 27N 117 28 E
utonghaolai, China 35 C11 42 50N 120 5 E
utongqiao, China 32 D5 29 22N 103 50 E
uwei, China 32 C5 37 57N 102 34 E
uxi, China 33 C7 31 33N 120 18 E
uxuan, China 34 F7 36 49N 112 50 E
uyang, China 34 H7 33 25N 113 35 E
uyi, China 34 F8 37 46N 115 56 E
uyi Shan, China 33 D6 27 0N 117 0 E
uyuan, China 34 D5 38 54N 111 48 E
uzhai, China 34 E6 38 54N 111 48 E
uzhi Shan, China 38 C7 18 45N 109 45 E
uzhong, China 34 E4 38 2N 106 12 E
uzhou, China 33 D6 23 30N 111 18 E
yaaba Cr. →, Australia 62 B3 16 27S 141 35 E
yalkatchem, Australia 61 F2 31 8S 117 22 E
yalusing, U.S.A. 85 E8 41 40N 76 16W
yandotte, U.S.A. 82 D4 42 12N 83 9W
yandra, Australia 63 D4 27 12S 145 56 E
yangala, L., Australia 63 E4 33 54S 149 0 E

yara, L., Australia 63 D3 28 42S 144 14 E
ycheproof, Australia 63 F3 36 5S 143 17 E
ye →, U.K. 13 F5 51 38N 2 40W
yemandoo, Australia 61 E2 28 28S 118 29 E
ymondham, U.K. 13 E9 52 35N 1 7 E
ymore, U.S.A. 80 E6 40 7N 96 40W
yndham, Australia 60 C4 15 33S 128 3 E
yndham, N.Z. 59 M2 46 20S 168 51 E
ynne, U.S.A. 81 H9 35 14N 90 47W
ynyard, Australia 63 G4 41 5S 145 44 E
ynyard, Canada 71 C8 51 45N 104 10W
yola L., Australia 61 E5 29 8S 130 17 E
yoming = Plympton-Wyoming,
Canada 84 D2 42 57N 82 7W
yoming □, U.S.A. 76 E10 43 0N 107 30W
yomissing, U.S.A. 85 F9 40 20N 75 59W
yong, Australia 63 E5 33 14S 151 24 E
ytheville, U.S.A. 82 G5 36 57N 81 5W

X

Xaafuun, Somali Rep. 47 E5 10 25N 51 16 E
Xaçmaz, Azerbaijan 19 F8 41 31N 48 42 E
Xai-Xai, Mozam. 57 D5 25 6S 33 31 E
Xainza, China 32 C3 30 58N 88 35 E
Xalapa, Mexico 87 D5 19 32N 96 55W
Xangongo, Angola 56 B2 16 45S 15 5 E
Xankändi, Azerbaijan 19 G8 39 52N 46 49 E
Xánthi, Greece 23 D11 41 10N 24 58 E
Xanxerê, Brazil 95 B5 26 53S 52 23W
Xapuri, Brazil 92 F5 10 35S 68 35W
Xar Moron He →, China 35 C11 43 25N 120 35 E
Xátiva, Spain 21 C5 38 59N 0 32W
Xau, L., Botswana 56 C3 21 15S 24 44 E
Xavantina, Brazil 95 A5 21 15S 52 48W
Xenia, U.S.A. 82 F4 39 41N 83 56W
Xeropotamos →, Cyprus 25 E11 34 42N 32 33 E
Xhora, S. Africa 57 E4 31 55S 28 38 E
Xhumo, Botswana 56 C3 21 7S 24 35 E
Xi Jiang →, China 33 D6 22 5N 113 20 E
Xi Xian, China 34 F6 36 41N 110 58 E
Xia Xian, China 34 G6 35 8N 111 12 E
Xiachengzi, China 35 B16 44 40N 130 18 E
Xiaguan, China 32 D5 25 32N 100 16 E
Xiajin, China 34 F9 36 56N 116 0 E
Xiamen, China 33 D6 24 25N 118 4 E
Xi'an, China 34 G5 34 15N 109 0 E
Xian Xian, China 34 E9 38 12N 116 6 E
Xiang Jiang →, China 33 D6 28 55N 112 50 E
Xiangcheng, Henan, China 34 H8 33 29N 114 52 E
Xiangcheng, Henan, China 34 H7 33 50N 113 27 E
Xiangfan, China 33 C6 32 2N 112 8 E
Xianggang = Hong Kong □,
China 33 G11 22 11N 114 14 E
Xianghuang Qi, China 34 C7 42 2N 113 50 E
Xiangning, China 34 G6 35 58N 110 50 E
Xiangquan, China 34 F7 36 30N 113 1 E
Xiangquan He = Sutlej →,
Pakistan 42 E4 29 23N 71 3 E
Xiangshui, China 35 G10 34 12N 119 33 E
Xiangtan, China 33 D6 27 51N 112 54 E
Xianyang, China 34 G5 34 20N 108 40 E
Xiao Hinggan Ling, China 33 B7 49 0N 127 0 E
Xiao Xian, China 34 G9 34 15N 116 55 E
Xiaoyi, China 34 F6 37 8N 111 48 E
Xiawa, China 35 C11 42 35N 120 38 E
Xiayi, China 34 G9 34 15N 116 10 E
Xichang, China 32 D5 27 51N 102 19 E
Xichuan, China 34 H6 33 0N 111 30 E
Xieng Khouang, Laos 38 C4 19 17N 103 25 E
Xifei He →, China 34 H9 32 45N 116 40 E
Xifeng, Gansu, China 34 G4 35 40N 107 40 E
Xifeng, Liaoning, China 35 C13 42 42N 124 45 E
Xifengzhen = Xifeng, China 34 G4 35 40N 107 40 E
Xigazê, China 32 D3 29 5N 88 45 E
Xihe, China 34 G3 34 2N 105 20 E
Xihua, China 34 H8 33 45N 114 30 E
Xili Shuiku, China 33 F10 22 36N 113 57 E
Xiliao He →, China 35 C12 43 32N 123 35 E
Ximana, Mozam. 55 F3 19 24S 33 58 E
Xin Xian = Xinzhou, China 34 E7 38 22N 112 46 E
Xinavane, Mozam. 57 D5 25 2S 32 47 E
Xinbin, China 35 D13 41 40N 125 2 E
Xing Xian, China 34 E6 38 27N 111 7 E
Xing'an, China 33 D6 25 38N 110 40 E
Xingcheng, China 35 D11 40 40N 120 45 E
Xinghe, China 34 D7 40 55N 113 55 E
Xinghua, China 35 H10 32 58N 119 48 E
Xinglong, China 35 D9 40 25N 117 30 E
Xingping, China 34 G5 34 20N 108 28 E
Xingtai, China 34 F8 37 3N 114 32 E
Xingu →, Brazil 93 D8 1 30S 51 53W
Xingyang, China 34 G7 34 45N 112 52 E
Xinhe, China 34 F8 37 30N 115 15 E
Xining, China 32 C5 36 34N 101 40 E
Xinjiang, China 34 G6 35 34N 111 11 E
Xinjiang Uygur Zizhiqu □, China 32 C3 42 0N 86 0 E
Xinjin = Pulandian, China 35 E11 39 25N 121 58 E
Xinkai He →, China 35 C12 43 32N 123 35 E
Xinken, China 33 F10 22 39N 113 36 E
Xinle, China 34 E8 38 25N 114 40 E
Xinlitun, China 35 D12 42 0N 122 8 E
Xinmin, China 35 D12 41 59N 122 50 E
Xintai, China 35 G9 35 55N 117 45 E
Xinwan, China 33 F10 22 47N 113 40 E
Xinxiang, China 34 G7 35 18N 113 50 E
Xinzhan, China 35 C14 43 50N 127 18 E
Xinzheng, China 34 G7 34 20N 113 45 E
Xinzhou, China 34 E7 38 22N 112 46 E
Xiongyuecheng, China 35 D12 40 12N 122 5 E
Xiping, Henan, China 34 H8 33 22N 114 5 E
Xiping, Henan, China 34 H6 33 25N 111 8 E
Xique-Xique, Brazil 93 F10 10 50S 42 40W
Xisha Qundao = Paracel Is.,
S. China Sea 36 A4 15 50N 112 0 E
Xiuyan, China 35 D12 40 18N 123 11 E
Xixabangma Feng, China 41 E14 28 20N 85 40 E
Xixia, China 34 H6 33 25N 111 29 E
Xixiang, China 34 H4 33 0N 107 44 E
Xiyang, China 34 F7 37 38N 113 38 E
Xizang Zizhiqu □, China 32 C3 32 0N 88 0 E
Xlendi, Malta 25 C1 36 1N 14 12 E
Xochob, Mexico 87 D7 19 8N 89 9W
Xuan Loc, Vietnam 39 G6 10 56N 107 14 E
Xuanhua, China 34 D8 40 40N 115 2 E

Xuchang, China 34 G7 34 2N 113 48 E
Xun Xian, China 34 G8 35 42N 114 33 E
Xunyang, China 34 H5 32 48N 109 22 E
Xunyi, China 34 G5 35 8N 108 20 E
Xúquer →, Spain 21 C5 39 5N 0 10W
Xushui, China 34 E8 39 2N 115 40 E
Xuyen Moc, Vietnam 39 G6 10 34N 107 25 E
Xuzhou, China 35 G9 34 18N 117 10 E
Xylophagou, Cyprus 25 E12 34 54N 33 51 E

Y

Ya Xian, China 38 C7 18 14N 109 29 E
Yaamba, Australia 62 C5 23 8S 150 22 E
Yaapeet, Australia 63 F3 35 45S 142 3 E
Yablonovy Ra. = Yablonovyy
Khrebet, Russia 29 D12 53 0N 114 0 E
Yablonovyy Khrebet, Russia 29 D12 53 0N 114 0 E
Yabrai Shan, China 34 E2 39 40N 103 0 E
Yabrūd, Syria 46 B5 33 58N 36 39 E
Yabucoa, Puerto Rico 89 d 18 3N 65 53W
Yacambú △, Venezuela 89 E6 9 42N 69 27W
Yacheng, China 33 E5 18 22N 109 6 E
Yacuiba, Bolivia 94 A3 22 0S 63 43W
Yacuma →, Bolivia 92 F5 13 38S 65 23W
Yadgir, India 40 L10 16 45N 77 5 E
Yadkin →, U.S.A. 83 H5 35 29N 80 9W
Yaeyama-Rettō, Japan 31 M1 24 30N 123 40 E
Yagodnoye, Russia 29 C15 62 33N 149 40 E
Yahila, Dem. Rep. of the Congo 54 B1 0 13N 24 28 E
Yahk, Canada 70 D5 49 6N 116 10W
Yahuma, Dem. Rep. of the Congo 52 D4 1 0N 23 10 E
Yaita, Japan 31 F9 36 48N 139 56 E
Yaiza, Canary Is. 24 F6 28 57N 13 46W
Yakima, U.S.A. 76 C3 46 36N 120 31W
Yakima →, U.S.A. 76 C3 47 0N 120 30W
Yakobi I., U.S.A. 70 B1 58 0N 136 30W
Yakovlevka, Russia 30 B6 44 26N 133 28 E
Yaku-Shima, Japan 31 J5 30 20N 130 30 E
Yakumo, Japan 30 C10 42 15N 140 16 E
Yakutat, U.S.A. 68 C6 59 33N 139 44W
Yakutia = Sakha □, Russia 29 C13 66 0N 130 0 E
Yakutsk, Russia 29 C13 62 5N 129 50 E
Yala, Thailand 39 J3 6 33N 101 18 E
Yalboroo, Australia 62 J6 20 50S 148 40 E
Yale, U.S.A. 84 C2 43 8N 82 48W
Yalgoo, Australia 61 E2 28 16S 116 39 E
Yalgorup △, Australia 61 D2 24 34S 115 2 E
Yalinga, C.A.R. 52 C4 6 33N 23 10 E
Yalkubul, Punta, Mexico 87 C7 21 32N 88 37W
Yalleroi, Australia 62 C4 24 3S 145 42 E
Yalobusha →, U.S.A. 81 J9 33 33N 90 10W
Yalong Jiang →, China 32 D5 26 40N 101 55 E
Yalova, Turkey 23 D13 40 41N 29 15 E
Yalta, Ukraine 19 F5 44 30N 34 10 E
Yalu Jiang →, China 35 E13 40 0N 124 22 E
Yam Ha Melah = Dead Sea, Asia 46 D4 31 30N 35 30 E
Yam Kinneret, Israel 46 C4 32 45N 35 35 E
Yamada, Japan 31 H5 33 33N 130 49 E
Yamagata, Japan 30 E10 38 15N 140 15 E
Yamagata □, Japan 30 E10 38 30N 140 0 E
Yamaguchi, Japan 31 G5 34 10N 131 32 E
Yamaguchi □, Japan 31 G5 34 20N 131 40 E
Yamal, Poluostrov, Russia 28 B8 71 0N 70 0 E
Yamal Pen. = Yamal, Poluostrov,
Russia 28 B8 71 0N 70 0 E
Yamanashi □, Japan 31 G9 35 40N 138 40 E
Yamanie Falls △, Australia 62 B4 18 29S 146 9 E
Yamantau, Gora, Russia 18 D10 54 15N 58 6 E
Yamba, Australia 63 D5 29 26S 153 23 E
Yambarran Ra., Australia 60 C5 15 10S 130 25 E
Yâmbiô, Sudan 51 H11 4 35N 28 16 E
Yambol, Bulgaria 23 C12 42 30N 26 30 E
Yamdena, Indonesia 37 F8 7 45S 131 20 E
Yame, Japan 31 H5 33 13N 130 35 E
Yamethin, Burma 41 J20 20 29N 96 18 E
Yamma-Yamma, L., Australia 63 D3 26 16S 141 20 E
Yampa →, U.S.A. 76 F9 40 32N 108 59W
Yampi Sd., Australia 60 C3 16 8S 123 38 E
Yampil, Moldova 17 D15 48 15N 28 15 E
Yampol = Yampil, Moldova 17 D15 48 15N 28 15 E
Yamuna →, India 43 G9 25 30N 81 53 E
Yamunanagar, India 42 D7 30 7N 77 17 E
Yamzho Yumco, China 32 D4 28 48N 90 35 E
Yana →, Russia 29 B14 71 30N 136 0 E
Yanagawa, Japan 31 H5 33 10N 130 24 E
Yanai, Japan 31 H6 33 58N 132 7 E
Yan'an, China 34 F5 36 35N 109 26 E
Yanaul, Russia 18 C10 56 25N 55 0 E
Yanbu 'al Baḥr, Si. Arabia 44 F3 24 0N 38 5 E
Yancheng, Henan, China 34 H8 33 35N 114 0 E
Yancheng, Jiangsu, China 35 H11 33 23N 120 8 E
Yanchep Beach, Australia 61 F2 31 33S 115 37 E
Yanchi, China 34 F4 37 48N 107 20 E
Yanchuan, China 34 F6 36 51N 110 10 E
Yanco Cr. →, Australia 63 F4 35 14S 145 35 E
Yandoon, Burma 41 L19 17 0N 95 40 E
Yang Xian, China 34 H4 33 15N 107 30 E
Yangambi, Dem. Rep. of
the Congo 54 B1 0 47N 24 24 E
Yangcheng, China 34 G7 35 28N 112 22 E
Yangch'ü = Taiyuan, China 34 F7 37 52N 112 33 E
Yanggao, China 34 D7 40 21N 113 55 E
Yanggu, China 34 F8 36 8N 115 43 E
Yangliuqing, China 35 E9 39 2N 117 5 E
Yangon = Rangoon, Burma 41 L20 16 45N 96 20 E
Yangpingguan, China 34 H4 32 58N 106 5 E
Yangquan, China 34 F7 37 58N 113 31 E
Yangtse = Chang Jiang →, China 33 C7 31 48N 121 10 E
Yangtze Kiang = Chang Jiang →,
China 33 C7 31 48N 121 10 E
Yangyang, S. Korea 35 E15 38 4N 128 38 E
Yangyuan, China 34 D8 40 1N 114 10 E
Yangzhou, China 33 C6 32 21N 119 26 E
Yanji, China 35 C15 42 59N 129 30 E
Yankton, U.S.A. 80 D6 42 53N 97 23W
Yanonge, Dem. Rep. of
the Congo 54 B1 0 35N 24 38 E
Yanqi, China 32 B3 42 5N 86 35 E
Yanqing, China 34 D8 40 30N 115 58 E
Yanshan, China 35 E9 38 4N 117 22 E
Yanshou, China 35 B15 45 28N 128 22 E
Yantabulla, Australia 63 D4 29 21S 145 0 E

Yantai, China 35 F11 37 34N 121 22 E
Yantian, China 33 F11 22 35N 114 16 E
Yanzhou, China 34 G9 35 35N 116 49 E
Yao Noi, Ko, Thailand 39 a 8 7N 98 37 E
Yao Xian, China 34 G5 34 55N 108 59 E
Yao Yai, Ko, Thailand 39 a 8 0N 98 35 E
Yaoundé, Cameroon 52 D2 3 50N 11 35 E
Yaowan, China 35 G10 34 15N 118 3 E
Yap, Pac. Oc. 64 G5 9 30N 138 10 E
Yapen, Indonesia 37 E9 1 50S 136 0 E
Yapen, Selat, Indonesia 37 E9 1 20S 136 10 E
Yapero, Indonesia 37 E9 4 59S 137 11 E
Yappar →, Australia 62 B3 18 22S 141 16 E
Yaqui →, Mexico 86 B2 27 37N 110 39W
Yar-Sale, Russia 28 C8 66 50N 70 50 E
Yaraka, Australia 62 C3 24 53S 144 3 E
Yaransk, Russia 18 C8 57 22N 47 49 E
Yare →, U.K. 13 E9 52 35N 1 38 E
Yaremcha, Ukraine 17 D13 48 27N 24 33 E
Yarensk, Russia 18 B8 62 11N 49 15 E
Yari →, Colombia 92 D4 0 20S 72 20W
Yarkand = Shache, China 32 C2 38 20N 77 10 E
Yarker, Canada 85 B8 44 23N 76 46W
Yarkhun →, Pakistan 43 A5 36 17N 72 30 E
Yarlung Ziangbo Jiang =
Brahmaputra →, Asia 32 D3 23 40N 90 35 E
Yarmouth, Canada 73 D6 43 50N 66 7W
Yarmūk →, Syria 46 C4 32 42N 35 40 E
Yaroslavl, Russia 18 C6 57 35N 39 55 E
Yarqa, W. →, Egypt 46 F2 30 0N 33 49 E
Yarra Yarra Lakes, Australia 61 E2 29 40S 115 45 E
Yarram, Australia 63 F4 38 29S 146 39 E
Yarraman, Australia 63 D5 26 50S 152 0 E
Yarras, Australia 63 E5 31 25S 152 20 E
Yartsevo, Russia 29 C10 60 20N 90 0 E
Yarumal, Colombia 92 B3 6 58N 75 24W
Yasawa Group, Fiji 59 C7 17 0S 177 23 E
Yaselda, Belarus 17 B14 52 7N 26 28 E
Yasin, Pakistan 43 A5 36 24N 73 23 E
Yasinski, L., Canada 72 B4 53 16N 77 35W
Yasinya, Ukraine 17 D13 48 16N 24 21 E
Yasothon, Thailand 38 E5 15 50N 104 10 E
Yass, Australia 63 E4 34 49S 148 54 E
Yāsūj, Iran 45 D6 30 31N 51 31 E
Yatağan, Turkey 23 F13 37 20N 28 10 E
Yates Center, U.S.A. 81 G7 37 53N 95 44W
Yathkyed L., Canada 71 A9 62 40N 98 0W
Yatsushiro, Japan 31 H5 32 30N 130 40 E
Yatta Plateau, Kenya 54 C4 2 0S 38 0 E
Yauco, Puerto Rico 89 d 18 2N 66 51W
Yavari →, Peru 92 D4 4 21S 70 2W
Yávaros, Mexico 86 B3 26 42N 109 31W
Yavatmal, India 40 J11 20 20N 78 15 E
Yavne, Israel 46 D3 31 52N 34 45 E
Yavoriv, Ukraine 17 D12 49 55N 23 20 E
Yavorov = Yavoriv, Ukraine 17 D12 49 55N 23 20 E
Yawatahama, Japan 31 H6 33 27N 132 24 E
Yazd, Iran 45 D7 31 55N 54 27 E
Yazd □, Iran 45 D7 32 0N 55 0 E
Yazd-e Khvāst, Iran 45 D7 31 31N 52 7 E
Yazman, Pakistan 42 E4 29 8N 71 45 E
Yazoo →, U.S.A. 81 J9 32 22N 90 54W
Yazoo City, U.S.A. 81 J9 32 51N 90 25W
Ybycuí △, Paraguay 94 B4 26 5S 56 46W
Ybytyruzú △, Paraguay 95 B4 25 51S 56 11W
Yding Skovhøj, Denmark 9 J13 55 59N 9 46 E
Ye Xian, China 34 H7 33 35N 113 25 E
Yebyu, Burma 38 E2 14 15N 98 13 E
Yechŏn, S. Korea 35 F15 36 39N 128 27 E
Yecla, Spain 21 C5 38 35N 1 5W
Yécora, Mexico 86 B3 28 20N 108 58W
Yedintsy = Edineţ, Moldova 17 D14 48 9N 27 18 E
Yegros, Paraguay 94 B4 26 20S 56 25W
Yehuah, Indonesia 37 J17 8 23S 114 45 E
Yehuda, Midbar, Israel 46 D4 31 35N 35 15 E
Yei, Sudan 51 H12 4 9N 30 40 E
Yekaterinburg, Russia 28 D7 56 50N 60 30 E
Yelarbon, Australia 63 D5 28 33S 150 38 E
Yelets, Russia 18 D6 52 40N 38 30 E
Yelizavetgrad = Kirovohrad,
Ukraine 19 E5 48 35N 32 20 E
Yell, U.K. 11 A7 60 35N 1 5W
Yell Sd., U.K. 11 A7 60 33N 1 15W
Yellow Sea, China 35 G12 35 0N 123 0 E
Yellowhead Pass, Canada 70 C5 52 53N 118 25W
Yellowknife, Canada 70 A6 62 27N 114 29W
Yellowknife →, Canada 70 A6 62 31N 114 19W
Yellowstone △, U.S.A. 76 D9 44 40N 110 30W
Yellowstone →, U.S.A. 76 B8 47 59N 103 59W
Yellowstone L., U.S.A. 76 D8 44 27N 110 22W
Yelsk, Belarus 17 C15 51 50N 29 10 E
Yemen ■, Asia 47 E3 15 0N 44 0 E
Yen Bai, Vietnam 38 B5 21 42N 104 52 E
Yenangyaung, Burma 41 J19 20 30N 95 0 E
Yenbo = Yanbu 'al Baḥr,
Si. Arabia 44 F3 24 0N 38 5 E
Yenda, Australia 63 E4 34 13S 146 14 E
Yenice, Turkey 23 E12 39 55N 27 17 E
Yenisey →, Russia 28 B9 71 50N 82 40 E
Yeniseysk, Russia 29 D10 58 27N 92 13 E
Yeniseyskiy Zaliv, Russia 28 B9 72 20N 81 0 E
Yennádhi, Greece 25 C9 36 2N 27 56 E
Yenyuka, Russia 29 D13 57 57N 121 15 E
Yeo →, U.K. 13 G5 51 2N 2 49W
Yeo, L., Australia 61 E3 28 0S 124 30 E
Yeo I., Canada 84 A3 45 24N 81 48W
Yeola, India 40 J9 20 2N 74 30 E
Yeoryioúpolis, Greece 25 D6 35 20N 24 15 E
Yeovil, U.K. 13 G5 50 57N 2 38W
Yeppoon, Australia 62 C5 23 5S 150 47 E
Yerbent, Turkmenistan 28 F6 39 30N 58 50 E
Yerbogachen, Russia 29 C11 61 16N 108 0 E
Yerevan, Armenia 19 F7 40 10N 44 31 E
Yerington, U.S.A. 76 G4 38 59N 119 10W
Yermak, Kazakhstan 28 D8 52 2N 76 55 E
Yermo, U.S.A. 79 L10 34 54N 116 50W
Yerólakkos, Cyprus 25 D12 35 11N 33 15 E
Yeropol, Russia 29 C17 65 15N 168 40 E
Yeropótamos →, Greece 25 D6 35 3N 24 50 E
Yeroskipos, Cyprus 25 E11 34 46N 32 38 E
Yershov, Russia 19 D8 51 23N 48 27 E
Yerushalayim = Jerusalem, Israel 46 D4 31 47N 35 10 E
Yes Tor, U.K. 13 G4 50 41N 4 0W
Yesan, S. Korea 35 F14 36 41N 126 51 E
Yeso, U.S.A. 81 H2 34 26N 104 37W
Yessey, Russia 29 C11 68 29N 102 10 E
Yetman, Australia 63 D5 28 56S 150 48 E
Yeu, Î. d', France 20 C2 46 42N 2 20W

Yevpatoriya, Ukraine .... 19 E5 45 15N 33 20 E
Yeysk, Russia .... 19 E6 46 40N 38 12 E
Yezd = Yazd, Iran .... 45 D7 31 55N 54 27 E
Yhati, Paraguay 94 B4 25 45S 56 35W
Yhú, Paraguay 95 B4 25 0S 56 0W
Yi →, Uruguay 94 C4 33 7S 57 8W
Yi 'Allaq, G., Egypt .... 46 E2 30 22N 33 32 E
Yi He →, China .... 35 G10 34 10N 118 8 E
Yi Xian, Hebei, China ...... 34 E8 39 20N 115 30 E
Yi Xian, Liaoning, China ... 35 D11 41 30N 121 22 E
Yialiás →, Cyprus .... 25 D12 35 9N 33 44 E
Yialousa, Cyprus .... 25 D13 35 32N 34 10 E
Yianisádhes, Greece .... 25 D8 35 20N 26 10 E
Yiannitsa, Greece .... 23 D10 40 46N 22 24 E
Yibin, China .... 32 D5 28 45N 104 32 E
Yichang, China .... 33 C6 30 40N 111 20 E
Yicheng, China .... 34 G6 35 42N 111 40 E
Yichuan, China .... 34 F6 36 2N 110 10 E
Yichun, China .... 33 B7 47 44N 128 52 E
Yidu, China .... 35 F10 36 43N 118 28 E
Yijun, China .... 34 G5 35 28N 109 8 E
Yıldız Dağları, Turkey ..... 23 D12 41 48N 27 36 E
Yilehuli Shan, China .... 33 A7 51 20N 124 20 E
Yimianpo, China .... 35 B15 45 7N 128 2 E
Yinchuan, China .... 34 E4 38 30N 106 15 E
Yindarlgooda, L., Australia . 61 F3 30 40S 121 52 E
Ying He →, China .... 34 H9 32 30N 116 30 E
Ying Xian, China .... 34 E7 39 30N 113 10 E
Yingkou, China .... 35 D12 40 37N 122 18 E
Yining, China .... 28 E9 43 58N 81 10 E
Yinmabin, Burma .... 41 H19 22 10N 94 55 E
Yiofiros →, Greece .... 25 D7 35 20N 25 6 E
Yirga Alem, Ethiopia .... 47 F2 6 48N 38 22 E
Yirrkala, Australia .... 62 A2 12 14S 136 56 E
Yishan, China .... 32 D5 24 28N 108 38 E
Yishui, China .... 35 G10 35 47N 118 49 E
Yishun, Singapore .... 39 d 1 26N 103 50 E
Yíthion, Greece .... 23 F10 36 46N 22 34 E
Yitong, China .... 35 C13 43 13N 125 20 E
Yiyang, Henan, China .... 34 G7 34 27N 112 10 E
Yiyang, Hunan, China .... 33 D6 28 35N 112 18 E
Yli-Kitka, Finland .... 8 C23 66 8N 28 30 E
Ylitornio, Finland .... 8 C20 66 19N 23 39 E
Ylivieska, Finland .... 8 D21 64 4N 24 28 E
Yoakum, U.S.A. 81 L6 29 17N 97 9W
Yog Pt., Phil. .... 37 B6 14 6N 124 12 E
Yogyakarta, Indonesia ...... 36 F4 7 49S 110 22 E
Yoho △, Canada 70 C5 51 25N 116 30W
Yojoa, L. de, Honduras 88 D2 14 53N 88 0W
Yŏju, S. Korea .... 35 F14 37 20N 127 35 E
Yok Don △, Vietnam .... 38 F6 12 50N 107 40 E
Yokadouma, Cameroon .... 52 D2 3 26N 14 55 E
Yokkaichi, Japan .... 31 G8 34 55N 136 38 E
Yoko, Cameroon .... 52 C2 5 32N 12 20 E
Yokohama, Japan .... 31 G9 35 27N 139 28 E
Yokosuka, Japan .... 31 G9 35 20N 139 40 E
Yokote, Japan .... 30 E10 39 20N 140 30 E
Yola, Nigeria .... 51 G8 9 10N 12 29 E
Yolaina, Cordillera de, Nic. . 88 D3 11 30N 84 0W
Yoloten, Turkmenistan ...... 45 B9 37 18N 62 21 E
Yom →, Thailand .... 36 A2 15 35N 100 1 E
Yonago, Japan .... 31 G6 35 25N 133 19 E
Yonaguni-Jima, Japan .... 31 M1 24 27N 123 0 E
Yŏnan, N. Korea .... 35 F14 37 55N 126 11 E
Yonezawa, Japan .... 30 F10 37 57N 140 4 E
Yong Peng, Malaysia .... 39 L4 2 0N 103 3 E
Yong Sata, Thailand .... 39 J2 7 8N 99 41 E
Yongamp'o, N. Korea .... 35 E13 39 56N 124 23 E
Yongcheng, China .... 34 H9 33 55N 116 20 E
Yŏngch'ŏn, S. Korea .... 35 G15 35 58N 128 56 E
Yongding, China .... 34 F2 36 38N 103 25 E
Yŏngdŏk, S. Korea .... 35 F15 36 24N 129 22 E
Yŏngdŭngpo, S. Korea .... 35 F14 37 31N 126 54 E
Yonghe, China .... 34 F6 36 46N 110 38 E
Yŏnghŭng, N. Korea .... 35 E14 39 31N 127 18 E
Yongji, China .... 34 G6 34 52N 110 28 E
Yŏngju, S. Korea .... 35 F15 36 50N 128 40 E
Yongnian, China .... 34 F8 36 47N 114 29 E
Yongning, China .... 34 E4 38 15N 106 14 E
Yongqing, China .... 34 E9 39 25N 116 28 E
Yŏngwŏl, S. Korea .... 35 F15 37 11N 128 28 E
Yonibana, S. Leone 50 G3 8 30N 12 19W
Yonkers, U.S.A. 85 F11 40 56N 73 54W
Yonne →, France .... 20 B5 48 23N 2 58 E
York, Australia .... 61 F2 31 52S 116 47 E
York, U.K. 12 D6 53 58N 1 6W
York, Ala., U.S.A. 81 J10 32 29N 88 18W
York, Nebr., U.S.A. 80 E6 40 52N 97 36W
York, Pa., U.S.A. 82 F7 39 58N 76 44W
York, C., Australia .... 62 A3 10 42S 142 31 E
York, City of □, U.K. 12 D6 53 58N 1 6W
York, Kap, Greenland 4 B4 75 55N 66 25W
York, Vale of, U.K. 12 C6 54 15N 1 25W
York Haven, U.S.A. 84 F8 40 7N 76 46W
York Sd., Australia .... 60 C4 15 0S 125 5 E
Yorke Pen., Australia ...... 63 E2 34 50S 137 40 E
Yorkshire Dales △, U.K. 12 C5 54 12N 2 10W
Yorkshire Wolds, U.K. 12 C7 54 8N 0 31W
Yorkton, Canada 71 C8 51 11N 102 28W
Yorkville, U.S.A. 78 G3 38 52N 123 13W
Yoro, Honduras 88 C2 15 9N 87 7W
Yoron-Jima, Japan .... 31 L4 27 2N 128 26 E
Yos Sudarso, Pulau = Dolak,
  Pulau, Indonesia .... 37 F9 8 0S 138 30 E
Yosemite △, U.S.A. 78 H7 37 45N 119 40W
Yosemite Village, U.S.A. ... 78 H7 37 45N 119 35W
Yoshino-Kumano △, Japan .... 31 H8 34 12N 135 55 E
Yoshkar Ola, Russia .... 18 C8 56 38N 47 55 E
Yŏsu, S. Korea .... 35 G14 34 47N 127 45 E
Yotvata, Israel .... 46 F4 29 55N 35 2 E
Youbou, Canada 78 B2 48 53N 124 13W
Youghal, Ireland 10 E4 51 56N 7 52W
Youghal B., Ireland 10 E4 51 55N 7 49W
Young, Australia .... 63 E4 34 19S 148 18 E
Young, Canada 71 C7 51 47N 105 45W
Young, Uruguay 94 C4 32 44S 57 36W
Younghusband, L., Australia . 63 E2 30 50S 136 5 E
Younghusband Pen., Australia . 63 F2 36 0S 139 25 E
Youngstown, Canada 71 C6 51 35N 111 10W
Youngstown, N.Y., U.S.A. ... 84 C5 43 15N 79 3W
Youngstown, Ohio, U.S.A. ... 84 E4 41 6N 80 39W
Youngsville, U.S.A. 84 E5 41 51N 79 19W
Youngwood, U.S.A. 84 F5 40 14N 79 34W
Youyu, China .... 34 D7 40 10N 112 20 E
Yozgat, Turkey .... 19 G5 39 51N 34 47 E
Ypacaraí △, Paraguay 94 B4 25 18S 57 19W
Ypané →, Paraguay 94 A4 23 29S 57 19W
Ypres = Ieper, Belgium ..... 15 D2 50 51N 2 53 E

Yreka, U.S.A. 76 F2 41 44N 122 38W
Ystad, Sweden .... 9 J15 55 26N 13 50 E
Ysyk-Köl, Kyrgyzstan .... 28 E8 42 25N 77 15 E
Ythan →, U.K. 11 D7 57 19N 1 59W
Ytyk-Kyuyel, Russia .... 29 C14 62 30N 133 45 E
Yu Jiang →, China .... 33 D6 23 22N 110 3 E
Yu Xian = Yuzhou, China .... 34 G7 34 10N 113 28 E
Yu Xian, Hebei, China ...... 34 E8 39 50N 114 35 E
Yu Xian, Shanxi, China ..... 34 E7 38 5N 113 20 E
Yuan Jiang →, China .... 33 D6 28 55N 111 50 E
Yuanqu, China .... 34 G6 35 18N 111 40 E
Yuanyang, China .... 34 G7 35 3N 113 58 E
Yuba →, U.S.A. 78 F5 39 8N 121 36W
Yuba City, U.S.A. 78 F5 39 8N 121 37W
Yūbari, Japan .... 30 C10 43 4N 141 59 E
Yūbetsu, Japan .... 30 B11 44 13N 143 50 E
Yucatán □, Mexico 87 C7 21 30N 86 30W
Yucatán, Canal de, Caribbean . 88 B2 22 0N 86 30W
Yucatán, Península de, Mexico . 66 H11 19 30N 89 0W
Yucatán Basin, Cent. Amer. . 66 H11 19 0N 86 0W
Yucatan Channel = Yucatán,
  Canal de, Caribbean 88 B2 22 0N 86 30W
Yucca, U.S.A. 79 L12 34 52N 114 9W
Yucca Valley, U.S.A. 79 L10 34 8N 116 27W
Yucheng, China .... 34 F9 36 55N 116 32 E
Yuci, China .... 34 F7 37 42N 112 46 E
Yuen Long, China .... 33 G11 22 26N 114 2 E
Yuendumu, Australia .... 60 D5 22 16S 131 49 E
Yülin, Hainan, China .... 39 C7 18 10N 109 31 E
Yulin, Shaanxi, China ...... 34 E5 38 20N 109 30 E
Yuma, Ariz., U.S.A. 79 N12 32 43N 114 37W
Yuma, Colo., U.S.A. 80 E3 40 8N 102 43W
Yuma, B. de, Dom. Rep. 89 C6 18 20N 68 35W
Yumbe, Uganda .... 54 B3 3 28N 31 15 E
Yumbi, Dem. Rep. of the Congo . 54 C2 1 12S 26 15 E
Yumen, China .... 32 C4 39 50N 97 30 E
Yun Ho →, China .... 35 E9 39 10N 117 10 E
Yun Xian, Australia .... 61 E2 28 20S 115 0 E
Yuncheng, Henan, China ..... 34 G8 35 36N 115 57 E
Yuncheng, Shanxi, China .... 34 G6 35 2N 111 0 E
Yungas, Bolivia 92 G5 17 0S 66 0W
Yungay, Chile 94 D1 37 10S 72 5W
Yunnan □, China .... 32 D5 25 0N 102 0 E
Yunta, Australia .... 63 E2 32 34S 139 36 E
Yunxi, China .... 34 H6 33 0N 110 22 E
Yupyongdong, N. Korea ...... 35 D15 41 49N 128 53 E
Yuraygir △, Australia ...... 63 D5 29 45S 153 15 E
Yurga, Russia .... 28 D9 55 42N 84 51 E
Yurimaguas, Peru 92 E3 5 55S 76 7W
Yurubí △, Venezuela 89 D6 10 26N 68 42W
Yuscarán, Honduras 88 D2 13 58N 86 45W
Yushe, China .... 34 F7 37 4N 112 58 E
Yushu, Jilin, China .... 35 B14 44 43N 126 38 E
Yushu, Qinghai, China ...... 32 C4 33 5N 96 55 E
Yutai, China .... 34 G9 35 0N 116 45 E
Yutian, China .... 35 E9 39 53N 117 45 E
Yuxarı Qarabağ = Nagorno-
  Karabakh □, Azerbaijan ... 19 F8 39 55N 46 45 E
Yuxi, China .... 32 D5 24 30N 102 35 E
Yuzawa, Japan .... 30 E10 39 10N 140 30 E
Yuzhno-Sakhalinsk, Russia .. 29 E15 46 58N 142 45 E
Yuzhnyy □, Russia .... 28 E5 44 0N 40 0 E
Yuzhou, China .... 34 G7 34 10N 113 28 E
Yvetot, France .... 20 B4 49 37N 0 44 E

Z

Zaanstad, Neths. .... 15 B4 52 27N 4 50 E
Zāb al Kabīr →, Iraq .... 44 C4 36 1N 43 24 E
Zāb aş Şaghīr →, Iraq ...... 44 C4 35 17N 43 29 E
Zabaykalsk, Russia .... 29 E12 49 40N 117 25 E
Zābol, Iran .... 45 D9 31 0N 61 32 E
Zābol □, Afghan. .... 40 D5 32 0N 67 0 E
Zābolī, Iran .... 45 E9 27 10N 61 35 E
Zabrze, Poland .... 17 C10 50 18N 18 50 E
Zacapa, Guatemala 88 D2 14 59N 89 31W
Zacapu, Mexico 86 D4 19 50N 101 43W
Zacatecas, Mexico 86 C4 22 49N 102 34W
Zacatecas □, Mexico 86 C4 23 30N 103 0W
Zacatecoluca, El Salv. 88 D2 13 29N 88 51W
Zacoalco, Mexico 86 C4 20 14N 103 33W
Zacualtipán, Mexico 87 C5 20 39N 98 36W
Zadar, Croatia .... 16 F8 44 8N 15 14 E
Zadetkyi Kyun, Burma .... 39 G1 10 0N 98 25 E
Zafarqand, Iran .... 45 C7 33 11N 52 29 E
Zafra, Spain 21 C2 38 26N 6 30W
Żagań, Poland .... 16 C8 51 39N 15 22 E
Zagaoua, Chad .... 51 E10 15 30N 22 24 E
Zagazig, Egypt .... 51 B12 30 40N 31 30 E
Żagħen, Iran .... 45 D7 30 40N 56 50 E
Zagreb, Croatia .... 16 F9 45 50N 15 58 E
Zāgros, Kūhhā-ye, Iran ..... 45 C6 33 45N 48 5 E
Zagros Mts. = Zāgros, Kūhhā-ye,
  Iran .... 45 C6 33 45N 48 5 E
Zahamena ○, Madag. .... 57 B8 17 37S 48 49 E
Zāhedān, Fārs, Iran .... 45 D7 28 46N 53 52 E
Zāhedān, Sīstān va Balūchestān,
  Iran .... 45 D9 29 30N 60 50 E
Zahlah, Lebanon .... 46 B4 33 52N 35 50 E
Zaïre = Congo →, Africa .... 52 F2 6 4S 12 24 E
Zaječar, Serbia & M. .... 23 C10 43 53N 22 18 E
Zaka, Zimbabwe .... 57 C5 20 20S 31 29 E
Zakamensk, Russia .... 29 D11 50 23N 103 17 E
Zakhodnaya Dzvina =
  Daugava →, Latvia .... 9 H21 57 4N 24 3 E
Zākhū, Iraq .... 44 B4 37 10N 42 50 E
Zákinthos, Greece .... 23 F9 37 47N 20 54 E
Zakopane, Poland .... 17 D10 49 18N 19 57 E
Zákros, Greece .... 25 D8 35 6N 26 10 E
Zalaegerszeg, Hungary ...... 17 E9 46 53N 16 47 E
Zalău, Romania .... 17 E12 47 12N 23 3 E
Zaleshchiki = Zalishchyky,
  Ukraine .... 17 D13 48 45N 25 45 E
Zalew Wiślany, Poland ...... 17 A10 54 20N 19 50 E
Zalingei, Sudan .... 51 F10 12 51N 23 29 E

Zalishchyky, Ukraine .... 17 D13 48 45N 25 45 E
Zama L., Canada 70 B5 58 45N 119 5W
Zambeke, Dem. Rep. of
  the Congo .... 54 B2 2 8N 25 17 E
Zambeze →, Africa .... 55 F4 18 35S 36 20 E
Zambezi = Zambeze →, Africa . 55 F4 18 35S 36 20 E
Zambezi, Zambia .... 53 G4 13 30S 23 15 E
Zambezi △, Zimbabwe .... 55 F2 17 54S 25 41 E
Zambezia □, Mozam. .... 55 F4 16 15S 37 30 E
Zambia ■, Africa .... 55 F2 15 0S 28 0 E
Zamboanga, Phil. .... 37 C6 6 59N 122 3 E
Zamora, Mexico 86 D4 20 0N 102 21W
Zamora, Spain 21 B3 41 30N 5 45W
Zamość, Poland .... 17 C12 50 43N 23 15 E
Zandvoort, Neths. .... 15 B4 52 22N 4 32 E
Zanesville, U.S.A. 84 G2 39 56N 82 1W
Zangābād, Iran .... 44 B5 38 26N 46 44 E
Zangue →, Mozam. .... 55 F4 17 50S 35 21 E
Zanjān, Iran .... 45 B6 36 40N 48 35 E
Zanjān □, Iran .... 45 B6 37 20N 49 30 E
Zanjān →, Iran .... 45 B6 37 8N 47 47 E
Zante = Zákinthos, Greece .. 23 F9 37 47N 20 54 E
Zanthus, Australia .... 61 F3 31 2S 123 34 E
Zanzibar, Tanzania .... 54 D4 6 12S 39 12 E
Zaouiet El-Kala = Bordj Omar
  Driss, Algeria .... 50 C7 28 10N 6 40 E
Zaouiet Reggâne, Algeria ... 50 C6 26 32N 0 3 E
Zaozhuang, China .... 35 G9 34 50N 117 35 E
Zap Suyu = Zāb al Kabir →, Iraq . 44 C4 36 1N 43 24 E
Zapadnaya Dvina = Daugava →,
  Latvia .... 9 H21 57 4N 24 3 E
Západné Beskydy, Europe .... 17 D10 49 30N 19 0 E
Zapala, Argentina 96 D2 39 0S 70 5W
Zapaleri, Cerro, Bolivia ... 94 A2 22 49S 67 11W
Zapata, U.S.A. 81 M5 26 55N 99 16W
Zapolyarnyy, Russia .... 8 B24 69 26N 30 51 E
Zaporizhzhya, Ukraine ...... 19 E6 47 50N 35 10 E
Zaporozhye = Zaporizhzhya,
  Ukraine .... 19 E6 47 50N 35 10 E
Zara, Turkey .... 44 B3 39 58N 37 43 E
Zaragoza, Coahuila, Mexico . 86 B4 28 30N 101 0W
Zaragoza, Nuevo León, Mexico . 87 C5 24 0N 99 46W
Zaragoza, Spain 21 B5 41 39N 0 53W
Zarand, Kermān, Iran .... 45 D8 30 46N 56 34 E
Zarand, Markazī, Iran ...... 45 C6 35 18N 50 25 E
Zaranj, Afghan. .... 40 D2 30 55N 61 55 E
Zarasai, Lithuania .... 9 J22 55 40N 26 20 E
Zárate, Argentina 94 C4 34 7S 59 0W
Zard, Kūh-e, Iran .... 45 C6 32 22N 50 4 E
Zāreh, Iran .... 45 C6 35 7N 49 9 E
Zaria, Nigeria .... 50 F7 11 0N 7 40 E
Zarneh, Iran .... 44 C5 33 55N 46 10 E
Zarós, Greece .... 25 D6 35 8N 24 54 E
Zarqā', Nahr az →, Jordan .. 46 C4 32 10N 35 37 E
Zarrīn, Iran .... 45 C7 32 46N 54 37 E
Zaruma, Ecuador 92 D3 3 40S 79 38W
Żary, Poland .... 16 C8 51 37N 15 10 E
Zarzis, Tunisia .... 51 B8 33 31N 11 2 E
Zaskar →, India .... 43 C7 34 13N 77 20 E
Zaskar Mts., India .... 43 C7 33 15N 77 30 E
Zastron, S. Africa .... 56 E4 30 18S 27 7 E
Zāvāreh, Iran .... 45 C7 33 29N 52 28 E
Zave, Zimbabwe .... 57 B5 17 6S 30 1 E
Zavitinsk, Russia .... 29 D13 50 10N 129 20 E
Zavodovski, I., Antarctica . 5 B1 56 0S 27 45W
Zawiercie, Poland .... 17 C10 50 30N 19 24 E
Zāwiyat al Bayḍā = Al Bayḍā,
  Libya .... 51 B10 32 50N 21 44 E
Zāyā, Iraq .... 44 C5 33 33N 44 13 E
Zāyandeh →, Iran .... 45 C7 32 35N 52 0 E
Zaysan, Kazakhstan .... 28 E9 47 28N 84 52 E
Zaysan, Oz., Kazakhstan .... 32 D4 28 48N 97 27 E
Zayü, China .... 32 D4 28 48N 97 27 E
Zazafotsy, Madag. .... 57 C8 21 11S 46 21 E
Zbarazh, Ukraine .... 17 D13 49 43N 25 44 E
Zdolbuniv, Ukraine .... 17 C14 50 30N 26 15 E
Zduńska Wola, Poland .... 17 C10 51 37N 18 59 E
Zeballos, Canada 70 D3 49 59N 126 50W
Zebediela, S. Africa .... 57 C4 24 20S 29 17 E
Zeebrugge, Belgium .... 15 C3 51 19N 3 12 E
Zeehan, Australia .... 63 G4 41 52S 145 25 E
Zeeland □, Neths. .... 15 C3 51 30N 3 50 E
Zeerust, S. Africa .... 56 D4 25 31S 26 4 E
Zefat, Israel .... 46 C4 32 58N 35 29 E
Zeil, Mt., Australia .... 60 D5 23 30S 132 23 E
Zeila, Somali Rep. .... 47 E3 11 21N 43 30 E
Zeist, Neths. .... 15 B5 52 5N 5 15 E
Zeitz, Germany .... 16 C7 51 2N 12 7 E
Zelenograd, Russia .... 18 C6 56 1N 37 12 E
Zelenogradsk, Russia .... 9 J19 54 53N 20 29 E
Zelienople, U.S.A. 84 F4 40 48N 80 8W
Zémio, C.A.R. .... 54 A2 5 2N 25 5 E
Zempoala, Mexico 87 D5 19 27N 96 24W
Zemun, Serbia & M. .... 23 B9 44 51N 20 25 E
Zenica, Bos.-H. .... 23 B7 44 10N 17 57 E
Žepče, Bos.-H. .... 23 B8 44 28N 18 2 E
Zevenaar, Neths. .... 15 C6 51 56N 6 5 E
Zeya, Russia .... 29 D13 53 48N 127 14 E
Zeya →, Russia .... 29 D13 51 42N 128 53 E
Zêzere →, Portugal 21 C1 39 28N 8 20W
Zghartā, Lebanon .... 46 A4 34 21N 35 53 E
Zgorzelec, Poland .... 16 C8 51 10N 15 0 E
Zhabinka, Belarus .... 17 B13 52 13N 24 2 E
Zhailma, Kazakhstan .... 28 D7 51 37N 61 33 E
Zhambyl = Taraz, Kazakhstan . 28 E8 42 54N 71 22 E
Zhangaqazaly, Kazakhstan ... 28 E7 45 48N 62 6 E
Zhangbei, China .... 34 D8 41 10N 114 45 E
Zhangguangcai Ling, China .. 35 B15 45 0N 129 0 E
Zhangjiakou, China .... 34 D8 40 48N 114 55 E
Zhangwu, China .... 35 C12 42 43N 123 52 E
Zhangye, China .... 32 C5 38 50N 100 23 E
Zhangzhou, China .... 33 D6 24 30N 117 35 E
Zhanhua, China .... 35 F10 37 40N 118 8 E
Zhanjiang, China .... 33 D6 21 15N 110 20 E
Zhannetty, Ostrov, Russia .. 29 B16 76 43N 158 0 E
Zhanyi, China .... 32 D5 25 38N 103 48 E
Zhanyu, China .... 35 B12 44 30N 122 30 E
Zhao Xian, China .... 34 F8 37 43N 114 45 E
Zhaocheng, China .... 34 F6 36 22N 111 38 E
Zhaotong, China .... 32 D5 27 20N 103 44 E
Zhaoyuan, Heilongjiang, China . 35 B13 45 27N 125 0 E
Zhaoyuan, Shandong, China .. 35 F11 37 20N 120 23 E
Zhashkiv, Ukraine .... 17 D16 49 15N 30 5 E
Zhashui, China .... 34 H5 33 40N 109 8 E
Zhayyq →, Kazakhstan .... 19 E9 47 0N 51 48 E
Zhdanov = Mariupol, Ukraine . 19 E6 47 5N 37 31 E
Zhecheng, China .... 34 G8 34 7N 115 20 E

Zhejiang □, China .... 33 D7 29 0N 120 0 E
Zheleznodorozhnyy, Russia .. 18 B9 62 35N 50 55 E
Zheleznogorsk-Ilimskiy, Russia . 29 D11 56 34N 104 8 E
Zhen'an, China .... 34 H5 33 27N 109 9 E
Zhengding, China .... 34 E8 38 8N 114 32 E
Zhengzhou, China .... 34 G7 34 45N 113 34 E
Zhenlai, China .... 35 B12 45 50N 123 5 E
Zhenping, China .... 34 H7 33 10N 112 16 E
Zhenyuan, China .... 34 G4 35 35N 107 30 E
Zhetiqara, Kazakhstan ...... 28 D7 52 11N 61 12 E
Zhezqazghan, Kazakhstan .... 28 E7 47 44N 67 40 E
Zhidan, China .... 34 F5 36 48N 108 48 E
Zhigansk, Russia .... 29 C13 66 48N 123 27 E
Zhilinda, Russia .... 29 C12 70 0N 114 20 E
Zhitomir = Zhytomyr, Ukraine . 17 C15 50 20N 28 40 E
Zhlobin, Belarus .... 17 B16 52 55N 30 0 E
Zhmerinka = Zhmerynka, Ukraine . 17 D15 49 2N 28 2 E
Zhmerynka, Ukraine .... 17 D15 49 2N 28 2 E
Zhob, Pakistan .... 42 D3 31 20N 69 31 E
Zhob →, Pakistan .... 42 C3 32 4N 69 50 E
Zhodino = Zhodzina, Belarus . 17 A15 54 5N 28 17 E
Zhodzina, Belarus .... 17 A15 54 5N 28 17 E
Zhokhova, Ostrov, Russia ... 29 B16 76 4N 152 40 E
Zhongdian, China .... 32 D4 27 48N 99 42 E
Zhongning, China .... 34 F3 37 29N 105 40 E
Zhongshan, Antarctica ...... 5 C6 69 0S 39 50 E
Zhongshan, China .... 33 G9 22 26N 113 20 E
Zhongshankong, China .... 33 G9 22 35N 113 29 E
Zhongtiao Shan, China ...... 34 G6 35 0N 111 10 E
Zhongwei, China .... 34 F3 37 30N 105 12 E
Zhongyang, China .... 34 F6 37 20N 111 11 E
Zhoucun, China .... 35 F9 36 47N 117 48 E
Zhouzhi, China .... 34 G5 34 10N 108 12 E
Zhuanghe, China .... 35 E12 39 40N 123 0 E
Zhucheng, China .... 35 G10 36 0N 119 27 E
Zhugqu, China .... 34 H3 33 40N 104 30 E
Zhuhai, China .... 33 G10 22 17N 113 34 E
Zhujiang Kou, China .... 33 G10 22 20N 113 45 E
Zhumadian, China .... 34 H8 32 59N 114 2 E
Zhuo Xian = Zhuozhou, China . 34 E8 39 28N 115 58 E
Zhuolu, China .... 34 D8 40 20N 115 12 E
Zhuozhou, China .... 34 E8 39 28N 115 58 E
Zhuozi, China .... 34 D7 41 0N 112 25 E
Zhytomyr, Ukraine .... 17 C15 50 20N 28 40 E
Ziārān, Iran .... 45 B6 36 7N 50 32 E
Ziarat, Pakistan .... 42 D2 30 25N 67 49 E
Zibo, China .... 35 F10 36 47N 118 3 E
Zichang, China .... 34 F5 37 18N 109 40 E
Zidi = Wandhari, Pakistan .. 42 F2 27 42N 66 48 E
Zielona Góra, Poland .... 16 C8 51 57N 15 31 E
Zierikzee, Neths. .... 15 C3 51 40N 3 55 E
Zigey, Chad .... 51 F9 14 43N 15 50 E
Zigong, China .... 32 D5 29 15N 104 48 E
Ziguinchor, Senegal 50 F2 12 35N 16 20W
Zihuatanejo, Mexico 86 D4 17 38N 101 33W
Žilina, Slovak Rep. .... 17 D10 49 12N 18 42 E
Zillah, Libya .... 51 C9 28 30N 17 33 E
Zima, Russia .... 29 D11 54 0N 102 5 E
Zimapán, Mexico 87 C5 20 54N 99 20W
Zimba, Zambia .... 55 F2 17 20S 26 11 E
Zimbabwe, Zimbabwe .... 55 G3 20 16S 30 54 E
Zimbabwe ■, Africa .... 55 F3 19 0S 30 0 E
Zimnicea, Romania .... 17 G13 43 40N 25 22 E
Zinave △, Mozam. .... 57 C5 21 35S 33 40 E
Zinder, Niger .... 50 F7 13 48N 9 0 E
Zinga, Tanzania .... 55 D4 9 16S 38 49 E
Zion △, U.S.A. 77 H7 37 15N 113 5W
Ziros, Greece .... 25 D8 35 5N 26 8 E
Zirreh, Gowd-e, Afghan. .... 40 E3 29 45S 62 0 E
Zitácuaro, Mexico 86 D4 19 28N 100 21W
Zitundo, Mozam. .... 57 D5 26 48S 32 47 E
Ziwa Magharibi = Kagera □,
  Tanzania .... 54 C3 2 0S 31 30 E
Ziway, L., Ethiopia .... 47 F2 8 0N 38 50 E
Ziyang, China .... 34 H5 32 32N 108 31 E
Zlatograd, Bulgaria .... 23 D11 41 22N 25 7 E
Zlatoust, Russia .... 18 C10 55 10N 59 40 E
Zlín, Czech Rep. .... 17 D9 49 14N 17 40 E
Zmeinogorsk, Kazakhstan .... 28 D9 51 10N 82 13 E
Znojmo, Czech Rep. .... 16 D9 48 50N 16 2 E
Zobeyrī, Iran .... 44 C5 34 10N 46 40 E
Zobia, Dem. Rep. of the Congo . 54 B2 3 0N 25 59 E
Zoetermeer, Neths. .... 15 B4 52 3N 4 30 E
Zolochev = Zolochiv, Ukraine . 17 D13 49 45N 24 51 E
Zolochiv, Ukraine .... 17 D13 49 45N 24 51 E
Zomba, Malawi .... 55 F4 15 22S 35 19 E
Zongo, Dem. Rep. of the Congo . 52 D3 4 20N 18 35 E
Zonguldak, Turkey .... 19 F5 41 28N 31 50 E
Zonqor Pt., Malta .... 25 D2 35 57N 14 34 E
Zorritos, Peru 92 D2 3 43S 80 40W
Zou Xiang, China .... 34 G9 35 30N 116 58 E
Zouar, Chad .... 51 D9 20 30N 16 32 E
Zouérate = Zouîrât, Mauritania . 50 D3 22 44N 12 21W
Zouîrât, Mauritania 50 D3 22 44N 12 21W
Zoutkamp, Neths. .... 15 A6 53 20N 6 18 E
Zrenjanin, Serbia & M. ..... 23 B9 45 22N 20 23 E
Zufār, Oman .... 47 D5 17 40N 54 0 E
Zug, Switz. .... 20 C8 47 10N 8 31 E
Zugspitze, Germany .... 16 E6 47 25N 10 59 E
Zuid-Holland □, Neths. ..... 15 C4 52 0N 4 35 E
Zuidbeveland, Neths. .... 15 C3 51 30N 3 50 E
Zuidhorn, Neths. .... 15 A6 53 15N 6 23 E
Zula, Eritrea .... 47 D2 15 17N 39 40 E
Zumbo, Mozam. .... 55 F3 15 35S 30 26 E
Zumpango, Mexico 87 D5 19 48N 99 6W
Zunhua, China .... 35 D9 40 18N 117 58 E
Zuni, U.S.A. 77 J9 35 4N 108 51W
Zunyi, China .... 32 D5 27 42N 106 53 E
Zurbātīyah, Iraq .... 44 C5 33 9N 46 3 E
Zürich, Switz. .... 20 C8 47 22N 8 32 E
Zutphen, Neths. .... 15 B6 52 9N 6 12 E
Zuurberg △, S. Africa ...... 56 E4 33 12S 25 32 E
Zuwārah, Libya .... 51 B8 32 58N 12 1 E
Zūzan, Iran .... 45 C8 34 22N 59 53 E
Zverinogolovskoye, Russia .. 28 D7 54 26N 64 50 E
Zvishavane, Zimbabwe .... 55 G3 20 17S 30 2 E
Zvolen, Slovak Rep. .... 17 D10 48 33N 19 10 E
Zwelitsha, S. Africa .... 53 L5 32 55S 27 22 E
Zwettl, Austria .... 16 D8 48 35N 15 9 E
Zwickau, Germany .... 16 C7 50 44N 12 30 E
Zwolle, Neths. .... 15 B6 52 31N 6 6 E
Zwolle, U.S.A. 81 K8 31 38N 93 39W
Żyrardów, Poland .... 17 B11 52 3N 20 28 E
Zyryan, Kazakhstan .... 28 E9 49 43N 84 20 E
Zyryanka, Russia .... 29 C16 65 45N 150 51 E
Zyryanovsk = Zyryan, Kazakhstan . 28 E9 49 43N 84 20 E
Żywiec, Poland .... 17 D10 49 42N 19 10 E
Zyyi, Cyprus .... 25 E12 34 43N 33 20 E

World: Regions in the News

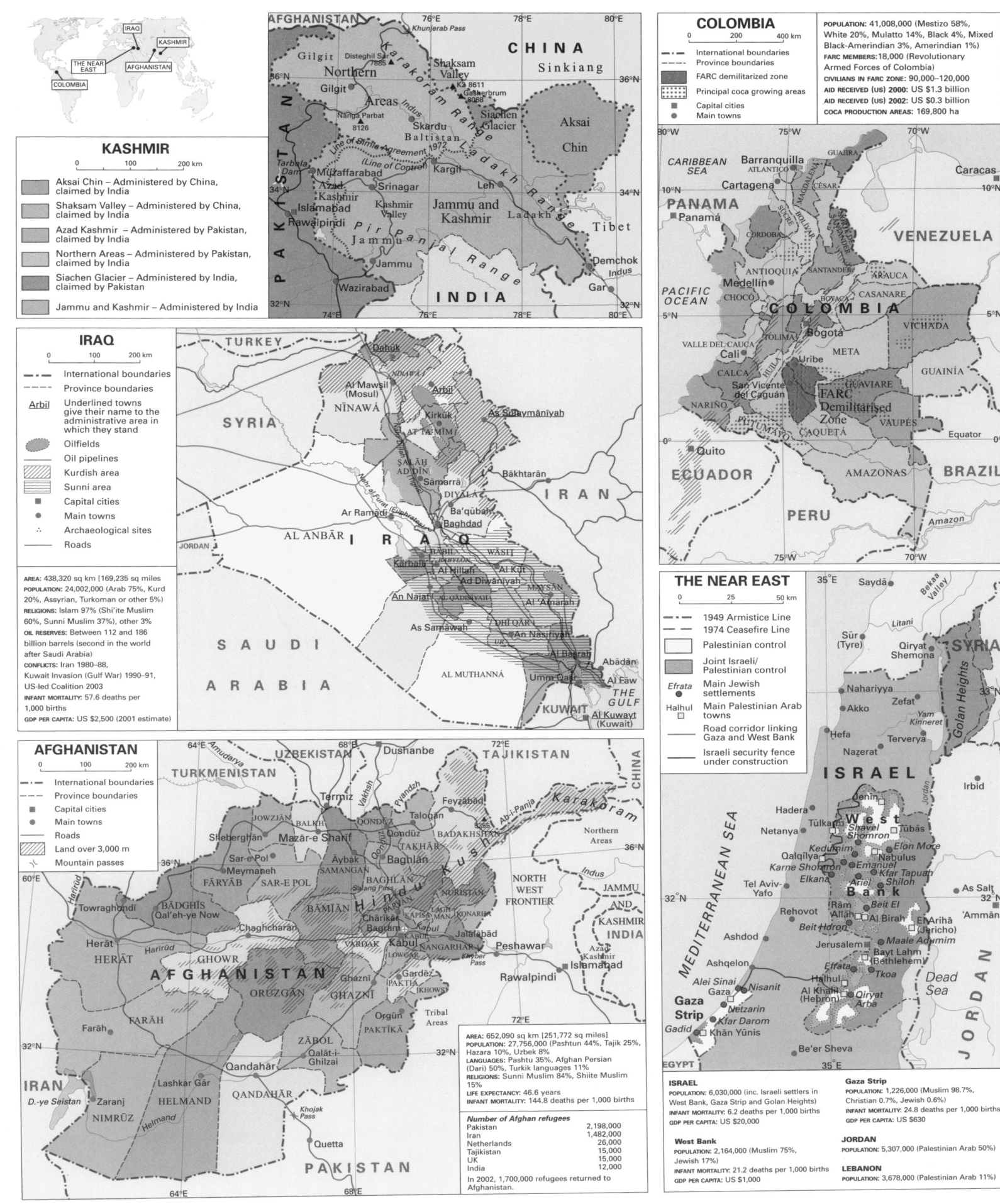

KASHMIR

0   100   200 km

- Aksai Chin – Administered by China, claimed by India
- Shaksam Valley – Administered by China, claimed by India
- Azad Kashmir – Administered by Pakistan, claimed by India
- Northern Areas – Administered by Pakistan, claimed by India
- Siachen Glacier – Administered by India, claimed by Pakistan
- Jammu and Kashmir – Administered by India

IRAQ

0   100   200 km

- — · · — International boundaries
- — — — Province boundaries
- Arbīl Underlined towns give their name to the administrative area in which they stand
- Oilfields
- Oil pipelines
- Kurdish area
- Sunni area
- Capital cities
- Main towns
- Archaeological sites
- Roads

AREA: 438,320 sq km [169,235 sq miles]
POPULATION: 24,002,000 (Arab 75%, Kurd 20%, Assyrian, Turkoman or other 5%)
RELIGIONS: Islam 97% (Shi'ite Muslim 60%, Sunni Muslim 37%), other 3%
OIL RESERVES: Between 112 and 186 billion barrels (second in the world after Saudi Arabia)
CONFLICTS: Iran 1980–88, Kuwait Invasion (Gulf War) 1990–91, US-led Coalition 2003
INFANT MORTALITY: 57.6 deaths per 1,000 births
GDP PER CAPITA: US $2,500 (2001 estimate)

AFGHANISTAN

0   100   200 km

- — — — International boundaries
- — — — Province boundaries
- Capital cities
- Main towns
- Roads
- Land over 3,000 m
- Mountain passes

AREA: 652,090 sq km [251,772 sq miles]
POPULATION: 27,756,000 (Pashtun 44%, Tajik 25%, Hazara 10%, Uzbek 8%)
LANGUAGES: Pashtu 35%, Afghan Persian (Dari) 50%, Turkik languages 11%
RELIGIONS: Sunni Muslim 84%, Shiite Muslim 15%
LIFE EXPECTANCY: 46.6 years
INFANT MORTALITY: 144.8 deaths per 1,000 births

Number of Afghan refugees

Pakistan	2,198,000
Iran	1,482,000
Netherlands	26,000
Tajikistan	15,000
UK	15,000
India	12,000

In 2002, 1,700,000 refugees returned to Afghanistan.

COLOMBIA

0   200   400 km

POPULATION: 41,008,000 (Mestizo 58%, White 20%, Mulatto 14%, Black 4%, Mixed Black-Amerindian 3%, Amerindian 1%)
FARC MEMBERS: 18,000 (Revolutionary Armed Forces of Colombia)
CIVILIANS IN FARC ZONE: 90,000–120,000
AID RECEIVED (US) 2000: US $1.3 billion
AID RECEIVED (US) 2002: US $0.3 billion
COCA PRODUCTION AREAS: 169,800 ha

- — — — International boundaries
- — · — Province boundaries
- FARC demilitarized zone
- Principal coca growing areas
- Capital cities
- Main towns

THE NEAR EAST

0   25   50 km

- — — — 1949 Armistice Line
- — · — 1974 Ceasefire Line
- Palestinian control
- Joint Israeli/Palestinian control
- Efrata Main Jewish settlements
- Halhul Main Palestinian Arab towns
- Road corridor linking Gaza and West Bank
- Israeli security fence under construction

ISRAEL
POPULATION: 6,030,000 (inc. Israeli settlers in West Bank, Gaza Strip and Golan Heights)
INFANT MORTALITY: 6.2 deaths per 1,000 births
GDP PER CAPITA: US $20,000

West Bank
POPULATION: 2,164,000 (Muslim 75%, Jewish 17%)
INFANT MORTALITY: 21.2 deaths per 1,000 births
GDP PER CAPITA: US $1,000

Gaza Strip
POPULATION: 1,226,000 (Muslim 98.7%, Christian 0.7%, Jewish 0.6%)
INFANT MORTALITY: 24.8 deaths per 1,000 births
GDP PER CAPITA: US $630

JORDAN
POPULATION: 5,307,000 (Palestinian Arab 50%)

LEBANON
POPULATION: 3,678,000 (Palestinian Arab 11%)

KEY TO EUROPEAN MAP PAGES

 **Large scale maps**
(>1:2 500 000)

 **Medium scale maps**
(1: 2 800 000 – 1:9 900 000)

 **Small scale maps**
(<1:10 000 000)

Arctic Circle

WORLD COUNTRY INDEX

Country	Page
Afghanistan	40
Albania	23
Algeria	50
Angola	52–53
Argentina	94, 96
Armenia	19
Australia	60–63
Austria	16–17
Azerbaijan	19
Bahamas	88–89
Bahrain	45
Bangladesh	41
Barbados	89
Belarus	17, 18–19
Belgium	15
Belize	88
Benin	50
Bhutan	41
Bolivia	92
Bosnia-Herzegovina	22–23
Botswana	56
Brazil	92–93, 95
Brunei	36
Bulgaria	23
Burkina Faso	50
Burma (Myanmar)	41
Burundi	54
Cambodia	38–39
Canary Is.	24
Cameroon	52
Canada	68–73
Central African Republic	52
Chad	51
Chile	94, 96–97
China	32–35
Colombia	92
Congo	52
Congo, Dem. Rep.	
of the	52–53, 54–55
Costa Rica	88
Croatia	22–23
Cuba	88–89
Cyprus	25
Czech Republic	16–17
Denmark	9
Djibouti	47
Dominican Republic	89
Ecuador	92
Egypt	51
El Salvador	88
England	12–13
Equatorial Guinea	52
Eritrea	47
Estonia	9
Ethiopia	47, 52
Fiji	59
Finland	8–9
France	20–21
French Guiana	93
Gabon	52
Gambia	50
Georgia	19
Germany	16
Ghana	50
Greece	23
Greenland	4
Guadeloupe	88
Guatemala	88
Guinea	50
Guinea-Bissau	50
Guyana	92
Haiti	89
Honduras	88
Hungary	17
Iceland	8
India	40–43
Indonesia	36–37
Iran	44–45
Iraq	44–45
Irish Republic	10
Israel	46
Italy	22–23
Ivory Coast	50
Jamaica	88
Japan	30–31
Jordan	46
Kazakhstan	28
Kenya	54
Korea, North	35
Korea, South	35
Kuwait	44–45
Kyrgyzstan	28
Laos	38
Latvia	9
Lebanon	46
Lesotho	57
Liberia	50
Libya	51
Lithuania	9
Luxembourg	15
Macedonia	23
Madagascar	57
Malawi	55
Malaysia	36–37, 39
Mali	50
Malta	25
Martinique	88
Mauritania	50
Mexico	86–87
Moldova	17
Mongolia	32
Morocco	50
Mozambique	55, 57
Namibia	56
Nepal	43
Netherlands	15
New Zealand	59
Nicaragua	88
Niger	50–51
Nigeria	50–51
Northern Ireland	10
Norway	8–9
Oman	47
Pakistan	40, 42
Panama	88
Papua New Guinea	64
Paraguay	94–95
Peru	92
Philippines	37
Poland	16–17
Portugal	21
Puerto Rico	89
Qatar	45
Romania	17
Russia	18–19, 28–29
Rwanda	54
St. Lucia	89
Samoa	59
Saudi Arabia	44–45, 47
Scotland	11
Senegal	50
Serbia and Montenegro	23
Sierra Leone	50
Singapore	39
Slovak Republic	17
Slovenia	22
Solomon Is.	64
Somali Republic	47
South Africa	56–57
Spain	21
Sri Lanka	40
Sudan	51
Suriname	92–93
Swaziland	57
Sweden	8–9
Switzerland	16
Syria	44, 46
Taiwan	33
Tajikistan	28
Tanzania	54–55
Thailand	38–39
Togo	50
Tonga	59
Trinidad and Tobago	93
Tunisia	50–51
Turkey	19
Turkmenistan	28
Uganda	54
Ukraine	18–19
United Arab Emirates	47
United Kingdom	10–13
USA	74–85
Uruguay	94–95
Uzbekistan	28
Vanuatu	64
Venezuela	92–93
Vietnam	38–39
Wales	12–13
Yemen	47
Zambia	55, 56–57
Zimbabwe	55